# International Dictionary of
# BALLET

# International Dictionary of BALLET

**VOLUME 1**

**A – K**

EDITOR
MARTHA BREMSER

ASSISTANT EDITOR
LARRAINE NICHOLAS

PICTURE EDITOR
LEANDA SHRIMPTON

St J

St James Press

Detroit London Washington DC

*Front Cover* – Richard Cragun in *Forsythe's Daphne*, 1977
(© Leslie Spatt)



ST JAMES PRESS
835 Penobscot Bldg.
Detroit, MI 48226-4094
or
PO Box 699
Cheriton House
North Way
Andover
Hants SP10 5YE

ST JAMES PRESS is an imprint of Gale Research Inc.

**Library of Congress Cataloging-in-Publication Data**
International dictionary of ballet / editor, Martha Bremser;
picture editor, Leanda Shrimpton.
p. cm.
Includes bibliographical references and index.
Contents: Vol. 1. A-K — v. 2. L-Z.
ISBN 1-55862-084-2 (set)
ISBN 1-55862-157-1 (Volume 1)
ISBN 1-55862-158-X (Volume 2)
1. Ballet — Encyclopedias. I. Bremser, Martha.
GV1585.I57 1993
792.8'03 — dc20 93-25051
CIP

A CIP catalogue record for this book is available from the British Library.

Printed in the United States of America.
Published simultaneously in the United Kingdom.

The paper used in this publication meets the minimum requirements of American National Standard for Information Sciences—Permanence Paper for printed Library Materials, ANSI Z39.48-1984. ∞™

# CONTENTS

# EDITOR'S NOTE

The *International Dictionary of Ballet* is in two volumes, and includes some 750 entries arranged in a single alphabetical sequence. The selection of entries is based on the recommendations of the advisers listed on page ix, and is both historical (from the Renaissance to the present) and international in scope, with inevitable emphasis on those areas (Russia, Europe, North America) whose contribution to the development of classical ballet has been the strongest. While modern dance itself does not fall within the parameters of this dictionary, a few selected leading modern dance choreographers, whose works have figured prominently in the repertories of international ballet companies, are represented here.

There are three types of entry in the dictionary: entries on individual artists, entries on individual ballets, and entries on ballet companies.

Entries on individual artists comprise the greatest number of entries in the dictionary, and include dancers, choreographers, designers, composers, librettists, and teachers. Because of the dictionary's emphasis on the performance aspect of the art, the great majority of individuals in the dictionary, both historical and comtemporary, belong to the first two categories. Each of the individual artist entries includes a career biography, a comprehensive list of roles (for dancers) and/or works (for choreographers, composers, designers, and librettists), and a list of relevant publications, followed by a signed critical essay by one of the dictionary's 160 contributors.

In the case of **ROLES** lists, the abbreviation (cr) refers to a "created" role. The information provided for every role, whether created or not, refers to the dancer's first appearance in that particular role. In the case of **WORKS** lists, the year given is that of the premiere performance, even if the choreography, music, design, or libretto was created earlier. Every effort has been made in these sections to provide as comprehensive a list as possible; however, entries will inevitably reflect the amount of source information available on the particular subjects.

Entries on individual ballets include full details of the ballet's premiere (choreography, music, design, location, date), a listing of other significant productions of the same ballet, a list of relevant publications, and a signed critical and historical analysis of the ballet. In most cases the section headed **Other productions include** covers those productions — be they restagings of the original choreography or completely new versions — which have been set to the original ballet score. Except in a few special cases, ballets with the same title but different music are not included here. In the few cases where a ballet libretto is based on a pre-existing story — such as myth, Shakespeare, or folktale — there is a separate section (**Other choreographic treatments of story**) referring to those works which, regardless of score, are related by virtue of their common subject matter.

Company entries make up a small proportion of the dictionary entries and include only companies of international standing, in either a historical or a contemporary context. These entries contain a synopsis of the company's history, a list of publications, and a substantial historical and critical essay by an expert in the field. All companies, whether their importance is historical or current, are listed by their most recent title or incarnation; cross-references are provided to avoid confusion regarding the numerous company titles.

## A NOTE ON SOURCES

All entries have a **PUBLICATIONS** list, which includes books, articles, and other written sources of relevance to the subject. As a rule, obituaries and reviews, unless part of more substantial or in-depth pieces, are not included. General encyclopedias, ballet dictionaries, and other standard reference works are not listed in the individual publications lists, but are acknowledged below.

There are several seminal works in the field of ballet history, without which this ballet dictionary would have been impossible. A few selected sources, such as Cyril Beaumont's essential *Complete Book of Ballets* and its various supplements, are listed wherever they apply in the individual publications lists. Many other fundamental reference works, simply because they would have to be listed in almost every entry, do not appear in each list. The most important of these are mentioned here with humble thanks to their authors and editors for making successive efforts in ballet research possible: *Enciclopedia dello Spettacolo* (9 vols. plus supplement; Rome, 1954-66), *The London Stage 1660-1800* (5 parts in 11 vols.; Carbondale, Illinois, 1960-68), *The Dance Encyclopedia* (ed. Anatole Chujoy and P.W. Manchester; New

York, 1967), *A Biographical Dictionary of Actors, Actresses, Musicians, Dancers, Managers and other Stage Personnel in London 1660-1800* (Carbondale, Illinois, 1973- ), *A Dictionary of Ballet* (ed. P.W. Manchester; London, 1974), *A Dictionary Catalogue of the Dance Collection* (New York Public Library; 10 volumes, plus annual supplements; New York, 1974- ), *The Concise Oxford Dictionary of Ballet* (ed. Horst Koegler; Oxford, 1977, 1982), *The Encyclopedia of Dance and Ballet* (ed. Mary Clarke and David Vaughan; New York, 1977), *The Phaidon Book of Ballet* (originally published as *Il Balletto: Repertorio del teatro di danza dal 1581*; English edition, Milan, 1981), *The New Grove Dictionary of Music and Musicians* (London, 1980), *The Royal Ballet — The First Fifty Years* (Alexander Bland, with production information compiled by Sarah C. Woodcock; London, 1981), *Ballet Encyclopedia* (Moscow, 1981).

## ACKNOWLEDGMENTS

I would like to thank the following for their invaluable help in the completion of this project: all of the advisers and contributors; the living entrants who cooperated by providing information about their careers; the many ballet companies, impossible to list here, who answered our numerous queries about their dancers and productions; Denise Collett-Simpson and the Library of the Royal Academy of Dancing; Peter Bassett and the Library of the Laban Centre for Movement and Dance; Westminster Reference Library; Harvard Theatre Collection; the New York Public Library; and the researchers Régine Astier, Maureen Needham Costonis, Birthe Johansen, Elizabeth Souritz, Nina Alovert, and Monique Babsky for helping compile very difficult roles lists.

I would like to make a special mention of the following unofficial collaborators, on whose assistance and encouragement I was completely reliant: Sarah C. Woodcock; Kathrine Sorley Walker; and Jane Pritchard. Finally, thanks to Daniel Kirkpatrick, under whose expert guidance the project originated; Mark Hawkins-Dady, whose continuous support I could not do without; and all of my friends and colleagues at St. James.

# ADVISERS

Sonia Arova
Erik Aschengreen
Ann Barzel
Peter Brinson
Richard Buckle
Françoise Carter
Mary Clarke
Debra Craine
Arlene Croce
Iris Fanger
Angelika Gerbes
Robert Greskovic
Ivor Guest
Dale Harris
Penelope Jowitt
C. Sandra Kemp
Elizabeth Kendall
Joan Lawson
Alastair Macaulay
Keith Money
Erik Näslund
Madeleine Nichols
Richard Ralph
Allen Robertson
Bent Schønberg
Carolyn Sheehy
Kathrine Sorley Walker
Elizabeth Souritz
Christine Temin
Edward Thorpe
Nancy Walker
David Vaughan

# CONTRIBUTORS

Richard Adama
Mindy Aloff
Nina Alovert
Sasha Anawalt
Jeannette Andersen
Jack Anderson
Jessica Arah
Erik Aschengreen
Régine Astier
Monique Babsky
Nancy van Norman Baer
Ann Barzel
Geoffrey Baskerville
Peter Bassett
Kristin Beckwith
Irmgard E. Berry
Susan F. Bindig
Ingrid Brainard
Martha Bremser
Alan Brissenden
Lynn Matluck Brooks
Judith F. Burns
Françoise Carter
Kenneth Chalmers
John Chapman
Judith Chazin-Bennahum
Amanda Chisnell
Virginia Christian
Melanie Trifona Christoudia
Marie-Françoise Christout
Mary E. Corey
Maureen Needham Costonis
Gilberte Cournand
Michael Crabb
Debra Craine
Karen Dacko
Beth Dean
Arsen Degen
Tony Devereux
Mike Dixon
George Dorris
Jeannine Dorvane
Carol Egan
Vicki Fairfax
Iris M. Fanger
William E. Fark
Anita Finkel
Jennifer Fisher
Norma Sue Fisher-Stitt
Bruce Fleming
Vadim Gaevsky
Joseph Gale
Vicente García-Márquez
Pamela Gaye
Rosaline George
Richard Glasstone
Noël Goodwin
Malve Gradinger
Harris Green
John Gregory
Robert Greskovic
Jessica Griffin

Irina Gruzdeva
Alice Helpern
Doris Hering
Monica Hetherington
Dawn Lille Horwitz
Elizabeth Hudson
Marilyn Hunt
Concetta Lo Iacono
Madeleine Inglehearn
George Jackson
Birthe Johansen
Robert Johnson
Susan Jones
Stephanie Jordan
Penelope Jowitt
Angela Kane
Larry Kaplan
Deirdre Kelly
C. Sandra Kemp
Yvonne Kendall
Kathryn Kerby-Fulton
Leo Kersley
Jane King
Marie-Louise Kjølbye
Helma Kloos
Kim Kokich
Géza Körtvélyes
Vera Krasovskaya
Patricia Laughlin
Joan Lawson
Jody Leader
Susan Lee
Irène Lidova
Lee Lourdeaux
Alastair Macaulay
Eric Maier
Emma Manning
Sylvia Marinari
Katy Matheson
Alanna Matthew
Joseph H. Mazo
Anne McClymont
Don McDonagh
Adrienne L. McLean
Alexander Meinertz
Keith Money
Gay Morris
Myrtill Nádasi
Erik Näslund
James E. Neufeld
Larraine Nicholas
Ole Nørlyng
Alfred Oberzaucher
Ou Jian-ping
Donna Perlmutter
Rosalind Pierson
Freda Pitt
Michelle Potter
Jane Pritchard
Rachel S. Richardson
Frank W.D. Ries
Ine Rietstap
Allen Robertson
Agnes Roboz
E. Amelia Rogers
Janice Ross
Richard Rutledge
Lesley-Anne Sayers
Tim Scholl
Bent Schønberg
Laura H. Shucart
Majbrit Simonsen
Herbert M. Simpson
Janet Sinclair
Kathrine Sorley Walker
Elizabeth Souritz
Debra Sowell
Louise Stein
Claudia B. Stone
Otis Stuart
Igor Stupnikov
Julia Sutton
Anna Swan
Mary Grace Swift
Christine Temin
Evelyn Téri
Elizabeth Terzian
Rose Anne Thom
Edward Thorpe
Kenji Usui
David Vaughan
Jenny J. Veldhuis
Horst Vollmer
Mary Jane Warner
Paige Whitley-Bauguess
Sally Whyte
Margaret Willis
Leland Windreich
Hans-Theodor Wohlfahrt
Sarah C. Woodcock
Martin Wright

# International Dictionary of
# BALLET

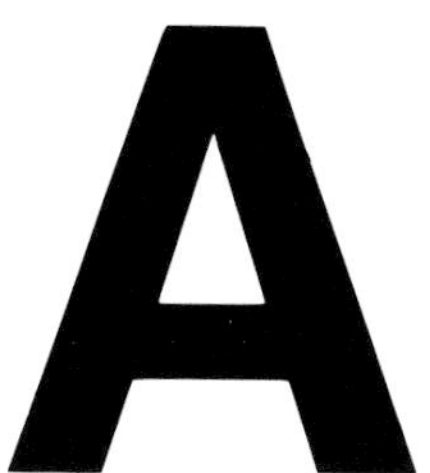

## ADAM, ADOLPHE

French composer. Born Adolphe Charles Adam in Paris, 24 July 1803. Educated at day-school in Paris; entered the Conservatoire in 1817; studied the organ and harmonium under François Benoist, later François Adrien Boieldieu. Began to compose comic opera under Boieldieu, also writing music for vaudeville theatre, Paris; first own dramatic composition, *Pierre et Catherine* (one-act operetta), performed at the Opéra-Comique in 1829; composed *Danilowa* (three-act opera), 1830; composed first own ballet score, *Faust*, 1833; first ballet for the Paris Opéra, 1836; travelled to St. Petersburg, 1839, and Berlin, 1840; founded own operatic theatre, Théâtre National, Paris, 1847 (closed the following year during the Revolution); elected Member of the Institute, 1844; made Professor of Composition at the Conservatoire, 1849. Recipient: Honourable Mention, Prix de Rome, 1824; Second Prix de Rome, 1824. Died in Paris, 3 May 1856.

### WORKS (Ballets)

1830 *La Chatte blanche* (pantomime-ballet in collaboration with C. Gide), Nouveautés
1833 *Faust* (chor. Deshayes), King's Theatre, London
1836 *La Fille du Danube* (chor. F. Taglioni), Opéra, Paris
1837 *Les Mohicans* (chor. Guerra), Opéra, Paris
1840 *L'Ecumeur de mer* (chor. F. Taglioni), Bolshoi Theatre, St. Petersburg
*Die Hamadryaden* (opera-ballet; chor. P. Taglioni), Königliche Opernhaus, Berlin
1841 *Giselle; ou, Les Wilis* (chor. Coralli, Perrot), Opéra, Paris
1842 *La Jolie Fille de Gand* (chor. Albert), Opéra, Paris
1843 *Le Diable à quatre* (chor. Mazilier), Opéra, Paris
1845 *The Marble Maiden* (chor. Albert), Drury Lane Theatre, London
1848 *Griseldis; ou, Les Cinq sens* (chor. Mazilier), Opéra, Paris
1849 *La Filleule des fées* (with H.F. de Saint-Léon; chor. Perrot), Opéra, Paris
1852 *Orfa* (chor. Mazilier), Opéra, Paris
1856 *Le Corsaire* (chor. Mazilier), Opéra, Paris

**Other ballets using Adam's music:** *Katerina* (Lavrovsky, 1935), *Beatrix* (J. Carter, 1966), *Le Diable à quatre Pas de deux* (Harkarvy, 1967), *Pas de quatre* (Gore, 1973), *L'Air d'esprit* (Arpino, 1978).

### PUBLICATIONS


By Adam:
*Souvenirs d'un musicien*, Paris, 1857
*Derniers d'un musicien*, Paris, 1859

About Adam:
Halévy, Fromental, *Notice sur la vie et les ouvrages de M. Adolphe Adam*, Paris, 1859; as "Adolphe Adam" in Halévy, *Souvenirs et portraits*, Paris, 1861
Mirecourt, E. de, *Adolphe Adam*, Paris, 1868
Pougin, A., *Adolphe Adam: Sa vie, sa carrière, ses memoires artistiques*, Paris, 1876
Evans, Edwin, "The Composer of *Giselle*", *Dancing Times* (London), November 1939
Beaumont, Cyril, *The Ballet Called Giselle*, London, 1944
Fiske, Robert, *Ballet Music*, London, 1958
Studwell, William E., "The Choreographic Chain: 70 Years of Ballet Music", *Dance Scope* (New York), Spring/Summer 1976
Ries, Frank W.D., "In Search of *Giselle*: Travels with a Chameleon Romantic", *Dance Magazine* (New York), August 1979
Guest, Ivor, *The Romantic Ballet in Paris*, revised edition, London, 1980
Jordan, Stephanie, "The Role of the Ballet Composer at the Paris Opera 1820–1850", *Dance Chronicle* (New York), vol. 4, no. 4, 1982


* * *

Adolphe Adam is now remembered almost entirely as the composer of *Giselle* (1841), although that was only the seventh of fourteen scores he wrote for ballet. He was also a prolific composer of operas, light operas, and vaudevilles: *Le Postillon de Longjumeau* (1836) and *Si j'étais roi* (1852) have music that is still occasionally heard. Influenced by a friendship with Ferdinand Hérold (composer of the best-known version of *La Fille mal gardée*), Adam decided at an early age and against parental wishes to compose for the theatre, and studied at the Paris Conservatoire with that in mind.

**Adolphe Adam**

Encouraged by his composition teacher, François Boieldieu, he began contributing songs to theatre shows from the age of twenty, and by 1830 had already composed 28 theatre works in various forms, including some dances. His first music for dance alone was *La Chatte blanche* (1830), written in collaboration with Casimir Gide, a fellow composer, followed in 1833 by a *Faust* ballet for the ballet master André Deshayes in London, where Adam's brother-in-law, Pierre Laporte, was manager of the King's Theatre.

The *Faust* music has disappeared, but it is known that some of it was used again in *Giselle*; his first ballet music for the Paris Opéra was for Marie Taglioni in her father's *La Fille du Danube* (1836). The ballet was not well received, but Adam's music was commended for its melodies and, more significantly, for its dramatic touches in the hero's "mad scene". *Les Mohicans* (Antonio Guerra) was staged at the Opéra the next year, following which Adam was invited to provide the music for *Giselle*.

He tailored it closely to detailed requirements from Perrot and Coralli, and his facility enabled it to be composed quickly (his memoirs claim eight days for the sketch and three weeks for the full work). Written almost as if it were a wordless opera, in the Italian cantilena style of Bellini and Donizetti, it has far fewer borrowings from existing music than comparable ballet scores of that time. There is an early use of leitmotiv (a phrase associated with a certain character or feeling), and of musical reminiscence for dramatic effect, while the short sections are varied in speed or expressive character to achieve dramatic contrast and developing purpose.

Adam had no control over the extra music by Frédéric Burgmüller added for the first performance (the "Peasant Pas de deux"), which remained part of the score, or over the cuts and later additions by Ludwig Minkus for productions in St. Petersburg. Only a piano score was printed in 1841; orchestrations were made from this until an orchestral score edited by Henri Busser and published in 1924 consolidated the music then in use at the Paris Opéra. This and the piano score together have variously supplied the basis for all later productions, with minor differences of detail (mainly of instrumentation) between one production and another.

Some of Adam's later scores are musically comparable to *Giselle*, including *La Jolie Fille de Gand* (François Albert, 1842), *Le Diable à quatre* (Joseph Mazilier, 1843), and Adam's last two ballets, both for Mazilier: *Orfa* (1852) and *Le Corsaire* (1856), the latter staged four months before the composer died. This was taken by Perrot to St. Petersburg and given there in 1858, but Adam's music became increasingly diluted or replaced by the work of other hands, including Pugni, Drigo, Minkus, and Prince Oldenburg, as well as Delibes for the *Pas des fleurs* in 1867, and the music of the Leningrad Kirov Ballet's present-day production is a motley assortment from all these. *La Jolie Fille de Gand* was newly orchestrated by Joseph Horovitz as *Beatrix*, a ballet by Jack Carter choreographed on the same scenario for London Festival Ballet in 1966.

In a memorial tribute in *Le Moniteur* after Adam's death, the respected critic Pier Angelo Fiorentino wrote that Adam achieved in ballet "a complete, dazzling and unchallengeable supremacy. There he is absolute master and he knew no rivals. It is in the ballet that he revealed his great poetic feeling . . . and he brought to this type of music all the flexibility of writing and all the diversity of style which he had shown elsewhere. The score of *Orfa* has real grandeur, that of *Le Corsaire* is powerfully dramatic, while *Le Diable á quatre* contains the vivacity of comedy . . ."

Adam provided a musical counterpart to the Romantic ballet on the Paris stage that enhanced visual content with expressive character and feeling. He sought no great depth of invention, nor originality of structure or harmony, but certainly in *Giselle* he left a musical portrait of one of the great moments in ballet history.

—Noël Goodwin

---

**ADAMS, Diana**

American dancer and teacher. Born in Staunton, Virginia, 29 March 1926. Studied with Emily Hadley in Memphis, Tennessee, at the Garden School for Girls and Ballet Arts School, New York, pupil of Edward Caton and Agnes de Mille; later studied with Antony Tudor, Ballet Theatre, New York. Married (1) British dancer Hugh Laing, 1947 (div. 1953); (2) Ronald Bates (div.). Stage début in the musical *Oklahoma!* (chor. Agnes de Mille), 1943; entered Ballet Theatre, at the invitation of Tudor, 1943: promoted to soloist, 1945; ballerina, New York City Ballet, 1950–63; also dancer in films, performing with Danny Kaye in *Knock on Wood* (dir. Panama and Frank, 1954) and Gene Kelly in *Invitation to the Dance* (dir. Kelly, 1956); teacher at the School of American Ballet, New York, after retiring from stage; was also active in selecting Ford Foundation scholarship students for School of American Ballet. Died in San Andreas, California, 10 January 1993.

**ROLES**

1944 Pas de trois in *Waltz Academy* (Balanchine), Ballet Theatre, Boston

1944/45 Myrtha in *Giselle* (Petipa after Coralli, Perrot; staged Dolin), Ballet Theatre
A Lover-in-Experience in *Pillar of Fire* (Tudor), Ballet Theatre
Rosaline in *Romeo and Juliet* (Tudor), Ballet Theatre
1945 Title role in *Helen of Troy* (Lichine), Ballet Theatre, New York
Cybele (cr) in *Undertow* (Tudor), Ballet Theatre, New York
Rich Lady (cr) in *Gift of the Magi* (Semenov), Ballet Theatre, Opera House, Boston
Principal dancer (cr) in *Graziana* (Taras), Ballet Theatre, New York
Tsarevna in *Firebird* (Taras), Ballet Theatre, New York
1946 Principal dancer (cr) in *Facsimile* (Robbins), Ballet Theatre, New York
Friend in *Les Patineurs* (Ashton), Ballet Theatre, New York
1948 Principal dancer (cr) in *Shadow of the Wind* (Tudor), Ballet Theatre, New York
Mother (cr) in *Fall River Legend* (de Mille), Ballet Theatre, New York
1949 Principal dancer (cr) in *The Dear Departed* (pas de deux; Tudor), Jacob's Pillow Festival, Massachusetts
1950 Principal dancer in *Designs With Strings* (Taras), Ballet Theatre, New York
The Dream (cr) in *Nimbus* (Tudor), Ballet Theatre, New York
Sacred Love in *Illuminations* (Ashton), New York City Ballet, New York
Principal dancer in *Symphonie Concertante* (Balanchine), New York City Ballet, New York
1951 Eurydice in *Orpheus* (Balanchine), New York City Ballet, New York
Fifth and Sixth Waltz (cr) in *La Valse* (Balanchine), New York City Ballet, New York
Marguerite Gautier (cr) in *Lady of the Camellias* (Tudor), New York City Ballet, New York
Principal dancer (cr) in *The Pied Piper* (Robbins), New York City Ballet, New York
Calliope in *Apollo, Leader of the Muses* (new production of *Apollon musagète*; Balanchine), New York City Ballet, New York
1952 Principal dancer (cr) in *Caracole* (later *Divertimento no. 15*; Balanchine), New York City Ballet, New York
One of the Starched White People (cr) in *Bayou* (Balanchine), New York City Ballet, New York
The Dancer in Gray (cr) in *La Gloire* (Tudor), New York City Ballet, New York
Iseult (cr) in *Picnic at Tintagel* (Ashton), New York City Ballet, New York
Principal dancer (cr) in *Concertino* (Balanchine), New York City Ballet, New York
1953 Principal dancer (cr) in *Valse Fantaisie* (Balanchine), New York City Ballet, New York
The Mare (cr) in *The Filly* (Bolender), New York City Ballet, New York
1954 First Time (cr) in *Opus 34* (Balanchine), New York City Ballet, New York
Dewdrop Fairy in *The Nutcracker* (Balanchine), New York City Ballet, New York
Sugar Plum Fairy in *The Nutcracker* (Balanchine), New York City Ballet, New York
Allegro (cr) in *Western Symphony* (Balanchine), New York City Ballet, New York
"Over the Pavements" (cr) in *Ivesiana* (Balanchine), New York City Ballet, New York
1956 Principal dancer (cr) in *Divertimento no. 15* (Balanchine), New York City Ballet, Stratford, Connecticut
1957 Pas de deux (cr) in *Agon* (Balanchine), New York City Ballet, New York
1958 Third Campaign: "Rifle Regiment" (cr) in *Stars and Stripes* (Balanchine), New York City Ballet, New York
1959 Five Pieces (cr) in *Episodes* II (Balanchine), New York City Ballet, New York
1960 Principal dancer (cr) in *Sinfonia no. 5* (Balanchine) in *Panamerica* (Balanchine, Contreras, Moncion, Taras, d'Amboise), New York City Ballet, New York
Lady of the Isles (cr) in *The Figure in the Carpet* (Balanchine), New York City Ballet, New York
Principal dancer (cr) in *Monumentum pro Gesualdo* (Balanchine), New York City Ballet, New York
Principal dancer (cr) in *Liebeslieder Walzer* (Balanchine), New York City Ballet, New York
Principal dancer (cr) in *Ragtime* I (Balanchine), New York City Ballet, New York
1961 Principal dancer (cr) in *Modern Jazz: Variants* (Balanchine), New York City Ballet, New York
Principal dancer (cr) in *Electronics* (Balanchine), New York City Ballet, New York

**Other roles include:** for New York City Ballet—The Siren in *Prodigal Son* (Balanchine), principal dancer in *Serenade* (Balanchine), principal dancer in *Allegro Brillante* (Balanchine), principal dancer in *Concerto Barocco* (Balanchine), Choleric in *The Four Temperaments* (Balanchine), Terpsichore in *Apollo* (Balanchine), Eurydice in *Orpheus* (Balanchine), Queen and Being Beauteous in *Illuminations* (Ashton), Rondo in *Western Symphony* (Balanchine), principal dancer in *Pas de Trois* (Balanchine), First and Second Movements in *Symphony in C* (Balanchine), Bourrée Fantasque, Prelude in *Bourrée Fantasque* (Balanchine), Caroline in *Lilac Garden* (*Jardin aux lilas*; Tudor), principal dancer in *Scotch Symphony* (Balanchine), principal dancer in *Gounod Symphony* (Balanchine).

## PUBLICATIONS

By Adams:
"Diana Adams on Suzanne Farrell", interview with David Daniel, *Ballet Review* (New York), Winter 1982
Interview in Tracy, Robert, *Balanchine's Ballerinas*, New York, 1983

About Adams:
Owen, Walter, "On Their Toes", *Dance Magazine* (New York), April 1946
LeCocq, Rhoda, "Baby Ballerinas", *Dance Magazine* (New York), October 1946
Owen, Walter, "Three Young Dancers Look Back", *Dance Magazine* (New York), April 1951
Chujoy, Anatole, *The New York City Ballet*, New York, 1953
Reynolds, Nancy, *Repertory in Review*, New York, 1977
Croce, Arlene, *Afterimages*, New York, 1978
Hering, Doris, "Ballet Theatre in Review", *Dance Magazine* (New York), July 1979
Denby, Edwin, *Dance Writings*, edited by Robert Cornfield and William Mackay, New York, 1986

* * *

Diana Adams took her early training with her stepmother, a former dancer, and continued with Agnes de Mille when her

**Diana Adams in *Scotch Symphony***

father moved the family to New York from her birthplace in Staunton, Virginia. De Mille put her on stage in 1943, when she was seventeen, in the long-running musical, *Oklahoma!* Subsequently, Adams joined the cast of *One Touch of Venus*, and seemed destined for a successful career on the popular stage.

But Adams was seen in this production by Antony Tudor, who arranged for her to join the five-year-old Ballet Theatre (later American Ballet Theatre) and her career became centered in classical ballet. When she joined the company there were some reservations as to whether she could become a "traditional" ballerina. At age twenty she was large (5′7″, 124 pounds), wore a size-14 dress, and did not fit the traditional image of the petite, ethereal, romantic ballet heroine.

She was instead the fore-runner of a newer breed of dancer which combined the leggy beauty of a Broadway chorine with an assured classical technique. It was casting to type when she was given the role of Helen ("The face that launched a thousand ships") in David Lichine's *Helen of Troy*. In short order Tudor began using her in his ballets. She was one of the Lovers-in-Experience in *Pillar of Fire*, Rosaline, Romeo's first infatuation, in *Romeo and Juliet*, and the lascivious mother in *Undertow*. She was also memorable as the haughtily beautiful Queen of the Wilis in *Giselle*.

Her long, delicately proportioned body attracted the attention of fellow dancer Michael Kidd, who was preparing his first ballet *On Stage!* and cast her in a minor role. She also attracted the attention of another fellow dancer, John Taras, who included her in his first ballet, *Graziana*. And she was thoroughly comfortable with the dramatic requirements of Tudor's psychologically intense ballets at the time that she, her husband Hugh Laing, and Tudor joined the fledgling New York City Ballet in 1950.

Tudor continued to cast her in his older ballets and to create new roles for her, notably in *Nimbus*. At this period the company boasted the combined artistic talents of Balanchine, Frederick Ashton, and Jerome Robbins, as well as Tudor's. Each of them created ballets for Adams. Ashton selected her as his Iseult, the beautiful queen of the Tristan and Iseult legend, for his *Picnic At Tintagel*. Balanchine gave her the fifth waltz in the premiere of *La Valse* in 1951, and made her Calliope in his revival of *Apollo* that same year.

Diane Adams had been compared to Felia Doubrovska in her graceful proportions and, in particular, for her long expressive legs and sensitively arched feet. It was not long before Balanchine cast her most memorably in the role of the Siren, a part that Doubrovska danced originally in the Diaghilev company's premiere of *The Prodigal Son*. In addition to her dramatically long legs, Adams had the rare quality of returning to stage level from a lift without indicating an abrupt change from air to the solidity of the floor: the transition was so smooth that it appeared as a long continuum.

The greatest difficulty Adams had in joining Balanchine's company was in changing her orientation from the dramatic presentation of movement so valued by Tudor to the sustaining musical line that is the hallmark of Balanchine ballets. For several years she mentally saw herself as a Tudor dancer and argued with Balanchine over the ballets that he cast her in. When Tudor discontinued his association with the company her problem was eased, and by 1954 she had become so completely transformed and committed to the new direction that Balanchine began to cast her in his most vanguard ballets, such as *Opus 34*, *Ivesiana*, and the landmark pas de deux in *Agon*.

The years at New York's City Center Theater were the most creative in Balanchine's career, and by the end of the 1950s, Adams had become the focus of the choreographer's creative attention. In addition to these "advanced" ballets, he also created roles for her in the humorous *Western Symphony* and *Stars and Stripes*, as well as in the refined *Caracole*, its successor *Divertimento No. 15*, and *Liebeslieder Walzer*.

Her career outside of the ballet stage included a short run on the dramatic stage in a 1957 production of Euripides' *The Trojan Women*. She also appeared in two films. The first (hilarious) one was with comedian Danny Kaye in *Knock On Wood*, choreographed by her old Ballet Theater fellow trooper Michael Kidd. The second film was *Invitation To The Dance*, choreographed by Gene Kelly, in which she played a hat-check girl in a stunning black costume.

After a successful dancing career, Adams played an important part in securing the future strength of her adopted company. With the assistance of a Ford Foundation grant in the 1960s, a national talent search was initiated to bring gifted students to study at the School of American Ballet. Adams was one of the examiners who travelled the country in search of talent and thus was the one who discovered Suzanne Farrell, and recommended her to Balanchine.

Ironically, Adams never danced the last ballet that Balanchine choreographed for her. *Movements for Piano and Orchestra* was an extremely spare score composed by Stravinsky, but before its first performance Adams was confined to bed. Balanchine selected Farrell to replace her. With hand gestures, verbal descriptions, and the assistance of her partner Jacques d'Amboise, Adams taught the role to Farrell. Adams had danced for twelve years with New York City Ballet and she subsequently taught at the School of American Ballet after her retirement from performing.

—Don McDonagh

---

## AFTERNOON OF A FAUN

**Choreography:** Jerome Robbins
**Music:** Claude Debussy
**Design:** Jean Rosenthal (set and lighting), Irene Sharaff (costumes)
**First Production:** New York City Ballet, City Center, New York, 14 May 1953
**Principal Dancers:** Francisco Moncion and Tanaquil LeClercq

**Other productions include:** Ballets: U.S.A. (restaged Robbins), with Kay Mazzo and John Jones; London, 1959. Royal Ballet (restaged Robbins), with Antoinette Sibley and Antony Dowell; London, 14 December 1971. Dance Theatre of Harlem, 1972. Paris Opéra Ballet; Paris, 3 October 1974. National Ballet of Canada; Toronto, 17 February 1977. Royal Danish Ballet; Copenhagen, 1976. Australian Ballet (staged Francisco Moncion), 1978. Zurich Ballet, 1980. La Scala Ballet; Milan, 1980. San Francisco Ballet, 1989. Norwegian National Ballet; Oslo, 1991.

### PUBLICATIONS

Reynolds, Nancy, *Repertory in Review*, New York, 1977
Balanchine, George, with Mason, Francis, *Balanchine's Complete Stories of the Great Ballets*, Garden City, N.Y., 1977
Siegel, Marcia, *The Shapes of Change*, Boston, 1979
"L'Après-midi d'un faune", *L'Avant-scène: Ballet/Danse* (Paris), no. 7, 1982

***Afternoon of a Faun*, with Anthony Dowell and Antoinette Sibley, Royal Ballet, London, 1971**

Years after his *Afternoon of a Faun* had become a perennial in the repertory of New York City Ballet, Jerome Robbins told Edward Villella that he had been its inspiration. Robbins had been visiting the School of American Ballet one afternoon and had seen him alone at the barre in a sunlit classroom, languidly stretching and luxuriating in the pleasure of his physical fitness, a splendid example of the All-American Teenager. "Although I was very flattered by that story," Villella said later, "I was glad that I had been unaware of it when I first danced the role." The obligation of performing this pas de deux is daunting enough for a man without having to bear the knowledge of having been even partially responsible for it.

There are no opportunities for technical fireworks for the dancer performing as Robbins's "faun". Instead the man must deliver continuity at the leisurely pace Debussy maintained in his *Prélude*, lifting his partner to his shoulder and then lowering her to the floor while matching its deliquescent legato. Because he is never offstage, he also bears the brunt of the responsibility for preventing the narcissism, constantly sensed beneath the shimmering surface of the ballet, from breaking into the open to pollute one of the more pristine works in the modern repertory.

Robbins treats the proscenium as a one-way mirror through which we in the audience observe dancers in a classroom observing themselves. At curtain's rise we first see nothing but a milky scrim. Then a room with a skylight and barres comes into view behind it. At the repeat of Debussy's harp glissando, the scrim rises. The room—muslin walls and ceiling backed by a blue cyclorama—is flooded with golden light.

A young man, shirtless in black tights, lies dozing on the floor. Matching the languid phrases of flute and oboe with slow stretchings, he strikes a series of poses—some of which recall those of Nijinsky's Faun—while dispassionately observing himself in the "mirror". When he is stretched out once more on the floor, a young woman enters, on pointe, to a mildly agitated section for winds and plucked strings. Oblivious to anything but her own reflection, she doesn't notice the young man until he sits up.

Without any outright acknowledgement of each other's presence—but with constant resort to the "mirror" to see how it looks—they perform, or rather sketch in, an elementary pas de deux. He partners her, or at least supports her; they retreat to opposite corners of the room for their "solos", which consist of slowly sidling towards one another for their "coda". He forms a circle with his arms through which she slips, to be held momentarily as if for a swimming lesson. Finally, when both are kneeling, he leans forward to kiss her lightly on the cheek. Watching her reflection all the while, the young woman rises and backs out of the classroom. As the languorous music of the opening returns, the young man repeats some of his initial stretching. He appears to be dozing again as the curtain descends.

Reaction to *Afternoon* apparently depended on how quickly the review had to be filed. The morning after its premiere John Martin in the *Times* was incensed by its lacking any "sense of continuity of phrased movement, and except for three or four beautifully contrived adagio lifts and their resolutions, there is nothing whatever of choreographic texture", though he conceded that Robbins "does no violence to Debussy's music". Walter Terry in the *Herald Tribune* was concerned that "whether Mr. Robbins intended it or not, his ballet suggests that the dancer is, or tends to be, in love with himself". Neither gave more than passing mention to the two unique dancers who created the work: Francisco Moncion, whose powerful presence could make immobility resonate, and Tanaquil LeClercq, who projected a fragility that was instantly contradicted by her dancing.

Writers for monthly publications found more to praise and less that shocked. P. W. Manchester in *Dance News* applauded the dancers for walking "with superb assurance, the tightrope between reality and fantasy", and admired Robbins for discarding "everything except the sensuousness implicit in the music [to make] a ballet which, in effect, is both an exposition and an exploitation of the essential narcissism of the dancer". Doris Hering in *Dance News* described Moncion and LeClercq as "exceedingly sensitive" and thought the ballet "a work of great awareness and wry insight and one that shimmers with atmosphere from beginning to end".

City Ballet's public welcomed *Afternoon of a Faun* from the start. The ballet has rarely missed a season in repertory in either the old City Center home or the present, grander New York State Theater at Lincoln Center, where its lack of pretension and subtle musicality keep it unfailingly fresh. The original production, with its simple, unimprovable costumes by Irene Sharaff and airy, light-shot setting by Jean Rosenthal, is equally defiant of time and fashion. Robbins brought it to London in 1971 when he set it on the Royal Ballet; Anthony Dowell and Antoinette Sibley starred.

Villella got his opportunity to dance the role he inspired soon after he joined City Ballet for the 1957–58 season. He recalled that Robbins spoke to him in sensuous terms, as a stage director would, suggesting a young man, just out of the shower, putting on cologne: "It's summer, late afternoon, and you're lying in a shaft of sunlight." Villella recounted no overt discussion of narcissism, but it is fairly safe to presume that this work will remain in active repertoires as long as there are mirrors in classrooms.

—Harris Green

---

## AGON

**Choreography:** George Balanchine
**Music:** Igor Stravinsky
**First Production:** New York City Ballet, City Center, New York, 1 December 1957 (preview at benefit performance, New York, 27 November 1957)
**Principal dancers:** Diana Adams and Arthur Mitchell; Melissa Hayden, Todd Bolender

**Other productions include:** San Francisco Ballet; San Francisco, 10 April 1967. Stuttgart Ballet; Stuttgart, 6 June 1970. Dance Theatre of Harlem; Spoleto Festival, July 1971. Royal Ballet (staged Patricia Neary after Balanchine), with Vergie Derman, David Wall, Wendy Ellis, Anthony Dowell; London, 25 January 1973. Paris Opéra Ballet; Paris, 13 March 1974. Dutch National Ballet; Amsterdam, 16 June 1974. Hamburg Ballet (staged Neary after Balanchine); Hamburg, 12 September 1976. German Opera Ballet (staged Neary after Balanchine); Berlin, 5 November 1977. Zurich Opera Ballet (staged Neary after Balanchine); Zurich, 9 September 1978.

German Opera Ballet (new version; chor. Tatiana Gsovsky); Berlin, 3 May 1958. Royal Ballet (new version; chor. Kenneth MacMillan, design Nicholas Georgiadis), with David Blair, Anya Linden; London, 20 August 1958. Royal Danish Ballet (new version; chor. Eske Holm); Copenhagen, 27 January 1967.

### PUBLICATIONS


Brundage, Christine, "*Agon*: Its Future Importance", *Dance Magazine* (New York), September 1958

Denby, Edwin, "Three Sides of *Agon*", *Evergreen Review* (New York), Winter 1959; reprinted in Denby, *Dancers, Buildings and People in the Streets*, New York, 1965

Kirstein, Lincoln, *Movement and Metaphor*, New York, 1970

Balanchine, George, with Mason, Francis, *Balanchine's Complete Stories of the Great Ballets*, Garden City, New York, 1977

Siegel, Marcia, *The Shapes of Change*, Boston, 1979

Alm, Irene Marion, *Stravinsky, Balanchine and Agon: The Collaborative Process*, PhD., University of California, Los Angeles, 1985

Drewal, Margaret T., "Constructionist Concepts in Balanchine's Choreography", *Ballet Review* (New York), Fall 1985


* * *

*Agon* is a dance for twelve dancers—eight women and four men clad in black and practice clothes—whose title is taken from the Greek word for "combat". It is one of the most astringently beautiful works of the twentieth century, one of Balanchine's seminal works which, were his others lost, would allow us to intuit all the rest.

The piece is divided into twelve sections following its score, a masterwork of Stravinsky's seventies composed especially for this ballet. The music was inspired by a book of French court dances; the dancing echoes in the same way its origins in courtly divertissements, in part through some of its configurations (the four trios near the end) and in part through the constant gestures of ritual politeness of the dancers. The male solo in the Sarabande, for example, ends with a bow and a hand held across the chest; the two women of the subsequent Galliarde engage in an exchange of flourishes that evokes exaggerated politeness: you, no you, no you. And underneath the music can be heard intermittently, as if submerged and floating to the surface, strains of court dances.

The movement as well is a mixture of classical patterns and distinctly twentieth-century variations upon them. The opening of the piece includes flexed ankles for the four men along with their fugue-like 1-2-3-4 kicks, macho-walks with broadly swinging arms, and jumps with flexed legs forming two

***Agon*, with Diana Adams and Arthur Mitchell, New York City Ballet, 1957**

repeating curves in the air like quotation marks. The eight women enter in the second section to agitated music for oboe and strings, their unceasing kicks making them look like a swarm of insects. In the Bransle Simple of the second pas de trois, two men manipulate a woman: the men never lose contact with her, showing her off as if she were a jewel in a setting while she, for her part, twists like a worm on a hook. In the first pas de trois, the gender roles are reversed. The lone man offers a supporting hand to first one woman, then the other, ending up with crossed arms—a joke in ballet terms, yet a movement which somehow looks beautiful, almost tender. In his subsequent solo the man follows a beautiful feathery kick with a gesture that looks like the squashing of a bug on the floor. But so meditatively does he do it that this move too ends by seeming elegant.

The solo for his female counterpart, the lone woman of the second pas de trois, is performed to castanets—a tour de force of seamless dance done without a net. The dancer looks as if she is demonstrating the technique in a movement style which is unknown to the audience but ingrained in herself: she spins out a line of motion to the inexorable clicking, her arms reaching out into the air and twice echoing the motions of the castanets that propel her. Then suddenly she is through, as if a tape had simply run out of a machine.

That part of the dance which viewers tend to remember the most intensely, however, is the pas de deux that ends the second of the work's three major sub-divisions (also containing the two pas de trois). In this section the man both manipulates and is in thrall to the woman, and the result is at once erotic and anaphrodisiac, simultaneously old-fashioned and futuristic, both reminiscent of machines and deeply human. Like liquid moving to fill in spaces defined for it, the woman moves to the man's hands or flows into the strange positions he assumes, her pretzel-like twists around him and head-back-to-toe bends like the motions of a fist clasping and unclasping. At times, the woman seems to be seeking help from the man as she hides her head against his body; at times the two echo each others' movements. Finally, they break apart briefly; then the man sidles over again and takes the woman's hand. The music becomes agitated, the dancers intertwine again, and the dance ends with the man on his knees before the woman, bodies folded around each other.

*Agon* has been recognized as a masterpiece since its first performance.

—Bruce Fleming

---

**ALBERT, Monsieur**

French dancer and choreographer. Born François Decombe (later adopted name of Albert) in Bordeaux, 15 April 1787. Studied with Lefebvre while engaged at the Théâtre de la Gaîté, Paris, and with Jean-François Coulon, at L'Académie royale de musique (Paris Opéra). Married Louise Albert-Himm: daughter, Elisa Albert-Bellon, a pupil and dancer of the Paris Opéra. Theatre début dancing in Bordeaux, 1799; also performed at Théâtre de la Gaîté, Paris; dancer, Paris Opéra, from 1803 (official début, 1808); premier sujet, from 1811, premier danseur, 1817–35, also performing frequently at King's Theatre, London; first choreography (*Le Séducteur au village*), 1818; maître des ballets adjoint, Paris Opéra, from 1822: maître de ballet, 1829–42; also produced ballets in Lyon, 1921, King's (later Her Majesty's) Theatre, London, 1821–22, 1832, 1837, Teatro San Carlo, Naples, 1825, Hofoper, Vienna, 1830, Brussels, 1838–40, and Drury Lane Theatre, London, 1844–45. Died in Fontainebleau, 19 July 1865.

## ROLES

1806 Paul (cr) in *Paul et Virginie* (P. Gardel), Court Theatre, Saint-Claude (later staged Opéra, Paris)
1813 Germeuil (cr) in *Nina* (Milon), Opéra, Paris
1815 Zéphire in *Flore et Zéphire* (Didelot), Opéra, Paris
1818 Mathieu in *La Servante justifiée* (P. Gardel), Opéra, Paris
Mectal (cr) in *Le Seducteur au village* (also chor.), Opéra Paris
1820 Duke of Mevilla (cr) in *Clari; ou, La Promesse de mariage* (Milon), Opéra, Paris
1821 Principal dancer in *Dansomanie* (P. Gardel), Opéra, Paris
1822 Title role (cr) in *Alfred le grand* (Paris production; Aumer), Opéra, Paris
Prince (cr) in *Cendrillon* (also chor.), King's Theatre, London (staged and performed Paris Opéra, 1823)
1826 Mars in *Mars et Vénus* (J.B. Blache), Opéra, Paris
1827 Astolphe (cr) in *Astolphe et Joconde; ou, Les Coureurs d'aventures* (Aumer), Opéra, Paris
Alphonse (cr) in *Le Sicilien; ou, L'Amour peintre* (A. Petit), Opéra, Paris
1828 Amyntas (cr) in *Lydie* (new version of *La Coquette soumise*; Aumer), Opéra, Paris
1833 Divertissement in *Inès de Castro* (Cortesi), King's Theatre, London
1841 Youth (cr) in *Aglaë; ou, L'Élève d'amour* (F. Taglioni), Her Majesty's Theatre, London
1842 The Marquis de San Lucar (cr) in *La Jolie Fille de Gand* (also chor.), Opéra, Paris
1845 Massachio (cr) in *The Marble Maiden* (also chor.), Drury Lane Theatre, London

**Other roles include:** Title role in *Achille* (P. Gardel), Pâris in *Le Jugement de Pâris* (P. Gardel).

## WORKS

1818 *Le Séducteur au village* (mus. Schneitzhoeffer), Opéra, Paris
1821 *Oenone et Pâris*, King's Theatre, London
*Finette et l'éveillé*, King's Theatre, London
*Alcide* (with Deshayes), King's Theatre, London
1822 *Cendrillon* (mus. A. Sor), King's Theatre, London (revived Paris Opéra, 1823)
1830 *Daphnis und Céphise* (mus. L. de Saint-Lubin), Hofoper, Vienna
*Der Zauberring* (mus. Gallenberg), Hofoper, Vienna
1832 *Une Heure à Naples* (mus. Costa), King's Theatre, London
*L'Anneau magique* (new production of *Der Zauberring*; mus. Gallenberg), King's Theatre, London
*Amynthe et l'Amour*, King's Theatre, London
1837 *Le Corsaire* (mus. N. Bochsa), King's Theatre, London
1840 Divertissements in *La Favorite* (opera; mus. Donizetti), Opéra, Paris
1842 *La Jolie Fille de Gand* (mus. Adam), Opéra, Paris
1843 Divertissements in *Dom Sébastien de Portugal* (opera; mus. Donizetti), Opéra, Paris
1844 *Le Corsaire* (revised version; mus. Bochsa), Drury Lane Theatre, London

**Monsieur Albert (François-Decombe) with Emilie Bigottini in *Cendrillon*, Paris Opéra, 1823**

1845 *The Marble Maiden* (mus. Adam), Drury Lane Theatre, London

## PUBLICATIONS

By Albert:
*L'art de la danse à la ville et à la cour, manuel à l'usage des maîtres a danser, des mères de famille et maîtresses de pension*, Paris, 1834

About Albert:
Beaumont, Cyril, *Complete Book of Ballets*, revised edition, London, 1951
Moore, Lillian, "Forgotten Dancers of the Nineteenth Century", *Dance Magazine* (New York), December 1953
Guest, Ivor, *The Romantic Ballet in England*, London, 1954
Guest, Ivor, "*La Jolie Fille de Gand*", *Dancing Times* (London), August 1966
Guest, Ivor, *The Romantic Ballet in Paris*, London, 1966
Chapman, John, "Auguste Vestris and the Expansion of Technique", *Dance Research Journal* (New York), Summer 1987

* * *

The early part of the nineteenth century was an exciting time for dance, a period of transition still rooted in the aristocratic styles and approaches of the eighteenth century, but already moving with the currents created by the romantic voyage into the sublime and the ridiculous. No dancer's career reflected these cross-currents better than that of Monsieur Albert. For he was the last great "danseur noble", dancing life into a highly traditional, aristocratic style that had already started to fade during the French Revolution. Yet at the same time he was among those teachers whose innovative training methods made the romantic ballet possible.

Albert began dancing in his home town of Bordeaux, where he probably saw the exemplary works of Jean Dauberval, and at the Théâtre de la Gaîté in Paris, where dancing was less strict than at the Opéra. His innovations as a teacher, and his willingness to embrace new approaches as a ballet master, may well have been the result of these early experiences outside the Paris Opéra.

Though he began appearing as an apprentice dancer at the Opéra in 1803, Albert had to wait until 1808 for an official Opéra début. It was a time when almost all his young colleagues were following the example of the brilliant Auguste Vestris, who had merged the three traditional genres of dance in order to execute more difficult, technically complex steps. General audiences cheered the athleticism. Connoisseurs despaired, for the most valued and beautiful of all styles, the danse noble, was being abandoned. Thus, when the handsome, noble Albert appeared in 1808, the cognoscenti breathed a collective sigh of relief, and hailed the future defender of the order.

Geoffroy, critic for *Le Journal des Débats* and one of the cognoscenti, wrote about that début, underlining Albert's natural gifts for the noble genre: "Nature has singularly favoured M. Albert; a beautiful face and physique, a great vigour, a superb elevation, brilliant legs, and feet such as art demands." It was not long before Albert was recognized by the élite as "the most beautiful dancer in Europe". His noble stage presence went to his very soul, for he maintained the essence of his style outside the theatre as well as within. He was well-educated in the arts and a model of social behaviour. Bournonville, who studied in Paris in the 1820s and 1830s, knew him:

> He was a complete gentleman, both offstage and on. Music and painting had formed his taste, and study of the classics had clarified his aesthetic views. He was a true artist . . . I have always retained the feeling of respect which his rare talent, combined with his whole manner, inspired in me during the early years of my youth. The word 'gentleman-like' fully describes Albert's demeanour as a dancer: noble, vigorous, gallant, modest, ardent, friendly, gay . . .

Thus Albert embodied the qualities that had distinguished the dance of the eighteenth century, a dance expressive of man at his most perfect. The intrinsic nobility of Albert's style meant that he was especially fine in the roles of the classical repertoire—Achille in Pierre Gardel's *Achille*, and Pâris in his *Le Jugement de Pâris*, and Mars in J.B. Blache's *Mars et Vénus*. He was also suited to royal characters, such as the Prince in his own *Cendrillon* and King Alfred in Jean Aumer's *Alfred le grand*.

As a teacher, Albert joined with men like Filippo Taglioni to introduce "a new gymnastic, more scientific, better applied, a well-directed method that discarded none of the principles that were recognized as being excellent, but that added to it new combinations, long, hard and progressive enchaînements, whose results were to form the chest, give control to the legs, and harden the whole body for the most difficult and complicated movements". These new methods imparted the strength and stamina necessary to the mastery of the highly athletic technique that typified the romantic era. Ironically, the style that resulted rendered Albert's own genre obsolete.

Albert was also a ballet master (maître des ballets adjoint at the Opéra from 1822) but, though competent, did not show in this role the brilliance that characterized his dancing and teaching. He produced only three works at the Opéra, *Le Séducteur au village* (1818), *Cendrillon* (1823), and *La Jolie Fille de Gand* (1842). Their subjects indicate a forward-looking artist, sensitive to the tastes of the periods of their creation. As with his teaching, Albert did not attempt to keep old traditions alive for their own sake.

Albert's works also reflected contemporary practices in his emphasis on dance and spectacle. Of his *Cendrillon*, the *Constitutionnel* critic wrote that the décor, costumes, and dancing were brilliant, but that the pantomime, or story-telling part of the ballet, was underdeveloped. The same paper wrote of his *Jolie Fille* that it possessed "excellent dances, ravishing steps and a spectacle full of grace, elegance and brilliance". It was thus that ballet masters broke the older *ballet d'action* mould, emphasizing dance over the representation of a dramatic action, and thus that Albert once again abandoned the neo-classical past in favour of approaches that were expanding the place of dance in ballets.

Though Paris was the centre of Albert's activities, he worked as ballet master and dancer in many European centres, such as London, Naples, Vienna, and Brussels. He was an energetic, highly talented, skilled, and forward-looking dance artist whose activities contributed much to the development of European ballet technique in the nineteenth century.

—John Chapman

---

**ALLARD, Marie**

French dancer. Born in Marseilles, 14 August 1742 (some sources say 1738). Studied as an apprentice at Comédie de Marseille; later studied with Gaetano Vestris, Paris. One son, by dancer and choreographer Gaetano Vestris, dancer Auguste Vestris, born 1760. Early stage appearances as actress, Comédie de Marseille, from c. 1752; prima ballerina, Opera House, Lyons, from c. 1754; moved to Paris, 1756; dancer, corps de ballet, Comédie Française, from 1756; Paris Opéra début, in *Zaïs* (ballet héroïque; mus. Rameau), 1761, becoming leading danseuse; first danced with leading Opéra danseur, Jean Dauberval, 1766; also choreographer: thought to have staged her own entrées and divertissements; recipient of royal pension, as a dancer of ballets de la cour, 1780; retired from the stage in 1781. Died in Paris, 14 January 1802.

**ROLES**

1761 Dancer in *Zaïs* (ballet-héroïque; mus. Rameau), Opéra, Paris
Dancer in *Armide* (tragédie-lyrique; mus. Lully), Opéra, Paris
Une Matelotte in *Les Indes galantes* (ballet-héroïque; mus. Rameau), Opéra, Paris
1762 Dancer in *Iphigénie en Tauride* (tragédie-lyrique; mus. Desmarets, Campra, Berton), Opéra, Paris
Dancer (cr) in *L'Opéra de société* (ballet; mus. Giraud), Opéra, Paris
La Statue animée in *Pygmalion* (fifth entrée in *Le Triomphe des arts*, ballet; mus. La Barre, Rameau), Opéra, Paris
1763 Dancer (cr) in *Polyxène* (tragédie-lyrique; mus. Dauvergne), Opéra, Paris
1764 Dancer in *Castor et Pollux* (tragédie-lyrique; mus. Rameau), Opéra, Paris
Terpsichore in *Les Fêtes d'Hébé; ou, Les Talents lyriques* (ballet; mus. Rameau), Opéra, Paris
Dancer in *Naïs, opéra pour la paix* (ballet-héroïque; mus. Rameau), Opéra, Paris
1765 Dancer (cr) in *Bacchus et Hégémone* (mus. Dauvergne), Opéra, Paris
Une Pastourelle in *Le Devin du village* (intermède; mus. Rousseau), Opéra, Paris
Une Sauvagesse in *Les Fêtes de l'Hymen et de l'Amour* (ballet-héroïque; mus. Rameau), Opéra, Paris
Une Furie in *Thésée* (tragédie-lyrique; mus. Lully), Opéra, Paris
1766 Dancer in *Les Fêtes lyriques* (fragments of various ballets), Opéra, Paris
Une Nymphe (cr) in *Sylvie* (ballet; mus. Berton, Trial), Opéra, Paris
1767 Terpsichore in *Le Carnaval du Parnasse* (opéra-ballet; mus. Mondonville), Opéra, Paris
Une Pastourelle in *La Terre* (act from *Les Eléments*, ballet; mus. Destouches), Opéra, Paris
Dancer (cr) in *Ernelinde* (tragédie-lyrique; mus. Philidor), Opéra, Paris
Terpsichore in *Les Fêtes grecques et romaines* (ballet héroique; mus. de Blamont), Opéra, Paris
Une Matelotte, Une Chasseresse in *Hippolyte et Aricie* (tragédie-lyrique; mus. Rameau), Opéra, Paris
Dancer (cr) in *Théonis* (pastorale; mus. Berton, Trial), Opéra, Paris
1768 Dancer in *Daphnis et Alcimadure* (pastorale; mus. Mondonville), Opéra, Paris
Dancer (cr) in *Titon et l'Aurore* (pastorale; mus. Mondonville), Opéra, Paris
Dancer in *La Vénitienne* (ballet; new mus. Dauvergne), Opéra, Paris
1769 Un Plaisir in *Anacréon* (ballet-héroïque; mus. Rameau), Opéra, Paris
Dancer in *Dardanus* (tragédie-lyrique; mus. Rameau), Opéra, Paris
Une Bacchante in *Enée et Lavinie* (tragédie-lyrique; new mus. Dauvergne), Opéra, Paris
1770 Médée in *Médée et Jason* (ballet; Noverre), Opéra, Paris
Dancer in *Zoroastre* (tragédie-lyrique; mus. Rameau), Opéra, Paris
1771 Dancer in *Alcione* (tragédie-lyrique; mus. Marais), Opéra, Paris
Dancer (cr) in *La Cinquantaine* (pastorale; mus. Laborde), Opéra, Paris
Dancer (cr) in *La Fête de Flore* (ballet; mus. Trial), Opéra, Paris
Dancer in *Pyrame et Thisbé* (tragédie-lyrique; mus. Rebel, Francoeur), Opéra, Paris
1772 Dancer (cr) in *Adèle de Ponthieu* (tragédie-lyrique; mus. Laborde, Berton), Opéra, Paris
Dancer in *Aline, reine de Golconde* (ballet-héroïque; mus. Monsigny), Opéra, Paris
Dancer (cr) in *Églé* (ballet; mus. Lagarde), Opéra, Paris
1773 Dancer in *Les Sauvages* (ballet; mus. Rameau), Opéra, Paris
Dancer (cr) in *L'Union de l'amour et des arts* (opera-ballet; mus. Floquet), Opéra, Paris
Principal dancer in *Zélindor, roi des Sylphes* (ballet; mus. Rebel, Francoeur), Opéra, Paris
1776 Une Bergère in *Les Romans* (ballet; mus. Niel, Cambini), Opéra, Paris
1778 Dancer (cr) in *La Chercheuse d'esprit* (ballet; M. Gardel), Opéra, Paris
Une Bergère (cr) in *Les Petits Riens* (ballet; Noverre), Opéra, Paris
1779 Dancer in *Alceste* (tragédie-lyrique; new mus. Gluck), Opéra, Paris

**A drawing of Marie Allard as a bacchante (costume design by Louis Boquet)**

Une Pastourelle (cr) in *Echo et Narcisse* (pastorale; mus. Gluck), Opéra, Paris

1780 Dancer (cr) in *Laure et Pétrarque* (pastorale; mus. Candeille), Opéra, Paris

### PUBLICATIONS

Grimm, Frederic Melchior, *Correspondance de Grimm et de Diderot*, Paris, 1829

Campardon, Emile, *L'Académie royale de musique*, 2 volumes, Paris, 1881

Capon, Gaston, *Les Vestris*, Paris, 1908

Migel, Parmenia, *The Ballerinas*, New York, 1972

* * *

Marie Allard, born in Marseilles, is famous as the dancer mother of the renowned French dancer Auguste Vestris, the result of her brief liaison with Opéra choreographer Gaetano Vestris. However, as a performer in her own right, she was one of the most popular female dancers of the second half of the eighteenth century, adored by audiences, critics, and non-partisan observers alike—and her small body, pretty face, and buoyant technique made her the archetypal French ballerina of the time. Parmenia Migel, the twentieth-century dance writer, comments that "her dancing had the piquant, sparkling and very feminine flavor which we tend to associate nowadays not only with the best French danseuses, but with Parisian charmers in general".

Although most sources say that Allard was born in 1742, her baptismal certificate says 1738; her parents are listed as Pierre and Catherine Feuiller Allard. She evidently had a most unhappy childhood and was apprenticed by her parents to the Comédie de Marseille at a very early age. From there she went to the opera at Lyons and then to the corps de ballet of the Comédie Francaise in Paris. Shrewd, self-sufficient, and ambitious, she set the ballet at the Paris Opéra as her goal, and in order to achieve this went to study with the popular and influential dancer Gaetano Vestris. It was after the birth of their son, Marie-Jean Augustin (or Auguste) Vestris, that she finally made her successful début at the Opéra, in the third act of *Zaïs*, in a 1761 revival of the heroic Cahusac ballet to music by Rameau.

Allard's quick movement and vivacious personality were credited by one contemporary observer as inspiring joy in the audience as soon as she made her appearance on stage, a sentiment her talent and technical ability vindicated. She was especially adept at executing rigaudons, gavottes, tabourins, and loures, which put her into the category of what was then known as a "gay" dancer, something we might now call "allegro". She was particularly admired for her performance of the gargouillade, a difficult ballet step which combines a pas de chat with a rond de jambe en l'air.

Marie Allard appeared in 35 different roles in her first ten years at the Opéra, and also found time to work with Vestris in training their son. Among other things, she danced in revivals of *Les Indes galantes*, *Les Fêtes de l'Hymen et de l'Amour*, and *Anacréon*, and danced Médée in Noverre's *Médée et Jason*, which she performed with Vestris. She was actively dancing when the tragic mask was supposedly first discarded by Gardel in 1773, a momentous event in the history of dance.

In the famous and tremendously popular pas de deux she performed with Jean Dauberval in the ballet *Sylvie* (1766), Allard is thought to have choreographed her own entrées. There is a beautiful engraving of this pair, she in the role of a nymph, which exudes the charm of both the dancers and the period.

Allard's private life, which could be termed promiscuous, or, at best, frivolous, was actually typical of a professional dancer in her position at the time. Her several pregnancies often prevented her from fulfilling her dance obligations and she began to put on weight at an early age—none of which deterred either her admiring audience or her devoted patrons. Among the latter were the Duc de Mazarin, who reportedly gave her a life annuity, and a Monsieur de Bontems, a valet of the King, for whom she evidently really cared.

By the time Allard appeared as one of two shepherdesses (the other was Guimard) in *Les Petis Riens*—the 1778 collaboration between Noverre and a very young Mozart—even her most faithful admirers were beginning to think she should retire. This she did in 1781, with a pension of 2,000 francs. (The King had granted her an equal amount as a dancer at court the previous year.) She moved away from Paris and died in 1802 as a result of a stroke.

—Dawn Lille Horwitz

---

## ALMA
(*La Fille de Feu*)

**Choreography**: Fanny Cerrito and Jules Perrot
**Music:** Sir Michael (Michele) Costa
**Design**: William Grieve (scenery)
**Libretto**: A.J.J. Deshayes
**First Production:** Her Majesty's Theatre, London, 23 June 1842
**Principal Dancers:** Fanny Cerrito (Alma) and Jules Perrot (Belfegor)

### PUBLICATIONS

Beaumont, Cyril, *Complete Book of Ballets*, revised edition, London, 1951

Guest, Ivor, *Fanny Cerrito*, London, 1956

Guest, Ivor, *The Romantic Ballet in England*, London, 1954, 1972

Guest, Ivor, *Jules Perrot: Master of the Romantic Ballet*, London, 1984

* * *

In the nineteenth-century ballet *Alma*, the statue of the title is endowed with life, her purpose to enchant and fascinate mankind. So long as she resists the love and passion that she arouses, she will remain alive—but if she succumbs, she will return to stone. Accompanied by the demon Periphite, she first fascinates the people of a German town, and then those at a French ball, where her charms ensnare Emazor, a Moorish prince. Finally, in Granada, she is offered as a prize at a tournament; the winner is Emazor, who is raised to the throne following a sudden revolt against the Spaniards. Alma falls in love with him, but as she is crowned his bride she is turned back to stone.

Although nominally the work of the then ballet master at Her Majesty's Theatre, Deshayes, and with interpolations by Fanny Cerrito, who danced the title role, *Alma's* importance lay in those parts choreographed by Jules Perrot. Of all the episodes in the ballet, the most significant was also the high point for the audience—Perrot's choreography for the "pas de fascination" in the second scene. Here Perrot was the evil demon inciting

**Fanny Cerrito in *Alma*, 1842**

the girls to surrender themselves to the dance, and Cerrito was Alma, mesmerizing all by her passionate yet controlled abandon. In his choreography for Cerrito, Perrot subtly implied Alma's bewitching power, which gradually becomes less controlled as she abandons herself to the passion and excitement. This was no mere interpolated dance episode; Perrot not only carried forward the plot and atmosphere of the ballet in dance terms alone (one of his earliest experiments in this direction), but also made clear through the sequence Alma's hypnotic power and the relationship between her and Periphite, whose mission it is to make Alma yield to temptation and, eventually, love.

In many previous works the action, expressed in mime, had been separate from the danced episodes, but Perrot was now learning to advance the action through dance alone. This form was one he was to develop in subsequent ballets choreographed at Her Majesty's, notably *Ondine* and *La Esmeralda.*

At a time when the ballerina was the undisputed star of the ballet, with her male counterpart consequently falling from favour, Perrot created a dominant role for the male dancer, showing that he could still play a major role in ballet, without becoming the mere background partner and foil to the ballerina. All the same, as Alma, Cerrito fascinated more than her stage companions; audiences went wild, and "Cerritomania" reached its height in London. Indeed many, including Benjamin Lumley, considered the real highlight of the ballet to be Cerrito's own pas de trois, composed by the ballerina herself to great audience acclaim. As historian Ivor Guest has described it, quoting contemporary reviews,

> In her choreography for the *pas de trois*, Cerrito brought out in turn all her voluptuous grace and brilliant attack. The slow movement, in which she evinced "the most refined perception of the beautiful in the arrangement of groups", threw into strong relief the succeeding *allegro* passage with its culminating sequence of *tours*, of a most dazzling rapidity, in which she was described as "flying round the stage and whirling as she flies".

*Alma* was also notable for its completeness as a stage work, successfully blending choreography, music, and décor into a satisfying whole. Costa's score was stronger than most ballet music of the time, and Grieve's sets were a triumph. But victory belonged to Perrot, and the success of *Alma* was such that he was invited to become ballet master at Her Majesty's Theatre.

—Sarah C. Woodcock

---

**ALONSO, Alicia**

Cuban dancer, choreographer, and ballet director. Born Alicia Ernestina de la Caridad del Cobre Martínez y del Hoyo in Havana, 21 December 1921. Studied flamenco dance in Spain as a child; studied ballet at the Sociedad Pro-Arte Musical, Havana, pupil of Nikolai Yavorsky, from 1931, with Alexandra Fedorova, Anatole Vilzak, and Enrico Zanfretti, New York, and at the School of American Ballet, New York, from 1938; also studied with Vera Volkova, London. Married dancer Fernando Alonso, 1937 (div.): one daughter, Laura; married Pedro Simón, 1975. Early career in Broadway musicals: stage début in *Great Lady*, New York, 1938; dancer, Lincoln Kirstein's Ballet Caravan, 1939–40, and Ballet Theatre (later American Ballet Theatre), 1940, returning to Pro-Arte, Havana, 1941–43; ballerina, Ballet Theatre (later American Ballet Theatre), 1943–48; guest ballerina with various companies, including Ballet Russe de Monte Carlo, 1955–60, and on world concert tours, especially in partnership with Igor Youskevitch; guest performer, Soviet Union (first Western ballerina to be invited), 1957–58, 1960; also guest artist with Royal Danish Ballet, Paris Opéra Ballet, Les Grands Ballets Canadiens, and Ballet du XXe Siècle; has continued to tour regularly, including to South America, Russia, China, Eastern Europe, and Africa, and to appear as occasional guest through her 70s, returning to American Ballet Theatre for 50th Anniversary Gala, 1990; has performed at various international arts festivals, including in France, 1966 and 1970, Nervi Festival, Italy, 1974, and Edinburgh Festival in Scotland, 1979, and 1991; has also appeared on film, including as title role in *Giselle* (Ballet Nacional de Cuba, 1963); also choreographer and ballet director: staged numerous ballets, including own works, Pro-Arte, Havana, from 1943; founder and director, Ballet Alicia Alonso, Havana, from 1948 (becoming Ballet de Cuba, 1955, and Ballet Nacional de Cuba, 1959); also staged ballets for many other companies, including Ballet Theatre, 1951, Paris Opéra Ballet, 1972, 1974, Central (National) Ballet of China, Peking, 1964, Vienna State Opera Ballet, and Teatro San Carlo, Naples; regular International Ballet Competition adjudicator, Varna, Moscow, and Tokyo. Recipient: Decoration of Carlos Manuel de Céspedes, 1947; *Dance Magazine* Award, 1958; Grand Prix de la Ville de Paris, 1966 and 1970; Prix Pavlova, 1966; Gold Medal of the Grand Teatro Liceo de Barcelona, 1971; Honorary Doctorate of Arts, University of Havana, 1973; National Hero of Labor, Cuban Workers' Union, 1976; Order "Felix Varela", State Council of the Republic of Cuba, 1981; Honorary Doctorate of Arts, Instituto de Arte, Cuba, 1987; "Great Honour" Award, Japan, 1991.

**ROLES**

1937 Odette/Odile in *Swan Lake* (Petipa, Ivanov; staged Yavorsky), Sociedad Pro-Arte Musical, Havana
1940 Maja (cr) in *Goya Pastoral* (Tudor), Ballet Theatre, New York
Mother/Sweetheart in *Billy the Kid* (Loring), Ballet Theatre, Chicago
1941 Carlotta Grisi in *Pas de quatre* (Dolin after Lester), Ballet Theatre, New York
1943 Waltz and Mazurka in *Les Sylphides* (Fokine), Ballet Theatre, New York
Title role in *Giselle* (Petipa after Coralli, Perrot; staged Dolin), Ballet Theatre, New York
1944 Mother in *Barn Dance* (Littlefield), Ballet Theatre, New York
Pas de deux in *Graduation Ball* (Lichine), Ballet Theatre, Montreal
Episode in his Past in *Jardin aux Lilas* (Tudor), Ballet Theatre, New York
A Wife of Bluebeard in *Bluebeard* (Fokine), Ballet Theatre
Principal dancer in *Capriccio Espagnol* (Massine), Ballet Theatre, New York
1945 Ate (cr) in *Undertow* (Tudor), Ballet Theatre, New York
Principal dancer (cr) in *Graziana* (Taras), Ballet Theatre, New York
Sugar Plum Fairy in *The Nutcracker* Pas de deux (Dolin after Ivanov), Ballet Theatre, New York
Juliet in *Romeo and Juliet* (Tudor), Ballet Theatre, New York
Principal dancer in *Bluebird Pas de deux* (Dolin after Petipa), Ballet Theatre
Girl in Pink in *On Stage!* (Kidd), Ballet Theatre
Kitri in *Don Quixote* Pas de deux (Obukhov after Petipa), Ballet Theatre
1946 Principal dancer (cr) in *Pas de deux* (Obukhov), Ballet Theatre, New York
Terpsichore in *Apollon Musagète* (*Apollo*; Balanchine), Ballet Theatre, New York
The Black Swan (Odile) in *Black Swan Pas de deux* (Petipa; staged Balanchine), Ballet Theatre, New York
Taglion in *Pas de quatre* (Lester), Ballet Theatre, London
The Girl in *Le Spectre de la rose* (Fokine), Ballet Theatre
Principal dancer in *Waltz Academy* (Balanchine), Ballet Theatre
La Déesse de la danse from Milan in *Gala Performance* (Tudor), Ballet Theatre
1947 Odette in *Swan Lake*, Act II (Ivanov; staged Dolin), Ballet Theatre, New York
Principal dancer, lead couple (cr) in *Theme and Variations* (Balanchine), Ballet Theatre, New York
Ballerina in *Petrushka* (Fokine), Ballet Theatre, New York
1948 The Accused (cr; replacing Kaye) in *Fall River Legend* (de Mille), Ballet Theatre, New York
Principal dancer (cr) in *Shadow of the Wind* (Tudor), Ballet Theatre, New York
Title role in *Princess Aurora* (divertissements from *The Sleeping Beauty*; Dolin after Petipa), Ballet Theatre
Swanilda in *Coppélia* (also chor.; after Petipa), Ballet Alicia Alonso, Havana
1949 The Swan in *The Dying Swan* (after Fokine), Ballet Alicia Alonso, Havana
1950 Lise in *La Fille mal gardée* (D. Romanoff), Ballet Theatre
1951 Principal dancer in *Concerto* (also called *Constantia*; Dollar), Ballet Theatre, New York
Principal dancer (cr) in *Schumann Concerto* (Nijinska), Ballet Theatre, New York
Principal dancer in *Tropical Pas de deux* (revival of *Fiesta Negra*; Martinez), Ballet Theatre, New York
1956 Columbine (cr) in *Harlequinade* (B. Romanov), Ballet Russe de Monte Carlo, Chicago
1958 Juliet (cr) in *Romeo and Juliet* (Alberto Alonso), Ballet de Cuba, Havana
1960 Liberty (cr) in *Despertar* (Martínez), Ballet Nacional de Cuba, Havana
Juana (cr) in *Juana en Rouen* (Leontieva), Ballet Nacional de Cuba, Havana
1963 Principal dancer in *Melódia* (Messerer), Ballet Nacional de Cuba, Havana
Miller's Wife in *Le Tricorne* (Massine; staged Rodríguez), Ballet Nacional de Cuba, Havana
1964 The Soldier in *La Avanzada* (Plisetskaya), Ballet Nacional de Cuba, Havana
The Wife in *La Nueva Odisea* (Köhler-Richter), Ballet Nacional de Cuba, Havana
1965 The Woman (cr) in *La Carta* (also chor.), Ballet Nacional de Cuba, Havana
1966 La Mestiza (cr) in *Mestiza* (Monreal), Ballet Nacional de Cuba, Havana
1967 Carmen in *Carmen Suite* (Alberto Alonso), Ballet Nacional de Cuba, Havana
1969 Julieta (cr) in *Un Retablo para Romeo y Julieta* (Alberto Alonso), Ballet Nacional de Cuba, Havana
1970 Julieta (cr) in *Un Retablo para Romeo y Julieta* (new version; Alberto Alonso), Ballet Nacional de Cuba, Havana
Jocasta (cr) in *Oedipus Rex* (Jorge Lefebre), Ballet Nacional de Cuba, Havana
Pas de deux from *The Flames of Paris* (after Vainonen), Ballet Nacional de Cuba, Havana
1971 Margarita (Marguerite) (cr) in *Nos Veremos ayer Noche, Margarita* (Méndez), Ballet Nacional de Cuba, Havana
1972 Principal dancer (cr) in *A Santiago* (Alberto Alonso), Ballet Nacional de Cuba, Santiago de Cuba
1974 Leading role (cr) in *Mujer* (Méndez), Ballet Nacional de Cuba, Havana
1975 Leading role in *Salomé* (Lefebre), Ballet Nacional de Cuba, Havana
Principal dancer (cr) in *Yagruma* (Lefebre), Ballet Nacional de Cuba, Havana
1976 Principal dancer in *Cecilia Valdés* (Herrera), Ballet Nacional de Cuba, Havana
Title role (cr) in *La Perí* (pas de deux; Méndez), Ballet Nacional de Cuba, Havana
1977 Principal dancer in *Canción para la extraña flor* (Méndez), Ballet Nacional de Cuba, Havana
Principal dancer (cr) in *Los Pinos Nuevos* (Herrera), Ballet Nacional de Cuba, Havana
1978 Principal dancer (cr) in *Ad Libitum* (Méndez), Ballet Nacional de Cuba, Havana
Principal dancer in *In the Night* (Robbins), Ballet Nacional de Cuba, Havana
Principal dancer (cr) in *Remembranza* (Macdonald), Ballet Nacional de Cuba, Havana
Principal dancer (cr) in *Spartacus* (pas de deux; Plisetskaya), Ballet Nacional de Cuba, Havana
1979 Cleopatra in *La Muerte de Cleopatra* (Biagi), Ballet Nacional de Cuba, Havana

**Alicia Alonso as Giselle**

Principal dancer (cr) in *Danza con la Guitarra* (Méndez), Ballet Nacional de Cuba, Havana
1980 Sor Helena (cr) in *Roberto el Diablo* (Méndez), Ballet Nacional de Cuba, Guanajuato
Lady Macbeth in *La Corona Sangrienta* (Tenorio), Ballet Nacional de Cuba, Charleston, South Carolina
Thoris (cr) in *Misión Korad* (also chor.), Ballet Nacional de Cuba, Havana
Principal dancer (cr) in *Canon* (Méndez), Ballet Nacional de Cuba, Havana
1981 Lucrecía (cr) in *Lucrecía Borgia* (Méndez), Ballet Nacional de Cuba, Havana
1982 Title role (cr) in *La Diva* (Méndez), Ballet Nacional de Cuba, Havana
Katy (cr) in *Cumbres Borrascosas* (Alberto Alonso), Ballet Nacional de Cuba, Havana
Title role in *Medea* (Nemecek), Ballet Nacional de Cuba, Havana
1983 Principal dancer (cr) in *Tributo a José White* (Alberto Alonso), Ballet Nacional de Cuba, Havana
1984 The Harmony (cr) in *La Saeta Dorada* (Méndez), Ballet Nacional de Cuba, Havana
Title role (cr) in *Fedra* (Tenorio), Ballet Nacional de Cuba, Havana
1985 Principal dancer in *Devaneo* (Magalhaes), Ballet Nacional de Cuba, Havana
1986 The Actress (cr) in *Diario Perdido* (Alberto Alonso), Ballet Nacional de Cuba, Havana
Ana de Glavaris (cr) in *La Viuda Alegre* (Méndez), Ballet Nacional de Cuba, Havana
1988 Barbara (cr) in *Jardín* (Riveros), Ballet Nacional de Cuba, Havana
Title role (cr) in *Dido Abandonada* (also chor.), Ballet Nacional de Cuba, Havana
1989 Principal dancer (cr) in *Amaris* (Lambrou), Ballet Nacional de Cuba, Havana
1990 Principal dancer (cr) in *Azor* (Méndez), Ballet Nacional de Cuba, Havana
Love (cr) in *Poema del Amor y del Mar* (Méndez), Ballet Nacional de Cuba, Palma de Mallorca, Spain
Principal dancer (cr) in *Sinfonía de Gottschalk* (also chor.), Ballet Nacional de Cuba, Havana
Principal dancer (cr) in *Retrato de un Vals* (also chor.), Ballet Nacional de Cuba, Havana

**Other roles include:** Principal dancer in *Grand Pas classique* (pas de deux; V. Gsovsky), the Sylph in *La Sylphide* (after Bournonville), title role in *Paquita* (after Petipa), principal dancer in *Raymonda* Pas de deux (after Petipa).

## WORKS

1943 *La Condesita* (mus. Nin), Sociedad Pro-Arte, Havana
*La Tinaja* (mus. Ravel), Sociedad Pro-Arte, Havana
1950 *Ensayos Sinfónicos* (mus. Brahms), Ballet Alicia Alonso, Havana (staged as *Ensayo Sinfónico* for Ballet Theatre, New York, 1951)
1951 *Lydia* (mus. A. Nugué), Ballet Alicia Alonso, Havana
1952 *El Pillete* (mus. Sibelius), Ballet Alicia Alonso, Havana
1955 *Narciso y Eco* (mus. Debussy), Ballet de Cuba, Havana
1965 *La Carta* (mus. Mántici), Ballet Nacional de Cuba, Havana
1967 *El Circo* (mus. Mántici), Ballet Nacional de Cuba, Havana
1978 *Genesis* (mus. Nono), Ballet Nacional de Cuba, Havana
1980 *Misión Korad* (mus. arranged Alvarez), Ballet Nacional de Cuba, Havana
1987 *El Caminante* (mus. Sanchez de Fuentes), Opera de Cuba
1988 *Dido Abandonada* (mus. Angiolini), Ballet Nacional de Cuba, Havana
1990 *Sinfonía de Gottschalk* (mus. Gottschalk), Ballet Nacional de Cuba, Havana
*Pretextes* (mus. Marbhant), Ballet Nacional de Cuba, Havana
*Retrato de un Vals* (mus. Lecuona), Ballet Nacional de Cuba, Havana

Also staged:
1945 *Giselle* (after Petipa, Coralli, Perrot; mus. Adam), Sociedad Pro-Arte Musical, Havana (staged Ballet Alicia Alonso, Havana, 1948; Teatro Colón, Buenos Aires, 1958; Los Angeles Ballet, 1958; Paris Opéra Ballet, 1972; Vienna State Opera Ballet, 1980; Teatro San Carlos, Naples, 1981; National Ballet of Czechoslovakia, 1989)
*(Grand) Pas de quatre* (after Lester; mus. Pugni), Ballet Alicia Alonso, Havana (staged Central Ballet of China, Peking, 1964; Paris Opéra Ballet, 1973; Teatro de Bellas Artes, Mexico, 1976; Grand Theatre, Warsaw, 1980; Rome Opera Ballet, 1987)
1950 *Don Quixote* Pas de deux (after Petipa, Obukhov; mus. Minkus), Ballet Alicia Alonso, Havana
*The Nutcracker* Pas de deux (Act I, after Ivanov; mus. Tchaikovsky), Ballet Alicia Alonso, Havana
1952 *La Fille mal gardée* (after Dauberval; mus. Hertel), Ballet Alicia Alonso, Havana (staged Central Ballet of China, 1964; Teatro de Bellas Artes, Mexico, 1976; National Theatre, Prague, 1980; Sofia Opera, 1985; Ballet de Cali, Colombia, 1991)
1954 *Swan Lake* (after Petipa, Ivanov; mus. Tchaikovsky), Ballet Alicia Alonso, Havana (staged Teatro de Bellas Artes, Mexico, 1976)
1957 *Coppélia* (after Petipa; mus. Delibes), Los Angeles Ballet, Los Angeles (staged Teatro de Bellas Artes, Mexico)
1968 *Grand Pas classique* (after V. Gsovsky), Ballet Nacional de Cuba, Havana
1970 *Raymonda* Pas de deux (after Petipa; mus. Glazunov), Ballet Nacional de Cuba, Havana
*The Flames of Paris* (after Vainonen; mus. Asafiev), Ballet Nacional de Cuba, Havana
1974 *The Sleeping Beauty* (after Petipa; mus. Tchaikovsky), Paris Opéra Ballet, Paris (staged La Scala, Milan, 1983)
*Le Corsaire* Pas de deux (after Petipa; mus. Drigo), Ballet Nacional de Cuba, Havana
1981 "Kingdom of the Shades" scene from *La Bayadère* (after Petipa; mus. Minkus), Ballet Nacional de Cuba, Havana
1984 *Paquita Grand Pas* (after Petipa; mus. Minkus), Ballet Nacional de Cuba, Havana
1987 *Diana and Acteon* Pas de deux (from *La Esmeralda*; after Vaganova, Petipa; mus. Pugni), Ballet Nacional de Cuba, Havana

## PUBLICATIONS

By Alonso:
"Performing *Giselle*", in Payne, Charles, *American Ballet Theatre*, New York, 1978

*Alicia Alonso*, Barcelona, 1981
Interview in Newman, Barbara, *Speaking of Dance: Dancers Talk About Dancing*, Boston, 1982
*Diálogos con la danza*, Havana, 1986

About Alonso:
Percival, John, "Caribbean Classic", *Dance and Dancers* (London), January 1967
Lidova, Irène, "Alicia Alonso", *Les Saisons de la danse* (Paris), November 1970
Gamez, Tana de, *Alicia Alonso at Home and Abroad*, New York, 1971
Goldner, Nancy, "Alicia Alonso", *Dance News* (New York), June 1971
Horosko, Marian, "Alicia Alonso, the 'Flower of Cuba'", *Dance Magazine* (New York), August 1971
Anderson, Jack, "An American Beauty", *Dance Magazine* (New York), October 1976
Cabrera, Miguel, *Orbita del Ballet Nacional de Cuba 1948–1978*, Havana, 1978
Maynard, Olga, "Alicia Alonso and the National Ballet of Cuba", *Dance Magazine* (New York), June 1978
Payne, Charles, *American Ballet Theatre*, New York, 1978
Siegel, Beatrice, *Alicia Alonso*, New York and London, 1979
Terry, Walter, *Alicia and her Ballet Nacional de Cuba*, Garden City, N.Y., 1981
Simón, Pedro, *Alicia Alonso—Vladimir Vasiliev—Giselle*, Havana, 1982
Baquero, Joaquin, *Alicia Alonso*, Havana, 1984
Percival, John, "A Living National Treasure", *Dance and Dancers* (London), May 1984
Denby, Edwin, *Dance Writings*, edited by Robert Cornfield and William Mackay, New York, 1986
Maynard, Olga, *El Legado de Alicia Alonso*, Havana, 1988
De Mille, Agnes, "Cuba's National Treasure: ¡Viva Alicia!", *Dance Magazine* (New York), August 1990
Sinclair, Janet, "O Rare Alicia Alonso", *Dance and Dancers* (London), August 1991

* * *

Alicia Alonso, prima ballerina assoluta of the Ballet Nacional de Cuba, started her professional career while still in her teens, in American musicals. She received her early training in her home town of Havana, where ballet was taught for the first time in Cuba (in the 1930s) by Nikolai Yavorski, a Russian emigré and former officer in the Czarist army. On arrival in New York she took classes with Fedorova and Zanfretti, and developed an exceptional technique which took her swiftly from *Stars in Your Eyes* to Kirstein and Balanchine's Ballet Caravan—and thence, only a year later, to the new Ballet Theatre (later American Ballet Theatre, or ABT).

In 1943, shortly after Alonso's return from Havana, where serious eye trouble had held her prostrate for many months, she made her first appearance as Giselle with Ballet Theatre, partnered by Anton Dolin. (Prima ballerina Alicia Markova had been taken ill.) Edwin Denby, who reviewed all her appearances at this time, described her as "a meticulous stylist . . . of classic precision and lightness", and as "a very Latin Giselle".

Denby admired Alonso as much for her lyrical qualities in such works as Fokine's *Les Sylphides*, Balanchine's *Apollo*, and Tudor's *Lilac Garden*, as in the dramatic roles of Lizzie Borden in de Mille's *Fall River Legend*, and Ate in Tudor's *Undertow*: in the relatively minor role of "this hideous creature with obscene features who leads all men into evil", he described her performance as "phenomenal".

The richest period of Alonso's dancing career began when Igor Youskevitch joined Ballet Theatre and became her partner in 1946. For them Balanchine created *Theme and Variations* in 1947, and Nijinska choreographed *Schumann Concerto* on them in 1951; both were abstract pieces which exploited to the full their refined classical virtuosity and the warmth of their combined personalities. While dancing together for fourteen years all over the world, Alonso and Youskevitch worked constantly on their interpretation of *Giselle*, which became, in the opinion of many, the greatest partnership of the century in this work. Youskevitch still speaks today of Alonso as "the greatest Giselle I ever danced with", and recalls "her vitality and lightness . . . her physical and spiritual integration with the role".

A profound study of romanticism in all its aspects, combined with a firm commitment to making ballet an art for all in the twentieth century, characterizes Alonso's production of this work for the Ballet Nacional de Cuba, which integrates the emotions of real life with the delicate fantasy of the ballet's original style. In the 1960s Arnold Haskell called this Giselle "the first perfect production I have ever seen in my long career. Now more than ever I believe in the ballet." Alonso has since mounted her *Giselle* on companies around the world.

An invitation to perform in the USSR in 1957–58 gave Alonso and her husband, Fernando, insights into Soviet methods of ballet education which, together with what she had learned in the United States from Fokine, Massine, Tudor, Balanchine, and de Mille, were to prove invaluable in the development of the Ballet Nacional de Cuba. The seeds of this company had been sown in Havana ten years before, with the creation of the Ballet Alicia Alonso.

In 1959, Alonso was at the height of her powers and personality, admired equally in the communist East and the capitalist West. The U.S. *Dance Magazine* had awarded her its Silver Trophy "for illuminating the purity of the classic dance with her radiant warmth". 1959 was also the year of the Cuban Revolution. A passionate patriot and revolutionary from her earliest years, Alonso was free to return home. With an immediate and generous state subsidy, she was able to devote all her phenomenal energies to the creation of her long-envisaged Cuban school of ballet, and a national company with its own choreographers and its own repertoire reflecting the diverse cultural influences of music-and-dance-loving, Latin-American, Afro-Caribbean Cuba.

Since 1959 Alonso has been teacher, choreographer, director, and prima ballerina assoluta. She has mounted and danced in all the jewels of the classical repertory with the company, which has grown to include 135 dancers. Pupils of the Cuban school of ballet have, since Varna in 1964, won golden opinions and gold medals from New York to Japan. As a choreographer, Alonso has used themes ranging from classical mythology (*Dido Abandonada*) to science fiction (*Misión Korad*). One of her first pupils, the choreographer Alberto Méndez, has created for her roles as diverse as Lucrezia Borgia and the Merry Widow, with Lady Macbeth, Marguerite Gautier, Maria Callas, and a seductively enigmatic nun, Sister Helena (*Roberto el Diablo*) among other wicked, heroic, romantic, or witty characters from mythology, history, and literature which feature in her repertoire.

Essentially a dramatic dancer-actress, Alonso is, she says, "always searching for the character". After Giselle, the character with whom she seems to have identified most vividly is Carmen, in Alberto Alonso's version of the ballet by this name. Sensual, alluring, arrogant, and tragic—nothing could be more different from her delicately romantic Giselle; nothing could illustrate more conclusively her range both as dancer and actress.

"A living legend" is the phrase that critics love to use when writing nowadays of Alicia Alonso, whether with reference to her Giselle, her Carmen, her unremitting determination to conquer blindness or, in her own country, to her courageous resistance to the Batista regime. The history of ballet will certainly record that on 14 January 1990, at the Metropolitan Opera House, New York, the Cuban ballerina Alicia Alonso danced the great Act II pas de deux from *Swan Lake* with her partner, Orlando Salgado, on the occasion of the fiftieth anniversary of American Ballet Theatre. Alonso was the one founder member of ABT still dancing, and of all the ballerinas known to history the one with the longest international career. She was rewarded on that occasion, as on so many others, with a standing ovation.

—Jane King

---

**AMBOISE, Jacques d'** *see* **D'AMBOISE, Jacques**

---

## AMERICAN BALLET THEATRE

American ballet company based in New York. Founded by Lucia Chase (chief sponsor) and Richard Pleasant (managing director) as Ballet Theatre, incorporating dancers from the Mordkin Ballet (founder Mikhail Mordkin), 1940; company performed as American Ballet Theatre (ABT) from 1957, with official home at the Metropolitan Opera House, New York, from 1977; also tours extensively in the continental United States. Official school associated with company, the American Ballet Theatre School, based in New York City, with own performing group, Ballet Repertory Company, established 1972. Current artistic director of American Ballet Theatre (succeeding directors Jane Hermann and Oliver Smith), Kevin McKenzie, from 1992.

### PUBLICATIONS

Amberg, George, *Ballet in America*, New York, 1949

Maynard, Olga, *The American Ballet*, Philadelphia, 1959

Cohen, Selma Jeanne, and Pischl, A.J., "The American Ballet Theatre: 1940–60", *Dance Perspectives* (New York), no. 6, 1960

Barnes, Clive, *Inside American Ballet Theatre*, New York, 1977

Palmer, Winthrop, *Theatrical Dancing in America: The Development of the Ballet from 1900*, revised edition, South Brunswick, New Jersey, and London, 1978

Payne, Charles, *American Ballet Theatre*, New York, 1978

Fraser, John, and Arnold, Eve (photographer), *Private View: Inside Baryshnikov's American Ballet Theatre*, New York, 1988

Croce, Arlene, "At the Supermarket", *The New Yorker* (New York), 17 July 1989

Barnes, Clive, "Showing the Flag", *Dance and Dancers* (London), August 1991

* * *

Until 1940 there was virtually no American tradition of ballet, and it was Ballet Theatre (as ABT was known from 1940 to 1957) that successfully established the notion of a native company as a viable, flourishing thing. Under Lucia Chase's direction the art form truly gained recognition and identity in America.

Ballet Theatre did not begin out of grandiose plans. It was first meant to be a more solid extension of the Mordkin Ballet, a come-and-go troupe centred on Mikhail Mordkin's studio that had been in existence since 1926, and when the idealistic, enthusiastic Richard Pleasant involved himself in the company's future, they expanded further and changed form. Pleasant wished to see a company that would equal European companies in scale, grandeur, and prestige. He inspired Chase with this dream and, with Mordkin as one of the many participants, the new "Ballet Theatre" crystallized as an entity that would display the work of a variety of choreographers.

Ballet Theatre burst upon the dance world in January 1940 with an extraordinary assemblage of works and credentials. There was Fokine's *Les Sylphides*; there was Dolin's *Giselle*; there was Nijinska's *La Fille mal gardée*; there was a joint work by Eugene Loring and dramatist William Saroyan that grabbed the headlines of the day, *The Great American Goof*; and, most of all, there was Antony Tudor's *Jardin aux Lilas*, *Dark Elegies*, and *Judgment of Paris*.

Ballet Theatre began its existence on an unprecedented wave of critical acclaim. Antony Tudor had come from Ballet Rambert at the Mercury Theatre in London, where he had several successful works to his credit when Chase and Pleasant invited him to New York. When Tudor accepted, he brought with him the dancer Hugh Laing, and a series of chamber-sized, delicate, and finely modelled ballets composed in a unique style that blended suggestions of serious narrative content with great formal beauty. Laing was central in making them all work in the new environment.

Tudor showed the relationship of uncompromised classical principles to contemporary social and cultural concerns—to modern times, to serious times. Today, with the experience of 50 more years of ballet-watching, we see additional reasons why Tudor's work is great; we see its qualities of formal beauty, of structured perfection, of classical decorum in its most highly sophisticated and unsentimental form.

In 1943 the young Jerome Robbins saved a lagging season at the Metropolitan Opera House, where Ballet Theatre now performed, with *Fancy Free*—both a popular success and a *succès d'estime*. On the strength of its appeal, the company's season at the Met was extended so the work could be given twelve more times. Like Robbins, who created many works for Ballet Theatre, Agnes de Mille was a praised and popular contributor of ballets, and their works were appreciated by critics and public. But still, it was Tudor who over time and through a steady, unmistakably demanding and serious tone, established the company's foundations most securely. In the same year a new administration, headed by Chase and designer Oliver Smith, came into being. It guided the company until 1980.

In 1947 a new period of acclaim began with the triumph of Balanchine's *Theme and Variations*. It was another turning point for ballet in America. In his previous New York artistic ventures, Balanchine's attempts at establishing a company had been frustrated. Chase and Smith approached him with a commission for a new work for their new star Igor Youskevitch, just out of the U.S. Navy and unsuited to the Tudor-Robbins repertoire. They suggested the "theme and variations" section of Tchaikovsky's third orchestral suite, and Balanchine's setting of the piece provided Ballet Theatre with its next greatly acclaimed success. A style of work that had never been accepted before—a pure, classical divertissement in regal style—now communicated its greatness to the New York dance world. A year later Balanchine staged the third act of *The Sleeping Beauty* for Ballet Theatre.

Touring had always been an important part of Ballet Theatre's existence: without a home in New York, the company toured in order to present more than a few weeks of performances a year. By the end of its first decade, it had built audiences for itself in Chicago, San Francisco, Los Angeles, Washington, and dozens of other cities. There were tours abroad, too, to South America and Europe. As the 1950s proceeded, these tours became more and more important. In fact, for the period between 1952 and 1964, when the company went to 50, 60, 90, 100 cities—they became Ballet—that is, *American* Ballet Theatre.

In 1964 the New York State Theater, a theatre for dance, opened and in 1965 saw the premiere of Jerome Robbins's staging of Stravinsky's *Les Noces*. Suddenly ABT was in full possession of another critical success—once more it enjoyed commendation and wide acclaim, a recognition of its place of value in the world of dance. The company followed through in 1967, with a long-wished-for production of the complete four-act *Swan Lake*. That same year, young Eliot Feld made a sensational début as a choreographer and a young dancer, Cynthia Gregory, emerged as a star and a ballerina.

In 1970 Natalia Makarova, who had left the Kirov Ballet in London, joined ABT; four years later she staged a production of the Petipa classic *La Bayadère*, Act II, "The Kingdom of the Shades". It was one of those productions that focused ABT's history and projected the company in a new direction. The way Makarova made the company work in this ballet, and the methods of classical execution she demonstrated and taught them, were recognized as something new and important in the development of the company. *The New Yorker*'s Arlene Croce called the event "Makarova's Miracle" and described it: "There is now in *Bayadère* an alert, disciplined, and expressive corps de ballet, trembling with self-discovery. Never, in my experience, had the company danced a classical piece in so strict a style, on so broad a scale, and with such clarity of rhythm."

Two more things happened in 1974; Mikhail Baryshnikov left Russia and joined ABT, and Antony Tudor rejoined the company as associate director. Tudor's return was more than ceremonial. In 1975 he created *The Leaves Are Fading*, his first work for ABT in 25 years and a work that equalled the greatest of his ballets of the 1930s and 1940s.

These were years of flourishing creativity once more. In 1976, Twyla Tharp created *Push Comes to Shove* and Jerome Robbins made *Other Dances*. Along with Tudor's new masterpiece and *La Bayadère*, these works defined a new period of identity and triumph for ABT. Ballet Theatre was dominated by a generation of dancers embodying the changes the company itself had made possible.

The last years of the Chase-Smith directorship saw ABT establish itself as the official ballet company of the Kennedy Center in Washington, D.C. (1971) and return to the Met as a New York home base (1977). Tours continued, but to fewer cities and for longer stays in each.

In the autumn of 1980, Mikhail Baryshnikov assumed the role of artistic director of ABT. The years of his directorship showed a development of the classical impulse in repertoire and dancing. The commissions for new works were ambitious and wide-ranging. ABT produced its first original full-length ballet—*Cinderella*—in 1984, and staged Kenneth MacMillan's three-act *Romeo and Juliet* in 1985. The giants of modern dance, Paul Taylor and Merce Cunningham, contributed works, while other choreographers from the modern field, including David Gordon, Karole Armitage, and Mark Morris, created new pieces for ABT.

A major element of the Baryshnikov administration was the refoundation of technical exactitude and definition in the dancers. In 50 years a lot goes on. But the highlights of the company's history all go in one direction, toward a surer statement of the power of classical dancing. There have been interruptions, but the development has proceeded and is still proceeding.

In 1989 Baryshnikov left the company amid some controversy, and Jane Hermann and Oliver Smith assumed co-directorship of the company. In 1992, ex-principal Kevin McKenzie took over the leadership of American Ballet Theatre, returning the company's artistic direction to the hands of a dancer.

—Anita Finkel

(*A version of this essay originally appeared in American Ballet Theatre's 1989–90 Souvenir Book.*)

---

**ANANIASHVILI, Nina**

Georgian/Soviet dancer. Born Nina Gedevanovna Ananiashvili in Tbilisi, 19 March 1964. Studied at the State Choreographic School of Georgia, Tbilisi, 1973–77, Moscow Choreographic School, from 1971; graduated 1981. Début, while still a student, as Swanilda in *Coppélia* (Bolshoi school production), 1980; soloist, Bolshoi Ballet, from 1981; guest artist, New York City Ballet, 1988, Boston Ballet, Royal Danish Ballet, Royal Ballet (London), National Ballet of Finland, 1990; has also appeared in Soviet ballet films, including *Such a Short Life*, *Your Turn Nina*, *Nina Ananiashvili Dancing*. Recipient: Gold Medal, International Ballet Competition, Varna, 1980; Gold Medal (Junior Competition), Moscow International Ballet Competition, 1981; Gold Medal (Senior Competition), Moscow International Ballet Competition, 1985; People's Artist of the Russian Federation, 1986; People's Artist, GSSR.

**ROLES**

1980 Swanilda in *Coppélia* (Gorsky), Bolshoi School Production, Bolshoi Theatre, Moscow

1982 Dancer in *Chopiniana* (Fokine), Bolshoi Ballet, Moscow
Kitty in *Anna Karenina* (Ryzhenko, Smirnov-Golovanov), Bolshoi Ballet, Moscow
The Fairy in *The Wooden Prince* (Petrov), Bolshoi Ballet, Moscow
Odette/Odile in *Swan Lake* (Petipa, Ivanov), Bolshoi Ballet, Hamburg

1983 Spanish dance in *Swan Lake* (Petipa, Ivanov), Bolshoi Ballet, Moscow
The Rose in *The Little Prince* (Maiorov), Bolshoi Ballet, Moscow
Myrtha in *Giselle* (Petipa after Coralli, Perrot; staged Lavrovsky), Bolshoi Ballet, Moscow

1984 Kitri in *Don Quixote* (Gorsky), Bolshoi Ballet, Moscow

1985 Title role in *Raymonda* (Grigorovich after Petipa, Gorsky), Bolshoi Ballet, Moscow
Title role in *Giselle* (Petipa after Coralli, Perrot; staged Lavrovsky), Bolshoi Ballet, Moscow

1986/87 Aurora in *The Sleeping Beauty* (Grigorovich after Petipa), Bolshoi Ballet, Odessa
Masha in *The Nutcracker* (Grigorovich), Bolshoi Ballet, Helsinki

1987 Juliet in *Romeo and Juliet* (Grigorovich), Bolshoi Ballet, Moscow

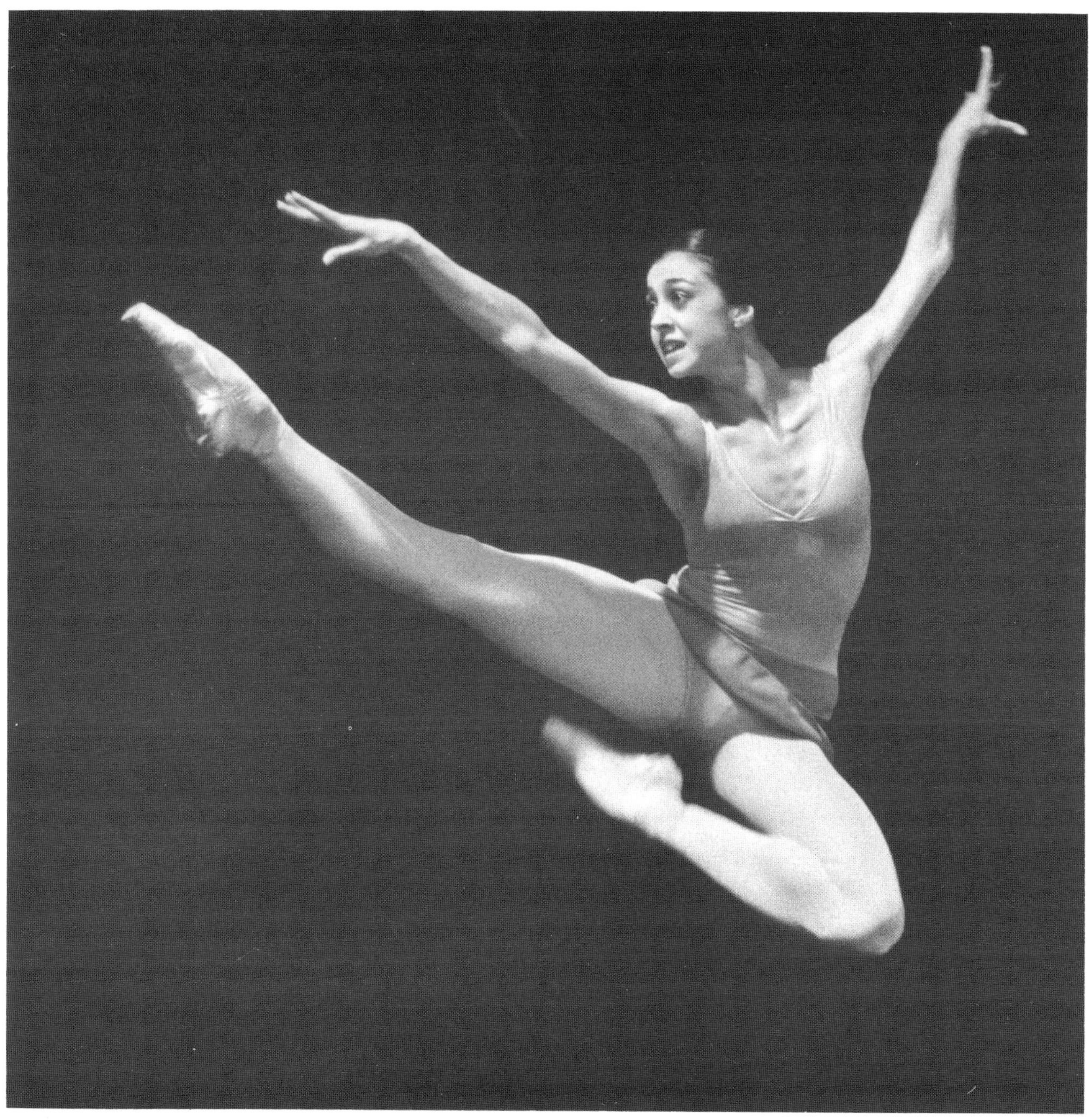

**Nina Ananiashvili**

Nikiya in "Kingdom of the Shades" from *La Bayadère* (Petipa), Bolshoi Ballet, Moscow
1988 Principal dancer in *Raymonda Variations* (Balanchine), New York City Ballet, New York
Second Movement in *Symphony in C* (Balanchine), New York City Ballet, New York
Principal dancer in *Apollo* (Balanchine), New York City Ballet, New York
Rita in *The Golden Age* (Grigorovich), Bolshoi Ballet, Moscow
1989 Mlada's Ghost (cr) in *Mlada* (opera; mus. Rimsky-Korsakov), Bolshoi Opera and Ballet, Moscow
Principal dancer in *Paquita: Grand Pas* (Petipa), Bolshoi Ballet, Moscow
1990 Kitri in *Don Quixote* (after Petipa), Royal Danish Ballet, Copenhagen
Title role in *La Sylphide* (Bournonville), Royal Danish Ballet, Copenhagen
Princess Rose in *The Prince of the Pagodas* (MacMillan), Royal Ballet, London
1991 Juliet in *Romeo and Juliet* (Lavrovsky), Kirov Ballet, Leningrad
Lise in *La Fille mal gardée* (Ashton), Royal Ballet, London
1992 Juliet in *Romeo and Juliet* (MacMillan), Birmingham Royal Ballet, Birmingham

## PUBLICATIONS

By Ananiashvili:

Interview with Tamara Finch, "An Interview with Nina Ananiashvili", *Dancing Times* (London), June 1989

Interview in "The Classics are Alive", *Dance and Dancers* (London), March 1992

About Ananiashvili:

Mainietse, Violette, "Birth of a Ballerina", *Muzykalnaya Zhizn* (Moscow), no. 5, 1985

Bisset, Alexander, "Four Bolshoi Giselles", *Dance and Dancers* (London), December 1986

Alovert, Nina, "Favored Swan", *Dance Magazine* (New York), March 1988

Flatow, Sheryl, "Ananiashvili and Liepa at the NYCB: Glastnost in Action", *Dance Magazine* (New York), June 1988

Clarke, Mary, "The Bolshoi Ballet: Part II", *Dancing Times* (London), September 1989

Willis, Margaret, "Nina Ananiashvili . . . and Juliet", *Dance Magazine* (New York), July 1992

Merrett, Sue, "Spotlight on Nina Ananiashvili", *Dancing Times* (London), February 1993

* * *

Nina Ananiashvili was born in Tbilisi, the capital of the Georgian Republic, and began her artistic career as an ice skater, becoming junior champion of Georgia at the age of nine. Her natural grace and expression led to her being offered a place at the State Choreographic Institute of Georgia a year later where she studied for three years. At thirteen, she was transferred to the Bolshoi School—the Moscow Choreographic Institute—where she trained with Natalia Zolotova, whose enthusiasm, insistence on detail, and supreme love of ballet rubbed off on her pupil. At seventeen, she won a gold medal at the Varna international ballet competition and performed the leading role of Swanilda in *Coppélia* in the Bolshoi School's production.

Upon graduation in 1981, Ananiashvili was immediately accepted into the Bolshoi Ballet as a soloist, where she has danced every famous Russian ballerina role in the company's repertoire. (Her first *Swan Lake* was performed in Hamburg in 1982 and received a 26-minute ovation). She brings to the balletic stage a strong sense of professionalism rooted in the highest degree of technical ability and artistry. Her graceful appearance is enhanced by her youthfulness and exotic beauty.

At the Bolshoi Theatre, Nina is taught by two of the greatest teachers in the Soviet Union, Raisa Struchkova and Marina Semenova, respected doyennes of the Russian and Soviet traditions. After brilliant careers of their own on stage, they now dedicate themselves to handing down their knowledge and understanding to a select few of the next generation of Russian dancers. Their diametrically opposed personalities have brought out different facets of Nina's artistry. With Raisa Struchkova, it is the dramatic presence—flamboyant, realistic acting, large, stage-encompassing movements, and a sense of bravado and exuberance, needed for such roles as Kitri (*Don Quixote*) and Odile (*Swan Lake*). With octogenarian Marina Semenova, who originally came to the Bolshoi from the Kirov in the 1930s, Nina is coached in the purer refinements of the Russian classical style with emphasis on lyricism, placement, and plasticity of the upper body.

As a result, Nina's performances offer a combination of tested values, plus a meticulous blending of precision—evidenced in her expressive arms, strong legs, fast turns, and pirouettes that spin like tops—with emotional acting and character projection. Her leaps have a lightness and lyricism; they end gently and softly. Her thoughtful presentations reveal a presence which commands the scene yet complements rather than dominates her partner.

At school and early in her career, she danced with Andris Liepa, in a partnership which caught the imagination of the Moscow ballet world. Her dark, regal looks and his fair, handsome youth gave an aura of romantic idealism to the ballets they performed. Together they also successfully entered international ballet competitions in Moscow and Jackson, Mississippi, and in 1988 they were invited to perform with the New York City Ballet—the first Soviet dancers to work with an American company. There they performed Balanchine's *Apollo*, *Symphony in C*, and *Raymonda Variations*. The latter were somewhat challenging for they were both accustomed to the traditional Petipa–Gorsky–Grigorovich production at the Bolshoi, in which lyricism and slowly unfolding poses contribute to the romantic, medieval Hungarian scenario. In Balanchine's plotless version to the same score, it was speed, sudden changes of direction, and playful movements which blended music and dance. Nina's elegance and eagerness to learn the new style won her much praise.

Nina Ananiashvili brings to her roles differing facets of her talent. As Aurora, she becomes a self-assured and joyful princess, a jewel in the eyes of her family and her people. As Giselle, she is an innocent peasant girl whose heart overflows with love as she eagerly anticipates the meeting with her mysterious Albrecht. As a Wili, she is compassionate and forgiving, ethereally wafting in and out of Albrecht's presence. As Myrtha, the Queen of the Wilis, she is cold and commanding, unrelenting and authoritative. As the Swan Queen, she is regal but vulnerable, delicately fragile in her encounters with the Prince yet bird-like in her flutterings. As Odile, she is audacious and manipulative, pouring forth her bewitching magneticism.

In recent years, Nina's most regular partner has been Aleksei Fadeyechev, son of the great danseur noble, Nikolai Fadeyechev, the partner of Ulanova. Together the young pair offer a sophisticated and elegant partnership, both exemplary exponents of the Russian ballet.

Ananiashvili has made guest appearances with most of the top European ballet companies and in May 1990 premiered the Boston Ballet's Soviet-American production of *Swan Lake*, dancing with Fernando Bujones.

—Margaret Willis

---

## ANASTASIA

**Choreography:** Kenneth MacMillan
**Music:** Bohuslav Martinů, Petr Ilyich Tchaikovsky
**Design:** Barry Kay
**Libretto:** Kenneth MacMillan
**First production:** Royal Ballet, Royal Opera House, London, 22 July 1971
**Principal Dancers:** Lynn Seymour (Anastasia), Derek Rencher (Tsar Nicholas II), Svetlana Beriosova (Tsarina), Antoinette Sibley (Mathilde Kschessinska), Antony Dowell (Her Partner)

**Other productions include:** German Opera Ballet (original production: one-act version), with Lynn Seymour; Berlin, 25

**Lynn Seymour in *Anastasia*, Royal Ballet, London, 1971**

June 1967. Stuttgart Ballet (revival of one-act version) with Marcia Haydée (Anastasia); Stuttgart, 14 April 1976. American Ballet Theatre (one-act version; restaged MacMillan); New York, 1985. English National Ballet, with Seymour; London, 19 June 1989.

**PUBLICATIONS**

Crisp, Clement, "*Anastasia*: Kenneth MacMillan talks to Clement Crisp about his new Ballet", *About the House* (London), vol. 3, no. 9, Summer 1971

Clarke, Mary, "*Anastasia* in Three Acts", *Dancing Times* (London), September 1971

Williams, Peter, "Anastasia", *Dance and Dancers* (London), September 1971

Crisp, Clement, *Ballet and Modern Dance*, London, 1974

Thorpe, Edward, *Kenneth MacMillan: The Man and his Ballets*, London, 1985

* * *

Inspired by the book *I, Anastasia*, Kenneth MacMillan's ballet delves into the mind and memory of Anna Anderson, a patient in a Berlin hospital who believes herself to be the Grand Duchess Anastasia. Originally created as a one-act ballet soon after MacMillan became artistic director of the German Opera Ballet, *Anastasia* juxtaposes past and present, fact and ambiguity. Events from Anastasia's childhood—the Ekaterinburg killings, a soldier who saved her, and their short-lived happiness together—are recalled in a series of flashbacks. Film, voices, and a succession of characters—Tsar Nicholas II and the Tsarina, Rasputin, Anastasia's sisters and the Tsarevitch, relatives of the Imperial family who visit the hospital—disturb Anna's consciousness. Sequence and characters are confused. Dancers duplicate roles. Incidents are recalled anachronistically as Anna attempts to recall her past and to provide proof of her Romanov identity.

In movement and design, the ballet conveys a sense of going in circles. A pas de trois for the Tsarina, Rasputin, and Anna's soldier husband is set in a side-stepping figure-of-eight form. Their interweaving, both in terms of spatial patterns and in the confusion of characters from different time periods, echoes Anna's desperate attempts to organize her thoughts and establish her identity. Several nurses enter, one behind the other, and as the progression of their line files forward, each successive pair circles around itself. In this spatial contrasting of straight lines and circles, MacMillan suggests that things are not what they seem.

In Berlin, Barry Kay's designs made full use of the theatre's revolving stage. When MacMillan extended *Anastasia* for the Royal Ballet in 1971, Kay developed the idea of circles and spirals further. The ballet created in Berlin became the last act of a three-act production in which events from Anastasia's childhood and the growing unrest in pre-revolutionary Russia foreshadow the hospitalized Anna's plight. Both music and design allude to the changing social order and to the contrasts between Anastasia's happy childhood and Anna's alienation. To music by Tchaikovsky, Acts I and II are set, respectively, at an Imperial family picnic and a Winter Palace ball. Like MacMillan's other large-scale ballets, action shifts between exterior and interior locations. Act II opens with a brief scene set in the St. Petersburg streets. Slogan-scrawled cloths, cold, starving peasants, and revolutionary fervour contrast sharply with the formal grandeur and gaiety of the ballroom scene which follows. And, like many MacMillan ballets, acts climax in crisis. Act I ends with news brought to the Tsar of the outbreak of the first world war; the ballroom festivities of Act II conclude abruptly as revolutionaries storm the palace.

The sterile hospital setting of the third act marks a change in time, place, and personality. The solitary bed, the open stage with lighting rigs exposed and hanging screens on to which film of the Imperial family is projected, the opening sound collage and dissonant Martinů symphony—all contribute to the incongruity between events past and the stark reality of Anna's present.

In *Anastasia*, MacMillan explores a recurring theme in his choreography—that of the outsider. Earlier works such as *Laiderette*, *The Burrow*, and *Las Hermanas* showed a particular interest in contemporary ideas revealed through a classical medium. Rejection, oppression, claustrophobia are the subjects of several MacMillan ballets. And, in *Anastasia*, a sense of alienation makes Anna's search for identity more acute. Surrounded by memories, she appears isolated. Relatives shun her; even the nurses distance themselves from her. Imaginary or real recollections? MacMillan offers no resolution. The ballet ends enigmatically—like Anderson herself, MacMillan's Anna is resolute in her claim to identity, but as she circles the stage on her hospital bed, a haggard, solitary figure, only she recognizes this to be true.

In Berlin, and for the extended Royal Ballet version, the role of Anna/Anastasia was created by Lynn Seymour. It is a role which requires extremes in dramatic interpretation and an ability to transcend ballet's technical conventions. When the ballet was extended to three acts, the title role became even more challenging. Initially, Anastasia is adolescent and innocent (in the three-act *Anastasia*, Seymour first entered on roller skates). She is playful and unaware of life's harsh realities, those beyond her Imperial surroundings and those of ensuing events. In Act II, she is excited and bemused by her coming-of-age celebrations. In Act III, all childhood happiness has been expunged, and she is aged and bereft by events.

The three-act *Anastasia* was revived by the Royal Ballet in 1978. In 1989, the original one-act version of the ballet was taken into the repertory of English National Ballet. Again, Seymour returned to the role of Anna/Anastasia. Older, heavier, but with all her former power and conviction, Seymour conveyed the psychological turmoil and suffering of MacMillan's most equivocal character.

—Angela Kane

---

**ANDERSEN, Frank**

Danish dancer, teacher, and ballet director. Born in Copenhagen, 15 April 1953. Studied at the Royal Danish Ballet School, Copenhagen, from 1960; also studied with Nora Kiss, Paris, and Stanley Williams, New York, with additional training in Leningrad. Married dancer Eva Kloberg, 1983. Early stage appearances, while still a student, in child roles for the Royal Danish Ballet, from 1961; dancer, Royal Danish Ballet, from 1971, becoming solo dancer (principal), from 1977; co-founder, with Dinna Bjørn, and principal dancer, international touring group, Soloists of the Royal Danish Ballet (also known as "The Bournonville Group"), from 1976, touring the United States, 1976–79, 1982, 1983, 1985, 1986, Central America, 1978, France, Italy, and Israel, 1979, Hong Kong, the Philippines, and Thailand, 1980; also international guest artist, including for Jacob's Pillow Festival in Massachusetts; has also appeared in Hamburg, Tokyo, and New York; teacher, and director of annual Bournonville Summer Academy; Royal ballet master (artistic director), Royal Danish Ballet, from 1985.

## ROLES

1970 Dancer in *Phases* (Kølgaard), Royal Danish Ballet, Copenhagen
A Cavalier in *Gala Performance* (Tudor), Royal Danish Ballet, Copenhagen
Dancer in *Helios* (von Rosen), Royal Danish Ballet, Copenhagen
1971 Fool in *Quatre Images* (Cranko), Royal Danish Ballet, Copenhagen
Dancer in *Opus 1* (Cranko), Royal Danish Ballet, Copenhagen
Pastorale in *Night Shadow* (*La Sonnambula*; Balanchine), Royal Danish Ballet, Copenhagen
Hungarian dance in *Swan Lake* (Petipa, Ivanov; staged Flindt), Royal Danish Ballet, Copenhagen
Franz in *The Nutcracker* (Flindt), Royal Danish Ballet, Copenhagen
1972 Trepak in *The Nutcracker* (Flindt), Royal Danish Ballet, Copenhagen
Dancer in *Triumph of Death* (Flindt), Royal Danish Ballet, Copenhagen
Dancer in *Concerto Prokofiev* (Blaska), Royal Danish Ballet, Copenhagen
Czardas in *Coppélia* (Brenaa after Saint-Léon), Royal Danish Ballet, Copenhagen
Coachman in *Petrushka* (Fokine), Royal Danish Ballet, Copenhagen
Bandit in *Carmen* (Petit), Royal Danish Ballet, Copenhagen
Third movement in *Jeu de cartes* (Cranko), Royal Danish Ballet, Copenhagen
One of Kostchei's men in *Firebird* (Holm), Royal Danish Ballet, Copenhagen
Second movement in *Jeu de cartes* (Cranko), Royal Danish Ballet, Copenhagen
1973 Flagellant in *Felix Luna* (Flindt), Royal Danish Ballet, Copenhagen
Young man in *Trio* (Flindt), Royal Danish Ballet, Copenhagen
Moor in *The Whims of Cupid and the Ballet Master* (Galeotti), Royal Danish Ballet, Copenhagen
Dancer in *Wednesday's School* (Bournonville; staged Ralov), Royal Danish Ballet, Copenhagen
1974 Assaulter in *The Miraculous Mandarin* (Flindt), Royal Danish Ballet, Copenhagen
Trumpet in *Fanfare* (Robbins), Royal Danish Ballet, Copenhagen
Heinz's friend in *Chronicle* (Holm), Royal Danish Ballet, Copenhagen
Antonio in *Romeo and Juliet* (Neumeier), Royal Danish Ballet, Copenhagen
1975 Dancer in *The Butterfly Mask* (Bjørn), Royal Danish Ballet, Copenhagen
Dancer in *The Dreamer* (Cullberg), Royal Danish Ballet, Copenhagen
Young man in *The Butterfly Mask*, Royal Danish Ballet, Copenhagen
Dancer in *The Four Seasons* (Flindt), Royal Danish Ballet, Copenhagen
Ballabile in *Napoli* (Bournonville), Royal Danish Ballet, Copenhagen
Dancer in *Proximities* (Louis), Royal Danish Ballet, Copenhagen
Clown in *Hoopla* (Louis), Royal Danish Ballet, Copenhagen
Tarantella in *Napoli* (Bournonville), Royal Danish Ballet, Copenhagen
Harlequin in *Visions* (Walbom, Brenaa) Danish television
The Soldier (cr) in *The Tinder Box* (Flindt), Danish television
1976 Aramis in *The Three Musketeers* (Flindt), Royal Danish Ballet, Copenhagen
Jester in *Swan Lake* (Petipa, Ivanov; staged Flindt), Royal Danish Ballet, Copenhagen
Harlequin in *Night Shadow* (Balanchine), Royal Danish Ballet, Copenhagen
Otto in *The Life Guards on Amager* (Bournonville), Royal Danish Ballet, Copenhagen
Pas de trois in *Swan Lake* (Petipa, Ivanov; staged Flindt), Royal Danish Ballet, Copenhagen
Benvolio in *Romeo and Juliet* (Neumeier), Royal Danish Ballet, Copenhagen
1977 Planchet in *The Three Musketeers* (Flindt), Royal Danish Ballet, Copenhagen
First Junior Cadet in *Graduation Ball* (Lichine), Royal Danish Ballet, Copenhagen
Dancer in *Septet Extra* (Manen), Royal Danish Ballet, Copenhagen
Dancer in *Interplay* (Robbins), Royal Danish Ballet, Copenhagen
Pas de sept in *A Folk Tale* (Bournonville), Royal Danish Ballet, Copenhagen
Male soloist in *Études* (Lander), Royal Danish Ballet, Copenhagen
Melancholic in *The Four Temperaments* (Balanchine), Royal Danish Ballet, Copenhagen
1978 Pedro in *The Toreador* (Bournonville/Flindt), Royal Danish Ballet, Copenhagen
Dancer in *Konservatoriet* (Bournonville), Royal Danish Ballet, Copenhagen
1979 Pas de deux from *Flower Festival in Genzano* (Bournonville), Royal Danish Ballet, Copenhagen
Geert in *The Kermesse in Bruges* (Bournonville), Royal Danish Ballet, Copenhagen
Gurn in *La Sylphide* (Bournonville), Royal Danish Ballet, Copenhagen
Jockey dance from *From Siberia to Moscow* (Bournonville), Tivoli Concert Hall, Copenhagen
Pas de trois in *La Ventana* (Bournonville), Royal Danish Ballet, Copenhagen
1980 Dancer in *Songs Without Words* (Manen), Royal Danish Ballet, Copenhagen
Pas de deux from *William Tell* (Bournonville), Royal Danish Ballet, Copenhagen
Puck in *A Midsummer Night's Dream* (Neumeier), Royal Danish Ballet, Copenhagen
1981 Dancer in *Memoria* (Ailey), Royal Danish Ballet, Copenhagen
Franz in *Coppélia* (Brenaa after Saint-Léon), Royal Danish Ballet, Copenhagen
Third Movement in *Symphony in C* (Balanchine), Royal Danish Ballet, Copenhagen
1982 Harlequin in *Night with Waning Moon* (Bruce), Royal Danish Ballet, Copenhagen
French dance in *The Whims of Cupid and the Ballet Master* (Galeotti), Royal Danish Ballet, Copenhagen
Pas de deux from *Le Corsaire* (Petipa; staged Bruhn),

Royal Danish Ballet, Copenhagen
1983 Jig in *Don Quixote* (Petipa, Gorsky), Royal Danish Ballet, Copenhagen
Basil in *Don Quixote* (Petipa, Gorsky), Royal Danish Ballet, Copenhagen
Señor in *La Ventana* (Bournonville), Royal Danish Ballet, Copenhagen
Soloist in *Bournonville Exercises* (Ralov after Bournonville), Royal Danish Ballet, Copenhagen
1984 The Moor in *Petrushka* (Fokine), Royal Danish Ballet, Tivoli Concerthall, Copenhagen
1985 Pulcinella in *Pulcinella and Pimpinella* (Cullberg), Royal Danish Ballet, Tivoli Concerthall, Copenhagen
Dancer in *Sad Songs* (Christe), Royal Danish Ballet, Midland, Michigan
1987 Mercutio in *Romeo and Juliet* (Neumeier), Royal Danish Ballet, Copenhagen
1990 Pas de deux in *Top Hat* (Gennaro), Royal Danish Ballet, Copenhagen

**PUBLICATIONS**

Hunt, Marilyn, "Dancing Bournonville Now", *Ballet News* (New York), November 1979
Guy, John, "The Royal Danish Ballet", *Dancing Times* (London), April 1985
Hardy, Camille, "Young Director, Old Tradition", *Dance Magazine* (New York), February 1986
Guy, John, "Spotlight on Frank Andersen: Ballet Master to the Queen", *Dancing Times* (London), August 1991

* * *

When Frank Andersen was appointed artistic director of the Royal Danish Ballet at the age of 32, he seemed only a boy. Actually, such illustrious predecessors as August Bournonville, Harald Lander, and Flemming Flindt had been even younger when they assumed the same post, but until Andersen's appointment, it seemed that only a smiling vivacity and a boyish charm had marked his career. In fact, this was not entirely the case. His Puck in John Neumeier's *A Midsummer Night's Dream*, as well as his Harlequin in Christopher Bruce's *Night with Waning Moon* and his Moor in *Petrushka*, had shown his ability to portray characters of a far more complex, and even difficult, nature.

Frank Andersen was not the stranger to management that he might have seemed at first. He has always shown a strong will, as a dancer as well as in the role of company director. Early in his career, he set out in the world not only to perfect his skill, but also (and perhaps even more importantly) to make contacts. He was trained in New York, Paris, and Leningrad, and he has danced as a principal dancer with many major international companies. Artistically, however, Frank Andersen has never had the bearing of an international superstar. He is, first and last, essentially Danish.

It was no coincidence, then, that Andersen took part (in 1976) in the formation of a special Bournonville performing group, called Soloists of the Royal Danish Ballet; and it is also no coincidence that he later headed the annual Bournonville summer academy. He was one of the most exemplary Bournonville dancers of his generation—cheerful, smiling, and high-flying. Above all, he never left any doubt in the minds of his spectators that he loved dancing.

Andersen has been a brilliant solo performer in all the Bournonville classics, and his demi-caractère charm has been successfully applied to a rich variety of wanton lads and cunning fools in the repertoire. He was funny, sweet, and moving as the First Cadet in Lichine's *Graduation Ball*, and equally charming as Planchet, the whistling servant in Flemming Flindt's *The Three Musketeers*. He was effective as Franz in *Coppélia*, and above all as the simple-minded Geert in the classic Bournonville ballet, *The Kermesse in Bruges*, where, with his magic ring, he makes all the ladies fall in love with him.

As artistic director (officially called the Royal Ballet Master) of the Royal Danish Ballet, Frank Andersen has succeeded in conveying his own ambitions as a dancer to the company he is leading. He wants "his" dancers to cover the widest possible span of classical and modern ballets. Since taking over the Royal Danish Ballet he has brought back into the repertoire such varied works as Jerome Robbins's *Afternoon of a Faun*, John Cranko's *Jeu de cartes*, and Cullberg's *Moon Reindeer*, while company premieres have included first performances of Balanchine's *Agon*, Cranko's *Onegin*, and Lar Lubovitch's *Rhapsody in Blue*. After his first years in the director's chair, he even stopped performing himself, and instead began teaching. He has also been a major force behind DANCE—Danish American National Culture Exchange—providing young dancers from Denmark and America with opportunities for student exchange.

Andersen is devoted to the old traditions of the Royal Theatre, where he grew up, and, lacking the talent to make ballets of his own, he has naturally taken to directing and preserving Bournonville's ballets. Keeping the Danish dance tradition alive might well become his own way of preserving a kind of eternal youth.

—Birthe Johansen

---

**ANDERSEN, Ib**

Danish dancer and choreographer. Born in Copenhagen, 14 December 1954. Studied at the Royal Danish Ballet School, Copenhagen, pupil of Kirsten Ralov, Hans Brenaa, Flemming Ryberg, Vera Volkova, from 1962; also studied in Germany and France, and with George Balanchine, New York. Apprentice, Royal Danish Ballet, 1972–73: dancer, corps de ballet, from 1973; principal dancer, from 1975, touring North America, 1976; joined New York City Ballet as principal dancer, 1980; retired from performing in 1990; also choreographer: first work, for Royal Danish Ballet, staged 1987, also choreographing for New York City Ballet, 1988. Recipient: Nijinsky Prize, 1979/80.

**ROLES**

1972 Dancer in *Concerto Prokofiev* (Blaska), Royal Danish Ballet, Copenhagen
One of Köstchei's men in *The Firebird* (Holm), Royal Danish Ballet, Copenhagen
Third Movement in *Jeu de cartes* (Cranko), Royal Danish Ballet, Copenhagen
Spanish Dance in *The Nutcracker* (Flindt), Royal Danish Ballet, Copenhagen
1973 Young Man, Soldier in *Felix Luna* (Flindt), Royal Danish Ballet, Copenhagen
Pas de deux in *Coppélia* (Brenaa after Saint-Léon), Royal Danish Ballet, Copenhagen
The Boy (cr) in *Monument for a Dead Boy* (van Dantzig),

**Ib Andersen**

Royal Danish Ballet, Copenhagen
First dancer in *Wednesday's School* (Ralov after Bournonville), Royal Danish Ballet, Copenhagen
1974 Principal dancer in *Elektro Bach* (Blaska), Royal Danish Ballet, Copenhagen
Patient in *Asylum* (Marks), Royal Danish Ballet, Copenhagen
Romeo in *Romeo and Juliet* (Neumeier), Royal Danish Ballet, Copenhagen
1975 Principal dancer in *The Four Seasons* (Flindt), Royal Danish Ballet, Copenhagen
Pas de six in *Napoli* (Bournonville), Royal Danish Ballet, Copenhagen
The Young Man in *The Young Man Must Marry* (Flindt), Royal Danish Ballet, Copenhagen
Principal dancer in *Proximities* (Louis), Royal Danish Ballet, Copenhagen
Clown in *Hoopla* (Louis), Royal Danish Ballet, Copenhagen
The Man in *Blue Eyes* (Jacobsen), Royal Danish Ballet, Copenhagen
1976 Male Soloist in *Études* (Lander), Royal Danish Ballet, Copenhagen
Ivan Tsarevich in *The Firebird* (Holm), Royal Danish Ballet, Copenhagen
D'Artagnan in *The Three Musketeers* (Flindt), Royal Danish Ballet, Copenhagen
1977 Junior Cadet in *Graduation Ball* (Lichine), Royal Danish Ballet, Copenhagen
Principal dancer in *Septet Extra* (van Manen), Royal Danish Ballet, Copenhagen
Principal dancer in *Interplay* (Robbins), Royal Danish Ballet, Copenhagen
Pas de deux classique in *Graduation Ball* (Lichine), Royal Danish Ballet, Copenhagen
Bridegroom in *Les Noces* (Lubovitch), Royal Danish Ballet, Copenhagen
The Prince in *The Nutcracker* (Flindt), Royal Danish Ballet, Copenhagen
1978 Title role (cr) in *The Toreador* (Flindt after Bournonville), Royal Danish Ballet, Copenhagen
Pas de deux from *Flower Festival at Genzano* (Bournonville), Royal Danish Ballet, Copenhagen
Principal dancer in *Greening* (Tetley), Royal Danish Ballet, Copenhagen
The Chosen in *Le Sacre du printemps* (Tetley), Royal Danish Ballet, Copenhagen
Principal dancer in *Ricercare* (Tetley), Royal Danish Ballet, Copenhagen
1979 Principal dancer in *Divertimento No. 15* (Balanchine), Royal Danish Ballet, Copenhagen
Carelis in *Kermesse in Bruges* (Bournonville), Royal Danish Ballet, Copenhagen
Albrecht in *Giselle* (Petipa after Coralli, Perrot; staged Bruhn), Royal Danish Ballet, Copenhagen
Vilhelm in *Far From Denmark* (Bournonville), Royal Danish Ballet, Copenhagen
Junker Ove in *A Folk Tale* (Bournonville), Royal Danish Ballet, Copenhagen
Principal dancer in *Jockey Dance* (from *From Siberia to Moscow*; Bournonville), Tivoli Concert Hall, Copenhagen
1980 Principal dancer in *Calcium Light Night* (Martins), New York City Ballet, New York
First Movement in *Symphony in C* (Balanchine), New York City Ballet, New York
Principal dancer (cr) in *Ballade* (Balanchine), New York City Ballet, New York
Spring in *The Four Seasons* (Robbins), New York City Ballet, New York
Principal dancer in *Ballo della Regina* (Balanchine), New York City Ballet, New York
Principal dancer in *Afternoon of a Faun* (Robbins), New York City Ballet, New York
Jockey Dance and Pas de trois from *La Ventana* in *Bournonville Divertissements* (Williams after Bournonville), New York City Ballet, New York
Principal dancer in *Dances at a Gathering* (Robbins), New York City Ballet, New York
Principal dancer, Fourth Couple (cr) in *Robert Schumann's Davidsbündlertänze* (Balanchine), New York City Ballet, New York
Aria I in *Stravinsky Violin Concerto* (Balanchine), New York City Ballet, New York
Principal dancer (cr) in *Lille Suite* (Martins), New York City Ballet, New York
Title role in *Apollo* (Balanchine), New York City Ballet, New York
Rubies in *Jewels* (Balanchine), New York City Ballet, New York
Principal dancer in *Goldberg Variations* (Robbins), New York City Ballet, New York
Cavalier in *The Nutcracker* (Balanchine), New York City Ballet, New York
1981 Principal dancer in *Scotch Symphony* (Balanchine), New York City Ballet, New York
Oberon in *A Midsummer Night's Dream* (Balanchine), New York City Ballet, New York
Principal dancer in *Raymonda Variations* (Balanchine), New York City Ballet, New York
Principal dancer (cr) in *Suite from Histoire du Soldat* (Martins), New York City Ballet, New York
Principal dancer in *La Source* (pas de deux; Balanchine), New York City Ballet, New York
James in *La Sylphide* (Bournonville), Royal Danish Ballet, Copenhagen

Principal dancer (cr) in *Mozartiana* (new version; Balanchine), New York City Ballet, New York
Principal dancer (cr) in *Pas de deux* (later called *Andantino*; Robbins), New York City Ballet, New York
Variation VI (cr) in *Trio in A Minor* (Taras) in *Tempo di Valse* (Balanchine, d'Amboise, Robbins, Taras), New York City Ballet, New York
Principal dancer (cr) in *Piano Pieces* (Robbins), New York City Ballet, New York

1982 Principal dancer in *Opus 19/The Dreamer* (Robbins), New York City Ballet, New York
Pas de deux from *William Tell* in *Bournonville Divertissements* (Williams after Bournonville), New York City Ballet, New York
Principal dancer in *Sonatine* (Balanchine), New York City Ballet, New York
Luke in *The Magic Flute* (Martins), New York City Ballet, New York
Principal dancer in *Donizetti Variations* (Balanchine), New York City Ballet, New York
Principal dancer (cr) in *Concerto for Two Solo Pianos* (Martins), New York City Ballet, New York
Frantz in *Coppélia* (Danilova, Balanchine after Petipa), New York City Ballet, New York

1983 Title role in *Orpheus* (Balanchine), New York City Ballet, New York
Pas de deux from *The Kermesse in Bruges* in *Bournonville Divertissements* (Williams after Bournonville), New York City Ballet, New York
Principal dancer in *Tzigane* (Balanchine), New York City Ballet, New York
Principal dancer in *Agon* (Balanchine), New York City Ballet, New York
Principal dancer in *Other Dances* (Robbins), New York City Ballet, New York
Principal dancer in *Gershwin Concerto* (Robbins), New York City Ballet, New York
Principal dancer in *Ballet d'Isoline* (Tomasson), New York City Ballet, New York
Principal dancer in *I'm Old Fashioned* (Robbins), New York City Ballet, New York

1984 Harlequin in *Harlequinade* (Balanchine), New York City Ballet, New York
Principal dancer (cr) in *A Schubertiad* (Martins), New York City Ballet, New York
"Frühlingstimmen" and "Der Rosenkavalier" in *Vienna Waltzes* (Balanchine), New York City Ballet, New York
Principal dancer in *Liebeslieder Walzer* (Balanchine), New York City Ballet, New York
Principal dancer (cr) in *Brahms/Handel* (Tharp, Robbins), New York City Ballet, New York

1985 Principal dancer in *Square Dance* (Balanchine), New York City Ballet, New York
Principal dancer (cr) in *Eight Lines* (Robbins), New York City Ballet, New York
Principal dancer in *Gounod Symphony* (Balanchine), New York City Ballet, New York
Principal dancer (cr) in *Valse Triste* (Martins), New York City Ballet, New York
Principal dancer in *Cortège Hongrois* (Balanchine), New York City Ballet, New York
Principal dancer in *Divertimento from Le Baiser de la fée* (Balanchine), New York City Ballet, New York
Principal dancer (cr) in *Shadows* (Bonnefoux), New York City Ballet, New York
Principal dancer in *Brahms-Schoenberg Quartet* (Balanchine), New York City Ballet, New York

1986 Title role in *Prodigal Son* (Balanchine), New York City Ballet, New York

1987 Principal dancer (cr) in *Sinfonia Mistica* (Mejia), New York City Ballet, New York
Principal dancer in *Chaconne* (Balanchine), New York City Ballet, New York
The Poet in *La Sonnambula* (Balanchine), New York City Ballet, New York

1988 Principal dancer in *Theme and Variations* from *Tchaikovsky Suite No. 3* (Balanchine), New York City Ballet, New York

1989 Principal dancer in *Tea Rose* (Martins), New York City Ballet, New York

1990 Principal dancer in *Duo Concertant* (Balanchine), New York City Ballet, New York

**Other roles include:** for Royal Danish Ballet—Franz's Friend in *Coppélia* (Brenaa after Saint-Léon), Pas de trois in *Swan Lake* (Flindt after Petipa, Ivanov), First solo in *La Sylphide* (Bournonville), Pas de trois in *The Life Guards at Amager* (Bournonville), Prince Siegfried in *Swan Lake* (Flindt after Petipa, Ivanov); for New York City Ballet—principal dancer in *The Steadfast Tin Soldier* (Balanchine), principal dancer in *Symphony in Three Movements* (Balanchine), principal dancer in *(Tchaikovsky) Pas de deux* (Balanchine), principal dancer in *Fanfare* (Robbins).

## WORKS

1987 *1-2-3—1-2* (mus. Schoenberg, orchestrated J. Strauss, Jr. and Liszt), Royal Danish Ballet, Copenhagen

1988 *Baroque Variations* (mus. Foss), New York City Ballet, New York

1990 *Fête Galante* (mus. Couperin), Royal Danish Ballet, Copenhagen

## PUBLICATIONS

By Andersen:
Interview in Cunningham, Katharine, "A Conversation with Ib Andersen", *Ballet Review* (New York), Fall 1981

About Andersen:
Sutton, Valerie, "Spotlight on Ib Andersen and Mette-Ida Kirk", *Dance Magazine* (New York), August 1976
Aschengreen, Erik, *The Royal Danish Ballet and Bournonville*, Copenhagen, 1979
Croce, Arlene, *Going to the Dance*, New York, 1982
Tobias, Tobi, "Top of NYCB's Danish Line: Ib Andersen", *Dance Magazine* (New York), January 1985
Kaplan, Larry, "Dancing Balanchine's Legacy", *Ballet Review* (New York), Winter 1985
Maiorano, Robert, *Balanchine's Mozartiana: The Making of a Masterpiece*, New York, 1985
Croce, Arlene, *Sight Lines*, New York, 1987

* * *

Until his retirement in 1990, Ib Andersen's dancing was notable for its clarity, precision, buoyancy, musicality, and brilliance. A self-effacing personality and performer, Andersen nonetheless possessed a lively and powerful stage presence.

Of moderate height for a male ballet star (approximately 5′

10″), he is lean, slight of build, and nicely proportioned. He has a fine-featured face, a friendly smile, and a demeanor that is frequently described as either "elfin" or "angelic".

Trained at the Royal Danish Ballet School in Copenhagen, Andersen became a master of the Bournonville style, with its brilliant allegro work and buoyant leaps, as well as a strong performer in a variety of roles by modern choreographers. He achieved his initial success one year after joining the company, when choreographer Rudi van Dantzig chose the young dancer to create the principal role in *Monument for a Dead Boy* in 1973. A year later, he was chosen for the role of Romeo in John Neumeier's *Romeo and Juliet*, and by 1979 he had performed the role of Albrecht in *Giselle*. Applauded on his tours to the United States with company and soloists, Andersen decided to join the New York City Ballet in 1980, following in the footsteps of several other distinguished Royal Danish Ballet émigrés.

During his tenure at the New York City Ballet, Andersen mastered over 60 roles, many of which were created on him, in ballets by George Balanchine, Jerome Robbins, Peter Martins, and others. In his first year with the company, he learned an astonishing number of roles, not all of which were performed. He stepped in immediately to replace injured dancers, to perform in the television taping of Martins' first ballet, *Calcium Light Night*, and to partner Merrill Ashley in Balanchine's *Ballo della Regina* and the premiere of his *Ballade*. That same year he was part of the creation of *Robert Schumann's Davidsbündlertänze*. In the following year he was integral to the development of *Mozartiana*, considered to be Balanchine's last great work.

In the wide-ranging challenges of over 30 Balanchine works, Andersen's signature success was perhaps in *Apollo*, which he had learned but never performed when he was with the Royal Danish Ballet. Noted especially for the youthful quality he brought to the role, he developed it consistently and performed it to the same acclaim on his retirement. He also took on, and was noted for, the more overt drama of the title roles in *Orpheus* and *Prodigal Son*, the more sublimated passions of *Liebeslieder Walzer*, and the role of the Poet in *La Sonnambula*. Equally, he was successful in the comic characterizations of Franz in *Coppélia* and Harlequin in *Harlequinade*, while bringing a mercurial ephemerality to the character of Oberon in *A Midsummer Night's Dream*. Andersen took his dramatic skills elsewhere only once, after joining the New York City Ballet, when he made his début in 1981 as James in *La Sylphide* as a guest artist with the Royal Danish Ballet. His wit, brilliance, and energy were also evident in his interpretations of such roles as "Rubies" in *Jewels*, *Tzigane*, and *Cortège Hongrois*.

Although critic Arlene Croce noted initially that Andersen had an androgynous quality, so that "he did not mate well", he none the less proved to be a sensitive, reliable, and generous partner. He performed with many of the company's female stars, notably Suzanne Farrell in *Mozartiana* and *Tzigane*. He was a steady partner for both Patricia McBride and Heather Watts, and he also worked with Merrill Ashley, Kyra Nichols, Darci Kistler, Maria Calegari, Karin von Aroldingen, Judith Fugate, Stephanie Saland, and finally Margaret Tracey.

In the Robbins repertory, he was frequently seen in *Afternoon of a Faun* and *Dances at a Gathering* and he created roles in *Piano Pieces* and *Andantino* (originally called *Pas de Deux*). As already noted, he also worked with Martins from the beginning and created roles in such diverse works as *Lille Suite*, *A Schubertiad*, *Concerto for Two Solo Pianos*, and *Valse Triste*, as well as performing in *Tea Rose* and as Luke in *The Magic Flute*.

The death of Balanchine was, of course, a loss to Andersen's career, as it was to many. Then in 1988 a hip injury began to curtail his performance activities. After a valiant process of therapy, he attempted to come back to the stage, performing a number of his favorite roles and making his début in *Duo Concertant* with Darci Kistler. But the rigors of performance were too intense and he decided to retire.

Andersen has choreographed three works to critical acknowledgement, if not exactly acclaim. *Baroque Variations*, for the New York City Ballet, was seen only briefly. Both *1-2-3—1-2*, to an odd combination of music (a Schoenberg orchestration of Johann Strauss Jr., and a work by Liszt), and *Fête Galante*, to music of Couperin for the Royal Danish Ballet, were small chamber works (for four couples) described by critics as "musical" and "competent".

—Katy Matheson

---

**ANDREYANOVA, Elena**

Russian dancer. Born Elena Ivanova Andreyanova in St. Petersburg, 13 July (1 July old style) 1819. Studied at the St. Petersburg Theatre School, graduated 1837; later studied under Carlo Blasis. Dancer, Bolshoi Theatre, St. Petersburg, 1837–54; guest ballerina Hamburg, London, Paris, Milan, 1845, London, 1852; leading artist, touring company, performing in Russia, including in Odessa, Kharkov, Kiev, Poltava, Voronezh, 1852–55; retired to France, 1855. Died in Paris, 26 October 1857.

**ROLES**

1840 Title role in *La Gitana* (Taglioni), Bolshoi Theatre, St. Petersburg
Elvira in *Don Juan* (A. Blache), Bolshoi Theatre, St. Petersburg
1842 Title role in *Gerta* (Taglioni), Bolshoi Theatre, St. Petersburg
Title role in *Giselle* (Coralli, Perrot), Bolshoi Theatre, St. Petersburg
1844 Title role in *La Péri* (Frederick after Coralli), Bolshoi Theatre, St. Petersburg
1846 Berthe in *Il Diavolo a quattro* (Casati after Mazilier), La Scala, Milan
1847 Title role (cr) in *Paquita* (Petipa after Mazilier), Bolshoi Theatre, St. Petersburg
1848 Title role in *Satanilla* (M. and J. Petipa after Mazilier), Bolshoi Theatre, St. Petersburg
1850 The Black Fairy (cr) in *La Filleule des fées* (new production; Perrot), Bolshoi Theatre, St. Petersburg
Berthe in *Le Diable à quatre* (Mazilier), Bolshoi Theatre, St. Petersburg
1851 Giannina (cr) in *The Naiad and the Fisherman* (Perrot), Bolshoi Theatre, St. Petersburg
Principal dancer (cr) in *Les Tribulations d'un maître de ballet* (Perrot), Bolshoi Theatre, St. Petersburg
1852 Vlasta (cr) in *The War of the Women; or, the Amazons of the Ninth Century* (Perrot), Bolshoi Theatre, St. Petersburg
Blanche in *Vert-Vert* (Mazilier), Bolshoi Theatre, St. Petersburg
1853 Narda (cr) in *Gazelda; or, the Tsiganes* (Perrot), Bolshoi Theatre, St. Petersburg

**Other roles include:** Elena in *Robert the Devil* (opera; mus. Meyerbeer), Fenella in *La Muette de Portici* (opera; mus Auber,

**Elena Andreyanova, in a lithograph by John Brandard, London, 1852**

chor. after Aumer), Rokotskaya in *La Chaumière Hongroise* (Didelot), title role in *Catarina; ou, La Fille du bandit* (Perrot).

## PUBLICATIONS

Pleshcheev, Aleksandr, *Our Ballet*, St. Petersburg, 1899
"Two Forgotten Russian Danseuses", *Annual of Imperial Theatres* (St. Petersburg), no. 4, 1909
Krasovskaya, Vera, *Russian Ballet Theatre from its Origin to the Middle of the Nineteenth Century*, Leningrad and Moscow, 1958
Roslavleva, Natalia, *Era of the Russian Ballet*, London, 1966
Guest, Ivor, *Jules Perrot: Master of the Romantic Ballet*, New York, 1984

* * *

Elena Andreyanova's talent was formed in the years of the triumph of romantic ballet, and it was her fate to appear for an entire five years on the St. Petersburg stage alongside Marie Taglioni herself. Following the great ballerina's departure in 1842, the situation which prevailed in Russian ballet was described by the critic Rafail Zotov, as follows: "Taglioni went away and the public were despondent. All these charming ballets which excited us remained behind as orphans about whom everybody always sympathises but nobody consoles. And what happened? Madame Andreyanova decided to take upon herself these great and difficult roles . . . She did not wish to present herself as an equal to Taglioni, but to show that a Russian dancer would not be unworthy of any of these roles, even after following behind a first-class European talent; to show that she, with her enthusiasm and love of work, had attained the highest level of accomplishment. And Madame Andreyanova did all this with rare artistry."

The first performance on the Russian stage of the role of Giselle (in 1842) was a test for Andreyanova. Contemporaries' reactions were by no means unanimous. "In the first act she performed the mad scene excellently, and in the second, she was exciting for the first minute after turning into a Wili," writes one. Another: "Madame Andreyanova is superlative where dance passes from the region of exquisite art into pure mastery. The distinctive features of her dance are strength, liveliness, and victory over difficulties—and therefore she excels in character dance."

The differences in the assessment of Andreyanova's talent were not accidental. They reflected both personal infatuation and the extremes produced by inevitable battles between factions of supporters. Andreyanova's name in the Russian society of those times was connected with her "friendship" of many years with the all-powerful director of the Imperial Theatres, Aleksandr Gedeonov. Although this evidently had little effect on the ballerina's undoubted stage successes, passions, scandals, and incidents constantly simmered around her.

Even successful tours beyond the boundaries of Russia did not convince the ballerina's adversaries of her talent. Nevertheless, according to Krasovskaya, "Andreyanova's success in Paris was equal to the successes of Taglioni and Fanny Elssler in St Petersburg." Let us quote a French critic's assessment of her guest tour at the Paris Opéra: "The features of Madame Andreyanova are filled with charm, mildness, and worthiness. We immediately recognize the pupil of Taglioni in the elegance of her figure, the correctness of her poses, and the flexibility of her movements; but to the qualities acquired in such a superlative school Madame Andreyanova unites further qualities unique to herself: extraordinary strength, mobility, and flexibility of movement—all highly rated by connoisseurs. They find this dancer's figure irreproachable, with arms rounded to perfection, and her poses distinguished by fullness and daring. In a word, Madame Andreyanova's début was crowned with full success." In Milan, in honour of the ballerina, a medal was struck with her profile.

In 1847, Marius Petipa produced the ballet *Paquita* for his début in St. Petersburg, and chose Andreyanova as his partner. In the role of the Spanish Paquita, the ballerina performed classical and character dances alike and performed the mime scenes with great dramatic strength. Andreyanova had her greatest success in the principal role of the ballet *Satinella* where, depending on the storyline, she appeared at one moment in the form of a demon beauty, at another in the form of a page, and at another in the form of a bayadère. Eye-witness Fedor Koni reported, "This role is very difficult; it all rests on mime-play, on the living personification of the idea of hell battling passionately with ardent love for the woman who is this fallen angel in her human form. Satinella must frighten the spectator and at the same time compel sympathy for herself. Madame Andreyanova attains this double effect through her well-thought-out and eloquent performance."

In addition to successful performances of major roles in ballets, the ballerina had a predilection for individual dances in opera ballets. The already-mentioned Zotov noted, "Andreyanova, following her personal inspiration, created a special type of dance known by the name of 'character'—full of life, fire, and conception. And it was impossible not to see the enthusiasm with which she performed these dances and the enthusiasm with which the public greeted her in the bolero, saltarello, khaleg, jota, zapateado, and in all character dances."

Andreyanova's last appearance on the stage was in Voronezh in November 1855 during a tour of the Russian provinces. The ballerina, then seriously ill, went to Paris where she died. In the cemetery of Père Lachaise a tomb is preserved with a memorial to this exceptional Russian dancer.

—Arsen Degen

---

**ANGIOLINI, Gaspero**

Italian dancer, choreographer, ballet master, and composer. Born Domenico Maria Gaspero Angiolini (baptismal name: Domenico Maria Angiolo Gasparini) in Florence, 9 February 1731. First music and dance lessons probably in Florence, under father, Francesco Angiolini; later studied with Franz Hilverding, Vienna, from early 1750s on. Married dancing partner Maria Teresa Fogliazzi, 1754: three sons (surviving into adulthood), Francesco, Giuseppe, Pietro. Dancer in Venice and northern Italy, 1747–50; dancer, Teatro San Moise, Venice (appearing in ballets by Domenico Minelli Dadati), 1748–50; also guest performer, Milan, Spoleto, Turin, and Padua; dancer at the inauguration of Teatro di Spoleto, and in Padua, 1751; choreographer in Rome, 1752; first dancer, Hoftheater, Vienna, from c.1752, dancing in Hilverding's ballets; choreographer for Teatro Regio, Turin, carnaval 1757; ballet master (succeeding Hilverding), Vienna, 1758–62; assistant to Hilverding in Russia, 1762, returning to Vienna, 1763–66; ballet master and court choreographer (again succeeding Hilverding), St. Petersburg, 1766–72; choreographer in Venice, Padua, and Milan, 1772–3; ballet master (succeeding Noverre), Vienna, 1774–76; choreographer for Russian court, 1776–78; ballet master at La Scala, Milan (working also in Venice, Verona, and Turin), 1778–82; ballet master and also director of ballet school, St. Petersburg 1783–86; choreographer at La Scala, Milan, 1788–89, Regio Teatro, Turin, 1790, Venice, 1791, La Scala, Milan, 1797; exiled from Milan to Cattaro, because of political activities, 1799–1801; also composer, creating the music for many of his own ballets including *Les Chinois en Europe* (1767); also writer, publishing treatise on pantomime ballet (1765). Died in Milan, 6 February 1803.

## WORKS

1757 *Diana ed Endimione* (ballet; mus. Gioanetti), Teatro Regio, Turin
*Balli di contadini* (ballet; mus. Gioanetti), Teatro Regio, Turin
*Ballo de'caratteri col giuoco della gatta-cieca* (ballet; mus. Gioanetti), Teatro Regio, Turin
*Soldati e vivandiere* (ballet; mus. Gioanetti), Teatro Regio, Turin
*Scoperta dell'America da Cristoforo Colombo* (ballet; mus. Gioanetti), Teatro Regio, Turin
*Ballo di nazioni diverse* (ballet; mus. Gioanetti), Teatro Regio, Turin
1759 *La Foire de Lyon*, Hoftheater, Vienna
1760 Dances in *Alcide al Bivio* (opera; mus. Hasse), Vienna
1761 *Don Juan; ou, Le Festin de Pierre* (pantomime ballet; mus. Gluck), Burgtheater, Vienna
1761/66 *Cid*, Vienna
*Ninfe*, Vienna
*Ritorno opportuno*, Vienna
*Teseo in Creta*, Vienna
1762 Dances in *Il Trionfo di Clelia* (opera; mus. Hasse), Vienna
Dances in *Artaserse* (opera; mus. G. Scarlatti), Vienna
Dances in *La Cythère assiégée* (opera; mus. Gluck), Burgtheater, Vienna
*Dance[s] of the Elysian Fields* in *Orfeo ed Euridice* (opera; mus. Gluck), Burgtheater, Vienna
Dances (with Hilverding) in *L'Olimpiade* (opera; mus. Manfredini), Moscow
1763 Dances in *Ezio* (opera; mus. Gluck), Vienna
1763/65 *Cleopatra* (heroic ballet), Vienna
*Teti e Peleo* (heroic ballet), Vienna
*Iphigenia* (heroic ballet), Vienna
*Le Avventure del seraglio* (mus. G. Scarlatti), Vienna
1764 *Le Muse protette dal genio d'Austria* (pantomime ballet; also mus.), Burgtheater, Vienna
Dances in *La Rencontre imprévue; ou, Les Pélerins de la Mecque* (opéra-comique; mus. Gluck), Burgtheater, Vienna
*Andromeda*, Vienna
1765 *Semiramis* (*Semiramide*; pantomime ballet; mus. Gluck), Burgtheater, Vienna
1765/66 *Iphigenia in Aulide*, Vienna
1766 *Alessandro* (ballet; mus. Gluck), Vienna
*Le Départ d'Énée; ou, Didon abandonnée* (heroic ballet; also mus.), Court Theatre, St. Petersburg
1767 *Les Chinois en Europe* (ballet; also mus.), Court Theatre, St. Petersburg
*La Costance récompensée* (ballet; mus. Manfredini) in *La Governante astuta e il tutore sciocco e geloso* (opera; mus. Galuppi), Moscow
*Un Amour d'Alexandre; ou, Plaisir et Amour* (ballet pantomime, new version of *Alessandro*; mus. Gluck), in *La Governante astuta e il tutore sciocco e geloso* (opera; mus. Galuppi), Moscow
*Divertissements des fêtes de Noël* (also mus.), Court Theatre, Moscow
1768 Dances in *Ifigenia in Tauride* (opera; mus. Galuppi), St. Petersburg
*Le Préjuge vaincu* (pantomime ballet; also mus.), Court Theatre, St. Petersburg
1769 Dances in *L'Olimpiade* (opera; mus. Traetta), St. Petersburg
*Armide et Renaud* (ballet; mus. Raupach), Court Theatre, St. Petersburg
1770 *L'Asile de Cupidon* (also *Le Refuge de Cupidon*, ballet; mus. Raupach), St Petersburg
*Les Nouveaux Argonautes* (ballet; mus. Springer), St. Petersburg
*Telemaco* (ballet; also mus.), St. Petersburg
1772 *Semira* (ballet; also mus.), St. Petersburg
c.1772 *L'Arte vinta dalla natura ovvero il Pittore* (ballet; also mus.), St. Petersburg
*L'Orphelin de la Chine* (ballet), St. Petersburg
*La Forza sottomessa all Ragione* (ballet), St Petersburg
1772/73 Intermezzo in *Armida* (opera; mus. Naumann), Padua
*Il Re alla caccia* (*La Caccia di Enrico IV*; ballet), Teatro San Benedetto, Venice
*Scene episodiche* (ballet), Teatro San Benedetto, Venice
*Il disertore francese* (ballet), Teatro San Benedetto, Venice
1773 *Il Sagrificio di Dirces* (heroic pantomime ballet; also mus.), Regio Ducal Teatro, Milan
*Soliman II; o, La Francese trionfante* (ballet; also mus.), Regio Ducal Teatro, Milan
*Arianna nell'isola di Nasso* (ballet), Regio Ducal Teatro, Milan
*La Contadina in Corte* (ballet), Regio Ducal Teatro, Milan
Dances in *Zon Zon* (opera; mus. Gazzaniga), Regio Ducal Teatro, Milan
Dances in *Andromeda* (opera; mus. Paisiello), Regio Ducal Teatro, Milan
Dances in *Il Cavalier parigino* (opera; mus. Monza), Regio Ducal Teatro, Milan
Dances in *La Pescatrice* (opera; mus. Piccini), Regio Ducal Teatro, Milan
Dances in *L'Incognita perseguitata* (opera; mus. Anfossi), Regio Ducal Teatro, Milan
Dances in *Le Pazzie d'Orlando* (opera; mus. Gugliemi), Regio Ducal Teatro, Milan
Dances in *Il Finto pazzo per amore* (opera; mus. Sacchini), Regio Ducal Teatro, Milan
Dances in *La Contessina* (opera; mus. Guzman), Regio Ducal Teatro, Milan
1774 *L'Orphelin de la Chine* (ballet; mus. Gluck), Vienna
*Le Roi et le fermier* (mus. Angiolini), Vienna
1775 *Montezuma; ou, La Conquête du Mexique* (ballet), Vienna
*Teseo in Creta* (ballet), Vienna
1776 *Thésée et Ariane* (ballet; also mus.), St. Petersburg
1777 Dances (mus. Steinbock) in *Nitteti* (opera; mus. Paisiello), St Petersburg
*L'Orphelin de la Chine* (ballet; also mus.), St. Petersburg
Dances in *Lucinda ed Armidoro* (opera; mus. Paisiello), St. Petersburg
1778 Dances in *Achille in Scirio* (opera; mus. Paisiello), St. Petersburg
1779 *Lo Scoprimento di Achille* (pantomime ballet; also mus.), La Scala, Milan
*Il Cavaliere benefico ossia Annet e Lubin* (pantomime

ballet; also mus.), La Scala, Milan
1780 *Alessandro trionfante nelle Indie* (heroic pantomime ballet), Teatro Filarmonico, Verona
*Pastorale* (ballet), Teatro Filarmonico, Verona
*Ciacciona* (ballet; also mus.), La Scala, Milan
*Demofoonte; ossia, Il Sagrificio di Dircea* (heroic pantomime ballet; new version of *Il Sagrificio di Dircea*; also mus.), La Scala, Milan
*La Morte di Cleopatra* (tragic pantomime ballet; also mus.), La Scala, Milan
*L'Amore e l'azzardo* (anacreontic pantomime ballet; also mus.), La Scala, Milan
*Divertimento in Giardino* (ballet; also mus.), La Scala, Milan
1781 *Attila* (tragic pantomime ballet; also mus.), La Scala Milan
*Il Castigo de' Bonzi* (ballet; also mus.), La Scala, Milan
*Solimano* (ballet; also mus.), La Scala, Milan
*Despina e Ricciardetto* (tragic pantomime ballet; also mus.), La Scala, Milan
*Lauretta* (pantomime ballet; also mus.), La Scala, Milan
*Gli Scherzi* (ballet; also mus.), La Scala, Milan
*Alzira ossia gli americani* (tragic pantomime ballet; also mus.), La Scala, Milan
*Il Diavolo a quattro; o, La Doppia metamorfosi* (*Le Diable à quatre*; comic pantomime ballet; also mus.), La Scala, Milan
*La Mascherata* (ballet; also mus.), La Scala, Milan
1782 *L'amicizia alla prova* (pantomime ballet; also mus.), Milan
*Il Trionfo d'amore* (ballet; also mus.), La Scala, Milan
*Il Genii riuniti* (heroic pantomime ballet; also mus.), La Scala, Milan
*Solimano II* (ballet; also mus.), La Scala, Milan
*Teseo in Creta* (heroic pantomime ballet; also mus.), La Scala, Milan
*La Vendetta spiritosa* (comic pantomime ballet; also mus.), La Scala, Milan
*L'amore al cimento ossia il Sofi generoso* (heroic pantomime ballet; also mus.), La Scala. Milan
1783/86 *Il Mondo della luna* (ballet; mus. Paisiello), St. Petersburg
*Pollinia* (ballet; mus. Sacchini, Sarti), St. Petersburg
1788 *Un Divertimento campestre* (ballet; also mus.), La Scala, Milan
1789 *Fedra* (tragic ballet; also mus.), La Scala, Milan
*Lorezzo* (comic-heroic ballet; also mus.), La Scala, Milan
*Le Nozze de' Sanniti* (ballet; also mus.), La Scala, Milan
*Dorina e l'uomo selvatico* (ballet; also mus.), La Scala, Milan
*Amore e Psiche* (heroic pantomime ballet; also mus.), La Scala, Milan
1790 *Sargine* (heroic ballet; also mus.), Regio Teatro, Turin
*Lorezzo* (comic-heroic ballet; also mus.), Regio Teatro, Turin
*I Vincitori dei Giuochi Olimpici* (ballet; also mus.), Regio Teatro, Turin
*Il tutore sorpresa* (ballet; also mus.), Regio Teatro, Turin
*Rinaldo e Armida*, La Scala, Milan
*Una Fiera*, La Scala, Milan
1791 *Tito; o, La Partenza di Berenice* (heroic pantomime ballet), Venice
*La Vendetta ingegnosa; o, La Statua di Condillac* (ballet), Venice
1797 *Deucalione e Pirra* (staged Paracca after Angiolini), La Scala, Milan
*Silvio; o, Il Vero patriotta* (ballet), La Scala, Milan
*Il Repubblicano* (ballet), La Scala, Milan
*Il Santissimo massacro; o, Le Vittime del Vaticano ovvero la fuga da Roma dell'ambasciatore Bonaparte* (ballet), La Scala, Milan
*Il Sogno di un democratico* (ballet), La Scala, Milan

**PUBLICATIONS**

By Angiolini:
Programme notes for premiere performance of *Le Festin de pierre* (*Don Juan*), Vienna, 1761; also in Gluck, C.W., *Sämtliche Werke*, edited by R. Gerber, G. Croll, et al., Kassel and Basel, 1951
*Dissertazione*, published with programme for *La Cythère assiégée*, Vienna, 1762
*Dissertation sur les ballets pantomimes des Anciens, publiée pour servir de programme au Ballet Pantomime Tragique de Sémiramis*, 1765; facsimile with foreword by W. Toscanini, Milan, 1965
*Lettere di Gaspero Angiolini a Monsieur Noverre sopra i balli pantomimi*, Milan, 1773
*Riflessioni sopra l'uso dei Programmi nei Balli Pantomimi*, 1775
*Dissertazione per servire di risposta all'invito del Ministro degli affari interni*, 1797

Ballet scores:
*Le Muse protette del genio d'Austria* (1764), *Didon abandonnée* (*Didone abbandonata*; 1766), *Les Chinois en Europe* (1767), *L'arte vinta della natura* (1772), *Il Re alla caccia* (1772)

About Angiolini:
Toscanini, W., "Gaspare Angiolini", *Metropolitan Opera News* (New York), 8 April 1955
Kirstein, Lincoln, *Movement and Metaphor: Four Centuries of Ballet*, New York, 1970
Tozzi, Lorenzo, *Il balletto pantomimo del settecento: Gaspare Angiolini*, L'Aquila, 1972
Winter, Marian Hannah, *The Pre-Romantic Ballet*, London, 1974
Carones, L., "Noverre and Angiolini: Polemical Letters" in *Dance Research* (London), vol. 5, no. 42, 1987

* * *

It appears that Gaspero Angiolini received his first dance training from his father, Francesco, in Florence. Between 1747 and 1750 he was engaged as dancer at the Teatro di San Moisé in Venice, with occasional guest appearances in Milan, Spoleto, Turin, and Padua. His first venture into choreography seems to have taken place in Rome in 1752. Soon after that Angiolini went to Vienna, attracted by the reputation of the Imperial ballet master Franz Hilverding, who was to become his mentor and model. Angiolini danced as soloist in Hilverding's ballets from about 1752; his partner was the prima ballerina Maria Teresa Fogliazzi, who became his wife in 1754. Fogliazzi, offspring of a distinguished Parma family, was greatly admired by major personalities at court and in the theatre; her connections opened many doors for her husband once his career as one of the leading choreographers of the day had been launched. Initially, however, Angiolini excelled as premier danseur in Vienna and Turin.

When Hilverding accepted the position of Imperial ballet master to the Russian court at St. Petersburg (1758), Angiolini became his successor in Vienna. His early choreographic works show his indebtedness to the style of Hilverding, but he is searching for his own, personal choreographic idiom ("la mia maniera"). His first major triumph was the tragic ballet *Don Juan; ou, Le Festin de Pierre*, based on Molière's *Dom Juan*, with music by C.W. Gluck; Angiolini himself danced the title role. Although the tragic ending shocked the audiences, who were accustomed to the light-hearted divertissements of the preceding decades, the fame of *Le Festin de Pierre* spread quickly, and performances in Paris, Hamburg, Frankfurt, and other German and Italian theatres followed soon.

Between 1762 and 1766 Angiolini created a number of ballets and arranged dance scenes for operas in performance on the Viennese stages, including several to the music of the court composer Gluck; on occasion he composed the music himself, as for his ballet *Le Muse protette*, which was presented as part of the festive events celebrating the coronation of Joseph II in 1764. Another milestone in the choreographer's career was the "ballet-pantomime tragique", *Semiramis*, based on Voltaire's drama of the same name, with music by Gluck. Rejected outright by those present at the performance because of its uncompromisingly brutal story-line ("soggetto il più terribile"), the work established its creator, once and for all, as one of the leading representatives of the new "ballet tragique", or *ballet d'action*.

In August 1765, Emperor Franz Stephan died. The Viennese theatres closed. Angiolini's friend and supporter, Count Durazzo, had left Vienna the year before, and *Semiramis* had failed. Thus, when the call to the Tsarist court in St. Petersburg came, the ballet master went gladly, as successor to Hilverding. Between September 1766 and 1772 Angiolini choreographed nine ballets and numerous divertissements for Italian operas in performances at the Winter Palace.

In 1772 he resigned from his post in St. Petersburg and went to Venice—not, however, without a stop-over in Vienna, where in the meantime Jean-Georges Noverre had established himself. The two men met in what appears to have been a civilized encounter; there was no sign as yet of the bitter controversy between them that would soon erupt and drag on for years to come. In Venice (1773) Angiolini produced six ballets to be performed in conjunction with the Italian *opera seria*; some of these were revivals of older materials (*Semiramis*, *Didon abandonnée*), others were newly created for Venice (e.g. *Il Re alla caccia*, *Il Disertore francese*). That same year saw the publication, in Milan, of Angiolini's *Lettere di G.A. a Monsieur Noverre sopra i balli pantomimi*, in which he challenged Noverre's claim to be the inventor of the ballet d'action and gave credit to Hilverding instead. Noverre responded sharply the following year (1774) with his *Petite Réponse aux grandes lettres du Sr. Angiolini* (in the introduction to the libretto of the ballet *Les Horaces et les Curiaces*). Angiolini countered with his *Riflessioni sopra l'uso dei programmi ne'balli pantomimi* (1775).

In the spring of 1774 Angiolini returned to Vienna to replace Noverre, who had been invited to Milan. He remained there for a short time only; in June 1775 he made a guest appearance in Pavia, where he crossed paths with Noverre in anything but a friendly encounter. Discouraged by the partisanship of the Viennese public in favor of Noverre, Angiolini left in 1776 for another two-year engagement in St. Petersburg. By 1779 he was back in Italy, working in Venice, Verona, Turin, and at La Scala in Milan, and on 17 December 1782 Angiolini signed a new four-year contract with St. Petersburg (his duties now including the directorship of a ballet school). He left Russia for good, late in 1786.

The final sojourn of Angiolini's life was in Italy once again. At La Scala he produced seven of his own ballets during the 1788–89 carnival season and in April of 1789; there then followed engagements at the Regio Teatro in Turin, La Scala, and Venice. On 31 October 1792 his wife died. Some years after that, he apparently became involved in political controversy, and because he expressed sympathies for the democratic ideas of the French was imprisoned in 1799 and subsequently exiled. He returned home in the summer of 1801 and died in Milan at the age of 71.

A brilliant dancer and mime himself, Angiolini was a passionate advocate of the total oeuvre for the ballet stage, in which a substantial dramatic story-line, music that supports the action in every detail, well-designed stage sets and machinery, and, above all, the expressiveness of the dancer's entire body ("la rhétorique muette") would work together in perfect unity. Only if all the arts collaborated in equal measure would, in the choreographer's opinion, the perfect "azione completa pantomima" be the result: the "ballet pantomime tragique" or "ballet d'action" of which he was the first true representative.

Angiolini's thoughts concerning this and more are formulated in three important discourses that were published in conjunction with the synopses of his Viennese ballets *Don Juan*, *Semiramis*, and *La Cythère assiégée*. The intellectual climate of Vienna in the 1760s was ideally suited to a choreographer of Angiolini's talents: C.W. Gluck and his librettist Count Rainero de Calzabigi were in the process of reforming the opera along similar lines, their efforts supported by the ballet master Franz Hilverding, whose ideas concerning the ballet d'action prepared the way for the innovative approach of his gifted pupil.

In his choreographies, as he himself states, Angiolini proceeded from the more traditional national dances, balli storici, and fables to comedy and drama and, finally, to the "complete tragedy in pantomime *dans le goût des Anciens*"—his *Don Juan* of 1761. Even though he occasionally made a concession to the taste of his public who preferred a "lieto fine" (a case in point is the lost ballet-tragique *Iphigénie en Aulide*), Angiolini firmly believed in the principles of classical Greek tragedy, employing only a limited number of soloists and using the corps de ballet in the manner of a Greek chorus. Of his dancing actors he demanded expressiveness of gesture, face, and movement in addition to an impeccable technique; he advises his students to read the classics, to study architecture, painting and sculpture, mathematics, geometry, and music. Unlike Noverre, whose ballet programmes contained lengthy descriptions of the plots (Angiolini was sharply critical of this practice, as his *Riflessioni* shows), Angiolini preferred to give merely an outline of the story to be told, insisting that the dancers' "silent speech" should be strong and clear enough to convey the tale as well as the meaning and the emotions to the audience.

Even though we do know that he thought about the possibility of fixing his choreographies in writing, no notations for Angiolini's tragic ballets have been found thus far. We shall therefore, to our infinite regret, never be able to recapture fully the beauty and the power of the works created by this remarkable artist of the eighteenth-century ballet theatre.

—Ingrid Brainard

---

**ANISIMOVA, Nina**

Russian dancer and choreographer. Born Nina Aleksandrovna Anisimova in St. Petersburg, 27 January (14 January old style) 1909. Studied at the Petrograd, later Leningrad, Choreographic School, pupil of Maria Romanova, Aleksandr Shiryaev, and Agrippina Vaganova; graduated in 1926; also studied character dancing under Aleksandr Monakhov, 1926–

27. Artist of the Maly Theatre of Opera and Ballet, 1926–27; dancer, State Academic Theatre for Opera and Ballet (GATOB), later the Kirov Ballet, 1927–58; first choreography (*Spanish Suite*) in 1935; continued to stage ballets until 1964, including *Swan Lake*, Copenhagen, 1964; teacher, Choreographic Department of the Leningrad Conservatory, 1963–74. Honoured Artist of the Russian Federation, 1944; People's Artist of the Bashkirskaia ASSR and Honoured Arts Worker of the Russian Federation, 1957; State Prize of the USSR, 1949. Died in Leningrad, 23 September 1979.

## ROLES

1932 Thérèse (cr) in *The Flames of Paris* (Vainonen), State Academic Theatre of Opera and Ballet (GATOB), Leningrad
1937 Nastia (cr) in *Partisan Days* (Vainonen), Kirov Ballet, Leningrad
1942 Aisha (cr) in *Gayané* (also chor.), Kirov Ballet, Perm

**Other roles include:** Nerilla in *The Talisman* (Petipa), Mercedes in *Don Quixote* (Gorsky), Siamka in *Bolt* (Lopukhov), Radmilla in *Militsa* (Vainonen). Character roles include Ukrainian, Slav, Rhapsody in *The Little Humpbacked Horse* (Saint-Léon; staged Gorsky), Saracen, Mazurka, Panaderos in *Raymonda* (Petipa; staged Sergeyev), Spanish Dance in *Swan Lake* (Petipa, Ivanov), Gypsy and Spanish Dance in *Don Quixote* (Gorsky), Hindu Dance in *La Bayadère* (Petipa; staged Ponomarev, Chabukiani), Gypsy in *Katerina* (Lavrovsky), Flamenco and Dance with the Castanets in *Laurencia* (Chabukiani), Spanish Dance in *The Nutcracker* (Vainonen), Dance on a Plate in *The Red Poppy* (Lopukhov), Cracoviak and Mazurka in the opera *Ivan Susanin* (mus. Glinka, chor. Andrei Lopukhov, S. Koren).

## WORKS

1935 *Spanish Suite* (mus. Albéniz, Granados, Sarasate), Grand Hall, Leningrad Philharmonia, Leningrad
1936 *Andalusian Wedding* (with S. Koren; mus. Albéniz, Granados, Chabrier), Leningrad Choreographic School Graduation Performance, Leningrad
1942 *Gayané* (mus. Khachaturian), Kirov Ballet, Perm
1944 *Crane's Song* (mus. Stepanov, Ismagilov), Bashkir Opera, Ufa
1947 *The Magic Veil* (mus. Zaranek), Maly Theatre, Leningrad
1949 *Coppélia* (new version; mus. Delibes), Maly Theatre, Leningrad
1950 *Schéhérazade* (new version; mus. Rimsky-Korsakov), Maly Theatre, Leningrad
1957 *Willow Tree* (mus. Yevlakhov), Maly Theatre, Leningrad
1963 *Cinderella* (mus. Prokofiev), Opera Ballet, Belgrade
*The Legend of the Lake* (mus. Vladigerov), State Opera Ballet, Sofia

Also staged:
1945 *The Fountain of Bakhchisarai* (after Zakharov; mus. Asafiev), State Opera Ballet, Sofia
1964 *Swan Lake* (after Petipa, Ivanov), Royal Danish Ballet, Copenhagen

## PUBLICATIONS

Chernova, N., *From Geltser to Ulanova*, Leningrad, 1951
Frangopulo, M., *N. Anisimova*, Leningrad, 1951
Keldish, Y., "A New Production of *Gayané*", *Sovetsky Muzyka* (Moscow), no. 2, 1954
Roslavleva, Natalia, *Era of the Russian Ballet*, London, 1966
Swift, Mary Grace, *The Art of the Dance in the USSR*, Notre Dame, Ind., 1968
Stupnikov, Igor, "Seventy-Five Years from Nina Anisimova's Birth", *Sovetsky Balet Teatr* (Moscow), no 4, 1984

* * *

An outstanding character dancer of exceptional temperament, Nina Anisimova was the creator of full-blooded "national" types on stage. In Anisimova's art, what was typical was the union of dance technique with unique expressiveness; her style of gesture was sweeping and striking, and her rhythm always impulsive and dynamic—whirlwind tempos usually dominated. Her dancing was electrifying; it all but attacked the spectator. Yet, as Krasovskaya said, "Anisimova's dance, with all its temperament, was marked by a great nobility acquired from the best masters of the school of Russian character dancing."

Anisimova was extremely popular with audiences; when she was at the height of her career, and her name appeared on the programme, people often waited for hours outside the theatre just to see her dance. For example, in the old faithful *Don Quixote*, she would perform either the gypsy dance in the second act (staged by Anisimova herself to the music of Pugni), or the Spanish march in the last act (a quite acrobatic piece created for her by the American dancer, Pauline Koner)—and even before she danced, when the audience knew she was about to appear, thunderous applause filled the house, as though an avalanche had fallen. Anisimova's gypsy dance featured a set of fouttée-like turns, done on heeled character shoes; such a virtuoso display demonstrated perfectly the combination of qualities inherent in her dancing: she could appear a gypsy and a classical dancer at the same time.

Anisimova's choreographic creativity was initially the artist's reaction against the limited character roles then available in Leningrad theatres; her special talent was unable to blossom in the ballet repertoire. Her first attempt at choreography was *Spanish Suite* in 1935, followed by *Andalusian Wedding*, performed at the graduation performance of the Leningrad Choreographic Academy in 1936. As a choreographer, Anisimova attained creative maturity in *Gayané*—her most famous work—where her mastery of character dance was united with a classicism that made for a complete and convincing artistic whole. Her best productions confirmed the significance of national dance, and showed its ability to resolve the potential conflict between "classical" and "character" styles in a single ballet.

After Anisimova's performing career was finished, she continued teaching, and also travelled abroad as a choreographer to stage ballets in Yugoslavia, Bulgaria, and other countries. Her partner, Joseph Gerbek, retired later than she did; and she returned to the stage to perform the famous Spanish march with him. In many ways it was merely a shadow of the former Anisimova which we saw; yet, when she rushed on to the stage, it was a moment which made one think, "We will never have another character dancer like her." And indeed, since her day the role of character dance in the Soviet Union has become something of a problem; sadly, choreographers like Grigorovich, Belsky, or Vinogradov have not used it in the way that Russia had grown accustomed to—in the way that Petipa, for instance, used it. In Grigorovich's *Swan Lake*, therefore, pointe shoes have replaced heeled character shoes in all of the national dances. It is certainly interesting to

*Apollon musagéte*, **Diaghilev's Ballets Russes, Paris, 1928**

see the Mazurka or the Spanish dance performed on pointe; but it seems a strange tendency in late twentieth-century Russian choreography to ignore, or dismiss, character dancing.

With the exception perhaps of Irina Gensler, Anisimova was the last great character dancer on the Soviet stage. Later generations have tried to imitate her, but they have only proven very good copies, not the original.

—Igor Stupnikov

---

## APOLLO

(Original title: *Apollon musagète*)

**Choreography:** George Balanchine
**Music:** Igor Stravinsky
**Design:** André Bauchant
**Libretto:** Igor Stravinsky
**First Production:** Diaghilev's Ballets Russes, Théâtre Sarah Bernhardt, Paris, 12 June 1928

**Principal Dancers:** Serge Lifar (Apollo), Alice Nikitina (Terpsichore; alternating with Alexandra Danilova), Lubov Tchernicheva (Polyhymnia), Felia Doubrovska (Calliope).

**Other productions include:** Chamber Music Society (first production to Stravinsky's score; chor. Adolph Bolm, design Nicholas Remisoff), with Bolm (Apollo), Ruth Page, Berenice Holmes, Elise Reiman (Muses); Washington, D.C., 27 April 1928. Royal Danish Ballet (restaged Balanchine, design Kjeld Abell), with Lief Ørnberg (Apollo); Copenhagen, 18 January 1931. American Ballet (restaged Balanchine; design Stewart Chaney), with Lew Christensen (Apollo), Elise Reiman (Terpsichore), Daphne Vane (Calliope), Holly Howard (Polyhymnia); New York, 27 April 1937. Teatro delle Arti (new version; chor. Aurel Milloss); Rome, 12 April 1941. Teatro Colón (restaged Balanchine, design Pavel Tchelitchev); Buenos Aires, 1942. Ballet Theatre (restaged Balanchine, design Barbara Karinska), as *Apollo*, with André Eglevsky (Apollo), Vera Zorina (Terpsichore), Nora Kaye (Polyhymnia), Rosella Hightower (Calliope); New York, 25 April 1943. New York City Ballet (revised Balanchine, costumes Karinska), as *Apollo, Leader of the Muses*, with André Eglevsky (Apollo), Maria Tallchief (Terpsichore), Diana Adams (Calliope), Tanaquil

***Apollo*, with Desmond Kelly in Royal Ballet ("New Group") production, 1971**

LeClerq (Polyhymnia); New York, 15 November 1951 (performed by New York City Ballet as *Apollo* from 1957, without scenery from 1979). La Scala Ballet (new version; chor. Lifar, design Georgio de Chirico), as *Apollo musagète*; Milan, 10 March 1956. Royal Ballet (staged John Taras after Balanchine; design John Craxton), as *Apollon musagète*, with Donald MacLeary (Apollo), Svetlana Beriosova (Terpsichore), Monica Mason (Polyhymnia), Georgina Parkinson (Calliope); London, 15 November 1966.

### PUBLICATIONS


Kirstein, Lincoln, "Balanchine Musagète", *Theatre Arts* (New York), November 1947

Barnes, Clive, "*Apollo*, Balanchine and Stravinsky", *About the House* (London), Christmas 1966

Kirstein, Lincoln, *Movement and Metaphor: Four Centuries of Ballet*, New York, 1970

Balanchine, George, with Mason, Francis, *Balanchine's Festival of Ballet*, Garden City, N.Y., 1977

Gruen, John, "An Olympian Apollo: Balanchine and Stravinsky", *Dance Magazine* (New York), April 1981

Borovsky, Victor, and Schouvaloff, Alexander, *Stravinsky on Stage*, London, 1982

Croce, Arlene, *Going to the Dance*, New York, 1982

Garis, Robert, "Balanchine-Stravinsky: Facts and Problems", *Ballet Review* (Brooklyn, N.Y.), Fall 1982

Au, Susan, "*Apollo*: The Transformation of a Myth", *Dance as Cultural Heritage*, CORD Dance Research Annual (New York), vol. 1, 1983

Jowitt, Deborah, *The Dance in Mind*, New York, 1985

Johnson, Robert, "White on White: The Classical Background of *Apollon musagète*", *Ballet Review* (New York), Fall 1985

Denby, Edwin, *Dance Writings*, edited by Robert Cornfield and William Mackay, New York, 1986

Gruen, John, "Mounting Olympus", *Dance Magazine* (New York), June 1987


* * *

The first production of Stravinsky's *Apollon musagète*, choreographed by Adolph Bolm and first performed in Washington, D.C. as a commission for Elizabeth Sprague Coolidge, attracted little notice. In fact, Stravinsky had reserved the European rights to the ballet for Serge Diaghilev, perhaps anticipating that the ballet would reach its full potential under Diaghilev's Ballets Russes.

It was the second version of *Apollon musagète*, performed in Paris with choreography by George Balanchine, that became legendary, heralding the birth of neoclassicism in ballet. It also marked the beginning of perhaps the most inspired artistic collaboration in the history of modern ballet: that of Stravinsky and Balanchine.

Stravinsky's scenario tells the story of the birth of the god Apollo, his education by the Muses of poetry, mime, and dancing (Calliope, Polyhymnia, and Terpsichore, respectively), and his ascension to the home of the gods on Mount Olympus. Balanchine created movement for four dancers that was beautifully in sympathy with Stravinsky's refined music (which was almost Mozart-like in style). But blended in with the pristine classical ballet sequences were moments of unexpected modernism—dancers shuffling in a line with flexed feet; a seated-position pirouette on pointe; Apollo prone on the floor, supporting Terpsichore in a full-pointe arabesque; and a flashing hand gesture for Apollo that was inspired by a city street sign. Here was the classical dancing of Petipa and the Maryinsky Theatre with a new twist.

*Apollo* (the title was shortened in the 1950s) reverberates with layers and layers of meaning, intended or otherwise. For instance, there is a moment when the three Muses, seated on the floor, reach up to link their arms around Apollo's forearm. One by one, they lunge forward and away from Apollo on pointe, their arms still tethered by Apollo's. They look like charms on a bracelet or sun-seeking flowers on a vine.

One can view this little scene as the Muses' attempt to guide and teach the young god in the ways of their arts. It can also be seen as a symbol of Apollo's power over the Muses and his struggle to train and mould them. In a much larger sense, the scene represents the allegorical text of the entire ballet—how poetry, mime, and dance fuse with music to create classicism. But ultimately, the tableau is simply an inspired moment of neoclassical dancing—form, line, elegance, lyricism, and discipline all merging into one bit of whimsy.

The latter perspective defines Balanchine's true aesthetic: ballet as a visual, rather than an intellectual, art. Ballet is a fantasy, he said. It has nothing to do with life. "We are trained to dance and perform for the idea of beautiful things." Balanchine believed that ballet was not an emotional art. If dance moves a person to tears, it is only by the beauty of the dancing. And yet *Apollo* is also about the birth of creativity and imagination, about the struggle of the artist. In many ways it is autobiographical. There is a point in the pas de deux where Apollo wearily lets his head fall into the cupped hands of Terpsichore. The gesture is repeated later with all three Muses. Perhaps Balanchine only felt comfort and inner peace in the hands of his muse, when he was creating dance.

With *Apollo*, Balanchine began to strip down ballet, clearing away the multiple choices to the one choice that was inevitable, unique to each piece. He was influenced by Stravinsky, who believed the highest expression in dance was absolute purity—dancing with no meaning apart from itself. The choreographer was, in effect, also building on the theories of Nijinsky, who said that the aim of dance technique was clarification. Balanchine realized for the first time that just as notes in music and colours in fine art belong to different families, so do gestures belong to their own groups. All the choreography he did after *Apollo* was affected by this realization.

Balanchine revised *Apollo* many times, cutting both music and dance sections. In its present form, the ballet begins with the education of Apollo (omitting the birth scene) and ends with the now-familiar tableau of Apollo reaching forward, the three Muses clinging to him and fanning out their legs in ever-ascending arabesques. Some critics have complained that this ending omits the tragic aspect of the ballet—Apollo ascending to Mount Olympus while his mother, Leto, swoons in sorrow. Balanchine defended his changes, saying that the ballet becomes interesting only when there is dancing. "That's what all my ballets are about."

—Jody Leader

---

## APPARITIONS

**Choreography:** Frederick Ashton
**Music:** Franz Liszt, arranged by Constant Lambert and orchestrated by Gordon Jacob
**Design:** Cecil Beaton
**Libretto:** Constant Lambert
**First Production:** Vic-Wells Ballet, Sadler's Wells Theatre, London, 11 February 1936
**Principal Dancers:** Robert Helpmann (The Poet), Margot Fonteyn (The Woman in Ball Dress)

**Other productions include:** Sadler's Wells Theatre Ballet (staged Ashton, design revised Beaton), with John Field (The Poet), Anne Heaton (Woman in Ball Dress); Stratford-upon-Avon, 28 January 1957.

## PUBLICATIONS

Alexander, Peter, "The Ballets of Frederick Ashton", *Dancing Times* (London), May 1939
Beaumont, Cyril, *The Complete Book of Ballets*, revised edition, London, 1951
Vaughan, David, *Frederick Ashton and His Ballets*, London, 1977
Vaughan, David, "Birthday Offering", *Ballet News* (New York), October 1979
Percival, John, "Years of Achievement", *Dance and Dancers* (London), February 1986
Macaulay, Alastair, "The Inconstant Muse", *Dance Theatre Journal* (London), Autumn 1987

* * *

Much was made at the time of the premiere of *Apparitions* of the coincidence that while Ashton and Lambert were doing the preliminary work on the ballet, the story of which was based on the libretto of Berlioz's *Symphonie fantastique*, the Russian choreographer Léonide Massine was working simultaneously on a ballet to the actual Berlioz score, which was first given some five months later than the Ashton work. At the time, it was stated both in the press and privately by partisans of the Vic-Wells Ballet that the modest little company based somewhere in a London slum had managed to produce a work similar, but in fact superior, to that presented by the choreographic genius of the period, Léonide Massine. It was a judgement, though, which some felt to be exaggerated, however appealing the theme, music, choreography, décor, and cast of *Apparitions* may have appeared (and did) at the time of its very successful first performance.

***Apparitions*, with Margot Fonteyn, 1949 revival**

*Apparitions* in 1936 had a magic of its own, a romantic magic of the 1930s; the ballet was an early instance of the neo-romantic movement which was to occupy a dominant position in the art world in England for the next two or three decades. And this magic firmly established Frederick Ashton as a figure to be reckoned with in English ballet, while also beginning the magical partnership of Ashton and Fonteyn which was to continue unbroken for almost 30 years. He first made a role for her, during the previous season, in his version of *Le Baiser de la fée*, in which she played second fiddle to the fabulously beautiful Pearl Argyle—and, whether by accident or design, the role given to the very young Margot Fonteyn accentuated her almost gauche inexperience. It was not until Fonteyn created the Woman in Ball Dress in *Apparitions* that the two artists began to find the measure of one another's capabilities, and to establish a rapport which was to produce some of the most breathtakingly beautiful moments to be seen on the twentieth-century ballet stage.

How much of a rapport was ever established between Ashton and his other *Apparitions* collaborator, Robert Helpmann, is arguable; but Ashton certainly also gave a remarkable opportunity to the Poet, a role which might have been no more than posturing in the hands of a lesser artist, but which, as performed by Helpmann, seemed the personification of every romantic poet in history. Neither he nor Fonteyn were given technically difficult steps, so one was conscious of nothing but the individual characterizations—and if one was never completely convinced by the sixteen-year-old Fonteyn as a femme fatale, Ashton gave her such elegant, seductive movements that it was enough for her to wear the beautiful dress (created for her by Cecil Beaton) and to move in her own individual style for the audience to believe that this was the most seductive of women in the ballet repertoire.

The story of the ballet is easy to follow. A Poet sees a vision of a beautiful woman and falls in love with her. Finding it hard to express his feelings in poetry, he takes laudanum, and dreams of her—first in a ballroom, next on a bare plain, where the body being carried by a procession of monks is hers, and finally in a cave (brilliantly designed using the simplest of means), where her beauty is transformed to an ugly mask. When he awakens, his beloved is gone and he kills himself in despair, whereupon the grieving Woman and her companions come to carry him away. Choreographically the ballet is uneven: the opening scene, with the Poet swooning after dosing himself with laudanum, and the first dream of a ballroom, set and dressed to absolute perfection by Beaton in his first design for ballet, hit a high spot not entirely sustained later in the work; those tedious Bells might have been arranged by a third-rate nineteenth-century choreographer in an off moment, and the third dream ("A Cavern") presented a remarkably conventional orgy. However, *Apparitions* was produced in accordance with Diaghilev's precept of equal partnership between choreographer, musician (or arranger), and designer, and was of great importance in the progress not only of choreographer and dancers, but also of the little English company in Islington which proved that it could produce a work, if not so spectacular as those presented by the visiting Russians, then at least one brimming with speed, movement, colour, and dramatic effect. It would not stand reproduction half a century later, even if the impulse to "improve" were prevented from destroying its individual qualities. This does not affect the fact that in its time, *Apparitions* was a vital contribution to the development of British ballet.

—Janet Sinclair

---

## L'APRÈS-MIDI D'UN FAUNE
(*The Afternoon of a Faun*)

**Choreography:** Vaslav Nijinsky
**Music:** Claude Debussy
**Design:** Léon Bakst
**Libretto:** Vaslav Nijinsky
**First Production:** Diaghilev's Ballets Russes, Théâtre du Châtelet, Paris, 29 May 1912
**Principal Dancers:** Vaslav Nijinsky (Faun), Lydia Nelidova (Principal Nymph)

**Other productions include:** Ballet Club (later Ballet Rambert; staged Leon Woizikowsky after Nijinsky), with William Chappell (Faun) and Diana Gould (Principal Nymph); London, 20 April 1931. (De Basil's) Ballets Russes de Monte Carlo, with Léonide Massine and Tamara Sidorenko; London, 2 October 1933. Paris Opéra (staged and revised Serge Lifar), with Lifar (Faun; solo); Paris, 18 March 1935. Ballet Theatre (staged Yurek Lazovsky after Nijinsky), with George Skibine (Faun) and Jeanette Lauret (Principal Nymph); Mexico City, 4 November 1941. Rome Opera Ballet (new version; chor. Aurel Milloss); Rome, 16 September 1944. New York City Ballet (new version; "contemporary variation" on Nijinsky, chor. Jerome Robbins, design Jean Rosenthal, costumes Irene Sharaff), as *Afternoon of a Faun*, with Francisco Moncion and Tanaquil LeClercq; New York, 14 May 1953. London Festival Ballet (after Lifar, Nijinsky); 8 May 1959, and again (staged Alicia Markova after Nijinsky) 6 September 1962. Paris Opéra Ballet (staged Léonide Massine, assisted by Romola Nijinsky; design Bakst); Paris, 3 March 1976. Joffrey Ballet (reconstructed Elizabeth Schooling and William Chappell after Nijinsky), with Rudolf Nureyev (Faun); New York, 6 March 1979. Béjart Ballet (new version; chor. Maurice Béjart), as *Prélude à L'Après-midi d'un faune*; Lausanne, 1987. Les Grands Ballets Canadiens (reconstructed from Nijinsky's own notation by Ann Hutchinson Guest and Claudia Jeschke); Montreal, 27 October 1989.

### PUBLICATIONS

Beaumont, Cyril, *Complete Book of Ballets*, revised edition, 1951
Kirstein, Lincoln, *Movement and Metaphor*, New York, 1970
"*L'Après-midi d'un faune*" (collection of articles), *L'Avant-scène: Ballet/Danse* (Paris), no. 7, 1982
De Meyer, Baron Adolf, *L'Après-midi d'un faune: Vaslav Nijinsky 1912*, with essays by Richard Buckle, Jennifer Dunning, Ann Hutchinson Guest; London and New York, 1983
Acocella, Joan, "Photo Call with Nijinsky: The Circle and the Center", *Ballet Review* (New York), Winter 1987
Nectoux, J.-M. (ed.), *Afternoon of a Faun*, translated by Maximilian Vos, New York, 1989
Garafola, Lynn, "Finding Faun", *Dance Magazine* (New York), October 1989
Garafola, Lynn, *Diaghilev's Ballets Russes*, New York, 1989
Guest, Ann Hutchinson, "Nijinsky's 'Faune' Restored", *Ballet Review* (New York), Summer 1990
Guest, Ann Hutchinson, and Jeschke, Claudia, *Nijinsky's Faune Restored*, Philadelphia, 1991

* * *

Nijinsky's first ballet was inspired by a trip to Greece with Léon Bakst, chief designer of Les Ballets Russes. Together they

**The nymphs in *L'Après-midi d'un faune*, Diaghilev's Ballets Russes, Paris, 1912**

produced the idea of a ballet that was to be a moving bas-relief based on Claude Debussy's *Prélude à l'après-midi d'un faune* (1894), which itself was inspired by Stephane Mallarmé. The rehearsals were conducted behind closed doors, and when the twelve-minute ballet made its tumultuous début, it resulted in Diaghilev's first "succès de scandale". Nijinsky danced barefoot, and his movements were accentuated by rigid and angular poses. The role of the faun, with its hints of sensuality and languor, eclipsed the more virtuoso parts on which Nijinsky's reputation in Western Europe originally rested.

The story concerns a faun (a mythological creature, half-boy, half-beast), lazily playing on his flute on a hot summer's day, who is taken unawares by some nymphs (mythological water spirits) who are on their way to bathe. He becomes amorously entangled with one of them before she, too, leaves the stage, after which he lustily fondles the scarf she has dropped. A highly stylized, frieze-like evocation of an innocent sensual encounter, the ballet scandalized its opening-night audience with its auto-erotic ending.

The music has been re-choreographed several times, also as a solo dance (Serge Lifar, 1935). But the most popular version is a contemporary ballet by Jerome Robbins called *Afternoon of a Faun*, a ballet in one act which was made on Tanaquil LeClercq and Francisco Moncion of the New York City Ballet. Robbins used Debussy's music as a source of inspiration, echoing the delicate, impressionistic score with classical movement that differs from Nijinsky's heavy, frieze-like steps. But like Nijinsky's original, Robbins's ballet is about unconscious sexual attraction, translating faun and nymph into two young dancers, male and female, in a ballet studio.

Nijinsky's first ballet is a landmark in the history of Diaghilev's Ballets Russes. It marked the end of an era dominated by Mikhail Fokine (who, for Diaghilev, represented the past) and the emergence of the dancer Nijinsky (who represented the future) as a choreographer whose ideas, no doubt stimulated by Diaghilev, lay outside and counter to the classical tradition of St. Petersburg. As the first ballet not to use a proscenium stage—there is no single point of view, the perspective is flat and the action simultaneous—it is also a revolutionary piece of choreography. *Faune* is also one of the first modern ballets, compelling its dancers to think not of just presenting movement, but of using movement to convey emotions and hidden states of mind.

The ballet took the first step in the process of liberating the theatre arts from nineteenth-century conventions. It achieved unusual images and a new expressiveness of the dancer's body, not least of which was the image of the dancer as a sexually expressive being. The ballet's brazen depiction of sexuality deeply shocked the whole of Paris upon its début in 1912. The city quickly split itself into two factions: the pro-Faunists, led by the sculptor Rodin, and the anti-Faunists, lead by the newspaper *Le Monde*, which decried the ballet in a front-page denouncement of its flagrant disregard for morality. The anti-Faunists were eventually silenced by Diaghilev who, after the first storm of disapproval subsided, had the courage to ask the audience at the Théâtre du Châtelet to sit through the twelve-minute ballet once more. Only five days after the ballet's premiere, *Le Figaro* noted approvingly that "Monsieur Nijinsky has changed the mime at the end of *L'Après-midi d'un faune*." This anticipated the New York performance by

Nijinsky that was revised and performed by Nijinsky in 1916. It appears that by this time the offensive masturbatory ending was altered, or, as the *New York Times* observed, was performed "more gracefully, less jerkily". The newspaper does not say how it was changed, but the *New York Sun* reports in January 1916: "The Faun takes [the scarf] up, presses it to his lips and lies down to sleep with his face buried in the robe." The following autumn, when Nijinsky again performed the ballet, critics detected no change in the ending.

Nijinsky recorded the choreography in his own system of notation while placed under house arrest in Budapest during World War I. This is significant because of the four extant Nijinsky ballets (*The Rite of Spring*, *Till Eulenspiegel*, and *Jeux* are the others), it is the only one known to have a written score. Nijinsky based his method on the Stepanov system, which he had studied at the Imperial Theatre School and then modified. Nijinsky, who in 1918 suffered a mental breakdown which ended his career, never provided a key for decoding his highly idiosyncratic style of notation. As a result, the ballet, as he originally conceived it, was never seen again until Les Grands Ballets Canadiens presented its reconstruction by dance scholars Ann Hutchinson Guest and Claudia Jeschke in Montreal in 1989. Guest was able to crack the code after her husband, writer Ivor Guest, discovered the Cecchetti exercises and the Luca della Robbia bas-relief "Cantoria" which Nijinsky notated at the same time that he did *Faune*, and which his wife Romola later gave to the Paris Opéra library. With the code broken, Guest and Jeschke could reconstruct the ballet as closely as possible to the original, revealing it to be more subtle than the increasingly corrupted versions handed down by memory and by those inspired by Baron Adolph de Meyer's photographs of the original cast.

—Deirdre Kelly

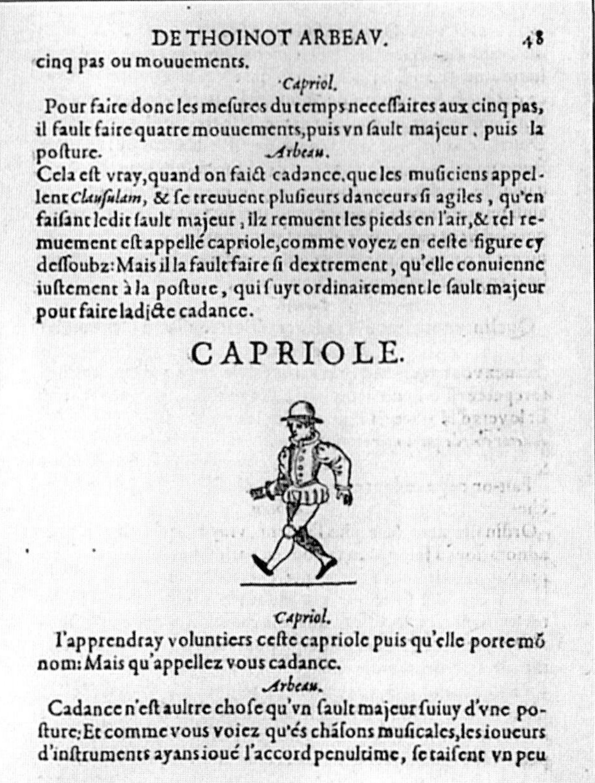

DE THOINOT ARBEAV. 48

cinq pas ou mouuements.

*Capriol.*

Pour faire donc les mesures du temps necessaires aux cinq pas, il fault faire quatre mouuements, puis vn sault majeur, puis la posture.

*Arbeau.*

Cela est vray, quand on faict cadance, que les musiciens appellent *Clausulam*, & se treuuent plusieurs danceurs si agiles, qu'en faisant ledit sault majeur, ilz remuent les pieds en l'air, & tel remuement est appellé capriole, comme voyez en ceste figure cy dessoubz: Mais il la fault faire si dextrement, qu'elle conuienne iustement à la posture, qui suyt ordinairement le sault majeur pour faire ladicte cadance.

CAPRIOLE.

*Capriol.*

I'apprendray voluntiers ceste capriole puis qu'elle porte mõ nom: Mais qu'appellez vous cadance.

*Arbeau.*

Cadance n'est aultre chose qu'vn sault majeur suiuy d'vne posture: Et comme vous voiez qu'és chãsons musicales, les ioueurs d'instruments ayans ioué l'accord penultime, se taisent vn peu

**A page from Thoinot Arbeau's *Orchésographie*, 1588**

---

**ARBEAU, Thoinot**

French dance writer and cleric. Born Jehan Tabourot in Dijon, 17 March 1520. Educated in Dijon, Poitiers, and possibly Paris, receiving Licentiate of Laws; dance training unknown: probably studied dance in Poitiers. Embarked on ecclesiastical career from early age: treasurer of the chapter at Langres, 1542; canon of Langres Cathedral, from 1547; canon-treasurer at Bar-sur-Aube, 1565; became *official* (ecclesiastical judge), *chantre scoliarque* (inspector of diocesan schools), and director of cathedral restoration after damage by lightning; appointed vicar-general of the diocese; published famous dance manual *Orchesographie* in Langres, 1588, describing and entabulating numerous dance steps with music; also published works on non-dance topics under the name of Jean Vostet Breton. Died in Langres, 23 July 1595.

**PUBLICATIONS**

By Arbeau:

*Kalendrier des bergers*, Langres, 1582

*Compot et manuel kalendrier*, Paris, 1588

*Orchesographie: et traicte en forme de dialogue, par lequel toutes personnes peuvent facilement apprendre & practiquer l'honneste exercice des dances*, Langres, 1589; reprinted as *Orchesographie, Metode et teorie en forme de discours et tablature pour apprendre à dancer, battre Tambour, Jouer du fifre & arigot, tirer des armes et escrimer, avec autres honneste exercices fort convenables à la Jeunesse*, Langres, 1596/R1972

*Orchesographie*, translated by Cyril Beaumont, London, 1925; reprinted New York, 1968

*Orchesography*, translated by M.S. Evans, London, 1948; reprinted with introduction, corrections, and notes by Julia Sutton, Labanotation by Mireille Baker, New York, 1967

About Arbeau:

Perrenet, Pierre, *Etienne Tabourot, sa famille et son temps*, Dijon, 1926

Barker, E. Phillips, "Master Thoinot's Fancy", *Music and Letters* (London), vol. 11, 1930

Barker, E. Phillips, "Some Notes on Arbeau", *The Journal of the English Folk Dance Society* (London), series 2, no. 3, 1930

Mary, André, "*L'Orchésographie de Thoinot Arbeau*", in Dacier, E., *Les Trésors des bibliothèques de France*, Paris, 1935

Dolmetsch, Mabel, *Dances of England and France 1450–1600*, London, 1949; reprinted 1975

Wood, Melusine, *Historical Dances*, London, 1952

Heartz, Daniel, *Preludes, Chansons and Dances for Lute Published by Pierre Attaingnant, Paris (1529–1530)*, Neuilly-sur-Seine, 1964

* * *

A member of a good family of Burgundy whose name, Tabourot, and crest of three tabours suggest that they once served as drummers to royalty, Thoinot Arbeau was surrounded by relatives who included writers, architects, and musicians (an uncle, Jean Pignard, was master of music of the cathedral at Langres in the first half of the century). Arbeau studied in Dijon, Poitiers, and perhaps Paris, receiving a Licentiate of Laws. His dance training is unknown, but he mentions his teacher at Poitiers, speaks of his own dancing skill as a young man, and refers several times to Antonius Arena's dance manual, *Ad suos compagnones studiantes* . . . (?1529). Arbeau's ecclesiastical career is recorded in a series of successful promotions, and he went from being treasurer of the chapter at Langres at the age of 22 to being eventually the vicar-general of his diocese. He is also known to have published two other works unrelated to dance under the pseudonym of Jean Vostet Breton. But he is known above all as the writer of the seminal tract on dance and dance technique, *Orchesographie*.

Arbeau's positive attitude toward dancing, as both beneficial to health and fun in the search for a mate, as well as his neo-Platonic conceit that dance on earth mirrors the dance of the universe, places him in the earthy ecclesiastic tradition of Rabelais. He says, for instance, that puritans who oppose dancing "deserve to be fed upon goat's meat cooked in a pie without bacon".

The significance of his *Orchesographie* is manifold. Arbeau was one of three lively old men who published important dance manuals at this time—the others were Fabritio Caroso and Cesare Negri—and his imaginary dialogue with his student, Capriol, sums up his knowledge of dance practice from at least 1550. His manual is the only one of that era to give tabulations correlating dance steps exactly with music, the only one in French, and the only north-European source to permit reasonably accurate realizations (the other northern sources, the so-called *MSS* of the Inns of Court, have cryptic shorthands which neither describe steps nor provide music). Arbeau is also unique in emphasizing the intimate connections between dance and the martial arts, for they frame his book, first with a variety of marching techniques and drum rhythms, and last with his longest and most complex dance, the strenuous men's sword dance *Les bouffons* (or mattachins), for which he provides the only extant choreography. *Orchesographie* is the sole sixteenth-century manual to describe so many *branles* in detail (24 types), some of which have movements pointing strongly to peasant origins (e.g., *Branle des Lavandières*); the only source for choreographies of *La Volte* and *Morisque* (his form of moresca, and the sole dance in the sixteenth-century manuals specified for a member of the lower classes); and the first to supply choreographies of a gavotte, an allemande, and a courante (though his versions of these dances are nevertheless problematic).

In addition to the dance types cited above, Arbeau describes others in varying detail: the *basse danse*, variations on the tordion and galliard, the canary (in duple rather than the usual triple time), and *Pavane d'Espagne*. He also defines the passamezzo, but without giving a choreography.

The dances in *Orchesographie* are typical of all the late-sixteenth-century manuals in that they are primarily social dances—whether circle dances for as many couples as will (branles), solo-couple dances (e.g., galliards), playful kissing games (e.g., gavottes), simple mixers (e.g., *Branle de la Torche*), humorous miming dances (e.g., *Branles des Hermites*), or that vaulting, intimate dance, *La Volte*. Some dances originated in theatrical performances (e.g., *Branle de Malte*, which Arbeau states came from a court mascherade, and *Les Bouffons*). Arbeau seemingly gives a greater variety of dance types than either Caroso or Negri, and many of his dances are simple enough for beginners, which theirs are not. Yet most of his choreographies are very brief, though he hints at variation; often also they are incomplete, such as the *Branle de Guerre*, which omits warlike gestures. Thus the advantages of Arbeau's manual are somewhat illusory.

Arbeau notes none of the complete, lengthy, and well-developed choreographies of social dance types that dominate the manuals of Caroso and Negri—the balletto suites of several movements, the complex figure dances for two or more couples, or the long sets of variations on famous dance types like the passamezzo, or canary. Arbeau's technical demands and step vocabulary are simpler than the Italians', and his style is also somewhat different: knees and ankles are more relaxed in kicking movements, and arms are somewhat freer. Many of his steps, however, are similar to those in the Italian books, so doubtless Arbeau knew the international European language of his time; this is even clearer in his strong emphasis on the Renaissance artistic tradition of improvisation and variation on standard models.

Arbeau also presents unique musical information; his book is the only known manual of Renaissance drum rhythms, and the only source of music for extemporizing on the fife. He gives important clues to musical performing practice for dance accompaniment, appropriate instrumentation, and instrument construction; he also includes sung dances and names collections of dance music. He emphasizes the strong improvisational skills required of Renaissance musicians, saying, "those who play improvise to please themselves".

*L'Orchesographie* supplies much insight into social ambience, proper comportment, and the interaction of musicians, dancers, and onlookers at a ball. Capriol, his student, is advised to keep his "head and body erect and appear self-possessed"; to "spit and blow [his] nose sparingly"; and to "converse affably". The well-bred young lady is told how to prevent her skirts from flying up immodestly during *La Volte*, and admonished never to "refuse him who does her the honour of asking her to dance".

Arbeau's manual, nevertheless, poses some serious questions. While it is obviously valid for northern European dance of the late sixteenth century, we do not know with certainty whether its style and dances in fact mirror French court practices (Arbeau was after all a provincial), nor how far into the seventeenth century it applies—de Lauze, publishing in 1623, shows marked changes of style. Despite these questions, however, *L'Orchesographie* remains a valuable, important, and timely source on an art much beloved in its day.

—Julia Sutton

---

**ARGYLE, Pearl**

South African dancer. Born Pearl Wellman in Johannesburg, 7 November 1910. Studied with Nikolai (Nicolas) Legat and Marie Rambert in London. Married Curtis Bernhardt, 1938. Dancer, Marie Rambert's company (later Ballet Club, eventually Ballet Rambert), from 1926; ballerina, Camargo Society, 1930–33, also performing with Les Ballets 1933; principal dancer, Vic-Wells (later Sadler's Wells) Ballet, 1935–38; also appeared in stage musicals and revues, including Cochran revue *Magic Nights* (mus. various; chor. Bradley and Ashton, 1932) and *Ballyhoo* (mus. Walker, chor. Bradley and Ashton, 1933); moved to U.S. after marriage in 1938: performer in Broadway musicals, including *One Touch of Venus* (mus. Weill, chor. de Mille, 1943). Died in New York, 29 January 1947.

**ROLES**

1927 Dance of Fairies, Dance of the Followers of Night, Dance of Haymakers, and Chaconne (cr) in *The Fairy Queen* (opera; mus. Purcell, chor. Rambert, Ashton),

Pupils of Marie Rambert with Purcell Opera Society and Cambridge Amateur Dramatic Society, London

1928 Gavotte Joyeuse, Passepied and Courante (cr) in *Nymphs and Shepherds* (Ashton), Marie Rambert Dancers, London

A Naiad (cr) in *Leda* (Ashton and Rambert), Marie Rambert Dancers, London

1929 Venus (cr) in *The Ballet of Mars and Venus* in *Jew Süss* (play by Ashley Dukes; chor. Ashton), Opera House, Blackpool

1930 Entrée de Cupidon (cr) in *Dances from Les Petits Riens* (probably a revision of *Nymphs and Shepherds*; chor. Ashton), Marie Rambert Dancers, London

A Nymph (cr) in *Leda and the Swan* (new production of *Leda*; chor. Ashton), Marie Rambert Dancers, London

Basse Danse (cr) in *Capriol Suite* (Ashton), Marie Rambert Dancers, London

1931 A Companion (cr) in *La Péri* (Ashton), Ballet Club, London

Valse (cr) in *Façade* (Ashton), Camargo Society, London

Title role (cr) in *The Lady of Shalott* (Ashton), Ballet Club, London

Adeline (cr) in *The Lord of Burleigh* (Ashton), Camargo Society, London

1932 Récamier (cr) in *An 1805 Impression* (later called *Récamier*; Ashton) in *Magic Nights*, Charles B. Cochran Revue, London

1933 Wife (cr) in *Les Masques* (Ashton), Ballet Club, London

Sita (cr) in *Atalanta of the East* (Tudor), Ballet Club, London

Principal dancer (cr) in *L'Errante* (*The Wanderer*; Balanchine), Les Ballets 1933, Paris

Hebe (cr) in *The Marriage of Hebe* (Doone), Ballet Club, London

Madame Récamier (cr) in *Récamier* (originally *An 1805 Impression* in revue *Magic Nights*; chor. Ashton), Ballet Club, London

1934 Title role (cr) in *Mermaid* (Howard and Salaman), Ballet Club, London

La Fille au bar (cr) in *Bar aux Folies-Bergère* (de Valois), Ballet Club, London

Mortal under Venus (cr) in *The Planets* (Tudor), Ballet Club, London

1935 Title role (cr) in *Cinderella* (Howard), Ballet Rambert, London

Phryné (cr) in *Valentine's Eve* (Ashton), Ballet Rambert, London

Hebe (cr) in *The Descent of Hebe* (Tudor), Ballet Rambert, London

Belinda (cr) in *The Rape of the Lock* (Howard), Ballet Rambert, London

The Fairy (cr) in *Le Baiser de la fée* (Ashton), Vic-Wells Ballet, London

1936 Principal dancer (cr) in *Siesta* (pas de deux; Ashton), Vic-Wells Ballet, London

The Serving Maid (cr) in *The Gods Go a-Begging* (de Valois), Vic-Wells Ballet, London

Principal dancer (cr) in *Siesta* (Ashton), Vic-Wells Ballet, London

1937 Odette in *Swan Lake*, Act II (Ivanov; staged Sergeyev), Vic-Wells Ballet, London

1938 The Empress (cr) in *Le Roi nu* (*The Emperor's New Clothes*; de Valois), Vic-Wells Ballet, London

Venus (cr) in *The Judgment of Paris* (Ashton), Vic-Wells Ballet, London

**Other roles include:** for Ballet Club/Ballet Rambert—Pavane in *Capriol Suite* (Ashton), L'Etoile in *Foyer de danse* (Ashton), Marguerite in *Mephisto Waltz* (Ashton), Terpsichore in *Mercury* (Ashton), Chiarina in *Carnaval* (Fokine), Young Girl in *Le Spectre de la rose* (Fokine), Prelude and Waltz in *Les Sylphides*, Myrrhina in *Lysistrata* (Tudor), Aurora in *Aurora's Wedding* (Petipa), Nymph in *L'Après-midi d'un faune* (after Nijinsky).

## PUBLICATIONS

Bradley, Lionel, *Sixteen Years of Ballet Rambert*, London, 1946

"The Sitter Out", *Dancing Times* (London), March 1947

Rambert, Dame Marie, "Pearl Argyle", *Ballet* (London), March/April 1947

Clarke, Mary, *Dancers of the Mercury: The Story of Ballet Rambert*, London, 1962

Anthony, Gordon, "Pioneers of the Royal Ballet: Pearl Argyle", *Dancing Times*, February 1970

Vaughan, David, *Frederick Ashton and his Ballets*, London, 1977

* * *

A pupil of Nicolas Legat and of Marie Rambert, the English ballerina Pearl Argyle was an early muse for the choreographers Frederick Ashton and Andrée Howard, and a close friend of both. She also created notable roles for Antony Tudor and Ninette de Valois.

Not technically strong, Argyle gained her reputation as a dancer in the early days of British ballet on the strength of her ravishing beauty, charm, and star quality. A woman with large, expressive eyes, she worked as hard at her appearance as at her dancing. At a time when most dancers left their careers very much to chance developments, Argyle was concerned with self-improvement and self-promotion. She was among the first dancers to acquire an agent.

Although her technique was limited, she brought a unique sensitivity to her roles, and many were created expressly for her. She was a musical dancer of restrained but radiant lyricism, and it is small wonder that she appeared as a number of legendary beauties. She was Venus both in Ashton's *Mars and Venus* and in his *Judgement of Paris*; Mme Récamier; and Belinda in *The Rape of the Lock*. Ashton described Argyle as being like a flower, and contrasted her with his other muse of the early 1930s, Alicia Markova, whom he likened to a brilliant diamond. "She was a great stylist and used her arms and hands more beautifully than any other dancer," said Ashton of Argyle. This quality would be shown in the title roles in Ashton's *The Lady of Shalott* and Howard's *Mermaid*. Similarly her looks and lyricism were effectively used as the Wife wielding her large fan in *Les Masques* and as the oriental Sita in Tudor's *Atalanta of the East*.

Given Argyle's beauty, it is not surprising that her career both in the commercial theatre and in films was as significant as that with the developing Ballet Club and Vic-Wells Ballet. For the impresario C.B. Cochran she starred (often with, or in choreography by, Ashton) in the midnight cabaret at the Trocadero, as well as featuring in Reinhardt/Massine's *Helen* and the revues *Ballyhoo* and *The Flying Trapeze*. These roles were primarily dancing ones, but this wider exposure built up her personal following, and her stage experience led to her being cast as Manet's Fille au bar in de Valois' *Bar aux Folies-Bergerè* at the Ballet Club, although it was a younger dancer (Elisabeth Schooling) whose similarity to the painted figure had initiated the ballet's creation.

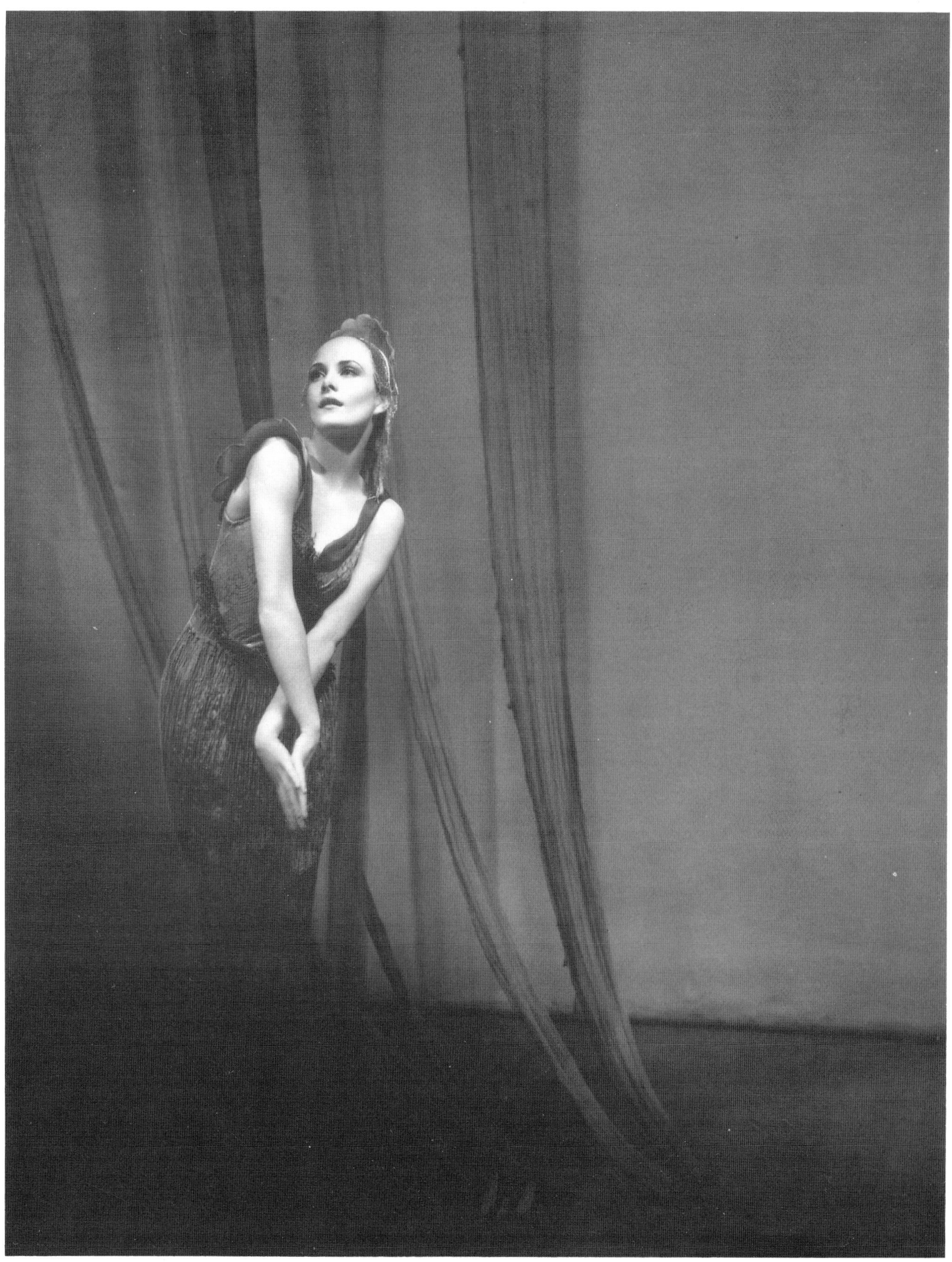

**Pearl Argyle in *Mermaid*, 1934**

It has been suggested that Argyle lacked the ability to project in large theatres and appeared happier on smaller stages. Nevertheless, her range of roles was wide. To take two of her later roles for the Vic-Wells Ballet, for instance, we see how the cold, aloof Fairy of Ashton's *Le Baiser de la fée* contrasts with the warmth and delicacy of feeling of the maidservant in de Valois's *The Gods Go a-Begging*.

Arnold Haskell noted that she was wise to retire when she did, emigrating to the United States to devote herself to her German-born film-director husband and their son. This enabled her to be remembered as a pioneer of memorable beauty without forcing comparisons with the more technically accomplished dancers who succeeded her. Tudor failed to tempt her out of retirement in America to appear as his Juliet with Ballet Theatre.

Although her performing career was brief, Argyle was never forgotten by those who saw her. Her stunning appearance is preserved in photographs by Paul Tanqueray and Gordon Anthony as well as in poetic descriptions. Perhaps one of the most significant tributes paid to her came in Ashton's obituary of his friend. He wrote: "I preferred to dance with her than with anybody else for, apart from being wonderfully responsive and unruffled as a partner, she was an inspiration in herself, and one became drunk with her beauty so to speak."

—Jane Pritchard

---

**AROLDINGEN, Karin von** *see* **VON AROLDINGEN, Karin**

---

**ARPINO, Gerald**

American dancer, choreographer, teacher, and ballet director. Born Gennaro Peter Arpino in Staten Island, New York, 14 January 1925. Studied at Ivan Novikoff Studio, with Mary Ann Wells, Seattle, and at School of American Ballet, New York, pupil of Felia Doubrovska, Antonia Tumkovsky, Muriel Stuart; also studied modern dance with Martha Graham. Dancer, May O'Donnell and Company, 1949–53, Nana Gollner/Paul Petroff Company, touring South America, 1952; also performed on Broadway, in musical *Bless You All* (chor. Tamiris); co-founder and principal dancer, Robert Joffrey Theatre Dancers (becoming Robert Joffrey Ballet), from 1956; first choreography for company, 1961; assistant director, Robert Joffrey Ballet (becoming City Center Joffrey Ballet), from 1965, also becoming principal choreographer; director, Joffrey Ballet (on death of Robert Joffrey), from 1988; also co-founder and teacher, American Ballet Center (now Joffrey Ballet School), from 1953. Recipient: *Dance Magazine* Award, 1973.

**WORKS**

1961 *Ropes* (mus. Ives), Robert Joffrey Ballet Concert, New York
*Partita for Four* (mus. Rieti), Robert Joffrey Ballet Concert, New York
1962 *Sea Shadow* (mus. Ravel; later changed to Colgrass), Robert Joffrey Ballet Concert, Damascus
*Incubus* (mus. Webern), Robert Joffrey Ballet Concert, Lisbon
1963 *The Palace* (mus. Harkness), Robert Joffrey Ballet Concert, Leningrad
1965 *Viva Vivaldi* (mus. Vivaldi), Robert Joffrey Ballet, New York
1966 *Night Wings* (mus. La Montaine), City Center Joffrey Ballet, New York
*Olympics* (mus. Mayuzumi), City Center Joffrey Ballet, New York
1967 *Cello Concerto* (mus. Vivaldi), City Center Joffrey Ballet, Tacoma, Washington
*Elegy* (mus. Panufnik), City Center Joffrey Ballet, New York
*Arcs and Angels* (mus. Lawes), City Center Joffrey Ballet, New York
1968 *A Light Fantastic* (mus. Britten, arranged Wright), City Center Joffrey Ballet, New York
*Fanfarita* (mus. Chapi y Lorente, adapted Wright), City Center Joffrey Ballet, New York
*Secret Places* (mus. Mozart), City Center Joffrey Ballet, New York
*The Clowns* (mus. Kay), City Center Joffrey Ballet, New York
1969 *Animus* (mus. Druckman), City Center Joffrey Ballet, New York
*The Poppet* (mus. Henze), City Center Joffrey Ballet, New York
1970 *Solarwind* (mus. Druckman), City Center Joffrey Ballet, New York
*Confetti* (mus. Rossini), City Center Joffrey Ballet, Chicago
*Trinity* (mus. Ralph, Holdridge), City Center Joffrey Ballet, Berkeley, California
1971 *Valentine* (mus. Druckman), City Center Joffrey Ballet, New York
*Reflections* (mus. Tchaikovsky), City Center Joffrey Ballet, New York
*Kettentanz* (mus. J. Strauss, Mayer), City Center Joffrey Ballet, Berkeley, California
1972 *Chabriesque* (mus. Chabrier), City Center Joffrey Ballet, Chicago
*Sacred Grove on Mount Tamalpais* (mus. Ralph), City Center Joffrey Ballet, New York
1973 *Jackpot* (mus. Druckman), City Center Joffrey Ballet, Chicago
1974 *The Relativity of Icarus* (mus. Samuel; text Larson), City Center Joffrey Ballet, Lewiston, N.Y.
1975 *Drums, Dreams and Banjos* (mus. Foster), City Center Joffrey Ballet, New York
1976 *Orpheus x Light 2* (mus. Serebrier), City Center Joffrey Ballet, New York
1977 *Touch Me* (mus. Cleveland), Joffrey Ballet, San Francisco
1978 *L'Air d'Esprit* (mus. Adam), Joffrey Ballet, Chicago
*Suite Saint-Saëns* (mus. Saint-Saëns, arranged Kaplan), Joffrey Ballet, New York
*Choura* (mus. Drigo), Joffrey Ballet, New York
1979 *Epode* (mus. Shostakovich), Joffrey Ballet, San Antonio, Texas
1980 *Divertissement* (mus. Verdi), Joffrey Ballet, San Francisco
1981 *Light Rain* (mus. Adams, Gauthier), Joffrey Ballet, New York
1983 *Round of Angels* (mus. Mahler), Joffrey Ballet, New York
*Quarter-Tones for Mr. B* (mus. Macero), Joffrey Ballet, New York
*Italian Suite* (mus. Wolf-Ferrari), Joffrey Ballet, New York
1984 *Jamboree* (mus. Macero, orchestrated Henderson),

**Gerald Arpino in rehearsal, early 1950s**

Joffrey Ballet, New York
1986 *Birthday Variations* (mus. Verdi), Joffrey Ballet, Chicago
*Anniversary Pas de Deux*, Gala Performance, New York
1987 Waltz of the Snowflakes, Waltz of the Flowers in *The Nutcracker* (after Ivanov), Joffrey Ballet, Iowa City, Iowa
1989 *The Oantages and the Palace Present TOW-A-DAY* (mus. Harkness, Kaplan), Joffrey Ballet, Washington, D.C.

## PUBLICATIONS


By Arpino:
Interview in Gruen, John, *The Private World of Ballet* (New York), September 1975

About Arpino:
Goodman, Saul, "Gerald Arpino", *Dance Magazine* (New York), October 1959
Fatt, A., "The Capricorn Combine", *Dance Magazine* (New York), October 1970
Maynard, Olga, "Arpino and the Berkeley Ballets", *Dance Magazine* (New York), September 1973
Philp, Richard, "Arpino's Icarus: Confrontation with the Fall", *Dance Magazine* (New York), January 1975
Daniels, Don, "Kept Promises", *Ballet Review* (New York), Spring 1986
Anawalt, Sasha, "Gerald Arpino and the Joffrey Ballet: No Compromise", *Dance Magazine* (New York), May 1992


* * *

Gerald Arpino started ballet lessons when he was seventeen at Ivan Novikoff's studio in Seattle, Washington, where Robert Joffrey was also enrolled. In 1944, they switched schools locally and were instructed for the next four years by Mary Ann Wells. She was harsh on Arpino and, because of her high expectations, he not only took her advanced classes for aspiring professionals, but the children's courses as well. The result was that Arpino developed an independent system of learning and a facility for creating original combinations.

As a teacher later on, when he and Joffrey founded their own school in 1953 (the American Ballet Center in New York City), Arpino insisted on giving children's classes, which provided the Joffrey Ballet with a dependable and much-needed income. He was resourceful and judicious with money, an ideal counterbalance to Joffrey.

Still, it was through Wells, whose imaginative scope was broad—she incorporated Graham floor-work into her daily routines—that Arpino was awakened to the flexible, almost porous nature of classical dance. He matured believing that ballet was non-elitist and had the potential to speak directly to the public.

Acknowledged for his versatility and dramatic enthusiasm, Arpino became Joffrey's principal male dancer in Robert Joffrey Theatre Dancers, which he co-founded in 1956. Until 1962, the ensemble toured over 400 small American towns and cities. In jocular response to its audiences, who were most familiar with Russian luminaries of Denham's Ballet Russe, Arpino was known backstage as "Arpinsky, the Poor Man's Nijinsky". His bravura talent lit up the stage.

On 18 May 1961, Arpino presented his first ballets, *Partita for Four* and *Ropes*, at a concert given with John Wilson & Company at the 92nd Street YMHA's Kaufmann Auditorium in New York. *Ropes*, a contemporary rite of passage, featured Brunilda Ruiz and six men hanging from a web of ropes, torturing her with psychologically weighted gestures. To the Ives score, Arpino had responded with stark and unforgiving movement, and *Ropes* signalled his direction as a choreographer who was intuitively to put his finger on society's pulse.

In 1962, he created *Sea Shadow*, a dream-like pas de deux for a mortal man who encounters a sea nymph beneath the ocean. Their lovemaking in this imaginary fluid environment gave Arpino license to push the limits of his dancers' extensions, making a choreographic feature out of the suppleness of their limbs and spines. His aesthetic, as it evolved thereafter, often spotlighted 180-degree penchée arabesques and ballerinas balanced prone on their pubic bones with arms and legs "swimming" behind them. Overt sexuality combined with a strong spiritual strain (particularly Christian) became one of Arpino's trademarks.

In spring of 1962, Arpino sustained a back injury that terminated his dancing career, and he turned fully to choreography. His next piece was a modern story ballet, *Incubus*, about a piteous girl destroyed by a nightmare. Other theatrically plotted works later followed, including *The Poppet* in 1969, depicting Salem witch trials, and *The Relativity of Icarus* in 1974, an erotic dramatization of the father-and-son myth.

Increasingly, Arpino was encouraged and relied upon by Joffrey to come up with works specifically designed to fill gaps in the company's programming. As chief choreographer and associate director, Arpino created on demand in whatever style was needed, sometimes fund-raising on his own and using dancers left out of other ballets. This baffled and irritated some critics, who felt it was a sign of weakness for him not to stick to one type of ballet. But international and national audiences championed him; Arpino's ballets have been the company's—and possibly America's—most popular.

Several of his works revolutionized the company's image and influenced such contemporary choreographers as William Forsythe and Laura Dean. His *Viva Vivaldi*, with its non-stop energy and Spanish flavor, persuaded observers that Joffrey Ballet must continue to exist when, after patroness Rebekah Harkness had abandoned the troupe in 1964, the company was compelled either to re-establish itself or fold. *Viva Vivaldi* at Central Park's Delacourt Theater alerted the public to Joffrey's incomparable pool of young virtuosos, many of whom possessed physical characteristics unsuitable for pure classical technique.

Arpino further distinguished the Joffrey Ballet as different from other major ballet troupes with his all-male *Olympics*. The company became a home to male dancers who wanted to experience a certain onstage equality with women. Arpino celebrated the rare talents of Robert Blankshine in 1968 with *The Clowns* (the first ballet to address the theme of nuclear holocaust), and of Gary Chryst, Christian Holder, and Dermot Burke with the 1970 rock ballet, *Trinity*.

*Trinity*, inspired by the Vietnam-era peace marches as witnessed by Arpino in Berkeley, California, during the company's residencies there, became Joffrey Ballet's signature work. In 1971, *Kettentanz*, Arpino's lyrical homage to Vienna, presented another hit that was paralleled in 1978 by *Suite Saint-Saëns*. Again creating a "pure dance" piece, Arpino showered the stage in *Saint-Saëns* with fleet combinations that suggested the dancers continuously moving at high velocity even when hidden in the wings. With *Light Rain* in 1981, Arpino's reputation for unembarrassed sensualism was clinched.

In 1982, Arpino's musical assistant, James Howell, died—and the choreographer created *Round of Angels* in dedication to his friend a year later. This work, featuring a swooning chorus of men lifting a single woman against a starlit background, accompanied by Mahler's Adagietto from the Fifth Symphony, is one of Arpino's most romantic. He went on to choreograph five more works, including *Italian Suite* and *Birthday Variations*, and sections of a full-length *The Nutcracker*—all successful, but hard earned.

If Howell's death slowed Arpino's prolific pace to half speed, Joffrey's death in March 1988 may have almost stopped it. Arpino inherited the directorship of the Joffrey Ballet, and his attention was forced almost exclusively on to the company's troubled administration. Internal unrest within the Joffrey Ballet's board came to a head on 1 May 1990, when Arpino resigned, taking his and Joffrey's ballets with him. Those board members and administrators who had instigated such a division soon resigned as well, and by the end of May Arpino had returned to direct the company.

By 1992, Arpino had consolidated a management team, two-thirds of whom were new to the Joffrey Ballet. His ballets were still the scaffolding of the company's identity, but they were revivals and not freshly minted creations.

In keeping with Joffrey's model, Arpino has continued reconstructing twentieth-century masterpieces. For example, it was his idea to revive Massine's 1933 ballet, *Les Présages*, asking Tatiana Leskova and Nelly Laport to stage the work for the company's 1992 spring season (though this was postponed as a result of cash-flow problems and disruptions caused by the Los Angeles riots).

Arpino is determined to maintain the Joffrey Ballet as a hothouse for young American choreographers by commissioning ballets from Charles Moulton, Peter Pucci, Margo Sappington, Alonzo King, Christopher d'Amboise, and Laura Dean among others. He anticipates returning to choreography himself, having produced 44 ballets, many of which are responsible for converting a vast and once skeptical public to ballet.

—Sasha Anawalt

---

**ASHLEY, Merrill**

American dancer. Born Linda Michelle Merrill in St. Paul, Minnesota, 2 December 1950. Studied with Sybil de Neergaard in Rutland, Vermont, Phyllis Marmein in Schenectady, New York, and at the School of American Ballet, New York City, from 1964. Married Kibbe Fitzpatrick, 6 September 1980. Dancer, corps de ballet, New York City Ballet, from 1967: soloist, from 1974; principal dancer, from 1977, with international tours including to Eastern Europe and China; performed at the White House, Washington, D.C., 1978, and as U.S. representative, 40th Anniversary Gala of UNESCO, Bolshoi Theatre, Moscow, 1986; toured U.S. with small company headed by Jacques d'Amboise, 1969–73; has also appeared on television, including for Public Broadcasting Service (PBS) "Dance in America" Series, and "Gala of Stars", 1980, 1982, 1984; guest artist, Sadler's Wells Royal Ballet, London, 1987; director and principal dancer of own group, Merrill Ashley and Dancers, touring Hawaii, 1980, 1981. Recipient: *Dance Magazine* Award, 1987.

**ROLES**

1968 Third Variation in *Divertimento no. 15* (Balanchine), New York City Ballet, New York

1969 Harp Variation in *Raymonda Variations* (previously *Valses et Variations*; Balanchine), New York City Ballet

**Merrill Ashley with Daniel Duell in *The Four Seasons***

1970 "Stairway to Paradise" in *Who Cares?* (Balanchine), New York City Ballet, New York
Principal dancer in *Stravinsky Symphony* (Clifford), New York City Ballet, New York
1972 Principal dancer (cr) in *Requiem Canticles (II)* (Robbins), New York City Ballet, New York
Thème Variée, fourth variation (cr) in *Danses Concertantes* (new version; Balanchine), New York City Ballet, New York
Principal dancer in *Symphony in E-Flat* (Clifford), New York City Ballet, New York
"My One and Only" in *Who Cares?* (Balanchine), New York City Ballet, New York
1973 Principal dancer in *Dances at a Gathering* (Robbins), New York City Ballet, New York
Variation III (cr) in *Cortège Hongrois* (Balanchine), New York City Ballet, New York
1974 Principal dancer (cr) in *Saltarelli* (d'Amboise), New York City Ballet, New York
Dawn (cr) in *Coppélia* (new production; Balanchine, Danilova after Petipa), New York City Ballet, Saratoga Springs, New York
Rondo in *Brahms-Schoenberg Quartet* (Balanchine), New York City Ballet, New York
Tema con Variazioni in *Tchaikovsky Suite No. 3* (Balanchine), New York City Ballet, New York
Principal dancer in *Tchaikovsky Piano Concerto No. 2* (previously *Ballet Imperial*; Balanchine), New York City Ballet, New York
Diamonds in *Jewels* (Balanchine), New York City Ballet, New York
Principal dancer in *Valse-Fantaisie* (Balanchine), New York City Ballet, New York
1975 Sanguinic in *The Four Temperaments* (Balanchine), New York City Ballet, New York
Sixth Variation in *Divertimento No. 15* (Balanchine), New York City Ballet, New York
1976 Chloe in *Daphnis and Chloe* (Taras), New York City Ballet, New York
Sugar Plum Fairy and Dewdrop Fairy in *The Nutcracker* (Balanchine), New York City Ballet, New York
Principal dancer in *Square Dance* (Balanchine), New York City Ballet, New York
1977 Emeralds in *Jewels* (Balanchine), New York City Ballet, New York
Rubies in *Jewels* (Balanchine), New York City Ballet, New York
Principal dancer in *Tchaikovsky Pas de Deux* (Balanchine), New York City Ballet, New York
Principal dancer in *Donizetti Variations* (Balanchine), New York City Ballet, New York
*La Ventana* Pas de trois in *Bournonville Divertissements* (Williams after Bournonville), New York City Ballet, New York
1978 Classical Pas de deux in *Cortège Hongrois* (Balanchine), New York City Ballet, New York
Principal dancer (cr) in *Ballo della Regina* (Balanchine), New York City Ballet, New York
Pas Degas (cr) in *Tricolore* (Martins, Bonnefous, Robbins), New York City Ballet, New York
Pas de deux in *Agon* (Balanchine), New York City Ballet, New York
Principal dancer in *In the Night* (Robbins), New York City Ballet, New York
1979 Spring in *The Four Seasons* (Robbins), New York City Ballet, New York
1980 Principal dancer (cr) in *Ballade* (Balanchine), New York City Ballet, New York
Odette in *Swan Lake* (one-act version; Balanchine after Ivanov), New York City Ballet, New York
Principal dancer in *Chaconne* (Balanchine), New York City Ballet, New York
1982 Principal dancer (cr) in *Chamber Works* (later *Concertino*; Robbins), New York City Ballet, New York
1983 Principal dancer in *Ballet d'Isoline* (Tomasson), New York City Ballet
Principal dancer in *Serenade* (Balanchine), New York City Ballet
1984 Principal dancer (cr) in *Brahms/Handel* (Tharp, Robbins), New York City Ballet, New York
The Siren in *The Prodigal Son* (Balanchine), New York City Ballet, New York
1985 Title role in *Firebird* (Balanchine, Robbins), New York City Ballet, New York
1986 "The Man I Love" in *Who Cares?* (Balanchine), New York City Ballet, New York
1987 Princess Aurora in *The Sleeping Beauty* (Petipa, Ashton; staged MacMillan), Sadler's Wells Royal Ballet, London
Title role in *Paquita* (Petipa; staged Samsova), Sadler's Wells Royal Ballet, London
1988 Principal dancer (cr) in *Barber Violin Concerto* (Martins), New York City Ballet, New York
Eurydice in *Orpheus* (Balanchine), New York City Ballet, New York
1989 Principal dancer in *Movements for Piano and Orchestra* (Balanchine), New York City Ballet, New York
Principal dancer in *Monumentum Pro Gesualdo* (Balanchine), New York City Ballet, New York
1990 Principal dancer (cr) in *Fearful Symmetries* (Martins), New York City Ballet, New York
1991 Carabosse (cr) in *The Sleeping Beauty* (new production; Martins after Petipa), New York City Ballet, New York

**Other roles include:** Principal dancer in *Symphony in Three Movements* (Balanchine), Third Movement in *Tchaikovsky Suite No. 2* (previously *Tchaikovsky Suite*; d'Amboise), principal dancer in *Allegro Brillante* (Balanchine), Fourth Campaign in *Stars and Stripes* (Balanchine), First, Second, and Third movements in *Symphony in C* (Balanchine), Emeralds in *Jewels* (Balanchine), principal dancer in *Concerto Barocco* (Balanchine), Divertissement and Helena in *A Midsummer Night's Dream* (Balanchine), principal dancer in *Irish Fantasy* (d'Amboise), principal dancer in *Haydn Concerto* (Taras), principal dancer in *La Source* (Balanchine), principal dancer in *Vienna Waltzes* (Balanchine), principal dancer in *In G Major* (Robbins), Polyhymnia in *Apollo* (Balanchine), principal dancer in *Kammermusik No. 2* (Balanchine).

## PUBLICATIONS

By Ashley:

Interview in Newman, Barbara, *Striking a Balance: Dancers Talk about Dancing*, Boston, 1982
Interview in Stuart, Otis, "Declaration of Independence", *Ballett International* (Cologne), September 1983
*Dancing for Balanchine*, New York, 1984
Interview with Newman, Barbara, "Speaking of Dance: Merrill Ashley", *Dancing Times* (London), June 1987
Interview in Kaplan, Larry, "A Conversation with Merrill Ashley", *Ballet Review* (New York), Spring 1989

About Ashley:
Tobias, Tobi, "All-American Ashley", *Dance Magazine* (New York), June 1979
Hodgson, Moira, "New York City Ballet's Merrill Ashley", *Dance News* (New York), June 1979
Croce, Arlene, *Going to the Dance*, New York, 1982
Kaplan, Larry, "Merrill Ashley and Balanchine's *Ballade*", *Ballet Review* (New York), Winter 1983
Tracy, Robert, *Balanchine's Ballerinas*, New York, 1983
Jacobson, Robert, "Full Speed Ahead", *Ballet News* (New York), July 1984
Croce, Arlene, *Sight Lines*, New York, 1987
Percival, John, "The Royal's All-American Guest", *Dance and Dancers* (London), March/April 1987
Croce, Arlene, "Victory", *The New Yorker* (New York), 22 May 1989

* * *

Merrill Ashley is one of the last New York City Ballet dancers to have been trained and developed under George Balanchine's active supervision. A virtuoso ballerina, Ashley is an exemplar of the Balanchine style, and language invoked to characterize her is invariably identical with that used to describe the New York City Ballet itself. Ashley's dancing is usually praised for its energy, its speed and attack, its pristine clarity, and for being intensely musical. Renowned above all for her prodigious allegro technique, Ashley has throughout her career consistently developed the lyrical and dramatic facets of her performing style.

For a dancer of her talent and accomplishment, Ashley spent rather a long time in the corps de ballet, nearly seven years. During that time, however, Balanchine singled her out for solos in *Divertimento No. 15*, *Raymonda Variations*, and various other ballets. By the time she appeared in two different roles in *Who Cares?* and Balanchine had created solos for her in *Cortège Hongrois* and *Coppélia*, she was beginning to make an impact on the repertory. Dancing at high speed, she was able to carve out in space each step she performed without distorting the choreography, and critics called her "electrifying". Her performances in *Tchaikovsky Piano Concerto* (formerly *Ballet Imperial*) and *Theme and Variations* (in *Tchaikovsky Suite No. 3*), two roles which have figured prominently in her career, made it clear that she was something of a technical wonder. Her astonishing and brilliant technical mastery significantly revealed itself in two other important Balanchine roles, Sanguinic in *The Four Temperaments* and the female lead in *Square Dance*, which Balanchine more or less revived for her in 1976.

Balanchine's ultimate showcase for Ashley's allegro powers is *Ballo della Regina*, in which her delicate and precise footwork is integrated into choreography calling for a grand, almost heroic style. Lincoln Kirstein called her an "ideal high-soprano dancer . . . moving with more speed, cutting her profiles with greater diamond-edged sharpness, intensity, precision, and strength than almost any dancer within recent memory". *Ballade*, which Balanchine choreographed for her in 1980, two-and-a-half years after *Ballo*, presented a more romantic portrayal of Ashley's art, one which, despite the propulsive pace of the ballet, revealed the lyricism inherent in her style. In these years Ashley also displayed her lyrical gifts in Balanchine's "Emeralds" in *Jewels*, and as the Girl in Mauve in Jerome Robbins's *Dances at a Gathering*.

The presentation of herself as a more lyrical and dramatic dancer has been the overriding motif of the last decade of Ashley's career, and in this vein she has added major Balanchine roles to her repertory, such as the lead in *Firebird* and the Siren in *The Prodigal Son*. But it was in such important Balanchine ballets as *Concerto Barocco* (first violin), *Chaconne*, *Symphony in C* (second movement), *Swan Lake*, *Jewels* ("Diamonds"), *Raymonda Variations*, *Donizetti Variations*, and *Gounod Symphony* that she revealed the full dimension of her art. In these ballets her musicality, her immaculate footwork, and her beautiful line are complemented by the conscious effort she has made to soften her attack and to make her upper body more flexible and expressive. Her evolving and expansive adagio technique has in fact reinforced the overall impact of her dancing. And having performed *Paquita* and Aurora in *The Sleeping Beauty* in the United States and in England, she has integrated into her dancing some of Petipa's precepts, which also influenced her performances in these Balanchine masterworks.

Ashley revealed the grandeur of her classical style in the Spring section of Jerome Robbins's *The Four Seasons* as well as in *Brahms/Handel*, which Robbins co-choreographed for her with Twyla Tharp. NYCB ballet master-in-chief Peter Martins enshrined Ashley as a classical goddess, with a warm and sensual heart beating under a chaste exterior, in his *Barber Violin Concerto* in 1988. In 1990 he made a new role for her in *Fearful Symmetries* in which he seemed content to portray her simply as a leading lady.

In 1982 Jennifer Dunning writing in the *New York Times* said that Ashley's dancing in *Ballade* "sets standards for greatness", and in 1989 Arlene Croce in *The New Yorker* described two Ashley performances in *Tchaikovsky Piano Concerto* in the most exalted language. "Ashley came on and reached a kind of sanctity rare in the career of any artist . . . she danced the whole concerto in a state of pure and fervent grace, so far into the music and away from the usual performance strategies as to seem transfigured. Why do we love Balanchine? Because he makes possible this condition of absolute transparency, this state of oneness with the music. And ballerinas are best who can throw themselves away and find that condition, that inner equilibrium which brings bliss to an audience. In the second of the Ashley performances, the company seemed to have caught on to what she was doing . . . What a ballet it is . . . Ashley showed us its tragic seriousness."

—Larry Kaplan

---

**ASHTON, Frederick**

British dancer, choreographer, and ballet director. Born William Mallandaine in Guayaquil, Ecuador, 17 September 1904. Studied with Léonide Massine, London, c.1923–24, and with Marie Rambert, from 1924; later studied under Bronislava Nijinska in Paris. First choreography (*A Tragedy of Fashion*) for Marie Rambert's Dancers, 1926; dancer, Ida Rubinstein's Company, Paris, 1928–29; choreographer, Rambert's company (later Ballet Club, and eventually Ballet Rambert) and Camargo Society, London, from 1929; also staged dances for revues and musical comedies, London, from 1932, and for opera in the U.S., 1934; resident choreographer and dancer (at invitation of Ninette de Valois), Vic-Wells Ballet (later Sadler's Wells, now Royal Ballet), from 1935: principal choreographer, from 1946; also staged ballets for Ballet Russe de Monte Carlo, 1939, New York City Ballet, 1950 and 1952, Royal Danish Ballet, 1955, La Scala Ballet, 1958; director (succeeding de Valois), Royal Ballet, Covent Garden, 1963–70; continued association with Royal Ballet with title of Founder Choreographer, and also appeared in character roles, from 1970. Commander of the Order of the British Empire,

**Frederick Ashton rehearsing Katherine Healy and Peter Schaufuss in *Romeo and Juliet*, London Festival Ballet**

1950; Queen Elizabeth II Coronation Award, Royal Academy of Dancing, London, 1959; Legion of Honour (France), 1960; Knighthood, 1962; Order of Dannebrog, Denmark, 1964; Companion of Honour, 1970; Honorary Doctor of Music, London University, 1970, and Oxford University, 1976; Order of Merit, 1977. Died in London, 18 August 1988.

## WORKS

1926 *A Tragedy of Fashion; or, The Scarlet Scissors* (mus. Goosens, arranged Irving), added to revue *Riverside Nights* (produced Nigel Playfair), Lyric Theatre, London

1927 Dances (with Marie Rambert) in *The Fairy Queen* (opera; mus. Purcell), Purcell Opera Society and Cambridge Amateur Dramatic Society, London

*Pas de deux* (mus. Kreisler), presented by Marie Rambert, Imperial Society of Teachers of Dancing Annual Dance Festival, London

*Argentine Dance* (mus. Artello), presented by Marie Rambert, Imperial Society of Teachers of Dancing Annual Dance Festival, London

1928 *Nymphs and Shepherds* (mus. Mozart), Marie Rambert Dancers, London

*Leda* (with Marie Rambert; mus. Gluck), Marie Rambert Dancers, London

1929 *The Ballet of Mars and Venus* in *Jew Süss* (play by Ashley Dukes; mus. Scarlatti, orchestrated by Lambert), Opera House, Blackpool

1930 *Capriol Suite* (mus. Warlock), Marie Rambert Dancers, Lyric Theatre, London (performed Camargo Society and Sadler's Wells Theatre Ballet, 1948)

*Dances from Les Petits Riens* (possibly a revision of *Nymphs and Shepherds*; mus. Mozart), Marie Rambert Dancers, London

*Mars and Venus* (revised version of *The Ballet of Mars and Venus*, 1929; mus. Scarlatti, orchestrated by Lambert), Marie Rambert Dancers, London (staged Camargo Society, 1931)

*Saudade do Brésil* (mus. Milhaud), Marie Rambert Dancers, London

*Mazurka des Hussars* (mus. Borodin), Marie Rambert Dancers, London

Dances in *Marriage à la Mode* (comedy by John Dryden; mus. Reynolds), Lyric Theatre, London

*Pomona* (mus. Lambert), Camargo Society, London

*"Follow Your Saint": The Passionate Pavan* (mus. Dowland) and *Dances on a Scotch Theme* (mus. Boyce, arranged Lambert) in The Masque presented by Arnold L. Haskell, Arts Theatre Club, London

*A Florentine Picture* (mus. Corelli), Marie Rambert Dancers, London

1931 *La Péri* (mus. Dukas), Ballet Club, London

*Façade* (mus. Walton), Camargo Society, London

*Mercury* (mus. Satie), Marie Rambert Dancers, London
*Regatta* (mus. Gavin Gordon), Vic-Wells Ballet, London
*The Lady of Shalott* (mus. Sibelius), Ballet Club, London
*A Day in a Southern Port* (later *Rio Grande*; mus. Lambert), Camargo Society, London
*The Lord of Burleigh* (mus. Mendelssohn), Camargo Society, London
1932 *Pompette* (mus. arranged Hugh Bradford), Ballet Club
*An 1805 Impression* (mus. Schubert), ballet in *Magic Nights*, Charles B. Cochran Revue, London
*High Yellow* (with Buddy Bradley; mus. Hughes), Camargo Ballet, London
*Foyer de danse* (mus. Lord Berners), Ballet Club, London
1933 *Pas de deux* (for Markova, Dolin; mus. Rameau), Coliseum, London
*Les Masques; ou, Changement de dames* (mus. Poulenc), Ballet Club, London
*Pavane pour une infante défunte* (mus. Ravel), Ballet Club, London
*Récamier* (also performed as *La Valse chez Madame Récamier*; new production of ballet originally choreographed for Charles B. Cochran revue *Magic Nights*, 1932; mus. Schubert), Ballet Club, London
*Les Rendezvous* (mus. Auber, arranged by Lambert), Vic-Wells Ballet, London
1934 *Mephisto Valse* (mus. Liszt), Ballet Club, London
*Pas de deux classique* (mus. Glazunov), Hippodrome, London
1935 *Valentine's Eve* (mus. Ravel), Ballet Rambert, London
*Le Baiser de la fée* (mus. Stravinsky), Vic-Wells Ballet, London
1936 *Siesta* (mus. Walton), Vic-Wells Ballet, London
*Apparitions* (mus. Liszt), Vic-Wells Ballet, London
*Nocturne* (mus. Delius), Vic-Wells Ballet, London
1937 *Perpetuum mobile* (mus. Strauss jun.), Vic-Wells Ballet, London
*Harlequin in the Street* (mus. Couperin, arranged Lambert), Arts Theatre, Cambridge
*Les Patineurs* (mus. Meyerbeer, arranged by Lambert), Vic-Wells Ballet, London
*A Wedding Bouquet* (mus. Lord Berners), Vic-Wells Ballet, London
1938 *Horoscope* (mus. Lambert), Vic-Wells Ballet, London
*The Judgment of Paris* (mus. Berkeley), Vic-Wells Ballet, London
*Harlequin in the Street* (new version; mus. Couperin, arranged by Lambert), Vic-Wells Ballet, London
1939 *Pas de deux* (mus. Chopin), Liverpool Ballet Club, Liverpool
*Cupid and Psyche* (mus. Lord Berners), Vic-Wells Ballet, London
*Devil's Holiday* (*Le Diable s'amuse*; mus. Tommasini, on themes by Paganini), Ballet Russe de Monte Carlo, New York
1940 *Dante Sonata* (mus. Liszt, orchestrated by Lambert), Vic-Wells Ballet, London
*The Wise Virgins* (mus. Bach, arranged by Lambert, orchestrated by Walton), Vic-Wells Ballet, London
1941 *The Wanderer* (mus. Schubert), Sadler's Wells Ballet, London
*The Quest* (mus. Walton), Sadler's Wells Ballet, London
1946 Garland Dance, Florestan and his Two Sisters in *The Sleeping Beauty* (Petipa; staged Sergeyev, with additions de Valois; mus. Tchaikovsky), Sadler's Wells Ballet, London
*Symphonic Variations* (mus. Franck), Sadler's Wells Ballet, London
*Les Sirènes* (mus. Lord Berners), Sadler's Wells Ballet, London
*The Fairy Queen* (masque after William Shakespeare; mus. Purcell), Covent Garden Opera and Sadler's Wells Ballet, London
1947 *Valses nobles et sentimentales* (mus. Ravel), Sadler's Wells Ballet, London
1948 *Scènes de ballet* (mus. Stravinsky), Sadler's Wells Ballet, London
*Don Juan* (mus. Strauss), Sadler's Wells Ballet, London
*Cinderella* (mus. Prokofiev), Sadler's Wells Ballet, London
1949 *Le Rêve de Léonor* (mus. Britten, orchestrated by Oldham), Les Ballets de Paris, London
1950 *Illuminations* (mus. Britten, orchestrated Oldham), New York City Ballet, New York
1951 *Daphnis and Chloë* (mus. Ravel), Sadler's Wells Ballet, London
*Tiresias* (mus. Lambert), Sadler's Wells Ballet, London
1952 *Picnic at Tintagel* (mus. Bax), New York City Ballet, New York
*Vision of Marguerite* (mus. Liszt), London Festival Ballet, London
*Sylvia* (mus. Delibes), Sadler's Wells Ballet, London
Act I Valse (pas de six), Act III Neapolitan Dance in *Swan Lake* (Petipa, Ivanov; staged Sergeyev, revised de Valois); Sadler's Wells Ballet, London
1953 *Homage to the Queen* (mus. Arnold), Sadler's Wells Ballet, London
1954 *Entrada de Madame Butterfly* (*Entry of Madame Butterfly*; mus. Sullivan), Granada Festival, Jardines del Generalife, Granada
*Trepak* (from *The Nutcracker*, Act II; mus. Tchaikovsky), Granada Festival, Jardines del Generalife, Granada
1955 *Rinaldo and Armida* (mus. Arnold), Sadler's Wells Ballet, London
*Variations on a Theme by Purcell* (mus. Britten), Sadler's Wells Ballet, London
*Madame Chrysanthème* (mus. Rawsthorne), Sadler's Wells Ballet, London
*Romeo and Juliet* (mus. Prokofiev), Royal Danish Ballet, Copenhagen
1956 *La Péri* (mus. Dukas), Sadler's Wells Ballet, London
*Birthday Offering* (mus. Glazunov, arranged by Irving), Sadler's Wells Ballet, London
1958 *La Valse* (mus. Ravel), La Scala, Milan
*Ondine* (mus. Henze), Royal Ballet, London
1959 Scène d'amour from *Raymonda* (mus. Glazunov), Royal Ballet, Royal Academy of Dancing Gala, London
1960 *La Fille mal gardée* (mus. Hérold), Royal Ballet, London
1961 *Les Deux Pigeons* (*The Two Pigeons*; mus. Messager, orchestrated by Lanchbery), Royal Ballet Touring Company, London
*Poème tragique* (mus. Stravinsky), Royal Ballet, London
*Persephone* (mus. Stravinsky), Royal Ballet, London
1963 *Marguerite and Armand* (mus. Liszt, orchestrated by Searle), Royal Ballet, London
1964 *The Dream* (mus. Mendelssohn, arranged Lanchbery), Royal Ballet, London
1965 *Monotones* (pas de trois; mus. Satie, orchestrated by Debussy and Roland-Manuel), Royal Ballet Gala, London
1966 *Monotones* (extended version of 1965 ballet; mus. Satie), Royal Ballet, London

1967 *Sinfonietta* (mus. Williamson), Royal Ballet Touring Company, Stratford-upon-Avon
1968 *Jazz Calendar* (mus. Bennett), Royal Ballet, London
*Enigma Variations (My Friends Pictured Within)* (mus. Elgar), Royal Ballet, London
Fairy of Joy (Prologue), Garland Dance (new version), Prince Florimund's Variation, Pas de deux (Awakening Scene), Gold and Silver pas de deux in *The Sleeping Beauty* (new production; Wright after Petipa), Royal Ballet, London
1970 *Lament of the Waves* (mus. Masson), Royal Ballet, London
*The Creatures of Prometheus* (mus. Beethoven), Royal Ballet Touring Company, Bonn
1971 *Tales of Beatrix Potter* (film-ballet; dir. Reginald Mills; mus. Lanchbery), Artists of the Royal Ballet
*Meditation from 'Thaïs'* (mus. Massenet), Gala Performance, Adelphi Theatre, London
1972 *Siesta* (mus. Walton), Royal Ballet, London
*The Walk to Paradise Garden* (mus. Delius), Royal Ballet, London
1974 *Fashion Show* (mus. popular songs), Royal Ballet School, London
1975 *Scène dansante* (mus. Offenbach), Artists of the Royal Ballet, Aldeburgh
*Brahms-Waltz* (after Isadora Duncan; mus. Brahms), Nijinsky Gala, Hamburg Ballet, Hamburg
1976 *A Month in the Country* (mus. Chopin), Royal Ballet, London
*Five Brahms Waltzes in the Manner of Isadora Duncan* (mus. Brahms), Ballet Rambert, London
1979 *Salut d'amour à Margot Fonteyn* (mus. Elgar), Royal Ballet, London
1980 *Rhapsody* (mus. Rachmaninov), Royal Ballet, London
1981 *Voices of Spring* (mus. Strauss), Royal Ballet, London
*Soupirs* (mus. Elgar), Sadler's Wells Royal Ballet, London
1982 *Pas de légumes* (mus. Rossini), Sadler's Wells Royal Ballet, London
1983 *Varii Capricci* (mus. Walton), Royal Ballet, New York
1985 *La Chatte métamorphosée en femme* (mus. Offenbach), Royal Ballet, London

Also staged:

1951 *The Nutcracker* (after Ivanov; mus. Tchaikovsky), Sadler's Wells Theatre Ballet, London
1960 *Giselle* (after Petipa, Coralli, Perrot, in collaboration with Tamara Karsavina; mus. Adam), Royal Ballet, New York

**Other works include:** *Radio Waves, The Bell Boys Stampede* (mus. Handy), *Carrambolina* and *The Ballet of Spring* in *A Kiss in Spring* (comedy, after Brammer and Grünwald's operetta *Das Veilchen vom Montmartre*, 1932), Dances (with Buddy Bradley) in *Ballyhoo* (revue; mus. Walker, 1932), *The Legend of Berenice* and *Rumba* in *How d'You Do*? (revue; mus. Hamilton, 1933); *The Orchid and the Cactus* (mus. Cochrane) and *Wall Street* (mus. Leslie-Smith) in *After Dark* (revue by Ronald Jeans, 1933); Dances in *Gay Hussar* (musical play; mus. Posford, 1933); *Cavalcoward* (mus. Coward), *Valse de concert* (mus. Glazunov), and *Triptych* (mus. Corelli) in *Nursery Murmurs* (revue; 1933); Dances in *Four Saints in Three Acts* (opera to words by Gertrude Stein; mus. Thomson; Hartford, Connecticut, 1934); *I'm Dancing with a Ghost* in *Jill Darling!* (musical comedy by Marriott Edgar; mus. Ellis, 1934); Dances in *Escape Me Never* (film, after play by Margaret Kennedy; dir. Paul Czinner, 1935); Dances (with Buddy Bradley and Tony Smythe) in *The Flying Trapeze* (musical after Müller's *Zirkus Aimé*; mus. Benatzky and Wayne, 1935); *A Flower Market, The Very Merry Widow* (mus. Lehár), *Olde London Towne: Buy My Cherries* (mus. McDougall), *Vauxhall Gardens, 1750, The Moth and the Flame, The Lady in Red* (mus. Dixon and Wrubel) in *Round About Regent Street* (revue; produced by George Black, 1935); *Love is a Dancing Thing, Cuba, Polonaise, The First Shoot* (mus. Walton), *Dangerous You, Sleigh Bells* in *Follow the Sun* (Charles B. Cochran revue, 1935); *The Hat* (mus. Ellis) in *The Town Talks* (revue by Vivien Ellis and Arthur Macrae; produced by André Charlot, 1936); Dances in *Die Fledermaus* (opera; mus. Johann Strauss jun., 1936); Scenes in *Home and Beauty* (Charles B. Cochran's Coronation Revue, 1936); *Waltz, Dancing with the Daffodils, Sir Thomas Beeton in the Kitchen* (mus. Frankel) in *Floodlight* (revue by Beverly Nichols, produced by C. Denis Freeman, 1937); *The Chinese Ballet* in *Running Riot* (musical by Douglas Furber; mus. Ellis, 1938); Ballet in *Tannhäuser* (opera; mus. Wagner; 1938); Dances in *A Midsummer Night's Dream* (play by Shakespeare; dir. Nevill Coghill, 1945); Dances in *Manon* (mus. Massenet; 1947); Dances in *Albert Herring* (opera; mus. Britten; 1947); Dances in *La Traviata* (opera; mus. Verdi; 1948); Dances (with Léonide Massine) in *The Tales of Hoffman* (film; dir. Powell, 1951); Dances in *The Story of Three Loves* (film; dir. Reinhardt and Minnelli, 1952); Dances in *Orpheus* (opera; mus. Gluck; 1953); Dances in *Orfeo ed Euridice* (opera; mus. Gluck; Milan, 1958); Dances in *Death in Venice* (opera; mus. Britten; New York, 1974); *Harlequinade* (with de Valois) in *World of Harlequin* (ballet-play by Peter Brinson; mus. arranged Lade, 1973); Dances in *Death in Venice* (opera; mus. Britten; New York, 1974); *Étude* (mus. Chopin) in *The Turning Point* (film; dir. Ross, 1977).

**PUBLICATIONS**

By Ashton:

"A Word about Choreography", *Dancing Times* (London), May 1930
"Notes on Choreography" in Sorell, Walter, *The Dance Has Many Faces*, second edition, New York, 1966
Interview in "A Conversation with Sir Frederick Ashton", *York Dance Review* (Ontario), Spring 1978
Interview in Macaulay, Alastair, "Ashton at Eighty", *Dance Theatre Journal* (London), Autumn 1984

About Ashton:

Sandon, Joseph, *Façade and Other Early Ballets by Frederick Ashton*, London, 1954
Barnes, Clive, "Frederick Ashton and his Ballets", *Dance Perspectives* (New York), no. 9, 1961
Dominic, Zoë (photographer) and Gilbert, John Selwyn, *Frederick Ashton: A Choreographer and his Ballets*, London, 1971
Fonteyn, Margot, *Margot Fonteyn: An Autobiography*, London, 1975
Vaughan, David, *Frederick Ashton and his Ballets*, London, 1977
Macaulay, Alastair, *Some Views and Reviews of Ashton's Choreography*, Guildford, Surrey, 1987
Anderson, Jack, *Choreography Observed*, Iowa City, 1987

* * *

Born in Ecuador, a child of the English upper middle class, and converted to dance by seeing Anna Pavlova perform in 1917,

Frederick Ashton did not begin studying ballet until about 1923. What makes this late start extraordinary is that he went on to become a main architect of British ballet style, and one of the most influential classical choreographers of the twentieth century. Another unusual feature of his career is that, unlike almost all other major classical choreographers or creators of dance styles, he was never a dance teacher.

Ashton's first dance teachers were Léonide Massine and—from around 1924—Marie Rambert. From them he learned the Cecchetti style of academic ballet that became central to his choreography. His original intention, however, was always to be a great dancer; and it is likely that, when he realized that his capacities as a classical dancer were limited, choreography became the sublimation of his original ambition.

It was Rambert who spotted choreographic potential in Ashton's inventiveness as a mime. He was the first of the choreographers whom she so nurtured. She then coaxed, challenged, and educated him in developing his choreographic art, and his first work, *A Tragedy of Fashion*, was given at her company's first performance (1926). This also began his long collaboration with the designer Sophie Fedorovitch, who was to be a crucial friend and counsellor. Henceforth, though Ashton remained a classical dancer for several more years, he devoted himself to choreography. An important stage of his apprenticeship occurred in the late 1920s, when he joined Ida Rubinstein's company as a dancer and absorbed himself in the teaching and choreography of Bronislava Nijinska. The novel accents she gave to academic ballet—in particular, her vivid way of making the upper body move as intensely as the lower—influenced him deeply.

When British ballet began to burgeon in the 1930s, Ashton was well situated to develop further as a choreographer. He choreographed not only for the Rambert dancers, but also for the Camargo Society and for the Vic-Wells Ballet. Among the ballets he made then are some still performed today—*Capriol Suite*, *Façade*, and *Les Rendezvous*. Much of his work at this time also brought him into collaboration with Constant Lambert, whose talents as composer, arranger, conductor, and pianist were of vital use to Ashton and whose critical faculties made him a signal influence on Ashton's work. As Ashton acquired a reputation for making sophisticated, elegant, and witty dances, he was invited to choreograph for the commercial West End theatre from 1932 on, and in particular for the producer Charles B. Cochran (as had Balanchine in the years 1929–31). In 1934 Ashton visited the U.S. and choreographed the dances for the opera *Four Saints in Three Acts* by Gertrude Stein and Virgil Thomson. Back in London, in 1935, he accepted Ninette de Valois's invitation to become resident choreographer for the Vic-Wells Ballet. Henceforth that company—later the Sadler's Wells Ballet, and from 1956 the Royal Ballet—would be the canvas for most of his choreography. There he soon discovered his new muse, the young Margot Fonteyn, whom he featured in most of the works he created from 1935 to 1959.

At that time the dominant choreographic influence in England was Massine, then making his grandiose symphonic ballets. Antony Tudor (at Rambert's Ballet Club) and de Valois were both developing strains of ballet expressionism. Ashton, though his talent for making charming and polished dances was widely recognized, was criticized for his fashionable lightness or frivolity, as shown in works already mentioned and in *Les Patineurs* and *A Wedding Bouquet* (both 1937). Only later was it generally recognized that he had been the sole true classicist of British choreography, the one who had kept the danse d'école alive at the heart of his works. During the Second World War (in which he fought from 1941 on), the tone and content of his ballets darkened; and after the war, when the Sadler's Wells Ballet moved to Covent Garden, he achieved a newly authoritative and ample kind of neoclassicism, exemplified in *Symphonic Variations*, *Scènes de ballet*, and *Cinderella*. The plotless *Symphonic Variations* was a conscious demonstration that the subject matter of ballet is dancing—a deliberate answer to the literary and histrionic vein of choreography that had become prevalent and popular during the war, especially in Robert Helpmann's early work. It was now that Ashton adopted Petipa as one of his main choreographic models (although surely Petipa had been an indirect influence on him from the first). He coached dancers in Petipa roles and made several supplementary dances for stagings of the old ballet classics. Since de Valois had made the nineteenth-century classics a cornerstone of the Sadler's Wells repertory, the evident Ashton–Petipa connection became the central column of the company's style.

From 1950 on, Ashton's primacy among choreographers in Britain was at last unmistakable. Tudor had moved to the U.S. in 1940; Helpmann's later works never achieved the success of his wartime ballets; de Valois gave up regular choreography after 1950; and Massine, whom de Valois had brought to Covent Garden in 1947, left in 1949. Moreover, Ashton became acknowledged as one of the world's leading choreographers and, in response to invitations from several major ballet companies, went abroad to make such works as *Illuminations* (New York City Ballet), *Romeo and Juliet* (Royal Danish Ballet), and *La Valse* (La Scala). At home—despite the double blow struck by the deaths of Fedorovitch (1951) and Lambert (1953)—his authority grew, he became a keen influence on the early choreographic efforts of John Cranko and Kenneth MacMillan, and he continued to extend the musical, lyrical, and virtuosic gifts of Fonteyn in such works as *Daphnis and Chloë*, *Sylvia*, *Birthday Offering*, and *Ondine*.

For almost thirty years, de Valois and Ashton worked together to make their troupe one of the world's few leading classical companies, and this collaboration is remarkable. De Valois, though not mainly a classical choreographer, shaped the company's pedagogy; Ashton, though not a teacher, shaped its main choreographic identity. Though there may have been private tensions between the two on matters of repertory and dancers, de Valois nonetheless respected Ashton to the extent that she would occasionally modify Royal Ballet School academic practice to conform with Ashton's choreographic initiative. Later, several of Ashton's favourite dancers taught at the Royal Ballet School, and passed on certain of his specific stylistic preferences to their students.

In 1959, Fonteyn became a guest artist at Covent Garden. Though she remained the leading interpreter of his work and though he made six other dances for her between 1963 and 1984, Ashton now turned his attention to other Royal Ballet dancers and refined his style yet further. The triumphant results included *La Fille mal gardée*, *The Two Pigeons*, *The Dream*, *Monotones*, and *Enigma Variations*. Such dancers as Nadia Nerina, Svetlana Beriosova, and David Blair reached new peaks in his work; and a new generation of dancers, led by the great partnership of Antoinette Sibley and Anthony Dowell, brought Ashton's classicism to new peaks of intricacy, detail, and fluency. The Royal's corps de ballet also reached its zenith in this era.

In the years that followed his departure from office in 1970, Ashton lived in semi-retirement until his death in 1988. He choreographed a large number of short pieces, and a few more substantial ballets—notably *A Month in the Country* (1976) and *Rhapsody* (1980). Though there were many excellent performances of Ashton ballets in this era, Ashton's significance to the Royal Ballet now began gradually and inevitably to wane. During the 1980s the Cecchetti style, which had been central to

Ashton's and de Valois's work, was superseded at the Royal Ballet School by the Vaganova method; and Ashton ballets were danced less frequently by the two Royal Ballet companies. He did, however, contribute to revivals of his ballets even in the last months of his life.

Many of Ashton's ballets, plotless or narrative, focus on a close community, with few distinctions of rank. They seldom display the grand hierarchy of Petipa's or Balanchine's ballets. A frequent theme is male–female love, lyrically expressed and often shown with literal or metaphorical gestures of sensuality. The ballet style shown in Ashton's ballet is a particularly intricate one, with upper and lower body maintaining a lively activity, and many internal embellishments of head, arms, épaulement, and footwork. Though many features of Ashton style prove elusive, many Ashton ballets are danced by companies around the world.

—Alastair Macaulay

---

## AS TIME GOES BY

**Choreography:** Twyla Tharp
**Music:** Franz Josef Haydn
**Design:** Jennifer Tipton (lighting) and Chester Weinberg (costumes)
**First Production:** City Center Joffrey Ballet, New York, 24 October 1973
**Principal Dancers:** Beatriz Rodriguez, Larry Grenier

**Other productions include:** Twyla Tharp Dance Company (restaged Tharp); New York, 1988. Paris Opéra Ballet (restaged Tharp); Paris, February 1989.

### PUBLICATIONS

Siegel, Marcia, "Tharpitis", *Dance Magazine* (New York), December 1973
Balanchine, George, with Mason, Francis, *Balanchine's Complete Stories of the Great Ballets*, Garden City, New York, 1977
Croce, Arlene, *Afterimages*, New York, 1977
Siegel, Marcia, *The Shapes of Change*, Boston, 1979
Tharp, Twyla, *Push Comes to Shove* (autobiography), New York, 1992

* * *

*As Time Goes By* was created by Twyla Tharp for the Joffrey Ballet just a year after her highly original and successful *Deuce Coupe* to music by the Beach Boys. *As Time Goes By* was both a radical departure and the logical next step for Tharp. It was danced solely by the Joffrey dancers, and therefore, the first work she created not using her own company. She choreographed for the women on pointe. The music was not drawn from twentieth-century American popular styles, as much of her previous work had been. She chose the last two movements of Haydn's Symphony no. 45 in F-sharp minor, the "Farewell Symphony". The originality of her responses to this music—the refreshing blend of apparent spontaneity and perfect order in her rich and witty choices of movement—as well as the surprising brevity of the ballet, contribute to its charm and impact. The look of *As Time Goes By* is chic. The women wear sophisticated, sleeveless, calf-length, fluid jersey dresses in shades of brown, beige, and slate. The men wear off-white shorts and pullovers.

As she had done in her dances to popular music, Tharp used Haydn's music as a structural and thematic inspiration. She increased and decreased the numbers of dancers on stage in response to what Haydn had done with the instrumentalists of the orchestra. The ballet begins with a female solo, expands into a sextet, eventually includes seventeen men and women on stage, and then winds down to a male solo.

The choreography bears all the characteristics of Tharp's technically demanding nonchalant style, but with a difference. It is punctuated by perfectly placed multiple turns, dramatically poised extensions, and clean, decorative allegro. Point work allows Tharp to make split-second directional changes, to give the dancers new height and line and, literally, a new point of balance. Tharp had juxtaposed her loose-limbed, dynamically unpredictable dancing and the refinement of ballet in *Deuce Coupe*, but the styles were represented by different performers. In *As Time Goes By*, both possibilities of moving wrestle in the same body. She fractures the familiar arrangements of the body and redesigns them. The results are in turn whimsical, giddy, breathtaking, or poignant.

The first solo sets the tone. It is frenetic, the dancer's limbs pitching at every angle, her legs whipping through familiar allegro, her torso buckling, the action abruptly speeding up or slowing down. Suddenly, the familiar line of a perfect classroom position asserts itself. As quickly, it dissolves into something undefinable. The dancer's deadpan expression denies the lack of transitions, preparations, and other balletic conventions. The effect is heightened as five other dancers join her. Unison movement disintegrates. A supported dancer is suddenly left to her own wits. A lift is begun and then abandoned. One dancer is passed rather unceremoniously to another. Dancers rearrange each other's limbs as if correcting. More dancers join them. Superficially, the effect is one of pandemonium. But the flow of energy in one dancer's body appears connected to another's. Multiple activity creates a richness, a density of motion, that accelerates and accumulates. The stage pulsates with the vital actions of individuals, while all together they weave a tapestry of shape and design, complex and satisfying.

The ballet ends with the adagio, in which the pace of activity diminishes and dancers gradually leave the stage. One lingering male dancer is left curling and stretching his limbs, undulating his torso, through slow-motion turns in an adagio of self-absorption. A contrast to the opening solo, it is equally compelling.

In the first and subsequent performances of the ballet the Joffrey dancers excelled. The fiery Beatriz Rodriguez danced the opening solo with extraordinary clarity, while Larry Grenier ended the ballet with an ease that bordered on indolence. When the Tharp company performed the piece almost fifteen years after its premiere, the dancers' point work was disappointing. The work lost its crisp definition.

As a milestone in Tharp's career, the ballet stands as a rite of passage. With *Deuce Coupe*, Tharp became the mistress of pop ballet, a chronicler of her time and a darling of press and audiences. With *As Time Goes By*, she established herself as one of the most innovative choreographers working with the ballet vocabulary.

—Rose Anne Thom

---

**ASYLMURATOVA, Altynai**

Soviet dancer. Born Altynai Abduachimovna Asylmuratova in Alma-Ata, 1 January 1961. Studied at the Leningrad Choreographic (Vaganova) School, pupil of Inna Zubkovskaya; graduated in 1978. Married Kirov dancer Konstantin Zaklinsky. Dancer, Kirov Ballet, from 1978; principal dancer from 1982, touring Canada with the Kirov, 1986; guest artist, American Ballet Theatre, New York, 1988, Royal Ballet, London, various seasons, from 1989; has appeared in video-films *Backstage at the Kirov* (1984) and *The Magic of the Kirov* (1989). Honoured Artist of the Russian Federation, 1983.

**ROLES**

1979 Persidka in *Khovanschina* (opera; mus. Mussorgsky, chor. Lopukhov)
Fairy of Courage in *The Sleeping Beauty* (Petipa, staged Sergeyev), Kirov Ballet, Leningrad
1980 Juanita in *Don Quixote* (Gorsky after Petipa), Kirov Ballet, Leningrad
1981 Lilac Fairy in *The Sleeping Beauty* (Petipa, staged Sergeyev), Kirov Ballet, Leningrad
1981/82 Esmeralda in *Esmeralda Pas de Six* (Vaganova after Petipa), Kirov Ballet, Leningrad
1982 Shirin in *The Legend of Love* (Grigorovich), Kirov Ballet, Leningrad
Odette/Odile in *Swan Lake* (Petipa, Ivanov, staged Sergeyev), Kirov Ballet, Leningrad
1983 Title role in *Giselle* (Petipa after Coralli, Perrot), Kirov Ballet, Leningrad
Raymonda's friend in *Raymonda* (Petipa, staged Sergeyev), Kirov Ballet, Leningrad
1984 Title role (cr) in *Asiyat* (Vinogradov), Kirov Ballet, Leningrad
1985 Kitri in *Don Quixote* (Gorsky after Petipa), Kirov Ballet, Leningrad
Nikiya in *La Bayadère* (Petipa, Chabukiani, Ponomarev), Kirov Ballet, Leningrad
Aegina in *Spartacus* (Yakobson), Kirov Ballet, Leningrad
1986 Neslan-Daredzhan in *The Knight in Tigerskin* (Vinogradov), Kirov Ballet, Leningrad
Title role in *La Sylphide* (von Rosen after Bournonville), Kirov Ballet, Leningrad
1987 Eve (cr) in *Adam and Eve* (Béjart), Kirov Ballet, Leningrad
Soloist (cr) in *Bachty* (Béjart), Kirov Ballet, Leningrad
Medora (cr) in *Le Corsaire* (new production; Gusev after Petipa), Kirov Ballet, Leningrad
1988 Mary Magdalen (cr) in *The Rehearsal* (Fodor), Kirov Ballet, Leningrad
Nikiya in *La Bayadère* (Makarova after Petipa), American Ballet Theatre, New York
1989 Soloist in *Theme and Variations* (Balanchine, staged F. Russell), Kirov Ballet, Leningrad
1991 Title role in *Manon* (MacMillan), Royal Ballet, London
Natalia in *A Month in the Country* (Ashton), Royal Ballet, London
1991/92 Caroline in *Jardin aux lilas* (Tudor; staged Hynninen), Maryinsky Theatre Ballet (previously the Kirov), Leningrad/St. Petersburg
1992 Juliet in *Romeo and Juliet* (MacMillan), Royal Ballet, London

**PUBLICATIONS**

Croce, Arlene, *Sight Lines*, New York, 1987
Tobias, Toby, "The Beautiful and the Damned", *New York Magazine* (New York), 8 June 1987
Macaulay, Alastair, "She Who Dances", *The New Yorker*, 13 June 1988
Clarke, Mary, "The Kirov Ballet", *Dancing Times* (London), September 1988
Willis, Margaret, "Kiroviana: The Glasnost Difference", *Dance Magazine* (New York), July 1989
Reynolds, Nancy, "Setting Balanchine in Leningrad", *Ballet Review* (New York), Summer 1989
Pierpont, Claudia Roth, "Voices of Petersburg", *Ballet Review* (New York), Winter 1990

* * *

Now that "glasnost" has become commonplace, and the cultural constraints of the old Soviet Union seem a thing of the distant past, it is not unusual to see Russian ballet dancers as guest artists—or indeed as newly appointed permanent members—of ballet companies all around the world. But when Altynai Asylmuratova first appeared on the Western scene, there was great excitement: here was not only one of the treasures of the Vaganova school who, in earlier times, might have been kept hidden from the West, but here also was a truly exhilarating, great ballerina in her own right, a dancer still in her early twenties whom the non-Russian world might be allowed to watch in her development.

Asylmuratova was first "spotted" by Western critics in 1982 during the Kirov's Paris tour. Then a mere 21, she dazzled audiences with her exquisite beauty (a dark-eyed Audrey Hepburn look, heightened by a touch of Eastern exoticism), and assured style. There was the expected Kirov perfection of line and unified flow of upper body, arms, and head; there was the predictable awe-inspiring Russian technique (though with the occasional, somehow endearing, quirks)—but more than anything else, there was a combination of delicate gracefulness with an almost unbelievable power of attack and conviction. In excerpts from *Esmeralda*, in 1982, she showed such intensity and yet such perfect lyricism that one well-known critic was prompted to remark on the ballerina's capacity be both "huge" and "deliciously subtle" at the same time. Later, when paired with the fiery Tartar Farukh Ruzimatov—whose own style of attack pushes the boundaries of classical line to the utmost—Asylmuratova, as if spurred by her counterpart, thrilled audiences with her capacity for leaping in head first, as it were, submerging herself utterly and giving radical interpretations to such signature roles as Nikiya in *La Bayadère*. Arlene Croce, observing Asylmuratova for the first time in 1982, wrote, "Asylmuratova is the real thing . . . [She] is the most prodigiously endowed ballerina the Kirov has shown us in 20 years". And British critic Alastair Macaulay, writing about Asylmuratova in *The New Yorker* in 1988, called Asylmuratova "one of the most glorious and original dancers of our day".

Asylmuratova's technique, coldly analyzed, is not perfect, and might be said to be surpassed in some particulars by her Kirov/Maryinsky colleagues. Her hit-or-miss record with pirouettes was noticed early on; obviously not a natural turner, Asylmuratova none the less throws herself into her pirouettes with the same abandon she exercises in everything else, resulting in the occasional brilliant spin and the occasional last-minute rescue from near-disaster. (On on occasion, during one of her London visits, she finished a series of solo turns flatly facing the back of the stage; but, ultimate performer and charmer that she is, she threw her head over her shoulder,

**Altynai Asylmuratova with Farukh Ruzimatov in *Le Corsaire*, Kirov Ballet**

flashed a brilliant smile, and convinced the audince that it was in the choreography.)

Asylmuratova has also shown some of the stylistic affectations more typically associated with her one-time partner Ruzimatov, who shamelessly distorts line, particularly of the back, for the sake of such dramatic poses as an extraordinarily deep and plunging arabesque. Alastair Macaulay diagnosed this problem as one of the "retracted pelvis", calling it "Kirov style as deformed by Béjart"—but other less erudite viewers might see a similarity in posture with Olga Korbutt, or any other in a long line of gymnasts who imitated her strange exaggeration of lifted chin and chest, such that the back appears nearly folded in two (this usually accompanied by a triumphant smile). But such mannerisms, in Asylmuratova's case, seem reserved for showpieces like the pas de deux from *Le Corsaire*, where, one might argue, the audience expects this sort of exhibitionism. Where classical purity is required, Asylmuratova rises to the occasion: her Aurora, as seen in the Kirov's 1990 London tour, was beautiful, assured, regal, and utterly true to Petipa. Her Giselle is not only dramatically real but shows an innate understanding of the essence of Romantic style and spirit, with her lovely arms and sensitive musicality in particular making her utterly convincing as an ethereal being in the second act.

Perhaps even more impressively, Asylmuratova has shown her ability to adapt to—and ultimately to absorb entirely—other choreographic styles, not just the debatable gymnastics of Béjart but the dramatic ballets of other great twentieth-century choreographers. As a frequent guest of the Royal Ballet in London, Asylmuratova has proven equally successful in works by those two hugely different English choreographers, Kenneth MacMillan and Frederick Ashton. In the overtly dramatic and passionate ballets of MacMillan, which require a physical as much as emotional abandon, Asylmuratova has shown herself more than equal to the tempestuous speed, acrobatic pas de deux, and expansive style of MacMillan's choreography, giving a rich and moving account of the tragedy of *Manon*. At the same time, the understated, delicate, yet profoundly suggestive choreography of Ashton's *A Month in the Country* seemed made for Asylmuratova, whose affecting portrayal of Natalia Petrovna may not have come from a lifetime's schooling in the "English" style, but perhaps had deeper roots in an understanding of the Chekhov which inspired Ashton in the first place.

In the abstract neo-classicism of Balanchine, first brought to Russia by the Kirov director Oleg Vinogradov (who arranged for the first legitimate Russian stagings of several Balanchine works), Asylmuratova adapted well to the fleet footwork and mercurial speed of Balanchine's choreography, if not with the same ease as the New York City Ballet dancers who have been brought up on the Balanchine style. Nancy Reynolds, an expert on the Balanchine repertory who travelled to Leningrad to observe these stagings, wrote of Asylmuratova's open admission that the steps seemed at first "too hard", for while her Russian training emphasized the use of the entire body, Balanchine's required that the legs be worked separately, and at unaccustomed speed. But, as Reynolds wrote of Asylmuratova in Balanchine's *Theme and Variations*, "She devours his movements with the avidity of one with an appetite for more". Consequently, Asylmuratova triumphed: "The vulnerable Asylmuratova of the serene legato line, who so captivated New York critics in *La Bayadère* last year, is not presently to be found on the Kirov stage," wrote Reynolds. "In her place is an imperial ballerina, strong, dynamic, and precise. She skims above all the tiny steps, and majesty colors her adagio."

What Reynolds identified as Asylmuratova's "hunger" in taking on new roles and new styles is perhaps the key to her success. Undoubtedly her foundation is her superb training in the Kirov tradition, but technique is far from everything. Her artistry is not learned but innate, something that is as much a part of her as her beauty and her spectacular, yet natural, smile—and she applies it to each new role she takes on with utter and searching conviction. And she simply has that rare thing, an enchanting stage personality. Running on stage for Aurora's first appearance in *The Sleeping Beauty*, for example, and flashing that exquisite smile to the rafters, Asylmuratova brings a palpable hush to the auditorium, even before she has danced a step. One feels the excitement and sense of heightened response in the theatre, as to something quite extraordinary: it is as if all who are there know that they are in the presence of greatness.

—Martha Bremser

---

**ATANASSOFF, Cyril**

French dancer. Born in Puteaux, 30 June 1941. Studied at Paris Opéra School, pupil of Roger Ritz, Serge Peretti, L. Legrand, Victor Gsovsky, Alexander Kalioujny, Harald Lander, Raoul Bari, and Gilbert Mayer, 1953–57. Married dancer Claude Tourneur: one daughter, Nathalie, b. 1967. Dancer, Paris Opéra Ballet, from 1957: second quadrille, 1957; coryphée, 1957–59; petit sujet, 1959–60; grand sujet, from 1960; premier danseur, from January 1962; danseur étoile, from 1964; toured with Paris Opéra Ballet to Russia, 1970, Cuba and London, 1971; guest artist, Brantôme Festival, 1959, 1960, and 1964; also performed in Berlin, 1964, Mexico, 1965, Festival de Sens, 1967, Teheran, Budapest, and Avignon, 1968, London, 1969, Venice, 1978, Japan, Brazil, Italy, Spain, Portugal, and Bordeaux, 1979; appeared at numerous international arts festivals, including at Provence, Orange, Nice-Cimiez, Carpentras, and Brantôme Festivals; also appeared with American Classical Ballet, 1971, "Groupe des 7", 1971 and 1975, London Festival Ballet, 1972, Opera du Rhin, 1976, Ballet de la Wallonie at Sisteron and Carpentras Festivals, and Vienna, 1980; farewell performance at Opéra, 1986; has since returned as guest artist; also teacher, CNSMD (Conservatoire Supérior), Paris, after retiring from the stage. Recipient: Chevalier de l'Ordre du Merite, 1972; Prix Petipa, 1973; Seconde Croisière de la Danse, 1980.

**ROLES**

1959 Principal dancer (cr) in *Concertstück* (Van Dyk), Brantôme Festival
Principal dancer (cr) in *L'Echarpe* (Van Dyk), Brantôme Festival
Principal dancer in *Grand Pas* (Lifar), Paris Opéra Ballet, Paris
Principal dancer in *Pas et lignes* (Bessy), French television
1960 Pas de quatre and Czardas in *Swan Lake* (Petipa, Ivanov; staged Burmeister), Paris Opéra Ballet, Paris
Principal dancer in *Clairière*, French television
Principal dancer in *Études* (Lander), Paris Opéra Ballet, Paris
1962 Principal dancer (cr) in *Pas de deux de Jolivet* (Bestonso), T.E.D.
1963 Principal dancer (cr) in *Danses brêves* (Skibine), Opéra-Comique, Paris

Principal dancer in *Concerto Barocco* (Balanchine), Paris Opéra Ballet, Paris
1964 The Young Man (cr) in *La Damnation de Faust* (Béjart), Paris Opéra Ballet, Paris
Principal dancer (cr) in *Les Paladins* (Descombey), Marais Festival, Paris
Principal dancer (cr) in *Sarracenia* (Descombey), Paris Opéra Ballet, Paris
Principal dancer (cr) in *Adage à la rose* (Brieux), Paris Opéra Ballet, Paris
Principal dancer in *Play-Bach* (Bessy), Opéra-Comique, Paris
Albrecht in *Giselle* (Petipa after Coralli, Perrot; staged Lifar), Paris Opéra Ballet, Paris
Principal dancer in *Le Palais de cristal* (Balanchine), Paris Opéra Ballet, Paris
Principal dancer in *Scotch Symphony* (Balanchine), Paris Opéra Ballet, Paris
Principal dancer in *Diable à la Kermesse* (Corelli), French television
1965 Principal dancer (cr) in *Amduscias* (Mosena), Rouen
The Chosen One in *Le Sacre du printemps* (Béjart), Paris Opéra Ballet, Paris
The Prince (cr) in *The Nutcracker* (Rayne), Opéra-Comique, Paris
Principal dancer in *Prisonnier du Caucase* (Skibine), Paris Opéra Ballet, Paris
Frollo (cr) in *Notre Dâme de Paris* (Petit), Paris Opéra Ballet, Paris
Adage in *Suite en blanc* (Lifar), Paris Opéra Ballet, Paris
Principal dancer in *But* (Descombey), Paris Opéra Ballet, Paris
Siegfried in *Swan Lake* (Petipa, Ivanov; staged Burmeister), Paris Opéra Ballet, Paris
Principal dancer in *Carmen* (Rayne), French television
1966 Franz (cr) in *Coppélia* (Descombey), Paris Opéra Ballet, Paris
Principal dancer (cr) in *Sarabande* (Labis), Paris Opéra Ballet, Paris
The Man in *Les Mirages* (Lifar), Paris Opéra Ballet, Paris
Quasimodo in *Notre Dâme de Paris* (Petit), Paris Opéra Ballet, Paris
1967 Principal dancer in *Bacchus et Ariadne* (Descombey), Paris Opéra Ballet, Paris
Principal dancer (cr) in *Equivalences* (Descombey), Théâtre de l'Est, Paris
1968 Principal dancer (cr) in *Fleur carnivore* (Rayne), French television
Principal dancer in *Hommage à S.B.* (Bessy), French television
1971 Principal dancer (cr) in *Saisons* (Parres), Festival Grand Rue
Principal dancer (cr) in *Combat de Tancrède* (Schmucki), Festival Provins
Principal dancer (cr) in *Aor* (Schmucki), Paris Opéra Ballet, Paris
1972 James (cr) in *La Sylphide* (Lacotte after Taglioni), Paris Opéra Ballet, Paris
Principal dancer (cr) in *Danse du Samourai* (Kudo), French television
Principal dancer (cr) in *Spirale* (Deshauteurs), French television
Principal dancer (cr) in *Dyade* (Charrat), Opéra-Comique, Paris
1973 Principal dancer (cr) in *Jeux* (Flindt), Paris Opéra Ballet, Paris
Principal dancer (cr) in *Amériques* (Butler), Paris Opéra Ballet, Paris
Principal dancer (cr) in *Intégrales* (Butler), Paris Opéra Ballet, Paris
The Prince (cr) in *L'Oiseau de feu* (Skibine), Capitole, Toulouse
Principal dancer in *Arcana* (Rusillo), French television
Principal dancer in Pas de deux in *Momente* (Rusillo), French television
1974 Pas de deux in *Agon* (Balanchine), Paris Opéra Ballet, Paris
Principal dancer (cr) in *Variations Diabelli* (Macdonald), Paris Opéra Ballet, Paris
Prince Désiré in *The Sleeping Beauty* (Petipa; staged Alonso), Paris Opéra Ballet, Paris
Principal dancer (cr) in *Astronomy* (Sparemblek), French television
1975 Principal dancer (cr) in *Pas de Dieux* (G. Kelly), Paris Opéra Ballet, Paris
1976 Le Comte Muffat (cr) in *Nana* (Petit), Paris Opéra Ballet, Paris
Title role in *Ivan the Terrible* (Grigorovich), Paris Opéra Ballet, Paris
Principal dancer in *Tzigane* (Balanchine), Paris Opéra Ballet, Paris
Principal dancer in *La Valse* (Balanchine), Paris Opéra Ballet, Paris
1978 Principal dancer in *The Four Seasons* (MacMillan), Paris Opéra Ballet, Paris
Principal dancer in *Sirène* (Schmucki), Creteil Festival
1979 Principal dancer in *Concerto* (Charrat), Ballet Théâtre Français, Nancy
Principal dancer in *Hopop* (Sanders), Ballet Théâtre Français
Orion in *Sylvia* (Lifar; staged Darsonval), Paris Opéra Ballet, Paris
1980 Principal dancer (cr) in *Une Dimanche à l'Aube* (Skouratoff), Bordeaux
1981 Colas (cr) in *La Fille mal gardée* (Spoerli), Paris Opéra Ballet, Paris
Basil (cr) in *Don Quixote* (new production; Nureyev after Petipa), Paris Opéra Ballet, Paris
Principal dancer in *Three Preludes* (Stevenson), Paris Opéra Ballet, Paris
1982 Principal dancer in *Leitmotiv* (Choo San Goh), Opéra, Monte Carlo
1983 Abdérâme in *Raymonda* (Petipa; staged Nureyev), Paris Opéra Ballet, Paris
1984 Spada in *Marco Spada* (Lacotte), Paris Opéra Ballet, Paris
Principal dancer in *Violin Concerto* (Balanchine), Paris Opéra Ballet, Paris
Pantalon in *Carnaval* (Fokine), Opéra-Comique, Paris
1985 Siegfried in *Swan Lake* (Petipa, Ivanov; staged Nureyev), Paris Opéra Ballet, Paris
1986 Tybalt in *Romeo and Juliet* (Nureyev), Paris Opéra Ballet, Paris
1987 Principal dancer in *Prisme du Chaman*, Opéra-Comique, Paris
1990 Dr. Coppélius in *Coppélia* (after Saint-Léon), Paris Opéra Ballet School, Opéra-Comique, Paris
1992 Destiny in *Le Rendez-vous* (Petit), Paris Opéra Ballet, Paris
The Corregidor in *Le Tricorne* (Massine), Paris Opéra Ballet, Paris

**Other roles include**: Faune in *L'Après-midi d'un faune* (Lifar),

Pas de deux from *The Nutcracker* (after Ivanov), principal dancer in *Concerto* (Skibine), Pas de deux from *Le Corsaire* (after Petipa), Daphnis in *Daphnis and Chloë* (Skibine), Pas de deux from *Flower Festival at Genzano* (Bournonville), principal dancer in *Grand Pas Classique* (also *Grand Pas d'Auber*; Gsovsky), Chief Warrior in *Polovstian Dances from Prince Igor* (Fokine), Romeo in *Romeo and Juliet* (Nureyev), principal dancer in *Tchaikovsky Pas de deux* (Balanchine).

## PUBLICATIONS

By Atanassoff:

Interview in Cabrera, Miguel, "Cyril Atanassoff in Cuba", *Cuba en el ballet* (Havana), January 1972

Interview in Lavolé, Jean-Pierre, "Cyril Atanassoff", *Pour la danse* (Marseille), February/March 1978

Interview in Planell, Martine, "L'âme du Chaman", *Pour la danse* (Marseille), June 1987

About Atanassoff:

Hersin, Adré Philippe, "Cyril Atanassoff", *Les Saisons de la danse* (Paris), November 1968

Niehaus, Max, *Ballet Faszination*, Munich, 1972

Christout, Marie-Françoise, "*Ivan the Terrible*", *Dance and Dancers* (London), December 1976

*Cyril Atanassoff: Présenté par Claude Bessy*, Paris, 1979

Mannoni, Gerard, and Jouhaud, Pierre, *Les Étoiles de l'Opéra de Paris*, Paris, 1981

Diénis, Jean-Claude, "Salut l'artiste!", *Danser* (Paris), July/August 1986

* * *

Cyril Atanassoff, a dancer gifted with a remarkable stage presence, gave early evidence of an original personality and a faultless technique. His long career was dedicated to the Paris Opéra, which he followed across the world, only very occasionally accepting the many invitations he received to dance with other international dance companies.

Soon after Atanassoff graduated from the Opéra Ballet School, an excellent example of both its strict training and at the same time its respect for individuality, he entered the corps de ballet and progressed rapidly through the ranks. From 1959 he distinguished himself particularly in Serge Lifar's *Grand Pas*, Peter van Dyk's *Concertstück*, and Harald Lander's *Études*. Balanchine appreciated Atanassoff's perfectly controlled technique, admiring the faultless precision of the dancer's performances in *Concerto Barocco*, *Palais de cristal* and *Scotch Symphony*, and later in *Agon* and (with Elisabeth Platel) *Violin Concerto*. However, Atanassoff was not able to display his powerful temperament and youthful ardour (which he still had when he left the Opéra in 1986) in abstract dance, being better suited to scenarios which allowed him to make use of his deep dramatic sense. Maurice Béjart recognized this gift when he created the role of the Young Man for Atanassoff in *The Damnation of Faust* and when he gave him the role of the Chosen One in *The Rite of Spring*. Atanassoff brought to the latter role an internal truth, a musicality, and a rhythmic spontaneity which emphasized the vulnerability of the adolescent overwhelmed by sexual urges. In the same way, with a seemingly endless spontaneity, Atanassoff confronted the "Mirages" of Lifar's ballet, showing how easily enticed is the man who is desperate to forget his deep and harrowing solitude and his mortality in the face of indifferent nature.

Linking dance closely with mime, Atanassoff was a passionate Albrecht, going from the carefree liveliness of the nobleman captivated by the peasant girl Giselle, to the realization of his fatal betrayal, and finally to the remorse which tears him from the world, throwing him at his beloved and driving him ultimately into madness. His innate noble bearing and masculine authority made him a moving Siegfried in *Swan Lake* in which, as in all the classical roles he danced, he was a most attentive and reliable partner. Among the ballerinas he partnered were Yvette Chauviré, Alicia Alonso, Jacqueline Rayet, Noëlla Pontois, and Dominique Khalfouni, whose first steps on stage he helped to guide.

Although by nature generous and modest, Atanassoff was able to portray characters who were ambiguous, complex, and sometimes antipathetic. Therefore, after creating the role of Frollo, the depraved priest in Roland Petit's *Notre Dâme de Paris*, Atanassoff danced with equal success the role of Quasimodo, the tender-hearted freak who is won over by Esmeralda. Petit also gave him the role of the Count Muffat, who is bewitched by the overpowering sexuality of the voluptuous *Nana*. In Yuri Grigorovich's *Ivan the Terrible* Atanassoff painted a terrifying and sinister picture of the cruel despot. In *Romeo and Juliet* he evoked the provocative and aggressive jealousy which underlies Tybalt's cruelty. Lastly, following in the tradition of Serge Lifar, he brought a sensual and voluptuous animalism to his interpretation of *Faun*, which was altogether Dionysian.

Well equipped to bring such a variety of roles to life, Cyril Atanassoff remains one of the most "complete" dancers in the history of ballet, owing to the way in which he has combined a complete mastery of the technique with expressive masculine strength.

—Marie-Françoise Christout

---

**AUMER, Jean-Louis**

French dancer and choreographer. Born in Strasbourg, 21 April 1774 (some sources say 1776). Studied under Jean Dauberval in Bordeaux. Appeared with Dauberval's company in London, 1791–92; dancer with Noverre's company, London, 1794, and under Giocomo Onorati, King's Theatre, London, 1795; début at L'Académie royale de musique (Paris Opéra), 1798; maître de ballet, Théâtre de la Porte-Saint-Martin, Paris, 1804–06; ballet master, Lyons, 1807; invited to produce a ballet (*Les Amours d'Antoine et de Cléopâtre*) at the Opéra, 1808; engaged by King of Westphalia as maître de ballet at Kassel, 1809–14; ballet master, Lyons, and then for court opera in Vienna, 1814–20; maître de ballet, Paris Opéra, 1820–31; also ballet master at King's Theatre, London, various intervening seasons, 1823–25; retired to Normandy, 1831. Died in St. Martin, July 1833.

## ROLES

1793 Egisthus in *Iphigenia in Aulide* (Noverre), King's Theatre, London

1794 Dancer (cr) in *Adélaide; ou, La Bergère des Alpes* (Noverre), King's Theatre, London

Dancer (cr) in *Le Bon Prince; ou, Les Infortunés Vertueux* (D'Egville), King's Theatre, London

Divertissement (cr) in *Don Giovanni* (opera; mus. Mozart, Gazzaniga; chor. Noverre), King's Theatre, London

Principal dancer (cr) in *L'Union des bergères* (Noverre), King's Theatre, London

Principal dancer (cr) in *Giustino I, Imperatore dei Romani* (Onorati), King's Theatre, London
Principal dancer (cr) in *L'Espiègle Soubrette; ou, Le Tableau mouvant* (Onorati), King's Theatre, London
1795 Principal dancer (cr) in *L'Amant retrouvé* (Onorati), King's Theatre, London
Principal dancer in *Paul et Virginie* ("new" ballet; chor. Onorati), King's Theatre, London
Bertrand in *The Deserter* (*Le Déserteur*; Dauberval), King's Theatre, London
Principal dancer (cr) in *L'Odio vinto dell'Eroismo* (Onorati), King's Theatre, London
1798 Principal dancer (Opéra debut) in *Le Déserteur* (Dauberval), Opéra, Paris
1800 Title role in *Pygmalion* (Milon), Opéra, Paris
1801 Don Quichotte in *Les Noces de Gamache* (Milon), Opéra, Paris
1815 Herzog (cr) in *Die Pagen des Herzogs von Vendôme* (also chor.), Hoftheater, Vienna
1820 Duc de Vendôme (cr) in *Les Pages du Duc de Vendôme* (new staging of 1815 production; also chor.), Opéra, Paris
1821 Hungarian Count (cr) in *La Fête hongroise* (also chor.), Opéra, Paris
1822 Denulf (cr) in *Alfred le Grand* (also chor.), Opéra, Paris
1823 Sigiskar (cr) in *Aline, Reine de Golconde* (also chor.), King's Theatre, London (performed and restaged for Opéra, Paris, later in 1823)
1827 Bailiff (cr) in *Astolphe et Joconde, ou Les Coureurs d'aventures* (also chor.), Opéra, Paris
1830 Synelet (cr) in *Manon Lescaut* (also chor.), Opéra, Paris

## WORKS

1804 *La Fille mal gardée* (after Dauberval; mus. various), Théâtre de la Porte-Saint-Martin, Paris
1805 *Rosina et Lorenzo; ou, Les Gondoliers de Venise*, Théâtre de la Porte-Saint-Martin, Paris
*Robinson Crusoe*, Théâtre de la Porte-Saint-Martin, Paris
*Le Page inconstant* (after Dauberval), Théâtre de la Porte-Saint-Martin, Paris
1806 *Jenny; ou, Le Mariage secret* (mus. Darondeau), Théâtre de la Porte-Saint-Martin, Paris
*Les Deux Créoles* (mus. Darondeau), Théâtre de la Porte-Saint-Martin, Paris
1807 *Antoine et Cléopâtre*, Lyons
1808 *Les Amours d'Antoine et de Cléopâtre* (mus. Kreutzer), Opéra, Paris
*Antoine et Cléopâtre*, Grand Theatre, Lyons
1814 *Divertissement*, Hoftheater, Vienna
*Zephir und Flora* (divertissement), Hoftheater, Vienna
*Luise und Alexis; oder, Der Deserteur* (after Dauberval's *Le Déserteur*), Hoftheater, Vienna
*Myrsile und Anteros; oder, Amors Macht* (mus. Kreutzer), Hoftheater, Vienna
1815 *Das Rosenfest; oder, Der Preis der Tugend*, Hoftheater, Vienna
*Die Bajaderen* (mus. Gyrowetz), Hoftheater, Vienna
*Die Hochzeit auf dem Lande* (divertissement; mus. Kinsky), Hoftheater, Vienna
*Die Feier der Grazien* (divertissement; mus. Kinsky), Hoftheater, Vienna
*Die Pagen des Herzogs von Vendôme* (divertissement; mus. Gyrowetz), Hoftheater, Vienna
*Das Ländliche Fest im Walde bei Kis-ber* (divertissement; mus. Gyrowetz), Hoftheater, Vienna
1816 *Ein Ritterliches Divertissement*, Hoftheater, Vienna
*Die Hochzeit der Thetis und des Peleus* (mus. Gyrowetz), Hoftheater, Vienna
*Die zwei Tanten; oder, Ehemals und heute* (mus. Gyrowetz), Hoftheater, Vienna
*Die Toilette von Alcibiades* (divertissement), Hoftheater, Vienna
*Ehre der Frauen* (divertissement; mus. Weigl and Persius), Hoftheater, Vienna
1817 *Amor und Psyche*, Hoftheater, Vienna
*Die zwei kleinen Savoyarden* (mus. Gyrowetz), Hoftheater, Vienna
*Das Sonnenfest* (divertissement; mus. Kinsky), Hoftheater, Vienna
*Erigone; oder, Der Triumph des Bacchus* (mus. Gyrowetz and Kinsky), Hoftheater, Vienna
1818 *Der Zauberschlaf* (mus. Gyrowetz and Persius), Hoftheater, Vienna
*Aline, Königen von Golkonda* (mus. Blum), Hoftheater, Vienna
*Achilles* (mus. Blum), Hoftheater, Vienna
1819 *Ossian* (French mus. adapted by Kinsky), Hoftheater, Vienna
*Der flatterhafte Page; oder, Figaros Hochzeit* (after Dauberval's *Le Page inconstant*; new mus. Gyrowetz), Hoftheater, Vienna
1820 *Emma; oder, Die heimliche Ehe* (new version of *Jenny*; mus. Kinsky), Hoftheater, Vienna
*Alfred der Grosse* (mus. Gallenberg), Hoftheater, Vienna
*Les Pages du Duc de Vendôme* (after 1815 Vienna production; mus. Gyrowetz), Opéra, Paris
1821 *Johann d'Arc* (mus. Gallenberg), Hoftheater, Vienna
*La Fête hongroise* (divertissement; mus. Gyrowetz), Opéra, Paris
1822 *Alfred le Grand* (new version; mus. Dugazon and Gallenberg), Opéra, Paris (staged King's Theatre, London, 1823)
1823 *Aline, reine de Golconde* (mus. Blum), King's Theatre, London
*Aline, reine de Golconde* (new version; mus. Dugazon, after Berton and Monsigny), Opéra, Paris
*Le Page inconstant* (after Dauberval; new mus. arranged Habeneck), Opéra, Paris
1824 *Le Songe d'Ossian*, King's Theatre, London
1825 *Cléopâtre, reine de Égypte* (mus. Kreutzer et al.), King's Theatre, London
1827 *Astolphe et Joconde; ou, Les Coureurs d'aventures* (mus. Herold), Opéra, Paris
*La Somnambule; ou, L'Arrivée d'un nouveau seigneur* (mus. Herold), Opéra, Paris
1828 Dances in *La Muette de Portici* (opera; mus. Auber), Opéra, Paris
*Lydie* (mus. Hérold), Opéra, Paris
*La Fille mal gardée* (revised version after Dauberval; new mus. Hérold), Opéra, Paris
1829 *La Belle au bois dormant* (mus. Hérold), Opéra, Paris
Dances in *Guillame Tell* (opera; mus. Rossini), Opéra, Paris
1830 *Manon Lescaut* (mus. Halévy), Opéra, Paris

## PUBLICATIONS

Beaumont, Cyril, *The Complete Book of Ballets*, revised edition, London, 1951
Guest, Ivor, *The Romantic Ballet in England*, London, 1954

Guest, Ivor, *The Romantic Ballet in Paris*, London 1966
Kirstein, Lincoln, *Movement and Metaphor: Four Centuries of Ballet*, New York, 1970
Winter, Marian Hannah, *The Pre-Romantic Ballet*, London, 1974

* * *

Aumer made his mark as a ballet master in Paris during the decade preceding the romantic ballet. A disciple of the great *ballet d'action* ballet master, Jean Dauberval, with whom he danced in London and Bordeaux during the French Revolution, Aumer never gave up the principles learned from his mentor. Indeed, he produced several of Dauberval's ballets for their Paris premieres. Some felt that, during his early career anyway, Aumer followed his teacher too closely. Noverre wrote in 1807: "Aumer, respecting his model, has added nothing." By this time Aumer had been dancing at the Opéra for ten years (since 1798) and had produced several ballets at the Théâtre de la Porte-Saint-Martin. His most successful was the first Parisian production of Dauberval's *La Fille mal gardée* (Bordeaux, 1789; Paris, 1804). His most famous was *Les Deux Créoles* (1806), created as an out-and-out challenge to Opéra ballet master Pierre Gardel, who had just produced a work on the same theme at the Opéra, *Paul et Virginie*. Aumer's only Paris Opéra ballet during his time there as a dancer was the neo-classical *Les Amours d'Antoine et de Cléopâtre* of 1808.

His early works, like his later ballets, achieved their impact through the power of their dramatic action as conveyed by silent acting or pantomime. One contemporary critic's description of his *Robinson Crusoe* (1805) sums up the appeal of these ballets, with their "succession, varied and infinite, of adventures and incidents which are weighty without shocking, which, always motivated without ever being predictable, astonish the mind, captivate the attention and agitate the soul . . .". The most serious of critics, Geoffroy, went so far as to assert that *Les Amours* was instructive and morally uplifting—the ultimate aim of any neo-classical, *ballet d'action* ballet master if art's most important task was to educate the viewer, and make him a better person.

*Les Amours* earned Aumer the admiration of Napoleon's brother, who invited him in 1809 to his court in Kassel. From there Aumer moved to Lyons, and then to Vienna, where he created several of the ballets he would present in Paris and London during the 1820s.

Aumer's return to Paris in 1820 was met with considerable enthusiasm by audiences and critics who were more than ready for a change after the long dominance of Gardel and Milon, the creators of all but two of the new ballets given at the Opéra since *Les Amours*. But Aumer did not live up to expectations. With the exception of two ballets created during his eleven years at the Opéra, his works failed in their main aim, the representation of a moving dramatic action. His first Opéra work, a production of *Alfred le Grand* (which had its premiere in Vienna) was typical of many. Its plot was long, involved, illogical, and confusing; its mise-en-scène was spectacular; its various elements were not integrated into a coherent whole. One observer, criticizing Aumer's unrealized dramatic intentions and his often absurd action (a village fête in the middle of a war), commented: "The piece has gained the only genre of success to which it has claim: one has applauded the dancers, sometimes the composer, three times M. Ciceri, because there were three changes of decorations; finally one has applauded M. Aumer . . .".

Aumer spent three seasons working in London during Opéra holidays. English critics reacted in a similar fashion to their continental counterparts. *Alfred* was judged the "most grotesque and absurd spectacle" as far as its dramatic action went, but was commended for its dances, music, dresses, and scenery. *Les Amours d'Antoine et Cléopâtre*, retitled *Cléopâtre, reine d'Egypte*, showed Aumer's "great skill in . . . groupings and *coups de theatre*. . . . Otherwise we cannot say much in praise, for the subject . . . abounds with action rather than dancing, and has the common defect of representing characters with whom the dancing mania seems perfectly inconsistent. Why should . . . Octavia in one scene be all agony at the desertion of her husband, and in the next join in a sprightly dance with the most perfect nonchalance?"

Aumer managed to avoid most of the usual shortcomings in his most successful Opéra work, *La Somnambule* (1827). It was the quintessence of the sentimental pantomimic ballet, presenting as it did a virtuous young girl wrongfully accused of faithlessness. In the end she is vindicated as, walking in her sleep, she is about to step into a whirling millwheel. It was ". . . a little drama, perfect in its ensemble, delicious in its details . . . touching and pathetic . . .". But it achieved its dramatic strength through the isolation of most of the dancing in the first act. (Indeed, those who danced did not perform the main roles.) The rest of the ballet was silent acting (pantomime). Furthermore, a new practice was tried: a second party wrote the scenario, in this instance the popular playwright Eugène Scribe. Much of the credit for the dramatic unity must go to him.

Aumer's inability to integrate dance and plot was the most convincing justification of the Opéra's indifference to his departure in the spring of 1831. A year after this, *La Sylphide* would demonstrate the power of dance to express character and atmosphere, showing the central role dance could play in creating poetic illusion—the very idea upon which romantic ballet was to be based. Yet Aumer learned his craft at a time when dances were for show, pantomime for expression, and ballets for the representation of drama. He had little to offer the likes of Marie Taglioni, Fanny Elssler, or Carlotta Grisi, dancers who would be central to the theatrical eloquence of ballet.

—John Chapman

---

## AUREOLE

**Choreography:** Paul Taylor
**Music:** George Frederick Handel
**Design:** Thomas Skelton (lighting)
**First Production:** Paul Taylor Dance Company, Connecticut College, New London, Connecticut, 4 August 1962
**Principal Dancers:** Paul Taylor, Elizabeth Walton, Dan Wagoner, Sharon Kinney, Renee Kimball

**Other productions include:** Royal Danish Ballet; Copenhagen, 25 May 1968. Paris Opéra Ballet; Paris, 1974.

## PUBLICATIONS

Horst, Louis, "The American Dance Festival", *Dance Observer* (New York), August–September 1962
Maskey, Jacqueline, "Paul Taylor Dance Company", *Dance Magazine* (New York), February 1964
Kerensky, Oleg, "The Paul Taylor Dance Company", *Dancing Times* (London), January 1965

***Aureole* performed by The Paul Taylor Company, with Paul Taylor, 1962**

Siegel, Marcia, *The Shapes of Change*, Boston, 1977
Taylor, Paul, *Private Domain*, New York, 1987

* * *

*Aureole* typifies the lighter, more lyrical side of Paul Taylor's style. Yet when the work was first performed in 1962 it was considered atypical, not just of Taylor's choreography but, more fundamentally, of the subject matter and movement emphases of American modern dance. Created at a time when modern dance seemed synonymous with social comment, and when post-modern dance was emerging as pedestrian, task-oriented, and centred in non-proscenium spaces, *Aureole* explored movement-music-stage space associations. Its unfussy white costumes, simple lighting, and Handel score were the antithesis of the highly theatrical approach preferred by many of Taylor's modern dance contemporaries.

Commissioned by the American Dance Festival where, according to Taylor, "anything old is out", *Aureole* marked a new development. Appropriately, its title alludes to brightness. In *Aureole*, Taylor introduced the idea that modern dance need not be angst-ridden or cerebral. Unashamedly Utopian, the world that *Aureole* inhabits is untouched by suffering or conflict. It is a non-narrative world where dancing is all-absorbing. The physical pleasure of moving with such spatial freedom, the rising optimism in the dance's rhythmic progression, the amity of the dancers' numerous meetings and partings make *Aureole* a work which glorifies both choreography and performers.

From a basic lexicon of steps, the choreography builds by accumulation. Successive side cabrioles and skimming sissonnes—performed with legs parallel rather than classically turned-out—travelling step-lunges, bent-kneed bourrées, and simple coupé turns propel the dancers through space. Often their trajectories are diagonal. The unbroken flow of motion as they enter and exit suggests infinite space. Arms either swing easily or are held softly—often high to the sides in the recurring Taylor "V" position. It is a dance in which movement—its source and the dancers' assimilation of it—appears easy.

Taylor's interest in upper-lower body duality, in which fast legwork contrasts with tilting, twisting torsos, is akin to Merce Cunningham's concern for asymmetry and complexity. But in *Aureole*'s symmetrical structure and in the momentum which Taylor draws from the music, there is a Balanchinian parallel. The dance's five sections are set closely to the tempi and phrasing of Handel's music. And, like Balanchine, Taylor goes beyond simple structural analogies. In *Aureole*, both the mood and the relationship of the five dancers to each other stem from the surface formality and underlying humour of the eighteenth-century accompaniment.

In the opening section, for the dance's three women and one of its two men, encounters are playful and conversational. Critics have described this first section as game-like. The man chases after the women or, set apart from them, he engages in brief displays of gusto. The second section, a solo for the second man, is more introspective. Created for Taylor himself, this role has been described by him as "some kind of earth father who goes round blessing things".

A rehearsal film was made of *Aureole* during the 1962 American Dance Festival. A copy of the film (minus sound, in the New York Public Library of the Performing Arts) records Taylor's performance. His large, powerful frame, his open, spreading arms, and his one-legged balances certainly suggest a sense of omnipresence and security.

It is in *Aureole* that Taylor's evolving choreographic style becomes evident. His is a style of contradictions. His preceding work, *Insects and Heroes*, along with *Scudorama*, the next work following *Aureole*, confirm his interest in dark-light alternatives. Significantly, Taylor's performance in *Aureole* provides clues to his subsequent movement concerns. Tall, broad, and strong, he moves easily and swiftly. There is a duality not only in upper-lower body movement but also in his weighty yet buoyant momentum. Knees bend deeply, and the body's centre of gravity is low and earthy. But the action of shaping through space is undulating rather than into the floor. Throughout, the upper body is uplifted. Arm gestures—and even held positions—emanate from deep within the torso. Their upward emphasis gives *Aureole* its Apollonian quality.

The dance's third section begins with a solo (created originally for Elizabeth Walton). In contrast to Taylor's solo in size, accent, and tempo, it begins in place with small hip movements from side to side. The gentle swinging action provides the impulse for larger movements which also retain a sideways progression. As in the man's solo, Taylor introduces the ensemble towards the end. (It is at the end of the man's solo that all five dancers are seen on stage together for the first time.)

The idea of a group is paramount. Of *Aureole*, Taylor says, this was "the dance that caused me to decide to take on the responsibilities of a full-time company". And *Aureole* is testimony to Taylor's interest in choreography created for dancers to enjoy. In his autobiography, *Private Domain*, he provides a further insight into his interest in particular dancers. Of *Aureole*'s fourth section—for the most part, a duet created for Taylor and Walton—he says, "The duet is built on my own feelings for Liz—part fantasy and part real." Whatever his fantasies were, the reality of the relationship is clear. Walton sits hammock-like across his torso. Throughout, there is a closeness and confidence in partnering. Taylor lifts and carries Walton with an ease that comes from knowing someone well. And in subsequent performances of *Aureole* it is a relationship which other Taylor company dancers also affirm.

In the final section, former groupings and glimpses of earlier phrases are recalled. But movements are more quirky and off-balance. Diagonal pathways—the longest distance a dancer can travel on stage—are reiterated. *Aureole's* final image is of Taylor leading the other four dancers in a series of long-reaching grands jetés along the upstage left-downstage right diagonal. As the curtain comes down on this follow-the-leader formation, the lasting impression is of the dancers' on-going momentum: all is infinite space and infinite motion.

—Angela Kane

---

## THE AUSTRALIAN BALLET

Australian ballet company based in Melbourne. Founded by Peggy van Praagh, incorporating dancers from the former Borovansky Ballet (founder Edouard Borovansky), 1962; funded at its origins by Australian Federal Government grant; performs within Australia as a national company, with many tours abroad, including to the Far East and Soviet Union. Official school associated with company, Australian Ballet School, founded and based in Melbourne, from 1964. Current artistic director of the Australian Ballet: Maina Gielgud, from 1983.

### PUBLICATIONS

Van Praagh, Peggy, *Ballet in Australia*, Melbourne, 1965
Formby, David, *Australian Ballet*, Sydney, 1976
Pask, Edward H., *Ballet in Australia: The Second Act 1940–1980*, Melbourne, 1982
Baum, Caroline, *Artists of the Australian Ballet*, 1989

* * *

The Australian Ballet is now considered one of the most dynamic of the internationally known companies. In 1990, after 28 years under its present title and steady annual seasons, it has achieved this reputation despite its having been coloured by the tastes of five quite different artistic directors.

Under Peggy van Praagh there was a period of "British-oriented" repertoire along with the standard classics; Sir Robert Helpmann was for a time joint artistic director with Dame Peggy (as a result of her ill health), bringing more of a British flavour to the company. The John Cranko influence came with the next director, Anne Wooliams, as a result of her background with his Stuttgart Company. Within her rather short tenure, an outstanding legacy was left. Then came a nostalgic and welcome nod by Marilyn Jones toward the Borovansky Ballet era. The present Australian Ballet repertoire is eclectic and thoroughly catholic thanks to the wide-ranging tastes of Maina Gielgud and her European background. She chose a young, malleable group. Following a useful re-shuffle of departments and duty demarcations, the Australian Ballet is now, under the present administrator Noel Pelly, displaying a tremendous homogeneity, with an *esprit de corps* among the group that engenders a strong and lively creativity. This vitality is due in part to Miss Gielgud's policy of providing opportunities for company members (sometimes even corps dancers) to perform solo roles, rather than importing soloists. Her courage has been amply rewarded: she can now rely on a strong company of dancers trained to fulfill a multitude of roles.

Gielgud's system of exchange between her own dancers (within a "no star" system) and overseas "name stars" coming to Australia works better these days than did the earlier system of an echelon of stars above a reliable but essentially nameless corps de ballet. Throughout these past decades the company has enjoyed numerous successful overseas tours, as well as full seasons in Australia, and the young dancers cultivated by Gielgud have received much praise.

The Australian Ballet has its roots in the pioneering work of the Borovansky Ballet. Edouard Borovansky, of Ballets Russes antecedents, was known as "The Father of Ballet in Australia". For twenty years he worked with energy and dogged perseverance in an unsubsidized commercial setting to establish ballet in Australia. This situation meant disbanding his company as each season ended, and beginning anew for the next Australasian tours. He died on 18 December 1959, having produced dancers who in their turn had created an audience for classical ballet in Australia. When Peggy van Praagh, the distinguished English teacher and producer, arrived in February 1960 to take over the Borovansky Ballet, she inherited fine Australian soloists and principals. Van Praagh campaigned strongly for government subsidy, saying she would return in 1961 only if there could be guarantees of the continuity of a company which the Australians could term "national". Her eloquence gained a Federal Government grant under the auspices of the Elizabeth Theatre Trust and the commercial J.C. Williamsons Theatres, with whom Borovansky had always worked.

As artistic director, van Praagh was a diplomat—a necessary attribute for steering the course of a new company. She emphasized the classics within the repertoire because, as she said, "Guest artists can more easily fit in, and the classics do, of course, measure the dancers' progress against parallel historic performances." She proved the wisdom of her policy with the acclaim she received when her new production for the company, *Giselle* (presented in Paris in 1965), was awarded the Grand Prix of the City of Paris at the International Festival of Dance.

Sir Robert Helpmann—a theatre genius in many spheres—achieved publicity easily when he became artistic director. The Australian press loved his flamboyance and his quotable one-liners. He created a number of works for the company which had strong impact, with perhaps the most significant being *The Display*. It is a distinctly Australian ballet with a dramatic focus, based on his sighting of lyre birds in a Victorian sanctuary. He also remained proud of having lured Rudolf Nureyev to Australia to produce the highly successful *Don Quixote* for the company. Starring Nureyev and Lucette Aldous, first on stage and then later on film, this ballet, with the expansive dancing and brilliant personality of its leads, drew the attention of crowds of people new to classical ballet.

Anne Woolliams's tenure after Sir Robert's departure was significant, as she brought the genius of several of Cranko's ballets to the company. Under her direction and production Cranko's *Romeo and Juliet* had a profound impact, and her *Swan Lake* was a marvel of reason, logic, and beauty. On her several visits since her resignation she has remounted her production of Cranko's masterpiece *Onegin* and has also brought *The Taming of the Shrew* into the repertoire.

When Woolliams resigned, Dame Peggy van Praagh agreed to return for one season, and then in 1978 Marilyn Jones was appointed the new director. But the difficulties that had been building between administration and artistic direction, which had resulted in the premature resignation of Woolliams, remained, so this versatile and superb ballerina inherited a troubled company. Her great forte was in performance, and she found it extremely awkward to be working, in her new status as director, with the very dancers who had been with her on stage.

In 1978 two members of the company, Marilyn Rowe and Kelvin Coe, were invited by the Bolshoi Ballet to dance as guests in Moscow. Their delicate pas de deux from *La Fille mal gardée* had won a silver medal in 1973 at the International competitions in Moscow. Another dancer from the company, Danilo Radojevic, had won the solo gold medal there in 1977. These performances, and subsequent critical acclaim, have added to the ever-growing reputation of the Australian company.

Maina Gielgud's present tenure as artistic director began in 1983. It has been a triumph. She has chosen such luminaries as Galina Ulanova, among other imported artists, to coach the dancers in certain roles. Irina Kolpakova has been guest teacher for classes and Ekaterina Maximova danced a very special Tatiana in *Onegin* with the company. In these performances the sense of unified purpose and artistic unity within the Australian Ballet was outstanding, the dancers supporting and equalling Maximova in her own depth of interpretation.

With her seasoned company now possessing a huge repertoire and having achieved real acclaim in Moscow and London (where her *Sleeping Beauty* inspired Clive Barnes to write, "These Australians have become a company to cherish"), Gielgud is directing a company of truly international stature.

At 30 years of age, the Australian Ballet has become an artistic entity, filled with predominately young, enthusiastic dancers who dance with a gracious lack of egoism. There are no old-world mannerisms here: these dancers are of the New World, and exude physical joyousness in their strength and stamina. They honour the goals of art by communicating with their viewers, working humbly yet proudly to reach the heights that are possible within this dynamic company.

—Beth Dean

---

**AYUPOVA, Zhanna**

Soviet dancer. Born Zhanna Ismailovna Ayupova in Petrosavodsk, 12 October 1966. Studied at the Leningrad Choreographic (Vaganova) School, pupil of N. Kurgapkina; graduated in 1984. Married painter Kirill Golubenkov, 1987: son, Fedor, b. 1991. Dancer, Kirov Ballet, from 1984: principal dancer from 1985; has also toured with the Kirov in France, the United Kingdom, the United States, and Canada. Recipient: Bronze Medal, Fifth International Ballet Competition, Moscow, 1985.

**ROLES**

1978 Masha (as a child) in *The Nutcracker* (Vainonen), Kirov Ballet, Leningrad

1984 Masha in *The Nutcracker* (Vainonen), School Graduation Performance, Kirov Theatre, Leningrad

Naiad in *The Naiad and the Fisherman* (Perrot, Petipa; staged Gusev), Kirov Ballet, Leningrad

Title role in *Giselle* (Petipa after Coralli, Perrot), Kirov Ballet, Leningrad

Pas de trois (friends of the Prince) in *Swan Lake* (Petipa, Ivanov; staged Sergeyev), Kirov Ballet, Leningrad

Mazurka, Seventh Waltz in *Chopiniana* (Fokine), Kirov Ballet, Leningrad

1985 Aurora in *The Sleeping Beauty* (Petipa; staged Sergeyev), Kirov Ballet, Leningrad

1986 Princess Florine in *The Sleeping Beauty* (Petipa; staged Sergeyev), Kirov Ballet, Leningrad

1987 One of three Odalisques in *Le Corsaire* (new production; Gusev after Petipa), Kirov Ballet, Leningrad

1988 Nikiya in *La Bayadère* (Ponomarev, Chabukiani after Petipa), Kirov Ballet, Leningrad

Title role in *La Sylphide* (von Rosen after Bournonville), Kirov Ballet, Leningrad

Odette/Odile in *Swan Lake* (Petipa, Ivanov; staged Sergeyev), Kirov Ballet, Leningrad

1989 Medora in *La Corsaire* (Gusev after Petipa), Kirov Ballet, Leningrad

The Girl in *Le Spectre de la rose* (Fokine), Kirov Ballet, Benefit for Farukh Ruzimatov, Leningrad

1990 Soloist in *Theme and Variations* (Balanchine; staged Russell), Kirov Ballet, Leningrad

Maria in *The Fountain of Bakhchisarai* (Zakharov), Kirov Ballet, Leningrad

**Zhanna Ayupova as Giselle**

**PUBLICATIONS**

By Ayupova:
Interview in Dunning, Jennifer, "Three Young Stars and their Paths to the Kirov", *The New York Times,* 14 July 1989.

About Ayupova:
Kisselgoff, Anna, "New *Giselle*, New Star from the Kirov", *The New York Times*, 9 July 1989

* * *

Zhanna Ayupova possesses a unique talent for our time: she is a born Romantic ballerina. As a musician has perfect pitch, Ayupova has an absolute feeling for the style of performing Romantic ballets of the past. She is a ballerina of medium height. Her small head, the gentle line of her neck, her big dark eyes, and her sloping shoulders give her a similarity to antique portraits. Her cunning glance and her capacity for sudden joy, like that of a modern young girl, combined with a charming old-fashioned delicacy, lend a particular spice to her stage countenance. Romantic etherealness, lightness, and weightless leaps combine in her performances with firm pointe-work, a flawless execution of terre-a-terre dance, masterful pirouettes, and other professional qualities. This combination of strong professionalism and a naturally romantic style of dance constitutes the stylistic particulars of Ayupova as a ballerina.

Her best roles are in *La Sylphide* and *Chopiniana*, as Aurora and Princess Florine in *Sleeping Beauty*, and Masha in *The Nutcracker*. A brilliant performer of classical variations, Ayupova had already drawn attention to herself in a variation of one of the Odalisques in *Le Corsaire* before she danced Medora. But to this day the pinnacle of her work remains her performance of Giselle. The twentieth-century public has seen so many different dancers perform Giselle that it is difficult to draw attention to oneself in this role. Ayupova nevertheless provides a truly unforgettable and outstanding performance of Giselle that will surely rank among the best of the late twentieth century.

In the first act, her performance of Giselle's dance is pure and harmonious, like Giselle's soul. She evokes the idyllic world of the peasant ballet to perfection. Her interpretation, therefore, does not so much suggest a heart that has been wounded by betrayal and cannot bear the grief, as an ideal spiritual world that cannot bear to come into contact with cruel reality. Ayupova dances the mad scene poetically and luminously. Repeating her first dance with Albrecht in this inverse, chaotic scene, the girl, even with her reason clouded, remembers only the happy moments. And only occasionally does a grimace of pain suddenly overtake her beautiful face. Ayupova's Giselle dies, like a butterfly that has landed on a flame, from the touch of an Albrecht who has already become, for her, deadly.

The thread of sincerity with which Ayupova connects the two acts is unusual, too. Ayupova's Giselle comes up out of the grave with a face devoid of any signs of life. Her lowered eyelids eclipse her vision, and she joins the nocturnal life of the Wilis gradually. Throughout the entire second act, Ayupova's performance is full of stunning intuitive details as, for example, when she first sees Albrecht. Running silently past the grieving figure, Ayupova's Giselle stops short for a second, like a white cloud. The last minute before she tears herself away and disappears, Ayupova turns her head slightly and looks at her former lover. Then she lowers her eyelids, douses the glance, and disappears. What remains in the memory is the inhuman glance of a being from another world.

Ayupova has not yet danced in contemporary ballets (apart from Balanchine's *Theme and Variations*), but her place in today's ballet world will undoubtedly be of growing importance. Her appearance on the stage in these modern times is somehow a reminder to the audience of romance and beauty.

—Nina Alovert

---

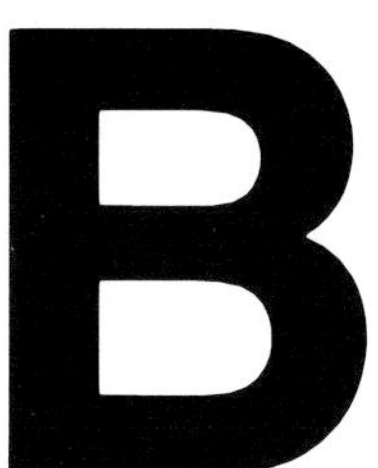

**BABILÉE, Jean**

French dancer, choreographer, and actor. Born Jean Gutmann in Paris, 3 February 1923. Studied at the Paris Opéra School, pupil of Gustave Ricaux, from 1936; also studied privately with Boris Kniaseff, Alexandre Volinin, and Victor Gsovsky, Paris, 1936–45. Served in the French resistance during World War II. Married dancer Nathalie Philippart, 1946 (sep.): one daughter, Isabelle. Début in Cannes, 1940, dancing with Ballets de Cannes during the war; dancer, corps de ballet, graduating to second quadrille, Paris Opéra Ballet, 1943–44; also performed with Paris Soirées de danse, 1944; principal dancer, Ballets des Champs-Elysées, 1945–50, and Ballets de Paris, from 1954; étoile, Paris Opéra Ballet, 1953; international guest artist, including for Ballets Milloss, Ballet Theatre (later American Ballet Theatre), New York, 1950–52, Maggio Musicale (Festival), Florence, 1951, La Scala, Milan, 1954; also choreographer: first ballet, *Sérénité*, for Soirées de danse, 1944; also staged ballets for Ballet Theatre, 1951, and Théâtre de Monte Carlo, 1955; founder, Les Ballets Jean Babilée, 1955–59; worked for a season with Lazzini at Marseilles Opera, 1966–67; director, Ballet du Rhin, Strasbourg, 1972–73; also actor, appearing on stage and in films including *La Ligne d'Ombre* (dir. Franju, 1971) and *Duelle* (dir. Rivette, 1975). Recipient: *Dance Magazine* Award, 1979.

**ROLES**

1940 The Spirit of the rose in *Le Spectre de la rose* (Fokine), Ballets des Cannes
Bluebird pas de deux from *The Sleeping Beauty* (Petipa), Ballets des Cannes
1945 Joker (cr) in *Jeu des cartes* (Charrat), Ballets des Champs-Elysées, Paris
The Young Man (cr) in *Le Déjeuner sur l'herbe* (Petit), Ballets des Champs-Elysées, Paris
Death (cr) in *Le Rendezvous* (Petit), Ballets des Champs-Elysées, Paris
1946 Mercury (cr) in *Les Amours de Jupiter* (Petit), Ballets des Champs-Elysées, Paris
The Young Man (cr) in *Le Jeune Homme et la mort* (Petit), Ballets des Champs-Elysées, Paris
1947 Principal dancer (cr) in *Portrait de Don Quichotte* (Milloss), Ballets des Champs-Elysées, Paris
1948 The Choreographer in *La Création* (Lichine), Ballets des Champs-Elysées, London
Oedipus (cr) in *La Rencontre* (*Oedipe et le sphinx*; Lichine), Ballets des Champs-Elysées, Paris
Eros (cr) in *L'Amour et son amour* (also chor.), Ballets des Champs-Elysées, Paris
1949 Title role (cr) in *Till Eulenspiegel* (also chor.), Ballets des Champs-Elysées, Paris
1951 Principal dancer (cr) in *Mysteries* (Milloss), Palais de Chaillot, Paris
1953 Albrecht in *Giselle* (Petipa after Coralli, Perrot; staged Lifar), Paris Opéra Ballet, Paris
Principal dancer (cr) in *Hop-Frog* (Lander), Paris Opéra Ballet, Paris
1954 Title role (cr) in *Pulcinella* (Beriozoff), La Scala, Milan
1955 Principal dancer (cr) in *Balance à trois* (also chor.), Les Ballets Jean Babilée, Monte Carlo
1956 King (cr) in *Le Caméléopard* (also chor.), Les Ballets Jean Babilée, Paris
Mario (cr) in *Mario et le mage* (Massine), La Scala, Milan
1957 Principal dancer (cr) in *Maratona di danza* (Sanders), Municipal Opera, Berlin
1963 Dancer in *La Reine verte* (play; chor. Béjart), Théâtre Hebertot, Paris
1967 Title role in *The Prodigal Son* (Lazzini), Marseilles Opera
Principal dancer (cr) in *A Soldier's Tale* (also chor.), Spoleto Festival
1971 Title role in *Pulcinella* (Massine), La Scala, Milan
1979 Principal dancer (cr) in *Life* (Béjart), Ballet du XXe Siècle, New York
1987 Principal dancer (cr) in *Inventaire* (Charrat, Germain), Compagnie Alain Germain

**Other roles include:** Faune in *L'Après-midi d'un faune* (after Nijinsky); leading acting roles in *Le Balcon* (play by Genet), *Orpheus Descending* (play by Tennessee Williams), *La Belle Dame sans merçi* (staged Tassencourt), *L'Histoire du Soldat* (Ramuz; staged Simon), *Tryptyque* (staged Simon), *Frigid* (Fleisser; staged Tikova, Babilée), *Salomé* (play by Wilde), *Je m'appelle Erik Satie* (staged Confortès).

**WORKS**

1944 *Serenité* (mus. Beethoven), Soirées de Danse, Paris

**Jean Babilée with Nathalie Phillipart rehearsing *Le Jeune homme et la mort***

1948 *L'Amour et son amour* (mus. Franck), Ballets des Champs-Elysées, Paris
1949 *Till Eulenspiegel* (mus. Strauss), Ballets des Champs-Elysées, Paris
1954 *Divertimento* (mus. Damase), Enghien Festival
1955 *Balance à trois* (mus. Damase), Les Ballets Jean Babilée, Monte Carlo
1956 *Sable* (mus. Le Roux), Ballets Jean Babilée, Paris
*Le Caméléopard* (mus. Sauguet), Ballets Jean Babilée, Paris
1957 *La Boucle* (mus. Damase), Ballets Jean Babilée, Paris
1964 *Le Roi des Gourmets* (mus. Rossini), Rome Opera, Rome
1967 *A Soldier's Tale* (mus. Stravinsky), Spoleto Festival
1969 *Hai-Kai* (mus. Webern), Ballet Théâtre Contemporain, Amiens
1972 *On n'est pas sérieux quand on a 18 ans* (mus. Duhamel), Ballet du Rhin, Strasbourg
1973 *Dances in M. Major* (mus. Dvǒrák), Ballet du Rhin
1976 *Camera Oscura* (mus. Bayle), Festival de musique contemporaine, Metz
1982 *Pas de deux* (mus. Bach), Spoleto Festival

**Other works include:** dances in *Falstaff* (opera; mus. Verdi; 1961), *Les Fêtes d'Hébé* (opera; mus. Rameau; 1964), *Charlie* (musical comedy; 1969), *Aïda* (opera; mus. Verdi); works for television—*Les Contes d'Offman* (mus. Offenbach; 1965), *Le Golem, La Fille du Tambour major* (mus. Offenbach; 1966), *Orphée aux Enfers* (mus. Offenbach; 1966), *L'Enfant et les sortilèges* (mus. Ravel; 1967); choreography in theatre productions *L'Histoire du soldat* (Ramuz, staged Simon; mus. Stravinsky), *Tryptyque* (staged Simon; 1978).

## PUBLICATIONS

By Babilée:
*Hommage à Balanchine*, with Serge Lifar, Irène Lidova, and Dinah Maggie, Paris, 1952
Interview in Passet, Dominique, "Jean Babilée, un retour en force", *Danser* (Paris), September 1984

About Babilée:
Lidova, Irène, "Quatre visages de la danse française", *Ballet Annual* (London), vol. 3, 1949
Brahms, Caryl, "Jean Babilée" in Swinson, Cyril, *Dancers and Critics*, London, 1950
Lidova, Irène, *17 Visages de la danse française*, Paris, 1953
Chardans, J.-C., "Jean Babilée", *Paris Théâtre* (Paris), October 1954
Davidson, Gladys, *Ballet Biographies*, revised edition, London, 1954
Beaumont, Cyril, *Ballets Past and Present*, London, 1955
Boll, André, *Jean Babilée*, Paris, 1956
"Personality of the Month: Jean Babilée", *Dance and Dancers* (London), August 1956
Cournand, Gilberte, *Beauté de la danse*, Paris, 1977
Stoop, Norma McLain, "Babilée", *Dance Magazine* (New York), July 1979
Koenig, John Franklin, *La Danse contemporaine*, Paris, 1980
Croce, Arlene, *Going to the Dance*, New York, 1982
Glasstone, Richard, "Poet and Dancer", *Dancing Times* (London), December 1989

* * *

A dancer is often remembered for one role in particular, and to some extent this is the case with Jean Babilée and *Le Jeune Homme et la mort*. The impact of this haunting and concisely constructed ballet in 1946 was unforgettable, and fortunately it has been captured effectively on film.

Nevertheless, Babilée has proved to be far more than a one-part star. A pupil of the Paris Opéra Ballet School, he was sixteen when World War II broke out. In 1940, when France capitulated to Germany, he found himself stranded in Avignon. He turned south, and was taken on as a dancer in Cannes, where he first showed his remarkable technical prowess and elevation in the Bluebird pas de deux and *Le Spectre de la rose*. An accident to his knee proved a blessing in disguise—restricting his dancing, it meant that he watched other artists and ballets and learned more about stagecraft. Later he would say: "To create a role, we need not only agility but also a clear head so that we can maintain a precise vision of our interpretation."

On his return to occupied Paris in 1942, he was restless and disturbed and at last left the Opéra, spending the years from 1943 to the Liberation as part of the resistance in Touraine. He came back to a very different ballet scene. The end of World War II saw a resurgence of artistic energy, and Babilée's reappearance as a dancer was with a young group that included Roland Petit and Renée Jeanmaire in recital at the Théâtre Sarah Bernhardt. This was the beginning of the exciting company, Les Ballets des Champs-Elysées, directed by Petit, whose repertoire of small works was of the highest artistic quality. The dancers were a hand-picked group, and Babilée found himself partnering ballerinas like Irène Skorik, Nathalie Philippart (later his wife), and Janine Charrat.

One of Babilée's first successes was as the Joker in Charrat's version of Stravinsky's *Jeu de cartes*, to which he brought a slightly malicious fluency. Again, he had a sinister role in Petit's *Le Rendezvous*, as Death lying in wait at street corners for the Young Man (Petit). Death was again featured in *Le Jeune Homme et la mort*, but this time Babilée was the Young Man and Death was Philippart as a sensuous, ruthless female who comes to him in his lonely attic bedroom.

Conceived by Jean Cocteau, *Le Jeune Homme* was choreographed by Roland Petit with masterly economy, and the dancers carried it magnificently. The movement was modern and acrobatic, admirably tailored to Babilée's smooth, athletic coordination. The sense of despair mounting to the point of suicide, followed by the romantic-gothic image of the woman leading the young man out over the rooftops, never failed to make a histrionic impact.

When Petit left Les Ballets de Champs-Elysées to set up Les Ballets de Paris at the end of 1947, Babilée remained with the former company for which David Lichine was invited to choreograph. Babilée appeared to great effect in *La Création*, an experimental work without music or sound accompaniment, and was cast in *La Rencontre*, a pas de deux for himself and Leslie Caron as Oedipus and the Sphinx. His power and precision in this role were remarkable. Babilée had become interested in creating his own ballets, and the opportunity now came for him to embark on choreography. *L'Amour et son amour* (1948) was a duet for himself and Philippart. The title came from Cocteau, who acted as adviser and guide, and the chosen music was César Franck's symphonic poem *Psyche*. It was a mystical and medieval work, but for his next ballet Babilée turned to the tantalizing theme and music of Richard Strauss's supreme joker Till Eulenspiegel.

Les Ballets des Champs-Elysées closed in 1950 and after that Babilée danced with the Ballets Milloss in Italy and with American Ballet Theatre before returning to the Paris Opéra Ballet to appear in *Giselle* and *Le Spectre de la rose* in 1953. As no stimulating new work was offered there, however, he moved again, returning briefly to Roland Petit before setting up his own company, Les Ballets Jean Babilée, which lasted for a few years. Two works from that period are remembered with admiration. *Balance à trois*, a highly virtuoso ballet about a trio of athletes in a gymnasium, was for himself, Alexandre Kalioujny, and Yvette Chauviré. *Le Caméléopard* was about a decadent civilization and a king who thought himself a god—a highly theatrical role which only a dancer of Babilée's charisma could make acceptable.

In later years Babilée has danced with various companies, but perhaps his most astounding appearances came when Maurice Béjart created *Life* for him—a work that was shown at the Minskoff Theatre in New York during a season of the Ballets du XXè siècle in 1979. In a highly physical role based on gymnastic disciplines with climbing frames, he proved that at the age of 56 he was as able as he had been in his youth to captivate audiences and critics by the magnetism of his performance.

—Kathrine Sorley Walker

---

**BACCELLI, Giovanna**

Italian dancer. Born Giovanna (sometimes called Gianetta) Francesca Antonia Guiseppe Zanerini in Venice, c. 1753. One son, by John Frederick Sackville, the Duke of Dorset. Début at the King's Theatre, London, 1774, remaining featured dancer there until 1783; Paris Opéra debut as guest danseuse of Noverre's London company, 1782; according to some sources, prima ballerina at Teatro San Benedetto, Venice, 1783–84, with Venice début in *Adriano in Siria* (D. Lefevre) at Carnaval, 1783; returned to King's Theatre, London, 1786; danced at the Paris Opéra, 1788; may have returned to Venice, 1788, making last performance there in 1789; was painted by Gainsborough and Reynolds. Died in London, 7 May 1801.

**ROLES**

1774 Dancer in *Pirhame et Thisbée*, King's Theatre, London
Rose in *Le Ballet des fleurs* (divertissement from Rameau's *Les Indes galantes*), King's Theatre, London
1774/75 Dancer in *New Pastoral Ballet* (divertissement), King's Theatre, London
Dancer in *Grand Chacone* (divertissement), King's Theatre, London
1775 Galatea in *Pigmalion amoureux de la statue* (Bouqueton), King's Theatre, London
Clytemnestra in *Oreste et Electre* (Vallouy), King's Theatre, London
The Victim in *Le Triomphe d'Euthime sur le génie de liba*, King's Theatre, London
Divertissement in *Didone* (opera; mus. Sacchini et al., chor. Boqueton), King's Theatre, London
Diane in *Diane et Endymion* (probably after Noverre), King's Theatre, London
1776 Dancer in *Serious Ballet* (divertissement), King's Theatre, London
Principal dancer (cr) in *La Générosité de Scipion*, King's Theatre, London
1777 Grand Chaconne, Pas de Deux (cr) in (*New*) *Serious Ballet* (possibly also chor., with Simonet), King's Theatre, London
Dancer (cr) in *La Clochette*, King's Theatre, London
Dancer in *New Ballet* (Simonet), King's Theatre, London
Dancer (cr) in *La Polonaise favourite*, King's Theatre, London
1778 Pas de Deux du Masque (cr) in *La Sérénade interrompue* (Simonet), King's Theatre, London
Minuet de la Cour, Gavotte in *L'Amour Artigiano* (opera; mus. Gassman), King's Theatre, London
Dancer (cr) in *Les Amants unis par l'Hymen*, King's Theatre, London
1779 Ballet by the Fairies (cr) in *Zemira e Azore* (opera; mus. Grétry), King's Theatre, London
Atalante (cr) in *Hippomène e Atalante*, King's Theatre, London
Iris (cr) in *La Fête du ciel*, King's Theatre, London
Minuet (cr) in *La Bravoure des femmes* (Simonet), King's Theatre, London
1780 Divertissement in *Quinto Fabio* (opera; mus. Bertoni), King's Theatre, London
Pas Seul (cr) in *La Fête pastorale* (Favre-Guiardel), King's Theatre, London
Dancer (cr) in *Les Amants surpris* (Simonet), King's Theatre, London
1781 Nancy in *Ninette à la cour* (G. Vestris after M. Gardel), King's Theatre, London
Galathée in *Les Caprices de Galathée* (G. Vestris after Noverre), King's Theatre, London
Creusa (cr) in *Medée et Jason* (G. Vestris after Noverre), King's Theatre, London
Divertissement (cr) in *L'Omaggio* (opera; mus. Bianchi, Rauzzini, Giordani, chor. G. Vestris), London
Inès (cr) in *Les Amantes réunis* (Noverre), King's Theatre, London
Dancer in *Les Petits Riens* (Noverre), King's Theatre, London
Dancer (cr) in *The Rural Sports* (Simonet), King's Theatre, London
1782 Iris in *Le Triomphe de l'amour conjugal* (Noverre), King's Theatre, London
Lucinde in *Rinaldo and Armida* (Noverre), King's Theatre, London
Herpin in *La Rosière de Salency* (Noverre), King's Theatre, London
Dancer in *Adela of Ponthieu* (Noverre), King's Theatre, London
Dancer (cr) in *Apollon et les muses* (Noverre), King's Theatre, London
Dancer (cr) in *New Dance* (Noverre), King's Theatre, London
Dancer (cr) in *Mirsa* (M. Gardel and G. Gardel), King's Theatre, London
Divertissement in *Électre* (opera; mus. le Moyne), Opéra, Paris
1783 Two Pas Seuls (cr) in *The Amours of Alexander and Roxana* (Le Picq), King's Theatre, London
Pas de deux (cr) added to *Le Tuteur trompé* (Le Picq), King's Theatre, London
1786 Principal dancer (cr; with Vestris) in *Le Premier Navigateur ou La Force de l'amour* (A. Vestris, after M. Gardel), King's Theatre, London
Principal dancer (cr) in *L'Amour jardinier* (D'Egville), King's Theatre, London
Pas de trois from *L'Epreuve villageoise* (opera; mus. Grétry, chor. A. Vestris), King's Theatre, London
Pas de quatre from *Panurge* (opera; chor. A. Vestris), King's Theatre, London
Principal dancer (cr) in *Les Deux Solitaires* (Giroux), King's Theatre, London

**Giovanna Baccelli in *Les Amants surpris*, 1781**

**ROLES** (attributed to Baccelli)

1784 Medea in *Giasone e Medea* (Vestris after Noverre, staged Lefebvre), Teatro San Benedetto, Venice
Principal dancer in *Gli Amori di Mirtillo e Silvanzia* (Lefebvre), Teatro San Benedetto, Venice
1789 Clytemnestra in *Il Ritorno d'Agamennone* (F. Clerico), Teatro San Benedetto, Venice
Dancer in *I Nasti d'amore* (Clerico), Teatro San Benedetto, Venice
Dancer in *I Sacrifizi di Tauride* (Clerico), Teatro San Benedetto, Venice
Dancer in *Il Filosofo deriso* (Clerico), Teatro San Benedetto, Venice
Dancer in *Alessio ed Eloisa; o sia Il Disertore* (P. Angiolini), Teatro San Benedetto, Venice
Dancer in *Le Due rivali; o sia La Prova del vero amore* (P. Angiolini), Teatro San Benedetto, Venice

**PUBLICATIONS**

Damerini, G., *Settecento veneziano*, Milan, 1939
Guest, Ivor, "The Italian Lady of Knole", *Ballet Annual* (London), no. 11, 1957
Einberg, Elizabeth, *Gainsborough's Giovanni Baccelli*, Tate Gallery, London, 1976
Wilson, George Buckley Laird, "Off Stage!", *Dancing Times* (London), January 1977

* * *

In an era in which the male dancer predominated, few women can have had such an illustrious career as Giovanna Baccelli—leading dancer at London's famous King's Theatre, mistress of the Duke of Dorset, and sitter to such eminent artists as Gainsborough and Reynolds.

Little is known of Baccelli's early life, other than that she was born in Venice as Giovanna Francesca Antonia Guiseppe Zanerini. Baccelli, her stage name, was also that of her mother—and of a singer, Domenico Baccelli, mentioned in the annals of the Paris Opéra in the 1760s and 1770s. Although it is not known whether the latter was a relative, it is indeed possible that Giovanna Baccelli was trained in France. She was a fluent French speaker; most dancers in Europe at that time were French or had French training, and French ballet masters such as Noverre and the Vestris were exercising an increasing influence over the development of ballet, turning it from an operatic interlude of minor importance to an art form rivalling opera itself.

It was in England, however, that the *ballet d'action*, with its emphasis on plot and dramatic effect, appeared in one of its earliest forms, when *The Loves of Mars and Venus*, "a Dramatic Entertainment of Dancing, Attempted in Imitation of the Pantomimes of the Ancient Greeks and Romans" (according to its creator and producer, John Weaver) was staged at London's Theatre Royal, Drury Lane, in 1717. This heralded a period in which dramatic skills would become as important in ballet as technical virtuosity, aided by the transition in female costume from the restrictive pannier and wigs to simpler dresses and heelless shoes, which must have permitted freer expression in movement. London's theatres were in the vanguard of this revolution.

Giovanna Baccelli made her début at London's King's Theatre, Haymarket, in 1774, and was a featured dancer there until 1783. Between 1783 and 1786 she may have danced in Italy—she frequently performed outside England—but returned to London to dance with Vestris at the King's Theatre in March 1786. Four months later she gave her last performance at that theatre, which was destroyed by fire in 1789. By this time, Baccelli's dancing career seems to have ended.

The critics of the time seem unanimous in their adulation of Baccelli, of her "youthful charms" as well as her excellent dancing, although a letter from one of her admirers, Henry, 10th Earl of Pembroke, qualifies this praise—"Le Grand Serieux n'est pas son genre. Nature & Art both have joined to make her the Demi caractere." This impression is reinforced by contemporary portraits of Baccelli; Gainsborough paints her against a rural background, a tambourine and a bunch of roses dropped with careful artlessness at her feet, and Reynolds portrays her with the scanty draperies, vine-leaves, and loose hair of a Bacchante, while in the sculpture by John Baptist Locatelli she wears nothing but a smile.

Baccelli's charm enabled her to occupy as important a position in fashionable society as that which she occupied in her profession; by October 1779 she was living at Knole, Sevenoaks, as mistress of John Frederick Sackville, 3rd Duke of Dorset. In 1783 the Duke was appointed British Ambassador to Paris, where he had few serious political responsibilities. When he received the Order of the Garter in 1788, Baccelli danced at the Paris Opéra wearing the Garter ribbon as a bandeau around her head. This hedonistic existence came to an end in 1785 when the Duke fell victim to depression after a slight stroke. After the French Revolution, he returned to England, where he led a dramatically changed existence managing his estate, curbing his spending, and marrying an heiress. This inevitably brought about an end to his affair with Baccelli, albeit an amicable one, and she left Knole in 1789, though not accompanied by her son by the Duke, probably born in 1779. In 1794 Baccelli moved to London (to Sackville Street, off Piccadilly), with a Mr. James Carey and her servants, who remained with her throughout her life and were among the beneficiaries of her will when she died in 1801.

—Jessica Griffin

---

**LE BAISER DE LA FÉE**
(*The Fairy's Kiss*)

**Choreography:** Bronislava Nijinska
**Music:** Igor Stravinsky
**Design:** Alexandre Benois
**Libretto:** Igor Stravinsky (after Hans Christian Andersen's *The Ice Maiden*)
**First Production:** Ida Rubinstein's Company, Paris Opéra, Paris, 27 November 1928
**Principal Dancers:** Ida Rubinstein (The Fairy), Anatole Vilzak (The Young Man), Ludmila Schollar (The Fiancée)

**Other productions include:** Vic-Wells Ballet (new version; chor. Frederick Ashton, design Sophie Fedorovitch), with Pearl Argyle (Fairy), Harold Turner (Young Man), Margot Fonteyn (Fiancée); London, 26 November 1935. American Ballet (new version; chor. George Balanchine, design Alice Halicka), with Kathryn Mullowney (Fairy), William Dollar (The Bridegroom), Giselle Caccialanza (The Bride); New York, 27 April 1937. Ballet Russe de Monte Carlo (restaged Balanchine); New York, 10 April 1940. Paris Opera Ballet (restaged Balanchine, design Hali); Paris, 2 July 1947. New York City Ballet (restaged Balanchine), as *The Fairy's Kiss*, with Maria Tallchief

**MacMillan's *Le Baiser de la fée*, with Lynn Seymour, Donald MacLeary and Svetlana Beriosova, Royal Ballet, London, 1960**

(Fairy), Nicholas Magallanes (Bridegroom), Tanaquil Le-Clercq (Bride); New York, 28 November 1950. Royal Ballet (new version; chor. Kenneth MacMillan, design Kenneth Rowell), with Svetlana Beriosova (The Fairy), Donald MacLeary (Young Man), Lynn Seymour (Fiancée); London, 12 April 1960. Dutch National Ballet (new version; chor. Ronald Hynd); The Hague, 1968. Frankfurt Ballet (new version; chor. and revised libretto John Neumeier, with additional music Tchaikovsky, design Jürgen Rose); Frankfurt, 2 January 1972. New York City Ballet (new version; chor. Balanchine), as *Divertimento from "Le Baiser de la fée"*, with Patricia McBride, Helgi Tomasson; New York, 21 June 1972.

## PUBLICATIONS

Chujoy, Anatole, "Ballet Russe de Monte Carlo", *Dance News* (New York), March 1946

Barnes, Clive, "*Le Baiser de la fée*", *Dance and Dancers* (London), April 1962

Balanchine, George, with Mason, Francis, *Balanchine's Complete Stories of the Great Ballets*, Garden City, N.Y., 1977

Reynolds, Nancy, *Repertory in Review*, New York, 1977

Anderson, Jack, *The One and Only: The Ballet Russe de Monte Carlo*, New York, 1981

Borovsky, Victor, and Schouvaloff, Alexander, *Stravinsky on Stage*, London, 1982
Garis, Robert, "Balanchine-Stravinsky: Facts and Problems", *Ballet Review* (Brooklyn, N.Y.), Fall 1982
Thorpe, Edward, *Kenneth MacMillan: The Man and the Ballets*, London, 1985
Baer, Nancy van Norman, *Bronislava Nijinska: A Dancer's Life*, San Francisco, 1986

* * *

There are numerous versions of *Le Baiser de la fée*, including those by Nijinska, Ashton, Balanchine (who staged it several times), and MacMillan. It is an allegorical ballet in four tableaux based on Hans Christian Andersen's fairy tale "The Ice Maiden", with a libretto by the composer, Igor Stravinsky.

Stravinsky was, according to the programme notes of the first performance, "inspired by the muse of Tchaikovsky", which, he claimed, gave the ballet its allegorical significance: Tchaikovsky's muse imprinted a fatal kiss on Tchaikovsky at birth which "made itself felt in all the work of that great artist and eventually led him to immortality". This is paralleled by the events Stravinsky selected from Andersen's tale: the ice maiden comes down from the sky to claim a small boy abandoned in the snow, whom she kisses to seal his eternal devotion to her. The boy grows up with no recollection of this, and the prophecy is tragically fulfilled when the ice maiden reclaims him and carries him away from his fiancée, later to relent and return him to his bride.

Stravinsky composed the music for this ballet at the request of Russian dancer and impresario Ida Rubinstein. Choreography was by Bronislava Nijinska, with design by another Russian and frequent collaborator, Alexandre Benois. Stravinsky was concerned that the form should be classical as *Apollo* had been, with "the fantastic roles . . . danced in white ballet-skirts, and the rustic scenes taking place in a Swiss landscape". The first performance of this version, conducted by Stravinsky, was at the Paris Opéra in November 1928, with subsequent performances in other European capitals. One of the dancers in this original production was Frederick Ashton, who later choreographed a version of his own for the Vic-Wells Ballet. This was first performed in 1935 and gave Margot Fonteyn one of her first created roles as the Fiancée; other principal dancers were Pearl Argyle and Harold Turner.

The score has continued to inspire choreographers throughout the twentieth century, despite the inherent difficulties of the predetermined libretto. Another British version was Kenneth MacMillan's own restaging of *Le Baiser de la fée*, performed at the Royal Opera House some 25 years after Ashton's first staging, now with Svetlana Beriosova, Donald MacLeary, and Lynn Seymour as principal dancers. The choreography, as MacMillan's biographer Edward Thorpe has pointed out, ". . . was the closest [MacMillan] had yet come to using the 'pure' classical vocabulary"—no doubt a result of the "mellifluous" score and the more traditional demands of a fairy-tale libretto.

*Le Baiser de la fée* was also part of the heritage from the Diaghilev era that George Balanchine took with him to America. His time with the Ballets Russes had sown the seeds of a lifelong friendship and collaboration between himself and Stravinsky, and *Baiser* was one of the early works created by the choreographer for his new company in America. It was performed at the Metropolitan Opera House in New York, where Balanchine's American Ballet was the resident company from 1935 to 1938. In his *Complete Stories of the Great Ballets*, Balanchine writes of some of the problems encountered in staging the ballet, which partly stem from its episodic form. The audience, he explains, must somehow perceive that the bridegroom of the second tableau is the child of the first and that the gypsy is the fairy in disguise. The magical ending requires a "stage high and deep for the achievement of full illusion", recalling the more spectacular productions of the Diaghilev years, but also presenting difficulties for whatever company is staging the ballet.

Various revivals of the Balanchine ballet were staged, each time with the choreographer tinkering with his work, apparently never quite satisfied. The 1950 version, called *The Fairy's Kiss* and performed at the City Center, New York, had Maria Tallchief in the lead role. As Nancy Reynolds writes in *Repertory in Review*, "The revival was welcomed in principle, but in the end *Baiser* was once again judged a beautiful, worthy, but imperfect work."

The Stravinsky Festival of 1972 provided the setting for another version of *Baiser*, when Balanchine arranged some new dances to the original music under the title of *Divertimento from "Le Baiser de la fée"* to celebrate the composer's ninetieth birthday. This was characteristic of the later Balanchine in being a "plotless pure-dance excerpt", as critic Anna Kisselgoff called it, but unusual in that the male dancer seemed to overshadow the female. Kisselgoff traces this back to the man's role as protagonist in the original version.

—Amanda Chisnell

---

## BAKST, Leon

Russian designer. Born Lev Samoilovich Rosenberg in Grodno, 19 May (27 April old style) 1866. Educated at the Sixth Gymnasium in St. Petersburg, 1874–83; studied art under Isaac Asknazi, Karl Wenig, Pavel Chistiakov, St. Petersburg Academy of Arts, 1883–87; resigned from Academy, 1887; also studied under Albert Edelfield and Jean-Louis Jérôme, 1893. Married Lubov Gritsenko, 1903 (div. 1910): one son, Andrei, b. 1907. First international exhibition, Berlin, 1896; co-founder of artistic association and chief designer of journal *Mir Iskusstva* (*The World of Art*), 1898; designer of costumes for Delibes' *Sylvia* (with Benois and Korovine; never produced), 1901; first stage design for Marius Petipa's *Le Coeur de la Marquise*, 1902; began collaboration with Mikhail Fokine, 1907, becoming designer for Diaghilev's Ballets Russes, 1909–22; also designer for opera, including for Diaghilev's productions of *Judith* (mus. Serov; 1909), and *Boris Godunov* (mus. Mussorgsky; 1913); also collaborated with choreographer and dancer Ida Rubinstein, beginning with *Antigone*, St. Petersburg, 1904, and later in Paris, from 1911; exiled from Russia, 1912; jury panel member, Paris Society of Decorative Arts, 1911; full member, St. Petersburg Academy of Arts, 1914. Died in Paris, 27 December 1924.

### WORKS (Ballet design)

1902 *Le Coeur de la Marquise* (chor. Petipa), Hermitage Theatre, St. Petersburg
1903 *The Fairy Doll* (chor. N. and S. Legat), Hermitage Theatre, St. Petersburg
1907 *Eunice* (costume for Kshessinskaya; chor. Fokine), Maryinsky Theatre, St. Petersburg
*Chopiniana* (costumes; chor. Fokine), Maryinsky Theatre, St. Petersburg

**A costume design by Leon Bakst for a lady-in-waiting, *The Sleeping Princess*, 1921**

*The Dying Swan* (costume for Pavlova; chor. Fokine), Maryinsky Theatre, St. Petersburg
*Torch Dance* (costume for Karsavina; chor. Fokine), Maryinsky Theatre, St. Petersburg
1908 *Egyptian Nights* (costumes, with Oreste Allegri; chor. Fokine), Maryinsky Theatre, St. Petersburg
*Bal poudré* (costumes; chor. Fokine), Pavlov Hall, St. Petersburg
*Salomé* (costumes only; play by Oscar Wilde, staged Ida Rubinstein; chor. Fokine), Mikhailovsky Theatre, St. Petersburg
1909 *Le Festin* (including "Firebird", or Bluebird Pas de deux; costumes, in collaboration with Benois; chor. Fokine and others), Diaghilev's Ballets Russes, Paris
*Cléopâtre* (new version of *Egyptian Nights*; chor. Fokine), Diaghilev's Ballets Russes, Paris
1910 *Bacchanale* (costume for Pavlova; chor. Fokine), Hall of the Assembly of the Nobility, St. Petersburg
*Danse siamoise* (costumes; later part of *Les Orientales*; chor. Fokine), Maryinsky Theatre, St. Petersburg
*Carnaval* (costumes; chor. Fokine), Pavlov Hall, St. Petersburg (several costumes probably from *Bal poudré* and *Fairy Doll*; new sets and costumes for Diaghilev's Ballets Russes' staging, Berlin, 1910)
*Kobold* (costume for Nijinsky; chor. Fokine), Maryinsky Theatre, St. Petersburg
*Carnaval* (new sets and costumes; chor. Fokine), Diaghilev's Ballets Russes, Berlin
*Schéhérazade* (chor. Fokine), Diaghilev's Ballets Russes, Paris
*L'Oiseau de feu* (*The Firebird*; costumes only; chor. Fokine), Diaghilev's Ballets Russes, Paris
1911 *Carnaval* (new set; chor. Fokine), Maryinsky Theatre, St. Petersburg
*Le Spectre de la rose* (chor. Fokine), Diaghilev's Ballets Russes, Monte Carlo
*Narcisse* (chor. Fokine), Diaghilev's Ballets Russes, Monte Carlo
*Le Martyre de Saint-Sébastien* (mystical play by d'Annunzio; chor. Fokine), Ida Rubinstein's Company, Paris
*Sadko* (costumes; mus. Rimsky Korsakov), Diaghilev's Ballets Russes, Paris
*La Péri* (costumes), Diaghilev's Ballets Russes (not produced)
*The Sleeping Beauty* Pas de deux (costumes for Pavlova and Nijinsky; chor. Petipa), Royal Opera House, London
1912 *Hélène de Sparte* (verse-play by Emile Verhaeren), Ida Rubinstein's Company, Paris
*Le Dieu bleu* (chor. Fokine), Diaghilev's Ballets Russes, Paris
*Thamar* (chor. Fokine), Diaghilev's Ballets Russes, Paris
*L'après-midi d'un faune* (chor. Nijinsky), Diaghilev's Ballets Russes, Paris
*Daphnis et Chloë* (chor. Fokine), Diaghilev's Ballets Russes, Paris
*Salomé* (play by Oscar Wilde; chor. Fokine), Ida Rubinstein's Company, Paris
*Les Papillons* (chor. Fokine), Maryinsky Theatre, St. Petersburg (revived by Diaghilev's Ballets Russes, Monte Carlo, 1914)
1913 *Jeux* (chor. Nijinsky), Diaghilev's Ballets Russes, Paris
*La Pisanelle, ou, La Mort parfumée* (play by d'Annunzio; chor. Fokine), Ida Rubinstein's Company, Paris
*Oriental Fantasy* (chor. Zajlich), Pavlova's Company, London
*L'Oiseau de feu* (new costumes for the Firebird and Ivan; chor. Fokine), Diaghilev's Ballets Russes
1913/15 *Orpheus* (mus. Roger-Ducasse), Maryinsky Theatre, St. Petersburg (not produced)
1914 *La Légende de Joseph* (costumes; chor. Fokine), Diaghilev's Ballets Russes, Paris
1915 *The Sleeping Beauty* (for the Enchantment scene; chor. Petipa), Diaghilev's Ballets Russes, Paris
1915/16 *Schéhérazade* (new sets and costumes; chor. Fokine), Diaghilev's Ballets Russes
1916 *The Sleeping Beauty* (chor. after Petipa), Anna Pavlova's Company, New York
1917 *Les Papillons* (new set and costumes; chor. Fokine), Diaghilev's Ballets Russes, Rome
*Sadko* (costumes; opera by Rimsky-Korsakov) (not produced)
*Les Femmes de bonne humeur* (chor. Massine), Diaghilev's Ballets Russes, Rome
1918 *La Boutique fantasque* (costumes; chor. Massine), Diaghilev's Ballets Russes (not used; Bakst replaced by Derain)
1920 *Aladin; ou, La Lampe merveilleuse* (costumes; revue), Théâtre Marigny, Paris
1921 *The Sleeping Princess* (chor. Petipa, Ivanov; staged Sergeyev, with additions by Nijinska), Diaghilev's Ballets Russes, London
1923 *Phaedre* (play by d'Annunzio), Ida Rubinstein's Company, Paris
1924 *Istar* (chor. Staats), Ida Rubinstein's Company, Paris

**PUBLICATIONS**

Peledan, Josephin, "Les Arts du Théâtre: Un Maître de Costume et du Décor: Léon Bakst", *L'Art Décoratif* (Paris), no. 25, 1911
Alexandre, Arsène, *L'Art décor de Léon Bakst*, Paris, 1913
Ritter, William, "Balletskizzen von Léon Bakst", Paris, 1913; as *The Decorative Art of Léon Bakst*, translated by Harry Melville, London, 1913
Levinson, André, *Bakst: The Story of the Artist's Life*, London, 1923
Beaumont, Cyril, *The Diaghilev Ballet in London*, London, 1940
Lister, Raymond, "Léon Bakst (1866–1924): A Bibliography and some notes", *Theatre Research/Récherches Théâtrales* (Glasgow), vol. 8, no. 3, 1967
*An Exhibition for the Centenary of Léon Bakst*, Milan, Rome, and Munich, 1967
Siordet, Gerard C., "Léon Bakst's Designs for Scenery and Costumes", *The Studio* (London), 1973
Spencer, Charles, *Léon Bakst*, London, 1973
Pruzhan, Irina, *Lev Samoilovich Bakst*, Leningrad, 1975
Mayer, Charles S., "The Influence of Léon Bakst on Choreography", *Dance Chronicle* (New York), vol. 1, no. 2, 1978
Borisovskaya, Anatolevna, *Lev Bakst*, Moscow, 1979
Pruzhan, Irina, *Léon Bakst: Set and Costume Designs*, Harmondsworth, 1987
Schouvaloff, Alexander, *Set and Costume Designs for Ballet and Theatre* (catalogue of the Thyssen-Bornemisza collection), London, 1987
Baer, Nancy van Norman, *The Art of Enchantment: Diaghilev's Ballets Russes 1909–1929*, San Francisco, 1988
Garafola, Lynn, *Diaghilev's Ballets Russes*, New York, 1989
Garafola, Lynn, "Léon Bakst", *Ballet Review* (New York), Fall, 1989

Schouvaloff, Alexander, *Léon Bakst: The Theatre Art*, London, 1991

* * *

Bakst was a principal figure in the pantheon of Ballets Russes artists (both those of Diaghilev's troupe and those associated with Ida Rubinstein), and his work expounded most of the themes that became the Ballets Russes' stock-in-trade: Orientalism, classicism renewed, a decadent, late romanticism, and even modernism. Bakst demonstrated that he was a master of all these genres, except perhaps the last. His designs helped bring them to life, and he imbued almost every production on which he worked with a typical sensuality.

This sensuality was revealed to the world first in the artist's Orientalist productions—*Salomé* for Rubinstein in 1908, the heart-stopping *Cléopâtre* of 1909, *Schéhérazade*, and many more. Bakst's facility in devising pseudo-oriental costumes and in fabricating exotic settings that stimulated an audience's erotic fantasy has often been ascribed to his Semitic origins, yet this is a highly unlikely proposition. Though sex surely thrived in the shtetl, as in other places, the odalisques and concubines of Bakst's imagination would have surprised the residents of his birthplace, Grodno, had they suddenly appeared there on the village street. The continual references of the designer's contemporaries to his Jewish origins, rather, are an unbecoming sign of their envy. Bakst, perhaps in spite of his Jewishness, was immeasurably successful in appropriating a mainstream European tradition—the projection of lascivious sexual desires on foreign and supposedly inferior races. The mantles of Delacroix and of Ingres, whose colourism and whose linear technique Bakst emulated, respectively, fit the Russian designer perfectly. Like these painters, Bakst profited from the explorations and overseas establishments of colonial Europe and, helped additionally by Art Nouveau's turn-of-the-century revolution in style, he raised to new heights the use of foreign design elements and untraditional combinations of colours, couching it all in a luxurious eroticism that was distinctively his own. The shocking success of the Ballets Russes' first seasons was, in part, due to Bakst's polished realization of ideals that Western European artists had pursued for a long time but had never captured in quite the same way.

Ironically, though the world remembers Bakst primarily for his Orientalist designs, the artist describes himself as a classicist in his own writings. Bakst's classicism, to be sure, was not the sugared distillation of the eighteenth century. Inspired by a primitive Hellas, and by the discoveries of the archeologists Evans and Halbherr in Crete, Bakst's vision of the antique world reflects the general shift of the arts in the nineteenth century toward Greek, and away from Roman, models. Specifically, his vision reflects the interests of contemporaries such as Vyacheslav Ivanov and the passion of ancient authors such as Sophocles and Euripides, whose dramas Bakst outfitted on stage and with whom he must have identified. Bakst admired the way in which antique art grounded itself in real forms, and his sensual nature took delight in the freedom of the ancients to adore the human nude in all its beauty. Like all his theatre apparel, the costumes that Bakst sketched for ballets such as *Daphnis et Chloë*, *Narcisse*. *Hélène de Sparte*, and *L'Après-midi d'un faune* were designed to reveal the body, extending its kinetic power, rather than concealing and restricting it. Nevertheless, his drawings of human figures are not confined by a narrow realism. Bakst knew how to exaggerate the body's forms or modify its proportions in such a way as to heighten its sensuality and create a sense of life in movement.

Though Bakst may have felt most at home describing Hellenist spectacles, he was also well acquainted with the historicist and decadent trends of late romanticism. The eclectic medieval and renaissance styles of his costume designs for *La Légende de Joseph* and of his costume and set designs for *Le Martyre de Saint-Sébastien* made these ballets into chivalric romances gone awry. Simultaneously recalling Ossian and the Marquis de Sade, they created an atmosphere of mystery, overcast by the awareness of impending death. These works explored, with an interest typical of the fin-de-siècle, themes of the hidden and direly forbidden. The shameful lust of Potiphar's wife for Joseph, the shameful lust of the emperor Hadrian for Sebastian, in fact, all the shameful lusts of Bakst's Parisian audience were rendered in these works with exquisite precision and care for historical detail. And with what tender nostalgia the bourgeois public remembered how its desires had awakened, seeing the fragile young woman of *Le spectre de la rose*, elegantly dressed by Bakst, transformed by a still amorphous vision of love that mirrored her own unfolding sexuality! Never has decadence been so tastefully expressed.

At the same time, Bakst was able to recreate the excess of mid-nineteenth-century fashion, the bell-shaped dresses with their ruffles, their pleats, their multiple petticoats and ribbons—all without ever appearing coarse. His Papillons, wearing pounds of clothing, remained light and unencumbered, ready to fly away. In *The Sleeping Princess* of 1921, Bakst enlivened another historical setting with his vivid palette of colours and the unique dynamism of his designs.

As a modernist Bakst was less successful, though his costumes for *Jeux*, by transferring classical values of simplicity and formal purity to designs for modern life, prefigured the work of constructivist artists in Russia and foreshadowed a major trend of modern design in general. The extent of his influence in this area still remains a subject in need of research. Certainly his conception of the stage space as a kinetic environment adapted to the scale of its human inhabitants and their actions, plus his introduction of radical diagonal perspectives, helped to bring stage design into the modern age. Also successful was his use of typical Art Nouveau or Jugendstil elements, when appropriate. Though Bakst's art, by centring itself on the human figure, consistently rose above mere decoration, he employed flat, crystalline patterns to great effect: in his costumes for the undersea creatures in *Sadko*, for example. If indeed there was a point beyond which Bakst could not go, the artist can hardly be faulted for remaining loyal to his own vision as the twentieth century progressed. Bakst was an extraordinary innovator, a wholly original talent whose advances made possible the efforts of his successors, without ever being equalled by them.

—Robert Johnson

---

**BALANCHINE, George**

Russian/American dancer, choreographer, and ballet director. Born Georgi Melitonovich Balanchivadze in St. Petersburg, 22 January (9 January old style) 1904. Studied at the Imperial Theatre School, St. Petersburg (later the Petrograd Theatre School), pupil of Sergei Andreyanov, Pavel Gerdt, 1913–21 (interrupted during the Revolution, 1917/18): graduated in 1921. Married (1) dancer Tamara Geva; (2) dancer Vera Zorina, 1938; (3) dancer Maria Tallchief, 1946; (4) dancer Tanaquil LeClercq, 1952 (div. 1969). Début, while still a student, Maryinsky Theatre, 1915; first choreography for ballet school concerts, 1919; dancer, State Academic Theatre for

Opera and Ballet (GATOB; formerly the Maryinsky Theatre and the State Maryinsky Theatre), from 1921; co-founder and leading dancer/choreographer, Young Ballet, 1922–24; founder, with Vladimir Dimitriev, Russian State Dancers, touring Europe, 1924; dancer, Diaghilev's Ballets Russes, performing as Georges Balanchine, 1924–29; first choreography for Ballets Russes, 1925, continuing as company choreographer until 1929; also staged dances for Charles B. Cochran 1930 Revue, London; guest choreographer, Royal Danish Ballet, 1930; ballet master and choreographer, Ballets Russes de Monte Carlo, 1932, also choreographing dances for opera at Opéra de Monte Carlo; founder, with Boris Kochno, and choreographer, Les Ballets 1933; moved to United States, on invitation of Lincoln Kirstein, 1933: founder, with Kirstein and Dimitriev, School of American Ballet, New York, from 1934; founder, with Kirstein, and chief choreographer, American Ballet, 1935–38, touring Eastern America, 1935, and performing as resident company (under name of American Ballet Ensemble) for Metropolitan Opera, New York; also choreographer for Broadway musicals, from 1936, Hollywood films, from 1937, Ballet Caravan (touring company founded by Kirstein, 1936), Original Ballet Russe (director de Basil), 1941, Teatro Colón in Buenos Aires, 1942, Ballet Theatre (later American Ballet Theatre), from 1943, Paris Opéra Ballet, 1947, Grand Ballet du Marquis de Cuevas, 1948, Sadler's Wells Ballet, 1950; choreographer for American Ballet Caravan (established with Kirstein from dancers of American Ballet and Ballet Caravan), touring South America, 1941; resident choreographer, Ballet Russe de Monte Carlo, 1944–46; founder, with Kirstein, and chief choreographer, Ballet Society, 1946–48, becoming New York City Ballet, from 1948; also choreographer for New York City Opera (with New York City Ballet as resident company), 1948–49; founder, James A. Doolittle–George Balanchine Ballet, Los Angeles, 1964–66; also director of numerous opera productions, including for NBC Opera Theatre telecast, 1956, Hamburg State Opera, from 1962, and choreographer for television, from 1949. Recipient: *Dance Magazine* Award, 1964; Handel Medallion of the City of New York, 1970; Order of the Légion d'Honneur, France, 1975; Knight of Dannebrog, First Class, 1978; National Gold Medal Award of National Society of Arts and Letters, 1980; Medal of Freedom, 1983. Died in New York, 30 April 1983.

## WORKS

1920 *La Nuit* (later *Romance*; mus. Rubinstein), *Schön Rosmarin* (mus. Kreisler), Petrograd Theatre School
1921 *Poème* (mus. Fibich), Petrograd Theatre School
1922 *Waltz* (mus. Drigo), *Waltz and Adagio* (mus. Balanchine), Petrograd Theatre School Graduation Performance, Petrograd
*Romanza* (mus. Balanchine), probably staged in Pavlovsk
*Waltz*, *Valse Triste* (mus. Sibelius), *Matelotte* (also *Sailor's Hornpipe*; mus. arranged Zuev), Concert Performance, Setroretsk
1923 *Valse Caprice* (mus. Rubinstein), *Columbine's Veil* (mus. von Dohnanyi), Petrograd
*Adagio* (mus. Saint-Saëns), *Spanish Dance* (mus. Glazunov), *Marche Funèbre* (mus. Chopin), Young Ballet, Petrograd
1923/24 *Étude* (mus. Scriabin), *Oriental Dance* (mus. Mussorgsky), *Elegy* (mus. Rachmaninov), Young Ballet, Petrograd
1924 *Pas de deux* (mus. Glazunov), State Theatre for Opera and Ballet (GATOB), Petrograd
*Invitation to the Dance* (mus. Weber), probably staged in Open-air Theatre, Pavlovsk
1925 *L'Enfant et les sortilèges* (mus. Ravel), Diaghilev's Ballets Russes, Monte Carlo
*Le Chant du rossignol* (mus. Stravinsky), Diaghilev's Ballets Russes, Paris
*Barabau* (mus. Rieti), Diaghilev's Ballets Russes, London
1926 *La Pastorale* (mus. Auric), Diaghilev's Ballets Russes, Paris
*Jack in the Box* (mus. Satie), Diaghilev's Ballets Russes, Paris
*The Triumph of Neptune* (mus. Berners), Diaghilev's Ballets Russes, London
1927 *La Chatte* (mus. Sauguet), Diaghilev's Ballets Russes, Monte Carlo
1928 *Apollon musagète* (later called *Apollo, Leader of the Muses*, and now called *Apollo*; mus. Stravinsky), Diaghilev's Ballets Russes, Paris
*The Gods Go a-Begging* (mus. Handel), Diaghilev's Ballets Russes, London
1929 *Le Bal* (mus. Rieti), Diaghilev's Ballets Russes, Monte Carlo
*Le Fils prodigue* (later *Prodigal Son*; mus. Prokofiev), Diaghilev's Ballets Russes, Paris
1930 *Aubade* (mus. Poulenc), Les Ballets Russes de Vera Nemchinova, Paris
1931 *La Légende de Joseph* (mus. Strauss), Royal Danish Ballet, Copenhagen
1932 *Cotillon* (mus. Chabrier), Ballets Russes de Monte Carlo, Monte Carlo
*La Concurrence* (mus. Auric), Ballets Russes de Monte Carlo, Monte Carlo
*Le Bourgeois Gentilhomme* (mus. R. Strauss), Ballets Russes de Monte Carlo, Monte Carlo
*Suites de danse* (mus. Glinka), Ballets Russes de Monte Carlo, Monte Carlo
1933 *Mozartiana* (mus. Tchaikovsky), Les Ballets 1933, Paris
*Les Songes* (mus. Milhaud), Les Ballets 1933, Paris
*The Seven Deadly Sins* (*Les Sept Péchés capitaux*; mus. Weill), Les Ballets 1933, Paris
*Errante* (later *The Wanderer*; mus. Schubert), Les Ballets 1933, Paris
*Fastes* (mus. Sauguet), Les Ballets 1933, Paris
*Les Valses de Beethoven* (mus. Beethoven), Les Ballets 1933, Paris
1934 *Serenade* (mus. Tchaikovsky), Students of the School of American Ballet, Estate of Felix Warburg, White Plains, New York (restaged American Ballet, New York, 1935)
*Dreams* (new staging of *Songes*; new mus. Antheil), Students of the School of American Ballet, Estate of Felix Warburg, White Plains, New York (restaged American Ballet, New York, 1935)
*Alma Mater* (mus. Kay Swift, arr. Morton Gould), Producing Company of the School of American Ballet, Hartford, Connecticut (restaged American Ballet, New York, 1935)
*Transcendence* (mus. Liszt, orch. Antheil), Producing Company of the School of American Ballet, Hartford, Connecticut (restaged American Ballet, New York, 1935)
1935 *Reminiscence* (mus. Godard, orchestrated Brant), American Ballet, New York
1936 *The Bat* (mus. J. Strauss the younger), American Ballet Ensemble, New York

*Orpheus and Eurydice* (opera-ballet; mus. Gluck), American Ballet Ensemble and Metropolitan Opera, New York

1937 *Le Baiser de la Fée* (mus. Stravinsky), American Ballet, New York

*Card Game* (or *Card Party*; mus. Stravinsky), American Ballet, New York

1941 *Balustrade* (mus. Stravinsky), Original Ballet Russe, New York

*Ballet Imperial* (later called *Tchaikovsky Piano Concerto no. 2*; mus. Tchaikovsky), American Ballet Caravan, Rio de Janeiro, Brazil

*Concerto Barocco* (mus. Bach), American Ballet Caravan, Rio de Janeiro, Brazil

*Divertimento* (mus. Rossini), American Ballet Caravan, Rio de Janeiro, Brazil

*Fantasia Brasileira* (mus. Mignone), American Ballet Caravan, Santiago, Chile

1942 *Concierto de Mozart* (also *Concierto*; mus. Mozart), Teatro Colón, Buenos Aires, Argentina

1944 *Danses Concertantes* (mus. Stravinsky), Ballet Russe de Monte Carlo, New York

*Waltz Academy* (mus. Rieti), Ballet Theatre, Boston

1945 *Pas de Deux* (also called *Grand Adagio*; mus. Tchaikovsky), Ballet Russe de Monte Carlo, New York

1946 *Night Shadow* (*La Sonnambula*; mus. Bellini, arranged Rieti), Ballet Russe de Monte Carlo, New York

*The Four Temperaments* (mus. Hindemith), Ballet Society, New York

*The Spellbound Child* (new version of *L'Enfant et les sortilèges*; mus. Ravel), Ballet Society, New York

1947 *Renard* (mus. Stravinsky), Ballet Society, New York

*Divertimento* (mus. Haieff), Ballet Society, New York

*Le Palais de Cristal* (later called *Symphony in C*; mus. Bizet), Paris Opera Ballet, Paris

*Symphonie Concertante* (mus. Mozart), Ballet Society, New York (originally performed by students of School of American Ballet, 1945)

*Theme and Variations* (later part of *Tchaikovsky Suite No. 3*; mus. Tchaikovsky), Ballet Theatre, New York

1948 *The Triumph of Bacchus and Ariadne* (ballet-cantata: mus. Rieti), Ballet Society, New York

*Orpheus* (mus. Stravinsky), Ballet Society, New York

*Pas de Trois Classique* (mus. Minkus), Grand Ballet du Marquis de Cuevas, Monte Carlo

1949 *Firebird* (mus. Stravinsky), New York City Ballet, New York

*Bourrée Fantasque* (mus. Chabrier), New York City Ballet, New York

1950 *Pas de Deux Romantique* (mus. Weber), New York City Ballet, New York

*Jones Beach* (with Robbins; mus. Andriessen) with Robbins, New York City Ballet, New York

*Trumpet Concerto* (mus. Haydn), Sadler's Wells Theatre Ballet, Manchester

*Mazurka from "A Life for the Tsar"* (mus. Glinka), New York City Ballet, New York

*Sylvia: Pas de Deux* (mus. Delibes), New York City Ballet, New York

1951 *Pas de Trois* (new version of *Pas de Trois Classique*; mus. Minkus), New York City Ballet, New York

*La Valse* (mus. Ravel), New York City Ballet, New York

*Capriccio Brillant* (mus. Mendelssohn), New York City Ballet, New York

*A La Françaix* (mus. Françaix), New York City Ballet, New York

*Tyl Ulenspiegel* (mus. R. Strauss), New York City Ballet, New York

1952 *Caracole* (mus. Mozart), New York City Ballet, New York

*Bayou* (mus. Thomson), New York City Ballet, New York

*Scotch Symphony* (mus. Mendelssohn), New York City Ballet, New York

*Metamorphoses* (mus. Hindemith), New York City Ballet, New York

*Harlequinade Pas de Deux* (mus. Drigo), New York City Ballet, New York

*Concertino* (mus. Françaix), New York City Ballet, New York

1953 *Valse Fantaisie* (mus. Glinka), New York City Ballet, New York

1954 *Opus 34* (mus. Schoenberg), New York City Ballet, New York

*The Nutcracker* (mus. Tchaikovsky), New York City Ballet, New York

*Western Symphony* (mus. Kay), New York City Ballet, New York

*Ivesiana* (mus. Ives), New York City Ballet, New York

1955 *Roma* (mus. Bizet), New York City Ballet, New York

*Pas de Trois II* (mus. Glinka), New York City Ballet, New York

*Pas de Dix* (mus. Glazunov), New York City Ballet, New York

*Jeux d'Enfants* (with Moncion, Milberg; mus. Bizet), New York City Ballet, New York

1956 *Allegro Brillante* (mus. Tchaikovsky), New York City Ballet, New York

*Divertimento No. 15* (mus. Mozart), New York City Ballet, Stratford, Connecticut

*A Musical Joke* (mus. Mozart), New York City Ballet, Stratford, Connecticut

1957 *Square Dance* (mus. Vivaldi, Corelli), New York City Ballet, New York

*Agon* (mus. Stravinsky), New York City Ballet, New York

1958 *Gounod Symphony* (mus. Gounod), New York City Ballet, New York

*Stars and Stripes* (mus. Sousa, arranged Kay), New York City Ballet, New York

*Waltz-Scherzo* (mus. Tchaikovsky), New York City Ballet, New York

*The Seven Deadly Sins* (new version; mus. Weill), New York City Ballet, New York

1959 *Native Dancers* (mus. Rieti), New York City Ballet, New York

*Episodes* (Part II by Balanchine, Part I by Martha Graham; mus. Webern), New York City Ballet, New York (Part II later staged alone)

1960 *Panamerica* (with Contreras, Moncion, Taras, d'Amboise; mus. Escobar, Chávez, Orbón), New York City Ballet, New York

*Pas de Deux* (also called *Tchaikovsky Pas de Deux*; mus. Tchaikovsky), New York City Ballet, New York

*The Figure in the Carpet* (mus. Handel), New York City Ballet, New York

*Variations from Don Sebastian* (later called *Donizetti Variations*; mus. Donizetti), New York City Ballet, New York

*Monumentum Pro Gesualdo* (mus. Stravinsky), New York City Ballet, New York

*Liebeslieder Walzer* (mus. Brahms), New York City Ballet, New York

*Ragtime (I)* (part of *Jazz Concert*; mus. Stravinsky), New York City Ballet, New York
1961 *Modern Jazz: Variants* (mus. Schuller), New York City Ballet, New York
*Electronics* (mus. Gassman, Sala), New York City Ballet, New York
*Valses et Variations* (later called *Raymonda Variations*; mus. Glazunov), New York City Ballet, New York
1962 *A Midsummer Night's Dream* (mus. Mendelssohn), New York City Ballet, New York
1963 *Bugaku* (mus. Mayuzumi), New York City Ballet, New York
*Movements for Piano and Orchestra* (mus. Stravinsky), New York City Ballet, New York
*Meditation* (mus. Tchaikovsky), New York City Ballet, New York
1964 *Tarantella* (mus. Gottschalk), New York City Ballet, New York
*Clarinade* (mus. Gould), New York City Ballet, New York
1965 *Pas de Deux and Divertissement* (incorporating *Sylvia: Pas de Deux*, 1950; mus. Delibes), New York City Ballet, New York
*Harlequinade* (mus. Drigo), New York City Ballet, New York
*Don Quixote* (mus. Nabokov), New York City Ballet, New York
1966 *Variations* (mus. Stravinsky), New York City Ballet, New York
*Brahms-Schoenberg Quartet* (mus. Brahms, orch. Schoenberg), New York City Ballet, New York
*Élégie* (solo; mus. Stravinsky), New York City Ballet, New York
*Ragtime (II)* (pas de deux; new version of *Ragtime (I)*; mus. Stravinsky), Philharmonic Hall, New York (restaged New York City Ballet, 1967)
1967 *Trois Valses Romantiques* (mus. Chabrier), New York City Ballet, New York
*Jewels* (mus. Fauré, Stravinsky, Tchaikovsky), New York City Ballet, New York (*Rubies* sometimes staged alone as *Capriccio*)
*Glinkiana* (mus. Glinka), New York City Ballet, New York
1968 *Metastaseis and Pithoprakta* (mus. Xenakis), New York City Ballet, New York
*Requiem Canticles* (mus. Stravinsky), New York City Ballet, New York
*Slaughter on Tenth Avenue* (mus. Rogers, orchestrated Kay), New York City Ballet, New York
*La Source* (pas de deux; mus. Delibes), New York City Ballet, New York (later incorporating part of *Pas de Deux and Divertissement*)
1969 *Valse Fantaisie* (formerly part II of *Glinkiana*; mus. Glinka), New York City Ballet, New York
1970 *Who Cares?* (mus. Gershwin, orchestrated Kay), New York City Ballet, New York
*Firebird* (new version, with Robbins; mus. Stravinsky), New York City Ballet, New York
*Suite No. 3* (later called *Tchaikovsky Suite No. 3*; mus. Tchaikovsky), New York City Ballet, New York (incorporating *Theme and Variations* as final movement)
1971 *Concerto for Jazz Band and Orchestra* (with Mitchell; mus. Liebermann), New York City Ballet and Dance Theatre of Harlem, New York
*PAMTGG* (mus. Kellaway), New York City Ballet, New York
1972 *Symphony in Three Movements* (mus. Stravinsky), New York City Ballet, New York
*Violin Concerto* (later called *Stravinsky Violin Concerto*; mus. Stravinsky), New York City Ballet, New York
*Danses Concertantes* (new version; mus. Stravinsky), New York City Ballet, New York
*Divertimento from "Le Baiser de la Fée"* (mus. Stravinsky), New York City Ballet, New York
*Scherzo à la Russe* (mus. Stravinsky), New York City Ballet, New York
*Duo Concertant* (mus. Stravinsky), New York City Ballet, New York
*Pulcinella* (with Robbins; mus. Stravinsky), New York City Ballet, New York
*Choral Variations on Bach's "Von Himmel Hoch"* (mus. Stravinsky), New York City Ballet, New York
1973 *Tchaikovsky Piano Concerto No. 2* (new production of *Ballet Imperial*; mus. Tchaikovsky), New York City Ballet, New York
*Cortège Hongrois* (mus. Glazunov), New York City Ballet, New York
1974 *Variations pour une Porte et un Soupir* (mus. Henry), New York City Ballet, New York
1975 *Sonatine* (mus. Ravel), New York City Ballet, New York
*Le Tombeau de Couperin* (mus. Ravel), New York City Ballet, New York
*Pavane* (solo; mus. Ravel), New York City Ballet, New York
*Tzigane* (mus. Ravel), New York City Ballet, New York
*Gaspard de la Nuit* (mus. Ravel), New York City Ballet, New York
*Rhapsodie Espagnole* (mus. Ravel), New York City Ballet, New York
*The Steadfast Tin Soldier* (mus. Bizet), New York City Ballet, Saratoga Springs, New York
1976 *Chaconne* (new version of finale of *Orpheo ed Euridice*; mus. Gluck), New York City Ballet, New York
*Union Jack* (mus. Kay), New York City Ballet, New York
1977 *Étude for Piano* (mus. Scriabin), Spoleto Festival, Charleston, South Carolina
*Vienna Waltzes* (mus. J. Strauss the younger, Lehár, R. Strauss), New York City Ballet, New York
1978 *Ballo della Regina* (mus. Verdi), New York City Ballet, New York
*Kammermusik No.2* (mus. Hindemith), New York City Ballet, New York
1980 *Ballade* (mus. Fauré), New York City Ballet, New York
*Walpurgisnacht Ballet* (originally staged in opera *Faust*, 1975; mus. Gounod), New York City Ballet, New York
*Robert Schumann's "Davidsbündlertänze"* (mus. Schumann), New York City Ballet, New York
1981 *Mozartiana* (new version; mus. Tchaikovsky), New York City Ballet, New York
*Hungarian Gipsy Airs* (mus. Menter, orchestrated Tchaikovsky), New York City Ballet, New York
*Symphony No. 6—Pathétique: Fourth Movement, Adagio Lamentoso* (with Robbins; mus. Tchaikovsky), New York City Ballet, New York
1982 *Tango* (mus. Stravinsky), New York City Ballet, New York
*Perséphone* (with Taras, Zorina; mus. Stravinsky), New York City Ballet, New York
*Variations for Orchestra* (mus. Stravinsky), New York City Ballet, New York

**George Balanchine rehearsing Suzanne Farrell, 1968**

Also staged:

1930 *Le Tricorne* (rechoreographed version of original ballet by Massine; mus. de Falla), Royal Danish Ballet, Copenhagen

*Schéhérazade* (rechoreographed version of original ballet by Fokine; mus. Rimsky-Korsakov), Royal Danish Ballet, Copenhagen

*La Boutique fantasque* (rechoreographed version of original ballet by Massine; mus. Rossini, orchestrated Respighi), Royal Danish Ballet, Copenhagen

*Polovtsian Dances from Prince Igor* (after Fokine; mus. Borodin), Royal Danish Ballet, Copenhagen

1946 *Raymonda* (with Danilova, after Petipa; mus. Glazunov), Ballet Russe de Monte Carlo, New York

1949 *Princess Aurora* (after Petipa; mus. Tchaikovsky), Ballet Theatre, Chicago

*Don Quixote* Pas de deux (after Petipa; mus. Minkus), Ballet Theatre, tour

*Black Swan* Pas de deux (from *Swan Lake*, after Petipa; mus. Tchaikovsky), Ballet Theatre, on tour

1951 *Swan Lake* (Act II, after Ivanov; mus. Tchaikovsky), New York City Ballet, New York

1969 *Swan Lake* (full-length version, after Petipa, Ivanov, Beriozoff; mus. Tchaikovsky), Ballet du Grand Théâtre, Geneva

1974 *Coppélia* (with Danilova, after Petipa, Cecchetti; mus. Delibes), New York City Ballet, Saratoga Springs, New York

**Other works include:** *Pizzicato Polka* (after Astafieva; mus. Delibes; included in divertissement *Le Festin*; 1925), *Valse Caprice* (after Astafieva) and *Lezghinka from Le Démon* (mus. Rubinstein; included in divertissement *L'Assemblée*; 1925), Entr'acte in Nijinska's *Romeo and Juliet* (mus. Lambert, entr'acte in silence; 1926), *The Creature of Prometheus* (with Lifar; mus. Beethoven; 1929), *Serenata: Magic* (mus. Mozart; 1936), *Pas de Trois for Piano and Two Dancers* (mus. Chanler; 1942), *Cinderella* (for television; mus. Tchaikovsky; 1949), *One, Yuletide Square* (version of *Coppélia* for television; mus. Delibes; 1952), *Noah and the Flood* (dance-drama, for television; mus. Stravinsky; 1962, with stage version, 1982), *Sonata* (mus. Stravinsky; 1972); Dances in operas *Le Coq d'or* (mus. Rimsky-Korsakov; 1923, 1937), *Carmen* (mus. Bizet; 1925, 1932, 1935, 1948), *Thaïs* (mus. Massenet; 1925), *Manon* (mus. Massenet; 1925, 1932, 1936), *Le Hulla* (mus. Samuel-Rousseau; 1925), *Fay-Yen-Fah* (mus. Redding; 1925, 1932), *Faust* (mus. Gounod; 1925, 1932, 1935, 1945, 1975), *Hérodiade* (mus. Massenet; 1925, 1932), *The Damnation of Faust* (mus. Berlioz; 1925, 1927), *Boris Godunov* (mus. Mussorgsky; 1926), *Judith* (mus. Honegger; 1926), *L'Hirondelle* (mus. Puccini; 1926), *Lakmé* (mus. Delibes; 1926, 1932, 1935), *Tales of Hoffmann* (mus. Offenbach; 1926, 1932, 1949), *Jeanne d'Arc* (mus. Gounod; 1926), *Hamlet* (mus. Thomas; 1926), *Samson et Dalila* (mus. Saint-Saëns; 1927, 1932, 1936, 1945), *La Traviata* (mus. Verdi; 1927, 1932, 1935, 1948), *Turandot* (mus. Puccini; 1927, 1932), *Ivan the Terrible* (mus. Gunsbourg; 1927), *Obéron* (mus. Weber; 1927), *Venise* (mus. Gunsbourg; 1928), *Sior Todéro Brontolon* (mus. Malipiero; 1928), *Un Bal Masquée* (mus. Verdi; 1928), *Don Giovanni* (mus. Mozart; 1928, 1938, 1948), *La Fille d'Abdoubarahah* (mus. Sanvel; 1928), *Roméo et Juliette* (mus. Gounod; 1929, 1932, 1937), *La Gioconda* (mus. Ponchielli; 1929, 1937), *Rigoletto* (mus. Verdi; 1929, 1932), *La Femme Nue* (mus. Février; 1929), *Martha* (mus. Flotow; 1929), *La Croisade des Dames* (mus. Schubert; 1929), *Orpheus in the Underworld* (mus. Offenbach; 1931), *Tannhäuser* (mus. Wagner; 1932, 1935), *Le Prophète* (mus. Meyerbeer; 1932), *Une Nuit à Venise* (mus. J. Strauss the younger; 1932), *Aïda* (mus. Verdi; 1932, 1935, 1945, 1948), *La Périchole* (mus. Offenbach; 1932), *Mignon* (mus. Thomas; 1936), *La Juive* (mus. Halévy; 1936), *The Mastersingers* (mus. Wagner; 1936), *The Bartered Bride* (mus. Smetana; 1936), *Lucia di Lammermoor* (mus. Donizetti; 1936), *Caponsacchi* (mus. Hageman; 1937), *Mârouf* (mus. Rabaud; 1937), *Rosalinda* (operetta after *Die Fledermaus*; mus. J. Strauss the younger; 1942), *La Vie Parisienne* (mus. Offenbach; 1942), *The Queen of Spades* (mus. Tchaikovsky; 1942), *The Fair at Sorochinsk* (mus. Moussorgsky; 1942), *The Merry Widow* (mus. Lehár; 1943), *Troubled Island* (mus. William Grant Still; 1949), *Adriana Lecouvreur* (mus. Cilea; 1953), *Ruslan and Ludmila* (mus. Glinka; 1969).

**Other stage works include:** for cabaret (Bat Theatre of Moscow)—*Grotesque Espagnol* (mus. Albéniz; 1927) and *Sarcasm* (mus. Prokofiev; 1927); for revue and musical comedy—*Wake up and Dream* (with Losch, Rivers; mus. Porter; 1929), *Charles B. Cochran's 1930 Revue* (with Lifar, Reader; ballet mus. Berners, Sauguet), *Charles B. Cochran's 1931 Revue* (with Bradley, Pierce; mus. Coward and others), *Sir Oswald Stoll's Variety Shows* (various items; 1931), *Ziegfeld Follies: 1936 Edition* (with modern dances by Alton; mus. Vernon Duke), *On Your Toes* (mus. Rodgers; 1936), *Babes in Arms* (mus. Rodgers; 1937), *I Married an Angel* (mus. Rodgers; 1938), *The Boys From Syracuse* (mus. Rodgers; 1938), *Great Lady* (mus. Loewe; 1938), *Keep off the Grass* (mus. McHugh, Duke; 1940), *Louisiana Purchase* (with modern dances by Carl Randall; mus. Berlin; 1940), *Cabin in the Sky* (with Dunham; mus. Duke; 1940), *The Lady Comes Across* (mus. Duke, Latouche; 1942), *What's Up* (mus. Loewe; 1943), *Dream With Music* (with tap routines by Henry Le Tang; mus. various, arranged Warnick; 1944), *Song of Norway* (operetta; mus. Grieg adapted Wright, Forrest; 1944), *Mr. Strauss Goes to Boston* (mus. Stolz; 1945), *The Chocolate Soldier* (operetta; mus. Oscar Straus; 1947), *Where's Charley?* (mus. Loesser; 1948), *Courtin' Time* (mus. Lawrence, Walker; 1951); for film—*Dark Red Roses* (dir. Hill; Tartar Ballet, mus. Mussorgsky; 1929), *The Goldwyn Follies* (dir. Marshall; mus. Gershwin, Duke; 1938), *I Was An Adventuress* (dir. Ratoff; *Swan Lake* scene, mus. Tchaikovsky; 1940).

**PUBLICATIONS**

By Balanchine:

"Notes on Choreography", *Dance Index* (New York), February and March 1945

"The Dance Element in Strawinsky's Music", in "Strawinsky in the Theatre: A Symposium", edited by Lederman, Minna, *Dance Index* (New York), October and December 1947; reprinted in Lederman, Minna, *Stravinsky in the Theatre*, New York, 1949

"Diaghileff and His Period", *Dance News* (New York), August 1949

*Balanchine's Complete Stories of the Great Ballets*, with Mason, Francis (ed.), New York, 1954; revised and enlarged (also published as *Balanchine's Festival of Ballet*), 1977

Volkov, Solomon, *Balanchine's Tchaikovsky: Interviews with George Balanchine*, New York, 1985

About Balanchine:

Amberg, George, *Ballet in America: The Emergence of an American Art*, New York, 1949

Chujoy, Anatole, *The New York City Ballet*, New York, 1953

Maynard, Olga, *The American Ballet*, Philadelphia, 1959

Koegler, Horst, *Balanchine und das moderne Ballet*, Velber, 1964

Kirstein, Lincoln, *Movement and Metaphor: Four Centuries of Ballet*, New York, 1970

Taper, Bernard, *Balanchine: A Biography*, New York and London, 1974; revised edition, New York, 1984

Slonimsky, Yuri, "Balanchine: The Early Years", translated by John Andrews, *Ballet Review* (New York), vol. 5, no. 3, 1975–76

Croce, Arlene, *Afterimages*, New York, 1977

Reynolds, Nancy, *Repertory in Review: Forty Years of the New York City Ballet*, New York, 1977

Kirstein, Lincoln, *Thirty Years: Lincoln Kirstein's The New York City Ballet*, New York, 1978

Siegel, Marcia, *The Shapes of Change: Images of American Dance*, Boston, 1979

Croce, Arlene, *Going to the Dance*, New York, 1982

*Choreography by George Balanchine: A Catalogue of Works*, edited by Leslie George Katz, Nancy Lassalle, and Harvey Simmonds, New York, 1983

McDonagh, Don, *George Balanchine*, Boston, 1983

Tracy, Robert, *Balanchine's Ballerinas: Conversations with the Muses*, New York, 1983

Ashley, Merrill, *Dancing for Balanchine*, New York, 1984

Maiorano, Robert, *Balanchine's Mozartiana: The Making of a Masterpiece*, New York, 1985

Dunning, Jennifer, *"But First a School": The First Fifty Years of the School of American Ballet*, New York, 1985

Shearer, Moira, *Balletmaster: A Dancer's View of George Balanchine*, London, 1986

Croce, Arlene, *Sightlines*, New York, 1987

Anderson, Jack, *Choreography Observed*, Iowa City, 1987

Buckle, Richard, *George Balanchine, Ballet Master: A Biography*, London, 1988

* * *

George Balanchine once identified the element of pointe work as a primary motivation for his career as choreographer. "If no pointes existed," he said to Walter Terry in 1962, "I would not be a choreographer. I would not be anything, probably. Perhaps a musician. The pointe made me."

As Balanchine tells it, it was seeing three ballerinas at work on pointe in the Imperial Theatre School around 1915 that gave him the epiphanal sense of ballet's extraordinary powers. The academically trained dancer and aspiring ballet master came of age in an era of modernism, where the rigors of classical dance were frequently deemed too old-fashioned for the new-world aspirations of twentieth-century art. However, unlike those practitioners who sought other, non-pointe methods for showing their modernity, the expatriate Russian, who left his homeland in 1924, took ballet into the modern day by embracing, and advancing, its accumulated technical expertise—not the least of which was the fairly recent ability for its ballerinas to work confidently on the tips of their toes. What Balanchine rejected were the extra-dance encumbrances that had attended ballet's development out of its opera/spectacle beginnings. Balanchine's ballet became modern by way of its independence from pantomime and literary/narrative concerns.

Of Serge Diaghilev, for whose Ballets Russes Balanchine worked as both dancer and choreographer, the innovative ballet master has said: "If it wasn't for him, I wouldn't be here." During his earliest years outside Russia, Balanchine used the Ballets Russes to advance his modernist theories of ballet. In this atmosphere of European theatre traditions, where the "book" was still very much part of a ballet's programme, Balanchine worked to emphasize ballet dancing's uniquely poetic powers of expression and to show dancers as something more than diversionary players.

When, at the behest of Lincoln Kirstein, Balanchine arrived in the United States of America, where no strict traditions for opera house dance theatre existed, he concentrated simultaneously on the training of dancers and on the creation of suitable dances for these artists to perform. He founded the School of American Ballet in 1934 and, after various companies of its dancers came and went, established the New York City Ballet in 1948. During his nearly 50-year-long career in the U.S., the Russian émigré established a secure ballet tradition where there had been none to speak of, and in so doing helped changed the face of ballet dancing worldwide.

Balanchine's values, whether displayed in opera productions, musical comedy theatre, Hollywood movies, or in his original ballet creations, consistently reflected the hallmarks of classicism: legibility, clarity, harmony, and nobility of stature. Especially when he concentrated almost exclusively on ballets for his own dancers in his own specially designed headquarters—Lincoln Center's New York State Theater designed by Philip Johnson—Balanchine promoted ballet as the art of big, gracious, articulate individuals.

Balanchine is on record as admiring large-scale elements of theatrical dance, particularly after he was situated with his company in the large-scale New York State Theater: "I like tall people . . . because you can see more," he said. Similarly, he appreciated, and preferred, large hands and long feet. Overall his credo was "more"—more breadth, more speed, more control, more sharpness, more softness, more reach, more pirouettes, more finely closed and more expansively open positions.

The one extra-dance element that Balanchine consistently concentrated on was music. His tastes ranged from the Offenbachian marches of John Philip Souza (*Stars and Stripes*) to the austere tonalities of Anton Webern (*Episodes*, a collaborative project with Martha Graham). The common thread in all his personal but wide-ranging musical tastes was music's ability to support dancing, to be what the French call "dansant".

Costuming and scenery came next, respectively, in Balanchine's order of dance theatre priorities. Though popular opinion frequently has it that he neglected these two areas, in fact it was often budgetary consideration that prevented him from "dressing" his ballets with more than minimal accessories. Balanchine was not against costumes or settings; he was opposed to heaviness of any kind, and aimed to have his dance and his dancers seen to their maximum degree.

The female dancer, at her most expert—i.e. on pointe—predominantly motivated and inspired Balanchine throughout his career. "I like woman" was the familiar phrase with which Balanchine expressed his vision of ballet (consider especially the repertory created for Tanaquil LeClercq, Diana Adams, and Suzanne Farrell). However, the male dancer also played a distinct part, albeit in lesser numbers, in the Balanchine canon. "Man is to serve," the ballet master would say, noting the place of the male dancer, the escort, in his world of ballet. So, while Balanchine's oeuvre has substantial examples of male dancer virtuosity and technical advancement, it also provides a textbook of cavalier deportment that sustains ballet's lineage to courtly, chivalrous, aristocratic behavior (as in the roles originated by André Eglevsky, Jacques d'Amboise, and Edward Villella).

Throughout his catalogue of works—an official volume, published just before his death, numbers 425 separate creations—Balanchine also concentrated on ensemble work, or the art of "groupings", so prominent in nineteenth-century ballet spectacle. Though the choreographer could decorate/orchestrate his dances with some of the most intricate and elaborate groupings of dancers—oftentimes these were infinitely more lush than any scenery could ever be—his corps de ballet was no simple background element. His supposed company of "no stars" was more accurately a company of all stars, where even corps de ballet dancers showed virtuoso ability.

—Robert Greskovic

---

## LE BALLET COMIQUE DE LA REINE

(also *Le Balet comique de la Royne*)

**Choreography**: Balthasar de Beaujoyeulx (Baldassarino di Belgiojoso)
**Music**: Lambert de Beaulieu, Jacques Salmon, Thibault de Courville
**Design**: Jacques Patin (scenery and costumes)
**Libretto:** La Chesnaye (verses)
**First production:** Palais Bourbon, Paris, 15 October 1581

### PUBLICATIONS

Beaujoyeulx, Balthazar de, *Le Balet-Comique de la Royne*, Paris, 1582; facsimile, with introduction by Margaret McGowan, Binghampton, N.Y., 1982
Lacroix, Paul (ed.), *Ballets et mascarades de cour*, vol. 1, Geneva, 1868
Pruniéres, H., *Le Ballet de Cour en France*, Paris, 1914
Welsford, Enid, *The Court Masque*, Cambridge, 1927
Kirstein, Lincoln, *Dance: A Short History of Classic Theatrical Dancing*, New York, 1935
Yates, Frances, *The French Academies of the Sixteenth Century*, in *Studies of the Warburg Institute* (London), vol. 15, 1947
McGowan, Margaret, *L'Art du Ballet de Cour en France 1581–1643*, Paris, 1963
Kirstein, Lincoln, *Movement and Metaphor: Four Centuries of Ballet*, New York, 1970

**The Four Virtues from *Le Ballet Comique de la Reine*, in an engraving by Jacques Patin, 1581**

MacClintock, C. and L., *Le Balet comique de la Royne*, Rome, 1971

Miller, James, "The Philosophical Background of the Renaissance", *York Dance Review* (North York, Ontario), Spring 1976

Sorrell, Walter, *Dance in its Time*, New York, 1981

* * *

Staged in October 1581 at the Palais Bourbon next to the Louvre, *Le Ballet Comique de la Reine*, or more properly, *Le Balet Comique de la Royne*, was commissioned by Queen Louise, wife of Henri III. The ballet formed part of the lavish entertainments in honour of the marriage of the Queen's sister, Marguerite of Lorraine, to the Duc de Joyeuse (favorite of Henri III, Catherine's third son).

In his preface to the reader Beaujoyeulx wrote that to have presented a simple play (comédie) would have been insufficiently dignified as an honour to such a great Queen, who had requested a magnificent and triumphant spectacle. Accordingly, he decided to mix music and poetry, but gave first place to the dance. He explained clearly why he had called the ballet "comique", fully realizing that some people might find the title puzzling. The reason, he wrote, is that it has a happy and tranquil ending, even though almost all the characters are gods and goddesses or heroic personages. He could, therefore, have called his ballet "héroique" or "épique", since according to classical artistic theory comedy was about ordinary people, whose failings rendered them ridiculous. The essence of the comic mode is the movement from disorder to order, chaos to harmony.

The plot of the ballet is based on the Circe myth and revolves around the struggle between reason and passion, a popular theme of the debates at the Palace Academy. The myth is used as a political allegory depicting the destructive power of the passions which lead to civil disorder, and the stability and superior power of reason and virtue.

In the text Beaujoyeulx described the scene in the great hall, surrounded on three sides by two galleries for the spectators. At one end of the hall was a dais three feet high with seats for the King, the Queen Mother, princes, and princesses. On each side were seats for the Ambassadors. Behind the royal dais were 40 steps stretching the whole width of the hall, with seats for the court ladies. In the dancing area to the right of the King was a small raised wood with a grotto for Pan, Nymphs, and Dryads. On the left was a long vault made of wood, the "Voulte Dorée", partially concealed by billowing clouds. Its interior was gilded and brightly illuminated by candlelight, and contained singers and musicians divided into ten "concerts de musique". Those amongst the audience who were better instructed in Platonic discipline, writes Beaujoyeulx, considered the music and singing to be the true celestial harmony, by which all created things are conserved.

At the far end of the hall opposite the King was a raised, geometrically patterned garden on a raked stage, filled with rare flowers and fruit and with a magnificent trellis hung with grapes. Behind the garden was a town (represented in perspective) and a castle, the home of the enchantress Circe, who was seen sitting in the doorway holding her golden wand. The set was lit by oil lamps made of different coloured glass, the garden by a hundred white candles. Beaujoyeulx estimated that there were easily nine or ten thousand spectators assembled in the hall, but this is probably an exaggeration.

The performance began at ten in the evening with a musical overture, followed by a gentleman who ran out of Circe's garden in terror, begging the King to put an end to her power. Circe appeared searching for him, failed to find him, and returned to her palace in a fury. A magnificent chariot disguised as a fountain and containing twelve Naiads led by Queen Louise then circled the hall, stopping before the King. After several songs the chariot exited and the Naiads returned to dance the first entrée, followed by the second entrée which opened with a "snail" figure, winding first one way, then another. When these had arrived opposite the king, the ballet continued with twelve different geometric figures, ending in a crescent facing the King. An enraged Circe rushed into the hall, touching each of the nymphs and musicians in turn with her wand, whereupon they were immobilized like statues, and she returned triumphant to her garden.

Mercury then descended to rescue the Naiads, bringing with him the juice of the magic herb moly which he sprinkled over them, restoring them to life. They resumed their dance but Circe returned, turning them back into statues, and mocking the illusions men have of restoring the golden age. She led the Naiads and Mercury into her garden. Eloquence alone, as depicted by Mercury, proves to be insufficient without Divine Reason. The satyrs and wood-nymphs appeal to Pan to rescue Circe's victims, but Pan, the universal world of nature, cannot resist Fate or break Circe's charms.

Next entered four ladies as the Four Cardinal Virtues, singing in praise of the King who has enabled these virtues to flourish in his kingdom. Minerva entered on a magnificent chariot led by a huge serpent. She then invoked the aid of Jupiter, who slowly descended in a cloud, accompanied by beautiful singing and music. All joined forces to attack Circe. Jupiter was shown striking her with a thunderbolt, taking her prisoner, and freeing her victims.

Circe's capture was then celebrated with the "grand Balet", composed first of fifteen passages or geometric figures, each one ending with the dancers facing the King. This was followed by a ballet of 40 geometric figures, in square, circular, and triangular formations. Each time the twelve Naiads completed a passage, it was broken by the four Dryads so that one figure flowed into the next. Halfway through the ballet a chain, consisting of four different kinds of interlacing, was danced. The music was extremely varied, some dances grave, others gay, some in triple time, and others gentle and slow.

After the "grand Balet" the Queen and ladies curtsied to the King and gentlemen, and presented them with symbolic medallions, after which followed the "grand Bal", the social dancing in which the audience was drawn into and became part of the idealized world cleansed of evil which had been presented by the ballet. The festivities ended at 3:30 a.m. with branles and other dances appropriate for such great occasions.

Although the King did not perform in the actual ballet (like James I in the later Stuart court masques), he was, in effect, the central character. He was placed centrally in the auditorium and all the action revolved around him, celebrating his divine presence, and praising his superior power from which all political, artistic, and social harmony stems. This was not simply flattery, but a means of instructing through praise and informing the monarch of his subjects' hopes and expectations.

Beaujoyeulx claimed that he had invented a new genre, inspired by the now lost Greek choric drama, although his ballet was more a culmination of earlier attempts at artistic unity, notably those of Lorenzo de Medici in Florence. But in general we can say that the *Balet comique* differs from earlier mascarades, carnivals, and ballets in two important ways. First, its component parts have been more carefully linked, and it has unity and consistent plot. Music and dance are not simply divertissements interrupting the plot, but are essential to the dramatic development of the theme. Each of the components—poetry, songs, ballets, pantomime—is necessary to the plot and to the overall design. It is a unified work of art. The second very important innovation is the publication, the following year, of the printed text with its lavish illustrations, which was circulated throughout the courts of Europe. Although such spectacular and costly ballets were not staged again in France for many years, as a result of political and financial instability, this ballet became the prototype for large-scale court entertainments and great state occasions. Ben Jonson had his own copy of the text, and through his work the *Balet comique* was to have immense influence on the Stuart court masque. Aurelian Townshend shows his debt to the *Balet comique* in his masque *Tempe Restor'd*. As far as we know, it has never been performed in its entirety since 1581.

—Francoise Carter

---

## LE BALLET DE LA NUIT

**Choreography**: Chancy, Mollier, Manuel, Vertpré, Jean-Baptiste Lully

**Music:** Jean de Cambefort, Jean-Baptiste Boësset, Michel Lambert, Jean Baptiste Lully

**Design:** Giacomo Torelli (machine effects), Henry de Gissey (costumes)

**Libretto:** Isaac de Benserade (verses)

**First Production:** Salle de Petit Bourbon, Paris, 23 February 1653

**Principal Dancers:** included Jean-Baptiste Lully, Pierre Beauchamps, and King Louis XIV (as The Sun)

### PUBLICATIONS

Lacroix, Paul (ed.), *Ballets et mascarades de cour*, vol. 1, Geneva, 1868

Fournel, François Victor, "Théâtre de la cour: ballets et mascarades" in *Les Contemporains de Molière* (reprint), 3 vols., Geneva, 1967

Christout, Marie-Françoise, *Le Ballet de Cour de Louis XIV 1643–1672*, Paris, 1967

Kirstein, Lincoln, *Movement and Metaphor: Four Centuries of Ballet*, New York, 1970

* * *

This important and highly successful ballet, which had six repeat performances, marks the end of the Fronde and opposition to Anne of Austria, the Queen-Mother, and Cardinal Mazarin. Invited by Parliament, the fifteen-year-old Louis XIV entered Paris in triumph on 21 October 1652. Louis had already demonstrated his talent for dancing, notably in the *Ballet de Cassandre* in 1651.

*Le Ballet de la nuit* was composed of 45 entrées, depicting

**A drawing of a musician from *Le Ballet de la Nuit*, 1623**

twelve hours (from 6:00 p.m. to 6:00 a.m.), divided into four vigils, each one of three hours. The first section (6:00–9:00 in the evening) depicts events which normally take place at this time in country and town. The scene first represents a distant landscape near the sea. The Sun sets and Night appears in a chariot of clouds drawn by owls and accompanied by twelve Hours. While Night converses with the Hours, four of them, including the King, dance the first entrée. Proteus leads his marine flocks to his cave and undergoes several metamorphoses. Five sea-nymphs await his orders. Six tired huntsmen return from the chase with a dead stag on a horse; two shepherds and two shepherdesses bring home their flocks of sheep. Four bandits (one of whom was the Duke of Buckingham) rob a haberdasher. The scene changes to a town with shops and shopkeepers, where two gallants and their ladies descend from coaches to buy ribbons and jams. The coachmen remind them of the lateness of the hour and they leave, while little boys disguised as animals dance. Six gypsies tell fortunes and pick pockets; two knife-grinders return home; the shops close; lamp-lighters light the lamps. The scene changes once more to represent the Cour des Miracles, a seedy Parisian quarter, once a retreat for beggars and vagabonds. Here legless cripples and beggars are suddenly cured of their ailments and misery, and dance a lively dance.

In the 9:00 p.m. to midnight section, Venus descends from heaven bringing Sports (danced by the King), Mirth, and Comus, god of cheer. Venus chases away the Three Fates, Old Age, and Sadness, since it is now the time for revelling. Characters from Ariosto's *Orlando Furioso* dance old-fashioned courantes and branles. They are entertained by two ballets within the ballet: first, the *Mariage de Thetis*, an amusing pantomime with mythological characters, followed by *Amphytriton* mimed in the style of the *commedia dell'arte*. The fête ends with a sarabande danced by five children dressed as Spaniards.

From midnight until 3:00 a.m., The Moon rises, surrounded by stars who retire so that she can admire Endymion. A cloud discreetly hides the lovers from view. The ancient astrologers Ptolemy and Zoroaster study the sudden eclipse and are consulted by four anxious peasants. Six Corybantes attempt to bring back the Moon by striking cymbals. Then follows a witches' sabbath in which four small monsters fly through the air and the witches cover themselves in grease in order to follow them. (It was a common belief at that time that the grease helped them to fly.) The witches' sabbath vanishes; a house catches fire, and half-naked men and women escape carrying children, cats, and monkeys while the arsonists are taken prisoner.

Between 3:00 and 6:00 a.m., Sleep and Silence are woken by the renown of the King, then lie down at the entrance to the cave of Dreams. First come the four elements—Fire, Air, Water, and Earth—representing the four bodily humours—choleric, sanguinic, phlegmatic, and melancholic—and each has dreams appropriate to his particular nature. Bashful lovers consult an oracle; three counterfeiters leave their den; blacksmiths begin work. The Day-Star appears, followed by Aurora in her chariot surrounded by the twelve Hours of the day, who retire on seeing the rising sun, performed by the King. He dances the "grand ballet" with the spirits of Honour, Grace, Love, Valour, Victory, Favour, Fame, and Peace, all of whom come to pay homage to him. In this final magnificent tableau, Louis is heralded as the Sun King, blessed with all qualities, and the bringer of all these benefits to his people.

It would seem that nothing was omitted from this ballet—burlesque, social comedy, allegory, classical mythology, pastoral and romance characters, monsters, animals—all followed one after the other, with sumptuous scene changes and lavish costumes. There were strong elements of the type of burlesque ballet-mascarades enjoyed by Louis XIII. But in spite of the hotch-potch of genres and characters, there is a definite theme which joins the seemingly disparate parts together. There is a clear-cut division of the progression of night and of the activities appropriate to each section. The numerous transformation scenes depict the gradual removal of strife and the overthrow of disorder, leading to the final climax and apotheosis—the rising of the sun upon a new day, a new age cleansed of disorder, suffering, and crime.

Since 1649, Louis had been called the Sun King, and in *Le Ballet de la nuit* this title is publicly confirmed. Louis heralds not only the golden age traditionally restored by a new monarch, but also the golden age of French Court ballet under the enthusiastic patronage of an elegant and refined dancer-King. The ballet also had considerable influence upon English theatrical dance after the Restoration of Charles II in 1660. Both the Dukes of York and Buckingham danced in it, and it is probable that the exiled Charles attended the performance.

—Francoise Carter

---

## BALLET IMPERIAL

(later *Tchaikovsky Piano Concerto No.2*, or *Concerto No. 2*)

**Choreography:** George Balanchine
**Music:** Petr Ilyich Tchaikovsky
**Design:** Mstislav Doboujinsky (set and costumes)
**First Production:** American Ballet Caravan, Teatro Municipal, Rio de Janeiro, 25 June 1941 (preview at Hunter College, New York, 29 May 1941)
**Principal Dancers:** Marie-Jeanne, William Dollar; Gisella Caccialanza, Fred Danieli, Nicholas Magallanes

**Other productions include:** Ballet Russe de Monte Carlo (restaged Balanchine), with Mary Ellen Moylan, Nicholas Magallanes, Maria Tallchief; Chicago, 4 October 1944. Sadler's Wells Ballet (restaged Balanchine; design Eugene Berman), with Margot Fonteyn, Michael Somes, Beryl Grey; London, 5 April 1950. Ballet of La Scala (restaged Balanchine); Milan, 25 March 1952. New York City Ballet (restaged Balanchine; new scenery Rouben Ter-Arutunian, new costumes Barbara Karinska), with Suzanne Farrell, Colleen Neary, Jacques d'Amboise; New York, 15 October 1964. German Opera Ballet; Berlin, 1 November 1968. New York City Ballet (new production; restaged and revised Balanchine; no scenery, new costumes Karinska), as *Tchaikovsky Piano Concerto No. 2*, with Patricia McBride, Peter Martins, Colleen Neary; New York, 12 January 1973.

### PUBLICATIONS

Beaumont, Cyril, "Balanchine's *Ballet Imperial*", *Ballet* (London), May 1950
Beaumont, Cyril, *Complete Book of Ballets*, revised edition, London 1951
Barnes, Clive, "Ballet Imperial", *Dance and Dancers* (London), March 1958
Balanchine, George, with Mason, Francis, *Balanchine's Complete Stories of the Great Ballets*, Garden City, New York, 1977
Reynolds, Nancy, *Repertory in Review*, New York, 1977
Crisp, Clement, "*Ballet Imperial*", *Dancing Times* (London), April 1985
Goodwin, Noël, "Tired Remnants of Glory", *Dance and Dancers* (London), April 1985
Kaplan, Larry, "Corps Choreography by Balanchine", *Ballet Review* (New York), Winter 1988

***Ballet Imperial*, with Susan Jaffe and Ross Stretton of American Ballet Theatre**

George Balanchine, responding to an invitation from the U.S. State Department to tour South America with his newly-formed American Ballet Caravan, created *Ballet Imperial* to Tchaikovsky's Second Piano Concerto. "It may not be the greatest music," Balanchine had stated, "but it's perfect for dancing." After several years of working on Broadway productions and Hollywood films, Balanchine in 1941 had returned to the Russian classicism of his early schooling in St. Petersburg. Having the resources of the School of American Ballet and of the company itself to draw upon, he was now able to provide the repertory with a work that would be the equivalent of a Russian classic, yet would be stylistically right for American dancers.

*Ballet Imperial* is a tribute to the Imperial Ballet School of the Maryinsky Theatre and to Marius Petipa. The original décor and costumes for the American Ballet Caravan by Mstislav Doboujinsky evoked the grandeur of the Winter Palace; subsequent productions have included Eugene Berman's for the Sadler's Wells Ballet (1950), and Rouben Ter-Arutunian's for the New York City Ballet (1964). The settings employed chandeliers, royal emblems, and draperies of brilliant blue, gold, and white; satin tunic costumes, layered tutus, and coronets were worn by the dancers who honoured, in mime, the court manners of a nineteenth-century aristocracy.

If the spirit of *Ballet Imperial* looked back to the century past, the choreography looked forward. It was a classical vocabulary, but reflected the music visually with a new speed and clarity. *Ballet Imperial* uses all three movements of the piano concerto and calls for two principal ballerinas of exceptional virtuosity, a male soloist, two female demi-soloists, and a corps of sixteen women and eight men. At the premiere staging, Balanchine had in Marie-Jeanne a dancer of remarkable speed and stamina, and he matched her special skills to the solo piano and cadenzas.

The ballet itself tells no story, but when the prima ballerina, as Princess, is led by her Cavalier to acknowledge the corps, her retinue, we are not far from Petipa. No longer did the corps remain in the background, but it was put in constant motion with a succession of turns and repeat turns duplicating the soloists. The second movement, marked andante, found the Cavalier searching for his Princess, who appeared from the corps, engaged him in an adagio, then disappeared, leaving him alone again; it was the visionary motif, somewhat distilled, of nineteenth-century romantic ballet. (Balanchine used the "searching male" theme again to great effect in the élégie of his *Tchaikovsky Suite No. 3* ballet.)

*Ballet Imperial* has been staged around the world. Individual productions and performances have varied. London's Sadler's Wells dancers brought the necessary aristocratic mien to the stage, Beryl Grey and Michael Somes being cited in particular; Ballet Russe de Monte Carlo had Mary Ellen Moylan and Maria Tallchief brilliantly executing the dual ballerina roles. Comparisons to the original 1941 cast were inevitable, however, and often unfavourable towards later companies' efforts. Many of the steps for the prima ballerina were revised or eliminated and critics pointed out that the dancers, particularly the Americans, were not very adept at portraying nobility.

Balanchine, not uncharacteristically, went about changing his work. The 1963 production for the Royal Ballet saw some of the mime disappear, only to reappear for the New York City Ballet version in 1964. But when *Ballet Imperial* was produced in New York in 1973 and re-titled simply the *Tchaikovsky Piano Concerto No. 2*, the choreographer's message had become clear: movement to music, unadorned. The revised version presented a new stage picture; gone were the chandeliers and tutus. Much of the court mime for the dancers was eliminated. Before a plain blue cyclorama was set the corps of women in chiffon dresses. Emphasis lay on allegro movements and tempi seemed faster, as did the dancers themselves in their new costumes. (Costumer Barbara Karinska had designed similar dresses for two previous Tchaikovsky/Balanchine ballets, *Allegro Brillante* and the solo *Tchaikovsky Pas de Deux*.) With the flowing movement of the material, the beauty of their line was extended to the musical phrases. A new lyrical quality that caught the sweep and bravura of the piano concerto was evident. Both stagings are still intact, and still being performed. Each version, the Russianized *Ballet Imperial* and the re-titled neo-classic, takes on a validity of its own.

—Richard Rutledge

---

## BALLET NACIONAL DE CUBA

Cuban ballet company based in Havana. Founded by Alicia and Fernando Alonso, with chief choreographer Alberto Alonso; first performances as the Ballet Alicia Alonso, 1948, assuming title of Ballet de Cuba, 1955, and Ballet Nacional de Cuba (as a result of the Revolution), 1959; has continued to be identified throughout its history with Alicia Alonso, who remains prima ballerina; junior company, La Joven Guardia, also performs and tours. Official school associated with the company, based in Havana, established 1959. Current artistic director of the Ballet Nacional de Cuba: Alicia Alonso.

### PUBLICATIONS

*El Ballet Nacional de Cuba en Europa*, Havana, 1969

Goldner, Nancy, "National Ballet of Cuba", *Dance News* (New York), September 1971

*Cuba en el ballet* (Havana), September 1973

Parera-Villalon, Celida, *Historia concisa del ballet en Cuba*, New York, 1974

Maynard, Olga, "Alicia Alonso and the Ballet Nacional de Cuba", *Dance Magazine* (New York), June 1978

Baker, Robert, "Ballet Nacional de Cuba", *Dance Magazine* (New York), October 1978

Jackson, George, "Ballet Nacional de Cuba", *Dance News* (New York), September 1978 and October 1979

Small, Linda, "Ballet Nacional de Cuba", *Dance Magazine* (New York), October 1979

Lidova, Irene, "Ballet Nacional de Cuba", *Les Saisons de la danse* (Paris), January 1980

Kirchner, Birgit, "Triumphs and Afflictions of the Revolution: The Cuban Dance Scene 30 Years On", *Ballett International* (Cologne), Zeitgeist/Handbook, 1990

* * *

In 1948, Alicia and Fernando Alonso brought together a small group of dancers from Havana's Sociedad Pro-Arte Musical and friends from the young Ballet Theatre, of which Alicia was at that time a ballerina, to form Cuba's first-ever professional ballet company. It was called the Ballet Alicia Alonso. After the Revolution of 1959 the company acquired the status of National Ballet of Cuba, together with a generous state subsidy. At the same time a National Ballet School was founded and funded.

Cuba's dancers have won international recognition ever since. At the Varna competitions in 1965, Arnold Haskell recognized "a new school—the Cuban School of Ballet" and dancers who "with their dances have taken their place in the history of centuries of ballet". Alicia Alonso, from whose extensive experience and passionately Cuban persona this school derives, describes it as an "escuela abierta"—open, and constantly assimilating elements of other schools. Its uniquely Cuban quality has developed, she claims, through a process of "adaptation to the academic technique of our physique, our way of saying things and expressing ourselves". The emphasis on "preserving our Cuban identity"—the vigorous fusion of Spanish and African cultures known as Cubania—goes side by side with an insistence on "respect for the essence of the period" in the performance of classical works.

Cuba's dancers have swift feet, elegant extensions, and spectacularly high, light jumps. The fluent "Russian" quality of their arms has made their *Giselle*, *Swan Lake*, and *Les Sylphides* among the most poetic in the world. But technique is regarded as a means, not an end in itself. Great attention is paid to characterization: every gesture must have its dramatic motivation. Whatever the style or the mood the corps de ballet, distinguished for its discipline, is always sensitively involved in the action. Every pas de deux is a romantic dialogue, a passionate encounter. Every dancer develops his or her individual interpretation.

The women combine their strength and high jumps with a seductive femininity. The men are tall, daring, and courteous. Walter Terry wrote of the Cuban men: "they wear their virility like a cloak of honour . . . they are the men of the Spanish dance where they proclaim their pride in their manhood". What Terry failed to mention was that many of these men, in a racially integrated company, proclaim their pride also in their African descent. Cuba was the first country to dispel the myth that ballet is for whites only. Here Albrecht and Siegfried, Basilio and Hamlet, are as likely to be black as white.

Today's company numbers 135 dancers, 80 women, and 55 men, with a repertoire extending from the one-act *La Fille mal gardée* through all the great French and Russian classics to William Forsythe's *Steptext*. Alonso herself is responsible for the historical reconstructions and, together with the company's five choreographers, for the majority of the twentieth-century pieces. The company also dances works by Balanchine (*Theme and Variations*), Tudor (*Lilac Garden*), Robbins (*In the Night*), Béjart (*Bakhti*), and Gades (*Bodas de Sangre*), among others.

The Cuban identity is everywhere apparent in the work of the home-grown choreographers. Alberto Mendez uses the music of the Cuban composer Leucona for his lyrical period piece, *Tarde en la Siesta*; he bases his *El Rio y el Bosque* on African legend. Herrera's *Cecilia Valdés* is inspired by a popular novel, and his *Electra Garrigó* by the work of Cuba's first writer for the Theatre of the Absurd; the music is by a young Cuban electronic composer. Alberto Alonso is the choreographer of the famous *Carmen* and a number of works based upon the rumba and the rhythms and folklore of Afro-Cuban dance. In 1988 a new and very successful version of *Don Quixote* was choreographed by two ballerinas, Marta Garcia and Maria Elena Llorente, and the maître de ballet Karemia Moreno. In every production the national characteristics are reinforced by the designers' vivid use of colour and symbolism.

A junior group, La Joven Guardia, consisting of 40 members of the corps de ballet and final-year students from the school, is directed by Alonso's daughter Laura. The extra tuition that these young dancers receive in pas de deux work and small-scale new choreography produces a technique and a maturity which qualifies them early for leading roles. The Joven Guardia gain valuable additional experience by giving special performances on the stage of Havana's García Lorca Theatre, and on tours throughout the island and abroad. The group contains a number of international competition medal winners, and the exceptional standards of its members bring still more Cuban vitality and character to the productions of the National Company.

The National Ballet, whose home is the magnificent 150-year-old Gran Teatro de La Habana, tours the world with its extensive repertoire which increases constantly, by an average of ten new works a year. The company also spends time giving performances in the provinces, often to thousands in the open air, with lecture demonstrations in schools, factories, and military establishments. Education is a special concern: there is a weekly one-hour radio programme and the ballet is frequently to be seen on television. The company's magazine, *Cuba en el Ballet*, reached its twentieth anniversary in 1990. Children with learning difficulties and behaviour problems, as well as the visually and hearing-impaired, are treated by means of Psicoballet, a form of dance therapy administered jointly by the ballet company and the psychiatric hospital.

The biennial International Ballet Festival of Havana, which is attended by hundreds of dancers, critics, and dance-lovers from almost every country, is a showcase for new Cuban choreography and provokes an intense and valuable exchange of experiences. Cuban teachers and choreographers are much sought after abroad, particularly in Latin America, where the Cuban influence is especially strong. Havana is the centre for the new Latin-American and Caribbean Dance Foundation, of which Alicia Alonso was unanimously elected president at the International Ballet Festival in 1988.

—Jane King

---

**BALLET RAMBERT** *see* **RAMBERT DANCE COMPANY**

---

## BALLET RUSSE DE MONTE CARLO

(Denham's Ballet Russe de Monte Carlo)

Touring ballet company, originally based in Monte Carlo and moving permanently to America, 1939. Origins in Colonel de Basil's Ballets Russes (performing also as Ballets Russes de Monte Carlo, Covent Garden Russian Ballet, and eventually the Original Ballet Russe), founded 1932, and directed by Colonel Wassily de Basil and René Blum; separation between de Basil and Blum, resulting in Blum's establishment of Ballets de Monte Carlo (chief choreographer Mikhail Fokine) 1936–37, followed by founding of Ballet Russe de Monte Carlo (artistic director Léonide Massine, managing director Serge Denham), 1938; inaugural season, Monte Carlo, April 1938, succeeded by famous London season, June 1938, and New York season, October 1938; last performances in Europe, 1939; toured the United States extensively, with regular New York seasons until 1950; became touring concert company, with no new repertoire, seasons 1952–54; re-established 1954, with first New York season since refounding in 1957; disbanded 1962.

### PUBLICATIONS

Haskell, Arnold, *Balletomania*, London, 1934; revised edition, London, 1977

Coton, A.V., *A Prejudice for Ballet*, London, 1938
Haskell, Arnold, *Ballet*, London, 1945
Lynham, Deryck, *Ballet Then and Now*, London, 1947
Amberg, George, *Ballet in America*, New York, 1949
De Mille, Agnes, *Dance to the Piper*, Boston, 1952
Maynard, Olga, *The American Ballet*, Philadelphia, 1959
Anderson, Jack, *The One and Only: The Ballet Russe de Monte Carlo*, New York, 1981
Sorley Walker, Kathrine, *De Basil's Ballets Russes*, London, 1982
Taper, Bernard, *Balanchine: A Biography*, revised edition, New York, 1984
Denby, Edwin, *Dance Writings*, New York, 1986

* * *

The Ballet Russe de Monte Carlo both perpetuated a cosmopolitan balletic style and contributed to the development of ballet as an American art. It was born as a result of quarrels between Léonide Massine (and the dancers and arts patrons who supported him) and the management of Colonel W. de Basil's Ballets Russes. At its inception in Monte Carlo in 1938, it was decidedly international in personnel. The onset of World War II significantly altered its orientation. It left Europe, never to return, in 1939, established headquarters in New York City, and devoted itself to touring the United States and Canada. At its demise in 1962, most of its dancers were Americans.

The Ballet Russe de Monte Carlo enjoyed two periods of sustained accomplishment: the first (1938–42) under the artistic leadership of Massine, the second (1944–46) when George Balanchine served as resident choreographer. For the Ballet Russe, Massine choreographed the phenomenally popular comedy, *Gaîté Parisienne* (1938), as well as ballets in a remarkable range of styles. They included *St. Francis* (*Nobilissima Visione*; 1938), a serious retelling of legends associated with the medieval saint; two important symphonic ballets, *Seventh Symphony* (1938) and *Rouge et Noir* (1939); and two controversial collaborations with Salvador Dali, *Bacchanale* (1939) and *Labyrinth* (1941).

The Ballet Russe allowed Balanchine to explore abstraction. He created *Danses Concertantes*, a major abstraction, in 1944, and revived such plotless pieces as *Ballet Imperial*, *Mozartiana*, and *Concerto Barocco*. He also choreographed *Night Shadow* (*La Sonnambula*; 1946), a morbid dramatic work that was likened to a Gothic horror story.

The Ballet Russe emphasized variety in its programming. Over the years, it produced such nineteenth-century classics as *Giselle*, *Coppélia*, and the second act of *Swan Lake*, and it introduced America to *The Nutcracker*, *Raymonda*, the *Paquita* divertissements, and the third act of *Swan Lake*. The Diaghilev era was represented by such achievements as *Les Sylphides*, *Petrushka*, *Le Spectre de la rose*, *Prince Igor*, *L'Après-midi d'un faune*, *Schéhérazade*, *The Three-Cornered Hat*, and *La Boutique fantasque*.

Whereas these productions reflected ballet's nineteenth-century heritage and its links with early twentieth-century modernism, the Ballet Russe, especially in its earlier years, also showed an awareness of more recent trends. With the premiere of Agnes de Mille's *Rodeo* in 1942, it demonstrated the validity of Americana as balletic subject matter. Later, in 1947, it became the first American ballet company to offer a work by a modern dancer by presenting Valerie Bettis's *Virginia Sampler*.

Just as the Ballet Russe affirmed ballet's ability to absorb diverse influences, so it assimilated dancers of varied backgrounds. Its stars included the legendary Russian ballerina Alexandra Danilova and her ebullient British partner Frederic Franklin. Among other notable dancers during its history were such Europeans as Alicia Markova, Mia Slavenska, Tamara Toumanova, Nathalie Krassovska, Yvette Chauviré, Nina Novak, Igor Youskevitch, André Eglevsky, Roman Jasinski, Oleg Tupine, and George Zoritch, and such North Americans and Latin Americans as Alicia Alonso, Ruthanna Boris, Mary Ellen Moylan, Irina Borowska, Gertrude Tyven, Leon Danielian, Nicholas Magallanes, Robert Lindgren, James Starbuck, and Alan Howard. Four ballerinas of American Indian descent were at one time or another members of the company: Rosella Hightower, Maria Tallchief, Moscelyne Larkin, and Yvonne Chouteau. And when it hired Raven Wilkinson in 1956, the Ballet Russe became the first touring American ballet company to employ a black dancer.

For many American dancers, the Ballet Russe was a company one wanted to join, because acceptance in it meant being part of a great tradition. By the 1960s, its largely American personnel could be considered evidence that America had become one of the homes of that tradition.

The company traveled everywhere across the United States and Canada. Its annual tours were often long and grueling. For instance, during the 1949–50 season there were 191 performances in 86 cities, and in 1954–55 there were 188 performances in 104 cities. Few later companies would dare to tour on such a scale. The company performed in small towns as well as in big cities. Its annual visits were eagerly awaited, and scores of people developed a fondness for dance because of the fact that once, when they were young, they had seen the Ballet Russe.

After about 1950, the Ballet Russe slipped slowly into an artistic decline. Serge Denham, the Russian-born banker who was its director, lacked the knack of developing important new choreographers. The rigors of touring caused some of the company's productions to grow shabby. Rising costs necessitated a shrinking of repertoire, until the company confined itself largely to a few tried-and-true favorites. Although it made much of the fact that its 1961–62 season was its 25th anniversary, by that time it was only a shadow of the glamorous and creatively vital troupe that had delighted sophisticates in 1938.

Nevertheless, until the end of the company's days, the members of the Ballet Russe danced their hearts out. By living in constant proximity to one another during their annual tours, these dancers became a kind of family, and a remarkable *esprit de corps* developed. To an amazing degree, the alumni of the Ballet Russe continue to play an important part in American dance. They can be found on the faculties of ballet schools across the continent, and several have founded important regional ballet companies.

Through its transcontinental tours, the Ballet Russe helped introduce ballet to North American communities. And by settling and working in some of those same communities, Ballet Russe dancers have helped make ballet flourish.

—Jack Anderson

---

**LES BALLETS RUSSES DE MONTE CARLO**

(also Ballets Russes de Colonel Wassily de Basil and eventually the Original Ballet Russe)

Russian emigré ballet company, initially based in Monte Carlo. Founded by Col. Wassily de Basil (a director of L'Opéra Russe à Paris), and René Blum (director of ballet at Théâtre de Monte Carlo); participated in opera productions at Casino Theatre (Théâtre de Monte Carlo), Monte Carlo, from January 1932, with first ballet season commencing 12 April 1932; continued as joint venture of Blum and de Basil until participation of Blum and Théâtre de Monte Carlo ceased officially in 1935; performed under a number of different names, including Les Ballets Russes de Col. W. de Basil, from 1934, the Monte Carlo Ballet Russe (New York), 1933–35, the Russian Ballet (also known as the Covent Garden Russian Ballet), presented by Educational Ballets Ltd. (director, Victor Dandré, de Basil having temporarily lost control), 1938–39, and finally the Original Ballet Russe, from 1939; toured Europe, with major summer seasons in London, from 1933: performed at Covent Garden, 1934–39, and 1947; also undertook three tours of Australia (with a second company, based on Léon Woizikovsky's troupe), 1936–37, as Educational Ballets Ltd., 1938–39, and 1939–40; also made regular winter tours of North America, 1933–38, 1941, 1946–47, South America, 1942–46; toured Spain, 1948; last performance, Palma de Mallorca, 6 November 1948 (a revived company briefly toured England, 1951–52).

## PUBLICATIONS


Beaumont, Cyril, *The Monte Carlo Russian Ballet*, London, 1934

Coton, A.V., *A Prejudice for Ballet*, London, 1938

Victorica, Victoría García, *El Original Ballet Russe en America Latina*, Buenos Aires, 1948

Krokover, Rosalyn, *The New Borzoi Book of Ballets*, New York, 1956

Sorley Walker, Kathrine, *De Basil's Ballets Russes*, London, 1982

Garcia-Márquez, Vicente, *The Ballets Russes: Colonel de Basil's Ballets Russes de Monte Carlo 1932–1952*, New York, 1990


* * *

When Diaghilev died in 1929, it seemed impossible to the shocked ballet community that this would mean an end to the spirit of his company. There was, after all, a large group of dancers now unemployed, many of them unable to return to Russia after the revolution, owing an almost patriotic allegiance to the gypsy life of the company. There was, above all, a repertory of ballets, with their scenery and costumes—ballets which audiences still wanted to see. Despite some ineffectual efforts to keep Diaghilev's company going, nothing comparable was to emerge until April 1932 at the Théâtre de Monte Carlo. Many of the dancers from that company, and much of its repertoire, derived from the ballet troupe of L'Opéra Russe à Paris, a company which was directed by Colonel Wassily de Basil and which was beginning to enjoy some success in independent ballet seasons, firstly under ballet director Bronislava Nijinska, and then under Boris Romanov.

The new company was jointly directed by Colonel de Basil and René Blum. The latter, as director of ballet programming, was able to offer the new company the financial stability of a contract and a home base in Monte Carlo, the old home of Diaghilev's company; but he was increasingly marginalized by the autocratic de Basil. When the company enjoyed an enormous success in London in 1934, advertised as Ballets Russes de Col. W. de Basil—a title which acknowledged neither Blum nor the company's origin in Monte Carlo—the split became irrevocable. The tension between the two men continued to be manifest when Blum founded his own Ballets de Monte Carlo in 1936; de Basil's company was later named the Original Ballet Russe as a form of retort. The rivalry between the two companies, whipped up by the press and taken up by partisan fans, was yet another feature of the exotic culture that surrounded the Ballets Russes.

In the first season, some of the familiar Diaghilev ballets were performed in the versions staged by L'Opéra Russe—Romanov's *Chout* and *Pulcinella*, and Woizikovsky's staging of Fokine's *Petrushka*. After Balanchine, the company's first maître de ballet, Massine and then Fokine took over the post, and supervised accurate revivals of their own works. At other times this continuity was ensured by the régisseur, Serge Grigoriev, and his wife Lubov Tchernicheva, both of whom had been with Diaghilev. It was Tchernicheva who supervised the teaching of the Diaghilev revivals.

By 1934 de Basil had acquired the scenery and costumes for a very large number of Diaghilev ballets. Works such as *Les Matelots*, *Schéhérazade*, *Le Tricorne*, *L'Après-midi d'un faune*, and *Thamar* would become an essential part of the repertoire, not only because they were popular but also because they were cost-effective. In terms of its repertoire, de Basil's company almost literally inherited the mantle of Diaghilev.

In other ways, de Basil's company was very different in style from the late period of Diaghilev's Ballets Russes. The frantic experimenting with new ideas in the visual arts was not to be a major trend, although leading visual artists would work successfully with the company—such as Joán Miró, who designed *Jeux d'enfants*, and Giorgio de Chirico, who designed *Protée* (1938). At the core of the appeal of de Basil's company was to be the dance itself. The company style is encapsulated in Massine's *Le Beau Danube* (new version, 1933), packed with demonstration numbers showing off the abilities of the cast, rushing to an exhilarating finale, but at the same time conveying characterization and narrative tellingly through the danced movement.

Balanchine, Massine, Fokine, and Nijinska, the most significant choreographers who worked for de Basil, were all formerly of Diaghilev's company. Works such as Balanchine's *Cotillon* and *La Concurrence* (both 1932), Nijinska's *Les Cent Baisers* (1935), and Fokine's *Paganini* (1939), provided the company with popular items which sustained its reputation for many years; but it is only Massine amongst these who embarked upon a period of enhanced creativity with de Basil. Apart from the demi-caractère works—*Le Beau Danube* and *Union Pacific* (1934), and the much admired *Jeux d'enfants* (1932)—he created his controversial series of symphonic ballets, *Les Présages*, *Choreartium* (both 1933), and *Symphonie fantastique* (1936). By using the musical form as choreographic material, these works developed the range of balletic subjects, and pointed the way towards non-narrative, "abstract" ballet.

Of new choreographers nurtured from within the company itself, only David Lichine proved to be a significant talent. With the support of Massine and the financial backing of Count Etienne de Beaumont, Lichine's first works, *Nocturne* (1933) and *Les Imaginaires* (1934), met with little success. But with *Francesca de Rimini* (1937), his reputation was established. *Graduation Ball* (1940) has turned out to be his most lasting work, and his version of *The Prodigal Son* in 1938 was considered by many to be superior to Balanchine's.

If the emphasis in Diaghilev's company was on his leading male dancers, the repertoire of de Basil's company was to revolve around the female stars. It is said to have been Balanchine's idea to underline youth and newness by employing the three "baby ballerinas", Tamara Toumanova, Irina Baronova, and Tatiana Riabouchinska. Coming from schools of Russian emigré teachers in Paris—Toumanova and Baronova (both aged thirteen) from the studio of Olga Preobrazhenska, and Riabouchinska (aged sixteen) from Mathilde Kchesinskaya—the three were a publicity man's dream. It was not so much their extreme youth which was astounding, but the maturity of their artistry, and the intuitive subtlety of their interpretations, which delighted audiences and critics alike. They were also individual in looks and style, inspiring not only rivalries among factions in their audiences, but providing the company choreographers with a wide palette of expressive qualities.

Other ballerinas also made distinguished contributions to the company. Two who should be mentioned are Alexandra Danilova, who made famous the memorable role of the Street Dancer in *Le Beau Danube*, and Nina Verchinina, whose distinctive style, influenced by European modern dance, was used so effectively by Massine in the symphonic ballets.

Though frequently on the verge of financial collapse, the company survived for sixteen years, and it is a tribute to de Basil's tenacity that he managed to hold it together. The years 1942–46, during which the company was continuously touring in South America, took a tremendous toll on the dancers. The critic Edwin Denby, who had praised them lavishly in 1941, pronounced the troupe that re-appeared in New York in 1946 "depressingly second-rate", relying on their guest artists to pull them through. Although the dancers retrieved some of their previous form, the real problem was that the era of the Ballets Russes had passed. In America and Britain, national companies were now being established. French ballet was experiencing a regeneration. Such companies had choreographers of their own and ballets in tune with the times. The colonel never had been able to emulate Diaghilev in his knowledge of, and canny involvement with, artistic trends of the day.

However, de Basil's Ballets Russes was an important force in the popularization of ballet: many of the fledgling companies now emerging would depend to some extent on the eager audiences which the Ballets Russes had helped to build. Not just an enthusiasm for ballet, but greater attention to professional training followed in the company's wake, as dancers decided to leave the company, settle down, and set up their own ballet schools. This was a particularly important phenomenon in Australia, where Edouard Borovansky opened his school—the nursery of what was to become the Australian Ballet—and in America, where many former dancers, including Lichine and Riabouchinska, contributed to the development of the national and regional companies.

—Larraine Nicholas

---

## LES BALLETS RUSSES DE SERGE DIAGHILEV

(Diaghilev's Ballets Russes)

Russian ballet company touring outside Russia, 1909–29. Founded by Russian impresario Serge Diaghilev, to present summer seasons of Russian Opera and Ballet in Paris, 1909, with début at Théâtre du Châtelet, May 1909; became a permanent ballet company under Diaghilev's name, 1911, touring throughout Europe, with first visit to London in 1911, South America, 1914, North America, 1916–17; based in Monte Carlo, 1922–29; company disbanded on Diaghilev's death, 1929.

### PUBLICATIONS


Propert, W.A., *The Russian Ballet in Western Europe 1909–1920*, London, 1921

Propert, W.A., *The Russian Ballet 1921–1929*, London, 1931

Lieven, Peter, *The Birth of the Ballets Russes*, translated by L. Zarine, London, 1936

Beaumont, Cyril, *The Diaghilev Ballet in London*, London, 1940

Benois, Alexandre, *Reminiscences of the Russian Ballet*, London and New York, 1941

Beaumont, Cyril, *Complete Book of Ballets*, revised edition, London, 1951

Grigoriev, Serge, *The Diaghilev Ballet 1909–1929*, translated by Vera Bowen, London, 1953

Buckle, Richard, *In Search of Diaghilev*, London, 1955

Sokolova, Lydia, *Dancing for Diaghilev*, London, 1960

Kochno, Boris, *Diaghilev and the Ballets Russes*, translated by Adrienne Foulkes, New York, 1970

Spencer, Charles, *The World of Serge Diaghilev*, London, 1974

Macdonald, Nesta, *Diaghilev Observed by Critics in England and the United States 1911–1929*, London and New York, 1975

Buckle, Richard, *Diaghilev*, London, 1979

Percival, John, *The World of Diaghilev*, revised edition, 1979

Baer, Nancy van Norman (ed.), *The Art of Enchantment: Diaghilev's Ballets Russes 1909–1929*, San Francisco, 1988

Garafola, Lynn, *Diaghilev's Ballets Russes*, New York, 1989

Pozharskaya, Militza, and Volodine, Tatania, *The Art of the Ballets Russes*, translated by V.S. Friedman, London, 1990


* * *

Diaghilev's Ballets Russes, bursting forth from Russia on the Western world in 1909, presented ballet as a *gesamtkunstwerk* and continued to astonish Western audiences for twenty years. It was the product of one of history's greatest impresarios, Serge Diaghilev, and became an international company of great artists over the years.

Although the Ballets Russes was governed at first by a "committee" which included designers, musicians, critics, balletomanes, members of nobility, and dancers, it was nevertheless always Diaghilev who had the final say. It was also he who recognized the market for Russian art, and was able to appoint the perfect collaborators with uncanny foresight.

Not only did the Ballets Russes set new standards for ballet technique, it also contributed a level of choreographic achievement which allowed ballet to make the transition from a classical to a modern art form. The fact that many of the works created for the Ballets Russes remain in the repertories of ballet companies throughout the world today attests to this fact.

Perhaps a more immediate and obvious influence of the Ballets Russes was that which it had on fashion and the decorative arts. The Parisian art and design world was overwhelmed by the colour, fabric, and fashion displayed, particularly in *Schéhérazade* (1910), that sensual epitome of oriental splendour. Credit for this must go to the ballet's designer, Léon Bakst. The results were seen not only in the fashion world, where harem trousers and skirts and voluminous turbans soon became the rage, but also in the jewellery industry, where Bakst's dazzling bold colours inspired new combinations of precious gems.

Thanks to Mikhail Fokine's choreographic originality, the West was able to enjoy the revolutionary works of the Ballets Russes, which, following Fokine's principles, attempted to unify theme with décor, music, and the dance. The new ballets were usually short (one act as opposed to three or four), based on Russian or other exotic motifs, and devoid of meaningless pantomime scenes.

The Ballets Russes brought about remarkable collaborations, not the least of which was *L'Oiseau de feu* (*The Firebird*), a Fokine work with the first musical score of Igor Stravinsky's to be commissioned especially for a ballet. From the time of that 1910 landmark work, Stravinsky was to become one of the

**A poster for Diaghilev's Ballets Russes, Paris season, 1923**

ballet world's most prolific and important composers.

Of great interest to contemporary dance audiences are the two extant works of Nijinsky, both of which created momentous scandals at their premieres. *L'Après-midi d'un faune* (1912) and *Le Sacre du printemps* (1913) inaugurated a new era in the history of dance, the age of the modern ballet. Recent revivals of both works, whether they are exact or approximate reconstructions of the original choreography, still show such integrity, originality, and power that it is difficult to imagine that they are nearly eighty years old. By comparison, Fokine's ballets, colourful and charming as they are, hold far less choreographic interest for us today.

Other landmark works which remain crucial to the development of ballet were Nijinska's *Les Noces* (1923), *Les Biches*, and *Le Train Bleu* (both 1924), all of which can be seen in the repertories of several companies today, Balanchine's signature pieces, *Apollon musagète* (1928) and *Le Fils prodigue* (*The Prodigal Son*, 1929), and the famous, though financially disastrous, revival of *The Sleeping Beauty*, renamed *The Sleeping Princess* by Diaghilev and presented in London in 1921. This last marked the first full production of a complete Petipa ballet outside Russia, and it presented many of the dancers who had originally appeared in the ballet, though in different roles more suitable for their age. The impression this production made on English balletomanes, critics, and dancers was lasting and had much to do with the future development of ballet in Britain.

During its twenty-year existence, the original Ballets Russes served as a training ground for many artists. Over the years the dispersal of the company members and collaborators enriched the formation of ballet schools and companies in the West, particularly in France, Britain, and the U.S. The French gained Lifar, whose influence on the development of ballet at the Paris Opéra was enormous; Britain celebrated the return of Ninette de Valois, Anton Dolin, and Alicia Markova and welcomed Marie Rambert and Tamara Karsavina; and America, most fortunate of all perhaps, adopted George Balanchine and Igor Stravinsky, along with Fokine and numerous other Ballets Russes veterans.

Following Diaghilev's death in 1929, many of the original company members were reunited when René Blum and Colonel de Basil formed the Ballets Russes de Monte Carlo in 1932. Many repertory pieces from the Diaghilev company were retained and performed for many more years. When the Blum/de Basil partnership broke up several years later, Blum enlisted Massine as artistic director and pursued many more successful years of touring, primarily in the U.S. Both the Ballet Russe de Monte Carlo (the Blum/Massine company) and Colonel de Basil's Original Ballet Russe offered many performances to ever-increasing audiences in Europe, the Americas, and Australia, while providing a "home" for some of the world's best dancers and choreographers.

Although the Ballets Russes as directed by Diaghilev ceased to exist over 60 years ago, many of the works created for that company still form an important body in the contemporary repertoire and continue to delight audiences worldwide.

Revivals of works by Fokine, Nijinsky, and Nijinska provide us with a precious glimpse of that golden period in dance history. It is our privilege to be able to enjoy the very ballets which forged the link between nineteenth-century classicism and the modernism which characterizes twentieth-century art.

—Carol Egan

---

## LES BALLETS SUÉDOIS

Swedish ballet company based in Paris, 1920–25. Founded by art patron Rolf de Maré, with dancers from Royal Swedish Ballet and Royal Danish Ballet, 1920; first performance, solo recital for dancer Jean Börlin, in Paris, March 1920, from which sprang larger company, Les Ballets Suédois, with Börlin as principal choreographer and dancer; also involved leading artists of the day, including Léger, Bonnard, and de Chirico, as collaborators; toured internationally, 1920–24; disbanded 1925.

### PUBLICATIONS

Macdougall, Allan Ross, "Ballets Russian and Swedish", *Shadowland*, October 1923

"The Swedish Ballet from France", *Literary Digest*, 15 December 1923

De Maré, Rolf (ed.), *Les Ballets Suédois dans l'art contemporain*, Paris, 1931

*Archives internationales de la danse* (magazine published by the Archives), 20 issues: Paris, 1932–36

Beaumont, Cyril, *Complete Book of Ballets*, revised edition, London, 1951

*Modern Swedish Ballet*, Catalogue of the Victoria and Albert Museum, London, 1970

Clarke, Mary, and Crisp, Clement, *Design for Ballet*, London, 1978

Banes, Sally, "An Introduction to the Ballets Suédois", *Ballet Review* (New York), vol. 7, nos. 2–3, 1978–79

Garafola, Lynn, *Diaghilev's Ballets Russes*, New York, 1989

Häger, Bengt, *Ballets Suédois*, translated by Ruth Sharman, London, 1990

Percival, John, "The Forgotten Company", *Dance and Dancers* (London), April 1991

* * *

Les Ballets Suédois, founded and directed by Rolf de Maré, a wealthy Swede, established itself with its 1920 Paris season as the artistic successor to Diaghilev's declining Ballets Russes. The Ballets Suédois presented ballets derivative of works by its Russian precursor as well as original ballets on themes of Swedish folklore, but the company made its mark with modern ballets in which Swedish choreographer and dancer Jean Börlin collaborated with the avant-garde artists, librettists, and composers of Paris. The Ballets Suédois successfully drew the attention of important European artists of the early 1920s, such as Jean Cocteau, Erik Satie, and Frances Picabia, to the ballet.

*L'Homme et son désir*, first performed by the Ballets Suédois in 1921, was originally conceived in 1917 for the Ballets Russes by poet Paul Claudel, composer Darius Milhaud, and designer Andrée Parr. Diaghilev, however, disliked the ballet's symbolism, dramatic content, and music, and Nijinsky's disintegrating mental health made it impossible for him to dance the leading role which had been created with him in mind. Consequently Claudel, Milhaud, and Parr took their ballet—about a man who spends a night in the Brazilian rain forest—to the Ballets Suédois, believing it to be a more artistically experimental company. The ballet presented a popular avant-garde notion of "the primitive", depicting an exotic place where life consists of a basic struggle between man and nature. The innovative set was constructed with platforms on four levels, and characters included the Moon, the Hours of the Night, Desire, and Exile.

*Les Mariés de la Tour Eiffel* with libretto by Jean Cocteau, music by "Les Six", masks by Jean Hugo, choreography by Jean Börlin, and sets by Irène Lagut, introduced the Dada movement, already gaining ground in the worlds of art and literature, to the dance world. The absurd scenario centres upon a photographer's attempts to catch the "birdie" which has escaped from inside his camera during the taking of a wedding-party photograph. Other characters include a bathing beauty, a lion, and the couple's future child. This ballet incorporates typical Dada themes: intentional absurdity, attack on bourgeoise values, mechanical imagery, and the transposition of ordinary objects to unusual contexts in order to remove preconceptions and to question definitions.

*La Création du monde*, presented by the Ballets Suédois in October 1923, was among the first pieces to bring the avant-garde fascination with black art from Africa and America to the European dance world. Blaise Cendrars, who had just published a book on black folklore, wrote the scenario. Darius Milhaud based his score for jazz orchestra on music he had heard in Harlem clubs, and Fernand Léger created African-inspired animal costumes.

In *Within the Quota*, the Ballets Suédois satirized the American dream. In the ballet, a Swedish immigrant to the United States encounters stereotypical American movie characters, and is ultimately "discovered" and transformed into a movie star by Mary Pickford herself. Börlin's choreography used steps from popular dances of the day, such as the shimmy and the foxtrot, to complement the jazz and ragtime-influenced Cole Porter score.

The Ballets Suédois' final work, *Relâche*, was another Dada-influenced piece. An incredible conglomerate of creative minds collaborated to create this most imaginative and controversial ballet. Conceived by Frances Picabia, composed by Erik Satie, and choreographed by Jean Börlin, the ballet featured a film made by René Clair to be shown between its two acts. Characters in the first act included a smoking fireman and a woman who danced only when there was no music playing. The film, entitled *Entr'acte*, featured a chess match between Man Ray and Marcel Duchamp and shots of a dancer photographed from below a transparent floor. In the second act, the fireman poured water from one container to another and Erik Satie drove on to the stage in a small car. After stretching the definition of ballet to its limits with *Relâche*, Jean Börlin and Rolf de Maré realized they could go no further and dissolved the company.

The Ballets Suédois took the artistic and expressive style of ballet started by the Ballets Russes and carried it to its artistic limits. In the summer of 1923, the people of Paris looked forward to seeing Isadora Duncan, the Ballets Russes, and the Ballets Suédois all on their stages during one season, causing one observant Parisian to note, "Paris is about to have the opportunity of seeing the Cause, the Effect, and the After-Effect".

—Claudia B. Stone

---

**BALLON (Balon), Claude**
(mistakenly called Jean by some modern writers)
French dancer, dancing master, and choreographer. Born in Paris, son of court dancing master François Ballon, probably in 1671. Dance training unknown: may have studied with father. Married dancer Marie Dufort, 4 July 1696: three children. First known appearance as dancer in *Orontée*, Chantilly, 1688; début at L'Académie royale de musique (Paris Opéra), 1690; performed in London, April 1699; retired from Opéra, c. 1712, to become dancer and resident choreographer for the Duchesse du Maine's theatre, Sceaux, c.1713–18; appointed dancing master to Louis XV, 1715, Compositeur des Entrées des ballets du Roi (Composer of the King's Ballets), and director of the Académie royale de danse, succeeding Beauchamps, from 1719; Maitre-à-Dancer des Enfants de France (Dancing master to the Children of France), from 1731; also directed private dancing school with his father, Paris, 1696–1699: private pupils included Marie Sallé and her brother, Monsieur Sallé. Died in Versailles, 9 May 1744.

## ROLES

1688 A Little Faun and Amour (cr) in *Orontée* (tragédie-lyrique; mus. Lorenzani, chor. Pécour), Chateau de Chantilly

1689 A Zephir (cr) in *Le Palais de flore* (ballet; chor. probably Beauchamps), Trianon

1690 Dancer in *Cadmus et Hermione* (tragédie-lyrique; mus. Lully, chor. probably Pécour), Opéra, Paris

1691 Tailleur, and Cuisinier in *Le Bourgeois Gentilhomme* (comédie-ballet by Moliére, chor. Pécour), Court Theatre

"Important" in *Ballet des Nations* (second entrée in *Le Bourgeois Gentilhomme*; comédie-ballet; mus. Lully, chor. Pécour), Court Theatre

Ensemble and Menelas (solo; cr) in *Ballet des passions* (ballet; chor. Pécour), Collège Louis le Grand

1692 Un Berger (cr) in *Le Ballet de Villeneuve St. George* (ballet; mus. Colasse, chor. probably Pécour), Villeneuve St. Georges

1697 Faune (cr) in *Issé* (pastorale-héroique; mus. Destouches, chor. Pécour), Opéra, Paris

Espagnol and More (duets; cr) in *L'Europe galante* (opéra-ballet; mus. Campra, chor. Pécour), Opéra, Paris

1698 Un Français and Pan (solos; cr) in *Ballet de la paix* (ballet), Collège Louis le Grand

1699 Un Captif (solo; cr) in *Amadis de Grèce* (tragédie-lyrique; mus. Destouches, chor. Pécour), Opéra, Paris

Plaisir burlesque, Habitant de l'Ile fortune, Habitant de l'Ile inconnue in *Intermèdes de la comédie des fées* (mus. Lalande), Fontainebleau

Un Dieu (solo; cr) in *Marthésie, Reine des Amazones* (tragédie-lyrique; mus. Destouches, chor. Pécour), Fontainebleau

Zephir (solo) in *Atys* (tragédie-lyrique; mus. Lully, chor. Pécour), Opéra, Paris

1700 Seigneur Scythe (solo) in *Mascarade des Amazones* (ballet-mascarade), Court Theatre, Marly

A Faun in *Impromptu* (ballet-mascarade), Chateau de St. Maur

Le Marié (duet) in *La Noce de village* (ballet-mascarade; mus. Philidor) Court Theatre, Marly

Matelot Basque (duet) in *Mascarade du Vaisseau Marchand* (ballet-mascarade; mus. Philidor), Court Theatre, Marly

Dieu du Ruisseau (solo; cr) in *Canente* (tragédie-lyrique; mus. Colasse, chor. Pécour), Opéra, Paris

Hero (solo; cr) in *Hésione* (tragédie-lyrique; mus. Campra, chor. Pécour), Opéra, Paris

1701 Entrée (cr) in *Scylla* (tragédie-lyrique; mus. Théobald), Opéra, Paris

Suivant de Pluton (solo; cr) in *Aréthuse* (ballet; mus. Campra, chor. Pécour), Opéra, Paris

Chef de milice, Un dragon (solos; cr) in *Jason* (ballet; chor. Pécour), Collège Louis le Grand

Lydien (cr) in *Omphale* (tragédie-lyrique; mus. Destouches, chor. Pécour), Opéra, Paris

1702 Triton (solo) in *Phaeton* (tragédie-lyrique; mus. Lully, chor. Pécour), Opéra, Paris

Peuple d'Europe, Habitant d'Anticyre (cr) in *Médus, Roi des Mèdes* (tragédie-lyrique; mus. Bouvard, chor. Pécour), Opéra, Paris

Mercure (solo; cr) in *L'Empire de l'imagination* (ballet; chor. Pécour), Collège Louis le Grand

Matelot (cr) in *Fragments de Monsieur de Lully* (ballet; mus. Lully, Campra, chor. Pécour), Opéra, Paris

More, Peuples de Palestine (cr) in *Tancrède* (tragédie-lyrique; mus. Campra, chor. Pécour), Opéra, Paris

1703 Jeux Junonien in *Persée* (tragédie-lyrique; mus. Lully, chor. Pécour), Opéra, Paris

Habitant de Damas (solo), Habitant Champètre (duet) in *Armide* (tragédie-lyrique; mus. Lully, chor. Pécour), Opéra, Paris

1704 Chef de la feste marine (solo), La Danse (duet), Masque (duet) (cr) in *Le Carnaval et la folie* (comédie-ballet; mus. Destouches, chor. Pécour), Opéra, Paris

Berger (solo) in *Isis* (tragédie-lyrique; mus. Lully, chor. Pécour), Opéra, Paris

Scythe (cr) in *Iphigénie en Tauride* (tragédie-lyrique; mus. Desmarets, Campra, chor. Pécour), Opéra, Paris

Suivant de Polymène (solo) in *Acis et Galatée* (pastorale-héroique; mus. Lully, chor. Pécour), Opéra, Paris

Peuples de Carthage (duet) in *Didon* (tragédie-lyrique; mus. Desmarets, chor. Pécour), Opéra, Paris

Duet (cr) in *Le Prince de Cathay* (comédie-ballet; mus. Mathau, chor. Pécour), "Divertissement de Sceaux", given for the Duchesse de Maine at Chatenay

Fête marine (duet), Berger in *Télémaque* (tragédie-lyrique; mus. Colasse, Campra, Charpentier, Desmarets, Rebel, chor. Pécour), Opéra, Paris

1705 Triton (solo; cr) in *Alcine* (tragédie-lyrique; mus. Campra, chor. Pécour), Opéra, Paris

Insulaire (solo) and Le Marié (duet) in *Roland* (tragédie-lyrique; mus. Lully, chor. Pécour), Opéra, Paris

Chef de la fête (solo; cr) in *La Vénitienne* (comédie-ballet; mus. La Barre, chor. Pécour), Opéra, Paris

Un Suivant d'Alcide (solo), Zéphir (duet) in *Alcide; ou, La Mort d'Hercule* (tragédie-lyrique; mus. Lully, Marais, chor. Pécour), Opéra, Paris

Solo (cr) in *La Tarantole* (comédie-ballet; mus. Matho, chor. Pécour), "Divertissement de Sceaux", given for the Duchesse de Maine at Chatenay

Sauvage (solo; cr) in *L'Empire du temps* (ballet; chor. Pécour), Collège Louis le Grand

Fête marine (duet; cr) in *Philomène* (tragédie-lyrique; mus. de la Coste, chor. Pécour), Opéra, Paris

Triton, Berger in *Le Triomphe de l'amour* (ballet; mus. Lully, chor. Pécour), Opéra, Paris

1706 Faune and Triton (solos; cr) in *Alcione* (tragédie-lyrique; mus. Marais, chor. Pécour), Opéra, Paris

Mycénien (solo; cr) in *Cassandre* (tragédie-lyrique; mus.

**Claude Ballon**

Bertin, Bouvard, chor. Pécour) Opéra, Paris
Dancer (cr) in *Divertissement de Sceaux* (comédie-ballet; mus. Gilliers), for Duchesse du Maine, Chatenay
La Danse (duet; cr) in *Le Professeur et la folie* (divertissement; mus. Destouches, chor. Pécour), Opéra, Paris
Demon (solo) in *Alceste* (tragédie-lyrique; mus. Lully, chor. Pécour), Chatenay
1707 Solo in (cr) in *Bradamante* (tragédie-lyrique; mus. de la Coste, chor. Pécour), Opéra, Paris
Intermèdes (cr) in *Mostellaria* (comédie-ballet by Malézieu after Plautus), "Divertissement de Sceaux", given for the Duchesse de Maine at Chatenay
Indien (solo), Berger in *Ballet des Saisons* (revival of *Les Saisons*, 1695; mus. Lully, Colasse, chor. Pécour), Opéra, Paris
Berger (duet) in *Thésée* (tragédie-lyrique; mus. Lully, chor. Pécour), Opéra, Paris
1708 Sauvage (solo; cr) in *Hippodamie* (tragédie-lyrique; mus. Campra, chor. Pécour), Opéra, Paris
L'Amérique (solo) in *Thetis et Pélée* (tragédie-lyrique; mus. Colasse, chor. Pécour), Opéra, Paris
Africain, Songe agréable (duet) in *Atys* (tragédie-lyrique; mus. Lully, chor. Pécour), Opéra, Paris
1709 Aegypans (duet), Peuples (cr) in *Sémélé* (tragédie-lyrique; mus. Marais, chor. Pécour), Opéra, Paris
Faune (cr) in *Méléagre* (tragédie-lyrique; mus. Baptistin, also known as Stuck), Opéra, Paris
1710 Matelot (duet), Berger (cr) in *Diomède* (tragédie-lyrique; mus. Bertin, chor. Pécour), Opéra, Paris
Matelot, Gondolier (duet; cr) in *Fêtes Vénitiennes* (ballet; mus. Campra, chor. Pécour), Opéra, Paris
1714 Horace (duet) in *Apollon et les muses* (divertissement from *Les Horaces*, play by Corneille; mus. La Motte, Mouret, chor. probably Ballon, Prévost), Fête for the Duchesse du Maine, Sceaux
1720 Ordonnateur de la fête (duet), Bohémien, Le Marié (cr) in *L'Inconnu* (ballet; mus. Lalande, chor. Ballon), Tuileries, Paris
Matelot (duet; cr) in *Les Folies de Gardenio* (ballet; mus. Lalande, chor. Ballon), Tuileries, Paris
1721 Chasseur (cr) in *Les Éléments* (ballet; mus. Lalande, Destouches, chor. Ballon), Tuileries

## WORKS

1714 *Le Comte de Gabalis et les peuples élémentaires* (grand divertissement; mus. Bourgeois), Sceaux
1720 *L'Inconnu* (ballet; mus. Lalande), Tuileries, Paris
*Les Folies de Gardenio* (ballet; mus. Lalande), Tuileries, Paris
1721 *Les Éléments* (ballet; mus. Lalande, Destouches), Tuileries, Paris
1722 *Les Éléments* (ballet; mus. Lalande, Destouches), Opéra, Paris
1728 *Monsieur de Pourceaugnac* (comédie-ballet by Molière), Versailles

**Other works include:** Ballroom dances recorded in the Feuillet notation, and published in *Recueil de danses Feuillet Dezais—La Sylvie, La Dombes* (1712); *La Mélanie* (1713); *La Gavotte de Sceaux, Le Rigaudon* (1714); *La Transilvanie* (1715); *La Clairmont, La Gavotte du Roi, La Bourée nouvelle* (1716); *La de Bergue* (1717); *La Brissac, La Czarienne* (1718); *La Montpensier, La Lorraine* (1719); *La Poitevine, La Modène, La Villeroi, La Boufflers* (1720); *Gaillarde de M. Ballon, Minuet de M. Ballon* (date unknown); in *A collection of new ball and stage dances composed by several masters*, c.1720—*La Mattelotte*; in *Méthode pour apprendre soi-mesme la Chorégraphie*, 1757—*La Czarienne.*

## PUBLICATIONS


Weaver, John, *An Essay Towards an History of Dancing*, London, 1712
Trévoux, A., *Les Divertissements de Sceaux*, 1722
Rameau, Pierre, *Le Maître à danser*, Paris, 1725; as *The Dancing Master*, translated by Cyril Beaumont, London, n.d.
Parfaict, les Frères (Claude et François), *Dictionnaire des théâtres*, 7 volumes, Paris 1756
Jal, A., *Dictionnaire critique de biographies et d'histoire*, Paris, 1867
Lawson, Joan, *A History of Ballet and its Makers*, London, 1964
Winter, Marian Hannah, *The Pre-Romantic Ballet*, London, 1974
Ferguson, Ian, "Who was Monsieur Balon?", *Dancing Times* (London), December 1982
Astier, Régine, "La vie quotidienne des danseurs sous l'ancien régime", *Les Gouts réunis*, no. 3, January 1983
Astier, Régine, "Claude Ballon, Dancing-master to Louis XV", *La Recherche en danse* (Paris), no. 3, 1984


* * *

Inexplicably called "Jean" by all modern dance historians, Claude Ballon made a spectacular career at the Paris Opéra in the early eighteenth century before moving on to even more prestigious court appointments—dancing master to the Duchesse du Maine and resident choreographer at her Sceaux theatre, and dancing master to Louis XV and composer of the king's ballets at Versailles. He was said to have had dazzling good looks, intelligence, great charm, and ease of manners alongside an outstanding performing talent. As partner to prima ballerina Subligny, he had first established his reputation as a "danseur noble, a specialty he was to define further and refine until his style became the yardstick by which other dancers were judged. The frères Parfaict attempted to describe his qualities: "He was of a size below average which is perhaps better fitting for the dance, he had a perfect ear, beautiful legs and admirable arms. To these [qualities], were added lightness, vitality and a certain air of tenderness which pervaded all his attitudes—especially in the pas-de-deux. One will not be surprised at the reputation which this dancer acquired at the Opéra and still enjoys to day."

Through his subsequent partnership with Françoise Prévost, Ballon came to experiment with the dramatization of dance, and seems to have gained in stature as an interpreter. An engraving representing him masked, dancing in a "grotesque" entrée from the *Carnaval et la folie*, together with his renowned experiments at Sceaux, evidently leading to the concept of the "*ballet d'action*", point to his versatility as a performer. His English colleague, ballet master John Weaver, wrote that "although an excellent dancer, he pretended to nothing more than a graceful motion of the body, with strong and nimble risings and the casting of his body into several agreeable postures . . . But for expressing anything in nature but modulated notions, it was never in his head."

It is to be surmised that Ballon made profit of his London season and went on to experiment at home with the innovative concepts he had encountered on his English tour. No solo for Claude Ballon has been recorded in the Feuillet notation, but the loure which he performed with Mr. Labbé "before his Majesty King William", during his London season, seemed to have been devised to set off the whole gamut of his virtuoso skills. With its heavily ornamented steps facing in all directions, its swift jumps, pirouettes, and sustained ronds-de-jambes, the dance demands perfect aplomb, superb control, and elegance. In 1701, the *Post-Boy* reported: "There is great expectation from the boy that this day dances at the King's playhouse ... He being equal to Monsieur Ballon." What better testimony to the lasting effect Claude Ballon had in England than this simple remark!

Seven duets with Marie Thèrése de Subligny have survived in the Feuillet notation, but unfortunately there is nothing left of any dance with Mlle Prévost, which makes it difficult to substantiate the idea of an evolution of his style. Nor are there any existing choreographic scores for the ballets he composed for the French court; and, as far as his annual collection of ballroom dances (engraved by Dezais) is concerned, it is not significantly different from that of Pécour. Dezais assured us that Ballon's dances were "the talk of the court" (Preface to the 1719 collection), possibly because many were choreographed as "suites" instead of as the more traditional type of dance with a single rhythm.

Claude Ballon's life style was lavish and he may have been the first male dancer to conduct himself as a celebrity, demanding, receiving, and spending huge fees, eliciting dubious publicity, hobnobbing with the great and the mighty, and altogether setting up a precedent for "star" treatment for generations to come.

—Régine Astier

**La Barberina, in an engraving by C.B. Glassbach**

---

**BARBERINA, La**

Italian dancer. Born Barbara Campanini in Parma, Italy, 1721. Studied with Neapolitan comic dancer Antonio Rinaldi, known as Fossan, or Fossano (often referred to in modern sources as Rinaldi Fossano). Married Carl Ludwig von Cocceji, 1749 (div. 1788). First appearance at L'Académie royale de musique (Opéra), Paris, 1739; performed at royal court, Fontainebleau, 1739, and danced in special performances at Versailles with troupe from the Comédie-Française, 1740; engaged by John Rich to perform in London, performing at Covent Garden and Lincoln's Inn Fields, season 1740–41; returned to Opéra, Paris, 1741, dancing again in London, 1741–42; appeared at Smock Alley Theatre, Dublin, 1742; went to Venice, 1743; engaged as première danseuse (at the request of Frederick II), Prussian Court, Berlin, 1744–49; became Comtesse de Campanini; abbess of institution for Poor Ladies of Good Birth until her death. Died in Barschau, Silesia, 7 June 1799.

**ROLES**

1739 Second entrée, La Musique (cr) in *Les Festes d'Hébé; ou, Les Talents lyriques* (ballet; mus. Rameau), Opéra, Paris
Principal dancer in *Zaïde, Reine de Grenade* (opera; mus. Royer), Opéra, Paris
Le Bouffon (with Fossan) in *Momus amoureux* (entrée), added to *Zaïde* (mus. Royer), Opéra, Paris
Plaisir in *Jeux et plaisir*, ballet in *Dardanus* (tragédie; mus. Rameau), Opéra, Paris

1740 Principal dancer in *Italian Peasants* (divertissement), Covent Garden, London
Principal dancer in *Le Tirolesi* (divertissement), Covent Garden, London
Danseuse in *Mars and Venus* (pantomime-ballet; probably after Weaver), Covent Garden, London

1741 Génies du feu in *L'Empire de l'amour* (mus. Moncrif), Opéra, Paris
Terpsichore in *Les Festes grecques et romaines* (ballet héroique; mus. Colin de Blamont), Opéra, Paris

1744 Principal dancer in *Catone in Utica* (mus. Graun), Comédie-Française, Berlin
Principal dancer in *Artaserse* (mus. Hasse), Hofoper, Berlin
Principal dancer in *La Clemenza di Tito* (mus. Hasse), Hofoper, Berlin
Principal dancer in *Alessandro e Poro* (mus. Graun), Hofoper, Berlin

1745 Principal dancer in *Lucio Papirio* (mus. Graun), Hofoper, Berlin
Principal dancer in *Adriano in Siria* (mus. Graun), Hofoper, Berlin
The Statue in *Pygmalion* (Lany), Hofoper, Berlin

1746 Principal dancer in *Domofoonte re di Tracia* (mus. Graun), Hofoper, Berlin
Principal dancer in *Cajo Fabricio* (mus. Graun), Hofoper, Berlin

1747 Principal dancer in *Arminio* (mus. Hasse), Hofoper, Berlin
Principal dancer in *Le Feste galanti* (mus. Graun), Hofoper, Berlin

1748 Principal dancer in *Cinna* (mus. Graun), Hofoper, Berlin
Principal dancer in *L'Europa galante* (mus. Graun), Hofoper, Berlin

## PUBLICATIONS

Röseler, W., *Die Barbarina*, Berlin, 1890
Dacier, E., *Mlle Sallé*, Paris, 1909
MacGormack, Gilson, B., "La Barberina", *Dancing Times* (London), December 1930
Winter, Marian Hannah, *The Pre-Romantic Ballet*, London, 1974
Dall'Ongaro, Giuseppe, *La Barberina*, Novara, 1987

* * *

The life of the eighteenth-century Italian-born dancer Barbara Campanini, "La Barberina", inspired not only a film but also a ballet, more than two centuries after her death. This was not on the strength of her dancing alone; La Barberina's meteoric rise owed as much to her shrewdly-conducted liaisons with influential men as to technical expertise.

Barbara Campanini was born in 1721 in Parma, where she studied with Antonio Rinaldi, known as Fossano. In 1739 Campanini made her début, partnered by Fossano, at the Académie royale (the Opéra) in Paris. She was an immediate success, partly because she faced little serious competition; Camargo had temporarily retired from the stage and Marie Sallé was about to retire (some liked to claim as a result of Barberina's success). La Barberina's confidence and almost acrobatic style, typically Italian, were all the better received. Her entrechats, pirouettes, and jetés battus were noted in particular. It was not long before she became the mistress of the Prince de Carignan, Inspecteur Genéral of the Opéra, who kept her in an apartment in the rue Vivienne. Unfortunately he was not her only visitor there, and their relationship evidently soured when de Carignan found La Barberina entertaining Lord Arundell.

La Barberina's reputation spread beyond Paris, and in 1740 she went to London at the invitation of John Rich, producer and director of the opera at Covent Garden, where she received as warm a reception as she had experienced in Paris. Her audience on opening night included King George II himself, and in the following ten days there were two command performances for the Prince of Wales.

In 1741 the chief designer at the Paris Opéra, Jean-Nicolas Servandoni, was sent to London to persuade La Barberina to renew her Opéra contract and return to France. She accepted the invitation, but returned to Paris to find that de Carignan had died and another dancer, Marianne Cochois, was the centre of attention. Disliking competition, La Barberina returned to England. In the following two years she made further appearances at Covent Garden, in programmes tailored to the English taste for the crude or comic—a taste which seems to have been shared by the royal family, who continued to attend La Barberina's performances. In 1742 she danced at Smock Alley Theatre, Dublin.

Meanwhile the new King of Prussia, the future Frederick the Great, was establishing an opera company designed to rival the Paris Opéra itself. He decided to engage La Barberina as première danseuse. At this point, La Barberina's romantic and professional commitments threatened to clash disastrously. She signed an agreement to appear in Berlin early in 1744, but when the time came, preferred to stay in Venice with her lover, the English Lord Stuart Wortley Mackenzie. Frederick, however, forced the Republic of Venice to conduct La Barberina to the Austrian frontier, from which point she was taken to Berlin. This episode seems to have been forgotten by the time of La Barberina's highly successful Berlin début on 13 May, which inspired the king to hire a corps de ballet (in which the young Noverre started his career) and award his première danseuse a three-year contract with the enormous salary of 7,000 thalers a year, on condition that she remained unmarried during this time.

Her position as royal favourite did not, however, prevent La Barberina from becoming involved with Carl Ludwig von Cocceji, the son of the king's chancellor, within four years of her arrival in Berlin. The affair resulted in a scandal so serious that Cocceji's parents requested his banishment, presumably for his own protection. Cocceji and La Barberina, however, were married secretly in 1749 and left Berlin for Silesia. According to Casanova, who visited Potsdam Palace in 1764, Frederick was heartbroken but was soon consoled by his new première danseuse, Marianne Cochois, the dancer who had usurped La Barberina's position in the limelight of the Paris Opéra.

La Barberina's marriage to Cocceji lasted only until 1759, when they were formally separated. Their divorce did not become official until 1788, when the king allowed La Barberina to remain Comtesse de Campanini. At the end of her life, La Barberina endowed a convent for impoverished gentlewomen, over which she presided as prioress until her death on 7 June 1799.

—Jessica Griffin

---

**BARONOVA, Irina**

Russian/British dancer. Born 13 March 1919 in Petrograd. Studied in Romania, and with Olga Preobrazhenska, Paris. Married (1) German Sevastianov, 1936 (div.); (2) Cecil G. Tennant, 1946 (d. 1967): three children; (3) German Sevastianov (remarried). Soloist, Paris Opéra, 1930, and Théâtre Mogador, 1931; engaged by Balanchine (at age thirteen) as ballerina, Ballets Russes de Monte Carlo, 1932, remaining with company (various Ballets Russes companies under the direction of de Basil), until 1939; ballerina, Original Ballet Russe, 1940–41, and Ballet Theatre (later American Ballet Theatre), New York, 1941–42; also performed with Roxy Theater, New York, 1943, and Massine's Ballet Russe Highlights, 1945; guest artist, Original Ballet Russe, touring Cuba and Rio de Janeiro, 1946; also appeared in several films, including *Florian* (dir. Edwin L. Marin, 1940) and *Yolanda* (Mexico, 1942); and appeared in plays and musicals, including as Anna Viskinova in *Follow the Girls* (musical by G. Bolton and E. Davies; chor. C. Littlefield), London, 1945; as ballerina in *Bullet in the Ballet* (play by C. Brahms and S. Simon), British tour, 1946; and as Tania Karpova in *Dark Eyes* (comedy by E. Miranova and E. Leontovich), U.S., 1947, and London, 1948; member, Technical Committee, and occasional teacher, Royal Academy of Dancing, London.

## ROLES

1931 Grand Ballet des Nymphes (cr) in *Orphée aux enfers* (opera; mus. Offenbach; chor. Balanchine), Théâtre Mogador, Paris

1932 Young Girl in *La Concurrence* (Balanchine), Ballets Russes de Monte Carlo, Monte Carlo

Ensemble, Valse (cr) in *Suites de danse* (Balanchine), Ballets Russes de Monte Carlo, Monte Carlo

Pas de quatre in *Chout* (Romanov), Ballets Russes de Monte Carlo

1933 Passion (cr) in *Les Présages* (Massine), Ballets Russes de Monte Carlo, Monte Carlo
The Rose Maid (cr) in *Beach* (Massine), Ballets Russes de Monte Carlo, Monte Carlo
Josephina (cr) in *Scuola di Ballo* (Massine), Ballets Russes de Monte Carlo, Monte Carlo
The First Hand (cr) in *Le Beau Danube* (revised version; Massine), Ballets Russes de Monte Carlo, Monte Carlo
The First Betrothed Pair (cr) in *Nocturne* (Lichine), Ballets Russes de Monte Carlo, Paris
The Top in *Jeux d'enfants* (Massine), de Basil's Ballets Russes, London
Odette in *Swan Lake*, (one-act version; after Ivanov), Ballets Russes de Monte Carlo, London
1934 Swan Princess in *Les Contes russes* (revival; Massine), de Basil's Ballets Russes de Monte Carlo, London
Ballerina in *Petrushka* (Fokine), de Basil's Ballets Russes
1935 Princess (cr) in *Les Cent baisers* (Nijinska), de Basil's Ballets Russes, London
Girl in *Le Spectre de la rose* (Fokine), de Basil's Ballets Russes, London
1936 The Young Lady (cr) in *Le Pavillon* (Lichine), de Basil's Ballets Russes, London
1937 The Queen of Shemakhan (cr) in *Le Coq d'or* (new production; Fokine), de Basil's Ballets Russes, London
1939 The Divine Genius (cr) in *Paganini* (Fokine), Covent Garden Russian Ballet (de Basil's company), London
1941 Title role (cr) in *Slavonika* (Psota), Ballet Theatre, Mexico City
Boulotte (cr) in *Bluebeard* (Fokine), Ballet Theatre, Mexico City
Aurora in *Princess Aurora* (suite from *The Sleeping Beauty*; Dolin after Petipa), Ballet Theatre, Mexico City
One of Seven Variations in *Princess Aurora* (suite from *The Sleeping Beauty*; Dolin after Petipa), Ballet Theatre, Mexico City
1942 Swanilda in *Coppélia* (Semenoff after Saint-Léon), Ballet Theatre, Mexico City
Aphrodite/Helen (cr) in *Helen of Troy* (Lichine), Ballet Theatre, Detroit
1945 Principal dancer in *Polish Festival*, *Russian Dance*, *Strange Sarabande* (Divertissements; Massine), Massine's Ballet Russe Highlights, U.S. tour
Peasant Girl (cr) in *Leningrad Symphony* (Massine), Massine's Ballet Russe Highlights, New York

**Other roles include:** for the Ballets Russes—Principal dancer in *Les Sylphides* (Fokine), Lady Gay in *Union Pacific* (Massine), Street Dancer in *Le Beau Danube* (Massine), Tarantella in *La Boutique fantasque* (Massine), Columbine in *Le Carnaval* (Fokine), Young girl in *Cotillon* (Balanchine), Guinevere in *Francesca da Rimini* (Fokine), Shuttlecock in *Jeux d'enfants* (Massine), leading guest in *Les Noces* (Nijinska), Aurora in *Aurora's Wedding* (after Petipa), Zobeïde in *Schéhérazade* (Fokine), title role in *Firebird* (Fokine), Mariuccia in *The Good-Humoured Ladies* (Massine), first and second movements in *Choreartium* (Massine), Lucille in *Le Bourgeois Gentilhomme* (Balanchine), Snow Maiden in *Le Soleil de nuit* (Massine), the Beloved in *Symphonie fantastique* (Massine); for Ballet Theatre—Lisette (Lise) in *La Fille mal gardée* (staged Nijinska), Can-Can in *The Fantastic Toyshop* (*La Boutique fantasque*; Massine).

**PUBLICATIONS**

By Baronova:
"Dancing for de Basil", *About the House* (London), June 1964
Interview in Finch, Tamara, "Working with Great Choreographers", *Dancing Times* (London), January 1989

About Baronova:
Haskell, Arnold, "The De Basil Ballet, 1930–1935", *Dancing Times* (London), October 1935
Barzel, Ann, "Irina Baronova", *Dance* (East Stroudsburg, PA), February 1940
Davidson, Gladys, *Ballet Biographies*, revised edition, London, 1954
Anthony, Gordon, "The Baby Ballerinas", *Dancing Times* (London), April 1973
Walker, Kathrine Sorley, *De Basil's Ballets Russes*, London, 1982
Terry, Walter, "Baby Ballerinas", *Ballet News* (New York), January 1982
García-Márquez, Vicente, *Les Ballets Russes*, New York, 1990

* * *

Every age can boast dancers who came to fame at absurdly young ages, but only de Basil's Ballets Russes could boast three such prodigies at one time, Irina Baronova and Tamara Toumanova (both thirteen when they joined de Basil in 1932) and Tatiana Riabouchinska (fifteen), whose fame did not fade, but grew with the years. As performers, these "Baby Ballerinas" were never judged as children; their performances were, technically and emotionally, adult, and their talents did not fade over the years, but matured and deepened. The rivalry between them, whether real or fostered by partisan audiences, added an extra frisson to performances and, although different in character and style, they were frequently compared and contrasted with each other.

It was Balanchine who discovered Baronova with Toumanova in the Paris studio of Olga Preobrazhenska. Through a mixture of outstanding natural ability, hard work, and a desire to compete with her contemporaries, Baronova's technique was already formidable, but so controlled that the most intricate difficulties appeared effortless. But, from her first appearances on stage, it became clear that this was not just a technical brilliance. Technique was always used expressively, in the service of the particular role; thus the fouettés which Baronova and Toumanova could execute so effortlessly were used in *Jeux d'enfants* in combinations of doubles and singles to express the characteristics of the Top. Audiences were always amazed when the mature young woman they had seen on stage was revealed at the stage door as a short-socked schoolgirl, clutching her teddy bear.

The lack of a normal childhood, inevitable in the life of a rootless Russian refugee, meant that Baronova was experienced beyond her years. Early in her career, she became aware of her responsibilities—to her audience, to the company, her teachers, and her parents—and determined to live up to her early successes and the faith that de Basil had placed in her. Her artistic development was helped by contact with the world-famous musicians and artists who worked with the company, including Stravinsky, Derain, Bérard, and Miro. Her interpretative and emotional development, her understanding of period style, as well as the development of theatre skills like make-up and hairdressing, owed much to Lubov Tchernicheva. Cast as Passion in the second movement of *Les Présages*, Baronova had to ask Tchernicheva to explain the emotion. To this, she added

**Irina Baronova in *Le Beau Danube*, Ballets Russes de Monte Carlo, London, 1933**

her own extraordinarily intuitive response to the choreography and the music. The result was an extraordinary evocation of young love, overlaid with the knowledge and anguish of parting.

Baronova's roles encompassed a remarkably wide range, emotionally and stylistically. Not for her the luxury of a single choreographer devoted to exploiting her particular talents. She embraced with equal success the very different styles of Balanchine, Massine, Nijinska, Fokine, Petipa, and Ivanov. Her range of expression was extraordinary, extending from the passion of *Les Présages* to the jealousy of the Top in *Jeux d'enfants*; from the light comedy of *Le Beau Danube* and *Scuola di Ballo* to the romanticism of the Girl in *Le Spectre de la rose*. She understood the delicate balance between puppet and woman of the Ballerina in *Petrushka* as well as the insouciant Lady Gay in *Union Pacific*. Her imperious, sulky Princess in Nijinska's *Les Cent Baisers*, with its intricate, complicated footwork and batterie, was in complete contrast to her transformation into Fokine's exotic, smouldering, taunting Queen of Shemakhan in *Le Coq d'or*, characterized by its sinuous Oriental movements. All this might argue a demi-caractère dancer, but in *Swan Lake* and *Aurora's Wedding*, she revealed herself as a ballerina in the great classical tradition.

Baronova is remembered for her warmth, joyfulness, and gaiety, for her brio and sense of style, and for her total confidence and willingness to take risks. Her line, described by Haskell as "reaching into the infinite", was clean and classical, her unbroken flow of movement like rich cream. Of the three "Baby Ballerinas", she had the greatest range and sense of character. She developed true ballerina authority without its mannerisms, allied to a warm womanliness.

She left de Basil in 1939. Aged only 20, she had danced, in nine years, more than most principals of today do in a lifetime, and at an age when many dancers today are still at school with perhaps three lessons a week, she was bearing the responsibility of a ballerina, dancing every night with the world's leading international company. It was not surprising that this intelligent young woman should suffer a natural reaction against dancing and look outside ballet for new artistic and emotional experiences.

For Baronova this included a spell in Hollywood, before she joined Ballet Theatre. At first she appeared to have been badly influenced by Hollywood; there was a tendency to over-project and rely upon "star" status, but these faults were soon eradicated, and her natural sumptuousness, authority, and ease returned. After touring with Massine's Ballet Russe Highlights and making guest appearances with de Basil, however, Baronova returned to England to marry, retiring from the stage to devote herself to her family. It was Fonteyn who persuaded her out of retirement to serve on the Technical Committee of the Royal Academy of Dancing, and she also undertook some teaching and coaching.

Baronova's career was brief and brilliant, but her contribution to the development and popularization of ballet must not be underestimated. Audiences for ballet before the 1930s were limited, drawn from relatively narrow social strata. With the coming of the de Basil Ballets Russes and the "Baby Ballerinas", the press seized upon the seeming glamour of the company, enticing audiences from the theatre and from the cinema to see ballet for the first time. Public interest in ballet reached hitherto unknown heights, and created a new, wider audience, drawn from all walks of life, from which dance all over the world would eventually benefit.

—Sarah C. Woodcock

---

## BARTÓK, Béla

Hungarian composer. Born in Nagyszentmiklós, 25 March 1881. First piano lessons with mother, Paula Voit; entered gymnasium at Nagyvárad (now Oradea, Romania), 1891, and continued music studies with Ferenc Kersch; studied piano with Ludwig Burger, Pozsany; later studied with Laszló Erhal and Anton Hyrtl; attended Budapest Academy of Music, 1899–1903. Married (1) pupil Márta Ziegler, 1909 (div.); (2) pupil Ditta Pásztory, 1923. Earliest compositions, most of them dances, at age nine; appointed to piano professorship, Budapest Academy of Music, 1907; first major theatre work, opera *Duke Bluebeard's Castle*, composed in 1911; completed ballet, *The Wooden Prince* (*A fából faragott királyfi*), 1917 (premiere same year at Budapest Opera House); visited London and Paris, 1922; premiere of *The Miraculous Mandarin*, Cologne, 1926; further performances banned; toured the United States, winter 1927–28, and Soviet Union, winter 1928–29; relieved of teaching duties at Budapest, 1934: appointed member of Hungarian Academy of Sciences; farewell concert, Budapest, 1940; left Hungary for United States: appointed visiting assistant in music, Columbia University, New York, 1941–42; last public performance, January 1943. Member, Légion d'honneur, 1931; recipient: Honorary Doctorate, Columbia University, 1940. Died in New York, 26 September 1945.

### WORKS (Ballets)

1917 *The Wooden Prince* (chor. Zöbisch), Budapest State Opera, Budapest

1926 *The Miraculous Mandarin* (chor. Steinbach), State Theatre, Cologne

**Other ballets using Bartók's music**: *The Wooden Prince* (new version: Harangozó, 1939; also Milloss, 1950; Walter, 1962; Eck, 1965; Seregi, 1970; Cauley, 1981), *Corybantic* (Humphrey, 1948), *Vagary* (Dudley, 1949), *Caprichos* (Ross, 1950), *Gypsy* (Hoyer, 1950), *Medea* (Cullberg, 1950), *Sonata* (Dudley, 1950), *Sonata* (Hoyer, 1951), *The Miraculous Mandarin* (new version: Harangozó, 1945; also Bolender, 1951; Rodrigues, 1956; Lavrovsky, as *Night City*, 1961; Eck, 1965; Flindt, 1967; Seregi, 1970; Pistoni, 1981), *Concerto Burlesco* (Gore, 1946), *Mystères* (Milloss, 1951), *Threshold of Time* (Milloss, 1951), *Afflicted Children* (Scott, 1953), *Dance Concerto* (O'Donnell, 1954), *Sonate de l'angoisse* (Milloss, 1954), *Concerto aux étoiles* (Lander, 1956), *Hungarica* (Milloss, 1956), *Journey* (MacMillan, 1957), *The Prisoners* (Darrell, 1957), *Sonate à trois* (Béjart, 1957), *Place of Panic* (Trisler, 1958), *Theatre for Fools* (Nagrin, 1959), *The Venus Flower* (Worth, 1959), *Yesterday's Papers* (Sanders, 1959), *Suite en noir et blanc* (Béjart, 1961), *A Wedding Present* (Darrell, 1962), *Estro barbarico* (Milloss, 1963), *Opus 12* (Van Manen, 1964), *Saracenis* (Descombey, 1964), *Music for Strings, Percussion and Celeste* (Eck, 1964), *Home* (Darrell, 1965), *Concerto* (Eck, 1965), *Dualis* (Van Manen, 1967), *Kommen und Gehen* (Kylián, 1970), *Revolt* (Cullberg, 1973), *Rituals* (MacMillan, 1975), *Three Pictures* (Corder, 1981), *The Hunchback of Notre Dame* (Wells, 1981).

### PUBLICATIONS

Haraszti, E., *Béla Bartók: His Life and Works*, Paris, 1938

Stevens, H., *The Life and Music of Béla Bartók*, New York, 1953

Sabin, R., "Béla Bartók and the Dance", *Dance Magazine* (New York), April 1961

Ujfalussy, J., *Bartók*, Budapest, 1965; English translation, 1971

Kroo, György, *A Guide to Bartok*, London, 1974
Griffiths, Paul, *Bartók*, London, 1984
Lambert, Vera, et al., *The New Grove Modern Masters: Bartók, Stravinsky, Hindemith*, New York, 1984

* * *

Béla Bartók was not a man of the theatre. As a person, he was a very private individual; as a composer, he wrote only three works directly for theatre performance—but the dance-like pulse underlying almost all his music, from chamber works to concertos, has proved attractive to choreographers around the world as a stimulus to dance movement.

His three theatre works, all of single-act length, are the opera *Duke Bluebeard's Castle*, composed in 1911, the ballet *The Wooden Prince*, and a balletic mime-drama, *The Miraculous Mandarin*. *The Wooden Prince* was directly composed to form a double bill with the opera; when *Mandarin* was added, Bartók hoped it would make a theatrical triple bill. Since 1945, the three works have been so presented by the Hungarian State Opera and Ballet, and occasionally elsewhere (such as by the English National Opera with London Festival Ballet in 1981), but Bartók did not live to see this happen.

All three works require a large orchestra for performance, and show a close relationship between the stage action and the music. *The Wooden Prince* (more literally, "The Wood-carved Prince") was composed to a libretto by Béla Balázs (who also wrote the opera's libretto) as a fairy-tale with allegorical associations. Its music is an arch-like structure of seven numbered dances and linking interludes, enclosed within a Prelude and Postlude. The opening 60 bars are spun almost entirely from the notes of the C major triad to suggest the nature-scene of the fable, and much of the writing conveys resplendent tone-pictures in the manner of Richard Strauss, whom Bartók greatly admired.

"Three parts are clearly distinguishable," he wrote, "and these in turn can be further divided. The first part extends to the end of the dance between the Princess and the wooden puppet. The second, considerably calmer than the first, bears the typical characteristics of an inner movement and lasts until the reappearance of the puppet. The third part is like a repetition of the first, but the order of the sections is reversed to correspond with the text." *The Wooden Prince* was first performed in advance of the opera, and became Bartók's first major success with the public.

*The Miraculous Mandarin* met a different fate, the lurid expressionism of Menyhért Lengyel's scenario bringing a ban on performance at Budapest until after Bartók's death, though it was seen earlier in Cologne (in 1926) and Prague (in 1927). The music is another symmetrical structure, wherein three descriptive episodes twice follow fierce rhythmic action closely related to the narrative.

Instruments have character-association: a clarinet for the Girl's eroticism, a trombone for an elderly rake, an oboe for a timid youth; chords on trombone and tuba herald the Mandarin, whose Orientalism is suggested at one point by the cellos playing quarter-tones, and whose survival of a hanging should bring the eerie sound of a wordless chorus vocalizing in minor thirds. These are two of the more unusual aspects of music that acquires character from the contrast of sharp-featured instrumental solos with colourful and sometimes violent ensemble writing.

*The Miraculous Mandarin* poses a challenge to choreographers which has seldom, if ever, been satisfactorily met. Of particular difficulty is the lengthy orchestral fugue to which the Mandarin is meant to chase the terrified Girl. To stage this without it looking silly before the fugue is spent, and to show the following three attempts to kill the Mandarin without unwanted comedy, is a problem which has proven a repeated obstacle to successful stage performance. (It is of interest to note that Bartók's own "concert suite" simply lops off all the music that follows the fugue.)

Bartok's field research into Hungarian and other folk music brought forth his *Romanian Folk Dances* (1917), and *Transylvanian Dances* (orchestrated in 1931 from a piano sonatina). A *Dance Suite* (1923) comprises five dances and a finale which makes use of various folk styles (Magyar, Romanian, quasi-Arabic) but is his own original invention. This music became a frequent stimulus to choreography, as have also, in particular, the *Music for Strings, Percussion and Celeste*, the *Divertimento* for strings, the piano suite *Mikrokosmos*, the second and third Piano Concertos, and the *Concerto for Orchestra*.

—Noël Goodwin

---

## BARYSHNIKOV, Mikhail

Russian/American dancer, choreographer, and ballet director. Born in Riga, Latvia, 28 January 1948. Studied at the Riga Opera Ballet School and at the Leningrad Choreographic School (The Vaganova School), pupil of Aleksandr Pushkin. Soloist, becoming principal dancer, Kirov Ballet, 1967–74; defected to the West while on tour with "Stars of the Bolshoi", Toronto, 1974; principal dancer, American Ballet Theatre, 1974–78, New York City Ballet, 1978–79; returned to American Ballet Theatre, becoming artistic director, 1980–89; also international guest artist, with appearances for the Royal Ballet, London, Paris Opéra Ballet, Hamburg Ballet, Stuttgart Ballet, National Ballet of Canada, Teatro Colón in Buenos Aires, Alvin Ailey Company, Paul Taylor Dance Company, and Théâtre de la Monnaie/Mark Morris, Brussels; founder and principal dancer, White Oak Dance Project (artistic collaborator Mark Morris), from 1990; also actor, with Broadway stage début in *Metamorphosis* (play by Stephen Berkoff after Kafka), 1989; has also appeared in films, including in *The Turning Point* (dir. Ross, 1977), *White Nights* (dir. Ross, 1985), *Dancers* (dir. Ross, 1987), *The Cabinet of Dr. Ramirez* (dir. Sellers, 1991), and on television, including numerous Public Broadcasting Service (PBS) television specials, from 1976, in "Baryshnikov at the White House" (1979), "Baryshnikov on Broadway" (ABC television, 1980), and "Baryshnikov in Hollywood" (CBS television, 1982). Recipient: Gold Medal, International Ballet Competition, Varna, Bulgaria, 1966; Gold Medal, First International Ballet Competition, Moscow, 1969; Nijinsky Prize, Paris, 1969; *Dance Magazine* Award, 1978; Emmy Award, 1979; Honorary Doctorate, Yale University, 1979; Best Actor Award, Outer-Circle Drama Critics, 1989.

### ROLES

1967 Pas de deux from *Don Quixote* (Gorsky after Petipa), Leningrad Choreographic School graduation performance, Leningrad

Peasant Pas de deux in *Giselle* (Petipa after Coralli, Perrot), Kirov Ballet, Leningrad

Principal dancer in *Eternal Spring* (pas de deux; Yakobson), Kirov Ballet, Leningrad

1968 Asiat's Friend in *Goryanka* (Vinogradov), Kirov Ballet, Leningrad

**Mikhail Baryshnikov in Murdmaa's *Daphnis and Chloë*, Leningrad, 1974**

Pas de trois in *Swan Lake* (Petipa, Ivanov; staged K. Sergeyev), Kirov Ballet, Leningrad
1969 "The Youth" in *Chopiniana* (Vaganova after Fokine), Kirov Ballet, Leningrad
Title role (cr) in *Vestris* (Yakobson), International Ballet Competition, Moscow
Basil in *Don Quixote* (Gorsky after Petipa), Kirov Ballet, Leningrad
Mercutio in *Romeo and Juliet* (Chernyshev), Irina Kolpakova Choreographic Evening, Leningrad
1970 Principal dancer in *Symphony in C* (Balanchine), concert performance with Natalia Makarova
Prince Désiré in *The Sleeping Beauty* (Petipa; staged K. Sergeyev), Kirov Ballet, Leningrad
Title role (cr) in *Hamlet* (K. Sergeyev), Kirov Ballet, Leningrad
1971 Adam (cr) in *The Creation of the World* (Kasatkina, Vasiliev), Kirov Ballet, Leningrad
The Dance of the Bird from *The Ice Maiden* (Lopukhov), Concert in Honour of Fedor Lopukhov, October Concert Hall, Leningrad
1972 Albrecht in *Giselle* (Petipa after Coralli, Perrot), Kirov Ballet, Leningrad
Prince Salamander in *The Prince of the Pagodas* (Vinogradov), Kirov Ballet, Leningrad
1974 Daphnis (cr) in *Daphnis and Chloë* (Murdmaa), Baryshnikov Choreographic Evening, Leningrad
Title role (cr) in *The Prodigal Son* (Murdmaa), Baryshnikov Choreographic Evening, Leningrad
1975 Principal dancer (cr) in *Medea* (pas de deux; Butler), Spoleto Festival, Italy
Principal dancer (cr) in *Awakening* (pas de deux; Weiss), American Ballet Theatre, New York
The Boy with the Matted Hair in *Shadowplay* (Tudor), American Ballet Theatre, New York
Romeo in *Romeo and Juliet* (MacMillan), Royal Ballet, London
1976 Hamlet (cr) in *Hamlet Connotations* (Neumeier), American Ballet Theatre, New York
Principal dancer (cr) in *Push Comes to Shove* (Tharp), American Ballet Theatre, New York
Principal dancer (cr) in *Pas de Duke* (Ailey), Alvin Ailey Company, New York
Principal dancer (cr) in *Other Dances* (pas de deux; Robbins), Gala, Metropolitan Opera House, New York
Principal dancer (cr) in *Once More Frank* (Tharp), American Ballet Theatre, New York
Principal dancer in *The Rite of Spring* (Tetley), American Ballet Theatre
The Prince (cr) in *The Nutcracker* (also chor.), American Ballet Theatre, Washington, D.C.
1977 Principal dancer (cr) in *Variations on "America"* (Feld), Eliot Feld Ballet, New York
Colas in *La Fille mal gardée* (Ashton), Royal Ballet, London
Romeo in *Romeo and Juliet* (Tchernichov), Maryland Ballet, Baltimore
Title role in *The Prodigal Son* (Balanchine), International Dance Festival of Stars, Chicago
1978 Hermann (cr) in *La Dame de pique* (Petit), Ballet de Marseille, Paris
Basilio (cr) in *Don Quixote* (*Kitri's Wedding*) (new version; also chor., after Gorsky, Petipa), American Ballet Theatre
Title role in *Apollo* (Balanchine), International Dance Festival of Stars, Chicago
1978/79 Franz in *Coppélia* (Danilova, Balanchine after Petipa), New York City Ballet, Saratoga Springs, New York
Second Movement in *Symphony in C* (Balanchine), New York City Ballet, New York
Oberon in *A Midsummer Night's Dream* (Balanchine), New York City Ballet, New York
Principal dancer in *Afternoon of a Faun* (Robbins), New York City Ballet, New York
Title role in *Orpheus* (Balanchine), New York City Ballet, New York
Principal dancer in *Dances at a Gathering* (Robbins), New York City Ballet, New York
Principal dancer in *Tchaikovsky Pas de Deux* (Balanchine), New York City Ballet, New York
Rubies in *Jewels* (Balanchine), New York City Ballet, New York
Harlequin in *Harlequinade* (Balanchine), New York City Ballet, New York
The Poet in *La Sonnambula* (Balanchine), New York City Ballet, New York
Pearly King, Costermonger Pas de deux in *Union Jack* (Balanchine), New York City Ballet, New York
Principal dancer in *Donizetti Variations* (Balanchine), New York City Ballet, New York
The Prince in *The Nutcracker* (Balanchine), New York City Ballet, New York
1979 Principal dancer (cr) in *The Four Seasons* (Robbins), New York City Ballet, New York
Principal dancer (cr) in *Opus 19* (later called *Opus 19/The Dreamer*; Robbins), New York City Ballet, New York
Principal dancer in *Eatin' Rain in Space* (Tanner), International Dance Festival, Chicago
1980 Principal dancer (cr) in *Rhapsody* (pas de deux; Ashton), Royal Ballet, London
1981 Grand Pas Hongrois from *Raymonda* (also chor.; after Petipa), Petipa Gala, American Ballet Theatre
Don José in *Carmen* (Petit), American Ballet Theatre
Principal dancer (cr) in *Configurations* (Choo San Goh), American Ballet Theatre, Washington, D.C.
Title role (cr) in *The Wild Boy* (MacMillan), American Ballet Theatre, Washington, D.C.
1983 Principal dancer (cr) in *Follow the Feet* (McFall), American Ballet Theatre, Washington, D.C.
Principal dancer (cr) in *The Little Ballet* (also called *Once Upon a Time*; Tharp), American Ballet Theatre, Minneapolis
1984 Principal dancer (cr) in *Sinatra Suite* (Tharp), American Ballet Theatre, Washington, D.C.
1985 Beliaev in *A Month in the Country* (Ashton), Royal Ballet, London
1986 Principal dancer (cr) in *Murder* (Gordon), American Ballet Theatre, San Francisco
Principal dancer (cr) in *The Mollino Room* (Armitage), American Ballet Theatre, Washington, D.C.
1988 Principal dancer (cr) in *Drink to Me Only with Thine Eyes* (Morris), American Ballet Theatre, New York
1989 Principal dancer (cr) in *Wonderland* (Morris), Théâtre de la Monnaie/Mark Morris, Brussels
1992 Principal dancer in *Duo Concertante* (Balanchine), New York City Ballet, New York
Principal dancer in *Three Preludes* (solo; Morris), New York City Ballet, New York

**Other roles include:** for American Ballet Theatre—title role in *Petrushka* (Fokine), principal dancer in *Theme and Variations* (Balanchine), Romeo in *Romeo and Juliet* (MacMillan), Solor in

"Kingdom of the Shades" from *La Bayadère* (Makarova after Petipa), the Spirit of the Rose in *Le Spectre de la rose*, James in *La Sylphide* (Lander after Bournonville), pas de trois from *The Guards of Amager* (Bournonville), solo variation in *Les Patineurs* (Ashton), principal dancer in *Le Corsaire* Pas de deux (after Petipa), the Devil in *Three Virgins and a Devil* (De Mille), the Young Man in *Le Jeune Homme et la Mort* (Petit); for the Eliot Feld Company—principal dancer in *Santa Fe Saga* (Feld); for the Paul Taylor Company—principal dancer in *Airs* (Taylor), and in *From Sea to Shining Sea* (Taylor); for the Martha Graham Dance Company—Husbandman in *Appalachian Spring* (Graham), Oedipus in *Night Journey*, title role in *El Penitente* (Graham); for the White Oak Dance Project—Duet from *Concerto Six Twenty-two* (Lubovitch), Punch in *Punch and Judy* (Gordon), "Fool to Care" and "Sabre Dance" in *Waiting for the Sunrise* (Lubovitch); principal dancer in *Canonic 3/4 Studies* (Morris), *A Lake* (Morris), *Ten Suggestions* (solo; Morris), *Cavalcade* (Morris), *Pas de Poisson* (Morris).

## WORKS

1976 *The Nutcracker* (mus. Tchaikovsky), American Ballet Theatre, Washington, D.C.
1983 *Cinderella* (with Anastos; mus. Prokofiev), American Ballet Theatre, Washington, D.C.

Also staged:
1978 *Don Quixote* (*Kitri's Wedding*; after Gorsky, Petipa; mus. Minkus), American Ballet Theatre, Washington, D.C.
1980 *Raymonda*, Acts II and III divertissements (after Petipa; mus. Glazunov), American Ballet Theatre
*The Sleeping Beauty*, Act III (after Petipa; mus. Tchaikovsky), American Ballet Theatre
*Giselle* (after Petipa, Coralli, Perrot), American Ballet Theatre
1988 *Swan Lake* (after Petipa, Ivanov; mus. Tchaikovsky), American Ballet Theatre, Orange County, N.Y.

## PUBLICATIONS

By Baryshnikov:
*Baryshnikov at Work*, edited by Charles France, New York, 1976
*Baryshnikov in Color*, New York, 1980

About Baryshnikov:
Thomas, Victor (ed.), *The Making of a Dance: Mikhail Baryshnikov and Carla Fracci in Medea*, New York, 1976
Goodman, Saul, *Baryshnikov: A Most Spectacular Dancer*, New York, 1979
Smakov, Gennady, "Russian Relations at New York's City Ballet: Baryshnikov and Balanchine", *Dance Magazine* (New York), February 1981
Smakov, Gennady, *From Russia to the West*, New York, 1981
Croce, Arlene, *Going to the Dance*, New York, 1982
Alovert, Nina, *Baryshnikov in Russia*, New York, 1984
Croce, Arlene, *Sight Lines*, New York, 1987
Fraser, John, *Private View: Inside Baryshnikov's American Ballet Theatre*, Toronto, 1988
Aria, Barbara, *Misha: The Mikhail Baryshnikov Story*, New York, 1989

* * *

Mikhail Baryshnikov's extraordinary dance career opened with a "veni, vidi, vici" directness. In 1963, the fifteen-year-old Russian came from Latvia to study ballet in Leningrad. In 1966, after the first of his three school years in the class of the renowned pedagogue Aleksandr Pushkin, he saw the way to international recognition by taking the gold medal in the Varna International Ballet Competition. In 1967, he conquered a whole new world. Writing a diary from the Soviet Union on a visit from the United States, Clive Barnes called Baryshnikov "the most perfect dancer I have ever seen", and noted how Galina Ulanova made glowing reference to "the little boy" in Leningrad.

With a Kirov Ballet season in London during the summer of 1970, the little boy from Leningrad started to become the biggest name in ballet since Nureyev. Natalia Makarova defected from the tour that first showed Baryshnikov to the West, when the company included the great Yuri Soloviev, but there was still plenty of attention given to the 22-year-old newcomer. Four years later, while part of a small tour of Soviet dancers in Canada, Baryshnikov defected as dramatically as had Nureyev and Makarova, and began his mature career.

If this Russian dancer's talent was never really in question, the nature of his gifts and skills did present some puzzlement to pre-existing notions of ballet dancing, especially for his Soviet mentors in his formative years. His Leningrad début performance was in the so-called "Peasant Pas de deux" from *Giselle*. For his U.S. début with American Ballet Theatre, the company to which he became more closely linked than any other, the one-time performer of the nameless peasant danced the leading role of Albrecht, the complex nobleman who dominates *Giselle*. He had already performed the role in Leningrad, but not after some struggle to convince the administration that there was more in him than a virtuoso solo dancer.

Acting upon the "artistic freedom" catch-phrase that increasingly surrounded Soviet defectors, the powers that be in the ballet world scrambled to give Baryshnikov the opportunities he had lacked in Russia. He performed with numerous companies and frequently had new works fashioned for him. Most of these premieres proved to be of no more than passing interest, holding the public's attention largely as excuses to see Baryshnikov perform. A few, notably Jerome Robbins's *Other Dances* and Twyla Tharp's *Push Comes to Shove, Sinatra Suite*, and *The Little Ballet*, as well as, arguably, Frederick Ashton's *Rhapsody*, showed more lasting substance.

During these halcyon years, from the mid-1970s to the mid-1980s, Baryshnikov danced just about anything he wanted. The only restraints put on his repertory of new roles were those he put upon himself. Something of the type-casting that obtained in the Kirov company stayed with him. For example, quintessential nineteenth-century cavalier roles, such as Prince Siegfried in *Swan Lake* and Prince Désiré in *The Sleeping Beauty*, held only a small place in his large repertory. His well-proportioned, but short-statured physique deemed him less than ideal for certain leading-man parts.

After four years with ABT as a base, and with sundry similarly constituted companies as supplementary hosts, Baryshnikov joined New York City Ballet, a company built by George Balanchine for his own dancers. Here, in a world-famous enclave, the eager Russian dancer hoped to work directly with the august Russian ballet master. Though he danced about as much of the company's repertory as any single male dancer could, Baryshnikov did not get to work with Balanchine on a new role. For a good part of Baryshikov's tenure at NYCB, Balanchine, who was able to give him tutelage and coaching, was not in sufficiently good health to create a new ballet. While there, the mainstay of his repertory was in roles originated for Edward Villella.

Baryshnikov left Balanchine's company, enriched if not renewed, to assume the directorship of ABT. He stayed with his directorial job for ten years, counteracting the company's somewhat backward-looking thrust with a contempory, youthful bent. He stressed clean classical dancing and showed an interest in refreshing the standard repertory with new design and youthful casting. He also choreographed or restaged several familiar ballets for ABT's repertory. Few of these met with solid critical success; and some, like *Cinderella*, co-choreographed with Peter Anastos, and *Swan Lake*, with Pier Luigi Samaritani's integral design scheme, were withdrawn before they had time to get into their stride.

Baryshnikov's appetite for dancing beyond ballet's purview and for theatrical work outside dancing itself also grew during his career outside Russia. He starred in a couple of television specials. He was featured in four movies, and eventually acted in a theatre work based on Kafka's *Metamorphosis*. He also worked with so-called modern and even post-modern dance practitioners, such as Alvin Ailey, Paul Taylor, Martha Graham, and David Gordon. The most lasting of these relationships developed with Mark Morris, who created a ballet for Baryshnikov at ABT and then other works once the dancer had left the company. Starting in the autumn of 1990, after his classical ballet dancing days were curtailed by injuries, Baryshnikov led a group called the White Oak Dance Project, which performed an all-Morris repertory.

The standards set by Baryshnikov in his nearly twenty-year-long career in the West have yet to be met, let alone bettered. His dancing remained distinguished by an impeccable clarity and a terrific force. His strong points were the very strong points of ballet technique: gyroscopic pirouettes, vaulting jumps, and precise, definite footwork. A good time after he gave up the pyrotechnical fancies of Chabukiani-type roles, such as Solor in "The Kingdom of Shades" from *La Bayadère*, he was still setting new standards of virtuosity in the role of Albrecht in the second act of *Giselle*. Some of his greatest late classical dancing came in the role of the "youth" in Fokine's *Les Sylphides*. Here with unerring control igniting rapturously expansive abandon, Baryshnikov embodied the ineffable "evocation poètique" at the heart of this and all true ballets blancs.

—Robert Greskovic

---

**BASIL, Colonel de** *see* **DE BASIL, Colonel**

---

## LA BAYADÈRE

(original Russian title: *Bayaderka*)

**Choreography**: Marius Petipa
**Music:** Aloisius Ludwig (Léon) Minkus
**Design**: Ivan Andreyev, Mikhail Bocharov, Piotr Lambin, Andrey Roller, Matvey Shishkov, Heinrich Wagner
**Libretto**: Sergei Khudekhov and Marius Petipa (after dramas of Indian classics by Kalidasa, Sakuntala and The Carl of Clay)
**First Production:** Bolshoi Theatre, St. Petersburg, 4 February 1877
**Principal Dancers**: Ekaterina Vazem (Nikiya), Lev Ivanov (Solor; mime role), Pavel Gerdt (Grand pas de deux), Maria Gorshenkova (Gamzatti)

**Other productions include:** Maryinsky Theatre (restaged Marius Petipa); St. Petersburg, 1900. Bolshoi Theatre (staged Aleksandr Gorsky after Petipa); Moscow, 25 January 1904. Bolshoi Theatre (new version; chor. Gorsky); Moscow, 19 March 1917. Bolshoi Theatre (first three acts: chor. Gorsky after Petipa; Act IV, "Kingdom of the Shades": staged Vassily Tikhomirov after Petipa); Moscow, 31 January 1923. State Academic Theatre of Opera and Ballet (GATOB; chor. Agrippina Vaganova after Petipa); Leningrad, 13 December 1932. Kirov Ballet (after Petipa, with new dances by Vakhtang Chabukiani and Nikolai Zubkovsky), with Natalia Dudinskaya (Nikiya); Leningrad, 10 February 1941. Royal Ballet ("Kingdom of the Shades" scene; staged Rudolf Nureyev after Petipa), with Margot Fonteyn (Nikiya) and Rudolf Nureyev (Solor); London, 27 November 1963 (same production later mounted for Paris Opéra Ballet, 1974). American Ballet Theatre ("Kingdom of the Shades" scene; staged Natalia Makarova after Petipa); New York, 3 July 1974. American Ballet Theatre (complete ballet; staged Makarova after Petipa); New York, 2 May 1980. Paris Opéra Ballet (complete ballet; staged Nureyev after Petipa); Paris, 8 October 1992.

**Other choreographic treatments of story:** Filippo Taglioni (choreography in opera by Auber entitled *Le Dieu et la bayadère*), Paris, 1830.

### PUBLICATIONS


Benois, Alexandre, *Reminiscences of the Russian Ballet*, London, 1941
Beaumont, Cyril, *Complete Book of Ballets*, revised edition, London, 1951
Petipa, Marius, *The Memoirs of Marius Petipa, Russian Ballet Master*, edited by Lillian Moore, London, 1958
Barnes, Clive, Goodwin, Noël, and Williams, Peter, "*La Bayadère*", *Dance and Dancers* (London), January 1964
Karsavina, Tamara, "A Blue Transparency of Night", *Dancing Times* (London), February 1964
Roslavleva, Natalia, *Era of the Russian Ballet*, London, 1966
Balanchine, George, and Mason, Francis, *Balanchine's Complete Stories of the Great Ballets*, Garden City, N.Y., 1977
Croce, Arlene, *Afterimages*, London, 1978
Anastos, Peter, "Ballet Relics: The Shroud of Leningrad", *Ballet Review* (New York), vol. 8, nos. 2–3, 1980
Smakov, Gennady, "The Tale of *La Bayadère*", *Ballet News* (New York), May 1980
Scherer, B.L., "Maligned Minstrel: Putting in a Good Word for Ludwig Minkus, Composer of La Bayadère", *Ballet News* (New York), May 1980
Vazem, Yekaterina, "Memoirs of a Ballerina of the St. Petersburg Bolshoi", part 3, *Dance Research* (London), Spring 1987
Barnes, Clive, "Treasure from the Past", *Dance and Dancers* (London), May 1989
René, Natalia, "*La Bayadère*", *Dance and Dancers* (London), May 1989
Pritchard, Jane, "Bits of *Bayadère* in Britain", *Dancing Times* (London), September 1989
Macaulay, Alastair, "In Death's Dream Kingdom", *Dancing Times* (London), November 1989
Wiley, Roland John (ed. and trans.), *A Century of Russian Ballet: Documents and Accounts 1810–1910*, Oxford, 1990


* * *

*La Bayadère*, created for the Bolshoi Theatre in St. Petersburg,

***La Bayadère*, with Martine van Hamel and Kevin McKenzie of American Ballet Theatre**

was a particularly spectacular ballet set in India with a complicated plot of love and intrigue. Solor, an Indian warrior, betrays Nikiya, the temple dancer (or bayadère) he has sworn to love forever, by agreeing to marry the Rajah's daughter, Gamzatti. On learning of Solor's love for Nikiya, Gamzatti connives at her rival's death. The bayadère is bitten by a venomous snake hidden in a basket of flowers as she dances at the betrothal celebration. She is too proud to accept the antidote offered by the High Brahmin when she realizes Solor intends to go through with his formal marriage. Her death distresses Solor, who takes refuge in opium and sees in a drug-induced vision multiple images of his beloved emerging from a mountain crevice and descending a slope in the Himalayas. Eventually the shade of Nikiya forgives him. Returning to reality, Solor is forced to marry Gamzatti; but during the ceremony, the shade of Nikiya appears to Solor. The temple collapses, crushing everyone to death—but in an apotheosis Nikiya is seen leading Solor to paradise.

*La Bayadère* was typical of the large-scale, full-evening productions (of which Marius Petipa was a leading exponent) that appealed to Russian audiences during the latter part of the nineteenth century. It was a notably lavish production with exotic Indian settings by Roller, Wagner, Shishkov, and Bocharov. The costumes were partly derived from ethnic dress or decorated with Indian motifs, but the score, by the Viennese composer Ludwig Minkus, showed no influence of Indian music; and the choreography, even in the character numbers, made barely a gesture to Indian dance forms. The betrothal and wedding scenes (described so vividly in Alexandre Benois's *Reminiscences*) provided opportunities not only for divertissements of classical and character dancing but also for impressive processions. The monumental nature of these scenes—the betrothal procession, which included a bejewelled elephant and royal tiger, had as many as 36 entrances—has led to comparisons of *La Bayadère* with Verdi's *Aïda*, first staged in St. Petersburg (and also with choreography by Petipa) only a few months after the former's premiere.

Aptly tagged "*Giselle*, East of Suez", *La Bayadère* both pays homage to romantic ballet and follows romantic ballet conventions. Petipa's inclusion of the shade of Nikiya (only visible to Solor) at the beginning of the wedding is reminiscent of a similar situation in Taglioni's *La Sylphide*. Typical of the romantic element is the combination of the ballet's exotic Indian location with the ethereal world of the bayadère-shades. The Kingdom of the Shades, inspired by Gustav Doré's illustrations for Dante's *Paradiso*, gives the choreographer the chance to show his dancers forsaking natural movement for pointe technique, in a scene of classical purity that contrasts with the drama that surrounds it. To diffuse the image of the shades and create a dream-like atmosphere, this scene is often performed behind a scrim or a succession of gauzes. Although the ballet conforms overall to contemporary notions of construction, this scene is particularly notable for choreography which extended the very frontiers of classical dance. It may be regarded as the precursor to Ivanov's lakeside scenes in *Swan Lake* and to many plotless but evocative ballets of the twentieth century, from Fokine's *Les Sylphides* to works by George Balanchine. Indeed, it is self-sufficient as a ballet in its own right, the ideal showcase for a talented corps de ballet. While the complete ballet, in which pantomime separates passages of dance, seems quaint and hackneyed to today's audiences, the Kingdom of the Shades retains all the appeal of its lyrical calm and classical precision.

The ballet's precise origins are not clear. India had already provided the setting for several ballets, including Taglioni's *Le Dieu et la bayadère* of 1830 (also known as *The Maid of Cashmere*); Marius Petipa's brother Lucien had created *Sacountala* (1858) for the Paris Opéra. The narratives are not identical, but triangular relationships (so beloved of romantic choreographers) involving a temple dancer and the similarity of locations suggest certain links. *La Bayadère* also bears comparison with other works in the Russian repertory. Nikiya's situation parallels that of the gypsy dancer, Esmeralda, in the ballet to which the latter gives her name, and dramatic motifs in *La Bayadère* are repeated from Petipa's first spectacular success, *Pharaoh's Daughter*.

*La Bayadère* has remained in the Russian repertory since its creation in 1877. It received a notable revival by Marius Petipa in St. Petersburg in 1900, and continued to be performed by the Maryinsky–Kirov company although it underwent several significant revisions. After the Revolution the spectacular collapse of the temple was dropped and the ballet ended with the Kingdom of the Shades. In 1932, Vaganova's authoritative revival extended the use of pointe work throughout the ballet, and in the next decade Chabukiani added new choreography to develop the role of Solor for virtuoso dancers. The spectacular solo for the Golden Idol by Nikolai Zubkovsky was also added.

*La Bayadère* had already undergone alterations in Moscow where, on the eve of the 1917 Revolution, Gorsky revised the whole ballet, drawing on ethnographical sources to introduce poses from Indian art. Where he failed was in the staging of the Kingdom of the Shades, when he put the bayadères in national costume rather than in the conventional tutus necessary to show off the choreography to advantage.

Although extracts of the ballet have repeatedly been performed in the West, and the "Kingdom of the Shades" has been popularized by Kirov tours in the 1960s and by numerous productions staged by Russians for Western companies, it was not until 1980 that a complete *La Bayadère* entered the Western repertory. In her staging for American Ballet Theatre, Natalia Makarova reverted to the full narrative but dispensed with the character dancing. It remains today, as in the nineteenth century, a peculiarly theatrical view of India—complete with a statue of the Buddha in a Hindu temple. Its survival depends on the opportunities it offers to dancers to combine dramatic acting with the purest classical technique.

—Jane Pritchard

---

**BAYLIS, Lilian**

English theatre manager. Born in London, niece of Victoria Theatre manager Emma Cons, 1874. Educated privately in South Africa and England. Early experience as arts manager, and organizer of ladies' orchestra, in Johannesburg; returned to England, at invitation of Emma Cons: assistant to manager, becoming acting manager, Victoria Theatre (The Old Vic), London, from 1898: full manager (on death of Emma Cons) from 1912, helping to establish opera and theatre companies; engaged Ninette de Valois as choreographer, Old Vic Theatre, 1926; manager, Sadler's Wells Theatre, from 1931, enabling the establishment of resident company, Vic-Wells Ballet, and Sadler's Wells Ballet School, 1931. Recipient: Companion of Honour, 1929; Honorary Master of Arts, Oxford; Honorary Doctor of Laws, Birmingham. Died in London, 25 November 1937.

**PUBLICATIONS**

Hamilton, Cicely and Baylis, Lilian, *The Old Vic*, London, 1926
"All About the Vic-Wells Ballet", *Dancing Times* (London), March 1932
De Valois, Ninette, "Lilian Baylis", *Dancing Times* (London) January 1938
Williams, Harcourt (ed.), *Vic-Wells: The Work of Lilian Baylis*, London, 1938
Thorndike, Sybil and Russell, *Lilian Baylis*, London, 1938
Williams, Harcourt, *Old Vic Saga*, London, 1949
Clarke, Mary, *The Sadler's Wells Ballet*, London, 1955
Findlater, Richard, *Lilian Baylis, The Lady of the Old Vic*, London, 1975

* * *

Photographs of Lilian Baylis convey a solid worthiness; she looks like a teacher, a Victorian philanthropist, or a social worker, and in many ways she was—but her medium of education, of reform, of "doing good", was the theatre. She inherited only a theatre-turned-temperance coffee house, known as the Old Vic, situated in an unfashionably poor district of south London. She had no money, and public subsidy of the arts was unknown in her day; but she was determined that the local people should have "the best" in entertainment—and this, she was told, meant grand opera, Shakespeare and, eventually, ballet. She believed in the power of great music and drama to enrich the lives of the poor and her aim was a true people's theatre that entertained without condescension.

She was completely monomaniacal, and had no interests outside her theatres; indeed, it is doubtful if she ever saw a performance by another company. Her taste was not impeccable; she loved opera, but in its lighter rather than its higher manifestations; she had probably never read Shakespeare, nor seen any of the great dancers who visited London. Yet from these unpromising beginnings were to grow a native-born English opera company presenting opera in English (the Sadler's Wells Opera, now the English National Opera), a theatre company that was to be the forerunner of the Royal National Theatre, and, at a time when ballet was seen as the prerogative of the Russian companies, a native-born British ballet—the Sadler's Wells Ballet (now the Royal Ballet).

Both opera and drama were well established at the Old Vic by the 1920s. Indeed, throughout the 1920s and 1930s, when Shakespeare had almost died out on the West End stage, the Old Vic attracted a new generation of young actors who came to learn how to play the classics, among them Sybil Thorndike, Edith Evans, John Gielgud, Peggy Ashcroft, Maurice Evans, Emlyn Williams, and Charles Laughton.

By the 1920s, Lilian Baylis was looking for a second theatre to relieve overcrowding at the Old Vic, and also to take her pioneering work to another district of London. It would also allow her to inaugurate another dream and fulfil a promise. This was nothing less than the foundation of a native British ballet company. In 1926 she had been approached by Ninette de Valois, who at that time was running a dance school. De Valois knew that a ballet company founded in the commercial theatre would be doomed to failure; she needed a theatre with a sympathetic regular audience that could provide for ballet evenings, while at the same time giving her students stage experience in walking on in plays or dancing in opera ballets. Hence she turned to the repertory theatres. It was Baylis who had the foresight to respond positively and take de Valois and her school into the organization. She gave them the chance of appearing in the opera ballets and performing the occasional ballet until such time as the second theatre, Sadler's Wells, could be rebuilt. De Valois also taught movement to the Old Vic drama students and, a most original concept at that time, to the opera chorus.

The opening of Sadler's Wells and the setting up of a ballet company there could only be described as an act of faith. There were no funds and the building debt was to cripple the theatre for many years. But without this stable home, de Valois would not have been able to create a company on a solid foundation so quickly. Baylis lived to see the Vic-Wells Ballet firmly established, with its own choreographers, de Valois and Ashton, and its own stars in the making in Fonteyn and Helpmann.

By the time of her death in 1937, Lilian Baylis had become a legend in the theatre, partly because of her work, partly because of her character. She was an original eccentric, blunt sometimes to the point of rudeness, and straightforward. Her celebrated penny-pinching derived from a natural frugality, but was also necessary to keep the theatres open at a time when state subsidy was unknown. Early productions at the Vic may often have been shabby and looked impoverished, but they were presented with commitment and love. Her famous prayer "Dear God, please send me some good actors cheap" was answered a hundred-fold. She prayed for everything, including guidance, money, and faith to keep the enterprises going. Her devout Christianity was of an intensely practical nature.

Baylis's greatest assets were her faith in God and the rightness of her cause, a gift for getting money out of people, an amazing instinct for finding the right collaborator at the right time, and the ability to ignore the height of any mountain that threatened to get in the way of her dream of a people's theatre, presenting the best at popular prices. She was no theorist. There had been schemes for a National Theatre and an English ballet before her, but they always got bogged down in committees and reports. Baylis had no high ideals of founding national companies, but her determination was to present only the best—and that is exactly what she achieved.

—Sarah C. Woodcock

---

**BEAUCHAMPS** (Beauchamp), **Pierre**
(mistakenly called Charles-Louis by some writers)
French dancer, choreographer, teacher, musician, composer, and conductor. Born in Paris (baptized 30 October), into a professional musical family, 1631. Studied as the apprentice of Monsieur Jourdain, and also possibly with his father. Dancing début as court dancer (in *Le Dérèglement des passions*), 1648, soon becoming solo dancer; first choreography c. 1655; became the first "Intendant des Ballets du Roi", responsible for the production of all court ballets, 1661; also director of ballets de college at Jesuit seminary; maître de ballet and joint director, with Jean-Baptiste Lully, of L'Académie royale de musique (Paris Opéra), 1672; appointed Chancellor, L'Académie royale de danse, 1680; retired from the Opéra on Lully's death, 1687, continuing as court choreographer; also devised a dance notation system: sued Raoul Feuillet for plagiarism, 1704 (but lost his case); also a leading teacher; pupils include Pécour, Favier, Faure, Blondy, Magny. Died in Paris, c. 1705.

**ROLES**

1648 Statue (duet), Marinier (duet), Nymphe, Sémélée in *Ballet des Dérèglements des passions* (ballet), Salle du Palais Royal, Paris

1653 Pas de quatre (cr) in *Balet royale de la nuit* (ballet; mus. Cambefort, Boesset), Salle de Petit-Bourbon, Paris

1654 Fou, More, Attaquant, Espagnol in *Ballet des Proverbes* (ballet), Louvre

Moment, Siècle d'Or, Printemps, Zephir in *Ballet du Temps* (ballet; mus. Mollier, Boesset), Louvre

Furie, Dryade, Académiste (cr) in *Les Noces de Pélée et de Thétis* (ballet in opera by Caproli; airs by Lully), Salle du Petit-Bourbon

1655 Jeune Berger, Chasseurs, Egyptien, Débauché, Suivant Armé (cr) in *Ballet des plaisirs* (ballet; also chor.), Louvre

Parties du Monde, Don Quichotte (cr) in *Ballet des Bienvenus* (ballet; mus. Lully), Compiègne

1656 Vent, Parfumeur, Insensé, Esclave More (cr) in *Ballet de Psyché* (ballet; also chor.), Louvre

Génie de France (solo), Roi More (cr) in *Ballet à la gloire de la Reine de Suède* (ballet, also known as *Ballet d'Essonnes*; also chor.), Essonnes

Entrée à Quatre (cr) in *La Galanterie du temps* (ballet-mascarade; mus. Lully), Louvre

Parties du Monde, Esclave, Platon, Sage de la Grèce in *Les Déguisements inopinés* (ballet-mascarade), Louvre

1657 Jeux, Maitre (solo), Mari Jalou, Paysan, Espion Espagnol (cr) in *Les Plaisirs troublés* (ballet-masquerade; also chor.), Louvre

Suivant, Chercheur de Trésor, Alchimiste, Suivant du Marié (cr) in *Ballet de l'amour malade* (ballet; mus. Lully), Grande Salle du Louvre

1658 Désespoir (solo), Polexandre (solo), and other entrées (cr) in *Ballet royal d'Alcidiane* (ballet; also chor.), Petit Bourbon, Paris

1659 Paysan, Ivrognes, Raison, Adroits (cr) in *Ballet de la Raillerie* (ballet; mus. Lully, Boesset), Louvre

1660 Basque Français, Esclave, Sylvain, Paysan Dansant (cr) in *Xerse* (ballet intermèdes, mus. Lully, in opera by Cavalli), Louvre

1661 Suite du Grand, Plaideur, Chevalier, Démon (cr) in *Ballet royal de l'impatience* (ballet; also chor.), Louvre

Moissoneur, Gallant (cr) in *Ballet des Saisons* (ballet; mus. Lully), Fontainebleau

1662 Foudre, Songe, Enseigne, Heure de la Nuit (cr) in *Hercule amoureux* (ballet; mus. Lully, in opera by Cavalli), Salle des Machines des Tuileries, Paris

1663 Le Marié, Valet, Officier (cr) in *Les Noces de village* (mascarade ridicule; mus. Lully), Château de Vincennes

Pirate (cr) in *Ballet des arts* (ballet; also chor. with Verpré), Palais Royal, Paris

1664 Un Plaisant, Un Galant, Un Magicien (solo) (cr) in *Le Mariage forcé* (comédie by Molière; also chor.), Louvre

Amour, La Renommé (solo), Guerrier (cr) in *Ballet des amours déguisés* (ballet; mus. Lully), Palais-Royal, Paris

Maure, Roger (solo; cr) in *Ballet du Palais d'Alcine* in *Les Plaisirs de l'île enchantée* (comédie-ballet by Molière; mus. Lully), Versailles

1665 Pollux, Berger, Philosophe, Pluton (cr) in *Ballet de la naisance de Vénus* (ballet; also chor.), Palais-Royal, Paris

Ecuyer, Paysans in *La Reception* (ballet-mascarade), Palais Royal, Paris
Dancer (cr) in *L'Amour médecin* (comédie by Molière; mus. Lully), Versailles
1666 Théagène (solo), Nymphe, Alexandre (cr) in *Ballet des muses* (ballet; also chor.), Saint Germain-en-Laye
1667 Egyptien Jouant de la Guitare in *Pastorale comique* (playlet by Molière) added to *Ballet des Muses* (also chor.) Saint-Germain-en-Laye
Maure (cr) in *Le Sicilien; ou, L'Amour peintre* (comédie by Molière; mus. Lully), Saint-Germain-en-Laye
1668 Plaisir, Masque Sérieux et Magnifique (cr) in *Le Carnaval* (ballet-mascarade, also called *Mascarade royale*; mus. Lully), Louvre (some sources say Tuileries)
Berger, Batelier, Suivant de Bacchus (cr) in *La Feste de Versailles* (*Grand Divertissement royal*; also chor., with Dolivet), Versailles
1669 L'Eau (solo; cr) in *Ballet de flore* (ballet; mus. Lully), Grand Salon, Tuileries
Page, Matassin (cr) in *Divertissement de Chambord* (also *Monsieur de Pourceaugnac*, comédie by Molière; mus. Lully), Chambord
1670 Dieu Marin, Pantomime, Faune, Jeunes Gens (cr) in *Divertissement royal* (with *Les Amants magnifiques*, comédie by Molière; also chor. with Dolivet), Saint-Germain
Turc Dansant, Espagnol (duet), Scaramouche (duet) in *Ballet des Nations* (cr) in *Le Bourgeois Gentilhomme* (comédie-ballet by Molière; also chor.), Chambord
1671 Cyclope, Furie, Enseigne (cr) in *Le Grand Ballet de Psyché* (tragédie-ballet; also chor.), Tuileries, Paris
Pêcheur, Sylvain, Turc, Scaramouche, Enseigne (cr) in *Ballet des Ballets* (mus. Lully), Saint-Germain-en-Laye
1672 Dancer (cr) in *Les Festes de l'Amour et de Bacchus* (pastorale; Debrosses), Jeu de Paume de Bel Air, Paris
1673 Africain, Comus (solos; cr) in *Cadmus et Hermione* (tragédie-lyrique; also chor.), Jeu de Paume de Bel Air, Paris
1674 Combattant, Démon (solo; cr) in *Alceste* (tragédie-lyrique; also chor.), Opéra, Paris
1675 Un Grand Seigneur de la Cour d'Égée (cr) in *Thésée* (tragédie-lyrique; also chor.), Saint-Germain-en-Laye
1676 Un Songe Funestre (cr) in *Atys* (tragédie-lyrique; also chor.), Saint-Germain-en-Laye
1677 Les Sept Arts Libéraux (cr) in *Isis* (tragédie-lyrique; also chor.), Saint-Germain-en-Laye
Dancer (cr) in *Psyché* (tragédie-lyrique; also chor.), Opéra, Paris
1679 Sorcier (solo; cr) in *Bellérophon* (tragédie-lyrique; also chor.), Opéra, Paris
1680 Suivant de la Discorde, Divinité Infernale (cr) in *Proserpine* (tragédie-lyrique; also chor.), Saint-Germain
1681 Mars (cr) in *Le Triomphe de l'amour* (ballet; also chor.), Château de Saint-Germain-en-Laye (performed later the same year at the Palais royal, Paris)
1682 Dancer (cr) in *Persée* (tragédie-lyrique; also chor.), Opéra, Paris
1683 Dancer (cr) in *Phaéton* (tragédie-lyrique; also chor.), Versailles
1684 Dancer (cr) in *Amadis de Gaule* (tragédie-lyrique; also chor.), Opéra, Paris
1685 Dancer (cr) in *Roland* (tragédie-lyrique; also chor.), Versailles
Dancer (cr) in *L'Eglogue de Versailles* (new version of *La Grotte de Versailles*; also chor.), Opéra, Paris
Sauvage Américain (cr) in *Le Temple de la paix* (ballet; also chor.), Fontainebleau
1686 Dancer (cr) in *Armide et Renaud* (tragédie-lyrique; also chor.), Opéra, Paris
Dancer (cr) in *Acis et Galatée* (pastorale héroique; also chor.), for the Duc de Vendôme, Anet
1687 Dancer in *Le Canal de Versailles* (divertissement; also chor.), Versailles
1689 Le Donneur de Livres in *Le Bourgeois Gentilhomme* (comédie-ballet by Molière; also chor.), Chambord
Plaisir Dansant (solo) in *Le Palais de Flore* (ballet), Trianon
1699 Danseur in *Intermèdes de la comédie des fées* (also chor.), Fontainebleau

## WORKS

1655 *Ballet des plaisirs* (ballet; mus. Lully, Boesset), Louvre
1656 *Ballet à la gloire de la reine de Suède* (*Ballet d'Essonnes*; mus. Mollier), Essonnes
*La Galanterie du temps* (ballet mascarade; mus. Lully), Louvre
*Ballet de Psyché* (ballet; mus. Lully, Boesset), Louvre
1657 *Ballet des plaisirs troublés* (ballet-mascarade; also mus., with Mollier, Lully), Louvre
1658 *Ballet d'Alcidiane* (mus. Lully, Mollier, Boesset), Louvre
1659 *Chacun fait le métier d'autruy* (ballet; mus. Lully), Château de Berny
1661 *Ballet royal de l'impatience* (ballet; mus. Lully, airs Dolivet, Beauchamps), Louvre
*Les Fâcheux* (comédie-ballet by Molière; mus. and chor. Beauchamps), Château de Vaux
1663 *Ballet des Arts* (ballet, chor. with Verpré; mus. Lully, Lambert), Palais Royal, Paris
1664 *Le Mariage forcé* (comédie by Molière; mus. Lully), Louvre, Paris
*Les Amours déguisés* (chor. possibly Beauchamps; mus. Lully), Palais Royal, Paris
1665 *Ballet de la naissance de Vénus* (ballet; mus. Lully), Palais Royal, Paris
1666 *Ballet des muses* (ballet; mus. Lully), Saint-Germain-en-Laye
1670 *Les Amants magnifiques* (part of *Divertissement Royal*; comédie by Molière; chor. with Dolivet, mus. Lully), Saint-Germain-en-Laye
*Le Bourgeois Gentilhomme* (comédie-ballet by Molière; mus. Lully), Chambord
1671 *Pomone* (pastorale; mus. Cambert), Théâtre Guénégaud, Paris
*Le Grand Ballet de Psyché* (tragédie-ballet by Molière, Corneille, Quinault; mus. Lully), Tuileries
1672 *Les Peines et plaisirs de l'amour* (pastorale; mus. Cambert), Théâtre Guénégaud, Paris
*Le Collier de perles* (comédie italienne; also mus.), Théâtre Italien, Paris
*Les Fêtes de l'Amour et de Bacchus* (pastorale by Molière, Quinault, Benserade; mus. Lully), Opéra, Paris
1673 *Cadmus et Hermione* (tragédie-lyrique; mus. Lully), Jeu de Paume de Bel Air, Paris
*Sédécias et Zénobie* (tragédie, with Lesuer; also mus.), Maison de M. Filz, Paris
1674 *Alceste; ou, Le Triomphe d'Alcide* (tragédie-lyrique; mus. Lully), Opéra, Paris

1675 *Thésée* (tragédie-lyrique, with Dolivet; mus. Lully), Opéra, Paris
*Le Carnaval* (ballet; mus Lully), Opéra, Paris
1676 *Atys* (tragédie-lyrique, with Dolivet; mus. Lully), Saint-Germain-en-Laye
1677 *Isis* (tragédie-lyrique; mus. Lully), Saint-Germain-en-Laye
1678 *Psyché* (tragédie-lyrique; mus. Lully), Opéra, Paris
1679 *Bellérophon* (tragédie-lyrique; mus. Lully), Opéra, Paris
1680 *Proserpine* (tragédie-lyrique; mus. Lully), Saint-Germain-en-Laye
1681 *Le Triomphe de l'amour* (ballet with Pécour; mus. Lully), Château de Saint-Germain-en-Laye
1682 *Persée* (tragédie-lyrique; mus. Lully), Opéra, Paris
1683 *Phaéton* (tragédie-lyrique; mus. Lully), Versailles
1684 *Amadis de Gaule* (tragédie-lyrique; mus. Lully), Opéra, Paris
1685 *Roland* (tragédie-lyrique; mus. Lully), Versailles
*L'Églogue de Versailles* (new version of *La Grotte de Versailles*; mus. Lully), Opéra, Paris
*Le Temple de la paix* (ballet; mus. Lully), Fontainebleau
1686 *Le Canal de Versailles* (divertissement; mus. Philidor), Versailles
*Ballet de la jeunesse* (ballet; mus. Lalande), Versailles
*Armide et Renaud* (tragédie-lyrique; mus. Lully), Opéra, Paris
*Acis et Galatée* (pastorale héroïque; mus. Lully), Anet

**Other works include:** ballets de collège—*Ballet du destin* (also mus., 1669), *Ballet de la paix* (also mus., 1679), *La France victorieuse sous Louis le Grand* (1680), *Plutus Dieu de richesses* (also mus., 1682), *Le Triomphe de la modération* (also mus., with Desmatins, Colasse, 1685), *Ballet des arts* (also mus., 1685), *Les Travaux d'Hercule* (also mus., 1686), *Ballet de Didon* (also mus., 1687), *Ballet de la jeunesse* (also mus., 1697).

## PUBLICATIONS

Parfaict, Claude et François, *Histoire du théâtre français*, 15 volumes, Amsterdam, 1735–49
Jal, A., *Dictionnaire critique de biographie et d'histoire*, Paris, 1872
Richardson, P.J.S., "The Beauchamp Mystery", *Dancing Times* (London), March–April, 1947
Christout, Marie-Françoise, *Le Ballet de cour de Louis XIV 1643–1672*, Paris, 1967
Derra de Moroda, Friderica, "Chorégraphie, the Dance Notation of the Eighteenth Century: Beauchamps or Feuillet?", *Book Collector* (London), vol. 16, 1967
Kunzle (Astier), Régine, "The Illustrious Unknown Choreographer, Pierre Beauchamp", *Dance Scope* (New York), 2 parts: vol. 8, no. 2, 1974; vol. 9, no. 1, 1975
Kunzle (Astier), Régine, "Pierre Beauchamps et les ballets de collège", *Dance Chronicle* (New York), vol. 6, no. 2, 1983; also printed in *La Recherche en danse* (Paris), vol. 3, 1983
Kunzle (Astier), Régine, "When Fiddlers Danced to their Own Tunes: The Beauchamps Scores", in *The Marriage of Dance and Music*, London, 1992
Kunzle (Astier), Régine, "Louis XIV, Premier danseur" in *Sun King: The Ascendancy of French Culture during the Reign of Louis XIV*, Washington, Toronto, and London, 1992

* * *

Pierre Beauchamps, called "the father of all ballet masters", set high teaching standards for ballet, which have been handed down to present generations. He applied logic to the art of dance. First of all, as Rameau tells us, he codified the five ballet positions of arms and feet. This formed a rational basis for systematizing the teaching of ballet, which had hitherto been dependent upon the idiosyncracies of dancing masters who might even, according to Louis XIV, do "irreparable harm" to students. Furthermore, Beauchamps worked for 30 years to invent an efficient system of dance notation at the King's behest. His methodology was adopted by Feuillet, who extensively published dances notated in this system without permission. When Beauchamps brought suit for infringement of property rights, witnesses acknowledged him as originator, but the court declined to assign him exclusive rights. Dismayed, Beauchamps protested his "vexation of having not only been deprived of the fruit of [his] labour, but most of all the honour of having carried out the king's orders". Beauchamps' worst fears were realized, in that the system is known today as "Feuillet notation".

Even worse, as Régine (Astier) Kunzle has pointed out, Beauchamps has been long mis-identified in the literature as Charles-Louis Beauchamp rather than Pierre. His father was a member of the King's violinists, as were countless cousins and his grandfather before him. Beauchamps made his début as a court dancer in the *Ballet des dérèglements des passions* on 23 February 1648. By 1655 he had acquired a reputation as a choreographer, and in 1661 was appointed "Intendant des Ballets du Roi".

That same year he proved himself a man of many talents as the composer, musical conductor, and choreographer for Molière's first comedy-ballet, *Les Fâcheux*. He continued to collaborate with Molière, choreographing many experiments in this new genre, including *Le Mariage forcé* and *Le Bourgeois Gentilhomme*. He composed music for over 150 ballets or divertissements, mostly after he was appointed director of the "ballets de college" at the Jesuit seminary, from the 1660s until his death.

Only a few years older than Louis XIV, Beauchamps became one of the King's favourite dancing partners in the ballets de cour and, much later, personal coach to His Majesty. Even though not himself an aristocrat, Beauchamps was selected for the signal honour of dancing a pas de quatre with the fourteen-year-old King in the first entrée of Benserade's *Le Balet royale de la nuit* (1653). An Italian musician named Lully made his début as a comic dancer in that ballet. Not long after that, Lully the composer, Benserade the librettist, Beauchamps the dancer and choreographer, and the King in the guise of both patron and performer, worked as a team in practically every court ballet given until Louis XIV's retirement from the stage in around 1669.

Beauchamps was not only involved in private court ballets and comedy-ballets, but also in the public performances of the earliest French operas. On 19 March 1671, he choreographed *Pomone*, the first opera produced at L'Académie de l'opéra, an institution that was later to develop into L'Académie royale de musique—more familiarly known as the Paris Opéra. After the King granted Lully a monopoly on opera production, Beauchamps became ballet master and was the interpreter of choice for Lully's operas and opera-ballets. He choreographed and probably danced in the premieres of Lully's works until the composer's death in 1687, including *Ballet royal de l'impatience*, *Les amours déguisés*, *Ballet de la naisance de Vénus*, *Psyché*, *Les Festes de l'Amour et de Bacchus*, *Thésée*, *Atys*, *Isis*, and *Le Triomphe de l'amour*. Beauchamps utilized professional female dancers in public performances for the first time in *Le Triomphe de l'amour*, where he danced the role of Mars.

In addition to all these honours and activities, the King appointed Beauchamps to head L'Académie royale de danse, an institution dedicated to the attempted "perfection" of the art of dance. Contrary to published reports, Beauchamps was not a founding member of that establishment in 1661.

By 1704, the old man was still known as Intendant des Ballets du Roi and director of L'Académie royale de musique. Although he had retired some time after 1702, he still retained the ability to perform the difficult step called a "tour billon", which involved a turning leap with the feet kicked forwards. Noted for the fire and vigour of his "grotesque" dances, Beauchamps could also perform in the "danse noble" or heroic style when necessary. Loret, in his *La Muse historique*, described "the incomparable" dancer, who was reputed to be one of the greatest dancers in all France, as "endowed with marvellous suppleness and elevation". The Parfaict brothers related how complex choreographic formations in Beauchamps' ballets were inspired by watching the random movements of his pet pigeons when he tossed corn kernels into their pens.

This highly esteemed dancer, choreographer, composer, and musician was regarded as a favourite of the King in that he was bestowed with many royal honours, some quite personal in nature. In addition to his unusually broad range of creative talents, Beauchamps was regarded as a discriminating collector of the fine arts. His private collection was acknowledged to be the best in Paris, and today his former possessions (including two Raphael Madonnas) hang in the Louvre, the Metropolitan Museum, El Prado, the Hermitage, and the National Gallery.

—Maureen Needham Costonis

---

## LE BEAU DANUBE

(original title: *Le Beau Danube bleu*)

**Choreography:** Léonide Massine
**Music:** Johann Strauss and Josef Lanner, arranged by Roger Desormière
**Design:** Vladimir and Elizabeth Polunin (scenery, after Constantin Guys), Comte Etienne de Beaumont (costumes)
**Libretto:** Léonide Massine
**First Production:** Comte Etienne de Beaumont's "Soirées de Paris", Théâtre de la Cigale, Paris, 17 May 1924
**Principal Dancers:** Lydia Lopokova (The Street Dancer), Léonide Massine (The Hussar)

**Other productions include:** Ballets Russes de Monte Carlo (new version, revised and staged Massine) with Nina Tarakanova (Street Dancer), Léonide Massine (Hussar), Tatiana Riabouchinska (Daughter), Irina Baronova (First Hand), David Lichine (King of the Dandies); Monte Carlo, 15 April 1933. Original Ballet Russe (new version; unattributed to Massine, "arranged by" Serge Lifar), as *Le Danube bleu*, with Olga Morosova (Street Dancer), David Lichine (Hussar); Sydney, 9 February 1940. Royal Danish Ballet (staged Massine), as *Den Skonne Donau*, with Erik Bruhn (Hussar); Copenhagen, 20 March 1948. Metropolitan Ballet (restaged Massine), with Alexandra Danilova (Street Dancer), Léonide Massine (Hussar), Svetlana Beriosova (First Hand); London, June 1949. London Festival Ballet (restaged Massine), with John Gilpin (Hussar); Southsea, 14 August 1950, and again London, 13 April 1971. Joffrey Ballet (staged Massine, with Alexandra Danilova coaching), with Alaine Haubert (Street Dancer), Dennis Wayne (Hussar); New York, 4 October 1972.

### PUBLICATIONS

Coton, A.V., *A Prejudice for Ballet*, London, 1933
Deakon, Irving, *To the Ballet*, New York, 1935
Beaumont, Cyril, *Complete Book of Ballets*, revised edition, London, 1951
Mauthner, Maria, "Queen of the Waltzes: The Centenary of *Le Beau Danube*", *Dancing Times* (London), August 1967
Massine, Léonide, "My First Sin", interview in *Dance and Dancers* (London), April 1971
Balanchine, George, and Mason, Francis, *Balanchine's Complete Stories of the Great Ballets*, Garden City, N.Y., 1977
Sorley Walker, Kathrine, *De Basil's Ballets Russes*, London, 1982
García-Márquez, Vicente, *Les Ballets Russes*, New York, 1990

* * *

*Le Beau Danube*, which together with *Mercure* was one of two sole survivors of five pieces made by Massine in 1924 for the "Soirées de Paris" of Comte Étienne de Beaumont, is a prime example of the genre of ballet best described as "delightful entertainment", and forms one in the long chain of successful ballets by Massine which seek to delight, amuse, and interest, while yet remaining faithful to the choreographer's own exacting standards. Its historical importance lies in the fact that it was the first ballet to earn itself a permanent place in the twentieth-century ballet repertoire after being made by a choreographer at the time of, or shortly after, a break with Diaghilev. Such a break when it occurred in connection with other choreographers could result in partial or total paralysis of the creative abilities, not—as in this case—in the creation of works which would survive, and bear revival decades later.

*Le Beau Danube*, at least in the version presented by the Blum/de Basil Ballets Russes on 15 April 1933 in Monte Carlo, is a perfect example of the fusion of different equally important elements, resulting in a flawless work of art, on no matter what level. The story is just plausible enough to hold the audience's interest, sitting lightly as it does on the somewhat ephemeral structure provided by the music. The décor and costumes are tasteful, suitable, and never loud or obtrusive; the choreographic structure is inventive, romantic, comic, and pathetic, in proportions exactly blended to produce a lightly whipped soufflé which melts in the mouth and leaves a faint, delicious taste behind—as befits a moral tale (free of all moralizing, one must hasten to add) of an older man of the world, whose engagement to an innocent young girl is put in jeopardy by the reappearance of a former mistress.

Though the ballet was originally produced with Lydia Lopokova as the Street Dancer, she only performed the role in Paris, and the ballerina with whom the character was most associated was Alexandra Danilova, whose piquant, vivid personality was the only one in the 1930s which could hold its own completely when contrasted with that of Massine, and which also provided a perfect foil to her rival in the ballet, the fiancée, as danced by Tatiana Riabouchinska. The dazzling "First Hand" of Irina Baronova and the other smaller parts were given with the meticulous attention to detail which always characterized Massine's work, and the light-hearted atmosphere of *Le Beau Danube* made it the ideal conclusion to an evening at the ballet, while the choreographer himself as the Hussar added one more to his amazingly comprehensive roster of fully differentiated characters. His mastery of the theatre—manifested in this ballet at the moment when the Hussar, left alone by his distraught fiancée, stands motionless centre stage and slowly raises his hand while the audience sits riveted—was one of the many facets of his personality which helped to make

*Le Beau Danube*, with Tatiana Riabouchinska and Léonide Massine in a Ballets Russes de Monte Carlo revival, London, 1933

him a legend in his own lifetime.

The ballet itself has triumphantly survived reproduction by many other companies, notably London Festival Ballet (now English National Ballet), in whose revival John Gilpin made an extremely dashing figure of the Hussar, even if his portrayal was not quite so sophisticated as that of the role's creator. Those who remember the production by Metropolitan Ballet will not easily forget the "in joke" provided by the spectacle of the First Hand, portrayed by Svetlana Beriosova, flirting with the Strong Man, portrayed by her father, Nicholas Beriozoff.

—Leo Kersley

---

**BEAUGRAND, Léontine**

French dancer. Born in Paris, 26 April 1842. Studied at the School of L'académie royal de musique (Paris Opéra), pupil of Mme. Dominique and Marie Taglioni, from 1850. Stage début, at age eleven, as page in *Jovita*, Paris Opéra; dancer, corps de ballet, Paris Opéra, 1857–60; coryphée, 1860–64; principal dancer, 1864–80. Died in Paris, 27 May 1925.

**ROLES**

1857 Ensemble (cr) in *Marco Spada* (Mazilier), Opéra, Paris
1858 Ensemble (cr) in *Sacountala* (L. Petipa), Opéra, Paris
A "Flying Sylph" (corps de ballet) in *La Sylphide* (revival; Taglioni), Opéra, Paris
1859 Divertissement, ensemble (cr) in *Herculanum* (opera; mus. David, chor. Mazilier), Opéra, Paris
1860 Divertissement, ensemble (cr) in *Pierre de Medicis* (opera; Poniatowski), Opéra, Paris
Pas de Ninivienne (cr) in *Semiramis* (opera; mus. Rossini, chor. L. Petipa), Opéra, Paris
Pas de trois (cr) in *Le Papillon* (M. Taglioni), Opéra, Paris
1863 Pas de quatre (cr) in *Diavolina* (Saint-Léon), Opéra, Paris
Peasant Pas de deux in *Giselle* (Coralli, Perrot), Opéra, Paris
1864 Title role in *Diavolina* (Saint-Léon), Opéra, Paris
1864/66 Divertissement in *Le Roi d'Yvetot* (L. Petipa), Opéra, Paris
Divertissement in *La Muette de Portici* (opera; mus. Auber), Opéra, Paris
Divertissement in *Guillaume Tell* (opera; mus. Rossini), Opéra, Paris
Divertissement in *La Juive* (opera; mus. Halévy), Opéra, Paris
1866 Danse Tacquetée (cr) in *Don Juan* (opera; mus. Mozart, chor. Saint-Léon), Opéra, Paris
Pas (cr) in *La Source* (Saint-Léon), Opéra, Paris
1867 The White Pearl (cr) in *Le Ballet de la reine* (Divertissement) in *Don Carlos* (opera; mus. Verdi, chor. L. Petipa), Opéra, Paris
1869 Hélène in Ballet in *Faust* (opera; mus. Gounod, chor. Justament), Opéra, Paris
1870 Dancer (cr) in *L'Invitation à valse* (Divertissement) in *Le Freychütz* (opera; mus. Weber, chor. Saint-Léon), Opéra, Paris
1871 Swanilda in *Coppélia* (revival; Saint-Léon), Opéra, Paris
1873 Dancer (cr) in *Gretna-Green* (Mérante), Opéra, Paris
1877 Carmencita (cr) in *Le Fandango* (Mérante), Opéra, Paris

**Léontine Beaugrand in *Le Papillon***

1880 Principal dancer in *La Fête du Printemps* (Divertissement) in *Hamlet* (opera; mus. Thomas, chor. L. Petipa), Opéra, Paris

**Other roles include:** Zulma (Lead Wili) in *Giselle* (Coralli, Perrot).

**PUBLICATIONS**

Fourcauld, Louis Boussés de, *Léontine Beaugrand*, Paris, 1881
Vieil abonné, Un (Mahalin, Paul), *Ces Demoiselles de l'Opéra*, Paris, 1887
Bernay, B., *La Danse au théâtre*, Paris, 1890
Beaumont, Cyril, *Three French Dancers of the Nineteenth Century*, London, 1935
Richardson, Philip, "Some *Coppélia* Memories", *Dancing Times* (London), October 1944
Migel, Parmenia, *The Ballerinas: from the Court of Louis XIV to Pavlova*, New York, 1972
Guest, Ivor, *The Ballet of the Second Empire*, London, 1974

* * *

Dancers have long struggled against a prevailing provincial attitude which discredits native talent performing on home turf. French ballerina Léontine Beaugrand, whose career was confined to the Paris Opéra's stage, was no exception to the phenomenon. Having neither an international reputation, a powerful protector, nor beauty and exotic appeal, Beaugrand, one of the Second Empire's better dancers, achieved only minor recognition through limited exposure in major roles—despite her considerable proficiency and artistry.

It was the Opéra, which persisted in promoting imported talent, and not the Press, which usually idolized physical beauty, that deterred Beaugrand's career. Despite her plain features, she attracted favourable commentary and warm praise from the critics, including a poem lamenting her retirement. Renowned writer Théophile Gautier had recognized her handicap as a "local" dancer and noted that a star could not be produced from a "garden fly". But, following her progress, he judged, "To-day a bud is unfolding which . . . will become a charming flower." And, remarking upon her viability as a "front rank" dancer he wryly observed, ". . . yet the powers that be still persist in borrowing stars of lesser worth from distant skies".

Slowly rising from the petite classe to principal stature, the skinny, homely Beaugrand had her début at the Opéra as a substitute page in Joseph Mazilier's *Jovita*, drafted for want of a prettier choice. Her official début as coryphée was in Marie Taglioni's *Le Papillon*, where she performed in a pas de trois—the type of role which was to characterize her career. Although Charles Nuitter, the Paris Opéra's archivist and *Coppélia*'s scenarist, conceived Swanilda for Beaugrand, Opéra manager Emile Perrin, doubting her box office potential, awarded the role to one of Beaugrand's classmates, a young Italian dancer called Giuseppina Bozzacchi (from whom Beaugrand eventually inherited the part).

Technically an accomplished ballerina—precise, strong, and rhythmic—Beaugrand was praised for her expressive phrasing and for her crisp, agile pointe work. Although noted for grace, lightness, and elevation, she also moved with energy and athleticism, as was appropriately displayed in Arthur Saint-Léon's *L'Invitation à valse*, a divertissement in *Le Freychütz*. Beaugrand frequently featured as a soloist in divertissements, and was lauded for masterful performances in Act II of Saint-Léon's *La Source* and in an interpolated variation in *Don Juan*. Successfully interpreting the leads in Saint-Léon's *Diavolina* and *Coppélia*, Beaugrand won accolades for her sparkling performances, which were highlighted by her instinct for comedy.

Beaugrand possessed a nervous, temperamental disposition, but was witty off-stage as well as on, and was known for her clever retorts to her colleagues' catty remarks. But she was kind by nature, as witnessed by her genuine friendliness towards her rival Bozzacchi, and she was a humanitarian, actively involved in the relief effort during the Franco-Prussian War.

Beaugrand's career was marked by irony. Overlooked in Paris for being local talent, the dancer whose technique exemplified the French school and whose miming aptitude was suitable to French tastes only danced secondary roles, while imported stars (especially the Italians, who were heavily criticized) often failed to satisfy the public's expectations.

Dedicated to the Opéra and to her art, Beaugrand was conscientious and hard-working, and persevered despite numerous disappointments. Motivated by self-discipline, she continued to practise in her apartment during the siege of Paris (which consequently closed the Opéra), and was prepared to perform when the theatre reopened. Despite her loyalty, however, the politics which inhibited her artistic potential also ended her career, forcing her into premature retirement.

The greatest irony, however, was in her favour. After the Franco-Prussian War, with no competition remaining, Beaugrand was finally cast in the role initially intended for her—Swanilda in *Coppélia*. An unequivocal success, it was the triumph of her career.

—Karen Dacko

---

**BEAUJOYEULX** (Beaujoyeux), **Balthasar de**

Italian violinist, composer, dancing master, and choreographer. Born Baldassare de Belgiojoso (later becoming known as Beaujoyeulx, or Beaujoyeux), before c.1535. Travelled to France with group of Piedmontese musicians, under Maréchal de Brissac, c.1555; musican and dancing master in the service of various royal households, and organizer of royal fêtes; valet de chambre to Catherine de Medici; participated in arrangement of court mascarades, including possibly *Paradis d'Amour* (1572), and *Le Ballet des Polonais* (1573); most famous work, *Ballet Comique de la Reine* (or *Balet Comique de la Royne*), produced at the Louvre, Paris, 1581; retired in 1584. Died in Paris, c.1587.

## PUBLICATIONS

By Beaujoyeux:

*Le Balet Comique de la Royne*, Paris, 1582

*Le Balet Comique de la Royne*, translated by Carol MacClintock and Lander MacClintock, American Institute of Musicology, New York, 1971

*Le Balet Comique de la Royne*, facsimile reproduction, with introduction by Margaret M. McGowan, New York, 1982

About Beaujoyeux:

Lacroix, P., *Ballets et Mascarades de Cour de Henri II à Louis XIV*, vol. 1, Geneva, 1868

Prunières, H., *Le Ballet de Cour en France*, Paris, 1914

Kirstein, Lincoln, *Dance: A Short History of Classic Theatrical Dancing*, New York, 1935

Walker, D.P., "The Aims of Baïf's Académie de Poésie et de Musique", *Musica Disciplina*, vol. 1, no. 2, 1946

Yates, Frances, *The French Academies of the Sixteenth Century*, 1947

McGowan, Margaret M., *L'Art du Ballet de Cour en France 1581–1643*, Paris, 1963

Kirstein, Lincoln, *Movement and Metaphor: Four Centuries of Ballet*, New York, 1970

Anthony, J.R., *French Baroque Music from Beaujoyeulx to Rameau*, revised edition, London, 1973

Miller, James, "The Philosophical Background of Renaissance Dance", *York Dance Review* (North York, Ontario), Spring 1976

* * *

The sixteenth-century Italian violinist, dancing master, and choreographer Baldassare de Belgiojoso went to France from Savoy in about 1555 in the suite of the Maréchal de Brissac, and was employed by several royal households. He was rapidly noted for his talent at organizing court entertainments, and was appointed valet de chambre to Catherine de Medici, wife of Henri II. He served her and her three sons for 30 years.

Beaujoyeulx possibly collaborated in the mascarade *Paradis d'Amour* (1572). The following year he choreographed *Le Ballet des Polonais* to celebrate the election of Catherine's second son,

***Ballet aux ambassadeurs polonais*, arranged by Balthasar Beaujoyeulx, 1573**

the Duc d'Anjou, as King of Poland. His most famous work is *Le Ballet Comique de la Reine* (1581), which Queen Louise discussed with him personally beforehand. He too was responsible for the libretto of the ballet, published the following year.

Beaujoyeulx is generally acknowledged to be the father of French Court ballet. He was much influenced by the theories of the Académie de Musique et de Poésie (1571), led by the poet, Jean-Antoine de Baïf. In this society, poets, artists, musicians, and choreographers exchanged ideas in their desire to emulate the artistic achievements of antiquity. Inspired by the aims of the Académie to recreate classical drama and "vers et musique mesurés a l'antique", in which verse, music, and dance were closely correlated, Beaujoyeulx attempted to synthesize dance steps with each musical note and phrase. Following the Pythagorean–Platonic belief that the underlying principle of the universe is to be found in numbers, he created his choreography according to mathematical and geometric floor patterns which had mystical and symbolic meanings. These patterns were designed to be seen from above, so that their meaning could be clearly understood. He described dance as the geometrical arrangements of several people dancing in a group, to the varying harmony of several instruments. His love of music is attested to by his frequent references to the beauty and novelty of the music of the *Ballet Comique*—in particular, that of the consorts in the *Voulte Dorée*. He compares it to the celestial music of the spheres, which ravishes the soul with its exquisite harmonies. This praise suggests that the Academicians had made great progress in their attempts to create a more expressive musical style which would have beneficial ethical and emotional effects upon the listener.

Beaujoyeulx's choreography was envisaged as a visual expression of this celestial music, an imitation of the movements of the heavenly spheres, in which the courtly ladies exhibited cosmic order and harmony on earth. The emphasis was on accuracy of timing and absolute precision in the use of space and floor patterns. The stylistic qualities were those of grace, charm, and elegance of movement. Beaujoyeulx praises the dexterity of the ladies' dancing in the *Ballet Comique de la Reine*, saying that one would have thought they were in battle formation, so well did they keep in time to the music and in their place—everyone thought that Archimides himself would not have had a better understanding of geometrical proportions than did these princesses and ladies in this ballet. It has been suggested that the dancing in the court ballets was no different from ordinary social dancing. But although the same steps were used, the dances were especially choreographed for a specific occasion and theme. The description of the numerous figured dances in the *Ballet Comique de la Reine* shows the considerable complexity of the choreography.

In a laudatory poem on the publication of *Ballet Comique*, Billard addressed Beaujoyeulx as "Geometre, inventif, unique en ta science". Geometrically patterned dance was not, in fact, a new invention. In the *Ballet des Polonais*, for example, the dancers trace figures in triangular and square formations. From earliest times and right through the Middle Ages, mathematics and number symbolism had been accorded a mystical status. But Beaujoyeulx's harmonizing of music, verse, and dance was generally acknowledged to be a new invention, one in which the Academy's aim to achieve a unity of the arts was fully realized. Moreover, this collaboration of poets, composers, and scenic designers under his overall direction marks the central importance of the choreographer in sixteenth-century French court ballet.

—Françoise Carter

---

**BEAUMONT, Comte Etienne de** *see* **DE BEAUMONT, Comte Etienne**

---

**BECK, Hans**

Danish dancer, choreographer, and ballet master. Born in Haderslev, Denmark, 31 May 1861. Studied at the Royal Danish Ballet School, Copenhagen, pupil of Georg Brodersen, from 1869. Début in 1879: solo dancer (principal dancer), Royal Danish Ballet, from 1881, partnering Valborg Borchsenius from 1890; ballet master, Royal Danish Ballet, 1894–1915: staged Danish production of *Coppélia*, 1896, and own ballet, *The Little Mermaid*, 1909; retired in 1915, continuing as rehearsal coach and adviser on Bournonville productions until his death. Died in Copenhagen, 10 June 1952.

**ROLES**

1876 Heimdal in *The Valkyrie* (Bournonville), Royal Danish Ballet, Copenhagen

**Hans Beck as James in *La Sylphide*, c.1882**

1880 The Bridegroom in *Wedding in Harlander* (Bournonville), Royal Danish Ballet, Copenhagen
A Warrior (cr) in *Aditi* (Hansen), Royal Danish Ballet, Copenhagen
1881 Pas de deux in *Flower Festival at Genzano* (Bournonville), Royal Danish Ballet, Copenhagen
1882 Antonio in *The Festival of Albano* (Bournonville), Royal Danish Ballet, Copenhagen
Ulf Drabant in *Valdemar* (Bournonville), Royal Danish Ballet, Copenhagen
James in *La Sylphide* (Bournonville), Royal Danish Ballet, Copenhagen
1884 Minnesanger in *Valdemar* (Bournonville), Royal Danish Ballet, Copenhagen
Alonso in *The Toreador* (Bournonville), Royal Danish Ballet, Copenhagen
Principal dancer in *The Whims of Cupid and the Ballet Master* (Galeotti), Royal Danish Ballet, Copenhagen
1886 Edmond in *Night Shadow* (*La Sonnambula*; Bournonville after Aumer), Royal Danish Ballet, Copenhagen
Fabriccio in *Pontemolle* (Bournonville), Royal Danish Ballet, Copenhagen
Alexis in *Konservatoriet* (Bournonville), Royal Danish Ballet, Copenhagen
Skirner in *The Lay of Thrym* (Bournonville), Royal Danish Ballet, Copenhagen
1887 Halvor in *Wedding in Harlander* (Bournonville), Royal Danish Ballet, Copenhagen
1888 Danish Sailor, Chinese Dance, and Lieutenant Vilhelm in *Far From Denmark* (Bournonville), Royal Danish Ballet, Copenhagen
1889 Junker Ove in *A Folk Tale* (Bournonville), Royal Danish Ballet, Copenhagen
1891 Carelis in *The Kermesse in Bruges* (Bournonville), Royal Danish Ballet, Copenhagen
1893 Title role in *Valdemar* (Bournonville), Royal Danish Ballet, Copenhagen
1894 Helge in *The Valkyrie* (Bournonville), Royal Danish Ballet, Copenhagen
1895 Loke in *The Lay of Thrym* (Bournonville), Royal Danish Ballet, Copenhagen
1896 Franz (cr) in *Coppélia* (also chor., with Glasemann, after Saint-Léon), Royal Danish Ballet, Copenhagen
1903 Ola in *Wedding in Hardanger* (Bournonville), Royal Danish Ballet, Copenhagen
Madge (the Witch) in *La Sylphide* (Bournonville), Royal Danish Ballet, Copenhagen
1904 Jokey, Provençal, Wine Peasant, Lieutenant Ivanov in *From Siberia to Moscow* (Bournonville), Royal Danish Ballet, Copenhagen
1905 Chauvin in *Pontemolle* (Bournonville), Royal Danish Ballet, Copenhagen
Volunteer, Dirk the Peasant, Edouard du Puy in *The King's Volunteers at Amager* (Bournonville), Royal Danish Ballet, Copenhagen
1906 Pierrot (cr) in *Les Millions d'Arlequin* (Walbom after Petipa), Royal Danish Ballet, Copenhagen
1907 Axel Hvide in *Valdemar* (Bournonville), Royal Danish Ballet, Copenhagen
1909 Geert in *The Kermesse in Bruges* (Bournonville), Royal Danish Ballet, Copenhagen
Principal dancer (cr) in *The Little Mermaid* (also chor.), Royal Danish Ballet, Copenhagen
1910 The Prince (cr) in *Cinderella* (Walbom), Royal Danish Ballet, Copenhagen

## WORKS

1909 *The Little Mermaid* (mus. Henriques), Royal Danish Ballet, Copenhagen

Also staged:
1896 *Coppélia* (with Glasemann, after Saint-Léon; mus. Delibes), Royal Danish Ballet, Copenhagen
1901 *Napoli* (after Bournonville; mus. Paulli, Helsted, Gade, Lumbye), Royal Danish Ballet, Copenhagen (revised and restaged several times subsequently)

## PUBLICATIONS

By Beck:
*From My Life and Dancing*, Copenhagen, 1944

About Beck:
Reumert, Elith, *The History of the Danish Ballet*, Copenhagen, 1922
Kragh-Jacobsen, Svend, and Krogh, Torben (eds.), *Den Kongelige Danske Ballet*, Copenhagen, 1952
Kragh-Jacobsen, Svend, *The Royal Danish Ballet: An Old Tradition and a Living Present*, London, 1955

Van Haven, Mogens, *The Royal Danish Ballet*, Copenhagen, 1961
Ralov, Kirsten, *The Bournonville School*, New York, 1979
Lundgren, Henrik, "Bournonville in Denmark and Abroad", in *Perspektiv på Bournonville*, Copenhagen, 1980

* * *

Hans Beck succeeded Louis Gade and Emil Hansen as the third ballet master at the Royal Danish Ballet after August Bournonville. Although not a pupil of Bournonville's himself, he remained faithful to the master's work and spirit. At Beck's début two days before Bournonville's death, the old man was very favourably impressed: "For this young man's sake I might have wanted still to work at the theatre, for his talents are unique", he was quoted as saying by his daughter Charlotte.

Beck's blond, boyish figure and outstanding masculine vitality made him ideal for the male Bournonville roles. From the heroic Nordic types of *Valdemar* and later *A Folk Tale*, to the fiery Latin Alonso of *The Toreador* and Gennaro the fisherman of *Napoli*, Beck was a virile and powerful stage presence. He performed all without affectation and with excellent characterization and dedication. Eventually, all the main roles of the Bournonville repertory became Beck's natural property: James in *La Syphide* (later Madge the witch became his as well, being traditionally played by a male dancer); the dancing master of *Konservatoriet*; Helge in *The Valkyrie*; Edouard in *The King's Volunteers on Amager*, and many more. The serpent-like, ambiguous Loke in *The Lay of Thrym*, a complex mime role, was the culmination of a career mostly containing heroic roles.

As ballet master, Beck dedicated his work to preserving Bournonville's ballets and to promoting the great choreographer's ideas of joy and naturalness of movement. Thus he made Bournonville's choreographic legacy his own in his memoirs, *From My Life and Dancing*. Beck formalized the Bournonville steps into classes, one for each day of the week, thus securing the tradition for future generations of students and dancers. Thanks to his faithfulness to the repertoire, Beck lost only one of the sixteen ballets that Bournonville himself had thought fit to survive him. (The lost ballet is *From Siberia to Moscow*.) Beck's eminent sense of the Bournonville style even enabled him to arrange and choreograph variations which arguably came quite close to the master's own intentions. Thus, the present form of the celebrated third act of *Napoli* is actually Beck's work.

By the time Beck retired in 1915, he had managed to keep the Royal Danish Ballet free from the influence of the revolutionary balletic ideas sweeping over Europe with Diaghilev's Ballets Russes. Beck stepped aside, acknowledging a need for innovation, but having secured a tradition for his Danish company. However, with his departure, the problem of the Bournonville heritage began. Fortunately, in the 1930s and 1940s ballet master Harald Lander asked Beck to assist him and Valborg Borchsenius, Beck's own former partner, to reconstruct a number of Bournonville's ballets. These, thankfully, remain in the Danish repertoire today.

—Marie-Louise Kjølbye

---

**BEDELLS, Phyllis**

English dancer and teacher. Born in Bristol, 9 August 1893. Studied with Theodore Gilmer in Nottingham, and in London with Madame Cavallazzi, from 1907, Alexander Genée, from 1908, Adolph Bolm and Enrico Cecchetti, 1911, and Anna Pavlova, 1912. Married Major Ian Macbean, 1918; one son, David, and one daughter, dancer Jean Bedells. Professional début in *Alice in Wonderland*, Prince of Wales Theatre, 1906; dancer, Empire Theatre, London, from 1907, becoming premiere danseuse, 1914–15; principal dancer in revues produced by Albert de Courville, including *Razzle Dazzle* (Drury Lane Theatre, 1916); also danced in films including *The Mystery Road* (Lasky Famous Players, 1920), and in plays, including *A Merry Death* (dir. Komisarzhevsky for Lahda Society, 1919/20); performed on concert tours with Laurent Novikoff, 1919/20, and Anton Dolin, 1926–27; dancer, choreographer, and committee member, Camargo Society, 1930–33; retired from stage, 1935; founding committee member and examiner, Association of Operatic Dancing (becoming Royal Academy of Dancing), from 1920; teacher, opening first school in Bristol, 1923, and later opening school in London; Vice-President, Royal Academy of Dancing, from 1946. Recipient: Queen Elizabeth II Coronation Award, Royal Academy of Dancing, 1958; Fellow of the Royal Academy of Dancing, 1971. Died in Henley-on-Thames, 2 May 1985.

**ROLES**

1907 The Naughty Pupil in *The Débutante* (Farren), Empire Theatre, London
Tiny Trippit (cr) in *The Belle of the Ball* (Farren), Empire Theatre, London
1908 Poppy (cr) in *A Day in Paris* (Farren), Empire Theatre, London
1910 Red Riding Hood Pas de deux from *The Sleeping Beauty* (after Petipa), Empire Theatre, London
The Head Pupil in *The Dancing Master* (Act I of *The Débutante*; Farren), Empire Theatre, London
The Débutante in *The Dancing Master* (Farren), Empire Theatre, London
1911 Ianthe in *Sylvia* (Farren), Empire Theatre, London
Title role in *Sylvia* (Farren), Empire Theatre, London
1912 The Slave of the Ring (cr; also chor.) in *Aladdin* (pantomime), Empire Theatre, London
1913 First Fairy (cr) in *Titania* (Kyasht), Empire Theatre, London
Sun Ray (cr) in *The Reaper's Dream* (Kyasht), Empire Theatre, London
Title role in *Titania* (Kyasht), Empire Theatre, London
"Pavlova" (cr) in *Nuts and Wine* (ballet in revue; also chor.), Empire Theatre, London
1914 Principal dancer (cr) in *Carnaval de Venise* (Cecchetti), ballet in *The Passing Show* (revue), Palace Theatre, London
Mademoiselle Paris (cr) in *Europe* (E. Espinosa), Empire Theatre, London
1915 The Spirit of the Vine (cr) in *The Vine* (Farren), Empire Theatre, London
Taglioni (cr) in *La Sylphide*, ballet in *Watch Your Step* (revue), Empire Theatre, London
Giroflée, A Country Girl (cr) in *Pastorale* (Majilton), Empire Theatre, London
1919/20 The Young Girl in *Le Spectre de la rose* (after Fokine), Charity Ball, Royal Opera House, London
Moon Maiden (cr) in *Pierrot of the Minute* (Gavrilov), Royal Opera House, London
Principal dancer (cr) in *Naïl* (opera; chor. Gavrilov), Royal Opera House, London

**Phyllis Bedells, 1926**

1920 Principal dancer (cr) in *A Fisherman's Love* (Novikoff), Lahda Society, London
Pas de deux from *Swan Lake* Act II (after Ivanov), Lahda Society, London
1926 Principal dancer (cr) in *Clair de Lune* (also chor.), ballet in *By the Way* (revue), Apollo Theatre, London
1927 Bluebird Pas de deux from *The Sleeping Beauty* (after Petipa), Variety tour with Dolin, London
1928 English Rose (cr) in *Pro Patria* (Espinosa), Winter Gardens, London
1929 Principal dancer in *Hiawatha* (pageant-opera; chor. Euphan Maclaren), Royal Albert Hall, London
Swanilda in *Coppélia* (after Petipa, Cecchetti), Association of Operatic Dancing, London
1930 The Abbess in *Ballet of the Nuns* (staged Alexander Genée), from *Robert the Devil* (opera; mus. Meyerbeer), Camargo Society, London
1931 Principal dancer (cr) in *Straussiana* (N. Legat), Camargo Society, London
Principal dancer (cr) in *Fête Polonaise* (de Valois), Camargo Society, London
Principal dancer (cr) in *Ballade in A Flat* (also chor.), Camargo Society, London
1932 Nocturne and Solo Valse in *Les Sylphides* (after Fokine), Association of Operatic Dancing, Copenhagen
1934 A Heavenly Messenger and Salomé (cr) in *The Messiah* (dramatized oratorio; also chor.), Sheffield

**Other roles include:** for concert performances with Novikoff—*Gopak*, *Caprice*, *The Prince and the Groom*, *Serenade*, *Krakoviak*; with Dolin—*Exercises*, *Rugger*, *Movement* (de Valois).

## WORKS

1912 The Slave of the Ring (solo) in *Aladdin* (pantomime); later used in *Everybody's Doing It* (revue by Grossmith and Bovill; mus. Clarke), Empire Theatre, London
1913 "Pavlova" in *Nuts and Wine* (revue; mus. Tours), Empire Theatre, London
Dances in *Love and Laughter* (operetta; mus. Oscar Straus), Lyric Theatre, London
Dances in *The Laughing Husband* (musical play; mus. Eysler), New Theatre, London
1926 *Clair de lune*, ballet in *By The Way* (revue by Jeans and Simpson; mus. Ellis), Apollo Theatre, London
1931 *Ballade in A flat* (mus. Chopin, orchestrated Bax), Camargo Society, London
1933 *The Débutante* (mus. Clarke), Association of Operatic Dancing, London
1934 Dances in *The Messiah* (dramatized oratorio; mus. Beethoven, Saint-Saëns), Sheffield

## PUBLICATIONS

By Bedells:
"The Future of Ballet", with various co-authors, *Dancing Times* (London), December 1920
Articles on ballet technique, *Dancing Times* (London), from January 1942
*My Dancing Days*, London, 1954
"From my Scrapbook", *Dance and Dancers* (London), December 1956
"Phyllis Bedells' Scrapbook", *Dance and Dancers* (London), January 1957

About Bedells:
"Little Biographies of Famous Dancers", *Dancing Times* London), December 1917
Perugini, Mark, *A Pageant of Dance and Ballet*, London, 1935
"Schools and Teachers: Phyllis Bedells", *Dance and Dancers* (London), December 1956
Dolin, Anton, "Fifty Years of Service: Phyllis Bedells' Jubilee", *Dance and Dancers* (London), December 1956
"Honouring Phyllis Bedells", *Dancing Times* (London), February 1957
Guest, Ivor, *The Empire Ballet*, London, 1962
Borgnis, Jennifer, "The Forgotten Ballerina", *Dance and Dancers* (London), May 1982

* * *

By the time Phyllis Bedells died in 1985, it had been fifty years since her official farewell performance, ample time for collective memories of her stage career to die, and for her high reputation as teacher, examiner, and vice-president of the Royal Academy of Dancing to overshadow her theatrical successes. From her first London engagement as a child performer in 1906, she had risen, by 1913, to become the first British premiere danseuse at the Empire Theatre, succeeding to the Danish Adeline Genée and the Russian Lydia Kyasht, and performing their roles in the popular Empire ballets of the day, such as *The Débutante* (also known as *The Dancing Master*) and *Titania*. But Bedells' initiation into the life of the "ballerina" had been quite different from that of the next generation of English dancers, whose careers were made possible largely by the efforts of personalities such as herself.

Having given up formal education at the age of twelve in order to train at Theodore Gilmer's school in Nottingham, Bedells was earning a living as a seasoned professional before her fourteenth birthday. Her first training undoubtedly derived partly from the French: Gilmer's father is said to have studied at the Paris Opéra Ballet School. Later, in London, she would become familiar with what the other national schools had to offer: she was trained in the Italian style by Madame Cavallazi, in the Danish style by Alexander Genée, and in the Russian style by Adolph Bolm, Enrico Cecchetti, and Anna Pavlova.

As inspirational as those teachers may have been, it was still a piecemeal approach to acquiring technique, necessitated by the conditions of the time. Later, as a teacher and founder member of the Association of Operatic Dancing (to become the Royal Academy of Dancing), Bedells was to be an important figure in the development of a more systematic approach to the teaching of ballet in Britain, helping to lay down a syllabus which combined the best of the major continental schools while adapting to the special circumstances of Britain, and which established a system for examining and certifying teachers to ensure standards for the future.

As a dancer, Bedells had a talent to entertain which was ideal for the broad appeal of the Empire Theatre. One or two ballets would be presented on a bill alongside variety acts, and a ballet generally provided a rather superficial pretext for spectacle and amusing incident. At the same time, the written criticism of the day could be well-informed on the niceties of classical technique, and gives us a picture of Phyllis Bedells as a dancer without the continental brilliance of execution, but with an appealing warmth of performance. At the time of her taking on the title role of *Sylvia*, in 1911, she was described in these terms by J.E. Crawford Flitch: "Her training, so far as it goes, has been painstaking, but what chiefly distinguishes her performance from the routine work of the average English dancer is an unaffected zest, almost a vividness of delight, which the obvious troublesomeness of the technique is unable to depress."

Whether dancing the part of a child with a skipping rope in *A Day in Paris* (1908), or as the gleefully wicked spirit in *The Vine* (1915), or dancing Genée's old role of the understudy unexpectedly taking the ballerina's role in *The Débutante*, she was a sparkling performer.

Gradually, revue came to supersede variety at the Empire, incorporating ballet numbers but not giving the opportunity for more developed works. Bedells had the necessary versatility to make this change. Singing, acting, and comedy were all within her range. For some years after leaving the Empire in 1915, revues gave her most of her employment.

There was a greater change, though, which was implicit in the times. Kyasht and Bolm, Pavlova and Mordkin, but most of all the season by Diaghilev's Ballets Russes in 1911, revealed levels of artistry and technique surpassing her previous experience. When she first joined the Empire Theatre, even an artist of the stature of Adeline Genée rarely appeared there with a male partner, and the romantic hero's part in a ballet was taken by a female dancer. Until 1908, when Lydia Kyasht and Adolph Bolm arrived at the Empire, neither Bedells nor most of her fellow dancers had seen supported pas de deux. Within a few years, appearances by Russian dancers would become commonplace, and Bedells, with her constant application to learning all that she could from whomever came along, went on to become the partner of two prominent male dancers, Anton Dolin and Laurent Novikoff. Roles from the classical canon thus only came into her repertoire later in her career. Her favourite concert piece became "The Bluebird Pas de deux", which she first performed with Dolin in 1927; and she learned *Coppélia* from Alexander Genée in 1929.

Her career might have been different. Had she persisted with lessons at Astafieva's studio, for example, she might have joined Diaghilev. She would have liked to have accepted a place in Pavlova's company in 1913, but her contract at the Empire could not be broken. In any case, she felt no overwhelming desire to work abroad. There was about her a kind of English insularity; she might not have flourished elsewhere. The needs of her family came very high on her priorities, and besides, she saw much to admire in the ballet scene at home, not only in the new developments in British ballet in the 1930s, but in those long-forgotten Empire ballets, which she compared favourably with the works of Massine and de Valois. Her concern became that British dancers should receive the training and recognition they deserved. In order to raise that profile she committed herself fully, as dancer, choreographer, and committee member, to the work of the Camargo society, as a public platform for British ballet in the early 1930s.

In his appreciation of Bedells, written in 1956, Dolin suggests that she was not a "great" dancer but a "good" one, and that "goodness" manifested itself as a habit of public service. In putting herself as a celebrity fully behind the development of British ballet, Phyllis Bedells was a foundation stone upon which Rambert and de Valois could build the more obvious successes of the 1930s.

—Larraine Nicholas

---

**BÉJART, Maurice**

French dancer, choreographer, and ballet director. Born Maurice Jean Berger in Marseilles, 1 January 1927. Educated at the Lycée de Marseille; studied dance at the Marseilles Opera Ballet School, and with Lubov Egorova, Madame Rousane, Nora Kiss, and Léo Staats, Paris; also studied with Vera Volkova, London. Dancer, corps de ballet, Marseilles Opera, from 1945; principal dancer, Mona Inglesby's International Ballet, 1949–50, Cullberg Ballet, and Royal Swedish Ballet, Stockholm, 1951–52; choreographer from 1946, becoming artistic director, choreographer, and principal dancer, Ballets Romantiques (later Ballet de l'Étoile), 1952; founder, choreographer, and director, Ballet Théâtre de Paris de Maurice Béjart, from 1957; artistic director of newly assembled company at Théâtre de la Monnaie, Brussels, becoming Ballet du XXe Siècle, 1960–87; artistic director, Béjart-Ballet Lausanne, 1987–92; also director, MUDRA (name given to the École de Danse et d'Interpretation Artistique), affiliated with Ballet du XXe Siècle, 1971–88; director of Performing Arts, John F. Kennedy Memorial Centre, Paris, 1981; director, newly established RUDRA (combining MUDRA dance school and small affiliated company), from 1992. Recipient: Grand Prix de Choréographie au Théâtre des nations, 1960; Medal of the Syndicat professionel de la critique, 1960; Diploma of the Cercle de la Jeune Critique, 1960; Grand Prix de l'Université de la danse, 1960; Grand Prix au Théâtre les nations, 1961; Prix de la Fraternité, 1966; Grand Prix national de la musique, 1970; *Dance Magazine* Award, 1974; Erasmus Prize, 1974; Honorary Doctorate of the Free University of Brussels, 1979; Grand Prize of Société des auteurs, 1980; Chevalier des arts et des lettres, Commandeur de l'ordre de Léopold et Grand Officier de la Couronne, Belgium; Medal of the Order of the Rising Sun, Japan.

**ROLES**

1946 Principal dancer (cr) in *Petit Page* (also chor.), Gala, Rouen

1948 Principal dancer (cr) in *'Adame Miroir* (Charrat), Ballets de Paris

Musician in *Les Demoiselles de la nuit* (Petit), Ballets de Paris

Rose Adagio from *The Sleeping Beauty* (extracts; after Petipa), Ballets de Paris

Clown (cr) in *L'Ecuyère* (Lifar), Gala, Salle Pleyel, Paris

1949 Bluebird in *The Sleeping Beauty* (Petipa; staged Sergeyev), International Ballet

Siegfried in *Swan Lake* (Petipa, Ivanov; staged Sergeyev), International Ballet

Principal dancer in *Gaîté parisienne* (Massine), International Ballet

Poet in *Les Sylphides* (Fokine), International Ballet

1950 Principal dancer (cr) in *Le Répétition au violon* (also chor.), Palais Chaillot, Paris

Jason (cr) in *Medea* (Cullberg), Cullberg Ballet, Gaevle, Sweden

Principal dancer (cr) in *L'Inconnu* (also chor.), Royal Swedish Ballet, Stockholm

1953 Principal dancer (cr) in *Les Sept Tentations du diable* (also chor.), Ballets Romantiques

Hamlet/Romeo (cr) in *Le Songe d'une nuit d'hiver* (also chor.), Ballets Romantiques, Paris

1954 Le Valet Grumio (cr) in *La Mégère apprivoisée* (also chor.), Ballet de l'Étoile, Paris

Principal dancer (cr) in *La Lettre* (also chor.), Ballet de l'Étoile, Paris

Principal dancer (cr) in *Chaussons rouges* (also chor.), Ballet de l'Étoile, Paris

Pas de deux from *Coppélia* Act III (Sergeyev after Petipa), Ballet de l'Étoile

**Maurice Béjart**

L'Homme (cr) in *Symphonie pour un homme seul* (also chor.), Ballet de l'Étoile, Paris
Pas de trois (cr) in *Arcane I* (also chor.), Fontaine Quatre Saisons, Paris
1956 Principal dancer (cr) in *Voila l'homme* (also chor.), Fontaine Quatre Saisons, Paris
Principal dancer (cr) in *Le Balayeur* (also chor.), Gala, Enghien
Principal dancer (cr) in *Le Teck* (also chor.), Ballet de l'Étoile, Marseilles
1957 Principal dancer (cr) in *Sonate à trois* (also chor.), Ballet de l'Étoile, Essen
Principal dancer (cr) in *Chapeaux* (also chor.), Ballet Théâtre de Maurice Béjart, Paris
Title role (cr) in *Pulcinella* (also chor.), Ballet Théâtre de Maurice Béjart, Belgian television
1958 Poet (cr) in *Orphée* (also chor.), Ballet Théâtre de Maurice Béjart, Liège television
"Choreographer" (cr) in *Études rythmiques* (also chor.), Ballet Théâtre de Maurice Béjart, Devon
Solo (cr) in *La Voix* (also chor.), Ballet Théâtre de Maurice Béjart
1959 Title role (cr) in *Pulcinella* (second version; also chor.), Ballet Théâtre de Maurice Béjart, Monte Carlo
Speaker (text) (cr) in *La Mer* (also chor.), Ballet Théâtre de Maurice Béjart, Berlin
1960 Principal dancer (cr) in *La Douceur du tonnerre* (also chor.), Ballet du XXe Siècle, Belgian television
1962 Principal dancer (cr) in *Temps*, part of *Suite Viennoise* (also chor.), Ballet du XXe Siècle, Brussels
1965 Principal dancer (cr) in *Prospective: Erotica* (also chor.), Ballet du XXe Siècle, Brussels
1968 L'Aimé (cr) in *La Nuit obscure* (also chor.), Ballet du XXe Siècle, Avignon
1974 Choreographer/Master of Ceremonies (cr) in *Seraphite* (also chor.), Ballet du XXe Siècle, Brussels
1975 Mephistopheles, Old Faust (cr) in *Notre Faust* (also chor.), Ballet du XXe Siècle, Brussels
1977 Principal dancer in *Le Molière imaginaire* (also chor.), Ballet du XXe Siècle, Paris
1980 Principal dancer in *Casta Diva* (also chor.), IRCAM International, Paris
1981 Principal dancer (cr) in *Les Chaises* (also chor.), Rio de Janeiro
1982 Greek Dancer (cr) in *Thalassa Mare Nostrum* (also chor.), Arles

## WORKS

1946 *Petit Page* (mus. Rachmaninov, Chopin), Gala, Rouen
1950 *L' Inconnu* (mus. Piaf, Fontenay), Royal Swedish Opera House, Stockholm
*La Répétition au violon* (mus. Offenbach), Gala, Palais Chaillot, Paris
*Les Patineurs* (mus. Waldteufel), Gala, Palais Chaillot, Paris
1952 *L'Oiseau de feu* (mus. Stravinsky), Swedish television
1953 *Redemption* (mus. Lizst), Gala, Bordeaux
Cavalier/Poet (cr) in *Pas des déesses* (Brieux), Ballet de l'Étoile
1955 Principal dancer (cr) in *La Nuit de la Saint-Jean* (also chor.), Gala, Palais Chaillot, Paris
Principal dancer (cr) in *La Belle au boa* (also chor.), Ballet de l'Étoile, Paris
Principal dancer in *Capriccio Italien* (also chor.), Gala, Palais Chaillot, Paris

*Les Sept Tentations du diable* (mus. Chopin), Ballets romantiques
*La Songe d'une nuit d'hiver* (mus. Chopin), Ballets romantiques, Paris
*L'Etrangère* (mus. Chopin), Ballets Romantiques, Paris
1954 *La Lettre* (mus. Schubert), Ballet de l'Étoile, Paris
*La Mégère apprivoisée* (mus. Scarlatti), Ballet de l'Étoile, Paris
*Les Chaussons rouges* (mus. Berlioz), Ballet de l'Étoile, Paris
1955 *La Nuit de la Saint-Jean* (mus. Swedish folksongs), Gala, Palais Chaillot, Paris
*La Belle au boa* (mus. Rossini), Ballet de l'Étoile, Paris
*Capriccio Italien* (mus. Tchaikovsky), Gala, Palais Chaillot, Paris
*Symphonie pour un homme seul* (mus. Schaeffer, Henry), Ballet de l'Étoile, Paris
*Voyage au coeur d'un enfant* (mus. Henry), Ballet de l'Étoile, Paris
Dances in *Mort d'un poète* (opera; mus. Delannoy), Cie Feres, Venice
Dances in *L'Amour et la folie* (opera; mus. Defaye), Cie Feres, Venice
*Arcane* (mus. Prévert, Henry), Fontaine Quatre Saisons, Paris
*Brève Rencontre* (mus. Constant), French television
1956 *Voilà l'homme* (mus. Arthuys), Fontaine Quatre Saisons, Paris
*Conseils à une jeune parisienne* (poem by Musset), J.M.F., Salle Pleyel, Paris
*Haut Voltage* (mus. Constant, Henry), Ballets Janine Charrat, Metz
*Concertino* (pas de deux; mus. Albinoni), Danse et la culture, Maison de la Chimie, Paris
*Le Cercle* (mus. Bach, Henry), Netherlands Ballet
*Tanit* (mus. Ohana), Gala, Enghien
*Le Balayeur* (mus. Bessières), Gala, Enghien
*Le Parfum de la dame en rouge* (mus. Calvi), Gala, Enghien
*Promethée* (mus. Ohana), Ballets 1956, Lyons
*CISP I* (mus. Schoffer), Ballet de l'Étoile, Marseilles
*Le Teck* (mus. Mulligan), Ballet de l'Étoile, Marseilles
1957 *Sonate à trois* (mus. Bartok), Ballet Théâtre de Maurice Béjart, Essen
*L'Étranger* (mus. Villa-Lobos), Ballet Théâtre de Maurice Béjart, Paris
*Chapeaux* (mus. Copland), Ballet Théâtre de Maurice Béjart, Paris
*Pulcinella* (mus. Stravinsky), Ballet Théâtre de Maurice Béjart, French television
*Concerto pour percussion et orchestre* (mus. Milhaud), Ballet Théâtre de Maurice Béjart, Berlin
1958 *Orphée* (mus. Henry), Ballet Théâtre de Paris de Maurice Béjart, Liège television
*Études rythmiques* (percussion), Ballet Théâtre de Paris de Maurice Béjart, Devon
*Juliette* (text and sound montage), Ballet Théâtre de Paris de Maurice Béjart, Devon
*La Voix* (sound effects), Ballet Théâtre de Paris de Maurice Béjart
*Arcane* (second version; pas de trois; mus. Henry), Ballet Théâtre de Maurice Béjart, Brussels
1959 *Violetta* (pas de deux; mus. Verdi), Ballet Théâtre de Paris de Maurice Béjart, Monte Carlo
*Pulcinella* (second version; mus. Vivaldi), Ballet Théâtre de Maurice Béjart, Monte Carlo
*Thème et variations* (mus. jazz), Ballet Théâtre de Paris

de Maurice Béjart, Berlin
*Equilibre* (mus. Brill), Ballets de l'Etoile, Berlin
*La Mer* (pas de deux; mus. Binert, with spoken texts), Ballet Théâtre de Paris de Maurice Béjart, Berlin
*Signes* (mus. Henry), Ballets Théâtre de Paris de Maurice Béjart, Geneva
*Fanfares* (mus. sixteenth-century), Ballet Théâtre de Paris de Maurice Béjart, Spain
*Le Sacre du printemps* (new version; mus. Stravinsky), Ballet Théâtre de Paris de Maurice Béjart, Brussels

1960 Dances in *Aniara* (opera; mus. Bloomdahl), Théâtre Royal de la Monnaie, Brussels
*La Douceur du tonnerre* (mus. Ellington), Ballet de XXe Siècle, Belgian television
*Premier Amour* (pas de deux; mus. Brill), Belgian television

1961 *Boléro* (mus. Ravel), Ballet du XXe Siècle, Brussels
*Webern* (mus. Webern), Ballet du XXe Siècle, Brussels
*Fanfares* (second version; mus. sixteenth-century), Ballet du XXe Siècle, Paris
*Les Sept Péchés capitaux* (mus. Weill), Ballet du XXe Siècle, Brussels
*Divertimento* (mus. Schirren, Belda, Lambo), Ballet du XXe Siècle, Brussels
*Les Quatre Fils Aymon* (with Charrat; mus. fifteenth and sixteenth-century), Ballet du XXe Siècle, Brussels
*Bacchanale de Tannhäuser* (mus. Wagner), Ballet du XXe Siècle, Bayreuth
*Gala* (mus. Scarlatti), Soloists of the Ballet du XXe Siècle, Venice
*Le Chevalier romain et la dame espagnol* (mus. Scarlatti), Ballet du XXe Siècle, Venice
*Don Juan* (revised version; mus. Vittona and Spanish madrigals), Ballet du XXe Siècle, Seville
*Suite en noir et blanc* (mus. Bartok), Ballet du XXe Siècle, Brussels
Dances in *Les Contes d'Hoffmann* (opera; mus. Offenbach), Théâtre Royal de la Monnaie, Brussels
*Suite viennoise*, including *Temps* (mus. Schönberg), *Espace* (mus. Webern), *Matière* (mus. Berg), Ballet du XXe Siècle, Brussels

1962 *Le Voyage* (mus. P. Henry), Cologne Opera House, Cologne
*Les Noces* (mus. Stravinsky), Ballet du XXe Siècle, Salzburg
*A la recherche de Don Juan* (revised version; mus. sixteenth-century), Ballet du XXe Siècle, Brussels
*Divertimento* (mus. Schirren), Ballet du XXe Siècle
*Prière* (mus. Negro spirituals), Ballet du XXe Siècle

1963 *Venusberg* (second version; mus. Wagner), Ballet du XXe Siècle, Baalbeck
*Fanfares* (third version; mus. Mouret), Ballet du XXe Siècle, Baalbeck
*Promethée* (second version; mus. Ohana), Ballet du XXe Siècle
*La Reine verte* (play; mus. Henry), Théâtre Hebertot, Paris
Dances in *La Veuve joyeuse* (operetta; mus. Lehar), Théâtre Royal de la Monnaie, Brussels
*Serenade* (mus. Toselli), Ballet du XXe Siècle, Brussels

1964 *La Damnation de Faust* (mus. Berlioz), Paris Opéra Ballet, Paris
*Fiesta* (mus. Mexican), Ballet du XXe Siècle, Brussels
*L'Oiseau de feu* (second version; mus. Stravinsky), Ballet du XXe Siècle, Brussels
*Neuvième Symphonie* (mus. Beethoven), Ballet du XXe Siècle, Brussels

1965 *Wagner ou l'amour fou* (mus. Wagner, Bernard), Ballet du XXe Siècle, Brussels
*Renard* (mus. Stravinsky), Paris Opéra Ballet, Paris
*Chatchouka* (mus. Tunisian), Hammammet
*Les Oiseaux* (opera-ballet; mus. Hadjidakis), Ballet du XXe Siècle, Brussels
*Prospective*, including *Erotica* (mus. Baird), *L'Art de la barre* (mus. Bach), *Le Cygne* (mus. Hindu, with text by Tagore), *Variations pour un porte et un soupir* (mus. Henry), Ballet du XXe Siècle, Brussels

1966 *Cantates* (mus. Webern), Ballet du XXe Siècle, Brussels
*Webern Opus V* (mus. Webern), Ballet du XXe Siècle, Brussels
*Histoire du soldat* (mus. Stravinsky), Rome
*Romeo and Juliet* (mus. Berlioz), Ballet du XXe Siècle, Brussels

1967 *La Tentation de Saint-Antoine* (mus. Flaubert), Barrault Company, Odeon, Paris
*Comedie*, including *Aubade*, *L'Heure exquise* (mus. Lehar), *Serenade II* (mus. Toselli), Ballet du XXe Siècle, Brussels
*Messe pour le temps present* (*Mass for Our Time*; mus. sound montage), Ballet du XXe Siècle, Avignon Festival

1968 *Ni Fleurs ni couronnes* (mus. Tchaikovsky), Ballet du XXe Siècle, Grenoble
*Le Voyage* (second version; mus. Henry), Ballet du XXe Siècle, Grenoble
*Baudelaire* (mus. Wagner, Debussy, jazz), Ballet du XXe Siècle, Grenoble
*A la recherche de . . .*, including *Cantates* (mus. Webern), *La Nuit obscure* (St. Jean de la Croix), *Bakhti* (mus. Hindu), Ballet du XXe Siècle, Avignon Festival
*Improvisations* (mus. Schirren), Ballet du XXe Siècle, Brussels

1969 *Concert de danse*, including *Prélude* (collective chor.; no music), *Nomos Alpha* (mus. Xenakis), *Variations* (mus. Webern), *Hi Kyo* (mus. Fukushima), *Lettera amorosa* (mus. Monteverdi), Ballet du XXe Siècle, Royan
*Salomé*, French television
*Les Quatre Fils Aymon* (second version; with Bortoluzzi and Lorca Massine), Ballet du XXe Siècle, Avignon
*Les Vainqueurs* (mus. Wagner), Ballet du XXe Siècle, Brussels
*Actus Tragicus* (mus. Bach), Ballet du XXe Siècle, Brussels

1970 *Comme la Princesse, Salomé est belle de soir* (mus. Strauss), Opéra-Comique, Paris
*Serait-ce la mort?* (mus. Strauss), Ballet du XXe Siècle, Marseilles
*L'Oiseau de feu* (mus. Stravinsky), Paris Opéra Ballet, Paris
*Sonate* (mus. Bach), Ballet du XXe Siècle, Brussels

1971 *Offrande chorégraphique* (collective chor.; mus. Bach, Schirren), Ballet du XXe Siècle, Brussels
*Erotica* (second version; mus. Baird), Ballet du XXe Siècle, Brussels
*Le Chant du compagnon errant* (*Song of a Wayfarer*; mus. Mahler), Ballet du XXe Siècle, Brussels
*Les Fleurs du mal* (mus. Debussy), Ballet du XXe Siècle, Vienna
*Nijinsky, clown de Dieu* (mus. Tchaikovsky, Henry), Ballet du XXe Siècle, Brussels

1972 *L'Ange heurtebise* (mus. Hadjidakis), Ballet du XXe Siècle, Brussels
*Ah! vous dirai-je maman?* (mus. Mozart), Ballet du XXe Siècle, Brussels

*Stimmung* (mus. Stockhausen), Ballet du XXe Siècle, Brussels
1973 *Le Marteau sans maître* (mus. Boulez), Ballet du XXe Siècle, Milan
Dances in *La Traviata* (opera; mus. Verdi), Théâtre Royal de la Monnaie, Brussels
*Golestan; ou, Le Jardin des roses* (mus. Iranian), Ballet du XXe Siècle, Persepolis
*Mallarmé III* (mus. Boulez), Ballet du XXe Siècle, Shiraz
*Tombeau* (mus. Boulez), Ballet du XXe Siècle, Brussels
*Farah* (mus. Iranian traditional), Ballet du XXe Siècle, Brussels
1974 *Seraphite* (mus. Mozart), Ballet du XXe Siècle, Brussels
*I Trionfi di Petrarcha* (mus. Berio), Ballet du XXe Siècle, Florence
*Ce que l'amour me dit* (mus. Mahler), Ballet du XXe Siècle, Monte Carlo
1975 *Chants d'amour et de guerre* (mus. Mahler), Les Ballets Beranger, Boulogne-sur-Seine
*Notre Faust* (mus. Bach), Ballet du XXe Siècle, Brussels
*Acqua alta* (mus. various), Ballet du XXe Siècle and MUDRA, Venice
*Pli Selon Pli* (mus. Boulez), Ballet du XXe Siècle, Brussels
1976 *Le Molière imaginaire* (text Molière, mus. Rota), Ballet du XXe Siècle, Paris
*Isadora* (mus. Beethoven), Ballet du XXe Siècle, Monte Carlo
*Heliogabale* (mus. Verdi and others), Ballet du XXe Siècle, Naqshe Rostam, Iran (revised version staged La Scala, Milan)
1977 *Clair de lune* (mus. Debussy), Lille International, Lille
*La Plus que lente* (mus. Debussy), Gand
*Petrouchka* (mus. Stravinsky), Ballet du XXe Siècle, Brussels
*V Comme* (Verdi), Ballet du XXe Siècle, Verona
1978 *Gaîté parisienne* (mus. Offenbach, Rosenthal), Ballet du XXe Siècle, Brussels
*Dichterliebe* (mus. Schumann), Ballet du XXe Siècle, Brussels
*Ce que l'amour me dit* (mus. Mahler), Ballet du XXe Siècle, Monte Carlo
*Ce que la mort me dit* (mus. Mahler), Ballet du XXe Siècle, Brussels
*Le Spectre de la rose* (mus. Weber), Ballet du XXe Siècle, Brussels
*Six Personnages en quête d'auteur*, Bolshoi Ballet, Moscow
*Le Minotaure*, Bolshoi Ballet, Moscow
1979 *Leda* (mus. Japanese), Ballet du XXe Siècle, Brussels
*Les Illuminations* (mus. Henry, oriental), Ballet du XXe Siècle, Luxor
*Life* (mus. Bach, Crocker), Ballet du XXe Siècle, New York
*Variations Don Giovanni* (mus. Mozart, Chopin), Ballet du XXe Siècle, Brussels
*Mephisto Valse* (mus. Liszt), Monte Carlo Opera, Monte Carlo
*Leda* (new version; mus. traditional), Bolshoi Ballet, Palais des Congrès, Paris
*Boléro* (second version; mus. Ravel), Palais de sports, Paris
*Boléro* (third version; mus. Ravel), Paris Opéra Ballet, Paris
1980 *Casta Diva* (mus. A. Louvier), IRCAM, Paris
*Eros-Thanatos* (mus. various), Ballet du XXe Siècle, Brussels
*Les Plaisirs de l'isle enchantée* (text Molière; mus. Lully), Comédie-Française, Paris
1981 *La Flute enchantée* (mus. Mozart), Ballet du XXe Siècle, Brussels
*Les Chaises* (mus. Wagner), Municipal Theatre, Rio de Janeiro
*La Muette* (mus. Donizetti and others), Ballet du XXe Siècle, Brussels
*Divine* (mus. Tuxedo Moon), Ballet du XXe Siècle, Brussels
*Light* (mus. Vivaldi, Tuxedo Moon), Ballet du XXe Siècle, Brussels
1982 *Wien, Wien nur du Allein* (mus. Schoenberg, Beethoven, and others), Ballet du XXe Siècle, Brussels
*L'Histoire du soldat* (second version; mus. Stravinsky), Ballet du XXe Siècle, Brussels
*Concerto pour violion* (mus. Stravinsky), Ballet du XXe Siècle, Brussels
*Thalassa-Mare Nostrum* (mus. Theodorakis), Ballet du XXe Siècle, Arles Festival
*Petrouchka* (second version; mus. Stravinsky), Ballet du XXe Siècle, Brussels
1983 *Messe pour le temps futur* (mus. Wagner, Beethoven), Ballet du XXe Siècle, Brussels
*Vie et la mort d'une marionnette humaine* (mus. Japanese), Ballet du XXe Siècle, New York
Dances in *Salomé* (opera; mus. Strauss), Grand Theatre, Geneva
1984 *Fragments* (mus. Wagner), Ballet du XXe Siècle, Paris
*La Luna* (mus. Bach), Teatro Nuova, Turin
*Dionysos* (mus. Wagner, Bach), Ballet du XXe Siècle, Milan
*Cinq Nô modernes* (text Mishima), Ballet du XXe Siècle, Brussels
1985 *Le Concours* (mus. Le Bars and others), Ballet du XXe Siècle, Paris
*Le Baiser de la fée* (mus. Stravinsky), Palais de Sports, Gand
*Mouvement-Rythme-Étude* (mus. Henry), Paris Opéra Ballet, Paris
*Operetta* (mus. Lehar, Strauss, Lecocq), Stuttgart Ballet, Stuttgart
1986 *Arepo* (mus. Gounod, H. Le Bars), Paris Opéra Ballet, Paris
*Kabuki* (mus. Toshiro Mayuzumi), Tokyo Ballet, Tokyo
*Le Martyre de Saint Sebastien* (mus. Debussy), Ballet du XXe Siècle, Milan
*Malraux; ou, La Métamorphose des dieux* (mus. Beethoven, Le Bars, traditional), Ballet du XXe Siècle, Brussels
*Seven Greek Dances* (mus. Theodorakis), Ballet du XXe Siècle, Paris
*Salomé* (mus. Drigo), Paris Opéra Ballet, Paris
1987 *Prélude à l'après-midi d'un faune* (mus. Debussy), Béjart Ballet Lausanne
*Trois Études pour Alexandre* (mus. Shostakovitch, traditional African), Ballet du XXe Siècle, Paris
*Conte russe* (mus. Tchaikovsky), Béjart Ballet Lausanne
*1830* (mus. Meyerbeer, Verdy), Béjart Ballet Lausanne
*Souvenir de Leningrad* (mus. Tchaikovsky and others), Béjart Ballet Lausanne, Lausanne
*Cantique* (mus. Jewish traditional), Béjart Ballet Lausanne
*Et Valse* (mus. Ravel), Béjart Ballet Lausanne, Lausanne
1988 *Fiche signaletique* (mus. Lully), Béjart Ballet Lausanne
*Patrice Chereau* (mus. Wagner, Le Bars), Béjart Ballet

Lausanne, Brussels
*Dybbuk* (mus. Schoenberg, Hassidic folk music), Béjart Ballet Lausanne, Lausanne
*Piaf* (mus. Piaf), Béjart Ballet Lausanne, Tokyo
*Kurozuka* (mus. various), Tokyo Ballet, Tokyo
*A force de partir je suis resté chez moi* (mus. Mahler), Béjart Ballet Lausanne, Lausanne
*Bugaku* (mus. Mayuzumi), Tokyo Ballet, Tokyo
1989 *1789 et nous* (mus. Beethoven, Le Bars), Béjart Ballet Lausanne, Paris
*Hamlet* (mus. Ellington, Purcell), Béjart Ballet Lausanne, Brussels
*Chaka* (Brazilian/Ivory Coast folk music), Béjart Ballet Lausanne, Paris
*Elégie pour elle*, Béjart Ballet Lausanne, Paris
*L'Aile* (mus. Sibelius), Béjart Ballet Lausanne, Brussels
1990 *Ring um den Ring* (mus. Wagner), German Opera Ballet, Berlin
*Pyramide* (traditional Egyptian music), Béjart Ballet Lausanne, Cairo
*Mozart-Tango* (mus. Mozart), Béjart Ballet Lausanne, Lausanne
1991 *Tod in Wien* (mus. Mozart), Béjart Ballet Lausanne, Vienna
*Death in Vienna—W.A. Mozart* (mus. Mozart), Béjart Ballet Lausanne, Vienna
*La Mort subite* (mus. various), Béjart Ballet Lausanne, Paris
*La Tour* (mus. various), Béjart Ballet Lausanne, Lausanne

**Other works include:** for film and television—*La Belle au boa*, *Chapeaux*, *La Reine verte*; also *Le Teck* (British television), *La Vie d'un danseur* (French television, 1968), *L'Invité du dimanche* (French television, 1969), *Je suis né à Venise* (television programme, 1977), *Je t'aime, tu danses* (television programme, 1977), *La Nuit Blanche de la danse* (television co-production, Leningrad, 1988), *Paradox sur le comedien* (television film, 1991).

## PUBLICATIONS

By Béjart:
*Mathilde*, Paris, 1962
*La Reine verte* (play), Paris, 1963
Interview in Gruen, John, *The Private World of Ballet*, New York, 1970
*L'Autre chante de la danse*, 1974
*Béjart par Béjart*, Paris, 1979
*Un instant dans la vie*, Paris, 1979
Interview in Whyte, Sally, "A Traveller Through Dance", *Dance and Dancers*, March 1990
*La Morte subite*, 1991

About Béjart:
Lobet, Marcel, *Panorama du ballet d'aujourd'hui*, Brussels, 1956
Lobet, Marcel, *Le Ballet français d'aujourd'hui*, Paris, 1958
Lobet, Marcel, *Dix années de ballets a la télévision belge*, Brussels, 1964
Stengele, R., *A la récherche de Béjart*, Brussels, 1968
Livio, Antoine, *Béjart*, Lausanne, 1969
"Maurice Béjart", *Les Saisons de la danse* (Paris), May 1970 (supplement, January 1970)
Geitel, Klaus, *Das Abenteuer Béjart*, Berlin, 1970
Aranais, Mireille, *Un journée avec Béjart*, Brussels, 1970
Mathis, Thierry, *Une visite chez Béjart*, 1972
Garaudy, Roger, *Danser sa vie*, Paris, 1973
Stengele, R., *Béjart et la danse*, Brussels, 1975
Boccon-Gobod, Thierry, *Béjart à l'Opéra de Paris*, Paris
Jackson, George, "Speaking up for Béjart", *Ballet News* (New York), September 1983
Nussac, Sylvie de, *Béjart aux travail*, Paris, 1984
Mannoni, G., *Maurice Béjart, l'avant-scène ballet*, Paris, 1985
Christout, Marie-Françoise, *Béjart*, revised edition, Paris, 1987
Muriset, Y., and Pastori, J.P., *Béjart, le tournant*, Lausanne, 1988
Mannoni, G., *Maurice Béjart*, Paris, 1991

* * *

French dancer–choreographer Maurice Béjart's early experience with the Cullberg Ballet and the International Ballet of Mona Inglesby enabled him to travel throughout Europe, dancing the standard classical repertory, and choreographing for Cullberg his first *L'Oiseau de feu*.

When, in 1955, Béjart became the first choreographer to use electronic music as an accompaniment for ballet (in *Symphonie pour un homme seul*), he was establishing a base for many of the attitudes, gestures, sound dynamics, and themes which we see in his choreography today. *Le Sacre du printemps*, whose primitive movements, based on classicism and developed in a linear fashion in parallel with Stravinsky's musical score, was abstractly conceived around the theme of sacrifice of the chosen couple, who must risk being absorbed by the collective personality of the group. Masterworks both, *Le Sacre* and *L'Oiseau de feu* are developed circularly, deriving their appeal from a tight choreography which opposes, through intricate patterns of repetition and counterpoint, the theme of the individual and that of the collective.

Béjart conceives of each ballet as part of a massive tapestry, a "work-in-progress", which reveals a striking diversity of form. Whereas such seminal works as *Le Sacre* stand apart, all the works together treat the same themes: love, pacifism, superiority of intuition, and religion—of which Béjart states, "You have to put religion everywhere, if you are a dancer". Yet all follow an intensely personal thread, having been backed up by research and a profound personal identification with their subject, such as in *Notre Faust*, *Nijinsky, clown de Dieu*, and the more recent *Malraux*.

Béjart's conception of ballet as theatre has allowed him to create a different type of dance audience and dancer. In the 1960s and 1970s, his Brussels-based company was the first to espouse dramatic changes in dress (such as flesh-coloured leotards and long hair), to use sports arenas as stages, and to make political use of themes through often tritely conceived slogans. "Make Love, Not War", echoed in Béjart's *Romeo and Juliet* in the 1960s, is not so distant from the emotional chant of *Revolution/Evolution* ("Abandonnez les usines") performed in the Grand Palais in Paris in the 1980s.

Béjart's "new" dancer—one who, in the words of a former Béjart dancer, is able to "sing Swan Lake" or, like the classically trained danseur-chanteur "Mudrist" of Brussels, to move impelled by gesture to the chant of guttural sound—often challenges technique with interpretative range.

If the new Béjart resembles the old, he may be said to have constructed a new dance form, a hybrid, out of the vestiges of late nineteenth-century theatre and contemporary film, borrowing as well from his own forays into theatre and into opera. With Béjart, nothing is superficial; his work with actors (as with *Cinq Noh modernes* of Yukio Mishima, performed first in Brussels and then in Paris with the Compagnie Renauld-Barrault), or with singers, only brings him back to dance, making the end result richer. "Through my contact with actors,

I have learned very much, but this is not my future. The body of the dancer is much more important."

As a showman, Béjart intends to shock and does so by the manipulation of basic stage relationships to reveal his often symbolic meaning. The relationship of décor to scenic action in *Loves of a Poet*, the relationship of dialogue to on stage action in *Seraphite*, the relationship of lighting to space in *I Trionfi*—are all prime examples of his craft. Yet the critical difference of opinion posed by his *oeuvre* would seem to lie in its conception of dance consisting merely of a static series of unrelated movement frames which contain both classical and modern phrases, sparsely conceived, or of balletic vocabulary presented as a vital link in a new, yet alternative tradition.

Frequently, Béjart reworks a ballet until it develops into a masterwork, as is the case of *Eros-Thanatos*, which was changed from its original 1980 version five or six times. More often he is prone to render a free interpretation of his subject matter, often reworking or even "violating" a masterpiece. In the psychological portrait of Nijinsky (*Nijinsky, clown de Dieu*), Béjart's aim was to present a psychological portrait, through scattered fragments portrayed in the dancer's diary, and to allow his audience their own conclusion. In *Piaf* he sought to reveal a portrait in dance, using songs and spoken scenes of the French chanteuse as an acoustic background. His choreography did not interpret the songs and, through the use of certain images, it actually satirized the singer's life.

Béjart's ultimate spectacle occurred in 1989 at the celebration of the French Revolution at the Grand Palais in Paris. *La Revolution*, equated with *Le Cirque*, evolves around four main dance extravaganzas set to Beethoven symphonies which evoke four main events: The Convocation of the States General, the Storming of the Bastille, the Declaration of Human Rights, and the Return of Louis XVI to Paris. As "total theatre", his four choreographic axes are supported by text which speaks of such disparate imagery as "trees without leaves", "women in the front line of war", "men dressed as women", and "Buffalo Bill on a Horse". *Revolution/Evolution* is punctuated by such dance combinations as a trio of Nobility, Church, and Third Estate (danced by Ruben Bach, Patrick Happy de Banc, and Gil Roman) as well as the Béjart-invented character of Bim (spirit of eternal youth, danced by Xavier Ferda). The work incorporates startling stage effects through the character of Volange, who descends from the dome of the Palais on a crimson ball (Michel Dussaert), and the performance of Calicot, the sans-culotte (Jorge Donn).

Today, it is the thrill of spectacle, revealed in *Revolution/Evolution*, the art of the master showman as shown by Béjart's reworking of the classical repertory with his own vision, which have made the Ballet du XXe Siècle and Béjart Ballet Lausanne of timely significance to varied world audiences.

—Pamela Gaye

---

**BELSKY, Igor**

Soviet dancer, choreographer, and ballet director. Born Igor Dmitrievich Belsky in Leningrad, 28 March 1925. Studied at the Leningrad Choreographic School, pupil of L. Petrov, A. Bocharov, and A. Lopukhov; graduated in 1943; also later attended Actors' Faculty of the State Institute for Theatrical Art (GITIS), 1957. Married Kirov dancer Lyudmila Alekseeva. Début (while still a student) with Kirov Ballet in Perm; official début at Kirov Theatre, Leningrad, 1943; artist, Kirov Ballet, 1943–63, becoming leading character dancer; also dancer in opera and films; teacher of character dance, Leningrad Choreographic School, 1946–48; chief choreographer, Maly Theatre of Opera and Ballet, 1962–73; teacher in the choreographic department of the Leningrad Conservatory, 1962, 1964–66; artistic director, Kirov Ballet, 1973–77, Cairo Ballet 1977–78; chief ballet master, Leningrad Music Hall, from 1979.

**ROLES**

1942 Principal dancer (cr) in *Creole Dance* (choreographic miniature; Yakobson), Kirov Ballet, Leningrad
1944 Principal dance (cr) in *Hungarian Gypsy Dance* (choreographic miniature; Yakobson), Kirov Ballet, Leningrad
1946 Principal dancer (cr) in *Alborada* (choreographic miniature; Yakobson), Kirov Ballet, Leningrad
1947 Ognen in *Militsa* (Vainonen), Kirov Ballet, Leningrad
1948 Panaderos in *Raymonda* (Sergeyev after Petipa), Kirov Ballet, Leningrad
1950 Shurale (cr) in *Ali-Batyr* (*Shurale*; Yakobson), Kirov Ballet, Leningrad
1955 Petro (cr) in *Taras Bulba* (Fenster), Kirov Ballet, Leningrad
1960 The Unknown (cr) in *Masquerade* (Fenster), Kirov Ballet, Leningrad
1956 The Athenian Fool (cr) in *Spartacus* (Yakobson), Kirov Ballet, Leningrad
1957 Severyan (cr) in *The Stone Flower* (Grigorovich), Kirov Ballet, Leningrad
1958 Mako (cr) in *The Path of Thunder* (Sergeyev), Kirov Ballet, Leningrad

**Other roles include:** Ostap in *Taras Bulba* (Lopukhov), Nur-Ali in *The Fountain of Bakhchisarai* (Zakharov), Li-Shan-Fu in *The Red Poppy* (Zakharov), the Fool and Menshikov in *The Bronze Horseman* (Zakharov), Tybalt, the Duke, and the National Dance in *Romeo and Juliet* (Lavrovsky), Rothbart and Spanish, Polish, and Hungarian dances in *Swan Lake* (Petipa, Ivanov, staged Sergeyev), Espada, Gypsy Dance, and Spanish March in *Don Quixote* (also chor.), Abderakhman, the Mazurka in *Raymonda* (Petipa, staged Sergeyev), the Hindu Dance in *La Bayadère* (Petipa, Chabukiani, Ponomarev), Dance with Castanets and the Flamenco in *Laurencia* (Chabukiani), Basque Dance in *The Flames of Paris* (Vainonen), Spanish Dance in *The Nutcracker* (Vainonen), Ukrainian Dance in *The Little Humpbacked Horse* (also chor.), the Polovtsian in "Polovtsian Dances" from *Prince Igor* (opera; music Borodin, chor. Fokine).

**WORKS**

1959 *The Coast of Hope* (mus. Petrov), Kirov Ballet, Leningrad
1961 *Leningrad Symphony* (mus. Shostakovich), Kirov Ballet, Leningrad
1963 *The Little Humpbacked Horse* (mus. Pugni), Maly Theatre, Leningrad
1966 *Eleventh Symphony* (mus. Shostakovich), Maly Theatre, Leningrad
1967 *Gadfly* (mus. Chernov), Maly Theatre, Leningrad
1969 *The Nutcracker* (mus. Tchaikovsky), Maly Theatre, Leningrad
1974 *Icarus* (mus. Slonimsky), Kirov Ballet, Leningrad

**PUBLICATIONS**

By Belsky:
"Ballet—A Form of Symphony", *Sovetsky Balet* (Moscow), no. 6, 1962
"Observations of a Choreographer", *Sovetskaya Muzyka* (Moscow), no. 3, 1964
"Problems of the Ballet Theatre—Dialogues", *Music and Choreography of Contemporary Ballet* (first edition), Leningrad, 1974
"Gabriella Komlyeva", *Sovetsky Balet* (Moscow), no. 3, 1983

About Belsky:
Belinski, A., "Igor Belsky", *Teatralnyi Leningrad* (Leningrad), no. 21, 1957
Lvov-Anokhin, Boris, "Bright Expressive Character", *Teatralnyi Leningrad* (Leningrad), no. 36, 1957
René, Natalia, "New Choreographer in Leningrad", *Dance and Dancers* (London), March 1961
Medvedev, A., "Again *Little Humpbacked Horse*", *Sovetskaya Muzyka* (Moscow), no 6, 1964
Swift, Mary Grace, *The Art of Dance in the USSR*, Notre Dame, Ind., 1968
Demidov, Aleksandr, "Doll's House", *Teatr* (Moscow), no. 3, 1970
Demidov, Aleksandr, *The Russian Ballet Past and Present*, London, 1978
Shmyrova, T., "Igor Belsky", *Sovetsky Balet* (Moscow), no. 3, 1983

* * *

Igor Belsky was an outstanding character dancer and a master of the "grotesque". A boisterous, mischievous boy as a student, he developed into a top dancer in the ranks of the Kirov. His art was distinguished by enormous stage presence: he possessed extraordinary acting gifts and an extremely individual performing style. He was the best known, and probably the most highly acclaimed performer of the roles of Shurale, Ostap, Severyan, and Nur-Ali. As a young dancer he danced almost all of the roles in the classical repertoire, but he was also always attracted to new ventures, and often did his own recitals at various places of culture in Leningrad. He often appeared with his regular partner, Nina Anisimova, in special concert programmes and creative evenings in the city, performing choreographic scenes and miniatures.

Belsky was a gifted choreographer, and he created two major works: *The Coast of Hope*—a ballet with almost no décor, simple staging, and what was then called "modern" choreography—and *Leningrad Symphony* (or *Seventh Symphony*) to the music of Shostakovich. *The Coast of Hope* centred upon a very basic story of a Soviet fisherman lost in a storm, but showed a powerful blend of classical and modern in telling a moving tale through dance. The Soviet ballet historian Yuri Slonimsky, pointing to the fact that "drama-ballet" had been driven nearly to extinction in the Soviet Union, wrote that "Yuri Grigorovich's *The Stone Flower* gave notice for the first time that a new era in the development of Soviet choreography had started. After it, like swallows of a new summer, Belsky's white seagulls appeared on a blue stage free of props. . . . *The Coast of Hope* announced the appearance not only of a talented choreographer but of an artist with a fresh understanding of the nature of balletic realism, actively battling for the fulfilment of the Soviet theme in the art of choreography."

The second of these ballets, *Leningrad Symphony*, was very unusual for the Kirov at the time; Shostakovich's symphony is dedicated to Leningrad during the 900 difficult days of blockade, and the ballet is choreographed to the first movement of the symphony. The ballet begins in early morning, with several couples appearing on stage, seeming at first to resemble seagulls and then turning into young boys and girls, dancing on the banks of the Niva. This peaceful scene is interrupted by the sense of an unknown and dangerous presence approaching—in short, the beginning of World War II for Russia. It was a powerful ballet, and used an effective form of symbolism for a very realistic theme. The Nazi invasion depicted in the ballet, for example, is represented in a general way by anonymous figures with horned helmets: it is not a particular people or nationality, but just an unidentified Enemy, which is trying to capture the city. The ballet was a great success, but it proved to be the only real example, along with *The Coast of Hope*, of Belsky's genius—for, apart from stagings of other ballets, Belsky did not choreograph another major original work for the Kirov after this.

Fundamentally, Belsky's true teacher and guide was Fedor Lopukhov. The essential principals of Lopukhov's *Dance Symphony* were grasped by Belsky, and the best scenes of *The Coast of Hope*, *Leningrad Symphony*, and *Eleventh Symphony* were constructed in the genre of dance symphonism. Belsky's *The Little Humpbacked Horse* also recreates the link with the "Kingdom of the Mummers" created by Lopukhov in his ballets; Belsky wittily develops the satire through continuous danced action.

Even though Belsky choreographed only two major ballets for the Kirov, they have assumed an important place in Soviet ballet, even world ballet. Later in his career, Belsky branched out and did work for music halls and drama theatres, eventually retiring after twenty years of work on the Kirov stage. He has been the chief choreographer for many smaller companies in Leningrad, as well as ballet master at the Leningrad Music Hall.

—Igor Stupnikov

---

**BENOIS, Alexandre**

Russian stage designer and painter. Born Aleksandr Nikolaevich Benua in St. Petersburg, 3 May (17 May old style) 1870. Studied law at St. Petersburg University, 1890–94; studied art as an external student at Academy of Arts, from 1887. Married Atia Kind, 1894. Exhibited at Society of Russian Watercolour Artists in St. Petersburg, 1893–96; first sets and costumes, for Glück's *Orpheus* (not produced), 1895; first visit to Paris and Versailles, 1896; contributed to magazine *Mir Iskusstva* (*The World of Art*), co-founded by Serge Diaghilev, St. Petersburg, 1899–1904; also contributed to *The Golden Fleece*, 1906–08, to *Moskovsky Ezhenedelnik* (*Moscow Weekly*), 1907–08, to *Starie Godi* (*Old Times*), 1907–13, and to *Rech* (*Speech*), 1908–17; curator of Hermitage Museum, St. Petersburg, 1918–26; began collaboration with Diaghilev's Ballets Russes in Paris, with *Le Pavillon d'Armide*, 1907, becoming Diaghilev's chief artistic adviser until 1911; returned to Moscow, working as designer for the Art Theatre, 1912–15; collaborated with dancer/producer Ida Rubinstein, Paris, from 1923; left Russia permanently to settle in Paris, 1926; designed for many ballet companies, including (de Basil's) Ballets Russes de Monte Carlo (later known as the Original Ballet Russe), Ballet of La Scala, Milan, Sadler's Wells Ballet, (Blum's) Ballet Russe de Monte Carlo, and London Festival Ballet; also designed for opera, theatre, and film. Died in Paris, 9 February 1960.

**Alexandre Benois's curtain design for *Petrushka* (night scene with fantastic creatures in the sky), 1925**

**WORKS** (Ballet design)

1901 *Sylvia* (set for Act I), St. Petersburg (not produced)
1907 *Le Pavillon d'Armide* (chor. Fokine), Maryinsky Theatre, St. Petersburg (restaged with revised designs by Diaghilev's Ballets Russes, Paris, 1909)
1908 *The Cheated Buyer* (ballet; mus. Clementi), Russian Merchant's Club, St. Petersburg
1909 *Les Sylphides* (*Chopiniana*) (chor. Fokine), Diaghilev's Ballets Russes, Paris
*Le Festin* (costumes, with Bakst and others; chor. Fokine), Diaghilev's Ballets Russes, Paris
1910 *Giselle* (chor. Petipa after Coralli, Perrot; staged Fokine), Diaghilev's Ballets Russes, Paris (designs revised for numerous other productions, including Paris Opéra, 1924 and 1949, and La Scala, Milan, 1951)
1911 *Petrushka* (chor. Fokine), Diaghilev's Ballets Russes, Paris (designs re-used or revised for numerous other productions, including State Maryinsky Theatre, Petrograd, 1920, Bolshoi Theatre, Moscow, 1920, Royal Danish Ballet, 1925, La Scala, Milan, 1947, Paris Opéra, 1948, Royal Ballet, London, 1957)
1912 *Les Fêtes* (ballet by Debussy; not produced)
1914 *Le Rossignol* (opera; chor. Romanov), Diaghilev's Ballets Russes, Paris
1922 *Le Mariage d'Aurore* (with Goncharova, using designs from *Le Pavillon d'Armide*, 1909; chor. Petipa, staged Nijinska), Diaghilev's Ballets Russes, Paris
1927 *The Sleeping Beauty* (chor. after Petipa), Casino, Paris
*Le Coq d'or* (opera-ballet; mus. Rimsky-Korsakov), Opéra, Paris
1928 *Les Noces de Psyché et de l'Amour* (chor. Nijinska), Ida Rubinstein's Company, Paris
*La Bien-Aimée* (chor. Nijinska), Ida Rubinstein's Company, Paris
*Bolero* (chor. Nijinska), Ida Rubinstein's Company, Paris
*Le Baiser de la fée* (chor. Nijinska), Ida Rubinstein's Company, Paris
*Nocturne* (chor. Nijinska), Ida Rubinstein's Company, Paris
*La Princesse Cygne* (chor. Nijinska), Ida Rubinstein's Company, Paris
*David* (chor. Nijinska), Ida Rubinstein's Company, Paris
1929 *Les Enchantements d'Alcine* (chor. Massine), Ida Rubinstein's Company, Paris
*La Valse* (chor. Nijinska), Ida Rubinstein's Company, Monte Carlo
1930 *Sadko* (opera; mus. Rimsky-Korsakov), Opéra, Paris
*Sadko* (opera; mus. Rimsky-Korsakov), Teatro Reale, Rome
1931 *La Valse* (new chor. Nijinska), Ida Rubinstein's Company, Paris
*Amphion* (chor. Massine), Ida Rubinstein's Company, Paris
1932 *Le Bourgeois Gentilhomme* (chor. Balanchine), Ballets

Russes de Monte Carlo, Monte Carlo

1934 *Diane de Poitiers* (chor. Fokine), Ida Rubinstein's Company, Paris

*Sémiramis* (chor. Fokine), Ida Rubinstein's Company, Paris

1935 *Psyché* (chor. Fokine), Olga Spessivtseva Concert, Opéra-Comique, Paris

1938 *The Nutcracker* (chor. after Ivanov), La Scala, Milan

1940 *Graduation Ball* (chor. Lichine), Original Ballet Russe, Sydney

*The Nutcracker* (chor. Fedorova after Ivanov), Ballet Russe de Monte Carlo, New York

1945 *Swan Lake* (chor. after Petipa, Ivanov), Ballet Russe de Monte Carlo, New York (designs revised for production at La Scala, Milan, 1950)

1946 *Raymonda* (chor. Danilova, Balanchine after Petipa), Ballet Russe de Monte Carlo, New York

1949 *Le Moulin enchantée* (chor. Lichine), (de Cuevas') Grand Ballet de Monte Carlo

1950 *Les Sylphides* (chor. Fokine), La Scala, Milan

1955 *Le Spectre de la rose* (chor. Fokine), La Scala, Milan

1957 *The Nutcracker* (substantially revised designs; chor. Lichine), London Festival Ballet, London

*Graduation Ball* (substantially revised designs; chor. Lichine), London Festival Ballet, London

## PUBLICATIONS

By Benois:

*Reminiscences of the Russian Ballet*, translated by Mary Britnieva, London, 1941

"The Story Behind *Petrushka*", *Dance and Dancers* (London), March 1957

*Memoirs*, translated by Moura Budberg, 2 vols: London, 1960 and 1964

*My Recollections*, Moscow, 1980

"*The Sleeping Beauty*", from Benois's *Reminiscences* in Wiley, Roland John (ed. and trans.), *A Century of Russian Ballet: Documents and Accounts 1810–1910*, Oxford, 1990

About Benois:

Levinson, André, "Un chef d'école: Alexandre Benois", *L'Art vivant* (Paris), 1 December 1926

*Mostra dei Benois* (catalogue), Como, 1955

*Mostra commemorativa di Alessandro Benois* (catalogue), Milan, 1960

Ustinov, Peter, "My Great-Uncle Alexandre", *The Queen* (London), 5 January 1960

Karsavina, Tamara, "Benois the Magician", *Ballet Annual* (London), no. 15, 1961

Etkind, Mark, *Aleksandr Nikolaevich Benois: 1870–1960*, Leningrad and Moscow, 1965

Kennedy, Janet, *The "Mir Iskusstva" Group and Russian Art, 1898–1912*, London and New York, 1972

Bowlt, John, *The Silver Age: Russian Art of the Early Twentieth Century and the "World of Art" Group*, Newtonville, Massachusetts, 1976

Clarke, Mary, and Crisp, Clement, *Design for Ballet*, London, 1978

Buckle, Richard, *Thoughts on Alexandre Benois* (introduction to catalogue), London, 1980

Wiley, Roland John, "Alexandre Benois' Commentaries on the First Saisons Russes", *Dancing Times* (London), 8 parts: October 1980–May 1981

Schouvaloff, Alexander, *Set and Costume Designs for Ballet and Theatre* (catalogue of the Thyssen-Bornemisza collection), London, 1987

Baer, Nancy van Norman, *The Art of Enchantment: Diaghilev's Ballets Russes 1909–1929*, San Francisco, 1988

Pozharskaya, Militsa, and Volodina, Tatiana, *The Art of the Ballets Russes: The Russian Seasons in Paris 1909–29*, London, 1990

* * *

In summing up his approach to art, Benois remarked that he was attracted most of all to "that which it is customary to call realism". Moreover, he referred to himself as a "passéiste", maintaining that his attitude to the past was "more tender, more loving" than it was to the present. Without exception his designs for the ballet reflect both this realism and this attraction to the past.

Benois' work for the theatre was prolific, and included designs for operatic and dramatic productions as well as works for the ballet. Although he had been engaged as chief designer for *Sylvia*, the proposed 1901 production by Prince Volkonsky and Serge Diaghilev, his real début for the ballet was in 1907, when he designed, and was responsible for the scenario of, *Le Pavillon d'Armide* with choreography by Mikhail Fokine and music by Nikolai Tcherepnin. After this work his major designs for the ballet were for *Les Sylphides* for Diaghilev's first Paris season in 1909, *Giselle* (1910), *Petrushka* (1911), and *Le Rossignol* (1914), all for the Ballets Russes.

*Le Pavillon d'Armide* was one of Benois' most successful productions. First produced at the Maryinsky Theatre in 1907, it entered the repertoire of Diaghilev's Ballets Russes and became a staple item with that company. In designing *Le Pavillon*, set in early eighteenth-century France, Benois was required to draw on his erudite historical knowledge and provided, in the sets and costumes, reconstructions of the period which were accurate to the finest detail. It was probably his success with *Le Pavillon* which encouraged him to pursue his theatrical vocation for, although his interest in the theatre dated back to his childhood, Benois was accomplished and accepted as a writer, illustrator, and artist before he began any of his theatrical commissions.

His best-known work for the ballet was *Petrushka*, for which he designed curtain, sets and costumes. In conjunction with its composer, Igor Stravinsky, Benois also devised the scenario. Set in St. Petersburg in 1830 during Butterweek Fair, the ballet, with choreography by Fokine, evoked elements from Benois' childhood memories and provided him with an ideal theme in which, once again, he could display his ability to recreate accurately an historical period. *Petrushka* has always been regarded as the high point of Benois' theatrical career. However, while his designs for *Petrushka* have become icons of ballet history, they cannot be said to be innovative. Like the rest of his designs, they use decoration as a static element and their importance lies mostly in the fact that they are integrated with great coherence into the overall conception of the ballet.

In his work for the theatre, Benois adopted a variety of historical styles to suit specific demands. *Giselle*, *Les Sylphides*, and *Le Rossignol* all received the same careful attention to detail as had *Le Pavillon d'Armide* and *Petrushka*. This ability to move from style to style reflected Benois' erudition and his interest in the past, traits which he had developed even in childhood and certainly as a member of the celebrated *World of Art* group. Strangely, despite his exceptional involvement with the theatre and with Diaghilev's Ballets Russes in particular, Benois remarked in his reminiscences that he was not "a devotee of the ballet, or even a balletomane", and as a designer his contribution to the twentieth century in which he worked

**A costume sketch by Christian Bérard for Harlequin in *La Nuit*, 1930**

was limited. Benois was at his best when retreating into a make-believe world which he could decorate.

—Michelle Potter

---

**BÉRARD, Christian**

French painter and designer. Born Christian-Jacques Bérard in Paris, 20 August 1902. Educated at the Lycée de Sailly, 1915–19; studied art at the Académie Ranson, pupil of Jean-Edouard Vuillard and Maurice Denis, 1920–23, and at the Académie Julien, 1924–25. First exhibition at the Galerie Drout, Paris, 1925; became associated with so-called "neo-Romantic" or "neo-humanist" painters Eugène Berman and Pavel Tchelitchev, Paris, 1926–30; met Serge Diaghilev, 1927, and began designing for the theatre, 1930: designed ballets for choreographers George Balanchine, Serge Lifar, Léonide Massine, Mikhail Fokine, Roland Petit, and David Lichine, 1930–48; co-founder, with Roland Petit and Boris Kochno, Les Ballets des Champs-Elysées, 1945; also designed for the theatre, including for Jean-Louis Barrault and Jean Cocteau, and for film, including for Cocteau films *La Belle et la bête* (1946), *L'Aigle a deux têtes* (1948), and *Les Parents terribles* (1948); contributor to *Vogue* magazine, Paris, from 1933. Died in Paris, 12 February 1949.

**WORKS** (Ballet design)

1929 *Coppélia* (after Petipa, Cecchetti), Diaghilev's Ballets Russes (not produced)
1930 *La Nuit* (chor. Lifar), Cochran Revue, Manchester and London
1932 *Cotillon* (chor. Balanchine), Ballets Russes de Monte Carlo, Monte Carlo
1933 *Mozartiana* (chor. Balanchine), Les Ballets 1933, Paris
1936 *Symphonie fantastique* (chor. Massine), de Basil's Ballets Russes, London
1937 *Les Elfes* (new production; chor. Fokine), Ballets de Monte Carlo, Monte Carlo
1938 *Seventh Symphony* (chor. Massine), Ballet Russe de Monte Carlo, Monte Carlo
1945 *Les Forains* (chor. Petit), Ballets des Champs-Elysées, Paris
1946 *La Sylphide* (chor. V. Gsovsky), Ballets des Champs-Elysées, Paris
1948 *Clock Symphony* (chor. Massine), Sadler's Wells Ballet, London
*La Rencontre; ou, L'Oedipe et le Sphinx* (chor. Lichine), Ballets des Champs-Elysées, Paris

**PUBLICATIONS**

By Bérard:
Illustrations in Cocteau, Jean, *Les Monstres sacrés*, Paris, 1940

About Bérard:
Amberg, George, *Art in Modern Ballet*, London, 1946
Hastings, Baird, *Christian Bérard: Painter, Decorator, Designer* (catalogue), Boston, 1950
Beaton, Cecil, and James, Philip, *Christian Bérard: An Exhibition of Paintings and Décors* (catalogue), London, 1950
Beaumont, Cyril, "Christian Bérard", *Studio* (London), October 1959
Rischbieter, Henning, *Bühne und Bildende Kunste im XX*, Hanover, 1968
Clarke, Mary, and Crisp, Clement, *Design for Ballet*, London, 1978
Strong, Roy, *Designing for the Dancer*, London, 1981
Buckle, Richard, *Spotlight* (catalogue), London, 1981
Harris, Dale, "Christian Bérard", *Architectural Digest* (New York), April 1989
García-Marquez, Vicente, *The Ballets Russes*, New York, 1990

* * *

Christian Bérard as a painter belonged to the school of "neo-humanism", a movement opposed to the dehumanizing aspects of such contemporary art movements as Cubism or abstract painting. It was a movement based upon feeling rather than form and was, with its emphasis on the human personality, peculiarly suited to theatrical design.

To the theatre, Bérard brought a new conception of space, based upon the theories of Appia and Craig, their austerity softened by his innate romanticism—not a sentimental romanticism, but one based firmly in a love and admiration for classic principles. He created not locations in his settings, but atmospheres, his spare, often monochrome, décors offset by the subtle beauty of his costumes. Often commonplace themes or objects were invested with an air of mystery and poignant sadness that raised them to a world of poetic beauty, as with the strolling players of *Les Forains*. To bring out a magic, beauty, and elegance from the commonplace or squalid was a particular characteristic of Bérard's art.

With its ability to convey the atmosphere and attributes of a place through its bare essentials, ballet was an ideal medium for Bérard. In *Seventh Symphony*, he evoked, by the simplest means, some pre-Christian Mediterranean period, the changes of mood effected by the lighting of the backcloth in evocative colours—first the yellow hue of autumn, then the cobalt of a spring sky, and finally fiery red. In all his theatrical designs he was very concerned with the structure of a work and saw it as his responsibility to provide a visual background that would accompany and augument the action. Eventually, in *Le Rencontre*, he dispensed with formal décors completely, reducing the set to the bare props demanded by the choreography and creating atmosphere by light alone—thus raising the circus ring in which the protagonists meet onto a universal plane.

It was an art of extreme subtlety. His lyrical, yet spare, use of colour was often diffused; in a dress the colour would be concentrated on the under-skirts, dissipated by or contrasting with the tone of the top-skirts. Overall muted tones would often be accented by a subtle use of pure colour. He had a unique sense of space, not only in the stage setting, but also in the architecture of the costumes that moved in that space. Thus in *Cotillon*, décor and costume perfectly complemented and expanded the mystery inherent in the choreography. Bérard provided the most basic of ballrooms with discreet alcoves and brocade chairs in which drifted the sea-green, lemon, cyclamen, rose, and lime dresses of the girls, offset by the black evening coats of the men, except for three dressed in ochre, jade green, and maroon. Here he achieved the perfect marriage between the romantic ballet tutu and the ball-dress, the subtle fusion perfectly expressing the mixture of adolescent sophistication and mystery that permeated the ballet.

There was nothing direct or obvious about Berard's art; his designs were models of subtle suggestion rather than direct statement, and he relied upon the dressmaker to translate those designs into tangible form. Although basically romantic, his costumes were no impractical fantasies, but were evocations of character and mood expressed in colour, line, and texture.

Bérard was master of all the decorative arts and excelled in every field that he attempted—he was stage designer, illustrator, fashion artist, interior and exhibition designer as well as painter. His influence upon a generation of stage designers, notably Vertes and Cecil Beaton, was profound.

—Sarah C. Woodcock

---

**BERIOSOVA, Svetlana**

Lithuanian/British dancer. Born in Kaunas, Lithuania, daughter of dancer/choreographer Nicholas Beriozoff, 24 September 1932. Studied with Beriozoff, at Vilzak–Schollar School of Ballet, New York, with Olga Preobrazhenska, Paris, and with Vera Volkova, London. Married Masuh Khan (div. 1974). Début with Ballet Russe de Monte Carlo, 1941; professional début, Ottawa Ballet Company, 1947; dancer (de Cuevas's) Grand Ballet de Monte Carlo, 1947; soloist, English Metropolitan Ballet, 1948–49; soloist, Sadler's Wells Theatre Ballet, from 1950; transferred to Sadler's Wells Ballet (later the Royal Ballet), 1952: ballerina, from 1955; also performed as guest ballerina around the world, including in Belgrade, Milan, Vienna, Stuttgart, and Australia; appeared on television, including in *Stars of the Ballet* (BBC, 1949); retired from the stage in 1975.

**ROLES**

1948 Principal dancer (cr) in *Designs with Strings* (Taras), Metropolitan Ballet, Edinburgh
Title role (cr) in *Fanciulla delle Rose* (Staff), Metropolitan Ballet, London
1948/49 Odette in *Swan Lake* (after Petipa, Ivanov), Metropolitan Ballet, London
1949 The First Hand in *Le Beau Danube* (Massine), Metropolitan Ballet, London
Principal dancer (cr) in *Ballamento* (Howard), Metropolitan Ballet, London
Title role in *Giselle*, Act II (after Petipa, Coralli, Perrot), Metropolitan Ballet, London
1950 The Lady in *Assembly Ball* (Howard), Sadler's Wells Theatre Ballet, London
Sugar Plum Fairy in *The Nutcracker*, Act II (Ivanov; staged Sergeyev), Sadler's Wells Theatre Ballet, tour
Odette in *Swan Lake*, Act II (Ivanov; staged Sergeyev), Sadler's Wells Theatre Ballet, tour
Bather in *Summer Interlude* (Somes), Sadler's Wells Theatre Ballet, London
Naila in *Selina* (Howard), Sadler's Wells Theatre Ballet, tour
Principal dancer (cr) in *Trumpet Concerto* (Balanchine), Sadler's Wells Theatre Ballet, Manchester
Lumilia (cr) in *Pastorale* (Cranko), Sadler's Wells Theatre Ballet, London
1951 Bride in *La Fête étrange* (Howard), Sadler's Wells Theatre Ballet, London
Swanilda in *Coppélia* (Petipa, Ivanov, Cecchetti; staged Sergeyev), Sadler's Wells Theatre Ballet, London
A Dancer in *The Prospect Before Us* (de Valois), Sadler's Wells Theatre Ballet, London
1952 Lilac Fairy in *The Sleeping Beauty* (Petipa; staged Sergeyev, revised de Valois), Sadler's Wells Ballet, London
A Young Wife in *Don Juan* (Ashton), Sadler's Wells Ballet, London
Principal dancer in *Ballet Imperial* (Balanchine), Sadler's Wells Ballet, London
Mazurka, Prelude in *Les Sylphides* (Fokine), Sadler's Wells Ballet, London
1953 The Youth's Romantic Love (cr) in *The Shadow* (Cranko), Sadler's Wells Ballet, London
Title role in *Sylvia* (Ashton), Sadler's Wells Ballet, New York
1954 Queen of the Waters in *Homage to the Queen* (Ashton), Sadler's Wells Ballet, London
Tsarevna in *The Firebird* (Fokine; staged Grigoriev, Tchernicheva), Sadler's Wells Ballet, Edinburgh
Odette/Odile in *Swan Lake* (Petipa, Ivanov; staged Sergeyev), Sadler's Wells Ballet, London
Princess Aurora in *The Sleeping Beauty* (Petipa; staged Sergeyev, Ashton, de Valois), Sadler's Wells Ballet, London
La Favorita in *Veneziana* (Howard), Sadler's Wells Ballet, London
1955 Armida (cr) in *Rinaldo and Armida* (Ashton), Sadler's Wells Ballet, London
1956 Principal dancer (cr) in *A Birthday Offering* (Ashton), Sadler's Wells Ballet, London
Title role in *Giselle* (Petipa after Coralli, Perrot; staged Sergeyev), Sadler's Wells Ballet, London
1957 Princess Belle Rose (cr) in *The Prince of the Pagodas* (Cranko), Royal Ballet, London
La Capricciosa in *The Lady and the Fool* (Cranko), Royal Ballet, London
Title role in *The Firebird* (Fokine), Royal Ballet, tour
Black Queen in *Checkmate* (de Valois), Royal Ballet, London
1958 Title Role in *Cinderella* (Ashton), Royal Ballet, London
1959 Title role (cr) in *Antigone* (Cranko), Royal Ballet, London
1960 Fairy (cr) in *Le Baiser de la fée* (MacMillan), Royal Ballet, London
1961 Principal dancer in *Diversions* (MacMillan), Royal Ballet, London
Title role in *Ondine* (Ashton), Royal Ballet, London
Title role (cr) in *Persephone* (Ashton), Royal Ballet, London
1962 Pas de deux in *Birthday Offering* (Ashton), Royal Ballet, London
Pas de deux and Variation (cr) from *Raymonda* (Ashton after Petipa), Royal Ballet, London
1963 The Lady of High Birth and Station (cr) in *Night Tryst* (Carter), Royal Ballet, London
1964 Rag Mazurka ("Hostess") in *Les Biches* (Nijinska), Royal Ballet, London
"When Love Begins to Sicken" (cr) in *Images of Love* (MacMillan), Royal Ballet, London
Principal dancer in *Serenade* (Balanchine), Royal Ballet, London
1966 The Bride in *Les Noces* (Nijinska), Royal Ballet, London
Terpsichore in *Apollo* (Balanchine), Royal Ballet, London
1968 Caroline in *Lilac Garden* (Tudor), Royal Ballet, London
Wednesday's Child in *Jazz Calendar* (Ashton), Royal Ballet, London
C.A.E. (cr) in *Enigma Variations* (Ashton), Royal Ballet, London

**Svetlana Beriosova as Odile in *Swan Lake*, Royal Ballet, London, 1968**

Clara in *The Nutcracker* (Nureyev), Royal Ballet, London
1969 Nikiya in *La Bayadère* (Nureyev after Petipa), Royal Ballet, London
1970 The Woman (cr) in *Checkpoint* (MacMillan), Royal Ballet Touring Company, Manchester
1971 Tsarina (cr) in *Anastasia* (MacMillan), Royal Ballet, London

**Other roles include:** for Sadler's Wells Theatre Ballet—Chiarina in *Carnaval* (Fokine), Variation "Prayer" in *Coppélia* (Petipa, Ivanov, Cecchetti; staged Sergeyev).

### PUBLICATIONS


Davidson, Gladys, *Ballet Biographies*, revised edition, London, 1954
Williams, Peter, "The Ascending Curve", *Dance and Dancers* (London), July 1952
"Portrait: Svetlana Beriosova", *Dance and Dancers* (London), July 1952
Swinson, Cyril, *Svetlana Beriosova*, London, 1956
Franks, A.H., *Svetlana Beriosova: A Biography*, London, 1958
Woodcock, Sarah, *The Sadler's Wells Royal Ballet*, London, 1991


* * *

From her earliest years, Svetlana Beriosova attracted attention as a potential world-class ballerina with her aristocratic line, her lissom port de bras, and her natural poise. These were qualities obvious from her first performances with Metropolitan Ballet in the late 1940s, and she developed them as a leading dancer with the Sadler's Wells Theatre Ballet in the early 1950s before she moved to the Sadler's Wells Ballet at Covent Garden. By the end of the decade, she was being hailed as the natural successor to Margot Fonteyn.

Beriosova's Russian training had developed in her a wonderful amplitude of movement, a beautiful back, and eloquent, unforced arms. Instead of flashy Russian virtuosity, all her work was infused with a poetic lyricism, and showed her use of dance to express drama and emotion. During her great years she was the grandest of Odettes and Auroras along with Fonteyn, the classical ballerina par excellence of the Royal Ballet.

At the beginning of her career, Beriosova could seem remote and withdrawn; but as she came to maturity she developed a warmth and humanity, which was coupled with a gracious feminity. It was this humanity that set her interpretations apart—the tenderness of the bewitched princess in *The Firebird*, the rapt apprehensiveness of the Bride in *Les Noces* (a role in which she remains unrivalled), the gentle, loving anxiety of Elgar's wife in *Enigma Variations*, in anguish because she cannot reach into the isolation of her husband's creative genius, the tragic Tsarina in *Anastasia*, or the gentle warmth that elevated the sentiment of *The Lady and the Fool* into a poignant human drama.

It was perhaps ironic that Beriosova, entirely Russian-trained, should be hailed after Fonteyn as exemplifying the Royal Ballet style. She enshrined the finest qualities of the great classical dancer, with her natural aristocracy, lyrical flow, and masterly phrasing complemented by an exceptional musicality—but it was also her warmth, charm, and humanity that enslaved audiences. Speed and hard brilliance did not come naturally to her. She was never a versatile dancer; her range was limited, and although she was an enchanting Swanilda during her years with the Sadler's Wells Theatre Ballet, and a perfect tragedy queen as Wednesday's Child in *Jazz Calendar*, she was not a natural comedienne.

Beriosova was an inspiration to younger dancers, not only in her performing, but in her professionalism and dedication. She was held in affection by audiences everywhere and did much, in her appearances with the Royal Ballet Touring Company in the 1960s, to win new audiences for ballet. Since retiring, she has built a career as a teacher and coach of professional dancers, with a special talent for passing on her own understanding of the architecture and meaning of the choreography of the great classical roles.

—Sarah C. Woodcock

---

**BERIOZOFF** (Beriosoff), **Nicholas**

Lithuanian/British dancer, choreographer, teacher, and ballet director. Born in Kaunas, Lithuania, 16 May 1906. Studied at National Ballet School, Prague, pupil of Kasimir Remislavsky, from c. 1920. Married dancer Doris Catana. Dancer, performing mostly character roles, National Theatre, Prague, from 1920; dancer, Lithuanian National Ballet, Kaunas, 1930–35, René Blum's Ballet de Monte Carlo, 1936–38, Ballet Russe de Monte Carlo, 1938–44; ballet master, (Marquis de Cuevas's) Ballet International, 1944, Metropolitan Ballet, 1948, Grand Ballet de Marquis de Cuevas, 1947 and again 1956, 1962, La Scala, Milan, 1950–51, London Festival Ballet, 1951–54; ballet director, Stuttgart Ballet, 1957–60, Finnish National Ballet, Helsinki, 1962–64, Zurich Ballet, 1964–71, Teatro San Carlo, Naples, 1971–73; Head of Ballet Department, Indiana University, late 1970s; since then freelance choreographer and guest ballet master, staging (mostly Fokine) ballets for companies throughout the world including National Ballet of Canada, 1979, 1980, 1982, NAPAC Ballet, South Africa, 1990, and American Ballet Theatre, 1991.

### WORKS

1954 *La Esmeralda* (mus. Pugni), London Festival Ballet, London
1958 *Le Baiser de la fée* (mus. Stravinsky), Stuttgart Ballet, Stuttgart
1962 *Promenade à deux* (mus. Rossini, Britten), London Festival Ballet
1962/64 *Le Sacre du printemps* (mus. Stravinsky), Finnish National Ballet, Helsinki
1965 *Ondine* (mus. Henze), Zurich Ballet, Zurich
1966 *Romeo and Juliet* (mus. Prokofiev), Zurich Ballet, Zurich
1967 *Cinderella* (mus. Prokofiev), Zurich Ballet, Zurich
1978 *The Nutcracker* (mus. Tchaikovsky), Teatro Reale, Turin

Also staged:
1951 *The Nutcracker* (after Ivanov; mus. Tchaikovsky), London Festival Ballet
*Petrushka* (after Fokine; mus. Stravinsky), London Festival Ballet
*Polovtsian Dances from Prince Igor* (after Fokine; mus. Borodin), London Festival Ballet
1952 *Schéhérazade* (after Fokine; mus. Rimsky-Korsakov), London Festival Ballet

**Nicholas Beriozoff as the Chief Eunuch in *Schéhérazade***

1957 *The Sleeping Beauty* (after Petipa; mus. Tchaikovksy), Stuttgart Ballet, Stuttgart
1962/64 *Swan Lake* (after Petipa, Ivanov; mus. Tchaikovsky), Finnish National Ballet, Helsinki
*Les Sylphides* (after Fokine; mus. Chopin), Finnish National Ballet, Helsinki
1976 *The Golden Cockerel* (*Le Coq d'or*; partly after Fokine; mus. Rimsky-Korsakov), London Festival Ballet
1979 *Le Spectre de la rose* (after Fokine; mus. Weber), National Ballet of Canada, Toronto
1982 *Don Quixote* (after Petipa; mus. Minkus), National Ballet of Canada, Toronto

**Other works include:** stagings of *L'Epreuve d'amour* (after Fokine; mus. Cette).

## PUBLICATIONS

Crowle, Pigeon, "Nicholas Beriozoff", *Ballet Today* (London), November 1954
Franks, A.H., *Svetlana Beriosova*, London, 1958
Anderson, Jack, "Who is a Ballet Master?", *Dance Magazine* (New York), January 1968
Braunsweg, Julian, *Ballet Scandals*, London, 1973
Wilson, G.B.L, "Beriozoff at 75", *Dancing Times* (London), July 1981
Merrett, Sue, "Beriozoff at 85", *Dancing Times* (London), August 1991

* * *

A father-figure to ballet factions on two continents, "Poppa" Beriozoff is revered for his passionate dedication to the two forces which shaped his career: the classical repertoire of the Russian Imperial Ballet and the genius of his mentor, Mikhail Fokine.

Born in Kaunus, Lithuania, and transported to Prague with a group of Russian-speaking children after the First World War, Beriozoff became familiar with the classical ballets in faithful reproductions performed in the Czech capital, and as an apprentice at the National Theatre he aspired to become a great dancer. The Petipa ballets, transmitted to Prague via Warsaw at the turn of the century, were fastidiously maintained in their pure versions.

As a young man he had the opportunity to perform in many of the Petipa works as a soloist with the National Ballet in Lithuania, which also resisted the Soviet tendencies to update and modify the classics. A trained musician as well, Beriozoff applied a prodigious memory to the productions of *Swan Lake*, *Don Quixote*, *Giselle*, and *Raymonda* which he had first absorbed on stage in Kaunus.

His association with Fokine began in 1936 when he left Lithuania, with fellow artists Vera Nemchinova and Nicholas Zverev, to join René Blum's short-lived ballet company in Monte Carlo. A large repertoire of Fokine ballets, old and new, were made available to him over the next several years, and when the Blum company dissolved most of these works were maintained in the Massine-directed company which succeeded it, the Ballet Russe de Monte Carlo. Recognizing Beriozoff's remarkable recall and intense sympathy with his work, Fokine assigned him the role of répétiteur of his ballets, a position he maintained unofficially over the next six decades. Through a method of detailed notation he was able, decades later, to restore the popular Fokine ballets from the Diaghilev repertoire and such latter-day creations as *Le Coq d'or* and *L'Epreuve d'amour*.

It was in a Fokine trifle called *Igrouchki* that Beriozoff sustained the injury that in 1938 brought an abrupt halt to his career as a dancer, though through his ongoing affiliations with Ballet Russe factions he continued to perform as a mime.

His mature years would find him working in a multiple capacity—as ballet master, répétiteur, choreographer, and company director. In some circumstances he performed all four functions concurrently, notably in the cities of Stuttgart and Zurich, where as director of state companies he developed vital and enthusiastic ballet audiences in communities where dance had existed merely to serve the needs of opera.

Beriozoff's original ballets failed to achieve immortality. His production of an essentially new version of Jules Perrot's 1844 ballet, *La Esmeralda*, 110 years later for London Festival Ballet, failed to survive, and his personal versions of the two Prokofiev ballets—*Romeo and Juliet* and *Cinderella*—and of the Henze *Ondine* were undistinguished. Shorter creations to Stravinsky music, *Le Baiser de la fée* and *Le Sacre du printemps*, did not compete with other more popular stagings. It was with his faithful restorations of Petipa and Fokine masterpieces that he enriched the resources of those companies which he personally directed or served as a visiting ballet master over the years, bringing his benign presence and vast stores of knowledge to ballet communities small and large. He travelled as far as Capetown, Oakland, California, Helsinki, Toronto, and Indianapolis, working in situations ranging from large state theatres to small civic companies and academic institutions.

In 1981, at age 75, "Poppa" Beriozoff defined his destined position as follows: "A man is made ballet master usually because he is the oldest member of the company and is blessed with a good memory which helps him recall not just the steps of a ballet, but the individual interpretations the great artists of the past gave to them." It is a modest self-assessment for a man whose role in preserving the great ballets of the nineteenth and twentieth century has been so crucial.

—Leland Windreich

---

## BERNSTEIN, Leonard

American composer, pianist, and conductor. Born in Lawrence, Massachusetts, 25 August 1918. Educated at Harvard University, pupil of Edward Ballantine, Edward Burlinghame Hill, A. Tillman Merritt, and Walter Piston, 1935–39, receiving B.A.; studied at Curtis Institute, pupil of Isabella Vengerova (piano), Renée Longy (score-reading), Randall Thompson (orchestration), winters 1939–40, 1940–41; also studied at Berkshire Music Centre (conducting with Sergei Koussevitzky), summers 1940, 1941. Married Felicia Montealegre Cohn, 1951 (d. 1978): 2 sons, 1 daughter. Member of Revuers show troupe, 1942; assistant conductor, New York Philharmonic Orchestra, 1943; composed first ballet, *Fancy Free* (chor. Jerome Robbins), 1944, collaborating with Robbins in 1946 and again 1974; also contributed music to Broadway musicals, including *On the Town* (chor. Robbins, 1944), *Wonderful Town* (chor. Robbins, 1953), *Candide* (chor. Robbins, 1956), and *West Side Story* (chor. Robbins, 1957); music director, New York City Symphony Orchestra, 1945–47; also teacher: member of faculty, Berkshire Music Center, 1948–55, and head of conducting department, 1951–55; musical adviser/conductor, Israel Philharmonic Orchestra, 1948–49; music director, Brandeis University, 1951–56; co-conductor (with Dmitri Mitropoulos), New York Philharmonic Orchestra Young People's Concerts broadcasts 1958–71; laureate conductor, New York Philharmonic, from 1969; president, London Symphony Orchestra, 1987–90. Recipient: Chevalier, Légion d'honneur, France, 1968; Officier, 1978, Commandeur, 1985; Cavaliere, Order of Merit, Italy, 1969; Commander's Cross of the Order of Merit, West Germany, 1987; Honorary doctorates from Yale University, 1966, Harvard University, 1967, Tel Aviv University, Johns Hopkins University, 1980, Hebrew University, Israel, 1981. Died New York, 14 October 1990.

### WORKS (Ballets)

1944 *Fancy Free* (chor. Robbins), Ballet Theatre, New York
1946 *Facsimile* (chor. Robbins), Ballet Theatre, New York
1974 *Dybbuk* (later *Dybbuk Variations*; chor. Robbins), New York City Ballet, New York

**Other ballets using Bernstein's music:** *The Age of Anxiety* (Robbins, 1950; also Neumeier, 1979), *Prelude, Fugue, and Riffs* (Clifford, 1969), *Mass* ("theatre piece"; Ailey, 1971), *Serenade* (Seregi, 1977), *On the Town* (Seregi, 1977), *Songfest* (Neumeier, 1979), *Suite of Dances* (Robbins, 1980), *Voyager* (Bolender, 1984).

### PUBLICATIONS

By Bernstein:
*Findings*, New York, 1982

About Bernstein:
Coleman, Francis A., "Leonard Bernstein", *Dance Magazine* (New York), May 1945
Edmunds, J., and Boelzner, G., *Some Twentieth-Century American Composers*, New York, 1960
Cone, M., *Leonard Bernstein*, New York, 1970
Weber, J.F., *Leonard Bernstein*, Utica, N.Y., 1975
Reynolds, Nancy, *Repertory in Review*, New York, 1977
Balanchine, George, with Mason, Francis, *Balanchine's Complete Stories of the Great Ballets*, Garden City, N.Y., 1977
Robinson, Paul, *Bernstein*, London, 1982
Peyser, Joan, *Bernstein: A Biography*, New York, 1987
Freedland, Michael, *Leonard Bernstein*, London, 1987
Gottlieb, Jack, *Leonard Bernstein: A Complete Catalogue of his Works*, New York, 1988
Goodwin, Noël, "Street Side Story", *Dance and Dancers* (London), December 1990

**Leonard Bernstein with Jerome Robbins**

The qualities most readily associated with Bernstein the performer are the extrovert ones of energy and enthusiasm. His physical involvement in conducting and playing, as caught on film, shows a response to music that is already close to dance, and of course this is only one aspect of the man that seems larger than life. Another is the extraordinary way in which his conducting ability brought him sudden fame: he stepped in to replace an indisposed Bruno Walter at a broadcast concert by the New York Philharmonic in 1943 and immediately his name was made.

The figure of the dancing conductor is too easily matched to the composer of *Fancy Free* in 1944, the first ballet for both Bernstein and its choreographer Jerome Robbins. Both artists operated in the middle ground characteristic of music and theatre in New York at the time, between the serious pretensions of the Broadway theatre and the popularizing mood of the classical music establishment. This was the middle ground Gershwin sought too, in works like *Rhapsody in Blue* and the *Piano Concerto*: America seemed to need home-grown classical music that could easily be appreciated by all its citizens. Bernstein's mentor was Aaron Copland, a composer who had invented a rural American sound in the 1930s by incorporating native elements—hymns and country dances—into traditional musical forms.

The half-hour ballet *Fancy Free* shows three sailors on a night out in New York City in the "present" of the ballet's first performance (1944). The scenario is realistic, urban, and modern: the sailors step into a bar for a drink, while away the time on a street corner, and try to catch the attention of girls walking by. The urban setting prompts jazz-inspired music from Bernstein and, together with Robbins's vigorous choreography, the work stands as a city equivalent to the rural Americana of *Oklahoma!* The ballet's enormous success led to the stage musical, *On the Town*. Bernstein and Robbins developed the idea of the ballet into a full evening's entertainment with a plot, dialogue, and new songs—not least of which was the inspired "New York, New York". A follow-up ballet from Bernstein and Robbins, *Facsimile*, described as a "choreographic observation", appeared two years later in 1946.

Once again the setting is contemporary—a stretch of beach where a woman in a bathing suit sits idly. A man approaches and she flirts with him. The arrival of a second man allows her to play one off against the other, and a fight is the result. However, she is not genuinely interested in either man, and the work ends with her alone once again. Perhaps this desultory tale could not inspire Bernstein to the same heights as *Fancy Free*. It is significant that Lincoln Kirstein described the earlier ballet as "the sturdiest characteristic national work"—terms that could not be used for the more sensitive follow-up. That Bernstein and Robbins accorded with these necessary characteristics of "sturdiness" and "American-ness" was proved once and for all in the musical *West Side Story* (1957). This immensely popular work seems to encapsulate a mid-century American urban reality—physically in the energetic dance and aurally in the eclectic melting-pot of Bernstein's music. There are elements of Berg and Bartók, Stravinsky and jazz, and the essential flavour of Broadway musical. Yet, however clear the sources and models for the music may be, the resulting mix has a freshness and confidence that transform the separate elements into something identifiably American.

Bernstein's touch seemed to grow less sure in the compositions which followed. Ballets have been created from other music of his—the *Age of Anxiety* symphony was choreographed by Robbins in 1950 and again by Neumeier in 1979. *Prelude, Fugue and Riffs* (1969) was choreographed by John Clifford, but the next piece to be composed with a specific dance element was the *Mass* of 1971. By this time Bernstein's mentor Copland had adopted serial procedures in his work; despite his attempts to follow suit, Bernstein felt unable to do so and kept firmly to his familiar terrain of extended diatony. If anything, the *Mass* is the high point of his eclecticism—a theatre work incorporating dancers, chorus, orchestra, and rock musicians. Composed for the opening of the John F. Kennedy Center in Washington, D.C., the piece created a great deal of controversy and had a mixed critical response.

*Dybbuk Variations* (1974) was the last ballet score and again the choreographer was Robbins. The subject, originally considered by both men at the time of *Fancy Free*, is drawn from a play by the Yiddish writer S. Ansky. There is thus a strong narrative burden on the music, much more demanding than the casual story-telling of the earlier works. Discussing the work, Bernstein commented that the experience of Jewishness was the basis for what he and Robbins had achieved. For a time this was a central element in his compositions—the "Kaddish" symphony and the Chichester Psalms, for example.

In later years Bernstein was better known as a conductor than as a composer, and his recordings in particular of Mahler showed an increasing preoccupation with late Romantic music. These thoughtful and, in some cases, staggeringly slow performances seem far removed from the animated work of the young composer, whose infectious, inventive, rhythmic language had made his music so perfect for dance.

—Kenneth Chalmers

---

**BESSMERTNOVA, Natalia**

Soviet dancer. Born Natalia Igorevna Bessmertnova in Moscow, 19 July 1941. Studied at the Moscow Choreographic School from 1952, pupil of Sofiya Golovkina; graduated in 1961; later coached by Marina Semenova. Married choreographer Yuri Grigorovich. Soloist, Bolshoi Ballet, from 1961; toured U.S. and Canada with great success, 1962; début as *Giselle*, 1963; also participated in numerous concert performances, with such partners as Nikita Dolgushin, Maris Liepa, and Mikhail Baryshnikov. Recipient: Gold Medal, International Ballet Competition, Varna, 1965; Anna Pavlova Prize, Paris, 1970; title of People's Artist of the USSR, 1976; State Prize of the USSR, 1977.

**ROLES**

1961 Seventh Waltz in *Chopiniana* (Vaganova after Fokine), Bolshoi Ballet, Moscow

The Daughter of Andre (cr) in *Pages from a Life* (Lavrovsky), Bolshoi Ballet, Moscow

1963 Title role in *Giselle* (Petipa after Coralli, Perrot), Bolshoi Ballet, Moscow

1964 Leili (cr) in *Leili and Medzhnun* (Goleizovsky), Bolshoi Ballet, Moscow

1965 Shirin (cr) in *The Legend of Love* (Moscow version; Grigorovich), Bolshoi Ballet, Moscow

1967 The Girl in *Le Spectre de la rose* (Fokine; staged M. Liepa), Bolshoi Ballet, Moscow

1968 Masha in *The Nutcracker* (Grigorovich), Bolshoi Ballet, Moscow

Phrygia in *Spartacus* (Grigorovich), Bolshoi Ballet, Moscow

Juliet (cr) in *Romeo and Juliet* (Ryzhenko, Smirnov-Golovanov), Bolshoi Ballet, Moscow

**Natalia Bessmertnova as Giselle, Bolshoi Ballet, 1962**

1969 Odette/Odile in *Swan Lake* (Grigorovich after Petipa), Bolshoi Ballet, Moscow
1970 Kitri in *Don Quixote* (Gorsky after Petipa), Bolshoi Ballet, Moscow
1974 Title role in *Giselle* (Petipa after Coralli, Perrot; staged Sergeyev), Kirov Ballet, Leningrad
1975 Anastasia (cr) in *Ivan the Terrible* (Grigorovich), Bolshoi Ballet, Moscow
1976 Valentina (cr) in *Angara* (Grigorovich), Bolshoi Ballet, Moscow
1979 Juliet (cr) in *Romeo and Juliet* (Grigorovich), Bolshoi Ballet, Moscow
1982 Rita (cr) in *The Golden Age* (Vainonen), Bolshoi Ballet, Moscow
1984 Title role (cr) in *Raymonda* (Grigorovich after Petipa), Bolshoi Ballet, Moscow

**Other roles include:** Maria in *The Fountain of Bakhchisarai* (Zakharov), Aurora, Princess Florine in *The Sleeping Beauty* (Grigorovich after Petipa), Juliet in *Romeo and Juliet* (Lavrovsky).

## PUBLICATIONS

Roslavleva, Natalia, "Natalia Bessmertnova", *Muzykalnaya Zhizn* (Moscow), no. 10, 1973
Greskovic, Robert, "The Grigorovich Factor and the Bolshoi", *Ballet Review* (Brooklyn, N.Y.), vol. 5, no. 2, 1975–76
Lvov-Anokhin, Boris, "Bessmertnova", *Master Artists of the Bolshoi Theatre*, Moscow, 1976
Demidov, Alexander, *The Russian Ballet Past and Present*, London, 1978
Gaevsky, Vadim, "Bessmertnova", *Divertissement*, Moscow, 1981
Smakov, Gennady, *The Great Russian Dancers*, New York, 1984
Alovert, Nina, *Baryshnikov in Russia*, New York, 1985
Demidov, Alexander, *A Bolshoi Ballerina: Natalia Bessmertnova*, translated by Yuri Shirokov, London, 1986
Macaulay, Alastair, "The Bolshoi's *Giselle*", *Dancing Times* (London), May 1987
Clarke, Mary, "Return of the Bolshoi", *Dancing Times* (London), August 1989

* * *

Bessmertnova belongs to that rare breed of sylph-like ballerinas whose line began with the legendary Marie Taglioni. In the history of the Bolshoi Theatre there are few such ballerinas. Not only Bessmertnova's external characteristics (delicate figure, elongated arms and legs, a refined silhouette), but also her poetic expressiveness, as if carrying forth the very yearnings of the soul, and her gifts of elevation and airborne speed, have all predisposed her to become a romantic dancer of the grand style. Other purely psychological features unique to Bessmertnova—nervous energy, impulsiveness, and mercurial emotions—have endowed her art with a sharply individual quality and with obvious contemporary relevance.

The character and scale of Bessmertnova's talent was apparent as early as 1963, when the still-young dancer, though technically not very equipped, was given the leading role in the ballet *Giselle* for the first time. There she revealed her immense lyricism and musical sensitivity. *Giselle* became her highest achievement and her performance became an original standard for dancers of the following generation. Nevertheless Bessmertnova never confined herself to the romantic repertoire, and her artistic destiny proved to be bound up with the choreographic destiny of Yuri Grigorovich, whom she married, and in whose ballets she danced all of the principal female roles over many years. Until Grigorovich's creative skill began to fail him, Bessmertnova attained considerable heights in these roles and in these ballets.

Any list of her important roles would have to include, in the first instance, *The Legend of Love*, *The Nutcracker*, and *Spartacus*, where she doubled for other ballerinas with great success; but we should also mention *Ivan the Terrible*, where Bessmertnova danced the role specially created for her, that of the poisoned Tsarina Anastasia, with remarkable mastery. However, following the productions of *Angara*, *Romeo and Juliet*, and *The Golden Age*, the new production of *Raymonda* did not bring great acclaim either to Bessmertnova or to her husband, Grigorovich. Nevertheless, it would not be correct to assert that Bessmertnova sacrificed her unique talent and opportunities for its expansion in other directions, for the sake of loyalty to Grigorovich—because it is not at all clear how her career would have developed in the Bolshoi Theatre had it not been for the special position she enjoyed there.

—Vadim Gaevsky

---

**BESSY, Claude**

French dancer, choreographer, and teacher. Born Claude Duraud in Paris, 20 October 1932. Studied at Paris Opéra School, pupil of Gustave Ricaux, Albert Aveline, Carlotta Zambelli, Lubov Egorova, and Serge Peretti, from 1942. Married (1) Max Bozzoni; (2) Michel Rayne. Dancer, Paris Opéra Ballet, from 1945: second quadrille, 1945–46; first quadrille, from 1946; petit sujet, from 1947; grand sujet, from 1949; première danseuse, from 1952; étoile, from 1956; guest artist with American Ballet Theatre, 1958 and 1959; toured Australia and Russia, performing with Bolshoi Ballet, Moscow, 1961; toured South America, 1962; also appeared in films, including *Invitation to the Dance* (dir. Gene Kelly, 1956), *Vive les vacances*, and *Terrain vague* (chor. Adret; Aix-les-Bains Festival, 1957), and on television, including *L'Homme et l'enfant* (French television, 1956), *Joie de vivre de Serge Lifar* (French television, 1956), *Ma Mère l'oye* (French television, 1960), and *Salomé* (French television, 1962); choreographer, staging ballets for Opéra Comique, Paris Opéra School, and Comédie Française; staged dances for musical *My Fair Lady* (mus. Loewe; 1984); also teacher: director, Paris Opéra Ballet School, from 1972. Recipient: Prix Pavlova, 1961; Member of Légion d'honneur, 1972.

## ROLES

1947 Snowflake in *Le Baiser de la fée* (Balanchine), Paris Opéra Ballet, Paris
Principal dancer in *Le Palais de cristal* (Balanchine), Paris Opéra Ballet, Paris
Principal dancer in *Serenade* (Balanchine), Paris Opéra Ballet, Paris
1950 "She" (cr) in *Septuor* (Lifar), Paris Opéra Ballet, Paris
1951 Principal dancer (cr) in *Terrain vague* (Adret), Gala
The Dragonfly (cr) in *Blanche-Neige* (Lifar), Paris Opéra Ballet, Paris
1952 Norwegian Couple in *Les Caprices de Cupidon* (Lander), Paris Opéra Ballet, Paris
La Magie (cr) in *Trésor et magie* (Lifar), Gala, Paris

**Claude Bessy with George Skibine in *Daphnis et Chloé*, Paris Opéra, 1959**

La Rose (cr) in *Les Indes galantes* (Lifar, Aveline, Lander), Paris Opéra Ballet, Paris
Principal dancer in *Études* (Lander), Paris Opéra Ballet, Paris
Principal dancer (cr) in *L'Aiglon* (divertissement; Aveline), Paris Opéra Ballet, Paris
1953 Jeanette McDonald (cr) in *Cinema* (Lifar), Paris Opéra Ballet, Paris
Tarantella (cr) in *Hop-Frog* (Lander), Paris Opéra Ballet, Paris
1954 Pas de deux (cr) in *Pas et lignes* (Lifar), Aix-les-Bains
1955 Titania (cr) in *La Tempête* (Lifar), Gala
Oceanide (cr) in *Les Noces fantastiques* (Lifar), Paris Opéra Ballet, Paris
La Danse (cr) in *L'Âme et la danse* (Lifar), Jeunesses musicales de France
Venus (cr) in *La Belle Hélène* (Cranko), Paris Opéra Ballet, Paris
1956 Principal dancer in *Faust* (divertissement; Aveline), Paris Opéra Ballet, Paris
1957 Principal dancer (cr) in *Mozart* (pas de deux; Lifar), Gala
Principal dancer (cr) in *Fête chez Thérèse* (pas de deux; Lifar), Gala
Third Movement (Pastorale) in *Symphonie fantastique* (Massine), Paris Opéra Ballet, Paris
Femme en rouge (cr) in *Chemin de lumière* (Lifar), Paris Opéra Ballet, Paris
Pas de deux (cr) in *Idylle et jeux* (Lifar), Gala, Le Mans
La Femme (cr) in *Le Bel Indifférent* (Lifar), Paris Opéra Ballet, Monte Carlo
1958 Principal dancer in *Le Bel Indifférent* (Lifar), Opéra Comique, Paris
Pas de deux (cr) in *Toi et moi* (Lifar), Paris Opéra Ballet, Monte Carlo
Chloé (cr) in *Daphnis et Chloé* (Lifar), Brussels Festival
Antinea (cr) in *L'Atlantide* (Lifar, Skibine), Paris Opéra Ballet, Paris
1959 Dame in *La Dame à la licorne* (Rosen), Paris Opéra Ballet, Paris
Chloé (cr) in *Daphnis et Chloé* (Skibine), Paris Opéra Ballet, Paris
Eurydice (cr) in *Orphée* (Van Dyk), Opéra Comique, Paris
1960 Principal dancer in *Le Combat* (Dollar), Opéra Comique, Paris
Venus (cr) in *Pas de dieux* (Kelly), Paris Opera Ballet, Paris
1961 La Belle (cr) in *La Belle de Paris* (Etchevery), Opéra Comique, Paris
Principal dancer in *Le Combat* (Charrat), Aix-en-Provence
Odette/Odile in *Swan Lake* (Petipa, Ivanov; staged Burmeister), Paris Opéra Ballet, Paris
1962 Principal dancer (cr) in *La Symphonie concertante* (Descombey), Paris Opéra Ballet, Paris
Title role in *Giselle* (Petipa after Coralli, Perrot; staged Lifar), Paris Opéra Ballet, Paris
1963 Principal dancer (cr) in *Entrelacs* (Labis), Jeunesse musicales de France
La Femme (cr) in *Reflets* (Rayne), Opéra Comique, Paris
1964 La Fée (cr) in *Les Paladins* (Descombey), Festival du Marais, Paris
La femme (cr) in *Sarracenia* (Descombey), Paris Opéra Ballet, Paris
*Le Miroir à trois faces*, French television
*Moi j'aime . . .* (Studio 60), French television
1965 Sugar Plum Fairy (cr) in *The Nutcracker* (Rayne), Opéra Comique, Paris
1966 Swanilda in *Coppélia* (Descombey), Paris Opéra Ballet, Paris
1967 Title role (cr) in *La Mer* (Lichine), Opéra Comique, Paris
1969 La Panthère (cr) in *Les Bandar Log* (Skibine), Opéra Comique, Paris
Principal dancer in *Istar* (Lifar), Paris Opéra Ballet, Paris
1971 La Mort (cr) in *Aor* (Schmucki), Paris Opéra Ballet, Paris

**Other roles include:** principal dancer in *Grand Pas classique* (also *Grand Pas d'Auber*, pas de deux; Gsovsky); leading roles in *La Symphonie pour six*, *Printemps à Vienne* (Lander), *Suite en blanc* (Lifar); the Woman in *Les Mirages* (Lifar); title role in *Phèdre* (Lifar), Waltz, Mazurka, and Pas de deux in *Les Sylphides* (Fokine), Pas de deux from *Don Quixote* (after Petipa).

## WORKS

1959 *Studio 60* (mus. Bergmann), Opéra, Monte Carlo
1962 *Play-Bach* (mus. Bach), Festival de Metz

1963 *Valse triste* (mus. Sibelius), Jeunesses Musicales de France (J.M.F.), Salle Pleyel, Paris
1966 *Les Fourmis* (mus. Sancan), Opéra Comique, Paris
1972 *Le Bourgeois Gentilhomme* (after comédie-ballet by Molière), Comédie Française, Paris
1980 *Classical Symphony* (mus. Prokofiev), Paris Opéra Ballet School, Paris
1985 *Concerto in Re* (Bach), Paris Opéra Ballet School, Paris

Also staged:
1985 *La Fille mal gardée* (after Romanov; mus. Hérold and others), Paris Opéra Ballet School, Paris

## PUBLICATIONS

By Bessy:
Interview in Gaubert, Henri, "Avant la répétition générale", *Musica-Disques* (Paris), December 1958
*Danseuse-Étoile*, Paris, 1961
*La Danse et l'enfant: L'École de danse de l'Opéra de Paris*, Paris, 1981
"Etre danseur" in Hoffmann, André, *Le Ballet*, Paris, 1982
Interview in Lartigue, "Rencontre avec Claude Bessy", *Opéra de Paris* (Paris), January 1983

About Bessy:
Livio, A., "Claude Bessy", in *Étoiles et ballerines*, Bienne, 1965
Hersin, A.P., "Claude Bessy", *Les Saisons de la danse* (Paris), March 1969
"Claude Bessy: Une Nouvelle École de danse de l'Opéra" *Danse* (Paris), February 1979
Hanotel, Valérie, "Une Journée avec les petits rats", *Danser* (Paris), January 1985

* * *

For more than twenty years and with unusual skill, Claude Bessy has directed the hundred-year-old ballet school of the Paris Opéra, which as a result has become one of the foremost schools in the world. Thanks to her energy and enthusiasm, modern, comfortable premises were built at Nanterre, creating perfect working conditions for her "petits rats", who previously had occupied cramped quarters in the old Opéra-Garnier. Bessy expanded the teaching programme, introducing modern dance, mime, folk, and character dance and organizing a professional performance annually. She also took her pupils on a successful tour of Japan and New York.

Active and glowing with health, Bessy still has the attraction of the seductive, captivating, and flirtatious beauty that she was at the height of her career with the Opéra in 1956, when she was made danseuse étoile. During the 1960s she worked first under the direction of Serge Lifar, then Michel Descombey and George Skibine. She was typical of the smiling, feminine dancer, engaging and sensual. She never attempted *Giselle* or *Swan Lake*, preferring roles in ballets like *Coppélia* and *The Nutcracker*. Contemporary choreographers created roles for her; Serge Lifar made her a seductive Océanide in his *Noces fantastiques*, while George Skibine made the most of her in *Daphnis and Chloë*, with décor by Marc Chagall. Gene Kelly's first work for the Paris Opéra, *Pas de dieux*, was especially created for Claude Bessy—a light-hearted, witty work in the style of an American musical.

Claude Bessy will always remain faithful to the theatre. She was not particularly well-known on the international stage, but in France she was one of the greatest stars of her time and an outstanding example of the temperament and character of the French school. She had numerous admirers and, with her fairness and radiant smile, and with the shapely lines of her gently rounded body, she represented a type of ballerina that has become more and more rare today when androgyny prevails over femininity and charm.

—Irène Lidova

---

## LES BICHES

**Choreography:** Bronislava Nijinska
**Music:** Francis Poulenc
**Design:** Marie Laurencin (scenery and costumes)
**First Production:** Diaghilev's Ballets Russes, Théâtre de Monte Carlo, 6 January 1924
**Principal Dancers:** Vera Nemchinova (Adagietto; or "La Garçonne"); Léon Woizikovsky, Anatole Vilzak, Nicolas Zverev (Chanson Dansée; or the three "Athletes"); Bronislava Nijinska (Rag Mazurka; or the "Hostess"); Lubov Tchernicheva, Lydia Sokolova (Chanson Dansée; or "Girls in Grey").

**Other productions include:** Markova-Dolin Ballet (restaged Nijinska), as *The House Party*, with Alicia Markova ("La Garçonne"), Anton Dolin (leading "Athlete"), and Diana Gould ("Hostess"); English tour, 1937. Grand Ballet du Marquis de Cuevas, with Marjorie Tallchief ("La Garçonne"), George Skibine ("Athlete"); Paris, 1947. Dance Theater of Harlem (staged Irina Nijinska; design John Gilkerson after Laurencin), with Virginia Johnson ("La Garçonne"); New York, 27 January 1983. Royal Ballet (revival; staged Nijinska), with Georgina Parkinson, David Blair, Svetlana Beriosova; London, 2 December 1964.

## PUBLICATIONS

Cocteau, Jean, *Les Biches*, Paris, 1924
Nijinska, Bronislava, "Reflections about the Production of *Les Biches*", *Dancing Times* (London), February 1937
Poulenc, Francis, "Francis Poulenc on his Ballets", *Ballet* (London), September 1946
Beaumont, Cyril, *Complete Book of Ballets*, revised edition, London, 1951
Grigoriev, Serge, *The Diaghilev Ballet*, translated by Vera Bowen, London, 1953
Anderson, Jack, "The Fabulous Career of Bronislava Nijinska", *Dance Magazine* (New York), August 1963
Croce, Arlene, "Bronislava Nijinska", *Ballet Review* (Brooklyn, N.Y.), vol. 4, no. 2, 1972
Balanchine, George, with Mason, Francis, *Balanchine's Complete Stories of the Great Ballets*, Garden City, N.Y., 1977
Buckle, Richard, *Buckle at the Ballet*, London, 1980
Dolin, Anton, "*Les Biches*: A Misconception", *Dancing Times* (London), February 1980
Miguel, Parmenia, "Bronislava Nijinska: The Artistic Genius Behind *Les Biches*", *Dance Magazine* (New York), December 1982
Vaughan, David, "Those Bright Young Things", *Ballet News* (New York), January 1983
Baer, Nancy van Norman, *Bronislava Nijinska: A Dancer's Legacy*, San Francisco, 1986

**Anton Dolin and Vera Nemchinova in *Les Biches*, Diaghilev's Ballets Russes, Monte Carlo, 1924**

"Bronislava Nijinska: Dancers Speak", *Ballet Review* (New York), Spring 1990

Merrett, Sue, "Bronislava Nijinska Remembered", *Dancing Times* (London), May 1991

* * *

Poulenc, pleased to have finally found what he felt was exactly the right title for this ballet, described it to Diaghilev as "so Marie Laurencin". *Les Biches* translates as "The Does" (or female deer), such as were depicted on Laurencin's original backdrop. But like everything else about this ballet, the title is beguiling; *Les Biches* is a work of gentle suggestion and ambiguity.

The setting is a drawing room of delicate pastel shades. The spirit is one of sophistication and Parisian chic, but here the formalities of polite society are merely a façade, and the object of Nijinska's satire. Ninette de Valois, on whom Nijinska worked out the choreography of the Hostess (a role Nijinska was to dance herself), later urged her dancers to consider the novels of Colette in order to understand the atmosphere of the period. She might also have referred them to the plays of Noël Coward. *Les Biches* depicts and satirizes a world which depends on an air of indifference and disinterest to maintain a sophisticated sense of shallowness. It is quintessentially a ballet of the 1920s. Poulenc, who was only 24 when he wrote the score, delighted in the sexual innuendo of the work. He wrote that *Les Biches* is a ballet without a plot because had it a plot it would have caused a scandal. He related the ballet to the wantonness of Watteau's paintings "which you sense if you are corrupted but which an innocent-minded girl would not be conscious of".

Laurencin's design of a very short jerkin for the girl in blue (this was reputedly the product of Diaghilev's own intervention rather than Laurencin's original design) was considered indecent by some important personages at the time, who wanted a skirt or tutu to be added for the sake of decency. If these objectors had looked further than the costumes they might have found even more to concern them. The girl in blue is essentially an androgynous figure, who struts through the work with polished self-absorption. She is often referred to as "La Garconne", for she is a figure of ambiguous sexuality. Her costume resembles that of a page-boy and she forms a clear point of contrast to the more mature, undulating revelry of the Hostess, who flaunts herself expansively across the stage space, complete with ostrich feather and long cigarette-holder.

The ladies of *Les Biches* are a far cry from the innocent virginal types that populate more traditional ballets; they have a very knowing quality and clearly revel in their sexuality. No doubt because the work was choreographed by a woman (an unusual occurrence in ballet, and particularly so at this time), there is a degree to which traditional roles in ballet are reversed. Certainly it is the sexuality of the women that propels the work along its course; it is a female world, a female context, and the men appear as decorative objects, amusing little things with which to while away a playful afternoon. The three athletic-looking men parade absurdly in their swim-suit costumes and are ridiculously self-absorbed. Two of them are impervious to the women's attempts at seduction, while a third joins up with his female counterpart, the girl in blue. Nijinska parades them like mannequins in some interesting and amusing pas de deux. The heterosexual courting that forms the basis of the dancing and games, however, scarcely veils the work's gentle hints at more homo-erotic images and narcissistic preoccupations. It is a work about disguises, about the mask of social mores behind which decadence and lasciviousness are enjoying free rein.

The success and appeal of *Les Biches* comes from its delightful ambiguity. This has been perfectly summarized by critic Richard Buckle who, following the revival at Covent Garden in 1964, wrote: "Have the three athletes who enter this whispering world of women just dropped in from the beach, or are they customers? Is the older woman with the Chanel pearls a hostess or a madam? Is the female dancer in the blue *gilet* with white gloves, who gets off with the leading man, meant to be a page boy? Are the two blue grey girls having an affaire? When the two athletes slump on the sofa are they exhausted with sex or female nattering? In fact, is everybody making love or conversation? It is so delightful not to know."

It is a work which continues to delight audiences, but delight them perhaps in a different way than was intended by the original work. Buckle points out that both Cecil Beaton and Sokolova, who remembered the original production, considered the work in revival to lack some of the qualities of the original. Sokolova maintained that the original had a mystery and sophistication which banished all question of laughs. Perhaps a modern, post-1960s and post-sexual-revolution audience could never in any case see the work as it might originally have been experienced.

*Les Biches* has nevertheless been an influential as well as a popular work. It certainly influenced Frederick Ashton, who claimed his early work, *A Tragedy of Fashion*, was directly inspired by it. Above all perhaps, it is a wonderful representative of Diaghilev's more fashionable and frivolous productions. But *Les Biches* is more than a trifle; Nijinska manages to infuse the movement language of the work with the innuendo and ambiguity of her subject matter. There is a fascinating combination of classical complexity and a beguiling slant at the hips taken into the upper body. As well as distorting the classical technique for her satirical ends, Nijinska manages to make the slightest movement express several possibilities; she can be sharp and precise while at the same time powerfully evocative, rich, and sensual in her choreography. When performed, as it often is, alongside *Les Noces*, which is so vastly different and undoubtedly Nijinska's greatest work, *Les Biches* holds its own and is at the very least a testament to the considerable range of Diaghilev's only woman choreographer.

—Lesley-Anne Sayers

---

## BILLY THE KID

**Choreography:** Eugene Loring
**Music:** Aaron Copland
**Design:** Jared French (scenery and costumes)
**Libretto:** Lincoln Kirstein
**First Production:** Ballet Caravan, Civic Theatre, Chicago, 16 October 1938
**Principal Dancers:** Eugene Loring (Billy), Marie-Jeanne (Mother/Sweetheart), Lew Christensen (Pat Garrett), Todd Bolender (Alias)

**Other productions include:** Ballet Theatre (restaged Loring), with Loring (Billy), Alicia Alonso (Mother/Sweetheart), Richard Reed (Pat Garrett), David Nillo (Alias); Chicago, 8 December 1940. Dance Players (restaged Loring) with Loring, Christensen; New York, 21 April 1942. Los Angeles Dance Theatre (restaged Loring); Pasadena, 20 October 1973. Oakland Ballet (restaged Loring); Oakland, 21 October 1976. Australian Ballet (restaged Loring); February 1977. Ballet West (restaged Loring); Salt Lake City, July 1979. Louisville Ballet (staged Patrice Whiteside); Louisville, 20 April 1983.

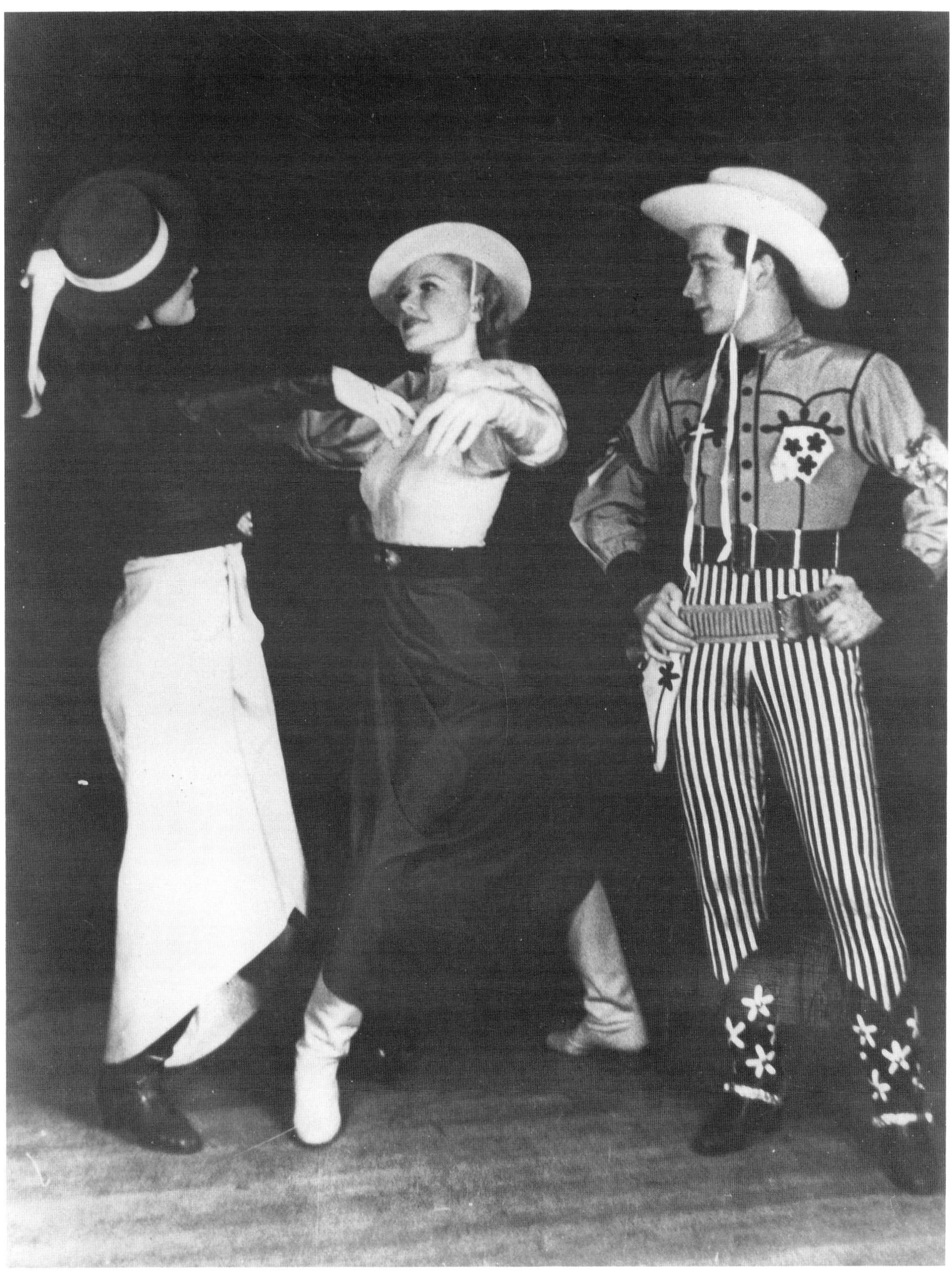

**Eugene Loring as Billy with the Ranchers' wives in *Billy The Kid*, Ballet Caravan, 1938**

Dance Theatre of Harlem (staged Whiteside, design Robert Fletcher); 28 June 1988. Joffrey Ballet (staged Whiteside); New York, 2 November 1988.

## PUBLICATIONS

Beaumont, Cyril, *Supplement to Complete Book of Ballets*, London, 1945

Denby, Edwin, *Looking at the Dance*, New York, 1949

Lloyd, Margaret, and Cohen, S.J., "Eugene Loring's Very American School of Dance", *Dance Magazine* (New York), August 1956

Maynard, Olga, *The American Ballet*, Philadelphia, 1959

Hindman, Anne A., *The Myth of the Western Frontier in American Dance and Drama 1930–43*, PhD, University of Georgia, 1972

"Billy is 35: Loring's Ballet Revisited", *Dance Magazine* (New York), February 1973

Balanchine, George, with Mason, Francis, *Balanchine's Complete Stories of the Great Ballets*, Garden City, N.Y., 1977

Payne, Charles, *American Ballet Theatre*, New York, 1977

Reynolds, Nancy, *Repertory in Review*, New York, 1977

Kirstein, Lincoln, *Thirty Years: The New York City Ballet*, New York, 1978

Siegel, Marcia, *The Shapes of Change*, Boston, 1979

Maynard, Olga, "Eugene Loring's American Classic: The Legend of Billy the Kid", *Dance Magazine* (New York), December 1979

Kirstein, Lincoln, *Ballet, Bias and Belief*, New York, 1983

Philp, Richard, "Billy the Kid turns 50", *Dance Magazine* (New York), November 1988

* * *

*Billy the Kid* represents a landmark in the development of American ballet. In depicting the American frontier and one of its most famous gun-fighters, *Billy the Kid* employed uniquely American thematic material. The ballet received wide critical acclaim when it was first performed by Ballet Caravan, and it continues to appear in the repertory of many major American ballet companies.

The frontier setting is given a sense of realism by its assortment of people from all walks of life, and Loring's ability to draw life-like characters can be seen in the care he took to define them in a movement vocabulary. The characters are revealed not only by their costumes and by such identifying short dances as the Mexican girls' dance; they are also defined by the characteristic movements with which they traverse the frontier streets. The housewives lean forward as they trudge through the streets, the result of a life of hard work, while the dance-hall girls strut proudly, showing off their legs and hips. Cowboys move as if riding horses, and their characteristic stance—legs in parallel and feet apart—suggests a life spent on horseback.

Once these characters are established by the movement that relates to their life experience, they are further defined by their reactions to one another. The housewives gossip in shocked agitation as the dance-hall girls entice the men of the town, and the girls themselves react to the housewives' prudery by addressing bumps and grinds in the housewives' direction. Billy himself is first seen as a young wide-eyed boy, holding the hand of his housewife mother, and his impulsive reaction to the accidental shooting death of his mother results in his first murder.

Loring's ability to make his characters seem real by connecting them to their environment is contrasted in his characterization of Billy. Except for the first appearance of Billy as a boy, he is often alienated from the larger action, appearing as a rather solitary figure. He is the only character to have an extended solo, and his killings are often set with only two characters present—Billy and Alias (a figure whose identity changes with each scene). Although Billy is seen with three other outlaws in the campfire and gun battle scenes, he pays little attention to them. Billy relates directly only to his mother, his sweetheart, and, briefly, to Pat Garrett.

Loring created his movement vocabulary from a wide spectrum of dance styles, and his choices were closely associated with the drama of the moment. Loring explained the appearance of the classically based double pirouette, followed by a double tour en l'air, that precedes all of Billy's adult murders as a representation of the fury Billy must have experienced. Even within this short movement phrase, a mixture of styles is evident, as the movement is from the classical dance but dispenses with the classical turn-out of the legs. The use of tap-dance movements in the fight over a card game between Billy and Pat Garrett mimics an angry dialogue between the two former friends. Although much of *Billy the Kid* does not use steps from the classical ballet, the pas de deux for Billy and his Sweetheart employs pointe work for the Sweetheart. Loring justified this use of pointe work by relating it to the dream-like essence of the Sweetheart's character.

From a formal point of view, much of the ballet is choreographed using what Loring would later teach as the "block method" at his American School of Dance. This method referred to the creation of movement motifs or phrases, which could then be manipulated in various ways. In *Billy the Kid*, recurring phrases with overlaps in timing or alterations in space lend density and variety to the scene, while the complexity of the image can be reduced to one or more relatively simple phrases. In addition, unison or near-unison movement is generally reserved for dancers who share the same character (such as the three dance-hall girls) or for points in the drama when the characters lose their individuality and are identified together as a crowd (as in the fight scene just prior to the Mother's death).

*Billy the Kid* is an intricate, complex ballet, filled with references to the great American west. Its strong characterization through the dance medium and its connection to the American experience have given it a long life on the ballet stage.

—Mary E. Corey

---

## BINTLEY, David

British dancer and choreographer. Born David Julian Bintley in Huddersfield, England, 17 September 1957. Educated at Holme Valley Grammar School; studied dance with Audrey Spencer, Dorothy Stevens, and at Royal Ballet Upper School, from 1974. Married Jennifer Catherine Ursula Mills, 1981: one son. Dancer, Sadler's Wells Royal Ballet, from 1976; first choreography for Sadler's Wells Royal Ballet, 1978; resident choreographer, Sadler's Wells Royal Ballet (later Birmingham Royal Ballet), 1983–85; resident choreographer, Royal Ballet, from 1986; has also staged ballets for San Francisco Ballet, 1990, 1992. Recipient: *Evening Standard* Award for Ballet, 1983; Laurence Olivier Award, 1984; *Manchester Evening News* Award, 1988.

**The Royal Ballet in David Bintley's *The Planets*, London, 1990**

## ROLES

1977 Widow Simone in *La Fille mal gardée* (Ashton), Sadler's Wells Royal Ballet, Glasgow
1978 Alaskan Rag in *Elite Syncopations* (MacMillan), Sadler's Wells Royal Ballet, Bournemouth
1979 Alain in *La Fille mal gardée* (Ashton), Sadler's Wells Royal Ballet, Sheffield
1980 The Red King in *Checkmate* (de Valois), Sadler's Wells Royal Ballet, London
1982 Bottom in *The Dream* (Ashton), Sadler's Wells Royal Ballet, Milton Keynes
1983 The Rake in *The Rake's Progress* (de Valois), Sadler's Wells Royal Ballet, Norwich
1984 Title role in *Petrushka* (Fokine), Sadler's Wells Royal Ballet, Eastbourne
1987 Ugly Sister in *Cinderella* (Ashton), Royal Ballet, London

**Other roles include:** Dr. Coppélius in *Coppélia* (Sergeyev after Petipa, Cecchetti; staged de Valois).

## WORKS

1978 *The Outsider* (mus. Bohác), Sadler's Wells Royal Ballet, Birmingham
*Take Five* (mus. Brubeck), Sadler's Wells Royal Ballet, London
1979 *Meadow of Proverbs* (mus. Milhaud), Sadler's Wells Royal Ballet, Birmingham
*Punch and the Street Party* (mus. Lord Berners), Sadler's Wells Royal Ballet, Edinburgh
1980 *Homage to Chopin* (mus. Panufnik), Sadler's Wells Royal Ballet, Stratford
*Adieu* (mus. Panufnik), Royal Ballet, London
*Polonia* (mus. Panufnik), Sadler's Wells Royal Ballet, London
1981 *Night Moves* (mus. Britten), Sadler's Wells Royal Ballet, London
1982 *The Swan of Tuonela* (mus. Sibelius), Sadler's Wells Royal Ballet, London
1983 *Choros* (mus. Meyer), Sadler's Wells Royal Ballet, London
*Consort Lessons* (mus. Stravinsky), Royal Ballet, London
1984 *Metamorphosis* (mus. McGowan), Sadler's Wells Royal Ballet, London
*Young Apollo* (mus. Britten, Crosse), Royal Ballet, London
1985 *Flowers of the Forest* (mus. Britten), Sadler's Wells Royal Ballet, Birmingham
*The Sons of Horus* (mus. McGowan), Royal Ballet, London
1986 *The Snow Queen* (mus. Tovey after Mussorgsky), Sadler's Wells Royal Ballet, Birmingham
*Galanteries* (mus. Mozart), Royal Ballet, Vancouver
1987 *Allegri Diversi* (mus. Rossini), Sadler's Wells Royal Ballet, London
1988 *Still Life at the Penguin Café* (mus. Jeffes), Royal Ballet, London
*The Trial of Prometheus* (mus. Burgon), Royal Ballet, London
*The Spirit of Fugue* (mus. McGowan), Royal Ballet, London
1989 *Hobson's Choice* (mus. Reade), Sadler's Wells Royal Ballet, London
1990 *The Planets* (mus. Holst), Royal Ballet, London
*Brahms Handel Variations* (mus. Brahms), Birmingham

Royal Ballet, Birmingham
*The Wanderer Fantasy* (mus. Schubert, Lizst), San Francisco Ballet, San Francisco
1991 *Cyrano* (mus. Josephs), Royal Ballet, London
1992 *Job* (mus. Vaughan Williams), San Francisco Ballet, San Francisco

## PUBLICATIONS


Davies, Richard, "Bintley: In the Steps of the Banished Poet", *Classical Music* (London), 3 October 1981
Goodwin, Noël, "Ritual and Identity", *Dance and Dancers* (London), December 1985
Meisner, Nadine, "SWRB's David Bintley", *Dance Magazine* (New York), February 1986
Macaulay, Alastair, "Beauty or the Beast: Choreography and the Royal Ballet", *Dance Theatre Journal* (London), Spring 1987
Macaulay, Alastair, "Twilight of the Gods: Bintley after Ashton", *Dancing Times* (London), December 1988
Goodwin, Noël, "A Matter of Form", *Dance and Dancers* (London), February 1989
Mackrell, Judith, "David Bintley", *Dance Theatre Journal* (London), Spring 1989
"Young Classical Choreographers", (Dance Study Supplement), *Dancing Times* (London), January 1990


* * *

David Bintley's talents, both as choreographer and as character dancer, were first noticed while he was still a student. Since then, his rapid rise through the hierarchy of the Royal Ballet has been largely due to the fact that his skills lie in areas where talent is hard to find.

His name as a dancer is closely identified with a number of character roles. For instance, Alain and Widow Simone from Ashton's *La Fille mal gardée*, together with the parts of Dr. Coppélius and Petrushka, link his name with some of the great character artists and dancers of the past, such as Stanley Holden, Alexander Grant, and Vaslav Nijinsky.

As a choreographer, Bintley can be seen to be more of a traditionalist than an innovator. Many of his works exemplify pastiche or overt quotations as he alludes to and acknowledges the great masters such as Balanchine, Petipa, and Fokine. He created his first professional ballet, *The Outsider*, at the age of twenty, very much in the shadow of his predecessors Ashton, Cranko, and MacMillan. In those initial years, it was the Sadler's Wells Royal Ballet which fostered and nurtured his ambitions, helping him to explore and develop his own particular choreographic style and mode of presentation.

Over a decade later and with more than a score of ballets to his credit, Bintley has created a number of narrative works, for example *Metamorphosis* and *Hobson's Choice*. Although unusual when compared to other modern-day choreographers, this skill is very suited to the Royal Ballet, whose traditions lie in the dance-drama or "ballet d'action". At the same time, Bintley has also systematically worked his way through a whole spectrum of other ballet types, exploring themes, moods, or atmospheres in *Homage to Chopin*, or turning to the plotless or pure dance work in *Galanteries*.

It is clear that Bintley has respect for the kind of artistic collaboration which was best exemplified by Diaghilev's Ballets Russes. A number of his works are to commissioned scores and designs, such as the lively jazzy music for *Choros* by Aubrey Meyer, and the abstract backcloths for *Young Apollo* by the painter Victor Pasmore. In typical de Valois vein, he often employs indigenous talent, for example the composer Paul Reade for *Hobson's Choice*, and more specifically, "in-house" expertise within the Royal Opera House, such as scenic artist Mike Becket and designer Terry Bartlett.

De Valois's influence can also be seen in the episodic structuring of some of Bintley's early works, such as *The Outsider* and *Meadow of Proverbs*, and in his use of expressionism, as in *Metamorphosis*. The patriotic *Punch and the Street Party* and Bintley's dedication of his very English work *Hobson's Choice* to "Madam", also serve to show his respect for the founder of the Royal Ballet in whose ballets he has often danced himself.

For his work, Bintley seeks ideas and inspiration from a number of different sources, including art, literature, film, architecture, fairy tale, drama, nature, and mythology. Narrative pieces, such as his three-act ballet *The Snow Queen*, often include strong theatrical and dramatic techniques and a dénouement which diverges from the original novel or story.

In *The Outsider*, his first professional piece, Bintley shows the strong influence of MacMillan, both in the choice of subject material and in the movement content. Based on a plot full of sordid sex and violence, the ballet relies on crude, erotic movements and a certain degree of sensationalism. Various motifs or positions are inverted or performed at all angles and levels in true MacMillan fashion. The use of "splits", both unsupported and in partnered sequences, and a stabbing use of the pointe can be seen to be strongly amplified in later works when a more Balanchine-like style is adopted.

This change in focus occurred after Bintley's three-month sabbatical to America and Germany in 1982. The three ballets which quickly followed display this new tone—*Choros* and *Consort Lessons* and *Young Apollo*. These works present dancers performing difficult combinations of movements focusing on quick, precise footwork, a density of steps within phrases, complex weight changes, and unorthodox hip movements. *Allegri Diversi*, however, shows Bintley drawing on Petipa's structural devices and floor patterns as well as traditionally classical steps to extend his dancers in a very different and challenging mode. Although *Choros* reveals an interesting form in the use of reversed trios and quartets, some of his other works, namely *Meadow of Proverbs* and *Consort Lessons*, are somewhat predictable in their overuse of canonic phrases.

Despite his many and considerable talents, Bintley has yet to produce a real masterpiece for posterity. He is now an established choreographer who has stated that his primary function is "to extend the classical vocabulary". This can only be achieved by true choreographic inventiveness. None the less, Bintley can be seen to be an artist who "keeps one foot in the past and places the other in the future". This quality is an asset revered by de Valois and may be very necessary for the acknowledged heir-apparent to MacMillan.

—Monica Hetherington

---

## BIRMINGHAM ROYAL BALLET

(formerly Sadler's Wells Royal Ballet)

English ballet company based in Birmingham, and established as "sister company" to the Royal Ballet at Covent Garden, London. Founded by Ninette de Valois as Sadler's Wells Opera Ballet, based at Sadler's Wells Theatre (on the move of the first company to the Royal Opera House, Covent Garden), 1946; performed as Sadler's Wells Theatre Ballet, 1947–57, with official base at Sadler's Wells Theatre, but policy of extensive tours within Britain; performed as Royal Ballet Touring Company (also known as Royal Ballet Touring Section), 1957–77, with short-lived period as Royal Ballet New Group, a small touring section of the main company, established 1970; assumed title of Sadler's Wells Royal Ballet, from 1976; official base moved to city of Birmingham, with company title becoming the Birmingham Royal Ballet, from 1990. Current artistic director (initially associate director) of the Birmingham Royal Ballet: Peter Wright, from 1970.

## PUBLICATIONS

Beaumont, Cyril, *The Sadler's Wells Ballet*, revised edition, London, 1947

Clarke, Mary, *The Sadler's Wells Ballet*, London, 1955

Haskell, Arnold, et al., *Gala Performance*, London, 1955

Fisher, Hugh, *The Sadler's Wells Theatre Ballet*, London, 1956

Bland, Alexander, *The Royal Ballet: The First Fifty Years*, London, 1981

Sorley Walker, Kathrine, *Idealist Without Illusions: Ninette de Valois*, London, 1983

"Chameleon Company" and other articles, *Dance and Dancers* (London), November 1990

Woodcock, Sarah C., *The Sadler's Wells Royal Ballet, Now the Birmingham Royal Ballet*, London, 1991

* * *

The history of the Birmingham Royal Ballet falls into clearly defined periods, each marked by a change of director and a change of policy.

As the Sadler's Wells Opera Ballet, it was the company set up by Ninette de Valois in 1946 to fill the gap created when the Sadler's Wells Ballet left the theatre of its name for Covent Garden. The function of the new company was to appear in the opera ballets, give the occasional evening of ballet, and undertake some touring—but it was also to act both as a training ground for dancers before they moved to Covent Garden and as a nursery for young choreographers.

The company proved exceptionally successful in achieving these aims. In under two years, it had become the Sadler's Wells Theatre Ballet, and under the sympathetic guidance of Peggy van Praagh, many dancers who later achieved maturity at Covent Garden were developed; these included Nadia Nerina, Anne Heaton, Svetlana Beriosova, David Blair, Pirmin Trecu, and Maryon Lane. But the Theatre Ballet was no mere transit station between the Sadler's Wells Ballet School and the Royal Opera House; it developed its own individuality, based on the vitality and youthful attraction of dancers who were to find fulfilment within the company, like Patricia Miller, David Poole, and Donald Britton.

Andrée Howard was the company's first resident choreographer, but within its first decade, the company had developed two major choreographic talents itself. The first, John Cranko, created a number of distinguished works, the most popular being his comic masterpiece *Pineapple Poll* and the romantically sentimental *The Lady and the Fool*. After his transfer to Covent Garden, the mid 1950s saw the emergence of Kenneth MacMillan, who in *Danses Concertantes* and *The House of Birds* gave the first indications of his very individual qualities.

In 1951, the company undertook a major American tour, for which it acquired its first full-length ballet, *Coppélia*, and slowly began to outgrow its "nursery" status. Touring began to assume an ever-increasing role as it took over much provincial and some overseas touring from the Sadler's Wells Ballet; by the mid 1950s the company was spending most of its life on the road with only occasional London seasons.

The year 1956 saw the appointment of John Field as director and a change in the aims of the company. It left Sadler's Wells and, with the creation of the Royal Ballet in 1957, the enlarged company, under the eventual name of the Royal Ballet Touring Company, became the touring arm of the new organization. The company was now the Royal Ballet's showcase outside London and abroad (except in America). Although the occasional new ballet was created, notably MacMillan's *The Invitation* and Ashton's *The Two Pigeons*, the repertory for the next decade became centred upon the nineteenth-century classics, which the company introduced to many provincial audiences for the first time. It also performed ballets shared with the Covent Garden company, like Ashton's *The Dream*. It developed its own straightforward approach to the classics, stressing narrative rather than technique, as befitted a company appearing mainly to uninitiated audiences.

A new generation of dancers had emerged from the company—most notably Donald MacLeary, Lynn Seymour, and Christopher Gable—before it transferred to the Royal Opera House; but now many Covent Garden principals, including Beriosova, Nerina, Linden, and Page, appeared with the company on tour. Still, by the end of the 1960s, the company had developed its own stars in Doreen Wells and David Wall, and the glamour of their partnership did much to attract new audiences. With Brenda Last, Shirley Grahame, Patricia Ruanne, Paul Clarke, Margaret Barbieri, and Nicholas Johnson also taking leading roles, the company had never looked stronger.

By the end of the decade, however, it was felt that a large touring company was no longer viable and that audiences were tiring of the classics. A major restructuring of the Royal Ballet took place in 1970, and John Field moved to Covent Garden, briefly to assume directorship with Kenneth MacMillan. In an attempt to bring the Royal Ballet into line with current developments in dance, the Touring Company was disbanded and in its place a small "experimental" company, eventually known as the Royal Ballet New Group, was established under the direction of Peter Wright. This was not successful with audiences on tour, although the repertory was considerably enriched by the acquisition of ballets by distinguished contemporary choreographers, including Glen Tetley and Hans van Manen, and by a new generation of dancers including Marion Tait, Alain Dubreuil, and Stephen Jefferies.

Slowly, Wright began to build the company back into a major force in British ballet. Beginning with *Coppélia*, he reintroduced the classics, which stretched the dancers technically. He also expanded the repertory to make the company a storehouse of the best choreography available, and fostered choreographic talent within the company.

In 1976, the company again made Sadler's Wells Theatre its base, taking the name of the Sadler's Wells Royal Ballet. Its ever-growing success since that date has been based upon a high standard of performance and a wide-ranging repertory, which includes, in Wright's production, one of the most imaginative stagings of *Swan Lake* to be seen today, as well as ballets by choreographers from many sources, including Petipa, Ashton, and Balanchine. Led by Barbieri, Tait, and David Ashmole, younger dancers like Karen Donovan, Sandra Madgwick, Miyoko Yoshida, Roland Price, and Michael O'Hare have developed. Choreographers were again encouraged to develop from within the company, notably David Bintley, whose success inevitably led to his transfer to Covent Garden.

In 1990 the company moved from London to a permanent home at the Birmingham Hippodrome and became The

Birmingham Royal Ballet, though remaining part of the Royal Ballet organization.

The Royal Ballet has always been fortunate in having two companies, one of classical pre-eminence, the other with what might be called a demi-caractère liveliness. The second company has, throughout its life, been an ambassador for the Royal Ballet in England and abroad, with its own particular character based upon energy, creative drive, and enjoyment in performing—something which has endeared it to audiences everywhere. Throughout its life, it has unselfishly fed the Covent Garden company with both dancers and choreographers, to the enrichment of British ballet, while former members of the company are to be found worldwide as company directors, dancers, ballet masters, and teachers.

—Sarah C. Woodcock

## BIRTHDAY OFFERING

**Choreography:** Frederick Ashton
**Music:** Aleksandr Glazunov, arranged and orchestrated by Robert Irving
**Design:** André Levasseur (costumes)
**First Production:** Sadler's Wells Ballet, Royal Opera House, London, 5 May 1956
**Principal Dancers:** Margot Fonteyn, Beryl Grey, Violetta Elvin, Nadia Nerina, Rowena Jackson, Svetlana Beriosova, Elaine Fifield, Michael Somes, Alexander Grant, Brian Shaw, Philip Chatfield, David Blair, Desmond Doyle, Bryan Ashbridge

**Other productions include:** Margot Fonteyn World Tour (abridged version); Athens, 10 August 1963. American Ballet Theatre (staged Faith Worth after Ashton); Houston, 25 October 1989.

### PUBLICATIONS

Balanchine, George, with Mason, Francis, *Balanchine's Complete Stories of the Great Ballets*, Garden City, N.Y., 1977
Vaughan, David, *Frederick Ashton and his Ballets*, London, 1977
Croce, Arlene, *Going to the Dance*, New York, 1982
Vaughan, David, "ABT's *Birthday Offering*", *Ballet Review* (New York), Fall 1990

* * *

*Birthday Offering* was made by Ashton as a "pièce d'occasion", the occasion being the twenth-fifth birthday of the Vic-Wells Ballet in May of 1956, shortly before it became the Royal Ballet. In 1989 it was set on American Ballet Theatre to commemorate another occasion and another birthday, ABT's fiftieth anniversary in 1990.

The vocabulary of the piece is drawn from that of high Russian classicism, which is to say from Petipa. Indeed, audiences have on more than one occasion found the piece simply derivative; the critic Arlene Croce reported the tepid responses of New York audiences to performances in the 1970s

The Royal Ballet in a revival of *Birthday Offering*

by the Royal Ballet. Yet though it is indebted to Petipa, the piece is more than merely a rehash of the past. Instead, it is like an old story told by a new narrator, so that the listener hears both the old and the new simultaneously. What the viewer of this ballet sees is a mixture of originality and appropriation that may be taken as a metaphor of the classical ballet in general.

*Birthday Offering* is a pas de quatorze for a lead couple and six ancillary ones. There is an entrance and a finale for all fourteen dancers; in between, each woman dances a variation, followed by a mazurka for the men and a pas de deux for the principals. The male-female relationships are those Ashton inherited from Petipa: men are used as supports for the women; it is the women who dance more than the men and who are more individualized. (In its first season this was as much due to the lack of strong male dancers as to design; the scholar David Vaughan notes that male variations were added later for David Blair and Rudolf Nureyev.) The backdrop is grey, relieved only by three pairs of glowing candelabra on the flats; the costumes are standard nineteenth-century prince and princess tutus by André Levasseur—vaguely Eastern European for the men, to go with the mazurka.

For all this air of the standard, however, Ashton manages both to highlight the natural tendencies of the classical style that he is utilizing—an artistic achievement in itself—and to put his own stamp on the motion that constitutes it. This style celebrates symmetry and order, a world in which individuality is a ripple on the surface of a larger whole. In this spirit, the Entrée and Finale bracket the work like bookends, the men sweeping the women across the stage in snaking lines into attitudes posées en avant and arrière. Even during the variations in the middle, the men take up symmetrical positions on the low steps at the back of the stage, with their hands across their chests in a gesture of waiting adoration.

It is in the variations that individuality has its brief moment of prominence, emphasized in each case by the carefully chosen snippets from Glazunov, to whose music the entire piece is set. Yet even here the ballerina's particularity is expressed through the faintest of echoes of and references to Petipa/Ivanov. The first solo, to xylophone music, recalls the Sugar Plum Fairy's dance to the celeste and produces some of the same sense of tripping lightness, with a few of the head-tilts of *The Nutcracker's* Chinese dancers thrown in for good measure. The second involves great swings of the upper torso and seems faintly Spanish in flavour, while the third, to a languid tune for strings, takes on the allure of *The Nutcracker*'s Arab divertissement. The last variation, for the lead ballerina (originally Margot Fonteyn), is expansive and playful, covering the stage in what is not surprisingly the technically most complex of the variations.

Even in the pas de deux that follows, the individual gives way to the other; ego is subsumed by superego. The lead couple, dressed in white and gold, enters on the diagonal, with the man supporting the woman around the waist and just off the floor as she crosses the floor in bourrées; the woman leans her head slightly towards the man as he does so, as if to acknowledge his help—making an emotional fact of the constant contact with a partner that in so many works in the classical tradition is merely a fact of the style. Motion in the pas de deux as a whole, in fact, is strikingly horizontal, with no lifting, so that the man and woman seem much more like equals than is usually the case, and the movement a celebration of the human rather than of longing towards the divine.

—Bruce Fleming

---

**BISSELL, Patrick**

American dancer. Born Walter Patrick Bissell in Corpus Christi, Texas, 1 December 1957. Studied with Bud Kerwin, from 1968, and Tania Smith, Toledo, Ohio, at the National Academy of Dance, Champaign, Illinois, at North Carolina School of the Arts, and at School of American Ballet, pupil of Stanley Williams, New York. Married dancer Jolinda Menendez, 1982. Dancer, becoming soloist, Boston Ballet, 1975–76; dancer, American Ballet Theatre, New York, from 1977: soloist, from 1978, principal dancer, from 1979; left American Ballet Theatre, 1980; guest artist, National Ballet of Canada, Toronto, 1980, Scottish Ballet, Edinburgh Festival, 1980, Pacific Northwest Ballet, Seattle, 1980, returning to American Ballet Theatre as principal dancer, 1981; also international guest artist, appearing with Hamburg Ballet, 1978, with Stars of World Ballet, Australian tour, 1979, and in concert performances with Natalia Makarova, Manila and Hong Kong, 1979; toured Latin America, 1982. Died (of drug overdose) in Hoboken, New Jersey, 28/29 December 1987.

**ROLES**

1978 Solor in "Kingdom of the Shades" from *La Bayadère* (Makarova after Petipa), American Ballet Theatre, Los Angeles
Nutcracker Prince in *The Nutcracker* (Baryshnikov), American Ballet Theatre, Chicago
Principal dancer in *Theme and Variations* (Balanchine), American Ballet Theatre, New York
Espada in *Don Quixote* (*Kitri's Wedding*; Baryshnikov after Petipa), American Ballet Theatre, New York
Principal dancer (cr) in *Élégie* (Neumeier), Hamburg Ballet, Hamburg
Principal dancer (cr) in *The Tiller in the Fields* (Tudor), American Ballet Theatre, Washington, D.C.

1978/79 Prince Siegfried in *Swan Lake* (Petipa, Ivanov; staged Blair), American Ballet Theatre
Prince Florimund in *The Sleeping Beauty* (Petipa; staged Skeaping), American Ballet Theatre
Principal dancer in *Holberg Suite* (Cranko), Hamburg Ballet, Hamburg
Principal dancer in *Études* (Lander), American Ballet Theatre

1979 Dancer (cr) in *Contredances* (Tetley), American Ballet Theatre, Washington, D.C.
Principal dancer in *Voluntaries* (Tetley), American Ballet Theatre
Principal dancer (cr) in *Concert Waltzes* (Levans), American Ballet Theatre

1980 Romeo in *Romeo and Juliet* (Cranko), National Ballet of Canada, Toronto
Title role (cr) in *Chéri* (Darrell), Scottish Ballet, Edinburgh Festival, Edinburgh
Solor in *La Bayadère* (full-length version; Makarova after Petipa), American Ballet Theatre

1981/82 Don José in *Carmen* (Petit), American Ballet Theatre

1983 Principal dancer (cr) in *Estuary* (Taylor-Corbett), American Ballet Theatre, Miami Beach, Florida
Principal dancer in *Symphonie Concertante* (Balanchine), American Ballet Theatre, Washington, D.C.
Prince Charming (cr) in *Cinderella* (Baryshnikov, Anastos), American Ballet Theatre, Washington, D.C.

**Other roles include:** for American Ballet Theatre—Albrecht in

*Giselle* (Petipa after Coralli, Perrot; staged Baryshnikov), Prince Désiré in *The Sleeping Beauty* (Petipa; staged MacMillan), principal dancer in *Raymonda Divertissements* (Petipa; staged Baryshnikov), principal dancer in *Sylvia: Pas de Deux* (Balanchine), Basilio in *Don Quixote* (*Kitri's Wedding*; Baryshnikov after Petipa), Romeo in *Romeo and Juliet* (MacMillan); as guest artist (Korea)—title role in *Apollo* (Balanchine).

**PUBLICATIONS**

By Bissell:
Interview in Gruen, John, "From Punk to Prince: Patrick Bissell", *Dance Magazine* (New York), April 1979; reprinted in Gruen, *People Who Dance*, New York, 1988
Interview in Flotow, Sheryl, "Flying High: Patrick Bissell", *Ballet News* (New York), June 1983

About Bissell:
Greskovic, Robert, "Portrait of the Artist as a Young Dancer", *Ballet Review* (New York), vol. 8, nos. 2–3, 1980
Sandler, Ken, "On the Comeback Trail", *Ballet News* (New York), August 1982
Croce, Arlene, *Going to the Dance*, New York, 1982
Greskovic, Robert, "Matinee Idol: ABT's Patrick Bissell", *Ballet News* (New York), June 1983
Croce, Arlene, *Sightlines*, New York, 1987

* * *

(Walter) Patrick Bissell had a story-book career. Unfortunately his story ended on a tragic note, and even more unfortunately, it was this tragedy that gained this gifted and exemplary dancer a prominence his special talents alone did not. Blessed with beauty, drive, and a wealth of opportunities, the underprivileged young man from Texas made his determined way as a stellar ballet dancer in a country where male dancers will probably never be in abundance. After some local and big-city ballet schooling, he entered the School of American Ballet, the most prestigious academy in the United States, and moved into the top ranks of American Ballet Theatre (ABT) at a rapid pace.

The tall, dark, and handsome Bissell caught immediate notice in the so-called workshop or graduation performances given by the School of American Ballet. In the two programmes the school gave in 1977, Bissell headed three of the five works given. Balletomanes looking for perfection of academic detail thought the nineteen-year-old very green and unfinished; other less pedantic star-watchers were struck by his inherent warmth and appealing grand manner. That summer he danced in the corps de ballet of Boston Ballet and that autumn became a member of ABT.

Within a year's time, he was performing Solor in the "Kingdom of the Shades" (from *La Bayadère*). His power, projection, and impetuous attack gained him attention with both the press and his company directors. At six feet, two inches in height and with an unaffectedly dashing manner, he was soon in great demand as partner for ballerinas of all sorts, especially tall women for whom suitable partners were always scarce. He kept ABT as his base, and was cast opposite almost all of its ballerinas during his ten years with the company. These included Martine van Hamel, Cynthia Gregory, Gelsey Kirkland, Susan Jaffe, Leslie Browne, and Alessandra Ferri. He also made many guest appearances, partnering ballerinas such as Natalia Makarova, Karin Kain, and Galina Samsova.

The list of ballerinas with whom he danced is long, and the range of ballets in which he performed leading roles is wide, but during the ten-year span of his career he got almost more media attention for his reckless misbehavior off-stage than for his sterling cavalier deportment on stage. This notoriety climaxed with the publication of Kirkland's memoir, *Dancing on My Grave*, in which she recounted in graphic detail her intimate, stormy, and drug-abusing relationship with Bissell while the two were at ABT. (Ironically, the two young dancers were initally brought together by Antony Tudor, in whose new ballet, *The Tiller in the Fields*, Kirkland and Bissell were to create leading parts. The work, with its Tudor pedigree, remains a major entry, on paper, in the past of both dancers. In fact, the one-act work was short-lived, and not kept around long enough to reveal any particular substance.) While the truth of Kirkland's horror story is not in question, neither was the truth of Bissell's very real dance power.

While his performances were somewhat variable in quality (and with hindsight the wonder is that they were not more so), Bissell showed a chivalrous bearing and generosity that were rarely less than remarkable. Empowered by the inherent strength in his sturdy, but not thick, physique, Bissell's classical dancing combined the palpable energy of the famous Belvedere torso with the statuesque calm of the equally famous Belvedere Apollo. He was not what School of American Ballet insiders call a "monster of perfection", in so far as precision and control of classical dancing are concerned. But Bissell was a master of performance and a gentlemanly consort who presented and tended ballerinas with perfection of strength and deftness. What his dancing lacked in ultimate finesse it made up for in power, sweep, and spontaneity. He had an unselfconscious understanding of knightly and princely demeanor, something particularly rare in American-born danseurs. In the roles of Solor and Basilio, as well as Espada (in *Don Quixote*), Don José (in Petit's *Carmen*), and Prince Charming (a role he originated in the Anastos/Baryshnikov *Cinderella*), Bissell colored all the specific classical dancing with a physical flamboyance and a musical lushness that were his alone. In the more staid roles of Albrecht, Siegfried, and Désiré he showed a more delicately gauged flair, but one, nevertheless, that vivified each character with dimensions beyond the predictable and usual.

Perhaps the role that best encapsulated the breadth, beauty, and intensity of Bissell's classical artistry was that of the solitary male in Balanchine's *Symphonie Concertante*. In this simple showcase of pristine classical vocabulary, the cavalier enters in the second movement to support and attend the work's two leading ballerinas simultaneously. What some danseurs have treated as a non-role, Bissell treated as a plum. Beaming radiantly, with a beloved ballerina in each hand, he shaped this andante passage into one of riveting intimacy and rich harmony. During the final presto movement he returned, sometimes with ballerinas, and, other times, briefly, alone. During his select solo passages he enlivened the proceedings with an urgent power and a happy thrust that, while musically obedient as well as theatrically spontaneous, were Bissell trademarks.

He was found dead of substance abuse in 1987 in his apartment in New Jersey. It was the end of his formidable but not necessarily overly appreciated artistic career, and the beginning of his elevation into the annals of art scandal. In the wake of his death, various self-serving individuals, including Kirkland, tried to promote themselves under the guise of I-told-you-so's about drug abuse. His distraught mother appeared in print and on television regarding the fact that she was an abusive parent. Those who admired his dancing will ever miss it and never forget it—for itself.

—Robert Greskovic

**BJØRNSSON, Fredbjørn**

Danish dancer, choreographer, and teacher. Born in Copenhagen, 10 September 1926. Studied at the Royal Danish Ballet School, Copenhagen, from 1935; also studied in Paris, London, and New York. Married dancer Kirsten Ralov. Dancer, Royal Danish Ballet, from 1944: solo dancer (principal), from 1949; toured the United States and Europe with Inge Sand and dancers of the Royal Danish Ballet, early 1950s; continued to perform character roles into the 1980s; also choreographer: first work for Royal Danish Ballet, 1954; has also staged ballets for Danish television and for Tivoli Theatre, Copenhagen, as well as for musicals and revue, opera, and the dramatic stage; teacher, Royal Danish Ballet School, and international guest teacher and coach of Bournonville repertoire, including in the United States and Canada, and for the Royal Swedish Ballet, Stockholm. Recipient: Knight of the Order of Dannebrog.

**ROLES**

1937 The Chimney Sweeper in *The Shepherdess and the Chimney Sweeper* (Lander), Royal Danish Ballet, Copenhagen

1943 Polovtsian warrior in *Polovtsian Dances from Prince Igor* (Fokine; staged Lander), Royal Danish Ballet, Copenhagen

Dancer in *La Valse* (Lander), Royal Danish Ballet, Copenhagen

1944 Circus servant in *The Dethroned Lion Tamer* (Larsen), Royal Danish Ballet, Copenhagen

1946 Wilfred in *Giselle* (Petipa after Coralli, Perrot; staged Volinine), Royal Danish Ballet, Copenhagen

Steir dance in *The Whims of Cupid and the Ballet Master* (Galeotti), Royal Danish Ballet, Copenhagen

1947 Tramp (cr) in *Kolingen* (B. Ralov), Royal Danish Ballet, Copenhagen

Ganymede in *Thorvaldsen* (Lander), Royal Danish Ballet, Copenhagen

The Boy in *The Land of Milk and Honey* (Lander), Royal Danish Ballet, Copenhagen

Angry wave in *The Sorcerer's Apprentice* (Lander), Royal Danish Ballet, Copenhagen

Dirk in *The Life Guards on Amager* (Bournonville), Royal Danish Ballet, Copenhagen

Greek dance in *The Whims of Cupid and the Ballet Master* (Galeotti), Royal Danish Ballet, Copenhagen

1948 Dancer (cr) in *Étude* (Lander), Royal Danish Ballet, Copenhagen

Faun (cr) in *Sylvia* (Larsen), Royal Danish Ballet, Copenhagen

Dandy in *Le Beau Danube* (Massine), Royal Danish Ballet, Copenhagen

Dancer in *Episode of an Artist's Life* (*Symphonie fantastique*; Massine), Royal Danish Ballet, Copenhagen

1949 Worker in *The Widow in the Mirror* (Ralov), Royal Danish Ballet, Copenhagen

Gypsy (cr) in *Morning—Noon—Evening* (Lander), Royal Danish Ballet, Copenhagen

Eskimo dance in *Salute to August Bournonville* (Bournonville; staged Lander), Royal Danish Ballet, Copenhagen

Suitor in *Aurora's Wedding* (from *The Sleeping Beauty*; Petipa, staged Brenaa), Royal Danish Ballet, Copenhagen

One of the Three Ivans in *Aurora's Wedding* (Petipa; staged Brenaa), Royal Danish Ballet, Copenhagen

1950 The Aggressive One (cr) in *Metaphor* (Theilade), Royal Danish Ballet, Copenhagen

Principal dancer (cr) in *Concerto* (Theilade), Royal Danish Ballet, Copenhagen

February in *Twelve by the Post* (B. Ralov), Royal Danish Ballet, Copenhagen

Principal dancer (cr) in *Symphonie classique* (Bartholin), Royal Danish Ballet, Copenhagen

The Red Man in *Morning—Noon—Evening* (Lander), Royal Danish Ballet, Copenhagen

1951 Frantz in *Coppélia* (Lander after Saint-Léon), Royal Danish Ballet, Copenhagen

Pas de deux in *Desire* (Larsen), Royal Danish Ballet, Copenhagen

Tybalt in *Romeo and Juliet* (Bartholin), Royal Danish Ballet, Copenhagen

Acteon in *Diana* (Lander), Royal Danish Ballet, Copenhagen

Gennaro in *Napoli*, Act III (Bournonville), Royal Danish Ballet, Copenhagen

The Blue Bird in *Aurora's Wedding* (Petipa; staged Brenaa), Royal Danish Ballet, Copenhagen

Carelis in *The Kermesse in Bruges* (Bournonville), Royal Danish Ballet, Copenhagen

1952 First Junior Cadet in *Graduation Ball* (Lichine), Royal Danish Ballet, Copenhagen

Principal dancer in *Design with Strings* (Taras), Royal Danish Ballet, Copenhagen

Bios (cr) in *Idolon* (Schaufuss), Royal Danish Ballet, Copenhagen

1953 Principal dancer (cr) in *Concertette* (Bruhn), Royal Danish Ballet, Copenhagen

Businessman (cr) in *The Courtesan* (B. Ralov), Royal Danish Ballet, Copenhagen

The student in *Parisiana* (Bartholin), Royal Danish Ballet, Copenhagen

1954 French dance in *The Whims of Cupid and the Ballet Master* (Galeotti), Royal Danish Ballet, Copenhagen

Vittorio (cr) in *Capricious Lucinda* (Larsen), Royal Danish Ballet, Copenhagen

1955 The Moor in *Night Shadow* (Balanchine), Royal Danish Ballet, Copenhagen

Fandango in *The Marriage of Figaro* (opera; mus. Mozart, chor. Bournonville), Royal Theatre, Copenhagen

Polovtsian Chief in *Polovtsian Dances from Prince Igor* (Fokine; staged Larsen), Royal Danish Ballet, Copenhagen

Young coachman in *Petrushka* (Fokine), Royal Danish Ballet, Copenhagen

1956 Alvar in *Far from Denmark* (Bournonville), Royal Danish Ballet, Copenhagen

Percussion in *Fanfare* (Robbins), Royal Danish Ballet, Copenhagen

Tybalt (cr) in *Romeo and Juliet* (Ashton), Royal Danish Ballet, Copenhagen

Señor in *La Ventana* (Bournonville), Royal Danish Ballet, Copenhagen

The Drummer in *Graduation Ball* (Lichine), Royal Danish Ballet, Copenhagen

1957 Vals in *The Sleeping Beauty* (Petipa; staged Ashton), Royal Danish Ballet, Copenhagen

Pas de deux from *The Flower Festival at Genzano* (Bournonville), Royal Danish Ballet, Copenhagen

Hawtorn (cr) in *Vision* (Larsen), Royal Danish Ballet, Copenhagen

Principal dancer (cr) in *Roguery* (also chor.), Tivoli

Concert Hall, Copenhagen
Naïden (cr) in *Moon Reindeer* (Cullberg), Royal Danish Ballet, Copenhagen
1958 Pas de deux from *Don Quixote* (Petipa; staged F. Schaufuss), Royal Danish Ballet, Copenhagen
Violet man (cr) in *Spectrum* (Vangsaa), Royal Danish Ballet, Copenhagen
First movement (cr) in *La Jeunesse* (Bartholin), Royal Danish Ballet, Copenhagen
Pierrot in *Harlequin's Millions* (Walbom), Royal Danish Ballet, Copenhagen
Pablo (cr) in *Happiness on Journey* (also chor.), Royal Danish Ballet, Copenhagen
1959 Peasant pas de deux in *Giselle* (Petipa after Coralli, Perrot; staged Bruhn), Royal Danish Ballet, Copenhagen
Principal dancer (cr) in *Festa* (Bruhn), Royal Danish Ballet, Copenhagen
First cock (cr) in *Cock's Leg* (Cullberg), Royal Danish Ballet, Copenhagen
1960 Bandit in *Carmen* (Petit), Royal Danish Ballet, Copenhagen
Beggar and Death in *Blood Wedding* (Rodrigues), Royal Danish Ballet, Copenhagen
Gypsy (cr) in *The Shadow* (Bartholin), Royal Danish Ballet, Copenhagen
The Devil's dance in *The Soldier's Tale* (Larsen), Copenhagen Municipal Park Theatre, Copenhagen
1961 Rageneau in *Cyrano de Bergerac* (Petit), Royal Danish Ballet, Copenhagen
The Wag in *The Burrow* (MacMillan), Royal Danish Ballet, Copenhagen
"Dance for the Joy of Life" in *The Little Mermaid* (Beck, Brenaa), Royal Danish Ballet, Copenhagen
1962 Zephyr in *Les Victoires de l'amour* (Lander), Royal Danish Ballet, Copenhagen
Principal dancer (cr) in *The Door* (K. Ralov), Royal Danish Ballet, Copenhagen
Disc jockey (cr) in *The White Melody* (also chor.), Danish television
1963 Mercutio in *Romeo and Juliet* (Ashton), Royal Danish Ballet, Copenhagen
First Movement in *Bourrée fantasque* (Balanchine), Royal Danish Ballet, Copenhagen
Phlegmatic in *Four Temperaments* (Balanchine), Royal Danish Ballet, Copenhagen
Gennaro in *Napoli* (Bournonville), Royal Danish Ballet, Copenhagen
1964 Alain in *La Fille mal gardée* (Ashton), Royal Danish Ballet, Copenhagen
Principal dancer (cr) in *Moods* (Brenaa), Royal Danish Ballet, Copenhagen
The Dancing Teacher in *The Lesson* (Flindt), Royal Danish Ballet, Copenhagen
Hungarian dance in *Swan Lake* (Petipa, Ivanov), Royal Danish Ballet, Copenhagen
First Pierrot (cr) in *The White Supper* (also chor.), Danish television
1965 Dr. Coppélius in *Coppélia* (Brenaa after Saint-Léon), Royal Danish Ballet, Copenhagen
Alexis in *Konservatoriet* (Bournonville), Royal Danish Ballet, Copenhagen
Man in *Sonate à trois* (Béjart), Copenhagen Ballet Theatre, New Theatre, Copenhagen
1966 The General in *Graduation Ball* (Lichine), Royal Danish Ballet, Copenhagen
Louis XIII (cr) in *The Three Musketeers* (Flindt), Royal Danish Ballet, Copenhagen

**Fredbjorn Bjørnsson as Mercutio in *Romeo and Juliet***

Geert in *The Kermesse in Bruges* (Bournonville), Royal Danish Ballet, Copenhagen
1967 Man about Town (cr) in *The Miraculous Mandarin* (Flindt), Royal Danish Ballet, Copenhagen
Ballet master in *Aimez-vous Bach?* (Macdonald), Royal Danish Ballet, Copenhagen
Giacomo in *Napoli* (Bournonville), Royal Danish Ballet, Copenhagen
Man in *Tango Chikane* (Flindt), Royal Danish Ballet, Copenhagen
Father-in-law in *The Young Man Must Marry* (Flindt), Royal Danish Ballet, Copenhagen
1968 Title role in *Petrushka* (Fokine), Royal Danish Ballet, Copenhagen
Fabulous monster (cr) in *Fresco* (Theilade), Royal Danish Ballet, Copenhagen
1969 Viderik in *A Folk Tale* (Bournonville), Royal Danish Ballet, Copenhagen
Anger in *The Seven Deadly Sins* (Cramér), Royal Danish Ballet, Copenhagen
1970 Companion in *Luggage* (Tomaszewski), Royal Danish Ballet, Copenhagen
1971 Bootface in *The Lady and the Fool* (Cranko), Royal Danish Ballet, Copenhagen
Thays in *The Life Guards on Amager* (Bournonville), Royal Danish Ballet, Copenhagen
Drosselmeyer in *The Nutcracker* (Flindt), Royal Danish Ballet, Copenhagen

Wooden doll in *The Nutcracker* (Flindt), Royal Danish Ballet, Copenhagen
1972 Aigisthos in *Orestes* (Holm), Royal Danish Ballet, Copenhagen
Dancer in *Triumph of Death* (Flindt), Royal Danish Ballet, Copenhagen
1974 Fool (cr) in *Chronicle* (Holm), Royal Danish Ballet, Copenhagen
Principal dancer in *Dreamland* (Flindt), Royal Danish Ballet, Copenhagen
1978 José in *The Toreador* (Bournonville; staged Flindt), Royal Danish Ballet, Copenhagen
1980 Snug in *A Midsummer Night's Dream* (Neumeier), Royal Danish Ballet, Copenhagen
1982 Old Folks' dance in *The Whims of Cupid and the Ballet Master* (Galeotti), Royal Danish Ballet, Copenhagen
Servant in *The Judgment of Paris* (Tudor), Royal Danish Ballet, Copenhagen
Bill (cr) in *Dawn* (La Cour), Royal Danish Ballet, Copenhagen
Man in *Acte sans parole* (Beckett), Royal Danish Ballet, Copenhagen
1983 Sancho Panza in *Don Quixote* (Petipa, Gorsky), Royal Danish Ballet, Copenhagen
1985 Ringmaster in *Circus Polka* (Robbins), Royal Danish Ballet, Copenhagen
1986 Omar in *Abdallah* (Bournonville, Marks), Royal Danish Ballet, Copenhagen
1988 Peppo in *Napoli* (Bournonville), Royal Danish Ballet, Copenhagen

## WORKS

1954 *Behind the Curtain* (mus. Schmidt), Royal Danish Ballet, Copenhagen
1957 *Roguery* (mus. Halvorsen), Tivoli Theatre, Copenhagen
1958 *Happiness on Journey* (mus. Sark), Royal Danish Ballet, Copenhagen
1962 *The White Melody* (mus. various), Danish television
1964 *The White Supper* (mus. Bjerre), Danish television
1965 Dances in *Maskarade* (opera; mus. Nielsen), Royal Danish Opera, Copenhagen
Dances in *The Italian Girl in Algiers* (opera; mus. Rossini), Royal Danish Opera, Copenhagen
1967 *Rendezvous* (mus. Svendsen), Hotel d'Angleterre, Copenhagen
1972 Dances in *L'Elisir d'amore* (opera; mus. Donizetti), Royal Danish Opera, Copenhagen
Dances in *The Grand Duchess's Farewell* (opera; mus. Costa), Royal Danish Opera, Copenhagen
1974 Dances in *Carmen* (opera; mus. Bizet), Royal Danish Opera, Copenhagen
1980 Dances in *The Threepenny Opera* (opera; mus. Weill), Royal Danish Opera, Copenhagen

Also staged:
1973 *Konservatoriet* (after Bournonville; mus. Paulli), Royal Swedish Ballet, Stockholm
1979 *Bournonville* (*The Wednesday School*, after Bournonville exercises; with K. Ralov), Boston Ballet, Boston

**Other works include:** Dances in *Paris-Copenhagen* (revue; 1955), *Blood Wedding* (play by García Lorca; 1956), *On the Slackrope* (revue; 1956), *Rinse Your Mouth, Please* (revue; 1961), *The Skin of our Teeth* (play by Wilder; 1962), *Teenager Love* (play by Olsen; 1962 and 1963), *A T.V. Nightmare* (play by Olsen; 1964), *A Scent of Flowers* (Saunders; 1965), *The Killer* (play by Ionesco; 1965), *Jacques Brel is Alive and Well* (revue; mus. Brel; 1971), *Donna Johanna* (play by Olsen; 1971), *Operetta* (play by Gombrowiecz; 1973), *Erik XIV* (play by Strindberg; 1974), *The Poetical Craze* (play by Olsen; 1976), *Spoke Song* (play by Parker; 1978).

## PUBLICATIONS

Lawson, Joan, "The Royal Danish Ballet Festival", *Dancing Times* (London), July 1951
Palatsky, Eugene, "Survival of the Fittest: A Look at the Annual Examination of the Royal Ballet School", *Dance Magazine* (New York), August 1961
Kragh-Jacobsen, Svend, *Twenty Solo Dancers of The Royal Danish Ballet*, Copenhagen, 1965
Cunningham, Katharine, "Watching Bournonville", *Ballet Review* (New York), vol. 4, no. 6, 1974
Aschengreen, Erik, "Fredbjørn Bjørnsson", *Dansk Biografisk Leksikon*, vol. 2, Copenhagen, 1979

* * *

Throughout his lifelong career, Fredbjørn Bjørnsson has been an outstanding ambassador of the Danish ballet tradition, both as a brillant and charming ballet dancer and as a Bournonville teacher of high repute.

Fredbjørn Bjørnsson entered the Royal Danish Ballet School in 1935 and became an extremely talented young dancer under the guidance of Harald Lander. He had his official début in the role of the Boy in *The Land of Milk and Honey* in 1947; and indeed, boyish charm was Fredbjørn Bjørnsson's trademark in the early years of his career. He started out as a joyful and vivid Frantz in *Coppélia*, a lighthearted Carelis in *The Kermesse in Bruges*, and a shy cadet in *Graduation Ball*.

But Fredbjørn Bjørnsson's talent kept growing, as his ability to adapt to new role types developed. In *Napoli* he danced a Gennaro glowing with passion and with an explosive Italian temperament. In *Carmen* he developed the role of the bandit to such perfection that Roland Petit picked Bjørnsson to perform the part when *Carmen* was filmed in Paris. He was demonic as the dance teacher in *The Lesson*, touching and heartbreaking as *Petrushka*, amusing and eccentric as the dear old Doctor Coppélius.

Humour and charm have, more than anything else, been central elements in Fredbjørn Bjørnsson's art, for instance when he danced the simpleminded Geert in *The Kermesse in Bruges*, or the somewhat senile general in *Graduation Ball*, or the fat shuffling eunuch Omar in *Abdallah*. And sometimes he combined humour with an unmistakable vulnerability, creating moments of unforgettable genius.

Most famous are undoubtedly his portrayals of the funny Doctor Coppélius in *Coppélia* and of the lovable troll Viderik in *A Folk Tale*, as which he has appeared as a guest artist with several foreign companies.

Fredbjørn Bjørnsson grew up with the Bournonville repertory at the Royal Danish Ballet and knows the Bournonville ballets by heart. As a child he was one of the children standing on the bridge in Act I of *Napoli*, and later he danced in the pas de six, and as Gennaro; and he has also been Peppo as well as Giacomo. All of the roles he danced in *Napoli* alone serve as an example of Fredbjørn Bjørnsson's extensive knowledge of the Bournonville tradition. But still, he was not limited to the Danish style: he also studied in Paris, London, and New York.

In the 1950s Bjørnsson toured the United States and Europe with Inge Sand and members of the Royal Danish Ballet, making Danish ballet known to the world. He danced in many different ballets and created several remarkable character roles, but his speciality has always been Bournonville.

In 1973 Bjørnsson staged a successful production of *Konservatoriet* in Stockholm for the Royal Swedish Ballet, but mainly he has worked in collaboration with his wife, Kirsten Ralov, former solo dancer and associate artistic director of the Royal Danish Ballet. Together they have staged Bournonville in most of the world, including in New Zealand, Russia, Europe, and the United States.

As a teacher at the Royal Ballet School Bjørnsson taught mime and the Bournonville technique. As such he gained a worldwide reputation as a Bournonville teacher, and he has been in demand as a guest teacher in Canada, the United States and Sweden.

—Majbrit Simonsen

---

**BLAIR, David**

British dancer, teacher, and ballet director. Born David Butterfield in Halifax, Yorkshire, 27 July 1932. Studied with Amy Ibbetson, Halifax, and (on scholarship) at the Sadler's Wells Ballet School, from 1946. Married dancer Maryon Lane. Dancer, Sadler's Wells Theatre Ballet, 1947–53: soloist, Sadler's Wells Ballet (later the Royal Ballet), from 1953; principal dancer, from 1955, becoming Margot Fonteyn's regular partner, 1961; guest artist, La Scala, Milan, 1957; also performed with Margot Fonteyn's Concert Ballet, 1958–59, and on British and American television; staged ballets for Atlanta Civic Ballet, Georgia, 1965, 1966, and American Ballet Theatre, 1967, 1968; teacher, Royal Ballet, from 1970; freelance teacher and coach, 1973–76; appointed artistic director of the Norwegian National Ballet, 1976, but died before taking up the post. Commander of the Order of the British Empire, (C.B.E.), 1964. Died in London, 1 April 1976.

**ROLES**

1948 Sailor in *Tritsch-Tratsch* (Cranko), Sadler's Wells Theatre Ballet, tour
The Golliwog in *Children's Corner* (Cranko), Sadler's Wells Theatre Ballet, London
Tom in *Selina* (Howard), Sadler's Wells Theatre Ballet, tour
1949 The Nutcracker Prince in *The Nutcracker*, Act III (Sergeyev after Ivanov), Sadler's Wells Theatre Ballet, London
Son (cr) in *Sea Change* (Cranko), Sadler's Wells Theatre Ballet, London
Popular Song in *Façade* (Ashton), Sadler's Wells Theatre Ballet, tour
Variation, Adagio of Lovers in *Les Rendezvous* (Ashton), Sadler's Wells Theatre Ballet, tour
Principal dancer in *Valses nobles et sentimentales* (Ashton), Sadler's Wells Theatre Ballet, tour
1950 Bather (cr) in *Summer Interlude* (Somes), Sadler's Wells Theatre Ballet, London
Principal Dancer (cr) in *Trumpet Concerto* (Balanchine), Sadler's Wells Theatre Ballet, Manchester
Damon (cr) in *Pastorale* (Cranko), Sadler's Wells Theatre Ballet, London
Master of Ceremonies in *Assembly Ball* (Howard), Sadler's Wells Theatre Ballet
1951 Captain Belaye (cr) in *Pineapple Poll* (Cranko), Sadler's Wells Theatre Ballet, London
Harlequin (cr) in *Harlequin in April* (Cranko), Sadler's Wells Theatre Ballet, London
Franz in *Coppélia* (Ivanov, Cecchetti; staged Sergeyev), Sadler's Wells Theatre Ballet, London
1952 Prince Siegfried in *Swan Lake*, Act II (Ivanov; staged Sergeyev), Sadler's Wells Ballet, London
The Mariner (cr) in *Ile des sirènes* (Rodrigues), Sadler's Wells Theatre Ballet, London
1953 The Innocent Suspect (cr) in *The Great Detective* (Dale), Sadler's Wells Theatre Ballet, London
1954 First Red Knight in *Checkmate* (de Valois), Sadler's Wells Ballet, London
Consort to Queen of the Earth in *Homage to the Queen* (Ashton), Sadler's Wells Ballet, London
The Caricaturist in *Mam'zelle Angot* (Massine), Sadler's Wells Ballet, London
The Miller in *The Three-Cornered Hat* (Massine), Sadler's Wells Ballet, tour
1955 Principal dancer (cr) in *Variations on a Theme by Purcell* (Ashton), Sadler's Wells Ballet, London
Tango: A Dago in *Façade* (Ashton), Sadler's Wells Ballet, London
Can-Can dancer in *La Boutique fantasque* (Massine), Sadler's Wells Ballet, London
Mazurka in *Les Sylphides* (Fokine), Sadler's Wells Ballet, London
Prince Florimund in *The Sleeping Beauty* (Petipa; staged Sergeyev, de Valois, Ashton), Royal Ballet, tour
1956 Albrecht in *Giselle* (Petipa after Coralli, Perrot; staged Sergeyev), Royal Ballet, London
Prince Siegfried in *Swan Lake* (Petipa, Ivanov; staged Sergeyev, de Valois, Ashton), Sadler's Wells Ballet, London
Prince in *Cinderella* (Ashton), Royal Ballet, London
Daphnis in *Daphnis and Chloë* (Ashton), Royal Ballet, London
Principal dancer (cr) in *Birthday Offering* (Ashton), Royal Ballet, London
Principal dancer in *Symphonic Variations* (Ashton), Royal Ballet, London
Principal dancer in *Scènes de ballet* (Ashton), Royal Ballet, London
1957 Title role (cr) in *The Prince of the Pagodas* (Cranko), Royal Ballet, London
Principal dancer in *Ballet Imperial* (Balanchine), Royal Ballet, London
Male solo in *Solitaire* (MacMillan), Royal Ballet, London
1958 Principal dancer (cr) in *Agon* (MacMillan), Royal Ballet, London
1959 Title role in *Petrushka* (Fokine), Royal Ballet, London
Polynices (cr) in *Antigone* (Cranko), Royal Ballet, London
Satan in *Job* (de Valois), Royal Ballet, London
1960 Colas (cr) in *La Fille mal gardée* (Ashton), Royal Ballet, London
1961 Ivan Tsarevich in *The Firebird* (Fokine), Royal Ballet, London
1962 Principal dancer in *Flower Festival at Genzano* (Bournonville), Royal Ballet, London
1963 Orestes (cr) in *Elektra* (Helpmann), Royal Ballet, London

**David Blair with Nadia Nerina in *La Fille mal gardée*, 1960**

1964 Chanson dansée ("Athlete") in *Les Biches* (Nijinska), Royal Ballet, London
Principal dancer in *Serenade* (Balanchine), Royal Ballet, London
1965 Principal dancer in *Birthday Offering* (Ashton, with new solo for Blair), Royal Ballet, London
Mercutio (cr) in *Romeo and Juliet* (MacMillan), Royal Ballet, London
1967 Jean de Brienne in *Raymonda* (Nureyev after Petipa), Royal Ballet Touring Company
1971 Husband in *The Invitation* (MacMillan), Royal Ballet, London
Fourth Song in *Song of the Earth* (MacMillan), Royal Ballet, London

**Other roles include:** Rake in *The Rake's Progress* (de Valois), principal dancer in *Don Quixote* Pas de deux (after Petipa), principal dancer in *Grand pas classique* (Gsovsky), principal dancer in (*Tchaikovsky*) *Pas de deux* (Balanchine).

## WORKS

Staged:
1965 *Swan Lake* (after Petipa, Ivanov; mus. Tchaikovsky), Atlanta Civic Ballet, Atlanta, Georgia
1966 *The Sleeping Beauty* (after Petipa, mus. Tchaikovsky), Atlanta Civic Ballet, Atlanta, Georgia
1967 *Swan Lake* (new production; after Petipa, Ivanov; mus. Tchaikovsky), American Ballet Theatre, Chicago
1968 *Giselle* (after Petipa, Coralli, Perrot; mus. Adam), American Ballet Theatre, Washington, D.C.

## PUBLICATIONS

Beaumont, Cyril, "Some Dancers of the Sadler's Wells Theatre Ballet", part 2, *Foyer* (London), Autumn/Winter 1951–52
"David Blair", *Ballet* (London), June 1952
Goodman, Saul, "Brief Biographies: David Blair", *Dance Magazine* (New York), February 1956
Swinson, Cyril, *Six Dancers of Sadler's Wells*, London, 1956
Percival, John, "Jack of all Ballet Trades", *Dance and Dancers* (London), March 1958
Percival, John, "Accent on the Male, 5: David Blair", *Dance and Dancers* (London), June 1958
"David Blair: A Profile", *About the House* (London), February 1963
Woodcock, Sarah, *The Sadler's Wells Royal Ballet*, London, 1991

* * *

David Blair was foremost among the group of male dancers developed by the Sadler's Wells Ballet organization in the immediate post-war period. He made his name with the newly-established Sadler's Wells Theatre Ballet, attracting attention with his well-formed technique and jovial, extrovert personality. By the time he moved to the Covent Garden company in 1953, he was being hailed as one of the most brilliant dancers of his generation.

He seemed at ease in every style, but despite his brilliance as a partner in the classics and as a character dancer, he was essentially in the great tradition of demi-caractère dancers—a style which suited his natural bluff Yorkshire good humour. In three roles choreographed for him, he has never been surpassed: as Captain Belaye in John Cranko's *Pineapple Poll*, as Colas in Frederick Ashton's *La Fille mal gardée*, and as Mercutio in Kenneth MacMillan's *Romeo and Juliet*. Here he was at his best; such roles enshrined his brilliant technique and his flair for establishing character through the choreography, exploiting his breezy self-possession and high spirits. Even today, no one has ever approached his breathtaking, witty account of Belaye's Hornpipe, nor the pacing and phrasing of Mercutio's difficult Ballroom solo.

A notable partner in the classics (he had learned his partnering technique from Dolin), he lacked self-effacement and saw the male dancer as the equal of the ballerina, to an extent that prevented him from being considered a great "danseur noble". But he was an excellent and flamboyant partner, notably to Elvin, while his consideration and experience steered many a young ballerina through her début in the great classics. He brought drama and commitment to the classical Princes and helped consolidate the idea that the classics were a dialogue between the leading players, rather than a mere vehicle for the ballerina.

Uniting as he did the qualities of artist and athlete, Blair helped win a new respect for the male dancer in England during the 1950s. By the end of the decade, he had won a position in the company second only to Michael Somes, and it was generally assumed that he would succeed Somes as Fonteyn's partner. But, when it happened, the partnership proved less than ideal, and soon afterwards Nureyev arrived, usurping Blair's position in the Royal Ballet. Several unhappy years followed for Blair, including a period of semi-retirement.

In the mid-1960s, Blair mounted important productions of the classics in America, based upon the Sergeyev productions with which he was familiar from the Royal Ballet. He showed a notable talent as a producer, but it was a gift he did not develop. He also did valuable work for the Royal Academy of Dancing, including revision of the syllabus. He returned to the Royal Ballet from time to time, making his official farewell in June 1973 as Colas. Then he was appointed director of the Norwegian Ballet, and it looked as though a new career was opening up for him when he died in 1976.

—Sarah C. Woodcock

---

## BLASIS, Carlo

Italian dancer, choreographer, and teacher. Born in Naples, 4 November 1795. Studied with Jean Dauberval and Pierre Gardel. Married Annunciata Ramaccini, c. 1832. Début at age twelve in Marseilles; dancer, Grand Théâtre, Bordeaux, 1816–17; Paris Opéra début, 1817; solo dancer (primo ballerino serio), under ballet master Salvatore Viganò, La Scala, Milan, 1818–22; choreographer, creating first ballets for productions of operas, Milan, 1819; dancer, touring Italy, 1822–26; soloist, King's Theatre, London, 1827, also working in England as choreographer, including for celebrations for the Duchess of St. Albans, Highgate, 1828; solo dancer, La Fenice, Venice, 1830; choreographer, Modena, 1834, Florence and Milan, 1835, Mantua, 1836, Naples, 1837; director and teacher of the "Class of Perfection", Ballet School of La Scala, Milan, 1837–50, also continuing as choreographer of dances for students; also guest teacher in various other European cities, including Warsaw, 1856, Lisbon, 1857–58, and Paris, 1859–60, becoming one of most celebrated teachers of his time: students include Fanny Cerrito, Carolina Rosati, Elena Andreyanova, and Augusta Maywood; choreographer and teacher, Bolshoi Theatre, Moscow, 1861–64; theorist and codifier of ballet technique, publishing books on own dance theories, 1820, 1828. Died in Cernobbio, Como, 15 January 1878.

## ROLES

1816/17 Archduke Leopold in *Teniers au village* (Barrès), Grand Théâtre, Bordeaux
Principal dancer in *La Folle par amour* (Blache), Grand Théâtre, Bordeaux
1817 Pas de deux in *Les Bayadères* (opera; mus. Catel, chor. P. Gardel), Opéra, Paris
Dancer in *La Caravane du Caire* (opera; mus. Grétry), Opéra, Paris
Dancer in *Castor et Pollux* (opera; mus. Winter), Opéra, Paris
1818 Dancer in *Dedalo* (Viganò), La Scala, Milan
Dancer in *La Spada di Kenneth* (Viganò), La Scala, Milan
Principal dancer (cr) in *La Scuola del Villaggio* (Viganò), La Scala, Milan

**An illustration from *Traité élémentaire*, by Carlo Blasis, 1820**

Pilade (cr) in *Pirro ed Ermione* (Fabris), La Scala, Milan
Principal dancer (cr) in *L'Ingegno supra l'età; ossia, L'Eridità rapita e riacquistata* (Gioja), La Scala, Milan
1819 Principal dancer (cr) in *Amore e dovere* (Galzerani), La Scala, Milan
Principal dancer in *La Spada di Kenneth* (Viganò), La Fenice, Venice
Principal dancer in *La Mirra* (Viganò), La Fenice, Venice
1820 Principal dancer (cr) in *I Titani* (Viganò), La Scala, Milan
1821 Principal dancer (cr) in *Alfredo il Grande* (Aumer), La Scala, Milan
Principal dancer (cr) in *Ballabile* (Bocci), La Scala, Milan
1822 Principal dancer in *Paggi del duca di Vendôme* (Aumer), La Scala, Milan
Principal dancer (cr) in *Apelle e campaspe* (Gioja), La Scala, Milan
1823 Principal dancer in *Kenilworth* (Gioja), La Scala, Milan
1824 Principal dancer in *Ero e Leandro* (Galzerani), Teatro Regio, Turin
Principal dancer in *L'Astuzia fortunata* (Galzerani), Teatro Regio, Turin
1826 Principal dancer in *Castello del diavolo* (Cortesi), Teatro Regio, Turin
Principal dancer in *Giovanna d'Arco* (Viganò), Reggio Emilia
1827 Principal dancer in *The Slave of Baghdad* (D'Egville), King's Theatre, London
Principal dancer in *La Vestale* (Viganò), King's Theatre, London
Principal dancer in *La Siège de Cythère* (Viganò), King's Theatre, London
1833 Principal dancer (cr) in *Leocadia* (also chor.), Modena

## WORKS

1819 *Il Finto feudatorio* (mus. F.A. Blasis), La Scala, Milan
1827 *Pandora*, Oxford Music Festival, Oxford
1833 *Leocadia*, Modena
1834 *Gli Intrighi amorosi*, Modena
1835 *L'Equivoco comico*, Teatro della Pergola, Florence

*Una Notte di carnevale*, Teatro della Pergola, Florence
*Gli Amori di Adone e Venere*, Teatro della Pergola, Florence
*Elina*, Canobbiana, Milan
1836 *La Scaltra fattoressa*, Teatro Nuovo, Mantua
1838 Pas de cinq in *Cambio del coscritto* (chor. Galzerani), La Scala, Milan
1839 Pas de cinq in *Assedio di Faenza* (chor. Rugali), Canobbiana, Milan
1840 *La Styrienne*, La Scala, Milan
Dances in *Mosè* (opera; mus. Rossini), La Scala, Milan
Pas de cinq in *Alì pascià di Giannina* (chor. Galzerani), La Scala, Milan
1841 Pas de deux in *Mazeppa* (chor. Cortesi), La Scala, Milan
Pas de cinq in *Astuzia contro Astuzia* (chor. Cortesi), La Scala, Milan
1842 Pas de trois in *Scimmia riconoscente* (chor. Paradisi), La Scala, Milan
1843 Pas de cinq in *Luisa Strozzi* (chor. Hus), La Scala, Milan
1846 Ballabile in *Roberto il diavolo* (opera; mus. Meyerbeer), La Scala, Milan
1847 *The Pretty Sicilian* (mus. F.A. Blasis, Senna, Bajetti), Drury Lane, London
*The Spanish Gallantries* (mus. F.A. Blasis), Drury Lane, London
*La Pléiade de Terpsichore*, Drury Lane, London
Pas de deux in *Odalisque* (chor. Albert), Covent Garden, London
Pas de deux in *La Bouquetière de Venise* (chor. Albert), Covent Garden, London
*La Salamandrina* (mus. Curmi), Covent Garden, London
*La Nouvelle Cachucha*, St. James's Theatre, London
*Pas villageois*, St. James's Theatre, London
*Flore et Zéphyr* (divertissement), Covent Garden, London
*La Bayonnaise* (mus. Donizetti), Covent Garden, London
*Gli Amori di una stella*, Teatro Comunale, Trieste
1848 Dances in *Stradella* (opera; mus. Flotow), Canobbiana, Milan
1849 Dances in *Macbeth* (opera; mus. Verdi), La Scala, Milan
Pas de trois in *Gisella* (chor. Cortesi), La Scala, Milan
*La Ninfa Eco*, Canobbiana, Milan
Pas de six in *Macbeth* (opera; mus. Verdi), La Scala, Milan
*La Due Zingare*, Canobbiana, Milan
Pas de deux in *La Silfide* (chor. F. Taglioni, mus. Panizza), Milan
Scottish pas de quatre and pas de six in *Macbeth* (opera; mus. Verdi), Carcano
1851 *Hermosa; o, La Danzatrice spagnuola*, La Fenice, Venice
1852 *Cagliostro*, La Fenice, Venice
*Il Prestigiatore*, La Fenice, Venice
Ballabile dei Pattinatori in *Profeta* (opera; mus. Meyerbeer), Parma
1853 *Manfredo; ossia, Disperazione ed illusione* (mus. Bajetti, Panizza, Viviani, Pugni, Hérold, De Royer, F.A. Blasis), Parma
*Le Gelosie ovvero la prova delle amanti*, Parma
*Il Figliuol prodigo*, Parma
*Le Galanterie parigine*, Teatro della Pergola, Florence
*Raffaello e la Fornarina*, Teatro della Pergola, Florence
1854/55 *Il Folletto*, Teatro Filarmonico, Verona
*Lodowiska*, Teatro Filarmonico, Verona
1856 Divertissement in *La Favorita* (opera; mus. Donizetti), Warsaw
*Faust* (new version), Warsaw
*Fiorina*, Warsaw
1857/58 *Galateia* (divertissement; mus. Ortori), Teatro de São Carlos, Lisbon
*Polca* (Divertissement), Teatro de São Carlos, Lisbon
*La Danzatrice veneziana* (divertissement), Teatro de São Carlos, Lisbon
*Le Quattro Nazioni* (divertissement), Teatro de São Carlos, Lisbon
*Diavolina* (divertissement), Teatro de São Carlos, Lisbon
Dances in *I Vespri Siciliani* (opera; mus. Verdi), Teatro de São Carlos, Lisbon
Dances in *Il Trovatore* (opera; mus. Verdi), Teatro de São Carlos, Lisbon
Dances in *La Sonnambula* (opera; mus. Bellini), Teatro de São Carlos, Lisbon
1860 Divertissement in *Histoire du drapeau*, Théâtre Imperial du Cirque, Paris
*Une Fête à Versaille*, Divertissement in *Le Cheval fantôme*, Théâtre Imperial du Cirque, Paris
1861 *Faust* (mus. Panici, Pugni), Bolshoi Theatre, Moscow
1862 *Meteor* (mus. Pinch, Pugni), Bolshoi Theatre, Moscow
*Two Days in Venice* (mus. Minkus et. al.), Bolshoi Theatre, Moscow
*Orfa* (mus. Adam, Minkus), Bolshoi Theatre, Moscow
1863 *Pigmalion i Galateja* (mus. Starzer), Bolshoi Theatre, Moscow

## PUBLICATIONS

By Blasis:

*Traité élémentaire, théoretique et pratique de l'art de la danse*, Milan, 1820; as *Trattato elementare, teorico-pratico sull' arte del ballo*, translated into Italian by Pietro Campilli, Forlì, 1830; as *Elementary Treatise*, translated and edited by M. Stewart Evans, New York, 1944

*The Code of Terpsichore*, translated by R. Barton, London, 1828; as *Manuel complet de la danse*, Paris, 1830; second edition, 1866; as *Nouveau manuel complet de la danse*; Paris, 1884

*Studi sulle arti imitatrici*, Milan, 1844

*Notes upon Dancing, Historical and Practical*, London, 1847

*Del carattere della musica sacra e del sentimento religioso*, Milan, 1854

Articles (*L'Analogie qui doit exister entre la danse et les beaux arts*, *De l'art et de l'esprit de la danse*, *De l'art et de l'esprit de la pantomime*, *Le Chorégraphe*, *De la musique rythmique, de la musique propre à la danse et au ballet*) in *L'Europe artiste*, Paris, 1855–57

*L'Uomo fisico, intellettuale e morale*, Milan, 1857

*La Raccolta di varj articoli letterarj di Carlo Blasis*, Milan, 1858

About Blasis:

Bournonville, August, *Mit Theaterliv*, 3 volumes: Copenhagen, 1848, 1865, 1877; as *My Theatre Life*, translated by Patricia McAndrew, Middletown, Connecticut, 1979

Berri, C., *Cenni Biografici di Carlo de Blasis*, Milan, 1871

Perugini, Mark E., "Carlo Blasis: Master of Masters", *Dancing Times* (London), 2 parts: September, October 1927

Kirstein, Lincoln, *Dance: A Short History of Classic Theatrical Dancing*, New York, 1935

Moore, Lillian, *Artists of the Dance*, New York, 1938

Carrieri, Raffaele, *La Danza in Italia 1600–1900*, Milan, 1946

Moore, Lillian, "Blasis to Bournonville", *Dance Magazine* (New York), February 1964

Sorrell, Walter, *Dance in its Time*, New York, 1981

* * *

Until the late eighteenth or early nineteenth century, dancers' arm movements were governed, in the main, by the functional rule of natural opposition. Following the lead set by Auguste Vestris (son of Gaetano), the so-called "new school" of early nineteenth-century ballet masters allowed this rule to be broken in their search for more decorative shapes. These came to be called arabesques, a term nowadays reserved for variants of one specific pose, but used initially to denote a great variety of sculptural poses and groupings. A number of these are described and illustrated in the dance manuals of Carlo Blasis.

This new preoccupation with the shapes made in space by the dancer's body (as opposed to the importance of the rhythmic elements and the floor patterns characteristic of court dance) went hand in hand with the changes in dress that came in the wake of the French Revolution. The advent of lighter costumes, more revealing of the dancer's figure, not only gave nineteenth-century women the freedom of movement already enjoyed by male dancers; it also emphasized the importance of line, establishing it as an essential component of ballet training.

In his *Code of Terpsichore*, under the heading "New Method of Instruction", Blasis describes his theories relating to the geometrical study of line as part of a dancer's training. He talks of composing a sort of alphabet of lines ". . . comprising all the positions of the limbs in dancing, giving these lines and their respective combinations their proper appellation, viz. perpendiculars, horizontals, obliques, right, acute and obtuse angles, etc., a language which I deem almost indispensible in our lessons".

Arguably the most influential force in the development of ballet training, Blasis codified the technique of ballet in his *Traité élémentaire, théorique et pratique de l'art de la danse* (1820) and *The Code of Terpsichore* (1828). As well as stressing the importance of balanced, harmonious lines, he insisted on maximum turn-out from the hips and discussed ways of coping with various anatomical difficulties. He wrote about the teaching of batterie and of pirouettes, claiming to have invented the pirouette in attitude—a pose he derived from Giambologna's statue of Mercury.

Blasis also formulated guidelines for the correct structuring of a ballet class and, in his *Notes upon Dancing* (1847), he laid down the most suitable age for commencing vocational training. He put these theories into practice as director of the Ballet School in Milan, where no pupil was admitted before the age of eight or after the age of twelve (fourteen for boys).

The study of mime was an essential part of the academy's curriculum, and in his writings Blasis places great emphasis on this aspect of a dancer's schooling. In addition to chapters on mime in the books already mentioned, Blasis wrote extensively on this subject in his *Studio sulle arti imitatrici* (1844) and *L'Uomo fisico, intellettuale e morale* (1857). The latter treatise deals in particular with the manner of expressing feelings and emotions.

Another area to which Blasis devotes particular attention is that of the three genres. This concerns the strict division which used to exist between the three categories (or genres) of Serious, Demi-caractère, and Comic dancers. Each category not only called for particular physical characteristics, but also had its own specific repertoire of suitable movements.

Although he was a prolific creator of ballets, none of Blasis's theatre works survives; yet, as a pedagogue, his influence is still tangible today. The importance of the Italian school in general, and of Blasis in particular, to the development of ballet remains fundamental. The galaxy of brilliant Italian dancers trained by him in Milan dazzled Europe for the best part of the nineteenth century, spreading the virtuosic Italian style to Russia and to France. There is a direct line of descent from Blasis via Lepri to Enrico Cecchetti, and so from him to British ballet via Ninette de Valois and Marie Rambert, and to Soviet ballet via the great teacher Agrippina Vaganova.

—Richard Glasstone

---

## BLISS, Arthur

English composer. Born Arthur Drummond Bliss in London, 2 August 1891. Studied composition with Charles Wood at Cambridge, graduating in 1913; also studied conducting with Stanford at the Royal College of Music, London, 1913–14. Married Gertrude Hoffmann, 1925. Served in the Royal Fusiliers and the Grenadier Guards during World War I. Early involvement in musical and theatrical performances in London, from 1919: arranger and composer of pieces for productions by Nigel Playfair at the Lyric Theatre, Hammersmith; organizer of series of concerts, Lyric Theatre, 1919, and composer of music for production of *The Tempest*, 1921; conductor, Portsmouth Philharmonic Society, from 1921; moved to California, 1923–25; also composer of music for films, including *Things to Come* (dir. Menzies, 1935); first ballet, *Checkmate*, written to own scenario in close collaboration with Ninette de Valois and Vic-Wells company, performed 1937; specialist in composing and conducting film and theatre music; intermittent visitor to United States, teaching at University of California at Berkeley, 1939–41; director of music, British Broadcasting Corporation (BBC), 1942–44; Master of the Queen's Music, 1953–75. Knight of the British Empire, 1950. Died in London, 27 March 1975.

### WORKS (Ballets)

1937 *Checkmate* (chor. de Valois), Vic-Wells Ballet, Paris
1944 *Miracle in the Gorbals* (chor. Helpmann), Sadler's Wells Ballet, London
1946 *Adam Zero* (chor. Helpmann), Sadler's Wells Ballet, London
1958 *The Lady of Shalott* (chor. Christensen), San Francisco Ballet, Berkeley, California

**Other ballets using Bliss's music**: *Rout* (de Valois, 1928), *Diversions* (Macmillan, 1961), *Frontier* (Neumeier, 1969), *Royal Offering* (de Warren, 1977).

### PUBLICATIONS

By Bliss:
*As I Remember*, London, 1970

About Bliss:
Haskell, Arnold, *Ballet Music since 1939*, London, 1946
Robertson, A., *British Music of our Time*, London, 1947
Hopkins, A., "The Ballet Music of Arthur Bliss", *Ballet Annual* (London), vol. 1, 1947
Crisp, Clement, "The Ballets of Arthur Bliss", *Musical Times* (London), August 1966
"For Arthur Bliss's 75th Birthday", Catalogue of Works, *Musical Times* (London), August 1966

Foreman, Lewis, *Arthur Bliss: A Catalogue and Critical Survey*, London, 1979
Goodwin, Noël, "Bliss at the Ballet", *Dance and Dancers* (London), August 1991

* * *

Arthur Bliss came to prominence in the 1920s and 1930s, soon occupying the forefront of British music; and between 1937 and 1958 he composed four original scores for ballet. Before these, his *Rout* (1920)—for instrumental ensemble and wordless soprano—was heard as a musical interlude in the London programmes of Diaghilev's Ballets Russes, and an arrangement of this for voice and two pianos was choreographed under the same title by Ninette de Valois (1928). First performed by students of her Academy of Choreographic Art in London, *Rout* joined the repertory of the emergent Vic-Wells Ballet up to 1932. In common with other Bliss works of that period, *Rout* showed influences from Stravinsky, Ravel, and the French school of "Les Six", and incorporated elements of jazz, an idiom the composer continued to favour.

Bliss was commissioned by de Valois to compose *Checkmate* for the Sadler's Wells Ballet, to have its Paris premiere on their first foreign tour in 1937. The composer devised his own scenario depicting chess pieces personified in dramatic conflict, and the music was composed in twelve separate numbers that relate to specific incidents (Dance of the Red Pawns, Entry of the Black Queen, Red Knight's Mazurka, The Attack, The Duel, and so on). Forceful rhythms and bold instrumental colours in a large orchestra played a large part in the ballet's success, and led to its frequent revival through the 1980s.

For Robert Helpmann's *Miracle in the Gorbals*, a more detailed scenario by Michael Benthall—which centred on the appearance of a Christ figure reborn in urban slums—necessitated a more strictly organized musical design, and was composed as an Overture and seventeen numbers. Some are in specific forms, such as rondo, waltz, or passacaglia with variations, or have allusions to others, like pavane and saraband, but they are freely treated and unified by thematic cross-references linked to the ballet's characters.

The tonal scheme, opening and closing in an ominous D minor, dramatically pointed up events and their development, and thereby coloured the choreography with its harmonic character and instrumental variety. Particular attention was drawn to a Dance of Deliverance after a Young Girl is revived from apparent suicide, where Bliss was seen as employing the idiom of spirituals and jazz with an almost revivalist religious fervour. The music helped the ballet's powerful impact on wartime audiences, many of whom were new to ballet.

Benthall also provided the scenario for Helpmann's *Adam Zero*, an allegorical fantasy in which the actual process of creating a ballet is related to seasons of the year and the human life-cycle of Adam as principal dancer. Bliss composed a score in sixteen numbers, of which some are narrative and others are allegorical illustration in terms of the seasons; the orchestra is of standard theatre size.

*Adam Zero's* most prominent features are the powerful rhythmic impulse, generated from the stage-setting scene (scene 2) which propels the forward progress, and the expressive character of seasonal dances tracing Adam's life-cycle before and after "Awakening to Love" and "Bridal Ceremony". A "Night Club Scene" between Autumn and Winter dances is written in a jazz idiom that paralleled Bernstein's *Fancy Free* of the same decade. *Adam Zero*, however, failed to hold its place in repertory and the music lapsed accordingly.

Bliss composed his last ballet, *The Lady of Shalott*, as a commission from the May T. Morrison music festival at the University of California, for Lew Christensen and the San Francisco Ballet. Based on Tennyson's romantic poem, the music was praised at the time for its richness of medieval colour, effective orchestration, and lyrical expression, and for its evocative contrasts of courtly and folk styles, but the ballet did not continue in repertory.

Some concert works have attracted other choreography, notably Kenneth MacMillan's *Diversions* (1961) to the *Music for Strings* (1935), John Neumeier's *Frontier* (1969) to the Quintet for Oboe and Strings (1927), and Robert de Warren's *Royal Offering* (1977) to *A Colour Symphony* (1922). Bliss published his autobiography, *As I Remember*, in 1970.

—Noël Goodwin

---

**BLONDY, Michel**

French dancer, teacher, and choreographer. Born in 1675, probably the nephew of dancer and choreographer Pierre Beauchamps. Début, L'Académie royale de musique (Paris Opéra), 1691; premier danseur, Paris Opéra (also occasionally referred to as M. Blonde, or Blondi), succeeding Louis Pécour as *compositeur des ballets* (ballet master), 1729; also celebrated teacher, Paris Opéra, with pupils including Marie Camargo, Marie Sallé, and Franz Hilverding. Died in Paris, 6 August 1739.

**ROLES**

1695 Dancer (cr) in *Les Saisons* (ballet; mus. Lully, Colasse, chor. Pécour), Opéra, Paris
1697 Dancer (cr) in *Issé* (pastorale-héroïque; mus. Destouches, chor. probably Pécour), Trianon
1700 Dancer (cr) in *Hésione* (tragédie-lyrique; mus. Campra, chor. Pécour), Opéra, Paris
1701 Loure pour deux hommes (cr) in *Scylla* (tragédie-lyrique; mus. Théobalde), Opéra, Paris
Dancer (cr) in *Omphale* (tragédie-lyrique; mus. Destouches, chor. Pécour), Opéra, Paris
1702 Saraband à deux (cr) in *Tancrède* (tragédie-lyrique; mus. Campra, chor. Pécour), Opéra, Paris
1705 Dancer in *Roland* (tragédie-lyrique; mus. Lully, chor. Pécour), Opéra, Paris
Dancer in *Bellérophon* (tragédie-lyrique; mus. Lully), Opéra, Paris
1706 Dancer in *L'Europe galante* (ballet; mus. Campra), Opéra, Paris
1707 Dancer in *Thésée* (tragédie-lyrique; mus. Lully, chor. Pécour), Opéra, Paris
1710 Dancer in *Phaéton* (tragédie-lyrique; mus. Lully), Opéra, Paris
Dancer in *Persée* (tragédie-lyrique; mus. Lully), Opéra, Paris
Entrée de Deux Hommes (cr) in *Les Fêtes vénitiennes* (opera-ballet; mus. Campra, chor. Pécour), Opéra, Paris
1711 Dancer in *Apollon législateur; ou, Le Parnasse reformé* (chor. Pécour), Opéra, Paris
1712 Dancer in *Achille et Polixène* (tragédie-lyrique; mus. Lully, Colasse), Opéra, Paris

1713 Entrée de Cithe (cr) in *Les Amours déguisés* (ballet; mus. Bourgeois), Opéra, Paris
Dancer (cr) in *Médée et Jason* (tragédie-lyrique; mus. Salomon), Opéra, Paris
1715 Dancer in *Proserpine* (tragédie-lyrique; mus. Lully), Opéra, Paris
1716 Dancer (cr) in *Ajax* (tragédie-lyrique; mus. Bertin), Opéra, Paris
Dancer (cr) in *Les Fêtes de l'été* (ballet; mus. Montéclair), Opéra, Paris
Dancer (cr) in *Hypermnestre* (tragédie-lyrique; mus. Gervais), Opéra, Paris
Dancer in *Alceste* (tragédie-lyrique; mus. Lully), Opéra, Paris
1717 Dancer in *Isis* (tragédie-lyrique; mus. Lully), Opéra, Paris
1718 Un Démon (cr) in *Sémiramis* (tragédie-lyrique; mus. Destouches), Opéra, Paris
1720 Dancer (cr) in *L'Inconnu* (ballet; mus. Lalande, chor. Ballon), Opéra, Paris
Dancer (cr) in *Polidore* (tragédie-lyrique; mus. Baptistin), Opéra, Paris
Un Chinois, Un Matelot (cr) in *Les Folies de Cardénio* (ballet; mus. Lalande, chor. Ballon), Opéra, Paris
Un Habitant des Enfers in *Thésée* (tragédie-lyrique; mus. Lully), Opéra, Paris
1721 Dancer (cr) in *Les Éléments* (ballet; mus. Lalande, Destouches, chor. Ballon), Tuileries, Paris
1722 Dancer in *Persée* (tragédie-lyrique; mus. Lully), Opéra, Paris
Un Sacrafin in *Renaud; ou, La Suite d'Armide* (tragédie-lyrique; mus. Desmarets), Opéra, Paris
Un Esclave in *Les Fêtes de Thalie* (ballet; mus. Mouret), Opéra, Paris
1723 Dancer (cr) in *Piritoüs* (tragédie-lyrique; mus. Mouret), Opéra, Paris
1726 Dancer (cr) in *Pyrame et Thisbé* (tragédie-lyrique; mus. Rebel, Francoeur, chor. Pécour), Opéra, Paris
1727 Dancer in *Le Jugement de Paris* (pastorale-héroïque; mus. Bertin), Opéra, Paris
Dancer (cr) in *Les Amours des dieux* (ballet- héroïque; mus. Mouret), Opéra, Paris
1728 Dancer (cr) in *Tarsis et Zélie* (tragédie-lyrique; mus. Rebel, Francoeur), Opéra, Paris
1729 Dancer in *Le Bourgeois Gentilhomme* (comédie-ballet by Molière; mus. Lully, chor. Ballon), Versailles
Dancer in *Pas de trois* (mus. Rebel), Versailles
Dancer (cr) in *Les Amours des déesses* (ballet-héroïque; mus. Quinault, chor. Blondy), Opéra, Paris
1730 *Phaeton* (tragédie-lyrique, new version; mus. Lully), Opéra, Paris
1731 *L'Empire à la mode*, Collège Louis le Grand
1732 *Callirhoé* (tragédie-lyrique, new version; mus. Destouches), Opéra, Paris
*Les Sens* (ballet; mus Mouret), Opéra, Paris
*Acis et Galathée* (divertissement), Opéra, Paris
*Scylla* (tragédie-lyrique, new version; mus. Théobalde), Opéra, Paris
1733 *Les Fêtes grècques et romaines* (ballet-héroïque, new version; mus. de Blamont), Opéra, Paris
1734 *Les Éléments* (ballet, new version; mus. Lalande, Destouches), Opéra, Paris
*Piritoüs* (tragédie-lyrique, new version; mus. Mouret), Opéra, Paris
*Les Plaisirs champêtres* (divertissement; mus. Rebel), Opéra, Paris
*Iphigénie en Tauride* (tragédie-lyrique, new version; mus. Desmarets, Campra), Opéra, Paris
1735 *Les Indes galantes* (chor. probably by Blondy, with Sallé; mus. Rameau), Opéra, Paris
1736 *Les Voyages de l'amour* (ballet; mus. Boismortier, chor. Blondy), Opéra, Paris
*Le Bourgeois Gentilhomme* (comédie-ballet by Molière, new version; mus. Lully), Comédie Francais, Paris
1739 *Alceste* (tragédie-lyrique, new version; mus. Lully), Opéra, Paris

## WORKS

1714 *Les Fêtes de Thalie* (opera-ballet; mus. Mouret), Opéra, Paris
*Le Mariage de Ragonde et de Colin* (ballet; mus. Mouret), for the Duchess of Maine, Sceaux
1721 *Les Fêtes vénitiennes* (opera-ballet; mus. Campra), Opéra, Paris
1722 *Le Ballet des vingt-quatre heures*
1728 *La Princesse d'Élide* (ballet-héroïque; mus. Villeneuve), Opéra, Paris
*Hypermnestre* (tragédie-lyrique; mus. Gervais), Opéra, Paris
1729 *Les Amours des déesses* (ballet-héroïque; mus. Quinault), Opéra, Paris
*Le Parnasse* (fragments), Versailles

## PUBLICATIONS

Rameau, Pierre, *Le Maitre à danser*, Paris, 1734
Parfait, *Histoire de l'académie royale de musique*, Paris, 1745
Noinville, *Histoire de l'académie royale de musique*, Paris, 1752
Clément, Jean Marie, and Laporte, Joseph de, *Anecdotes dramatiques*, Paris, 1775
Winter, Marian Hannah, *The Pre-Romantic Ballet*, London, 1974
Ferguson, Ian, "Notes on the Blondy Family", *Dancing Times* (London), February 1983

* * *

It is unfortunate that more is not known of this dancer who played such an important role in the development of dance in Paris at the beginning of the eighteenth century. His relationship with Beauchamps, most likely his uncle, no doubt made entry into the profession easier, but he appears to have earned his reputation as a dancer on his own merits. In speaking of the dancer Marcel, Rameau says "the pas de deux which he has danced and still dances every day with Blondy are scenes in which the pictures are so exact and the colours so alive that one cannot help but admire them". Parfait, in *Histoire de l'academie royale de musique* (1745), describes Blondy as "the greatest dancer in Europe for the classical dance and the roles of furies", and a study of the surviving notation of those dances performed by Blondy and Marcel show amazing technical complexity, including a multitude of beats, pirouettes, entrechats—ranging from trois to sept, often with a tour en l'air at the same time—and sequences of rapid beaten steps interspersed with slow sustained ronde de jambs en l'air. There is no doubt that young dancers today would find these dances extraordinarily demanding.

Blondy is also known to have been a notable teacher. According to both Clément and Babault, Camargo had become very upset by Prévost's attempts to keep her in the background. She went to Blondy for advice and he suggested that she leave

Prévost and become his pupil. He then arranged for her to appear at Court as his student, and in view of his reputation Prévost could do nothing to prevent it. Kirstein suggests that Blondy was Camargo's lover, but other scholars claim to have found no evidence for this; and even Letainturier-Fradin, whose life of Camargo (1908) is unfortunately more concerned with scandal than fact, makes no mention of such a relationship, simply reporting Blondy's offer to become her teacher. Blondy was also the teacher of Franz Hilverding, who later became dancing master to the Empress Maria Theresa of Austria, the first in a line of distinguished dancing masters to work in Austria. Hilverding later moved at the request of the Empress Elizabeth to St. Petersburg and was responsible for developing ballet in Russia to a high standard, and, according to Angiolini, it was Hilverding rather than Noverre who introduced the reforms in ballet with a return to the pantomimes of the ancients.

It is interesting that Noverre (in his *Lettre XIII*), states that Blondy forbade his students to study choreography (which Noverre identifies as "the art of writing dance with the aid of different signs"). Noverre outlines the dance notation as published by Feuillet but finds no particular value in it, especially for the dancers and ballet masters of his day. He feels that dances have become so much more complex that this notation can no longer serve to notate it. In any case he seems to see no value in writing down dances at all, claiming that notation cannot express the emotions and character of the dance and is therefore an empty shell. It is curious that in support of his cause he should cite Blondy, the nephew of the very man who invented this particular form of notation.

—Madeleine Inglehearn

## BLUM, René

French ballet impresario. Born in Paris, 13 March 1878. Educated in Paris. Co-founder, magazines *La Revue blanche*, *Le Banquet*; co-editor and art critic, *Gil Blas* arts journal, 1910–14; also directed several theatres in Paris; organized first season in Monte Carlo, 1923; director of plays and operettas, Théâtre de Monte-Carlo, 1924–29; on Diaghilev's death, appointed ballet director, Monte Carlo, from 1929: joined forces with Colonel Wassily de Basil to form Les Ballets Russes de Monte Carlo, 1932, serving as manager, 1932–34; artistic director, Ballets Russes de Monte Carlo (also performing as Ballets Russes de Col. W. de Basil, or de Basil's Ballets Russes), 1932–34; broke with de Basil, 1935: founder and director, Ballets de Monte Carlo (ballet master Mikhail Fokine), 1936–38; co-director, with Massine, Ballet Russe de Monte Carlo, 1938–40; arrested during Nazi occupation in 1941; deported to Auschwitz, 1942. Died in Auschwitz, 28 September 1942.

### PUBLICATIONS

Haskell, Arnold, "The De Basil Ballet, 1930–1935", *Dancing Times* (London), October 1933

Huisman, Georges, "René Blum", *The Ballet Annual* (London), vol. 7, 1953

Davis, Janet Rowson, "René Blum: A Centenary Tribute", *Dancing Times* (London), March 1978

Sorley Walker, Kathrine, *De Basil's Ballets Russes*, London, 1982

**René Blum, New York, 1940**

Davis, Janet, "René Blum, 1878–1942", *Society of Dance History Scholars Proceedings* (11th Annual Conference), 1988

* * *

René Blum, with his impeccable taste, keen intelligence, and scholarly but enthusiastic approach to all the arts, was perhaps the quintessential embodiment of twentieth-century European culture up until World War I. It is due, in large part, to his efforts that so much of the Diaghilev heritage still exists, and he is of major importance to dance historically, not only for his knowledge and preservation of this material, but because he was the only individual who really knew the enigmatic and often manipulative Colonel de Basil. This information is still not available—and may never be—due to the disappearance of the manuscript of Blum's autobiography.

Born in Paris as the youngest of five boys, Blum was raised in an orthodox Jewish home. He and his brother Léon, who was to become a noted critic and eventually the Prime Minister of France, were always interested in the arts and were very much a part of Left Bank society.

Blum was co-founder of the magazines *La Revue blanche* and *Le Banquet* and for many years was co-editor of *Gil Blas*, a literary paper. At the age of twenty he founded a publishing house which brought out the works of decorative artists and wood engravers. He organized numerous exhibitions, and promoted young artists. As a friend and collaborator of poets and writers, he worked with Gabriele d'Annunzio on the translation of one of his novels, and was instrumental in getting *Du côté de chez Swann*, the first volume of Marcel Proust's *A la recherche du temps perdu*, published.

His sense of theatre led to his directing several theatres in Paris. His deep knowledge of music included knowing entire scores by memory, as well as what was involved in the complete production of an opera. Blum's interests also included cinema; he headed the first Cinema Club in France, and later, its more professional successor. During World War I he volunteered as an English interpreter, but ended up in charge of the safety of works of arts, winning a Croix de Guerre in the process.

It was when René Blum was brought to Monte Carlo in 1924 as manager of the Theatre of the Monte Carlo Casino, and made responsible for all entertainments in Monaco (during which time he presented dozens of authors and musicians and co-authored several productions himself), that his involvement with and knowledge of dance increased. He and Serge Diaghilev had numerous occasions on which to meet (Diaghilev was responsible for providing choreography for the operas under Blum's aegis) and their relationship seems to have been cordial. (Blum probably had even more taste than Diaghilev, but not his drive.)

When Diaghilev died in 1929, Blum took over the responsibility for dance in the operas, as well as that of the ballet seasons at Monte Carlo. It took him two years to form a new company for the purposes of keeping the Diaghilev repertory, offering employment to the artists, and encouraging new choreography. During this time he brought in many small dance groups, one of which was the Ballet de l'Opéra à Paris, headed by Col. Wassily de Basil. Blum was obviously impressed with de Basil, possibly because the latter possessed many of the characteristics Blum did not: a flair for publicity, a certain recklessness, the ability to make absurd promises and to use people for his own ends. In 1932 Blum made him co-director of the company, calling it Les Ballets Russes de Monte Carlo de René Blum and Col. de Basil. Blum evidently did not travel with the company when it was on tour, with the result that he was not known outside Monte Carlo, and de Basil (whom Blum once called the "gangster Colonel") was left in control. De Basil was increasingly irresponsible financially; Blum put a great deal of his own money into the company, eventually becoming artistic director and leaving de Basil as general director. The company and the relationship ended in April 1935, and de Basil left to form another group.

In 1936 Blum formed another company. International in character, it included Vera Nemchinova, Helene Kirsova, Anatole Vilzak, and André Eglevsky. When Balanchine turned down his invitation to join him, stating in a warm letter that, although a collaboration with Blum was one of the things he had always desired, he could not leave the United States, Blum signed Fokine. During two very successful seasons they continued to present the Diaghilev ballets, with Fokine restaging his own ballets as well as creating three new works. Blum was tired, in poor health, and gradually running out of money, when, at Léonide Massine's urging, he sold the rights to the name and repertory to World Art, Inc., with the understanding that he was to remain (and be billed as) founder and director, with Massine as artistic director. The company had a successful season in Paris in June 1939, and by the outbreak of the war was in the United States, where no mention was ever made of Blum in either programmes or publicity.

When the Nazis occupied France, Blum insisted upon staying in his Paris flat, spurning many offers of refuge outside the country and arguing that he had to remain courageous as the brother of the jailed ex-Prime Minister. He was arrested during a roundup of Jewish intellectuals in December 1941, deported to Auschwitz on 23 September, 1942, and died on 28 September—whether due to ill health or the gas chambers is unknown. Jean Jacques Bernard, son of the dramatist Tristan Bernard, was arrested with him, and when word came before the deportation that efforts to get Blum released would be successful, Blum convinced doctors to send Bernard out instead, feeling he was young, in good health, and, as a writer, could tell the world what was happening.

By all accounts, René Blum as a critic, editor, writer, patron, lecturer, and organizer was unbelievably knowledgeable about and interested in all the arts, and extremely supportive of new and emerging artists. It is difficult from this perspective to discern whether his quiet modesty and erudite charm, aided by a warm and generous sense of humour, were truly representative of a disinterest in official recognition and power or whether he was always in awe of his famous older brother. (Often referred to as "Le Blumet" to distinguish him from Léon, he supposedly turned down the directorship of the Paris Opéra, saying one Blum in the spotlight was enough.)

Prior to his death, Blum was planning to spend more time writing. His memoirs were to have been published by Frederick Muller of London; mysteriously neither their copy nor the one in Paris could be found after the war. In addition, he had begun work on a book about dance. The loss of his manuscripts leaves a large gap in our knowledge of twentieth-century dance, but the art still owes much to this remarkable man.

—Dawn Lille Horwitz

---

## BOCCA, Julio

Argentinian dancer. Born in Buenos Aires, 6 March 1967. Early studies with mother, Nancy Bocca; studied at the Instituto Superior de Arte del Teatro Colón, Buenos Aires, from 1974, pupil of Gloria Kazda, José Parés, Ninel Jultyeva, Karemina Moreno, and Luis Aguilar; later studied with Maggie Black and Wilhelm Burmann. Principal dancer, Fundación Teresa Carreño de Venezuela, Caracas, and Ballet del Teatro Municipal de Rio de Janeiro, from 1982; guest artist in Russia, appearing with Bolshoi Ballet, Moscow, Kirov Ballet, Leningrad, and Novisibirsk Ballet, 1985; principal dancer, American Ballet Theatre, from 1986; has toured internationally with American Ballet Theatre, performing in United States, Europe, and Asia; international guest artist, including for Royal Ballet in London, Stuttgart Ballet, Ballet of La Scala in Milan, Paris Opéra Ballet, Royal Danish Ballet, Oslo Opera Ballet, English National Ballet, and Teatro Colón of Buenos Aires; founder, with Eleonora Cassano, Ballet Argentino, touring Argentina, Latin America, and Europe, from 1990. Recipient: Gold Medal, Fifth International Ballet Competition, Moscow, 1985; "Dancer of the Year", *The New York Times*, 1986; Gino Tanni Award for the Arts, Rome, 1990; Léonide Massine Positano-Italiana 1991.

### ROLES

1982 The Spirit of the Rose in *Le Spectre de la rose* (Fokine), Caracas

1983 Colas in *La Fille mal gardée*, Ballet del Teatro Municipal, Buenos Aires
The Prince in *The Nutcracker* (after Ivanov), Ballet del Teatro Municipal, Buenos Aires
Franz in *Coppélia* (after Petipa, Cecchetti), Ballet del Teatro Municipal, Buenos Aires
Mercutio in *Romeo and Juliet* (Biaggi), Teatro Colón, Buenos Aires
Principal dancer in *The River* (Ailey), Caracas

1984 Peasant Pas de deux in *Giselle* (after Petipa, Coralli, Perrot), Teatro Colón, Buenos Aires

**Julio Bocca**

Bluebird in *Aurora's Wedding* (Divertissement from *The Sleeping Beauty*; after Petipa), Teatro Colón, Buenos Aires

Principal dancer in *Conservatoire* (*Konservatoriet*; Bournonville), Teatro Colón, Buenos Aires

1985 Basil in *Don Quixote* (Petipa, Gorsky), Novosibirsk Ballet, Novosibirsk

The Prince in *The Nutcracker* (Vainonen), Novosibirsk Ballet, Novosibirsk

Pas de deux from *Le Corsaire* (after Petipa), Bolshoi Ballet, Moscow

1986 The Nutcracker Prince in *The Nutcracker* (Baryshnikov), American Ballet Theatre, Orange County, New York

1987 Principal dancer in *Sylvia Pas de deux* (Balanchine), American Ballet Theatre, Miami

Principal dancer in *Donizetti Variations* (Balanchine), American Ballet Theatre, San Francisco

Prince Désiré in *The Sleeping Beauty* (MacMillan after Petipa), American Ballet Theatre, Chicago

The Bronze Idol in *La Bayadère* (Makarova after Petipa), American Ballet Theatre, Los Angeles

Principal dancer in *Études* (Lander), American Ballet Theatre, New York

James in *La Sylphide* (Bournonville; staged Bruhn), American Ballet Theatre, New York

Principal dancer (cr) in *Drink to Me Only with Thine Eyes* (Morris), American Ballet Theatre, New York

1988 The Peruvian in *Gaîté parisienne* (Massine), American Ballet Theatre, Chicago

Basil in *Don Quixote* (Baryshnikov after Petipa), American Ballet Theatre, Los Angeles

Romeo in *Romeo and Juliet* (MacMillan), American Ballet Theatre, New York

Solor in *La Bayadère* (Makarova after Petipa), American Ballet Theatre, New York

Dancer in *Afternoon of a Faun* (Robbins), Royal Danish Ballet, Copenhagen

Joker in *Jeu de cartes* (Cranko), Royal Danish Ballet, Copenhagen

1990 Principal dancer (cr) in *Brief Fling* (Tharp), American Ballet Theatre, New York

Jean de Brienne in *Raymonda*, Act III (after Petipa), Ballet Argentino, Buenos Aires

The Young Man in *Le Jeune Homme et la mort* (Petit), Ballet Argentino, Buenos Aires

Leading role (cr) in *Birdy* (Aviotte), Ballet Argentino, Buenos Aires

Principal dancer (cr) in *Kuarahy* (López), Ballet Argentino, Buenos Aires
1991 Franz in *Coppélia* (new production; Martinez), American Ballet Theatre, New York
Principal dancer in *Other Dances* (Robbins), American Ballet Theatre, New York
1992 Principal dancer in *Tchaikovsky Pas de deux* (Balanchine), Teatro Breton, Logroño, Spain
Principal dancer in Divertissement from *William Tell* (Bournonville), Royal Danish Ballet, Copenhagen
Principal dancer in *Floresto do Amazonas* (Onero), Ballet Municipal de Rio de Janeiro

## PUBLICATIONS

By Bocca:
Interview in Acocella, Joan, "Julio Bocca", *New York Magazine*, February 1991

About Bocca:
Hunt, Marilyn, "Argentina's Golden Boy: Julio Bocca", *Dance Magazine* (New York), March 1987
Macaulay, Alastair, "In Death's Dream Kingdom", *Dancing Times* (London), November 1989
Gruen, John, "Julio Bocca: Argentinian Ace", *Dance Magazine* (New York), November 1990

* * *

Julio Bocca stands in the front rank of international stardom while still in his early twenties. Boyish, thick-legged, and short (about the height of Mikhail Baryshnikov), the young Argentine is known for his go-for-broke audacity, a determination to go himself one better, which is yet accompanied by a natural generosity and sweetness.

Bocca did not dance outside South America until 1985, when he won the gold medal at the Fifth International Ballet Competition in Moscow. The prestigious award instantly made him a national hero in Argentina. And in the ballet world the award brought him to the attention of major companies; within a year he was appointed principal dancer at American Ballet Theatre.

Bocca's swift record of success stems from years of dogged hard work. His first class was at age four with his mother, a ballet teacher at the National Dance School in Buenos Aires. Later he studied with his father, who teaches Argentine folk dancing.

For his repertoire, Bocca has consistently preferred the nineteenth-century classics; apart from *Swan Lake*, he had performed in them all by the age of 24. His first big ballet was at age 16, when he cut his teeth on *La Fille mal gardée* at the Municipal Ballet Theatre of Rio de Janeiro. Several years later in Moscow, he thrilled Soviet audiences with *Le Corsaire* and *The Nutcracker*. A year later, at Ballet Theatre, he carved a comic niche for himself as Basil in *Don Quixote*. In that role, wrote Anna Kisselgoff of *The New York Times*, Bocca projected "an elastic quality of movement, very Spanish in flair".

Bocca's experience with contemporary choreography is more limited. First, he tried Mark Morris's *Drink to Me Only with Thine Eyes* and found it "fairly easy". But Twyla Tharp's jaunty *Brief Fling* tested his mettle with the way it undercuts classical style.

Bocca's technique, which includes a vaulting jump and Soviet-style flourishes, is widely praised. (As a youth, he admired Vladimir Vasiliev.) When Bocca first arrived at Ballet Theatre in 1986, he was not yet fully formed as an artist. The New York critics found him "promising", while on the west coast Martin Bernheimer of *The Los Angeles Times* described him as "flamboyant but somewhat untidy". Three years later, the New York press had nothing but praise for Bocca's performances. And ballerina Alessandra Ferri, Bocca's partner in *Giselle* and *Romeo and Juliet*, has said that his Romeo has acquired much more depth and nuance than it had in their earlier performances together.

But Bocca's career has not been a smooth road of self-improvement. When Baryshnikov still ran Ballet Theatre in 1988, the Argentine wunderkind grew dispirited because he could not get coaching from his renowned director. Performing only once every ten days, or less, Bocca finally left the company for a string of European engagements. But in 1990 Bocca's relation to the company changed abruptly for the better when Jane Hermann was appointed co-director. Mindful of Bocca's star status, she offered him exceptional incentives to return to the fold: more frequent performances and six to eight months advanced notice of scheduling. (Only one other dancer at Ballet Theatre has been extended similar terms.) When Bocca is not performing with the company, he can sign on for engagements elsewhere.

Because of Bocca's increasingly international status and growing maturity, "there are many who even seem him as the new Mikhail Baryshnikov", as Anna Kisselgoff wrote. On the other hand, Bocca's intense concentration on his career has limited his life experiences; he rarely takes a vacation (once in five years) and has yet to visit a New York museum or see Central Park. With room for personal growth, the former prodigy can look forward to even greater maturity on stage.

—Lee Lourdeaux

---

**BOGDANOVA, Nadezhda**

Russian dancer. Born Nadezhda Konstantinova Bogdanova, daughter of Bolshoi Theatre dancers Tatyana Karpakova and Konstantin Bogdanov, in Moscow, 2 September 1836. Early training with father, with stage début at age 12; later trained in Paris, including at the Paris Opéra School. Dancer with family company from 1848, touring Russian provinces 1848 and 1850, and to France with family in 1850; Paris Opéra début, 1851: principal dancer, Paris Opéra, 1851–55, 1865, also performing in Vienna and Berlin; ballerina, Bolshoi Theatre, St. Petersburg, 1856–64; visiting ballerina, touring Russian and European cities including Budapest, 1858, Naples, 1859, Moscow, 1862, Warsaw, 1866, 1867, until retirement, 1867. Died in Warsaw, 15 September 1897.

## ROLES

1851 Kathi in *La Vivandière* (Saint-Léon), Opéra, Paris
Hungarian dance in *Vert-Vert* (Mazilier), Opéra, Paris
1852 Divertissement in *Le Juif errant* (opera; mus. Halévy), Opéra, Paris
Voluspa in *Orfa* (Mazilier), Opéra, Paris
1853 Divertissement in *La Fronde* (opera; mus. Niedermeyer), Opéra, Paris
Dancer in *Aelia et Mysis* (Mazilier), Opéra, Paris
1854 Title role in *Giselle* (after Coralli, Perrot), Vienna
Divertissement in *La Nonne Sanglante* (opera; mus. Gounod), Opéra, Paris

1856 Title role in *Giselle* (Coralli, Perrot), Bolshoi Theatre, St. Petersburg
Marguerite in *Faust* (Perrot), Bolshoi Theatre, St. Petersburg
Title role in *La Esmeralda* (Perrot), Bolshoi Theatre, St. Petersburg
Title role in *Gazelda* (Perrot), Bolshoi Theatre, St. Petersburg
1857 Clorinda (cr) in *La Débutante* (Russian version; Perrot), Bolshoi Theatre, St. Petersburg
Title role in *La Sylphide* (Taglioni), Bolshoi Theatre, St. Petersburg
Pas de deux (with brother, Nikolai Bogdanov), Théâtre Italien, Paris
1858 Title role in *Catarina; ou, La fille du bandit* (Perrot), Bolshoi Theatre, St. Petersburg
1861 Title role in *La Météore* (Saint-Léon), Bolshoi Theatre, St. Petersburg
1865 Title role in *Giselle*, Act I, (Coralli, Perrot), Opéra, Paris

**Other roles include:** Title role in *The Orphan Teolinda*, (Saint-Léon), title role (grande scène mimique) in *La Sonnambula* (opera; mus. Bellini).

## PUBLICATIONS

Pleshcheev, Aleksandr, *Our Ballet*, St. Petersburg, 1859
Chaffée, George, "The Ballettophile", *Dance Magazine* (New York), April 1945
Guest, Ivor, *The Ballet of the Second Empire, 1847–1858*, London, 1955
Roslavleva, Natalia, *Era of the Russian Ballet*, London, 1966
Guest, Ivor, *Jules Perrot: Master of the Romantic Ballet*, London, 1984
Wiley, Roland John (ed. and trans.), *A Century of Russian Ballet: Documents and Accounts, 1810–1910*, Oxford, 1990

* * *

Nadezhda Bogdanova was born into a theatrical family. Her mother was Tatyana Karpokova, ballerina of the Moscow Bolshoi Theatre, and her father was Konstantin Bogdanov, leading dancer and later régisseur, or rehearsal director, of the same theatre. She was taught by her father and began her stage career early. In 1848 and 1850, as part of a family company, she toured the Russian provinces. However, by the time she was only fourteen, on the advice of Fanny Elssler, Bogdanova was travelling to Europe to complete her studies in Paris; and in 1851 she made her début on the stage of the Paris Grand Opéra. Soon afterwards she appeared in Paris and Vienna with great success—and it was in Vienna that she danced her first *Giselle*. This was followed by a successful four years on the stage of the Paris Opéra.

Bogdanova had returned to her native country by 1855, and in St. Petersburg she appeared at the Moscow Bolshoi Theatre in a varied repertoire including *Giselle*, *La Sylphide*, and *La Esmeralda*. Nevertheless, she did not break her link with Paris. She danced in Italian opera and made frequent guest tours in Germany, Italy, and Hungary. The ballerina's last appearance was in 1867 in Warsaw, after which she left the stage at the age of 31 and in the full flowering of her talent.

Bogdanova was a ballerina of expressive, lyrical beauty. A contemporary critic wrote, after her first season in St. Petersburg, "Joyful, contrastingly sad, and even timid feelings appear in Madame Bogdanova's dancing, and are especially effective thanks to the tenderness of their expression. In such feelings is always so much that is natural, so much that is warm and sincere. On the other hand, strong movements are always moderated by her gracefulness, which in her is always combined with softness and tenderness. It is remarkable that not in a single role does she contradict her own character. Whatever varied roles we see her in, she is always able to subordinate them to her character without in the least violating the whole conception." At the same time, Aleksandr Pleshcheev observed that Bogdanova's technique was reminiscent of that of the best European dancers, and that her movements and poses were always charming. "Nothing awkward was to be seen in them; they were smooth, even gracious, and light."

Naturally Bogdanova, the performer of all the major roles in the Romantic repertoire, had other colours in her artistic palette. For example, in a fragment from a piece of Warsaw criticism by Pavlischev, we are told that one of the most striking features of Bogdanova's dancing was her supported lifts. "It is impossible to imagine the spring and daring and height with which she raises herself above her partner's head, in the position of a horizontally flying figure." The writer goes on to point out that her points were also excellent but that character dances and small pas with turns did not suit her.

Among the major Russian ballerinas of the nineteenth century, Bogdanova occupies a very special position thanks both to her Russo-French schooling and to her deliberately chosen destiny as an eternal touring artist, the favourite of the public in the various towns and cities she visited.

—Arsen Degen

---

## BOLENDER, Todd

American dancer, choreographer, and ballet director. Born in Canton, Ohio, 27 February 1914. Studied with Chester Hale, Anatole Vilzak, and at the School of American Ballet, New York. Dancer, (Lincoln Kirstein's) Ballet Caravan (later American Ballet Caravan), from 1936, participating in South American tour, 1941; principal dancer, Ballet Society, from 1946, and New York City Ballet (successor to Ballet Society), from 1948; also appeared with Littlefield Ballet, Ballet Theatre (later American Ballet Theatre), 1944, and Ballet Russe de Monte Carlo, 1945–46; founder member and director, American Concert Ballet, 1943; choreographer, Ballet Society, and later New York City Ballet, from 1946; also staged ballets for Emily Frankel and Mark Ryder Company, Theater an der Werk, Ankara Opera House in Turkey, Dallas Opera, and Metropolitan Opera, New York; ballet director, Cologne Opera, 1963–66, and Frankfurt Ballet, 1966–69; also staged ballets for Harkness Ballet, 1974; founder, with Janet Reed, Pacific Northwest Ballet, 1975–77; director of ballet company, Ataturk Opera House, Turkey, 1977–80; artistic director, Kansas City Ballet, from 1981, becoming State Ballet of Missouri, from 1986; has also staged ballets for the Lyric Opera of Kansas City, Missouri.

## ROLES

1936 Title role in *The Bat* (Balanchine), American Ballet Caravan, New York
1938 The State Trooper (cr) in *Filling Station* (L. Christensen), Ballet Caravan, Hartford, Connecticut
Alias (cr) in *Billy the Kid* (Loring), Ballet Caravan, Chicago

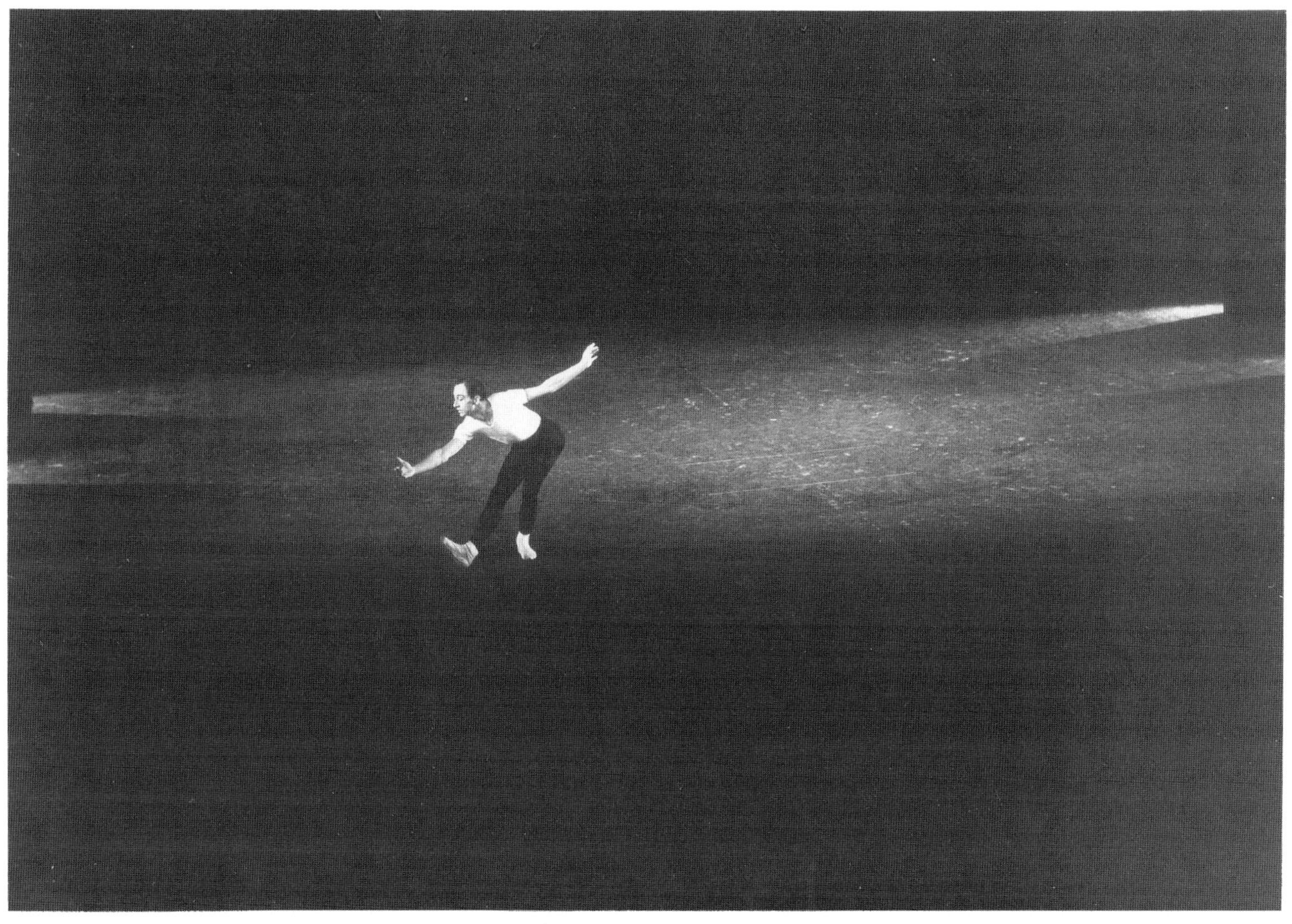

**Todd Bolender in *The Four Temperaments*, New York City Ballet**

1939 A Father (cr) in *City Portrait* (Loring), Ballet Caravan, Mobile, Alabama

1940 Principal dancer (cr) in *A Thousand Times Neigh!* (Dollar), Ballet Caravan, Flushing Meadow, New York

1941 Dancer (cr) in *Pastorela* (L. Christensen, J. Fernandez), American Ballet Caravan, Rio de Janeiro
March: King (cr) in *Divertimento* (Balanchine), American Ballet Caravan, Rio de Janeiro

1943 Hop o' my Thumb (cr) in *Mother Goose Suite* (also chor.), American Concert Ballet

1946 Phlegmatic (cr) in *The Four Temperaments* (Balanchine), Ballet Society, New York

1947 The Fox (cr) in *Renard* (Balanchine), Ballet Society, New York
Principal dancer (cr) in *Divertimento* (no relation to 1941 ballet; Balanchine), Ballet Society, New York
Gemini: Moon (cr) in *Zodiac* (also chor.), Ballet Society, New York
Groom (cr) in *Highland Fling* (Dollar), Ballet Society, New York
Andante (cr) in *Symphonie Concertante* (Balanchine), Ballet Society, New York

1949 Title role in *Jinx* (L. Christensen), New York City Ballet, New York

1950 Principal dancer (cr) in *The Age of Anxiety* (Robbins), New York City Ballet, New York

1951 The Joker in *The Card Game* (revival of *The Card Party*; Balanchine), New York City Ballet, New York
Title role in *The Miraculous Mandarin* (also chor.), New York City Ballet, New York
Title role in *Tyl Ulenspiegel* (Balanchine), New York City Ballet, New York
Principal dancer (cr) in *The Pied Piper* (Robbins), New York City Ballet, New York

1952 Principal dancer (cr) in *Metamorphoses* (Balanchine), New York City Ballet, New York
Principal dancer (cr) in *Kaleidoscope* (Boris), New York City Ballet, New York
Second movement in *Interplay* (Robbins), New York City Ballet, New York

1953 The Youth in *The Five Gifts* (Dollar), New York City Ballet, New York
Percussion (cr) in *Fanfare* (Robbins), New York City Ballet, New York

1954 Third Movement (cr) in *Quartet* (Robbins), New York City Ballet, New York
"The Unanswered Question", "In the Inn" (cr) in *Ivesiana* (Balanchine), New York City Ballet, New York

1955 A Man About Town (cr) in *Souvenirs* (also chor.), New York City Ballet, New York

1956 Principal dancer (cr) in *The Concert* (Robbins), New York City Ballet, New York

1957 First pas de trois: Sarabande (cr) in *Agon* (Balanchine), New York City Ballet, New York

**Other roles include:** Rich Boy in *Filling Station* (L. Christensen),

Beast in *Mother Goose Suite* (also chor.), Bourrée Fantasque in *Bourrée Fantasque* (Balanchine), principal dancer in *A la Françaix* (Balanchine), Scherzo in *Western Symphony* (Balanchine).

## WORKS

1943 *Mother Goose Suite* (mus. Ravel), American Concert Ballet (staged New York City Ballet, 1948)
1945 *Comedia Balletica* (mus. Stravinsky), Ballet Russe de Monte Carlo, New York
1947 *Zodiac* (mus. R. Revil), Ballet Society, New York
1948 *Capricorn Concerto* (mus. Barber), Ballet Society, New York
1951 *The Miraculous Mandarin* (mus. Bartók), New York City Ballet, New York
1953 *The Filly; or, A Stableboy's Dream* (mus. J. Coleman), New York City Ballet, New York
1955 *Souvenirs* (mus. Barber), New York City Ballet, New York
*At the Still Point* (mus. Debussy), Dance Drama Company of Emily Frankel and Mark Ryder, New York
1956 *The Still Point* (new production of *At the Still Point*; mus. Debussy), New York City Ballet, New York
*The Masquers* (mus. Poulenc), Dance Drama Company of Emily Frankel and Mark Ryder, New York (staged New York City Ballet, 1957)
1960 *Creation of the World* (mus. Milhaud), New York City Ballet, New York
1963 *Theme and Variations* (mus. Blacher), Cologne Opera Ballet, Cologne
1964 *Contrasts* (mus. Zimmermann), Cologne Opera Ballet, Cologne (restaged American Ballet Theatre, 1966)
*Dance 1—Dance 2* (mus. Copland), Cologne Opera Ballet, Cologne
1966 *Kontraste* (mus. Zimmermann), American Ballet Theatre, New York
1967 *Time Cycle* (mus. Foss), Frankfurt Ballet, Frankfurt
1972 *Serenade in A* (mus. Stravinsky), New York City Ballet, New York
*Piano-Rag-Music* (mus. Stravinsky), New York City Ballet, New York
1981 *Tchaikovsky Suite* (mus. Tchaikovsky), Kansas City Ballet, Kansas City
1982 *Classical Symphony* (mus. Prokofiev), Kansas City Ballet, Kansas City
*Galatea* (mus. von Suppe), Kansas City Ballet, Kansas City
1983 *Grand Tarantella* (mus. Gottschalk), Kansas City Ballet, Kansas City
1984 *Folktale* (mus. Stravinsky, *Le Baiser de la fée*), Kansas City Ballet, Kansas City
*Voyager* (mus. Bernstein), Kansas City Ballet, Kansas
*Concerto in F* (mus. Gershwin), Kansas City Ballet, Kansas City
1987 *An American in Paris* (mus. Gershwin), State Ballet of Missouri, Kansas City
1989 *Celebration* (mus. Gershwin), State Ballet of Missouri, Kansas City
1992 *Tchaikovsky Dances* (mus. Tchaikovsky), State Ballet of Missouri, Kansas City

**Other works include:** Dances in operas *L'Elisir d'amore* (mus. Donizetti; New York, 1954), *Die Meistersinger* (mus. Wagner; New York, 1958), *Thaïs* (mus. Massenet; Dallas, 1961), *Die Meistersinger* (mus. Wagner; New York, 1962), *Les Troyennes* (mus. Berlioz; New York, 1971), *Tannhaüser* (mus. Wagner; Kansas City, 1988), *Samson and Delilah* (mus. Saint-Saëns; Kansas City, 1990).

## PUBLICATIONS

By Bolender:

Contribution to Mason, Francis (ed.), *I Remember Balanchine*, New York, 1991

About Bolender:

Barzel, Ann, "Bright Young Men", *Dance Magazine* (New York), April 1946
Hastings, Baird, "Todd Bolender", *Chrysalis* (New York), vol. 3, nos. 5–6, 1950
Chujoy, Anatole, *The New York City Ballet*, New York, 1953
Todd, Arthur, "The Conquering Hero", *Dance Observer* (New York), April 1961
"Todd Bolender", *Tanzblätter* (Vienna), October 1976
Reynolds, Nancy, *Repertory in Review*, New York, 1977
Balanchine, George, with Mason, Francis, *Balanchine's Complete Stories of the Great Ballets*, Garden City, N.Y., 1977
Denby, Edwin, *Dance Writings*, edited by Robert Cornfield and William Mackay, New York, 1986
Barzel, Ann, "Todd Bolender: A Decade in Kansas City", *Dance Magazine* (New York), October 1991

* * *

Although Todd Bolender danced with American Ballet Theatre (then known as Ballet Theatre) as well as with the Littlefield Ballet and the Ballet Russe de Monte Carlo, his most consistent development both as dancer and choreographer came during his fifteen years with Ballet Society and its successor, the New York City Ballet.

He was by no means the typical Balanchine male dancer. He lacked the speed and precision of Robert Barnett, or the strength and classical presence of Edward Villella or Jacques d'Amboise. Physically Bolender was narrow-shouldered and unusually flexible. This gave his dancing a look of softness not suited to classical partnering. But Balanchine knew how to use him most effectively in the comic or slightly eccentric aspects of character dance. The roles Balanchine created especially for Bolender have remained indelibly his, and have never been quite so distinctive on subsequent dancers.

Outstanding among these roles was the Phlegmatic Variation in *The Four Temperaments*. It was a solo in which the feet executed tricky rhythms while the remainder of the body moved in a languid manner, which the French call "désossé". A similar quality was required for the Sarabande of Balanchine's *Agon*. Only here, a touch of humor and a look of riskiness was added, as when Bolender was required to pull away from strange off-balance stances, or to plant one foot and use the other to pivot around it. Again, Bolender's suppleness was used in deliberate contrast to the hard-edged dancing of the other principals.

Balanchine's *Ivesiana* provided Bolender with an unusual dramatic challenge. It occurred in the section titled "The Unanswered Question". A woman (Allegra Kent) was slowly carried by four darkly clad men. They lifted her in all manner of strange and tantalizing positions, never once allowing her body to touch the ground and never allowing a worshipful male, portrayed by Bolender, to touch her. Frantically he followed or preceded the cortège—reaching, falling on his back as she was passed over him, repeatedly trying to embrace this beautiful creature with the long, flowing hair. Clad only in tights, and with his torso and feet bare, Bolender created a poetic counterpart to this chilly enigma.

Todd Bolender was also a superb comedian with a penchant for high camp. Choreographer Jerome Robbins used this particular quality to telling effect in *The Concert* and in *Fanfare*. In the former, Bolender was a henpecked husband who constantly escaped into daydreams of sexual conquest. Clad in a vest and long underwear, and chewing on a huge cigar, he was the prototype of James Thurber's short story character, J. Walter Mitty.

In *Fanfare*, a festive delineation of the instruments of the orchestra (based upon Benjamin Britten's *A Young Person's Guide to the Orchestra*), Bolender led the percussion section. Anyone who saw him can never forget his gleeful leer as he was carried about crashing imaginary cymbals, or the flirtatious way he shook his shoulders to the chattering of castanets.

As a choreographer, Bolender does not often resort to humor. His bent is lyrical. *Souvenirs* is, however, a hilarious exception. It satirizes the antics of a group of guests in an Edwardian hotel, and it does so with the pacing and style of a silent film. In fact, the high point is a seduction scene for a hissing Siren and her slick-haired paramour. There is also a room-to-room chase, an assignation or two, and some cavorting bathing beauties. *Souvenirs* becomes momentarily sentimental as three little wallflowers wistfully dream of their ideal beau. This vignette typifies Bolender's insight into the feelings of young women. The same insight occurs in the role of the Young Girl in his *Mother Goose Suite* and in that of the tormented protagonist of *The Still Point*.

Certainly Bolender's best known work, *The Still Point*, was created for the Frankel-Ryder Comany the year before it was taken into the New York City Ballet repertoire. It has since been acquired by several other companies. In form, *The Still Point* is deceptively simple. An adolescent girl is rejected by her frolicsome contemporaries. In the midst of her anguished solitude, a young stranger offers her tenderness and compassion. Perhaps because of its spareness, the ballet drew exceptionally sensitive performances from its original principals, Melissa Hayden and Jacques d'Amboise. D'Amboise in particular was required to express the man's entire personality by means of a few simple and direct gestures.

Bolender has also created a number of abstract ballets, all of them well crafted but lacking in daring. To a degree this is also true of the repertoire he has structured for the Missouri State Ballet, which he has directed since 1981. It includes a firm foundation of Balanchine ballets, as well as works by Lew Christensen, Jacques d'Amboise, Francisco Moncion, William Dollar, Tom Ruud, and Bolender himself. For the most part they form a cross section of what was prevalent in the 1950s and 1960s.

—Doris Hering

---

**BOLM, Adolph**

Russian/American dancer, choreographer, and teacher. Born Adolf Rudolfovich Bolm in St. Petersburg, 25 September (some sources say 23 September) 1884. Studied at the Imperial Theatre School, St. Petersburg, pupil of Platon Karsavin and Nikolai Legat; graduated in 1903; later studied with Enrico Cecchetti. Dancer, soon becoming soloist, Maryinsky Theatre, St. Petersburg, from 1904; organized first Pavlova tour with dancers of the Imperial Theatre, performing Riga, Copenhagen, Stockholm, 1908, and Prague, Berlin, 1909; also performed with Lydia Kyasht, London tour, 1908, 1910; danced with Diaghilev's Ballets Russes, first seasons, Paris, 1909, 1910; resigned from St. Petersburg Imperial Theatres, 1911, rejoining Diaghilev's company as leading dancer and choreographer; toured U.S. with Diaghilev's Ballets Russes, 1916, 1917, staying in U.S. after second tour, 1917: founder, Ballet Intime, from 1917; principal dancer and choreographer, Metropolitan Opera, New York, 1917–18, and Chicago Opera, 1919, 1922–24; ballet director, Chicago Opera, 1924; director, Chicago Allied Arts Ballet, 1924–27, also performing in New York, 1925, and Buenos Aires (working also as choreographer), 1925; choreographer, Chamber Music Society, Washington, D.C., 1928; worked in Hollywood from 1931, creating ballets for films, including *The Mad Genius* (1931), *The Men in her Life* (1941), *The Life of Cellini*; choreographer, San Francisco Opera, 1933, Ballet Theatre, New York, 1940, 1945, and San Francisco Ballet, 1947; also teacher: ballet master, Ballet Theatre, 1942–43; private teacher, Los Angeles, 1938–40, and Hollywood, late 1940s. Recipient, Swedish Order of Literis et Artibus from King Gustav of Sweden, 1908. Died in Los Angeles, 16 April 1951.

**ROLES**

1908 Pierre in *Cavalry Halt* (Petipa), "Imperial Ballet of St. Petersburg" tour, Stockholm
Prince Siegfried in *Swan Lake*, Act II (Ivanov), "Imperial Ballet of St. Petersburg" tour, Stockholm
Pas de deux (with Kyasht) from *The Little Humpbacked Horse* (Saint-Léon), Empire Theatre, London
1909 Chief Warrior (cr) in *Polovtsian Dances from Prince Igor* (Fokine), Diaghilev's Ballets Russes, Paris
1909/12 Moor in *Petrushka* (Fokine), Diaghilev's Ballets Russes
Ivan Tsarevich in *Firebird* (Fokine), Diaghilev's Ballets Russes
Amoun in *Cléopâtre* (Fokine), Diaghilev's Ballets Russes
Title role in *Petrushka* (Fokine), Diaghilev's Ballets Russes
1910 Pierrot (cr) in *Le Carnaval* (Fokine), Diaghilev's Ballets Russes, Paris
"Les Papillons de l'Orient" (pas de deux; cr) in *East and West* (new version of *Round the World*; Farren), Empire Theatre, London
Slave (cr) in *Fantasie Chorégraphique* (also known as *Dance Idylls*; also chor.), Empire Theatre, London
1911 Viscount de Beaugency in *Le Pavillon d'Armide* (Fokine), Coronation Gala, Covent Garden, London
1912 Prince (cr) in *Thamar* (Fokine), Diaghilev's Ballets Russes, Paris
Darkon (cr) in *Daphnis et Chloë* (Fokine), Diaghilev's Ballets Russes, Paris
Leading dancer (cr) in *La Fête d'Hébé* (opera; mus. Rameau, chor. Bolm), Opéra de Monte Carlo, Monte Carlo
1914 King Dorkon (cr) in *Le Coq d'or* (Fokine), Diaghilev's Ballets Russes, Paris
Title role (cr) in *Midas* (Fokine), Diaghilev's Ballets Russes, Paris
1915 Prince in *La Princesse enchantée* (Bluebird pas de deux from *The Sleeping Beauty*; Petipa), Diaghilev's Ballets Russes, Paris
1916 Title role (cr) in *Sadko* (also chor.), Diaghilev's Ballets Russes, San Sebastián
1917 Wind (cr) in *Falling Leaves* (or *Poem Choreographic*; also

chor., probably after Pavlova) in *Miss 1917* (Broadway revue), Century Theatre, New York
1918 King Dodon in *Le Coq d'or* (also chor.), Metropolitan Opera House, New York
1919 Title role in *Petrushka* (also chor., after Fokine), Metropolitan Opera House, New York
The Dwarf (cr) in *The Birthday of the Infanta* (also chor.), Chicago Opera, Chicago
1922/24 Leading roles in dances (also chor.) in *The Snow Maiden* (opera; mus. Rimsky-Korsakov), *Cléopâtre* (opera; mus. Massenet), *L'Africaine* (opera; mus. Meyerbeer), *The Jewess* (*La Juive*; opera, mus. Halévy), Chicago Opera, Chicago
1928 Apollo (cr) in *Apollon musagète* (also chor.) Chamber Music Society, Washington, D.C.

## WORKS

1910 *Fantasie Choreographique* (also known as *Dance Idylls*), Empire Theatre, London
"Les Papillons de l'Orient" (pas de deux) in *East and West* (new version of *Round the World*; Farren), Empire Theatre, London
1912 Dances in *La Fête d'Hébé* (opera; mus. Rameau), Opéra de Monte Carlo, Monte Carlo
1913 Persian Dances in *Khovanshchina* (opera; mus. Mussorgsky), Diaghilev's Ballets Russes, Paris
1914 Dances in *May Night* (opera; mus. Rimsky-Korsakov), Diaghilev's Ballets Russes, Paris
1916 *Sadko* (mus. Rimsky-Korsakov), Diaghilev's Ballets Russes, San Sebastián
1917 *White Peacock* (mus. Griffes), Ballet Intime, tour
*Falling Leaves* (or *Poem Choreographic*, probably after Pavlova; mus. Glazunov), in *Miss 1917* (Broadway revue), Century Theatre, New York
1918 *Le Coq d'or* (mus. Rimsky-Korsakov), Metropolitan Opera House, New York (also later staged for San Francisco Opera)
1919 *The Birthday of the Infanta* (mus. Carpenter), Chicago Opera, Chicago
1922 *Krazy Kat* (jazz-pantomime; mus. Carpenter), New York
Dances in *The Snow Maiden* (opera; mus. Rimsky-Korsakov), Chicago Opera, Chicago
1923 Dances in *Cléopâtre* (opera; mus. Massenet), Chicago Opera, Chicago
1924 Dances in *L'Africaine* (opera; mus. Meyerbeer), Chicago Opera, Chicago
Dances in *The Jewess* (*La Juive*; opera; mus. Halévy), Chicago Opera, Chicago
*Elopement* (mus. Mozart), Chicago Allied Arts Ballet, Chicago
*Foyer de la danse* (mus. Chabrier), Chicago Allied Arts Ballet, Chicago
1925 *El Amor Brujo* (new version; mus. de Falla), Chicago Allied Arts Ballet, Chicago
*Christmas Carol* (mus. Vaughan Williams), Chicago Allied Arts Ballet, Chicago
*Little Circus* (mus. Offenbach), Chicago Allied Arts Ballet, Chicago
*The Rivals* (mus. Eicheim), Chicago Allied Arts Ballet, Chicago
*Mandragora* (mus. Szymanowsky), Chicago Allied Arts Ballet, Chicago
*Bal de marionettes* (mus. Satie), Chicago Allied Arts Ballet, Chicago
1926 *Parnassus au Montmartre* (mus. Satie), Chicago Allied Arts Ballet, Chicago
*La Farce du pont neuf* (mus. Hersher), Chicago Allied Arts Ballet, Chicago
*Pierrot lunaire* (mus. Schoenberg), Chicago Allied Arts Ballet, Chicago
*Vision mystique* (mus. Skriabin, arranged Lamont), Chicago Allied Arts Ballet, Chicago
1927 *Tragedy of the Cello* (mus. Tansman), Chicago Allied Arts Ballet, Chicago
*Harmony*, Chicago Allied Arts Ballet, Chicago
1928 *Apollon musagète* (mus. Stravinsky), Chamber Music Society, Washington, D.C.
*Harlequinade* (mus. Mondonville), Chamber Music Society, Washington, D.C.
*Pavane pour une infante défunte* (mus. Ravel), Chamber Music Society, Washington, D.C.
*Alt Wien* (mus. Beethoven), Chamber Music Society, Washington, D.C.
1932 *Ballet mécanique* (based on *Iron Foundry*, originally choreographed for film *The Mad Genius*, 1931; mus. Mosolov), Hollywood Bowl, Hollywood
1934 *Patterns* (mus. Tcherepnin), San Francisco Ballet, San Francisco
1935 *Bach Cycle*: *Danse noble*, *Lament*, *Consecration* (mus. Bach), San Francisco Ballet, San Francisco
1940 *Peter and the Wolf* (mus. Prokofiev), Ballet Theatre, New York
*Firebird* (mus. Stravinsky), Hollywood Bowl, Hollywood
1945 *Firebird* (new version; mus. Stravinsky), Ballet Theatre, New York
1947 *Mephisto* (mus. Lizst), San Francisco Ballet, San Francisco

Also staged:
1919 *Petrushka* (after Fokine; mus. Stravinsky), Metropolitan Opera House, New York

## PUBLICATIONS

By Bolm:
"A Dancer's Days: The Memoirs of a Russian Dancer Who Tells of His Life and Adventures", *Dance Magazine* (New York), 3 parts: September, October, November 1926

About Bolm:
Amberg, George, *Ballet in America*, New York, 1949
Beaumont, Cyril, *Complete Book of Ballets*, revised edition, London, 1951
Barzel, Ann, and Beaumont, Cyril, "Adolph Bolm", *Ballet Annual* (London), vol. 6, 1952
Dougherty, J., "Perspective on Adolph Bolm", *Dance Magazine* (New York), 3 parts: January, February, March 1963
Money, Keith, *Anna Pavlova: Her Life and her Art*, London, 1982
Garafola, Lynn, *Diaghilev's Ballets Russes*, New York, 1989

* * *

Although he spent more than half of his adult life in America, Adolph Bolm's artistic point of view was grounded in the avant-garde of turn-of-the-century Russia, where his career started, and in the avant-garde atmosphere of the early seasons of the Diaghilev Ballet in which he was prominent. He chose to live and work in America and adored its institutions; but his milieu, his artistic circle in New York, Chicago, and California, consisted of Russian émigrés—Stravinsky, Roer-

**Adolph Bolm in California, late 1930s**

ich, Anisfeld, Tcherepnine, Remisov, Chaliapin. He was an intellectual interested in politics, literature, architecture, music, and painting, and his outlook was cosmopolitan.

As a dancer he was uniquely virile. In his various roles Bolm was never the boyish jeune premier. He was a man, strong and mature. References to his dancing at the beginning of his career mention his superlative elevation. It was his great jump, coupled with the abandon he assumed in performing the Chief Warrior in Fokine's *Prince Igor*, that made him and the Diaghilev Ballet the sensation of the first Diaghilev season in Paris. He was usually categorized as a "character dancer", but he also danced classical roles, especially with Pavlova on the 1908 tour he arranged for the great ballerina in Scandinavia and England. During his performing career he excelled in roles that emphasized the grotesque, the exotic, and the dramatic—and when he was artistic director of any company he created ballets with such roles.

Bolm was the Slave to Karsavina's *Thamar*, Sadko in his underseas ballet of that title, the Dwarf in his *The Birthday of the Infanta*. He was noted for his heart-breakingly disconsolate Pierrot in Fokine's *Carnaval*. Perhaps it was that role that inspired him to base a number of his later dances, such as *Harlequinade*, on *commedia dell'arte* characters. Puppets, too, were in his range. He danced the puppet Petrushka and also the role of the Moor in that Fokine ballet.

Soon after his graduation from the Imperial Ballet School, Adolph Bolm travelled abroad to the capitals of Europe. During the several summers of his travels he visited Paris, Vienna, and Milan, and noted the decadent state of classical ballet. He was inspired to show western Europe Russia's high level of ballet, and that led to the tour with Pavlova. He joined Diaghilev for the famous opening season in 1909 and was with the company for its exciting first years.

Bolm's inquisitive nature, adventurous in life and art, led him to leave Russia permanently and to move on from the Diaghilev company. He remained in America, where he participated in a number of types of dance presentations. At the time, there were no ballet companies in America: classical ballet dancers were found only in the opera companies of New York, Boston, and Chicago. As a prestigious former director and principal dancer of Diaghilev's Ballets Russes, Bolm was invited to present ballets in New York's Metropolitan Opera. His productions of *Petrushka* (after Fokine) and of *Le Coq d'or* became part of the Met repertoire. He danced the title role in *Petrushka* and King Dodon in *Le Coq d'or*, the latter his own version of the Rimsky-Korsakov work. Some years later Bolm staged his *Coq d'or* for the San Francisco Opera.

When not working in the operas, Bolm was involved in other dance projects in New York. There was his ballet, *Falling Leaves*, to Glazunov's music for a Broadway revue, *Miss 1917*. (He danced the role of The Wind.) He pioneered the "prologue to the movie", live dance divertissements on the stages of elaborate "cinema palaces". This type of entertainment became the fashion in hundreds of film theatres throughout America and Europe.

Always active, Bolm organized his Ballet Intime, a small troupe that presented concert programmes of original dances. Bolm was principal dancer, choreographer, and director. He recruited an ensemble and added guest artists of several dance styles, including Japanese, Hindu, Norwegian, and Swedish dancers. Ballet Intime functioned in America and England, and in its latter days in the 1930s, Bolm tours included modern dancer Martha Graham and eclectic dancer Agnes de Mille.

During his first years in New York, Bolm met the American composer-businessman John Alden Carpenter, who was instrumental in having the renowned dancer invited by the Chicago Opera to stage and dance *The Birthday of the Infanta*, based on an Oscar Wilde fairytale. Robert Edmond Jones designed the elaborate décor. The ballet was a great success and was subsequently presented in New York at the Met. In New York, Bolm choreographed a second ballet to a Carpenter score, *Krazy Kat*, based on a popular cartoon. This was one of the first American theme ballets of the twentieth century.

The success of these ballets led to an invitation (in 1924) to direct the ballet of the Chicago Opera. Given a free hand, a large ballet ensemble, and a broad opera repertoire, Bolm gave opera ballet episodes a spirit and theatrical importance they never had before or since. Among the outstanding ballets were those in *L'Africaine*, *The Jewess*, *Cléopâtra*, and especially, in Rimsky-Korsakov's *Sneguritchka* (*The Snow Maiden*). The great basso Fedor Chaliapin directed and sang the lead in the opera, while Nicholas Roerich, famous for his décors for Diaghilev, designed the sets and costumes. Bolm choreographed the ballets and partnered ballerina Anna Ludmila in the dances. This all-Russian collaboration was a sensation and a success. But the Chicago Opera's singers, the great divas and tenors of the period, were jealous of the prominence accorded the dance by press and public, and after two seasons of superlative opera ballet, Bolm's contract was not renewed.

By this time Bolm had a school and developed artist-dancers, and was characteristically looking to higher goals. With the financial sponsorship of local philanthropists, he founded the Allied Arts Ballet, a company based on the Diaghilev philosophy of ballet as a collaboration of dance, music, and painting. Bolm was artistic director and choreographer of the company which presented original dance works and also played avant-garde symphonic works. Tamara Karsavina was guest artist the first season and Ruth Page was premiere danseuse. Interesting guest artists were always included, such as oriental dancer Vera Mirova, Spanish dancer Maria Montero, and modern dancer Ronny Johnsson. The Allied Arts Ballet, the first repertory ballet company in America, lasted several seasons and when philanthropists vanished with the Great Depression, it disbanded. Bolm maintained his school and directed a concert group for which he created all the dances and performed the leading roles. This small group toured large cities and remote towns, often sponsored by women's clubs. The programmes, plus the lectures often added by Bolm, inspired local dancers and teachers, and were instrumental in building audiences. Bolm's example encouraged young males to become dancers.

In 1933, Bolm was invited to direct the ballet for the San Francisco Opera, where his most important accomplishment was founding the ballet school, which still exists and contributes in an important way to American ballet. The Russian spent the remainder of his life in California. In Hollywood he created ballets for films, some of which found their way to the screen in distorted form. Most notable was *The Iron Foundry*, choreographed at the invitation of Bolm's friend John Barrymore for his film *The Mad Genius*. The ballet, set to music by Russian composer Mosolov, was cut out of the picture because the film company would not pay for the expected music rights. However, presented later in the Hollywood Bowl as *Ballet mécanique*, the piece drew tremendous audiences and had great success.

When Ballet Theatre (later American Ballet Theatre) was founded, Bolm was invited to choreograph a ballet to Prokofiev's *Peter and the Wolf* in 1940. The piece followed the story explicitly in Bolm's mimetic style, and was a popular item in the repertoire for two decades. Also for American Ballet Theatre, and again collaborating with Russian artists, Bolm choreographed a new version of *Firebird* to the Stravinsky score with new décor by Marc Chagall. Alicia Markova danced the premiere; but the ballet was not a success.

As a teacher, Adolph Bolm left a far-reaching legacy: many American teachers studied with him, and carried on his precepts in their own teaching. His background and foundation was the classicism of the Imperial Russian academy (he was also in Cecchetti's class during his Diaghilev years), but when he became a teacher, his classes veered from the purely technical. It was not that he did not advocate technique, but he left the inculcating of these fundamental elements of classical ballet to his assistants. He found barre work uninteresting and gave it short shrift. The major part of his class was in the centre, dancing the enchainements he created, often to unusual and intricate rhythms. He emphasized the importance of character dances, and usually ended his class with a mazurka or czardas. He also encouraged his students to study Spanish dancing as a road to style.

Bolm is not often credited with pioneering the above-mentioned activities in America, but uncredited or not, his influence was broad. Overall, his importance to American ballet is immeasurable.

—Ann Barzel

---

## BOLSHOI BALLET

Russian ballet company based in Moscow. Origins traced to 1776, in foundation of private company of actors and dancers in Moscow from which grew the dancers who performed at the Petrovsky Theatre, established in 1780, and moving to the New Imperial Theatre (upon destruction of Petrovsky Theatre by fire), from 1802, and finally the New Bolshoi Petrovsky Theatre, the current Bolshoi Theatre, established 1825 (renovated after fire, 1856); company now the official resident ballet company of the Bolshoi Theatre for Opera and Ballet, known more commonly as the Bolshoi Ballet. School affiliated with the company, with origins in first Moscow ballet school, established at the Home of Education (an orphanage), 1773: now known as the Bolshoi Ballet School or, more correctly, the Moscow Choreographic School. Artistic Director of the Bolshoi Ballet (from 1964): Yuri Grigorovich.

### PUBLICATIONS

*The Moscow Bolshoi Theatre, 1825–1925: A Collections of Articles and Other Materials*, Moscow, 1925

Bellew, Hélène, *Ballet in Moscow Today*, London, 1956

Krasovskaya, Vera, *Russian Ballet Theatre from its Beginning to the Middle of the Nineteenth Century*, Leningrad and Moscow, 1958

Gozenpud, Akim, *The Musical Theatre in Russia, from its Origins to Glinka's Time*, Leningrad, 1959

Slonimsky, Yuri, *The Bolshoi Ballet*, second edition (in English), Moscow, 1960

Krasovskaya, Vera, *Russian Ballet Theatre of the Second Half of the Nineteenth Century*, Leningrad and Moscow, 1963

Roslavleva, Natalia, *Era of the Russian Ballet*, London, 1966

Krasovskaya, Vera, *Russian Ballet Theatre of the Early Twentieth Century*, 2 volumes: *Choreographers*, Leningrad, 1971; *Dancers*, Leningrad, 1972

Lvov-Anokhin, Boris, *Masters of the Bolshoi Ballet*, Moscow, 1976

Demidov, Alexander, *The Russian Ballet Past and Present*, London, 1978

Pokrovsky, Boris, and Grigorovich, Yuri, *The Bolshoi*, translated by Daryl Hislop, New York, 1979

Souritz, Elizabeth, *The Art of Choreography in the 1920s*, Moscow, 1979; as *Soviet Choreographers in the 1920s*, translated by Lynn Visson, Durham, N.C., and London, 1990

* * *

The building which currently houses the Bolshoi was constructed in 1825, on the site of the former Petrovsky Theatre, and for that reason 1825 has been regarded, until recently, as the year of the theatre's birth. However, today's scholars have put the date of the Bolshoi's foundation back to 1776, due to a definite continuity of style which existed among various companies which performed on various stages before 1825. These companies often included the same actors and had a similar repertoire. In 1776 a private company, owned by Prince Urusov and an Englishman called Maddox, was set up with dancers among its members. The first Moscow ballet dancers received their professional training in the dance classes at the Home of Education (a Moscow orphanage), where dancing had been taught since 1773.

The first Russian choreographer to work in Moscow was a visitor from St. Petersburg, Ivan Valbergh, who worked in the city from 1806 to 1807. Already at that early stage Moscow ballet had its own distinctive features, as distinguished from the St. Petersburg school: there was more folk dancing incorporated into ballet performances in Moscow, comic ballets were particularly successful, and dramatic acting prevailed over pure dance.

In the first quarter of the nineteenth century, a major influence was Adam Glushkovsky, who managed the Bolshoi company from 1812 to 1839. His productions featured a variety of genres, from melodramas much loved by the Muscovites to patriotic divertissements with plenty of folk dancing, which were in great demand during and immediately after the Napoleonic Wars. Glushkovsky's ballets, using stories from Russian literature, were particularly prominent, such as those based on Pushkin's works. On the other hand, Félicité Hullin-Sor, a dancer, instructor, and choreographer who worked at the Bolshoi from 1823 until 1839, introduced Russian ballet to the Romantic style and staged a number of French productions, including *La Sylphide*. In the 1850s Fanny Elssler was a major success at the Bolshoi Theatre and she introduced the public to Jules Perrot's ballets.

In 1853, the Bolshoi House burnt down and was re-opened in 1856. Thus started a new and rather controversial phase in the theatre's life. The Romantic productions—specifically the Perrot ones, full of dramatic possibilities and rich in emotional dancing and mime acting—became a thing of the past. The Bolshoi company still consisted of first-rate dancers, but all those decades the company was headed by foreigners who failed to grasp its stylistic character and to make use of its potential. In 1861–64 the company's director was Carlo Blasis, who turned out to be a valuable teacher at the Theatre School. The most frequently staged ballets were those by Arthur Saint-Léon, transferred from St. Petersburg (such *The Little Humpbacked Horse*, 1866). The only considerable Moscow achievement was *Don Quixote*, staged in 1869 by Marius Petipa. It was the first version of a ballet which was later to become famous, and it differed largely from the ones which followed in St. Petersburg, particularly in its emphasis on character dancing.

In 1871 the management decided to invite another foreign choreographer, Wenzel Reisinger, the creator of the ill-fated first production of Tchaikovsky's *Swan Lake*. Reisinger was followed as chief choreographer by Joseph Hansen (1879–82),

Aleksei Bogdanov from St. Petersburg (1883–89), and Joseph Mendez (1889–98). A crisis in Moscow Ballet loomed large, and by the end of the century the situation became critical. There was even some talk about the Bolshoi's closure, and, though this never happened, the company was cut almost by half in 1882.

The reason for the crisis was not only the fact that for several decades the Bolshoi suffered from the lack of talent among its own chief choreographers; mainstream Russian ballet at that time was too far removed from the traditions of the Moscow company. The St. Petersburg choreographers Saint-Léon, and later Petipa and Lev Ivanov, followed the trend towards a greater complexity of dance and thus more sophisticated ballet technique. Dancing became more abstract, losing touch with pantomime, becoming its own raison d'être, and reflecting only the most general ideas of the choreographer—hence the balletic compositions in *La Bayadère* (the "Shades", 1877), the ensembles in *The Sleeping Beauty* (1890), "Snow Flakes" in *The Nutcracker* (1892), and the "Swan Scenes" in *Swan Lake* (1895). But this pure dance style was closer to the St. Petersburg than to the Moscow school. The Bolshoi company wanted, and needed, a more dramatic style of dancing with plenty of character, closer to pantomime.

A new era for the Bolshoi Ballet was started by Aleksandr Gorsky. In 1899 he staged his own version of *Don Quixote* and in 1902 he was appointed the company's chief choreographer, the position which remained his for twenty years. Gorsky's work brought about a true renaissance in the Bolshoi Theatre. His work was close, on the one hand, to the ideas of the Moscow Art Theatre which opened in 1898 under Stanislavsky and advocated "realism"—that is, historical and psychological verisimilitude. On the other hand, Gorsky was undoubtedly impressed by the Russian brand of "art nouveau" and it showed in his choreography, where asymmetry prevails and, unlike Petipa's works, there are plenty of intricate curves and elaborate contrasts. A number of original productions were staged by Gorsky in the Bolshoi (the most memorable of them being *Gudule's Daughter*, 1902; *Salammbô*, 1910; *Love is Quick!*, 1913); he also produced versions (often with completely overhauled choreography) of the old ballets such as *La Bayadère*, *Le Corsaire*, *Giselle*, and *Swan Lake*. Among Gorsky's followers were the dancers who owed him their first leading parts; however, Gorsky had strong opponents in his company who objected to his innovations—among them the leading dancer of the company, Vasily Tikhomirov, and the prima ballerina Ekaterina Geltser (though the latter did collaborate with Gorsky on several occasions).

The 1920s in Russia were the decade of experiment and of the emergence of new forms in all arts. Ballet workshops, which at that time opened in Moscow by the dozen, were rich in innovation and followed a large variety of trends such as Duncanist (after the American dancer Isadora Duncan), rhythmical, plastique, "Machine Dancing" after Foregger, and so on. However, the innovative choreography was not admitted on to the Bolshoi stage, where the conservative wing was quite strong. Only one experimental ballet, *Joseph the Beautiful* (1925) by Kasyan Goleizovsky, was staged in the Bolshoi, featuring "constructivist" stage designs by Boris Erdman and a number of purely choreographic innovations. Goleizovsky's work was not, however, regarded by the Bolshoi's management as the major achievement of the post-revolutionary years. Instead, they were excessive in promoting *The Red Poppy* by Vasily Tikhomirov and Lev Laschilin, in which the leading role was danced by Ekaterina Geltser, and in which the supposedly more accessible, "modern" story was meant to express state ideology.

The slogan "art must be easy for the people to understand" stayed in force for a long time afterwards. From the 1930s up to the mid-1950s the main trend in the Soviet ballet was "nearer to a realistic drama". The productions made at that time, which they called "dram-ballets", had to have a detailed story behind them which would evolve during three or four acts. As for the dancing itself, it was fairly uncomplicated and was often replaced by a danced pantomime. The most celebrated dram-ballets were produced in Leningrad by Rostislav Zakharov (*The Fountain of Bakhchisarai*) and Leonid Lavrovsky (*Romeo and Juliet*), and later restaged in Moscow. Moscow ballet at that time was traditionally regarded as "provincial", but because Moscow became the capital after the October revolution, the official policy was to give it special support. Among the Moscow choreographers active in the 1930s to the 1940s were Igor Moiseyev and the choreographic trio Aleksandr Radunsky, Nikolai Popko, and Lev Pospekhin. The leading dancers at that time were Asaf Messerer, Mikhail Gabovich, and Olga Lepeshinskaya.

During World War II the Bolshoi company was evacuated to Kuibyshev. After its return to Moscow, the company was joined by the outstanding ballerina Galina Ulanova, and Leonid Lavrovsky became the chief choreographer. During the next decade, as well, Zakharov staged a number of successful productions (*Cinderella*, *The Bronze Horseman*). However, the deficiencies of dram-ballet, which was gradually losing its better qualities, became obvious at the beginning of the 1950s. There was a reaction against its illustrative nature, and there were ever more calls for a greater complexity in the dance itself. This became possible due to the changes in political atmosphere after the death of Stalin, and for the first time in many years it was possible to discuss alternative avenues in art. In addition, the touring companies from abroad which began coming to the Soviet Union provided much material for discussion.

Consequently, a group of young choreographers insisted on the urgent need for change. One of them, Yuri Grigorovich, whose first productions were staged in Leningrad in the late 1950s, came to work in Moscow in the early 1960s. His works, like *The Stone Flower* and *A Legend of Love*, were received as a great innovation at the time because characterization and artistic message were expressed through dance itself. Grigorovich received much support from the younger members of the company, and his productions were made famous by Maya Plisetskaya, Natalia Bessmertnova, Ekaterina Maximova, Vladimir Vasiliev, Maris Liepa, Nina Timofeyeva, and others.

The Bolshoi is often referred to as "the main theatre of the country", thus emphasizing its grandeur and its somewhat pompous character. The Bolshoi Ballet repertoire is orientated towards a wide range of public tastes, largely international, because international tours have lately played a major part in the company's life, while in Moscow a ticket to the Bolshoi is a rare commodity almost unobtainable for an ordinary Muscovite, for a great percentage of the seats are filled by tourists from abroad. Essentially, the Bolshoi speaks to its public by using a highly emotional language of pageantry. Grigorovich's ballets are large-scale, highly dramatic, dynamic, and full of big mass scenes; they require a great deal of expressiveness and a slightly elevated style of dancing. But the dominance of this type of production has led to a certain uniformity of repertoire. There are few old ballets or works by other choreographers than Grigorovich. Comic ballets, which used to be part of the Moscow tradition, have completely disappeared. The company employs few character or mime dancers.

A number of Grigorovich's productions from the late 1970s to the early 1980s (like *Angara* and *Romeo and Juliet*) have proven unsuccessful. They repeated the old discoveries and contained no new ideas or devices. Since the late 1970s, critics and people in the profession have been voicing the opinion that the monopoly of one choreographer impedes the progress of the Bolshoi Ballet. As a result, Maya Plisetskaya began to order or stage new productions tailor-made for herself, while artists like Vladimir Vasiliev urgently insisted on the necessity for change within the theatre (though later he had to sever his links with the Bolshoi almost completely). There have been few new productions at the Bolshoi in recent years. The last original production by Grigorovich (*The Golden Age*) was staged in 1982, while the attempt to invite a major choreographer from abroad (Roland Petit with *Cyrano de Bergerac*) proved unsuccessful. A show which consisted of miniature ballets by Goleizovsky and Bournonville (1989) was only performed a few times, partly because the existing members of the company do not feel at home in an unfamiliar style. The leading dancers of the Bolshoi in recent years have been Nadezhda Pavlova, Ludmila Semenyaka, Nina Ananiashvili, Alla Mikhaltchenko, Vyatcheslav Gordeyev, Irek Mukhamedov, and Andris Liepa, though the last two have recently moved on to pursue their careers elsewhere.

—Elizabeth Souritz

---

**BÖRLIN, Jean**

Swedish dancer and choreographer. Born in Härnösand, Sweden, 13 March 1893. Studied at the Royal Theatre School, Stockholm, pupil of Gunhild Rosen, 1902–05; later studied with Mikhail Fokine, Copenhagen, and José Otero, Madrid, 1918–20. Dancer, Royal Theatre, Stockholm, 1905–1918: second soloist, from 1913; after period of independent study and experiments in choreography, leading dancer in recital financed by Rolf de Maré, Paris, 1920, leading to establishment of company: sole choreographer and principal dancer, Ballets Suédois, founded and financed by de Maré, based in Paris and touring widely in Europe and U.S., 1920–25; also appeared in two films directed by René Clair, *Entr'acte* (1924) and *Le Voyage imaginaire* (1925); dancer, Théâtre des Champs Élysées, Paris, 1925, also touring in recitals, including North and South America; leading dancer in recital with his own pupils, Paris, 1929. Died in New York, 6 December 1930.

## ROLES

1909 Dancer in *Die Puppenfee* (mus. Bayer), Royal Theatre, Stockholm

1911 Dancer in *Theresa's Party* (Stichel, Zöbisch), Royal Theatre, Stockholm

1913 Satyr in *Cléopâtre* (Fokine), Royal Theatre, Stockholm

1914 Eusebius in *Carnaval* (Fokine), Royal Theatre, Stockholm

1915 Dancer in *Dance Pictures* (divertissement; Gunhild Rosen), Royal Theatre, Stockholm

1920 Dancer (cr) in *Sculpture nègre* (also chor.), Börlin solo concert, Paris
Principal dancer (cr) in *Iberia* (also chor.), Ballets Suédois, Paris
Dancer (cr) in *Jeux* (also chor.), Ballets Suédois, Paris
Country Youth (cr) in *Nuit de Saint-Jean*, (also chor.), Ballets Suédois, Paris
The Prince (cr) in *Maison de fous* (also chor.), Ballets Suédois, Paris
Minuet and Rigaudon (cr) in *Le Tombeau de Couperin* (also chor.), Ballets Suédois, Paris
Dervish (cr) in *Derviches* (also chor.), Ballets Suédois, Paris
Bridegroom (cr) in *Les Vierges folles* (also chor.), Ballets Suédois, Paris
The Young Man (cr) in *El Greco* (also chor.), Ballets Suédois, Paris

1921 Man in (cr) *L'Homme et son désir* (also chor.), Ballets Suédois, Paris
Principal dancer (cr) in *Dansgille* (also chor.), Ballets Suédois, tour

1922 Madman (cr) in *Skating Rink* (also chor.), Ballets Suédois, Paris

1923 The Birdseller (cr) in *Marchand d'oiseaux* (also chor.), Ballets Suédois, Paris
Man (cr) in *La Création du monde* (also chor.), Ballets Suédois, Paris
Immigrant (cr) in *Within the Quota* (also chor.), Ballets Suédois, Paris

1924 Khedad (cr) in *Le Roseau* (also chor.), Ballets Suédois, Paris
Youth (cr) in *La Jarre* (also chor.), Ballets Suédois, Paris
A Man (cr) in *Relâche* (also chor.), Ballets Suédois, Paris

## WORKS

1920 *Sculpture nègre* (mus. Poulenc), Börlin solo concert, Paris
*Iberia* (mus. Albéniz), Ballets Suédois, Paris
*Jeux* (mus. Debussy), Ballets Suédois, Paris
*La Nuit de Saint Jean* (mus. Alfvén), Ballets Suédois, Paris
*Maison de fous* (mus. Dahl), Ballets Suédois, Paris
*Le Tombeau de Couperin* (mus. Ravel), Ballets Suédois, Paris
*El Greco* (mus. Inghelbrecht), Ballets Suédois, Paris
*Derviches* (mus. Glazunov), Ballets Suédois, Paris
*Les Vierges folles* (mus. Atterberg), Ballets Suédois, Paris
*Pas de deux* (mus. Chopin), Ballets Suédois, Paris

1921 *La Boite à Joujoux* (mus. Debussy), Ballets Suédois, Paris
*L'Homme et son désir* (mus. Milhaud), Ballets Suédois, Paris
*Les Mariés de la Tour Eiffel* (mus. Tailleferre, Auric, Honegger, Milhaud, Poulenc), Ballets Suédois, Paris
*Dansgille* (also called *Danses villageoises*; mus. trad. Swedish music, arranged Bigot), Ballets Suédois, tour

1922 *Skating Rink* (mus. Honegger), Ballets Suédois, Paris

1923 *Offerlunden* (*Sacred Grove*, pantomime staged Börlin; mus. Haquinius), Ballets Suédois, Paris
*Marchand d'oiseaux* (mus. Tailleferre), Ballets Suédois, Paris
*La Creation du monde* (mus. Milhaud), Ballets Suédois, Paris
*Within the Quota* (mus. Cole Porter), Ballets Suédois, Paris

1924 *Le Roseau* (mus. Lazarus), Ballets Suédois, Paris
*Le Porcher* (mus. traditional, orchestrated Ferroud), Ballets Suédois
*Le Tournoi singulier* (mus. Roland-Manuel), Ballets Suédois
*La Jarre* (after *La Giarra*, by Pirandello; mus. Casella), Ballets Suédois, Paris
*Relâche* (mus. Satie), Ballets Suédois, Paris

**Jean Börlin in "Danse Arabe", a recital solo, c.1922**

1929 *Cercle éternel* (recital; mus. Tansman), Théâtre des Champs-Élysées, Paris

## PUBLICATIONS

De Maré, Rolf (ed.), *Les Ballets Suédois dans l'art contemporain*, Paris, 1931
Beaumont, Cyril, *Complete Book of Ballets*, revised edition, London, 1951
Institute Suédois, *Cinquantenaire des Ballets Suédois*, exhibition catalogue, Stockholm, 1970
Banes, Sally, "An Introduction to the Ballets Suédois", *Ballet Review* (New York), vol. 7, nos. 2–3, 1978–79
Häger, Bengt, *Ballets Suédois*, translated by Ruth Sharman, London, 1990

* * *

Jean Börlin, a Swedish ballet dancer who studied Bournonville and Italian techniques before training with Mikhail Fokine in Stockholm and Copenhagen, was the principal dancer and choreographer for the Ballets Suédois. In that capacity he collaborated with some of the foremost composers and artists of his time—including Erik Satie, Jean Cocteau, Francis Picabia, Fernand Leger, and Paul Claudel—to create some of the most innovative ballets of the early twentieth century.

Rolf de Maré, the founder of the Ballets Suédois, hired Börlin in 1920 and based his company in Paris. Apart from de Maré, Börlin, and a few dancers from the Stockholm Royal Opera, there was not much else that was Swedish about the Ballets Suédois. Originally de Maré had wanted to use the company as a vehicle for translating Swedish folk themes into modern theatre, but the Ballets Suédois made a name for itself with avant-garde ballets combining the choreography of Jean Börlin with the work of French librettists, composers, and painters.

With its first Paris season in 1920, the Ballets Suédois established itself as the artistic successor to Diaghilev's declining Ballets Russes. Comparisons of Börlin to Vaslav Nijinsky, the principal dancer of the Ballets Russes, were inevitable. In fact, Paul Claudel conceived *L'Homme et son désir* in 1917 as a vehicle for Nijinsky, who, it turned out, could not perform the role because of his disintegrating mental health. In 1921, after seeing Jean Börlin and the Ballets Suédois, Claudel and his collaborators offered the ballet to the new company. Whether or not Börlin's dancing was like Nijinsky's, his choreography was certainly similar to Fokine's.

Börlin's choreography adhered closely to the "five principles" Fokine had formulated for the Ballets Russes: movement corresponded to subject matter, period, and musical style; dance and gesture advanced dramatic action; dancers' entire bodies were used; the corps de ballet was integral to the ballet rather than just ornamental; and the dance was combined with other arts. Börlin's movement was described by some critics as very much like pantomime and not very "dancey", reflecting his emphasis on expression rather than a traditional dance vocabulary. His use of popular dances such as the shimmy and the foxtrot in *Within The Quota*, to music by Cole Porter, is an example of movement corresponding to subject matter, period, and musical style.

After staging their most ambitious piece, *Relâche*, in 1924, de Maré and Börlin decided to disband the Ballets Suédois. Börlin gave recitals in South America and two more concerts in Paris before he died in New York at the age of 37.

—Claudia B. Stone

---

**BOROVANSKY, Edouard** (Eduard)
Czechoslovakian/Australian dancer, choreographer, teacher, and ballet director. Born Eduard Josef Screcek in Přerov, Moravia, 2 February 1902. Studied ballet privately in Prague, and also as a member of Olomouc Opera Company, and with Augustin Berger, National Theatre, Prague; later studied with Olga Preobrazhenska and Lubov Egorova, Paris. Married dancer Xenia Nikolaeva Smirnova, 1933. Singer and dancer, becoming solo dancer, Olomouc Opera Company, 1921–23; member of corps de ballet, National Theatre, Prague, 1923–25; dancer (performing as Borowanski), becoming principal mime-dancer, Anna Pavlova company, 1926–31, briefly teaching in Prague, 1931; member of Woizikowsky company, Opéra-Comique, Paris, 1934; soloist (performing as Edouard Borovansky), Ballets Russes de Monte Carlo (later de Basil's Ballets Russes and Covent Garden Russian Ballet), 1932–39, noted particularly for character roles; also responsible for training supernumeraries for Ballets Russes; left company during Australian tour, 1939: founder, with wife Xenia, Academy of Russian Ballet, Melbourne, Australia, 1939; founder and director of student company, Borovansky Australian Ballet (Borovansky Ballet), supported by Melbourne Ballet Club from 1940, performing its first professional season, 1944, and undergoing numerous disbandings and re-organizations; also choreographer, mostly of small chamber pieces for his companies; left behind large repertoire and company, directed by Peggy van Praagh after his death: many dancers incorporated into Australian Ballet, 1962. Died in Sydney, 18 December, 1959.

## ROLES

1933 The Strong Man (Athlete) (cr) in *Le Beau Danube* (new version; Massine), Ballets Russes de Monte Carlo, Monte Carlo
A Triton, A Bather, The Maharajah, The Old Gentleman (cr) in *Beach* (Massine), Ballets Russes de Monte Carlo, Monte Carlo
Fabrizio (cr) in *Scuola di Ballo* (Massine), Ballets Russes de Monte Carlo, Monte Carlo
First Movement (cr) in *Choreartium* (Massine), Ballets Russes de Monte Carlo, London
Pierrot in *Le Carnaval* (Fokine), Ballets Russes de Monte Carlo, London
1934 A Mexican, A Capitalist (cr) in *Union Pacific* (Massine), de Basil's Ballets Russes, Philadelphia
Shopkeeper's Assistant in *La Boutique fantasque* (Massine), de Basil's Ballets Russes, London
1935 The King (cr) in *Les Cent Baisers* (Nijinska), de Basil's Ballets Russes, London
1936 Passion, An Executioner, A Devil (cr) in *Symphonie fantastique* (Massine), de Basil's Ballets Russes, London
1937 Girolamo (cr) in *Francesca da Rimini* (Lichine), de Basil's Ballets Russes, London
Polkan (cr) in *Le Coq d'or* (Fokine), de Basil's Ballets Russes, London
The Painter (cr) in *Le Lion amoureux* (Lichine), de Basil's Ballets Russes, London
1943 Officer (cr) in *Capriccio Italien* (also chor.), Borovansky Ballet, Melbourne

**Other roles include:** for National Theatre, Prague—Pas de trois in *Aida* (opera; mus. Verdi), a cavalier in *The Sleeping Beauty* (after Petipa), Russian Dance in *The Nutcracker* (after Ivanov), von Rothbart in *Swan Lake* (after Petipa, Ivanov); for the

Pavlova company—Archaeologist's Assistant in *The Romance of a Mummy* (Clustine, Novikov), Pierrot in *The Coquetries of Columbine* (Legat), pas de deux in *Champions*, Enrique (Hilarion) in *Giselle* (after Petipa, Coralli, Perrot); for de Basil's Ballets Russes—a Tailor in *La Concurrence* (Balanchine), Chief Eunuch in *Schéhérazade* (Fokine), King Dodon in *Le Coq d'or* (Fokine).

## WORKS

1939 *Étude* (mus. Debussy), Students of the Academy of Russian Ballet, Melbourne
1940 *Australia* (mus. Nedbal), Students of the Academy of Russian Ballet, Cavalcade of Empire Pageant, Melbourne
*Vltava* (mus. Smetana), Borovansky Australian Ballet, Melbourne
*L'Amour ridicule* (mus. Albéniz), Borovansky Australian Ballet, Melbourne
1941 *Fantasy on Grieg's Concerto in A Minor* (mus. Grieg), Borovansky Australian Ballet, Melbourne
1943 *Capriccio Italien* (mus. Tchaikovsky), Borovansky Ballet, Melbourne
1946 *Terra Australis* (mus. E. Rofe), Borovansky Ballet
Dances in *Gay Rosalinda* (operetta; mus. J. Strauss), Borovansky Ballet, Melbourne (including divertissement *Minuit à bal*, also staged as independent work)
1949 *The Black Swan* (mus. Sibelius), Borovansky Educational Ballet Club, Melbourne (staged for Borovansky Ballet, 1951)
1951 *The Outlaw* (mus. Williams), Borovansky Ballet

Also staged:
1939 *Petite Mozartiana* (after Pavlova; mus. Mozart), Students of Academy of Russian Ballet, Melbourne
1940 *Autumn Leaves* (after Pavlova; mus. Chopin), Borovansky Australian Ballet, Melbourne
1944 *Giselle* (after Petipa, Coralli, Perrot), Borovansky Ballet, Adelaide

**Other works include:** Stagings of *La Boutique fantasque* (after Massine; mus. Rossini), *Petrushka* (after Fokine; mus. Stravinsky), *Coppélia* (two-act version, after Petipa; mus. Delibes).

## PUBLICATIONS

By Borovansky:
"Australian Ballets", *Opera, Ballet, Music Hall in the World* (Paris), no.2, Winter 1952
"The Borovansky Ballet: Australia", *Ballet Annual 8*, London, 1953

About Borovansky:
"An Australian Ballet", *Dancing Times* (London), November 1944
Lawrence, Margaret, "Ballet in Australia", *Dancing Times* (London), December 1946
MacGeorge, Norman, *The Borovansky Ballet in Australia and New Zealand*, Melbourne, 1946
O'Brien, John, "Who is Borovansky?", *Ballet Today* (London), February 1955
Salter, Frank, *Borovansky: The Man Who Made Australian Ballet*, Sydney, 1980
Pask, Edward H., *Ballet in Australia: The Second Act 1940–1980*, Melbourne, 1982
García-Márquez, Vicente, *The Ballets Russes*, New York, 1990

The decision by Edouard Borovansky to remain in Australia in 1939 at the conclusion of a tour with the Ballets Russes was courageous. His reasons for doing so were twofold; he was realistic enough to perceive that war was rapidly approaching in Europe, and Australia seemed a safe distance away from such conflict. He was also idealistic and driven by the ambition of forming an Australian ballet company. This ambition, at that time in history, was almost as outlandish as putting men on the moon.

He had a priceless asset in his wife, Xenia, who was a fine, experienced ballet teacher, and when the Borovanskys opened their Academy of Russian Ballet in Melbourne in May 1939, it was Xenia Borovansky who was in charge of classical training. Borovansky himself gave character dance classes. As well as her teaching skill, Xenia Borovansky possessed a calm, matter-of-fact personality which was an important balance for her husband's volatile moods.

If Xenia Borovansky was the anchor, Borovansky was the flier. His aims were high—he wanted not just to have the best ballet school in Australia, but to begin his Australian ballet company as soon as possible. The school quickly became a magnet for any promising young dancers who had managed to acquire a reasonable basic training (which was not easy then, as good teachers in Australia had been few and far between). Also, many young people who had become enthusiastic about ballet after seeing the Ballets Russes were attracted to the Borovansky school, as it represented a link with the companies they so much admired.

Borovansky's personality was as alien to his students as was his broken English. He could rage and deride, but also be amusing and charming. His complex character combined daring, stubborn determination, vision, autocracy, idealism, and genuine enthusiasm—and his students were swept along with him, as they too became convinced that they could be the nucleus of the first Australian ballet company.

To underline the difficulty of his task, it should be pointed out that until then Australians suffered from what is still called "cultural cringe", and were convinced that only imported performing artists were of any quality. Native-born Australians were only considered worth seeing if they had achieved fame "overseas".

Nevertheless, the high standard of even the earliest, most tentative public performances by Borovansky's students was publicly noted. From the outset Borovansky was completely single-minded about his students; he was not interested simply in having a school full of well-trained dancers, but in training performers as well.

In 1942 he converted one of his studios into a tiny performing area, with a stage and rostra for seating. Regular Sunday night performances were given here, which became a focal point for Melbourne dance-lovers. At this time Borovansky's idealism was at its height and he encouraged his students to create original choreography and young artists to try their hands at stage design. Everything seemed possible for this visionary man and his ambitious young dancers.

Over the next couple of years, the Borovansky Australian Ballet Company gave several public seasons in Melbourne theatres and the unbelievable happened. The public packed the theatres and clamoured for more. This was partly due to the high standard of performance Borovansky was providing, but it was also very largely due to the fact that World War II was preventing any visits by touring companies. Ballet had become very popular as a result of the Ballets Russes tours; the public craved such entertainment and was pleasantly surprised to discover that a local company could provide an acceptable substitute.

J. C. Williamson Theatres Limited owned nearly all the

theatres in Australia and New Zealand. To succeed in any theatrical venture it was essential to gain their cooperation. In peace-time, Williamson's imported most of its artists, but this was not possible in war-time and, having observed the public interest in Borovansky's ballet company, it offered to contract the company to tour nationally under Williamson's auspices. Thus in 1944, only five years after opening his studio, Borovansky and his Australian Ballet Company became professional.

In those early years the company performed original ballets by several talented company members and Borovansky created many himself. He was not a great choreographer but he could put together acceptable ballets, and if the choreography was somewhat derivative few people noticed.

From the beginning of his association with Williamson's, Borovansky had to learn to compromise artistically and forget some of his idealism. Being commercially minded, the management wanted productions of proven successes, not experimentation. The company already performed Fokine's *Les Sylphides* and among ballets added to the repertoire were *Giselle*, *Le Beau Danube*, *Schéhérazade*, Act II of *Swan Lake*, and *Coppélia*. In the 1950s the Borovansky Ballet performed the full *Sleeping Beauty*, *Swan Lake*, and *Nutcracker* to great public acclaim.

Having spent several years with Anna Pavlova's company, Borovansky knew about artistic compromise in a repertoire aimed at surefire success and, if this did not quite follow his original ideals for the company, he was sufficiently realistic to accept the fact that he had to produce what the management wanted or not perform at all.

During his twenty years in Australia, Borovansky produced many fine dancers, despite his reputation amongst them as a "monster". In his book *Borovansky, The Man who made Australian Ballet*, Frank Salter writes "but he was a monster who encouraged his dancers into becoming brilliant performers, who bullied them into finding their own identities as artists, and who terrified them into becoming major personalities in the Australian theatre".

Between 1944 and 1959 the Borovansky Ballet had an erratic career, touring Australia and New Zealand for a couple of years, then being disbanded by the management. They would reform after about twelve months and follow the same procedure. This was, of course, unsatisfactory for the dancers and not what Borovansky had wanted for his company. The fact that all their seasons were hugely successful helped sugar the pill, but as time wore on his health deteriorated. He suffered a heart attack and died in December 1959, only a few weeks after launching yet another version of his company.

Perhaps at that time, Borovansky's days as the linchpin of Australian ballet were numbered. Moves were already afoot to seek government backing for a national ballet company, and his autocratic style would have been at odds with such things as boards of directors. It should never be forgotten, however, that it was Edouard Borovansky's mixture of single-minded determination, enthusiasm, vision, and skill that made the impossible possible. He was the right man, in the right place, at the right time.

When the Australian Ballet made its début in 1962, its first stars—Kathleen Gorham, Marilyn Jones, and Garth Welch—were Borovansky's last stars. It inherited about half of Borovansky's dancers, some key staff, and an established touring structure from the Borovansky Ballet, plus an audience whom Borovansky had convinced that Australian ballet and its dancers were equal to any.

—Patricia Laughlin

---

**BORTOLUZZI, Paolo**

Italian dancer and ballet director. Born in Genoa, 17 May 1938. Studied with Ugo Dell'Ara in Genoa; later studied with Victor Gsovsky, Asaf Messerer, and Maurice Béjart in Brussels. Married dancer Jaleh Kerendi, 1970: 2 children, Vanessa and Alexis. Début, Nervi Festival, 1957; dancer, Ugo Dell'Ara's Ballet Italien, 1957–60; appeared with Léonide Massine's Balletto Europeo, 1960; soloist, soon becoming principal dancer, (Béjart's) Ballet du XXe Siècle, 1960–73; guest artist, American Ballet Theatre, New York, from 1972; also appeared as guest artist with La Scala, Milan, Tokyo Ballet, German Opera on the Rhine, Düsseldorf, Royal Ballet in London, Rome Opera, San Francisco Ballet, and Ballet de Marseille; appeared on films and television, including in Cologne television films *Nomos Alpha* (1971), *Portrait: Paolo Bortoluzzi* (1971), *Apollo* (1974), *Moment of Memory* (1975); ballet director, Milan, 1978, Rome Opera, and German Opera on the Rhine, Düsseldorf, 1984–90, Grand Theatre, Bordeaux, from 1990; also teacher: founder and director, with wife Jaleh Kerendi, of ballet school in Turin, from 1973. Recipient: Nijinsky Prize, Paris; Prix de la Critique, Munich.

**ROLES**

1957 Principal dancer (cr) in *Ouverture per le Regine* (Dell'Ara), Nervi Festival

1958 Don Juan (cr) in *Le Dernier Don Juan* (Dell'Ara), Ballet Italien, Milan

**Paolo Bortoluzzi in Maurice Béjart's *L'Oiseau de feu*, c.1970**

Principal dancer (cr) in *Lune de miel* (Dell'Ara), Ballet Italien, Milan
Franz in *Coppélia* (Novaro), Teatro Massimo, Catania
1960 Principal dancer (cr) in *La Commedia umana* (Massine), Balletto Europeo, Nervi Festival, Genoa
Principal dancer in *Le Bal des voleurs* (Massine), Balletto Europeo, Nervi Festival, Edinburgh
Principal dancer in *Choreartium* (revival; Massine), Balletto Europeo, Nervi Festival, Edinburgh
Soloist (cr) in *Bolero* (Béjart), Ballet du XXe Siècle, Brussels
1961 Principal dancer in *Temps* (part of *Suite Viennoise*; Béjart), Ballet du XXe Siècle, Brussels
Principal dancer (cr) in *Étude* (pas de deux, part of *Divertimento*; Béjart), Ballet du XXe Siècle, Brussels
Principal dancer (cr) in *La Leçon de danse* (Messerer), Gala Performance, Brussels
The Prince in *The Sleeping Beauty* (pas de deux; Petipa), Gala Performance, Brussels
Principal dancer (cr) in *Le Chevalier romain et la dame espagnole* (Béjart), Ballet du XXe Siècle, Venice
Solo variation (cr) in *Les Etapes* (Belova), Belgian television
1963 Apollo in *Marsia* (Milloss), Gala performance, Brussels
Solo variation (cr) in *Fanfares* (new version; Béjart), Ballet du XXe Siècle, Baalbeck
The Poet in *Les Demoiselles de la nuit* (Petit), Ballet of La Scala, Milan
Chout in *Il Buffone* (Novaro), Ballet of La Scala, Milan
1964 Prince Siegfried in *Swan Lake* (Beriozoff after Petipa, Ivanov), Ballet of La Scala, Milan
Principal dancer (cr) in *Passacaglia* (Sparemblek), Ballet du XXe Siècle, Nervi
Principal dancer (cr) in *Ninth Symphony* (Béjart), Ballet du XXe Siècle, Brussels
1965 Principal dancer (cr) in *Mathilde* (Béjart), Ballet du XXe Siècle, Brussels
Le Cygne (cr) in *Les Oiseaux* (Béjart), Ballet du XXe Siècle, Brussels
Solo variation (cr) in *L'Art de la barre* (part of *Prospective*; Béjart), Ballet du XXe Siècle, Brussels
Principal swan (cr) in *Le Cygne* (part of *Prospective*; Béjart), Ballet du XXe Siècle, Brussels
1966 Principal dancer (cr) in *String Quartet no. 1* (Walter), German Opera on the Rhine, Düsseldorf
Creature (cr) in *The Creatures of Prometheus* (Walter), German Opera on the Rhine, Düsseldorf
Romeo (cr) in *Romeo et Juliette* (Béjart), Ballet du XXe Siècle, Brussels
1967 Principal dancer (cr) in *Messe pour le temps présent* (Béjart), Ballet du XXe Siècle, Avignon
Prince in *Cinderella* (Walter), German Opera on the Rhine, Düsseldorf
1968 Principal dancer (cr) in *Ni Fleurs ni couronnes* (Béjart), Ballet du XXe Siècle, Grenoble
Title role (cr) in *Baudelaire* (Béjart), Ballet du XXe Siècle, Grenoble
Principal dancer (cr) in *Cantates, Bhakti* (parts of *A la récherche de ...*; Béjart), Ballet du XXe Siècle, Avignon
1969 Principal dancer (cr) in *Nomos Alpha* (solo; Béjart), Ballet du XXe Siècle, Royan
Principal dancer (cr) in *Suite no. 1 for Violoncello* (Walter), German Opera on the Rhine, Düsseldorf
1971 Principal dancer (cr) in *Songs of a Wayfarer* (Béjart), Ballet du XXe Siècle, Brussels
The Rose (cr) in *Nijinsky, clown de dieu* (Béjart), Ballet du XXe Siècle, Brussels
1972 Title role in *Le Spectre de la rose* (after Fokine), American Ballet Theatre
Principal dancer in *Variations for Four* (Dolin), American Ballet Theatre
1973 Daphnis (cr) in *Daphnis and Chloë* (Walter), German Opera on the Rhine, Düsseldorf
The Man (cr) in *Peraspera* (Milloss), Vienna State Opera Ballet, Vienna
1974 Prince (cr) in *The Sleeping Beauty* (new version; Walter after Petipa), German Opera on the Rhine, Düsseldorf
Principal dancer (cr) in *Relazioni fragili* (Milloss), Vienna State Opera Ballet, Vienna

**Other roles include:** Principal dancer in *Fantasie concertante* (Charrat), Can-Can dancer in *La Boutique fantasque* (Massine), Basil in *Don Quixote Pas de deux* (after Petipa), principal dancer in *Les Sylphides* (Fokine), Albrecht in *Giselle* (after Petipa, Coralli, Perrot), Prince in *The Nutcracker* (after Ivanov), title role in *Orfée* (Béjart), Valet in *Jeu de cartes* (Charrat), the Duke in *Pulcinella* (Massine).

## WORKS

1961 *Suite en si mineur* (mus. Bach), Ballet du XXe Siècle, Brussels
1962 *Suite en ré majeur* (mus. Bach), Ballet du XXe Siècle, Brussels
*Cinq Etudes* (mus. Debussy)
1963 *Introduction et allegro* (mus. Ravel), Ballet du XXe Siècle, Brussels
1964 *Ricercare* (pas de deux; mus. Weber), Ballet du XXe Siècle, Brussels
1965 *La Valse* (mus. Ravel), Ballet du XXe Siècle, Brussels (restaged German Opera on the Rhine, Düsseldorf, 1969)
*Siegfried Idyll* (part II of Béjart's *Wagner, ou l'amour fou*; mus. Wagner), Ballet du XXe Siècle, Brussels
1968 *L'Orage* (pas de deux; mus. Rossini), Ballet du XXe Siècle, Brussels
1978 *Les nuits d'été* (mus. Berlioz), Teatro Comunale, Florence
1980 *Cinderella* (mus. Prokofiev), Ballet of La Scala, Milan
*I Vespri Siciliani* (mus. Verdi), Teatro Comunale, Florence
1981 *Picasso* (mus. Xenakis, Hindemith, Ligeti), La Scala, Milan
1985 *Clair de lune* (mus. Debussy), Torino Danza, Turin
*Dialogue* (mus. Grieg), German Opera on the Rhine, Düsseldorf
1988 *Face à face* (mus. Satie), Torino Danza, Turin
1989 *Butterfly* (mus. Puccini, Philip Glass), Torino Danza, Turin
1990 *... E cosi via* (mus. Charpentier), La Scala, Milan
1991 *Les Saisons* (mus. Vivaldi), Grand Theatre, Bordeaux
*Strauss* (mus. Strauss), Grand Theatre, Bordeaux
1992 *Beauty and the Beast* (mus. Büchner), Grand Theatre, Bordeaux

## PUBLICATIONS

About Bortoluzzi:

Herf, Estelle, "The Story of Paolo Bortoluzzi", *Ballet Today* (London), September–October 1969

Rossel, L., "Paolo Bortoluzzi", *Les Saisons de la danse* (Paris), August 1969
Niehaus, Max, *Ballet Faszination*, Munich 1972
*Paolo Bortoluzzi*, Paris, 1979

* * *

Although Paolo Bortoluzzi has had a long and varied career, he is most likely to be remembered for the roles made for him by Maurice Béjart, when the dancer was one of the most prominent leading lights of the company then known as the Ballet du XXe Siècle. However, his talents had been clearly discernible before then, first in his native Genoa, and in the ill-starred company Léonide Massine put together for the 1960 festival at nearby Nervi, and then in Milan. When he appeared with Carla Fracci in Roland Petit's cat ballet, *Les Demoiselles de la nuit*, at La Scala in 1963, the elegance of his style aroused immediate notice. Not having the ideal build for a danseur noble, being too chunky around the midriff, Bortoluzzi nevertheless appeared with success in Italy in such roles as Siegfried and Albrecht.

He was seen at his best, though, in roles made to measure for him by Béjart, such as the pseudo-Indian *Bhakti* (the pas de deux from the last section of which has become popular gala fare), as the "other half" to Rudolf Nureyev in the Mahler duo, *Songs of a Wayfarer*, and in the fearsomely taxing virtuoso solo to an ear-troubling accompaniment by Xenakis, *Nomos Alpha*. The Mahler piece, which has proved an outstandingly durable item in the international repertory, has changed its identity somewhat since the early performances, when according to Béjart's initial programme note the two roles represented the two halves of the contradictory personality of a single individual. Since it was impossible to express this concept clearly in dance, the choreographer modified his commentary in a later note. While in later years, with other companions, Nureyev tended to seem the more vulnerable member of the rather nebulous duo, this was not so in the original cast, partly because of Bortoluzzi's slighter figure and partly because Nureyev at that time invariably dominated a stage.

While that was a role requiring a classical smoothness of execution, *Nomos Alpha* was anti-classical in nearly every way, although probably only a classical virtuoso could have performed it. As well as virtuosity, it demanded exceptional stamina, for in its 20 minutes or so, involving a sequence of mood-changes, Bortoluzzi was required to use just about every muscle in his body, writhing, doubling himself up, and constantly changing facial expression as well, from quirkily humorous to whimsical, to gleeful, perturbed, or wrathful.

After Bortoluzzi left the Béjart company, the pas de deux from *Bhakti* was danced by many others, and his role in Romeo and Juliet, as in many other ballets (as well as the Mahler duo), were taken over by his successors; but *Nomos Alpha* remained his alone, for it depended on his physique and personality. It is therefore no longer performed.

In the 1960s, amid guest appearances with La Scala in Milan and Erich Walter's company at Düsseldorf, Bortoluzzi launched himself as a choreographer, an occupation in which he gradually became more active as he performed less. A drifting Berlioz pas de deux for himself and Luciana Savignano cannot be claimed to have revealed any conspicuous choreographic talent, but his name sufficed for the theatre management. Like several other Italian male dancers past their prime, Bortoluzzi gradually achieved a workmanlike mastery of his means, while never becoming a choreographer of real creative talent. A certain musical insensitivity should perhaps be ascribed to the years spent with Béjart, to whom the movements devised by Bortoluzzi also frequently owe a debt.

Bortoluzzi's partnership with Savignano continued with *Cinderella*, which was dominated by Beni Montresor's scenery, and which largely ignored the romantic element in Prokofiev's music. The couple continued to appear together over several years. A ballet called *Butterfly*, which he made for Savignano and the company of the Teatro Nuovo in Turin, toured the country widely in 1989 and 1990. Using—indeed exploiting—extracts from the recording of *Madama Butterfly* that has Maria Callas singing the title role, with interpolations by Philip Glass, it earned many plaudits for Savignano, despite the rather muddled treatment. In April 1990, Bortoluzzi made and appeared in another piece for the Scala Ballet, with the odd title of . . . *E così via* (*And so on*), but it added nothing to his reputation.

Once Bortoluzzi had left the Brussels company, it was to Germany that he turned increasingly. At the invitation of Eric Walter, who created roles for him, he was invited to the German Opera on the Rhine both to dance and to choreograph, and on Walter's death he took over as director of the company. Even if his choreography was not always highly esteemed by the more knowledgeable section of the public, he kept the company going successfully until 1990, when—at the time of a directors' merry-go-round—he was invited to take over the ballet company of the Grand Théâtre in Bordeaux, thus opening the way to a new adventure, while enabling him to return to the language of his most successful years.

His reputation as a dancer will, at all events, survive; that as a ballet-master and choreographer is less certain.

—Freda Pitt

---

## LE BOURGEOIS GENTILHOMME

**Choreography:** Pierre Beauchamps
**Music:** Jean Baptiste Lully
**Design:** Carlo Vigarani (scenery and costumes)
**Libretto:** Molière
**First Production:** Chambord, 14 October 1670

**Other productions include:** Court revival (chor. Louis Pécour), with Claude Ballon and Mlle. La Fontaine; 1691.

**Other choreographic treatments of story:** George Balanchine (Monte Carlo, 1932; New York, 1944 and 1979), Antony Tudor (Manchester, 1968).

### PUBLICATIONS

Christout, Marie-Françoise, *Le Ballet de Cour de Louis XIV 1643–1672*, Paris, 1967
Mongrédien, G., "Molière et Lulli", *Revue du XVIIe siècle*, 98–9, 1973
Anthony, J., *French Baroque Music from Beaujoyeulx to Rameau*, London, 1972; revised edition, 1978
Molière, *Oeuvres Complètes*, edited by Georges Mongrédien, vol. 4, Paris, 1979
McBride, Robert, "The Triumph of Ballet in *Le Bourgeois Gentilhomme*", *Form and Meaning: Aesthetic Coherence in Seventeenth-century French Drama*, Amersham, 1982
Turnbull, M., "Louis XIV and Lully: The Early Years", *Newsletter of the Society for Seventeenth-century French Studies*, 1983

McBride, Robert, "Ballet: A Neglected Key to Molière's Theatre", *Dance Research* (London), Spring 1984

Abraham, Claude, "Farce and Ballet: *Le Bourgeois Gentilhomme* Revisited", *Cahiers de dix-septième* (Paris), vol. 2, no. 1, 1988

* * *

Performed in 1670 at Chambord before the King and court, *Le Bourgeoise gentilhomme* is Molière's most famous comedy-ballet with music by Jean-Baptiste Lully, choreography by Pierre Beauchamps, and décor by Vigarani. The Turkish costumes were supervised by d'Arvieux, who also helped Molière with the Turkish mascarade. He had recently visited the Orient and had amused the Court with tales of his travels and strange Turkish customs.

The play is in five acts, and is a burlesque parody of the pretentious seventeenth-century social climbers who bought offices conferring nobility or land from impoverished nobles, often taking their names as well. The plot revolves around Monsieur Jourdain, played by Molière, an ignorant, gullible, and rich bourgeois who wishes to pass himself off as a gentleman by acquiring gentlemanly accomplishments, clothes, and friends. A summary of the plot will show how closely comedy, song, music, and dance are interwoven.

The first two acts show Jourdain attempting to "improve" himself. At the same time the greed, vanity, and pretentiousness of those he hires are ridiculed. Act I opens with the music and dancing masters and their pupils who perform a song and demonstrate dance steps. In Act II Jourdain tries to learn a minuet and a reverence to impress the marquise Dorimène, with whom he is infatuated. The fencing master arrives to give his lesson. All three masters begin quarrelling over the merits of their respective arts, and are chased away by the philosophy master who gives a lesson in vowel pronunciation. The tailor arrives and his four assistants ceremoniously attire Jourdain in his extravagant new clothes and wig. He pays them handsomely and they dance for joy.

In Act III we meet the count Dorante, Dorimène's suitor, who borrows money from Jourdain and pretends to give Jourdain's gifts to Dorimène on Jourdain's behalf. Madame Jourdain, a down-to-earth bourgeoise, wishes her daughter Lucile to marry Cléonte; Nicole, her lively maid, wishes to marry Cléonte's quick-witted manservant, Covielle. Jourdain refuses his daughter's hand to Cléonte since he has high hopes of his daughter becoming a marquise. Covielle thinks up a plan to overcome the opposition. The scene ends with Jourdain preparing a lavish dinner for Dorante and Dorimène (having dispatched his wife to her sister). Six cooks dance the third interlude, then bring on a table covered with dishes.

Act IV opens with the dinner party during which is sung the famous "Chanson à Boire", Lully's favourite song. The party is brusquely ended by the return of a furious Madame Jourdain. The highlight of the act and of the whole comedy-ballet is the arrival of Cléonte, disguised as the son of the Turkish Sultan who wishes to marry Lucile. Jourdain has the title of *Mamamouchi* conferred on him by the Mufti, danced by Lully, and accompanied by four Dervishes, six Turkish dancers, and six musicians playing Turkish instruments. The mascarade is a fantastic and hilarious extravaganza.

In the final act, Dorante, who has been party to the trick, asks Dorimène to join in the deception. She tells him that she will marry him to prevent him from ruining himself by giving her so many expensive gifts. Lucile is summoned and at first refuses to marry the Turk, but on recognizing Cléonte, immediately agrees to obey her father. Madame Jourdain, horrified at the sight of her husband in Turkish robes and turban, is informed of the ruse, and the notary is rapidly summoned to perform a double wedding. Jourdain gives Nicole to Covielle who has acted as interpreter throughout the ceremony. While they wait for the notary—Jourdain still totally unaware of the outrageous trick that has been played on him—they are entertained by the *Ballet des Nations* consisting of six entrées, including Spanish, Italian, and French dances and songs.

*Le Bourgeois Gentilhomme* is a perfect example of the comedy-ballet genre, in which music, song, and dance are integral to the characterization and the development of the plot. If we compare it to Molière's first attempt, *Les Fâcheux*, we can see how brilliantly he has developed the genre. Music and dance are as important as the play; indeed it was even described as a ballet composed of six entrées accompanied by comedy (*Gazette de Paris*, 1670), so outstanding was the dancing.

But comedy and ballet were soon to be separated. In 1671 Lully managed to buy the sole rights to produce ballet and opera, so that the dance element in Molière's plays disappeared. However, the basic structure of the comedy-ballet was later to be adopted by the opéra-comique.

—Françoise Carter

---

**BOURMEISTER, Vladimir** *see* **BURMEISTER, Vladimir**

---

**BOURNONVILLE, August**

Danish dancer, choreographer, ballet director, and teacher. Born in Copenhagen, son of dancer (later ballet director) Antoine Bournonville, 21 August 1805. Studied at the school of the Royal Theatre, Copenhagen, pupil of father and Vincenzo Galeotti; later studied with Pierre Gardel and Auguste Vestris, Paris, 1820, 1824–29. Married Charlotte Bournonville. Début as a child, Royal Theatre, Copenhagen, in *Lagertha* (Galeotti), 1813, becoming leading dancer, 1820–23; dancer, Paris Opéra, 1826–28, becoming partner of Marie Taglioni; dancer with French troupe, King's Theatre, London, 1828, also touring in Europe; solo dancer, teacher, and choreographer, Royal Theatre, Copenhagen, from 1828, retiring from the stage, 1848; ballet master, Royal Theatre, Copenhagen, 1830–1877, with only two brief periods abroad: ballet master, Court Opera, Vienna, 1855–56; "intendant", Royal Opera House, Stockholm, 1861–64. Died in Copenhagen, 30 November 1879.

**WORKS**

1829 *Gratiernes Hyldning* (*Acclaim to the Graces*; mus. Caraffa, Gallemberg, Sor), Royal Theatre, Copenhagen

Dances in *Fidelio* (opera; mus. Beethoven), Royal Theatre, Copenhagen

*Søvngaengersken* (*The Night Shadow*, after Aumer's *La Somnambule*; mus. Hérold), Royal Theatre, Copenhagen

*Soldat og Bonde* (*Soldier and Peasant*; mus. Keck), Royal Theatre, Copenhagen

**August Bournonville's *Sylphiden (La Sylphide)*, with Anna Tychsen and Hans Beck, Copenhagen, c.1882**

1830 Dances (with Funck) in *Den Stumme i Portici* (*La Muette de Portici*, opera; mus. Auber), Royal Theatre, Copenhagen

*Hertugen af Vendômes Pager* (*Les Pages du Duc de Vendôme*, after Aumer; mus. Gyrowetz), Royal Theatre, Copenhagen

*Paul og Virginie* (*Paul et Virginie*, after P. Gardel; mus. Kreutzer), Royal Theatre, Copenhagen

1831 Dances in *Bruden* (*La Fiancée*, opera; mus. Auber, Royal Theatre, Copenhagen

*Victors Bryllup; eller, Faedrene-Arnen* (*Victor's Wedding; or, The Ancestral House*; mus. Keck), Royal Theatre, Copenhagen

1832 *Faust* (mus. arranged Keck), Royal Theatre, Copenhagen

Dances in *Ravnen* (*The Raven*, opera; mus. Hartmann), Royal Theatre, Copenhagen

1833 *Veteranen; eller, Det Gaestfrie Tag* (*The Veteran; or, The Hospital House*; mus. Zinck), Royal Theatre, Copenhagen

*Romeo og Giulietta* (*Romeo and Juliet*, after Galeotti; mus. Schall), Royal Theatre, Copenhagen

Pas de deux added to *Carnaval de Venise* (Milon), Royal Theatre, Copenhagen

1834 Dances in *Guerillabanden* (*Les Guérillas*, opera; mus. Bredal), Royal Theatre, Copenhagen

Dances in *Tempelherren og Jodinden* (*Der Templer und die Jüdin*, opera; mus. Marschner), Royal Theatre, Copenhagen

*Nina; eller, Den Vanvittige af Kaerlighed* (*Nina; ou, La Folle par amour*, after Milon; mus. Persuis), Royal Theatre, Copenhagen

Dances in *Klerkevaenget* (*Le Pré aux clercs*, opera; mus. Hérold), Royal Theatre, Copenhagen

1835 *Tyrolerne* (*The Tyrolians*; mus. Frøhlich, Rossini), Royal Theatre, Copenhagen

*Valdemar* (mus. Frøhlich), Royal Theatre, Copenhagen

1836 Dances in *Hans Heiling* (opera; mus. Marschner), Royal Theatre, Copenhagen

*Sylfiden* (*La Sylphide*; mus. Løvenskjold), Royal Theatre, Copenhagen

1837 *Don Quixote ved Camachos Bryllup* (*Don Quixote at Camacho's Wedding*; mus. arranged Zinck), Royal Theatre, Copenhagen

Dances in *Postillonen i Lonjumeau* (*Le Postillon de Lonjumeau*, opera; mus. Adam), Royal Theatre, Copenhagen

1838 *Herthas Offer* (*Hertha's Offering*; mus. arranged Frøhlich), Royal Theatre, Copenhagen

Dances in *Fiorella* (opera; mus. Auber), Royal Theatre, Copenhagen

*Fantasiens ø eller, Fra Kinas Kyst* (*Isle of Phantasy*; mus.

Hartmann, Auber, and others), Royal Theatre, Copenhagen

1839 Dances in *Eventyret paa Maskaraden; eller, Den sorte Domino* (*Le Domino noir*, opera; mus: Auber), Royal Theatre, Copenhagen

*Festen i Albano* (*The Festival in Albano*; mus. Frøhlich), Royal Theatre, Copenhagen

1840 *Faedrelandets Muser* (*National Muses*; mus. Frøhlich, Gade), Royal Theatre, Copenhagen

*Toreadoren* (*The Toreador*; mus. Helsted), Royal Theatre, Copenhagen

1841 Dances in *Brama og Bayadern* (*Le Dieu et la bayadère*, opera; mus. Auber), Royal Theatre, Copenhagen

1842 *Napoli; eller, Fiskeren og hans Brud* (*Naples; or, The Fisherman and his Bride*; mus. Paulli, Helsted, Gade, Lumbye), Royal Theatre, Copenhagen

Dances in *William Tell* (opera; mus. Rossini), Royal Theatre, Copenhagen

*Polka Militaire* (mus. Lumbye), Royal Theatre, Copenhagen

1843 *Erik Menveds Barndom* (*The Childhood of Erik Menved*; mus. Frohlich), Royal Theatre, Copenhagen

Dances in *Kronjuvelerne* (*Les Diamants de la couronne*, opera; mus. Auber), Royal Theatre, Copenhagen

Dances in *Moses* (opera; mus. Rossini), Royal Theatre, Copenhagen

1844 Dances in *Figaros Bryllup* (*Le Nozze di Figaro*, opera; mus. Mozart), Royal Theatre, Copenhagen

Dances in *Hugenotterne* (*Les Huguenots*, opera; mus. Meyerbeer), Royal Theatre, Copenhagen

*Bellman; eller, Polskdansen paa Grönalund* (*Bellan; or, The Dance at Grönalund*; mus. arr. Paulli), Royal Theatre, Copenhagen

*En Børnefest* (*Children's Party*; mus. Paulli), Royal Theatre, Copenhagen

*Hamburger Dans* (pas de deux; mus. Lumbye), Royal Theatre, Copenhagen

1845 *Parisian Polka*, benefit performance, Royal Theatre, Copenhagen

Dances in *Don Juan* (*Don Giovanni*, opera; mus. Mozart), Royal Theatre, Copenhagen

*Kirsten Piil; eller, To Midsommerfester* (*Kirsten Piil; or, Two Mid-Summer Festivals*; mus. Helsted), Royal Theatre, Copenhagen

*Rafael* (mus. Frøhlich), Royal Theatre, Copenhagen

1846 Dances in *Uthal* (opera; mus. Méhul), Royal Theatre, Copenhagen

*Polacca Guerriera* (pas de deux; mus. Lumbye), Royal Theatre, Copenhagen

Dances in *Czaren og Tømmermanden* (*Czaar und Zimmermann*, opera; mus. Lortzing), Royal Theatre, Copenhagen

1847 *Den Nye Penelope* (*The New Penelope; or, Spring Festival in Athens*; mus. Løvenskjold), Royal Theatre, Copenhagen

Dances in *Diamantkorset* (*Das Diamantkreuz*, opera; mus. Salomon), Royal Theatre, Copenhagen

*Maritana* (mus. Lumbye), Royal Theatre, Copenhagen

*Den Hvide Rose; eller, Sommeren i Bretagne* (*The White Rose; or, Summer in Brittany*; mus. Paulli), Royal Theatre, Copenhagen

1848 *Søndags Echo: Amagerdands* (*Echo of Sunday: An Amager Dance*; mus. Paulli), performed by children, Royal Theatre, Copenhagen

Dances in *Federigo* (opera; mus. Rung), Royal Theatre, Copenhagen

Dances in *Dronningens Livgarde* (*Les Mousquetaires de la reine*, opera; mus. Halévy), Royal Theatre, Copenhagen

*Gamle Minder; eller, En Laterna magica* (*Old Memories; or, The Magic Lantern*; mus. arranged Helsted), Royal Theatre, Copenhagen

1849 Dances in *Brylluppet ved Comosoen* (*Wedding at Lake Como*, opera; mus. Glaeser), Royal Theatre, Copenhagen

*Konservatoriet; eller, Et Avisfrieri* (*The Dancing School; or, A Proposal by Advertising*, mus. Paulli), Royal Theatre, Copenhagen

*Pas des trois cousines* (divertissement), Casino Theatre, Copenhagen

*Holmens faste Stok* (*Holmen's Old Guard*, divertissement), Royal Theatre, Copenhagen

*Husardans* (*Hussar Dance*; mus. Lumbye), Rosenborg Gardens, Copenhagen

1850 *De Uimodstaaelige* (*The Irresistibles*; mus. Lumbye), Royal Theatre, Copenhagen

*Psyche* (mus. Helsted), Royal Theatre, Copenhagen

1851 *Kermessen i Brügge; eller, De Tre Gaver* (*The Kermesse in Bruges; or, The Three Gifts*; mus. Paulli), Royal Theatre, Copenhagen

1852 *Zulma; eller, Krystalpaladset* (*Zulma; or, The Crystal Palace in London*; mus. Paulli), Royal Theatre, Copenhagen

1853 Dances in *Nøkken* (*The Nix*, opera; mus. Glaeser), Royal Theatre, Copenhagen

*Brudefaerden i Hardanger* (*Wedding in Hardanger*; mus. traditional, arranged Paulli), Royal Theatre, Copenhagen

1854 *Et Folkesagn* (*A Folk Tale*; mus. Gade, Hartmann), Royal Theatre, Copenhagen

Dances in *Det hemmelige Aegteskab* (*Il Matrimonio segreto*, opera; mus. Cimarosa), Royal Theatre, Copenhagen

*La Ventana* (mus. Lumbye), Royal Theatre, Copenhagen (final seguidilla after P. Taglioni added 1856)

1855 *Abdallah* (mus. Paulli), Royal Theatre, Copenhagen

1856 *Den Alvorlige Pige* (*The Serious Maiden*; mus. Lincke), Royal Theatre, Copenhagen

1857 *I Karpatherne* (*In the Carpathians*; mus. Paulli), Royal Theatre, Copenhagen

Dances in *Lucia di Lammermoor* (opera; mus. Donizetti), Royal Theatre, Copenhagen

1858 Dances in *Liden Kirsten* (opera; mus. Hartmann), Royal Theatre, Copenhagen

*Polketta* (duet; mus. Lumbye), Casino, Copenhagen

*Blomsterfesten i Genzano* (*Flower Festival in Genzano*; mus. Helsted, Paulli), Royal Theatre, Copenhagen

*Fiskerpigerne* (*The Fishergirls*; mus. Lumbye), Casino, Copenhagen

*El Caprichio* (danced in the vaudeville *En Caprice*; mus. Lumbye), Casino, Copenhagen

1859 *Galop Militaire* (duet; mus. Lumbye), Casino, Copenhagen

*Tarantella Napolitana* (duet; mus. Lumbye), Casino, Copenhagen

*La Polonaise* (duet; mus. Lumbye), Casino, Copenhagen

Dances in *Lucrezia Borgia* (opera; mus. Donizetti), Royal Theatre, Copenhagen

*Fjelstuen; eller, Tyve Aar* (*The Mountain Hut; or, Twenty Years*; mus. Winding, Hartmann), Royal Theatre, Copenhagen

1860 *Fjernt fra Danmark; eller, Et Costumebal Ombord* (*Far from Denmark; or, A Costume Ball Onboard*; mus. Glaeser, Lumbye, Lincke), Royal Theatre,

Copenhagen
1861 Dances in *Iphigenia i Aulis* (opera; mus. Gluck), Royal Theatre, Copenhagen
*Valkyrien* (*The Valkyrie*; mus. Hartmann), Royal Theatre, Copenhagen
1865 Gypsy Dance in *Troubadouren* (opera, mus. Verdi; divertissement mus. Lumbye), Royal Theatre, Copenhagen
1866 *Pontemolle: et Kunstnergilde i Rom* (*Pontemolle: An Artist's Party in Rome*; mus. Holm, Lincke, Neruda), Royal Theatre, Copenhagen
1867 Dances in *De Lystige Koner i Windsor* (*The Merry Wives of Windsor*, opera; mus. Nicolai), Royal Theatre, Copenhagen
Dances in *Elverpigen* (*The Elf-Maid*, opera; mus. Hartmann), Royal Theatre, Copenhagen
1868 *Thrymskvilden* (*The Lay of Thrym*; mus. Hartmann), Royal Theatre, Copenhagen
1869 Dances in *Tryllefløjten* (*Die Zauberflöte*, opera; mus. Mozart), Royal Theatre, Copenhagen
Dances in *Paschaens Datter* (*The Pascha's Daughter*, opera; mus. Heise), Royal Theatre, Copenhagen
1870 *Cort Adeler i Venedig* (*Cort Adeler in Venice*; mus. Heise), Royal Theatre, Copenhagen
*Bouquet Royal* (mus. Lumbye), divertissement performed at a "Casino", including *Skandinavisk Quadrille*, later performed at the Royal Theatre, Copenhagen
Dances in *Lohengrin* (opera; mus. Wagner), Royal Theatre, Copenhagen
Dances in *Villars Dragoner* (*Les Dragons de Villars*, opera; mus. Maillard), Royal Theatre, Copenhagen
1871 Dances in *Broncehesten* (*Le Cheval de Bronze*, opera; mus. Auber), Royal Theatre, Copenhagen
*Livjaegerne paa Amager* (*The King's Lifeguards on Amager*; mus. Holm), Royal Theatre, Copenhagen
*Udfaldet i Classens Have* (*The Sally from Classen Have 1807*; tableau), Royal Theatre, Copenhagen
*Et Eventyr i Billeder* (*A Fairy-Tale in Pictures*; mus. Holm), Royal Theatre, Copenhagen
1872 Dances in *Mestersangerne i Nürnberg* (*Die Meistersinger von Nürnberg*, opera; mus. Wagner), Royal Theatre, Copenhagen
1873 Dances in *Robert af Normandiet* (*Robert le diable*, opera; mus. Meyerbeer), Royal Theatre, Copenhagen
Dances in *Korsikaneren* (*The Corsican*, opera; mus. Hartmann), Royal Theatre, Copenhagen
*Mandarinens Døttre* (*The Daughters of the Mandarin*; mus. Holm), Royal Theatre, Copenhagen
1874 *Weyses Minde* (*In Memory of Weyse*; mus. arr. Holm), Royal Theatre, Copenhagen
Dances in *Ifigenia i Tauris* (*Iphigénie en Tauride*, opera; mus. Gluck), Royal Theatre, Copenhagen
*Farvel til det Gamle Theatre* (*Farewell to the Old Theatre*; mus. various), Royal Theatre, Copenhagen
1875 Dances in *Tannhäuser* (opera; mus. Wagner), Royal Theatre, Copenhagen
*Arcona* (mus. Hartmann), Royal Theatre, Copenhagen
*Fra det Forrige Aarhundrede* (*From the Last Century*; mus. arr. Holm), Royal Theatre, Copenhagen
1876 Dances in *Den Bjasergtagne* (*The Bewitched*, opera; mus. Hallström), Royal Theatre, Copenhagen
*Fra Siberien til Moskau* (*From Siberia to Moscow*; mus. Moller), Royal Theatre, Copenhagen
1879 *Mindet Krans for Danmarks Store Digter* (*A Memorial Wreath to Denmark's Great Poet*, tableaux; mus. Moller), Folk Theatre, Copenhagen

**PUBLICATIONS**

By Bournonville:

*Mit Theater Liv* (autobiography), 3 volumes: Copenhagen, 1848, 1865, 1877; as *My Theatre Life*, translated by Patricia McAndrew, Middletown, Connecticut, 1979
*Études choréographiques*, Copenhagen, 1861

About Bournonville:

Kraagh-Jacobsen, Sven, *The Royal Danish Ballet*, London, 1955
Bruhn, Erik, with Moore, Lillian, *Bournonville and Ballet Technique*, London, 1961
Fog, Dan, *The Royal Danish Ballet 1760–1958 and August Bournonville: A Chronological Catalogue*, Copenhagen, 1961
McAndrew, Patricia, "Bournonville à Paris", *Dance Chronicle* (New York), vol. 2, no. 3, 1978
Aschengreen, Erik, "August Bournonville", *Les Saisons de la danse* (Paris), November 1979
McAndrew, Patricia, "Bournonville: Citizen and Artist", *Dance Chronicle* (New York), vol. 3, no. 2, 1979
Terry, Walter, *The King's Ballet Master*, New York, 1979
Ralov, Kirsten (ed.), *The Bournonville School*, New York, 1979
Fridericia, Allan, *Auguste Bournonville*, Copenhagen, 1979
Aschengreen, Erik, *The Royal Danish Ballet and Bournonville*, Copenhagen, 1979
Aschengreen, Erik, Hallar, Marianne, and Heiner, Jorgen, *Perspectiv på Bournonville*, Copenhagen, 1980
Aschengreen, Erik, "The Ballet Poems of August Bournonville: The Complete Scenarios", translated by Patricia McAndrew, *Dance Chronicle* (New York), vol. 3, no. 2–vol. 6, no. 1, 1979–83
Guest, Ann Hutchinson, "The Bournonville Style", *Dance Chronicle* (New York), vol. 4, no. 2, 1981
Jürgensen, Knud Arne, "New Light on Bournonville", *Dance Chronicle* (New York), vol. 4, no. 3, 1981
Glasstone, Richard, "Dance Research and Bournonville", *Dancing Times* (London), April 1985
Aschengreen, Erik, "Bournonville Style and Tradition", *Dance Research* (London), Spring 1986
Jürgensen, Knud Arne, *The Bournonville Ballets: A Photographic Record 1844–1933*, London, 1987
Guest, Ivor, "Perrot and Bournonville", *Dancing Times* (London), November 1988
Hallar, Marianne, and Scavenius, Alette (eds.), *Bournonvilleana*, translated by Gaye Kynoch, Copenhagen, 1992

* * *

The Royal Danish Ballet's secure position on the international ballet scene is first and foremost a result of the work of August Bournonville. In 1830, at the age of only 25, he became responsible for ballet at the Royal Danish Theatre; and he held this position with little interruption until 1877. He was trained by Vincenzo Galeotti, the Italian dancer and choreographer who became the founder of the Royal Danish Ballet, as well as by his father, the accomplished French dancer Antoine Bournonville, who had arrived in Copenhagen from Stockholm in 1792.

In the Paris of the 1820s Bournonville continued his training with the most important pedagogues of ballet, such as Pierre Gardel and Auguste Vestris, and after his exams he was engaged at the Paris Opéra. As a dancer he excelled in demi-caractère roles, performing with life and vigour; and he could have had an international career. But he chose to go back to Copenhagen—no doubt because he felt loyal to Denmark, but also because he was not satisfied with the prospects the international ballet world had to offer a young male dancer during the Romantic period. August Bournonville was brought up by male dancers who had themselves been stars in their active dancing careers; now, however, the ballerinas had invaded the stage, putting the male dancer in the shadow. Bournonville did not want to be a mere prop to the ballerina, more or less hidden behind her tutu. His aim was to be more than a mere "porteur des dames". In Denmark he could decide his career for himself, and he became, for almost 50 years, the all-powerful artistic director of the ballet company in Copenhagen.

In Paris Bournonville had been impressed and influenced by the new ideas about theatre staging as they developed at the Opéra and at the boulevard theatres between 1820 and 1830. Here he saw fantastic Romantic scenes with great numbers of people on the stage. In Bournonville's ballets we still experience this Romantic *mise-en-scène*. Bournonville also brought back to Copenhagen the French dancing style, in which elegance and grace dominated. The style then virtually disappeared all over Europe, but has been kept alive to this day in Copenhagen, where about ten of Bournonville's ballets are still performed as part of an unbroken tradition. In *Konservatoriet*, for example, the choreographer dramatized memories of his years of study in Paris and put on the stage the "danse d'école", where the key word is harmony and grace. And in Bournonville's ballets the harmony of the dance reflects the harmony of the soul: ballet steps are infused with joyful exuberance. It is perhaps this joy of dance, just as infectious now, more than a hundred years after his death, as it was then, which has caused Bournonville's work to triumph in the age of technology; he stands as an irrepressible representative of the exhilaration and human warmth which we still cannot do without.

Bournonville was well aware of the demands and standards of the international world of ballet. He raised the Danish ballet to an international level of ability and at the same time gave it a unique national quality which remains its distinctive characteristic, and gives it continuing interest abroad. It was due to him that Danish dancers achieved social equality with the artists of the theatre and the citizens of the town. Through his own excellent dancing and through the important position male dance was given in his ballets, Bournonville created a tradition for Danish male dance of the highest standard. Although the level of male dance degenerated in most of Europe, it remained strong in Denmark.

August Bournonville staged about 50 ballets, as well as numerous divertissements in opera and drama. He was a sublime man of the theatre, and one of the few in Denmark in the nineteenth century who continually kept up to date with international theatrical developments. He knew what was going on in Europe, but, great personality that he was, he went his own way, creating his own ballets in many genres. He produced straightforward and uncomplicated idyllic ballets like *Far from Denmark* and *The King's Lifeguards on Amager*. He created delightful works based on folklore, such as the merry Flemish *Kermesse in Bruges* or the oriental *Abdallah*, and in addition he created Norwegian, Italian, and Spanish ballets. In *The Valkyrie* and *The Lay of Thrym*, he created ballets based on Nordic myths, but the major works—fortunately among the dozen or so ballets still performed—are *La Sylphide, Napoli*, and *A Folk Tale*. These three have become treasures of the Danish ballet repertoire, and they represent the essence of Bournonville's artistic outlook.

Despite the strong influence of France and French Romanticism, Bournonville's art was very Danish. The attitude to life represented by his works is as far as could be imagined from European Romanticism and its preoccupation with disintegration and disharmony. With a firm foundation in the Danish Biedermeier tradition, Bournonville maintained that art should be positive, its purpose to elevate us and make us harmonious human beings. In these ideas he concurs with Danish writers and other artists of the time, who regarded art as a means to connect this world with a higher one. Bournonville in his ballets dedicates himself to a world of order, meaning, beauty, and harmony, where the strongly erotic and the dramatic are cast away or defeated, and happy balance prevails.

—Erik Aschengreen

---

## BOURRÉE FANTASQUE

**Choreography:** George Balanchine
**Music:** Emmanuel Chabrier
**Design:** Barbara Karinska (costumes)
**First Production:** New York City Ballet, City Center, New York, 1 December 1949
**Principal Dancers:** Tanaquil LeClercq, Jerome Robbins (Bourrée fantasque), Maria Tallchief, Nicholas Magallanes (Prélude), Janet Reed, Herbert Bliss (Fête Polonaise)

**Other productions include:** London Festival Ballet, with Marylyn Burr, Belinda Wright, Olga Ferri, John Gilpin, Ronald Emblen; London, 18 August 1960. Paris Opéra Ballet (restaged Balanchine); Paris, 18 December 1963. Royal Danish Ballet; Copenhagen, 1963. American Ballet Theatre; Washington, D.C., 8 December 1981.

### PUBLICATIONS

Balanchine, George, with Mason, Francis, *Balanchine's Complete Stories of the Great Ballets*, Garden City, New York, 1977
Reynolds, Nancy, *Repertory in Review*, New York, 1977
Kirstein, Lincoln, *30 Years: The New York City Ballet*, New York, 1978
Croce, Arlene, *Sight Lines*, New York, 1987

* * *

For many years perhaps the chief interest in *Bourrée Fantasque*, which fell into neglect for some twenty years until revived by American Ballet Theatre in 1981, lay in its supposed resemblances to and differences from the still more legendary and lost *Cotillon*, Balanchine's 1932 ballet to music by Chabrier. The differences and similarities, as the two works became known in revival, proved to be provocative indeed.

*Bourrée Fantasque*, as its title suggests, is a far more frolicsome, light, effervescent ballet, largely lacking the edge of fatality and mystery that was *Cotillon*'s signature. Though the second movement, to the *Gwendolyne*, consists of a cavalier's pursuit and loss of a mysterious beauty, it is enclosed in two movements of great brightness and frivolity. Yet to the devotee, the essential emotional quality of *Cotillon*—the alternating moods, the contrasting colours and swirls of movement, the romantic conviction—are very much detectable in *Bourrée Fantasque*.

The look of the ballet is most striking and "French", with the women of the first and third movements wearing black, stiff, perky tutus set off with elegantly cut bodices in matte velvet—turquoise, amethyst, and topaz. The men wear berets.

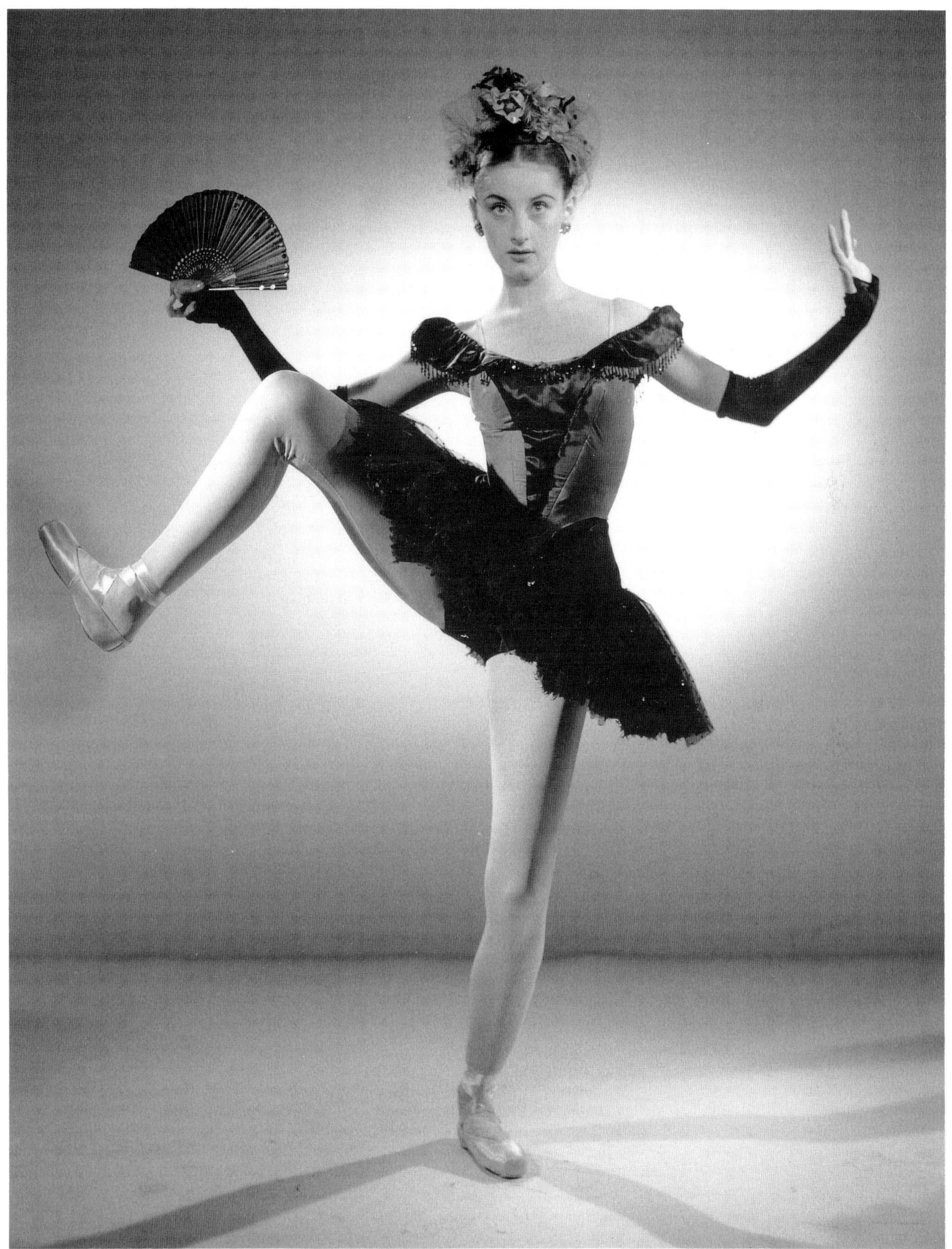

**Tanaquil LeClercq in *Bourrée fantasque*, New York City Ballet, c.1950**

**Serge Lifar and Alexandra Danilova in *La Boutique fantasque*, 1919**

All three sections contain pas de deux of differing tones but all display, in a manner calling to mind Balanchine's later masterwork *Jewels*, a different facet of the ballerina. In contemporary performance, the first movement poses a problem, for the tone appears to be at once comic, wry, and devastatingly chic—a combination of qualities apparently possessed by the originator, Tanaquil LeClercq, but elusive to those who have come after her. The interaction with a somewhat too short and too gauche partner has today become broadened into slapstick that misfires, but what endures and remains magnificent is the imagery of the fan that Balanchine develops in the eight women of the corps (they are supported by four men). Throughout the dance they form patterns, closing and opening, fluttering and turning, that present endlessly imaginative developments of the image of the fan carried by the flirtatious ballerina.

The mood of the second movement is lyrical and romantic. A corps of eight women and two demi-soloists, all in long silver-grey and faintly blue silk tutus adorned with serpentine black appliqué designs on the bodices, form various screens through which the ballerina and cavalier wander, glimpse, find, and lose each other. In its recollection of the vision scene of *The Sleeping Beauty*, this movement most distinctly recalls the interlacing lines of women in *Cotillon* as well as the seductive mystery of the Hand of Fate episode in that ballet.

The veil is dispelled in the third movement, led by an athletic duo who perform breathtaking gymnastic lifts against the backdrop of a full corps. As the movement proceeds, it displays the full riches of the company, with soloists and corps of each movement joining together to produce spectacular mass effects—particularly when each of the three ballerinas leads her "troop"—her corps—in two series of grands jetés across the stage.

Yet the frivolity of this grand finale seems, when set against the elegiac mood of the central action, almost defiant, and faintly but definitely tinged with desperation. In this way, it is most definitely linked again to *Cotillon* and to the circular, feverish finale of that work and its family of descendants.

—Anita Finkel

---

## LA BOUTIQUE FANTASQUE

**Choreography:** Léonide Massine
**Music:** Giacomo Rossini, arranged and orchestrated by Ottorino Respighi
**Design:** André Derain (scenery and costumes)
**Libretto:** André Derain
**First Production:** Diaghilev's Ballets Russes, Alhambra Theatre, London, 5 June 1919
**Principal Dancers:** Enrico Cecchetti (The Shopkeeper), Stanislas Idzikovsky (The Snob), Lydia Sokolova, Léon Woizikovsky (Tarantella Dancers), Vera Nemchinova (Mazurka: Queen of Hearts), Lubov Tchernicheva (Mazurka: Queen of Clubs), Lydia Lopokova, Léonide Massine (Can-Can Dancers).

**Other productions include:** Royal Danish Ballet (new version; chor. George Balanchine, design Kjeld Abell), with Kirsten Nellemose, Borge Ralov (Can-Can Dancers); Copenhagen, 12 October 1930. (De Basil's) Ballets Russes de Monte Carlo (revival, staged Massine), with Alexandra Danilova, Léonide Massine (Can-Can Dancers), Yurek Shabelevsky (Snob), Tamara Toumanova, Roman Jasinsky (Tarantella Dancers); London, 16 July 1934. Rome Opera (new version; chor. Aurel Milloss, design M. Pompei), with Milloss, Attilia Radice (Can-Can Dancers); Rome, 21 January 1939. La Scala Ballet (new version; chor. Nives Poli), as *La Bottega fantastica*; Milan, 18 December 1940. Netherlands Ballet (restaged Massine); Rotterdam, 4 March 1958. Sadler's Wells Ballet (restaged Massine), with Moira Shearer, Léonide Massine (Can-Can Dancers), Alexis Rassine (Snob), Julia Farron, Harold Turner (Tarantella Dancers); London, 27 February 1947. Ballet Theatre (restaged Massine), as *The Fantastic Toy Shop*, with Simon Semenoff (Shopkeeper), Irina Baronova, Léonide Massine (Can-Can Dancers), Richard Reed (Snob), Nora Kaye, Yura Lazovsky (Tarantella Dancers); Omaha, Nebraska, 4 January 1943. Royal Ballet Touring Company (restaged Massine), with Doreen Wells, Ronald Emblen (Can-Can Dancers); Stratford upon Avon, 31 January 1968.

### PUBLICATIONS

"The Sitter Out", *Dancing Times* (London), June 1919
Coton, A.V., *A Prejudice for Ballet*, London, 1938
Beaumont, Cyril, *The Diaghilev Ballet in London*, London, 1940
Beaumont, Cyril, *Complete Book of Ballets*, revised edition, London, 1951
"*The Fantastic Toyshop*: The Story of a Ballet", *Dance Magazine* (New York), December 1951
Grigoriev, Serge, *The Diaghilev Ballet*, translated by Vera Bowen, London, 1953
Massine, Léonide, *My Life in Ballet*, London and New York, 1968
Williams, Peter, "The Case for Massine", *Dance and Dancers* (London), March 1968
Goodwin, Noël, "Rossini's Fantasques, *Dance and Dancers* (London), June 1968
Balanchine, George, with Mason, Francis, *Balanchine's Complete Stories of the Great Ballets*, Garden City, N.Y., 1977
Garafola, Lynn, *Diaghilev's Ballets Russes*, New York, 1989

* * *

*La Boutique fantasque* was one of two Massine ballets that had their premieres at the Alhambra Theatre, London, during the first Diaghilev season after the end of the first world war. The other was *Le Tricorne*. Earlier ballets by Massine had been shown in London during the Diaghilev company's season as part of the music-hall entertainment presented by Sir Oswald Stoll at the Coliseum, so his novel style of choreography—presenting the comic, the satirical, the grotesque, and the national/character dance intermingled, with only an occasional polite nod in the direction of the classical—did not come as too much of a shock to the audience. So the speedy, heady, concentrated style of *La Boutique fantasque* was welcomed by a public painlessly assimilating the stylistic changes in the Ballets Russes since the departure of choreographers Fokine and Nijinsky and the advent of Massine, while also welcoming such brilliant newcomers to Diaghilev's company as Lopokova, Nemchinova, Woizikowsky, and Idzikowski.

*La Boutique fantasque* was enormously successful at its premiere (and indeed for the next twenty years), and it is not hard to understand why. Both *Boutique* and *Tricorne* were in tune with the times in which they were created. The world was anxious to forget the misery of the trenches of the first war: those who had survived were anxious to enjoy life and, in particular, the glorious future for returning heroes in which they all believed. The general public in London discovered the

Ballets Russes in their thousands, and *La Boutique fantasque* gave them a bright, fast-moving, airy, idiosyncratic treat, brilliantly danced by a plethora of great artists—from Enrico Cecchetti as the Shopkeeper, to Lukine (Leighton Lucas, later the conductor) as the Son of the Russian family, via Massine, Lopokova, Grigoriev, Idzikowski, Tchernicheva, Nemchinova, Sokolova, Gavrilov, Zverev, and also Vera Clark (Savina), who was to cause Massine's break with Diaghilev when she and Massine married some two years later.

Lopokova was particularly admired in her role as the leading Can-Can Dancer, along with Massine. Cyril Beaumont wrote:

> Lopokova was delightful. Her resemblance to a doll was extraordinary. It was a totally different conception from the angular, stiffly-jointed puppet of the dancer in *Petrouchka.* Her rounded limbs, pale face, full cheeks, curved pouting lips, and innnocent expression recalled one of those china dolls so beloved by children of the Victorian era.

According to Beaumont, no successor of Lopokova's could ever quite recapture "that delicious piquant blend of ingenuousness and naughtiness that was Lopokova's creation"—although Danilova was a notable performer in her role, both for Diaghilev (after Lopokova had gone), and later for the Ballets Russes de Monte Carlo. Massine, who was to Beaumont "equally superb" in the Can-Can,

> . . . danced with all that sinuous, cat-like grace and seemingly india-rubber limbs which history has accorded to the notorious Valentin Désossé, and radiated a similar raffishness which at once suggested a background of gas-lit globes and the glare of chandeliers reflected in countless mirrors.

In addition to a remarkable cast, perfectly fitted into their roles with Massine's usual grasp of individual potential, the witty, quirky arrangements made by Respighi of the original Rossini tunes were a source of fascination to the musical members of the audience, while the brilliant designs of André Derain (whose assignment to this task had caused a quarrel between Diaghilev and Bakst, the former's original inappropriate choice as décor artist) completed the perfectly balanced whole—even though Serge Grigoriev remarks in his memoirs that he found the décor "completely unsuitable".

If *La Boutique fantasque*, which held its place in the Ballets Russes repertory between the two world wars and was always rapturously received when performed at Covent Garden, was not quite so successful on its revival by the Royal (then Sadler's Wells) Ballet at Covent Garden in 1947 as was the choreographer's *Le Tricorne*, it has yet received well over 300 performances by the two Royal companies and has given first-rate dancing opportunities, taken with success by many of its various casts. Perhaps the intellectual concentration which went into the composition of the choreography, the varying styles of dance required, are not quite in tune with the young artist of today, who is rarely encouraged to be conscious of the possibility of dancing in any style other than the classical.

Nevertheless, *La Boutique fantasque* is a fine example of the genre of perfectly conceived, amusing ballets developed by Massine, and, like so many others of this type by this choreographer, the interest and attention is held throughout the ballet, which is by no means a short one. This is just where so many of Massine's imitators fail, for they cannot sustain the light touch throughout; it was in this ability that an important facet of his genius was demonstrated.

—Janet Sinclair

## BOZZACCHI, Giuseppina

Italian dancer. Born in Milan, 23 November 1853. Studied in Milan, becoming protégée of Milan prima ballerina Amina Boschetti; studied with Mme. Dominique (Caroline Lassiat), Paris, and at L'Académie royale de musique (Paris Opéra), from 1865. Dancer, Paris Opéra, creating role of Swanilda in first production of *Coppélia* (Saint-Léon), 1870. Died (aged 17, of fever contracted during German siege) in Paris, 23 November 1870.

### PUBLICATIONS

Guest, Ivor, "*Coppélia*", *Ballet* (London), December 1946
Beaumont, Cyril, *Complete Book of Ballets*, revised edition, London, 1951
Guest, Ivor, "In Memory of Giuseppina", *Dancing Times* (London), November 1953
Guest, Ivor, "The Birth of *Coppélia*", *Dance Magazine* (New York), February 1958
Guest, Ivor, *Two Coppélias*, London, 1970
Migel, Parmenia, *The Ballerinas*, New York, 1972
Guest, Ivor, *The Ballet of the Second Empire*, London, 1974

* * *

Giuseppina Bozzacchi, a charming, brown-haired girl with a pale complexion and a warm, lively personality, achieved the ultimate career fantasy—the direct ascent from student to ballerina.

Although the "prodigy" phenomenon existed long before the discovery of Bozzacchi in 1862, and has not yet ceased to produce gifted young artists, this ballerina's talent was supplemented with luck, both good and ill.

Fatefully, dancer Léontine Beaugrand, envisioned by *Coppélia*'s scenarist Charles Nuitter as the first Swanilda, was bypassed by the Paris Opéra's management owing to lack of box-office appeal. Choreographer Arthur Saint-Léon's own candidate, Adèle Grantzow, was prevented from performing by illness and injury. When composer Léo Delibes's talent search in Italy proved in vain, Emile Perrin, director of the Paris Opéra, offered fifteen-year-old Bozzacchi, who had no previous stage experience, a chance at stardom.

Initially enrolled in classes in her native Milan, Bozzacchi caught the attention of La Scala's reigning prima ballerina, Amina Boschetti. Through Boschetti's intercession, Bozzacchi, who emigrated to Paris, was accepted by Mme. Dominique (Caroline Lassiat) as a student.

Discerning Bozzacchi's endurance, natural physical abilities, and developing talent as qualities inherent in a distinguished performer, Mme. Dominique favored the child with her personal attention. Relatively petite, Bozzacchi was coached by the equally diminutive Mme. Dominique to compensate for the lack of physical stature (a condition which would be much more difficult to overcome today). Prior to arranging Bozzacchi's audition in 1865 before Perrin and Saint-Léon, Mme. Dominique built upon the Milanese dancer's primary technical foundation, tempering the Italian school's gymnastic approach with the nobility, moderation, and clarity of the classical French method. Saint-Léon was impressed with Bozzacchi's technique. Perrin was motivated to offer her a six-year contract with a stipulation prohibiting her from performing for the initial two years.

At the time of her engagement, the glory of the Romantic era was fading, as was the predominance of Paris as Europe's ballet centre. The star system that had supplanted the Opéra's established tradition, and segregated performers into three

Giuseppina Bozzacchi in *Coppélia*, 1870

divisions—noble, demi-caractère, and comique—had proved self-destructive. Ironically, it was the flagging system that provided Bozzacchi's opportunity. With the availability of prominent ballerinas declining and with the public's increasing disdain for male virtuosity, the Opéra had sought in Bozzacchi a vehicle to infuse excitement into the theatre. She inspired new hope for the rebirth of an art form which was waning in popularity and deteriorating in artistic content.

Although Bozzacchi's style had not yet crystallized, she evidently demonstrated a mastery of nineteenth-century technical developments and innovations in ballet, refined to suit Parisian tastes. At her début, she was favorably compared to Emma Livry and proclaimed as a Carlotta Grisi in the making. By today's technical standards, Bozzacchi would have much to learn, but with her reputed strength and natural balance, she probably could have achieved some competence had she been allowed the chance.

Supple, delicate, yet tireless, Bozzacchi possessed the assurance of a seasoned ballerina, and was hailed for her technical strength, steadiness, agility, and facility of movement. Light and graceful, she was said to display firm, precise, fleet pointes. What she lacked in elevation and "ballon", she compensated with natural verve and acting ability. The Parisian critics, always quick to condemn the flamboyant Italian miming style, found Bozzacchi to be a witty actress, adept at employing her instinctive gestures and expressive features to convey the spirit of her role with confidence, feeling, and intelligence.

Unlike many of Bozzacchi's successors, who portray Swanilda as aggressive and sulky, her character, more of a minx than a brat, aptly reacted with hope, uneasiness, and anger to the ear of corn's silence. In Act II Bozzacchi excelled in the transformation from a mechanical automaton to a lively, mischievous lass, playfully (rather than cruelly) wreaking havoc on Dr. Coppélius's workshop.

Unspoiled by her immediate success, Bozzacchi retained her simplicity and humility. A sparkling personality both on and off the stage, she won the hearts of the critics, the admiration of her teachers and, to some degree—in a jealous, competitive field—the affection of other dancers.

The good fortune that propelled Bozzacchi to stardom came to an abrupt halt with the outbreak of the Franco-Prussian War, the closing of the Opéra, and her death from smallpox on her seventeenth birthday.

Bozzacchi holds the distinction of having proved herself as a capable artist worthy of the opportunity she was afforded, of having created the leading role in ballet's comic masterpiece, and having been nineteenth-century Paris's last ballerina.

—Karen Dacko

---

**BRENAA, Hans**

Danish dancer and teacher. Born Hans Pedersen in Copenhagen, 9 October 1910. Studied at the Royal Danish Ballet School, Copenhagen, from 1918; also coached by Lubov Egorova. Married (1) Erica Voigt, 1939: one child; (2) Bodil Steen, 1952 (div. 1956). Début, while still a student, Royal Theatre, Copenhagen, 1920; dancer (performing as Hans Brenaa), Royal Danish Ballet, from 1928; dancer, Ballets de la Jeunesse, Paris, 1938–39; began performing solo and principal roles, Royal Danish Ballet, from 1942, becoming solo dancer (principal), 1945; final performance, 1955; became established as expert on modern productions of Bournonville ballets, staging Bournonville repertoire for companies around the world; co-producer, with Allan Fridericia, of television series featuring six Bournonville classes, 1963; also teacher, Royal Danish Ballet School, Copenhagen, from 1942; guest teacher, Ballet Rambert, London, and Netherlands Dance Theatre, The Hague. Died in Copenhagen, 14 April 1988.

**ROLES**

1925 One of the automata (clowns) in *Coppélia* (Beck after Saint-Léon), Royal Danish Ballet, Copenhagen
A Spirit (cr) in *A Poet's Dream* (play by J. Magnusson; chor. Uhlendorff), Royal Theatre, Copenhagen
Indian War Dance in *Far from Denmark* (Bournonville; staged Uhlendorff), Royal Danish Ballet, Copenhagen

1926 A Warrior in *Polovtsian Dances from Prince Igor* (Fokine), Royal Danish Ballet, Copenhagen
"For Old and Young" in *Dream Pictures* (divertissement; Walbom) Royal Danish Ballet, Copenhagen
A Butterfly (cr) in *Butterfly* (Uhlendorff), Royal Danish Ballet, Copenhagen

1927 Allegro (cr) in *A Colour Game* (Uhlendorff), Royal Danish Ballet, Copenhagen

Fandango in *Far From Denmark* (Bournonville; staged Lander), Royal Danish Ballet, Copenhagen
A Gentleman in *From the Ballet Class* (from Act I of *Konservatoriet*; Bournonville), Royal Danish Ballet, Copenhagen
A Gentleman, an Indian (cr) in *Danish Folk Dances* (Uhlendorff), Royal Danish Ballet, Copenhagen
Dance of the Tapestries (cr) in *The Kiss* (ballet-pantomime; Jorgen-Jensen), Royal Danish Ballet, Copenhagen
Temptation in *The Little Mermaid* (Beck), Royal Danish Ballet, Copenhagen
1928 One of Harlequin's friends in *Harlequin's Millions* (Walbom), Royal Danish Ballet, Copenhagen
Pulchinelle's Tarantella Gallop in *Dream Pictures* (Walbom), Royal Danish Ballet, Copenhagen
An Indian in *Firebird* (Kaj Smith after Fokine), Royal Danish Ballet, Copenhagen
Jota Dance in *The Toreador* (Bournonville; staged Jorgen-Jensen), Royal Danish Ballet, Copenhagen
Spring Dance in *Wedding Festival in Hardanger* (Bournonville; staged K. Smith), Royal Danish Ballet, Copenhagen
1930 Jabloschko (cr) in *Potpourri* (divertissement; K. Smith), Royal Danish Ballet, Copenhagen
Cake-Walk in *Potpourri* (divertissement; K. Smith), Royal Danish Ballet, Copenhagen
Grand Polonaise (cr) in *Hybris* (Jorgen-Jensen), Royal Danish Ballet, Copenhagen
Courante du Roy, Frier in *Hybris* (Jorgen-Jensen), Royal Danish Ballet, Copenhagen
Mazurka, Tarantelle in *La Boutique fantasque* (Balanchine after Massine), Royal Danish Ballet, Copenhagen
Negro Slave in *Schéhérazade* (Balanchine after Fokine), Royal Danish Ballet, Copenhagen
1931 A Soldier in *Barabau* (Balanchine), Royal Danish Ballet, Copenhagen
One of Joseph's brothers (cr) in *Legend of Joseph* (Balanchine), Royal Danish Ballet, Copenhagen
1932 Isidor Brown in *Gaucho* (Lander), Royal Danish Ballet, Copenhagen
Johann Strauss (cr) in *Strauss in Paris* (Jorgen-Jensen), Royal Danish Ballet, Copenhagen
Gypsy Dance II (cr) in *Tata* (Lander), Royal Danish Ballet, Copenhagen
Gypsy Csala in *Tata* (Lander), Royal Danish Ballet, Copenhagen
Solo dance (Act III) in *Napoli* (Bournonville; staged Lander), Royal Danish Ballet, Copenhagen
Negro Dance (cr) in *Asra* (Knudsen after Heine), Royal Danish Ballet, Copenhagen
1933 Apollo (cr) in *The Battle of the Goddesses* (Lander), Royal Danish Ballet, Copenhagen
Fred in *Pierrette's Veil* (ballet-pantomime; Beck), Royal Danish Ballet, Copenhagen
A Dog (cr) in *Diana* (Lander), Royal Danish Ballet, Copenhagen
A Gentleman (cr) in *Football* (Lander), Royal Danish Ballet, Copenhagen
Greek Dance in *The Whims of Cupid and the Ballet Master* (Galeotti; staged Lander), Royal Danish Ballet, Copenhagen
Solo dance (Act I) in *Konservatoriet* (Bournonville; staged Lander), Royal Danish Ballet, Copenhagen
1934 Dance of the Peasants (cr) in *The Zaporoges* (Lander), Royal Danish Ballet, Copenhagen
The Diplomat, "The Sound of Kroll's Ball" in *Dream Pictures* (divertissement; Walbom), Royal Danish Ballet, Copenhagen
Mazurka in *Les Sylphides* (extracts; Fokine), Royal Danish Ballet, Copenhagen
Adagio Bride's Companion (cr) in *The Widow in the Mirror* (Ralov), Royal Danish Ballet, Copenhagen
Dancer in *Bolero* (Lander), Royal Danish Ballet, Copenhagen
The Dream in *Once Upon an Evening* (Lander), Royal Danish Ballet, Copenhagen
1935 Chinese in *Far From Denmark* (Bournonville; staged Lander), Royal Danish Ballet, Copenhagen
1936 The Butler (cr) in *The Swineherd* (Lander), Royal Danish Ballet, Copenhagen
Lightning, "Dance of the People", "Temptation", "Dance of Joy" (cr) in *The Little Mermaid* (new version; Lander; "Dance of Joy" chor. Beck), Royal Danish Ballet, Copenhagen
A Faun (cr) in *Psyche* (Theilade), Royal Danish Ballet, Copenhagen
The Ballet Master, A Gentleman (cr) in *The Seven Deadly Sins* (Lander), Royal Danish Ballet, Copenhagen
Eros in *Psyche* (Theilade), Royal Danish Ballet, Copenhagen
Czardas in *Coppélia* (Lander after Saint-Léon), Royal Danish Ballet, Copenhagen
1937 Hungarian solo II in *Coppélia* (Lander after Saint-León), Royal Danish Ballet, Copenhagen
Harlequin in "Waltz of the Sylphides" in *Dream Pictures* (divertissement; Walbom), Royal Danish Ballet, Copenhagen
A Peasant Lad, Pas de deux in *Coppélia* (Lander after Saint-Léon), Royal Danish Ballet, Copenhagen
Young Coachman in *Petrushka* (Fokine; staged Lander), Royal Danish Ballet, Copenhagen
Czardas in *Tata* (Lander), Royal Danish Ballet, Copenhagen
1938 Huntsman, Waltz I in *Swan Lake* (Petipa, Ivanov; staged Lander), Royal Danish Ballet, Copenhagen
"Maidens and Men", "Frivolity" (cr) in *The Circle* (Theilade), Royal Danish Ballet, Copenhagen
1939 Harald Hildetand, A Monk in *The Valkyrie* (Bournonville; staged Lander), Royal Danish Ballet, Copenhagen
Dancer in *H.C. Lumbye-Fantasy* (divertissement; Walbom and Lander), Royal Danish Ballet, Copenhagen
Blue Waltz in "Romance", Student in "Our Own Times" (cr) in *The Denmark-Ballet* (Lander), Royal Danish Ballet, Copenhagen
Gossip in *Le Malade imaginaire* (comédie-ballet by Molière; chor. Ralov), Royal Danish Ballet, Copenhagen
1940 Principal dancer (cr) in *La Valse* (Lander), Royal Danish Ballet, Copenhagen
Hercules (cr) in *Thorvaldsen* (Lander), Royal Danish Ballet, Copenhagen
An Angry Wave (cr) in *The Sorcerer's Apprentice* (Lander), Royal Danish Ballet, Copenhagen
1941 Mr. Mogens in *A Folk Tale* (Bournonville; staged Lander), Royal Danish Ballet, Copenhagen
Solo Variation (Act I) in *La Sylphide* (Lander after Bournonville), Royal Danish Ballet, Copenhagen
Golfo in *Napoli* (Bournonville; staged Lander), Royal Danish, Ballet, Copenhagen
1942 September, a Painter (cr) in *The Twelve Passengers*

(Ralov), Royal Danish Ballet, Copenhagen
Robin Hood in *El Dorado* (Lander), Royal Danish Ballet, Copenhagen
A Whaler (cr) in *Qarrtsiluni* (Lander), Royal Danish Ballet, Copenhagen
"Crinoline-Polka-Mazurka" in *Dream Pictures* (divertissement; Walbom), Royal Danish Ballet, Copenhagen
Dancer (cr) in *Festive Polonaise* (Lander), Royal Danish Ballet, Copenhagen
A Young Man in White (cr) in *Spring* (Lander), Royal Danish Ballet, Copenhagen
1943 Van der Steen in *The Kermesse in Bruges* (Bournonville; staged Lander), Royal Danish Ballet, Copenhagen
1944 Coupé de Champagne in *The Eternal Triangle* (Ralov), Royal Danish Ballet, Copenhagen
Nocturne (cr) in *Passiones* (Ralov), Royal Danish Ballet, Copenhagen
1945 October, a Huntsman in *The Twelve Passengers* (Ralov), Royal Danish Ballet, Copenhagen
Prince Siegfried in *Swan Lake* (one-act version; Lander after Petipa, Ivanov), Royal Danish Ballet, Copenhagen
Destiny in *Quasi una Fantasia* (Lander), Royal Danish Ballet, Copenhagen
The Deputy Commander in *Far from Denmark* (Bournonville; staged Uhlendorff), Royal Danish Ballet, Copenhagen
Don Alzarez in *Far From Denmark* (Bournonville; staged Uhlendorff), Royal Danish Ballet, Copenhagen
1946 Hans Christian in *Dream Pictures* (divertissement; Walbom), Royal Danish Ballet, Copenhagen
The Happy Merchant in *Petrushka* (Fokine; staged Lander), Royal Danish Ballet, Copenhagen
Space (cr) in *The Phoenix* (Lander), Royal Danish Ballet, Copenhagen
French Dance in *The Whims of Cupid and the Ballet Master* (Galeotti; staged Lander), Royal Danish Ballet, Copenhagen
1947 The Uncle in *El Dorado* (Lander), Royal Danish Ballet, Copenhagen
1948 Solo (cr) in *Étude* (Lander), Royal Danish Ballet, Copenhagen
Cupid in *Sylvia* (Larsen), Royal Danish Ballet, Copenhagen
1949 A Gentleman (cr) in *Valse triste* (Lander), Royal Danish Ballet, Copenhagen
Principal dancer (cr) in *Rhapsody* (Lander), Royal Danish Ballet, Copenhagen
Polka Militaire in *Salute to Auguste Bournonville* (suite of dances; staged Lander, Beck after Bournonville), Royal Danish Ballet, Copenhagen
Steffen in *The King's Lifeguards on Amager* (Bournonville; staged Lander), Royal Danish Ballet, Copenhagen
1950 The Prince in *Aurora's Wedding* (divertissements from *The Sleeping Beauty*; Petipa, Nijinska; staged Brenaa), Royal Danish Ballet, Copenhagen
Peppo in *Napoli* (Bournonville; staged Lander), Royal Danish Ballet, Copenhagen
1952 The Old General in *Graduation Ball* (Lichine), Royal Danish Ballet, Copenhagen
Giacomo in *Napoli* (Bournonville; staged Lander), Royal Danish Ballet, Copenhagen
1955 Vincenzo Galeotti in *Capricious Lucinda* (Larsen), Royal Danish Ballet, Copenhagen

## WORKS

1964 *Atmospheres* (mus. Liszt), Royal Danish Ballet, Copenhagen

Also staged:
1950 *Aurora's Wedding* (divertissements from *The Sleeping Beauty*; after Petipa), Royal Danish Ballet, Copenhagen
1966 *Napoli*, Act III (after Bournonville; mus. Paulli, Helsted, Gade, Lumbye), Boston Ballet, Boston (also staged Norwegian Ballet, 1966; Bonn Opera Ballet, 1966)
1969 *Konservatoriet* (after Bournonville; mus. Paulli), City Center Joffrey Ballet, New York (also staged Bonn Opera Ballet, 1973; Paris Opéra Ballet, 1976)
*Guillaume Tell* (after Bournonville; mus. Rossini), City Center Joffrey Ballet, New York
1971 *Flower Festival at Genzano* (pas de deux, after Bournonville; mus. Helsted, Paulli), Paris Opéra Ballet, Paris
1973 *La Ventana* (after Bournonville; mus. Lumbye), Bonn Opera Ballet, Bonn
1975 *La Sylphide* (after Bournonville; mus. Lovenskjøld), CAPAB Ballet, South Africa

**Other works include:** for Royal Danish Ballet—numerous restagings of Bournonville ballets; *The Whims of Cupid and the Ballet Master* (after Galeotti), *Coppélia* (after Beck, Glasemann).

## PUBLICATIONS

Schonberg, Bent, *Hans Brenaa: Danish Ballet Master*, translated by Joan Tate, London, 1990

* * *

In 1918, Hans Brenaa entered the school of the Royal Danish Ballet and in 1920 he made his début in the Children's Dance from *Hill of the Elves* with Margot Gerhardt (later Lander), whose favourite partner he was until she left the stage in 1950.

Appointed principal dancer in 1945, he showed certain very distinctive features in his work. His strength was pirouettes of any kind, whereas his jumps were not at all spectacular. He had acquired his turning skill in 1928 when a pupil of Lubov Egorova in Paris. Until that time, Brenaa—like all other dancers in Denmark—only knew the Bournonville pirouettes, in which the head followed the body and in which the dancer turned only twice. Now, Brenaa began his career as a teacher, when, after his return, he taught the entire company in Copenhagen how to turn.

As a partner, Brenaa was second to none in his day. Tall and very strong, he sacrificed himself entirely to the ballerina, responding to the subtle changes in her dancing from performance to performance. He left the stage in 1955, having taken the main roles in *Les Sylphides, Widow in the Mirror, Spring, The Phoenix, Étude, Aurora's Wedding*, and *Graduation Ball.*

It is, however, as a teacher and a preserver of the Bournonville repertoire that Brenaa made his greatest impact. None of his generation could remember steps from the old ballets as well as Brenaa could. As a child, he saw all of Bournonville's ballets each time they were danced and, even when he was much older, he could remember works he had not seen for decades. He taught the Bournonville style all over the world—in America, England, Russia, Sweden, Germany,

France, Italy, Holland, and Belgium—and he was an extremely precise instructor. He could pass on to all of the young dancers the steps as originally set by Bournonville, though he was not against an evolution of the Bournonville style. Also in contrast to the old master, he cherished the idea of the "danseur noble"—indeed, he had been a dancer of that genre himself.

Significantly, Brenaa was opposed to the use of pure Bournonville technique. He himself had an intuitive response to the Bournonville school, unlike Harold Lander's purely analytical understanding. Brenaa found a general usefulness for modern dancers in the technique. It is an irony of fate that Brenaa is remembered only as an enthusiastic defender of that school, for he did in fact try to develop it by incorporating some of the modern dance ideas of his day. This was clearly demonstrated by his teaching at the Netherlands Dance Theatre in The Hague, when he not only changed the original music but also deliberately altered many of the steps.

For Danish television, Brenaa filmed all six of the Bournonville classes (a different class for each working day of the week) with dancers of the Royal Theatre. But his main achievement was to restage Bournonville's classical ballets—notably, *La Sylphide*, *A Folk Tale*, *Napoli*, and *La Ventana*—and to revive two other classics—*The Whims of Cupid and the Ballet Master* (1786), and the Max Glasemann-Hans Beck version of *Coppélia*, often considered to be the best version of the ballet in existence. The former is the world's oldest ballet with the original choreography by the founder of the Royal Danish Ballet, the Italian Vincenzo Galeotti.

—Bent Schønberg

---

## BRIANZA, Carlotta

Italian dancer and teacher. Born in Milan, 1867. Studied at Imperial Academy (La Scala School), Milan, pupil of Carlo Blasis. Dancer, becoming ballerina, Ballet of Teatro alla Scala, Milan; toured America in 1883; went to Russia, appearing in St. Petersburg, 1887, and Moscow, 1888; ballerina under ballet master Marius Petipa, Maryinsky Theatre, St. Petersburg, 1889–91, creating most famous role, Princess Aurora in *The Sleeping Beauty*, 1890; returned to Italy, appearing as prima ballerina at La Fenice, Venice, 1895, and La Scala, Milan, 1895, 1896, 1900; also appeared at Empire Theatre, London, 1888, and Opéra-Comique, Paris, 1903/04; invited by Diaghilev to appear in Ballets Russes production of *The Sleeping Princess*, London, 1921; also teacher in Paris and Nice, from 1891. Died c. 1935.

### ROLES

1887 Civilization in *Excelsior* (Cecchetti after Manzotti), Arcadia Theatre, St. Petersburg

1888 Marguerite in *Faust* (after Perrot), Bolshoi Theatre, Moscow
Spirit of Gamleh in *The Girl I Left Behind Me* (Lanner), Empire Theatre, London

1889 Emma in *The Tulip of Haarlem* (Petipa, Ivanov), Maryinsky Theatre, St. Petersburg
Title role in *La Esmeralda* (Petipa after Perrot), Maryinsky Theatre, St. Petersburg

1890 Princess Aurora (cr) in *The Sleeping Beauty* (Petipa), Maryinsky Theatre, St. Petersburg
Title role (cr) in *Nénuphar* (Petipa), Maryinsky Theatre, St. Petersburg

1891 Nisia in *King Candaule* (Petipa), Maryinsky Theatre, St. Petersburg
Marietta/Draginiatza (cr) in *Kalkabrino* (Petipa), Maryinsky Theatre, St. Petersburg

1895 Title role in *Sylvia* (after Mérante), La Scala, Milan
Ballerina in *Nozze slave* (Graeb), La Scala, Milan
Ballerina in *La Maledetta* (Seramo), La Scala, Milan
Ballerina in *Tanzmärchen* (Gaul, Hassreiter), Teatro alla Fenice, Venice

1896 Title role (cr) in *Sylvia* (new production; Saracco after Mérante), La Scala, Milan
Ballerina in *Day Sin* (after F. Pratesi), La Scala, Milan
Swanilda in *Coppélia* (after Saint-Léon), La Scala, Milan
Princess Aurora in *La Bella del bosco dormente* (*The Sleeping Beauty*; Saracco after Petipa), La Scala, Milan

1900 Title role in *Sieba* (Manzotti), La Scala, Milan
Ballerina in *Le Scarpette rosse* (Hassreiter), La Scala, Milan

1903/04 Dancer in *Lakmé* (opera; mus. Delibes, chor. Mariquita), Opéra-Comique, Paris
Dancer in *Manon* (opera; mus. Massenet; chor. Mariquita), Opéra-Comique, Paris

1921 Carabosse in *The Sleeping Princess* (Petipa; staged Sergeyev, with additions Nijinska), Diaghilev's Ballets Russes, London

### PUBLICATIONS

Pleshcheev, Alexander, *Our Ballet*, St. Petersburg, 1899
Skalkovsky, K., "Carlotta Brianza", in *The World of Theatre*, St. Petersburg, 1899
Khudekov, Sergei, *The History of Dancing*, Petrograd, 1918
"Tchaikovsky-Bakst: The Sleeping Princess", *The Sketch* (London), 16 November 1921
Benois, Alexandre, *Reminiscences of the Russian Ballet*, London, 1941
Slonimsky, Yuri, "Marius Petipa", translated by Anatole Chujoy, *Dance Index* (New York), May–June 1947
Beaumont, Cyril, *Complete Book of Ballets*, revised edition, London, 1951
Lifar, Serge, *A History of Russian Ballet from its Origins to the Present Day*, London, 1954
Jackson, G. and Gogel, P., "The Italian (Sleeping) Beauty of 1896: The First Full Production in the West", *Ballet Review* (New York), 1969
Krasovskaya, Vera, "Marius Petipa and the Sleeping Beauty", *Dance Perspectives* (New York), no. 49, 1972
Wiley, Roland John, *Tchaikovsky's Ballets*, Oxford, 1985
Wiley, Roland John (ed. and trans.), *A Century of Russian Ballet: Documents and Accounts 1810–1910*, Oxford, 1990

* * *

During the latter half of the nineteenth century, ballet audiences in Russia were treated to performances by a galaxy of Italian ballerinas. Trained at La Scala, Milan, according to methods laid down by dancing master Carlo Blasis, these dancers were more technically accomplished than their Russian counterparts and able to perform multiple pirouettes and sustained pointework, assisted by the innovation of blocked pointe shoes. Amongst these dancers was Carlotta Brianza, whose performances drew a large and enthusiastic audience, fascinated by her prodigious virtuosity.

Brianza made her début in Russia in 1887, appearing in Manzotti's *Excelsior* (originally choreographed in 1881) at the Arcadia Theatre in the Livadia Park, St. Petersburg. She danced the role of Civilization, which was to become an important part of her repertoire after subsequent performances in both Paris and Russia had increased her stature amongst the St. Petersburg balletomanes. The management of the Maryinsky Theatre was aware of Brianza's growing reputation and thus engaged her in 1889. A year later she was to be given the role of Princess Aurora in *The Sleeping Beauty*, which was to prove the pinnacle of her career.

Brianza was fortunate that the leading figures who created this ballet, namely Marius Petipa and Petr Tchaikovsky, were warmly disposed towards her. Petipa had always preferred choreographing for female dancers, and with the role of Aurora he sought to highlight Brianza's gifts, creating dances with intricate, dazzling movements retaining a characteristic femininity. Tchaikovsky's admiration for Brianza's artistry and musicality inspired him to compose one of his greatest ballet scores.

Contemporary reviews of *The Sleeping Beauty* note the qualities which made Brianza such an outstanding ballerina. The critic Skalkovsky was particularly elated by her dancing, stating that "All her dances—entrée, adagio, and variations on pointe—are extremely elegant, masterfully and accurately executed".

Such praise was especially prompted by the Rose Adagio, where Princess Aurora was supported in turn by each of her four suitors. The manner in which she balanced unsupported on one toe in an attitude (a pose evidently derived by her tutor Blasis), while each suitor came forward in turn to offer her his arm and then revolve her slowly in the same pose, exhibited Brianza's adeptness.

The role established Brianza's legendary status in the dance world so well that in 1921, when the great Russian impresario Serge Diaghilev set about mounting a new version of *The Sleeping Beauty* entitled *The Sleeping Princess* (staged by Sergeyev after Petipa, with additional numbers by Nijinska), he proposed that Brianza should dance the leading role. However, when it was pointed out that by now she was in her sixties, he realized that it was an impossible request. Instead Brianza, who by now had retired from performing to devote her time to teaching in Paris, offered to dance the role of the wicked fairy Carabosse, and the contract was duly signed.

Diaghilev's Ballets Russes rehearsed at the Drill Hall, off Tottenham Court Road in London. Here Brianza conducted the daily class, maintaining the traditions of her classical background, and passing on her knowledge and expertise to a younger, upcoming generation of dancers.

There was great expectation surrounding the work in preparation, with newspapers and periodicals of the time speculating on this event to be staged at the Alhambra Theatre. Many writers focused on the ballet's historical link with the Maryinsky production, noting that the original Aurora, Carlotta Brianza, would be appearing on the London stage. The *Sketch* of 16 November 1921 featured an article which included a photograph of Brianza as the wicked fairy arriving at the christening. This interest continued with a picture of Brianza on the front cover of the Christmas edition of *The Dancing Times*, recording her last performances as a dancer.

This periodical's association with Brianza was renewed in more recent times (July and August 1978) with regard to the later years of this ballerina's life. Initially it had been thought Brianza died in 1930 in Paris, possibly committing suicide. However, when G.B.L. Wilson was browsing through some old copies of a quarterly review called the *Archives Internationales de la danse*, he came across an advertisement inserted by Carlotta Brianza in the April 1934 edition for her "Cours de danses classiques et numéro" at the Studio Wacker, Paris, describing herself as "du Théâtre Imperiale de Petrograd, de la Scala de Milan et de l'Opéra Comique". Further doubts over the exact date of Brianza's death were raised by a letter received by G.B.L. Wilson from Pieter Van der Sloot, the head of a ballet school in Germany. He told Wilson that Madame Brianza had placed an even larger advertisement for her classes in the July 1934 and April 1935 issues, though none appeared in the July 1935 edition, suggesting that Brianza may have died in the early part of that year.

Considering Brianza was the first Aurora in *The Sleeping Beauty*, a role which for over a century has remained an indelible part of a ballerina's repertoire linking a long line of illustrious dancers to Brianza, it is surprising that so little documentation exists on the latter years of her life. This makes her an even more intriguing personality in the history of dance, and one worthy of further investigation.

—Melanie Trifona Christoudia

---

## THE BRONZE HORSEMAN

(original Russian title: *Mednyi vsadnik*)

**Choreography:** Rostislav Zakharov
**Music:** Reinhold Glière
**Design:** Mikhail Bobyshov
**Libretto:** Petr Abolimov, after the poem by Aleksandr Pushkin
**First Production:** Kirov Ballet, Leningrad, 14 March 1949
**Principal Dancers:** Konstantin Sergeyev (Evgeny), Natalia Dudinskaya (Parasha)

**Other productions include:** Bolshoi Ballet, with Aleksei Yermolaev and Olga Lepeshinskaya; Moscow, 27 June 1949.

### PUBLICATIONS

Roslavleva, Natalia, "*The Bronze Horseman*: How a Ballet is Made", *Ballet Today* (London), 2 parts: March 1950, April–May 1950
Zakharov, Rostislav, *The Choreographer's Art*, Moscow, 1954
Beaumont, Cyril, *Ballets Past and Present*, London, 1955
Belza, I.F., and Glière, Reinhold, "*The Bronze Horseman*", *Balet*, Leningrad, 1961
Crisp, Clement, *Making a Ballet*, London, 1975

* * *

"From the darkness of the woods, from the depths of crime", the energy and will of Peter the First gave birth to the beautiful city of St. Petersburg. It took more than 100 years. The young lovers Evgeny and Parasha meet at the monument to Peter, and then joyfully spend their time together at a small house at the outskirts of the city. But their happiness is destroyed by a terrible flood, during which Parasha dies. From the dullness and misery of Evgeny's grief arises an image of the Bronze Horseman—Peter the First's statue—galloping through the empty streets of the city. The frenzied youth, believing that the statue is pursuing him, at last loses his strength and falls lifelessly to the ground.

*The Bronze Horseman* played a very important part in the history of the Kirov Theatre. It was staged by Rostislav

Zakharov to commemorate one of the anniversaries of Aleksandr Pushkin's birthday. For 40 years his ballet has been on the stage of the Kirov, and the public has loved it for several reasons. First of all, it was a St. Petersburg ballet, dedicated to the city and to its founder, Peter the Great. Secondly, it was based on the poem by the great Russian poet Pushkin. All of the creators of the ballet—Zakharov himself, along with the composer Reinhold Glière and the scenery designer Mikhail Bobyshov—did their best to create a true rendition of the great poem by means of plastic form and active choreography. Zakharov somehow managed to follow faithfully the traditions of classical ballet; he very cleverly combined the dance and mime, the pictorial effects on stage, and the narrative methods so that it was a production in the tradition of the Kirov Theatre, where all the various elements are joined together in a harmonious whole.

It is a big ballet, in three acts, and from the start it was understood both by adults and by children, because the poem "The Bronze Horseman" is familiar to everyone. The title refers to the statue of Peter the Great, which still stands right in the centre of Leningrad, as well as to the famous Pushkin poem. The poem deals with the experience of a small man and a great tsar; and of course the life of the small man is crushed by the imperial city and, to be exact, by the terrible inundation which sweeps over him. The heroine, a symbol of his happiness, dies, and he, her lover, a petty government official, is left to go mad, as it appears to him in his nightmares that the great statue has come down from its pedestal and pursued him.

Everything is recognizable in the ballet; it is easy, in a sense, to follow each step. Zakharov's choreography is both appealing and accessible to an audience. It is not very difficult, but it includes such classical forms as the waltz, the pas de deux, and variations. The story takes place at the beginning of the eighteenth century, when in fact the city was founded (1703), and then switches suddenly to the middle of the nineteenth century, recalling the historic flood of St. Petersburg in 1824. It is a very tragic tale, done in a sort of epic choreographic language. From the duet of the lovers in the middle of the square, to the variations of the tsarina at the ball arranged by Peter the Great, to the dances of jesters surrounding Peter the Great, or the group dances near the house where Parasha lives—all the elements together create a very beautiful choreographic picture as well as a moving tale of grand proportions.

The mechanics of the stage effects have always been popular as well; usually the audience applauds the flood scene, which is done in a way similar to the opening shipwreck of *Le Corsaire*. We see enormous waves, created by yards of billowing fabric, boats thrown about on the river, people trying to save the lives of the drowning, Evgeny swimming hard to reach the house of Parasha, but in vain.

*The Bronze Horseman* is recognized as one of the best examples of its period, and is one of the best representations of what is now called choreographic drama. Very often this term is used pejoratively; but in the case of *The Bronze Horseman*, it indicates a very logical and effective combination of mime, dancing, and acting. It remains in the repertoire of the Kirov Ballet to this day.

—Igor Stupnikov

---

**BROWNE, Leslie**

American dancer. Born in New York, daughter of American Ballet Theatre dancers Isabel and Kelly Browne, 29 June 1958. Studied at the Phoenix School of Ballet, Phoenix, Arizona, 1965–72, and at the School of American Ballet, New York, 1972–74. Dancer, corps de ballet, New York City Ballet, 1974–76; soloist, American Ballet Theatre, New York, from 1976, becoming principal dancer from 1986; also performed at the Spoleto Festival with Edward Villella, Charleston, S.C., 1978, and with Chicago Ballet, 1978; guest artist, Ballet Philippines, Manila, 1982; toured with Baryshnikov and Company, 1985, 1986, 1987; has also appeared in films, including as Emilia in *The Turning Point* (dir. Herbert Ross, 1977), Romola Nijinsky in *Nijinsky* (dir. Ross, 1980), and Nadine in *Dancers* (dir. Ross, 1987); has appeared on national television, including for Public Broadcasting Service (PBS) series "Live from Lincoln Center", 1987, "Great Performances", 1988, and "A Tudor Evening", 1990. Nomination, Best Supporting Actress (for *The Turning Point*), American Academy Awards, 1978.

## ROLES

1975 Dancer (First violin) in *Concerto Barocco* (Balanchine), School of American Ballet Workshop, New York
Elise in *Konservatoriet* (Bournonville), School of American Ballet Workshop, New York
Odette in *Swan Lake*, Act II (after Ivanov), Arizona Ballet Theatre, Phoenix

1976 Pas de trois in *Swan Lake* (Ivanov, Petipa; staged Blair), American Ballet Theatre, Washington, D.C.
Fairy of the Wood in *The Sleeping Beauty* (Petipa; staged Skeaping), American Ballet Theatre, Washington, D.C.
Clara in *The Nutcracker* (Baryshnikov), American Ballet Theatre, Washington, D.C.

1977 Variation: Prayer in *Coppélia* (Martinez after Saint-Léon), American Ballet Theatre, New York
Principal dancer in *Voluntaries* (Tetley), American Ballet Theatre, New York
Caroline in *Jardin aux lilas* (Tudor), American Ballet Theatre, Los Angeles
Tsarevna in *Firebird* (Fokine; staged Newton), American Ballet Theatre, Washington, D.C.

1978 Solo Variation (Third Shadow) in "The Kingdom of the Shades" from *La Bayadère* (Makarova after Petipa), American Ballet Theatre, Houston
Pas de deux in *Graduation Ball* (Lichine), American Ballet Theatre, Houston
Nocturne, Prelude, and Waltz in *Les Sylphides* (Fokine), American Ballet Theatre, Los Angeles
Principal dancer in *The Leaves are Fading* (Tudor), American Ballet Theatre, Santa Barbara
Principal dancer in *Danses concertantes* (MacMillan), American Ballet Theatre, Washington, D.C.
Mercedes in *Don Quixote* (*Kitri's Wedding*; Baryshnikov after Petipa), American Ballet Theatre, Washington, D.C.
Lisette in *La Fille mal gardée* (Nault), Chicago Ballet, Chicago
Principal dancer in *The Overgrown Path* (pas de trois; Villella), Spoleto Festival, Charleston, S.C.

1980 Pas de trois in *Les Rendezvous* (Ashton), American Ballet Theatre, Washington, D.C.
Grand Pas Hongrois in *Raymonda Divertissement* (Acts II, III; Baryshnikov after Petipa), American Ballet Theatre, Washington, D.C.

1981 First movement in *Concerto* (MacMillan), American Ballet Theatre, Minneapolis
The Sleepwalker in *La Sonnambula* (Balanchine),

American Ballet Theatre, Syracuse, N.Y.
The Coquette in *La Sonnambula* (Balanchine), American Ballet Theatre, Washington, D.C.
Solo Variation (First Shadow) in *La Bayadère* (Makarova after Petipa), American Ballet Theatre, New York
Sapphire Variation in *The Sleeping Beauty* (Petipa; staged Skeaping), American Ballet Theatre, New York
The Lover in *Les Patineurs* (Ashton), American Ballet Theatre, Detroit
First Movement in *Bourrée Fantasque* (Balanchine), American Ballet Theatre, Washington, D.C.

1982 The Woman in *The Wild Boy* (MacMillan), American Ballet Theatre, New York
The Youngest Sister in *Pillar of Fire* (Tudor), American Ballet Theatre, Los Angeles
Principal dancer in *Great Galloping Gottschalk* (Taylor-Corbett), American Ballet Theatre, New York
The Sugar Plum Fairy in *The Nutcracker* (after Ivanov), Ballet Philippines, Manila

1983 Principal dancer in *Symphonie Concertante* (Balanchine), American Ballet Theatre, New York
Gamzatti in *La Bayadère* (Makarova after Petipa), American Ballet Theatre, New York

1984 First Variation in *Paquita* (Nureyev after Petipa), American Ballet Theatre, New York

1985 Juliet in *Romeo and Juliet* (MacMillan), American Ballet Theatre, Washington, D.C.
The Lady with Him in *Dim Lustre* (Tudor), American Ballet Theatre, New York
Myrtha in *Giselle* (Petipa after Coralli, Perrot; staged Blair), American Ballet Theatre, New York

1986 Principal dancer (cr) in *The Mollino Room* (Armitage), American Ballet Theatre, Washington, D.C.
Principal dancer in *Requiem* (MacMillan), American Ballet Theatre, Chicago

1987 First Aria in *Stravinsky Violin Concerto* (Balanchine), American Ballet Theatre, Miami
Lilac Fairy in *The Sleeping Beauty* (MacMillan after Petipa), American Ballet Theatre, San Francisco
Title role in *Giselle* (Petipa after Coralli, Perrot; staged Blair), American Ballet Theatre, Los Angeles
Hagar in *Pillar of Fire* (Tudor), American Ballet Theatre, New York
Second Song in *Dark Elegies* (Tudor), American Ballet Theatre, New York
First Movement (cr) in *Bruch Violin Concerto No. 1* (Tippet), American Ballet Theatre, Orange County, N.Y.
Kitri in *Don Quixote* (Baryshnikov after Petipa), American Ballet Theatre, Los Angeles
Title role in *Paquita* (Nureyev after Petipa), American Ballet Theatre, Los Angeles

1988 La Reine de la danse (from Moscow) in *Gala Performance* (Tudor; staged Wilson), American Ballet Theatre, Orange County, N.Y.
Principal dancer in *Ballet Imperial* (Balanchine), American Ballet Theatre, New York
Fifth Variation in "Grand Pas Classique" from *Raymonda* (Petipa; staged Baryshnikov), American Ballet Theatre, New York
Principal dancer in *Drink to Me Only with Thine Eyes* (Morris), American Ballet Theatre, New York

1989 Odette/Odile in *Swan Lake* (Baryshnikov after Petipa, Ivanov), American Ballet Theatre, Chicago
Title role in *La Sylphide* (Bruhn after Bournonville), American Ballet Theatre, New York

1990 Principal dancer in *Nine Sinatra Songs* (Tharp), American Ballet Theatre, Washington, D.C.
Principal dancer in *Push Comes to Shove* (Tharp), American Ballet Theatre, Washington, D.C.
Ballerina (in green) in *Birthday Offering* (Ashton), American Ballet Theatre, Miami

1991 Mercedes in *Don Quixote* (Vasiliev), American Ballet Theatre, Los Angeles
Aurora in *Coppélia* (Martinez), American Ballet Theatre, New York
Third Movement in *Concerto* (MacMillan), American Ballet Theatre, New York

## PUBLICATIONS

By Browne:

Interview in Fields, Sidney, "Only Human", *New York Daily News* (New York), 15 November 1977

Interview in Lawson, Carol, "New Face Leslie Browne: Dance, Ballerina Dance", *New York Times* (New York), 23 December 1977

About Browne:

Stoop, Norma McLain, "Leslie Browne of American Ballet Theatre and *The Turning Point*", *Dance Magazine* (New York), October 1977

Croce, Arlene, *Going to the Dance*, New York, 1982

Fraser, John, and Arnold, Eve (photographer), *Private View: Inside Baryshnikov's American Ballet Theatre*, New York, 1988

* * *

Leslie Browne was catapulted to fame at an early age, when she starred in the 1977 Herbert Ross film *The Turning Point*, the first mainstream commercial film since *The Red Shoes* to make the ballet world its central subject (and the first of several Hollywood films to capitalize on the name of Mikhail Baryshnikov). Replacing the mercurial and unpredictable ballerina Gelsey Kirkland, for whom the role was originally intended, the previously unknown Browne quieted most charges of nepotism (she was god-daughter to the husband-and-wife team of Herbert Ross and Nora Kaye) by dancing rather nicely and by proving that, in spite of an absurd story-line and an appalling script, her acting was not all that bad. This is not so surprising in retrospect, given that Browne's greatest claim is as a dramatic ballerina.

Some might take issue with the notion that Browne was an unknown before her foray into Hollywood (although even after the movie Arlene Croce wrote, rather waspishly, that "Leslie Browne is still an unknown"). Balletomanes had already taken note of Browne's promise after her distinguished performance at the annual School of American Ballet workshop, and in the year before the release of *The Turning Point* she had danced Clara in Baryshnikov's version of *The Nutcracker*. Apart from the appeal of her youthful innocence—the quality that Hollywood had exploited as her "dewy freshness"—Browne showed a solid technique, including well-arched feet and an impressively high jump.

After returning from Hollywood to the far less glamorous world of the ballet rehearsal studio, Browne slowly climbed to the top of the ladder, becoming principal dancer only after another nine years. Unlike Gelsey Kirkland from whom she stole her early movie fame, Browne could never be hailed as one of the world's greatest ballerinas: the exquisite qualities that made Kirkland so exciting were a rare combination of talents and temperament seen none too often on the ballet stage today. But next to the notorious Kirkland, whose artistic inconsistency, emotional instability, and infamous involvement with drugs have become legend, Browne has been the comparative model of dependability. Apart from breaks due to injury or illness, she has remained with her mother company throughout her career, and if her name does not necessarily cause a flutter when it appears on the programme, at least it engenders confidence, for Browne's solid technique and artistry have certainly been reliable.

Partly because of her facial characteristics (tending towards the over-serious) and partly because of her dancing style, Browne has never been an "ingénue" type, despite her fresh-faced appearance as a baby ballerina in *The Turning Point*. She is perhaps more memorable as Myrtha than as the title role in *Giselle*; she has a commanding, forbidding presence as the Queen of the Wilis, showing a majestic control of the stage and a sense of the drama of the role which is more in her line than the waif-like character of Giselle. Her Gamzatti in *La Bayadère*, similarly, makes use of her authority and technical strength, making this a more natural role for her than Nikiya, which has gone to other ballerinas of her age and status at American Ballet Theatre. Kitri in *Don Quixote* perhaps displays Browne to her best advantage, allowing her to show off both her natural dramatic flair and her impressive leaps.

Like many of the ballerinas at American Ballet Theatre, which regularly churns out the full-length classics and has not had a resident choreographer of import for any real length of time, Browne has not had many roles created for her. She danced in the premieres of Clarke Tippet's *Bruch Violin Concerto No. 1* and Karen Armitage's *The Mollino Room*, and she participated in the creation of Mark Morris's *Drink to Me Only with Thine Eyes*, although she was unable to dance at the premiere.

It is as a dramatic ballerina that Browne, slowly but surely, has cut out a niche for herself, most importantly in the ballets of Antony Tudor. Perhaps it is appropriate that the role which Browne has made her own is the role created by her godmother, Nora Kaye—that of Hagar in *Pillar of Fire*. In this psychological study of repression and thwarted passion, Kaye gave such a moving interpretation of the tragic role of Hagar that she and Tudor were given 28 curtain calls at the ballet's premiere. Some 45 years later, audiences are not as stunned by the daring intensity of Tudor's work, but they still respond to the dramatic power of Browne's portrayal, which has grown in depth and meaning over the years that she has performed the role. As New York critic Jack Anderson wrote in 1992, "Antony Tudor has [recently] been honoured by some fine performances of his work", crediting it not least of all to the presence of Leslie Browne. Pointing out that "Leslie Browne is now giving a distinctive personal interpretation of Hagar in *Pillar of Fire*", Anderson wrote of the ballerina's own way of ". . . making the very act of approaching or retreating from a person a sign of this woman's longings and her distrust of her own worth". Browne has also been outstanding as Caroline in *Jardin aux lilas*, drawing on her ability to express character and emotion through the highly symbolic language of movement that is Tudor's extension of the ballet vocabulary. Tudor has also chosen Browne as the lead for revivals of his 1975 ballet, *The Leaves are Fading*; indeed, Browne's greatest tribute from the choreographer may well have been his choice to have her perform the pas de deux from this ballet in Washington, D.C., when he was the recipient of the Kennedy Center Award.

In some senses, Browne might better have been served by the choreographers and companies of her godmother's day, when the many possibilities of psychological ballet were being explored, and the term "dramatic ballerina" (indeed a term said to be coined for Nora Kaye) represented the highest achievement for a dancer. Today an American dramatic ballerina like Browne falls into something of a vacuum: she fits neither into the abstract neo-classical repertoire of a Balanchine company, nor very happily into the standard menu of nineteenth-century ballets which have been the staple of American Ballet Theatre, apart from Baryshnikov's attempts to expand the repertoire in the 1980s. Fortunately the Tudor legacy has given Browne a group of ballets in which to define herself; but one cannot help wondering how she might have developed under a choreographer like Kenneth MacMillan (who incidentally chose Browne as his first-cast Juliet for the American Ballet Theatre staging of his *Romeo and Juliet*), or any other more dramatically inclined choreographers.

Now that Baryshnikov—whose policy of developing "home" ballerinas undoubtedly helped Browne's career—has left Ballet Theatre, Browne's future is looking uncertain. Apparently undervalued by the new management, Browne for the first time in her professional career looks like a ballerina without a home. But the necessity of developing her career outside American Ballet Theatre might well hold the possibility for the artistic fulfilment which, so far, seems to have eluded her.

—Virginia Christian

---

**BRUCE, Christopher**

British dancer, choreographer, and producer. Born in Leicester, England, 3 October 1945. Studied in Scarborough and at the Rambert School, London. Married Marian Meadowcroft, 1967: two sons and one daughter. Début with Walter Gore's London Ballet, 1963; dancer, Ballet Rambert, from 1963, becoming leading dancer in modern roles, from 1966; choreographer, Ballet Rambert (now Rambert Dance Company), from 1969, becoming associate choreographer, 1975–87, and associate director, 1975–79; associate choreographer, London Festival Ballet (becoming English National Ballet), 1986–91; resident choreographer, Houston Ballet, since 1989; has also staged works for Royal Ballet, Scottish Ballet, Batsheva Dance Company, Munich Opera Ballet, Gulbenkian Ballet Company, Australian Dance Theatre, Royal Danish Ballet, Royal Swedish Ballet, Tanz Forum, Cologne, Nederlands Dans Theater, and Kent Opera; has worked as choreographer/producer for opera, musicals, television, film, and theatre, including as choreographer for *Mutiny!* (mus. Essex; Piccadilly Theatre, 1985). Recipient: *Evening Standard* Inaugural Dance Award, 1974.

**ROLES**

1965 Principal dancer (cr) in *The Realms of Choice* (Morrice), Ballet Rambert, London
1966 Principal dancer (cr) in *Diversities* (Taylor), Ballet Rambert, London
1967 Pierrot in *Pierrot Lunaire* (Tetley), Ballet Rambert, London
Principal dancer (cr) in *Hazard* (Morrice), Ballet Rambert, London
1968 Principal dancer (cr) in *Embrace Tiger and Return to Mountain* (Tetley), Ballet Rambert, London
Principal dancer (cr) in *The Act* (Hodes), Ballet Rambert, London

1969 Principal dancer (cr) in *Blind Sight* (Morrice), Ballet Rambert, London
1971 Principal dancer (cr) in *That is the Show* (Morrice), Ballet Rambert, London
1972 Principal dancer (cr) in *Stop-Over* (Scoglio), Ballet Rambert, London
1977 The Poet (cr) in *Cruel Garden* (also chor., with Kemp), Ballet Rambert, London
1979 Prospero (cr) in *The Tempest* (Tetley), Ballet Rambert Swetzingen, Germany
1986 Tchaikovsky/Drosselmeyer (cr) in *The Nutcracker* (new production; Schaufuss), London Festival Ballet, London
1988 Title role in *Petrushka* (Fokine), London Festival Ballet, London

**Other roles include:** for Ballet Rambert—Faune in *L'Apres-midi d'un faune* (Nijinsky), principal dancer in *Ziggurat* (Tetley), principal dancer in *tutti-frutti* (Falco), principal dancer in *Celebration* (Siobhan Davies), principal dancer in *Ricercare* (Tetley).

## WORKS

1969 *George Frederic* (mus. Handel), Ballet Rambert, Edinburgh
*Living Space* (poems by Robert Cockburn), Ballet Rambert, Guildford
1970 *Wings* (mus. Bob Downes), Tanz Forum, Cologne
1972 *for these who die as cattle* (no music), Ballet Rambert, London
*There Was a Time* (mus. Hodgson), Ballet Rambert, London
1973 *Duets* (mus. Hodgson), Ballet Rambert, London
1974 *Weekend* (mus. Hodgson), Ballet Rambert, London
*Unfamiliar Playground* (mus. Hymas), Sadler's Wells Royal Ballet, London
1975 *Ancient Voices of Children* (mus. Crumb), Ballet Rambert, London
1976 *Black Angels* (mus. Crumb), Ballet Rambert, Horsham
*Girl with a Straw Hat* (mus. Brahms), Ballet Rambert, London
*Promenade* (mus. Bach), Ballet Rambert, Exeter
*Echoes of a Night Sky* (mus. Crumb), Batsheva Dance Company, Israel
*Voices* (mus. Kodaly), Batsheva Dance Company, Israel
1977 *Cruel Garden* (with Lindsey Kemp; mus. Miranda), Ballet Rambert, London
*Responses* (no music), EMMA Dance Company
1979 *Labyrinth* (mus. Subotnick), Australian Dance Theatre, Melbourne
*Night with Waning Moon* (mus. Crumb), Ballet Rambert, London
*Sidewalk* (mus. Lambert), Ballet Rambert, Oxford
1980 *Interactions* (mus. Carpenter), Springplank (Nederlands Dans Theater apprentice group), The Hague
*Preludes and Songs* (mus. Hymas), Ballet Rambert, Cheltenham
1981 *Dancing Day* (mus. Holst), Rambert Academy, London (first performance by Ballet Rambert, 1981, Venice)
*Cantata* (mus. Stravinsky), Tanz Forum (of Cologne), London
*Ghost Dances* (mus. South American folk songs, arranged Carr), Ballet Rambert, Bristol
*Holiday Sketches* (mus. Billie Holiday recordings), London Contemporary Dance School, London (performed by Janet Smith and Dancers, 1982)
*Village Songs* (mus. Bartók), Nederlands Dans Theater, Sheveningen
1982 *Berlin Requiem* (mus. Weill), Ballet Rambert, London
*In Alium* (mus. Taverner), Nederlands Dans Theater, The Hague
1983 *Concertino* (mus. Janáček), Ballet Rambert, Norwich
*Curses and Blessings* (mus. Eben), Nederlands Dans Theater, Sheveningen
1984 *Intimate Pages* (mus. Janáček), Ballet Rambert, Birmingham
*Sergeant Early's Dream* (mus. folk songs), Ballet Rambert, Canterbury
1985 *Remembered Dances* (mus. Janáček), Scottish Ballet, Glasgow
*Silence is the End of our Song* (Chilean poems), Royal Danish Ballet, Danish television commission
*Land* (mus. Nordheim), London Festival Ballet, London
1986 *Ceremonies* (mus. Shipley), Ballet Rambert, London
*The World Again* (mus. Burgon), London Festival Ballet, London
*The Dream is Over* (mus. John Lennon songs), Cullberg Ballet, London Weekend Television (staged London Festival Ballet, London, 1987)
1987 *Swansong* (mus. Chambon), London Festival Ballet, Bilbao
1989 *Les Noces* (mus. Stravinsky), Gulbenkian Ballet, Lisbon
*Guatama Buddha* (mus. Naresh Sohal), Houston Ballet
*Symphony in Three Movements* (mus. Stravinsky), English National Ballet, Bristol
1990 *Journey* (mus. Mickleburg), Houston Ballet, Houston
1991 *Rooster* (mus. Rolling Stones), Grand Theatre, Geneva
1992 *Nature Dances* (mus. Chambon), Houston Ballet, Houston

**Other works include:** for Kent Opera—dances in operas *Il Ballo del Ingrate* (mus. Monteverdi), *Il Conbattimento di Tancredi e Clorinda* (mus. Monteverdi), *Venus and Adonis* (mus. John Blow), *Agrippina* (mus. Handel); movement and dance in *A Winter's Tale* (play by Shakespeare; staged 1987), and *The Changeling* (play by Middleton; staged 1988); dances in musical *Joseph and His Amazing Technicolour Dreamcoat* (dir. Dunlop).

## PUBLICATIONS

By Christopher Bruce:
Interview in "The Anatomy of Pierrot", *Dance and Dancers* (London), December 1969
Interview in "Curtain Up", *Dance and Dancers* (London), June 1986

About Christopher Bruce:
Dodd, Craig, "The Return of Springtime", *Dancing Times* (London), May 1969
Gow, Charles, "Christopher Bruce", *Dancing Times* (London), March 1973
Austin, Richard, *The Birth of a Ballet*, London, 1976
Dougill, David, "Where Bruce Gets his Ideas From", *Classical Music* (London), 2 October 1976
Brinson, Peter, and Crisp, Clement, *Ballet and Dance: A Guide to the Repertory*, London, 1981
"Man with a Purpose", in "Curtain Up", *Dance and Dancers* (London), June 1986
Kane, Angela, "Christopher Bruce's Choreography: Inroads or Re-tracing Old Steps", *Dancing Times* (London), October 1991

**Christopher Bruce in *Pierrot lunaire*, Ballet Rambert, 1967**

Christopher Bruce's very individual quality of movement and imagination made him the perfect interpreter of the leading role in *Pierrot Lunaire* at its British premiere in 1967. He was then 22. A dancer of rare magnetism—he calls it "a concentrated presence that every dancer should develop"—and a choreographer with a deep commitment to the problems of the real world, he earned a glowing reputation early in his career, both at home and abroad. His training with Rambert had been classical, but when the company re-organized in 1966, adopting modern American methods and establishing an entirely new repertory, he proved capable of assimilating the two styles into one of his own, with which he could express the poetry and the pain which characterize all his major works.

Bruce has made more than 40 ballets, 23 of them for Rambert. He has worked with more than fifteen companies abroad, and has choreographed for opera, musicals, theatre, and film. He and his works have appeared frequently on British television and he has created works for television in Denmark and Sweden.

Audiences found Bruce's "concentrated presence" riveting, whether as a member of an abstract, anonymous group, as in Tetley's *Ziggurat* and *Embrace Tiger and Return to Mountain*, or in such intensely personal roles as Faune, Pierrot Lunaire, and the poet García Lorca in *Cruel Garden*. Critics referred to him in the 1970s as "the Nureyev of Modern Dance"; but while he had the charisma he had none of the flamboyance, and no taste for publicity. Nevertheless, a jury of leading critics selected him for the first-ever *Evening Standard* Dance Award in 1974, and Clement Crisp of the *Financial Times* spoke of him as "a dancer with a touch of genius, and a choreographer of enormous talent".

The works which earned Bruce this recognition were, in true Rambert tradition, innovatory. They revealed a talent for creating movement images related to deeply held convictions rarely expressed before in dance, and requiring a new language. "I have to feel quite strongly to make things work", said Bruce when interviewed on the subject of his first serious work, *Wings*; "I work instinctively from knowing and feeling. I don't just put steps together". Abstract in form, *Wings* yet conveyed a powerful sense of the tragic vulnerability of the human body, a theme which became more explicit, and was conveyed in still more challenging form, in the next two pieces: *for these who die as cattle*, inspired by the First World War poetry of Wilfred Owen, and *There Was a Time*, an interpretation of the ten-year Trojan War. Both these pieces, performed on a thrust stage, the first in silence, the second accompanied throughout by an electronic whine like a malignant wind, drew sculpturally powerful performances of absolute integrity from a young cast. The unfamiliar form and sound provoked one leading critic to an apoplectic outburst, while others wrote of Bruce's "concern with the human condition" and his "ability to fix emotional states with movement of real sensitivity".

Bruce has never relied upon spectacle or familiar music: at this period he worked almost exclusively with the designer Nadine Baylis and the lighting designer John B. Read (both at the beginning of their immensely successful careers) in order to create spare, luminous patterns to reinforce the meaning of the movement. He was one of the first in Britain to choreograph to electronic scores, by Bob Downs and Brian Hodgson; he made four works to scores by George Crumb, two of them with texts by Federico García Lorca, with whom Bruce has a close affinity. It is as both choreographer and dancer of the role of the tragic Spanish poet in *Cruel Garden* that Bruce will perhaps be most vividly remembered.

*Cruel Garden* was a spectacle, performed in the round in a converted engine shed, a surrealistic drama devised by the mime Lindsay Kemp and based on the life and works of García Lorca. Bruce brought to the choreography both his classical elegance and his contemporary realism, showing an actor's observation and imagination, in his passionate portrayal of the poet's concern for the oppressed. Bryan Robertson wrote in the *Spectator* that Bruce "with amazing strength and delicacy . . . is in a rare state of grace. *Cruel Garden* is a great masterpiece of the English stage."

Bruce retired from dancing at the age of 34. His career had been dogged by severe knee problems, culminating in two operations which kept him from performing for several months at a time; but his creativity remained unimpaired. Inspired by a concert of Andean music given by the exiled Chilean group Inti Illimani he produced what has proved to date his most popular work, *Ghost Dances*, a haunting piece with strong folk influences, dedicated "to the innocent people of Latin America, from the time of the Spanish conquests continuously devastated by political oppression". This short, intense piece, danced to an arrangement of South American folk songs, is in the repertoire of companies from Sweden to Australia.

*Berlin Requiem*, based on Brecht's harsh, satirical commentary on twentieth-century urban society and set to Kurt Weill's brazen score, treated the theme of oppression with movement more violent than Bruce had ever created before, resulting in a disturbing piece for which audiences seemed unprepared. But two of the last ballets Bruce made before leaving Ballet Rambert were among his most accessible. *Intimate Pages*, danced to Janáček's String Quartet no. 2, contains some of his most lyrical writing, and is exquisitely designed by Walter Nobbe, with whom Bruce has since worked successfully a number of times. *Sergeant Early's Dream*, a piece about emigration and nostalgia, draws upon the music of British, Irish, and American folk songs, their legends and their dances. It is full of energy, humour, and sweet sorrow, with designs again by Walter Nobbe; nothing could have been more different from the Cunningham-directed style which was beginning to be introduced into the Rambert company after the death of its founder.

In 1985, Bruce undertook to produce six works in three years for the classical London Festival Ballet. *Cruel Garden* was revived to acclaim, and four one-act pieces—*Land*, *The World Again*, *The Dream is Over* (to eight songs by John Lennon), and *Swansong*—saw the dancers seize upon the opportunities of dramatic expression and motivated movement that Bruce gave them, to perform as never before.

Since 1988 Bruce has been resident choreographer with the Houston Ballet, for whom he has created *Guatama Buddha*, an attempt to "distill the essence of the quality of the man, his life and his philosophy", and *Journey*, choreographed at the request of the composer, Palle Millelborg, in memoriam to Erik Bruhn, with sets by Walter Nobbe.

Christopher Bruce's ballets have created a category all their own. There are "no limits, no boundaries", as he has said himself, finding it "exciting to move in all sorts of directions". Classical, contemporary, folk, and a host of other influences, whether choreographic, literary, musical, or theatrical, continue to enrich the work of a man described by Noël Goodwin as one "whose sensibility and talent, warmth of feeling and instinct for movement can take dancers to their limits and beyond".

—Jane King

---

**BRUHN, Erik**

Danish dancer, choreographer, and ballet director. Born Belton Evers in Copenhagen, 3 October 1928. Studied at the Royal Danish Ballet School, 1937–47; also studied with Stanislas Idzikowski, London. Dancer, Royal Danish Ballet, Copenhagen, from 1947: solo dancer (principal) from 1949; guest artist, Metropolitan Ballet, England, 1947–49; dancer, American Ballet Theatre, from 1949: soloist, from 1951, and principal dancer from 1955, returning to perform with Royal Danish Ballet, from 1952; guest artist, New York City Ballet, 1959–60, Royal Ballet, 1962, Stuttgart Ballet, 1962, Australian Ballet, 1962, La Scala, Milan, 1962, Harkness Ballet, 1964, National Ballet of Canada, 1965, and Ruth Page Ballet; choreographer, Rome Opera House, 1966; director, Royal Swedish Ballet, Stockholm, 1967–71; resident producer, National Ballet of Canada, 1973–76, returning as artistic director, 1983–86; also choreographer: first work, *Concertette*, staged in Copenhagen, 1953; restaged many of the classics for various international companies, including Royal Danish Ballet, Royal Swedish Ballet, Munich (Bavarian State Opera) Ballet, Harkness Ballet, and National Ballet of Canada; appeared in film, *Hans Christian Andersen* (dir. Vidor, chor. Petit, 1952), and made acting début in Copenhagen, 1974; also author, with Lillian Moore, of book on Bournonville ballet technique. Recipient: Nijinsky Prize, Paris, 1963; title of Knight of Dannebrog, 1963; Election to the Roll of Honour, Students' Association of Denmark, 1965; *Dance Magazine* Award, 1968; Diplôme d'honneur, Canadian Conference of the Arts, 1974; Litteris et Artibus Medal, Stockholm, 1980. Died in Toronto, 1 April 1986.

**Erick Bruhn in *La Sylphide*, 1967**

**ROLES**

1942 Principal dancer in *Napoli* (Bournonville), Royal Danish Ballet School, Copenhagen

1946 Indian Dance in *Far From Denmark* (Bournonville), Royal Danish Ballet, Copenhagen

Greek Dance in *The Whims of Cupid and the Ballet Master* (Galeotti), Royal Danish Ballet, Copenhagen

Adonis in *Torvaldsen* (Lander), Royal Danish Ballet, Copenhagen

1947 Principal dancer (cr) in *Lover's Gallery* (F. Staff), Metropolitan Ballet, Blackpool, England

1947/48 Prince Siegfried in *Swan Lake* (Ivanov), Metropolitan Ballet, tour

Bluebird in *Bluebird Pas de deux* (from *The Sleeping Beauty*; after Petipa), Metropolitan Ballet, tour

Pas de deux from *The Sleeping Beauty*, Act III (after Petipa), Metropolitan Ballet, tour

The Poet in *Les Sylphides* (Fokine; staged V. Gsovsky), Metropolitan Ballet, tour

The Spirit of the rose in *Le Spectre de la rose* (Fokine), Metropolitan Ballet, tour

Principal dancer in *Dances of Galatea and Pygmalion* (V. Gsovsky), Metropolitan Ballet, tour

Pas de trois in *Swan Lake* (Act I; after Petipa), Metropolitan Ballet, tour

1948 Principal dancer (cr) in *Designs with Strings* (Taras), Metropolitan Ballet, Edinburgh

Principal dancer (cr) in *The Pilgrim's Progress* (Howard), Metropolitan Ballet, London

The Hussar in *Le Beau Danube* (Massine), Royal Danish Ballet, Copenhagen

1948/49 Soloist in *Konservatoriet* (Bournonville), Royal Danish Ballet, Copenhagen

Principal dancer in *Napoli* (Bournonville), Royal Danish Ballet, Copenhagen.

The Dandy in *Le Beau Danube* (Massine), Royal Danish Ballet, Copenhagen

Shepherd in *Symphonie fantastique* (Massine), Royal Danish Ballet, Copenhagen

Dancer in *Études* (Lander), Royal Danish Ballet, Copenhagen

Officer and Adagio Dancer in *The Widow in the Mirror* (Ralov), Royal Danish Ballet, Copenhagen

James in *La Sylphide*, Act II (Bournonville), Royal Danish Ballet, Copenhagen

Czardas in *Coppélia* (Lander), Royal Danish Ballet, Copenhagen

1949 Principal dancer (cr) in *Rhapsodie* (Lander), Royal Danish Ballet, Copenhagen

Orestes in *Helen of Troy* (Lichine), Ballet Theatre, New York

Paris in *Romeo and Juliet* (Tudor), Ballet Theatre, New York

1950 Pas de deux from *The Nutcracker* (Ivanov), Ballet Theatre, New York

1951 Principal dancer (cr) in *Schumann Concerto* (Nijinska), Ballet Theatre, New York

Principal dancer in *Concerto* (*Constantia*; Dollar), Ballet Theatre

Prince Sapphire in *Bluebeard* (Fokine), Ballet Theatre

Principal dancer in *Don Quixote* Pas de deux (Obukhov after Petipa), Ballet Theatre

Lover in *Les Patineurs* (Ashton), Ballet Theatre

James in *La Sylphide* (Bournonville), Royal Danish Ballet, Copenhagen

Solo dancer in *Études* (Lander, after Bournonville), Royal Danish Ballet, Copenhagen

Romeo in *Romeo and Juliet* (Bartholin), Royal Danish Ballet, Copenhagen

1952 Principal dancer (cr) in *Idolon* (Schaufuss), Royal Danish Ballet, Copenhagen

Third Movement in *Symphony in C* (Balanchine), Royal Danish Ballet, Copenhagen

Ove in *A Folk Tale* (Bournonville), Royal Danish Ballet, Copenhagen

1953 Prince (cr) in *La Courtisane* (Ralov), Royal Danish Ballet, Copenhagen

A Student (cr) in *Parisiana* (Bartholin), Royal Danish Ballet, Copenhagen

1954/55 The Man She Must Marry in *Jardin aux Lilas* (Tudor), Ballet Theatre

Prince Siegfried in *The Black Swan* pas de deux (Petipa), Ballet Theatre

Title role in *Aleko* (Massine), Ballet Theatre

Principal dancer in *Theme and Variations* (Balanchine), Ballet Theatre

Pas de deux in *Graduation Ball* (Lichine), Ballet Theatre

Paris in *Helen of Troy* (Lichine), Ballet Theatre

Caricaturist in *Mam'zelle Angot* (Massine), Ballet Theatre

Albrecht in *Giselle* (Petipa after Coralli, Perrot; staged Dolin), Ballet Theatre

1955 Romeo in *Romeo and Juliet* (Ashton), Royal Danish Ballet, Copenhagen

1956 Saint-Léon in *Pas des Déesses* (Joffrey), Ballet Theatre Workshop, New York

1957 Principal dancer (cr) in *Journey* (MacMillan), Ballet Theatre Previews, New York

The Youth (cr) in *La Muerte Enamorada* (Martinez), Ballet Theatre Previews, New York

The Troubadour (cr) in *The Careless Burghers* (Sanders), Ballet Theatre Previews, New York

Principal dancer (cr) in *Paquita Pas de deux* (Fedorova after Petipa), American Ballet Theatre, Washington, D.C.

The Bridegroom in *Blood Wedding* (Rodrigues), Ballet Theatre Previews, New York

Junior Cadet in *Graduation Ball* (Lichine), Ballet Theatre

1958 Principal dancer (cr) in *Concerto* (Ross), American Ballet Theatre, New York

Principal dancer (cr) in *Tristan* (pas de deux; Ross), American Ballet Theatre, New York

Jean in *Miss Julie* (Cullberg), American Ballet Theatre, New York

Principal dancer in *Variations for Four* (Dolin), American Ballet Theatre, New York

1959 Principal dancer (cr) in *Duet* (also chor.), Bellas Artes, Guatemala City, Guatemala

Prince Siegfried in *Swan Lake* (one-act version; Balanchine after Ivanov), New York City Ballet, New York

Principal dancer in *Divertimento No. 15* (Balanchine), New York City Ballet, New York

Principal dancer in *Pas de Dix* (Balanchine), New York City Ballet, New York

Cavalier in *The Nutcracker* (Balanchine), New York City Ballet, New York

1960 Preludios Para Percusión (Colombia; cr) in *Panamerica* (Balanchine, Contreras, Moncion, Taras, d'Amboise), New York City Ballet, New York

The Young Man (cr) in *Helios* (Von Rosen), Danish television

The Poet in *Night Shadow* (*La Sonnambula*; Balanchine), New York City Ballet, New York

Seaman in *Lady from the Sea* (Cullberg), American Ballet Theatre, New York

Don José in *Carmen* (Petit), Royal Danish Ballet, Copenhagen

1961 The Gangster in *La Chaloupée* (Petit), Royal Danish Ballet, Copenhagen

Principal dancer in *Grand Pas Glazounov* (from *Raymonda*; Balanchine), American Ballet Theatre, New York

Pas de deux from *Flower Festival at Genzano* (Bournonville), Jacob's Pillow Dance Festival, Massachusetts

1962 Principal dancer (cr) in *Fantaisie* (also chor.), Bruhn/Nureyev Company, Cannes

Principal dancer (cr) in *Toccata and Fugue* (also chor.), Bruhn/Nureyev Company, Cannes

Principal dancer (cr) in *Serenade* (also chor.), Bavarian Opera Ballet, Munich

Daphnis in *Daphnis and Chloë* (Cranko), Stuttgart Ballet, Stuttgart

Principal dancer (cr) in *Pas de deux* (also chor.), Tivoli Gardens, Copenhagen, Denmark

Prince Florimund in *The Sleeping Beauty* (Petipa; staged Sergeyev, Ashton, de Valois), Royal Ballet, London

Franz in *Coppélia* (Van Praagh after Petipa, Cecchetti), Australian Ballet, Sydney

1964 Daphnis in *Daphnis and Chloë* (Skibine), Paris Opéra Ballet, Paris

1965 Principal dancer (cr) in *Scottish Fantasy* (also chor.), Harkness Ballet, Cannes

Principal dancer (cr) in *The Abyss* (Hodes), Harkness Ballet, Cannes

1966 Romeo (cr) in *Romeo and Juliet* (pas de deux; also chor.), Rome Opera Ballet, Rome

1967 Solo (cr) in *Morning, Noon and Night* (Akesson, Gundersen), Swedish television

1971 Pas de deux (cr) added to *The River* (Ailey), American Ballet Theatre, New York

Title role in *The Miraculous Mandarin* (Gadd), American Ballet Theatre, New York

1974 Madge the Witch in *La Sylphide* (also chor., after Bournonville), National Ballet of Canada, Toronto

1975 Principal dancer (cr) in *Epilogue* (pas de deux; Neumeier), American Ballet Theatre, New York

Dr. Coppélius in *Coppélia* (also chor.), National Ballet of Canada, Toronto

Abdul-Rakhaman in *Raymonda* (Nureyev after Petipa), American Ballet Theatre, New York

Principal dancer in *La Ventana Pas de trois* (also chor., after Bournonville), American Ballet Theatre, New York

The Man in *Las Hermanas* (MacMillan), American Ballet Theatre, New York

1976 Claudius in *Hamlet Connotations* (Neumeier), American Ballet Theatre, New York

Title role in *Petrushka* (Fokine), American Ballet Theatre, New York

1977 The Moor in *The Moor's Pavane* (Limón), American Ballet Theatre

1978 Rasputin (cr) in *Rasputin—The Holy Devil* (Clouser), Fort Worth Ballet and James Clouser's Space/Dance/Theater, Fort Worth, Texas

1979 Principal dancer (cr) in *The Mist* (pas de deux; Patsalas), Wolf Trap, Virginia

**WORKS**

1953 *Concertette* (mus. Gould), Royal Danish Ballet, Copenhagen
1957 *Festa* (mus. Rossini), American Ballet Theatre, New York
1959 *Duet* (mus. A. Beriot), Bellas Artes, Guatemala City, Guatemala
*Festa* (new version; mus. Rossini), Royal Danish Ballet, Copenhagen
1962 *Toccata and Fugue* (mus. J. S. Bach), Nureyev/Bruhn Company, Théâtre du Casino Municipale, Cannes
*Fantaisie* (mus. traditional Spanish), Nureyev/Bruhn Company, Théâtre du Casino Municipale, Cannes
*Serenade* (mus. O. Olsen), Bavarian Opera Ballet, Munich
*Pas de Deux*, Tivoli Gardens Centenary, Tivoli Gardens, Copenhagen
1965 *Scottish Fantasy* (mus. G. Crum), Harkness Ballet, Cannes
1966 *Romeo and Juliet* (pas de deux; mus. Prokofiev), Rome Opera Ballet, Rome
1978 *Here We Come* (mus. American marches), National Ballet of Canada School, Toronto

Also staged:
1962 *Napoli* Pas de six (after A. Bournonville; mus. Paulli and others), Royal Ballet, London
*Flower Festival at Genzano* Pas de deux (after A. Bournonville; mus. Helsted, Paulli), Royal Ballet, London (staged Australian Ballet, 1962; Royal Swedish Ballet, 1966; National Ballet of Canada, 1974)
1964 *Giselle* (after Coralli and Perrot; mus Adam), Royal Danish Ballet, Copenhagen (staged Royal Swedish Ballet, 1969)
*La Sylphide* (after A. Bournonville; mus. H. Løvenskjold), National Ballet of Canada, Toronto (staged Rome Opera Ballet, 1966; Royal Swedish Ballet, 1968; American Ballet Theatre, 1983; Australian Ballet, 1985)
1966 *Swan Lake*, Act II (after Ivanov; mus. Tchaikovsky), Rome Opera Ballet, Rome
1967 *Swan Lake* (after Petipa, Ivanov, with some dances from Bolshoi Ballet production; mus. Tchaikovsky), National Ballet of Canada, Toronto
1972 *Les Sylphides* (after Fokine; mus. Chopin), Royal Danish Ballet, Copenhagen
1973 *Coppélia* (mus. Delibes), National Ballet of Canada, Toronto
1975 *La Ventana* Pas de trois (after Bournonville; mus. Lumbye), American Ballet Theatre, New York
1979 *Swan Lake* (revised version; after Petipa, Ivanov; mus. Tchaikovsky), National Ballet of Canada, London

**PUBLICATIONS**

By Bruhn:
*Bournonville and Ballet Technique*, with Lillian Moore, London, 1961
"Ballon and the Bournonville Style", with Lillian Moore, *Dancing Times* (London), November 1961
Interview in "Erik Bruhn Talks", *Dance and Dancers* (London), June 1962
Interview in Maynard, Olga, "Erik Bruhn", *Dance Magazine* (New York), January 1966
*Beyond Technique*, Dance Perspectives no. 36 (New York), 1968
Interview in Gruen, John, *The Private World of Ballet*, New York, 1975
"Restaging the Classics", in Payne, Charles, *American Ballet Theatre*, New York, 1978
Conversations with John Gruen, printed posthumously in Gruen, John, *People Who Dance*, Pennington, New Jersey, 1988

About Bruhn:
Goodman, Saul, "Brief Biographies: Erik Bruhn", *Dance Magazine* (New York), May 1955
Crowle, Pigeon, "Erik Bruhn", *Ballet Today* (London), October 1956
"Bruhn, Bournonville, and Ballet", *Dance Magazine* (New York), February 1962
Moore, Lillian, "Profile: Erik Bruhn", *Dancing Times* (London), May 1964
Kragh-Jacobsen, Svend, *Aereskunstneren Erik Bruhn*, Copenhagen, 1965
Terry, Walter, "Beyond Technique", *Saturday Review* (New York), 22 February 1969
Lidova, Irène, "Erik Bruhn", *Les Saisons de la danse* (Paris), October 1969
Siegel, Marcia, "One Thousand Roses", *The Hudson Review* (New York), January 1975
"Royal Dane", *Dancing Times* (London), June 1975
Gruen, John, *Danseur Noble: Erik Bruhn*, New York, 1979
Como, William, "Tribute to Erik Bruhn, the Dancer's Dancer", *Dance Magazine* (New York), May 1981
Bland, Alexander, and Percival, John, *Men Dancing: Performers and Performing*, London, 1984

* * *

Erik Bruhn, the leading danseur noble of his generation and the first real ballet superstar to emerge after the Second World War, rewrote the traditional ballet scenario by demonstrating that, in classical dance, a man could be as much the centre of attention as a woman. He gleaned his ideas from the Royal Danish Ballet School in Copenhagen, where he was immersed in the traditions of one of Europe's oldest and most respected ballet institutions. Those traditions were established by the great Danish ballet master August Bournonville, who believed that dance could, with the aid of music, raise itself to the heights of poetry through the appearance of ease in virtuoso performance. "The summit of talent is to know how to conceal the mechanism through the calm harmony which is the foundation of true grace." Bournonville wrote these words but Bruhn lived them. His entire career can be said to be the mastery of the Bournonvillean illusion of noble simplicity.

Bruhn's dancing, while strong and expressive, was characterized by supreme taste and artistry. He was the consummate Prince in ballets like *Swan Lake* and the ultimate James in his own version of Bournonville's *La Sylphide*, giving a crisp, musical, richly expressive performance. His dramatic talents made him a formidable presence in such contemporary ballets as Birgit Cullberg's *Miss Julie* and Roland Petit's *Carmen*. And his formidable partnering skills made him the favourite of many of the world's leading ballerinas: Alicia Markova, Nora Kaye, Alicia Alonso, Maria Tallchief, Violette Verdy, Natalia Makarova, Kirsten Simone, Sonia Arova (to whom he was once briefly engaged), and Carla Fracci can be numbered among the great dancers with whom he performed. With Fracci, Bruhn formed one of the greatest dancing partnerships this century. His Scandanavian cool and her Italian sprightliness was like a meeting of ice and fire. In May 1984, more than ten years after his official retirement from dancing, Bruhn rejoined Fracci on stage in a special gala performance in New York of the second act of *La Sylphide* which drew a standing ovation from the packed Metropolitan Opera House. Such enthusiastic responses to his dancing were not uncommon. In Toronto, in 1964, he gave a performance in the National Ballet of Canada's production of his *La Sylphide* that received 25 curtain calls. It was the beginning of a long love affair between Bruhn and the Toronto company.

Bruhn was an innovative thinker, a pioneer in his own field. But his ideas were not always popular. He believed that complacency in anyone's career was death, and he was always looking for ways to challenge himself, and others, through new roles and new styles. When he was artistic director of the Royal Swedish Ballet, Bruhn found himself battling against an entrenched bureaucracy in Stockholm and a general unwillingness to accept his new approaches to running a classical company. In the end he won, but the toll on his energies was heavy, leading him to exclaim, "Never again". The National Ballet of Canada, however, presented him with a different and more sympathetic challenge, one that made him revoke his earlier resolution. Within a year of taking over the company, Bruhn had already changed its image significantly. The key signal was his choice of guests for a gala evening in 1984. Instead of the standard formula—a string of popular pas de deux by international superstars—Bruhn chose to emphasize Canadian artists Danny Grossman, Robert Desrosiers, and David Earle, choreographers not working in ballet, but in modern dance. Later he commissioned some of the same choreographers to create new works for the National Ballet's dancers, thereby asserting his belief in the value of contemporary movement styles for classically trained ballet dancers.

Bruhn's version of *Swan Lake* also sparked controversy when it made its début with the National Ballet of Canada in 1967. Bruhn completely reworked the role of the Prince according to his own belief in lending new credibility to the male dancer. His Prince is a fully developed, three-dimensional character with a recognizable psychological profile. The role, to be acted as much as danced, takes the male dancer from being merely a porteur to being an integral part of the ballet.

This was long Bruhn's ambition: to make himself, as a male dancer, the heart of everything he danced. He did this out of love for ballet and out of a deep need to realize himself through his art. "There have been certain moments on the stage where I suddenly had a feeling of completeness," Bruhn once said to his biographer John Gruen. "I had the indescribable sensation of being everywhere and nowhere. I had the sense of being universal." Those who watched Bruhn dance experienced something of the same—a being beyond the ordinary who inspired joy and wonder for the heights he reached.

—Deirdre Kelly

---

**BUDAPEST BALLET** *see* **HUNGARIAN STATE OPERA BALLET**

---

## BUGAKU

**Choreography:** George Balanchine
**Music:** Toshiro Mayuzumi
**Design:** David Hays (scenery and lighting), Barbara Karinska (costumes)
**First Production:** New York City Ballet, City Center, New York, 20 March 1963
**Principal Dancers:** Allegra Kent, Edward Villella

**Other productions include:** Dance Theatre of Harlem, with Lydia Abarca, Ronald Perry; New York, 1975. Zurich Opera Ballet; Zurich, 12 April 1980.

### PUBLICATIONS

Balanchine, George, with Mason, Francis, *Balanchine's Complete Stories of the Great Ballets*, Garden City, N.Y., 1977
Reynolds, Nancy, *Repertory in Review*, New York, 1977
Kirstein, Lincoln, *30 Years: The New York City Ballet*, New York, 1978

* * *

Balanchine's philosophical gift was simplicity, even in the most complex of situations. In *Bugaku*, as in a number of his other masterpieces, he combined and extended classical technique and cultural style beyond the boundaries of their time, and he did it simply.

*Bugaku* is a portrait of the courtship and marriage ritual, of its outward formalities and inner truths. It is perhaps Balanchine's most erotic ballet. Inspired by Japanese Gagaku Court dancers of the Imperial household, it overcame initial negative criticism about "Western" stereotypical interpretation of Eastern cultures because of its ultimate integrity.

Visually, the sets by David Hays for *Bugaku* are minimalistic and only suggestive of Japanese style. The traditional red and green of Japanese Gagaku are represented by two red boards, in the slight curve of a pagoda, suspended by white ropes against a blue-grey backdrop, and green carpeting. The curtain is up while the overture is played. Slow, gently ascending violin strings begin the opening theme.

Balanchine commissioned Toshiro Mayuzumi to fashion the music in the spirit of Japanese court music. It is quite a remarkable score, at times powerfully evocative with its lush dramatics and harmonious sweep. Although one critic likened the score to a series of air-raid warnings, a review by Thomas Willis dated 10 August 1963, praised it lovingly:

> Above all, Balanchine begins with scores. This one . . . is fascinating for its crossbreeding of east and west. Strings begin in eerie glissando, basses and cellos pluck so hard the strings slap the fingerboard. Winds are used for softly trilling color, or shrill accent. Percussion can ornament in delicate tracery or mark a heroic masculine beat. Even its strongest impact points have a vital moment of preparation.

It is Eastern music, in short, that can be danced in European style.

Five women enter in an orderly line from stage left and quietly, obediently perform a variation alone that is gently coquettish. They wear sparsely adorned black Japanese ceremonial wigs. They are in toe shoes, but often in moments of transition their feet flex and knees turn in. Their stiff tutus are shaped like lotus petals, and their variation includes bows of honour, kneeling, inclined heads, doll-like arm movements, and occasional surprises of extension and stretch.

Five men follow, also in line, in traditional wigs with braided ponytail. They are clad in short white kimonos, and perform a kind of czardas, where the marching lunge in each direction

**_Bugaku_ with Allegra Kent and Edward Villella (left), New York City Ballet, 1963**

takes on the significance of a warrior dance against a chilling musical backdrop. A collective adagio briefly hints at the question of physical dominance, and then the couples in white stop their dance. The formality of classical ballet symmetry in this variation blends naturally with the formality of oriental ceremony.

The dancers leave the stage quickly and neatly, their simple walk an eloquent expression of the beauty of natural control. After a short interlude, all the dancers return, in similar procession but in different costumes: diaphanous robes and white bikini body stockings for the women, and for the men robes covering sleeveless white shirts and white tights. After an initial greeting, danced in the robes, the betrothed couple separates and the men surround the Groom as the women surround the Bride to remove these robes. Carrying the robes aloft, the attendants line up again, and the men and women then separate and exit, leaving the couple alone.

The ensuing pas de deux is one of the most strenuous in ballet today. When the dancers keep that strain to themselves it can be powerfully sensual. However, if the principals fail to trust the choreography, its sexuality can become vulgar. The encounter ends with a ceremonial bow. The four couples return to the stage and perform the final adagio en masse, building on the thematic shapes of the ritualistic dance.

The opening night cast was led by Allegra Kent and Edward Villella. Sharing the roles in other performances were Mimi Paul and Arthur Mitchell. These principals were exceptionally flexible, technically superior, and naturally sensual dancers. They remain the standard for excellence in this work.

After its début at New York's City Center on 20 March 1963, *Bugaku* received radically mixed reviews. A few criticized the music harshly for its unfamiliar atonal couplings. Some were upset by the contradiction between ballet's pointed toes and the tradition of flat-footed Japanese dancing. Others deplored its acrobatics, saying it was antithetical to anything Japanese, and that it contained ugly and unseemly positions. Yet these criticisms in themselves are products of the kind of predisposed thinking that fosters stereotype. The longevity of this ballet (it is still being performed, although it was retired from the New York City Ballet repertoire at least once) attests to Balanchine's genius for translating one culture's beauty into terms another can understand.

Of *Bugaku*, Louis Biancolli wrote, "only genius can account for its unified beauty of content and idiom". Comparing it with *Apollo*, with which *Bugaku* shared the bill one night, he concluded that despite a gap of "three and a half decades, the ballets have in common that absolute integrity of pace and mood that never veers from the twin dictates of music and dance".

—Kim Kokich

---

**BUJONES, Fernando**

American dancer and choreographer. Born in Miami, Florida, 9 March 1955. Studied at the School of Ballet Nacional de Cuba, and at the School of American Ballet (scholarship student), New York, from 1967, pupil of Stanley Williams and André Eglevsky; has also been coached by Zeida Cecilia Mendez. Married (1) Marcia Kubitschek, 1980: one daughter, Alejandra (b. 1983); (2) dancer Maria Arnillas, 1991. Professional début with André Eglevsky's company, Long Island, 1970; dancer, American Ballet Theatre, New York, from 1972: member of the corps de ballet, 1972–73; soloist, from 1973; principal dancer, from 1974; resigned, 1985; guest artist, Paris Opéra, 1981, Rome Opera Ballet, 1977, Vienna State Opera Ballet, 1978–79, Tokyo Ballet, 1979, Royal Ballet, London, 1985–86, and Bolshoi Ballet, Moscow (first American dancer to be invited by director Yuri Grigorovich), 1987; other international guest appearances include with National Ballet of Canada, 1976, Teatro Municipal in Rio de Janeiro, 1976, Edinburgh Festival, 1977, German Opera Ballet, Berlin, 1977, Stuttgart Ballet, 1979, Ballet du XXe Siècle, 1987; permanent guest artist, Boston Ballet, from 1987; principal guest artist, American Ballet Theatre, from 1990; has also appeared on television and films, including for "Dance in America" television series for the Public Broadcasting Service (PBS), 1976, 1985, and in the film *The Turning Point* (dir. Ross, 1978); also choreographer and director, creating first choreography for American Ballet Theatre, 1985; associate artistic director, and choreographer, Rio de Janeiro Opera House, 1986–87; has staged ballets for companies including Boston Ballet, Turin Opera Ballet, American Ballet Theatre, and National Ballet of Canada, from 1988. Recipient: Gold Medal, International Ballet Competition, Varna, Bulgaria, 1974; Outstanding Young Men of America Award, 1980; *Dance Magazine* Award, 1982; *New York Times* Award for Outstanding Artistic Talent of Florida, 1986; Hispanic Heritage Award, 1989; Library of Congress Honor Day (20th anniversary), 1991.

**ROLES**

1973 Sailor in *Fancy Free* (Robbins), American Ballet Theatre
The Lover in *Jardin aux Lilas* (Tudor), American Ballet Theatre
Pas de deux, "Diana and Acteon" from *La Esmeralda* (Nureyev after Petipa), American Ballet Theatre

**Fernando Bujones in *Le Corsaire***

Principal dancer in *Les Sylphides* (Fokine), American Ballet Theatre
The Transgressor in *Undertow* (Tudor), American Ballet Theatre
1974 Principal dancer in *Theme and Variations* (Balanchine), American Ballet Theatre, Chicago
Boy in Green in *Les Patineurs* (Ashton), American Ballet Theatre
1975 Solor in *La Bayadère*, Act IV (Makarova after Petipa), American Ballet Theatre, New York
Pas de deux from *Le Corsaire* (Nureyev after Petipa), American Ballet Theatre, New York
Jean de Brienne in *Raymonda* (Nureyev after Petipa), American Ballet Theatre, Houston
Prince Siegfried in *Swan Lake* (Petipa, Ivanov; staged Blair), American Ballet Theatre, Portland, Oregon
James in *La Sylphide* (Bruhn after Bournonville), American Ballet Theatre, Washington, D.C.
1976 Prince in *The Nutcracker* (Baryshnikov), American Ballet Theatre, Washington, D.C.
Prince Désiré in *The Sleeping Beauty* (Petipa; staged Skeaping), American Ballet Theatre, New York
1977 Albrecht in *Giselle* (Petipa after Coralli, Perrot; staged Blair), American Ballet Theatre, New York
Franz in *Coppélia* (Parés after Saint-Léon), German Opera Ballet, Berlin
1978 Basilio in *Don Quixote* (Nureyev after Petipa), Vienna State Opera Ballet, Vienna
1981 James in *La Sylphide* (Lacotte after Petipa, Coralli, Perrot), Paris Opéra Ballet, Paris
1982 Principal dancer (cr) in *Clair de Lune* (pas de deux; Anastos), American Ballet Theatre, New York
1983 Don José in *Carmen* (Petit), American Ballet Theatre, Miami
Pas de deux from *La Fille mal gardée* (Petipa; staged Joffe), American Ballet Theatre
1984 Billy in *Billy the Kid* (Loring), American Ballet Theatre, New York
Principal dancer (cr) in *Bach Partita* (Tharp), American Ballet Theatre, New York
1987 Alexandre (cr) in *Trois Etudes pour Alexandre* (Béjart), Béjart Ballet, Lausanne
1988 D'Artagnan in *The Three Musketeers* (Prokovsky), Australian Ballet
1990 Principal dancer in *Abdallah* (Bournonville), Boston Ballet, Boston

**Other roles include:** principal dancer (lead couple) in *Theme and Variations* (Balanchine), principal dancer in *Interludes* (McFall), The Man She Must Marry in *Jardin aux Lilas* (Tudor), principal dancer in Grand Pas from *Paquita* (Nureyev after Petipa), Variation, Adagio in *Les Rendezvous* (Ashton), principal dancer in *Grand Pas Classique* (pas de deux; Gsovsky), Jean in *Miss Julie* (Cullberg); also created title role in *Narcissus* (Eduardo Recalt), pas de deux in *Concertino* (Lynne Taylor-Corbett), principal dancer in *Rendezvous* (pas de deux; van Hoff).

## WORKS

1985 *Grand Pas Romantique* (mus. Adam, *Le Diable à Quatre*), American Ballet Theatre, New York (staged Torino Opera Ballet 1989)

Also staged:
1985 *Raymonda*, Act III (after Petipa; mus. Glazunov), Opera House, Rio de Janeiro, Brazil (staged Turin Opera Ballet, 1988; Boston Ballet, 1989; American Ballet Theatre, 1991)
1988 Pas de deux, "Diana and Acteon", from *La Esmeralda* (after Petipa; mus. Pugni), National Ballet of Canada
1990 *Paquita* (Grand Pas, after Petipa; mus. Deldevez, Minkus), Turin Opera Ballet

## PUBLICATIONS

By Bujones:
Interview with Brubach, Holly, in *Ballet News* (New York), October 1980
*Fernando Bujones* (autobiography; in English and Portuguese), Rio de Janeiro, 1984

About Bujones:
Gruen, John, "Spotlight on Bujones", *Dance Magazine* (New York), October 1976
Stoop, Norma McLain, "Fernando Bujones", *Dance Magazine* (New York), December 1979
Brubach, Holly, and Petitjean, Pierre (photographer), *Ten Dancers*, New York, 1982
Taub, Eric, "That Championship Season", *Ballet News* (New York), September 1984
Gruen, John, "Gregory and Bujones", *Dance Magazine* (New York), September 1984
"Guest Shot", *Ballet News* (New York), November 1985
Fanger, Iris, "Fernando Bujones", *Dance Magazine* (New York), May 1991

* * *

Fernando Bujones was a prodigy when he first burst on to the American dance scene. He was the first American to win the gold medal at the International Ballet Competition, and the youngest principal dancer in the history of American Ballet Theatre. He was quickly catapulted to international fame on the basis of a rock-solid technique that to this day still inspires awe. His jumps are extraordinary high and his jetés are expansive, often embellished with brilliant tours and beats. A danseur noble with a slight demi-caractère physique, Bujones has an extravagantly elegant line that makes him the perfect choice for the princely roles of the classical repertoire. Yet one could argue that he lacks the dramatic projection to give these roles depth. His strength instead lies in virtuosity, and bravura dancing of the highest order.

While Bujones has partnered many of the great ballerinas of the day—Natalia Makarova, Carla Fracci, Cynthia Gregory, Gelsey Kirkland, Marcia Haydée, and Yoko Morishita, with whom he has a special rapport—he is not recognized for his partnering skills. Critics have decried his presentational style, pointing to a tendency to lead with the chin and to punctuate phrases with a bravura expansion of arms and torso, and claiming that such displays often takes precedence over partnering the ballerina. He has also come under fire for immodesty. "Baryshnikov has the publicity, I have the talent", was his famous claim to the press, after his dazzling win at the 1974 International Ballet Competition was eclipsed by the media attention lavished on Baryshnikov, who was defecting to the West at the same time as Bujones was impressing the judges in Varna. A rivalry between the two dancers soon ensued when Baryshnikov joined American Ballet Theatre. Bujones, ever outspoken, complained that foreign guest artists were taking the plum roles away from American dancers.

Baryshnikov apparently never forgot the brashness of

Bujones. Shortly after taking over American Ballet Theatre in 1980, he and Bujones were at loggerheads. Bujones eventually quit the company in a rage after Baryshnikov refused to acknowledge his star qualities. With Baryshnikov himself leaving Ballet Theatre in the autumn of 1989, Bujones began re-establishing his roots; in 1990 he appeared frequently with the company as a guest artist.

If Bujones is immodest, at least he has talent to stand on. Speaking in his own defence, Bujones once said that he wasn't arrogant so much as self-confident. And anyone who has seen him dance can attest to the fact that this tremendous belief in his own ability, combined with a deep love of the art, is what makes his performances so thrilling. "I know very well just how good I am", he explained to writer John Gruen in 1976. "When I go on stage to perform I feel secure and confident. I know what I can do, and it's a very exhilarating feeling . . . so I just let myself go. I don't think that's arrogance." There are undoubtedly many members of the audience who would have agreed with this assessment.

What is more, Bujones has undoubtedly matured, both artistically and personally, in recent years. Some, like the Boston critic Iris Fanger, attribute this to his experience with the Boston Ballet, where he has been a fairly regular presence since 1987, as much as to personal changes. As Fanger wrote in May 1990, "During the four years with Boston, Bujones seems to have softened his persona, giving way to a sharing of the stage with the younger dancers. His elevation is no less startling nor has his detailed footwork faltered, but it's his fully rounded characterizations—James in *La Sylphide*, Jean in *Miss Julie*, Prince Siegfried—that now leave the greatest impression. His concentration onstage is total, and he seems to be as concerned with presenting his partner as himself." This is certainly a change from the Bujones of earlier days.

Finally, with Bujones showing an increasing interest in choreography, perhaps even with an ambition to direct his own company some day, the obsession with bravado in performance might be making way for more varied and balanced artistic concerns. His importance as a world-class dancer is undisputed, but his contribution to the art in other ways may yet be determined.

—Deirdre Kelly,
with Virginia Christian

---

## BURMEISTER, Vladimir

Russian/Soviet dancer and choreographer. Born Vladimir Pavlovich Burmeister in Vitebske, 15 July (2 July old style) 1904. Studied at the Moscow School of Choreography (then named Lunacharsky Theatre Technicum), 1925–29. Married dancer Antonina Krupenina. Character dancer (while still a student), concerts of the "Studio of Drama-Ballet" (dir. N. Gremina), 1925–29; soloist, Viktorina Kriger's Moscow Art Ballet, later part of Stanislavsky and Nemirovich-Danchenko Lyric Theatre, from 1930, performing in Paris for company's first Western tour, 1956; chief choreographer of the same company, 1941–60 and 1963–71, guest choreographer, Paris Opéra Ballet, 1961, 1962, London Festival Ballet, 1961. Recipient: State Prize of the USSR, 1946; title of People's Artist of the USSR, 1970. Died in Moscow, 5 March 1971.

### ROLES

1932 Louis XV in *The Carmagnole* (Bolotov, Virsky), Moscow Art Ballet, Moscow

1933 Niquese in *The Rivals* (Kholfin), Moscow Art Ballet, Moscow

1936 Nurali in *The Fountain of Bakhchisarai* (Zakharov), Moscow Art Ballet, Moscow

Korrekhidor (cr) in *Treurolka* (Kholfin), Moscow Art Ballet, Moscow

### WORKS

1938 *The Christmas Eve* (with Lopukhov; mus. Asafiev), Stanislavsky and Nemirovich-Danchenko Ballet, Moscow

Dances in *La Belle Hélène* (operetta; mus. Offenbach), Stanislavsky and Nemirovitch-Danchenko Ballet, Moscow

1939 *The Grenade Launchers* (concert piece; mus. Albéniz), Moscow Ballet School, Moscow

1940 Dances in *La Périchole* (operetta; mus. Offenbach), Stanislavsky and Nemirovich-Danchenko Ballet, Moscow

1941 *Straussiana* (mus. Strauss), Stanislavsky and Nemirovich-Danchenko Ballet, Moscow

1942 *The Merry Wives of Windsor* (mus. Oransky), Stanislavsky and Nemirovich-Danchenko Ballet, Moscow

1943 *Lola* (mus. Vasilenko), Stanislavsky and Nemirovich-Danchenko Ballet, Moscow

1944 *Shéhérazade* (mus. Rimsky-Korsakov), Stanislavsky and Nemirovich-Danchenko Ballet, Moscow

1946 *Carnaval* (mus. Schumann), Stanislavsky and Nemirovich-Danchenko Ballet, Moscow

1947 *Tatyana* (mus. Krein), Kirov Ballet, Leningrad

1948 *The Coast of Happiness* (with Ivan Kurilov; mus. Spadavecchia), Stanislavsky and Nemirovich-Danchenko Ballet, Moscow

1950 *Esmeralda* (mus. Pugni, Glière, Vasilenko), Stanislavsky and Nemirovich-Danchenko Ballet, Moscow

1953 *Swan Lake* (new chor. Acts I, III, IV; Act II after Ivanov; mus. Tchaikovsky), Stanislavsky and Nemirovich-Danchenko Ballet, Moscow (staged for company tour, Paris Opéra, 1956, and for Paris Opéra Ballet, 1960)

1957 *Jeanne D'Arc* (mus. Peiko), Stanislavsky and Nemirovich-Danchenko Ballet, Moscow

1961 *The Snow Maiden* (mus. Tchaikovsky), London Festival Ballet, London (staged for Stanislavsky and Nemirovich-Danchenko Ballet, 1963)

1962 *Sur un thème* (mus. Bizet), Paris Opéra Ballet, Paris

1967 *The Red Devils* (mus. Dunaevsky, Knushevitsky), Stanislavsky and Nemirovich-Danchenko Ballet, Moscow

1970 *Apassionata* (mus. Beethoven), Stanislavsky and Nemirovich-Danchenko Ballet, Moscow

*A Lonely White Sail* (mus. Yurovsky), Stanislavsky and Nemirovich-Danchenko Ballet, Moscow

### PUBLICATIONS

By Burmeister:

"Tradition and Innovation: Notes on Ballet", Interview, *Sovetskaya Muzyka* (Moscow), no 6, 1964

"A Search for Truth in the Ballet Theatre", extracts from

Vladimir Burmeister's Notes connected with his version of *Swan Lake*, with an introduction by Nadezhda Vikhreva, *Sovetsky Balet* (Moscow), no 4, 1984

About Burmeister:
Williams, Peter, "Classical Landscape with Figures", *Dance and Dancers* (London), July 1961
"Personality of the Month: Vladimir Bourmeister", *Dance and Dancers* (London), August, 1961
Eliash, Nikolai, "Obsessed with an Ideal: A Tribute to V.P. Burmeister, on his 60th Birthday", *Teatralnaya Zhizn* (Moscow), no 13, 1964
Roslavleva, Natalia, *Era of the Russian Ballet*, London, 1966
*The Ballet Company of the Music Theatre Named after K.S. Stanislavsky and V.I. Nemirovich-Danchenko*, Moscow, 1975
Sheremetevskaya, N., "Newly Established Ballet Theatres", *Sovetsky Baletni Teatr* (Moscow), 1976
Golantseva, G., "Giving a Tune: In Memoriam V.P. Burmeister", *Muzykalnaya Zhizn* (Moscow), no. 23, 1979
Vikhreva, N., Morozov, M., Edelman, V., "On Burmeister's Productions of *Esmeralda*, *The Merry Wives of Windsor* and *Lola*", *Sovetsky Balet* (Moscow), no. 3, 1985
Kazenin, Igor, "A Long and Happy Life: On Burmeister's Production of *Swan Lake*", *Teatr* (Moscow), no. 11, 1986

* * *

Choreographer Vladimir Burmeister was trained at the Choreography Department of the Moscow Theatre College named after Lunacharsky. In that school, new methods of teaching the future dancers and choreographers were used, quite different from a typical ballet school curriculum. The students took an extensive course in dramatic acting as well as in the history of various artistic genres. The quality of teaching was extremely high. At the Choreography Department, there was an experimental group which was constantly developing new forms of dramatic performance based on dancing, or pantomime with a story behind it. While still a student, Burmeister began to appear in variety and music-hall shows, performing choreographic sketches and character dances (such as Spanish dances).

In 1930, Vladimir Burmeister joined the Moscow Art Ballet (directed by the dancer Viktorina Kriger), a company whose members were mostly former students of the Lunacharsky College. There Burmeister performed a series of solo mime roles. In 1933, the company became part of the Music Theatre directed by Vladimir Nemirovich-Danchenko, an innovative theatre with the productions of operas and operettas based upon the most advanced methods of directing drama.

It was then that Burmeister made his first steps as a choreographer, staging dances in Jacques Offenbach's operettas *La Périchole* and *La Belle Hélène*. Working in close contact with several drama directors involved in the company, the famous Nemirovich-Danchenko among them, proved to be a great formative influence on the beginner's artistic individuality.

1941 saw Burmeister as the head of the Theatre's ballet company, which did not follow most other Moscow theatres into wartime evacuation. After his two comic ballet productions, *Straussiana* and *The Merry Wives of Windsor* (based on Shakespeare's play), Burmeister created one of his best works, *Lola*, in 1943. It was a ballet to the music of Sergei Vasilenko and several Spanish composers. The story was about the Spanish people's fight against the Napoleonic invasion and had as its central character a girl called Lola, who sacrificed her life in that fight. The production became immensely popular, evoking direct associations with the war which was still going on in Russia. From that time on, Burmeister was established as the company's head, and he was to remain in that capacity for nearly 30 years.

Burmeister's work belonged entirely to the genre of "dram-ballet" (balletic drama), a trend which dominated the Soviet ballet theatre in the 1930 to the 1940s. A typical "dram-ballet" was a performance in several acts, often with a plot based on a well-known work of literature (by Shakespeare, Gogol, Pushkin, Balzac, and so on). The story in such a ballet would be reproduced in great detail, as if it were a play. In fact, this kind of performance imitated the drama theatre, the only difference being that instead of words there was pantomime, rhythmical movement, and, occasionally, dancing. Extensive dancing scenes were only allowed in "dram-ballet" when the characters were supposed to dance according to the plot (at celebrations, weddings, balls, and so on). Ballet of this kind was officially declared to be closest to the principles of socialist realism and its proponents claimed its total supremacy.

At the time when Burmeister was working, official critics and bureaucrats kept insisting that ballet performances should portray our Soviet contemporaries and their lives. Burmeister created a number of such ballets: *The Coast of Happiness* (about the Soviet youth during the war and in peaceful times), *Tatyana* (about a young guerilla girl), and *A Lonely White Sail* (about the revolutionary events in Odessa in 1917) are among them. These ballets were constantly being awarded government prizes, but they did not last long in the repertoire because they were totally unpopular with the public. The productions of this kind were superficial and were, in fact, stripped of all specifically balletic means of expression. The best of Burmeister's works with a modern theme was a short concert piece, *The Grenade Launchers*, created in 1939 during the Civil War in Spain and performed for many years afterwards.

Burmeister's fairy-tale ballets (*The Snow Maiden* to the music by Tchaikovsky) and his new versions of the classic productions (*Esmeralda*, *Swan Lake*) had a longer and happier life. The *Swan Lake* he created in 1953 has been given over 1,000 times, was reproduced in many cities of the USSR and even in the Grand Opéra in Paris (1960) where it was also a great success. Using Tchaikovsky's original score, Burmeister restored several cuts usually made in the music. He turned the Overture into a Prologue with acting and dancing, and changed the scenario considerably. He created his own choreographic versions of Acts I, III, and IV, while Act II retained its original choreography by Lev Ivanov. As a result of these changes, the development of the plot became logical and unequivocal—but musically, the ballet was far removed from Tchaikovsky's original conception.

In the Prologue, the evil magician was actually shown turning Odette into a swan. Act II presented a "genre picture" of the flippant Prince and his friends entertaining themselves with peasant girls. The suite of dances in the third act was choreographed by Burmeister most successfully. Even so, he tried to squeeze it into the rigid framework of the plot, making various national dances demonstrate Odile's varying appearances: in the phantasmagoria staged by von Rothbart, she appeared to the Prince first as a Polish, then as a Spanish or Venetian girl.

Such simplification of the plot and the "oversaturation" of the production with mime acting could not but clash with the multi-dimensional character of the music. But at the time when the production was created this approach was apparently regarded as natural and did not cause any protest, even among the specialists. Some people even suggested that Burmeister should revise Act II in the same "realistic" manner, which he actually did in the later version of his production staged in Tallinne.

Whatever can be said about his choreography, Burmeister's indisputable achievement is the formation of the ballet company of the Moscow Stanislavsky and Nemirovich-Danchenko Music Theatre, where he has fostered a whole generation of dancers.

—Irina Gruzdeva

---

**BUSSELL, Darcey**

British dancer. Born in London, 27 April 1969. Studied at the Arts Educational School, Tring, Hertfordshire, and Royal Ballet Schools, 1982–87. Dancer, Sadler's Wells Royal Ballet, 1987–88; soloist, Royal Ballet (at Covent Garden), from 1988: first soloist, from September 1989; principal dancer, from December 1989, touring United States in 1991; has also made several television appearances. Recipient: Prix de Lausanne, 1986; Sir James Garreras Award for the Most Promising Newcomer of 1990; *Evening Standard* Ballet Award, 1990; *Dance and Dancers* Dancer of the Year, 1990; joint winner of *Cosmopolitan* Achievement Award in the Performing Arts, April 1991; Laurence Olivier Award, 1992.

## ROLES

1986 Principal dancer in *Concerto* (MacMillan), Royal Ballet School Performance, London

1987 Myrtha in *Giselle* (Petipa after Coralli, Perrot; staged Wright), Sadler's Wells Royal Ballet, London

1988 Lilac Fairy in *The Sleeping Beauty* (Petipa, Ashton; staged de Valois), Royal Ballet, London

Principal dancer (cr) in *The Spirit of Fugue* (Bintley), Royal Ballet, London

1989 Princess Rose (cr) in *The Prince of the Pagodas* (MacMillan), Royal Ballet, London

Gamzatti in *La Bayadère* (Makarova after Petipa), Royal Ballet, London

Principal dancer in *Capriccio for Piano and Orchestra* (*Rubies* from *Jewels*; Balanchine), Royal Ballet, London

Principal dancer (Agnus Dei) in *Requiem* (MacMillan), Royal Ballet, London

1990 Odette/Odile in *Swan Lake* (Petipa, Ivanov; staged Dowell), Royal Ballet, London

Principal dancer in *Laurencia* Pas de six (Nureyev after Chabukiani), Royal Ballet, London

Principal dancer (cr) in *Farewell* (pas de deux, later incorporated into *Winter Dreams*; MacMillan), Royal Ballet, London

Bethena Waltz in *Elite Syncopations* (MacMillan), Royal Ballet, London

Title role in *Raymonda* Act III (Nureyev after Petipa), Royal Ballet, London

Principal dancer in *Song of the Earth* (MacMillan), Royal Ballet, London

Principal dancer (cr) in *Bloodlines* (Page), Royal Ballet, London

Sugar Plum Fairy in *The Nutcracker* (Wright), Royal Ballet, London

Aria I in *Stravinsky Violin Concerto* (Balanchine), Royal Ballet, London

1991 Masha (cr) in *Winter Dreams* (MacMillan), Royal Ballet, London

Title role in *Raymonda* Act III (Petipa), Royal Ballet, London

Rag Mazurka ("Hostess") in *Les Biches* (Nijinska), Royal Ballet, London

Pas de deux in *Agon* (Balanchine), Royal Ballet, London

Principal dancer (cr) in *Present Histories* (Tuckett), Royal Ballet, London

Second Movement in *Symphony in C* (Balanchine), Royal Ballet, London

1992 Principal dancer (Trois Gymnopédies) in *Monotones* (Ashton), Royal Ballet, London

Principal dancer in *In the Middle, Somewhat Elevated* (Forsythe), Royal Ballet, London

Title role in *Manon* (MacMillan), Royal Ballet, London

Nikiya in *La Bayadère* (Makarova after Petipa), Royal Ballet, Japanese tour

1993 Princess Aurora in *The Sleeping Beauty* (Petipa, Ashton; staged de Valois), Royal Ballet, London

**Other roles include:** Winter Fairy in *Cinderella* (Ashton), Lady Mary in *Enigma Variations* (Ashton), principal dancer in *Galanteries* (Bintley), Harlot in *Romeo and Juliet* (MacMillan), Second Solo ("Kingdom of the Shades") in *La Bayadère* (Makarova after Petipa), principal dancer in *Pursuit* (Page).

## PUBLICATIONS


Jordan, Stephanie, "Dispiriting Fugue", *Dance and Dancers* (London), February 1989

"The Royal Ballet: Biographies", *Ballet in London Yearbook 1989/90*, London, 1989

Hunt, Marilyn, "Reviews", *Dance Magazine* (New York), March 1990

Hunt, Marilyn, "Darcy Bussell", *Dance Magazine* (New York), September 1991

Clarke, Mary, "Royal Ballet—A New Manon", *Dancing Times* (London), April 1992


* * *

"Every choreographer needs a muse", wrote one British critic in 1989, by way of explaining the sudden prominence of the young (and previously unknown) dancer Darcey Bussell. As both the last and the youngest-ever muse to choreographer Kenneth MacMillan after Alessandra Ferri left London for New York, Darcey Bussell played an important role at the Royal Ballet in the late 1980s and early 1990s. Bussell was plucked out of the corps of the Sadler's Wells Royal Ballet, the Royal's sister company, to create the leading role in Kenneth MacMillan's *Prince of the Pagodas* at the age of twenty—and virtually ever since she has been a central box office draw for a company which, to many minds, had slid into dangerous doldrums in the years previous.

While holding on to its reputation as one of the leading classical companies in the world, the Royal Ballet was perceived by many to be in a serious slump in the 1980s, not least of all because of its failure to produce any exciting new stars. This has all changed: whatever one might feel about the company's current artistic direction, Covent Garden has at last come up with some names that attract attention and sell tickets. Director Antony Dowell has brought in stars like Sylvie Guillem and Laurent Hilaire of the Paris Opéra; young dancers like Viviana Durante and Errol Pickford have come into their own; and the wunderkind Darcey Bussell spurred Kenneth Macmillan into a late creative phase in his long and prolific career.

**Darcy Bussell with Irek Mukhamedov in *Winter Dreams*, London, 1990**

Darcey Bussell has the height and long-limbed beauty that is more usually associated with American dancers—more specifically, with Balanchine dancers. Indeed, with the Royal Ballet companies recently taking a number of Balanchine works into their repertoires, Bussell has had a chance to put her flexible body and extended lines to good purpose: and it was in the Balanchine repertory with the Sadler's Wells Royal Ballet that she first began to attract notice. Later, when the the main company took on one of the masterpieces of the Stravinsky/Balanchine canon, *Agon*, Bussell was perfectly cast in the gymnastic and angular pas de deux, looking particularly effective when matched with guest artist Eddie Shelman of the Dance Theatre of Harlem.

Some of the more purist British critics, worried about the influence of "New World" athleticism and the increased emphasis on Russian training at the Royal Ballet School, have been hesitant in their praise of Bussell, unable to find anything resembling the cherished "English" style of a Margot Fonteyn or an Antoinette Sibley. Fed up, too, with the Royal's promotion of showy guest artists like Guillem, whose extraordinary technique can be said to display the possibilities for the truly grotesque in long-legged pyrotechnics, critics looking for subtle artistry have been continually frustrated.

Bussell was not born a great dramatic actress. In the beginning she resembled a young colt, rather reminiscent of the young Suzanne Farrell, or any other Balanchine protégée put on stage when still green. But this, none the less, was part of her charm. American critics were not entirely happy with Bussell's début as Odette/Odile in the United States, perhaps because they were expecting impossibly great things from Britain's legendary Royal Ballet—but perhaps, also, because they were simply nonplussed by the legs and extensions of a ballerina whose "look" is more typically American than English. And up until then, her gifts had mostly been displayed in works that did not demand the artistic maturity, as well as the sheer strength, of the great classics like *Swan Lake*.

But the important thing about Darcey Bussell has been her development, in recent years, from slightly awkward ingénue into a more mature artist searching deeper within for dramatic expression and meaning. In *Winter Dreams*, MacMillan's 1990 ballet based on Chekhov's *Three Sisters*, Bussell unleashed a surprisingly passionate and emotional performance in the role of Masha, the frustrated and unfulfilled wife who is tortured by her impossible love for Vershinin, played with equal conviction and depth by ex-Bolshoi star Irek Mukhamedov. Another much-heralded début was Bussell's first performance in MacMillan's intensely dramatic three-act ballet, *Manon*, where she had again been paired with Mukhamedov. Scheduled for Autumn 1991, Bussell's appearance was cancelled virtually on the eve of her début, apparently because of difficulties posed by the young ballerina's height. At last, a partner tall enough was found in Hungarian dancer Zoltan Solymosi, and Bussell's performance as Manon was widely praised.

With this performance, in a sense, Darcey Bussell established herself as a true ballerina and an artist of significance. Mary Clarke wrote in the *Guardian*, "Of her dancing I need hardly speak. Technically, it is so pure, so beautiful, that there is joy to be found in every movement." But, as Clarke went on to point out, the dancer's understanding of the dramatic aspect of her role was evident: ". . . through her dancing, through MacMillan's choreography, Manon's character very clearly emerges". Calling Bussell's portrayal of the many moods and changes of Manon "deeply moving", Clarke concluded, "Darcey Bussell, therefore, fully justified MacMillan's faith with a performance of rare beauty and integrity. She has joined the extraordinary roster of Manons who preceded her."

Bussell's range continues to expand, thanks largely to the Royal Ballet's recent efforts to stage a variety of contemporary works, from both outside choreographers and homegrown talents. In William Tuckett's intriguing *Present Histories*, a deliberately enigmatic little mini-drama of modern social behaviour, Bussell easily adapted to the dramatic requirements of a subtle sketch that called for very little balletic technique; while in William Forsythe's showy, exuberant, and exhibitionist modern ballet, *In the Middle, Somewhat Elevated*, she showed impressive command over the demanding choreography, revealing a sort of stage savvy and easy confidence which completely erased the image of the shaky, coltish ingénue, and which was just right for the part.

If the late Kenneth MacMillan had continued in the 1990s to add more new ballets to his already impressively long list of works, then Bussell would probably have been assured a prominent position at the Royal Ballet, if not to say in the history of one of Britain's most important choreographers. But even without MacMillan, Bussell has now proven her value as a dancer of impressive range and artistry whose exciting potential is still revealing itself.

—Martha Bremser

---

**BUTLER, John**

American dancer, choreographer, and ballet director. Born John Nielson Butler in Memphis, Tennessee, 29 September 1920. Studied at the Graham School and American School of Ballet, New York. Dancer in Broadway musicals and with Martha Graham Company, 1942–55; choreographer of dances for Broadway and off-Broadway shows, 1947–49; choreographer, New York City Opera, 1951–54; founder, director, and choreographer, John Butler Dance Theatre, from 1953, performing at Festival of Two Worlds, Spoleto, Italy, from 1958, as American Dance Theatre, Spoleto, 1959; also dance director, Spoleto Festival, 1958; freelance choreographer, staging works for New York City Ballet, from 1957, American Ballet Theatre, from 1958, New York City Opera Company, 1959–61, Metropolitan Opera, New York, from 1958, Nederlands Dans Theater, from 1962, Pennsylvania Ballet, from 1964, Harkness Ballet from 1966, Australian Ballet, 1968, Alvin Ailey Dance Theater, from 1972, Batsheva Dance Company, from 1972, and Paris Opéra Ballet, 1973; also choreographer of numerous works for television. Recipient: *Dance Magazine* Award, 1964.

**WORKS**

1953 *Masque of the Wild Man* (mus. Glanville-Hicks), John Butler Dance Theatre, Jacob's Pillow Dance Festival, Lee, Massachusetts

*Malocchio* (mus. Provenzano), John Butler Dance Theatre, American Dance Festival, New London, Connecticut

1954 *The Brass World* (mus. Jolivet), John Butler Dance Theatre, Brooklyn, New York

*Three Promenades with the Lord* (mus. American folk), John Butler Dance Theatre, Jacob's Pillow Dance Festival, Lee, Massachusetts

*The Adventure* (mus. Barber), John Butler Dance Theatre, U.S. television (CBS)

1955 *Frontier Ballad* (mus. traditional American folk), John Butler Dance Theatre, Brooklyn, New York

**John Butler's *Medea*, with Carla Fracci and Mikhail Baryshnikov, American Ballet Theatre, 1975**

*The Haunted World* (revision of *The Brass World*; mus. Jolivet), John Butler Dance Theatre, Brooklyn, New York

*Clowns and Angels* (mus. Bowles), John Butler Dance Theatre, Nervi Dance Festival, Genoa

Dances in *Salomé* (play by Oscar Wilde; mus. Bernstein), "Omnibus", U.S. television (CBS)

1956 *Democratic Vistas* (mus. Scott), "Camera Three", U.S. television (CBS)

*The Unicorn, the Gorgon and the Manticore* (mus. Menotti), Coolidge Auditorium (under auspices of Library of Congress), Washington, D.C. (staged New York City Ballet, 1957)

1957 *Seven Faces of Love* (mus. Kenton), Ballet Theatre Workshop, New York

1958 *The Glory Folk* (mus. traditional American folk), John Butler Dance Theatre, Spoleto Festival

*Triad* (also called *Da Hospita*; mus. Prokofiev, Glanville-Hicks, Tailleferre, Ellington), John Butler Dance Theatre, Spoleto Festival

*The Unquiet Graves* (mus. Hollingsworth), John Butler Dance Theatre, Spoleto Festival

*The Letter and the Three* (mus. jazz, arranged Shirley), Geoffrey Holder and Company, New York
*Creation and Fall*, John Butler Dance Company, "Look Up and Live", U.S. television
1959 *Carmina Burana* (scenic cantata; mus. Orff), New York City Opera, New York
*In the Beginning* (mus. Barber), New York City Opera, New York
*The Sybil* (mus. Surinach), American Dance Theatre, Spoleto Festival
*The Five Senses* (mus. Schuller, Starer, Lees, Siday, traditional folk songs), American Dance Theatre, Spoleto Festival
*Brief Encounter* (mus. Bowles), American Dance Theatre, Spoleto Festival
*Amusement Park* (mus. Bowles), American Dance Theatre, Spoleto Festival
*Album Leaves*, John Butler Dance Theatre, Spoleto Festival
1960 *Turning Point* (mus. Evans, Lewis, Hopkins), Idlewild Festival of the Arts, California
*Portrait of Billie* (mus. Billie Holiday songs), Jacob's Pillow Dance Festival, Lee, Massachusetts
*Saul and the Witch of Endor* (mus. Glanville-Hicks), "Lamp unto My Feet", U.S. television (CBS)
*David and Bathsheba* (mus. Surinach), "Lamp unto My Feet", U.S. television (CBS)
1961 *Willie the Weeper* in *Ballet Ballads* (mus. Moross; chor. with Tetley, Ray), East 47th Street Theatre, New York (originally part of *Nausicaa*, opera by Glanville-Hicks, Athens International Festival)
*Psalms*, "Lamp unto My Feet", U.S. television (CBS)
*Esther* (mus. Laderman), "Lamp unto My Feet", U.S. television (CBS)
*Ballet of the Nativity* (mus. Wernick), "Lamp unto My Feet", U.S. television (CBS)
1962 *Alone*, Freda Miller Memorial Concert, New York
*Hadrianas* (mus. Starer), Netherlands Dance Theatre, Rotterdam
*Brief Dynasty* (mus. Starer), "Lamp unto My Feet", U.S. television (CBS)
1963 Dances in *Jeanne d'Arc au Bucher* (dramatic oratorio; mus. Honegger), Santa Fe Opera, Santa Fe
*Sebastian* (mus. Menotti), Netherlands Dance Theatre, Amsterdam
*The Mark of Cain* (mus. Ravel), U.S. television (CBS)
1964 *Catulli Carmina* (mus. Orff), Caramoor Festival, Katonah, New York
*Ceremonial* (mus. Bartók), Caramoor Festival, Katonah, New York
*Ceremony of Innocence* (mus. Harrison), "Lamp unto My Feet", U.S. television (CBS)
*L'Enfance du Christ* (mus. Berlioz), John Butler Dance Theatre, U.S. television (CBS)
1965 *Chansons de Bilitis* (mus. Debussy), Festival of Two Worlds, Spoleto
1966 *Jepthah's Daughter* (mus. Glanville-Hicks), U.S. television (CBS)
*Villon* (mus. Starer), Pennsylvania Ballet Company, Second Harper Festival, Chicago
1967 *Aphrodite* (mus. Lees), Boston Ballet, Boston
*Five Ballets of the Five Senses* (mus. Schuller, Starer, Lees, Siday, traditional folk songs by Bibb), Lincoln Center/Stage 5 series, U.S. public television (NET)
*After Eden* (mus. Hoiby), Harkness Ballet, New York
*A Season in Hell* (mus. Glanville-Hicks), Harkness Ballet, New York
*Landscape for Lovers* (mus. Hoiby), Harkness Ballet, New York
*The Captive Lark* (mus. Starer), Village Theatre
1968 *Threshold* (mus. Durko, Bacewicz), Australian Ballet, Sydney
*The Initiate* (mus. Bacewicz, Durko), Repertory Dance Theater, University of Utah, Salt Lake City
*Encounters* (mus. Subotnick), Repertory Dance Theater, University of Utah, Salt Lake City
*Labyrinth* (mus. Somers), Royal Winnipeg Ballet, Winnipeg
1970 *The Minotaur* (mus. Carter), Boston Ballet, Boston
*Journeys* (mus. von Webern), Pennsylvania Ballet, Brooklyn, New York
*Itinéraire* (mus. Berio), Ballet-Théâtre contemporaine, Paris
1971 *Hi-Kyò* (mus. Fukushima), Ballet-Théâtre contemporaine, London
1972 *Tragic Celebration* (*Hara-Kiri*; mus. Fukushima), Gala Benefit for the Dance Collection of the New York Public Library, New York
*According to Eve* (mus. Crumb), Alvin Ailey Dance Theater, New York
*La Voix* (mus. Crumb), Ballet du Rhin
*Moon Full* (mus. Tzui Auni), Batsheva Dance Company
1973 *Black Angel* (mus. Crumb), Pennsylvania Ballet, Philadelphia
*Trip* (mus. Berio), Les Grands Ballets Canadiens, Montreal
*Integrales* (mus. Varèse), Paris Opéra Ballet, Paris
*Amériques* (mus. Varèse), Paris Opéra Ballet, Paris
1974 *Cult of the Night* (mus. Schoenberg), Frankfurt
*Puppets of Death* (after Shakespeare's *Othello*; mus. Schoenberg), Batsheva Dance Company, Tel Aviv
1975 *Medea* (mus. Barber), Festival of Two Worlds, Spoleto
1976 *Les Noces* (mus. Stravinsky), The Dance Company (of New South Wales), Sydney
*Facets* (mus. various songs), Solo for Judith Jamison, Alvin Ailey Dance Theater, New York
*Othello* (mus. Crumb), Pittsburgh Ballet Theatre, Pittsburgh
1977 *Icarus* (ice ballet; mus. Crosse), John Curry Theatre of Skating, Palladium, London
1978 *Les Doubles* (mus. Dutilleux), Bavarian State Opera Ballet, Munich
*Othello* (mus. Dvořák), Ballet of La Scala, Milan
1979 *The Commitment* (mus. Bernstein), Solo for Judith Jamison, Kansas City Ballet, Kansas City
1980 *Dawns and Dusks* (mus. Hoddinott), Ballet of the German Opera on the Rhine, Duisburg
1981 *George Sand—A Landscape* (mus. Chopin), Bat-Dor Dance Company, Tel Aviv
1983 *Quest* (mus. Ruggieri), Les Grands Ballets Canadiens
1987 *Romeo and Juliet* ("chamber version"; mus. Prokofiev), Princeton Ballet, Princeton

**Other works include:** for New York City Opera—Dances in operas *The Consul* (mus. Menotti; 1950), *Bluebeard's Castle* (mus. Bartók; 1952), *La Cenerentola* (mus. Rossini; 1953), *Die Fledermaus* (mus. Strauss; 1953), *La Traviata* (mus. Verdi; 1953), *The Tender Land* (mus. Copland; 1954), *The Marriage of Figaro* (mus. Mozart; 1959); also individual works *The Letter* (mus. Ravel), *The Old Woman Laments Her Youth* (mus. Starer), *Ritual* (mus. Starer), *Hypnos* (mus. Evans), *Shadow of Madness* (mus. Castellnuovo), *La Testament* (mus. Pound), *Tragic Celebration* (mus. Starer), *Alone* (mus. Guiffre), dances in *Amahl and the Night Visitors* (mus. Menotti).

**PUBLICATIONS**

By Butler:
"Confessions of a Choreographer", in Nadel, M.H. (ed.). *The Dance Experience*, New York, 1970
Interview in Loney, Glenn, "All the Strange Things: John Butler on Opera Choreography", *Dance Magazine* (New York), August 1971

About Butler:
Terry, Walter, *The Dance in America*, New York, 1956
Caradente, G., "Ballet at the Spoleto Festival", *Dance Magazine*, October 1959
Hering, Doris, "*Carmina Burana*", *Dance Magazine* (New York), November 1959
Terry, Walter, "The Legacy of Isadora Duncan and Ruth St. Denis", *Dance Perspectives* (New York), Winter 1960
Terry, Walter, "Erotic Dances in the Starlight", *Saturday Review*, 22 July 1967
Terry, Walter, "Beautiful Bodies", *Saturday Review*, 24 February 1968
Loney, Glenn, "Busy John Butler Reports on Roving Choreography", *Dance Magazine*, (New York), January 1974
McDonagh, Don, *The Complete Guide to Modern Dance*, Garden City, New York, 1976
Victor, Thomas (photographer), *The Making of a Dance: Mikhail Baryshnikov and Carla Fracci in Medea*, with an introduction by Clive Barnes, New York, 1976

* * *

Since World War II, the division between ballet and modern dance has narrowed considerably. Every classical company has at least a token modern piece in its repertoire, and the younger ballet choreographers often combine the forms. In the United States, no one has contributed more to this homogenization of forms than John Butler. His works are performed by so many ballet companies that few remember he was a modern dancer and choreographs in that form.

Butler has not only created dances for classical companies; he has influenced both modern and ballet through his students and associates. Lar Lubovitch, who has headed his own modern company for 20 years, lists Butler among his "great teachers". Lubovitch also danced in Butler's short-lived company. Glen Tetley studied and danced with Butler as well. That association shows in the modern movements in Tetley's ballets.

Butler studied with Martha Graham and performed in her company, but his style is his own. Like Graham, he emphasizes emotional motivation, particularly erotic drives. And he creates strong roles for men.

Butler has also been unusually prolific. In little more than two decades, he choreographed some 60 pieces. In one year alone, he created eight new works and restaged two, for almost as many companies. At times he was commuting across the Atlantic, working in Boston, Utah, the Netherlands, New York City, Athens, Spoleto, Italy, and Venezuela.

The 40-year old *Carmina Burana* is the work most people identify with Butler. A choral-dance piece set to Carl Orff's "dramatic cantata", it is one of the most theatrical events in ballet or modern dance. The source is a collection of thirteenth-century verses celebrating the joys of life: gambling, drinking, and sex. The manuscript, written in a bawdy, colloquial German-Latin, was discovered in a Bavarian monastery, and is obviously the work of seminarians in a less than religious mood. Orff's music is driving and passionate, qualities which Butler realized in his choreography.

The dance forms range from folk to formal, with numerous body-to-body contacts for company and principals. The piece begins and ends with the priests in proper habits and behaving circumspectly. The middle section is sensual, so much so that several critics objected.

Despite, or perhaps because of this, *Carmina Burana* was an instant hit in its premiere performance at the New York City Center in September 1959. It has since been performed extensively in America and Europe and the Middle East.

Butler staged the work for the Netherlands Dance Theatre during his season in residence with that company, and supervised a filming of the ballet at a ruined castle in Holland. He also set it on Rosella Hightower's dancers in Marseilles and the Gulbenkian Ballet of Lisbon.

When he returned to America, Butler mounted *Carmina Burana* for the Pennsylvania Ballet and the Alvin Ailey American Dance Theatre. The Grands Ballets Canadiens in Montreal dances the work, and it is in the repertoire of the Ballet Nacional de Venezuela. And prior to the present theocracy and the prohibition of all things Western, it was performed by the Imperial Ballet of Iran. In recent years, several smaller regional companies in the United States have also performed the piece.

Butler has had the good fortune to work closely with the composers in several of his ballets. He choreographed the television opera *Amahl and the Night Visitors* by Gian Carlo Menotti, which has become almost as much a part of the American Yuletide season as holly and mistletoe. He choreographed other Menotti compositions—*Sebastian* for the Harkness Ballet, *The Unicorn, the Gorgon and the Manticore* for television—and he served as dance director for Menotti's annual Festival of Two Worlds in Spoleto.

Lee Hoiby composed the music for Butler's pas de deux *After Eden*; and *Medea*, the first piece commissioned for Baryshnikov after he defected from the Kirov Ballet, has music by Samuel Barber. One of Butler's major commissions was to choreograph *Paradise Lost*, Kristof Penderecki's monumental work for Chicago Lyric Opera.

Some critics have disparaged Butler's association with these "less serious" composers. But "they are no less serious about their music than their predecessors", the choreographer has said. "They are popular, true, and their music reaches audiences far greater than Beethoven or Mozart ever dreamed about. It's 'bread and butter' to the public. And who knows? Given satellite communications, TV, cassettes and all the marketing techniques of today, the Old Masters might have achieved the same kind of popularity. Would that have made them 'less serious'?"

That assessment might easily apply to Butler's work as well. His modern works are no less serious than the creations of Petipa or Bournonville. And like them, he has enriched ballet.

—William E. Fark

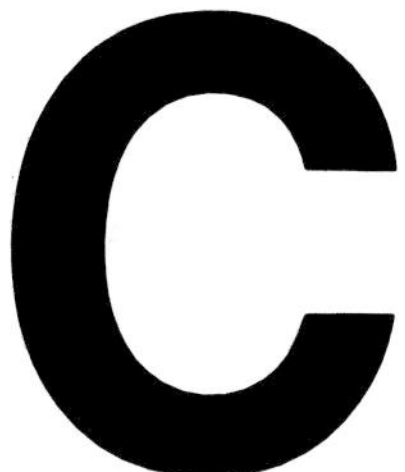

## THE CAGE

**Choreography:** Jerome Robbins
**Music:** Igor Stravinsky
**Design:** Ruth Sobotka (costumes), Jean Rosenthal (set and lighting)
**Libretto:** Jerome Robbins
**First Production:** New York City Ballet, City Center, New York, 14 June 1951
**Principal Dancers:** Nora Kaye (The Novice), Yvonne Mounsey (The Queen), Nicholas Magallanes, Michael Maule (The Intruders)

**Other productions include:** Pacific Northwest Ballet; Seattle, October, 1984.

### PUBLICATIONS


Stahl, Norma G., "Choreographing the Battle of the Sexes", *Dance Magazine* (New York), August 1953

Beaumont, Cyril, *Ballets of Today*, revised edition, London, 1954

Sabin, Robert, "The Creative Evolution of *The Cage*", *Dance Magazine* (New York), August 1955

Maynard, Olga, *The American Ballet*, Philadelphia, 1959

Balanchine, George, with Mason, Francis, *Balanchine's Complete Stories of the Great Ballets*, Garden City, N.Y., 1977

Reynolds, Nancy, *Repertory in Review*, New York, 1977


* * *

During the early 1950s, New York City Ballet choreographer Jerome Robbins turned to introspection as the impetus for his ballets. Among the strongest in this vein were *Age of Anxiety* (1950), *The Cage* (1951), and *Afternoon of a Faun* (1953). Surely the most potent was, and is, *The Cage*.

At that time Robbins was ostensibly grappling with his own sexual orientation. The dramatic ballerina Nora Kaye was an extremely close friend; they were even rumoured to be contemplating marriage. *The Cage* expressed an extremely ambivalent and disturbing attitude towards women.

Like all true artists, he was able to cast his misgivings in symbolic and consequently universal terms. The female participants in *The Cage* were insects—resembling black widow spiders who, after the act of mating, killed their male counterparts. Inevitability shadowed their on-stage adventure.

To parallel the choreography, Robbins selected Igor Stravinsky's Concerto in D for Strings. Like much of Stravinsky's music during this particularly fertile period, it alternated a pizzicato terseness with spans of soaring lyricism. The piece seemed to have been written especially for *The Cage*, as though its subtitle, "Basler", might well have been changed to "The Cage".

The ballet opened in near darkness. As the musicians attacked their strings with a resonating "plunk", an ominous network of ropes, horizontally suspended over the stage, began slowly to rise. This weighted, confining environment was devised by lighting designer Jean Rosenthal. It might be noted that had she chosen to pursue a stage designing career, it would have been a distinguished one.

A corps of terrifyingly beautiful women appeared. They wore flesh-coloured leotards decorated with a textured, excrescent-looking pattern. It emphasized the women's breasts, navel, and pubic area. The costumes were designed by Ruth Sobotka, a dancer with the company. The women's hair was teased into huge, random nests. Led by the statuesque Yvonne Mounsey as their Queen, they lifted their knees sharply and then stabbed the ground, using their pointes like stilettos. Their arms resembled poisonous feelers.

Nora Kaye as the Novice was brought forth by the Queen. With her frail knees bent and drawn together and with a caul of cloth over her head, she appeared wet with new birth. When the Queen removed the cloth, her short hair was slicked forward and glistening. Left alone, she tentatively tried her limbs.

A male (Michael Maule) appeared. Called a First Intruder, he attempted to mate with her. Abstractedly, almost automatically, she jabbed his sides, squeezed his head between her twisting thighs, and called to her companions. They got rid of the corpse. After a brief celebratory dance, they left her to the ultimate test. A Second Intruder (Nicholas Magallanes) entered. He and the Novice embarked upon an exquisite mating ritual whose love gestures, while insectile, reached the level of pure poetry. With tremulous fingers they caressed each other's fingertips, and the moment of climax found her outstretched between his knees with the tops of her shoes drumming the floor.

Her companions returned. Instinct and the needs of the individual were thrown into fierce rivalry. Gradually they impelled her to deal the fatal sting. Afterward she coldly wiped the insides of her thighs and took her place among her sisters. Her knees were bent and turned in; her arms were sharply angled. All tenderness was forgotten.

And so Jerome Robbins exorcised a personal misgiving into a ballet of consummate originality and universality.

—Doris Hering

***The Cage*, with Nora Kaye and Nicholas Magallanes, New York City Ballet, 1951**

**CAHUSAC, Louis de**

French librettist, dance historian, and theorist. Born in Montauban into a noble family, 6 April 1706. Studied law at Toulouse. Became one of the founders of the literary society of Montauban, 1730; went to Orléans, becoming secretary to the intendant Pajot, 1730; went to Paris to prepare his work *Pharamond* for production at court, 1733; wrote another tragedy, *Le Comte de Warwick* (which was a failure), 1742; secretary to the Count of Clermont, 1743; wrote and staged the comedy *Zénéide*, 1743, leading to successful career as librettist of opéra-ballets at the Opéra, Paris, 1743–59; also theorist and writer on dance, contributing articles on "ballet", "danse", "décoration", "merveilleux", and "figurant" for Diderot's *Encyclopédie* (in 17 volumes, published 1751–65); also author of major work on the history of dance, *La danse ancienne et moderne; ou, Traité historique de la danse*, published in 1754; granted the office of the Royal Censor, as well as a pension from the court. Died in Paris, 22 June 1759.

**WORKS** (libretti)

1745 *Les Fêtes de Polymnie* (mus. Rameau) Opéra, Paris
1747 *Les Fêtes de l'Hymen et de l'Amour* (ballet-héroique; mus. Rameau), Versailles
1748 *Zaïs* (ballet; mus. Rameau), Opéra, Paris
1749 *Naïs, opéra pour la paix* (ballet-héroique; mus. Rameau), Opéra, Paris
*Zoroastre* (tragédie; mus. Rameau), Opéra, Paris
1752 *Les Amours de Tempé* (ballet; mus. Dauvergne, chor. M. Gardel), Opéra, Paris
1754 *La Naissance d'Osiris; ou, La Fête pamilie* (ballet allégorique; mus. Rameau), Opéra, Paris
*Anacréon* (ballet héroique; mus. Rameau), Fontainebleau

## PUBLICATIONS

By Cahusac:

Articles in Diderot, Charles (ed.), *Encyclopédie*, 17 volumes: Paris, 1751–65

*La Danse ancienne et moderne; ou, Traité historique de la danse*, 3 volumes: La Haye, 1754

About Cahusac:

La Porte, Abbé Joseph de, *Anecdotes dramatiques*, Paris, 1775

Noverre, Jean-Georges, *Lettres sur les arts imitateurs en général et sur la danse en particulier*, 2 volumes: Paris and La Haye, 1807

Collé, Charles, *Journal et mémoires*, 3 volumes: Paris, 1868

Grimm, Friedrich Melchior, *Correspondance littéraire*, 16 volumes: Paris, 1877–82

Girdlestone, Cuthbert, *Jean-Philippe Rameau*, London, 1957

Oliver, Alfred Richard, *The Encyclopedists as Critics of Music*, New York, 1966

Winter, Marian Hannah, *The Pre-Romantic Ballet*, London, 1974

Chazin-Bennahum, Judith, "Cahusac, Diderot, and Noverre: Three Revolutionary French Writers on the Eighteenth-Century Dance", *Theatre Journal* (Baltimore), May 1983

Chazin-Bennahum, Judith, *Livrets of Ballets and Pantomimes during the French Revolution (1787–1801)*, Ph.D. Dissertation, University of Michigan, 1983

Pitou, Spire, *The Paris Opera*, 2 volumes: London, 1985

* * *

Louis de Cahusac is a major figure in the history and aesthetics of eighteenth-century dance. His informative articles for the *Encyclopédie* and his inspirational *Traité de la danse* reveal both the historian and the theorist. Well-documented and educational, Cahusac's works show his erudition. He was acquainted with the works of the Jesuit Le Jay, Père Ménestrier, Abbé du Bos, and Batteux. Throughout his writings, Cahusac manifests an interest in the development of public taste and of personal artistic style. His lucidity of thought as well as his clarity of expression conform to the spirit of the Enlightenment. Moreover, his collaboration with Rameau on seven of his opéra-ballets provide the embodiment of his theories and those of his age.

As a historian, Cahusac puts into practice Aristotle's theory: "He who considers things in their first growth and origin will obtain the clearest view of them." In his articles on dance and ballet and in his *Traité*, Cahusac gives a history of this art from the earliest times to 1750. He begins his articles with a clear definition followed by a rational classification of dances into the sacred, secular, and theatrical categories. He analyzes the etymology of the word "ballet", defines it, and divides it into three distinct genres: historical, fabulous, and poetic.

Cahusac finds in ballet the origin of opera. For him, opera in France evolved from the local *fêtes* rather than from the Italian opera. The order of progression from ballet to opera developed from Molière's comédie-ballet to La Motte's lyric-ballet, and finally to Rameau's opéra-ballet. According to Cahusac, Rameau's opéra-ballet was the highest expression of ballet.

In his analytical approach to dance history, Cahusac outlines the elements of ballet, of which the most significant is the unity of design. To achieve unity and coherence, the action of the ballet should be divided into five acts. Each act should be made up of three, six, nine, and sometimes twelve *entrées*. Poetry is merely used to explain the action being represented. The other elements are, in the order of their importance: dance steps to set figures, instrumental and vocal music, decoration, and machinery.

To illustrate his point of view, Cahusac describes specific ballets. He considers *L'Europe galante*, *Les Eleménts*, *Les Amours des dieux*, and *Les Fêtes grecques et romaines* as resourceful. His selection is based on criteria aligned with his own purposes and theories.

Cahusac makes a significant historical statement. He explains the secondary role of dance in Quinault's operas by two factors. First, female dancers did not appear on the operatic stage in France until the year 1681, in the Lully-Quinault opera *Le Triomphe de l'amour*. Second, the number of dancers at Quinault's disposal was smaller than in 1750. Thus, Cahusac draws connections, finding causal antecedents to important historical facts.

As a theorist, Cahusac clearly emphasizes his artistic principles throughout his writings. He devotes the first chapter of his *Traité* to the necessity of a theory to enlighten the artist, to correct the overindulgence of art, and to help the progress of ballet.

Cahusac's first principle, "Dance as imitation of Nature", represents the aesthetic emblem of the Age of Enlightenment, in which fidelity to nature and respect for the great classics remain the highest virtues. In all things, Nature must be the guide; and art must seek to imitate Nature. Music must also imitate Nature, expressing a definite feeling or a specific mood. Even the music for the entr'acte should continue the illusion of the spectacle.

Cahusac's second principle deals with the theory of dramatic ballet. He stresses the importance of a plot. Dance should not be used solely as a pleasurable entertainment. It should be intimately linked to the main action. All the parts must be in relation to the principal action and each dance must be part of the action. Cahusac criticizes the self-centeredness of certain dancers who liked to appear in solo more than once, regardless of the general action of the piece. In his libretti Cahusac attempts to integrate all the arts. In *Zoroastre*, he used the chorus with great effect.

To achieve a cohesive theatrical action, a composer of ballet must select appropriate subjects for the theatre. Important historical actions may not necessarily be suitable. Cahusac suggests actions drawn from ancient history, fables, and mythology. Such actions require a clear exposition, an ingenious knot, and a well-presented denouement. To reach the desired effect, further rules must be observed: these are precision of gesture and rapidity of action. Gesture is more precise than speech. It portrays a situation instantly, in a single movement. Therefore, useless *entrées*, figures, or steps should be avoided.

Cahusac often explains through comparison, sometimes merging the historian with the theorist and the critic. He compares the *danse en action* to the *danse simple*. He argues that the *danse en action* has the superiority of a beautiful historical picture to simple cut-out figures of flowers. The first is orderly, composed; the second is mechanically arranged. Cahusac made use of the *danse en action* in Rameau's *Les Fêtes de Polimnie*, *Zaïs*, *Naïs*, and *Les Fêtes de l'Hymen et de l'Amour*.

Cahusac repeatedly affirms his third artistic principle, that of dance as expression of passions. He emphasizes the requirement of a moving plot. A composer of ballet must study men thoroughly before "painting" them and must examine passions closely before expressing them. Cahusac considers the virtuosity of the dancers of his time irreproachable but finds them lacking in expression.

In addition to drama, music, and dance, the decoration must constantly present elements of surprise and illusion. This is realized through the fantastic element, *le merveilleux*, the cornerstone of eighteenth-century French opera. *Le merveilleux* depends for its subject-matter upon mythology. It includes the giving of supernatural powers to characters and the making of extravagant metamorphoses. "The scenery," writes Abbé La Porte, "the theatrical machines, the lighting, the costumes in the opera *Zoroastre* were magnificent, surpassing even the most beautiful things which one had seen in this theatre since its foundation."

Although the proliferation of dances is the most outstanding aspect of the opéra-ballet era, Cahusac fails to mention the use of technique in dance. This is partially due to the limited dance vocabulary of his time. For the eighteenth-century French audience, dance is the development of the beautiful proportions of the body requiring precision in the execution of gestures, grace in the movements of arms, lightness in the performance of steps.

Cahusac's reaction against the conservative elements of the "grand siècle", perpetuated after Lully's death, invited the criticism of his contemporaries. Grimm found in his *Traité de la danse* curious research and interesting details, but thought Cahusac had only indicated the weakness of contemporary dance. On the other hand, Noverre commended him for revealing the beauties of the art of dance, for proposing necessary embellishments, and for showing the dancers the sure way to success.

—Elizabeth Terzian

---

**CALEGARI, Maria**

American dancer. Born in New York, 30 March 1957. Studied at the Ballet Academy, Queens, and at the School of American Ballet, New York, from 1971, pupil of Alexandra Danilova, Stanley Williams, Felia Doubrovska, Suki Schorer, and Muriel Stuart. Dancer, corps de ballet, New York City Ballet, from 1974: soloist, from 1981; principal dancer, from 1983, touring with company both in the United States and abroad; has also appeared on television, including for Public Broadcasting Service (PBS) "Dance in America" series, 1985, 1986. Recipient: Professional Children's School Alumni Award, 1986.

**ROLES**

1977 Dewdrop Fairy in *The Nutcracker* (Balanchine), New York City Ballet, New York
1978 Principal dancer in *Divertimento No. 15* (Balanchine), New York City Ballet, New York
Élégie in *Tchaikovsky Suite No. 3* (Balanchine), New York City Ballet, New York
Principal dancer in *Serenade* (Balanchine), New York City Ballet, New York
1980 Ricercata in *Episodes II* (Balanchine), New York City Ballet, New York
Fourth Movement in *Symphony in C* (Balanchine), New York City Ballet, New York
Principal dancer in *Goldberg Variations* (Robbins), New York City Ballet, New York
Sugar Plum Fairy in *The Nutcracker* (Balanchine), New York City Ballet, New York
1981 Calliope in *Apollo* (Balanchine), New York City Ballet, New York
Principal dancer (cr) in *Suite from "Histoire de Soldat"* (Martins), New York City Ballet, New York
Principal dancer in *Souvenir de Florence* (Taras), New York City Ballet, New York
October—Chant d'Automne (cr) in *Piano Pieces* (Robbins), New York City Ballet, New York
Principal dancer in *Suite No. 1 in D major* (Duell), New York City Ballet, New York
Sanguinic in *The Four Temperaments* (Balanchine), New York City Ballet, New York
Pas de trois in *Agon* (Balanchine), New York City Ballet, New York
Principal dancer in *Tchaikovsky Piano Concerto No. 2* (previously *Ballet Imperial*; Balanchine), New York City Ballet, New York
Principal dancer in *In the Night* (Robbins), New York City Ballet, New York
1982 Principal dancer in *Capriccio Italien* (Martins), New York City Ballet, New York
Principal dancer (cr) in *Gershwin Concerto* (Robbins), New York City Ballet, New York
Principal dancer (Girl in Mauve) in *Dances at a Gathering* (Robbins), New York City Ballet, New York
Choleric in *The Four Temperaments* (Balanchine), New York City Ballet, New York
First Movement in *Symphony in C* (Balanchine), New York City Ballet, New York
Principal dancer in *Symphony in Three Movements* (Balanchine), New York City Ballet, New York
Principal dancer (cr) in *Four Chamber Works* (later *Chamber Works*; Robbins), New York City Ballet, New York
Principal dancer in *In G Major* (Robbins), New York City Ballet, New York
Principal dancer (cr) in *La Création du monde* (Duell), New York City Ballet, New York
1983 Odette in *Swan Lake* (one-act version; Balanchine after Ivanov), New York City Ballet, New York
Pas de trois from *La Ventana* in *Bournonville Divertissements* (Williams after Bournonville), New York City Ballet, New York
Royal Canadian Air Force and WRENS in *Union Jack* (Balanchine), New York City Ballet, New York
Principal dancer (Girl in Green) in *Dances at a Gathering* (Robbins), New York City Ballet, New York
Principal dancer (cr) in *Glass Pieces* (Robbins), New York City Ballet, New York
Principal dancer in *Rossini Quartets* (Martins), New York City Ballet, New York
Principal dancer in *Who Cares?* (Balanchine), New York City Ballet, New York
Emeralds in *Jewels* (Balanchine), New York City Ballet, New York
1984 Principal dancer in *I'm Old Fashioned* (Robbins), New York City Ballet, New York
Third Movement in *Western Symphony* (Balanchine), New York City Ballet, New York
Principal dancer (cr) in *A Schubertiad* (Martins), New York City Ballet, New York
Principal dancer (cr) in *Antique Epigraphs* (Robbins), New York City Ballet, New York
Principal dancer in *Piano-Rag-Music* (Martins), New York City Ballet, New York
Principal dancer (Girl in Pink) in *Dances at a Gathering* (Robbins), New York City Ballet, New York

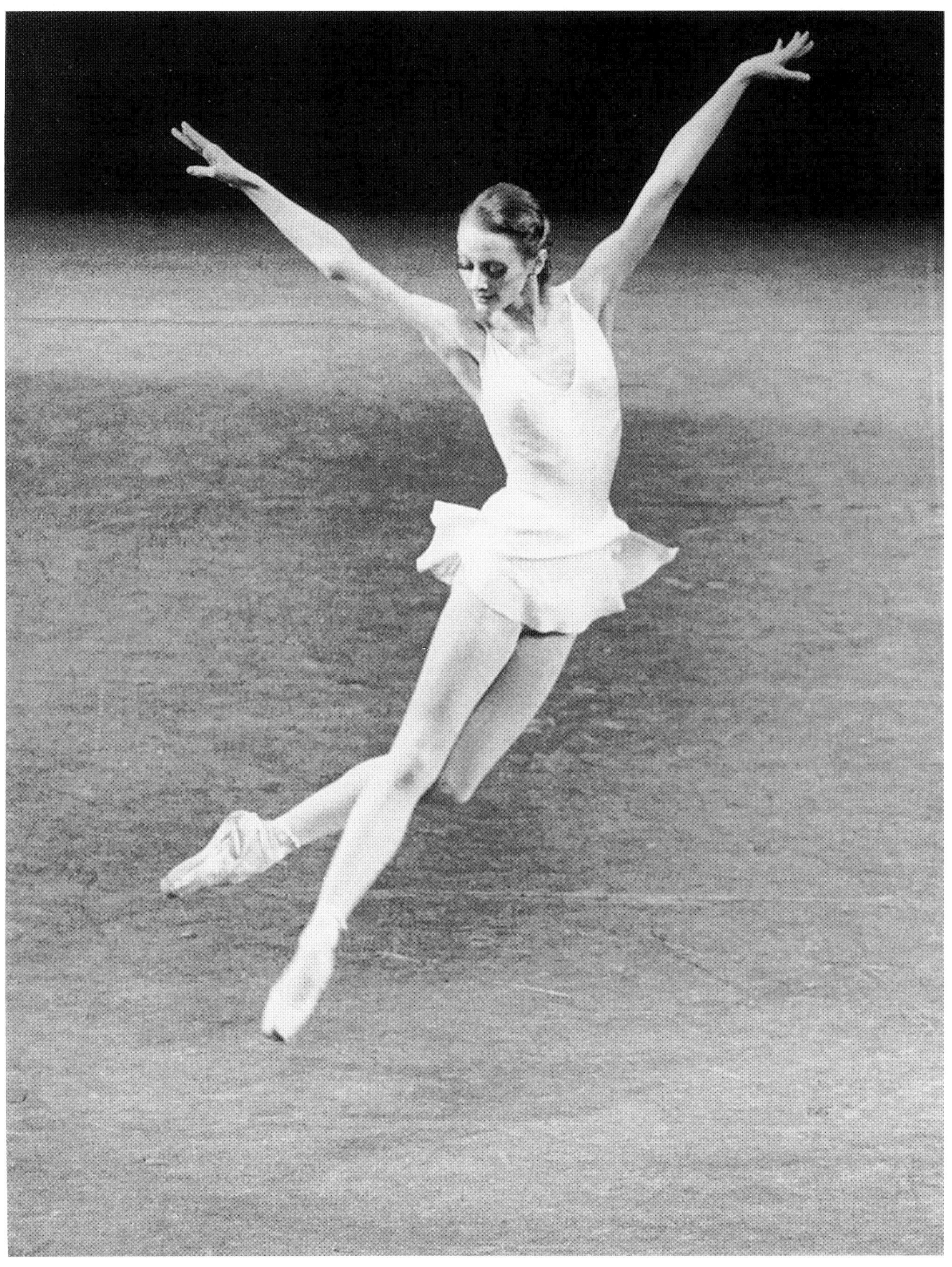

**Maria Calegari in *Gershwin Concerto*, New York City Ballet**

Principal dancer in *Afternoon of a Faun* (Robbins), New York City Ballet, New York
Principal dancer in *Liebeslieder Walzer* (Balanchine), New York City Ballet, New York
Principal dancer (cr) in *Brahms/Handel* (Tharp, Robbins), New York City Ballet, New York
Principal dancer in *Concertino* (Robbins), New York City Ballet, New York
Fall in *The Seasons* (Robbins), New York City Ballet, New York
Principal dancer in *Menuetto* (Tomasson), New York City Ballet, New York
1985 Principal dancer in *Stravinsky Violin Concerto* (Balanchine), New York City Ballet, New York
Principal dancer (cr) in *Eight Lines* (Robbins), New York City Ballet, New York
Principal dancer in *Bugaku* (Balanchine), New York City Ballet, New York
Titania in *A Midsummer Night's Dream* (Balanchine), New York City Ballet, New York
The Novice in *The Cage* (Robbins), New York City Ballet, New York
Allegro in *Brahms-Schoenberg Quartet* (Balanchine), New York City Ballet, New York
1986 Principal dancer in *Robert Schumann's "Davidsbündlertänze"* (Balanchine), New York City Ballet, New York
Principal dancer in *Kammermusik No. 2* (Balanchine), New York City Ballet, New York
Principal dancer in *Piccolo Balletto* (Robbins), New York City Ballet, New York
Pas de deux in *Agon* (Balanchine), New York City Ballet, New York
1987 "Gold and Silver Waltz" and "Der Rosenkavalier" in *Vienna Waltzes* (Balanchine), New York City Ballet, New York
The Door in *Variations pour une porte et un soupir* (Balanchine), New York City Ballet, New York
Strip-Tease Girl in *Slaughter on Tenth Avenue* (Balanchine), New York City Ballet, New York
Principal dancer in *Mozartiana* (Balanchine), New York City Ballet, New York
1988 Principal dancer in *Chaconne* (Balanchine), New York City Ballet, New York
Second Movement in *Symphony in C* (Balanchine), New York City Ballet, New York
Fourth Movement in *Western Symphony* (Balanchine), New York City Ballet, New York
Principal dancer (cr) in *Five* (Bonnefoux), New York City Ballet, New York
Eurydice (cr) in *Into the Hopper* (Cook), New York City Ballet, New York
Principal dancer (cr) in *Ives Songs* (Robbins), New York City Ballet, New York
1990 Principal dancer in *Echo* (Martins), New York City Ballet, New York
1991 The Siren in *Prodigal Son* (Balanchine), New York City Ballet, New York
Second Waltz (cr) in *Waltz Trilogy* (LaFosse), New York City Ballet, New York
Lilac Fairy in *The Sleeping Beauty* (Martins after Petipa), New York City Ballet, New York
1992 Principal dancer (cr) in *Flötezart* (Cook), New York City Ballet, New York

**PUBLICATIONS**

By Calegari:
Interview in Gruen, John, "Maria Calegari: Enigma Variations", *Dance Magazine* (New York), June 1990

About Calegari:
Taub, Eric, "Maria Calegari", *Ballet News* (New York), May 1982
Gruen, John, "She Means What She Dances", *Dance Magazine* (New York), February 1983
Macaulay, Alastair, "Balanchine's World", *Ballet Review* (New York), Spring 1984
Reiter, Susan, "Turning Point", *Connoisseur* (New York), November 1984
Croce, Arlene, *Sight Lines*, New York, 1987
Karkar, Waltraud, *And They Danced On*, Wausau, Wisconsin, 1989
Finkel, Anita, "Three Dancers Today", *The New Dance Review* (New York), January–March 1990

* * *

Tall, extremely slender, and long-limbed, Maria Calegari is further distinguished by her strawberry blonde hair and very pale skin. As a dancer, she is intelligent and sensitive in her interpretations of a repertory that is unusually diverse for a ballerina with the New York City Ballet. Descriptions of her frequently show striking contrasts—delicate but strong, understated but lively, fire but ice, elegant but tough.

Since she is extremely limber, Calegari can accomplish astonishingly beautiful shapes with her body; since she is extremely smart and strong, she can control them. The clarity of her arabesque is practically a signature. But, more important, as critic Arlene Croce has noted, she has the capacity to shape phrases and movements, not just shape steps. Her musicality, her awareness of the importance of the details and transitions of movement, all lend her the quality of portrayal that defines the elusive term "ballerina".

After having started dance classes at age three in Queens, New York, Calegari suffered a year of injury before coming to the School of American Ballet at age fourteen. Although considered a late-comer there, she made steady progress, joining New York City Ballet three years later. She worked her way through the corps de ballet, at first receiving increasing attention from Balanchine, then losing it, then regaining it. She began to come into her own in the late 1970s and to emerge fully in the early 1980s, becoming a soloist in 1981 and a principal dancer in 1983.

Calegari has sustained a large number of roles in the repertory over the years, frequently appearing in more than one ballet in a performance. What distinguishes the range of her repertory is not only that she has worked with each of the major choreographers of New York City Ballet, but that, as Croce has noted, she has performed in roles designed originally for ballerinas with widely differing qualities. For example, she has taken on the elegant fluidity of Violette Verdy's role in "Emeralds" (*Jewels*) as well as the lyrical charm of her role in *Dances at a Gathering*; she understands the dramatic abstraction of Tanaquil LeClerq's Choleric role in *The Four Temperaments* as well as the witty insouciance of her role in *Western Symphony*; she can demonstrate the classical poise of Suzanne Farrell's role in *Chaconne* as well as the zesty charm of her roles in *Union Jack*; and she excels in the glamour of Karin von Aroldingen's role in *Vienna Waltzes* as well as the athletic surprises of her role in *Kammermusik No. 2*. In a number of ballets, Calegari has mastered more than one of the principal parts: for example, she has danced the first, second, and fourth movements of *Symphony in C*; the pas de trois and pas de deux of *Agon*; the mauve, green, and pink roles of *Dances at a Gathering*; and the third and fourth movements of *Western Symphony*.

Calegari's repertory included from very early on the "dark angel" role in *Serenade* and Calliope in *Apollo*. It ranges from the graciousness of *Liebeslieder Walzer*, to the passion of *Robert Schumann's "Davidsbündlertänze"*, to the understated grace of Titania in *A Midsummer Night's Dream*. It includes the astringent angularity and wit of so-called "leotard" ballets such as *Stravinsky Violin Concerto* and *Episodes*. More recently Calegari has taken on the cool eroticism of *Bugaku*, the coy enchantment of the Strip-Tease Girl in *Slaughter on Tenth Avenue*, and the sensuous Siren of *Prodigal Son*.

Calegari has also proven herself capable of mastering works based in the nineteenth-century repertory. Early in her career she took on the classical charm of the Petipa-based Sugar Plum Fairy in *The Nutcracker* and more recently she danced the role of the Lilac Fairy in Peter Martins' new production of *The Sleeping Beauty*. Perhaps the great highlight of her career has been her sensitive, subtle, and poignant interpretation of Odette in Balanchine's staging of the Ivanov "white act" of *Swan Lake*. She discussed the work with the ailing master shortly before his death. Although he never created a new role for her, he coached her in this role from his hospital bed through words and by demonstrating with his hands.

Despite her strengths as a classical ballerina, Calegari is equally at home in many works by Jerome Robbins, depicting glamour, flow, and sophistication in *Gershwin Concerto*, *I'm Old Fashioned*, and *In the Night*. She has created a number of roles in his works, including the ultra-modern *Glass Pieces*, the mysterious hieroglyphic *Antique Epigraphs*, and the surprising Robbins–Tharp collaboration, *Brahms/Handel*. She has also taken on and created roles in works by Martins, Bonnefoux, Cook, Joseph Duell, LaFosse, Taras, and Tomasson.

Although she continues to perform many of her roles, Calegari has been through some difficult periods in recent years. The death of Balanchine in 1983 and the suicide of her close friend and fellow dancer Joseph Duell in 1986 contributed to a loss of emotional strength and some deterioration of physical health. Her searches for spiritual support, especially by means of a psychic, have been controversial. However, periods of recovery give hope that she will fully regain and further fulfill her extraordinary gifts as a dancer.

—Katy Matheson

---

**CAMARGO, Marie-Anne**

French dancer. Born Marie-Anne de Cupis in Brussels, 15 April 1710. First studied with father, musician and dance teacher Ferdinand-Joseph de Cupis; also studied with Mlle (Françoise) Prévost, Paris, from the age of 10, and later with Michel Blondy and Louis Pécour, L'Académie royale de musique (Paris Opéra), Paris. Two children by Louis de Bourbon, Comte de Clermont. Début in Brussels, c. 1720, resulting in three-year contract with the Théâtre royal de la Monnaie; dancer, Rouen Opera, 1725; first performance at Opéra, Paris (performing under the name of Camargo), in *Les Caractères de la danse*, 1726, soon becoming premiere danseuse (and famous rival to Marie Sallé); also choreographer, staging own solos; retired 1735, but returned to stage 1740; naturalized as French citizen, 1739; last Paris Opéra performance, 5 March 1751; retired with largest pension ever given to a dancer. Died in Paris, 28 April 1770.

**ROLES**

1726 Dancer in *Les Caractères de la danse* (mus. Rebel), Opéra, Paris
Une Matelotte (cr) in *Ajax* (tragédie-lyrique; mus. Bertin), Opéra, Paris
Une Grâce in *Les Amours déguisés* (ballet; mus. Bourgeois), Opéra, Paris

1727 Une Matelotte, Une Bergère, Une Bacchante (cr) in *Les Amours des dieux* (ballet-héroïque; mus. Mouret), Opéra, Paris
Une Matelotte in *Le Jugement de Pâris* (pastorale-héroïque; mus. Bertin), Opéra, Paris
Habitante de la Seine, Une Amante Heureuse, Une Matelotte in *Médée et Jason* (tragédie-lyrique; mus. Salomon), Opéra, Paris
Une Amante Contente, La Mariée in *Roland* (tragédie-lyrique; mus. Lully), Opéra, Paris

1728 Une Matelotte in *Alceste; ou, Le Triomphe d'Alcide* (tragédie-lyrique; mus. Lully), Opéra, Paris
Une Matelotte in *Les Amours de Protée* (ballet; mus. Gervais), Opéra, Paris
Une Paysanne in *Bellérophon* (tragédie-lyrique; mus. Lully), Opéra, Paris
Une Naïade, Une Matelotte in *Hypermnestre* (tragédie-lyrique; mus. Gervais), Opéra, Paris
Une Scythe, Une Nymphe de Diane (cr) in *Orion* (tragédie-lyrique; mus. La Coste), Opéra, Paris
Une Elève de Terpsichore, Une Bohémienne (cr) in *La Princess d'Élide* (ballet-héroïque; mus. Villeneuve, chor. Blondy), Opéra, Paris
Une Habitante des Rives du Pénée, Une Suivante de la Sibylle Delphique (cr) in *Tarsis et Zélie* (tragédie-lyrique; mus. Rebel, Francoeur), Opéra, Paris

1729 Une Bergère, Terpsichore (cr) in *Les Amours des déesses* (ballet-héroïque; mus. Quinault, chor. Blondy), Opéra, Paris
Une Matelotte (cr) in *Nouveaux Fragments* (ballet; mus. Campra), Opéra, Paris
Une Magicienne, Une Nymphe, Une Moresse in *Tancrède* (tragédie-lyrique; mus. Campra), Opéra, Paris
Une Bergère, Une Vieille in *Thésée* (tragédie-lyrique; mus. Lully), Opéra, Paris

1730 Une Matelotte, Une Néréide in *Alcione* (tragédie-lyrique; mus. Marais), Opéra, Paris
Terpsichore, Une Bacchante, Une Jeune Fille de la Suite de Diane (cr) in *Les Caprices d'Erato; ou, Les Caractères de la musique* (divertissement added to *Alcione*; mus. de Blamont), Opéra, Paris
Une Matelotte in *Le Carnaval et la folie* (comédie-ballet; mus. Destouches), Opéra, Paris
Une Egyptienne in *Phaëton* (tragédie-lyrique; mus. Lully, chor. Blondy), Opéra, Paris
Une Grecque, Une Nymphe de Thétis (cr) in *Pyrrhus* (tragédie-lyrique; mus. Royer), Opéra, Paris
Une Matelotte in *Télémaque* (tragédie-lyrique; mus. Destouches), Opéra, Paris

1731 Une Suivante d'Urgande in *Amadis de Gaule* (tragédie-lyrique; mus. Lully), Opéra, Paris
Un Plaisir (cr) in *Endymion* (pastorale-héroique; mus. de Blamont), Opéra, Paris
Une Bohémienne, Un Masque Galant in *Les Fêtes*

**Marie Camargo (engraving after a painting by Nicolas Lancret)**

*vénitiennes* (ballet; mus. Campra), Opéra, Paris
Une Matelotte, Une Bergère in *Idoménée* (tragédie-lyrique; mus. Campra), Opéra, Paris

1732 Une Bergère, Une Bacchante (cr) in *Le Ballet des sens* (ballet; mus. Mouret, chor. Blondy), Opéra, Paris
Une Matelotte, Une Amante Heureuse (cr) in *Biblys* (tragédie-lyrique; mus. La Coste), Opéra, Paris
Une Dryade, Une Bergère, Une Calydonienne in *Callirhoé* (tragédie-lyrique; mus. Destouches, chor. Blondy), Opéra, Paris
Une Suite de la Jeunesse, Une Bergère in *Isis* (tragédie-lyrique; mus. Lully), Opéra, Paris
Une Israélite (cr) in *Jephté* (tragédie-lyrique; mus. Montéclair), Opéra, Paris

1733 Une Bergère, Un Génie, Une Bacchante (cr) in *L'Empire de l'amour* (ballet-héroïque; mus. de Brassac), Opéra, Paris
Une Matelotte, Une Bergère (cr) in *Hippolyte et Aricie* (tragédie-lyrique; mus. Rameau), Opéra, Paris
Une Bergère, Une Dryade in *Issé* (pastorale; mus. Destouches), Opéra, Paris
Une Grecque, La Prêtresse de l'Amour in *Omphale* (tragédie-lyrique; mus. Destouches), Opéra, Paris
Terpsichore, Une Bergère in *Les Fêtes greques et romaines* (ballet-héroïque; mus. de Blamont, chor. Blondy), Opéra, Paris

1734 Une Matelotte, Une Suivante de Pomone in *Les Éléments* (ballet; mus. Lalande, Destouches, chor. Blondy), Opéra, Paris
Une Femme du Peuple de la Grèce (cr) in *La Fête de Diane* (divertissement added to *Les Fêtes greques et romaines*; mus. de Blâmont), Opéra, Paris
Une Néréide in *Iphigénie en Tauride* (tragédie-lyrique; mus. Desmarets, Campra), Opéra, Paris
Une Bacchante in *Les Fêtes nouvelles* (ballet; mus. Duplessis), Opéra, Paris
Un Démon transformé en Songe, Une Danseuse dans une Fête de Village in *Pirithoüs* (tragédie-lyrique; mus. Mouret), Opéra, Paris
Une Bacchante, Une Matelotte in *Philomèle* (tragédie-lyrique; mus. La Coste), Opéra, Paris

1735 Une Suivante de Nisus, Une Bergère in *Scylla* (tragédie-lyrique; mus. Théobalde), Opéra, Paris

1740 Une Naïade in *Atys* (tragédie-lyrique; mus. Lully), Opéra, Paris

1742 La Danseuse dans une Noce in *Les Amours de Ragonde* (ballet-burlesque; mus. Mouret), Opéra, Paris
Une Bergère, une Nymphe (cr) in *Isbé* (pastorale; mus.

Mondonville), Opéra, Paris

1743 Une Suite de l'Amour et de la Folie, Une Habitante de Cythère (cr) in *Les Caractères de la folie* (opéra-ballet; mus. Bury), Opéra, Paris

Une Pastourelle (cr) in *Don Quichotte chez la Duchesse* (opéra-ballet; mus. Boismortier), Opéra, Paris

Une Ombre d'Héroine, Une Phrygienne in *Hésione* (tragédie-lyrique; mus. Campra), Opéra, Paris

Une Matelotte, La Rose in *Les Indes galantes* (ballet-héroïque; mus. Rameau), Opéra, Paris

Doris in *Le Pouvoir de l'amour* (ballet; mus. Royer), Opéra, Paris

1744 Une Phrygienne in *Dardanus* (tragédie-lyrique; mus. Rameau), Opéra, Paris

Une Bergère in *Acis et Galathée* (pastorale-héroïque; mus. Lully), Opéra, Paris

Une Habitante d'Ochalie in *Alcide* (tragédie-lyrique; mus. Louis Lully, Marais), Opéra, Paris

Un Masque in *L'École des amants* (ballet; mus. Nieil), Opéra, Paris

Une Thyrinthienne in *Les Grâces* (ballet-héroïque; mus. Mouret), Opéra, Paris

1745 Une Matelotte in *Amadis de Grèce* (tragédie-lyrique; mus. Destouches), Opéra, Paris

Une Nymphe (cr) in *Les Fêtes de Polymnie* (ballet; mus. Rameau), Opéra, Paris

La Mariée, Une Provençale in *Les Fêtes de Thalie* (ballet; mus. Mouret), Opéra, Paris

Une Bacchante, Une Romaine (cr) in *Le Temple de la gloire* (ballet; mus. Rameau), Opéra, Paris

Une Chasseresse in *Zaïde, reine de Grenade* (ballet; mus. Royer), Opéra, Paris

Une Sylphide (cr) in *Zélindor, roi des Sylphes* (ballet; mus. Rebel, Francoeur), Opéra, Paris

1746 Un Démon transformé in *Armide* (tragédie-lyrique; mus. Lully), Opéra, Paris

Une Ethiopienne in *Persée* (tragédie-lyrique; mus. Lully), Opéra, Paris

Une Bergère, Une Femme du peuple de Sicile (cr) in *Scylla et Glaucus* (tragédie-lyrique; mus. Leclair), Opéra, Paris

Une Néréide in *Le Triomphe de l'harmonie* (ballet-héroïque; mus. Grenet), Opéra, Paris

1747 Une Matelotte (cr) in *Daphnis et Chloë* (pastorale; mus. Boismortier), Opéra, Paris

Une Pastourelle in *L'Europe galante* (opéra-ballet; mus. Campra), Opéra, Paris

Pas de trois, Pas de six in *Églé* (act from *Les Fêtes d'Hébé; ou, Les Talents lyriques*, ballet; mus. Rameau), Opéra, Paris

1748 Une Sauvagesse, Pas de cinq (cr) in *Les Fêtes de l'Hymen et de l'Amour* (ballet-héroïque; mus. Rameau), Opéra, Paris

Une Sylphide (cr) in *Zaïs* (ballet-héroïque; mus. Rameau), Opéra, Paris

Une Marinière in *Fragments de differents ballets* (mus. various), Opéra, Paris

1749 Une Provençale in *Les Caractères de l'amour* (ballet-héroique; mus. de Blâmont), Opéra, Paris

Terpsichore in *Le Carnaval du Parnasse* (opéra-ballet; mus. Mondonville), Opéra, Paris

Une Divinité des Mers déguisé en Matelotte (cr) in *Naïs, opéra pour la paix* (ballet-héroïque; mus. Rameau), Opéra, Paris

Une Mage (cr) in *Zoroastre* (tragédie-lyrique; mus. Rameau), Opéra, Paris

1750 Une Matelotte (cr) in *Léandre et Héro* (tragédie-lyrique; mus. Brassac), Opéra, Paris

Une Européenne in *Thétis et Pélée* (tragédie-lyrique; mus. Collasse), Opéra, Paris

1751 Une Nymphe (cr) in *Titon et l'aurore* (ballet; mus. Bury), Opéra, Paris

## PUBLICATIONS


Parfait (Claude et François), *Dictionnaire des Théâtres*, 7 volumes, Paris, 1756

Noverre, Jean-Georges, *Lettres sur la danse et les ballets*, Stuttgart and Lyons, 1760; as *Letters on Dancing and Ballets*, translated by Cyril Beaumont, London, 1930

Jal, Auguste, *Dictionnaire critique de biographie et d'histoire*, Paris, 1872

Campardon, Emile, *L'Académie royale de musique au XVIIIe siècle*, Paris, 1884

Letainturier-Fradin, Gabriel, *La Camargo*, Paris, 1907; reissued 1950

Dacier, Émile, *Une danseuse de l'Opéra sous Louis XV, Melle Sallé*, Paris, 1909

Beaumont, Cyril, *Three French Dancers of the Eighteenth Century*, London, 1934

Kirstein, Lincoln, *Dance: A Short History of Classic Theatrical Dancing*, New York, 1935

Moore, Lillian, *Artists of the Dance*, New York, 1938

Migel, Parmenia, *The Ballerinas*, New York, 1972

Prudhommeau, Germaine, "Camargo–Sallé: Duel au pied levé," *Danser* (Paris), March 1986


* * *

The name of Marie Camargo shines so gloriously in ballet history that it has come to symbolize the eighteenth century to which she so fittingly belonged. The subject of adulation, gossip, and vicarious interest, she led an extravagant and unconventional life which provided constant scandal for the social chroniclers of her time. Fashions, hair-styles, and dishes were named after her. Charisma of such magnitude always eludes explanation, and Noverre's description of the ballerina's attributes does not clear the mystery: "Melle Camargo was neither pretty, nor tall nor well formed . . . but her mind was good . . . and it prompted her to select a style [of dancing] suitable to her physique . . . a lively and vivacious style which left no time for the spectators to detect the faults in her anatomy." Those spectators who did notice these shortcomings, however, never seemed to care. After Camargo's triumphant début in *Les Caractères de la danse* the Parisian journal *Mercure* noted that ". . . she has still much to learn", and the actress Lecouvreur, who sat in the audience, reported that "her greatest merit was her youth and her vigour". Nevertheless, both agreed that the public had been kept in total rapture. "Her dancing was quick, light, brilliant, and full of liveliness," said Noverre. "She could perform jettés battus, the royale, clean-cut entrechats, with extreme facility. She only danced to lively music, and since such fast tempi do not permit the display of grace, she replaced it with speed, ease and gaiety." In pursuit of the greater freedom she needed to suit this dancing style, the ballerina reportedly discarded the heels from her shoes, shortened her skirts, and invented precautionary drawers—this alone would have been enough innovation to send an eighteenth-century audience into a frenzy.

To the modern historian remains the task of unravelling facts from fantasy, and reality from legend, in order to assess Camargo's worth and influence in the absence of such tangible data as would be provided by choreographic scores. One gavotte only by Camargo, recorded in the dancer Despréaux's notebooks, is disappointingly plain and conventional. The fact remains, however, that Camargo was its author, indicating that the dancer made use of the Opéra privilege which granted premiers danseurs the right to choreograph their solos. Noverre made a passing remark regarding the preservation of Camargo's choreography in his chapter on notation (Lettre XIII), but this has gone unnoticed by Camargo's biographers. However, it would throw a different light on Camargo's career if she had indeed formulated most of her brilliant vocabulary.

In earlier times, other female dancers had risen to the same choreographic challenge, for example Mlle Lafontaine in the late seventeenth century, and Mlles Subligny, Prévost, and Guyot at the beginning of the eighteenth—especially the latter, who was Camargo's direct predecessor in the genre known as "Haute danse". No less than thirteen choreographies for Mlle Guyot have been preserved in the Feuillet notation, four of which were solos most certainly composed by herself. These muzettes, canaris, gavottes, and entrées for bacchantes or scaramouchettes stand out from the choreography reserved for female dancers: they sparkle with intricate cabrioles, entrechats, and fast pirouettes, and are showcases for the display of an outstanding technique. Camargo must have seen Guyot dance, since her first teacher had been Prévost, Guyot's most frequent partner, and her second mentor was Blondy, another brilliant exponent of the genre.

Camargo must have set her mind to outshine her famous predecessors. Voltaire flatly stated that "Melle Camargo was the first female to dance like a man", and this may be where Camargo's difference lies: she dared to invade the male dancer's territory. Dance was traditionally divided into two genres—"danse basse", reserved for the noble style, and "danse haute", for demi-caractère, caractère, and comique dancing. The dances of the latter category, as recorded in the Feuillet notation, show noticeable differences between male and female technique. Mlle Guyot turned one pirouette when Blondy turned two, she danced "entrechats-quatre" after her cabrioles, while he beat "entrechats-six" with sustained ronds de jambes en dehors and en dedans. One has the impression that Guyot could have gone further but that she did not dare to challenge (or did not think of challenging) the sternly observed notions of stage propriety, mandatory in female dancing. In 1707, Pasch had voiced strong disapproval of women dancers attempting "tours de force" (*Beschreibung vahrene tanz kunst*, Frankfurt, 1707), and he was simply echoing the sentiments of most dance theorists of his own and earlier times. Modesty was the cardinal virtue to be fostered in women if the fabric of a correct social order was to be preserved. "Haute dance" was the realm of devils and furies—the roles traditionally reserved for males.

Camargo defied these norms. In the 25 years of her career, she was only once cast as a grace; she appeared mostly as sailoress, hunteress, bacchante, or demon. Her dark complexion suited the roles of Bohemians, Moorish sultanas, Greek shepherdesses, and Ethiopian or Egyptian princesses, roles which lent themselves to open interpretation. No doubt this "foreign" material, which was less bound by rules of performance, helped her find the courage to break the conventions. It is obvious that history has yet to do justice to Marie Camargo's undaunted self-confidence, vision, and perseverance. In challenging the limits of her own body and mind, as well as her art, she set a precedent that spurred other women on to explore hitherto unheard-of technical possibilities. She bravely paved the way for the Barberinas, Lanys, Vestris, Esslers, and Cerritos, of the future.

—Régine Astier

---

**CAMPANINI, Barbara** *see* **BARBERINA, La**

---

**CANADIAN NATIONAL BALLET** *see* **NATIONAL BALLET OF CANADA**

---

## CARMEN

**Choreography:** John Cranko
**Music:** Georges Bizet (arranged by Wolfgang Fortner and Wilfried Steinbrenner)
**Design:** Jacques Dupont (scenery and costumes)
**Libretto:** John Cranko
**First Production:** Stuttgart Ballet, Staatstheater, Stuttgart, 28 February 1971
**Principal Dancers:** Marcia Haydée (Carmen), Richard Cragun (Escamillo), Egon Madsen (Don José)

**Other choreographic treatments of story:** Marius Petipa (Madrid, 1845), Kasyan Goleizovsky (Moscow, 1931), Roland Petit (Paris, 1949; see *Carmen*, Petit), Ruth Page (New York, 1976), Miroslav Kura (Prague, 1978), Oleg Danovski (Wiesbaden, 1979), Erwin Kosek (Luneburg, 1980), Dieter Ammann (Lucerne, 1980), Antonio Gades (Paris, 1983).

### PUBLICATIONS

Percival, John, "*Carmen*: Cranko's New Ballet", *Dance and Dancers* (London), May 1971
Balanchine, George, *Balanchine's Complete Stories of the Great Ballets*, Garden City, N.Y., 1977
Percival, John, *Theatre in my Blood: A Biography of John Cranko*, London, 1983

* * *

The picture that John Cranko draws of Carmen is essentially quite different from that presented by countless other choreographers before him, ever since Marius Petipa's *Carmen et son torero* in Madrid, in 1845 (two years before Prosper Merimée's novella *Carmen* was published), and Georges Bizet's famous opera of 1875. John Cranko did not see *Carmen* as the story of a man-eating "femme fatale", but as the tragedy first and foremost of a social outcast struggling for recognition: the "heathen" gypsy Carmen is a stranger among supposedly Christian Spaniards. As a homosexual, Cranko himself felt part of a social minority, and he intended to present in an exemplary and timeless fashion, through the *Carmen* material, the fate of one despised. As Cranko said: "Merimée describes a problem which can easily be projected into our own time; the blacks among the whites, a Jewish girl in Nazi-dominated society".

Correspondingly, Cranko demanded a set for *Carmen* which only hinted at a Spanish flavour, and commissioned Wolfgang Fortner (and his co-worker Wilfried Steinbrenner) to write a score which would indeed draw from the music of Bizet, but at the same time alienate it. The *Bizet-collages* of Fortner and Steinbrenner quote the popular melodies of Bizet and preserve their Spanish flavour as they do the marked Habanera and Seguidilla rhythms. At the same time, however, they vary and ironize the original. The use of strong, forceful, rhythmic percussion is notable.

Cranko avoided including "original" Spanish folk dance. His *Carmen* is based almost entirely on stage dance. In order to turn the attention of the audience more towards the (timeless) social drama, Cranko created an "artificial Spain". For the premiere he wrote: "You will indeed find atmosphere, castanets and a few dances, but they are alienated by the underlying Greek rhythms, for example."

The ballet, which lasts only about 80 minutes, is split into seven scenes. Cranko concentrates mainly on the pair of protagonists, Carmen and Don José (similar to Roland Petit's treatment in his *Carmen* ballet of 1949, which, in contrast to Cranko's work, does not point to the social aspects and only deals with the changing feelings of love and hate between Carmen and Don José). Other figures who play important roles in Merimée's and Bizet's works have either been cut out altogether (such as Micaela) or relegated to minor roles, as with the toreador, who, in Cranko's version, is nameless and merely serves to embody the persona of Carmen's lover, one integrated into society, and her own desire for general acceptance.

Characteristic of Cranko's style of production are the highly dramatic pas de deux, unequalled in their artful compression and force of expression. In *Carmen* they also form the true narrative framework. The story of Carmen and Don José is reflected in their dances, without the need for the illustrative function of crowd scenes. Cranko's *Carmen* is also a true costume drama: to begin with, Carmen, the worker in a cigarette factory, is poorly dressed when she comes across Don José in his smart sergeant's uniform. José arrests Carmen after an argument with the factory supervisor. While Don José falls into decline and becomes a thief and murderer for her, his uniform is exchanged for rags, while Carmen's rise in society at the side of her toreador finds expression in bright robes. Thus they meet in the final scene: Don José, who sacrificed his former existence for Carmen, and whom she has now left, stabs her, after she has enjoyed but a brief glimpse of longed-for happiness with the toreador, while the ovation of a crowd fêtes the toreador and his companion after a successful bullfight.

John Cranko's *Carmen* shares the fate of *Onegin*, created six years later, in that the choreographer was never entirely satisfied with the work after the premiere. Only a year after the first performance, Cranko removed the piece from the Stuttgart Ballet's programme, with the intention of reworking it completely. His unexpected death in 1973 prevented this. There were no official records of the original either in dance notation or on film. In 1978, however, the discovery of an illegal recording of a performance of *Carmen* by the Stuttgart Ballet in New York permitted the company to include the work in their repertoire once more. Ten years later, at the height of a flamenco and *Carmen* boom unleashed by the dance film of the same name (by Carlos Saura and Antonia Gades in 1983), a new production by Marcia Haydée followed. Haydée, the first Carmen, choreographed new sections "in the spirit of John Cranko" for this production, above all introducing variations, solos, duets, and group dances for the corps. The original sets by Jacques Dupont were correspondingly reworked and recreated. In contrast to other full-length ballets by John Cranko, *Carmen* has never been included in the repertoire of another company.

—Horst Vollmer

---

## CARMEN

**Choreography:** Roland Petit
**Music:** Georges Bizet (arranged from the opera *Carmen*)
**Design:** Antoine Clavé (scenery and costume)
**Libretto:** Roland Petit (based on opera by Henri Meilhac and Ludovic Halévy)
**First Production:** Les Ballets de Paris (de Roland Petit), Prince's Theatre, London, 21 February 1949
**Principal Dancers:** Renée Jeanmaire (Carmen), Roland Petit (Don José), Serge Perrault (Toreador)

**Other productions include:** Royal Danish Ballet (restaged Petit), with Kirsten Simone, Flemming Flindt, Henning Kronstam; Copenhagen, 15 January 1960. American Ballet Theatre, with Natalia Makarova, Renée Jeanmaire, Mikhail Baryshnikov; Washington, D.C., 16 December 1981. London Festival Ballet, with Alessandra Ferri; London, 20 June, 1986. Paris Opéra Ballet (restaged Petit), with Isabelle Guérin, Laurent Hilaire; Paris, April 1990.

Ruth Page's Chicago Opera Ballet (new version; chor. Ruth Page, mus. arranged Isaac van Grove, design Nicolai Remisoff); Iowa, 11 January 1960 (restaged with new design Bernard Daydé; Michigan, 8 January 1962). Bolshoi Ballet (new version: chor. Alberto Alonso, mus. rescored by Rodion Schedrin, scenery Boris Messerer, costumes Salvador Fernandez), as *Karmen Siuita*, or *Carmen Suite*; Moscow, 20 April 1967. Dance Theatre of Harlem (new version; chor. Ruth Page, design André Delfau); Chicago, 12 May 1972. Nevada Dance Theatre (new version; chor. Vassily Sulich, mus. arranged Rodion Schedrin); Las Vegas, 17 November 1978. Scottish Ballet (new version; chor. Peter Darrell, mus. arranged Dominic Muldowney, new libretto Darrell after Prosper Merimée, design Terry Bartlett); Edinburgh, August 1985. Ballet Royale de Wallonie (new version; chor. Jorge Lefebre, design Joelle Roustan and Roger Bernard); Charleroi, 18 March 1989.

**Other choreographic treatments of story:** Marius Petipa (Madrid, 1845), Kasyan Goleizovsky (Moscow, 1931), John Cranko (Stuttgart, 1971; see *Carmen*, Cranko), Ruth Page (New York, 1976), Miroslav Kura (Prague, 1978), Oleg Danovski (Wiesbaden, 1979), Erwin Kosek (Luneburg, 1980), Dieter Ammann (Lucerne, 1980), Antonio Gades (Paris, 1983).

### PUBLICATIONS

Beaumont, Cyril, *Ballets of Today*, London, 1954
Barnes, Clive, "*Carmen*", *Dance and Dancers* (London), October 1961
Balanchine, George, with Mason, Francis, *Balanchine's Complete Stories of the Great Ballets*, Garden City, N.Y., 1977
Alovert, Nina, "José Baryshnikov and Twin Carmens", *Dance Magazine* (New York), April 1982
Mannoni, Gérard, *Roland Petit, une chorégraphie et ses peintres*, Paris, 1990

* * *

Roland Petit's *Carmen* is one of those ballets whose ingredients so exactly match public needs and tastes at the time of its first performance that its success preserves the ballet long after its normal span of life, thus enabling it to outlive several other versions of the same story. It was first performed by Roland Petit's Ballets de Paris in London in 1949 and instantly turned a

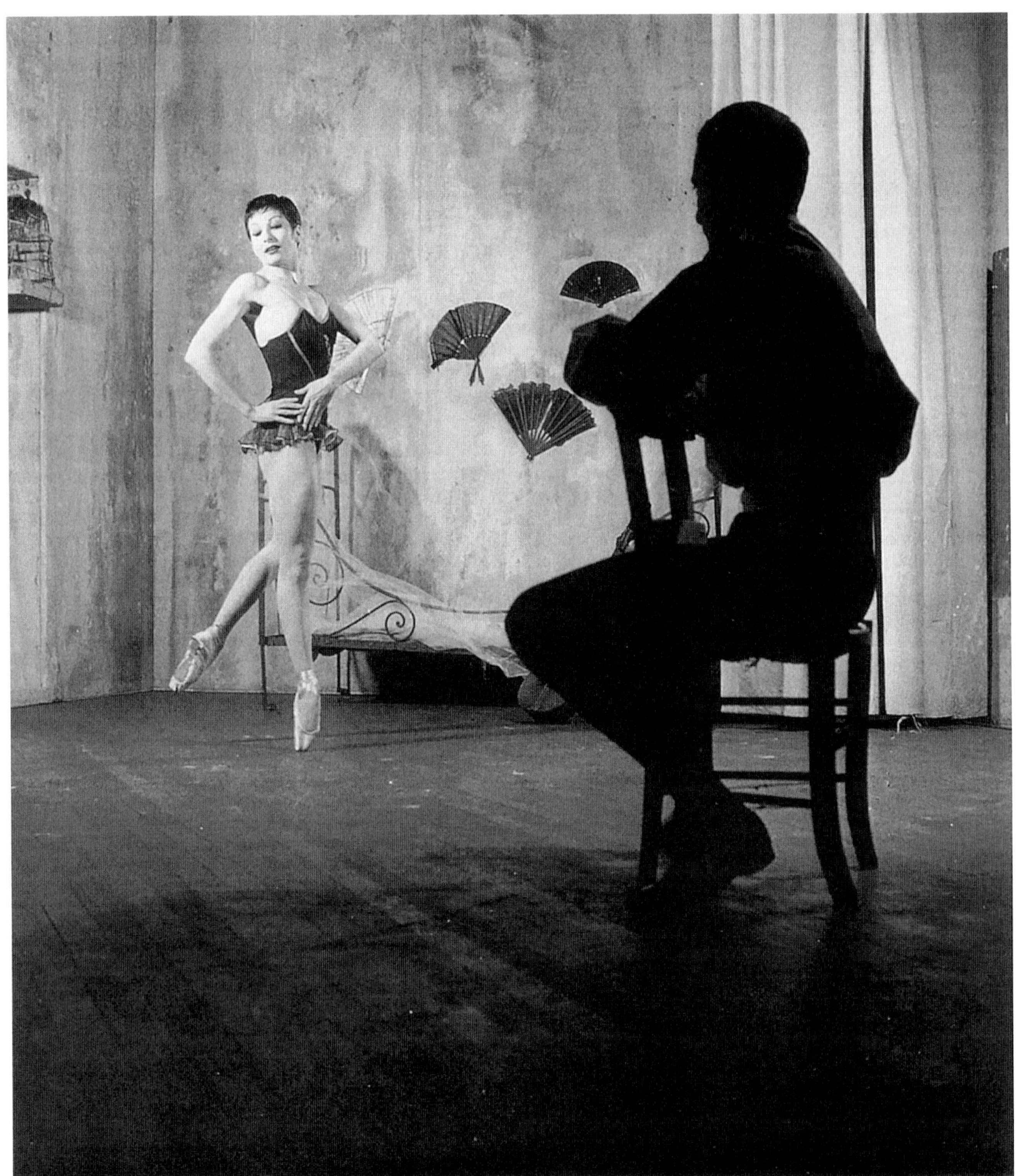

***Carmen*, with Renée Jeanmaire and Roland Petit, 1956**

flagging season (Petit's first without the supervision of Kochno) into a financial success. This success made the company instantly newsworthy, taking them to New York and even to Hollywood to make a film, which never materialized. The appeal of *Carmen* to both the general public and the dance critics was immediate, its colourful, exotic, sexy glamour making an exciting contrast to the more austere offerings of the then Sadler's Wells Ballet. The action had the exciting atmosphere of half-submerged sexual freedom, experienced by many during the Second World War. There was also, for the intellectually inclined, a whiff of some of the new French philosophical movements to be found in the attitudes of the characters in the ballet. In its middle years, *Carmen* also appealed as a piece of tourist nostalgia to a wider audience whose opportunities for travel had opened up so widely during the 1960s.

It is the characterizations required by the leading roles, plus the familiarity of the story and music, that have carried the ballet through nearly 50 years of performance. Both Carmen and Don José have provided the opportunity for a number of dancers to reveal more full-bloodedness than classical ballets normally allow; they can indulge in a thoroughly passionate, sexy affair in which the final strangling is a much more satisfying climax than anything that has taken place in the infamous and—for its period—extremely realistic bedroom pas de deux. Anticipation by audiences of such a lack of inhibition provides another reason for the long life of the ballet. Good dancers in the roles establish an atmosphere of abandoned passion. Brilliant dancers can reveal a whole range of finer nuances about the physical attraction, and complementary revulsion, of these characters for each other. In contrast to all this larger-than-life passion, subsidiary characters, such as the bandits, are treated as sophisticated but cheerful teenagers, and the Toreador is a comic creation wallowing in the adulation of his fans—one of the funniest entrées of any ballet.

The choreographic basis of the ballet is in Petit's familiar style—inverted inward movements that are interlaced with conventional ballet steps used to heighten excitement. For the corps de ballet, repeated shouts and rhythmical stamps also add to the momentum. Natural gestures are used a great deal (Danish audiences always reacted with horror to Don José *wiping his hands* on the curtain in the bedroom scene) and it is difficult to avoid the feeling that the whole intention of the ballet is to shock the audience.

Despite the ballet's instant success and acceptance in London, Petit has been harshly criticized, especially in France, for his treatment of the story and for his reorganization of Bizet's music for different purposes. Both story and music have been adapted to further the impact of the ballet in the theatre, however, and a slavish adherence to the originals would have weakened Petit's conception.

Antonio Clavé's designs, mostly black costumes against white sets with startling splashes of brilliant colour, are both flattering to the dancers and atmospheric. His costume for Jeanmaire in the bedroom pas de deux—basically a seductive black corset—together with her urchin hairstyle (which started a new fashion) are everything that is considered to be French and erotic. It gave her an image that was hers for life and which she was still successfully exploiting in the 1980s. Clavé's sets also create an extraordinary sense of heat and menace, especially the silently revolving cartwheels of the assassination and robbery scene. Unfortunately, the built-up construction has often caused lengthy pauses between the scenes, detracting from the overall momentum of the ballet.

*Carmen* was the prototype for many ballets, exploring the psychological manifestation of sexual attraction by means of the pas de deux. With its sexual realism it contributed to the destruction of the artificial fantasy world of ballet; it certainly introduced a whole range of new fantasies in which its audiences could indulge. And this, despite the less than inventive choreography, the crudely drawn subsidiary characters, and the long waits between scenes, ensures that it continues to succeed in the theatre.

—Peter Bassett

---

## LE CARNAVAL

(Original Russian title: *Karnaval*)

**Choreography:** Mikhail Fokine
**Music:** Robert Schumann, orchestrated by Aleksandr Glazunov, Nikolai Rimsky-Korsakov, Anatole Liadov, Aleksandr Tcherepnin
**Design:** Léon Bakst (costumes)
**Libretto:** Mikhail Fokine
**First Production:** Dancers of the Imperial Ballet, Pavlov Hall, St. Petersburg, 5 March (20 February old style) 1910
**Principal Dancers** (uncredited at the time): Tamara Karsavina (Columbine), Leonid Leontiev (Harlequin), Vera Fokina (Chiarina), Ludmila Schollar (Estrella), Bronislava Nijinska (Papillon), Vsevolod Meyerhold (Pierrot), Vasily Kiselev (Florestan), Aleksandr Shiryaev (Eusebius)

**Other productions include:** Diaghilev's Ballets Russes (new sets and costumes Bakst), with Lydia Lopokova (Columbine), Vaslav Nijinsky (Harlequin); Teater des Westens, Berlin, 20 May 1910. Marie Rambert Dancers (staged Léon Woizikovsky and Tamara Karsavina), with Karsavina (Columbine), Woizikovsky (Harlequin); London, 30 December 1930. Teatro Colón (restaged Fokine); Buenos Aires, 1931. Latvian National Opera (staged Anatole Vilzak after Fokine); Riga, 1932. Ballets Russes de Monte Carlo (staged Woizikovsky), with Alexandra Danilova (Columbine); London, 14 September 1933. Vic-Wells Ballet (staged Wanda Evina after Fokine, design Elizabeth and Marsh Williams); London, 24 October 1933. Ballet Theatre (restaged Fokine), with Patricia Bowman (Columbine), William Dollar (Harlequin), Adolph Bolm (Pierrot); Center Theater, New York, 13 January 1940. Stanislavsky and Nemirovich-Danchenko Ballet (staged Vladimir Burmeister after Fokine); Moscow, 1946. Royal Swedish Ballet (staged Mary Skeaping after Fokine); Stockholm, 1957. Kirov Ballet (staged Konstantin Sergeyev after Fokine); Leningrad, 15 December 1962. Western Theatre Ballet (staged Karsavina, Elizabeth Schooling after Fokine); Rotherham, 18 May 1961. (Eliot Feld's) American Ballet Company (staged Yurek Lazowsky after Fokine); New York, 24 October 1969.

### PUBLICATIONS

Beaumont, Cyril, *Complete Book of Ballets*, revised edition, London, 1951
Skeaping, Mary, "Fokine in Sweden", *Dance and Dancers* (London), May 1957
Barnes, Clive, "*Le Carnaval*", *Dance and Dancers* (London), 2 parts: April, May 1958
Fokine, Michel, *Fokine: Memoirs of a Ballet Master*, translated by Vitale Fokine, London, 1961
Dalton, Elizabeth, "In Search of Bakst", *Dancing Times* (London), June 1967
Anderson, Jack, "Legends in the Flesh", *Ballet Review* (Brooklyn, N.Y.), vol. 3, no. 2, 1969
Buckle, Richard, *Nijinsky*, London and New York, 1971
Vaughan, David, "Fokine in the Contemporary Repertory", *Ballet Review* (New York), vol. 7, nos. 2–3, 1978–79
Horwitz, Dawn Lille, *Michel Fokine*, Boston, 1985
Baer, Nancy van Norman, *The Art of Enchantment: Diaghilev's Ballet Russes, 1909–29*, San Francisco, 1988
Garafola, Lynn, *Diaghilev's Ballets Russes*, New York and London, 1989

* * *

***Le Carnaval*, with Vera Fokina and Mikhail Fokine, Berlin, c.1910**

*Le Carnaval* was created in three spontaneous rehearsals in 1910 for a charity performance in Pavlov Hall, St. Petersburg, to benefit the magazine *Satyricon*. When Fokine was approached by two young men involved in the publication (Mikhail Kornfeld, later to be its publisher, and the later-famous poet Potemkin) they gave him free rein, although they mentioned that the theme of the event was to be carnival. The choreographer immediately thought of Schumann's *Carnaval Suite for Piano*, which he had long admired.

The score has musical references (to Chopin and Paganini), literary ones (to the four *commedia dell'arte* characters Harlequin, Columbine, Pierrot, and Pantalone), and stage directions written in after it was completed. There are also autobiographical references to Ernestine Von Frichen, with whom Schumann was in love when he was very young, to Clara Schumann, his wife, and in the final section of the music, entitled "Marche des Davidsbündler contre les Philistines", to the composer's advocacy of the "new" art, as against the conservatism of the old. (The "Davidsbund" was an artistic society invented by Schumann as a foil to the conservative musical establishment.)

The libretto, put together by Fokine and Léon Bakst, has no real plot; rather it is a series of light, humorous, and joyous incidents combined with some moments of poignancy and an undercurrent of satire. The four characters of the *commedia* are complemented by Florestan, representing the impulsive side of Schumann's nature, Eusebius, the thoughtful solitary side, Estrella (Ernestine), Chiarina (Clara), Papillon, a fluttering lady, six light-hearted couples, and four Philistines.

For the gallant males, coquettish females, and lovers who teasingly accept and reject each other, Fokine devised numerous pas de deux, pas de trois, and pas seuls. The curtain rises on three ladies pursued by three swains. Then Chiarina and Estrella appear. Suddenly Pierrot peers anxiously through a curtain and dances with long sleeves flapping, as if in search of love. Harlequin bounds in and teases him. There is a scene with the dreamy Eusebius and Chiarina, one with Estrella and Florestan, and another with Pierrot trying (and failing) to catch Papillon in his hat. Columbine and Harlequin tease the pompous Pantalone and are eventually betrothed. The Philistines are routed by all the dancing couples, and Harlequin binds Pantalone with Pierrot's sleeves. For the benefit performance, the chasing of the Philistines took place in the audience but this action later took place on stage.

Among the outstanding variations were the solo by Harlequin, where he finished one series of pirouettes by slowing down and sitting on the final chord, a pas de trois by Estrella and two friends, and a duet by Harlequin and Columbine, in which his steps were performed to the melody of the flute and clarinet and hers, in counterpoint, to the strings.

The costumes and sets for *Le Carnaval* illustrate another instance where the role of the designer, in this case Bakst, was of utmost importance. His sketches for the costumes gave Fokine further inspiration for the finely etched characters he created. The simple set—the ante-room of a ballroom delineated by a curtain running all around the stage and up to the flies, with two chandeliers and two small striped sofas—as well as the costumes, were designed in the style of Biedermeier. Even the traditional *commedia* figures were altered slightly to fit this viewpoint. The set evidently had the effect of making the dancers appear smaller—thus making the audience feel even more strongly that they were watching a finely tuned miniature.

*Carnaval* seems to have been the most delicate, most exquisite ballet Fokine ever created, as well as the most difficult to pinpoint. As was the case in many of his works, the roles depended to a large degree upon the talents of the original performers, and if one looks at just the steps (except for the one Harlequin solo) they are almost simplistic. It was the infusion of lightness, gaiety, coyness, and self-absorbtion, combined with an underlying sadness—all of which must be contributed by the dancers—that resulted in what most critics of the time regarded as a most effective adaptation of Schumann's music and characters. Recent attempts to reconstruct the work in England, Sweden, and the United States have had varying degrees of success. This is because the roles must be created from within each individual performer, not from externally imposed steps or gestures. They require someone like Fokine himself to elicit this from the dancers—an almost impossible task.

—Dawn Lille Horwitz

---

## CAROSO, Fabritio

(Fabritio Caroso da Sermoneta)

Italian dancing master, theorist, choreographer, and author of dance manuals. Born in Sermoneta, near Rome, c. 1526/35. Studies unknown; oral history suggests early sponsorship by the Caetani, ancient ducal family of Sermoneta and Rome. Established reputation as dancing master for noble families in Rome; wrote two dance manuals, containing rules for social dance as well as own and other choreographies with music, published as *Il Ballarino* in Venice, 1581, and *Nobiltà di dame* in Venice, 1600, 1605; reissued second manual as *Raccolta di varij balli* in Rome, 1630. Died after 1605.

### PUBLICATIONS

By Caroso:

*Il Ballarino*, Venice, 1581

*Nobiltà di dame*, Venice 1600, 1605; as *Raccolta di varij balli*, Rome, 1630

*Nobiltà di dame*, translated and edited by Julia Sutton, with music transcribed and edited by F. Marian Walker, Oxford, 1986

Music:

*Biblioteca di rarità musicali*, vol. I: *Danze del secolo XVI trascritte in notazione moderne dalle opere: 'Nobiltà di dame' del Sig. F. Caroso da Sermoneta; 'Le Gratie d'Amore' di C. Negri, milanese detto il Trombone*, transcribed and edited by Oscar Chilesotti, Milan, 1884

*Fabritio Caroso 'Il Ballarino'*, transcribed and edited by Helmut Mönkemeyer, Rodenkirchen/Rhein, 1971

About Caroso:

Alessandri, Felippo de gli [sic], *Discorso sopra il ballo*, Terni, 1620

Wood, Melusine, *Some Historical Dances*, London, 1952

Dolmetsch, Mabel, *Dances of Spain and Italy 1400–1600*, London, 1954; reprinted New York, 1954

Moe, Lawrence, *Dance Music in Printed Italian Lute Tablatures in the 16th Century*, Ph.D. Dissertation, Harvard University, 1956

Wood, Melusine, *More Historical Dances*, London, 1956

Sutton, Julia, *Renaissance Revisited: Twelve Dances in Labanotation with Music and Commentary*, with notation by K. Wright Dunkley, New York, 1972

Feves, Angene, "Caroso's Patronesses", *Proceedings of the*

14

AVSTRIA GONZAGA

BALLETTO;

IN LODE DELLA SERENISS.MA SIG.RA

DVCHESSA DI MANTOVA.

'HVOMO in questo Balletto ha da pigliar la Dama per la man'ordinaria, cioè per la sinistra, come si ha nel disegno, facendo insieme Riuerenza minima, con due Continenze, poi passeggiando, si hanno da fare quattro Seguiti ordinarij; col piegare alquanto le ginocchia nel fine dell'vltimo Seguito, à modo di meza Riuerenza; & lasciando la mano in quell'instante, s'hanno da fare due Seguiti volti alla mano sinistra; con vn'altro Seguito innanzi con tre Trabuchetti incontro, & due Puntate, l'una innanzi, & l'altra in dietro, & la Riuerenza graue insieme.

Nel secondo tempo l'huomo solo ha poi da far due Seguiti fiancheggiati in dietro con due Passi graui fiancheggiati, & altri due presti innanzi similmente fiancheggiati, & vn Trabuchetto col fianco sinistro per dentro à piè pari in punta di piedi leggiermente, principiandoli col piè sinistro. Il medesimo si ha da far vn'altra volta principiandoli col piè destro. Dopò insieme si voltano due Seguiti alla sinistra, scorrendone vn'altro, col toccar la fè destra, & far Riuerenza minima col piè destro. Il medesimo si fa voltando alla man destra, principiando li due Seguiti col piè destro, ma però facendo la Riuerenza minima col piè sinistro, & toccando la fè sinistra.

Nel terzo tempo, la Dama ha da far il medesimo che ha fatto l'huomo, & insieme si fanno i due Seguiti con l'altre cose dette.

d 2 Alla

**An opening from Fabritio Caroso's *Il Ballarino*, 1581, showing the balletto *Austria Gonzaga***

*Dance History Scholars Conference*, Riverside, California, 1986

Maloney, M. Paul, *The Art of Dancing in 1600: The Balletti of Fabrizio Caroso*, M.A. Thesis, Monash University, Australia, 1986

Sutton, Julia, "Triple Pavans: Clues to Some Mysteries in Sixteenth-Century Dance", *Early Music* (Oxford), no. 14, 1986

Feves, Angene, "Fabritio Caroso and the Changing Shape of the Dance 1500–1600", *Dance Chronicle* (New York), vol. 14, no. 2/3, 1991

* * *

Fabritio Caroso, an important Italian dancing master of the late sixteenth century, is best known as the author of two large manuals giving rules for dance style, steps, and etiquette, and including approximately one hundred choreographies with music (in mensural notation and Italian lute tablature) that sum up Italian dance practice of the second half of the sixteenth century.

Caroso was contemporary with Thoinot Arbeau, Cesare Negri, Livio Lupi, and Prospero Lutij, authors of other manuals of the time. Negri and Lupi quoted directly from *Il Ballarino*, but there is no evidence that they studied with Caroso. The presence of his books in distant libraries (as in the royal libraries of England) suggest even wider geographic validity for Caroso's dances and style. A continuance of his style in southern Europe through the first quarter of the seventeenth century seems likely: Felippo de gli [sic] Alessandri (*Discorso sopra il ballo*, 1620) mentions Caroso and nine of his dances; and *Nobiltà di dame* was reissued as *Raccolta di varij balli* in 1630.

Caroso's manuals, like his contemporaries', reflect accepted practice rather than attempts at choreographic originality. He was in the mainstream of the dance tradition of Italy, but close ties between his dances and other sources support a view that there was a basic western European dance style, with regional or national differences.

As the first known Italian dance manual in nearly a century, *Il Ballarino* is unique, for it includes the first detailed instructions, with music, for many sixteenth-century dance types whose names go back to the fifteenth century (*ballo*, *balletto*, *bassa*, *alta*, and *tordiglione*), thus giving some insights into one hundred years of change. *Il Ballarino* also has the first examples of some dance types of sixteenth-century origins and popularity (*pavan*, *pavaniglia*, *passo e mezzo*, *galliard*, and *canary*). Even more significantly, Caroso's two books are the sole sources of some dance types named in literary and musical sources (*Saltarello*, *Contrapasso*, *Chiaranzana*, *Spagnoletta*, and *Ballo del Fiore*), and have many examples of a fast triple dance termed *cascarda* only by Caroso.

*Il Ballarino* (80 dances and 54 rules for step patterns) may have been the better known of Caroso's books in his day, but *Nobiltà di dame* (49 dances and 68 rules for steps) is the more useful to twentieth-century dance scholars because it redefines and corrects much of the terminology and many of the choreographies of the first book. Its terms for, and definitions of, the steps incorporate and explain time values more precisely, its musical notation is more careful, and the punctuation in the choreographic text is more systematically employed to coincide with musical phrasing and repetition.

Although Caroso claimed that *Nobiltà di dame* was simply a second edition of *Il Ballarino*, its greater clarity may well facilitate our understanding of all sixteenth-century materials. *Nobiltà di dame* also has new steps and choreographies, and a lengthy, unique section primarily on ballroom etiquette.

All of Caroso's choreographies are intended for social dancing. Most, in fact, are for the quintessential social unit of one couple (possibly even one couple at a time). Of dances for more participants, small numbers prevail (three or six are the most common), and unusual numbers occur rarely (as in "Ballo del Fiore", a mixer for five); one dance is in longways formation for any number of couples ("Chiaranzana"). Although he has no theatrical dances, Caroso's step vocabulary appears in those sources, thus validating his teachings for dance in spectacle.

Caroso's dances are playful, flirtatious, charming, and courtly, but also skilful, vigorous, and sophisticated. They are the dances of young gentlemen for whom dance was one of the manly arts, demanding as much prowess as fencing and riding, of young ladies for whom dance was a chance to display their charms gracefully but energetically, and of aristocrats who adorned their surroundings and pleased observers while pleasing themselves. Most of the dances are abstract. The only miming dances, "Torneo Amoroso" and all versions of "Barriera", evoke aspects of the tournament, a common metaphor for amorous engagement. The paths of the dancers are always taken in relation to their partners or other dancers. A typical couple dance, such as "Rosa Felice", might consist of opening honours; a lead-in figure that traverses the ballroom (both to attract attention and to acknowledge the onlookers); the giving of right hands round, left hands round, and both hands round; a reverse S-shaped figure in which the partners exchange places, and a leading-out figure with honours (the similarity to eighteenth-century dances is striking, especially to the minuet). Another scheme combines figures danced simultaneously with those in which the partners take turns dancing before each other (for example, "Passo e mezzo"); a third possibility has the couple traversing the hall side-by-side (as in "Pavaniglia"); and still another employs a refrain of steps and/or paths at the end of each figure ("Alta Regina"). Dances for more than one couple often add circles and various kinds of hays (for example, "Contrapasso Nuovo").

The basic aspects of Caroso's dance style are the same for both sexes, and are suited to the dress and social positions of young nobility. Gentlemen are hatted and gloved, with capes and swords. Ladies are on high *pianelle* (pantoufles or slippers), and their skirts with short trains are supported by farthingales and layers of petticoats; their hands hold handkerchiefs, gloves, and muffs, or toy with their jewellery. Rules for handling all this paraphernalia are found in Caroso's notes on etiquette. Posture is erect, with the arms graceful and quiet at the sides; an elegant strutting (*pavoneggiare*) sways the cape or skirt and accentuates pride of bearing; flanking and pivoting movements toward and away from partners (*fiancheggiare*), as in fencing, abet flirtation; only the feet touch the floor, of course. The numerous step patterns require vigorous, complex, and rapid footwork, endurance, and elevation, and are accomplished with flexed ankle, straight leg, and slight plié. Turnout is expressly forbidden ("... keep your toes parallel, not ... one toe pointing east the other west"); hands take or clap partner's hands, or hold the hilt of a sword or a handkerchief; arms are rarely raised above the head and have no purely ornamental gestures.

Differences in style between the sexes reflect social mores. The gentlemen undertake the most difficult feats, such as multiple capers or turns in the air. In such technical demands Caroso is a moderate, certainly more sophisticated and demanding than Arbeau, but not approaching the brilliant male pyrotechnics Negri details. While all the masters agree that dancers should be able to improvise appropriately upon accepted models, Caroso is the only one to insist, especially in *Nobiltà di dame*, that in so doing one must follow a *vera regola* (true rule) of perfect symmetry, to ensure that all step patterns and figures are in keeping with neo-Platonic aesthetic doctrine.

Aside from symmetry, the formal principle of variation dominates Caroso's choreographies. All his dances vary figures to music that is repeated as needed (for example "Celeste Giglio"). The complex forms that can result when the principle of variation is applied in different ways, and sometimes combined with rondo or ternary forms in the dance or in the music, or in both, reveal mastery of compositional techniques.

The music in Caroso's manuals is anonymous "music for use". The pieces vary greatly in quality. Most with only lute tablature are essentially skeletal chord progressions, on which the expert players employed by all noble families would improvise variations. The music is simple, homophonic, and formulaic, with only occasional rubrics to guide the correlation between it and the text. Many dance pieces seem patched together of small re-usable melodic and harmonic units chosen for their temporal durations, or are built on well-known ostinato basses, chord schemes, or melodies with basses (e.g. *passo e mezzo*), which were common throughout sixteenth-century Europe. Fortunately, many of the problems of correlating text and music are yielding to study and permitting systematic reconstruction, thereby enabling the dances of this period of high art and culture to take their rightful place in Renaissance courtly life.

—Julia Sutton

---

**CARTER, Alan**

British dancer, choreographer, and ballet director. Born in London, 24 December 1920. Studied with Serafina Astafieva and Nikolai Legat, and at the Italia Conti School, London. Served in the British Forces during World War II. Married dancer Julia Claire. Dancer, Vic-Wells (later Sadler's Wells) Ballet, from 1937: soloist, 1938–41, becoming principal dancer (after war service) with Sadler's Wells Opera Ballet (later Sadler's Wells Theatre Ballet), 1946–47; first choreography, for same company, 1946; founder and director, St. James Ballet, 1948–50; ballet director, Empire Theatre, London, 1951–53; choreographer and ballet director, Bavarian State Opera, Munich, 1954–59, Amsterdam Ballet, 1959, and in Tel-Aviv, 1960; guest teacher and choreographer, Royal Ballet Touring Company, 1962–63; ballet director, Wuppertal Opera, 1964–68, Grand Theatre, Bordeaux, 1968–70, Finnish National Ballet, Helsinki, 1971–72, and Icelandic Ballet, 1973–75; also teacher: director, State Ballet School, Istanbul, 1970–71; artistic co-director, Elmhurst Ballet School, London, 1976–80, and director of own school in Bournemouth; also ballet master for several films, including *The Red Shoes* (dir. Powell, 1948), *The Tales of Hoffmann* (dir. Powell, 1951), *Invitation to the Dance* (dir. Gene Kelly, 1953), and choreographer for *The Man Who Loved Redheads* (dir. French, 1955).

**ROLES**

1937 A Peasant Boy, A Gendarme (cr) in *A Wedding Bouquet* (Ashton), Vic-Wells Ballet, London

Chessplayer (Love) (cr) in *Checkmate* (de Valois), Vic-Wells Ballet, Paris
Pas de six in *Les Rendezvous* (Ashton), Vic-Wells Ballet, London
1938 Gemini (cr) in *Horoscope* (Ashton), Vic-Wells Ballet, London
Harlequin (cr) in *Harlequin in the Street* (Ashton), Vic-Wells Ballet, London
A Minister (cr) in *Le Roi nu* (*The Emperor's New Clothes*; de Valois), Vic-Wells Ballet, London
1939 Cavalier to the Breadcrumb Fairy in *The Sleeping Princess* (Petipa; staged Sergeyev), Vic-Wells Ballet, London
The Rake in *The Rake's Progress* (de Valois), Vic-Wells Ballet, London
1940 Ensemble (cr) in *Dante Sonata* (Ashton), Vic-Wells Ballet, London
Monsieur Didelot (cr) in *The Prospect Before Us* (de Valois), Vic-Wells Ballet, London
Variation ("Blue Boy") in *Les Patineurs* (Ashton), Vic-Wells Ballet, tour
1941 Dancer (cr) in *The Wanderer* (Ashton), Sadler's Wells Ballet, London
Popular Song in *Façade* (Ashton), Sadler's Wells Ballet, London
Adagio and Pas de deux in *Fête polonaise* (de Valois), Sadler's Wells Ballet, London
1946 The Prince in *The Nutcracker*, Act III (Sergeyev after Ivanov), Sadler's Wells Theatre Ballet, London
Tango: A Dago in *Façade* (Ashton), Sadler's Wells Theatre Ballet, tour
Principal dancer in *Les Sylphides* (Fokine), Sadler's Wells Theatre Ballet, tour
A Nobleman in *The Gods Go a-Begging* (de Valois), Sadler's Wells Theatre Ballet, London
The Lover (cr) in *The Vagabonds* (Burke), Sadler's Wells Theatre Ballet, London
The Elder Brother (cr) in *The Catch* (also chor.), Sadler's Wells Theatre Ballet, London
1947 The Master of Treginnis in *The Haunted Ballroom* (de Valois), Sadler's Wells Theatre Ballet, London
Peasant (cr) in *Bailemos* (Franca), Sadler's Wells Theatre Ballet, London

## WORKS

1946 *The Catch* (mus. Bartok), Sadler's Wells Theatre Ballet, London
1948 *Visions* (mus. Chopin), St. James' Ballet
*Ritornel* (mus. Hawkins), St. James' Ballet
1955 *The Miraculous Mandarin* (mus. Bartok), Bavarian State Opera Ballet, Munich
*House of Shadows* (mus. Britten), Bavarian State Opera Ballet, Munich
*Concertino* (mus. Pergolesi), Bavarian State Opera Ballet, Bayreuth
*Flight of the Dove* (mus. Schilling), Bavarian State Opera Ballet, Munich
*Mister Scrooge* (mus. Suk), Bavarian State Opera Ballet, Munich
1956 *Les Parapluies* (mus. Wooldridge), Bavarian State Opera Ballet, Munich
*Comedietta* (mus. Mozart), Bavarian State Opera Ballet, Munich
1957 *Capriccio* (mus. Stravinsky), Bavarian State Opera Ballet, Munich
*Herr Orpheus* (mus. Stravinsky), Bavarian State Opera Ballet, Munich
*Feuilleton* (mus. Stravinsky), Bavarian State Opera Ballet, Munich
*Salade* (mus. Milhaud), Bavarian State Opera Ballet, Munich
1958 *The Prince of the Pagodas* (mus. Britten), Bavarian State Opera Ballet, Munich
*Changement de pieds* (mus. Martin), Edinburgh International Ballet, Edinburgh
1959 *Ondine* (mus. Henze), Bavarian State Opera Ballet, Munich
*The Empty Stage* (mus. Britten), Amsterdam Ballet, Amsterdam
*Variations on a Theme* (mus. Dohnányi), Amsterdam Ballet, Amsterdam
1962 *Toccata* (mus. Bach), Royal Ballet Touring Company, Newcastle
1963 *Night Tryst* (mus. Purcell), Royal Ballet, London

Also staged:
1955 *The Nutcracker* (after Ivanov; mus. Tchaikovsky), Bavarian State Opera Ballet, Munich
1956 *Giselle* (after Petipa, Coralli, Perrot; mus. Adam), Bavarian State Opera Ballet, Munich
*The Rake's Progess* (chor. de Valois; mus. Gordon), Bavarian State Opera Ballet, Munich

## PUBLICATIONS

By Carter:
"Odious Comparisons! Ballet here, Germany, and there, Britain", *Ballet Annual* (London), vol. 13, 1959

About Carter:
Regner, Otto Friedrich, "New Era in Munich", *Dance and Dancers* (London), May 1955
Corathiel, Elisabeth, "The Work of Alan Carter", *Ballet Today* (London), September 1956
Wilson, G.B.L., "The English Dancing Master in Europe", *Ballet Annual* (London), vol. 13, 1959

* * *

A bright and promising talent emerged from Sadler's Wells Ballet School in the 1930s with all the basic elements for a great future. A Londoner, Alan Carter already showed, in a delightful role created for him by Frederick Ashton in *Harlequin in the Street*, an easy and quicksilver technique and considerable charm of presentation. It was a minor ballet, but stylish and witty. Set to music by Couperin, it was designed by André Derain, with an eighteenth-century street scene as background, and exquisitely coloured period costumes. Carter's role was the familiar one of Harlequin the mischief maker, troubling the waters of a love affair between Monsignor (Michael Somes) and La Superbe (June Brae). His character was expressed in aerial leaps and pirouettes and a brilliant use of batterie, contrasting admirably with the graver andante movement of Somes and Brae.

As with all the young British male dancers of the time, Carter's career was torn apart by World War II. From 1940 to 1946 he was in the armed forces, and no amount of talent and hard work could make up, where dancing was concerned, for the lost years. In 1946, however, Ninette de Valois launched the "second company", Sadler's Wells Opera (later Theatre) Ballet at Sadler's Wells Theatre, and Carter was engaged as a principal dancer. He created a memorable role as one of the tragic gypsy lovers in Anthony Burke's *The Vagabonds* and danced The Master of Treginnis in a revival of *The Haunted Ballroom*. His style and schooling were always apparent as was his considerable dramatic ability.

Although Sadler's Wells Theatre Ballet was definitely a company for encouraging choreographers, Carter only contributed one divertissement number, a lively peasant piece called *The Catch*, and he did not stay long at Sadler's Wells. He was engaged as ballet master for the film *The Red Shoes*, and was then asked to direct a small group backed by the Arts Council called the St. James' Ballet. This was followed by a similar job, as director of a ballet company based on the Empire Cinema in Leicester Square, for which he choreographed various pieces, and he functioned again as ballet master for the film *The Tales of Hoffmann*. In 1954, he received his first major directorial appointment as choreographer and ballet director at the Bayerischer Staatsoper, Munich, where he remained for five years.

In Munich, where he had an excellent company of dancers, he established a splendidly varied repertoire. He produced classics like *Giselle* and *The Nutcracker*, he created many admirable short ballets (among them *House of Shadows* to Benjamin Britten's *Variations on a Theme* by Frank Bridge), and was given permission by de Valois for the first staging of her *The Rake's Progress* by another company—he had danced a remarkably effective Rake at Sadler's Wells in 1939. He also produced his own versions of two three-act ballets, *The Prince of the Pagodas* and *Ondine*. In a letter to *The Dancing Times* in 1990 he recounts how Britten, on a visit to Munich in 1957, invited him to be the first person (after John Cranko) to choreograph *Pagodas*.

Carter's talents are many, and his influence was widespread, as he took up posts in cities ranging from Tel Aviv to Amsterdam. A painter as well as a choreographer, he has often exhibited paintings and designs. In 1962 he returned briefly to England as guest teacher and choreographer for the Royal Ballet Touring Company, staging *Toccata* for them. This was a relaxed and entirely enjoyable creation to a J.S. Bach fantasia-toccata that was, for its time, avant-garde in its freely imaginative mixture of dance styles and choreographic jokes. A.H. Franks wrote in 1963, "I find this nonsense delightful, the humour gentle and the movement in keeping with our time . . . the whole work is one of more than passing enchantment." Unfortunately it had a short life, and Carter moved on to take up an appointment in Wuppertal, thereafter working in Bordeaux, Istanbul, and Helsinki. He settled in England again in 1976 as co-director of Elmhurst Ballet School, Camberley, and later directed his own studio in Bournemouth.

Carter belongs to the influential body of Sadler's Wells Ballet dancers who went out as valuable missionaries to foreign fields, as artistic directors, ballet masters, and teachers. The contributions of John Cranko in Stuttgart, Celia Franca in Canada, Peggy van Praagh in Australia, and Kenneth MacMillan in West Berlin are all well known, but Carter's more itinerant life also had important results.

—Kathrine Sorley Walker

---

**Jack Carter with Norman McDowell in *The Witch Boy*, Amsterdam, 1956**

## CARTER, Jack

English dancer and choreographer. Born in Shrivenham, England, 8 August 1923. Studied at Sadler's Wells Ballet School from 1938, and later with Vera Volkova and Anna Severskaya in London, and Olga Preobrazhenska in Paris. Served in the British Forces, World War II. Dancer, Ballet Guild, London, 1946, then with Continental Ballet, 1948, Original Ballet Russe, 1950, Ballet Rambert, 1951; choreographer, with early works for Molly Lake, Continental Ballet, and Ballet Workshop, London; company choreographer, Ballet der Lage Landen, Amsterdam, 1954–57; resident choreographer, London Festival Ballet, 1965–70, also staging ballets for London Dance Theatre, Western Theatre Ballet (later Scottish Ballet), and Royal Ballet touring company; international guest choreographer, staging ballets in Europe, North America, South America, Australia, New Zealand, South Africa, and Japan; choreographer and producer of ballets for film and television, in England, Belgium, and France.

### WORKS

1946 *Fantaisies* (also called *Episode*; mus. Chopin), Molly Lake's Embassy Ballet, London
1949 *Impromptu for Twelve* (mus. Rossini), Continental Ballet
1950 *Stagioni* (mus. Verdi), Ballet Workshop, London
1951 *L'Homme et sa vie* (mus. various), Ballet Workshop, London
*Living Image* (mus. Salzedo), British Broadcasting Corporation (BBC) television
*Por Tres Personas* (mus. Manuel), Ballet Workshop, London
1952 *Ouverture* (mus. Bloch), Ballet Workshop, London

1953 *Past Recalled* (restaging of *Ouverture*; mus. Bloch), Ballet Rambert, London
*Psalmus Tenebrae* (mus. Busoni), Ballet Workshop, London
1954 *Love Knots* (mus. Hummel, arranged Salzedo), Ballet Rambert, London
*The Life and Death of Lola Montez* (mus. Verdi, orchestrated Salzedo), Ballet Workshop, London (staged Ballet Rambert, same year)
1956 *The Witch Boy* (mus. Salzedo), Ballet der Lage Landen, Amsterdam
1959 *London Morning* (mus. Coward), London Festival Ballet, London
*Señora de Mañara* (mus. Tchaikovsky), Milorad Miskovitch company, Paris
1960 *Grand Pas des fiancées* (mus. Tchaikovsky), London Festival Ballet, London
1962 *Improvisations* (mus. Copland), London Festival Ballet, London
1963 *Les Invités du soir* (mus. Tchaikovsky), Geneva Ballet, Geneva
1964 *Agrionia* (mus. Salzedo), London Dance Theatre, Newcastle
1966 *Beatrix* (*La Jolie Fille de Gand*; mus. Adam, Horovitz), London Festival Ballet, London
1967 *Cage of God* (mus. Rawsthorne), Western Theatre Ballet, London
1969 *The Unknown Island* (mus. Berlioz), London Festival Ballet, Rome
1973 *Pythoness Ascendant* (mus. Berio), New London Ballet, Hong Kong
*Three Dances to Japanese Music* (mus. Katada), Scottish Ballet, Glasgow
1975 *Shukumei* (mus. Stomu Yamash'ta), Royal Ballet Touring Company, Stratford-on-Avon
1976 *Lulu* (mus. Milhaud), Sadler's Wells Royal Ballet, London

Also staged:
1963 *Swan Lake* (after Petipa, Ivanov; mus. Tchaikovsky), Teatro Colón, Buenos Aires
1965 *Coppélia* (after Saint-Léon, Petipa; mus. Delibes), Teatro Colón, Buenos Aires
*The Nutcracker* (after Ivanov; mus. Tchaikovsky), London Festival Ballet
1967 *The Sleeping Beauty* (after Petipa; mus. Tchaikovsky), Teatro Colón, Buenos Aires
1968 *Coppélia* (new production; after Saint-Léon, Petipa; mus. Delibes), London Festival Ballet
1974 *Dancing Floor* (mus. Subotnik), Scottish Ballet, Glasgow
1978 *Quodlibet* (mus. Ponchielli), Maryland Ballet, Baltimore
1980 *Summer Day* (mus. Debussy), Theatre Ballet of London, Edinburgh
1986 *Melodrame* (mus. Weill), Royal New Zealand Ballet, Wellington
1988 *Natives of Dreamland* (mus. d'Indy), Louisville Ballet, Louisville, Kentucky
1990 *Namouna* (mus. Lalo), Asami Maki Ballet, Tokyo
1991 *Cinderella* (mus. Prokofiev), Royal New Zealand Ballet, Wellington

## PUBLICATIONS

Jackson, Frank, *They Make Tomorrow's Ballets*, London 1953
Sinclair, Janet, "Choreographers of Today: Jack Carter", *Ballet Today* (London), April 1960
"Swan Lake Re-Assessed", *Dancing Times* (London), January 1963
"Years of Achievement: The Making of The Witch Boy", *Dance and Dancers* (London), July/August 1986
Sinclair, Janet, "Not Without Honour", *Dance and Dancers* (London), April 1989

* * *

As he was born nearly a decade after Antony Tudor, it was to be expected that Jack Carter should be influenced by the work of the older man, for, like Tudor, Carter has never been interested in presenting the purely decorative for its own sake. He prefers to put on stage some original comment of his own on humans and humanity, whether serious or comic. He has rarely produced a conventional dance work, and that only when circumstances forced him to do so: and even in such a ballet as *Beatrix* his enormous sense of humour, and his refusal to take either himself or his project too seriously, made much of the otherwise conventional pastiche both amusing and interesting.

After surviving parental disapproval and army service in the Second World War, Carter, who had dabbled in musical composition and even had one of his works played on the BBC, made his first choreography by accident when the creator of a ballet in which he was dancing suffered a mental block. His subsequent first complete work remained in the repertoire for four seasons.

Throughout his career Carter, like Tudor, has always been at his best when working with small groups of dedicated dancers—groups such as Angela and David Ellis's Ballet Workshop, which developed young choreographers on a shoestring, the Amsterdam Ballet der Lage Landen, Western Ballet, and the company founded by Norman McDowell, London Dance Theatre, for which he produced one of his most memorable works, *Agrionia*. All these small pioneering groups were impecunious, if not always quite at starvation level; the performers were there for the work, not the money, looking only for a driving inspiration to make them feel they were doing something worthwhile. To work with dancers in this category, to get to know exactly what they could do and give it to them, was Carter's forte.

It was Carter's bad luck to be born too late to join in the birth of English ballet, at which point his work might well have been immediately accepted, together with that of Ashton, Tudor, and de Valois. Coming to choreography when he did, after the Second World War, Carter suffered from the prevalence of the "abstract" mystique, which has proliferated in England since the mid-1940s almost to the exclusion of all other dance forms. This is an idiom in which he has never worked and which, one may assume, has never held much attraction for him. In other styles, however, his versatility is remarkable, contrasting the exciting melodrama of *The Witch Boy* with the philosophical *Cage of God*, the humour of *Stagioni* with the brilliantly observed psychological statement of *Agrionia*, his own favourite among his extensive repertoire.

Though it is in ensemble work that Carter is at his best, yet star dancers such as Galina Samsova, John Gilpin, and Marian St. Claire have brought out facets of his choreographic talent which were both a challenge and a delight to dancer, choreographer, and audience. In line with Massine's principle, he has rarely chosen to embark upon an original work without something new to say, and his ballets are all distinctively contrasted, though the choreographic style is unmistakably his own: he never repeats himself, or, indeed, anyone else. Unusually among many contemporary choreographers, he enjoys working to a composed score, and his collaboration with Leonard Salzedo produced two of his most dramatically effective works. His other notable collaborator was the dancer and designer Norman McDowell, who danced leading roles in many of his ballets and designed costumes and sets for the majority of them.

Carter should be choreographing at regular intervals for a company young enough, small enough, and enthusiastic enough to give him the commitment he needs and indeed has earned. It was unfortunate that his encounter with the Royal Ballet should have followed exactly the pattern of Tudor's—that is, one success, made for the company at Covent Garden, followed by one (critical) flop, made for the touring company at Sadler's Wells, after which neither returned to the Royal Ballet companies. Fortunately, though some of his finest works seem gone for ever, the hypnotic *Three Dances to Japanese Music* holds its place triumphantly in more than one repertoire in England, while other Carter ballets are to be seen abroad, notably in South Africa.

—Janet Sinclair

---

**CECCHETTI, Enrico**

Italian dancer, choreographer, and teacher. Born in Rome, son of dancer and choreographer Cesare Cecchetti, 21 June 1850. Studied at Academy of Dance, Florence, pupil of Baratti and Giovanni Lepri. Married dancer Giuseppina de Maria, 1878. Début as a child, performing with parents in Ronzani Ballet, American tour, 1857; official début at the Teatro Pagliano, Florence, 1868, then touring internationally with small troupe of dancers; début at La Scala, Milan, 1870; performed in Denmark, Norway, Holland, Germany, Austria, and Russia, with St. Petersburg début in 1874; principal dancer, La Scala, Milan, from 1885; principal dancer, leading own company and performing at Arcadia Theatre, St. Petersburg, 1887; principal dancer and second ballet master, Maryinsky Theatre, St. Petersburg, from 1887; principal dancer, Empire Theatre, London, 1888, 1891–92; choreographer and rehearsal director, Maryinsky Theatre, from 1892; teacher, St. Petersburg Theatre School, 1892–1902, Warsaw Opera House, 1902–06, and privately in St. Petersburg, 1906–11; teacher, rehearsal supervisor, and character performer, Diaghilev's Ballets Russes, 1911–21; teacher and rehearsal director, Anna Pavlova tour, 1913; teacher in London, 1918–23, and in Milan, from 1925; recognized as leading teacher of his time; pupils include Vera Trefilova, Mathilde Kshesinskaya, Anna Pavlova, Olga Preobrazhenska, Tamara Karsavina, Vaslav Nijinsky, Marie Rambert, Mikhail Fokine, Agrippina Vaganova, Boris Romanov, Aleksandr Gorsky, Adolph Bolm, Mikhail Mordkin, Serge Lifar, Ninette de Valois, Alexandra Danilova, Alicia Markova; teaching methods codified and published by Cyril Beaumont and Stanislas Idzikowski, 1922; Cecchetti Society founded in London, 1922. Died in Milan, 12 November 1928.

**Enrico Cecchetti as Catalabutte in *The Sleeping Princess***

## ROLES

1885 Spirit of Darkness in *Excelsior* (Manzotti), La Scala, Milan
Principal dancer (cr) in *Messalina* (Danesi), La Scala, Milan
Principal dancer (cr) in *A Villa to be Sold* (comic divertissement; also chor.), Her Majesty's Theatre, London

1886 Principal dancer (cr) in *Amor* (Manzotti), La Scala, Milan

1887 Principal dancer (cr) in *Rolla* (Manzotti), La Scala, Milan
The Artist in *An Artist's Dream* (also chor.; after Perrot), Arcadia Theatre, St. Petersburg
Principal dancer in *The Power of Love* (also chor.), Arcadia Theatre, St. Petersburg
Principal dancer in *The Tulip of Haarlem* (Petipa, Ivanov), Maryinsky Theatre, St. Petersburg
Principal dancer (cr) in *Dilara* (Lanner), Empire Theatre, London

1888 The Elf (cr) in *Rose d'Amour* (Lanner), Empire Theatre, London

1889 Vayou, God of the Wind (cr) in *The Talisman* (Petipa), Maryinsky Theatre, St. Petersburg

1890 Bluebird (cr) and Carabosse (cr) in *The Sleeping Beauty* (Petipa), Maryinsky Theatre, St. Petersburg

1891 Reuben (cr) in *Kalkabrino* (Petipa), Maryinsky Theatre, St. Petersburg
Malignity in *Orfeo* (Lanner), Empire Theatre, London

1892 Principal dancer in *Versailles* (Lanner), Empire Theatre, London

1893 Pignerolle (cr) in *Cinderella* (also chor., with Petipa, Ivanov), Maryinsky Theatre, St. Petersburg

1910 Pantalon (cr) in *Le Carnaval* (first version; Fokine), Pavlov Hall, St. Petersburg
Chief Eunuch (cr) in *Schéhérazade* (Fokine), Diaghilev's Ballets Russes, Paris
Köstchei (cr) in *The Firebird* (Fokine), Diaghilev's Ballets Russes, Paris
1911 The Old Showman (cr) in *Petrushka* (Fokine), Diaghilev's Ballets Russes, Paris
1913 The Marquis in *The Magic Flute* (Ivanov), Anna Pavlova Company, tour
1914 The Astrologer (cr) in *Le Coq d'or* (Fokine), Diaghilev's Ballets Russes, Paris
1917 Marquis di Luca (cr) in *Les Femmes de bonne humeur* (Massine), Diaghilev's Ballets Russes, Rome
1919 The Shopkeeper (cr) in *La Boutique fantasque* (Massine), Diaghilev's Ballets Russes, London
1920 The Doctor (cr) in *Pulcinella* (Massine), Diaghilev's Ballets Russes, Paris

## WORKS

1885 *A Villa to be Sold* (comic divertissement), Her Majesty's Theatre, London
1887 *The Power of Love*, Arcadia Theatre, St. Petersburg
1892 Dances, Act III of *Mlada* (with Ivanov; mus. Rimsky-Korsakov), Maryinsky Theatre, St. Petersburg
1893 *Cinderella* (with Petipa, Ivanov; mus. Schel), Maryinsky Theatre, St. Petersburg
1902/05 *Dopo il ballo* (mus. Köhler), Warsaw Opera Ballet, Warsaw
*Piplet* (mus. Mardoglio), Warsaw Opera Ballet, Warsaw
*Eva*, Warsaw Opera Ballet, Warsaw
1905 Polish Dance in *Halka* (opera; mus. Moniuszko), Teatro Lirico, Milan
Dances in *La Damnation de Faust* (opera; mus. Berlioz), Rome
1906 Dances in *La Juive* (opera; mus. Halévy), Rome

Also staged:
1887 *Excelsior* (shortened version, after Manzotti), Arcadia Theatre, St. Petersburg
*Sieba* (shortened version, after Manzotti), Arcadia Theatre, St. Petersburg
*An Artist's Dream* (*Le Délire d'un peintre*, after Perrot; mus. Pugni), Arcadia Theatre, St. Petersburg
1888 *Catarina; ou, La Fille du bandit* (after Perrot; mus. Pugni), Maryinsky Theatre, St. Petersburg
1894 *Coppélia* (after Petipa; mus. Delibes), Maryinsky Theatre, St. Petersburg
1913 *The Magic Flute* (with Pavlova, after Ivanov; mus. Drigo), Anna Pavlova Company, London

**Other works include:** for the students of the Imperial School, St. Petersburg—*L'Héroine des Alpes* (1891), *Emma Flourans* (1893), *Le Triomphe de Terpsichore* (1893), *Après un bal joyeux* (1897), *Leçon à l'auberge* (1898), *Le Songe de Phidias* (1899), *Les Ombres séduites* (1900), *De la lune au Japon* (1900), *Gipsy* (1900).

## PUBLICATIONS

By Cecchetti:
"Letters from the Maestro: Enrico Cecchetti to Gisella Caccialanza", *Dance Perspectives* (New York), no. 45, 1946
*Letters from the Maestro: Enrico Cecchetti to Gisella Caccialanza*, translated by Gisella Caccialanza, edited by Sally Bailey, New York, 1971

About Cecchetti:
Pleshcheev, Aleksandr, *Our Ballet*, St. Petersburg, 1899
Racster, Olga, *The Master of the Russian Ballet*, London, 1922
Beaumont, Cyril and Idzikowski, Stanislas, *A Manual of the Theory and Practice of Classical Theatrical Dancing—méthode Cecchetti*, London, 1922; revised edition 1940; New York, 1975
Beaumont, Cyril, *Enrico Cecchetti: A Memoir*, London, 1929
Craske, Margaret, and Beaumont, Cyril, *The Theory and Practice of Allegro in Classical Ballet (Cecchetti Method)*, London, 1930
Moore, Lillian, *Artists of the Dance*, London, 1938
Celli, Vincenzo, "Enrico Cecchetti", *Dance Index* (New York), vol. 5, no. 7, 1946
Beaumont, Cyril, "Cecchetti's Legacy to the Dance", *Ballet Annual* (London), no. 2, 1948
Moore, Lillian, "Enrico Cecchetti: 1850–1928", *Dance Magazine* (New York), 2 parts: September, October 1953
Krasovskaya, Vera, *The Russian Ballet Theatre of the Second Half of the Nineteenth Century*, Leningrad and Moscow, 1963
Krasovskaya, Vera, *The Russian Ballet Theatre of the Early Twentieth Century*, Leningrad, 1971, 1972
Rossi, Luigi, *Enrico Cecchetti: Il Maestro dei Maestri*, Vercelli, 1978
Glasstone, Richard, "Ashton, Cecchetti, and the English School", *Dance Theatre Journal* (London), Autumn 1984

* * *

A pupil of Lepri, who was himself a student of the early nineteenth-century codifier of ballet technique, Carlo Blasis, Enrico Cecchetti developed the Blasis method further, devising an extraordinarily wide range of exercises which he divided into six groups, one for each day of the working week. This ensured that his students covered, weekly, the full gamut of movements comprising the classical canon. A combination of very basic technical exercises and highly complex choreographed pirouettes, adages, and allegro enchaînements, the bulk of this work was in a set format, repeated according to a regular programme. However, it is all too often forgotten that Cecchetti also strongly advocated that this set work should always be supplemented by several new enchaînements in each class. His programme of study was designed essentially for professional dancers. It requires great precision of execution and fosters a highly developed sense of rhythmic coordination and awareness of purity of line.

Although he is now remembered especially as a pedagogue, Cecchetti was both a brilliant virtuoso dancer and a gifted mime artist. Full use of this dual talent was made by Petipa when, in the first production of *The Sleeping Beauty* at the Maryinsky (1890), he had Cecchetti create both the character part of Carabosse and the virtuoso role of the Bluebird. When Diaghilev formed his Ballets Russes in 1909, Cecchetti (by now in his late fifties) not only became the company teacher, but also continued his career as a performer, creating a wide range of character roles in ballets by Fokine and Massine.

Cecchetti also choreographed a number of ballets and although none of these has survived, something of this aspect of his work is known to us through his restagings of various existing nineteenth-century ballets which have been handed down to us, notably his charming dances for Swanilda and her friends in *Coppélia*. The adagio and allegro enchaînements he arranged for the classroom are little choreographic gems and have served as source material for other choreographers, in particular Ashton. Motifs from Cecchetti's classroom choreography are to be seen in Ashton ballets such as *Les Rendezvous* and *Les Patineurs*, while one of Ashton's earliest works,

*Valentine's Eve*, made extensive use of steps from the maestro's Saturday class.

But it is as a pedagogue that Cecchetti's place in history is assured. Together with other Italian dancers, he introduced the element of virtuosity into the Imperial Russian Ballet and then went on to become teacher for the Class of Perfection at the Maryinsky school. Pavlova engaged him as her private tutor and he coached all the great stars of the Diaghilev company. He taught both Marie Rambert and Ninette de Valois and thus had a formative influence on the fledgeling British ballet.

Students only started working with the maestro once they had mastered the basic classical technique—often under the tutelage of his wife. In 1922, at the instigation of Cyril Beaumont, the Cecchetti Society was founded in London to preserve and promote his work. Later, the Society devised a graded system of study for children, as a lead into the Maestro's own professional programme of work. The latter was subsequently divided up into examination syllabi of varying levels of difficulty. One of the (unintentional) effects of this has been a tendency for students and teachers to lose sight of the full, rich expanse of the method as a whole, as it was conceived and taught by Cecchetti.

With a number of important exceptions (including notably Margaret Craske and Peggy van Praagh) the work has all too often been handed down by teachers lacking the theatrical flair essential to a true understanding of its essence. This problem has been compounded both by tying the teaching of the method to a system of graded examinations and also by the fact that although it was recorded in great detail, in longhand (a true labour of love), by Beaumont, Idzikowski, Craske, and de Moroda, this method of recording is able to give only a limited indication of timing, rhythm, and dynamics. This was subsequently remedied to a large extent by the publication in Benesh dance notation of the method, as taught by Nora Roche for nearly a quarter of a century at the Royal Ballet School. Roche learnt the method from Craske, to whom Cecchetti had entrusted its dissemination.

To the renowned virtuosity and strength of the Italian school, Cecchetti added an expressive dimension of his own. This is seen particularly in his famous exercises for ports de bras, with their harmoniously balanced arm lines and subtle use of head movement, of which Ashton wrote: "If I had my way, I would always insist that all dancers should daily do the wonderful ports de bras. It inculcates a wonderful feeling for line and correct positioning and the use of head movement and épaulement, which—if properly absorbed—will be of incalculable use throughout a dancer's career."

—Richard Glasstone

---

## CENTRAL BALLET OF CHINA

(also known as the National Ballet of China)

Chinese ballet company based in Beijing (Peking). Founded as performing group of Beijing Dance School, directed by Soviet teacher Petr Gusev, 1959; first performed as the Experimental Ballet Society of the Beijing Ballet School, becoming independent performing company, directed by Dai Ai-lian, 1963; established as resident company of the Central Opera and Ballet Theatre, Beijing; became known (by official directorate from the Chinese Ministry of Culture) as the Central Ballet of China, 1980. Official school associated with the company now known as the Beijing Dance Academy. Artistic director of the Central Ballet of China: Jiang Zuhui.

### PUBLICATIONS

Grey, Beryl, *Through the Bamboo Curtain*, London, 1965

Atlas, H., "China Dances to Revolutionary Tune", *Dance News* (New York), September/October 1972

Lloyd, Maude, et al., "Dancers in China", *Dance and Dancers* (London), February 1986

Percival, John, "Dancing out of China", *Dance and Dancers* (London), September 1986

Percival, John, "Dancing Their Own Way", *Dance and Dancers* (London), November 1986

Jianning, Ma, "Report/China: There Come the Chinese Ballet Dancers", *Ballet International* (Cologne), November 1986

Robertson, Allen, and Hutera, Donald, *The Dance Handbook*, London, 1988

* * *

Founded in 1959, the first Chinese national ballet company was originally named the Experimental Ballet Society of the Beijing Dance School and was made up of the first group of graduates from the school's Ballet Major, set up under the direct guidance of the Russian ballet expert Petr Gusev, with Dai Ai-lian its first director. The year 1963 witnessed the company's independence from the Beijing Dance School and its beginnings as a full-scale professional ballet company. Nevertheless, it was established within a traditional Russian framework, becoming the Affiliated Ballet of the Central Opera and Ballet Theatre, an arrangement which lasted throughout the Cultural Revolution from 1966 to 1976. Its signature "collective" work, the first on a Chinese theme, was the full-length "revolutionary model ballet", *The Red Detachment of Women*, in 1964. The company performed under the short-lived title of the Chinese Ballet Troupe simply to fit the needs of presenting this one representative work of the Chinese repertoire, and finally was granted its present name officially by the Ministry of Culture in 1980. The company has a strong team of about 100 dancers, a resident orchestra, and a talented stage art workshop which has been able to provide not only the stage sets, costumes, and so on, but also the dancers' pointe and soft shoes.

The Chinese company, in addition to its previous privileges of the Beijing-based Central Government's full support and the ability to take in the most talented graduates from the Beijing Dance Academy, was given a brand-new image and an independent identity as a result of the Central Government's "Reform and Open Policy". It was thus allowed the opportunity to invite world-famous dancers, teachers, and choreographers like Dame Margot Fonteyn, Sir Anton Dolin, Dame Beryl Grey, Alan Hooper, Ben Stevenson, Belinda Wright, Lycette Darsonval, Celia Franca, Mikhail Baryshnikov, Rudolf Nureyev, Violette Verdy, Karin von Aroldingen, and many others to give classes, coach the dancers, and stage new works. In this way, on the solid basis the Russian ballet masters helped to establish the company has built up a comprehensive repertoire of world classics, such as *La Fille mal gardée*, *Swan Lake*, *Le Corsaire*, *Giselle*, *The Fountain of Bakh-chisarai*, *Sylvia*, and *Don Quixote*. Meanwhile, the company has spared no pains to create ballets with a distinctly Chinese theme and spirit, thus producing some quite innovative full-length works, such as *Ode to the Yimeng Mountain*, *Son and Daughter of the Grassland*, *The Maid of the Sea*, *The New Year's Sacrifice*, *Li Dai-Yu*, *Trilogy of Searching for Light*, *Lan Hua-Hua*, *Yang Gui-Fei*, and interestingly enough, the experimental 1990 *Mountain Forest*, with American modern choreographer Norman Walker doing a half-hour piece to Chinese contemporary music by Liu Dunnan.

The dancers of this most national and yet international

**Central Ballet of China (then called "Chinese Ballet Troupe") performing *Red Detachment of Women*, 1970**

Chinese ballet company have travelled extensively to cities at home and to major cities in Burma, the former Yugoslavia, Romania, Albania, Germany, Austria, the Philippines, Japan, Algeria, Tunisia, the United States of America, the United Kingdom, and the former Soviet Union, winning praise and critical acclaim from all quarters. Moreover, they have won a total of 22 medals to date at the international ballet competitions in Varna, Moscow, Osaka, Jackson, and Lausanne, as well as 53 prizes in the national dance competitions. The principal dancers have been invited to dance in eleven different countries as guest artists, with the company's teachers and choreographers going abroad to teach or stage Chinese ballets in five different countries: all this has convincingly brought the Central Ballet of China on to the world stage, compared by critics like Clive Barnes to the National Ballet of Canada, but with a stronger corps and top international-class principals.

During an average of 120 performances each year, most of the dancers have the chance to be on stage; and the present problems are how to set up a reasonable and feasible retirement system for the older dancers, how to obtain more competitive new works and more opportunities to dance, and most of all, how to keep on the dancers who make up the backbone of the company. Perhaps all these closely related artistic problems will not be solved properly until the Central Government's "Reform and Open Policy" has led to a feasible programme which will meet the international needs of a ballet company.

One of Gusev's former assistants, Li Cheng-xiang, has taken up the position of the company's artistic director, also serving as a company choreographer since 1980. Another productive choreographer and deputy director has been Moscow-based Jiang Zuhui, who has staged three full-length ballets, *Laurencia*, *La Esmeralda*, and *The New Year's Sacrifice*, and has contributed choreography to stagings of *The Red Detachment of Women* and *The Song of Chinese Revolution*. The most representative Chinese ballerina, as well as the first Chinese Swan Queen, has been Bai Shu-xiang, who is still dancing and who is also a company deputy director. Her own artistic ups and downs have been the exact reflection of New China's 40-year history.

The Central Ballet of China has initiated a children's ballet class, mainly for educational purposes and not for training apprentices, as the company can only take in the strictly trained Ballet Major graduates from the Beijing Dance Academy. Nevertheless, these boys and girls are selected through auditions in primary and middle schools in Beijing, and some of them have appeared with the company, for instance in the crowd scenes in *Don Quixote*; all have opportunities occasionally to dance before the public.

The Central Ballet of China has truly and successfully introduced ballet, this crystallization of Western civilization, into China and into other Eastern countries as well, thus enriching both Chinese and other Eastern peoples' aesthetic experience and cultural taste. The company has always tried its utmost to create Chinese ballets by all possible means, leading ultimately to the establishment of the school of Chinese ballet, and making ballet an important part of Chinese life and culture. The great success of the Beijing-based Central Ballet of China has not only led to the births of the Shanghai Ballet, the Liaoning Ballet, and the training programme for the future Inner Mongolian Ballet, but has also proved to be the best experiment which convincingly demonstrates that the Chinese Central Government's "Reform and Open Policy" is both wise and long-sighted. There is something beautiful, revelatory, and moral about an art which is able to transcend any racial, linguistic, historical, or political obstacles.

—Ou Jian-ping

---

## CERRITO, Fanny

Italian dancer and choreographer. Born Francesca Teresa Guiseppa Raffaela in Naples, 11 May 1817. Studied at the Ballet School of the Teatro San Carlo, Naples; graduated in 1832; also studied with Jules Perrot in Vienna, 1837, Carlo Blasis at La Scala, Milan, 1838–40, and Arthur Saint-Léon. Married dancer and choreographer Arthur Saint-Léon, 1845 (separated 1851); one daughter, Matilde (b. 1853) by the Marqués de Bedmar. Stage début at Teatro del Fondo, Naples, July 1832; performed in Rome, Carnival Season, 1833, and Florence, 1833–34; prima ballerina assoluta, Teatro Valle, Rome, Spring and Autumn, 1834; prima ballerina, Teatro Carignano and Teatro Regio, Turin, 1835–36; Vienna début, 1836; Milan début, 1838; prima ballerina, La Scala, Milan, various seasons, 1838–40; London début, 1840, performing in London, Liverpool, and Manchester, 1841; prima ballerina, partnered by Arthur Saint-Léon, Vienna, 1841–42; ballerina, under ballet master Jules Perrot, Her Majesty's Theatre, London, 1842–48; Paris début, 1847, performing at the Opéra, various seasons, 1848–55; Madrid début, 1851; returned to Vienna, 1853; finished association with the Opéra, 1855; went to Russia: St. Petersburg début, 1855; Moscow début, 1856; last appearance at Lyceum Theatre, London, 1857; also choreographer, staging own dances and producing own ballet, *Gemma*, for Paris Opéra, 1854. Died in Paris, 6 May 1909.

### ROLES

1832 Pas de deux in *L'Oroscopo* (Galzerani), Teatro del Fondo, Naples

1833 Dancer in *I Tre Gobbi di Damasco* (Galzerani), *Gli Empirici* (Galzerani), *Buondelmonte* (Galzerani), Teatro di Tordinova, Rome
- Danza delle Ombre (cr) in *L'Ombra di Tsen-Ven* (S. Taglioni), Teatro San Carlo, Naples
- Pas de cinq (cr) in *Bianca di Messina* (S. Taglioni), Teatro San Carlo, Naples

1834 Pas de trois (cr) in *L'Eredità* (S. Taglioni), Teatro del Fondo, Naples
- Pas de trois (cr) in *L'Assedio di Negroponte* (Monticini), Teatro San Carlo, Naples
- Pas de cinq (cr) in *Tolomeo Evergete* (S. Taglioni), Teatro San Carlo, Naples

1835 Pas de trois (cr) in *I Due Prigionieri* (S. Taglioni), Teatro del Fondo, Naples
- Iride (cr) in *Amore e Psiche* (S. Taglioni), Teatro San Carlo, Naples
- Pas de trois in *La Selvaggia nell'isola deserta* (Bianchi), Teatro del Fondo, Naples
- Dancer in *Cunegonda*, *Ildebrando Duca di Spoleto* (Astolfi), *Gli Automi* (Astolfi), Teatro Carignano, Turin
- Dancer in *Ezzolino sotte le Mure di Bassano* (Serafini), Teatro Regio, Turin

1836 Pas de trois in *Mose* (opera; mus. Rossini), Kärntnertor Theater, Vienna
- Principal dancer in *Der Korsar* (Galzerani), *Die Waise aus Genf* (Galzerani), *Die Charlatane* (Galzerani), *Die Spanier in Peru* (Galzerani), Kärntnertor Theater, Vienna
- Ninetta in *Die Lustige Jagd Partie*, Kärntnertor Theater, Vienna
- Louise in *Liebe Staerker als Zaubermacht*, Kärntnertor Theater, Vienna

1837 Pas de cinq (also chor.) in *Die Wohltaetige Fee* (divertissement; Campilli), Kärntnertor Theater, Vienna
- Tarantella in *La Bal masqué* (*Gustave*; opera by Auber), Kärntnertor Theater, Vienna
- Amalie in *Ottavio Pinelli* (Samengo), Kärntnertor Theater, Vienna
- Pas "La Gitana" in *Der Hinkende Teufel* (Arnel), Kärntnertor Theater, Vienna
- Principal dancer in *Emma di Salerno* (G. Albini), Teatro Comunale, Trieste

1838 Principal dancer (cr) in *I Veneziana in Constantinopoli* (divertissement; Monticini), La Scala, Milan
- Fenella in *La Muta di Portici* (*La Muette de Portici*; opera; mus. Auber), La Scala, Milan

1839 Principal dancer in *I Viaggiatori all'isola de'amore* (Monticini), La Scala, Milan
- Title role in *Esmeralda* (Monticini; "grand ballabile" staged Blasis), La Scala, Milan
- Zulma in *La Rivolta delle donne del seraglio* (B. Vestris, after Taglioni's *La Révolte au sérail*), La Scala, Milan
- Principal dancer in *La Conquista di Granada* (Galzerani), La Scala, Milan

1840 Principal dancer in *Il Cambio del conscritto*, *Romanow* (S. Taglioni), *L'Assedio di Schiraz* (S. Taglioni), La Scala, Milan
- Divertissement (including "La Lituania") in *Une Nuit de bal* (Guerra), Her Majesty's Theatre, London
- Pas de quatre (cr) in *Le Lac des fées* (Guerra), Her Majesty's Theatre, London
- Pas de trois (also chor.) added to Divertissement from *La Gitana* (Guerra after Taglioni), Her Majesty's Theatre, London
- Principal dancer in *Le Brigand de Terracina* (Deshayes), Her Majesty's Theatre, London
- Divertissements, including "La Castellana" (cr) in *Le Toréador* (Guerra), Her Majesty's Theatre, London
- Principal dancer (cr) in *Il Genio e la maga* (Monticini), Bologna
- Pas de trois (cr) in *L'Ebrea di Toledo* (Cortesi), La Scala, Milan

1841 Title role (cr) in *La Silfide* (Cortesi after Taglioni), La Scala, Milan
- Cupid's Pupil in *Aglaé; ou, L'Élève d'amour* (Taglioni), Her Majesty's Theatre, London
- Aerine (cr) in *Die Wiederbelebte Sylphide* (B. Vestris), Kärntnertor Theater, Vienna

**Fanny Cerrito with Arthur Saint-Léon in *Lalla Rookh*, c.1846**

Pas de deux in *Le Diable boîteux* (Aniel after Coralli), Kärntnertor Theater, Vienna
Dancer (cr) in *Der Soldat und die Marketenderin in Steiermark* (character pas de deux; also chor.), Kärntnertor Theater, Vienna
Title role (cr) in *Amors Zögling* (also chor.), Kärntnertor Theater, Vienna
Pas de deux (cr; Guerra) in *Der Pact mit der Unterwelt* (B. Vestris), Kärntnertor Theater, Vienna
Zelia in *Der Feen-See* (*Le Lac des fées*; Guerra), Kärntnertor Theater, Vienna

1842 Title role (cr) in *Alma; ou, La Fille de feu* (Perrot, Deshayes, with some *pas* by Cerrito), Her Majesty's Theatre, London
Dancer in *Double Cachucha* and *Varsovienne* (pas de caractère) added to *Une Soirée de Carnaval* (Perrot), Her Majesty's Theatre, London

1843 Title role (cr) in *Gisella* (Cortesi), La Scala, Milan
Principal dancer in *Les Houris* (divertissement; Perrot), Her Majesty's Theatre, London
Title role (cr) in *Ondine; ou, La Naiade* (Perrot), Her Majesty's Theatre, London
Dancer in *Pas de deux* (with Elssler; chor. Perrot), Her Majesty's Theatre, London
The Lady in *Un Bal sous Louis XIV* (Perrot), Her Majesty's Theatre, London
Principal dancer in *La Vivandiera ed il postiglione* (Saint-Léon, probably with Cerrito), Teatro Alibert, Rome

1844 Dancer in *La Manola* (Aragonese dance; also chor., with Saint-Léon), Her Majesty's Theatre, London
Kathi (cr) in *La Vivandière* (new production of *La Vivandiera* to new mus. Pugni; also chor.), Her Majesty's Theatre, London
Title role (cr) in *Zélia; ou, Les Nymphes de Diane* (Perrot), Her Majesty's Theatre, London

1845 Principal dancer (cr) in *La Vendetta d'Amore*, Teatro di Apollo, Rome
Polka da sala in *La Festa in maschera*, Teatro di Apollo, Rome
Dancer (cr) in *La Vincita al Latto* (divertissement; also chor.), Teatro di Apollo, Rome
Title role (cr) in *Rosida; ou, Les Mines de Syracuse* (also chor.), Her Majesty's Theatre, London
Ballerina (cr) in *Pas de quatre* (Perrot), Her Majesty's Theatre, London

1846 Principal dancer (cr) in *La Encantadora de Madrid* (Astolfi), Teatro Regio, Madrid
Title role (cr) in *Lalla Rookh* (Perrot), Her Majesty's Theatre, London
A Goddess (cr) in *Le Jugement de Pâris* (Perrot), Her Majesty's Theatre, London

1847 Title role in *La Esmeralda* (Saint-Léon after Perrot), Königstheater, Berlin
Title role (cr) in *Das Blümenmädchen im Elsass* (Saint-Léon), Königstheater, Berlin
Dancer (cr) in *Das Maskenball* (divertissement), Königstheater, Berlin
The Air (cr) in *Les Éléments* (Perrot), Her Majesty's Theatre, London
Fatma (cr) in *La Fille de marbre* (new version of *Alma*; Saint-Leon), Opéra, Paris

1848 Title role (cr) in *Giovanna Maillotte* (Galzerani), La Fenice, Venice
Passo dell'angelo (cr) in *Tartini il Violinista* (Saint-Léon), La Fenice, Venice
Chiara (cr) in *L'Anti-Polista ed i Polkamani* (Saint-Léon), La Fenice, Venice
Spring (cr) in *Les Quatre Saisons* (Perrot), Her Majesty's Theatre, London

1849 Hélène de Vardeck (cr) in *Le Violon du diable* (new production of *Tartini*; Saint-Léon), Opéra, Paris

1850 Title role (cr) in *Stella; ou, Les Contrebandiers* (Saint-Léon), Opéra, Paris

1851 Title role (cr) in *Pâquerette* (Saint-Léon), Opéra, Paris
Dancer (cr) in *La Sal Andaluza* (pas de deux), Teatro Real, Madrid

1852 Title role in *Nathalie* (Massot), Teatro Real, Madrid
Title role (cr) in *Orfa* (Mazilier), Opéra, Paris

1854 Title role (cr) in *Gemma* (also chor.). Opéra, Paris
Fenella in *La Muette de Portici* (opera; mus. Auber), Opéra, Paris

1855 Title role (cr) in *Eva* (Desplaces), Royal Italian Opera, Covent Garden, London
Title role (cr) in *Armida* (Perrot), Bolshoi Theatre, St. Petersburg

1856 Alma in *La Fille de marbre* (Saint-Léon; staged and with additional dances Perrot), Bolshoi Theatre, St. Petersburg
Title role in *Gazelda* (revival; Perrot), Winter Court, St. Petersburg
Principal character in *L'Ile des muets* (comedy by Deligny; chor. Perrot), Bolshoi Theatre, St. Petersburg

1857 Red Indian Girl (cr) in *La Brésilienne* (Desplaces), Lyceum, London
Minuet in *Don Giovanni* (opera; mus. Mozart), Lyceum Theatre, London

## WORKS

1837 Pas de cinq in *Die Wohltaetige Fee* (divertissement; Campilli), later included in *Clorinde* (Aniel), Kärntnertor Theater, Vienna

1841 *Der Soldat und die Marketenderin in Steiermark* (character pas de deux), Kärntnertor Theater, Vienna
*Amors Zögling*, Kärntnertor Theater, Vienna

1842 Pas in *Alma; ou, La Fille de feu* (chor. Perrot, Deshayes; mus. Costa), Her Majesty's Theatre, London
*L'Élève d'amour* (expanded version of *Amors Zögling*), Her Majesty's Theatre

1843 *L'Allieva d'amore* (*L'Élève d'amour*; mus. Rolland), Teatro Alibert, Rome
*Il Lago delle fate* (*Le Lac des fées*; after Guerra), Teatro Alibert, Rome
*La Vivandiera ed il postiglione* (attributed to Saint-Léon; probably chor. with Cerrito; mus. Rolland), Teatro Alibert, Rome

1844 *La Manola* (Aragonese dance; with Saint-Léon), Her Majesty's Theatre, London
*La Vivandière* (new production of *La Vivandiera*; new mus. Pugni), Her Majesty's Theatre, London

1845 *La Vincita al latto* (divertissement; mus. Rolland), Teatro di Apollo, Rome
*Rosida; ou, Les Mines de Syracuse* (mus. Pugni), Her Majesty's Theatre, London

1854 *Gemma* (mus. Gabrielli), Opéra, Paris

## PUBLICATIONS

*Fanny Cerrito in Rome*, Rome, 1843
J.D.D.S., *Biographie de M. et Mme Fanny Cerrito-Saint-Léon*, Paris, 1850

Vieil Abonné, Un (Mahalin, Paul), *Ces Demoiselles de l'Opéra*, Paris, 1887
Moore, Lillian, *Artists of the Dance*, New York, 1938
Moore, Lillian, "Cerrito and *Ondine*", *Dancing Times* (London), June 1943
Chaffee, George, "The Romantic Ballet in London", *Dance Index* (New York), September–December 1943
Chaffee, George, "Three or Four Graces", *Dance Index* (New York), November 1944
Beaumont, Cyril, *Complete Book of Ballets*, revised edition, 1951
Guest, Ivor, "The *Pas de Quatre*", *Ballet* (London), August 1951
Guest, Ivor, *The Romantic Ballet in England*, London, 1954
Guest, Ivor, *Fanny Cerrito: The Life of a Romantic Ballerina*, London, 1956
Guest, Ivor, *The Romantic Ballet in Paris*, London, 1966
Migel, Parmenia, *The Ballerinas*, New York, 1972
Guest, Ivor, *The Ballet of the Second Empire*, London, 1974
Saint-Léon, Arthur, *Letters from a Ballet Master: The Correspondence of Arthur Saint-Léon*, edited by Ivor Guest, New York, 1981

* * *

The Neapolitan ballerina Fanny Cerrito began dancing at an early age with her parents' blessing and encouragement. Although she showed little talent at first, her natural gifts emerged over the years as her technique developed and improved. In 1832 she joined the company at the Teatro San Carlo in Naples and was immediately recognized as a unique artist. Several years later, while engaged to dance in Vienna, she spent several months further improving her technique under the ballet master Jules Perrot, who would later become a close collaborator during the many years she spent dancing in London.

Returning to Italy from Vienna, Cerrito spent two valuable years at Milan's La Scala, dancing and training under Carlo Blasis. By 1840 she possessed outstanding elevation, speed, and lightness, with an ability for strong pointe work and good balance. Her style of dancing was marked by unusual abandon (to the point where some critics believed she was improvising), complemented by her own personal charm, physical beauty, and vivacity. Her weakest point was her apparent lack of dramatic ability when it came to acting rather than pure dancing.

By 1842 Cerrito was firmly established as the leading ballerina at Her Majesty's Theatre in London. While some critics compared her to Marie Taglioni, others pitted her against Fanny Elssler. The London public was so devoted to Cerrito, however, that she dared dance *La Sylphide*, that ballet so closely associated with its originator, Marie Taglioni, in 1841. Cerrito wisely avoided comparison with Taglioni by interpreting the role quite differently, making it more playful, passionate and voluptuous—and *The Times* critic found it to be "... perhaps her best achievement".

Like many other dancers of her day, Cerrito was often called upon to choreograph parts or all of the ballets in which she appeared. Her efforts in this direction, most remarkably *Alma* which she created in collaboration with Jules Perrot in London in 1842, were lauded by press and public. Late in her career she collaborated with Théophile Gautier on the libretto for *Gemma*, a Paris Opéra production for which she also created the choreography and danced the leading role.

During her years in London she performed in many of Perrot's finest ballets, the most beloved being *Ondine*. This ballet, though flawed in some ways, showed both Perrot and Cerrito at the height of their creative careers, and is perhaps most memorable for the famous "Pas de l'ombre", in which Cerrito danced charmingly with her shadow. "Wit and poetry were so nicely blended in this dance", writes ballet historian Ivor Guest, "as to make it one of the most perfect gems of choreography in the history of ballet, a gem that survives today only as legend." Guest goes on to say:

> In no other *pas*, and in no other ballet, did Fanny's magic weave such a spell over those who watched her. It was a spell that lingered long after the curtain had fallen, like the aftermath of a dream, as one witness put it, in which there had glided and glistened in a world of moonlight, roses, and crystal, "A delicious creation with all the loveableness of the woman combined with all the airiness of the fairy".

Cerrito also danced in a number of popular divertissements, beginning with a pas de deux with her most serious rival, Fanny Elssler, and followed by the famous *Pas de quatre*, which brought the greatest ballerinas of the day—Cerrito, Taglioni, Grisi, and Grahn—on to the stage at the same time. This was in turn followed by the ultimate production, *Le Jugement de Pâris*, which made use both of Perrot's choreographic genius and of the audiences' fascination with the ballerinas' rivalries, pitting the ballerinas against one another in a divertissement that depicted Taglioni, Cerrito, and Grahn as goddesses vying for the golden apple of Pâris, danced by Arthur Saint-Léon.

Under Perrot's careful coaching, Cerrito's technique reached its zenith. Although her technical feats were lauded by critics from Italy to England, Gautier—keen observer and aficionado of the Romantic Ballet—found Cerrito's talents to be utterly natural and therefore not worthy of comparison with Taglioni, Elssler, or Grisi. Upon seeing her dance for the first time (in 1846), he wrote: "In an art which has rigid rules, despite the apparent frivolity, she represents the flowering of natural gifts, fantasy and caprice." Cerrito had no "école", wrote Gautier, meaning it as no insult, but deliberately departing from a classical evaluation of the ballerina's technique and style:

> ... Mlle Cerrito owes more to nature than to application; she dances by inspiration, and indeed in my belief her qualities would even disappear if she devoted herself to study in the hope of perfecting her technique, for the "gift" would then be lost, not acquired. Her qualities consist of freshness, ease of movement, and a naïveté which makes one forgive a fault for its grace. At certain moments she seems to be improvising, there is such happy inspiration in her steps. Just as some singers have voices whose main attraction lies in the *timbre*, and which it would be wrong to impair by study, so Mlle Cerrito has, in a sense, a silvery and youthful *timbre* of dancing which fatigue might crack.

From 1845 until 1851 Cerrito was wife and partner of Arthur Saint-Léon, one of the leading male dancers of his time who was also a gifted musician and choreographer. During their marriage they appeared as leading dancers at theatres in London and Paris, as well as giving numerous guest appearances throughout western Europe. Together they created many charming national and folk dances such as the Redowa Polka, the Polka de Sala (the Polka being the ballroom dance craze of the moment), and the Sicilienne. For many viewers Cerrito's best performances were linked to these short and charming character dances.

After spending many years in quiet retirement, Cerrito died in Paris in May 1909, shortly before the historic début of

Diaghilev's Ballets Russes which heralded a new era in the history of ballet.

—Carol Egan
with Elizabeth Hudson

---

**CHABUKIANI, Vakhtang**
Soviet dancer, choreographer, teacher, and ballet master. Born Vakhtang Mikhailovich Chabukiani in Tbilisi, 12 March (27 February old style) 1910. First ballet training at the studio of M. Perrini, Tbilisi; later attended evening courses at the Leningrad Choreographic School, pupil of Viktor Semenov, graduating in 1928; student, day department of the Leningrad Choreographic School, pupil of Vladimir Ponomarev, L. Leontiev, A. Monakhov; graduated 1929. Dancer, State Theatre of Opera and Ballet (GATOB; later the Kirov), from 1929; leading soloist until 1941; guest performer, with Tatiana Vecheslova, in Latvia, Estonia, Italy, and the U.S. (first Soviet dancers to tour the U.S.), 1934; soloist, teacher, choreographer, and artistic director, Paliashvili Theatre of Opera and Ballet, Tbilisi, 1941–73; ballet master and director of the Tbilisi Choreographic Academy, 1950–73; also performer in films, including *Stars of the Ballet*, 1946, and *Othello*, 1960. Honoured Artist of the Russian Federation, 1939; Honoured Arts Worker of the Georgia SSR, 1943; People's Artist of the USSR, 1950; Recipient: State Prize of the USSR, 1941, 1948, 1951; Lenin Prize, 1958. Died in Tbilisi, 5 April 1992.

**ROLES**

1929 Winter Bird in *The Ice Maiden* (Lopukhov), State Theatre of Opera and Ballet (GATOB), Leningrad
1930 Principal dancer in *The Golden Age* (Vainonen), GATOB, Leningrad
1931 Albrecht in *Giselle* (Petipa after Coralli and Perrot), GATOB, Leningrad
1932 Bluebird in *The Sleeping Beauty* (Petipa, staged Lopukhov), GATOB, Leningrad
Jerome (cr) in *The Flames of Paris* (Vainonen), GATOB, Leningrad
1933 The Count (cr) in *Swan Lake* (Vaganova after Petipa, Ivanov), GATOB, Leningrad
1934 Vaslav (cr) in *The Fountain of Bakhchisarai* (Zakharov), GATOB, Leningrad
1935 Acteon (cr) in *Esmeralda* (Vaganova after Petipa, Perrot), GATOB, Leningrad
1936 The Premier Danseur (cr) in *Lost Illusions* (Zakharov), Kirov Ballet, Leningrad
1937 Kerim (cr) in *Partisan Days* (Vainonen), Kirov Ballet, Leningrad
1938 Dzhardzhi (cr) in *Heart of the Hills* (also chor.), Kirov Ballet, Leningrad
1939 Frondoso (cr) in *Laurencia* (also chor.), Kirov Ballet, Leningrad
1940 Andrei (cr) in *Taras Bulba* (Lopukhov), Kirov Ballet, Leningrad
1947 Avtandil (cr) in *Sinatle* (also chor.), Paliashvili Theatre, Tbilisi
1950 Title role (cr) in *Gorda* (also chor.), Paliashvili Theatre, Tbilisi
1953 Sergei Sokolov (cr) in *For Peace* (also chor.), Paliashvili Theatre, Tbilisi

**Vakhtang Chabukiani**

1957 Title role (cr) in *Othello* (also chor.), Paliashvili Theatre, Tbilisi
1961 Title role (cr) in *The Demon* (also chor.), Paliashvili Theatre, Tbilisi
1962 Principal dancer (cr) in *Bolero* (also chor.), Paliashvili Theatre, Tbilisi

**Other roles include:** The Youth in *Chopiniana* (Vaganova after Fokine), Harlequin in *Carnaval* (Fokine), Basil in *Don Quixote* (Gorsky), Prince Siegfried in *Swan Lake* (Petipa, Ivanov; staged Vaganova), Vaslav in *The Fountain of Bakhchisarai* (Zakharov), Jerome in *The Flames of Paris* (Vainonen), Vladimir in *Katerina* (Lavrovsky), Koloman in *Raymonda* (Petipa, staged Vainonen), Solor in *La Bayadère* (Petipa, Chabukiani, Ponomarev), Genie of the Waters in *The Little Humpbacked Horse* (Gorsky after Saint-Léon), Acrobat and Phoenix in *The Red Poppy* (Lopukhov), Merchant and Slave in *Le Corsaire* (Petipa, staged Vaganova; slave variation Chabukiani), Sportsman in *The Golden Age* (Vainonen), the Polo Dance in *Carmen* (opera; mus. Bizet, chor. Chabukiani).

**WORKS**

1929 *Dance of Fire* (concert piece; mus. Rubinstein), Concert Programme, GATOB, Leningrad
1937 *Heart of the Hills* (mus. Balanchivadze), Paliashvili Theatre of Opera and Ballet, Tbilisi (staged Kirov Theatre, Leningrad, 1938)

1939 *Laurencia* (mus. Krein), Kirov Ballet, Leningrad (staged Paliashvili Theatre, Tbilisi, 1978)
1942 "Walpurgis Night" in *Faust* (opera; mus. Gounod), Paliashvili Theatre, Tbilisi
1947 *Sinatle* (mus. Kiladze), Paliashvili Theatre, Tbilisi
1948 Dances in *Carmen* (opera; mus. Bizet), Kirov Theatre, Leningrad
1950 *Gorda* (mus. Toradze), Paliashvili Theatre, Tbilisi
1953 *For Peace* (mus. Toradze), Paliashvili Theatre, Tbilisi
1957 *Othello* (mus. Machavariani), Paliashvili Theatre, Tbilisi (staged Kirov Theatre, Leningrad, 1960)
1961 *The Demon* (mus. Sinadze), Paliashvili Theatre, Tbilisi
1962 *Bolero* (mus. Ravel), Paliashvili Theatre, Tbilisi
1966 *Cinderella* (mus. Prokofiev), Paliashvili Theatre, Tbilisi
1971 *Hamlet* (mus. Gabichvadze), Paliashvili Theatre, Tbilisi
1980 *Appassionata* (mus. Beethoven), Paliashvili Theatre, Tbilisi

Also staged:
1942 *Giselle* (after Petipa, Coralli, Perrot), Paliashvili Theatre, Tbilisi
*Chopiniana* (after Fokine), Paliashvili Theatre, Tbilisi
1943 *Don Quixote* (after Gorsky), Paliashvili Theatre, Tbilisi
1944 *Esmeralda* (after Vaganova), Paliashvili Theatre, Tbilisi
1945 *Swan Lake* (after Petipa, Ivanov), Paliashvili Theatre, Tbilisi
1947 *La Bayadère* (with Ponomarev, after Petipa), Kirov Ballet, Leningrad
1959 *The Sleeping Beauty* (after Petipa), Paliashvili Theatre, Tbilisi
1968 *La Bayadère* (with Ponomarev, after Petipa), Paliashvili Theatre, Tbilisi

**PUBLICATIONS**

By Chabukiani:
"The Dramatic Pattern in Ballet", *Rabochy i Teatr* (Leningrad), no. 11, 1937
"My Experience: Argument and Discussion", *Sovetsky Balet* (Moscow), no. 5, 1986

About Chabukiani:
Morley, Iris, *Soviet Ballet*, London, 1945
Krasovskaya, Vera, *Vakhtang Chabukiani*, Moscow, 1956, 1960
Kriger, Viktorina, *Vakhtang Chabukiani*, Moscow, 1960
Burtikashvili, A., *Magician of the Dance*, Tbilisi, 1960
Gugushvili, E., *Theatre Portraits*, Tbilisi, 1961
Roslavleva, Natalia, *Era of the Russian Ballet*, London, 1966
Christout, Marie-Françoise, and Percival, John, "The View from Tbilisi", *Dance and Dancers* (London), February 1967
Chernova, N., *From Geltser to Ulanova*, Moscow, 1979
Smakov, Gennady, *The Great Russian Dancers*, New York, 1984
Stupnikov, Igor, "Born for Dance", *Teatralnaya Zhizn* (Moscow), no. 18, 1985

* * *

Vakhtang Chabukiani was a Georgian boy who came to Leningrad to study dance. He was then about eighteen years old (having already spent a year as an artist with the Paliashvili Theatre in Tbilisi), and was past the age of entering the regular school—so he joined the evening classes of the Leningrad Choreographic School, where Vladimir Ponomarev was fortunately then teaching. It was a strong class of dancers, yet within a short time Chabukiani was one of the most outstanding pupils there. Within three years he was dancing with the company, and soon afterwards he was performing leading roles.

Chabukiani mastered the air itself; people compared him to an eagle because he appeared to accomplish the flight of a soaring bird. Watching old films of Chabukiani, one can find many faults from a technical point of view—especially when one considers the advance of male ballet technique today—but the spirit, the attack, and the energy from within were extraordinary. Chabukiani wanted the male dancer to conquer the stage, to overtake the entire space in a few leaps; his turns and jumps were stupendous, even if in strictly practical terms his elevation was not especially high. But that sense of stretching, of almost pausing, in the air created the impression that he was flying. Tatyana Vecheslova wrote, "He was born and created for the dance. Never in a single performance was he removed from it. At one moment, like a steel spring, he sped up his rotation, then gradually slowed it down, as if obeying some internal command. Nature had not given him a large jump, but his flight was compared to the flight of an eagle. From a leap, he never fell on to the stage, but came down on it simply to fly up again."

Chabukiani wanted the male roles to be much stronger, and he sought to reconstruct many of the classic ballets in order to provide the male dancer with fuller and more intricate movements, as well as a stronger presence. Together with his teacher Ponamarev, he decided to restage Petipa's *La Bayadère*, and with the older dancer's help he re-created the male roles: all the variations of Solor which are familiar today, for example, do not belong to Petipa but are the creations of Chabukiani. And thanks to Chabukiani even the structure of the male dancer changed: the dancer developed strong, muscular legs (which surprised the English public in the 1950s and early 1960s when the Soviet companies first came to the West), and well-developed upper bodies. The work of the arms no longer lay merely in partnering the ballerina, but in contributing overall to a general athleticism and strength.

Chabukiani's first choreography was a production of separate numbers created during his student years. His first independent ballet, *Heart of the Hills*, was created in Tbilisi in 1937 and produced at the Kirov Theatre in 1938. In 1939, Chabukiani created *Laurencia*, a ballet that remained in the company's repertoire for many years. Up until 1941, he produced dances for the operas *Carmen* and *Faust*, and of course he revived, jointly with Ponamarev, the ballet *La Bayadère*. In 1941, when many of the dancers were evacuated from Leningrad, Chabukiani returned to his native Tbilisi, where he continued to create successful ballets and powerful roles for himself. Particularly memorable examples were *Othello*, to the music of the Georgian composer Machavariani, and *The Demon*, based on the poem by Lermontov. Many remember the performance, when Chabukiani was over 50, of *Othello*, which was revived on the Kirov stage in 1957: he was in his best form, and audiences were surprised by how slender and how energetic he was—he was still the archetype of the heroic male dancer on the Soviet stage.

When we speak of Chabukiani's influence, we speak not necessarily of a direct influence but of the carrying on of a tradition; and Chabukiani's legacy exists in more ways than we may at first realize. When Nureyev first burst on the world stage, for example, he was actually repeating many of the stylistic qualities that had first been seen in the earlier master: that savage attack on stage and that uninhibited male energy is something that began with Chabukiani.

—Igor Stupnikov

**CHADWICK, Fiona**

British dancer. Born in Morecambe, England, 13 May 1960. Studied at the Royal Ballet Lower School, 1971–76, and Royal Ballet Upper School, London, 1976–78. Married dancer Antony Dowson, 17 March 1990: one daughter, Emily, b. 1991. Dancer, Royal Ballet, London, from 1978, performing also for lecture-demonstration group, Ballet For All, 1978; soloist, Royal Ballet, from 1981; principal dancer from 1984; has toured internationally with the Royal Ballet, including the United States, 1991, and Japan, 1992.

**ROLES**

1980 Title role in *Firebird* (Fokine), Royal Ballet, London

1982 Entrée ("Blue Girls") in *Les Patineurs* (Ashton), Royal Ballet, London
Myrtha in *Giselle* (Petipa after Coralli, Perrot; staged de Valois), Royal Ballet, London
Princess Aurora in *The Sleeping Beauty* (Petipa, Ashton; staged Wright), Royal Ballet, London

1983 Lescaut's Mistress in *Manon* (MacMillan), Royal Ballet, London
Pas de trois in *Les Patineurs* (Ashton), Royal Ballet, London
Odette/Odile in *Swan Lake* (Petipa, Ivanov; staged Dowell), Royal Ballet, London
Principal dancer (cr) in *Midsummer* (Ashton), Royal Ballet, London

1984 Principal dancer in *Song of the Earth* (MacMillan), Royal Ballet, London
Blue Pas de deux in *Return to the Strange Land* (Kylián), Royal Ballet, London
Principal dancer in *Young Apollo* (Bintley), Royal Ballet, London
Calliope Rag in *Elite Syncopations* (MacMillan), Royal Ballet, London
Rag Mazurka ("Hostess") in *Les Biches* (Nijinska), Royal Ballet, London
Juliet in *Romeo and Juliet* (MacMillan), Royal Ballet, London
Principal dancer in *Scènes de ballet* (Ashton), Royal Ballet, London
Sugar Plum Fairy in *The Nutcracker* (Wright), Royal Ballet, London

1985 Title role in *Giselle* (Petipa after Coralli, Perrot; staged Wright), Royal Ballet, London
Katia in *A Month in the Country* (Ashton), Royal Ballet, London

1986 Principal dancer (cr) in *Galanteries* (Bintley), Royal Ballet, London
Mary Vetsera in *Mayerling* (MacMillan), Royal Ballet, London
Principal dancer in *Gloria* (MacMillan), Royal Ballet, London
The Fairy in *Le Baiser de la fée* (MacMillan), Royal Ballet, London
Principal dancer in *Symphonic Variations* (Ashton), Royal Ballet, London

1987 Principal dancer (cr) in *Pursuit* (Page), Royal Ballet, London
The Chosen Maiden in *The Rite of Spring* (MacMillan), Royal Ballet, London

1988 Principal dancer (cr) in *The Trial of Prometheus* (Bintley), Royal Ballet, London
Principal dancer in *Serenade* (Balanchine), Royal Ballet, London
Divertissement (Neapolitan Girl) in *Ondine* (Ashton), Royal Ballet, London
Title role in *Cinderella* (Ashton), Royal Ballet, London

1989 Gamzatti in *La Bayadère* (Makarova after Petipa), Royal Ballet, London
Nikiya in *La Bayadère* (Makarova after Petipa), Royal Ballet, London
Pas de trois (cr) in *Piano* (Page), Royal Ballet, London
Princess Epine (cr) in *The Prince of the Pagodas* (MacMillan), Royal Ballet, London

1990 Principal dancer in *Laurentia* Pas de six (Nureyev after Chabukiani), Royal Ballet, London
Mercury (cr) in *The Planets* (Bintley), Royal Ballet, London
Neptune in *The Planets* (Bintley), Royal Ballet, London

**Other roles include:** Mazurka in *Les Sylphides* (Fokine), Winter Fairy in *Cinderella* (Ashton), Mitzi Caspar in *Mayerling* (MacMillan), Gypsy Girl in *The Two Pigeons* (Ashton), Lise in *La Fille mal gardée* (Ashton), title role in *Raymonda*, Act III (Nureyev after Petipa).

**PUBLICATIONS**

By Chadwick:

Interview in Levene, Louis, "We Do as We're Told", *Dance and Dancers* (London), June 1990

About Chadwick:

"Dancers You Will Know: Bryony Brind, Fiona Chadwick", *Dance and Dancers* (London), October 1981

Finch, Tamara, "Dance Portrait: Fiona Chadwick", *Dancing Times* (London), June 1987

Shaw, Robert, "Stravinsky Ballets", *Dance and Dancers* (London), December 1987

Percival, John, "Reviews", *Dance and Dancers* (London), April 1989

"The Royal Ballet: Biographies", *Ballet in London Yearbook 1989/90*, London, 1989

* * *

Fiona Chadwick first encountered ballet when her mother took her to Manchester Opera House to see Fonteyn and Nureyev in *The Sleeping Beauty* when she was six years old. She was soon taken to a local ballet school, and then moved down from her family home in Morecambe to London in order to join the Royal Ballet School at White Lodge in 1971. She made her début on the Royal Opera House stage early in 1972, when she appeared as a Page in the Prologue of *The Sleeping Beauty*. She subsequently worked her way through the Upper School, watching as many performances as possible by taking advantage of the free standing passes offered to students at the Royal Ballet School. She danced the Second Variation in *Birthday Offering*, and the Mazurka in *Les Sylphides* (coached by Alicia Markova) in the Royal Ballet School's annual performance in 1978, and graduated into the Royal Ballet immediately.

Chadwick spent the first six months in the company working with Ballet For All, the now defunct lecture-demonstration group which used to tour small towns and colleges with an educational programme. Once in the main company at Covent Garden, Chadwick was promoted to soloist in 1981 after being plucked from the corps on 29 November to dance *The Firebird*. She made history by being, at 21, the youngest Royal Ballet dancer to undertake this famous Fokine role, and her reviews

**Fiona Chadwick in MacMillan's *Prince of the Pagodas*, 1989**

announced a triumph. She was further promoted to principal dancer in 1984.

Fiona Chadwick is a very compact dancer, neatly proportioned and of an average height without any extremes about her. Her greatest asset is her strong technique, which is always engineered with precision. She shines most brilliantly in roles which require an exactitude, and her interpretation of Raymonda's solo in Act III is riveting for the sharp edge she gives each step.

She has, however, danced nearly all the ballerina roles in the Royal Ballet's classical repertoire, including *Swan Lake*, *The Sleeping Beauty*, *Giselle*, *The Nutcracker*, and *La Bayadère*—in which she dances both Nikiya and Gamzatti, two vastly different leading female roles. This mastering of both roles underlines her versatility as well as her open-mindedness about trying to portray a diversity of characters. Many claim that she is particularly suited to the role of Princess Aurora, as in some ways she epitomizes the "English Rose" ballerina. (Not surprisingly, her own heroine is Dame Margot Fonteyn, the definitive Aurora of all time.) Chadwick's secure balances, purity of line, and clarity of phrasing are fine tributes to the Petipa choreography. She is also exceptionally dependable, and if another ballerina becomes indisposed at short notice, Chadwick's good will is inevitably called upon, for she is a truly reliable performer.

In Ashton ballets, Chadwick has been cast in the title role of *Cinderella* (also performing as the Winter Fairy, which she dances with a crisp, icy precision), as Lise in *La Fille mal gardée*, both the "Blue Girl" and the "Red Girl" in *Les Patineurs*, Katia in *A Month in the Country*, the Neapolitan Girl in *Ondine*, the provocative Gypsy Girl in *Two Pigeons*, and as a leading dancer in *Symphonic Variations* and *Scènes de ballet*.

All the same, Chadwick cites Kenneth MacMillan as her favorite choreographer. He chose her to re-create the role of the Fairy in his reworking of *Le Baiser de la fée* (1986), also choosing her to create Princess Epine in his most recent full-length ballet, *The Prince of the Pagodas* (1989), which has been preserved on film. Her other MacMillan roles include Juliet, which she plays with a touching innocence, holding on to her childhood long after other dancers in the same role have matured into knowing, yearning young women; both Mary Vetsera and Mitzi Caspar in *Mayerling*; the Calliope Rag from *Elite Syncopations*; Lescaut's Mistress in *Manon*; and leading female roles in *Gloria* and *Song of the Earth*. Undoubtedly, however, the MacMillan ballet that taxed Chadwick's physical strength more than any other was *The Rite of Spring*, in which she danced the Chosen Maiden in 1987 with what seemed almost inexpendable energy. (One could perhaps even complain that she dances the role with such strength that she does not give any hint of the Chosen Maiden's helpless exhaustion.) In Chadwick the Royal Ballet might have the best female successor to Monica Mason, the original creator of the role.

Although she has danced repeatedly with several partners, Chadwick has never forged a real stage partnership with any single male dancer, although she did share the title "Dancer of the Year" (1986/87 season) with Patrick Armand, in a survey conducted by *Dance and Dancers* magazine. Perhaps more of a soloist than a pas de deux dancer, Chadwick shows an utter and complete calm on stage which verifies her strength and independence as a dancer.

—Emma Manning

---

## CHANT DU COMPAGNON ERRANT *see* SONG OF A WAYFARER

*see* SONG OF A WAYFARER

---

## LE CHANT DU ROSSIGNOL
(*The Song of the Nightingale*)

**Choreography:** Léonide Massine
**Music:** Igor Stravinsky (extracted from his opera *Le Rossignol*)
**Design:** Henri Matisse (scenery and costumes)
**Libretto:** Igor Stravinsky and Léonide Massine, after Hans Christian Andersen
**First Production:** Diaghilev's Ballets Russes, Opéra, Paris, 2 February 1920
**Principal Dancers:** Tamara Karsavina (Nightingale), Lydia Sokolova (Death), Stanislas Idzikovsky (Mechanical Nightingale)

**Other productions include:** Diaghilev's Ballets Russes (first production to Stravinsky's score; opera-ballet, chor. Boris Romanov, design Alexandre Benois), as *Le Rossignol*, with Tamara Karsavina (Nightingale); Paris, 26 May 1913. Diaghilev's Ballets Russes (revival; new chor. George Balanchine, and new Nightingale costume Matisse), with Alicia Markova (Nightingale); Paris, 17 June 1925. Bavarian State Opera Ballet (new version; chor. John Cranko, design Dorothea Zippel); Munich, 23 February 1968. New York City Ballet (new version; chor. Taras, design Rouben Ter-Arutunian), as *The Song of the Nightingale*, with Gelsey Kirkland (Nightingale); New York, 22 June 1972.

### PUBLICATIONS

Barr, Alfred, *Matisse, His Art and His Public*, New York, 1951
Grigoriev, Serge, *The Diaghilev Ballet*, translated by Vera Bowen, London, 1953
Sokolova, Lydia, *Dancing for Diaghilev*, London, 1960
Massine, Léonide, *My Life in Ballet*, London and New York, 1968
Kochno, Boris, *Diaghilev and the Ballets Russes*, translated by Adrienne Foulke, New York, 1970
Baer, Nancy van Norman, *The Art of Enchantment: Diaghilev's Ballets Russes 1909–1929*, San Francisco, 1988
Garafola, Lynn, *Diaghilev's Ballets Russes*, New York, 1989

* * *

The story of *Le Chant du rossignol* is a simple parable: the Emperor of Japan presents a mechanical song-bird to the Emperor of China, who becomes so enamoured of his gift that he sends his real nightingale away. A short time later, the Emperor becomes ill, and it seems that nothing can cure him, but at the last moment the nightingale flies in. Its beautiful song saves the Emperor's life.

The 1920 production of *Le Chant du rossignol*, with music by Igor Stravinsky, choreography by Léonide Massine, and sets and costumes by Henri Matisse, was the third version of Hans Christian Andersen's fairytale *The Nightingale* to be commissioned by Serge Diaghilev. In 1914 the Ballets Russes first produced *Le Rossignol* as an opera, with music and libretto by Stravinsky, designs by Alexandre Benois, and choreography by Boris Romanov. Performed in both Paris and London, the production fell out of repertory when, during the First World War, the costumes and sets perished while stored in the cellars of the Theatre Royal, Drury Lane (London). In 1916, Diaghilev decided to adapt Stravinsky's opera to a ballet and commissioned production designs from the Italian futurist artist Fortunato Depero. Depero's radical designs, composed of geometrically derived forms—cones, cylinders, arc segments, and disks—were rejected by Diaghilev because they were choreographically confining, in addition to being too cumbersome for touring.

Three years later, in 1919, Diaghilev invited Matisse to design a new version of *Le Chant du rossignol* (as the ballet version of *Le Rossignol* became known). No overall photograph or design of the stage survives, but according to the scene painter Vladimir Polunin (who was responsible for the execution of Matisse's designs), the orientally inspired set was simple, if not austere, and harmonious in its use of a subdued palette. The critic Arnold Haskell was in awe of this refined design, which "on account of its colour and perfect proportions . . . [gives] the impression of great oriental grandeur and luxury."

The restrained nature and elegant simplicity of Matisse's set influenced, and was influenced by, the ballet's streamlined choreography. Both suggested a modernist sensibility in the use of simplified form and the abstraction of mood and place. In creating the dances for *Le Chant du rossignol*, which he described as a "formalized Oriental fantasy", Massine readily acknowledged his use of poses, movements, and groupings taken from Chinese art. The ingenious arrangement of dancers in close-knit groups and vertical human pyramids, for example, were derived from figure combinations found on lacquered screens and carved ivory boxes.

Massine's sculptural poses and ensemble movements were well served by the uniform costumes created by Matisse for the corps de ballet. In contrast to the set, they displayed a wide range of colour, some in brilliant hues, some in pastels, and some in stark midnight blue and white. Simply cut robes and tunics for the most part, they were made of silk, satin, felt, and velvet—fabrics chosen for their shimmering and absorbent qualities under the stage lights. The Mourners' all-encompassing white felt cloaks and hoods, appliquéd with dark velvet chevrons and triangles, converted the dancer's figure into a planar surface—an abstract shape—as did the saffron yellow satin robes of the Mandarins. According to the critic Walter A. Propert, Massine caused these alternately shimmering and absorbent surfaces to move "silently before the pale background . . . like spirits passing at dawn".

By designing costumes that deliberately masked the curves of the body, Matisse transformed the dancers into building blocks of Massine's accumulative architectonic structures. When the costumes were isolated and placed in movement by the figures inside, they became part of an overall fluctuating pattern of stylized shape and colour. In his biography, Massine confirmed the shared point of view on the part of designer and choreographer: "I worked closely with Matisse to create a fusion of costumes, décor, and choreography, and I found this ballet one of my most successful efforts at collaboration with a designer."

With critics and public, however, *Le Chant du rossignol* was an equivocal success, and it vanished from the Ballets Russes

**A costume for a mourner in *Le Chant du Rossignol*, designed by Henri Matisse, 1920 (Castle Howard Costume Galleries)**

repertory the same year that it was first presented. Even Diaghilev criticized Massine's hermetic choreography, and Stravinsky accused Matisse of doing little more than "copy the china in the shops on the rue de la Boétie". For the public that still associated the Ballets Russes with lavish spectacle, *Le Chant du rossignol* was a confusing disappointment. In 1925, the ballet was revived with new choreography by George Balanchine, and Matisse designed a new costume for the leading role of the Nightingale danced by Alicia Markova. According to Boris Kochno, "Balanchine managed admirably the arduous task of reviving an unsuccessful ballet", but, like the 1920 original, it remained in repertory for only one season.

—Nancy van Norman Baer

---

**CHAPPELL, William**

British dancer, designer, and producer. Born in Wolverhampton, 27 September 1908. Educated at the Chelsea School of Art; studied dance under Marie Rambert, London. Served in the British Army, 1940–45. Stage début, 1929; dancer, with Ida Rubinstein's company, touring Europe 1929–30, with Ballet Club, later Ballet Rambert (one of its first members), 1929–34, Camargo Society, 1931, and Vic-Wells Ballet (later Sadler's Wells Ballet), 1934–40; designer of scenery and costumes for Marie Rambert Dancers (becoming Ballet Club and eventually Ballet Rambert), from 1928, and for Vic-Wells/Sadler's Wells Ballet, from 1934; also designed for Anthony Tudor's London Ballet and Mona Inglesby's International Ballet; producer of plays and revues, London, from 1951; also worked as director and choreographer for operas and revues; teacher and adviser for Nureyev season, 1979, Joffrey Ballet, 1979; also illustrator of several books.

**William Chappell (left) with Walter Gore and Antony Tudor in *Lysistrata*, 1932**

**ROLES**

1927 Dance of the Monkeys (cr) in *The Fairy Queen* (opera; mus. Purcell, chor. Ashton, Rambert), Purcell Opera Society, Cambridge Amateur Dramatic Society and Marie Rambert Dancers, London

1928 Passepied and Courante (cr) in *Nymphs and Shepherds* (Ashton), Marie Rambert Dancers, London
Ganymede (cr) in *Leda* (Ashton, Rambert), Marie Rambert Dancers, London

1930 Entrée de Cupidon (cr) in *Dances from Les Petits Riens* (probably a revision of *Nymphs and Shepherds*; Ashton), Marie Rambert Dancers, London
Dancer (cr) in *Capriol Suite* (Ashton), Marie Rambert Dancers, London
Zephyr (cr) in *Leda and the Swan* (new version of *Leda*; Ashton), Marie Rambert Dancers, London
Batsman (cr) in *Le Cricket* (Salaman), Marie Rambert Dancers, London

1931 Jodelling Song, Popular Song (cr) in *Façade* (Ashton), Camargo Society, London
Principal dancer in *Follow Your Saint* (*The Passionate Pavane*; originally in 1930 Masque presented by Arnold Haskell; chor. Ashton), Camargo Society, London
American Champion (cr) in *Le Boxing* (Salaman), Ballet Club (later Ballet Rambert), London
Apollo (cr) in *Mercury* (Ashton), Ballet Club, London
One of Seven Sons, War, A Comforter (cr) in *Job* (de Valois), Camargo Society, London
A Young Man (cr) in *Regatta* (Ashton), Vic-Wells Ballet, London
A Reaper (cr) in *The Lady of Shalott* (Ashton), Ballet Club, London
A Creole Boy (cr) in *A Day in a Southern Port* (*Rio Grande*; Ashton), Camargo Society, London
Title role (cr) in *The Lord of Burleigh* (Ashton), Camargo Society, London

1932 Pas de quatre (cr) in *An 1805 Impression* (later called *Récamier*; Ashton), in *Magic Nights*, Charles B. Cochran Revue, London
Joey, a Stranger (cr) in *High Yellow* (Bradley, Ashton), Camargo Society, London

1933 Principal dancer (cr) in *Pavane pour une infante défunte* (Ashton), Ballet Club, London

1934 Prince (cr) in *Mermaid* (Howard, Salaman), Ballet Club, London
The Stranger Player (cr) in *The Haunted Ballroom* (de Valois), Vic-Wells Ballet, London
Adolphe (cr) in *Bar aux Folies-Bergère* (de Valois), Ballet Club, London
Young Man with a Guitar (cr) in *The Jar* (de Valois), Vic-Wells Ballet, London
Mortal under Venus (cr) in *The Planets* (Tudor), Ballet Club, London
Elihu in *Job* (de Valois), Vic-Wells Ballet, London
Entrance in *Les Rendezvous* (new production; Ashton), Vic-Wells Ballet, London

1935 Sylvestre (cr) in *Valentine's Eve* (Ashton), Ballet Rambert, London
The Rake's Friend (cr) in *The Rake's Progress* (de Valois), Vic-Wells Ballet, London
The Man in *La Création du monde* (de Valois), Vic-Wells Ballet, London

1936 A Shepherd (cr) in *The Gods Go a-Begging* (de Valois), Vic-Wells Ballet, London
A Friend (cr) in *Prometheus* (de Valois), Vic-Wells Ballet, London

1937 John (cr) in *A Wedding Bouquet* (Ashton), Vic-Wells Ballet, London
Second Red Knight (cr) in *Checkmate* (de Valois), Vic-Wells Ballet, Paris
1938 Mercury (cr) in *The Judgment of Paris* (Ashton), Vic-Wells Ballet, London
A Tailor in *Le Roi nu* (*The Emperor's New Clothes*; de Valois), Vic-Wells Ballet, London
Pas de deux in *Les Patineurs* (Ashton), Vic-Wells Ballet, London
1939 Cavalier to Violet Fairy, Third Prince in *The Sleeping Princess* (Petipa; staged Sergeyev), Vic-Wells Ballet, London
One of the Townspeople (cr) in *Cupid and Psyche* (Ashton), Vic-Wells Ballet, London

**Other roles include:** for Ballet Club/Ballet Rambert—Spirit of the Rose in *Spectre de la rose* (Fokine), Faun in *L'Après-midi d'un faune* (Nijinsky), Pavane in *Capriol Suite* (Ashton), a Personage in *Les Masques* (Ashton), The Player in *Le Rugby* (Salaman); for Vic-Wells/Sadler's Wells Ballet—the Stranger Player in *The Haunted Ballroom* (de Valois), the Rake's Friend in *The Rake's Progress* (de Valois), Chinese Dance in *The Nutcracker* (Sergeyev after Ivanov).

## WORKS (Ballet Design)

1928 *Leda* (costumes only; later revised as *Leda and the Swan*; chor. Ashton), Marie Rambert Dancers, London
1930 *Mars and Venus* (originally part of *Jew Süss*, play by Ashley Dukes; new costumes Chapell, 1930; chor. Ashton), Marie Rambert Dancers, London
*Capriol Suite* (costumes only; chor. Ashton), Marie Rambert Dancers, London
*Saudade do Brésil* (costumes only; chor. Ashton), Marie Rambert Dancers, London
*Follow Your Saint: The Passionate Pavane* and *Dances on a Scotch Theme* (costumes only in Masque presented by Arnold Haskell; chor. Ashton), Arts Theatre Club, London
1931 *Cephalus and Procris* (chor. de Valois), Camargo Society, London
*Le Boxing* (chor. Salaman), Ballet Club (later Ballet Rambert), London
*La Péri* (chor. Ashton), Ballet Club, London
*The Dance of the Hours* (costumes only; chor. Ashton, Fleming), The Regal Ballet, London
*Mercury* (chor. Ashton), Ballet Club, London
*Regatta* (chor. Ashton), Vic-Wells Ballet, London
*The Lady of Shalott* (costumes only; chor. Ashton), Ballet Club, London
*The Jackdaw and the Pigeons* (chor. de Valois), Vic-Wells Ballet, London
*The Dancer's Reward* (costumes only, after Aubrey Beardsley; chor. de Valois), Camargo Society, London
1932 *Narcissus and Echo* (chor. de Valois), Vic-Wells Ballet, London
*Nursery Suite* (with Nancy Allen; chor. de Valois), Vic-Wells Ballet, London
*Lysistrata* (chor. Tudor), Ballet Club, London
*The Origin of Design* (design after Inigo Jones; chor. de Valois), Camargo Society, London
*An 1805 Impression* (later *Récamier*; chor. Ashton), in *Magic Nights*, Charles B. Cochran Revue, London
*High Yellow* (costumes only; chor. Bradley and Ashton), Camargo Society, London
*Foyer de danse* (costumes only; chor. Ashton), Ballet Club, London
*Ballyhoo* (revue; costumes only, with Norman Edwards; chor. Bradley and Ashton), Comedy Theatre, London
1933 *Pride* (chor. de Valois; solo), Vic-Wells Ballet, London
*Atalanta of the East* (chor. Tudor), Ballet Club, London
*The Wise and Foolish Virgins* (chor. de Valois), Vic-Wells Ballet, London
*Les Rendezvous* (Ashton), Vic-Wells Ballet, London (redesigned for new productions 1937, 1947)
*The Sleeping Princess: Bluebird Pas de deux* (costumes only; chor. after Petipa), Vic-Wells Ballet, London
1934 *Paramour* (costumes only; London production; chor. Tudor), Ballet Rambert, London
*Bar aux Folies-Bergère* (chor. de Valois), Ballet Rambert, London
*The Jar* (chor. de Valois), Vic-Wells Ballet, London
1935 *Giselle* (chor. Petipa, Coralli, Perrot; staged Sergeyev, revision of 1934 production), Vic-Wells Ballet, London
1936 *The Sleeping Princess*, Act III (*Aurora Pas de deux*; costumes only; chor. after Petipa), Vic-Wells Ballet, London
1937 *Perpetuum Mobile* (costume for Joy Newton; chor. Ashton), Vic-Wells Ballet, London
*Les Patineurs* (chor. Ashton), Vic-Wells Ballet, London
1938 *The Judgment of Paris* (chor. Ashton), Vic-Wells Ballet, London
1940 *Coppélia* (chor. Petipa, Ivanov, Cecchetti; staged Sergeyev), Vic-Wells Ballet, London (redesigned for same company, 1946)
*The Seasons* (chor. Staff), London Ballet, London
1941 *Pavane pour une infante défunte* (chor. Staff), Ballet Rambert, London
*Bartelmas Dances* (chor. Gore), Oxford Ballet Club (later staged by Ballet Rambert)
*Swan Lake*, Act II (chor. Ivanov; staged Sergeyev), International Ballet, Glasgow
*Amoras* (chor. Inglesby), International Ballet, London
1943 *Everyman* (costumes only; chor. Inglesby), International Ballet, London
1947 *Swan Lake* (Petipa, Ivanov; staged Sergeyev), International Ballet, London
1948 *Capriol Suite* (new production; Ashton), Sadler's Wells Theatre Ballet, London
1980 *Rhapsody* (chor. Ashton), Royal Ballet, London
1985 *La Chatte métamorphosée en femme* (solo; chor. Ashton), Royal Ballet

## PUBLICATIONS

By Chappell:
*Studies in Ballet*, London, 1948
*Fonteyn: Impressions of a Ballerina*, London, 1951
"A Fragment from an Autobiography", in Crisp, Clement, et al. (eds.), *Ballet Rambert: 50 Years On*, revised edition, London, 1981
*Edward Burra: A Painter Remembered by his Friends* (editor and joint author), London, 1982
*Well, Dearie: The Letters of Edward Burra* (editor), London, 1985

About Chappell:
Haskell, Arnold, *The Marie Rambert Ballet*, London, 1931

"The Man Who Pleases the Eye", *Carnaval* (London), March/April 1947
Noble, Peter (ed.), *British Ballet*, London, c.1949
Davidson, Glenys, *Ballet Biographies*, revised edition, London 1954
Clarke, Mary, *Dancers of Mercury: The Story of Ballet Rambert*, London, 1962
Anthony, Gordon, "William Chappell", *Dancing Times* (London), May 1970
Anthony, Gordon, *A Camera at the Ballet*, Newton Abbot, 1976

* * *

William Chappell is a unique figure in dance, an English dancer and designer whose career spans the whole history of British ballet in the twentieth century. After studying ballet with Marie Rambert in the 1920s, he obtained professional employment as a dancer with Ida Rubinstein's company in Paris in 1929 (in common with the then equally unknown Frederick Ashton and David Lichine), returned to England to appear with the newly-titled Ballet Club (later Ballet Rambert), and subsequently joined the Camargo Society and the Vic-Wells Ballet.

Chappell had also studied at Chelsea Art School, and it is for his ballet designs that his name will retain a permanent place in the early history of ballet in England. In contrast to the somewhat more flamboyant styles of dancers like Hugh Laing, Frederick Ashton, Leslie Edwards, or Walter Gore, Chappell seemed to personify a small oasis of quiet, for he had that peaceful temperament which tends to observe others in silence, rather than to take active part in events if not actually required to do so. (This temperament could have expected to be treated to a hard time in the army, for which Chappell was the first member of the Vic-Wells Ballet to volunteer in 1940: but the story goes that during the first period of drill the other new recruits were on the floor after half an hour, while he was still going, not even out of breath, at the end, which caused the others to regard him with a healthy respect which he might otherwise not have received from them.)

Although he could never at any stage have been described as a virtuoso, Chappell's dancing was sufficiently competent to enable him to create roles in the early repertoire in ballets which survived for several decades, including de Valois's *The Rake's Progress*, *The Haunted Ballroom*, and *Checkmate*, and Ashton's *Façade*, *Capriol Suite*, and *A Wedding Bouquet*. Moreover, it was undoubtedly his artist's eye for style which made his performances in *L'Après-midi d'un faune* and *Le Spectre de la rose* picturesque, if not presented with quite the force or projection which these roles often receive. Where his dance training and experience stood him in good stead, obviously, was in his costume designs for ballet, since he knew from personal experience not only how important it was to a dancer to be able to move freely, but exactly what to design for a dancer to enable him/her to be able to do so. He designed costumes for seventeen early Ashton ballets and seven de Valois ballets before the outbreak of war in 1939, with costume design also thrown in for Tudor, Staff, and Salaman; later Gore and Inglesby used his work, and he also designed *Coppélia* and *Swan Lake*. His most famous designs are undoubtedly for *Les Patineurs*—which have remained unchanged (save for Robert Helpmann's hat) since the opening night, and *Les Rendezvous*—which has been redesigned more times than one can hope to detail here.

Chappell's final collaboration with Frederick Ashton came in 1980, when he designed that choreographer's *Rhapsody* for the Royal Ballet at the Royal Opera House, Covent Garden. During the intervening 40 years he worked extensively in the world of revue, musical theatre, and straight drama, both as designer and director. For Joan Cross, he has designed the operas *Peter Grimes* and *Mitridate, Re di Ponto* in Oslo, and *La Traviata* at Sadler's Wells.

—Leo Kersley

---

**CHARRAT, Janine**

French dancer, choreographer, ballet director, and teacher. Born in Grenoble, 24 July 1924. Married (1) Gerard Bourret; (2) Michel Humbert. Studied with Jeanne Ronsay, Alexandre Volinin, Olga Preobrazhenska, and Lubov Egorova, Paris. Début in film, *La Mort du cygne*, 1937; performer, in connection with the Diaghilev Exhibition, Musée des Arts Decoratifs, 1939; leading dancer, recitals with Roland Petit, 1941–44, and Les Nouveaux Ballets de Monte Carlo, touring 1946; étoile, Grand Ballet du Marquis de Cuevas, 1946–47, 1950, also performing at Budapest Opera, 1947, and for Petit's Ballets de Paris; choreographer, staging own solos for concert recitals when still a student; first complete ballet for Les Ballets des Champs-Elysées, 1944, later staging works for companies including Petit's Ballets de Paris, German Opera Ballet, Berlin, Stockholm, and Amsterdam opera companies; founder, Les Ballets Janine Charrat, 1951, becoming Le Ballet de France, 1953–55; freelance choreographer, staging works in Milan and Buenos Aires, 1956, for Grand Ballet du Marquis de Cuevas, 1957; founder and choreographer of own company for Palermo Festival, 1957, touring in North and South America, Europe, Africa, and Japan, 1958–59; artistic director, Ballet of the Grand Théâtre (Geneva Ballet), Geneva, 1962–64; co-founder, Ballet International de Paris, 1965; also independent choreographer, staging works for numerous companies including the Paris Opéra Ballet, Théâtre Royal de la Monnaie, Brussels, Vienna Opera Ballet, Harkness Ballet, Bavarian State Opera Ballet and Hanover Ballet; appeared on television, including in 12 short films by Benoit-Levy for American television, 1951; director of dance, Centre Pompidou, Paris, 1979–91; founder of new company, Civic Theatre, Nice, 1983; also teacher: founder, Académie de Danse Janine Charrat, Paris, from 1970; member of the UNESCO Conseil International de la Danse. Recipient: Oscar du Courage (survived serious burns while making television production of ballet), 1961; Chevalier des Arts et des Lettres, 1961; Gold Medal of the Festival of Dance, Théâtre des Champs-Elysées, 1964; Légion d'Honneur, 1973; Officier de la Légion d'Honneur, 1991.

**ROLES**

1942 Principal dancer (cr) in *Britannicus* (Lifar), Gala
Principal dancer (cr) in *Nuit d'aout* (Lifar), Gala
1943 Virginie (cr) in *Paul et Virginie* (Petit), Gala, Salle Pleyel, Paris
Principal dancer (cr) in *Avant le bal* (Lifar), Gala, Paris
1944 Eurydice (cr) in *Orphée et Eurydice* (Petit), Gala, Salle Pleyel, Paris
Principal dancer (cr) in *La Jeune Fille endormie* (also chor., with Petit), Gala, Salle Pleyel, Paris
Principal dancer (cr) in *Les Masques* (Lifar), Gala
1945 Ballerina (cr) in *Jeu de cartes* (also chor.), Ballets des Champs-Elysées, Paris
Principal dancer (cr) in *Carnet de bal* (Lifar), Gala, Paris

1946 Principal dancer (cr) in *Cressida* (also chor.), Nouveau Ballet de Monte Carlo
Tinatine (cr) in *Chota Roustaveli* (Lifar), Nouveau Ballet de Monte Carlo, Monte Carlo
Principal dancer (cr) in *Passion* (Lifar), Nouveau Ballet de Monte Carlo, Monte Carlo
Principal dancer in *Prière* (Lifar), Nouveau Ballet de Monte Carlo, Monte Carlo
1947 Principal dancer (cr) in *Concerto* (also chor.), Opéra Comique, Paris
1948 Principal dancer (cr) in *La Femme et son ombre* (also chor.), Ballets de Paris, Paris
1949 Clorinda (cr) in *Le Combat* (pas de deux; Dollar), Ballets de Paris, London
Principal dancer (cr) in *Flocons de neige* (Volinine), Ballets des Champs-Elysées, Paris
Principal dancer (cr) in *Thème et variations* (also chor.), Ballets de Paris
Principal dancer in *Le Beau Danube* (Massine), Grand Ballet du Marquis de Cuevas, Monte Carlo
Archiposa (cr) in *Abraxas* (also chor.), Municipal Opera Ballet, Berlin
1950 Title role in *Giselle* (Petipa after Coralli, Perrot; staged Lifar), (Marquis de Cuevas's) Grand Ballet de Monte Carlo
Juliet in *Romeo and Juliet* (Lifar), Grand Ballet du Marquis de Cuevas
1951 Queen of the Amazons (cr) in *Le Massacre des Amazones* (also chor.), Ballets Janine Charrat, Grenoble
Principal dancer (cr) in *L'Etrangère à Paris* (also chor.), Ballets Janine Charrat, Grenoble
Dancer in White (cr) in *Concerto de Grieg* (also chor.), Ballets Janine Charrat, Grenoble
1953 Principal dancer (cr) in *Grand Pas royal* (Brieux), Le Ballet de France, Paris
Catherine (cr) in *Les Algues* (also chor.), Le Ballet de France, Paris
Principal dancer (cr) in *Le Colleur d'affiches* (also chor.), Le Ballet de France, Paris
1954 Principal dancer (cr) in *Première Symphonie* (also chor.), Le Ballet de France, Sarrebruck
1957 The Woman (cr) in *Les Liens* (also chor.), Le Ballet de France, Toulouse
1958 Title role (cr) in *La Chimière* (also chor.), Le Ballet de France, Paris
1961 Anna in *Sept Péchés capitaux* (Béjart), Théâtre Royal de la Monnaie, Brussels

## WORKS

1945 *Jeu de cartes* (mus. Stravinsky), Ballets des Champs-Elysées, Paris
1946 *Cressida* (mus. Aubin), Nouveau Ballet de Monte Carlo, Monte Carlo
1947 *Concerto* (mus. Prokofiev), Opéra-Comique, Paris
1948 *L'Âme heureuse* (mus. Koechlin), Opéra Comique, Paris
*Allegro* (mus. Ravel), Budapest Opera Ballet, Budapest
*'adame Miroir* (mus. Milhaud), Ballets de Paris, Paris
*La Femme et son ombre* (mus. Tcherepnine), Ballets de Paris, Paris
1949 *Thème et variations* (mus. Tchaikovsky), Ballets de Paris
*La Nuit* (mus. Sauguet), Ballets des Champs-Elysées, Paris
*Abraxas* (mus. Egk), Municipal Opera Ballet, Berlin
*Hérodiade* (mus. Hindemith), Ballets des Champs-Elysées, Berlin

**Janine Charrat in her own ballet, *Les Algues*, Paris, 1953**

1950 *Nuit et jour* (pas de deux; mus. Tchaikovsky), Palais de Chaillot, Paris
Dances in *Oberon* (opera; mus. Weber), Amsterdam Opera, Amsterdam
*Le Passage de l'étoile* (mus. Jean Villeard), Théâtre du Jorat, Mézières
1951 *Orfeo* (mus. Lupi), Festival of Venice
*Le Dernier Jugement* (mus. Sauguet), Ballets des Champs-Elysées, Paris
*Le Massacre des Amazones* (mus. Semenoff), Ballets Janine Charrat, Grenoble
*Danseuse de Degas* (mus. Semenoff), Ballets Janine Charrat, Grenoble
*L'Etrangère à Paris* (mus. Wiener), Ballets Janine Charrat, Grenoble
*Concerto de Grieg* (pas de deux; mus. Grieg), Ballets Janine Charrat, Grenoble
*Christopher Colombus* (oratorio; mus. Egk), State Opera, Berlin
1952 *Armida* (mus. Rossini), Maggio Musicale, Florence
*Rumba classique* (mus. Semenoff), Ballets Janine Charrat
*Suite Ravel–Debussy*, Ballets Janine Charrat, Paris
*Rêve d'amour* (mus. Liszt), Ballets Janine Charrat, Cannes
1953 *Geste pour un genie* (mus. Jarre), Ballets Janine Charrat, Amboise
*La Mécanique* (mus. Garret), Ballets Janine Charrat, Amboise

*Les Algues* (mus. Bernard), Le Ballet de France, Paris (staged Harkness Ballet, 1967)
*Héraklès* (mus. Thiriet), Le Ballet de France, Paris
*Le Colleur d'affiches* (mus. Van Parys), Le Ballet de France, Paris
1954 *Première Symphonie* (mus. Beethoven), Ballets Janine Charrat, Sarrebruck
*Orphée* (opera-ballet; mus. Gluck), Théâtre Empire, Paris
1955 *La Valse* (mus. Ravel), Le Ballet de France, Santander
1956 *Les Sept Péchés capitaux* (mus. Weill), La Scala, Milan
*Le Joueur de flute* (mus. Rhallys, Constant), Teatro Colón, Buenos Aires
*Persephone* (mus. Stravinsky), Ballet of the Teatro Massimo, Palermo
1957 *Les Liens* (mus. Semenoff), Le Ballet de France, Toulouse
*Diagramme* (mus. Bach), Grand Ballet de Marquis de Cuevas, Paris
*Persephone* (mus. Stravinsky), Palermo Festival, Palermo
*Arlequin* (mus. Stirn), Ballet de France, Montreal
*Le Leader* (mus. Delarue), Le Ballet de France, New York
1958 *La Chimère* (mus. Thiérac), Le Ballet de France, Paris
1960 Dances in *Le Roi David* (opera; Honneger), Paris Opéra Ballet, Paris
*Electre* (mus. Pousseur), Théâtre Royale de la Monnaie, Brussels
1961 *Les Quatre Fils Aymon* (with Béjart; mus. Schirren), Ballet du XXe Siècle, Brussels
1962 *Zone interdite* (mus. K. Sipuch), Ballets Janine Charrat, Stamford
*Champagne Party* (mus. Strauss), Ballets Janine Charrat, Stamford
1963 *Tu auras nom . . . Tristan* (mus. Maes), Geneva Ballet, Geneva
*Pour le temps présent* (mus. Schibler), Geneva Ballet, Geneva
1964 *Alerte . . . Puits 21* (mus. Wissmer), Geneva Ballet, Geneva
*L'Enfant et les sortilèges* (mus. Ravel), Vienna State Opera Ballet, Vienna
*Paris* (mus. Sauguet), Ballets Janine Charrat, Paris
*La Répétition de Phèdre* (mus. Josephs), Ballets Janine Charrat, Paris
1966 *Le Cycle* (mus. Wirren), Ballets Janine Charrat, Paris
*Rencontres* (mus. Lai), Ballets Janine Charrat, Paris
1968 *Au Mendiant du ciel* (mus. Landowski), Chaillot
*Persephone* (mus. Stravinsky), Essen Opera, Gelsenkirchen
*Up to Date*, Ballets Janine Charrat, Paris
1969 *L'Oiseau de feu* (mus. Stravinsky), Vienna State Opera Ballet, Vienna
*Casanova in London* (mus. Egk), Bavarian State Opera Ballet, Munich
1972 *Séquence* (mus. Handel), Lille
*Les Collectionneurs* (mus. Malec), Opéra Comique, Paris
*Dyade* (mus. Prokofiev), Opéra Comique, Paris
1973 *Offrandes* (mus. Varese), Paris Opéra Ballet, Paris
*Hyperprism* (mus. Varese), Paris Opéra Ballet, Paris
1979 *Diacronies* (Varese), Paris Opéra Ballet, Paris
1981 *Concerto pour la main gauche* (mus. Ravel), Toulouse
1982 *D'Hecube* (mus. Courtiouse), Bordeaux Festival
1984 *Salade* (mus. Milhaud), Nice Opera Ballet, Nice
1985 *Janine Charrat and Centre Pompidou* (mus. various), Pompidou Centre, Paris
1987 *Palais des glaces* (mus. d'Aisme), Ballets de Janine Charrat, Paris
*Inventaire*, Compagnie Alain Germaine, Paris
1988 *'adame Miroir* (new version; mus. Milhaud), Ballets Janine Charrat, Paris
*Bach Preludes* (mus. Bach), Ballets Janine Charrat, Paris

**Other works include:** concert pieces—*Tabou*, *Le Charmeur de serpents*, *La Berceuse equatoriale*, *Salomé* (solos), *La Cathédrale engloutie* (mus. Debussy).

## PUBLICATIONS

Lidova, Irène, "Janine Charrat" in *15 Danseurs et danseuses*, Paris, 1948
Lidova, Irène, *17 Visages de la danse française*, Paris, 1953
Beaumont, Cyril, *Ballets of Today*, London, 1954
Livio, A., "Janine Charrat" in *Étoiles et ballerines*, Bienne, 1965
"Ballet de France: Janine Charrat", *Dance and Dancers* (London), February 1965
Humbert, M., *Janine Charrat: Antigone de la danse*, Paris, 1970
Lidova, Irène, "Janine Charrat", *Les Saisons de la danse* (Paris), August 1970

* * *

Janine Charrat was already a star by the age of twelve. She was a slender child, with a face like a little fox, who appeared in a film called *La Mort du cygne*. In this, she played the part of a "petit rat" at the Opéra who commits a crime out of adoration for one of the ballerinas. This was Charrat's first contact with any kind of dance and it led her towards choreography. Her first dance teacher, Jeanne Ronsay, was an orientalist, and this influenced the first works of her young student prodigy. At fourteen, Charrat gave her first recitals in small halls in Paris. Her choreography amazed the experts. Her solos, with a definite oriental flavour, were called *Tabou*, *Le Charmeur de serpents*, *La Berceuse equatoriale*; but she also danced to *La Cathédrale engloutie* by Debussy, in which she seemed to lose herself in passionate prayer.

Janine Charrat came from a middle-class family with no interest in the arts. She spent her childhood in the fire station of the 17th district of Paris, where her father held an important position. In her bedroom she sculpted and drew pictures of her idol, Serge Lifar. Janine's first classical dance teacher, Lubov Egorova, guessed at the uncommon talents of her strange pupil, who refused to submit to the strict discipline of an ordinary class, seeing dance purely as an expression of her state of mind. Charrat was always a distinctive dancer, far removed from the usual ballet framework. She never belonged to any company other than her own and, apart from works by Serge Lifar and a few other choreographers, she danced only her own choreography. By refusing gratuitous virtuosity, she developed her own personal technique. Her sensuous body achieved a complete fluidity; her arms and hands had a dramatic expressiveness which was quite often violent. A moving and serious dancer, she was not suited to a lightweight repertoire. Her best roles were the young mad woman in her own masterpiece *Les Algues*, and the white dancer in her *Concerto de Grieg*.

Small, wiry, and fragile-looking, Janine Charrat was normally a calm, gentle person, but when in the grips of her art she became authoritarian and indefatigable. Led much more by instinct than by thought, Charrat used her imagination in composing original and expressive enchaînements. Her beginnings as a choreographer in the 1940s were linked to her collaboration with Roland Petit, with whom she gave a series of recitals acclaimed by the artistic and dramatic audiences in Paris. These performances formed the basis of the creation in 1945 of the Ballets des Champs-Elysées. Charrat, who was then twenty, created a sensation in Stravinsky's *Jeu de cartes*, a ballet which launched the unknown dancer, Jean Babilée, in the role of the Joker.

A few years later Charrat formed her company—Les Ballets Janine Charrat, briefly called Le Ballet de France—but few of her ballets have survived. Her best work of these was *Les Algues*, which she created in collaboration with the designer and producer Bertrand Castelli. Sadly, this brought her bad luck. While filming a scene for television her long ballet skirt caught fire after brushing against a lighted candelabra. Janine Charrat came close to death, suffering severe burns, but with remarkable courage she came back to life and to dance after a lengthy convalescence.

For a while Charrat directed the ballet company of the Grand Theatre in Geneva, and then joined up with Milorad Miskovitch for tours in Africa, South America, and the Far East, arranging a few short ballets—among them the solo *Salomé*, which she danced herself with remarkable dramatic energy. More recently she has been dance adviser at the Centre Pompidou. But Charrat's need to create has remained alive, as has her youthful enthusiasm for the dance.

—Irène Lidova

---

**CHASE, Lucia**

American dancer and ballet director. Born in Waterbury, Connecticut, 24 March 1907. Educated at St. Margaret's School, Waterbury; studied acting at the Theatre Guild School, and ballet with Mikhail Mordkin, Mikhail (Michel) Fokine, Antony Tudor, Bronislava Nijinska, and Anatole Vilzak, New York. Married Thomas Ewing, 1926 (d. 1933). Stage début in corps de ballet, Mikhail Mordkin's company, New York, 1932; professional début as principal dancer with newly established Mordkin Ballet, 1937–39; co-founder, with Richard Pleasant, and dancer, Ballet Theatre (later American Ballet Theatre), 1940, becoming principal dancer (and also chief financial investor): co-director, with Oliver Smith, from 1945; retired from stage, 1960; retired as company director, 1980. Recipient: *Dance Magazine* Award, 1957; Capezio Award, 1968; Handel Medallion of the City of New York, 1975; honorary doctorates, Long Island University, 1979, and Yale University, 1980; U.S. Medal of Freedom, 1980; Norman Lloyd Award, North Carolina School of the Arts, 1981. Died in New York, 9 January 1986.

**ROLES**

1937 Princess Aurora in *The Sleeping Beauty* (Petipa; staged Mordkin), Mordkin Ballet, Waterbury, Connecticut
Title role in *Giselle* (Petipa after Coralli, Perrot; staged Mordkin), Mordkin Ballet, Scranton, Pennsylvania
Fisherman's Wife in *The Goldfish* (Mordkin), Mordkin Ballet, Scranton, Pennsylvania
1938 The Child in *Trepak* (Mordkin), Mordkin Ballet, New York
Lisette (Lise) in *La fille mal gardée* (Mordkin), Mordkin Ballet, New York
1940 Film Star / L'Etoile (cr) in *Quintet* (Dolin), Ballet Theatre, New York
Little girl (cr) in *The Great American Goof* (Loring), Ballet Theatre, New York
Prelude in *Les Sylphides* (Fokine), Ballet Theatre, New York
Fourth Song in *Dark Elegies* (Tudor), Ballet Theatre, New York
Minerva in *The Judgment of Paris* (Tudor), Ballet Theatre, New York
Principal dancer (cr) in *Capriccioso* (new version of *Italian Suite*; Dolin), Ballet Theatre, Chicago
1941 Greedy Virgin in *Three Virgins and a Devil* (de Mille), Ballet Theatre, New York
Grisette in *The Beloved* (*La Bien Aimée*; Nijinska), Ballet Theatre, Mexico City
Queen Clementine (cr) in *Bluebeard* (Fokine), Ballet Theatre, Mexico City
Marushia (cr) in *Slavonika* (Psota), Ballet Theatre, Mexico City
1942 Eldest Sister (cr) in *Pillar of Fire* (Tudor), Ballet Theatre, New York
Fortune teller (cr) in *Aleko* (Massine), Ballet Theatre, Mexico City
Athena in *Helen of Troy* (Fokine, Lichine), Ballet Theatre, Mexico City
Athena / Bachos (cr) in *Helen of Troy* (Lichine), Ballet Theatre, Detroit
1943 Asturian Fandango in *Capriccio Espagnol* (Massine, La Argentinita), Ballet Theatre, San Francisco
Juliet's Nurse (cr) in *Romeo and Juliet* (Tudor), Ballet Theatre, New York
Khivria (cr) in *Fair at Sorochinsk* (Lichine), Ballet Theatre, New York
1944 The Innocent (cr) in *Tally-ho!; or, The Frail Quarry* (de Mille), Ballet Theatre, Los Angeles
1945 Principal dancer (cr) in *Rendezvous* (pas de deux; Nijinska), Ballet Theatre, New York
Polyhymnia (cr) in *Undertow* (Tudor), Ballet Theatre, New York
1946 Fanny Cerrito in *Pas de Quatre* (Lester), Ballet Theatre, Boston
1951 Fiona in *The Thief who Loved a Ghost* (Ross, Ward), Ballet Theatre, New York
1957 Mother in *Blood Wedding* (A. Rodrigues), Ballet Theatre Previews, New York
1967 Mother in *Las Hermanas* (MacMillan), American Ballet Theatre, New York
Princess-Mother in *Swan Lake* (Petipa, Ivanov; staged Blair), American Ballet Theatre, Chicago

**Other roles include:** Ballerina in *Petrushka* (Fokine), Columbine in *Carnaval* (Fokine), Stepmother in *Fall River Legend* (de Mille).

**PUBLICATIONS**

By Chase:

"Directing a Ballet Company", in Payne, Charles, *American Ballet Theatre*, New York, 1978
Interview (published posthumously) in Gruen, John, *People Who Dance*, Pennington, New Jersey, 1988

About Chase:

Dolin, Anton, "Lucia Chase is America's National Ballet Theatre", *Dance and Dancers* (London), July 1953

**Lucia Chase with Rudolf Bing and dancers, New York, c.1940**

Coleman, Emily, "Lucia Chase: Director in Spite of Herself", *Theatre Arts* (New York), September 1958
Terry, Walter, "America's Ballet Royalty", *Saturday Review* (New York), 28 October 1967
Maynard, Olga, "Lucia Chase: First Lady of American Ballet", *Dance Magazine* (New York), August 1971
Gruen, John, "Close-up: Lucia Chase", *Dance Magazine* (New York), January 1975
Payne, Charles, *American Ballet Theatre*, New York, 1978
Terry, Walter, "Make Way for Lucia", *Ballet News* (New York), September 1979
Hunt, Marilyn, "Lucia Chase", *Dance Magazine* (New York), March 1986
"Lucia Chase Remembered", *Ballet Review* (New York), Spring 1990

* * *

Lucia Chase once said, "Acting was my first love, music second, and dancing a hobby"—yet of all these things, it was ballet that gave her many years of "glorious artistic and personal fulfilment".

Her devotion to the difficult life of the dancer and ballet director is all the more surprising in the light of her comfortable and conventional New England upbringing. However, her family were keen patrons of the arts and encouraged Lucia in her initial choice of career—acting. She studied drama at New York's Theatre Guild School, attending singing lessons and—after a meeting with Mikhail Mordkin, the former partner of Pavlova—ballet lessons. Lucia received encouragement in all her theatrical interests from her husband, Thomas Ewing Jr., whom she had married in 1926, but in 1933 he died of pneumonia. The support that Lucia received from Mordkin after this tragic event persuaded her to devote herself to ballet. Eventually she became a leading dancer with the Mordkin Ballet (which she also helped to fund), dancing principal roles in such ballets as *Les Sylphides*, *Petrushka*, and *Pas de quatre*. It seems, however, that she soon realized that she would never be a true classical dancer (her ballet training began too late for her to develop the necessary technique). She ceased dancing classical roles and for the remainder of her dancing career she concentrated on dramatic roles such as the Eldest Sister in Antony Tudor's *Pillar of Fire* and the Stepmother in Agnes de Mille's *Fall River Legend*. The critic Walter Terry described her as "a superb dramatic dancer and a brilliant comedienne". Chase continued to dance until 1960.

In 1940 Chase and Richard Pleasant, who had also been with the Mordkin Ballet, co-founded Ballet Theatre, later to become American Ballet Theatre. Their plan was to invite guest choreographers to work with the company rather than having one choreographer at its head, so that it would be, in Lucia Chase's words, "a gallery of the dance . . . a great international company but American in spirit". In the first year, the eleven guest choreographers included Mordkin, Mikhail Fokine, Antony Tudor, and Agnes de Mille. The company had financial difficulties from the start, and Pleasant resigned his directorship in 1941. In 1945, after a period under the management of impresario Sol Hurok, Lucia Chase was asked to become the company's director. Chase had helped to fund Ballet Theatre from its foundation, though she later said that she had done so with great reluctance. She accepted the offer of the directorship, but on condition that she share the post with stage designer Oliver Smith, and that she resign after one year, by which time a permanent director should have been chosen. In fact, she stayed until 1980. In 1975, Antony Tudor joined the team as associate director.

As director of American Ballet Theatre, Chase's responsibilities included choosing the dancers, selecting ballets, and setting programmes and casting, with the help of her regisseurs and choreographers. She insisted on watching all rehearsals and performances, even after her retirement. Her strong will resulted in many arguments, but in other ways she refused to be treated any differently from the other members of the company, travelling on the company bus and sharing rooms with other dancers while on tour, remaining a union member and lining up to collect her dancer's salary like all the others. Chase not only introduced important foreign choreographers and dancers to America, including Antony Tudor and Mikhail Baryshnikov, but also encouraged homegrown talent, including Jerome Robbins, Michael Kidd, Glen Tetley, and Twyla Tharp. In the 1950s and early 1960s some questioned her qualifications as a director, but by the 1970s she had proven herself through her judicious choice of productions, from re-creations of such classics as *Swan Lake*, *La Bayadère*, and *La Fille mal gardée* to new works such as Herbert Ross's *Caprichos* and *The Maids*, and José Limòn's *The Moor's Pavane*.

Lucia Chase died in 1986, six years after she had relinquished the directorship of American Ballet Theatre to Mikhail Baryshnikov. At a Dance Collection memorial in 1986, her colleagues, friends, and members of her family spoke of her many talents—artistic, administrative, and nurturing—but above all they remembered her devotion to the company she had helped to create.

—Jessica Arah

---

**CHAUVIRÉ, Yvette**

French dancer and teacher. Born in Paris, 22 April 1917. Studied at the Paris Opéra School, pupil of L. Couat, Carlotta Zambelli, Van Gothem, Mme. Rousane, Albert Aveline, Serge Lifar, Boris Kniaseff, and Victor Gsovsky, 1927–1931. Dancer, Paris Opéra Ballet: second quadrille, from 1930; première danseuse, from 1937; étoile, from 1941; ballerina, Nouveau Ballet de Monte Carlo, 1946–47, returning to Paris Opéra Ballet, 1947, and touring the United States, 1948; international guest artist, performing in London, 1949, La Scala, Milan, 1950 and 1952, Ballet Russe de Monte Carlo, New York, 1950–51, Ballets de Marigny, 1951–52, London Festival Ballet, 1952, Rome Opera Ballet, 1953–54, Vichy Festival, 1955, Ballets des Champs-Elysées, Stuttgart Ballet, 1958, Royal Ballet, London, 1958 and 1962–63; ballerina, Grand Ballet de Marquis de Cuevas, 1961–1962; also toured the Soviet Union, 1958, 1960, and 1966, Central America, 1959, South America, 1962, Johannesburg, 1966; retired from Paris Opéra, 1972; also appeared in films, including *La Morte du cygne* (chor. Lifar, 1937), *Carousel Napoletano* (chor. Massine, 1954), and *Une Étoile pour l'exemple* (prod. Delouche, 1988); choreographer, Ballets des Champs-Elysées, from 1950; artistic and technical counsellor, Paris Opéra Ballet, 1963–68; director, Académie internationale de danse, Paris, 1981–82, and teacher, Paris Opéra School; president of Paris International Dance Competition, 1984; president of Association of Artists and Friends of the Paris Opéra, 1986. Recipient: Chevalier de la Légion d'honneur, 1964; Officier de la Légion d'honneur, 1974; Commandeur de l'Ordre national du mérite; Commandeur des arts et des lettres et Membre du conseil de cet ordre, 1975; Commandeur de la Légion d'honneur, 1988.

Yvette Chauviré as Giselle, late 1940s

**ROLES**

1936 Principal dancer (cr) in *Le Roi nu* (Lifar), Paris Opéra Ballet, Paris
1937 Melchore (cr) in *David Triomphant* (Lifar), Paris Opéra Ballet, Paris
The Jewess (cr) in *Alexandre le Grand* (Lifar), Paris Opéra Ballet, Paris
1938 Principal dancer in *Les Santons* (Aveline), Paris Opéra Ballet, Paris
Principal dancer in *Adelaide* (Lifar), Paris Opéra Ballet, Paris
1939 Young girl in *La Spectre de la rose* (Fokine), Paris Opéra Ballet, Paris

1940 La Bohemienne in *Les Deux Pigeons* (Mérante; staged Aveline), Paris Opéra Ballet, Paris
1941 Dame noble (cr) in *Le Chevalier et la demoiselle* (Lifar), Paris Opéra Ballet, Paris
Title role (cr) in *Istar* (Lifar), Paris Opéra Ballet, Paris
Title role in *Sylvia* (Lifar), Paris Opéra Ballet, Paris
1942 Florence (cr) in *Joan de Zarissa* (Lifar), Paris Opéra Ballet, Paris
La Femme in *Les Animaux modèles* (Lifar), Paris Opéra Ballet, Paris
Djali (cr) in *Les Deux Pigeons* (new production; Aveline), Paris Opéra Ballet, Paris
1943 Pas de trois (cr) in *Suite en blanc* (Lifar), Paris Opéra Ballet, Paris
Title role in *Giselle* (Petipa after Coralli, Perrot; staged Sergeyev), Paris Opéra Ballet, Paris
Swanilda in *Coppélia* (Petipa, Cecchetti; staged Larthe), Paris Opéra Ballet, Paris
1945 Odette in *Swan Lake*, Act II (V. Gsovsky after Ivanov), Paris Opéra Ballet, Paris
1946 Dame (cr) in *Dramma per musica* (Lifar), Nouveau Ballet de Monte Carlo
Princess Daredjan (cr) in *Chota Roustaveli* (Lifar), Nouveau Ballet de Monte Carlo, Monte Carlo
Principal dancer (cr) in *Cressida* (Charrat), Nouveau Ballet de Monte Carlo
1947 Leucothéa (cr) in *Nautéos* (Lifar), Nouveau Ballet de Monte Carlo, Paris
L'Ombre (cr) in *Les Mirages* (Lifar), Paris Opéra Ballet, Paris (first performed at répétition générale, 1944)
1948 Title role (cr) in *L'Ecuyère* (Lifar), Salle Pleyel, Paris
1949 Juliette in *Roméo et Juliette* (Lifar), Opéra, Paris
1950 Title role (cr) in *L'Ucello di fuoco* (*Firebird*; Wallmann), Ballet of La Scala, Milan
Odette/Odile in *Swan Lake* (Petipa, Ivanov; staged Bulnes), Ballet of La Scala, Milan
Principal dancer (cr) in *Grand Pas classique* (also *Grand Pas d'Auber*; pas de deux; Gsovsky), Ballets des Champs-Elysées, Paris
"She" in *Nocturne* (V. Gsovsky), Ballet des Champs-Elysées, Paris
1951 Principal dancer (cr) in *Mystères* (Milloss), Palais de Chaillot, Paris
The Doll in *Petrushka* (Fokine; staged Beriozoff), London Festival Ballet
Sugar Plum Fairy in *The Nutcracker* (Beriozoff, Lichine), London Festival Ballet, Paris
1953 Principal dancer in *Suite en Re* (Lifar), JMF, Théâtre de Champs-Elysées, Paris
Flore in *Zéphire et Flore* (Massine), Paris Opéra Ballet, Rome
1954 Principal dancer in *Rondo Capriccioso* (Lifar), Enghien Festival
Leucothéa (cr) in *Nautéos* (revised version; Lifar), Paris Opéra Ballet, Paris
1955 Hélène (cr) in *La Belle Hélène* (Cranko), Paris Opéra Ballet, Paris
Principal dancer (cr) in *Balance à trois* (Babilée), Monte Carlo
Title role in *Le Cygne* (*The Dying Swan*; also chor., after Fokine), Paris Opéra Ballet, Paris
Title role (cr) in *La Péri* (also chor.), Vichy Festival
1956 La Danseuse (cr) in *Divertissement à la cour* (Lifar), Monte Carlo
Principal dancer (cr) in *Concerto aux étoiles* (Lander), Paris Opéra Ballet, Paris
1957 Title role (cr) in *L'Indécise* (Lifar), Enghien Festival
Principal dancer in *Adagio d'Albinoni* (Lifar), Monte Carlo
Carlotta Grisi in *Pas de quatre* (Dolin), Nervi Festival
Marguerite (cr) in *La Dame aux camelias* (T. Gsovsky), Berlin Ballet, Berlin
Title role in *La Péri* (Lifar), Paris Opéra Ballet, Paris
1958 Princess Aurora in *The Sleeping Beauty* (Petipa; staged Sergeyev, Ashton, de Valois), Royal Ballet, London
1959 Juliet in *Romeo and Juliet* (T. Gsovsky), Berlin Ballet, Berlin
Principal dancer in *Belle et la Bête* (pas de deux; Reinholm), Enghien Festival
Principal dancer in *Orphée* (pas de deux; T. Gsovsky), Enghien Festival
Principal dancer in *Joan de Zarissa* (pas de deux; T. Gsovsky), Enghien Festival
1960 Principal dancer (cr) in *Songe d'une nuit de Nice* (Lifar), Nice
Marguerite (cr) in *La Dame aux camélias* (expanded version; T. Gsovsky), Paris Opéra Ballet, Paris
Juliette in *Roméo et Juliette* (T. Gsovsky), Berlin Ballet, Berlin
1961 Principal dancer in *Esther* (Skibine), Versailles Ballet
1964 Principal dancer in *Adage à la rose* (Brieux), Paris Opéra Ballet, Paris
1965 Juliet in *Romeo and Juliet* (Parlić), Marais Festival, Paris
1969 Principal dancer (cr) in *Constellations* (Lifar), Paris Opéra Ballet, Paris
1984 Countess de Doris in *Raymonda* (Nureyev after Petipa), Paris Opéra Ballet, Paris
1986 Lady Capulet in *Romeo and Juliet* (Nureyev), Paris Opéra Ballet, Paris
1990 Maude (cr) in *Harold and Maude* (Frey), Sinopa, Switzerland

**Other roles include:** Waltz, Mazurka and Pas de deux in *Les Sylphides* (Fokine), principal dancer in *Seagull* (Gai).

## WORKS

1948 *Solitude et prelude* (mus. Bach), Gala Pleyel
1950 *Suite romantique* (mus. Chopin), Ballets des Champs-Elysées
1951 *Romeo et Juliette* (mus. Tchaikovsky), Florence
*Clair de lune* (mus. Beethoven), Gala, Paris
1952 *Pour les enfants sages*, Ballet de Marigny
*Le Rendez-vous sentimental*, Ballet de Marigny
1955 *La Péri* (mus. Dukas), Vichy
1957 *Arabesque* (mus. Debussy), JMF, Salle Pleyel, Paris
1971 *Suite en Re* (mus. Bach), Théâtre des Champs-Elysées

## PUBLICATIONS

By Chauviré:
"Yvette Chauviré Looks at the Role of Giselle", *Dance and Dancers* (London), February 1958
"Yvette Chauviré Creates a Modern Role", *Dance and Dancers* (London), March 1958
*Je suis ballerine*, Paris, 1960

About Chauviré:
Guillot de Rode, F., "Yvette Chauviré", *Quinze Danseurs et danseuses*, Paris, 1948

Lidova, Irène, "Yvette Chauviré", in Swinson, Cyril (ed.), *Dancers and Critics*, London, 1950
Moore, Lillian, "A New Choreographer", *Dancing Times* (London), June 1950
Beaumont, Cyril, "Four Giselles", *Ballet* (London), March 1951
Davidson, Gladys, *Ballet Biographies*, revised edition, London, 1954
Austin, Richard, "Yvette Chauviré", *Ballet Today* (London), November 1959
Nemenschousky, Léon, *A Day with Yvette Chauviré*, London, 1960
Livio, A., "Yvette Chauviré", in *Étoiles et ballerines*, Bienne, 1965
Lidova, Irène, "Yvette Chauviré", *Les Saisons de la danse* (Paris), February 1968
Pepys, Tom, "Curtain Up", *Dance and Dancers* (London), February 1977

* * *

The Paris Opéra Ballet was so proud of Yvette Chauviré that she was affectionately termed "La Chauviré nationale". Pre-eminent as an interpreter of the company's repertoire, whether in the traditional classics or in contemporary ballets, she was a prima ballerina of outstanding technical refinement and an interpreter of the richest emotional depth. She had an unusual ability for uniting classical style and Romantic feeling. Infinite variety characterized both her work and her personality.

Chauviré, who was trained at the Paris Opéra Ballet School from 1927, made her début in 1935 in a solo, *Impressionisme*, which she herself arranged. Even at that early stage she attracted critical acclaim—Pierre Michaut wrote: "Pour elle, la danse est bien un langage, un moyen d'expression, elle en use et en joue avec aisance et confiance." Chauviré was closely identified with the prolific choreographic talent of Serge Lifar during his long years of dominance in Paris, and her first major creation was in his ballet *David Triomphant* (1937). Their collaboration was marked by mutual esteem: she said, "Il était inspiré et brûlait d'une flamme créatrice . . . les poses, les lignes qu'il dessinait dans l'espace étaient pour moi l'esprit même de la danse."

In 1937 Chauviré became widely known outside France as one of the stars of the remarkable film *La Mort du cygne*. In this she plays the idol of the little pupil (Janine Charrat) who tries to help her against a rival ballerina (Mia Slavenska) with disastrous results when Slavenska falls through a trap-door. In 1941 Chauviré made an immense impression on Parisian audiences by the brilliance and stamina with which she created what was practically a solo tour de force in the eighteen-minute ballet *Istar*, for which she was rewarded by promotion at the age of 24 to the rank of danseuse étoile.

Other successes followed, right through the years of World War II—*Le Chevalier et la demoiselle*, *Joan de Zarissa*, and *Suite en blanc*—and Chauviré also became celebrated as one of the great Giselles of all time. In 1945, however, when Lifar's regime at Paris was interrupted by political feeling, Chauviré accompanied him to Monaco where they worked for the Nouveau Ballet de Monte Carlo. For this company Chauviré created a role in *Dramma per musica* and danced in several other Lifar ballets. She returned with Lifar to Paris in October 1947 and almost immediately starred in his great ballet *Les Mirages*, a highly romantic and fantastic piece in which her role of "The Shadow" was conveyed through pure classical movement. The following year, she visited the United States for the first time with the Paris Opéra Ballet, where she was much praised, and after 1949 she carried on a peripatetic career, to great international acclaim, as a guest artist with such companies as Milan's La Scala Ballet, London's Royal Ballet and Festival Ballet, and the Ballet Russe de Monte Carlo. Her repertoire was confined mainly to classics like *Giselle* and *Swan Lake*. Sadly, the range of contemporary roles for which she was admired in France was never understood by audiences abroad.

When Chauviré returned to the Paris Opéra Ballet, she delighted her public with a new look in *La Belle Hélène*, choreographed with youthful audacity and wit by John Cranko in 1955. She was provocative, petulant, and brilliant in a style far removed from the romantic lyricism of her remarkable Giselle. Although appearing at the Opéra, she continued to make guest appearances abroad and at regional festivals; but in 1963 she was recalled to Paris as director of the Paris Opéra Ballet School. There she exerted a remarkable influence on the new generation of young ballerinas, and later became director of the Académie internationale de danse. For her farewell performance at the Paris Opéra on 20 November 1972 there was no question as to which of her many roles should be chosen—she danced Giselle, which she had made so much her own.

In 1988 an admirable documentary film was shown of Chauviré's work as teacher and coach. *Yvette Chauviré: Une Étoile pour l'exemple* was made by Dominique Delouche, and in it Chauviré hands on to young dancers her knowledge and experience of great roles. She taught *Istar* to Isabelle Guérin and *Giselle* to Florence Clerc; she coached Dominique Khalfouni in *La Mort du cygne* and Marie-Claude Pietragalla in the original version of *Les Deux Pigeons* which she herself had learned from its creator Carlotta Zambelli. Such continuity is of the utmost value, but the charm of the film is to see one of the greatest prima ballerinas of our time in her native setting of the Paris Opéra.

—Kathrine Sorley Walker

---

## CHECKMATE

**Choreography:** Ninette de Valois
**Music:** Sir Arthur Bliss
**Design:** Edward McKnight Kauffer
**Libretto:** Sir Arthur Bliss
**First Production:** Vic-Wells Ballet, Théâtre des Champs-Elysées, Paris, 15 June 1937
**Principal Dancers:** Harold Turner (First Red Knight), June Brae (The Black Queen), Pamela May (The Red Queen), Robert Helpmann (The Red King)

**Other productions include:** Royal Ballet Touring Company, with Desmond Doyle (First Red Knight), Beryl Grey (The Black Queen), Henry Legerton (The Red King), Barbara Remington (The Red Queen); Tokyo, 18 April 1961. Vienna State Opera Ballet; Vienna, April 1964. Turkish State Ballet; 1964. Rome Opera Ballet; Rome, 1964. The Australian Ballet, with Robert Helpmann (The Red King); Sydney, 6 May 1986.

### PUBLICATIONS

Coton, A.V., *A Prejudice for Ballet*, London, 1938
Beaumont, Cyril, *Supplement to Complete Book of Ballets*, London, 1945

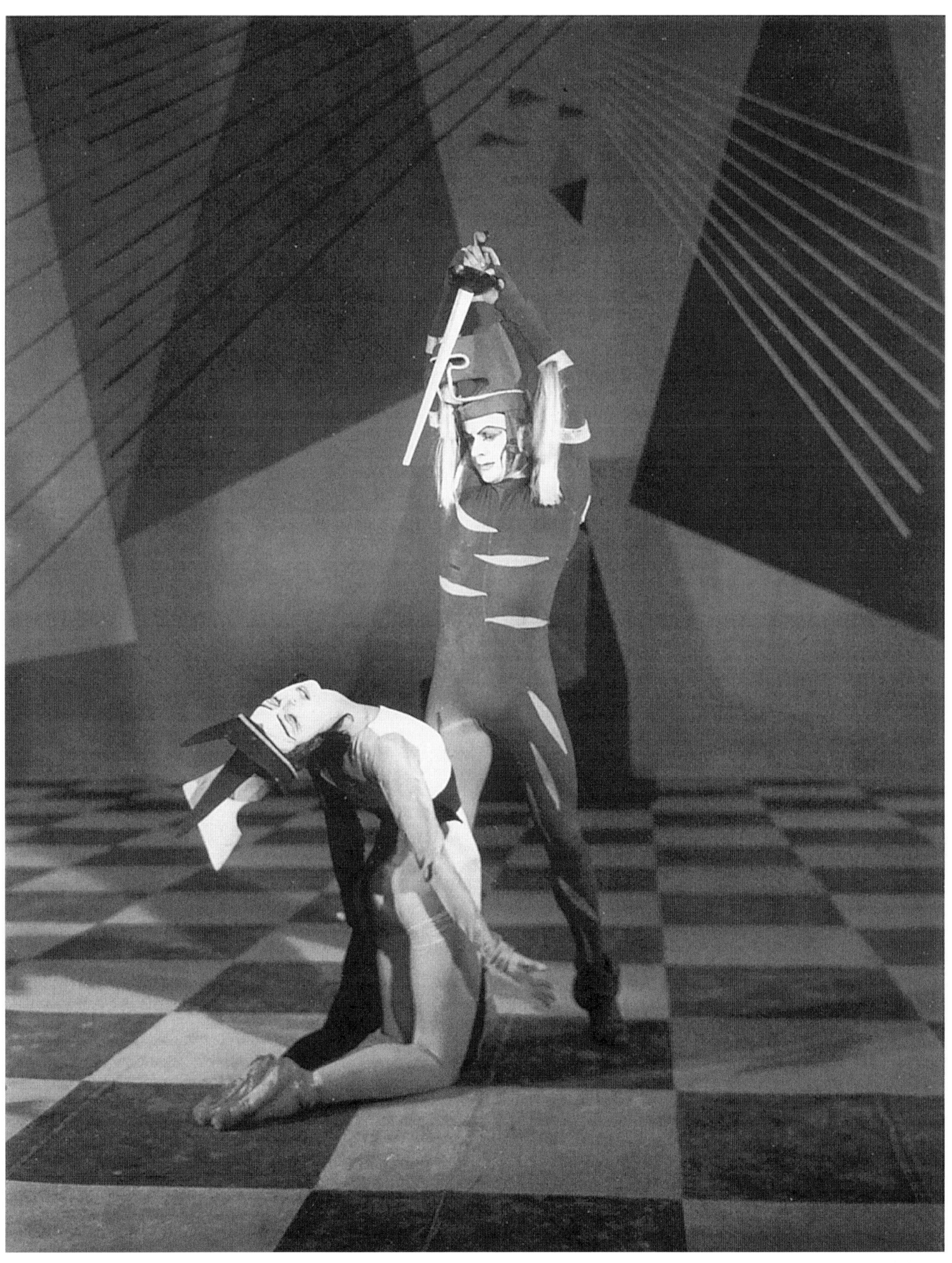

***Checkmate*, with Harold Turner and Pamela May in a Sadler's Wells Ballet revival, London, 1947**

Robertson, Marion, *"The Rake's Progress" and "Checkmate"*, London, 1949
Williams, Peter, and Goodwin, Noel, "Games of Love and Death", *Dance and Dancers* (London), November 1975
Sorley Walker, Kathrine, *Ninette de Valois: Idealist without Illusions*, London, 1987
Sinclair, Janet, "A Gripping Collaboration", *Dance and Dancers*, June 1987
Goodwin, Noël, "Bliss at the Ballet", *Dance and Dancers* (London), August 1991

* * *

*Checkmate* is, together with *The Rake's Progress*, the surviving record for posterity of the choreography of Ninette de Valois. Since the ballet's premiere in Paris in 1937, the leading roles of Black and Red Queen, Red Knight and Red King—though seldom so brilliantly performed as they were then by June Brae and Pamela May, Harold Turner and Robert Helpmann—have, during the following half century, offered endless opportunities to their successors, which have been taken with worthwhile results by scores of performers. This is de Valois's strength as choreographer; unlike the ballets of her colleague Ashton, her works are not indelibly stamped by the personalities of those who created them, but can be handed on from generation to generation, to offer continuing artistic rewards to their successive interpreters.

*Checkmate*, a work set in the mould established by Fokine (and out of fashion at the present time), aims to tell a story in movement, and, on the way, to provide the spectator with one or two ideas about human behaviour. By placing the choreographer, musician, and designer on equal terms, the aim of ballet in the Diaghilev and immediately post-Diaghilev era was to present a spectacle perfectly balanced in all elements—and this *Checkmate* effortlessly (or apparently effortlessly) achieved. Like its forerunner, *The Rake's Progress*, the ballet contains no technical feats for their own sake, although the Red Knight's solo mazurka has winded nearly everyone who has ever danced it (nowadays the dancer leaves the stage to get his breath back, which did not happen in the days of Harold Turner). Since the ballet's premiere in Paris, the music of Arthur Bliss, discreetly cut by the choreographer when first setting the work, has all been restored, not always to advantage. However, it must be admitted that the stirring score which Bliss provided to accompany this work, together with the startlingly effective décor and costumes of the poster artist McKnight Kauffer, did mesh successfully with the inspired choreography of de Valois, to provide a spectacle described in a newspaper of the time as ". . . not chess, but passionate metaphysics".

The story of *Checkmate*, though vaguely tied to the idea of the game by naming the characters Pawns, Castles, Knights, Kings, and Queens, in fact bears little relation to a formal game of chess, but uses the characters to tell a familiar tale of a beautiful woman who uses her feminine charms to deflect a hapless male from his duty. With hindsight at a distance of over 50 years, it is easy to distinguish some of the extraneous factors which governed the choreography and structure of the ballet, just as one can recognize them in *Job* and *The Rake*. One must admire the deft professionalism with which de Valois used every talent available to her in precisely the manner which would display it to best advantage, whether it was Helpmann's dramatic force, Brae's luscious personality, the technical strength of the two leading Black Pawns, Mary Honer and Margot Fonteyn, May's potent pathos, Turner's comprehensive technique and rugged charm, or the not so strong technical capabilities of the more minor cast members. This was a "company ballet", and the cheers which echoed round Sadler's Wells Theatre after its performances showed just how much audiences appreciated the singleness of purpose which united its constituent parts.

At the beginning of the final decade of the twentieth century, the genre of *Checkmate*, with its balance among the elements of dance, music, and décor in order to say something which could not be said more effectively in any other medium, is out of fashion with most choreographers. However, audiences still go to see *Checkmate* and still applaud loud and long at curtain-fall; and, even though the four leading characters have become simplified with the passage of time into something more conventional than they were when originally performed, the choreography is still strong, original, and idiosyncratic enough to survive the stereotyping imposed upon it by dancers who have not fully grasped the subtleties of their original conception by one of the choreographic masters of English ballet.

—Janet Sinclair

---

**CHINESE NATIONAL BALLET** *see* **CENTRAL BALLET OF CHINA**

---

**CHIRIAEFF, Ludmilla**

Latvian/Canadian dancer, choreographer, and ballet director. Born in Riga, Latvia, 1923. Studied with Alexandra Nikolaeva, Berlin; later studied with Mikhail Fokine and Léonide Massine. Dancer, Colonel de Basil's Ballets Russes, 1936–37; dancer, Berlin State Opera Ballet, 1939–44; soloist and ballet mistress, Lausanne; teacher, opening own school in Geneva, from 1948; founder, Les Ballets des arts, Geneva; emigrated to Canada, 1952: choreographer, creating ballets (with Jean Boisvert) for Radio Canada Television, from 1952; founder and director, Les Ballets Chiriaeff, Montreal, 1955, becoming Les Grands Ballets Canadiens, from 1957; also founder of associated touring troupe, Les Compagnons de la danse, 1971; retired as company director, 1974; director, Académie des Grands Ballets Canadiens, from 1957; founder, L'École supérieure de danse des Grands Ballets Canadiens, 1966, becoming L'École supérior de danse du Québec, 1980.

**WORKS**

1952 *Tziganes* (mus. traditional folk), Canadian television
1953 *Caucasienne* (mus. Ivanov, Khachaturian), Canadian television
*Boeuf sur le toit* (mus. Milhaud), Canadian television
*Cage d'or*, Canadian television
*L'Ineffable M. Triquet* (mus. Weber), Canadian television
*Cendrillon* (mus. Prokofiev, Mozart), Canadian television
*Pierrot de la lune* (*Au Clair de la lune*; mus. Arensky), Canadian television
1954 *Jeu de cartes* (mus. Prokofiev), Canadian television
*Epouvantail* (mus. Copland), Canadian television
*Danses symphoniques* (mus. Hindemith), Canadian television
*Esquisse* (mus. Villa-Lobos), Canadian television
*Kaleidoscope* (mus. Mercure), Canadian television

*Pierre et le loup* (mus. Prokofiev), Canadian television
*Pulcinella* (mus. Stravinsky), Canadian television
*Les Quatres saisons* (mus. Vivaldi), Canadian television
1955 *Une Nuit sur le Mont Chauve* (mus. Mussorgsky), Les Ballets Chiriaeff, Canadian television
*Les Clowns* (mus. Françaix), Les Ballets Chiriaeff, Canadian television
*Variations sur un thème enfantin* (mus. Dohnanyi), Les Ballets Chiriaeff
*Les Noces* (mus. Stravinsky), Les Ballets Chiriaeff
*Variations en blanc* (mus. Arensky), Les Ballets Chiriaeff
*Pas de trois* (mus. Glazunov), Les Ballets Chiriaeff
*Histoire du soldat* (mus. Stravinsky), Les Ballets Chiriaeff
*Les Ruses d'amour* (mus. Glazunov), Les Ballets Chiriaeff
*Contes de Perrault* (mus. Dohnanyi), Les Ballets Chiriaeff
1956 *Tarantelle* (mus. Rossini, Respighi), Les Ballets Chiriaeff
*L'Oiseau phoenix* (mus. Pépin), Les Ballets Chiriaeff
*Valse caprice* (mus. Contant), Les Ballets Chiriaeff
*Ti-Jean* (mus. Perrault), Les Ballets Chiriaeff
*Suite (Valses) en blanc* (mus. Tchaikovsky), Les Ballets Chiriaeff
1957 *Carnaval des animaux* (mus. Saint-Saëns), Les Ballets Chiriaeff
*Suite canadienne* (mus. Perrault), Les Ballets Chiriaeff
*Étude caractère* (mus. Dvořák), Les Ballets Chiriaeff
*L'Enfant et les sortilèges* (mus. Ravel), Les Ballets Chiriaeff
1958 *Farces* (early music), Les Grands Ballets Canadiens
*Étude* (mus. Schumann), Les Grands Ballets Canadiens
*Horoscope* (mus. Matton), Les Grands Ballets Canadiens
1959 *La Belle Rose* (mus. Perrault), Les Grands Ballets Canadiens
*Nonagone-Essai* (mus. Bach, Perrault), Les Grands Ballets Canadiens
1960 *Memoires de Camille* (with E. Caton; mus. Verdi), Les Grands Ballets Canadiens
1961 *Canadiana* (mus. Perrault, Avarmaa), Les Grands Ballets Canadiens
*La Fille mal gardée* (with Hyrst, Nault; mus. Hertel), Les Grands Ballets Canadiens
*Jeux d'Arlequin* (mus. Gretry), Les Grands Ballets Canadiens
*Quatrième Concert royal* (mus. Couperin), Les Grands Ballets Canadiens
1962 *Payse* (mus. Vallerand), Les Grands Ballets Canadiens
1963 *Exercises* (mus. Bartók), Les Grands Ballets Canadiens
1964 *Fête Hongroise* (mus. Brahms), Les Grands Ballets Canadiens
1970 *Initiation à la danse* (with Gradus, Belhumeur; mus. Rachmaninov, Legety, Schumann), Les Compagnons de la danse, Montreal
1976 *Artère* (mus. and text Charpentier), Les Grands Ballets Canadiens

Also staged:
1957 *Petrushka* (with MacPherson, after Fokine; mus. Stravinsky), Les Grands Ballets Canadiens
1959 *The Black Swan* (from *Swan Lake*, after Petipa; mus. Tchaikovsky), Les Grands Ballets Canadiens

**Other works include:** *Les Cent Baisers* (mus. Field), *Chemin de la croix*, *Quiproquo* (mus. Lalo), *Scuolo di ballo* (mus. Boccherini).

**PUBLICATIONS**

Maynard, Olga, "Ludmilla Chiriaeff and Les Grands Ballets Canadiens", *Dance Magazine* (New York), April 1971
Citron, Paula, "The French Canadian Experience", *Dance Magazine* (New York), April 1982
Crabb, Michael, "Les Grands Ballets Canadiens", *Dancing Times* (London), July 1982
"Out of the Box: The Improbable Adventures of Canada's French Ballet Company", *Dance and Dancers* (London), August 1982

* * *

It says much about Ludmilla Chiriaeff's vision and determination that in 1957 she gave the ambitious name "Les Grands Ballets Canadiens" to a two-year-old company with only sixteen dancers, and that under her guidance this company proved itself worthy of the name.

Ballet was part of Ludmilla Chiriaeff's world from her early years; Mikhail Fokine, with whom she would later work, was a friend of her father's. Chiriaeff received her early ballet training from Nikolaeva in Berlin and entered Colonel de Basil's Ballets Russes in 1936. During World War II she danced with the Berlin State Opera Ballet, leaving to work as a dancer, choreographer, and ballet mistress in Geneva.

In 1952 Ludmilla Chiriaeff decided to emigrate to Canada. She first settled in Toronto, but soon moved to the more welcoming city of Montreal. Here she became involved in the attempts of several young television producers to bring ballet to a mass audience through this relatively new medium. She formed Les Ballets Chiriaeff, a group of dancers which began its life in the rarified atmosphere of the television studio, but by 1955 was appearing on stage. In 1957 it became known as Les Grands Ballets Canadiens.

As director, Chiriaeff gave the company a classical foundation but at the same time did her utmost to give it a truly French-Canadian character, using indigenous folklore as the subject of her early choreography and frequently employing Canadian choreographers, designers, and composers—a tradition which has since been maintained by her successors.

Madame Chiriaeff also recognized the importance of ensuring a well-trained supply of homegrown dancers, and to this end established the Académie des Grands Ballets Canadiens. After her retirement in 1974, she spent much time on improving training and succeeded in making ballet classes part of the school curriculum in Quebec. Part of her legacy also is the École supérior de danse du Québec, so named in 1980, thirteen years after it was founded as the École supérior of Les Grands Ballets Canadiens, at the instigation of the Quebec Minister of Cultural Affairs.

Ludmilla Chiriaeff was the backbone of her company for many years, and choreographed a large number of ballets, both for stage and television, which provided the basis of her dancers' repertoire. Although her works were never recognized as particularly distinguished or original, Chiriaeff was none the less capable of constructing good, workable pieces which suited her dancers and made the best of their talents. And her continued determination, despite the odds against her and her fledgeling company (including a powerful Catholic church opposed to the exposure of too much flesh on stage), meant that her company survived its setbacks and was allowed to carry on in the tradition that she established. Canadian critic Michael Crabb wrote in 1982, "Ludmilla was and is a lady of vision and courage. At fifty-eight, she remains a stylish woman of great beauty with a personality wrapped in a slightly wistful, almost tragic air. This aura entirely belies the tough core without which its owner could never have endured the heartache and exasperation inevitably involved in building a ballet company." Like Canada's other "pioneering women"—Gweneth Lloyd and Betty Farrally of the Royal Winnipeg Ballet and Celia Franca of the National Ballet of Canada—says Crabb, "Ludmilla Chiriaeff had to be a figher and a survivor". This is exactly what she was, and her determination has paid off.

—Jessica Arah

---

## CHIRICO, Giorgio de

Italian painter and designer. Born in Volos, Greece, of Italian parents, 10 July 1888. Educated in Volos; studied drawing with Mavrudis, 1897–99, and with Carlos Barbieri and Gilleron, 1899; studied under Bolonakis and Jacobidis at Polytechnic School, Athens, 1900–06, and at Academy of Art, Munich, 1906–08. Married (1) Raissa Calza, c. 1925; (2) Isabella Packswer (nom de plume: Isabella Far), 1933. Lived in Milan, 1908–10, Florence, 1910–11, and Paris, 1911–15, exhibiting own paintings, and meeting Apollinaire, Reynal, and Picasso; clerk in the Italian army, 1915–18; associated with Carlo Carrà and "Scuola Metafisica", and "Valori Plastici" group, 1917; lived in Rome, 1919–25, and in Paris, 1925–31, becoming associated with the Surrealists; first work for the theatre, *La Giara* (*The Jar*), for the Ballets Suédois, 1924; visionary novel *Hebdomeros* published, 1929; broke with earlier style, returning to realism, 1930; later did stage designs for de Basil's Ballets Russes, Paris Opéra, and La Scala, Milan, dividing time between Paris, Italy, and United States; settled in Rome, 1945. Died in Rome, 20 November 1978.

### WORKS (Ballet design)

1924 *La Giara* (*The Jar*; chor. Börlin), Ballets Suédois, Paris
1925 *La Morte di Niobe* (chor. Krohl), Teatro Odelaschi, Rome
1929 *Le Bal* (chor. Balanchine), Diaghilev's Ballets Russes, Monte Carlo
1931 *Pulcinella* (chor. Romanov), Ballet de L'Opéra Russe à Paris, Monte Carlo
*Bacchus and Ariane* (chor. Lifar), Opéra, Paris
1937 *Les Bacchantes* (chor. Iolas), Athens
1938 *Protée* (chor. Lichine), (de Basil's) Russian Ballet, London
1944 *Amphion* (chor. Milloss), Ballet of La Scala, Rome
1945 *Danze di Galanta* (chor. Milloss), Teatro Adriano, Rome
1949 *Orfeo* (opera; mus. Monteverdi, chor. Romanov), Maggio Musicale, Florence
1951 *La Leggenda di Giuseppe* (*The Legend of Joseph*; chor. Wallmann), Ballet of La Scala, Milan
1952 *Mephistopheles* (chor. Milloss), Ballet of La Scala, Milan
1956 *Apollon musagète* (chor. Lifar), Opéra, Paris

### PUBLICATIONS

By de Chirico:
*Hebdomeros, le peintre et son génie chez l'écrivain*, Paris, 1929
*Memorie della mia vita*, 2 vols: Rome, 1945–62; as *Memoirs*, London, 1971; as *De Chirico by de Chirico*, New York, 1972
*Commedia dell'arte moderna* (with Isabella Far), Rome, 1945

About de Chirico:
De Maré, Rolf (ed.), *Les Ballets Suédois dans l'art contemporain*, Paris, 1931
Soby, James Thrall, *The Early Chirico*, New York, 1941
Stegen, I., *Die Ecole de Paris und das Theater* (dissertation), Vienna, 1966
Bruni, Claudio, *De Chirico: Catalogo generale*, 15 vols., Venice, 1971–83
*De Chirico* (catalogue), 2 vols., Rome, 1981
Strong, Roy, *Designing for the Dancer*, London, 1981
Martin, Marianne, "On de Chirico's Theater", *De Chirico: The Tate Gallery*, London and New York, 1982
Fagiolo Dell'Arco, Maurizio, *L'Opera completa di De Chirico*, Milan, 1984
Häger, Bengt, *Les Ballets Suédois*, London, 1989

* * *

The theatrical works of Giorgio de Chirico constitute a largely neglected aspect of his *oeuvre* as an artist, although he designed for over twenty productions following his theatrical début in 1924. Of his works for the ballet, three demand attention: *La Giara* (1924), his first work for the theatre, *Le Bal* (1929), and *Protée* (1938), all of which show the development of his particular attitude to theatrical space.

De Chirico's first designs for the theatre were for *La Giara*, created in 1924 for Les Ballets Suédois. With a score by Alfredo Casella, choreography by Jean Börlin, and libretto adapted by Luigi Pirandello from one of his short stories, the ballet is reputed to have been created at the wish of Rolf de Maré, director of Les Ballets Suédois, as an Italian ballet to rival Serge Diaghilev's Spanish-flavoured *Le Tricorne*. The story-line concerned a Sicilian potter, and de Chirico provided costumes which clearly recalled Sicilian peasant dress. More interesting was his set, which showed a farmhouse behind parted stage curtains, a feature which, by establishing a double space beyond the already existing stage space, questioned the nature of spatial representation in the theatre. It was this ambiguity of space to which de Chirico would constantly return in his later theatrical works.

De Chirico's best-known designs for the ballet were for *Le Bal*, a work which had its premiere in Monte Carlo in 1929 by Serge Diaghilev's Ballets Russes. With choreography by George Balanchine, music by Vittorio Rieti, and scenario by Boris Kochno, the ballet elaborated on the idea of different levels of reality, and on the relationship between appearance and reality. Such a scenario made it easy for de Chirico to continue his explorations of the ambiguous space of the stage.

With his backdrop for Scene II of *Le Bal*, de Chirico depicted a room whose space at first glance appeared closed, but which was in fact invaded by a multitude of mysterious and visionary objects and openings extending its reality into the metaphysical. On the costumes he painted architectural features, mostly classical elements such as columns and archways. These architectural features recalled the imagery used on the backcloth. By moving the static architectural elements of the backcloth into the actual stage space and, furthermore, onto moving bodies, de Chirico further questioned spatial representation and the relationship between appearance and reality.

In 1938, de Chirico designed *Protée* for the Covent Garden season of the Russian Ballet of Educational Ballets Ltd. (the temporary name for de Basil's Ballets Russes). The work was described as a choreographic tableau by David Lichine and Henry Clifford, and was performed to music by Claude Debussy. Set in a temple by the sea, the ballet concerned the god Proteus, prophet of the sea, and the unsuccessful attempts

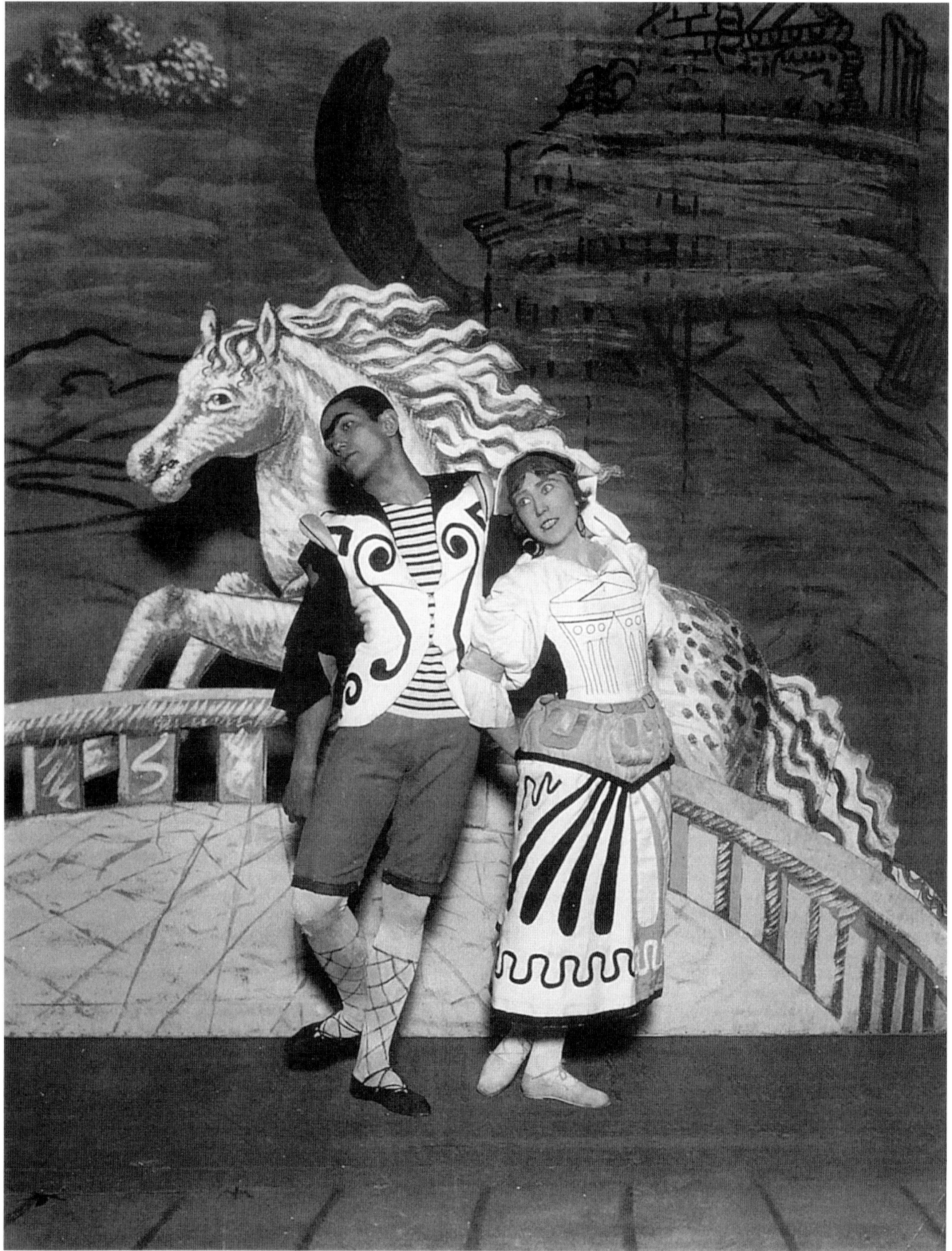

**Serge Lifar and Lydia Sokolova in *Le Bal*, 1929, with sets and costumes designed by Giorgio de Chirico**

by a group of maidens to catch him in order to learn their destiny.

De Chirico created a backdrop for *Protée* which was evocative of the prophetic role of Proteus, his associations with the classical world, and his elusiveness in the ballet. This he achieved by setting up an ambiguous relationship between objects and the space they occupied with imagery in which the sea was a force at once invading the stage space and yet gently recoiling from it, and in which classical allusions were suggested rather than stated. De Chirico's costumes for *Protée* repeated the imagery of the backcloth and, as with *Le Bal*, created further ambiguities.

In his work outside the theatre, de Chirico consistently questioned reality by painting seemingly real scenes which, on closer investigation, contained unreal elements. *La Giara* brought his explorations into the nature of reality to the stage. With *Le Bal* and *Protée* de Chirico expanded upon these investigations, focusing especially on spatial ambiguity in a way that was not possible on a two-dimensional canvas.

—Michelle Potter

---

## CHOREARTIUM

**Choreography:** Léonide Massine
**Music:** Johannes Brahms (Symphony no. 4 in E minor)
**Design:** Konstantin Tereshkovich and Eugène Lourié
**First Production:** Ballets Russes de Monte Carlo, Alhambra Theatre, London, 24 October 1933
**Principal Dancers:** Irina Baronova, Alexandra Danilova, Tatiana Riabouchinska, Nina Verchinina, Vera Zorina, Roman Jasinsky, David Lichine, Paul Petrov, Yurek Shabelevsky

**Other productions include:** Teatro Colón (revival; staged Massine); Buenos Aires, 1959. Balletto Europeo (restaged Massine); Edinburgh, 5 September 1960. Birmingham Royal Ballet (revival; staged Tatiana Leskova after Massine); Birmingham, 25 October 1991.

### PUBLICATIONS

Coton, A.V., *A Prejudice for Ballet*, London, 1938
Evans, Edwin, "The Music of *Choreartium*", *Dancing Times* (London), August 1939
Beaumont, Cyril, *Complete Book of Ballets*, revised edition, 1951
Barnes, Clive, "Massine Goes North", *Dance and Dancers* (London), November 1960
Massine, Léonide, *My Life in Ballet*, London and New York, 1968
Sorley Walker, Kathrine, *De Basil's Ballets Russes*, London, 1982
Sinclair, Janet, "*Choreartium*: Massine's Lost Ballet of 1933", *Dance and Dancers* (London), January 1986
García-Márquez, Vicente, *Les Ballets Russes*, New York, 1990
Sinclair, Janet, "*Choreartium* Born Again", *Dance and Dancers* (London), October 1991

* * *

During the course of an exceedingly prolific choreographic career, a career which for decades dominated the contemporary ballet scene, Léonide Massine always tried to follow the principles of the Diaghilev era by ensuring that the work of the choreographer, the musician (dead or alive), and the designer were treated, during the creation of a new ballet, as being of equal importance. And despite the fact that the composer in this case was long dead, yet the principle still showed quite clearly in *Choreartium*, the ballet which demonstrated to the world the possibilities inherent in "abstract, "symphonic", "plotless" ballet (descriptive adjectives were legion).

It would have been simple, even obvious (and probably at the time original and modish) to dress this ballet entirely in the leotards which were to be so frequently used for *Choreartium*'s subsequent imitations—just as it would have been simpler to play the ballet against a skycloth, possibly borrowing some ideas from the marvellously inventive lighting used by Ballets Jooss, which was just beginning to be seen outside Germany at the time. However, Massine chose to employ artists of reputation to design the sets and costumes, and the contributions of Tereshkovich and Lourié provided exactly the clean, clear, vivid, and painlessly inventive designs needed to parallel the clean, clear music of Brahms and the vivid, painlessly inventive choreography of Massine.

Massine had devoted almost two years to the creation, mental and physical, of his first "symphonic" ballet, *Les Présages*. A gamble in an entirely new style, the work in the event was an instantaneous success, and within three months of its London premiere, its successor *Choreartium* was presented. (Between these two creations, Massine had mounted a reproduction of *Le Beau Danube* and presented new works *Beach* and *Scuola di Ballo*.) A furore ensued. The audience greeted the new ballet with roars of applause. Many music critics—though not all, Ernest Newman the notable exception—tore the work to pieces, taking the odd attitude that it was in some way "wrong" to dance to a "pure" musical score (for "wrong", read "somehow immoral"), or at any rate "wrong" to dance to a symphony of Brahms, however acceptable it had become to dance to piano compositions of Chopin or Schumann and to "programme music" of Rimsky-Korsakov or Balakirev, none expressly composed for dance. Constant Lambert was one of the most vocal, and expressed the opinion that merely to graft abstract movement on to abstract music was a side alley down which ballet, if it took that course, would destroy itself as a positive art form. Some may feel that the events of the subsequent 50 years have vindicated these apprehensions, but that should not obscure the facts of the matter, which are that during the 1930s (in England at any rate), *Choreartium* was regarded as a masterpiece. Its influence on other choreographers was far-reaching—affecting, among many others, the work of the young Ashton, who produced two of his most successful works very much in line with the choreographic principles of Massine's "symphonic" ballet—*Dante Sonata* and *The Wanderer*, to the music of Liszt and Schubert.

To the audience of the 1930s the amazing thing about *Choreartium* had nothing to do with the sacrilege involved in ballet-dancing to a symphony by Brahms. What was amazing—even disconcerting, at first sight—was that here was a ballet without any trace of a theme, story, mood, place, time, period, even period costume: surely a divertissement? But that could not be so, for the dancers attacked their roles with the utmost seriousness: they did not even acknowledge that an audience was sitting there watching them, let alone grin at the stalls, or bow and curtsy to the audience before the curtain had fallen at the very end of the ballet. This absolute refusal to acknowledge the public in any way until the whole symphony was finished was the most immediately surprising thing about

**Léonide Massine and Tamara Toumanova in *Choreartium*, Ballets Russes de Monte Carlo, 1933**

*Choreartium*, and it lent an air of absolute seriousness to the performance which evoked the utmost concentration in the spectators.

None of these considerations, however, could have held much weight had it not been for the fact that the actual choreographic structure was sufficiently interesting to grasp and hold the audience's attention in the course of a long, complex work. In fact, the more often one watched this ballet, the more one realized and appreciated the mastery with which Massine sketched in his own contrasts of light and shade, strength and sweetness, in parallel to what Brahms was doing with the orchestra, and the absolute professionalism with which he manoeuvred his large and brilliant cast of dancers so that they all looked at their best, while at the same time were stretched to their full capabilities.

—Janet Sinclair

---

**CHRISTENSEN, Lew**

American dancer, choreographer, teacher, and director. Born in Brigham City, Utah, brother of dancers Harold and William (later Willam) Christensen, 9 May 1908 (some sources say 1909). Studied with uncle, Lars Christensen, and Stefano Mascagno, Utah, and at School of American Ballet, New York, from 1936; also studied with Mikhail (Michel) Fokine, Luigi Albertieri, New York. Served in the United States Army during World War II. Married ballerina Gisella Caccialanza: one son, Christopher. Early career in vaudeville with Christensen brothers, touring with Willam Christensen in vaudeville-ballet act, 1927–32; joined Albertina Rasch musical, *The Great Waltz*, 1935; soloist, American Ballet (performing at the Metropolitan Opera House as American Ballet Ensemble), 1936–37; soloist and choreographer, Ballet Caravan, 1936–40, becoming American Ballet Caravan, and touring South America, 1941; soloist, Dance Players, 1941–42; dancer, choreographer, ballet master, Ballet Society (later New York City Ballet), 1946–48; also appeared in film of musical *On Your Toes* (mus. Rodgers, chor. Balanchine; dir. Enright, 1939); also teacher: faculty member, School of American Ballet, New York, from 1946; principal choreographer, teacher, and director, San Francisco Ballet, from 1952; co-director, with Michael Smuin, San Francisco Ballet, from 1974; also ballet master, San Francisco Opera. Died in Burlingham, California, 9 October 1984.

## ROLES

1936 The Boy (cr) in *Serenata: Magic* (Balanchine), Hartford Festival, Hartford, Connecticut
Allegro Vivace (cr) in *Concerto* (later called *Classic Ballet*; Dollar, Balanchine), American Ballet Ensemble, New York
Title role (cr) in *The Bat* (Balanchine), American Ballet Ensemble, New York
Orpheus (cr) in *Orpheus and Eurydice* (opera; music Gluck, chor. Balanchine), American Ballet Ensemble and Metropolitan Opera, New York
Pas de deux (cr) in *Encounter* (also chor.), Ballet Caravan, Bennington, Vermont
Captain Zorbino (cr) in *Harlequin for President* (Loring), Ballet Caravan, Bennington, Vermont
Apollo (cr) in *Promenade* (Dollar), Ballet Caravan, Bennington, Vermont
John Rolfe (cr) in *Pocahontas* (also chor.), Ballet Caravan, Bennington, Vermont
The Bullfighter (cr) in *The Soldier and the Gypsy* (D. Coudy), Ballet Caravan, Keene, New Hampshire
Air (cr) in *Show Piece* (E. Hawkins), Ballet Caravan, Saybrook, Connecticut
Mac, the Attendant (cr) in *Filling Station* (also chor.), Ballet Caravan, Hartford, Connecticut

1937 Apollo (cr) in *Apollon Musagète* (new production of *Apollo, Leader of the Muses*; Balanchine) American Ballet, New York

1938 Principal dancer (cr) in *Air and Variations* (Dollar), Ballet Caravan, Winthrop College, Rock Hill, South Carolina
Oberon (cr) in *A Midsummer Night's Dream* (also chor.), San Francisco Opera Ballet, Portland
Pat Garrett (cr) in *Billy the Kid* (Loring), Ballet Caravan, Chicago, Illinois

1939 Wilmer J. Smith (cr) in *Charade; or, The Débutante* (also chor.), Ballet Caravan, Lancaster, Pennsylvania

1940 Prince Siegfried (cr) in *Swan Lake* (new production; W. Christensen after Petipa, Ivanov), San Francisco Opera Ballet, San Francisco

1941 Boyfriend in *Time Table* (Tudor), American Ballet Caravan, Rio de Janeiro
Lucifer (cr) in *Pastorela* (also chor., with Fernandez), American Ballet Caravan, Rio de Janeiro
Football Hero (cr) in *Juke Box* (Dollar), American Ballet Caravan, Rio de Janeiro

1946 Theme (cr) in *The Four Temperaments* (Balanchine), Ballet Society, New York

1947 The Rooster (cr) in *Renard* (*The Fox*) (Balanchine), Ballet Society, New York
Principal dancer (cr) in *Divertimento* (Balanchine), Ballet Society, New York
Puppeteer and Devil (cr) in *Punch and the Child* (Danieli), Ballet Society, New York

1948 Major-domo (cr) in *The Triumph of Bacchus and Ariadne* (Balanchine), Ballet Society, New York
Fourth Movement in *Symphony in C* (new production of *Le Palais de cristal*; Balanchine), Ballet Society, New York

**Other roles include:** The Father in *Prodigal Son* (Balanchine).

## WORKS

1936 *Encounter* (mus. Mozart), Ballet Caravan, Bennington, Vermont
*Pocahontas* (mus. E. Carter), Ballet Caravan, Bennington, Vermont

1938 *Filling Station* (mus. V. Thomson), Ballet Caravan, Hartford, Connecticut
*A Midsummer Night's Dream* (mus. Mendelssohn), San Francisco Opera Ballet, Portland

1939 *Charade; or, The Débutante* (mus. American melodies, arranged by T. Rittmann), Ballet Caravan, Lancaster, Pennsylvania

1941 *Pastorela* (with José Fernandez; mus. P. Bowles), American Ballet Caravan, Rio de Janeiro

1942 *Jinx* (mus. Britten), Dance Players (restaged New York City Ballet and San Francisco Ballet, 1949)

1947 *Blackface* (mus. C. Harman), Ballet Society, New York

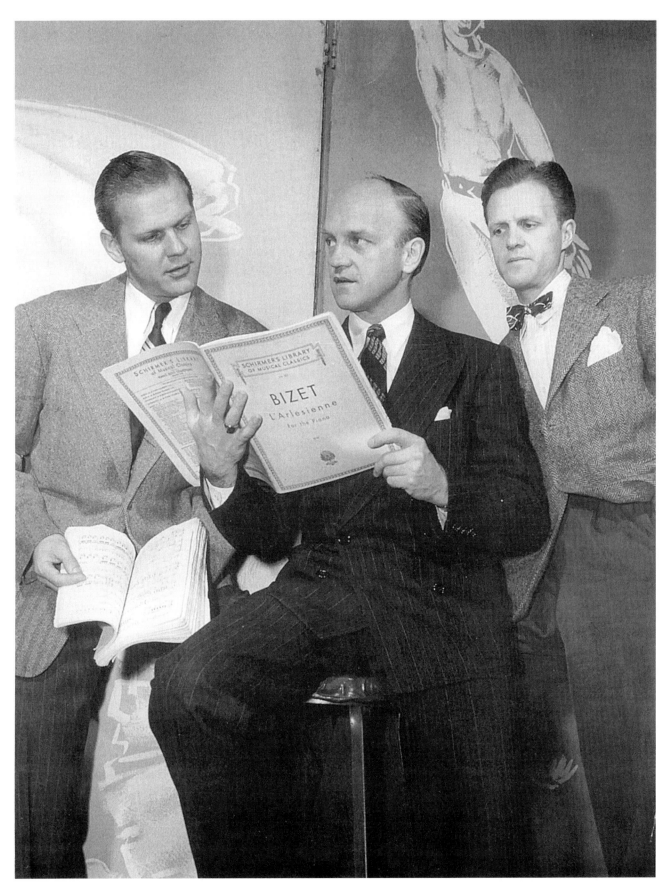

**The Christensens, from left to right: Lew, Willam and Harold Christensen, c.1940**

1949 *The Story of a Dancer* (mus. Handel; narration Lew Christensen), San Francisco Ballet, San Francisco
1950 *Prelude: To Performance* (revised version of *The Story of a Dancer*; mus. Handel; narration Lew Christensen), San Francisco Ballet, San Francisco
1951 *Divertimenti* (with W. Christensen, after Petipa; mus. Tchaikovsky), San Francisco Ballet, San Francisco
*Le Gourmand* (mus. Mozart), San Francisco Ballet, San Francisco
1952 *American Scene* (mus. Harman), San Francisco Ballet, San Francisco
1953 *Con Amore* (mus. Rossini), San Francisco Ballet, San Francisco (restaged New York City Ballet, 1953)
*The Festival* (mus. Mozart), San Francisco Ballet, San Rafael
1954 *Heuriger* (mus. Mozart), San Francisco Ballet, San Francisco
*The Dryad* (mus. Schubert), San Francisco Ballet, San Francisco
*Beauty and the Shepherd* (later called *A Masque of Beauty and the Shepherd*; mus. Gluck), San Francisco Ballet, San Francisco
*The Nutcracker* (mus. Tchaikovsky), San Francisco Ballet, San Francisco
1955 *The Tarot* (mus. Tchaikovsky), San Francisco Ballet, San Francisco
1957 *Emperor Norton* (mus. Duke), San Francisco Ballet, San Francisco
1958 *The Lady of Shalott* (mus. Bliss), San Francisco Ballet, Berkeley, California
*Beauty and the Beast* (mus. Tchaikovsky), San Francisco Ballet, San Francisco
1959 *Sinfonia* (mus. Boccherini), San Francisco Ballet, Vallejo, California
*Divertissement d'Auber* I (mus. Auber), San Francisco Ballet, Vallejo, California
*Caprice* (mus. von Suppé), San Francisco Ballet, Vallejo, California
1960 *Danza Brillante* (mus. Mendelssohn), San Francisco Ballet, San Francisco
*Esmeralda: Pas de deux* (mus. Pugni), San Francisco Ballet, San Francisco
*Variations de Ballet* (with Balanchine; mus. Glazunov), San Francisco Ballet, San Francisco
1961 *Original Sin* (mus. Lewis), San Francisco Ballet, San Francisco
*St. George and the Dragon* (mus. Hindemith), San Francisco Ballet, San Francisco
*Shadows* (mus. Hindemith), San Francisco Ballet Theatre (Workshop), San Francisco
*Prokofiev Waltzes* (mus. Prokofiev), San Francisco Ballet Theatre (Workshop), San Francisco
1962 *Jest of Cards* (mus. Krenek), San Francisco Ballet, San Francisco
*Bach Concert* (mus. Bach), San Francisco Ballet, San Francisco
1963 *Divertissement d'Auber* II (mus. Auber), San Francisco Ballet, Phoenix, Arizona
*Fantasma* (mus. Prokofiev), San Francisco Ballet, Tucson, Arizona
*Dance Variations* (mus. Rieti), San Francisco Ballet Theatre (Workshop), San Francisco
1965 *Life: A Do it Yourself Disaster* ("A Pop Art Ballet"; mus. Ives), San Francisco Ballet, San Francisco
*Lucifer* (mus. Hindemith), San Francisco Ballet, San Francisco
1966 *Pas de Six* (mus. Lumbye), San Francisco Ballet, Merced, California
1967 *Symphony in D* (mus. Cherubini), San Francisco Ballet, San Francisco
*Il Distratto* (mus. Haydn), San Francisco Ballet Theatre (Workshop), San Francisco
*The Nutcracker* (new version; mus. Tchaikovsky), San Francisco Ballet, San Francisco
1968 *Three Movements for the Short-haired* (mus. Lewis), San Francisco Ballet, San Francisco
*The Magical Flutist* (mus. Ponchielli), San Francisco Ballet, San Francisco
1971 *Airs de Ballet* (mus. Grétry), San Francisco Ballet, San Francisco
1972 *Tingel-tangel-taenze* (mus. Johann Strauss Jr. and Sr., Josef Strauss, Lumbye), San Francisco Ballet, San Francisco
1973 *Cinderella* (with Smuin; mus. Prokofiev), San Francisco Ballet, San Francisco
*Don Juan* (mus. Rodrigo), San Francisco Ballet, San Francisco
1976 *Stravinsky Pas de Deux* (mus. Stravinsky), San Francisco Ballet, San Francisco
1977 *The Ice Maiden* (mus. Stravinsky), San Francisco Ballet, San Francisco
1979 *Scarlatti Portfolio* (mus. Scarlatti, orchestrated Lees), San Francisco Ballet, San Francisco
1981 *Vivaldi Concerto Grosso* (mus. Vivaldi), San Francisco Ballet, San Francisco

Also staged:
1955 *Renard* (after Balanchine; mus. Stravinsky), San Francisco Ballet, San Francisco
1959 *Danses Concertantes* (after Balanchine; mus. Stravinsky), San Francisco Ballet, San Francisco
1964 *The Seven Deadly Sins* (after Balanchine; mus. Weill), San Francisco Ballet, San Francisco

**Other works include:** For San Francisco Opera—Dances in operas *La Gioconda* (mus. Ponchielli; 1948), *Carmen* (mus. Bizet; 1951, 1960, 1962), *Romeo and Juliet* (mus. Gounod; 1951), *Boris Godunov* (mus. Mussorgsky; 1951), *La Forza del Destino* (mus. Verdi; 1951), *La Traviata* (mus. Verdi; 1951), *Rigoletto* (mus. Verdi; 1951, 1954, 1961), *Lucia di Lammermoor* (mus. Donizetti; 1954, 1961), *The Portuguese Inn* (mus. Cherubini; 1954), *Manon* (mus. Massenet; 1954), *The Marriage of Figaro* (mus. Mozart; 1954), *Joan of Arc at the Stake* (chor. with W. Christensen; mus. Honegger; 1954), *Louise* (mus. Charpentier; 1955), *Don Giovanni* (mus. Mozart; 1955), *Andrea Chenier* (mus. Giordano; 1955), *Aida* (mus. Verdi; 1960, 1961), *Cosi Fan Tutte* (mus. Mozart; 1960), *Blood Moon* (mus. Dello Joio; 1961), *Un Ballo in Maschera* (mus. Verdi; 1961), *Faust* (mus. Gounod; 1962), *The Daughter of the Regiment* (mus. Donizetti; 1962), *Falstaff* (mus. Verdi; 1962); for Pacific Opera Company—*Hansel and Gretel* (mus. Humperdinck; 1951).

## PUBLICATIONS

By Christensen:

"Story and Storyless Ballets", *Dance Magazine* (New York), July 1956
"An Informal Interview", *Dance Digest* (San Jose, California), 2 parts: February, March 1958
Interview in Newman, Barbara, *Striking a Balance: Dancers Talk About Dancing*, Boston, 1982
Contribution to Steinberg, Cobett, *The San Francisco Ballet: The First 50 Years*, San Francisco, 1983

About Christensen:
Barzel, Ann, "A Gallery of American Dancers: Lew Christensen", *Dance Magazine* (New York), June 1942
Beaumont, Cyril, *Supplement to Complete Book of Ballets*, London, 1945
Maynard, Olga, *The American Ballet*, Philadelphia, 1959
Como, B., and Philp, R., "The Christensen Brothers", *Dance Magazine* (New York), June 1973
Maynard, Olga, "The Christensen Brothers: An American Dancing Dynasty", *Dance Magazine* (New York), June 1973
Reynolds, Nancy, *Repertory in Review*, New York, 1977
Ross, Janice, "Lew Christensen: An American Original", *Dance Magazine* (New York), December 1981
Von Buchau, S., "Native Dancer", *Ballet News* (New York), May 1982
Kirstein, Lincoln, *Ballet: Bias and Belief*, New York, 1983
Leivick, L., "Knocking Down Doors: San Francisco Ballet Turns Fifty", *Dance Magazine* (New York), February 1983
Steinberg, Cobett, *The San Francisco Ballet: The First 50 Years*, San Francisco, 1983
Kirstein, Lincoln, "American Apollo", *Ballet News* (New York), January 1985
Mason, Francis, "Lew Christensen", *Ballet Review* (New York), Winter 1985

* * *

The youngest of the Christensen brothers, Lew began serious ballet training at an earlier age than either Willam or Harold. Driven by Willam's vision and determination, Lew acquired the most advanced technique of the three brothers. His virtuosity formed the centerpiece of the vaudeville act in which he toured with Willam (and later, Harold) and their partners. Over six feet tall, blond, and strikingly good-looking, Lew was known early on for his ability to execute quick, well-placed pirouettes and multiple tours.

That virtuosity was honed by Balanchine, who welcomed Lew and Harold into the American Ballet Ensemble during its controversial residency at the Metropolitan Opera. In title roles in *Orpheus and Eurydice* and *Apollon Musagète*, Lew gained fame as America's first "home grown" danseur noble of the twentieth century. As the first American to dance the role of Apollo, Lew set a standard for future performers. According to Kirstein, "His distinguished interpretation of this difficult part was more golden baroque, more the Apollo Belvedere than Serge Lifar's dark, electric, archaic animalism of nine years before. But at last here was an American dancer with his own individual classical attitude, using his six feet of height with a suave and monumental elegance which was wholly athletic, frank, musical, and joyful, and wholly unlike the smaller-scaled grace of the Russian prototype."

Lew's obvious talent and unaffected style had a strong impact on Lincoln Kirstein and contributed to the founding of Ballet Caravan, an all-American company dedicated to proving the viability of American themes and dancers in an art form then associated almost exclusively with Europe and Russia. A charter member and leading dancer of the Caravan, Lew also served as the troupe's ballet master and created several ballets for its repertory, including *Filling Station*, one of the first ballets to feature stock American characters rather than European ones.

Along with his wife, Balanchine ballerina Gisella Caccialanza (one of Enricho Cecchetti's last protégées), Lew figured prominently in the forerunners to New York City Ballet: the American Ballet, Ballet Caravan, the 1941 American Ballet Caravan, and, after World War II, Ballet Society. Lew's rise to stardom within the Balanchine companies was cut short by World War II, which he endured as an infantry soldier in France. Returning to the Kirstein/Balanchine fold after the war, Lew regained a measure of his former technique, created new roles, and served as Ballet Society's ballet master. Kirstein saw Lew as the logical heir to Balanchine's company at some future date, but Lew was eventually drawn back into the family circle; he left New York to join Willam and Harold in San Francisco.

The relative geographical isolation of San Francisco allowed Lew to develop as a company director and choreographer without the influence exerted by Balanchine's genius. Between 1950 and his death, he choreographed over 70 ballets and operas, experimenting in a variety of styles: the tongue-in-cheek, neo-Romantic *Con Amore*; other narrative ballets such as *The Lady of Shalott*, *Beauty and the Beast*, *The Nutcracker*, and the jazzy and titillating *Original Sin*; *Jest of Cards*, to Ernest Krenek's avant-garde score; the Pop-Art-inspired *Life: A Do It Yourself Disaster*; and technically demanding neo-classical works such as *Sinfonia*, *Divertissement d'Auber*, and *Stravinsky Pas de Deux*. Many critics felt he never shook off the influence of Balanchine's style, although Lew himself felt there were major differences between his creative work and that of his most influential teacher. Drawing on his experience as a virtuoso performer, he created demanding roles for men, from "Mac" in *Filling Station* to the solo "Hoop Dance" in *Scarlatti Portfolio*, which won a bronze medal for choreography at the International Ballet Competition in Jackson, Mississippi (1979).

As a teacher working with Harold, who directed the San Francisco Ballet (SFB) School from the 1940s through to the 1970s, Lew developed SFB's first generation of neo-classical dancers. Lew's success as a teacher made his job as company director more difficult; over the years he lost some of his best dancers—including Conrad Ludlow, Cynthia Gregory, and Terry Orr—to larger companies in New York. But receipt of Ford Foundation grants in the late 1950s and early 1960s consolidated San Francisco's importance as a center for ballet training outside of New York City, and constituted an important step in the decentralization of ballet in America.

—Debra Sowell

---

**CHRISTENSEN, Willam**

American dancer, choreographer, teacher, and ballet director. Born William (later changed name to Willam) F. Christensen in Brigham City, Utah, 27 August 1902. Studied social and folk dances with father, Chris Christensen; studied ballet with uncle, Lars Peter Christensen, California, 1920–26, and with Stefano Mascagno, 1922–26; also studied and performed with Mikhail Fokine, Summer 1934. Married (1) Mignon Trieste Lee, 1929; 2 children: William Lee Christensen and Roxanne Gisella Christensen Selznick; (2) Florence Goeglein, 1973. Early career in vaudeville with brother, Lew Christensen, touring 1927–32; founder, director, and teacher, William F. Christensen Ballet, Portland, Oregon, 1932–37; soloist, San Francisco Opera Ballet, 1937; ballet master, San Francisco Opera Ballet, 1938–42; director, San Francisco Ballet, 1942–51; professor of Dance, University of Utah, Salt Lake City, 1951–67; director, Utah Civic Ballet and Ballet West, Salt Lake City, 1963–78. Recipient: Distinguished Teaching Award, University of Utah, 1965; Distinguished Research Professor, University of Utah, 1970–71; Fellow, Utah Academy of Sciences, Arts and Letters, 1972; Honorary Doctorate of Fine

Arts, Utah State University, 1973; Capezio Dance Award, 1984.

## WORKS

1935 *Chopiniana* (or *Chopinade*, after Fokine; mus. Chopin), Portland Creative Theatre and School of Music and Dancing, Portland, Oregon (staged San Francisco Opera Ballet, 1937)
1936 *Les Visions de Massenet* (mus. Massenet, arranged by Mischa Pelz), William F. Christensen Ballet, Municipal Auditorium, Portland, Oregon
*A Spanish Romance* (mus. Rimsky-Korsakov), William F. Christensen Ballet, Portland, Oregon
*A Roumanian Wedding Festival* (mus. Enesco), William F. Christensen Ballet, Portland, Oregon
*Coeur de Glace* (*The Princess With the Frozen Heart*; mus. Mozart), William F. Christensen Ballet, Portland, Oregon
*L'Amant Rêvé* (*The Dream Lover*; mus. Weber), Municipal Auditorium, Portland, Oregon
*Ballet from The Bartered Bride* (mus. Smetana), William F. Christensen Ballet, Portland, Oregon
*Bolero* (mus. Ravel), William F. Christensen Ballet, Portland, Oregon
1937 *Promenade and Minuet* (mus. Gluck), William F. Christensen Ballet, Portland, Oregon
*Gigue Variations* (mus. Gluck), William F. Christensen Ballet, Portland, Oregon
*Bourrée Fantasque* (mus. Chabrier), William F. Christensen Ballet, Portland, Oregon
*Capriccio Espagnol* (mus. Rimsky-Korsakov), San Francisco Opera Ballet, Santa Cruz, California
1938 *Romeo and Juliet* (mus. Tchaikovsky), San Francisco Opera Ballet, Sacramento
*Ballet Impromptu* (*A Bach Suite*; mus. Bach), San Francisco Opera Ballet, San Francisco
*In Vienna* (also *In Old Vienna*; mus. Strauss), San Francisco Opera Ballet, San Francisco
*Le Coq d'Or* (opera-ballet; mus. Rimsky-Korsakov), San Francisco Opera Ballet, San Francisco
1939 *Faust* (mus. Gounod), San Francisco Opera Ballet, San Francisco
*American Interlude* (mus. Turner), San Francisco Opera Ballet, San Francisco
1940 *A Midsummer Night's Dream* (mus. Mendelssohn), San Francisco Opera Ballet, San Francisco
*And Now the Brides* (mus. Berens), San Francisco Opera Ballet, Burlingame, California
1941 *Tarantella* (mus. Respighi), Stern Grove, San Francisco
1942 *Scènes de Ballet* (Suite of Divertissements; mus. Beethoven and others), San Francisco Ballet, San Francisco
*Winter Carnival* (mus. Strauss, arranged Fritz Berens), San Francisco Ballet, San Francisco
*Amor Espagnol* (mus. Massenet), San Francisco Ballet, San Francisco
1943 *Sonata Pathétique* (mus. Beethoven), Garden Court, Palace Hotel, San Francisco
*Hansel and Gretel* (mus. Humperdinck), San Francisco Ballet, San Francisco
1944 *Triumph of Hope* (mus. Franck), San Francisco Ballet, San Francisco
*Prince Siegfried* (mus. Tchaikovsky), San Francisco Ballet, San Francisco
*Le Bourgeois Gentilhomme* ("Ballet Pantomime"; mus. Lully), War Memorial Opera House, San Francisco
*The Nutcracker* (mus. Tchaikovsky), San Francisco Ballet, San Francisco
1945 *Pyramus and Thisbe* (mus. Berens), San Francisco Ballet, San Rafael, California
*Blue Plaza* (mus. Copeland with Jose Manero), San Francisco Ballet, San Francisco
1947 *Dr. Pantalone* (mus. Scarlatti, arranged Berens), San Francisco Ballet, San Francisco
*Parranda* (mus. Gould), San Francisco Civic Ballet, San Francisco
1949 *Vivaldi Concerto* (mus Vivaldi), San Francisco Ballet, San Francisco
*Danza Brillante* (mus. Mendelssohn), San Francisco Ballet, San Francisco
1950 *The Nothing Doing Bar* (mus. Milhaud), University Theatre Ballet, San Francisco
1951 *Les Maîtresses de Lord Byron* (mus. Liszt), San Francisco Ballet, San Francisco
1952 *The Snow Queen* (mus. Tyrell), Young People's Theatre, University of Utah, Salt Lake City
1953 *Le Chausseur Maudit* (mus. Franck), University of Utah Theatre Ballet, Salt Lake City
*The Creatures of Prometheus* (mus. Beethoven), San Francisco Ballet, San Francisco
1955 *Tchaikovsky Ballet* (also *Divertimenti from Tchaikovsky Ballets*; mus. Tchaikovsky), University of Utah Theatre Ballet, Salt Lake City
1956 *Concerto* (mus. Bach), University of Utah Theatre Ballet, Salt Lake City
1957 *Crown of Joy* (mus. Mendelssohn), University of Utah Theatre Ballet, Salt Lake City
*Something in the Wind* (mus. Stravinsky), University of Utah Theatre Ballet, Salt Lake City
*Caprice de Paree* (mus. Ibert), University of Utah Theatre Ballet, Salt Lake City
1959 *Symphonia* (mus. Mozart), University of Utah Theatre Ballet, Salt Lake City
1960 *Variations in Contrast* (mus. Mozart), University of Utah Theatre Ballet, Salt Lake City
*La Fille Naïve* (mus. Auber), University of Utah Theatre Ballet, Salt Lake City
1962 *Garden of Evil* (mus. Shostakovitch), University of Utah Theatre Ballet, Salt Lake City
1963 *Blue Tournament* (mus. Handel), University of Utah Theatre Ballet, Salt Lake City
*Toxcatl* (mus. Hatton), University of Utah Theatre Ballet, Salt Lake City
1964 *La Valse* (mus. Ravel), Utah Civic Ballet, Salt Lake City
1965 *Pas de Six* (mus. Nicolai), Utah Civic Ballet, Salt Lake City
1967 *Romantica* (mus. Dvořák), Utah Civic Ballet, Salt Lake City
*Firebird* (mus. Stravinsky), Utah Civic Ballet, Salt Lake City
1969 *Bravura* (mus. Chabrier), Ballet West, Merced, California
1970 *Cinderella* (mus. Prokofiev), Ballet West, University of Utah, Salt Lake City
1972 *Mozartiana* (mus. Tchaikovsky), Ballet West, University of Utah, Salt Lake City
1974 *Jubilee* (mus. Shostakovitch), Ballet West, University of Utah, Salt Lake City
*Women Remembered* (mus. James Prigmore), Ballet West, University of Utah, Salt Lake City

Also staged:
1940 *Swan Lake* (after Petipa, Ivanov; mus. Tchaikovsky), San Francisco Opera Ballet, San Francisco
1944 *Coppélia* (after Petipa, Cecchetti; mus. Delibes), San Francisco Opera Ballet, San Francisco
1951 *Divertimenti* (with Lew Christensen, after Petipa), San Francisco Ballet, San Francisco
1969 *La Bayadère*, Act IV (after Petipa; mus. Minkus), Ballet West, University of Utah, Salt Lake City
1971 *Paquita* Pas de Deux (after Petipa; mus. Minkus), Ballet West, University of Utah, Salt Lake City

**Other works include:** for San Francisco Opera—dances in operas *Andrea Chenier* (mus. Giordano; 1938), *Don Giovanni* (mus. Mozart; 1938), *Martha* (mus. Flotow; 1938), *Die Meistersinger* (mus. Wagner; 1938), *La Forza del Destino* (mus. Verdi; 1938), *Rigoletto* (mus. Verdi; 1939), *La Traviata* (mus. Verdi; 1939), *Lakme* (mus. Delibes; 1940), *The Masked Ball* (mus. Verdi; 1940), *Carmen* (mus. Bizet; 1940), *Aida* (mus. Verdi; 1940), *Tannhäuser* (mus. Wagner; 1941), *The Daughter of the Regiment* (mus. Donizetti; 1941), *The Bartered Bride* (mus. Smetana; 1942), *Lucia di Lammermoor* (mus. Donizetti; 1942), *Faust* (mus. Gounod; 1942), *Die Fledermaus* (mus. Strauss; 1942), *Samson et Dalila* (mus. Saint-Saëns; 1943), *La Forza del Destino* (mus. Verdi; 1943), *The Tales of Hoffman* (mus. Offenbach; 1945), *Boris Godunov* (mus. Mussorgsky; 1946), *Romeo and Juliet* (mus. Gounod; 1947), *Falstaff* (mus. Verdi; 1948), *La Gioconda* (mus. Ponchielli; 1948), *The Marriage of Figaro* (mus. Mozart; 1950), *Hansel and Gretel* (mus. Humperdinck; 1951), *Mefistofele* (mus. Boito; 1952), *Turandot* (mus. Puccini; 1953), *The Portuguese Inn* (mus. Cherubini; 1954), *Joan of Arc at the Stake* (mus. Honegger; chor. with Lew Christensen; 1954), *Macbeth* (mus. Verdi; 1955), *Il Trovatore* (mus. Verdi; 1956), *The Elixir of Love* (mus. Donizetti; 1956), *Orfeo ed Euridice* (mus. Gluck; 1959).

## PUBLICATIONS

Maynard, Olga, *The American Ballet*, Philadelphia, 1959
Hey, Nigel, "Professor in Ballet Slippers", *Dance Magazine* (New York), May 1963
Maynard, Olga, "The Christensens: An American Dance Dynasty", *Dance Magazine* (New York), June 1973
Steinberg, Cobett, *San Francisco Ballet: The First Fifty Years*, San Francisco, 1983

* * *

The oldest of the three dancing Christensen brothers from Utah, Willam began serious ballet training in his teens after a thorough education in music and social dancing. From their relatives and from the family's chief instructor, Stefano Mascagno, Willam and his brothers (Harold and Lew) inherited a strong bias favoring the classical tradition in dance, a mindset that put them in opposition to the experimental forms of the early twentieth century and gave direction to their lives' work. Willam's ardent desire for a performing career, coupled with the need to supplement the family income, propelled him into the vaudeville circuits, which he and Lew (later, Harold and Lew) and their partners toured in a ballet act studded with dramatic tours de force.

Throughout his career, Willam functioned as an instigator, a builder of companies and a promoter of ballet away from the traditional cultural centers of the American East Coast. When his wife's illness forced them to give up vaudeville, Willam not only started up a successful ballet school in Portland, but also founded a fledgeling company there. Upon his move to San Francisco, he soon added the responsibilities of ballet master of the San Francisco Opera Ballet to the originally offered position of First Dancer. When World War II caused the Opera to dismantle its ballet troupe, Willam and Harold bought the opera's ballet school and established the independent San Francisco Ballet. Together they succeeded in keeping the school and company functioning through the shortages of the war years and through later periods of fluctuating patronage and unstable community support. Willam's idealistic commitment to ballet was matched by a warm and generous personality, impeccable manners, and the ability to work congenially with others in promoting the fortunes of his company.

As a dancer, Willam excelled in demi-caractère roles which benefited from his gift for mimicry and character delineation. As a choreographer he gained inspiration from his study with Fokine (Willam choreographed his own version of *Les Sylphides*, entitled *Chopiniana*, and a version of *Le Spectre de la Rose* entitled *L'Amant Rêvé*) and from the example of Massine's narrative ballets, which provided models for works such as *In Vienna* and *Winter Carnival*. Willam's strength as a choreographer lay in his ability to make even inexperienced dancers look good on stage and to suggest broadly-drawn characterizations in a repertory that tended toward the demi-caractère. He also choreographed successfully for the San Francisco Opera, providing choreography for opera productions another seventeen years after San Francisco Ballet became an independent entity.

The San Francisco years were the high point of Willam's career; there he achieved the distinction of being the first American choreographer to stage full-length productions of *Coppélia*, *Swan Lake*, and *The Nutcracker*. To keep the company functioning between opera seasons, he insisted on touring. Never one to minimize his talents or opportunities, Willam's goal was a large touring company modelled on the various incarnations of the Ballet Russe. While, realistically, he could not hope to match the Ballet Russe companies in star power or elaborate productions, his grass-roots tours throughout the west and mid-west introduced thousands of Americans to the classics he revived. Although early in his career he changed his name from "William" to "Willam" to meet the expectations of those who considered ballet a foreign art form, he promoted American dancers through his companies, and challenged Russian hegemony by staging his own versions of Russian classics. At the same time, he reinforced the traditions of glamour and company hierarchies associated with the classical dance.

The final phase of Willam's career, his transfer from the economically uncertain world of professional ballet to the more stable environment of a university, was again prompted by his wife's steadily declining health. Consciously separating himself from the academic tradition in which modern dance was taught in departments or colleges of physical education, Willam established conservatory-style ballet training within the University of Utah's Theatre Department. Employing tactics similar to those that had promoted his companies in Portland and San Francisco, he established a student performing group, marshalled community support, orchestrated local performances and extended tours, and finally received a prestigious Ford Foundation grant which allowed him to turn the student group into a professional company (now Ballet West).

Willam's legacy as a builder of companies is matched by his contribution as a teacher. In Portland he discovered and nurtured the talents of Janet Reed and Mattlyn Gavers; from his San Francisco company the likes of James Starbuck, Onna White, Peter Nelson, Jocelyn Vollmar, Harold Lang, Scott

Douglas, Norman Thompson, and Carolyn George went east to build reputations in larger companies; and in Utah he provided early training for Michael Smuin, Kent Stowell, Finis Jhung, Bart Cook, and Jay Jolley.

—Debra Sowell

---

## CINDERELLA

**Choreography:** Frederick Ashton
**Music:** Sergei Prokofiev
**Design:** Jean-Denis Malclès (scenery and costumes)
**Libretto:** Frederick Ashton (after the fairy tale by Charles Perrault)
**First Production:** Sadler's Wells Ballet, Royal Opera House, London, 23 December 1948
**Principal Dancers:** Moira Shearer (Cinderella), Michael Somes (Prince), Frederick Ashton, Robert Helpmann (Stepsisters), Alexander Grant (The Jester)

**Other productions include:** Royal Ballet (new production; restaged and revised Ashton, designs Henry Bardon and David Walker, additional music Prokofiev, orchestrated John Lanchbery), with Margot Fonteyn (Cinderella), David Blair (Prince), Ashton and Helpmann (Stepsisters); London, 23 December 1965. Australian Ballet (staged Robert Mead, design Kristian Fredrikson), with Lucette Aldous (Cinderella); Sydney, 17 March 1972. PACT Ballet (staged John Hart), with Dawn Weller (Cinderella); Johannesburg, 25 August 1972.

Bolshoi Ballet (original production to score; chor. Rostislav Zakharov, design Peter Williams), as *Zolushka*, with Olga Lepeshinskaya (Zolushka) and Mikhail Gabovich (Prince); Moscow, 21 November 1945. Kirov Ballet (new version; chor. Konstantin Sergeyev, design Boris Erdman), as *Zolushka*, with Natalia Dudinskaya (Zolushka) and Konstantin Sergeyev (Prince); Leningrad, 8 April 1946. Ballet of La Scala (new version; chor. Alfred Rodrigues), with Violette Verdy (Cinderella); Milan, 15 December 1955. Théâtre des Champs-Elysées (new version; chor. Vaslav Orlikovsky); Paris, 4 December 1963. National Ballet of Canada (new version; chor. Celia Franca); Toronto, 15 April 1968. National Ballet of Washington (new version; chor. Ben Stevenson, design Edward Haynes and Norman McDowell), with Gaye Fulton (Cinderella) and Desmond Kelly (Prince); Washington D.C., 24 April 1970. Ballet of La Scala (new version; chor. Paolo Bortoluzzi); Milan, 16 March 1977. Paris Opéra Ballet (new version; chor. Rudolf Nureyev), as *Cendrillon*, with Sylvie Guillem (Cendrillon); Paris, 25 October 1986. Ballet Theatre of the Kremlin (new version; chor. Vasily Vasiliev); Moscow, 1991.

**Other choreographic treatments of story:** François Decombe Albert (London, 1822), Marius Petipa, Enrico Cecchetti, and Lev Ivanov (St. Petersburg, 1893), Fred Farren and Alexander Genée (London, 1906), Andrée Howard (London, 1935), Mikhail Fokine (London, 1938), Robert de Warren (Manchester, 1979), Peter Darrell (Aberdeen, 1979), Walter Gore (Brisbane, 1975).

### PUBLICATIONS


Dmitriev, Nikolai, "A New Moscow Ballet", *Dancing Times* (London), December 1944

Volkov, Nikolai Dmitrievitch, "*Cinderella*: New Soviet Ballet", *Theatre World* (London), March 1946

Barnes, Clive, "*Cinderella*", *Dance and Dancers* (London), January 1961

Balanchine, George, with Mason, Francis, *Balanchine's Complete Stories of the Great Ballets*, Garden City, N.Y., 1977

Vaughan, David, *Frederick Ashton and His Ballets*, London, 1977

Milnes, Rodney, "Prokofiev's Ballet Scores: Part II", *Dance Gazette* (London), October 1984


* * *

There are many versions of the story of Cinderella (the earliest was written down in China in the ninth century), and it has been the basis for a long list of pantomimes, operas, and ballets. The earliest *Cinderella* ballet proper was by Duport in Vienna in 1813, although Drury Lane's *Cinderella* ten years earlier had a ballet divertissement of Loves and Graces, introduced by Venus. London's first complete *Cinderella* ballet was seen in 1822, the year Paris first heard Rossini's opera *La Cenerentola*. Petipa choreographed *Cinderella* for the Maryinsky in 1893—it was in this splendid production that Pierina Legnani first performed in Russia her celebrated feat of 32 consecutive fouettés—but none of the choreography has survived. Adeline Genée first danced Cinderella at the Empire, Leicester Square, on Twelfth Night 1906, and 29 years later to the day Andrée

Ekaterina Maximova with the Bolshoi Ballet in Zakharov's *Cinderella*, Moscow, 1971

**Robert Helpmann and Frederick Ashton as the sisters in Ashton's *Cinderella*, London, 1949**

Howard choreographed her one-act *Cinderella* (in which Ashton was the elegant Prince) for Rambert's Ballet Club at the Mercury Theatre, Notting Hill. Certainly Ashton was influenced in his own *Cinderella* by Howard's version, and his decision to have two men dance the Ugly Sisters owes more to Fokine's example in his *Cinderella*, choreographed for de Basil's Ballet Russe and first seen in London at the Royal Opera House on 19 July 1938, than it does to pantomime tradition.

Prokofiev had begun composition on the score for *Cinderella* in 1941 but, because of the war and his opera *War and Peace*, the orchestration was not completed until 1944. The music was choreographed first for the Bolshoi by Rostislav Zakharov in 1945 and then for the Kirov by Konstantin Sergeyev in 1946. Olga Lepeshinskaya created Cinderella in Moscow (where Ulanova, who alternated with her, had great success in the role) and Dudinskaya first danced it in Leningrad. Prokofiev and his collaborators were guided by Perrault's version of the story and by the great Tchaikovsky ballet scores which themselves served the structure of Petipa's choreography. Prokofiev wrote that he conceived *Cinderella* (which he dedicated to Tchaikovsky) "as a classical ballet with variations, adagios, pas de deux, etc. I see Cinderella not only as a fairy-tale character but also as a real person, feeling, experiencing, and moving among us", and again: "What I wished to express above all in the music of *Cinderella* was the poetic love of Cinderella and the Prince, the birth and flowering of that love, the obstacles in its path and finally the dream fulfilled."

Frederick Ashton first considered the idea of composing a full-evening ballet as early as 1939 when the Vic-Wells *Sleeping Princess* had proved so successful, but because of the war these ambitions were shelved. Early in 1946, though, in a speech at the Soviet Theatre Exhibition, de Valois said she could not wait to see the first full-length English classical ballet, and during 1946 and 1947 there were constant rumours of possible three-act ballet scores. At one point Delibes' *Sylvia* seemed the most likely choice (that came in 1952 and was Ashton's second full-length ballet), but in the late spring of 1948 Prokofiev's *Cinderella* was selected as the score Ashton would choreograph.

Ashton had heard—and liked—quite a lot of the Prokofiev music and he thought Perrault's story a good one. In the event Ashton cut some of the music, notably the third-act scene showing the Prince's journey in search of Cinderella (a pretext for a divertissement of national dances) and a shorter dance of Grasshoppers and Dragonflies after the Fairy Summer's variation in the first act.

Ashton's *Cinderella* is his own realized dream of a Petipa ballet, and the ballet itself enacts the realization of dreams, notably Cinderella's own. When we first see her she is a demi-caractère dancer dreaming of being a ballerina—that seems to be the balletic point of her solo with the broomstick in the kitchen—and it is as a ballerina that she magically enters the ballroom, stepping on pointe down the stairs and advancing in pas de bourrée to the front of the stage. Back in the kitchen she recalls the slipper (or rather the pointe shoe) that she carries in her apron; the shoe is the clue to her dream and persuades her it was true. The Prince finds Cinderella, but in his arms she discovers her own identity as a ballerina: her dream of herself has been realized.

The choreography of *Cinderella* is full of dreams, some most definitely unfulfilled. In the ballroom, the put-upon, shy Ugly

Sister—significantly Ashton's own role—performs a Petipa figure that amounts to her dream of being Odile at Siegfried's ball or the Sugar Plum Fairy. She is in fact full of choreographic dreams, and that is the clue to her character (as is the fact that she has Edith Sitwell's nose). Again in the ballroom the bossy Ugly Sister does a fish-dive with her suitor, a dream of the final pas de deux in *The Sleeping Beauty*.

Ashton's *Cinderella* may have its faults—the first act seems long, the third rather short—but it contains superlative choreography, most notably in the divertissement for the Fairies of the Seasons. *Cinderella* may serve as a danced pantomime for children, but more importantly it engages the adult mind.

—Martin Wright

---

**CLAUSS, Heinz**

German dancer. Born in Esslingen, 17 February 1935. Studied with Hans von Kusserow and Robert Mayer, Theatre-Ballet School, Stuttgart, 1949–57; also studied with Nora Kiss and Olga Preobrazhenska, Paris. Dancer, becoming first soloist (principal dancer), Württemberg State Theatre (Stuttgart Ballet), 1951–57; first soloist, Zürich State Opera Ballet, 1957–59, Hamburg State Opera Ballet, 1959–67, Stuttgart Ballet, 1967–76, touring internationally with Stuttgart company including to the U.S., Australia, England, Japan, Brazil, Russia, Israel, France, Greece, and Lebanon; has also staged many Balanchine and Cranko works internationally, including in Rome, Oslo, Stockholm, Amsterdam, Stuttgart, and New York; also teacher: director, John Cranko Ballet School, Stuttgart, 1976–90. Recipient: John Cranko Medal, 1987.

**ROLES**

1955 Franz in *Coppélia* (Mayer after Petipa), Stuttgart Ballet, Stuttgart
Title role in *The Prodigal Son* (Mayer), Stuttgart Ballet, Stuttgart
1957 Prince in *The Firebird* (Mayer after Fokine), Stuttgart Ballet, Stuttgart
1958 Romeo (cr) in *Romeo and Juliet* (Mayer), Zürich State Opera Ballet, Zürich
1959 Grand pas de deux from *Don Quixote* (after Gorsky, Petipa), Hamburg State Opera Ballet, Hamburg
Prince in *Cinderella* (Mayer), Zürich Ballet, Zürich
1960 Principal dancer in *Serenade* (Balanchine), Hamburg State Opera Ballet, Hamburg
Principal dancer (cr) in *Struktur nach studie 1* (Cebron), Hamburg State Opera Ballet, Hamburg
1961 Paris (cr) in *Romeo and Juliet* (new version; van Dyk), Hamburg State Opera Ballet, Hamburg
1962 Phlegmatic in *Four Temperaments* (Balanchine), Hamburg State Opera Ballet, Hamburg
Title role in *Apollo* (Balanchine), Hamburg State Opera Ballet, Hamburg
Principal dancer in *Concerto Barocco* (Balanchine), Hamburg State Opera Ballet, Hamburg
1963 Prince Siegfried in *Swan Lake* (Van Dyk after Petipa, Ivanov), Hamburg State Opera Ballet, Hamburg
1965 Prince (cr) in *Cinderella* (van Dyk), Hamburg State Opera Ballet, Hamburg
First movement in *Symphony in C* (Balanchine), Hamburg State Opera Ballet, Hamburg
1967 Principal dancer in *Holbergs Zeiten* (Cranko), Stuttgart Ballet, Stuttgart
Principal dancer in *Études* (Lander), Hamburg State Opera Ballet, Hamburg
Title role in *Onegin* (revised version; Cranko), Stuttgart Ballet, Stuttgart
1968 Don Quixote (cr) in *Présence* (Cranko), Stuttgart Ballet, Stuttgart
A Man (cr) in *The Sphinx* (MacMillan), Stuttgart Ballet, Stuttgart
1969 Lucentio (cr) in *The Taming of the Shrew* (Cranko), Stuttgart Ballet, Stuttgart
Petrucchio in *The Taming of the Shrew* (Cranko), Stuttgart Ballet, Stuttgart
1970 Principal dancer (cr) in *Brouillards* (Cranko), Stuttgart Ballet, Stuttgart
Fiancé (cr) in *Fräulein Julie* (MacMillan), Stuttgart Ballet, Stuttgart
Soloist (cr) in *Poème de l'extase* (Cranko), Stuttgart Ballet, Stuttgart
One of two soloists in *Ebony Concerto* (Cranko), Stuttgart Ballet, Stuttgart
1971 Don José (cr) in *Carmen* (Cranko), Stuttgart Ballet, Stuttgart
Summer (cr) in *Die Jahreszeiten* (*The Seasons*, new version; Cranko), Stuttgart Ballet, Stuttgart
1972 Adagio (cr) in *Initials R.B.M.E.* (Cranko), Stuttgart Ballet, Stuttgart
Prince (cr) in *Swan Lake* (new production; Cranko after Petipa, Ivanov), Stuttgart Ballet, Stuttgart
1973 Principal dancer in *L'Estro armonico* (Cranko), Stuttgart Ballet, Stuttgart
The Man (cr) in *Spuren* (*Traces*; Cranko), Stuttgart Ballet, Stuttgart
Adagio (cr) in *Concerto* (MacMillan), Stuttgart Ballet, Stuttgart
1974 A Cavalier in *The Lady and the Fool* (Cranko), Stuttgart Ballet, Stuttgart
Principal dancer (cr) in *Rückkehr ins fremde Land* (*Return to the Strange Land*, first version; pas de trois; Kylián), Stuttgart Ballet, Stuttgart
1975 Principal dancer in *Intermezzo* (Feld), Stuttgart Ballet, Stuttgart
1976 Second movement in *Symphony in C* (Balanchine), Stuttgart Ballet, Stuttgart

**PUBLICATIONS**

By Clauss:
Interview in Kemper, Ferry, "Die John-Cranko-Schule", in *Neue Zeitschrift für Musik*, March–April 1980
Interview with Garske, Rolf, in "The Students Must Take the Initiative Themselves", *Ballett International* (Cologne), September/October 1987

About Clauss:
Regner, O.F., *Ballettführer*, Stuttgart 1956, 1972
Geitel, K., *Der Tänzer heute*, Berlin, 1964
Herf, Estelle, "Heinz Clauss", *Ballet Today* (London), January–February 1966
Geitel, K., "Heinz Clauss", *Ballet 1967*, Velber, 1967
Stoop, Norma McLain, "Stuttgart Snowball", *After Dark* (New York), November 1969
Niehaus, Max, *Ballett-Faszination*, Munich, 1972
*John Cranko*, Stuttgart, 1973
Cranko, John, *Über den Tanz*, Frankfurt, 1974

**Heinz Clauss as Apollo, Stuttgart Ballet**

Kilian, H., *Stuttgarter Ballet*, Weingarten, 1980

* * *

When still a teenager Heinz Clauss became a member of the Ballet Company of the Württemberg State Theatre in Stuttgart (the Stuttgart Ballet), first as an apprentice, later as a member of the corps de ballet, and then as a principal. While in Stuttgart, he danced Franz in *Coppélia*, the title role in *Prodigal Son*, and the Prince in *The Firebird*. In 1957 he joined the ballet company of the Opera House in Zürich, where his roles included the Prince in *Cinderella* and *Firebird* as well as Romeo in Mayer's *Romeo and Juliet*. Two years later he was a principal dancer with the ballet company of the Hamburg State Opera. Here, apart from the strictly classical roles, such as the Princes in *Swan Lake* and *Cinderella*, or the virtuoso solo part in *Études*, he danced in many ballets by Balanchine, such as *Concerto Barocco*, *The Four Temperaments*, *Apollo*, and *Symphony in C*. In 1967 Clauss staged *Apollo* for the Stuttgart Ballet at the Wurttemberg State Theatre and danced the title role. From that year, and at the invitation of John Cranko, Clauss danced as a principal with the Stuttgart Ballet. During those years he went on various international tours with the company, and created several leading roles in ballets by Cranko. Clauss danced the title role in the revised version of *Onegin*, Don Quixote in *Présence*, Lucentio and Petrucchio in *The Taming of the Shrew*, and the Bridegroom in Kenneth MacMillan's *Miss Julie*.

During the early 1960s Heinz Clauss was recognized nationwide as the leading German Balanchine dancer of his generation. In response to Clauss's interpretation of Apollo, the German dance critic Klaus Geitel wrote in 1967, "art and technique unite and create this beautiful harmonic structure, which we call ballet". For Clauss, artistic subtlety took priority over pure technical showmanship. As his technique was so clean and perfect, he could easily concentrate on the character and meaning of each part. Later, when he worked with John Cranko, who inspired great creativity in so many dancers, Onegin and Romeo became his greatest triumphs. Here he could develop his personality and could believe in a part; he not only had to dance, but also to portray character.

Clauss's discretion and modesty, and his deep understanding and honesty towards his art, made it impossible for him to abandon the standards he had set himself throughout his entire career. He was never the typical classical prince or the breathtaking virtuoso dancer, but an artist who distinguished himself through a dignified rather than an obsessive attitude towards the dance. Despite having staged many works by Balanchine and Cranko worldwide, he never longed to choreograph himself, with the exception of a single pas de deux. Instead, it was in teaching that Clauss found his other calling. In 1976, when Anne Woolliams suggested that he succeed her as director of the state-owned John Cranko Ballet School (at this time the only qualified school of its kind in the whole of Western Germany), he decided reluctantly that it might be time for a change. He accepted the offer and for the next fifteen years divided his time equally between the administration and intensive teaching. Thanks to his dedication, the school not only achieved a high reputation, but maintained a satisfying relationship with the Stuttgart Ballet. In 1990, for reasons of health, Heinz Clauss was forced to step down from his position and to hand over the school to his long-time colleague Axel Ursuliak.

—Hans-Theodor Wohlfahrt

---

## CLÉOPÂTRE

(Original Russian title: *Egipetskie nochi*, or *Egyptian Nights*)

**Choreography:** Mikhail Fokine
**Music:** Anton Arensky
**Design:** Léon Bakst
**Libretto:** Mikhail Fokine
**First Production:** Maryinsky Theatre, St. Petersburg, 21 March 1908
**Principal Dancers:** Anna Pavlova (Veronika), Elizaveta Time (Cléopâtre), Pavel Gerdt (Mark Antony), Olga Preobrazhenskaya, Vaslav Nijinsky (Slaves), Mikhail Fokine (Amoun), Tamara Karsavina (Jewish Dance)

**Other productions include:** Diaghilev's Ballets Russes (extended version, with additional music by Taneyev, Rimsky-Korsakov, Glinka, Glazunov), as *Cléopâtre*, with Anna Pavlova (Ta-Hor), Ida Rubinstein (Cléopâtre), Mikhail Fokine (Amoun), Tamara Karsavina, Vaslav Nijinsky (Favourite Slaves); Paris, 2 June 1909. Diaghilev's Ballets Russes (revised version; additional choreography Léonide Massine, new design Robert Delaunay), with Lubov Tchernicheva (Cléopâtre) and Léonide Massine (Amoun); London, 5 September 1918. Fokine Ballet (restaged Fokine); New York, 1927. De Basil's Ballets Russes (revival), with Lubov Tchernicheva (Cléopâtre), Yurek Shabelevsky (Amoun), Alexandra Danilova (Ta-Hor); Philadelphia, 10 November 1936.

### PUBLICATIONS

Beaumont, Cyril, *Cléopâtre*, London, 1918
Beaumont, Cyril, *Complete Book of Ballets*, revised edition, 1951
Grigoriev, Serge, *The Diaghilev Ballet*, translated by Vera Bowen, London, 1953
Hering, Doris, "Against the Tide", *Dance Magazine* (New York), 2 parts: August, September 1961
Spencer, Charles, *Leon Bakst*, New York, 1973
Mayer, Charles S., "The Influence of Léon Bakst on Choreography", *Dance Chronicle* (New York), vol. 1, no. 2, 1978
Pruzhan, Irina, *Léon Bakst: Set and Costume Designs*, Harmondsworth, 1987
Baer, Nancy van Norman, *The Art of Enchantment: Diaghilev's Ballets Russes 1909–29*, San Francisco, 1988
Garafola, Lynn, *Diaghilev's Ballets Russes*, New York, 1989

* * *

Though it has not survived as a staple element in the repertoire of classical ballet companies, in the manner of several other important creations for Diaghilev's Ballets Russes (such as *Le Spectre de la rose*, *Petrushka*, or the *Danses Polovetsiennes*), Fokine's *Cléopâtre* was also one of the outstanding successes of the company's first Paris season in 1909. It created an immediate sensation among both audiences and contemporary critics, remaining in the Diaghilev repertoire for several seasons. As such it occupies an important place in ballet history as one of the key works in which Ballet Russes's innovations helped liberate classical dance from the conventions of the day, and for the assurance with which it demonstrated the possibility of achieving an impressive dramatic structure in cumulative danced tableaux, without relying totally on actual "steps".

Much of its original impact came from the extraordinary harmony of elements brought together for its creation, the piece

**Ida Rubinstein in *Cléopâtre*, Diaghilev's Ballets Russes, Paris 1911**

being one of the most extreme examples of both Diaghilev's and Fokine's willingness to fuse the best of different aspects of theatre art in order to achieve an overwhelming effect. The ballet was thus as much the success of its designer, Bakst, as of its choreographer, and the impact of this work on the contemporary art scene in Paris was considerable. It central role was also a dramatic impersonation, rather than a dance one, and gave its creator Ida Rubinstein one of the greatest successes of her career. The major dance roles were originally taken by Fokine as Amoun, Pavlova as Ta-Hor, and Karsavina and Nijinsky as Cléopâtre's two leading slaves (although their principal "duet" was cut from the ballet in subsequent seasons).

*Cléopâtre* was a reworking of Fokine's earlier *Egyptian Nights*, mounted for the Maryinsky in 1908, which in itself incorporated a solemn procession led by the High Priest from a version of *Une Nuit d'Egypte*, created by Lev Ivanov for Stanislav Gillert in 1901. The music was by Arensky, as in the 1908 version, but with additional material by Glazunov (the Bacchanale), Taneyev, Rimsky-Korsakov, and Glinka. Bakst's décor retained the archaic Egyptian style of the earlier production, but gave it a different appearance with strikingly different colours and designs.

There were very few true dancing "*pas*" in the ballet: its choreographic effect was in the arrangement of groupings in bas-relief formation against a background of tall columns and statues, and as such it was was essentially a theatrical romance in stylized movement, with two main dramatic focuses. The first concentrated on the spectacular entrance procession of Cléopâtre, carried by Nubian slaves in a sarcophagus set on a catafalque. Rubinstein was revealed only gradually, as screens hiding the sarcophagus were drawn aside and successive layers of multi-coloured veils removed by attendants to disclose the tall, half-naked body of the Queen beneath. The second was the climax, in which the slave Amoun must inevitably die, once Cléopâtre has yielded to his desire.

While Nijinsky apparently cut a panther-like figure as the favoured slave at Cléopâtre's feet, it was evidently Rubinstein—with elongated eyes and covered in turquoise-green paint—who dominated the piece. The individuality of her gestures, which Nijinska described as "adaptable only to the structure of *her* body", coupled with her unique presence and particular beauty, gave the ballet a quality that has not enabled it to survive beyond Rubinstein's performance of the role. The music, also, which was much criticized at the time for being a pot-pourri of several composers, has none of the stature of some of Diaghilev's commissioned scores, sufficient to keep its memory alive in the concert hall away from a theatre staging.

As with several other works by Fokine created with specific artists in mind, it is frequently hard now to evaluate the contemporary impact of a piece, especially when the (actually slight) "choreographic" content relies heavily on gesture, atmosphere, and subtle dramatic pacing to achieve its effect. Though it was Fokine's desire to break with the conventions of the Imperial classical ballet and establish new values in the presentation of movement and danced drama in the theatre, *Cléopâtre* must today be numbered among the body of his works which achieved that aim, without retaining the magic of their first impact for suceeding generations.

—Geoffrey Baskerville

---

**COCTEAU, Jean**

French writer, poet, film-maker, designer, and ballet librettist. Born in Maisons-Laffitte, near Paris, 5 July 1889. Educated at Lycée Condorcet, Paris, and privately. Published first volume of verse at age 19; designed posters and wrote scenarios and publicity material for Diaghilev's Ballets Russes; author of libretti for Fokine's *Le Dieu bleu* (1912), Massine's *Parade* (1917), and Nijinska's *Le Train bleu* (1924) for Diaghilev, also influencing the scenarios for *Les Biches* (mus. Poulenc, chor. Nijinska, 1924) and *Les Fâcheux* (mus. Auric, chor. Nijinska, 1924); also librettist for Fratellini Brothers, 1920, Jean Börlin and the Ballets Suédois, 1921, Ballets des Champs-Elysées, Paris Opéra, and Theater am Gärtnerplatz, Munich; writer of numerous essays and articles on dance as well as playwright and novelist; writer and director of films, including *Le Sang d'un poète* (1932), *La Belle et la bête* (1946), *Les Enfants terribles* (1950), *Orphée* (1950), and *Le Testament d'Orphée* (1950); co-founder of *Shéhérazade* magazine; president, Jazz Academy;

honorary president, Cannes Film Festival. Recipient: Louions-Delluc Prize, 1946; Avant-garde Film Grand Prize, 1950; honorary doctorate, Oxford University, 1956; member of Académie française, 1955, and Royal Academy of Belgium; honorary member, American Academy and German Academy; commander, Legion of Honour, 1961. Died in Milly-le-Forêt, 11 October 1963.

**WORKS** (Ballet scenarios, libretti, and designs)

1912 *Le Dieu bleu* (libretto, with Frédéric de Madrazo), Diaghilev's Ballets Russes, Théâtre du Châtelet, Paris
1917 *Parade* (libretto; chor. Massine, mus. Satie, design Picasso), Diaghilev's Ballets Russes, Théâtre du Châtelet, Paris
1920 *Le Boeuf sur le toit* (libretto and production; mus. Milhaud, design Guy-Pierre Fauconnet and Raoul Dufy), Fratellini Brothers, Comédie des Champs-Elysées, Paris
1921 *Les Mariés de la Tour Eiffel* (libretto; chor. Börlin, mus. Auric, Milhaud, Tailleferre, Honegger, and Poulenc, design Irène Lagut and J. Hugo), Ballets Suédois, Théâtre des Champs-Elysées, Paris
1924 *Le Train bleu* (libretto; chor. Nijinska, mus. Milhaud), Diaghilev's Ballets Russes, Théâtre des Champs-Elysées, Paris
1946 *Le Jeune Homme et la mort* (libretto, costumes, and production; chor. Petit, mus. Bach), Ballets des Champs-Elysées, Théâtre des Champs-Elysées, Paris
1948 *L'Amour et son amour* (décor; libretto and chor. Babilée, mus. Franck), Théâtre des Champs-Elysées, Paris
1950 *Phèdre* (libretto and décor; chor. Lifar, mus. Auric), Paris Opéra Ballet, Paris
1953 *La Dame à la licorne* (libretto and décor; chor. Rosen, mus. J. Chailley), Theater am Gärtnerplatz, Munich

**PUBLICATIONS**

By Cocteau (relating to dance):
*Les Mariés de la Tour Eiffel*, Paris, 1921
*Les Biches*, with George Auric, Georges Braque, and Louis Laloy, Paris, 1924
*Les Fâcheux*, with Marie Laurencin, Darius Milhaud, and Francis Poulenc, Paris, 1924
*Paris Album 1900–1914*, Paris, 1956
*Entre Picasso et Radiguet*, Paris, 1967

About Cocteau:
Mauriac, C., *Jean Cocteau, ou la vérité du mensonge*, Paris, 1945
Priddin, D., *The Art of French Literature from Théophile Gautier to P. Valéry*, London, 1952
Millecam, J.-P., *L'Etoile de Jean Cocteau*, Monaco, 1952
Oxenhandler, N., *Scandal and Parade: The Theatre of Jean Cocteau*, 1957
Bancroft, David, "A Critical Reassessment of Cocteau's *Parade*", *Journal of the Australasian Universities Language and Literature Association*, 25–26, 1966
Knapp, Bettina, *Jean Cocteau*, New York, 1970
Steegmuller, Francis, *Cocteau: A Biography*, Boston, 1970
Wildmann, Carl, "Jean Cocteau and the Ballet", *Dancing Times* (London), October 1973
Ries, Frank W.D., "Acrobats, Burlesque, and Cocteau", *Dance Scope* (New York), Fall/Winter 1976–77
Anderson, Alexandra, and Saltus, Carol (eds.), *Jean Cocteau and the French Scene*, New York, 1984
Ries, Frank W., *The Dance Theatre of Jean Cocteau*, Ann Arbor, Michigan, 1986
Aschengreen, Erik, *Jean Cocteau and the Dance*, translated by Patricia McAndrew and Per Avsum, Copenhagen, 1986
Daniels, Don, "Cocteau's Poésie", *Ballet Review* (New York), Fall 1989

* * *

Ten years after Cocteau's death Carl Wildman gave the following analysis of the poet's career in *The Dancing Times*:

> His contribution to the ballet has been crucial, diverse, his action catalytic; the veins which he explored are still being mined. Though a number of his works have a place in theatrical history rather than in repertoire, it is by the ramifications of his influence that his presence is chiefly known.

Not everyone would agree with this statement, although most would have to admit that Cocteau's involvement in dance was wide-ranging: designing posters, costumes, or sets, writing scenarios, commissioning music scores, writing reviews and/or critical analyses of various works, even giving interviews which informed the public how they should react to certain ballets. Often this style of involvement was thought of as self-serving or just irritating, as the memoirs of Igor Stravinsky, Misia Sert, and others would attest.

Cocteau was, however, an important catalyst for many artists to change and experiment, and his writings continually reiterate his loathing of repetition, monotony, and boredom. His work in ballet reflects this mental mobility and dextrous versatility, although it is difficult to make generalizations, since his role as catalyst could contract or expand, depending on his collaborators and how dominant a role Cocteau played in a particular production. In *Parade* he quickly lost control to Satie, and then Picasso, but in *Le Train bleu* he was able to convince Diaghilev that his ideas should take precedence over Nijinska's. These ideas could only be taken so far, however, since Cocteau was not a dancer and, therefore, inexperienced at choreography; he had always to leave the realization of the steps to someone else. This frustration was eventually overcome when he began to direct in cinema, and many film critics and historians have frequently remarked how Cocteau "choreographed" his films—for example, the "celestial ceiling" in *La Sang d'un poète*, or Beauty floating down Beast's hall in *La Belle et la bête*.

Walter Sorell, in an obituary notice published in 1964, captured succinctly Cocteau's thematic desires:

> In retrospect it becomes altogether clear that Jean Cocteau was a pioneer in transferring the reflection of everyday life onto the dance stage. Instead of the spectacular sequence of heightened unreality, the fairy tale atmosphere on which ballet has fed for so long, he broke with the cliché and he offered the gesture of heightened reality. What we have accepted as avant-garde dance in the fifties and sixties has been built, in more ways than one, on Cocteau's living and dying, and living again.

The transferral and transformation of the commonplace or mundane was key to nearly all of Cocteau's dance compositions: the artist's garret in *Le Jeune Homme et la mort*, the American prohibition in *Le Boeuf sur le toit*, swimmers cavorting with Kodak cameras on the beach in *Le Train bleu*, even the sound of a typewriter in *Parade*.

In many ways these "effects" could be considered the

**Jean Cocteau (centre) after a performance of *Le Jeune Homme et la mort*, with, from left to right, Jean Babilée, Boris Kochno, Nathalie Philippart, Roland Petit and Georges Wakhevitch, Paris, 1946**

affectations of a social dilettante who was still following Diaghilev's dictum of "Astonish me!" But while this remark can be considered the catalyst that helped launch Cocteau on his varied and diversified career, it was not the overriding factor. He was simply trying out different ways of expressing himself while remaining true to his theory that everything could be poetry—it only depended on the presentation: "Poetry borrows astonishing contrasts by chance, it transplants things, it accidently sets up a new order."

Cocteau obviously loved dance, since he continued to contribute to the field even into the 1950s; his last major contribution was the scenario, sets, and costumes for *La Dame à la licorne*, choreographed by Heinz Rosen in 1953. Cocteau felt that dance could reach a wider audience than certain other arts and this appealed to him greatly. He claimed, "Dance is the universal language where the corps are charged to express themselves and make darkness light for the waiting audience." Through its language plastique Cocteau felt that dance could reach "a superior realism, a higher expression which speaks more than traditional pantomime". Speaking of dance in the female gender, which he did with all his "muses", Cocteau said, "She is an 'esperanto' in the contemporary babelism. She traverses the walls of idioms. She gives, in addition, the direct translation of a poetry which abandons all terms." This concept of dance as "visual poetry" was one of Cocteau's most frequently reiterated philosophies.

Cocteau's penchant for publicity, even notoriety, frequently overshadowed his work, and this has often made it difficult to assess his contributions clearly. Although he is probably better known for his drawings and films, his contributions to and involvement with dance have, in recent years, gained increased recognition.

—Frank W. D. Ries

---

**Lesley Collier as Lise in Ashton's *La Fille mal gardée***

**COLLIER, Lesley**

British dancer. Born in Orpington, Kent, 13 March 1947. Studied with Irene Ayres in Kent, and at Royal Academy of Dancing and Royal Ballet School (scholarship pupil), London. Married (1) Geoffrey Price, (divorced); (2) Nicholas Dromgoole, (divorced); twin sons, Peter and Benjamin, b. 1989. Dancer, Royal Ballet, from 1965: soloist, from 1970; principal dancer, from 1972; has appeared on television and film, including in *Tales of Beatrix Potter* (chor. Ashton, 1976), and *Stories from a Flying Trunk* (chor. Ashton, 1979), *The Dancing Princesses* and *Dizzy Feet* (both chor. Maen). Recipient: Dancer of the Year, *Dance and Dancers* Magazine, 1986; *Evening Standard* Award, 1987.

**ROLES**

1965 Young Girl in *The Two Pigeons* (Ashton), Royal Ballet School Performance, London
1967 Bluebird in *The Sleeping Beauty* (Petipa, Ashton; staged MacMillan), Royal Ballet, tour
White Cat in *The Sleeping Beauty* (Petipa, Ashton; staged MacMillan), Royal Ballet
1970 Dancer in *Birthday Offering* (Ashton), Royal Ballet, London
Title role in *Anastasia* (MacMillan), Royal Ballet, London
1971 Lise in *La Fille mal gardée* (Ashton), Royal Ballet, London
Dancer in *Dances at a Gathering* (Robbins), Royal Ballet, London
Tuesday in *Jazz Calendar* (Ashton), Royal Ballet, London
1972 Principal dancer in *Les Sylphides* (Fokine), Royal Ballet, London
1973 Juliet in *Romeo and Juliet* (MacMillan), Royal Ballet, London
Odette/Odile in *Swan Lake* (Petipa, Ivanov, Ashton; staged de Valois), Royal Ballet, London
Bransle Gay (Pas de trois) in *Agon* (Balanchine), Royal Ballet, London
Third Song in *Song of the Earth* (MacMillan), Royal Ballet, tour
Lilac Fairy in *The Sleeping Beauty* (Petipa, Ashton; staged MacMillan), Royal Ballet, London
Principal dancer in *Scènes de ballet* (Ashton), Royal Ballet, London
Anna II in *The Seven Deadly Sins* (MacMillan), Royal Ballet, tour
1974 Stop-Time Rag (cr) in *Elite Syncopations* (MacMillan), Royal Ballet, London
Princess Aurora in *The Sleeping Beauty* (Petipa, Ashton; staged MacMillan), Royal Ballet, London
Clara in *The Nutcracker* (Nureyev), Royal Ballet, London
Principal dancer in *Don Quixote* Pas de deux (after Petipa), Royal Ballet, London
Title role in *Giselle* (Petipa after Coralli and Perrot; staged Sergeyev), Sadler's Wells Royal Ballet, Leeds
Dorabella in *Enigma Variations* (Ashton), Royal Ballet, London
The Young Girl in *The Two Pigeons* (Ashton), Royal Ballet, London
1975 Principal dancer (cr) in *Four Schumann Pieces* (van Manen), Royal Ballet, London
Spring (cr) in *The Four Seasons* (MacMillan), Royal Ballet, London
Principal dancer in *Symphony* (MacMillan), Royal Ballet, London
1976 Principal dancer in *Voluntaries* (Tetley), Royal Ballet, London
1977 Katherina in *The Taming of the Shrew* (Cranko), Royal Ballet, tour
Principal dancer in *Symphonic Variations* (Ashton), Royal Ballet, London
The Girl in *The Invitation* (MacMillan), Royal Ballet, London
Principal dancer in *Pavane* (MacMillan), Royal Ballet, London
1978 Principal dancer (cr) in *Tweedledum and Tweedledee* (Ashton), Royal Ballet, London
Principal dancer in *Serenade* (Balanchine), Royal Ballet, London
Mary Vetsera in *Mayerling* (MacMillan), Royal Ballet, London
Title role in *Manon* (MacMillan), Royal Ballet, London
Second Song in *Song of the Earth* (MacMillan), Royal Ballet, London
Principal dancer in *Façade* (Ashton), Royal Ballet, London
1979 Principal dancer in *La Fin du jour* (MacMillan), Royal Ballet, London
Title role in *Cinderella* (Ashton), Royal Ballet, London
Principal dancer in *Liebeslieder Walzer* (Balanchine), Royal Ballet, London
Titania in *The Dream* (Ashton), Royal Ballet, London
The Chosen One in *The Rite of Spring* (MacMillan), Royal Ballet, London
The Bride in *A Wedding Bouquet* (Ashton), Royal Ballet, London
1980 Principal dancer in *Mam'zelle Angot* (Massine), Royal Ballet, London
Third Sister in *My Brother, My Sisters* (MacMillan), Royal Ballet, London
Principal dancer (cr) in *Rhapsody* (Ashton), Royal Ballet Gala, London
Title role in *The Firebird* (Fokine), Royal Ballet, London
Principal dancer (cr) in *Dances of Albion* (Tetley), Royal Ballet, London
1981 Principal dancer in *Napoli* Pas de six and Tarantella (Beck after Bournonville), Royal Ballet, London
1982 Miranda (cr) in *The Tempest* (Nureyev), Royal Ballet, London
1983 Principal dancer (cr) in *Consort Lessons* (Bintley), Royal Ballet, London
1984 Sugar Plum Fairy in *The Nutcracker* (new production; Wright), Royal Ballet London
1985 Principal dancer (cr) in *Number Three* (Corder), Royal Ballet, London
Elizabeth (cr) in *Frankenstein, The Modern Prometheus* (Eagling), Royal Ballet, London
Isis Mourning (cr) in *Sons of Horus* (Bintley), Royal Ballet, London
1986 Principal dancer (cr) in *Galanteries* (Bintley), Royal Ballet, Vancouver
1989 Princess Epine in *The Prince of the Pagodas* (MacMillan), Royal Ballet, London
1990 Nikiya in *La Bayadère* (Makarova after Petipa), Royal Ballet, London
1991 Roxane (cr) in *Cyrano* (Bintley), Royal Ballet, London
Principal dancer (lead pas de deux) in *Scènes de ballet* (Ashton), Royal Ballet, London
First Movement in *Symphony in C* (Balanchine), Royal Ballet, London

Title role in *Raymonda* Act III (Nureyev after Petipa), Royal Ballet, London

## PUBLICATIONS

Goodman, Saul, "Lesley Collier", *Dance Magazine* (New York), August 1972
Clarke, Mary, "Royal Dancers", *Dancing Times* (London), February 1975
Clarke, Mary, "Sleeping Beauties", *Dancing Times* (London), December 1977
Rigby, Cormac, "Fleet of Foot, Melting Hearts", *Dance and Dancers* (London), November 1986

* * *

Lesley Collier's popularity during her 25 years with the Royal Ballet speaks for itself. As the mother of twins at age 41, who then returned successfully to the stage, Collier shows a stamina and strength of character which are but a few of the many qualities that have made her career at the top so enduring.

As a young dancer in training, Collier successively won three scholarships, to the Irene Ayres School of Dancing, the Royal Academy of Dancing, and the Royal Ballet School. Joining the company in 1965, she spent three years in the corps and danced her first solos in the Bluebird and White Cat pas de deux. As a coryphée she danced many roles in the classics, including *Raymonda* and *La Bayadère*, before being promoted to soloist during the 1970 New York season.

As a soloist Collier danced her first Lise in *La Fille mal gardée*, a role with which she has since become closely identified. In one of the most technically demanding roles in ballet, one sees only the seemingly effortless assurance of her sunny interpretation, particularly in the mime scene; she shows us "an adoringly loving and warm-hearted Lise", as the critic Cormac Rigby wrote. In fact, this sentiment can be applied to many of Collier's performances; a sense of fun and total enjoyment pervades her interpretations. Even her Odette suggests not so much tragedy as an attempt to make her character more human; John Percival of *The Times* wrote of her début, "a plucky little Swan Queen", while Fernau Hall of *The Daily Telegraph* wrote, "Her fine intelligence and imagination will bring her Odette up to the remarkable standard of her Odile". However divided the critics were over her *Swan Lake*, they were united in praise of Collier's first Juliet with Wayne Eagling in 1973. To be given both Odette/Odile and Juliet in her first year as a principal was an indication of Collier's fluent progress. Of her début as Juliet, critic Nicholas Dromgoole wrote, "Now we can sit back and watch a great ballerina develop in our midst".

Collier's dramatic ability equals her technical assurance, and though she dislikes the assumption that the latter gives her the freedom to concentrate on interpretation, the combination is only part of the allure. The elusive qualities which no amount of technical bravura can make up for—individuality, charm, and expressiveness—create a formidable synthesis in Collier. Reliable and versatile, she dances all the ballerina roles in the classics as well as in a diverse repertoire of works ranging from Fokine to Bintley.

A petite physique gives Collier force of motion and fast-footed clarity. Though not ideally suited in technique to the nineteenth-century "sylph" ballets, she compensates for this in character and musicality. Her *Giselle* is subtle and vivacious in Act I, giving way to a compelling portrayal of vulnerability by the end of the mad scene.

Many outstanding roles have been created on Collier, but probably the most dazzling was with Baryshnikov in Ashton's *Rhapsody*, specially commissioned for the Queen Mother's 80th birthday in 1980. A virtuoso show piece, set to music by Rachmaninov, it displayed the incomparable talents of both Baryshnikov and Collier. "If Baryshnikov is all gold", wrote Alexander Bland, "Collier glitters with diamanté, darting through her fiendishly fast and difficult solos like a little firecracker". She has also danced with Baryshnikov in *La Fille mal gardée* and *Romeo and Juliet*.

Other choreographers who have created ballets for Collier include MacMillan, Nureyev, van Manen, Tetley, Bintley, and Eagling. Though not typecast as a MacMillan dancer, Collier has had much success in many of his works, with her great adaptability no doubt contributing to her ability to portray MacMillan heroines with feeling. In Bintley's elegant 1986 ensemble piece, *Galanteries*, she showed an expressive lyricism and an innate feeling for the music. More recently she has performed in *Symphony in C*, a Balanchine ballet acquired for the first time by the Royal Ballet in 1991, and in David Bintley's rather ill-fated but interesting dramatic ballet, *Cyrano*.

—Anna Swan

---

# THE CONCERT
(subtitled *The Perils of Everybody*)

**Choreography:** Jerome Robbins
**Music:** Frédéric Chopin (partly orchestrated by Hershy Kay)
**Design:** Irene Sharaff (costumes)
**First Production:** New York City Ballet, City Center, New York, 6 March 1956
**Principal Dancers:** Tanaquil LeClercq, Yvonne Mounsey, Wilma Curley, Todd Bolender, Robert Barnett, Richard Thomas, John Mandia

**Other productions include:** Ballets: U.S.A. (restaged and revised Robbins; backdrops by Saul Steinberg); Spoleto Festival, 8 June 1958. Royal Ballet (costumes Irene Sharaff, curtain Edward Gorey), with Lynn Seymour, Michael Coleman, Georgina Parkinson, John Fletcher; London, 4 March 1975. The Australian Ballet; Sydney, 10 May 1979. San Francisco Ballet (staged Tom Abbot, 1987; restaged Sara Leland); San Francisco, 15 April 1988.

## PUBLICATIONS

Franks, Arthur Henry, "A New Experience", *The Dancing Times* (London), October 1959
Barnes, Clive, and Williams, Peter, "That Was Ballets: USA That Was", *Dance and Dancers* (London), November 1959
Barnes, Clive, and Williams, Peter, "Transatlantic Return", *Dance and Dancers* (London), October 1961
Brinson, Peter, and Crisp, Clement, *Ballet for All*, London, 1970
Terry, Walter, "Dancer Laughter", *Saturday Review* (New York), 1 January 1972
Balanchine, George, with Mason, Francis, *Balanchine's Complete Stories of the Great Ballets*, Garden City, N.Y., 1977
Reynolds, Nancy, *Repertory in Review*, New York, 1977

* * *

**Merle Park and Michael Coleman in *The Concert*, Royal Ballet, London, c.1978**

The sub-title of *The Concert*, "The Perils of Everybody", echoes the silent-movie serial called "The Perils of Pauline", where the heroine was dangled over ledges, tied to railroad tracks, and generally victimized by all manner of comically melodramatic menaces. Although this sub-title may prepare the viewer for many of the sillier goings-on of this most diverting of comic ballets, it does not prepare him or her for the underlying strain of real sadness and truth on which its humour is based.

The point of departure for *The Concert* is Robbins's touching observation of one form of human vulnerability, namely the fact that that people's minds tend to wander at concerts. Or, as he puts it more kindly in his programme note: "One of the pleasures of attending a concert is the freedom to lose oneself in listening to the music. Quite unconsciously, mental pictures and images form . . .". A self-important pianist enters from upstage left to cross all the way to his instrument, set at the other corner. His audience enters, carrying chairs: it consists of two young women disturbing a young man who wants to concentrate on the music, a girl in a large hat who sits leaning on the piano rim, a bossy wife, and her husband, a shy young man. A problem with tickets causes wholesale seat-changing, during which an aggressive woman pulls the chair out from under the girl in the big hat, leaving her—in one of the piece's best sight gags—still sitting in the same position on pointe, her arms cradled on the rim of the piano. Finally all the audience members are on their feet; they pick up their chairs and go off.

Some of the sections that follow are merely slapstick, though we laugh all the same: the girl in the big hat proves too energetic a partner for the shy boy, who in desperation hits her over the head with a truncheon hidden in the piano. The henpecked husband tries to kill his wife, but finds that the dagger that is rubber on her turns real when turned on himself; six men and the husband partner the girl in the big hat to the strains of a mazurka, the husband kicking her constantly in the behind. Finally, the "Butterfly Prelude" that ends the piece has the dancers flapping about with gauzy wings under their arms and ending up being chased by the pianist, waving a huge butterfly net. Some sections are so off-beat as to be brilliant: the opening of one of the celebrated musical pieces, known to ballet-goers from *Les Sylphides*, is set to a woman trying on hats.

Yet some sections are tinged with truth rather than with the silliness of mere sight gags. A number of commentators have seen Robbins' treatment of the so-called "Raindrop Prelude" as a comment on mass influence: dancers open the furled umbrellas they are carrying because they see a single person with an open one. Finally they are all clustered in a mass under a single umbrella and break up only when the girl in the floppy hat determines, by sticking out a hand, that the rain has stopped.

The so-called "Mistake Waltz", as another example, is set as a student ballet performance clearly inspired by *Les Sylphides*. The hapless girls, however, cannot get things right: one is flapping up while the others are flapping down, another ends upright rather than to the side and must slowly, unobtrusively, drift to the correct position. This section is not, strictly speaking, justified by the conceit of audience members acting out their fantasies: at least these girls do not appear in the original group of dancers. And who would dream of an unsuccessful ballet performance, save as a nightmare? Yet what is touching here is not only our empathy with these not-ready-for-prime-time dancers, but the very fact that their efforts to stay in step and keep together are for an audience, such as we are down below.

This section about dancers, that is, makes clear the self-referentiality implicit in its silent-movie humour: we too are audience members. And the final tableau makes this perfectly clear. The dancers from the first section position their chairs facing the audience before a Saul Steinberg backdrop of a theatre audience. Since the first backdrop had been of a stage, the tables have now been turned—and the dancers are ready to watch us act out our own fantasies, which we call life.

—Bruce Fleming

---

## CONCERTO

**Choreography:** Kenneth MacMillan
**Music:** Dmitri Shostakovich
**Design:** Jürgen Rose (scenery and costumes)
**First Production:** German Opera Ballet, Berlin, 30 November 1966
**Principal Dancers:** Didi Carli, Falco Kapuste, Lynn Seymour, Rudolf Holz, Silvia Kesselhelm

**Other productions include:** American Ballet Theatre (restaged MacMillan, lighting Jean Rosenthal), with Eleanor D'Antuono, Scott Douglas, Toni Lander, Bruce Marks, Cynthia Gregory; Jacksonville, Florida, 28 March 1967. Royal Ballet Touring Company, with Elizabeth Anderton, David Wall, Doreen Wells, Richard Farley, Jane Landon; London, 26 May 1967. Royal Ballet, with Jennifer Penney, Michael Coleman, Alfreda Thorogood, Kerrison Cooke, Monica Mason; London, 17 November 1970. Stuttgart Ballet; Stuttgart, 22 December 1973. Royal Danish Ballet (restaged MacMillan with Monica Parker); Copenhagen, 24 October 1991.

### PUBLICATIONS

Clarke, Mary, "Minor MacMillan", *Dancing Times* (London), July 1967

Goodwin, Noël, Percival, John, and Williams, Peter, "Berlin Export/67", *Dance and Dancers* (London), July 1967

"Royal Ballet—USA, Royal Ballet—UK", *About the House* (London), August 1967

Brinson, Peter, and Crisp, Clement, *Ballet for All*, London, 1970

Thorpe, Edward, *Kenneth MacMillan: The Man and his Ballets*, London, 1985

* * *

*Concerto* was created by Kenneth MacMillan as one of two new ballets to form a triple-bill with *The Invitation* for his first programme in West Berlin. This followed his appointment as director of ballet at the Berlin German Opera (Deutsche Oper) in 1966. (The other new work was to Ravel's *Valses nobles et sentimentales*, made in a hurry and dropped almost as quickly.) As in his *Symphony* (Royal Ballet, 1963) MacMillan chose music by Shostakovich—the Piano Concerto No. 2, Op. 102—and created plotless dancing for a principal couple, two further couples and a single woman soloist, three "second" pairs, and corps de ballet.

Shostakovich composed this Concerto in 1957 primarily as a graduation work for his son Maxim, the soloist at the Concerto's performance with the Moscow Youth Orchestra in the Conservatory. The orchestra was given relatively modest writing to support various aspects of virtuoso technique for the pianist in each of three movements. It offered MacMillan a ready-made musical ground-plan in clearly defined sections and lyrical or rhythmically buoyant textures; he equated principal dancers generally but not rigidly with the solo piano, the remainder with the orchestra.

The design by Jürgen Rose is for working tights and skirted tunics in shades of yellow, orange, and Venetian red seen against wings and a backcloth in dappled beige, on which lighting related to musical moods shines a pale "sun" to start the middle movement. The opening Allegro begins immediately on the music with brisk, open dancing by the principal pair and corps; the three second pairs are added to diversify the texture and often take up steps initiated by the principals.

At the climax of the music's sonata-form development, MacMillan, instead of letting the movement become correspondingly congested, restricts the stage to four pairs only, from which the principals then detach themselves to dance the piano's solo cadenza (which itself evolves from the preceding music). The full ensemble is brought back at the moment of re-statement of the music's initial main themes, by which time the pseudo-military feel of the first theme has visibly and wittily infected the dancers. At the end the principals march off in step with the rest, but instantly return backwards for the man to catch the woman waist-high at the closing chord.

Against the prevailing C minor of the central Andante, the piano opposes a lyrical, reflective melody in C major, and this becomes the basis of the long, sweeping pas de deux recognized as the chief glory of the ballet. MacMillan's acknowledged inspiration for the pas de deux was the sight of Lynn Seymour warming up independently at the barre while he was rehearsing others; her bending and stretching movements became the start of the pas de deux with her partner's arms supporting, then gently lifting and changing her pose. Their steps are later echoed at a distance by three supporting pairs but the interest remains focused on the principals, ending with the woman in arabesque penchée supported on the man's back inclined forwards.

A single female soloist makes a high-kicking entry to begin the third movement, again Allegro, a jaunty rondo with one main melodic motif in 2/4 time and another contriving an "out of step" effect in 7/8. The solo woman is seen in contrast to the two pairs of principals from the previous movements, with a fuller corps de ballet brought in at the music's linking passages (these fashioned from piano exercises in a teaching manual). The tight, restricted steps in unison block movements for the corps, who are at times huddled in opposite diagonals of the

**Galina Samsova and Desmond Kelly in *Concerto*, Sadler's Wells Royal Ballet, London, 1979**

stage, are the only weak element in an otherwise joyous ballet.

The ballet's initial success in Berlin led the Royal Ballet to offer its directorship to MacMillan—he would assume this role on Frederick Ashton's intended retirement three years later. MacMillan accepted the offer. *Concerto* made a quick transition to the Royal Ballet Touring Company in Britain six months later, eight days after it was staged by American Ballet Theatre in New York. It has since been produced by other companies, including the Stuttgart, Royal Swedish, and Australian Ballets; the central movement danced entirely as a pas de deux has been detached successfully and performed on its own in gala and school graduation programmes.

—Noël Goodwin

---

## CONCERTO BAROCCO

**Choreography:** George Balanchine
**Music:** Johann Sebastian Bach
**Design:** Eugene Berman (scenery and costumes)
**First Production:** Ballet Caravan, Teatro Municipal, Rio de Janeiro, 27 June 1941 (preview Hunter College, New York, 29 May 1940)
**Principal Dancers:** Marie-Jeanne, Mary Jane Shea, William Dollar

**Other productions include:** Grand Ballet du Marquis de Cuevas (restaged Balanchine); Monte Carlo, 1948. New York City Ballet (restaged Balanchine), with Marie-Jeanne, Ruth Gilbert, Francisco Moncion; New York, 11 October 1948. Ballet Russe de Monte Carlo (restaged Balanchine; danced in practice costumes), with Marie-Jeanne, Patricia Wilde, Nicholas Magallanes; New York, 9 September 1945. San Francisco Ballet, with Nancy Johnson, Sally Bailey, Gordon Paxman; San Francisco, 10 April 1953. Royal Danish Ballet (staged John Taras); Copenhagen, 9 January 1955. Hamburg Ballet; Hamburg, 11 October 1960. National Ballet of Canada (staged Una Kai); Ottawa, 21 November 1961. La Scala Ballet; Milan, 1961. Paris Opéra Ballet (restaged Balanchine); Paris, 18 December 1963. Bavarian State Opera Ballet; Munich, 18 May 1969. Dance Theatre of Harlem, 1971. Houston Ballet (staged Victoria Simon); Houston, September 1972. Sadler's Wells Royal Ballet; Cambridge, 26 August 1977. Zurich Opera Ballet (staged Patricia Neary); Zurich, 21 October 1978. Basel Ballet (staged Neary); Basel, December 1989.

**Marjorie Tallchief and George Skibine in *Concerto Barocco*, Grand Ballet de Monte Carlo, 1948**

**PUBLICATIONS**

Balanchine, George, with Mason, Francis, *Balanchine's Complete Stories of the Great Ballets*, Garden City, N.Y., 1977
Reynolds, Nancy *Repertory in Review*, New York, 1977
Siegel, Marcia, *The Shapes of Change*, Boston, 1979
Anderson, Jack, *The One and Only: The Ballet Russe de Monte Carlo*, London, 1981
Kaplan, Larry, "Corps Choreography by Balanchine", *Ballet Review* (New York), Winter 1988
Selleck, Nancy, "Barocco turns 50", *Ballet Review* (New York), Spring 1991

* * *

*Concerto Barocco* is the closest Balanchine ever came to choreographing an abstract ballet. Everything about it is strict, precise, and completely rooted in the musical structure of Bach's Double Violin Concerto in D Minor that is its accompaniment.

A concerto consists of one, two, or three solo instruments backed by an orchestra. The ballet contains three major solo artists, the two female principals, and a male principal who appears only in the central movement. The eight-woman corps is on stage throughout the length of the ballet, framing and reflecting the actions of the principals. The word "Barocco" suggests the intricate and imaginatively varied design which is demonstrated throughout the work. The term also suggests the term "baroco", a coined word in logic that refers to the syllogism, a form of philosophic reasoning that consists of three assertions. The ballet has three sections, as does the score.

The intertwining musical melodies of the violins are continually reflected by the paired movements of the two female principals, who circle and pierce the lines of the corps. All of the women are dressed identically in short white tunics. Originally, the ballet had a backdrop and more elaborate costumes, including headpieces. Simple black tunics without headpieces replaced them in 1951 and the décor was eliminated. The present costumes were first seen in the early 1960s.

There is a classical serenity both in the movements of the dancers and in the simple geometric patterns in which they are placed. An emotional note is introduced in the middle section, when a man enters to dance a duet with the first of the two principal women. The duet is an unusual one and consists in great part of stylized walking and smooth, at times soaring, lifts. In the walking segments the couple form arches with their arms above the lines of the corps, who duck beneath them.

There is no individual variation for either of them demanding virtuoso technique, yet the man's role is traditionally assigned to a principal dancer. During the course of the movement, the man entwines all of the corps around him in two intricate spirals. The lifts of the opening moments are repeated at the conclusion of the section and the principals gracefully exit to opposite sides of the stage. The man has provided a hint of romance in what had been a chaste world of women.

That world, now invigorated with jazzy, syncopated movement, dominates the concluding segment. The dualities inherent in the score are vigorously presented by pairs of the corps women moving swiftly outward from a spoke formation and then as quickly re-forming in other balanced groupings. All drop to one knee with an arm extended to conclude. The principals do the same facing one another in a mirror image.

The classical decorum of the opening movement is restored, but in a slightly altered configuration. The presence of a man who passed through and momentarily became a factor in this all female elysium has animated it to other and even more exciting symmetries.

—Don McDonagh

---

**CONSERVATOIRE, Le** *see* **KONSERVATORIET**

---

**COPLAND, Aaron**

American composer. Born in Brooklyn, New York, 14 November 1900. Educated at the Boys' High School, New York; studied piano with Leopold Wolfsohn, Victor Wittgenstein, and Clarence Adler; studied composition with Rubin Goldmark, from 1917, and Nadia Boulanger, Paris, 1921–24. First large-scale composition, the ballet *Grohg* (never performed), 1925; founder of contemporary music series, Copland-Sessions Concerts, New York, 1928–31; teacher, modern music course for laymen, New School for Social Research, New York, 1927–37; first commissioned ballet score, *Hear Ye! Hear Ye!*, 1934, continuing to compose ballets for leading American choreographers Eugene Loring, Agnes de Mille, and Martha Graham; lecturer, Harvard University, 1935, 1944; faculty chairman, becoming head of composition, Berkshire Music Center Summer schools, 1940–65; Charles Eliot Norton Professor, Harvard University, 1951–52; frequent broadcaster, 1959–72; also composer of influential film scores, including *Of Mice and Men* (dir. Milestone, 1939), *Our Town* (dir. Wood, 1940), *North Star* (dir. Milestone, 1948), *The Red Pony* (dir. Milestone, 1948), and *The Heiress* (dir. Wyler, 1949). Recipient: Guggenheim Fellowship, 1925–27; RCA Victor Award (for *Dance Symphony*), Pulitzer Prize, and New York Music Critics' Circle Award (for *Appalachian Spring*), 1945; Oscar for Best Musical Score (*The Heiress*), 1950; U.S. Medal of Freedom, 1964; Commander's Cross of the Order of Merit, Germany, 1970; Kennedy Center Award, 1979; honorary doctorates from Princeton University, 1956, Oberlin College, 1958, University of Hartford, 1959, Harvard University, 1961, New York University 1970, Columbia University, 1971, and University of York, England, 1971. Died in New York, 2 December 1990.

**WORKS** (Ballets)

1925 *Grohg* (never produced; extracts incorporated into *Dance Symphony*, 1930)
1934 *Hear Ye! Hear Ye!* (chor. Page), Chicago Opera Ballet, Chicago
1938 *Billy the Kid* (chor. Loring), Ballet Caravan, Chicago
1942 *Rodeo* (chor. de Mille), Ballet Russe de Monte Carlo, New York
1944 *Appalachian Spring* (chor. Graham), Martha Graham Company, Washington, D.C.
1963 *Ballet in Seven Movements* (score revised from *Dance Panels*; chor. Rosen), Bavarian State Opera Ballet, Munich

**Other ballets using Copland's music:** *Time Table* (Tudor, 1941), *El Salon Mexico* (Humphrey, 1943), *Day on Earth* (Humphrey, 1947), *The Pied Piper* (Robbins, 1951), *Chapeaux* (Béjart, 1957),

**Aaron Copland, 1918**

*Improvisations* (J. Carter, 1962), *Dance Symphony* (Koner, 1963), *Dance 1—Dance 2* (Bolender, 1964), *Shadow'd Ground* (Taras, 1965), *Lessons in Love* (Darrell, 1966), *Ballet for a Theatre* (Ulrich, 1973), *Polyandrion* (Ruud, 1973), *Tzaddik* (Feld, 1974), *Hamlet: Connotations* (Neumeier, 1976), *Windsor Pas de Deux* (Kudelka, 1979).

**PUBLICATIONS**


By Copland:

*What to Listen for in Music*, New York, 1939, 1957

*Our New Music*, New York, 1941; revised as *The New Music 1900–1960*, New York, 1968

*Music and Imagination*, Cambridge, Mass., 1952

*Copland on Music*, New York, 1960

*Copland: 1900 through 1942* (autobiography), with Vivian Perlis, New York, 1984

About Copland:

Heylbut, R., "America Goes to the Ballet", *Etude* (Philadelphia), July 1948

Berger, Arthur, *Aaron Copland*, New York, 1953

Smith, Julia, *Aaron Copland: His Work and Contribution to American Music*, New York, 1955

Goldman, R., "Aaron Copland", *Musical Quarterly* (New York), no. 157, 1961

Goodwin, Noël, "Copland's Musical Americana", *Dance and Dancers* (London), November 1990

Kennicott, P., "Aaron Copland: Mythical Americana", *Dance Magazine* (New York), November 1990


* * *

Aaron Copland is largely considered America's foremost twentieth-century composer. As early as the mid-1920s, he was intent on composing works that would be recognized immediately as American in character. He strove to discover the quintessential American idiom, using jazz and folk music. He realized that if modern American music was to get anywhere, it had to speak to common people in a language and through a medium they could understand. Thus he began composing for radio, film, and ballet in a simple, plain style.

Copland helped create the first distinctly American ballets, too. His first efforts were negligible. *Grohg*, composed at a time when Serge Diaghilev's productions were all the rage, was inspired by the German expressionist art film *Nosferatu.* Copland and his friend Harold Clurman wrote the scenario, a gruesome story about a magician vampire who has the power to make corpses come to life. It was Copland's first and last effort at ballet scenario-writing and his most ambitious undertaking up until that time. The ballet has never been performed.

Nonetheless, the work foreshadowed Copland's preoccupation with jazz. The opening section ("Cortège Macabre"), in particular, contains Copland's first use of polyrhythms. Also, elements emerge in the finale which have become known as typically Copland—uneven eighth-note groupings and independent rhythms. The work is most important as a forerunner to his more successful ballets.

Commissioned and choreographed by American dancer Ruth Page for the Chicago Opera Ballet, *Hear Ye! Hear Ye!* was Copland's first experience writing music for a ballet that he knew in advance would be staged. Page wrote the scenario, a satirical treatment of an American court of justice attempting to find the murderer of a nightclub dancer. Copland's score matched the story perfectly, providing a running commentary on the action. For instance, the opening and ending musical theme is a parody of the American national anthem, representing the distortion of American justice. The score also includes a parody of Mendelssohn's "Wedding March", emphasizing the cynicism behind the innocence of the newlywed couple, two of the dozens of characters that populate the courtroom.

Critics raved, saying that the score demonstrated Copland's instinct for the theater. They saw the music as thoroughly representative of the American scene, noting its modernist harmonies and rhythms. The ballet encouraged Copland to write more works for the stage.

Copland's biggest successes in the ballet form were *Billy the Kid*, *Rodeo*, and *Appalachian Spring*. Commissioned by Lincoln Kirstein for Ballet Caravan and choreographed by Eugene Loring, *Billy the Kid* was based on the life of outlaw William Bonney. For the score, Copland freely adapted cowboy songs and folk melodies to capture the spirit of the old West. The appearance of this ballet marked the crystallization of the American folksong style in music.

Copland's *Billy* score is incredibly photographic. In the first scene, a pastoral theme played by the woodwinds conveys the wide expanse and nostalgic loneliness of the open prairie. To create a rollicking, frontier-town street scene, Copland put fresh, unconventional harmonies on several, well-known cowboy melodies, including "The Old Chisholm Trail", "Git Along Little Dogies", and "Good-Bye, Old Paint". For the fight scenes, low-pitched percussion interspersed with the double-tonguing of muted trumpets make for fast pistol shots. And the celebration after Billy's death is fashioned from garish, dance-hall saloon melodies, creating the humorous effect of a player-piano out of tune. Critic Edwin Denby wrote that the score "was at every point a decisive help in realizing the poetic meaning of *Billy the Kid*". Unanimously praised, the ballet became the first, full-fledged "American" ballet in style, form, and content, and a prototype for later American West ballets.

*Rodeo* was Copland's second cowboy ballet, capturing with humor and pathos an episode from life in the West. It was choreographed and based on a scenario by Agnes de Mille for the Ballet Russe de Monte Carlo. Just as de Mille used cowboy roping movements and other gestures to evoke the flavor of American domestic manners, so did Copland draw on square-dance tunes and other indigenous music forms. He used jazz polyrhythms (some from the Charleston) to illustrate the first scene, "Buckaroo Holiday". In the "Saturday Night Waltz" scene, he put an American cadence on that distinctly European dance form, the waltz. And in the final hoedown, probably the best-known music from *Rodeo*, Copland quoted American square-dance tunes "Bonyparte" and "McLeod's Reel".

*Appalachian Spring* is Copland's most critically acclaimed work. Inspired by Martha Graham's scenario, the composer created the flavor of Shaker hymns and dance songs, using only one direct quotation—"Simple Gifts". The score is more contrapuntal in texture than any of his previous works, evoking a kind of American baroque. Conductor-composer Leonard Bernstein, Copland's close friend, has described this work as a self-portrait of Copland, because of its plainness. Clean, diversified rhythms, sensitive use of tone color, and an economic variation technique make this Copland's most important American music.

Although originally commissioned by Jerome Robbins, *Dance Panels* (*Ballet in Seven Movements*) had its first performance with choreography by Heinz Rosen, ballet master of the Bavarian State Opera in Munich. The work was conceived by Copland as a ballet without a story, stylistically direct and simple. It is rarely performed with choreography. Parts of the music are very diatonic. The lyrical sections are plain, without complexities of texture. To wit, the piece opens with a slow waltz, followed by a light, transparent scherzo. A melancholy and nostalgic pas de trois leads to a section characterized by brisk rhythms and jazzy drum patterns. The sixth section is lyrical and, after a finale in jagged, irregular rhythms, the work ends as quietly as it began.

Copland is no Stravinsky, who made his mark by creating memorable ballet scenarios. For the most part Copland's talent, as far as the dance world is concerned, lies in illustrating exactly a choreographer's vision with wit, sensitivity, and a distinctly American outlook. Finally, it should be noted that choreographers throughout this century have used Copland's works—those pieces not expressly composed for dance—to fashion remarkable ballets and modern dances. *Music for Theatre*, for example, has inspired dozens of choreographers, including Doris Humphrey, Antony Tudor, Peter Darrell, Jochen Ulrich, and Eliot Feld.

—Jody Leader

---

## COPPÉLIA

(also *La Fille aux yeux d'émail*)

**Choreography:** Arthur Saint-Léon
**Music:** Léo Delibes
**Design:** Charles Cambon, Edouard Despléchin, and Antoine Lavastre (scenery), Alfred Albert (costumes)
**Libretto:** Charles Nuitter and Arthur Saint-Léon (after E.T.A. Hoffmann)
**First Production:** Théatre Impérial de L'Opéra, Paris, 25 May 1870
**Principal Dancers:** Giuseppina Bozzacchi (Swanilda) and Eugénie Fiocre (Franz)

**Other productions include:** Theâtre de la Monnaie (staged Joseph Hansen after Saint-Léon); Brussels, 29 November 1871. Moscow Bolshoi Theatre (staged Hansen after Saint-Léon); Moscow, 5 February (24 January old style), 1882. Empire Theatre (one-scene version; staged A. Bertrand after Saint-Léon); London, 8 November 1884. Metropolitan Opera House, with Marie Guiri and Felicita Carozzi; New York, 11 March 1887. Maryinsky Theatre (chor. Petipa, revised by Enrico Cecchetti); St. Petersburg, 7 February (26 January old style) 1894. Royal Danish Ballet (staged G. Glasemann and Hans Beck); Copenhagen, 27 December 1896. Munich Hoftheater (staged Alexander Genée), with Adeline Genée (Swanilda); Munich, 21 November 1896. Empire Theatre (new production; restaged Alexander Genée), with Adeline Genée (Swanilda); London, 14 May 1906. Vic-Wells Ballet (two-act version; chor. Nicholas Sergeyev after Petipa and Cecchetti, design Edwin Calligan), with Lydia Lopokova (Swanilda) and Stanley Judson (Franz); London, 21 March 1933. Sadler's Wells Ballet (three-act version; chor. Sergeyev after Petipa and Cecchetti, design William Chappell), with Mary Honer (Swanilda), Robert Helpmann (Franz); London, 15 April 1940. Ballet Theatre (one-act version; chor. Simon Semenoff after Saint-Léon), with Irina Baronova (Swanilda), Anton Dolin (Franz), and Simon Semenoff (Dr. Coppélius); New York, 22 October 1942. London Festival Ballet (chor. Harald Lander after Glasemann and Beck), with Belinda Wright (Swanilda) and John Gilpin (Franz); London, 31 August 1956. Ballet Rambert (after Petipa and Cecchetti, design Mstislav Doboujinsky), with Violette Verdy (Swanilda), Norman Dixon (Franz), and Norman Morrice (Dr. Coppélius); London, 1 August 1957. Paris Opéra Ballet (new version; chor. Michel Descombey, design Clayette); Paris, 29 June 1966. Paris Opéra Ballet (reconstruction of original; chor. Pierre Lacotte after Saint-Léon); Paris, 1974. New York City Ballet (chor. Alexandra Danilova and George Balanchine after Petipa, Cecchetti); Saratoga Springs, N.Y., 17 July 1974. Ballet de Marseille (new version; chor. Roland Petit), with Karen Kain (Swanilda), Roland Petit (Dr. Coppélius); Paris, 18 September 1975.

### PUBLICATIONS

Robert, Grace, *The Borzoi Book of Ballets*, New York, 1946
Beaumont, Cyril, *Complete Book of Ballets*, revised edition, London, 1951
Lawson, Joan, *Mime*, New York, 1957
Denby, Edwin, *Looking at the Dance*, New York, 1968
Guest, Ivor, *Two Coppélias*, London, 1970
Kirstein, Lincoln, *Movement and Metaphor: Four Centuries of Ballet*, New York, 1970
Guest, Ivor, *The Ballet of the Second Empire*, London, 1974
Buckle, Richard, *Buckle at the Ballet: Selected Criticism*, New York, 1980
Saint-Léon, Arthur, *Letters from a Ballet Master: the Correspondance of Arthur Saint-Léon*, edited by Ivor Guest, New York, 1981
Bland, Alexander, *Observer of the Dance*, London, 1985

* * *

*Coppélia*, born in the aftermath of Romanticism, was created in Paris as France was losing its predominance as Europe's dance capital. With ballet's popularity declining, fewer ballerina stars available, and women "en travestie" usurping the male

***Coppélia*, as staged for Sadler's Wells Royal Ballet by Peter Wright, with Margaret Barbier and David Ashmole**

contingent, *Coppélia* starred an unknown child prodigy, Giuseppina Bozzacchi, partnered by Eugénie Fiocre (who reportedly looked fetching in male attire), and featured a mechanical doll, rather than an ethereal creature, as the "other woman". Pointe work served the earthbound. Although local colour provided by the robust peasants still tied the ballet to the Romantic formula, its artistic cohesiveness and inventiveness foreshadowed the classical ballet of the late nineteenth century. The individual contributions of composer Léo Delibes, choreographer Arthur Saint-Léon, and scenarist Charles Nuitter, commissioned by the Paris Opéra's director, Emile Perrin, formed an integrated work, proportionally combining music, dance, and story.

Musically, Delibes advanced the use of leitmotif to identify the characters, employed lyric melody to inspire movement, incorporated colour and tone to establish atmosphere, and attempted to formulate the music to serve the action. A masterpiece acclaimed for its originality and high quality, the score revolutionized balletic composition and set precedents for the evolution of classical ballet.

Choreographically, Saint-Léon—who built his reputation upon his strong sense of rhythm, his ability to mould choreography to the star's talents, and his aptitude for assimilating ethnic material—developed a sparkling divertissement, charming solos, refined ensemble passages, and an ingenious use of national dances, notably the Hungarian czardas. Ironically, the very choreographer who devised a system of dance notation did not record his own choreography for *Coppélia*. Ensconced in the Paris Opéra's active repertory, interrupted only by the Franco–Prussian War and the temporary closing of the theatre, Saint-Léon's choreography has in some form been preserved in the house's production.

Nuitter, a structurally conscientious scenarist, adapted a well-formulated, innovative story line from E.T.A. Hoffmann's *Der Sandmann* for *Coppélia*. Treading lightly upon the original tale's macabre elements, Nuitter's scenario drew more from *La Fille mal gardée*'s comedy than from Gothic terror. A comic trifle, witty and intellectually uncomplicated, Nuitter's libretto focused on human characters, an automaton, and a hint of enchantment with the requisite happy ending. The work, which popularized the mechanical doll as a thematic device, re-established the credibility of the *ballet d'action*.

Although *Coppélia* was enthusiastically received and scored a personal triumph for its promising young star, Bozzacchi (who appeared in eighteen performances), the ballet had one major flaw—"The Festival of the Bell", the divertissement preceding the finale. Problematic in its conceptualization, the suite was criticized as extraneous to the story line. Following the ballet's premiere at the Opéra, the dances were shortened, then deleted (though reinstated 90 years later). Other choreographers in subsequent versions have grappled with Act III, abbreviating, omitting, or redesigning it.

The problem is intrinsic in the well-drawn libretto, which closely conforms to the action. Although there are some choreographic detours in the first act and digressions in the second, the main plot dominates. The underdeveloped subplot of the festival is introduced in the first act, but without strong reinforcements injected elsewhere, the thematic thread quickly unravels and is forgotten. The climactic moment, when Franz and Coppélius realize their respective follies, is dramatically fulfilling. As Swanilda and Franz flee the workshop, the story-telling reaches an extremely satisfying conclusion. But, for etiquette's sake, reparations may be offered to Coppélius. Theatrically, the swirl of dancing peasants is a justified device to bring down the curtain. The anti-climactic divertissement, however, merely serves as a technical display.

The psychological need, expressed by some critics, to see a mature Swanilda transformed in Act III into a prima ballerina, partnered but controlled by the equally matured Franz, arises from a classical ballet orientation, which dictates the inclusion of a grand pas de deux framed by preliminary divertissements.

Although a precursor to the genre, Saint-Léon's *Coppélia* is not a classical ballet. With Franz "en travestie", provisions were not made for a grand pas de deux between the leading characters. (Interestingly, an 1887 production seen in Boston and New York included an Act II adagio for Swanilda and the festival's bell-ringer, a character now deleted.) Classical influence was probably introduced to *Coppélia* during its first Russian incarnations. The improvement effected by the interpolation is debatable—the choreography for what has become *Coppélia*'s "traditional" grand adagio is intricately awkward, uninspiring, and graceless.

*Coppélia*'s dramatic elements are entrusted to Doctor Coppélius, the ballet's most complex and paradoxical character. Because he is often portrayed as a doddering old fool, eccentric, absent-minded, and ridiculous, there is a tendency to gloss over the sinister, dark facets of his personality. Coppélius may be a lonely man, aching for reciprocated affection, but his modus operandi is psychologically warped. Scientist, master mechanic, and sorcerer, he consciously attempts to steal a young man's life-force in order to humanize his creation. Despite his selfishness, he must also propel the ballet's comic premise.

Of the three main characters, the most underdeveloped, both conceptually and mentally, is Franz, whose comic heritage descends from *commedia dell'arte* through *La Fille mal gardée*'s Colin. Shallow, self-satisfied, easily duped, and fickle, he also seems to be a first cousin to James, Albrecht, and Siegfried. Franz is unequivocally a fool.

Swanilda, on the other hand, is unsophisticated but clever. She should be saucy and mischievous, not overbearing and cruel. Like her ancestor from *La Fille mal gardée*, Lisette, she is playfully unruly and coyly manipulative. The role requires a capable technician and an accomplished comic actress.

To sustain credibility, *Coppélia* demands an understanding of the demi-caractère genre and a feeling for the late Romantic period. Otherwise, the comic elements are reduced to forced silliness and the ensemble passages deteriorate into a meaningless string of dances.

*Coppélia* owes its longevity to its inspired, very danceable score. But the ballet is also remarkable for its perennial appeal and for its historical significance as Romanticism's grand finale and classical ballet's prologue.

—Karen Dacko

---

## LE COQ D'OR

(Original Russian title: *Zolotoi petushok*, or *The Golden Cockerel*)

**Choreography:** Mikhail Fokine
**Music:** Nikolai Rimsky-Korsakov (opera *The Golden Cockerel*, performed as opera-ballet)
**Design:** Natalia Gontcharova (scenery and costumes)
**Libretto:** Vladimir Belsky (poem by Aleksandr Pushkin, as revised by Alexandre Benois)
**First Production:** Diaghilev's Ballets Russes, Théâtre National de l'Opéra, Paris, 24 May 1914
**Principal Dancers:** Tamara Karsavina (Queen of Shemakhan), Aleksis Bulgakov (King Dodon), Enrico Cecchetti (Astrologer)

**Other productions include:** Metropolitan Opera (new version; chor. Adolph Bolm), with Bolm (Dodon) and Rosina Galli (Queen of Shemakhan); New York, 1918. Metropolitan Opera and American Ballet Ensemble (new version; chor. George Balanchine, uncredited); New York, 4 February 1937. De Basil's Ballet Russe (new version, without singers; staged Fokine), with Irina Baronova (Queen of Shemakhan), Tatiana Riabouchinska (title role), Marc Plotoff (King Dodon), Harcourt Algeranov (Astrologer); London, 17 July 1937. San Francisco Opera Ballet (new version; chor. Willam Christensen); San Francisco, 3 November 1938. Rome Opera Ballet (new version; chor. Aurel Milloss); Rome, 29 February 1940. Ballet de Wallonie (staged George Skibine; design André Delfau); 3 October 1974. London Festival Ballet (staged Nicholas Beriozoff after Fokine; design Delfau, Guy after Gontcharova), as *The Golden Cockerel*; London, 6 May 1976.

### PUBLICATIONS

Downes, Edwin Owen, "*Coq d'or* in Three Versions", *The New York Times*, 21 November 1937
"The Sitter Out", *Dancing Times* (London), September 1947
Beaumont, Cyril, *Complete Book of Ballets*, revised edition, 1951
Grigoriev, Serge, *The Diaghilev Ballet*, translated by Vera Bowen, London, 1953
Fokine, Michel, *Fokine: Memoirs of a Ballet Master*, translated by Vitale Fokine, London, 1961
Horwitz, Dawn Lille, *Michel Fokine*, Boston, 1985
Garafola, Lynn, *Diaghilev's Ballets Russes*, New York, 1989

* * *

Pushkin's poem, recounting the folk tale of the Golden Cockerel who always rewards those who keep their promises, is full of satirical, robust humour as well as delicate fantasy. It is the contrast between peasant naïveté and artistic imagination that is the keynote to Rimsky-Korsakov's opera, which interprets the poem in a prologue and three acts.

In the prologue, the court Astrologer tells the audience how he will make the ageing King Dodon a gift of a magic Golden Cockerel who, in exchange for a suitable reward, will always save him from danger. The curtain then rises on the King and his sons, who are in council, arguing clumsily about how best to fight their enemy. The Astrologer appears and offers his gift. The King accepts, and the Cockerel crows, ordering his sons to battle; when the King falls asleep he is roused by the Cockerel again, who orders him forth as well. The King and his "ill-trained retinue" go forth eagerly, only to find that his sons have been killed in battle; but, from the midst of his despair the King sees a mysterious tent arise, from which appears the beautiful Queen of Shemakhan and her court. She entices him to dance, after which, exhausted, he falls at her feet and begs her to marry him. But as the couple set forth, the Astrologer appears in a clap

*Le Coq d'or* **(Beriozoff after Fokine), performed by London Festival Ballet, 1976**

of thunder, demanding his reward—the Queen. Dodon refuses and attempts to give back the Golden Cockerel before striking the Astrologer on the head with his sceptre. The Cockerel then flies at the King and kills him. The court is left in disarray, and the Queen and the Cockerel disappear as the Astrologer sings, "Those who do not keep their promises will never flourish".

Rimsky-Korsakov was one of the five composers known as the "Mighty Heap" who were determined to further the cause of a distinctly Russian music, as opposed to the classical formula following in the line of Bach, Beethoven, and Brahms. His continued interest in folk music permeates his fifteen operas, inspired as they are by the history and folk tales which form the basis of Pushkin's poems. Rimsky-Korsakov used folk tunes to depict the world of reality, and contrasted these with original melodies, created from elements inherent in those tunes, for his world of fantasy. This was a technique which his pupil Stravinsky was to employ later with his ballet scores.

Both Diaghilev and Benois had seen the first production of the opera *Le Coq d'or* in Moscow (1908), and were intrigued by its broad humour and appealing fantasy. When the Ballets Russes were to stage their annual season at the Paris Opéra in 1914, Diaghilev suggested that Benois should produce this opera, with the help of Fokine, who had now returned to the company. As Benois was fully occupied with staging and designing a play for the Moscow Art Theatre, as well as Stravinsky's opera-ballet *Le Rossignol*, he invited Natalia Gontcharova to supply a traditional and colourful set and costumes. But more importantly, he persuaded Fokine to set choreography through which dancers interpreted Pushkin's poem as it was sung by an on-stage chorus and soloists. The singers were from the Bolshoi, and were grouped around the edge of the stage as a framework to the dance.

Benois's production was a triumphant success. Each solo singer was paired with a dancer, and because each performer was Russian the relation between words and gestures was abundantly clear—the melodies for each were similarly phrased, just as the costumes of singers and dancers were similarly coloured. Particularly outstanding were Tamara Karsavina as the Queen of Shemakhan and Aleksis Bulgakov as the old King Dodon. The Golden Cockerel did not appear: only her high soprano call commanded the stage. As the music critic Edwin Evans said, "Her voice was the magic of Pushkin".

As Fokine later explained in his memoirs, this sort of treatment of an opera was extremely unusual. He wrote:

> I staged this opera the same way as I staged a ballet: that is, I demonstrated each position, each movement, each gesture.

(Opera, of course, had never before been staged by anyone in this manner.) All action on the stage was carefully composed and set, as is done with orchestra scores. Nothing was left to chance or to improvisation.

The joint participation of dancers and singers (which, according to Fokine, must have been the result of Diaghilev's greatest persuasive powers, for the singers had to be talked into relinquishing their accustomed places centre-stage) meant that, as Fokine put it, "With this division of labour, two results were achieved: one, the perfection of a vocal rendition; and two, the beauty of the mimico-balletic intepretation."

In 1937, Fokine restaged the opera for De Basil's company. He eliminated the singers and placed greater emphasis on the humour of the story, reinforcing the clumsy antics of Dodon and his court. He also created a greater contrast between the worlds of reality and fantasy by making the Queen and the Cockerel dance on pointe, as distinguished from the rest. These two roles were danced brilliantly by Riabouchinska as the Cockerel and Baronova as the Queen. Adolph Bolm staged his version of the opera, closely following the Benois–Fokine production, in several opera houses in America, beginning with his first staging for the Metropolitan Opera in New York in 1918. Bolm had been in the original Ballets Russes production for Diaghilev, dancing the role of the Vicomte.

—Joan Lawson

---

**CORALLI, Jean**

Italian dancer and choreographer. Born Giovanni (Jean) Coralli Peracini into Bolognese family in Paris, 15 January 1779. Studied at the Paris Opéra School. Married (second marriage) Teresa Coralli, solo dancer at Vienna Kärntnertor Theater. Début as dancer, Paris Opéra, 1802; performer with Sebastien Gallet's company in London, 1802–03; primo ballerino serio (in partnership with Teresa Coralli), La Scala, Milan, 1809, 1810, dancing with companies under Lorenzo Panzieri and Domenico Fabris, 1811; also dancer, La Scala, 1812, 1814–15, and 1820, La Fenice, Venice, 1813 and 1820, and Teatro San Carlos, Lisbon, 1817; début as choreographer, Vienna: ballet master, Hofburgoperntheater (Hofoper), Vienna, 1805–7; also choreographer in Milan, 1813–15, Marseilles, 1815 and 1822, and Lisbon, 1817; ballet master, Théâtre de la Porte-Saint-Martin, Paris, 1825–29; ballet master, Paris Opéra, 1831–50, collaborating with Jules Perrot in staging of first production of *Giselle*, 1841; founder, with Filippo Taglioni, Association philanthropique de secours mutuels des artistes de l'opéra, Paris, 1835; retired in 1848. Died in Paris, 1 May 1854.

**WORKS**

1806 *Paul und Rosette; oder, Die Winzer,* Hofoper, Vienna (restaged with mus. Umlauf, 1813)
*Der Grossmütige Kalif,* Hofoper, Vienna
*Amphion; oder, Der Zölig der Musen,* Hofoper, Vienna
*Die Abenzerragen und Zegris; oder, Die feindlichen Volkstämme* Hofoper, Vienna
1807 *Die Inkas; oder, Die Eroberung von Peru* (mus. Gyrowetz), Hofoper, Vienna
*Helena und Paris* (mus. J.N. Hummel), Hofoper, Vienna
1815 *Imene deificato,* La Scala, Milan
*La Mania del ballo,* La Scala, Milan
1816 Dances in *Il Ritorno d'Astrea* (cantata), La Scala, Milan
*Le Nozze di Zefiro e Flora,* La Scala, Milan
1825 *La Statua di Venera,* La Scala, Milan
*Belisa* (mus. Grossoni), La Scala, Milan
*Lisbell; ou, La Nouvelle Claudine* (mus. Grossoni), Théâtre de la Porte-Saint-Martin, Paris
*Les Ruses espagnoles* (mus. Pâris), Théâtre de la Porte-Saint-Martin, Paris
1826 *Monsieur de Pourceaugnac* (mus. Piccini, Lully), Théâtre de la Porte-Saint-Martin, Paris
*Gulliver* (mus. Piccini), Théâtre de la Porte-Saint-Martin, Paris
*La Visite à Bedlam* (mus. Piccini), Théâtre de la Porte-Saint-Martin, Paris
1827 *Le Mariage de raison* (mus. Piccini), Théâtre de la Porte-Saint-Martin, Paris
*La Neige* (mus. Chautagne, Ferrand), Théâtre de la Porte-Saint Martin, Paris
1828 *Les Hussards et les jeunes filles,* Théâtre de la Porte-Saint-Martin, Paris
*Léocadie; ou, Cinq ans après* (mus. Béancourt, Miller), Théâtre de la Porte-Saint-Martin, Paris
1829 *Les Artistes* (mus. Piccini), Théâtre de la Porte-Saint-Martin, Paris
1830 *Die Nachwandlerin* (mus. various), Hofoper, Vienna
*Die Heirat aus Vernunft* (mus. various), Hofoper, Vienna
*Childerich, König der Franken* (mus. Riotte, Gyrowetz), Hofoper, Vienna
1831 *L'Orgie* (mus. M. Carafa), Opéra, Paris
1832 Dances (mus. Gide) in *La Tentation* (opera; Halévy), Opéra, Paris
1833 Dances in *Ali-Baba* (opera; mus. Cherubini; some dance mus. Halévy), Opéra, Paris
1834 *La Tempête; ou, L'Ile des génies* (mus. Schneitzhoeffer), Opéra, Paris
Dances in *Don Juan* (opera; mus. Mozart), Opéra, Paris
1836 *Le Diable boîteaux* (mus. Gide), Opéra, Paris
1837 *La Chatte métamorphosée en femme* (mus. de Montfort), Opéra, Paris
Dances in *Stradella* (opera; mus. Niedermeyer), Opéra, Paris
1839 Dancs in *Le Lac des fées* (opera; mus. Auber), Opéra, Paris
*La Tarentule* (mus. Gide), Opéra, Paris
1840 Dances in *Les Martyrs* (opera; mus. Donizetti), Opéra, Paris
1841 *Giselle; ou, Les Wilis* (with J. Perrot; mus. Adam), Opéra, Paris
Dances in *La Riene de Chypre* (opera; mus. Halévy), Opéra, Paris
1843 *La Péri* (mus. Burgmüller), Opéra, Paris
1844 *Eucharis* (mus. Deldevez), Opéra, Paris
Dances in *Marie Stuart* (opera; mus. Niedermeyer), Opéra, Paris
1845 Dances in *L'Etoile de Séville* (opera; mus. Balfe), Opéra, Paris
1846 Dances in *David* (opera; mus. Mermet), Opéra, Paris
Dances in *L'Âme en peine* (opera; mus. Flotow), Opéra, Paris
1847 *Ozaï; ou, L'Insulaire* (mus. Gide), Opéra, Paris

**Other works include:** for Théâtre de la Porte-Saint-Martin—dances in *Mandrin* (melodrama by Antier, Arago, Cosiner; 1827), *Faust* (drama by Béraud, Merle, Nodier; 1828), *Marino Falieri* (tragedy by Dalavigne; 1830).

Giovanni Coralli

## PUBLICATIONS


Saint-Léon, Arthur, *La Sténochorégraphie, ou l'art d'écrire promtement la danse,* Paris, 1852

Castil-Blaze, *La'Académie impériale de musique*, Paris, 1855

Gautier, Théophile, *The Romantic Ballet as seen by Théophile Gautier*, translated by Cyril Beaumont, London, 1932

Lifar, Serge, *Carlotta Grisi*, Paris, 1941

Lifar, Serge, *Giselle*, Paris, 1942

Beaumont, Cyril, *The Ballet Called Giselle*, London, 1944

Beaumont, Cyril, *Complete Book of Ballets*, revised edition, London, 1951

Guest, Ivor, *The Romantic Ballet in England*, London, 1954

Guest, Ivor, *The Romantic Ballet in Paris*, London, 1966

Winter, Marian Hannah, *The Pre-Romantic Ballet*, London, 1974


* * *

If ever a ballet master was in the right place at the right time, and in possession of the right skills and experience, it was Jean Coralli, who turned up in Paris on the eve of the era we now call the era of the Romantic Ballet. He came in 1825 to serve as choreographer at that perennial proving ground for would-be Opéra ballet masters, the Théâtre de la Porte-Saint-Martin. Initial dance training at the Paris Opéra and two decades of work throughout Western Europe had honed his skills and sharpened his theatrical perceptions. He was ready and waiting in 1831 when the brilliant entrepreneur, Louis Véron, took over the Opéra directorship, and began looking for artists who would form the foundation of his theatrical empire. Marie Taglioni served as one cornerstone; Jean Coralli was another. He held the post of ballet master at the Paris Opéra under Véron from 1831 to 1835, and then continued under a succession of directors until 1850. It was an auspicious time to be ballet master at the Opéra, to work for audiences avid for ballet, and to create ballets for dancers like Fanny Elssler (for whom he created four works) and Carlotta Grisi (for whom he created one).

Coralli's vision of ballet fit well with Véron's contention that audiences wanted spectacle, rapid action, variety, grandeur, and star dancers, for Coralli eschewed strict adherence to popular *ballet d'action* principles. Instead of devoting all the elements of ballet—dancing, pantomime, machinery, décor, costumes, and music—to the depiction of a coherent dramatic action, he used them to create a succession of striking stage pictures. Though Coralli apparently could be difficult to work with, he appears to have been a master of collaboration, giving designers, musicians, and dancers ample opportunities to display their genius. He knew how to bring all the diverse elements that went to make a ballet together into a single integrated picture. The critic "J. T.", writing of *La Tempête*, summed it up neatly: ". . . today ballets inhabit a different realm of ideas than did those of composers of other times: balletic action is hardly more than a vehicle for grouping dancers, a sort of frame which serves to show the décor" (*La Quotidienne*, 20 September 1834). Critic Jules Janin was delighted with the result, describing the inferno scene in *La Tentation* with relish—"a beautiful tumult, a sublime bacchanal, a picture from hell, an admirable cacophony of shapes, of sounds, of masks, of dances" (*Le Journal des Debats*, 27 June 1832). Many shared Janin's delight, for Coralli enjoyed considerable success in works such as *La Tentation* (where St. Anthony struggled against sensuality and the tumultuous forces of hell), *La Tempête* (with its supernatural mystery and shipwreck), and *La Péri* (in which oriental mysticism and eroticism served as the background).

Coralli gave full reign to the imaginations of brilliant designers like Ciceri and machinists like Constant, whose exploitation of new methods of lighting and scenery-painting enhanced the overall illusion of fantastic realities. There was the grand staircase in *La Tentation* that stretched into the depths of Hell, "supported by two monsters, muzzles gaping . . . All hell's troops descend there: drums, trumpets, foot soldiers, hussars, artillery . . .". There was the flight of Ariel and Lea in *La Tempête* (based on the Shakespeare play) which was, as *La Quotidienne* described it, "performed with great lightness. The aerial perspective of the forest . . . is painted with great skill, and is lit in a piquant manner. . . . verisimilitude has never been so closely approached." A favourite scene in this work represented the sun rising, setting, and filtering through a forest.

Coralli did more than supply a vehicle for the display of other artists' talents. His dances were central to the creation of the illusion, whether it be that of a picturesque Italian village (*La Tarentule*), of the seething chaos of Hell (*La Tentation*), or the gentle moonlit mystery of a spirit-haunted forest (*Giselle*). As demonstrated in *Giselle*, he was a master craftsman who melded his dances into the fabric of ballets. Like other choreographers of the Romantic period (Filippo Taglioni for instance), he used dance not as incidental divertissement, but as a tool for the enhancement of atmosphere and illusion. His character dances in particular were highly popular during a period when anything foreign stimulated imaginations. J.T. found those in *Le Diable boîteux* "voluptuous, intoxicating, sweet, tender, lively and passionate." They not only depicted all the emotions of love, but contained the spirit of the Spanish people. Likewise, Hippolyte Prévost recognized the true talent behind the success of *La Péri*. "It is not therefore M. Gautier [writer of the scenario], but M. Coralli who is the true magician of this fairy tale. M. Gautier has repeated what others have made before him; M. Coralli, he has imagined a thousand delicious groups, a thousand charming pas. . . . Honour therefore to M. Coralli!" (*Le Constitutionnel*, 19 July 1834).

Coralli's ability to create illusion through dance was most evident from his collaboration on *Giselle*. The great Jules Perrot created the dances for Giselle (Carlotta Grisi), but Coralli, as far as we can tell, contributed the corps dances. *Giselle* was not typical of Coralli's ballets in that its story required only two simple scenes, no grandeur, no rapid changes, and no bewildering stage transformations. Coralli rose to the occasion, especially in the second act, where it was his dances for the white, tulle-clad wilis that created the atmosphere of poetic mystery and sentimental femininity that had critics and audiences in raptures. The image of cool spirits wafting through moonlit mists relied upon the regular soloists and corps de ballet, that is on Coralli's work, not Perrot's. Hippolyte Prévost wrote in 1841, "Nothing is purer in design and truer in realization and character than the chorus dances." Another critic commented on the effect of Coralli's second act dances this way: ". . . here are charming dances and divinely light and vaporous groups; here is a delicate, fine and dainty fantasy. All these wilis' dances are true little masterpieces which impart the greatest honour to M. Coraly."

—John Chapman

---

**CORNAZANO, Antonio**

Italian dance theorist, writer, poet, and possibly dancing master. Born into noble family in Piacenza, c. 1430. Educated privately; also studied at the Studio di Siena, 1443–48, and with dancing master and theorist Domenico di Piacenza, Piacenza. Married Taddea de Varro, c. 1479. Secretary, teacher, and "consigliore" to house of Francesco Sforza, Piacenza, 1454–66, writing dance treatise, *Libro dell'arte del danzare*, 1455; military adviser to General Bartolommeo Colleone, Venice, 1466–c.1477, returning to Piacenza, 1477–79; called to services of Ercole I d'Este, Ferrara, from 1479. Died in Ferrara, December 1484.

**PUBLICATIONS**

By Cornazano:

*Libro dell'arte del danzare*, 1455; second version, 1465 (one known copy of manuscript at Biblioteca Apostolica Vaticana, Rome)

*The Book on the Art of Dancing*, translated by Madeleine Inglehearn and Peggy Forsyth, London, 1981

About Cornazano:

Poggiali, C., *Memorie per la storia di Piacenza*, vol. 1, Piacenza, 1789

Zannoni, "Il Libro dell'arte del danzare di Antonio Cornazano (1465)", *Rendiconti della Reale Accademia dei Lincei*, series 4, vol. 6, 1890

Mazzi, C., "*Il Libro dell'arte del danzare* di Antonio Cornazano", *La Bibliofilia*, vol. 17, 1915–16

Michel, Artur, "The Earliest Dance Manuals", *Medievalia et humanistica*, 3, 1945

Bianchi, D., "Tre maestri di danza alla corte di Francesco Sforza", *Archivo storico lombardo*, series 9, vol. 2, 1962–64

Meylan, R., *L'Énigme de la musique des basses danses du quinzième siècle*, Berne and Stuttgart, 1968

Brainard, Ingrid, "Bassedanse, Bassandanza and Ballo in the Fifteenth Century", *Dance History Research* (New York), vol. 64, 1970

* * *

Antonio Cornazano was a humanist and poet of considerable renown in Renaissance Italy. A cultured and refined gentleman of letters, he is unlikely to have been a professional dancer or dancing master, although in the dedicatory poem at the beginning of his treatise on dance he says, "Love has rightly ordained that I should set down in writing for you the art which I have already taught so that it may not be lost." It is more likely that Cornazano was that mainstay of the dance teacher, an enthusiastic amateur. His references to Duke Borso and Lady Beatrice d'Este show that he had spent time at the court of Ferrara, where the great dancing master Domenico taught, and indeed Cornazano refers to Domenico as "my only master and compatriot".

Cornazano's treatise is dedicated to Hyppolita Sforza, and we know that when she married and moved to Naples, she took with her the dancing master Johannes Ambrosio, who also claimed to have studied with Domenico of Ferrara. It is possible, therefore, that while Ambrosio was her official dancing master and taught her technique and style, as well as choreographing dances for the Sforza court in general, Cornazano taught her some of his favourite dances as learned from Domenico.

Another possibility is that Cornazano's work was in part a transcript of Domenico's treatise, with a few added thoughts of his own, written for the young Hyppolita to study. It is certainly very much closer to Domenico's in format than those of Guglielmo and Ambrosio, though more practical and lacking the beautifully poetic similes employed by Domenico. Cornazano also boasts that "having heard it [a new dance] described or seen it danced only once, that was sufficient for me to join into the dance *dicto facto* and without further ado perform the same without a single error of judgement"—and yet some of his dance instructions fit very awkwardly with the music. A glance at Domenico's treatment of the same dances shows the hand of a real craftsman, with steps and music blending together with grace and elegance.

Cornazano provides some musical clues regarding the treatment of the *bassadanza*. None of the other sources give music for these dances, although they are obviously very popular. Cornazano, however, gives three pieces of music which he says are "best and more often used than all the others" for the *bassadanza* and *saltarelli*. This suggests that any suitable music can be used for dancing the *bassadanza*, whereas the *balli* each had their own composed music.

The real value of Cornazano is that he provides another source for a period in which material is very sparse, and only by being able to compare all these sources can we begin to build up a picture, not only of specific dances, but of the place of dance in the courtly life of Renaissance Italy.

—Madeleine Inglehearn

---

**LE CORSAIRE**

**Choreography:** Joseph Mazilier
**Music:** Adolph Adam
**Design:** Edouard Desplèchin, Charles Cambon, and Joseph

Thierry (scenery) and A. Martin (costumes), Sacré (machinery)
**Libretto:** H. Vernoy de Saint-Georges and Joseph Mazilier (after "The Corsair", poem by Lord Byron)
**First Production:** Théatre Impérial de L'Opéra, Paris, 23 January 1856
**Principal Dancers:** Carolina Rosati (Medora), Claudina Cucchi (Gulnare), Domenico Segarelli (Conrad)

**Other productions include:** St. Petersburg Bolshoi Theatre (chor. Jules Perrot and Marius Petipa after Mazilier, with additional mus. Pugni), with Ekaterina Friedberg (Medora) and Marius Petipa (Conrad); St. Petersburg, 24 January (12 January old style) 1858. St. Petersburg Bolshoi Theatre (restaged Petipa, with additional mus. Delibes), with Marie Petipa (Medora); St. Petersburg, 6 February (25 January old style) 1868. Maryinsky Theatre (new version; restaged Petipa, with additional mus. Drigo and Minkus), with Pierina Legnani (Medora); St. Petersburg, 25 January (13 January old style) 1899. Moscow Bolshoi Theatre (new version; restaged Aleksandr Gorsky, with additional mus. Frédéric Chopin and Petr Tchaikovsky), with Ekaterina Geltser (Medora) and Vasily Tikhomirov (Conrad); Moscow, 15 January 1912. Kirov Ballet (staged Agrippina Vaganova after Petipa); Leningrad, 15 May 1931. Maly Theatre (new version; chor. Petr Gusev, libretto Yuri Slonimsky); Leningrad, 31 May 1955. Stanislavsky and Nemirovich-Danchenko Ballet (staged Nina Grishina after Petipa), with Maris Liepa; Moscow, 1957. Kirov Ballet (new production; staged Konstantin Sergeyev after Petipa); Leningrad, 5 July 1973.

**Other choreographic treatments of story:** Giovanni Galzerani (Milan, 1826), François Decombe Albert (London, 1837; revived London, 1844).

## PUBLICATIONS


Karsavina, Tamara, *Theatre Street*, London, 1930
Slonimsky, Yuri, "Jules Perrot", translated by Anatole Chujoy, *Dance Index* (New York), December 1945
Beaumont, Cyril, *Complete Book of Ballets*, revised edition, London, 1951
Petipa, Marius, *The Memoirs of Marius Petipa, Russian Ballet Master*, edited by Lillian Moore, London, 1958
Roslavleva, Natalia, *Era of the Russian Ballet*, London, 1966
Guest, Ivor, *The Ballet of the Second Empire*, London, 1974
Balanchine, George, and Mason, Francis, *Balanchine's Complete Stories of the Great Ballets*, Garden City, N.Y., 1977
Smakov, Gennady, *The Great Russian Dancers*, New York, 1984
Guest, Ivor, *Jules Perrot: Master of the Romantic Ballet*, London, 1984
Vazem, Yekaterina, "Memoirs of a Ballerina of the St. Petersburg Bolshoi Theatre", *Dance Research* (London), 3 parts: Autumn 1985, Spring 1986, Spring 1987
Vaughan, David, "Annals of *Le Corsaire*: The Kirov 1988", *Ballet Review* (New York), Fall 1987
Percival, John, "The Corsair Sails Again", *Dance and Dancers* (London), January 1988


* * *

Byron's poem *The Corsair*, first published in 1814, seemed an ideal source for a spectacular ballet. Its location—Greece was still under Ottoman domination in the nineteenth century—was romantic and barbaric, and scenes in the slave market, the pirates' cavern, and the seraglio, not to mention the dramatic shipwreck for a final climax, all had exotic appeal. Before the ballet Joseph Mazilier choreographed for the Paris Opéra (1856), Byron's poem had inspired Berlioz's swashbuckling overture (1831) as well as several ballets. Galzerani's for La Scala in Milan (1826) was the first, but Albert's for the King's Theatre Haymarket (revised seven years later at the Theatre Royal, Drury Lane) is perhaps better known. Albert followed Byron's original narrative but Mazilier realized that to make the ballet more appealing he needed to keep the names, characters, and spirit of the original while altering the scenario—such that Medora was no longer the stay-at-home wife of the corsair, Conrad, but an independent heroine who fought for her liberty and the right to choose her own partner.

The score, commissioned from Adolph Adam (his last ballet) was praised for its dramatic inspiration and the whole production acclaimed. A contemporary reviewer exclaimed, "All Paris will go to see the scene of the ship sinking beneath the waves amid the lightning flashes and violence of the storm." The great dramatic ballerina Carolina Rosati brought grace, intelligence, and wit to the role of Medora, Mlle. Cucchi a sparkling humour to Gulnare's outwitting of the Pasha, and Domenico Segarelli, who specialized in "terrible and menacing looks", was Conrad.

*Le Corsaire* was an instant success, and within six months Rosati repeated her triumph at Her Majesty's Theatre in London. The following season the ballet was staged in Italy (Turin and Milan), the United States (Boston), and Russia (St. Petersburg), following Vernoy de Saint George's scenario for Mazilier and drawing on his original choreography. After Rosati's retirement from the stage, *Le Corsaire* was dropped from the Opéra's repertoire, and the original sets and costumes were among those destroyed by fire in 1861. However, in 1867, Mazilier was persuaded to restage the complete work in Paris, adding a pas des fleurs as entertainment for the character Pasha Seyd, to newly composed music by Leo Delibes.

In many respects *Le Corsaire* is typical of successful nineteenth-century works in which spectacular effects were all-important; the principal roles called for mimetic as well as dancing skills. Originally performed throughout the West, it only survived in active repertoire in Russia, where Byron's poems were immensely popular. Here its repeated stagings reflected shifts in audiences' tastes. Initially mounted at the request of the theatre's administration for St. Petersburg's Bolshoi Theatre by Jules Perrot (1858), it had effects (supervised by Andrei Roller, in collaboration with designers Wagner and Petrov), which were even more impressive than in the Parisian original, whose complicated scenario was still being followed.

In the story of *Le Corsaire*, Medora is sold by her guardian, a bazaar-keeper by the name of Lanquedem, to the lecherous Pasha Seyd (performed by Perrot himself) when none of the slave girls takes his fancy. She is rescued by Conrad (Marius Petipa, who subsequently staged four productions of the ballet) who becomes her lover. In the corsairs' lair the rescued slave girls entertain their new masters and persuade Conrad to free them. In revenge Conrad's henchman, Birbanto, plots with Lanquedem to re-capture Medora after rendering Conrad unconscious with drugged lotus-blossoms.

Rival sultanas Zulma and Gulnare are overshadowed in Seyd's harem by the arrival of Medora. Gulnare seizes the opportunity to impersonate Medora at her marriage to the Pasha, enabling Conrad to rescue Medora again. Aboard ship the corsairs celebrate their return. After Medora has exposed Birbanto as a traitor, a storm builds up and the stricken vessel sinks beneath the waves. All are drowned except Conrad and

*Le Corsaire*, **Act III, performed by the Kirov Ballet**

Medora, who are seen embracing on a solitary rock surrounded by a now calm sea.

Within this narrative structure there were opportunities for sustained dancing; there were character dances for the slave girls and corsairs, a famous pas d'eventail to entertain the pirates, and the dance of the odalisques to entertain Pasha Seyd. With each revival the choreography was altered and new music was composed to the choreographers' requirements or inserted from other sources. Thus parts of the ballet are now attributable to Cesare Pugni, Prince Peter von Oldenburg, and Riccardo Drigo as well as to Adam and Delibes. Tchaikovsky's music for Sobeschanskaya's 1877 *Swan Lake* pas de deux was rediscovered in the score for Gorsky's 1912 Moscow staging of the ballet.

It is not easy to trace the evolution of *Le Corsaire* through the nineteenth century, but whereas Perrot drew inspiration from the paintings of Eugène Delacroix for his groupings, Petipa made his stage picture more symmetrical. The most vivid descriptions of the ballet appear in the autobiographies of two great Russian Medoras. Ekaterina Vazem recalls the naturalistic acting of Petipa, and describes Saint-Leon's desire to elaborate further the "Jardin animée" so that the audience was sprayed with perfume. Tamara Karsavina describes her own role, including Medora's mimetic dance "en travestie" (originally performed in Greek skirt and bolero but by the turn of the century in Turkish trousers) ending with the nautical command "en borde". She also gives an amusing description of hired sailors crawling on all fours beneath the canvas sea before rising to run on two legs as the waves grow higher.

For many years, Western audiences only knew the ballet from such written descriptions and from the few classical extracts performed in divertissements—the pas de deux, the pas d'esclave, the odalisques' trio, and "Le Jardin animée"—but since 1987 the Kirov has toured its most recent and highly entertaining reconstruction, providing a new focus of interest in the old ballet. This covers only half the narrative with a simplified shipwreck now serving as prologue to Conrad's adventures. It has revealed, however, the context for one of the most popular pas de deux in the repertory and reminded audiences that this was originally created by Petipa as a pas de trois for Medora (Legnani), Conrad, and a slave. Its development as a showpiece dates from performances by the virtuoso dancer Vakhtang Chabukiani, who eliminated the ballet's hero from the trio and based his own interpretation on Michelangelo's slaves bursting the bonds that imprison them. Such nonsensical social comment, designed for 1930s Soviet audiences, does not detract from the bravura embellishment of the role which later gave Nureyev a showcase in the West for his own "sleek barbarity and magnetic power".

—Jane Pritchard

---

## COTILLON

**Choreography:** George Balanchine
**Music:** Emmanuel Chabrier (orchestrated by Chabrier, Felix Mottl, Vittorio Rieti)
**Design:** Christian Bérard
**Libretto:** Boris Kochno
**First Production:** Gala in Honour of Prince Louis II of Monaco,

**Lubov Rostova and David Lichine in *Cotillon*, Ballets Russes de Monte Carlo, 1932**

Monte Carlo, 17 January 1932 (company premiere: Les Ballets Russes de Monte Carlo, Monte Carlo, 12 April 1932)
**Principal Dancers:** (roles not originally identified) Tamara Toumanova (Daughter of the House), Nathalie Strakhova (Her Friend), George Balanchine (one performance, followed by David Lichine; The First Guest), Valentina Blinova (Mistress of Ceremonies), Léon Woizikovsky (Master of Ceremonies), Lubov Rostova and Valentin Froman ("Hands of Fate" pas de deux)

**Other productions include:** Joffrey Ballet (reconstructed by Millicent Hodson and Kenneth Archer, after Balanchine), with Tina LeBlanc (Young Girl), Edward Stierle (Young Man), Leslie Carothers (Mistress of Ceremonies), Jerel Hilding (Master of Ceremonies); New York, 26 October 1989.

## PUBLICATIONS

Coton, A.V., *A Prejudice for Ballet*, London, 1938
Gowing, Lawrence, "*Cotillon* and the English Ballet", *Dancing Times* (London), August 1938
Beaumont, Cyril, *Complete Book of Ballets*, revised edition, 1951
Archer, Kenneth, "The Quest for *Cotillon*", *Ballet Review* (New York), Summer 1988
Barnes, Patricia, "The Past Recalled", *Dance and Dancers* (London), February 1989
McDonagh, Don, "Lost Balanchine Rediscovered", *Ballet Review* (New York), Fall 1989
Kochno, Boris, *Christian Bérard*, New York, 1990
Jacobs, Laura, "*Cotillon* Revived", *Ballet Review* (New York), Winter 1990
García-Márquez, Vicente, *Les Ballets Russes*, New York, 1990

* * *

The action of *Cotillon* takes place in a ballroom. The programme prefixed each episode with an explanatory title and short description of the action:

> *The Toilet.* The Dance Room where the final preparations are interrupted by the arrival of the guests. *The Introductions.* The Conductor of the Dance runs in late. *The Pleasure Garden.* The Conductor and the Conductress demonstrate the figures of the first dance, which are repeated by all the guests. *Novel Entrance and Dance of Hats.* Harlequins, Jockeys and Spaniards. *The Hand of Fate.* The Cavalier approaches to choose his partner from amongst the ladies, but is stopped by the hand of destiny, gloved in black, which suddenly appears. *The Magic Lantern.* A young girl tells the future to the guests. Appearance of the "Chauve-Souris" and "la Coupe de Champagne". *Grand Rond and end of Cotillon.*

A young girl puts the finishing touches to her toilet helped by a friend; an early guest admires her, but they are interrupted by the arrival of the guests. In the absence of the Conductor of the Cotillon, his partner makes the introductions. The Conductor arrives, breathless and agitated, and begins to organize the guests. Following the first figure of the Cotillon, favours are distributed, leading to a series of character vignettes taking their style from the various hats. The Cavalier comes up to the curtain to choose one of the hands revealed above it, but is stopped by the sudden appearance of Destiny, who forces him to dance with her. The young girl tells fortunes; she is rebuffed by the Conductress of the Dance. Destiny, as the bat, flies away with her partner. The young girl returns and fouettés centre stage, her spins accentuated by the guests sweeping around her in a counterpointing circle as the curtain falls.

In *Cotillon*, Balanchine and Kochno devised a ballet less important for its obvious surface action than for its atmosphere. Beyond the framework of people meeting at a social occasion and the formal structure of the Cotillon, the work exuded a subtle poetry, so delicate as to be only half-perceived, and all the more potent for being merely suggested and never explained. To many, *Cotillon* engendered a sense of bittersweet decay, a strange mixture of youth and sophistication, full of poignancy and unspoken tragedy. Running like an undercurrent beneath the surface was an impression of foreboding that the revellers might sense but which they could not understand, and over which they had no control. It engendered an intense yet mysterious and delicate emotion that transformed the surface action into something rich and strange, and exuded strange contrasts, mixing gaiety and warning, sweetness and bitterness, loveliness and corruption. Some saw a desperation in the gaiety, a "sense of sweet sin implicit in every move and gesture" (A.V. Coton).

The principal pas de deux, the Hand of Fate, conveyed no passion, only a vague sexuality, its effect heightened by being communicated by hands and eyes alone. Gestures had their basis in the contemporary and ageing social dance form, but were given individual twists which reinforced the singular atmosphere; calm and formal sequences would be broken by sudden, quirky gestures, jutting hips, or a flick of the wrist.

The role of the young girl was created for the thirteen-year-old Tamara Toumanova, her extreme youth in disturbing contrast to the maturity of her stage persona. The ballet was created for a predominently young company, and for some, the ballet expressed the heady quality of young people at their first ball, with all youth's mixture of innocence and sophistication, confidence hiding insecurity, composure masking heartbreak.

*Cotillon* was a triumphant collaboration between Balanchine, Kochno, and their designer, Christian Bérard. Bérard's understated setting of a few red-curtained boxes, gilt chairs, and subtly coloured and decorated romantic ball dresses for the girls and evening dress for the men, the leading dancers picked out by their brightly coloured tail coats, reflected the paradoxical atmosphere of reality and mystery. Using existing music by Chabrier, Balanchine revealed its undertones of haunting nostalgia; and music, libretto, choreography, and design fused into a seamless whole.

*Cotillon* owed much to the subtlety of Kochno's libretto, but the undercurrents were implicit in the choreography, and not obvious from the surface action alone. So subtle was the atmosphere that it almost defied expression in words and, indeed, went unperceived by many, who saw the ballet as nothing more than a pleasant divertissement.

—Sarah C. Woodcock

---

**CRAGUN, Richard**

American dancer. Born in Sacramento, California, 5 October 1944. Studied tap dance with Jean Lucille; studied ballet with Barbara Briggs, then at the Banff School of Fine Arts, Canada, pupil of Gweneth Lloyd and Betty Farally, and at the Royal Ballet School, pupil of Errol Addison and Harold Turner, London, 1961–62; also studied with Vera Volkova, Copenhagen. Dancer, Stuttgart Ballet, from 1962: principal dancer (solo dancer), from 1965, creating numerous roles under choreographer John Cranko and forming celebrated partnership with ballerina Marcia Haydée; international guest artist, including with Boston Ballet, 1968, Royal Ballet Touring Company, England, 1968 and 1970, American Ballet Theatre, 1976, 1978, 1983, Chicago Ballet, 1980, Ballet du XXe Siècle, 1983, Feld Ballet/NY, 1984, and Bavarian State Opera Ballet, Munich, 1986; has also appeared with German Opera Ballet of Berlin, (East) Berlin State Opera Ballet, Royal Danish Ballet, Royal Swedish Ballet, Dutch National Ballet, National Ballet of Canada, Vienna State Opera Ballet, Tokyo Festival Ballet, and Ballet of La Scala, Milan. Recipient: German Order of Merit (Bundesverdienstkreuz), 1985; *Dance Magazine* Award, 1985; title of "Kammertänzer" conferred by Minister President of Baden-Württemberg; German Golden Shoe Award, 1987.

**ROLES**

1962 Summer in *The Seasons* (Cranko), Stuttgart Ballet, Stuttgart
Principal dancer in *The Great Peacock* (Wright), Stuttgart Ballet, Stuttgart
Wedding pas de deux (cr) in *Romeo and Juliet* (new version; Cranko), Stuttgart Ballet, Stuttgart
1963 Benvolio in *Romeo and Juliet* (Cranko), Stuttgart Ballet, Stuttgart
Romeo in *Romeo and Juliet* (Cranko), Stuttgart Ballet, Stuttgart
Principal dancer (cr) in *L'Estro Harmonico* (Cranko), Stuttgart Ballet, Stuttgart
Reflection (cr) in *The Mirror Walkers* (Wright), Stuttgart Ballet, Stuttgart
Principal dancer (cr) in *Die Reise nach Jerusalem* (*Musical Chairs*; Cranko), Stuttgart Ballet, Stuttgart
Principal dancer (cr) in *Quintet* (Wright), Stuttgart Ballet, Stuttgart
Principal dancer in *House of Birds* (MacMillan), Stuttgart Ballet, Stuttgart
Principal dancer (cr) in *Variationen* (*Trade Variations*; (Cranko), Stuttgart Ballet, Stuttgart
Pepe in *Las Hermanas* (MacMillan), Stuttgart Ballet, Stuttgart
1964 Principal dancer in *Diversions* (MacMillan), Stuttgart Ballet, Stuttgart
Mercutio in *Romeo and Juliet* (Cranko), Stuttgart Ballet, Stuttgart
Principal dancer (cr) in *Design for Dancers* (Wright), Stuttgart Ballet, Stuttgart
Tsarevitch in *The Firebird* (Cranko), Stuttgart Ballet, Stuttgart
Principal dancer in *The Force* (Killar), Noverre Society, Stuttgart
1965 First Movement (cr) in *Bouquet Garni* (Cranko), Stuttgart Ballet, Stuttgart
Principal dancer in *Allegro Brillante* (Balanchine), Stuttgart Ballet, Stuttgart
Third Movement in *La Valse* (Balanchine), Stuttgart Ballet, Stuttgart
Principal dancer (cr) in *Opus 1* (Cranko), Stuttgart Ballet, Stuttgart
Fourth Song (cr) in *Das Lied von der Erde* (*Song of the Earth*; MacMillan), Stuttgart Ballet, Stuttgart
Prince Siegfried in *Swan Lake* (Cranko after Petipa, Ivanov), Stuttgart Ballet, Stuttgart
The Man in *Das Lied von der Erde* (MacMillan), Stuttgart Ballet, Stuttgart
1966 Lensky in *Onegin* (Cranko), Stuttgart Ballet, Stuttgart
Principal dancer (cr) in *Concerto for Flute and Harp* (Cranko), Stuttgart Ballet, Stuttgart
Albrecht in *Giselle* (Petipa after Coralli, Perrot; staged Wright), Stuttgart Ballet, Stuttgart
Principal dancer (cr) in *Pas de quatre* (Cranko), Stuttgart Ballet, Stuttgart
The Prince in *The Nutcracker* (Cranko), Stuttgart Ballet, Stuttgart
1967 Joker in *Jeu de cartes* (Cranko), Stuttgart Ballet, Stuttgart
Title role in *Onegin* (Cranko), Stuttgart Ballet, Stuttgart
The Catalyst in *Katalyse* (Cranko), Stuttgart Ballet, Stuttgart
Title role in *Apollo* (Balanchine), Stuttgart Ballet, Stuttgart
Principal dancer (cr) in *Namouna* (Wright), Stuttgart Ballet, Stuttgart
1968 Roi Ubu (cr) in *Présence* (Cranko), Stuttgart Ballet, Stuttgart
Principal dancer (cr) in *The Sphinx* (MacMillan), Stuttgart Ballet, Stuttgart
Prince Siegfried in *Swan Lake* (Petipa, Ivanov; staged Sergeyev, de Valois, Ashton), Royal Ballet Touring Company, London
Principal dancer in *Weg nach Innen* (*The Way Inward*; Rille), Noverre Society, Stuttgart
1969 Petrucchio (cr) in *The Taming of the Shrew* (Cranko), Stuttgart Ballet, Stuttgart

**Richard Cragun in Forsythe's *Daphne*, 1977**

1970 Prince Florimund in *The Sleeping Beauty* (Petipa, Ashton; staged Wright), Royal Ballet Touring Company, Manchester
Pickwick (cr) in *Brouillards* (Cranko), Stuttgart Ballet, Stuttgart
Principal dancer (cr) in *Poème de l'extase* (Cranko), Stuttgart Ballet, Stuttgart
Third Movement in *Agon* (Balanchine), Stuttgart Ballet, Stuttgart
Principal dancer (cr) in *Kommen und Gehen* (Kylián), Stuttgart Ballet, Stuttgart
1971 Escamillo (cr) in *Carmen* (Cranko), Stuttgart Ballet, Stuttgart
Don José in *Carmen* (Cranko), Stuttgart Ballet, Stuttgart
1972 R. (cr) in *Initials R.B.M.E.* (Cranko), Stuttgart Ballet, Stuttgart
Principal dancer (cr) in *Legend* (pas de deux; Cranko), Stuttgart Ballet, Munich
Principal dancer (cr) in *−1 + 6* (Cranko), Stuttgart Ballet, Stuttgart
1973 Prisoner (cr) in *Spuren* (*Traces*; Cranko), Stuttgart Ballet, Stuttgart
Principal dancer in *Arena* (Tetley), Stuttgart Ballet, Stuttgart
Principal dancer (cr) in *Voluntaries* (Tetley), Stuttgart Ballet, Stuttgart
1974 Principal dancer (cr) in *Ritual Album* (Berg), Stuttgart Ballet, Stuttgart
Principal dancer in *Gemini* (Tetley), Stuttgart Ballet, Stuttgart
Principal dancer (cr) in *Nacht* (Neumeier), Stuttgart Ballet, Stuttgart
1975 Principal dancer in *Laborintus* (Tetley), Stuttgart Ballet, Stuttgart
Principal dancer in *Intermezzo* (Feld), Stuttgart Ballet, Stuttgart
Daphnis (cr) in *Daphnis und Chloë* (Tetley), Stuttgart Ballet, Stuttgart
Brighella in *Pierrot Lunaire* (Tetley), Stuttgart Ballet, Stuttgart
Principal dancer (cr) in *Alegrias* (Tetley), Stuttgart Ballet, Stuttgart
Principal dancer in *Symphony in C* (Balanchine), Stuttgart Ballet, Stuttgart
1976 The Sacrifice in *Le Sacre du Printemps* (Tetley), Stuttgart Ballet, Stuttgart
Principal dancer in *Songs of a Wayfarer* (Béjart), Stuttgart Ballet, Stuttgart
King Claudius (cr) in *Der Fall Hamlet* (new version of *Hamlet Connotations*; Neumeier), Stuttgart Ballet, Stuttgart
Second Movement (cr) in *Requiem* (MacMillan), Stuttgart Ballet, Stuttgart
1977 Apollo (cr) in *Daphne* (Forsythe), Stuttgart Ballet, Stuttgart
Principal dancer (cr) in *Innere Not* (Montagnon), Stuttgart Ballet, Stuttgart
The Fool in *The Lady and the Fool* (Cranko), La Scala, Milan
1978 Principal dancer (cr) in *Glocken* (*Bells*; Montagnon), Stuttgart Ballet, Stuttgart
Principal dancer (cr) in *Concertino* (Helliwell), Stuttgart Ballet, Stuttgart
The Brother (cr) in *My Brother, My Sisters* (MacMillan), Stuttgart Ballet, Stuttgart
Des Grieux (cr) in *Die Kameliendame* (*The Lady of the Camellias*; Neumeier), Stuttgart Ballet, Stuttgart
The Young Man from the House Opposite in *Pillar of Fire* (Tudor), American Ballet Theatre, New York
Third Sailor (Rumba) in *Fancy Free* (Robbins), American Ballet Theatre, New York
1979 Title role (cr) in *Orpheus* (Forsythe), Stuttgart Ballet, Stuttgart
Principal dancer in *Exultate, Jubilate* (Lubovitch), Stuttgart Ballet, Stuttgart
1980 Principal dancer (cr) in *Die Fenster* (*The Window*; Helliwell), Stuttgart Ballet, Stuttgart
Title role (cr) in *Richard III* (*IV, 1*) (Scholz), Stuttgart Ballet, Stuttgart
Wagner in *Träume* (*Dreams*; Spoerli), Stuttgart Ballet, Stuttgart
Principal dancer (cr) in *Das Märchen* (*Fairytales*; pas de trois; Scholz), Stuttgart Ballet, Stuttgart
Von Eisenstein in *Die Fledermaus* (Page), Chicago Ballet
1981 First Movement (cr) in *Forgotten Land* (Kylián), Stuttgart Ballet, Stuttgart
Pierrot in *Pierrot in the Dead City* (Shawn), Jacob's Pillow Festival, Lee, Massachusetts
Principal dancer in *Fetish* (Mumaw), Jacob's Pillow Festival, Lee, Massachusetts
1982 Principal dancer in *Twilight* (pas de deux; van Manen), Stuttgart Ballet, Stuttgart
James in *La Sylphide* (Bournonville; staged Schaufuss), Stuttgart Ballet, Stuttgart
Title role in *Petrushka* (Béjart), Stuttgart Ballet, Stuttgart
1983 Papa in *Gaité Parisienne* (Béjart), Stuttgart Ballet, Stuttgart
Stanley Kowalski (cr) in *A Streetcar Named Desire* (Neumeier), Stuttgart Ballet, Stuttgart
The Prince in *The Nutcracker* (Baryshnikov), American Ballet Theatre, New York
Principal dancer (cr) in *La Danse* (Béjart), Ballet du XXe Siècle
1984 Principal dancer in *Straw Hearts* (Feld), Feld Ballet/NY, New York
1985 Principal dancer (cr) in *Operette* (Béjart), Stuttgart Ballet, Stuttgart
Principal dancer (cr) in *Abschied* (Spoerli), Stuttgart Ballet, Stuttgart
1986 Principal dancer in *Canto Vital* (Plissetski), Stuttgart Ballet, Stuttgart
Aschenbach (cr) in *Death in Venice* (Vesak), Bavarian State Opera Ballet, Munich
1987 Principal dancer in *Sarcasms* (*Piano Variations II*, pas de deux; van Manen), Stuttgart Ballet, Stuttgart
Carabosse in *The Sleeping Beauty* (Haydée after Petipa), Stuttgart Ballet, Stuttgart
Principal dancer (cr) in *ENAS* (Haydée), Stuttgart Ballet, Stuttgart
1988 King (cr) in *Wie Antigone* (*Like Antigone*, new version; Mats Ek), Stuttgart Ballet, Stuttgart
Principal dancer in *Chambre séparée* (Béjart), Stuttgart Ballet, Stuttgart
1989 Hilarion in *Giselle und die Wilis* (Haydée after Coralli, Perrot), Stuttgart Ballet, Stuttgart
1990 Principal dancer in *Wien, Wien, nur du allein* (Béjart), Stuttgart Ballet, Stuttgart
Junior in *On Your Toes* (musical by Rodgers and Hart; chor. Fuller), Forum Theatre, Ludwigsburg

1991 Principal dancer (cr) in *Stati d'animo* (Zanella), Stuttgart Ballet, Stuttgart

Saturn (cr) in *The Planets* (Haydée), Stuttgart Ballet, Stuttgart
Principal dancer in *Moon* (van Manen), Stuttgart Ballet, Stuttgart
Graf (cr) and Madame (cr) in *Bürger als Edelmann* (Kurz), Stuttgart Ballet, Stuttgart
1992 Principal dancer (cr) in *Man in the Shadows* (Zanella), Stuttgart Ballet, Stuttgart

**Other roles include:** principal dancer in *Tritsch Tratsch* (Cranko), principal dancer in *Hommage à Bolschoi* (pas de deux; Cranko), principal dancer in *La Source* (pas de deux; Cranko), the Poet in *Les Sylphides* (Fokine), the Prince in *The Lady and the Fool* (Cranko), Armand in *The Lady of the Camellias* (Neumeier), Faun in *L'Après-midi d'un faune* (Nijinsky), principal dancer in *Something Special* (pas de deux; Aschcar), the Man in *The Interrogation* (*Die Befragung*; Cranko), Jean in *Miss Julie* (MacMillan), principal dancer in *Bolero* (Béjart), principal dancer in *Mahler Symphony No. 3* (Neumeier), Paris in *Das Urteil des Paris* (Scholz), title role in *The Hunchback of Notre Dame* (Petit), Proust in *Notre Proust* (Petit).

**PUBLICATIONS**

By Cragun:
Interview with Regitz, Hartmut, "Wenn Marcia Haydée einmal den falschen Schuh erwischt", *Ballett: Chronik und Bilanz des Balettjahres* (Zürich), 1983

About Cragun:
Geitel, K., "Des Ungestümen Zähmung durch sich selbst", *Ballett*, 1969
Niehaus, Max, *Ballett Faszination* (Munich), 1972
Gruen, John, "Stuttgart Profiles: Marcia Haydée and Richard Cragun", *Dance Magazine* (New York), August 1975
Terry, Walter, *Great Male Dancers of the Ballet*, New York, 1978
Taub, Eric, "Richard Cragun", *Ballet News* (New York), May 1982
Pikula, Joan, "Richard Cragun", *Dance Magazine* (New York), August 1983
Percival, John, and Bland, Alexander, *Men Dancing: Performers and Performances*, London, 1984
Hardy, Camille, "Richard Cragun", *Dance Magazine* (New York), July 1985

* * *

When the Stuttgart Ballet staged the Broadway musical *On Your Toes* in September 1990, Richard Cragun celebrated his fortieth year on stage. For Cragun, a circle was completed with the role of the New York music professor Phil Dolan III, known as "Junior". In *On Your Toes* he not only had the opportunity to show his outstanding qualities as a classical dancer; more than that, he revealed his immense skill as a tap dancer—and it was with tap that his life as a dancer had begun in Sacramento, California.

For more than three decades Cragun has maintained his position as a premier danseur of world class. His technical abilities are as far-reaching as is his variety of expression. It is difficult to compare him to other dancers of his type, yet such attempts have often been made. At one of Cragun's appearances, one critic found himself reminded of "Nureyev's leaps, Dowell's accuracy and Wall's enthusiasm" (John Percival in 1969), while another made the pithy remark: "[Cragun] belongs in the category of a Nureyev or a Villella" (Clive Barnes, on the New York premiere of John Cranko's *The Taming of the Shrew*, in 1969). Yet what makes Cragun unique as a dancer is something more than the combination of an unusual technique and a gift for expression. The fact is that in the course of his career he has developed a unique, and unrivalled, style and character of his own.

Cragun himself credits this not least to the unusually varied training he received as a dancer, which did not take place in a single school devoted to a particular style. After the tap-dancing lessons and early ballet classes with Barbara Briggs in California and Canada, he completed a year at the Royal Ballet School in London. Then, also for the space of a year, he took private lessons with Vera Volkova in Copenhagen. He had his first professional engagement at the end of that year (1962) with John Cranko's Stuttgart Ballet, where he has remained ever since.

Straight away Cranko recognized the talent of the young Richard Cragun. From the beginning he entrusted him with small solo parts in his ballets. Cragun's rise to his position as one of the most proficient male soloists of the international dance scene began with the end of Ray Barra's career, when the older dancer was forced by injury to retire as principal soloist of the Stuttgart company. Cragun gradually took on the leading roles which Barra had created in Cranko ballets such as *Romeo and Juliet* and *Onegin*. In 1965, Cragun made his mark at the side of Birgit Keil with his interpretation of the male solo part in Cranko's abstract piece *Opus 1* (with music by Anton von Webern).

As with Marcia Haydée (and other Stuttgart soloists), it is thanks to choreographer and ballet director John Cranko that Richard Cragun became an international star. Indeed, the famous role of Petrucchio in Cranko's *The Taming of the Shrew* has undoubtedly become "Cragun's role". In the title of his work *Initialen R. B. M. E.* (choreographed in 1972 to Brahms), Cranko created a homage to "his" soloist—*R.* stands for Richard. Cragun danced in countless dramatic and abstract works by Cranko, as well as in the traditional works of the classical romantic repertoire. He interpreted roles in the (few) Stuttgart Balanchine productions and in the important works created for the Stuttgart Ballet by choreographers such as Kenneth MacMillan, Glen Tetley, Peter Wright, Jiří Kylián, and William Forsythe.

More recently, choreographers as varied as Maurice Béjart, Hans van Manen, and John Neumeier have made use of Cragun's wide-ranging artistic abilities. One of the outstanding full-length productions by John Neumeier for the Stuttgart Ballet, *A Streetcar Named Desire* (based on the play by Tennessee Williams), was created for the Cragun–Haydée partnership, which, after more than 25 years, is the most enduring and harmonious dance partnership in international ballet. Moreover, Marcia Haydée has created some spectacular choreography for Richard Cragun in her own productions, such as Carabosse in her version of *The Sleeping Beauty* (1987). Both as a member of the Stuttgart Ballet and as a guest solo artist, Cragun has danced throughout the world and with almost every ballerina of importance in his era.

On stage Cragun possesses an extremely masculine presence. His interpretations are characterized by virility, whether the piece be abstract or dramatic. His style is robust and powerful, his virtuosity still undiminished after several decades on stage. At the same time, Cragun has become the father figure of the "Cranko family", as the members of the Stuttgart Ballet still see themselves some two decades after Cranko's death in 1973. As a serious and analytical personality, Cragun has gradually grown into the responsibilities of this role, which he fulfils at the side of Marcia Haydée, now director of the company, and intermittent partner in life. Above all it is thanks to Haydée and Cragun that the Stuttgart Ballet has continued to be led, after Cranko's death, in Cranko's spirit, as an international company of class and distinction.

—Horst Vollmer

---

**CRAMÉR, Ivo**

Swedish dancer, choreographer, and ballet director. Born Martin Ivo Frederick Carl Cramér in Gothenburg, Sweden, 5 March 1921. Studied with Vera Alexandrova, Birgit Cullberg, Vera Volkova, and Sigurd Leeder, including period of study in England. Married dancer and choreographer Tyyne Talvo, 1948. Dancer, Cullberg Group, Sweden, 1944; founder, Cramér Ballet, 1945, briefly touring Sweden; co-director, with Cullberg, Swedish Dance Theatre, 1946–47; choreographer, from 1947, and director, Verde Gaio folk dance company, Lisbon, 1948–49; freelance choreographer of ballets, operettas, and stage musicals, including in Oslo, from 1946; dancer and choreographer with Scandinavian companies, touring Europe during the 1950s, including Ny Norsk Balett (New Norwegian Ballet), 1952; resident choreographer, Bergen Festival, 1958, 1959, 1960; founder and artistic director of new touring company, Cramér Ballet, state-funded by the Swedish National Theatre Centre (Riksteatern), Stockholm, 1968–75, 1980–86; artistic director, Royal Swedish Ballet, 1975–80; leading producer of early ballets, staging numerous historical reconstructions, some in collaboration with Mary Skeaping. Recipient: Second Prize, International Choreographic Competition, Copenhagen, 1947.

**WORKS**

1945 *Biblical Pictures* (mus. Gluck, Handel), Cramér Ballet, Stockholm
*The Girl Who Trampled on Bread* (mus. Cramér), International Choreography Competition, Stockholm
1946 *The Lost Sun* (mus. Söderlundh), Swedish Dance Theatre, Swedish tour
*Swedish Suite* (mus. Söderlundh), Cramér Ballet, Stockholm
1947 *Endless Night* (*Noite sem fim*; mus. Mussorgsky), Verde Gaio, Lisbon
1948 *Adventures of Harlequin* (mus. Scarlatti), Verde Gaio, Lisbon
*Balada* (mus. Ravel), Verde Gaio, Lisbon
*Para la dó oriente* (mus. Prokofiev), Verde Gaio, Lisbon
*A Menina e os fantoches* (mus. Prokofiev), Verde Gaio, Lisbon
*Quatre danças* (mus. Rameau), Verde Gaio, Lisbon
1949 *St. John's Eve* (*Johannesnatten*; mus. de Frumerie), Stora Theatre, Gothenburg
1950 *Family Concert* (*Familjekonserten*; mus. Mozart), Stora Theatre, Gothenburg
*The Emperor of Portugal* (mus. Söderlundh), Stora Theatre, Gothenburg
*Peter and the Wolf* (mus. Prokofiev), Stora Theatre, Gothenburg
*Truffaldino*, New Norwegian Ballet, Oslo
1957 *The Prodigal Son* (new version; mus. Alfvén), Royal Swedish Ballet, Stockholm
1958 *The Linden Tree* (mus. Larsson), Royal Swedish Ballet, Stockholm
1959 *Romantic Suite* (mus. Grieg), Bergen Festival, Bergen
*Bendik and Arolilja* (mus. Sönstevold), Norwegian National Ballet, Oslo
1960 *Bluebeard's Nightmare* (mus. Saeverud), Norwegian National Ballet, Oslo
1962 *Catharsis* (mus. Nordheim), The National Scene, Bergen, Norway
1967 *Zodiak* (mus. Werle), Royal Swedish Ballet, Stockholm
*The New Narcissus* (with Skeaping; mus. Dupuy), Drottningholm Ballet, Sweden
1969 *A Plate of Pea Soup* (mus. Lundsten), Cramér Ballet, Orebro
*Cat's Journey* (*Kattresen*; mus. von Koch), Cramér Ballet, Stockholm
1971 *Good Evening, Beautiful Mask* (mus. Lundsten), Cramér Ballet, Södertälje
*Father Spring* (*Fader vår*; mus. Lundsten), Cramér Ballet, Stockholm
1972 *Peasant Gospel* (mus. traditional), Cramér Ballet, Stockholm
1973 *The Nix* (*The Water Sprite*; mus. Lundsten), Royal Swedish Ballet, Stockholm
*Do You Know Fia Jansson?* (mus. traditional), Cramér Ballet, Södertälje
1982 *Pierrot in the Park* (after the *commedia dell'arte*; mus. eighteenth-century), Cramér Ballet, Open Air Theatre, Drottningholm
1983 *Golgatha*, Cramér Ballet, Ostersund

Also staged:

1971 *The Fishermen; or, The Girl from the Archipelago* (with Skeaping, after Antoine Bournonville libretto, 1789; mus. Kraus), Royal Swedish Ballet, Drottningholm
1976 *La Dansomanie* (with Skeaping, after Gardel libretto, 1800; mus. Méhul, arranged Farncombe), Royal Swedish Ballet, Drottningholm
1980 *The False Phantom* (with Skeaping after Terrade libretto), Cramér Ballet, Drottningholm
1981 *Harlequin, Magician of Love* (reconstruction after Marcadet 1793; mus. du Puy, arranged Farncombe), Royal Swedish Ballet, Drottningholm
*Harlequin's Death* (with Skeaping, after Terrade libretto, 1796; mus. anonymous) Royal Swedish Ballet, Drottningholm
1989 *La Fille mal gardée* (reconstruction after Dauberval 1789; mus. anon. 1789, arranged Farncombe), Nantes Opera Ballet, Nantes
1992 *Médée et Jason* (reconstruction after Noverre; mus. Jean-Joseph Rodolphe), Ballet du Rhin, Strasbourg
*Figaro; or, Love and Almaviva* (after Duport's *Le Barbier de Seville*; mus. eighteenth-century), Royal Swedish Ballet, Drottningholm

**PUBLICATIONS**

By Cramér:

"Gustavian Dances in the Commedia dell'arte Tradition", in *Gustavian Opera*, Stockholm, 1991

About Cramér:

Flagg, T., "Ivo Cramer", *After Dark*, January 1970
Ståhle, Anna Greta, "Dans taler med: Ivo Cramér", *Dans* (Stockholm), October 1975

Ståhle, Anna Greta, "Cramérbaletten", *Dancing Times* (London), August 1983
Goodwin, Noël, "Masks and Bergamasks", *Dance and Dancers* (London), December 1983
Sjögren, Margareta, *Skandinavisk balett*, Stockholm, 1988
Guest, Ivor, "Ivo Cramér's *La Fille mal gardée* at Nantes", *Dancing Times* (London), April 1989

* * *

In all of Ivo Cramér's long career, there can be nothing so satisfying as the knowledge of his recent international recognition as restorer of historical ballets, in particular of works from the eighteenth century. His production of *La Fille mal gardée* (for Nantes Opera Ballet in 1989), which was staged to coincide with both the bicentennials of Dauberval's production at Bordeaux and of the French Revolution itself, brought this aspect of his career to the attention of the world ballet community. He was able to follow up this success in 1992 with a Noverre ballet, *Medeé et Jason*, staged for the Ballet du Rhin. In both, he showed that scholarly reconstructions can also be entertaining spectacles for the twentieth-century audience.

With *La Fille mal gardée*, Cramér based the reconstruction of the technique on published eighteenth-century manuals, such as Gennaro Magri's 1779 treatise. The discovery of a set of orchestral parts in the Stockholm archives gave indications of the relationship of stage action to music. With this as a basis, he then had to create the choreography himself, using his own particular talent to recapture the spirit of the age, as embodied in movement.

Cramér's first reconstructions were in cooperation with Mary Skeaping, at one time the director of the Royal Swedish Ballet and an expert on accurate ballet reconstruction in her own right. Together they mounted a number of ballets at the Drottningholm Court Theatre near Stockholm, making use of the theatre's intact eighteenth-century stage machinery. Their production of *The Fishermen; or, The Girl from the Archipelago*, after an Antoine Bournonville work staged in the same year as *La Fille mal gardée*, has been delighting audiences at Drottningholm since 1971. But it was perhaps only when two Drottningholm ballets, *Harlequin, Magician of Love* and *La Dansomanie*, were successfully restaged for the Paris Opéra Ballet, starring Rudolf Nureyev, that the rest of the world began to see that these were not just curiosities of a local interest only.

Cramér has had a varied career, choreographing for every sort of group, including with Birgit Cullberg for the Jooss-influenced Swedish Dance Theatre, the Verde Gaio folk dance company in Lisbon, and the Royal Swedish Ballet. He is predominantly a man of the theatre, whose priority is to communicate to the audience, in whatever movement language he is using. A constant element in his career, however, has been the development of his own company, Cramér Ballet, which toured Scandinavia for nearly twenty years. Its style embraced folk dance, pantomime, and modern dance technique. The repertoire, exploring Scandinavian themes and musical styles, developed its own devoted audience. He wrote, "We give our audience a domestic alternative to imported culture. We offer something which has roots in our own environment without being just national." When Cramér's company appeared in London in 1983, however, it was not a success. It simply did not fit in with the international style and repertoire which the dance public now expects.

In line with his company manifesto, Cramér's choreography has generally explored national and homely themes. In *Biblical Pictures*, *The Prodigal Son*, and *Golgatha*, he interprets the bible stories as unsophisticated narratives, giving rise to humour or pathos. Of these, *The Prodigal Son*, staged for the Royal Swedish Ballet, is considered to be his master work. Both the stage design and movement are derived from traditional decorative and figurative wall-paintings, which were a feature of Swedish peasant architecture. Cramér has also explored Swedish history. *Good Evening, Beautiful Mask* is based on the assassination of King Gustav III (the founder of the Royal Swedish Ballet) in his own opera house. Cramér has also seen the importance of making works especially for children, such as *Peter and the Wolf*.

In trying to make connections between the two Cramérs—the folk nationalist and the historical expert—we can perhaps see that the same qualities inform both sets of choreography. The understanding of dance as a binding factor between people at the most human level is what enables him to recreate dance characters from the past with a freshness that delights modern audiences.

—Larraine Nicholas

---

## CRANKO, John

South African dancer, choreographer, and ballet director. Born in Rustenburg, South Africa, 15 August 1927. Studied at Cape Town University Ballet School, from 1942, and at the Sadler's Wells Ballet School, London, from 1946. Début as dancer and choreographer in South Africa, staging works for University of Cape Town Ballet and Cape Town Ballet Club; dancer and choreographer, Sadler's Wells Theatre Ballet, London, from 1947, becoming resident choreographer, 1950; also choreographer for Sadler's Wells (becoming Royal) Ballet; choreographer and director of London revues *Cranks* (1955), and *New Cranks* (1960); opera director, staging first production of *A Midsummer Night's Dream* (mus. Britten), Aldeburgh, 1960; guest choreographer, Stuttgart Ballet, 1960, returning as artistic director, Stuttgart Ballet, 1961–73; chief choreographer, Bavarian State Opera, Munich, 1968–71, also continuing as choreographer, Stuttgart Ballet, 1971–73. Died 26 June 1973.

### WORKS

1944 *The Soldier's Tale* (mus. Stravinsky), Cape Town Ballet Club, Cape Town
1945 *Suite, Opus 3* (also known as *Aus Holbergs Zeit*; mus. Grieg), University of Cape Town Ballet
*Primavera* (mus. Debussy), University of Cape Town Ballet
1946 *Tritsch-Trasch* (mus. J. Strauss), University of Cape Town Ballet (restaged Sadler's Wells Theatre Ballet, 1947)
1947 *Adieu* (mus. Scarlatti), Vic-Wells Ballet, London
*Morceaux enfantins* (*Children's Corner*; mus. Debussy), Royal Academy of Dancing Production Club, London (restaged Sadler's Wells Theatre Ballet, 1948)
1948 *The School for Nightingales* (mus. Couperin), St. James Ballet, Chatham
1949 *Sea Change* (mus. Sibelius), Sadler's Wells Theatre Ballet, Dublin
*Beauty and the Beast* (mus. Ravel), Sadler's Wells Theatre Ballet, London
1950 *The Witch* (mus. Ravel), New York City Ballet, London

**John Cranko, c.1950**

*Pastorale* (mus. Mozart), Sadler's Wells Theatre Ballet, London
1951 *Pineapple Poll* (mus. Sullivan, arranged Mackerras), Sadler's Wells Theatre Ballet, London
*Harlequin in April* (mus. Arnell), Sadler's Wells Theatre Ballet, London
Dances in *The Fairy Queen* (mus. Purcell), Covent Garden Opera, London
1952 *Bonne-Bouche* (mus. Oldham), Sadler's Wells Ballet, London
*Umbrellas* (mus. Lanchbery), Kenton Theatre, Henley-on-Thames
*The Forgotten Room* (mus. Schubert), Kenton Theatre, Henley-on-Thames
*Paso Doble* (mus. arranged Lanchbery), Kenton Theatre, Henley-on-Thames
*L'Après-midi d'Emily Wigginbotham* (mus. Lanchbery), Kenton Theatre, Henley-on-Thames
*Dancing* (mus. Shearing), Kenton Theatre, Henley-on-Thames
*Reflection* (mus. Gardner), Sadler's Wells Theatre Ballet, Edinburgh
1953 *The Shadow* (mus. Dohnányi), Sadler's Wells Ballet, London
Dances in *Gloriana* (opera; mus. Britten), Covent Garden Opera, London
1954 *The Lady and the Fool* (mus. Verdi, arranged Mackerras), Sadler's Wells Theatre Ballet, Oxford
*Variations on a Theme* (mus. Britten), Ballet Rambert, London
1955 *La Belle Hélène* (mus. Offenbach, arranged Aubert, Rosenthal), Paris Opera Ballet, Paris
*Dances Without Steps* (mus. Casella), London Ballet Circle, London
*Corps, cous, coudes et coeur* (mus. Stravinsky), London Ballet Circle, London
1957 *The Prince of the Pagodas* (mus. Britten), Royal Ballet, London
*The Angels* (mus. Arnell), Royal Ballet Touring Company, London
1958 *Romeo and Juliet* (mus. Prokofiev), Ballet of La Scala, Milan
*Secrets* (mus. Poulenc), Edinburgh International Ballet, Edinburgh
*Cat's Cradle* (mus. Addison), Grand Ballet du Marquis de Cuevas
1959 *La Reja* (mus. Scarlatti), Ballet Rambert, London
*Antigone* (mus. Theodorakis), Royal Ballet, London
*Sweeney Todd* (mus. Arnold), Royal Ballet Touring Company, Stratford-upon-Avon
1961 *Divertimento* (mus. Mozart), Stuttgart Ballet, Stuttgart
*Familienalbum* (mus. Walton), Stuttgart Ballet, Stuttgart
*Intermezzo* (mus. Shearing, Lee), Stuttgart Ballet, Stuttgart
*The Catalyst* (mus. Shostakovich), Stuttgart Ballet, Stuttgart
1962 *Scenes de Ballet* (mus. Stravinsky), Stuttgart Ballet, Stuttgart
*The Seasons* (mus. Glazunov), Stuttgart Ballet, Stuttgart
*Daphnis and Chloë* (mus. Ravel), Stuttgart Ballet, Stuttgart
*Romeo and Juliet* (new version; mus. Prokofiev), Stuttgart Ballet, Stuttgart
1963 *L'Estro armonico* (mus. Vivaldi), Stuttgart Ballet, Stuttgart
*Die Reise nach Jerusalem* (*Musical Chairs*; mus. Stolze), Stuttgart Ballet, Stuttgart
*Variations* (mus. Trede), Stuttgart Ballet, Stuttgart
1964 *The Firebird* (mus. Stravinsky), German Opera Ballet, Berlin
*La Source* (pas de deux; mus. Delibes), Stuttgart Ballet, Stuttgart
*Hommage à Bolschoi* (pas de deux; Glazunov), Stuttgart Ballet, Stuttgart
*Concerti Grossi* (mus. Handel), Cologne City Ballet, Cologne
1965 *Bouquet Garni* (mus. Rossini, Britten), Stuttgart Ballet, Stuttgart
*Jeu de Cartes* (mus. Stravinsky), Stuttgart Ballet, Stuttgart
*Onegin* (mus. Tchaikovsky, Stolze), Stuttgart Ballet, Stuttgart
*Raymonda* (pas de deux; mus. Glazunov), Stuttgart Ballet, Stuttgart
*Jeux de vagues* (pas de deux; mus. Debussy), Stuttgart Ballet, Stuttgart
Dances in *Carmina burana* (mus. Orff), Stuttgart Festival, Stuttgart
*Opus 1* (mus. Webern), Stuttgart Ballet, Stuttgart
1966 *Brandenburg 2 & 4* (mus. Bach), Royal Ballet, London
*Concerto for Flute and Harp* (also known as *Mozart Concerto*; mus. Mozart), Stuttgart Ballet, Stuttgart
*Pas de Quatre* (mus. Glinka), Stuttgart Ballet, Stuttgart
*The Nutcracker* (mus. Tchaikovsky), Stuttgart Ballet, Stuttgart
1967 *The Interrogation* (mus. Zimmermann), Stuttgart Ballet, Stuttgart
*Oiseaux Exotiques* (mus. Messiaen), Stuttgart Ballet, Stuttgart

*Quatre Images* (mus. Ravel), Stuttgart Ballet, Stuttgart
*Onegin* (revised version; mus. Tchaikovsky, arranged Stolze), Stuttgart Ballet, Stuttgart
*Holberg Suite* (pas de deux; mus. Grieg), Stuttgart Ballet, Stuttgart
1968 *Encounter in Three Colours* (mus. Stravinsky), Munich State Opera Ballet, Munich
*Song of the Nightingale* (mus. Stravinsky), Munich State Opera Ballet, Munich
*Fragmente* (mus. Henze), Stuttgart Ballet, Stuttgart
*Présence* (mus. Zimmermann), Stuttgart Ballet, Stuttgart
*Kyrie Eleison* (mus. Bach, Stolze), Stuttgart Ballet, Stuttgart
*Salade* (mus. Milhaud), Stuttgart Ballet, Stuttgart
1969 *The Taming of the Shrew* (mus. Stolze after Scarlatti), Stuttgart Ballet, Stuttgart
*Triplum* (mus. Fortner), Munich State Opera Ballet, Munich
*Grund zum Tanzen* (mus. Grund), Munich State Opera Ballet, Munich
*Fête Polonaise* (mus. Chabrier), Munich State Opera Ballet, Munich
*Französische Suite—une Fête Galante* (mus. Egk), Munich State Opera Ballet, Munich
1970 *Brouillards* (mus. Debussy), Stuttgart Ballet, Stuttgart
*Poème de l'extase* (mus. Scriabin, Fortner), Stuttgart Ballet, Stuttgart
*Orpheus* (mus. Stravinsky), Stuttgart Ballet, Stuttgart
*Cous, coudes, corps & coeurs* (new version; mus. Stravinsky), Stuttgart Ballet, Stuttgart
*Ballade* (mus. Fauré), Stuttgart Ballet, Stuttgart
*Ebony Concerto* (mus. Stravinsky), Munich State Opera Ballet, Munich
1971 *Carmen* (mus. Fortner, Steinbrenner), Stuttgart Ballet, Stuttgart
*Song of My People* (mus. Ben-Zvi, Sternberg), Batsheva Dance Company
1972 *Initials R.B.M.E.* (mus. Brahms), Stuttgart Ballet, Stuttgart
*Legende* (mus. Wieniawsky), Stuttgart Ballet, Munich
*−1 + 6* (mus. Haydn), Stuttgart Ballet, Stuttgart
*Ariel* (mus. Chabrier), Stuttgart Ballet, Stuttgart
1973 *Green* (Debussy), Stuttgart Ballet, Stuttgart
*Traces* (mus. Mahler), Stuttgart Ballet, Stuttgart

Also staged:
1962 *Coppélia* (after Petipa, Cecchetti; mus. Delibes), Stuttgart Ballet, Stuttgart
1963 *Swan Lake* (after Petipa, Ivanov; mus. Tchaikovsky), Stuttgart Ballet, Stuttgart (restaged and revised 1970, 1972)

## PUBLICATIONS


Jackson, Frank, *They Make Tomorrow's Ballets*, London, 1953
Siegel, Marcia, *Watching the Dance Go By*, Boston, 1977
Koegler, Horst, "John Cranko", *Les Saisons de la danse* (Paris), March 1972
Schäfer, J.C. and W.E., *Gespräche uber den Tanz*, Frankfurt, 1974
Winkler-Betzendahl, Madeline, and Dominic, Zoë (photographer), *John Cranko und das Stuttgarter Ballett*, revised edition, Pfullingen, 1975
Schäfer, Walter Erich, *Bühne eines Lebens*, Stuttgart, 1975; extracts, translated by Jean Wallis, *Dancing Times* (London), May–October 1976
Kilian, Hannes, and Geitel, Klaus, *John Cranko: Ballet für die Welt*, Sigmaringen, 1977
Koegler, Horst, *Stuttgart Ballet*, London, 1978
Brinson, Peter, and Crisp, Clement, *Ballet and Dance: A Guide to the Repertory*, London, 1980
Percival, John, *Theatre in My Blood: A Biography of John CrankoCranko*, London, 1983
Woodcock, Sarah C., *The Sadler's Wells Royal Ballet*, London, 1991


* * *

John Cranko's unexpected death (of a heart attack) during his company's return flight from the United States inflicted a shock on the Stuttgart Ballet from which it only recovered by a long and difficult process lasting several years. Cranko had built up the Stuttgart ensemble and led it to the forefront of the ballet companies of Western Germany (the then Federal Republic), helping the city to become an international success as one of the "capital cities" of classical dance. He was the father of the so-called "Stuttgart ballet miracle". He was also a father-figure to the members of the company; his ability to integrate and to develop dancers individually is well remembered. The loss of this unique personality left a gap which could not be without artistic consequences—and these were made manifest in the subsequent administration. Glen Tetley's directorship, which lasted from 1974 to 1976, remained in the final analysis unsuccessful and unfortunate, in spite of the fact that Tetley created several important pieces during this time. During Cranko's term of office, the life of the Stuttgart Ballet was too heavily influenced by his personality for a new style of leadership to be accepted both on stage and behind the scenes. Only when Marcia Haydée took on directorship of the Stuttgart Ballet as Tetley's successor, and clearly declared her intention to nurture and continue the Cranko inheritance, did the ensemble's lack of direction come to an end.

John Cranko was no unknown quantity when he came to Stuttgart. On the contrary, he already had a name for himself in Great Britain as a young and promising choreographer; and he had already produced Prokoviev's *Romeo and Juliet* in 1958 with the Milan La Scala company. It was his premiere production of Benjamin Britten's *The Prince of the Pagodas*, created for the Royal Ballet in 1957, which earned him an invitation in 1960 to the Württemburg (now known as the Stuttgart) Theatre as guest choreographer. The theatre director, Walter-Erich Schafer—without whose contribution the later success of Cranko and his company is barely conceivable—installed Cranko as the new ballet director of his theatre from 1961 onwards, after the production of *The Prince of the Pagodas*. Before Cranko, who held this position until his death, along with that of chief choreographer for the Bavarian State Opera Ballet in Munich at intermittent periods, Nicholas Beriozoff had already done a great deal of foundation work. But in spite of this, Stuttgart was more or less unknown in the ballet world, like the rest of post-war Germany. John Cranko, in an example to other West German towns, was encouraged to smooth the way for a balletic tradition which could survive the death of its founder. In all probability, he would never have had such an opportunity in Great Britain.

John Cranko, who had already begun to choreograph as a student in Kapstadt, was possessed of a particular talent for the multiple-act, narrative ballet. He added many such works to the international repertoire, which have come to be regarded as classics of the genre. Cranko was convinced that the narrow base of the existing repertoire should be expanded continually. His most outstanding contributions are productions such as Prokofiev's *Romeo and Juliet* (in the Stuttgart version, for which, in 1962, he won the recognition of press and public alike with the title of ballet director), *Onegin*, choreographed to a collage of music by Tchaikovsky (premiered in 1965, and reworked in 1967), and *The Taming of the Shrew* (created in 1969 to music by Domenico Scarlatti, adapted by Cranko's associate Kurt-Heinz Stolz). The ballets are danced by numerous international companies, while other full-length Cranko ballets such as *Swan Lake*, *The Nutcracker*, and *Carmen* were important in Stuttgart to the image of the ensemble and its repertoire.

The Stuttgart Ballet's regular work with other choreographers—for instance Peter Wright, the company's ballet master at the time, who brought his notable production of *Giselle* on to the stage in 1966, and Kenneth MacMillan—was part of Cranko's strategy. What is more, he improved the technical level of the company, and was a decisive force in the careers of dancers such as Marcia Haydée, Ray Barra, Birgit Keil, Egon Madsen, Richard Cragun, and Heinz Clauss. Supported by the energetic Noverre Society, he paid particular attention to the promotion of young choreographic talent such as that of John Neumeier, Ashley Killar, Gray Veredon, and Jiří Kylián. In addition, he used the Noverre Society to educate broad sections of the audience and convert them into connoisseurs of classical dance.

Along with the early creations *Pineapple Poll* (1951) and *The Lady and the Fool* (1954), both of which were originally presented with the Sadler's Wells Theatre Ballet, several Stuttgart pieces stand out among Cranko's one-act short ballets—these include *Jeu de Cartes*, *Opus 1* (both created in 1965), and *Brouillards* (1970). Cranko's delight in experimentation was particularly apparent in *Presence* (1968), which arose out of a collaboration with the contemporary German composer Bernd Alois Zimmermann, and which illustrated, among other works, Cranko's sense of humour and fun in movement, which never lost its Englishness even in Germany. *Die Befragung* (1967) and *Spuren* (1973) exemplify Cranko's commitment to social criticism. On the other hand, *Initialen R.B.M.E* (1972) is the choreographer's individual homage to "his" soloists, Richard Cragun (R.), Birgit Keil (B.), Marcia Haydée (M.), and Egon Madsen (E.).

John Cranko did not have a strong stylistic influence in terms of the development of a new language of dance. He worked on the foundation of classical dance, which he sought to modify as befitting the times. George Balanchine's neo-classicism is recognizable as the pattern for all of Cranko's concert pieces (for example *L'estro Armonico* to Vivaldi, 1963). However, it is the highly dramatic and expressive pas de deux which may be considered "typical Cranko", as they are to be found in the full-length ballets. Apart from these, Cranko's abilities as leader of a ballet company and creator of new full-length ballets have had the most influence of all—not least on the current director of the Hamburg Ballet, John Neumeier. In Cranko's time, numerous choreographers, directors, ballet masters, educationalists, and dancers emerged from the environment of the Stuttgart Ballet, and they in turn made a vital contribution to the development of classical dance in the Federal Republic. The ballet school attached to the Württemburg Theatre, which Cranko built up with the help of his ballet mistress Anne Woolliams after the fashion of the big international schools, was the first truly professional academy of its kind in the Federal Republic. John Cranko's influence, not just in Germany but on the international dance scene, cannot be overestimated; and in that sense his presence continues to be felt today.

—Horst Vollmer

---

**CRASKE, Margaret**

British dancer and teacher. Born in Norfolk, 26 November 1892. Studied with Madame Vandyck, c. 1915, and with Enrico Cecchetti, London, 1918–23; also studied with Meher Baba, India, 1931, 1939–46. Dancer, Diaghilev's Ballets Russes, 1920; dancer, touring in small group with Ninette de Valois, 1922/23; teacher of Cecchetti system in London, 1924–31, and 1938–39; moved to United States, 1939: ballet mistress, at invitation of Antony Tudor, American Ballet Theatre, New York, from 1946; teacher at Juilliard School and Metropolitan Opera Ballet School, 1950–66; assistant director, Metropolitan Opera Ballet School until 1968; also teacher at Jacob's Pillow Summer Dance Festivals, and founder of own school, Manhattan School of Dance, 1961–86; co-author of two manuals on classical technique. Died in Myrtle Beach, South Carolina, 18 February 1990.

**PUBLICATIONS**

By Craske:

*The Theory and Practice of Allegro in Classical Ballet (Cecchetti Method)*, with Cyril Beaumont; London, 1930

*Practice of Advanced Allegro in Classical Ballet*, with F. Derra de Moroda; London, 1956

*The Dance of Love*, Myrtle Beach, South Carolina, 1980

*Still Dancing with Love*, Myrtle Beach, South Carolina, 1990

About Craske:

Miguel, Parmenia, "Ninetieth Birthday Celebrations", *Dance Magazine* (New York), November 1982

Vander Wef, K., "Uncompromising Champion", *Ballet News* (New York), January 1983

* * *

When Enrico Cecchetti left England to retire to his native Italy, he entrusted his London school and the dissemination of his teaching method to Margaret Craske. Renowned as one of the major dance pedagogues of the twentieth century, Craske had also been an excellent dancer, although her career as a performer was cut short by injury. Her equal expertise in performing and in teaching Cecchetti's work was unique, and won her the Maestro's special admiration and esteem.

Craske was to collaborate with Cyril Beaumont and later with Derra de Moroda in recording Cecchetti's exercises and enchaînements, and although she originally worked with others in the London-based Cecchetti Society on the task of dividing up the Maestro's weekly programme of study into several syllabus programmes linked to dance examinations at various levels, she later distanced herself from this graded system.

Few teachers have had as wide an influence on the development of ballet as Margaret Craske; none has been equally influential in both Britain and the United States. In London her studio was frequented by many of those who were to be instrumental in forming and developing the English style of ballet, including Frederick Ashton, Antony Tudor, and Peggy van Praagh, while Ninette de Valois engaged her as ballet mistress to her newly formed company. Future pedagogues such as Nora Roche, who was to train a whole generation of dancers at the Royal Ballet School, were students of Miss Craske, and the establishment of ballet schools and companies in many British commonwealth countries was largely undertaken by other former Craske pupils.

When, in 1946, Antony Tudor invited her to join what is now the American Ballet Theatre as ballet mistress, Craske embarked on a new phase in her career and one which was to be of fundamental importance to the development of dance in the United States.

To many people it is Balanchine's name that is synonymous with American classical ballet. His influence has certainly been enormous, largely due to his prolific and distinguished choreographic invention. But it was Craske who was to teach many of those who were to become America's leading dancers. She was particularly noted for her superlative teaching of pointe work, adhering strictly to Cecchetti's method of making the dancer rise on the pointes with a little spring, distinctly pushing off the floor. This develops the elasticity of the instep and teaches the concentration of the body on one spot. Melissa Hayden—to name but one of America's ballerinas—owed her astonishing strength on pointe and the fleetness of her footwork to Craske's coaching.

But what was unique about Miss Craske was that not only ballet dancers but also a whole generation of American modern dancers flocked to her Manhattan studio. She had also taught for many years at the Metropolitan Opera Ballet School and at the Juilliard School, as well as regularly joining the faculty at the Jacob's Pillow Summer Dance Festivals. This is where she first taught dancers like Paul Taylor and Jean Cébron—the latter was to become a close associate of Kurt Jooss at the Volkwangschule in Germany.

The nineteenth-century classical/romantic ballet which formed Cecchetti's own background may seem worlds apart from the modernism of Merce Cunningham. Yet many of Cunningham's best dancers—notably Viola Farber and Carolyn Brown—were ardent Craske devotees. The combination of superlative rhythmic coordination and absolute precision in the placement and positioning of the whole body, necessary to the performance of Cunningham's choreography, were perfectly served by the equivalent demands of the Cecchetti work taught by Craske. Both are characterized by rapid changes of direction, sudden bursts of speed, and a finely tuned sense of balance.

Whereas Craske's teaching in England was much involved with the faithful preservation of Cecchetti's work in the exact form in which he had taught it, in the United States she gradually distanced herself from that approach, seeking to condense and distil what she had learnt from the Maestro. She preserved the essence of his work, based as it is on anatomical truth, but selected key aspects of Cecchetti's own settings and, where necessary, adapted them to the needs of specific pupils.

Margaret Craske knew how to use the body with a maximum of effort and a minimum of distortion. Much loved by her students, she was rigorous and unremitting in her pedagogic demands, perspicacious in her assessment of the capabilities of individual dancers, and immensely wise in her understanding of people—a wisdom no doubt gained from her long and devoted study of the teaching and philosophy of the Indian guru Meher Baba.

—Richard Glasstone

---

## THE CREATURES OF PROMETHEUS

(also *Gli uomini di Prometeo* and *Die Geschöpfe des Prometheus*)

**Choreography:** Salvatore Viganò
**Music:** Ludwig van Beethoven
**Design:** Alessandro Sanquirico
**Libretto:** Salvatore Viganò
**First Production:** Burg Theatre, Vienna, 28 March 1801
**Principal Dancers:** Maria Cassentini and Salvatore Viganò (Creatures), Mme. Brendi (Terpsichore), and Cesari (Prometheus)

**Other productions include:** Teatro alla Scala (new version; chor. Viganò, with additional mus. Haydn, Mozart, Weigl, and Gluck, scenery Pasquale Canna, costumes and machinery Giacomo Pregliasco), as *Prometeo*, with Luigi Costa (Prometheus); Milan, 22 May 1813. Paris Opéra Ballet (new version, chor. Serge Lifar, design Quelvée); Paris, 30 December 1929. Augsburg Municipal Theatre (chor. Aurel Milloss after Viganò); Augsberg, 23 September 1933 (restaged Rome Opera Ballet, 1940). Vic-Wells Ballet (new version; chor. Ninette de Valois, design John Banting); London, 13 October 1936. Royal Swedish Ballet (new version; chor. Elsa Marianne von Rosen); Stockholm, 13 October 1936. Düsseldorf Opera Ballet (new version; chor. Yvonne Georgi); Düsseldorf, 21 May 1952. Ballet of the German Opera on the Rhine (new version; chor. Erich Walter); Düsseldorf, 25 November 1966. Royal Ballet Touring Company (new version; chor. Frederick Ashton, design Ottowerner Meyer), with Doreen Wells and Kerrison Cooke (Creatures), Brenda Last (Terpsichore), and Hendrik Davel (Prometheus); Bonn, 6 June 1970.

### PUBLICATIONS


Ritorni, Carlo, *Commentaria della vita e delle opera coreodrammatiche di Salvatore Viganò*, Milan, 1838

Prunières, Henry, "Salvatore Viganò", *Numéro spécial de la Revue musicale: Le Ballet au XIXe Siècle* (Paris), September 1921

Hadland, F.A., "Beethoven and the Ballet: An Approaching Centenary", *Dancing Times* (London), January 1927

Levinson, André, "Le Ballet de Prométhée: Beethoven et Viganò", *La Revue musicale* (Paris), April 1927

Beaumont, Cyril, *Complete Book of Ballets*, revised edition, London, 1951

"Ballet Backgrounds, 1: Two Creatures of One Prometheus", *Ballet Today* (London), July 1953

Gatti, C., *Il Teatro alla Scala 1778–1963*, 2 volumes, Milan, 1964

Christout, Marie Françoise, "Beethoven, Musicien de ballet", *Les Saisons de la danse* (Paris), November 1970

Howes, Frank, "Prometheus = Creator – Beethoven", *Dancing Times* (London), January 1971

Vaughan, David, *Frederick Ashton and his Ballets*, London, 1977

Raimondi, Ezio, *Il Sogno del Coreodramma*, Reggio Emilia, 1984


* * *

*The Creatures of Prometheus*, a heroic-allegorical ballet in two acts, was choreographed by Salvatore Viganò to music by Ludwig van Beethoven, and was first performed in Vienna in March 1801. A theatre bill, found in Nottebohm's second posthumous Beethoveniana, announced the ballet for the 21st of March, but it was first performed on the 28th, for the benefit of the prima ballerina Mademoiselle Cassentini. This was followed by sixteen performances that same year, and thirteen others the following year. This was enough evidence of its success.

The scenario of the ballet is based on one of the stories of the creation of man in Greek mythology. Prometheus—the name means forethought—was a wise titan who brought down a life-giving fire from the sun to give life to men. The theme of

Prometheus is symbolic of the goodness of nature, the potentialities of man, and the sublimity of his destiny. It represents the autonomy of man and stresses the importance of education.

Of the 1801 version, only Beethoven's score remains. The scenario can be reconstructed vaguely from the annotations found on the musical score, which consist of an overture, an introduction, and sixteen numbers. The overture and the introduction set the mood of the ballet depicting, with heavy accents, the peal of thunder and the fury of the elements. Frantic rapid eight-notes and climactic dynamics make a powerful opening. Prometheus has outraged the gods by helping himself to the celestial fire. He runs through the forest towards his inanimate figures. He applies the fire to the hearts of his creatures who acquire life and motion, and become men and women. This movement unfolds in a pleasant melody. Prometheus is delighted at his success but soon realizes that his creatures have neither reason nor heart. The uncertainty of the situation materializes in the form of musical tempo. A dramatic adagio is followed by a brilliant allegro. The statues become hostile and resist Prometheus's attempts to seize them. As the first-act curtain falls, Prometheus is seen dragging them away.

Act II begins with a majestic movement appropriate to the setting: it is Mount Parnassus, where Apollo, attended by the Muses and Graces, Bacchus, Orpheus, Terpsichore, and other deities, is seen on the steps of the temple of Apollo. Prometheus appears and presents his creatures to Apollo. He hopes the gods will instruct them in the arts and sciences. This scene is perhaps better defined as a symphonic tableau both musically and choreographically. The symphonic nature of Beethoven's music parallels the polyphonic orchestration of Viganò's choreography. In order to give visual form to this colossal canvas of characters, Viganò arranged them in pyramidal groups as in a tableau by Raphael. The interaction between the creatures and the gods is illustrated in a series of dances. Euterpe begins to play, supported by Amphion. Arion and Orpheus join them, and finally Apollo himself. A harp is heard as nowhere else in Beethoven. The creatures begin to respond to music and express joy and gratitude. Terpsichore initiates them in the art of dance, and Bacchus teaches them a Bacchanale. Melpomene, the muse of tragedy, interrupts their joy with her dagger. She reveals to the creatures the harsh truth about death. She rushes on Prometheus and stabs him. Thalia, the muse of comedy, intervenes and holds masks before the weeping faces of the horrified creatures. Prometheus returns to life during a pastorale led by Pan. Festive dances as solos for the male and female dancers follow. The cheerful finale of the concluding tableau presents one of Beethoven's most famous themes. It is introduced in the *Variations and Fugue in E flat* (op. 35) and in the finale of the *Eroica* symphony.

This mythological ballet provided ample material both for the choreographer and composer within its historical context. It reflects the taste of the Napoleonic era, first in its theme of the saviour of mankind, second in the grandiose spectacular effects, picturesque tableaux, processions, and marches. The theories of the eighteenth-century Enlightenment, along with the influences of the French Revolution and Napoleon's rise to power undoubtedly had a tremendous effect on the arts at the dawn of the nineteenth century.

The details of the collaboration of Viganò and Beethoven are very obscure. That early and unrenewed association between the two creators—both at the beginning of their careers—cannot be assumed to have been motivated artistically. In 1813, Viganò produced a new version of the ballet with music by different composers. *Prometeo* had its premiere at La Scala in Milan on 22 May 1813. The choreographer then expanded the ballet into six acts. This development required additional music. For his new version, Viganò used music by Haydn, Mozart, Weigl, Gluck, and Beethoven. The question as to why he went back to his former practice of using a pastiche of works, which sounds like an accompaniment to a silent movie, remains unanswered.

Viganò's 1813 *Prometeo* was a sort of choreographic oratorio compared to the Viennese "Little Prometeo". Viganò altered the ending of the ballet in which Prometeo is chained to a rock on the Mount Caucasus, to have his liver devoured by an eagle. He introduced new characters such as Geography, Agriculture, Architecture, and Astronomy, offering each time a new tableau. Only a theatre such as La Scala had the elaborate stage machinery necessary for the development of Viganò's choreographic ideas. The scene in which Prometeo and Minerva pass through the clouds was reminiscent of Dante's *Commedia*, wrote Ritorni. The abundance of spectacular details was the object of both positive and negative criticism. The echoes of Viganò's popularity and the enthusiastic comments of the press inspired a series of letters, *Lettere critiche intorno al Prometeo*, in which the author discusses the morality, the philosophy, and the religion of *Prometeo*'s subject.

Despite the laudatory reviews of the critics and the glowing accounts of Stendhal, the Milanese *Prometeo* lacks coherence and homogeneity. *The Creatures of Prometheus* remains a landmark in Viganò's career and in the history of ballet, both stylistically and musically. It spurred him into producing such notable works as *I Titani* and *Dedalo*, thus continuing as a prototype for his Milanese mythological masterpieces. Unity through variety and contrast, along with harmony of form and content—these were the qualities Viganò tried to maintain in his ballet.

—Elizabeth Terzian

---

**CUBAN NATIONAL BALLET** *see* **BALLET NACIONAL DE CUBA**

---

**CUEVAS, Marquis George de** *see* **DE CUEVAS, Marquis George**

---

**CULLBERG, Birgit**

Swedish dancer, choreographer, and ballet director. Born in Nyköping, Sweden, 3 August 1908. Married Anders Ek, 1942 (div.): son, dancer Niklas (b. 1943); twins, dancer/choreographer Mats, and Malin (b. 1945). Studied literature at Stockholm University; studied dance with Vera Alexandrova, Jeanna Falk, and Trude Engelhardt, then with Kurt Jooss and Sigurd Leeder at Dartington Hall, England, 1935–1939; later studied dance with Lillian Karina and Martha Graham. Dancer and choreographer, concerts and revues, Stockholm, from 1939, also founding first group in same year; founder and choreographer, Cullberg Group, 1944, taking part in Swedish National Theatre Centre tours; founder, with Ivo Cramér, Swedish Dance Theatre, 1946–47, touring widely in Europe;

founder, with Elsa Marianne von Rosen, of new company, Cullberg Ballet, 1949; resident choreographer, Royal Swedish Ballet, 1952–1956; member of the artistic council to the Royal Swedish Ballet, 1963; also choreographer and guest producer for American Ballet Theatre, the Royal Danish Ballet, and other companies in Scandinavia and Germany; director and choreographer, Stockholm City Theatre, 1960; founder and artistic director, Cullberg Ballet, 1967–81, funded by the Swedish National Theatre Centre; has choreographed many works for television, including *The Evil Queen* (mus. Wiren; Swedish television, 1961), and *Red Wine in Green Glasses* (mus. Beethoven; Swedish television, 1971). Recipient: Top prize, Second International Choreography Competition, organized by the Archives internationale de la danse, Stockholm, 1945; Swedish King's Fellowship, 1958; Order of Vasa, 1961; Prix d'Italia (for *The Evil Queen*), 1961 and (for *Red Wine in Green Glasses*), 1971; honorary title of Professor, 1979.

## WORKS

1942 *Kulturpropaganda* (solo dance in revue; mus. Penny), Stockholm
1944 *Regatta*, Cullberg Group, Stockholm
*The Tree*, Cullberg Group, Stockholm
*Occupation*, Cullberg Group, Stockholm
*Offensive*, Cullberg Group, Stockholm
*Hercules at the Crossroads* (mus. Söderman), Cullberg Group, Stockholm
*Romeo and Juliet* (mus. Prokofiev), Cullberg Group, Stockholm
1945 *Rhythms of Life* (mus. Söderman), Cullberg Group, International Choreography Competition, Stockholm
1946 *Reap, Reap, Oats* (mus. Söderman), Swedish Dance Theatre
1947 *The Three Musketeers* (mus. Verdi), Swedish Dance Theatre, Stockholm
1948 *Famous Lovers* (mus. Wagner and others), Cullberg Group, Swedish tour
1949 *Flower, Seed, and Fruit* (mus. Milhaud), Cullberg Ballet, Östersund
1950 *Miss Julie* (mus. Rangström), Cullberg Ballet, Västerås, Sweden
*Medea* (mus. Bartók, arranged Sandberg), Cullberg Ballet, Gaevle, Sweden
*Oscar's Ball* (mus. Wirén), Royal Swedish Ballet, Stockholm
*Stone Portal* (mus. Prokofiev), Open Air Theatre, Stockholm
1952 *The Swain and Six Princesses* (mus. Nystroem), Royal Swedish Ballet, Stockholm
*Serenade* (mus. Wirén), Royal Swedish Ballet, Stockholm
1953 *Pas de coq* (mus. Rossini), Royal Swedish Ballet, Stockholm
1955 *Romeo and Juliet* (new version; Prokofiev), Royal Swedish Ballet, Stockholm
1956 *Circle of Love* (mus. Hallnäs), Gothenburg Opera Ballet, Gothenburg
1957 *Moon Reindeer* (mus. Riisager), Royal Danish Ballet, Copenhagen
1959 *Odysseus* (mus. Englund), Finnish National Ballet, Worcester, Massachusetts
1960 *The Lady from the Sea* (mus. Riisager), American Ballet Theatre, New York
1961 *Eden* (pas de deux, also called *Adam and Eve*; mus. Rosenberg), American Ballet Theatre, New York
*The Evil Queen* (mus. Wirén), Swedish television
1963 *The Seven Deadly Sins* (mus. Weill), Open Air Theatre, Stockholm
1964 *Salome* (mus. Rosenberg), Royal Swedish Ballet, Stockholm
1966 *I am not you* (mus. Brustad), Norwegian television
*Dionysos* (mus. Blomdahl), Städtische Bühnen, Dortmund
1967 *I am not you* (new version, also called *Fedra*; mus. Rosenberg), Cullberg Ballet
*Spawning Ground* (*Lekrattnet*; mus. Carlos, Raiijmakers), Cullberg Ballet, Stockholm
1968 *Eurydice is Dead* (mus. Moricone, Pontorcovo), Cullberg Ballet, Örebro
1969 *Romeo and Juliet* (third version; mus. Prokofiev), Cullberg Ballet, Stockholm
1973 *Revolt* (mus. Bartók), Cullberg Ballet, Swedish television (stage version same year)
1974 *The School for Wives* (mus. Rossini), Cullberg Ballet, Swedish television (stage version same year)
*The Dreamer* (mus. by Creative Sound Studio, Copenhagen), television production, Wisconsin, U.S.A.
1975 *The War Hero* (stage version of *The Dreamer*), Royal Danish Ballet
1976 *Report* (mus. Petersson), Cullberg Ballet, Stockholm
*Peer Gynt* (mus. Sonstevold), Norwegian television
1977 *At the Edge of the Backwoods* (mus. Petersson), Cullberg Ballet, Bergen Festival
1979 *War Dances* (mus. Petersson), Royal Swedish Ballet, Stockholm
1982 *Medea's Children* (with Carbone, revised version of *Medea*), Teatro Regio, Turin
*Pulcinella and Pimpinella* (mus. Stravinsky), Swedish television
1984 *Abballet* (mus. Abba), Swedish television
1985 *Family Portraits* (mus. Tchaikovsky), Verona Ballet, Verona
1988 *Don Quixote's Dreams*, Il Balletto di Venezia, Vignale

## PUBLICATIONS

By Cullberg:
"Why Study Ballet?", *Dance Magazine* (New York), May 1961
"The Influence of Television Techniques on the Creation of Ballets", *Dancing Times* (London), November 1965
"Television Ballet", in *The Dance has Many Faces*, second edition, New York, 1966
"Ballet: Flight and Reality", translated by Laura de la Torre Bueno, *Dance Perspectives* (New York), Spring 1967
"Ballet in Television" (in English), *Monde de la danse* (Paris), vol. 1, no. 1, 1976
*Dance in New Dimensions*, with Måns Reuterswärd and Bertil Lauritzen, Stockholm 1987

About Cullberg:
Beaumont, Cyril, "Swedish Ballet", *Ballet* (London), May 1951
Beaumont, Cyril, *Ballets of Today*, London, 1954
Lipschütz, Dan, "Present Trends in Swedish Ballet", *World Theatre* (Brussels), Spring 1955
Goodman, Saul, "Lady from Nyköping", *Dance Magazine* (New York), June 1960
Loney, Glenn, "Sons and Mothers: Niklas Ek and Birgit Cullberg", *Dance Magazine* (New York), April 1970
Lidova, Irène, "Birgit Cullberg", *Les Saisons de la danse* (Paris), May 1972
Näslund, Erik, *Birgit Cullberg*, Stockholm, 1978

Näslund, Erik, "Alles ist leben: für Birgit Cullberg ist das alter kein thema", *Ballet: Chronik und Bilanz des Balletjahres* (Zurich), 1985

Törnqvist, Egil, and Jacobs, Barry, *Strindberg's "Miss Julie": A Play and its Transpositions*, Norwich, 1988

* * *

The great dance luminaries of the earlier decades of this century were to have a decisive influence on many young people in their choice of life path. Ashton and Tudor were only two of many youths whose lives were changed by Pavlova. In the modern dance field, Wigman, Kreutzberg, and Jooss had similar effects. Birgit Cullberg's life changed when she saw the Jooss Ballet perform *The Green Table* in Stockholm. Suddenly it became clear to her that dance could have a stronger meaning and could be a reflection of modern times. Cullberg, who had danced since childhood and had continued to study classical and modern dance on an amateur basis as an adult while studying literature at the University of Stockholm, suddenly decided at the age of 27 to devote her life to dance. She went to study with Jooss in England in 1935 and stayed for four years, returning to Sweden to establish herself as dancer and choreographer, and founding her first little Cullberg group in the autumn of 1939. Her works in the 1940s consisted of solos and small group compositions in different genres, and Cullberg was to become especially famous for her biting satire and humour, as well as for her political awareness. Many of her works were rooted in literature, making use of her university studies. Ever since, Cullberg has used themes from the great works of literature as inspiration for her ballets.

Sensing the limitations of the Jooss–Leeder technique, Cullberg took up her studies in classical ballet in the 1940s, using her experiences in her innovatory ballet *Miss Julie* in 1950. Cullberg was one of the first to work on the fusion between classical and modern idioms, something which has since come to dominate the ballet scene. *Miss Julie* was inspired by Petit's *Carmen* (which she had seen in Paris in 1949), in which Cullberg saw the possibilities of using classical ballet to portray complicated human relations. *Miss Julie* was thus created out of the psychological-realistic ballet drama which was developed in Europe and America in the 1930s and 1940s. It proved to be a triumphant success and won both ballet and choreographer, as well as ballerina Elsa Marianne von Rosen, an engagement with the Royal Swedish Ballet in the autumn of 1950. Cullberg then served as resident choreographer for the company until 1956.

*Miss Julie* and Cullberg's next ballet drama, *Medea*, were born out of a very personal situation, the trauma created by the choreographer's divorce from actor Anders Ek. Dance has always functioned as a safety valve for Cullberg, and without being too subjective, one can perhaps state that she has achieved the best results when she has had the starting point in a personal situation. But one need not know the personal background to understand the theatrical result. Cullberg has proved her greatness as an artist in her ability to transform the very private into the universal. She is capable of taking a step to one side in order to assume the unsentimental role of the observer. Here literature has served as a necessary mask for the very personal. This filtering of her art through the experiences of her own life is of course the key to Cullberg's very direct way of speaking to the audience.

There are several reasons for the great exposure and popularity Cullberg's ballets have had all over the world since her first breakthrough with *Miss Julie* in 1950. The most important is of course the fact that her themes are so universal and her ballets have an attractive dramatic and emotional force. But a further reason is the fact that her works can be staged very easily, using completely new dancers and different companies. This does not mean that Cullberg is less personal than other choreographers, whose works are more difficult to transfer to other dancers. For Cullberg the choreography comes first, not the dancers. She hardly ever works out the choreography on the dancers she has at hand when she is about to create a new ballet, but prepares everything beforehand on herself. The dancers nevertheless have very rewarding roles to dance, since the choreographer wishes to portray human relations and conflicts in dance. The parts in Cullberg's ballets, especially Miss Julie and Jean the butler, have changed many a dancer's career. Hidden dramatic powers have come to the fore, making stage personalities richer and more mature. Erik Bruhn, Violette Verdy, Cynthia Gregory, and Fernando Bujones are only some of many dancers whose careers have reached a turning point as a result of appearing in Cullberg's works.

Cullberg has also found another way of speaking very directly to audiences—via television. She is a pioneer in the field of television dance and her tremendous work in this area for more than three decades has been rewarded with many international prizes and awards. Cullberg is the only choreographer who plans all the camera work herself, as well as choreographing directly for television. Everything is prepared in a notebook, image after image, camera angle after camera angle. As soon as she started to work with the new medium in the early 1960s, she understood the distinction between the stage and the television medium. She started to look at the small screen and realized that this was the basic condition: not the stage, not the T.V. studio, but a small square screen that has to be filled with life, like a painting. It was a revolutionary discovery which Cullberg has stuck to ever since in all her works for television.

"Nothing is so dreadful as a gesture without meaning", declared François Delsarte, the nineteenth-century forerunner of modern dance. It is an opinion to which Cullberg and her mentor Kurt Jooss have also subscribed. Although she is at times inclined to use a more abstract approach to dance, the "dance is about dance" view—as embraced by Balanchine, Cunningham, and their followers—has never found an advocate in Cullberg. And her ballet dramas have continued to hold a grip on audiences all over the world. *Miss Julie* is a modern classic that is still one of ballet history's most performed works, and in sheer output of ballet productions Cullberg is, of the choreographers of our times, surpassed only by George Balanchine.

—Erik Näslund

---

**CUNNINGHAM, Merce**

American dancer, choreographer, and company director. Born Mercier Cunningham in Centralia, Washington, 16 April 1919. Educated at Centralia High School; studied tap and ballroom dancing with Maude M. Barrett; also attended George Washington University, Washington, D.C., Cornish School (now Cornish College), Seattle, Washington, Bennington College School of Dance summer session, and Mills College, Oakland, California. Dancer, Martha Graham Dance Company, New York, 1939–45; first independent choreography (in concert shared with Jean Erdman and Nina Fonaroff), 1942; first solo concert with composer John Cage, 1944; dancer, concerts in Paris, summer 1949; founder, Merce

Cunningham Dance Company, Black Mountain College, North Carolina, 1953, with first tour of United States, 1955, and annual tours thereafter; world tour, 1964; staged *Un jour ou deux*, Paris Opéra, 1973; began annual seasons at City Center Theater, New York, 1973; also collaborator on series of dance videos from 1974, first with Charles Atlas, later with Elliot Caplan; has appeared on television, including for Public Broadcasting Service (PBS) series "Dance in America", 1977; also director, *Points in Space* (with Elliot Caplan), co-produced with British Broadcasting Corporation (BBC) Television, 1986; subject of *Cage/Cunningham*, film portrait (dir. Caplan, 1991). Recipient: John Simon Guggenheim Memorial Foundation fellowships, 1953 and 1959; honorary D. Litt., University of Illinois, 1972; Samual H. Scripps/American Dance Festival Award for lifetime achievement, 1982; Commandeur de l'Ordre des arts et des lettres, 1982; honorary member of American Academy and Institute of Arts and Letters, 1984; MacArthur Foundation fellowship, 1985; Kennedy Center Honors, 1985; Laurence Olivier Award, 1985; Algur H. Meadows Award, Southern Methodist University, Dallas, Texas, 1987; Légion d'honneur, 1989; National Medal of Arts, U.S., 1990; Digital Dance Premier Award, London, 1990.

## ROLES

1939 Acrobat (cr) in *Every Soul is a Circus* (Graham), Martha Graham Company, New York
1940 Christ Figure (cr) in *El Penitente* (Graham), Martha Graham Company, New York
March (cr) in *Letter to the World* (Graham), Martha Graham Company, New York
1941 Pegasus (cr) in *Punch and Judy* (Graham), Martha Graham Company, New York
1943 Poetic Beloved (cr) in *Deaths and Entrances* (Graham), Martha Graham Company, New York
1944 Revivalist (cr) in *Appalachian Spring* (Graham), Martha Graham Company, New York
1948 Jonas, a Mechanical Monkey in *The Ruse of Medusa* (comedy by Erik Satie; translated M.C. Richards; chor. Cunningham), Black Mountain College, North Carolina

**Other roles include:** Solos (cr) in own works, from 1942–1990s.

## WORKS

1942 *Seeds of Brightness* (with Jean Erdman; mus. Lloyd), Bennington, Vermont
*Credo in Us* (with Jean Erdman; mus. Cage), Bennington, Vermont
*Ad Lib* (with Jean Erdman; mus. Tucker (mus. Cage from 1946), Bennington, Vermont
*Renaissance Testimonials* (solo; mus. Powers), Bennington, Vermont
*Totem Ancestor* (solo; mus. Cage), Humphrey-Weidman Studio, New York
1943 *In the Name of Holocaust* (solo; mus. Cage), Chicago
*Shimmera* (solo; mus. Cage), Chicago
*The Wind Remains* (Zarzuela after García Lorca; mus. Bowles), Cunningham, Erdman and others, New York
1944 *Triple-Paced* (solo; mus. Cage), New York
*Root of an Unfocus* (solo; mus. Cage), New York
*Tossed as it is Untroubled* (solo; mus. Cage), New York
*The Unavailable Memory of* (solo; mus. Cage), New York
*Spontaneous Earth* (solo; mus. Cage), New York
*Four Walls* (dance-play; mus. Cage), Cunningham, Harris, and others, Perry Mansfield Workshop, Steamboat Springs, Colorado
*Idyllic Song* (solo; mus. Satie, arranged Cage), Richmond, Virginia
1945 *Mysterious Adventure* (solo; mus. Cage), New York
*Experiences* (solo; mus. Cage, Gearhart), New York
1946 *The Encounter* (solo; mus. Cage), New York
*Invocation to Vahakn* (solo; mus. Hovhaness), New York
*Fast Blues* (solo; mus. Baby Dodds), New York
*The Princess Zondilda and her Entourage* (mus. Haieff), Cunningham, Bosler, and Litz, New York
1947 *The Seasons* (mus. Cage), Ballet Society, New York
*The Open Road* (solo; mus. Harrison), New York
*Dromenon* (mus. Cage), with group, New York
1948 *Dream* (solo; mus. Cage), Columbia, Missouri
Dances in *The Ruse of Medusa* (mus. and libretto Erik Satie), Cunningham and others, Black Mountain College, North Carolina
*A Diversion* (mus. Cage), Cunningham, Hamill, and Lippold, Black Mountain College, North Carolina
*Orestes* (solo; mus. Cage), Black Mountain College, North Carolina
1949 *Effusions avant l'heure* (later called *Games*, also *Trio*; mus. Cage), Cunningham, Le Clercq, and Nichols, Paris
*Amores* (duet; mus. Cage), Cunningham and LeClercq, Paris
*Duet* (for Betty Nichols and Milorad Miskovitch), Garden Fête, Paris
*Two Step* (solo; mus. Satie), New York City Dance Theatre, New York
1950 *Pool of Darkness* (mus. Weber), Cunningham and others, New York
*Before Dawn* (solo), New York
*Waltz* (mus. Satie), Louisiana State University student group, Baton Rouge
*Rag-Time Parade* (mus. Satie), Louisiana State University student group, Baton Rouge
*Waltz* (solo; mus. Satie), New York
1951 *Sixteen Dances for Soloist and Company of Three* (mus. Cage), Cunningham and group, Millbrook, New Jersey
*Variation* (solo; mus. Feldman), Seattle, Washington
*Boy Who Wanted to be a Bird* (solo), Martha's Vineyard, Massachusetts
1952 *Suite of Six Short Dances* (solo; mus. various, arranged Jennerjahn), Black Mountain College, North Carolina
*Excerpts from Symphonie pour un homme seul* (later called *Collage*; mus. Schaeffer, Henry), Cunningham and group, Creative Arts Festival of Brandeis University, Waltham, Massachusetts
*Les Noces* (mus. Stravinsky), Cunningham and group, Creative Arts Festival of Brandeis University, Waltham, Massachusetts
*Theater Piece* (by John Cage; mus. Tudor), Black Mountain College, North Carolina
1953 *Suite by Chance* (mus. Wolff), Merce Cunningham Dance Company, Urbana, Illinois
*Solo Suite in Space and Time* (solo; mus. Cage), Baton Rouge, Louisiana
*Demonstration Piece*, Louisiana State University Student group, Baton Rouge, Louisiana

**Merce Cunningham rehearsing *Summerspace* with Patricia Neary, New York City Ballet, 1966**

*Epilogue* (mus. Satie), Louisiana State University Student group, Baton Rouge, Louisiana

*Banjo* (mus. Gottschalk), Merce Cunningham Dance Company, Black Mountain College, North Carolina

*Dime a Dance* (mus. various, arranged Tudor), Merce Cunningham Dance Company, Black Mountain College, North Carolina

*Septet* (mus. Satie), Merce Cunningham Dance Company, Black Mountain College, North Carolina

*Untitled Solo* (mus. Wolff), Black Mountain College, North Carolina

*Fragments* (mus. Boulez), Merce Cunningham Dance Company, New York

1954 *Minutiae* (mus. Cage), Merce Cunningham Dance Company, Brooklyn

1955 *Springweather and People* (mus. Brown), Merce Cunningham Dance Company, Annandale-on-Hudson, New York

1956 *Lavish Escapade* (solo; mus. Wolff), Merce Cunningham Dance Company, South Bend, Indiana

*Galaxy* (mus. Brown), Merce Cunningham Dance Company, South Bend, Indiana

*Suite for Five in Space and Time* (later called *Suite for Five*; mus. Cage), Merce Cunningham Dance Company, South Bend, Indiana

*Nocturnes* (mus. Satie), Merce Cunningham Dance Company, Jacob's Pillow Dance Festival, Massachusetts

1957 *Changeling* (solo; mus. Wolff), Merce Cunningham Dance Company, Brooklyn

*Labyrinthian Dances* (mus. Hauer), Merce Cunningham Dance Company, Brooklyn

*Picnic Polka* (mus. Gottschalk), Merce Cunningham Dance Company, Brooklyn

1958 *Collage III* (solo; mus. Schaeffer, Henry), Pittsburgh, Pennsylvania

*Antic Meet* (mus. Cage), Merce Cunningham Dance Company, New London, Connecticut

*Summerspace* (mus. Feldman), Merce Cunningham Dance Company, New London, Connecticut

*Night Wandering* (duet; mus. Nilsson), Royal Opera House, Stockholm

1959 *From the Poems of the White Stone* (mus. Chou Wen-Chung), Merce Cunningham Dance Company, Urbana, Illinois

*Gambit for Dancers and Orchestra* (mus. Johnston), Merce Cunningham Dance Company, Urbana, Illinois

*Rune* (mus. Wolff), Merce Cunningham Dance Company, New London, Connecticut

1960 *Theater Piece* (duet; mus. Cage), Composers' Showcase, New York
*Crises* (mus. Nancarrow), Merce Cunningham Dance Company, New London, Connecticut
*Hands Birds* (mus. Brown), Carolyn Brown solo, Venice
*Waka* (mus. Ichiyanagi), Carolyn Brown solo, Venice
*Music Walk with Dancers* (duet; mus. Cage), Venice
1961 *Suite de Danses* (for television, dir. John Mercure; mus. Garrant), Merce Cunningham Dance Company, Canadian Broadcasting Corporation (CBC), Montreal
*Aeon* (mus. Cage), Merce Cunningham Dance Company, Montreal
1963 *Field Dances* (mus. Cage), Merce Cunningham Dance Company, Los Angeles
*Story* (mus. Ichiyanagi), Merce Cunningham Dance Company, Los Angeles
1964 *Open Session* (solo), Hartford, Connecticut
*Paired* (duet; mus. Cage), Merce Cunningham Dance Company, Hartford, Connecticut
*Winterbranch* (mus. Young), Merce Cunningham Dance Company, Hartford, Connecticut
*Cross Currents* (mus. Nancarrow, arranged Cage), Merce Cunningham Dance Company, London
*Museum Event no. 1*, Merce Cunningham Dance Company, Vienna
1965 *Variations V* (mus. Cage), Merce Cunningham Dance Company, New York
*How to Pass, Kick, Fall and Run* (mus. Cage), Merce Cunningham Dance Company, Chicago
1966 *Place* (mus. Mumma), Merce Cunningham Dance Company, Saint-Paul de Vence
1967 *Scramble* (mus. Ichiyanagi), Merce Cunningham Dance Company, Chicago
1968 *Rainforest* (mus. Tudor), Merce Cunningham Dance Company, Buffalo, New York
*Walkaround Time* (mus. Behrman), Merce Cunningham Dance Company, Buffalo, New York
*Assemblage* (film for television; mus. Cage, Tudor, Mumma), Merce Cunningham Dance Company, KQED-TV, San Francisco
1969 *Canfield* (mus. Oliveros), Merce Cunningham Dance Company, Rochester, New York
1970 *Tread* (mus. Wolff), Merce Cunningham Dance Company, Brooklyn
*Second Hand* (mus. Cage), Merce Cunningham Dance Company, Brooklyn
*Signals* (mus. Tudor, Mumma, Cage), Merce Cunningham Dance Company, Paris
*Objects* (mus. Lucier), Merce Cunningham Dance Company, Brooklyn
1971 *Loops* (solo; mus. Mumma), Museum of Modern Art, New York
1972 *Landrover* (mus. Cage, Mumma, Tudor), Merce Cunningham Dance Company, Brooklyn
*TV Rerun* (mus. Mumma), Merce Cunningham Dance Company, Brooklyn
*Borst Park* (mus. Wolff), Merce Cunningham Dance Company, Brooklyn
1973 *Un jour ou deux* (mus. Cage), Paris Opera Ballet, Paris
1974 *Westbeth* (work for video, dir. Atlas and Cunningham; mus. Cage), Merce Cunningham Dance Company, New York
1975 *Exercise Piece*, Merce Cunningham Dance Company, New York
*Changing Steps* (mus. Cage), Merce Cunningham Dance Company, Detroit
*Rebus* (mus. Behrman), Merce Cunningham Dance Company, Detroit
*Solo* (mus. Cage), Merce Cunningham Dance Company, Detroit
*Sounddance* (mus. Tudor), Merce Cunningham Dance Company, Detroit
1976 *Torse* (mus. Amacher), Merce Cunningham Dance Company, Princeton, New Jersey
*Squaregame* (mus. Kosugi), Merce Cunningham Dance Company, Adelaide, Australia
*Video Triangle* (part of event for television, dir. Brockway; mus. Tudor), WNET, New York
1977 *Travelogue* (mus. Cage), Merce Cunningham Dance Company, New York
*Inlets* (mus. Cage), Merce Cunningham Dance Company, Seattle
*Fractions* (for video, dir. Atlas and Cunningham; mus. Gibson) (staged Merce Cunningham Dance Company, 1978)
1978 *Exercise Piece I*, Merce Cunningham Dance Company, New York
*Exercise Piece II* (mus. Cage), Merce Cunningham Dance Company, Toronto
*Exchange* (mus. Tudor), Merce Cunningham Dance Company, New York
*Tango* (solo; mus. Cage), New York
1979 *Locale* (for video, dir. Atlas and Cunningham; mus. Kosugi), New York (staged Merce Cunningham Dance Company, 1979)
*Roadrunners* (mus. Tone), Merce Cunningham Dance Company, Durham, North Carolina
1980 *Exercise Piece III* (mus. Cage), Merce Cunningham Dance Company, New York
*Duets* (mus. Cage), Merce Cunningham Dance Company, New York
*Fielding Sixes* (mus. Cage), Merce Cunningham Dance Company, London
*Channels/Inserts* (filmdance, dir. Atlas and Cunningham; mus. Tudor), New York (staged Merce Cunningham Dance Company, 1981)
1981 *10's With Shoes* (mus. Kalve), Merce Cunningham Dance Company, New York
*Gallopade* (mus. Kosugi), Merce Cunningham Dance Company, London
1982 *Trails* (mus. Cage), Merce Cunningham Dance Company, New York
*Quartet* (mus. Tudor), Merce Cunningham Dance Company, Paris
1983 *Coast Zone* (for video, dir. Atlas and Cunningham; mus. Austin), New York (staged Merce Cunningham Dance Company, 1983)
*Inlets 2* (mus. Cage), Merce Cunningham Dance Company, Lille-Roubaix
*Roaratorio* (mus. Cage), Merce Cunningham Dance Company, Lille-Roubaix
1984 *Pictures* (mus. Behrman), Merce Cunningham Dance Company, New York
*Doubles* (mus. Kosugi), Merce Cunningham Dance Company, Durham, North Carolina
*Phrases* (mus. Tudor), Merce Cunningham Dance Company, Angers
1985 *Native Green* (mus. King), Merce Cunningham Dance Company, New York
*Arcade* (mus. Cage), Pennsylvania Ballet, Philadelphia
1986 *Grange Eve* (mus. Kosugi), Merce Cunningham Dance Company, New York
*Points in Space* (for video, dir. Caplan and Cun-

ningham; mus. Cage), London (staged Merce Cunningham Dance Company, 1987)
1987 *Fabrications* (mus. Pimenta), Merce Cunningham Dance Company, Minneapolis
*Shards* (mus. Tudor), Merce Cunningham Dance Company, New York
*Carousel* (mus. Kosugi), Merce Cunningham Dance Company, Jacob's Pillow, Massachusetts
1988 *Eleven* (mus. Ashley), Merce Cunningham Dance Company, New York
*Five Stone* (mus. Cage, Tudor), Merce Cunningham Dance Company, Berlin
*Five Stone Wind* (mus. Cage, Kosugi, Tudor), Merce Cunningham Dance Company, Avignon
1989 *Cargo X* (mus. Kosugi), Merce Cunningham Dance Company, Austin, Texas
*Field and Figures* (mus. Tcherepnin), Merce Cunningham Dance Company Minneapolis
*August Pace* (mus. Pugliese), Merce Cunningham Dance Company, Berkeley, California
*Inventions* (mus. Cage), Merce Cunningham Dance Company, Berkeley, California
1990 *Polarity* (mus. Tudor), Merce Cunningham Dance Company, New York
1991 *Neighbors* (mus. Kosugi), Merce Cunningham Dance Company, New York
*Trackers* (mus. Pimenta), Merce Cunningham Dance Company, New York
*Beach Birds* (mus. Cage), Merce Cunningham Dance Company, Zurich
*Loosestrife* (mus. Pugliese), Merce Cunningham Dance Company, Paris
1992 *Change of Address* (mus. Zimmermann), Merce Cunningham Dance Company, Austin, Texas

## PUBLICATIONS

By Cunningham:
"Space, Time and Dance", *trans/formation* (New York), 1952
"The Impermanent Art", *7 Arts* (Indian Hills, Colorado), 1955
*Changes: Notes on Choreography*, edited by Frances Starr, New York, 1968
"A Collaborative Process Between Music and Dance" in *TriQuarterly 54* (Evanston, Illinois), Spring 1982
*Le danseur et la danse*, entretiens avec Jacqueline Lesschaeve, Paris, 1980; as *The Dancer and the Dance*, Merce Cunningham in conversation with J. Lesschaeve, London and New York, 1985

About Cunningham:
Denby, Edwin, *Looking at the Dance*, New York, 1949
Cohen, Selma Jeanne (ed.), "Time to Walk in Space", *Dance Perspectives 34* (New York), Summer 1968
Tomkins, Calvin, *The Bride and the Bachelors*, New York, 1968
Klosty, James (ed.), *Merce Cunningham*, New York, 1975
Croce, Arlene, *Going to the Dance*, New York, 1982
Croce, Arlene, *Sight Lines*, New York, 1987
Adam, Judy (ed.), *Dancers on a Plane: Cage/Cunningham/Johns*, London, 1989
De Gubernatis, Raphaël, *Cunningham*, Paris, 1990

* * *

Merce Cunningham's career as a choreographer spans almost half a century. At the outset, he was seen by many as a supremely gifted dancer who wasted his talents on frivolous, even perverse experimentation. Four decades later, his position as leader of the modernist movement in dance is unassailable.

Cunningham was born and grew up in a small town in the northwest United States, and became a full-time dance student in the late 1930s at the Cornish School in Seattle, Washington, where his teacher, Bonnie Bird, engaged John Cage as the dance department's musician. Cage introduced the students to unorthodox ideas about the relationship of dance and music. Cunningham left Cornish after two years; Martha Graham saw him at a summer school at Mills College (Oakland, California) in 1939 and invited him to join her company in New York. He danced with her for six years, creating leading roles in many of her dances.

In the meantime, Cage also moved to New York and in the summer of 1942 composed a score for *Credo in Us*, jointly choreographed and danced by Cunningham and Jean Erdman for a concert they shared with Nina Fonaroff at Bennington College. Two years later, Cunningham and Cage presented a concert of solo dances and music for prepared piano in New York. At that time, dance and music shared a common rhythmic structure, coming together only at certain points. As time went on, dance and music became more and more independent of each other; by the early 1950s, their only relationship was that of simultaneity of performance.

Cunningham proposed other radical formal innovations: that any point in the dance space could be as important as any other and that "anything could follow anything". He followed Cage in the use of chance processes, abandoning the usual principles governing dance structure, whether narrative (cause and effect, conflict and resolution) or musical (the imitation of musical forms). Any movement could be used in choreography: in 1952, when Cunningham choreographed excerpts from *Symphonie pour un homme seul*, a "musique concrète" score by Pierre Schaeffer and Pierre Henry, he prepared gamuts of possible movements from which selections were made by chance that included not only recognizable dance steps (social as well as theatrical dance), but also everyday movement and gesture.

The use of chance, Cunningham believes, frees him from the limitations of habit and intuition, opening up movement possibilities that might not otherwise occur to him. Both he and Cage wish to "imitate nature in the manner of her operations". It is not that Cunningham's dances are lacking in structure—the structure is organic, not imposed.

In the summer of 1953, Cunningham was invited to teach in the summer session at Black Mountain College, the progressive liberal arts school in the Smoky Mountains of North Carolina, and took with him a group of dancers who had been studying with him in New York—including Carolyn Brown, Viola Farber, Remy Charlip, and Paul Taylor. They rehearsed and performed a repertory of dances, and Cunningham decided to keep the group together as the Merce Cunningham Dance Company, which gave its first New York season the following winter.

John Cage and David Tudor were the company musicians; Tudor, like Cage, has continued to work with the company throughout its history. They developed a form of live electronic music that has provided most of Cunningham's sound scores. The company has commissioned scores from many contemporary composers: the only instruction given to a composer is the proposed duration of the work.

Cunningham has extended to designers the same freedom that he has to musicians. Robert Rauschenberg was resident designer from 1954 to 1964; in 1967 Jasper Johns was appointed artistic advisor, in which capacity he not only designed several works himself but invited such artists as Frank Stella, Andy Warhol, Marcel Duchamp, Robert Morris, and Bruce Nauman to contribute designs; Johns was succeeded in 1980 by Mark Lancaster, who was in turn succeeded by William Anastasi and Dove Bradshaw in 1984.

In the early years, performances were few and far between, but in the summer of 1964 the company embarked on a world tour that was to last six months. Engagements in Paris and London—where a week's season was extended into a month—won the kind of considered critical comment, as well as enthusiastic audience response, that the company rarely received at home. Word began to get back to the United States of this reception, and by the time the company returned—having danced in both western and eastern Europe, India, Thailand, and Japan—there was a new curiosity about the work.

The company began to tour more widely in the United States under the auspices of the National Endowment for the Arts and the New York State Council on the Arts, and to be seen in extended seasons in New York City, rather than the single performances of earlier years. Tours abroad became an almost annual part of the company activity.

Cunningham has never refused the challenge of performing in non-theatrical venues such as museums, gymnasiums, stadiums, or even public spaces like the Piazza San Marco in Venice or Grand Central Station in New York, where he has given performances he calls "Events"—excerpts from his repertory arranged into a seamless sequence, without intermission, to suit the location. This flexibility has enabled him to adapt to yet another kind of space, that seen by the camera, and to choreograph several works specifically for video or film, in collaboration first with Charles Atlas, then with Elliot Caplan, thus defining a grammar of dance on screen. In a reversal of the usual practice (of adapting or "reconceiving" stage works for the screen), Cunningham later adapted most of his film/video dances for the stage.

Cunningham's works are now to be found in the repertories of both ballet and modern dance companies in Europe and the United States, including the Rambert Dance Company, the Paris Opéra Ballet, American Ballet Theatre, and Pacific Northwest Ballet.

—David Vaughan

---

**CYGNE, Le** *see* **DYING SWAN, The**

---

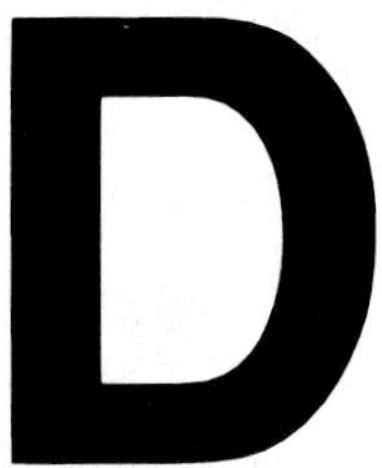

**D'AMBOISE, Jacques**

American dancer, choreographer, and teacher. Born Joseph Jacques Ahearn in Dedham, Massachusetts, 28 July 1934. Studied at the School of American Ballet, New York, pupil of Anatole Obukhov, Pierre Vladimirov, Muriel Stuart, Vecheslav Swoboda, Felia Doubrovska, and George Balanchine. Married dancer Carolyn George: 4 children, including dancer Christopher d'Amboise (b. 1960). Stage début, when still a student, with Ballet Society (precursor to New York City Ballet), 1947; dancer, New York City Ballet, from 1949: principal dancer, from 1953, creating many Balanchine roles, and participating in all tours abroad until 1984–85 season; international guest artist, including for Joffrey Ballet, San Francisco Ballet, Munich Ballet, Hamburg Ballet, Pacific Northwest Ballet, and Ballet de San Juan; has also appeared in films, including *Seven Brides for Seven Brothers* (dir. Stanley Donen, chor. Michael Kidd, 1954), *Carousel* (dir. Henry King, chor. Agnes de Mille, 1956), and *The Best Things in Life are Free* (dir. Michael Curtiz, 1956); first choreography, for New York City Ballet, in 1960; has also choreographed for television and for musicals, often acting as director; teacher, School of American Ballet, from 1970; founder and director, National Dance Institute (encouraging pre-vocational dance training), from 1976, with special interest in teaching and choreography for deaf students. Recipient: six Honorary Doctorates; Paul Robeson Award; Governors Award; MacArthur Scholarship; New York State Regents Award; New York City Historical Society Award; Capezio Dance Award, 1990.

**ROLES**

1947 St. Michael in *Pastorela* (L. Christensen, J. Fernandez), Ballet Society, New York

1950 "Being Beauteous" ensemble (cr) in *Illuminations* (Ashton), New York City Ballet, New York

Bald Head (cr) in *The Witch* (Cranko), New York City Ballet, London

1951 A Man (cr) in *The Miraculous Mandarin* (Bolender), New York City Ballet, New York

1952 Tristram (cr) in *Picnic at Tintagel* (Ashton), New York City Ballet, New York

Principal dancer (cr) in *Interplay* (Robbins), New York City Ballet, New York

Orion (cr) in *La Gloire* (Tudor), New York City Ballet, New York

1953 Another Youth (cr) in *The Five Gifts* (Dollar), New York City Ballet, New York

The Bandit in *Con Amore* (L. Christensen), New York City Ballet, New York

Mac in *Filling Station* (L. Christensen), New York City Ballet, New York

Viola (cr) in *Fanfare* (Robbins), New York City Ballet, New York

1954 Second movement (cr) in *Quartet* (Robbins), New York City Ballet, New York

Rondo (cr) in *Western Symphony* (Balanchine), New York City Ballet, New York

"Halloween" (cr) in *Ivesiana* (Balanchine), New York City Ballet, New York

1956 Principal dancer (cr) in *The Still Point* (new version of *At the Still Point*; Bolender), New York City Ballet, New York

1957 A Soldier in *The Masquers* (Bolender), New York City Ballet, New York

Title role in *Apollo* (previously *Apollo, Leader of the Muses*; Balanchine), New York City Ballet, New York

1958 Principal dancer (cr) in *Gounod Symphony* (Balanchine), New York City Ballet, New York

Fourth Campaign (cr) in *Stars and Stripes* (Balanchine), New York City Ballet, New York

Jason in *Medea* (Cullberg), New York City Ballet, New York

1959 Principal dancer (cr) in *Native Dancers* (Balanchine), New York City Ballet, New York

Five Pieces (cr) in *Episodes II* (Balanchine), New York City Ballet, New York

1960 Prince of Persia (cr) in *The Figure in the Carpet* (Balanchine), New York City Ballet, New York

Ensemble (cr) in *Variations from Don Sebastian* (later called *Donizetti Variations*; Balanchine), New York City Ballet, New York

Principal dancer in *Tchaikovsky Pas de Deux* (Balanchine), New York City Ballet, New York

1961 Principal dancer (cr) in *Electronics* (Balanchine), New York City Ballet, New York

Principal dancer (cr) in *Valses et Variations* (later called *Raymonda Variations*; Balanchine), New York City Ballet, New York

1963 Principal dancer (cr) in *Movements for Piano and Orchestra* (Balanchine), New York City Ballet, New York

Principal dancer (cr) in *Meditation* (pas de deux; Balanchine), New York City Ballet, New York

Principal dancer in *Waltz Scherzo* (Balanchine), New York City Ballet, New York

1964 Principal dancer in *Ballet Imperial* (Balanchine), New York City Ballet, New York

Principal dancer (cr) in *Quatuor* (also chor.), New York City Ballet, New York

Cavalier in *The Nutcracker* (new production; Balanchine), New York City Ballet, New York

1965 Title role in *Don Quixote* (Balanchine), New York City

**Jacques D'Amboise with Kay Mazzo in *Movements for Piano and Orchestra*, 1963**

Ballet, New York

1966 Rondo alla Zingarese (cr) in *Brahms-Schoenberg Quartet* (Balanchine), New York City Ballet, New York

1967 Diamonds (cr) in *Jewels* (Balanchine), New York City Ballet, New York

1969 Principal dancer (cr) in *Pas de Deux* (also chor.), New York City Ballet, New York

1970 "The Man I Love", "Embraceable You", "Who Cares?", "Liza", "Clap Yo' Hands" (cr) in *Who Cares?* (Balanchine), New York City Ballet, New York

Prince Ivan (cr) in *The Firebird* (new production; Balanchine, Robbins), New York City Ballet, New York

1973 Classical pas de deux (cr) in *Cortège Hongrois* (Balanchine), New York City Ballet, New York

1975 Principal dancer (cr) in *Alborada del Gracioso* (also chor.), New York City Ballet, New York

1976 Dress MacLeod (cr) in *Union Jack* (Balanchine), New York City Ballet, New York

1980 Principal dancer (Second Couple) (cr) in *Robert Schumann's "Davidsbündlertänze"* (Balanchine), New York City Ballet, New York

**Other roles include:** Sanguinic in *The Four Temperaments* (Balanchine), First Movement in *Symphony in C* (Balanchine), Fête Polonaise in *Bourrée Fantasque* (Balanchine), principal dancer in *Sylvia: Pas de Deux* (Balanchine), principal dancer in *Scotch Symphony* (Balanchine), principal dancer in *Interplay* (Robbins), principal dancer in *Afternoon of a Faun* (Robbins), Divertissement in *A Midsummer Night's Dream* (Balanchine), principal dancer in *Irish Fantasy* (also chor.), principal dancer in *Pas de Deux and Divertissement* (Balanchine), First Movement in *Tchaikovsky Suite No. 2* (also chor.).

## WORKS

1960 *Sinfonia no. 2* (*Uruguay*; mus. Tosar) in *Panamerica* (chor. Balanchine, Contreras, Moncion, Taras; mus. various, arranged Chávez), New York City Ballet, New York

1963 *The Chase* (mus. Mozart), New York City Ballet, New York

1964 *Quatuor* (mus. Shostakovich), New York City Ballet, New York

*Irish Fantasy* (mus. Saint-Saëns), New York City Ballet, Los Angeles

1967 *Prologue* (mus. Byrd, Farnaby, et al., arranged Irving), New York City Ballet, New York

1969 *Tchaikovsky Suite* (later called *Tchaikovsky Suite no. 2*; mus. Tchaikovsky), New York City Ballet, New York

*Pas de Deux* (mus. von Webern), New York City Ballet, New York

*Saltarelli* (mus. Vivaldi), Ballet de San Juan, Puerto Rico

1975 *Sinfonietta* (mus. Hindemith), New York City Ballet, New York

*Alborada del Gracioso* (mus. Ravel), New York City Ballet, New York

*Sarabande and Danse* (mus. Debussy, orchestrated by Ravel), New York City Ballet, New York

1981 *Scherzo Opus 42* (mus. Tchaikovsky), New York City Ballet, New York

*Valse-Scherzo* (part of *Tempo di Valse*; mus. Tchaikovsky), New York City Ballet, New York

*Concert Fantasy* (mus. Tchaikovsky), New York City Ballet, New York

1982 *Celebration* (mus. Mendelssohn), New York City Ballet, New York

**Other works include:** for Ballet West—*Meditation from Thaïs* (pas de deux; mus. Massenet); for Ballet Spectacular—*You are Love*, *Pas de trois Twenties*; for Ballet de San Juan—*Firebird* (mus. Stravinsky); for Kennedy Theatre for Children—*Peter and the Wolf* (mus. Prokofiev); for television—*Peanut Ballet* (nominated for Emmy Award, 1989); dances in musicals *Lady in the Dark* (with Palmer, Tolan), *Peter Pan* (with Palmer, Irving), *Roberta* (with Newway, Hickman, Horton).

## PUBLICATIONS

By d'Amboise:

Interview in Maynard, Olga, "Jacques d'Amboise: An Interview", Dance Magazine (New York), October 1969

*Teaching the Magic of Dance*, with Hope Cook and Carolyn George, New York, 1983

About d'Amboise:

Woody, R., "Brilliant Young Dancer", *Dance Magazine* (New York), January 1954

Joel, Lydia, "Jacques d'Amboise", *Dance Magazine* (New York), February 1957

Goodman, Saul, "Spotlight on Melissa Hayden and Jacques d'Amboise", *Ballet Today* (London), May–June 1970

Goodman, Saul, "An Extraordinary Anniversary", *Dance Magazine* (New York), November 1970

Reynolds, Nancy, *Repertory in Review*, New York, 1977

Croce, Arlene, *Afterimages*, New York, 1979

Solway, Diane, "Follow the Leader", *Ballet News* (New York), May 1983

Farrell, Suzanne, *Holding on to the Air* (autobiography), New York, 1991

Gere, David, "Jacques d'Amboise", *Dance Magazine* (New York), May 1991

* * *

Wearing a beard, which added solemnity to his otherwise boyish face, Jacques d'Amboise made his solo début with the New York City Ballet in 1952. Sir Frederick Ashton had been commissioned to create *Picnic at Tintagel* for the company, and he selected the seventeen-year-old d'Amboise to portray Tristram. Diana Adams was Iseult in this flashback version of the tragic story.

Pure dramatic roles like that of Tristram were not often assigned to d'Amboise during his 34 years with the company. The only other which comes to mind is that of Jason in Birgit Cullberg's 1958 version of *Medea*. Instead, he rapidly became the company's ranking danseur noble.

His six-foot stature was a decided asset in partnering the tall ballerinas whom George Balanchine was developing. D'Amboise was also a virtuoso dancer who knew instinctively how much energy to release into a phrase, so that it never seemed either driven or truncated, never appeared disproportionate to the music. As if that weren't enough, he had a casual, manly charm which enabled him to present his partners most advantageously.

Balanchine was greatly stimulated by d'Amboise's easy-flowing technique. He created more new roles for the young man than for any other dancer in the company. He also revived roles for him. The most important was that of Apollo, which became the dancer's sole province for several years. He was the ideal incarnation of Balanchine's neo-classical god. The choreographer's treatment of the theme is both reverent and playful. As the action unfolds and the god progresses from cavorting with his three muses to facing his destiny as their leader, he simultaneously progresses from inchoate infancy to glowing manhood. Jacques d'Amboise embarked upon this choreographic journey with an endearing simplicity, and yet physically he was so masterful that the ascent to Parnassus seemed to be his rightful heritage. In later years, when other dancers assumed the role, the image of d'Amboise remained indelible.

Jacques d'Amboise was by no means a comedian, but he could be playful. And so it was natural to revive Lew Christensen's *Filling Station* for him. He was perfectly suited to the role of Mac, the genial, all-American gas station attendant. But probably his most amusing assignment was the pas de deux he shared with Melissa Hayden in Balanchine's *Stars and Stripes*. They jokingly dubbed themselves "Ike and Mamie" as they sailed through the intricacies of this showpiece to John Philip Sousa's "El Capitan" march. There were endless entrechats with flexed feet, grands jetés punctuated with saucy salutes, enchaînements which easily encircled the New York State Theatre's spacious stage. In addition to its heartiness, the pas de deux required a dizzying speed.

Even in d'Amboise's more elegant partnering assignments like the "Diamonds" section of Balanchine's *Jewels*, or *Movements for Piano and Orchestra*, or *Robert Schumann's Davidsbündlertänze*, there was an underlying current of energy. It was perhaps responsible for the impressive length of his dancing career.

During his second decade with the company, d'Amboise began to create ballets. His output included *The Chase*, *Quatuor*, *Irish Fantasy*, *Prologue*, *Tchaikovsky Suite No. 2*, *Saltarelli*, and *Alborada del Gracioso*. With the exception of *Irish Fantasy*, they lasted briefly. *Irish Fantasy* (Saint-Saëns) enjoyed a more substantial career, but it is no longer in the repertoire, despite the soundness of its structure and the warmth of its style.

Occasionally d'Amboise took time off to appear in films. The most memorable was *Seven Brides for Seven Brothers*. Its challenging dances by Michael Kidd and the dashing manner in which they were performed by d'Amboise and his six on-screen brothers have made it a classic among cinema musicals.

As d'Amboise matured, his joy in dancing became channeled in another direction. In 1976 he founded the National Dance Institute, and in 1984 he left the New York City Ballet to devote his time to this non-profit project. It assembles children (and occasionally a group of adults) from all parts of New York City, gives them basic dance training, and unites them in an annual performance at the Felt Forum of Madison Square Garden. While the participants are not necessarily motivated toward a career in dance, this opportunity to perform enhances their self-confidence. It also makes them aware of dance as a natural and satisfying means of expression.

—Doris Hering

---

## DANCES AT A GATHERING

**Choreography:** Jerome Robbins
**Music:** Frédéric Chopin
**Design:** Joe Eula (costumes), Thomas Skelton (lighting)
**First Production:** New York City Ballet, New York State Theatre, New York, 22 May 1969 (gala benefit preview 8 May 1969)
**Principal Dancers:** Allegra Kent, Sara Leland, Kay Mazzo, Patricia McBride, Violette Verdy, Anthony Blum, John Clifford, Robert Maiorano, John Prinz, Edward Villella

**Other productions include:** Royal Ballet (restaged Robbins); London, 19 October 1970. Paris Opéra Ballet (restaged Robbins); Paris, 16 November 1991.

### PUBLICATIONS

"Jerome Robbins Discusses *Dances at a Gathering* with Edwin Denby", *Dance Magazine* (New York), July 1969
Sealy, Robert, "Mr. Robbins, Mr. Balanchine, Mr. Boelzner", *Ballet Review* (Brooklyn, N.Y.), vol. 3, no. 3, 1970
Clarke, Mary, "*Dances at a Gathering*", *Dancing Times* (London), December 1970
Williams, Peter, et al., "*Dances at a Gathering*", *Dance and Dancers* (London), December 1970
Balanchine, George, with Mason, Francis, *Balanchine's Complete Stories of the Great Ballets*, Garden City, N.Y., 1977
Reynolds, Nancy, *Repertory in Review*, New York, 1977

* * *

A number of ballets by Jerome Robbins could justifiably be entitled *Dances at a Gathering*. A group of apparent strangers coming happily together to flirt, interact, and dance is almost a Robbins trademark: the narcissistic pas de deux *Afternoon of a Faun* (1953), *In The Night* (1970), and the comic mayhem of *The Concert* (1956) are ostensibly very different works, yet all contain this particular element. With these and other works by Robbins, the inspiration lies, principally, in the apparently spontaneous response of the dancers to the music as it is being played. The participants are confident, joyful, and spirited. *Dances at a Gathering* has all the afore-mentioned elements, and in many respects is the apex of Robbins's achievements in this particular genre for the New York City Ballet. Certainly it has been hailed as a work of genius on both sides of the Atlantic.

The piece evolved from Robbins's desire to create a pas de deux to Chopin's music for Patricia McBride and Edward Villella, after he had been inspired by their performances in his *Afternoon of a Faun*. At the time he also had the 25th Anniversary City Center Gala in mind as the most appropriate occasion to unveil the work. As rehearsals for the ballet progressed, a creative valve opened and, with Balanchine's encouragement, Robbins created more and more dances to the Chopin piano music he had chosen. When *Dances at a Gathering* had its premiere at the New York State Theater in 1969, it featured ten performers: five male, five female. The ballet was dedicated to the memory of Jean Rosenthal, who had died seven days earlier.

The curtain rises on an empty stage with simple black side tabs and a vivid blue cyclorama representing the sky. The lighting by Thomas Skelton evokes a meadow in the late afternoon and changes to match shifts in the character of the music. A man in a white shirt and brown tights walks dreamily on to the stage as if listening to the music; his walk flows naturally into a dance which is part joyful, part reverie. As he leaves the stage he resumes his meditative mood. He is followed by a couple whose pas de deux is initially tentative but finally exuberant, concluding with a run into the wings with the girl supported on the man's shoulder. In solos, pairs, and groups of never more than six, the dancers occupy the stage in playful,

*Dances at a Gathering*, **performed by New York City Ballet, 1969**

ecstatic, amorous, or enquiring mood. Each character remains positive, secure, and friendly; the mood remains happy throughout.

In the final section, all ten dancers come together for the first time to the music of the Nocturne, Opus 15 No. 1. In subdued early evening light, the young man in brown who began the proceedings looks around him and, in a curious gesture, touches the ground with his hand. In sympathetic reaction the dancers look at him and each other, and then upwards at the sky. They appear to be looking and listening intently for a moment and then move away, breaking into pairs and then dividing finally towards the back of the stage: men at one side, women at the other. They bow to each other as the curtain falls.

While the atmosphere of the ballet is unremittingly uplifting, many have commented on the sense of impending apocalypse in the pregnant moment where the performers gaze up at the sky. Like all great works of art, *Dances at a Gathering* is open to many interpretations. The thoughtful aspect of the ballet engenders a like thoughtfulness in its audience, and frequently the viewer's own preoccupations can be projected on to what is essentially an abstract piece.

Robbins, irritated by speculation about the "meaning" of his creation, said: "There are no stories to any of the dances in *Dances at a Gathering*. There are no plots and no roles. The dancers are themselves dancing with each other to that music in that space."

The cast at the first performance was an impressive one, including Patricia McBride, Allegra Kent, Violette Verdy, and Edward Villella. The simple costumes by Joe Eula featured blue, pink, dusty rose, apricot, and mauve as identifying colours for the featured women, and salmon, gold, mauve, green, and brown for the men. Subsequent casts for New York City Ballet have featured Merrill Ashley, Stephanie Saland, Bart Cook, Sean Lavery, Peter Martins, and Mikhail Baryshnikov. Robbins created *Other Dances* in 1976 as a sequel, but while it was a success it never achieved the modern classic status of its predecessor.

—Mike Dixon

---

**DANCE THEATRE OF HARLEM**

American ballet company based in New York. Origins in the school established in Harlem district of New York City by Arthur Mitchell and Karel Shook, 1969; first professional performance of company, 1971; has since toured internationally, including several visits to London, and tour of the Soviet Union, 1988. Official school associated with company, Dance Theatre of Harlem School, still based in Harlem, with small training company, Dance Theatre of Harlem (DTH) School Ensemble, participating in local tours and collaborating with DTH Choreographers' Workshop. Current artistic director of Dance Theatre of Harlem: Arthur Mitchell.

**The Dance Theatre of Harlem performing their own version of *Giselle*, Act I**

## PUBLICATIONS

Maynard, Olga, "Arthur Mitchell and the Dance Theatre of Harlem", *Dance Magazine* (New York), March 1970
Greskovic, Robert, "The Dance Theatre of Harlem: A Work in Progress", *Ballet Review* (New York), vol. 4, no.6, 1974
"Dance Comes to Harlem", interview with Arthur Mitchell and Karel Shook, *Dance and Dancers* (London), October 1974
Williams, Peter, et al., "Harlem Comes to London", *Dance and Dancers* (London), October 1974
Steinbrink, M., "Dream Factory", *Ballet News* (New York), February 1981
Barnes, Clive, "Building a Repertory", *Dance and Dancers* (London), August 1987
Kendall, Elizabeth, "Dance Theatre of Harlem at Twenty", *Dance Magazine* (New York), June 1989
Wolfahrt, Hans, "Arthur Mitchell" (interview), *Ballett Journal* (Cologne), October 1989
West, Martha Ullman, "On the Brink: DTH Men in Crisis", *Dance Magazine* (New York), October 1990

* * *

The Dance Theatre of Harlem is one of those inspiring artistic ventures which has defied all odds to become an international success. Founded by Arthur Mitchell in direct response to the assassination of Martin Luther King, Jr. in 1968, the company's self-proclaimed aim from the beginning has been to serve the black community in Harlem and, on a wider scale, to prove to the world that black dancers can excel in an art form which has traditionally been a somewhat precious, whites-only preserve.

Mitchell himself was a leading dancer with Balanchine's New York City Ballet, where as the only black premier danseur on the ballet stage during the 1950s he had already proven false any prejudices about the unsuitability of black dancers for ballet. Purists may argue (as some have done) that Mitchell was still marginalized, typecast in such token roles as Puck in Balanchine's *A Midsummer Night's Dream*—but Balanchine certainly believed in the value of Mitchell's superb technique and stage presence, casting him, for example, as the lead opposite Diana Adams in his neo-classical Stravinsky masterpiece, *Agon* (1957). All the same, in his rise to the top Mitchell can only have been made forcibly aware of the total lack of black dancers in the world of professional ballet.

Mitchell's first aim, before he could even dream of directing a professional company, was to start a school. The Dance Theatre of Harlem (DTH) School was founded in 1969, with the late dancer/teacher Karel Shook as artistic adviser and with the assistance of a Ford Foundation grant; and its first classes were held in the basement of a Harlem church. Mitchell's mission, as the publicity for the school now proclaims, was "to introduce young people, particularly those who were economically and culturally disadvantaged, to the beauty and discipline of dance". Ballet was not the sort of thing that attracted the average Harlem youth off the streets, but Mitchell lured enough students into the studio (soon moved to a disused auto garage) to justify maintaining a permanent school. By the end of the first summer season, the original class of 30 had expanded to 400. Two years later, Mitchell had an ensemble capable of putting on an full-length evening of classical ballet.

The Dance Theatre of Harlem's professional début was in 1971, at the Guggenheim Museum in New York City. The company performed mostly in small chamber pieces choreographed by Mitchell himself, but it was soon to take on a number of Balanchine ballets—a fortuitous result of Mitchell's previous association with the choreographer and an acquisition which ultimately helped to define the so-called "neo-classical" style of the company. The dancers leading this troupe were by no means technical virtuosos, but the most immediately palpable quality about their dancing was the visible energy and enthusiasm of their attack. In an art form which, for all its tremendous physical demands, can often be accused of staid and predictable mannerism, this vitality and eagerness was hugely refreshing. After twenty years, the company still retains this exciting energy.

DTH, it must be said, was lucky to have its share of strong dance personalities who played a large part in defining the company's early identity. The ballerinas who came to prominence in the early years of the company were the classically perfect Lydia Abarca and later on the extremely versatile Virginia Johnson, a ballerina who continues to be at the centre of DTH's image and reputation. Both had the joint burden and honour of being groomed for their roles from a very early age (in the early 1970s the average age among company dancers was nineteen)—and therefore both displayed a poise and self-assurance on stage which was impressive for their relative lack of experience. By the time of the company's 1974 London tour, the British critics were pointing to Abarca's and Johnson's having "the serene perfection that we look for in the best Balanchine dancers".

At the same time, Mitchell certainly did not stop at Balanchine's dictum that "ballet is woman", producing a series of exciting male dancers who, like Mitchell himself, combined grace and athleticism, artistic finesse and masculinity. Paul Russell, delivering what critics called "electric" performances in the "Rose from Spanish Harlem" dance from Louis Johnson's *Forces of Rhythm*, or leaping through the air in the male solo from the *Le Corsaire* pas de deux (staged by Karel Shook), had the early makings of a "star". Other male DTH dancers who helped to establish its reputation were Ronald Perry, William Scott, Derek Williams, and Joseph Wyatt. After the company's 1974 spring season in New York, local critic Robert Greskovic was rhapsodizing,

> DTH is proof that ballet dancing is not a matter of race, but a matter of selection and direction. It's not a matter of We (whites) who have it and They (blacks) who don't. Human bodies and personalities vary; some can be made into classical dancers and some can't. In making up for lost time, Mitchell seems to have had an especially keen eye. So clear is his success that anyone watching DTH should be over the Black point in about three minutes. . . . Considering the company's four-year existence and its youth, . . . its claim to fame in the dance capital of the world [is] remarkably justified.

Since then, the Dance Theatre of Harlem has simply grown in stature and reputation. One cannot exactly claim that it has gone "from strength to strength", given that, like almost every other small dance company trying to survive in an era of ever-decreased arts funding, it has had its share of bankruptcy, temporary closure, cancelled seasons, and rebirth under new organization. Artistically, however, the Dance Theatre of Harlem can hardly be faulted.

The repertoire has grown steadily, exemplifying, as always, the remarkable range and versatility of the Harlem dancers. As well as expanding the Balanchine repertory, Mitchell has taken on a number of dramatic works, including Valerie Bettis's balletic version of *A Streetcar Named Desire* and the Agnes de Mille classic, *Fall River Legend*. The Dance Theatre of Harlem has also joined enthusiastically in the recent trend for revivals of early twentieth-century works, putting on a particularly successful programme of Bronislava Nijinska works, including her two famous ballets for Diaghilev, *Les Noces* and *Les Biches*. It has also continued to support black choreographers and to stage works (often with a more contemporary or jazz-dance emphasis) which point to the dancers' own important African heritage.

Perhaps most famous of all the company ventures has been Arthur Mitchell's and Frederic Franklin's restaging of that archetype of nineteenth-century Romantic ballet, *Giselle*, in which the setting was moved from a rather indistinct Ruritania of the last century to the American south before the Civil War. This "Creole" *Giselle* was meticulously researched and extremely effective in its new setting, yet at the same time utterly true to the Romantic spirit and required early nineteenth-century balletic style. Considered now almost a trademark of the company, this *Giselle* won unanimous praise at its 1984 premiere, winning the Olivier Award in London for Best New Production of the year.

The Dance Theatre of Harlem, now past its twentieth anniversary, has undoubtedly established itself as one of the leading ballet companies of the world. Its only vulnerability, perhaps, lies in its dependence on the vision and direction of its founder and leader, Arthur Mitchell, without whom the company could well lose its focus in the future. Nevertheless, after the financial problems of the late 1980s and the re-establishment of a company with a glossier, more international image, the company looks well positioned to continue as a strong ballet presence into the twenty-first century.

—Martha Bremser

---

**DANIELIAN, Leon**

American dancer, choreographer, and teacher. Born in New York City, 31 October 1920. Studied with Mikhail Mordkin, Ballet Arts, and American Ballet School, New York; also studied with Mikhail (Michel) Fokine, Anton Dolin, Antony Tudor, Igor Schwezoff, Seda Suny, and Vecheslav Swoboda. Début as corps dancer with Mordkin Ballet, 1937; soloist, Ballet Theatre (later American Ballet Theatre), 1939–41, and Colonel de Basil's Original Ballet Russe, 1941/42; principal dancer, Ballet Russe de Monte Carlo, 1943–51, 1952–57: principal guest artist, various seasons, 1958–60; partner to Yvette Chauviré on a tour of North Africa and the south of France, 1951; guest artist (Roland Petit's) Ballet des Champs-Elysées, Paris, season 1951–52, and San Francisco Ballet, 1953, 1957, and 1959; also appeared in Broadway musicals, including *I Married an Angel* (mus. Rodgers; chor. Balanchine, 1938), and in operetta, including *Song of Norway* (operetta after Grieg; chor. Balanchine, 1944), and for opera companies of Pittsburgh and St. Louis; choreographer, Ballet Russe de Monte Carlo, from 1956; director and choreographer, Leon Danielian Ballet Group, 1960; teacher, Ballet Russe de Monte Carlo School, New York, from 1948, also teaching at own school in White Plains, New York, during the 1950s; director, American Ballet Theatre School, from 1967; Assistant Dean of Dance, Purchase

State University of New York, from 1980; Professor of Dance, University of Texas at Austin, from 1982. Recipient: Best Performing Male Dancer of the Year Award, East Coast Critics, 1949; Dance Masters of America Annual Award, 1971.

## ROLES

1939 Harlequin in *Carnaval* (Fokine), Ballet Theatre, New York
Pas de trois from *Swan Lake* (Petipa, Ivanov; staged Dolin), Ballet Theatre
The Huntsman in *Lady Into Fox* (Havard), Ballet Theatre, New York
1940 Principal dancer (cr) in *Capriccioso* (new version of *Italian Suite*; Dolin), Ballet Theatre, Chicago
Count Azagra (cr) in *Goyescas* (Fernandez), Ballet Theatre, New York
Dictator (cr) in *Quintet* (Dolin), Ballet Theatre, New York
The Lamplighter in *Voices of Spring* (Mordkin), Ballet Theatre, New York
1941/42 Bluebird in *Le Mariage d'Aurore* (divertissements from *The Sleeping Beauty*; after Petipa), Original Ballet Russe
Principal dancer in *Choreartium* (Massine), Original Ballet Russe
Principal dancer in *Les Présages* (Massine), Original Ballet Russe
Principal dancer in *Cimarosiana* (Massine), Original Ballet Russe
1944 Dancer (cr) in *The Red Poppy* (Schwezoff), Ballet Russe de Monte Carlo, New York
Principal dancer (cr) in *Danses Concertantes* (Balanchine), Ballet Russe de Monte Carlo, New York
Harlequinade (cr) in *Le Bourgeois Gentilhomme* (new version; Balanchine), Ballet Russe de Monte Carlo, New York
1945 Principal dancer (cr) in *Comedia Balletica* (Bolender), Ballet Russe de Monte Carlo, New York
1946 Blackamoor (cr) in *Night Shadow* (*La Sonnambula*; Balanchine), Ballet Russe de Monte Carlo, New York
Pas de trois (cr) in *Raymonda* (new production; Balanchine, Danilova after Petipa), Ballet Russe de Monte Carlo, New York
1947 Frontiersman (cr) in *Virginia Sampler* (Bettis), Ballet Russe de Monte Carlo, New York
El Bonito (cr) in *Madroños* (Lobos), Ballet Russe de Monte Carlo, New York
Principal dancer (cr) in *Cirque de Deux* (Boris), Ballet Russe de Monte Carlo, Hollywood
1948 The Romantic One in *Love Song* (R. Page), Ballet Russe de Monte Carlo, Rochester, New York
Bonaventuri (cr) in *Quelques Fleurs* (Boris), Ballet Russe de Monte Carlo, New York
1949 The Husband in *The Mute Wife* (Cobos), Ballet Russe de Monte Carlo, New York
The Cadet in *Graduation Ball* (Lichine), Ballet Russe de Monte Carlo, New York
Leader of the Ball in *Birthday* (Chamié) Ballet Russe de Monte Carlo, New York
1951 Pas de deux from *Don Quixote* (after Petipa), Ballet des Champs-Elysées, Paris
Principal dancer in *The Black Swan* Pas de deux (from *Swan Lake*; after Petipa), Ballet des Champs-Elysées, Paris
Principal dancer in *Impromptu au Bois* (Page), Ballet des Champs-Elysées, Paris
1953 The Bandit (cr) in *Con Amore* (L. Christensen), San Francisco Ballet, San Francisco
Tennis Player in *A la Françaix* (Balanchine), San Francisco Ballet, San Francisco
1954 Ko-Ko (cr) in *The Mikado* (Cobos), Ballet Russe de Monte Carlo, Baltimore
The Poet (cr) in *Harold in Italy* (Massine), Ballet Russe de Monte Carlo, Boston

**Other roles include**: for Ballet Theatre—Benno and Siegfried in *Swan Lake*, Act II (Dolin after Ivanov), Mazurka and Pas de deux in *Les Sylphides* (Fokine); for Original Ballet Russe—leading roles in *Le Coq d'or* (Fokine), *Francesca da Rimini* (Massine); for Ballet Russe de Monte Carlo—Spirit of the Rose in *Le Spectre de la rose* (Fokine), Peruvian in *Gaîté Parisienne* (Massine), Slave in *Schéhérazade* (Fokine), Faun in *L'Après-midi d'un faune* (Nijinsky), Franz in *Coppélia* (Petipa, Ivanov, Cecchetti; staged Sergeyev), Cavalier in *The Nutcracker* (one-act version; Fedorova after Ivanov), Hussar and King of the Dandies in *Le Beau Danube* (Massine), Frankie in *Frankie and Johnny* (Page), principal dancer in *Serenade* (Balanchine).

## WORKS

1956 *Sombreros* (mus. Mexican folk music, orchestrated by Boutnikoff), Ballet Russe de Monte Carlo, Washington, D.C.
1957 *The Mazurka* (mus. Chopin, Tchaikovsky, Strauss, arranged Boutnikoff), Ballet Russe de Monte Carlo, Hartford
1961 *España* (mus. Breton, Chapi, Granados), Ballet Russe de Monte Carlo, Chicago

## PUBLICATIONS

By Danielian:
"Impressions of a Sojourn in Paris", *Dance Magazine* (New York), March 1952
Interview in Gruen, John, *The Private World of Ballet*, New York, 1975

About Danielian:
"American Stars of the Ballet Russe", *Dance Magazine* (New York), September 1944
Denby, Edwin, *Looking at the Dance*, New York, 1949
Gale, Joseph, "Meanwhile, Back in the Classroom", *Dance Magazine* (New York), April 1972
Gold, R., "Leon Danielian and the American Ballet Theatre School", *Dance Magazine* (New York), January 1975
Gale, Joseph, *Behind Barres: The Mystique of Masterly Teaching*, New York, 1980
Anderson, Jack, *The One and Only: The Ballet Russe de Monte Carlo*, London, 1981

* * *

Born in New York City in 1920, Leon Danielian was a first-generation American: his father was Armenian, his mother Georgian. He grew up in Manhattan, spending part of his childhood in New Jersey. He studied dance as a child with a friend of his mother's, Mme. Seda (also the teacher of Jacques d'Amboise and Janet Shibata). By the time Danielian was twelve years old, Seda believed she had taught him all she could; so she sent him to study with Mikhail Mordkin, her former teacher, who had a school in New York.

Mordkin began creating a ballet company in 1935, which actually materialized in 1937. Danielian made his professional début with the Mordkin Ballet, having already performed Russian dancing in film houses and church halls with his sister, Hercelia. He joined Ballet Theatre as a soloist at its inception in 1939, along with eight other dancers from the Mordkin Ballet who were transferred to the new company. In addition to works by Mordkin, he performed ballets by Fokine, Dolin, and Tudor. He remained in Ballet Theatre through the end of 1941.

Danielian was invited to join Colonel de Basil's Original Ballet Russe in 1941 as premier danseur. He remained until that company left for a tour of South America, where they remained during the war years. He then became a principal dancer with the Ballet Russe de Monte Carlo in 1943, working steadily with that company for some eight years, also appearing in summer stock and operettas. After appearing as guest artist with Roland Petit's Ballet des Champs-Elysées in Paris, and then touring southern France and northern Africa with Yvette Chauviré, Danielian returned to Ballet Russe for most of the 1950s, serving as choreographer from 1956. Sadly, he became seriously disabled with osteoarthritis in the late 1950s and retired from performing.

Leon Danielian was one of two American-born premier danseurs in the United States in his generation. (The other was John Kriza.) The majority of principal dancers in Ballet Theatre and Ballet Russe were Russian or English; during the 1940s there was a preference for Russian training, Russian stars, and Russianized names.

Danielian's virtuoso style encompassed classical and demi-caractère roles. He was well known for his exceptional speed, purity of line, theatricality, and lyricism. Critics underlined his perfect tours en l'air, exceptional beats, and high grands jetés, as well as his excellent arm movements and elegant manner. He was the first American dancer to perform an entrechat huit.

His enormous amount of touring with major companies, primarily the Ballet Russe and San Francisco Ballet, made Danielian well known all over the United States and abroad. In classical roles, he was an elegant partner to several important ballerinas, including Alexandra Danilova, Nathalie Krassovska, Anna Istomina, Mary Ellen Moylan, Ruthanna Boris, Yvette Chauviré, and Moscelyne Larkin. He was considered a model of classical style for the male dancer. Of his demi-caractère roles, he was best known for his performance as the Peruvian in *Gaîté Parisienne*.

His first-hand knowledge and experience of the works of Fokine, Massine, Mordkin, Dolin, Balanchine, Loring, and Tudor made him an invaluable company member, ballet master, and master teacher. His interest in teaching ballet made it possible for him to continue actively in the field after an early end to his performing career. A dedicated teacher, he was responsible for training many principal dancers in the Ballet Russe de Monte Carlo, American Ballet Theatre, and other professional ballet and modern companies. He became known for his eloquence in teaching of technique and style, his high professional standards, and his sharp wit and humor. "A highly intelligent man", as John Gruen wrote in 1975, "he brings to the classroom enormous knowledge, flavored by an irrepressible wit. He is clearly an American teacher training American dancers, but this forthright quality is suffused with a theatricality garnered from his years with European companies." And, as Danielian himself has said, ballet is not just abstract art or a form of athletics; "the dance is theatre".

—Alice Helpern

---

**DANILOVA, Alexandra**

Russian/American dancer, choreographer, and teacher. Born Aleksandra Dionisievna Danilova in Peterhof (Leninsk), 20 November 1903 (some sources say 1904). Studied at the Theatre School, St. Petersburg/Petrograd, from 1911: pupil of Vera Zukova, Elisaveta Gerdt, Viktor Semenov, Agrippina Vaganova, Olga Preobrazhenskaya; graduated in 1920. Married (1) Guiseppe Massera, 1933 (d. 1937); (2) dancer Casimir Kokich, 1941. Dancer, State Academic Theatre for Opera and Ballet (GATOB; previously the Maryinsky Theatre), Petrograd, 1921–24: soloist, from 1922; dancer, "Young Ballet" (Molodoi Balet), 1923; toured Western Europe with troupe of dancers (including George Balanchine) organized by Vladimir Dmitriev, performing as "The Soviet State Dancers" in Germany and London, 1924; engaged by Diaghilev in Paris: dancer, Diaghilev's Ballets Russes, 1924–29; ballerina, from 1927; dancer, Ballet de l'Opéra de Monte Carlo, 1925, 1929–30; leading dancer in Sir Oswald Stoll's musical *Waltzes from Vienna* (chor. A. Rasch), London, 1931–32; ballerina, de Basil's Ballets Russes, 1933–38; prima ballerina, (Denham's) Ballet Russe de Monte Carlo, 1938–52, and as guest artist, 1957; guest ballerina for numerous companies, including Sadler's Wells Ballet, London, 1949, London Festival Ballet, 1951, and Slavenska-Franklin Ballet, 1952–53, touring Japan, 1953; founder and ballerina, Great Moments of Ballet, touring North and South America, South Africa, and Japan, 1954–56; appeared in operettas and stage musicals, including *Song of Norway* (chor. Balanchine, 1944), *Oh, Captain!* (dir. José Ferrer, 1958); also choreographer, staging opera ballets for Metropolitan Opera, New York, 1959–61, and staging ballets for Ballet Russe de Monte Carlo (in collaboration with Balanchine), 1946 and 1949, La Scala, Milan, 1961, Washington (D.C.) Ballet, 1961, New York City Ballet (in collaboration with Balanchine), 1974, and Tokyo Ballet, 1981; teacher, Edith James School, Dallas, from 1953, also teaching in Japan, 1957; permanent faculty member, School of American Ballet, New York, 1964–89; appeared in film *The Turning Point* (dir. Ross), 1977, and in documentary *Reflections of a Dancer: Alexandra Danilova, Prima Ballerina Assoluta* (1986). Recipient: Capezio Award, 1958; *Dance Magazine* Award, 1984; Lion of the Performing Arts Award, New York Public Library, 1986; Kennedy Center Award, 1989; Handel Medallion, New York City, 1986.

**ROLES**

1919/20 Pas de trois from *Paquita* (Petipa), Imperial Theatre School Performance, St. Petersburg
Pas de deux from *Sylvia* (Preobrazhenskaya), Imperial Theatre School Performance, St. Petersburg

1920/21 Maiden in *Eros* (Fokine), State Academic Theatre for Opera and Ballet (GATOB), Petrograd
Peasant pas de deux in *La Fille mal gardée* (Petipa, Ivanov), GATOB, Petrograd

1921 Variation "Prayer" in *Coppélia* (Ivanov, Cecchetti after Saint-Léon), GATOB, Petrograd
Principal dancer (cr) in *Poème* (Balanchine), Concert Performance, Petrograd Theatre School, Petrograd
Ta-Hor in *Egyptian Nights* (Fokine), GATOB, Leningrad

1922 Adagio (cr) in *The Creation of the World* (Lopukhov), GATOB, Petrograd

1923 Principal dancer (cr) in *Marche funèbre* (Balanchine), Young Ballet, Petrograd

1924 Principal dancer in *Adagio* (Balanchine), Young Ballet, Pavlovsk

**Alexandra Danilova in *Le Beau Danube*, Ballets Russes de Monte Carlo, London, 1933**

Title role in *Firebird* (Lopukhov after Fokine), GATOB, Leningrad
Diamond Fairy in *The Sleeping Beauty* (Petipa, staged Lopukhov), GATOB, Leningrad
Pas de trois in *Le Corsaire* (Petipa), GATOB, Leningrad
Lead Wili in *Giselle* (Petipa after Coralli, Perrot), GATOB, Leningrad
Komarik in *Les Contes russes* (Fokine), Diaghilev's Ballets Russes, London

1924/26 Estrella in *Le Carnaval* (Fokine), Diaghilev's Ballets Russes
Candide Fairy in *Aurora's Wedding* (from *The Sleeping Beauty*; Petipa, staged Nijinska), Diaghilev's Ballets Russes

1925 A Muse (cr) in *Zéphire et Flore* (Massine), Diaghilev's Ballets Russes, Monte Carlo
Shepherdess and Butterfly (cr) in *L'Enfant et les sortilèges* (Balanchine), Diaghilev's Ballets Russes, Monte Carlo
A Servant of Barabau (cr) in *Barabau* (Balanchine), Diaghilev's Ballets Russes, London
Bluebird pas de deux in *Aurora's Wedding* (from *The Sleeping Beauty*; Petipa, staged Nijinska), Diaghilev's Ballets Russes, London

1926 Ballerina in *Petrushka* (Fokine), Diaghilev's Ballets Russes
Girl in *Les Matelots* (Massine), Diaghilev's Ballets Russes, Paris
The Black Dancer (cr) in *Jack in the Box* (Balanchine), Diaghilev's Ballets Russes, Paris
Princess in *Swan Lake* (one-act version; after Petipa, Ivanov), Diaghilev's Ballets Russes, London
Fairy Queen (cr) in *The Triumph of Neptune* (Balanchine), Diaghilev's Ballets Russes, London

1926/27 Can-Can in *La Boutique fantasque* (Massine), Diaghilev's Ballets Russes
Snow maiden in *Le Soleil de nuit* (Massine), Diaghilev's Ballets Russes
Aurora in *Aurora's Wedding* (Petipa, staged Nijinska), Diaghilev's Ballets Russes

1927 Young Woman Worker (cr) in *Le Pas d'acier* (Massine), Diaghilev's Ballets Russes, Paris
Young girl in *Le Spectre de la rose* (Fokine), Diaghilev's Ballets Russes, Monte Carlo
Principal dancer in *Les Sylphides* (Fokine), Diaghilev's Ballets Russes

1928 Pas de deux (cr) in *Ode* (Massine), Diaghilev's Ballets Russes, Paris
Terpsichore in *Apollon musagète* (Balanchine), Diaghilev's Ballets Russes, Paris (created on Danilova; danced by Nikitina at premiere)
The Serving Maid (cr) in *The Gods Go a-Begging* (Balanchine), Diaghilev's Ballets Russes, London
The Lady (cr) in *Le Bal* (Balanchine), Diaghilev's Ballets Russes, Monte Carlo

1933 Street Dancer in *Le Beau Danube* (revival; Massine), Ballets Russes de Monte Carlo, Monte Carlo
Titania (cr) in *Nocturne* (Lichine), Ballets Russes de Monte Carlo, Paris
Columbine in *Le Carnaval* (Woizikovsky after Fokine), Ballets Russes de Monte Carlo, London
Principal dancer (cr) in *Choreartium* (Massine), Ballets Russes de Monte Carlo, London

1934 Principal dancer in *Beethoven Variations* (Nijinska), Théâtre de la Danse Nijinska and Ballets Russes de Monte Carlo, Monte Carlo
Principal dancer in *Bolero* (Nijinska), Théâtre de la Danse Nijinska and Ballets Russes de Monte Carlo, Monte Carlo

1935 Mariucca in *Les Femmes de bonne humeur* (revival; Massine), de Basil's Ballets Russes, London
Rich couple, pas de six (cr) in *Jardin public* (Massine), de Basil's Ballets Russes, Chicago

1936 The Young Lady in *Le Pavillon* (Lichine), de Basil's Ballets Russes, London
Principal dancer in *Danses slaves et tziganes* (Nijinska), de Basil's Ballets Russes, New York
Pas de trois in *Cimarosiana* (divertissement from *Le Astuzie femminile*; Massine), de Basil's Ballets Russes, New York
Gaiety, a Witch (cr) in *Symphonie fantastique* (Massine), de Basil's Ballets Russes, London

1937 Guinevere (cr) in *Francesca da Rimini* (Lichine), de Basil's Ballets Russes, London

1938 Glove Seller in *Gaîté Parisienne* (Massine), Ballet Russe de Monte Carlo, Monte Carlo
Swanilda in *Coppélia* (Sergeyev after Petipa, Cecchetti), Ballet Russe de Monte Carlo, Monte Carlo
Myrtha in *Giselle* (Petipa after Coralli, Perrot; staged Lifar), Ballet Russe de Monte Carlo, London

1939 Peasant couple (cr) in *Capriccio Espagnol* (Massine, La Argentinita), Ballet Russe de Monte Carlo, Monte Carlo
Daughter (cr) in *Devil's Holiday* (Ashton), Ballet Russe de Monte Carlo, New York

1940 Bride in *Le Baiser de la fée* (Balanchine), Ballet Russe de Monte Carlo, New York
Queen of Spades in *Jeu de cartes* (Balanchine), Ballet Russe de Monte Carlo, New York
Débutante (cr) in *Vienna: 1814* (Massine), Ballet Russe de Monte Carlo, New York
Girl in *The New Yorker* (Massine), Ballet Russe de Monte Carlo, New York

1941 Young Girl (cr) in *Saratoga* (Massine), Ballet Russe de Monte Carlo, New York
Sugar Plum Fairy in *The Nutcracker* (Fedorova after Ivanov), Ballet Russe de Monte Carlo, New York

1942 Principal dancer in *Chopin Concerto* (Nijinska), Ballet Russe de Monte Carlo, New York
Spring in *The Snow Maiden* (Nijinska), Ballet Russe de Monte Carlo, New York
Title role in *Giselle* (Petipa after Coralli, Perrot), Ballet Russe de Monte Carlo, San Francisco

1943 Sierra (cr) in *The Cuckold's Fair* (Lopez), Ballet Russe de Monte Carlo, Cleveland, Ohio
Tai-Hoa (cr) in *The Red Poppy* (Schwezoff), Ballet Russe de Monte Carlo, Cleveland
Russian Princess (cr) in *Ancient Russia* (Nijinska), Ballet Russe de Monte Carlo, Cleveland

1944 Principal dancer (cr) in *Danses Concertantes* (Balanchine), Ballet Russe de Monte Carlo, New York
Adelina in *Song of Norway* (operetta; mus. Grieg, adapted Wright and Forrest; chor. Balanchine), Imperial Theatre, New York

1945 Adagio and Variations in *Mozartiana* (Balanchine), Ballet Russe de Monte Carlo, New York
Principal dancer (cr) in *Pas de Deux* (also called *Grand Adagio*; Balanchine), Ballet Russe de Monte Carlo, New York

1946 The Sleepwalker (cr) in *La Sonnambula* (Balanchine), Ballet Russe de Monte Carlo, New York
Title role (cr) in *Raymonda* (new production; Balanchine and Danilova after Petipa), Ballet Russe de Monte Carlo, New York

Bride in *The Bells* (R. Page), Ballet Russe de Monte Carlo, New York
1947 Title role in *Lola Montez* (E. Caton), Ballet Russe de Monte Carlo, New York
1948 Mrs. Potiphar in *Billy Sunday* (R. Page), Ballet Russe de Monte Carlo, York, Pennsylvania
Cerrito in *Pas de quatre* (Dolin after Perrot), Ballet Russe de Monte Carlo, New York
1949 Title role in *Paquita* (also chor.; after Petipa), Ballet Russe de Monte Carlo, New York
1950 The Guest Ballerina (cr) in *Prima Ballerina* (Chamié), Ballet Russe de Monte Carlo, Chicago
1952 Principal dancer in *Ballerina* (Slavenska), Slavenska-Franklin Ballet, New York

**Other roles include:** for Diaghilev's Ballets Russes—Young Girl in *Les Matelots* (Massine), dancer in *Cimarosiana* (Massine), Chanson dansée ("Grey Girl") in *Les Biches* (Nijinska), Wedding Guest in *Les Noces* (Nijinska), Slave Girl in *Cléopâtre* (Fokine), Odalisque in *Schéhérazade* (Fokine), and dances (chor. Balanchine) in operas *Manon* (mus. Massenet), *Les Contes d'Hoffman* (mus. Offenbach), *Hamlet* (mus. Ambroise Thomas), *Turandot* (mus. Puccini), *Venise* (mus. Gunsbourg), *La Gioconda* (mus. Ponchielli), *La Femme Nue* (mus. Février); for Ballet Russe de Monte Carlo—principal dancer in *Pictures at an Exhibition* (Nijinska), *Bolero* (Nijinska).

## WORKS

1958 Dances in *La Gioconda* (opera; mus. Ponchielli), Metropolitan Opera, New York
1959 *Les Diamants* (mus. de Beriot), Metropolitan Opera Ballet, New York
1960 Dances in *The Gypsy Baron* (opera; mus. Strauss), Metropolitan Opera, New York
1961 Dances in *Boris Godunov* (opera; mus. Mussorgsky), Metropolitan Opera, New York
*The Nutcracker* (mus. Tchaikovsky), Washington Ballet, Washington, D.C.

Also staged:
1946 *Raymonda* (with Balanchine, after Petipa; mus. Glazunov), Ballet Russe de Monte Carlo, New York (later staged for Minnesota Dance Theatre)
1949 *Paquita* (after Petipa; mus. Deldevez, Minkus), Ballet Russe de Monte Carlo, New York (later staged for Cincinnati Ballet and Dance Theatre of Harlem)
1972 *Chopiniana* (*Les Sylphides*; after Fokine), New York City Ballet, New York (also staged for Pennsylvania Ballet as *Les Sylphides*)
1974 *Coppélia* (in collaboration with Balanchine, after Petipa; mus. Delibes), New York City Ballet, Saratoga Springs, New York
1981 *Coppélia* (after Petipa; mus. Délibes), Asami Maki Ballet, Tokyo

**Other works include:** for the Metropolitan Opera—Dances in *La Périchole* (operetta; mus. Offenbach), *Adriana Lecouvreur* (opera; mus. Cilea); for the School of American Ballet—*Aurora's Wedding* (after Petipa; mus. Tchaikovsky), *Les Saisons* (mus. Glazunov), *Scènes de Ballet* (mus. Stravinsky).

## PUBLICATIONS

By Danilova:
Interview, "A Conversation with Danilova", *Ballet Review* (Brooklyn, N.Y.), 2 parts: vol. 4, nos. 4 and 5, 1973
Interview in Gruen, John, *The Private World of Ballet*, New York, 1975
Interview in Philp, Richard, "Danilova on Balanchine", *Dance Magazine* (New York), July 1983
*Choura: The Memoirs of Alexandra Danilova*, New York, 1986

About Danilova:
Twysden, A.E., *Alexandra Danilova*, London, 1945
Davidson, Gladys, *Ballet Biographies*, revised edition, London, 1954
Hagin, B.H., and Denby, Edwin, "The Art of Danilova", *Chrysalis* (Boston), vol. 12, nos. 1–4, 1959
Anthony, Gordon, "Alexandra Danilova", *Dancing Times* (London), June 1976
Fay, Anthony, "The Belle of the Ballet Russe: Alexandra Danilova", *Dance Magazine* (New York), October 1977
Anderson, Jack, *The One and Only: The Ballet Russe de Monte Carlo*, London, 1981
Anderson, Jack, "Danilova and Franklin", *Ballet Review* (New York), Winter 1982
Sorley Walker, Kathrine, *Les Ballets Russes de Monte Carlo*, London, 1982
García-Márquez, Vicente, *Les Ballets Russes*, New York, 1990

* * *

Alexandra Danilova has been an extremely important dancer and ambassadress of ballet thanks to her charming personality, her classical refinement, and her long association with both the classical tradition of her St. Petersburg Maryinsky training and the most advanced contemporary ballet of the Diaghilev and Ballet Russe companies—most obviously that of George Balanchine, with whom she worked from his earliest years as a choreographer. On long tours of the United States, she converted audiences to ballet, giving her best even in the smallest towns: she said she always felt there might be some future artist in the audience. Later, as a teacher, she passed on her heritage to countless new generations of dancers.

The choreographer Léonide Massine, who created several of the witty roles for which Danilova was especially known, captured her aura in one word: champagne. Her joy in dancing and her vivacity were contagious; the quick, sharp wit of her dancing, expressed with beautiful legs and feet, was irresistible. A lady of the world, on stage and off, she combined elegance and unmannered refinement in her dancing with a feminine and witty sex appeal, conveyed in the subtle turn of a shoulder or the timing of a step.

Danilova's qualities were especially set off in Massine's light, bubbling works. She had tremendous success as the lovely Glove Seller in *Gaîté Parisienne*, as the big-hearted Street Dancer in *Le Beau Danube*, and as the Can-Can Dancer in *La Boutique fantasque*. The mischievous Swanilda in *Coppélia* was another of her comedy successes. Even after she had performed these roles for many years, as the American critic Edwin Denby wrote of her in *Le Beau Danube*, "She is still the most radiant and the freshest dancer in the piece". She was famous, for example, for playing with her full skirts in a way that was charming rather than vulgar, and it never became hackneyed.

With her musicality and strong technique and pointe work, Danilova was also a versatile dancer, on whom Balanchine made several of his early ballets—most notably using her mysterious, elusive quality in *La Sonnambula* (*Night Shadow*). The role of Terpsichore in his *Apollo* was originally intended for her (although Nikitina danced at the premiere), and she alternated in the ballet's early performances. Among her created roles was the Daughter in Frederick Ashton's short-lived *Devil's Holiday*. She was a notable, melancholy Swan Queen, a lovely lead in classical showpieces like *The Nutcracker* and *Raymonda* (which she staged with Balanchine), and an imperious Myrtha. She had a long partnership with the ebullient and debonair Frederic Franklin.

As a teacher for many years at Balanchine's School of American Ballet, from which she retired in 1989, Danilova handed on the Russian heritage and continued to set an example of ballerina elegance. Most significant were her women's variations classes and her stagings for the annual workshop performances. She taught Fokine dances, but above all those of Petipa, as the purest embodiment of the classical tradition. Her aim was to give an artistic finish to the students and teach them "how to express themselves—you don't just dance like a machine." For the New York City Ballet she staged *Chopiniana* (*Les Sylphides*) and, along with Balanchine, *Coppélia*.

In 1989, Danilova received the prestigious Kennedy Center Honors, becoming the first dancer who was not also a choreographer to be honored in this way.

—Marilyn Hunt

---

## DANSES CONCERTANTES

**Choreography:** George Balanchine
**Music:** Igor Stravinsky
**Design:** Eugene Berman (scenery and costumes)
**First Production:** Ballet Russe de Monte Carlo, City Center, New York, 10 September 1944
**Principal Dancers:** Alexandra Danilova, Leon Danielian

**Other productions include:** Sadler's Wells Theatre Ballet (new version; chor. Kenneth MacMillan, design Nicholas Georgiadis), with Maryon Lane, David Poole; London, 18 January 1955. San Francisco Ballet (new version; chor. Lew Christensen, design Tony Duquette); San Francisco, 13 October 1959. Cologne Opera Ballet (new version; chor. Todd Bolender, costumes Ed Wittstein); Cologne, 9 July 1964. Ballet-Théâtre Contemporain (new version; chor. Félix Blaska, costumes Sonia Delaunay); Amiens, 1968. German Opera Ballet (new version; chor. John Taras); Berlin, 1 December 1971. New York City Ballet (restaged and revised substantially by Balanchine), with Linda Yourth and John Clifford; New York, 20 June 1972.

### PUBLICATIONS


Coleman, Francis, "A Talk with Igor Stravinsky", *Dance Magazine* (New York), April 1945

Denby, Edwin, *Looking at the Dance*, New York, 1949

Barnes, Clive, "*Dances Concertantes*", *Dance and Dancers* (London), March 1959

Balanchine, George, with Mason, Francis, *Balanchine's Complete Stories of the Great Ballets*, Garden City, N.Y., 1977

Reynolds, Nancy, *Repertory in Review*, New York, 1977

Anderson, Jack, *The One and Only: The Ballet Russe de Monte Carlo*, London, 1981

Garis, Robert, "Balanchine and Stravinsky: Facts and Problems", *Ballet Review* (New York), Fall 1982

Barnes, Clive, "Echoes from the Past", *Dance and Dancers* (London), September 1989


Although *Danses Concertantes* is best known as a Balanchine creation, Stravinsky's music has been staged by several other choreographers, including Kenneth MacMillan, Félix Blaska, Todd Bolender, and Lew Christensen. Whether the music itself originally had been meant for a Balanchine ballet is not certain; Balanchine's production for the Ballet Russe de Monte Carlo came two years after the concert premiere of *Danses Concertantes* in 1942. But the rhythmically complex music, in five sections and for 24 instruments, is clearly a work for the theatre.

For Balanchine, the Stravinsky piece suggested the Italian spirit of *commedia dell'arte*, and in designer Eugene Berman he found an artist to match the wit and tongue-in-cheek humour of the music. Setting the tone was Berman's colourful front curtain, which rose to reveal the fourteen dancers who paraded and introduced themselves as travelling players, perhaps circus acrobats. The original Ballet Russe version, which included marches and a pas d'action, focused on a central pas de deux danced with great élan and sophistication by Alexandra Danilova and Leon Danielian (later replaced by Frederic Franklin). When the Stravinsky/Balanchine *Rubies* was first danced, it was said to resemble in mood and tone this same pas de deux.

In each interpretation of *Danses Concertantes* there was a uniformity of response to Stravinsky's brash vitality that utilized the classical vocabulary of ballet with bright, flashy, sharply accented movements. Critic Edward Denby noted that the Balanchine figures were "glittering, twittering, stalking", as though they were giant birds. The bird motif was evident also in MacMillan's choreography, originally intended for the Sadler's Wells Theatre Ballet and later revived by the Royal Ballet. Less lyrical and formal than the Balanchine, the MacMillan made its appeal in brilliant angular forms and youthful freshness. While it was favourably received by the critics, it nevertheless did not remain long in the Royal Ballet's repertory.

Félix Blaska's *Danses Concertantes* for the Ballet-Théâtre Contemporain (1968) was not a critical success, though it caught some of the dynamics and rhythmic cadences of its two predecessors.

All three stagings were noticeable for the employment of distinguished painters; décor and costumes were designed to make an immediate pictorial impact. Eugene Berman's elegant costumes in five colours were retained for subsequent mountings in New York; the MacMillan version introduced Nicholas Georgiadis to the ballet world, his costumes striking a note of levity. Sonia Delaunay's red, black, white, and blue abstractions highlighted the French production for the Théâtre Contemporain and proved more memorable than the choreography.

*Danses Concertantes* saw life again when Todd Bolender adapted the tricky score for the Cologne Opera Company in 1964 while another American dancer/choreographer, Lew Christensen, provided a mounting for the San Francisco Ballet Company, first in 1959 and later for a gala performance in 1986 when Beni Montresor's silver metallic setting enlivened the stage.

In 1972, when Balanchine staged *Danses Concertantes* for the New York City Ballet Stravinsky Festival, he wanted to do something different and the work was re-choreographed. This may have been a necessity since the Ballets Russes de Monte Carlo's version, choreographed more than 25 years before, had slipped from memory. (Ballet Russe had found it difficult to find musicians to play the Stravinsky score while touring and had danced it less and less.) The 1972 re-creation featured a series of pas de trois, each with an individuality and colour of its own, each with "people who are here now," as Balanchine

*Danses Concertantes*, performed by New York City Ballet, 1989

remarked. Still not an unqualified success with the critics or the audience, it became—in the eyes of many—a "problem" ballet. *Danses Concertantes* reappeared in 1989, however, with happier results. The City Ballet seemed to have found the key to its irony and to its exuberance.

*Danses Concertantes* will probably never be a popular standard. Its five-part composition results in a fragmentation difficult to bind, though Balanchine had a wonderful adhesive in the Eugene Berman designs.

—Richard Rutledge

---

## LA DANSOMANIE

**Choreography:** Pierre Gardel
**Music:** Etienne Nicholas Méhul
**First Production:** Théâtre de l'Académie royale de musique (Paris Opéra), 14 June 1800
**Principal Dancer:** Pierre Gardel

**Other productions include:** Royal Swedish Theatre (staged Louis Deland after Gardel), with Filippo Taglioni; Stockholm, 1804. Vienna Hoftheater (staged Filippo Taglioni after Gardel); Vienna, 4 October 1805. Royal Swedish Ballet (reconstruction; staged Ivo Cramér and Mary Skeaping after Gardel); Drottningholm, 1976. Paris Opéra Ballet (restaged Cramér), with Rudolf Nureyev (Duléger); Paris, 1986.

### PUBLICATIONS

Guest, Ivor, *The Romantic Ballet in Paris*, London, 1966
Winter, Marian Hannah, *The Pre-Romantic Ballet*, London, 1974
Guest, Ivor, "*La Dansomanie*", *Dancing Times* (London), November 1985
Chazin-Bennahum, Judith, *Dance in the Shadow of the Guillotine*, Carbondale and Edwardsville, 1988

* * *

*La Dansomanie*'s premiere left many of the more serious members of the audience wondering about chief ballet master Pierre Gardel's judgement, if not his sanity. The year was 1800. The Paris Opéra had just come through the uncertainty and hardship of the French Revolution. During a six-year period, from 1793 to 1798, no new ballets had been produced. There were times when the ballet artists had gone unpaid. And at this point in time, after years of drought, Gardel rejected all the popular grand and noble subjects that would have imparted to his reappearance the resounding tone of great significance, and chose a farce.

During the early Revolution, Gardel, like his colleague, the painter Jacques Louis David, had shown his support of the new order with *Télémaque* (1790), a work that reflected the republican virtues of antiquity, virtues that were taken as models by the Revolution. And during the long dry spell he had cherished the dream of producing a tribute to freedom, *William Tell.* Now that the Revolution was over, he abandoned the neoclassical gods and heroes and the romantic victims of oppression, and focused on the common man. In so doing he displayed his breadth of vision, his desire to experiment, and his unwillingness to take himself too seriously. *La Dansomanie* is about a wealthy gentleman who is so fanatical about dance that he requires his entire household to follow the dictates of Terpsichore. Even the suitors seeking his daughter's hand must dance to win her.

Why choose such a subject? one might ask. In 1800, France was regaining a sense of security. Perhaps in parodying his own art, Gardel was stating that the time had come to relax a little, to take a more balanced view of life. In his "Author's Reflections" (at the beginning of the libretto), he describes *La Dansomanie* as "a trifle, a veritable witticism, a nothing with no kind of pretension other than that of offering, under the mask of gaiety, the graces and the divine talents [i.e. the dancers of the Paris Opéra] that the Public cherishes so justifiably". The quality of the ballet, and its success, suggest that though Gardel was aware that his audiences considered ballets such as *La Dansomanie* to be inferior, he took his parody ballet more seriously than he makes out in his "Reflections".

But Gardel was correct in anticipating criticism. No less an authority than Jean-Georges Noverre felt that Gardel had gone too far in parodying his art; critic Geoffroy considered the ballet too trifling for the Opéra. Never the less, success with the general audience was overwhelming and the ballet was frequently revived. In 1811 the *Journal de Paris* critic claimed that *La Dansomanie* "always has the same success as it did when new; it is one of the most pleasing productions of M. Gardel . . .". In 1819 it served as the centre-piece for Gardel's benefit performance. The 1824 revival drew the observation that it was "the most original and the most intelligent" work in the repertoire of genre ballets.

*La Dansomanie's* lack of seriousness represented a serious challenge to traditional tastes since its success demonstrated that a wider range of subjects would be possible. However, as Napoleon's power rapidly increased, it was his tastes that came to rule, and his vision was dominated by the heroes, gods, and demi-gods of antiquity. Genre subjects did not become common until the second decade of the new century.

*La Dansomanie* was more than an opportunity for audiences to "lighten up". It was also a clever way of doing one of the things Gardel liked doing best, presenting dances. Ever since Noverre's story-orientated *ballet d'action* approach had become popular amongst ballet masters, the place of dancing in ballets had become a touchy issue, for it was through pantomimic action, not dancing, that ballet stories were most clearly represented. And as Noverre demanded that everything in a ballet contribute to the unity of the dramatic impact, it left little room for dancing. Gardel solved the problem by simply rejecting strict *ballet d'action* practice and introducing dances whenever he felt it was appropriate. What was different about *La Dansomanie* was that its dances told its story. Its dramatic unity, the way in which the dances furthered the action, was one of its most powerful features, one that audiences and critics appreciated enormously. One critic paid *La Dansomanie* the compliment of calling it a "true comedy" and asserting that "the piece would gain little if it were written in prose or verse". At a time when poetry was the zenith of the arts, and literature the yardstick by which all else was measured, no higher compliment could be paid to a ballet's dramatic strength. Clearly, some critics saw through the lightness of *La Dansomanie's* theme to its core of artistic genius.

—John Chapman

---

**DANTZIG, Rudi van** *see* **VAN DANTZIG, Rudi**

---

## DAPHNIS ET CHLOE

**Choreography:** Mikhail Fokine
**Music:** Maurice Ravel
**Design:** Léon Bakst (scenery and costumes)
**Libretto:** Mikhail Fokine (after Greek pastoral by Longus)
**First Production:** Diaghilev's Ballets Russes, Théâtre du Châtelet, Paris, 8 June 1912
**Principal Dancers:** Tamara Karsavina (Chloe), Vaslav Nijinsky (Daphnis), Adolph Bolm (Dorkon)

**Other productions include:** Paris Opéra (restaged Fokine); Paris, 20 June 1921. Philadelphia Ballet (new version; chor. Catherine Littlefield); Philadelphia, 31 March 1937. Berlin State Opera Ballet (new version; chor. Tatiana Gsovsky); Berlin, 1946. Rome Opera Ballet (new version; chor. Aurel Milloss, design E. Prampolini); Rome, February 1951. Sadler's Wells Ballet (new version; chor. Frederick Ashton, design John Craxton), with Margot Fonteyn (Chloe), Michael Somes (Daphnis), John Field (Dorkon); London, 5 April 1951. Paris Opéra Ballet (new version; chor. Serge Lifar, design Marc Chagall); Brussels, 8 July 1958. Paris Opéra Ballet (new version; chor. George Skibine, design Marc Chagall), with Skibine (Daphnis), and Claude Bessy (Chloe); Paris, 3 June 1959. Stuttgart Ballet (new version; chor. John Cranko, design Nicholas Georgiadis); Stuttgart, 15 July 1962. La Scala Ballet (staged Serge Lifar and Nicholas Zverev after Fokine); Milan, 21 December 1962. Frankfurt Ballet (new version; chor. John Neumeier, design Jürgen Rose); Frankfurt, 2 January 1972. Dutch National Ballet (new version; chor. Hans van Manen, to second suite only; design Vroom); Amsterdam, 14 December 1972. Stuttgart Ballet (new version; chor. Glen Tetley, design Willa Kim), with Richard Cragun (Daphnis) and Marcia Haydée (Chloe); Stuttgart, 17 May 1975. New York City Ballet (new version; chor. John Taras, design Joe Eula), with Peter Martins (Daphnis) and Nina Fedorova (Chloe); New York, 22 May 1975.

### PUBLICATIONS

Beaumont, Cyril, *Michel Fokine and his Ballets*, London, 1935
Hussey, Dyneley, "Ravel's *Daphnis and Chloe*", *Dancing Times* (London), 2 parts: August, September 1948
Beaumont, Cyril, *Complete Book of Ballets*, revised edition, London, 1951
Goddard, Scott, "Ravel's *Daphnis et Chloe*", *Ballet Annual* (London), vol. 6, 1952
Barnes, Clive, "*Daphnis and Chloe*", *Dance and Dancers* (London), 2 parts: July, August, 1958

**Tamara Karsavina as Chloe in *Daphnis et Chloe*, 1914**

Fokine, Michel, *Fokine: Memoirs of a Ballet Master*, translated by Vitale Fokine, London, 1961
Balanchine, George, with Mason, Francis, *Balanchine's Complete Book of the Great Ballets*, Garden City, N.Y., 1977
Vaughan, David, *Frederick Ashton and his Ballets*, London, 1977
Horwitz, Dawn Lille, *Michel Fokine*, Boston, 1985
Garafola, Lynn, *Diaghilev's Ballets Russes*, New York, 1989
Bowden, Jill Anne, "John Craxton, *Daphnis and Chloe*, and Greece", *Dancing Times* (London), June 1992

* * *

The libretto for *Daphnis and Chloe*, in virtually every version which has been performed this century, derives in some way from Mikhail Fokine's translation to the stage of the Greek pastoral recorded by Longus. Fokine's staging of the story, which was not performed until 1912, in turn dates back to the choreographer's earliest aesthetic experiments at the beginning of the century: in 1904, the young Fokine had submitted his libretto to the management of the Russian Imperial Theatres, with an attached preface explaining his reasons for "producing a Greek ballet in the spirit of the age". The proposal was turned down, but the idea remained with Fokine until he could at last bring it to fruition with Diaghilev's Ballets Russes in 1912.

The tale is a simple love story: Daphnis, a shepherd, and Chloe, his lover, are led from innocence to joyous knowledge by the god Pan, who instructs them in lovemaking. Embellishments to the mythological tale over the centuries have included the addition of such characters as Dorkon, an amorous herdsman, and Lykanion, a temptress, both of whom Fokine used in the development of the action. Also included in the two-act ballet were the capture of Chloe by pirates, a contest between Dorkon and Daphnis, and celebratory dances to Pan, along with such additional characters as shepherds, goddesses, fauns, and bacchantes all contributing to the overall effect of a Greek tableau.

Fokine's choice of a Greek legend as the basis of a ballet was extremely important to his own aesthetic, as much as his envisioned ancient setting was revolutionary for the Imperial stage. Scorning the use of ballet libretti as mere vehicles for frothy divertissement, often in the well-worn style of court pageantry, Fokine sought naturalism and unity in his use of dance. In his first submission of the *Daphnis and Chloe* libretto, in effect one of his early manifestos about the liberation of ballet from stale nineteenth-century conventions, Fokine wrote:

> No ballet master could commit the following mistake: arrange dances for Russian peasants in the style of Louis XV or . . . create dances in the manner of the Russian trepak to a French theme. Then why permit the constant error in productions based on subjects from Ancient Greece: shall Greeks dance the French way?

The Imperial Theatre was obviously not willing to go as far as Fokine was; but the avant-garde atmosphere of Diaghilev's Ballets Russes would seem ideal for Fokine's development of his Greek ballet idea. An appropriately dream-like and atmospheric score by Ravel had been commissioned in 1909, and Bakst created equally evocative sets and costumes (although these were used in 1911 for *Narcisse*, so that new ones had to be made for the ballet's eventual premiere). But sadly, Fokine's plans for *Daphnis and Chloe* were continually frustrated—and by the time the ballet was actually performed, most critics agree, the work did not receive its due.

When Fokine was finally able to stage *Daphnis and Chloe*, his rift with Diaghilev was nearly complete. The impresario, largely because of his new (and almost obsessional) fascination with the development of Nijinsky as a choreographer, gave Fokine's ballet little attention. Diaghilev did all that he could to postpone the premiere, and the scandal and resultant disruption caused by Nijinsky's *L'Après-midi d'un faune* in May 1912 meant that Fokine's work remained in the shadow. As Serge Grigoriev, the company régisseur, later wrote, Fokine's ballet ". . . deserved better treatment than it received—for it had everything to recommend it". Pointing to Ravel's "distinguished score" (which has since become a classic in its own right), Bakst's "delightful setting", and the ballet's highly effective dramatic climax, Grigoriev claimed that the ballet would have had a greater impact if Diaghilev had given it more attention. But *Daphnis and Chloe* was completed in a strained and unhappy atmosphere, and by the end of the summer of 1912 Fokine had left Diaghilev's company and returned to Russia.

After Fokine's initial efforts with this ballet, numerous choreographers have been attracted to Ravel's evocative score and to the story which is so intricately linked to the music. Perhaps the most important version to follow Fokine's is Frederick Ashton's (choreographed for Margot Fonteyn and Michael Somes in 1951), which Ashton scholar David Vaughan has called the choreographer's "first fully mature work, and the first of a series of great ballets about love that he was to make in the next two decades".

Ashton, while following Fokine fairly closely in the interweaving of libretto and score, departed from his predecessor in the use of modern rather than Greek dress, and in putting the dancers on pointe. Declaring himself bored with barefoot pseudo-Hellenic ballets involving "tunics and veils and scarves" (Fokine's influence was greater than he could have dreamed in 1904), Ashton wanted a ballet that was believable in a modern context, "as though it could still happen today". By departing from the then-familiar neo-classicism of "mythological" ballet, claims Vaughan, Ashton was affirming his belief and faith in the principles of classical ballet, and in so doing created a work that was both timeless and contemporary. Ashton had "the courage to be simple, to work against the lush impressionism of the score, creating a tension that gives the ballet its structural strength".

Also important to the ballet's genesis was Margot Fonteyn, at this stage just at the beginning of her twenty-year career as Ashton's most important muse. Ashton was later to say that he enjoyed working on *Daphnis and Chloe* almost more than on anything else, because it was so difficult—"I had to dig deeply into myself to do it"—and the one who returned his effort step for step was Fonteyn, in what Vaughan called "one of her most personal roles". Later interpreters of the Ashton role have included the lovely and expressive Antoinette Sibley, but Ashton late in his life remarked that it was in *Daphnis and Chloe* more than in any other ballet that he missed Margot Fonteyn.

Other modern balletic interpretations of Ravel's *Daphnis and Chloe* have included John Cranko, John Neumeier, Glen Tetley, and John Taras.

—Virginia Christian

---

## DARK ELEGIES

**Choreography:** Antony Tudor
**Music:** Gustav Mahler (*Kindertotenlieder*)
**Design:** Nadia Benois (scenery and costumes)
**Libretto:** Antony Tudor (after text of *Kindertotenlieder*, Friedrich Rückert)
**First Production:** Ballet Rambert, Duchess Theatre, London, 19 February 1937
**Principal Dancers:** Maude Lloyd, Antony Tudor, Peggy van Praagh

**Other productions include:** Ballet Theatre (restaged Tudor, design Raymond Sovey after Nadia Benois), with Nina Stroganova, Miriam Golden, Antony Tudor, Hugh Laing; New York, 24 January 1940. National Ballet of Canada (design Kay Ambrose after Benois); Kingston, Ontario, 15 November 1955. Royal Swedish Ballet (design Roland Svensson); Stockholm, 6 September 1961. Hamburg Ballet (staged Sonia Arova); Hamburg, 9 September 1970. Dutch National Ballet, 19 January 1972. Royal Ballet (staged Airi Hynninen after Tudor); London, 27 November 1980. Paris Opéra Ballet (staged Sallie Wilson after Tudor); Paris, 18 February 1985. Houston Ballet (staged Wilson after Tudor); Houston, 28 May 1987. San Francisco Ballet (staged Wilson after Tudor); San Francisco, March 1991.

### PUBLICATIONS

Percival, John, *Antony Tudor: A Young Man's Ballets*, Dance Perspectives 17, London, 1963
Anderson, Jack, "The View from the House Opposite: Some Aspects of Tudor", *Ballet Review* (Brooklyn, N.Y.), vol. 4, no. 6, 1974
Balanchine, George, with Mason, Francis, *Balanchine's Complete Stories of the Great Ballets*, Garden City, N.Y., 1977
Huxley, Michael, "A History of a Dance: Analysis of *Dark Elegies*" in Adshead, Janet, et al., *Dance Analysis: Theory and Practice*, London, 1988
Chazin-Bennahum, Judith, "Shedding light on *Dark Elegies*", Society of Dance History Scholars, Proceedings, 1988
Perlmutter, Donna, *Shadowplay: The Life of Antony Tudor*, London, 1991

* * *

*Dark Elegies* was Antony Tudor's last major work for Ballet Rambert; later the same year he broke away to form his own company, and soon after that left for America, where he was to remain for the rest of his life. The idea for the ballet had been in his mind for two years before Marie Rambert finally agreed to allow him to go ahead with it, after seeing the pas de deux of the second song which Tudor danced with Maude Lloyd (who created leading roles in several of his ballets).

Set to Mahler's song-cycle *Kindertotenlieder*, the ballet explores individual and communal responses to grief and bereavement, as young parents mourn the loss of their children as a result of an unspecified tragedy. The ballet is not narrative; rather, it reveals different facets of the human experience through solos, a duo, and ensemble dances, as the community gradually progresses through lamentation to the beginnings of acceptance and resignation. The two scenes are indeed entitled "Lamentations of the Bereaved" and "Resignation". There are five songs in the cycle, and each of these is given over to solos or group dances which flow into and out of each other without a break. At no time is there only one dancer on stage; some members of the community are always present as witnesses to the action, so that the sense of community is strong. Each song is a setting of a poem by Rückert which itself is a meditation on an aspect of bereavement, but the dances do not "act out" the words; rather, they embody a response to the underlying mood of the whole song-cycle.

Images in the ballet are rich but non-specific; many different readings are possible within the range of experience explored. Some, for example, suggest the rocking to sleep of a small child; others, more outwardly focused, suggest searching or reaching for a lost child, while others simply convey a sense of bewildered or angry questioning. To look for direct relationships between particular dance images and their supposed meanings, however, is to miss the point of the ballet as a whole. Through the structuring of these images into solo, duo, and ensemble dances, the ballet explores the ways in which individuals respond differently to the tragedy, and explores the significance of the role of the community in terms of its capacity to offer mutual support, encouragement, and fellow-feeling. The common tragedy unites the community in a strong bond, but at the same time the loneliness of grief comes across—not only in the different movement styles of individuals, but also in their different relationships with the rest of the group, and the degree to which they are able to accept support.

Tudor described it as his favourite ballet, and many consider it to be his greatest. In terms of choreographic style, it is perhaps the most difficult of his ballets to pin down, drawing, as it does, on various dance forms for movement ideas (some

***Dark Elegies* with, from left to right, Antony Tudor, Maude Lloyd, Peggy van Praagh, Agnes de Mille, and Walter Gore, Ballet Rambert, London, 1937**

have commented on the possible influence of Jooss, as well as noting that ideas were drawn from various national dance styles, and even tap dancing), and presenting powerful and moving images related to its theme without the support of a narrative. Nothing happens in the ballet; nothing has changed at the end, except in as much as there is a sense of acceptance and the beginnings of hope in the possibility of new life as the second scene draws to a close.

The discipline of the structure and the starkness of the movement vocabulary combine to provide a telling counterpart to the richly romantic music of Gustav Mahler. Nothing is allowed to overflow into excess or melodrama; all is contained and controlled with a sense of inner strength and fortitude on the part of the dancers. Grief is expressed more through the struggle to contain and overcome it than through any indulgent wallowing in easy emotion.

As with all of Tudor's ballets, the manner of performance is of crucial importance to the correct interpretation of the work. In recent years, some companies have found it difficult to achieve the required sense of weight in the movement; the characters are peasants and thus intimately related to the land in which they live, and in addition to this natural tendency the burden of grief has the effect of literally weighing people down. The effort to overcome this burden of grief and suffering is conveyed most poignantly when dancers are able to give the upwardly focused movements that sense of triumphing over death, or of lifting themselves up through a great effort of will in order to cry out against the cruelty of providence.

The critics were divided on the ballet's merits at its first performance, although generally the reaction was negative—the music was considered unsuitable for ballet, and the theme too sombre. The movement style itself bemused many, and the "Sitter Out" in the *Dancing Times* wrote that it was "not a ballet which will have a general appeal, but . . . as an experiment has a definite value". The dancers themselves, however, were convinced of its beauty and value (as Patricia Clogstoun recorded in her diary at the time), and the ballet has proved to have a lasting relevance in the years since. It has been in the repertoire of a number of companies, including the Royal Swedish Ballet, the Royal Danish Ballet, American Ballet Theatre, and the Royal Ballet, as well as Ballet Rambert.

—Rachel S. Richardson

---

**DARRELL, Peter**

English dancer, choreographer, and ballet director. Born Peter Skinner in Richmond, England, 16 September 1929. Studied at the Sadler's Wells Ballet School, London. Dancer, Sadler's Wells Ballet, 1944–46, Sadler's Wells Opera Ballet (becoming

Sadler's Wells Theatre Ballet), 1946–47, and London Festival Ballet, 1951–52, also performing with Malmö Opera Ballet, Sweden, and in musical shows in Paris and London; first choreography, for Ballet Workshop, 1951; also choreographer for London Festival Ballet, 1952, 1970, 1973, Royal Winnipeg Ballet, Canada, 1963, Zurich State Opera Ballet, 1966, German Opera Ballet, Berlin, 1968, Irish Ballet, 1974; staged dances for musical shows and pantomime, including *A Wish for Jamie* (Glasgow, 1966), and for television, including *Cool for Cats* (Granada Television, 1959); co-director, with Elizabeth West, and principal choreographer, Western Theatre Ballet, from 1957: sole director, from 1962; founder, artistic director, and chief choreographer, Scottish Theatre Ballet (incorporating Western Theatre Ballet, and later known as Scottish Ballet), 1969–86, remaining principal choreographer until his death. Recipient: Commander of the Order of the British Empire, 1984. Died in Glasgow, 2 December 1987.

**WORKS**

1951 *Midsummer Watch*, Ballet Workshop, London
1952 *The Telltale Heart* (mus. Hobson), Ballet Workshop, London
*Farewell* (mus. Françaix), Ballet Workshop, London
*Harlequinade* (mus. Drigo), London Festival Ballet
1953 *Les Chimères* (mus. Hobson), Ballet Workshop, London
*Trio* (mus. Vivaldi), Ballet Workshop, London
1954 *Magic* (mus. Hobson), Ballet Workshop, London
*Fountain* (mus. Fauré), Ballet Comique of London, Oxford
1955 *The Gift* (mus. Fauré), Ballet der Lage Landen
1956 *Vampaera* (musique concrète), Bristol School of Dancing, Bristol
*Celeste and Celestinha* (mus. Seixas), Bristol School of Dancing, Bristol (first professional performance, Western Theatre Ballet, 1957)
1957 *The Prisoners* (mus. Bartók), Western Theatre Ballet, Dartington
*Non-Stop* (mus. Williams, Palmer), Western Theatre Ballet, Bristol
1958 Dances in *The Unicorn, the Gorgon and the Manticore* (opera; mus. Menotti), Western Theatre Ballet and New Opera Company, London
*The Enchanted Garden* (mus. Glazunov), Western Theatre Ballet, Oxford
*Impasse* (mus. Holmes), Western Theatre Ballet, Bristol
1959 *Chiaroscuro* (mus. Milhaud), Western Theatre Ballet
*Quatre quartières* (mus. Albimoor), Western Theatre Ballet and Béjart Company, Théâtre Royale de la Monnaie, Brussels
1960 *Bal de la victoire* (mus. Kuhlau, Lumbye), Western Theatre Ballet, Ostende, Belgium
*Sound Barrier* (mus. Rugulo), Sunday Ballet Club, London
1961 *Salade* (mus. Milhaud), Western Theatre Ballet, Edinburgh Festival
*Ode* (mus. Stravinsky), Western Theatre Ballet, Guildford
1962 *A Wedding Present* (mus. Bartók), Western Theatre Ballet, Sunderland
1963 *Jeux* (mus. Debussy), Western Theatre Ballet, Croydon
*Mayerling* (mus. Fauré), Royal Winnipeg Ballet, Winnipeg
*Elegy* (mus. Fauré), Western Theatre Ballet, London
*Mods and Rockers* (mus. The Beatles), Western Theatre Ballet, London
1964 *Lysistrata* (mus. Dankworth), Western Theatre Ballet, Bath
*Houseparty* (mus. Poulenc's *Les Biches*), Western Theatre Ballet, British television
1965 *Home* (mus. Bartók), Western Theatre Ballet, Sunderland
*A Man Like Orpheus* (mus. Leppard), Western Theatre Ballet, British television
1966 *Sun into Darkness* (mus. Williamson), Western Theatre Ballet, London
*Lessons in Love* (mus. Copland), Zurich State Opera Ballet, Zurich
1967 *Francesca* (mus. Roussel), Western Theatre Ballet, London
Dances in *Orpheus and Eurydice* (opera; mus. Gluck), Sadler's Wells Opera and Western Theatre Ballet, London
1968 *Ephemeron* (mus. Milhaud), Western Theatre Ballet, London (originally staged Sadler's Wells Opera Ballet, same year)
*Catulli Carmina and Carmina Burana* (mus. Orff), German Opera Ballet, Berlin
1969 *Beauty and the Beast* (mus. Musgrave), Scottish Theatre Ballet, London
1970 *Herodias* (mus. Hindemith), Scottish Theatre Ballet, London
*La Vida* (mus. Auber), London Festival Ballet, London
1971 *Four Portraits* (mus. Prokofiev), Scottish Theatre Ballet, Callander
*Garden Party* (mus. Bach, orchestrated Stoker), Charity Gala, London
*Othello* (mus. Liszt), New London Ballet, Trieste
1972 *Tales of Hoffmann* (mus. Offenbach, arranged Lanchbery), Scottish Ballet, Edinburgh
*Variations for a Door and a Sigh* (mus. Pierre Henry), Scottish Ballet, Glasgow
1973 *Scorpius* (mus. Musgrave), Scottish Theatre Ballet, Glasgow
*La Péri* (mus. Dukas), London Festival Ballet, London
*In Nightly Revels* (mus. Bach), Jacob's Pillow Dance Festival, Lee, Massachusetts
*The Nutcracker* (mus. Tchaikovsky), Scottish Ballet, Edinburgh
1974 *Grand Pas Gitane* (mus. Saint-Saëns), Irish Ballet, Cork
*Asparas* (pas de deux; mus. Massenet), Irish Ballet, Cork
*O Caritas* (mus. Toumazi, Jeremy Taylor, Cat Stevens), Scottish Ballet Workshop
*An Engagement Party* (mus. Janáček), New London Ballet, British television
1975 *The Scarlet Pastorale* (mus. Frank Martin), Scottish Ballet, Edinburgh
*Voyage* (solo; mus. Mendelssohn), Scottish Ballet, Aberdeen
*Songs Without Words* (mus. Mendelssohn), Students from Scottish Ballet Scholarship Classes, Glasgow
1976 *Mary, Queen of Scots* (mus. McCabe), Scottish Ballet, Glasgow
1978 *Five Rückert Songs* (mus. Mahler), Scottish Ballet, Ballet for Scotland tour, Falkirk
*Picnic* (mus. Poulenc), Scottish Ballet Workshop, Schools Programme
1979 *Such Sweet Thunder* (mus. Ellington), Scottish Ballet, Glasgow
*Cinderella* (mus. Rossini), Scottish Ballet, Aberdeen
*Tristan and Iseult* (mus. Lizst), New London Ballet, York

1980 *Chéri* (mus. Earl), Scottish Ballet, Edinburgh
1982 *Carriages at Midnight* (mus. Kreisler), Scottish Ballet, Glasgow
*Midnight Masquerade* (mus. Richard Rogers), Scottish Ballet, Aberdeen
*Variations on a Rococo Theme for Cello and Orchestra Opus 33* (mus. Tchaikovsky), Scottish Ballet, Glasgow
1983 *Gardens of the Night* (mus. Chopin), Scottish Ballet, Glasgow
1985 *Carmen* (mus. Bizet, arranged Muldownie), Scottish Ballet, Edinburgh

Also staged:
1971 *Giselle* (assisted by Graeme; after Petipa, Coralli, Perrot; mus. Adam), Scottish Theatre Ballet, Aberdeen
1977 *Swan Lake* (after Petipa, Ivanov; mus. Tchaikovsky), Scottish Ballet, Edinburgh

**Other works include**: for Scottish Ballet—*Valses de concert* (mus. Glazunov), *Economy in a straitjacket but still room for movement* (mus. Bach), *Offenbach Variations* (mus. Offenbach, arranged Lanchbery).

## PUBLICATIONS


By Darrell:
Interview in "Peter Darrell Talks to Dance and Dancers", *Dance and Dancers* (London), June 1963
Interview in "Settling over the Border", *Dance and Dancers* (London), June 1979

About Darrell:
"Personalities of the Month: Elizabeth West and Peter Darrell", *Dance and Dancers* (London), May 1958
"Peter Darrell: Profile", *Dancing Times* (London), September 1964
Brinson, Peter, and Crisp, Clement, *Ballet for All*, London, 1970
Goodwin, Noël, *A Ballet for Scotland*, Edinburgh, 1979
Sandler, Ken, "Peter Darrell", *Ballet News* (New York), May 1981
Massie, Annette, "Elizabeth West and Western Theatre Ballet", *Dance Research* (London), Spring 1988


* * *

The first generation of Sadler's Wells Theatre Ballet dancers contained an astonishing number of artists later of influence throughout the world. They included Kenneth MacMillan, John Cranko, Peter Wright (now director of Birmingham Royal Ballet), and Peter Darrell, whose name will always be identified with Scottish Ballet.

Peter Darrell (born Peter Skinner) was a student of Sadler's Wells Ballet School before joining the company in 1944. He was transferred to the new Sadler's Wells Opera (later Theatre) Ballet in 1946 as a founding member, and stayed with it for nearly two years. He danced in musicals, with London Festival Ballet, and the Malmo Opera Ballet, and began choreographing with Ballet Workshop in 1951. His compositions gave little idea of his true talent, and he had no major work until 1957, when he became co-founder and choreographer for Western Theatre Ballet, a small company based in Bristol.

He and his co-director, Elizabeth West, put Western Theatre Ballet on the map, building up a reputation for the company as a very up-to-date, spirited, and interesting organization. They recruited excellent young dancers who worked together as a recognizable team. With them, Darrell found his true metier as a choreographer. Influences from theatre and film (especially the French films of the 1950s) inclined him to work with strongly dramatic themes that were relevant to the period, as in ballets like *The Prisoners*, a tough tale about two escapees who become enemies, and *Mods and Rockers*, which reflected group conflicts of the 1960s.

In 1962, Elizabeth West was killed in a tragic mountain accident, and Darrell took sole charge. Not only did the company survive, but it went on to become famous. He maintained its reputation for varied and stimulating work and its dancers were greatly admired. At this time the tide was turning strongly towards the establishment of regional ballet, and the city of Glasgow decided to look for an existing company that could be transferred to Scotland. Western Theatre Ballet was their choice, Darrell came to terms with them, and Scottish Theatre Ballet (later Scottish Ballet) began its life in 1969.

From then until his death, Darrell was principal choreographer and artistic director of a company whose reputation increased steadily both in Britain and on tours overseas. He had a considerable gift for creating and recruiting dancers, and although he composed many ballets in the repertoire, he also acquired works in very divergent styles from leading choreographers, among them Rudi van Dantzig, Flemming Flindt, Jack Carter, and Walter Gore.

Every company needs the classics, but Darrell was adventurous in his staging of them. Often, indeed, he intentionally ran into controversy. There was a *Swan Lake* in 1977 in which Siegfried was a nineteenth-century opium-eater. Using the music in its original 1877 sequence, Darrell wrote a new scenario that left out the fairytale elements of enchanted princesses and a magician. Siegfried's evil genius was his friend Benno, and Odette and the swans were merely part of drug-induced dreams. On the other hand, Darrell could arrange for excellent orthodox stagings, such as Bournonville's *Napoli* by Poul Gnatt, and *La Sylphide* by Hans Brenaa.

Audiences love full-evening ballets these days, and Darrell created an adventurous series. None of them had the daring and intensity of the one he staged for Western Theatre Ballet on the theme of pagan rituals surviving in a Cornish village, *Sun into Darkness*. He catered admirably, however, for the general public with a delightful version of *Tales of Hoffmann*, for which he prepared an excellent scenario. The characters of Nicholas and Schlemil were discarded, as was the character of Coppélius, and Antonia inevitably is a would-be ballerina rather than a singer. The ballet was a splendid vehicle for his company ballerinas, the charmingly contrasted Elaine McDonald and Marian St Claire. A later ballet, *Chéri*, stylishly designed by Philip Prowse, was a fluent and impassioned translation of Colette's novels in terms of dance.

As an artistic director, Darrell managed to remain on good terms with dancers, public, and administrators. He had the vision to provide Scotland with the kind of ballet company it needed, offering an excellent list of productions that ranged from traditional classics to avant-garde works. He drew on choreographers from the modern dance world as well as from classical ballet, and regularly tried out new talent in workshop seasons. He established a company school, and small groups of dancers were regularly despatched to take glimpses of ballet to the remoter areas of the Highlands and islands of Scotland.

—Kathrine Sorley Walker

**DARSONVAL, Lycette**

French dancer, choreographer, and ballet director. Born Alice Perron, sister of dancer Serge Perrault, in Coutances, 12 February 1912. Studied at the Paris Opéra Ballet School, pupil of Mlle. Couat and Carlotta Zambelli, from 1925; later studied with Lubov Egorova, Olga Preobrazhenska, and Madame Rousanne (Rousanne Sarkissian). Petit sujet, Paris Opéra Ballet, 1930; leading dancer and guest artist, touring North America with Serge Lifar, 1933–34, central Europe with Ballets Russes d'Esprilova, and Algeria, 1935, returning to Opéra, 1936: première danseuse, 1936–40; danseuse étoile, 1940–60, performing in Germany, 1945, Europe, 1948, South America and Italy, 1950; also appeared on television, including in *The Sleeping Beauty* (British television, 1952), and in film, including in *Symphonie en blanc* (chor. Lifar, 1943); founder of own small touring company, performing in Europe and the United States, from 1953; director, Paris Opéra Ballet School, 1957–59; maîtresse de ballet, Nice Opéra Ballet, 1963–64; professor of dance, Nice Conservatory, 1971–76; also founder and teacher of own school in Nice; professor, Course de Perfectionnement, Paris Opéra School, from 1975; jury member, Concours International de Danse, 1970; vice president of Jury for Concours International de Danse at Varna, 1978. Recipient: Premier Prix de Danse Classique au Grande Concours International de Varsovie (Warsaw), 1933; Chevalier de la Légion d'Honneur, 1959; Officier de la Légion d'Honneur, 1980; Commandeur de l'Ordre National du Mérite; Chevalier des Arts et des Lettres.

**ROLES**

1929 Muse in *Sylvia* (Staats), Paris Opéra Ballet, Paris
Shepherdess in *The Creatures of Prometheus* (Lifar), Paris Opéra Ballet, Paris
1936 Title role in *Giselle* (Petipa after Coralli, Perrot; staged Lifar), Paris Opéra Ballet, Paris
Divertissement in *Castor et Pollux* (Guerra), Paris Opéra Ballet, Paris
1937 Sorceress (cr) in *David triomphant* (Lifar), Paris Opéra Ballet, Paris
Title role in *Elvire* (Aveline), Paris Opéra Ballet, Paris
1938 Oriane (cr) in *Oriane et le Prince d'Amour* (Lifar), Paris Opéra Ballet, Paris
Pamela (cr) in *Adelaide* (Lifar), Paris Opéra Ballet, Paris
Principal dancer (cr) in *Vie et lumière* (pas de deux; Aveline), Paris Opéra Ballet, Paris
1939 Laurette (cr) in *La Nuit vénitienne* (also chor.), Paris Opéra Ballet, Paris
1941 Title role (cr) in *Sylvia* (Lifar), Paris Opéra Ballet, Paris
Chloe in *Daphnis et Chloe* (Fokine), Paris Opéra Ballet, Paris
Princess (cr) in *La Princesse au jardin* (Lifar), Paris Opéra Ballet, Paris
Young girl in *Le Spectre de la rose* (Fokine), Paris Opéra Ballet, Paris
1942 Gourouli (cr) in *Les Deux Pigeons* (Aveline), Paris Opéra Ballet, Paris
Principal dancer in *Suite de danse* (Clustine), Paris Opéra Ballet, Paris
Isabeau (cr) in *Joan de Zarissa* (Lifar), Paris Opéra Ballet, Paris
1943 Principal dancer (cr) in *Suite en blanc* (Lifar), Paris Opéra Ballet, Zurich
Lucia (cr) in *L'Amour sorcier* (Lifar), Paris Opéra Ballet, Paris
Thaïs in *Ballet de la tentation* (Lifar), Paris Opéra Ballet, Paris
1944 Swanilda in *Coppélia* (Aveline after Saint-Léon), Paris Opéra Ballet, Paris
Principal dancer in *La Nuit* (Lifar), Paris Opéra Ballet, Paris
Title role in *La Grisi* (Aveline), Paris Opéra Ballet, Paris
Principal dancer in *Les Petits Riens* (Lifar), Paris Opéra Ballet, Paris
1945 Juliette in *Romeo et Juliette* (pas de deux; Lifar), Paris Opéra Ballet, Paris
1946 Rosine in *Précaution Inutile* (Etchevery), Opéra-Comique, Paris
Waltz, Mazurka in *Les Sylphides* (Fokine; staged Tcherkas), Opéra-Comique, Paris
1947 Odette in *Swan Lake* (Act II extracts; Gsovsky after Ivanov), Paris Opéra Ballet, Paris
The Fairy in *Le Baiser de la fée* (Balanchine), Paris Opéra Ballet, Paris
First Movement (cr) in *Le Palais de cristal* (Balanchine), Paris Opéra Ballet, Paris
Sugar Plum Fairy in *The Nutcracker* (Act II; Etchevery), Opéra-Comique, Paris
Pas d'action (cr) in *The Sleeping Beauty* (Act III; Tcherkas after Petipa), Opéra-Comique, Paris
1948 Pas d'action in *Divertissement* (Lifar), Paris Opéra Ballet, Paris
Principal dancer (cr) in *Zadig* (Lifar), Paris Opéra Ballet, Paris
La Princesse infernale (cr) in *Lucifer* (Lifar), Paris Opéra Ballet, Paris
1949 Artemis (cr) in *Endymion* (Lifar), Paris Opéra Ballet, Paris
Principal dancer in *Ballade* (Lifar), Paris Opéra Ballet, Paris
1950 Mimi (cr) in *La Grande Jatte* (Aveline), Paris Opéra Ballet, Paris
Dulcinea (cr) in *Le Chevalier errant* (Lifar), Paris Opéra Ballet, Paris
Oenone (cr) in *Phèdre* (Lifar), Paris Opéra Ballet, Paris
Title role in *Phèdre* (Lifar), Paris Opéra Ballet, Paris
1951 Principal dancer in *Black Swan* Pas de deux (from *Swan Lake*; Petipa, staged Tcherkas), Opéra-Comique, Paris
1952 Princess Aurora in *The Sleeping Beauty* (after Petipa), British television
1953 Principal dancer (cr) in *Variations* (Lifar), Paris Opéra Ballet, Paris
The Vamp (cr) in *Cinema* (Lifar), Paris Opéra Ballet, Paris
1954 Salomé (cr) in *La Tragédie de Salomé* (Aveline), Paris Opéra Ballet, Paris
1957 Clorinde (cr) in *Combats* (also chor.), Paris Opéra Ballet, Paris
The Swan in *La Mort du cygne* (Lifar), Opéra-Comique, Paris
1959 Taglioni in *Pas de quatre* (Dolin), Paris Opéra Ballet, Paris

**WORKS**

1939 *La Nuit vénitienne* (mus. Thiriet), Paris Opéra Ballet, Paris
1952 *Rondo Capriccioso* (mus. Saint-Saëns), Palais de Chaillot, Paris
1957 *Combats* (mus. Banfield), Paris Opéra Ballet, Paris (also staged Nice Opéra Ballet)

Also staged:
1979 *Sylvia* (after Lifar, Mérante; mus. Delibes), Paris Opéra Ballet, Paris (also staged for the Central Ballet of China, Peking, 1980)

**PUBLICATIONS**

By Darsonval:
"L'Amerique en dansant", *La Danse* (Paris), February 1957
Interview in Roy, Sylvie, "Jai interviewé Lycette Darsonval", *Musica: Disques* (Paris), November 1958
*Ma Vie sur les pointes*, Paris, 1988

About Darsonval:
Vaillat, L., *Le Ballet de l'Opéra de Paris*, 3 volumes: Paris, 1943, 1947, 1951
Cadieu, Martine, *Lycette Darsonval*, Paris, 1951
"Lycette Darsonval," *Ballet* (London), February 1952
Guest, Ivor, "Fair Exchange: The Stars of the Paris Opera", *Dance and Dancers* (London), September 1954
Fabre, Dominique, *Lycette Darsonval*, Paris, 1956
Christout, Marie-Françoise, "Lycette Darsonval", *Dance and Dancers* (London), February 1960

* * *

Lycette Darsonval, whose real name was Alice Perron, was born in Coutances in Normandy; she had three brothers, one of whom, Serge Perrault, was a dancer. Lycette was a very lively, undisciplined child who expressed herself by dancing as soon as she heard music. When she was eight years old her family moved to the Montmartre area of Paris, which was still very much a village in those days. One day, when Lycette was dancing in the street to the music of a barrel organ, a passer-by stopped and stared in amazement: she was a friend of Cléo de Mérode and the ballerina Camille Bos. A few days later the woman came to see Lycette and her mother, spoke very highly of the little girl's talents, and proposed to enrol her in the Opéra Ballet school.

Lycette was twelve years old and was accepted because of her perfect proportions. Her mother enrolled her under the name of Alice Leplat. At the age of fourteen she was taken into the ballet and became Carlotta Zambelli's favourite pupil. From her, Lycette learnt "le taqueté"—speed and lightness on her feet—together with an invaluable artistic inheritance—*Sylvia*, *Giselle*, *Coppélia*, and *Le Deux Pigeons*. Lycette Darsonval also worked with Nicolas Guerra and Albert Aveline; she was the great hope of the Opéra. Apart from an extraordinary technique and "diamond" pointes, she possessed the beauty of Diana the huntress as portrayed by Jean Goujon—a regal bearing, a radiantly fair complexion, and a dazzling stage presence. In 1930 the journalist L.L. Martin sketched a portrait of her in *Les Demoiselles de l'Opéra*, saying, "more than any of her companions, Lycette Leplat possesses the brilliance of the stage. There is nothing mechanical about her, nothing willed or skilfully contrived; but above all spirit, spirit in her legs, spirit in her pointes etc. . . . Oh, how I forgive her for not always submitting to discipline!"

In 1930, Darsonval became a "petit sujet"; disappointed at not being made a sujet despite a brilliant exam, she left the Opéra. She got married, travelled extensively in Equatorial Africa, and then returned to Paris and to the ballet studio—in particular to classes given by Lubov Egorova, Olga Preobrazhenska, and Madame Rousanne. She perfected her fouettés and her petits tours on pointe, which she introduced to the Opéra, where they had always been done on demi-pointe. In 1933 Darsonval (who now went by this name), competed in the first International Classical Dance Competition in Warsaw, and won first prize. A long tour in the United States with Serge Lifar further consolidated her talents. She danced as a guest artist in 1935 with the Russian ballet company Ballets d'Esprilova, then appearing in Europe and North Africa.

The following year, Serge Lifar advised Darsonval to return to the Opéra Ballet. The director, Jacques Rouché, agreed on condition that she started again as a petit sujet and took the exams; she accepted. That same year, Serge Lifar organized a competition to find a new *Giselle*, as Olga Spessivtseva had left the Opéra. The finalists were Lycette Darsonval (petit sujet), Paulette Dynalix, and Marie-Louise Didion (sujets). Lycette Darsonval was the winner and remained the holder of the role of *Giselle* for fifteen years. She was made a première danseuse without having to go through the soloists' class and three years later she was promoted to étoile. In his memoirs, Serge Lifar credits himself with having given the Opéra its first French *Giselle* and its first French étoile. He extols her beauty, her artistic sense, her faultless virtuosity in *Oriane et le Prince d'Amour*, *Joan de Zarissa*, *Sylvia* (one of her greatest roles), *Romeo et Juliette*, *Le Chevalier errant*, *Endymion*, and *Suite en blanc*. The variations arranged for Darsonval in *Suite en blanc* have been analyzed by the critic Leandre Vaillat in *Le Ballet de l'Opéra*: "The 'étoile', Lycette Darsonval, describes a skilful pattern of pas courus, glissades, fouettés, finishing with petits tours and pirouettes without any preparation. The accumulation of difficulties, with their breathless rhythm and unrelenting succession, is such that the virtuosity which links these elements smoothly, gives the dancer the air of an inhuman and detached idol!"

Darsonval's choice of partners was first of all Serge Lifar, followed by Michel Renault, Alexandre Kalioujny, Attilio Labis, and Henri Danton. In 1954, she gave a masterly demonstration of her dramatic talents in *La Tragédie de Salomé* (choreographed by Aveline), in which the beauty and expressiveness of her body were stunning.

Lycette Darsonval also did some choreography for the Opéra and was, in fact, the first woman to do so, staging *La Nuit vénitienne* (1939) and *Combats* (1959). She introduced "performance lectures" at the Sorbonne in 1941. Her theme, "Three centuries of dance at the Opéra", formed the basis of the programme she arranged for the company she founded in 1953 and which she took on several tours, including the United States. She danced her farewell performance at the Opéra in *Giselle* in 1959—she was still dazzling. While on stage, she was presented with the Order of the Chevalier d'Honneur by the Minister for Culture, André Malraux. (She was promoted to Officer in 1980.)

Lycette Darsonval remained at the Opéra as teacher of the class of grands sujets. She was also, at this time, the first female principal of the Opéra Ballet School. She also built up a career away from the Opéra, as ballet mistress of the Nice Opéra and as director and teacher at the Nice Conservatory. Many excellent and successful dancers passed through her classes, going on to win competitions and become étoiles: Frédéric Olivieri and Jean Pierre Aviotte were just two of them. Darsonval also founded her own ballet school in Nice.

In 1975 Claude Bessy entrusted Darsonval with the "classe de perfectionnement" of the Opéra Ballet School. But the crowning point of her career was the reworking of the choreography of *Sylvia* for the Opéra in 1979, which was also staged for the Central Ballet of Peking in 1980.

—Gilberte Cournand

**DAUBERVAL, Jean**

French dancer and choreographer. Born Jean Bercher in Montpellier, son of Comédie-Française actor Etienne-Dominique Bercher, 19 August 1742. Studied at l'Académie royale de musique (Paris Opéra), pupil of Jean-Georges Noverre. Married the dancer Mlle Théodore (Marie-Madeleine Crespé), before 1783. Early career in Bordeaux, also performing in Lyons, 1757; choreographer, Teatro Regio di Torino, Carnival season, 1759; Paris Opéra debut as dancer in *Zaïs* (ballet-héroïque; mus. Rameau), 1761; premier danseur, dancing under Noverre, Stuttgart, 1762–64; leading dancer and choreographer, King's Theatre, London, 1763–64, and also 1784; premier danseur demi-caractère, Opéra, Paris, from 1763; premier danseur noble and joint assistant maître de ballet (with Maximilien Gardel), from 1773, becoming involved in antagonism with Noverre, after Noverre's appointment as chief maître de ballet, 1776, and expelled briefly from Opéra, 1779; resigned, due to differences with Gardel (then chief maître de ballet), 1783; ballet master, King's Theatre, London, 1783–84; maître de ballet, Bordeaux, 1785–90; ballet master and principal dancer, Pantheon Theatre, London, 1791–92. Died in Tours, 14 February 1806.

**ROLES**

1757 Dancer in *La Toilette de Venus* (Noverre), Opéra, Lyons

1761 Dancer in *Zaïs* (ballet-héroïque; mus. Rameau), Opéra, Paris

Dancer in *Armide* (tragédie-lyrique; mus. Lully), Opéra, Paris

1762 Un Polonais in *Les Indes galantes* (ballet héroique; mus. Rameau), Opéra, Paris

Dancer in *Acis et Galatée* (pastorale-héroïque; mus. Lully), Opéra, Paris

Dancer in *Les Fêtes grecques et romaines* (ballet; mus. de Blâmont), Opéra, Paris

Dancer in *Iphigénie en Tauride* (tragédie-lyrique; mus. Desmarets, Campra, Berton), Opéra, Paris

Dancer (cr) in *L'Opéra de société* (ballet; mus. Giraud), Opéra, Paris

1763 Dancer (cr) in *Polyxène* (tragédie-lyrique; mus. Dauvergne), Opéra, Paris

Principal dancer in *New Dance*, King's Theatre, London

Dancer (cr) in *The Turkish Coffee House* (also chor.), King's Theatre, London

1764 Dancer (cr) in *Le Mariage du village* (also chor.), King's Theatre, London

"Polchoise" (cr) in *La Masquerade* (also chor.), King's Theatre, London

Un More in *Tancrède* (tragédie-lyrique; mus. Campra), Opéra, Paris

1765 Dancer (cr) in *Bacchus et Hégémone* (mus. Dauvergne), Opéra, Paris

Dancer in *Castor et Pollux* (tragédie-lyrique; mus. Rameau), Opéra, Paris

Un Pâtre in *Le Devin du village* (intermède; mus. Rousseau), Opéra, Paris

Dancer in *Les Fêtes d'Hymen et de l'Amour* (ballet-héroïque; mus. Rameau), Opéra, Paris

Un Berger in *Thésée* (tragédie-lyrique; mus. Lully), Opéra, Paris

1766 Un Turc in *La Turquie* (act from *L'Europe galante*, ballet; mus. Campra), Opéra, Paris

Dancer in *Les Fêtes lyriques* (fragments from various works), Opéra, Paris

Un Cyclope, Bacchus (cr), "Pas de deux pantomime" (cr; also chor.) in *Sylvie* (opéra-ballet; mus. Berton, Trial), Opéra, Paris

1767 Un Pâtre in *La Terre* (act from *Les Éléments*, ballet; mus. Destouches, Lalande), Opéra, Paris

Dancer (cr) in *Ernelinde* (tragédie-lyrique; mus. Philidor), Opéra, Paris

Un Matelot, Un Chasseur in *Hippolyte et Aricie* (tragédie-lyrique; mus. Rameau), Opéra, Paris

Dancer (cr) in *Théonis* (pastorale; mus. Berton, Trial, Grenier), Opéra, Paris

1768 Dancer in *Daphnis et Alcimadure* (pastorale; mus. Mondonville), Opéra, Paris

Dancer in *Titon et l'aurore* (pastorale; mus. Mondonville), Opéra, Paris

Dancer in *La Vénitienne* (ballet; new mus. Dauvergne), Opéra, Paris

1769 Un Plaisir in *Anacréon* (ballet-héroïque; mus. Rameau), Opéra, Paris

Dancer in *Enée et Lavinie* (tragédie-lyrique; new mus. Dauvergne), Opéra, Paris

1770 Dancer in *Zaïde* (ballet; mus. Royer), Opéra, Paris

Dancer in *Zoroastre* (tragédie-lyrique; mus. Rameau), Opéra, Paris

1771 Dancer (cr) in *La Fête de Flore* (ballet; mus. Trial), Opéra, Paris

1772 Dancer (cr) in *Adèle de Ponthieu* (tragédie-lyrique; mus. Berton, Laborde), Opéra, Paris

Dancer in *Aline, reine de Golconde* (ballet; mus. Monsigny), Opéra, Paris

Dancer in *La Cinquantaine* (pastorale; mus. Laborde), Opéra, Paris

Dancer (cr) in *Eglé* (ballet; mus. Lagarde), Opéra, Paris

1773 Dancer in *Zélindor, roi des sylphes* (ballet; mus. Rebel, Francoeur), Opéra, Paris

Dancer in *Les Sauvages* (ballet; mus. Rameau), Opéra, Paris

Dancer (cr) in *L'Union de l'amour et des arts* (ballet; mus. Floquet), Opéra, Paris

1774 Dancer (cr) in *Azolan; ou, Le Serment indiscret* (ballet; mus. Floquet), Opéra, Paris

Dancer (cr) in *Sabinus* (tragédie-lyrique; mus. Gossec), Opéra, Paris

Dancer in *Le Carnaval du Parnasse* (opéra-ballet; mus. Mondonville), Opéra, Paris

1775 Dancer (cr) in *Cythère assiégée* (ballet; mus. Gluck, ballet music Berton), Opéra, Paris

Dancer in *La Provençale* (act from *Les Fêtes de Thalie*, ballet; mus. Mouret), Opéra, Paris

Dancer in *Erosine* (act from *Les Fêtes de Thalie*, ballet; mus. Berton), Opéra, Paris

1777 Dancer (cr) in *Alain et Rosette; ou, La Bergère ingénue* (ballet; mus. Ponteau), Opéra, Paris

L'Éveillé (cr) in *La Chercheuse d'esprit* (ballet; M. Gardel), Choisy

1778 Dancer (cr) in *Les Petits Riens* (Opéra version, ballet; mus. Mozart, chor. Noverre), Opéra, Paris

Créon in *Médée et Jason* (ballet-pantomime; mus. Noverre), Opéra, Paris

1779 Dancer (cr) in *Amadis de Gaule* (tragédie-lyrique; new version, mus. J.C. Bach), Opéra, Paris

Dancer (cr) in *Echo et Narcisse* (pastorale; mus. Gluck, chor. Noverre), Opéra, Paris

1782 Un Paysan (cr) in *La Double Epreuve; ou, Colinette à la cour* (opéra-comique; mus. Grétry), Opéra, Paris

1784 Old Age (cr) in *The Four Ages of Man* (also chor.), King's Theatre, London

**Jean Dauberval with Marie Allard in *Sylvie*, 1766**

Dancer (cr) in *Le Réveil du bonheur* (also chor.), King's Theatre, London
Skirmish (cr) in *Le Déserteur; ou, La Clémence royale* (also chor.), King's Theatre, London

## WORKS

1759 *Trionfo di Bacco in Tracia* (mus. G.A. Le Messier), Teatro Regio, Turin
*Metamorfosi dei compagni d'Ulisse nell'isola di Circe* (mus. Le Messier), Teatro Regio, Turin
*Disposizioni per l'assalto generale d'una città assediata* (mus.Le Messier), Teatro Regio, Turin
*La Fontana del ringiovanimento* (mus. Le Messier), Teatro Regio, Turin
*Festa fiamminghe* (mus. Le Messier), Teatro Regio, Turin
*Feste del gran sultano* (mus. Le Messier), Teatro Regio, Turin

1763 *The Turkish Coffee House*, King's Theatre, London
*A Tyrolese Wedding*, King's Theatre, London

1764 *Le Matelot Provençal*, King's Theatre, London
*The Encampment*, King's Theatre, London
*Le Mariage du village*, King's Theatre, London
*La Femme maitresse*, King's Theatre, London
*Le Tambourine*, King's Theatre, London
*La Masquerade*, King's Theatre, London

1766 "Pas de deux pantomime" in *Sylvie* (opéra-ballet; mus. Berton, Trial), Opéra, Paris

1771 *Le Nozze villereccie* (mus. Le Messier), Teatro Regio, Turin
*L'Unione d'Amore e d'Imeneo* (mus. Le Messier), Teatro Regio, Turin
*Le Feste in onore di Minerva* (mus. Le Messier), Teatro Regio, Turin
*Il Naufragio fortunato* (mus. Le Messier), Teatro Regio, Turin
*Il Ritorno da caccia* (mus. Le Messier), Teatro Regio, Turin

*Il Trionfo della vittoria* (mus. Le Messier), Teatro Regio, Turin
*Attacco a sorpresa di un parco d'equipaggi militari* (mus. Le Messier), Teatro Regio, Turin
*Popoli taurini e allobrogi festeggianti* (mus. Le Messier), Teatro Regio, Turin
1775 *Torneo di Filippo Augusto alla Regina Bianca*, Teatro Regio, Turin
*Festa di Marli*, Teatro Regio, Turin
1780 *Les Fêtes de Gamache* (with Noverre; mus. Montreuil), Opéra, Paris
Dances in *Andromaque* (tragédie-lyrique; mus. Grétry), Opéra, Paris
Dances in *Le Seigneur bienfaisant* (comédie-lyrique; mus. Floquet, chor. with Noverre, M. Gardel), Opéra, Paris
1783 *The Pastimes of Terpsichore* (mus. Barthélemon), King's Theatre, London
*Friendship Leads to Love*, King's Theatre, London
1784 *Le Réveil du bonheur* (mus. Barthélemon), King's Theatre, London
*Le Coq du village; ou, La Loterie ingénieuse*, King's Theatre, London
*Orpheo* (mus. Barthélemon), King's Theatre, London
*Le Magnifique*, King's Theatre, London
*The Four Ages of Man* (mus. Handel et al.), King's Theatre, London
*Pygmalion* (mus. J.J. Rousseau), King's Theatre, London
*Le Déserteur; ou, La Clémence royale*, King's Theatre, London
1785 *Le Bonheur est d'aimer* (mus. Barthélemon), Grand Theatre, Bordeaux
*L'Heureuse recontre; ou, La Reine de Golconde*, Grand Theatre, Bordeaux
1787 *Le Page inconstant* (after *Le Mariage de Figaro*), Grand Theatre, Bordeaux
*Les Jeux d'Églé*, Grand Theatre, Bordeaux
*L'Épreuve villageoise*, Grand Theatre, Bordeaux
1788 *La Toilette de Véus*, Grand Theatre, Bordeaux
*Dorothée*, Grand Theatre, Bordeaux
*Psyché*, Grand Theatre, Bordeaux
1789 *L'Oracle accompli*, Grand Theatre, Bordeaux
*Amphion élève des muses*, Grand Theatre, Bordeaux
*Momus vaincu*, Grand Theatre, Bordeaux
*La Fille mal gardée* (originally called *Le Ballet de la Paille*, and also known as *Il n'est qu'un pas du mal au bien*; mus. French airs), Grand Theatre, Bordeaux
1791 *Divertissement*, Pantheon, London
*Amphion et Thalie; ou, L'Elève des muses* (possibly a version of *Amphion élève des muses*), Pantheon, London
*Telemachus in the Island of Calypso* (mus. Mazzinghi), Pantheon, London
*Le Triomphe de la folie*, Pantheon, London
*Le Siège de Cythère*, Pantheon, London
*L'Amant déguisé*, Pantheon, London
*La Fontaine d'amour*, Pantheon, London
*Le Fête villageoise* (mus. Mazzinghi), Pantheon, London
1792 *Le Volage fixé* (new production; mus. Mazzinghi), Haymarket Theatre, London
*La Foire de Smirne; ou, Les Amants réunis* (mus. Mazzinghi), Haymarket Theatre, London

**Other works include:** *Paphos assiégé par les Scythes* (revived by D'Egville, London, 1802); *Annette et Lubin* (revived by Aumer, Théâtre de la Porte-Saint-Martin, Paris, 1804).

**PUBLICATIONS**

Noverre, Jean-Georges, *Lettres sur la danse et les ballets*, Stuttgart and Lyons, 1760; as *Letters on Dancing and Ballets*, translated by Cyril Beaumont, London, 1930
Saint-Léon, Arthur, *La Stenochorégraphie*, Paris, 1852
Jullien, Adolphe, *L'Opéra secret au XVIIIe Siècle*, Paris, 1880
Campardon, Emile, *L'Académie royale de musique au XVIIe siècle*, Paris, 1884
Beaumont, Cyril, *Complete Book of Ballets*, revised edition, London, 1951
Guest, Ivor, *The Romantic Ballet in England*, London, 1954
Guest, Ivor, *La Fille mal gardée*, London, 1960
Guest, Ivor, "The Legacy of Dauberval", *Ballet Annual* (London), vol. 15, 1961
Guest, Ivor, *The Romantic Ballet in Paris*, London, 1966
Winter, Marian Hannah, *The Pre-Romantic Ballet*, London, 1974
Guest, Ivor, "*La Fille mal gardée*: New Light on the Original Production", *Dance Chronicle* (New York), vol. 1, no. 1, 1977
Costonis, Maureen Needham, "Dauberval's *Le Siège de Cythère*, 1791: A Commentary in Translation", *Dance Chronicle* (New York), vol. 14, no. 2/3, 1991

* * *

Jean Bercher, or "Dauberval"—demi-charactère dancer, influential teacher, and choreographic reformer—is today revered as the creator of *La Fille mal gardée*, the only eighteenth-century ballet in the current repertoire of ballet companies from Russia to the United States. In his own time, he was as famous as a joyful and dramatically expressive dancer as he was as a choreographer. According to Noverre, his 1766 "Pas de deux pantomime", created for Berton and Trial's opera *Sylvie* at the Paris Opéra, was "full of dramatic action and interest ... [which] expressed all the sentiments that love can inspire". In Carmontelle's engraving of the scene, Dauberval is depicted in elaborate costume, beplumed and bewigged, draped in blue damask and russet-coloured silk bows. While his costume may appear absurd to contemporary eyes, the same would not be noted of his technique: his muscular legs are properly turned out from the hip, his fingers curved gracefully without artifice, and his head turned in profile with eyes focused intently ahead. He and his partner lean away from each other; their poses, while entirely different, were designed as complementary variations on a rococo curving line.

In all, Dauberval danced in 49 operas and ballets at the Paris Opéra from 1761 to 1782, including in the premieres of many operas (such as Berton's *Adèle de Ponthieu*, Gossec's *Sabinus*, and Grétry's *Double Epreuve, ou Colinette à la cour*) and ballets (Mozart's *Les Petits riens*, Gardel's *La Chercheuse d'esprit*, Gluck's *Echo et Narcisse*, and Mondonville's *Le Carnaval de Parnasse*), in addition to performing in revivals of works by Lully and Rameau.

Noverre, with uncharacteristic kind words for another choreographer, lavished praise upon Dauberval as his favourite pupil, and even went so far as to address the *Lettres sur la danse et les arts imitateurs* (1807 edition) to him. Their relationship dated back to 1757, when Noverre engaged him as first dancer at Lyons, and Dauberval danced in *La Toilette de Venus* (18 November 1757), his first known starring role. Later he took leave of the Paris Opéra to dance at Stuttgart under Noverre from 1762 to 1764 and at London in 1764. In 1773, Dauberval was engaged as assistant ballet-master at the Paris Opéra; he had every expectation of promotion until Marie Antoinette interceded in favour of Noverre. Even though Gardel and he joined forces to oust the interloper, Dauberval still collaborated with Noverre in the choreography for *Les Fêtes de Gamache*.

Dauberval revealed early promise as a choreographer, and began this aspect of his career at the age of seventeen. He composed three ballets for the Turin opera house in 1759, and returned to the Savoy court in 1771 and 1775. The Turin repertoire was composed almost entirely of heroic and pastoral ballets peopled by Greek divinities. He choreographed a pastoral ballet (and, it would appear, some comical ones as well) for the King's Theatre, London, in 1764, and was engaged as ballet master for the Pantheon, presenting mythological ballets such as *Le Siège de Cythere*, divertissements during the opera, and some light-hearted ballets. Approximately two-thirds of his total *oeuvre* were of the serious genre, whereas the comical "ballets villageoises" such as *La Fille mal gardée* represented a significantly smaller proportion of his output. His wife described him as a master of all genres, claiming that "there is nothing in his art that this man could not accomplish".

Unfortunately, Dauberval was prevented from composing ballets during his stay at the Paris Opéra, and thus his engagement at Bordeaux's Grand Theatre (1785–90) unloosed a great burst of creativity. He resigned from the Paris Opéra, ostensibly for medical reasons, but more likely to join his bride, Mlle. Théodore, who was to dance leading roles in all his new ballets. Dauberval's reputation was greatly enhanced by the ballets composed after 1785; several were revived and mounted by his pupils, even some 40 years after their creation. His devoted disciples enabled *La Fille mal gardée* (1789) to be disseminated throughout Europe: D'Egville revived it in London in 1799; Eugène Hus staged it in Paris in 1803 and in Bordeaux in 1807; Aumer presented it with great care and accuracy for the Paris Opéra in 1828; and Didelot produced it in St. Petersburg in 1827. Bournonville jokingly referred to Bordeaux as a "nursery", where Dauberval's creations grew to maturity and henceforward set forth to conquer the world of ballet.

Noverre credited Dauberval as "the first to have the courage to battle against stereotypes and prejudices, to triumph over the Opéra's outmoded rules, to throw away masks, to adopt realistic costumes, and to demonstrate Nature's most engrossing traits", reforms Noverre had advocated in his 1760 *Lettres*. While Dauberval incorporated these ideas into his own programme, he envisioned other changes that his master had not anticipated. Noverre preferred to separate the danced finale from the pantomime action seen throughout the ballet, while Dauberval wove the pantomime into the dance to such an extent that, were the dance removed, the dramatic action of the whole would have collapsed.

For these reasons, as well as for the fact that he trained the most important choreographers of the next generation (including Viganò, Didelot, Aumer, and Hus), Dauberval should be seen as the most significant choreographic reformer between Noverre and Taglioni. Nineteenth-century artists of the dance fully recognized his importance in this respect: even as late as 1830, when Romanticism was in the air, Blasis held up his works composed 40 years previously as perfect models for both serious and comical ballets.

Didelot deemed Dauberval to be the "Molière of ballet". Filled with gratitude to his former teacher, he described Dauberval's greatest talent as the ability to "portray character" in "true and profound" ways. Dauberval's expressed goal for his ballets was couched in more modest terms: he only wanted, he said in his preface to *Telemachus in the Island of Calypso*, "to interest the heart" of the spectator rather than "to dazzle the eye".

—Maureen Needham Costonis

---

## DAVIDSBÜNDLERTÄNZE

(full title: *Robert Schumann's "Davidsbündlertänze"*)

**Choreography:** George Balanchine
**Music:** Robert Schumann
**Design:** Rouben Ter-Arutunian
**First Production:** New York City Ballet, New York State Theatre, New York, 19 June 1980 (gala preview 12 June 1980)
**Principal Dancers:** Suzanne Farrell, Karin von Aroldingen, Heather Watts, Kay Mazzo, Jacques d'Amboise, Adam Lüders, Peter Martins, Ib Andersen

### PUBLICATIONS

Levy, Suzanne, "The Dark Side of the Mirror", *Washington Dance View* (Washington, D.C.), December 1980/January 1981
Haieff, Alexei, "Balanchine and Schumann", *Ballet Review* (Brooklyn), Summer 1981
Pierpont, Claudia Roth, "Balanchine's Romanticism", *Ballet Review* (New York), Summer 1984

* * *

Three years before his death, George Balanchine produced a dance that took the ballet world by surprise. Named not only after the piece of music to which it was set but also after that music's composer, its unwieldy title was *Robert Schumann's "Davidsbündlertänze"*, *Dances of the Band of David*. Critics saw that it was (in one of their most often-used phrases) a deeply romantic ballet, and hence something of a shock for those who had come to think of the master only in terms of his neo-classical, ascerbic-Stravinsky mode.

Set to the eighteen pieces of Schumann's 1837 score that is played by a piano on stage, the ballet is a dance for four couples. Each couple contacts the other couples only briefly, and within each couple the man and woman are constantly breaking apart and wheeling away from each other. Two of the couples seem more clearly delineated than the others, and their dances seem to set up clearly dramatic situations. But what?

Critics in 1980 grasped after the few straws Balanchine threw them in an interview with Anna Kisselgoff of *The New York Times*: one of the four couples, danced by Adam Lüders and Karin von Aroldingen, represented the composer and his wife, Clara Wieck, to whom Schumann was engaged when he wrote the score, and from whom his madness later estranged him. The other couples were, critics extrapolated, perhaps further aspects of the composer; it was suggested that the other main pair, danced by Balanchine muse Suzanne Farrell and her partner Jacques d'Amboise, represented Robert and Clara as young lovers. Something strange was going on, at any rate: the backdrop, designed by Rouben Ter-Arutunian, showed a misty Gothic cathedral inspired—so Balanchine told Kisselgoff—by the paintings of the German Romantic Caspar David Friedrich, with a gnarled tree on the left and great cracking ice floes leading up to it.

The idea that this was a Balanchine ballet with a programme—and most strangely, a submerged one, lost in the tenebrous mists of psychology where the master had not often wandered—seemed most justified at the end of the piece, where Lüders retreated backwards into a diminishing spotlight of blue light, holding out his hands in fruitless supplication and farewell to von Aroldingen, who buried her face in her hands, lit up bright against the darkness, as the curtain fell. So too for the five almost comic black-clad silhouettes that menaced the

**Peter Martins and Heather Watts in Davidsbündlertänze, New York City Ballet, 1980**

Schumann character shortly before: men wearing top-hats and cloaks, and wielding huge metre-high quill pens like enormous paper cut-outs. Surely these "represented" the critics who so plagued Schumann.

Yet if all the couples were aspects of the same two people, how to deal with the fact that the four pairs dance a rigid square dance, changing partners, and three men toast each other with invisible glasses? Clearly they are as much social acquaintances and real friends as phantoms of the mind. And why the Art-Nouveau chandeliers, the fact that the women change to pointe shoes only after after each couple has danced a pas de deux in ballroom shoes? Perhaps this was a gathering of "real" people after all.

Yet, like most other Balanchine ballets, it may ultimately be that the programme is to be found primarily in the movement itself. Almost totally gone is the on-centre classicism Balanchine inherited from Petipa, the world of order and balance that even the neo-classical ballet adopts. Instead, the couples twirl off-centre, hide their faces in their arms or seek obsessively to confirm contact by touching each others' faces, do delicate inter-twining dances where their arms seem turned to nuzzling snakes, spend entire sections without contacting one another at all, and engage in lonely solos. Only briefly, and when it seems a blatant contrast, does the music become four-square, and the dancers with it; only as an exception that proves the rule does a man hold the woman around the waist in order to partner her in conventional fashion. This is a dance both of failed relationships and of movements whose centre is missing; it is both composed of and "about" the glancing motions of people who, despite their desperate efforts, cannot reach the still point at the centre of the moving wheel.

—Bruce Fleming

---

**DAYDÉ, Liane**

French dancer. Born in Paris, 27 February 1932. Studied at Studio Lamartine, Paris, and at the Paris Opéra School, pupil of Mme. d'Alessandri, Mlle. Cesbron, Suzanne Lorcia, Albert Aveline, Carlotta Zambelli, Blanche d'Alessandri, Alexandre Volinin, and Boris Kniaseff, 1942–44. Married impresario and ballet director Claude Giraud, 1961: one son, Alain. Dancer, Paris Opéra Ballet: deuxieme quadrille from 1945; coryphée

**Liane Daydé in *Blanche-Neige*, Paris Opéra, 1951**

from 1947; petit sujet from 1948; premiere danseuse from 1949, étoile from 1950, touring the Soviet Union, 1958; left the Opéra, 1960; also international guest artist, appearing at Royal Opera House, London, La Scala, Milan, Rome Opera, Rio de Janeiro, Teatro Colón in Buenos Aires, Royal Theatres in Copenhagen and Oslo, and Helsinki Opera; guest artist, Grand Ballet de Marquis de Cuevas, 1961; artistic director and étoile, Grand Ballet Classique de France, from 1962, touring Middle and Far East; professor and advisor of studies at Paris Conservatoire, 1979; also member of many examination and appointments boards in France; jury member, International Ballet Competition, Varna, Bulgaria. Recipient: Officier de l'Ordre national du mérite; Chevalier des arts et des lettres; Officier du Ouissam Alaouite (Morocco); Officier du Nicham Iftkar (Tunisia); Mandarin of the Royal Order of Cambodia; Bronze and Gold Medals du Patinage; Prix Pavlova, Paris; Prix Marquis de Cuevas; Prix de l'Université de la danse, Paris.

## ROLES

1949 Fairy Candide in *Divertissement* (from *The Sleeping Beauty*; Lifar after Petipa), Paris Opéra Ballet, Paris
La Petite Fille in *Elvire* (Aveline), Paris Opéra Ballet, Paris
Principal dancer in *Le Festin d'araignée* (Aveline), Paris Opéra Ballet, Paris
The Hen in *Les Animaux modèles* (Aveline), Paris Opéra Ballet, Paris
Principal dancer in *Suite en blanc* (Lifar), Paris Opéra Ballet, Paris

1950 Principal dancer (cr) in *Passion* (Lifar), Paris Opéra Ballet, Paris
Une Grâce in *Les Fêtes d'Hébé* (Aveline), Paris Opéra Ballet, Versailles
La Jeune fille (cr) in *L'Inconnue* (Lifar), Paris Opéra Ballet, Paris
Aricie (cr) in *Phèdre* (Lifar), Paris Opéra Ballet, Paris

1951 Title role (cr) in *Blanche-Neige* (Lifar), Paris Opéra Ballet, Paris
La Damoiselle in *Le Chevalier et la damoiselle* (Lifar), Paris Opéra Ballet, Paris

1952 Swanilda in *Coppélia* (Saint-Léon), Paris Opéra Ballet, Paris
Coraline (cr) in *Fourberies* (Lifar), Paris Opéra Ballet, Paris
Title role in *Giselle* (new production; Romanov after Petipa, Coralli, Perrot), Rome Opera Ballet, Rome
Le Papillon (cr) in "Les Fleurs" in *Les Indes galantes* (Lander), Paris Opéra Ballet, Paris

1953 Title role in *Giselle* (Petipa, Coralli, Perrot; staged Lifar), Paris Opéra Ballet, Paris
La Petite Fiancée du monde (cr) in *Cinema* (Lifar), Paris Opéra Ballet, Paris
Principal dancer (cr) in *Variations* (Lifar), Paris Opéra Ballet, Paris
Tripetta (cr) in *Hop-Frog* (Lifar), Paris Opéra Ballet, Paris
The Young Girl in *Le Spectre de la rose* (Fokine), Paris Opéra Ballet, Paris

1954 Polka (cr) in *Printemps à Vienne* (Lander), Paris Opéra Ballet, Paris
Dancer in *Romeo and Juliet Pas de deux* (Lifar), Paris Opéra Ballet, London

1955 Juliet (cr) in *Romeo and Juliet* (new version; Lifar), Paris Opéra Ballet, Paris

1956 La Danseuse de Degas in *Entre deux rondes* (Lifar), Paris Opéra Ballet, Paris

1957 Principal dancer (cr) in *Duo* (Lifar), Geneva

1958 Title role in *Annabel Lee* (Skibine), Opéra-Comique, Paris
Principal dancer (cr) in *Symphonie classique* (Lifar), Paris Opéra Ballet, Paris
Sugar Plum Fairy in *The Nutcracker* Pas de deux (after Ivanov), Paris Opéra Ballet, Paris

1959 The Unicorn in *La Dame à la Licorne* (Rosen), Paris Opéra Ballet, Paris
The Princess (cr) in *Isoline* (Skibine), Opéra-Comique, Paris

1961 Princess Aurora in The *Sleeping Beauty* (Petipa, Nijinska; staged Helpmann), Grand Ballet de Marquis de Cuevas, Paris

1963 Principal dancer (cr) in *Dance Panels in Seven Movements* (Rosen), Bavarian State Opera Ballet, Munich

**Other roles include:** Ballerina in *Pas de quatre* (Dolin), Bluebird Pas de deux from *The Sleeping Beauty* (Petipa), Waltz and Mazurka in *Les Sylphides* (Fokine) ballerina in *Études* (Lander).

**PUBLICATIONS**

Guest, Ivor, "Impressions of the Paris Opéra Ballet", *Ballet* (London), October 1951

Goodman, Saul, "Brief Biographies: Liane Daydé", *Dance Magazine* (New York), June 1955

Coquelle, Jean, "Liane Daydé", *Ballet Today* (London), August/September 1957

"Portrait de Liane Daydé", *Journal musical français* (Paris), October 1957

Silvant, J., *Liane Daydé,* Paris, 1970

"Liane Daydé", *Pour la danse* (Paris), July/August/September 1970

* * *

A true child of the Paris Opéra, Liane Daydé held the title of youngest "étoile" for nine years, nominated at the age of seventeen—in the same year as her notable performance, beside Tamara Toumanova, in *Phèdre* by Jean Cocteau and Serge Lifar. Small, fragile, and delicate, with a child-like face, this tiny ballerina delighted small girls who dreamed of becoming dancers. Daydé danced with no apparent effort, relaxed as though she were amusing herself at improvising her steps. As a young "petit rat" at the Opéra school under the tutelage of the great Italian, Carlotta Zambelli, she really discovered her art thanks to another great Italian teacher, Blanche d'Alessandri, a severe but dedicated teacher who was in the habit of rapping her pupils with a stick.

*Blanche-Neige* (1951) was Daydé's first important new role, for which Serge Lifar exploited her child-like charm and freshness as well as her brilliant technique. Her innocence might have been a bit false, and her smiles perhaps a little too forced; but her performance was stunning all the same. Other new roles followed: she excelled in *Entre deux rondes*, where she seemed to have stepped out of a Degas engraving, and in *Romeo and Juliet* in 1955, where her gifts as an actress became apparent.

In 1958 Daydé conquered the Soviet public with her performance of *Giselle* at the Bolshoi with the Paris Opéra Ballet. The press loved *Entre deux rondes* and also *Études* by Harald Lander. In 1960, after dancing the role of the Unicorn in the Jean Cocteau/Heinz Rosen ballet *La Dame à la licorne* Daydé left the Paris Opéra once and for all, and launched herself into the career of an international star, covering Europe and America in a highly successful recital tour with Michel Renault, étoile at the Opéra, in which she played on her acrobatic style a great deal and won audiences with her smiles. The escapade earned her a court case with the Opéra, which she won, moreover.

Engaged by the Marquis de Cuevas in 1961, Daydé was one of the most charming and delightful Princesses Aurora, dancing with Serge Golovine in Raymundo de Larrain's famous production of *The Sleeping Beauty* at the Théâtre Champs Elysées. When the Marquis de Cuevas's company disappeared, Liane Daydé organized her own, the Grand Ballet Classique de France, administered by her husband, the impresario Claude Giraud, and generously funded by the Ministry for Foreign Affairs. The repertoire was drawn from that of both the de Cuevas company and the Opéra (including, for example, *Entre deux rondes* by Lifar). Le Grand Ballet Classique toured abroad for several years, visiting the Philippines, Iran, and China. Rosella Hightower and Michel Renault numbered among her principals.

Another important activity was Daydé's participation in the events held on the outskirts of Paris at the end of the 1960s, known as "Le Rayonnement du Théâtre", in which she appeared along with Milorad Miskovitch and his ensemble of soloists. This project allowed small communities deprived of dance the opportunity to see first-class performers. The repertoire included *Romeo and Juliet* (the Serge Lifar/Tchaikovsky version) and *Annabel Lee* by Georges Skibine, among others. From the 1970s onwards, while continuing her career as a dancer, Liane Daydé gave herself over to teaching, a career which she has since pursued by directing the dance department of the Regional Conservatory of the City of Paris.

—Irène Lidova

---

## DE BASIL, Colonel Wassily

Russian ballet director. Born Vasily Grigorievich Voskresensky in Kaunas, 1888. Married (1) dancer Nina Leonidova; (2) dancer Olga Morosova. Served as a Cossack officer; aide-de-camp to General Bicherakov, Persian Campaign of 1916. First experience as manager, organizing small touring group (including first wife Nina Leonidova), performing at variety theatres in France, Switzerland, and Italy, early 1920s; met Georgian impresario Prince Alexis Zereteli; founded artists' agency, Paris, 1925, and became co-director, with Zereteli and Michel Kachouk, of L'Opéra Russe à Paris; founder (with René Blum), Les Ballets Russes de Monte Carlo, 1932, becoming Les Ballets Russes de Col. W. de Basil (or de Basil's Ballets Russes), 1934; sole director (after split with René Blum), Ballets Russes de Col. W. de Basil, 1935–39, becoming Original Ballet Russe, 1939–51. Died in Paris, 27 July 1951.

**PUBLICATIONS**

Haskell, Arnold, "The de Basil Ballet, 1930–35", *Dancing Times* (London), October 1935

"Secrets of the Russian Ballet", *Windsor Magazine* (London), January 1937

Haskell, Arnold, "Colonel Wassily de Basil", *Ballet Annual* (London), vol. 6, 1952

Manchester, Phyllis, "The Legacy of Ballet Russe", *Dance News Annual* (New York), 1953

Haskell, Arnold, *Ballet*, revised edition, London, 1955

Sorley Walker, Kathrine, *De Basil's Ballets Russes*, London, 1982

García-Márquez, Vicente, *Les Ballets Russes*, New York, 1990

* * *

A Cossack officer with an adventurous career during World War I, Vasily Grigorievich Voskresensky was one of the most improbable people to have had an influence on ballet. Under his simplified name of Colonel W. de Basil, however, he was a powerful force during the 1930s and 1940s, directing in a highly personal style a company whose dancers and repertoire were an important cultural influence throughout the world.

Like all career soldiers who are exiled from their countries at the end of a great war, de Basil found himself with no qualifications for civilian life. He made his way to Paris and got a job driving a van for a film studio. He was joined there by his wife and her sister, who were both theatre dancers, and they began to get work in France and Italy. De Basil borrowed money to start them in a little group of their own, added a couple of classical ballet dancers, and toured with some success through regional France. Soon, however, with exiled Georgian impresario Prince Alexis Zereteli and Ignaty Zon, who had owned a café chantant in Moscow, de Basil opened an artists' agency in Paris, and a few years later, became a director of L'Opéra Russe à Paris.

One of the company's engagements was in 1931 in Monte Carlo, where René Blum was director of ballet. Impressed by de Basil's energy and initiative, Blum discussed with him the possibility of forming a Russian ballet company at Monte Carlo, and this bore fruit later in the year, when they went into partnership to found the Ballets Russes de Monte Carlo.

This was the company that dominated the 1930s in Europe, the United States, and Australia. They engaged Diaghilev dancers and, as choreographer for the first season, George Balanchine. When Balanchine left in 1932, he was replaced by Léonide Massine, and Alexandra Danilova joined as prima ballerina. Three young dancers, however, caught most of the headlines. In the studios of the Russian emigré teachers in Paris, Balanchine had discovered the astonishing teenagers Tamara Toumanova, Irina Baronova, and Tatiana Riabouchinska—soon to become labelled in ballet history as the "baby ballerinas".

After a triumph in London in 1933 and New York in 1934, the Ballets Russes de Monte Carlo (known after a split between Blum and de Basil as the Ballets Russes du Col. W. de Basil and finally as the Original Ballet Russe) became the dominant factor in world ballet. Towards the end of the 1930s, their regular seasons in Europe and the United States (coast-to-coast tours) and their immensely successful visits to Australia were disrupted by various factors, not least by the outbreak of World War II in September 1939.

De Basil, a vigorous personality about whom controversies raged, was in no way a figurehead director. Life with him was an intensely human affair of rivalries, ambitions, camaraderie, temperamental outbursts, squabbles, and reconciliations—and never dull for a moment. He ran his company as he would have run a partisan brigade, treating them as a fighting force for the preservation and presentation of Russian ballet. This attitude was particularly noticeable during the war years in South America from 1942 to 1946, when he struggled against tremendous difficulties to keep the company together and functioning.

In many ways de Basil was misjudged. He was labelled an opportunist and to a great extent this was true, but the motive for all his actions was a sincere desire to promote Russian ballet. He was often believed to be a scheming business man interested only in making money, but in fact he had little idea of business, being quite outgunned by the shrewd impresarios with whom he had to deal, and he never made money at all. He died a poor man in Paris in 1951, but he had kept together for a surprising number of years, against desperate odds, a company that will never be forgotten, either by those who danced in it or the widely scattered audiences for whom it opened up a magic world.

—Kathrine Sorley Walker

---

## DE BEAUMONT, Comte Etienne

French ballet designer, librettist, and art patron. Born 8 March 1883. Studied Eurythmics with Paulet Thevenz, 1911. Organized Les Soirées de Paris at Théâtre de la Cigale, together with Jean Cocteau, Léonide Massine, and soloists of Diaghilev's Ballets Russes, Paris, May and June 1924; first stage designs (costumes) for Les Soirées de Paris, 1924; also commissioned designs for Massine ballets, including *Salade* (Georges Braque), 1924, *Mercure* (Pablo Picasso), 1924, and scores from Darius Milhaud and Erik Satie; designer, sponsor, and librettist, de Basil's Ballets Russes de Monte Carlo, 1933–34; sponsor of various performances, including Cocteau's *Le Boeuf sur le toit* and avant-garde films; also painter and fine artist, including as jewellery designer for Chanel. Died in Paris, 1956.

**WORKS** (Ballet design)

1924 *Le Beau Danube* (costumes; chor. Massine), Les Soirées de Paris, Paris
1933 *Scuola di Ballo* (chor. Massine), Ballets Russes de Monte Carlo, Monte Carlo
*Nocturne* (also libretto; chor. Lichine), Ballets Russes de Monte Carlo, Paris
1934 *Les Imaginaires* (also called *Les Formes*; chor. Lichine), de Basil's Ballets Russes, Paris
1938 *Gaîté Parisienne* (also libretto; chor. Massine), Ballet Russe de Monte Carlo, Monte Carlo
*Nobilissima Visione* (also called *St. Francis*; design with Tchelitchev; chor. Massine), Ballet Russe de Monte Carlo, London

**PUBLICATIONS**

Massine, Léonide, *My Life in Ballet*, London, 1968
Sorley Walker, Kathrine, *De Basil's Ballets Russes*, London, 1982
García-Márquez, Vicente, *Les Ballets Russes*, New York, 1990
Garafola, Lynn, "Les Soirées de Paris", in Keynes, Milo (ed.), *Lydia Lopokova*, London, 1983
Peters, Arthur King, *Jean Cocteau and his World*, London, 1987

* * *

Patron, designer, author of ballet libretti, and organizer of thematic costume balls, Comte Etienne de Beaumont was a passionate amateur of modern art with a particular interest in ballet. He was a wealthy and discriminating Parisian dilettante who surrounded himself with artists. Tall, slim, and elegant, this bisexual dandy was the model for the eponymous count in Raymond Radiguet's *Le Bal du Comte d'Orgel*. He sponsored a wide range of performances, including the Fratellini Brothers at the Cirque Medrano, Jean Cocteau's *Le Boeuf sur le toit* at the Comédie de Champs-Elysées, and several 1920s experimental films. He was generous when friends and artists fell on hard times: he was responsible for Erik Satie's care during his final illness, and he provided accomodation for Marie Laurencin during the Second World War. His own productions and elitist events were generally fund-raising activities for charitable organizations.

De Beaumont had a genuine interest in dance. In 1911, with his life-long friends Cocteau and Lucienne Daudet, he took classes in Eurythmics from Paulet Thevenz. He became an early and constant supporter of Diaghilev and his Ballets Russes, although briefly in 1924 he set out to rival them with his own "Soirées de Paris" at the Théâtre de la Cigale. These were a series of experimental performances (and an exhibition of works illustrating popular entertainment in circus and music hall) staged from 17 May to 30 June. Productions included Cocteau's adaptation of Shakespeare, *Roméo et Juliette*; Tristan Tzara's *Mouchoir de nuage*; light shows by Loïe Fuller (who also lit the productions); Spanish dance by Ida Rubinstein; jazz dance by Harry Wills; and ballets choreographed by Léonide Massine (temporarily estranged from Diaghilev). For these ballets de Beaumont, imitating Diaghilev's approach, commissioned new designs from George Braque (*Salade*), André Derain (*Gigue*), Marie Laurencin (*Les Roses*), and Pablo Picasso (*Mercure*), as well as new scores from Darius Milhaud, Henri Sauguet, and Erik Satie. The most interesting creation, sufficiently innovative (and upsetting to the surrealists) to create a Parisian "scandale", was Picasso's "Poses plastiques", *Mercure*. This ballet impressed Diaghilev, who acquired it for his own company in 1927. De Beaumont also sponsored the Ballets Russes' *Jack-in-the Box* (Balanchine), performed as a tribute to Satie in 1926.

During de Beaumont's Soiŕees de Paris, he reportedly turned his hand to choreography, creating, along with the dancer Rupert Doone, *Vogue*—which was so tasteless (and sexually ambiguous) that Lydia Lopokova (star of the ballets along with Stanislas Idzikovski and Massine himself) refused to appear in it. The season was criticized for being too "artistic". It was certainly a commercial failure, and de Beaumont made no concessions to popular appeal. The artists complained that he devoted more time to his charity balls than to the actual stage productions. Nevertheless, all the ballets, with the exception of *Vogue*, were revived, revised, or recreated for subsequent companies in London, Monte Carlo, and Paris.

De Beaumont never again operated on such a large scale, and after 1924 he limited his activities to sponsorship and to collaborating on specific ballets with choreographers Léonide Massine and David Lichine. In 1933, he supported the Blum/de Basil Ballets Russes de Monte Carlo as patron, librettist, and designer. (Designing décors and costumes was only one area of his personal artistic activity: he also designed costume jewellery for Chanel, painted, and created collages.) Most of his designs drew on historical sources or on the work of other artists. De Beaumont had been responsible for the costumes for *Le Beau Danube* for Les Soirées de Paris in 1924, and now in 1933 this ballet was substantially revised, becoming an immensely popular work for the Ballets Russes. Its costumes, like its settings, were derived from paintings by Constantin Guys. The year 1933 was a busy one for de Beaumont, for he also collaborated on the libretto and costumes for Massine's *Scuola di Ballo*, and for Lichine's first ballet *Nocturne* (inspired by *A Midsummer Night's Dream*). De Beaumont similarly collaborated on Lichine's second work, *Les Imaginaires* (or *Les Formes*), but most of his production work was for Massine.

The success of *Le Beau Danube*, to a score by Johann Strauss, led de Beaumont to suggest he collaborate with Massine on another lively character romp, this time to music by Offenbach. Whereas the Strauss ballet had been Massine's own idea, *Gaîté Parisienne* originated with de Beaumont, who proposed a ballet in the style of the painter Franz Xavier Winterhalter, with the suggested title of *Tortoni* (the name of a popular Second Empire café).

None of de Beaumont's other ballets had the success of his two operetta-style collaborations with Massine; and after the Second World War, although still organizing costume balls, he was a less important figure in the French dance world. It has been suggested that during the War he angled to take over the running of the Opéra.

As a personality, de Beaumont, and indeed his circle, continue to fascinate. When Ian Spink created a new production of *Mercure* for Ballet Rambert in 1986, he not only drew on the Greek mythology of the ballet's original narrative, but also mixed in references to the man (portrayed by Mark Baldwin) who commissioned the work.

—Jane Pritchard

---

**DEBUSSY, Claude**

French composer. Born in St-Germain-en-Laye, 22 August 1862. Studied with Guiraud and others at the Paris Conservatoire, 1872–84, winning Prix de Rome for composition *L'Enfant prodigue*, 1883. Married (1) Rosalie Texier, 1899; (2) amateur singer Emma Bardac, 1908: one daughter, Claude-Emma ("Chou-Chou") b. 1905. Tutor and musician in the household of Nadezhda von Meck, Tchaikovsky's patron, Russia, 1880 and 1881; resident in Rome during Prix de Rome scholarship, from 1885; returned to Paris, thereafter concentrating on composition, from 1887; first major success, concert of cantata *La Damoiselle élue*, 1893; music critic, *La Revue blanche*, *Gil Blas*, and other publications, from 1901; performed and conducted in England, Belgium, Holland, Austria, Hungary, Italy, and Russia, 1907–14; appointed to advisory board of Paris Conservatoire, 1909; initial discussions with Serge Diaghilev for a ballet *Masques et bergamasques* (not composed), 1910; ballet score, *Khamma*, commissioned by Maude Allan, 1911 (not performed until 1947); only major ballet score (also last major orchestral work), *Jeux*, 1913. Died in Paris, 25 March 1918.

**WORKS** (Ballets)

1911 *Le Martyre de Saint-Sébastien* (incidental music; text d'Annunzio, chor. Fokine), Ida Rubinstein's Company, Paris
1913 *Jeux* (chor. Nijinsky), Diaghilev's Ballets Russes, Paris
1914 *No-ja-li* (*Le Palais du silence*; scenario by G. de Feure; not performed)
1919 *La Boîte à joujoux* (chor. Hellé), Théâtre Lyrique de Vaudeville, Paris
1947 *Khamma* (chor. Etchevery), Opéra-Comique, Paris (original comission from Maude Allan, 1911)

**Other ballets using Debussy's music:** *L'Après-midi d'un faune* (Nijinsky, 1912; also Woizikovsky, Sokolova, after Nijinsky, 1931; Lifar, 1935; Robbins, 1953: see *Afternoon of a Faun*; Béjart, 1987), *Nuages* (Fuller, 1913), *Sirènes* (Fuller, 1913), *Jeux* (new version: Börlin, 1920; also Dollar, 1950; Darrell, 1963; Taras, 1966), *La Boite à joujoux* (new version: Börlin, 1921), *La Mer* (Fuller, 1925), *The Minstrel* (Littlefield, 1935), *Waltz* (Yacobson, 1938), *Protée* (Lichine, 1938), *Daylight's Dauphin* (Tetley, 1951), *Ballade* (Robbins, 1952), *Afternoon of a Faun* (Robbins, 1953), *L'Ange* (Skibine, 1953), *Night Island* (van Dantzig, 1955), *Pas et lignes* (Lifar, 1955), *Nuages et fêtes* (Lifar, 1955), *The Still Point* (Bolender, 1955), *Jeux de vagues* (Cranko, 1965), *La Damoiselle élue* (Walter, 1966), *Haiku* (Neumeier, 1966), *Wind's Bride* (Sequoio, 1967), *La Mer* (Schilling, 1968), *Baudelaire* (Béjart, 1968; mus. also Wagner, and jazz), *Brouillards* (Cranko, 1970), *Chansons de Bilitis* (Cauley, 1970), *Les Fleurs du mal* (Béjart, 1971), *Green* (Cranko, 1973), *Cathédrale engloutie* (Kylián, 1975), *Nuages* (Kylián, 1976, 1979), *La Plus que lente* (Béjart, 1977), *Claire de lune* (Béjart, 1977), *Faun* (van Schayk, 1978), *Soirée Debussy* (Petit, 1982), *Pelléas et Mélisande* (Petit, 1984), *La Mer* (Petit, 1984), *Children's Corner* (Petit, 1984), *Piano Variations V* (*Exposed*) (van Manen, 1984), *Le Martyre de Saint-Sébastien* (Béjart, 1986), *Silent Cries* (Kylián, 1986), *Debussy pour sept danseurs* (Petit, 1990), *Game* (Tuckett, 1990), *The Little Mermaid* (Slaughter, 1992).

**PUBLICATIONS**

Lockspeiser, Edward, *Debussy: His Life and Mind*, London, 2 volumes, 1962 and 1965

Lockspeiser, Edward, "The Martyrdom of St. Sebastian", *The Listener* (London), 5 May 1966
Austin, W., *Debussy: Prelude to The Afternoon of a Faun*, New York, 1970
Orledge, R., "Another Look inside Debussy's 'Toybox'", *Musical Times* (London), cxvii, 1976
Orledge, R, "Debussy's Second English Ballet: *Le Palais du silence* or *No-ja-li*", *Current Musicology* (New York), no. 22, 1976
Orledge, R., *Debussy and the Theatre*, Cambridge, 1982
Neagu, Philippe, et al., *Afternoon of a Faun: Mallarmé, Debussy, Nijinsky*, New York, 1989
Parks, Richard S., *The Music of Claude Debussy*, New Haven, 1989

* * *

Although Debussy showed little feeling for ballet as an art, he began talks on possible ballet projects in the 1890s with the writer Paul Valéry (for a ballet on an Amphion theme) and the writer Pierre Louÿs (for a *Daphnis et Chloë*, no less), but neither came to anything. In 1903, after attending a music-hall programme at London's Empire Theatre in which a ballet was included, he noted down thoughts on his "ideal" ballet conception.

This ideal ballet would have action defined only by "mysterious symbolism" inherent in the dancer or his/her body-rhythm, and "a dreamy imprecision" for scenery with changing lighting effects, not clear-cut lines. His ideas parallel the so-called impressionist musical style he developed, favouring line, colour, immediate sensations, and the expression of "waking dreams"—yet his first discussions with Diaghilev were for a *commedia dell'arte* ballet identified as *Masques et bergamasques*.

Debussy was sufficiently enthused to sketch out his own scenario, and was understandably offended when Diaghilev gave up the idea. However, the impresario used his charm to mollify the composer sufficiently to obtain approval for Nijinsky in 1912 to use the *Prélude à l'après-midi d'un faune*, composed nearly 20 years previously.

Debussy took no part in the making of a ballet that became visually notorious; it is known only that he viewed the dress-rehearsal with distaste. The sensuous flow of melody and harmony was remote from anything resembling conventional dance music at that time, but subsequent reconstructions suggest it was precisely the dichotomy between sight and sound that created a particular resonance. "Instead of the law-ordained married bondage between music and dance," explains Richard Buckle in his book *Diaghilev*, "the possibility of a freer union, a more felicitous concubinage, could now be perceived."

Incidental music for Gabriele d'Annunzio's *Le Martyre de Saint-Sébastien* (1911) was written at the instigation of Ida Rubinstein, who wanted to play the title role; the dance element was confined to music for Sebastian treading the burning coals. For the Canadian Maude Allan the same year he composed *Khamma* (though she never performed it); time pressed, and Debussy never orchestrated his work beyond the first few bars, turning the task over to Charles Koechlin. Within the opening and closing scenes of this "wretched little Anglo-Egyptian ballet", as he called it in a letter, Debussy composed characteristically fine ideas in sinuously twisting chromatic textures and abrupt fanfares. There are four dances of increasing tempo and intensity, from a measured saraband to a final dance of ecstasy; Debussy wrote that they incorporated "my latest discoveries in the chemistry of harmony".

Debussy's masterwork for dance (and his last major orchestral work) is *Jeux*, commissioned by Diaghilev for Nijinsky, whose scenario Debussy first dismissed as idiotic but later declared was "all that is needed to bring rhythm to birth in a musical atmosphere". The score is of unusual subtlety, the rhythmic metre elusive and the melodic motifs not so much developed as carried forward by a wave-like motion from one episode to the next; close analysis has identified more than twenty separate motifs during the duration of about seventeen minutes.

Of his elaborate orchestration Debussy wrote that he sought "un orchestre sans pied", an effect free of bass-register roots, with "orchestral colouring that seems to be lit up from behind". His imagination was vividly fired and he composed rapidly, seeking no help in orchestration—but the music won little admiration at the ballet's premiere and had to wait until the 1950s and 1960s for recognition as a musical masterwork.

Little more than a week before the premiere of *Jeux*, Debussy seemed not to have objected to Loie Fuller's use of *Fêtes* and *Nuages* (both from the orchestral *Nocturnes*) for one of her Paris programmes. Otherwise there was only the affectionate parody of music-box effects, folk-tunes, and some well-known quotations in the children's ballet, *La Boîte à joujoux*, to complete Debussy's contribution to ballet. Composed for piano in 1913 and only partly orchestrated when he died, this work was completed by André Caplet for production in 1919, but attracted little subsequent attention theatrically. Other concert works have stimulated later choreography, but of little lasting distinction.

—Noël Goodwin

---

**DE CUEVAS, Marquis George**

Chilean/American ballet director and patron of the arts. Born eighth Marquis de Piedrablanca de Guana de Cuevas in Santiago de Chile, 26 May 1885. Married Margaret Strong-Rockefeller. Sponsor of Masterpieces of Art exhibition at New York World's Fair, 1939–40; founder and director of Ballet Institute, 1943, and Ballet International, first performing in 1944; director (and chief financial backer), Nouveau Ballet de Monte Carlo (originally founded 1942), from 1947, renaming company the Grand Ballet de Monte Carlo, 1947–51, becoming Grand Ballet (also International Ballet) du Marquis de Cuevas, 1951–62; engaged Bronislava Nijinska as ballet mistress, 1947, and brought many American dancers to Europe, including Rosella Hightower, Marjorie Tallchief, and William Dollar; took company on numerous world tours, 1947–60, with company continuing briefly under nephew Raymundo de Larrain after the Marquis's death, 1961–62. Died in Cannes, 22 February 1961.

**PUBLICATIONS**

By de Cuevas:

"Why I am in Ballet, and what my Dancers say of my Being There", *Ballet Today* (London), March 1954

About de Cuevas:

Daguerre, P., *Le Marquis de Cuevas*, Paris, 1954
Aronin, Isobel, Joy, "The Marquis is a Showman", *Dance Magazine* (New York), May 1955

**Marquis Georges de Cuevas**

Tassart, Maurice, "Le Marquis: George de Cuevas", *Ballet Annual* (London), vol. 16, 1962
Lidova, Irène, "Hommage au Marquis de Cuevas", *Les Saisons de la danse* (Paris), January 1975

* * *

It has become usual to consider the Marquis de Cuevas as the last patron of ballet in our time, although this designation is inaccurate. The Marquis George de Cuevas was passionately fond of ballet; he was an aesthete who found in ballet a means to satisfy his thirst for beauty. He was married to Margaret Strong-Rockefeller (grand-daughter of John) and, thanks to her fortune, was able to maintain a magnificent company and to engage the very best dancers for more than ten years.

Although Chilean by birth, the Marquis de Cuevas was a true Parisian. His heart was in Paris and it was there that he based his company. Extravagant, capricious, and distinguished by aristocratic elegance, the Marquis became a newsworthy and popular figure in France. He lived in a magnificent flat on the quai Voltaire acquired from his friend, the actress Cécile Sorel. He used to receive his visitors—collaborators, dancers, hangers-on—lying on his bed, while beside him his "right-hand man" (nicknamed Orpheus) sorted through his visitors and got rid of the most insistent ones. He used to make spectacular entrances at the theatre swathed in a huge midnight-blue cape and surrounded by all his staff. His ear-splitting bravos would drown the sound of the orchestra. At the slightest opportunity he applauded his favourite dancer, Rosella Hightower, his "spiritual daughter" as he called her, whose virtuoso performances of the Black Swan entranced him.

The Marquis was loved by the public. He was very extrovert and was just as happy to kiss strangers as his friends. The Americans nicknamed him the "kissing Marquis". He would not stand for any competition and considered his company to be unique. He did not have a real sense of theatre and was easily persuaded, often by those who were incompetent, to create works with no future.

He only liked classical ballet and could recognize a good dancer. His ballet company included dancers of all nationalities. Thanks to the Marquis, French towns in the provinces were able to see excellent performances of the ballet classics. The company had long seasons in Cannes and Deauville at the invitation of M. André, director of the casinos there, and the company also danced two or three times a year in Paris. The Marquis always went on tour with the company. His presence was indispensable and no one was allowed to make a decision without first asking his advice. He was irascible, capricious, and easily upset. He adored popularity and glory. His much-publicized duel with Serge Lifar caused a lot of ink to flow, and his "Ball of the Century" in 1953, held near Biarritz, was an international event, giving rise to more than 5,000 articles in the world press. The Marquis appeared dressed as the Sun King, sceptre in hand, while his corps de ballet danced the second act of *Swan Lake* on a raft moored in the middle of a small lake.

The Marquis's last and most splendid offering to the Parisian public was a stupendous production of *The Sleeping Beauty*. The production was in the hands of his nephew by marriage, Raymundo de Larrain, who also designed the sets and costumes. The choreography was begun by Bronislava Nijinska, but she refused to complete it following a disagreement with de Larrain. Robert Helpmann completed the third act, and it was in this production that Rudolf Nureyev made his first appearance in the West. The Marquis was at this time very ill and attended the first night in a wheelchair. The company which had been home to so many well-known dancers collapsed in June 1962, little more than a year after the Marquis's death in 1961.

—Irène Lidova

---

## DELIBES, Léo

French composer. Born Clément Philibert Delibes in Saint-Germain du Val, 21 February 1836. Studied music at the Paris Conservatoire: studied voice training from 1848; studied piano, organ, harmony, and advanced composition, pupil of Adolphe Adam, among others. Married Léontine Estelle Denain, 1871. Accompanist, Théâtre-Lyrique, and organist, St. Pierre de Chaillot, from 1865; first stage work, *Deux sous de charbon* (light operetta) performed at Folies Nouvelles, 1856, followed by many other compositions in this genre; chorus master, Paris Opéra, 1864–71; first ballet composition, collaborating with Minkus, *La Source*, 1866; first complete ballet score, *Coppélia*, 1870; professor of composition, Paris Conservatoire, from 1881. Died in Paris, 16 January 1891.

**WORKS** (Ballets)

1866 *La Source; ou, Naïla* (with Minkus; chor. Saint-Léon), Opéra, Paris
1867 *Valse; ou, Pas des fleurs* (added to Adam's *Le Corsaire*; chor. Mazilier), Opéra, Paris
1870 *Coppélia; ou, La Fille aux yeux d'émail* (chor. Saint-Léon), Opéra, Paris

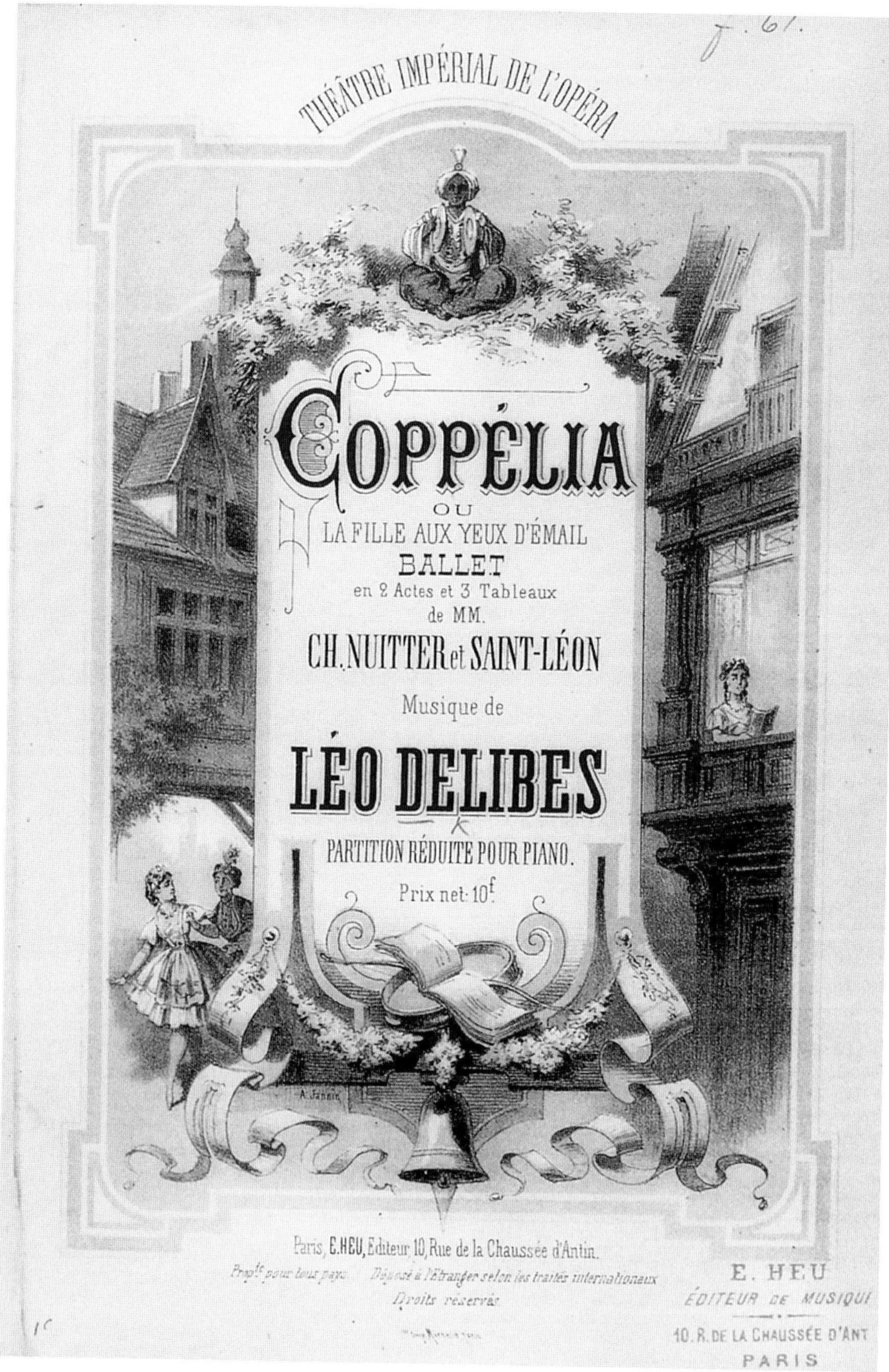


**A title-page from a piano score of *Coppélia*, by Léo Delibes, 1870**

1876 *Sylvia; ou, La Nymphe de Diane* (chor. Mérante), Opéra, Paris

**Other ballets using Delibes' music:** *Coppélia* (new production; Petipa, Cecchetti after Saint-Léon, 1884; also Glasemann and Beck, 1896; Genée, 1896; Sergeyev, 1933; Parlic, 1948; Georgi, 1952; Cranko, 1962; Descombey, 1966; Danilova and Balanchine, 1974; Petit, 1975, van Praagh, 1979), *Sylvia* (Farren, 1911; Staats, after Mérante, 1919; Lifar, 1941; Ashton, 1952; Seregi, 1972, Glasstone, 1981), *Soir de fête* (Staats, 1925), *Sylvia Pas de deux* (Balanchine, 1950), *La Source Pas de deux* (Cranko, 1964), *Pas de deux and Divertissement* (Balanchine, 1965), *La Source* (Balanchine, 1968), *Delibes Divertissement* (Martins, 1982).

## PUBLICATIONS


Hanslick, E., "Ballette von Léon Delibes", *Musikalische Stationen* (Berlin), 1885

Curzon, Henri de, *Léo Delibes*, Paris, 1926

Coquis, André, *Léo Delibes: sa vie et son oeuvre*, Paris, 1957

Fiske, Robert, *Ballet Music*, London, 1958

Guest, Ivor, *Two Coppélias*, London, 1970

Goldner, Nancy, *Coppélia*, New York, 1974

Guest, Ivor, *The Ballet of the Second Empire*, London, 1974

Studwell, William E., *Tchaikovsky, Delibes, Stravinsky: Four Essays on Three Masters*, Chicago, 1977

Dunn, Thomas, "Delibes and *La Source*: Some Manuscripts and Documents", *Dance Chronicle* (New York), vol. 4, no. 1, 1981

Studwell, William E., *Adolphe Adam and Léo Delibes: A Guide to Research*, New York, 1987


* * *

Léo Delibes was a composition student under Adolphe Adam at the Paris Conservatoire, and was increasingly drawn to the theatre while working as accompanist, piano teacher, and organist. Like Adam, he began with light operas and vaudevilles composed at the rate of about one a year, starting from the age of twenty, and going on for the next fifteen years. He became chorus-master at the Théâtre-Lyrique and, from 1864, took on the same post at the Opéra. A ceremonial cantata for Napoleon III was well liked, and led to an invitation to share with Minkus the composition of the music for Arthur Saint-Léon's *La Source* (1866).

Of the ballet's three acts Delibes composed the whole of the second, and the first scene of the third act; and after it was performed, he was considered to have done the better job. His divertissement, with its Andante horn solo and Danse circassienne finale, became part of the concert repertory; the Pas d'action anticipates the Chant bacchique in his later *Sylvia*; the Mazurka is exhilarating, and the scenes of ceremonial splendour and romantic apparition have appealing illustrative character.

In 1867, Delibes wrote a Pas des fleurs, mostly in waltz rhythm, to add to Adam's music when Mazilier's *Le Corsaire* was revived (and this music forms part of the surviving production by Russia's Kirov/St. Petersburg Ballet). The further favourable impression it made led to the sole commission for *Coppélia* (1870). Then in his early thirties, Delibes was very much the junior partner to Saint-Léon and Nuitter; but it is principally his music that has kept this ballet, in its many later adaptations, a mainstay of the international repertory.

Musically, *Coppélia* begins almost where *Giselle* left off, in a similar structure of short numbers arranged for colour and contrast, and extending the previous tentative experiments with leitmotif, themes that directly express and identify mood and/or character. Swanilda, Franz, and Dr. Coppélius are each presented through their themes (two in the case of Franz, these taking cognisance of the fact that the role was first danced by a woman *en travesti*), rather than just accompanied by them.

The widespread European trend, at that time, towards various kinds of musical nationalism finds expression in *Coppélia* in exuberant corps de ballet dances (Mazurka and Czardas, the latter for the first time in a theatre score), and a Slav "Thème varié" for Swanilda and friends, all in the first act. The final divertissement, Fête de la cloche, is often regrettably shortened instead of allowed to illustrate, as the music does in the six numbers that follow the Waltz of the Hours, the main uses for the village's newly presented bell.

Delibes was in a sense the first "impressionist" composer, in that he followed similar principles to those of the leading contemporary pictorial artists in making the different uses of colour the most important element in his composition. He also had the invaluable gift of combining an equal facility for illustrating detail, expressing emotional mood, and stimulating the sense of movement in a way that was more effective in ballet than in his operas.

He surpassed this achievement in *Coppélia* only with his one later and superior ballet score, *Sylvia* (for Louis Mérante in 1876). Here the technique of scene-painting is extended to what is virtually a descriptive tone-poem, again with some use of leading themes. Curiously, Sylvia herself is not separately identified in music, but the exultant, leaping theme of Diana's huntresses in general dominates the music, while the shepherd-lover Aminta is associated with a solo flute, and the evil Orion with a menacing horn.

No full orchestral score of *Sylvia* was published, but a piano score includes a number of stage directions and instrumentations, of which the alto saxophone in the Act III Barcarolle was then rare, and its effect is still haunting. The Intermezzo and Valse lente in the first act and the Pizzicato for strings that opens the divertissement in the third act became favourites in light music concerts; but it is Delibes' instinct for colour and movement overall which can make this score so exhilarating to hear in the theatre, and it is regrettable that opportunities to do so are few.

—Noël Goodwin

---

## DE MARÉ, Rolf

Swedish impresario and patron of the arts and ballet. Born in Stockholm, 9 May 1888. Educated privately. Developed strong interest in folk art, music, and dance, travelling in Europe, Asia, and Africa to build up collection of primitive art; went to Paris: sponsored performances by Swedish dancer and choreographer Jean Börlin, becoming founder and director, Les Ballets Suédois, Paris, 1920–25; produced, with Börlin as choreographer, numerous ballets bringing together leading artists and musicians of the day, including Jean Cocteau, the composers "Les Six", and artists Bonnard, de Chirico, Léger, and Picabia, among others; director, Théâtre des Champs-Elysées, Paris, 1924–27; founder, with Dr. Pierre Tugal, Les Archives internationales de la danse, Paris, 1931–50, and organizer of affiliated international choreographic competitions, 1932, 1945, 1947; attended many international conferences on ballet in Europe, 1935–36, and in the United States,

**Rolf de Maré, c.1939**

1937; made a cinematic record of dance in the Far East, 1938. Died in Barcelona, 28 April 1964.

## PUBLICATIONS

*Les Ballets Suédois dans l'art contemporain*, Paris, 1931

Banes, Sally, "An Introduction to the Ballets Suédois", *Ballet Review* (New York), vol. 7, nos. 2–3, 1978–79

Garafola, Lynn, *Diaghilev's Ballets Russes*, New York, 1989

Häger, Bengt, *Les Ballets Suédois*, Paris, 1989; translated by Ruth Sharman, London, 1990

* * *

Rolf de Maré was a wealthy dance aficionado whose ambition was to become "the Serge Diaghilev of Sweden". Perhaps at the urging of his friends Vera and Mikhail Fokine, de Maré set out to combine his interests in dance and Swedish folk art to create a ballet company presenting works based on traditional Swedish themes. He aimed to have the great artists of Europe translate Swedish folklore into modern theatre in the same way that Diaghilev, the impresario of the Ballets Russes, had translated Russian culture into a new style of dance. Ultimately, however, de Maré's Ballets Suédois made a name for itself with ballets which were not Swedish in origin.

De Mare hired Jean Börlin, a Swede who had studied with Fokine at the Stockholm Royal Opera and in Copenhagen, as the company's choreographer. Börlin, in turn, hired several dancers away from the Stockholm Royal Opera, but they represented the extent of Swedish contributors to the Ballets Suédois. The company was based in Paris, and French librettists, composers, and painters contributed the scenarios, music, and sets for most Ballets Suédois productions, prompting one American critic to describe the company as "more French than Swedish".

With its first Paris season in 1920, the Ballets Suédois established itself as the artistic successor to Diagilev's declining Ballets Russes. The Ballets Suédois presented ballets derivative of work by its Russian forebear as well as original ballets on themes of Swedish folklore, but the company made its mark with avant-garde works that reflected such current movements in art as Dadaism and Surrealism. A number of contemporary artists became interested in working in ballet because of the Ballets Suédois. Jean Cocteau, Erik Satie, and Francis Picabia were among those who contributed to the company's repertoire. The Ballets Suédois disbanded in 1925 after its last and most innovative production, *Relâche*.

Six years later, Rolf de Maré established the Archives internationales de la danse, in memory of the Ballets Suédois and its choreographer Börlin, in June 1931. The archives housed a vast library of books, magazines, and souvenir programmes dealing with dance history and hosted lectures, demonstrations, and exhibitions until it closed in 1950. The Archives internationales de la danse also published a magazine from 1932 to 1936, and sponsored an international choreography competition (of which Kurt Jooss was the first winner, in 1932, with *The Green Table*). After 1950, most of de Maré's vast collection was given to the Paris Musée de l'Opéra and the Stockholm Dansmuseet.

Although Rolf de Maré may not have had the influence or creative initiative of Serge Diaghilev, he was able to create a company that took off where the Ballets Russes had started. His company elevated ballet to the level of contemporary movements in art and music, and de Maré himself contributed to the study of dance history with the establishment of an important dance archive.

—Claudia B. Stone

---

## DE MILLE, Agnes

American dancer and choreographer. Born in New York City, niece of filmmaker Cecil B. de Mille, 18 September 1905 (some sources say 1908 or 1909). Educated at University of California at Los Angeles (B.A. in English); studied dance at Theodore Koslov School of Imperial Russian Ballet, Los Angeles, from age 13, and with Marie Rambert, London, from 1932; also studied with Antony Tudor, Lydia Sokolova, Carmelita Moracci, Edward Caton, and Nina Stroganova. Married Walter F. Prude, 1943: one son, Jonathan. Toured United States and Europe as a solo dancer/choreographer, from 1928; first professional choreography, staging dances for Morley's *The Black Crook*, 1929; left the United States for Europe, 1932: toured Europe, with solo concerts in Paris, Brussels, and London; dancer and choreographer, Ballet Club (becoming Ballet Rambert), London, from 1932, Tudor's Dance Theatre (later becoming London Ballet), 1937–38; returned to the United States: resident choreographer, Ballet Theatre (later American Ballet Theatre), New York, from 1938; dancer and choreographer, Ballet Russe de Monte Carlo, 1942, Jooss Ballet, 1942; director and choreographer, Agnes de Mille Dance Theatre, touring 1953–54; guest choreographer, staging ballets for companies including Royal Winnipeg Ballet, Boston Ballet, and Harkness Ballet; choreographer for musicals, with first major Broadway success in *Oklahoma!*, 1943; continued as leading Broadway choreographer through 1960s, often working as director, including for Cole Porter's *Out of this World* (1950), and *Come Summer* (1971); also choreographer for film and television, including dance sequences in films *Romeo and Juliet* (dir. Cukor, 1936), and *London Town* (dir. Ruggles, 1945); narrator for Joffrey Ballet's lecture-demonstration *Conversations about the Dance*, broadcast by Public Broadcasting Service (PBS), 1980; Chairman of the National Council on the Arts Dance Panel, from 1965; first President of the Society of Stage Directors and Choreographers, incorporated 1965; founder, Heritage Dance Theatre, based at the North Carolina School of the Arts, 1953. Recipient: Donaldson Award, 1943, 1944, 1945, 1947; Woman of the Year Award, American Newspaper Women's Guild, 1946; Antoinette Perry Award, 1947; honorary doctorates from Mills College, 1952, Smith College, 1954, Hood College, 1959, and Northwestern University, 1960; Alumni Medal, University of California, 1953; *Dance Magazine* Award, 1957; Spirit of Achievement Award, Albert Einstein College of Medicine, Yeshiva University, 1958; Capezio Dance Award, 1966; Handel Medallion, New York City, 1976; Kennedy Center Achievement Award, 1980; Elizabeth Blackwell Award, 1982.

### ROLES

1937 Fourth Song (cr) in *Dark Elegies* (Tudor), Ballet Rambert, London
An Aristocrat (cr) in *Gallant Assembly* (Tudor), Ballet Rambert, London
1938 Principal dancer (cr) in *Seven Intimate Dances* (also chor., with Tudor), Westminster Theatre, London
Venus (cr) in *The Judgment of Paris* (Tudor), London Ballet, London
1941 The Priggish Virgin (cr) in *Three Virgins and a Devil* (new production; also chor.), Ballet Theatre, New York
1942 Cowgirl (cr) in *Rodeo* (mus. Copland), Ballet Russe de Monte Carlo, New York

**Other roles include:** solo dances (also chor.) performed at recitals from 1928—'49 (mus. traditional), *Stagefright, Ballet Class, May Day, Harvest Reel, Ouled Naïl, Witch Dance, Dance of Death, Hymn, Mountain White, Tryout, Elizabethan Suite, Gala Farewell, Striptease.*

### WORKS

1934 *Three Virgins and a Devil* (mus. Resphigi), in *Why Not Tonight?* (revue; mus. Hyden), Palace Theatre, London
1938 *Seven Intimate Dances* (with Tudor; mus. various), Westminster Theatre, London
1940 *Black Ritual* (mus. Milhaud), Ballet Theatre, New York
1941 *Drums Sound in Hackensack* (mus. Cohen), Jooss Ballet, New York
*Three Virgins and a Devil* (new production; mus. Resphigi), Ballet Theatre, New York
1942 *Rodeo* (mus. Copland), Ballet Russe de Monte Carlo, New York (staged Ballet Theatre, 1950)
1944 *Tally Ho; or, The Frail Quarry* (mus. Gluck, arranged Nordoff), Ballet Theatre, Los Angeles
1948 *Fall River Legend* (mus. Gould), Ballet Theatre, New York
1952 *The Harvest According* (mus. Thomson), Ballet Theatre, New York
1956 *Rib of Eve* (mus. Gould), Ballet Theatre, New York
1962 *The Bitter Weird* (suite of Scottish dances; mus. Loewe, songs from *Brigadoon*), Royal Winnipeg Ballet, Canada
1965 *The Wind in the Mountains* (mus. Rosenthal after American traditional songs), American Ballet Theatre, New York
*The Four Marys* (mus. Rittman), American Ballet Theatre, New York
*The Rehearsal* (mus. Gould), Royal Winnipeg Ballet, New York
1970 *A Rose for Miss Emily* (mus. Hovhaness), American Ballet Theatre, New York
1975 *Summer* (mus. Schubert), Boston Ballet, Boston
*Inconsequentials* (mus. Schubert), Richmond Ballet, Richmond
1976 *Texas Fourth* (mus. traditional, with songs by Schmidt, arranged Baker), American Ballet Theatre, New York

**Agnes de Mille, c.1930**

1978 *A Bridegroom Called Death* (new version of *Summer*; mus. Schubert), Joffrey Ballet, New York
1988 *The Informer* (mus. Celtic, arranged Rittman and others; orchestrated Brohn), American Ballet Theatre, Los Angeles

**Other works include:** for Heritage Dance Theatre—*Dances of Elegance* (mus. Arlen, Waldteufel, Strauss, Taylor), *Hell on Wheels* (mus. popular, arranged Rittman), *Conversations Pleasant and Unpleasant* (mus. Scarlatti, Handel, arranged Rittman), *Legends* (mus. popular, arranged Rittman, Kleiner), *Dances from the Golden Era* (mus. Délibes, Strauss, Meyerbeer), *Golden Age* (mus. Pitot, after Rossini); for television—*Gold Rush* (based on dances from *Paint Your Wagon*; CBS television, 1958), *Cherry Tree Carol* (NBC television, 1959); for film—dances in *Romeo and Juliet* (film after play by Shakespeare; dir. Cukor, 1937); for dramatic stage, Broadway, and revue—dances in *The Black Crook* (melodrama by J. and H. Paulton; 1929), *Nymph Errant* (musical by Cole Porter; London, 1932), mime and movement sequences in *Hamlet* (play by Shakespeare; dir. Leslie Howard, 1936), dances in *Hooray for What!* (musical; lib. Harburg, Lindsay, and Crouse, mus. Harburg and Arlen, 1937), *Swingin' the Dream* (musical; lib. after Shakespeare, mus. van Heusen, 1939), *Oklahoma!* (musical; lib. Hammerstein, mus. Rodgers, 1943), *One Touch of Venus* (musical; lib. Perelman and Nash, mus. Weill, 1943), *Bloomer Girl* (musical; lib. Herzig and Saidy, mus. Arlen; 1944), *Carousel* (musical; lib. Hammerstein, mus. Rodgers, 1945), *Brigadoon* (musical; lib. Lerner, mus. Loewe, 1947), *Allegro* (musical; lib. Hammerstein, mus. Rodgers, 1947), *Gentlemen Prefer Blondes* (musical after play by Loos; lib. Field, mus. Steyne, 1949), *Paint Your Wagon* (musical; lib. Lerner, mus. Loewe, 1951), *The Girl in Pink Tights* (musical; mus. Romberg, 1954), *Goldilocks* (musical; lib. Kerr, mus. Anderson, 1958), *Juno* (musical after O'Casey's *Juno and the Paycock*; lib. Stein, mus. Blitzstein, 1959), *Kwamina* (musical; lib. Arthur, mus. Adler, 1961), *110 in the Shade* (musical after Nash's *The Rainmaker*; lib. Jones, mus. Schmidt, 1963).

## PUBLICATIONS

By de Mille:

*Dance to the Piper* (autobiography), London, 1951; Boston, 1952
*And Promenade Home* (autobiography), Boston, 1956
*To a Young Dancer*, Boston, 1962
*The Book of the Dance*, New York, 1963

*Lizzie Borden: A Dance of Death*, Boston, 1968
Contributor to Terry, Walter, *The Dance in America*, New York, 1968
*Russian Journals*, Dance Perspectives Foundation, New York, 1970
*Speak to Me, Dance With Me* (autobiography), Boston, 1973
*Where the Wings Grow* (autobiography), New York, 1977
*America Dances*, New York, 1981
Interview in *Ballet News* (New York), September 1983
*Portrait Gallery: Artists, Impresarios, Intimates*, Boston, 1990
*Martha: The Life and Work of Martha Graham*, New York, 1991

About de Mille:
"New Ballerina", *Theatre Arts Monthly* (New York), May 1931
Denby, Edwin, *Looking at the Dance*, New York, 1949
Amberg, George, *Ballet in America*, New York, 1949
Maynard, Olga, *The American Ballet*, Philadelphia, 1959
Denby, Edwin, *Dancers, Buildings and People in the Street*, New York, 1965
Gale, Joseph, "Spirit of '76: The Agnes de Mille Heritage Dance Theatre", *Dance Magazine* (New York), June 1974
Payne, Charles, *American Ballet Theatre*, New York, 1978
Gruen, John, "Dance Vision", *Dance Magazine* (New York), February 1981

* * *

Agnes de Mille is a true original. In a career that encompassed several disciplines, she was the first to integrate the dances of musical comedy into the actual plot of the show (with *Oklahoma!* in 1943), changing the nature of musical theatre for all time. Prior to *Oklahoma!* and de Mille's later theatrical successes, show dances were extraneous to story lines. They constituted a diversion, and had their origins in the operas of earlier centuries, when dances were simply dropped in the midst of a work so that there might be something for everyone. In such contemporary shows as *Oklahoma!*, *Carousel*, *Brigadoon*, and *Paint Your Wagon*, de Mille's choreography not only entertained audiences, but advanced the action and enhanced emotion. The dance sequences were ethnically authentic, dealing with the not-so-common man in a manner that rang with truth, affection, and understanding.

This same principle applies to de Mille's work in ballet. De Mille was essentially a woman of the theatre, and theatricalism is a quality which pervades her ballets. She followed in the path of Antony Tudor, the great English choreographer whose works she performed in London in the 1930s, and whose ground-breaking achievements in dramatic dance undoubtedly influenced her own choreographic development. But where Tudor often explored the darkest depths of the human psyche, bringing dance into the realms of death, tragedy, and tortuous human passions, de Mille early on had a knack for gentle humour, protraying human emotion with what might be termed a lighter, more poignant touch.

Her greatest ballet success was *Rodeo* for the Ballet Russe de Monte Carlo in 1942, and it established the genre of what Edwin Denby was to call "the American local-color ballet", derived, as he put it, "from pantomime, and novel character-dance elements". (Eugene Loring's *Billy the Kid* came first, but as Denby explained, "What in *Billy* is local color in *Rodeo* is the main subject.") *Rodeo* continues to delight audiences to this day with its so-called local flavor, but more important is the fact that it tells a story and establishes character *through* dance, expanding the movement vocabulary of both dance and mime by using a sort of hybrid of both. (It must also be remarked that much of the ballet's original success came from de Mille's own performance of the central character, the Cowgirl; Denby put it simply: "Miss de Mille herself is wonderfully real on the stage; she is a great actress-dancer.")

De Mille was also to explore darker themes, most famously in *Fall River Legend*, the 1948 ballet which is based on the true story of Lizzie Borden, a nineteenth-century spinster accused of killing her stepmother with an axe. Here, in collaboration with the designer Oliver Smith, whose Americana set showed a domestic frame house and gallows combined in one structure, de Mille demonstrated her ability to build a work on sheer atmosphere, developing by apparently simple means an air of tension, oppression, and foreboding. A work which still remains in the active repertoire of American Ballet Theatre (for which it was created), *Fall River Legend* is unashamed melodrama, perhaps a bit dated now, but giving us yet another example of de Mille's powerful and instinctive sense of theatre.

De Mille has always sought to advance and promote American heritage in dance. These words constitute, in fact, the identity of her first dance company in 1953—the Heritage Dance Theatre. In a very real sense the pride and glorification of what she once called "The Intrinsic American" informs almost every choreographic highway along her journey. She is fundamentally a story-teller, one of the best her country has ever produced in dance. Nearly all of her works reflect permutations of the American ideal within a dramatic framework, from the wide-open spaces to smoke-filled night clubs. It is her background, her style, and her primary contribution.

De Mille's own words express it well:

> What a heritage is left us! How rich! How varied! How original and expressive! From the English derivatives, longways, round and squared, ambled or raced; through the clogs; to the whole remarkable literature of Black tap and jazz which is absolutely indigenous; the later urban forms of tap; Black bottom, jitterbug, rock (let us not despise these—nobody else does); the marvelously inventive theater forms—minstrel show, vaudeville, night club and Broadway musical (which foreigners consider our most creative theater), all ours, all irresistible; and beyond these the ethnic forms, and behind all, the great untapped source of American Indian magic waiting for its proper translator.

Still, Americana is not de Mille's only subject, as the wide range and variety of her work shows. Her innate ability is to take the traditional movements and dances of any culture—be it the society of eighteenth-century France in *Tally-ho* or the villages of Scotland in the musical *Brigadoon*—and show its direct connection to the heartbeat of the community. In *The Informer*, her setting is Ireland. The story is that of many informers during the period in Ireland known as "The Troubles", roughly from 1919 to 1921. The action is stark—doom is foretold from the opening curtain. The point, however, is that *The Informer* is constructed out of passion and conviction, as if the choreographer herself had been present in Dublin's drab back streets; mood, action, and choreography are informed by truth. Even the step-dancing has a power and a relevance: undoubtedly, careful research was carried out in order to establish accurate forms of folk movement; but the shape and remembrance of it have an authenticity and emotional truth drawn from de Mille's own knowledge of the role that folk dance plays in expressing the most fundamental of human feelings.

A woman of sharp wit and pronounced judgements, de Mille is also an accomplished author. She began writing books in 1952, and by 1990 had thirteen to her credit, all informed by her rare brand of intellect and filled with the epigrams which she delivers with an air of authority. She has unusually clear sight—one might say second-sight—in taking everyone's measure, including her own, and she is seldom chary of expressing her views.

Beginning with *Dance to the Piper*, most of de Mille's books are autobiographical. Their language is lyrical to the point of poetry, rising occasionally to inspiration comparable to the wildest flights of music. Her descriptions of the contemporary dance scene around her are also valuable histories of important eras in English and American dance.

Posterity may remember de Mille best as a trail-blazer, the choreographer who dared, who introduced real ballet into the musical theatre, and who introduced real theatre into the ballet. De Mille made it possible, or at least easier, for Jerome Robbins, Michael Kidd, Jack Cole, Bob Fosse, Michael Bennett, Tommy Tune, and others who formed an entire generation of great show choreographers, to expand the boundaries of dance and to build up on the foundation she laid.

—Joseph Gale
with Virginia Christian

## LES DEMOISELLES DE LA NUIT

**Choreography:** Roland Petit
**Music:** Jean Françaix
**Design:** Léonor Fini (scenery and costumes)
**Libretto:** Jean Anouilh
**First Production:** Les Ballets de Paris, Théâtre Marigny, Paris, 21 May 1948
**Principal Dancers:** Margot Fonteyn (Agathe), Roland Petit (Young Man), Gordon Hamilton (Baron de Grotius)

**Other productions include:** American Ballet Theatre, with Colette Marchand, John Kriza, Eric Braun; New York, 13 April 1951.

### PUBLICATIONS

"Roland Petit's Ballets de Paris", *Ballet* (London), June 1948
Beaumont, Cyril, *Ballets of Today*, London, 1954
Balanchine, George, with Mason, Francis, *Balanchine's Complete Stories of the Great Ballets*, Garden City, N.Y., 1977
Mannoni, Gérard, *Roland Petit, un chorégraphe et ses peintres*, Paris, 1990

* * *

*Les Demoiselles de la nuit* is a ballet about a cat transformed into a woman who is unable to restrain her natural impulses and eventually returns to the world of cats. Complete with a divertissement in the first scene, the detailed libretto reads like a scenario from the Romantic period (Fanny Elssler performed a solo on a very similar theme). However, the realization of the Petit ballet is very much of the twentieth century. It is constructed around two main characters, a musician and the cat/woman Agathe, and explores the ambivalent nature of Agathe, who is attracted romantically to the musician but is unable to resist both her feline instincts to attack small animals and the more basic sexual attractions represented by the tom-cat Baron, to whom she returns after a tender night with the musician. The final scene is set on the rooftops of Paris where, rather romantically, both the musician and Agathe plunge to their deaths in the street, watched by the cats.

**Eric Braun and Mary Ellen Moylan in *Les Demoiselles de la nuit*, Les Ballets de Paris**

Petit is, of course, exploring a very masculine view of femininity in the role of Agathe, portraying both the captivating and the cruel, inconstant sides of her nature. He managed, however, to avoid sentimentality and created an atmosphere of mystery and fantasy that forms a lasting memory of the ballet for many of its viewers. The central scene, a lyrical pas de deux, is one of his most admired pieces of choreography, and one that has all the emotional sexual charge with which he is associated.

Apart from the musician, who—other than his passions—appears to have little individuality or personality, the remainder of the cast are cats who provide the mystery and the fantastical element which are such vital ingredients in this ballet. The cats are given sufficient human personality to confuse the musician, and their personalities have that hint of sexual menace that is very typical of Petit's choreography, notably in the Baron (who is perhaps Agathe's true husband) and the Governess (who suggests protection and restraint). The cats and their guests also provide the opportunity for the fantastic divertissement in the first scene.

The chief significance of the ballet was the part it played in the development of Fonteyn as a ballerina; not only did it mark the beginning of her international reputation but it was generally felt, on her return to the Royal Opera House, that she had finally acquired the allure and glamour of a truly great ballerina. She obviously relished the opportunity to play an attractive, sexy role, but it was the whole chic ambience of the Ballets de Paris that enabled her to acquire that final degree of glamour. She seems to have adapted to the atmosphere of the company extremely well and it developed some of the gritty qualities that underlay her growing artistry. There are stories of a very Gallic response to a difficult head-dress—in a situation where temperamental display was probably the only effective response—but she also displayed a typically British calm when the elaborately constructed set for the last scene collapsed at the first performance.

*Les Demoiselles de la nuit*, although briefly produced by American Ballet Theatre, where the role of Agathe was danced by Colette Marchand, has not survived in the repertory. It was a ballet of atmosphere, greatly enhanced by Léonor Fini's sets, costumes, and cat masks, and the music of Jean Françaix. Its success was the result of the sum of its parts—a true collaboration between choreographer, designer, composer, and dancers—but ballets reliant on atmosphere rarely survive for a long time in the theatre.

—Peter Bassett

---

**DENARD, Michaël**

French dancer and ballet director. Born in Dresden, 5 November 1944. Studied at Conservatoire de Tarbes, and with Solange Golovine, Serge Peretti, and Jean-Pierre Franchetti, Paris. Dancer, corps de ballet, Capitole de Toulouse, 1963, Opéra de Nancy, 1964, and Lorca Massine's Ballets Européens, Paris, 1965; dancer, becoming soloist, Pierre Lacotte's Jeunesses Musicales de France (J.M.F), 1966; also dancer with various other companies, including those of Golovine and Dirk Sanders; surnumeraire, Paris Opéra Ballet, from 1966; coryphée from 1967; sujet from 1968; premier danseur from 1969; étoile from 1971, also performing frequently with the affiliated Groupe de Recherche Chorégraphique de l'Opéra de Paris (GRCOP), from 1981; retired from Opéra in 1989; international guest artist, including for American Ballet Theatre, Ballet du XXe Siècle, Bolshoi Ballet, Ballet de Marseille, Teatro Colón in Buenos Aires, Budapest Opera, and Théâtre du Silence; ballet director, State Opera, Berlin, from 1992; has also made frequent appearances on French television, including in *Portrait d'une étoile* (1973), and as Louis Mérante in video *The Ballerinas* (1985); also singer and actor, recording songs by Michel Mallory, and appearing in first acting role, 1980; jury member, Third Paris International Dance Competition, 1989. Recipient: Prix Nijinsky, 1971; Chevalier, Legion d'honneur, 1990.

**ROLES**

1965 Principal dancer in *Just Feelings* (Lorca Massine), Ballets Européens de Lorca Massine, Paris
Principal dancer in *Focus* (Lorca Massine), Ballets Européens de Lorca Massine, Paris
1966 Romeo in *Romeo and Juliet*, Ballet Jeunesses Musicales de France (J.M.F.), Paris
Principal dancer in *Bifurcation* (Lacotte), Ballet J.M.F., Paris
Oberon in *Songe d'une nuit d'eté* (Lacotte), Ballet J.M.F., Paris
Principal dancer in *Bacchianas* (J. Sanders), Ballet J.M.F., Paris
Title role in *Hamlet* (Lacotte), Ballet J.M.F., Paris
1967 Tancredi (cr) in *Combat* (Lacotte), Aix Festival
Principal dancer (cr) in *Interferences* (Mayer), A.J.A.C., Théâtre des Champs-Elysées, Paris
Dancer in *Jazz Suite*, Ballet Studio de l'Opéra, Le Havre
Principal dancer in *Echeveau* (Schmucki), Ballet Studio de l'Opéra, Le Havre
Dancer in *Symphonie classique* (Descombey), Ballet Studio de l'Opéra, Mexico
1969 Iskander in *Istar* (Lifar), Paris Opéra Ballet, Paris
Principal dancer (cr) in *Anaklasis* (Ariel), A.J.A.C., Théâtre Gémier, Paris
Principal dancer (cr) in *Fiat Lux* (Gernier), A.J.A.C., Théâtre Gémier, Paris
Principal dancer (cr) in "*7 × 1*" (collective choreography), Group des 7, Saint-Malo
Prince Siegfried (cr) in *Swan Lake* (new production; MacMillan after Petipa, Ivanov), German Opera Ballet, Berlin
Principal dancer in *Coppélia* (Descombey), Paris Opéra Ballet, Paris
Waltz, Mazurka in *Les Sylphides* (Fokine), Paris Opéra Ballet, Paris
Principal dancer (cr) in *Christina et ses chimères* (Descombey), French television
1970 Principal dancer (cr) in *Comme la Princesse Salomé est belle ce soir* (Béjart), Opéra-Comique, Paris
Principal dancer in *Serenade* (Balanchine), Paris Opéra Ballet, Paris
Principal dancer (cr) in *Visage* (Descombey), Opéra-Comique, Paris
Principal dancer (cr) in *La Favorite* (Lacotte), Venice
Dancer (cr) in *Ils Disent participer* (Garnier), Avignon
Title role (cr) in *L'Oiseau de feu* (Béjart), Paris Opéra Ballet, Paris
Principal dancer in *Grand Pas classique* (*Grand Pas d'Auber*; Gsovsky), Paris Opéra Ballet, Paris
Prisoner in *Prisoner of the Caucausus* (Skibine), Opéra-Comique, Paris
Pas de quatre in *Swan Lake* (Burmeister after Petipa, Ivanov), Paris Opéra Ballet, Paris
Romeo in *Romeo and Juliet* (Béjart), Ballet du XXe Siècle, Brussels
1971 Principal dancer (cr) in *Suite en Ré* (Chauviré), Théâtre des Champs-Elysées, Paris
Principal dancer (cr) in *Microcosmos* (Lefevre), Théâtre du Silence, Paris
Principal dancer (cr) in *Paquita* (Grand Pas; Nureyev after Petipa), American Ballet Theatre, New York
Principal dancer (cr) in *Delta T/L'Infini* (Schmucki), Gala, Avignon
Principal dancer in *Annabel Lee* (Skibine), Opéra-Comique, Paris
Principal dancer in *The River* (Ailey), American Ballet Theatre, New York
Principal dancer in *Études* (Lander), American Ballet Theatre, New York
Baron in *Gaîté Parisienne* (Massine), American Ballet Theatre, New York
1972 James (cr) in *La Sylphide* (new production; Lacotte after Taglioni), Paris Opéra Ballet, Paris
Principal dancer (cr) in *Dyade* (Charrat), Opéra-Comique, Paris
Principal dancer in *Webern Opus 5* (Béjart), Théâtre du Silence
Principal dancer in *Unfinished Symphony* (*La Symphonie inachevée*; van Dyk), American Ballet Theatre, New York
Phoebus in *Notre Dame de Paris* (Petit), Paris Opéra Ballet, Paris
Albrecht in *Giselle* (Petipa after Coralli, Perrot; staged Alonso), Paris Opéra Ballet, Lille
Paris in *Helen of Troy* (Lichine), American Ballet Theatre, New York
1973 Principal dancer (cr) in *Integrales* (Butler), Paris Opéra Ballet, Paris

Principal dancer (cr) in *Ameriques* (Butler), Paris Opéra Ballet, Paris
Solo in *Densité 21.5* (Carlson), Paris Opéra Ballet, Paris
Principal dancer (cr) in *Un Jour ou deux* (Cunningham), Paris Opéra Ballet, Paris
Principal dancer in *Suite de danses* (Vaussard after Clustine), Paris Opéra Ballet, Paris
Title role in *Le Roi de la nuit* (Lacotte), Paris Opéra Ballet, Nice

1974 Prince Siegfried in *Swan Lake* (Burmeister after Petipa, Ivanov), Paris Opéra Ballet, Paris
Principal dancer in *Variations for Four* (Dolin), American Ballet Theatre, New York
Franz in *Coppélia* (Lacotte), Paris Opéra Ballet, Paris
Principal dancer (cr) in *Schéhérazade* (Petit), Paris Opéra Ballet, Paris
Pas de deux in *Agon* (Balanchine), Paris Opéra Ballet, Paris
Principal dancer (cr) in *Variations Diabelli* (Macdonald), Paris Opéra Ballet, Paris
Saint Loup (cr) in *Les Intermittences du coeur* (Petit), Opéra de Monte Carlo, Monte Carlo
Title role (cr) in *L'Ange* (Garnier), Avignon
Principal dancer (cr) in *Grieg Pas de deux* (Sarelli), French television
Principal dancer in *Afternoon of a Faun* (Robbins), Paris Opéra Ballet, Paris
Principal dancer in *Orphée* (*Orpheus*; Balanchine), Paris Opéra Ballet, Paris
Title role in *Apollo* (Balanchine), American Ballet Theatre, New York
Her Lover in *Jardin aux lilas* (Tudor), American Ballet Theatre, New York
Principal dancer in *Napoli Divertissement* (Lander after Bournonville), American Ballet Theatre, New York
Melot (cr) in *Tristan* (Tetley), Paris Opéra Ballet, Paris

1975 The Poet (cr) in *Symphonie fantastique* (Petit), Paris Opéra Ballet, Paris
Solo (cr) in *Le Roi des Aulnes* (Garnier), French television (TF1)
Romeo in *Romeo and Juliet* (MacMillan), French television (TF1)
Dorian Gray (cr) in *Dorian* (Schmucki), French television (TF1)
Title role (cr) in *Michael* (Plasschaert), French television (TF1)
Prince Desiré in *The Sleeping Beauty* (Petipa; staged Alonso), Paris Opéra Ballet, Paris
Pas de deux from *Flower Festival at Genzano* (Bournonville), American Ballet Theatre, New York

1976 Kurbsky in *Ivan the Terrible* (Grigorovich), Paris Opéra Ballet, Paris
Principal dancer in *Sonatine* (Balanchine), Paris Opéra Ballet, Paris
Principal dancer in *Tzigane* (Balanchine), Paris Opéra Ballet, Paris
Principal dancer in *Tchaikovsky Pas de deux* (Balanchine), Ballet de Caracas, Paris
Colas in *La Fille mal gardée* (Romanov), Ballet de Wallonie
Principal dancer in *Rodin mis en vie* (Sappington), Ballet de Caracas, Paris
Principal dancer (cr) in *Stars* (Schmucki), Marseille

1977 Principal dancer in *Adagietto* (Araiz), Paris Opéra Ballet, Paris
Principal dancer in *Phèdre* (Lifar), Paris Opéra Ballet, Paris

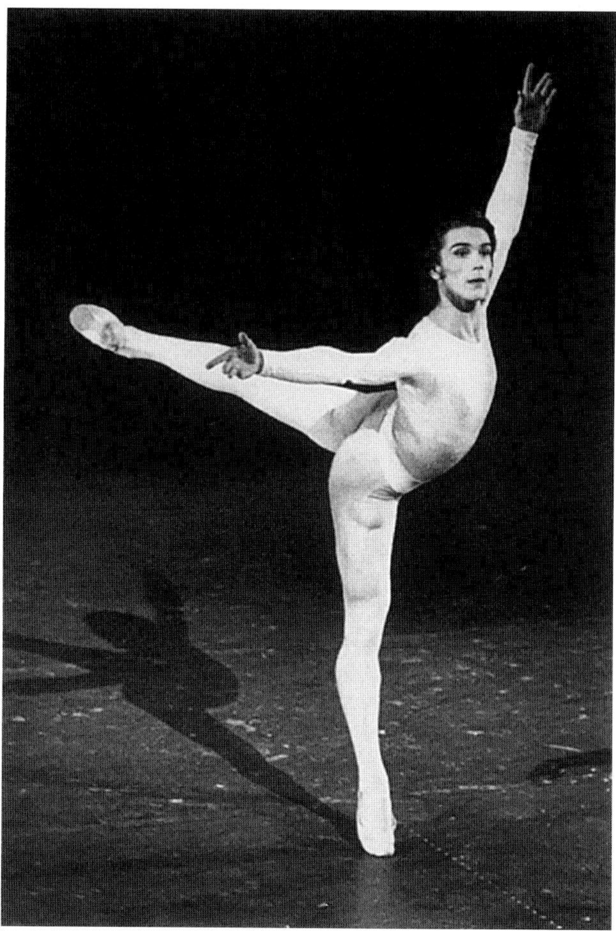

**Michael Denard in *Unfinished Symphony*, 1971**

The Young Man in *Les Mirages* (Lifar), Paris Opéra Ballet, Paris
Romeo in *Romeo and Juliet* (Skibine), Ballet de Wallonie

1978 Principal dancer in *Avalanche* (Lubovitch), Théâtre du Silence, Paris
Principal dancer in *La Fille du Danube* (Lacotte after Taglioni), Teatro Colón, Buenos Aires
Principal dancer in *The Four Seasons* (MacMillan), Paris Opéra Ballet, Paris
Title role in *Apollon Musagète* (*Apollo*; Balanchine), Paris Opéra Ballet, Paris

1979 The Man in *Serait-ce la mort?* (Béjart), Paris Opéra Ballet, Paris
Principal dancer in *Carnaval de Venise* (Lacotte after Petipa), Gala, Chicago
Amour in *Sylvia* (Darsonval after Petipa, Lifar), Paris Opéra Ballet, Paris

1980 Principal dancer (cr) in *L'Amour et la vie d'une femme* (Lefevre), Théâtre du Silence, Paris
Solo (cr) in *Medea* (Marty), Alain Marty Company, Creteil
Aminta in *Sylvia* (Darsonval after Petipa, Lifar), Paris Opéra Ballet, Paris
Principal dancer (cr) in *À Perrot* (collective choreography), Creteil
Principal dancer in *Nathalie* (Lacotte after Taglioni), GRCOP, Guanajuato Festival, Mexico
Principal dancer in *Summer Solstice* (Moreland), Paris Opéra Ballet, Paris

1981 Principal dancer in *Aunis* (Garnier), Groupe de Recherche Chorégraphique de l'Opéra de Paris (GRCOP), Paris
Frederici (cr) in *Marco Spada* (Lacotte), Rome Opera Ballet, Rome
Principal dancer (cr) in *Mad Rush* (Childs), GRCOP, Paris
1982 Principal dancer in *Leitmotiv* (San Goh), Paris Opéra Ballet, Paris
Drosselmeyer in *The Nutcracker* (Hightower), Paris Opéra Ballet, Paris
1983 Romeo in *Romeo and Juliet* (Cranko), Paris Opéra Ballet, Paris
1984 Frederici in *Marco Spada* (Lacotte after Mazilier), Paris Opéra Ballet, Paris
Principal dancer in *Violin Concerto* (Balanchine), Paris Opéra Ballet, Paris
Jim Morrison (cr) in *Au bord du précipice* (Ailey), Paris Opéra Ballet, Paris
Jean de Brienne in *Raymonda* (Nureyev after Petipa), Paris Opéra Ballet, Paris
Abderam in *Raymonda* (Nureyev after Petipa), Paris Opéra Ballet, Paris
Eusebius in *Le Bourgeois Gentilhomme* (Balanchine), Opéra-Comique, Paris
Principal dancer (cr) in *Voyage à Bayreuth* (Marty), Nantes
1985 Principal dancer in *À Coeur ouvert* (Garnier), Paris Opéra Ballet, Paris
Terrestrial in *Shadowplay* (Tudor), Paris Opéra Ballet, Paris
Second Movement in *Symphony in C* (Balanchine), Paris Opéra Ballet, Paris
The Man She Must Marry in *Jardin aux lilas* (Tudor), Paris Opéra Ballet, Paris
Principal dancer in *Dark Elegies* (Tudor), Opéra-Comique, Paris
1986 Principal dancer in *Grosse Fugue* (van Manen), Paris Opéra Ballet, Paris
Principal dancer (cr) in *Songe* (Maillot), La Romaine Festival
1987 Film Producer (cr) in *Cinderella* (Nureyev), Paris Opéra Ballet, Paris
Aristocrat (cr) in *Sans armes citoyens!* (van Dantzig), Paris Opéra Ballet, Paris
Principal dancer in *Quatre Derniers Lieder* (van Dantzig), Paris Opéra Ballet, Paris
Principal dancer in *Pavane* (Limon), Paris Opéra Ballet, Paris
1988 Sebastien in *Le Martyre de Saint-Sébastien* (Wilson), MJC, Bobigny
Principal dancer (cr) in *Comment Wang Po fut sauvé* (Marty), Montauban Festival
1989 The Beast in *Beauty and the Beast* (Tressera), Europa Ballet, Vicenza
Principal dancer in *Echec et mat* (Guelis), Ballets Noirs de Paris, Paris
Le Recitant in *Ring um den Ring* (Béjart), Ballet Lausanne, Berlin
1990 Principal dancer (cr) in *Re-creation* (Marty), Montauban Festival

## PUBLICATIONS

By Denard:

Interview in Lavolé, Jean-Pierre, "Michaël Denard", *Pour la danse* (Paris), February/March 1977
Interview in Vaccarino, Elisa, "Michaël Denard, La Bella Bestia", *Ballettoggi* (Milan), September 1989

About Denard:

Niehaus, Max, *Ballet Faszination*, Munich, 1972
Hersin, André Philippe, "Michaël Denard", *Les Saisons de la danse* (Paris), November 1974
Duvernay, Anne, "Michaël Denard", *Danse* (Paris), October 1979
Elsen, M.C., *Thesmar—Denard*, Paris, 1979
*Visions de la danse* (collection), Paris, 1979
Mannoni, Gérard, *Les Étoiles de l'Opéra de Paris*, Paris, 1982
Dienis, Jean Claude, "Michaël Denard", *Danse* (Paris), July/August 1985
Chaban, Sylvie, *Michaël Denard*, Paris, 1991
Guerrier, Claudine, *Michaël Denard: L'Interprète et la création*, Paris, 1992

* * *

Gifted with a perfectly proportioned physique, a rangy but muscular elegance, an expressive face, and an undeniable stage presence, Michaël Denard made a name for himself as one of the most distinguished dancers of his generation. However, he did not start studying ballet until he was seventeen, after he had passed his baccalaureat, and he also considered acting, a career to which he would successfully turn later. Adding hard work to his natural talents while becoming familiar with the stages of provincial theatres, he was soon noticed by his teacher Solange Golovine, as well as by Dirk Sanders and Pierre Lacotte. Entering the Ballet de l'Opéra in 1966 after winning a competition, Denard progressed rapidly through the ranks. In 1969 he was singled out by Serge Lifar, who entrusted him with the role of Iskander in *Istar* and awarded him the Prix Nijinsky in 1971. In 1977 Lifar was so taken with the dancer's youthful sincerity and emotion that he gave him the role of the young man in the revival of *Les Mirages*. Maurice Béjart, however, sensing in Denard a romantic musicality and a sense of theatre, created two very different ballets for him: *Comme la Princesse Salomé est belle ce soir* and *L'Oiseau de feu*, giving Denard the opportunity to switch from strength to fragility, authority to vulnerability, and changing him from a revolutionary chieftain into a huge crimson bird flying free. Béjart also gave Denard the role of an impassioned and impulsive Romeo with the Ballet du XXe Siècle, and at the Opéra gave him the role of the man in *Serait-ce la mort?*, in which Denard rather overdid the modest sobriety.

At the same time, the dancer asserted his personality in the major roles of the classical repertoire, in particular in Pierre Lacotte's version of *La Sylphide* and later his revival of *Coppélia*, in which Denard portrayed a moonstruck and dreamy Franz. His pure style and feeling for the music made him a Prince Siegfried lost in his dreams, while in *Giselle*, dancing with Jacqueline Rayet or Ghislaine Thesmar, his Albrecht went from selfish ingenuousness to frenzied despair. Roland Petit made the most of his technique and his powerful stage presence when he placed him opposite Zizi Jeanmaire in *Symphonie fantastique*. Denard also restored the subtle musicality and faultless technical precision of the pas de deux arranged by Peter van Dyk to Schubert's *Unfinished Symphony*.

Later on, Denard adapted his dancing to Balanchine's style with ease. He was a radiant *Apollo* and also danced in *Symphony in C*, *Orphée*, *Agon*, and Stravinsky's *Violin Concerto*, with great success. It was in this last ballet that he danced his farewell performance at the Palais Garnier in 1989. Denard was a faultless dancer and an attentive and reliable partner who was invited as a guest artist all over the world, partnering among others Maya Plisetskaya, Natalia Makarova, Cynthia Gregory, and Ghislaine Thesmar. He was a guest with American Ballet Theatre, dancing in numerous ballets including *Gaîté Parisienne* and *Helen of Troy*. Denard was also attracted to modern dance and created roles in works by John Butler and Merce Cunningham; he excelled in Jerome Robbins' version of *Afternoon of a Faun*, and in *Density 21.5* after Carolyn Carlson. In Alvin Ailey's *Au bord du précipice* he portrayed with unaffected sensitivity a two-faced, narcissistic rock idol. He performed frequently with Le Ballet Théâtre du Silence; he portrayed a cheerful sailor in Jacques Garnier's *Aunis*; and he played the part of another sailor, somewhat incongruously, in Robert Wilson's production of *Le Martyre de Saint-Sébastien* at the Opéra. After dancing the role of the husband in Tudor's *Jardin aux lilas Garden*, Denard turned more and more to the theatre, starting in classical tragedy. In Béjart's *Ring um den Ring* he was on stage for four and half hours giving an inspired recitation of Wagner's poem in old German.

Denard's elegance, courtesy, and kindness, together with his skill in different stage techniques, his cultured sensibility, and his natural stage presence, have made him a most engaging and appealing artist.

—Marie-Françoise Christout

---

## DERAIN, André

French painter and stage designer. Born in Chatou, 10 June 1880. Studied painting from 1895; inscribed in engineering at École de Mines, 1896, leaving to study at Académie Camillo, 1898, Académie Carrière, 1898–99, and Académie Julien, Paris, 1904. Married Alice Derain, 1907; also two illegitimate children. Exhibited at Salon d'Automne with Fauves, 1905; allied to Fauve, Cubist, and neo-classical painters, 1905–08, but adopted more traditional style after 1914; first stage design for *L'Annonce faite à Marie* by Claudel, 1919; met Massine, collaborating on design for *La Boutique fantasque*, 1919; travelled to Italy, 1921; designer of over 20 works for the theatre throughout his career, mostly for ballet, including for Diaghilev's Ballets Russes, the Ballets Russes de Monte Carlo, Petit's Ballets de Paris, Vic-Wells and Sadler's Wells Ballet, Paris Opéra, and Opéra-Comique, Paris; also designer for operas and theatre; librettist for many of the ballets he designed, as well as designer of ballet publicity and programmes; lived mainly in Chambourcy from the 1930s, with visit to Germany with Vlaminck, 1941, for which branded a collaborator. Died in Chambourcy, 8 September 1954.

### WORKS (Ballet design)

1919 *La Boutique fantasque* (chor. Massine), Diaghilev's Ballets Russes, London
1924 *Gigue* (chor. Massine), "Les Soirées de Paris", presented by Comte Etienne de Beaumont, Paris (restaged for Cochran Revue, Manchester, 1926)
1926 *Jack-in-the-Box* (chor. Balanchine), Diaghilev's Ballets Russes, Paris
1932 *La Concurrence* (also libretto; chor. Balanchine), Ballets Russes de Monte Carlo, Monte Carlo
1933 *Les Songes* (also libretto; chor. Balanchine), Les Ballets 1933, Paris (costumes re-used for Balanchine's *Dreams*, 1934, *Divertimento*, 1941, and Bolender's *Mother Goose Suite*, 1948)
*Les Fastes* (also libretto; chor. Balanchine), Les Ballets 1933, Paris
1935 *Salade* (chor. Lifar), Paris Opéra Ballet, Paris
1936 *L'Epreuve d'amour* (or *Chung-Yang et le Mandarin Cupide*; chor. Fokine), Ballets Russes de Monte Carlo, Monte Carlo
1937 *Harlequin in the Street* (also libretto; chor. Ashton), Arts Theatre, Cambridge
1938 *La Nymphe Endormie* (chor. Fokine), de Basil's Russian Ballet (presented by Educational Ballets, Ltd.; never performed)
1947 *Mam'zelle Angot* (new designs for revised 1943 ballet; chor. Massine), Sadler's Wells Ballet, London
1948 *Que le Diable l'emporte* (chor. Petit), Ballets de Paris, Paris
1949 *Les Femmes de bonne humeur* (new designs for 1917 ballet; chor. Massine), (de Cuevas's) Grand Ballet de Monte Carlo, Paris
1950 *La Valse* (chor. Massine), Opéra-Comique, Paris
*La Boutique fantasque* (new designs; chor. Massine), Opéra-Comique, Paris

### PUBLICATIONS

By Derain:
*Les Songes* (programme of "Les Ballets 1933"), Paris, 1933

About Derain:
Kahnweiler, Daniel-Henry, *Derain*, Leipzig, 1920
Cogniat, Raymond, *Les Décors de théâtre*, Paris, 1930
Ayrton, Michael, "André Derain as Designer for the Ballet", *Ballet Annual* (London), vol. 5, 1951
Detaille, G., and Mulys, G., *Les Ballets de Monte Carlo 1911–1944*, Paris, 1954
Boll, A., *Serge Diaghilev et la décoration théâtrale*, Paris, 1955
Buckle, Richard, *Modern Ballet Design*, London, 1955
Gosling, Nigel, "Matisse and Derain", *Ballet Annual* (London), vol. 10, 1956
Sutton, Denys, *Derain* (catalogue), London, 1967
Rischbieter, H. (ed.), *Art and Stage in the Twentieth Century*, New York, 1971
*Diaghilev's Designers: The Second Generation* (catalogue), Canberra, c.1986
Kahane, M., *L'Artistes et l'Opéra de Paris: dessins de costums*, Paris, 1987
*Les Ballets 1933*, The Royal Pavilion Art Gallery and Museum, Brighton, 1987
Garafola, Lynn, *Diaghilev's Ballets Russes*, Oxford and New York, 1989
García-Márquez, Vicente, *The Ballets Russes*, New York, 1990

* * *

André Derain was one of the greatest designers of theatrical décors and costumes in the twentieth century, and most of his design work was undertaken for dance. From the time of his first commission for *La Boutique fantasque* (1919), Derain could frequently be found in theatres, and often took part in the actual painting of the scenery. Not only did he design ballets, but at times he also wrote or collaborated on their scenarios. When working for companies he would also contribute graphics and illustrations for publicity material and souvenir programmes.

Derain was not a great innovator for the stage—he continued the traditional practice of painted cloths—but he deserves greater recognition than he has received for the quality of his

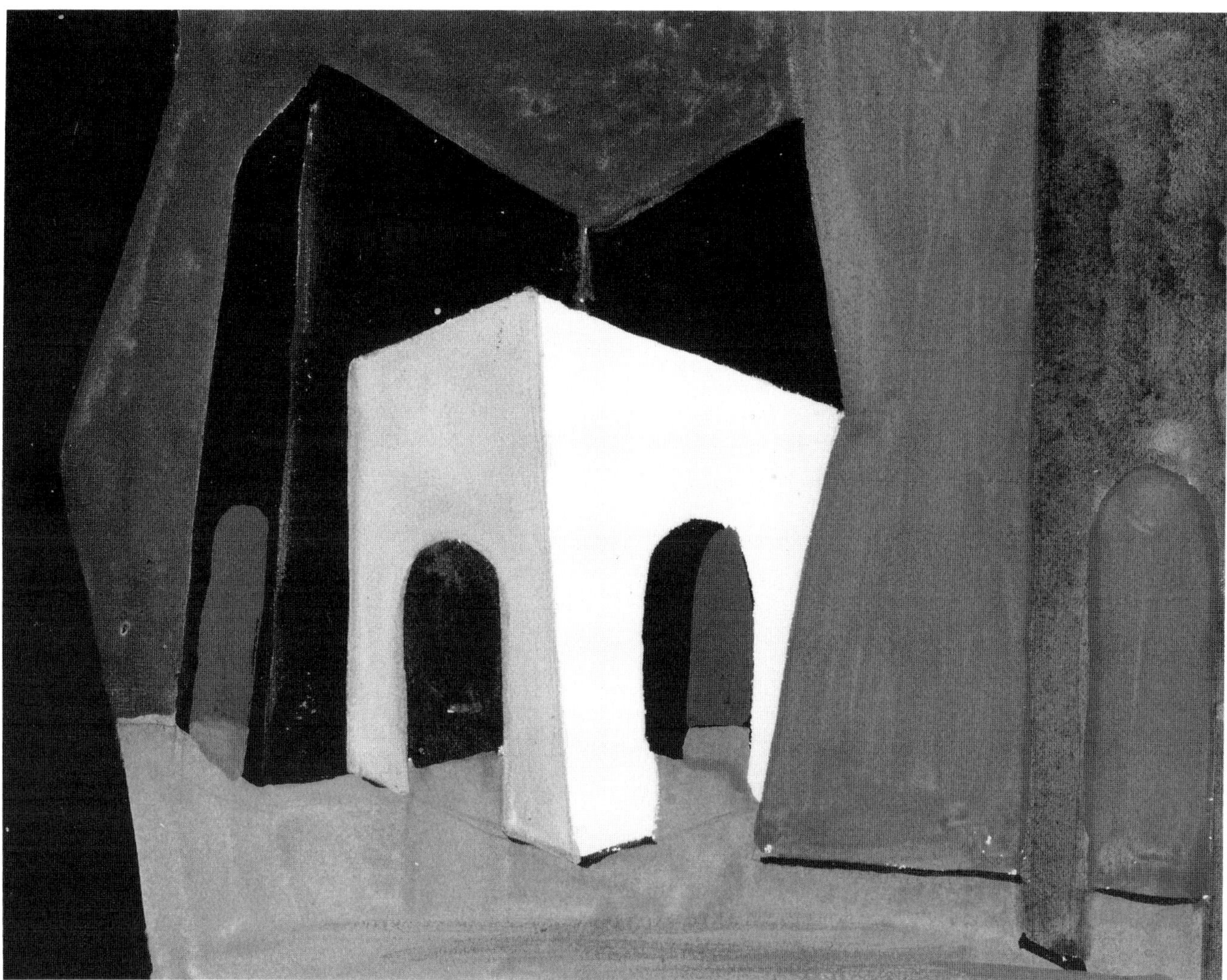

**A set design by André Derain for *Jack In The Box*, 1926**

work. He was a notable colourist (his designs lose their impact when seen only in black-and-white reproductions or photographs) and a designer of imagination and wit.

Derain frequently created front cloths for his ballets. These decorative curtains served to establish the mood of the works rather than evoking the ballets' location or subject. Thus, for *La Boutique fantasque*, masquers are seen in front of a curtain through which a landscape is glimpsed; for *La Concurrence* various *commedia* characters, including an equestrienne standing on a dappled horse, overlook a view; for *Mam'zelle Angot* clowns and monkeys are capering before a brilliant sky.

Derain was introduced to the balletic world by Serge Diaghilev, who was enlarging his company's range of designers, hitherto almost exclusively Russian, to include French-based artists. With his colourful work which adapted popular art forms, Derain was an apt choice. Although his work may initially seem child-like, it is surprisingly sophisticated; by an astute use of colour and stylized perspectives Derain throws the dancers into sharp relief against their setting.

Derain only worked for Diaghilev on one other occasion, and then at the insistence of Etienne de Beaumont, owner of the rights to Erik Satie's music for the short, witty *Jack-in-the-Box*. For this Derain created his most abstract setting; and his imaginatively designed tutus are a good example of his inventive approach to conventional dance costumes. Derain had previously worked for de Beaumont on the settings and costumes for *Gigue*, the most highly acclaimed work presented during the Soirées de Paris (and subsequently included in Cochran's 1926 revue). More has been written on Picasso's *Mercure* for Les Soirées—an example of a work in which the design element overpowers the production—but in *Gigue*, Derain's delicious designs complemented perfectly the performers and the choreography.

Derain's settings are most frequently exterior locations, rural or urban, and his backcloths are carefully designed with a succession of horizontal levels so that they can be appreciated by audiences throughout the theatre. For costumes he frequently drew on historical sources—fashion plates for *La Concurrence*; images from Epinal for *Les Songes*; Etruscan painted murals from the Tomb of the Triclinium for *Les Fastes*; Chinese porcelain for *L'Epreuve d'amour*. For each he simplifies and stylizes the "reality" of his source material, retaining a certain nostalgia but producing designs that are modern and unsentimental. Evidence survives that he was willing to modify his designs so that costumes were generally easy for the dancer to move in.

Derain collaborated with the leading choreographers of his time—Massine, Balanchine, Fokine, Ashton, Lifar, and Petit. On several occasions the designs he created were subsequently used for revised or new ballets—the most obvious example being the re-use of the costumes for *Les Songes* (created for Les Ballets 1933) in three successive ballets in the United States.

Not all the ballets for which Derain created designs were new works. Towards the end of his career he was invited to re-design several established ballets, such as *Mam'zelle Angot* (his designs were superior to the originals by Doboujinsky) and *Les Femmes de bonne humeur* (originally by Bakst, and possibly Derain's least successful ballet). Also at this time he reworked his own designs for *La Boutique fantasque* for the Paris Opéra, and designed a completely new, narrative version of *La Valse* inspired by Lermontov's play *Masquerade*.

Derain's theatre work was much admired by the Bloomsbury circle, and his influence is clearly detected in Duncan Grant's designs for the ballet. It was Maynard Keynes who invited Derain to work at Cambridge in 1937, designing *Harlequin in the Street* at the Arts Theatre with Lopokova and Ashton; and after the Second World War, Keynes brought back the team of Massine and Derain to work at the Royal Opera House at Covent Garden, marking Derain's return to theatrical work after an absence of a decade.

—Jane Pritchard

---

## DESHAYES, André-Jean-Jacques

French dancer and choreographer. Born in Paris, son of dancer, choreographer, and teacher Jacques-François Deshayes, 24 January 1777. Studied at the ballet school of l'Académie royale de musique (Paris Opéra), from 1788. Married the dancer Elisabeth Duchemin (performed as Mme Deshayes). Stage début in child roles, Opéra, Paris, 1790s; dancer, Paris Opéra, from 1794, becoming premier danseur demi-caractère, dancing under maître de ballet Pierre Gardel; premier danseur, Lisbon, 1799; London début (in Dauberval's *Les Jeux d'Eglé*), 1800; left the Paris Opéra, 1802; first dancer, La Scala, Milan, 1802–03; also leading dancer in Naples, Germany, and Vienna; principal dancer, King's Theatre (later Her Majesty's), London, 1800, 1804–11, 1821, 1829–31, 1833, 1835–38, 1842; official choreographer for the King's Theatre, 1821, 1829–31, 1833, 1835–8, 1842. Died in Batignolles, 19 December 1846.

### WORKS

1806 *La Dansomanie* (after P. Gardel), King's Theatre, London
1807 *L'Enlèvement d'Adonis* (mus. Venua), King's Theatre, London
1810 *Psyche* (after P. Gardel; mus. Venua), King's Theatre, London
1811 *Figaro* (after Duport; mus. Venua), King's Theatre, London
1821 *Le Prix*, King's Theatre, London
*Le Paysanne supposée* (mus. Venua), King's Theatre, London
*Alcide* (with Albert), for coronation of George IV, King's Theatre, London
*Le Seigneur généreux* (mus. Sor), King's Theatre, London
1824 *Zémire et Azor* (mus. Schneitzhoeffer), Opéra, Paris
1829 *La Somnambule* (after Aumer), King's Theatre, London
*Masaniello* (mus. D. Auber), King's Theatre, London
*Les Déguisements imprévus* (mus. Bochsa), King's Theatre, London
1831 *Kenilworth* (mus. Costa), King's Theatre, London
*La Bayadère* (mus. Auber, arranged Musard), King's Theatre, London
1833 *Faust* (mus. Adam), King's Theatre, London
1835 *Zéphir berger*, King's Theatre, London
1836 *Le Rossignol* (mus. Nadaud), King's Theatre, London
*Beniowsky* (mus. Bochsa), King's Theatre, London
1837 *Le Brigand de Terracina* (mus. Auber, Pilati), Her Majesty's Theatre, London
1838 *Le Chalet* (mus. Adam, Pilati), Her Majesty's Theatre, London
1842 *Giselle* (with Perrot; music Adam), Her Majesty's Theatre, London
*La Fête des nymphes*, Her Majesty's Theatre, London
*Alma* (with Perrot, Cerrito; mus. Costa), Her Majesty's Theatre, London

### PUBLICATIONS

By Deshayes:
*Idées generales sur l'Académie royale de musique, et plus specialement sur la danse*, Paris, 1822

About Deshayes:
Baron, *Lettres sur la danse*, Paris, 1925
Beaumont, Cyril, *Bibliography of Dancing*, London, 1937
Chaffee, George, "The Romantic Ballet in London: 1821–1858", *Dance Index* (New York), vol. 2, 1943
Guest, Ivor, *The Romantic Ballet in England*, London, 1954
Winter, Marian Hannah, *The Pre-Romantic Ballet*, London, 1974
Chapman, John, "Ballet in Early Nineteenth-Century London as seen by Leigh Hunt and Henry Robertson", *Dance Chronicle* (New York), vol. 1, no. 2, 1978
Chapman, John, "Dance in Transition 1809–1830", *Dancing Times* (London), March 1978

* * *

André-Jean-Jacques Deshayes was the son of the celebrated teacher Jacques-François Deshayes, who was director of the Paris Opéra and Comédie-Française ballet schools as well as maître de ballet at the Comédie. André-Jean-Jacques, along with his brother, trained at the Paris Opéra school and frequently appeared in children's parts in Opéra productions.

Upon graduation, the talented Deshayes was given an Opéra contract. However, he was a restless and ambitious youth who sought varied opportunities to broaden his dancing career. In 1799, he made guest appearances in Lisbon, and the following year he accepted a London engagement. In 1802, he requested a further leave from the Opéra to perform in Milan, but the current ballet master, Pierre Gardel, refused his application. Deshayes, valuing his independence more than financial security, broke his contract and, with his wife, former classmate Elisabeth Duchemin, travelled to Milan to perform at La Scala.

The bulk of Deshayes' career, however, was spent in London at the King's Theatre, where he was engaged as principal dancer from 1804 to 1811. Under the leadership of ballet master and choreographer James d'Egville, the King's Theatre featured many fine French artists, including Mlles. Parisot and Hilligsberg, and Messrs. Boisgirard and Laborie. Along with Deshayes, these dancers possessed dignity, grace, ease, and nobility which allowed them to give meaning to dance through the expressive quality of their dancing. Deshayes too possessed elegance and grace, but he was set above these artists by what contemporary reports called "his steps and changes . . . distinguished for neatness and strength", which enabled him to gain audience approval for his masterful technique.

By 1809, most of these elegant dancers, who represented the old school, had left or retired to be replaced by a younger generation of virtuoso dancers who specialized in multiple pirouettes, spectacular jumps, and extended balances that delighted audiences, if not the critics. The *Examiner* wrote that "[Armand] Vestris and [Fortunata] Angiolini though considerably improved since their arrival have unluckily directed their attention to an inferior branch of the art, the rapid execution of steps; and have not attempted, or attempted without success, to equal the elegance of Monsieur and Madame Deshayes, whose performance possesses something sentimental that appeals to the mind as well as the eye, while that of Vestris is mere bodily exertion, only superior to the feats of the equestrians and rope dancers."

During his tenure at the King's, Deshayes also tried his hand at choreography with considerable success. His early work, *Figaro*, was praised in 1811 as "one of the most entertaining ballets that have been produced for many seasons".

During the Napoleonic Wars, Deshayes worked on the continent, including a rather unsuccessful stint at the Paris Opéra. In 1821, he was engaged once again by the King's Theatre, for the new manager, John Ebers, insisted on hiring only the finest French dancers and choreographers available to mount new works. Between 1821 and 1842, Deshayes created a number of important ballets there—*Masaniello*, *La Somnambule*, *La Bayadère*, *Beniowsky*, and *Le Brigand de Terracina*—as well as collaborating on the London productions of *Giselle* and *Alma* with Jules Perrot.

Deshayes' own works were built on strong story-lines expressed in mime and developed through careful staging embellished with incidental dances. His ballets were imaginative and varied in style, ranging from the lively Spanish dances of *Masaniello* to the warlike dances of *Kenilworth*. His innovative and refreshing stage works were a forerunner to the Romantic ballet, with their emphasis on exotic or historical settings and melodrama. Such gentle touches as his *pas seul* before a looking glass for Pauline Duvernay in *Le Brigand de Terracina* foreshadowed the work of Jules Perrot.

In 1842, Deshayes retired and returned to Paris to live out his final years. Shortly after his death it was written of him that "A more amiable or more courteous personage never existed in the realms of the fantastic toe, nor was he devoid of inventive talent".

—Mary Jane Warner

---

## DESIGNS WITH STRINGS
(also *Design for Strings* and *Dessins pour six*)

**Choreography:** John Taras
**Music:** Petr Ilyich Tchaikovsky
**Design:** George Kirsta
**First Production:** Metropolitan Ballet, Edinburgh, Scotland, 6 February 1948
**Principal Dancers:** Svetlana Beriosova, Sonia Arova, Celia Franca, Delysia Blake, Erik Bruhn, David Adams

**Other productions include:** Ballet Theatre (costumes Irene Sharaff), with Diana Adams, Norma Vance, Lillian Lanese, Dorothy Scott, Erik Bruhn, Michael Lland; New York, 25 April 1950. Royal Danish Ballet (restaged Taras), as *Variationer*; Copenhagen, 22 April 1952. German Opera Ballet; Berlin, 4 October 1964. Dance Theatre of Harlem, as *Design for Strings*; New York, 25 April 1974.

### PUBLICATIONS

"The Sitter Out", *Dancing Times* (London), July 1948
Brinson, Peter, and Crisp, Clement, *Ballet for All*, London, 1970
Percival, John, "The Metropolitan Ballet", *Dance and Dancers* (London), February 1960
Balanchine, George, with Mason, Francis, *Balanchine's Complete Stories of the Great Ballets*, Garden City, New York, 1977

* * *

In 1948 *Designs with Strings* was an early example of the plotless ballet, which today is the type most frequently seen on our stages. Happily, it followed the mood of the music so sympathetically that it was emotionally as well as intellectually engaging throughout. The ballet got off to such a good start that it is still running, but few present-day ballet-goers, surfeited as they are with "new ballets" that are nothing more than the same old legs-up exercises to any old piece of music, could appreciate just how good a start that was.

In 1948 most ballets had plots and could be considered subjects for intelligent conversation after the show. But at the same time much was beginning to be heard about the importance of the as yet unseen plotless works of Balanchine in America: unseen, that is, except his untypical *Theme and Variations*, also to a lush Tchaikovsky score, and danced with such verve, panache, and projection by Alonso and Youskevitch that it hardly seemed "plotless" at all, simply a work full of character about which someone had forgotten to print the story in the programme. So *Designs with Strings* was the English audience's first encounter with a new trend.

Metropolitan Ballet, which first performed the work, was a lively touring company not two years old, composed of exciting young dancers from many different backgrounds, whose youthful exuberance gave the company its distinctive flavour. The young cast was eager to try out this new species of ballet, made by a choreographer who had seen its dramatic growth in popularity in New York during the previous five years. It was an impressive cast: the restrained, reserved fifteen-year-old Beriosova from New York, already dancing with a control and smoothness that entirely concealed her remarkable technique; Delysia Blake from South Africa, with the long legs and fair colouring of the archetypal "blonde bombshell", and as sophisticated as Beriosova was ingenuous; David Adams and Erik Bruhn, both aged nineteen but otherwise at different ends of the spectrum. Adams was of an extrovert and no-nonsense temperament, while Bruhn, at that time still dancing entirely in the old French Bournonville manner in which he had been trained, was just about to embark on his five-year love-affair with the Russian and Italian techniques, and danced with unforgettable clarity and unassuming command of the stage. The two remaining members of the cast had seen the worst of the war years touring England—Sonia Arova, from Bulgaria via Paris, a dazzling technician with a vivid personality to match, and the Londoner Celia Franca, Rambert- and Tudor-trained, intelligent, attractive, and musical.

Taras had quite a palette to paint with. And somehow, with

these different dancers from different backgrounds, he successfully created (together with Tchaikovsky, at that time the most popular composer in England) that most unusual type of dance work—a ballet of a mood. The young dancers travelled happily with Taras down this unfamiliar path, in a sense representing young people everywhere, fresh from the conclusion of the war and brimming with new optimism. This was the time when the foundation of the Arts Council, such that artistic events could be subsidized as they were on the Continent, or the establishment of a national health service, made the future seem rosy indeed to a country exhausted from years of bombs and blackout conditions. At the time, and still more at a distance of nearly half a century, *Designs with Strings* seemed to epitomize and celebrate not only the eternal optimism of youth, but also its sadness, its inexplicable changes of mood, and its ability to rise above all obstacles.

*Designs with Strings* also benefited from the fact that audiences could make of it what they liked, for the slight, elusive suggestion, a cloud no bigger than a man's hand, of a sad conclusion in the ballet's last moments enabled viewers to see in the earlier passages exactly what they wished and to draw their own conclusions, thus making the ballet everything to everyone who watched it.

—Leo Kersley

---

## LES DEUX PIGEONS

**Choreography:** Louis Mérante
**Music:** André Messager
**Design:** Auguste-Alfred Rubé, Chaperon, J.B. Lavastre (sets), Bianchini (costumes)
**Libretto:** Henry Régnier and Louis Mérante
**First Production:** Théâtre de l'Opéra, Paris, 18 October 1886
**Principal Dancers:** Rosita Mauri (Gourouli), Marie Sanlaville (Pepio), Mélanie Hirsch (Djali)

**Other productions include:** Paris Opéra (one-act version; chor. Albert Aveline), with Carlotta Zambelli (Gourouli); Paris, 1919. Covent Garden Theatre (shortened version, with score adapted by Messager; chor. François Ambroisiny); London, 21 June 1906. Royal Ballet Touring Company (new version; chor. Frederick Ashton, mus. arranged John Lanchbery, design Jacques Dupont), with Christopher Gable (The Young Man), Lynn Seymour (The Young Girl); London, 14 February 1961 (see Ashton's *The Two Pigeons*).

### PUBLICATIONS

Beaumont, Cyril, *Complete Book of Ballets*, revised edition, London, 1951
Guest, Ivor, "*Les Deux Pigeons*: The History", *Dancing Times* (London), February 1961
Brinson, Peter, and Crisp, Clement, *Ballet and Dance*, Newton Abbot, 1980

* * *

It was his teacher Saint-Saëns who recommended André Messager to Vaucorbeil, the director of the Paris Opéra, and it was Vaucorbeil himself who chose La Fontaine's fable as a suitable subject for a ballet. *Les Deux Pigeons* was Messager's first ballet score and it was recognizably in the tradition of Delibes. The second-act variation for Gourouli is a pizzicato, very like that Delibes created for *Sylvia*.

Henri Régnier devised the three-act scenario, which he set in eighteenth-century Thessaly. His "two pigeons" were two young lovers, Gourouli and Pepio. Pepio is drawn by what he imagines are the pleasures of a gypsy life and leaves Gourouli. But she follows him and, after she has disguised herself as a gypsy, Pepio is fascinated by her. The other gypsies rob Pepio and he returns home to be forgiven by Gourouli.

Unfortunately for Messager, Vaucorbeil died in 1884, Régnier resigned at the end of the year, and the new directors showed little interest in the new work which waited twelve months before it went into rehearsal. The choreographer was Louis Mérante, who had been responsible for *Sylvia* ten years earlier. The first performance eventually took place on 18 October 1886, when it shared the bill with Donizetti's four-act opera *La Favorita*. The poet Stéphane Mallarmé was in the audience and recorded his impressions in *Crayonné au théâtre*.

The ballet was designed for the Spanish ballerina Rosita Mauri (as Gourouli) who was partnered by Marie Sanlaville (as Pepio) "en travestie". The gypsy girl Djali was Mélanie Hirsch, and Louis Mérante himself, though aged 58, danced the First Gypsy in the second act. (*Les Deux Pigeons* was Mérante's last ballet. Nine months after it opened, although feeling unwell, he partnered Mauri at a charity performance. He suffered a relapse and died on 17 July 1887, after seventeen remarkable years as the Opéra's maître de ballet.)

*Les Deux Pigeons* was a great success for Mauri. In the first and third acts she wore a blond wig (in contrast to her gypsy disguise) and at her first entrance was unrecognized even by her claque. In the second act, *Le Figaro* reported, she came into her own, "with her magnificent black hair floating on her shoulders, and the whiteness of her skin emerging from a flame-coloured satin bodice, giving her a look of devilish wantonness". Her "stunning" pizzicato variation had to be repeated "by the acclaim of the entire audience".

Largely because of Messager's music, *Les Deux Pigeons* remained in the Opéra's repertory. The first revival of 1894 omitted the third act—the lovers were reunited at the end of the second—and changed the setting to Hungary. In 1912 Carlotta Zambelli was Gourouli, a role she had learned from Mauri herself. Albert Aveline made new choreography for the ballet in 1919 (still with Zambelli), but not until 1942 was its travesty tradition broken and Pepio danced by a man, Serge Peretti, whose Gourouli was Lycette Darsonval. The most recent revival was in 1980 for the students of the Paris Opéra school.

*Les Deux Pigeons* never had the international success of *Coppélia* or *Sylvia*, but it was seen in London at Covent Garden in 1906 when Messager was artistic director there. He shortened his original score for this production, which had choreography by François Ambroisiny. Sir Frederick Ashton's version of the ballet, to John Lanchbery's arrangement of Messager's music, was first seen at the Opera House on 14 February 1961.

—Martin Wright

---

## DE VALOIS, Ninette

Irish/British dancer, choreographer, teacher, and ballet director. Born Edris Stannus in Baltiboys, Ireland, 6 June 1898. Studied with Lila Field, Edouard Espinosa, Enrico Cecchetti, and Nikolai (Nicolas) Legat. Dancer in pantomime, Lyceum

Theatre, London, 1914–18; principal dancer, Beecham Opera and Ballet Company, and with Lopokova and Massine companies, London, 1918–23; principal dancer, Covent Garden Opera, 1919; dancer, Ballets Russes de Serge Diaghilev, 1923–25: guest artist, 1926 and 1928; principal dancer, Anton Dolin's company, 1926, and Covent Garden Opera, 1928; principal dancer and choreographer, Abbey Theatre, Dublin, 1928–34; principal dancer and choreographer, Festival Theatre, Cambridge, 1926–31; founder and principal, Academy of Choregraphic [sic] Art, London, 1926–31, Abbey Theatre Ballet School, Dublin, from 1927, Sadler's Wells Ballet School (becoming Royal Ballet School), from 1931; choreographer, Camargo Society, Ballet Club (later Ballet Rambert), Vic-Wells (later Sadler's Wells) Ballet, from 1930; founder and director, Vic-Wells Ballet (becoming Sadler's Wells Ballet and Royal Ballet), 1931–63, and Sadler's Wells Opera (later Theatre) Ballet, from 1946; founder and director, Turkish School of Ballet, Ankara, 1948, and Turkish State Ballet, 1956. Recipient: Chevalier de la Légion d'Honneur, 1950; Honorary Doctorates in Literature from Sheffield University, 1955, Oxford University, 1955, and Dublin University, 1957; Honorary Doctorate in Music, Reading University, 1951; Honorary Doctorate in Law, Aberdeen University, 1958; title of Commander of the Order of the British Empire, 1947; Dame Commander of the Order of the British Empire, 1951; Albert Medal of the Royal Society of Arts, 1964; Erasmus Prize, 1974; Companion of Honour, 1983; Critics' Circle Award, 1989.

## ROLES

1914 "Grand Fairyland Ballet" in *Jack and the Beanstalk* (revue), Lyceum Theatre, London

1915 Principal dancer in *Robinson Crusoe* (revue), Lyceum Theatre, London

1916 Principal dancer in *Mother Goose* (revue), Lyceum Theatre, London

1917 Solo variations in *Music, Dancing and Pictures*, Devonshire Park, Eastbourne

1918 Scenes from *Faust*, *Phoebus and Pan*, *Carmen*, Beecham Opera and Ballet, London Palladium

Principal dancer in *Cinderella* (revue), Lyceum Theatre, London

1919 Principal dancer in *Laughing Eyes* (revue), Theatre Royal, Newcastle

Dances in *La Traviata* (opera; mus. Verdi), *Thaïs* (opera; mus. Massenet), *Aida* (opera; mus. Verdi), Grand Opera Season, Covent Garden Opera, London

1920 Principal dancer in *Oh! Julie!* (musical; mus. Brooke and Darewski), Shaftesbury Theatre, London

1922 Principal dancer in *Cupidon* (solo), *Fanatics of Pleasure*, *Passe-pied* (pas de deux), *Gopak*, *Three Graces*, *The Cockatoo's Holiday*, *Gavotte* (pas de deux), *Finale*, *Czardas* (pas de trois), *The Masquerade*, *Les Elegantes*, *Pavane*, Massine-Lopokov Russian Ballet season, London

1923 Principal dancer (cr) in *You'd Be Surprised* (revue; chor. Massine), Covent Garden, London

Finger variation and Red Riding Hood in *Aurora's Wedding* (Nijinska after Petipa), Diaghilev's Ballets Russes, Monte Carlo

1924 Ensemble (cr) in *Les Biches* (Nijinska), Diaghilev's Ballets Russes, Monte Carlo

A Nymph in *L'Après-midi d'un faune* (Nijinsky), Diaghilev's Ballets Russes, Monte Carlo

A Shuttlecock (cr) in *Les Fâcheux* (Nijinska), Diaghilev's Ballets Russes, Monte Carlo

**Ninette de Valois**

Une Poule (ensemble; cr) in *Le Train bleu* (Nijinska), Diaghilev's Ballets Russes, Paris

Florestan Pas de trois (cr; added by Nijinska) in *Aurora's Wedding* (Nijinska after Petipa), Diaghilev's Ballets Russes, tour

Pas de quatre (cr; added by Nijinska) in *Cimarosiana* (Massine), Diaghilev's Ballets Russes, tour

Pasquina in *The Good Humoured Ladies* (Massine), Diaghilev's Ballets Russes, tour

1925 A Neighbour in *Le Tricorne* (Massine), Diaghilev's Ballets Russes, London

Papillon in *Carnaval* (Fokine), Diaghilev's Ballets Russes, Monte Carlo

Gossip in *Les Fâcheux* (Nijinska), Diaghilev's Ballets Russes, on tour

A Lady of the Court (cr) in *Le Rossignol* (Balanchine), Diaghilev's Ballets Russes, London

Dorotea in *Les Femmes de bonne humeur* (Massine), Diaghilev's Ballets Russes

The Favourite Slave in *Cléopâtre* Fokine), Diaghilev's Ballets Russes

1926 Nurse in *Romeo and Juliet* (Nijinska, with entr'acte by Balanchine), Diaghilev's Ballets Russes, Paris

Felicia in *Les Femmes de bonne humeur* (Massine), Diaghilev's Ballets Russes, London

Principal dancer in *Lacquer*, *Little Boy Blue*, *Jack and Jill* (pas de deux), *Variation* (solo), Anton Dolin company, London

Rag Mazurka ("Hostess") in *Les Biches* (Nijinska), Diaghilev's Ballets Russes, London

1927 Principal dancer (cr) in *Rout* (also chor.), Festival Theatre, Cambridge
1928 Rosalind in *Les Petits Riens* (also chor.), Old Vic, London
1929 Fand (cr) in *Fighting the Waves* (dance-drama; also chor.), Abbey Theatre, Dublin
1931 The Jackdaw (cr) in *The Jackdaw and the Pigeons* (also chor.), Vic-Wells Ballet, London
Aurora in *Cephalus and Procris* (de Valois), Vic-Wells Ballet, London
A Foreign Visitor (cr) in *Regatta* (Ashton), Vic-Wells Ballet, London
Principal dancer (cr) in *The Dancer's Reward* (also chor.), Camargo Society, London
1932 Berthe in *Giselle* (after Petipa, Coralli, Perrot), Camargo Society, London
The Young Girl in *Le Spectre de la rose* (Fokine), Vic-Wells Ballet, London
The Courtesan (cr) in *The Enchanted Grove* (Doone), Vic-Wells Ballet, London
Principal dancer (cr) in *Fête polonaise* (also chor.), Vic-Wells Ballet, London
The Tight-Rope Dancer (cr) in *Douanes* (also chor.), Vic-Wells Ballet, London
Débutante (cr) in *The Origin of Design* (also chor.), Vic-Wells Ballet, London
Katie Willows in *The Lord of Burleigh* (Ashton), Vic-Wells Ballet, London
1933 Procris (cr) in *Cephalus and Procris* (also chor.), Vic-Wells Ballet, London
Swanilda in *Coppélia* (Acts I and II; Petipa, Cecchetti; staged Sergeyev), Vic-Wells Ballet, London
Ilina (cr) in *Bluebeard* (dance drama; also chor.), Abbey Theatre, London
The Guardian of the Well (cr) in *At the Hawk's Well* (dance-drama by W.B. Yeats; also chor.), Abbey Theatre, Dublin
Pas de trois (cr) in *Les Rendezvous* (Ashton), Vic-Wells Ballet, London
1934 Peasant pas de deux in *Giselle* (Petipa after Coralli, Perrot; staged Sergeyev), Vic-Wells Ballet, London
The Bride (cr) in *The Wise and Foolish Virgins* (also chor.), Vic-Wells Ballet, London
The Queen (cr) in *The King of the Great Clock Tower* (dance-drama by W.B. Yeats; also chor.), Abbey Theatre, Dublin
1935 Columbine in *Carnaval* (Fokine), Vic-Wells Ballet, London
1936 The Peasant Woman (cr) in *Barabau* (de Valois), Vic-Wells Ballet, London
1937 Webster (cr) in *A Wedding Bouquet* (Ashton), Vic-Wells Ballet, London

**Other roles include:** for Diaghilev's Ballets Russes—A Nymph in *Narcisse* (Fokine), Swan and Czardas in *Swan Lake*, Acts II and III (Fokine after Petipa, Ivanov), Lisinion in *Daphnis and Chloë* (Fokine), Young Woman in *Le Sacre du printemps* (Massine), a Baroness in *Les Tentations de la bergère* (Nijinska), a Friend in *La Boutique fantasque* (Massine).

## WORKS

1918 Solo in *Scenes from Phoebus and Pan* (mus. Bach), Beecham Opera and Ballet, London
1921 *Albumblatt no. 7* (mus. Grieg), and other pieces, de Valois group, Camberwell Palace
1923 "Chicken à la King" (mus. unknown) in *You'd Be Surprised* (revue; chor. Massine), Covent Garden, London
1925 *The Art of the Theatre* (mus. Ravel), Sunshine Matinée (charity matinée), London
1927 *Beauty and the Beast* (mus. Ravel), Festival Theatre, Cambridge
*A Daughter of Eve* (solo; mus. Arensky), Festival Theatre, Cambridge
*Rout* (mus. Bliss), Festival Theatre, Cambridge
*Nautical Nonsense* (mus. Bach), Festival Theatre, Cambridge
*Poisson d'or* (mus. Debussy), Festival Theatre, Cambridge
*Rhythm* (mus. Beethoven), Festival Theatre, Cambridge
*Russe fantastique* (mus. Rebikov), Festival Theatre, Cambridge
*Pride* (solo; mus. Scriabin), Festival Theatre, Cambridge
1928 *Venetian Suite* (mus. Respighi), Abbey Theatre, Dublin
*Les Bouffons* (mus. Liadov), Abbey Theatre, Dublin
*Rituelle de feu* (mus. Falla), Abbey Theatre, Dublin
*The Faun* (mus. White), Abbey Theatre, Dublin
*Scène de ballet* (mus. Gluck), Academy of Choregraphic Art, London
*The Scorpions of Ysit* (mus. Hamilton, later Gordon), Academy of Choregraphic Art, London
*Les Petits Riens* (mus. Mozart, arranged Lambert), Old Vic, London
1929 *The Picnic* (mus. Vaughan Williams), Old Vic, London
*Hommage aux belles Viennoises* (mus. Schubert, arranged Franklin), Association of Operatic Dancing, London
Dances in *Fighting the Waves* (dance-drama by W.B. Yeats; mus. Anthiel), Abbey Theatre, Dublin
1930 *Suite de danses* (mus. Bach, arranged Goossens), Old Vic, London
*Cephalus and Procris* (mus. Grétry, arranged Evans), Camargo Society, London
1931 *La Création du monde* (mus. Milhaud), Camargo Society, London
*The Jackdaw and the Pigeons* (mus. Bradford), Vic-Wells Ballet, London
*Job* (A masque for dancing; mus. Vaughan Williams), Camargo Society, London
*Fête polonaise* (mus. Glinka), Vic-Wells Ballet, London
Dances in *The Dreaming of the Bones* (dance-drama by W.B. Yeats; mus. Larchet), Abbey Theatre, Dublin
*The Dancer's Reward* (mus. Lambert), Camargo Society, London
*The Jew in the Bush* (mus. Jacob), Vic-Wells Ballet, London
1932 *Narcissus and Echo* (mus. Bliss), Vic-Wells Ballet, London
*Nursery Suite* (mus. Elgar), Vic-Wells Ballet, London
*The Origin of Design* (mus. Handel, arranged Beecham), Camargo Society, London
*Douanes* (mus. Toye), Vic-Wells Ballet, London
1933 *The Birthday of Oberon* (choral ballet; mus. Purcell, arranged Lambert), Vic-Wells Ballet, London
Dances in *At the Hawk's Well* (dance-drama by W.B. Yeats; mus. McCarthy), Abbey Theatre, Dublin
*The Wise and Foolish Virgins* (mus. Atterberg), Vic-Wells Ballet, London
1934 *The Haunted Ballroom* (mus. Toye), Vic-Wells Ballet, London
*Bar aux Folies-Bergères* (mus. Chabrier, arranged

Lambert), Ballet Club, London
Dances in *The King of the Great Clock Tower* (dance-drama by W.B. Yeats; mus. Duff), Abbey Theatre, Dublin
1935 *The Rake's Progress* (mus. Gordon), Vic-Wells Ballet, London
1936 *The God Go a-Begging* (mus. Handel, arranged Beecham), Vic-Wells Ballet, London
*Barabau* (mus. and text Rieti), Vic-Wells Ballet, London
*Music for Ballet* (mus. Sargent), Cambridge Theatre Gala, London
*Prometheus* (mus. Beethoven, arranged Lambert), Vic-Wells Ballet, London
1937 *Checkmate* (mus. Bliss), Vic-Wells Ballet, Paris
1938 *Le Roi nu* (*The Emperor's New Clothes*; mus. Françaix), Vic-Wells Ballet, London
1940 *The Prospect Before Us* (mus. Boyce, arranged Lambert), Vic-Wells Ballet, London
1941 *Orpheus and Eurydice* (mus. Gluck), Vic-Wells Ballet, London
1943 *Promenade* (mus. Haydn, arranged Evans, Jacob), Vic-Wells Ballet, Edinburgh
1946 Dance of "The Three Ivans" in *The Sleeping Beauty* (staged de Valois, Ashton after Petipa, Sergeyev; mus. Tchaikovsky), Sadler's Wells Ballet, London
1950 *Don Quixote* (mus.Gerhard), Sadler's Wells Ballet, London
*Keloglan Masali* (mus. Ulvi Cemal Erin), Turkish State Ballet School
1962 *The Muses* (mus. Arensky), Royal Ballet School, London
1964 *At the Fountainhead* (mus. Tüzün), Turkish State Ballet
1966 *Sinfonietta* (mus. Kodalli), Turkish State Ballet
Dance of the Fiancées in *Swan Lake* (Petipa, Ivanov; mus. Tchaikovsky), Turkish State Ballet
1971 Peasant dance (Act I) in *Swan Lake* (after Petipa, Ivanov; mus. Tchaikovsky), Royal Ballet, London
Garland Dance in *The Sleeping Beauty* (Petipa; mus. Tchaikovsky), Turkish State Ballet
1973 *The Wedding of Harlequin; or, Harlequin Revived* (with Ashton), Ballet for All, Felixstowe

## PUBLICATIONS

By de Valois:
*Invitation to the Ballet*, London, 1937
*Come Dance With Me*, London, 1957
*Step by Step*, London, 1977

About de Valois:
Beaumont, Cyril, *The Sadler's Wells Ballet*, revised and enlarged edition, London, 1947
Clarke, Mary, *The Sadler's Wells Ballet*, London, 1955
Bland, Alexander, *The Royal Ballet: The First Fifty Years*, London, 1981
Sorley Walker, Kathrine, "The Festival and the Abbey: Ninette de Valois' Early Choreography 1925–1934", *Dance Chronicle* (New York), 2 parts: vol. 7, no. 4, 1984–85, and vol. 8, no. 1/2, 1985
Sorley Walker, Kathrine, *Ninette de Valois: Idealist Without Illusions*, London, 1987
Woodcock, Sarah, *The Sadler's Wells Royal Ballet*, London, 1991

* * *

Few people in the dance world have excelled in so many fields as did Ninette de Valois—she was dancer, choreographer, teacher, artistic director, administrator, and writer—but she will primarily be remembered as the architect of the Royal Ballet. Her talent, vision, drive, and administrative genius established, within 25 years, an organization recognized as the national ballet whose achievements could stand comparison with the long-established state companies. Without her drive and vision, it is unlikely that British ballet could have reached such a high standard in so short a time.

As a soloist with the Diaghilev Ballet, de Valois had the opportunity to observe at first hand the running of a major company. Typically, she observed dispassionately its weaknesses as well as its strengths, and so evolved her own plan for the establishment of a repertory British ballet.

She first established a school which would feed a company and where there could develop a recognizably English school of dancing. Her next move was to give her students a footing within the professional theatre, where they would have the chance to mature slowly, without over-performing or being overexposed to public scrutiny. She found the ideal in Lilian Baylis's Old Vic Theatre, where her dancers could appear in the opera ballets and, once Sadler's Wells Theatre had reopened in 1931, could give the occasional full evening of ballet. Here, alongside the new works created by herself and Frederick Ashton, she established the Petipa–Ivanov classics, thus providing her company with links to ballet's mainstream development and a foundation on which both dancers and repertory could build. It was the first time outside Russia that these ballets had formed a regular part of a company's repertory, and was the beginning of their present world-wide popularity.

De Valois's flair for picking the right collaborators was seen in her selection of Alicia Markova as first ballerina of the new company, and of Frederick Ashton as resident choreographer and Constant Lambert as musical director, to be followed by the development of Robert Helpmann and Margot Fonteyn as leading dancers.

By the early 1930s, de Valois was one of England's most experienced choreographers, having worked not only in opera and the commercial theatre, but also at Dublin's Abbey Theatre and the avant-garde Festival Theatre in Cambridge. She passionately believed in ballet's place alongside the other theatre arts, and in her own works she exploited the dramatic potential of dance. Much of her inspiration came from literature or painting—Blake's illustrations to the Book of Job for *Job*, Hogarth's *The Rake's Progress*, and Cervantes' *Don Quixote*—and was allied to a strong musical and visual sense so that her ballets were a perfect unity of the elements. She selected her composers and designers with great skill—Arthur Bliss and McKnight Kauffer for *Checkmate*, Gavin Gordon and Rex Whistler for *The Rake's Progress*, Roberto Gerhard and Edward Burra for *Don Quixote*. Her choreography was characterized by meticulous significant movements, all worked out in advance of rehearsal, with an emphasis upon dramatic expressiveness. She excelled at creating male roles, and only in *Checkmate* was the female dominant. Though her own training was in the classical dance, she was aware of developments elsewhere, and her work clearly showed the influence of the Central European School.

Nothing could stand in de Valois's way, and even seeming disaster turned into eventual triumph. The war could have destroyed the company, but under her guidance it undertook years of hard provincial touring that established it as the national ballet, in a way that London performances could never have done. Thus, in 1946, the Sadler's Wells Ballet was chosen to be resident at the Royal Opera House, formally recognized as Britain's premier company.

The Royal Opera House, with its boards of governors and committees, was a new world. Here de Valois's grasp of administration and the tactics of the board room were revealed—and she dealt with politicians and businessmen as readily as she had with creative artists. It was she who, perceiving the tenuous relationship between the Royal Opera House and the Sadler's Wells Ballet, conceived the granting of the Royal Charter, thus creating the Royal Ballet and establishing the independence and future of her company.

De Valois's abilities were based upon a mixture of intuitive genius, remarkable intelligence, and practical common sense. If there were talents that she overlooked, it was not as a result of failure of perception on her part, but because of a secure knowledge of the precise needs of her company at any particular time if her plan was to succeed. With typical humility and understanding of the relative importance of things, she gave up dancing once there were others to take her place, and choreography once Ashton was securely established, so that she could dedicate herself to developing and running the company. Knowing where to direct her energies at any particular time has always been one of her strengths. She was, and had to be, ruthless in pursuing her aims. But those aims were for the company, not personal glory—and she was willing to sacrifice whatever was necessary for the success of the whole.

De Valois's insight and critical faculties have never wavered. Her interest has never been in the past, but only in the future—hence her life-long devotion to the School, to which she returned after retiring from directorship of the company in 1963. Even today, she is tireless in her encouragement of young dancers and choreographers. She views the extraordinary organization that she has created dispassionately and never indulgently, bringing an unsentimental, hard-headed common sense to bear on the problems before the boards and committees on which she still sits.

De Valois's influence has spread beyond Britain; she was responsible for establishing ballet in Turkey, and ex-Royal Ballet dancers, directors, and choreographers throughout the world have confessed how much they owe to her example in their own work. Yet she is the first to acknowledge the debt she owes to others. It may take, as de Valois herself once snapped to a ballet audience anxious to acclaim her, more than one to make a ballet company: but without that one, the Royal Ballet would never have been established on the solid, professional basis that brought it, in so short a time, to such an eminent position on the world scene.

—Sarah C. Woodcock

---

## LE DIABLE À QUATRE

**Choreography:** Joseph Mazilier
**Music:** Adolph Adam
**Design:** Pierre-Luc-Charles Ciceri, Edouard-Désiré-Joseph Despléchin, Charles Séchan, Jules-Pierre-Michel Diéterle (scenery), Paul Lormier (costumes)
**Libretto:** Adolphe de Leuven (after Coffey's farce *The Devil to Pay; or, The Wives Metamorphosed*)
**First Production:** Théâtre de L'Académie royale de musique (Paris Opéra), Paris, 11 August 1845
**Principal Dancers:** Carlotta Grisi (Mazourka), Lucien Petipa (Count Polinski), Joseph Mazilier (Mazourki), Maria Jacob (Countess)

**Other productions include:** Drury Lane Theatre (staged Jean Baptiste Barrez after Mazilier), as *The Devil to Pay*; London, 24 November 1845. Broadway Theatre, New York, 1848.

### PUBLICATIONS

Lifar, Serge, *Carlotta Grisi*, Paris, 1941
Beaumont, Cyril, *Complete Book of Ballets*, revised edition, London, 1951
Guest, Ivor, *The Romantic Ballet in Paris*, London, 1966
Miguel, Parmenia, *The Ballerinas*, New York, 1972

* * *

Based on an English farce, *Le Diable à quatre* contrasts the lives of two women—the haughty, spoiled, and capricious Countess and the kind, gentle Mazourka, married to the hard-drinking Mazourki. The Countess offends a magician, disguised as a blind fiddler, but Mazourka treats him kindly. To punish the Countess, the magician causes her to change places with Mazourka for a day. Mazourka's gentle character astonishes the Count and his servants; but the Countess, although spiritedly standing up to Mazourki, is suitably chastened by her experience. She promises to reform her manner and is restored to her former state, Mazourki promises not to beat his wife in future, and the couples are reunited.

The subject of the ballet represented a new departure, for comedy ballets were rare in the Romantic era. Its subject was the manners and mores of the real world, with the minimum of supernatural characters. In comparison with many of the ballets of the time, it was an uncomplicated and realistic plot, with recognizable characters and episodes based on the ever-popular theme of the eternal battle between husband and wife. It was also hailed for its instructive, moralizing attitude.

Paris critic Hippolyte Lucas, writing in *La Siècle* in August 1845, found it a good thing that a ballet ". . . should be based on a popular idea. A folk tale, a tradition or an old farce that everyone knows has a greater chance of success than the most original flights of poetry". He went on to explain:

> The mythological ballet had the advantage that when it was in vogue, the loves of Mars and Venus and the annoyance of Vulcan still intrigued a number of minds. Mythology has now gone out of fashion. The fantastic ballet succeeded it and enjoyed its day; sylphides glided in the air, wilis lightly brushed the ground, and romantic apparitions took the place of nymphs and gods. Ballet became more obscure, but it gained something misty and aerial. Now, at the present moment, it seems to want to come to the aid of man's wisdom. *Le Diable à quatre* has set out to illustrate a proverb. . . . Joking apart, it is not a bad thing to lead ballet back, from time to time, to the simple laws of good sense.

In his choreography, Mazillier paid more attention than was usual in Paris to the dances for the ensemble. The Parisian corps de ballet had become rather undisciplined, posing rather than performing, and it was a novel experience for the audiences to see them concentrating on becoming an integral part of the drama.

The ballet was a particular triumph for Carlotta Grisi. Heretofore, she had been regarded as a lyrical and poetic dancer, but as Mazourka, she had the chance to reveal a charming wit and sparkle. The role gave her the opportunity of creating virtually two characters—the gentle, roguish village girl and the noble lady. It was an important development for her. As historian Ivor Guest has written, "Carlotta had

**Carlotta Grisi and Lucien Petipa in *Le Diable à quatre*, 1845**

returned from London with her reputation greatly enhanced after dancing in the great *Pas de Quatre* with Taglioni, Cerrito, and Grahn. Now, in the role of Mazourka, she revealed a new side to her talent, both as a dancer and as an actress." Guest goes on to quote a contemporary reviewer, who said of Grisi that "In her other roles she proved that she possessed all the poetry of dance. Today she has proved that she possesses wit to the highest degree. One might say she has almost invented it, for in our time the *ballet bouffe* had to give place to the *ballet mélancholique*, no doubt for want of worthy interpreters." Carlotta Grisi accomplished a rare feat—that of making the Paris audience laugh.

—Sarah C. Woodcock

---

## LE DIABLE BOITEUX
(also *The Devil on Two Sticks*)

**Choreography:** Jean Coralli
**Music:** Casimir Gide
**Design:** Feuchères, Charles Séchan, Jules-Pierre-Michel Diéterle, Charles-Antoine Cambon, Humanité-René Philastre (scenery), Eugène Lami (costumes)
**Libretto:** Edmond Burat de Gurgy, Adolphe Nourrit
**First Production:** Théâtre de L'Académie royale de musique (Paris Opéra), Paris, 1 June 1836
**Principal Dancers:** Fanny Elssler (Florinda), Jean-Baptiste Barrez (Asmodeus), Joseph Mazilier (Cleophas), Amélie Legallois (Dorotea), Pauline Leroux (Paquita)

**Other productions include:** Drury Lane Theatre (probably staged Joseph Mazilier after Coralli), as *The Devil on Two Sticks*, with Pauline Duvernay (Florinda); London, 1 December 1836. Her Majesty's Theatre, as *The Devil on Two Sticks*, with Fanny Elssler (Florinda); London, 9 August 1838. Maryinsky Theatre, as *The Lame Magician*; St. Petersburg, 11 October 1839.

### PUBLICATIONS

Beaumont, Cyril, *Fanny Elssler*, London, 1931
Gautier, Théophile, *The Romantic Ballet as Seen by Théophile Gautier*, translated by Cyril Beaumont, London, 1932
Beaumont, Cyril, *Complete Book of Ballets*, revised edition, London, 1951
Guest, Ivor, *The Romantic Ballet in England*, London, 1954
Guest, Ivor, *The Romantic Ballet in Paris*, London, 1966
Guest, Ivor, "The Cachucha Reborn", *Dancing Times* (London), October 1967
Guest, Ivor, *Fanny Elssler*, London, 1970
Hutchinson-Guest, Anne, *Fanny Elssler's Cachucha*, London, 1981
Cruickshank, Judith, "Fanny Elssler's Cachucha", *Dance and Dancers* (London), March 1982
Hutchinson-Guest, Anne, "A Gala For Fanny", *Dancing Times* (London), October 1985

* * *

In the nineteenth century, industrialization resulted in profound social upheaval and with it emerged a new romantic ideology as people sought to escape from the realities of everyday life. This was reflected in ballets of the period, such as Filippo Taglioni's *Le Dieu et la bayadère* (1830) and *The Revolt of the Harem* (1833), whose themes and choreographic content exhibited the public's growing fascination for foreign locations and folklore. *Le Diable boîteux*, choreographed in 1836 by Jean Coralli, is a key example of this trend. Set in Madrid, it utilizes the colourful national dances of Spain and the concurrent vogue for all things Spanish as instigated by leading figures of the Romantic movement, Alexandre Dumas and Victor Hugo.

The ballet was based on a well-known novel of the same title written by Le Sage. Divided into three acts, it follows the adventures of a young student Cleophas, who frees the limping devil Asmodeus from a bottle in which he has been imprisoned. He is rewarded with money and introductions to three ladies whom he has previously met at a masked ball—the wealthy Dorotea, dancer Florinda, and penniless Paquita. At first Cleophas pursues Florinda, but is interrupted by her ballet master and another admirer. He thus turns his attentions to Dorotea, but here again his efforts are thwarted, since he is challenged to a duel by a young officer and gambles his entire fortune away. In the concluding scene, Asmodeus reveals that the officer was Florinda in disguise, and she then presents Paquita with a purse full of gold to share with Cleophas as they decide to embark on a life together.

The premiere performance of *Le Diable boîteux* caused much excitement amongst its Parisian audience. Fanny Elssler danced the role of Florinda, and her dancing of the "cachucha" bewitched onlookers, becoming the rage in Paris, with *Le Diable boîteux* referred to as "Le Ballet de la mode". Pauline Duvernay, who appeared in the London premiere of the work in 1836 at the King's Theatre (its title translated as *The Devil on Two Sticks*), also caught the imagination of her audience, amongst whom were the Duchess of Kent and the future Queen of England, Princess Victoria. Duvernay received rapturous encores and the *Times* complimented her for a skilful execution of steps.

The success of Elssler and Duvernay was largely due to Coralli's choreography, in which he captured the flavour of Spain better than any choreographer had done previously. Taking the rhythm of the traditional Spanish melody known as the cachucha, Coralli created a solo beginning with graceful movements, developing into a vivacious and passionate dance. The solo afforded the ballerina opportunities for intricate tacqueterie—the stamping of heels, tapping of toes, the turn-in-turn-out of a foot to make the skirt sway—and for coquettish glances accompanied by a resilient arching waist. In choreographing the final scenes of the ballet, Coralli drew upon the knowledge he had gained from visits to Paris by leading Spanish dancers including Dolores Serral, Francisco Font, and Manuela Dubinon, in order to produce a series of dances recalling the zapateado, tarzico, manchegas and jaleo. Here the dancers competed against one another in an exuberant display, punctuating their movements with the clicking of heels and jingling of tambourines.

The authentic rendering of Spanish dancing was assisted by the design of the ballet, in which each of the three acts was peppered with symbols suggestive of its locale. The audiences of *Le Diable boîteux* journeyed from a Moorish palace surrounded by a garden of flowers, to the Madrid Opera House, a Spanish square, and a landscape of the Manzanares banks, with the Toledo bridge spanning its waters.

The dancers' costumes also reflected the ballet's Spanish theme, with contemporary reviews and illustrative memorabilia encapsulating its atmosphere. A great deal of this material focuses on Elssler's rendition of the cachucha, emphasizing the prominence of ballerinas in romantic ballets as she incarnated her audience's dreams and was thus elevated to celebrity status.

**Fanny Elssler in *Le Diable boiteaux*, 1836**

Gautier (in *Les Beautés de l'Opéra*, 1845) refers to Elssler's dress trimmed with broad flounces of black lace, a big comb and rose adorning her hair, while Jean-Auguste Barre's statuette depicts her costumed as a Spanish dancer wearing heeled shoes and clasping castanets in each hand.

In recent times such documentation has enabled present-day audiences to appreciate some of Coralli's choreography—for the cachucha, the choreographic centrepiece of *Le Diable boîteux*, has been reconstructed by leading dance notation expert Ann Hutchinson Guest. This came about when her husband, dance historian Ivor Guest, presented her with a copy of the book entitled *Grammatik der Tanzkunst* (*Grammar of the Art of Dancing*), written in 1887 by Friedrich Albert Zorn, who worked out a system of notation inspired by Saint-Léon and included the cachucha in his manual. Hutchinson-Guest studied Zorn's notation and sought the advice of Felicia Victoria, a specialist on Spanish dance, and together they set about reconstructing the cachucha for a modern-day ballerina to perform. The completed reconstruction was performed in 1967 by Virginia Wakelyn and subsequently filmed in 1981 with Margaret Barbieri recreating the dance Coralli originally composed for Elssler. Interestingly, Barbieri commented that she found many of the passages and repetitions of motifs involving swift footwork very difficult, affirming that Coralli's choreography for *Le Diable boîteux* demanded dancers of the highest standard, and contributed greatly to the development of dance technique.

—Melanie Trifona Christovdia

---

**DIAGHILEV, Serge**

Russian ballet impresario. Born Sergei Pavlovich Dyagilev (Diaghilev) in Novgorod, 31 March (19 March old style) 1872. Educated (in law) in St. Petersburg, from 1890. Co-founder, progressive art magazine *Mir Iskusstva* (*The World of Art*), 1899; appointed artistic adviser, Maryinsky Theatre, St. Petersburg, 1899, editing theatre *Annual* and participating in productions of *Sadko* and *Sylvia*: resigned in 1901; organizer of Russian art exhibitions in Paris and St. Petersburg, 1904–08; producer of *Boris Godunov*, Paris, 1908, leading to invitation to stage Paris season of Russian opera and ballet: founder, producer, and effective artistic director, Diaghilev's Ballets Russes, 1909–29, with seasons in Paris, Berlin, Vienna, Budapest, Monte Carlo, London, Spain, North and South America; choreographers commissioned or developed by Diaghilev include Mikhail Fokine, Léonide Massine, Vaslav Nijinsky, Bronislava Nijinska, and George Balanchine; composers include Igor Stravinsky, Maurice Ravel, Francis Poulenc, Darius Milhaud, Eric Satie; designers include Léon Bakst, Alexandre Benois, Pablo Picasso, Natalia Gontcharova, Mikhail Larionov, Pavel Tchelitchev, Henri Matisse, Jean Cocteau (also librettist). Died in Venice, 19 August 1929.

**WORKS** (as producer)

1909 *Le Pavillon d'Armide* (mus. Tcherepnine; chor. Fokine; design Benois), Diaghilev's Ballets Russes, Paris
*Polovtsian Dances from Prince Igor* (mus. Borodin, orchestrated by Rimsky-Korsakov, Glazunov; chor. Fokine; design Roerich), Diaghilev's Ballets Russes, Paris
*Le Festin* (suite of dances; mus. Glazunov, Glinka, Mussorgsky, Rimsky-Korsakov, Tchaikovsky; new chor. Fokine, with other dances by Petipa, Gorsky, Goltz, Kshesinsky; design Korovin, with costumes by Bakst, Benois, Bilibin), Diaghilev's Ballets Russes, Paris
*Les Sylphides* (new version of *Chopiniana*; mus. Chopin, orchestrated by Glazunov, Stravinsky, Taneyev; chor. Fokine; design Benois), Diaghilev's Ballets Russes, Paris
*Cléopâtre* (mus. Arensky and others; chor. Fokine; design Bakst), Diaghilev's Ballets Russes, Paris

1910 *Le Carnaval* (new production of St. Petersburg 1910 ballet; mus. Schumann, orchestrated by Arensky, Glazunov, Liadov, Rimsky-Korsakov, Tcherepnine; chor. Fokine; design Bakst), Diaghilev's Ballets Russes, Berlin
*Schéhérazade* (mus. Rimsky-Korsakov; chor. Fokine; design Bakst), Diaghilev's Ballets Russes, Paris
*Giselle* (new production; mus. Adam; chor. Petipa after Coralli, Perrot, with revisions by Fokine; design Benois), Diaghilev's Ballets Russes, Paris
*L'Oiseau de feu* (*Firebird*; mus. Stravinsky; chor. Fokine; design Golovin, with additional costumes by Bakst), Diaghilev's Ballets Russes, Paris
*Les Orientales* (mus. Arensky, Borodin, Glazunov, with Grieg, Sinding orchestrated by Stravinsky; chor. Fokine; design Korovin, with additional costumes by Bakst), Diaghilev's Ballets Russes, Paris

1911 *Le Spectre de la rose* (mus. Weber, orchestrated by Berlioz; chor. Fokine; design Bakst), Diaghilev's Ballets Russes, Monte Carlo
*Narcisse* (mus. Tcherepnin; chor. Fokine; design Bakst), Diaghilev's Ballets Russes, Monte Carlo
*Sadko* (mus. Rimsky-Korsakov, from opera *Sadko*; chor. Fokine; design Anisfeld, with additional costumes Bakst), Diaghilev's Ballets Russes, Paris
*Petrouchka* (*Petrushka*; mus. Stravinsky; chor. Fokine; design Benois), Diaghilev's Ballets Russes, Paris
*Swan Lake* (two-act version; mus. Tchaikovsky; chor. Petipa, Ivanov, with revisions by Fokine; design Korovin, Golovin), Diaghilev's Ballets Russes, London

1912 *Le Dieu bleu* (mus. Hahn; chor. Fokine; design Bakst), Diaghilev's Ballets Russes, Paris
*Thamar* (mus. Balakirev; chor. Fokine; design Bakst), Diaghilev's Ballets Russes, Paris
*L'Après-midi d'un faune* (mus. Debussy; chor. Nijinsky; design Bakst), Diaghilev's Ballets Russes, Paris
*Daphnis et Chloë* (mus. Ravel; chor. Fokine; design Bakst), Diaghilev's Ballets Russes, Paris

1913 *Jeux* (mus. Debussy; chor. Nijinsky; design Bakst), Diaghilev's Ballets Russes, Paris
*Le Sacre du printemps* (mus. Stravinsky; chor. Nijinsky; design Roerich), Diaghilev's Ballets Russes, Paris
*La Tragédie de Salomé* (mus. Schmitt; chor. Romanov; design Soudeikine), Diaghilev's Ballets Russes, Paris

1914 *Papillons* (new production of 1912 ballet; mus. Schumann, orchestrated by Tcherepnine; chor. Fokine; design Dobuzhinsky, with costumes by Bakst), Diaghilev's Ballets Russes, Monte Carlo
*The Legend of Joseph* (mus. Strauss; chor. Fokine; design Sert, with costumes by Bakst), Diaghilev's Ballets Russes, Paris
*Le Coq d'or* (opera-ballet; mus. Rimsky-Korsakov; chor. Fokine; design Goncharova), Diaghilev's Ballets Russes, Paris

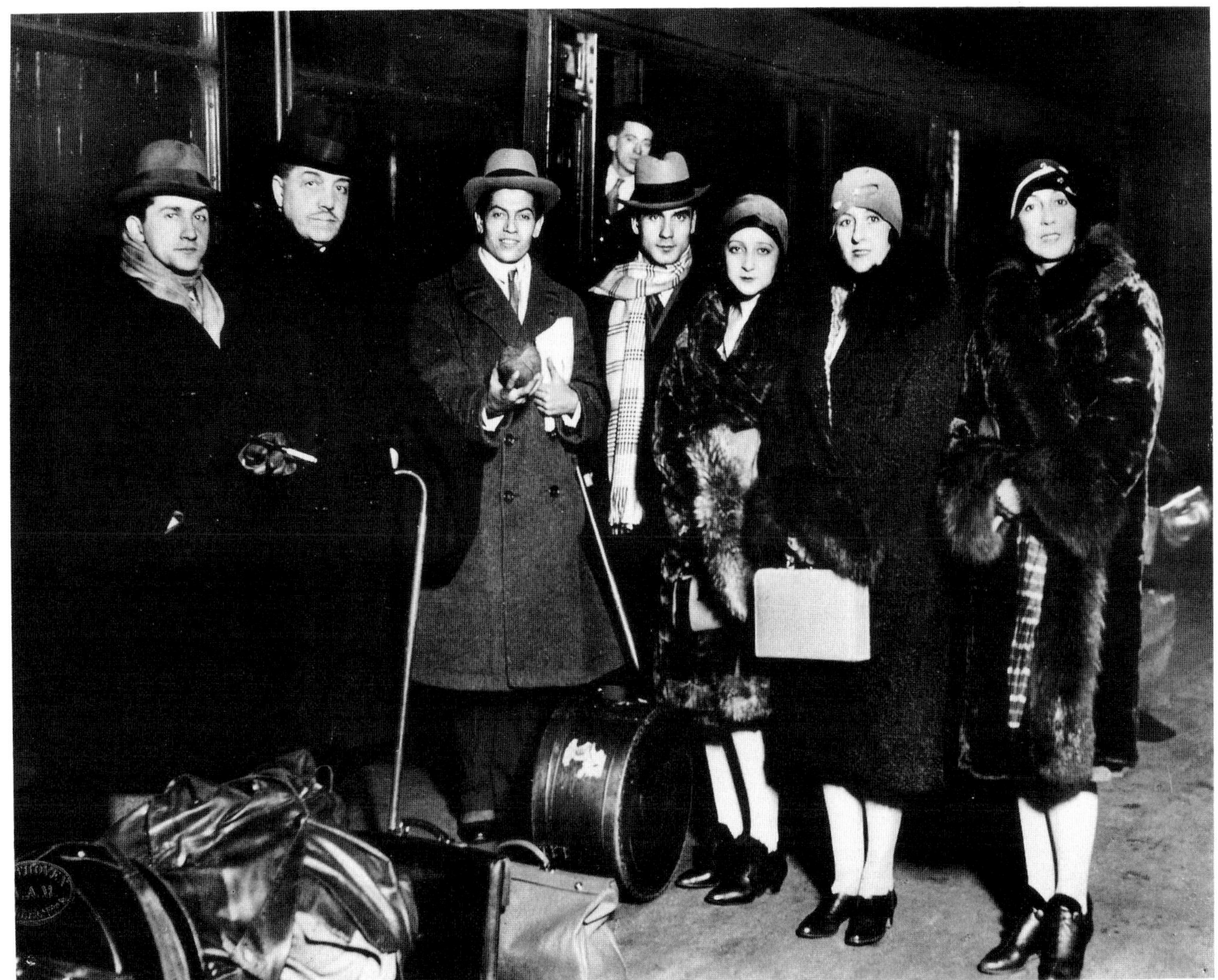

**Serge Diaghilev with members of Les Ballets Russes, London, 1928. From left to right: Roger Desmorière, Serge Diaghilev, Serge Lifar, Boris Kochno, Alexandra Danilova, Lubov Tchernicheva and Felia Doubrovska**

*Midas* (mus. Steinberg; chor. Fokine; design Dobuzhinsky), Diaghilev's Ballets Russes, Paris

1915 *Le Soleil de nuit* (mus. Rimsky-Korsakov; chor. Massine; design Larionov), Diaghilev's Ballets Russes, Geneva

1916 *Las Meninas* (mus. Fauré; chor. Massine; design Socrate, with costumes by Sert), Diaghilev's Ballets Russes, San Sebastián

*Kikimora* (mus. Liadov; chor. Massine; design Larionov), Diaghilev's Ballets Russes, San Sebastián

*Till Eulenspiegel* (mus. Strauss; chor. Nijinsky; design Jones), Diaghilev's Ballets Russes, New York

1917 *Les Femmes de bonne humeur* (*The Good-Humoured Ladies*; mus. Scarlatti, orchestrated by Tommasini; chor. Massine; design Bakst), Diaghilev's Ballets Russes, Rome

*Contes Russes* (mus. Liadov; chor. Massine; design Larionov, assisted by Gontcharova), Diaghilev's Ballets Russes, Paris

*Parade* (mus. Satie; chor. Massine; design Picasso), Diaghilev's Ballets Russes, Paris

1919 *La Boutique fantasque* (mus. Rossini, orchestrated by Respighi; chor. Massine; design Derain), Diaghilev's Ballets Russes, London

*Le Tricorne* (mus. de Falla; chor. Massine; design Picasso), Diaghilev's Ballets Russes, London

1920 *Le Chant du rossignol* (ballet adapted from opera; mus. Stravinsky; chor. Massine; design Matisse), Diaghilev's Ballets Russes, Paris

*Pulcinella* (mus. Stravinsky, after Pergolesi; chor. Massine; design Picasso), Diaghilev's Ballets Russes, Paris

*Le Astuzie femminili* (opera-ballet; mus. Cimarosa, orchestrated by Respighi; chor. Massine; design Sert), Diaghilev's Ballets Russes, Paris

1921 *Chout* (mus. Prokofiev; chor. Slavinsky, Larionov; design Larionov), Diaghilev's Ballets Russes, Paris

*The Sleeping Princess* (after Petipa's *The Sleeping Beauty*; mus. Tchaikovsky; chor. Petipa, with additional dances Nijinska; design Bakst), Diaghilev's Ballets Russes, London

1922 *Le Mariage de la belle au bois dormant* (also *Aurora's Wedding*; mus. Tchaikovsky; chor. Petipa, with additions by Nijinska; design Benois, with additional costumes by Gontcharova), Diaghilev's Ballets Russes, Paris

*Le Renard* (mus. Stravinsky; chor. Nijinska; design Larionov), Diaghilev's Ballets Russes, Paris

1923 *Les Noces* (mus. Stravinsky; chor. Nijinska; design Gontcharova), Diaghilev's Ballets Russes, Paris

1924 *Les Tentations de la bergère; ou, L'Amour vainqueur* (mus. Montéclair, orchestrated by Casadesus; chor. Nijinska; design Gris), Diaghilev's Ballets Russes, Monte Carlo

*Les Biches* (mus. Poulenc; chor. Nijinska; design Laurencin), Diaghilev's Ballets Russes, Monte Carlo

*Cimarosiana* (suite of dances from *Le Astuzie femminili*; mus. Cimarosa, chor. Massine; design Sert), Diaghilev's Ballets Russes, Monte Carlo

*Les Fâcheux* (mus. Auric; chor. Nijinska; design Braque), Diaghilev's Ballets Russes, Monte Carlo

*Night on Bald Mountain* (ballet from opera *Sorochintsy Fair*; mus. Mussorgsky; chor. Nijinska), Diaghilev's Ballets Russes, Monte Carlo

*Le Train bleu* (mus. Milhaud; chor. Nijinska; design Laurens, with costumes by Chanel), Diaghilev's Ballets Russes, Paris

1925 *Le Festin* (suite of dances; mus. Glazunov, Arensky, Mussorgsky, Satie, Delibes, Tcherepnin; chor. Balanchine, Fokine, and others), Diaghilev's Ballets Russes, Monte Carlo

*Les Contes des fées* (suite of dances from *The Sleeping Princess*; mus. Tchaikovsky; chor. Nijinska after Petipa; costumes Gontcharova), Diaghilev's Ballets Russes, Monte Carlo

*L'Assemblée* (suite of dances; mus. Gounod; chor. Balanchine and others), Diaghilev's Ballets Russes, Monte Carlo

*Le Bal du Lac de cygnes* (suite from *Swan Lake*; mus. Tchaikovsky; chor. Petipa; costumes Golovin), Diaghilev's Ballets Russes, Monte Carlo

*Zéphire et Flore* (mus. Dukelsky; chor. Massine; design Braque), Diaghilev's Ballets Russes, Monte Carlo

*Les Matelots* (mus. Auric; chor. Massine; design Pruna), Diaghilev's Ballets Russes, Paris

*Barabau* (mus. Rieti; chor. Balanchine; design Utrillo), Diaghilev's Ballets Russes, London

1926 *Romeo and Juliet* (mus. Lambert; chor. Nijinska, with entr'acte by Balanchine; design Ernst, Miró), Diaghilev's Ballets Russes, Monte Carlo

*La Pastorale* (mus. Auric; chor. Balanchine; design Pruna), Diaghilev's Ballets Russes, Paris

*Jack-in-the-Box* (mus. Satie; chor. Balanchine; design Dérain), Diaghilev's Ballets Russes, Paris

*The Triumph of Neptune* (mus. Berners; chor. Balanchine; design adapted by Prince Shervashidze, with costumes by Pruna), Diaghilev's Ballets Russes, London

1927 *La Chatte* (mus. Sauget; chor. Balanchine; design Gabo, Pevsner), Diaghilev's Ballets Russes, Monte Carlo

*Mercure* (mus. Satie; chor. Massine; design Picasso), Diaghilev's Ballets Russes, Paris

*Le Pas d'acier* (mus. Prokofiev; chor. Massine; design Yakulov), Diaghilev's Ballets Russes, Paris

1928 *Ode* (mus. Nabokov; chor. Massine; design Tchelitchev), Diaghilev's Ballets Russes, Paris

*Apollon musagète* (mus. Stravinsky; chor. Balanchine; design Bauchant), Diaghilev's Ballets Russes, Paris

*The Gods Go a-Begging* (mus. Handel, arranged by Beecham; chor. Balanchine; design Bakst, from *Daphnis and Chloë*, with costumes by Gris, from *Les Tentations de la bergère*), Diaghilev's Ballets Russes, London

1929 *Le Bal* (mus. Rieti; chor. Balanchine; design de Chirico), Diaghilev's Ballets Russes, Monte Carlo

*Le Fils prodigue* (*Prodigal Son*; mus. Prokofiev; chor. Balanchine; design Rouault), Diaghilev's Ballets Russes, Paris

**Other works include:** opera productions (as impresario)—*Boris Godunov* (mus. Mussorgsky, revised by Rimsky-Korsakov; Paris, 1908), *Ivan the Terrible* (mus. Rimsky-Korsakov; Paris, 1909), *Ruslan and Ludmila*, Act I (mus. Glinka; Paris, 1909), *Judith*, Act III (mus. Serov; Paris, 1909), *Khovanshchina* (mus. Mussorgsky, orchestrated by Rimsky-Korsakov, Ravel, Stravinsky; chor. Bolm; Paris, 1913), *Le Rossignol* (mus. Stravinsky; chor. Romanov; Paris, 1914), *May Night* (mus. Rimsky-Korsakov; chor. Bolm; London, 1914), *La Colombe* (mus. Gounod, with additions Poulenc; Monte Carlo, 1924), *Le Médecin malgré lui* (mus. Gounod, with additions Satie; Monte Carlo, 1924), *Philémon et Baucis* (mus. Gounod; Monte Carlo, 1924), *Une Education manquée* (mus. Chabrier, with additions Milhaud; Monte Carlo, 1924), *Oedipus Rex* (mus. Stravinsky; Paris, 1927).

## PUBLICATIONS

Haskell, Arnold, and Nouvel, Walter, *Diaghileff: His Artistic and Private Life*, London, 1935

Lieven, Prince Peter, *The Birth of the Ballets Russes*, translated by L. Zarine, London, 1936

Beaumont, Cyril, *The Diaghilev Ballet in London*, London, 1940

Benois, Alexandre, *Reminiscences of the Russian Ballet*, translated by Mary Britnieva, London, 1941

Grigoriev, Serge, *The Diaghilev Ballet*, translated by Vera Bowen, London, 1953

Lifar, Serge, *Serge de Diaghilev*, Paris, 1954

Buckle, Richard, *In Search of Diaghilev*, London, 1956

Kochno, Boris, *Diaghilev and the Ballets Russes*, translated by Adrienne Foulke, New York, 1970

Percival, John, *The World of Diaghilev*, London, 1971

Macdonald, Nesta, *Diaghilev Observed by Critics in England and the United States 1911–1929*, London and New York, 1975

Buckle, Richard, *Diaghilev*, London, 1979

Baer, Nancy van Norman, *The Art of Enchantment: Diaghilev's Ballets Russes*, San Francisco, 1988

Garafola, Lynn, *Diaghilev's Ballets Russes*, New York, 1989

* * *

Serge Diaghilev, a name that to many suggests a kind of Svengali of the dance, was in great part responsible for the universal acceptance of ballet as a popular form of art in the first decades of this century. The fact that Diaghilev had never studied or taught dance, and was neither dancer nor choreographer, did not deter him from establishing one of the greatest dance companies the world had ever seen.

Thanks to his already well-earned reputation as a highly gifted entrepreneur, Diaghilev was able to enlist administrative and financial support for his programmes from the very first season in Paris in 1909. Ever since childhood, Diaghilev had been a clever manipulator of those around him. During the early years of his career he had also learned to pit one faction against another, always to his own advantage. In addition to these skills in diplomacy and political manoeuvring, Diaghilev harboured a deep desire to "own" a company, much as the Tsars owned the Imperial Ballet or other Russian nobility and wealthy merchants owned opera, ballet, and theatre companies. This desire, added to the aforementioned skills, enabled Diaghilev to accomplish the nearly impossible task of establishing and continuing over twenty years to direct a ballet company which, though affiliated eventually with the Opera House at Monte Carlo, remained an autonomous institution, dependent upon the box office and upon the support of whomever Diaghilev could entice.

In the earliest years of the Ballets Russes, the dancers were merely on loan to Diaghilev from the Imperial Ballet, restricting the first few seasons to limited engagements in Paris during the summer vacation. However, after 1911 the core group—Nijinsky, Fokine, Bolm, Nijinska, Schollar, and others who formed a company in exile—was offered an escape both from a turbulent Russia, beset by political and economic problems, and from a restrictive and waning Imperial Ballet.

Just as anxious as the Russians were to go West, the Europeans, and later the Americans, were delighted to receive them. Paris, in particular, was only too eager to witness the exotic, passionate, and brilliant Slavs, wild creatures from the East who displayed a level of dance never before seen in the West. Diaghilev had recognized this market as early as 1907, when he first brought an exhibition of Russian art to Paris. From the unequalled success of that exhibition and the following year's opera and musical concerts—especially the famed production of *Boris Godunov*, which introduced Feodor Chaliapin to Western audiences—Diaghilev recognized the hunger for Russian and oriental culture abroad and consciously set about satisfying it. He produced a series of short ballets based on Russian and other exotic themes, ballets such as *The Firebird*, *Petrushka*, *Schéhérazade*, *Le Sacre du printemps*, and *Les Noces*. Passions were so aroused that police had to be called into the theatres to prevent rioting. This was particularly true of the infamous 1913 premiere of *Le Sacre du printemps*, not only marked by a modernist style of choreography by Nijinsky, but especially distinguished by the insistent percussive rhythms of Stravinsky's revolutionary score.

Although Diaghilev's primary goal was not to cause scandals, he was certainly not averse to public outcry, particularly when it boosted box office receipts. His major goal, however, continued to be that of serving his public with the kind of work it wanted, while continuing to explore and experiment in all areas of ballet production. His gift for recognizing talent, developing it, and thereby bringing about some of the most productive artistic collaborations known to the history of theatre, was unique.

A discussion of Diaghilev would not be complete without mentioning two of his strongest personality traits: his homosexuality and his Pygmalion complex. Along with his desire to create was an equally strong need to possess. There can be no better evidence of his success in this area than the three dancer/choreographers who were each, at various times in Diaghilev's life, objects of his love and subjects for his creativity. Neither Nijinsky, Massine, nor Lifar would probably have developed as choreographers without the encouragement, prompting, and manipulative direction of Diaghilev. If Diaghilev could not produce the works of art, he could certainly produce the artists who would eventually create them.

Diaghilev's great love for the visual arts and music is apparent in all Ballets Russes productions. His collaborations with long-time colleagues such as Léon Bakst, Alexandre Benois, and Nicholas Roerich were augmented by the discovery of new talent such as Stravinsky, Picasso, and Cocteau. Although his treatment of the artists was often harsh, many remained loyal to him to the end. Exceptions were, however, notable—particularly the break with Nijinsky, precipitated by the dancer's marriage during a South American tour. Diaghilev's jealousy was easily aroused by any of his artists becoming independent or joining forces with another company. His habit of setting people against each other was also evident and often quite destructive, as in his handling of certain designers (Bakst versus Benois, for example) and choreographers (Fokine versus Nijinsky, Nijinska versus Balanchine).

Diaghilev moved much further ahead than his contemporaries, producing ballets which incorporated themes or styles that were quite avant-garde for their time. This was certainly the case with Nijinsky's ballets, *L'Après-midi d'un faune*, *Jeux*, and *Le Sacre du printemps*. It was also true in the case of the Cubist ballet, *Parade* and the 1921 revival of *The Sleeping Beauty*, a production so financially disastrous it nearly caused the demise of the Ballets Russes. The irony was that within twelve years the company had come full cycle—from the Imperial Ballet days of lavish, full-length classical ballets, through a long period of modernist one-act works, to return to the classicism of Petipa once again.

Perhaps Diaghilev's greatest discovery occurred late in his life and career. In 1924 he hired a small troupe of Russian émigré dancers headed by George Balanchine. The group included Alexandra Danilova and Tamara Geva. After proving his talent by choreographing several opera ballets and a revival of Stravinsky's *Le Chant du rossignol*, Balanchine proved his genius by creating *Apollon musagète*, a collaboration with Stravinsky which was to set a standard for neo-classicism, in both ballet and music, which has rarely been equalled since.

During the last two years of his life, Diaghilev's interest in ballet diminished while his passion for book-collecting increased, until his library of rare first-edition Russian manuscripts and scores became one of the finest in the world. The collection was shared by his companion, secretary, and biographer, Boris Kochno.

In the twenty years of its existence, Diaghilev's Ballets Russes accomplished more in the development of the art form than any single institution in history. Although never content to rest on his laurels and always in fear of being thought of as old-fashioned, Diaghilev undoubtedy realized the extent of his contribution and, even within his own lifetime, knew the wide-ranging effect of his accomplishments.

—Carol Egan

---

**DIAGHILEV'S BALLETS RUSSES** *see* **BALLETS RUSSES DE SERGE DIAGHILEV**

---

**DIDELOT, Charles-Louis**

French dancer, choreographer, and teacher. Born Charles-Louis Frédéric Didelot in Stockholm, son of French choreographer and dancer of the Royal Swedish Theatre, Charles Didelot, 1767. Studied with Louis Frossard in Stockholm; later studied with Jean Dauberval, Jean-Barthélemy Lany, André Jean-Jacques Deshayes and Jean-Georges Noverre, Paris, from 1776, and with Gaetan and Auguste Vestris, Paris, from 1787. Married (1) dancer Marie Rose Paul (Pole), called Mlle Rose (d. 1803); (2) Marie Rose Colinette, in Russia, c.1805/06: son, Karl (Charles) Karlovich Didelot. Child dancer, Théâtre de l'Ambigue Comique, Paris; dancer, while still a student, L'Académie royale de musique (Paris Opéra), from 1783; returned to Stockholm, dancing in opera productions at Royal Swedish Theatre, from 1786; leading dancer, under Noverre,

King's Theatre, London, 1787–89; dancer, under ballet master Dauberval, Bordeaux, 1789–90; leading dancer, Pantheon Theatre, London, 1791; official Paris Opéra debut (in Gardel's *Le Premier Navigateur*), August 1791; leading dancer, Théâtre Montansier, Paris, 1793, performing with wife, Mlle Rose, at Théâtre des Terreaux, Lyons, 1795; choreographer, with first recorded choreography in Stockholm, 1786–87; staged *La Métamorphose*, later to develop into *Zéphire et Flore* (or *Flore et Zéphire*), Lyons, 1795; choreographer, King's Theatre, London, 1796–81, producing most famous version of *Flore et Zéphire*, 1796; ballet master, St. Petersburg, 1801–11; choreographer in London and Paris, 1811–16; returned to St. Petersburg 1816, remaining in Russia for remainder of career: differences with Emperor Nicholas I led to arrest in 1829, official dismissal 1830, actual retirement 1834. Died in Kiev, 7 November 1837.

## WORKS

1786 *Pas de deux*, Royal Opera House, Stockholm
1788 *La Bonté du Seigneur*, King's Theatre, London
*Richard Coeur-de-lion*, King's Theatre, London
1789 *New Divertissement*, King's Theatre, London
*L'Embarquement pour Cythère*, King's Theatre, London
1795 *La Métamorphose* (early version of *Zéphire et Flore*), Théâtre des Terreaux, Lyons
1796 Pas de deux in *A Divertissement*, King's Theatre, London
Pas de deux and Pas de trois in *Le Bouquet* (ballet by Onorati; mus. Mazzinghi), King's Theatre, London
*Little Peggy's Love* (mus. Bossi), King's Theatre, London
*The Caravan at Rest*, King's Theatre, London
*L'Amour vengé; ou, La Métamorphose*, King's Theatre, London
*Flore et Zéphire* (one-act version; mus. Bossi), King's Theatre, London
*L'Heureux Naufrage; ou, Les Sorcières écossaises*, (mus. Bossi), King's Theatre, London
1797 *Sappho et Phaon* (mus. Mazzinghi), King's Theatre, London
*Acis et Galathée* (one-act version; mus. Bossi), King's Theatre, London
1800 *Laura et Lenza; ou, Le Troubadour* (mus. Bossi), King's Theatre, London
1801 *Alonzo the Brave and the Fair Imogen* (mus. Bossi, Federici), King's Theatre, London
*Ken-si and Tao* (mus. Bossi), King's Theatre, London
1802 *Apollo and Daphne*, Hermitage Theatre, St. Petersburg
1803 *Roland and Morgana* (mus. Cavos), Imperial Theatres, St. Petersburg
*Le Pâtre et l'hamadryade*, Imperial Theatres, St. Petersburg
1804 *Zéphire et Flore* (extended one-act version), Hermitage Theatre, St. Petersburg
1807 *Medée et Jason* (five-act version, after Le Picq), Imperial Theatres, St. Petersburg
1808 Dances in *The Sea Pier* (divertissement), Imperial Theatres, St. Petersburg
*Don Quixote*, Imperial Theatres, St. Petersburg
*Golden Wedding* (divertissement), Imperial Theatres, St. Petersburg
1809 *Psyche et l'Amour*, Hermitage Theatre, St. Petersburg
*Solange Rose*, Imperial Theatres, St. Petersburg
*Zélis et Alcindor; ou, La Forêt aux aventures* (mus. Cavos), Tavritsky Palace, St. Petersburg
1810 *Laura and Henry; or, The Defeat of the Moors*, Hermitage Theatre, St. Petersburg
*Dove of Zélis* (new version of *Zélis et Alcindor*), Pupils of the Imperial Theatre School, St. Petersburg (staged c.1810)
1812 *Zélis; ou, La Forêt aux aventures* (mus. Venua), King's Theatre, London
*L'Epreuve; ou, La Jambe de bois* (mus. Venua), King's Theatre, London
*Zéphyr inconstant puni et fixe; ou, Les Noces de Flore* (new one-act version of *Zéphyr et Flore*; mus. Venua), King's Theatre, London
*La Reine de Golconde* (mus. Venua), King's Theatre, London
*Russian Dance* in *Le Bal champêtre* (divertissement; mus. Venua), King's Theatre, London
1813 *Le Pâtre et l'hamadryade* (mus. Venua), King's Theatre, London
*Une Soirée d'été* (divertissement), King's Theatre, London
*La Chaumière hongroise; ou, Les Illustres Fugitifs* (two-act version, later *The Hungarian Hut*; mus. Venua), King's Theatre, London
*Les Amants péruviens* (divertissement), King's Theatre, London
*Kacheli* (Russian divertissement; mus. Fiorillo), King's Theatre, London
*L'Indorf et Rosalie; ou, L'Heureuse Ruse* (later *Rosalie et Dozinval*; mus. Mortellari), King's Theatre, London
*Le Troubadour* (divertissement from *Laura et Lenza*; mus. Venua), King's Theatre, London
1814 *Thamaida et Alonzo; ou, L'Isle sauvage* (mus. Jouve), King's Theatre, London
*Karl et Lisbeth; ou, Le Déserteur malgré lui* (mus. Horn), King's Theatre, London
*New Spanish Divertissement*, King's Theatre, London
*Le Bazzard d'Algier; ou, Le Retour du corsair*, King's Theatre, London
1815 *Zéphire et Flore* (two-act version; mus. Venua, Hus-Desforges, Lefèvre), Opéra, Paris (staged Hermitage Theatre, St. Petersburg, 1818)
1816 *Return of the Heroes*, Imperial Palace, Pavlovsk
*Acis et Galathée* (two-act version; mus. Cavos), Imperial Theatres, St. Petersburg
*Holiday in the Seraglio* (divertissement), Imperial Theatres, St. Petersburg
1817 *The Unexpected Return; or, Evening in the Garden* (divertissement), Imperial Theatres, St. Petersburg
*The Young Milkmaid; or, Nicette and Luke* (mus. Antonolini), Imperial Theatres, St. Petersburg
*Apollo and the Muses* (divertissement), Imperial Theatres, St. Petersburg
*Don Carlos and Rozalba; or, The Lover, the Doll, and the Model* (mus. Cavos), Imperial Theatres, St. Petersburg
*Theseus and Ariadne; or, The Defeat of the Minotaur* (mus. Antonolini), Imperial Theatres, St. Petersburg
*La Chaumière hongroise; ou, Les Illustres Fugitifs* (four-act version; with Auguste (Poirot); mus. Venua), Imperial Theatres, St. Petersburg
1818 Dances in *Apollon and Pallada in the North* (prologue; text Sheller, mus. Cavos), opening of Bolshoi Theatre, St. Petersburg
*The Young Island Girl; or, Leon and Tamaida* (mus. Cavos), Imperial Theatres, St. Petersburg
*The Caliph of Bagdad; or, The Youthful Adventures of Harun Al-Rashid* (mus. Antonolini), Imperial The-

atres, St. Petersburg
*A Hunting Adventure* (mus. Cavos), Imperial Theatres, St. Petersburg
1819 *Medée et Jason* (four-act version, after Le Picq), Imperial Theatres, St. Petersburg
*Raoul de Créquis; or, Return from the Crusades* (mus. Cavos), Imperial Theatres, St. Petersburg
*The Sea Victory; or, Liberation of the Captives* (mus. Antonolini et al.), Imperial Theatres, St. Petersburg
*Bazaar* (divertissement), Imperial Theatres, St. Petersburg
*Ken-Si and Tao; or, The Beauty and the Beast* (new version; mus. Antonolini), Imperial Theatres, St. Petersburg
*Laura and Henry; or, The Troubadour* (new version; mus Cavos), Imperial Theatres, St. Petersburg
*Raoul Barbe-Bleue* (after Valberg, with Auguste; mus. Cavos, Antonolini), Imperial Theatres, St. Petersburg
1820 *Inès de Castro* (with Auguste; mus. Boieldieu), Imperial Theatres, St. Petersburg
*The Abduction: or, Robert Ataman of the Robbers* (with Auguste), Imperial Theatres, St. Petersburg
*Karl et Lisbeth; ou, Le Déserteur malgré lui* (new version; mus. Turik), Imperial Theatres, St. Petersburg
*Cora and Alonso; or, The Virgin of the Sun* (mus. Antonolini), Imperial Theatres, St. Petersburg
*Euthyme et Eucharis; or, The Vanquished Shade of Libas* (mus. Jomas), Imperial Theatres, St. Petersburg
1821 *Alcestis; or, The Descent of Hercules into the Underworld* (mus. Antonolini), Imperial Theatres, St. Petersburg
*Roland and Morgana; or, The Destruction of the Enchanted Island* (new version; mus. Antonolini), Imperial Theatres, St. Petersburg
*The Return from India; or, The Wooden Leg* (mus. Venua), Imperial Theatres, St. Petersburg
*Algerian Bandits*, Imperial Theatres, St. Petersburg
1822 *L'Offrande à l'Amour*, Imperial Theatres, St. Petersburg
*The Princess of Trebizond; or, The Island of the Dumb* (with Shakovskoi; mus. Cavos), Imperial Theatres, St. Petersburg
1823 *Lily of Narbonne; or, The Knight's Vow* (with Shakovskoi; mus. Cavos), Imperial Theatres, St. Petersburg
*The Prisoner of the Caucasus; or, Shade of the Bride* (mus. Cavos), Imperial Theatres, St. Petersburg
*Anacreon and Cupidon* (mus. Cavos), Imperial Theatres, St. Petersburg
*Spanish Diversion; or, Masks* (divertissement), Imperial Theatres, St. Petersburg
*The Abduction* (with Auguste; mus. various), Imperial Theatres, St. Petersburg
1824 *The European Saved by a Savage; or, The Broken Idol* (mus. Turik), Imperial Theatres, St. Petersburg
*New Slavic Folk Dance and Comic Harlequin Scene*, Imperial Theatres, St. Petersburg
*Cendrillon* (mus. Cavos), Imperial Theatres, St. Petersburg
*La Forêt noire* (with Auguste; mus. Paris), Imperial Theatres, St. Petersburg
*Ruslan and Ludmila; or, The Overthrow of Chernomor the Evil Sorceror*, (with Auguste, after Glushkovsky; mus. Sholtz), Imperial Theatres, St. Petersburg
1825 *Phaedra* (mus. Cavos, Turik, Shelikhov), Imperial Theatres, St. Petersburg
Harem divertissement in *Kerim-Girei* (romantic trilogy; mus. Cavos), Imperial Theatres, St. Petersburg
Divertissement and final ballet in *Satan and All His Devices: or, The Lesson of the Sorcerer* (based on the opera *Le Diable à quatre*; mus. Cavos, Turik, Shelikhov), Imperial Theatres, St. Petersburg
1826 *The Dream Realized* (national divertissement), Imperial Theatres, St. Petersburg
1827 *Fête villageoise* (with Auguste; mus. Cavos, arr. Turik, Shelikhov), Kamenny Island Theatre
*Liza and Colin; or, Vain Precautions* (after Dauberval's *La Fille mal gardée*), Imperial Theatres, St. Petersburg
1828 *Dido; or, The Destruction of Carthage* (with Auguste, after Le Picq; mus. Soler et al., arranged Cavos), Imperial Theatres, St. Petersburg
1829 *The Mad Woman; or, The Coming of the New Lord* (mus. Hérold), Imperial Theatres, St. Petersburg
*The New Heroine; or, The Cossack Woman* (with Auguste: mus. arrangements of Titov and others), Imperial Theatres, St. Petersburg
*Piramo e Tisbe* (with Auguste; mus. Canziani), St. Petersburg

**Other works include:** dances in operas—*Frigga* (mus. Ahlström; Stockholm, 1787), *Chimène* (mus. Sacchini; Bordeaux, 1790), *Zémire et Azor* (mus. Grétry; London, 1796), *Le Calife de Bagdad* (mus. Boieldieu; St. Petersburg, 1806), *Télémaque dans l'Isle de Calypso* (mus. Boieldieu; St. Petersburg, 1806), *Aline, reine de Golconde* (mus. Boieldieu; St. Petersburg, 1816), *Belmonte and Constanze* (*Die Entfürung aus dem Serail*; mus. Mozart; St. Petersburg, 1816), *Le Sacrifice interrompu* (mus. Winter; St. Petersburg, 1817), *Le Prince de Catane* (mus. Isouard; St. Petersburg, 1817), *Le Caravane de Caire* (mus. Grétry; St. Petersburg, 1817), *Télémaque dans l'isle de Calypso* (mus. Boieldieu; St. Petersburg, 1817), *Roxus Pumpernickel; or, He Came to Get Married and Didn't* (St. Petersburg, 1818), *Lodoiska; ou, Les Tartares* (mus. Kreutzer; St. Petersburg, 1818), *Zoraïme et Zulnare* (mus. Boieldieu; St. Petersburg, 1818), *The Ruins of Babylon; or, The Triumph and Fall of Giafar Barmecide* (mus. Cavos; St. Petersburg, 1818), *Dobrynia Nikitich; ou, Le Château terrible* (mus. Cavos, Antonolini; St. Petersburg, 1818), *La Vestale* (mus. Spontini; St. Petersburg, 1819), *Le Petit Chaperon rouge* (mus. Boieldieu; St. Petersburg, 1819), *La Clochette* (mus. Hérold; St. Petersburg, 1819), *Ferdinand Cortes; or, The Conquering of Mexico* (mus. Spontini; St. Petersburg, 1820), *Les Bayadères* (mus. Catel; St. Petersburg, 1820), *Alexander of Macedon in India* (mus. Neukomm; St. Petersburg, 1821), *Toberne: ou, Le Pêcheur suédois* (mus. Bruni; St. Petersburg, 1822), *Naina; or, The Magic Rose-Leaf* (mus. Boieldieu, Isouard, Cavos; St. Petersburg, 1822), *The Firebird; or, The Adventures of Tsarevich Ivan* (mus. Cavos, Antonolini; St. Petersburg, 1822), *Svetlana; or, A Hundred Years in One Day* (mus. Catel; St. Petersburg, 1822), *Jeanne d'Arc; or, The Maid of Orleans* (mus. Carafa; St. Petersburg, 1823), *The Genie Iturbiel; or, The Thousand Years and Two Days of Vizier Haroun* (mus. Cavos, Antonolini, Méhul, Isouard; St. Petersburg, 1823), *Roger de Sicile* (mus. Berton; St. Petersburg, 1824), *The Secret Patron* (mus. Kreutzer; St. Petersburg, 1825), *La Neige* (mus. Auber; St. Petersburg, 1826), *Miroslava; ou, Le Bucher de la Mort* (mus. Antonolini, Cavos, Shelikov; St. Petersburg, 1827); dances in plays and spectacles—*Marguerite d'Anjou* (historic drama; St. Petersburg, 1816), *Semélé; ou, La Vengeance de Junon* (mythological presentation; mus. Cavos, Antonolini; St. Petersburg, 1818), *Le Marchand de Smyrne* (opera-vaudeville; St. Petersburg, 1819), *The Banquet of John Lackland* (analogical prologue; St. Petersburg, 1821), *Charade in Action* (mus. Verstovsky, Maurer; St. Petersburg, 1823), *The Pirate* (romantic comedy; St. Petersburg, 1823), *Finn* (comedy in verse; St. Petersburg, 1824), *The Return of Prince Pozharsky to His Estate* (analogical divertissement; mus. Cavos; St.

Petersburg, 1826), *Joy of the Moldavians; or, Victory* (mus. Cavos, Eizerich; St. Petersburg, 1828).

## PUBLICATIONS

Mundt, N.P., *Karl Ludovik Didlo, Repertory of the Russian Theatre*, vol. 1, part 3, 1840
Saint-Léon, Arthur, *La Sténochorégraphie*, Paris, 1852
Kirstein, Lincoln, *Dance: A Short History of Classic Theatrical Dancing*, New York, 1935
Rey, Ian, *Charles Louis Didelot*, Prague, 1937
Glushkovsky, Adam, *Memoirs of a Ballet Master*, Moscow, 1940
Beaumont, Cyril, *Complete Book of Ballets*, revised edition, London, 1951
Guest, Ivor, *The Romantic Ballet in England*, London, 1954
Hall, Fernau, *World Dance*, New York, 1955
Slonimsky, Yuri, *Didelot*, Leningrad, 1958
Krasovskaya, Vera, *Russian Ballet Theatre of the First Half of the Nineteenth Century*, Moscow and Leningrad, 1958
Roslavleva, Natalia, *Era of the Russian Ballet*, London, 1966
Kirstein, Lincoln, *Movement and Metaphor: Four Centuries of Ballet*, New York, 1970
Swift, Mary Grace, *A Loftier Flight: The Life and Accomplishments of Charles-Louis Didelot, Balletmaster*, Middletown, Connecticut and London, 1974
Lawson, Joan, *A History of Ballet and its Makers*, London, 1976

* * *

Didelot was a pivotal figure in the history of ballet. In his youth, male dancers—no matter what part they played—were used to wearing buckled, heeled shoes, powdered wigs, and knee breeches. In the ballet *Bacchus et Ariadne* (1791), Didelot dared to dance in flesh-coloured tights with a tiger skin thrown over his shoulder and grape leaves in his hair. Later in 1791, he appeared in the ballet *Corisande* in a gauzy tunic, while his partner, Mlle. Chevigny, also wore a Greek-type costume. In his early ballets, some dancers appeared in Greek-type cothurnes. More importantly, in his later ballets, dancers began to dance sur les pointes, thought it is difficult to document at exactly what time this practice began.

Early in life, Didelot's face was disfigured by smallpox scars. His physique was hardly that of a "danseur-noble"; on the contrary, it was wiry and sinewy. He concentrated, therefore, on speed, on performing dazzling pirouettes and other movements to distract from his physical shortcomings. It was not for his dancing, however, but for his choreography and teaching that Didelot gained his most lasting fame. His arrival in Russia in 1801 was a landmark in the history of Russian ballet. Didelot injured himself severely in 1805 and from that point, his energy was spent pre-eminently in choreography and teaching. In St. Petersburg, there was fertile ground for his great creativity to blossom. In 1802 he had his Russian début as a choreographer with his ballet *Apollo and Daphne*. From 1801 to 1811, he gained a wide following among the capital's balletomanes, but troubles and disagreements with administration, as well as the burning of the Imperial Theatre, urged him to return to London.

There, Didelot enjoyed fame and good pay, but his heart was always in Paris. When the opportunity came in 1815 to stage his lovely *Zéphire et Flore* at the Opéra, he accomplished it with astounding success, but he could never cope with the cliques and machinations of the Opéra's administration, so he turned again to Russia for the last phase of his career.

In Russia he enjoyed the luxury of having a subsidized ballet school to train dancers for his productions. Before Didelot's time, the well-endowed state theatres had assiduously imported expensive foreign stars to dance the main parts in ballets. Ultimately, his school produced a sufficient number of competent performers to allow the administration had to rely less on imported talent. His pupils never forgot their master, for his methods were draconian and severe, often enforced with the aid of a stick. In private dealings with his pupils, however, Didelot was compassionate and defensive of their personal well-being when this could be threatened by exploitative theatre administrators.

Didelot not only developed the dancers' technical expertise in performing astounding physical feats for their day, but he also emphasized intense training in mime, urging his dancers to achieve a "soulful" performance, to *act* their parts with feeling and expression instead of performing mere mechanical feats. In this he was eminently successful, and was a prime force in establishing a tradition in Russian ballet which emphasized the dramatic potential of the dancer's role. The Russian poet Alexander Pushkin immortalized Didelot in his poem *Eugene Onegin*, referring to the "soulful flights" performed by Avdotia Istomina, one of the most famous ballerinas to grace his Russian productions.

In his productions, Didelot went to great lengths to bring astounding, realistic effects to the stage, another characteristic of Russian ballet that has endured to the present. In the ballet *Cora and Alonso*, for example, a live volcano was depicted on the stage. His works were also characterized by the use of intricate stage machinery to produce "flights" of his dancers.

Didelot appeared on the artistic scene at a time when classicism was giving way to romanticism. While he employed many classical, mythological themes in his works, such as *Zéphire et Flore* (his most famous and enduring work), he entered fully into the new romantic spirit, utilizing folk themes with local colour in a number of works, such as *The Prisoner of the Caucasus*.

Didelot never found it easy to practise the obsequiousness toward officialdom that was necessary in the ballet world of his day, and in 1834, after many altercations with the management, his contract with the Imperial Theatres was terminated. He journeyed to Kiev for his health, and there he died, leaving behind many disconsolate balletomanes in St. Petersburg.

—Mary Grace Swift

---

## DIVERTIMENTO NO. 15

**Choreography:** George Balanchine
**Music:** Wolfgang Amadeus Mozart
**Design:** James Stewart Morcom (scenery), Barbara Karinska (costumes)
**First Production:** New York City Ballet, New York State Theatre, New York, 19 December 1956 (preview at American Shakespeare Theatre, Stratford, Connecticut, 31 May 1956)
**Principal Dancers:** Diana Adams, Melissa Hayden, Yvonne Mounsey, Patricia Wilde, Barbara Milberg, Nicholas Magallanes, Roy Tobias, Jonathan Watts

**Other productions include:** New York City Ballet (earlier version of ballet: chor. Balanchine, costumes Christian Bérard), as *Caracole*, with Maria Tallchief, Melissa Hayden, Patricia Wilde, Diana Adams, Tanaquil LeClercq, André

Eglevsky, Nicholas Magallanes, Jerome Robbins; New York, 19 February 1952. New York City Ballet (new scenery David Hays, new costumes Barbara Karinska); New York, 27 April 1966. Vienna State Opera Ballet; Vienna, 26 May 1969. Bavarian State Opera Ballet; Munich, 20 December 1970. Dutch National Ballet, 17 June 1971. Geneva Ballet, with guest artists from New York City Ballet; Geneva, 1971. Hamburg Ballet, 16 November 1971. Royal Danish Ballet; Copenhagen, 9 February 1978. Paris Opera Ballet (as *Divertimento*); Paris, 31 March 1978. San Francisco Ballet (staged Francia Russell); San Francisco, 15 October 1979. Les Grands Ballets Canadiens; Montreal, 15 November 1979. Birmingham Royal Ballet (staged Victoria Simon); Birmingham 13 October 1989. Finnish National Ballet (staged Patricia Neary); Helsinki, January 1992.

## PUBLICATIONS

Balanchine, George, with Mason, Francis, *Balanchine's Complete Stories of the Great Ballets*, Garden City, N.Y., 1977

Reynolds, Nancy, *Repertory in Review*, New York, 1977

Kirstein, Lincoln, *30 Years: The New York City Ballet*, New York, 1978

Croce, Arlene, *Going to the Dance*, New York, 1982

* * *

*Divertimento No. 15* is one of George Balanchine's most intricate, limpid, and luminous creations; it is also one of the ballet master's earliest clinical titles. Balanchine had given his dances the names of their music before, but except in the case of his 1954 *Opus 34*, a now lost exercise in grotesquerie, he hadn't given the catalogue number as well. Actually, the first time he fashioned a dance from this particular Mozart composition, he gave it a fanciful name, *Caracole*. That was in 1952, and the choreography displayed five ballerinas, three cavaliers, and an ensemble of eight women—precisely the same configuration as that of the 1956 *Divertimento*. For designs, the first ballet to this iridescent Mozart confection used Christian Bérard's costume scheme for Balanchine's 1933 *Mozartiana*. The references in those costumes, like the reference in the title, evoked images of horse ballets.

For his second serving up of this Mozart composition (which Balanchine is said to have considered the finest Divertimento ever written), the choreographer devised new dances, finding he had forgotten his *Caracole* version. The old *Caracole* title was initially used for the very first performance of the new staging, then changed to the *Divertimento* some months later. Whatever the specific choreographic changes, some relationship between the two ballets remained, especially in the case of material performed by dancers who were in both stagings. Diana Adams, Melissa Hayden, Tanaquil LeClercq, Patricia Wilde, and Nicholas Magallanes were in the first performances of both creations. (Wilde and Magallanes changed their place in the ballet's hierarchy—in *Divertimento* each assumed the central role after having performed a lesser role in *Caracole*—but everyone else remained in a consistent role.)

In both works Balanchine used the score in the same way, structuring his ballet according to the musical movements, omitting in each case its second minuet (the fifth movement), and the andante from its sixth movement. *Divertimento No. 15* is thus arranged as follows: Allegro (for the full cast), Theme and Variations (alternating solo dances for the two side cavaliers and successive solos for the five ballerinas and the central cavalier), Minuet (for the ensemble), Andante (pas de deux for each of the ballerinas partnered by one of the three men), and Finale (full cast, climax and recapitulations). In the late 1960s, Balanchine amplified his Andante by creating a grand promenade and reverence for the men and women, accompanied by a specially arranged cadenza for violin and viola composed by John Colman.

Although Balanchine gave his sublime show of classical dancing an almost clinical title in 1956, he initially surrounded it with scrolled and floral trappings reminiscent of its rococo eighteenth-century milieu. At first it was performed with a backdrop by James Stewart Morcom, originally used to decorate the stage of *Symphonie Concertante* (1947), another of Balanchine's rare Mozart ballets. Subsequently he had his dance decorated with a surround of trellises and floral details designed by David Hayes. The costumes for this version were consistently the work of Barbara Karinska, who used a palette of creamy yellows and whites accented with light blues. The men were in formally decorated and bi-coloured tunics with tights, with the women in satin-skirted tutus which had the look of floral beds (on the leads) and scallop shells (on the ensemble).

Eventually, all Balanchine felt his audiences needed to see was his prettily dressed dancers and their dancing, and he did away with all semblance of décor. Plainly titled and plainly presented, *Divertimento No. 15* remained anything but a plain work of art. In pace, plastique, and complexity of invention, this ballet keeps opening up and expanding, giving off in the process of solo, duo, and grouped moments an intoxicating perfume at once delicate and definite.

Having eliminated the specific references imparted by his first title and indicated by details of setting, Balanchine left his dancers' elaborate moves and chivalrous manners to speak for themselves. His ballet is a poem of individualized timeless beauty, a classical work of art about classical values untethered by specific locale or situation. His dramatic, uneven set-up of five women and three men maintains itself, even when the two sexes meet for interrelated dances, mainly pas de deux. The ballerinas of *Divertimento No. 15* are all aspects of love and are never reduced to partners of one lover. The pairing of the ballerinas with cavaliers is neither fixed nor final. While one ballerina has central pride of place in the overall scheme of the groupings and in terms of sequence and virtuoso material in solo-dancing, she does not remain consistently paired with the cavalier who occupies a similarly central position amid his fellow danseurs. Balanchine does not reduce Mozart's divertimento to a situation about particular lovers; he illuminates it as a paean to eternal love.

—Robert Greskovic

---

## DOLGUSHIN, Nikita

Russian dancer, choreographer, and teacher. Born Nikita Aleksandrovich Dolgushin in Leningrad, 8 November 1938. Studied at the Leningrad Choreographic (Vaganova) School, pupil of M. Mikhailov, Aleksandr Pushkin; graduated in 1959. Married Aleksandra Dulgushina, 1960. Dancer, Kirov Ballet, 1959–61; principal dancer, Novosibirsk Ballet (dir. Gusev), 1961–66, Moiseyev's Young Ballet (State Concert Ensemble), 1966–68; also guest artist, Australian Ballet, 1961, Kirov Ballet, 1968 (performing with Natalia Makarova), 1972, 1982; principal dancer, Maly Theatre Ballet, 1968–83, performing also in London, Paris, Vienna, Canada, Germany, India, and appearing as well in films and on television, including *Ballet Miniatures* (Leningrad television, 1971) and *Nikita Dolgushin Dancing* (Leningrad television, 1982); also choreographer and

**Nikita Dolgushin in rehearsal**

teacher, graduating from the Leningrad Conservatory, 1980: professor, Choreographers' Faculty, and artistic director, Student Ballet, Leningrad Conservatory, from 1983; director, Choreographers' Faculty, from 1986; guest instructor, International Ballet Symposium, Towson State University, Baltimore, Maryland, 1989; also member of editors' collegium, *Sovetsky Balet* magazine, Moscow. Recipient: Gold Medal, International Ballet Competition, Varna, 1964; title of Honoured Artist of the Russian Federation, 1964; People's Artist of the USSR, 1976; D.H.L., Towson State University, 1991.

## ROLES

1959 Liszt (cr) in *Lisztiana* (Goleizovsky), Graduation Performance, Leningrad Choreographic School, Leningrad
- Satyr in *Spartacus* (Yakobson), Kirov Ballet, Leningrad
- Principal dancer in *The Kiss* (choreographic miniature; Yakobson), Kirov Ballet, Leningrad
- Principal dancer in *The Blind Girl* (choreographic miniature; Yakobson), Kirov Ballet, Leningrad
- Troubadour, Paris in *Romeo and Juliet* (Lavrovsky), Kirov Ballet, Leningrad

1960 The Youth in *Chopiniana* (Fokine), Kirov Ballet, Leningrad
- The Prince in *The Nutcracker* (Vainonen), Kirov Ballet, Leningrad
- Pas de trois in *Swan Lake* (Sergeyev after Petipa, Ivanov), Kirov Ballet, Leningrad
- Troubadour in *Raymonda* (Sergeyev after Petipa), Kirov Ballet, Leningrad
- Albrecht in *Giselle* (Petipa after Coralli, Perrot), Kirov Ballet, Leningrad
- Mephistopholes in *Masked Ball* (Fenster), Kirov Ballet, Leningrad
- Principal dancer in *Waltz* (choreographic miniature; Yakobson), Kirov Ballet, Leningrad

1961 Smith in *The Path of Thunder* (Sergeyev), Kirov Ballet, Leningrad
- Ferkhad in *The Legend of Love* (Grigorovich), Novosibirsk Ballet, Novosibirsk

1962 Young Man in *Leningrad Symphony* (Belsky), Novosibirsk Ballet, Novosibirsk
- Ferkhad in *The Legend of Love* (Grigorovich), Novosibirsk Ballet, Novosibirsk

1963 Bakhram (cr) in *Seven Beauties* (Gusev), Novosibirsk Ballet, Novosibirsk

Jean de Brienne in *Raymonda* (Vainonen after Petipa; staged Gusev), Novosibirsk Ballet, Novosibirsk
Prince Siegfried in *Swan Lake* (Petipa, Ivanov, staged Vinogradov, Gusev), Novosibirsk Ballet, Novosibirsk
1964 Prince (cr) in *Cinderella* (Vinogradov), Novosibirsk Ballet, Novosibirsk
Solor in *La Bayadère* (Petipa), Novosibirsk Ballet, Novosibirsk
1965 Romeo (cr) in *Romeo and Juliet* (Vinogradov), Novosibirsk Ballet, Novosibirsk
The Slave in *Le Corsaire* (Petipa, staged Gusev), Novosibirsk Ballet, Novosibirsk
1966 Prince Désiré in *The Sleeping Beauty* (Petipa, staged Gusev), Novosibirsk Ballet, Novosibirsk
Soloist (cr) in *Bolero* (Blinov after Tangieva-Bereznak), Novosibirsk Ballet, Novosibirsk
1967 Principal dancer (cr) in *Two Preludes* (Goleizovsky), Concert for Nikita Dolgushin, Tchaikovsky Concert Hall, Moscow
1968 Albrecht in *Giselle* (Petipa after Coralli, Perrot), Kirov Ballet, Leningrad
Cavalier in *Paquita* (Petipa, staged Boyarsky), Maly Theatre Ballet, Leningrad
1969 Hamlet (cr) in *Meditations* (also chor.), Maly Theatre Ballet, Leningrad
Principal dancer (cr) in *Concert in White* (also chor.), Maly Theatre Ballet, Leningrad
Soloist in *Pas de Deux* (also chor.), Maly Theatre Ballet, Leningrad
Prince (cr) in *The Nutcracker* (Belsky), Maly Theatre Ballet, Leningrad
1971 Cavalier (cr) in *Mozartiana* (also chor.), Maly Theatre Ballet, Leningrad
Colin (cr) in *La Fille mal gardée* (Vinogradov), Maly Theatre Ballet, Leningrad
Romeo (cr) in *Romeo and Juliet* (also chor.), Maly Theatre Ballet, Leningrad
Soloist (cr) in *Chamber Suite* (also chor.), Maly Theatre Ballet, Leningrad
1972 Toreador in *Carmen Suite* (Zamuel), Maly Theatre Ballet, Leningrad
Title role in *Hamlet* (Sergeyev), Kirov Ballet, Leningrad
1973 Franz (cr) in *Coppélia* (Vinogradov), Maly Theatre Ballet, Leningrad
1974 Prince Igor (cr) in *Yaroslavna* (Vinogradov), Maly Theatre Ballet, Leningrad
1975 James in *La Sylphide* (von Rosen after Bournonville), Maly Theatre Ballet, Leningrad
1976 The Poet in *The Crossroads* (Lebedev), Maly Theatre Ballet, Leningrad
1977 Tutor (cr) in *Educational Poem* (Vinogradov), Maly Theatre Ballet, Leningrad
1978 Title role (cr) in *Tsar Boris* (Boyarchikov), Maly Theatre Ballet, Leningrad
1981 Phoebus in *Esmeralda* (Boyarchikov after Perrot, Petipa), Maly Theatre Ballet, Leningrad
1982 Basil in *Don Quixote* (Gorsky after Petipa), Kirov Ballet, Leningrad
Carl (cr) in *The Robbers* (Boyarchikov), Kirov Ballet, Leningrad
1984 Title role (cr) in *Narcissus* (Aleksidze), Leningrad Conservatory Student Ballet, Leningrad
Soloist (cr) in *Monologue of Jude* (Aleksidze), Leningrad Conservatory Student Ballet, Leningrad
The Moor in *The Moor's Pavanne* (also chor., after Limón), Leningrad
Soloist in *Andante Sostenuto* (also chor.), Leningrad Conservatory Student Ballet, Leningrad
1985 Title role in *Don Juan* (Aleksidze), Leningrad Conservatory Student Ballet, Leningrad
1986 Soloist in *The Dream* (also chor.), Leningrad Conservatory Student Ballet, Leningrad
1988 Title role in *Hamlet* (also chor.; new production), Leningrad Conservatory Student Ballet, Leningrad
1991 Prince (cr) in *Cinderella* (also chor.), Towson State University, Baltimore

**Other roles include:** for the Maly Theatre Ballet—title role in *Le Spectre de la rose* (Fokine), soloist in Grand Pas from *Flower Festival at Genzano* (Bournonville, staged von Rosen); for the Novosibirsk Ballet—Solor in *La Bayadère* (Petipa), the Youth in *Chopiniana* (Fokine).

## WORKS

1967 *Impulse* (mus. Schumann), Tchaikovsky Concert Hall, Moscow
1969 *Meditations* (*Hamlet*; mus. Tchaikovsky), Maly Theatre Ballet, Leningrad
*Concert in White* (mus. Tchaikovsky), Maly Theatre Ballet, Leningrad
*Pas de Deux* (mus. Rossini), Maly Theatre Ballet, Leningrad
1970 *Mozartiana* (mus. Tchaikovsky), Maly Theatre Ballet, Leningrad
1971 *Romeo and Juliet* (mus. Tchaikovsky), Maly Theatre Ballet, Leningrad
*Chamber Suite* (mus. Schedrin), Maly Theatre Ballet, Leningrad
1972 *Clytemnestra* (mus. Gluck), Maly Theatre Ballet, Leningrad
1976 *Pas de deux* (mus. Tchaikovsky), Maly Theatre Ballet, Leningrad
1980 *Romeo and Juliet* (new production; mus. Tchaikovsky), Leningrad Conservatory Student Ballet, Leningrad
1984 *Andante Sostenuto* (mus. Tchaikovsky), Leningrad Conservatory Student Ballet, Leningrad
1986 *The Dream* (mus. Shosson), Leningrad Conservatory Student Ballet, Leningrad
1988 *Hamlet* (new production; mus. Tchaikovsky), Leningrad Conservatory Student Ballet, Leningrad
1990 *King Lear* (with Aleksidze; mus. Nasidze), Leningrad Conservatory Student Ballet, Leningrad
1991 *Cinderella Suite* (mus. Prokofiev), Towson State University, Baltimore

Also staged:
1973 *Giselle* (after Petipa, Coralli, Perrot; mus. Adam), Maly Theatre Ballet, Leningrad
1975 Grand Pas from *Paquita* (after Petipa; mus. Minkus), Maly Theatre Ballet, Leningrad
1984 *The Moor's Pavanne* (after José Limón; mus. Purcell), Leningrad Conservatory Student Ballet, Leningrad
1991 *La Sylphide* (after Bournonville), Tbilisi Ballet, Tbilisi

## PUBLICATIONS

By Dolgushin:
Interview with Katy Matheson, "Training Russian Choreographers", *Dance Theatre Journal* (London), Summer 1988

About Dolgushin:
René, Natalia, "Siberian Thaw", *Dance and Dancers* (London), November 1963
Lvov-Anokhin, Boris, "Nikita Dolgushin", *Teatr* (Moscow), no. 10, 1964
Krasovskaya, Vera, *Nikita Dolgushin*, Leningrad, 1965
Smakov, Gennady, *The Great Russian Dancers*, New York, 1984
Alovert, Nina, *Baryshnikov in Russia*, Winston, N.Y., 1984
Greskovic, Robert, "Dancing in the Dark—Discovering Nikita Dolgushin", *Dance Theatre Journal* (London), Spring 1988
Mazo, Joseph, "Nikita Dolgushin", *Dance Magazine* (New York), June 1990
Matheson, Katy, "Nikita Dolgushin: Work, Love, and Spirituality", *Dance Magazine* (New York), June 1990

* * *

Nikita Dolgushin, an important exemplar of Russian ballet, began his career with precise and uncanny parallels to that of Rudolf Nureyev. Both were born in 1938, both studied with Aleksandr Pushkin, the great ballet pedagogue in Leningrad, and both had decisive career moves in 1961. In that year, while Nureyev left the Leningrad Kirov Ballet company to make his career outside the Soviet Union, Dolgushin, as a result of petty ballet politics, was "transferred" from the prestigious Kirov company to the one attached to the Novosibirsk Opera, in Siberia. The rest of this duality is now history. Nureyev became just about the biggest known in the ballet world and Dolgushin became the biggest unknown.

Connoisseurs, inside and outside the Soviet Union, gave some indication of Dolgushin's extraordinary artistry as a dancer, but these observations, by such individuals as Natalia Makarova, Mikhail Baryshnikov, Aleksandr Demidov and Vera Krasovskaya, mostly served to deepen the Dolgushin mystery. Who was this dancer and what was he like? How did his dancing stand out in the context of the incomparably formidable lineage of Russian male dancers?

Once reports of Dolgushin built up some momentum, and when, late in his career, around 1979, the BBC finally televised him in his capacities as both director and leading dancer of Leningrad's Maly Theatre Ballet, the greater ballet world ended up learning something substantive about a uniquely stellar Russian dancer. Or did it? His winning of the first prize gold medal in 1964, the inaugural year of the Varna Ballet Competition, didn't gain him international attention as it did subsequent medallists. By the time actual evidence of Dolgushin's dancing got before the public outside the Soviet Union—he had in fact performed live in Sydney, London, and Paris in the late 1960s—the world outside Russia already had its fixed notions about Russian male dancing. Nijinsky set the tone and Nureyev capitalized on it: in between, other Russian men more or less matched up to it.

But Dolgushin was not only largely unknown as an individual; he was also nearly unheard of as a dance stylist. Handsome, lanky, and serene, he was a danseur noble out of Russia in the Western European line of Erik Bruhn or Henning Kronstam. Even the Russians who admired him didn't quite know how to describe him. The word "intellectual" kept cropping up in their commentary.

Physically, with his ideal ballet dancer proportions—slender but not shapeless limbs, long legs, arms, and neck, strongly featured head, and large hands and feet—Dolgushin departs from the norm of the Slavic physique. In its way his is almost as atypical a build for a Russian male dancer as Tamasaburo Bando's is for a Kabuki onnagata. The label of "intellectual" probably means to separate Dolgushin's unfiery approach to dancing from that of other, "passionate" Russian dancers. But, his "other" approach does not mean one of coldness or mere athletic efficiency. Dolgushin's nobility results from his personal combination of physical prowess and performance accent. His plastique reveals impeccable line without calculation or strain. Maximal pride of stature and pose appear to him as givens, part of his inborn coordination, not as airs, signalling acquired affectation. The clarity, precision, and up-scale size of his movements—turns, jumps, beats—give his dancing a virtuosity utterly lacking in showy effort or haughty self-awareness.

The photographs and video documents that eventually came to light from late in his career tell a story of a gracious nobleman who both carried on the formidable line of great Russian dancing and individualized that tradition in remarkable ways. With his lean physique and long proportions Dolgushin appears even taller than his actual height. While his big jumps are not especially large-scale by Russian ballet standards, his elevation is clean and clear. So are all aspects of his dancing. Dolgushin is the kind of showman who glories in showing as clearly and precisely as he can every detail of his artful moves. His legs and feet work with the clarity of a scalpel, acting with calm and strict definition to dramatize the openings and closings of classical dancing's select vocabulary. Dolgushin's dancing doesn't boom or bellow through time and space; it courses with a delicate and unmistakable momentum that accumulates an overreaching clarity out of an array of smaller clear parts.

The finespun articulation and simple momentum with which Dolgushin renders classical dancing were either threatening or misunderstood, or both, during his formative years. The bulk and force associated with Russian male dancing were beautifully contrasted by his individual way of working. His renderings of princes, poets, and troubadours told of an unusual classical "voice". The spareness of his physicality and articulation acted, much as a related spareness had for Anna Pavlova, to re-invent a longstanding tradition. Dolgushin's danseur noble cleared the way for a whole new standard of classical refinement. Even without the kind of exposure his original and remarkable abilities deserved, he made his mark, and male classical dancing will never be the same.

—Robert Greskovic

---

**DOLIN, Anton**

British dancer, choreographer, and ballet director. Born Sydney Francis Patrick Chippendall Healey-Kay, in Slinfold, England, 27 July 1904. Studied with Grace and Lily Cone, Brighton, 1914–15, and at the Italia Conti Stage School, London, 1915–16; also studied with Serafina Astafieva, from 1917, Bronislava Nijinska, 1924, and with Enrico Cecchetti. Stage début as a child performer in *Bluebell in Fairyland*, 1916; dancer (performing as Patrickieff), corps de ballet of *The Sleeping Princess*, Diaghilev's Ballets Russes, London, 1921; first solo appearance, performing as Anton Dolin, Astafieva's Anglo-Russian Ballet, London, 1923; soloist, Diaghilev's Ballets Russes, 1923–25, and 1929; leading dancer in revues and various concert tours, partnering Phyllis Bedells, Tamara Karsavina, Vera Nemchinova, and Ninette de Valois, 1925–27; co-founder, with Nemchinova, and choreographer, the Nemchinova–Dolin Ballet, touring Europe, 1927–29; founder member and dancer, the Camargo Society, London, from 1930;

principal dancer, de Basil's Ballets Russes de Monte Carlo (later appearing as the Covent Garden Russian Ballet, and eventually the Original Ballet Russe), 1933, 1938–39; principal guest artist, Vic-Wells Ballet, London, also appearing in stage revues, 1931–35; founder, with Alicia Markova, Markova–Dolin Ballet, performing in Britain, 1935–38, and United States, 1945–49; principal dancer and choreographer, Ballet Theatre (later American Ballet Theatre), New York, 1940, remaining guest artist until 1946; also choreographer and principal dancer in Billy Rose revue *The Seven Lively Arts*, New York, 1944–45; guest artist, Sadler's Wells Ballet and Ballet Russe de Monte Carlo, 1948; founder, principal dancer, and artistic director, Festival Ballet (later becoming London Festival Ballet, now the English National Ballet), 1950–61; artistic director, Rome Opera Ballet, 1961–64; freelance choreographer and guest producer, staging ballets worldwide, 1964–83; also actor, appearing as St. George in *Where the Rainbow Ends*, London, various seasons 1949–58; appeared on film, including in first full-length talking film made in Britain, *Dark Red Roses* (dir. Hill, chor. Balanchine, 1929), in *Invitation to the Waltz* (1934), and as Cecchetti in *Nijinsky* (dir. Ross, 1980). Recipient: Queen Elizabeth II Coronation Award, Royal Academy of Dancing, 1954; Order of the Sun (Peru), 1958; Knighthood, 1981; *Dance Magazine* Award, 1981. Died in Neuilly-sur-Seine, Paris, 25 November 1983.

## ROLES

1923 Dancer in *Hymn to the Sun* (solo; also chor.), and *Danse Russe* (solo; also chor.), Astafieva's Anglo-Russian Ballet, London

Bacchanale in *Cléopâtre* (Fokine), Diaghilev's Ballets Russes, Monte Carlo

Polovtsian Warrior in *Polovtsian Dances from Prince Igor* (Fokine), Diaghilev's Ballets Russes, Monte Carlo

1924 Daphnis in *Daphnis et Chloë* (Fokine, with new pas de deux added by Nijinska), Diaghilev's Ballets Russes, Monte Carlo

A Count (cr) in *Les Tentations de la bergère; ou, L'Amour vainqueur* (Nijinska), Diaghilev's Ballets Russes, Monte Carlo

Chanson Dansée ("Athlete") in *Les Biches* (Nijinska), Diaghilev's Ballets Russes, Monte Carlo

L'Elégant (cr) in *Les Fâcheux* (Nijinska), Diaghilev's Ballets Russes, Monte Carlo

Pas de deux in *Cimarosiana* (divertissement from *Le Astuzie Femminili*; Massine), Diaghilev's Ballets Russes

Beau Gosse (cr) in *Le Train bleu* (Nijinska), Diaghilev's Ballets Russes, Paris

Mazurka, Waltz in *Les Sylphides* (Fokine), Diaghilev's Ballets Russes

Bluebird Pas de deux in *Aurora's Wedding* (from *The Sleeping Beauty*; Petipa; staged Sergeyev), Diaghilev's Ballets Russes

1924/25 Prince Charming in *Aurora's Wedding* (Petipa, staged Sergeyev), Diaghilev's Ballets Russes

1925 The Spirit of the Rose in *Le Spectre de la rose* (Fokine), Diaghilev's Ballets Russes, Monte Carlo

Prince Siegfried in *Le Bal du "Lac des cygnes"* (*Swan Lake*, Act III; Petipa, staged Sergeyev), Diaghilev's Ballets Russes, Monte Carlo

Zéphyr (cr) in *Zéphyr et Flore* (Massine), Diaghilev's Ballets Russes, Monte Carlo

Eusebius in *Carnaval* (Fokine), Diaghilev's Ballets Russes, London

1926 Principal dancer in *Movement*, *Little Boy Blue* (pas de deux), *Clair de lune* (pas de deux), *Jack and Jill* (pas de deux; also chor.), *In a Classroom* (also chor.), *Exercises* (also chor.), Concert tour with Phyllis Bedells

1927 Student (cr) in *The Nightingale and the Rose* (also chor.), Nemchinova–Dolin Ballet, London

Pas de deux from *The Nutcracker* (after Ivanov), Concert performance with Karsavina

1928 Jazz (cr) in *Rhapsody in Blue* (also chor.), Nemchinova–Dolin Ballet, London

Spirit of Revolution (cr) in *Revolution* (also chor.), Nemchinova–Dolin Ballet, London

Principal dancer (cr) in *Danse Espagnol* (solo; later danced for Vic-Wells Ballet as *Spanish Dance*; also chor.), London Coliseum

1929 American Sailor in *Les Matelots* (Massine), Diaghilev's Ballets Russes

The Young Man (cr) in *Le Bal* (Balanchine), Diaghilev's Ballets Russes, Monte Carlo

A Confidant (cr) in *Le Fils prodigue* (*Prodigal Son*; Balanchine), Diaghilev's Ballets Russes, Paris

Pas de trois in *Swan Lake* (two-act version; Petipa, Ivanov; staged Fokine), Diaghilev's Ballets Russes, Cologne

The Moor in *Petrushka* (Fokine), Diaghilev's Ballets Russes

Harlequin in *Carnaval* (Fokine), Diaghilev's Ballet Russes

Title role in *Petrushka* (Fokine), Diaghilev's Ballet Russes

Principal dancer (cr) in *Pas de deux* (later *Moods*; Balanchine), Variety Programme, Coliseum, London

1930 Vertumnus (cr) in *Pomona* (Ashton), Camargo Society, London

1931 Satan (cr) in *Job* (de Valois), Camargo Society, London

1932 Cook's Man in *Douanes* (de Valois), Vic-Wells Ballet, London

Eros (cr) in *The Enchanted Grove* (Doone), Vic-Wells Ballet, London

Prince Siegfried in *Swan Lake*, Act II (Sergeyev after Ivanov), Vic-Wells Ballet, London

Title role in *The Lord of Burleigh* (Ashton), Vic-Wells Ballet, London

Georgie Porgie, Prince (cr) in *Nursery Suite* (de Valois), Vic-Wells Ballet, London

Polydore (cr) in *The Origin of Design* (de Valois), Camargo Society, London

Gavotte in *Suite of Dances* (de Valois), Vic-Wells Ballet, London

Principal dancer (cr) in *The Love Song* (pas de deux; also chor., with Genée), Charity Gala, Drury Lane Theatre, London (staged for Ballet Theatre, 1940)

Albrecht in *Giselle* (Petipa after Coralli, Perrot; staged Sergeyev), Camargo Society, London

Adam (cr) in *Adam and Eve* (Tudor), Camargo Society, London

1933 Jânos in *The Whitsun King* (Török, de Moroda), Coliseum, London

1935 The Prince in *The Nutcracker*, Act II (Sergeyev after Ivanov), Vic-Wells Ballet, London

The Master of Treginnis in *The Haunted Ballroom* (de Valois), Vic-Wells Ballet, London

Title role (cr) in *David* (Lester), Markova–Dolin Company, Newcastle

Aucassin (cr) in *Aucassin and Nicolette* (Toye), Markova–Dolin Company, Liverpool

**Anton Dolin in *Les Présages*, 1948**

Third Entrée in *Grand Valse* (Lester), Markova–Dolin Company, tour
Principal dancer in *Blue Danube Waltz* (Markova), Markova–Dolin Company, tour

1936 The Musician in *The Beloved* (*La Bien-Aimée*; Nijinska), Markova–Dolin Company, London
Dancer in *Spanish Peasant Dance* (solo; also chor.), Markova–Dolin Company, tour

1937 Chanson dansée ("Athlete"), Andantino in *The House Party* (*Les Biches*; Nijinska), Markova–Dolin Company, tour

1938 Title role in *Protée* (Lichine), De Basil's Ballets Russes
Ivan Tsarevitch in *The Firebird* (Fokine), De Basil's Ballets Russes
Title role (cr) in *Le Fils prodigue* (Lichine), (de Basil's) Covent Garden Russian Ballet, Sydney
A Young Musician in *Symphonie fantastique* (Massine), (de Basil's) Covent Garden Russian Ballet, Sydney

1938 The Golden Slave in *Schéhérazade* (Fokine), (de Basil's) Covent Garden Russian Ballet, tour
The Traveller in *Jeux d'enfants* (Massine), (de Basil's) Covent Garden Russian Ballet, Melbourne

1940 Principal dancer (cr) in *Capriccioso* (new version of *Italian Suite*; also chor.), Ballet Theatre, Chicago
Brother (cr) in *Quintet* (also chor.), Ballet Theatre, New York

1941 Title role (cr) in *Bluebeard* (Fokine), Ballet Theatre, Mexico City
Principal dancer in *The Sylphide and the Scotsman* (pas de deux), Jacob's Pillow Festival, Lee, Massachusetts

1942 Title role (cr) in *Don Domingo de Don Blas* (Massine), Ballet Theatre, Mexico City
Title role in *Aleko* (Massine), Ballet Theatre, New York
Paris (cr) in *Helen of Troy* (Lichine), Ballet Theatre, Detroit
Franz in *Coppélia* (one-act version; S. Semenoff after Saint-Léon), Ballet Theatre, Mexico City
A Youth (cr) in *Romantic Age* (also chor.), Ballet Theatre, New York

1943 Red Coat (cr) in *Fair at Sorochinsk* (Lichine), Ballet Theatre, New York

1944 Prince (cr) in *Tally-ho; or, The Frail Quarry* (de Mille), Ballet Theatre, Los Angeles
Principal dancer (cr) in *Scènes de ballet* (also chor.) in *The Seven Lively Arts* (Billy Rose revue), Ziegfeld Theatre, New York

1945 Ivan Tsarevitch in *Firebird* (Bolm), Ballet Theatre, New York

1946 Armand (cr) in *Camille* (Taras), Original Ballet Russe, New York

1947 Des Grieux (cr) in *Lady of the Camellias* (also chor.), Markova–Dolin Company, Mexico City
Principal dancer (cr) in *Pas de trois* (Robbins), Original Ballet Russe, New York

1948 Prince Florimund in *The Sleeping Beauty* (Petipa; staged Ashton, de Valois), Sadler's Wells Ballet, London
Pas de deux from *Don Quixote* (after Petipa), Sadler's Wells Ballet, London

1950 Principal dancer in *Chopiniana* (Markova, Dolin, Cone), London Festival Ballet, Monte Carlo

1951 Principal dancer (cr) in *Ballet des parfums* (Lichine), London Festival Ballet, Monte Carlo
Second Movement (cr) in *Symphonic Impressions* (Lichine), London Festival Ballet, Monte Carlo

1952 Principal dancer (cr) in *Pas de rêve* (also chor.), London Festival Ballet, London

1953 Baron Popoff (cr) in *Vilia* (*The Merry Widow*; Page), London Festival Ballet, Manchester

1954 Frollo (cr) in *La Esmeralda* (Beriozoff), London Festival Ballet, London

1955 Principal dancer in *Mlle Fifi* (Solov), London Festival Ballet, Barcelona
Principal dancer in *Études* (Lander), London Festival Ballet, London

1957 The Preacher in *The Witch Boy* (J. Carter), London Festival Ballet, Manchester
Drosselmeyer in *The Nutcracker* (Lichine), London Festival Ballet, London

1959 Gentleman in the Bathchair (cr) in *London Morning* (J. Carter), London Festival Ballet, London

1977 King Herod (acting role) in *Salomé* (Kemp), Lindsay Kemp company, London

**Other roles include:** in concert performances—dancer in *Bolero* (solo; also chor.), *Pas de deux—Blues* (Balanchine); for Diaghilev's Ballets Russes—Coviello in *Pulcinella* (Massine); for the Markova-Dolin companies—principal dancer in *Mr. Puppet* (Fonaroff), *Blue Mountain Ballads* (Sadler), *Mephisto Valse* (also chor., with Markova), *Vestris* (Celli); for revues and musical shows—principal dancer in *The Punch Bowl* (also chor.; London, 1925), *Palladium Pleasures* (London, 1926), *The Charlot Show of 1926* (London, 1926), *Vaudeville Vanities* (London, 1926), *White Birds* (also chor.; London, 1927), *La Féerie blanche* (Paris, 1928), *International Revue* (New York, 1930), *Charlot's Masquerade* (London, 1930), *Stand Up and Sing* (London, 1930), *The Tales of Hoffmann* (operetta; dir. Reinhardt, chor. Dolin; Berlin, 1931), *Ballerina* (London, 1933), *West End Scandals* (London, 1934), *Mother Goose* (divertissement in pantomime; London, 1936), *All the Best* (Blackpool, 1938), *The Seven Lively Arts* (also chor., including *Scènes de ballet*; New York, 1944–45).

## WORKS

1923 *Hymn to the Sun* (mus. Rimsky-Korsakov), Astafieva's Anglo-Russian Ballet, London
*Danse Russe* (mus. Kolin), Astafieva's Anglo-Russian Ballet, London
*Mazurka* (mus. Chopin), Astafieva's Anglo-Russian Ballet, London

1926 *Jack and Jill*, *In a Classroom*, *Exercises* (mus. Grainger), Concert tour with Phyllis Bedells

1927 *The Nightingale and the Rose* (after story by Oscar Wilde), Nemchinova–Dolin Ballet, London
*Revolution* (mus. Chopin), Nemchinova–Dolin Ballet, London
*Rhapsody in Blue* (mus. Gershwin), Nemchinova–Dolin Ballet, London
*Danse espagnole* (solo, later *Spanish Dance*; mus. Albéniz), London Coliseum

1931 Dances in *The Tales of Hoffmann* (operetta; mus. Offenbach; dir. Reinhardt), State Opera, Berlin

1940 *Capriccioso* (mus. Cimarosa, Rossini, Britten), Ballet Theatre, New York
*Quintet* (mus. Scott), Ballet Theatre, New York

1941 *Pas de quatre* (after Lester; mus. Pugni), Ballet Theatre, New York
*Romantic Age* (mus. Bellini), Ballet Theatre, New York

1944 *Scènes de ballet* (mus. Stravinsky), in *The Seven Lively Arts* (Billy Rose revue), Ziegfeld Theatre, New York

1947 *Lady of the Camellias*, Markova–Dolin Company, Mexico City

1949 *Chopiniana* (with Markova, Cone; mus. Chopin), Markova–Dolin Ballet
*Chopin Suite* (*Suite in White*; with Markova and Cone, after Fokine; mus. Chopin, arranged Biezard), Markova–Dolin Ballet
1952 *Pas de rêve* (mus. Bruch), London Festival Ballet, London
1955 *Harlequinade* (Pas de deux romantique; mus. Drigo), London Festival Ballet, London
1957 *Variations for Four* (mus. Keogh), London Festival Ballet, London
1959 *The Enchanted Stream* (mus. Debussy), London Festival Ballet, Dublin
1967 *Pas de Deux for Four* (mus. Adam), London Festival Ballet, Southsea
1971 *Variations for Four* (solo version; mus. Keogh), London Festival Ballet

Also staged:
1940 *Swan Lake*, Act II (after Ivanov; mus. Tchaikovsky), Ballet Theatre, New York
*Giselle* (after Petipa, Coralli, Perrot; mus. Adam, arranged Dorati), Ballet Theatre, New York
1941 *Princess Aurora* (divertissement from *The Sleeping Beauty*, after Petipa; mus. Tchaikovsky), Ballet Theatre, Mexico City

## PUBLICATIONS

By Dolin:
*Divertissement* (autobiography), London, 1931
*Ballet Go Round* (autobiography), London, 1938
*Pas de Deux: The Art of Partnering*, New York, 1949; London, 1950
*Alicia Markova: Her Life and Art*, London and New York, 1953
*Autobiography*, London, 1960
*The Sleeping Ballerina: The Story of Olga Spessivtseva*, London, 1966

About Dolin:
Haskell, Arnold, *Balletomania*, London, 1934
Beaumont, Cyril, *Complete Book of Ballets*, revised edition, London, 1951
Grigoriev, Serge, *The Diaghilev Ballet*, translated by Vera Bowen, London, 1953
Selby-Lowndes, Joan, *Blue Train: The Story of Anton Dolin*, London, 1958
Anthony, Gordon, "Pioneers of the Royal Ballet: Anton Dolin", *Dancing Times* (London), June 1970
Wheatcroft, Andrew, *Dolin, Friends and Memories*, London 1982
Nerina, Nadia (ed.), *A Pictorial Tribute to Sir Anton Dolin, The First British Ballet Star 1904–1983*, London, 1984
Gerafola, Lynn, *Diaghilev's Ballets Russes*, New York, 1989

* * *

Anton Dolin's career encompassed several forms of theatre, from children's plays to musical comedy, but he is best remembered as the first British premier danseur of this century. In this capacity he was also important as a role model for other British male dancers, who had the talent and determination to overcome the general prejudice which prevailed during the first decades of this century against classical dance as a profession for men.

It was Dolin's Irish-born mother who encouraged him in his desire for a stage career, which became centred on dance after she had taken him to see Serafina Astafieva perform at the London Coliseum. Dolin's first major engagement as a dancer then came when he was chosen, among Astafieva's pupils, to perform as an extra in Serge Diaghilev's spectacular production of *The Sleeping Princess* at the Alhambra Theatre in 1921. Chief amongst the many impressions received through this close acquaintance with one of the greatest artistic organizations in the Western world was watching Olga Spessivtseva prepare for the role of Aurora. "Her dancing", he once said, "was an inspiration which has stayed with me all my life." His own assiduous application to his art led him to rejoin Diaghilev's company, first as a member of the corps de ballet and later as a soloist and principal. His greatest success came with the leading male role in Bronislava Nijinska's sophisticated ballet *Le Train bleu*, revealing him as a dancer of considerable technique and presence.

After two seasons with the Ballets Russes, Dolin left to enjoy a celebrity status in revue and musical comedy. Then, in 1927, he formed his own small dance company with Vera Nemchinova in a venture which enjoyed an extended tour of several European cities; but the group was finally disbanded with a financial loss. There followed another engagement with the Ballets Russes, during which time Dolin partnered the young British ballerina Alicia Markova in the beginning of what was to be a famous life-long partnership.

In the late summer of 1929 news came of Diaghilev's death in Venice, and thus the end of a great era of dance and the scattering of his great assemblage of artists throughout the world. A year later Dolin sailed for New York, the first of many visits to America. However, his contract to appear in revue turned out to be disastrous and he was soon back in London as a founder-member of the Carmargo Society, presenting subscription performances to British balletomanes and keeping the art of ballet alive until Marie Rambert founded the company which would become Ballet Rambert and Ninette de Valois founded the Vic-Wells (later Sadler's Wells) Ballet in the early 1930s.

With Markova as his partner, Dolin was the leading dancer in de Valois's embryo company (ultimately to become the Royal Ballet) until 1935, when the two dancers left to form their own troupe, initially presenting major classics like *Swan Lake* and *Giselle* and later introducing modern works into the repertoire. Four years later, with Britain at war, Dolin sailed for America, performing throughout the war years with the newly formed Ballet Theatre and dancing with several of the company's leading ballerinas (scoring a particular success in the title role of Fokine's *Bluebeard*).

At the end of the war Dolin and Markova decided to reform their own company, with which they toured the United States and South America with considerable success. They returned to Britain to appear in *Giselle* and *Swan Lake* as guests with the Sadler's Wells ballet in its new home at Covent Garden, providing a chance for a whole new generation of ballet-goers to see two artists who had developed something of a legendary reputation on both sides of the Atlantic.

In 1949, Dolin and Markova planned the formation of a new company with the impresario Dr. Julian Braunsweg. As the Festival of Britain was also about to begin, Markova suggested calling the company the Festival Ballet, a name which remained in more or less the same form for 39 years, until the title was changed to English National Ballet.

In 1952 Markova left the company, but Dolin continued as artistic director for another ten years before handing over to John Gilpin. During the next twenty years Dolin revived a number of ballets, including his famous reconstruction of the *Pas de quatre*, originally danced in 1845 by Marie Taglioni,

Carlotta Grisi, Fanny Cerrito, and Lucile Grahn. He also continued to teach, direct, and act in America, France, Italy, Australia, and Britain. In 1981 he received a knighthood, at the age of 77; within three years he had died, the victim of a heart attack.

Dolin's importance to British ballet cannot be underestimated. His technical gifts as a dancer were never in question, although throughout his career various critics were to complain about his tendency towards mannerism and theatricality, at the expense of an artistry which was undoubtedly a natural asset. Purists worried about his various digressions into vaudeville, musical comedy, and revue early in his career, "spending his days and energy", wrote A. V. Coton in 1938, "in divertissement items in variety bills and revues at the Coliseum, Palladium, and in the provinces".

When Dolin had first appeared in London, the teenage prodigy of the Astafieva company, the *Daily Sketch* critic J. T. Grein had written,

> A new dancer, Anton Dolin, carried us away in enthusiasm. . . . Dolin is as light as a feather, as graceful as a fawn, as wing-footed as Mercury. I for one believe that Dolin, wholly unaffected, immersed in his art, will ere long be proclaimed the rival and successor of Nijinsky, and, if he remains unspoilt, he may be the greater of the twain, for so far his work is entirely free of pose.

British balletomane Arnold Haskell later quoted these enthusiastic words, no doubt to demonstrate the important point about remaining "unspoilt" as much as to emphasize just how impressively talented the young dancer was for his time. As Haskell went on to point out, Dolin's later success was all the more extraordinary for the fact that "he should have ruined his career time and time again through his flirtations with the commercial stage, with banality and bad taste". Dolin's professionalism was consummate; Haskell had to admit that even in these other ventures " . . . he has always done the thing supremely well". And furthermore, Dolin was aware of the pitfalls himself; he was adaptable and practical. As Haskell said, "He has done dreadful things, vapid, meaningless, flashy things; he knows it, and so far can always recover in time, and in the right surroundings."

Dolin maintained his command of the ballet stage, and his importance to the success of fledgeling ballet companies in the 1930s, 1940s, and 1950s must not be forgotten. As star attraction with Markova, he helped draw early audiences to de Valois's new Vic-Wells Ballet, and hence to develop a permanent English ballet audience; as one of the early stars and choreographers of the new Ballet Theatre in America in 1940, he helped launch one of America's earliest and most successful companies; and as founder and director of the Festival Ballet, he helped bring ballet to audiences in the provinces who might never have otherwise had the chance to appreciate it. He also left an important legacy in his various stagings of the classics.

Dolin's skill and sensitivity in partnering was often noted and emulated, and his ability to spot potential ballet stars, such as David Lichine, was legendary. But perhaps most of all, his dancing, as Dame Ninette de Valois wrote, "... brought a spark of virility to the male classical dance picture".

—Edward Thorpe
with Elizabeth Hudson

---

**DOLLAR, William**

American dancer, choreographer, ballet director, and teacher. Born William Henry Dollar in St. Louis, Missouri, 20 April 1907. Studied with Catherine Littlefield, Philadelphia, and with Mikhail (Michel) Fokine, Mikhail Mordkin, and Pierre Vladimirov, New York; also studied at the School of American Ballet, pupil of George Balanchine, 1934, and with Alexandre Volinine, Paris. Married dancer Yvonne Patterson. Début, Municipal Opera, St. Louis, 1930; principal dancer, Philadelphia Opera Ballet, from 1933; soloist, becoming principal dancer, American Ballet, 1935–37, performing as American Ballet Ensemble with the Metropolitan Opera, New York; principal dancer, Ballet Theatre, 1940, American Ballet Caravan, touring South America, 1941, and New Opera Company, New York, 1942; guest artist, American Ballet Theatre, and various foreign companies, including Ballet International, 1944, and Grand Ballet du Marquis de Cuevas; also performer in musicals and in film, including *The Goldwyn Follies* (dir. Marshall, chor. Balanchine, 1938); choreographer, Ballet Caravan, from 1936; choreographer and dance director, Ford Ballet, New York World's Fair, 1940; co-founder and ballet master, American Concert Ballet, 1943; ballet master, Ballet Society, 1946, Grand Ballet de Monte Carlo (later Grand Ballet du Marquis de Cuevas), 1948; founder, choreographer, and supervisor, Iranian National Ballet, from 1956; guest choreographer, staging ballets for numerous companies including Les Ballets de Paris de Roland Petit, 1949, Teatro Municipal, Rio de Janeiro, 1965, Le Théâtre d'Art du Ballet, Paris, 1965, and Detroit City Ballet, and New York City Opera; also teacher, American Concert Ballet, from 1943, Ballet Society, New York, from c.1946, and Ballet Theatre School, New York, from 1950. Died in Flourtown, Pennsylvania, 28 February 1986.

**ROLES**

1935 Principal dancer in *Serenade* (Balanchine), American Ballet, New York
The Villain (cr) in *Alma Mater* (Balanchine), American Ballet, New York
A Man (cr) in *Errante* (Balanchine), American Ballet, New York
Pas de trois (cr) in *Reminiscence* (Balanchine), American Ballet, New York
The Acrobat (cr) in *Dreams* (new production of *Songes*; Balanchine), American Ballet, New York
The Man in Black in *Transcendence* (Balanchine), American Ballet, New York

1936 Principal dancer in *Concerto* (later *Classic Ballet*; also chor., with Balanchine), American Ballet, New York
A Gypsy (cr) in *The Bat* (Balanchine), American Ballet, New York
Amor (cr) in *Orpheus and Eurydice* (opera; mus. Gluck, chor. Balanchine), American Ballet, New York

1937 The Joker in *The Card Party* (later *Card Game*; Balanchine), American Ballet, New York
Bridegroom (cr) in *Le Baiser de la Fée* (Balanchine), American Ballet, New York

1940 Wolf (cr) in *Peter and the Wolf* (Bolm), Ballet Theatre, New York
Harlequin in *Carnaval* (Fokine), Ballet Theatre, New York
Dancer (cr) in *A Thousand Times Neigh!* (also chor.), Ballet Caravan, World's Fair, Flushing Meadow, New York

1941 Principal dancer (cr) in *Ballet Imperial* (later *Concerto*

William Dollar

No. 2; Balanchine), American Ballet Caravan, Rio de Janeiro
Principal dancer (cr) in *Concerto Barocco* (Balanchine), American Ballet Caravan, Rio de Janeiro
Man with Nickels (cr) in *Juke Box* (Dollar), American Ballet Caravan, Rio de Janeiro

1946 Black Cat (cr) in *The Spellbound Child* (Balanchine), Ballet Society, New York
Melancholic (cr) in *The Four Temperaments* (Balanchine), Ballet Society, New York

1947 Gemini (Sun) Twin (cr) in *Zodiac* (Bolender), Ballet Society, New York

1950 Principal dancer in *The Duel* (*Le Combat*; also chor.), New York City Ballet, New York
War with Mosquitoes (cr) in *Jones Beach* (Robbins, Balanchine), New York City Ballet, New York

1954 Herr Drosselmeyer (cr) in *The Nutcracker* (Balanchine), New York City Ballet, New York

**Other roles include:** Mac in *Filling Station* (L. Christensen), principal dancer in *Air and Variations* (also chor.); for American Ballet Ensemble at the Metropolitan Opera—principal dancer in operas (chor. Balanchine) *Aida* (mus. Verdi; 1935), *Mignon* (mus. Thomas; 1936), *La Juive* (mus. Halévy; 1936), *The Bartered Bride* (mus. Smetana; 1936), *Caponsacchi* (mus. Hageman; 1937); for the New Opera Company—principal dancer in *The Fair at Sorochinsk* (mus. Mussorgsky, chor. Balanchine; 1942), and in operas (also chor.) *La Vie Parisienne* (mus. Offenbach; 1942), *The Queen of Spades* (*Pique Dame*; mus. Tchaikovsky; 1942), *Macbeth* (mus. Verdi; 1942).

**WORKS**

1936 *Concerto* (with Balanchine; called *Classic Ballet* from 1937; mus. Chopin), American Ballet, New York
*Promenade* (mus. Ravel), Ballet Caravan, Bennington, Vermont

1938 *Air and Variations* (mus. Bach), Ballet Caravan, Winthrop College, Rock Hill, South Carolina

1940 *A Thousand Times Neigh!* (mus. Bennett), Ballet Caravan, World's Fair, Flushing Meadow, New York

1941 *Juke Box* (mus. Wilder), American Ballet Caravan, Rio de Janeiro

1942 Dances in *La Vie Parisienne* (opera; mus. Offenbach), New Opera Company, New York
Dances in *The Queen of Spades* (*Pique Dame*; opera; mus. Tchaikovsky), New Opera Company, New York
Dances in *Macbeth* (opera; mus. Verdi), New Opera Company, New York

1943 *Five Boons of Life* (mus. Dohnanyi), American Concert Ballet, New York

1944 *Constantia* (revision of *Concerto*; mus. Chopin), Ballet International, New York

1947 *Highland Fling* (mus. Bate), Ballet Society, New York

1948 *The Five Gifts* (revision of *Five Boons of Life*; mus. E. Dohnanyi), Grand Ballet de Monte Carlo

1949 *Le Combat* (mus. de Banfield), Les Ballets de Paris de Roland Petit, London
*Ondine* (mus. Vivaldi), New York City Ballet, New York

1950 *The Duel* (revision of *Le Combat*; mus. de Banfield), New York City Ballet, New York
*Jeux* (mus. Debussy), Ballet Theatre, New York

1952 Dances in *Four Saints in Three Acts* (play by G. Stein; mus. V. Thomson), American National Theatre, New York

1953 *The Leaf and the Wind* (pas de deux; mus. P. Ramseier), Ballet Theatre, Dallas, Texas

1954 *Mendelssohn Concerto* (mus. Mendelssohn), Ballet Theatre Workshop, New York
*Larghetto and Mazurka* (mus. Chopin), Ballet Theatre Workshop, New York

1955 *Annabel Lee* (mus. Hindemith), Kaufman Theatre, New York

1958 *The Parliament of the Birds* (mus. Respighi), Ballet Theatre Workshop, New York
*Angrismenc* (mus. Stravinsky), Ballet Theatre Workshop, New York

1961 *Serenata*, Teatro Municipal, Rio de Janeiro
*Divertimento–Rossini* (mus. Rossini), American Ballet Theatre, New York

1964 *La Dame aux camélias* (mus. Verdi), Paris

**Other works include:** for New York City Opera—dances in operas *Andrea Chénier* (mus. Giordano), *Rigoletto* (mus. Verdi), *Carmen* (mus. Bizet), *La Traviata* (mus. Verdi).

**PUBLICATIONS**

"Two American Biographies", *Dance Magazine* (New York), November 1944
Chujoy, Anatole, *The New York City Ballet*, New York, 1953
Balanchine, George, with Mason, Francis, *Balanchine's Complete Stories of the Great Ballets*, Garden City, N.Y., 1977
Reynolds, Nancy, *Repertory in Review*, New York, 1977

Hunt, Marilyn, "William Dollar", *Dance Magazine* (New York), September 1980
Asinof, Lynn, "Where It All Began", *Ballet News* (New York), November 1980

* * *

The 1930s and 1940s were an exciting and contradictory time in the development of American ballet. Russian expatriate teachers exercised a strong influence on their American students, and yet these same students were often pressured into creating ballets dealing with American folk themes. Typical were ballets like Eugene Loring's *Billy the Kid*, Lew Christensen's *Filling Station* and *Pocahontas*, and Catherine Littlefield's *Barn Dance*. William Dollar avoided this pattern. His early choreography developed consistently from his background.

His principal teachers and aesthetic influences were indeed Russian. They included Mikhail Fokine, Mikhail Mordkin, George Balanchine, Pierre Vladimirov, and in Paris, Alexandre Volinine. From Fokine he acquired his expressive use of arms and head, and from Balanchine and Volinine he acquired his deep affection for classical purity. Dollar's dancing was buoyant, yet precise. His ballets made varied and confident use of classical patterns.

In 1936, at the age of 29, Dollar made his choreographic début in a collaboration with his mentor George Balanchine. Using the Chopin Piano Concerto in F Minor, they created *Concerto*. Dollar was responsible for the first and third movements and Balanchine for the second. It was performed by the American Ballet, one of the four companies which formed the New York City Ballet lineage.

*Concerto* led a peripatetic life. Credited solely to Dollar and renamed *Constantia*, it turned up in the 1944 repertoire of Ballet International, and it was subsequently acquired by the Original Ballet Russe, the Grand Ballet de Monte Carlo, Ballet Theatre, and American Ballet Theatre. *Concerto* was the kind of work which lent stability to any repertoire, for within its nicely balanced structure there was ample challenge for the dancers.

Dollar's first independent piece of choreography was *Promenade* to Ravel's *Valses nobles et sentimentales*. It was staged in 1936 for Ballet Caravan. *Promenade* was essentially a pure dance work set in the Empire period (with costumes in the style of the painter Horace Vernet). Like the art of that period, its atmosphere was perfumed with Greek classical allusions.

Although George Balanchine gave him every opportunity to teach and to make ballets, Dollar was at that time much more preoccupied with dancing. He and Lew Christensen were the principal male classical dancers of the Balanchine–Kirstein sequence of companies. Among the roles Dollar created in Balanchine ballets were the Bridegroom in *Le Baiser de la Fée* and the leading male roles in *Concerto Barocco* and *Ballet Imperial*. By the 1950s, however, Dollar's dancing career was cut short by arthritis of the hip. It was an ironic fate for a dancer known for his strong technique and unfettered elevation.

Dollar's choreographic career began to include dramatic works, among them *The Five Gifts* (also known as *Five Boons of Life*), *Highland Fling*, *Jeux*, *Ondine*, *Lady of the Camellias*, *Angrismene*, and *Juke Box*. None of these remained long in the repertoires for which they were created. The one ballet which has endured and has made its way successfully from company to company is *Le Combat*. It was originally staged in 1949 for Roland Petit's Ballets de Paris, and was at that time an extended pas de deux for Janine Charrat and Vladimir Skouratoff.

Perhaps influenced by the theatricality of this French company, the ballet was both pungent and sentimental. With décor by Marie-Laure de Noailles and a spirited score by Rafaello de Banfield, *Le Combat* was based on Tasso's *Jerusalem Delivered*. It told of the struggle between the Christian knight Tancredi and his love, the Saracen maiden Clorinda. With their visors down, they pursued each other and did not recognize each other until she was mortally wounded, throwing off her helmet before dying.

The ballet was first performed in the United States by Colette Marchand and Milorad Miskovitch. The following year (1950), it was renamed *The Duel*. Three additional knights were woven into the choreography, and it entered the New York City Ballet repertoire. Although first performed by Dollar with Melissa Hayden, it soon became an impressive vehicle for Hayden and Francisco Moncion. In 1958 it was retitled *The Combat* and became part of the Ballet Theatre repertoire, where it was a signature vehicle for Lupe Serrano. It was subsequently acquired by the Dance Theatre of Harlem.

After his career as dancer came to an end, Dollar expanded his teaching activities by helping to establish the State Ballet School of Tehran in 1956, and becoming ballet master and guest choreographer of the Teatro Municipal de Rio Janeiro in 1965. He also began to guest at teachers' organizations like the Cecchetti Council and to stage ballets for regional companies like the Detroit City Ballet. Unlike many of his contemporaries, he never directed a company of his own. Perhaps the gentle disposition which made him a poetic dancer did not suit him to the rigours of artistic direction.

—Doris Hering

---

## DOMENICO de PIACENZA

(also known as Domenico da Ferrara)

Italian dancer and teacher. Born in Piacenza, c. 1425–30. Became established as dancing master, most likely teaching in Piacenza, from c. 1440s; arranged and performed dances for court festivities and weddings, including with Johannis Ambrosio for wedding festivities in Forli, January 1456, and dances for wedding of Ippolita Sforza to Alfonso Duke of Calabria, May 1465, and wedding of Constanzio Sforza and Camilla d'Aragon, Ferrara, 1465; codified theories in *De arte saltandi et choreas ducendi*, treatise which refers to Domenico in the third person (most likely dictated to scribes), c. 1460. Died after 1465.

### PUBLICATIONS

By Domenico:

*De arte saltandi et choreas ducendi. De la arte di ballare e danzare*, c. 1460; manuscript in Bibliothèque Nationale, Paris

About Domenico:

Kinkeldey, Otto, "A Jewish Dancing Master of the Renaissance: Guglielmo Ebreo", *Studies in Jewish Bibliography and Related Subjects in Memory of Abraham Solomon Freidus*, New York, 1929
Wood, Melusine, *Some Historical Dances*, London, 1952
Dolmetsch, Mabel, *Dances of Spain and Italy 1400–1600*, London, 1954; reprinted New York, 1975
Amaya, Mario, "When was Ballet Born: The Dance in Art 5", *Dance and Dancers* (London), December 1961
"Tre maestri di danza alla core Sforzesca", *Archivo Storico Lombardo*, no. 89, 1962

Bianchi, Dante, "Un trattato inedito de Domenico de Ferrara", *La Bibliofilia* (Florence), no. 65, 1963
Brainard, Ingrid, "The Role of the Dancing Master in Fifteenth-Century Courtly Society", *Fifteenth Century Studies* (New York), vol. 2, 1979
Inglehearn, Madeleine, "A Little-known Fifteenth-century Italian Dance Treatise", *Music Review* (Cambridge), August-/November 1981
Padovan, Maurizio, "Guglielmo Ebreo da Pesaro e i maestri del XV secolo", *Mesure et Arte del Danzare* (Pesaro), 1987

* * *

Domenico de Piacenza, also referred to as Domenico da Ferrara, lived in the mid-fifteenth century. He is referred to in one treatise as having been a Jew, but if so, he must have been converted to Christianity, as he is given the title Cavaliero by his contemporaries. Little is known about his life. The writer Antonio Cornazano produced a dance treatise in 1455 in which he refers to Domenico as his revered and honoured teacher. There are references in the treatise of Johannis Ambrosio to Domenico dancing with him at wedding festivities in Forli on 25 January 1456, and also dancing a morescho and many balli at the wedding of Ippolita Sforza to Alfonso Duke of Calabria on 16 May 1465. There are no further references to him. It is therefore assumed by scholars that he was teaching and performing in the mid fifteenth century, and his date of birth can be placed at c. 1425–30.

Domenico of Ferrara was the founder of the "Lombard School" of fifteenth-century dance. He is referred to by other contemporary writers as their teacher, and as such seems to have been highly respected by them. The treatise *De arte saltandi et choreas ducendi*, attributed to Domenico, is in fact written in the third person and states that "the honoured and noble knight Domenichino of Piacentino wishing to write with great reverence, entreats Him who by His holy humanity deigns to help the said performer and writer in this subject". This opening prayer seems to indicate that although Domenico is not writing himself, he is the author of the ideas contained in the text. It is possible, therefore, that he dictated the material to a scribe. (In fact, there are two or three changes of handwriting towards the end which suggest more than one scribe, and the very last dance is scribbled almost as an afterthought.)

The problem with all the fifteenth century dance treatises is that they were written for people who were already very experienced dancers, having learned the art from an early age along with the other accomplishments deemed important to a nobleman or lady. In many respects, therefore, they are frustratingly vague. Details such as how to perform the steps of the dance are either glossed over or not given at all.

Domenico, however, gives many enlightening comments—if not on the mechanics, at least on the spirit of the dances. He describes dance as a "gentle art" but one which requires intelligence and hard work if it is to be well done, and he sets out six main headings for a good dancer. These are Memory, Measure, Manner, Lightness of Spirit, Movement of the Body, and Use of the Floor-space. Most of these headings are self-explanatory and apply to any dancer in any age. Every dancer must remember the dance, keep time with the music, use the floor-space fully, and be cheerful and pleasant to watch. Domenico illustrates some of his points very dramatically. For example, under Manner he compares a dancer to a gondola which, driven by two oars over a quiet sea, lifts gently with the wave and suddenly drops as the wave passes. Other writers simply refer to this as "undulating". Domenico also suggests that a dancer can vary the quality of movement so that sometimes he will pause abruptly as though he had seen the head of Medusa and been turned to stone, and in the next instant swoop away like a falcon searching for prey.

It is with these elegant illustrations that Domenico illuminates the courtly dances of the fifteenth century for us, and presents a living picture of the art which is far more enlightening than the more mundane—if factually more detailed—accounts given by his followers. He also lists the four main dance tempi: Bassa danza, Saltarello, Quadernaria, and Piva, illustrating their relationship to each other by means of a ladder, defining the relationship between music and steps, and explaining when a dance should begin on the up beat (vuodo) and when on the down beat (pieno).

Domenico gives instructions for seventeen Balli and four Bassa danze. The Ballo as a dance type may have been Domenico's own particular invention, since his contemporaries usually include twelve or more of his Ballo choreographies in their work, but only three or four of their own, whereas he appears to have choreographed few Bassa danze compared with the others. The Ballo was usually a dance of mixed rhythms, though some are in duple time throughout, as distinct from the Bassa danza which is always in compound duple (6/8). Some of the Balli also have a dramatic element—for example Mercantia, where one lady smiles in turn upon each of the three suitors who come to dance with her, or Sobria, where the lady refuses to dance with any man but her partner. The fact that Domenico favoured this type of mime dance indicates that he was an actor as well as a dancer, and as such, the forerunner of dancers like Weaver, Sallé, and Noverre.

Domenico's choreographies are for small units of dancers, most frequently for one couple or for two men and one woman, unlike the dances being practised in the rest of Europe at this time, which appear to have been processional dances for as many couples as wished to dance. This use of small numbers of dancers meant that more elaborate floor patterns could be created, and thus laid the ground work for the elaborate dances of Caroso and Negri and the even more intricate patterns of the late seventeenth and early eighteenth-century French dances. He also opened up the possibility of using a greater variety of steps, although regretfully neither he nor his contemporaries give sufficient technical information about these to enable us to reconstruct them with great accuracy. The theories propounded by Domenico can be said to have laid the foundations for European social and theatrical dance for over 300 years.

—Madeleine Inglehearn

---

## DON JUAN

(also *Le Festin de Pierre*)

**Choreography:** Gaspero Angiolini
**Music:** Christoph Willibald Gluck
**Design:** Giovanni Maria Quaglio
**Libretto:** Raniero di Calzabigi and Angiolini, after Molière's 1665 play, *Dom Juan; ou, Le Festin de Pierre*
**First Production:** Burgtheater, Vienna, 17 October 1761

**Other productions include:** Regio Teatro Ducale (staged Vicenzo Galeotti after Angiolini); Milan, 1766. Royal Danish Theatre (restaged Galeotti); Copenhagen, 29 October 1781. King's Theatre (staged Charles LePicq after Angiolini) as *Il Convitato di Pietra*; London, 12 March 1785. Haymarket Theatre (staged Carlo Delpini); London, 15 April 1785.

Vienna State Opera Ballet (new version; chor. Heinrich Kröller); Vienna, 1924. Tanzbühne Theater (new version; chor. Aurel Milloss, "inspired" by Angiolini); Augsburg, 23 September 1933 (restaged Düsseldorf 1935, Florence 1951, and La Scala, Milan, 1971). (René Blum's) Ballets de Monte Carlo (new version; chor. Mikhail Fokine, design Mariano Andreu, libretto Eric Allatini and Fokine), with Anatole Vilzak (Don Juan), Jeanette Lauret (Dona Elvira), and André Eglevsky (Chief Jester and Demon); Alhambra Theatre, London, 25 June 1936. German Opera on the Rhine (new version; chor. Otto Kruger); Düsseldorf, 27 January 1958. Teatro alla Scala (new version; chor. Léonide Massine, with scenario by Massine after Molière), as *Don Giovanni*; Milan, 7 March 1959. Frankfurt Ballet (new version; chor. John Neumeier, with additional music de Victoria); Frankfurt, 25 November 1972.

**Other choreographic treatments of story:** Onorato Viganò (Venice, 1787), Heinrich Kroller (Vienna, 1924), Rudolf von Laban (Hamburg, 1925), Tatiana Gsovsky (Berlin, 1938), Nina Jirsíková (Prague, 1941), Frederick Ashton (London, 1948), Léonide Massine (Milan, 1959), Erich Walter (Wiesbaden, 1963), Richard Adama (Vienna, 1969), Lew Christensen (San Francisco, 1973), Bernd Schindowski (Gelsenkirchen, 1988), Peter Breuer (Berlin, 1989).

## PUBLICATIONS


Michel, A., "The Ballet d'action before Noverre", *Dance Index* (New York), March 1947

Hussey, Dyneley, "Gluck and the Reform of Ballet", *Dancing Times* (London), 2 parts: December 1948, January 1949

Beaumont, Cyril, *Complete Book of Ballets*, revised edition, London, 1951

Kirstein, Lincoln, *Movement and Metaphor: Four Centuries of Ballet*, New York, 1970

Winter, Marian Hannah, *The Pre-Romantic Ballet*, London, 1974

Maynard, Olga, "Don Juan and his Artistic Metamorphosis", *Dance Magazine* (New York), January 1977

Gertsman, Lois, "Musical Character Depiction in Gluck's *Don Juan*", *Dance Chronicle* (New York), vol. 1, no. 1, 1977

"*Don Juan* in Wien", *Tanzblätter* (Vienna), vol. 2, no. 15, April 1978

Russel, C.C., "The Libertine Reformed: *Don Juan* by Gluck and Angiolini", *Music and Letters* (London), January 1984


* * *

Don Juan is a character who has appeared in literature, paintings, and on stage, and has inspired numerous musical compositions. Considered the first anti-hero, and made legendary by countless theatrical adaptations—the most famous being Molière's *Dom Juan* in 1665—Don Juan is a philandering adventurer whose exploits form the substance of a tale embodying the moral debate of good versus evil, and addressing itself (often ambiguously) to the question of repentence.

This legendary figure was first represented in ballet in 1761 by Gaspero Angiolini, a former pupil of the Viennese Franz Hilverding, whose pioneering theories of the *ballet d'action* were concerned with creating movement as a vehicle for expressing emotion. Previously ballet had been largely based on popular dances—such as the gavotte or minuet—of the period; there was little distinction between social and theatrical dance, and ballet had not asserted itself sufficiently to attain artistic independence from opera. However, in the middle of the eighteenth century, advocates of the *ballet d'action*, including Angiolini and Jean-Georges Noverre, helped to liberate the choreographer, giving him new creative power—which he had not enjoyed in court ballets and opera-ballets—to produce works in which every element contributed to the development of the main theme.

The story of *Don Juan* was immediately attractive to Angiolini, unencumbered as it was with subplots, and allowing the choreographer to explore the motivations of human behaviour. In creating the ballet Angiolini was assisted by two like-minded individuals, the librettist Raniero Calzabigi and the composer Christoph Gluck, who shared the choreographer's desire to present ballets with a strong dramatic narrative.

In keeping with this intention, a fourteen-page foreword to the programme, signed by Angiolini, was handed out to audiences at the premiere performance of *Don Juan* on 17 October 1761; in it, the choreographer expounded his theories about the dance of ancient Greece and Rome, and included a summary of the ballet's story.

Unfortunately, nothing survives of the original choreography. Descriptions of the action exist only in the diary of Karl Graf Zinzendorf, written in 1761, and in a detailed scenario located at the Paris Opéra. Nevertheless, by considering the relationship of the story and musical composition of the work, it is possible to ascertain the historical significance of the ballet, which sought to emphasize the importance of theatrical dance, as distinct from purely technical dance.

In presenting a story Angiolini recognized the advantage of dividing up a ballet into acts. *Don Juan* is divided into three acts, a division emphasized by Gluck who set the music in different keys for each. In Act I, Don Juan is in the Commander's house in Madrid, where he serenades Elvira in an attempt to seduce her. His amorous advances are thwarted by Elvira's father, the Commander, who draws a sword and embarks on a duel with Don Juan, only to be fatally wounded. Here Angiolini fully exploited the dramatic potential of the situation, choreographing a vigorous danced duel. The score hints at the movement composition probably employed by Angiolini, conjuring up images of broad leaps and turns. Furthermore, it demonstrates the extent of the choreographer's collaboration with Calzabigi and Gluck in order to achieve a fusion between plot, choreography, and music.

The second act takes place at Don Juan's house where a grand banquet is being held, with the music evoking the gavotte, country minuet, contredanse, and fandango, suggesting that Angiolini made use of court dances not merely for display but to set the scene. At different intervals guests continue to arrive, until Don Juan opens the door to be met by the statue of the Commander. Here the music changes with trombones conveying the tension of the situation and horror of the onlooking guests.

However, it is in the final act of *Don Juan* that the full triumph of Angiolini and his fellow collaborators is most markedly achieved. At this stage in the plot Don Juan visits the Commander's tomb set in a dismal graveyard. Gluck's score conveys a sinister atmosphere, combining a strange sound of pizzicato in the bass, a sustained horn note, and repetition in the upper strings building to a dramatic finale. In the concluding scene, in which the Commander implores Don Juan to repent, demons perform the "Dance of the Furies" as they come to take Don Juan to hell. The music adopts the traditional form of the chaconne, but the composer gave it extra dramatic power and suspense with a series of variations on a ground bass. This allowed Angiolini plenty of opportunity to choreograph dancing full of stirring action.

It is easy to imagine how absorbed the audience must have

been as it witnessed this unfolding drama, but on one occasion the action on stage was equalled by events offstage, when during this dance the Vienna theatre actually caught fire. The mishap did not detract from the ballet's popularity and it remained in the repertory for more than 40 years.

The influence of *Don Juan* has been long-lasting, with numerous choreographers inspired to present their own versions of the ballet. Other eighteenth-century choreographers who restaged the Angiolini ballet included Domenico Ballon, Guiseppe Banti, Carlo Bianciardo, Gasparo Burci, Carlo Bendini, Filippo Beretti, Antonio Campioni, Francesco Clerico, Louis Dupen, Paolo Franci, Nicola Ferlotti, Michele Fabiani, Sébastien Gallet, Charles LePicq, Eusebio Luzzi, Giovanni Monticini, Giacomo Onorati, Domenico Rossi, and Giuseppe Traffieri. Among twentieth-century choreographers who have been inspired to stage their own versions of the classic story have been Aurel Milloss, Mikhail Fokine, Léonide Massine, and John Neumeier, all of whom used the original eighteenth-century Gluck score.

—Melanie Trifona Christoudia

---

**DONN, Jorge Itovitch**

Argentinian dancer and ballet director. Born in Buenos Aires, 28 February 1947. Studied at the Ballet School of the Teatro Colón, Buenos Aires, 1952–62. Dancer, performing small roles at Teatro Colón and on television; left South America for Europe: dancer, becoming principal dancer and creating numerous roles for choreographer Maurice Béjart, Ballet du XXe Siècle, from 1963; also international guest artist, including for Bolshoi Ballet, Moscow; artistic director, Yantra Company, 1976; artistic director, Ballet du XXe Siècle, 1980; director, Vichy Ballet, 1989, returning to Béjart Ballet Lausanne after failure of Vichy company; also appeared in ballet films, including *Le Danseur* (Béjart, 1968), *Je suis né à Venise* (Béjart, 1977), *Coleur Chair* (Weyergans, 1978), *Les Uns et les autres* (Lelouch, 1981), and *Lettre à un jeune danseur* (also chor., 1987), and on television, including in *La Vie d'un danseur* (French television, 1968). Recipient: Critics Prize (Buenos Aires), 1968; *Dance Magazine* Award. Died in Lausanne, 1 December 1992.

**ROLES**

1964 Dancer (cr) in *Neuvième Symphonie* (Béjart), Ballet du XXe Siècle, Brussels
1965 A Swan in *Cygne* (Béjart), Ballet du XXe Siècle, Brussels
1966 Principal dancer (cr) in *Webern Opus 5* (Béjart), Ballet du XXe Siècle, Brussels
Romeo (cr) in *Romeo and Juliet* (Béjart), Ballet du XXe Siècle, Brussels
1967 Principal dancer (cr) in *Messe pour le temps présent* (Béjart), Ballet du XXe Siècle, Avignon
Aubade (cr) in *Soirée Comédie* (Béjart), Ballet du XXe Siècle, Brussels
1968 Le Poète (one of the figurations) (cr) in *Baudelaire* (Béjart), Ballet du XXe Siècle, Grenoble
The Chosen One in *Le Sacre du printemps* (Béjart), Ballet du XXe Siècle, Paris
Principal dancer (cr) in *Le Voyage* (second version; Béjart), Ballet du XXe Siècle, Brussels
Principal dancer (cr) in *La Nuit obscure* and *Bhakti*, second and third parts of *A la recherche de . . .* (Béjart), Ballet du XXe Siècle, Avignon
1969 Principal dancer (cr) in *La Lettra amorosa* in *Concert de danse* (Béjart), Ballet du XXe Siècle
He (cr) in *Les Vainqueurs* (Béjart), Ballet du XXe Siècle, Brussels
Principal dancer (cr) in *Actus Tragicus* (Béjart), Ballet du XXe Siècle, Brussels
1970 Principal dancer (cr) in *Serait-ce la mort?* (Béjart), Ballet du XXe Siècle, Marseilles
Title role in *L'Oiseau de feu* (Béjart), Ballet du XXe Siècle, Brussels
Principal dancer in *Sonate No. 5* (Béjart), Ballet du XXe Siècle, Brussels
1971 Title role (cr) in *Nijinsky, Clown de Dieu* (Béjart), Ballet du XXe Siècle, Brussels
Principal dancer (cr) in *Ni fleurs ni couronnes* (Béjart), Ballet du XXe Siècle, Brussels
Principal dancer (cr) in *Offrande chorégraphique* (Béjart), Ballet du XXe Siècle, Brussels
Principal dancer (cr) in *Fleurs du mal* (Béjart), Ballet du XXe Siècle, Vienna
1972 Title role (cr) in *L'Ange heurtebise* (Béjart), Ballet du XXe Siècle, Brussels
1973 Principal dancer (cr) in *Le Marteau sans maître* (Béjart), Ballet du XXe Siècle, Milan
The Carrier of the Light (cr) in *Golestan* (Béjart), Ballet du XXe Siècle, Persepolis
Principal dancer in *Chant du compagnon errant* (Béjart), Gala, Paris
1974 Petrarca (cr) in *I Trionfi del Petrarca* (Béjart), Ballet du XXe Siècle, Florence
The Poet (cr) in *Ce que l'amour me dit* (Béjart), Ballet du XXe Siècle, Monte Carlo
1975 The Soldier in Love (cr) in *Acqua Alta* (Béjart), Ballet du XXe Siècle, Venice
Lucifer (cr) in *Notre Faust* (Béjart), Ballet du XXe Siècle
1976 Louis XIV (cr) in *Le Molière imaginaire* (Béjart), Ballet du XXe Siècle, Paris
1977 Principal dancer in *Heliogabale* (Béjart), Ballet du XXe Siècle, Paris
"Der Rosenkavalier" (cr) in *Vienna Waltzes* (Balanchine), New York City Ballet, New York
1978 The Boy in *Petrushka* (Béjart), Ballet du XXe Siècle, Brussels
Father (cr) in *Gaîté Parisienne* (Béjart), Ballet du XXe Siècle, Brussels
The Poet (cr) in *Dichterliebe* (Béjart), Ballet du XXe Siècle, Brussels
Zeus (cr) in *Leda* (Béjart), Ballet du XXe Siècle, Brussels
He (cr) in *Ce que la mort me dit* (Béjart), Ballet du XXe Siècle, Brussels
1979 Principal dancer (cr) in *Les Illuminations* (Béjart), Ballet du XXe Siècle, London
Mephisto (cr) in *Mephisto Valse* (Béjart), Monte Carlo Opera, Monte Carlo
Principal dancer in *Boléro II* (Béjart), Ballet du XXe Siècle, Paris
Principal dancer in *Boléro III* (Béjart), Paris Opéra Ballet, Paris
1980 Bolero, La Mélodie (cr) in *Eros-Thanatos* (Béjart), Ballet du XXe Siècle, Brussels
1981 Tamino (cr) in *La Flute enchantée* (Béjart), Ballet du XXe Siècle, Brussels
The Poor One (cr) in *Light* (Béjart), Ballet du XXe Siècle, Brussels

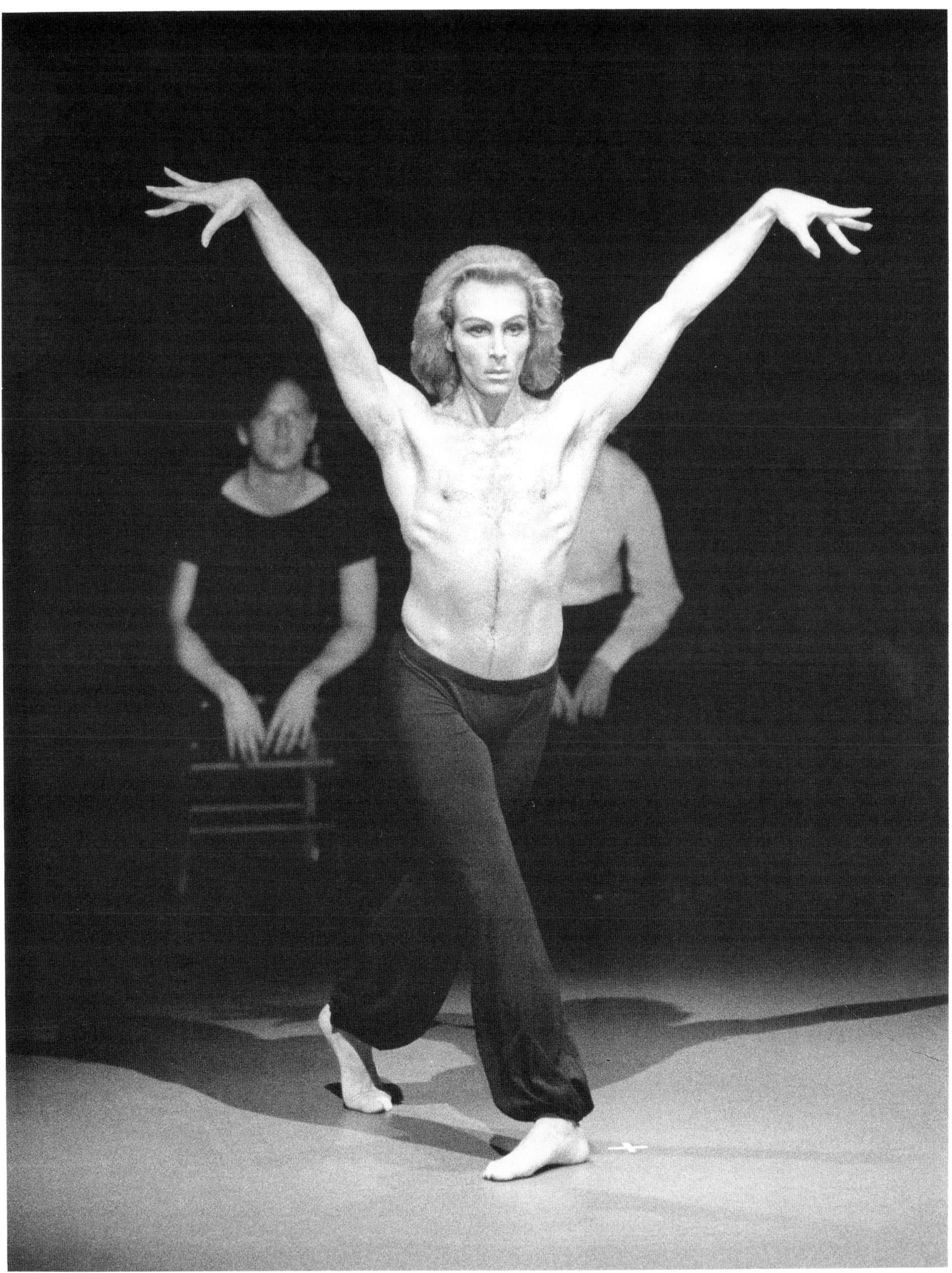

**Jorge Donn in *Bolero***

The Blind Man (cr) in *La Muette* (Béjart), Ballet du XXe Siècle
Principal dancer (cr) in *Divine* (Béjart), Ballet du XXe Siècle
1982 Ludwig in *Wien Wien nur du Allein* (Béjart), Ballet du XXe Siècle, Brussels
1983 Principal dancer (cr) in *Messe pour le temps futur* (Béjart), Ballet du XXe Siècle, Brussels
The Dancer (cr) in *Vie et mort d'une marionette humaine* (solo; Béjart), New York
1984 Principal dancer (cr) in *Fragments* (*1984!*) (Béjart), Ballet du XXe Siècle
Le Comédien/Wagner (cr) in *Dionysos* (Béjart), Ballet du XXe Siècle, Milan
1985 Police Inspector (cr) in *Le Concours* (Béjart), Ballet du XXe Siècle, Paris
1986 The Hero (cr) in *Malraux; ou, La Métamorphose des Dieux* (Béjart), Ballet du XXe Siècle
1987 La Musique (cr) in *Souvenir de Leningrad* (Béjart), Béjart Ballet Lausanne, Lausanne
Principal dancer (cr) in . . . *Et Valse* (Béjart), Béjart Ballet Lausanne, Lausanne
1988 Messenger, Tzaddikin (cr) in *Dybbuk* (Béjart), Béjart Ballet Lausanne, Jerusalem
Principal dancer (cr) in *A force de partir je suis resté chez moi* (Béjart), Béjart Ballet Lausanne, Lausanne
1989 Principal dancer (cr) in *1789 . . . et nous* (Béjart), Béjart Ballet Lausanne, Paris
1990 Title role in *Nijinsky, Clown de Dieu* (theatre version; Béjart), Show devised for Donn by Béjart

## PUBLICATIONS


By Donn:

Interview in Gruen, John, *The Private World of Ballet*, New York, 1975

Dupuis, Simone, "Jorge Donn", *Les Saisons de la danse* (Paris), February 1981

About Donn:

Herf, Estelle, "Jorge Donn of Béjart's 20th-Century Ballet", *Ballet Today* (London), November/December 1969

Hersin, André-Philippe, "Jorge Donn", *Les Saisons de la danse* (Paris), February 1974

Ferran, France, and Catany, Toni, *Jorge Donn danse Béjart*, Paris, 1977

Stoop, Norma McLain, "The Creator and the Interpreters", *Dance Magazine* (New York), March 1979

Philp, Richard, "Donn", *Dance Magazine* (New York), January 1984

Mannoni, Gérard, *Béjart, l'avant-scène ballet danse*, 1985

Bland, Alexander, and Percival, John, *Men Dancing: Performers and Performances*, London, 1989


* * *

When asked what dance represented for him, Jorge Donn replied: "It's everything, it's my life." These few simple words reveal the passion which drove the dancer in his search for perfection.

After discovering the Ballet du XXe Siècle in Buenos Aires in 1963, Donn's interest took a definite shape. With the seriousness of his age (he was sixteen) he fought his shyness, overcame obstacles, and joined Maurice Béjart's company, which from then on became his world. Discreet, almost secretive, Jorge did not open up easily, but Béjart discovered hidden talents in him and sensed a strong personality waiting to be developed. Donn's looks attracted the eye, his sincerity was moving, and his dramatic sense quickly took him up among the top dancers.

One of his first major roles was in *Romeo and Juliet*. Donn lived the role of Romeo with great intensity; his youth brought the role to life, his gentleness and ardour shaping Romeo's character, his rare smile illuminating the moments of joy, only to be quickly overcome by anxiety. The charming games played with Juliet revealed his tenderness, as well as the lyricism of a passion whose tragic beauty was sealed with death.

In Bejart's *Le Voyage*, inspired by the Tibetan *Book of the Dead* (previously choreographed by Lothar Hoffgen), Jorge Donn found a role that suited him perfectly. During this initiation he seemed to find the gestures which led him from hell to a new birth. His muscles, sensitive and flexed, seemed to speak of fear, hope, and the sufferings of a return to life. His reserve disappeared on stage, forgotten for a time, and his involvement was total. The effort demanded by Béjart of his dancers marked them deeply, probably forever. In *Messe pour le temps présent* (*Mass for our Time*) the choreographer created for Donn a Nietzschean meditation dedicated to the night, an intense evocation of pain and solitude that the dancer made his own from the depths of his soul.

In 1960 the dancer Duska Sifnios, raised up on a large round table as the image of femininity offered to man, gave herself up to the driving rhythm of Ravel's *Bolero*, choreographed by Béjart. In 1979 Jorge Donn took the dancer's place in the centre of the table and the ballet took on a whole new significance. Surrounded by women, like priestesses in a ritual, Donn stood alone, moved by an irrepressible force linking him with the cosmos. The vibrations that he released induced a superhuman exaltation until the final annihilation.

In the final scene of *Nijinsky, Clown de Dieu* the choreographer produced another powerful image: the dancer was trapped in the middle of a milling crowd when an arm emerged, thrusting upwards. Into the outstretched hand, his friend the little clown placed a rose, symbol of hope and joy. Donn put all his soul into his interpretation, as he did also in *Dichterliebe*—radiant, sorrowful, and comical.

Caught between wisdom and madness, inspired by a tragic fate, the dancer shared his intense emotion with us; he was able to reach the audience through dance, free of all dramatic trappings; the precision of his line and steps conveyed an interpretation which was uniquely his own. The musical image, as it were, filled his whole body. Expansive movements, in which the dancer seemed stretched towards infinity, opening out with the grace of an unfolding flower, were seen at their best in adage—for instance in the last movement of Gustave Mahler's Third Symphony, "What love tells me". In this a remarkable pas de deux Donn danced with Luciana Savignano, mirrored by six other couples. The music's vibrant harmonies and waves of gentleness were broken by sudden moments of tension which had a powerful lyricism in themselves, borne out by the choreography. The beauty of the dancer who could have been the inspiration for one of Michelangelo's slaves made his vulnerability all the more poignant.

—Jeannine Dorvanne

---

## DON QUIXOTE

**Choreography:** Marius Petipa
**Music:** Léon (Aloisius Ludwig) Minkus

**Design:** Pavel Isakov, F. Shenian, I. Shagin
**Libretto:** Marius Petipa, after Miguel de Cervantes
**First Production:** Bolshoi Theatre, Moscow, 26 October (14 October old style) December 1869
**Principal Dancers:** Wilhelm Vanner (Don Quixote), Anna Sobeshchanskaya (Kitri), Sergei Sokilov (Basil), Polina Karpakova (Dulcinea), Vassily Geltser (Sancho Panza), Leon Espinosa (Harlequin), Dmitri Kuznetsov (Gamache)

**Other productions include:** St. Petersburg Bolshoi Theatre (restaged Petipa), with Alexandra Vergina (Kitri), Timofei Stukolkin (Don Quixote), Lev Ivanov (Basil); St. Petersburg, 21 November (9 November old style) 1871. Moscow Bolshoi Theatre (staged Aleksandr Gorsky, design Aleksander Golovin and Konstantin Korovin), with Lyubov Roslavleva (Kitri), Vassily Tikhomirov (Basil), Mikhail Mordkin (Espada); Moscow, 18 December (6 December old style) 1900 (revived 1906). Maryinsky Theatre (restaged Gorsky), with Mathilda Kshesinskaya (Kitri), Nikolai Legat (Basil), Aleksei Bulgakov (Don Quixote); St Petersburg, 1 February (20 January old style) 1902. State Academic Theatre for Opera and Ballet (GATOB, later Kirov Ballet; staged Fedor Lopukhov, partly after Gorsky); Petrograd, 30 September 1923. Bolshoi Theatre (staged Kasyan Goleizovsky and Rotislav Zakharov, design Vadim Ryndin); Moscow, 10 February 1940. Ballet Rambert (staged Witold Berkowski after Gorsky, Petipa), with Lucette Aldous (Kitri), Kenneth Bannerman (Basil), John Chesworth (Don Quixote); London, 26 July 1962. Vienna State Opera Ballet (chor. Rudolf Nureyev after Petipa); Vienna, 1966 (revived for Australian Ballet, 1970). American Ballet Theatre (staged Mikhail Baryshnikov after Gorsky, Petipa), as *Don Quixote* (*Kitri's Wedding*); Washington, D.C., 28 March 1978.

**Other choreographic treatments of story:** Franz Hilverding (Vienna, 1740), Jean-Georges Noverre (Vienna, 1768), Louis-Jacques Milon (Paris, 1801), Charles Didelot (St. Petersburg, 1808), James Harvey D'Egville (London, 1809), August Bournonville (Copenhagen, 1837), Paul Taglioni (Berlin, 1839), Aurel Milloss (Paris, 1947), Tatiana Gsovsky (Berlin, 1949), Ninette de Valois (London, 1950), Serge Lifar (Paris, 1950), George Balanchine (New York, 1965).

## PUBLICATIONS

Beaumont, Cyril, *Complete Book of Ballets*, revised edition, London, 1951

Krassovskaya, Vera, "*Don Quixote*: A Dramatic Ballet", in *The Russian Ballet Theatre of the Early Twentieth Century*, Leningrad and Moscow, 1963

Denby, Edwin, "About *Don Quixote*", *Dance Magazine* (New York), July 1965

Krassovskaya, Vera, "*Don Quixote* in Moscow and *Don Quixote* in Petersburg", in *The Russian Ballet of the Early Twentieth Century*, Leningrad, 1971

* * *

The ballet *Don Quixote* has a long and somewhat complicated history. Its premiere took place in 1869 at Moscow's Bolshoi Theatre, with the action divided into four acts and the choreography, by Marius Petipa, set to the music of Minkus. Less than two years later, in 1871, a new version by Petipa was shown at the St. Petersburg Bolshoi Theatre. It now consisted of five acts (eleven episodes, a prologue, and an epilogue), and used the same designs as the first production. In 1900, a new production by Aleksandr Gorsky was staged, consisting again of four acts, in which Petipa's scenario and, in some places, his choreography was preserved. A Spanish dance and a fandango, set to the original music by Minkus, were added to the fourth act.

In 1902 this last production was staged at the Maryinsky Theatre in St. Petersburg. The cast was an eminent one: Kitri was danced by Mathilda Kshesinskaya, Basil by Nikolai Legat, Don Quixote by Aleksei Bulgakov, Sancho Panza by Enrico Cecchetti, and Gamache by Pavel Gerdt, with the roles of the Street Dancer, Amor, and Juanita taken by the young ballerinas Olga Preobrazhenskaya, Tamara Karsavina, and Anna Pavlova respectively.

The ballet became part of the permanent repertoire both of the Moscow Bolshoi Theatre (the most famous productions being those by Aleksandr Gorsky in 1906, and by Rostislav Zakharov and Kasyan Goleizovsky in 1940) and the Leningrad Kirov Theatre (which saw productions by Fedor Lopukhov in 1923, with new choreography for the fandango, and by Petr Gusev in 1946, with the scenario modified by Yuri Slonomsky and with new dances introduced by Nina Anisimova). The ballet as it derives from the Russian Petipa version was staged in many Soviet theatres throughout the first half of the twentieth century, and made its way abroad from the 1940s onward.

The plot of the ballet *Don Quixote* is taken from Cervantes' novel of the same name. It concerns the unsuccessful attempt by a rich man, Comacho (called Gamache in the ballet) to marry the beautiful Quiteria (Kitri), who in turn is in love with Basilio (Basil), a young man from her village. Petipa was not the first choreographer to be attracted to the Cervantes novel; his most important predecessor was Franz Hilverding, who staged Gluck's *Don Juan* in Vienna in 1740. Nor was Petipa the first to turn the Kitri–Basil episode into a ballet. An earlier version, *Gamache's Wedding*, had been staged by Louis Milon in Paris in 1801, and Petipa could also have known Charles Didelot's, Paul Taglioni's, and August Bournonville's ballets based on the same plot. However, all of these earlier works have sunk into oblivion long since, while the Petipa–Gorsky–Minkus masterpiece has been kept alive for over a century. Many Russian ballerinas have made outstanding appearances as Kitri, from Pavlova, Karsavina, and Trefilova through to Natalia Dudinskaya, Maya Plisetskaya, and Ekaterina Maximova; and such danseurs as Mikhail Mordkin, Vakhtang Chabukiani, and of course Rudolf Nureyev and Mikhail Baryshnikov have gone down in ballet history as superb Basils.

Today *Don Quixote* is considered one of the most joyous and festive of the classical ballets, brimming with spectacular virtuoso dancing. At the same time this abundance of dancing is well organized, showing a clear choreographic and dramatic vision (particularly in the Kirov version). A short prologue based on mime action is followed by an episode called "A Square in Barcelona", in which classical choreography imitating the "Spanish Style" is predominant, with a sprinkling of character dances. The second episode, "The Gypsy Camp", comes as a sharp contrast—here pantomime and character dancing reign supreme (although some fifteen years ago this scene also contained a lyrical pas de deux for the two main characters). The next episode, "Dulcinea's Garden", is a purely classical one in which only female dancers appear. This is followed by "A Tavern in Seville"; once again, there is plenty of character dancing and acting—and traditionally, even the ballerina wears heeled shoes in this scene. The final wedding celebration is an extended classical grand pas with the now famous pas de deux of the main characters.

The characters of the ballet do much more than just perform their numerous variations, however; they express their thoughts and emotions through dancing, and each character

***Don Quixote*, Act III pas de deux, as performed by Elisabetta Terabust and Patrice Bart, London Festival Ballet**

has his or her own idiosyncrasies which are expressed in the choreography itself. *Don Quixote* is also distinguished by what might be called its democratic spirit: the only "noble cavalier" in the ballet is Gamache, and he is the butt of everyone's jokes and tricks. Don Quixote himself is treated with an increasing irony, friendly though it may be. By contrast, Kitri and Basil are heroes of the people; they belong to the crowd and the crowd interferes in their lives without any second thoughts.

Critical opinions differ concerning the changes made by Aleksandr Gorsky in his production of Petipa's *Don Quixote* in 1900, but his undoubted achievement was an innovative approach to the choreography of the crowd scenes. In an interview given before the ballet's first night in St. Petersburg the choreographer said, "The main difference between traditional ballet productions and mine is that I make lots of people move about the stage all the time without any order or symmetry. People on the right may be doing one thing, people on the left something else, and in the background yet another thing may be going on, so that every section of the stage attracts the spectators' attention." Gorsky made conscious attempts to rejuvenate classical ballet by borrowing new concepts from the Moscow Art Theatre, as well as from contemporary Russian painting, and some consider his version a completely separate work from Petipa's.

It is no coincidence that the Gorsky *Don Quixote* is to this day inseparable from the evocative scenery created by Golovin ("A Square in Barcelona" and the Wedding scenes), Korovin ("The Gypsy Camp" and "A Tavern in Seville"), and Baron Klodt ("Dulcinea's Garden"). These settings embody a typically Russian idea of Spain as a country of bright colours, hot temperaments, and high-running passions, and these things permeate the whole ballet.

Outside Russia, the most well-known versions of the ballet have come from Nureyev and Baryshnikov, who have more or less brought the St. Petersburg/Kirov version—the direct descendant of Petipa—to the West. Prior to their stagings, Witold Berkowski had mounted a production for England's Ballet Rambert in 1962. The *Don Quixote Pas de Deux*, a familiar concert piece, has been performed by countless companies around the world.

—Arsen Degen

**DOUBROVSKA, Felia**

Russian/American dancer and teacher. Born Felizata Dluzhnevska in St. Petersburg, 1896. Studied at the Imperial Theatre School, St. Petersburg, pupil of Kulichev; graduated in 1913. Married Russian dancer Pierre Vladimirov (Vladmiroff), 1922. Dancer, Maryinsky Theatre, St. Petersburg, becoming soloist, 1913–20; emigrated (with Vladimirov) to Paris, 1920: ballerina, Diaghilev's Ballets Russes, 1920–29, also performing as guest artist, Mordkin Ballet, U.S., 1927; dancer, Anna Pavlova's company, 1929–31; ballerina, performing at the Teatro Colón, Buenos Aires, 1931, for Ballet de l'Opéra Russe à Paris, Monte Carlo and London, 1931, with Ballets Russes de Monte Carlo, 1932, Ballets Serge Lifar, London, 1933, Bronislava Nijinska company, 1934, and Léon Woizikowsky company, 1935; guest artist, American Ballet, 1936, de Basil's Ballets Russes, London, 1937; prima ballerina, Metropolitan Opera Ballet, New York, 1938–39; teacher, School of American Ballet, New York, 1949–80. Died in New York, 18 September 1981.

**ROLES**

1921 Fairy of the Pine Woods, Sister Anne (cr) in *The Sleeping Princess* (new production; Petipa, staged Sergeyev, additional dances Nijinska), Diaghilev's Ballets Russes, London
Enchanted Princess (Bluebird pas de deux) in *The Sleeping Princess* (new production; Petipa, staged Sergeyev, additional dances Nijinska), Diaghilev's Ballets Russes, London
1923 Bride (cr) in *Les Noces* (Nijinska), Diaghilev's Ballets Russes, Paris
1925 Rondeau (cr) in *Les Biches* (Nijinska), Diaghilev's Ballets Russes, Monte Carlo
A Muse (cr) in *Zéphire et Flore* (Massine), Diaghilev's Ballets Russes, Monte Carlo
1926 Pas de trois (cr), Entr'acte (Balanchine) in *Romeo and Juliet* (Nijinska), Diaghilev's Ballets Russes, Monte Carlo
The Film Star (cr) in *Pastorale* (Balanchine), Diaghilev's Ballets Russes, Paris
Dancer (cr) in *Jack-in-the-Box* (Balanchine), Diaghilev's Ballets Russes, Paris
1928 Dancer (cr) in *Ode* (Massine), Diaghilev's Ballets Russes, Paris
Dancer (cr) in *La Fille d'Abdoubarahah* (opera; Sanvel, chor. Balanchine), Diaghilev's Ballets Russes, Monte Carlo
Polyhymnia (cr) in *Apollon musagète* (Balanchine), Diaghilev's Ballets Russes, Paris
One of two ladies (cr) in *The Gods Go a-Begging* (Balanchine), Diaghilev's Ballets Russes, London
1929 Dawn (cr), The Dance of the Hours, in *La Gioconda* (opera; mus. Ponchielli, chor. Balanchine), Diaghilev's Ballets Russes, Monte Carlo
Principal dancer (cr) in *La Croisade des dames* (opera; mus. Schubert, chor. Balanchine), Diaghilev's Ballets Russes, Monte Carlo
Spanish entrance (cr) in *Le Bal* (Balanchine), Diaghilev's Ballets Russes, Monte Carlo
The Siren (cr) in *Le Fils prodigue* (*Prodigal Son*; Balanchine), Diaghilev's Ballets Russes, Paris
Title role in *L'Oiseau de feu* (Fokine), Diaghilev's Ballets Russes, Paris
1929/30 Myrtha in *Giselle* (after Petipa, Coralli, Perrot), Anna Pavlova's Company, tour
1931 Title role in *Giselle* (after Petipa, Coralli, Perrot), Teatro Colón, Buenos Aires
Pimpinella (cr) in *Pulcinella* (Romanov), Ballet de l'Opéra Russe à Paris
Adagio, "Snowflakes" from *The Nutcracker* (after Ivanov), Ballet de l'Opéra Russe à Paris, London
Premiere danseuse, Aurora (cr) in *Orphée aux enfers* (opera; mus. Offenbach, chor. Balanchine), Théâtre Mogador, Paris
1932 Swan Queen (Odette) in *Swan Lake* (one-act version; after Ivanov), Ballets Russes de Monte Carlo, European tour
1933 Principal dancer (cr) in *Dans l'Elysée* (probably Balanchine), Ballets Serge Lifar, London
1936 Lady (cr) in *Serenata: Magic* (Balanchine), American Ballet, Hartford, Connecticut
1938/39 Fury in *Orfeo* (opera; mus. Gluck, chor. Romanov), Metropolitan Opera House, New York
Principal dancer in *Thaïs* (opera; mus. Massenet, chor. Romanov), Metropolitan Opera House, New York
Principal dancer in *Tannhäuser* (opera; mus. Wagner, chor. Romanov), Metropolitan Opera House, New York

**Other roles include:** for Diaghilev's Ballets Russes—Rag Mazurka ("Hostess") in *Les Biches* (Nijinska); for Ballets Russes de Monte Carlo—principal dancer in *Les Sylphides* (Fokine), Princess Florine in Bluebird pas de deux from *The Sleeping Beauty* (Petipa).

**PUBLICATIONS**

By Doubrovska:
"In the Shadow of the Russian Tradition", as told to Marian Horosko, *Dance Magazine* (New York), February 1971
Interview in Gruen, John, *The Private World of Ballet*, New York, 1975
"Doubrovska Remembers", as told to Gerald Ackerman and Susan Cook, *Ballet News* (New York), August 1980
Interview in Newman, Barbara, *Striking a Balance*, Boston, 1982

About Doubrovksa:
Grigoriev, Serge, *The Diaghilev Ballet*, translated by Vera Bowen, London, 1953
Moore, Lillian, "From Artist to Student", *Dance Magazine* (New York), May 1954
"Diaghilev Teachers in America", *Ballet Annual* (London), vol. 10, 1956
Kochno, Boris, *Diaghilev and the Ballets Russes*, New York, 1970
Huckenpahler, Victoria, "Felia Doubrovska: Imperial Ballerina", *Dance Chronicle* (New York), vol. 5, no. 4, 1982–83
Tracy, Robert, *Balanchine's Ballerinas*, New York, 1983

* * *

Felia Doubrovska was part of La Belle Epoque, and as such emerged as a principal ballet dancer of great individuality and grace. Her dancing bridged classical and modern styles by virtue of her elegance, suppleness, and precision. After retiring from the stage, Doubrovska became a highly respected and distinguished faculty member at the School of American Ballet in New York, where she taught until a year before her death.

Doubrovska graduated at the top of her class with Olga Spessivtseva from the Imperial Theatre School in St. Peters-

**Felia Doubrovska in *Les Noces*, 1923**

burg, and joined the Maryinsky in 1913. For a dancer of the day she was considered tall (at 5′6″), and her thin, elongated form made her appear taller than she was; yet she possessed incomparable control of her long legs, which were tapered by perfectly arched feet.

Although she ascended beyond the corps de ballet of the Maryinsky, Doubrovska was not cast in any major classical roles, because her unusual height was considered inappropriate for a ballerina. By 1920, she was still a soloist, and after surviving three lean years of the revolution, she escaped with her mother and others across the Finnish border on skis.

She resettled in Paris, where her dancing in a theatrical revue at the Théâtre des Champs-Elysées received excellent critical notice. This piqued the interest of the impresario Serge Diaghilev, who was looking for new dancers to add to his Ballet Russes. A meeting was arranged and he asked her to repeat what she had done at the Champs-Elysées, after which Doubrovska was invited to join his company as a soloist.

Her European début occured during the 1921 London season in a new production of *The Sleeping Beauty* (retitled *The Sleeping Princess*), where she danced the Fairy of the Pine Woods and the Bluebird.

In those early days with the Diaghilev company, Doubrovska became dissatisfied with what she said were "very, very small" roles offered to her, and so left to tour with Anna Pavlova's company. A letter from Boris Kochno, Diaghilev's adviser and spokesman, convinced her that she was needed back, and so after only six weeks away, she returned. Says Kochno:

> When she first came to Diaghilev to take the part of a fairy in *The Sleeping Princess*, she necessarily subordinated her personality to the need for uniformity within the group. . . . It took the creations of Balanchine and Massine choreographed on my scenarios (*La Pastorale*, *Ode*, *Le Fils prodigue*), to develop and fully realize Doubrovska's unique potential. . . . Only then did this classically-based dancer with a contemporary flair come into her own.

Doubrovska also sparked the interest of Bronislava Nijinska, who created the role of the Bride in *Les Noces* on her in 1923. Her great success with Massine came in his *Ode*, which had its premiere in 1928. She had an amazing ability to accomodate the unusual configurations and unconventionality of George Balanchine's particular vision and he cast her as the Film Star in his 1926 ballet, *La Pastorale*. Thereafter it was Doubrovska who served as Balanchine's favorite "guinea pig".

Balanchine, who said he liked tall dancers because the audience could see more, appreciated the clean lines of Doubrovska's slender body and her willingness to try the oddly contortionistic movement that characterized his style. Alexandra Danilova adds that he also admired Doubrovska's dramatic talent. He used Doubrovska to create the roles of Polyhymnia (Polymnia), the Muse of Mime, in *Apollon musagète* (*Apollo*), and the Siren in *Prodigal Son* (*Le Fils prodigue*).

Felia Doubrovska once admitted that she admired Anna Pavlova so much that she tried to copy her. Yet while certain physical parallels can be drawn, Doubrovska's unique charm and plaintive beauty created a wholly new kind of dancer. Although she felt uneasy about the Siren's suggestive movements in Balanchine's *Prodigal Son*, her seduction scene was praised for its dramatically serpentine quality. In a review written for *The Nation and Athenaeum* on 6 July 1929, dancer and critic Lydia Lopokova wrote, "Doubrovska as an unbelievably fantastic seductress was thin, strong, and enticing. But what would the old ballerinas have said to anyone who asked them to do with their bodies the things she has to do! She had a great success—it is a part no one will ever be able to take from her."

Following Diaghilev's death in 1929, Felia Doubrovska appeared with other groups of former Diaghilev dancers, including Nijinska's company in 1934. She danced with the Ballet de l'Opéra Russe à Paris, the Leon Woizikovsky company, and the de Basil Ballet Russe. When war threatened to break out in Europe, she and her husband Pierre Vladimirov (a partner to Pavlova and a premier danseur classique) moved to the United States where, for a short time, she continued to perform as a prima ballerina with the Metropolitan Opera when Balanchine was its director.

By the age of 43, Doubrovska had decided to leave the stage and said that she "wanted the memory of [her] dancing to remain as pleasant as possible". She settled into domestic life, living with her husband and mother, who died in 1947. She maintained her friendship with Balanchine, who had hired Vladimirov to teach at his School of American Ballet (SAB) when it opened in 1934. Balanchine eventually persuaded Doubrovska to teach there as well, because he knew she could train women dancers the way he needed them to be trained—classically, and with an eye to increased stamina and malleable grace.

Doubrovska joined the faculty at SAB in 1948 and remained an active teacher there for 32 years. She told John Gruen that teaching her first class at the school was terrifying, as she was assigned the advanced women's classes and had to face all of Balanchine's former ballerinas and wives there. Those who were fortunate enough to have taken her class quickly discovered that she was confident and authoritative about the technique and artistry that she was passing down to them.

As a teacher Doubrovska was very strict and her corrections were always useful. Her appearance was meticulously maintained, and she was never sloppy or dishevelled. Her luminous eyes were always generously made up and she used them in the ways of a silent film star. Whoever was in her class, whether a ballet star or unknown student, was treated as a student, and corrected and criticized as Doubrovska saw fit.

—Kim Kokich

---

**DOWELL, Anthony**

British dancer and ballet director. Born in London, 16 February 1943. Studied with June Hampshire, and at Royal Ballet School, from 1953. Dancer, Covent Garden Opera Ballet, 1960, and Royal Ballet, from 1961; principal dancer, Royal Ballet, from 1966, touring Italy, 1965, Eastern Europe, 1966, New York, 1968, 1969, 1972, Japan, 1975; principal guest artist, American Ballet Theatre, New York, 1977–80; also guest artist for the Joffrey Ballet, New York, 1979, and National Ballet of Canada, Toronto, 1979, 1981; starred in Anthony Dowell Ballet Gala for charity, Palladium Theatre, London, 1980; has also appeared on television, including BBC *Omnibus* programme, "All the Superlatives" (dir. Colin Nears, 1976); assistant director, Royal Ballet, 1984: associate director, 1985; artistic director, from 1986; has staged ballets for the company, including new production of *Swan Lake*, 1987. Recipient: *Dance Magazine* Award, 1972; Commander of the Order of the British Empire, 1973.

**ROLES**

1962 Principal dancer in *Napoli* Divertissement (Bruhn after Bournonville), Royal Ballet, London

1963 Country Boy in *La Fête étrange* (Howard), Royal Ballet, London

1964 Principal dancer in *Diversions* (MacMillan), Royal Ballet, London

Oberon (cr) in *The Dream* (Ashton), Royal Ballet, London

1965 Cousin in *The Invitation* (MacMillan), Royal Ballet, Tour

Principal dancer (cr) in *Monotones* (no. 2: Trois Gymnopédies; Ashton), Royal Ballet, London

Benvolio (cr) in *Romeo and Juliet* (MacMillan), Royal Ballet, London

Romeo in *Romeo and Juliet* (MacMillan), Royal Ballet, London

1966 Principal dancer in *Brandenburg Concertos nos. 2 and 4* (Cranko), Royal Ballet, London

Friend in *Les Noces* (Nijinska), Royal Ballet, London

The Joker in *Card Game* (Cranko), Royal Ballet, London

Principal dancer in *Monotones* (*nos. 1 and 2*; Ashton), Royal Ballet, London

The Messenger of Death in *Song of the Earth* (MacMillan), Royal Ballet, London

1967 The Boy With the Matted Hair (cr) in *Shadowplay* (Tudor), Royal Ballet, London

The Prince in *Cinderella* (Ashton), Royal Ballet, London

Albrecht in *Giselle* (Petipa after Coralli, Perrot; staged Sergeyev, Ashton), Royal Ballet, London

Prince Siegfried in *Swan Lake* (Petipa, Ivanov, Ashton; staged Helpmann), Royal Ballet Touring Company

Principal dancer in *Symphonic Variations* (Ashton), Royal Ballet, London

1968 Troyte (cr) in *Enigma Variations* (Ashton), Royal Ballet, London

Friday in *Jazz Calendar* (Ashton), Royal Ballet, London

Her Lover in *Lilac Garden* (*Jardin aux lilas*; Tudor), Royal Ballet, London

Drosselmeyer/The Prince in *The Nutcracker* (Nureyev after Vainonen), Royal Ballet, London

Prince Florimund in *The Sleeping Beauty* (Petipa, Ashton; staged Wright), Royal Ballet, London

1969 Daphnis in *Daphnis and Chloe* (Ashton), Royal Ballet, London

Jean de Brienne in *Raymonda* Act III (Nureyev after Petipa), Royal Ballet, London

1970 Principal dancer in *Dances at a Gathering* (Robbins), Royal Ballet, London

Principal dancer in *Scènes de ballet* (Ashton), Royal Ballet, London

1971 Principal dancer in *Afternoon of a Faun* (Robbins), Royal Ballet, London

Mathilde Kschessinska's Partner (cr) in *Anastasia* (3-act version; MacMillan), Royal Ballet, London

Principal dancer (cr) in Meditation from *Thaïs* (pas de deux; Ashton), Royal Ballet, London

1972 The Boy (cr) in *Triad* (MacMillan), Royal Ballet, London

1973 Principal dancer (cr) in *Pavanne* (MacMillan), Royal Ballet, London

Sanguinic in *The Four Temperaments* (Balanchine), Royal Ballet, London

Sarabande in *Agon* (Balanchine), Royal Ballet, London

Solor in *La Bayadère* (Nureyev after Petipa), Royal Ballet, London

Colas in *La Fille mal gardée* (Ashton), Royal Ballet, London

Principal dancer in *In the Night* (Robbins), Royal Ballet, London

1974 Des Grieux (cr) in *Manon* (MacMillan), Royal Ballet, London

Lescaut in *Manon* (MacMillan), Royal Ballet, London

1975 Principal dancer (cr) in *Four Schumann Pieces* (Van Manen), Royal Ballet, London

Autumn (cr) in *The Four Seasons* (MacMillan), Royal Ballet, London

Mercutio in *Romeo and Juliet* (MacMillan), Royal Ballet, London

Principal dancer in *Don Quixote* Pas de Deux (after Petipa), Royal Ballet, London

1976 Beliaev (cr) in *A Month in the Country* (Ashton), Royal Ballet, London

1978 Solor (cr) in *La Bayadère* (new production; Makarova after Petipa), American Ballet Theatre, New York

1979 Principal dancer (cr) in *Contredanses* (Tetley), American Ballet Theatre, New York

The Narrator in *A Wedding Bouquet* (after Ashton), Joffrey Ballet, New York

1982 The Fisherman (cr) in *Le Rossignol* (Ashton), Metropolitan Opera House, New York

Prospero (cr) in *The Tempest* (Nureyev), Royal Ballet, London

1983 Lo Straniero (cr) in *Varii Capricci* (Ashton), Royal Ballet, New York

1984 The Prince (cr) in *The Nutcracker* (new production; Wright), Royal Ballet, London

**Anthony Dowell in *The Sleeping Beauty***

1985 Imsety (cr) in *The Sons of Horus* (Bintley), Royal Ballet, London
1988 Palemon in *Ondine* (Ashton), Royal Ballet, London
The High Brahmin in *La Bayadère* (Makarova after Petipa), Royal Ballet, London
Carabosse in *The Sleeping Beauty* (Petipa; staged de Valois), Royal Ballet, London
1990 The Aged Emperor (cr) in *The Prince of the Pagodas* (MacMillan), Royal Ballet, London
1991 Kulygin (cr) in *Winter Dreams* (MacMillan), Royal Ballet, London

## WORKS

Staged:
1987 *Swan Lake* (after Petipa, Ivanov; mus. Tchaikovsky), Royal Ballet, London

## PUBLICATIONS

By Anthony Dowell:
"Anthony Dowell Talks to *Dance and Dancers*", *Dance and Dancers* (London), April 1969
Interview in Gruen, John, *The Private World of Ballet*, New York, 1975
Interview in Hodgson, Moira, "Dowell Discusses his Move to ABT", *Dance News* (New York), December 1978

About Anthony Dowell:
Goodman, Saul, "Anthony Dowell: Brief Biography", *Dance Magazine* (New York), June 1967
Spatt, Leslie (photographer), *Sibley and Dowell*, London, 1976
Monahan, James, "Anthony Dowell", *Dancing Times* (London), October 1978
Hunt, Marilyn, "Anthony Dowell", *Dance Magazine* (New York), March 1979
Harris, Dale, "Spreading His Wings", *Ballet News* (New York), September 1979
Bland, Alexander, *The Royal Ballet: The First 50 Years*, London, 1981
"The Royal Ballet: The Biographies" in *Ballet in London Yearbook 1989/90*, London, 1989
Percival, John, "Swans in their Setting", *Dance and Dancers* (London), July 1989
Sorley Walker, Kathrine, "Royal Ballet Worries", *Dancing Times* (London), December 1989

* * *

From being the finest premier danseur so far produced by the Royal Ballet system, Anthony Dowell has risen successfully to become artistic director of the company. It has been a career as smooth, untrammelled, and seemingly effortless as the perfect classical virtuosity which made him world-renowned as a dancer. Unlike the case of so many of his contemporaries, there were no on-stage or off-stage dramas to feed the media, no revelatory biographies to be written, no temperamental clashes to feed the gossip of balletomanes. The only controversies surrounding his career to date seem likely to be the policies he has pursued thus far in formulating the company's repertoire.

In his youth, Dowell's natural facility at ballet had led him to go from school into the Royal Ballet School. That same facility allowed him to sail through the daily dance curriculum with comparative ease, although he was bored by the academic classes. From the Royal Ballet Upper School, Dowell graduated into the Covent Garden Opera Ballet which, at that time, was considered the appropriate place for an apprentice artist before joining one of the two Royal Ballet companies. There is no doubt, however, that his exceptional technique, natural poise, and elegant dancing had marked him out early for careful nurturing as a future company premier danseur noble.

Dowell was drafted into the ranks of the Royal Ballet at Covent Garden to make up the company numbers on its second visit to the Soviet Union in 1961. His first major role with the company came a year later, when he was chosen to dance in Erik Bruhn's production of dances from *Napoli*. At a time when Nureyev had burst upon the international scene and was fast becoming a role model for all young male dancers in the West, Dowell, by contrast, was showing many of Erik Bruhn's attributes: a cool perfection of classical line and finish, a nobility of bearing, and a virtuosity at the service of artistic expression, rather than bravura display for its own sake.

Two years after *Napoli*, Frederick Ashton chose Dowell to dance Oberon in his new production of *The Dream*, matching him with Antoinette Sibley as Titania in a pairing that was to initiate one of the world's great dance partnerships over the next two decades. These two dancers complemented one another perfectly, almost as the Geminian halves of one being. Both of them scored great personal triumphs in *The Dream*—it is true to say that their performances have never been matched, far less surpassed—and, although the ballet achieved a certain success in London, the enthusiasm which the work engendered in New York was even greater, due in no small part to the performances of these young soloists, who helped confirm the ballet's permanent place in the repertoire.

In 1965 Kenneth MacMillan produced his version of *Romeo and Juliet*, in which Dowell created the minor role of Benvolio. Once again he was perfectly cast, his noble manner and serious mien a perfect foil to Mercutio's more volatile character. In later years, Dowell was to prove one of the great Romeos, combining his naturally aristocratic reserve with a youthful passion which he was able to portray with increasing depth through his years as a performer.

Two years later, Dowell was cast in the leading role of Antony Tudor's enigmatic ballet *Shadowplay*, a work partly based on Kipling's *Jungle Book* and reflecting Tudor's great personal interest in Buddhism. Tudor was a choreographer who expected his dancers to think very closely about their roles, considering the psychological motivation behind each move and the reason for every glance or gesture. Working on this part, Dowell has said, was the first time he had really thought about the interpretation of a given role. This experience, and the intellectual discipline Tudor imposed, initiated a period of interpretive performances that placed Dowell in the front rank of international ballet artists.

Throughout the late 1960s Dowell became the great British exemplar of the classical style, making impressive débuts in *Swan Lake*, *The Sleeping Beauty*, and *Giselle*. He also appeared in contemporary classics, such as Ashton's *Symphonic Variations* and MacMillan's *Song of the Earth*, in which he first danced the technically and emotionally demanding role of the Messenger of Death. In the late 1960s and early 1970s he also created a number of important roles, for example in Ashton's *Jazz Calendar* and *Enigma Variations*, and MacMillan's *Triad* and full-length version of *Anastasia*.

In March 1974 MacMillan produced his third full-length ballet, *Manon*, with Dowell and Sibley in the leading roles: Sibley as the eponymous, amoral heroine and Dowell as her besotted lover, Des Grieux—parts which may be considered the apotheosis of their partnership. Indeed, at this time, although Margot Fonteyn and Rudolf Nureyev were still making occasional appearances with the company as guest artists, Dowell and Sibley could be said to be leading the Royal Ballet.

Some two years later, Dowell created the role of Beliaev in Ashton's new ballet, *A Month in the Country* (1976), with Lynn Seymour as the heroine Natalia Petrovna. The ballet was a great success, but Dowell was beginning to feel that he was in need of a change of scene, having triumphed in all the major roles available to him in the Royal Ballet repertoire. Accordingly he took an "extended leave of absence" from the Royal Ballet to dance with American Ballet Theatre, where his regular partner was the great Kirov Ballet artist Natalia Makarova. There is no doubt that Dowell's three years with ABT were beneficial, extending his repertoire and interpretive abilities. He returned to the Royal Ballet to lead the company's Fiftieth Anniversary celebrations in 1981. One of the last roles that he created was that of the somewhat gigolo-like character in Ashton's rather trivial work *Varii Capricci*—a work which did, at least, revive his partnership with Sibley, which continued for another few years in such ballets as *The Dream, Manon*, and *A Month in the Country*.

In September 1984 Dowell was appointed assistant to Norman Morrice, then director of the Royal Ballet. A year later, he was made associate director, and in 1986 he succeeded Morrice as director of the company. Well aware of what an administrative and artistic burden the appointment can be, he none the less placed his reputation on the line within six months with a wholly new version of *Swan Lake*. It proved a controversial production, mainly because of the supposed excesses of the design; but some observers found reassurance in the quality of the dancing, particularly welcome as the company had received some fierce criticism in the preceding year or two because of noticeable evidence of falling standards of performance.

Dowell's directorship of the company has received further criticism (which must be the lot of any director), but his policy of carefully guiding the careers of a new generation of dancers, while introducing a number of illustrious guest artists as a stimulus to both young dancers and audience attendance, appears to be achieving positive results. He still makes occasional appearances as a dancer: in 1990, he created the role of the Emperor in MacMillan's new version of *The Prince of the Pagodas*, and in May of that year he assumed his original role of Beliaev in *A Month in the Country* in order to partner distinguished guest star Sylvie Guillem in her début as Natalia Petrovna.

—Edward Thorpe

---

## THE DREAM

**Choreography:** Frederick Ashton
**Music:** Felix Mendelssohn, arranged by John Lanchbery
**Design:** Henry Bardon (scenery), David Walker (costumes)
**Libretto:** Frederick Ashton (after Shakespeare's *A Midsummer Night's Dream*)
**First Production:** Royal Ballet, Royal Opera House, London, 2 April 1964
**Principal Dancers:** Antoinette Sibley (Titania), Anthony Dowell (Oberon), Keith Martin (Puck), Alexander Grant (Bottom)

**Other productions include:** Royal Ballet Touring Company (design Peter Farmer), with Doreen Wells (Titania), David Wall (Oberon); Oxford, 2 December 1966. Australian Ballet (staged Elphine Allen, design Peter Farmer), with Elaine Fifield (Titania), Kelvin Coe (Oberon), Paul Saliba (Puck), Alan Alder (Bottom); Sydney, 11 July 1969. Joffrey Ballet (staged John Hart, design David Walker), with Rebecca Wright (Titania), Burton Taylor (Oberon), Russell Sultzbach (Puck), Larry Grenier (Bottom); Wolftrap Performing Arts Center, Virginia, 9 August 1973. Royal Swedish Ballet (design Walker), with Kerstin Lidstrom (Titania), Jens Graff (Oberon), Klas Rickman (Puck), Nisse Winqvist (Bottom); Stockholm, 14 October 1975. National Ballet of Canada, with Karen Kain (Titania); Toronto, 15 February 1978. Ballet West (staged John Hart); Salt Lake City, 1985.

**Other choreographic treatments of story:** Marius Petipa (St. Petersburg, 1876), Mikhail Fokine (St. Petersburg, 1906), David Lichine (Paris, 1933), George Balanchine (New York, 1962: see *A Midsummer Night's Dream*), John Neumeier (Hamburg, 1977), Robert de Warren (Manchester, 1981).

### PUBLICATIONS

Williams, Peter, Barnes, Clive, and Goodwin, Noël, "*The Dream*", *Dance and Dancers* (London), May 1964
Balanchine, George, with Mason, Francis, *Balanchine's Complete Stories of the Great Ballets*, Garden City, N.Y., 1977
Vaughan, David, *Frederick Ashton and his Ballets*, London, 1977
Newman, Barbara, "Sibley Talks About Dancing", *Ballet Review* (Brooklyn), Summer 1981
Macaulay, Alastair, "A Summer Night's Ashton", *Dancing Times* (London), August 1986

* * *

Ashton's *The Dream* was the direct result of Shakespeare's quatercentenary in April 1964. The Royal Ballet decided to celebrate with a triple bill. They already had Helpmann's *Hamlet* in the repertoire, although not in regular performance, and they wanted to add works by Ashton and MacMillan. MacMillan staged *Images of Love*, based on some of the Sonnets, and Ashton, true romantic, chose to make a one-act ballet out of *A Midsummer Night's Dream*. He also decided to set it to Mendelssohn's incidental music for the play. This had been used in 1937 for a magical staging of the play directed by Tyrone Guthrie for the Old Vic, with Vivien Leigh and Robert Helpmann as Titania and Oberon and choreography by Ninette de Valois, and again in 1954 when it was directed by Michael Benthall for Moira Shearer and Helpmann, a version for which Ashton had choreographed the Nocturne.

The music was a perfect choice for the scenario as mapped out by Ashton with John Lanchbery, who arranged the music. Theseus and Hippolyta were discarded along with old Egeus, and Bottom and his fellow "mechanicals" were severely cut down. It is, however, a narrative ballet, with brilliant choreography furthering the narrative at every stage.

Ashton has evoked the Romantic era with keen sympathy, so that most of the Fairy ensembles recall nineteenth-century lithographs; there is even an echo of the 1845 *Pas de quatre* in one grouping of girls. The choreography, sometimes deliciously demi-caractère and comic and at others purely classical and technically virtuoso, sustains the highest standard of invention. The roles of Oberon and Puck are fiercely challenging for male dancers; Titania's part in the fine pas de deux of reconciliation with Oberon requires the utmost delicacy and sensitivity from a ballerina; and the dances for the lovers conjure up the

**Antoinette Sibley and Anthony Dowell in *The Dream*, Royal Ballet, London, 1964**

Shakespearean character of each of the four.

The ballet begins with the quarrel between Oberon and Titania, when he demands from her the changeling boy, and on her refusal despatches Puck for the magic flower whose juice will alter people's affections. Thereafter it deals with the comedy of misunderstandings between the two pairs of runaway lovers and Titania's infatuation with Bottom, who has been transformed by Puck into a donkey; and all ends on the idyllic note of renewed love between the King and Queen of Fairyland and wedded bliss for the mortals. Over the years it has had fine performances in every role. None, however, has surpassed the original casting of Antoinette Sibley and Anthony Dowell as Titania and Oberon, with Alexander Grant as Bottom.

Lanchbery's Mendelssohn score for the ballet uses the Overture composed in 1826 and the later Suite. The song "You spotted snakes" is included, although not always chorally sung. Various sets and costumes have been used, all of which preserve, in the case of the immortals, the enchanting style of the first designs by Henry Bardon and David Walker—which in turn owed much to those of Oliver Messel for the Old Vic/Guthrie production of the play in 1937.

—Kathrine Sorley Walker

---

## DRINK TO ME ONLY WITH THINE EYES

**Choreography:** Mark Morris
**Music:** Virgil Thomson
**Design:** Santo Loquasto (costumes)
**First Production:** American Ballet Theatre, Metropolitan Opera House, New York, 31 May 1988
**Principal Dancers:** Mikhail Baryshnikov, Shawn Black, Julio Bocca, Isabella Podovani, Robert Hill, Susan Jaffe, Carld Jonassaint, Lucette Katerndahl, Kathleen Moore, Martine van Hamel, Robert Wallace, Ross Yearsley

### PUBLICATIONS

Macaulay, Alastair, "Vivamus Atque Amenus", *The New Yorker* (New York), 20 June 1988
Mason, Francis, "Forewords and Afterwords", *Ballet Review* (New York), Summer 1988
Garafola, Lynn, "Mark Morris and the Feminine Mystique", *Ballet Review* (New York), Fall 1988
Temin, Christine, "The Triumph of Mark Morris", *Boston Globe Magazine* (Boston), 19 February 1989
Acocella, Joan, "Mark Morris and the Classical Vision", *Art in America* (New York), January 1991

* * *

Mark Morris's *Drink to Me Only With Thine Eyes* came into being out of a commission from Mikhail Baryshnikov, then artistic director of American Ballet Theatre. By 1987, when he began creating the ballet, Morris—who had been making dances for himself and his various groups of dancers for some fifteen years—had previously fulfilled only two ballet commissions. His first was *Mort Subite* for the Boston Ballet; his second was *Esteemed Guests* for the Joffrey Ballet. Both had their premiere performances in 1986, the former in February and the latter in September. The time was one in which diverse practitioners of so-called modern dance were increasingly being called on to create works for classical ballet companies. The term "crossover choreography" was regularly coined when discussing such works. Because of his widely admired dances in the modernist vein, Morris became sought after, in spite of his relative youth (he was 29 when he made *Mort Subite*), as the exemplar of such crossover works.

*Drink to Me Only With Thine Eyes* takes its name from the famous seventeenth-century song of the same name, which Virgil Thomson uses as the basis of one of his piano études. Called "Tenor Lead", it closes the suite of thirteen Thomson études that Morris uses for his ballet's score. Especially as seen in the context of American Ballet Theatre (the only company now performing it), Morris's *Drink* looks as if it could be nicknamed *Études*. Like Harald Lander's *Études*, long identified with American Ballet Theatre, Morris's ballet is a stark, white-on-black picture of ballet dancing arranged as studies of steps from the danse d'école alongside studies of fingerings for the piano. Where Lander's work is reminiscent of the classroom and somewhat simplistic, Morris's is sometimes diabolically complex and eventually dramatic. Lander's dancers are dressed in traditional tutus or vest-topped tights; Morris's dancers are in white dance-wear that looks like casual clothing.

Performing on a stage with a piano in the centre back, the cast of twelve dancers—six men and six women—frequently projects the straightforwardness of pupils at a recital. Early on, some of the women are carried on in overhead horizontal lifts, in which they look somewhat like ancient statuary. The cut-off tights beneath their skirted leotards even give a sense of the truncated limbs associated with antique sculptures. This austere and measured opening soon gives way to the fancy flights and coursings Morris has devised for the variously coloured and textured musical numbers. "Repeating Tremolo", the second étude, is a series of solo entrances and exits that introduces all the dancers and establishes the distinctively arranged poses that will characterize their statuesque plastique here. "Double Glissando", the fourth section, brings on the dancer who was originally Baryshnikov. Here, and subsequently, this role is made of vaulting jumps, precisely centred pirouettes, and gyroscopic turns that are distinguished by both their whirling amplitude and their pin-point finishes.

Just past the ballet's middle, for "Double Sevenths", the full cast makes one charging circuit around the piano, and thus the musician and the musical instrument become memorably part of the work's cast and décor. "Parallel Chords", the tenth segment, is a trio of male solos in a tango mood, with the Baryshnikov role standing out by way of turns and extensions hot with emphatic concentration.

The women, who have been precisely and playfully picking their way through their études on pointe, have stately postures in lifts that drape them sleepily yet strongly over their partner's shoulders. The most prominent women's section is "Ragtime Bass", the eleventh étude, in which three women point and counterpoint their toework intricately yet playfully, and end up making a little grouping reminiscent of some of Merce Cunningham's most felicitous friezes.

The suite ends with "For the Weaker Fingers", a pianissimo étude amazingly arranged here for some men doing huge jumps. The capping segment, Thomson's variation on "Drink to Me Only With Thine Eyes", is essentially a recapitulation of all that has transpired before. The effect is not only one of theatrical closure, but one of dramatic and emotional denouement. The lifts, postures, and steps that have graphically and formally dramatized these piano études now become grave, almost melancholy, like the song being played. The overhead carries, the over-the-shoulder lifts, the torsioned and back-

***Drink To Me Only With Thine Eyes*, American Ballet Theatre, 1988**

leaning poses, the little lengths of running steps and pivots all glow luminously beyond their physical impact.

With ABT's premiere of *Drink to Me Only With Thine Eyes*, Baryshnikov's faith in Mark Morris was justified. *The New York Times* critic Anna Kisselgoff, commenting on the "effective theatrical atmosphere" of the essentially plotless work, called *Drink* "a ballet that keeps the eye and mind alert". Dale Harris (of *The Wall Street Journal*) went even further: "The impression [these dancers] make", he wrote, "is frankly dazzling. There is no finer classical dancing to be seen anywhere today."

The particularly studied dances that Morris created in response to Thomson's music studies have, ultimately, done more than entertain their public and engage their inspiring dancers. They have created their own little world, one in which myriad emotions are presented and in which words are utterly superfluous. The figures struck by the calm and still women carried on stage remind us in the end of more than anonymous statues; they have become representations of the muses of dance and music.

—Robert Greskovic

---

**DUDINSKAYA, Natalia**

Ukrainian/Soviet dancer and teacher. Born Natalia Mikhailovna Dudinskaya in Kharkov, 21 August 1912. First lessons with mother, Natalia Tagliori; studied at the Leningrad Choreographic School, pupil of Agrippina Vaganova; graduated in 1931. Married dancer and choreographer Konstantin Sergeyev. Début (while still a student) as Princess Florine in *The Sleeping Beauty*; performed principal roles soon after becoming artist of the State Academic Theatre for Opera and Ballet (GATOB, later the Kirov); leading artist, Kirov Theatre, 1931–62; teacher, Kirov Class of Perfection, 1951–70; Repetiteur, Kirov Ballet, 1963–78; teacher, Leningrad Choreographic School, from 1964; has also appeared frequently in films and on Soviet television, including Carabosse in *The Sleeping Beauty* (dir. Sergeyev), 1964. Recipient: title of Honoured Artist of the Russian Federation, 1939; State Prize of the USSR, 1941, 1947, 1949, 1951; title of People's Artist of the Russian Federation, 1951; People's Artist of the USSR, 1957.

**ROLES**

1932 Mireille de Poitiers (cr) in *The Flames of Paris* (Vainonen), State Academic Theatre for Opera and Ballet (GATOB), Leningrad

**Natalia Dudinskaya, Leningrad, late 1930s**

1938 Title role in *Raymonda* (Vainonen after Petipa), Kirov Ballet, Leningrad
1939 Title role (cr) in *Laurencia* (Chabukiani), Kirov Ballet, Leningrad
1940 Pannochka (cr) in *Taras Bulba* (Lopukhov), Kirov Ballet, Leningrad
1942 Title role (cr) in *Gayané* (Anisimova), Kirov Ballet, Perm
1945 Title role (cr) in *Gayané* (new version; Anisimova), Kirov Ballet, Leningrad
Odette/Odile in *Swan Lake* (Petipa, staged Lopuhkov), Kirov Ballet, Leningrad
1946 Title role (cr) in *Cinderella* (Sergeyev), Kirov Ballet, Leningrad
Principal dancer (cr) in *Alborada* (choreographic miniature; Yakobson), Kirov Ballet, Leningrad
1947 Title role (cr) in *Militsa* (Vainonen), Kirov Ballet, Leningrad
Snow White (cr) in *Spring Fairy Tale* (Lopukhov), Kirov Ballet, Leningrad
Principal dancer (cr) in *Sentimental Waltz* (choreographic miniature; Yakobson), Kirov Ballet, Leningrad
1948 Title role (cr) in *Raymonda* (new production; Sergeyev after Petipa), Kirov Ballet, Leningrad
1949 Parasha (cr) in *The Bronze Horseman* (Zakharov), Kirov Ballet, Leningrad
Principal dancer (cr) in *Choreographic Etude* (choreographic miniature; Yakobson), Kirov Ballet, Leningrad
1950 Syuimbike (cr) in *Ali-Batyr* (*Shurale*; Yakobson), Kirov Ballet, Leningrad
1953 Galya (cr) in *Native Fields* (Andreyev), Kirov Ballet, Leningrad
1955 Pannochka (cr) in *Taras Bulba* (Fenster), Kirov Ballet, Leningrad
1956 Baronness Strahl (cr) in *Masquerade* (Fenster), Kirov Ballet, Leningrad
1957 Sari (cr) in *Path of Thunder* (Sergeyev), Kirov Ballet, Leningrad
1959 Principal dancer (cr) in *The Absent Lover* (choreographic miniature; Yakobson), Kirov Ballet, Leningrad

**Other roles include:** Nikiya in *La Bayadère* (Petipa, Ponomarev, Chabukiani), Aurora and Princess Florine in *The Sleeping Beauty* (Petipa, staged Lopukhov, later Sergeyev), Kitri and the Street Dancer in *Don Quixote* (Gorsky after Petipa), title role in *Giselle* (Petipa after Coralli, Perrot), Coralli in *Lost Illusions* (Zakharov), Medora in *Le Corsaire* (Petipa, staged Vaganova), title role in *Katerina* (Lavrovsky), Maria in *The Fountain of Bakhchisarai* (Zakharov), Seventh Waltz and Mazurka in *Chopiniana* (Vaganova after Fokine), the Butterfly in *Carnaval* (Fokine), Bacchanalian in *Faust* (opera; mus. Bizet, chor. Chabukiani), principal dancer in *Viennese Waltzes* (Yakobson).

## PUBLICATIONS

By Dudinskaya:
"Unforgettable Lessons" in *Agrippina Vaganova*, Leningrad, 1958
"Alla Sizova", *Muzykalnaya Zhizn* (Moscow), no. 2, 1967
"My Life is Dance", *Dance and Dancers* (London), October 1970
"About Agrippina Yakovlevna Vaganova", *Teatr* (Moscow), no. 6, 1983

About Dudinskaya:
Slonimsky, Yuri (ed.), *The Soviet Ballet*, New York, 1947
Movshenson, A., *Natalia Mikhailovna Dudinskaya*, Leningrad, 1951
Vaganova, Agrippina, *Volume of Materials and Memoirs*, Leningrad, 1958
Kremshevskaya, G., *Natalia Dudinskaya*, Leningrad and Moscow, 1964
Golovashenko, I., "N. Dudinskaya", *Teatr* (Moscow), no. 9, 1968
Gregory, John, "Natalia Dudinskaya", *Dancing Times* (London), October 1970
Makarova, Natalia, *A Dance Autobiography*, New York, 1979
Chernova, N., *From Geltser to Ulanova*, Moscow, 1979
Krasovskaya, Vera, "The Youth of Dudinskaya", *Teatr* (Moscow), no. 9, 1982
Smakov, Gennady, *The Great Russian Dancers*, New York, 1984

* * *

Dudinskaya was a classical ballerina, a pre-eminent dancer of the heroic style who dedicated her life to the purity of ballet technique. A pupil of Vaganova, she understood from the start the principles taught by the great professor of dance, and she was one of Vaganova's favourite and best-loved dancers. In her art, the basic features of Vaganova's school were displayed with especial clarity. The choreographer and teacher Fedor Lopukhov wrote of her, "Dudinskaya reached the heights of virtuousity in classical dance. Here is a case where one can say that a great love of work forms a good half of the talent and guarantees its development." One of Dudinskaya's few shortcomings was that she was not a great actress; but she was astute enough to realize this, and she worked hard on mime and dramatic expression, perfecting these qualities all her dancing life.

As a technician, Dudinskaya was superb; complicated ballet technique presented absolutely no difficulty for her. Indeed, it was as if she were forever trying to invent ever more difficult movements and technical feats, to do things no other dancer had done or could do. As Lopukhov pointed out, Dudinskaya possessed a powerful jump, which she executed without any show of tension—her "ballon" was seemingly effortless. Describing the special qualities of Dudinskaya's style, and her mastery of technique, Bogdanov-Berezovski wrote that "The striking tempos of her dance were a remarkable feature of her individual style. These tempos were all the more striking because they were achieved in enchainements of enormous complexity."

Vakhtang Chabukiani had an enormous influence on the formation of Dudinskaya's career. He was her partner for many years, and her birth as a ballerina came with her creation of Laurencia in his ballet of that name. After 1945, Dudinskaya's partner became Konstantin Sergeyev (whom she married), and he created roles especially for her in several of his ballets. With Sergeyev this ballerina took part in the creation of new ballets by Soviet composers Prokofiev, Glière, Soloviev-Sedy, and Karaev. At the same time, the classical repertoire played a significant part in her dancing life and she was a superlative performer in the roles of Kitri, Nikiya, Odile, and Raymonda.

At the height of her career, in the 1940s and 1950s, Dudinskaya was essentially the First Lady of the company, and she did not retire from leading roles until the age of 52. Of course there were other ballerinas in the company of equal status, many of whom—such as Galina Ulanova and Alla Shelest—were superior as dramatic and expressive dancers. Dudinskaya was always aware of this, and worked tremendously hard to equal her rivals in dramatic roles. For much of her prime she virtually ruled the company; she did not allow anyone else to dance *Giselle* but herself, and the fact that she was the only Giselle on the Leningrad stage for years obviously hindered the development of the company.

All the same, Dudinskaya's contribution is without question. After her performing career was over, she and her husband Sergeyev were transferred to the Vaganova school as senior teacher and artistic director of the school; there they produced many important dancers. They knew both classical and modern choreography extremely well and passed their valuable knowledge on to their pupils. Dudinskaya still teaches a great deal, and at 80 she continues to epitomize the virtues of energy, dedication, and hard work. Her classes are always very well disciplined; her pupils perform difficult steps at an early age, and young students in exams can execute the combinations that are usually done only by senior classes. As a teacher she demands energy, discipline, and mental as well as physical agility: Dudinskaya is regarded as the true inheritor of the Vaganova tradition, and no one can question her lifelong sense of responsibility to her art.

—Igor Stupnikov

---

## DUPOND, Patrick

French dancer and ballet director. Born in Paris, 14 March 1959. Studied at Paris Opéra School, pupil of Max Bozzoni, from 1971. Dancer, Paris Opéra Ballet: corps de ballet, from 1975; coryphée, from 1977; sujet, from 1978; premier danseur, from 1979; étoile, from 1980, also appearing in Carpentras and Nuits de Lerins Festivals and with Groupe des cadets de l'Opéra, and touring America with Groupe des 7 de Janine Charrat, 1979; international guest artist, including for Ballet-Théâtre Français de Nancy, 1978 and 1984–88, Ballet du Rhin at Carpentras, 1981; has also appeared at Spoleto Festival, with American Ballet Theatre, New York, and with Ballet Concert Lily Laskine; founder and director of own group, Patrick Dupond and Stars, 1985; principal guest artist, Paris Opéra Ballet, from 1985, also continuing to appear with other companies including in Japan, with Ballet du XXe Siècle, and Twyla Tharp Company, New York, 1992; has also appeared in films and on television, including in *She Dances Alone* (television film, with Kyra Nijinska, 1980), and as subject of video entitled *Dancing Machine*, 1990; director, Ballet-Théâtre Français de Nancy, 1988–90; artistic director, Paris Opéra Ballet, from 1990. Recipient: Grand Prix and Gold Medal (Junior category), Varna International Ballet Competition, 1976; Grand Prix national de la danse, 1982; Prix Belmondo, 1986; Commandeur des arts et lettres, 1988.

### ROLES

1976 Georges (cr) in *Nana* (Petit), Paris Opéra Ballet, Paris
Pas de deux from *Don Quixote* (after Petipa), Opéra-Comique, Paris
1977 Hippolyte in *Phèdre* (Lifar), Paris Opéra Ballet, Paris
Kourbski in *Ivan the Terrible* (Grigorovich), Paris Opéra Ballet, Paris
1978 Mercutio in *Romeo and Juliet* (Grigorovich), Paris Opéra Ballet, Paris
Principal dancer in *Mahler's Songs* (Araiz), Paris Opéra Ballet, Paris
Title role in *Le Fils prodigue* (*Prodigal Son*; Balanchine), Paris Opéra Ballet, Paris
The Jester in *Swan Lake* (Petipa, Ivanov; staged Burmeister), Paris Opéra Ballet, Paris
Principal dancer (cr) in *La Barre* (Schmucki), Chicago Gala
Title role (cr) in *Le Petit Pan* (Schmucki), Gala, Chicago
The Messenger of Death in *Chant de la terre* (*Song of the Earth*; MacMillan), Paris Opéra Ballet, Paris
Principal dancer in *Les Quatre Saisons* (*The Four Seasons*; MacMillan), Paris Opéra Ballet, Paris
Dancer (cr) in *Metaboles* (MacMillan), Paris Opéra Ballet, Paris
Principal dancer in *Symphonie pour cinq* (Goubé), Créteil
1979 Principal dancer (cr) in *Diachronies* (Charrat), Opéra-Comique, Paris
Principal dancer (cr) in *Variations* (Verdy), Opéra-Comique, Paris
Principal dancer (cr) in *Sonatine bureaucratique* (Pendleton), Opéra-Comique, Paris
Principal dancer (cr) in *Relâche* (Pendleton), Opéra-Comique, Paris
Principal dancer in *Parade* (Massine), Opéra-Comique, Paris
Title role (cr) in *Vaslav* (Neumeier), Hamburg Ballet, Hamburg
Daphnis in *Daphnis and Chloe* (Neumeier), Hamburg

**Patrick Dupond in *Études***

Ballet, Hamburg
Solor in *La Bayadère*, Act II (Petipa, Nureyev), Paris Opéra Ballet, Paris
Principal dancer in *Bolero* (Béjart), Paris Opéra Ballet, Paris
Carabosse in *The Sleeping Beauty* (Petipa; staged Hightower), Paris Opéra Ballet, Paris
Principal dancer in *Adagietto* (Araiz), Chicago Gala
Hermann in *La Dame de Pique* (Petit), Rome Opera Ballet, Rome

1980 Title role in *L'Oiseau de feu* (Béjart), Paris Opéra Ballet, Paris
Principal dancer in *Études* (Lander), Paris Opéra Ballet, Paris
Solor in *La Bayadère* (Petipa; staged Makarova), American Ballet Theatre, New York
The Spirit of the Rose in *Le Spectre de la rose* (Fokine), French television
Young Man (cr) in *Le Fantôme de l'Opéra* (Petit), Paris Opéra Ballet, Paris
Principal dancer (cr) in *Schema* (Nikolais), Paris Opéra Ballet, Paris

1981 Basil in *Don Quixote* (after Petipa), Oslo Royal Ballet
Basil in *Don Quixote* (Nureyev after Petipa), Paris Opéra Ballet, Paris
Albrecht in *Giselle* (Petipa after Coralli, Perrot; staged Lifar), Paris Opéra Ballet, Paris
Principal dancer (cr) in *Le Bal masqué* (Cacciuleanu), Opéra-Comique, Paris
Franz in *Coppélia* (after Saint-Léon), Ballet du Rhin
Alain in *La Fille mal gardée* (Spoerli), Paris Opéra Ballet, Paris

1982 Prince Désiré in *The Sleeping Beauty* (Petipa; staged Hightower), Paris Opéra Ballet, Paris
Title role in *Petrushka* (Neumeier), film Delouche
Puck in *A Midsummer Night's Dream* (Neumeier), Paris Opéra Ballet, Paris
Prince (cr) in *The Nutcracker* (Hightower), Paris Opéra Ballet, Paris

1983 Principal dancer in *Au bord du précipice* (Ailey), Paris Opéra Ballet, Paris
Mercutio in *Romeo and Juliet* (Cranko), Paris Opéra Ballet, Paris
Principal dancer in *Capriccio* (*Rubies* from *Jewels*; Balanchine), Paris Opéra Ballet, Paris
Spaniard (cr) in *Raymonda* (new production; Nureyev after Petipa), Paris Opéra Ballet, Paris
Principal dancer in *Pas de Duke* (Ailey), Ailey Company, New York
St-Loup in *Intermittences du coeur* (Petit), Ballets de Marseille, New York
The Young Man in *Le Jeune Homme et la mort* (Petit), Ballet de Marseille, New York

1984 Title role in *Icare* (Lifar), Paris Opéra Ballet, Paris
Principal dancer in *Arlequin, magicien par amour* (Cramer), Opéra-Comique, Paris
Harlequin in *Carnaval* (Fokine), Opéra-Comique, Paris
Principal dancer in *No Man's Land* (Van Dantzig), Paris Opéra Ballet, Paris
Caliban in *The Tempest* (Nureyev), Paris Opéra Ballet, Paris
Cléonte in *Le Bourgeois Gentilhomme* (Balanchine), Opéra-Comique, Paris
Title role in *Marco Spada* (Lacotte), Paris Opéra Ballet, Paris
Principal dancer in *Danses concertantes* (MacMillan), Paris Opéra Ballet, Paris
Romeo (cr) in *Romeo and Juliet* (Nureyev), Paris Opéra Ballet, Paris

1985 Principal dancer in *Symphonie pour un homme seul* (Béjart), Ballet du XXe Siècle, New York
Principal dancer (cr) in *Salome* (Béjart), Ballet du XXe Siècle, New York
Title role (cr) in *Le Chat botté* (Petit), Ballet de Marseille, Paris
Morris in *Washington Square* (Nureyev), Paris Opéra Ballet, Paris

1986 Prince in *Cinderella* (Nureyev), Paris Opéra Ballet, Paris
Principal dancer in *Boléro* (Béjart), Ballet of La Scala, Milan

1987 Principal dancer in *Arc en ciel* (*Schema* extracts; Nikolais), Paris Opéra Ballet, Paris
Title role in *Petrushka* (after Fokine), Ballet-Théâtre Français de Nancy, Nancy
Principal dancer (cr) in *Soon* (Ezralow), Paris Opéra Ballet, Paris
Principal dancer in *Roméo et Juliette* Pas de deux (Lifar), Ballet-Théâtre Français de Nancy
Prince in *The Nutcracker* (Beriozoff), Verona Festival

1988 Principal dancer (cr) in *Démago-Megalo* (also chor.), Ballet-Théâtre Français de Nancy
Principal dancer in *Martyr de St-Sebastien* (Wilson, Darde), Paris Opéra Ballet, Bobigny
Principal dancer (cr) in *Faits et gestes* (Dove), Ballet-Théâtre Français de Nancy
Principal dancer (cr) in *Bad Blood* (Dove), Ballet-Théâtre Français de Nancy
Principal dancer (cr) in *Vespers* (Dove), Ballet-Théâtre Français de Nancy
Principal dancer (cr) in *White Silence* (Dove), Ballet-Théâtre Français de Nancy
Principal dancer (cr) in *Illuminations* (Malandain), Ballet-Théâtre Français de Nancy

1989 Principal dancer (cr) in *Rouge Poisson* (Darde), Ballet-Théâtre Français de Nancy
Faun in *L'Après-midi d'un faune* (after Nijinsky), Paris Opéra Ballet, Paris
Principal dancer (cr) in *Idmen* (Larrieu), Ballet-Théâtre Français de Nancy, Strasbourg
Principal dancer (cr) in *I Vespri Siciliani* (opera; mus. Verdi, chor. Van Hoecke), La Scala, Milan

1990 Title role in *Apollo* (Balanchine), Ballet-Théâtre Français de Nancy
Principal dancer in *L'Arlésienne* (pas de deux; Petit), Paris Opéra Ballet, Paris
The Young Man in *Les Mirages* (Lifar), Paris Opéra Ballet, Paris

1991 Principal dancer in *Dances at a Gathering* (Robbins), Paris Opéra Ballet, Paris
Principal dancer in *Push Comes to Shove* (Tharp), Paris Opéra Ballet, Paris
Principal dancer (cr) in *Grand Pas: Rhythm of the Saints* (Tharp), Paris Opéra Ballet, Paris

1992 The Young Man in *Le Rendezvous* (Petit), Paris Opéra Ballet, Paris
The Miller in *Le Tricorne* (Massine), Paris Opéra Ballet, Paris

**Other roles include:** principal dancer in *Aureole* (Taylor), pas de deux from *Don Quixote* (after Petipa), principal dancer in *Grand Pas classique* (pas de deux; also *Grand Pas d'Auber*; Gsovsky), principal dancer *Le Corsaire Pas de deux* (after Petipa).

## WORKS

1988 *Démago-Mégalo*, Ballet-Théâtre Français de Nancy

Also Staged:
1991 *Giselle* (after Petipa, Coralli, Perrot; mus. Adam), Paris Opéra Ballet, Paris

## PUBLICATIONS

Geitel, Klaus, "17 × Patrick Dupond", *Ballett: Chronik und Bilanz des Ballettjahres* (Zurich), 1981

Pastori, Jean-Pierre, *Patrick Dupond, la fureur de danser*, Lausanne, 1982

Flatow, Sheryl, "Enfant Terrible: Patrick Dupond of the Paris Opera Ballet", *Ballet News* (New York), July 1983

Sedro, Véronique, "Dupond Superstar", *Opéra de Paris*, February 1984

Stoop, Norma McLain, "Opera Étoile Patrick Dupond", *Dance Magazine* (New York), July 1984

Thuilleux, J., *Les Années Dupond au Ballet Français de Nancy*, 1990

* * *

Few dancers have experienced as rapid a rise to fame as Patrick Dupond, whose natural gifts singled him out for notice while he was still a student. The ease of his soft, high jumps on the one hand, and his evident enjoyment of challenges to his virtuosity on the other, allied with his quickly developed "naughty boy" image to bring him instant popularity when he was taken into the corps de ballet of the Paris Opéra at the age of sixteen. (When, after that, he was awarded the Gold Medal at the Varna competition in 1976, it was still in the "Junior" category.) Dupond did not stay long on the lowest rung: only a year later, he was entrusted with his first solo role, in Roland Petit's *Nana*. It is not surprising that it should have been Petit who thus favoured him: ever since the early days of the Ballets des Champs-Elysées, when Jean Babilée was the leading danseur of the company, Petit had chosen to work with young virtuoso dancers of strong personality whenever possible. In 1980, Petit cast Dupond in a more important created role, as the young man in *Le Fantôme de l'Opéra*, with Peter Schaufuss as the unhappy haunter and Dominique Khalfouni (not yet Petit's muse in Marseille) as the young girl. More notable still, though not widely known, was when he took over the role of Hermann in the same choreographer's *La Dame de Pique* (*The Queen of Spades*) at the Rome Opera when Mikhail Baryshnikov had suffered a serious injury, and Denys Ganio was unable to replace him any longer. Not only did Dupond wholeheartedly meet the daunting technical demands of the solos made for Baryshnikov, but he showed how congenial to him was the role of the young man, caught up in an intricate web of deceit as an obsessive gambler and unenthusiastic lover.

This capacity of his to identify himself with various "mixed-up kids" (though Hermann's case was more complex) has been exploited by at least two other choreographers—Alvin Ailey and Thierry Malandain. Ailey's *Au bord du précipice* had all the Opéra dancers concerned, with Dupond leading, throwing off the shackles of their strict classical training with great verve.

Before considering the Malandain work, which belongs to a later chapter in Dupond's crowded career, two other roles which Dupond performed while he was still at the Opéra need to be mentioned. John Neumeier's *Vaslav* was made for him in Hamburg, but it rapidly entered the Opéra repertory. Despite the impossibility of believing in Dupond as, in any way, the reincarnation of the enigmatic Polish genius, and despite the difficulty of accepting that in the ballet he was moulding the other dancers for a creation of his own, the work made a strong impression. What made Dupond a candidate for the role of Nijinsky must have been—particularly in the film *She Dances Alone*, in which he danced *Le Spectre de la rose*—his seemingly effortless, springy, and high jumps.

Dupond worked with Neumeier again when the latter staged his full-evening *A Midsummer Night's Dream* for the Paris company. Dupond was in his element performing Puck's mischievous tricks. It has to be admitted that occasionally the dancer's rather self-conscious winsomeness has risked toppling over into mawkishness, as in the solo *Le Petit Pan*, made for him by Norbert Schmucki and much applauded at galas round the world. Another work that is saved for the more critical spectator only by Dupond's sense of humour is his own *Démago-Megalo* (in which his little dog also appears). Theoretically about the tribulations of a touring company, it was made when he was already artistic director of the Ballet de Nancy—a responsibility that was to prove unexpectedly short-lived.

When the Opéra gave an evening of ballets by Kenneth MacMillan in 1978, Dupond had a new solo made for him in *The Four Seasons*, and also an original part to play (wearing tails) in the underrated *Metaboles*, in which he was one of the group of men hungering for Dominique Khalfouni.

An idol for audiences—automatically applauded on his entrance in France and Italy, and no doubt elsewhere—and spoiled and wilful as a result, Dupond was unlikely to be a favourite with Rudolf Nureyev when the Russian arrived as artistic director of the Paris company, so Dupond's departure could have been foreseen.

Touring with the Ballet de Nancy and having to take, or share in, important decisions, undoubtedly gave Dupond a greater maturity, without visibly diminishing the joy in dancing that instantly communicates itself to audiences and is so winning. Of the many occasions on which this has been particularly evident, one could cite his endearing performance as the half-pathetic, half-playful Jester in the Burmeister production of *Swan Lake*, and also his guest performances with Carla Fracci at La Scala, Milan, in December 1989, when the rather static production of *I Vespri Siciliani* sprang suddenly into life when Dupond made his entry with a mischievous smile, one which that meant that he would make everyone sit up. This he did, reaping more applause than anyone except the conductor, Riccardo Muti.

It is partly this attitude, but also Dupond's build, that makes him less than ideal for the roles of classical princes, although he has performed them. What was clear in the Verdi opera, but also in the Malandain work, *Illuminations* (in which, as a desperately unhappy young man he sat clutching his head melodramatically), and in *Démago-Mégalo*, is that Dupond is still, first and foremost, a star performer.

Although Dupond made some sage comments on his intentions when announcing the programmes for his first season (1990–91) as director of the Paris Opéra company, his decisions were made in agreement with the two maîtres de ballet who were acting as directors pending the appointment of a successor to Nureyev. Dupond's predilection for change and variety have to be curbed when he is in charge in Paris—where, in any case, he is obliged to spend only eight months a year, in order to enable him to pursue an independent career elsewhere. In view of his eclectic tastes—he has recently made a film with Alain Delon, he has appeared several times on French television in programmes featuring him, and a few years ago he even recorded some songs—he can be counted on to take full advantage of the other four months.

—Freda Pitt

---

**DUPORT, Louis-Antoine**

French dancer, choreographer, and ballet director. Born in Paris, 1781. Studied with Jean-François Coulon, Paris. Married the Viennese ballerina Therese Neumann, 1813. Début at l'Académie royale de musique (Paris Opéra), 1797: leading dancer, Opéra, 1797–1808, becoming rival to reigning premier danseur August Vestris; also choreographer, staging own works at the Opéra, 1805 and 1806; left Paris in 1808, performing in Vienna and then Russia: St. Petersburg début, August 1808, remaining as leading dancer until 1812; choreographer and dancer, Kärntnertor Theater, Vienna, from 1812, also appearing in Naples, 1817; returned to London, producing ballets and dancing at the King's Theatre, 1819; appeared for last time as premier danseur in Naples, 1820; returned to Vienna: entered partnership as director with opera producer/impresario D. Barbaja, Kärntnertor Theater, Vienna, 1821–36. Died in Paris, 19 October 1853.

## ROLES

1801 Zéphire in *Psyché* (P. Gardel), Opéra, Paris
A Villager (cr) in *Les Noces de Gamache* (Milon), Opéra, Paris
1803 Principal dancer in *Héro et Léandre* (Milon), Opéra, Paris
Principal dancer in *Le Retour de Zéphyr* (P. Gardel), Opéra, Paris
1804 Aiace (cr) in *Achille à Scyros* (P. Gardel), Opéra, Paris
1805 Principal dancer (cr) in *Acis et Galathée* (also chor.), Opéra, Paris
1806 Principal dancer (cr) in *Figaro* (also chor., after Blache's *Almaviva et Rosine*), Opéra, Paris
Principal dancer (cr) in *L'Hymen de Zéphyr; ou, Le Volage fixé* (also chor.), Opéra, Paris
1808 Zephyr in *Zéphyr et Flore* (Didelot), Hermitage Theatre, St. Petersburg
Principal dancer in *Les Amours de Vénus et Adonis; ou, La Vengeance de Mars* (also chor., with Didelot), Imperial Theatres, St. Petersburg
1809 Principal dancer in *La Fête chez le hobereau*, Imperial Theatre, St. Petersburg
Principal dancer in *Les Américains; ou, L'Heureux Naufrage* (Didelot), Imperial Theatre, St. Petersburg
1810 Principal dancer in *Mélora et Sulima*, Imperial Theatre, St. Petersburg
Principal dancer in *Solange Rose* (Didelot), Imperial Theatre, St. Petersburg
Principal dancer in *Le Troubadour* (Didelot), Imperial Theatre, St. Petersburg
Principal dancer in *Le Jugement de Pâris* (after P. Gardel), Imperial Theatre, St. Petersburg
1814 Colin in *La Fille mal gardée* (also chor.; after Dauberval), Hofoper, Vienna
1819 Adolphe in *Adolphe et Mathilde* (also chor.) King's Theatre, London
Principal dancer in *La Rose* (also chor.), King's Theatre, London
Principal dancer in *Les Ingénus* (also chor.), King's Theatre, London

## WORKS

1805 *Acis et Galathée* (ballet-pantomime; mus. Darondeau, Gianella), Opéra, Paris
1806 *Figaro* (ballet-pantomime, after J.B. Blache's *Almaviva et Rosine*; also called *Le Barbier de Seville*, and *Figaro; ou, La Précaution inutile*), Opéra, Paris
*L'Hymen de Zéphyr; ou, Le Volage fixé* (divertissement), Opéra, Paris
1808 *Figaro; oder, Der Barbier von Sevilla* (restaging of Paris production), Kärntnertor Theater, Vienna
*Les Amours de Vénus et Adonis; ou, La Vengeance de Mars* (with Didelot), St. Petersburg
1812 *Zephyr; oder, Der wiederkehrende Frühling*, Kärntnertor Theater, Vienna
*Die Spanische Abendunterhaltung*, Kärntnertor Theater, Vienna
*Der Blöde Ritter; oder, Die Macht der Frauen*, Kärntnertor Theater, Vienna
1813 *Telemach auf der Insel Kalypso*, Kärntnertor Theater, Vienna
*Der Ländliche Tag*, Kärntnertor Theater, Vienna
*Die Maskerade; oder, Der Ball des Gutsherrn*, Kärntnertor Theater, Vienna
*Acis und Galathea; oder, Der Riese Polifem*, Kärntnertor Theater, Vienna
*Die Erziehung des Adonis; oder, Dessen Aussöhnung mit Venus*, Kärntnertor Theater, Vienna
1814 *La Fille mal gardée* (after Dauberval), Kärntnertor Theater, Vienna
1817 *Le Virtu premiata* (mus. Gallenberg), Teatro San Carlo, Naples
1819 *Adolphe et Mathilde* (staged by Guillet), King's Theatre, London
*Les Ingénus* (also *Les Six Ingénus*), King's Theatre, London
*La Rose*, King's Theatre, London
1831 *L 'Ottavino*, scene in *Conquista di Malacca; ossia, I Portoghesi nell'indie* (chor. Taglioni), Teatro Regio, Turin

## PUBLICATIONS


Baron, M., *Lettres sur la danse*, Paris, 1826
Castil-Blaze, *Histoire de l'Académie imperial de musique*, Paris, 1855
Desharbres, N., *Deux siècles à l'Opéra*, Paris, 1868
d'Alheim, P., *Sur les pointes*, Paris, 1897
Vuiller, G., *La Danse*, Paris, 1898
Lifar, Serge, *Histoire du Ballet Russe*, Paris, 1950
Krasovskaya, Vera, *Russian Ballet Theatre in the First Half of the Nineteenth Century*, Leningrad and Moscow, 1958
Moore, Lillian, "The Duport Mystery", *Dance Perspectives* (New York), no. 7, 1960
Winter, Marian Hannah, *The Pre-Romantic Ballet*, London, 1974
Swift, Mary Grace, *A Loftier Flight: The Life and Accomplishments of Charles-Louis Didelot*, Middletown, Connecticut, 1974
Chapman, John, "Auguste Vestris and the Expansion of Technique", *Dance Research* (London), Summer 1987

Though he was ballet master, opera house director, and teacher during his career, Louis Duport made his most significant impact as a dancer during the first two decades of the nineteenth century. After training with one of the most renowned Parisian masters, Jean-François Coulon, Duport made his Paris Opéra debut in 1797. It was a pivotal moment in the development of ballet, for the barriers between the traditional three genres, or styles, were being broken down by the brilliant Auguste Vestris, who dazzled audiences with his athletic jumps, turns, and footwork. To the delight of Opéra audiences, the young Duport was soon challenging the previously unassailable Vestris. The contest that ensued so enhanced the already considerable popularity of the expanded dance style that almost all the younger generation of dancers emulated the two virtuosi, whose successes ensured that dance technique would continue to go in the direction of enhanced athleticism.

Duport's dancing prowess was remarkable. No less an authority than Jean-Georges Noverre wrote of him: "He surprises with his directness and his brilliance, with his boldness and his vivacity, with his vigour and his suppleness: his execution is full of rapid and difficult steps that he performs with infinite ease; he pirouettes out of sight, and with such velocity, that the eye is dazzled." After many touchy negotiations Duport and Vestris finally agreed to appear on stage at the same time. It was the end of October 1804—the year that saw Napoleon crown himself emperor. "Never", wrote one witness, "have the combats of the [Roman] circus, nor the old jousts, excited a livelier curiosity . . ." Another wrote that "It would take a Virgil to describe this combat". Most critics refused to designate a winner.

Perhaps modelling himself after the new emperor Napoleon, Duport set out to make the Opéra his empire. Not satisfied with only challenging Vestris, he set out to unseat the reigning ballet master Pierre Gardel. After much intriguing, Duport managed to show three ballets at the Opéra, *Acis et Galathée* (1805), *Figaro* (after J.B. Blache, 1806), and *L'Hymen de Zéphyr; ou, Le Volage fixé* (1806). Though he possessed some skill for the creation of dances that showed off dancers' technique, he did not have the genius to overthrow Gardel. The full range of his ambitions thwarted, he fled the country in 1808 disguised as a woman. He went to St. Petersburg, where he was received most graciously as a victim of Napoleon's tyranny. Russian audiences adored him as had the French. However, Charles Didelot, the head of the St. Petersburg company, complained bitterly about Duport's uncooperative and demanding nature.

Most of Duport's later career was spent at the Kärntnertor Theater in Vienna where he was co-director with Barbaja from 1821 to 1836. He was a good director, so much so that when the Paris Opéra was seeking a director of its own, it was rumoured that Duport was a candidate. Fanny Elssler, who danced at the Kärntnertor, wrote about Duport, attesting to his abilities as a director and to his mediocrity as a ballet master: "We are working with both hands and feet to get rid of Herr Duport, because he never gives the public anything new, but I feel that, if this succeeds, it will be difficult to find a better Director." In 1836 Duport returned to Paris and withdrew from public life.

—John Chapman

---

## DUPRÉ, Louis

French dancer, choreographer, and ballet master. Born c. 1697. Studied at L'Académie royale de musique (Paris Opéra), pupil of Louis Pécour. Married (wife's identity unknown). May have appeared (as "le petit Dupré") in child roles at Opéra, Paris, 1701–06; possibly member of the orchestra in a Rouen theatre, before entering Paris Opéra; official début, Opéra, 1714, soon becoming leading dancer; may have been ballet director, presenting group of students at Lincoln's Inn Fields, London, 1725 (although likely to have been another Dupré, such as James Dupré), possibly remaining in London until 1729; reportedly travelled to London, Dresden, and Court of King Augustus, various seasons while absent from Opéra cast lists, 1724–30; premier danseur, Opéra, Paris, from 1730; retired officially as dancer, 1751, but returned for some later appearances; maître de ballet (succeeding Michel Blondy), Opéra, Paris, from 1739; choreographer, staging works for Paris Opéra, Opéra-Comique, and Collège de Louis le Grand; director of ballet school, Opéra, Paris, until 1743: pupils included Gaetan Vestris, Jean-Georges Noverre, Maximilien Gardel, and Jean-Baptiste Hus; reportedly taught in Poland, 1756-62; member of Académie royale de la danse. Died in late December 1774.

### ROLES

1714 Pas de deux, Prêtres, Bergers, Grecques (cr) in *Télémaque* (tragédie-lyrique; mus. Destouches), Opéra, Paris

1715 Un Forgeron, Un Buveur, Un Masque sérieux (cr) in *Les Plaisirs de la paix* (ballet; mus. Bourgeois), Opéra, Paris

1716 Un Masque (cr) in *Les Fêtes de l'eté* (ballet; mus. Monteclair), Opéra, Paris

1717 Mars in *The Loves of Mars and Venus* (ballet; mus. Symonds and Fairbanks), London (unconfirmed; possibly performed by another Dupré)

Un Vosque (cr) in *Camille* (tragédie-lyrique; mus. Campra), Opéra, Paris

Un Berger, Un Guerrier, Un Homme du peuple d'Amathonte (cr) in *Vénus et Adonis* (tragédie-lyrique; mus. Desmarets), Opéra, Paris

1718 Un Démon, Un Faune, Un Babylonien, Un Peuple elémentaire, Un Prêtre (cr) in *Sémiramis* (tragédie-lyrique; mus. Destouches), Opéra, Paris

Un Berger in *Amadis de Gaule* (tragédie-lyrique; mus. Lully), Opéra, Paris

Un Berger in *Les Ages* (opéra-ballet; mus. Campra), Opéra, Paris

1719 Un Magicien in *Alcione* (tragédie-lyrique; mus. Marais), Opéra, Paris

Un Berger, Un matelot (cr) in *Les Plaisirs de la campagne* (ballet; mus. Bertin), Opéra, Paris

1720 Un Thrace, Un Magicien, Un Grec (cr) in *Polydore* (tragédie-lyrique; mus. Baptistin), Opéra, Paris

Un Magicien in *Scylla* (tragédie-lyrique; mus. Théobalde), Opéra, Paris

Un Sacrificateur, Un Habitant des Enfers in *Thésée* (tragédie-lyrique; mus. Lully), Opéra, Paris

1721 Un Espagnol in *Les Fêtes vénitiennes* (ballet; mus. Campra, chor. Blondy), Opéra, Paris

Un Jeu, Un Magicien in *Omphale* (tragédie-lyrique; mus. Destouches), Opéra, Paris

Une Suite de Saturne, L'Eté in *Phaëton* (tragédie-lyrique; mus. Lully), Opéra, Paris

1722 Une Suite de la Fortune, Un Fantôme in *Persée* (tragédie-lyrique; mus. Lully), Opéra, Paris

Un Masque, Un Suivant d'Apollon in *Les Saisons* (ballet; mus. collasse), Opéra, Paris

Un Esclave, Un Matelot in *Les Fêtes de Thalie* (ballet; mus. Mouret), Opéra, Paris

Un Plaisir, Un Sacrafins, Un Démon (cr) in *Renaud; ou, La Suite d'Armide* (tragédie-lyrique; mus. Desmarets, Opéra, Paris
Un Matelot in *La Provençale* (pièce lyrique; mus. Mouret), Opéra, Paris

1723 Un Grec (cr) in *Les Fêtes grecques et romaines* (ballet-héroïque; mus. de Blamont), Opéra, Paris
Un Guerrier, Un Suivant de la Jalousie in *Philomèle* (tragédie-lyrique; mus. Lacoste), Opéra, Paris
Un Berger héroïque, Un Magicien (cr) in *Pirithoüs* (tragédie-lyrique; mus. Mouret), Opéra, Paris
Un Vent in *Thétis et Pelée* (tragédie-lyrique; mus. Collasse), Opéra, Paris

1724 Un Génie, Un Démon in *Amadis de Grèce* (tragédie-lyrique; mus. Destouches), Opéra, Paris

1725/29 God of the Woods, Demon, Countryman, Earth, in *The Rape of Proserpine*, Lincoln's Inn Fields, London (unconfirmed; may have been another Dupré)
Masquerader in *Italian Jealousy*, Lincoln's Inn Fields, London (unconfirmed; may have been another Dupré)

1730 Un Indien, Une Furie in *Phaëton* (tragédie-lyrique; mus. Lully, chor. Blondy), Opéra, Paris
Un Suivant de Diane (cr) in *Les Caprices d'Erato; ou, Les Caractères de la musique* (divertissement added to *Alcione*; mus. de Blamont), Opéra, Paris

1731 Un Faune (cr) in *Endymion* (pastorale; mus. de Blamont), Opéra, Paris
Le Maître de danse, Un Vénitien in *Les Fêtes Vénitiennes* (opéra-ballet, mus. Campra), Opéra, Paris
Un Captif in *Amadis de Gaule* (tragédie-lyrique; mus. Lully) Opéra, Paris
Un Suivant de la Jalousie in *Idoménée* (tragédie-lyrique; mus. Campra), Opéra, Paris

1732 Un Babylonien (cr) in *Le Ballet des sens* (opéra-ballet; mus. Mouret, chor. Blondy), Opéra, Paris
Un Milésien, Un Amant malheureux (cr) in *Biblis* (tragédie-lyrique; mus. Lacoste), Opéra, Paris
Une Divinité des Richesses, La Guerre in *Isis* (tragédie-lyrique; mus. Lully), Opéra, Paris

1733 Un Dieu du Ciel, Un Génie (cr) in *L'Empire de l'amour* (ballet-héroïque; mus. Brassac), Opéra, Paris
Un Démon Transformé (cr) in *Les Caractères de l'amour* (ballet; mus. de Blamont), Opéra, Paris
Un Lutteur in *Les Fêtes grecques et romaines* (ballet-héroïque; mus. de Blamont, chor. Blondy), Opéra, Paris
Un Démon (cr) in *Hippolyte et Aricie* (tragédie-lyrique; mus. Rameau), Opéra, Paris
Un Européen in *Issé* (pastorale; mus. Destouches), Trianon
Un More in *Omphale* (tragédie-lyrique; mus. Lully), Opéra, Paris

1734 Un Chevalier Romain in *Les Eléments* (ballet; mus. Lalande, Destouches, chor. Blondy), Opéra, Paris
Un Homme du peuple de la Grèce (cr) in *La Fête de Diane* (divertissement added to *Les Fêtes grecques et romaines*; mus. de Blamont), Opéra, Paris
Un Suivant d'Ulysse (cr) in *Les Fêtes nouvelles* (ballet; mus. Duplessis), Opéra, Paris
Un Grec in *Iphigénie en Tauride* (tragédie-lyrique; mus. Desmarets, Campra, chor. Blondy), Opéra, Paris
Un Courtisan in *Philomèle* (tragédie-lyrique; mus. Lacoste), Opéra, Paris

1735 Un Captif, Un Masque in *Les Fêtes de Thalie* (ballet; mus. Mouret), Opéra, Paris
Un Cyclope (cr) in *Achille et Déïdamie* (tragédie-lyrique; mus. Campra), Opéra, Paris
Un Byzantin (cr) in *Les Graces* (ballet; mus. Mouret), Opéra, Paris
Un Bostangi (cr) in *Les Indes galantes* (ballet-héroïque; mus. Rameau), Opéra, Paris

1736 Un Masque, Un Espagnol in *L'Europe galante* (ballet; mus. Campra), Opéra, Paris
Un Sauvage, Un Esprit elémentaire, Un Gnome, Un Tyrien (cr) in *Les Voyages de l'amour* (ballet; mus. Boismortier), Opéra, Paris
Un Sauvage in *Les Indes galantes* (ballet-héroïque; mus. Rameau), Opéra, Paris
Un Guerrier in *Médée et Jason* (tragédie-lyrique; mus. Salomon), Opéra, Paris
Un Italien, Un Suivant de Minerve in *Les Romans* (ballet; mus. Cambini), Opéra, Paris

1737 Une Planète (cr) in *Castor et Pollux* (tragédie-lyrique; mus. Rameau), Opéra, Paris
Un Suivant de l'Harmonie, Un Démon, Une Furie, Une Divinité (cr) in *Le Triomphe de l'harmonie* (ballet-héroïque; mus. Grenet), Opéra, Paris
Un Courtisan de Céphée et de Persée in *Persée* (tragédie-lyrique; mus. Lully), Opéra, Paris
Un Faune in *Les Amours de dieux* (ballet-héroïque; mus. Mouret), Opéra, Paris

1738 Un Magicien in *Tancrède* (tragédie-lyrique; mus. Campra), Opéra, Paris
Un Argien dansant (cr) in *Le Ballet de la paix* (tragédie-lyrique; mus. Rebel, Francoeur), Opéra, Paris
Un Phrygien in *Atys* (tragédie-lyrique; mus. Lully), Opéra, Paris
Un Magicien, Un Satyre in *Les Fêtes de l'Amour et de Bacchus* (pastorale; mus. Lully), Opéra, Paris

1739 Un Suivant de Zéphyr et de Flore (cr) in *Les Amours du Printemps* (ballet-héroïque; mus. de Blamont), Opéra, Paris (originally performed at Fontainebleau, 1737)
Un Plaisir (cr) in *Dardanus* (tragédie-lyrique; mus. Rameau), Opéra, Paris
Un Abencerrage, Un Chasseur (cr) in *Zaïde, reine de Grenade* (ballet; mus. Royer), Opéra, Paris
Une Divinité infernale in *Alceste* (tragédie-lyrique; mus. Lully), Opéra, Paris

1740 Un Héros in *Amadis de Gaule* (tragédie-lyrique; mus. Lully), Opéra, Paris
Un Israëlite in *Jephté* (tragédie-lyrique; mus. Monteclair), Opéra, Paris
Un More in *Pyrame et Thisbé* (tragédie-lyrique; mus. Rebel, Francoeur), Opéra, Paris

1741 Un Prêtre in *L'Empire de l'amour* (ballet; mus. Brassac), Opéra, Paris
Un Prêtre d'Isis (cr) in *Ninétis* (tragédie-lyrique; mus. Myon), Opéra, Paris
Un Magicien in *Alcione* (tragédie-lyrique; mus. Marais), Opéra, Paris
Un Songe, Un Européen in *Issé* (pastorale; mus. Destouches), Trianon
Un Habitant de Sicile in *Proserpine* (tragédie-lyrique; mus. Lully), Opéra, Paris

1742 Un Grec in *Les Ages* (opera-ballet; mus. Campra), Opéra, Paris
Un Faune (cr) in *Isbé* (tragédie-lyrique; mus. Mondonville), Opéra, Paris
Un Indien, Un Fantôme in *Phaëton* (tragédie-lyrique; mus. Lully), Opéra, Paris
Un Grec in *Ajax* (tragédie-lyrique; mus. Bertin), Opéra, Paris

1743 Un Vent Souterrain in *Hésione* (tragédie-lyrique; mus.

Campra), Opéra, Paris
Un Phrygien (cr) in *Le Pouvoir de l'amour* (ballet; mus. Royer), Opéra, Paris
Le Père de la Mariée in *Roland* (tragédie-lyrique; mus. Lully), Opéra, Paris

1744 Un Grec in *Thésée* (tragédie-lyrique; mus. Lully), Opéra, Paris
Un Suivant d'Alcide in *Alcide* (tragédie-lyrique; mus. L. Lully, Marais), Opéra, Paris
Un Chasseur, Un Vénetien, Un Chinois (cr) in *L'Ecole des amants* (ballet; mus. Nieil), Opéra, Paris
Un Argien in *Les Graces* (ballet; mus. Mouret), Opéra, Paris

1745 Jeux et Plaisirs (cr) in *Zelindor, roi des sylphes* (tragédie-lyrique; mus. Rebel, Francoeur), Versailles
Le Père de la Mariée, Troupe de Masques, Jeux and Plaisirs in *Les Fêtes de Thalie* (ballet; mus. Mouret), Opéra, Paris
Un Romain (cr) in *Le Temple de la gloire* (ballet; libretto Voltaire, mus. Rameau), Opéra, Paris
Jeux et Plaisirs (cr) in *Les Fêtes de Polymnie* (ballet; mus. Rameau), Opéra, Paris

1746 Un Berger héroïque in *Zelisca* (comédie-ballet; mus. Jélyote), Versailles
Ministre de Circé in *Scylla et Glaucus* (tragédie-lyrique; mus. Leclair), Opéra, Paris
Un Amant fortuné in *Armide* (tragédie-lyrique; mus. Lully), Opéra, Paris
Un Argien in *Hypermnestre* (tragédie-lyrique; mus. Gervais), Opéra, Paris
Un Sauvage (solo) in *Le Triomphe de l'harmonie* (ballet-héroïque; mus. Grenet), Opéra, Paris
Une Divinité Infernale, Un Courtisan de Céphée in *Persée* (tragédie-lyrique; mus. Lully), Opéra, Paris

1747 Un Egyptien (cr) in *Les Fêtes de L'Hymen et de L'Amour* (ballet-héroïque; mus. Rameau), Opéra, Paris

1748 Un Suivant de la Fortune (cr) in *Aeglé* (ballet; mus. La Garde), Versailles
Un Suivant de la Folie in *Le Carnaval et la Folie* (comédie-ballet; mus. Destouches), Opéra, Paris
Les Huit Génies du Prologue (cr) in *Zaïs* (ballet-héroïque; mus. Rameau), Opéra, Paris
Un Afriquain (cr) in *Almasis* (ballet; mus. Royer), Versailles

1749 Un Démon en plaisir in *Les Caractères de l'amour* (ballet; mus. de Blamont), Opéra, Paris
Bacchus, Un Masque galant (cr) in *Le Carnaval du Parnasse* (opera-ballet; mus. Mondonville), Opéra, Paris
Un Athlète pour la lutte (cr) in *Naïs, opéra pour la paix* (ballet-héroique; mus. Rameau), Opéra, Paris
Un Satyre, Un Dryade (cr) in *Platée* (ballet; mus. Rameau), Opéra, Paris
Un Peuple elémentaire (cr) in *Zoroastre* (tragédie-lyrique; mus. Rameau), Opéra, Paris
Magicien, Corinthien in *Médée et Jason* (tragédie-lyrique; mus. Salomon), Opéra, Paris

1750 Un More in *Tancrède* (tragédie-lyrique; mus. Campra), Opéra, Paris
Bacchus in *Thétis et Pelée* (tragédie-lyrique; mus. Collasse), Opéra, Paris
Un Bohémien in *Les Fêtes vénitiennes* (opera-ballet; mus. Campra), Opéra, Paris
Un Chasseur (cr) in *Léandre et Héro* (tragédie-lyrique; mus. Brassac), Opéra, Paris

1751 Un Génie, suivant d'Oröés (cr) in *Acante et Céphise* (pastorale-héroïque; mus. Rameau), Opéra, Paris
Un Suivant du génie de l'Afrique (cr) in *Les Génies tutélaires* (divertissement; mus. Rebel, Francoeur), Opéra, Paris
Un Péruvien, Un Sauvage in *Les Indes galantes* (ballet-héroïque; mus. Rameau), Opéra, Paris

1752 Un Ombre d'amants légers (cr) in *Les Amours de Tempé* (ballet; mus. Dauvergne, chor. M. Gardel), Opéra, Paris
Un Faune in *Daphnis et Chloé* (opera-ballet; mus. Boismortier), Opéra, Paris
Suite de Neptune in *Acis et Galatée* (pastorale-héroïque), Opéra, Paris

**ROLES** (attributed to "Le Petit Dupré")

1701 A Child in *Scylla* (tragédie-lyrique; mus. Théobalde), Opéra, Paris

1702 A Child in *Phaëton* (tragédie-lyrique; mus. Lully), Opéra, Paris
Un Petit More in *Omphale* (tragédie-lyrique; mus. Destouches), Trianon

1703 "Les Deux Petits Garçons" (with petit Pierrot) in *Les Muses* (ballet; mus. Campra), Opéra, Paris
Un Amour in *Ulysse* (tragédie-lyrique; mus. Rebel), Opéra, Paris

1706 Matelots (with D. Dumoulin) in *Alceste* (tragédie-lyrique; mus. Gluck), Opéra, Paris

**WORKS**

1748 *Portrait du Grand Monarque*, Collège de Louis le Grand, Paris
1749 *Catilina*, Collège de Louis le Grand, Paris
1750 *Le Temple de la fortune*, Collège de Louis le Grand, Paris
1751 *Le Génie*, Collège de Louis le Grand, Paris
1754 *Les Spectacles du Parnasse*, Collège de Louis le Grand, Paris
1755 *La Prosperité*, Collège de Louis le Grand, Paris

**PUBLICATIONS**

By Dupré:
*Méthode trés facile et fort nécessaire pour apprendre soi-même la chorégraphie*, Le Mans, 1756 (authorship unconfirmed)

About Dupré:
Cahusac, Louis, *Traité historique de la danse*, 3 volumes: Le Haye, 1754
Parfait (Claude et François), *Dictionnaire des théâtres de Paris*, 7 volumes: Paris, 1756–67
Noverre, Jean-Georges, *Lettres sur la danse et sur les ballets*, Stuttgart, 1760; as *Letters on Dancing and Ballets*, translated by Cyril Beaumont, London, 1930
Dorat, Claude-Joseph, *La Déclamation Théâtrale*, Paris, 1767
Castil-Blaze, *La Danse et des ballets depuis Bacchus jusqu' à Mademoiselle Taglioni*, Paris, 1832
Campardon, Emile, *L'Académie royale de musique au XVIIIe siècle*, Paris, 1884
Moore, Lillian, "The Great Dupré", *Dance Magazine* (New York), June 1960
Winter, Marian Hannah, *The Pre-Romantic Ballet*, London, 1974
Marsh, Carol, *French Court Dance in England 1706–1740*, Ph.D. Dissertation, City University of New York, 1985

Ralph, Richard, *The Life and Works of John Weaver*, New York, 1985

* * *

Louis Dupré, dancer of the Paris Opéra in the eighteenth century, was both hailed and criticized for his flawless but unvaryingly noble, rather than dramatic, style throughout an exhaustive career of more than 50 years. Given the flattering nickname "le Dieu de la danse" by his admirers and referred to also as le grande Dupré—a name alluding to his prominence as well as distinguishing him from Jean-Denis Dupré (1706–82), a dancer shorter in height and less proficient than Louis—Dupré began his career in the early 1700s, when he seems to have appeared in children's roles at the Opéra with, among others, la petite Prévost (Françoise). Although he retired officially in 1751 (Gaetan Vestris took over his position as premier danseur as well as his title "le Dieu de la danse"), Dupré continued to dance for a short while, including in a notable performance at Fontainebleau with Marie Sallé, who had also reappeared out of retirement. Until his death in 1774, Dupré maintained his position as one of the prestigious thirteen members of the Académie royale de la danse.

Despite his reputation for being an uncompromising danseur noble, Dupré portrayed a wide variety of roles, including that of shepherd, faun, savage, ghost, and demon (the *Dictionnaire encyclopédique* indicates that although Dupré achieved less elevation than his successors Gaetan and Auguste Vestris, he performed brilliant gargouillades in this role). Dupré was also warrior, fury, magician, cyclops, Roman, Spaniard, Indian, African, and many more. During his tenure at the Opéra, he appeared in the works of numerous composers, including the many revivals of tragic operas by J.B. Lully and premieres of opéra-ballets by André Campra and Jean-Philippe Rameau. It is indeed exciting to consider the influences Dupré experienced and elicited during the expanse of his career, studying under the illustrious teacher and choreographer Louis Pécour; sharing the stage with Françoise Prévost, Claude Ballon, Michel Blondy, the Dumoulin brothers, François Marcel, Marie-Anne Camargo, Marie Sallé, La Barbarina, Jean-Barthélemy and Louise Lany, Claude Javillier (l'ainé), and possibly with Hester Santlow and John Weaver (in Weaver's *ballet d'action* experiment *The Loves of Mars and Venus*); and instructing, among others, Jean-Georges Noverre, Gaetan Vestris, Maximilien Gardel, Jean-Baptiste Hus, and Marie Sallé's cousin, Marianne Cochois. He reportedly tutored members of the court in social dancing as well. Dupré's role as choreographer seems to be somewhat overshadowed by his reputation as a performer and teacher, although it was no less important. In addition to his choreographic duties at the Opéra, Dupré is known to have staged dances at the Opéra-Comique (where he directed Noverre) and at the College de Louis le Grand.

Much of what we know about Dupré's dancing talent and style is related through eye-witness accounts of his performances and poems alluding to this "God"—that "mingles in the dances of mortals" (Dorat)—"What grace in his every step" (anonymous). Noverre wrote in his *Lettres sur la danse* that his teacher's title, Dieu de la danse, was earned by the "rare harmony" of his every movement and that "in fact, he seemed a divinity rather than a man". The writer described a dancer whose every movement was "gentle and flowing" and whose muscles were "perfectly coordinated", achieving a "perfect whole". But Noverre warned that this perfect harmony was "due to a beautiful physique, precise arrangement, and a well-combined proportion of parts, resulting less on study and reasoning than on nature" and that it "cannot be attained unless one is so endowed". He complained that his teacher preferred to dance chaconnes and passacailles, which suited the great dancer's "taste, style, and noble stature", never varying his style—he was always Dupré. Jacques Casanova confirmed Noverre's observations in his *Mémoires*, describing Dupré's performance in *Les Fêtes vénitiennes* of 1750: the audience evidently clapped loudly at "the appearance of a tall, handsome dancer, wearing a mask and an enormous black wig which reached half-way to his waist, and wearing a costume open in the front which fell to his heels . . . I see that fine figure coming forward with measured steps, reaching the front of the stage, he slowly raises his rounded arms, moves them gracefully, extends and withdraws them, moves his feet with precision and lightness, takes some small steps, makes some *battements* at the calf, a *pirouette*, and disappears like a zephyr. The whole had not lasted half a minute. Applause and bravos burst from every part of the house; I was astonished, and asked my friend [Patu] the reason for it." Patu replied, "We applaud the grace of Dupré and the divine harmony of his movements. He is now sixty years of age, and those who saw him forty years ago say that he is always the same." Patu believed they had just witnessed "absolute perfection". Casanova wrote that Dupré returned at the end of Act II, and danced "exactly the same as before" but to different music.

Louis de Cahusac praised Louis in his *Traité historique de la danse* (1754), stating that no man had ever surpassed his "fine physique, elegant dancing, and noble positions". In 1762 Gallini wrote, "I have myself seen the celebrated Dupré, at near the age of sixty, dance at Paris, with all the agility and sprightliness of youth, and with such powers of pleasing, as if the graces *in him* had braved superannuation." Dupré's reputation survived well after his death, and in 1820 Carlo Blasis wrote that "our predecessors . . . were more eminent than we in the grave or serious style . . . Dupré and Vestris the elder were models in this valuable sphere and have had few worthy successors". He added that these dancers may have lacked a variety of steps but "what they did was done superlatively". The Louis Dupré being described—this Dieu de la danse—was perhaps the last vestige, or rather the epitome, of the noble, serious Opéra style that, Noverre complained, rendered technical virtuosity in the form of unrelated divertissements rather than as expressive dance or *ballet d'action* in which, he argued, dance should be completely expressive of and appropriate to the drama.

—Paige Whitley-Bauguess

---

## DURANTE, Viviana

Italian dancer. Born Viviana Paola Durante in Rome, 8 May 1967. Studied with Olga Amati in Italy, and at the Royal Ballet School, London. Dancer, Royal Ballet, from 1984: coryphée, 1986; soloist, from 1987; principal dancer, from February 1989, touring the United States, 1991; has also appeared in separate concert performances with Irek Mukhamedov and Company, touring Britain, 1992. Recipient: *Time Out* London Dance Award, 1989; Dancer of the Year Award, *Dance and Dancers*, December 1989; *Evening Standard* Ballet Award, 1990; Positano Prize, Italy, 1991.

### ROLES

1988 Odette/Odile in *Swan Lake* (Petipa, Ivanov; staged Dowell), Royal Ballet, Australian tour

Principal dancer (cr) in *The Spirit of Fugue* (Bintley), Royal Ballet, London
Principal dancer in *Rhapsody* (Ashton), Royal Ballet, London
Title role in *Cinderella* (Ashton), Royal Ballet, London
Princess Aurora in *The Sleeping Beauty* (Petipa, Ashton; staged Wright), Royal Ballet, London
1989 Title role in *Ondine* (Ashton), Royal Ballet, Bristol
First Sister in *My Brother, My Sisters* (MacMillan), Royal Ballet, London
Juliet in *Romeo and Juliet* (MacMillan), Royal Ballet, London
Nikiya in *La Bayadère* (Makarova after Petipa), Royal Ballet, London
Principal dancer (cr) in *Piano* (Page), Royal Ballet, Plymouth
Princess Rose in *The Prince of the Pagodas* (MacMillan), London
Sanctus in *Requiem* (MacMillan), Royal Ballet, London
Principal dancer in *Laurentia* Pas de six (Nureyev after Chabukiani), Royal Ballet, London
Principal dancer in *Rubies* (from *Jewels*; Balanchine), Royal Ballet, London
1990 Lise in *La Fille mal gardée* (Ashton), Royal Ballet, London
Principal dancer in *Gloria* (MacMillan), Royal Ballet, London
Principal dancer in *Galanteries* (Bintley), Royal Ballet, London
Sugar Plum Fairy in *The Nutcracker* (Wright), Royal Ballet, London
Aria II in *Stravinsky Violin Concerto* (Balanchine), Royal Ballet, London
Principal dancer (cr) in *Pursuit* (Page), Royal Ballet, London
Principal dancer (cr) in *Bloodlines* (Page), Royal Ballet, London
Golden Hours in *Elite Syncopations* (MacMillan), Royal Ballet, London
Saturn Pas de deux in *The Planets* (Bintley), Royal Ballet, London
1991 Title role in *Manon* (MacMillan), Royal Ballet, London
Irina (cr) in *Winter Dreams* (MacMillan), Royal Ballet, London
Principal dancer in *Scènes de ballet* (Ashton), Royal Ballet, Washington, D.C.
Principal dancer in *Thaïs* Pas de deux (Ashton), Royal Ballet, London
Adagietto ("La Garçonne") in *Les Biches* (Nijinska), Royal Ballet, London
Principal dancer (cr) in *Present Histories* (Tuckett), Royal Ballet, London
Principal dancer in *Danses concertantes* (MacMillan), Royal Ballet, London
Roxane in *Cyrano* (Bintley), Royal Ballet, London
1992 Title role in *Giselle* (Petipa after Coralli, Perrot; staged Sergeyev, Ashton), Royal Ballet, London
The Woman (cr) in *The Judas Tree* (MacMillan), Royal Ballet, London
Summer Pas de deux from *The Seasons* (MacMillan), Irek Mukhamedov and Company, British tour
Dancer in *Diana and Acteon* Pas de deux (from *Esmeralda*; Vaganova), Irek Mukhamedov and Company, British tour
Title role in *Cinderella* (Ashton), Royal Ballet, London

**Other roles include:** for the Royal Ballet—Vera in *A Month in the Country* (Ashton), Second variation in *Birthday Offering* (Ashton), Fairy Autumn in *Cinderella* (Ashton), Act I Pas de trois in *Swan Lake* (Petipa, Ivanov, Ashton; staged Dowell), Fairy of the Golden Vine in *The Sleeping Beauty* (Petipa, Ashton; staged de Valois), Florestan Pas de trois in *The Sleeping Beauty* (Petipa, Ashton; staged de Valois), Third solo variation ("Shades") in *La Bayadère* (Makarova after Petipa), Spring in *The Four Seasons* (MacMillan), Kitri in *Don Quixote* Pas de deux (after Petipa); for the Royal Opera, London—Voices of Spring Pas de deux in *Die Fledermaus* (opera; mus. J. Strauss).

## PUBLICATIONS

"A Year of Dance", *Dance and Dancers* (London), November 1986
"Dancer You Will Know", *Dance and Dancers* (London), August 1987
Pascal, Julia, "A Name of the Nineties", *Illustrated London News* (London), December 1988
Percival, John, "Steps to Perfection", *The Times* (London), 7 June 1989
Clarke, Mary, "Covent Garden's *Giselle*", *Dancing Times* (London), March 1992

* * *

A review of the Royal Ballet School's 1984 summer performances singled out Viviana Durante as "a dancer of great potential". She joined the Royal Ballet the same year and soon began to prove the wisdom of this press prediction.

Less extreme on stage than some of her contemporaries, Durante none the less has made great progress, characterized by a rigorous approach to all she has danced. Petite and extremely pliant, she has a rare talent for tempering movement to classical principles. Arabesques and attitudes radiate expansively, retirés are of perfect textbook proportion, and port de bras always complement lower body lines. Initially, dance technique overshadowed personality; but Durante is an exemplar of how dancers can learn through coaching and through repertory. Each new ballet and each repeated performance of a particular role has taught her a great deal about stage persona.

The breadth of the Royal Ballet's repertory provides its dancers with wide-ranging experience in characterization and dance style. Alongside works by contemporary choreographers, the nineteenth-century classics are an ongoing challenge. It is by these that a ballerina is traditionally tested. Durante's performances in *La Bayadère*, *The Sleeping Beauty*, and *Swan Lake* proved that she has the steely precision and polish of a true ballerina. As a Royal Ballet School student, she had performed various roles in *Aurora's Wedding* and it was as Aurora in the full-length *Sleeping Beauty* that London audiences first saw her tackle the classics. Her début in 1988 augured well, but it was only after gaining experience in Kenneth MacMillan's choreography and in Frederick Ashton's *Cinderella*, *La Fille mal gardée*, and *Ondine* that Durante fully grasped the demands of the classical repertory.

Since 1989, she has taken on and triumphed in a series of ballerina roles. Her promotion to principal dancer coincided with the return of MacMillan to Covent Garden and with a renewed enthusiasm for his ballets within the Royal's repertory. Durante has developed most in MacMillan's choreography; his narrative works in particular have coaxed out her interpretative skills.

Durante is ideally suited, physically and dramatically, to the

**Viviana Durante in *Les Biches*, 1991**

role of the teenage heroine in *Romeo and Juliet*. Adolescent shyness and exuberance conflict with Juliet's single-minded pursuit of true love. The role requires the technical mastery of a mature ballerina, and as in many of MacMillan's ballets, the greatest test is in concealing actual accomplishment in order to convince us of the character's innocence and vulnerability. As yet, Durante does not have the command of MacMillan's earlier muses in Juliet's crucial moments of stillness—but her pas de deux reveal real understanding of the character's contrasting responses to Paris and Romeo.

The role which confirmed Durante's rite of passage to ballerina status was Manon. It is a difficult role for a young dancer because, unlike Juliet, the character grows up socially as well as sexually. As the worldly courtesan, Durante is wily and seductive. Her command of the role is most marked by her timing of gesture and use of her eyes. The way that Manon manipulates her gaze signals her see-saw attention to Des Grieux and Monsieur GM. Durante develops the character's fickleness with irresistible charm and, after Manon finally gives up all illusions of grandeur for life with Des Grieux, she makes the transition from temptress to faithful lover rivetingly clear.

More recently, MacMillan provided Durante with her most interesting created roles. As Irina in *Winter Dreams*, she has fast, intricate choreography which conveys the more optimistic spirit of Chekhov's youngest sister. In *The Judas Tree*, Durante is the sole woman amid fourteen men in a modern-day metropolis. The male protagonist is danced by the former

Bolshoi dancer, Irek Mukhamedov, and MacMillan created tense, sometimes violent choreography for him and Durante.

Through MacMillan's ballets, an exciting partnership between these two dancers has emerged. Mukhamedov's powerful technique and sense of theatre have given Durante a new-found confidence in pas de deux and, by performing together on a regular basis, both are absorbing the respective strengths of Russian and British ballet styles.

A spin-off from this interchange has been a venture initiated by Mukhamedov in 1992. For three performances in Northampton, Oxford, and Bradford, a group of Royal Ballet dancers presented a divertissement programme under the collective title of Irek Mukhamedov and Company. Durante and Mukhamedov headed the cast, giving thrilling performances in the Summer pas de deux from MacMillan's *The Four Seasons* and in Vaganova's *Diana and Acteon*.

The Royal Ballet has benefitted enormously from recent policy changes and from the healthy competition which has been injected into the company from abroad. Of the present Royal principals, Durante is one of two ballerinas who have gained most. She and Darcey Bussell are the company's future stars—luminous, in the ascendant, and destined to go far.

—Angela Kane

---

**DUTCH NATIONAL BALLET**
(Het Nationale Ballet)
Dutch ballet company based in Amsterdam. Founded as a fusion of the Netherlands Ballet (artistic director Sonia Gaskell) and Amsterdam Ballet (itself a conglomeration of Ballet der Lage Landen and Netherlands Opera Ballet under Mascha ter Weeme), 1961; reorganized with Sonia Gaskell and Mascha ter Weeme as co-directors, with Gaskell soon becoming sole director; directorship assumed by choreographer Rudi van Dantzig, 1971–91; company based at Muziektheater, Amsterdam, with frequent tours both within the Netherlands and internationally. Artistic director of the Dutch National Ballet (succeeding Rudi van Dantzig): Wayne Eagling, from 1991.

**PUBLICATIONS**

Schultink, J., Boswinkel, W., and Koning, W., *Het Nederlands Ballet*, Antwerp, 1958

Goodwin, Noël, "Rudi van Dantzig", *About the House* (London), March 1970

Loney, G., "Rudi van Dantzig on the National Ballet of Holland", *Dance Magazine* (New York), March 1974

Utrecht, Luuk, *Het Nationale Ballet van 1961–1986*, Amsterdam, 1987

Merret, Sue, "Dutch National Ballet at the Crossroads", *Dancing Times* (London), June 1991

* * *

The Dutch National Ballet (Het Nationale Ballet) came into existence in 1961 after a long and somewhat unpalatable Dutch "ballet-war". The company was an amalgamation of the Netherlands Ballet and the two-year-old Amsterdam Ballet, the last being, in its turn, a forced fusion of the Ballet der Lage Landen and the Ballet van de Nederlandse Opera. Two artistic leaders, Sonia Gaskell and Mascha ter Weeme, were appointed, each the director of one of the old companies. The decision to fuse was not an artistic one. It was a political move inspired mainly by finances. The great differences in artistic policy made Mascha ter Weeme leave after one season, and Sonia Gaskell became the sole director.

The new company had three more or less self-imposed tasks: performing the international well-known classics from the nineteenth century, keeping alive the important works of twentieth-century choreographers like Fokine, Massine, Balanchine, and Kurt Jooss, and adding to the repertoire newly created ballets by contemporary national and international balletmakers. Furthermore, the Dutch National Ballet had to provide the dancers for opera productions when needed. The company was housed in the Municipal Theatre of Amsterdam, sharing that building with the Opera and the municipal drama company. Resident choreographers were Rudi van Dantzig and Robert Kaesen. Both were appointed co-artistic directors in 1965. The repertoire was eclectic. *Giselle*, *Swan Lake*, and *The Sleeping Beauty* were, in various versions, the returning classics. From the Diaghilev repertoire came *Petrushka*, *Firebird*, *Les Sylphides*, *Le Spectre de la rose*, and *Prodigal Son*. Jooss's *Green Table* was added, as were Balanchine ballets which now number 23. The repertoire also contained ballets by Harald Lander, Antony Tudor, and Frederick Ashton, along with modern danceworks by Pearl Lang, Paul Taylor, Maurice Béjart, Henryk Tomaszewski, and the Dutch avant-garde choreographer Koert Stuyf.

After years of mounting troubles between Gaskell and both her dancers and her board of directors, Gaskell left, leaving van Dantzig and Kaesen in charge of the company. Two years later Kaesen also left, his place being taken for one season by Benjamin Harkarvy. From 1971 van Dantzig was the sole director. The same artistic course was followed, but from then on a large part of the repertoire was filled by new works from Rudi van Dantzig, Toer van Schayk, and Hans van Manen, its resident choreographers. Thanks to them, the Dutch National Ballet has played an important part in the development of classical ballet, combining the tradional technique with elements from modern dance. In 1986, the company moved to the newly built Muziektheater, sharing its very well equipped new housing with the Nederlandse Opera. One season later Hans van Manen left.

In recent years, several choreographers from the world of modern dance have again created new works: these include Maguy Marin, Caroline Carlson, and Edouard Lock. The company is financed by the government and the city of Amsterdam. To stimulate the creative powers of the dancers, a yearly choreographic workshop is organized. From these John Wisman and Jan Linkens have come to the fore.

In the 1960s, Marianne Hilarides, Olga de Haas, Sonja van Beers, Irene de Vos, Sylvester Campbell, Simon Andre, and Conrad van de Weetering were the leading dancers. The 1970s saw the prominence of Maria Aradi, Sonja Marchiolli, Monique Sand, Han Ebbelaar, Henny Jurriens, Zoltan Peter, Francis Sinceretti, and Clint Farha. New soloists during the 1980s were Coleen Davis, Caroline Iura, Jeanette Vondersaar, Karin Schnabel, Fred Berlips, Alan Land, and Lindsy Fischer. From 1970, until her retirement in 1990, Alexandra Radius was the unofficial prima ballerina of the company. The Dutch National Ballet has performed in many countries all over the world. Rudi van Dantzig announced his retirement in 1991, and was succeeded by Wayne Eagling from England's Royal Ballet.

—Ine Rietstap

---

**Anna Pavlova in *The Dying Swan (Le Cygne)*, 1925**

## THE DYING SWAN

(*Le Cygne*; original Russian title: *Umirayushchy lebed*)

**Choreography:** Mikhail Fokine
**Music:** Camille Saint-Saëns (*Le Cygne* from *Le Carnaval des animaux*)
**Design:** Léon Bakst (costume)
**First Production:** Hall of Nobles, St. Petersburg, 22 December 1907 (several sources say 1905)
**Principal Dancer:** Anna Pavlova

**Other productions include:** Stagings by Pavlova for performances in New York, 1910; London, 1910; Berlin, c. 1913; Mexico City, 1919; for film taken at Fairbanks Studio, Hollywood, 1925; by Fokine, for Vera Fokina, Philadelphia, 1923; interpretations (chor. after Fokine; depending on the performer) by such ballerinas as Tamara Toumanova (staged Balanchine after Fokine), Alicia Markova, Galina Ulanova, Maya Plisetskaya, Yvette Chauviré, Natalia Makarova.

### PUBLICATIONS

Fokine, Mikhail, *The Dying Swan*, New York, 1925
Beaumont, Cyril, *Michel Fokine and his Ballets*, London, 1935
Beaumont, Cyril, *Anna Pavlova*, London, 1938
Franks, A.H., *Pavlova: A Collection of Memoirs*, London, 1956
Fokine, Michel, *Memoirs of a Ballet Master*, translated by Vitale Fokine, London, 1961
Dandré, Victor, *Anna Pavlova in Art and Life*, New York, 1972
Balanchine, George, with Mason, Francis, *Balanchine's Complete Stories of the Great Ballets*, Garden City, N.Y., 1977
Lazzarini, John and Roberta, *Pavlova: Repertoire of a Legend*, New York, 1980
Money, Keith, *Anna Pavlova*, London, 1982
Ries, Frank W.D., *Ballet Review* (New York), "Rediscovering Pavlova's Dances", *Ballet Review* (New York), Winter 1984

* * *

During the heyday of Anna Pavlova and for some years afterwards, every little girl who knew any ballet at all—and not a few large ones—learned to dance Pavlova's famous signature solo, *The Dying Swan* (*Le Cygne*). Its classical veneer and deceptive simplicity still lead young dancers, and even beauty pageant contestants, to try it; they sense, as do more practised interpreters, that this solo has become an emblem of the ethereal allure of ballet. They hope that by donning the white feathered tutu and waving their arms, they might participate in ballet's rarified magic and beauty. As if to encourage such ambition, the choreographer Mikhail Fokine once wrote a booklet outlining how to perform the solo, with step-by-step photos of his wife Vera demonstrating.

But *The Dying Swan*, known most often in Pavlova's day simply as *Le Cygne*, is rarely discussed as significant apart from the ability of the dancer to display her talents within it. Certainly, its perfect marriage to the bird-like, dramatic style of Pavlova, for whom it was created, and her endless repetitions of it during world tours, helped establish the dance's fame. But the solo endures in different ways without her. It is, in fact, unique in the ballet vocabulary for several reasons.

For Fokine, *The Dying Swan* was the beginning of what he hoped would be revolutionary reforms in ballet. In his memoirs he called the solo one of the first illustrations of a "new form of Russian ballet". When he first set the choreography on Pavlova—apparently in one brief rehearsal—it was for a charity benefit, performed outside the conservative Maryinsky Theatre in St. Petersburg. Away from the hidebound Imperial ballet establishment, he could experiment with the way stage space was employed, match gesture to character, and use the entire body expressively, breaking from restrictions that existed at the time. As Fokine later said, *The Dying Swan* aims "not so much at the eyes of the spectator, but at his soul, at his emotions".

Such talk brings to mind the fact that Isadora Duncan had been seen and admired by St. Petersburg dancers by 1905. But though the American dancer, with her free range of movement and emotional flair, may have encouraged Fokine's own liberating tendencies significantly, his solo is based firmly in the classical ballet vocabulary. Interestingly, however, major interpreters of *The Dying Swan* over the years—Alicia Markova, Galina Ulanova, Maya Plisetskaya, and Natalia Makarova among them—have never used exactly the same choreography, or even similar choreography at times, even though one could always turn to Fokine's authoritative notated version.

Unlike any other solo in classical ballet, *The Dying Swan* retains the name of its original choreographer, but no one seems compelled to use the same steps, as recorded versions show. However, this does not seem to affect the solo's popularity or recognizability. A basic pattern and characteristic movements are always used—bourrées criss-crossing the stage, undulations of the arms, a flagging of energy and a final floor pose—but many dancers add arabesques, various turns, and sustained segments on one knee.

The steps are not technically demanding, so that a great deal of acting is possible—indeed, required. A ballerina may even improvise easily as the mood of a particular performance dictates or allows. Often compared to a poem or monologue (it can be tedious or inspired, like Hamlet's "To be, or not to be"), *The Dying Swan* actually exists more as a concept—or perhaps as a ritual, with each enactment invested with the emotions of those present.

Like most rituals, *The Dying Swan* is connected with a strong mythology, having roots in the ancient belief that swans sing before they die. And the solo's power was amplified by the legend of Pavlova, who was herself known as "The Immortal Swan" and died, it was reported, asking for her Swan costume. Although the solo's protocol is not as strict as some rituals, it does share other features: it has a recognizable costume and music (much like a white wedding ritual), and deals with an important (in this case, ultimate) life transition. Nowadays, its repetitions often occur on special occasions, often representing an elegy at a memorial or tribute concert.

As is the case with any ritual, *The Dying Swan* can become hackneyed, but it also possesses tantalizing possibilities for the ballerina and her audience. In three minutes' time, it can symbolize strength, grief, resignation, transformation, and transcendence. Natalia Makarova has said the dance is "about life itself, and how we, like a swan, hold on to it with all our fading strength". American Ballet Theatre's Susan Jaffe thinks, as her swan dies, of letting go a part of herself in order to move on with her life. The Kirov's Galina Mezentseva knows only that it's what the audience wants to see—a beautiful death. Canadian ballerina Vanessa Harwood believes the dying swan never really dies, she is simply at peace with herself.

In any event, the solo doesn't seem to die; it keeps telling the story, one way or another, symbolizing a notion of the eternal, as well as the enduring possibilities of ballet itself.

—Jennifer Fisher

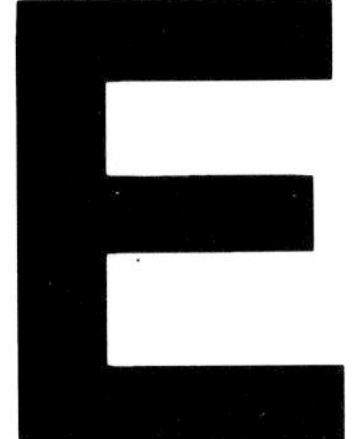

**EAGLING, Wayne**

Canadian dancer. Born in Montreal, Quebec, 27 November 1950. Studied with Patricia Ramsey, Studio of Dance Arts, California, and at Royal Ballet School, London, from 1966. Dancer, Royal Ballet, from 1969: soloist, from 1972; principal dancer, from 1975; also choreographer, with first works for Royal Ballet Choreographic Workshop; first full-length ballet, for Royal Ballet at Covent Garden, 1985; guest choreographer, Teatro alla Scala, Milan, 1990; has also appeared in films, including *Superstitious Man* (dir. Dark, 1983), and choreographed for music video by rock group Queen; left Royal Ballet, 1991: artistic director, Dutch National Ballet, Amsterdam, from 1991.

**ROLES**

1970 Dancer in *Field Figures* (Tetley), Royal Ballet, Nottingham

1971 Chanson dansée (An "Athlete") in *Les Biches* (Nijinska), Royal Ballet, London

1972 Younger Brother (cr) in *Triad* (MacMillan), Royal Ballet, London

Principal dancer in *Requiem Canticles* (Robbins), Royal Ballet, London

Bluebird pas de deux in *The Sleeping Beauty* (Petipa, Ashton; staged Wright), Royal Ballet, London

Dancer in *Dances at a Gathering* (Robbins), Royal Ballet, London

Dancer in *Laborintus* (Tetley), Royal Ballet, London

1973 Phlegmatic in *The Four Temperaments* (Balanchine), Royal Ballet, London

Romeo in *Romeo and Juliet* (MacMillan), Royal Ballet, London

Dancer in *Symphonic Variations* (Ashton), Royal Ballet, London

Pas de trois (Bransle Simple) in *Agon* (Balanchine), Royal Ballet, London

1974 Hothouse Rag (cr) in *Elite Syncopations* (MacMillan), Royal Ballet, London

Des Grieux in *Manon* (MacMillan), Royal Ballet, London

1975 Principal dancer (cr) in *Four Schumann Pieces* (van Manen), Royal Ballet, London

Spring (cr) in *The Four Seasons* (MacMillan), Royal Ballet, London

Neophyte (cr) in *Rituals* (MacMillan), Royal Ballet, London

Principal dancer (Gnossiennes) in *Monotones* (Ashton), Royal Ballet, London

Prince Siegfried in *Swan Lake* (Petipa, Ivanov; staged Sergeyev, Ashton, de Valois), Royal Ballet, London

The Prince in *Cinderella* (Ashton), Royal Ballet, London

Principal dancer in *Concerto* (MacMillan), Royal Ballet, London

Principal dancer in *Symphony* (MacMillan), Royal Ballet, London

1976 Principal dancer in *Twilight* (van Manen), Royal Ballet, London

Principal dancer in *Adagio Hammerklavier* (van Manen), Royal Ballet, London

The Cousin in *The Invitation* (MacMillan), Royal Ballet, London

Principal dancer in *Serenade* (Balanchine), Royal Ballet, London

Principal dancer in *Voluntaries* (Tetley), Royal Ballet, London

1977 Principal dancer (cr) in *Gloriana* (MacMillan), Royal Ballet, Queen's Silver Jubilee Gala, London

Dancer (cr) in *The Fourth Symphony* (Neumeier), Royal Ballet, London

The Voice of Spring (cr) in *Die Fledermaus* (opera; mus. Strauss, chor. Ashton), Royal Opera, London

Petruchio in *The Taming of the Shrew* (Cranko), Royal Ballet, London

Hamlet in *Hamlet with Ophelia* (also *Hamlet Prelude*, pas de deux; Ashton), Royal Ballet, tour

Colas in *La Fille mal gardée* (Ashton), Royal Ballet, London

Troyte in *Enigma Variations* (Ashton), Royal Ballet, London

Solor in *La Bayadère* (Petipa, Nureyev), Royal Ballet, tour

Prince Florimund in *The Sleeping Beauty* (Petipa, Ashton; staged MacMillan), Royal Ballet, London

Fourth Song in *Song of the Earth* (MacMillan), Royal Ballet, London

Mazurka, Pas de deux in *Les Sylphides* (Fokine), Royal Ballet, tour

1978 Friday in *Jazz Calendar* (Ashton), Royal Ballet, London

Crown Prince Rudolf in *Mayerling* (MacMillan), Royal Ballet, London

1979 Oberon in *The Dream* (Ashton), Royal Ballet, London

Principal dancer (cr) in *La Fin du jour* (MacMillan), Royal Ballet, London

1980 Principal dancer (cr) in *Gloria* (MacMillan), Royal Ballet, London

The Brother in *My Brother, My Sisters* (MacMillan), Royal Ballet, London

Albrecht in *Giselle* (Petipa after Coralli, Perrot; staged Sergeyev), Royal Ballet, London

Principal dancer (cr) in *Dances of Albion* (Tetley), Royal Ballet

1981 Title role in *Hamlet* (Helpmann), Royal Ballet, London

**Wayne Eagling as Romeo**

1982 The Young Man in *The Two Pigeons* (Ashton), Royal Ballet, London
The Boy with Matted Hair in *Shadowplay* (Tudor), Royal Ballet, London
The Dark Angel (cr) in *Orpheus* (MacMillan), Royal Ballet, London
Title role in *Orpheus* (MacMillan), Royal Ballet, London
Title role in *Apollo* (Balanchine), Royal Ballet, London
Ariel (cr) in *The Tempest* (Nureyev), Royal Ballet, London
Jean de Brienne in *Raymonda*, Act III (Nureyev), Royal Ballet, London
1983 Title role in *Prodigal Son* (Balanchine), Royal Ballet, London
Principal dancer in *Requiem* (MacMillan), Royal Ballet, London
Oscar Beregi in *Isadora* (MacMillan), Royal Ballet, London
Principal dancer (cr) in *Consort Lessons* (Bintley), Royal Ballet, London
Principal dancer in *Gluck Melody* (Messerer), Ballet Gala, London
Principal dancer in *The Flames of Paris* (Vainonen) Ballet Gala, London
1984 Woyzeck (cr) in *Different Drummer* (MacMillan), Royal Ballet, London
Principal dancer in *Return to the Strange Land* (Kylián), Royal Ballet, London
The Prince in *The Nutcracker* (Wright), Royal Ballet, London
1988 Principal dancer in *Bugaku* (Balanchine), Royal Ballet, London
Tirrenio in *Ondine* (Ashton), Royal Ballet, London
The Chosen One in *The Rite of Spring* (MacMillan), Royal Ballet, London
1989 Sanctus in *Requiem* (MacMillan), Royal Ballet, London

## WORKS

1983 *RBSque* (mus. Vangelis), Royal Ballet, Amnesty International Gala, London (staged Royal Ballet School, 1984)
1984 *A Broken Man* (mus. Vangelis), Royal Ballet Choreographic Workshop, London
1985 *Frankenstein, the Modern Prometheus* (mus. Vangelis), Royal Ballet, London
1986 *Beauty and the Beast* (mus. Vangelis), Royal Ballet, London
1988 *Byron* (mus. Tchaikovsky), La Scala Ballet, Italy
*Pavane* (mus. Fauré), Mantua Festival, Mantua
1989 *Senso* (mus. Bruckner), La Scala Ballet, Palermo
*Pas de deux* (mus. Donizetti, Liszt, Satie), Mondevision television, Naples
*Nijinsky* (mus. Debussy), Ballet of Naples, Naples
1990 Dances in *The Queen of Spades* (opera; mus. Tchaikovsky), La Scala Opera, Milan
*The Wall Concert* (mus. Pink Floyd), Berlin
*Mozart pas de deux* (mus. Mozart), Dancers of the Royal Ballet, tour

## PUBLICATIONS

By Eagling:

Interview in Leech, M., "Spotlight on Wayne Eagling, Royal Ballet Solo Artist," *Dance Magazine* (New York), August 1976
*The Company We Keep*, in collaboration with Robert Jude and Ross MacGibbon, London 1981

About Eagling:

Macaulay, Alastair, "Beauty or the Beast", *Dance Theatre Journal* (London), Spring 1987
"The Royal Ballet: The Biographies", *Ballet in London Yearbook 1988/89*, London, 1988

* * *

Primarily acclaimed as a Royal Ballet danseur noble, Wayne Eagling is now establishing himself as a choreographer of daring and innovative (if controversial) talent.

When he entered the company in 1969, his individuality, despite the drilled discipline of the corps, attracted much attention. During the MacMillan years (1970–77), his swift progress within the company, bringing him to principal dancer status within six years, encompassed an eclectic variety of leading and principal roles. While still in the corps he danced his first created role, that of the younger brother in MacMillan's *Triad* (1972), in which his speed and agility were particularly exploited, and he was also cast in a leading role in Jerome Robbins's *Requiem Canticles*. In September of that year he was promoted to soloist.

The following year Eagling made his début in *Romeo and Juliet*, dancing opposite Lesley Collier as Juliet. Though mostly well received, it led to a furore with the management after a cunningly edited interview appeared in a leading London magazine, nearly ending his Royal Ballet career. (Fortunately for all concerned this was not the case.) Not reticent about coming forward with his own views, Eagling has shown from the start an outspokenness which has not always endeared him to those in management. He has always been vocal about the appalling situation of dancers and money, pointing to the fact that the two are poles apart.

Eagling has been described as a "moving meteor", and it is easy to see why so many outstanding roles were created on him. It was in MacMillan's ballets that Eagling displayed his unique talents to their utmost, most notably in *Manon*, *Mayerling* (perhaps his most challenging role), and *My Brother, My Sisters*. He created roles in *Elite Syncopations*, *The Four Seasons*, *La Fin du jour*, and *Gloria*, MacMillan's elegy for "the lost generation" of World War I.

Eagling as a dancer was a favourite with audiences and some critics, with attention being drawn to his technical assurance, great elevation, suppleness, and speed. His versatility as a dancer, along with a more general stage presence, made him a dependable and popular member of the Royal Ballet. His flexibility, however, could present difficulties: having very loose joints gave him agility and a fluid line but it did have its drawbacks. His ankles are particularly prone to injury, and as a result he has had to undergo three operations on his right foot, the most recent in May 1990.

Great partnerships seem to be a thing of the past, and though Eagling has danced with many leading dancers he has never really had a partnership as such. His most frequent partners have been Merle Park, Lesley Collier, and Italian ballerina Alessandra Ferri (with whom he can be seen on video in *Romeo and Juliet*).

Eagling's relationship with British dance critics has not always been easy, and suggests that he is not, and has no desire to be, one of their darlings. His first major choreography for the Royal Ballet, *Frankenstein, the Modern Prometheus* (1985) was so enthusiastically received by the audience (and hence remains in the repertoire) that one unimpressed critic accused him of hiring his own "claque". Another called it "a misbegotten piece of vulgarity with intellectual pretensions". Nicholas Dromgoole of *The Sunday Telegraph*, on the other hand, wrote "With *Frankenstein*, Eagling has leapt to a distinctive place as a dance creator".

Eagling's fascination with the Opera House's well-equipped stage had led him to utilize the mechanical and technical facilities to maximum effect. His shock tactics with *Frankenstein* were intended, as he put it with characteristic bluntness, to "blow the whole of the Opera House backwards". He succeeded, and with similar effect he created his second work, *Beauty and the Beast*, in 1986. Again, critics complained—Alastair Macaulay summed it up by calling it "as naff and silly a work as all the critics said"—but the audiences flocked to see it.

In May 1990, Eagling choreographed three sections of Tchaikovsky's opera *The Queen of Spades* for La Scala, Milan. His association with the ballet company in Milan has resulted in several works for its prima ballerina Carla Fracci, notably *Byron*, created on Fracci and Richard Cragun, and the three-act *Senso*. He has also choreographed for Dance Umbrella (*A Broken Man*, a tribute to Michael Somes), the Young European Dancer of the Year Competition, the Royal Ballet Choreographic Workshop, and a music video for the rock band Queen; and in 1978 Eagling produced a Charity Gala for Mencap.

—Anna Swan

---

**EBREO, GUGLIELMO** *see* **GUGLIELMO EBREO**

---

## ECHOING OF TRUMPETS

(original Swedish title: *Ekon av Trumpeter*)

**Choreography:** Antony Tudor
**Music:** Bohuslav Martinů
**Design:** Birger Bergling (scenery and costumes)
**Libretto:** Antony Tudor
**First Production:** Royal Swedish Ballet, Royal Opera House, Stockholm, 28 September 1963
**Principal Dancers:** Gerd Andersson, Catharina Ericson, Viveka Ljung, Kerstin Lust, Hervor Sjostrand, Kari Sylwan, Anette Wiedersheim-Paul, Mario Mengarelli, Nils Johansson, Richard Wold, Svante Lindberg

**Other productions include:** Metropolitan Opera Ballet (restaged Tudor), as *Echoes of Trumpets*; New York, 27 March 1966. American Ballet Theatre; East Lansing, Michigan, 15 November 1967. London Festival Ballet; London, 27 April 1973.

### PUBLICATIONS

Ståhle, Anna Greta, "The Years in America and After", *Dance Perspectives* (New York), no. 18, 1963
Cohen, Selma Jeanne, "Time for Dance in Stockholm", *Saturday Review* (New York), 26 June 1965
Vaughan, David, "Tudor, Trumpets and Oracles", *Ballet Review* (Brooklyn), vol. 1, no. 4, 1966
Anderson, Jack, "Antony Tudor Talks about his New Ballets", *Dance Magazine* (New York), May 1966
Balanchine, George, with Mason, Francis, *Balanchine's Complete Stories of the Great Ballets*, Garden City, N.Y., 1977
Bliss, Sally Brayley, "Antony Tudor: Personal Reminiscences", *Choreography and Dance* (London), vol. 1, part 2, 1989
Szmyd, Linda, "Antony Tudor: Ballet Theatre Years", *Choreography and Dance* (London), vol. 1, part 2, 1989

* * *

In 1949 Antony Tudor went to Stockholm as artistic director of the Royal Swedish Ballet. His brief residence of one year brought him great success and he returned in 1962 to resume the directorship of the company and to set several ballets for them. In a letter to Lucia Chase in 1963, Tudor wrote from Sweden that "... the Martinů is giving me more difficulty than I could have possibly imagined and I am trying to accustom myself to the possibility of a 'still-born little bomb.'" Twenty days later, the premiere of *Echoing of Trumpets* overwhelmed the audience and brought Tudor back on to the map as a great dramatic choreographer.

The ballet depicts village women victimized by a brutal occupying army. In 1966, Jack Anderson interviewed Tudor, who admitted that most audiences associated the ballet with World War II, and that there were resemblances to the historical destruction of Lidice, Czechoslovakia, by the Nazis. But Tudor also said, "Perhaps it's more about how people always seem to want to dominate other people ... they never stop torturing each other with a kind of mild viciousness ... I've known some specialists in it ... even in ballet studios." He added, "Take the soldiers in my ballet. They don't really rape the women in the village. They just torment them until they make the women feel degraded and, in so doing, they degrade themselves." With this explanation, Tudor broadened the message of his ballet.

Tudor recalled that the Martinů music had deeply touched him, and that he chose it because as a child he had heard bombs falling, and later remembered the trumpets blaring from an army camp with a firing range near his home. Trumpets sound throughout the symphony.

Where possible, Tudor used theatrical settings for his ballets. In *Echoing of Trumpets* he chose a harsh, jagged, multi-level design that emphasized a feeling of entrapment, as there was only one place to enter and exit the stage. On the higher level he placed a woman who oversees the surroundings, as if watching to protect the town. Other women, dressed in simple dresses and wearing shawls, continue this sense of watchfulness. Fragile and tentative in their movements, the women seem without protection. Tudor's choreography often raises the women on their pointes, moving them slowly in mannequin-like steps. They come together, arms stiffly held at their sides, huddling in closely guarded patterns of movement. When the soldiers pour over the wall, dressed in uniforms and heavy boots, they do not execute "ballet" steps but hold each others' shoulders like Eastern European folk dancers in a strong and determined ring, a relentless force, frankly sexual in their attacks. When a woman brings bread to share, it is brutally knocked from her hand. She grabs for it, and a soldier mashes the bread into the ground. This encounter presages others of a more desperate manner.

The central moment of the ballet is a grotesque dance of death. The soldiers execute a villager, stringing him up by his feet on a gallows at the peak of the back wall where the viewer focuses on the vulnerable verticality of a hanging body, upside down, "jerking like a fish on a line". After the women cut the body down, the tormented wife dances with it. She tries to pull it on to her, to breathe life into it. She takes his clasped hands into hers and drags his limp body around in a circle. She then flings him away with such violence that one senses an anger far exceeding any sorrow.

Once again the soldiers enter. The women plot revenge and suddenly the shawls become weapons and they strangle a soldier, thus bringing down the wrath of their captors. In multiple pas de deux the women are tossed from one man to the other and are raised and stretched out as if on a rack. In the end only two women are left, wearily keeping watch. They know their fate. The trumpets call once more, and the stage goes dark.

In 1964 Clive Barnes, having seen the ballet at the International Festival of Dance in Paris, called *Echoing of Trumpets* "the long-awaited Tudor masterpiece". "He has given us", wrote Barnes, "a profoundly anti-romantic ballet about war—a ballet that is real, terrible and yet still beautiful in the scarlet way of tragedy. It has all that poignant immediacy associated with Tudor's early work. Bitter, perhaps pessimistic, it is one of those ballets that have been hewn out of a human soul . . .".

The American premiere of *Echoing of Trumpets* was danced by the Metropolitan Opera Ballet Company in 1966. Though the ballet was given only one performance at the Met, other ballet companies chose to recreate it, including American Ballet Theatre in 1967.

—Judith Chazin-Bennahum

---

**ECK, Imre**

Hungarian dancer, choreographer, and ballet director. Born in Budapest, 2 December 1930. Studied with Ferenc Nádasi, Budapest, from 1946. Married Zsuzsa Végvári, 1951: one daughter, Julia. Dancer, Budapest State Opera Ballet, 1946–60, becoming character solo dancer, 1950; first major choreography, for Budapest State Opera Ballet, in 1958; founder, artistic director, and choreographer, Ballet Sopianae, Pécs, 1960–69; chief choreographer, from 1969; also guest choreographer, staging works for numerous international companies, including Finnish National Ballet, Belgrade Opera Ballet, Boston Ballet, and Vienna State Opera Ballet. Recipient: Liszt Prize, 1962; Kossuth Prize, Hungary, 1976; title of Honoured Artist, Presidential Council of Hungary, 1978; Excellent Artist, Presidential Council of Hungary, 1987.

### ROLES

1950 Hilarion in *Giselle* (after Petipa, Coralli, Perrot), Budapest State Opera Ballet, Budapest
1952 Von Rothbart in *Swan Lake* (after Petipa, Ivanov), Budapest State Opera Ballet, Budapest
1954 Tybalt in *Romeo and Juliet* (Lavrovsky), Budapest State Opera Ballet, Budapest

**Other roles include:** for Ballet Sopianae—title role in *The Miraculous Mandarin* (also chor.), King Herod in *Salomé* (also chor.).

### WORKS

1958 *Csongor and Tünde* (mus. Weiner), Budapest State Opera Ballet, Budapest
1960 *The Ballad of Horror* (mus. Szokolay), Ballet Sopianae, Pécs
1961 *Variations on an Encounter* (mus. Vujicsics), Ballet Sopianae, Pécs
1962 *Hiroshima* (mus. Bukovy), Ballet Sopianae, Pécs
*As Commanded* (mus. Bukovy), Ballet Sopianae, Pécs
*Cobweb* (mus. Gulyás), Ballet Sopianae, Pécs
*Overture* (mus. Rossini), Ballet Sopianae, Pécs
1963 *Le Sacre du printemps* (mus. Stravinsky), Budapest State Opera Ballet, Budapest
1964 *Music for Strings, Percussion, and Celeste* (mus. Bartók), Budapest State Opera Ballet, Budapest
*Études in Blue* (mus. Vivaldi), Ballet Sopianae, Pécs
1965 *The Wooden Prince* (mus. Bartók), Ballet Sopianae, Pécs
*Concerto* (mus. Bartók), Ballet Sopianae, Pécs
*The Miraculous Mandarin* (mus. Bartók), Ballet Sopianae, Pécs
*Passacaglia* (mus. Petrovics), Ballet Sopianae, Pécs
1966 *Don Juan* (mus. Gluck), Ballet Sopianae, Pécs
1967 *Lulu* (mus. Berg), Ballet Sopianae, Pécs
1968 *Descent to Hell* (mus. Schubert, folk), Ballet Sopianae, Pécs
1969 *Undine* (after scenario of Ashton, de la Motte-Fouqué; mus. Henze), Budapest State Opera Ballet, Budapest
1970 *Summer Evening* (mus. Kodály), Ballet Sopianae, Budapest
1971 *Peacock Variations* (mus. Kodály), Ballet Sopianae, Pécs
*Hungarian Dolls* (mus. Weiner), Ballet Sopianae, Budapest
*Ties* (mus. Lajtha), Ballet Sopianae, Pécs
1972 *Sonata* (mus. Kodály), Ballet Sopianae, Pécs
1973 *Le Sacre du printemps* (new version; mus. Stravinsky), Ballet Sopianae, Pécs
*Faust Symphony* (mus. Liszt), Ballet Sopianae, Pécs
1974 *Tempest* (mus. Sibelius), Finnish National Ballet, Helsinki
1975 *Monsieur Molière* (mus. Grinblatt), Ballet Sopianae, Pécs
1976 *Requiem* (mus. Verdi), Ballet Sopianae, Pécs
*Kalevala* (mus. Sibelius), Finnish National Ballet, Helsinki
1978 *Sixth and Seventh Symphonies* (mus. Beethoven), Ballet Sopianae, Pécs
1979 *Salomé* (mus. Petrovics), Ballet Sopianae, Pécs
1989 *Carmina Burana* (mus. Orff), Ballet Sopianae, Pécs
*The Desert of Love* (mus. The East Ensemble), Ballet Sopianae, Pécs

### PUBLICATIONS

"A Chink in the Curtain", *Dance and Dancers* (London), April 1963
Franks, A.H., "Young Hungarians: Ballets Sopianae", *Dancing Times* (London), May 1963
Dienes, Gedeon, "Hungary: World Survey", *Dancing Times* (London), August 1963
Dienes, Gedeon, "The Choreographic Analysis of the Repertoire of the Ballet of Pécs", in *Essays on Dance 1967–68*, Budapest, 1968
Dallos, A., *A Pécsi Ballet Története*, Budapest, 1969
Vitányi, Iván, "New Endeavours in the Hungarian Dance Scene", in *Essays on Dance, 1969–70*, Budapest, 1970
Körtvélyes, Géza, "Contemporary Dance Tendencies in Hungarian Dance 1957–77", in *Essays on Dance 1978–79*, Budapest, 1979
Dienes, Gedeon, "Ballet in the Provinces, 1945–85", in *The History of Dance in the Theatre in Hungary*, Budapest, 1989

* * *

The significance and the character of Imre Eck's choreographic work can only be measured in the light of preceding events. In the 1950s the one and only ballet company in Hungary was the State Opera Company of Budapest (also known as the Hungarian National Ballet). It had in its repertoire Massine-type national character ballets, and it imported Russian classics and monumental Soviet ballet-dramas from the Soviet Union. Apart from this, there was a flourishing folk-dance movement in the country, but modern dance and Western-style ballets were banned by the cultural leadership. After the 1956 revolution, the artistic, ideological, and stylistic dictatorship gradually eased—and as a result, in 1960, Imre Eck founded a modern ballet company with twenty young, well-trained dancers at Pécs (a university town in southern Hungary).

During the era of the country's artistic isolation, Imre Eck started working without the knowledge of decades of achievement on the international scene, and created a repertoire which was, in Hungarian terms, avant-garde. In five years he mounted a series of 20- to 30-minute ballets with contemporary themes and outlook, in a particularly modern style. He created 25 new ballets; nineteen contemporary Hungarian composers wrote especially commissioned scores, and he also used four well-known Bartók pieces.

A philosophical approach, a conscious allegiance with intellectualism, the investigation of the social and private problems of the recent past, a sense of emotional reserve on the one hand, but strong, coarse eroticism on the other: this was the world of Imre Eck at that time. The themes were war and violence, the struggle of good and evil, ethical dilemmas, and the problems of finding a partner in life, and the position of man and his world—and these featured in one-act pieces, in ballets without narrative, in chamber works, and in miniatures. His more recent ballets are characteristically esoteric and symbolic, with multiple meanings and associations, coupled with abstract, symbolic, or naturalistic sets and effective lighting. As far as form is concerned, Eck's style came to consist, apart from academic dance and technique, of the complex use of "terre à terre" dancing, expressionist movements, and mime and jazz motifs. A dominant mode of his choreography is the character relief, using movements and poses of a broken, even deformed line, and the constant variation of the traditional ballet vocabulary with acrobatic and gymnastic elements, sometimes even at the price of dance fluency.

The above style, formed in the first decade of Eck's work, was altered and adapted with the use of older Hungarian music (mainly Franz Liszt), as well as works from the classical canon, mainly baroque and twentieth-century pieces. In many of Eck's smaller and larger works, this has brought with it a minimized use of character and folk-dance movement, and the strengthening of the poliphonic concept. Meanwhile, Eck has always interpreted his chosen music in an individual, often arbitrary manner. As an artistic director, he has preserved the company's musical and choreographic "workshop" atmosphere.

During the 1960s, Eck was a visiting choreographer in, among other places, Boston, Edinburgh, Vienna, Belgrade, and Helsinki. However, his most important ballets have been mounted for his own company. The most significant of these are *Variations on an Encounter*, *Cobweb*, *Études in Blue*, *The Miraculous Mandarin*, *Ties*, *Monsieur Molière*, *Requiem*, and *Salomé*. Among his rare appearances as a dancer in Pécs, the title role of *The Miraculous Mandarin*, and King Herod in *Salomé*, have been outstanding. Sadly, as a result of illness, Eck's creative output has declined in the last decade.

—Géza Körtvélyes

---

**EDWARDS, Leslie**

British dancer, teacher, and ballet director. Born in Teddington, London, 6 August 1916. Studied with Marie Rambert, Margaret Craske, Stanislas Idzikowski, Vera Volkova, and at the Sadler's Wells Ballet School. Dancer, Vic-Wells Ballet, from 1933, also dancing for Ballet Rambert, 1935–37; soloist, Sadler's Wells Ballet (later Royal Ballet), 1937–58, becoming leading mime and character dancer; also appeared in film *Tales of Beatrix Potter* (chor. Ashton, dir. Mills, 1971); teacher, Royal Ballet School, and ballet master to Royal Opera, from 1958; director, Royal Ballet Choreographic Group, from 1967; guest director, Washington Ballet, Washington, D.C., 1962. Recipient: Order of the British Empire, 1975.

**ROLES**

1935 Musician, Gambler, Creditor, King (cr) in *The Rake's Progress* (de Valois), Vic-Wells Ballet, London
Trapezist (cr) in *Circus Wings* (Salaman), Ballet Rambert, London

1935/37 Trainer in *Le Boxing* (Salaman), Ballet Rambert, London
Bowler in *Le Cricket* (Salaman), Ballet Rambert, London
Lover in *Le Jardin aux lilas* (Tudor), Ballet Rambert, London
A Personage in *Les Masques* (Ashton), Ballet Rambert, London
Mephisto in *Mephisto Waltz* (Ashton), Ballet Rambert, London

1936 A Nobleman (cr) in *The Gods Go a-Begging* (de Valois), Vic-Wells Ballet, London

1937 Red Castle, Black Castle (cr) in *Checkmate* (de Valois), Vic-Wells Ballet, Paris
Pas de huit (cr) in *Les Patineurs* (Ashton), Vic-Wells Ballet, London
Arthur (cr) in *A Wedding Bouquet* (Ashton), Vic-Wells Ballet, London

1938 Guard, peasant (cr) in *Le Roi nu* (*The Emperor's New Clothes*; de Valois), Vic-Wells Ballet, London

1939 Cavalier to Camellia Fairy in *The Sleeping Princess* (Petipa; staged Sergeyev), Vic-Wells Ballet, London

1940 Dancer (cr) in *Dante Sonata* (Ashton), Vic-Wells Ballet, London
An Angel (cr) in *The Wise Virgins* (Ashton), Vic-Wells Ballet, London
A Lawyer (cr) in *The Prospect Before Us* (de Valois), Vic-Wells Ballet, London

1941 Dancer (cr) in *The Wanderer* (Ashton), Sadler's Wells Ballet, London

1943 Archimago (cr) in *The Quest* (Ashton), Sadler's Wells Ballet, London
Popular Song in *Façade* (Ashton), Sadler's Wells Ballet, London
One of Les Merveilleuses (cr) in *Promenade* (de Valois), Sadler's Wells Ballet, London

1944 Beggar (cr) in *Miracle in the Gorbals* (Helpmann), Sadler's Wells Ballet, London
Pierrot in *Carnaval* (Fokine), Sadler's Wells Ballet, London
The Rake in *The Rake's Progress* (de Valois), Sadler's Wells Ballet, London

1946 The Mime (cr) in *Adam Zero* (Helpmann), Sadler's Wells Ballet, London
Dr. Coppélius in *Coppélia* (Petipa, Cecchetti; staged Sergeyev), Sadler's Wells Ballet, London

**Leslie Edwards as Catalabutte in *The Sleeping Beauty***

Catalabutte in *The Sleeping Beauty* (Petipa; staged Sergeyev, Ashton, de Valois), Sadler's Wells Ballet, London

Chauffeur (cr) in *Les Sirènes* (Ashton), Sadler's Wells Ballet, London

1947 The Red King in *Checkmate* (de Valois), Sadler's Wells Ballet, London

The American in *La Boutique fantasque* (Massine), Sadler's Wells Ballet, London

The Butcher in *Mam'zelle Angot* (Massine), Sadler's Wells Ballet, London

1948 The King (cr) in *Clock Symphony* (Massine), Sadler's Wells Ballet, London

King of Denmark in *Hamlet* (Helpmann), Sadler's Wells Ballet, London

The Hairdresser (cr) in *Cinderella* (Ashton), Sadler's Wells Ballet, London

1950 Priest (cr) in *Don Quixote* (de Valois), Sadler's Wells Ballet, London

1951 Title role in *Don Quixote* (de Valois), Sadler's Wells Ballet, London

A Goatman (cr) in *Donald of the Burthens* (Helpmann), Sadler's Wells Ballet, London

1952 Bilby (cr) in *Mirror for Witches* (Howard), Sadler's Wells Ballet, London

League of Light (cr) in *Bonne-Bouche* (Cranko), Sadler's Wells Ballet, London

The Governor in *The Three-Cornered Hat* (Massine), Sadler's Wells Ballet, London

1956 Hypnotist (cr) in *Noctambules* (MacMillan), Sadler's Wells Ballet, London

1957 Emperor of the Middle Kingdom (cr) in *The Prince of the Pagodas* (Cranko), Royal Ballet, London

1958 A Hermit (cr) in *Ondine* (Ashton), Royal Ballet, London

1959 Oedipus (cr) in *Antigone* (Cranko), Royal Ballet, London

1960 Thomas (cr) in *La Fille mal gardée* (Ashton), Royal Ballet, London

1963 A Duke (cr) in *Marguerite and Armand* (Ashton), Royal Ballet, London

1968 "B.G.N." (cr) in *Enigma Variations* (Ashton), Royal Ballet, London

1971 The Owl (cr) in *Tales of Beatrix Potter* (chor. Ashton, dir. Mills), British film

**Other roles include:** Hilarion in *Giselle* (Petipa after Coralli, Perrot; staged Sergeyev), the Father in *Prodigal Son* (Balanchine), Florestan in *Carnaval* (Fokine), Arabian Dance in *The Nutcracker* (Sergeyev after Ivanov), Carabosse in *The Sleeping Beauty* (Petipa; staged Sergeyev, de Valois, Ashton), Benno, Mazurka in *Swan Lake* (Petipa, Ivanov; staged Sergeyev), Ghost of Hamlet's Father in *Hamlet* (Helpmann).

## PUBLICATIONS

Davidson, Gladys, *Ballet Biographies*, revised edition, London, 1954

Swinson, Cyril, *Six Dancers of Sadler's Wells*, London, 1956

"Dancer of Today: Leslie Edwards", *Dance and Dancers* (London), June 1958

Anthony, Gordon, "Pioneers of the Royal Ballet: Leslie Edwards", *Dancing Times* (London), July 1970

Steinbrink, Mark, "Leslie Edwards", *Ballet News* (New York), September 1981

* * *

Leslie Edwards' career has not been a spectacular succession of leading roles, but a series of cameos, on which he has lavished the care that others would only have given to principal roles. To see another performer as any of the characters on which Edwards has set his unmistakable mark, is to realize the importance of experience, indisputable authority, and attention to detail.

When the young Vic-Wells Ballet first mounted the classics, the company suffered from a lack of mature artists to bring to life the kings, queens, nobles, and courtiers. Only time could fill the gap, and Edwards was one of the first generation of artists developed within the company who were to give life and solidity to many productions. His talents as a mime first attracted attention in 1943, when he created Archimago in Frederick Ashton's *The Quest*, a perfect study in evil hypocrisy. The following year he played the Beggar in Robert Helpmann's *Miracle in the Gorbals*, showing a tragic figure almost touched with religious understanding amid his squalid surroundings. From then, although Edwards was to appear in many leading roles, including an intelligent, absent-minded Dr. Coppélius, and a moving Red King in *Checkmate*, he was to make his name as an indispensible portrayer of the unspectacular, but no less important, small roles.

For many years, no Royal Ballet production was complete without Edwards' authority being brought to bear on another magnificent cameo role. Many choreographers were to use his talents, among them Ashton, MacMillan, Cranko, and Andrée Howard. To every role he brought a complete understanding of its importance in the ballet and a characterization that made it an immediately recognizable and individual human being. In the classics his impeccable stage manners illuminated Benno in *Swan Lake*, while his Hilarion in *Giselle* was full of jealous forboding that none the less did not lose sympathy for the character. Most of all, however, he will be remembered as Catalabutte in *The Sleeping Beauty*, master-minding the Christening, the Birthday, and the Wedding with magnificent assurance and dignity, showing a pomposity and self-satisfaction that raised the character from a mere "walk-on" part to being an integral part of the drama.

A strength of the Royal Ballet organization has always been the devotion it inspired in its first generations of dancers, and the use it has made of their talents over and above their performances. Not only have they passed on their experience to others, but they have, by their example, ensured that the first principals and traditions of the company have been transferred on to younger generations. Thus Edwards has both taught and rehearsed the Royal company, and has also acted as ballet master to the Royal Opera.

Edwards' most important work outside performing, however, was as Director of the Royal Ballet Choreographic Group, founded in 1967 as a workshop where aspiring choreographers could learn their craft. His practical encouragement and his own experience of working with many choreographers proved invaluable, and over the years the Group nursed the talents of more than one generation of new choreographers—including Ronald Hynd, Geoffrey Cauley, David Bintley, and Michael Corder.

—Sarah C. Woodcock

---

**EGLEVSKY, André**

Russian/American dancer and teacher. Born Andrei Evgenovich Eglevsky in Moscow, 21 December 1917. Educated in

French high school; studied ballet with Julie Sedova and Maria Nevelskaya (Nevelska), Nice, from c. 1925, and with Lubov Egorova, Mathilde Kshessinskaya, and Alexandre Volinine, Paris, and with Nikolai Legat, London; later studied at the School of American Ballet, New York, pupil of Pierre Vladimirov and Anatole Obukhov. Married dancer Leda Anchutina, 1938: two sons and daughter, dancer Marina Eglevsky. Dancer, soon becoming soloist, (de Basil's) Ballets Russes de Monte Carlo, 1931–34, joining Woizikowsky company, 1935, and (René Blum's) Ballets de Monte Carlo, 1936–37; principal dancer, American Ballet, 1937–38, Ballet Russe de Monte Carlo, 1939–42, Ballet Theatre (later American Ballet Theatre), 1942–43 and 1945–46, Marquis de Cuevas's Ballet International, 1944, Massine's Ballet Russe Highlights, 1945, de Basil's Original Ballet Russe, 1947, (de Cuevas's) Grand Ballet de Monte Carlo, 1947–50, New York City Ballet, 1951–58; also performed at Radio City Music Hall, New York, and in musical *Great Lady* (mus. Loewe, chor. Balanchine, 1938); appeared in film, *Limelight* (dir. Chaplin, 1952); teacher, School of American Ballet, New York, from 1958; founder and teacher, Eglevsky School, Long Island, New York: student company, the Eglevsky Ballet, founded 1961. Died in New York, 4 December 1977.

**André Eglevsky**

## ROLES

1933 Movement, A Destiny (cr) in *Les Présages* (Massine), Ballets Russes de Monte Carlo, Monte Carlo
A Salesman (cr) in *Le Beau Danube* (Massine), Ballets Russes de Monte Carlo, Monte Carlo
"Bathing Time", "Airs from the Casino" (cr) in *Beach* (Massine), Ballets Russes de Monte Carlo, Monte Carlo
Count Anselmi (cr) in *Scuola di ballo* (Massine), Ballets Russes de Monte Carlo, Monte Carlo
First Betrothed Pair (with Baronova; cr) in *Nocturne* (Lichine), Ballets Russes de Monte Carlo, Paris
First and Fourth Movements (cr) in *Choreartium* (Massine), Ballets Russes de Monte Carlo, London
Mazurka, Pas de deux in *Les Sylphides* (Fokine), Ballets Russes de Monte Carlo, London
A Spirit in *Jeux d'enfants* (Massine), Ballets Russes de Monte Carlo

1934 Surveyor of Irish Workmen (cr) in *Union Pacific* (Massine), de Basil's Ballets Russes, Philadelphia
Cossack Chief in *La Boutique fantasque* (Massine), de Basil's Ballets Russes, London

1935 Harlequin in *Carnaval* (Fokine), Les Ballets de Léon Woizikowsky, London
The Moor in *Petrushka* (Woizikowsky after Fokine), Les Ballets de Léon Woizikowsky, London
The Bluebird in *Bluebird Pas de deux* (from *The Sleeping Beauty*; after Petipa), Les Ballets de Léon Woizikowsky, London

1936 The Lover (cr) in *L'Épreuve d'amour* (Fokine), Blum's Ballets de Monte Carlo, Monte Carlo
Chief Jester/Chief Demon (cr) in *Don Juan* (Fokine), Blum's Ballets de Monte Carlo, London

1936/37 Polovtsian Warrior in *Polovtsian Dances from Prince Igor* (Fokine), Blum's Ballets de Monte Carlo
The Spirit of the Rose in *Le Spectre de la rose* (Fokine), Blum's Ballets de Monte Carlo

1937 Principal dancer (cr) in *Les Éléments* (Fokine), Blum's Ballets de Monte Carlo, London
Title role in *The Bat* (Balanchine), American Ballet, New York

1938 Premier danseur (cr) in *Great Lady* (musical comedy; mus. Frederick Loewe, chor. Balanchine), Majestic Theatre, New York

1939 Faun (cr) in *Bacchanale* (Massine), Ballet Russe de Monte Carlo, New York
The Prince in *Swan Lake*, Act II (after Ivanov), Ballet Russe de Monte Carlo, New York

1940 Bridegroom in *Le Baiser de la fée* (Balanchine), Ballet Russe de Monte Carlo, New York
Jack of Clubs in *Poker Game* (*Jeu de cartes*; Balanchine), Ballet Russe de Monte Carlo, New York
A Boy Friend (cr) in *The New Yorker* (Massine), Ballet Russe de Monte Carlo, New York
Prince in *The Nutcracker* (one-act version; Fedorova after Ivanov), Ballet Russe de Monte Carlo, New York

1941 Theseus (cr) in *The Labyrinth* (Massine), Ballet Russe de Monte Carlo, New York
Siegfried in *The Magic Swan* ("Black Swan" pas de deux; after Petipa), Ballet Russe de Monte Carlo, New York

1942/43 Paris (variation chor. Balanchine) in *Helen of Troy* (Lichine), Ballet Theatre
Albrecht in *Giselle* (Dolin after Petipa, Coralli, Perrot), Ballet Theatre

1943 Title role in *Apollo* (Balanchine), Ballet Theatre, New York
Gritzko (cr) in *Fair at Sorochinsk* (Lichine), Ballet Theatre, New York
Artist (cr) in *Mademoiselle Angot* (later *Mam'zelle Angot*; Massine), Ballet Theatre, New York
The Prince in *The Nutcracker Pas de deux* (Dolin after Ivanov), Ballet Theatre, New York

1944 Principal dancer (cr) in *Sentimental Colloquy* (also chor.), (de Cuevas') Ballet International, New York
Principal dancer (cr) in *Prince Goudal's Festival* (Romanov), Ballet International, New York
Apollo (cr) in *Brahms Variations* (Nijinska), Ballet International, New York
1945 Solo dancer (cr) in *The Warrior* (Massine), (Massine's) Ballet Russe Highlights, New York
Principal dancer (cr) in *Polish Festival* (Massine), Ballet Russe Highlights, New York
Principal dancer (cr) in *Graziana* (Taras), Ballet Theatre, New York
1946 Principal dancer (cr) in *Pas de deux* (Obukhov), Ballet Theatre, New York
1947 Principal dancer (cr) in *Pas de trois* (Robbins), Original Ballet Russe, New York
1948 Principal dancer (cr) in *Pas de trois classique* (Balanchine), Grand Ballet de Monte Carlo, London
1949 Principal dancer (cr) in *In Memoriam* (Nijinska), Grand Ballet de Monte Carlo, Paris
Principal dancer (cr) in *Le Moulin enchanté* (Lichine), Grand Ballet de Monte Carlo, Paris
1951 Principal dancer (cr) in *Pas de trois (I)* (new version of *Pas de trois classique*; Balanchine), New York City Ballet, New York
Title role in *Apollo, Leader of the Muses* (also called *Apollo*; Balanchine), New York City Ballet, New York
Principal dancer (cr) in *Capriccio Brillant* (Balanchine), New York City Ballet, New York
Principal dancer (cr) in *A la Françaix* (Balanchine), New York City Ballet, New York
Prince Siegfried (cr) in *Swan Lake* (Balanchine after Ivanov), New York City Ballet, New York
1952 Principal dancer (cr) in *Caracole* (later called *Divertimento no. 15*; Balanchine), New York City Ballet, New York
Principal dancer (cr) in *Scotch Symphony* (Balanchine), New York City Ballet, New York
Principal dancer (cr) in *Harlequinade Pas de Deux* (Balanchine), New York City Ballet, New York
Principal dancer (cr) in *Concertino* (Balanchine), New York City Ballet, New York
1954 Third Movement (cr) in *Western Symphony* (Balanchine), New York City Ballet, New York
1955 Principal dancer (cr) in *Roma* (Balanchine), New York City Ballet, New York
Principal dancer (cr) in *Pas de Trois (II)* (Balanchine; chor. attributed to Eglevsky in later stagings), New York City Ballet, New York
Principal dancer (cr) in *Pas de Dix* (Balanchine), New York City Ballet, New York
1958 Principal dancer (cr) in *Waltz-Scherzo* (pas de deux; Balanchine), New York City Ballet, New York

**Other roles include:** for de Basil's Ballets Russes/Original Ballet Russe—Golden Slave in *Schéhérazade* (Fokine), principal dancer in *Don Quixote Pas de deux* (after Petipa), First couple in *La Concurrence* (Balanchine), leading roles in *Seventh Symphony* (Massine), *Rouge et noir* (Massine), *Capriccio espagnole* (Massine), *Vienna 1814* (Massine); for Ballet Theatre—leading roles in *Bluebeard* (Fokine), *Aleko* (Massine), *Graduation Ball* (Lichine), The Prince in *The Nutcracker*; for Grand Ballet de Monte Carlo—principal roles in *The Five Gifts* (Dollar), *Constantia* (Dollar), *Mad Tristan* (Lichine); for New York City Ballet—principal dancer in *Sylvia Pas de deux* (Balanchine).

## WORKS

1944 *Sentimental Colloquy* (mus. Bowles), (de Cuevas's) Ballet International, New York

Also staged:
1977 *The Sleeping Beauty* (after Petipa; with additional chor. Balanchine), The Eglevsky Ballet, Hampstead, New York

## PUBLICATIONS

By Eglevsky:
Interview in Marsh, L., "Eglevsky: An Interview", *Dance Magazine* (New York), November 1943

About Eglevsky:
Buckle, Richard, "André Eglevsky", *Dancing Times* (London), July 1937
Beaumont, Cyril, *Supplement to Complete Book of Ballets*, London, 1942
Sheridan, H., "André Eglevsky: The Great Classical Dancer", *Chrysalis* (New York), 1949
Denby, Edwin, *Looking at the Dance*, New York, 1949
Raher, D., "Eglevsky: Paragon of Pirouettes", *Dance and Dancers* (London), June 1952
Davidson, Gladys, *Ballet Biographies*, revised edition, London, 1954
Reynolds, Nancy, *Repertory in Review*, New York, 1977
Rosen, Lillie, "Remembering André Eglevsky", *Dance Scope* (New York), vol. 12, no. 2, 1978
Manchester, P.W., "André Eglevsky 1917–1977", *Ballet Review* (Brooklyn, N.Y.), no. 1, 1978–79
Sorley Walker, Kathrine, *De Basil's Ballets Russes*, London, 1982
Denby, Edwin, *Dance Writings*, edited by Robert Cornfield and William Mackay, New York, 1986

* * *

André Eglevsky was one of the outstanding classical dancers of his generation. From the 1930s through the 1950s, he was one of the greatest and most influential of male dancers outside of the Soviet Union.

Eglevsky's career began when he was accepted, at the age of fourteen, into de Basil's Ballets Russes de Monte Carlo; he was the first great male dancer to have been produced by this post-Diaghilev era. In his early career, he was renowned for his technical virtuosity and, in particular, for the incredible number of pirouettes he could perform (at least twelve to fifteen). The arrival of Anton Dolin as guest artist with the company, however, was to have a great effect on Eglevsky. In order to emulate what he perceived as Dolin's great artistry in manner and style, he began to take lessons with the ex-Maryinsky dancer and renowned teacher Nikolai Legat, who was working in London. He stayed with Legat for two years, though this meant leaving the company and facing a great deal of financial hardship. It was a curious decision for a young star whose career within the world's leading ballet company was already clearly set; it points to a deep respect for his art, a perfectionism, and a capacity for self-criticism. Eglevsky realized that with Legat his artistry could develop and gain the polish of the Maryinsky tradition. It was a decision which was well rewarded, and in the 1940s he took over from Dolin as the leading interpreter of Albrecht in *Giselle*, showing audiences a refreshingly new interpretation of the part.

As with his training, Eglevsky's performing career came under a variety of important influences. He was fortunate in working with the most influential choreographers of this century—Fokine, Massine, and Balanchine. Probably Fokine was the choreographer with whom Eglevsky was in greatest sympathy. He created the role of the Lover in Fokine's *L'Epreuve d'amour* and the Chief Jester and Chief Demon in *Don Juan*. He was to become a guardian of Fokine's style, and throughout his career he had a deep respect for the original stylistic nuances of an interpretation, seeking to preserve them in later productions. Eglevsky saw technique as merely a springboard; he had a fine sense of mime, and was renowned for the creative insights of his characterizations. He was emphatic that a dancer must not just simply know how, but also why. This was an attitude which was not ideally suited to Balanchine's method of working, but nevertheless Eglevsky proved himself a brilliant interpreter of many of Balanchine's major works. In particular the choreographer gave Eglevsky the chance to broaden his range; for example, in creating *A La Françaix* for Eglevsky, Balanchine enabled him to reveal an ability for comedy.

During the 1940s and 1950s Eglevsky was a particular source of inspiration to male dancers; he was the epitome of the "danseur noble" with a virtuosity and soaring power that had not been seen since Nijinsky. Like Nijinsky, he was particularly successful at creating the illusion of hovering in the air. Critic Edwin Denby frequently wrote of his "soaring rhythm", and Eglevsky was renowned for his power and breadth as well as for his precision and grace. Although a large man, he created on stage the illusion of extreme lightness, ease, and elegance; he was able to bring out the sensuality as well as the academicism of the classical style. His attributes were combined to particular brilliance in the role of the favourite slave in *Schéhérazade*, but he had considerable range, excelling in roles as various as the Moor in *Petrushka*, the young god in Balanchine's *Apollo*, Paris in Lichine's *Helen of Troy*, and Albrecht in *Giselle*. As a partner Eglevsky was highly sensitive, with an understanding of the natural balance of the ballerina, and was renowned as the model of classical perfection and the grand style.

Eglevsky was also a gifted teacher, and after his retirement he taught both at the School of American Ballet and at his own school in Massapequa, Long Island. From his training with Alexandre Volinine and Nikolai Legat, Eglevsky embodied elements of the Bolshoi and Maryinsky traditions respectively; from this background and through his work with Fokine, Massine, and Balanchine, Eglevsky united the diverse traditions of the Russian schools. He recognized the value of this legacy and was committed to passing it on through teaching. In his youth he had been able to persuade Legat to write down some classes, and in his later life Eglevsky gave these classes, meticulously explaining their context and origin. He had been coached by Fokine for the title role in *Le Spectre de la rose* and was in turn able to teach the part to Baryshnikov; he also coached Ivan Nagy for his role as Apollo. His teaching drew principally on the methods of Fokine and Legat, and he is reported to have said that he owed his arm work to Fokine and his placement and combinations to Legat. Amongst his pupils were Fernando Bujones and his daughter, Marina Eglevsky. In 1961, he founded the Eglevsky Ballet Company out of his school.

—Lesley-Anne Sayers

---

**EGOROVA, Lyubov** (Lubov)

Russian dancer. Born Lyubov (Lubov) Nikolaevna Egorova in St. Petersburg, 8 August (27 July old style) 1880. Studied at the Imperial Theatre School, St. Petersburg, pupil of Enrico Cecchetti; graduated in 1898; later studied in Class of Perfection with Maria Gorshenkova, Ekaterina Vazem, Anna Johannsen. Married Prince Nikita Trubetskoy, 1917. Dancer, Maryinsky Theatre, 1898–1917: ballerina from 1914; toured with company of Anna Pavlova and Mikhail Mordkin in Scandinavia, Germany, Finland, 1908–09; leading dancer, performing with Pierre Vladimirov, Théâtre des Champs-Elysées, Paris, 1920, and with Diaghilev's Ballets Russes, Alhambra Theatre, London, 1921–22; teacher at own school, Paris, from 1923: students include Alexandra Danilova, Vera Nemchinova, Solange Schwarz, Alice Nikitina, Janine Charrat, Ethéry Pagava, Youly Algaroff, Serge Lifar, Anton Dolin; choreographer for the Nemchinova-Dolin Ballet, 1929; founder and director, Les Ballets de la Jeunesse, 1937–38; later taught for Royal Danish Ballet, Copenhagen, and International Ballet, London. Chevalier de l'Ordre des Arts et Lettres, Paris, 1964. Died in Paris, 18 August 1972.

## ROLES

1902/05 Ilka in *The Enchanted Forest* (Ivanov), Maryinsky Theatre, St. Petersburg
Lisa in *The Magic Flute* (Ivanov), Maryinsky Theatre, St. Petersburg
Tsikalia in *Don Quixote* (Petipa), Maryinsky Theatre, St. Petersburg
Clemence in *Raymonda* (Petipa), Maryinsky Theatre, St. Petersburg
Pierrette in *Harlequinade* (*Les Millions d'Arlequin*; Petipa), Maryinsky Theatre, St. Petersburg
Breadcrumb Fairy in *The Sleeping Beauty* (Petipa), Maryinsky Theatre, St. Petersburg
Candide Fairy in *The Sleeping Beauty* (Petipa), Maryinsky Theatre, St. Petersburg

1905 Title role in *The Blue Dahlia* (Petipa), Maryinsky Theatre, St. Petersburg

1906 Selesten in *Robert and Bertram; or, The Two Thieves* (new production; Gorsky after Kshesinsky, Mendez), Maryinsky Theatre, St. Petersburg

1907 Myrtha in *Giselle* (Petipa after Coralli, Perrot), Maryinsky Theatre, St. Petersburg

1910 Title role in *Raymonda* (Petipa), Maryinsky Theatre, St. Petersburg

1911 Nikiya in *La Bayadère* (Petipa), Maryinsky Theatre, St. Petersburg
Aspicia in *The Pharaoh's Daughter* (Petipa), Maryinsky Theatre, St. Petersburg
Fleur-de-Lis in *Esmeralda* (Perrot), Maryinsky Theatre, St. Petersburg
Princess Aurora in *The Sleeping Beauty* (Petipa), Maryinsky Theatre, St. Petersburg

1912 Sugar Plum Fairy in *The Nutcracker* (Ivanov), Maryinsky Theatre, St. Petersburg
Tsar Maiden in *The Little Humpbacked Horse* (Petipa after Saint-Léon; staged Gorsky), Maryinsky Theatre, St. Petersburg

1913 Odette/Odile in *Swan Lake* (Petipa, Ivanov), Maryinsky Theatre, St. Petersburg

1914 Title role in *Giselle* (Petipa after Coralli, Perrot), Maryinsky Theatre, St. Petersburg

1915 Francesca (cr) in *Francesca da Rimini* (Fokine), Maryinsky Theatre, Petrograd

1921 Aurora, Fairy of the Songbirds in *The Sleeping Princess* (Petipa; staged Sergeyev, with additional dances by Nijinska), Diaghilev's Ballets Russes, London

**Other roles include:** for the Maryinsky Theatre—Pas de trois in *Swan Lake*, Kitri in *Don Quixote* (Petipa), Princess Florine in *The Sleeping Beauty*, title role in *Camargo* (Ivanov after Petipa), Naila in *La Source* (Coppini after Saint-Léon), Medora and the Slave Girl in *Le Corsaire* (Petipa).

## WORKS

1929 *The Wind* (choreographed for Vera Nemchinova), Nemchinova-Dolin Ballet, London
1932 *La Flamme* (mus. Jaumeton-Epstein), Théâtre des Champs-Elysées, Paris

## PUBLICATIONS


Schever, L. Franc, "Les Ballets de la Jeunesse", *Dancing Times* (London), February 1938
Dolin, Anton, *Ballet Go Round*, London, 1938
Haskell, Arnold, *Balletomania*, London, 1943
Tugal, Pierre, "Witness of a Glorious Past: Lubov Egorova", *Dancing Times* (London), June 1952
Milford, Nancy, *Zelda Fitzgerald*, New York, 1970
Krasovskaya, Vera, *Russian Ballet Theatre of the Beginning of the Twentieth Century*, volume 2: Leningrad, 1972
Smakov, Gennady, *The Great Russian Dancers*, New York, 1984


* * *

Lyubov Egorova, a student of Cecchetti, graduated from the Theatre School of St. Petersburg in 1898 and entered the ballet company of the Maryinsky Theatre as a corps dancer. She remained with the St. Petersburg company for some eighteen years, performing in a wide range of ballets in the classical repertoire.

Notwithstanding her excellent external gifts—irreproachable figure, appealing face, shapely legs with high insteps, and, thanks to Cecchetti, sure mastery over her technical gifts—recognition came far from quickly for Egorova. She earned the title of ballerina only in 1914, after fifteen years on the stage. Critics reproached Egorova for inexpressiveness, and for the absence of individuality and feeling in her performance. Egorova's soft lyrical character and the special tenderness of her movements revealed themselves not immediately and not to all. The insignificant role of Francesca (in *Francesca da Rimini*) created by Fokine especially for Egorova did not bring the desired success. Only after dancing the roles of Giselle and Odette, in which dance dominates and gives scope for more expansive emotional expression, did the ballerina win her rightful claim to a place in Russian ballet.

Egorova was to leave Russia, performing with Diaghilev's Ballets Russes company in 1921–22, and eventually opening her own ballet school in Paris where she was teacher to many outstanding dancers. Among her pupils were Solange Schwarz, Janine Charrat, Ethéry Pagava, Youly Algaroff, and George Skibine. In 1937, Egorova founded "Les Ballets de la Jeunesse", a company to provide a showcase for her own pupils, which she directed for a year. Later she conducted classes in classical dance for the Royal Danish Ballet, and in London she taught for the International Ballet.

Egorova was a ballerina perhaps ahead of her time; certainly in Russia it was many years before the true nature of her gifts was understood and appreciated. The ballet historian Vera Krasovskaya, speaking of Egorova's gifts, confirms that: "Restrained dramatism, concealed in the simplicity and naturalness of [Egorova's] dancing, was not then in keeping with the times. Emphatic virtuosity was in the forefront. The search for the new oriented itself to the effect of picturesque passions and demanded explosions of temperament. The poetry of Egorova's dance, light and slightly enigmatic in its simplicity, did not find a response among contemporaries." Nevertheless, when the star of Galina Ulanova rose on the same stage twenty years later, the nature of her talent was then compared above all with the talent of Egorova.

—Arsen Degen

---

## EIFMAN, Boris

Russian choreographer and ballet director. Born Boris Yakovlevich Eifman in Rubtsovsk, 22 July 1946. Studied at Kishinev Ballet School; graduated in 1964; also studied at choreographers' department, Leningrad Conservatory, pupil of Georgi Aleksidze; graduated in 1972. Dancer, Kishinev Opera and Ballet Theatre, from 1964; ballet master, Leningrad Ballet School, 1972–77; artistic director and chief ballet master, Leningrad Theatre of Contemporary Ballet (also called New Ballet, 1977–78, and Leningrad Ballet Ensemble, 1978–80), from 1977, directing Leningrad (St. Petersburg) Boris Eifman Ballet Theatre, from 1990; first choreography, 1970; also choreographer for various Soviet ballet films, including *Variations on a Roccoco Theme* (1968), *Icarus* (1970), *The Crystal Palace* (1973), *Brilliant Divertissement* (for the Kirov, 1973), *Three Compositions* (1976), and for television, including *Bloody Sun* (Berlin, 1978); staged own ballets in Monte Carlo, 1989, 1990.

## WORKS

1972 *Gayané* (mus. Khachaturian), Maly Theatre Ballet, Leningrad
1975 *Firebird* (mus. Stravinsky), Kirov Ballet, Leningrad
1972/77 *Towards Life* (mus. Kabalevsky), Graduation Performance, Leningrad Ballet School, Leningrad
*The Meetings* (mus. Schedrin), Graduation Performance, Leningrad Ballet School, Leningrad
*The Beautiful Impulses of the Soul* (mus. Schedrin), Graduation Performance, Leningrad Ballet School, Leningrad
1977 *Only Love* (mus. Schedrin), New Ballet (Leningrad Theatre of Contemporary Ballet), Leningrad
*The Song Broken* (mus. Schedrin), New Ballet (Leningrad Theatre of Contemporary Ballet), Leningrad
*Bivocality* (mus. Pink Floyd), New Ballet (Leningrad Theatre of Contemporary Ballet), Leningrad
1978 *Firebird* (mus. Stravinsky), New Ballet (Leningrad Theatre of Contemporary Ballet), Leningrad
1979 *Movement Eternal* (mus. Khachaturian), Leningrad Ensemble (Theatre of Contemporary Ballet), Leningrad
*Boomerang* (mus. rock music), Leningrad Ensemble (Theatre of Contemporary Ballet), Leningrad
1980 *The Idiot* (mus. Tchaikovsky), Leningrad Theatre of Contemporary Ballet, Leningrad

1981 *Autographs* (mus. various), Leningrad Theatre of Contemporary Ballet, Leningrad
1982 *Day of Madness; or, The Marriage of Figaro* (mus. Rossini), Leningrad Theatre of Contemporary Ballet, Leningrad
*The Legend* (mus. Kogan), Leningrad Theatre of Contemporary Ballet, Leningrad
1983 *Metamorphoses* (mus. various), Leningrad Theatre of Contemporary Ballet, Leningrad
1984 *Twelfth Night* (mus. Donizetti), Leningrad Theatre of Contemporary Ballet, Leningrad
1985 *Second Lieutenant Romashov* (mus. Gavrilin), Leningrad Theatre of Contemporary Ballet, Leningrad
1986 *Intrigues of Love* (mus. Rossini), Leningrad Theatre of Contemporary Ballet, Leningrad
1987 *The Master and Margarita* (mus. Petrov), Leningrad Theatre of Contemporary Ballet, Leningrad
*Adagio* (originally part of *Autographs*, 1981; mus. Albinoni), Kirov Ballet, Leningrad
1989 *Pinnochio* (ballet for children; mus. Offenbach), Leningrad Theatre of Contemporary Ballet, Leningrad
*Les Intrigues de l'amour* (mus. Rossini), Les Ballets de Monte Carlo, Monte Carlo
1990 *Intrigues of Love* (new production; mus. Rossini), Boris Eifman Ballet Theatre, Leningrad
*The Passions of Man* (mus. Sarmanto), Boris Eifman Ballet Theatre, Leningrad
1991 *The Murderers* (mus. Raken), Boris Eifman Ballet Theatre, Leningrad

## PUBLICATIONS


Demidov, Aleksandr, "New Choreographers Emerging in the Soviet Union", *Dance News* (New York), March 1979

Ansett, Martine, "Le Concours de Moscow: les nuits blanches de Leningrad", *Pour la danse* (Paris), October 1981

Parks, Gary, "Soviet Artist in New Works", *Dance Magazine* (New York), July 1987

Sirvin, René, "Un Béjart Sovietique", *Le Figaro* (Paris), 29 July 1988

Vanslov, Viktor, "Leningrad Ballet Ensemble" (reprinted and translated from *Sovetsky Balet*, Moscow), *Dance Magazine* (New York), July 1989

Koegler, Horst, "One from Russia", *Dance and Dancers* (London), February 1990

*Ballet Théâtre de Leningrad: Boris Eifman* (pamphlet), Théâtre des Champs-Elysées Festival de Danse Sovietique, Paris, 1990

Whyte, Sally, "St. Petersburg Ballet Theatre: Prague Spring Festival", *Dance and Dancers* (London), August 1992


* * *

Boris Eifman is one of Leningrad/St. Petersburg's leading dance personalities, and an important force in contemporary Russian culture as the director of his own dance theatre. This theatre was established in Leningrad in 1977 and has gone by various names, including the "New Ballet", the "Leningrad Ballet Ensemble," the "Leningrad Theatre of Contemporary Ballet", and since 1990, the "Leningrad Boris Eifman Ballet Theatre", taking on the name of St. Petersburg when Leningrad reverted to its original name in 1992. The theatre's original aim was to attract young people to the ballet, and it is most likely for this reason that the innovative young ballet master Boris Eifman was invited to put the company together. The repertoire of the theatre consists entirely of ballets staged by this ballet master, and therefore its history is closely tied to Eifman's own creative background.

Eifman completed ballet school in Kishinev in 1964. In 1972, he completed his studies in the ballet master department of the Leningrad Conservatory (under the tutelage of Georgi Aleksidze) and became ballet master at the Leningrad School of Choreography. He staged two full-length ballets: *Gayané* (to the music of Khachaturian) at the Maly Theatre, and *Firebird* (to the music of Stravinsky) at the Kirov Theatre. Both productions were original versions of the ballets.

Eifman belonged to the generation of Soviet ballet masters (Igor Chernyshev, Georgi Aleksidze, later, Leonid Lebedev, and others) who tried at the end of the 1960s and the beginning of the 1970s to change traditional Russian ballet and make it more contemporary. The first programme at the new theatre (1977) consisted of ballet miniatures to music by contemporary composers: Schedrin's *Only Love*, Kalnin's rock-ballet *The Song Broken*, and a ballet entitled *Bivocality*, to the music of the rock group Pink Floyd. In 1978, Eifman revived his ballet *Firebird*. With the staging in 1980 of the ballet *The Idiot*, based on Dostoevsky's novel, to the music of Tchaikovsky's Symphony No. 6, a new stage in Eifman's work began, and with it the Theatre's creative life bloomed.

The Soviet ballet master Leonid Yakobson, and the Western choreographers Béjart, Petit, Neumeier, and Kylián greatly influenced Eifman's creative style. But Eifman's choreographic identity, from his very first ballets on the stage of the School of Choreography, was entirely his own. His choreography is called "modern", but the word does not mean the same as it does in the West. The foundation of Eifman's choreographic style is classical dance, but radically changed and technically complex, combined with a free plasticity and acrobatics. His choreography "attacks" the audience, and his duets are passionate, emotional, and aesthetically refined. Thus, in creating a contemporary choreographic language, Eifman remains faithful to one of the most important traditions of twentieth-century Russian ballet: the search for a new means of expression is not an end in itself, but rather a means to express emotional images and philosophical ideas. Eifman creates theatrical performances combining choreography and drama, but devoid of pantomime. The basis of his one-act ballets and miniatures is character clash, the hero's attempt at spirituality, and the eternal themes of good and evil, freedom and violence, and love and power. The repertoire of the Eifman Theatre consists of one-act ballet performances and two evenings of miniatures to the music of various composers such as *Autographs* and *Metamorphoses*.

His ballet performances are often fantasies on themes from works of literature, for example: *Second Lieutenant Romashov* (based on Kuprin's *The Duel*, to the music of Gavrilin) and *The Master and Margarita* (based on Bulgakov's novel of the same name, to the music of Petrov). The repertoire also includes Eifman's comedic, almost buffoonish ballets *Day of Madness* (based on Beaumarchais, to the music of Rossini) and *The Twelfth Night* (based on Shakespeare's play, to the music of Donizetti). In 1989, Eifman staged a children's ballet of *Pinocchio*, based on the Italian fairy tale and a literary adaptation by the Soviet writer A. Tolstoy, to the music of Offenbach.

The company is made up of 50 people. A particularly outstanding dancer, Valery Mikhailovsky, former premier dancer with the Odessa Ballet, has been with the company from its beginning. In 1978, Valentina Morozova, a former dancer with the Kuibyshev Ballet Theatre, became the prima ballerina of the Eifman Theatre. Over the years such stars of the Soviet ballet as Alla Osipenko, Maris Liepa, Nikita Dolgushin, and

Galina Mezentseva, as well as John Markovsky and Vadim Pisarev, have performed with the Theatre.

—Nina Alovert

---

## LES ÉLÉMENTS

**Choreography:** Jules Perrot
**Music:** Bajetti
**Design:** Charles Marshall
**Libretto:** Jules Perrot
**First Production:** Her Majesty's Theatre, London, 26 June 1847
**Principal Dancers:** Carlotta Grisi (Fire), Carolina Rosati (Water), Fanny Cerrito (Air)

### PUBLICATIONS

Michel, Arthur, "*Pas de Quatre* 1845–1945", *Dance Magazine* (New York), July 1945
Beaumont, Cyril, *Complete Book of Ballets*, revised edition, London, 1951
Guest, Ivor, *The Romantic Ballet in England*, London, 1954
Guest, Ivor, *Fanny Cerrito*, London, 1956
Guest, Ivor, *Jules Perrot: Master of the Romantic Ballet*, London, 1984

* * *

*Les Éléments* was the third Jules Perrot ballet produced for Her Majesty's Theatre, London, to exploit the competitive spirit that characterized the great Romantic ballerinas. *Pas de quatre* (1845) had delighted audiences with the novelty of presenting the reigning stars together on the same stage in a sort of Terpsichorean contest. A year later *Le Jugement de Pâris* (1846) firmly established the expectation that each season would include such a divertissement ballet by Perrot. In 1847, *Les Éléments* dutifully presented the impressive trio of Carlotta Grisi, Carolina Rosati, and Fanny Cerrito in a battle of Earth, Air, Fire, and Water (Earth was represented by the corps de ballet).

*Les Éléments* was the most complex of the divertissements presented thus far. It appears that not even Perrot, with his genius for creating pure dance, was able to refrain from elaboration, shifting away from the elegant simplicity that marked *Pas de quatre* as a masterpiece. The first scene of *Les Éléments* represented a woody landscape, at the back of which was a clump of foliage that divided to allow the entrance of a corps of yellow-clad nymphs representing Earth. After a short pas d'ensemble, the clump of foliage sank under the ground to

**Carolina Rosati, Carlotta Grisi and Fanny Cerrito in Les Éléments, London, 1847**

be replaced by a lake across which glided a boat bearing Rosati (Water), "surrounded", as a contemporary observer described it, "by dolphins and fabulous creatures of the piscatory race, and waited on by a second bevy of nymphs, decked out in robes of blue". The earth nymphs and water nymphs performed a dance, after which Rosati executed a swimming solo. Suddenly a volcano erupted, spilling onto the stage a host of red salamanders and their leader Grisi (Fire). Grisi too danced a solo, but unlike Rosati, she did "not attempt to mimic what she conceives to be the form and qualities of fire, contenting herself with a step in which the graces and wonders of her art are exquisitely developed". As the volcano disappeared, clouds rolled in bearing Cerrito (Air) and her company of nymphs in white transparent gauze. At first, there was antagonism between the elements. Fire shunned Water, but Air reconciled the enemies and they executed a beautiful pas de trois that began with a pose after Raphael's "Graces" (Perrot frequently drew inspiration for poses and groupings from famous paintings and sculptures). Further solos, pas de deux, and pas de trois followed, climaxing with the three ballerinas circling the entire stage.

Divertissement ballets such as *Les Éléments* were a radical departure from convention. Ever since the latter days of the eighteenth century, ballets told stories; dances shown in their own right were not considered worthy of serious consideration. The success of *Les Éléments* prompted one critic to assert: "The old historical ballet of action seems to have for ever departed." Predicting a bright future for ballet, he claims that the "aged deem this rebellion—the youthful revolution". He is pleased that the "classical and didactic" has been replaced by the "romantic and the ideal". But what he viewed as revolution was really the death throes of the romantic ballet in London. Stories disappeared, not because romanticism demanded it (after all, the romantic masterpieces *La Sylphide* and *Giselle* were highly dramatic), but because audiences were only interested in the glamourous star ballerinas, not the artistic substance of ballet. The tenuousness of the works, and their dependence on their stars for success, are underlined by the fact that none of the four great divertissements by Jules Perrot were performed after their initial runs (despite the oft-recognized brilliance of the choreography). Powerful as Perrot's choreography was, his divertissement ballets were not allowed to survive without their stars.

—John Chapman

---

## ELITE SYNCOPATIONS

**Choreography:** Kenneth MacMillan
**Music:** Scott Joplin, Scott Hayden, Paul Pratt, James Scott, Joseph F. Lamb, Max Morath, Donald Ashwander, Robert Hampton
**Design:** Ian Spurling (costumes)
**First Production:** Royal Ballet, Royal Opera House, London, 7 October 1974
**Principal Dancers:** Monica Mason (Calliope Rag), Jennifer Penney and David Wall (Golden Hours), Merle Park (Stop-Time Rag, Bethena Waltz), Vergie Derman and Wayne Sleep (Alaskan Rag), Donald MacLeary (Bethena Waltz), Michael Coleman (Friday Night)

**Other productions include:** Sadler's Wells Royal Ballet, with Marion Tait (Stop-Time Rag, Bethena Waltz), Lois Strike (Calliope Rag), Christine Aitken and Carl Myers (Golden Hours), Desmond Kelly (Bethena Waltz), Vivyan Lorrayne and Brian Bertscher (Alaskan Rag), David Ashmole (Friday Night); London, 10 February 1978. National Ballet of Canada, Toronto, 10 November 1978. Houston Ballet (staged Monica Parker after MacMillan); Houston, 6 September 1990.

### PUBLICATIONS

Vaughan, David, "The Royal Ballet in Munchkinland", *Dancing Times* (London), November 1974
Williams, Peter, and Goodwin, Noël, "*Elite Syncopations*", *Dance and Dancers* (London), December 1974
Balanchine, George, with Mason, Francis, *Balanchine's Complete Stories of the Great Ballets*, Garden City, N.Y., 1977
Brinson, Peter, and Crisp, Clement, *Ballet and Dance: A Guide to the Repertory*, London, 1980
Thorpe, Edward, *Kenneth MacMillan: The Man and his Ballets*, London, 1985

* * *

The idea of basing a ballet on ragtime music was suggested to MacMillan by Austin Bennett. At the time, MacMillan was too busy working on *Manon* to take up the suggestion; by the time his work on *Manon* was over, the film *The Sting*, with its popular ragtime score, had already been released, and a couple of dance works had already been choreographed to ragtime. MacMillan, however, was undeterred.

He chose twelve ragtime pieces, five by Scott Joplin (including the eponymous *Elite Syncopations*), two by Joseph F. Lamb, and one each by Donald Ashwander, Robert Hampton, Max Morath, Paul Pratt, and James Scott. To these, he choreographed dances which ranged from solos (such as *Friday Night Rag*) through duets (*Golden Hours Rag*) and a pas de quatre (*Hothouse Rag*) to ensembles such as the final *Cataract Rag*, in which the whole company participated. The Royal Ballet's leading dancers showed off their comic talents; the lofty Vergie Derman and the diminutive Wayne Sleep performed a slapstick pas de deux, Monica Mason appeared solo as a burlesque queen, and Merle Park and Donald MacLeary flaunted their virtuosity in a duet. For all its earthy humour, the choreography of *Elite Syncopations* called upon all the dancers' classical training.

MacMillan did not commission a new set for the ballet, preferring to open up the Covent Garden stage as far as the back wall of the theatre, where the flats and props for other ballets in the repertory were stacked. This suggested the seedy atmosphere of a New Orleans dance hall. Philip Gammon's twelve-piece band, complete with pianist/conductor, was placed centre back of the stage, and bentwood chairs stood in two rows to accommodate dancers whenever they were "sitting out".

Ian Spurling's costumes added to the comic effect. The dancers wore leotard costumes in brilliant colours, decorated with spots, stripes, hearts, arrows, and stars, and topped with outrageous hats. (The critic Richard Buckle complained that the costumes "prevented you from seeing the dancing" and were "so full of ingenious stylizations and learned, witty allusions that it is like singing 'The Waste Land' in a pub".)

At its opening, in a triple bill with *Scènes de Ballet* and *Song of the Earth*, the ballet provoked the audience to appreciative laughter. The critics, however, were less convinced of its appeal; most assumed that MacMillan had created the ballet in the aftermath of *The Sting*'s success and thought that it would not survive. Other critics disapproved of the ballet's "salon

**Elisabeth McGorian and Jonathan Burrows in *Elite Syncopations*, Royal Ballet, London**

vulgarity" and of the sight of "so many noble dancers poking their bottoms out". Nevertheless, the enthusiasm of the audience and the dancers themselves prevailed, winning the ballet a place in the repertoire of the Royal Ballet touring company. In 1978 *Elite Syncopations* was staged by the National Ballet of Canada.

—Jessica Arah

---

**ELSSLER, Fanny**

Austrian dancer and choreographer. Born Franziska Elssler, sister of dancer Thérèse Elssler, in Gumpendorf, 23 June 1810. Studied at the Ballet School (directed by Friedrich Horschelt) of Theater an der Wien; studied at Kärntnertor Theater, Vienna, pupil of Jean Aumer, from 1818; later studied with August Vestris, Paris. One son by Prince of Salerno, b. 1827; one daughter by dancer Anton Stuhlmüller, b. 1833. Début as child dancer (aged seven), Kärntnertor Theater, Vienna, 1818, continuing to perform in ballets by Taglioni, Henry, Armand Vestris, Vienna, also performing at Hoftheater, Vienna; dancer, Teatro San Carlo, Naples, 1825–27, returning to Kärntnertor Theater, 1827–30; leading ballerina, touring Europe, with appearances in Berlin, various seasons, 1830–32, London, 1833, 1834, Paris (Opéra début), 1834, Bordeaux, 1836, London, 1838, 1839; toured America, performing in New York, Boston, Philadelphia, Washington, D.C., Charleston, New Orleans, Havana, 1840–42; returned to Europe, dancing in Vienna, Berlin, Brussels, Dublin, Hamburg, and London, 1843, La Scala, Milan, 1844, Hungary, Dublin, Munich, and Turin, 1844, Venice, Florence, 1845, Covent Garden, London, and Padua, 1847; Russian début, Bolshoi Theatre, St. Petersburg, 1848, performing also in Moscow, 1848–51; last public performance, Vienna, 1851. Died in Vienna, 27 November 1884.

**ROLES**

1824 Iseult in *The Fairy and the Knight* (Armand Vestris), Kärntnertor Theater, Vienna
Louise in *Eleanore* (A. Vestris), Kärntnertor Theater, Vienna
Beda in *Bluebeard* (A. Vestris), Kärntnertor Theater, Vienna
A Page in *Les Pages du duc de Vendôme* (Aumer), Kärntnertor Theater, Vienna
1825 Dancer in *Cesare in Egitto* (Gioja), Teatro San Carlo, Naples

Rosalia (cr) in *Fedeltà e Trionfo* (Gioja), Teatro San Carlo, Naples

1826 Dancer (cr) in *Acbar, Gran Mogol* (S. Taglioni, Costa), Teatro San Carlo, Naples

Dancer in *Sofronimo e Caritea; ossia, Il Potere della bellezza* (Hus), Teatro San Carlo, Naples

Dancer in *Alcibiade* (S. Taglioni), Teatro San Carlo, Naples

Briseide in *L'Ira d'Achille* (S. Taglioni), Teatro San Carlo, Naples

Pas de huit in *Didone* (after Vigano), Teatro San Carlo, Naples

Pas de huit in *Giovanna d'Arco* (after Vigano), Teatro San Carlo, Naples

Dancer in *Selico; ossia, I Buon Figlio* (Henry), Teatro San Carlo, Naples

1827 Dancer in *Pernile* (Samengo), Teatro San Carlo, Naples

Giulietta (cr) in *Ottavio Pinelli* (Samengo), Kärntnertor Theater, Vienna

1829 Title role (cr) in *Matilde, Herzogin von Spoleto* (Astolfi), Kärntnertor Theater, Vienna

Cleopatra in *Cäsar in Egypten* (Astolfi), Kärntnertor Theater, Vienna

Amalie in *Ottavio Pinelli*, Kärntnertor Theater, Vienna

Ambrosia in *St. Clair* (Astolfi), Kärntnertor Theater, Vienna

Viviane in *The Fairy and the Knight* (Vestris), Kärntnertor Theater, Vienna

Emma in *Der Berggeist* (revival; Horschelt), Kärntnertor Theater, Vienna

1830 Pas de deux in *La Muette de Portici* (opera; Auber), Kärntnertor Theater, Vienna

Adeline (cr) in *Der Zauberring* (Albert), Kärntnertor Theater, Vienna

Leading role in *La Somnambule* (A. Titus after Aumer), Berlin

Title role in *The Swiss Milkmaid* (Titus after F. Taglioni), Berlin

Arsene in *Die Neue Amazone*, Berlin

Rosette in *Deux Mots* (opera; mus. Dalayrac), Berlin

1831 Armida in *Das befreyte Jerusalem* (Samengo), Kärntnertor Theater, Vienna

Title role (cr) in *Theodosia* (Samengo), Kärntnertor Theater, Vienna

Leading role (cr) in *Orpheus und Euridice* (Henry), Kärntnertor Theater, Vienna

Fenella in *La Muette de Portici* (opera; mus. Auber), Berlin

1832 Zoloe (cr) in *Le Dieu et la Bayadère* (opera; mus. Auber), Berlin

Lise in *La Fille mal gardée* (after Dauberval), Berlin

1833 Pas de deux in *Faust* (Deshayes), King's Theatre, London

Pas in *Flore et Zéphire* (Didelot), King's Theatre, London

Divertissement in *Ines de Castro* (Cortesi), King's Theatre, London

Viviane in *The Sorceress and the Knight* (*La Fée et le chevalier*; T. Elssler), King's Theatre, London

1834 Pas de deux (cr) in *Armide* (T. Elssler), King's Theatre, London

Alcine (cr) in *La Tempête; ou, L'Ile des génies* (Coralli), Opéra, Paris

Pas de deux (cr; chor. T. Elssler) in *Gustave* (opera; mus. Auber), Opéra, Paris

1835 Mathilde (cr) in *L'Ile des pirates* (Henry), Opéra, Paris

1836 Florinda (cr) including *La Cachucha* (solo; also chor.) in *Le Diable boîteux* (Coralli), Opéra, Paris

Principal dancer in *Natalie; ou, La Laitière suisse* (F. Taglioni), Grand Théâtre, Bordeaux

Principal dancer in *Le Carnaval de Venise* (Milon), Grand Théâtre, Bordeaux

Leading role in *La Somnambule* (Aumer), Grand Théâtre, Bordeaux

Title role in *Cendrillon* (Albert), Grand Théâtre, Bordeaux

Principal dancer in *Jean de Paris*, Grand Théâtre, Bordeaux

Title role in *La Sylphide* (Taglioni), Grand Théâtre, Bordeaux

Principal dancer in *Robert le diable* (opera; mus. Meyerbeer), Grand Théâtre, Bordeaux

1837 Title role in *Nina; ou, La Folle par amour* (Milon), Kärntnertor Theater, Vienna

Kié-li (cr) in *La Chatte métamorphosée en femme* (Coralli), Opéra, Paris

1838 Zoé (cr) in *La Volière; ou, Les Oiseaux de Boccace* (T. Elssler), Opéra, Paris

Zerlina in *Le Brigand de Terracina* (Deshayes), King's Theatre, London

Title role in *La Sylphide* (F. Taglioni), Opéra, Paris

Title role in *La Fille du Danube* (F. Taglioni), Opéra, Paris

1839 Sarah (cr), including *La Cracovienne* (solo, mazurka) in *La Gipsy* (Mazilier), Opéra, Paris

Lauretta (cr) in *La Tarentule* (Coralli), Opéra, Paris

1840 Principal dancer (cr) in *La Smolenska* (pas de caractère), Elssler's benefit performance, Opéra, Paris

Principal dancer in *L'Amour; ou, La Rose animée* (divertissement; Sylvain), Park Theatre, New York

1843 Title role in *Giselle* (Coralli, Perrot), Her Majesty's Theatre, London

Menuet and Gavotte (cr) in *Un Bal sous Louis XIV* (divertissement; Perrot), Her Majesty's Theatre, London

Principal dancer (with Cerrito; cr) in *Pas de deux* (Perrot), Her Majesty's Theatre, London

Blanche d'Oviedo (cr) in *Le Délire d'un peintre* (divertissement; Perrot), Her Majesty's Theatre, London

1844 Principal dancer in *Armida* (B. Vestris), La Scala, Milan

Principal dancer (cr) in *Venere ad Adone* (B. Vestris), La Scala, Milan

Principal dancer in *La Paysanne Grande Dame* (divertissement; Perrot), Her Majesty's Theatre, London

Title role in *La Esmeralda* (Perrot), Her Majesty's Theatre, London

1845 Beatrix in *La Jolie Fille de Gand* (Cortesi after Albert), La Scala, Milan

Title role in *Yelva; ou, L'Orpheline russe* (melodrama; Scribe), Josefstadt Theater, Vienna

Title role in *La Zingara* (Ronzani, after the scenario of *La Esmeralda*), Teatro Cumunitativo, Bologna

1847 Title role in *Catarina; ou, La Fille du bandit* (expanded version; Perrot), La Scala, Milan

Odetta (cr) in *Odetta; o, La Demenza di Carlo VI, re di Francia* (Perrot), La Scala, Milan

Principal dancer (cr) in *La Bouquetière de Venise* (divertissement; Albert), Royal Italian Opera, Covent Garden, London

Girl (cr) in *La Salamandrine* (Blasis), Royal Italian Opera, Covent Garden, London

Title role (cr) in *Manon Lescaut* (Casati after Aumer), Royal Italian Opera, Covent Garden, London

1848 Marguerite (cr) in *Faust* (Perrot), La Scala, Milan

**Fanny Elssler in *La Volière*, 1838**

1849/50 Ysaure in *La Filleule des fées* (Perrot), Bolshoi Theatre, St. Petersburg
1849 Pas de trois (cr; Perrot) added to *Lida* (Petipa; after *The Swiss Milkmaid*, Taglioni), Bolshoi Theatre, St. Petersburg
1850 Principal dancer (cr) in *The Butterfly and the Flowers* (divertissement; also chor.), Bolshoi Theatre, Moscow
Principal dancer in *La Paysanne lunatique* (Frédéric after Guérinot), Bolshoi Theatre, Moscow

## WORKS

1836 *La Cachucha* (solo) in *Le Diable boîteux* (Coralli), Opéra, Paris
1844 *Le Délire d'un peintre* (after Perrot; mus. Pugni), La Scala, Milan
1845 *La Tarantola* (after Coralli; mus. Gide), La Scala, Milan
1850 *The Butterfly and the Flowers* (divertissement), Bolshoi Theatre, Moscow

**Other works include:** *Maskerade* (with T. Elssler).

## PUBLICATIONS

Gautier, Théophile, *Portraits contemporains*, Paris, 1874
Erhard, August, *Fanny Elssler: Das Leben einer Tanzerin*, Munich, 1910
Moore, Lillian, *Artists of the Dance*, New York, 1938
Pirchan, Emil, *Fanny Elssler, Eine Wienerin Tanzt um die Welt*, Vienna, 1940
Guest, Ivor, *The Romantic Ballet in England*, London, 1954
Anderson, John Q., "Fanny Elssler and Ralph Waldo Emerson", *Dance Magazine* (New York), July 1954
Guest, Ivor, "Romantic Ballerinas in Dublin", *Dance and Dancers* (London), April 1960
Raab, Riki, *Fanny Elssler. Eine Weltfaszination*, Vienna, 1962
Guest, Ivor, *The Romantic Ballet in Paris*, London, 1966
Guest, Ivor, *Fanny Elssler*, London, 1970
*Fanny Elssler in America*, introduction and notes by Allison Delarue, New York, 1976
Oberzaucher, Alfred, and Schüller, Gunhild, "Trunkener Körper und Schwebender Geist," *Ballett: Chronik und Bilanze des Ballettjahres* (Velber), 1984
*Gautier on Dance*, edited by Ivor Guest, London, 1986
Costonis, Maureen Needham, "The Personification of Desire: Fanny Elssler and American Audiences", *Dance Chronicle* (New York), v. 13 no. 1, 1990

* * *

Fanny Elssler, a contemporary of Marie Taglioni and one of the greatest dancers of all time, won critical acclaim from balletomanes, critics, and fans from Moscow to Havana. She epitomized the earthy, dramatic side of Romantic ballet as opposed to the ethereal and spiritual aspect, the terre-à-terre versus the aerial.

A native of Vienna, Elssler trained there and in Italy, where her technique was strengthened considerably, particularly her pointe work. Before making her Paris début she was coached painstakingly by Auguste Vestris, the old God of the dance. His training gave her style and finish and prepared her to face the world's most critical ballet audience at the Paris Opéra, where Taglioni reigned as Queen of the dance.

Despite her considerable strength and virtuosity, Elssler's greatest gifts seemed to lie in her dramatic and pantomimic talents. She could build a character through mime, gesture, dance, and facial expression, creating unforgettable interpretations of major heroines such as Giselle, Esmeralda, and Lise in *La Fille mal gardée*. Perhaps her most famous parts, however, were in character solos such the *Cachucha*, arranged by Elssler herself for inclusion in Jean Coralli's early Romantic ballet *Le Diable boîteux*, and Mazilier's wonderful Mazurka, the *Cracovienne*, included in the ballet *La Gipsy*. While the latter was coquettish and frolicsome, the former, based on classical Spanish dancing, was sensual and flirtatious. Théophile Gautier, the leading dance critic of the time, compared Elssler to Taglioni on several occasions, calling Taglioni a Christian dancer as opposed to Elssler, the pagan dancer, and asserted that Elssler was a dancer for men, while Taglioni appealed more to women.

Elssler's partners over the years included many of the greatest dancers of the time. Anton Stuhlmüller, a fellow Viennese dancer, served as Colas to Elssler in her début appearance as Lise in Dauberval's *La Fille mal gardée* (Berlin, 1832). Jules Perrot, one of the finest dancers of the Romantic period, first partnered Elssler in London in 1834, while in St. Petersburg in 1848 it was Christian Johannson who filled the post. During her two-year American tour (1840–42), Elssler's partners were James Sylvain and Jules Martin, while members of her small troupe included the young American dancers Julia Turnbull and George Washington Smith. The impression she made on American audiences was strong and her extensive tours to many of the east coast and southern states, as well as to Havana in Cuba, resulted in regular outbursts of "Elsslermania". In Washington the Congress even adjourned early to enable the politicians to attend Elssler's first performance.

Although she was not the first Romantic ballerina to dance in Russia, Taglioni and others having preceded her by several years, Elssler's appearances in St. Petersburg and Moscow made a lasting impression on Russian audiences and dancers. She was particularly appreciated for her dramatic and miming skills as exhibited in *Giselle* and *La Fille mal gardée*. In the former, Elssler would inevitably be compared to the ballet's original Giselle, Carlotta Grisi; but London audiences, who saw Elssler's début in the role in 1843, thought the Austrian ballerina's rendering of the part equal, if not superior, to that of Grisi. Of particular note was Elssler's performance in the "mad scene" in the first act; as historian Ivor Guest has written, "Comparing the mad scenes of the two dancers, there was no doubt that Elssler's was vastly superior." Guest goes on to quote a contemporary review: "'The acting of Carlotta Grisi in this scene of delirious frenzy was of a totally different kind,' wrote the *Morning Herald*. 'It excited only occasional pity, with a passing admiration for the agility and cleverness of the dancer. Fanny Elssler does more. The situation in which she is placed exacts the sympathy, but the art—emphatic, classic art—with which she surrounds it demands the cool and deliberate respect due to original genius.'"

In *La Fille mal gardée*, Elssler again brought new meaning and expression to a ballet already made familiar by others; once more, her outstanding ability as an actress was what audiences and critics remembered. Although *Fille* had been in the St. Petersburg repertory for many years, it was given new life by Elssler. Her mime scene, when Lise is locked in the house by her mother, has been retained over the years and was recreated for Ashton's version in 1960 by Tamara Karsavina, who had danced the role in St. Petersburg in her youth.

Although their styles were diametrically opposed, Elssler's contributions to ballet equalled Taglioni's and presented the human side of the character as opposed to the spiritual. Perhaps not surprisingly, Elssler's only failure came when she performed *La Sylphide*, the ballet created for Taglioni which most perfectly displayed the ethereal grace for which she was known. Elssler's legacy remains in the tradition of dramatic ballerinas such as Karsavina, Fonteyn, Alonso, and Makarova, all of whom are renowned for their complete interpretations of ballet's greatest roles and their ability to combine technique with drama, creating memorable all-round performances.

—Carol Egan

---

**ELVIN, Violetta**

Russian/British dancer. Born Violetta Prokhorova in Moscow, 3 November 1925. Studied at the Moscow Choreographic School (Bolshoi Ballet School), pupil of Koschylova, Agrippina Vaganova, Elisaveta Gerdt, and Victor Semenov, 1934–42. Married (1) Harold Elvin, c.1945; (2) Fernando Savaressi: one child. Soloist, Bolshoi Ballet, 1942, State Theatre, Tashkent, 1943, Bolshoi Ballet at Kuibyshev (during World War II evacuation), 1944, and Moscow, 1945–46; principal dancer, Sadler's Wells Ballet, 1946–56, with début as Princess Florisse (Bluebird Pas de deux); guest artist, London Festival Ballet, 1950, La Scala, Milan, 1952 and 1953, Ballet Rambert, 1955; also appeared in Copenhagen, 1954, South America, 1955, Stockholm, 1956; performed in pantomime *Where the Rainbow Ends* (chor. K. Lester, 1955) and on television and films, including *The Queen of Spades* (dir. Dickinson, 1948), *Melba* (dir. Milestone, 1953); retired from stage to Italy: ballet director, Teatro San Carlo, Naples, 1985–86.

**ROLES**

1942 Odette/Odile in *Swan Lake* (after Petipa, Ivanov), Tashkent State Theatre, Tashkent
1946 Pas de deux in *Les Patineurs* (Ashton), Sadler's Wells Ballet, London
The Betrayed Girl in *The Rake's Progress* (de Valois), Sadler's Wells Ballet, London
Bluebird in *The Sleeping Beauty* (Petipa; staged Sergeyev, Ashton, de Valois), Sadler's Wells Ballet, London
1947 Black Queen in *Checkmate* (de Valois), Sadler's Wells Ballet, London
The Miller's Wife in *The Three-Cornered Hat* (Massine), Sadler's Wells Ballet, London
1948 The Fairy Summer (cr) in *Cinderella* (Ashton), Sadler's Wells Ballet, London
Title role in *Cinderella* (Ashton), Sadler's Wells Ballet, London
La Morte amoureuse in *Don Juan* (Ashton), Sadler's Wells Ballet, London
Odette in *Swan Lake*, Act II (Petipa, Ivanov; staged Sergeyev), Sadler's Wells Ballet, London
Princess Aurora in *The Sleeping Beauty* (Petipa; staged Sergeyev, Ashton, de Valois), Sadler's Wells Ballet, London
1950 Principal dancer (cr) in *Ballabile* (Petit), Sadler's Wells Ballet, London
Principal dancer in *Ballet Imperial* (Balanchine), Sadler's Wells Ballet, London
Dulcinea in *Don Quixote* (de Valois), Sadler's Wells Ballet, London
Odette/Odile in *Swan Lake* (Petipa, Ivanov; staged Sergeyev), Sadler's Wells Ballet, London
1951 Lykanion (cr) in *Daphnis and Chloë* (Ashton), Sadler's Wells Ballet, London
Title role in *Giselle* (Petipa after Coralli, Perrot; staged Sergeyev), Sadler's Wells Ballet, London
Title role in *Tiresias* (Ashton), Sadler's Wells Ballet, London
1952 Title role in *Sylvia* (Ashton), Sadler's Wells Ballet, London
Principal dancer in *Macbeth* (opera; mus. Verdi, chor. Milloss), La Scala, Milan
Title role in *La Gioconda* (Massine), La Scala, Milan
1953 Queen of the Waters (cr) in *Homage to the Queen* (Ashton), Sadler's Wells Ballet, London
La Favorita (cr) in *Veneziana* (Howard), Sadler's Wells Ballet, London
1956 Principal dancer (cr) in *Birthday Offering* (Ashton), Sadler's Wells Ballet, London
Title role in *The Firebird* (Fokine), Sadler's Wells Ballet, London

**Other roles include:** Fairy of the Crystal Mountain in *The Sleeping Beauty* (Petipa; staged Sergeyev, de Valois), Columbine in *Carnaval* (Fokine), Cossack Girl in *La Boutique fantasque* (Massine).

**PUBLICATIONS**

By Elvin:
"For Dancers", *Ballet Today* (London), November 1954
"Violetta Elvin Writes", *Ballet Today* (London), January 1955, July 1955

About Elvin:
Alvalez, Elka, "Meet Violetta Elvin", *Ballet Today* (London), June 1952
Swinson, Cyril, *Violetta Elvin*, London, 1953
Fisher, Hugh, *Violetta Elvin*, London, 1953
Davidson, Gladys, *Ballet Biographies*, revised edition, London, 1954
"Personality of the Month: Violetta Elvin", *Dance and Dancers* (London), June 1956
Briansky, Oleg, "A Day with Violetta Elvin", *Ballet Today* (London), March 1962

* * *

From its earliest years the Sadler's Wells Ballet had occasionally drawn upon the talents of Russian dancers who had been trained in the traditions of the Imperial Russian Ballet—most notably its first ballerina, Alicia Markova, and occasionally, Lydia Lopokova. The first Soviet-trained dancer to appear with the Sadler's Wells Ballet, indeed the first Russian-born dancer to become a permanent member of the company, was Violetta Prokhorova, who was later to change her name to Elvin.

She trained at the Bolshoi Ballet School, where her teachers included Elisaveta Gerdt and Agrippina Vaganova, and graduated to the Bolshoi Ballet as a soloist in 1942. A period at the Tashkent State Theatre followed, where the ballerina danced her first principal roles, including her début as Odette/Odile. She later returned to Moscow, where she met and married Englishman Harold Elvin, accompanying him to England in 1945. Elvin joined the Sadler's Wells Ballet just before it made its début at the Royal Opera House.

**Violetta Elvin**

The Royal Opera House had a considerably larger stage and auditorium than the Sadler's Wells Ballet dancers had been used to, and not surprisingly it took them a little time to adjust. It was Elvin, trained in the Soviet style and used to the huge spaces of the Bolshoi, who had the requisite attack to cover the stage and the projection necessary to carry to the farthest corners of the building.

At first, Elvin's strong, forthright style needed to develop subtlety, and her technique was not always secure; but her elegant carriage and beautiful proud arms hinted at what might develop. In the early 1950s, she achieved a new maturity, especially in the classics. If she was a somewhat exotic Giselle and did not exploit to the full the drama and emotion of the role, her Princess Aurora was a delightfully rounded interpretation, developing from a youthful charm in the first act to a steady heartfelt radiance in the last, and understanding to the full the splendour of the role. Most satisfying was her Odette, in which her proud, noble carriage, expressive arabesques, and fluid arms found perfect expression.

Ashton created for her the langorous Fairy Summer in *Cinderella*, and she was later a touching exponent of the title role, achieving at her transformation a gracious, happy radiance. She was also the first Lykanion in Ashton's *Daphnis and Chloë*, which exploited her exotic beauty. Elvin followed Margot Fonteyn into a number of roles, notably Sylvia, La Morte amoureuse in *Don Juan* (when she replaced an injured Fonteyn at the première), the female Tiresias, and Dulcinea-Aldonza Lorenzo in *Don Quixote*. Her dark, alluring beauty and fiery attack admirably suited the Miller's Wife in the revival of *The Three-Cornered Hat*. Through the years, Elvin's technique developed speed and brilliance, making her especially satisfying in *Ballet Imperial*.

She retired from dancing before reaching her final maturity as an artist, and her warmth and joyous attack were to be much missed by her faithful Opera House audience.

—Sarah C. Woodcock

---

## ENGLISH NATIONAL BALLET

(formerly London Festival Ballet)

British ballet company based in London. Origins in the Markova–Dolin company, founders Alicia Markova and Anton Dolin, 1935–37, performing as Gala Performances of Ballet, 1949; first performances as Festival Ballet, managed by impresario Dr. Julian Braunsweg and artistic director Anton Dolin, in Bournemouth, followed by season at Stoll Theatre, London, 1950; established regular seasons at Royal Festival Hall, London, from 1952, while also touring extensively within Britain and abroad; performed as London's Festival Ballet, from 1951, and as London Festival Ballet, from 1969; renamed English National Ballet, June 1989. Official school associated with company, English National Ballet School, based at Markova House, London, founded in 1988. Current artistic director of English National Ballet (succeeding Peter Schaufuss): Ivan Nagy.

### PUBLICATIONS


Swinson, Cyril, *London's Festival Ballet*, London, 1958

Dolin, Anton, *Autobiography*, London, 1960

Braunsweg, Julian, *Braunsweg's Ballet Scandals*, London, 1973

Hodgson, Moira, "London Festival Ballet: Looking at its First Quarter-Century, 1950–1975", *Dance Magazine* (New York), November 1976

Gillard, David, *Beryl Grey*, London, 1977

Gilpin, John, *A Dance with Life*, London, 1982

Percival, John, "A Hope for Festival", *Dance and Dancers* (London), November 1984

Teverson, Claire, "London Festival Ballet", in White, Joan (ed.), *Twentieth-Century Dance in Britain*, London, 1985

"Forty Years On", *Dance and Dancers* (London), July 1990

Pritchard, Jane, *English National Ballet* (booklet), London, 1990


* * *

The company now known as English National Ballet emerged from the British tours, from 1949, of "Gala Performances" designed to show off the talents of Alicia Markova and Anton Dolin. As a result of their experiences with successive Markova–Dolin companies in Britain and America, the stars agreed that the new group should not bear their names (which relieved them of the obligation to dance at every performance). 1951 was "Festival of Britain" year, and Markova proposed the title of Festival Ballet which, with the extra word London to identify the company's base, proved a more than satisfactory name for almost four decades. The company was renamed English National Ballet in 1989 to emphasize its importance both nationally and internationally.

In many respects the first Markova–Dolin company (1935–37) which had toured the British Isles extensively, giving eight performances a week, was the model for the new company. It also had a mixed repertory of nineteenth-century classics, works created by Diaghilev's choreographers, Fokine and Nijinska, and newly created ballets. English National Ballet has concentrated on major nineteeth-century ballets, adding to more familiar works an important Bournonville repertory. It also has a tradition of keeping alive those ballets created for the successive Ballets Russes companies, including masterworks by Fokine (supervised by Nicholas Beriozoff), Massine, and Lichine. Indeed, its rich Fokine repertory led to the company being used to portray Diaghilev's company in Herbert Ross's 1979 film *Nijinsky*. London Festival Ballet's repertory initially was modelled on those of the second-generation Ballets Russes companies, and links with their past were highlighted by London Festival Ballet's regular visits to Monte Carlo during the 1950s.

English National Ballet has never been a notably innovative company determined to challenge its audience. The creation of new ballets takes a secondary role in programme planning, although *The Snow Maiden* (1961) by Vladimir Burmeister and Rudolf Nureyev's vividly dramatic *Romeo and Juliet* (1977) were acclaimed full-evening works. Shorter, more contemporary creations have included Michael Charnley's jazz-style *Symphony for Fun* (1952), Barry Moreland's *The Prodigal Son (in Ragtime)* (1974)—one of the first ballets to use Scott Joplin's music—and Christopher Bruce's dramatic and disturbing *Swansong* (1987). Other choreographers who have contributed significantly to the repertory include Anton Dolin, Jack Carter, Ronald Hynd, and Ben Stevenson, all of whom have staged versions of the classics as well as their own choreography. The ballet most closely associated with English National Ballet must be *The Nutcracker*, which it has established as a popular Christmas treat in Britain, just as New York City Ballet has in America. It has been presented in seven different productions and has received almost 1,800 performances to date.

From the start the company's dancers came from many countries, and their training and experience did much to enrich ballet in Britain. With a focus on well-established works it was

**English National Ballet (previously London Festival Ballet) in Ashton's *Romeo and Juliet***

easy to promote a star system which brought in internationally acclaimed dancers as guests for short periods. The actual policy of the company has hardly changed from when it was established by the first artistic director, Anton Dolin, and his administrator, the Polish impresario Julian Braunsweg. Essentially it aimed to present popular ballet of high quality with international star casts at affordable prices to audiences throughout Britain. The company's international outlook attracted the attention of foreign promoters, and from 1951 London Festival Ballet toured extensively abroad as well as in Britain. Its raison d'être has always been to perform. In most years it has presented more performances than any other British company. In the early years the repertory was simply selected to suit the size of the venue; more recently, individual tours have catered for both larger and smaller stages.

The company's first London season was presented at the Stoll Theatre, one of the finest dance houses in the capital but one scheduled for demolition—so from 1952 Julian Braunsweg took advantage of the newly opened Royal Festival Hall for the company's London performing base. The Festival Hall was built primarily for orchestral concerts; although the company found the means to adapt it and build a proscenium stage, it has never been an ideal venue for ballet, and from 1969 the company was seen to greater advantage at the London Coliseum, which facilitated the introduction of more spectacular productions. This was important, as in the 1960s the company was responding to a change in the taste of its audience, who now demanded full-evening productions in preference to mixed bills.

Markova remained with London Festival Ballet as ballerina until 1952, and thereafter appeared as a regular guest until her retirement in 1964. She maintains her involvement with the company (of which she became president in 1986) and remains responsible for the current production of *Les Sylphides* (1976); she also coached the principal dancers for Peter Schaufuss's 1986 production of *The Nutcracker*. Dolin retired as artistic director in 1960, when he was giving up many of his favourite roles, but he retained a life-long interest guesting as Drosselmeyer until 1980. Braunsweg continued to pilot the company, funding it privately for twelve years, until forced out in 1965 by the need for it to become a primarily grant-aided organization. Donald Albery re-styled the company with artistic assistance from Norman McDowell and Jack Carter, who brought into it the residue of their London Ballet. They began the policy of restaging the classics, which continued under the directorships of Beryl Grey and John Field. These two former members of the Royal Ballet drew on their own backgrounds and the company rather lost some of its individuality, although both did a great deal to encourage and promote talent from within the organization.

Peter Schaufuss's appointment as artistic director emphasized the company's long-standing links with Denmark, evidenced by the long list of Danish dancers and choreographers who have worked with it. The company has performed Bournonville's ballets with admirably authentic style, and Harald Lander's *Études* has been its signature work since 1955. Schaufuss extended the range of the repertory but, as under his successor Ivan Nagy, the quality of the choreography was sometimes open to question.

The constant need to tour and the lack, until 1977, of a

permanent base have posed considerable challenges to the company—but it has built up its own partisan and enthusiastic following. It has always presented strong male dancers alongside its ballerinas (indeed, in 1957 Dolin choreographed a showpiece for four male virtuosos, *Variations for Four*). It has a wonderfully energetic spirit and an infectious joie de vivre which informs both light-hearted works, such as Lichine's *Graduation Ball*, and technically brilliant showpieces, like Lander's *Études* and Balanchine's *Bourrée fantasque*. A sense of real aristocratic grandeur was achieved with Nureyev's *The Sleeping Beauty* (1975), but the company's heart seems rather to be with romantic works, such as the two productions of *Giselle* by Dolin in 1950 and Mary Skeaping in 1971 respectively, and of *La Sylphide* by Schaufuss, which, together with Cranko's emotionally vivid *Onegin* and Ashton's lyrical *Romeo and Juliet*, have elicited enduringly memorable performances of the highest quality from company members and guests alike.

—Jane Pritchard

---

## ENIGMA VARIATIONS
(Subtitled *My Friends Pictured Within*)

**Choreography:** Frederick Ashton
**Music:** Edward Elgar
**Design:** Julia Trevelyan Oman (scenery and costumes)
**First Production:** Royal Ballet, Royal Opera House, London, 25 October 1968
**Principal Dancers:** Derek Rencher (Edward Elgar), Svetlana Beriosova (The Lady—Elgar's Wife), Stanley Holden (Hew David Steuart-Powell), Brian Shaw (Richard Baxter Townshend), Alexander Grant (William Meath Baker), Robert Mead (Richard P. Arnold), Vyvyan Lorrayne (Isabel Fitton), Anthony Dowell (Arthur Troyte Griffith), Georgina Parkinson (Winnifred Norbury), Desmond Doyle (A. J. Jaeger), Antoinette Sibley (Dora Penny-Dorabella), Wayne Sleep (George Robertson Sinclair), Deanne Bergsma (Lady Mary Lygon)

**Other productions include:** (Tudor's) London Ballet (earlier version to same music; chor. Frank Staff); Cambridge, 1940.

### PUBLICATIONS

Porter, Andrew, "*Enigma Variations*", *About the House* (London), March 1969
Monahan, James, "Reflections", *Dancing Times* (London), May 1969
Anderson, Jack, "Party Manners and Frederick Ashton", *Ballet Review* (Brooklyn, N. Y.), vol. 3, no. 4, 1970
Kirstein, Lincoln, *Movement and Metaphor*, New York, 1970
Balanchine, George, with Mason, Francis, *Balanchine's Complete Stories of the Great Ballets*, Garden City, N.Y., 1977
Vaughan, David, *Frederick Ashton and his Ballets*, London, 1977

* * *

Elgar's *Enigma Variations* are a series of character studies, thematically linked by the unstated "enigma" theme. Frank Staff had choreographed the score in 1940 but it was an abstract, if very imaginative, treatment—an approach which Ashton rejected: "I could have taken the music and done a series of dances. But this somehow didn't appeal to me. Then I hit upon the idea of using the actual people who were written about musically and this began to fascinate me. I did a lot of study on them and read biographies to try and get under the skin of it." Ashton went on to point out that when Elgar's daughter, who is now a very old lady, came to see it she said, "I don't understand how you did it because they were exactly like that." Certainly when Ashton wanted to be naturalistic and historically accurate he was, but for all the meticulous detail of Julia Trevelyan Oman's décor, the ballet transcends its specific context.

Various interpretations have been offered for *Enigma Variations*. Lincoln Kirstein saw in it "a metaphor for the success of British ballet" as well as a "commentary on the decline of an empire", and it is true that Ashton felt a certain nostalgia for Elgar's England. Andrew Porter took Ashton's theme to be "the loneliness of the creative artist, the sense of desolation which not the sunlight of friends, nor the moments of triumph, not even the shining steady ray of a loving helpmate, can dispel for long", a reading which squares with Ashton's own experience. The essential point is that *Enigma Variations* is a densely layered work and easily bears a weight of metaphor beyond the scope of any merely naturalistic work.

Undoubtedly *Enigma Variations* has a profoundly meditative quality. The setting includes both the outside and the inside of Elgar's house and it may well be, as David Vaughan remarks, that the action is "simultaneously interior and exterior in another sense—that it takes place in the memory of the protagonist rather than in actuality." In other words, Ashton presents Elgar's friends not literally as they were, but as he might have remembered them.

Elgar's—and Ashton's—subtitle is *My Friends Pictured Within*, and the ballet offers a series of portraits which are Chekhovian both in their range of idiosyncrasy and pathos, and in the affection which transmutes shortcoming into foible and quotidian virtue into a sort of unique glory. Undoubtedly Ashton drew on the individual and distinguished abilities of his original cast, and to a certain extent they too have a right to be thought of as the friends the choreographer pictured within his work.

*Enigma Variations* has a firm classical base which subsumes passages of gesture and movement—as naturalistic as children's games and bicycle-riding, as stylized as the Loïe Fuller-like manipulation of draperies in the final variation—and, often most significantly, stillness. The ballet breathes, the dance animates itself spontaneously yet with deep feeling. For instance the Nimrod variation, a duet that becomes a trio, moves from "real" walking into a simple but most eloquent dance which, in turn, as the moment of intensity passes, subsides back into walking. The choreography here, as throughout the ballet, is as economical as it is poignant. Ashton's subject is not some vivid passion but friendship, loyalty, support, affection, kindness, grace—the calm attendants equally of civilized living and of civilized art.

—Martin Wright

---

## L'EPREUVE D'AMOUR

**Choreography:** Mikhail Fokine
**Music:** Various composers c. 1838 (originally attributed to Mozart)

***Enigma Variations*, with Desmond Doyle, Derek Rencher, and Svetlana Beriosova, Royal Ballet, London, 1968**

**Design:** André Derain
**Libretto:** Mikhail Fokine
**First Production:** (René Blum's) Ballets de Monte Carlo, Monte Carlo, 4 April 1936
**Principal Dancers:** Vera Nemchinova (Chung-Yang), André Eglevsky (The Lover), Jean Jazvinsky (The Mandarin), Anatole Obukhov (Ambassador), Helene Kirsova (The Butterfly)

**Other productions include:** Finnish National Ballet (chor. George Gé after Fokine); Helsinki, 22 March 1956. Indiana University (chor. Nicholas Beriozoff after Fokine), 1980.

## PUBLICATIONS

Goodman, G.E., "Notes on Décor: Les Ballets de Monte Carlo", *Dancing Times* (London), June 1936
Coton, A.V., *A Prejudice for Ballet*, London, 1938
Beaumont, Cyril, *Complete Book of Ballets*, revised edition, London, 1951
Fokine, Michel, *Fokine: Memoirs of a Ballet Master*, translated by Vitale Fokine, London, 1961
Anderson, Jack, *The One and Only: The Ballet Russe de Monte Carlo*, London, 1981
Horwitz, Dawn Lille, *Michel Fokine*, Boston, 1985

* * *

*L'Epreuve d'amour* was the first new ballet Fokine choreographed for René Blum's company, Les Ballets de Monte Carlo. It had its premiere at the Théâtre de Monte Carlo in 1936. Categorized as a form of "chinoiserie"—the eighteenth-century European version of Chinese figures on porcelains and screens—the ballet was said to have been inspired by the discovery at Graz of an unknown score by Mozart. To date, however, no musicologist has credited the work to Mozart, and it is now believed to be the score to a divertissement, "The Recruit", with music by various composers and first performed in Vienna in 1838. The libretto, by Fokine and the painter André Derain, who also designed the décor, was suggested by the score. It is probable that Derain first designed some of the costumes, which in turn helped inspire him and Fokine in devising the libretto.

The story, in three scenes, centres on four main characters: a Mandarin, his daughter Chung-Yang, her lover, and an Ambassador from a Western country. The first scene opens on a Chinese landscape with a group of monkeys and the pompous Mandarin, who dismisses with his stick both the monkeys and a butterfly who darts about him. The Chinese maidens enter with the lover, whose duet with Chung-Yang is interrupted by the returning Mandarin, who also dismisses him with his stick. The next scene shows the arrival of the Western Ambassador, who sets up a tent, gives out gifts, and does a spectacular dance. The young girl is left behind by her father and when the Ambassador creeps out of his tent in an attempt to seduce her, he is attacked by a dragon (the lover). The Ambassador is left poor after the lover's friends rob him, and the Mandarin consents to Chung-Yang's marriage to her beloved when he discovers the Ambassador is no longer rich. When the latter's goods are returned, the Mandarin reverses his decision—but the Ambassador refuses to be loved for his money, the lovers are carried to their wedding, and the Mandarin is left alone with the monkeys, the butterfly, and his empty visions of wealth.

Vera Nemchinova danced Chung-Yang, with André Eglevsky as the lover and Anatole Obukhov as the Ambassador. Eglevsky recalled the work as a lovely ballet where every step was performed "double", always finishing in a turned-out plié in second, which, tongue-in-cheek, was supposed to represent the "Chinese" element.

A silent rehearsal film made by the Denham Company gives occasional glimpses of what most of the London critics regarded as a fresh, witty farce and a charming fantasy. (*The Sunday Times*, however, found it childish, the music at cross-purposes with the Chinese figures.) In the film, the maidens and the butterfly perform their many fast parallel runs en pointe, and the maidens often stop and politely give each other a darting kiss. Their later tiny hand-claps for the Ambassador's virtuosity are also obviously satirical. The Mandarin's walk is flat-footed, with the heel hitting first, and his lower back is curved forward, causing his buttocks to stick out. His strong poses (sometimes with clenched fists) and the maidens' often simpering ones give the feeling of an old-fashioned melodrama. The two lovers have one pas de deux in which one or both of them are in profile to the audience: sometimes he is on the floor while she is standing or kneeling. There are many slow turns where their curved torsos move together in half-circles, or one or the other turns under the arch made by their intertwined arms.

The ballet was a favourite with audiences, and Derain's décor, with its sparse architectural motif of a few red pagoda roofs and blue mountain peaks, was considered his masterpiece for the stage.

A.V. Coton, writing later, pointed out that the near-human antics of the monkeys and the flittings of the butterfly created an obvious comparison between human and animal characteristics. Cyril Beaumont considered it a carefully constructed and refined work, and praised the beautiful groupings, with every step and gesture emerging naturally from the development of the action.

When *L'Epreuve d'amour* was brought to the United States by Denham's Ballet Russe de Monte Carlo, it received poor reviews, possibly because it was very difficult to stage and was rather neglected by the company. It was revived by Nicholas Beriozoff, who had danced in it, at Indiana University in 1980.

—Dawn Lille Horwitz

---

## LA ESMERALDA

**Choreography:** Jules Perrot
**Music:** Cesare Pugni
**Design:** William Grieve (scenery), D. Sloman (machinery), Mme. Copère (costumes)
**Libretto:** Jules Perrot, after Victor Hugo's *Nôtre Dame de Paris*
**First Production:** Her Majesty's Theatre, London, 9 March 1844
**Principal Dancers:** Carlotta Grisi (Esmeralda), Jules Perrot (Gringoire), Arthur Saint-Léon (Phoebus), Adelaide Frassi (Fleur de Lys), Antoine Louis Coulon (Quasimodo)

**Other productions include:** Teatro alla Scala (restaged Perrot), with Fanny Elssler (Esmeralda), Perrot (Gringoire); Milan, 26 December 1844. Hippolyte Monplaisir's "French Ballet Company"; Broadway Theatre, New York, 18 September 1848. Bolshoi Theatre (restaged Perrot), with Elssler, Perrot; St Petersburg, 2 January 1849 (21 December 1848 old style). Maryinsky Theatre (staged Marius Petipa after Perrot, with additional mus. Riccardo Drigo), with Virginia Zucchi (Esmeralda); St. Petersburg, 29 December (17 December old style) 1886. Kirov Ballet (staged Agrippina Vaganova after Petipa), with Tatyana Vecheslova (Esmeralda), Leonid Leontiev (Gringoire); St Petersburg, 23 April 1935. London Festival Ballet (staged Nicholas Beriozoff, mus. arranged Geoffrey Corbett, design Nicola Benois), with Natalie Krassovska (Esmeralda), John Gilpin (Gringoire); London, 14 July 1954.

**Other choreographic treatments of story:** Antonio Monticioni (Milan, 1839), Aleksandr Gorsky (*Gudule's Daughter*; Moscow, 1902), Vasily Tikhomirov (Moscow, 1926), Vladimir Burmeister (Moscow, 1950), Roland Petit (*Nôtre Dame de Paris*; Paris, 1965), Bruce Wells (*The Hunchback of Nôtre Dame*; Melbourne, 1981).

### PUBLICATIONS


Beaumont, Cyril, *Complete Book of Ballets*, revised edition, London, 1951

Guest, Ivor, *The Romantic Ballet in England*, London, 1954

"Curtain up: Classic Returns after 110 years", *Dance and Dancers* (London), July 1954

Guest, Ivor, "*La Esmeralda*", *Dance and Dancers* (London), July 1954

Moore, Lillian, "*Esmeralda* in America; Festival Ballet Brings us a New Production of a Century-old Masterpiece", *Dance Magazine* (New York), October 1954

Kirstein, Lincoln, *Movement and Metaphor: Four Centuries of Ballet*, New York, 1970

Guest, Ivor, *Jules Perrot: Master of the Romantic Ballet*, London, 1984


* * *

Esmeralda consents to marry the poet Gringoire to save him from death at the hands of the Truands; she tells him, however, that she has married him out of pity, not love. She is desired by the evil priest, Frollo, who attempts to abduct her, but she is saved by the arrival of Phoebus and his troops. They capture Quasimodo, Frollo's henchman, but Esmeralda pleads for his release.

Despite his forthcoming marriage to Fleur de Lys, Esmeralda falls in love with Phoebus. Accompanied by Gringoire, she goes to dance at the celebrations where Phoebus, charmed by her, persuades her to dance with him.

Frollo spies upon a meeting between Phoebus and Esmer-

Mad^lle Carlotta Grisi and Mons^r Perrot
IN THE VERY ATTRACTIVE BALLET
LA ESMERALDA.


**Jules Perrot and Carlotta Grisi in *La Esmeralda*, 1844**

alda. Jealously, he stabs Phoebus and then escapes, so that Esmeralda is arrested for the murder. Frollo promises to save her if she will marry him, but Phoebus, whose wound was not mortal, appears, and declares her innocence. Frollo tries to stab Esmeralda, but is prevented by Quasimodo, who kills him.

*La Esmeralda* was the culmination of Perrot's work on the dramatic ballet that he had begun in *Ondine*. His selection of incidents from Hugo's immense work was skilful and dramatically effective. He focused upon the character of the gypsy girl, Esmeralda, and set her against a large and varied tapestry of characters. His construction was brilliant, and no part could have been removed without destroying the whole. As in *Ondine*, he alternated scenes before the drop curtain with scenes requiring the full stage, so that there was no break in the action. Ballet, which before had often been seen as a very ill-constructed theatrical form, was here a tightly knit unity, in which no character or movement was superfluous. Every individual and every movement had a part to play in the overall drama, and added to narrative, character, or atmosphere. Every role was psychologically true, expressed through its own characteristic movement, which ranged from the high aristocratic to low-life, as represented by the Truands.

The ballet was notable for its emphasis on the individual characters. Before, everything had concentrated on the ballerina, but now she was only one of a group of characters of equal importance to the story. For the first time, the corps de ballet became recognizable individuals reacting to events around them and with an important part to play in establishing the mood of the various episodes. Thus in the first scene they appeared as the raffish Truands, and in the last act as the people of Paris, exultant at the Feast of Fools, against which Esmeralda's despair as she was led to execution became all the more poignant. There were no great set pieces; the many processions and crowds did not appear only in order to give the principals a rest, as had been the case previously, but were an integral part of the whole work.

Compared with many ballets of the Romantic era, *Esmeralda* was intensely realistic, with no supernatural characters, and exotic location gave way to the teeming life of medieval Paris. As Esmeralda, Carlotta Grisi was highly praised. *The Times* hailed her as combining the "innocent playfulness of Cerrito—the arch coquetry of Elssler—and the quiet poetry of Taglioni". She created a fully three-dimensional character—a lively girl, compassionate, affectionate, coquettish, merry, pensive, and loving—but one that was part of the whole drama and not a mere "ballerina" role. The role was later taken over by Fanny Elssler, who brought to it her own particular intensity, but imbued Esmeralda with a sense of tragedy that made her less engaging than Grisi.

*Esmeralda* had the longest life of all Perrot's ballets. He mounted it in Russia in 1849, where the intense realism of his portrayal of individual characters and especially his sympathetic treatment of the mob brought him into conflict with the authorities. Even as late as 1902, when Gorsky mounted his own version, *Gudule's Daughter*, in Moscow, it was attacked as dangerous realism. The ballet underwent many revisions in Russia at the hands of Petipa, his definitive reworking for Zucchi taking place in 1886, and it was this version, as revised by Vaganova in 1935, that forms the basis of the ballet surviving in Russia today.

—Sarah C. Woodcock

---

## ÉTUDES
(Original title: *Étude*)

**Choreography:** Harald Lander
**Music:** Karl Czerny (arranged by Knudåge Riisager)
**Design:** Erik Nordgren
**First Production:** Royal Danish Ballet, Royal Theatre, Copenhagen, 15 January 1948
**Principal Dancers:** Margot Lander, Hans Brenaa, Svend Erik Jensen

**Other productions include:** Royal Danish Ballet (restaged, with some revisions, Lander); Copenhagen, 18 February 1951. Paris Opéra Ballet (restaged and revised Lander; design Moulene, costumes Fost), as *Études*, with Micheline Bardin, Michel Renault, Alexandre Kalioujny; Paris, 19 November 1952. London Festival Ballet (restaged and revised Lander; scenery Bernard Daydé); London, 8 August 1955. American Ballet Theatre (restaged and revised Lander; scenery Rolf Gerard, costumes Barbara Karinska); with Toni Lander, Royes Fernandez, Bruce Marks; New York, 5 October 1961. Danish television (restaged and revised Lander); Copenhagen, 1969.

### PUBLICATIONS

Barnes, Clive, with Hunt, David, and Williams, Peter, "New Ballet: *Études*", *Dance and Dancers* (London), February 1953
Beaumont, Cyril, *Ballets Past and Present*, London, 1955
Goodman, Saul, "Meet Harald Lander", *Dance Magazine* (New York), December 1961
Wilson, G.B.L., "A Gamble Pays Off: Success of *Études* in Cologne", *Dancing Times* (London), July 1965
Hersin, André Philippe, "A L'Opéra: *Études* et *Les Noces*", *Les Saisons de la danse* (Paris), April 1976

* * *

The idea of staging a ballet class seems to have originated with Bournonville, whose *Konservatoriet* (*The Conservatoire*, or *The Dancing School*) recalls his studies in Paris under Auguste Vestris. In 1948 Bournonville's compatriot Harald Lander used the same idea and, like Bournonville, traced the progress of the dancer from the young child working at the barre to the complex steps of the étoile. Acknowledging his source of inspiration, he included typical Bournonville steps in the choreography, such as the quarter turn, while Erik Nordgreen's original setting for the ballet (originally named *Étude*) was reminiscent of Bournonville's studio.

One of the difficulties of creating such a ballet is making it something more than a mere demonstration of technique. Other choreographers have avoided this by inserting a dramatic element into the dance-class framework. Bournonville's *Konservatoriet* was originally subtitled *A Proposal of Marriage Through a Newspaper* in reference to a sentimental sub-plot, which Lander and his collaborator Borchsenius discarded in their 1941 revival of the ballet. In Jerome Robbins's *Afternoon of a Faun* a boy and girl practise together in a classroom during the lunchbreak; the boy kisses the girl on the cheek, and she leaves the room, disturbed, while in Flemming Flindt's macabre *The Lesson*, based on a Ionesco play, a psychopathic ballet-master murders his pupil. Lander's ballet, by contrast, is purely and simply a display of ballet steps, varying only from the pattern of an ordinary ballet class in that the barres are occasionally rearranged and the dancers do not always perform the same movements at the same time. The dance critic Richard Buckle reports a conversation between a

***Études*, as performed by London Festival Ballet, 1955**

nine-year-old boy and his mother watching *Études* in 1951: '"Mummy, what are they doing?' He was answered 'The music is piano exercises and they are doing ballet exercises to them.' 'Yes, but Mummy, why are they doing them *now*?"'

This of course points to the central issue with such a work. *New Yorker* critic Arlene Croce perhaps explained it more thoroughly when she wrote in 1979:

> The ballet *Études* should have proved once and for all that classical *forms* have a structural coherence but are no more intrinsically dramatic than the harmonic series in music. The choreographer, Harald Lander, justly equates classroom combinations with Czerny keyboard exercises; the result is a smashing non-ballet.

Critics have always acknowledged the effectiveness of *Études* as a stage piece, but are hesitant to praise it as a "ballet". That shrewd observer of dance, Edwin Denby, had written in 1951 that "I thought *Études* very effective, but heavy and with little grace of spirit"; and two years later he reiterated his opinion by saying that *Études* ". . . seemed to me effective and clean, but not very distinguished".

But considered as an effective "non-ballet", as Croce would have it, *Études* is the best of its kind. It has always been immensely popular with audiences, and dancers undoubtedly relish the chance to demonstrate their craft in a straightforward, if unsubtle, fashion. Whether or not it is a compliment to its choreographer, *Études* is by far the best known of Lander's works.

—Jessica Arah

---

**EVDOKIMOVA, Eva**

American dancer. Born in Geneva, 1 December 1948. Studied at the Bavarian State Opera Ballet School, Munich, 1956–59, and at the Royal Ballet School, London, 1959–65; also studied with Maria Fay, London, Vera Volkova, Copenhagen, and with Natalia Dudinskaya, Leningrad. Married Michael Gregori, 1982. Dancer, Royal Danish Ballet, 1966–69; dancer, becoming soloist (principal), German Opera Ballet, Berlin, from 1969; international guest artist, from 1971, appearing with companies including the Kirov Ballet in Leningrad, London Festival Ballet (now English National Ballet), American Ballet Theatre, Ballet of La Scala, Milan, Tokyo Ballet, Teatro Colón in Buenos Aires, National Ballet of Canada, Zürich Ballet, Boston Ballet, and Warsaw Ballet. Recipient: Prizes at the International Ballet Competitions in Varna, 1968, and Moscow, 1969; Gold Medal, International Ballet Competition, Varna, 1970; Critics' Prize, Berlin, 1974.

**ROLES**

1966 A Lady of the Court in *The Three Musketeers* (Flindt), Royal Danish Ballet, Copenhagen
Divertissement in *The Kermesse in Bruges* (Bournonville), Royal Danish Ballet, Copenhagen
1967 Principal dancer in *Aspects* (F. Schaufuss), Royal Danish Ballet, Copenhagen
Pas de six and Tarantella in *Napoli* (Bournonville), Royal Danish Ballet, Copenhagen
1968 Pas de deux from *Flower Festival at Genzano* (Bournonville; staged von Rosen), Royal Danish Ballet, Copenhagen
Pas de quatre in *Études* (Lander), Royal Danish Ballet, Copenhagen
Pas de trois in *Donizetti Variations* (Balanchine), Royal Danish Ballet, Copenhagen
1969 Polish Dance in *Swan Lake* (Petipa, Ivanov; staged Lander), Royal Danish Ballet, Copenhagen
First and Fourth Movements in *Symphony in C* (Balanchine), German Opera Ballet, Berlin
The Tsarevna in *The Firebird* (Fokine), German Opera Ballet, Berlin
Principal dancer in *Concerto* (MacMillan), German Opera Ballet, Berlin
Principal dancer in *Episodes* II (Balanchine), German Opera Ballet, Berlin
Princess Aurora in *The Sleeping Beauty* (MacMillan after Petipa), German Opera Ballet, Berlin
1970 A Muse in *Apollo* (Balanchine), German Opera Ballet, Berlin
Waltz, Mazurka in *Les Sylphides* (Fokine), Monte Carlo Ballet
Ballerina in *Pas de quatre* (Dolin), Monte Carlo Ballet
Principal dancer (cr) in *The Scarecrows* (Luipart), German Opera Ballet, Berlin
Second Movement in *Symphony in C* (Balanchine), German Opera Ballet, Berlin
Title role in *Giselle* (Petipa after Coralli, Perrot), German Opera Ballet, Berlin
1971 Teresina in *Napoli*, Act III (Bournonville; staged von Rosen), Gothenburg Ballet, Sweden
Principal dancer in *Monotones* (Ashton), German Opera Ballet, Berlin
Title role in *La Sylphide* (Bournonville; staged Brenaa), Kathleen Crofton Ballet
Title role in *Paquita* (after Petipa), Monte Carlo Ballet
Principal dancer in *L'Histoire du soldat* (Baumann), German Opera Ballet, Berlin
Odette/Odile in *Swan Lake* (MacMillan after Petipa, Ivanov), German Opera Ballet, Berlin
Principal dancer in *Orfeo* (Walter), (Düsseldorf) German Opera on the Rhine, Saltzburg
1972 Principal dancer in *Tchaikovsky Concerto* (Balanchine), German Opera Ballet, Berlin
Principal dancer in *Fantaisies* (Clifford), German Opera Ballet, Berlin
Clemence, Raymonda's Friend in *Raymonda* (Nureyev after Petipa), Zürich Ballet
Clara/Princess in *The Nutcracker* (Flindt), Royal Danish Ballet, Copenhagen
1973 The Young Girl in *Le Spectre de la rose* (Fokine), Monte Carlo Ballet
Swanilda in *Coppélia* (Parés after Petipa), German Opera Ballet, Berlin
Juliet in *Romeo and Juliet* (Cranko), Munich State Opera Ballet
Odette/Odile in *Swan Lake* (Grey after Petipa, Ivanov), London Festival Ballet
1974 Mélisande in *Pelléas and Mélisande* (Walter), German Opera Ballet, Berlin
The Ballerina in *Petrushka* (Fokine; staged Taras), German Opera Ballet, Berlin
Juliet in *Romeo and Juliet* (Boyartchikov), German Opera Ballet, Berlin
1975 Title role in *Raymonda* (new production; T. Gsovsky, Beriozoff after Petipa), German Opera Ballet, Berlin
Nikiya in *La Bayadère* (after Petipa), German Opera Ballet, Berlin
Pas de deux from *Le Corsaire* (after Petipa), Ballet of La Scala, Milan
Kitri in *Don Quixote* (Borkovsky after Gorsky), London Festival Ballet
Princess Aurora in *The Sleeping Beauty* (Nureyev after Petipa), London Festival Ballet, London
1976 Principal dancer in *Adagio Hammerklavier* (van Manen), German Opera Ballet, Berlin
Girl in Pink in *The Sanguine Fan* (Hynd), London Festival Ballet, London
Louise (cr) in *The Nutcracker* (Hynd), London Festival Ballet, Liverpool
Pas de deux from *Spartacus* (Grigorovich), Moscow
Prelude in *Les Sylphides* (Fokine), London Festival Ballet, Birmingham
1977 The Sleepwalker in *Night Shadow* (*La Sonnambula*; Balanchine), London Festival Ballet, London
Juliet in *Romeo and Juliet* (Nureyev), London Festival Ballet
Principal dancer in *La Valse* (Balanchine), German Opera Ballet, Berlin
Principal dancer in *Daphnis and Chloë* (van Manen), German Opera Ballet, Berlin
Title role (cr) in *Cinderella* (Panov), German Opera Ballet, Berlin
Pas de deux in *Agon* (Balanchine), German Opera Ballet, Berlin
Principal dancer in *Opus 5* (Béjart), German Opera Ballet, Berlin
The Young Girl in *The Green Table* (Jooss), German Opera, Berlin
1978 Principal dancer in *Greening* (Tetley), London Festival Ballet, Oxford
Principal dancer in *Theme and Variations* (Balanchine), American Ballet Theatre
Elisa in *Conservatoire* (*Konservatoriet*; Bournonville), London Festival Ballet
Lise in *La Fille mal gardée* (Parés), German Opera Ballet, Berlin
1979 Title role in *The Firebird* (Cranko), German Opera Ballet, Berlin
Isolde in *Tristan* (Houlton), German Opera Ballet, Berlin
Nastasia (cr) in *The Idiot* (Panov), German Opera Ballet, Berlin
Title role in *Sphinx* (Tetley), London Festival Ballet, Bristol
Title role in *La Sylphide* (Schaufuss after Bournonville), London Festival Ballet, London
Clara in *The Nutcracker* (Nureyev), German Opera Ballet, Berlin
1980 Title role in *Miss Julie* (Cullberg), German Opera Ballet, Berlin
1981 A Sister in *Las Hermanas* (MacMillan), German Opera Ballet, Berlin

Principal dancer in *Childe Harold* (Spoerli), German Opera Ballet, Berlin
Ballerina in *Gala Performance* (Tudor), German Opera Ballet, Berlin
1982 Principal dancer in *Medea's Children* (Cullberg, Carbone), Teatro Regio, Turin
Teresina in *Napoli* (Bournonville; staged Schaufuss), National Ballet of Canada, Toronto
1983 Hilda in *A Folk Tale* (Bournonville; staged Schaufuss), German Opera Ballet, Berlin
1985 Lise in *La Fille mal gardée* (Ashton), Bavarian State Opera Ballet, Munich
Swanilda (cr) in *Coppélia* (Hynd), London Festival Ballet, London
1990 Odette/Odile in *Swan Lake* (Makarova after Petipa, Ivanov, Ashton), English National Ballet, London

**Other roles include:** Tatiana in *Onegin* (Cranko), the Swan in *The Dying Swan* (Fokine), Terpsichore in *Apollo* (Balanchine); principal dancer in *Grand Pas classique* (pas de deux; Gsovsky), *Unicorn* (Neumeier), *A Family Portrait* (Cullberg), *Carmencita* (Montagnon), *Transfigured Night* (Spoerli), *Undine* (Schilling).

## PUBLICATIONS

Geitel, K., "Alles über Eva", in *Ballett: Chronik und Bilanz des Balletjahres* (Velber), 1971
Kleinert, Annemarie, *Portrait of an Artist: Eva Evdokimova*, English edition, London, 1982
Barnes, Patricia, "All About Eva", *Ballet News* (New York), May 1983
Dupuis, S., "Eva Evdokimova: Une romantique du XXe siècle", *Les Saisons de la danse* (Paris), May 1983
Crisp, Clement, "Romantic Spirit", *Ballet News* (New York), May 1983

* * *

The art of Eva Evdokimova is the confluence of extraordinarily diverse international influences and training; born in Geneva of American and Bulgarian parents, she spent her childhood in Germany and England, studying at the Munich Opera Ballet School and at the Royal Ballet School. She received additional training, and her first real exposure to the Russian tradition, from Maria Fay; the Bournonville style was absorbed during her time as a member of the corps of the Royal Danish Ballet. Ulanova invited Evdokimova to study in Russia after seeing her perform at the Moscow Ballet Competition and later at Varna, where Evdokimova received the Gold Medal. In Leningrad she became the favourite pupil of Natalia Dudinskaya, who carried the flame of the Vaganova tradition at the Kirov.

The combination of Western and Eastern European schooling produced a ballerina who excelled in both styles and brought highly individual refinements from one to the other. She is known principally as a romantic dancer. Her physique appears to have a fragile porcelain delicacy, matching a face with large sensitive eyes. Her style, beautiful and limpid, recalls the photographs of Spessivtseva, with whom she has often been compared; and like Spessivtseva, she is a justly famous Giselle. Her interpretation is characterized by a poetic, abstract quality, a ravishing attenuated line, and exquisite ports de bras. Although she learned much from the coaching of Yvette Chauviré in the part, Evdokimova's Giselle is a unique achievement, acknowledging the Kirov tradition while remaining outside it.

**Eva Evdokimova as Giselle, c.1971**

Evdokimova was chosen to dance Aurora at the first performance of Nureyev's *The Sleeping Beauty* for London Festival Ballet in 1975. In this, as in other major classics, she achieved considerable success. She is a versatile dancer who can shine equally in Bournonville or Petipa, and even more remarkably, in a number of modern roles—of which Luipart's *Scarecrows* and Tetley's *Sphinx* are outstanding examples. She has the gift of being able to dance in the appropriate style of a particular school while still contributing a dimension that is completely her own.

An exceptionally musical dancer, Evdokimova is renowned for the softness of her jumps, apparently attributable to her habit of wearing old, soft ballet slippers when in class. Evdokimova brings directness and honesty to her roles and eschews unnecessary bravura in favour of artistic integrity.

—Mike Dixon

---

## EXCELSIOR

**Choreography:** Luigi Manzotti
**Music:** Romualdo Marenco
**Design:** Alfredo Edel (scenery and costumes)
**Libretto:** Luigi Manzotti
**First Production:** Teatro alla Scala, Milan, 11 January 1881
**Principal Dancers:** Bice Vergani (Spirit of Light), Carlo Montanara (Spirit of Darkness), Rosina Viale (Civilization)

**Other productions include:** Her Majesty's Theatre (staged Carlo

Coppi), with Giovannina Limido and Enrico Cecchetti; London, 22 May 1885. Arcadia Theatre (shortened version; staged Cecchetti after Manzotti); St. Petersburg, 1887. Teatro dei Piccoli (version for marionettes), 1895. Teatro San Carlo ("reproduced" and largely revised by Giovanni Pratesi); Naples, 1931. Maggio Musicale Fiorentino (new version, chor. Ugo Dell'Ara, mus. Fiorenzo Carpi, design Giulio Coltellacci), with Ludmilla Tcherina, Carla Fracci, Attilio Labis, and Ugo Dell'Ara; Florence, 27 June 1967. Teatro alla Scala (restaged Dell'Ara), with Fracci, Paolo Bortoluzzi, Elettra Morini, and Dell'Ara; Milan, September 1974.

## PUBLICATIONS

Evans, Edwin, "A Romantic Ballet—for Christmas?", *Dancing Times* (London), December 1942

Carrieri, Raffaele, *La Danza in Italia*, Milan, 1946

Beaumont, Cyril, *Complete Book of Ballets*, revised edition, London, 1951

Koegler, Horst, "Historic *Excelsior* Revived", *Dance and Dancers* (London), April 1975

* * *

*Excelsior* is not so much a ballet as a spectacle, prefiguring the group scenes of the big Hollywood musical comedies. It was, when new, a grandiose, rather nationalistic hymn to material progress.

Not only did it enjoy greater success than any other Italian ballet, but it is also the only Italian ballet to have survived into the twentieth century, albeit in a reduced production. By the time Manzotti and Marenco made *Excelsior*, they had already experienced great success in Turin with *Sieba* (in which Virginia Zucchi appeared) and knew they had won the approval of the public. By 1881, public taste had, indeed, declined lamentably, and it seemed that only such lavish entertainments, with their colourful scenery and costumes and virtuoso performances, would gain favour. In *Excelsior* Manzotti astutely exploited the mood of optimism that reigned in Italy at that time; the ballet is self-congratulatory as far as Italian achievements are concerned, as the scene with Alessandro Volta demonstrates. This is so ingenuous as to make us smile now, but it was taken seriously as an indication of progress in 1881, as was the scene in which French and Italian engineers work at their respective ends of the Mont Cénis tunnel until they get through and embrace one another amid general rejoicing.

There are two principal ballerina roles, the more important being that of Civilization, represented simply by a charming ballerina in a tutu, smiling benignly on all and partnered by a handsome young man. The other is the Spirit of Light, who wins all the battles against the Spirit of Darkness, foiling the latter's plans to frustrate human progress.

*Excelsior* was so popular that it was performed in several other countries. Boris Kochno records in his book *Le Ballet* that after seeing Elena Cornalba (a notably strong technician) in the role of Electricity at the Eden Theatre in 1883, the poet Mallarmé was so struck by her performance that he devoted several pages to her in his *Divergences*.

It is not surprising that Tchaikovsky was not impressed, because Marenco's score is just a medley of polkas and military-band music. On the other hand, Bernard Shaw was full of praise for the ballet when he saw it at Her Majesty's Theatre in May 1885, with Adelina Rossi and Enrico Cecchetti in the cast. Writing in *The Dramatic Review*, he said he found it "one of the pleasantest entertainments at present accessible in London", singling out the colourful scenery and costumes by Alfredo Edel, as well as Cecchetti's "amazing spins". *Excelsior* was really not as far removed from divertissement as Shaw imagined, but obviously he approved so heartily of the theme, which he referred to as "the victories of man over nature", that he overlooked other shortcomings. He also approved of the presence of so many men on the stage, for at that time in London good male dancers were rare.

The Scala stage is unusually large, and was thus able to accommodate literally hundreds of dancers for the original production. A far smaller number of dancers was employed in Ugo Dell'Ara's reworking for the Maggio Musicale Fiorentino at the Teatro Comunale in Florence in 1967, partly, no doubt, because corps de ballet dancers are somewhat better paid these days, but also because the Comunale stage is smaller and the Florence opera house has never had a large ballet company, at least not in recent decades. The original choreography has not survived, so the revival could only be an approximation. However, it was enormously successful and was afterwards given in Milan, Rome, Verona, and Naples, with changing casts. Audiences were delighted by the stage effects, particularly the skilful lighting, and enjoyed the scene with the scarlet-clad telegraph boys. A more blasé spectator might have found the ballet embarrassingly naïve, and the melodramatic contortions of the Spirit of Darkness, usually danced by Dell'Ara, could seem ludicrous, but evidently there were few such spectators in the theatre.

Carlo Colla's famous company of marionettes has *Excelsior* in its repertory, and their version is likely to be closer to the original, notwithstanding the limitations of the medium. The Spoleto Festival of Two Worlds included it in its 1990 programme, showing that interest in the work has not yet died.

—Freda Pitt

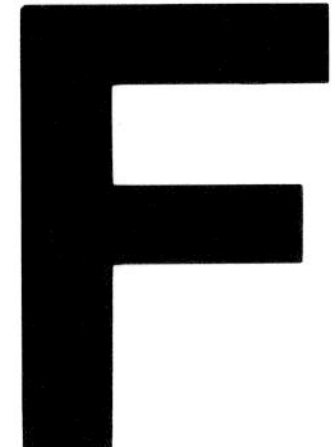

## FAÇADE

**Choreography:** Frederick Ashton
**Music:** William Walton (originally written as an accompaniment to poems by Edith Sitwell)
**Design:** John Armstrong (scenery and costumes)
**First Production:** Camargo Society, Cambridge Theatre, London, 26 April 1931
**Principal Dancers:** Antony Tudor (Scotch Rhapsody), Lydia Lopokova (Jodelling Song, Tango), Pearl Argyle (Valse), Alicia Markova (Polka), Frederick Ashton (Tango), William Chappell and Walter Gore (Popular Song)

**Other productions include:** Ballet Club (restaged Ashton) with original cast, apart from Andrée Howard (Jodelling Song), Alicia Markova (Tango); London, 4 May 1931. Vic-Wells Ballet (restaged and revised Ashton, design revised Armstrong), with Robert Helpmann (Scotch Rhapsody), Gwyneth Matthews (Jodelling Song), Margot Fonteyn (Polka), Pamela May (Waltz), Molly Brown (Tango: A Debutante), Frederick Ashton (Tango: A Dago), Harold Turner and William Chappell (Popular Song); London, 8 October 1935 (restaged and further revised Ashton, with new designs Armstrong, 23 July 1940). Sadler's Wells Opera Ballet, with Anne Heaton (Polka), Donald Britton and Alexander Grant (Popular Song), Ashton (Tango: A Dago), June Brae (A Debutante); London, 29 April 1946. Norwegian Ballet (staged Harold Turner); Oslo, 4 October 1960. City Center Joffrey Ballet (staged John Hart after Ashton); Chicago, 28 January 1969. Australian Ballet (staged Peggy van Praagh), with Robert Helpmann (A Dago); Melbourne, 8 September 1972. Teatro Regio Ballet (staged Faith Worth); Turin, January 1992.

### PUBLICATIONS


Hussey, Dyneley, "William Walton", *Dancing Times* (London), 3 parts: October, December 1949; January 1950

Beaumont, Cyril, *Complete Book of Ballets*, revised edition, London, 1951

Sandon, Joseph, *"Façade" and Other Early Ballets by Frederick Ashton*, London, 1954

Balanchine, George, with Mason, Francis, *Balanchine's Complete Stories of the Great Ballets*, Garden City, New York, 1977

Vaughan, David, *Frederick Ashton and his Ballets*, London, 1977

Clarke, Mary, "Ballet in War Time", *Dancing Times* (London), April 1990


*   *   *

Like his earlier *Capriol Suite*, Frederick Ashton's *Façade* is a witty sequence of dances with no linking plot. Both ballets are essentially divertissements, but whereas *Capriol Suite* looks with an amused modern eye at sixteenth-century French dances, *Façade* satirizes a wider range of folk, social, and theatrical forms. *Capriol Suite* and *Façade* are the two earliest Ashton works to have survived in the repertory and *Façade* remains one of his most popular works.

Although Edith Sitwell's poems *Façade* (1922) explore the rhythms of dance, Ashton disclaimed any connection with them—partly because Sitwell herself wanted nothing to do with his ballet. What Ashton choreographed were numbers selected from the score originally written by Walton to accompany a recitation of Sitwell's poems (first performed privately on 24 January 1922 and first performed in public on 12 June 1923), a self-styled "Entertainment" that variously recalls Schönberg's *Pierrot lunaire* (1912) and Stravinsky's *L'Histoire du soldat* (1918). Walton's music took on a life of its own, independent of Sitwell's poems, with the performance of five numbers as an interlude between ballets in Diaghilev's 1926 Lyceum season. Publication of the Concert Suite by Oxford University Press brought the score to a wider public and caught the attention of Günter Hess, who choreographed the first *Façade* ballet.

Ashton's *Façade* was first performed under the auspices of the Camargo Society—Ashton received £5 for the choreography—and immediately went into the repertory of Marie Rambert's Ballet Club, to which all the original dancers except Lydia Lopokova belonged. Rambert had paid £40 for the Camargo production's costumes and in return acquired the rights to the ballet. When Ashton joined the Vic-Wells company in 1935, Rambert continued to perform the original *Façade* (and indeed did so until 1969) while Ashton revised his choreography for Ninette de Valois, adding a new Country Dance. In 1940 he added two further new items, Noche Espagnola (Nocturne péruvienne) and Foxtrot. The first two additions have long been dropped and *Façade* as presently danced by the Royal Ballet consists of the following numbers: Scottish Rhapsody, a double parody of both Highland Dancing and a classical pas de trois; Yodelling Song, ingeniously contrived for three likely Tyrolien lads, a milkmaid, and her stool; Polka, an insouciant but very difficult solo, ending in a double tour en l'air which only Markova seems to have brought off with complete success; Foxtrot, for two 1920s couples, incorporating the Charleston, Black Bottom, and other period dances; Waltz, for four women making self-consciously tasteful patterns of arms and legs; Popular Song, a deadpan soft-shoe shuffle routine for a bored, boatered, and blazered music-hall double-act; Tango, for the ultimate oiled gigolo (Ashton's own original role) and the ultimate pea-brained débutante; and finally a hectic Tarantella, which brings all the dancers back on stage together.

***Façade*, as performed by Sadler's Wells Royal Ballet, London**

The John Armstrong sets and costumes that we now see are those he redesigned in 1940 after his original décor had been lost in the Nazi invasion of Holland. The new designs coarsened some of *Façade*'s humour and altered the point of some of its jokes, but in any case the ballet is danced more broadly nowadays than it was originally. *Façade* as a whole may have been funnier when, as David Vaughan remarks of the Tango, "its comedy was more subtle and its social comment slyer". Nevertheless it retains its popular appeal.

Ashton himself said of this surprisingly durable early work: "I always look back with particular pleasure upon *Façade*, because I really liked that collaboration with William Walton. It was a marvellous score by any standards and I had a marvellous cast for it and it was the first ballet that I'd done bringing humour into a piece that was classically based. I still do regard it as a rather particular landmark in my work." *Façade* points forward in Ashton's career to *Les Rendezvous* (1933) and *Les Patineurs* (1937).

—Martin Wright

---

## LES FÂCHEUX

**Choreography:** Pierre Beauchamp
**Music:** Pierre Beauchamp
**Design:** Charles Le Brun, Giacomo Torelli (machines)
**Libretto:** Molière (Jean-Baptiste Poquelin)
**First Production:** Vaux-le-Vicomte, 17 August 1661

**Other choreographic treatments of story:** Bronislava Nijinska (libretto Boris Kochno after Molière; Monte Carlo, 1924), Léonide Massine (Monte Carlo, 1927).

### PUBLICATIONS

Sazonova, Julia, "Molière et la danse", *Le Rythme et la danse*, 1937
Christout, Marie-Françoise, *Le Ballet de Cour de Louis XIV 1643–1672*, Paris, 1967
Kirstein, Lincoln, *Movement and Metaphor*, New York, 1970
Mongredien, Georges (ed.), *Molière: Oeuvres Complètes*, vol. 1, Paris, 1979

* * *

In August 1661, in the hope of regaining Louis XIV's favour, Fouquet, the Minister of Finance, requested Molière to put on an entertainment for the King at his splendid new chateau at Vaux-le-Vicomte. *Les Fâcheux* (*The Bores*) was performed in an open-air theatre with herms, jets of water, trees, and alleyways in perspective, taking advantage of the natural beauty of the park. The décor was by Charles Le Brun (the future decorator of Versailles), the machines by Torelli. Pierre Beauchamp was responsible for both music and choreography.

The plot of this three-act comédie-ballet is simple. Eraste loves Orphise but his suit is opposed by Damis, her guardian, who wants her to marry another suitor. Their attempts to meet secretly are continually frustrated by the intrusion of a series of bores: the pretentious bore at a play who explains the plot in a voice louder than the actors'; a music and dance enthusiast who attempts to teach Eraste the courante he has choreographed, making him dance the lady's part; a professional dueller; two affected ladies discussing the perfect lover; a tedious huntsman (included later at Fontainebleau and thought to be modelled on the marquis of Soyecourt at the suggestion of Louis XIV); a pedantic self-styled Greek scholar; an inventor with ridiculous ideas for building ports around the whole French coast—all typical characters taken from contemporary society and presented in a succession of farcical sketches. Finally Eraste saves Damis from the very men sent to punish Eraste for persisting in his suit, and a grateful Damis agrees willingly to the marriage.

Most of the dancing was loosely integrated into the plot between the acts and at the beginning and end of the play. In the prologue a naiad appears out of a shell and makes a declamatory speech written by Pellison in praise of the King. She commands several fauns, dryads, and satyrs to emerge from the trees and statues; they dance to the music of oboes and violins. At the end of Act I a group of "pall mall" players force Eraste to leave the alley where he is waiting for Orphise. In a second entrée, inquisitive people surround him and force him again to retire. At the end of Act II, bowls players perform a dance imitating the movements of the game. In the second entrée little boys with catapults interrupt the lovers and are chased away in the third entrée by cobblers, who in turn are put to flight by a gardener who performs a solo. At the end of Act III, the happy lovers are about to celebrate their nuptials, when a crowd of masquers with fiddles and tambourines burst in. They are driven out in the first entrée by Swiss guards with halberds, who retire for the last entrée, consisting of a ballet with four shepherds and one shepherdess—a graceful and

***Les Fâcheux*: an engraved frontispiece from a 1661 edition of Molière's works**

pleasing conclusion, restoring pastoral harmony and tranquillity to the scene.

In his foreword Molière explains that the original intention had been to include a separate ballet as part of the entertainment, but since there was a shortage of good dancers, he had decided to include the dances between the acts of the play so that the intervals would allow the dancers time to change their costumes and perform other roles. He had attempted to incorporate the dancing into the plot as best he could, uniting ballet and play, but because of the lack of time (he had only two weeks in which to write and direct the play) and the fact that the whole work was not conceived by one single person, there were times where perhaps the ballet did not mix with the plot as naturally as he would have liked. But, he adds, since the play had been well received, it was an idea which could be developed, given more time. The invention of comédie-ballet, then, happened by chance and necessity rather than by intention. A totally new genre was accidentally created.

The ballet was very well received and performed on several subsequent occasions, notably on 27 August at Fontainebleau, where a professional dancer, Mlle. Giraut, was much applauded for her gaiety and grace. Louis XIV was so impressed by Molière that he officially appointed him to provide court festivals and comedies. Almost a third of Molière's plays are comédie-ballets, in several of which the king himself danced. The most successful and famous of this genre is *Le Bourgeois Gentilhomme* (1670).

—Françoise Carter

---

## FADEYECHEV, Nikolai

Russian/Soviet dancer and teacher. Born Nikolai Borisovich Fadeechev (Fadeyechev) in Moscow, 27 January 1933. Studied at the Moscow School of Choreography, pupil of Aleksandr Rudenko and others, 1943–52. Married Bolshoi dancer Irina Holina: son, Bolshoi dancer Aleksei Fadeechev, b. 1960. Dancer, Bolshoi Ballet, 1952–77, touring U.S. and Canada, 1966; principal guest artist, Paris Opéra, 1961; répétiteur (rehearsal director), Bolshoi Ballet, from 1977; also has appeared in films and on television, including in *Swan Lake*, Act II (BBC, 1957), *Giselle* (with Nadia Nerina; BBC, 1958) and in Russian television documentaries *Maya Plisetskaya* (Moscow, 1964), *Ballerina* (Moscow, 1969), and *Raymonda* (Moscow, 1974). Recipient: title of People's Artist of the USSR, 1976.

### ROLES

1952 Prince in *The Nutcracker* (Vainonen), Bolshoi Choreographic School Performance, Moscow

1953 One of the four Phoenixes in *The Red Poppy* (Lavrovsky), Bolshoi Ballet, Moscow

Cavalier (Grand Pas) in *Raymonda* (Lavrovsky after Petipa), Bolshoi Ballet, Moscow

Bernard in *Raymonda* (Lavrovsky after Petipa), Bolshoi Ballet, Moscow

1954 Opal in *The Story of the Stone Flower* (Lavrovsky), Bolshoi Ballet, Moscow

Siegfried in *Swan Lake* (Dolinskaya, Messerer after Petipa, Ivanov), Bolshoi Ballet, Moscow

1955 Blue Bird in *The Sleeping Beauty* (Gabovich, Messerer after Petipa), Bolshoi Ballet, Moscow

Prince Désiré in *The Sleeping Beauty* (Gabovich, Messerer after Petipa), Bolshoi Ballet, Moscow

1958 The Youth in *Laurencia* (Chabukiani), Bolshoi Ballet, Moscow

Garmody (cr) in *Spartacus* (Moiseyev), Bolshoi Ballet, Moscow

1960 Romeo in *Romeo and Juliet* (Lavrovsky), Bolshoi Ballet, Moscow

Jean de Brienne in *Raymonda* (Lavrovsky after Petipa), Moscow

1962 Vaslav in *The Fountain of Bakhchisarai* (Zakharov), Bolshoi Ballet, Moscow

Armen in *Gayané* (Vainonen), Bolshoi Ballet, Moscow

1963 Prince Désiré in *The Sleeping Beauty* (Grigorovich after Petipa), Bolshoi Ballet, Moscow

1964 Ivan Tsarevich in *Firebird* (Vlasov, Simachov after Fokine), Bolshoi Ballet, Moscow

1967 Don José (cr) in *Carmen Suite* (Alonso), Bolshoi Ballet, Moscow

Ilyas (cr) in *Asel* (Vinogradov), Bolshoi Ballet, Moscow

**Nikolai Fadeyechev in *Swan Lake***

1968 Principal dancer (cr) in *Preludes and Fugues* (Kasatkina, Vasiliev), Bolshoi Ballet, Moscow
1969 Prince Siegfried (cr) in *Swan Lake* (new production; Grigorovich after Petipa, Ivanov), Bolshoi Ballet, Moscow
1972 Karenin (cr) in *Anna Karenina* (Plisetskaya, Ryzhenko, and Smirnov-Golovanov), Bolshoi Ballet, Moscow

**Other roles include:** principal dancer ("The Poet") in *Chopiniana* (*Les Sylphides*; Fokine).

## PUBLICATIONS

Gabovich, Mikhail, "Nikolai Fadeechev", *Teatr* (Moscow), no. 10, 1958
Hering, Doris, "And Still the Chasm", *Dance Magazine* (New York), November 1962
"The Bolshoi in London", *Dancing Times* (London), August 1963
Roslavleva, Natalia, *Era of the Russian Ballet*, London, 1966
Grishina, Elena, *Nikolai Fadeechev*, Moscow, 1990

* * *

Nikolai Fadeyechev, formerly a dancer and at present a rehearsal supervisor at the Bolshoi Theatre, was trained at the Moscow School of Choreography. As a boy, he was not regarded as particularly promising but later he met Aleksandr Rudenko, a first-rate teacher, who revealed and developed the youth's amazing natural gifts. It was Rudenko who prepared him for his very first appearance as the Prince in *The Nutcracker*, in a performance by the graduation class.

In 1952 Fadeyechev joined the Bolshoi Theatre and was immediately offered several parts in classical ensembles. Soon afterwards he was dancing Bernard in *Raymonda*, and the next season, Prince Siegfried in *Swan Lake*, a role which won him recognition both among the public and the critics.

It was, however, his début as Albrecht in *Giselle* that brought him real success—a début which took place during the

Bolshoi's first visit to London. The young dancer who partnered Galina Ulanova was not totally overshadowed by the great ballerina, and the English critics praised him highly. For instance, Clive Barnes wrote in the journal *Dance and Dancers*: "The young and relatively obscure Fadeyechev proved to be an excellent Albrecht; he is an elegant and masculine dancer, a strong and naturally considerate partner and already a marvellous artist."

In the wake of his London triumph the young dancer performed on the Bolshoi stage, one after another, nearly all the main romantic parts in the classical and modern ballets: Désiré (*The Sleeping Beauty*), The Poet (*Chopiniana*), Jean de Brienne (*Raymonda*), Romeo, and Vaslav (*The Fountain of Bakhchisarai*). All those characters were the so-called "rosy princes", but Fadeyechev knew how to avoid repetitiveness and to turn each of them into an individual character.

Fadeyechev's art happily combined technical excellence, good taste, and dramatic talent. He was a "flying" dancer. A leap, not particularly high, but supple and long, together with a soft landing, gave the impression of him soaring in the air. His posture was always correct, graceful, and statuesque. In some classical and modern variations, Fadeyechev managed to use such complex combinations of movements that they could never be repeated by any other dancer. But technical excellence never became self-justifying in his case. He did not emphasize technical difficulty for its own sake, and did not turn his dance into acrobatics: all his movements were natural and looked deceptively easy.

On top of this, Fadeyechev was a brilliant actor. His movements, gestures, and elements of mime acting were always meaningful, and helped to create an image or a character. Where it was at all possible (for instance in *Giselle* or in *Romeo and Juliet*), he tried to show a dynamic change in the character's personality, the development of his psyche. At the same time, he was a first-rate partner. He danced with many great ballerinas—Galina Ulanova, Maya Plisetskaya, Raisa Struchkova, Nina Timofeyeva—and they all regarded him as a very reliable and adaptable cavalier who was exceptionally sensitive to the ballerina's needs.

Fadeyechev came to dancing in modern choreographers' productions as an already experienced master, at a later stage in his career. Here he had to learn to speak a new choreographic language, mastering complex modern support techniques and creating characters with a specific national flavour. All this enriched the dancer's work and broadened his creative scope. An important landmark in the dancer's career was the 1966–67 season when he was to create two roles in new ballets: Ilyas in Oleg Vinogradov's *Asel* and Don José in Alberto Alonso's *Carmen Suite*.

The character of Ilyas, an ordinary young lorry driver, seemed strikingly unexpected in the career of such a pure lyrical dancer as Fadeyechev had shown himself to be by this time. However, much to the critics' surprise, this character proved to be utterly recognizable in Fadeyechev's presentation, with plenty of psychological reality and no sham.

In the other of the two modern parts, *Carmen Suite*, everything was new to Fadeyechev, including sharp musical rhythms, a strong presence of the grotesque, and unusual choreography. In this ballet Fadeyechev was particularly successful as a dramatic actor: he created a deeply tragic character in Don José by means of mime and gesture, almost without dancing.

The last role to be danced by Fadeyechev turned out to be Karenin in *Anna Karenina*, in the choreographic version by Maya Plisetskaya, Natalia Ryzhenko, and Viktor Smirnov-Golovanov. But the role of Karenin was almost completely the brainchild of Fadeyechev himself, born during the rehearsals through improvisation. At first, following Tolstoy's text, he imagined the role to be purely pantomimic: the trouble was, he said, that it was absolutely impossible to imagine Karenin dancing. But eventually, in certain scenes, he started to introduce elements of dance. As a result of this long process, a very unusual interpretation of this complex, contradictory character unfolded. In the mime scenes, where Fadeyechev often managed to achieve a complete psychological transformation, one saw an important Petersburg official, a stickler for the high society prejudice, "an evil machine". Yet, Karenin's inner life, the awakening of his soul, was shown through his duets with Anna, and in his meditations, as reflected through both mime and dance.

Fadeyechev retired early and started a teaching career. At present, he is a rehearsal supervisor at the Bolshoi. He has advised such leading figures of the Bolshoi ballet as Aleksandr Bogatyrev, Vyacheslav Gordeyev, his own son, Aleksei, and many others. The qualities of Fadeyechev the dancer—perfect technique and dramatic talent, an acute feeling for a choreographic style, and that special civilized manner of dancing which is getting ever rarer among Russian ballet dancers—all this makes his advice precious to the younger generations.

—Irina Gruzdeva

---

**FAIRY DOLL, The** *see* **PUPPENFEE, Die**

---

## FALL RIVER LEGEND

**Choreography:** Agnes de Mille
**Music:** Morton Gould
**Design:** Oliver Smith (scenery), Miles White (costumes)
**Libretto:** Agnes de Mille
**First Production:** Ballet Theatre, Metropolitan Opera House, New York, 22 April 1948
**Principal Dancers:** Alicia Alonso (The Accused), Diana Adams (The Mother), Peter Gladke (The Father), John Kriza (The Pastor), Muriel Bentley (The Stepmother), Ruth Ann Koesun (The Accused as a Child)

**Other productions include:** Ballet of the German Opera on the Rhine; Düsseldorf, 3 December 1980. Dance Theatre of Harlem (staged Enrique Martinez, costumes Stanley Simmons), with Virginia Johnson (The Accused); New York, 3 February 1983.

**Other choreographic treatments of story:** Frank Staff (South Africa, 1957).

### PUBLICATIONS

Krevitsky, N., "Ballet Theatre", *Dance Observer* (New York), June–July 1948
Beaumont, Cyril, *Ballets of Today*, London, 1954
Maynard, Olga, *The American Ballet*, Philadelphia, 1959
Goodman, Saul, "Nora Kaye", *Dance Magazine* (New York), February 1965
de Mille, Agnes, *Lizzie Borden: A Dance of Death*, Boston, 1968

***Fall River Legend*, as performed by Ballet Theatre, New York, 1948**

Balanchine, George, with Mason, Francis, *Balanchine's Complete Stories of the Great Ballets*, Garden City, N.Y., 1977

Barker, Barbara, "Agnes de Mille's Heroines of the '40's", Society of Dance History Scholars, Proceedings, 12th Conference, 1989

* * *

In 1948, six years after the success of *Rodeo*, her first great hit for the ballet stage, Agnes de Mille created *Fall River Legend*, a vastly different work from *Rodeo*, but still in the mainstream of Americana.

*Fall River Legend* compresses the sprawling story of Lizzie Borden, an unmarried woman of Fall River, Massachusetts, who was acquitted of murdering her father and stepmother with an axe in 1892.

The crime achieved international notoriety, and de Mille leaves no doubt of her own belief that Lizzie did it. In an admirable example of tight dramatic construction within the seamless framework of a prologue and eight successive scenes, the choreographer gives us the antecedents of the crime: the deterioration of Lizzie's mind under the pressures of her beloved mother's death, and the machinations of her domineering stepmother; her unaware and ineffectual father; and the saving grace of the town Pastor, who responds to Lizzie's reaching out for comfort, and perhaps romance. As a recent critic has pointed out, Lizzie Borden was acquitted, but ". . . de Mille convicts her heroine; she is more interested in why a spinster should commit such an act in a stifling New England town".

An axe embedded in a chopping-block set at the side of the stage, innocent in itself, dominates the ballet. In the Prologue, the Accused, as she is called, stands beside the Pastor near a gallows. As the foreman reads the jury's verdict, the gallows swings back (in Scene 1) to become the front of a New England house, revealing a sitting room and stairs leading to the second floor.

The Accused stands apart, contemplating the events of her life as a child dancing happily with her parents while townspeople—one of them a plain, cold woman dressed in black—pass by. The Accused vicariously experiences her mother's fainting attacks and death, and her father's turning to the forbidding woman in black, apparently a friend of the family, for consolation.

Soon, the woman becomes the stepmother of the Accused. The years follow in boredom, repression, and frustration. The father is completely under his second wife's domination. The pair are shown reading in their rocking chairs.

The Accused also sits with them, but finally runs upstairs. The stepmother whispers to the father and later to the Pastor, as if to suggest that the Accused is not in her right mind.

De Mille shows how the house, loveless and threatening, draws the Accused, yet repels her. In an escape into the open air she meets the young Pastor, and they become friends—and in the timeless compression of a stage work, joyfully and romantically involved.

The disapproving parents summon the Accused back into the house, and the pressure becomes palpable. The Accused suddenly rushes out and picks up the axe. The stepmother cringes in terror when the Accused appears holding the weapon, but the Accused had only been letting off steam by chopping wood. Nonetheless, the stepmother's reaction is a telling one.

In succeeding scenes, the Accused watches enviously as couples her age express their happiness; she dances with the Pastor, who gives her flowers and invites her to a picnic; she is accepted wholeheartedly and with love at a congregational meeting. But when the stepmother intervenes to bring her home again, her reason appears to leave her and again she picks up the axe.

There is a blackout followed by a dream in which the house has been replaced by a backdrop showing a bloodied room. The Accused's dress has been removed, and her underdress is bloody. She seeks comfort in the arms of a dream figure of her mother.

The scene shifts to the house. People are milling about. Something dreadful has happened, but no one seems to know what. The Accused rushes about trying to set the furniture in order, then dashes out the door. Two men enter the house and emerge shortly with the axe and a shawl that had been worn by the Accused's mother and later by the Stepmother. The Accused kisses the shawl and throws herself into the arms of the Pastor who has responded to the news.

In a reprise of the Prologue, the Accused accepts the verdict calmly as the Pastor extends his final blessing. She faces the gallows as the curtain falls.

*Fall River Legend* is the essence of theatre, a modern melodrama whose effect is heightened by Morton Gould's powerful score and by Oliver Smith's symbolic set combining frame house and gallows, and lit in the end by a blood-red sky. The parts are sharply drawn, requiring careful dramatic performances to magnify the impact of the ballet. The leading role has come to be identified with its greatest portrayer, Nora Kaye, although Sallie Wilson achieved equal success with it. In 1990, the choreographer herself felt that Cynthia Gregory, a classical ballerina essaying the role for the first time, was equally superb. New York critic Anna Kisselgoff, reviewing Gregory's performance, rightly pointed to the fact that in *Fall River Legend*, "It is the heroine's state of mind that is perpetually on view," requiring the ballerina to approach de Mille's "body-language style of choreography" with care and attention. Gregory succeeded admirably in this, adding to the popularity of a classic work which is at the center of renewed interest in the "dance drama". Muriel Bentley originated the role of the stepmother. Lucia Chase, who followed her, has remained memorable for her convincing evocation of evil. The first Pastor was John Kriza, and he has remained identified with the part.

—Joseph Gale

---

## FANCY FREE

**Choreography:** Jerome Robbins
**Music:** Leonard Bernstein
**Design:** Oliver Smith (scenery), Kermit Love (costumes)
**Libretto:** Jerome Robbins
**First Production:** Ballet Theatre, Metropolitan Opera House, New York, 18 April 1944
**Principal Dancers:** Harold Lang, John Kriza, and Jerome Robbins (Sailors), Janet Reed, Muriel Bentley, and Shirley Eckl (Passers-by), Rex Cooper (Bartender)

**Other productions include:** New York City Ballet (restaged Robbins); New York, 1980. Dance Theatre of Harlem (staged Sara Leland); Pasadena, 13 May, 1985.

Graz Opera Ballet (new version; chor. Fred Marteny); Graz, Austria, 1969. Komische Oper (Comic Opera) (new version; chor. Tom Schilling); East Berlin, 1971. Ballet of Marseille (new version; chor. Fred Marteny); 4 December 1971.

### PUBLICATIONS

Barrett, Dorothy, "Jerome Robbins", *Dance Magazine* (New York), May 1945
Coleman, Francis A., "Leonard Bernstein", *Dance Magazine* (New York), May 1945
Beaumont, Cyril, *Ballets of Today*, London, 1954
Maynard, Olga, *The American Ballet*, Philadelphia, 1959
Denby, Edwin, *Looking at the Dance*, New York, 1968
Kirstein, Lincoln, *Movement and Metaphor*, New York, 1970
Balanchine, George, with Mason, Francis, *Balanchine's Complete Stories of the Great Ballets*, Garden City, N.Y., 1977
Siegel, Marcia, *The Shapes of Change*, Boston, 1979
Tobias, Tobi, "Bringing Back Robbins's 'Fancy'", *Dance Magazine* (New York), January 1980
Goodwin, Noël, "Street Side Story", *Dance and Dancers* (London), November 1990

* * *

Jerome Robbins credits the inspiration for *Fancy Free* to the combined effect of seeing Paul Cadmus's sensational, controversial painting, *The Fleet's In*; to working in New York City during World War II when Times Square was thronged with sailors on leave, strutting about in groups of three; and to the frustration he felt as a corps member of Ballet Theatre in its "Russified" period under the management of Sol Hurok. (". . . For one whole year," he recalled, "I did not get out of boots, Russian bloomers, and a peasant wig.") American folk and popular dances could be as valid an inspiration as Russian dances, Robbins believed, and he set out to prove it in his first full-scale work.

Before he joined Ballet Theatre in 1940, Robbins had choreographed mostly solos for himself as an entertainer on "the borscht circuit", the Jewish summer resorts in upper New York State. By the time he was dancing solo roles, he was submitting ideas to director Alden Talbot, but none was accepted until 1943, after he took Anatole Chujoy's advice to propose "something small, with a few people and one set".

*Fancy Free* takes place in and outside of a Manhattan neighborhood bar. The first sound one hears is the bartender's radio, tuned to a station broadcasting Billie Holiday's recording of Leonard Bernstein's song "Big Stuff". When the radio is switched off, Bernstein's orchestra fires off a fusillade of percussive chords, and three American sailors bound into view. They are bursting with innocent toughness and spirits so buoyant that one of them inadvertently bolts straight upward. The other two automatically steady him in mid-air, but such camaraderie doesn't prevent a little collusion: the same sailor somehow always loses when they match to see who buys the drinks in the bar. The arrival of one striking female with a red pocketbook puts undue strain on their comradeship. After a childish bit of purse snatching, the girl stalks off with two of the men in pursuit.

The remaining sailor isn't alone for long, however. He quite literally bumps into a nice girl. She accepts his invitation to drinks in the convenient bar where they dance a sinuous pas de

***Fancy Free*, with, from left to right, Jerome Robbins, John Kriza, Harold Lang, Janet Reed and Muriel Bentley, Ballet Theatre, New York, 1944**

deux to a swooningly bluesy theme. Their growing intimacy is disrupted by the return of the other two sailors with the now amenable girl of the handbag. To a burst of chatter among the wind instruments, the women recognize each other. They insist upon remaining together, but the men decide that three escorts are one too many; to determine who must be odd man out, each sailor will dance a solo and the girls will pick the loser.

They dance but the girls refuse to judge them. Tempers flare and a slapstick brawl sends the boys tumbling over and behind the counter. As a fist and a foot and a wildly writhing body pop into view, the girls give up and walk out in disgust. Nursing skinned knuckles and sore jaws, the boys emerge and repeat their rituals of mateyness performed at their entrance. Out on the street once more, though, they fall under the magnetic sway of a passing girl. One by one they break away to scamper after her, each rounding the corner of the bar in a frantic, one-legged hop worthy of Charlie Chaplin or Harry Langdon.

Characterization is as important as steps to a successful performance of *Fancy Free*. Robbins tailor-made the roles to fit the personalities of his colleagues at Ballet Theatre. The girl with the purse, danced by Muriel Bentley, was sharp and savvy, while the second girl, danced by Janet Reed, was much less aggressive because, as Robbins said, "Muriel's a New Yorker; Janet isn't". Harold Lang was an agile show-off so his solo, the first and flashiest of the lot, opens with a double turn in the air that ends in a split. John Kriza, the sailor who always got stuck with the tab, was so genuinely sweet that he always did pay for everyone; his solo, the second, is a low-keyed, lyrical gambol that ends in a dreamy pose on the floor (a parody of Tudor, Edwin Denby noted). Robbins, who had studied dance of all kinds, was savoring Spanish and character forms when he choreographed the third solo; his sailor does a cheekily syncopated "rumba" with Mexican overtones (a jab at Massine, thought Denby).

Even with a less than convincing cast—and some of its 1940s popular steps are a bit alien to later generations—*Fancy Free* can still be galvanic fare if its score is played with due attention to its springy rhythms and the disparate influences (Copland, Shostakovitch, and jazz, among others) that Bernstein synthesized so distinctly. Robbins has said that he first approached Vincent Persichetti with the commission and was referred instead to Bernstein. Confident that he could fulfill the assignment while holding down his new post as assistant conductor of the Philharmonic Symphony Orchestra of New York, Bernstein accepted. He would make a sensational conducting début on 14 November 1943, when he replaced the indisposed Bruno Walter to lead the orchestra on its Sunday afternoon radio broadcast over CBS; but this thunderclap of fame did not disrupt his commitment to Robbins. He mailed him sections of the score while Robbins was on the road with Ballet Theatre in the winter of 1943–44, often including a recording of a four-handed piano version played by himself and Copland. Bernstein was in the pit at the old Metropolitan Opera House to conduct the world premiere and to share the torrential acclaim it triggered. Hurok extended the company's season by two weeks, scheduling *Fancy Free* for most performances.

Broadway producers showered the dynamic young duo with offers, but they wisely played it safe on their first venture into show business. They decided to do a musical about three sailors on leave in New York City. Directed by the veteran George Abbott, *On the Town* opened in December 1944 at the Adelphi Theatre for a respectable run of 463 performances. Bernstein's friends Betty Comden and Adolph Green wrote the book and lyrics and starred in the show, along with Nancy Walker and Sono Osato. Four and a half years later Gene Kelly and Stanley Donen co-directed the movie version for Metro-Goldwyn-Mayer.

No company other than Ballet Theatre (later American Ballet Theatre) danced Robbins's *Fancy Free* until 1980, when Robbins set it on New York City Ballet. A recording of "Big Stuff" by Dee Dee Bridgewater is heard on its bartender's radio. The work is also performed by the Dance Theatre of Harlem.

—Harris Green

---

**FARRELL, Suzanne**

American dancer. Born Roberta Sue Ficker in Cincinnati, Ohio, 16 August 1945. Studied with Marian La Cour, Conservatory of Music, Cincinnati, and at the School of American Ballet (on scholarship), New York, from 1960. Married dancer Paul Mejia, 1969. Dancer (under stage name Suzanne Farrell), New York City Ballet, from 1961, becoming soloist, from 1963, and principal dancer, 1965–69; left New York City Ballet: guest artist, National Ballet of Canada, 1969; principal dancer, Ballet du XXe Siècle, Brussels, 1970–74; returned to New York: principal dancer, New York City Ballet, from 1975; also international guest artist, including for Royal Danish Ballet, Copenhagen, 1976, and Chicago Ballet (director Paul Mejia), 1981; has appeared on television, including in all of the "Choreography by Balanchine" programmes on Public Broadcasting Service (PBS) "Dance in America" series; producer of Balanchine ballets since retiring from stage, including staging of *Scotch Symphony* for the Kirov Ballet, Leningrad, 1988; also teacher: member of the faculty, School of American Ballet, New York. Recipient: *Mademoiselle* Magazine Merit Award, 1965; University of Cincinnati Award of Merit in Creative and Performing Arts, 1965; *Dance Magazine* Award, 1976; New York City Award of Honor for Arts and Culture, 1980; Brandeis University Creative Arts Award in Dance, 1980; Hononary Doctorate, Middlebury College, Vermont, 1992.

**ROLES**

1962/63 Principal dancer (second solo) in *Concerto Barocco* (Balanchine), Friends of City Center, New York
Principal dancer in *Donizetti Variations* (Balanchine), Friends of City Center, New York
Principal dancer in *Serenade* (Balanchine), New York City Ballet, New York

1963 Young girl (cr) in *Arcade* (Taras), New York City Ballet, New York
Bacchante in *Orpheus* (Balanchine), New York City Ballet, New York
Principal dancer (cr) in *Movements for Piano and Orchestra* (Balanchine), New York City Ballet, New York
Principal dancer in *Liebeslieder Walzer* (Balanchine), New York City Ballet, New York
Titania in *A Midsummer Night's Dream* (Balanchine), New York City Ballet, New York
Principal dancer (cr) in *Meditation* (pas de deux; Balanchine), New York City Ballet, New York

1964 Terpsichore in *Apollo* (Balanchine), New York City Ballet, New York
Contrapuntal Blues (cr) in *Clarinade* (Balanchine), New York City Ballet, New York
Principal dancer in *Scotch Symphony* (Balanchine), Artists of the New York City Ballet, Arts Festival, Munich
Principal dancer in *Irish Fantasy* (d'Amboise), New York City Ballet, New York
Principal dancer in *Ballet Imperial* (later *Tchaikovsky Piano Concerto No. 2*; Balanchine), New York City Ballet, New York
Principal dancer in *Monumentum pro Gesualdo* (Balanchine), New York City Ballet, New York

1965 Dulcinea (cr) in *Don Quixote* (Balanchine), New York City Ballet, New York
Pas de deux in *Agon* (Balanchine), New York City Ballet, New York
Five Pieces in *Episodes II* (Balanchine), New York City Ballet, New York
Odette in *Swan Lake* (one-act version; Balanchine after Ivanov), New York City Ballet, New York

1966 Solo (cr) in *Variations* (Balanchine), New York City Ballet, New York
Rondo alla Zingarese (cr) in *Brahms–Schoenberg Quartet* (Balanchine), New York City Ballet, New York
Principal dancer (cr) in *Ragtime* II (new version of 1960 ballet; Balanchine), Philharmonic Hall, New York
Sugar Plum Fairy in *The Nutcracker* (Balanchine), New York City Ballet, New York
Principal dancer in *Bugaku* (Balanchine), New York City Ballet, New York

1967 Diamonds (cr) in *Jewels* (Balanchine), New York City Ballet, New York
Sanguinic in *The Four Temperaments* (Balanchine), New York City Ballet, New York

1968 Pithoprakta (cr) in *Metastaseis and Pithoprakta* (Balanchine), New York City Ballet, New York
Strip-tease Girl (cr) in *Slaughter on Tenth Avenue* (Balanchine), New York City Ballet, New York
Principal dancer (cr) in *Requiem Canticles* (Balanchine) (performed only once in honour of Martin Luther King), New York City Ballet, New York
Second Movement in *Symphony in C* (Balanchine), New York City Ballet, New York

1969 Principal dancer (cr) in *Sylvia Pas de deux* (Mejia), Concert performance, Manhasset
Nikiya in *La Bayadère* ("Kingdom of the Shades"; Valukin after Petipa), National Ballet of Canada, Toronto
Odette/Odile in *Swan Lake* (Petipa, Ivanov; staged Bruhn), National Ballet of Canada, Toronto

**Suzanne Farrell in *Vienna Waltzes*, 1977**

Sugar Plum Fairy in *The Nutcracker* (Franca after Ivanov), National Ballet of Canada, Toronto

1970 Principal dancer (cr) in *Sonate* (Béjart), Ballet du XXe Siècle, Brussels

Juliet in *Romeo and Juliet* (Béjart), Ballet du XXe Siècle, Brussels

1971 Principal dancer in *Erotica II* (Béjart), Ballet du XXe Siècle, Brussels

Principal dancer (cr) in *Les Fleurs de mal* (Béjart), Ballet du XXe Siècle, Brussels

The Girl in Pink (cr) in *Nijinsky, clown de dieu* (Béjart), Ballet du XXe Siècle, Brussels

Principal dancer in *Messe pour le temps present* (Béjart), Ballet du XXe Siécle, Brussels

Shiva in *Bhakti* (Béjart), Ballet du XXe Siècle, Brussels

1972 Principal dancer in *Alborada del Gracioso* (Mejia), Ballet du XXe Siècle, Brussels

The dancer (cr) in *Ah, vous dirais-je maman* (solo; Béjart), Ballet du XXe Siècle, Brussels

The Woman in *Symphonie pour un homme seul* (Béjart), Ballet du XXe Siècle

The Woman in *Le Sacre du printemps* (Béjart), Ballet du XXe Siècle

1973 True Rose (cr) in *Golestan* (Béjart) Ballet du XXe Siècle, Persepolis

Principal dancer (cr) in *Farah* (Béjart), Ballet du XXe Siècle, Brussels

Principal dancer in *Méditation* (Béjart), Ballet du XXe Siècle

Principal dancer in *Mathilde* (Béjart), Ballet du XXe Siècle

Principal dancer in *Le Marteau sans maître* (Béjart), Ballet du XXe Siècle

Principal dancer in *IXe Symphonie* (Béjart), Ballet du XXe Siècle

1974 Laura (cr) in *I Trionfi del Petrarce* (Béjart), Ballet du XXe Siècle, Florence

Principal dancer in *Bolero* (Béjart) Ballet du XXe Siècle

Estelle in *Sonate à trois* (Béjart), Ballet du XXe Siècle

1975 Principal dancer (cr) in *Tzigane* (Balanchine), New York City Ballet, New York

Principal dancer (cr) in *Concerto in G* (later called *In G Major*; Robbins), New York City Ballet, New York

Principal dancer (cr) in *Alborada del Gracioso* (d'Amboise), New York City Ballet, New York

1976 Principal dancer (cr) in *Chaconne* (Balanchine), New York City Ballet, New York

Royal Canadian Air Force, Wrens (cr) in *Union Jack* (Balanchine), New York City Ballet, New York

1977 "Rosenkavalier" Waltzes (cr) in *Vienna Waltzes* (Balanchine), New York City Ballet, New York

Pas de deux from *Flower Festival at Genzano* (Bournonville; staged Williams), New York City Ballet, New York

1980 Principal dancer (cr) in *Walpurgisnacht Ballet* (Balanchine), New York City Ballet, New York

Lucille (cr) in *Le Bourgeois Gentilhomme* (Balanchine), New York City Ballet, New York

Principal dancer, Second couple (cr) in *Robert Schumann's "Davidsbündlertänze"* (Balanchine), New York City Ballet, New York

1981 Preghiera, Theme et Variations (cr) in *Mozartiana* (new production; Balanchine), New York City Ballet, New York

Title role in *Cinderella* (Mejia), Chicago Ballet, Chicago

1982 Principal dancer (cr) in *Elégie* (solo; Balanchine), New York City Ballet, New York

Principal dancer (cr) in *Variations for Orchestra* (solo; Balanchine), New York City Ballet, New York

1983 Principal dancer (cr) in *Rossini Quartets* (Martins), New York City Ballet, New York

Principal dancer (cr) in *Ballet d'Isoline* (Tomasson), New York City Ballet, New York

1984 Principal dancer (cr) in *Rejouissance* (Martins), New York City Ballet, New York

1985 Principal dancer (cr) in *In Memory of . . .* (Robbins), New York City Ballet, New York

1988 Principal dancer (cr) in *Sophisticated Lady* (Martins), New York City Ballet, New York

1989 Principal dancer (cr) in *Echo* (Martins), New York City Ballet, New York

**Other roles include:** The Siren in *Prodigal Son* (Balanchine), Eighth Waltz, La Valse in *La Valse* (Balanchine), The Sleepwalker in *La Sonnambula* (Balanchine), principal dancer in *Raymonda Variations* (Balanchine), principal dancer in *Irish Fantasy* (d'Amboise), principal dancer in *Pas de Deux and Divertissement* (Balanchine), Jota Aragonese in *Valse Fantaisie* (Balanchine), principal dancer in *In the Night* (Robbins), Chloë in *Daphnis and Chloë* (Taras).

## PUBLICATIONS

By Farrell:

Interview in *Dance News* (New York), November 1970

Interview in Gruen, John, *The Private World of Ballet*, New York, 1975

Comments on Balanchine in Horosko, Marian, "See the Music, Hear the Dance", *Dance Magazine* (New York), July 1983

Interview in Kendall, Elizabeth, *Dancing* (New York), 1983

Interview in Tracy, Robert, "Balanchine's Ballerinas", New York, 1983

Interview in Garske, Rolf, "Suzanne Farrell, Ballerina par Excellence", *Ballett-International* (Cologne), September 1983

Interview in Brubach, Holly, "Pas Seul", *Ballet News* (New York), October 1983

Interview in Como, William, "Farrell on Farrell", *Dance Magazine* (New York), 3 parts: April 1985, May 1985, June 1985

*Holding on to the Air* (autobiography), with Toni Bentley, New York, 1990

About Farrell:

Sealy, R., "Paul and Suzanne", *Ballet Review* (New York), vol. 3, no. 1, 1975

Goldner, Nancy, "Suzanne Farrell: Chez Balanchine", *Les Saisons de la danse* (Paris), December 1975

Hersin, André-Philippe, "Suzanne Farrell: Chez Béjart", *Les Saisons de la danse* (Paris), December 1975

Croce, Arlene, *Afterimages*, New York, 1977

Reynolds, Nancy, *Repertory in Review*, New York, 1977

Maynard, Olga, "The Metamorphosis of a Balanchine Ballerina", *Dance Magazine* (New York), January 1979

Croce, Arlene, *Going to the Dance*, New York, 1982

Daniel, David, "Diana Adams on Suzanne Farrell", *Ballet Review* (New York), Winter 1982

Croce, Arlene, *Sight Lines*, New York, 1987

McDonagh, Don, "Suzanne Farrell", *Ballet Review* (New York), Winter 1990

* * *

George Balanchine referred to Suzanne Farrell as his Stradivarius. For him she was an expressive instrument—and first class of her kind. He meant the comparison in several senses. Farrell can't read a musical score but she possesses instinctive musicianship. She can trace musical phrasing and pick out climaxes by ear, she has a metronomic sense of timing, and she is so confident about her responses that she prides herself on never having danced to a given musical work the same way twice in a row. For Balanchine, Farrell was also a great instrument in practical terms: she could not only pick up steps very quickly but she could pick up on Balanchine's mere choreographic sugestions—and project them back to him as classical dancing with an empathy that struck observers as telepathic. Furthermore, as the critic David Daniel has observed, her physique is full of contradictory elements that permitted Balanchine to obtain theatrical effects he had not been able to achieve consistently before.

Farrell is tall—5′ 6¾″—yet her head is small, her shoulders are narrow, and her legs naturally taper down sleekly from the knee, lending her a fragile appearance. Also, her long foot gives her a regal elevation (she stands well over 6′ on pointe), and she is both quite loose in the hips and quite strong. It is possible for her to perform large, even vulgar movements and leave a delicate impression, a gift that Balanchine exploited in such roles for her as the Strip-tease Girl in *Slaughter on Tenth Avenue* or the Gypsy ballerina in the fourth movement of *Brahms-Schoenberg Quartet*. Farrell's years with the New York City Ballet (1961–69 and 1975–88) coincided with a period of intensive technical experimentation for Balanchine, as well as with an intensification of romantic themes inherent in his work. Her ability—and eagerness—to dance at her limits, continually courting loss of composure in pursuit of the Balanchinian "more" (more stretch, more speed, more energy) magnified his technical findings and extended the range of feelings in his work. Farrell was both the summation of Balanchine's achievements and the door to his hopes. It isn't suprising that, on every level, he adored her.

Suzanne Farrell, who took her stage name on entering the New York City Ballet, was born Roberta Sue Ficker in the midwestern United States. She began to study ballet at the Conservatory of Music in her native Cincinnati. In 1960, Diana Adams—at that time a ballerina with the New York City Ballet—visited Cincinnati as a scout for the School of American Ballet's new Ford Foundation program. She recommended that Farrell audition for the school (SAB) in New York; a few months later, Farrell, her mother, and her two sisters moved to New York City and Farrell was enrolled on a Ford Foundation scholarship.

She was taken into the company in 1961. The first new role made on her was by John Taras, for his 1963 *Arcade*. That same year she took on the ballerina role of a new Balanchine ballet, *Movements for Piano and Orchestra*, which the original exponent, Diana Adams, had to give up on short notice mid-rehearsal. And in December of 1963, Balanchine choreographed his first role especially for Farrell: the ballerina in *Meditation*, a pas de deux with Jacques d'Amboise. The following year, he revived one of his earlier masterpieces—*Ballet Imperial* (later known as *Tchaikovsky Piano Concerto No. 2*)—for her. In 1965, he made her his Dulcinea in his complex and ambitious evening-length ballet, *Don Quixote*. With this work, the love story of Balanchine and Farrell—a passion in which art and life seemed to be two faces of the same coin—was dramatized for the public as well as for the subjects themselves. With the "Diamonds" pas de deux in *Jewels* in 1967, Balanchine crystallized his appreciation of what he saw as Farrell's limitless capacities for classical dancing, as well as his reverence for her personally.

By 1969, however, Farrell had married Paul Mejia, another young dancer with the New York City Ballet, and her relationship with Balanchine became strained to the breaking point. In the spring of that year, it broke: both Farrell and Mejia left the company. For a brief period, Farrell danced as a guest star with the National Ballet of Canada, and then she and her husband moved to Belgium, where she joined Maurice Béjart's Ballet du XXe Siècle. With Béjart, she was a principal dancer—and a star. She performed with him until 1974, when she wrote to Balanchine and asked to return to the New York City Ballet. In 1975 she returned, in the ballerina role of the Second Movement of *Symphony in C*. Her effect on audiences and critics was powerful, and continued until her retirement from the stage in 1988—following a series of poignant performances with a new artificial hip.

During her second period at the New York City Ballet, Farrell created starring roles in Balanchine's *Tzigane*, *Union Jack*, *Vienna Waltzes*, *Walpugisnacht Ballet*, *Le Bourgeois Gentilhomme*, *Robert Schumann's "Davidsbündlertänze"*, and *Mozartiana*. His last two ballets ever were for her—they were solos, resettings of Stravinsky scores which he had choreographed for Farrell in the 1960s, *Élégie* and *Variations for Orchestra*. During this period, Farrell also linked up with Peter Martins to form one of the great ballet partnerships of the age: their performances in Balanchine's *Chaconne* and in "Diamonds" are perhaps the pinnacle of their work together.

Farrell has danced for Jerome Robbins and for Martins, but it is her relationship with Balanchine for which she is venerated. Her own view of that relationship is a curious mixture of blunt pragmatism and poetic vision. In 1990, she wrote in her autobiography, *Holding On to the Air*: "I was a kind of good jack-of-all trades, which could be very dull indeed except for the one thing I did have, probably the thing Diana had seen in Cincinnati: I could move, and if I could incorporate what Balanchine wanted with my movement, it might blossom into something—it could be anything. I think that was interesting to Balanchine. With no image to uphold and no glory in any single area of technique, I never had the debilitating worry that I might lose my strongest point." As Farrell so simply states it, she had no strongest point, "and the result was freedom and flexibility".

—Mindy Aloff

---

**FARRON, Julia**

British dancer and teacher. Born in London, 22 July 1922. Studied at the Cone-Ripman School and at Vic-Wells Ballet School, London. Married choreographer Alfred Rodrigues. Dancer (performing originally as Joyce Farron), Vic-Wells Ballet (later Sadler's Wells Ballet and Royal Ballet), 1936–61, making guest appearances in mime roles from 1964; teacher, Royal Ballet School, 1964–82; assistant director, Royal Academy of Dancing, 1982–83, and director, 1983–89.

**ROLES**

1934 Snowflake Fairy (cr) in *Cinderella* (pantomime), Drury Lane, London

1935 Little Bo-Peep (cr) in *Nursery Suite* (de Valois), Vic-Wells Ballet, London

1936 A Spirit (cr) in *Le Baiser de la fée* (Ashton), Vic-Wells Ballet, London

A Fairy in *The Nutcracker* (Ivanov; staged Sergeyev), Vic-Wells Ballet, London
Black Lackey in *The Gods Go a-Begging* (de Valois), Vic-Wells Ballet, London
A Belfry Spirit (cr) in *Apparitions* (Ashton), Vic-Wells Ballet, London
Pépé (cr) in *A Wedding Bouquet* (Ashton), Vic-Wells Ballet, London
1937 Pas de deux in *Les Patineurs* (Ashton), Vic-Wells Ballet, tour
Lilian in *The Lord of Burleigh* (Ashton), Vic-Wells Ballet, London
Young Treginnis in *The Haunted Ballroom* (de Valois), Vic-Wells Ballet, London
Red Pawn in *Checkmate* (de Valois), Vic-Wells Ballet, London
Spirit, Bridesmaid in *Le Baiser de la fée* (Ashton), Vic-Wells Ballet, London
Son of Morning in *Job* (de Valois), Vic-Wells Ballet, London
1938 Polka in *Façade* (Ashton), Vic-Wells Ballet, London
Columbine in *Carnaval* (Fokine), Vic-Wells Ballet, London
1939 Psyche (cr) in *Cupid and Psyche* (Ashton), Vic-Wells Ballet, London
Entrée ("Blue girl") in *Les Patineurs* (Ashton), Vic-Wells Ballet, London
Waltz in *Les Sylphides* (Fokine), Vic-Wells Ballet, London
Breadcrumb Fairy, Sapphire Fairy in *The Sleeping Princess* (Petipa; staged Sergeyev), Vic-Wells Ballet, London
Black Pawn in *Checkmate* (de Valois), Vic-Wells Ballet, London
1940 A Child of Light in *Dante Sonata* (Ashton), Vic-Wells Ballet, London
A Wise Virgin in *The Wise Virgins* (Ashton), Vic-Wells Ballet, London
Mademoiselle Theodore in *The Prospect Before Us* (de Valois), Vic-Wells Ballet, tour
1941 Eurydice in *Orpheus and Eurydice* (de Valois), Vic-Wells Ballet, tour
Principal dancer (cr) in *The Wanderer* (Ashton), Vic-Wells Ballet, London
1942 The Bride in *The Wise Virgins* (Ashton), Sadler's Wells Ballet, London
Alicia in *The Haunted Ballroom* (de Valois), Sadler's Wells Ballet, London
The Serving Maid in *The Gods Go a-Begging* (de Valois), Sadler's Wells Ballet, London
1943 Faith (cr) in *The Quest* (Ashton), Sadler's Wells Ballet, London
The Lady in *Comus* (Helpmann), Sadler's Wells Ballet, London
1944 The Betrayed Girl in *The Rake's Progress* (de Valois), Sadler's Wells Ballet, London
1945 Titania's train in *The Fairy Queen* (Ashton), Sadler's Wells Ballet, London
1946 The Queen of Denmark in *Hamlet* (Helpmann), Sadler's Wells Ballet, London
The Prostitute in *Miracle in the Gorbals* (Helpmann), Sadler's Wells Ballet, London
Titania's Train (cr) in *The Fairy Queen* (masque after Shakespeare; mus. Purcell, chor. Ashton), Covent Garden Opera and Sadler's Wells Ballet, London
1946/47 Lady Kitty in *Les Sirènes* (Ashton), Sadler's Wells Ballet, London
The Red Queen in *Checkmate* (de Valois), Sadler's Wells Ballet, London
Title role in *Mam'zelle Angot* (Massine), Sadler's Wells Ballet, London
Tarantella in *La Boutique fantasque* (Massine), Sadler's Wells Ballet, London
1948 An Amour in *Don Juan* (Ashton), Sadler's Wells Ballet, London
1951 Principal dancer in *Ballabile* (Petit), Sadler's Wells Ballet, London
Principal dancer in *Ballet Imperial* (Balanchine), Sadler's Wells Ballet, London
The Black Queen in *Checkmate* (de Valois), Sadler's Wells Ballet, London
The Fairy Godmother in *Cinderella* (Ashton), Sadler's Wells Ballet, London
A Nymph of Pan (cr) in *Daphnis and Chloë* (Ashton), Sadler's Wells Ballet, London
Lykanion in *Daphnis and Chloë* (Ashton), Sadler's Wells Ballet, London
The Aristocrat in *Mam'zelle Angot* (Massine), Sadler's Wells Ballet, London
Prelude in *Les Sylphides* (Fokine), Sadler's Wells Ballet, London
The Mother, The King's Guest (cr) in *Donald of the Burdens* (Massine), Sadler's Wells Ballet, London
1952 Hannah (cr) in *Mirror for Witches* (Howard), Sadler's Wells Ballet, London
Princess Florine (Bluebird) in *The Sleeping Beauty* (Petipa; staged Sergeyev, de Valois, Ashton), Sadler's Wells Ballet, London
Diana (cr) in *Sylvia* (Ashton), Sadler's Wells Ballet, London
Neapolitan Dance (cr; chor. Ashton) in *The Sleeping Beauty* (Petipa; staged Sergeyev, de Valois, Ashton), Sadler's Wells Ballet, London
1953 Principal dancer in *Homage to the Queen* (Ashton), Sadler's Wells Ballet, London
Tarantella (cr) in *Veneziana* (Howard), Sadler's Wells Ballet, London
1955 Sibilla (cr) in *Rinaldo and Armida* (Ashton), Sadler's Wells Ballet, London
1956 The Faded Beauty in *Noctambules* (MacMillan), Sadler's Wells Ballet, London
1957 Princess Belle Epine (cr) in *The Prince of the Pagodas* (Cranko), Royal Ballet, London
1958 Berta (cr) in *Ondine* (Ashton), Royal Ballet, London
1959 Jocasta (cr) in *Antigone* (Cranko), Royal Ballet, London
1965 Lady Capulet (cr) in *Romeo and Juliet* (MacMillan), Royal Ballet, London

**PUBLICATIONS**

Swinson, Cyril, *Six Dancers of Sadler's Wells*, London, 1956
"Dancers of Today: Julia Farron", *Dance and Dancers* (London), July 1957
"Julia Farron", *Ballet Today* (London), May 1958
"Personality of the Month: Julia Farron", *Dance and Dancers* (London), July 1961
Anthony, Gordon, "Pioneers of the Royal Ballet: Julia Farron", *Dancing Times* (London), August 1970
Anthony, Gordon, *A Camera at the Ballet*, London, 1975

* * *

Julia Farron was the first scholarship pupil of Ninette de

**Julia Farron as Lady Capulet in *Romeo and Juliet* with Anthony Dowell, c.1965**

Valois's ballet school after its establishment at Sadler's Wells Theatre in 1931. Aged nine at that time, she studied for only five years and in 1936 became the most junior member of the Vic-Wells Ballet, having already made her professional début at the age of twelve in pantomime at Drury Lane, followed a year later by her ballet début at the Wells, in de Valois's *Nursery Suite*. At fifteen, she appeared in her first created role, Pépé the dog in Ashton's *A Wedding Bouquet*, and, after a couple of small named parts, next inherited Markova's role of the *Façade* Polka and Karsavina's of Columbine in *Le Carnaval*. At that time, Farron's style of dancing was unusual within the Vic-Wells Ballet, in that in no way was it influenced by Fonteyn. Farron was entirely individual: her crisp, wide-eyed, pert manner, her highly-arched feet, and unusually long neck lent her an elegance and poise beyond her years, while her neat footwork and clarity of dancing showed her to be the ideal exponent of de Valois's choreography.

Farron's rapid progress in the company while still so young had well qualified her for the chance to create a leading role in a new ballet, and in 1938 she received the opportunity to do so. It was quite unbelievably bad luck that this leading role was that of Psyche in the first real flop of Frederick Ashton's career. *Cupid and Psyche* pleased no one; it achieved only four performances (to the accompaniment of some booing, an unwelcome novelty at the Wells); critics and public for once agreed that Michael Somes seemed to be performing in a separate world of his own, that Frank Staff looked as though he were wondering exactly what ballet he was in, and that the treatment of the Gods and Goddesses in the final scenes was quite inappropriate and not even very funny. Everyone liked Farron, whose special qualities were highlighted by the awfulness of what was going on around her: but her association with a complete failure did her future prospects no good at all. It was back to small supporting roles for a couple of seasons, until Ninette de Valois cast Farron in the leads, created by Pamela May, of *The Prospect Before Us* and *Orpheus and Eurydice*, and subsequently her *Haunted Ballroom* and *The Gods Go a-Begging*. In fact, the ill-fated Psyche was the one and only lead creation of Farron's entire career, and although she later proved worth her weight in gold in the creation of secondary roles (most notably Princess Belle Epine in John Cranko's *Prince of the Pagodas* and Berthe in Ashton's *Ondine*), she never again took the lead in a new creation by any choreographer.

Such a fate is, of course, that of many dancers, as most "house" choreographers prefer to work only with a few dancers of their own choice; it was Farron's bad luck which brought her to prominence in the company at just the time when de Valois was becoming more and more preoccupied with administration, and therefore never made especially for Farron new ballets which could have established her in the very top rank of contemporary ballerinas.

Ninette de Valois remarked in her *Invitation to the Ballet* (1927) "An old saying runs as follows: 'It takes three years to make a good pupil, five years a dancer, and eight years an artist.' This is apt, and allows for a child starting at the age of nine to be ready at fourteen to seek an engagement as a very young dancer, and at seventeen to be a performer of some responsibility towards his work." Julia Farron's career followed this schedule almost exactly and is, together with that of de Valois herself, along with Markova, Baronova, Grey, Beriosova, and many others, proof of the truth of the old saying. Julia Farron's responsibility to her work enabled her to survive several periods of neglect, alternating with other periods during which, for example, she bravely tackled the virtuoso role of the leading ballerina in *Ballet Imperial*—a role which was in theory technically beyond her but in which, cast in the sudden absence of other ballerinas rehearsed in the role, she succeeded through sheer determination (even, once the emergency was over, retaining the role for a further four performances).

To many, Farron's appearance as *Mam'zelle Angot* by far surpassed that of the original choice for the role in the revival of this typically Massine work, no less than Fonteyn herself: Farron was equally at home with the Aristocrat in the same ballet, while both Black and Red Queens in *Checkmate* were well within her capabilities. After continuing in mime roles from 1961 to 1965—making a career span with the same company of thirty years—she continued to work in teaching, only retiring in 1989, after a career in the ballet world which lasted more than half a century.

—Janet Sinclair

**FEDOROVA, Sophia** (Sofia)

Russian dancer. Born Sofia Vasilievna Fedorova in Moscow, 28 September (16 September old style) 1879. Studied at the Moscow Theatre School, pupil of Vasily Tikhomirov; graduated in 1899. Married opera singer and director Petr Oleinin. Dancer, Bolshoi Theatre, Moscow, 1899–1918, Diaghilev's Ballets Russes, 1909–13 and 1928, and Anna Pavlova's company, Paris, 1925–26; retired from dancing completely after nervous breakdown in 1930. Died in Neuilly, 3 January 1963.

**Sophia Fedorova in *Cléopâtre***

## ROLES

1900 Mercedes (cr) in *Don Quixote* (Gorsky after Petipa), Bolshoi Theatre, Moscow
1901 The Gypsy Dance (cr) in *The Little Humpbacked Horse* (Gorsky after Saint-Léon), Bolshoi Theatre, Moscow
1902 Esmeralda (cr) in *Gudule's Daughter* (Gorsky), Bolshoi Theatre, Moscow
1903 The Old Woman (cr) in *The Gold Fish* (Gorsky), Bolshoi Theatre, Moscow
1904 Gamzatti in *La Bayadère* (Gorsky after Petipa), Bolshoi Theatre, Moscow
1905 Lise in *Vain Precautions* (*La Fille mal gardée*; Gorsky after Petipa), Bolshoi Theatre, Moscow
The Slave Khita (cr) in *Pharaoh's Daughter* (Gorsky after Petipa), Bolshoi Theatre, Moscow
1906 Selesten (cr) in *Robert and Bertram*; *or*, *The Two Thieves* (Gorsky), Bolshoi Theatre, Moscow
1907 Pierette (cr) in *Harlequinade* (Gorsky after Petipa), Bolshoi Theatre, Moscow
1909 Polovtsian Maiden (cr) in *Polovtsian Dances* from *Prince Igor* (opera; mus. Borodin, chor. Fokine), Diaghilev's Ballets Russes, Paris
Bacchanalia in *Cléopâtre* (Fokine), Diaghilev's Ballets Russes, Paris
Ta-Hor in *Cléopâtre* (Fokine), Diaghilev's Ballets Russes, Paris
Czardas (cr) in *Le Festin* (Fokine and others, czardas by Gorsky), Diaghilev's Ballets Russes, Paris
1910 Almeya (cr) in *Schéhérazade* (Fokine), Diaghilev's Ballets Russes, Paris
Dancer with Snakes (cr) in *Salammbô* (Gorsky), Bolshoi Theatre, Moscow
1912 The Military Dance in *Le Corsaire* (Gorsky after Petipa), Bolshoi Theatre, Moscow
1913 Title role in *Giselle* (Petipa after Coralli, Perrot; staged Gorsky), Bolshoi Theatre, Moscow
1915 Mazurka (cr) in *Eunice and Petronius* (Gorsky), Bolshoi Theatre, Moscow

**Other roles include:** The White Cat in *The Sleeping Beauty* (Gorsky after Petipa), The Wife of Khan and the Ukrainian in *The Little Humpbacked Horse* (Gorsky after Saint-Léon), the Czardas in *Coppélia* (Petipa after Saint-Léon; staged Gorsky), Spanish Dance in *Swan Lake* (Gorsky after Petipa, Ivanov), the Hindu Dance in *La Bayadère* (Gorsky after Petipa), the Polka in *Harlequinade* (Petipa), Panaderos in *Raymonda* (Gorsky after Petipa); in operas—Mazurka in *A Life for the Tsar* (mus. Glinka; chor. Gorsky), Lezhginka in *Ruslan and Ludmila* (mus. Glinka, chor. Gorsky).

## PUBLICATIONS

Cocteau, Jean, *Le Saison Russe*, Paris, 1911
Grigorov, S., *Balletic Art and S. V. Fedorova*, Moscow, 1914
Roslavleva, Natalia, *Era of the Russian Ballet*, London, 1966
Krasovskaya, Vera, *Russian Ballet Theatre of the Beginning of the Twentieth Century*, vol. 2, Leningrad, 1972
Souritz, Elizabeth, *The Art of Choreography in the 1920s*, Moscow, 1979; as *Soviet Choreographers in the 1920s*, translated by Lynn Visson, Durham, N.C. and London, 1990

* * *

Sophia Fedorova was an extraordinary personality in Russian ballet at the beginning of the century. Fedor Lopukhov remembers, "Sophia Fedorova showed herself to be a great and most interesting actress. The range of her roles was extraordinarily wide, from the simple Lise in *Vain Precautions* to the tragic Esmeralda. A classical dancer, she also danced solo and character roles with success." Fokine, as Lopukhov points out, had spotted Fedorova in the Moscow Ballet and she went on to become one of the most popular Russian ballerinas in Paris, with the Bacchanalia in *Cléopâtre* noted as a particularly outstanding spectacle associated with her dancing. Lopukhov goes on: "Short, not beautiful, and it would seem, not very stage-worthy, Fedorova in moments of high tension seemed to grow on the stage. Her body, when seized by powerful emotion, shook, and her face lit up as if from the inside. She managed the condition of ecstasy or frenzy particularly well. Here was an actress who could extinguish her own personality without a remnant and could put an artistic image in its place. There have been few like her in the ballet theatre of my time." And one further important aspect of the dancer's gifts was what Grigorov called her original artistic pathos; as he put it, "a noble passion without the least tinge of cheap emotion."

Fedorova was also an outstanding character dancer. Her younger colleague on the Moscow stage, Viktorina Kriger, remembered, "In her performance was much fire and the genuine passion of dance. She went on the stage and the theatre instantly livened up. The dry mathematics of classicism paled before the living truth." Nevertheless Fedorova's dancing was not simply a regular variation on one and the same theme. All of the national dances which she performed were faithful to life and to their ethnic roots. Again, as Grigorov notes, they were distinguished not by costume or by various steps and poses, but by the essence of national mood they represented.

Still, Fedorova's talent could not be compressed in character roles and dances alone. For this reason, Fedorova's appearances in classical roles—into which she injected her own intense characterization—at times approached pure naturalism. As the historian Vera Krasovskaya writes, "Her Esmeralda, the little ragamuffin girl, looked out from under her brows wildly and mistrustfully. Only gradually, in the awkward timidity of movement, and in unexpected impulses, were the depths of the pure soul revealed." And the scene in *Esmeralda* after the torture was so convincingly acted by Fedorova that a shaken eye-witness, Yuri Belyaev, afterwards described the blind horror, dishevelled appearance, and glazed eyes of the dancer as if they had been real. "Cheeks, brow, and hands were smeared with blood and filth. Her head . . . on stretched neck with swelling veins, rolled from side to side, and one arm dragged along the floor."

Fedorova had long dreamed of performing *Giselle*, and she danced the role in 1913. The tragic potential of the role was carried to the limit; the psychological tragedy of the story brought out to the fullest. The way another eye-witness saw it was not unusual: "All this is so awfully true to life that it seizes you and gives you a nervous tremor. You wish to come out of this nightmare to remind yourself that you are at the ballet."

It is possible, then, that it was the very role of Giselle which became the final experience that broke the fragile, spiritual constitution of this delicate artist. Disease gradually progressed. In 1918, Fedorova was forced to cease appearing on the stage of her native theatre. In 1922, in the hope of a cure, she went to France. Serious attacks of spiritual malaise alternated with more hopeful periods, and then she again went on the stage, her last encounter with the public in one of the performances of the Diaghilev company in 1928. Eventually Fedorova suffered a breakdown, and she lived in relative obscurity until her death in 1963.

—Arsen Degen

---

**FEDOROVITCH, Sophie**
Russian/British stage designer. Born Sofiya Fedorovich (Fedorovitch) in Minsk, 15 December 1893. Studied painting at private school in Moscow, and later at the St. Petersburg Academy. Came to England after Russian Revolution, 1920, forming close collaboration with Frederick Ashton; exhibited paintings as non-member with London Group, 1920–32, with Seven and Five Group, London, and at Salon des Indépendants and Salon d'Automne, Paris, 1926–29; mounted own show at Beaux-Arts Gallery, London, 1928; first professional ballet designs for Ashton's *A Tragedy of Fashion*, staged by Marie Rambert's Dancers (later Ballet Rambert), 1926; designer for Ashton, Ninette de Valois, and other English choreographers, working for Vic-Wells (later Sadler's Wells) Ballet, London Ballet, and Ballet Rambert; also designer for opera productions at Covent Garden, London, and for theatre, including the Old Vic, London, and the Royal Shakespeare Theatre, Stratford-Upon-Avon; naturalized British subject, 1940; also member of artistic advisory panel, Sadler's Wells Ballet, 1951. Died in London, 25 January 1953.

**WORKS** (Ballet designs)

1925 *Les Nenuphars* (chor. James), Marie Rambert Studio Student Matinée, London
1926 *A Tragedy of Fashion; or, The Scarlet Scissors* (chor. Ashton), Rambert Dancers, London
1930/31 *Thumbelina* (not produced)
1932 *The Scorpions of Ysit* (chor. de Valois), Vic-Wells Ballet, London
1933 *Les Masques* (chor. Ashton), Ballet Club (later Ballet Rambert), London
1934 *Mephisto Valse* (chor. Ashton), Ballet Club, London

**Sophie Fedorovitch**

1935 *Valentine's Eve* (chor. Ashton), Ballet Rambert, London (designs reused for *Valse finale* (chor. Gore), Ballet Club, London, 1938)
*Douanes* (chor. de Valois), Vic-Wells Ballet, London
*Le Baiser de la fée* (chor. Ashton), Vic-Wells Ballet, London
1936 *Nocturne* (chor. Ashton), Vic-Wells Ballet, London
*Prelude* and *Symphonie Russe* in *To and Fro* (chor. Tudor), Peter Farquharson revue, Comedy Theatre, London
1937 *Lady into Fox* (chor. Tudor), Ballet Rambert, London (not produced)
1938 *Horoscope* (chor. Ashton), Vic-Wells Ballet, London
1939 *Endymion* (chor. Inglesby), Ballet de la Jeunesse Anglaise, London
1939/40 *Penny Royal* (Ruritanian musical extravaganza; not produced)
1940 *Concerto* (chor. Lester), Arts Theatre Ballet, London
*Dante Sonata* (chor. Ashton), Vic-Wells Ballet, London
*La Fête étrange* (chor. Howard), London Ballet, London
1941 *Orpheus and Eurydice* (chor. de Valois), Sadler's Wells Ballet, London
1942 *The Great Gate of Kieff* ("curtain-raiser" to Mussorgsky's opera *Sorochinsky Fair*; chor. De Viller), Jay Pomeroy production, London
1946 *The Concerto Ballet* (from *Song of Norway*; chor. Helpmann), Emile Littler Production, London
*Symphonic Variations* (chor. Ashton), Sadler's Wells Ballet, London
1947 *Valses nobles et sentimentales* (chor. Ashton), Sadler's Wells Theatre Ballet, London
1950 *Summer Interlude* (chor. Somes), Sadler's Wells Theatre Ballet, London
1952 *Clair de lune* (chor. Bartholin), Grand Ballet du Marquis de Cuevas (not produced)
1953 *Orpheus et Eurydice* (opera by Gluck; chor. Ashton), Sadler's Wells Ballet and Covent Garden Opera, London
*Veneziana* (chor. Howard), Sadler's Wells Ballet, London

**PUBLICATIONS**

Beaumont, Cyril, *Design for the Ballet*, London, 1937
Amberg, George, *Art in Modern Ballet*, London, 1946
Beaumont, Cyril, *Ballet Design: Past and Present*, London, 1946
Fleet, S., "Sophie Fedorovitch as a Ballet Designer", *Ballet Annual* (London), vol. 2, 1948
Rambert, Marie, "How They Began: Ballet Rambert", *Dancing Times* (London), August 1950
Rambert, Marie, "Sophie Fedorovitch", *Dance and Dancers* (London), March 1953
Buckle, Richard, "Sophie Fedorovitch", *Ballet Annual* (London), vol. 8, 1954
*Sophie Fedorovitch 1893–1953*: *Memorial Exhibition of designs for Ballet, Opera and Stage*, Victoria and Albert Museum (catalogue), London, 1955
Barnes, Clive, "Fedorovitch Memorial Exhibition", *Dance and Dancers* (London), February 1956
Vaughan, David, *Frederick Ashton and his Ballets*, London, 1977
Clarke, Mary, and Crisp, Clement, *Design for Ballet*, London, 1978
Schouvaloff, Alexander, *Set and Costume Designs for Ballet and Theatre* (catalogue of the Thyssen-Bornemisza collection), London, 1987

* * *

Sophie Fedorovitch was in at the start of British ballet, and she designed productions for both Marie Rambert's Ballet Club and Ninette de Valois's Vic-Wells Ballet. Both directors—as well as many dancers, choreographers, and fellow designers—valued her opinions, advice, and friendship. She earned special affection and respect from her colleagues for her steadiness of eye and mind, and her frank, perceptive manner. In the last two years of her life Fedorovitch was a member of the Sadler's Wells Ballet Advisory Board, but informally she had served in this capacity for nearly twenty years.

Fedorovitch left Russia during the upheavals that followed the Revolution, and came to join friends in London in 1920; but for the next decade she made herself equally at home in England, Italy, and France. In Paris, where she was involved with other emigrés, she even for a while drove a taxi at night to support her art. She exhibited her paintings in Paris and London with some success, but from 1932 she turned almost exclusively to stage design. She worked on operas and plays as well as ballets—but it is as a designer for dance that her skill remains unsurpassed. She made her main base in England (in Brancaster, Norfolk). She loved the spaciousness of that flat landscape as it met the sky, and it became a hallmark of many of her designs, notably her masterpieces *La Fête étrange*, *Dante Sonata*, and *Symphonic Variations*.

It was Marie Rambert who first recognized Fedorovitch's talent. They had met at rehearsals for the Ballets Russes's sumptuous production of *The Sleeping Princess* (1921) and at Cecchetti's studio where Fedorovitch sketched the dancers. In 1925, when Rambert's pupil Frances James was arranging ballets for a student matinée, she suggested that Fedorovitch might design the evocatively named *Les Nenuphars*. When a year later, Frederick Ashton was making his first choreography, *A Tragedy of Fashion*, Rambert again proposed Fedorovitch as the designer. Ashton's first professional creation was also Fedorovitch's, and they became, until her untimely accidental death in 1953, the closest friends, and Ashton often relied on her advice. They collaborated on a further ten ballets, in each of which the design was in complete accord with the choreography.

Fedorovitch understood the needs of the choreographer, and of dancers too. Her sets were uncluttered, and with a few telling details she could evoke a place and an atmosphere. As William Chappell observed, she created "proportioned voids"—" . . . the spectator seeing them needs to use his own mind, meet the designer half way and supply from his own imagination what he wishes or is stimulated to see in the disciplined simplicity shown to him". Columns bill-posted with announcements "un bal", linked by a balustrade beyond which opened out a carefully lit night sky, conjured up the Paris of Ashton's *Nocturne*. A backcloth of the wintry view seen from a terrace suggested the chateau of Andrée Howard's *La Fête étrange*, conveying all the melancholy and separation of the lost domain. The empty sky of the lagoon framed by pink walls and gilded lattices devised for Howard's *Veneziana* needed only costumes and four lanterns on poles to evoke carnival-time in Venice. Fedorovitch's interior settings showed the same deft imagination. For *A Tragedy of Fashion*, where a screen of mirrors extends beneath an arch of enormous scissors (suggestive of the Shears of Fate or even the Sword of Damocles), she established the chic, modish narcissisism of the couturier's salon. Scale always mattered to Fedorovitch, whether designing for the tiny Mercury or the Royal Opera House itself. When a ballet was transferred to a larger venue, mere enlargement of the design was not enough and Fedorovitch insisted on the opportunity to rework it. If she thought a setting had ceased to be effective, she asked for the ballet to be dropped from the repertory.

Economy of line and colour was the essence of Fedorovitch's design. The décor for *Symphonic Variations*, with its curved and broken lines on a green ground, distils the very rhythms and relationships of the ballet, and gives it a space that reflects both the English landscape and a classical Utopia. Fedorovitch's use of a restricted palette was masterly. Her black-and-white set and costumes for *Les Masques* was praised for its ingenuity, and even when black and white served in *Dante Sonata* to represent good and evil, she gave the symbolism all the urgency of the sinewy Flaxman illustrations that had inspired the work. Fedorovitch chose an unexpectedly narrow but exactly suitable colour range of rose pink, darkening to burgundy, for *Valses nobles et sentimentales*, but she could also use strong splashes of colour to focus attention on specific characters or to mark a change of mood.

Fedorovitch's costumes have the same qualities as her settings. All superfluous detail was stripped away to allow complete freedom of movement. Matilda Etches, the couturière who made up so many of Fedorovitch's designs, recalled how together they would drape fabric over a dancer to establish the general shape of the costume and then Fedorovitch would command the dancer to move. The designs on paper were in a sense no more than an aide-memoire; the real designing took place live. Fabric could thus be deployed to reveal as necessary, or even extend the choreography. Delius's music used for *Nocturne* suggested waves of movement to both Ashton and Fedorovitch, and the rippling trains of the Edwardian dresses she designed opened up further opportunities for the choreographer. Fedorovitch could convey character through costume. In *Mephisto Valse* Marguerite's chaplet of flowers, white dress, and apron appliqued with marguerites were a picture of innocence which contrasted with the red, black, and grey designs for the other dancers. For all her general timeless quality, she could also convey a topicality, as with the stylish "Rose d'Isphan" of *A Tragedy of Fashion*, which anticipates similar models that appeared later on the pages of *Vogue*.

Fedorovitch's designs are elementally simple, but their simplicity results from deep understanding and mature sophistication. She is often and rightly praised as a British-based equivalent of Christian Bérard, a designer she herself much admired.

—Jane Pritchard

---

**FELD, Eliot**

American dancer, choreographer, and ballet director. Born in Brooklyn, New York, 5 July 1942. Studied at the High School of Performing Arts, at the School of American Ballet, and with Richard Thomas, New York. Professional stage début in off-Broadway shows, from 1954; performed in first New York stage production of *West Side Story* (chor. Robbins, 1958), and other musical comedies on Broadway; also performed in modern dance companies under Pearl Lang, Sophie Maslow, Donald McKayle; dancer, American Ballet Theatre, 1963–68, and 1971–72; first choreography for American Ballet Theatre, 1967; founder, director, and choreographer, American Ballet Company, 1969–71; guest choreographer for companies including Royal Winnipeg Ballet, London Festival Ballet, New York City Ballet, Royal Swedish Ballet, and Royal Danish Ballet; founder, Eliot Feld Ballet, 1974 (becoming Feld Ballet, c. 1980, and Feld Ballets/NY, 1990), remaining principal choreographer and artistic director; has also appeared on television, including in Public Broadcasting Service (PBS) "Dance in America" series, and in documentary for German television (1970); also founder and director, The New Ballet School, New York, 1978; founder, Joyce Theater, a dance theatre remodelled from Elgin Cinema, and serving as home theatre for Feld Ballets/NY, New York, 1982. Recipient: *Dance Magazine* Award, 1990; Honorary Doctorate, Juillard School, 1991.

**WORKS**

1967 *Harbinger* (mus. Prokofiev), American Ballet Theatre, Miami, Florida
*At Midnight* (mus. Mahler), American Ballet Theatre, New York
1968 *Meadowlark* (mus. Haydn), Royal Winnipeg Ballet, Winnipeg
1969 *Intermezzo No. 1* (mus. Brahms), American Ballet Company, Spoleto, Italy
*Cortège Burlesque* (mus. Chabrier), American Ballet Company, Spoleto
*Pagan Spring* (mus. Bartók), American Ballet Company, Brooklyn, New York
1970 *Early Songs* (mus. Strauss), American Ballet Company, Brooklyn, New York
*A Poem Forgotten* (mus. Riegger), American Ballet Company, Brooklyn, New York

**Eliot Feld with his dancers**

*Cortège Parisien* (mus. Chabrier), American Ballet Company, Brooklyn, New York
*Consort* (mus. Dowland, Morley, Neusidler, and others), American Ballet Company, Brooklyn, New York
1971 *Romance* (mus. Brahms), American Ballet Company, Brooklyn, New York
*Theatre* (mus. R. Strauss), American Ballet Company, Brooklyn, New York
*The Gods Amused* (mus. Debussy), American Ballet Company, Brooklyn, New York
*A Soldier's Tale* (mus. Stravinsky), American Ballet Theatre, Washington, D.C.
*Eccentrique* (mus. Stravinsky), American Ballet Theatre, Washington, D.C.
1972 *Winter's Court* (mus. Elizabethan lute songs), Royal Danish Ballet, Copenhagen
1973 *Jive* (mus. Gould), City Center Joffrey Ballet, New York
1974 *Tzaddik* (mus. Copland), Eliot Feld Ballet, New York
*Sephardic Song* (mus. traditional, arranged Valls), Eliot Feld Ballet, New York
*The Real McCoy* (mus. Gershwin), Eliot Feld Ballet, New York
1975 *Mazurka* (mus. Chopin), Eliot Feld Ballet, Lewiston, New York
*Excursions* (mus. Barber), Eliot Feld Ballet, New York
1976 *Impromptu* (mus. Roussel), Eliot Feld Ballet, New York
1977 *Variations on "America"* (mus. Ives, W. Schumann), Eliot Feld Ballet, New York
*A Footstep of Air* (mus. Beethoven), Eliot Feld Ballet, New York
*Santa Fé Saga* (mus. Gould), Eliot Feld Ballet, Lewiston, New York
1978 *La Vida* (mus. Copland), Eliot Feld Ballet, New York
*Danzon Cubano* (mus. Copland), Eliot Feld Ballet, Vienna, Virginia
*Half Time* (mus. Gould), Eliot Feld Ballet, New York
1979 *Papillon* (mus. Offenbach), Eliot Feld Ballet, Lewiston, New York
1980 *Circa* (mus. Hindemith), Feld Ballet, Rochester, New York
*Anatomic Balm* (mus. ragtime), Feld Ballet, Purchase, New York
*Scenes for the Theater* (later called *Scenes*; mus. Copland), Feld Ballet, Purchase, New York
1981 *Song of Norway* (mus. Grieg, arranged Wright, Forrest), Feld Ballet and New York City Opera, New York
1982 *Play Bach* (mus. Bach), Feld Ballet, Washington, D.C.
*Over the Pavement* (mus. Ives), Feld Ballet, New York
*Straw Hearts* (mus. various), Feld Ballet, New York
1983 *Summer's Lease* (mus. Mahler), Feld Ballet, New York
*Three Dances* (mus. Cage), Feld Ballet, New York
1984 *The Jig is Up* (mus. the Bothy Band, Cunningham), Feld Ballet, New York
*Adieu* (mus. Wolf), Feld Ballet, New York
*Moon Skate* (mus. Ravel), John Curry Skating Company, New York

1985 *Intermezzo No. 2* (mus. Brahms), Feld Ballet, New York
*Against the Sky* (mus. Bartók), Feld Ballet, New York
*The Grand Canon* (mus. Reich), Feld Ballet, New York
*Medium: Rare* (solo; mus. Reich), Feld Ballet, New York
*Aurora I* (mus. Reich), Feld Ballet, New York
*Aurora II* (mus. Reich), Feld Ballet, New York
1986 *Echo* (solo; mus. Reich), Feld Ballet, New York
*Skara Brae* (mus. traditional), Feld Ballet, New York
*Bent Planes* (mus. Reich), Feld Ballet, New York
1987 *Embraced Waltzes* (mus. Chopin), Feld Ballet, New York
*A Dance for Two* (mus. Haydn), Feld Ballet, New York
1988 *Shadows Breath* (mus. Mozart), Feld Ballet, Philadelphia
*The Unanswered Question* (mus. Ives), New York City Ballet, New York
*Kore* (solo; mus. Reich), Feld Ballet, Nervi, Italy
*Petipa Notwithstanding* (mus. Riley), Feld Ballet, Nervi, Italy
1989 *Asia* (mus. Ravel), Feld Ballet, New York
*Love Song Waltzes* (mus. Brahms), Feld Ballet, New York
*Ah Scarlatti* (mus. Scarlatti), Feld Ballet, Virginia Beach, Virginia
*Mother Nature* (mus. Monteverdi), Feld Ballet, Philadelphia
1990 *Contra Pose* (mus. C.P.E. Bach), Feld Ballets/NY, Washington, D.C.
*Charmed Lives* (mus. Ravel), Feld Ballets/NY, New York
1991 *Ion* (solo; mus. Reich), Feld Ballets/NY, New York
*Fauna* (mus. Debussy), Feld Ballets/NY, New York
*Common Ground* (mus. J.S. Bach), Feld Ballets/NY, New York
*Savage Glance* (mus. Shostakovitch), Feld Ballets/NY, New York
1992 *Clave* (solo; mus. Reich), Feld Ballets/NY, New York
*Evoe* (mus. Debussy), Feld Ballets/NY, New York
*Endsong* (mus. R. Strauss), Feld Ballets/NY, New York
*Wolfgang Strategies* (mus. Mozart), Feld Ballets/NY, New York
*To the Naked Eye* (mus. Stravinsky), Feld Ballets/NY, New York
*Hello Fancy* (mus. traditional), Students of The New Ballet School, New York

## PUBLICATIONS

By Feld:
Interview in "Three up and Many More to Go", *Dance and Dancers* (London), January 1969
Interview in France, Charles, "A Conversation with Eliot Feld", *Ballet Review* (Brooklyn, N.Y.), vol. 3 no. 6, 1971
Interview in Gruen, John, *The Private World of Ballet*, New York, 1975
Interview in Ragosin, Elinor, *The Dance Makers: Conversations with American Choreographers*, New York, 1980
Interview in Cowser, R.L., "Eliot Feld Talks", *Dance Scope* (New York), vol. 14 no. 3, 1980
Interview in Mazo, Joseph H., "After 25 Years", *Elle* (New York), March 1992

About Feld:
Hering, Doris, "Two Eliot Felds?", *Dance Magazine*, January 1971
Siegel, Marcia, "Feld Re-Fielded", *Dance Magazine* (New York), March 1974
Anderson, Jack, "Talking to Myself About Eliot Feld", *Dance Magazine* (New York), February 1975; reprinted in Anderson, *Choreography Observed*, Iowa City, 1987
Pierpont, Claudia Roth, "Contradictions in Eliot Feld", *Dance Life* (New York), Summer 1976
Gruen, John, "Spotlight on: Eliot Feld", *Dance Magazine* (New York), June 1977
Jowitt, Deborah, *The Dance in Mind*, Boston, 1985
Tobias, Tobi, "Plus ça change . . .", *New York* (New York), 19 June 1990
Barnes, Clive, "A Modern Classic: Eliot Feld", *Dance Magazine* (New York), February 1992

* * *

Eliot Feld is a positive force in ballet, a mature choreographer with a substantial body of work behind him, and with the potential still for even greater achievements. Turning 50 in 1992, he has taken two decades-plus to develop a style that is now recognizably his. More importantly, he has learned to live in an arts culture that accommodates strong personalities grudgingly.

Feld's career is marked by various stages of maturation. The first image is that of precocity. He made his show-business début at the age of 12, off-Broadway, and made it to the "big time" four years later in the famous Broadway production of *West Side Story*.

Feld was an energetic and eclectic performer. By the time he joined American Ballet Theatre at age 22, he had played in three more Broadway shows, danced with the modern companies of Pearl Lang, Sophie Maslow, and Donald McKayle, and appeared in the film version of *West Side Story*.

His future seemed assured at ABT. He was charismatic and his talent extended beyond performing. His first ballet choreography, *Harbinger* (1967), received great acclaim. Some critics saw him as the greatest find since Jerome Robbins.

But Feld was also ambitious. After one more choreographic triumph, *At Midnight*, he left ABT in 1968 to form his own American Ballet Company, in residence at the Brooklyn Academy of Music.

Feld's next three years were a learning experience. He was unusually prolific, working at one stage on four ballets at the same time. He also learned that keeping a company afloat required more than talent and enthusiasm. He disbanded the group and worked as a freelance choreographer.

The Eliot Feld Ballet Company, founded in 1974, showed that he was more closely attuned to economic reality. Feld used taped music for most of the pieces, and toured. The company has subsequently not only survived, but grown over fifteen years. It is now affiliated with a school which offers free dance training to children in low-income families, and has attracted a modest but loyal audience.

Feld, too, has grown and changed without loss of energy. In the course of 25 years he has created over 60 ballets. During the early years, his ballet choreography was frequently closer to theatre dance than classical forms. Even his pieces set to serious music were often facetious or silly, designed as crowd pleasers. In one piece involving a chaise longue, the furniture was more active than the dancers.

From the combination of ballet, theatre, and drama, Feld has since arrived at a more definable personal style. He is a superior craftsman, sensitive to music and matching it to movement. His pieces still tend toward what might be called over-brightness (some call it "glitzy"). But while he does not explore to any appreciable depth, Feld is serious.

His work is contemporary, created for audience of the 1990s. His pieces show that Feld is in step with his changing times, and will change with them. Yesterday's brash youngster will no doubt some day be ballet's "Grand Old Man".

—William Fark

---

## LES FEMMES DE BONNE HUMEUR
*(The Good-Humoured Ladies)*

**Choreography:** Léonide Massine
**Music:** Domenico Scarlatti, arranged and orchestrated by Vincenzo Tommasini
**Design:** Léon Bakst
**Libretto:** Vincenzo Tomassini, after comedy *Le Donne di Buon Umore* by Carlo Goldoni
**First Production:** Diaghilev's Ballets Russes, Teatro Costanzi, Rome, 12 April 1917
**Principal Dancers:** Guiseppina Cecchetti (Marquise Silvestra), Lydia Lopokova (Mariuccia), Lubov Tchernicheva (Constanza), Léonide Massine (Leonardo), Enrico Cecchetti (Marquis di Luca), Stanislas Idzikowski (Battista), Sigmund Novak (Rinaldo), Léon Woizikowsky (Niccolo)

**Other productions include:** (de Basil's) Ballets Russes de Monte Carlo (restaged Massine), with Lara Obidenna (Silvestra), Alexandra Danilova (Mariuccia), Tamara Grigorieva (Constanza), Paul Petrov (Leonardo), Marian Ladre (Marquis di Luca), Yurek Shabelevsky (Battista); Philadelphia, 16 February 1935. Grand Ballet du Marquis de Cuevas (scenery André Derain), with Rosella Hightower (Mariuccia); London, 7 July 1949. Opéra Comique (design André Masson); Paris, 1952. La Scala (new version; chor. Luciana Novaro, design P. Pizzi), with Carla Fracci; Milan, 21 February 1960. Royal Ballet (restaged Massine), as *The Good-Humoured Ladies*, with Lydia Sokolova (Silvestra), Antoinette Sibley (Mariuccia), Anya Linden (Constanza), Brian Shaw (Battista), Ronald Hynd (Leonardo), Alexander Grant (Niccolo); London, 11 July 1962.

### PUBLICATIONS


Beaumont, Cyril, *The Good-Humoured Ladies*, London, 1918
Hussey, Dyneley, "*The Good-Humoured Ladies*: 1918–1949", *Dancing Times* (London), September 1949
Beaumont, Cyril, *Complete Book of Ballets*, revised edition, London, 1951
Kochno, Boris, *Le Ballet*, Paris, 1954
Massine, Léonide, *My Life in Ballet*, London, 1960
Barnes, Clive, "*The Good-Humoured Ladies*", *Dance and Dancers* (London), July 1962


***Les Femmes de bonne humeur*, with Lubov Tchernicheva, Léon Woizikowsky, Vera Nemchinova and Stanislas Idzikowski in a revival by Diaghilev's Ballets Russes, c.1924**

Clarke, Mary, "*The Good-Humoured Ladies*", *Dancing Times* (London), August 1962

Sokolova, Lydia, "*The Good-Humoured Ladies*", *About the House* (London), November 1962

Karsavina, Tamara, "Dancers of the Twenties", *Dancing Times* (London), February 1967

* * *

When Massine at 21 years of age created *Les Femmes de bonne humeur* (*The Good-Humoured Ladies*), based on Goldoni's play of the same name, neither he nor Diaghilev, who suggested the idea to him, can have had any idea that this ballet was to introduce an entirely new strand into the choreographic fabric of the twentieth century: a strand which was developed not only in the creation of many more works by Massine himself (*Le Tricorne*, *La Boutique fantasque*, *Pulcinella*, *Les Matelots*, *Le Beau Danube*, *Gaîté parisienne*, *Mam'zelle Angot*, etc.), but also in a whole series of ballets in the same genre by other choreographers, of which perhaps the most successful have been Lichine's *Graduation Ball*, Cranko's *Pineapple Poll*, and more recently David Bintley's *Hobson's Choice*.

*The Good-Humoured Ladies* was one of those apparently accidental felicitous occurrences which can develop within any art form and, if not transform it out of all recognition, at least add a new dimension not visualized by those responsible at the time of the work's creation. First of all, with *Le Soleil de nuit* the choreographer, at twenty, had been the youngest ever to be given the chance by Diaghilev to create a ballet, and—luckily for himself and for twentieth-century ballet—had made a piece sufficiently professional (it was still being performed twenty years later) to encourage Diaghilev to give the young man two further opportunities, followed by *The Good-Humoured Ladies*. Further, Massine had recently been immersing himself in the study of Pierre Rameau, Feuillet, and Blasis—his comment on the latter in his autobiography bearing repetition here: "Yet Blasis's aesthetic vision was not bounded by the purely technical aspects of ballet. He realized that all choreography must strive for an emotional and visual harmony, as he made clear when he quoted from Dauberval in his *Traîté de la danse*: 'It is not enough to please the eye. I wish also to interest the heart.'" Massine's choreography in *The Good-Humoured Ladies* followed this precept, as indeed it did in all his works, always bearing in mind that it was also frequently the intellect and not the heart alone at which he aimed his work. Also important is the fact that Massine was guided by Diaghilev in the choice of music. And finally, but in some ways most important of all, Massine had at his disposal a cast of sophisticated, mature dancers technically and temperamentally able to grasp what he was about and keen to put his ideas into action—Lopokova, Tchernicheva, Cecchetti and his wife, Idzikovski, Woizikovsky, and Massine himself: a cast which would be quite impossible to match in the ballet world today, three-quarters of a century later.

In addition to Massine's study of the written works of ballet authorities of the past, he was helped in his composition, as he tells us in his autobiography, by Diaghilev's suggestion that he study the works of Guardi, Watteau, Longhi, and their contemporaries—while the problems of translating the intricacies of the Goldoni play into movement were smoothed by the support of Scarlatti's elegant music. Though to weld all these elements together into a convincing whole would seem a daunting task for so young a choreographer, Massine succeeded admirably, despite the fact that he tells us "there were also moments when I was not able to sustain the continuity of the choreographic counterpoint". If so, any such failing was not apparent to the ordinary public, or indeed to the press, which was ecstatic and commented, for example, "not only a very brilliant work of art, but a most exhilarating entertainment", and "an artistic event of the first importance".

*The Good-Humoured Ladies* survived triumphantly beyond the Diaghilev era and was produced with great success by the Ballets Russes of Colonel de Basil, in which production many will remember the delightful Mariuccia of Danilova and the ravishing Constanza of Grigorieva (coincidentally, the daughter-in-law of the original creator of that role), and it remained in his repertoire for a considerable period. It was only when it was disastrously revived by the Royal Ballet in 1962 that it failed to please, and this largely because only Lydia Sokolova, who came out of retirement to play Silvestra at half-a-dozen performances, seemed to have the slightest grasp of what the choreographer wanted in the way of style. The ballet amazes and delights with inventive and idiosyncratic movement; each character has his or her individual quirks, down to the two minor characters who enter performing pas de chat starting from the back foot; and each character, if danced with concentration and commitment, provides a witty comment on human nature. But to attempt to present it without an entirely adult, committed cast was to invite disaster, and disaster duly ensued. The period in which *The Good-Humoured Ladies* was conceived and presented was probably unique in that it employed and appreciated dancers who were completely able to grasp what an original thinker was demanding of them; dancers are often dismissed as talented, stupid puppets, and indeed a few of them are, but stupidity is not an essential ingredient in any dancer's make-up, as the success of Massine's works in general, and this ballet in particular, clearly demonstrates.

—Janet Sinclair

---

## FERRI, Alessandra

Italian dancer. Born Alessandra Maria Ferri in Milan, 6 May 1963. Studied at the ballet school of the Teatro alla Scala, Milan, 1974–78, and at the Royal Ballet School, London, 1979–80. Dancer, Royal Ballet, London, from 1980, becoming soloist, 1982–83, and principal dancer, 1983–85; principal dancer, American Ballet Theatre, New York, from 1985; guest artist, London Festival Ballet, London, 1986, National Ballet of Canada, 1989, Ballet National de Marseille 1989, Maggio Musicale Fiorentino (festival), from 1989, Balletto Argentino, Buenos Aires, 1990, Maggiodanza and Aterballetto, Italy, 1991; has also appeared on television, including for British Broadcasting Corporation (BBC), American Public Broadcasting Service (PBS) series "Dance in America", 1989, Argentinian television, 1990, and French television, 1991, and in films, including in *Dancers* (dir. Ross, 1987). Recipient, Prix de Lausanne, 1980; Sir Laurence Olivier Award, 1983; Dancer of the Year, *Dance and Dancers*, 1983; Society of West End Theatres Award, London, 1983; Premio Aqui Danza, Italy, 1987; Premio Positano "Leonide Massine", Italy, 1990; Premio Bennetto Danza, Treviso, Italy, 1990.

## ROLES

1980 Principal dancer in *Concerto* (MacMillan), Royal Ballet, London

1981 Red Riding Hood in *The Sleeping Beauty* (Petipa, Ashton; staged de Valois), Royal Ballet, London

**Alessandra Ferri as Juliet in MacMillan's *Romeo and Juliet*, Royal Ballet, London**

Birdcage Woman in *Illuminations* (Ashton), Royal Ballet, London
Principal dancer in *Afternoon of a Faun* (Robbins), Royal Ballet, London
1982 Gypsy Girl in *The Two Pigeons* (Ashton), Royal Ballet, London
Principal dancer (cr) in *L'Invitation au voyage* (Corder), Royal Ballet, London
Principal dancer in *Napoli* (Pas de six and Tarantella; after Bournonville, Beck), Royal Ballet, London
Mary Vetsera in *Mayerling* (MacMillan), Royal Ballet, London
1983 Micol (cr) in *Valley of Shadows* (MacMillan), Royal Ballet, London
Fairy of the Crystal Fountain and Woodland Glade in *The Sleeping Beauty* (Petipa, Ashton; staged MacMillan), Royal Ballet, London
Principal dancer in *Voluntaries* (Tetley), Royal Ballet, London
Victorine in *Konservatoriet* (Bournonville), Royal Ballet, London
Title role in *Manon* (MacMillan), Royal Ballet, London
Anna (cr) in *The Seven Deadly Sins* (new version; MacMillan), British television
Principal dancer (cr) in *Chanson* (pas de deux; Dean), Royal Ballet, London
Principal dancer (cr) in *Consort Lessons* (Bintley), Royal Ballet, London
1984 Marie (cr) in *A Different Drummer* (MacMillan), Royal Ballet, London
Juliet in *Romeo and Juliet* (MacMillan), Royal Ballet, London
Principal dancer in *Return to the Strange Land* (Kylián), Royal Ballet, London
1985 Odette in *Swan Lake* (new production; Petipa, Ivanov; staged Hightower, produced Zeffirelli), Ballet of La Scala, Milan
Nikiya in *La Bayadère* (Makarova after Petipa), American Ballet Theatre, Vienna, Virginia
Clara in *The Nutcracker* (Baryshnikov), American Ballet Theatre, Los Angeles
1986 Title role in *Giselle* (Petipa after Coralli, Perrot; staged Baryshnikov), American Ballet Theatre, Chicago
Principal dancer in *Requiem* (MacMillan), American Ballet Theatre, San Francisco
Title role in *Carmen* (Petit), London Festival Ballet, London
1987 The Sleepwalker in *La Sonnambula* (Balanchine), American Ballet Theatre, New York
The Sylph in *La Sylphide* (Bruhn after Bournonville), American Ballet Theatre, Washington, D.C.
Aria I in *Stravinsky Violin Concerto* (Balanchine), American Ballet Theatre, Washington, D.C.
Princess Florine in *The Sleeping Beauty* (Petipa; staged MacMillan), American Ballet Theatre, New York
Principal dancer (cr) in *Bruch Violin Concerto No. 1* (Tippet), American Ballet Theatre, Orange County, New York
1988 Principal dancer in *In the Upper Room* (Tharp), American Ballet Theatre, Costa Mesa, California
La Fille de Terpsichore from Paris in *Gala Performance* (Tudor; staged Wilson), American Ballet Theatre, Orange County, California
Fifth Variation in *Birthday Offering* (Ashton), American Ballet Theatre, Houston
Kitri in *Don Quixote* (*Kitri's Wedding*) (Baryshnikov after Petipa), American Ballet Theatre, New York
Odette/Odile in *Swan Lake* (Petipa, Ivanov; staged Baryshnikov), American Ballet Theatre, Washington, D.C.
1989 Principal dancer in *Quartet* (Tharp), American Ballet Theatre, New York
Juliet in *Romeo and Juliet* (Cranko), National Ballet of Canada, Toronto
Chérubin (cr) in *Le Diable amoureux* (Petit), Ballet National de Marseille, Fiesole, Italy
Clara in *Lo Schiaccianoci* (Poliakov), Maggio Musicale Fiorentino, Florence
1990 Principal dancer in *Other Dances* (Robbins), American Ballet Theatre, San Francisco
Principal dancer in *Cheek to Cheek* (Petit), Treviso, Italy
The Accused in *Fall River Legend* (de Mille), American Ballet Theatre, Orange County, California
Principal dancer in *Sinfonietta* (Kylián), American Ballet Theatre, Washington, D.C.
Principal dancer (cr) in *Birdy* (Aviotte), Ballet Argentino, Buenos Aires
La Morte in *Le Jeune homme et la morte* (Petit), Balletto Argentino, Buenos Aires
1991 Principal dancer in *White Man Sleeps* (Ezralow), Maggio Musicale Fiorentino, Florence
Terpsichore in *Apollo* (Balanchine), Maggiodanza, Florence
Caroline in *Jardin aux lilas* (Tudor), Maggiodanza, Florence

**Other roles include:** for the Royal Ballet—Chanson dansée ("The Garçon") in *Les Biches* (Nijinska), Youngest Sister in *Pillar of Fire* (Tudor), Waltz, Mazurka in *Les Sylphides* (Fokine).

**PUBLICATIONS**

By Ferri:
Interview in Guatterini, Marinella, "Alessandra Ferri", *Ballettoggi* (Milan), November–December 1984
Interview in Gruen, John, *People Who Dance*, Princeton, N.J., 1988
Interview with Poletti, Sylvia, in *Danza & Danza* (Milan), January 1990

About Ferri:
"Dancer You Will Know: Alessandra Ferri", *Dance and Dancers* (London), June 1982
"Dancer of the Year: Alessandra Ferri", *Dance and Dancers* (London), March 1983
"Il Personaggio dell'Ano: Alessandra Ferri", *Danza & Danza* (Milan), January 1987
Gruen, John, "Ferri Tales Can Come True", *Dance Magazine* (New York), October 1987
Ottolenghi, V.C., "Alessandra Ferri", *Ballettoggi* (Milan), June 1988
Macaulay, Alastair, "Two Spring Seasons", *The New Yorker* (New York), 11 July 1988

* * *

Alessandra Ferri gives us a rare example of the sensuality of balletic line. This quality transforms what is asymmetrical—an arabesque for example—into a form more perfect than symmetry. She is the quintessential soubrette, a beautiful ballerina who is at her best portraying strong characters.

Her small physique (5′2″) is perfectly proportioned. Ferri has an astonishingly supple back, highly arched feet, and a remarkable stage presence. Her clean classic technique evolved through the three basic schools of ballet: Italian, English, and Russian.

Ferri's first ballet classes came once a week at her elementary school in Milan. She progressed to classes at Teatro alla Scala, and by age fifteen, with the support of her family, she left home to begin more serious training at The Royal Ballet School in London.

Her professional performing career began with the Royal Ballet, where she quickly ascended the ranks to soloist. Ferri has said that she never felt comfortable in the corps de ballet. This manner of self-confidence is evident on stage and gives a marvelous dramatic edge to her dancing.

Sir Kenneth MacMillan recognized Ferri's potential and developed it by casting her in major dramatic roles, from Juliet to Mary Vetsera in his *Mayerling*. She also attracted the interest of filmmaker Franco Zeffirelli, who produced *Swan Lake* in Milan with Ferri as Odette. Then, in 1985, Mikhail Baryshnikov invited her to join American Ballet Theatre as a principal dancer.

Ferri accepted the invitation during a period when the Royal Ballet was criticized for a decline in quality. Her reason for leaving, she explained, was that she wanted to perform more often and dance new roles. She spoke of wanting to dance with a company that was more focused about daily training, so she could improve her technique.

Her 1985 U.S. début as Nikiya in *La Bayadère* was well-received, although some critics faulted her for occasional wobbly balances and speed. One later noted that her Giselle, at times, omitted difficult steps. Yet over the next several years Ferri developed into an artist of technical purity and strength. Her fiery intensity has been known to captivate an audience and hold it willingly entranced until she exits the stage.

Ferri's great gift is her ability to take dramatic choreography and bring out its true essence, often adding an unexpected dimension to it. Her Juliet is not shy, but impulsive. Her Giselle is not timid, but playful. Again, in the case of Giselle, Ferri assumes the character so completely that as experience leads her into the hapless fate of the betrayed, she responds vividly and wildly, replacing playfulness with a reckless despair that is utterly convincing.

Ferri's deep brown eyes are particularly expressive, but she does not rely on face-acting; it is the entire body which acts. She has a way of wearing a character on her body so that her form is completely involved: she is never standing dead on the stage. Even something as minute and subtle as her quick intake of breath the moment her gaze meets Romeo's has a powerful impact. Some critics complain of her predilection for mannerism, and in plotless works, she occasionally seems lost; this is most likely because her natural impulse to act is suppressed.

Worldwide guest appearances seem to have enhanced Ferri's stamina in a way that has made her recent performances quite spectacular. One of the most interesting events of her recent career was her collaboration with Roland Petit's Ballet National de Marseille. Petit, who called Ferri one of the greatest ballerinas in the world today, created an unusual role specifically for her that treated the audience to her dramatic and physical range. The ballet, *Le Diable amoureux*, whose surrealistic plot is adapted from a story by eighteenth-century French writer Jacques Cazotte, revolves around three main characters: the Devil, his object of desire, the Jeune Homme, and the Devil's instrument, a young boy who is later revealed to be a woman, the Chérubin.

As Chérubin, Alessandra Ferri had to release all her femininity and dance as a man would. Her grand stride and broad-shouldered power gave every indication of being virile truth. Without the restraining delicacy of pointe shoes, Ferri's magnificent feet and legs were all expressive freedom and stark punctuation. Her portrayal was so honest that at no time did she ever give us cause to think she was something other than what she appeared to be, an admiring self-sacrificing page. Subsequently, her onstage transformation from boy to woman was a stunning transfiguration. Petit's combination of masculine and feminine movement as manipulated by Ferri gave as clear an image of the beauty of androgyny as could ever be imagined. If there had ever been any doubt of Alessandra Ferri's stature and talent before *Le Diable amoureux*, it was eradicated after these performances.

—Kim Kokich

---

## LA FÊTE ÉTRANGE

**Choreography:** Andrée Howard
**Music:** Gabriel Fauré (piano pieces and songs), selected by Ronald Crichton
**Design:** Sophie Fedorovitch (scenery and costumes)
**Libretto:** Ronald Crichton (after an episode in Alain-Fournier's *Le Grand Meaulnes*)
**First Production:** London Ballet, Arts Theatre, London, 23 May 1940
**Principal Dancers:** Frank Staff (The Country Boy), Maude Lloyd (The Châtelaine), David Paltenghi (The Bridegroom)

**Other productions include:** Ballet Rambert (restaged Howard), with same cast; London, 20 June 1940. Sadler's Wells Theatre Ballet (mus. orchestrated Lennox Berkeley), with Donald Britton (The Country Boy), June Brae (The Bride), Anthony Burke (The Bridegroom); London, 25 March 1947. Royal Ballet (mus. re-orchestrated Guy Warrack) with Pirmin Trecu (The Country Boy), Svetlana Beriosova (The Bride), Ronald Hynd (The Bridegroom); London, 11 December 1958. Scottish Ballet (staged Helen Starr after Howard), with Elaine McDonald (The Bride); Norwich, 30 September 1971.

### PUBLICATIONS

Beaumont, Cyril, *Supplement to Complete Book of Ballets*, London, 1945
Barnes, Clive, "*La Fête Étrange*", *Dance and Dancing* (London), January 1958
Crichton, Ronald, "*La Fête Étrange*", *Dancing Times* (London), January 1958
Monahan, James, "Reassessments, 2: *La Fête Étrange*", *Dancing Times* (London), January 1963
Sorley Walker, Kathrine, "The Choreography of Andrée Howard", *Dance Chronicle* (New York), vol. 13, no. 3, 1991
Pritchard, Jane, "The Choreography of Andrée Howard: Some Further Information", *Dance Chronicle* (New York), vol. 15, no. 1, 1992

* * *

In an episode from Alain-Fournier's novel, *Le Grand Meaulnes*, the eponymous hero—a country boy—has lost his way in the forest and stumbles upon a strange wedding feast: *La Fête étrange*. The fancy dress of the wedding guests adds to the

***La Fête étrange*, as performed by Margaret Barbieri, Desmond Kelly, and David Morse, Sadler's Wells Royal Ballet, London, c.1979**

pervading air of mystery as the country boy is irresistibly drawn into a love triangle with the beautiful châtelaine and her bridegroom. The subtlety of Alain-Fournier's prose is perfectly captured in the understatement of Andrée Howard's sensitive choreography.

In one of the most telling moments in all twentieth-century ballet, the three main protagonists remain absolutely still, the bridegroom standing on the château steps surveying the young intruder sitting, lovelorn, at the bride's feet. She stands motionless, trapped between the two men's steady gaze, as three girls glide across the stage to the exquisite sound of Fauré's song *Soir*.

This is a mood ballet, with none of the overt emotional conflict one might expect to find in a straightforward narrative work. That conflict is conveyed here in dance movement symbolic of emotion. As seen by Ronald Crichton in his scenario for this ballet, the sequence of events—together with the gradual changes of mood from anticipation through happiness to ecstasy, fading finally into sadness and disillusion—symbolizes the tragedy of sensitive adolescence. All ends in solitude and grief as the curtain falls on an empty stage.

The subtle changes of mood seem to flow naturally from the selection of Fauré's piano pieces which, together with two of his songs, make up the score. Both of these songs add immeasurably to the overall atmosphere: *Mandoline*, a joyous serenade to young love, and *Soir*, a poignant heralding of impending grief.

Sophie Fedorovich's wintry set—starkly simple, yet cleverly suggestive of the terrace of a French château lost in the depths of a forest—together with the subtle colouring of her elegant costumes creates the perfect ambience for Howard's intensely evocative choreography.

Frank Staff and Maude Lloyd headed the cast of the original London Ballet production of 1940. In the 1950s, the Sadler's Wells Theatre Ballet revived the work (which they had first staged in 1947) with Pirmin Trecu as a marvellously convincing country boy, and Margaret Hill and Sheilah O'Reilly both immensely touching in the role of the bride. Beriosova danced this role beautifully in the later Covent Garden revival of the work, but the large stage of the Opera House tended to dissipate the delicate atmosphere of this ballet. Other revivals, notably by the Scottish Ballet and the Sadler's Wells Royal Ballet, have helped preserve this unique but all too ephemeral work, one of the best one-act ballets to have been created by an English choreographer.

—Richard Glasstone

---

**FEUILLET, Raoul Auger**

French dancing-master, choreographer, author, and reputed inventor of the Feuillet dance notation. Born c. 1660. Dancing-master in Paris, teaching ballroom dances from studio in Rue de la Bussy; published his dance notation system in *Chorégraphie, ou l'art de décrire la danse par caractères, figures et signes démonstratifs*, 1700; unsuccessfully sued for plagiarism by Pierre Beauchamps and André Lorin, 1704; continued to publish engraved collections of ballroom dances for Parisian social seasons, 1700–10. Died 14 June 1710.

## PUBLICATIONS

By Feuillet:

*Chorégraphie, ou l'art de décrire la danse par caractères, figures et signes démonstratifs*, Paris, 1700, 1701, 1712, 1713

*Recueil de danses contenant un très grand nombre des meilleures entrées de M. Pécour, tant pour hommes que pour femmes dont la plupart ont été dansées à l'Opéra*, Paris, 1704; reprinted 1970

*Recueil de contredanses mises en chorégraphie d'une manière si aisée que toutes personnes peuvent facilement les apprendre sans le secours d'aucun maitre*, Paris, 1706; reprinted 1968; as *For the further improvement of dancing*, translated by John Essex, London, 1710; reprinted 1970

*Orchesography or the art of dancing by characters and demonstrative figures from the French by Mr. Feuillet*, translated by John Weaver, London, 1706, c. 1710, c. 1715

*Recueil de toutes les danses de bal qui ont été gravées depuis l'année 1700*, Annual Feuillet/Dezais collection of Ballroom Dances, 1700–22

*Rechtschaffener Tanzmesiter, oder grundliche erklarung der Franzosischen Tanz-Kunst*, translated and augmented by Gottfried Taubert, 3 volumes: Leipzig, 1717

Based on the Feuillet notation:

Rameau, Pierre, *Abrégé de la nouvelle méthode dans l'art d'écrire ou de tracer toutes sortes de danses de ville*, Paris, 1725

Tomlinson, Kellom, *The art of dancing explained by reading and figures*, London, 1735

Dupré, *Méthode pour apprendre de soi-mème la chorégraphie ou l'art de décrire les danses par caractères, figures et signes démonstratifs*, Au Mans, 1757

Minguet, P., *Arte de danzar a la francesa*, Madrid, 1758

Guillemin, *Chorégraphie ou l'art de décrire la danse*, Paris, 1784

About Feuillet:

Siris, Peter (after Feuillet), *The Art of Dancing Demonstrated by Characters and Figures ... done from the French of Mr. Feuillet, with many alterations in the figures*, London, 1706

Noverre, Jean-Georges, *Lettres sur la danse et sur les ballets*, Stuttgart and Lyons, 1760; as *Letters on Dancing and Ballets*, translated by Cyril Beaumont, London, 1930

Ritcheson, Shirley, *Feuillet's Chorégraphie and its Implications in the Society of France and England*, (dissertation), Ohio State University, 1965

Moroda, Derra de, "Chorégraphie—The Dance Notation of the Eighteenth Century: Beauchamp or Feuillet?", *The Book Collector* (London), Winter 1967

Wynne, Shirley, "Reconstruction of a Dance from 1700", *Dance History Research*, New York, 1970

Hilton, Wendy, *Dance of Court and Theatre: The French Noble Style, 1690–1725*, Princeton, 1981

Rebman, Elizabeth, "*Chorégraphie*": *An Annotated Bibliography of Eighteenth-century Printed Instruction Books*, M.A. Thesis, Stanford University, 1981

Raoul Auger Feuillet's publication in 1700 of *Chorégraphie, ou l'art de décrire la dance par caractères, figures et signes démonstratifs, avec lesquels on apprend facilement de soy-même toutes sortes de Dances* [sic] proved a milestone in the history of baroque dance. The treatise describes in a detailed but easily comprehensible manner the basics of the first known systematic dance notation by abstract symbol. Through the mid-eighteenth century, the system of *Chorégraphie* was employed widely for recording both court and theatrical dances, and enabled the rapid dissemination of the latest, most popular choreographies throughout Europe.

With the treatise, Feuillet was granted "le privilege du roy" (sic) for the exclusive publication of works in *Chorégraphie*, a privilege which he held for six years. Ironically, Feuillet did not invent the notation system. Pierre Beauchamps, dancing master to Louis XIV for approximately 22 years and "Compositeur des Ballets du Roi", created it apparently some twenty years earlier at Louis' request, but for reasons unclear, failed to publish the work. Equally unclear are the full circumstances surrounding his unsuccessful suit brought against Feuillet in 1704 in which he attempted to regain rights to the system.

Feuillet did not acknowledge Beauchamps in *Chorégraphie*, but his debt to Beauchamps and the substance of his own extensive contributions to the system received further confirmation through subsequent writings of other dancing masters. These publications attest that Feuillet did not duplicate Beauchamps' work, but that he expanded and improved upon the system. He set down rules and devised a method for its proper use.

Feuillet's later publications suggest that he had not completed his task with the 1700 manual. He published a second edition of *Chorégraphie* in 1701, augmenting the earlier work with a few new notation examples. *Traité de la Cadence* from 1704 discussed further the notation of the timing of steps in duple and triple meter. His 1706 *Recueil de contredances* [sic] added to the system symbols specifically related to the contredanse. With these publications, Feuillet firmly established his claim to the notation and his supremacy in the field, which perhaps explains Beauchamps's failed suit against him. By 1704, the system so clearly bore Feuillet's stamp that there was no question but that the "privilege du roy" should remain his possession.

The number of dances recorded in *Chorégraphie* alone is evidence of the notation system's value in the eyes of the early eighteenth-century dance world; but the numerous translations of Feuillet's treatises acknowledge its greater influence. With the expiration of his royal privilege in 1706 came two English translations of *Chorégraphie*: John Weaver's *Orchesography*, and *The Art of Dancing Demonstrated by Characters and Figures* by Peter Siris. Gottfried Taubert in his 1717 *Rechtschaffener Tantzmeister* translated into German both the second edition of *Chorégraphie* and *Traité de la Cadence*. Treatises inspired by *Chorégraphie*, though not exact translations of it, appeared also in Spanish and Italian.

Feuillet also made a mark as an able choreographer. With the first edition of *Chorégraphie*, he published two collections of dances to serve as working examples of the notation system. Fifteen of his own dances for the theatre comprised one collection, while popular ballroom dances by Louis Pécour, Beauchamps's successor at the Opéra, made up the other. Feuillet's compositions in this collection include solos and duets, and, particularly notable, a *Ballet de Neuf Danseurs*. Probably one of the most complex examples of dances recorded in *Chorégraphie*, it is what Wendy Hilton calls "a beautiful study in double symmetry". Until his death in 1709, Feuillet shared with Pécour the creation of ballroom dances for the

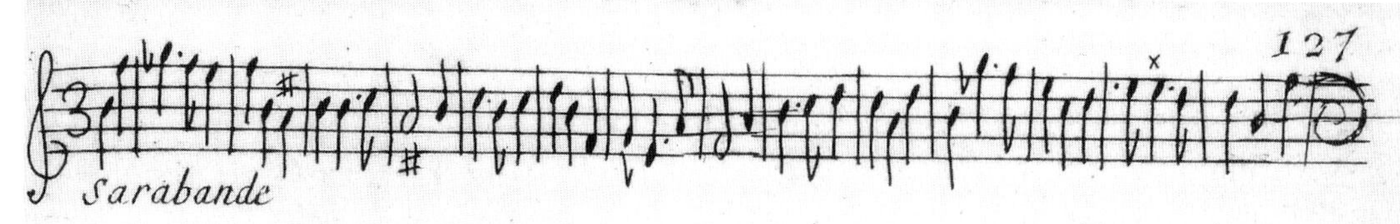

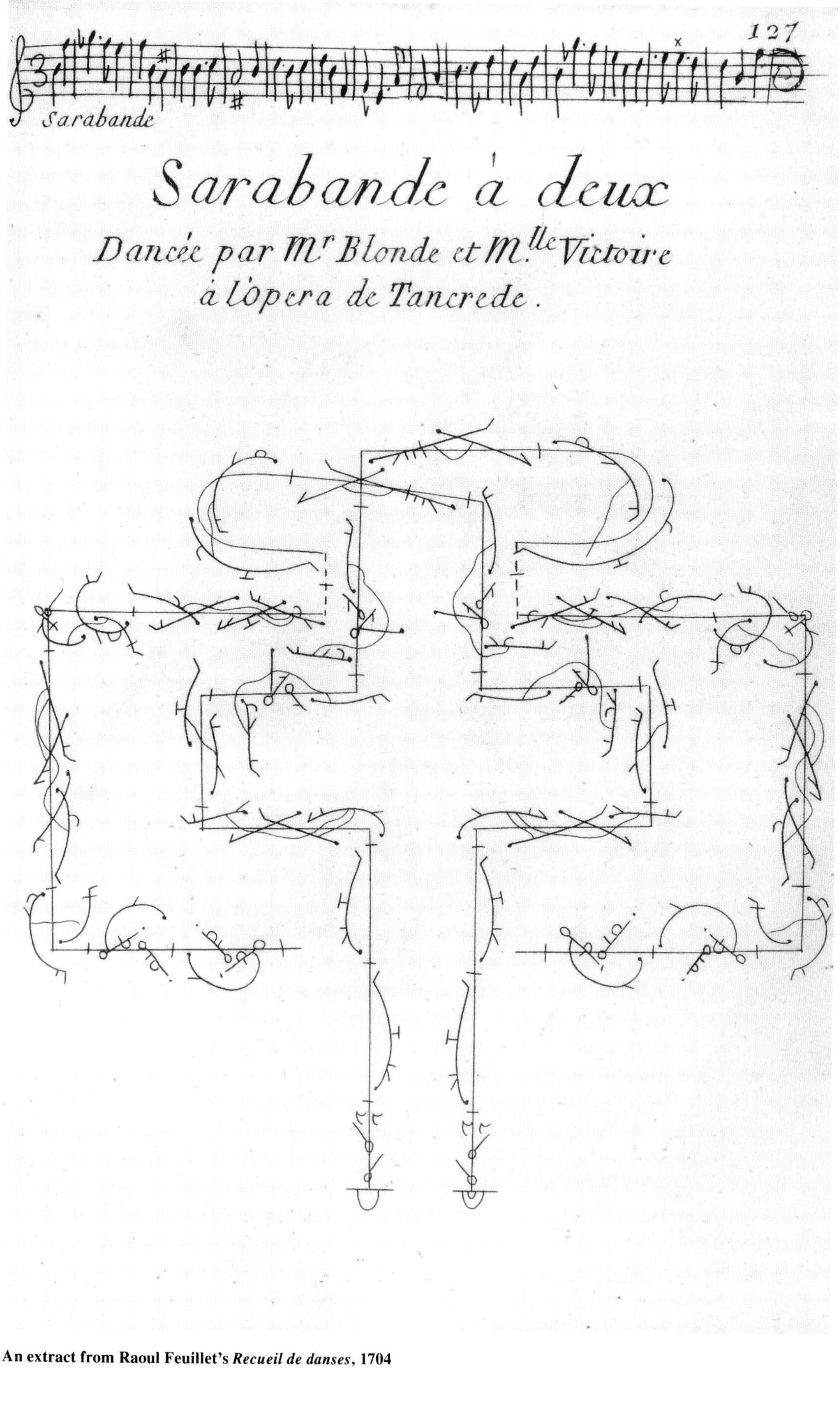

Sarabande à deux

Dancée par Mr Blonde et Mlle Victoire
à l'Opera de Tancrede.

**An extract from Raoul Feuillet's *Recueil de danses*, 1704**

annual collections, all of which he notated and published.

No assessments of his choreography by contemporaries remain. The inclusion of his works in treatises published outside France during the first half of the century, however, demonstrates Feuillet's enduring, international reputation as a choreographer. Taubert published a number of Feuillet's dances in his 1717 treatise. *Le Charmant Vainqueur*, from the 1709 annual collection of dances, appears as late as 1758 in Pablo Minguet's *El Noble Arte de Danzar a la Francesa* published in Madrid.

Feuillet's legacy to the contemporary dance world rests in an extensive repertory of notated choreographies in the French Baroque style and in his theoretical publications which enable the clear interpretation and reconstruction of these dances. His work in *Chorégraphie* provides a valuable glimpse of an early dance technique that helped form the foundation of contemporary ballet.

—Susan F. Bindig

---

**FIELD, John**

British dancer and ballet director. Born John Greenfield in Doncaster, 22 October 1921. Studied with Edna Slocombe and Shelagh Elliott-Clarke, Liverpool, and at Sadler's Wells School, London, 1939. Served in the Royal Air Force during World War II. Married dancer Anne Heaton, 1958. Début with Liverpool Ballet Club, 1938; dancer, Vic-Wells Ballet (later Sadler's Wells Ballet), from 1939, soon becoming principal dancer; toured with company in 1949, 1950–51, 1953 and 1954; also appeared in film, *The Black Swan*, partnering Beryl Grey, 1952; director, Sadler's Wells Theatre Ballet, from 1956: assistant director, and head of touring section, on company's merger with Sadler's Wells Ballet to become the Royal Ballet, from 1956; appointed co-director (with Kenneth MacMillan), Royal Ballet, 1970, resigning later same year; ballet director, La Scala, Milan, 1971–74; artistic director, Royal Academy of Dancing, London, 1975–78; director, from 1976; artistic director, London Festival Ballet, 1979–84; director of British Ballet Organization, 1984–91. Commander of the Order of the British Empire, 1967. Died in Esher, Surrey, 3 August 1991.

**ROLES**

1939 Dancer in *The Haunted Ballroom* (de Valois), Ballet Club, Liverpool

1940 Dancer holding Model of Pantheon (cr) in *The Prospect Before Us* (de Valois), Vic-Wells Ballet, London

1941 Dancer (cr) in *The Wanderer* (Ashton), Sadler's Wells Ballet, London

Popular Song in *Façade* (Ashton), Sadler's Wells Ballet, London

1942 Variation ("Blue Boy") in *Les Patineurs* (Ashton), Sadler's Wells Ballet, London

Mazurka in *Les Sylphides* (Fokine), Sadler's Wells Ballet, London

1947 Cossack Chief in *La Boutique fantasque* (Massine), Sadler's Wells Ballet, London

A Black Knight in *Checkmate* (de Valois), Sadler's Wells Ballet, London

Bootmaker in *Mam'zelle Angot* (Massine), Sadler's Wells Ballet, London

1948 Ensemble (cr) in *Scènes de ballet* (Ashton), Sadler's Wells Ballet, London

The Caricaturist in *Mam'zelle Angot* (Massine), Sadler's Wells Ballet, London

A Rival (cr) in *Don Juan* (Ashton), Sadler's Wells Ballet, London

Prince Siegfried in *Swan Lake*, Act II (Ivanov; staged Sergeyev), Sadler's Wells Ballet, London

1950 First Red Knight in *Checkmate* (de Valois), Sadler's Wells Ballet, London

Prince Florimund in *The Sleeping Beauty* (Petipa; staged Sergeyev, de Valois, Ashton), Sadler's Wells Ballet, London

Title role in *Don Quixote* (de Valois), Sadler's Wells Ballet, London

1951 Dorkon (cr) in *Daphnis and Chloë* (Ashton), Sadler's Wells Ballet, London

The Lover (cr) in *Tiresias* (Ashton), Sadler's Wells Ballet, London

Dancer in *Ballet Imperial* (Balanchine), Sadler's Wells Ballet, London

A Child of Light in *Dante Sonata* (Ashton), Sadler's Wells Ballet, tour

Principal dancer in *Symphonic Variations* (Ashton), Sadler's Wells Ballet, tour

1952 Siegfried in *Swan Lake* (Petipa, Ivanov; staged Sergeyev, de Valois, Ashton), Sadler's Wells Ballet, London

Principal dancer in *Scènes de ballet* (Ashton), Sadler's Wells Ballet, London

Aminta in *Sylvia* (Ashton), Sadler's Wells Ballet, London

Orion in *Sylvia* (Ashton), Sadler's Wells Ballet, London

1953 Consort to the Queen of Fire (cr) in *Homage to the Queen* (Ashton), Sadler's Wells Ballet, London

1954 Albrecht in *Giselle* (Petipa after Coralli, Perrot; staged Sergeyev), Sadler's Wells Ballet, London

1957 The Poet in *Apparitions* (Ashton), Royal Ballet, London

**PUBLICATIONS**

By Field:

Interview, "The Other Half of the Apple", *Dance and Dancers* (London), December 1966

Interview with Fernau Hall, "The Use of Benesh Notation in the Royal Ballet", *Dancing Times* (London), August 1968

About Field:

Beaumont, Cyril, *Ballets of Today*, London, 1954

Clarke, Mary, *The Sadler's Wells Ballet*, London, 1955

Roberts, Sonia, "Men in Ballet: John Field", *Ballet Today* (London), March 1956

"Personality of the Month: John Field", *Dance and Dancers* (London), April 1961

Buckle, Richard, "John Field", *About the House* (London), Christmas 1970

Woodcock, Sarah, *The Sadler's Wells Royal Ballet*, London, 1991

* * *

An important career as a principal dancer is not always the best foundation for work as an artistic director, but the two phases of John Field's working life prove that such a state of affairs

**John Field with Beryl Grey in *Aurora's Wedding***

can exist. Born in Doncaster, Field (whose real name was Greenfield) studied with one of the group of first-rate regional teachers of the time, Shelagh Elliott-Clarke, making his début in 1938 with the active and enterprising Liverpool Ballet Club. This Club had a close working friendship with Ninette de Valois and the Vic-Wells Ballet, and in 1939—the year World War II began—Field found a place in the Vic-Wells Ballet itself. In the couple of years before his calling-up to the armed forces, he made solid progress, developing from a tall, good-looking, dark-haired member of the corps de ballet, who was singled out by balletomanes as having decided style and potential, to a dancer of leading roles. Returning to the company at Covent Garden after the war, he quickly regained ground, moving effortlessly into the category of danseur noble as partner in the long classics to Beryl Grey, Violetta Elvin, and later Svetlana Beriosova. With Grey he made guest appearances abroad, as well as a stereoscopic film of *Swan Lake*, titled *The Black Swan*.

In 1956 Field was offered the chance of becoming director of Sadler's Wells Theatre Ballet, and decided to accept this and retire from dancing. It was an important step for British ballet—the ten-year-old company had flourished under its previous director, Peggy van Praagh, but under Field it was to become the favourite ballet company of the British regions. He developed a significant group of dancers, led by Doreen Wells and David Wall, whose delightful partnership in works like *La Fille mal gardée* and *The Two Pigeons* established them as firm favourites with the ballet public. When the company was merged with Sadler's Wells Ballet (based at Covent Garden) as the Royal Ballet in October 1956, his title changed to Assistant Director of the Royal Ballet in charge of the touring portion—and the touring portion became lovingly, if unofficially, known to the ballet public as "John Field's company".

This situation continued until 1970 when Sir Frederick Ashton retired from the directorship of the Royal Ballet, and it was decided that the touring company would be disbanded and replaced by a small experimental section called "The New Group". At the same time, a joint directorship was envisaged between Kenneth MacMillan and John Field—but as the roles of the two men were not made sufficiently clear, it came as a surprise to Field to discover that his work would be on the administrative rather than the artistic side. He immediately resigned, and shortly afterwards took up the position of director of ballet at La Scala, Milan. Finding conditions there difficult to accept, he was glad to leave after his three-year term. He went to the Royal Academy of Dancing, where he remained as director for four years, proving a stimulating force in the training and educational side of classical ballet. All the same, the opportunity of taking over London Festival Ballet as director, and regaining the type of work with a performing company and dancers that he had so much enjoyed with the Royal Ballet, was an enticing one, and he took this on in 1979.

He followed a policy closely akin to the one that had been so successful formerly—of producing new talent in dancing and choreography—but he did not establish such a good and close relationship with Festival's widely assorted artists. He left in 1984, and then directed British Ballet Organisation (BBO), an international teaching body founded by Edouard Espinosa, reworking the syllabus and altering and updating the general image.

—Kathrine Sorley Walker

---

FIELD MASS *see* SOLDIER'S MASS

---

FILLE DU PHARAON, La *see* PHARAOH'S DAUGHTER

---

## LA FILLE MAL GARDÉE

**Choreography:** Frederick Ashton
**Music:** Ferdinand Hérold, arranged John Lanchbery
**Design:** Osbert Lancaster
**Libretto:** Frederick Ashton after Jean Dauberval
**First Production:** Royal Ballet, Royal Opera House, London 28 January 1960
**Principal Dancers:** Nadia Nerina (Lise), David Blair (Colas), Alexander Grant (Alain), Stanley Holden (Widow Simone)

**Other productions include:** Royal Ballet Touring Company, with same cast; Bristol, 9 November 1962. Royal Danish Ballet (restaged Ashton), with Solveig Ostergaard (Lise), Niels Kehlet (Colas), Fredbjørn Bjørnsson (Alain), Niels Bjørn Larsen (Widow Simone); Copenhagen, 16 January 1964. Australian Ballet (staged Elphine Allen), with Marilyn Jones (Lise), Bryan Lawrence (Colas), Ray Powell (Widow Simone); Sydney, 12 October 1967. PACT Ballet (staged John Hart), with Merle Park (Lise), Anthony Dowell (Colas); Johannesburg, 4 September 1969. Hungarian State Opera Ballet (scenery Gabor Forray, costumes Tiradar Mark), with Zsuzsa Kun (Lise), Viktor Rona (Colas); Budapest, 28 March 1971. Bavarian State Opera Ballet (staged Annette Page, Ronald Hynd), with Gislinde Skroblin (Lise), Heinz Bosl (Colas); Munich, 18 May 1971. Royal Swedish Ballet, with Kirsten Lidstrom (Lise), Imre Dozsa (Colas); Stockholm, 1 April 1972. State Ballet of Turkey (staged Faith Worth); Ankara, 24 November 1973. San Francisco Ballet, San Francisco; 10 January 1978. Joffrey Ballet (staged Faith Worth, supervised by Alexander Grant); Los Angeles, 11 September 1986. Houston Ballet; Houston, 11 June 1992.

### PUBLICATIONS

Guest, Ivor, "Introducing *La Fille mal gardée*", *Dancing Times* (London), February 1960
Guest, Ivor, *La Fille mal gardée*, London, 1960
Guest, Ivor, "The Legacy of Dauberval", *Ballet Annual* (London), vol. 15, 1961
Lanchbery, John, and Guest, Ivor, "The Scores of *La Fille mal gardée*", *Theatre Research* (London), 3 parts: vol. 3, nos. 1–3, 1961
Barnes, Clive, "Ballet Perspectives 28: *La Fille mal gardée*", *Dance and Dancers* (London), January 1963
Percival, John, "La Fille mal gardée", *About the House* (London), Summer 1970
Kirstein, Lincoln, *Movement and Metaphor*, New York, 1970
Vaughan, David, *Frederick Ashton and his Ballets*, London, 1977
Brinson, Peter, and Crisp, Clement, *Ballet and Dance: A Guide to the Repertory*, London, 1980

* * *

Frederick Ashton's *La Fille mal gardée* is the supreme example of ballet-making at its most confident and skilled. Only a choreographer at the peak of his form could take such a simple, old-fashioned tale and turn it into a modern-day masterpiece. Based on Jean Dauberval's ballet of 1789, *Fille* recaptures the rustic joie de vivre of romanticism. Created in 1960, it is Ashton's testament to tradition—to the conventions of family life and community, and to the formal values of the danse d'école. It is also his testament to the accomplishments of the Royal Ballet after three decades of development.

*La Fille mal gardée* highlights the company's consummate style and also the lessons learned by Ashton from previous choreography. In *Sylvia* (1952) and *Ondine* (1958), he had shown how Romantic ballet scenarios could become starting-points for new work. In these, and in *Cinderella* (1948), he explored the dramatic and structural possibilities of the three-act form. The action in *Fille*, however, is concentrated into two acts (with Act I sectioned into two scenes). One of the ballet's strengths is its conciseness—dances for principals and corps de ballet all further the plot. Even character roles involve challenging solos which convey personality. And successive pas de deux have dual significance, confirming the central couple's increasing intimacy and also the ballet's major theme: the triumph of true love over maternal match-making.

Widow Simone arranges the marriage of her daughter Lise to Alain, the son of a well-to-do landowner, but Lise's heart has already been won by the young farmer Colas. Despite Simone's efforts to keep the two lovers apart, they steal moments together in each of the ballet's three scenes. In the farmyard, Lise and Colas "play horses" in a spirited pas de ruban. Here, Ashton introduces pink ribbons as leitmotiv and the pas de deux ends with the lovers drawn together in a "cat's cradle" knot.

In subsequent pas de deux, ribbons connect the couple more subtly. During the harvest scene, in the ballet's most virtuoso pas de deux, Lise performs a promenade en attitude, supported not by Colas but by a confluence of ribbons held overhead. Then, amid the bravura of their solo variations, a line of dancers criss-cross ribbons upstage. This trellis formation suggests the writing of kisses—an indication of the lovers' deepening relationship and of the community's consent. In the final scene of the ballet, ribbons criss-cross the bodice of Lise's wedding dress.

Two pas de deux occur inside Widow Simone's farmhouse. The first follows a mime scene in which Lise dreams of marriage to Colas. It is one of Ashton's most sensuous and tender love duets, and it marks the turning-point of the plot. From here on, the lovers' fate is driven by external forces. Lise's make-believe becomes real when Widow Simone agrees to their marriage and the final pas de deux culminates in Colas carrying his bride-to-be over the threshold.

Ashton created *La Fille mal gardée* at a crucial point in the Royal Ballet's history. Since World War II, his choreography

Frederick Ashton's *La Fille mal gardée*, with Merle Park and Rudolf Nureyev, Royal Ballet, London, 1974

had been synonymous with the Margot Fonteyn–Michael Somes partnership (and Fonteyn's next partnership with Rudolf Nureyev was yet to be forged). Many younger dancers were emerging and Ashton was clearly inspired by their talents. Significantly, *Fille* is a ballet about youthful endeavour. Life, love, and the future are viewed optimistically. Unlike his later period-style ballets, such as *Enigma Variations* and *A Month in the Country*, there is no tinge of nostalgia.

The role of Lise was created on Nadia Nerina, whose speed and elevation spurred Ashton to devise fast, filigree steps for each of her solos. Yet, from film of Nerina's dancing in *Fille*, what is even more striking is her wonderful plasticity, particularly in port de bras and épaulement, and her seamless legato phrasing. Nerina says, "*Fille* should be romantic. It's the sort of ballet that should make you laugh and cry at the same time. Alec [Alexander] Grant's Alain was always on the border, and the same with Mother—Stanley Holden never played for laughs."

Ashton's friends recall his witty impersonations at parties—studied, subtle, and amusing. Such careful characterization is evident in the roles of Alain and Widow Simone. Both demand dramatic sensitivity, in terms of pathos and pantomime, respectively. Although *Fille* is intentionally funny, Ashton draws a fine line between humour and slapstick. Moreover, with the exception of *Rhapsody* (1980), it contains the most technically complex choreography ever created by Ashton for the male dancer. The role of Alain requires the combined classical rigour and dramatic nuance of the finest demi-caractère dancer while that of Colas has challenged many great danseurs nobles.

The simplicity of subject and sentiment in *Fille* belies the complexity of Ashton's sources. The ballet draws upon Dauberval's scenario and several nineteenth-century productions. A musical arrangement by Ferdinand Hérold, introduced at the Paris Opéra in 1828, formed the basis of John Lanchbery's score. New choreography interpolated for Fanny Elssler in 1837 inspired the tripping taqueté steps of Ashton's harvest scene. Lise's mime scene, first included in a production by Lev Ivanov in 1885, was taught to Nerina by Tamara Karsavina. (She had danced the role of Lise in St. Petersburg.)

Ashton also acknowledges the pastoral influences of Beethoven's sixth symphony and the writings of Wordsworth's sister, Dorothy, in the ballet's rural calm. But it is his love of the Suffolk countryside which resonates most. Parallels between Ashton's time-weather perspective in *Fille* and the ever-summery scenes in Constable's paintings are clear. Even more striking is their similarly unaffected manner. Naturalness permeates both choreography and canvas. And, like Constable's country idylls, Ashton presents the ideal as "return-to-nature" realism.

*La Fille mal gardée*'s sunny locale, its uncomplicated plot, and easily identifiable characters make it one of Ashton's most accessible ballets. Choreographic—and historical—richness make it one of his greatest. *Fille* is the ultimate ballet to dispel bias between popular and high art.

—Angela Kane

---

## LA FILLE MAL GARDÉE

**Choreography:** Jean Dauberval
**Music:** popular French tunes, with additional music by unknown composer
**Libretto:** Jean Dauberval
**First Production:** Grand Théatre, Bordeaux, 1 July 1789, as *Le Ballet de la paille*
**Principal Dancers:** Mlle. Théodore (Mme. Dauberval) (Lison, now called Lise), Eugène Hus (Colas), M. Dupri (Alain), M. Brochard (Ragotte, now called Widow Simone)

**Other productions include:** Pantheon Theatre (restaged Dauberval), as *La Fille mal gardée*, with Mlle. Théodore, Charles Didelot, Salvatore Viganò, and Maria Medina; London, 30 April 1791. Teatro La Fenice (staged Salvatore Viganò after Dauberval); Venice, 1792. King's Theatre (staged James D'Egville after Dauberval), as *La Fille mal gardée* (also referred to as *Honi soi qui mal y pense*); London, 18 April 1799. Théâtre de la Porte-Saint-Martin (staged Eugène Hus after Dauberval); Paris, 13 October 1803. Royal Danish Theatre (staged Burlo after Dauberval); Copenhagen, 28 February 1819. Bolshoi Theatre (staged Charles Didelot after Dauberval), as *Liza and Colin; or, Vain Precautions*; St. Petersburg, 23 October (11 October old style) 1827. Théâtre de L'Académie royale de musique (Paris Opéra; staged Jean Aumer after Dauberval, mus. Louis Joseph Ferdinand Hérold); Paris, 17 November 1828. Paris Opéra (restaged with additional pas de deux, mus. Gaetano Donizetti), with Fanny Elssler; Paris, 15 September 1837. Bolshoi Theatre, with Fanny Elssler; Moscow, 1850. Königliche Opera House (chor. Paul Taglioni, mus. Peter Ludwig Hertel); Berlin, 7 November 1864. Bolshoi Theatre (chor. Marius Petipa and Lev Ivanov, mus. Hertel), with Virginia Zucchi and Pavel Gerdt; St. Petersburg, 27 December (15 December old style) 1885. Bolshoi Ballet (restaged Aleksandr Gorsky after Petipa); Moscow, 1901. Anna Pavlova Company (shortened version; staged Aleksandr Shiryaev after Petipa), with Anna Pavlova (Eliza), Laurent Novikov (Colas); Palace Theatre, London, 1911. Kirov Ballet (staged Leonid Lavronsky); Leningrad, 1937. Mordkin Ballet (restaged Mikhail Mordkin) with Lucia Chase (Lise), Dimitri Romanoff (Colin), Mikhail Mordkin (Simone); New York, 1938. Ballet Theatre (staged Bronislava Nijinska); New York, 19 January 1940 (revived as *The Wayward Daughter*, 1941, and *Naughty Lisette*, 1942). Nouveau Ballet de Monte Carlo (staged Alexandra Balashova); Monte Carlo, 1946. Ballet Theatre (staged Dmitri Romanoff); New York, April 1949. Royal Ballet (new version; chor. Frederick Ashton, mime restored Tamara Karsavina, mus. Hérold, adapted by John Lanchbery, design Osbert Lancaster), with Nadia Nerina (Lise), David Blair (Colas), Stanley Holden (Widow Simone), Alexander Grant (Alain); London, 28 January 1960 (see Ashton's *La Fille mal gardée*). Paris Opéra Ballet (new version; chor. Heinz Spoerli, mus. adapted J.-M. Damase); Paris, 1981. Nantes Opera Ballet (reconstruction: staged Ivó Cramér after Dauberval, mus. traditional airs arranged Farncombe), Nantes, 1989.

### PUBLICATIONS

Beaumont, Cyril, *Complete Book of Ballets*, revised version, London, 1951
Guest, Ivor, *La Fille mal gardée*, London, 1960
Guest, Ivor, "Introducing *La Fille mal gardée*", *Dancing Times* (London), February 1960
Guest, Ivor, "The Legacy of Dauberval", *Ballet Annual* (London), vol. 15, 1961
Lanchbery, John, and Guest, Ivor, "The Scores of *La Fille mal gardée*", *Theatre Research* (London), 3 parts: vol. 3, nos. 1–3, 1961
Barnes, Clive, "*La Fille mal gardée*", *Dance and Dancers* (London), January 1963

Guest, Ivor, *The Romantic Ballet in Paris*, London, 1966
Kirstein, Lincoln, *Movement and Metaphor: Four Centuries of Ballet*, New York, 1970
Percival, John, "*La Fille mal gardée*", *About the House* (London), Summer 1970
Winter, Marian Hannah, *The Pre-Romantic Ballet*, London, 1974
Guest, Ivor, "*La Fille mal gardée*: New Light on the Original Production", *Dance Chronicle* (New York), vol. 1, no. 1, 1977
Guest, Ivor, "Ivo Cramér's *La Fille mal gardée* at Nantes", *Dancing Times* (London), April 1989
Michel, Marcel, "*La Fille mal gardée*", *Pour la danse* (Paris), May 1989
Lamont, R.C., "Dancescape", *Dance Magazine* (New York), July 1989
Percival, John, "The Well-guarded Daughter", *Dance and Dancers* (London), June 1992

* * *

Born on the eve of the French Revolution, *La Fille mal gardée* was not a ballet to inspire audiences with feelings of liberté, egalité, and fraternité. It was about peasants, but not the suffering, dirty, sometimes unruly peasants of the French cities and countryside; its farm-boys and milkmaids were of the pretty, happy, contented variety favoured by the courtiers of Louis XVI. The ballet's creator, the highly sought-after ballet master Jean Dauberval, was intimate with the royal court and more than happy to share its pomp, luxury, and cultural richness. His rebellion was not against the social order, but against the artistic status quo in which ballet was considered the least important of the arts, inferior owing to its muteness.

Sharing Jean-Georges Noverre's belief that ballets could be serious dramatic entertainments, Dauberval adopted a *ballet d'action* approach. And unlike so many of his fellow late-eighteenth-century ballet masters, he managed the extremely difficult task of creating a work within which dance was an integral part of the dramatic action. Most ballet masters, Noverre among them, failed to achieve such a synthesis, for they could not make dance expressive and thus failed to make it contribute to the progress of their ballet stories. The result was that they either took the route of Salvatore Viganò and left it out of their ballets, or they introduced it as irrelevant divertissement. Dauberval, on the other hand, was so successful at integrating dance into his action that to remove a dance sequence from one of his ballets was to render the whole work meaningless. The result was a work that realized the central purpose of *ballet d'action*, the presentation of a unified action within which all the balletic elements—music, silent acting, costumes, scenery, machinery, and dancing—contributed to a coherent dramatic action.

In spite of its brilliant success, there was much that was not new about *La Fille mal gardée*, originally performed as *Le Ballet de la paille*. Its music consisted of the usual arrangement of popular airs, among them those of Haydn. Its story was based upon the popular theme of two young lovers who are thwarted by parental authority, and its characters were based upon those of the *commedia dell'arte*—Lise and Colas, the young lovers; Alain, the clown or zany; and Mother Simone, the pantaloon.

The difference between *Fille* and other ballets was that the story was uniquely suited to dance. First, it is simple, easily told through action. Within the straightforward structure there are many sentimental episodes. We are touched by the moments of love and tenderness and amused by the humour. The festive nature of harvest time allows for many dances to be woven naturally into the fabric of the ballet. And the simple passions and characterizations, youth, love, folly, sadness, and joy, can be represented by dancers. Ultimately, it is the ballet's danceability that has made it a continuing success.

Only two years after its premiere, *La Fille mal gardeé* was performed at the Pantheon Theatre in London under Dauberval's direction. The *Times* wrote: "... the ACTION throughout of DIDELOT and D'AUBERVAL renders totally unnecessary the descriptive word". The ballet was still thriving in London in 1826 at the Adelphi Theatre. In Paris the work was first performed in 1803 under the direction of Eugène Hus at the Théâtre de la Porte-Saint-Martin. Again it was the dramatic strength of the work that impressed observers. "The girl is alone in her house, convinced that she is safe from all danger," wrote a Parisian paper of the performance of one of the great forgotten Lises, Madame Queriau, "suddenly her lover appears, the poor girl is struck motionless with astonishment and fright. This lover, whom she had formerly had such pleasure to see, is to her eyes a serpent ready to devour her: the efforts she makes to escape him, the struggles of fear and love, offer a new spectacle." From 1828 to 1854, *Fille* played at the Paris Opéra, where Fanny Elssler was its greatest interpreter. Elsewhere in Europe productions proliferated, and the ballet proved particularly popular in St. Petersburg; it was first performed there in 1818, revived in 1827, and produced again in 1885 by Petipa and Ivanov (using music written by Hertel for an 1864 Berlin production by Paul Taglioni). It was in this latter production that the great designer Alexandre Benois remembered another famous Lise. "... [Virginia] Zucchi gave a strikingly sincere and realistic performance. Here was a genuinely inexperienced girl who first felt the danger of temptation and then, moved by her passion for Colas, gave in to his tender entreaties without losing her charming shyness."

Productions continued to abound in the twentieth century; one of the most successful being Frederick Ashton's for the Royal Ballet in 1960. Ashton based his production on the oldest known libretto (Porte-Saint-Martin, 1803) and upon an arrangement of the 1828 Hérold score. Ashton's vision was not too dissimilar to that of the eighteenth-century aristocrats whose tastes for the pastoral supplied Dauberval's aesthetic. "There exists in my imagination", wrote Ashton, "a life in the country of eternally late spring, a leafy pastorale of perpetual sunshine and the humming of bees.... But do not let us forget Dauberval: his is a masterly balletic conception, his characters are rounded and his action carries through to the end. His piece displays the most lively *sense du théâtre* in the clever arrangement of effective situations and charming tableaux. The interest is kept up to the end ...".

—John Chapman

---

**FIREBIRD** *see* **OISEAU DE FEU, L'**

---

## THE FLAMES OF PARIS

(original Russian title: *Plamya Parizha*)

**Choreography:** Vasily Vainonen
**Music:** Boris Asafiev (based on songs of the French Revolution)
**Design:** Vladimir Dmitriev
**Libretto:** Nicolai Volkov and Vladimir Dmitriev

*The Flames of Paris*

**First Production:** State Academic Theatre for Opera and Ballet (GATOB), Leningrad, 7 November 1932
**Principal Dancers:** Vakhtang Chabukiani (Jérome), Olga Jordan (Jeanne), Nina Anisimova (Thérèse), Natalia Dudinskaya (Mireille de Poitiers), Konstantin Sergeyev (Mistral)

**Other productions include:** Bolshoi Ballet, with Aleksei Yermolaev (Jérome), Anastasia Abramova (Jeanne), Nadezhda Kapustina (Thérèse), Marina Semenova (Mireille de Poitiers), Moscow, 6 July 1933.

## PUBLICATIONS

"The 'Danse des citoyens'", *Dancing Times* (London), January 1936
Raffé, W.G., "Ballet in the USSR", *Dancing Times* (London), January 1936
Beaumont, Cyril, *Complete Book of Ballets*, revised edition, London, 1951
*The Flames of Paris*, Moscow, 1951
Shaverdyan, A., *USSR Bolshoi Theatre*, Moscow, 1952
Roslavleva, Natalia, *Era of the Russian Ballet*, London, 1966

* * *

*The Flames of Paris* is a so-called "revolutionary" ballet, and takes as its subject the French Revolution, including in its scenario the storming of the Tuileries by the Marseillais and their victorious march on Paris. Although its setting is eighteenth-century France, it is a perfect illustration of Leningrad ballet in the 1920s and 1930s, during which time there was a determined effort to find subjects in world history which reflected the more immediate situation in Russia, and to show that the October Revolution was part of more universal movements and historical events.

The ballet opens in a forest near Marseilles, where the peasant Gaspard and his children—Jeanne and Pierre—are gathering brushwood. When a Count and his royal hunting party arrive, the peasants disperse, but Jeanne attracts the attention of the Count, who attempts to embrace her. When her father intervenes, he is beaten up by the Count's servant and taken away. Later, in the Marseilles Square, Jeanne tells the people what has happened to her father, and the people's indignation over the injustices of the aristocracy grows. They storm the prison, and free the prisoners of the Marquis de Beauregard.

Next, the court of Versailles in all its decadence is portrayed. After a performance at the court theatre which is followed by a lush banquet, the officers of the court write a formal petition to the King, requesting permission to deal with the unruly revolutionaries. The actor Antoine Mistral, discovering this secret document, is killed by the Marquis: but before he dies, he manages to pass the document on to Mireille de Poitiers, who escapes as the sound of the "Marseillaise" is heard from the windows.

The scene then shifts to a square in Paris, where an uprising and the storming of the palace is prepared. Mireille rushes in with the document revealing the conspiracy against the revolution, and her bravery is applauded. At the height of this scene, the officers of the Marquis arrive in the square; Jeanne, recognizing the man who insulted her in the wood, runs up and slaps him across the face. Following this, the crowd rushes upon the aristocrats. To the sound of revolutionary songs, the people storm the palace and burst into the staircase of the front hall. In the resulting skirmish, Jeanne attacks the Marquis, who is then killed by her brother, and the Basque Thérèse sacrifices her life for the Revolution. Finally, back in the square in Paris, the people celebrate their victory over the defenders of the old regime.

In composing the choreography for this rich four-act ballet, Vasily Vainonen drew upon many different sources, as did the composer, Boris Asafiev: *The Flames of Paris* blends classical and character dancing, court music and popular songs, solo performances and huge group scenes. The choreography is mostly classical, but for the part of Thérèse, for example, Vainonen chose the outstanding Leningrad character dancer, Nina Anisimova: she danced only character dances, displaying strong, expressive folk movements which symbolize the energy and the spirit of the crowd. Then on the other hand, the dances for Philippe, one of the Marseillais, and his bride are purely classical: the two characters dance a pas de deux which is done in the true St. Petersburg manner, after Petipa. In the scene at the palace of Louis XVI, we have a great deal of traditional mime, and Marie Antoinette dances a minuet which is a beautiful piece of choreography in itself. As a further technique for putting classical dancing on the stage, Vainonen invented the roles of the pair of actors, Mireille de Poitiers and Antoine Mistral, who have been invited by the King to perform at the banquet. These were originally performed by Natalia Dudinskaya and Konstantin Sergeyev, and are designed for outstanding ballet dancers who can display their virtuosity in a classical pas de deux. These actors are of course on the side of the revolutionary mob, so that after the storming of the palace they are joined by the group in dances which include variations, codas, and the participation of an enormous corps de ballet consisting of 24 and later 32 dancers.

*The Flames of Paris* was very popular with audiences, and also represented an important step in the development of male ballet technique in the early 1930s. Vainonen created an unusually large number of male characters who have "lead" roles in terms of dancing. The roles of the young men who participate in the Revolution—the "Marseillaise", Jérome and his friends, or the actor Mistral—were created on outstanding dancers like Vakhtang Chabukiani and Konstantin Sergeyev, who could perform stupendous things for their time. Their variations were exciting, consisting of unusual jumps, complicated tricks in the air, striking stretched jetés and turns—all creating a very strong and very vivid picture of male dancing as well as of the French Revolution they represented. The male variations from *The Flames of Paris* were often used later as concert pieces, for they make effective showcases of virtuoso dancing. Similarly, the pas de deux and grand divertissement from the final act have been performed separately by numerous dancers and companies, including outside the Soviet Union.

—Igor Stupnikov

---

## FLINDT, Flemming

Danish dancer, choreographer, and ballet director. Born in Copenhagen, 30 June 1936. Studied at the Royal Danish Ballet School, from 1946, pupil of Harald Lander and Vera Volkova; also studied at the Paris Opéra Ballet School, 1952–54. Married dancer Vivi Gelker, 1970. Dancer, becoming solo dancer (principal), Royal Danish Ballet, Copenhagen, from 1955: guest artist from 1962; international guest artist, including for London Festival Ballet, from 1955, Ballet Rambert, 1960, Ruth Page's Chicago Opera Ballet, 1962, Rome Opera Ballet, 1962, Royal Ballet, 1963, Vienna State Opera Ballet, 1963, Bolshoi Ballet, Moscow, 1968, and many other companies; premier danseur étoile, Paris Opéra Ballet, from 1961; artistic director (Royal Ballet Master), Royal Danish Ballet, 1966–78; founder of own company, Denmark, 1978, and director of own school, Copenhagen, 1978–81; guest choreographer and producer, staging ballets for companies including Paris Opéra Ballet, Ballet of La Scala, Milan, Metropolitan Opera, New York, National Ballet, Washington, D.C., and Royal Danish Ballet, Copenhagen; artistic director, Dallas Ballet, 1981–87, 1988–89. Recipient: Prix Italia for choreography of *The Lesson*, 1963; Knight of Dannebrog, 1974; Carina Ari Medal, 1975.

### ROLES

1950 Chimney-Sweep in *The Shepherdess and the Chimney-Sweep* (Lander), Royal Danish Ballet, Copenhagen

1954 Principal role in *Concertette* (Bruhn), Royal Danish Ballet, Copenhagen
Principal role in *Bag Tæppet* (*Behind the Curtain*; Bjornsson), Royal Danish Ballet, Copenhagen

1955 Harlequin in *La Sonnambula* (*Night Shadow*; Balanchine), Royal Danish Ballet, Copenhagen
Benvolio (cr) in *Romeo and Juliet* (Ashton), Royal Danish Ballet, Copenhagen
The Nutcracker Prince in *The Nutcracker* (Beriozoff, Lichine after Ivanov), London Festival Ballet, London
Gennaro in *Napoli* (Bournonville), London Festival Ballet
Soloist in *Études* (Lander), London Festival Ballet

1956 Prince Siegfried in *Swan Lake*, Act II (Dolin after Ivanov), London Festival Ballet
The Spirit of the rose in *Le Spectre de la rose* (Fokine), London Festival Ballet
Franz in *Coppélia* (Lander after Saint-Léon), London Festival Ballet

1957 The Drummer in *Graduation Ball* (Lichine), London Festival Ballet
Principal dancer (cr) in *Variations for Four* (Dolin), London Festival Ballet, London
Waltz, Mazurka in *Les Sylphides* (Fokine), London Festival Ballet

1958 Principal dancer in *Symphony in C* (Balanchine), Royal Danish Ballet, Copenhagen
Pas de deux from *Don Quixote* (Schaufuss after Petipa), Royal Danish Ballet, Copenhagen
Soloist in *Opus 13* (Schaufuss), Royal Danish Ballet, Copenhagen
Greek dance in *The Whims of Cupid and the Ballet Master* (Galeotti), Royal Danish Ballet, Copenhagen
Soloist in *La Jeunesse* (Bartholin), Royal Danish Ballet, Copenhagen
Nilas in *Moon Reindeer* (Cullberg), Royal Danish Ballet, Copenhagen
Harlequin in *Les Millions d'Arlequin* (Walbom after Petipa), Royal Danish Ballet, Copenhagen
James in *La Sylphide* (Bournonville), Royal Danish Ballet, Copenhagen

1960 Don José in *Carmen* (Petit), Royal Danish Ballet, Copenhagen
Leonardo in *Blood Wedding* (Rodrigues), Royal Danish Ballet, Copenhagen
Armand (cr) in *La Dame aux camélias* (Ralov), Royal Danish Ballet, Copenhagen
Romeo in *Romeo and Juliet* (Ashton), Royal Danish Ballet, Copenhagen

1961 Prince Siegfried in *Swan Lake* (Petipa, Ivanov; staged Burmeister), Paris Opéra Ballet, Paris
Albrecht in *Giselle* (Petipa after Coralli, Perrot; staged Lifar), Paris Opéra Ballet, Paris
Principal dancer in *Suite en blanc* (Lifar), Paris Opéra Ballet, Paris

Principal dancer in *The Four Temperaments* (Balanchine), Paris Opéra Ballet, Paris
Zephyr in *Les Indes galantes* (Lander), Royal Danish Ballet, Copenhagen
1962 Endymion (cr) in *Les Victoires de l'amour* (Lander), Royal Danish Ballet, Copenhagen
Soloist in *Études* (Lander), Royal Danish Ballet, Copenhagen
Soloist in *Sur un thème* (Burmeister), Paris Opéra Ballet, Paris
The Youth in *Les Mirages* (Lifar), Paris Opéra Ballet, Paris
Danilo in *The Merry Widow* (Page), Chicago Opera Ballet, Chicago
Pas de deux in *Annabel Lee* (Skibine), Danish television
Hero (cr) in *Hero et Leandre* (Corelli), French television
1963 Principal dancer in *Scotch Symphony* (Balanchine), Paris Opéra Ballet, Paris
Aminta in *Sylvia* (Ashton), Royal Ballet, London
Colas in *La Fille mal gardée* (Ashton), Royal Ballet Touring Company
The Ballet Master (cr) in *The Lesson* (also chor.), Danish television
Principal dancer in *Flower Festival at Genzano* (Bournonville; staged Bruhn), Royal Ballet, London
1965 Principal dancer (cr) in *The Young Man Must Marry* (also chor.), Danish television
1966 D'Artagnan in *The Three Musketeers* (also chor.), Royal Danish Ballet, Copenhagen
1967 Principal dancer in *Le Loup* (Petit), Royal Danish Ballet, Copenhagen
Principal dancer in *Tango Chikane* (also chor.), Royal Danish Ballet, Copenhagen
Leading role in *The Miraculous Mandarin* (also chor.), Royal Danish Ballet, Copenhagen
1968 Albrecht in *Giselle* (Petipa after Corelli, Perrot; staged Dolin), Royal Danish Ballet, Copenhagen
Title role in *The Prodigal Son* (Balachine), Royal Danish Ballet, Copenhagen
Senor in *La Ventana* (Bournonville; staged Brenaa), Royal Danish Ballet, Copenhagen
1970 Principal dancer in *Concerto Prokofiev* (Blaska), Royal Danish Ballet, Copenhagen
Principal dancer in *La Fête Polonaise* (Lander), Royal Danish Ballet, Copenhagen
1971 Principal dancer (cr) in *The Triumph of Death* (also chor.), Danish television
Eduard in *The Lifeguards on Amager* (Bournonville), Royal Danish Ballet, Copenhagen
Frantz in *Bagaget* (Tomaszewski), Royal Danish Ballet, Copenhagen
Gennaro in *Napoli* (Bournonville), Royal Danish Ballet, Copenhagen
1972 Principal dancer in *Orestes* (Holm), Royal Danish Ballet, Copenhagen

## WORKS

1963 *The Lesson* (mus. Delerue), Danish television (staged Royal Danish Ballet, Paris, 1964)
1965 *The Young Man Must Marry* (*Le Jeune homme à marié*; mus. Norgaard), Danish television (staged Royal Danish Ballet, Copenhagen, 1968)
*Faust* (mus. Gounod), Metropolitan Opera Ballet, New York
1966 *The Three Musketeers* (mus. Delerue), Royal Danish Ballet, Copenhagen
*Rosendrommen* (*The Dream of the Rose*; mus. von Weber), Royal Danish Ballet, Copenhagen
1967 *Gala Variations* (pas de deux; mus. Riisager), Royal Danish Ballet, Copenhagen
*The Miraculous Mandarin* (mus. Bartók), Royal Danish Ballet, Copenhagen
*Tango Jalousie* (mus. Gade), Danish television
*Ballet Royal* (mus. Riisager), Royal Danish Ballet, Copenhagen
*Tango Chikane* (mus. Norgaard), Royal Danish Ballet, Copenhagen (staged National Ballet, Washington, 1968)
1968 *Le Sacre du Printemps* (mus. Stravinsky), Danish television
1969 *Le Porcher* (mus. Riisager), Royal Danish Ballet, Copenhagen
1971 *The Triumph of Death* (mus. Koppel), Danish television (staged Royal Danish Ballet, Copenhagen, 1972)
*The Four Seasons* (mus. Vivaldi), Royal Danish Ballet, Copenhagen
*Summer Dances* (mus. Italian baroque, arranged Schultz), Royal Danish Ballet, Copenhagen
*The Nutcracker* (mus. Tchaikovsky), Royal Danish Ballet, Copenhagen
1972 *Trio* (mus. Norgaard), Royal Danish Ballet, Copenhagen
1973 *Felix Luna* (mus. Buch), Royal Danish Ballet, Copenhagen
*Jeux* (mus. Debussy), Royal Danish Ballet, Copenhagen
1974 *Dreamland* (mus. Koppl), Royal Danish Ballet, Copenhagen
1978 *Salomé* (mus. P.M. Davies), Flemming Flindt company, Circus Theatre, Copenhagen
1985 *Tarantella Classique* (mus. Mandernach), Dallas Ballet, Dallas
1987 *Phaedra* (mus. Glass), Dallas Ballet, Dallas
Dances in *William Tell* (opera; mus. Rossini), La Scala, Milan
1989 *The Overcoat* (mus. Shostakovich), Maggio Musicale, Florence
1991 *Caroline Mathilde* (mus. Davies), Royal Danish Ballet, Copenhagen

Also staged:
1963 Pas de deux from *Don Quixote* (after Petipa; mus. Minkus), Royal Danish Ballet, Copenhagen
1966 *The Kermesse in Bruges* (with Brenaa, after Bournonville; mus. Paulli), Royal Danish Ballet, Copenhagen
1967 *La Sylphide* (with Brenaa, after Bournonville; mus. Løvenskjold), Royal Danish Ballet, Copenhagen
*Napoli* (after Bournonville; mus. Paulli, Helsted, Gade, and Lumbye), Royal Danish Ballet, Copenhagen
1968 *La Ventana* (after Bournonville; mus. Lumbye), Royal Danish Ballet, Copenhagen
*Konservatoriet* (after Bournonville; mus. Paulli), Royal Danish Ballet, Copenhagen
1969 *A Folk Tale* (after Bournonville; mus. Gade, Hartmann), Royal Danish Ballet, Copenhagen
*Swan Lake* (after Petipa, Ivanov; mus. Tchaikovsky), Royal Danish Ballet, Copenhagen
1970 *The Life Guards on Amager* (after Bournonville; mus. Holm, Dupuy, Lumbye), Royal Danish Ballet, Copenhagen
1973 *Far From Denmark* (after Bournonville; mus. Glaeser, Gottschalk, Lumbye, Dupuy, Lincke), Royal Danish Ballet, Copenhagen

1975 *Wednesday's School* (after Bournonville), Royal Danish Ballet, Copenhagen
1977 *The Toreador* (after Bournonville; mus. arranged Helsted), Royal Danish Ballet, Copenhagen
1982 *Wedding Festival at Hardanger* (after Bournonville), Norwegian Ballet, Oslo
1985 *Coppélia* (after Saint-Léon; mus. Delibes), Dallas Ballet, Dallas

## PUBLICATIONS

By Flindt:
"Mesteren Bournonville", *Berlingske Tidende*, 26 February 1969
Interview in Stoop, Norma McLain, "Flemming Flindt and the Royal Danish Ballet", *Dance Magazine* (New York), May 1976

About Flindt:
Roberts, S., "Men in Ballet: Flemming Flindt", *Ballet Today* (London), March 1957
"Personality of the Month: Flemming Flindt", *Dance and Dancers* (London), September 1960
Goodman, Saul, "Brief Biographies: Flemming Flindt", *Dance Magazine* (New York), September 1960
Anderson, Jack, "Introducing Flemming Flindt", *Dance Magazine* (New York), November 1965
Aschengreen, Erik, "Flemming Flindt", *Les Saisons de la danse* (Paris), December 1970
Percival, John, "Danish Variety", *Dance and Dancers* (London), February 1974
Percival, John, "Copenhagen Dreamland", *Dance and Dancers* (London), November 1974
Duff, Helen, "Dancing in Copenhagen", *Dancing Times*, (London), December, 1978
Aschengreen, Erik, *Balletbogen*, Copenhagen, 1982
Lundgreen, Henrik, "50 år Flemming Flindt", *Politiken* (Copenhagen), 29 September 1986

* * *

Flemming Flindt is one of the most controversial figures in the history of the Royal Danish Ballet in this century. At the age of eighteen, he entered the company as a principal dancer without having been a member of the corps. Almost immediately he was launched into an international career that brought him to London's Festival Ballet, the Paris Opéra Ballet, where he was appointed premier danseur etoile, and many other European and American companies. As a danseur noble he danced all the major classical roles.

His greatest artistic achievements, however, came during his twelve-year tenure (1966–78) as ballet master of the Royal Danish Ballet. Only thirty years old, he took over a company that had been entirely devoted to the preservation of the Bournonville repertory, apart from a brief fling with modern ballet during the leadership of Harald Lander (1932–51). But since Lander's departure nothing new had happened; and the ballet had become a dusty Bournonville museum with a very small audience. Flindt was faced with the impossible task of bringing contemporary ballet to the company, and at the same time maintaining the Bournonville heritage.

Judging by ticket sales, Flindt was very successful in bringing the company out of its dusty hibernation. Ninety-two percent of all seats were sold out on ballet evenings, the highest percentage ever in the history of the company. It was especially his own ballets which drew large crowds. But Flindt not only brought people to the ballet; he also brought ballet to people all over the country through the many television productions he made. Several of his ballets were first created for television and then later adapted for the stage.

Flindt knew how to appeal to a broad audience. He presented restagings of the Bournonville repertory, reconstructed some of the Bournonville ballets no longer danced, and revived the classics. He staged an extremely successful *Nutcracker*, which is in the repertory of the Royal Danish Ballet today. He brought in dances by contemporary choreographers such as Robbins, Taylor, Limón, Tetley, Feld, and others, and he created his own ballets, which were more dance-dramas than ballets.

Flindt also wrote ballet history. In Taylor's *Aureole*, the Royal Danish Ballet danced barefoot for the first time ever, and in Flindt's *Triumph of Death*, the company—ballet master included—danced naked. The nude scenes created heated discussions, but the popularity of the ballet was due to the topical themes it dealt with, those of death and pollution. The score, by the Danish rock group Savage Rose, was the first rock score ever commissioned by the Royal Danish Theatre.

Flindt brought contemporary life into the ballet. Several of his ballets were based on plays or ideas by the French playwright Eugene Ionesco, with whom Flindt worked closely. And several of the scores he used were by contemporary composers. He brought in a new verve and vitality which the Royal Danish Ballet had hitherto not known.

The critics, however, were sceptical. They criticized Flindt's Bournonville restagings and reconstructions for being too flashy and showy, and too far removed from the originals. They acknowledged that he had brought modern ballet to the stage, but at the same time claimed that the diversity of the repertory had ruined the style and technique of the dancers.

In 1978 Flindt left his position as ballet master of the Royal Danish ballet, tired of being at the centre of a fierce, if fruitful, public discussion about his role as ballet master and his talents as choreographer. Furthermore, his power had become disconcerting to many. He was accused of favouring his own ballets too much and of preferring the modern-dancer type which his wife, Vivi Flindt (formerly Gelker), represented, to the classical type. He was also said to have ruined the careers of several of the female dancers, because they never had a chance to develop in the classical repertoire. By the time he left, Flindt felt artistically stunted. With the growing economic crisis of the 1970s, the budget of the solely state-subsidized theatre had been constantly cut, which had made it increasingly difficult to mount bigger productions.

As an epitaph to Flindt's career as ballet master, the Danish critic Henrik Lundgreen wrote in the Danish newspaper *Politiken* in 1986: "Flindt's period at the Royal Danish Ballet was the last time something happened. [He] put too much emphasis on his own ballets . . . But he managed to keep Copenhagen at the centre of the international dance scene . . . In this respect Flindt is missed thoroughly: as an international intermediary and dynamic initiator."

Flindt has often been compared to Bournonville. They both began with an international dance career, which they broke off to return to Denmark at a very young age to assume the position of ballet master. But whereas Bournonville practically erased the works of his predecessor Galeotti and left a heritage that has shaped the Royal Danish Ballet ever since, Flindt, although he is considered the most important Danish choreographer after Lander, has not left any lasting imprint on ballet. Except for his staging of *The Nutcracker*, which is still performed every Christmas, only a few of his ballets are occasionally revived. What Flindt is remembered for above all is the turmoil he created. This is perhaps a reflection of the true problem with the Royal Danish Ballet. As long as the Bournonville heritage is to be left unchanged, there is no room for real innovation.

After leaving the Royal Danish Ballet, Flindt and his wife ran their own ballet school in Copenhagen until 1981. In that year, he accepted the position as ballet master of the Dallas Ballet with the promise of artistic freedom. His aim was to make the company internationally renowned, but before he could fulfil his dream the company closed down for financial reasons.

Now Flindt is leading a truly international career, travelling all over the world staging ballets and occasionally choreographing new pieces. In 1991, he returned to the Royal Danish Ballet, who commissioned him to choreograph a historical ballet.

—Jeannette Andersen

---

## FLORE ET ZÉPHIRE

**Choreography:** Charles Louis Didelot
**Music:** Cesare Bossi
**Design:** Liparotti
**Libretto:** Charles-Louis Didelot
**First Production:** King's Theatre, London, 7 July 1796
**Principal Dancers:** Janet Hilligsberg (Cleonisa), Rose Collinet (Mme. Didelot; Flora), Charles Louis Didelot (Zephyrus)

**Other productions include:** Hermitage Theatre (restaged Didelot); as *Zéphire et Flore;* St. Petersburg, 1804 (revived at same theatre, with Louis Duport and Maria Danilova, 1808). King's Theatre (restaged Didelot; new music Venua), as *Zéphyr inconstant, puni et fixé; ou, Les Noces de Flore;* London, 7 April 1812. L'Académie royale de musique (Paris Opéra; two-act version, restaged Didelot; music Venua, design Ciceri, costumes Marches, machines Boulton), as *Zéphire et Flore*, with François Decombe Albert and Geneviève Gosselin; Paris, 12 December 1815. Hermitage Theatre (restaged Didelot; design Kondratiev, costumes Babini, machines Thibeault); St. Petersburg, 15 February (26 January old style) 1818. King's Theatre (revival, after Didelot; mus. Venua) with Marie Taglioni; London, 3 June 1830.

**Other choreographic treatments of story:** Léonide Massine (Monte Carlo, 1925).

### PUBLICATIONS

Van Noorden, C., "Thackeray and the Ballet", *Dancing Times* (London), May 1923
Beaumont, Cyril, *Complete Book of Ballets,* revised edition, London, 1951
Hall, Fernau, *World Dance,* New York, 1955
Roslavleva, Natalia, *Era of the Russian Ballet,* London, 1966
Kirstein, Lincoln, *Movement and Metaphor: Four Centuries of Ballet,* New York, 1970
Guest, Ivor, "Thackeray and the Ballet", *Dancing Times* (London), January 1972
Swift, Mary Grace, *A Loftier Flight: The Life and Accomplishments of Charles-Louis Didelot,* Middletown, Connecticut, 1974
Winter, Marian Hannah, *The Pre-Romantic Ballet,* London, 1974
Lawson, Joan, *A History of Ballet and its Makers,* London, 1976

*Flore et Zéphire,* Charles-Louis Didelot's 1796 masterpiece, had the distinction of ushering in the era of Romantic ballet, synthesizing as it did the theoretical, choreographic, and technical developments which took place under the great masters Jean-Georges Noverre, Jean Dauberval, and Auguste Vestris. Didelot's innovations enhanced the fantastic and expressive qualities of choreography, making it possible to convey a story through danced mime.

At the King's Theatre in London, where *Flore et Zéphire* was first produced, Didelot had at his disposal an improved flying machine invented by English mechanics which allowed choreographic flights to cover the length, breadth, and circumference of the stage on silent, invisible wires. For some time dancers had been attempting to rise higher onto the tips of the toes for increased speed and more spectacular feats of balance; but with the advent of the new flying machine, dancers could be supported for several moments en pointe before taking flight. *Flore et Zéphire* is assumed to be the first ballet to use this advance in technique. The machine also made possible simple but highly effective lifts whereby the traditional pas de deux, in which both dancers generally performed the same steps, became a dramatic, danced conversation between male and female dancers.

Didelot's desire to make the traditional Greek mythological subjects accessible to a wider range of London theatre-goers probably spurred his innovations to some extent. In the story of Zéphire and Flore, Zéphire—the God of Wind—descends from the sky to claim his beloved Flore, is distracted by another nymph, but ultimately returns to his true love and sweeps her away into the sky with him in a climactic moment of reciprocated love. By defining more sharply the different physical qualities of movement and the differences between steps more appropriate to male or female, and by exploiting dancers' natural abilities to express feeling through movement, Didelot was able to depict dramatic action in a new way. Rather than resorting to conventional gesture in the traditional "scènes d'action", he used a more fluid and natural type of mime which was actually danced mime. By reforming the costuming—the dancers wore Grecian tunics, flesh-colored tights, light slippers, and gossamer wings—movement became less restricted and more imaginative, natural, and poetic. Corps de ballet as well as principal dancers were expected to retain the characteristic style dictated by the setting; and by allowing a certain amount of individual movement within unusually picturesque groupings, the action was helped to unfold more realistically in this way, as well.

*Flore et Zéphire* vaulted Didelot into the ranks of the great choreographers and won him an invitation from Tsar Paul I to settle in Russia as a dancer, ballet master, and professor of dance. The ballet was presented at the Hermitage Theatre in St. Petersburg in 1808, with the names of the title reversed to reflect the emphasis placed on the role of Zéphire in the revised version (first seen in St. Petersburg in 1804). The new production was created for the illustrious guest artist Louis Duport, whose virtuosity was unequalled at that time. The choreography for Zéphire became breathtakingly ethereal as Duport's great elevation far exceeded that of the original Zéphire, Didelot himself. Didelot also changed the very essence of the original mythological story by endowing his characters with human feelings, which the Russian dancers in particular projected successfully through the choreography (it was one of Didelot's brilliantly talented Russian pupils, Maria Danilova, who was Duport's partner in the St. Petersburg *Zéphire et Flore*).

In 1815 Didelot at last realized his life's dream of presenting *Flore et Zéphire* at the Paris Opéra. His efforts had been repeatedly thwarted by the jealous intrigues and outright

***Flore et Zéphire*, with Marie Taglioni as Flore, 1831**

hostility of Pierre Gardel, the omnipotent ruler of the Opéra. However, thanks to the intervention of the Russian patrons who headed the allied troops which occupied Paris at the time, the ballet was finally produced to ecstatic acclaim. With one powerful stroke of genius, Didelot settled the score with Gardel and added European recognition to that awarded him by England and Russia. Gardel perhaps enjoyed a small satisfaction in that he required Didelot to bear the costs of production himself, and though Louis XVIII granted him the sum of 2,000 francs as a personal accolade, Didelot still had 400 francs to pay. The ballet became a classic, with 189 performances at the Opéra, and became an important vehicle for Marie Taglioni's debut in the 1830 London revival.

*Flore et Zéphire* falls squarely on the line between classicism and romanticism in ballet. Didelot failed to address certain limitations of the grand pantomimic spectacle even as he sought to enhance the poetic and expressive qualities of ballet. As the creative harbinger of Romantic ballet with its predominance of danced action, he introduced in *Flore et Zéphire* a new technique of dancing which made expression through exceptional choreographic images a possibility.

—Kristin Beckwith

---

**FOKINE, Mikhail** (Michel)

Russian dancer, choreographer, teacher, and ballet director. Born Mikhail (later called himself Michel) Mikhailovich Fokin (Fokine) in St. Petersburg, 5 May (23 April old style) 1880. Studied at the Imperial Theatre School, St. Petersburg, pupil of Platon Karsavin, Nikolai Volkov, Aleksandr Shiryaev, Pavel Gerdt; graduated in 1898. Married dancer Vera Antonova, 1905: one son, dancer and teacher (and editor of Fokine's memoirs) Vitale Fokine. Dancer, Maryinsky Theatre, St. Petersburg: soloist, from 1898, first soloist, from 1900; teacher, Imperial Theatre School, from 1902; first choreography, for Theatre School graduation performance, 1905; first Maryinsky Theatre choreography, *Le Pavillon d'Armide*, 1907; chief choreographer, Diaghilev's Ballets Russes, 1909–12, continuing as choreographer for the Imperial Theatres, St. Petersburg; broke with Diaghilev, 1912; returned to St. Petersburg and Maryinsky Theatre during World War I; left Russia for the last time, 1918: worked in Stockholm, performing and teaching also in Finland and Denmark, 1918–20; performed in New York and various American cities with wife Vera Fokina, 1920; freelance choreographer and performer, New York, including for Metropolitan Opera House, Hippodrome, Gertrude Hoffman's Company, Ziegfeld Follies, Carnegie Hall, and also in Boston, Philadelphia, and Newark, 1921–28; performed as Fokine Ballet, 1922, and as American Ballet, and Fokine Dancers, 1924, 1925; also staged ballets for Paris Opéra, 1921, His Majesty's Theatre, London, 1923, tours in Scandinavia and Germany, 1925, Théâtre des Champs-Elysées and Opéra Privé, Paris, 1929, Latvian National Opera House, Riga, 1929, Hollywood Bowl, 1929, Teatro Colón, Buenos Aires, 1931, Ida Rubinstein Company, Paris, 1934, Opéra Comique, Paris, 1935, and La Scala, Milan, 1936; chief choreographer, René Blum's Ballets de Monte Carlo, 1936–38; staged ballets for (de Basil's) Educational Ballets, performing as Russian Ballet and Covent Garden Russian Ballet, 1938–39, and for Ballet Theatre (later American Ballet Theatre), New York, 1941–42; also founder of Fokine School in New York, 1921. Died in New York, 22 August 1942.

**WORKS**

1905 *Acis and Galatea* (mus. Kadletz), Imperial Theatre School Performance, St. Petersburg
*Polka with a Little Ball* (mus. Herbert), Imperial Theatre School Performance, St. Petersburg
*Le Cygne* (also *The Dying Swan*; mus. Saint-Saëns), Hall of the Assembly of the Nobility, St. Petersburg (some sources say 1907)

1906 *The Flight of the Butterflies* (mus. Chopin), Hall of the Assembly of the Nobility, St. Petersburg
*Polka-Pizzicato* (mus. Strauss), Hall of the Assembly of the Nobility, St. Petersburg
*Sevillana* (mus. Albéniz), Hall of the Assembly of the Nobility, St. Petersburg
*A Midsummer Night's Dream* (after Petipa; mus. Mendelssohn), Imperial Theatre School Performance, St. Petersburg
*Divertissement—Valse fantasia* (mus. Glinka), Imperial Theatre School Performance, St. Petersburg
*La Vigne* (mus. Rubinstein), Maryinsky Theatre, St. Petersburg
*Spanish Dance* (mus. Bizet), Maryinsky Theatre, St. Petersburg
*Czardas* (mus. Brahms), Summer Theatre, Krasno Selo

1907 *Eunice* (mus. Shcherbachev), Maryinsky Theatre, St. Petersburg
*Chopiniana* (mus. Chopin, orchestrated Glazunov), Maryinsky Theatre, St. Petersburg
*The Animated Gobelin* (later part of *Le Pavillon d'Armide*; mus. Tcherepnin), Imperial Theatre School Performance, St. Petersburg
*Le Pavillon d'Armide* (mus. Tcherepnin), Maryinsky Theatre, St. Petersburg
*Dance with a Torch* (*Danse Assyrienne*; mus. Arensky), Charity Performance, Maryinsky Theatre, St. Petersburg

1908 *The Night of Terpsichore*, Maryinsky Theatre, St. Petersburg
*Danses sur la musique de Chopin* (later part of *Rêverie romantique*; mus. Chopin), Maryinsky Theatre, St. Petersburg
*Egyptian Nights* (also *Une Nuit d'Egypte*, later performed as *Cléopâtre*; mus. Arensky), Maryinsky Theatre, St. Petersburg
*Rêverie Romantique—Ballet sur la musique de Chopin* (second version of *Chopiniana*; mus. Chopin, orchestrated Keller, Glazunov), Maryinsky Theatre, St. Petersburg
*Bal poudré* (mus. Clementi, orchestrated Keller), Pavlov Hall, St. Petersburg
*The Four Seasons* (mus. Tchaikovsky), Imperial Theatre School, St. Petersburg
*Grand Pas sur la musique de Chopin* (mus. Chopin), Imperial Theatre School, St. Petersburg
*The Dance of the Seven Veils* in *Salomé* (play by Oscar Wilde, produced by Ida Rubinstein), Mikhailovsky Theatre, St. Petersburg

1909 *Le Pavillon d'Armide* (new production; mus. Tcherepnin), Diaghilev's Ballets Russes, Paris
*Polovtsian Dances from Prince Igor* (mus. Borodin, from the opera *Prince Igor*), Diaghilev's Ballets Russes, Paris
*Le Festin* (suite of dances, chor. Fokine with Petipa, Gorsky, Goltz, Kshesinsky), Diaghilev's Ballets Russes, Paris
*Les Sylphides* (new version of *Chopiniana*; mus. Chopin,

**Mikhail Fokine with Tamara Karsavina in *L'Oiseau de feu*, Paris, 1910**

orchestrated Glazunov, Stravinsky, Taneyev), Diaghilev's Ballets Russes, Paris
*Cléopâtre* (new version of *Egyptian Nights*; mus. Arensky, with additional music Glazunov, Glinka, Mussorgsky, Rimsky-Korsakov, Taneyev, Tcherepnin), Diaghilev's Ballets Russes, Paris

1910 *Bacchanale* (mus. Glazunov), Hall of the Assembly of the Nobility, St. Petersburg
*Carnaval* (mus. Schumann, orchestrated Arensky, Glazunov, Liadov, Rimsky-Korsakov, Tcherepnin), Pavlov Hall, St. Petersburg
*Danse siamoise* (mus. Sinding, orchestrated Stravinsky), Maryinsky Theatre, St. Petersburg
*Kobold* (mus. Grieg, orchestrated Stravinsky), Maryinsky Theatre, St. Petersburg
*Grotto of Venus* (mus. Wagner, from *Tannhäuser*), Maryinsky Theatre, St. Petersburg
*Schéhérazade* (mus. Rimsky-Korsakov), Diaghilev's Ballets Russes, Paris
*L'Oiseau de feu* (*The Firebird*; mus. Stravinsky), Diaghilev's Ballets Russes, Paris
*Les Orientales* (mus. Arensky, Borodin, Glazunov, Grieg, Sinding, orchestrated Stravinsky), Diaghilev's Ballets Russes, Paris

1911 *Le Spectre de la rose* (mus. Weber, orchestrated Berlioz), Diaghilev's Ballets Russes, Monte Carlo
*Narcisse* (mus. Tcherepnin), Diaghilev's Ballets Russes, Monte Carlo
Dances in *Le Martyre de Saint-Sébastien* (play by d'Annunzio), Ida Rubinstein's Company, Paris
*Sadko* (mus. Rimsky-Korsakov), Diaghilev's Ballets Russes, Paris
*Petrushka* (as *Pétrouchka*; mus. Stravinsky), Diaghilev's Ballets Russes, Paris
*Variations* (mus. Chopin), Maryinsky Theatre, St. Petersburg
Dances in *Orpheus and Eurydice* (opera; mus. Gluck), Maryinsky Theatre, St. Petersburg

1912 *Papillon* (mus. Schumann), Maryinsky Theatre, St. Petersburg
*Islamey* (also *Islamé*; mus. Balakirev), Maryinsky Theatre, St. Petersburg
*Le Dieu bleu* (mus. Hahn), Diaghilev's Ballets Russes, Paris
*Thamar* (mus. Balakirev), Diaghilev's Ballets Russes, Paris
*Daphnis et Chloë* (mus. Ravel), Diaghilev's Ballets Russes, Paris
Dances in *Salomé* (play by Oscar Wilde), Ida Rubinstein's Company, Paris (version of 1908 production)
Dances in *Judith* (opera; mus. Rubinstein), Maryinsky Theatre, St. Petersburg
Dances in *The Pearl Fishers* (opera; mus. Bizet), Maryinsky Theatre, St. Petersburg

1913 *The Seven Daughters of the Mountain King* (mus. Spendiarov), Anna Pavlova's Company, Berlin
*Les Préludes* (mus. Liszt), Anna Pavlova's Company, Berlin
Dances in *La Pisanelle ou la mort parfumée* (play by d'Annunzio; mus. Schumann), Ida Rubinstein's Company, Paris

1914 *The Legend of Joseph* (mus. Strauss), Diaghilev's Ballets Russes, Paris
*Le Coq d'or* (mus. Rimsky-Korsakov), Diaghilev's Ballets Russes, Paris
*Midas* (mus. Steinberg), Diaghilev's Ballets Russes, Paris

1915 *The Dream* (mus. Glinka), Maryinsky Theatre, Petrograd
*Francesca da Rimini* (mus. Tchaikovsky), Maryinsky Theatre, Petrograd
*Stenka Razin* (mus. Glazunov), Maryinsky Theatre, Petrograd
*Eros* (mus. Tchaikovsky), Maryinsky Theatre, Petrograd
*Prélude* (mus. Chopin), *Romance* (mus. Tchaikovsky), *Bacchus* (mus. Tcherepnin), *Tarantella*, Maryinsky Theatre, Petrograd

1916 *Andantino* (mus. Tchaikovsky), Maryinsky Theatre, Petrograd
*Khaitarma* (mus. Spendiarov), *Russian Songs*, Maryinsky Theatre, Petrograd
*Jota Aragonesa* (mus. Glinka), Maryinsky Theatre, Petrograd
*Princess Avriza* (mus. Mussorgsky), Maryinsky Theatre, Petrograd
*The Sorcerer's Apprentice* (mus. Dukas), Maryinsky Theatre, Petrograd

1917 *Abrek* (mus. traditional, orchestrated Asafiev), Maryinsky Theatre, Petrograd
Dances in *Ruslan and Ludmila* (opera; mus. Glinka), Maryinsky Theatre, Petrograd

1918 *The Four Seasons* (ballet for children; mus. Grieg, Schumann, Tchaikovsky), Stadium, Stockholm
*Moonlight Sonata* (ballet for children; mus. Beethoven), Stadium, Stockholm

1919 Dances, including "Bacchanale" in *Aphrodite* (musical; after Louys), Century Theatre, New York

1920 *Mecca* (mus. Asche), Century Theatre, New York

1921 *Le Rêve de la marquise* (mus. Mozart), Metropolitan Opera House, New York
"Thunder Bird", ballet in *Get Together* (revue; mus. Borodin, Glinka, Tchaikovsky), Hippodrome, New York
*The Shaytan's Captive* (or *Shaitan*; mus. Glazunov, from *Raymonda*), Gertrude Hoffman's Company, New York
*Russian Toys* (mus. Rimsky-Korsakov), Gilda Grey Company, New York

1922 *The Adventures of Harlequin* (mus. Beethoven), Fokine Ballet, Mark Strand Theatre, New York
*Voices of Spring* (mus. Strauss), Fokine Ballet, New York
*Chinese Dance* (mus. Rebikov), Fokine Ballet, New York
*Humoresque and Polka* (mus. Dvorak, Strauss), Fokine Ballet, New York

1923 *Frolicking Gods* (mus. Tchaikovsky, from *The Nutcracker*), Ziegfeld Follies, New York
*Farljandio* (mus. Herbert), Ziegfeld Follies, New York
Dances in *Hassan* (play by J. Elroy Flecker; mus. Delius), His Majesty's Theatre, London
"The Return from the Carnival", ballet in *Casanova* (play by Lorenzo di Azertis; mus. Taylor), Empire Theater, New York
*Santa Claus* (mus. Liadow), Gertrude Hoffman Company, Newark, New Jersey
*La Nuit ensorcelée* (mus. Chopin), Opéra, Paris

1924 *Olé Toro* (mus. Rimsky-Korsakov), American Ballet (Fokine company), New York
*Medusa* (mus. Tchaikovsky), American Ballet (Fokine company), New York
*Les Elfes* (mus. Mendelssohn), American Ballet (Fokine company), New York

*The Shemakhanskaya Tsaritsa* (mus. Rimsky-Korsakov), American Ballet (Fokine company), Philadelphia

1925 *The Immortal Pierrot* (mus. Beethoven), American Ballet (Fokine company), New York

*Fra Mino* (mus. Schumann), Fokine Ballet, Berlin

Dances in *A Midsummer Night's Dream* (play "after" Shakespeare; mus. Mendelssohn), Drury Lane Theatre, London

1927 *Prologue to Faust* (mus. Mussorgsky, Grieg), Madame Fokina and "Fokine Girls", Philadelphia

1928 "The Ballet of Flowers" in *Rosalie* (musical comedy), Ziegfeld Follies, New Amsterdam Theatre, New York

*South Island Sea Dance*, Grand Street Follies, New York

1931 *The Adventures of Harlequin* (new version; mus. Beethoven), Teatro Colón, Buenos Aires

*The Sorcerer's Apprentice* (new version; mus. Dukas), Teatro Colón, Buenos Aires

1934 *Diane de Poitiers* (mus. Ibert), Ida Rubinstein's Company, Paris

*Sémiramis* (mus. Honegger), Ida Rubinstein's Company, Paris

1935 *La Valse* (mus. Ravel), Ida Rubinstein's Company, Paris

*Bolero* (mus. Ravel), Ida Rubinstein's Company, Paris

*Psyché* (mus. Franck), Olga Spessivtseva Concert, Opéra-Comique, Paris

*Méphisto Waltz* (mus. Liszt), Olga Spessivtseva Concert, Opéra-Comique, Paris

1936 *The Love for Three Oranges* (mus. Sonzogno), La Scala, Milan

Dances in *Samson and Delila* (opera; mus. Saint-Saëns), La Scala, Milan

*L' Epreuve d'amour* (mus. various; originally thought to be Mozart), (René Blum's) Ballets de Monte Carlo, Monte Carlo

*Don Juan* (mus. Gluck), (René Blum's), Ballets de Monte Carlo, London

1937 *Les Elements* (mus. Bach), de Basil's Ballets Russes, London

1938 *Cendrillon* (mus. d'Erlanger), (de Basil's) Russian Ballet, London

1939 *Paganini* (mus. Rachmaninov), (de Basil's) Covent Garden Russian Ballet, London

1941 *Bluebeard* (mus. Offenbach), Ballet Theatre, Mexico City

1942 *Russian Soldier* (mus. Prokofiev), Ballet Theatre, New York

(*Helen of Troy*: mus. Offenbach; incomplete and finished after Fokine's death by Lichine; Ballet Theatre, Mexico City)

**PUBLICATIONS**

By Fokine:

*The Dying Swan*, New York, 1925

"The New Ballet" (*Argus*, 1916) and "Letter to *The Times*" (6 July 1914), in Beaumont, Cyril, *Michel Fokine and his Ballets*, London, 1935

"Fokine's Five Principles of Ballet" as set forth in his famous letter to *The Times*, 6 July, 1914; *Dancing Times* (London), October 1942

*Michel Fokine: Memoirs of a Ballet Master*, translated and edited by Vitale Fokine, London, 1961

About Fokine:

Svetlov, Valerian, "The Diaghilev Ballet in Paris", *Dancing Times* (London), 3 parts: December 1929; January, February 1930

Beaumont, Cyril, *Michel Fokine and his Ballets*, London, 1935

Lieven, Piotr, *The Birth of the Ballets Russes*, London, 1936

Beaumont, Cyril, *Complete Book of Ballets*, revised edition, London, 1951

Grigoriev, Serge, *The Diaghilev Ballet*, translated by Vera Bowen, London, 1953

Vaughan, David, "Fokine in the Contemporary Repertory", *Ballet Review* (New York), vol. 7, nos. 2–3, 1978–79

Horwitz, Dawn Lille, "A Ballet Class with Michel Fokine", *Dance Chronicle* (New York), vol. 3, no. 1, 1979

Kirstein, Lincoln, "Homage to Michel Fokine", in *Ballet, Bias and Belief*, New York, 1983

Copeland, Roger, and Cohen, Marshall, *What is Dance? Readings in Theory and Criticism*, New York, 1983

Horwitz, Dawn Lille, *Michel Fokine*, Boston, 1985

Garafola, Lynn, *Diaghilev's Ballets Russes*, New York, 1989

Koner, Pauline, "With Fokine", *Ballet Review* (New York), Spring 1989

* * *

Fokine has been called the father of twentieth-century ballet. The many changes he made in choreographic structure are still valid today. Yet his belief in classical dance as the basis on which to build was unwavering, as stated in an early letter to the press. "There can only be evolution in art, never revolution. Without firm technique and discipline there can only be anarchy." He held to this dictum throughout his career as dancer, mime, teacher, and choreographer.

Classical dance was not his only interest. Throughout his school days at the Imperial Academy he was preparing himself to become a choreographer of many styles. With his brothers he read Russian and international literature, enjoyed football and gymnastics, and sketched the movements and costumes of many eras, styles, and nationalities from art galleries and museums. He played the piano, mandolin, and balalaika. During holidays he travelled throughout Russia, Spain, Italy, and Scandanavia, adding to his notes and sketches of dance, customs, and behaviour. His outstanding talent was recognized by all his teachers, and he always came first or second in the annual academic and dance examinations.

He graduated into the Imperial Ballet of the Maryinsky at the age of eighteen as second soloist, and two years later became first Soloist, performing every kind of role from danseur noble partnering Pavlova and Karsavina to acting as a mime. More importantly, in 1902 he became a teacher and immediately set about making reforms both in classroom and on stage. When his first class was ready to graduate, he set out his ideas in an open letter. "I believe dance should express meaning and not degenerate into mere gymnastics. Dance should express meaning, the spirit of the actors, their emotions, characters and lives as they live them on stage. . . . In place of the dualism of mime and dance, ballet must become a harmonious blending of music, painting, and plastic art."

Fokine's first aim as choreographer was to do away with stereotyped scenes and pas d'action, as derived from seventeenth-century court ballet and followed by all later ballet masters. To do this he had to prepare dancers to make them capable of expressing mood, emotion, and action. As teacher he created exercises in which steps and gestures were fused to produce a continuous flow of movement conveying meaning firstly through the music. His students had "to listen to the call of the note and rise and fall of the melody whilst preserving a certain style and quality to make sense of the dance". Fokine believed: "All dance is based on gesture. . . . An arabesque can be a longing for height, an inclination of the whole body. . . . If there is not this feeling, only a lifting of the leg, it is intolerable nonsense."

Fokine's interpretation of music went much further than responding to note and phrase. The content of each score was equally important, as he realized that each composer had his own particular style. In a letter to John Martin, the American critic, he deplored Isadora Duncan's dancing in the same way whether to Bach, Mozart, Beethoven, or Chopin, saying, "It is meaningless and without feeling." He loved to work with composers, as he did when working out his choreographic design for *The Firebird* and *Petrushka*, with Stravinsky accompanying him and making valuable contributions from the piano. Later, when working with specially chosen composers such as Tchaikovsky (about whom he consulted Modeste, the brother) and Rachmaninov, with whom he discussed *Paganini* closely, he received in turn much advice on the outline of the plot, the style of dance and costume, and how best to assemble the score.

Fokine's first ballets were mostly staged for private parties or charitable events. These and the open letters to the press attracted the attention of those important Russian artists working for the magazine *The World of Art*, and Fokine soon became a member of their group. They appreciated his wide knowledge and understanding of the problems—later faced when helping to create Diaghilev's Ballets Russes—inherent in a philosophy where dance, music, and décor had to be subordinated to one another to produce a ballet of meaning and style.

Fokine's first ballets created in Russia demonstrated how he wove together conventional and characteristic gesture, into the dream worlds of *Les Sylphides*, *The Dying Swan*, and later, *Le Spectre de la rose*, as well as into the more worldly *commedia dell'arte* characters of *Carnaval*. These ballets were made for dancers whose special qualities Fokine fostered before they captured world attention: Karsavina, Pavlova, and Nijinsky.

Fokine's belief that "All dance is gesture" is seen at its most effective in the *Polovtsian Dances from Prince Igor*, *The Firebird*, *Petrushka*, and those in which he used traditional Russian folk dances to define how the human characters reacted to the fantasies enacted in their midst. His juxtaposition of reality and fantasy was reinforced by similar borrowings from folk sources by the composers Borodin and Stravinsky and the artists Roerich, Benois, and Gontcharova. The worldly dancing of the Polovtsian Warriors, the Betrothal dance of the Enchanted Princesses, and particularly the crowd dancing at the St. Petersburg Easter Fair, were in absolute contrast to the dancing of the characters from the world of fantasy. For these Fokine created what he called Mimed dance or Dance-mime, explaining that the difference between them was a matter of degree. Mimed dance was for those like Tamara Karsavina, who "have the gift of transforming their dance into the world of fantasy and can soar through the air like my Firebird and Golden Cockerel because they represent life and love". Dance-mime was for those few "who lose their own identity when they step on stage and become another being. The Kostchei and the Showman represent death, hate, or fate—they only act, they do not dance. In Petrushka I have empictured The Little Man, the anti-hero of so many European folk tales. No matter how often he gets slapped, he always rises again to give hope. Maybe my Petrushka is made of wood, canvas, and worked by strings, but he sees and feels."

Fokine was the first to create his own particular choreographic style, based on a distinct philosophy, to expose and express the "meaning" behind his artistic creations—some 80 ballets by the end of his career. These works were short, at most comprising one or two scenes—largely because Diaghilev expected him to produce three ballets for each nightly programme during the first years of the Ballets Russes. Even in the most spectacular, for example, *Cléopâtre* with eight divertissements for different slaves, Fokine only used dances to communicate something—here, to display the great Queen's wealth.

Fokine's discipline in choreographic design was not simple. By creating a particular style for a particular story, score, and décor, he proved that it was possible to mould classical dancers' movement to their characters, such that they appeared as themselves—Russians in all their exuberance (*Prince Igor*, *Petrushka*), Greeks, as seen on vases or frescos (*Narcisse*, *Daphnis and Chloë*), Spaniards (*Jota Aragonesa* and others), Botticelli-like Italians (*Francesca da Rimini*), or softly flowing Romantics (*Les Elphes* and others) as well as other characters from many eras, with typical behaviour, habits, and dances.

Any student working with this genius knew how much insight he gave into the roles he created, the tiny details he imparted to each step and gesture, its accent and phrasing—not only to the music, but also its part in the whole design. Each dancer was made to feel significant. You were just as important to the story when playing the little Girl with the muff, spell-bound by the Charlatan's tune before the tragic Petrushka appeared, as when you were dancing the Prelude in *Les Sylphides* where you had to listen to the call of the note before making your gesture. These gestures were the essence of his choreography. As Tamara Karsavina said: "To dance for Fokine was to understand how to tell the world a story in which you believed."

—Joan Lawson

---

## A FOLK TALE

(original Danish title: *Et Folkesagn*)

**Choreography:** August Bournonville
**Music:** Johann Peter Emilius Hartmann and Niels Wilhelm Gade
**Design:** Christensen, Lund, and Lehmann
**Libretto:** August Bournonville
**First Production:** Royal Theatre, Copenhagen, 20 March 1854
**Principal Dancer:** Juliette Price (Hilda)

**Other productions include:** German Opera Ballet (staged Peter Schaufuss after Bournonville, design David Walker); Berlin, 30 April 1983. London Festival Ballet (extracts; staged Schaufuss); 21 February 1988.

### PUBLICATIONS

Beaumont, Cyril, *Complete Book of Ballets*, revised edition, London, 1951
Crosland, Margaret, *Ballet Carnival*, London, 1955
Bournonville, August, *My Theatre Life*, translated by Patricia McAndrew, Middletown, Connecticut, 1979
Terry, Walter, *The King's Ballet Master*, New York, 1979
Aschengreen, Erik, Hallar, Marianne, and Heiner, Jorgen, *Perspectiv på Bournonville*, Copenhagen, 1980
"The Ballet Poems of August Bournonville: The Complete

***A Folk Tale*, as performed by the Royal Danish Ballet, 1952**

Scenarios", translated by Patricia McAndrew, *Dance Chronicle* (New York), vol. 4, no. 2, 1981
Croce, Arlene, *Sight Lines*, New York, 1987
Clarke, Mary, "A Real Royal Ballet: *A Folk Tale* in Copenhagen", *Dancing Times* (London), November 1991

* * *

Until 1979 Bournonville's *A Folk Tale* was hardly known outside its native Denmark, despite the fact that of all the choreographer's creations it was his favourite. Of all his ballets, it is the most deeply rooted in Danish folklore and tradition. Upon its performance in 1979 in the Bournonville centennial festival in Copenhagen, the ballet met an enthusiastic response from foreign critics. *A Folk Tale*'s charm lies in its fairy-tale quality, its simultaneous evocation of delight and fear. Bournonville's ballet echoes the supernatural qualities of *Giselle*, its predecessor by thirteen years; like the Wilis, Bournonville's elf-maidens dance around the hero Ove and try to lure him into the underworld.

Since the ballet's rediscovery, some have heralded it as a hitherto unrecognized classic, but according to some, such as the critic Arlene Croce, "It is one thing to experience the appeal of *A Folk Tale* and another to applaud it as a ballet masterpiece." In Croce's opinion, Bournonville's work cannot be compared in terms of poetic force to *Giselle* or to *The Sleeping Beauty*, created 36 years later. In true ballet classics, dance is the medium through which meaning is conveyed, and the story-line is of secondary importance. This is not the case with *A Folk Tale*, in which pantomime is more important than dance; in fact, its most successful scenes contain very little dancing. In some parts of the ballet, the dances—pleasing as they are—are little more than showpieces, for which the plot provides only the thinnest pretext. Traditionally the supernatural creatures of the ballet classics—swans, Wilis, sylphs—are ethereal and graceful, and for these classical dancing seems a natural medium. For the trolls of Bournonville's *A Folk Tale*, however, no medium could be less appropriate, and classicism instead becomes a metaphor for Christian virtue as personified by Hilda, the human child stolen by the trolls but uncorrupted by their greed.

Bournonville's moral message—the redemptive power of Christian love—is hammered home relentlessly; Hilda rescues Ove after his adventure with the elf-maidens by offering him a goblet of holy water. The trolls, however, are no mere cardboard cut-out representatives of supernatural evil; through them, Bournonville presents a satirical picture of humanity's baser instincts. This is particularly effective in the scene in which Birthe, the troll changeling left in Hilda's place, preens at her dressing-table like the lady of the manor she is supposed to be, while trying unsuccessfully to fight down her trollish impulses, represented by clawing movements and clumsy jumps.

The most successful productions of the ballet have emphasized its period charm with traditional costumes; those designed by Queen Margrethe II for the Royal Danish Ballet's 1991 production captured the necessary magical quality, unlike the less successful designs by Lars Juhl for the 1979 revival which were in an artificial, contemporary style without the trapdoors and other stage devices so popular with nineteenth-century choreographers.

—Jessica Arah

---

**FONTEYN, Margot**

British dancer. Born Peggy Hookham in Reigate, England, 18 May 1919. Studied as a child with Hilda Bosustov in Ealing, George Goncharov in Shanghai, and Nikolai Legat in London; studied with Serafina Astafieva, London, from 1933, and at the Sadler's Wells School, from 1934; also studied with Olga Preobrazhenska, Nicholas Sergeyev, Boris Kniaseff. Married Dr. Roberto Arias, 5 December 1955. Début in *The Nutcracker*, Vic-Wells Ballet, 1934; dancer with Vic-Wells Ballet (later Sadler's Wells and Royal Ballet), from 1934: principal dancer, from 1935, becoming company's chief ballerina, and creating many roles for choreographer Frederick Ashton; guest artist, Royal Ballet, from 1959, receiving title of prima ballerina assoluta, 1979; also international guest artist with many companies, including Ballets de Paris, 1948, and on worldwide tours partnered by Rudolf Nureyev from 1963; president, Royal Academy of Dancing, from 1954; Chancellor of Durham University, from 1982. Recipient: Commander of the Order of the British Empire, 1951; Dame Commander of the Order of the British Empire, 1956; Honorary Doctorate in Literature, University of Leeds, 1953; Honorary Doctorate in Music, London University, 1954, and Oxford University, 1959; Order of the Finnish Lion, 1960; *Dance Magazine* Award, 1962; Honorary Doctorate in Law, Cambridge University, 1962. Died in Panama City, 21 February 1991.

**ROLES**

1934 Snowflake in *The Nutcracker* (Sergeyev after Ivanov), Vic-Wells Ballet, London
Young Treginnis (cr) in *The Haunted Ballroom* (de Valois), Vic-Wells Ballet, London
1935 Alicia in *The Haunted Ballroom* (de Valois), Vic-Wells Ballet, London
Creole Girl in *Rio Grande* (new production of *A Day in a Southern Port*; Ashton), Vic-Wells Ballet, London
Fiancée (cr) in *Le Baiser de la fée* (Ashton), Vic-Wells Ballet, London
Polka in *Façade* (Ashton), Vic-Wells Ballet, London
Odette in *Swan Lake* (Petipa, Ivanov; staged Sergeyev), Vic-Wells Ballet, London
Variation/Adagio of Lovers in *Les Rendezvous* (Ashton), Vic-Wells Ballet, London
Waltz, Mazurka in *Les Sylphides* (Fokine), Vic-Wells Ballet, London
1936 The Woman in Ball Dress (cr) in *Apparitions* (Ashton), Vic-Wells Ballet, London
Columbine in *Carnaval* (Fokine), Vic-Wells Ballet, London
Sugar Plum Fairy in *The Nutcracker*, Act III (Ivanov; staged Sergeyev), Vic-Wells Ballet, London
Poor Girl (later Flower Girl; cr) in *Nocturne* (Ashton), Vic-Wells Ballet, London
Princess Aurora in *The Sleeping Princess* (*Aurora pas de deux*; Petipa, staged Sergeyev), Vic-Wells Ballet, London
1937 Title role in *Giselle* (Petipa after Coralli, Perrot; staged Sergeyev), Vic-Wells Ballet, London
Odette/Odile in *Swan Lake* (Petipa, Ivanov; staged Sergeyev), Vic-Wells Ballet, London
Pas de deux (cr) in *Les Patineurs* (Ashton), Vic-Wells Ballet, London
Title role in *Pomona* (Ashton), Vic-Wells Ballet, tour
Julia (cr) in *A Wedding Bouquet* (Ashton), Vic-Wells Ballet, London
1938 Young Woman (cr) in *Horoscope* (Ashton), Vic-Wells Ballet, London
Venus in *The Judgment of Paris* (Ashton) Vic-Wells Ballet, London
1939 Débutante in *Façade* (Ashton), Vic-Wells Ballet, tour
Aurora in *The Sleeping Princess* (Petipa; staged Sergeyev), Vic-Wells Ballet, London
1940 A Child of Light (cr) in *Dante Sonata* (Ashton), Vic-Wells Ballet, London
The Bride (cr) in *The Wise Virgins* (Ashton), Vic-Wells Ballet, London
1941 Principal dancer ("Lover"; cr) in *The Wanderer* (Ashton), Sadler's Wells Ballet, London
Love (cr) in *Orpheus and Eurydice* (de Valois), Sadler's Wells Ballet, London
1942 The Lady (cr) in *Comus* (Helpmann), Sadler's Wells Ballet, London
Swanilda in *Coppélia* (Petipa, Ivanov, Cecchetti; staged Sergeyev), Sadler's Wells Ballet, tour
Ophelia (cr) in *Hamlet* (Helpmann), Sadler's Wells Ballet, London
The Betrayed Girl in *The Rake's Progress* (de Valois), Sadler's Wells Ballet, London
1943 Rendezvous in *Promenade* (de Valois), Sadler's Wells Ballet, London
Una (cr) in *The Quest* (Ashton), Sadler's Wells Ballet, London
1944 The Young Girl in *Le Spectre de la rose* (Fokine), Sadler's Wells Ballet, London
1946 Title role in *Giselle* (Petipa after Coralli, Perrot; staged Sergeyev), Sadler's Wells Ballet, London
Principal dancer (cr) in *Symphonic Variations* (Ashton), Sadler's Wells Ballet, London
La Bolero (cr) in *Les Sirènes* (Ashton), Sadler's Wells Ballet, London
Spirit of the Air (cr) in *The Fairy Queen* (masque after Shakespeare; mus. Purcell, chor. Ashton), Covent Garden Opera and Sadler's Wells Ballet, London
1947 Title role in *Mam'zelle Angot* (Massine), Sadler's Wells Ballet, London
The Miller's Wife in *The Three-Cornered Hat* (*Le Tricorne*; Massine), Sadler's Wells Ballet, London
1948 Principal dancer (cr) in *Scènes de ballet* (Ashton), Royal Ballet, London
Agathe (cr) in *Les Demoiselles de la nuit* (Petit), Ballets de Paris, Paris
La Morte amoureuse (cr) in *Don Juan* (Ashton), Sadler's Wells Ballet, London
Title role in *Cinderella* (Ashton), Sadler's Wells Ballet, London
1950 Principal dancer in *Ballet Imperial* (Balanchine), Sadler's Wells Ballet, London
Dulcinea (cr) in *Don Quixote* (de Valois), Sadler's Wells Ballet, London

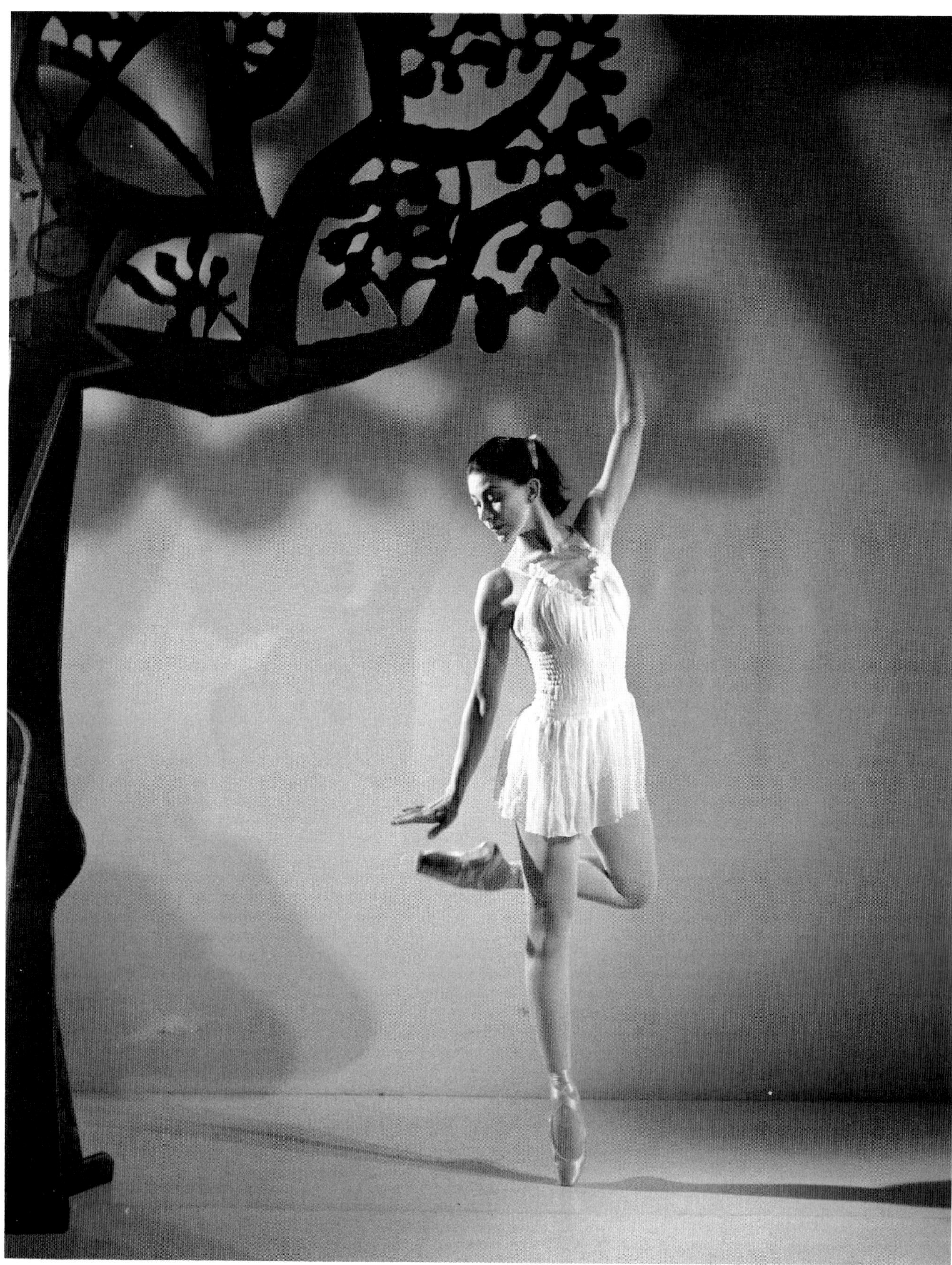

**Margot Fonteyn in Ashton's *Daphnis and Chloe*, 1951**

1951 Chloe (cr) in *Daphnis and Chloe* (Ashton), Sadler's Wells Ballet, London
Tiresias as a woman (cr) in *Tiresias* (Ashton), Sadler's Wells Ballet, London
1952 Title role (cr) in *Sylvia* (Ashton), Sadler's Wells Ballet, London
1953 Queen of the Air (cr) in *Homage to the Queen* (Ashton), Sadler's Wells Ballet, London
1954 Title role in *The Firebird* (Fokine) Sadler's Wells Ballet, Edinburgh
1956 Title role in *La Péri* (Ashton), Royal Ballet, London
Principal dancer (cr) in *Birthday Offering* (Ashton), Royal Ballet, London
1957 The Ballerina in *Petrushka* (Fokine), Royal Ballet, London
1958 Title role (cr) in *Ondine* (Ashton), Royal Ballet, London
1959 Principal dancer (cr) in *Raymonda: Scène d'amour* (pas de deux; Ashton), Royal Academy of Ballet Gala, London
Pas de deux from *Le Corsaire* (after Petipa), Royal Ballet, London
1963 Nikiya (cr) in *La Bayadère* (new production; Nureyev after Petipa), Royal Ballet, London
Marguerite (cr) in *Marguerite and Armand* (Ashton), Royal Ballet, London
1965 Juliet (cr) in *Romeo and Juliet* (MacMillan), Royal Ballet, London
1967 The Woman in *Paradise Lost* (Petit), Royal Ballet, London
1969 Mélisande in *Pélléas et Mélisande* (Petit), Royal Ballet, London
1970 Title role in *Raymonda*, Act III (Nureyev after Petipa), Royal Ballet, London
1972 The Diva (cr) in *Poème de l'extase* (Cranko), Royal Ballet, London
1975 Principal dancer (cr) in *The Scarlet Pastorale* (Darrell), Scottish Ballet
1976 Title role in *The Merry Widow* (Hynd), Australian Ballet, New York

**PUBLICATIONS**

By Fonteyn:
*Margot Fonteyn: An Autobiography*, London, 1975
*A Dancer's World*, London, 1978
*The Magic of Dance* (in conjunction with BBC series), London, 1980
*Pavlova Impressions*, London, 1984

About Fonteyn:
Clarke, Mary, *The Sadler's Wells Ballet*, London, 1955
Monahan, James, *Fonteyn: A Study of a Ballerina in her Setting*, London, 1957
Money, Keith, *The Art of Margot Fonteyn*, London, 1965
Crisp, Clement, "Margot Fonteyn", *Les Saisons de la danse* (Paris), December 1968
Money, Keith, *Fonteyn: The Making of a Legend*, London, 1973
"Portrait of Fonteyn", *Dance Magazine* (New York), July 1973
Vaughan, David, *Frederick Ashton and his Ballets*, London, 1977
Bland, Alexander, *Fonteyn and Nureyev: The Story of a Partnership*, London, 1979
Bland, Alexander, *The Royal Ballet: The First Fifty Years*, London, 1981
Stewart, Rachel, *Margot Fonteyn*, London, 1988
"Where Honour is Due", *Dance and Dancers* (London), May 1989

* * *

Theatrical legends are studded with the unlikely, and perhaps the only remarkable thing about Fonteyn's rise to the heights of international acclaim is that it should have been achieved with a deceptive cloak of English "good manners". In fact, this quiet take-over was based on a streak of indomitability from which the bearer was probably powerless to escape. This tenacity (not to be confused with mere ambition) was also a marked component of Anna Pavlova's personality, but whereas Pavlova was open about her mission, Fonteyn tended to suggest, always, that she was simply trapped in the expectations of others. The effects, however, were the same.

As a child, the interests of Peggy Hookham did not really extend beyond the amusements of "character dancing", but a succession of teachers (dotted along the route of the Hookham family's travels in America and the Far East) all recognized a combination of self-discipline and application that could propel a girl towards the higher realms of professional dancing. At fourteen she was accepted by Ninette de Valois's Vic-Wells Ballet in London, and quickly put into the corps de ballet as its youngest member, despite de Valois's concern about her feet: "She was not even standing on them properly!" Alicia Markova was the company's ballerina, greatly admired by the new recruit, now renamed Margot Fonteyn. Within a year the young dancer had been given Markova's role in a revival of Frederick Ashton's *Rio Grande*, and critics immediately predicted a future: "... there is no saying what this child of fifteen may not do".

There was an indefinable stage presence about Fonteyn, of which the principal characteristic was a seeming vulnerability which made an audience feel protective. While her effects were not large, she had a knack of avoiding doing anything out of key, and from the start displayed an intuitive sense of general measure in most matters. Her appearance was faintly exotic, with dark hair and eyes, and with her flawless body proportions it was really very difficult for her to make an unpleasing shape. Her instinctive sense of line was remarkable: pure yet mathematically complex. De Valois was quite convinced the girl had all the hallmarks of a true ballerina, and when Markova suddenly left the company in 1935, a worried young Fonteyn found herself precipitated into the remorseless glare of the centre spot.

After taking over the lead in *Les Rendezvous*, Fonteyn was reported in one newspaper as having "some of that intoxicating quality always associated with great dancers". The recipient of this unusual praise had no time to wonder what it was all about, for she was swept into a vortex of more and more demanding roles; in just over two years she completed first appearances in the leads of *The Nutcracker*, *Giselle*, *Swan Lake*, and *The Sleeping Princess*. If her view of herself was one of inadequacy, she had at least the belief and support of the team around her, and Nicholas Sergeyev, with his deep knowledge of the St. Petersburg school, assured de Valois that the girl was fully capable of the demands inherent in a role such as Aurora. Once on stage, she was fortunate in having as her partner Robert Helpmann, indubitably the real star of the company; he could sustain the theatrical excitement of a performance while at the same time nursing the young tyro through some of the more frightening technical passages.

Despite her own diffidence concerning these show-case roles of classical dancing, Fonteyn progressed steadily; in addition, she had won the respect of Frederick Ashton, who had begun to shape a whole string of ballets around her in roles which drew on varying shades of characterization, from pathos and innocence to hard-headed glamour and even dead-pan comedy. He was later to admit that her exceptional natural musicality, allied to her particularly expressive arms, led him to explore areas of lyrical movement he might otherwise have bypassed. She drew the eye, yet without fuss or contrivance. The key lay in the even distribution of her talents, which meant that no one particular highlight stood out; where other dancers might arrive at a series of peaks, Fonteyn's performance unfurled with a continuous dramatic tone, as if everything was filtered through some internal prism that released the colours evenly. Her triumph in America on her first appearance there in 1949 has passed into legend; thereafter, the 1950s saw the dancer securely established internationally. Michael Somes had been Fonteyn's handsome and reliable stage partner, and his retirement from strictly classical roles left her in a temporary limbo; people began speaking of their good fortune in catching one of Fonteyn's "last performances".

It was while she was heading a Royal Ballet tour in Russia in 1961 that there was excitement in Paris at the defection from the Kirov company of an exciting young dancer, Rudolf Nureyev. Fonteyn swiftly secured his presence for a London charity gala, though she herself declined to dance with one "so young". It was de Valois who overcame these reservations; she invited both Nureyev and Fonteyn to appear in *Giselle* at Covent Garden. In February 1962, in a truly historic performance, the cool Queen of British ballet melded her style with that of the volatile Russian pretender in an electrifying couple of hours. If the ingredients were unlikely, the mix was spine-tingling. Though both dancers were destined to appear with many other partners, the Fonteyn–Nureyev partnership became the international hot ticket during a giddy decade; in duration and in the sheer variety of works encompassed, nothing in ballet history really approaches this pairing.

Nureyev, accustomed to stealing the limelight rather effortlessly, found that Fonteyn could palm an audience as easily, and with that degree of parity, both felt freed as well as challenged, able to pour all their energies into the crucible of the performance. When Nureyev mounted the white act of *La Bayadère*, and later the full-length *Raymonda*, for the Royal Ballet, he forced Fonteyn to re-examine the bedrock of her technique, demanding from her an attack which she herself had thought was not her forté. Remarkably, in her forties she actually improved her basic technique. As her own public persona changed and expanded during her years as an internationally celebrated dancer, she could, if required, carry a grandeur on stage that was entirely uncontrived. In England, some purists and die-hards had begun to fret that *their* Fonteyn, a template for pure and cerebral classicism, was somehow changing her style—as if she should have remained set in aspic, ignoring the great breezes of the 1960s. Such anxieties overlooked a vital point: how should any ballerina progress through her forties, if she had no intention of retiring?

Ulanova, first seen in London at the age of 49, had been an inspiration for audiences and dancers alike, and Fonteyn certainly was one who recognized the message: that renewal must inevitably involve changes and risks. Indeed, as she progressed through her late forties, many of her *Swan Lake* performances had an epic quality quite beyond normal expectation, and the Odette role was somehow distilled and re-defined to an almost oriental abstraction of intensity. Fonteyn finally shed these big classics—albeit reluctantly—one by one, in order to avoid permanent injury from a problem knee and instep.

When Fonteyn was 57, the Australian Ballet mounted a production of *The Merry Widow*, which they took to America with Fonteyn as the lure, and one or two critics felt the production was trading on her past greatness to the detriment of the present. And yet, by the first night in New York, it was clear that her performance was a triumph. As usual, she had gauged exactly the style needed for that work in that place, delivering a performance of irresistible allure. She had never been a spectacular technician; she used no "tricks". On the other hand, she always achieved whatever was required of her, and with an impervious smoothness. She was not uniquely gifted as an actress, yet she could hold an audience like a demon fiddler. Her range appeared to be limitless. She danced for more than 40 years, in over 30 countries, with more than 30 partners, in over 80 roles. And what did people remember most about her performances? Usually, that at some point, for no apparent reason, they found themselves blinking through tears. If there was a trick, it was a simple one: she made all who saw her cry a little.

—Keith Money

---

## LES FORAINS

**Choreography:** Roland Petit
**Music:** Henri Sauget
**Design:** Christian Bérard
**Libretto:** Boris Kochno
**First Production:** Les Ballets des Champs-Elysées, Paris, 2 March 1945
**Principal dancers:** Roland Petit (The Ring Master), Ethéry Pagava (The Girl Acrobat), Nina Vyroubova (The Sleeping Beauty)

**Other productions include:** Les Ballets de Paris (restaged Petit). Ballet Théâtre Français de Nancy; 22 October 1981. Paris Opéra Ballet School; Paris, 24 March 1990.

### PUBLICATIONS

Beaumont, Cyril, *Ballets of Today*, London, 1945
"The Sitter Out", *Dancing Times* (London), May 1949
Hussey, Dyneley, "Some New French Ballets", *Dancing Times* (London), June 1949
"Since the End of the War in 1945 . . .", *Ballet Annual* (London), vol. 7, 1953
Balanchine, George, with Mason, Francis, *Balanchine's Complete Stories of the Great Ballets*, Garden City, N.Y., 1977
Kochno, Boris, *Christian Bérard*, London, 1988
Mannoni, Gérard, *Roland Petit: Un chorégraphe et ses peintres*, Paris, 1990

* * *

*Les Forains* is one of Roland Petit's earliest ballets. It was originally performed at a recital and its success encouraged Petit and Kochno to form Les Ballets des Champs-Elysées, where it became a signature ballet of the company. Basically it is a divertissement, but one that is subtly constructed by setting the dances in a context that is extremely sympathetic to audiences. The simple device of using a group of travelling circus artists setting up their pitch and performing for no return provides a framework that humanizes the divertissement and provides a contrast between on- and off-stage life. It is a bitter-sweet work and the dancers—some of whom, including Petit, had recently given up safe jobs at the Paris Opéra—must have made parallels with the difficulties and lack of rewards in their own lives.

Despite the ending, with the forgotten performing pigeons safely retrieved, Petit managed to avoid sentimentality by conveying both the excitement of performance and the exhaustion and hopeless resignation that follows. It was the first occasion on which he proved his ability to establish a distinctive atmosphere from the very rise of the curtain. As in so many of his works, it is the atmosphere that Petit created, rather than the details of steps, which his audiences remember; even after the first performance the unevenness of some of the dances was noticed by critics, and the English critics commented on the excessive use of technical feats and acrobatics for effect.

Although Boris Kochno organized the artistic elements of *Les Forains*, the ballet owes a considerable debt to Christian Bérard who provided the libretto and the sets and costumes, all of which displayed the effective simplicity and economy of his style—even if these were dictated by the limited finances available. His set, a simple arrangement of poles and sheets, and clever lighting aroused the greatest comment and has influenced theatre design since.

Henri Sauguet contributed a sad, melancholic score, evocative of fairground music, which suggested rather than reproduced true circus music. It included a particularly haunting waltz to which the artists arrived and departed.

Some of the most effective ballets have been conceived and produced over an extraordinarily short period. The essential work on *Les Forains*, it is said, took less than two weeks, during which time the participants worked together with intense creativity and inspiration. Its success in France resulted in the creation of the most effective and influential of the small independent companies which were so active in the 1940s and 1950s. In Britain the ballet was *the* outstanding success of the first season by a foreign ballet company after the artistic isolation of the Second World War; and it was seen, in its atmosphere and style and way in which technique was used for theatrical ends, to be indicative of the direction in which dance was developing. This was not entirely due to its being the one ballet in the repertory to appeal particularly to English tastes by using characterization to gain some of its effects. However, the growing emphasis on technique and abstract dance at the expense of characterization has ensured that, apart from the extremely rare revival, *Les Forains* has not lasted in the repertory of any company.

—Peter Bassett

---

## FORNAROLI, Cia

Italian dancer and teacher. Born in Milan, 16 October 1888. Studied at the Ballet School of the Teatro alla Scala, Milan, pupil of Enrico Cecchetti, Adelaide Vigano, Caterina Beretta, Achille Coppini, and Raffaele Grassi. Married Dr. Walter Toscanini. Prima ballerina, Metropolitan Opera Ballet, New York, 1910–14; guest ballerina, performing at Teatro Principal in Barcelona, Teatro Real in Madrid, and Teatro Colón, Buenos Aires, 1914–16; ballerina, Teatro Costanzi, Rome, 1916–20, with brief period at La Scala, 1918, and Teatro Colón, 1920; prima ballerina assoluta, La Scala, Milan, 1921–23, 1924–33; dancer with Italian-Wiener Ballet, Volksoper, Vienna, 1923; guest ballerina in tours in Italy and Europe, also dancing with Pavlova company; also actress, appearing in Italian silent films including Caesar films *L'Anello di Pierrot* (1917), *Cuori e tuffi* (1917), *Frou-Frou* (1918), *Nellina* (1918), and *Nanà* (1918); choreographer, Italian Chamber Ballets, 1933; ballet mistress, International Music Festival, Venice, and Italian Ballet of San Remo, 1933–34; director, succeeding Enrico Cecchetti, ballet school of La Scala, Milan, 1929–33; left Italy for United States: ballet mistress, Ballet Theatre, New York, from 1940; director of own ballet school, School of Classical Dancing (Cecchetti Method), New York, 1944–46. Died in New York, 16 August 1954.

**Roles include:** Ballerina in *Mahit* (mus. Pick-Mangiagalli), Clorinda in *Combattimento di Tancredi e Clorinda* (also chor.); dances in *La Leggenda di Sakuntala* (opera; mus. Alfano), *Louise* (opera; mus. Charpentier); leading roles in *Il Carillon magico*, *Il Convento veneziano* (Pratesi), *Vecchia Milano* (Pratesi), *Pietro Micca* (Manzotti), *Excelsior* (Manzotti), *Petrushka* (Romanov).

### WORKS

1924 Dances in *Orfeo* (opera; mus. Gluck), La Scala, Milan

1933 *La Primavera* (mus. Vivaldi), Balletti Italiani di camera
*Concerto dell'estate* (mus. Pizzetti), Balletti Italiani di camera

1933/34 *Gli Uccelli* (mus. Respighi), Balletto Italiano di San Remo
*Histoire d'un Pierrot* (mus. Costa), Balletto Italiano di San Remo
*La Berceuse* (mus. Pick-Mangiagalli), Balletto Italiano di San Remo

**Other works include:** *Combattimento di Tancredi e Clorinda* (mus. Monteverdi), *Le Couvent sur l'eau* (mus. Casella), *Pantea* (mus. Malipiero), *Napoli* (mus. Alfano).

### PUBLICATIONS

Martini, Gualtiero de, *Cia Fornaroli e l'arte della danza*, Milan, 1923

Gatti, Carlo, *La Scala rinnovata*, Milan, 1926

May, Helen, "With Cecchetti at La Scala", *Dancing Times* (London), July 1928

Celli, Vincenzo, "Serata d'onore: Cia Fornaroli", *Dance Magazine* (New York), January 1955

Moore, Lillian, "The Romance of a Dance Collection", *Dance Magazine* (New York), December 1955

Gatti, C., *Il Teatro alla Scala 1778–1963*, 2 volumes, Milan, 1964

Rossi, L., *Il Ballo alla Scala 1778–1970*, Milan, 1972

* * *

Today Cia Fornaroli is remembered for the collection of dance memorabilia donated by her husband Walter Toscanini to the New York Public Library. During her lifetime, however, she attempted to give new life to the traditional Italian school of ballet, battling against provincialism and bourgeois aestheticism, and at the same time paying no heed to the revolution of the Ballets Russes.

Fornaroli's musical and expressive movements owed more to the late nineteenth century than the twentieth, trained as she was by the famous Italian ballet masters—the last of whom, Cecchetti, was nevertheless to acknowledge the achievement of the Russian school. She began her career by taking minor roles

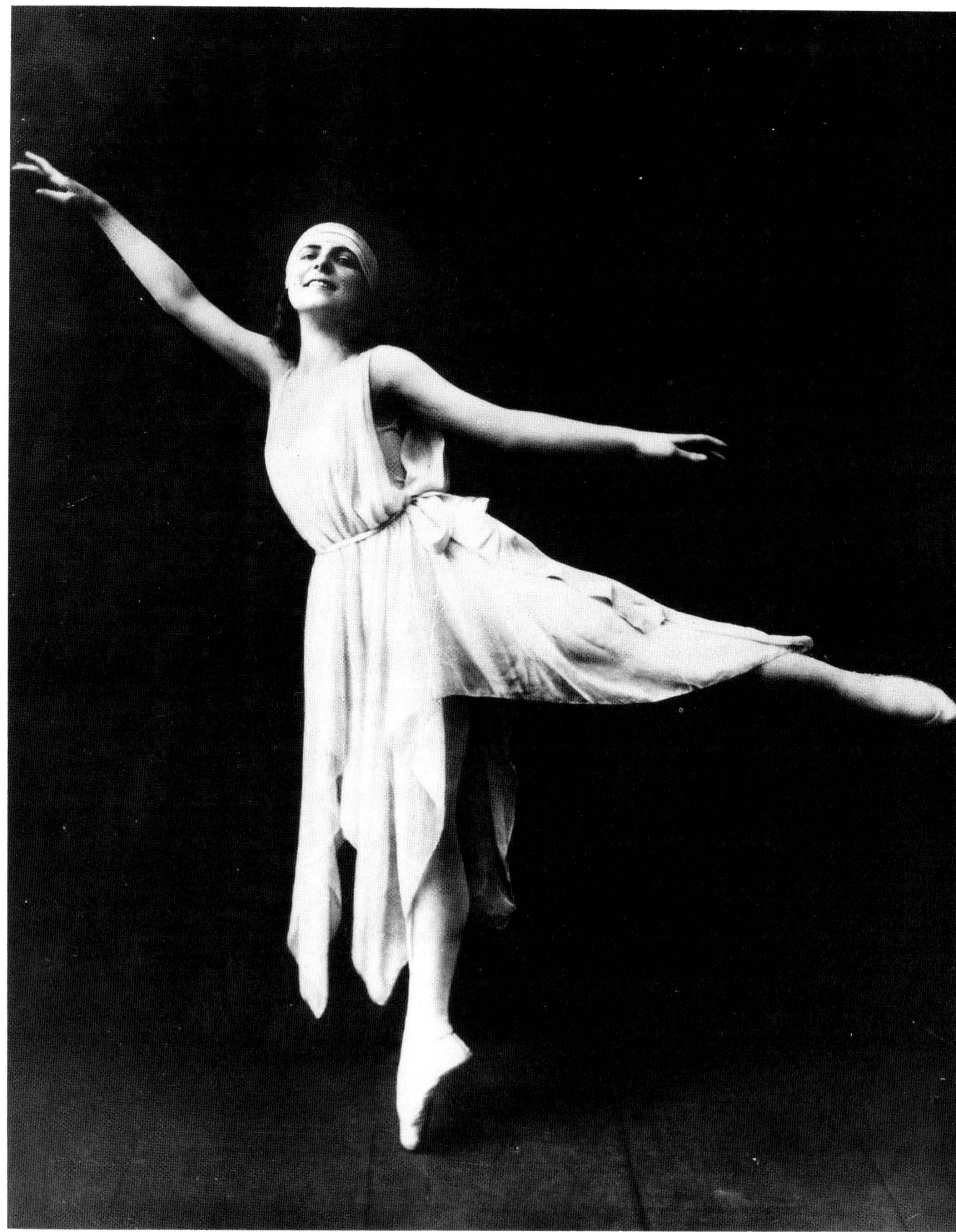

**Cia Fornaroli**

in the ballets of Manzotti and later danced in opera seasons at the Metropolitan, New York, and the Colón Theatre in Buenos Aires, the last theatres in which Italian dancers were still in demand.

During World War I, when the Milanese school was beset with political and social problems which would end in its closure, Fornaroli was engaged at the Rome Opera House. That she also made several film appearances is not surprising, as silent films often took inspiration from *ballets-féeries* and the music hall.

The return of ballet to La Scala was marked by the ballet *Il carillon magico*, inspired by the traditional Italian *commedia dell'arte*. Toscanini was appointed as director of the theatre, with Preobrazhenskaya in charge of the ballet school. She was succeeded by Cecchetti, assisted by Fornaroli. Although the musical rebirth of La Scala brought illustrious composers from all over the world to conduct their own works—among them, Richard Strauss and Igor Stravinsky—the emphasis on Italian tradition was maintained in ballets such as *Il Convento veneziano*, in which Fornaroli appeared. These received a better reception than the two versions of *Petrushka* staged at La Scala, in which Fokine's metaphysical drama (rechoreographed by Boris Romanov) was reduced to a simple tale of puppets. The second failure in Milan of Diaghilev's company inspired ideas of turning back to a more glorious time, and Cia Fornaroli's next appearance was in a far more popular work, *Vecchia Milano*, set in the Risorgimento era and celebrating the Italian theatre of bygone times.

On leaving La Scala in 1933, Fornaroli established her own company and ventured into choreography for the first time. Her efforts were not particularly original but were based on the music of contemporary composers such as Malipiero and Respighi who were attempting to reform Italian theatre. She enjoyed the friendship of d'Annunzio, who gave her suggestions for the dances in *Orfeo* and a cycle (never realized) of seven dances; he called her "Madonna Cia of the rhythmic hands".

Fornaroli's career was interrupted when her husband Walter Toscanini fell foul of the fascist regime—his antiquarian bookshop was a meeting place for intellectuals and anti-fascists. She was obliged to accompany Toscanini into voluntary exile in the United States. Here she established her own ballet school, building on a brilliant teaching career which had begun earlier, when she succeeded Cecchetti as director of the ballet school at La Scala in 1929. Her students had included Nives Poli, Attilia Radice, and Teresa Legnani. Graceful and elegant of gesture, lively and lyrical in style, and capable of the most delicate port de bras, Fornaroli is remembered as a teacher of intelligence and great understanding, who was driven by an almost religious devotion to the methods of Cecchetti.

—Concetta Lo Iacono

---

**FORSYTHE, William**

American dancer, choreographer, and ballet director. Born in New York, 30 December 1949. Studied at the Joffrey Ballet School, New York, pupil of Jonathan Watts, Maggie Black, and Finis Jhung, from 1969. Married former dancer Eileen Brady. Dancer, Joffrey Ballet, 1971–73, Stuttgart Ballet, 1973–80; first choreography for the Noverre Society Young Choreographers' Workshop, Stuttgart, 1976; choreographer, Stuttgart Ballet, 1976–81; freelance choreographer, staging ballets in Germany, Austria, Italy, Netherlands, 1980–82; choreographer, Frankfurt Ballet, 1982: director and chief choreographer, from 1984; has also choreographed for Basle Ballet, 1977, Bavarian State Opera (Munich) Ballet, 1979, Nederlands Dans Theater, 1980, 1983, German Opera Ballet, Berlin, 1981, Joffrey Ballet, 1983, Paris Opéra Ballet, 1983, Aterballetto, Italy, 1984, San Francisco Ballet, 1987, New York City Ballet, 1988. Recipient: Chevalier des Arts et Métiers, France, 1991; Laurence Olivier Award, London, 1992.

**WORKS**

1976 *Urlicht* (mus. Mahler), Noverre Society, Stuttgart (staged Stuttgart Ballet, 1977)
1977 *Daphne* (mus. Dvořák), Stuttgart Ballet, Stuttgart
*Bach Violin Concerto in A Minor* (mus. Bach), Basel Ballet, Basel
*Flore Subsimplici* (mus. Handel), Stuttgart Ballet, Stuttgart
1978 *From The Most Distant Time* (mus. Ligeti), Stuttgart Ballet, Stuttgart
*Dream Of Galilei* (mus. Penderecki), Stuttgart Ballet, Stuttgart
*Folia* (mus. H.W. Henze), Montepulciano Festival, Italy
1979 *Orpheus* (mus. Henze), Stuttgart Ballet, Stuttgart
*Side 2—Love Songs* (mus. popular), Stuttgart Ballet, Stuttgart
*Time Cycle* (mus. Foss), Stuttgart Ballet, Stuttgart
1980 *Joyleen Gets Up, Gets Down, Goes Out* (mus. Boris Blacher), Bavarian State Opera Ballet, Munich
*'Tis Pity She's a Whore* (mus. Thomas Jahn), Montepulciano Festival, Italy
*Famous Mothers Club* (no music), solo for Lynn Seymour, London
*Say Bye Bye* (mus. montage, arranged Forsythe), Nederlands Dans Theater, The Hague
1981 *Die Nacht Aus Blei* (mus. von Bose), German Opera Ballet, Berlin
*Whisper Moon* (mus. Bolcom), Stuttgart Ballet, Stuttgart
*Tancredi and Clorinda* (*Event 1,2,3;* mus. montage), Stuttgart International Arts Congress
1982 *Gänge 1—Ein Stuck über Ballett* (mus. Forsythe, Simon), Nederlands Dans Theater, The Hague
1983 *Gänge* (full-length version; mus. Jahn), Frankfurt Ballet, Frankfurt
*Mental Model* (mus. Stravinsky), Nederlands Dans Theater, The Hague
*Square Deal* (mus. William Forsythe), Joffrey Ballet, New York
*France/Dance* (mus. J.S. Bach), Paris Opéra Ballet, Paris
1984 *Berg AB* (mus. Alban Berg), film for the Vienna State Opera Ballet, Vienna
*Artifact* (mus. J.S. Bach, Crossman-Hecht), Frankfurt Ballet, Frankfurt
*Steptext* (mus. J.S. Bach), Aterballetto, Italy (staged Frankfurt Ballet, 1985)
1985 *LDC* (mus. Willems), Frankfurt Ballet, Frankfurt
1986 *Isabelle's Dance* (mus. Crossman-Hecht), Frankfurt Ballet, Frankfurt
*Skinny* (mus. Willems, Forsythe), Frankfurt Ballet, Frankfurt
*Die Befragung des Robert Scott* (mus. Willems), Frankfurt Ballet, Frankfurt
*Big White Baby Dog* (mus. Willems), Frankfurt Ballet, Frankfurt

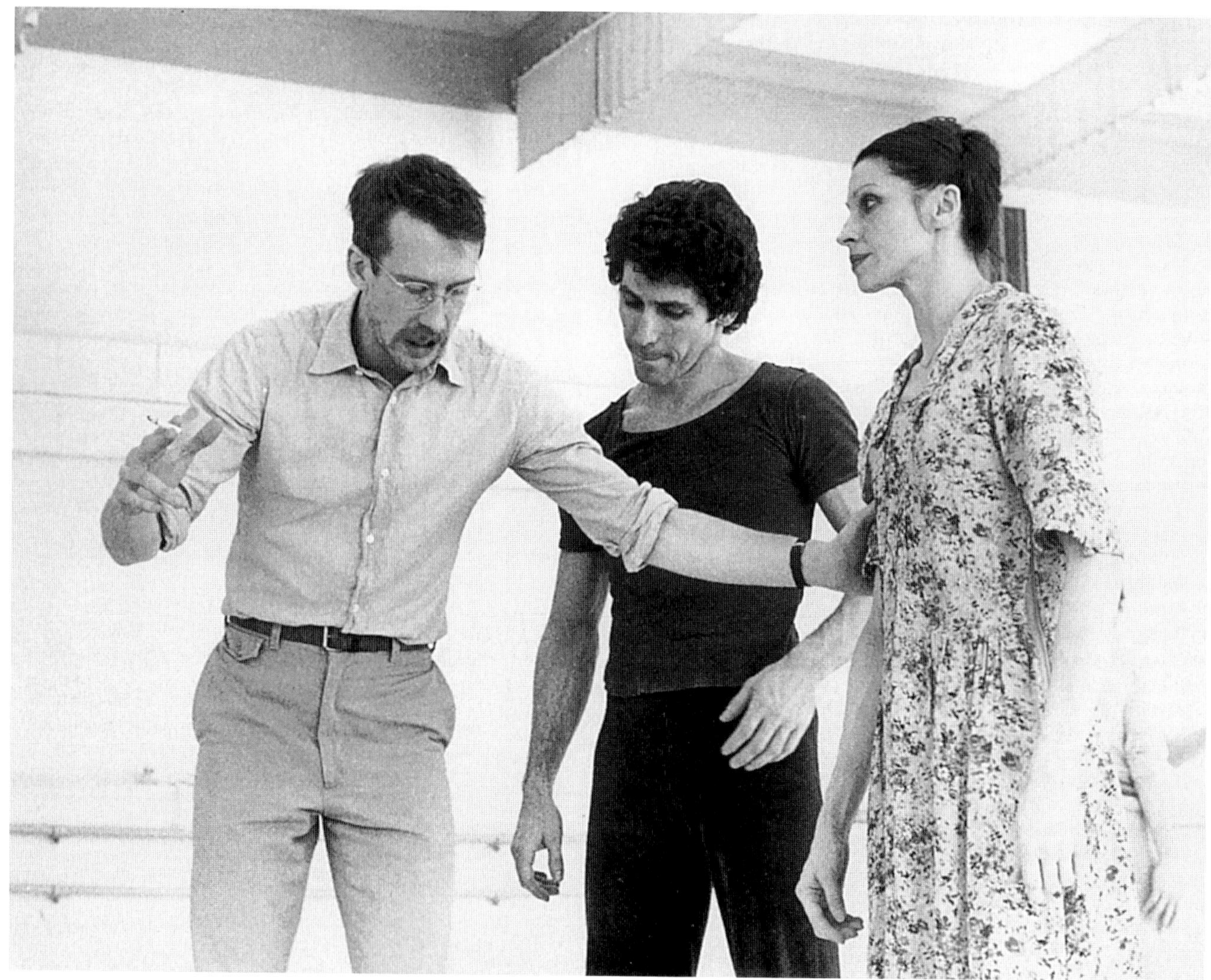

**William Forsythe rehearsing Richard Cragun and Birgit Keil in *Orpheus*, 1978**

*Baby Sam* (mus. Willems), Frankfurt Ballet, Bari
*Pizza Girl* (mus. Willems), Frankfurt Ballet, Frankfurt
1987 *New Sleep* (mus. Willems), San Francisco Ballet, San Francisco
*Same Old Story* (mus. Willems), Frankfurt Ballet, Hamburg
*The Loss Of Small Detail* (mus. Willems), Frankfurt Ballet, Frankfurt
1988 *In The Middle, Somewhat Elevated* (mus. Willems, Stuck), Paris Opéra Ballet, Paris
*Impressing The Czar* (including *In the Middle, Somewhat Elevated*; mus. Willems, Beethoven, Stuck, Crossman-Hecht), Frankfurt Ballet, Frankfurt
*Behind The China Dogs* (mus. Stuck), New York City Ballet, New York
*The Vile Parody Of Address* (mus. J.S. Bach), Frankfurt Ballet, Frankfurt
1989 *Enemy In The Figure* (mus. Willems), Frankfurt Ballet, Frankfurt
*Slingerland Teil I* (mus. Bryars), Frankfurt Ballet, Frankfurt
1990 *Limb's Theorem* (mus. Willems), Frankfurt Ballet, Frankfurt
*Slingerland Teil II and III* (mus. Willems, Bryars), Frankfurt Ballet, Amsterdam
*Slingerland Teil IV* (mus. Willems), Frankfurt Ballet, Paris
1991 *The Second Detail* (mus. Willems), National Ballet of Canada, Toronto
*Loss of Small Detail* (*Neufassung*) (mus. Willems), Frankfurt Ballet, Frankfurt
*Snap, Woven Effort* (mus. Willems), Frankfurt Ballet, Frankfurt
1992 *As a Garden in this Setting* (mus. Willems), Frankfurt Ballet, Frankfurt
*Herman Schmerman* (mus. Willems), New York City Ballet, New York

## PUBLICATIONS

By Forsythe:

Interview in Kirchner, Birgit, "Good Theatre of a Different Kind", *Ballett International* (Cologne), August 1984
Interview in Vaccarino, Elisa, *Balletto oggi* (Milan), November 1989
Interview in Driver, Senta, and others, "A Conversation with William Forsythe", *Ballet Review* (New York), Spring 1990

About Forsythe:
Whitney, Mary, "Prodigal Son", *Ballet News* (New York), October 1983
Langer, R., and Sikes, R., "New Directors, Part II: William Forsythe", *Dance Magazine* (New York), January 1986
Stuart, Otis, "Forsythe's Follies", *Ballet Review* (New York), Fall 1987
Macaulay, Alastair, "Acid Rain", *The New Yorker* (New York), 25 July 1988
Michel, Marcella, "Billy Side Story", *Pour la danse* (Paris), February 1989
Croce, Arlene, "Wise Guys", *The New Yorker* (New York), 31 July 1989
Meisner, Nadine, "Choreographer for Today", *Dance and Dancers* (London), April 1990
Meisner, Nadine, "Dangerous Dancing", *Dance and Dancers* (London), January/February 1992

* * *

William Forsythe belongs to the small number of choreographers who have continued to develop the classical vocabulary in contemporary times. Where Balanchine, Forsythe's great model, has blown the cobwebs from the classical, taking elements of jazz, folk, and Broadway into his style, Forsythe has ventured into funk, break-dancing, and "Afro" dance. Critics of his style maintain that he has become too far removed from tradition, that he violates both ballet and dancers. His admirers recognize in his work a daring neo-classicism that pushes beyond the established bounds, a contemporary style of ballet which exploits fully the possibilities of a super-trained dancer—a style which genuinely reflects something of the "go-get-it" mentality, and therefore reflects the hurriedness and pitilessness of our time.

It had already become apparent in Forsythe's first pieces in the late 1970s (*Urlicht*, to music by Mahler, *Flore Subsimplici*, to music by Handel, or *Dream of Galilei*, to music by Penderecki) that his was a forward thrust to new forms through the breaking up and smashing open of the old. In the solos and duets (*Time Cycle*, *Side 2—Love Songs*), dancers take a wild run-up for a pirouette or an arabesque. These classical lines explode in an outburst of rage, or collapse in resignation. They pull each other in opposite directions, out of balance. The men begin by leading their partners in a promenade, yet shake them at intervals or push them away, so that they fall crashing to the floor. *Say Bye Bye*, set to deafening rock-pop music, is a decadently boisterous party of young people in the 1950s who carry out a wild orgy in this brutal vocabulary of cut and thrust. The classical vocabulary, in such a broken form, becomes an expression of human passion, aggression, and despair.

By contrast, Forsythe's work can be characterized by aesthetic form, as seen in the abstract piece *In the Middle, Somewhat Elevated*. Protagonists of such pieces are dancers like Sylvie Guillem, who bring with them exceptional physical capabilities. The costumes are usually restricted to tight-fitting black or dark blue leotards and black sheer tights, in order to emphasize the contours and plastic qualities of the body. Torso and hips are displaced even more than in Balanchine's work; the axis of the body is forced to an even steeper angle. The legs are even more articulated and rise even higher from the hip. While Balanchine leaves his ballerinas a certain traditional feminine charm, Forsythe's women have an emancipated, virile quality. Where Balanchine choreographed quick footwork, Forsythe has his women perform daringly sculptural figures with acrobatic elegance. The woman is hardly ever held or carried by her partner: rather, woman and man wrestle competitively with each other. While Balanchine's ballets are carried forward by their own musicality, one must speak rather of an athletic dynamism in Forsythe's work. Here, movement and not music stands firmly in the fore. Best of all, Forsythe likes to work to rhythmically pointed synthesized music (usually by Tom Willems) whose echo-like beat functions purely and simply as an impulse to movement.

Forsythe relates no continuous narratives. The two story ballets—*Orpheus*, to the ballet composition by Hans Werner Henze, and *'Tis Pity She's a Whore* (*Schade, dass sie eine Hure ist*), after the drama by John Ford—were commissioned works and remain exceptions. His pieces are purely abstract, or else simply mixed with theatrical elements. Papier mâché animal figures and buildings (the Empire State Building, the Eiffel Tower) stand on the stage, a midget recites a few sentences in a serialistic manner (*France/Dance*), a woman speaks mechanically through a megaphone (*Big White Baby Dog*). Forsythe wants to move away from a "gracious rhetoric" through the disparity between the objects and people gathered together on stage. His choreographic principle is "active continuity". That means that he doesn't narrate in a chronological or causal manner, but lets various stories rise independently from the interaction of very varied objects ("movement-objects", "word-objects", "sound-objects").

In the combining of these objects again and again (most often by computer, in a similar way to Merce Cunningham), new constellations develop, and hence new possibilities of meaning—and meaning can signify, quite simply, atmosphere. For Forsythe has no desire to impart a message. He styles himself as a designer and architect, who merely puts diverse materials and building bricks together. *France/Dance* is a model example of this: the whole piece consists of passages and elements of Balanchine's *Apollo* rearranged into a new combination. The way in which he combines his "objects" and his building materials to which his own lighting designs belong, and the way in which he recognizes and selects the possibilities offered by the computer—these are indeed the stuff of his art.

—Malve Gradinger

---

## THE FOUNTAIN OF BAKHCHISARAI

(original Russian title: *Bakhchisaraisky Fontan*)

**Choreography:** Rostislav Zakharov
**Music:** Boris Asafiev
**Design:** Valentina Khodasevich (scenery)
**Libretto:** Nikolai Volkov (after poem of the same name by Aleksandr Pushkin)
**First Production:** State Academic Theatre for Opera and Ballet (GATOB), Leningrad, 28 September 1934
**Principal Dancers:** Galina Ulanova (Maria), Konstantin Sergeyev (Vatslav), Mikhail Dudko (Girei), Olga Iordan and Tatyana Vecheslova (alternating as Zarema)

**Other productions include:** Stanislavsky Nemirovich-Danchenko Theatre, with Angelina Urusova (Maria), Viktorina Kriger (Zarema); Moscow, 20 April 1936. Bolshoi Ballet, with Vera Vasileva (Maria), Lyubov Bank (Zarema), Petr Gusev (Girei); Moscow, 11 June 1936. Budapest State Opera (Hungarian) Ballet (restaged Zakharov); Budapest, 29 April 1952. Finnish National Ballet (restaged Zakharov), with Doris Laine (Maria); Helsinki, 1956.

***The Fountain of Bakhchisarai*: Galina Ulanova as Maria, with Tatiana Vecheslova and Mikhail Dudko, Leningrad, 1934**

## PUBLICATIONS

Bogdanov-Berezovsky, Valerian, Volkov, Nikolai, *The Fountain of Bakhchisarai*, Leningrad, 1934

Raffé, Walter G., "The Newer Soviet Ballet: *The Fountain of Bakhchisarai*", *Dancing Times* (London), August 1935

Beaumont, Cyril, *Complete Book of Ballets*, revised version, London, 1951

Zakharov, Rostislav, *The Choreographer's Art*, Moscow, 1954

Asafiev, B.V., *The Fountain of Bakhchisarai*, Moscow, 1955

Barnes, Clive et al., "Bolshoi Ballet: 'The Fountain of Bakhchisarai'", *Dance and Dancers* (London), December 1956

Roslavleva, Natalia, "Stanislavsky and the Ballet", *Dance Perspectives* (New York), no. 23, 1965

Lopukhov, Fedor, *Sixty Years in Ballet*, Moscow, 1966

* * *

Choreographed in 1934 by Zakharov to a score by Boris Asafiev, *The Fountain of Bakhchisarai* is based on a poem by Aleksandr Pushkin which tells of unrequited love, jealousy, and tragic death. At the centre of the story is the Polish princess Maria, who has unwittingly claimed the attentions of the Khan Gerei, smitten by her beauty from the first moment of seeing her. His entreaties fail, for she does not love him (her favourite, Vatslav, has been slain by the Khan himself in a battle between the Poles and the Tartars); but his love for Maria has sparked the jealousy of his chief wife, Zarema.

At first Zarema's agonized jealousy is soothed by the princess herself: slipping into Maria's bedchamber at night, and begging her to give the Khan back to his favourite wife, Zarema is soon calmed by the princess's sincere and heartfelt explanation that she does not, and never will, love Gerei. But Gerei has recently visited Maria, and, though his attempts to win her have been in vain, he has left behind his tyubeteyka (embroidered skull cap). The sight of this now enrages Zarema once more, and she rushes upon Maria, and stabs her. Gerei, who has arrived and attempted to restrain Zarema, watches his beloved Maria die. Unconsolable, and unmoved even by the victorious return of his Tartar armies, the Khan remains alone with his thoughts. Finally, in his torment and his grief, Gerei orders a "fountain of tears" to be built at Bakhchisarai in Maria's memory.

*The Fountain of Bakhchisarai* was Zakharov's first and most successful ballet. The well-know Russian composer Asafiev himself suggested that the young Zakharov work on the ballet, the music for which he had just completed. Zakharov set to work with a libretto by Nikolai Volkov, and the result was the extremely popular four-act ballet which is still performed in Russia today.

The strongest features of this work are its dramatic integrity, clarity, and the expressiveness of its staging. Zakharov created several memorable choreographic scenes, ranging from group ensembles, as in the dance of the Khan's wives in the harem, to pas de deux, like that between Maria and Vatslav, to solos, as in Zarema's jealous monologue, or her stealthy entrance in Maria's bedchamber. Zakharov also choreographed effective ensembles of national dance, like the Tartar dances in the final act, apparently inspired by a scene etched on a tarnished silver dish which the choreographer had seen in the Hermitage Museum.

But perhaps most important of all, Zakharov showed the possibilities for successful dramatic adaptions of literary themes to ballet (after this the poetry of Aleksandr Pushkin was to become a popular source for Russian ballet libretti) and he set the course for future Soviet developments upon the idea of "dramatic" ballet. Indeed, the work is considered to illustrate several of the principles of the Stanislavsky method and in many ways proved a model for Soviet ballet in the 1930s (though "dram-ballet" itself was ultimately to become a worn-out art form).

In addition to Zakharov's own effective blend of elements to form a compelling full-length ballet, *The Fountain of Bakhchisarai* also owes its particular success to Galina Ulanova, who danced the Polish princess Maria, and Tatyana Vecheslova, who created the part of Zarema—that is, to dancers who were capable, by virtue of their phenomenal artistry, of breathing life into even those moments of less choreographic expressivity. Ulanova's performance of Maria's death scene has become a legend in Russian ballet history. Her soft, fluid low arabesque, arching from the shoulder blade, and her arm slowly sliding down the column—Maria's last movement before death—have come to be associated with the image of Maria for every subsequent generation of performers. And equally, it seems that to this day every ballerina who dances the role of Zarema is lit with the flame of passion that racked Vecheslova as Zarema. It is a satisfying work for both performers and audience, and it is easy to see why the ballet remains in the repertoire of the Kirov Theatre to this day.

—Nina Alovert

---

## THE FOUR TEMPERAMENTS

**Choreography:** George Balanchine
**Music:** Paul Hindemith
**Design:** Kurt Seligmann (scenery and costumes)
**First Production:** Ballet Society, Central High School of Needle Trades, New York, 20 November 1946
**Principal Dancers:** William Dollar (Melancholic), Mary Ellen Moylan and Fred Danieli (Sanguinic), Todd Bolender (Phlegmatic), Tanaquil LeClerq (Choleric)

**Other productions include:** Royal Ballet, with Desmond Kelly (Melancholic), Ann Jenner and Antony Dowell (Sanguinic), Wayne Eagling (Phlegmatic), Deanne Bergsma (Choleric); London, 25 January 1973. Sadler's Wells Royal Ballet, London, 4 October 1976. New York City Ballet (restaged and revised Balanchine; performed in practice dress, with no décor); New York, 1951. Royal Swedish Ballet; Stockholm, 6 April 1960. Netherlands Ballet; Paris, 6 May 1960. La Scala Ballet; Milan, 1962. Hamburg Ballet; Hamburg, 27 March 1962. Royal Danish Ballet; Copenhagen, 15 May 1963. Paris Opéra Ballet (restaged Balanchine); Paris, 18 December 1963. Boston Ballet; Boston, January, 1968. National Ballet of Canada; Toronto, 24 March 1969. German Opera Ballet; Berlin, 23 November 1970. Geneva Ballet; Geneva, 17 March 1970. Frankfurt Ballet; Frankfurt, 21 April 1974. Ballet West, 1975. Dance Theatre of Harlem (restaged Victoria Simon); New York, 20 February 1979. San Francisco Ballet; Honolulu, 27 January 1974. Los Angeles Ballet, 1982.

### PUBLICATIONS

Hussey, Dyneley, "Paul Hindemith", *Dancing Times* (London), August 1947
Balanchine, George, with Mason, Francis, *Balanchine's Complete Stories of the Great Ballets*, Garden City, N.Y., 1977
Reynolds, Nancy, *Repertory in Review*, New York, 1977
Croce, Arlene, *Afterimages*, New York, 1979
Siegel, Marcia, *The Shapes of Change*, Boston, 1979
"Staging Balanchine's Ballets: A Symposium", *Ballet Review* (New York), Fall 1983
Graff, Ellen, "*The Four Temperaments* and *Orpheus*: Models of a Modern Classical Tradition", *Ballet Review* (New York), Fall 1985
Corey, Mary, "Before *Four Temperaments*", *Ballet Review* (New York), Spring 1987
Acocella, Joan, "The Four Humors", *Ballet Review* (New York), Winter 1987
"Celebrating *The Four Temperaments*", *Ballet Review* (New York), 2 parts: Winter 1987, Spring 1988

* * *

Balanchine's 1946 ballet, *The Four Temperaments*, is named after Paul Hindemith's *Theme with Four Variations (According to the Four Temperaments)*. Hindemith states the three parts of the theme, then offers variations on each of them as, respectively, Melancholic, Sanguinic, Phlegmatic, and Choleric—the four temperaments of medieval medicine. Balanchine gives the parts of the theme to three male/female pairs; the steps in the subsequent movements are developed, to a certain extent, from the lexicon of motions offered in this opening section.

At the beginning of this section, a woman gives her hand, as if in blind trust, to a man she does not look at; the first of the three parts of the theme is marked by arabesques in attitude with the woman's leg between the man's, and by the woman's repeatedly flexing foot. The second section of the theme introduces one of the best sight gags of the piece, a kind of H-shape with two dancers' arms, reminiscent of Siva and formed by the woman standing before the man with their arms at right angles, moving up and down. The third part of the theme introduces, among with other motions, a melted, more twisted version of these boxed arms where the bones seem turned to snakes.

The four movements that follow focus alternately on a principal male or female dancer; at the change of thematic sections the configuration of dancers alters, the dance always remaining structurally faithful to the music. The degree to which these movements reflect the temperament of their titles is more than trivial, yet less than absolute. The first movement, Melancholic, seems one of those more evidently coloured by its temperament. A male dancer wraps his arms around his own torso like tendrils, flees a group of four women who come on

***The Four Temperaments*, performed by Sadler's Wells Royal Ballet, London**

and seem to kick him backwards, reaches again and again to the heavens, and walks off in a backbend, his arms straight out and his head upside down. Balanchine clearly perceives melancholy as a kind of Romantic restlessness, a state in which the shell of the body is simply too slight for the powerful longings for the infinite that gush through it and render the person a social misfit.

Phlegmatic, the third movement, seems similarly coloured by its temperament. The principal man seems like a more athletic Hamlet, obsessed with himself and living in a world of phantoms: he picks up his own foot, does obeisance to an imaginary partner, and tries vainly to extricate himself from a cage whose bars are the legs of the four women who have come on with their arms out in "so what?" gestures made to hold up a disdainful plate of soup. The man jerks as if stung by bees, and scuttles about with his arms and legs hanging from his back like the limp extremities of a crippled crab.

Sanguinic and Choleric, movements two and four respectively, seem more complex in their relation to emotion, if indeed there is a point in following this connection at all. In Sanguinic, a boy and a girl get involved in a series of jumpy movement repetitions. He holds her in "swimming" lifts; four girls come in with their shoulders doing busy-busy flounces. At the end the principal female dancer is alone with the women. In Choleric, the three accompanying men attach themselves to the free extremities of a woman and manipulate her for a time, like cavaliers turned to encumbrances. The finale makes liberal use of the H-shaped arms; at the end the corps is stepping about in place while men lift women across the stage.

The visual complexity and sheer, compact inventiveness of this ballet are such that, when it is over, the viewer may have trouble saying what he or she has seen. Practically every step grabs the eye, and no movement is without its strange and sometimes contradictory associations. Yet the suggestions of emotion in the title and, to a certain extent, the movement, encourage the viewer to see this piece as more than just steps: perhaps as the attempt to classify all human behaviour? If so, Balanchine clearly sees the world as more complex, and more social than the easy quadropartite individual classification of the title. For Balanchine, we are who we are—not alone, but in the company of (or alienated from) others.

And this is a troubling world. In this ballet, people stick their extremities in others' intimate places without looking at one another, attach to others' legs as if weighting them down, twist and twine their arms and torsos without ever seeming to acknowledge that they have done so. In any case they are each time whisked off by the inexorable logic of the music to begin another theme, their motions controlled by powers higher than they.

These are not the clear, sunny Enlightenment creatures of other Balanchine ballets who look at each other and make the physical contact that is sanctioned by their Petipan world of supporter and supported, adorer and adored; instead they are the twisting horrors of Freud's subconscious. Their movements are both unspeakably intimate and completely impersonal; the whole seems to unfold as if in a dream. *The Four Temperaments* may not involve mothers-in-law (as Balanchine said ballet did not), but it is a dance made in the tenebrous depths of the human psyche; it is just movement, but because of the naked power, manipulation, and intrusion in its movement, it is considerably more.

The score, commissioned by Balanchine, dates from 1940; the choreography had its premiere in 1946.

—Bruce Fleming

---

**FRACCI, Carla**

Italian dancer. Born in Milan, 20 August 1936. Studied at the Ballet School of La Scala, Milan, from 1946: pupil of Edda Martignoni, Vera Volkova, Esmée Bulnes; graduated in 1954; also later studied with Felia Doubrovska, Robert Joffrey, New York. Married theatre director Beppe Menegatti, 1964: one son, Francesco (b. 1969). Dancer, Ballet of La Scala, Milan, from 1954: soloist, 1956–58, prima ballerina, from 1958; guest ballerina, London Festival Ballet, 1959, 1962, Royal Ballet, London, 1963, Rome Opera Ballet, various seasons, 1964–67, Stuttgart Ballet and Munich Ballet, 1965, Chicago Opera Ballet, 1966, 1968, Monte Carlo Ballet, 1967, 1968, and Royal Swedish Ballet, 1969; principal guest artist, frequently appearing with Erik Bruhn, American Ballet Theatre, New York, from 1967; has appeared on television, including in documentary *An Hour with Carla Fracci* (Italian television, 1973), and on film, including as Karsavina in *Nijinsky* (dir. Ross, 1980); actress: dramatic roles include Titania in *A Midsummer Night's Dream* (dir. Menegatti, chor. Gai, 1963), Ariel in *The Tempest* (dir. Menegatti, chor. Gai, 1964), the Moon in García-Lorca's *Blood Wedding* (dir. Menegatti, chor. Gai, 1965), title role in Goldoni's *Turandot* (dir. Menegatti, 1966). Recipient: Leopardo d'oro, 1959; Woman of the Year Award, *Mademoiselle* magazine, 1961; Prix Anna Pavlova, Paris, 1962; *Dance Magazine* Award, 1968.

**ROLES**

1955 The Young Girl in *Le Spectre de la rose* (Fokine), Ballet of La Scala, Milan
Spring Fairy (cr) in *La Cenerentola* (*Cinderella*; Rodrigues), Ballet of La Scala, Milan

1955/56 Silvestra in *Mario e il mago* (Massine), Ballet of La Scala, Milan
Title role in *La Cenerentola* (*Cinderella*; Rodrigues), Ballet of La Scala, Milan
La Cortigiana in *Sebastian* (Novaro), Ballet of La Scala, Milan

1957 Sugar Plum Fairy in *The Nutcracker* (Rodrigues), Ballet of La Scala, Milan
Cerrito in *Pas de quatre* (Dolin after Perrot), Nervi Festival
Pas de deux in *The Four Seasons* (*Glazunov Pas de deux*; Rodriguez), Nervi Festival, Genoa
Eve in *Rappresentazione di Adamo e Eva* (Milloss), Ballet of La Scala, Perugia

1958 Principal dancer in *Orfeo ed Euridice* (opera-ballet; mus. Gluck, chor. Ashton), Opera and Ballet of La Scala, Milan
Princess Belle Rose in *The Prince of the Pagodas* (Cranko), Ballet of La Scala, Milan
Juliet (cr) in *Romeo and Juliet* (Cranko), Ballet of La Scala, Venice
The Wife (cr) in *Secrets* (Cranko), Edinburgh International Ballet, Edinburgh
Title role in *Giselle* (Petipa after Coralli, Perrot; staged Dolin), London Festival Ballet, London

1959 Elvira (cr) in *Don Giovanni* (Massine), Ballet of La Scala, Milan
Queen of Clubs (cr) in *Jeu de cartes* (Novaro), Ballet of La Scala, Milan
Principal dancer in *Pièce d'occasion* (Cranko), London Festival Ballet, London
Principal dancer in *Harlequinade* ("Pas de deux romantique"; Dolin), London Festival Ballet

1960 Leading role (cr) in *The Good-Humoured Ladies* (Novaro), Ballet of La Scala, Milan
Principal dancer (cr) in *Fantasmi al Grand Hotel* (Massine), Ballet of La Scala, Milan
Principal dancer (cr) in *La Commedia umana* (Massine), Balletto Europeo, Nervi Festival, Genoa
Juliette (cr) in *Ballo dei ladri* (*Le Bal des voleurs*; Massine), Balletto Europeo, Nervi Festival, Genoa
The Young Girl in *Le Beau Danube* (Massine), Balletto Europeo, Nervi Festival, Genoa
Principal dancer in *Choreartium* (third and fourth movements; Massine), Balletto Europeo, Nervi Festival
Principal dancer in *Concerto Barocco* (Balanchine), Ballet of La Scala, Milan

1961 Principal dancer in *Bourrée fantasque* (Balanchine), Ballet of La Scala, Milan
Odette in *Swan Lake* (one-act version; Balanchine), Ballet of La Scala, Milan
Swanilda in *Coppélia* (Danilova, Franklin after Petipa), Ballet of La Scala, Milan
Principal dancer in *I Sette Peccati capitali* (Lecoq), Teatro Eliseo, Rome
Principal dancer in *Ballet Imperial* (Balanchine), Ballet of La Scala, Milan
Nela (cr) in *La Giara* (Novaro), Ballet of La Scala, Milan

1962 Title role in *La Sylphide* (Bournonville; staged Lander), Ballet of La Scala, Milan
A Goddess in *Le Jugement de Pâris* (Miskovitch after Perrot), Spoleto Festival
Principal dancer (cr) in *Teatrino di Cristobal* (Gades, Graeme), Spoleto Festival
Chloë in *Daphnis and Chloë* (Lifar, Zevrev after Fokine), Ballet of La Scala, Milan

1963 Principal dancer (cr) in *Le Songe d'une nuit d'éte* (Miskovitch), Ballet of La Scala, Milan
The Young Girl in *Le Loup* (Petit), Ballet of La Scala, Milan
Principal dancer in *La Chambre* (Petit), Ballet of La Scala, Milan
Principal dancer in *Rhapsodie espagnole* (Petit), Ballet of La Scala, Milan
Agathe in *Les Demoiselles de la nuit* (Petit), Ballet of La Scala, Milan
Pas de deux from *Flower Festival at Genzano* (after Bournonville), Royal Ballet Touring Company

1964 Principal dancer (cr) in *Pantea* (Gai), Ballet of La Scala, Milan
Principal dancer in *Follia d'Orlando* (T. Gsovsky), Ballet of La Scala, Milan

1965 Principal dancer in *Allegro Brillante* (Balanchine), Ballet of La Scala, Milan
Title role (cr) in *Francesca da Rimini* (Pistoni), Ballet of La Scala, Milan
Title role in *Giselle* (Petipa after Coralli, Perrot), Ballet

of La Scala, Milan
Princess Aurora in *The Sleeping Beauty* (Petipa; staged Helpmann), Ballet of La Scala, Milan
Title role in *Sylvia* (Ashton), Rome Opera Ballet, Rome

1966 Gelsomina (cr) in *La Strada* (Pistoni), Ballet of La Scala, Milan
Juliet (cr) in *Romeo and Juliet* (pas de deux; Bruhn), Rome Opera Ballet, Rome

1967 Civilization in *Excelsior* (Dell'Ara after Manzotti), Maggio Musicale, Florence
Ophelia (cr) in *La Pazzia di Ofelia* (*The Madness of Ophelia*; Labis), Ballet of La Scala, Milan

1968 Nina (cr) in *La Mouette* (*The Seagull*; Gai), Sienna Festival
Swanilda (cr) in *Coppélia* (new production; Rodriguez after Saint-Léon), American Ballet Theatre, Brooklyn, New York

1969 Lady Macbeth (cr) in *Macbeth* (Pistoni), Teatro San Carlo, Naples
Title role in *Miss Julie* (Cullberg), American Ballet Theatre, New York

1970 Title role in *Paquita* (extracts; Nureyev after Petipa), Ballet of La Scala, Milan
Mélisande (cr) in *Pélléas et Mélisande* (Gai), Ballet of La Scala, Milan
Caroline in *Jardin aux lilas* (*Lilac Garden*; Tudor), American Ballet Theatre, New York
Kitri in *Don Quixote Pas de deux* (after Petipa), Ballet of La Scala, Milan
Juliet in *Romeo and Juliet* (Tudor), American Ballet Theatre, New York
Terpsichore (cr) in *The Creatures of Prometheus* (Miskovitch), Genoa

1971 Cleopatra (cr) in *La Nuit egyptienne* (dell'Ara), Ballet of La Scala, Milan
Sugar Plum Fairy in *The Nutcracker* (Nureyev), Ballet of La Scala, Milan

1973 Katerina in *The Stone Flower* (Gai), Ballet of La Scala, Milan

1974 Odette/Odile in *Swan Lake* (Field after Petipa, Ivanov), Ballet of La Scala, Milan
Terpsichore in *Convento veneziano* (Fascilla), Venice
Ophelia in *Hamlet* (Fascilla), Teatre Romana, Verona
La Stella/Olympia/Antonia/Giulitta in *Tales of Hoffmann* (Darrell), American Ballet Theatre

1975 Title role (cr) in *Medea* (pas de deux; Butler), Spoleto Festival, Spoleto
The Fairy (cr) in *Le Baiser de la fée* (Gai), Ballet of La Scala, Milan

1977 Principal dancer (cr) in *Poem Nocturne* (Tetley), Spoleto Festival, Charleston, South Carolina
Principal dancer in *Bolero* (Béjart), Verona Festival
Daughter of the Bandit Chief (cr) in *Marco Spada* (Fascilla), Accademica Filarmonica, Rome
Desdemona in *Othello* (*La Voix*; Butler), Accademica Filarmonica, Rome

1979 Title role in *La Péri* (Gai), La Fenice, Venice
Princess Belle Rose (cr) in *The Prince of the Pagodas* (Wilson), Carla Fracci and company, Venice

1981 Title role (cr) in *Mirandolina* (Rodrigues), Carla Fracci and company, Bari

1980 Kitri in *Don Quixote* (Nureyev), Ballet of La Scala, Milan

1982 Bilitis (cr) in *Bilitis et le faune* (Bonnefous), Malibran Theatre, Venice

1983 Principal dancer (cr) in *Bergkristall* (van Hoecke), Rome Opera, Rome

1985 Odile in *Swan Lake* (new production; Petipa, Ivanov; staged Hightower, produced Zeffirelli), Ballet of La Scala, Milan

1986 Title roles (cr) in *Le Due Gemelle* (*The Twin Girls*; Gai), Teatro Filarmonico, Verona

1988 Principal dancer (cr) in *I Vespri siciliani* (opera; mus. Verdi, chor. van Heocke), La Scala, Milan

1990 Isadora (cr) in "Fate's Warning" (solo; reconstruction M. Hodson after Duncan) and other scenes (chor. Deane, Gai, and others) in *Adieu et au revoir* (dir. Menegatti), Teatro Mercadante, Naples
Title role (cr) in *Phaedra* (Deane, Eagling, Hodson), Teatro Massimo, Palermo
Principal dancer (cr) in *Il Vespro siciliano* (Deane), Teatro Massimo, Palermo

1991 The Accused in *Fall River Legend* (de Mille), American Ballet Theatre, New York

**Other roles include:** Waltz, Mazurka in *Les Sylphides* (Fokine), Princess Aurora in *The Sleeping Beauty* (Nureyev after Petipa), the Ballerina in *Petrushka* (Fokine), Juliet in *Romeo and Juliet* (Fascilla), principal dancer in *Portrait of Salomé*, principal dancer in *Symphony in C* (Balanchine), principal dancer in *Serenade* (Balanchine), La Capprichiosa in *The Lady and the Fool* (Cranko), Juliet in *Romeo and Juliet* (Nureyev), principal dancer in *William Tell* (opera; mus. Rossini, chor. Flindt).

## PUBLICATIONS

By Fracci:
*Ballet Handbook*, Milan
Interview in Gruen, John, *The Private World of Ballet*, New York, 1975
*La Mia Vita sulle punte*, Milan, 1978

About Fracci:
Corathiel, E., "Careers in Pictures: Carla Fracci", *Ballet Today* (London), November 1959
Pitt, Freda, "Carla Fracci's Future", *Dancing Times* (London), July 1970
Lidova, Irène, "Carla Fracci", *Les Saisons de la danse* (Paris), June 1972
Tobias, Tobi, "Visiting Fracci", *Dance Magazine* (New York), January 1974
Tobias, Tobi, "About Carla Fracci", *Dance Magazine* (New York), April 1976
Ottolenghi, Vittorio, "Madonna of the Dance", *Ballet News* (New York), July 1981
Terry, Walter, and Fitzgerald, Brendan, "Fracci Observed", *Ballet News* (New York), July 1981
Migel, Parmenia, "A Romantic Ballerina in our Time: Carla Fracci", *Dance Magazine* (New York), December 1984
Agostini, Alfio, "Carla Fracci, La Stellissime", *Danser* (Paris), April 1986

* * *

Carla Fracci is the one Italian ballerina who can be considered a "household name"; she was also the first Italian ballerina this century to achieve international fame. Possessing an unquestioned reputation at home (where she is never subjected to real criticism) such that almost any theatre or opera house is glad to invite her on the assumption that her presence will ensure large audiences, Fracci has frequently danced abroad as a guest, but never as an integral part of a foreign company. In the 1989–90 Milan season, at an age when most ballerinas have given up

**Carla Fracci in *La Sylphide*, 1967**

dancing (and Fracci makes no secret of her age), she appeared for the second time in La Scala's inaugural opera performance and announced her intention of doing so again the following year; she then opened the series of *Giselles* at the same theatre.

Giselle is a role that Fracci has appeared in all over Italy, as well as, less often, in England and the U.S., and it may be considered her signature work. Her partnership with Erik Bruhn, initiated at Ballet Theatre and pursued in Italy, marked the highest point not only of Fracci's performances of *Giselle* but also of her dancing of Romantic roles in general. Apart from *Giselle*, these include *La Sylphide*, which Harald Lander staged for La Scala Ballet in 1962, when Esmée Bulnes was in charge of the company. While in later years Fracci tended to over-act (from a Bournonvillean point of view) in the Act II death scene, much in the same way that her *Giselle* performances became overly self-conscious (one was uncomfortably aware of seeing Carla-Fracci-as-Giselle rather than simply "Giselle"), one remembered that before she became an institution in Italy, her portrayal of the role was touching and poignant in Act I and satisfyingly ethereal in Act II. When she danced with a great artist such as Bruhn, Fracci was at her best. Interestingly, for example, when Bruhn was unable to appear in the American Ballet Theatre Covent Garden season in 1970, her Giselle was received without enthusiasm by the London critics (ironic references being made, for one thing, to the excessive richness of her Act II costume), and both she and her manager-husband were deeply offended.

Fracci's marriage to theatre director Beppe Menegatti has had a fundamental influence on her career, for he masterminds all her performances. It was his behind-the-scenes influence on his friend Franco Zeffirelli that resulted in Odile's role, in the latter's eccentric production of *Swan Lake* at La Scala, being illogically enlarged to give his wife greater prominence than Odette. But his importance has been greater and more lasting in another way.

Ever since the early 1960s, Fracci's career has, indeed, shown a marked dichotomy. On the one hand there have been the productions in the opera houses that were part of their managements' planning; and on the other hand she has regularly appeared all around the country in works devised by her husband. As he seems to have limited confidence in dance as a means of expression, his productions have always tended to rely on speech, as well as on a theatrical or literary text for their subject. As Fracci's physical powers have waned, speech has taken an increasingly central role, as has for many years the engagement of young male dancers of talent to bear the brunt of the dancing load.

Menegatti's later productions have frequently taken on too strong a didactic air. Probably the best of these mélanges was the Nijinsky programme given at the San Carlo in Naples in 1989. Although the speech was of limited interest to that large part of the audience that knew little or nothing about Nijinsky's life, and was therefore unacquainted with most of the names referred to, and while it had little to offer to the minority who knew it all already, there were considerable compensations in the danced excerpts. Fracci appeared in many items, most successfully in *Giselle* and *Raymonda*. The presence of Vladimir Vasiliev and Eric Vu An made a memorable contribution to the production. One of the biggest advantages of this programme was that nearly all the choreography was by choreographers of real stature. Too often this has not been so, Fracci's roles being carefully tailored so that she can make an effect without being overstretched. Inevitably, the choreography has been entrusted only to those who are willing to be so directed.

This pinpoints Fracci's greatest misfortune as an artist. Apart from the first version of Cranko's *Romeo and Juliet* (the Stuttgart production is a revision), Fracci has had nothing created for her by a front-rank choreographer. Thus, for example, her very modern sense of irony has never been exploited, and although in works directed by her husband she has essayed many styles, even Isadora's, she remains for the majority stereotyped as a Romantic ballerina—in Italy, as *the* Romantic ballerina—ever since she took the Cerrito role in Anton Dolin's staging of the *Pas de quatre* at an early Nervi festival. The situation in the United States is slightly different, since Fracci has quite frequently appeared in works such as Antony Tudor's *Lilac Garden* with American Ballet Theatre.

If she has been unfortunate on the creative side, Fracci has been quite fortunate in her choice of partners. In 1966, she achieved what would have been the height of many a ballerina's ambition by appearing at the Teatro del l'Opera in Rome with both Rudolf Nureyev (in *La Sylphide*) and Erik Bruhn (in the Balcony pas de deux from *Romeo and Juliet*) in the same programme. In *Giselle* she has danced over the years not only with Bruhn, but also with Nureyev, Baryshnikov, Vasiliev, Henning Kronstam, John Gilpin, and Gheorghe Iancu (the latter being her regular partner for many years in Italy).

In *La Sylphide*, Fracci's first partner (at La Scala in 1962) had been Mario Pistoni, who then skilfully brought out her talent for conveying pathos in the role of Gelsomina, the waif-like, brutally ill-treated creature at the centre of *La Strada*, Pistoni's most famous and best ballet, which is based on Fellini's film of the same name. Menegatti has seemed to prefer to push her in the direction of strong drama, not always with success. She was required to speak in his production about Isadora Duncan and Eleonora Duse, given at the Teatro Mercadante in Naples in 1990 (and later in Milan and elsewhere), but she had previously shown her ability to do this in the film *Nijinsky*, in which her acting performance in the role of Tamara Karsavina was much praised. Fracci is blessed with good looks and charm, and these qualities were well used in Herbert Ross's film (which curiously enough has never been shown in Italy). She also appeared as Verdi's wife, the singer Giuseppina Strepponi, in an Italian television serial about the composer.

Fracci had many well-deserved successes abroad early in her career. In the late 1950s her dancing at the Edinburgh Festival showed a springlike freshness that had an immediate appeal, even if her technique was not especially strong. Her Giselle with the then Festival Ballet was very much liked also.

An intelligent woman, Fracci has usually known whose assistance to invoke in preparing a role. For example, she worked with Alicia Markova on *The Dying Swan* (for a television performance) and learned from Millicent Hodson the Isadora solo that was by far the best item in the Duncan–Duse show. When she appeared in the English National Ballet's 40th birthday gala in Spring 1990, she demonstrated (in the Balcony pas de deux from Cranko's *Romeo and Juliet*) that she was still able, by means of her artistry, to conquer even some of the harshest of the London critics.

—Freda Pitt

---

**FRANCA, Celia**

British dancer, choreographer, and ballet director. Born in London, 25 June 1921. Studied at the Guildhall School of Music, and at Royal Academy of Dancing, London, pupil of Stanislas Idzikowski, Judith Espinosa, Marie Rambert, and Antony Tudor. Married James William Morton, 1960. Stage début in *Spread it Abroad* (revue; chor. Gore), London, 1936; dancer, Ballet Rambert, 1936–39: soloist, from 1936, performing leading dramatic roles from 1938; dancer, Ballet des Trois Arts, London, 1939, Arts Theatre, London, 1940, International Ballet, London, 1941, Sadler's Wells Ballet (now Royal Ballet), London, 1941–46; guest artist and choreographer, Sadler's Wells Theatre Ballet, London, 1946–47; dancer and teacher, Ballets Jooss, 1947; dancer and ballet mistress, Metropolitan Ballet, London, 1947–49; leading dancer, Ballet Workshop, London, 1949–51; guest artist, Ballet Rambert, London, 1950; also choreographed for British television, 1949; moved to Canada: founder, National Ballet of Canada, Toronto, Ontario, 1951, serving as principal dancer, 1951–59, and artistic director, 1951–74; also teacher: co-founder and teacher, National Ballet School, Toronto, 1959; guest teacher and lecturer, People's Republic of China, 1978, 1980; co-artistic director and teacher, School of Dance, Ottawa, from 1978; also board member, Theatre Ballet of Canada (now Ottawa Ballet), 1980–88. Recipient: Civic Award of Merit, Toronto, 1963; Officer of the Order of Canada, 1967; Canada Dance Award, 1984; Companion of the Order of Canada, 1985; Order of Ontario, 1987.

**ROLES**

1936 Corps de ballet, Mars, in *The Planets* (Tudor), Ballet Rambert, London
1937 Pas de deux (cr) in *Suite of Airs* (Tudor), Ballet Rambert, London
Episode in his Past in *Jardin aux lilas* (Tudor), Ballet Rambert, Bath
Mazurka in *Les Sylphides* (Fokine), Ballet Rambert, Nice
1939 Dope Fiend (cr) in *Paris Soir* (Gore), Ballet Rambert, London
Medusa (cr) in *Perseus* (Regan), Ballet des Trois Arts, London
The Subconscious (cr) in *Midas* (also chor.), Ballets des Trois Arts, London
1940 Bird (cr) in *Peter and the Wolf* (Staff), Ballet Rambert, Cambridge
Marguerite in *Mephisto Valse* (Ashton), Ballet Rambert, Edinburgh
1941 Myrtha in *Giselle* (Petipa after Coralli, Perrot; staged Sergeyev), Sadler's Wells Ballet, Edinburgh
Dawn in *Coppélia* (Saint-Léon), Sadler's Wells Ballet, Edinburgh
Street Dancer in *The Prospect Before Us* (de Valois), Sadler's Wells Ballet, London
1942 Queen (cr) in *Hamlet* (Helpmann), Sadler's Wells Ballet, London
"Children of Darkness" in *Dante Sonata* (Ashton), Sadler's Wells Ballet, London
1943 Wrath (cr) in *The Quest* (Ashton), Sadler's Wells Ballet, London
1944 Spider (cr) in *Le Festin de l'araignée* (Howard), Sadler's Wells Ballet, London
Prostitute (cr) in *Miracle in the Gorbals* (Helpmann), Sadler's Wells Ballet, London
1947 First peasant (cr) in *Bailemos* (also chor.), Sadler's Wells Theatre Ballet, London
Young Girl (cr) in *Lovers' Gallery* (Staff), Metropolitan Ballet, Blackpool
1949 Street Girl (cr) in *Pleasuredrome* (Hightower), Metropolitan Ballet, Harrow
Salome (cr) in *Dance of Salome* (also chor.), BBC television
1955 Title role in *Lady from the Sea* (Leese), National Ballet of Canada, Washington D.C.
1967 Black Queen in *Swan Lake* (Bruhn after Petipa, Ivanov), National Ballet of Canada, Toronto

**Other roles include:** for Ballet Rambert—Neptune in *The Planets* (Tudor), La Goulue in *Bar aux Folies-Bergère* (de Valois), The Dancer in *The Rake's Progress* (de Valois), Russian Ballerina in *Gala Performance* (Tudor), Young Girl in *Le Spectre de la rose* (Fokine), Blue Bird in *Dances from Aurora's Wedding* (from *The Sleeping Beauty*; Petipa), the Bride in *Mermaid* (Howard), Nymph in *L'Après-midi d'un faune* (Nijinsky), Pavane in *Capriol Suite* (Ashton), Sports Girl in *Le Boxing* (Salaman), Polka in *Façade* (Ashton), Night in *The Descent of Hebe* (Tudor), the Wife and the Lady Friend in *Les Masques* (Ashton), Pas de trois in *Swan Lake* (Act II; after Ivanov), First Song in *Dark Elegies* (Tudor), Ursula in *The Haunted Ballroom* (de Valois), Daughter in *Job* (de Valois); for the Metropolitan Ballet—Gypsy Girl in *The Dances of Galanta* (Gsovsky), Swanilda in *Coppélia* (after Petipa); for the National Ballet of Canada—title role in *Giselle* (Petipa after Coralli, Perrot), Operetta Star in *Offenbach in the Underworld* (Tudor), Black Lady in *Winter Night* (Gore), Carabosse in *The Sleeping Beauty* (Nureyev after Petipa), Madge in *La Sylphide* (Bruhn after Bournonville), Lady Capulet in *Romeo and Juliet* (Cranko), the Pianist in *The Lesson* (Flindt).

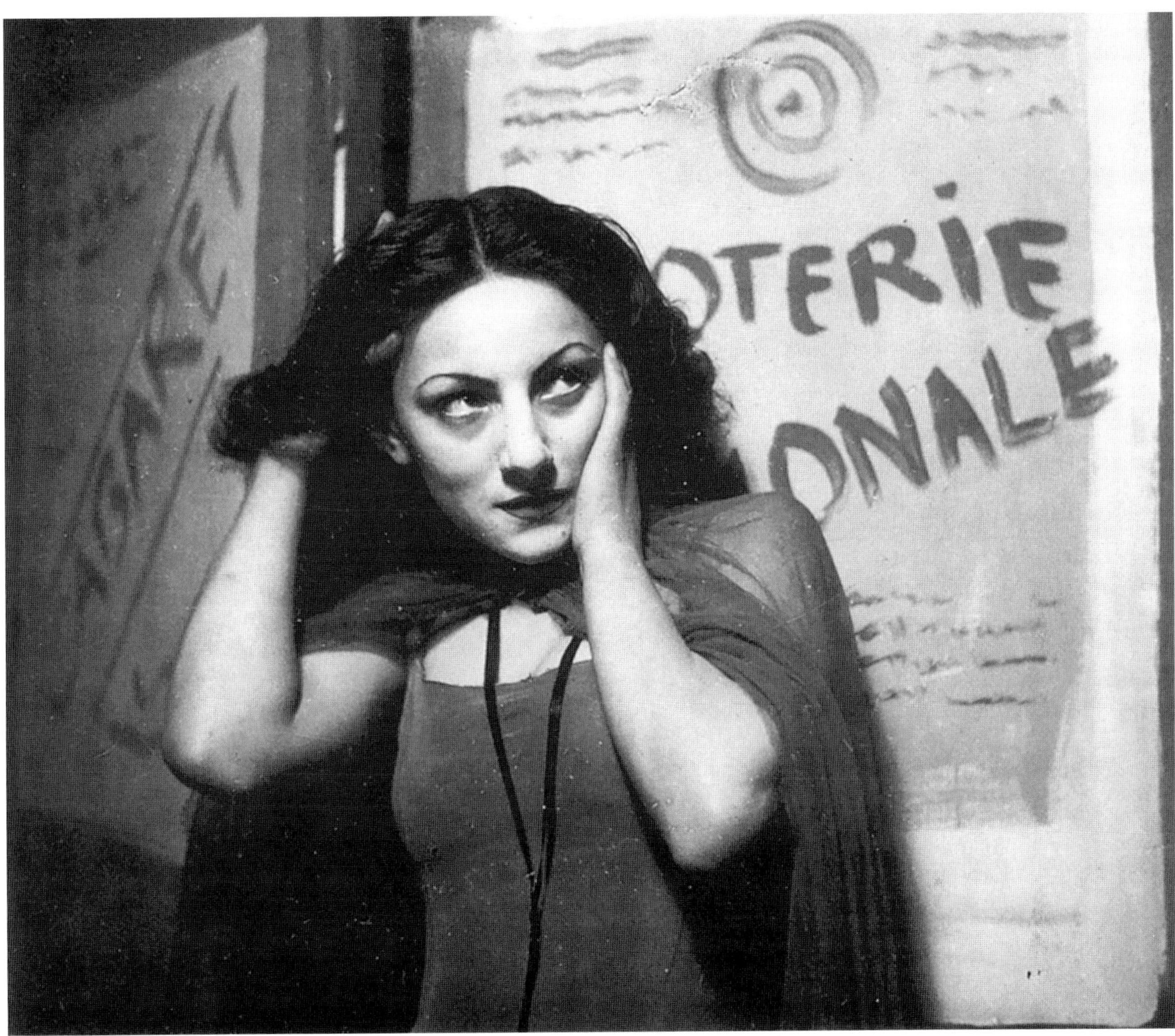


**Celia Franca as the Dope Fiend in *Paris Soir*, 1939**

## WORKS

1938 *Constanza's Lament* (mus. Beethoven), Ballet Rambert
1939 *Midas* (mus. Lutchens), Ballets des Trois Arts, London
1942 *Cancion* (mus. Turina), Ballet Guild, London
1946 *Khadra* (mus. Sibelius), Sadler's Wells Theatre Ballet, London
1947 *Bailemos* (mus. Massenet), Sadler's Wells Theatre Ballet, London
1949 *Dance of Salome* (mus. Hartley), BBC television
1950 *The Eve of St. Agnes* (mus. Lanchbery), BBC television
1951 *Colloque sentimental* (mus. Debussy), Ballet Workshop
*Dance of Salome* (new version; mus. Hartley), National Ballet of Canada, Toronto
1952 *L'Après-midi d'un faune* (mus. Debussy), National Ballet of Canada, Toronto
*Le Pommier* (mus. Grattan), National Ballet of Canada, Edmonton
1955 *Casse-Noisette* (mus. Tchaikovsky), National Ballet of Canada, Toronto
1964 *The Nutcracker* (new version; mus. Tchaikovsky), National Ballet of Canada, Toronto
1967 *EH!* (mus. Poulenc), National Ballet of Canada
1968 *Cinderella* (mus. Prokofiev), National Ballet of Canada, Toronto
1970 *Hansel and Gretel* (mus. Humperdinck), CBC Canadian television

Also staged:
1952 *Giselle* (after Petipa, Coralli, Perrot; mus. Adam), National Ballet of Canada, Toronto
*Coppélia* (after Petipa, Cecchetti; mus. Delibes), National Ballet of Canada, Toronto
1955 *Swan Lake* (after Petipa, Ivanov; mus. Tchaikovsky), National Ballet of Canada, Toronto
1960 *Princess Aurora* (selections from *The Sleeping Beauty*, after Petipa; mus. Tchaikovsky), National Ballet of Canada, Toronto
1975 *Les Sylphides* (with Bruhn, after Fokine; mus. Chopin), National Ballet of Canada, Toronto
*Offenbach in the Underworld* (chor. Tudor; mus. Offenbach), National Ballet of Canada, Toronto

**Other works include:** for Canadian Opera Company—dances in *Die Fledermaus* (Strauss), *Macbeth* (Verdi), *Aida* (Verdi), *Faust* (Gounod), and *The Merry Widow* (Lehár); for Edmonton Opera Association—dances in *La Traviata* (Verdi), *The Merry Widow* (Lehár).

## PUBLICATIONS

By Franca:

*The National Ballet of Canada: A Celebration* (with Ken Bell), Toronto, 1978

About Franca:

Bradley, Lionel, *Sixteen Years of Ballet Rambert*, London, 1946

Frost, Honor, *How a Ballet is Made*, London, 1948

Davidson, Gladys, *Ballet Biographies*, revised edition, London, 1954

Patterson, John, "National Ballet of Canada", *Dance Magazine* (New York), January 1960

Whittaker, Herbert, *Canada's National Ballet*, Toronto, 1967

Maynard, Olga, "Idea Image and Purpose: Ballet in Canada Today", *Dance Magazine* (New York), April 1971

Maynard, Olga, "Celia Franca and the National Ballet of Canada", *Dance Magazine* (New York), May 1974

* * *

Celia Franca's early commitment to a career in dance in her native England gave her a range and quality of experience from which she could draw almost indefinitely when, as a young woman, she left her home to take on the task that would become her life's work: the creation of the National Ballet of Canada. Her teachers, Antony Tudor and Stanislas Idzikowski, imbued her with a life-long respect for the principles of Enrico Cecchetti, while her professional experience with Ballet Rambert, Sadler's Wells, and the Metropolitan Ballet exposed her to the full range of the classical repertoire as well as the most recent developments in British choreography. A dramatic dancer of distinction, she appeared in the premiere of Tudor's *Dark Elegies* and from that time on felt a particular affinity for Tudor's work. She also experimented with choreography herself, for the Sadler's Wells Theatre Ballet and BBC television, among others.

In Canada she put all of this experience to use in building a professional company in a country that had virtually no indigenous tradition of professional dance. With scarce financial resources, she involved herself in every aspect of artistic administration in order to create a company which reflected her own ideals of ensemble playing, professional attention to detail, musicality, and authenticity of style. From the storehouse of her own memory, she mounted many works from the standard repertoire. She welcomed the advent of television in Canada as an opportunity to promote ballet in another medium and became expert at adapting the company's full-length works to the special needs of the camera. She also choreographed original ballets for the company, though she never laid claim to great distinction as a choreographer. Along with all these activities she continued to perform. Her interpretation of *Giselle* was seen across Canada and the United States, during the company's frequent tours. After her official retirement from dancing, she appeared as a powerful and highly individual character artist. Generations of spectators will remember forever her imperious, grief-torn Lady Capulet in Cranko's *Romeo and Juliet*.

The intensity and commitment of her on-stage personality carried over into her off-stage work for the cause of dance. Never one to sacrifice artistic principles to financial exigency, she fought with integrity and passion to realize her vision of a classically-based company for the nation. She was instrumental in the founding of the National Ballet School, which grew out of summer institutes sponsored by the young company, and has maintained her interest in education, since her retirement as artistic director, with free-lance teaching assignments across Canada and in the People's Republic of China. As an individual and as a member of the Canada Council, the country's federal granting body for the arts, she has had considerable impact as a spokesperson for the artistic community in her adopted country.

Boldness and daring characterized virtually every phase of her career. Once having established herself in the relative security of the English cultural climate, she ventured into a new environment where the very premises of her professional life were frequently called into question. There, undaunted by indifference or opposition, she won supporters to her side with the strength of her vision and the consistency of her purpose. The accurate measure of her achievement can be taken only by acknowledging the full range of her contributions to the field of dance and the tremendous odds against which she struggled to bring them to fruition.

—James E. Neufeld

---

**FRANKLIN, Frederic**

British-American dancer, choreographer, teacher, and ballet director. Born in Liverpool, England, 13 June 1914. Studied with Shelagh Elliott-Clarke, Liverpool, Lydia Kyasht and Nikolai (Nicolas) Legat, London, and Lubov Egorova, Paris. First stage experience as tap dancer, with "Lancaster Lads" troupe, London and Paris, 1931: professional début in cabaret with Mistinguette, Casino de Paris, 1931; dancer, with Wendy Toye, in cabaret and musical shows, London, from 1933; also performed in operetta, 1934; soloist, Markova–Dolin company, 1935–37; principal dancer, Ballet Russe de Monte Carlo, from 1938, becoming ballet master, 1944; guest star with Alexandra Danilova, Sadler's Wells (later Royal) Ballet, Covent Garden, 1949; founder (with Mia Slavenska) and principal dancer, Slavenska–Franklin Ballet, 1952–54, touring the United States and the Far East; returned to Ballet Russe de Monte Carlo as principal dancer and ballet master, 1954–56; toured South Africa with Danilova, 1956; director, Washington (D.C.) Ballet, the performing group of Washington School of Ballet, 1957–60; artistic adviser, American Ballet Theatre, New York, 1961; artistic director, National Ballet, Washington, D.C., 1962–74; co-artistic director, Pittsburgh Ballet Theatre, 1974–77, also working with Cincinnati Ballet, from 1974, and Chicago Ballet, 1976–77; resident choreographer, Cincinnati Ballet, from 1978, serving as acting director, 1984–87; has also staged ballets for La Scala, Milan, 1961, New York City Ballet, 1964, numerous regional American companies including Tulsa Ballet, Louisville Ballet, Richmond Ballet, and Boston Ballet, and for Dance Theatre of Harlem, from 1981, setting choreography for Arthur Mitchell's Creole *Giselle*, 1984, and currently serving as company artistic consultant; also member of advisory board, Tulsa Ballet. Recipient: Capezio Award, 1992.

## ROLES

1935/37 Bluebird in *Aurora's Wedding* (divertissements from *The Sleeping Beauty*; Dolin after Petipa), Markova–Dolin Ballet
Trepak solo in *The Nutcracker* (Divertissements; Dolin after Ivanov), Markova–Dolin Ballet

1938 Baron (cr) in *Gaîté Parisienne* (Massine), Ballet Russe de Monte Carlo, Monte Carlo
Spirit of Creation (cr) in *Seventh Symphony* (Massine), Ballet Russe de Monte Carlo, Monte Carlo
Knight and Wolf (cr) in *Nobilissima Visione* (Massine), Ballet Russe de Monte Carlo, London
Dobryna in *Bogatyri* (Massine), Ballet Russe de Monte Carlo, New York

1939 Red leader (cr) in *Rouge et noir* (Massine), Ballet Russe de Monte Carlo, Monte Carlo
Young Lover (cr) in *Devil's Holiday* (Ashton), Ballet Russe de Monte Carlo, New York
Ralston (cr) in *Ghost Town* (Platoff), Ballet Russe de Monte Carlo, New York
Day (cr) in *Nuages* (*Clouds*; Theilade), Ballet Russe de Monte Carlo, New York

1940 Joker in *Poker Game* (*Jeu de cartes*; Balanchine), Ballet Russe de Monte Carlo, New York
Secretary (cr) in *Vienna—1814* (Massine), Ballet Russe de Monte Carlo, New York
Principal dancer in *Serenade* (Balanchine), Ballet Russe de Monte Carlo, New York
Gossip Columnist (cr) in *The New Yorker* (Massine), Ballet Russe de Monte Carlo, New York

1941 Minotaur (cr) in *Labyrinth* (Massine), Ballet Russe de Monte Carlo, New York
Czardas soloist in *The Magic Swan* (*Swan Lake*, Act III; Fedorova after Petipa), Ballet Russe de Monte Carlo, New York
Jockey (cr) in *Saratoga* (Massine), Ballet Russe de Monte Carlo, New York

1942 Champion Roper (cr) in *Rodeo* (de Mille), Ballet Russe de Monte Carlo, New York

1942/43 Title role in *St. Francis* (*Nobilissima Visione*; Massine), Ballet Russe de Monte Carlo, San Francisco

1943 Principal dancer in *Étude* (Nijinska), Ballet Russe de Monte Carlo, Cleveland
Chivato in *The Cuckold's Fair* (Lopez), Ballet Russe de Monte Carlo, Cleveland
Russian Sailor (cr) in *The Red Poppy* (Schwezoff), Ballet Russe de Monte Carlo, Cleveland

1944 "Freddy and His Fiddle", "Chocolate Pas de Trois", "Song of Norway" (cr) in *Song of Norway* (operetta; mus. Grieg, arranged Wright and Forrest; chor. Balanchine), Philharmonic Auditorium, Los Angeles
Principal dancer in *Danses Concertantes* (Balanchine), Ballet Russe de Monte Carlo, New York
Cléonte in *Le Bourgeois Gentilhomme* (Balanchine), Ballet Russe de Monte Carlo, New York

1945 Adagio and Variations in *Mozartiana* (Balanchine), Ballet Russe de Monte Carlo, New York
Principal dancer (cr) in *Pas de Deux* (also *Grand Adagio*) (Balanchine), Ballet Russe de Monte Carlo, New York

1946 Bridegroom in *The Bells* (Page), Ballet Russe de Monte Carlo, Jacob's Pillow, Massachusetts
Eligible Young Bachelor (cr) in *Virginia Sampler* (Bettis), Ballet Russe de Monte Carlo, New York
El Menesteroso (cr) in *Madroños* (Cobos), Ballet Russe de Monte Carlo, New York

1947 Hero in *Lola Montez* (Caton), Ballet Russe de Monte Carlo, New York
Title role in *Billy Sunday* (Page), Ballet Russe de Monte Carlo, York, Pennsylvania

1950 Hunter in *Mort du Cygne* (Constantin Nepo after Lifar), Ballet Russe de Monte Carlo, New York
Romeo in *Roméo et Juliette* (Constantin Nepo after Lifar), Ballet Russe de Monte Carlo, New York
Premier Danseur in *Prima Ballerina* (Chamié), Ballet Russe de Monte Carlo, Chicago

1952 Stanley (cr) in *A Streetcar Named Desire* (Bettis), Slavenska–Franklin Ballet, Montreal

1954 Katisha (cr) in *The Mikado* (Cobos), Ballet Russe de Monte Carlo, Baltimore

**Other roles include:** for Ballet Russe de Monte Carlo—Albrecht in *Giselle* (after Petipa, Coralli, Perrot), Favourite Slave in *Schéhérazade* (Fokine), Franz in *Coppélia* (Sergeyev after Petipa, Cecchetti), Gypsy Youth in *Capriccio Espagnol* (Massine), the Poet in *Night Shadow* (*La Sonnambula*; Balanchine), Chief Warrior in *Polovtsian Dances from Prince Igor* (after Fokine).

## WORKS

1958 *Etalage* (mus. Liszt), Washington Ballet, Washington, D.C.

1960 *Hommage au Ballet* (mus. Gounod), Washington Ballet, Washington, D.C.

1961 *Tribute* (mus. Franck), Ballet Russe de Monte Carlo, Boston

1962 *Fantaisie Espagnole*, Ballet San Juan

1963 *Rhythm in 3*, National Ballet, Washington, D.C.

1964 *The Nutcracker* (mus. Tchaikovsky), National Ballet, Washington, D.C.

1966 *Danse Brillante* (also *Pas de Trois*; mus. Glinka), National Ballet, Washington, D.C.

1968 *Warmup*, National Ballet, Washington, D.C.

1976 *Prodigal Son* (mus. Prokofiev), Louisville Ballet, Louisville

1978 *Sylvia Pas de deux* (mus. Delibes), Cincinnati Ballet

1980 *Waltz Russe*, Ballet Metropolitan, Columbus, Ohio

1983 *Poème lyrique* (mus. Ravel), Cincinnati Ballet, Cincinnati

Also staged:

1948 *Giselle* (after Petipa, Coralli, Perrot; mus. Adam), Ballet Russe de Monte Carlo, New York (also staged for National Ballet of Washington, D.C., 1968)

1957 *Swan Lake*, Act II (after Ivanov; mus. Tchaikovsky), National Ballet, Washington, D.C.
*Les Sylphides* (after Fokine; mus. Chopin), National Ballet, Washington, D.C.
*Prince Igor* (*Polovtsian Dances*, after Fokine; mus. Borodin), Washington Ballet, Washington, D.C.

1961 *Grand Pas Glazunov* (Balanchine, Danilova; mus. Glazunov), American Ballet Theatre, Cleveland
*Coppélia* (after Petipa, Cecchetti; mus. Delibes), Ballet of La Scala, Milan

1964 *Ballet Imperial* (Balanchine; mus. Tchaikovsky), New York City Ballet, New York

1971 *La Sylphide* (after Bournonville; mus. Løvenskjold), Miami Ballet, Miami

1976 *Frankie and Johnny* (after Page, Stone; mus. Moross), Chicago Ballet, Chicago

**Frederic Franklin with Alexandra Danilova in *Danses Concertantes*, Ballet Russe de Monte Carlo, 1944**

1980 *Aurora's Wedding* (from *the Sleeping Beauty*, after Petipa; mus. Tchaikovsky), Cincinnati Ballet
1981 *Schéhérazade* (after Fokine; mus. Rimsky-Korsakov), Dance Theatre of Harlem, New York
1984 *Giselle* (new production, with revised scenario by Arthur Mitchell and Carl Michel; mus. Adam), Dance Theatre of Harlem, London

**Other works include:** stagings of *Raymonda Pas de dix* (mus. Glazunov), *La Sonnambula* (after Balanchine; mus. Bellini), *Paquita* (after Petipa; mus. Minkus), *Billy Sunday* (after Page; restaged with new music, 1976; staged with original Gassman music, 1983), *Pas de quatre* (after Dolin, Lester).

## PUBLICATIONS

Dolin, Anton, *A Ballet Go Round*, London, 1938
Maynard, Olga, "Frederic Franklin: A Life in the Theatre", *Dance Magazine* (New York), June 1974
Anderson, Jack, *The One and Only: The Ballet Russe de Monte Carlo*, New York, 1981
Anderson, Jack, "Danilova and Franklin", *Ballet Review* (New York), Winter 1982
Danilova, Alexandra, *Choura: The Memoirs of Alexandra Danilova*, New York, 1986
Denby, Edwin, *Dance Writings*, edited by Robert Cornfield and William Mackay, New York, 1986
Kerensky, Oleg, and Witherspoon, Charles, "A Dancer's Life", in "Curtain Up", *Dance and Dancers* (London), October 1989

* * *

In the studio or on the stage, Frederic Franklin is a vital force in ballet's promulgation and preservation. From his professional origins in British radio serializations and musical revues, Franklin developed into an eminent ballet master, choreographer, teacher, and artistic director, on top of his achievement as one of twentieth-century ballet's finest and most versatile performers. His expansive career is remarkable for its multi-faceted success and for the impact it has had on the art form's survival.

In his prime, Franklin was a capable technician and dynamic artist with assured carriage, elegant style, and large, clean, open lines, who always performed with graceful ease and rhythm. Though he was criticized for occasional upper-body rigidity, his confident, virile dancing was lauded for strength, athleticism, speed, agility, and precision, best demonstrated in *The Nutcracker*'s Trepak or in the Polovtsian Dances from *Prince Igor*. Virtuosity aside, Franklin's greatest assets were his versatility, enthusiasm, and dynamic stage presence. Although competent in classical roles, Franklin—gifted with dramatic abilities, a fine sense of timing, and comic flair—excelled in demi-caractère ballets. In these works he could best utilize his charm and ebullient personality, which could capture audiences and rescue mediocre choreography from disaster.

The ideal danseur of his era, Franklin was a masterful, gallant partner—skilled, sturdy, dependable, self-effacing, yet showing dash and finesse—and he cut a romantic figure in the 1940s and 1950s. Paired with Russian ballerina Alexandra Danilova, with whom he shared a powerful stage rapport, Franklin utilized his adaptability and sensitivity towards his partner to enhance their rare chemistry. The inexhaustible and dedicated duo traversed America with the Ballet Russe de Monte Carlo, never refusing to perform and never modifying choreography to compensate for fatigue. Danilova and Franklin, renowned for their performances of sweeping grandeur in Balanchine's *Grand Adagio*, swooning romanticism in Massine's *Gaîté Parisienne*, or robust comedy in *Coppélia*, were one of ballet's most sublime partnerships. Generating dance enthusiasm across the United States, they captivated audiences and established ballet as part of American culture.

Franklin's directorial talent, discovered by Léonide Massine and encouraged by George Balanchine, blossomed with his appointment as ballet master of the Ballet Russe de Monte Carlo, a company fraught by then with disorganization and lack of artistic continuity. Quick to institute an understudy policy and to clarify choreographic and stylistic confusion among the corps de ballet, Franklin preserved the company's repertory and educated new recruits.

Founding the short-lived Slavenska–Franklin Ballet and the National Ballet of Washington D.C., both of which, despite weak repertories, were artistically applauded, Franklin established his reputation for producing professional, exuberant, and technically proficient ensembles. Although he also guided the interim artistic stability of the Cincinnati Ballet, he prefers to freelance as a choreographer and director.

Working primarily with eclectic American companies, Franklin has set a broad spectrum of ballets, from the classics to period pieces. He possesses a phenomenal memory for patterns and steps, along with a reverence for original choreography and an uncanny musicality, and so he is the quintessential ballet master—thorough, efficient, and organized, with a strong sense of fair play. Consistently praised for his conscientious classical stagings, which are stylistically correct and technically precise, particularly in their display of clean, disciplined corps work, Franklin remains essentially faithful to his original sources—the repertories of the Markova–Dolin Ballet and Ballet Russe de Monte Carlo. The double-edged authenticity and historical significance of his productions challenges the artistry of contemporary technicians. For his setting of the Dance Theatre of Harlem's *Giselle*, Franklin won the 1984 Laurence Olivier Award as the year's best choreographer.

Guardian of the story ballet, Franklin as choreographer prefers to explore the plotless genre. His works, often noted for their affinity with Balanchine's concepts and for Soviet influence, are firmly based on academic classical technique, hallmarked by correctness, symmetry, and an orderly flow of movement. His *Sylvia Pas de Deux* displays lovely unsupported arabesque turns in the adagio and a memorable toss/catch bravura finale. *Tribute*, also noted for Balanchine/Soviet similarities, produces a feeling of airy spaciousness and brightness. Although his choreographic motivation may derive from academic inspiration, as in his *Etalage* and *Hommage à Ballet*, Franklin's works, tasteful, "dancey", and poetically structured, reflect his infallible musicality and his straightforward style.

A warm, friendly and articulate man, Franklin has boundless energy, which has enabled him to stimulate his dancers' potentials. As a teacher he gives a well-structured, inspired technique class. He possesses a sharp eye for errors, quickly finding flaws which other instructors fail to notice or mention. In the studio, he is a source of encouragement and knowledge.

As a mature performer, Franklin, whose instinctive acting talents contributed to his career's success, has developed dramatic excellence as a mime. He has always been noted for his ability to submerge himself in his roles (as he proved in Valerie Bettis's *A Streetcar Named Desire*), and he draws rich characterizations. Especially memorable as Father Lorenzo in *Romeo and Juliet*, Franklin emitted an aura of serenity and humility, his benevolence conveyed by simple gestures and unassuming movements. Also outstanding as *La Sylphide*'s

**Margarita Froman**

Madge, Franklin, wholly transformed into the malicious hag, provided a subtly forceful presence, whose deliberately emphasized actions effected lingering dramatic impact.

Although Franklin's career has taken him from London, across Europe, to the Far East and South Africa, his greatest artistic impact has been in the United States, where he willingly shares the knowledge and wealth of his theatrical wisdom with new generations of dancers, as well as with new audiences.

—Karen Dacko

---

**FROMAN, Margarita**

Russian dancer, choreographer, and teacher. Born Margarita Petrovna Froman in Moscow, 8 November (27 October old style) 1890. Studied at the Moscow Choreographic School (Bolshoi Ballet School). Dancer, Bolshoi Theatre, Moscow, 1909–21, performing with Ballets Russes de Serge Diaghilev, 1914, 1916, returning to Bolshoi Ballet, 1917, and becoming ballerina; ballet director and choreographer, State Opera Ballet, Zagreb (former Yugoslavia), from 1921; choreographer, State Opera Ballet, Belgrade, from c. 1937; also teacher: founder and director of schools in Zagreb and Belgrade, with students including Mia Slavenska; moved to the United States: teacher at own school in Connecticut, from early 1950s. Died in Boston, 24 March 1970.

**WORKS**

1922 *Polovtsian Dances from Prince Igor* (mus. Borodin), Zagreb State Opera Ballet, Zagreb
*Schéhérazade* (mus. Rimsky-Korsakov), Zagreb State Opera Ballet, Zagreb
*Les Papillons* (mus. Schumann), Zagreb State Opera Ballet, Zagreb
*The Jilted Pierrot* (mus. Weber), Zagreb State Opera Ballet, Zagreb
1923 *Thamar* (mus. Balakirev), Zagreb State Opera Ballet, Zagreb
*Coppélia* (mus. Delibes), Zagreb State Opera Ballet, Zagreb
*Petrushka* (mus. Stravinsky), Zagreb State Opera Ballet, Zagreb
*The Nutcracker* (excerpts; mus. Tchaikovsky), Zagreb State Opera Ballet, Zagreb
1924 *The Gingerbread Heart* (mus. Baranovic), Zagreb State Opera Ballet, Zagreb
*Carnaval* (mus. Schumann), Zagreb State Opera Ballet, Zagreb
*Capriccio espagnol* (mus. Rimsky-Korsakov), Zagreb State Opera Ballet, Zagreb
1927 *Box of Toys* (mus. Debussy), Zagreb State Opera Ballet, Zagreb
1928 *The Firebird* (mus. Stravinsky), Zabreb State Opera Ballet, Zagreb
1930 *The Three-Cornered Hat* (mus. de Falla), Zagreb State Opera Ballet, Zagreb
1932 *Les Noces* (mus. Stravinsky), Zagreb State Opera Ballet, Zagreb
*The Nutcracker* (full length; mus. Tchaikovsky), Zagreb State Opera Ballet, Zagreb
1937 *Imbrek-with-the-nose* (mus. Baranovic), Belgrade State Opera Ballet, Belgrade
*Harnasie* (mus. Symanowski), Belgrade State Opera Ballet, Belgrade
*Caucasian Sketches* (mus. Ippolitov-Ivanov), Belgrade State Opera Ballet, Belgrade
*Afternoon of a Faun* (mus. Debussy), Zagreb State Opera Ballet, Zagreb
1947 *The Legend of Ohrid* (mus. Hristic), Belgrade State Opera Ballet, Belgrade
1949 *Romeo and Juliet* (mus. Prokofiev), Zagreb State Opera Ballet, Zagreb

Also staged:
1921 *Swan Lake*, Act II (after Ivanov; mus. Tchaikovsky), Zagreb State Opera Ballet
1927 *Raymonda* (after Petipa; mus. Glazunov), Belgrade State Opera Ballet
1940 *Swan Lake* (after Petipa, Ivanov; mus. Tchaikovsky), Zagreb State Opera Ballet

**Other works include:** for Belgrade National Ballet—*The Humpbacked Horse* (mus. Pugni).

**PUBLICATIONS**

Marinkovic-Rakic, B., and Nikolajevic, R., *Ballet Jougoslave*, Belgrade, 1958
"Margarita Froman" (obituary), *Dance News* (New York), May 1970
Maynard, Olga, "The Dance in Yugoslavia", *Dance Magazine* (New York), May 1977

* * *

Margarita Froman was born and trained in Moscow in the years before the Russian revolution, graduating into the company of the Bolshoi Theatre in 1909. Although she did not make a very great impact as a leading dancer there, she obviously benefitted from a sound training in the Russian style, something which was to prove crucial to her later career as teacher, ballet mistress, and producer of the classics outside Russia. When Froman was 24, she left Russia temporarily to tour with Diaghilev's Ballets Russes in Europe and America (Western sources differ about this, and Froman's exact place in the Diaghilev company in the years 1914–16 is hard to determine). It was only on her return to the Bolshoi in 1917 that she was promoted to ballerina, thereafter dancing such leading roles as Kitri in *Don Quixote*, Swanilda in *Coppélia*, and the Lilac Fairy in *The Sleeping Beauty*.

Froman's greatest contribution to ballet, however, was not as a performer, but as teacher and ambassador of the classical Russian ballet style. Choosing to leave the new Soviet Union in 1921, Froman settled in Yugoslavia with her brother, Maximilian Froman, becoming leading ballerina and ballet mistress (with her brother as premier danseur) of the Zagreb State Opera Ballet. Here she instilled everything she knew from her Bolshoi and Ballets Russes backgrounds, establishing a ballet school and setting about staging the classics, from the nineteenth-century favourites (she began with the inevitable *Swan Lake* Act II) to the more recent Diaghilev/Fokine collaborations from the early Ballets Russes years, which she had learned first-hand when touring with the company.

Froman's energy was apparently endless, as she continued to stage several new productions a year, eventually expanding her ballet empire to Belgrade, where from 1937 she was ballet director, dividing her time between the two cities. Froman's impact on Yugoslavian ballet is immeasurable. As the dance historian Anatole Chujoy has written, "She had a decisive influence on the establishment and development of ballet in Yugoslavia. In the course of her years in Yugoslavia, she, first in Zagreb and then in Belgrade, succeeded in transplanting the tradition and the art of Russian ballet to the Yugoslav stage."

Froman's stagings were varied. As was quite common in Europe in the years following the tours of Diaghilev's Ballets Russes, Froman staged her own versions of the Diaghilev ballets, mounting an early production of the *Polovtsian Dances from Prince Igor* in 1922, and going on to arrange her own stagings of *Schéhérazade*, *Thamar*, *Petrushka*, and *The Firebird*. More important, however, she responded to the need for a national ballet which acknowledged local traditions and folk dance styles; in 1924 she created *The Gingerbread Heart*, set to a score by the Croatian composer Krešimir Baranović and using traditional folk songs and folk dances. *Harnasie* in 1937 borrowed Polish folk themes and dances, while *The Legend of Ohrid* returned to Yugoslav themes and music. The latter ballet, along with *The Gingerbread Heart* and *The Devil in the Village* by Pia and Pino Milaker, were said by Chujoy to be considered "the national ballets of Yugoslavia".

Froman's legacy in Yugoslavia was profound, and she holds an important place among those Russian expatriate dancers who contributed to the growth and development of twentieth-century ballet in Europe. Her influence, furthermore, spread even further than eastern Europe; after some 30 years as the leading ballet mistress in Yugoslavia, Froman emigrated to America, where she taught in Connecticut until her death in 1970.

—Elizabeth Hudson

---

## FUOCO, Sofia

Italian dancer. Born Maria Brambilla in Milan, 16 January 1830. Studied at the Ballet School of the Teatro alla Scala, Milan, pupil of Carlo Blasis, from c. 1837. Début, La Scala, Milan, 1839, performing in *I Riti indiani* and *Conquista di Granata*; prima ballerina assoluta, La Scala, from 1843; ballerina, Opéra, Paris, various seasons, 1846–50; toured Europe, with appearances in London, 1847, Madrid, 1848, Rouen, Bordeaux, Dieppe, Madrid, Granada, Malaga, and Venice, 1851, Rome, Modena, Venice, Florence, Padua, 1852–54, Livorno, 1855, Perugia and Trieste, 1856, and Bologna, 1858; probably retired from the stage in late 1850s. Died in Carate Lario, Lake Como, 4 June 1916.

### ROLES

1839 Dancer in *I Riti indiani*, La Scala, Milan
Dancer in *Conquista di Granata*, La Scala, Milan
1841 Title role (cr) in *Niobe; ossia La Vendetta di Latona* (Huss), La Scala, Milan
1843 Gisella in *Gisella; ossia, La Willi* (Cortesi), La Scala, Milan
1846 Principal dancer in *Pas de quatre* (Perrot; staged Taglioni), La Scala, Milan
Title role (cr) in *Betty; ou, La Jeunesse de Henry V* (Mazilier), Opéra, Paris
1847 Peasant Pas de deux in *Giselle* (Coralli, Perrot), Opéra, Paris
Divertissement (cr) in *Jérusalem* (opera; mus. Verdi; chor. Mazilier), Opéra, Paris
1848 Pas de treize (cr) in *Nisidia* (Mabille), Opéra, Paris
Divertissement (cr) in *Jeanne la folle* (opera; mus. Clapisson, chor. Mabille), Opéra, Paris
1852 Principal dancer (cr) in *Il Prestigiatore* (Blasis), La Fenice, Venice
Title role (cr) in *Zuleika* (Coppini), La Fenice, Venice
1853 Title role (cr) in *Palmina; ossia, La Figlia del Torrente* (Martin), La Scala, Milan
Title role in *Catarina; ou La Fille du bandit* (Perrot), La Scala, Milan
1854 Principal dancer (cr) in *La Nozze di Ninetta e Nane* (Fissi), Florence
Principal dancer (cr) in *Armilla; ossia, La Cetra incantata* (Monticini), La Fenice, Venice
Principal dancer (cr) in *Kabdelaj; o, La Figlia del profeta* (Viotti), Ancona

### PUBLICATIONS


Blasis, Carlo, *Notes upon Dancing, Historical and Practical*, London, 1847

*Cenni biografici intorno alla celebre danzatrice Sofia Fuoco*, Modena, 1853

*Ces demoiselles de l'Opéra*, second edition, Paris 1887

Rivalta, Camillo, *Il Tramonto di una diva* (*Sofia Fuoco*), Faenza, 1916

Gautier, Théophile, *The Romantic Ballet as seen by Théophile Gautier*, edited and translated by Cyril Beaumont, London, 1932

Michel, Arthur, "*Pas de Quatre* 1845–1945", *Dance Magazine* (New York), July 1945

Beaumont, Cyril, *Complete Book of Ballet*, revised edition, London, 1951

Guest, Ivor, *The Ballet of the Second Empire 1847–1858*, London, 1955

Guest, Ivor, *The Romantic Ballet in Paris*, London, 1966


* * *

Sofia Fuoco, who was born of a Milanese family called Brambilla, was one of the products of the school of the great Italian teacher, Carlo Blasis. She began her training at the unusually early age of seven (apparently breaking the rules to do so), and soon became one of Blasis's group of so-called "Pleiades". Her début on the stage of Milan's Teatro alla Scala came when she was only nine years old; by the age of thirteen, having replaced a ballerina disposed by illness, she became the theatre's prima ballerina assoluta.

From the start Fuoco (who adopted her stage name on her first appearance in 1843) had distinguished herself as a dancer of lively style, but equally impressive was her strong technique, that hallmark of the Italian school in the nineteenth century. Of especial note was her skill on pointes, such that at the height of her career she was known as "La Pointue". She was an immensely popular ballerina in her day, and her fame spread beyond her native Milan to various cities in Europe, where she toured successfully in the 1840s and 1850s, performing in Paris, London, Madrid, and Barcelona as well as in numerous cities in Italy.

Fuoco's youthful career as "prima ballerina assoluta" could not have had a more auspicious start: the very year she was given this title at La Scala, she performed in Antonio Cortesi's *Gisella; ossia, La Willi*, one of numerous stagings around Europe in the 1840s which took their inspiration from the

**Sofia Fuoco in *Tarantella***

famous Corralli/Perrot *Giselle*, first produced at the Paris Opéra in 1841. Cortesi's version, which used new music by Bajetti, expanded the action to five acts, and originally featured Fanny Cerrito in the title role. A few years later, in 1846, Fuoco participated in another historical event, when Marie Taglioni staged her version of Perrot's *Pas de quatre* for the Milan stage, thus presenting the only contemporary staging of the famed divertissement to be seen outside London at that time. The four ballerinas who danced in this production were Taglioni, Carolina Rosati (then performing as Carolina Galletti), Carolina Vente, and Fuoco herself.

That same year Fuoco made her Paris début, and again her success was complete. "Mlle Fuoco . . . bears a name of happy augury—*fire*! It might have been invented for her." So begins Théophile Gautier's description of the young Italian dancer's performance on her Paris début in *Betty; ou, La Jeunesse d'Henri V*. From the time of Fuoco's arrival in Paris, descriptions of her abilities on pointe had excited interest, with the new ballet quickly created for her by Mazilier to mark her début at the Opéra. *Betty*, with a score by Ambrose Thomas, had its premiere on 10 July 1846, and was by critical consensus an overly heavy and unnecessarily complicated production; but Fuoco's performance in it was unanimously judged a success.

Gautier's vivid portrait of the young ballerina's performance is worth repeating here:

> From her first appearance, Mlle. Sofia Fuoco made a distinct impression. She has the merit of originality, so rare in the dance, a limited art if ever there was one; she does not remind one of either Taglioni, Elssler, Carlotta, or Cerito.
>
> Her *pointes* in particular are astounding; she executes the whole of an *écho* without once lowering her heel to the ground. Her feet are like two steel arrows rebounding from a marble pavement; not a moment of weakness, not a vibration, not a tremor; that inflexible toe never betrays the light body it supports.
>
> Other dancers have been said to have wings, to have roamed the air amid clouds of muslin; Mlle. Fuoco flies too, but grazing the ground with the tip of her nail, alive, quick, dazzling in her rapidity.
>
> Dancing, it will be said, does not consist entirely of *pointes* and *taquetés*. True, but, in everything executed by Mlle. Fuoco, we have remarked that neatness, that finish, that precision which are to the dance what style is to poetry, we also believe that she possesses other qualities, in a lesser degree, undoubtedly, but sufficient.

This was "one of the most brilliant débuts in dancing . . . for a long time" claimed Gautier, with another contemporary critic complimenting the "gracefulness, vigour, precision and ease" of the "very youthful person" whose skills were being compared to those of the greatest ballerinas of the day. Fuoco was to have had another ballet at the Opéra created for her, provisionally titled *La Taïtienne*, but because of conflicts created by another engagement in Rome, followed by a knee injury, she was replaced by Adeline Plunkett in the title role of the Coralli ballet, which was eventually produced as *Ozaï* (1847). "As things turned out", writes Ivor Guest, "Carlotta could congratulate herself on not being associated with *Ozaï* . . ." —for the ballet, Coralli's last stage work for the Opéra, was a failure.

Fuoco's success at the Opéra continued another three years, when she performed in intermittent seasons while continuing to appear on stages throughout Europe. She danced in another Perrot revival, *Catarina*, staged at La Scala in 1853, and in numerous ballets by Italian choreographers, including those by Dario Fissi, himself a dancer and apparently Fuoco's inseparable partner.

After the late 1850s little is known about Fuoco's career. Her importance today undoubtedly lies in the fact that she was a dancer known almost entirely for her technique (and even that was said by some critics to be limited to pointe-work alone). As such, her career was pointing the way towards greater and greater emphasis on technical prowess in ballet, inevitably at the expense of artistry. Those very elements which made her a success at her Paris début, then, were also hinting at the coming decadence of French post-Romantic ballet. An increasing emphasis on technical facility, such as Fuoco's pointes, was ultimately to result in the decline of the great Romantic style, leading to what Ivor Guest has called the sacrifice of "aesthetic consideration for effect".

Fuoco probably retired at a relatively early age, and, according to most sources she died "a rich and well-loved old lady" in her villa on Lake Como.

—Elizabeth Hudson

**GABLE, Christopher**

British dancer, actor, and ballet director. Born in London, 13 March 1940. Studied at the Sadler's Wells (later Royal) Ballet School, London. Dancer, Covent Garden Opera Ballet, 1956, joining Royal Ballet Touring Company, 1957: soloist, from 1959; principal dancer, from 1961; soloist, Royal Ballet (at Convent Garden), 1963–67, leaving stage to pursue acting career; founder and director, Central School of Ballet, from 1982; artistic director, Northern Ballet Theatre, Yorkshire, from 1987; has appeared as actor in films, including title role in *The Boyfriend* (dir. Ken Russell, 1972), and as John in *The Slipper and the Rose* (dir. Russell, 1976); has appeared as actor on stage and television, including role of Lysander in *A Midsummer Night's Dream* (dir. Peter Brook, 1970). Recipient: Honorary Member of Royal Northern College of Music, Manchester; *Manchester Evening News* Award for Contribution to the Theatre (Horniman Award), 1989.

**ROLES**

1958 Popular Song in *Façade* (Ashton), Royal Ballet Touring Company

1959 Male solo in *Solitaire* (MacMillan), Royal Ballet Touring Company

Knight in *La Belle Dame sans merci* (Howard), Royal Ballet Touring Company, Leeds

1960 The Cousin (cr) in *The Invitation* (MacMillan), Royal Ballet Touring Company, Oxford

Pas de deux in *Solitaire* (MacMillan), Royal Ballet Touring Company

1961 Pas de deux in *Danses concertantes* (Balanchine), Royal Ballet, London

Prince Florimund in *The Sleeping Beauty* (Petipa, staged Sergeyev; with additions Ashton, de Valois), Royal Ballet Touring Company

Bluebird in *The Sleeping Beauty* (Petipa, staged Sergeyev; with additions Ashton, de Valois), Royal Ballet Touring Company

The Young Man (cr) in *The Two Pigeons* (Ashton), Royal Ballet Touring Company, London

1962 Colas in *La Fille mal gardée* (Ashton), Royal Ballet Touring Company

First Red Knight in *Checkmate* (de Valois), Royal Ballet, London

The Bridegroom in *Blood Wedding* (Rodrigues), Royal Ballet Touring Company

Pas de deux from *Flower Festival at Genzano* (Bournonville), Royal Ballet Touring Company

Adagio/Variations in *Les Rendezvous* (Ashton), Royal Ballet Touring Company

Fugue (cr) in *Toccata* (A. Carter), Royal Ballet Touring Company, Newcastle

1963 Franz in *Coppélia* (Sergeyev after Petipa, Cecchetti; staged de Valois), Royal Ballet, London

Colas in *La Fille mal gardée* (Ashton), Royal Ballet, London

Prince Siegfried in *Swan Lake* (Petipa, Ivanov, Ashton; staged Helpmann), Royal Ballet, London

Aminta in *Sylvia* (Ashton), Royal Ballet, London

The Boy in *House of Birds* (MacMillan), Royal Ballet Touring Company

1964 Solor in *La Bayadère* (Nureyev after Petipa), Royal Ballet, London

Daphnis in *Daphnis and Chloë* (Ashton), Royal Ballet, London

Title role in *Hamlet* (Helpmann), Royal Ballet, London

Two Loves I Have (cr) in *Images of Love* (MacMillan), Royal Ballet, London

The Caricaturist in *Mam'zelle Angot* (Massine), Royal Ballet, London

1965 Prince in *Cinderella* (Ashton), Royal Ballet, London

Albrecht in *Giselle* (Petipa after Coralli, Perrot; with additions Ashton), Royal Ballet Touring Company, London

Romeo (cr; danced at premiere by Nureyev) in *Romeo and Juliet* (MacMillan), Royal Ballet, London

Principal dancer in *Laurencia* Pas de six (Nureyev after Chabukiani), Royal Ballet, London

1966 Principal dancer (cr) in *Brandenburg Nos. 2 and 4* (Cranko), Royal Ballet, London

The Joker in *Card Game* (Cranko), Royal Ballet, London

1987 L.S. Lowry (cr) in *A Simple Man* (Lynne), Northern Ballet Theatre

1989 Don Quixote (cr) in *The Amazing Adventures of Don Quixote* (Moricone), Northern Ballet Theatre

**WORKS**

Staged:

1989 *The Amazing Adventures of Don Quixote* (chor. Moricone; mus. Minkus), Northern Ballet Theatre

1990 *Giselle* (after Petipa, Coralli, Perrot), Northern Ballet Theatre, Buxton

1991 *Romeo and Juliet* (chor. Moricone; mus. Prokofiev), Northern Ballet Theatre, Blackpool

1992 *Swan Lake* (after Petipa, Ivanov; mus. Tchaikovsky), Northern Ballet Theatre, Leeds

**Christopher Gable in *Swan Lake***

**PUBLICATIONS**

By Gable:
Interview in Newman, Barbara, *Striking a Balance: Dancers Talk About Dancing*, Boston, 1982
Interview with Morris, Geraldine, "Christopher Gable Talking About Teaching", *Dancing Times* (London), January 1984

About Gable:
"Christopher Gable", *Dance and Dancers* (London), May 1963
Dodd, Craig, "Christopher Gable", *Ballet Today* (London), July 1963
Goodman, Saul, "Brief Biography: Christopher Gable", *Dance Magazine* (New York), July 1965
Goodwin, Noël, "Passionate Pedagogue", *Dance and Dancers* (London), September 1982
"The Road to Manchester", *Dance and Dancers* (London), September 1987
Percival, John, "Rehabilitating Don Quixote", *Dance and Dancers* (London), July 1989
Woodcock, Sarah, *The Sadler's Wells Royal Ballet*, London, 1991

* * *

Christopher Gable's instinct for performing showed itself at an early age with a penchant for talent contests; as a child of London's East End, he would cheerfully launch himself into almost any category that was listed, from recitation to tap-dancing. It was said that he was sent to ballet classes simply because there was a school on the right side of the road which did not require him to cross through traffic. In the event, he went through the Lower and Upper Schools of Sadler's Wells, and graduated in the Opera in a pas de deux with a Canadian student, Lynn Seymour. She was earmarked subsequently for the Royal Ballet Touring Company, but Gable was to all intents and purposes discarded into the Opera ballet corps. (Sadler's Wells was gaining a reputation for overlooking its own most likely products.) Gable virtually gate-crashed his way into the touring company and survived because of mishaps to others ahead of him. This base, compared to the sheltered London company, traditionally provided five years' experience in one.

Gable had an unusual facility for turns *and* jumps; importantly, he was true danseur noble material, with a strong, graceful, well-proportioned body. He was blessed with a truly wonderful neck; indeed, Tchernicheva, coaching him for *Les Sylphides*, remarked that she had never seen anything like it since Nijinsky. His facial features somehow "read" easily from the furthest reaches of an auditorium; his looks were entirely glamorous, but in a thoroughly contemporary idiom: he was at once pretty and rugged.

But behind the surface charm lay a deep seriousness of purpose. In revolt against stereotypical ballet, wherein card-board princes were represented by paper-thin characterization, Gable devoured all Stanislavsky's precepts. He had a knack of utilizing moments of stillness, with the confidence sometimes to be "soft" on stage, utilizing a sort of Michelangelo plastique that drew the eye with its quiet harmony of line. When Kenneth MacMillan cast Gable and Lynn Seymour as the adolescents in *The Invitation*, it was a reunion of like-minded dancers who had a compatible and intense musicality which allowed them to launch into a duet with a certain lyrical abandon. Happily for Seymour's subsequent career, Gable was from the start an exceptionally strong as well as careful partner, cushioning her sometimes fragile technique and providing a security which allowed her to explore her innate dramatic expressiveness. Nevertheless, their pairing in Ashton's *The Two Pigeons* arose by chance; Gable replaced an injured colleague almost at the dress rehearsal. Initially, Seymour had been out of sympathy with the vocabulary of pastiche which Ashton was using for this ballet, but Gable immediately started playing his role "for real", so much so that one of Ashton's aides complained that the role of The Young Man was somehow being altered. "Leave him alone," said Ashton, seeing quicker than anyone just how much dramatic strength lay in the new colouring.

On the first night of *The Two Pigeons* in 1961, an exuberant solo from Gable drew a huge roar from the Covent Garden audience, which undoubtedly felt it had discovered a new star at that moment. Seymour, too, displayed an inimitable touch, and the final pas de deux was seen by a great many people through a mist of tears. This simulacrum of heartfelt ardour, performed in a way that actually caught people by the throat, was a startlingly new experience for many ballet-goers of that time. By the time Nureyev arrived in England, its audiences were already receptive to a strong Romantic flourish in male ballet roles. In his first full season with the Royal Ballet, Nureyev became fascinated by the way Gable and Seymour could grip an audience. Fonteyn admitted that she became unnerved by watching them, and significantly, the pair had a company listing as the only alternative cast for *Marguerite and Armand*, though the roles were never actually relinquished by Fonteyn and Nureyev. In a single extraordinary year, Covent Garden saw Gable partner no less than eight senior ballerinas (Fonteyn included), in roles right across the company's repertoire, but the partnership with Seymour unquestionably had an extra dimension.

Regrettably, the management lacked entirely any will to foster the partnership, and though MacMillan had built his *Romeo and Juliet* exclusively on Gable and Seymour, an unhealthy brew of impresario's lobbying from America, and managerial cowardice in London, meant they were denied the ballet's first night. (They had already danced the Balcony pas de deux for Canadian television, six months earlier.) This behind-the-scenes discord rumbled on for another two years, until Seymour decided to follow MacMillan to the Berlin Opera House, and Gable suddenly persuaded himself that his feet (which had been afflicted with arthritis) were about to cut short his dancing career.

In truth, Covent Garden had fumbled a priceless hand of cards. Newly determined on chasing a career in acting, the logical heir to Helpmann and Somes thus gave his last performances for the company (as Cinderella's prince) in 1967. It was a dazzling example of what might be considered the Royal Ballet's high tide of throw-away accomplishment. This prince was reckless, yet controlled, outgoing, yet marked by gravitas; it made Cinderella's story an entirely plausible romance. This kind of talent is not so commonplace that ballet can really afford to lose it. Fifteen years on, Northern Ballet Theatre acquired Gable as their director, and for them, he made a memorable return to dramatic ballet, with Moira Shearer, in Gillian Lynne's *A Simple Man*. It was a bitter-sweet reminder of two really exceptional dance talents, both of which could be said to have had too short a flowering in their parent company's history.

—Keith Money

---

**GABOVICH, Mikhail**

Russian/Soviet dancer. Born Mikhail Markovich Gabovich in the village of Velikie Guliaki, near Kiev, 7 December (24 November old style) 1905. Studied at the Moscow Choreographic School, pupil of Aleksandr Gorsky and Vasily Tikhomirov; graduated in 1924. Married Bolshoi dancer Mariana Bogolyubskaya: son, Bolshoi dancer Mikhail Gabovich, b. 1948. Soloist, Bolshoi Ballet, 1924–52; teacher, Moscow Choreographic School, from 1951, becoming artistic director, 1954–58; also the author of numerous articles in ballet criticism. Recipient: title of Honoured Artist of the USSR, 1937; State Prize, 1946, 1950; People's Artist of the Russian Federation, 1951. Died in Moscow, 12 July 1965.

## ROLES

1924 Charmant in *The Sleeping Beauty* (Tikhomirov after Petipa), Bolshoi Ballet, Moscow
Prince's Friend in *Swan Lake* (Gorsky after Petipa), Bolshoi Ballet, Moscow
1925 Slave in *Raymonda* (Gorsky, Petipa), Bolshoi Ballet, Moscow
1927 Bernard in *Raymonda* (Gorsky, Petipa), Bolshoi Ballet, Moscow
1928 Slave in *Le Corsaire* (Gorsky), Bolshoi Ballet, Moscow
1930 Bolero dancer in *Carmen* (opera; mus. Bizet, chor. Moiseyev), Bolshoi Ballet, Moscow
Title role in *The Footballer* (Moiseyev), Bolshoi Ballet, Moscow
Indian dance in *La Bayadère* (Gorsky after Petipa), Bolshoi Ballet, Moscow
Solor in *La Bayadère* (Gorsky after Petipa), Bolshoi Ballet, Moscow
Prince Désiré in *The Sleeping Beauty* (Gorsky after Petipa), Bolshoi Ballet, Moscow
1931 Miguel in *The Comedians* (Chekrygin), Bolshoi Ballet, Moscow
Basil in *Don Quixote* (Gorsky), Bolshoi Ballet, Moscow
1932 Espada in *Spanish Capriccio* (Zhukov), Bolshoi Ballet, Moscow
Prince in *Swan Lake* (Gorsky), Bolshoi Ballet, Moscow
Mato in *Salammbô* (Moiseyev), Bolshoi Ballet, Moscow
Youth in *Chopiniana* (Fokine, staged Chekrygin), Bolshoi Ballet, Moscow
1933 Prince Zéphire in *The Nutcracker* (Chekrygin, Monakhov), Bolshoi Ballet, Moscow
1934 Antoine (cr) in *The Flames of Paris* (Vainonen; Moscow version), Bolshoi Ballet, Moscow
Albert (Albrecht) in *Giselle* (Gorsky), Bolshoi Ballet, Moscow
1936 Jean de Brienne in *Raymonda* (Gorsky), Bolshoi Ballet, Moscow
Vatslav in *The Fountain of Bakhchisarai* (Zakharov), Bolshoi Ballet, Moscow
Blue Bird in *The Sleeping Beauty* (Tikhomirov after Petipa), Bolshoi Ballet, Moscow
1938 Ocean in *The Little Humpbacked Horse* (Gorsky after Saint-Léon), Bolshoi Ballet, Moscow
Vladimir (cr) in *The Prisoner of the Caucasus* (Zakharov), Bolshoi Ballet, Moscow
1941 Andrei (cr) in *Taras Bulba* (Zakharov), Bolshoi Ballet, Moscow
1945 Prince (cr) in *Cinderella* (Zakharov), Bolshoi Ballet, Moscow
1946 Kumai in *Prince Igor* (opera; mus. Borodin, chor. Goleizovsky), Bolshoi Ballet, Moscow
Romeo (cr) in *Romeo and Juliet* (Lavrovsky; Moscow version), Bolshoi Ballet, Moscow
1949 Evgeny in *The Bronze Horseman* (Zakharov), Bolshoi Ballet, Moscow
Mali-Chen in *The Red Poppy* (Lavrovsky), Bolshoi Ballet, Moscow

## PUBLICATIONS

By Gabovich:
*The Ballet School of the Bolshoi Theatre* (in collaboration with Ella Bocharnikova), Moscow, 1957
"Moscow Critic Analyses New York City Ballet", *Dance Magazine* (New York), December 1962
*Soul-Inspired Flight* (posthumous collection of essays), Moscow, 1966

About Gabovich:
Volkov, Nikolai, "Distinguished Artists of the Moscow Ballet", *Dancing Times* (London), October 1944
Zviagina, S., "The Generous Heart of the Artist: In Memoriam M.M. Gabovich", *Sovetskaya Muzyka* (Moscow), no. 5, 1966
Greskovic, Robert, "The Grigorovich Factor and the Bolshoi", *Ballet Review* (Brooklyn, N.Y.), vol. 5, no. 2, 1975–76
Vecheslova, Tatyana, "A Man of Beauty", *Teatr* (Moscow), no 3, 1976
*Mikhail Gabovich: Essays*, Reminiscences about M.M. Gabovich, Moscow, 1977
Razumnyi, V., "The Drama of a Happy Lot", *Sovetsky Balet* (Moscow), no 2, 1987

* * *

The whole life and work of Mikhail Gabovich was linked to the Moscow Bolshoi Theatre. He started his training in classical ballet at an exceptionally late age for someone who wanted to make it his career. At fourteen he went, quite by chance, to a concert given by Mikhail Mordkin. As a result, he became so interested in dance that he even started performing, in concerts, Mordkin's well-known choreographic piece *An Italian Beggar*. At the same time he entered a private ballet school, the director of which was Maria Gorshkova, a former ballerina of the Maryinsky and Bolshoi theatres. After a year Gorshkova suggested that Gabovich join a special school to provide him with professional training—a ballet school affiliated to the Bolshoi Theatre, in which classes were taught by Aleksandr Gorsky and Vasily Tikhomirov. After three years of working there with great enthusiasm, Gabovich mastered the techniques of classical ballet so well that he was able to join a ballet company.

During his first years in the theatre Gabovich performed several solo parts in the ballets of the classical repertoire, but soon he was dancing the leading roles. He was greatly gifted, and his elegant figure and good looks, as well as his technical excellence, brought him easy success as a classical leading dancer. His dancing was beautiful and musical, yet he was understated and far from ostentatious about his great skill.

His style of performance was perhaps more rational than emotional: his roles showed depth of characterization rather than passion, as he always tried to justify his every gesture and movement. This approach proved invaluable later, in the late 1930s, when he was dancing the leading roles in many "dram-ballets". At the beginning of his career it was mostly the various social types which he aimed to present through his dancing—for example, the character of the Young Communist in the ballet *The Footballer* (choreographed by Igor Moiseyev). In his

Mikhail Gabovich in *Raymonda*

more mature years, however, he learned to create roles with detailed psychological characterization, though not devoid of a social colouring.

His artistic apogee was in the roles he performed with Galina Ulanova: Albert (Albrecht) in *Giselle*, Romeo in *Romeo and Juliet*, the Prince in *Cinderella*. However, Gabovich's career as a dancer was abruptly brought to an end in 1949, after his leg was injured during a rehearsal of the ballet *The Ruby Stars*.

While being one of the Bolshoi Theatre's central figures, Gabovich never confined himself to dancing. He was a cultured person with varied interests. Naturally enough, he gave much thought to the history of ballet and its future. In his career, Gabovich had a chance of showing his skills as a manager and a critic. As early as 1925, while still a beginner at the Bolshoi, Gabovich became a leader of "the young people's revolt", an action of the Theatre's young artists supporting Kasyan Goleizovsky and his innovative productions against the management, which was interfering with the choreographer's work.

During the war, Gabovich was head of the half of the Bolshoi ballet which had not been evacuated, and he continued working in besieged Moscow. It was here that his energy and his talent as an organizer were fully employed. Thanks to his efforts, the company was able not only to keep up much of its repertoire but also to launch several new productions.

Gabovich was among those who, in the late 1940s and early 1950s, promoted, together with the critics Vladimir Golubov and Yuri Slonimsky, the concept of ballet performance based on dancing as opposed to the officially established "dram-ballet". He was one of the first to welcome Yuri Grigorovich's productions, which did not reject dramatic meaning, but sought to convey meaning and emotion through dance itself. Faithful to the traditions of the Moscow ballet, Gabovich also studied the work of the choreographer Aleksandr Gorsky in great detail. Late in his life Gabovich wrote several pieces of ballet criticism and analysis, which were collected and published the year after his death.

—Irina Gruzdeva

---

**GAD, Rose**

Danish dancer. Born in Copenhagen, 20 September 1968. Studied at the Royal Danish Ballet School, Copenhagen, from 1978. Dancer, Royal Danish Ballet, from 1985; solo dancer (principal), from 1991. Recipient: First Prize, Eurovision Ballet Competition, 1987; Erik Bruhn Prize (first recipient), 1988.

**ROLES**

1987 Title role in *La Sylphide* (Bournonville), Royal Danish Ballet, Copenhagen

1988 Eleonora in *The Kermesse at Bruges* (Bournonville), Royal Danish Ballet, Copenhagen

1989 The girl in *Afternoon of a Faun* (Robbins), Royal Danish Ballet, Copenhagen

Principal dancer in *Fête galante* (Ib Andersen), Royal Danish Ballet, Copenhagen

Principal dancer in *France/Dance* (Forsythe), Royal Danish Ballet, Copenhagen

Principal dancer in *Manhattan Abstraction* (Laerkesen), Royal Danish Ballet, Copenhagen

1990 Sigyn in *The Lay of Thrym* (Bournonville; staged von Rosen), Royal Danish Ballet, Copenhagen

Title role in *Giselle* (Petipa after Coralli, Perrot; staged Kronstam), Royal Danish Ballet, Copenhagen

1991 Clara/The Princess in *The Nutcracker* (Flindt), Royal Danish Ballet, Copenhagen

Title role (cr) in *Caroline Mathilde* (Flindt), Royal Danish Ballet, Copenhagen

Hilda in *A Folk Tale* (Bournonville), Royal Danish Ballet, Copenhagen

Principal dancer in *Theme and Variations* (Balanchine), Royal Danish Ballet, Copenhagen

Principal dancer in *(Tchaikovsky) Pas de Deux* (Balanchine), Royal Danish Ballet, Copenhagen

Terpischore in *Apollo* (Balanchine), Royal Danish Ballet, Copenhagen

Principal dancer in *Serenade* (Balanchine), Royal Danish Ballet, Copenhagen

1992 Principal dancer in *Polacca* (Laerkesen), Royal Danish Ballet, Copenhagen

**PUBLICATIONS**

Hunt, Marilyn, "The Pleasure of their Company: Jewels in the Danish Crown", *Dance Magazine* (New York), June 1992

Rose Gad could be said to be, like her name, a young rose, already a prominent figure among the many fine dancers of the Royal Danish Ballet. Slender-limbed and graceful, with exquisite musicality and technique, Rose Gad has already earned her place among the company's top dancers, despite her relative youth. Her blond, girlish beauty destined her for the great romantic parts from the beginning; and she has grown into that rare thing, a modern romantic ballerina.

A native child of the Bournonville school, Gad first showed her superior mastery of the Bournonville style when she won First Prize at the Eurovision Ballet Competition for young dancers in 1987, performing the great pas de deux from the second act of *La Sylphide* with partner Nikolaj Hübbe. Later in 1987, *La Sylphide* was her first main role in a full-length ballet. She was an enchanting Sylphide, at the same time coquettish and yet too innocent to realize the fatal consequences of her earthly love for James. As a sweetly sensual, life-loving Giselle, who is suddenly driven into heart-rending despair, she drew the unhappy romantic heroine close to our own time, showing us a young girl of flesh and blood. In 1991, the Danish choreographer Flemming Flindt created his contemporary dance-drama, *Caroline Mathilde*, especially for Rose Gad, who lent her combination of natural elegance and erotic attractiveness to the tragic title role of the young queen, wife of the mad King Christian VII.

Despite her success as a dramatic ballerina, Rose Gad's straight lines and superb classical technique have also fit excellently into abstract modern works, like William Forsythe's *France/Dance*, Ib Andersen's *Fête Galante*, and Anna Laerkesen's *Partita* and *Polacca*. She has also shown admirable skill and poise in Balanchine's *Apollo*, *Tchaikovsky Pas de Deux*, *Serenade*, and *Theme and Variations*. Rose Gad is still very young, but she is one of the great hopes of the Royal Danish Ballet, and her ability to shine both in the modern repertoire and in the great classics of the Bournonville tradition make her one of the important ballerinas of our day.

—Marie-Louise Kjølby

---

## GAÎTÉ PARISIENNE

**Choreography:** Léonide Massine
**Music:** Jacques Offenbach (arranged by Manuel Rosenthal)
**Design:** Comte Etienne de Beaumont (scenery and costumes)
**Libretto:** Comte Etienne de Beaumont
**First Production:** Ballet Russe de Monte Carlo, Monte Carlo, 5 April 1938
**Principal Dancers:** Nina Tarakanova (The Glove-Seller), Eugénie Delarova (The Flower Girl), Jeannette Lauret (La Lionne), Léonide Massine (The Peruvian), Frederic Franklin (The Baron), Igor Youskevitch (The Officer)

**Other productions include:** Royal Swedish Ballet (restaged Massine); Stockholm, 30 April 1956. American Ballet Theatre, with Toni Lander (Glove-Seller), Roni Mahler (Flower Girl), Betsy Erikson (La Lionne), Michael Smuin (Peruvian), Royes Fernandez (Baron), Han Ebelaar (Officer); Albuquerque, New Mexico, 12 January 1970. London Festival Ballet, with Maina Gielgud; London, 9 April 1973. Ballet du XXe Siècle (new version; chor. Maurice Béjart); Brussels, 27 January 1978. American Ballet Theatre (staged Lorca Massine after Léonide Massine; costumes Christian Lacroix, scenery Zack Brown), with Cheryl Yeager (Glove-Seller), Johan Renvall (Peruvian), Victor Barbee (Baron); Tampa, Florida, 19 January 1988. Les Ballets de Monte Carlo (staged Lorca Massine, assisted by Susanna della Pietra); Monte Carlo, December 1989.

### PUBLICATIONS

Beaumont, Cyril, *Supplement to Complete Book of Ballets*, London, 1942
Barnes, Clive, "Massine Rehearses in Stockholm", *Dance and Dancers* (London), August 1956
Massine, Léonide, *My Life in Ballet*, London, 1960
Anderson, Jack, *The One and Only: The Ballet Russe de Monte Carlo*, London, 1981
Agostino, Alfio, "Lo Spettro di Rossini", *Balletto Oggi* (Milan), January–February 1989

* * *

*Gaîté Parisienne* was made exactly half-way through the long creative life of Léonide Massine, one which began with *Soleil de nuit* (1916) and concluded with *La Commedia umana* (1960). No subsequent work of his has survived, with the sole exception of *Mam'zelle Angot* (1943). *Gaîté* is still going and still gives pleasure to its audiences, despite the 1943 verdict of Cyril Beaumont that "the standard of the choreography is not what one is entitled to expect from a choreographer of Massine's invention and artistry", and despite the most hideous designs (by Paris couturier Christian Lacroix) ever foisted upon a dead choreographer of taste when it was revived by American Ballet Theatre in the late 1980s.

*Gaîté Parisienne* was the first work which Massine created for the Ballet Russe de Monte Carlo in 1938. Both his other works in 1938 were of a serious nature (the *Seventh Symphony* of Beethoven, and *Noblissima Visione* by Hindemith), and possibly he took up the idea of Etienne de Beaumont of a Winterhalter/Offenbach ballet as a welcome relaxation from the others occupying his mind at the time. Massine reports in his autobiography that Beaumont had obtained from Offenbach's nephew the manuscript scores of more than 100 operettas, from which Beaumont and Massine chose enough music to make up a ballet lasting about half an hour, after which Massine invented a story to go with it. The story was flimsier than any other Massine comedy work: in fact, he describes it as "a light-hearted episode", with a French-farce plot serving solely as a peg upon which to hang a divertissement. *Gaîté Parisienne* was a work of sheer "entertainment"; yet it must not be forgotten that despite its superficiality it offered chances of humorous characterization to artists of the calibre of Danilova (in the role created by Tarakanova), Franklin, Youskevitch, and the choreographer himself, in yet another addition to that extraordinary gallery of characters whose variety no other dancer/choreographer in living memory can equal.

When considering *Gaîté Parisienne*, as many authorities and notably Cyril Beaumont tend to do, as a close relation of the choreographer's *Le Beau Danube*, it must be remembered that nearly fifteen years separate the two works, and that the attitudes of any 29-year-old are likely to alter radically by the time he reaches age 43. To complain that the later ballet does not embody the romantic attitudes which illuminated the earlier one is to bemoan the passage of time, a fruitless effort in any sphere but in none so fruitless as the sphere of art. In the case of this particular work of art, also, the choreographer was not in the slightest degree concerned with the objectives of *Le Beau Danube*, which told a sweet little story about two young lovers separated and reunited. The aim of *Gaîté Parisienne* was

***Gaîté Parisienne*, with Léonide Massine and Mia Slavenska, Ballet Russe de Monte Carlo (performing as Covent Garden Ballet Russe), London, 1939**

to create an ensemble work of vigour and vitality with opportunities for character dancing, with plenty of style and humour, taking place in a totally unreal world (in contrast to the reality of the scene in the park of *Le Beau Danube*)—the world of the Paris nightclub which only ever existed in the imagination of the tourist. Winterhalter may have been in the mind of Etienne de Beaumont when he put the idea to Massine, but what in fact emerged in the eventual stage picture was more an echo of Toulouse Lautrec as caricaturist (though the performers retained the charming faces of the conventional ballet dancer, as against the savage exaggerations and distortions of Lautrec's pictures of Paris night life).

The choreographic texture of *Gaîté* relates closely to the flowing conventionalities of the musical accompaniment; the ensembles, as ever with a Massine ballet, direct the eye of the spectator unerringly in the right direction and the work given to the soloists is always worth looking at, if only as a demonstration of the choreographer's ability to show dancers to an audience at their best, without pandering to any weaknesses.

In view of the fact that Massine, during his career as part of the Diaghilev ensemble and also subsequently, had the most impressive record of any choreographer of collaboration with great contemporary artists (Benois, Picasso, Chagall, Dali, Dufy, Gontcharova, Derain, Matisse, Bérard, Bakst, Tchelitchev, Laurencin, Braque, de Chirico, and many others beside), it does seem doubly insulting that when American Ballet Theatre revived *Gaîté Parisienne* in 1988, this choreographer's work of all others should have been the recipient of some of the most hideously vulgar and inappropriate costumes ever to have been perpetrated upon the ballet stage. Despite this, the ballet still held the interest of the audience and one can only hope that it may be retained in the repertoire—but re-dressed with the taste, style, and chic brought to its first production by the designs of the ballet's original begetter, Count Etienne de Beaumont.

—Janet Sinclair

---

## GALA PERFORMANCE

**Choreography:** Antony Tudor
**Music:** Sergei Prokofiev
**Design:** Hugh Stevenson (scenery and costumes)
**Libretto:** Antony Tudor
**First Production:** London Ballet, Toynbee Hall Theatre, London, 5 December 1938
**Principal Dancers:** Peggy van Praagh (La Reine de la danse, from Moscow), Maude Lloyd (La Déesse de la danse, from Milan), Gerd Larsen (La Fille de Terpsichore, from Paris), Antony Tudor, Guy Massey, and Hugh Laing (Cavaliers)

**Other productions include:** Ballet Rambert (restaged Tudor); London, 28 June 1940. Ballet Theatre (restaged and revised Tudor; design Nicolas de Molas), with Nora Kaye (La Reine de la danse), Nana Gollner (La Déesse de la danse), Karen Conrad (La Fille de Terpsichore), Antony Tudor, Hugh Laing (Cavaliers); New York, 11 February 1941. National Ballet of Canada (design Kay Ambrose); Ottawa, 18 November 1953. German Opera Ballet; Berlin, 12 October 1963. Royal Danish Ballet; Copenhagen, 9 December 1970. Australian Ballet (staged Sallie Wilson); Melbourne, 1990.

### PUBLICATIONS

Beaumont, Cyril, *Supplement to Complete Book of Ballets*, London, 1945
Menuhin, Diana, "The Varying Moods of Tudor", *Dance and Dancers* (London), July 1955
Percival, John, *Antony Tudor: A Young Man's Ballets*, Dance Perspectives 17, New York, 1963
Balanchine, George, with Mason, Francis, *Balanchine's Complete Stories of the Great Ballets*, Garden City, N.Y., 1977
Denby, Edwin, *Dance Writings*, edited by Robert Cornfield and William Mackay, New York, 1986
Clarke, Mary, "Rambert in Wartime", *Dancing Times* (London), July 1990
Perlmutter, Donna, *Shadowplay: The Life of Antony Tudor*, London, 1991
Merrett, Sue, "*Gala Performance*", *Dancing Times* (London), July 1992

* * *

Tudor made *Gala Performance* ballet for his own young company, the London Ballet, which gave fortnightly performances at the Toynbee Hall in London during 1938 and 1939. He felt that a classical ballet was required for the repertoire, but for a small company, with few experienced or truly accomplished dancers, a real nineteenth-century "classic" was out of the question. Clearly, in order to bring off a successful parody, which *Gala Performance* is, a high technical achievement was essential in the principals, but not in the corps, whose very amateurishness could add to the authentic flavour of this ballet. Tudor's principal dancers, Maude Lloyd, Peggy van Praagh, and Gerd Larsen, were used intelligently, their individual strengths exploited variously—just as the nineteenth-century ballerinas he sought to portray would have insisted, of course. There was a lack of proficient male dancers in the 1930s, but the cavaliers in *Gala Performance* are required to do little beyond supporting the ballerinas, with a small breathing space now and then.

The ballet is in two scenes. The first is backstage before a gala performance; warming up and last-minute practising are going on, and the star ballerinas themselves demonstrate their various claims to superiority by dictating imperiously to the conductor, flying about fluffily, or being oppressive to the dresser, generally exacting homage everywhere. The second scene is the performance itself, with the three stars demonstrating their individual skills and vying for audience acclaim.

The theme of the ballet, then, is ballet itself; its traditions are reflected in the nineteenth-century spectacle and in the three important national "schools" represented. The three ballerinas represent Moscow ("La Reine de la danse"), Paris ("La Fille de Terpsichore"), and Milan ("La Déesse de la danse"). The supremacy of the Ballerina, and of technique above all else, to no other end than display is perfectly demonstrated and sent up. We are shown the egotism of ballerinas, their idiosyncrasies, mannerisms, selfishness, and complete disregard for anything except their own glory and acclaim.

It is comic because of the subtle parody of both national styles and temperament; satiric because of the fact that it illustrates all that was weak and of small worth in nineteenth-century ballet—particularly through the individual characters portrayed, who, by virtue of their iron rule over all other things, are debasing the very art which they profess to serve. There are petty cruelties, such as the small but stinging slap to the hand of the dresser who allows concentration on the ballerina to falter for a moment; and there is essentially a complete lack of regard

*Gala Performance*, **performed by Ballet Rambert, London, 1938**

or consideration for any other person, be he or she conductor, dresser, partner, or coryphée.

Edwin Denby wrote of this ballet: "... Tudor invents a ballet style never seen elsewhere, but quite recognizable". Tudor's "invented" style exploits not only the movement characteristics of a certain type of nineteenth-century ballet and ballerina, but also the structural aspects. The ballerinas' solos are central, naturally, and all else in the second scene serves merely as a setting for these. Group tableaux are elaborate and extravagant and hilariously insecure; patterns of movement repeat, first across this diagonal, then across the other, then again, for good measure. There is no dramatic logic in the performance that is presented in the second scene; matters of theme, period, and setting are of no significance whatsoever; the ballerinas alone provide the raison d'être.

However, as so often with Tudor's ballets, the hidden agenda provides rich entertainment. The faceless coryphées of little worth are shown to have personalities of their own through little moments indicating small rivalries among themselves, as they vie for what small attention might be available; the cavaliers, a poor, downtrodden breed, are shown in their complete subservience and spinelessness as they are forced, by power of will, to kiss the hand of the glorious star, and to support their ballerinas while often being themselves partly or even wholly out of sight. One is injured during the performance, and limps stiffly offstage. One wonders, with some trepidation, what punishment may be in store for this dereliction of duty.

George Beiswanger suggested that this ballet represented an inverted manifesto of Tudor's beliefs, inasmuch as it encapsulates, with trenchant irony, all the elements of classical ballet which he intended to eschew entirely in his career. If that is true, perhaps it goes some way to explaining Tudor's growing dislike of *Gala Performance* over the years ("a lousy piece of work" he described it to Canadian students), despite its resistant popularity. Another reason would surely be the fact that it suffered much from exaggeration and over-statement in later productions, an inevitable result of larger stages, bigger audiences, and a hugely successful televisation in early 1939.

It is the small, apparently unconscious, gestures which give the real insight into the underlying drama of *Gala Performance*; the audience must feel let into the secret in a subtle way, as if each member of the audience is the only one who has noticed what is really happening under the glittering façade. This is true not only of Tudor's comedies, but also of his more serious dramatic works, such as *Jardin aux lilas* and *Pillar of Fire*; and over-statement has undoubtedly blunted the edge of a number of Tudor's ballets. All the same, *Gala Performance* has been performed with great success by the National Ballet of Canada and American Ballet Theatre, among other companies.

—Rachel S. Richardson

---

**GALEOTTI, Vincenzo**

Italian/Danish dancer, choreographer, ballet master, and teacher. Born Vincenzo Tomasselli in Florence, 5 March 1733. Studied with Gasparo Angiolini in Italy; also claimed to be a pupil of Jean Georges Noverre. Married dancer Antonia Guidi. Début as a solo dancer, Giuseppe Forti's company, Teatro San Moise, Venice, 1759; dancer, Teatro San Benedetto, 1761; possibly danced in Noverre's company, Stuttgart, 1763; first post as ballet master, Teatro San Benedetto, Venice, 1765; choreographer, Teatro Regio Ducale, Milan, 1766; ballet master, Teatro San Salvatore, Venice, 1766–67, and Teatro Regio, Turin, 1767, returning to Teatro San Benedetto, 1768; London début (dancing with wife Antonia Guidi), King's Theatre, 1769; dancer and ballet master, King's Theatre, 1770–71; returned to Italy, 1771/72; dancer and choreographer at theatres in Venice (under ballet master Angiolini), and Genoa; chosen by Pietro Scalabrini (representative sent to Italy by Copenhagen's Royal Theatre) for appointment in Denmark: ballet master and teacher, Royal Theatre, Copenhagen, 1775–1816; granted Danish citizenship, c. 1780. Died in Copenhagen, 16 December 1816.

## WORKS

1766 *Il Convitato di pietro* (*The Stone Guest*; ballet after Angiolini), Teatro Regio Ducale, Milan

1766/67 Divertissements in *Armida* (opera; mus. Traetta), Teatro San Salvatore, Venice

*Genii transformati in Piaceri ed amanti felici* (ballet), Teatro San Salvatore, Venice

1767 Dances in *Tancredi* (opera; mus. Bertoni), Teatro Regio, Turin

*Il Convitato di pietro* (ballet; mus. Gluck, arranged Le Messier), Teatro Regio, Turin

*Amore e Psiche* (*Cupid and Psyche*; mus. Le Messier), Teatro Regio, Turin

*La Fiera di Moncalieri* (*The Fair at Moncalieri*), Teatro Regio, Turin

*Il Giardino di Vaux Hall in Londra* (*Vauxhall Gardens in London*), Teatro Regio, Turin

*Siracusani festeggianti la liberazione della patria* (*Syracusans Celebrating the Liberation of their Country*), Teatro Regio, Turin

*Vendita di schiavi* (*Slave Merchant*), Teatro Regio, Turin

*Le Furie e loro seguaci* (*The Furies and their Followers*), Teatro San Salvatore, Venice

1770 Dances in *Orfeo* (opera; mus. Gluck, with additional mus. J.C. Bach), King's Theatre, London

1772/73 *La Bandiera*, Teatro San Moise, Venice

*Una Fiera*, Teatro San Moise, Venice

1774 *La Dolce Vendetta* (ballet), Genoa

*La Caccia di Enrico IV* (ballet; after Angiolini's *Il Re alla caccia*; mus. Angiolini), Genoa

1775 *Kongen paa Jagt* (*The King's Hunt*; new version of *La Caccia di Enrico IV*), Royal Theatre, Copenhagen

*Bønderne og Herrerne på Lystgaarden* (*Peasants and Masters at the Villa*; mus. Scalabrini, Schall), Royal Theatre, Copenhagen

1776 *Zigeunernes Leir* (*The Gypsies' Camp*), Royal Theatre, Copenhagen

*Slavindehandleren* (*The Slave Merchant*), Royal Theatre, Copenhagen

*Amors Søde Haevn* (*Cupid's Sweet Revenge*), Royal Theatre, Copenhagen

*Marybones Have i London* (*Marylebone Gardens in London*), Royal Theatre, Copenhagen

1777 *Den Bedragne Sofi* (*Jilted Sophy*), Royal Theatre, Copenhagen

*Den Forladte Dido* (*Dido Abandoned*, after Angiolini; mus. Angiolini), Royal Theatre, Copenhagen

*Betlersken* (*The Beggar-Woman*), Royal Theatre, Copenhagen

1778 *Kunsten Overvunden af Kaerlighed* (*Art Overcome by Love*, after Angiolini's *L'Arte vinta della natura*; mus. Angiolini), Royal Theatre, Copenhagen

*Statuen; eller, Det unyttige Hekseri* (*The Statue; or, The Vain Sorcery*), Royal Theatre, Copenhagen

1779 *Linna og Valvais* (*Linna and Valvais*), Royal Theatre, Copenhagen

*Den Aedelmodige Tyrk* (*The Noble-minded Turk*), Royal Theatre, Copenhagen

1780 *L'Orphelin de la Chine* (chor. and mus. after Angiolini), Royal Theatre, Copenhagen

*Harpespilleren* (*The Harper*), Royal Theatre, Copenhagen

*Kjaerligheds og Mistankens Magt* (*The Power of Love and Suspicion*; mus. Schall), Royal Theatre, Copenhagen

*Modehandlerinderne* (*Les Modistes*), Royal Theatre, Copenhagen

1781 *Savoyardinderne* (*Les Savoyardes*; mus. Schall), Royal Theatre, Copenhagen

*Don Juan* (mus. Gluck), Royal Theatre, Copenhagen

*Den Forraadte og Haevnede Amor* (*Cupid Betrayed and Revenged*; mus. Schall), Royal Theatre, Copenhagen

1782 *Hermann og Dolman; eller, Goddaedighed og Teknemlighed* (*Hermann and Dolman, or Charity and Gratitude*; mus. Schall), Royal Danish Theatre, Copenhagen

*Den Unventede Hjaelp* (*L'Aide insupposée*; mus. Schall), Royal Theatre, Copenhagen

*Den Mistaenkelige Kone* (*The Jealous Wife*; mus. Schall), Royal Theatre, Copenhagen

1783 *Heksemesteren og den Velgørende Fe* (*The Sorcerer and the Beneficient Nymph*), Royal Theatre, Copenhagen

*De To Elskende Beskyttede af Amor* (*The Two Lovers Protected by Cupid*), Royal Theatre, Copenhagen

1784 *Angelica og Medoro* (*Angelica and Medoro*; mus. Lolle), Royal Theatre, Copenhagen

*Den Straffede Vankundighed; eller, Kunstnernes Seir* (*Ignorance Chastised; or, The Victory of the Artists*; mus. Lolle), Royal Theatre, Copenhagen

*Amor og Psyche* (*Cupid and Psyche*; mus. Schall), Royal Theatre, Copenhagen

1785 *Laurette; eller, Den Forbedrede Forfører* (*Laurette; or, The Reformed Debaucher*; mus. Schall), Royal Theatre, Copenhagen

1786 *Amors og Balletmesterens Luner* (*The Whims of Cupid and the Ballet Master*; mus. Lolle), Royal Theatre, Copenhagen

1787 *Semiramis* (after Angiolini; mus. Darbès), Royal Theatre, Copenhagen

1788 *Vaskepigerne og Kedelflikkeren* (*The Laundry-maids and the Tinker*; mus. Schall), Royal Theatre, Copenhagen

*Afguden på Ceylon* (*The Idol in Ceylon*; mus. Schall), Royal Theatre, Copenhagen

*Hververen* (*The Recruiter*; mus. Schall), Royal Theatre, Copenhagen

1789 Dances in *Aline, reine de Golconde* (opera; mus. Schulz), Royal Theatre, Copenhagen

1790 *Den Forstilte Døve* (*The Man Pretending to be Deaf*), Royal Theatre, Copenhagen

1791 *Fanden er Løs* (*The Devil is Loose*, later *The Metamorphosis; or, the Devil is Loose*; mus. Schall), Royal Theatre,

Copenhagen
1792 Dances in *Kinafarene* (*The China Travellers*, opera; mus. Schall), Royal Theatre, Copenhagen
*Telemak på Calypsos O* (*Telemachus on the Isle of Calypso*, opera-ballet; mus. Ahlefeldt), Royal Theatre, Copenhagen
1793 *La Fiera d'Amsterdam*, Teatro La Fenice, Venice
1795 *Machinisten* (*Le Machiniste*; mus. Schall), Royal Theatre, Copenhagen
1796 *Den Vaegelsindede; eller, Det Forstyrrede Maleri* (*Inconstancy; or, The Destroyed Painting*; mus. Schall), Royal Theatre, Copenhagen
1797 *Annette og Lubin* (*Annette and Lubin*; mus. Schall), Royal Theatre, Copenhagen
1801 *Lagertha* (tragic pantomime; mus. Schall), Royal Theatre, Copenhagen
1802 *Biergbeboerne; eller, Börnene og Speilet* (*The Mountaineers; or, The Children and the Mirror*; mus. Schall), Royal Theatre, Copenhagen
*Nina; eller, Den Vanvittige af Kierlighed* (*Nina; ou, La Folle par amour*; mus. Schall), Royal Theatre, Copenhagen
1804 *Inez de Castro* (pantomime ballet; mus. Schall), Royal Theatre, Copenhagen
1806 *Pantomimisk Prolog* (*Pantomimic Prologue*, in Celebration of the King's and Crown Prince's Birthdays; mus. Schall), Royal Theatre, Copenhagen
1808 *Rolf Blaaskiaeg* (*Bluebeard*; mus. Schall), Royal Theatre, Copenhagen
1810 *Drømmen* (*The Dream*, pantomimic prologue; mus. Schall), Royal Theatre, Copenhagen
1811 *Romeo og Giulietta* (*Romeo and Juliet*; mus. Schall), Royal Theatre, Copenhagen
*Koromanien; eller, Dansesygen* (*Choromania; or, The Dancing Madness*; mus. Schall), Royal Theatre, Copenhagen
1812 Dances in *Faruk* (opera; mus. Weyse), Royal Theatre, Copenhagen
1813 Dances in *Alma og Elfride; eller, Skoven ved Hermanstad* (*La Forêt d'Hermanstad; ou, La Fausse Épouse*, opera; mus. Schall), Royal Theatre, Copenhagen
1814 Dances in *Hytten i Schwarzwald* (*The Hut in the Black Forest*, opera; mus. Braun), Royal Theatre, Copenhagen
1816 *Macbeth* (mus. Schall), Royal Theatre, Copenhagen

**Other works include:** dances in *Herman von Unna* (drama; mus. Vogler), *Peters Bryllup* (*Peter's Wedding*; singspiel, or "song-play"; mus Schultz), *Aften* (*The Evening*; singspiel; mus. Schall), *Eropolis* (lyrical drama; mus. Kunzen), *Danekvinderne* (*The Estimable Woman*; drama; mus. Kunzen), *Gyrithe; eller, Danmarks Frelse* (*Gyrithe; or, The Rescue of Denmark*; drama; mus. Kunzen), *Kaerlighed på Landet* (*Rustic Love*; singspiel; mus. Kunzen), *Azemia; eller, De Vilde* (*Azémia; ou, Les Sauvages*; singspiel; mus. d'Alayrac), *Soliman den Anden* (*Soliman II; ou, Les Trois Sultanes*, comedy; mus. Sarti, Walther).

## PUBLICATIONS

Kragh-Jacobsen, Svend, *The Royal Danish Ballet: An Old Tradition and a Living Present*, London, 1955
Beaumont, Cyril, *Ballets Past and Present*, London, 1955
Fog, Dan, *The Royal Danish Ballet, 1760–1958, and August Bournonville*, Copenhagen, 1961
Winter, Marian Hannah, *The Pre-Romantic Ballet*, London, 1974

* * *

Vincenzo Galeotti is usually considered the father of Danish ballet, despite his Italian ancestry. A Florentine, he left his medical studies to train as a dancer under Gasparo Angiolini, a leading figure in the development of the *ballet d'action*.

By 1759 Galeotti was a featured dancer at the Teatro San Moise in Venice. Early in his career, he danced in many European centres, but he frequently returned to his beloved Venice, where he progressed swiftly to the rank of principal dancer and ballet master. While directing his own company at Venice's Teatro Benedetto, he began mounting works, usually following the conventional staging of the period.

Around 1763 he met his future wife, Antonia Guidi, who had danced in Jean Georges Noverre's famous Stuttgart Company. Some seven years later, the couple were engaged at the King's Theatre in London, where Galeotti was featured dancer and ballet master and his wife was a dancer. He continued his choreographic work there, staging several works, including Gluck's *Orfeo*, as well as numerous ballet divertissements. Returning to Venice, again as ballet master at the San Moise, he embarked on a serious and intensive study of Angiolini's ballets and the principles of his *ballet d'action*, since Angiolini was also working in Venice.

In 1775, his future was set when he was invited by Pietro Scalabrini, music conductor at the Danish court, to go to Copenhagen as ballet master. By then in his forties, Galeotti had already had a satisfying career on the continent, but this new position inspired him to greater heights. His responsibilities were numerous, since he was hired to perform, teach corps de ballet dancers and soloists, and look after the repertory. Since the Danes were accustomed to a diet of short ballet divertissements on mythological and antique subjects, and popular dances from different nations, they found Galeotti's initial works in Angiolini's *ballet d'action* style both innovative and exciting. Galeotti thrived in his new environment and became a prolific choreographer.

Shortly after his wife's death in 1780, Galeotti was granted Danish citizenship. He found solace in his work and in his Danish companions. Although he went through a fallow period in his final years, he was stirred to new heights as he found stimulation in new themes. His masterpiece *Lagertha* was the first ballet on a Nordic theme, and his *Romeo and Juliet* received considerable praise, with one critic commenting that "It is not only in the solo parts that the emotions are touched. The large company is divided into sections which each express sorrow, joy, surprise, etc. in different nuances at the same time as they form picturesque groupings."

Galeotti's accomplishments were substantial. As a dancer, he was praised for his elegant and noble manner and his skills in mime. He danced until the ripe old age of 77, making his last appearance as Friar Lawrence. As a teacher, he was responsible for raising technical standards by insisting that all company dancers take his class; this ensured a uniformity of style which led eventually to the founding of the Royal Danish Ballet.

He popularized dance in Denmark by creating an extensive repertory of over 30 ballets. Although his first ballets were strongly influenced by Noverre's and Angiolini's theories, in time he diverged from their ideas to experiment with various styles and to develop his own form. An intelligent and educated man, he frequently selected literary themes from the works of Voltaire and Shakespeare, but he was able to rework them to give them a fresh and original feel. His ballets were always built on a strong story line, with good characterization developed through pantomime. He was particularly successful with crowd scenes, which one reviewer praised for their "rhythmic precision and kaleidoscopic symmetry". An unusual feature was the incorporation of choral singing into several of his ballets. Although his successors, Antoine and August Bournonville, found his work old-fashioned, his ballets were very popular during his own lifetime.

Today, Galeotti's only surviving ballet is *The Whims of Cupid and the Ballet Master*. This charming ballet was not considered memorable by Galeotti himself; it was merely a gentle comic work consisting of a suite of national character dances. But he had the innovative idea of linking the dances together through a small mischievous Cupid who blindfolded the lovers who came to his temple and then united the wrong ones, which led to a finale of "great confusion". Today, this piece is the oldest extant work in the ballet repertory, thus ensuring that Galeotti will be remembered.

—Mary Jane Warner

---

## GARDEL, Maximilien

French dancer, choreographer, and ballet master. Born Maximilien Léopold Philippe Joseph Gardel, son of ballet master Claude Gardel, in Mannheim, 18 December 1741. Studied at the Académie royale de musique (Paris Opéra), from 1755. Dancer, Paris Opéra, from 1755; official début, 1759; danseur seul by 1764/65; reputedly first dancer to appear without mask and wig (as Apollo in *Castor et Pollux*), 1772; appointed assistant maître de ballet, with Jean Dauberval, to maître de ballet Vestris, 1773; maître de ballet, Paris Opéra, replacing Noverre, 1781; also leading teacher: students include younger brother Pierre Gardel (b. 1758), premier danseur of the Paris Opéra; received pension from the King as Maître des ballets de la cour, 1782. Died in Paris, 11 March 1787.

**Pierre Gardel, from *Costumes et Annales des Grands Théâtres de Paris*, 1786**

### ROLES

1760 Chaconne in *Dardanus* (tragédie-lyrique; mus. Rameau, chor. G. Vestris), Opéra, Paris
- Dancer in *Ismène* (pastorale; mus. Rébel, Francoeur), Opéra, Paris
- Dancer (cr) in *Le Prince de Noisy* (ballet; mus. Rébel, Francoeur), Opéra, Paris
- Dancer in *Canente* (tragédie-lyrique; new mus. Dauvergne), Opéra, Paris

1761 Dancer in *Armide* (tragédie-lyrique; mus. Lully), Opéra, Paris
- Dancer in *Hercule mourant* (tragédie-lyrique; mus. Dauvergne), Opéra, Paris
- Dancer in *Jephté* (tragédie-lyrique; mus. Monteclair), Opéra, Paris
- Dancer in *Zaïs* (ballet-héroïque; mus. Rameau), Opéra, Paris

1762 Dancer in *Acis et Galathée* (pastorale-héroïque; mus. Lully), Opéra, Paris
- Dancer in *Les Fêtes grecques et romaines* (ballet-héroïque; mus. de Blamont), Opéra, Paris
- Dancer in *La Guirlande* (opéra-ballet; mus. Rameau), Opéra, Paris
- Dancer in *Iphigénie en Tauride* (tragédie-lyrique; mus. Desmarets, Campra, Berton), Opéra, Paris
- Dancer (cr) in *L'Opéra de société* (ballet; mus. Giraud), Opéra, Paris

1763 Dancer (cr) in *Polyxène* (tragédie-lyrique; mus. Dauvergne), Opéra, Paris
- Dancer in *Orfeo ed Euridice* (opéra; mus. Gluck, chor. Noverre), Hoftheater, Stuttgart

1764 Dancer in *Castor et Pollux* (tragédie-lyrique; mus. Rameau), Opéra, Paris
- Dancer in *Les Fêtes d'Hébé; ou, Les Talents lyriques* (ballet; mus. Rameau), Opéra, Paris
- Dancer in *Naïs, opéra pour la paix* (ballet-héroïque; mus. Rameau), Opéra, Paris
- Dancer in *Tancrède* (tragédie-lyrique; mus. Campra), Opéra, Paris

1765 Dancer in *Le Devin du village* (intermède; mus. Rousseau), Opéra, Paris
- Dancer in *Les Fêtes d'Hymen et de l'Amour* (ballet-héroïque; mus. Rameau), Opéra, Paris
- Dancer in *Thésée* (tragédie-lyrique; mus. Lully, chor. Laval, father and son), Opéra, Paris

1766 L'Amant volage (cr) in *Aline, reine de Golconde* (ballet-héroïque; mus. Monsigny), Opéra, Paris
- Dancer in *Les Fêtes lyriques* (fragments from various ballets), Opéra, Paris
- Un Chasseur, Adonis (cr) in *Sylvie* (ballet; mus. Berton, Trial), Opéra, Paris
- Un Gnome in *Zélindor, roi des sylphes* (ballet; mus. Rebel, Francoeur), Opéra, Paris

1767 Dancer in *Le Carnaval du Parnasse* (opéra-ballet; mus. Mondonville), Opéra, Paris
Dancer in *Le Feu* and *La Terre* (acts from *Les Eléments*, ballet; mus. Mouret), Opéra, Paris
Dancer (cr) in *Ernelinde* (tragédie-lyrique; mus. Philidor), Opéra, Paris
Un Berger in *Hippolyte et Aricie* (tragédie-lyrique; mus. Rameau), Opéra, Paris
Dancer (cr) in *Théonis* (pastorale; mus. Berton, Trial), Opéra, Paris
1768 Dancer in *Titon et l'Aurore* (pastorale; mus. Mondonville), Opéra, Paris
Dancer in *La Vénitienne* (ballet; mus. Dauvergne), Opéra, Paris
Dancer in *Daphnis et Alcimadure* (pastorale; mus. Mondonville), Opéra, Paris
1769 Oracle in *Zaïs* (ballet-héroïque; mus. Rameau), Opéra, Paris
Dancer in *Enée et Lavinie* (tragédie-lyrique; new mus. Dauvergne), Opéra, Paris
Dancer in *Erigone* (act from *Les Fêtes de Paphos*, ballet; mus. Mondonville), Opéra, Paris
1770 Dancer in *Hylas et Zélis* (pastorale; mus. Bury), Opéra, Paris
Dancer in *Zaïde, reine de Grenade* (ballet; mus. Royer), Opéra, Paris
Dancer in *Zoroastre* (tragédie-lyrique; mus. Rameau), Opéra, Paris
1771 Dancer in *Alcione* (tragédie-lyrique; mus. Marais), Opéra, Paris
Le Seigneur (cr) in *La Cinquantaine* (pastorale; mus. Laborde), Opéra, Paris
Dancer (cr) in *Ismène et Ismènias* (tragédie-lyrique; mus. Laborde), Opéra, Paris
Un Esprit terrestre in *Pyrame et Thisbé* (tragédie-lyrique; mus. Rebel, Francoeur), Opéra, Paris
1772 Apollo in *Castor et Pollux* (tragédie-lyrique; mus. Rameau), Opéra, Paris
Dancer in *Adèle de Ponthieu* (tragédie-lyrique; mus. Berton, Laborde), Opéra, Paris
Dancer (cr) in *Eglé* (ballet; mus. Lagarde), Opéra, Paris
Dancer in *Pygmalion* (entrée from *Le Triomphe des arts*, ballet; mus. La Barre, Rameau), Opéra, Paris
1773 Chaconne (cr) in *L'Union de l'amour et des arts* (opéra-ballet; mus. Floquet), Opéra, Paris
Dancer in *Les Sauvages* (ballet; mus. Rameau), Opéra, Paris
1774 Dancer (cr) in *Azolan; ou, Le Serment indiscret* (ballet-héroïque; mus. Floquet), Opéra, Paris
Dancer (cr) in *Orphée et Eurydice* (tragédie-lyrique, Paris version; mus. Gluck, chor. Noverre), Opéra, Paris
Dancer (cr) in *Sabinus* (tragédie-lyrique; mus. Gossec), Opéra, Paris
Dancer (cr) in *Iphigénie en Aulide* (tragédie-lyrique; mus. Gluck, chor. Noverre), Opéra, Paris
1775 Dancer (cr) in *Alexis et Daphné* (pastorale; mus. Gossec), Opéra, Paris
Dancer (cr) in *Cythère assiégée* (ballet; mus. Gluck, ballet mus. Berton), Opéra, Paris
1776 Dancer (cr) in *Alceste* (Paris version: tragédie-lyrique; mus. Gluck, chor. Noverre), Opéra, Paris
Alexandre (cr) in *Apelles et Campaspe* (ballet, Opéra version; Noverre), Opéra, Paris
Dancer in *Médée et Jason* (ballet; G. Vestris after Noverre), Opéra, Paris
1777 Vieil Horace (cr) in *Les Horaces* (ballet; Noverre), Opéra, Paris
Dancer (cr) in *Armide* (tragédie-lyrique; mus. Gluck, chor. Noverre), Opéra, Paris
1778 Alain, fils de M. Subtil (cr) in *La Chercheuse d'esprit* (ballet; also chor.), Opéra, Paris
1779 Dancer (cr) in *Amadis de Gaule* (tragédie-lyrique; new mus. J.C. Bach), Opéra, Paris

## WORKS

1777 *La Chercheuse d'esprit* (after comedy by Favart), Court Theatre, Versailles (restaged Paris Opéra, 1778)
*Ninette à la cour* (mus. Ciampi, Duni), Court Theatre, Choisy (restaged Paris Opéra, 1778)
1778 *Phaon* (opéra-lyrique; mus. Piccini), Court Theatre, Choisy
1779 *Mirza et Lindor* (mus. Gossec), Opéra, Paris
1780 Dances in *Le Seigneur bienfaisant* (comédie-lyrique, with Dauberval, Noverre; mus. Floquet), Opéra, Paris
1781 *La Fête de Mirza* (mus. Gossec, Grétry), Opéra, Paris
1782 Dances in *L'Embarras de richesses* (opéra-comique; mus. Grétry), Opéra, Paris
1783 Dances in *Renaud* (tragédie-lyrique; mus. Sacchini), Opéra, Paris
*La Rosière*, Opéra, Paris
1784 *L'Oracle*, Opéra, Paris
Dances in *La Caravane du Caire* (opera; mus. Grétry), Opéra, Paris
Dances in *Diane et Endymion* (opera; mus. Piccinni), Opéra, Paris
1785 *Le Premier Navigateur; ou, Le Pouvoir de l'amour* (mus. Grétry), Opéra, Paris
Dances in *Panurge dans l'île des lanternes* (opera; mus. Grétry), Opéra, Paris
1786 Dances in *Oedipe à Colone* (tragédie-lyrique; mus. Sacchini), Court Theatre, Versailles
Dances in *Phèdre* (tragédie-lyrique; mus. Lemoyne), Opéra, Paris
*Les Sauvages; ou, Le Pouvoir de la danse* (with P. Gardel), Opéra, Paris
*Le Déserteur* (mus. Miller), Court Theatre, Fountainebleau (restaged Paris Opéra, 1788)
1786/87 *Le Coq au village* (after comedy by Favart), Opéra, Paris
*Le Pied de Boeuf* (also mus.), Opéra, Paris

## PUBLICATIONS


Despréaux, J.-E., *Mes passe-temps: chansons suivies de l'art de la danse*, Paris, 1806

Noverre, Jean-Georges, *Lettres sur les arts imitateurs*, Paris, 1807

Baron, A., *Lettres entretiens sur la danse*, Paris, 1824

Castil-Blaze, François Henri Joseph, *La Danse et les ballets depuis Bacchus jusqu'à Mlle. Taglioni*, Paris, 1832

Saint-Léon, Arthur, *La Stenochorégraphie*, Paris, 1852

Saint-Léon, Arthur, *Portraits et biographies des plus célèbres maîtres des ballets et chorégraphes, anciens et nouveaux de l'école franqise et italien*, Paris, 1852

Castil-Blaze, *L'Académie impériale de musique*, Paris, 1855

Campardon, Émile, *L'Académie royale de musique au XVIIIe siècle*, Paris, 1884

Guest, Ivor, *The Romantic Ballet in Paris*, London, 1966

Winter, Marian Hannah, *The Pre-Romantic Ballet*, London, 1974

Maximilien Gardel made his Opéra début during the reign of Louis XIV. It was an exciting time in ballet, for there were bold new ideas in the air, ideas that aimed to transform ballet from a non-dramatic divertissement into a serious story-telling art. Only a year after Gardel's début, Jean-Georges Noverre published *Lettres sur la danse* (1760), a book that quickly became the definitive work on the *ballet d'action*. The young Maximilien Gardel was impressed with Noverre's ideas, but did not get a chance to demonstrate his support for some time; the Opéra was an institution rooted in tradition, and was not eager to change. Nevertheless, in 1772 Gardel was asked to replace Gaetan Vestris in *Castor et Pollux*. He agreed on the condition that he appear without a mask and heavy wig, both impediments to the expression of human feeling in action ballets. Three years later, in 1775, Gardel submitted to the Opéra administration a scenario for a ballet, *L'Avenement de Titus à L'Empire*, in which he included a "Preliminary Discourse" supporting *ballet d'action*. Like Noverre he believed that ballet masters could achieve the status of poets, painters, musicians, and the most celebrated artists if they studied the human passions and made them the focus of ballets. "*Ballet d'action*", he writes, "must be the animated painter of nature; in fact, nothing can better express the different feelings of the soul, than the face . . .". Gardel also followed Noverre's lead in his belief that dramatic continuity was all-important. "Unity of action", he writes, "a clear exposition, character and plot development which lead to interest and which result in a surprising denouement; these are the rules demanded by *Ballet d'action* . . .".

Noverre insisted that if ballet was to achieve the high respect it deserved, it had to draw its subjects from the most heroic classical sources. His *Médée et Jason* and *Les Horaces* are among his most ambitious works. But Maximilien Gardel was not so strict nor as uncompromising as Noverre. When he became ballet master with Jean Dauberval in 1781, he went to the popular Rococo comic operas of the period for his stories. He knew that, as much as audiences admired the grand and noble classics, they enjoyed the lighter sentimental tales of love and adventure better. Thus he made his name with works like *La Rosière* (1783) and *Le Déserteur* (first produced in 1786 at Fontainebleau, and staged in 1788 at the Opéra).

It is curious that Gardel is said to have been a key participant in the intrigue to get rid of Noverre, who was ballet master at the Opéra from 1776 to 1781, for not only did he admire Noverre's theories, but he wrote in *L'Avenement de Titus* that he was sorry that problems with the Opéra had forced the master to leave earlier in his career. At a time when everyone appears to have been involved in political manoeuvring against everyone else, it is difficult to assess exactly what role Maximilien Gardel played in Noverre's fall from power in 1781. Whatever the case, Gardel's own departure from the Opéra was far more dramatic than Noverre's. In 1787 he suffered a minor cut to his foot. It became infected, and he died. Pierre, his younger brother, took over the post of chief ballet master. He too, would show a willingness to bend the rules of *ballet d'action* in order to realize his vision.

—John Chapman

---

**GARDEL, Pierre**

French dancer, choreographer, ballet master, and teacher. Born Pierre Gabriel Gardel in Nancy, son of ballet master Claude Gardel and brother of dancer and choreographer Maximilien Gardel, 4 February 1758. Studied at the school of L'Académie royale de musique (Paris Opéra) in 1771; pupil of Maximilien Gardel. Married (1) dancer Anne-Jacqueline Coulon; (2) dancer Marie-Elisabeth-Anne Boubert, known as Mlle. Miller, 1795. Dancing début at the Opéra, 1772 (some sources say 1774), soon becoming leading dancer; promoted to premier danseur noble, 1780; leading dancer, Noverre's company at King's Theatre, London, 1781–82; assistant to maître de ballet en chef Maximilien Gardel, Paris Opéra, from 1783, choreographing first ballet, 1784; maître de ballet en chef (on Maximilien's death), from 1787; retired from performing, 1795, and from Opéra in 1829; received royal pension as dancer of ballets de la cour, 1785. Died in Paris, 18 October 1840.

**ROLES**

1771 Le Fils du Seigneur (cr) in *La Cinquantaine* (pastorale; mus. Laborde), Opéra, Paris

1772 Dancer in *Castor et Pollux* (tragédie-lyrique; mus. Rameau), Opéra, Paris

1773 Dancer (cr) in *L'Union de l'amour et des arts* (ballet; mus. Floquet), Opéra, Paris

1774 Dancer (cr) in *Iphigénie en Aulide* (tragédie-lyrique; mus. Gluck, chor. Noverre), Opéra, Paris

Dancer (cr) in *Azolan: ou, Le Serment indiscret* (ballet; mus. Floquet), Opéra, Paris

Dancer (cr) in *Orphée et Eurydice* (tragédie-lyrique, Paris version; mus. Gluck, chor. Noverre), Opéra, Paris

Dancer (cr) in *Sabinus* (tragédie-lyrique; mus. Gossec), Opéra, Paris

1775 Dancer (cr) in *Céphale et Procris* (tragédie-lyrique; mus. Grétry), Opéra, Paris

Dancer (cr) in *Philémon et Baucis* (ballet; mus. Gossec), Opéra, Paris

1776 Un Suivant de la fortune in *Les Romans* (ballet; mus. Nieil, Cambini), Opéra, Paris

1778 M. Narquois, savant (cr) in *La Chercheuse d'esprit* (ballet; M. Gardel), Opéra, Paris

1779 Lindor (cr) in *Mirza et Lindor* (ballet; M. Gardel), Opéra, Paris

1781 Principal dancer (cr) in *A Divertissement Dance* (Noverre), King's Theatre, London

Alphonso (cr) in *Les Amants réunis* (Noverre), King's Theatre, London

Dancer in *Les Petits Riens* (revival; Noverre), King's Theatre, London

Renaud (cr) in *Rinaldo e Armida* (Noverre), King's Theatre, London

1782 Admetus (cr) in *Le Triomphe d'amour conjugal* (Noverre), King's Theatre, London

Prince of Wales Minuet, Divertissement in *A Masked Ball* (Noverre), King's Theatre, London

Leading role in *La Rosière de Salency* (revival; Noverre), King's Theatre, London

Principal dancer in *Mirsa* (M. and P. Gardel), King's Theatre, London

Alexander in *Apelles and Campaspe; or, The Generosity of Alexander the Great* (revival; Noverre), King's Theatre, London

Dancer (cr) in *Adela of Ponthieu* (*Adèle de Ponthieu*; Noverre), King's Theatre, London

Jason in *Medea and Jason* (revival; Noverre), King's Theatre, London

1783 Un Prêtre du temple (cr) in *Alexandre aux Indes* (tragédie-lyrique; mus. Mireaux), Opéra, Paris

Le Seigneur (cr) in *La Rosière* (ballet; M. Gardel), Opéra, Paris

1784 Dancer (cr) in *La Caravane du Caire* (opera; mus. Grétry, chor. M. Gardel), Opéra, Paris

Dancer (cr) in *Tibulle* (act from *Les Fêtes grecques et romaines,* ballet-héroïque; new mus. Mlle Beaumesnil), Opéra, Paris

1785 Dancer (cr) in *Panurge dans l'île des lanternes* (opera; mus. Grétry, chor. M. Gardel), Opéra, Paris

Dancer (cr) in *Pizarre* (tragédie-lyrique; mus. Candeille), Opéra, Paris

Dancer (cr) in *Pénélope* (tragédie-lyrique; mus. Piccini), Opéra, Paris

1786 Dancer (cr) in *Phèdre* (tragédie-lyrique; mus. Lemoyne, chor. M. Gardel), Opéra, Paris

Dancer in *Roland* (tragédie-lyrique; new mus. Piccini), Opéra, Paris

Dancer (cr) in *Rosine* (opera; mus. Gossec), Opéra, Paris

Dancer (cr) in *Les Sauvages* (ballet; also chor. with M. Gardel), Opéra, Paris

1787 Dancer (cr) in *Alcindor* (opera; mus. Dézaides), Opéra, Paris

Dancer (cr) in *Oedipe à Colone* (tragédie-lyrique; mus. Sacchini), Opéra, Paris

1788 Dancer (cr) in *Amphitryon* (opera; mus. Grétry, chor. P. Gardel), Opéra, Paris

Dancer in *Arvire et Evélina* (opera; mus. Sacchini), Opéra, Paris

Dancer (cr) in *Démophon* (tragédie-lyrique; mus. Cherubini), Opéra, Paris

Title role (cr) in *Le Déserteur* (ballet; M. Gardel), Opéra, Paris

Dancer in *La Toison d'or; ou, Médée à Colchos* (tragédie-lyrique; mus. Vogel), Opéra, Paris

Dancer (cr) in *New Ballet* (Noverre), King's Theatre, London

Pas de quatre from *Panurge* (opera; chor. A. Vestris), King's Theatre, London

1789 Dancer (cr) in *Aspasie* (opera; mus. Grétry), Opéra, Paris

Dancer (cr) in *Démophon* (tragédie-lyrique; mus. Vogel), Opéra, Paris

Dancer (cr) in *Les Prétendus* (opera; mus. Lemoyne), Opéra, Paris

1790 Title role (cr) in *Télémaque dans l'île de Calypso* (ballet; also chor.), Opéra, Paris

Apollon (cr) in *Psyché* (ballet; also chor.), Opéra, Paris

1800 Principal dancer (cr) in *La Dansomanie* (also chor.), Opéra, Paris

## WORKS

1784 Dances in *Dardanus* (tragédie-lyrique; mus. Sacchini), Opéra, Paris

1786 *Les Sauvages; ou, Le Pouvoir de la danse* (with M. Gardel), Opéra, Paris

1787 Dances in *Tarare* (opera; mus. Salieri), Opéra, Paris

1788 Dances in *Amphitryon* (opera; mus. Grétry), Opéra, Paris

Dances in *Démophon* (tragédie-lyrique; mus. Cherubini), Opéra, Paris

1789 Dances in *Aspasie* (opera; mus. Grétry), Opéra, Paris

1790 *Télémaque* (mus. Miller), Opéra, Paris

*Psyché* (mus. Miller), Opéra, Paris

1791 *Bacchus et Ariane* (mus. Rochefort), Opéra, Paris

1793 *Le Jugement de Pâris* (mus. Haydn, Méhul, Pleyel), Opéra, Paris

*Fête pour l'inauguration des bustes de Marat et Le Peletieu* ("lyric scene"; mus. Gluck, Gossec, Philidor), Opéra Boulevard, Paris

1800 *La Dansomanie* (mus. Méhul), Opéra, Paris

1802 *Le Retour de Zéphire* (mus. Steibelt), Opéra, Paris

1803 *Daphnis et Pandore; ou, La Vengeance de l'amour* (mus. Mehul), Opéra, Paris

Dances in *Anacréon; ou, L'Amour fugitif* (opera; mus. Cherubini), Opéra, Paris

1804 *Une Demi-heure de caprice,* Opéra, Paris

*Achille à Scyros* (mus. Cherubini), Opéra, Paris

1805 Dances in *Don Giovanni* (opéra; mus. Mozart), Opéra, Paris

1806 *Paul et Virginie* (mus. Kreutzer), Court Theatre, Saint-Cloud (also performed at Opéra, Paris, 1806)

1807 Dances in *Vestale* (opera; mus. Spontini), Opéra, Paris

1808 *Vénus et Adonis* (mus. Lefebvre), Court Theatre, Saint-Cloud

*Alexandre chez Apelles* (mus. Catel), Opéra, Paris

Dances in *Fernando Cortez* (opera; mus. Spontini), Opéra, Paris

1809 *La Fête de Mars* (mus. Kreutzer), Opéra, Paris

1810 *Vertumne et Pomone* (mus. Lefebvre), Opéra, Paris

*Persée et Andromède* (mus. Méhul), Opéra, Paris

1812 *L'Enfant prodigue* (mus. Berton), Opéra, Paris

1813 Dances in *Les Abencérages* (opera; mus. Cherubini), Opéra, Paris

1814 *Le Retour des lys* (mus. Persuis), Opéra, Paris

1815 *L'Heureux Retour* (with Milon; mus. Persuis, Berton, Kreutzer), Opéra, Paris

1817 *Les Fiancés de Caserte; ou, L'Echange des roses* (with Milon; mus. Dugazon), Opéra, Paris

1818 *Proserpine* (mus. Schneitzhoeffer), Opéra, Paris

*Zirphile; ou, Cent Ans en un jour* (opéra-ballet; mus. Lefebvre), Opéra, Paris

*La Servante justifiée* (mus. Kreutzer), Opéra, Paris

1819 Dances in *Olympie* (opera; mus. Spontini), Opéra, Paris

1820 Dances in *Apasie et Périclès* (opera; mus. Daussoigne), Opéra, Paris

1821 Dances in *Blanche de Provence* (opera; mus. Berton, Boïeldieu, Cherubini, Kreutzer, Päer; chor. with Milon), Opéra, Paris

1822 Dances in *Aladin* (opera; mus. Isouard), Opéra, Paris

Dances in *Florestan* (opera; mus. M. Garcia; chor. with Milon), Opéra, Paris

Dances in *Sapho* (opera; mus. Reicha), Opéra, Paris

1823 Dances in *Virginie* (opera; mus. Berton), Opéra, Paris

Dances in *Vendôme en Espagne* (opera; mus. Auber, Boïeldieu, Hérold), Opéra, Paris

1824 Dances in *Ipsiboé* (opera; mus. Kreutzer), Opéra, Paris

Dances in *Les Deux Salem* (opera; mus. Daussoigne), Opéra, Paris

1825 Dances in *La Belle au bois dormant* (opera; mus. Carafa), Opéra, Paris

Dances in *Pharamond* (opera; mus. Boïeldieu, Berton, Kreutzer, Lesueur), Opéra, Paris

Dances in *Armide* (tragédie-lyrique; revival, mus. Gluck, chor. with Milon), Opera, Paris

1826 Dances in *Le Siège de Corinthe* (opera; mus. Rossini), Opéra, Paris

1827 Dances in *Moïse* (opera; mus. Rossini), Opéra, Paris

Dances in *Macbeth* (opera; mus. Chélard), Opéra, Paris

**PUBLICATIONS**

Bachaumont, *Mémoires,* Paris, 1781

Noverre, Jean-Georges, *Lettres sur les artes imitateurs,* Paris, 1807

Berchoux, J., *La Danse; ou, Les Dieux de l'opéra,* Paris, 1808

Baron, A., *Lettres et entretiens sur la danse,* Paris, 1824

Saint-Léon, Arthur, *La Sténochorégraphie*, Paris, 1852

Castil-Blaze, *L'Académie impériale de musique,* Paris, 1855

d'Heylé, G., *Foyer et coulisses,* Paris, 1875

Campardon, Émile, *L'Académie royale de musique au XVIIIe siècle,* Paris, 1884

Guest, Ivor, *The Romantic Ballet in Paris,* London, 1966

Winter, Marian Hannah, *The Pre-Romantic Ballet,* London, 1974

Chapman, John, "Forgotten Giant: Pierre Gardel", *Dance Research* (London), Spring 1987

* * *

Pierre Gardel, ballet master at the Paris Opéra during the Revolution, Empire, and early Restoration, has been accused of being everything from the Opéra's Robespierre, and its Napoleon, to its Louis XVIII—that is, its ruthless executioner, its power-hungry empire builder, and its stolid reactionary. Whatever the validity of these assertions, Gardel was an artist whose intense vision, innovative imagination, knowledge of audiences, and formidable creative skills set a standard that others could only imitate. He was a leader who led by the excellence of example, not just in art, but in loyalty to his country and the institution he served.

The highly negative image of Gardel is a modern one based on his resistance to other ballet masters creating works at the Paris Opéra where he was chief ballet master. Whether this was justifiable or not, Gardel's immense contributions as ballet master and director of the school attached to the Opéra far outweigh any damage he may have caused. Many of his contemporaries appear to agree with this conclusion. The great author and ballet master, Jean-Georges Noverre, who had many axes to grind and no reason to pander to the powers that be, wrote in 1807 that most of the dancers who merited applause came from Gardel's school and that the training produced "a perfectly executed ensemble, and a rare harmony of poses and movements of the body...". Confirming Noverre's assertion, no less a figure than August Bournonville sought Gardel as his teacher when he came to Paris in the early 1820s. The Dane wrote enthusiastically of Gardel's creative powers, saying that "One did not know which to admire most: his inexhaustible wealth of invention or the well-calculated use of time and energies at his excellent rehearsals." Another important younger contemporary, Carlo Blasis, cited Gardel as a high authority in his 1820 treatise on dancing. The popularity of Gardel's ballets attests to his great facility as an artist, for his works consistently drew the biggest audiences at the Opéra. The evidence in Gardel's favour is powerful.

Gardel was an innovator. His subject matter sometimes shocked more conservative ballet-lovers, and he caused some mild alarm—for example, by introducing everyday people in farcical circumstances in *La Dansomanie*; by utilizing an exotic setting and presenting a tragic ending in *Paul et Virginie*; or by going to the Biblical, rather than the classical, past in *L'Enfant prodigue.* A strong supporter of the Revolution who, unlike many of his colleagues, did not leave France (despite meagre creative opportunities) during the period of turmoil, Gardel cherished the idea of producing a ballet that would cry out for liberté, égalité, fraternité—*William Tell.* The project never came to fruition, but it demonstrates that Gardel was clearly open to romantic viewpoints as early as the 1790s.

Though he was eager to introduce popular, revolutionary, and romantic subjects, Gardel's earlier works followed the neo-classical tastes of the Revolution. He created the most successful of all the heroic and anacreontic ballets—*Psyché*, *Télémaque*, and *Le Jugement de Pâris*. And, in the introduction to his *Psyché* scenario, he demonstrated his insight and his strength of will, for here he observed that ballet audiences liked spectacle as much as stories and that his intentions were to soften the strict *ballet d'action* emphasis on dramatic action with beautiful dances, sets, and costumes. It must have taken some courage to go against, as he did, the almost universally accepted principles of his art laid down by Jean-Georges Noverre in his book, *Lettres sur la danse* (1760). Gardel was rewarded for keeping faith with his own artistic vision; *Psyché* alone ran for over 300 performances.

Gardel also led the way in the development of ballet music at the Opéra. Common practice in his day was to create scores by arranging well-known airs, partly in the belief that audience familiarity with the original context and/or words of the music would help explain the often confusing ballet story. *Le Retour de Zéphire* (to music by Steibelt) was the first of many ballets in which Gardel commissioned original music. His reasons for doing this are not clear, for critics complained whenever he did it. Perhaps he sought the continuity and artistic unity possible in such collaborations.

In the end, it is probably true to say that Pierre Gardel reflected the many varied facets of the men who led his age. He was probably at one time or another tyrant, genius, general, politician, revolutionary, reactionary, and father. The complex combination of traits these personae represent allowed him successfully to maintain his ballet company when the Opéra administrations themselves were rising and falling with breathtaking rapidity. It is doubtful that any other combination of personal qualities could have steered the Opéra with such sureness, consistency, and artistic success through the tumultuous seas of one of France's most brilliant and most difficult of voyages.

—John Chapman

---

**GASKELL, Sonia**

Lithuanian/Dutch dancer, teacher, choreographer, and ballet director. Born in Vilkaviskis, Lithuania, 14 April 1904. Studied in Kharkov, Ukraine, and with Lubov Egorova and Léo Staats, Paris, from 1925. Married (1) Abraham Goldenson, 1925 (div.); (2) Philippe Bauchhenss, 1939. Early career as cabaret dancer, touring France and Italy, 1930s; founder and choreographer, Les Ballets de Paris, 1936–39; teacher in Paris, 1936–39, and Amsterdam, from 1939; founder of own company, Ballet Studio '45, Amsterdam, becoming Ballet Recital I, 1945, and Ballet Recital II, 1952–54; founder, Netherlands Ballet Academy, The Hague, and artistic director, Netherlands Ballet, from 1954; artistic director, Dutch National Ballet (an amalgamation of Netherlands Ballet and the Amsterdam Ballet), 1961–68. Recipient: Knight of the Order of the Oranje Nassau, 1959; Officer of the Order of the Oranje Nassau, 1966; Silver Medal of the City of Amsterdam, 1969. Died in Paris, 9 July 1974.

**WORKS**

1948 *Intermezzo* (mus. Khachaturian), Ballet Recital I, The Hague
1949 *Odysseus and Calypso* (mus. Juda), Ballet Recital I, Amsterdam
1950 *Alles om een Mantel* (*All About a Coat*; mus. Stokvis), Ballet Recital I, Arnhem
*Ballet-suite* (mus. Gluck), Ballet Recital I, Arnhem
1951 *Judith* (mus. Andriessen), Ballet Recital I, Amsterdam
*Ritme en Klank* (*Rhythm and Sound*; mus. Bartók), Ballet Recital I, Amsterdam
1952 *De Liefde van Don Perlimplin en Belisa* (mus. Villa-Lobos), Ballet Recital II, The Hague
*Sonate* (mus. Mul), Ballet Recital II, The Hague
*Ragtime* (mus. Stravinsky), Ballet Recital II, The Hague
*Le Mariage forcé* (mus. Rameau), Ballet Recital II, Scheveningen
1953 *Luctor et Emergo* (mus. Frid), Ballet Recital II, Amsterdam
*Le Festin de l'araignée* (mus. Roussel), Ballet Recital II, Amsterdam
*Dansflitsen* (mus. Dresden), Ballet Recital II, The Hague
1954 *Het Ballet van der Lezer* (*The Readers' Ballet*; mus. Andriessen), Ballet Recital II, The Hague
*Paradou* (mus. Frid), Ballet Recital II, Utrecht
1955 *De Stoelen* (*The Chairs*; mus. Escher), Netherlands Ballet, The Hague
*Het is Heus Waar!* (*It's Really True!*; mus. Høffding), Netherlands Ballet, The Hague
1956 *Die Liebesprobe* (mus. Mozart), Netherlands Ballet, Schwetzingen, Germany
*Sphere* (mus. Badings), Netherlands Ballet, The Hague

**PUBLICATIONS**

Haskell, Arnold, "Sonia Gaskell Jubilee", *Dancing Times* (London), March 1966
Loney, Glenn, "Evolution of an Ensemble", *Dance Magazine* (New York), March 1974
Van de Weetering, Conrad, and Utrecht, Luuk, *Sonia Gaskell*, Zutphen, 1976
Scaik, Eva van, *Op Gespannen Voet: Geschiedenis van de Nederlandse Theaterdans*, Haarlem, 1981
Utrecht, Luuk, *Het Nationale Ballet: 25 Jaar*, Alphen aan de Rijn, 1987

* * *

Sonia Gaskell was born in Lithuania and grew up in Kharkov in Ukraine, where she attended her first ballet lessons. Due to the regular pogroms against the Jewish people, she fled to Palestine in 1921. Her marriage to scientist Abraham Goldenson brought her in 1925 to Paris, where she studied with Lubov Egorova and Léo Staats. Gaskell claims to have danced with the Diaghilev Ballet, but this has never been confirmed. What is certain is that she performed with several small companies, and toured with a colleague throughout France and Italy, performing an acrobatic piece in cabarets and nightclubs. She opened a ballet studio in Paris and assembled a small company, Les Ballets de Paris, for which she made her first choreographies. In 1939, Gaskell followed her second husband, the architect Philippe Bauchhenss, to Amsterdam. For health reasons she had stopped dancing and now devoted her time to teaching.

During the Second World War, Gaskell was forced to go into hiding, but continued to give ballet classes. After the war, she started a small company promoting classical dance. First it was called Ballet Studio '45, later becoming Ballet Recital I (1945–1951) and II (1952–1954). She was appointed artistic leader of the newly formed Netherlands Ballet in 1954, and was given the same position when this company was amalgamated with the Amsterdam Ballet in 1961 to become Het Nationale Ballet (Dutch National Ballet). But she withdrew in 1968, and left Holland for Paris, where she died.

**Sonia Gaskell at a rehearsal for *Othello* with the Netherlands Ballet, 1959**

Gaskell's ambition and aim was to give The Netherlands a ballet company that would and could perform the great classics, keep alive the important ballets of the first half of the twentieth century (mainly from the Diaghilev repertoire), and at the same time promote contemporary works by national and international balletmakers.

Her great erudition, energy, and drive made the realization of this ambition possible. In the beginning, when money was scarce, she had to provide her companies with her own choreographies. They showed sound craftmanship but revealed that she was not a choreographer by calling. When the financial tide turned for the better, Gaskell succeeded in attracting important people from the dance world to work with her company; Lichine, Massine, Béjart, Taras, Dolin, and several ballet masters from Moscow's Bolshoi Ballet, whose teaching methods and dancing style Gaskell greatly admired, were brought to Holland. From 1955, the company was given rights to perform ballets by Balanchine. Apart from the international great names, Gaskell also stimulated the dancers of the company to try their own hands at choreography, with Rudi van Dantzig and Jaap Flier emerging as the company's most important discoveries. In addition, Gaskell gave many talks and lecture-demonstrations, and in so doing built up a solid ballet audience.

Gaskell was undoubtedly a very controversial figure. She was both blindly adored and thoroughly hated. Her chaotic working methods and her strong, authoritarian character provoked much resistance, and while on the one hand she pushed and inspired her dancers to great achievement, she also on the other hand pushed many of them beyond their capacities, which led to many unnecessarily short careers.

During Gaskell's artistic leadership, severe disagreements between her and her dancers and board of directors were the order of the day, leading to a constant coming and going of dancers and company managers. A great clash of opinions resulted, in 1958, in the defection of nearly all of her soloists to form their own company, the Nederlands Dans Theater. Due to all these—often self-imposed—troubles, Gaskell's artistic leadership gave her less and less satisfaction; and in 1968, embittered, she left the company and the country.

Gaskell's influence on the development of dance in Holland has without a doubt been great. She belongs, along with Mascha ter Weeme, Hans Snoek, and Françoise Adret—dedicated leaders of the important early Dutch ballet companies—to the small number who can be called the founders of Dutch ballet.

—Ine Rietstap

---

## GAUTIER, Théophile

French poet, writer, ballet critic, and librettist. Born Pierre Jules Théophile Gautier in Tarbes, 30 August 1811. Educated in Paris. One son, by Eugénie Fort, b. 1836, and two daughters, by Ernesta Grisi (sister of ballerina Carlotta Grisi), b. 1845 and 1847. Member of circle of romantic French writers, and founder of own "petit cénacle", including Gérard de Nerval, Paris, 1830; poet, publishing first collection of verse, 1830; journalist, 1831–36, writing for the *Chronique de Paris*, from 1835; art and drama critic, *La Presse*, 1836–55, and *Le Moniteur*, from 1855; also writer for *Le Moniteur*, *Le Figaro*, and for reviews *Ariel*, *Le Cabinet de lecture*, *La France littéraire*; playwright, publishing first play, *Une larme du diable*, 1839; ballet librettist, with first and most famous work, *Giselle*, performed at the Paris Opéra, 1841; author of several collections of art criticism, including *Histoire de l'art dramatique en France*, 1858–59, and *Histoire du romantisme*, 1872. Died in Neuilly, 23 October 1872.

### WORKS (ballet libretti)

1841 *Giselle* (chor. Coralli and Perrot; mus. Adam; design Ciceri), Opéra, Paris
1843 *La Péri* (chor. Coralli; mus. Burgmüller; design Séchan, Diéterle, Philastre, Cambon), Opéra, Paris
1851 *Pâquerette* (chor. Saint-Léon; mus. Benoist; design Despléchin, Cambon, Thierry), Opéra, Paris
1854 *Gemma* (chor. Cerrito; mus. Gabrielli), Opéra, Paris
1858 *Sacountala* (chor. L. Petipa; mus. Reyer; design Martin, Nolan, Rubé), Opéra, Paris

### PUBLICATIONS

By Gautier:
*Les Beautés de l'Opéra*, with Jules Janin and Charles Philarète, Paris, 1845
*Poésies complètes*, Paris, 1845
*L'Art moderne*, Paris, 1856
*Histoire de l'art dramatique en France depuis vingt-cing ans*, 6 volumes, 1858–59
*Théâtre*, Paris, 1872
*Histoire du romantisme*, Paris, 1872
*The Romantic Ballet as seen by Théophile Gautier*, edited and translated by Cyril Beaumont, London, 1932
*Gautier on Dance*, edited by Ivor Guest, London, 1988

About Gautier:
Moore, Lillian, "The Ballets of Théophile Gautier", *Dancing Times* (London), February 1935
Beaumont, Cyril, *The Ballet Called Giselle*, London, 1944
Beaumont, Cyril, *Complete Book of Ballets*, revised edition, London, 1951
Richardson, Joanna, *Théophile Gautier: His Life and Times*, New York, 1959
Spencer, Michael Clifford, *The Art Criticism of Théophile Gautier*, 1969
Kermode, Frank, *Romantic Image*, London, 1971
Grant, Richard, *Théophile Gautier*, 1975
Guest, Ivor, *Gautier on Dance*, London, 1988
Chapman, John, "Silent Drama to Silent Dream: Parisian Ballet Criticism", *Dance Chronicle* (New York), vol. 11, no. 3, 1988

* * *

Theophile Gautier is usually remembered as the author of *Mademoiselle de Maupin*, as an aesthetician, poet, and art critic, and even for his Bohemian pink waistcoat, before he is remembered as the author of *Giselle*, or indeed for his many writings on dance. Studies of French Romanticism invariably pay their respects to Gautier's influence, but few mention the Romantic ballet. Even studies devoted to Gautier often ignore the significance of the ballet in his life and work beyond a passing reference to his enduring devotion to ballerina Carlotta Grisi. Yet, aside from his undoubted influence on ballet as an art form, the ballet became a focus for the realization of Gautier's Romantic aesthetics.

His famous dictum, "l'art pour l'art", became the battle cry of the French Romantics in their revolt against both the neo-classical ethics of art and the utilitarianism associated with the rise of the middle classes. Although it reflected the decline of the aristocracy in its wider range of subject type, Romanticism upheld certain aristocratic ideals, such as grace, and essentially sought escape from real life, locating the imagination as the true concern of art. Gautier turned to ballet during the 1830s when the new Romantic style, with its wonderful illusions of ethereality, was already established. Gautier's ballet scenarios sought to realize Romantic preoccupations with the supernatural and the exotic. The most important was *Giselle* (1841), which developed the themes of Adolphe Nourrit's *La Sylphide* (1832). *Giselle* epitomizes the Romantic ballet—yet an element of its subject matter, the poetic treatment of madness and death in a young woman, became a recurrent theme in later nineteenth-century painting, and much of Gautier's writing foreshadows the Aesthetic movement and the decadence of the "fin de siècle".

In his criticism Gautier was concerned to convey the sensual experience that a work offered. He was not concerned with choreography as such, and makes few references to technique; and the result is "impressionistic" or "appreciative" criticism. Gautier was a creative, artist–critic who predates modern conceptions of the critic as specialist, outside the artistic or creative sphere. Essentially his approach was to collude with the illusion created by the work and to identify the source of that pleasure, which was invariably located in the ballerina.

**A 19th-century engraving of a scene from *Giselle*, libretto by Théophile Gautier**

Marie Taglioni, he tells us, was not just a dancer, she was the dance itself, and it is around the dancer that Gautier centred his appreciation.

A certain proportion of Gautier's writing is little more than a voyeuristic discussion of the sexuality of the dancer. Yet his vocabulary draws on his experience of the plastic arts and he most often treats the ballerina's body and movements in terms of sensually significant form rather than simply as sexually provocative object. In late Romantic art, women were emblematic of an idealized Nature where a unity of body and soul was untouched by discredited intellect. Yeats's treatment of the dancer, in his poems, is in keeping with Gautier's appreciations, and both are manifestations of Romantic ideals.

Beauty was of primary importance to Romantic aesthetics and is a focal criterion in Gautier's appreciations. In early Romanticism beauty took the form of a masculine and virile ideal whereas Gautier's writing reflects the feminine ideals of later Romanticism in either its tragi-poetic form or that of the femme fatale, *la belle dame sans merci*. This dichotomy of feminine type is represented in the Romantic ballet by the opposition of Marie Taglioni's ethereal and spiritual qualities and the more earthy sexuality of Fanny Elssler, an opposition which Gautier encouraged, calling Taglioni a "Christian" and Elssler a "Pagan" dancer. In ballet, late Romantic aesthetics became trivialized in many respects and Gautier, with his many references to male ugliness, certainly encouraged the notion that the art was unsuitable for men. This attitude was not to be seriously challenged until the arrival of Nijinsky.

Gautier's influence on ballet certainly outlived the course of the Romantic ballet of which it was so much a part. Several of the ballets of Diaghilev's Ballets Russes were inspired by Gautier; *Le Spectre de la rose* was based on one of his poems, and *Le Pavillon d'Armide* on one of his stories, while *Cléopâtre* was originally an unrealized ballet scenario for Fanny Elssler. These ballets are quintessentially of the Diaghilev era, but it is not difficult to find in them the aesthetic ideals and imaginative world of Théophile Gautier. He believed that fairyland was the ideal location for a ballet, somewhere beyond the real, with exotic, mythical creatures. It was this aspect of ballet, its potential for such a realization, which captivated Gautier; his first interest was the pursuit of the Romantic image, and his interest in ballet resulted from this pursuit. Yet his insistence that dancing should aspire to the condition of music made visible may be said to anticipate the abstract ballet, even though there is no evidence that he consciously conceived of such a thing. His placing of the dance at the centre of the plot of *Giselle* perhaps encapsulates this stress on the poetics of dancing.

Through the translation of Cyril Beaumont, Gautier's writings have exerted a great influence on ballet criticism. A reverie in description, the collusion with the illusion of the work, the desire to render the experience poetically, the treatment of the ballet through a focus on the ballerina—all are found in early twentieth-century ballet criticism and are reminiscent of Gautier. While many of these aspects became trivialized when removed from the era of their Romantic context, Gautier's sensitivity of responsiveness and creative interaction with form and movement could continue to inspire.

Overall, Gautier's greatest contribution to the development of ballet was his emphasis on the poetic qualities of dancing itself; he enabled his readers to respond to the poetics of movement, giving them a language and a way of seeing that had significance to ballet appreciation beyond the Romantic ideals reflected. In addition to the importance of his scenarios and ideas, Gautier's criticism is a wonderfully vivid chronicle of the Romantic ballet through which we can also glimpse the contemporary imagination.

—Lesley-Anne Sayers

---

## GAYANÉ

**Choreography:** Nina Anisimova
**Music:** Aram Khachaturian
**Design:** Natan Altman (scenery), Tatyana Bruni (costumes)
**Libretto:** Konstantin Derzhavin
**First Production:** Kirov Ballet, Perm, 9 December 1942
**Principal Dancers:** Natalia Dudinskaya (Gayané), Nikolai Zubkovsky (Koren), Konstantin Sergeyev (Armen), Tatanya Vecheslova (Nune), Boris Shavrov (Giko)

**Other productions include:** Kirov Ballet (design V.F. Ryndin); Leningrad, 20 February 1945. Kirov Ballet (restaged and revised Anisimova; design Valery Dorrer), with Natalia Dudinskaya, Nikolai Zubovsky, Konstantin Sergeyev, Feya Balabina; Leningrad, 13 June 1952. Bolshoi Ballet (new version; chor. Vasily Vainonen); Moscow, 1957. Leningrad Maly Theatre (new version; chor. and libretto Boris Eifman); Leningrad, 1972. Bolshoi Ballet (restaged Anisimova); Moscow, 19 November 1961.

### PUBLICATIONS

Slonimsky, Yuri, *Soviet Ballet*, Moscow and Leningrad, 1950
Khachaturian, Aram, *Gayané* (booklet), Moscow, 1957
Entelis, L.A., *One Hundred Ballet Librettos*, Leningrad, 1971

* * *

*Gayané*, created by the Russian character dancer Nina Anisimova, is set on a collective farm in Armenia. The character Gayané, daughter of Avanes (the chairman of the Kolkhoz, or collective), helps to capture a stranger who has secretly penetrated the territory of the Soviet Army with the intention of discovering geological secrets. By doing this, the loving Gayané is coming to the aid of her friend, the youth Armen. Armen's rival, Giko, pays for his life for involuntarily helping the enemy. But all ends well, and the finale of the ballet is a celebration of the friendship of the peoples and nations of the Soviet Union.

The story is very simple and very naïve, reflecting the attitudes and sentiments of the 1940s, when the country was involved in world war. It is the tale of a spy caught, and of people who are weak and cannot at first resist his influence. But of course it is also about the final victory of the collective farmers, who overcome the troubles and triumphantly create their own collective, to live happily ever after.

*Gayané*, with Olga Zabotkina, Kirov Ballet, 1972

Essentially, it was understood at the time that this simple libretto was really just the necessary backdrop for the dancing itself, which was splendidly choreographed and staged by Anisimova (herself an outstanding character dancer, who performed in the original production). Anisimova thought in terms of character dancing, but she knew a surprising amount about classical dance. *Gayané* has survived for many years, and excerpts from it have been performed by numerous companies and schools, who borrow especially from the second act, in which a wedding takes place. Anisimova created wonderful duets and variations for Gayané and for her lover, Kasakov. It was very unusual choreography for its time, in that it combined classical dance with folk dance, particularly in the stylized use of arms and hands, reflecting the Armenian folklore and culture that form the background of the ballet. The composer, Khachaturian, wrote evocative music which is often performed separately by symphony orchestras the world over.

The premiere cast included Natalia Dudinskaya and Konstantin Sergeyev, the leading figures at the time in Leningrad ballet. Nina Anisimova, naturally, did not forget herself, and she danced the part of an Armenian girl in the ballet who appears on the stage as an image and symbol of socialist labour. She works hard; she knows how to produce the most from the fields; but she also knows how to enjoy life, spending her free time in dancing and in laughter. The suite of dances in the second act represents different nationalities in the Soviet Union, because at that time Armenia was already a mixed population. For this Anisimova created the famous Sabre Dance, which, performed separately as an extract, was to become a showpiece for companies in many countries. The style of movement in the dance is unusual, and quite unexpected, even for character dance—unusual bends of the body, inventive positions of the arms which do not come from the classical vocabulary, the overall structure of the body which is not balletic—but most of all, in keeping with the music of Khachaturian, everything is very temperamental, which suited the character of Anisimova herself.

The ballet was created when the company was in Perm (during the World War II evacuation), on the small stage of the Perm state theatre. But despite these limitations the effect was profound; in effect, the message was that the company still lived on, despite the very hard times. Anisimova invited different dancers to participate in her ballet, dancers who happened to be in the city at that time: there was a sense of camaraderie and combined effort which suited the positive feeling of the ballet itself. The composition, the music, the dancing—all together created something which, regardless of the weaknesses in the libretto, expressed the triumph of dancing and its many different possibilities.

In later years, when critics came to analyze *Gayané* more closely, they came to see that in strict terms, it does not stand as a completely successful whole because of its very naïve libretto, and because of what might be called its over-sociological emphasis. But all the same, choreographers, critics, and historians persuaded the Kirov Theatre to take on the excerpts from the ballet and to show them to the public, and they proved very successful. The variation of Gayané, the variation of Giko, the bad boy of the ballet, or the character dances of the people, for example, were all very effectively done and were subsequently shown often as concert numbers. After its Perm premeire, the ballet was restaged twice for the Kirov by Anisimova, with the 1952 version, after her revisions and additions, standing as the definitive version.

In the end, Anisimova did a very important thing on the stage of the Kirov—she proved that character dancing was still alive, and that it should be included in the world of classical ballet. *Gayané*'s use of dance did not really follow in the Petipa tradition, as for example in *Swan Lake*, where the audience is treated to national dance in separate divertissements, or "dances of le salon", as Petipa called it: here, by contrast, the force of character dance is felt throughout the ballet; it is a natural part of the people and of their story. Over the years, the ballet helped other choreographers to understand that it is very important for choreographic art, at least in Russia, to combine different parts of character dancing with the classical and mime tradition. *Gayané* established itself as a sound example of the way that excellent character dance and ballet can be combined; and as such, its value to Soviet choreography of the twentieth century is undoubtedly quite significant.

—Igor Stupnikov

---

## GELTSER, Ekaterina

Russian/Soviet dancer. Born Ekaterina Vasilievna Geltser, daughter of Bolshoi ballet master and mime artist Vasily Geltser, in Moscow, 14 November (2 November old style) 1876. Studied at the Moscow Choreographic School, pupil of I.D. Nikitin and José (Joseph) Mendez, 1884–94; also later trained with Christian Johansson, Marius Petipa, St. Petersburg. Married Bolshoi dancer and stage partner Vasily Tikhomirov. Dancer, corps de ballet, Bolshoi Theatre, Moscow, 1894, becoming second ballerina, 1895–96; ballerina, Maryinsky Theatre, St. Petersburg, 1896–98; returned to Bolshoi: first ballerina, from 1901; ballerina, Diaghilev's Ballets Russes, Paris, 1910, also touring in Brussels and Berlin; performed with Tikhomirov and Bolshoi dancers, Alhambra Theatre, London, 1911, with Mikhail Mordkin's All-Star Imperial Russian Ballet, Metropolitan Opera House, New York, 1911; also toured extensively in Russia after retirement from the Bolshoi, 1935; continued dancing until the late 1930s. Recipient: title of People's Artist of the USSR (first ballerina to be so awarded), 1925; State Prize of the USSR, 1943. Died in Moscow, 12 December 1962.

### ROLES

1894 Aspasia in *Walpurgis Night* (opera; mus. Gounod), Bolshoi Theatre, Moscow
Variation in *Catarina* (Petipa), Bolshoi Theatre, Moscow

1896 Spinner's Variation in *Coppélia* (Petipa, Ivanov), Maryinsky Theatre, St. Petersburg

1897/98 Jewel Fairy in *The Sleeping Beauty* (Petipa), Maryinsky Theatre, St. Petersburg

1898 Variation, Dream Scene, Grand Pas Hongroise (cr) in *Raymonda* (Petipa), Maryinsky Theatre, St. Petersburg

1899 White Cat in *The Sleeping Beauty* (Petipa), Bolshoi Theatre, Moscow
Naiad in *The Naiad and the Fisherman* (Petipa after Perrot), Bolshoi Theatre, Moscow
Teresa in *Cavalry Halt* (Petipa), Bolshoi Theatre, Moscow
Clairemond in *The Stars* (Clustine), Bolshoi Theatre, Moscow
Fairy Godmother in *Little Magic Slipper* (Reisinger), Bolshoi Theatre, Moscow

1900 Princess Aurora in *The Sleeping Beauty* (Petipa), Bolshoi Theatre, Moscow

1901 Title role in *Raymonda* (Petipa), Maryinsky Theatre, St. Petersburg

1905 Princess in *The Magic Mirror* (Gorsky after Petipa), Bolshoi Theatre, Moscow
Swanilda (cr) in *Coppélia* (new production; Gorsky after Saint-Léon), Bolshoi Theatre, Moscow

1906 Kitri in *Don Quixote* (Gorsky), Bolshoi Theatre, Moscow

1907 Colombine (cr) in *Harlequinade* (Gorsky after Petipa), Bolshoi Theatre, Moscow

1910 Queen Bint-Anta in *Pharaoh's Daughter* (Gorsky), Bolshoi Theatre, Moscow
Principal dancer in *Le Festin* (Fokine), Diaghilev's Ballets Russes, Paris
Principal dancer in *Les Orientales* (Fokine), Diaghilev's Ballets Russes, Paris
Principal dancer in *Les Sylphides* (Fokine), Diaghilev's Ballets Russes, Paris
Title role (cr) in *Salammbô* (Gorsky), Bolshoi Ballet, Moscow

1911 Ballerina (cr) in *The Dance Dream* (Gorsky), Alhambra Theatre, London
Odette/Odile in *Swan Lake* (after Petipa, Ivanov), Mordkin's All-Star Imperial Russian Ballet, New York

1912 Medora (cr) in *Le Corsaire* (Gorsky), Bolshoi Theatre, Moscow

1913 Fisherwoman (cr) in *Love is Quick!* (Gorsky), Bolshoi Theatre, Moscow

Doll (cr) in *Le Carnaval* (Gorsky), Bolshoi Theatre, Moscow
Ondine (cr) in *Schubertiana* (Gorsky), Bolshoi Theatre, Moscow
1914 Tsar-Maiden (cr) in *The Little Humpbacked Horse* (Gorsky), Bolshoi Theatre, Moscow
1915 Eunice (cr) in *Eunice and Petronius* (Gorsky), Bolshoi Theatre, Moscow
1916 Lise in *Vain Precautions* (*La Fille mal gardée*; Gorsky after Petipa), Bolshoi Theatre, Moscow
1924 Sylph in *La Sylphide* (Tikhomirov after Petipa), Bolshoi Theatre, Moscow
1926 Title role (cr) in *Esmeralda* (Tikhomirov), Bolshoi Theatre, Moscow
1927 Tao-Hoa (cr) in *The Red Poppy* (Tikhomirov, Lashchilin), Bolshoi Theatre, Moscow

**Other roles include:** Dancer in *Bacchanalia* (Gorsky), Polonaise, Mazurka in *Ivan Susanin* (opera; mus. Glinka), Nikiya in *La Bayadère* (Gorsky).

## PUBLICATIONS

Slonimsky, Yuri, *The Soviet Ballet*, New York, 1947.
*Ekaterina Vasilievna Geltser*, Moscow, 1954
René, Natalia, "Moscow Assoluta", *Dance and Dancers* (London), April 1963
Martynova, D.M., *Ekaterina Geltser*, Moscow, 1965
Krasovskaya, Vera, *Russian Ballet Theatre of the Early Twentieth Century*, Part 2: Leningrad, 1972
Chernova, N., *From Geltser to Ulanova*, Moscow, 1979
Smakov, Gennady, *The Great Russian Dancers*, New York, 1984
Souritz, Elizabeth, *The Art of Choreography in the 1920s*, Moscow, 1979; as *Soviet Choreographers in the 1920s*, translated by Lynn Visson, Durham, N.C. and London, 1990

* * *

Heroic is the word most frequently used to describe Ekaterina Geltser's performances. Of medium height, with stocky build and muscular legs, the Muscovite ballerina was a far from conventionally beautiful dancer. Nevertheless her technique and acting ability enabled her to impress audiences in a variety of roles, particularly the dramatic ballets staged by Aleksandr Gorsky; and she became the epitome of the Bolshoi ballerina of the first half of the twentieth century.

Ekaterina Geltser came from a theatrical family of German descent. Her father was the great mime artist Vasily Geltser, also a choreographer in his own right and a contributor to ballet scenarios, most notably for the original *Swan Lake*. His daughter's strong motivation and the encouraging opinions of her teachers overcame his reluctance for Ekaterina to adopt a career in the Imperial ballet. She acquired a strong Italian technique and "steel pointes" from her Bolshoi teacher José (Joseph) Mendez, but realized it was necessary to train in St. Petersburg to improve her épaulement and develop a softer, more graceful port de bras. She left the Bolshoi, where she was already dancing solo roles in *The Little Humpbacked Horse* and a Japanese dance in *Daita*, to spend a couple of years taking classes with Christian Johansson and to have the opportunity of rehearsing with Marius Petipa.

Petipa regarded Geltser as an interesting, individual dancer and coached her in variations from his *The Sleeping Beauty*. In her performance as the White Cat (a role she danced at the first Moscow performance of the ballet), he described her as being like a panther rather than a cat. Petipa created a variation for Geltser in *Raymonda* and when Italian ballerina Pierina Legnani left Russia, Geltser was invited to return to St. Petersburg to take over the title role.

Geltser was not widely known outside Russia. She appeared briefly with the Ballets Russes in 1910, and the following year undertook a short engagement at London's Alhambra in Gorsky's *The Dance Dream* (based on a hotch-potch of hits from the Bolshoi's repertoire). Later, in 1911, she took over from Julie Sedova as Odette/Odile in the first complete *Swan Lake* in America, presented by Mikhail Mordkin's All-Star Imperial Russian Ballet for the performances at New York's Metropolitan. Reviews for these performances all note Geltser's technical accomplishments but compare her physique unfavourably with other Russians dancing in the West. To a certain extent her repertoire did not show her to best effect.

Geltser was less impressive in lyrical ballets than in dramatic works. Although she chose to dance Odette/Odile, it was only in the ballroom and not in the lakeside acts that she made much impact. As a footnote to her appearances in *Swan Lake*, Geltser was one of the last dancers to perform an extract of the ballet's 1877 choreography, as she learnt the ballroom scene's Boyar Dance to the Melancholia from Sobeshchanskaya. This Russian dance she performed as a solo and interpolated into other ballets. She performed it as the Tsar Maiden in *The Little Humpbacked Horse* and appears to have danced it with Diaghilev's Ballets Russes and in the "Old Russia" scene from *The Dance Dream*.

In her youth, Geltser had greatly admired the actresses Maria Yermolova, Sarah Bernhardt, and Eleonora Duse, and her own forte was in roles charged with drama. This made her an ideal interpreter of Gorsky's stagings of notable ballets in Moscow. Among her roles were a fiery Kitri in *Don Quixote*, Medora in Gorsky's own *Le Corsaire*, Bint-Anta in *The Pharaoh's Daughter*, and the title roles in *Salammbô* and *Esmeralda*. She was also inimitable in what might be described as demi-caractère divertissements such as the Hebrew Bacchanale from the opera *Samson and Delilah* and the anti-German, 1914 propagandist *Spirit of Belgium* to Schubert's *Marche Militaire*. Her last great creation (still combining virtuosity with drama) came in 1927 as Tao-Hoa, the Chinese dancer in *The Red Poppy*. Geltser's regular partners included Aleksandr Volinin (until 1910), her husband and teacher Vasily Tikhomirov, and Leonid Zhukov.

Geltser was the only Russian prima ballerina assoluta who did not leave Russia during the First World War and Revolution. Together with Tikhomirov and supported by Anatole Lunacharsky (who described her as "the pearl of Russian ballet"), Geltser was instrumental in the preservation of traditional classical ballet in Moscow. In the post-Revolutionary experimental period, Geltser appeared conservative to those who favoured the work of Isadora Duncan or Kasyan Goleizovsky, but her performances at the Bolshoi and before audiences throughout the Soviet Union—dramatic and colourful choreodramas—provided moments of escape to audiences often deprived of food and heat. In recognition of her services and popularity, she was the first appointed "People's Artist of the USSR". Geltser also built up a remarkable collection of Russian paintings.

Geltser continued to dance until she was well over 60, although at the end her repertoire dwindled to the Polonaise and the Mazurka from Glinka's *Ivan Susanin* (*A Life for the Tsar*). Natalie René has described how she expected "a good laugh upon seeing the old dancer who refused to give up. Instead I was completely overwhelmed by her great artistry."

A short silent film of Geltser dancing *Moment Musicale* with Tikhomirov survives. Unfortunately both dancers and dancing

**Ekaterina Geltser with Vasily Tikhomirov and corps de ballet in *The Goldfish*, Bolshoi Ballet, Moscow**

look quaint and there is no sense of Geltser's celebrated personality. It remains, at best, a curiosity with little bearing on written descriptions of this formidable theatrical artist.

—Jane Pritchard

---

**GENÉE, Adeline**

Danish/British dancer. Born Anna Kirstina Margarete Petra Jensen in Hinnerup, Arhus, 6 January 1878. Studied with aunt and uncle, Antonia Zimmerman and Alexander Genée. Married Frank S.N. Isitt. First stage appearance at age of ten, Christiana (Oslo); official début (replacing Italian ballerina Antonia Dell 'Era), Berlin Court Opera, 1896; dancer, Munich Court Opera, 1896–97; principal dancer, Empire Theatre, London, 1897–1907, returning as guest ballerina, from 1908; also frequent guest ballerina, appearing with Hans Beck, Copenhagen, from 1902, touring independently, including in America, from 1908, and appearing with Alexandre Volinin, U.S. tour, 1912–13, and with Volinin and members of the Imperial Russian Ballet, touring Australia and New Zealand, 1913; leading dancer, London Coliseum, various seasons from 1912, also appearing at Alhambra Theatre, Drury Lane Theatre, and Royal Opera House, London; official farewell performance, 1914, continuing to appear for various seasons until 1917; returned to stage to perform with Anton Dolin, London, 1932–33; founder and president of London Association of Operatic Dancing (becoming the Royal Academy of Dancing), 1920–54; also founder member of Camargo Society, 1930; president, Anglo-Danish Society. Recipient: Honorary Doctorate of Music, University of London, 1946; Dame Commander of the British Empire, 1950; "Ingenio et Arti" from King of Denmark; Order of Dannebrog, 1953. Died in Esher, 23 April 1970.

**ROLES**

1896 Centifolie in *Die Rose von Schiras* (Graeb), Imperial Opera, Berlin
Swanilda in *Coppélia* (Alexander Genée after Saint-Léon), Hoftheater, Munich

1896/97 Snowflakes Waltz in *Der Kinder Weinnachtstraum* (pantomime divertissement; mus. Bayer), Hoftheater, Munich

1897 "Menuet Waltzer", Gavotte in *Rococo* (Jungmann), Hoftheater, Munich
Flower Fairy (cr) in *Der Blumen Rache* (Jungmann), Hoftheater, Munich
A Diamond (Waltz and Adage), and Variation (cr) added to *Monte Cristo* (one scene only; chor. Lanner), Empire Theatre, London

1898 The Liberty of the Press (cr) in *The Press* (Lanner), Empire Theatre, London
Fairy Good Fortune in *Alaska* (Lanner), Empire Theatre, London

1899 Lizette in *Round the Town Again* (Lanner), Empire Theatre, London

**Adeline Genée in *Coppélia***

1900 Variations (cr) in *Sea-Side* (Lanner), Empire Theatre, London
1901 Vanessa Imperialis, Queen of Butterfly Land (cr) in *Les Papillons* (Lanner), Empire Theatre, London
Adage (cr) in *Old China* (Lanner), Empire Theatre, London
1902 Grand Adagio, "The Roses of England" (cr) in *Our Crown* (divertissement for Coronation; Lanner), Empire Theatre, London
Divertissement from *Flower Festival at Genzano* (Bournonville), Royal Danish Theatre, Copenhagen
1903 Coquette (title role; cr) in *The Milliner Duchess* (Lanner, Alexander Genée), Empire Theatre, London
Pas de deux (chor. Alexander Genée) added to *The Duel in the Snow* (Martinetti, Lanner), Empire Theatre, London
Champagne dance (cr) in *Vineland* (Lanner), Empire Theatre, London
1904 Dances, including Hunting Dance, Cakewalk, "Merry Marguerite" (also chor.; cr) in *High Jinks* (Lanner), Empire Theatre, London
1905 Bebe (cr) in *The Dancing Doll* (Lanner), Empire Theatre, London
Bugler Boy (cr) in *The Bugle Call* (Farren, Alexander Genée), Empire Theatre, London
1906 Title role (cr) in *Cinderella* (Farren, Alexander Genée), Empire Theatre, London
Title role (cr) in *The Débutante* (Lanner), Empire Theatre, London
1907 Lady Dolly (cr) in *Sir Roger de Coverley* (Lanner), Empire Theatre, London
Stella Dane, Queen of the Dance, and Variations (cr) in *The Belle of the Ball* (new version; Farren, Alexander Genée), Empire Theatre, London
1908 Variations, Divertissement (cr) in *The Soul Kiss* (musical comedy and burlesque; also chor.), Chestnut Street Opera House, Philadelphia
Title role (cr) in *The Dryad* (also chor., originally performed privately), Empire Theatre, London
1909 Abbess Elena in the "Ballet of the Nuns" from *Roberto il Diavolo* (opera; mus. Meyerbeer, chor. Alexander Genée), Empire Theatre, London
Divertissements (cr) in *The Silver Star* (musical comedy by Harry Smith; chor. Alexander Genée), Forrest Theatre, Philadelphia
1910 Divertissements in *The Bachelor Belles* (musical comedy), Chestnut Street Theatre, Philadelphia
1912 Title role in *La Camargo* (also chor.), Coliseum, London
Principal dancer (cr) in *A Dream of Roses and Butterflies* (divertissement; also chor.), Coliseum, London
Principal dancer (cr) in *La Danse* (also chor., after the style of various historical ballerinas), Metropolitan Opera House, New York
Polka in *Les Millions d'Harlequin* (mus. Drigo), Metropolitan Opera House, New York
Waltz and Mazurka in *Les Sylphides* (after Fokine), Metropolitan Opera House, New York
1915 Minuet in *The School for Scandal* (play by Sheridan), Royal Opera House, Covent Garden, London
Principal dancer in *The Masque of War and Peace*, Drury Lane Theatre, London
Princess (cr) in *The Princess and the Pea* (ballet pantomime by Dora Bright), Coliseum, London
Ballerina (cr) in *The Dancer's Adventure* (also chor., with Bright), Coliseum, London
1916 "Spring" (divertissement; chor. Alexander Genée) in *Now's the Time* (revue), Alhambra Theatre, London
Patty (cr) in *The Pretty Prentice* (also chor., with MacLennan), Alhambra Theatre, London
1932 Principal dancer (cr) in *The Love Song* (suite of dances; also chor.), Coliseum, London

## WORKS

1904 Dances (including Hunting Dance, Cakewalk, "Merry Marguerite") in *High Jinks* (Lanner), Empire Theatre, London
1908 Variations, Divertissements in *The Soul Kiss* (musical comedy and burlesque), Chestnut Street Opera House, Philadelphia
*The Dryad* (mus. Bright), Empire Theatre, London (originally performed privately)
1911 *A Dream of Roses and Butterflies* (divertissement; mus. various), Coliseum, London
1912 *La Camargo* (mus. Bright), Coliseum, London
*La Danse* (mus. Bright), Coliseum, London
1915 *The Dancer's Adventure* (mus. Bright), Coliseum, London
1916 *The Pretty Prentice* (mus. Clark), Coliseum, London
1932 *The Love Song* (mus. Bright, arranged Rieti), Coliseum, London

## PUBLICATIONS


Crawford-Flitch, J.E., *Modern Dancing and Dancers*, London, 1912
Perugini, M.E., *The Art of Ballet*, London, 1915
Haskell, Arnold, *Balletomania*, London, 1934
Beaumont, Cyril, *Complete Book of Ballets*, revised edition, London, 1951
Bedells, Phyllis, *My Dancing Days*, London, 1954
Davidson, Gladys, *Ballet Biographies*, revised edition, London, 1954
Guest, Ivor, *Adeline Genée: A Lifetime of Ballet under Six Reigns*, London, 1958
Guest, Ivor, *The Empire Ballet*, London, 1962


* * *

Adeline Genée's long and distinguished career developed at a time when ballet was relegated to the music hall, considered entertainment rather than art. In England and America, Genée was an important link between the nineteenth-century traditions of ballet and its re-emergence as a serious art form in the twentieth century. Several ballerinas from the height of the Romantic ballet, including Taglioni, were still alive when Genée was born, and a part of her audience had seen Elssler dance in their youth—yet by Genée's death the dancing career of Margot Fonteyn was at its end. Genée's own enormously successful performing career was eclipsed by the arrival of the Russians in Europe and America, but to some extent she had prepared the way for them, and Genée was to go on to play an important part in the establishment of British ballet in the post-Diaghilev era.

Her early training in Denmark came from her uncle and aunt. Alexander Genée had studied in St. Petersburg under Marius Petipa and Christian Johansson, and Antonia Genée had studied in Hanover with the father and teacher of Adele Grantzow, the last ballerina to have performed the original version of *Giselle* at the Paris Opéra. Her early training was said to have been rigorous, giving her a strong technique while also developing her artistry.

Adeline Genée danced in several countries, but she made her home in England, where she was adored by critics and public alike, from royalty to the working classes. Her London début in 1897, the year of Queen Victoria's Silver Jubilee, was in a revival of *Monte Cristo* in which she danced the part of the Diamond. It was a time when ballet had sunk to its lowest ebb and was not considered a serious art. Nevertheless, its popularity is reflected in the fact that it enjoyed two lavish theatres, the Empire and the Alhambra, with resident corps de ballets. Genée was engaged at the Empire, where she was to perform for the next ten years.

The Empire was a music hall but its main attraction was the ballet which had, therefore, to have popular appeal. There was little room for experimentation, but the ballets were original and delightful. One of Genée's favourites was *The Milliner Duchess*, in which she had to develop from a naïve girl in a hat shop to a sophisticated woman who captivates a marquis. Classical ballets were out of fashion and nothing old or sad was wanted, but Genée did manage to reinstate *Coppélia*, insisting that it be included in her repertoire. It was successfully produced by her uncle, and Swanilda became the role with which Genée was always identified. In Copenhagen Genée performed *Coppélia* with Hans Beck as her partner; Beck had been a pupil of Bournonville and was responsible for conserving the Bournonville repertory.

Genée was renowned for her vivacity, her charm, and her lightness and grace as well as for her technical accomplishment. "She might pirouette on a daisy and it would not bend", wrote one critic, testimony not only to Genée's qualities but also to the fact that aspects of the Romantic style and imagery in dance appreciation had formed a firm alliance with Victorian sentiments. This is also apparent in Dora Bright's scenario of the ballet *The Dryad*, in which Genée danced the title role of an imprisoned wood nymph who seeks (but fails to find) the constant love of a mortal in order to gain her freedom.

When Genée arrived in the United States, ballet was virtually non-existent, and she had to dance in interludes in musicals. Her New York début was in 1908 (two years before the arrival of Anna Pavlova), in Ziegfeld's *The Soul Kiss*. This evidently created a furore and she was then in great demand for American musicals such as the *The Silver Star*, in which she spoke as well as danced. Genée was a great success in America and was later favourably compared to Pavlova, being described as prettier and more adaptable.

Throughout her career Genée had a high regard for the artistic legacy of her art. Working within the context of the music hall, she managed to heighten standards and appreciation for ballet while increasing its popularity. When she partnered Alexander Volinine at the Coliseum in 1914, London saw her for the first time with a first-class male dancer. Volinine was a Bolshoi-trained dancer who became a principal in Diaghilev's Ballets Russes in 1910 and later became Pavlova's partner. Thus in a sense, by appearing with Volinine, Genée linked London's ballet with the Russian ballet that London audiences were beginning to see and appreciate as a serious art form. Volinine was to become an influential teacher in Paris, where André Eglevsky, the great classical dancer of the 1940s and 1950s was one of his pupils.

There is always a sense in Genée's career of an important link between the past artistic traditions of ballet and its future; this was clearly something she took very seriously. For *La Danse* (a work which was seen and admired by Ted Shawn), in which Genée danced a series of portraits of four great earlier ballerinas—Taglioni, Prévost, La Camargo, and Marie Sallé—her research was said to have been extensive and meticulous. Genée's concern with the traditions and firm foundations of ballet as an art continued to exercise a profound influence after her dancing career was over. She was one of the founders of the Camargo Society in England in 1930, the aim of which was to create a national ballet after the demise of Diaghilev's Ballets Russes. She was also the first president of the Association of Operatic Dancing, founded in 1920, which was to become the Royal Academy of Dancing. Here Genée was active in furthering artistic standards and the standards of dance teaching, launching syllabi and examinations, and obtaining royal patronage.

—Lesley-Anne Sayers

---

**GEORGI, Yvonne**

German/Dutch dancer, choreographer, teacher, and ballet director. Born in Leipzig, 29 October 1903. Studied at the Dalcroze Institute, Hellerau, 1920, and at the Mary Wigman School, Dresden, from 1921; also studied ballet with Mme. Rousanne (Rousanne Sarkissian), Paris, 1950. Married Louis Arntzenius, 1932. Début as a concert dancer, Leipzig, 1923, also performing with Wigman group, with Harald Kreutzberg, and in solo concerts touring Europe and North America up to 1939; dancer, Kurt Jooss's company, Münster State Theatre, 1924–25; choreographer (ballet mistress), Reussisches Theater, Gera, 1925–26, Hanover Opera House, 1926–1931 and 1933–36; founder, dance school and performing group, Amsterdam, 1931, leading to formation of Ballets Yvonne Georgi, touring America, 1939, and becoming resident company at Amsterdam Opera House, 1941; choreographer, Board of City Theatres, Amsterdam, during World War II; choreographer (ballet mistress), Düsseldorf Opera House, 1951–54; ballet director, Hanover State Theatre, 1954–70; also guest choreographer, Vienna State Opera Ballet, 1959, also staging ballets in Wuppertal, Göttingen, Salzburg, Bayreuth, and Buenos Aires; also choreographer for the film *Ballerina* (dir. Berger, 1950), and for many operas including *Bluebeard's Castle* (mus. Bartók, 1953); director, Dance Department of the Hanover Academy of Music, until 1973. Died in Hanover, 25 January 1975.

**WORKS**

1925 *Der Dämon* (mus. Hindemith), Reussisches Theater, Gera
1926 *Saudades do Brasil* (mus. Milhaud), Reussisches Theater, Gera
*Barabau* (mus. Rieti), Reussisches Theater, Gera
*Pulcinella* (mus. Stravinsky), Reussisches Theater, Gera
1927/28 *Don Morte* (mus. Wilckens), Hanover Opera House, Hanover
1928 *Tanzsuite* (mus. Wellesz), Hanover Opera House, Hanover
*Das seltsame Haus* (mus. Hindemith), Hanover Opera House, Hanover
*Baby in der Bar* (mus. Grosz), Hanover Opera House, Hanover
*Robes, Pierre & Co* (mus. Wilckens), Hanover Opera House, Hanover
1931 *Le Train bleu* (mus. Milhaud), Berlin State Opera House, Berlin
1933 *Acis und Galathea* (mus. Lully), Amsterdam Wagner Society, Amsterdam
1935 *Goyescas* (mus. Granados), Hanover Opera House, Hanover

1936 *Diana* (mus. Voormolen), Amsterdam
1939 *Prometheus* (mus. Beethoven), Ballets Yvonne Georgi, Amsterdam
*Erinnerung* (mus. Turina), Ballets Yvonne Georgi, Amsterdam
1940/43 *Symphonie Fantastique* (mus. Berlioz), City Theatres, Amsterdam
*The Nutcracker* (mus. Tchaikovsky), City Theatres, Amsterdam
*Sylvia* (mus. Delibes), City Theatres, Amsterdam
*Coppélia* (mus. Delibes), City Theatres, Amsterdam
1944 *Carmina Burana* (scenic cantata; mus. Orff), Amsterdam
1951 *Apollon musagète* (mus. Stravinsky), Düsseldorf Opera Ballet, Düsseldorf
*Das Feuervogel* (mus. Stravinsky), Düsseldorf Opera Ballet, Düsseldorf
*Les Animaux modèles* (mus. Poulenc), Düsseldorf Opera Ballet, Düsseldorf
1952 *Die Geschöpfe des Prometheus* (mus. Beethoven), Düsseldorf Opera Ballet, Düsseldorf
*Das Goldfischglas* (mus. Andriessen), Düsseldorf Opera Ballet, Düsseldorf
*Die vier Temperamente* (mus. Hindemith), Düsseldorf Opera Ballet, Düsseldorf
*El Amor Brujo* (mus. de Falla), Düsseldorf Opera Ballet, Düsseldorf
*Coppélia* (mus. Delibes), Düsseldorf Opera Ballet, Düsseldorf
1953 *Wendungen*, Düsseldorf Opera Ballet, Düsseldorf
*Pas de coeur* (mus. von Einem), Düsseldorf Opera Ballet, Düsseldorf
*Le Sacre du printemps* (mus. Stravinsky), Düsseldorf Opera Ballet, Düsseldorf
1954 *Symphonie fantastique* (mus. Berlioz), Hanover State Opera, Hanover
*Gluck, Tod und Traum* (mus. von Einem), Alpach
1955 *Les Biches* (mus. Poulenc), Hanover State Opera Ballet, Hanover
*Human Variations* (mus. Gould), Hanover State Opera Ballet, Hanover
1956 *Der Mohr von Venedig* (mus. Blacher), Hanover State Opera Ballet, Hanover
1957 *Elektronisches Ballett* (mus. Badings), Hanover State Opera Ballet, Hanover
*Le Loup* (mus. Dutilleux), Hanover State Opera Ballet, Hanover
1958 *Agon* (mus. Stravinsky), Vienna State Opera Ballet, Vienna
*Evolutionen* (mus. Badings), Vienna State Opera Ballet, Vienna
1959 *Ruth* (mus. Erbse), Vienna State Opera Ballet, Vienna
*Das Einhorn, der drache und der Tigerman* (mus. Menotti), Hanover State Opera Ballet, Hanover
1960 *Die Frau aus Andros* (mus. Badings), Hanover State Opera Ballet, Hanover
1961 *Angst* (mus. Constant), Hanover State Opera Ballet, Hanover
1962 *Metamorphosen* (mus. R. Strauss), Hanover State Opera Ballet, Hanover
1964 *Demeter* (mus. Blacher), Schwetzingen
1965 *Der Golem* (mus. Burt), Hanover State Opera Ballet, Hanover
1968 *Paradis perdu* (mus. Constant), Hanover State Opera Ballet, Hanover
1970 *Jeux vénitiens* (mus. Lutoslawski), Hanover State Opera Ballet, Hanover
*Klein Zack, gennant Zinnober* (mus. Karetnikow), Hanover State Opera Ballet, Hanover
1971 *Trionfi* (mus. Orff), Teatro Colón, Buenos Aires
1973 *Skorpion* (mus. Gould), Hanover Ballet, Hanover

**Other works include:** *Bacchus and Ariadne* (mus. Roussel), *Ballade* (mus. von Einem), *Bolero* (mus. Ravel), *Orpheus and Eurydice* (mus. Badings), *Prisma, Opus 16* (mus. Schonberg), *Straw Hat* (mus. Ibert).

## PUBLICATIONS


By Georgi:
*Anmerkungen zum Theatertanz*, Dresden, 1934

About Georgi:
Jurgen, Hans, *Harald Kreutsberg, Yvonne Georgi*, Leipzig, 1930
Linick, Etta, "A Chat with the Germans", *The American Dancer* (Los Angeles), March 1931
Vickery, Katherine, "Yvonne Georgi", *Dance Observer* (New York), January 1936
Koegler, Horst, *Yvonne Georgi*, Velber, 1963
Schäfer, Rolf Helmut, *Yvonne Georgi*, Braunschweig, 1974


* * *

Yvonne Georgi, one of the most brilliant products of the Mary Wigman School, was a principal factor in Germany's dance renaissance in the 1950s and 1960s. Though she created a series of arresting solos for herself for performance in the concert hall, her lasting strength as a choreographer lay with her finely honed and musically subtle work for the corps de ballet of the theatre—"choreography" in the true sense of the word.

Her first loves were theatre and classical dance. Her relatively late start, at the age of seventeen, and her awareness of her own capabilities at that age, led her to Mary Wigman, who found in her an instinctive understanding of the Wigman aesthetic. But Georgi was never a revolutionary. She did not see the classical dance as a lifeless art form; she did not wish to bury the pointe shoe; and so her theatrical instinct led her early in her career back to the established theatre and its repertory of operas, operettas, and dance evenings performed by a permanent dance group. Within this form she practised the innovations which were to give new life to a stultified German dance.

For a time she seemed to live two lives: on the one hand, she was the international concert artist, dancing solo recitals (and duet evenings with Harald Kreutzberg) to enthusiastic audiences, while on the other, she was the choreographer, developing her aesthetic within the German theatrical scene—and to equal acclaim.

Though one tends to date her increasing return to classical dance as a post-war phenomenon, she was choreographing for, and collaborating with, ballet master Victor Gsovsky in the mid-1930s. (The rumour that she spent months in Paris at that time studying ballet remains just that.)

As early as 1952, Georgi had begun working with Richard Adama, who taught her dancers various pieces of the classical repertoire, unused in performance until she staged *The Nutcracker* and included the Ivanov "Pas de deux" in choreography otherwise by Georgi. During the 1950s and 1960s, Adama staged *Les Sylphides*, *Le Spectre de la rose*, *Giselle*, and a complete *Swan Lake* for her ever-improving Hanover Company.

Georgi's own choreography, however, became more erratic in its solo inventions, and ever more illuminating in its group

**Yvonne Georgi**

work. It seemed as if her respect for classical dance made her reluctant to apply her own innovations to an established and limited repertoire of steps, such that the stronger personalities among her principal dancers fought against a restricted choreographic idiom, with varying degrees of success. However, when working with dancers of international repute such as Dora Csinady, Adama, or Karl Musil, she arrived at a kind of choreographic balance, resulting in an artistic collaboration that could spark a role into life. At other moments, and with other dancers, her soloists seemed straitjacketed into an academism, that she, as a dancer, had never been guilty of. But her use of group movement became ever more confident, culminating perhaps in *Metamorphosen*, glowing in a kind of sunset; breathtaking in its seamless flow, it is certainly one of the great German ballets of the 1960s.

No evaluation of Yvonne Georgi could be complete without mentioning the influence of her husband, L.M.G. Arntzenius, a leading Dutch music critic. He gave support to her instinctive musicality, never interfering in the creative process, but constantly advising and guiding her selectivity. His connection with young composers of our time, and his impeccable feeling for what was valid as opposed to what was simply stylish, resulted in Yvonne Georgi's name being associated with many of the leading composers, over a period of several generations.

—Richard Adama

---

## GERDT, Elisaveta

Russian/Soviet dancer and teacher. Born in St. Petersburg, daughter of Maryinsky dancers Pavel Gerdt and Aleksandra Shaposhnikova, 29 April (17 April old style), 1891. Studied at the St. Petersburg Imperial Theatre School, pupil of Vera Zhokova and Mikhail Fokine; graduated in 1908. Married (1) dancer Samuel Andrianov; (2) conductor Aleksandr Gauk. Performed (while still a student) in Fokine's *Animated Gobelin*, 1907; dancer, Maryinsky Theatre, St. Petersburg, from 1908, dancing solo roles from 1910, and appointed ballerina 1919; retired from the stage in 1928; teacher, Class of Perfection, Leningrad Choreographic School, and ballerinas' class, State Academic Theatre of Opera and Ballet (GATOB), 1927–34: students include Alla Shelest; teacher, Moscow Choreographic School, 1935–42, 1945–60: students include Maya Plisetskaya, Raisa Struchkova, Ekaterina Maksimova. Recipient: title of Honoured Artist of the Russian Federation, 1925; Honoured Art Worker of the Russian Federation, 1951. Died in Moscow, 5 November 1975.

### ROLES

1907 Armide (cr) in *The Animated Gobelin* (scene from future *Le Pavillon d'Armide*; Fokine), Maryinsky Theatre, St. Petersburg

1908 Leading dancer in *Chopiniana* (second version; Fokine), Graduation Performance, Maryinsky Theatre, St. Petersburg

1911 Lilac Fairy in *The Sleeping Beauty* (Petipa), Maryinsky Theatre, St. Petersburg
1908/17 Aurora's Variation in *Coppélia* (Petipa, Cecchetti), Maryinsky Theatre, St. Petersburg
Columbine in *Carnaval* (Fokine), Maryinsky Theatre, St. Petersburg
1917 Isabelle in *The Trials of Damis* (*Les Ruses d'amour*; Petipa), State Academic Theatre for Opera and Ballet (GATOB), Petrograd (Leningrad)
1918 Anna (cr) in *Bluebeard* (Legat after Petipa; staged Monakhov, Chekrygin), GATOB, Petrograd (Leningrad)
1919/28 Odette/Odile in *Swan Lake* (Petipa, Ivanov), GATOB, Leningrad
Title role in *Raymonda* (Petipa), GATOB, Leningrad
Tsar-Maiden in *The Little Humpbacked Horse* (Petipa after Saint-Léon), GATOB, Leningrad
Masha in *The Nutcracker* (Ivanov), GATOB, Leningrad
Nikiya in *La Bayadère* (Petipa), GATOB, Leningrad
Aspiccia in *Pharaoh's Daughter* (Petipa), GATOB, Leningrad
1922 Aurora (cr) in *The Sleeping Beauty* (new production; Lopukhov after Petipa), GATOB, Leningrad
Soloist (cr) in *Chopiniana* (Chekrygin), GATOB, Leningrad
1923 Sugar Plum Fairy (cr) in *The Nutcracker* (Lopukhov, Shiryaev after Ivanov), GATOB, Leningrad
1924 The Radiant Power (cr) in *The Red Whirlwind* (Lophukhov), GATOB, Leningrad
1925 Smeraldina (cr) in *Pulcinella* (Lophukhov), GATOB, Leningrad

**Other roles include:** Myrtha in *Giselle* (Petipa after Coralli, Perrot), title role in *Paquita* (Petipa), Raymonda's Friend in *Raymonda* (Petipa), Queen of the Nereids in *The Little Humpbacked Horse* (Petipa after Saint-Léon).

## PUBLICATIONS

Volynsky, Akim, "Lily of Ballet", *Zhizn Iskussva* (Petrograd), no. 19, 1923
Borisoglebsky, Mikhail, *Materials on the History of Russian Ballet*, Leningrad, 1939
Struchkova, Raisa, "Remarkable Teacher of Classical Dance", *Teatr* (Moscow), no. 12, 1963
Roslavleva, Natalia, and Lawson, Joan, "Yelizaveta Gerdt", *Dancing Times* (London), May 1964
Krasovskaya, Vera, *Russian Ballet Theatre of the Beginning of the Twentieth Century*, volume 2: Leningrad, 1972
Chernova, Natalia, *From Geltser to Ulanova*, Moscow, 1979

* * *

When Elisaveta Gerdt first came to the class of Fokine, the young teacher was just beginning to overthrow the aesthetics of classical dance, and did not care much about the academic training of his pupils. But at least one of them opposed his innovatory views by virtue of the pure academicism of her own dancing. For Elisaveta Gerdt, the models of excellence were the school of Christian Johansson, the theatre of Marius Petipa, and the performing art of her own father. Throughout her career a blonde, svelte, and pretty dancer, Gerdt represented the pure, noble, and serene academic style of classical ballet. When Fokine staged *The Animated Gobelin* (the first version of his ballet *Le Pavillon d'Armide*) in the spring of 1907, he entrusted the role of the enchantress Armide to his young pupil Elisaveta Gerdt. That was the only work of Fokine which suited the noble and cold personality of Gerdt to perfection. On December 21, 1907, the critic of *Peterburgskaya Gazeta* wrote about the school performance and noticed that Gerdt "differs from other pupils by good pirouettes, elegance of dance, and pretty looks", but said that she had to be "more daring among the timid ones, and success will then follow".

Gerdt never took this advice: her dance always retained its reserved manner. The parts in her repertoire were "Sylphide" in *Chopiniana* (*Les Sylphides*), Columbine in *Carnaval*, Aurora's variation in *Coppélia*, and Isabella in *Les Ruses d'Amour*. One of the young dancer's best parts became the Lilac Fairy in *The Sleeping Beauty*, which she danced for the first time in 1911. In general, her dance evoked the images of spring flowers. At any rate, it gave the famous Russian critic, Akim Volinsky, the idea of comparing Gerdt with the lily of the valley. On December 28, 1912, he wrote about her variation in *Paquita*: "The white petals of lily of the valley touched me by their freshness", and further explained, "her cabrioles are irreproachable. The turns on the floor and in the air—perfect. The beats in entrechat-six give the visual sensation of lustre. And with all that the body of the artist lives in movement and trembles like a string. Her long arabesques in the coda with their wonderful passages from side to side shone with the colours of tender tinges." All of this made Gerdt a perfect Queen of the Wilis in *Giselle*.

In 1919, Gerdt was appointed ballerina and danced all the central parts of the classical ballets, such as Odette/Odile, Aurora, Raymonda, the Tsar-Maiden in *The Little Humpbacked Horse*, Masha in *The Nutcracker*, Nikiya in *La Bayadère*, Paquita, and Aspiccia in *Pharaoh's Daughter*. The revolutionary choreographer Fedor Lopukhov gave Gerdt roles in his ballets *Pulcinella* (Smeraldina) and *The Red Whirlwind* (The Radiant Power). Critics reprimanded Gerdt for the coldness of her dance, but praised her for the perfection of its form. In fact, Gerdt helped to preserve the academic culture of Russian ballet. For George Balanchine's eye, as his biographer Bernard Taper tells us, her dance "possessed a crystalline purity that was near perfection".

In 1928, Gerdt left the stage. For some five years she conducted the Class of Perfection in Leningrad's Choreographic School and the ballerinas' class in Leningrad's Theatre of Opera and Ballet. Gerdt was also a teacher at the Moscow Choreographical School, and from 1935 a teacher (or coach) for the professional dancers of the Bolshoi Theatre. Among her pupils were Alla Shelest, Maia Plisetskaia, Raisa Struchkova, and Ekaterina Maksimova.

—Vera Krasovskaya

---

### GERDT, Pavel

Russian dancer, choreographer, and teacher. Born Pavel (Pavel-Friedrich) Andreyevich Gerdt into German family in Volinkino, near St. Petersburg, 4 December (22 November old style) 1844. Studied at the Imperial Theatre School, St. Petersburg, pupil first of Aleksandr Pimenov and Jean Petipa, later (in graduation class) of Marius Petipa and Christian Johannsson; graduated in 1864. Married dancer Aleksandra Vasilievna Shaposhnikova, 1868: four children, including Maryinsky ballerina Elisaveta Gerdt (b. 1891). Début (while still a student), 1858: soloist, Bolshoi and Maryinsky Theatres, St. Petersburg, 1860–1916, receiving title of His Majesty's Soloist, 1901; teacher, Imperial Theatre School, 1880–1904: students include Elisaveta Gerdt, Anna Pavlova, Tamara

Karsavina, Agrippina Vaganova, Mikhail Fokine, Lydia Kyasht, Nikolai and Sergei Legat; also choreographer, composing ballet for Anna Pavlova's graduation performance, 1899, and for Maryinsky Theatre, 1901, 1902. Died in Vommala, Finland, 11 August 1917; buried in Leningrad.

## ROLES

1871 Apollo (cr) in *The Two Stars* (Petipa), Bolshoi Theatre, St. Petersburg
1872 Vestris (cr) in *La Camargo* (Petipa), Bolshoi Theatre, St. Petersburg
1874 Dance of the Butterfly (cr) in *Le Papillon* (Petipa), Bolshoi Theatre, St. Petersburg
1877 Classical variation, Grand Pas de deux (cr) in *La Bayadère* (Petipa), Bolshoi Theatre, St. Petersburg
1879 The Captain (cr) in *The Daughter of the Snows* (Petipa), Bolshoi Theatre, St. Petersburg
1880 Rudolph (cr) in *La Fille du Danube* (Petipa after Taglioni), Bolshoi Theatre, St. Petersburg
1881 Soliman (cr) in *Zoraya* (Petipa), Bolshoi Theatre, St. Petersburg
Lucien (cr) in *Paquita* (Petipa after Mazilier), Bolshoi Theatre, St. Petersburg
Jean (cr) in *Markitantka* (Petipa after Saint-Léon), Bolshoi Theatre, St. Petersburg
1884 Franz (cr) in *Coppélia* (Petipa after Saint-Léon), Bolshoi Theatre, St. Petersburg
1885 Colin (cr) in *Vain Precautions* (*La Fille mal gardée;* revival, Petipa, Ivanov), Bolshoi Theatre, St. Petersburg
1889 Nureddin (cr) in *The Talisman* (Petipa), Maryinsky Theatre, St. Petersburg
1890 Prince Désiré (cr) in *The Sleeping Beauty* (Petipa), Maryinsky Theatre, St. Petersburg
1891 Title role (cr) in *Kalkabrino* (Petipa), Maryinsky Theatre, St. Petersburg
1892 Prince Whooping Cough (cr) in *The Nutcracker* (Ivanov), Maryinsky Theatre, St. Petersburg
1893 Prince Charming (cr) in *Cinderella* (Petipa, Ivanov, Cecchetti), Maryinsky Theatre, St. Petersburg
Luke (cr) in *The Magic Flute* (Ivanov), Maryinsky Theatre, St. Petersburg
1895 Prince Siegfried (cr) in *Swan Lake* (Petipa, Ivanov), Maryinsky Theatre, St. Petersburg
1896 Pierre (cr) in *Cavalry Halt* (Petipa), Maryinsky Theatre, St. Petersburg
Raoul (cr) in *Bluebeard* (Petipa), Maryinsky Theatre, St. Petersburg
1898 Abderakhman (cr) in *Raymonda* (Petipa), Maryinsky Theatre, St. Petersburg
1900 Bacchus (cr) in *Les Saisons* (Petipa), Hermitage Theatre, St. Petersburg
Damis (cr) in *The Trials of Damis* (*Les Ruses d'amour;* Petipa), Hermitage Theatre, St. Petersburg
1903 Shopkeeper (cr) in *The Fairy Doll* (N. and S. Legat), Hermitage Theatre, St. Petersburg
1907 Petronio (cr) in *Eunice* (Fokine), Maryinsky Theatre, St. Petersburg
Vicomte de Beaugency (cr) in *Le Pavillon d'Armide* (Fokine), Maryinsky Theatre, St. Petersburg
Mark Lugano (cr) in *The Blood-Red Flower* (Legat), Maryinsky Theatre, St. Petersburg
1908 Antonio (cr) in *Egyptian Nights* (*Une Nuit d'Egypte*, later called *Cléopâtre*; Fokine), Maryinsky Theatre, St. Petersburg
1909 Akdar in *The Talisman* (Petipa, staged Legat), Maryinsky Theatre, St. Petersburg
1912 Khan (cr) in *The Little Humpbacked Horse* (St. Petersburg version of Gorsky after Petipa, Saint-Léon), Maryinsky Theatre, St. Petersburg
The King (cr) in *Islamé* (Fokine), Maryinsky Theatre, St. Petersburg
1916 Gamache in *La Bayadère* (Petipa), Maryinsky Theatre, Petrograd

**Other roles include:** Matteo in *The Naiad and the Fisherman* (Perrot), Oberon in *A Midsummer Night's Dream* (Petipa), Valentine in *Faust* (Perrot), James in *La Sylphide* (Petipa after Taglioni), Phoebus in *La Esmeralda* (Petipa after Perrot), Ta-Hor in *Pharaoh's Daughter* (Petipa), Conrad in *Le Corsaire* (Petipa), Lucien in *Paquita* (Petipa), title role in *King Candaule* (Petipa), Albrecht in *Giselle* (Petipa after Coralli, Perrot).

## WORKS

1899 *Imaginary Dryads* (mus. Pugni), Graduation Performance of Anna Pavlova, St. Petersburg
1901 *Sylvia* (continuing Ivanov's work; mus. Delibes), Maryinsky Theatre, St. Petersburg
1902 *Javotta* (mus. Saint-Saens), Maryinsky Theatre, St. Petersburg

## PUBLICATIONS

By Gerdt:
Interview in *Petersburgskaya Gazeta* (St. Petersburg), 22 November 1900

About Gerdt:
Svetlov, Valerian, *Terpsichore,* St. Petersburg, 1907
Shiryaev, Aleksandr, *St. Petersburg Ballet* (memoirs), Leningrad, 1941
Krasovskaya, Vera, *Russian Ballet Theatre in the Second Half of the Nineteenth Century,* Leningrad, Moscow, 1963
Lopukhov, Fedor, *Sixty Years in Ballet,* Moscow, 1966
Relkin, Abbi, "In Pavlova's Shadow", *Ballet News* (New York), January 1981
Smakov, Gennady, *The Great Russian Dancers,* New York, 1984
Gregory, John, "Legendary Dancers: Pavel Gerdt", *Dancing Times* (London), November 1987
Wiley, Roland John, *A Century of Russian Ballet: Documents and Eyewitness Accounts 1810–1910,* Oxford, 1990

* * *

Pavel Gerdt was educated at St. Petersburg's Imperial Theatre School. His first teacher, Aleksandr Pimenov, was a pupil of Charles-Louis Didelot; after this came Jean Petipa. In the graduation class, his teachers were Christian Johansson and Marius Petipa. From these teachers he acquired the best traditions of the European school, leading back through Johansson and Bournonville to Auguste Vestris, coupled with the original style of the Russian ballet. Gerdt's life was unclouded and more serene than the destiny of many of the princes from the ballets in his repertoire. He graduated in 1864, but according to the rules became a member of the ballet company of the Maryinsky Theatre as early as 1860, when he reached sixteen years of age. In 1868, he married a dancer, Aleksandra Vasilievna Shaposhnikova (1849–1930). They had three sons and a daughter, the ballerina Elisaveta Gerdt.

Pavel Gerdt never lived in poverty, as some of his colleagues did. From 1874 onwards he received a very high salary—1,143 roubles a year, 15 roubles for each performance, and one benefit night a season. In 1882, he received 5,000 roubles a year. In 1901, Gerdt was endowed with the rare title of His Majesty's Soloist.

During the second half of the nineteenth century, the duties of the male performer were strictly divided between dance and mime. So at the beginning of his career Gerdt appeared mostly as the nameless partner of ballerinas in virtuoso pas de deux, pas de trois, and other types of ballet divertissements. Then Petipa noticed the handsome young man with the noble bearing, tried him as a mime artist, and entrusted him with leading roles in many ballets. Soon Gerdt became the only partner to all the ballerinas; his repertory included more than 100 parts, mainly in Petipa ballets. The best were James Reuben in *La Sylphide*, Rudolph in *La Fille du Danube*, Phoebus de Chateaupers in *La Esmeralda*, Ta-Hor in *Pharaoh's Daughter*, Conrad in *Le Corsaire*, Lucien in *Paquita*, Solor in *La Bayadère*, and Albrecht in *Giselle*.

Several of Gerdt's heroes were known only in Russia, but they belonged to the creative genius of Marius Petipa. The naive plot of such ballets opened huge vistas for miming and dancing and the audiences of the 1870s asked for nothing more. The part of the Norwegian captain in the Minkus–Petipa ballet *The Daughter of the Snows*, first performed on 7 January 1879, might be cited as an example. At the end of the first act, the captain says farewell to his bride and leaves his native village for a polar expedition. Before leaving, he takes part in demi-character "Norwegian" dances. In the second act, his ship arrives in the kingdom of the snows. The hero realizes that there will be no way back. He mimes his despair and then his wonder and delight at the sudden appearance of the beautiful Snow Maiden. In the third act, the dying captain sees a vision of spring coming to the isle of frost; he dreams that his love melts the wicked heart of the daughter of the Snows. In this ballet, there were pure classical dances both for the principals and for a corps de ballet of flowers, consisting of nine dancers and 36 female students of the Imperial Ballet School. The final apotheosis came in a picture of the Captain and his crew, frozen to death.

Gerdt, who had been brought up in the aesthetics of the Petipa style, knew how to keep his noble presence and ease of manner even in less poetical works. Petipa's heyday came in 1890 with his staging of *The Sleeping Beauty*, when Gerdt was an elderly dancer of 46. Still, it was Gerdt who created the part of Prince Désiré. In the last act, he danced a short variation; "only a few bars of music," one critic wrote, "but what a beautiful dance." Then came the leading parts in Tchaikovsky's other ballets: Prince Siegfried in *Swan Lake* and Prince Koklush in *The Nutcracker*. In the Glazunov–Petipa ballets he performed the roles of the Saracen knight Abderakhman in *Raymonda*, Damis in *The Trials of Damis*, and Bacchus in *Les Saisons*. The part of Abderakhman was an outstanding one in Gerdt's repertoire. His Saracen came into the slow life of Raymonda's castle like a bird of prey. The passion of the musical theme impregnated every movement of this Abderakhman. When Raymonda's bridegroom came to her rescue, only the help of the White Lady—protectress of the noble family of Raymonda—allowed him to conquer the Saracen. In 1899 a critic wrote in *Petersburgskaya Gazeta* about an old balletomane, who came to the Maryinsky Theatre after fifteen years of absence and asked: "Tell me, please, if this is a son of Gerdt, whom I admired so many years ago?" On 27 November 1916, Gerdt appeared on stage for the last time in the comic role of Gamache in *Don Quixote*.

From 1880 until 1904, Gerdt was a teacher of classical dance at the Imperial Theatre School. Among his pupils were Anna Pavlova, Tamara Karsavina, Agrippina Vaganova, and Mikhail Fokine. As a choreographer, Gerdt created the ballet *Imaginary Dryads* for the graduation performance of his favourite pupil Anna Pavlova, as well as *Sylvia* and *Javotta* for the Maryinsky Theatre. Gerdt died in Vommala (Finland) on 11 August 1917. His death symbolically marked the end of a great epoch in Russian ballet.

—Vera Krasovskaya

---

## GIELGUD, Maina

British dancer, choreographer, teacher, and ballet director. Born Maina Julia Gordon Gielgud in London, 14 January 1945. Studied at the Hampshire School, London; also studied with Olga Preobrazhenska, Tamara Karsavina, Stanislas Idzikowski, Julie Sedova, Lubov Egorova, and Rosella Hightower. Dancer, Roland Petit's Ballets de Paris, 1961, and Grand Ballet du Marquis de Cuevas, 1961–62; soloist, Milorad Miskovitch Company, 1962, Grand Ballet Classique de France, 1963–1966, Béjart's Ballet du XXe Siècle, 1967–71; principal dancer with German Opera Ballet, Berlin, 1971–72, London Festival Ballet, 1972–75; also frequent guest artist, including for Sadler's Wells Royal Ballet, 1975–77; rehearsal director, London City Ballet, 1981–82; artistic director, Australian Ballet, Melbourne, from 1983. Honorary Member of the Royal Australian Order.

### ROLES

1962 La Flute in *Noir et blanc* (also *Suite en blanc*; Lifar), Grand Ballet Classique de France, Albi and Montauban Festival

1963 Lucille Grahn in *Pas de quatre* (Dolin), Grand Ballet Classique de France

Principal dancer in *Soirée musicale* (Taras), Rosella Hightower company, Vichy

Principal dancer in *Pas de trois* (Balanchine), Rosella Hightower company

Snow Queen (cr) in *The Little Match Girl* (Hightower), Rosella Hightower company, Cannes

1965 Mazurka, Pas de deux in *Les Sylphides* (Fokine), Grand Ballet Classique de France, tour

1967 Queen Mab in *Romeo and Juliet* (Béjart), Ballet du XXe Siècle, Brussels

Principal dancer in *Messe pour le temps présent* (Béjart), Ballet du XXe Siècle, Avignon

1968 Variation (cr) in *Baudelaire I* (Béjart), Ballet du XXe Siècle, Grenoble

Pas de deux (cr) in *Le Voyage II* (Béjart), Ballet du XXe Siècle, Grenoble

Pas d'action (cr) in *Ni Fleurs ni couronnes* (Béjart), Ballet de XXe Siècle, Grenoble

Principal dancer, Third Movement (cr) in *Bhakti* (Béjart), Ballet du XXe Siècle, Avignon

1969 Princess Aurora in *The Sleeping Beauty* (after Petipa), Ballet de Marseille, Barcelona

Principal dancer (cr) in *Les Quatres fils Aymon II* (Béjart), Ballet du XXe Siècle, Avignon

1970 Principal dancer (cr) in *Serait-ce la mort*? (Béjart), Ballet du XXe Siècle, Marseilles

**Maina Gielgud as the Black Queen in *Checkmate*, Sadler's Wells Royal Ballet, London, 1975**

1971 Odette/Odile in *Swan Lake* (Messerer after Petipa, Ivanov), Budapest State Opera Ballet, Budapest
1972 Choleric in *The Four Temperaments* (Balanchine), German Opera Ballet, Berlin
Myrtha in *Giselle* (after Petipa, Coralli, Perrot), German Opera Ballet, Berlin
Principal dancer in *Grand pas classique* (pas de deux; Gsovsky), German Opera Ballet, Berlin
Polyhymnia in *Apollo* (Balanchine), German Opera Ballet, Berlin
First Movement in *Symphony in C* (Balanchine), German Opera Ballet, Berlin
Principal dancer in *Episodes* (Balanchine), German Opera Ballet, Berlin
Odette/Odile in *Swan Lake* (Ivanov, Petipa; staged Grey), London Festival Ballet
Snow Fairy/Sugar Plum Fairy in *The Nutcracker* (Carter after Ivanov), London Festival Ballet, Bristol
Zobeide in *Schéhérazade* (Fokine), London Festival Ballet, Birmingham
1973 Principal dancer (cr) in *In Nomine* (Moreland), Fanfare for Europe
Street Dancer in *Le Beau Danube* (Massine), London Festival Ballet
Glove-Seller in *Gaité Parisienne* (Massine), London Festival Ballet
Principal dancer (cr) in *Dark Voyage* (Moreland), London Festival Ballet, Oxford
1974 The Ice Maiden in *The Fairy's Kiss* (Hynd), London Festival Ballet, London
Title role in *Giselle* (Petipa after Coralli, Perrot; staged Skeaping), London Festival Ballet
Kitri in *Don Quixote* (after Petipa, Gorsky), Ballet de Marseille, Marseilles
Lise in *La Fille mal gardée* (Ashton), Australian Ballet, Melbourne
1975 Juliet in *Romeo and Juliet* (Cranko), Australian Ballet, Sydney
Title role in *La Sylphide* (Bournonville), Gala for Rosella Hightower, Cannes
Title role in *Raymonda*, Act III (Nureyev after Petipa), Sadler's Wells Royal Ballet, London
Black Queen in *Checkmate* (de Valois), Sadler's Wells Royal Ballet, London
Siren in *The Prodigal Son* (Balanchine), Sadler's Wells Royal Ballet, London
1977 Swanilda in *Coppélia* (Wright after Petipa, Cecchetti), Sadler's Wells Royal Ballet, Cambridge

Gypsy girl in *Two Pigeons* (Ashton), Sadler's Wells Royal Ballet, tour
1978 Principal dancer (cr) in *Steps, Notes, and Squeaks* (also chor.), Open Space Theatre, London
1980 Princess (cr) in *The Soldier's Tale* (also chor.), Queen Elizabeth Hall, London

**Other roles include:** for Grand Ballet Classique de France—Sleeping Beauty in *Les Forains* (Petit), Cléopatre in *Faust Divertissement* (Mosena); for Ballet du XXe Siècle—Second Movement in *Ninth Symphony* (Béjart), principal dancer in *Webern Opus V* (Béjart), principal dancer in *Les Vainqueurs* (Béjart), principal dancer in *Forme et ligne* (Béjart); for Ballet Theatre of Joseph Rusillo—principal dancer in *Ketsu-Bokou* (Rusillo).

## WORKS

1973 *The Little Prince* (mus. Janáček), London Festival Ballet Choreographic Group, London
1978 *The Soldier's Tale* (mus. Stravinsky), Queen Elizabeth Hall, London
*Steps, Notes, and Squeaks* (mus. various), Open Space Theatre, London
1981 *Ghoulies and Ghosties* (mus. Debussy), London City Ballet, London

Also staged:
1985 *The Sleeping Beauty* (after Petipa; mus. Tchaikovsky), Australian Ballet
1987 *Giselle* (after Petipa, Coralli, Perrot; mus. Adam), Australian Ballet

## PUBLICATIONS

By Gielgud:
Interview in Laughlin, Patricia, "Gielgud's Challenges", *Dance Australia* (Sydney), December 1989–January 1990

About Gielgud:
Herf, E., "Maina Gielgud", *Ballet Today* (London), July/August 1968
Combescat, P., "Maina Gielgud", *Les Saisons de la Danse* (Paris), January 1969
Goodman, Saul, "Maina Gielgud", *Dance Magazine* (New York), May 1971
Murray, Jan, "Travels with a Tutu", *Observer Magazine* (London), 25 February 1979
Davies, R., "Maina Gielgud", *Classical Music* (London), 8 January 1983
Horosko, Marian, "Mainly Maina", *Dance Magazine* (New York), August 1985
Merrett, Sue, "Maina Gielgud and the Australian Ballet", *Dancing Times* (London), July 1988

* * *

Maina Gielgud's career has encompassed many areas in the world of dance; she has succeeded both as a classical and as a contemporary dancer, and as an indefatigable artistic director, and she has brought the Australian Ballet to international acclaim. But then theatre, if not actually dance, is in her blood: her mother is the Hungarian actress Zita Gordon; her great aunt was Ellen Terry; and her great-uncle is Sir John Gielgud.

As a dancer Gielgud was memorable for her energetic attack; she appeared to let nothing defeat her. Strong on personality and presentation, she resembled an athletic American ballerina rather than an English rose, and her exuberant, if sometimes brittle, style can be traced back to her training with the American dancer Rosella Hightower—she is very much a product of the Hightower school.

Hightower, however, was just one of Gielgud's many teachers (she claims to have studied with 35 different teachers before setting foot on the professional stage), and through this eclectic training she learned to adapt to a variety of styles. She was exposed to the traditions and style of the Russian school by Tamara Karsavina, and while Gielgud was rarely lauded as a romantic heroine—being at her most successful when cast as a hard, unkind character—Karsavina's influence is discernible in her dancing.

Initially she thought that she was destined to be a classical dancer, and her first professional engagements were with classical companies—Roland Petit, the Marquis de Cuevas, and the Grand Ballet Classique de France. However, her ideas were radically reformed when she saw Béjart's work. Attracted by the theatricality of the controversial choreographer's ballets, she joined his Ballet du XXe Siècle. After working with him for four years, Gielgud's body yielded to a contemporary, sensual, and often angular way of moving. In Béjart's *Bhakti* (one of several ballets he created on her) she made an exotic goddess, filling each step with a sense of mysterious intrigue. But the Béjart ballet with which she became associated was *Forme et ligne*. Her great sense of humour (which she tends to repress) was revealed in this piece (commonly called *Squeaky Door*), as were her steely balances, by-products of her technical grounding.

Béjart influenced her greatly (and she has, many years later, added a number of Béjart ballets to the Australian Ballet's repertoire); but her classical roots were drawn upon again when Rudolf Nureyev invited her to dance in *The Sleeping Beauty* with him in Barcelona.

Working subsequently with a host of companies worldwide (and most prominently with the London Festival Ballet and the Sadler's Wells Royal Ballet), she danced countless roles, finding the greatest affinity with those calling for a strong characterization. Her tall stature too lent itself to roles like the Black Queen in *Checkmate*, in which her powerful sense of dramatic theatre was especially appropriate, or the Queen of the Wilis, which in her interpretation was truly menacing. As the inexorable Ice Maiden in Ronald Hynd's *The Fairy's Kiss*, she was ravishingly icy, and she dressed the role of *Raymonda* with a charismatic authority. In *Swan Lake*, she was far more brilliant as the callous, diamond-edged Odile than as Odette in the white acts.

Marrying her dance ability with her innate sense of theatre and general enterprise, she created *Steps, Notes, and Squeaks*—a programme revealing the other side of the footlights to audiences—in 1978. Originally staged in London at the Open Space Theatre, it moved on to the West End to the Ambassadors Theatre for a short season. The programme opened with Gielgud demonstrating daily classwork, and then introduced a partner with whom she worked on a classical pas de deux (invariably from *The Sleeping Beauty*) under the critical eye of an eminent ballerina—a role frequently played by Svetlana Beriosova. Next the couple was seen tackling a new choreography, and the programme concluded with a performance of the classical pas de deux. *Steps, Notes, and Squeaks* was a big success for Gielgud, and subsequently toured to many major cities throughout the world. Inspired by this success, she decided to realize her choreographic inclinations, and she created *The Soldier's Tale* on Wayne Sleep, for a special performance with the National Theatre.

Diverting her energies away from performing, she took up

the post of rehearsal director with London City Ballet. For this company she created *Ghoulies* and *Ghosties*, which again demonstrated her sense of humour, and was directed at a young audience. Barely a year later, she was appointed artistic director of the Australian Ballet, taking the reins during a difficult period in the company's history. A dancers' strike had crippled the performance schedule and morale was low, but she was not daunted. Instead she is quoted as saying "My luck has been to find talent here that does not exist anywhere else in the world." She also claims to be able to spot an Australian dancer anywhere in the world because Australians are such "gutsy" dancers.

Raising the standard of dancing to an international level, Gielgud dared to take the company overseas, and brought it to the Royal Opera House, London, in 1988. Risking inevitable comparison with the Royal Ballet's *The Sleeping Beauty* (ranked as one of the company's hallmarks), Gielgud brought her own production of the Petipa classic to London, with the sound view that a company's true strength could only be analyzed in a full-length classic. While the Australian Ballet's designs for *The Sleeping Beauty* were perhaps too gaudy for European taste, and her alterations to the original choreography not particularly successful, her courage was rewarded as the company's dancers themselves received excellent reviews. "A sparkling and meticulously rehearsed performance" claimed the *Daily Telegraph*, while John Percival in *The Times* could not recall ever having seen a *Sleeping Beauty* "so consistently well danced from beginning to end".

Gielgud adamantly believes in the nurturing of young dancers and in giving them major roles while still young, and she is frequently criticized for pushing young dancers too soon. She has dedicated herself to the development of the Australian Ballet, and few performances go by without her watching vigilantly, scribbling notes throughout. Her drive is relentless, her gaze piercingly astute, and her devotion to dance unquestionable.

—Emma Manning

---

## GILMOUR, Sally

English dancer. Born in Malaya, 1921. Studied with Tamara Karsavina in London, 1930–33, and at the Rambert School. Married Dr. Alan Wynne in Australia, 1948. Début, Ballet Club (later Ballet Rambert), while still a student; dancer, becoming principal dancer, Ballet Rambert, from 1937, touring Australia, 1947–49, and remaining there until 1950; returned to Ballet Rambert, 1950–53; also appeared as Louise in musical *Carousel* (Rodgers and Hammerstein; Drury Lane Theatre, 1950), and as guest artist, London Festival Ballet, 1950.

### ROLES

1936 Nymph in *Mars and Venus* (Ashton), Ballet Club, London
1937 Pas de trois from *Swan Lake* (after Ivanov, Petipa), Ballet Rambert, London
Maria (cr) in *Cross-Garter'd* (new version; Toye), Ballet Rambert, London
A Mortal under Mars in *The Planets* (Tudor), Ballet Rambert
1938 Guest in *Valse finale* (Gore), Ballet Rambert, London
The Sport Girl in *Le Boxing* (Salaman), Ballet Rambert
Signes de Zodiaque/Polka (cr) in *Croquis de Mercure* (Howard), Ballet Rambert, London
Red Riding Hood in *Aurora's Wedding* (after Petipa), Ballet Rambert
A Wife (cr) in *La Péri* (Staff), Ballet Rambert, Cambridge
1939 A Lover (cr) in *Paris-Soir* (Gore), Ballet Rambert, London
The Creole in *Paris-Soir* (Gore), Ballet Rambert, London
Silvia (cr) in *Lady into Fox* (Howard), Ballet Rambert, London
Muse in *La Muse s'amuse* (Howard), Ballet Rambert, London
M'as tu vue (cr) in *Czernyana* (Staff), Ballet Rambert, London
Polka in *Façade* (Ashton), Ballet Rambert
1940 Granddaughter (cr) in *Cap over Mill* (Gore), Ballet Rambert, London
Duck (cr) in *Peter and the Wolf* (Staff), Ballet Rambert, Cambridge
Caroline in *Jardin aux lilas* (Tudor), Ballet Rambert
Title role in *The Mermaid* (Salaman, Howard), Ballet Rambert
Marguerite in *Mephisto Valse* (Ashton), Ballet Rambert
Maiden in *Death and the Maiden* (Howard), Ballet Rambert
A Mortal under Venus in *The Planets* (Tudor), Ballet Rambert
La Fille au bar in *Bar aux Folies-Bergère* (de Valois), Ballet Rambert
1941 The Châtelaine in *La Fête étrange* (Howard), Ballet Rambert, London
Visions (cr) in *Czerny 2* (Staff), Rambert-London Ballet, London
Principal dancer (cr) in *Bartlemas Dances* (Gore), Oxford University Ballet Club, Oxford
Principal dancer (cr) in *Confessional* (Gore), Oxford University Ballet Club, Oxford
1942 Juno in *La Belle Hélène* in *The Tales of Hoffmann*, Strand Theatre, London
1943 Girl with Birds (cr) in *Carnival of the Animals* (Howard), Ballet Rambert, London
The Little Girl in *Carnival of the Animals* (Howard), Ballet Rambert
Peter in *Peter and the Wolf* (Staff), Ballet Rambert
La Reine de la danse from Moscow in *Gala Performance* (Tudor), Ballet Rambert
Etoile in *La Foyer de la danse* (Ashton), Ballet Rambert
Title role in *Pompette* (Ashton), Ballet Rambert
1944 Younger Sister (cr) in *The Fugitive* (Howard), Ballet Rambert, Bedford
Hebe in *The Descent of Hebe* (Tudor), Ballet Rambert
Principal dancer (cr) in *Simple Symphony* (Gore), Ballet Rambert, Bristol
Swan Queen in *Swan Lake*, Act II (Nijinska after Ivanov), Ballet Rambert
Columbine (cr) in *Harlequinade* in *The Glass Slipper*, St. James Theatre, London
Juno in *The Judgment of Paris* (Tudor), Ballet Rambert
Mortal under Mercury in *The Planets* (Tudor), Ballet Rambert
1945 Title role in *Giselle*, Act II (after Petipa, Coralli, Perrot), Ballet Rambert, Birmingham
La Fille de Terpsichore from Paris in *Gala Performance* (Tudor), Ballet Rambert
Débutante in *Façade* (Ashton), Ballet Rambert

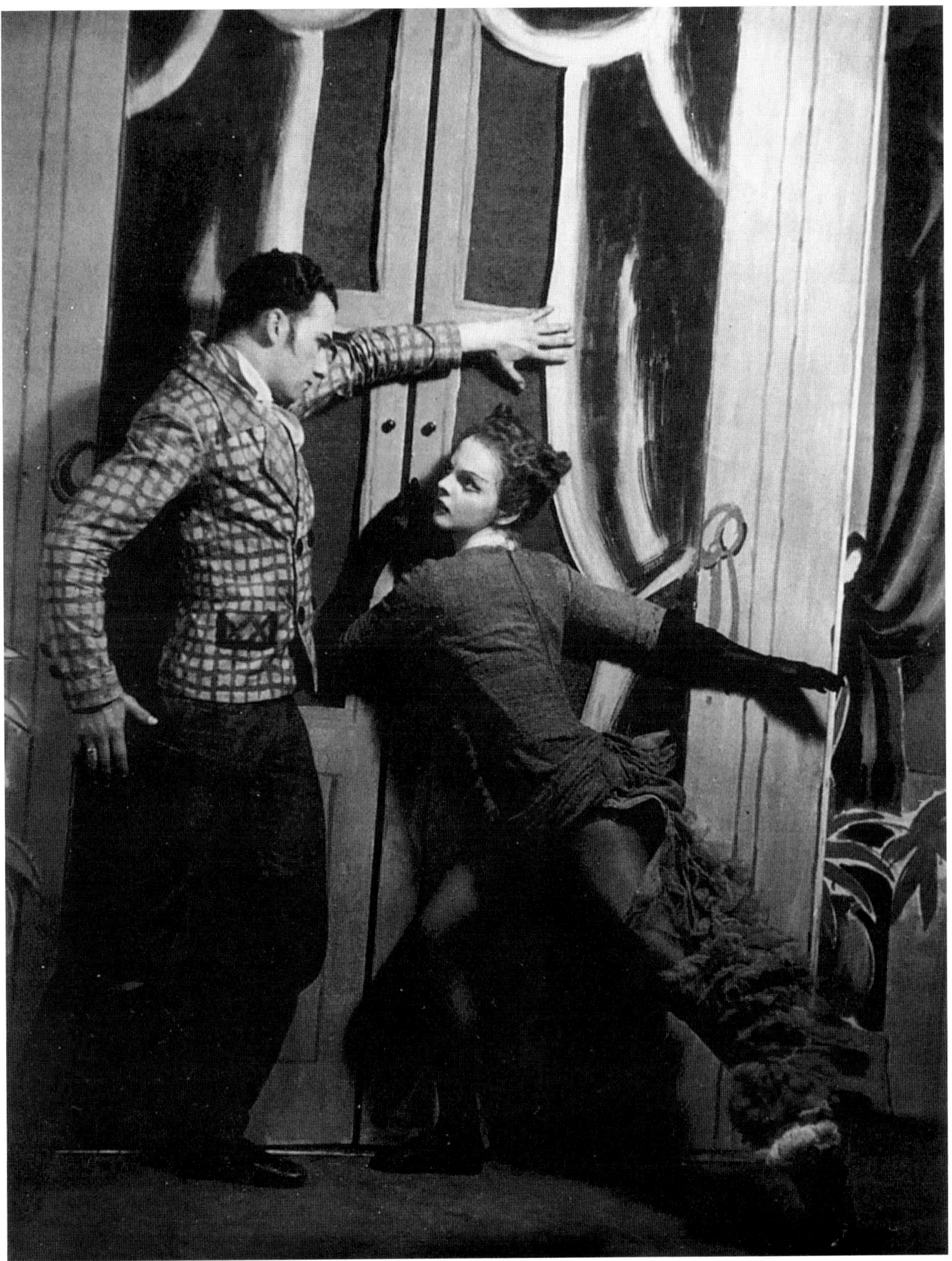

**Sally Gilmour with Charles Boyd in Andrée Howard's *Lady Into Fox*, Ballet Rambert, 1939**

1946 Title role in *Giselle* (after Petipa, Coralli, Perrot), Ballet Rambert, London
Hysterics (cr) in *Concerto Burlesco* (Gore), Ballet Rambert, London
Pretty Polly (cr) in *Mr. Punch* (Gore), Ballet Rambert, London
1947 Tulip (cr) in *The Sailor's Return* (Howard), Ballet Rambert, London
1948 Felice (cr) in *Winter Night* (Gore), Ballet Rambert, Melbourne
1951 Grace (cr) in *Orlando's Silver Wedding* (Howard), Festival of Britain, Pleasure Gardens Amphitheatre, London

**Other roles include:** Nymph in *L'Après-midi d'un faune* (Nijinsky; staged Woizikowsky), Scotch Rhapsody in *Façade* (Ashton), Attendant on Jupiter in *The Descent of Hebe* (Tudor), La Goulue in *Bar aux Folies-Bergère* (de Valois), A Fan in *Le Rugby* (Salaman), Columbine in *Carnaval* (Fokine), Danse de tendresse in *Croquis de Mercure* (Howard), Presque classique in *Czernyana* (Staff), First, Second, and Fourth Movements in *Dark Elegies* (Tudor), Myrrhina and Lampito in *Lysistrata* (Tudor), Tirolese in *Soirée musicale* (Tudor), Young Girl in *Le Spectre de la rose* (Fokine), Valse, Mazurka, and Prelude in *Les Sylphides* (Fokine), principal dancer in *The Tartans* (Staff).

## PUBLICATIONS

By Gilmour:
"Tribute" in Crisp, Clement, Sainsbury, Anya, and Williams, Peter (eds.), *Ballet Rambert: 50 Years and On*, revised edition, London, 1981
"Remembering Andrée Howard", *Dance Research* (London), Spring 1989

About Gilmour:
Bradley, Lionel, *Sixteen Years of Ballet Rambert*, London, 1946
Beaumont, Cyril, "Sally Gilmour", *Ballet* (London), July 1947
Noble, Peter, *British Ballet*, London, c.1949
Miller, Tatlock, "Sally Gilmour . . . The Fox Returns", *Dance and Dancers* (London), June 1950
Davidson, Gladys, *Ballet Biographies*, revised edition, London, 1954
Williams, Peter, "Creator of Characters", *Dance and Dancers* (London), May 1955
Clarke, Mary, *Dancers of Mercury: The Story of Ballet Rambert*, London, 1962

* * *

Sally Gilmour was a key figure in the development of the dramatic tradition within British ballet. She was pretty, but did not conform to the conventional image of a beautiful ballerina, and her technique was not impeccable. Nevertheless, Gilmour's expressive, individual talent made her one of the most important and best-loved dancers of the 1940s. She was regarded by some as second only to Margot Fonteyn as the leading female dancer in Britian.

A dramatic dancer rather than a classical ballerina, Gilmour has at times been placed in the demi-caractère category, but that does not allow for her versatility. She took on leading classical roles with Ballet Rambert and was a lyrical, moving Odette in *Swan Lake*, Act II. Rambert's acclaimed production of *Giselle* was staged for her benefit, and Gilmour made an indelible impression on those who saw her. Cyril Beaumont praised her performance for "its lyric qualities, its poetry, its pathos". He wrote, "Other interpreters of the role may excel her in technical ability, but not one of them equals her in expression."

Gilmour's range encompassed both comedy and tragedy. She could be zany and boyish as Peter in *Peter and the Wolf*, child-like as the Granddaughter in *Cap over Mill* and the girl in *Carnival of Animals*, and witty in *Le Boxing*, *Czernyana*, and *Gala Performance*. At the same time, she could move audiences to tears as the girl betrayed by the Inquisition in the ballet monologue to Robert Browning's *Confessional*, or as the innocent younger sister awakened by love in *The Fugitive*. She had the ability to grip the audience's attention even when motionless. She was a notable interpreter of Tudor's ballets and was particularly acclaimed as Caroline in *Jardin aux lilas* in which she captured the sense of frustrated young love.

Gilmour had been encouraged in her career by her father, who had taken her to watch Pavlova in Singapore and, when the family returned to London, arranged for her to have classes from Tamara Karsavina. From the age of twelve she trained with Marie Rambert, who quickly recognized Gilmour's talent and potential. While still a student she appeared with Ballet Club, her earliest roles being a Little Swan in the *Swan Lake* pas de quatre and an Attendant in Ashton's *Mars and Venus*. She soon began to create her own roles—including a lively, pert Maria in Wendy Toye's new version of *Cross-Garter'd*—but her real breakthrough came in 1939, when she danced the first performance of *Lady into Fox*. Andrée Howard had intended the role of Silvia for herself, but ill health forced her to create the part on Celia Franca. Shortly before the premiere Franca became unavailable, and at Rambert's suggestion Gilmour (originally cast as a Huntswoman) was carefully coached for the role, and became forever associated with Mr. Tebrick's Wife who is inexplicably transformed into a fox. This was the first of several fey or fanciful characters that Gilmour performed to perfection. It was also the first of a number of animal roles she created. Among these were the adorable, unfortunate, waddling duck in *Peter and the Wolf* (did the choreographer Frank Staff have a premonition of Gilmour's subsequent success in *Giselle* when he devised the Duck's ghostly return?); and a feline Grace in Howard's ballet based on *Orlando the Marmalade Cat*. She could take on all the characteristics of an animal, and even 25 years after she had last performed as Mrs. Tebrick, in a television interview, unaided by costume or makeup, she assumed for the camera the appearance of a fox while discussing the creation of *Lady into Fox*.

Many of Gilmour's greatest roles were specifically created for her talent. Andrée Howard and Walter Gore (also her most regular partner) in particular recognized her ability to express a variety of moods and characters. For Gore, Gilmour was the muse of many of his earliest ballets, and his works, from *Valse finale* and *Confessional* through to *Winter Night*, included roles for her. For Howard, Gilmour's enigmatic, highly sensitive personality made her the ideal interpreter, both of already established ballets—her interpretations of the suffering Mermaid was memorable and her delicate Maiden in *Death and the Maiden* equalled Howard's own—and of new works. As Tulip the Negro Princess in *The Sailor's Return*, Gilmour showed her wonderful power of sinking herself into a character. She developed from a girl who jumps with childish glee at her new finery to a mature widow desolate at the loss of her husband, son, home, and dignity.

When Gilmour took over established roles, she interpreted them afresh and made them her own. She found emotional depths in the innocent and tender Marguerite and was a sensitive Young Girl in *Le Spectre de la rose*. Even in roles not obviously suited to her own personality she would eventually find a way of portraying them with conviction; she brought, for example, new freshness and sparkle to the sophisticated La Goulue in *Bar aux Folies-Bergère*.

Most of Gilmour's performing career was spent with Rambert, to whom she has always acknowledged her debt. She was happiest performing in a family atmosphere and was one of the dancers who campaigned for Ballet Rambert's re-establishment in 1943. Even at the end of her performing career when, because of family commitments, she stopped regular touring, she still made guest appearances with the Rambert company. She also branched out and appeared as Louise in the musical *Carousel* and briefly in films. She turned down the offer to join the Ballets Russes with the possibility of dancing many of Riabouchinska's roles, but memorably substituted for an indisposed Markova in Festival Ballet's *Giselle*.

Gilmour was intelligent and had an exceptional memory. Her ability to recall choreography with precision contributed to the restaging of a number of ballets, particularly during Ballet Rambert's 1947–49 Australian tour. She was also called on to help revive ballets at other times, and it is her clear recollection of the 1937 staging of *Dark Elegies* (a work in which she danced all the leading women's parts as well as appearing in the corps de ballet) that has kept the original version of Tudor's ballet alive.

—Jane Pritchard

---

**GILPIN, John**

British dancer, teacher, actor, and ballet director. Born in Southsea, 10 February 1930. Studied with Tina Pearce, Swansea, and Barbara Spencer-Edwards, Devonshire, 1937–40, at Cone-Ripman School (on scholarship), from 1940, and Rambert School, London, from 1945; also coached by Tamara Karsavina. Married (1) Sally Judd, 1960: one daughter, Tracy; (2) Princess Antoinette of Monaco, 1983. Early stage, film, and radio career as child actor; dancer, soon performing solo roles, Ballet Rambert, 1945–48, touring Australia with Ballet Rambert, 1947–48; leading dancer, Roland Petit's Ballets de Paris, 1948–49; also performed with (Marquis de Cuevas's) Grand Ballet de Monte Carlo, 1950; principal dancer, (London) Festival Ballet, from 1950; guest artist, Royal Ballet, 1961, 1963, American Ballet Theatre, 1965, Chicago Ballet, 1966, Festival Ballet, 1969, and with many companies in Europe and America; assistant artistic director, London Festival Ballet, 1959–62: artistic director, 1962–65; artistic director, Pittsburgh Ballet Theatre, 1977; freelance teacher, often teaching abroad, including in Copenhagen, Tokyo, and Ankara; appeared in films, including in *We'll Meet Again* (dir. Brandon, 1942), and *They Were Sisters* (dir. Crabtree, 1945); also appeared in play *Invitation to the Dance* (Maxim Mazumdar), based on Gilpin's life, Newfoundland, 1980, and New York, 1981, and as Oberon in Lindsay Kemp's *Midsummer Night's Dream*, Italy, 1981. Recipient: Adeline Genée Gold Medal, London, 1943; Nijinsky Prize, Paris, 1957; Gold Medal, Paris International Dance Festival, 1964. Died in London, 5 September 1983.

**ROLES**

1945 Scotch Rhapsody in *Façade* (Ashton), Ballet Rambert, Brighton
Tyrolese in *Soirée musicale* (Tudor), Ballet Rambert, Brighton
1946 Spirit of the Rose in *Le Spectre de la rose* (Fokine), Ballet Rambert
Peasant pas de deux from *Giselle* (after Petipa, Coralli, Perrot), Ballet Rambert, London
Variation in *Czernyana* (Staff), Ballet Rambert
The Planet Mercury in *The Planets* (Tudor), Ballet Rambert
Guest in *The Fugitive* (Howard), Ballet Rambert
Jack Ketch (cr) in *Mr. Punch* (Gore), Ballet Rambert, London
Harlequin in *Carnaval* (Fokine), Ballet Rambert, Birmingham
Peter in *Peter and the Wolf* (Staff), Ballet Rambert, Birmingham
Canzone (cr) in *Concerto Burlesco* (Gore), Ballet Rambert, London
1947 Huntsman in *Lady into Fox* (Howard), Ballet Rambert, Belfast
Bluebird in *Bluebird Pas de deux* (after Petipa), Ballet Rambert, Bristol
Principal dancer (cr) in *Plaisance* (Gore), Ballet Rambert, Bristol
Charlie Ney, the Rabbit Catcher (cr) in *The Sailor's Return* (Howard), Ballet Rambert, London
Popular Song in *Façade* (Ashton), Ballet Rambert, Melbourne
1948 Tarantella in *Soirée musicale* (Tudor), Ballet Rambert, Australian tour
Mercury in *The Descent of Hebe* (Tudor), Ballet Rambert, Australian tour
Principal dancer in *Winter Night* (Gore), Ballet Rambert, Australian tour
1949 King of the Dandies in *Le Beau Danube* (Massine), Les Ballets de Paris
King of Nougat (cr) in *Le Rêve de Léonor* (Ashton), Les Ballets de Paris, London
Sailor in *'Adame miroir* (Charrat), Les Ballets de Paris
Bandit in *Carmen* (Petit), Les Ballets de Paris
Negro Page in *Que le diable l'emporte!* (Petit), Les Ballets de Paris
Principal dancer in *Concerto Barocco* (Balanchine), (de Cuevas's) Grand Ballet de Monte Carlo
1950 Principal dancer (cr) in *Perséphone* (Taras), Grand Ballet de Monte Carlo
Principal dancer in *Dessins pour les six* (*Designs with Strings*; Taras), Grand Ballet de Monte Carlo
Principal dancer in *Les Sylphides* (Fokine), Grand Ballet de Monte Carlo
Principal dancer in *Capriccioso* (Dolin, Cone), London Festival Ballet
Hussar in *Le Beau Danube* (Massine), London Festival Ballet, Southsea
Harlequin in *Harlequinade* (Lichine after Petipa), London Festival Ballet, London
The Prince in *The Nutcracker* (Dolin, Markova, Cone after Ivanov), London Festival Ballet
Albrecht in *Giselle* (Petipa after Coralli, Perrot; staged Dolin), London Festival Ballet
1951 Principal dancer in *Black Swan Pas de deux* (from *Swan Lake*; after Petipa), London Festival Ballet
Fourth Movement (cr) in *Symphonic Impressions* (Lichine), London Festival Ballet, Monte Carlo
1952 Principal dancer (cr) in *Concerto Grosso en ballet* (Lichine), London Festival Ballet, London
Faust (cr) in *Vision of Marguerite* (Ashton), London Festival Ballet, London
Principal dancer (cr) in *Symphony for Fun* (Charnley),

**John Gilpin**

London Festival Ballet, London
Principal dancer (cr) in *Harlequinade* (Darrell), London Festival Ballet
1953 Danilo in *Vilia* (R. Page), London Festival Ballet
The White Rabbit (cr) in *Alice in Wonderland* (Charnley), London Festival Ballet, Bournemouth
Principal dancer (cr) in *Concerto* (Lambrinos), London Festival Ballet, London
Principal dancer (cr) in *The Laurel Crown* (Lambrinos), London Festival Ballet
1954 Pierre Gringoire (cr) in *Esmeralda* (new production; Beriozoff), London Festival Ballet, London
Gennaro in *Napoli* (divertissement; Bournonville, staged Lander), London Festival Ballet, London
1955 Principal dancer in *Études* (Lander), London Festival Ballet, London
1956 Franz in *Coppélia* (Lander), London Festival Ballet
Principal dancer (cr) in *Homage to the Princess* (Charnley), London Festival Ballet, Monte Carlo
Dancer in *The Gift of the Magi* (Semenoff), London Festival Ballet, Monte Carlo
1957 Fourth solo (cr) in *Variations for Four* (Dolin), London Festival Ballet, London
Title role in *The Witch Boy* (J. Carter), London Festival Ballet, Manchester
Junior Cadet in *Graduation Ball* (Lichine), London Festival Ballet, Monte Carlo
1958 Solo (Cha-cha-cha) (cr) in *Octetto* (*Classico*; Stone), London Festival Ballet
Principal dancer in *Grand pas classique* (pas de deux; Gsovsky), London Festival Ballet
Principal dancer (cr) in *Pièce d'occasion* (Cranko), London Festival Ballet, London
1959 The Sailor (cr) in *London Morning* (J. Carter), London Festival Ballet, London
1960 Title role (cr) in *Bonaparte à Nice* (Lifar), London Festival Ballet, Nice
Prelude in *Bourrée fantasque* (Balanchine), London Festival Ballet
1961 Variation ("Blue Boy") in *Les Patineurs* (Ashton), Royal Ballet, London
1962 Principal dancer in *Promenade à deux* (Beriozoff), London Festival Ballet, Barcelona
Principal dancer in *Improvisations* (J. Carter), London Festival Ballet
1963 Title role (cr) in *Peer Gynt* (Orlikovsky), London Festival Ballet, Monte Carlo
Principal dancer in *Flower Festival at Genzano* (pas de deux; after Bournonville), Royal Ballet Touring Company
1964 The Devil in *Walpurgis Night* (Orlikovsky), London Festival Ballet
Prince Siegfried in *Swan Lake* (new production; Petipa, Ivanov; staged Orlikovsky), London Festival Ballet, Verona
1966 The Marquis (cr) in *Beatrix* (J. Carter), London Festival Ballet, London
Principal dancer in *Pas de deux romantique* (Carter), London Festival Ballet, Barcelona
1967 The Poet in *La Sonnambula* (Balanchine), London Festival Ballet, Venice
The Prince in *The Sleeping Beauty* (Stevenson after Petipa), London Festival Ballet, London
Principal dancer (cr) in *Pas de deux for Four* (Dolin), London Festival Ballet, Southsea
1969 Principal dancer in *The Unknown Island* (J. Carter), London Festival Ballet
1970 Principal dancer in *La Vida* (pas de trois; Darrell), London Festival Ballet

## PUBLICATIONS

By Gilpin:
Interview in Gruen, John, *The Private World of Ballet*, New York, 1975
*A Dance With Life* (autobiography), London, 1982

About Gilpin:
Davidson, Gladys, *Ballet Biographies*, revised edition, London, 1954
"John Gilpin", in *Dance and Dancers* (London), July 1954
"Personality of the Month: John Gilpin", *Dance and Dancers* (London), August 1957
Swinson, Cyril, *John Gilpin*, London, 1957
Swinson, Cyril, *Dancers of Today*, no. 12, London, 1957
Percival, John, "Accent on the Male, 2: John Gilpin", *Dance and Dancers* (London), January 1958
Percival, John, "Britain's Great Virtuoso", *Dance and Dancers* (London), January 1958
Corathiel, Elisabeth, "John Gilpin", *Ballet Today*, (London), February 1958
Lidova, Irène, "John Gilpin", *Les Saisons de la danse* (Paris), December 1972

* * *

A versatile performer, John Gilpin was a leading dancer of his generation, but his talent has subsequently been overlooked; he worked only briefly with the Royal Ballet, and his years as a guest artist were overshadowed by the arrival in the West of Rudolf Nureyev.

Gilpin began his career as a dancer early, joining Ballet Rambert at the age of 15 (having already won the Adeline Genée Gold Medal in 1943, the youngest recipient ever), and having been featured in pictorial magazines as a "new Nijinsky". He was already a successful actor in plays, in films, and on radio (he returned to acting at the end of his dancing career). His commitment to dance was such that he turned down a salary of £50 per week (in 1945) to create the title role in Terence Rattingan's *The Winslow Boy*, earning £6 per week instead as a featured dancer with Rambert.

Gilpin had a natural talent for classical ballet. Technique came easily to him and he possessed an unmatched perfection of line and a musicality which complemented his personal elegance. A virtuoso dancer, he rarely used his technique to show off. He is remembered as an unrivalled interpreter of a leading role in *Études*, in which he performed the full series of grands pirouettes and fouettés without a break. While still with Rambert, performing a repertoire that included the Pas de trois from *Swan Lake*, the Bluebird pas de deux, and the Peasant pas de deux from *Giselle*, he was hailed as a successor to Britain's previous principal virtuoso, Harold Turner.

Gilpin was a danseur noble, at home as the Prince in *Swan Lake*, *The Nutcracker*, and *The Sleeping Beauty*, as well as Albrecht in *Giselle* (a favourite role) and the Poet in *Les Sylphides*. Indeed, it was a report of his performances in *Les Sylphides* and *The Nutcracker* with the de Cuevas Company that persuaded Anton Dolin to invite the apparently aloof (but in fact rather shy) Gilpin to become a principal with (London's) Festival Ballet in 1950. He remained with Festival for most of his career. It has been said that Rambert developed him as an artist and Festival made him a star.

A skilled partner, Gilpin worked with most great ballerinas

**Fanny Elssler in the Cracovienne from *La Gipsy***

of his day, from Danilova, Riabouchinska, Toumanova, Chauviré, and Fonteyn to Gilmour, Lander, Fracci, Sibley, and Pontois. He also had a long-standing partnership with Belinda Wright. They both joined Ballet Rambert at the same time; he then followed her to Petit's Ballet de Paris and she in turn joined him at Festival Ballet.

Gilpin always regretted that few significant roles were created for him to show off his special talent. Andrée Howard choreographed the cameo of the Rabbit Catcher in *The Sailor's Return*, and his friend Noël Coward devised his only ballet, *London Morning* (choreography by Jack Carter) for him. Ashton created roles for Gilpin in *Le Rêve de Léonor* and the *Vision of Marguerite*, and Anton Dolin devised the final solo in his showpiece for four male dancers, *Variations for Four*; but most of Gilpin's created roles were in ballets that have failed to survive. His talent as a dramatic interpreter was rarely used, but none the less his performances in the title role of *The Witch Boy* (which he insisted was brought into Festival's repertoire) were memorable.

In 1959 he became assistant to the artistic director and subsequently artistic director of London's Festival Ballet. In 1977 he was artistic director of Pittsburg Ballet, but he had little talent for directorship. Gilpin's only attempts at choreography were solos for himself on a 1954 tour of India. Late in his career he did contribute, with his friend and mentor Anton Dolin, to memorable stagings of *Giselle*, *Variations for Four*, *Nutcracker* (after the 1957 Lichine–Benois staging), and *Le Spectre de la rose*. This last ballet was one with which he was particularly associated. He first appeared in it for Rambert with Sally Gilmour (having learned his role from William Chappell) and was subsequently coached for Festival by Anton Dolin and Tamara Karsavina. As the Spirit of the Rose, Gilpin was one of the few dancers to blot out audiences' image of what Nijinsky must have been like in this ballet, instead giving a strong interpretation himself.

Gilpin did undertake guest engagements including at La Scala in Milan with Carla Fracci; both Royal Ballet companies (notably as the virtuoso Blue Boy in *Les Patineurs* and in *The Sleeping Beauty*); and American Ballet Theatre for their 25th Anniversary Season. However, he preferred to develop within the family atmosphere of a permanent company.

The last twenty years of Gilpin's career were marred by personal and physical problems. The collapse of his marriage, the strain of developments within London's Festival Ballet, and repeated pain and operations for an arterial disease led to alcoholism (which he eventually overcame). His return stage performances included his appearance in a play based on his life especially written for him, *Invitation to the Dance*, and as Oberon with Lindsay Kemp's Company.

A dancer who respected history and tradition in ballet, Gilpin as a young soloist with the de Cuevas Company asked for a role in the corps de ballet in *Le Tricorne*, in order to be on stage with Toumanova and Massine. At the time of his death he was largely engaged in passing on his own years of experience to younger dancers.

—Jane Pritchard

---

## LA GIPSY

**Choreography:** Joseph Mazilier
**Music:** François Benoist, Ambroise Thomas, and Marco Aurelio Marliani
**Design:** Humanité-René Philastre and Charles-Antoine Cambon (scenery), Paul Lormier (costumes)
**Libretto:** Jules-Henri Vernoy de Saint-Georges and Joseph Mazilier
**First Production:** Théâtre de l'Académie royale de musique (Paris Opéra), Paris, 28 January 1839
**Principal Dancers:** Fanny Elssler (Sarah), Thérèse Elssler (Mab), Joseph Mazilier (Stenio)

**Other productions include:** Her Majesty's Theatre (restaged after Mazilier), with Fanny Elssler; London, 24 June 1839.

### PUBLICATIONS

Gautier, Théophile, *The Romantic Ballet as seen by Théophile Gautier*, translated by Cyril Beaumont, London, 1932
Pirchan, Emil, *Fanny Elssler*, Vienna, 1940
Beaumont, Cyril, *Complete Book of Ballets*, revised edition, London, 1951
Guest, Ivor, *The Romantic Ballet in Paris*, London, 1966
Guest, Ivor, *Fanny Elssler: The Pagan Ballerina*, London, 1970

* * *

*La Gipsy* was a gamble, the product of the collaboration of a ballet master who had not yet produced a major work at the Opéra and a playwright who had never written for dance. It was, however, a time for gambles; the three previous Opéra productions, *Les Mohicans* (Guerra, 1837), *La Chatte metamorphosée en femme* (Coralli, 1837), and *La Volière* (T. Elssler, 1838) had all been failures as ballets, though the dancing and décor were of the high standard typical of the Duponchel administration. Perhaps the Opéra was looking for new blood. Whatever the reasoning, it was the untried Joseph Mazilier and Jules-Henri Vernoy de Saint-Georges who joined forces as ballet master and scenarist to produce a work that stirred the blood of critics and audiences alike.

Joseph Mazilier was known as a highly expressive dancer. His enthusiasm for drama found more than ample outlet in Saint-Georges's *La Gipsy* scenario, based as it was on Cervantes' tragic *La Bohémienne*. Saint-Georges, a successful writer of light plays and comic operas, capitalized in *La Gipsy* on popular tastes for adventure and high passions; they were all there—kidnapping, mistaken identities, tragic love, and murders set in the romantic times of Cromwell's England. Sarah (Fanny Elssler), daughter of Lord Campbell, is saved from a wild animal by the fugitive roundhead (Mazilier) who is hiding in a band of gypsies. The two fall in love to the fury of Mab, queen of the gypsies (Thérèse Elssler). Mab has Sarah arrested; in the course of the trial, however, Sarah's true identity is discovered. Mab, enraged, has the roundhead shot, and is herself stabbed by the desolate Sarah.

It was an ambitious undertaking to tell such a story, long and complex, filled with outpourings of human passion, through the silent language of dancing. Similar attempts usually led to confusing dramatic action, interrupted by incidental dances, all highlighted by brilliant scenery and costumes. Mazilier triumphed over the obstacles; contemporary reviews proclaimed, "the ballet's action offers a lively dramatic interest sustained and developed with great scenic talent. It has, moreover, the advantage, rather rare in choreography, of being almost always intelligible without the aid of the scenario." So powerful were the dances that one critic commented that Mazilier puts "ideas into the legs of his dancers . . .".

There were two primary genres of ballet during the romantic period, those that relied on the development of a dramatic action, along the lines of Noverre's *ballets d'action*, and those like *La Sylphide* (1832) and *Giselle* (1841), that relied on the creation of a poetic illusion. Mazilier's *La Gipsy* was a masterpiece of the former genre, and took its place alongside other "action" ballets such as his famous *Le Corsaire* (1856) and *Paquita* (1846), as well as many of Jules Perrot's ballets—*La Esmeralda* (1844) and *Faust* (1848), for example. And for all Mazilier's skills as a creator of outstanding dances, much of *La Gipsy* was taken up with silent acting, or pantomime in the style of *ballet d'action*.

The star of *La Gipsy* was Gautier's "pagan ballerina", Fanny Elssler, whose abundant expressive gifts and fiery technique were suited to the depiction of the hot-blooded gypsy Sarah. Imagine the scene in which the dancing Sarah/Elssler tries to distract attention from her hidden fugitive lover. "Few things have been seen more fearful than the cold and measured grace of Mlle. Fanny Elssler in this juncture—than the manner in which every step was watched, every gesture allowed its right time—so that neither flurry nor faltering might be detected—than the set smile—the vigilant ear—the quivering lip controlling itself." Such moments, played out in innumerable small Boulevard theatres, were the bread and butter of many a French actress. To Elssler they were champagne and caviar, as were her character dances, without which no ballet featuring Elssler would be complete. *La Gipsy* offered audiences the delights of her "Cracovienne", a sprightly dance in which she appeared in a coquettish military costume, dancing to the sound of her own clicking spurs.

*La Gipsy* set the tone for Mazilier's works. Their impact would be achieved through their dramatic action and their dancing; mise en scène gave the action depth and brilliance. It was a fine beginning to an outstanding career. As one critic observed, "*La Gipsy* has very happily arrived to break the choreographic bad luck that has weighed for so long on the theatre of Rue Lepelletier [the Opéra]."

—John Chapman

---

## GISELLE

**Choreography:** Jean Coralli and Jules Perrot
**Music:** Adolphe Adam
**Design:** Pierre Ciceri (set) and Paul Lormier (costumes)
**Libretto:** Jules-Henri Vernoy de Saint-Georges, Théophile Gautier, Jean Coralli
**First Production:** Théâtre de l'Academie royale de musique (Paris Opéra), Paris, 28 June 1841
**Principal Dancers:** Carlotta Grisi (Giselle), Lucien Petipa (Albrecht), Adèle Dumilâtre (Myrtha)

***Giselle*, with Carlotta Grisi in the title role, Paris Opéra, 1841**

**Other productions include:** Her Majesty's Theatre (restaged and revised Perrot, André Jean-Jacques Deshayes), with Grisi, Perrot; London, 12 March 1842. St. Petersburg Bolshoi Theatre (staged Antoine Titus), with Elena Andreyanova; St. Petersburg, 30 December (18 December old style) 1842. Teatro alla Scala (chor. Antonio Cortesi, with additional mus. Bajetti), with Carlotta Grisi, Francesco Mérante; Milan, 17 January 1843. Howard Atheneum (staged Mary Ann Lee after Coralli, Perrot), with Mary Ann Lee, George Washington Smith; Boston, 1 January 1846. Bolshoi Theatre (restaged Perrot), with Fanny Elssler and Marius Petipa; St. Petersburg, 1848 (restaged Perrot, with additional chor. Marius Petipa, with Carlotta Grisi, 1850). Bolshoi Theatre (staged Petipa) with Maria Gorshenkova; St. Petersburg, 17 February (5 February old style) 1884. Moscow Bolshoi Theatre (staged and revised Aleksandr Gorsky), with Vera Karalli; Moscow, 12 October (30 September old style) 1907. Diaghilev's Ballets Russes (staged and revised Mikhail Fokine), with Tamara Karsavina, Vaslav Nijinsky; Paris, 17 June 1910. All-Star Russian Imperial Ballet (staged Mikhail Mordkin); New York, 15 October 1910. Anna Pavlova Company (staged Pavlova, Ivan Clustine); London, 1913. Olga Spessivtseva Concert (staged Nikolai Sergeyev), with Olga Spessivtseva, Albert Aveline; Opéra, Paris, 26 November 1924. Paris Opéra Ballet (staged Serge Lifar), with Olga Spessivtseva, Lifar; Paris, 11 March 1932. Camargo Society (staged Nikolai Sergeyev), with Olga Spessivtseva, Anton Dolin; London, 24 June 1932. Vic-Wells Ballet (staged Nikolai Sergeyev), with Alicia Markova, Anton Dolin; London, 1 January 1934. Ballet Theatre (staged Anton Dolin), with Annabelle Lyon, Anton Dolin; New York, 12 January 1940. Sociedad Pro-Arte Musical (staged Alicia Alonso), with Alonso; Havana, 5 June 1945 (staged Ballet Alicia Alonso, later the Ballet Nacional de Cuba, 1948). Ballet Rambert (Act II only; staged Marie Rambert after Sergeyev), with Sally Gilmour, Walter Gore; Birmingham, 31 July 1945. Original Ballet Russe (staged Anton Dolin); New York, 11 October 1946. Royal Danish Ballet (staged Alexandre Volinin); Copenhagen, 10 November 1946. Royal Swedish Ballet (staged Mary Skeaping); Stockholm, 1953. Australian Ballet (staged Peggy van Praagh); British tour, 1965. Dance Theatre of Harlem ("Creole" version, with revised scenario by Arthur Mitchell, Carl Michel; staged Frederic Franklin after Petipa, Coralli, Perrot); London, 18 July 1984. Stuttgart Ballet (staged Marcia Haydée), as *Giselle und die Wilis*; Stuttgart, May 1989.

**Other choreographic treatments:** Cullberg Ballet (modern dance

*Giselle*, **as performed by Anthony Dowell and Maria Almeida, Royal Ballet, London, 1985**

interpretation of original score; chor. Mats Ek, Danish television, 1990).

## PUBLICATIONS


Lifar, Serge, *Giselle*, Paris, 1942

Beaumont, Cyril, *The Ballet Called Giselle*, London, 1944

Beaumont, Cyril, "Four Productions of *Giselle*", *Ballet* (London), October 1946

Guest, Ivor, "A Note on *Giselle*", *Ballet* (London), May 1948

Beaumont, Cyril, *The Complete Book of Ballets*, revised edition, London, 1951

Karsavina, Tamara, "*Giselle*", *Dancing Times* (London), 3 parts: October, November, December 1953

Buckle, Richard, "Monsters at Midnight", *Dance and Dancers* (London), 3 parts: April, May, June 1966

Guest, Ivor, *The Romantic Ballet in Paris*, London, 1966

Guest, Ivor, "The Two Giselles of the Romantic Ballet", *Dancing Times* (London), December 1968

Anderson, Jack, "*Giselle*", *Dance Magazine* (New York), December 1968

Alonso, Alicia, "Performing *Giselle*", in Payne, Charles, *American Ballet Theatre*, New York, 1978

Chapman, John, "An Unromantic View of Nineteenth-century Romanticism", *York Dance Review* (Toronto), Spring 1978

Ries, Frank W.D., "In Search of *Giselle*", *Dance Chronicle* (New York), vol. 4, no. 2, 1981

Alderson, Evan, "Ballet as Ideology: *Giselle* Act II", *Dance Chronicle* (New York), vol. 10, no. 3, 1987

Smith, Marian, "What Killed Giselle?", *Dance Chronicle* (New York), vol. 13, no. 1, 1990


* * *

Romanticism had many faces, some born of the human spirit's need for a more beautiful and exciting world, others born of its fascination with the horrific, the degenerate, and the destructive. Though ballet dealt to some extent with both, it was uniquely suited to the representation of the former, and one ballet, perhaps more than any other, captured that yearning for the sublime, for a place beyond the limits of banal everyday existence. *Giselle* offered audiences an escape to a world of mystery, beauty, danger, and death, a vision that stirred the blood of poetic, as well as more prosaic, imaginations.

The rather muddled vision of poet and critic Théophile Gautier (inspired by a Heinrich Heine story) supplied the starting-point for this, the most popular of all romantic ballets. His complicated story outline was streamlined and focused by Jules-Henri Vernoy de Saint-Georges, a popular playwright who had enjoyed much success with scenarios for Joseph Mazilier's *La Gipsy* (1839) and *Le Diable amoureux* (1840). Even so, the first act was considered by many critics to be, for the most part, a rehash of old material—a virtuous, innocent girl is duped by a philandering aristocrat. The stroke of romantic genius was to substitute in the place of the usual happy ending, in which virtue is rewarded, a tragic death followed by a ghostly resurrection. Thus the audience is transported from the quaint Rhineland village where the sweet Giselle dwelt in pastoral peace to a world of dark, spirit-haunted forests. Here it is that the Wilis, girls betrayed by men, hunt at night, exacting terrible revenge on the sex that doomed them to that fate. And here it is that the desolate Albrecht is saved by the still faithful Giselle, now a Wili, from her femme fatale sisters.

*Giselle*'s power lay in the poignancy of its straightforward, tragic story and in the second act's creation of a vivid and convincing illusion of poetic fantasy. This coming-together of drama and illusion depended on the close collaboration of the ballet masters, designers, and composer, and on the use of dance itself to give depth to character portrayal and substance to the supernatural atmosphere. So consistent and convincing was the stage picture that the most poetic writers, men such as Jules Janin and Théophile Gautier himself, wrote in their reviews of *Giselle* as if they were describing reality, not a concoction of sets, costumes, music, and dances. "The night throws its soft vapours over the entire countryside," wrote Janin, "around us all is silent, even the forest nightingale . . . the silver lake murmurs its small complaint. . . . This vapour, it is the queen of the wilis, Myrtha in person. The first ray of September moon light has imparted to the beautiful Myrtha the fine contours of her beautiful body." So intense was the illusion, so susceptible was the audience, that they were lifted from everyday life into a sphere where dream was reality.

It is still not known for certain who choreographed what in *Giselle*, though the consensus is that Jean Coralli, ballet master at the Opéra, created all the dances with the exception of those for Carlotta Grisi (Giselle) herself. These were probably choreographed by Jules Perrot, Grisi's teacher and lover. Both choreographers were inspired. One critic wrote of Coralli's second-act dances: "All these wilis dances are true little masterpieces which bring considerable honour to M. Coraly [sic]." Perrot's genius is attested to by the brilliance of Grisi's reception. Her role demanded, as was common during this period, the skills of dancer and silent actress both. Hippolyte Prévost wrote in his review: ". . . Carlotta Grisi is no less distinguished as a mime than as a dancer. What lightness, grace and soft voluptuousness in her steps and her poses! What expression and charm in her pantomime!"

One of the unusual features of the *Giselle* reviews was that critics did not stop at their praise of the star ballerinas. It is a tribute to the overall soundness of the choreographic structure and the strength of the dances that other dancers were noticed. ". . . It is necessary", wrote *Le Constitutionnel*, "to cite a perfectly executed, charming dance by Mlle Fitzjames; not to mention all these pretty wilis, and among them, the pretty Mlle Adele Dumilatre." Even Lucien Petipa, who performed Albrecht, won notice. "Petipa, the young and handsome dancer," observed Prévost, "whose talent has been enjoyed and appreciated for a long time, has performed the role of Duke Albert as an actor full of intelligence. Mlle Nathalie Fitz-James and Mablie have also ravishingly executed a pas de deux very ingeniously conceived by M. Coraly [sic]."

Set designer Pierre Ciceri had been setting new standards of realism ever since the 1820s, his greatest work to date being the haunting designs for *La Sylphide*. In *Giselle* he had a similar canvas to work upon, highlighting even more the contrast between the first and second acts. Paul Lormier's costumes likewise followed the route from pretty peasant to mysterious Wili. The latter were veiled in layers of white tulle (in the style of *La Sylphide*) that, ghost-like, drifted around the spirits' aerial forms. The composer, Adolphe Adam, had worked on Filippo Taglioni's last Opéra ballet, *La Fille du Danube* (1836), as well as Guerra's *Les Mohicans* (1837), but *Giselle* was his masterpiece. The quality of his score was the most convincing statement yet in favour of composing music for ballets rather than arranging pre-existing melodies. It demonstrated what could be achieved by sensitive collaboration between a talented composer and a ballet master. Indeed, *Giselle*, the most widely performed of all Romantic ballets, demonstrated the art's potential for plumbing the depths of the human spirit and for depicting the essence of popular visions of the ideal. Its drama and its depiction of romantic yearnings have remained relevant throughout the century and a half of its existence.

—John Chapman

---

*Giselle* is the Romantic era's most enduring ballet. It has been danced by most of the world's leading ballet companies and, today, it remains a regular repertory favourite. The role of Giselle was created on Carlotta Grisi, and reviews of her performances, both in Paris in 1841 and in London the following year, hint at her Taglioni-like lightness. In Paris, the role was danced almost exclusively by Grisi, but in London, Fanny Elssler danced the role during the 1843 season at Her Majesty's Theatre. It was Elssler's more dramatic interpretation which influenced most later productions, and it is Elssler who is a significant link in the ballet's survival. The first Paris production had been a collaboration between Jean Coralli and Jules Perrot; at Her Majesty's Theatre, the choreography of the 1842 production was shared by Perrot and the London-based choreographer André Deshayes. A production of *Giselle* was staged by Antoine Titus in St. Petersburg the same year, but it was Perrot's re-working of the original Paris production, performed in St. Petersburg in 1848, which became the basis of subsequent Russian versions of the ballet. Fanny Elssler was the first Giselle in Perrot's St. Petersburg version and although Grisi, the creator of the role, made her St. Petersburg début in the ballet in 1850, it was Elssler's polarity of technical skills and her dramatic mad scene which Russian audiences favoured.

In Perrot's version for St. Petersburg, the role of Albrecht was danced by Marius Petipa. In 1850, Petipa assisted in Perrot's staging of *Giselle* for Grisi and, during the mid-1880s, while working as ballet master at the Maryinsky Theatre, he made a series of revisions. It is the Coralli–Perrot–Petipa legacy upon which most twentieth-century productions draw.

*Giselle* continued to be danced in Russia at a time when ballet declined in western Europe. The last Paris performances of the ballet were in 1868. It was Russian dancers, therefore, who re-introduced *Giselle* to Paris over 40 years later. In 1910, Serge Diaghilev included the ballet in the Ballet Russe's second Paris season. Alongside the new works presented by Mikhail Fokine, *Giselle* was considered old-fashioned by the chic Opéra audiences. (Serge Grigoriev, the company's regisseur, described the 1910 production of *Giselle* as "a comparative failure".) But, as interest in ballet was rekindled, *Giselle* became a ballet to covet again. Productions by Anna Pavlova's company and the Camargo Society helped to re-establish the work's popularity, and it is interesting to note that in the development of three major ballet companies—American Ballet Theatre, the Paris Opéra Ballet, and Britain's Royal Ballet—*Giselle* played an important part, serving as an early staple in their repertories. More recently, some choreographers have returned to the scenario, and Adam's score, to find new inspiration. Updated versions of the ballet include one by Frederic Franklin for Dance Theatre of Harlem. Here, the action is located in Louisiana, the Wilis' haunting ground a bayou rather than forest. Another version, by Mats Ek for

Sweden's Cullberg Ballet, is set in a lunatic asylum. The dancers wear modern dress, with Myrtha a nurse in white uniform. Extreme, perhaps, but proof that the Romantic ideas which first inspired *Giselle*—love, dualism, other worlds—are of ongoing appeal.

—Angela Kane

---

**GLAZUNOV, Aleksandr**

Russian composer. Born Aleksandr Konstantinovich Glazunov in St. Petersburg, 10 August (29 July old style) 1865. Educated at "Real" school, and at St. Petersburg University as unenrolled student; studied music with Elenovsky, from c.1864; later tutored privately (at recommendation of Balakirev) by Rimsky-Korsakov. First symphony written at age sixteen, and given at St. Petersburg Free School of Music, 1882; conductor for Paris Exhibition, 1889, and thereafter for Russian Symphony Concerts, St. Petersburg; composer for Imperial Theatres, St. Petersburg, collaborating with choreographer Marius Petipa, from 1898; professor, St. Petersburg Conservatory, from 1900, and director, from 1906, playing important role in reorganization of the Conservatory after Revolution; left Russia permanently, 1928: after tours in Spain and U.S., settled in Paris. Died in Paris, 21 March 1936.

**WORKS** (Ballets)

1898 *Raymonda* (chor. Petipa), Maryinsky Theatre, St. Petersburg

1900 *The Trials of Damis* (*Les Ruses d'amour*; chor. Petipa), Maryinsky Theatre, St. Petersburg

*Les Saisons* (chor. Petipa), Hermitage Theatre, St. Petersburg

1907 Orchestration of music for *Chopiniana* (later *Les Sylphides*; mus. Chopin; chor. Fokine), Maryinsky Theatre, St. Petersburg

**Other ballets using Glazunov's music:** *The Dance of the Seven Veils* (for the play *Salomé* by Oscar Wilde; chor. Fokine, 1908), *Cléopâtre* (revision of *Egyptian Nights*; music by Glazunov and others added to Arensky score; chor. Fokine, 1909), *Fifth Symphony* (Gorsky, 1916), *Stenka Razin* (Fokine, 1916), *Derviches* (Börlin, 1920), *Pas de deux classique* (Ashton, 1934), *The Seasons* (Staff, 1940; also Cranko, 1962, Hynd, 1981), *Le Forêt romantique* (Taras, 1955), *Pas de dix* (sometimes called *Raymonda Pas de dix*; Balanchine, 1955), *Birthday Offering* (Ashton, 1956), *The Enchanted Garden* (Darrell, 1958), *Variations de Ballet* (L. Christensen and Balanchine, 1960), *Valses et Variations* (later called *Raymonda Variations*; Balanchine, 1961), *Configuraçao* (Gore, 1967), *Cortège Hongrois* (Balanchine, 1973), *The Little Ballet* (*Once Upon a Time*; Tharp, 1983), *Eine Reise durch die Jahreszeiten* (Neumeier, 1988).

**PUBLICATIONS**

Belyaev, V., *A. Glazunov*, Petrograd, 1922
Calvocoressi, M.D., and Abraham, Gerald, "Glazunov", in *Masters of Russian Music*, London, 1936
Abraham, Gerald, *On Russian Music*, London, 1939
Fedorova, G., *A. Glazunov*, Leningrad, 1947
Fédorov, V., "Glazounov: Musicien russe, ou compositeur européen?", *Revue de Musicologie* (Paris), xli, 1958
Schwartz, B., *Music and Musical Life in Soviet Russia 1917–1970*, London, 1972
Molden, Peter L., "Glazunov and the Ballet", *Dancing Times* (London), 2 parts: July, August 1987
Mundy, Simon, *Alexander Glazunov*, London, 1987

* * *

Aleksandr Glazunov has retained a prominent profile in the history of Russian classical ballet, largely through the survival of a small number of works—most notably his masterpiece *Raymonda* (either in full or in part) now in the repertories of most major companies in the world. Widely respected personally and professionally in both musical and academic circles, Glazunov also had the good fortune to have Marius Petipa, then at the height of his mature powers, as choreographer—not only for this work but also for his two other principal commissioned ballet scores, *Les Saisons* and *The Trials of Damis*, also known as *Les Ruses d'amour* (though the latter has not maintained its place in the public domain).

Though *Raymonda* has secured its place in public affections and its music has many individual felicities (particularly in the symphonic manipulation, during the first two acts, of several themes of considerable beauty, as well as impressive orchestration attaining at times an almost Wagnerian voluptuousness), Glazunov stands, in fact, at the end of a tradition that was already in decline when he was brought to the dance stage by the Imperial Theatres. Then in mid-career, he surely seemed to the presiding powers the figure in Russian music most likely to fill the gap left by Tchaikovsky. The prevailing genre of large-scale narrative ballets, which might require music to suit themes of historical romance, magical fairy tale, or exotic amorous intrigue, was ideally suited to his talents as a composer. His extraordinary technical skill could command both symphonic breadth, ingenious rhythmic characterization, and rich oriental colouring; but ballets of this nature were to survive in their existing form only so long as Petipa and Ivanov were there to breathe life into them.

It is thus an irony of fate that Glazunov, who had begun his career as the new hope of the "modern" school in late nineteenth-century Russian composition, should have come by the end of his career to represent a bastion of traditionalism in the conservatoire, and to have been bypassed by his younger contemporaries both in the development of new forms of musical expression and in theatrical experiment. Though Diaghilev incorporated the "Bacchanale" from Autumn (*Les Saisons*) into Fokine's revision of *Cléopâtre* for the Ballets Russes, and Fokine choreographed his *Stenka Razin* in 1916, and Gorksy (founder, with Fedor Lopukhov, of the controversial but influential "symphonic" choreography movement in ballet) used his Fifth Symphony in the same year, Glazunov's brief impact on the course of ballet has remained limited to a handful of colourful but traditional pieces, and his memory today is held in greater esteem than his influence.

—Geoffrey Baskerville

---

**GLUSHKOVSKY, Adam Pavlovich**

Russian dancer, teacher, and choreographer. Born in St. Petersburg, 1793. Studied at the Imperial Theatre School, St. Petersburg, pupil of Ivan Valbergh and Charles-Louis Didelot;

completed Theatre School studies in 1809; also studied with French ballet master Louis Duport. Dancer in St. Petersburg, 1808–11, performing many of the virtuoso lead male roles; went to Moscow, 1812: principal dancer, director of ballet school, and chief choreographer, Bolshoi Theatre, Moscow, 1812–39; performed mostly character and pantomime roles later in career, retiring from the stage in 1831; choreographed own works and restaged fourteen Didelot ballets; also wrote memoirs of his life as a ballet master, first published in 1856. Died c. 1870.

## WORKS

1814 *The Profligate; or, The Robber's Lair* (mus. arranged Cherzelli), Bolshoi Theatre, Moscow
1815 *Filatka and Fedora at a Funfair in Novinskoye*, Bolshoi Theatre, Moscow
1816 *May Day; or, A Holiday in Sokolniki* (mus. Davidov), Bolshoi Theatre, Moscow
*The Triumph of the Russians; or, The Military Camp at Krasnoye* (mus. various), Bolshoi Theatre, Moscow
*The Death of Roger, the Most Horrible Chieftain of the Robbers* (mus. arranged Cherzelli), Bolshoi Theatre, Moscow
1817 *Cossacks on the Rhine* (mus. various), Bolshoi Theatre, Moscow
1821 *Ruslan and Lyudmila* (mus. Scholz), Bolshoi Theatre, Moscow
1826 *Three Belts; or, The Russian Cinderella* (mus. Scholtz), Bolshoi Theatre, Moscow
1831 *The Black Scarf; or Infidelity Punished* (mus. various), Bolshoi Theatre, Moscow

Also staged:
1817 *Zéphire et Flore* (after Didelot; mus. Cavos), Bolshoi Theatre, Moscow
1819 *The Hungarian Hut* (after Didelot; mus. Venua), Bolshoi Theatre, Moscow

**Other works include:** numerous divertissements on Russian folk themes; stagings of *The Prisoner of the Caucasus* (after Didelot; mus. Cavos), and other Didelot ballets.

## PUBLICATIONS

By Glushkovsky:
"Some Reminiscences about the Famous Choreographer Charles L. Didelot", *Moskvityanin* (Moscow), vol. 1, no. 4, 1856; as *Memoirs of a Ballet Master*, edited by Yuri Slonimsky, Moscow and Leningrad, 1940

About Glushkovsky:
Krasovskaya, Vera, *The Russian Ballet Theatre from its Beginnings to the Mid-Nineteenth Century*, Moscow and Lenningrad, 1958
Gozenpud, A., *Musical Theatre in Russia, from the Early Times to Glinka*, Leningrad, 1959
Roslavleva, Natalia, *Era of the Russian Ballet*, London, 1966
Swift, Mary Grace, *A Loftier Flight: The Life and Accomplishments of Charles-Louis Didelot, Balletmaster*, Middletown, Connecticut, 1974

* * *

Adam Glushkovsky trained at the Imperial Theatre School at St. Petersburg, and on graduating danced a number of (principally virtuoso) roles in the St. Petersburg company for several years. It is, however, with the Bolshoi Theatre in Moscow that his name is primarily associated. He was sent to Moscow in 1812 to take up the post of director of the Ballet School and chief choreographer of the Bolshoi Theatre, and while he also became a celebrated demi-caractère dancer, it is as a choreographer and teacher that he is now best remembered. His work with the students of the Ballet School helped to establish the standards of Russian ballet training, at a time when all the great figures in ballet tended to be French. Although the French and Italians continued to dominate until late in the century, and the grand Russian style was probably developed most definitively by the Frenchman Marius Petipa, the ballet in Russia could not have flourished as it did had there not been a basis of sound and systematized training, as inherited and then developed in Moscow by Adam Glushkovsky.

Glushkovsky's principal teacher and mentor in St. Petersburg had been Charles-Louis Didelot, with whom he had a particularly close association, Didelot acting as his guardian as well as his teacher, taking him into his own home and refusing any payment for his board. Glushkovsky thoroughly assimilated and codified all that his own teachers, especially Didelot, had imparted to him, and his memoirs provide a valuable commentary on the theory and practice of ballet in Russia in the early nineteenth century.

With Napoleon's marching on Russia in 1812, Glushkovsky managed to save the Ballet School by getting his students out of Moscow just days before the French invasion. Several of his early ballets expressed the intense patriotism aroused by the war of 1812, as the titles (such as *The Triumph of the Russians* or *Cossacks on the Rhine*) none too subtly suggest. These ballets incorporated an element of Russian folk dance, and the skilful assimilation of folk idiom into the stricter forms of classical ballet is one of his more important contributions to the development of Russian choreography. The long "gothic" ballets which he produced during the same period, with such self-explanatory titles as *The Death of Roger, the Most Horrible Chieftain of the Robbers*, have bequeathed somewhat less to posterity.

The close professional association with Didelot continued to flourish, Glushkovsky reviving all of Didelot's best ballets, including the celebrated *Zephyr and Flora* (*Flore et Zéphire*) in 1817. In 1821, Glushkovsky was the first to choreograph a ballet (*Ruslan and Lyudmila*) based on a poem by Pushkin, and Didelot acknowledged its importance by staging it, in a revised version, in St. Petersburg (1824). Glushkovsky's later ballet, *The Black Scarf* (1831), was also inspired by the Pushkin poem of that name, and he was responsible for the revival in Moscow of Didelot's own famous Pushkin-inspired ballet, *The Prisoner of the Caucasus*. The use of contemporary Russian literature, instead of the more conventional foreign (frequently classical) sources, is another aspect of Glushkovsky's expression of patriotism in balletic form.

In terms of artistry, Glushkovsky's ballets, like Didelot's, fell between the eighteenth-century *ballets d'action* and the nineteenth-century Romantic ballets, but his use of the themes and images of Russian Romantic poetry was an important aspect of his part in preparing the ground for the extraordinary Romantic revolution in ballet over the next two decades. This artistic foresight, as well as his masterful incorporation of Russian folk dance into the classical idiom and his invaluable work in the training of Russian classical dancers, has assured for Glushkovsky a lasting place in the history of Russian ballet.

—Penelope Jowitt

## THE GOLDEN AGE

(original Russian title: *Zolotoi Vek*)

**Choreography:** Yuri Grigorovich
**Music:** Dmitri Shostakovich, arranged by Yuri Simonov
**Design:** Simon Virsaladze
**Libretto:** Ivan Glikman and Yuri Grigorovich, partly after original libretto by A.V. Ivanovsky
**First Production:** Bolshoi Ballet, Moscow, 4 November 1982
**Principal Dancers:** Irek Mukhamedov (Boris), Natalia Bessmertnova (Rita), Geiminas Taranda (Jashka)

**Other productions include:** State Academic Theatre for Opera and Ballet (GATOB, later the Kirov; original production to score; libretto Ivanovsky, chor. Vasily Vainonen, Leonid Yakobson, Vladimir Chesnokov), with Galina Ulanova, Olga Iordan, Boris Shavrov; Leningrad, 26 October 1930. Kiev Theatre for Opera and Ballet (libretto V. Snirnov, chor. E. Vigile); Kiev, 1930. Odessa Theatre for Opera and Ballet, under title of *Dinamiada* (chor. Mikhail Moiseyev); Odessa, 1931.

### PUBLICATIONS

About original production:
Slonimsky, N., "Dmitri Dmitrievitch Shostakovich", *Musical Quarterly* (New York), October 1942
Beaumont, Cyril, *Complete Book of Ballets*, revised edition, London, 1951
Swift, Mary Grace, *The Art of Dance in the USSR*, Notre Dame, Indiana, 1968
Bogdanov-Berezovsky, Valerian, *The Leningrad Opera and Ballet Theatre named after Kirov*, Leningrad and Moscow, 1959
Armashevskaya, K., and Vainonen, N., *Balletmaster Vainonen*, Moscow, 1971

About the Grigorovich production:
Alovert, Nina, "The Soviet Dance Theatre of Yuri Grigorovich", *Dance Magazine* (New York), December 1987
Grigorovich, Yuri, and Davlekamova, Sania, *The Golden Age*, translated by Tim Coey, Neptune, N.J., 1989

* * *

***The Golden Age*, with Irek Mukhamedov and the corps de ballet of the Bolshoi Ballet**

The original version of *The Golden Age* by Vasily Vainonen told of a Soviet football team travelling abroad in the West, and its encounters and confrontations with bourgeois youth and elements of facism. Considered "ideologically destructive" for its views, it was removed from the repertoire after one season.

Grigorovich's ballet, created fifty years later, still holds to the political theme with its moral and social overtones, and it is set not in a capitalist country but in the newly-created Soviet state in 1923. Grigorovich gives another view of the good-versus-evil plot: the cause of the common man in challenging and overcoming the evil in society. As in his *Ivan the Terrible*, which deals with Russian history in the sixteenth century, Grigorovich has given his audiences another insight into Russian/Soviet history. *The Golden Age* depicts the political atmosphere in the post-revolutionary period when communism still contained aspects of pre-1917 bourgeois life. The ballet can thus be considered a historical view upon those times. Virsaladze's designs re-created the art-nouveau of the era, with sets of triangular patterns and painted slogans. His costumes range from fishermen's patchwork overalls and women's headscarves for the day to fancy hats and satin shimmies for the nightclub.

The ballet brims with vitality, entertainment, and fun. The choreography explodes with displays of athletic bravura based on classical form, yet focusing on the physical and dramatic rather than on the refinement of Russian balletic classicism—a quality to which some critics have strongly objected.

The action takes place at a small Soviet resort on the Black Sea in 1923, a time when young people, fired with enthusiasm for their new regime, organized festivals and educated citizens through the "Young Workers Agitprop Theatre" on how to uphold communist ideals. But Lenin's policies of those early days—the New Economic Policy (NEP)—also allowed limited capitalistic freedoms which resulted in a flourishing black market and, ideological purists argue, a lowering of moral values. It is the resultant struggle between right and wrong which the ballet highlights.

The scenario is simple—the hero wears white, the villain, black—and the scenes shift briskly from the sunny sea-side festivites of wholesome Soviet youth to the dark confines of the fox-trotting, tango-swaying clientele at the decadent nightclub, "The Golden Age". At a festival Boris, a young fisherman, meets and falls in love with a beautiful girl called Rita. She, he later discovers, is a cabaret dancer at the nightclub. Under the name of "Mademoiselle Margo" she performs with her partner, "Monsieur Jacques", who, unbeknown to her, is really Jashka, the leader of a gang of cut-throats. These brigands waylay the clientele on their way home to rob and kill them.

Boris persuades Rita to run away from the "Golden Age" and to join him and his friends in their pursuit of higher ideals. But the jealous Jashka sets his gang on Boris, beating him and wrapping him up in a fishing net. Rita summons help and the stage suddenly becomes alive as swarms of dancers leap around in an exhausting chase scene. The gang is captured and all ends in an exuberant display of flag-flying.

*The Golden Age* is stamped with all of Grigorovich's usual trade-marks: emphasis on male bravura and scenes contrasting mass dancing with gentle, intimate pas de deux. One moment great hordes of fisherfolk pour over the stage in vital, energetic ribbons of movement; the next, Boris and Rita are entwined in a flowing duet, gymnastic but visually beautiful. The ballet depends on its dancers, for it needs the enthusiasm and spontenaity of all, whether they be young Komsomols (Communist Youth members), athletes, muscular bandits, or bobbed-and-shingled, foppish tango dancers at the nightclub stepping out to strains of "Tea for Two" on a soprano saxaphone. The ballet's toe-tapping music uses a variety of rhythms and instruments—electric guitars, banjos, xylophones, solo piano—to set the mood of the 1920s. It is a ballet for and about the Bolshoi's expansive style and movement, and is a vehicle to show off the company's young, virile male dancers.

The role of Boris follows the structure of other Grigorovich heroes who make similar powerful entrances and solos. Yet here, and especially when danced by the Tartar dancer Irek Mukhamedov for whom the role was created, Boris becomes a superpowered, exciting extension of the traditional classical male. Mukhamedov's fierce heroism and prodigious technique showed him catapaulting across the stage in a series of powerful steps, many of them unseen before. Other dancers, such as Yuri Vasuchenko and Andris Liepa, have shown strong technical dancing but none has surpassed the verve and velocity of Mukhamedov. With such talented exponents in the Bolshoi company, *The Golden Age* met with success world-wide; with the departure of Mukhamedor to the West, it has perhaps lost some of its original power.

—Margaret Willis

---

## GOLEIZOVSKY, Kasyan

Russian dancer and choreographer. Born Kasyan Yaroslavovich Goleizovsky in Moscow, 5 March (22 February old style) 1892. Studied first in Moscow, pupil of Nikolai Domashev, then at the St. Petersburg Theatre School, pupil of Mikhail Obukhov, Mikhail Fokine, 1902–09. Married (1) Nina Sibiryakova; (2) Bolshoi soloist Vera Vasilieva. Dancer, Bolshoi Theatre, Moscow, 1909–18; choreographer, mostly of miniatures, Nikita Baliev's cabaret theatre, The Bat, from 1914/15; director of own studio, Moscow, from 1916, of Bolshoi Theatre School, from 1918, and own Moscow Chamber Ballet, from 1922; also choreographer for Moscow cabaret (called "Crooked Jimmy"), 1922, 1923, and Moscow circus; resigned from Bolshoi, 1927, continuing to stage ballets and dances in Ukraine, 1927–28, for Viktorina Kriger's Moscow Art Ballet, 1931, for Maly Opera Theatre, Leningrad, 1932, 1933, and for music halls in Moscow and Leningrad; returned to the Bolshoi, various seasons, from 1933; also occasional choreographer for Leningrad and Moscow Ballet Schools, from 1934, Yermolova Theatre, Moscow, 1945, 1953, and the Song and Dance Ensemble of the Ministry of the Interior (NKVD), from 1942. Recipient: title of Honoured Artist, Bylorussian SSR, 1940; Honoured Art Worker, Lithuanian SSR, 1945. Died in Moscow, 2 May 1970.

### WORKS

1916 *The Dance of the Nymphs and the Goatlegged* (mus. Satz), Intimate Theatre, Moscow
*The Choice of a Bride* (mus. and verse Kuzmin), Intimate Theatre, Moscow

1918 *The Evolution of Dance,* Moscow Ballet School, Moscow
*The Sonata of Death and Movement* (mus. Skriabin), Moscow Ballet School, Moscow
*The Sandmen* (ballet for children; mus. Schumann et al.), Goleizovsky's Studio, at the Children's Division of the Temusek, Ministry of Enlightenment (Narkompros), Moscow
*The Masque of Red Death* (never performed in public; mus. Tcherepnin), Bolshoi Ballet, Moscow
*Masks* (mus. Ber), Moscow Ballet School, Moscow

**A costume design by Kasyan Goleizovsky for the Pharoah in *Joseph the Beautiful*, 1925**

1919 *Snow White* (incomplete, never performed in full; mus. Rebikov), Temusek Children's Theatre, Moscow
*Harlequinade* (mus. Chaminade), Goleizovsky's Studio, Theatre Section of the Ministry of Enlightenment (Narkompros), Moscow
*Max and Moritz* (mus. Schytte), Goleizovsky's Studio, Theatre Section of the Ministry of Enlightenment (Narkompros), Moscow
1921 Concert miniatures including:
*Danse sacrée* (mus. Debussy), Goleizovsky's Studio, now called "The Quest", Moscow
*Cake-walk* (mus. Debussy), The Quest, Moscow
*Prologue* (duet; mus. Medtner), The Quest, Moscow
*Funeral March* (mus. Medtner), The Quest, Moscow
*Guirlande* (mus. Skriabin), The Quest, Moscow
*Flammes sombres* (mus. Skriabin), The Quest, Moscow
*Etudes* (mus. Skriabin), The Quest, Moscow
*Preludes* (mus. Skriabin), The Quest, Moscow
*Poème* (mus. Skriabin), The Quest, Moscow
1922 *Salomé* (mus. Strauss), Moscow Chamber Ballet, Moscow
*Faun* (mus. Debussy), Moscow Chamber Ballet, Moscow
*White Mass* (new version of *The Sonata of Love and Death;* mus. Skriabin), Moscow Chamber Ballet, Moscow
*Tragedy of the Masks* (mus. Ber), Moscow Chamber Ballet, Moscow
*Tombeau de Colombine* (mus. Ber), Moscow Chamber Ballet, Moscow
*Visions Fugitives* (mus. Prokofiev), Moscow Chamber Ballet, Moscow
*Dances* (mus. Skriabin), including *Désir*, *Caresse dansée*, *Valse langoureuse*, *Etudes and Mazurkas*, Moscow Chamber Ballet, Moscow
1923 *Etudes of Pure Dance* (mus. Skriabin), Moscow Chamber Ballet, Moscow
*Preludes* (mus. Lizst), Moscow Chamber Ballet, Moscow
1924 *Etudes of Pure Classicism* (mus. Chopin), Moscow Chamber Ballet, Moscow
*Death of Isolde* (mus. Wagner), Moscow Chamber Ballet, Moscow
*The City* (mus. Blanter), Moscow Free Theatre, Moscow
1925 *Teolinda* (mus. Schubert), Bolshoi Filial Theatre (Experimental Theatre), Moscow
*Joseph the Beautiful* (mus. Vasilenko), Bolshoi Filial Theatre, Moscow
*Lola* (never performed, cancelled by Bolshoi directorate; mus. Vasilenko), Bolshoi Ballet, Moscow
1926 *In the Sun's Rays* (mus. Vasilenko), Theatre of Opera and Ballet, Odessa
*Polovtsian Dances* from *Prince Igor* (mus. Borodin), Theatre of Opera and Ballet, Odessa
1927 *The Whirlwind* (mus. Ber), Bolshoi Filial Theatre, Moscow
1928 *The Imps* (mus. Schubert), Moscow Studio of Dramatic Ballet, Moscow
1929 *Suite* (ten dances; mus. Liszt), Bolshoi Concert Programme, Moscow
*Spanish Dances* (from *Lola*, 1925; mus. Vasilenko), Bolshoi Concert Programme, Moscow
*Choreofragments* (mus. Dunaevsky), Bolshoi Concert Programme, Moscow
1931 *Lisztiana* (mus. Liszt), Moscow Art Ballet (dir. Viktorina Kriger), Moscow
*Soviet Village* (mus. Bez), Moscow Art Ballet, Moscow
*Carmen Suite* (mus. Bizet), Moscow Art Ballet, Moscow
1932 Dances in *Die Meistersinger* (opera; mus. Wagner), Maly Opera Theatre, Leningrad
1933 *Charda* (national dances; mus. various), Bolshoi Ballet, Moscow
*Chopin* (mus. Chopin), Bolshoi Ballet, Moscow
*Dionysus* (mus. Shenshin), Bolshoi Ballet, Moscow
1934 *Polovtsian Dances* from *Prince Igor* (mus. Borodin), Bolshoi Ballet, Moscow
1935 *The Sleeping Beauty* (mus. Tchaikovsky), Theatre of Opera and Ballet, Kharkov
1936 *The Chickens* (mus. Mussorgsky), Moscow Ballet School, Moscow
*Les Sabots* (mus. Dunaevsky), Moscow Ballet School, Moscow
*Gnome* (mus. Mussorgsky), Moscow Ballet School, Moscow
1939 *The Fountain of Bakhchisarai* (mus. Asafiev), Theatre of Opera and Ballet, Minsk
1941 *Du Gul* (*Two Roses*; mus. Lensky), Decade of Art for Tadzhikistan, Moscow
1942 *The Fir Tree of Father Frost* (ballet for children; mus. Potapov) Moscow Ballet School, Vasilsursk
1943 *Drowsy Slumber* (mus. Chemberdzhi), Moscow Ballet School, Moscow
*Valse Fantasy* (mus. Glinka), Moscow Ballet School, Moscow
1949 *Spanish Dances* (mus. various), Concert for Maya Plisetskaya, Tchaikovsky Concert Hall, Moscow
*Song of Love* (mus. Liszt), Concert for Maya Plisetskaya, Moscow
*Spring* (mus. Rachmaninov), Concert for Maya Plisetskaya, Moscow
1950 *No to War* (mus. Chopin), Concert for Natalia Kinus, Tchaikovsky Concert Hall, Moscow
*To Peace* (mus. Rodine ), Concert for Natalia Kinus, Moscow
1960 *Dances* (mus. Skriabin et al.), including *Guirlande*, *Three Moods*, *Heroica*, *Tragic Poem*, Programme for Bolshoi Dancers, Tchaikovsky Concert Hall, Moscow
1962 *Skriabiniana* (suite of eight dances; mus. Skriabin), Bolshoi Theatre, Moscow
1963 Dances in *Rusalka* (opera; mus. Dargomyzhsky), Bolshoi Filial Theatre, Moscow
1964 *Leili and Medzhnun* (mus. Balasanian), Bolshoi Ballet, Moscow
1967 *Two Preludes* (mus. Bach), Concert for Nikita Dolgushin, Tchaikovsky Concert Hall, Moscow

## PUBLICATIONS

By Goleizovsky:
*Images of Russian Folk Choreography*, Moscow, 1964

About Goleizovsky:
Roslavleva, Natalia, *Era of the Russian Ballet*, London, 1966
Swift, Mary Grace, *The Art of Dance in the USSR*, Notre Dame, Indiana, 1968
Joffe, L., "Kasyan Goleizovsky", *Les Saisons de la danse* (Paris), March 1973
Mikhailov, Mikhail, "Kasyan Yaroslavovich Goleizovsky," *Music and Choreography of Contemporary Ballet*, Leningrad, 1974
Manor, G., "Before Balanchine: Kasyan Goleizovsky's Russian Revolution", *Dance Magazine* (New York), 2 parts: January, February 1989

Souritz, Elizabeth, *The Art of Choreography in the 1920s*, Moscow, 1979; as *Soviet Choreographers in the 1920s*, translated by Lynn Visson, Durham, N.C. and London, 1990

* * *

In Moscow during the 1920s, Kasyan Goleizovsky was the leader who encouraged the younger generation to experiment. He had been a student at the St. Petersburg Theatre School; he was accepted in 1902 and studied there for seven years alongside the future dancers of Diaghilev's Ballets Russes abroad. At this time, Mikhail Fokine was already working with the students and young dancers of the Maryinsky Theatre, and taught the women's equivalent to the class in which Goleizovsky studied.

In 1909 Goleizovsky was accepted into the Moscow ballet company, and until 1918 he danced at the Bolshoi Theatre. Here, he took part in several of Aleksandr Gorsky's experimental productions. Thus, the future choreographer's youth was linked with the two major reformers of the Russian ballet stage—Fokine and Gorsky. From them, on the one hand, he inherited a profound knowledge of classical ballet and a respect for it as the professional basis for the art of dance; on the other hand, he learned to distrust the supposed immutability of academic canons. Goleizovsky understood that Fokine and Gorsky were asking their dancers to swim against the current; and so, when he himself matured, he began to re-examine the ideas of his teachers with a critical eye.

In 1916 Goleizovsky opened a private school, and began to stage dances and sometimes even small ballets at theatres outside the Bolshoi, such as The Bat or the Mamonovsky Theatre of Miniatures. By 1917 he was already quite popular as a choreographer on the cabaret stage. The revolution then immediately opened up other prospects for artistic creativity. The ballet, that stronghold of tradition, slowly and arduously began to turn towards the new; and so, when an obviously talented young man appeared and announced that his goal was "to bring the art of ballet closer to the broad democratic masses", he was welcomed.

In the spring of 1918, Goleizovsky was invited to head the studio of the Bolshoi Theatre School, and his first programme, including a dance set to a sonata by Skriabin, aroused great interest, showing from the start the choreographer's interest in unconventional means of expression. At the beginning of the 1918–19 season, Goleizovsky left the Bolshoi in order to devote himself entirely to choreography. As well as working with a group of dancers which had grown out of his private studio, he also headed a children's performing group—and his first children's ballet, *The Sandmen*, was produced in the autumn of 1918.

But the most significant stage in Goleizovsky's development was his work with the Moscow Chamber Ballet, which grew out of his private studio. The dance studios of the 1920s were the places where most experimental work went on, and they ultimately contributed significantly to Soviet choreography. (Isadora Duncan opened her own school in Moscow in 1921, and many leaders of the private studios at the time were followers of Duncan.) Among the miniatures which Goleizovsky choreographed during this period were *Faun*, to the music of Claude Debussy, and *Salomé*—which became rather notorious for its eroticism—to the music of Richard Strauss.

During the Chamber Ballet period, the basic lines along which Goleizovsky was developing artistically began to show more clearly, and his choreographic signature took shape. Revolution had to be reflected in the theatre, and the desire for modernity was the thing which ruled. Goleizovsky was putting new ideas into form with his own dancers—and this was a formative influence on the young George Balanchine (then Balanchivadze), who later told his biographer Bernard Taper, "Seeing Goleizovsky is what gave me the courage to try something different on my own."

The culmination of Goleizovsky's experimental work in the Chamber Ballet period, and his most significant creative whole, was his 1925 ballet *Joseph the Beautiful*. This ballet, along with *Teolinda* (Goleizovsky's answer to Romantic ballet, performed to the music of Schubert), had its premiere at the Bolshoi's Experimental Theatre on 3 March 1925. *Joseph the Beautiful* was an ambitious work which explored the themes of human freedom, dignity, and individualism against the evils of power—and, although ultimately very controversial, was admitted even by its detractors to be a well composed and stylistically unified work.

In *Joseph the Beautiful* Goleizovsky had created a ballet with continuous choreographic action, intending that each dance should either introduce the audience to a new event or add new detail to the development of characters and action. In this respect, and in his liking for spectacle, he followed Fokine. But where Fokine often transformed the stage into a broad canvas, with the dancers as moving brush strokes, Goleizovsky in *Joseph the Beautiful* created choreography which suggested a sculpture with many figures. He positioned the dancers in pictorial poses and made complex configurations of groups—living bas reliefs, in a sense. Not interested in pure form for its own sake (as in, say, the abstract groupings of traditional corps de ballet), Goleizovsky instead formed expressive groups out of warm, living bodies—intending the audience to appreciate the beauty of a bare leg stretched, or a group of bodies placed, often on the floor, in attractive arrangements.

*Joseph the Beautiful* ultimately brought about a huge division in the Bolshoi Theatre, in essence pitting the old guard against the new on the issue of "new" choreography and the limits of experimentalism like Goleizovsky's. The "revolt" of the younger generation was largely in response to the attempts by traditionalists like Vasily Tikhomirov to throw *Joseph the Beautiful* out of the repertory. Angered and defiant, Goleizovsky himself eventually left Moscow and produced the ballet in the Ukraine. In the following years Goleizovsky created *Lola*, an attempt at a Spanish folk tragedy which was never performed, and *The Whirlwind*, shown at the end of 1927 only once, and badly received.

The decision was made by the Bolshoi not to continue staging *The Whirlwind*, and after this, Goleizovsky's other works were also dropped from the plans of the Bolshoi Theatre. Cut off from further work in academic ballet theatres, and working mostly in vaudeville (including music halls in Moscow and Leningrad), Goleizovsky continued to create concert programmes for the young dancers of the Bolshoi during the late 1920s and early 1930s. In these programmes he developed his earlier discoveries and sought new resolutions, but many of his most interesting ideas of the 1920s remained unfulfilled.

Goleizovsky lived to be 78, and while he always had difficulties in doing what he wanted to do, he did continue to work throughout the 1930s, 1940s and 1950s—and especially in the 1960s, when he had new chances to experiment in the changed atmosphere after Stalin's death. But he did not work in the traditional venues. On the rare occasions when he was invited by ballet theatres, it was to do *The Sleeping Beauty* (1935) or *The Fountain of Bakhchisarai* (1939)—traditional ballets which Goleizovsky in fact treated in completely non-traditional ways, thereby giving the establishment cause to frown upon his work again.

In the later 1930s Goleizovsky worked in various republics, helping to arrange folk dances for the so-called "Decades", festivals of national art in Moscow. This gave him the chance to study quite seriously the dances of various regions (which is shown in his 1964 book about Russian national dances). But he had no real opportunities for creating his own works and his talent was for the most part wasted. At last, in the 1960s, the Bolshoi administration asked for a suite of dances to Skriabin (*Skriabiniana*), and, as Goleizovsky had worked with Skriabin all his life, this was in a sense a culmination. But it was a huge disappointment—not least of all to George Balanchine, who saw the ballet while in Russia, and had hoped for so much more from the man who had first inspired him in 1922 in Petrograd.

But it is obvious what happened: the rest of the world, including Balanchine, had been moving forward all these years, while Goleizovsky, talented as he was, had been kept away from new ideas and artistic developments. Even his new ballet in 1964, *Leili and Medzhnun*, was no more than a variation on the old ideas about oriental dance, first developed in the 1920s. The man who had been such a bold aesthete, such a raffiné in the world of early twentieth-century Soviet art, was in the later part of his life forced to produce dances with titles like slogans, as in *Against the War*, or to produce numbers for the Song and Dance Ensemble of the Ministry of the Interior. The story of Kasyan Goleizovkskу is a tragedy of wasted talent and wasted opportunity, and sadly, it was the plight of many Soviet artists of his generation.

—Elizabeth Souritz

---

**GOLOVINE, Serge**

French dancer and teacher. Born in Monaco, 20 November 1924. Studied with Julie Sedova in Nice, from 1935; also studied with Gustave Ricaux in Monaco, and Carlotta Zambelli, Olga Preobrazhenska, and Alexandre Volinine in Paris. Dancer, Monte Carlo Opera Ballet (Nouveau Ballet de Monte Carlo, becoming Nouveaux Ballets de Monte Carlo), from 1941, becoming danseur étoile, 1945; dancer, becoming grand sujet, Paris Opéra Ballet, 1946–49; soloist, becoming principal dancer, Grand Ballet de Monte Carlo (later Grand Ballet du Marquis de Cuevas), 1949–61; first choreography *Feux rouges, feux verts*, 1953; founded own group, Les Compagnons de la danse, 1962, touring Europe, North Africa, and Central America; artistic director, choreographer, and principal dancer, Geneva Opera Ballet, 1964–69; retired from the stage in 1976; also teacher: founder of own school in Geneva, 1969; teacher, school of Solange Golovina, Paris, and at the Paris Opéra Ballet School.

**ROLES**

1941 Amore in *Le Bal masqué* (mus. Strauss), Monte Carlo Opera Ballet, Monte Carlo
1943 Principal dancer in *Les Sylphides* (Fokine), Monte Carlo Opera Ballet, Monte Carlo
1944 Title role in *Le Spectre de la rose* (Fokine), Monte Carlo Opera Ballet, Monte Carlo
Principal dancer in *Carnaval* (Fokine), Monte Carlo Opera Ballet, Monte Carlo
Franz in *Coppélia* (after Saint-Léon), Monte Carlo Opera Ballet, Monte Carlo
1947/49 Principal dancer in *Le Palais de cristal* (*Symphony in C*; Balanchine), Paris Opéra Ballet, Paris
1947 Principal dancer in *Serenade* (Balanchine), Paris Opéra Ballet, Paris
Danseur in *La Grisi* (Aveline), Paris Opéra Ballet, Paris
Le Coq noir in *Les Animaux modèles* (Lifar), Paris Opéra Ballet, Paris
Le Nègre in *Marouf* (opera; mus. Rabaud), Paris Opéra Ballet, Paris
1950 Leading role in *Perséphone* (Taras), (de Cuevas's) Grand Ballet de Monte Carlo
Mercutio (cr) in *Tragédie à Vérone* (Skibine), (de Cuevas's) Grand Ballet de Monte Carlo, Monte Carlo
Dancer in *The Black Swan* Pas de deux (Petipa), (de Cuevas's) Grand Ballet de Monte Carlo, Barcelona
The Bluebird in *Bluebird Pas de deux* (from *The Sleeping Beauty*; Petipa), (de Cuevas's) Grand Ballet de Monte Carlo
The Miller in *Le Moulin enchantée* (Lichine), (de Cuevas's) Grand Ballet de Monte Carlo
The Dandy in *Le Beau Danube* (Massine), (de Cuevas's) Grand Ballet de Monte Carlo
Principal dancer in *Les Femmes de bonne humeur* (Massine), (de Cuevas's) Grand Ballet de Monte Carlo
Prince Siegfried in *Swan Lake* (Act II; Ivanov; staged Nijinska), (de Cuevas's) Grand Ballet de Monte Carlo
1951 Principal dancer (cr) in *Le Bal des jeunes filles* (Taras), (de Cuevas's) Grand Ballet de Monte Carlo, London
Principal dancer in *Pas de trois classique* (Balanchine), Grand Ballet du Marquis de Cuevas
The Husband in *La Femme muette* (Cobos), Grand Ballet du Marquis de Cuevas
Principal dancer in *Don Quixote Pas de deux* (Gorsky, Petipa), Grand Ballet du Marquis de Cuevas
Principal dancer (cr) in *Symphonie allégorique* (*Les Saisons*; Massine), Grand Ballet du Marquis de Cuevas, Bordeaux
Principal dancer (cr) in *Tarasiana* (pas de deux; Taras), Grand Ballet du Marquis de Cuevas, Paris
1952 The Boy (cr) in *Cordélia* (Taras), Grand Ballet du Marquis de Cuevas, Paris
Dancer (cr) in *Un Nuit d'été* (Taras), Grand Ballet du Marquis de Cuevas, Paris
Title role in *Petrushka* (Fokine, staged Nijinska), Grand Ballet du Marquis de Cuevas
Iphias (cr) in *Piège de lumière* (Taras), Grand Ballet du Marquis de Cuevas, Paris
1953 The Fiancé (cr) in *L'Ange gris* (Skibine), Grand Ballet du Marquis de Cuevas, Deauville
The Hunter (cr) in *L'Aigrette* (new version; Gsovsky), Grand Ballet du Marquis de Cuevas, Paris
James in *La Sylphide* (Bournonville; staged Lander), Grand Ballet du Marquis de Cuevas, Paris
Streetseller (cr) in *Feux rouges, feux verts* (also chor.), Grand Ballet du Marquis de Cuevas, Paris
1954 Prince in *The Nutcracker* (after Ivanov), Grand Ballet du Marquis de Cuevas
Albrecht in *Giselle* (after Petipa, Coralli, Perrot), Grand Ballet du Marquis de Cuevas
Harlequin in *Arlequinade* (Nijinska after Petipa), Grand Ballet du Marquis de Cuevas
1955 Principal dancer (cr) *Le Lien* (Goubé), Grand Ballet du Marquis de Cuevas, Cannes
Paris (cr) in *Roméo et Juliette* (also chor., with Skibine, Skouratoff, Taras), Grand Ballet du Marquis de Cuevas, Paris
1956 Principal dancer (cr) in *Pastorale* (Skibine), Grand Ballet du Marquis de Cuevas, Paris
1957 The Emperor (cr) in *La Chanson de l'éternelle tristesse* (Ricarda), Grand Ballet du Marquis de Cuevas, Paris

**Serge Golovine**

The Man (cr) in *L'Amour et son destin* (Lifar, Parlic), Grand Ballet du Marquis de Cuevas, Vienna
Principal dancer in *Constantia* (Dollar), Grand Ballet du Marquis de Cuevas
1958 Mazurka in *Noir et blanc* (*Suite en blanc*; Lifar), Grand (International) Ballet du Marquis de Cuevas
Antonio in *La Lampara* (dell'Ara), Grand (International) Ballet du Marquis de Cuevas, Paris
Principal dancer (cr) in *Duetto* (pas de deux; Lifar), Grand (International) Ballet du Marquis de Cuevas, Paris
Narcisse (cr) in *La Mort de Narcisse* (also chor.), Grand (International) Ballet du Marquis de Cuevas, Paris
1959 Title role in *Tristan fou* (Massine), Grand (International) Ballet du Marquis de Cuevas
1960 Prince Florimund in *The Sleeping Beauty* (Helpmann, Nijinska after Petipa), Grand (International) Ballet du Marquis de Cuevas, Paris
1961 Principal dancer in *Grand Pas d'Auber* (*Grand Pas classique*; Gsovsky), Grand (International) Ballet du Marquis de Cuevas
Principal dancer in *Le Pas de la vestale* (Bournonville; staged von Rosen), Grand Ballet du Marquis de Cuevas
1962 The Faune in *L'Après-midi d'un faune* (after Nijinsky), Compagnons de la danse
Principal dancer in *Les Forains* (Petit), Compagnons de la danse
Principal dancer (cr) in *Symphonie classique* (first version; also chor.), Compagnons de la danse
Principal dancer in *Dessin pour les six* (Taras), Compagnons de la danse
1964 Principal dancer (cr) in *Présentation* (also chor.), Geneva Opera Ballet, Geneva
1965 Principal dancer (cr) in *L'Oiseau de feu* (also chor.), Geneva Opera Ballet, Geneva
Principal dancer (cr) in *Symphonie classique* (new version; also chor.), Geneva Opera Ballet, Geneva
Principal dancer in *Arcades* (Labis), Geneva Opera Ballet, Geneva
Principal dancer (cr) in *Répercussion* (also chor.), Geneva Opera Ballet, Geneva
1966 Principal dancer (cr) in *Petite Symphonie concertante* (also chor.), Geneva Opera Ballet, Geneva

**Other roles include:** principal dancer in *Variations for Four* (Dolin), the Poet in *La Sonnambula* (Balanchine).

## WORKS

1953 *Feux rouges, feux verts* (mus. Petit), Grand Ballet du Marquis de Cuevas, Paris
1955 *Roméo et Juliette* (with Skibine, Skouratoff, Taras; mus. Berlioz), Grand Ballet du Marquis de Cuevas, Paris
1958 *La Mort de Narcisse* (mus. Pothier), Grand (International) Ballet du Marquis de Cuevas, Paris
1962 *Symphonie classique* (first version; mus. Prokofiev), Compagnons de la danse
1964 *Présentation* (mus. Rossini), Geneva Opera Ballet, Geneva
1965 *L'Oiseau de feu* (mus. Stravinsky, Casado), Geneva Opera Ballet, Geneva
*Symphonie classique* (new version; mus. Prokofiev), Geneva Opera Ballet, Geneva
*Ressac* (mus. Métral), Geneva Opera Ballet, Geneva
*Répercussion* (mus. Métral), Geneva Opera Ballet, Geneva
*Le Mandarin merveilleux* (mus. Bartók), Geneva Opera Ballet, Geneva
1966 *Sebastian* (mus. Menotti), Geneva Opera Ballet, Geneva
*Petite Symphonie concertante* (mus. Martin), Geneva Opera Ballet, Geneva
*Métaphore* (mus. Bach), Geneva Opera Ballet, Geneva
*Oppression* (mus. Gould), Geneva Opera Ballet, Geneva
*Le Chant du Pavot* (mus. Landowski), Geneva Opera Ballet, Geneva
1967 *Contraste* (mus. Schibler), Geneva Opera Ballet, Geneva
*Academia* (mus. Czerny), Geneva Opera Ballet, Geneva
*L'Entremonde* (mus. Guyonnet), Geneva Opera Ballet, Geneva
1968 *Labyrinthe* (mus. Bartók), Geneva Opera Ballet, Geneva
*Roméo et Juliette* (mus. Prokofiev), Geneva Opera Ballet, Geneva

## PUBLICATIONS

Hervin, C., *Serge Golovine*, Paris, 1951
Lidova, Irène, "Deux Visages de la danse française", *Ballet Annual* (London), vol. 6, 1952
Reiss, Françoise, "Serge Golovine", *Chrysalis* (Boston), vol. 5, nos. 1–2, 1952
Zürner, Ineborg, "Serge Golovine", *Ballet Today* (London), December 1953
Daguerre, P., *Le Marquis de Cuevas*, Paris, 1954
Glotz, M., *Serge Golovine*, Paris, 1955
Barnes, Clive, "News from London", *Dance Magazine* (New York), October 1958
Lidova, Irène, "Serge Golovine", *Les Saisons de la danse* (Paris), April 1976

* * *

Serge Golovine was a dancer in the purest sense of the word. His body was chiselled by centuries of tradition and he displayed all the discipline of the classical school, developed over the generations.

Golovine was born in Monaco of parents from opposite sides of Europe: his father was from Russia and his mother from Brittany. His two younger brothers, Georges and Jean, were also dancers, and his sister Solange was a well-known teacher. His first teacher was Julie Sedova, a dancer from the Imperial Russian Ballet who then lived in Nice. Serge was a thin, fragile child, introspective and slightly mistrustful, as though he were afraid of letting the world know his secret—the overwhelming desire to become a dancer.

Life was not easy for the Golovine family and when war broke out, Serge had to practise alone in the courtyard of their house in a pair of worn-out ballet shoes. In 1942 Jean Babilée came to dance in the south of France and inspired the young Golovine to aim for perfection. He was helped in this by Gustave Ricaux, a teacher from the Paris Opéra who was living in Monaco during the German Occupation of Paris.

When he was not yet twenty, Golovine danced *Le Spectre de la rose* at the Monte Carlo Opéra where he received a tremendous welcome and became a local celebrity. He was on the brink of a brilliant career. A few years later he auditioned for the Paris Opéra. He was accepted, but had to begin at the bottom of the corps de ballet. The hierarchy of the Opéra was merciless, and his years with the Opéra were both humiliating and dull. In 1950 he decided to try his luck with the Marquis de

Cuevas's company, whose leading dancers were André Eglevsky and Georges Skibine. Fate was kind to him at last when, in 1950, on tour in Barcelona, he took Eglevsky's role as Rosella Hightower's partner in the *Black Swan* pas de deux. He was acclaimed by the public and a great dancer was born. He became the idol of Parisian audiences.

Serge Golovine was not tall, but was well proportioned, with narrow hips and long muscles. He had natural elevation and a youthful grace which appealed to the public. He danced with great openness, as though trying to give the best of himself. His greatest roles were the Bluebird, the Spectre de la rose, and the title role in *Petrushka*, which he studied with Bronislava Nijinska (whose favourite he was). In 1952 he created the role of Iphias in John Taras's *Piège de lumière*. This unusual role is that of an exotic butterfly, who fights to the death to save the Morphide who is threatened by man.

Golovine also had admirers beyond Paris. He enjoyed several triumphant seasons with the de Cuevas company in London, where critics praised his strong technique and stage presence. In 1958, Clive Barnes and Peter Williams of the London magazine *Dance and Dancers* commented enthusiastically on the young dancer's dramatic improvement, pointing to his stage presence, his manners, and "the lovely cleanness of his dancing". Praise was unqualified:

> In shape he bears a slight resemblance to the pictures of Vestris and undoubtedly, he is the 'Dieu of the Danse' of contemporary French ballet. His elevation is prodigious—he just soars in the air without any apparent preparation.

Calm and thoughtful, Golovine led an austere life devoted entirely to his art. His last role before the Ballet du Marquis de Cuevas broke up in 1962 was that of Prince Désiré in Raymundo de Larrain's memorable production of *The Sleeping Beauty*. He danced with Liane Daydé, a "ballerine miniature"; together they formed a ravishing couple.

Golovine never again found a place in a large-scale company. He settled eventually in Geneva where, for a few years during the late 1960s, he directed the ballet company of the Municipal Opera. Following this, he founded his own school, using his own very personal method of teaching. He has very few choreographed works to his name, being rather more of a teacher than a creator. Serge Golovine is now teaching at the Paris Opéra, and is one of the school's best teachers, also coaching the young men in the top class.

—Irène Lidova

---

**GOOD-HUMOURED LADIES, The** *see* **FEMMES DE BONNE HUMEUR, Les**

---

**GONTCHAROVA, Nathalie** (Natalia)

Russian/French painter and designer. Born Natalya Sergeevna Goncharova (Gontcharova) in Ladyzhino, Toula, 4 June 1881. Educated at the Fourth Gymnasium, Moscow, 1891–96; studied art at the Moscow Institute of Painting, Sculpture and Architecture, pupil of Prince Paul Trubetskoy, 1898–1902. Married artist and designer Mikhail Larionov, 1955. Painter, exhibiting at Union of Russian Artists, St. Petersburg, and contributing to Russian section at Salon d'Automne, Paris, 1906; co-founder, with Larionov, "Knave of Diamonds" group, 1910, "Donkey's Tail" group, 1912, and the "Target" group, 1913, becoming recognized as founder of theory of "rayonism"; first stage design, Moscow, 1909; began collaboration with Diaghilev's Ballets Russes with designs for *Le Coq d'or*, Paris, 1914; settled permanently in Paris, 1915, continuing to design for Diaghilev, various seasons 1916–26; costume designer for Olga Spessivtseva, Paris, 1934; designer for choreographers Serge Lifar, Mikhail Fokine, Boris Kniaseff, and for Ballet Russe de Monte Carlo; also designer for theatre and opera, including for Tairov's production of Goldoni's play *The Fan* and Rimsky-Korsakov's *Grad Kitezh*; member, Société des artists indépendants, Paris, 1921; acquired French nationality, 1938. Recipient: Gold Medal for Sculpture, School of Painting, Sculpture and Architecture, Moscow, 1902; Diploma of Honour, Exposition des Beaux Arts, Bordeaux, France, 1927. Died in Paris, 17 October 1962.

**WORKS** (Ballet design)

1914 *Le Coq d'or* (opera-ballet; chor. Fokine), Diaghilev's Ballets Russes, Paris
1915 *Liturgie* (chor. Massine) (not produced)
*The Invisible City of Kitezh* (mus. Rimsky-Korsakov) (not produced)
1916 *España* (mus. Ravel), Diaghilev's Ballets Russes (not produced)
*Triana* (mus. Albeniz), Diaghilev's Ballets Russes (not produced)
1917 *Contes russes* (costumes, with Larionov; chor. Massine), Diaghilev's Ballets Russes, Paris
*Sadko* (costumes; chor. Bolm), Diaghilev's Ballets Russes, San Sebastian
1921 *Igrouchki* (*Russian Toys*; chor. Fokine), Palace Theater, New York
1922 *Le Mariage de la Belle au bois dormant* (costumes, with Benois; chor. Petipa, staged Nijinska), Diaghilev's Ballets Russes, Paris
*Le Renard* (with Larionov; chor. Nijinska), Diaghilev's Ballets Russes, Paris
1923 *Les Noces* (chor. Nijinska), Diaghilev's Ballets Russes, Paris
1924 *La Nuit sur le mont chauve* (chor. Nijinska), Diaghilev's Ballets Russes, Monte Carlo
1925 *Les Contes de fées* (from Act III of *The Sleeping Princess*; Petipa, staged Nijinska), Diaghilev's Ballets Russes, Monte Carlo
1926 *The Firebird* (revival; chor. Fokine, staged Grigoriev and Tchernicheva), Diaghilev's Ballets Russes, London
1930 *Au Temps des Tartares* (chor. Kniaseff), Ballets Russes de Boris Kniaseff
1932 *Bolero* (chor. Nijinska), Théâtre de la danse Nijinska, Paris
*Sur la Borysthène* (costumes, with Larionov; chor. Lifar), Paris Opéra Ballet, Paris
*Divertissement* (chor. Lifar, after Petipa), Paris Opéra Ballet, Paris
1933 *Voyage d'une danseuse* (chor. Romanov), Theatre Chauve-Souris, New York
1935 *L'Amour sorcier* (costumes; chor. Woizikowsky), Les Ballets Léon Woizikowsky, European tour
*Méphisto Valse* (chor. Fokine), Olga Spessivtseva Concert, Opéra-Comique, Paris
1937 *Le Coq d'or* (ballet version; chor. Fokine), de Basil's Ballets Russes, London

**Nathalie Gontcharova's backcloth for *The Firebird*, 1926 revival**

1938 *Igrouchki* (*Russian Toys*, revival; chor. Fokine), Ballets de Monte Carlo
*Cendrillon* (*Cinderella*; chor. Fokine), Russian Ballet (de Basil's Ballets Russes), London
*Bogatyri* (chor. Massine), Ballet Russe de Monte Carlo, New York
1939 *La Tragédie de l'horloge* (chor. Leslie), Doris Nils Company
*Légende* (chor. Nils), Doris Nils Company
*Les Forces errantes* (chor. Nils), Doris Nils Company
1939/40 *Obsession* (revival; chor. Kniaseff), Ballets Russes de Boris Kniaseff, Paris
*La Foire de Sorotchinsky* (chor. Eltsov), Ballets Russes de Boris Kniaseff, Paris
1940 *Goyescas* (chor. T. Gsovsky), Ballets Russes de Boris Kniaseff, Paris
*Offrande pathétique* (chor. Kniaseff), Ballets Russes de Boris Kniaseff, Paris
*Piccoli* (chor. Kniaseff), Ballets Russes de Boris Kniaseff, Paris
1940/41 *Swan Lake* (chor. after Petipa, Ivanov), Ballets Russes de Boris Kniaseff, Paris
1942 *La Princesse des Ursins* (ballet; mus. Jolivet), Théâtre de la Cité, Paris
1943 *Goulnar* (ballet; mus. Djabadari) (not produced)
1949 *Un Coeur de diamant* (chor. Lichine), (de Cuevas's) Grand Ballet de Monte Carlo, Monte Carlo
*La Veillée* (chor. Kniasev), Teatro Politeama, Buenos Aires
1954 *Firebird* (chor. after Fokine), Sadler's Wells Ballet, Edinburgh
1957 *Igrouchki* (chor. after Fokine), Théâtre des arts du ballet, Monte Carlo
*Les Elfes* (chor. after Fokine), Théâtre des arts du ballet, Monte Carlo
*Eros* (chor. after Fokine), Théâtre des arts du ballet, Monte Carlo
*Islamey* (chor. after Fokine), Théâtre des arts du ballet, Monte Carlo
*The Sorcerer's Apprentice* (chor. after Fokine), Théâtre des arts du ballet, Monte Carlo
1958 *Carnaval* (chor. after Fokine), Théâtre des arts du ballet, Monte Carlo

**Other works include:** for Ballets Boris Kniaseff—designs for *Le Carnaval de Venise* (mus. Goldoni), *Le Temple egyptien* (mus. Arensky), *Vision antique* (mus. Gagotsky), *Coup de bambou* (mus. Satie).

## PUBLICATIONS


By Gontcharova:

*Les Ballets Russes de Serge Diaghilev et la Décoration théâtrale*, with Mikhail Larionov and Pierre Vorms, Belvès, France, 1930; revised edition, 1955

"The Creation of *Les Noces*", *Ballet and Opera*, September 1949

*Cinquante Ans à Saint Germain des Pres* (with Larionov), Paris, 1972

"The Metamorphoses of the Ballet *Les Noces*", *Leonardo* (London), no. 12, 1979

About Gontcharova:

Eganbury, Eli, *Natalia Gontcharova–Mikhail Larionov*, Moscow, 1913

Stephens, W., *The Soul of Russia*, London, 1916
Propert, W.A., *The Russian Ballet in Western Europe*, London, 1921
Gregor, Joseph, and Miller, René Fulop, *The Russian Theatre*, London, 1930
Beaumont, Cyril, *Design for the Ballet*, London, 1943
Beaumont, Cyril, *Ballet Design: Past and Present*, London, 1946
Amberg, George, *Art in Modern Ballet*, London, 1946
Chamot, Mary, "The Early Works of Goncharova and Larionov", *The Burlington Magazine* (London), June 1955
Waldemar, George, *Larionov*, Paris, 1966
Loguine, Tatiana, *Gontcharova et Larionov: Cinquante ans à Saint Germain des Pres*, Paris, 1971
Gray, Camilla, *The Russian Experiment in Art 1863–1922*, London, 1971
Chamot, Mary, *Natalia Gontcharova*, Paris, 1972
Chamot, Mary, *Gontcharova: Stage Designs and Paintings*, London, 1979
Schouvaloff, Alexander, *Set and Costume Design for Ballet and Theatre*, Catalogue of the Thyssen-Bornemisza Collection, London, 1987
Baer, Nancy van Norman, *The Art of Enchantment: Diaghilev's Ballets Russes 1909–1929*, San Francisco, 1988
Garafola, Lynn, *Diaghilev's Ballets Russes*, New York, 1989
Svetaeva, Marina, *Nathalie Gontcharova: Sa Vie et son oeuvre*, translated from the Russian by Véronique Lossky, Paris, 1990

* * *

"The ballet décor does not have as its sole purpose the establishment, according to the indications of a libretto, of the time and place of an action; the scrupulously historical reconstruction of this or that style is not the end assigned to it. Décor is above all an independent creation, supporting the spirit of the work to be performed; it is an autonomous art form with its own problems and subject to its own laws . . . "—thus proclaimed Natalia Gontcharova and Mikhail Larionov, two of twentieth-century ballet's most important designers.

Nathalie Gontcharova's commission from Diaghilev to design *Le Coq d'or* was ground-breaking in two respects; not only was she the first artist outside the close *Mir Iskusstva* circle to receive such a commission for the Ballets Russes, but she was also the first woman to do so. At the age of 33, Gontcharova was already a leading member of Moscow's artistic society, one of the founders of the rayonist movement and an associate of the Moscow futurists. In April 1913 she had held an exhibition of a decade's work in Moscow, containing no fewer than 768 works. Her paintings of this period combined the very modern—semi-abstract compositions influenced by the cubist and futurist movements—with traditional Russian folk art.

Gontcharova's knowledge of her country's folklore and history came from a childhood spent in the Russian countryside and from subsequent research, including visits to archaeological museums and interviews with Russian artisans. These were to be the strongest influences on her designs for Diaghilev's Ballets Russes, having undergone a significant transformation. The exotic and oriental elements of Russian art which had influenced Bakst's designs played no part in Gontcharova's or Larionov's work. Instead, they turned to an earlier Russia of folk tales and Orthodox ceremonies. These were represented in a stylized manner that rendered them at once primitive and modern. The naturalism of traditional ballet décor gave way to futurism—Gontcharova and Larionov replaced perspective and *trompe d'oeil* with flat representation and used geometric shapes in bright colours to represent natural objects and architecture.

At the same time, the status of the ballet designer began to change. No longer was design subservient to music and choreography; under Gontcharova and Larionov it reigned supreme. Massine's unrealized *Liturgie*, for example, is a series of tableaux based on Byzantine art and the Italian primitives, in which static poses take the place of movement. (During Massine's early years as a choreographer, Larionov acted as his editor, not only reviewing but also revising his work, often paring down the steps to a minimum). Futurism, via Gontcharova and Larionov, also influenced balletic movement itself, converting—or contorting—soft and fluid shapes into hard angles, which some critics and audiences found grotesque and even comical.

Cyril Beaumont commented on the "fantasy, brilliant colour, and richly decorative quality" of Gontcharova's designs for *Le Coq d'or*. The setting for the first scene had a folk tale quality, consisting of a walled town, the walls themselves decorated with imaginary animals and their pointed towers with a floral design, and fantastic trees with enormous flowers. Vivid colour and fantasy also distinguished Larionov's and Gontcharova's designs for *Contes russes*, based on Russian folk tales and containing the hideous demons Kikimora and Baba Yaga as well as fairytale heroines and groups of Russian peasants.

The designs for *Les Noces* were very different, demonstrating that the Gontcharova/Larionov insistence on freedom from the constraints of choreography was sometimes ill-judged. Diaghilev had commissioned the designs from Gontcharova and, when they were complete, took the choreographer Bronislava Nijinska to see them. Although Nijinska was impressed by Gontcharova's draughtsmanship and sense of colour, she later wrote that they "seemed to me to be diametrically opposed to the music of Stravinsky and also to my conception of the ballet. Once outside Gontcharova's studio, [Diaghilev] turned to me. 'Well, Bronia, you are very quiet. I hope the costumes for *Les Noces* delighted you.' 'Frankly', I replied, 'these costumes, in themselves, are magnificent and may be very good for a performance of a Russian opera, but completely impossible for any ballet and for *Les Noces* most of all.'"

Diaghilev's first response was to side with Gontcharova and drop Nijinska from the project, but he approached the latter the following spring, when she insisted that there should be "no colourful ostentation", saying "I see the costumes as being of the utmost simplicity and all alike." She also commented, tellingly, that the heaviness of the traditional costumes—full-length robes and high headdresses for the women, heavy boots for the men—concealed the dancers' movements, so that the body was "like a violin enclosed in its case". Diaghilev commissioned new designs from Gontcharova, who produced an austere set and uniform-like costumes in brown, grey, black, and white.

Beaumont found Gontcharova's decorative use of colour and design equally inappropriate in her new designs for *Firebird* (these did not include the costumes for the Firebird and the Tsarevna, which were by Bakst), on the grounds that they lacked the "fairy-like beauty" of Golovine's original designs for the ballet.

The influence of Gontcharova on twentieth-century ballet design cannot be underestimated. Her originality is without question, and her effect on subsequent concepts of design equally unquestionable. In Richard Buckle's words, "she was a fighter on the barricades of art".

—Jessica Arah

**GORE, Walter**

Scottish dancer and choreographer. Born Frederick Robert Taylor in Waterside, Scotland, 8 October 1910. Studied at the Italia Conti School, from 1924, and also with Léonide Massine and Marie Rambert. Served in the British Navy during World War II. Married dancer Paula Hinton, 1950. Début, Marie Rambert's Dancers (later Ballet Club, and eventually Ballet Rambert), first season, 1930, also performing with Camargo Society, 1931, 1932; dancer with Rambert's company, 1930–35; also appeared in stage musicals, including Cochran revue *Magic Nights* (mus. various; chor. Bradley and Ashton, 1932), *A Kiss in Spring* (mus. Brammer and Grünwald; chor. Ashton, 1932), and *Ballyhoo* (mus. Walker; chor. Bradley and Ashton, 1932); dancer, Vic-Wells Ballet, from 1934, leaving to choreograph for stage musicals, 1936, including for Herbert Farjeon revue *Spread it Abroad* (mus. Walker; Saville Theatre, 1936); principal dancer, Ballet Rambert, from autumn 1936, and choreographer, 1938–41, 1944–49; also choreographer and dancer for British Broadcasting Corporation (BBC) television, from 1937/38; guest choreographer, Ballet des Champs-Elysées, Paris, 1952; choreographer, New Ballet Company, 1952, also staging ballets for own and other companies, including Sadler's Wells Theatre Ballet, 1953; founder, Walter Gore Ballet, 1954, touring Australia under the name of Australian Theatre Ballet, 1955–56; guest choreographer, Norwegian Opera Ballet, various seasons, from c.1954, Ballet der Lage Landen, Amsterdam, 1956, and Miskovitch Company ("Les Ballets 1956"), Paris, 1956; ballet director and choreographer, Frankfurt Ballet, 1957–59; founder and director, London Ballet, 1961–63; ballet director, Gulbenkian Ballet (Grupo Gulbenkian de Bailado), Lisbon, 1965–69, Augsburg, 1971–72; Professor of Dance, Conservatorio Navarro de Musica, Pamplona, 1978–79. Died in Pamplona, 16 April 1979.

**ROLES**

1931 Jodelling Song and Popular Song (cr) in *Façade* (Ashton), Camargo Society, London
Sir Toby (cr) in *Cross-Garter'd* (Tudor), Ballet Club (later Ballet Rambert), London
One of Seven Sons, Pestilence, A Comforter (cr) in *Job* (de Valois), Camargo Society, London
A Young Man (cr) in *Regatta* (Ashton), Vic-Wells Ballet, London
Lover (cr) in *The Lady of Shalott* (Ashton), Ballet Club, London
Sailor (cr; later called The Stevedore) in *A Day in a Southern Port* (*Rio Grande*; Ashton), Camargo Society, London
Eustace (cr) in *The Lord of Burleigh* (Ashton), Camargo Society, London
1932 Cinesias (cr) in *Lysistrata* (Tudor), Ballet Club, London
Man (cr) in *The Garden* (Salaman), Ballet Club, London
Pas de quatre (cr) in *An 1805 Impression* (later called *Récamier*; Ashton), in *Magic Nights*, Charles B. Cochran revue, London
Title role in *Mercury* (Ashton), Camargo Society, London
Eddy, a Stranger (cr) in *High Yellow* (Bradley, Ashton), Camargo Ballet, London
Un Abonné (cr) in *Foyer de danse* (Ashton), Ballet Club, London
Dancer in *The Passionate Pavane* (revision of *Follow Your Saint*, 1930; Ashton), Camargo Society, London
1933 Buffoon (cr) in *Pavane pour une infante défunte* (Tudor), Ballet Club, London
Lover (cr) in *Les Masques* (Ashton), Ballet Club, London
Juggler (cr) in *Our Lady's Juggler* (new production; Howard and Salaman), Ballet Club, London
1934 Alexander (cr) in *Paramour* (Tudor), in *Dr. Faustus* (play by Marlowe), Oxford University Dramatic Society, Oxford (ballet also staged for Ballet Club, 1934)
Faust (cr) in *Mephisto Waltz* (Ashton), Ballet Club, London
Gustave (cr) in *Bar aux Folies-Bergère* (de Valois), Ballet Club, London
Zi Dima Lucasi (cr) in *The Jar* (de Valois), Vic-Wells Ballet, London
1935 Court Hairdresser (cr) in *Cinderella* (Howard), Ballet Rambert, London
Robert (cr) in *Valentine's Eve* (Ashton), Ballet Rambert, London
The Rake (cr) in *The Rake's Progress* (de Valois), Vic-Wells Ballet, London
Hilarion in *Giselle* (Petipa after Coralli, Perrot; staged Sergeyev), Vic-Wells Ballet, London
Trainer (cr) in *Circus Wings* (Salaman), Ballet Rambert, London
1937 Third Song (cr) in *Dark Elegies* (Tudor), Ballet Rambert, London
Malvolio (cr) in *Cross-Garter'd* (new version; Toye), Ballet Rambert, London
1938 Mercury (cr) in *Croquis de Mercure* (Howard), Ballet Rambert, London
Principal male (cr) in *Valse finale* (also chor.), Ballet Rambert, London
1939 Taxi Driver (cr) in *Paris-Soir* (also chor.), Ballet Rambert, London
Étude symphonique (cr) in *Czernyana* (Staff), Ballet Rambert, London
1940 Army Surgeon (cr) in *Cap Over Mill* (also chor.), Ballet Rambert, London
The Cat (cr) in *Peter and the Wolf* (Staff), Ballet Rambert, London
Principal dancer (cr) in *Bartlemas Dances* (also chor.), Oxford Ballet Club, Oxford
1941 Visions (cr) in *Czerny 2* (Staff), Ballet Rambert, London
Principal dancer (cr) in *Confessional* (also chor.), Oxford Ballet Club, Oxford
1944 Title role (cr) in *The Fugitive* (Howard), Ballet Rambert, Bedford
Principal dancer (cr) in *Simple Symphony* (also chor.), Ballet Rambert, Bristol
The Lover (cr) in *Un Songe* (Staff), Ballet Rambert, Norwich
1945 Albrecht in *Giselle*, Act II (after Petipa, Coralli, Perrot), Ballet Rambert, Birmingham
1946 Title role (cr) in *Mr. Punch* (also chor.), Ballet Rambert, London
1947 William Targett (cr) in *The Sailor's Return* (Howard), Ballet Rambert, London
Principal dancer (cr) in *Plaisance* (also chor.), Ballet Rambert, London
Robert (cr) in *Winter Night* (also chor.), Ballet Rambert, Melbourne
1949 Principal dancer (cr) in *Kaleidoscope* (also chor.), Ballet Rambert, London
Rafael (cr) in *Antonia* (also chor.), Ballet Rambert, London
1951 Harlequin (cr) in *The Gay Invalid* (play after Molière; also chor.), Princes Theatre, London

Walter Gore with Sally Gilmour in *The Fugitive*, Ballet Rambert, 1944

**Other roles include:** for Ballet Club/Ballet Rambert—Bluebird in *Aurora's Wedding* (after Petipa), Valentin in *Bar aux Folies-Bergère* (de Valois), The English Champion in *Le Boxing* (Salaman), Batsman, Bowler, and Umpire in *Le Cricket* (Salaman), Tordion in *Capriol Suite* (Ashton), Pantalon and Harlequin in *Carnaval* (Fokine), Se Habla Español in *Czerny 2* (Staff), Dago (Tango) in *Façade* (Ashton), Maître de ballet in *Foyer de danse* (Ashton), The Man She Must Marry and Lover in *Le Jardin aux lilas* (Tudor), Prince Siegfried in *Swan Lake* Act II (after Ivanov), Mr. Tebrick in *Lady into Fox* (Howard), Mars in *Mars and Venus* (Ashton), Prince in *Mermaid* (Howard and Salaman), Virtuoso in *La Muse s'amuse* (Howard), Iskender in *La Péri* (Staff), Mortals under Venus and under Mars in *The Planets* (Tudor), principal dancer in *Pavane pour une infante défunte* (Stone), The Player in *Le Rugby* (Salaman), Tirolese in *Soirée musicale* (Tudor), A Laddie in *The Tartans* (Staff), The Lover in *Night and Silence* (also chor.).

## WORKS

1938 *Valse finale* (later *Valses sentimentales*; mus. Ravel), Ballet Rambert, London
1939 *Paris-Soir* (mus. Poulenc), Ballet Rambert, London
1940 *Cap Over Mill* (mus. Bate), Ballet Rambert, London
1941 *Confessional* (mus. Sibelius), Oxford Ballet Club, Oxford
*Bartlemas Dances* (mus. Holst), Oxford Ballet Club, Oxford
*Porphyria* (mus. Rachmaninov), Oxford Ballet Club, Oxford
1944 *Simple Symphony* (mus. Britten), Ballet Rambert, Bristol
1946 *Mr. Punch* (mus. Oldham), Ballet Rambert, London
*Concerto Burlesco* (mus. Bartók), Ballet Rambert, London
1947 *Plaisance* (mus. Rossini), Ballet Rambert, London
1948 *Winter Night* (mus. Rachmaninov), Ballet Rambert, Melbourne
1949 *Kaleidoscope* (mus. Brahms, Paganini), Ballet Rambert, London
*Antonia* (mus. Sibelius), Ballet Rambert, London
1951 *Hoops* (mus. Poulenc), London Theatre Ballet, Eastbourne
*Tancredi e Clorinda* (mus. Monteverdi), English Opera Group, London (later staged for Ballet Workshop)
*La Damnée* (*Crucifix*; mus. Barber), Ballets des Champs-Elysées, Paris
*Pastorale for Today* (mus. Poulenc), Continental Ballet, British tour
*Armida* (mus. Cherepnin), British Broadcasting Corporation (BBC) Television

1952 *Theme and Variations* (mus. Tchaikovsky), National Ballet of Australia, Melbourne
*Street Games* (mus. Ibert), New Ballet Company, London
*Romantic Evening* (mus. Heller), New Ballet Company, London
*Peepshow* (mus. Françaix), Ballet Workshop, London
*Birthday Suite* (mus. Tippett), BBC Television
1953 *Light Fantastic* (mus. Chabrier), Walter Gore Ballet, Malvern
*The Gentle Poltergeist* (mus. Fauré), Walter Gore Ballet, London
*Classical Suite* (mus. Rossini), Walter Gore Ballet, Malvern
*Cyclasm* (mus. Addison), Walter Gore Ballet, London
*Carte Blanche* (mus. Addison), Sadler's Wells Theatre Ballet, Edinburgh
1955 *Grand Pas de trois classique* (mus. Rossini), Australian Theatre Ballet, Adelaide
*Musical Chairs* (mus. Berners), Australian Theatre Ballet, Adelaide
*Soft Sorrow* (mus. Fauré), Australian Theatre Ballet, Adelaide
1956 *Les Saisons* (mus. Glazunov), Les Ballets 1956, Paris
*Ginerva* (mus. Sibelius), Het Nederlands Ballets, The Hague
*De Eenzame* (mus. Busoni), Ballet der Lage Landen, Amsterdam
1957 *Suite for Two Dancers* (mus. Glazunov), Ballet der Lage Landen, Amsterdam
*Pavane for a Dead Lover* (mus. Bocai), Ballet der Lage Landen, Amsterdam
*Flugel des Schlafes* (mus. Debussy), Frankfurt Ballet, Frankfurt
*The Nutcracker* (mus. Tchaikovsky), Royal Gala, Ballet der Lage Landen, Amsterdam
1958 *Marionetten Flirt* (mus. Chabrier), Frankfurt Ballet, Frankfurt
*Die im Schatten Leben* (*Eaters of Darkness*; mus. Britten), Frankfurt Opera Ballet, Frankfurt
*Grand Soirée* (mus. Rossini), Frankfurt Ballet, Frankfurt
*The Assassin* (mus. Bach), Pilar Lopez Ballet, Barcelona
*Ballade* (mus. Fauré), Pilar Lopez Ballet, Barcelona
*Grand Pas de deux* (mus. Dvořák), Pilar Lopez Ballet, Barcelona
*Night and Silence* (mus. Bach, arr. Mackerras), Edinburgh Festival Ballet, Edinburgh
*Garten der Tränen* (mus. Franck), Frankfurt Ballet, Frankfurt
1959 *Der Grosse Kryg* (mus. Casella), Frankfurt Ballet, Frankfurt
*Don Ramiro* (mus. Nass), Frankfurt Ballet, Frankfurt
*Das Magische Wesen* (mus. Schuller), Frankfurt Ballet, Frankfurt
*The Four Temperaments* (mus. Hindemith), Frankfurt Ballet, Frankfurt
*Ljubovna Tragedy* (mus. Shostakovich), Zagreb Opera House Ballet
*Belfrielse* (mus. Barber), Norwegian Opera Ballet, Oslo
1960 *Schemering* (mus. Martin), Amsterdam Ballet, Amsterdam
*Parade* (mus. Britten), Amsterdam Ballet, Amsterdam
1961 *The Magical Suite* (mus. Josephs), London Ballet, London
*The Sassenach Suite* (mus. M. Arnold), London Ballet, Hintelsham
*The Fair Maid* (mus. Bizet), London Ballet, Edinburgh
*Les Joyaux* (mus. Poulenc), London Ballet, Oxford
1962 *The Magical Being* (mus. W. Josephs), London Ballet, Carlisle
*Suite for Two Dancers* (mus. Weber), London Ballet, Amsterdam
1964 *Sweet Dancer* (mus. F. Martin), Ballet Rambert, London
1965 *The Maskers* (mus. Foss), Western Theatre Ballet
1965/ *Limbo* (mus. Ravel), Gulbenkian Ballet, Lisbon
66 *O Casamento* (mus. Ibert), Gulbenkian Ballet, Lisbon
*Il Ballo dell'ingrate* (mus. Monteverdi), Gulbenkian Ballet, Lisbon
*O Bando* (mus. dello Joio), Gulbenkian Ballet, Lisbon
1967 *Configuracaõ* (mus. Glazunov), Gulbenkian Ballet, Lisbon
*Danças de Boyce* (mus. Boyce), Gulbenkian Ballet, Lisbon
*Feira* (mus. Ravel), Gulbenkian Ballet, Lisbon
*Suite de Verdi* (mus. Verdi), Gulbenkian Ballet, Lisbon
*Dance Pictures* (mus. Maros), Gulbenkian Ballet, Lisbon
1968 *O Campo da Morte* (mus. Searle), Gulbenkian Ballet, Lisbon
*Visoes Fugitivas* (mus. Rachmaninov), Gulbenkian Ballet, Lisbon
1969 *Desportistas* (mus. Poulenc), Gulbenkian Ballet, Lisbon
*Historia de Amor* (mus. Roussel), Gulbenkian Ballet, Lisbon
*Ensaio de Dança e Movimento* (mus. Bäkh, Rabe, Hambraeus), Gulbenkian Ballet, Lisbon
1972 *Beach* (mus. Rachmaninov), Bat-Dor Company, Tel Aviv
*Jeg en er Kloven* (mus. Addison), Norwegian Opera Ballet, Oslo
*Firebird* (mus. Stravinsky), Ballet Company, Perth, Australia
1973 *Embers of Glencoe* (mus. T. Wilson), Scottish Theatre Ballet
*Pas de quatre* (mus. Adam), National Ballet of Rhodesia
1975 *Cinderella* (mus. Rossini, Brumby), Queensland Ballet, Brisbane
*Victim* (mus. Ben Haim), Bat-Dor Company, Tel Aviv

**Other works include:** dances in *The Gay Invalid* (play after Molière), and *A Wedding in Paris* (musical; mus. Hans May); dances in operas *La Traviata* (mus. Verdi), *Iphigénie en Aulide* (mus. Gluck), *The Bartered Bride* (mus. Smetana), *The Merry Widow* (mus. Lehár), "Walpurgisnacht" in *Faust* (mus. Gounod); also stagings of *Les Sylphides* (after Fokine; mus. Chopin), *Carnaval* (after Fokine; mus. Schumann), *Giselle* (after Petipa, Coralli, Perrot; mus. Adam).

## PUBLICATIONS

By Gore:
"The Australian Ballet Today", *Ballet Today* (London), 2 parts; October 1956, November 1956
"German Somersault", *Dance and Dancers* (London), April 1957
"My Plans for Frankfurt", *Dance and Dancers* (London), May 1957
"Tribute", in Crisp, Clement, Sainsbury, Anya, and Williams, Peter (eds.), *Ballet Rambert: 50 Years and On*, revised edition, London, 1981

About Gore:
Bradley, Lionel, *Sixteen Years of Ballet Rambert*, London, 1946

Barnes, Clive, "Walter Gore", *Ballet Today* (London), October 1950
Williams, Peter, "Harlequin Gore Transcends Molière", *Dance and Dancers* (London), April 1951
Bradley, Lionel, "Walter Gore and Paula Hinton", *Ballet Today* (London), April 1952
Alvarez, Elka, "Meet Walter Gore and Paula Hinton", *Ballet Today* (London), January 1953
Williams, Peter, "Theatre in the Blood", *Dance and Dancers* (London), May 1953
Beaumont, Cyril, *Ballets of Today*, London, 1954
Franks, A.H., *Twentieth-Century Ballet*, London, 1954
Kersley, Leo, "Choreographers of Today: Walter Gore", *Ballet Today* (London), April 1961
Clarke, Mary, *Dancers of Mercury: The Story of Ballet Rambert*, London, 1962
"The Life and Work of Walter Gore: A Tribute", (Introduction by Clement Crisp), *Dance Research* (London), Spring 1988

* * *

So much attention has been paid to Frederick Ashton and Antony Tudor, the two star choreographers of Ballet Rambert, that Marie Rambert's other choreographic discoveries have often been unjustly neglected. One of these was Walter Gore, whose career began as a dancer in the early days of British ballet and extended to the moment he died during a teaching engagement in Pamplona, Spain, on Easter Day 1979.

Gore, a Scotsman whose real name was Frederick Robert Taylor, came from a family of musicians and actors and was a pupil of the famous Italia Conti Stage School from the age of fourteen, making his first stage appearance in 1924 in the children's play *Where the Rainbow Ends*. He showed natural dance ability, and went on to study with Massine and later Marie Rambert. Like others of his time, he was an able and attractive dancer with marked theatrical ability rather than virtuoso technique. He danced with Rambert's company from its first season at the Lyric Hammersmith in 1930 and with the Camargo Society in 1931, creating roles in many ballets. In 1934 he joined the Vic-Wells Ballet where he created the role of the Rake in Ninette de Valois' superb ballet *The Rake's Progress*, but soon afterwards he left to work in West End musicals and revues.

Always on the lookout for choreographers, Rambert gave him the opportunity in 1938 to create his first ballet, *Valse Finale*, but before he could advance very far in that field World War II began, and in 1941 he was called to active service in the Royal Navy. He had a tough war, being seriously injured when his ship was twice torpedoed on the same day. He was invalided out of the Forces and returned to Rambert in 1944, building up a fine reputation both as a dancer and as a choreographer. He appeared very successfully as Albrecht in *Giselle*, but his greatest strength lay in modern drama and comedy, as one of Britain's foremost demi-caractère dancers. He was one of the original interpreters of Antony Tudor's *Dark Elegies*, giving a deeply moving and sensitive performance, and his creation of William Targett in Andrée Howard's *The Sailor's Return* was a fine example of comic character dancing.

As a choreographer Gore had tremendous variety and an intensely personal style. He had a rare talent for works as light as soufflés, delicious little numbers for opening or closing a programme. The 1953 *Carte Blanche* (for Sadler's Wells Theatre Ballet) was one of these, while *Street Games*, for the New Ballet Company the year before, cleverly adapted traditional children's games—rope-skipping, hoop-rolling, hopscotch—in terms of classical dance. Equally, however, there was a dark and passionate side to his creative art. This had been shown as early as 1941 in a memorable solo work, *Confessional*, based on Robert Browning's poem and created for Sally Gilmour. It was continued in *Antonia*, for Paula Hinton (who later became his wife), where he used rhythmic footwork and passionate duets in a way that for the time was sexually very frank. *Crucifix*, again for Hinton, was a highly dramatic tale of murder and witch-burning. *Eaters of Darkness* (*Die im Schatten Leben*, for Frankfurt Ballet) was a stark study of a sane woman confined in a lunatic asylum, while ballets like *Winter Night* and *Night and Silence* were fluently lyrical and impassioned.

Gore left Rambert in 1950, after the company's very successful tour of Australia, and thereafter worked in many countries. He ran small companies of his own in Britain, principally the New Ballet Company, later called the Walter Gore Ballet, and the London Ballet, always frustrated by lack of money. He worked in Holland, Germany, France, Australia, and the United States, and fulfilled terms as director of the Frankfurt Ballet and the Grupo Gulbenkian de Bailado in Lisbon.

—Kathrine Sorley Walker

---

## GORSKY, Aleksandr

Russian dancer, choreographer, and teacher. Born Aleksandr Alekseevich Gorsky in St. Petersburg, 18 August (6 August old style) 1871. Studied at the Imperial Theatre School, St. Petersburg, from 1880, graduating in 1889. Dancer, Maryinsky Theatre, 1889–1900: second soloist, from 1895, first soloist, 1900; teacher, St. Petersburg Theatre School, 1896–1900, régisseur, Bolshoi Theatre, Moscow, from 1901, and ballet master and choreographer, Moscow Ballet School, 1902–24; also invited to London to stage own ballet for the Alhambra Theatre, in connection with coronation of George V, 1911. Recipient: Officier de l'Académie (French diploma), 1902; title of Honoured Artist of the Imperial Theatres, 1915. Died in Moscow, 20 October 1924.

### ROLES

1892 Chinese Dance in *The Nutcracker* (Ivanov), Maryinsky Theatre, St. Petersburg
1893 Footman in *The Magic Flute* (Ivanov), Maryinsky Theatre, St. Petersburg
1894 Ylas in *Offrande à l'amour* (Petipa, Ivanov), Maryinsky Theatre, St. Petersburg
Niqueuse (Alain) in *Vain Precautions* (*La Fille mal gardée*; Petipa, Ivanov), Maryinsky Theatre, St. Petersburg
1895 Aquilon in *The Awakening of Flora* (Petipa, Ivanov), Maryinsky Theatre, St. Petersburg
1896 Gavrilo in *The Little Humpbacked Horse* (Saint-Léon), Maryinsky Theatre, St. Petersburg
1897 Ka-ke-ki-go in *The Daughter of Mikado* (Ivanov), Maryinsky Theatre, St. Petersburg
1898 A Gypsy in *Fiametta* (Saint-Léon), Maryinsky Theatre, St. Petersburg
1900 A Satyr in *The Seasons* (Petipa), Maryinsky Theatre, St. Petersburg
Harlequin in *The Trials of Damis* (*Les Ruses d'amour*; Petipa), Maryinsky Theatre, St. Petersburg

**Aleksandr Gorsky's *Giselle*, Moscow, 1922**

## WORKS

1899 *The Sleeping Beauty* (after Petipa; mus. Tchaikovsky), Bolshoi Theatre, Moscow
*Clorinda, Queen of the Mountain Fairies* (mus. Keller), Imperial Theatre School Performance, Mikhailovsky Theatre, St. Petersburg
1900 *Raymonda* (after Petipa; mus. Glazunov), Bolshoi Theatre, Moscow
*Don Quixote* (new version; mus. Minkus), Bolshoi Theatre, Moscow (staged Maryinsky Theatre, St. Petersburg, 1902)
1901 *Swan Lake* (partly after Petipa, Ivanov, with additional new chor; mus. Tchaikovsky), Bolshoi Theatre, Moscow
*Vain Precautions* (*La Fille mal gardée*, after Petipa, Ivanov; mus. Hertel), Bolshoi Theatre, Moscow
*The Little Humpbacked Horse* (new version; mus. Pugni et al.), Bolshoi Theatre, Moscow (staged Maryinsky Theatre, St. Petersburg, 1912)
*Giselle* (partly after Petipa, Coralli, Perrot; mus. Adam), Bolshoi Theatre, Moscow
1902 *Gudule's Daughter* (mus. Simon), Bolshoi Theatre, Moscow
1903 *The Goldfish* (partly after Saint-Léon; mus. Minkus et al.), Bolshoi Theatre, Moscow
1904 *La Bayadère* (after Petipa; mus. Minkus), Bolshoi Theatre, Moscow
1905 *The Magic Mirror* (mus. Koreshenko), Bolshoi Theatre, Moscow
*Coppélia* (after Saint-Léon; mus. Delibes), Bolshoi Theatre, Moscow
*The Pharaoh's Daughter* (after Petipa; mus. Pugni), Bolshoi Theatre, Moscow
1906 *Robert and Bertram; or, The Two Thieves* (mus. Pugni), Bolshoi Theatre, Moscow
1907 *Giselle* (revised version of 1901 production; mus. Adam), Bolshoi Theatre, Moscow
*Nur and Anitra* (mus. Ilyinsky), Bolshoi Theatre, Moscow
*Harlequinade* (after Petipa; mus. Drigo), Bolshoi Theatre, Moscow
1908 *Etudes* (mus. Rubenstein, Grieg, Chopin, Stein et al.), Bolshoi Theatre, Moscow
*Raymonda* (new version; mus. Glazunov), Bolshoi Theatre, Moscow
1910 *Salammbô* (mus. Arends), Bolshoi Theatre, Moscow
1911 *The Red-Blood Flower* (mus. Hartman), Bolshoi Theatre, Moscow
*The Dance Dream* (mus. Brahms, Glazunov, Tchaikovsky, Luigini, Rubinstein), Alhambra Theatre, London

1912 *Le Corsaire* (completely new version; mus. Adam et al.), Bolshoi Theatre, Moscow
*Swan Lake* (after Petipa, Ivanov; mus. Tchaikovsky), Bolshoi Theatre, Moscow
1913 *Love is Quick!* (mus. Grieg), Bolshoi Theatre, Moscow
*Schubertiana* (mus. Schubert), Bolshoi Theatre, Moscow
*Le Carnaval* (divertissement; mus. various), Bolshoi Theatre, Moscow
1914 *Dances of the People* (mus. various), Bolshoi Theatre, Moscow
*The Little Humpbacked Horse* (revision of 1901 production; mus. Pugni), Bolshoi Theatre, Moscow
1915 *Eunice and Petronius* (mus. Chopin), Bolshoi Theatre, Moscow
1916 *Fifth Symphony* (mus. Glazunov), Bolshoi Theatre, Moscow
1917 *La Bayadère* (completely new version; mus. Minkus et al.), Bolshoi Theatre, Moscow
1918 *Night on the Bald Mountain* (mus. Mussorgsky), Bolshoi-Dancers, Theatre of the Aquarium Gardens, Moscow
*Lyric Poem* (mus. Glazunov), Bolshoi Dancers, Theatre of the Aquarium Gardens, Moscow
*En Blanc* (mus. Tchaikovsky), Bolshoi Dancers, Theatre of the Aquarium Gardens, Moscow
*Giselle* (revision of 1901, 1907 productions; mus. Adam), Bolshoi Dancers, Theatre of the Aquarium Gardens, Moscow
*Spanish Sketches* (mus. Glinka), Bolshoi Dancers, Theatre of the Aquarium Gardens, Moscow
*La Péri* (mus. Dukas), Bolshoi Dancers, Theatre of the Aquarium Gardens, Moscow
*Thamar* (mus. Balakirev), Bolshoi Dancers, Theatre of the Aquarium Gardens, Moscow
*Fairytale of the Viennese Wood* (mus. Strauss), Bolshoi Dancers, Theatre of the Aquarium Gardens, Moscow
*Stenka Razin* (mus. Glazunov), Bolshoi Dancers, Theatre of the Aquarium Gardens, Moscow
1919 *The Nutcracker* (mus. Tchaikovsky), Bolshoi Theatre, Moscow
1920 *Swan Lake* (new version; mus. Tchaikovsky), Bolshoi Theatre, Moscow
*Andalusian Summer* (mus. Sarasate), Dancers of Elirov's School, Volny Theatre, Moscow
*The Serf Muse* (mus. Nebolsin), Dancers of Elirov's School, Exam Performance, Moscow
1921 *Salomé's Dance* (mus. Strauss), Bolshoi Theatre, Moscow
*Chrysis* (mus. Glière), Bolshoi Dancers, General Rehearsal (not shown to the public)
*Invitation à la danse* (mus. Weber), Bolshoi Studio, Moscow
*Liszt's Second Rhapsody* (mus. Liszt), Bolshoi Studio, Moscow
1922 *Giselle* (new version; mus. Adam), Bolshoi Ballet, Novy Theatre, Moscow
*Les Petits riens* (mus. Mozart), Bolshoi Ballet, Novy Theatre, Moscow
*Ever-Fresh Flowers* (mus. Asafiev and others), Moscow Ballet School, Novy Theatre, Moscow
1923 *The Venus Grotto* (mus. Wagner), Bolshoi Theatre, Moscow

## PUBLICATIONS

By Gorsky (interviews):
*Peterburgskaya gazeta* (St. Petersburg), 20 January 1902
*Rampa i zhizn* (Moscow), 1 June 1914
*Rannoe utro* (Moscow), 1 June 1914
*Teatr* (Moscow), August, 1916
*Rannoe utro* (Moscow), 21 March, 1918

About Gorsky:
Bakhrushin, Yuri, *A.A. Gorsky*, Moscow and Leningrad, 1946
Roslavleva, Natalia, *Era of the Russian Ballet*, London, 1966
Krasovskaya, Vera, *The Russian Ballet Theatre of the Early Twentieth Century*, Part 1: Leningrad, 1971
Gabovich, Mikhail, "A.A. Gorsky: A Monograph", in *M.M. Gabovich: Essays*, Reminiscences About M.M. Gabovich, Moscow, 1977
Messerer, Asaf, *The Dance, the Thought, the Time*, Moscow, 1979; new edition 1990
Souritz, Elizabeth, *The Art of Choreography in the 1920s*, Moscow, 1979; as *Soviet Choreographers in the 1920s*, translated by Lynn Visson, Durham, N.C. and London, 1990

* * *

Aleksandr Gorsky joined the Maryinsky Theatre's ballet company in 1889, and for the most part he danced demi-caractère parts. He was also interested in working as a choreographer, however, and created his first ballet production, *Clorinda*, for a dance examination at the School of Theatre in 1899. At that time Gorsky was a great admirer of Stepanov's system of recording balletic steps, so that all parts in *Clorinda* have been recorded using that method.

In 1899, the Administration of Imperial Theatres commissioned Gorsky to reproduce Marius Petipa's production of *The Sleeping Beauty* in Moscow, and this was the beginning of his work in the Bolshoi Theatre. Gorsky found the Bolshoi company in a state of crisis. It had been losing prestige throughout the 1890s and its future now appeared totally unclear. Gorsky started implementing his plan of reforming the ballet theatre in Moscow. He tried to do away with the artistic conventions of classical ballet, such as the rigid norms of dramatic construction, the separation of dance and mime acting, the use of standard balletic forms, like pas de deux, and the wearing of traditional costumes, such as tutus. He also tried to achieve a consistency of action, expressivity, and general production style, thus bringing ballet into closer correspondence with real life.

Gorsky's innovations were part of a larger change which was then underway in Russian culture. With the activization of the whole of Russian society that had started in the mid-1890s, the arts and literature began to flourish, and new cultural movements cropped up and began conflicting with one another. Gorsky's work was greatly influenced by the crucial events in Moscow's artistic life, such as the opening of the Moscow Art Theatre by Stanislavsky and Nemirovich-Danchenko (he acknowledged this influence in his interview for the newspaper *Rampa i Zhizn* of 1 June 1914). He was also much impressed by the new Private Opera sponsored by Mamontov, in which advanced methods of directing and modern stage design were used, as well as by the painting and architecture of the Russian Art Nouveau.

In the many years of his work in the Bolshoi Theatre, Gorsky completely changed its repertoire, creating new ballets and revising old productions (mostly in collaboration with the designer Konstantin Korovin). After his own version of *Don Quixote* (1900) which had made him the focus of everyone's interest, Gorsky staged *Gudule's Daughter* (1902), the first production created entirely by himself. The ballet was based on Victor Hugo's novel *The Hunchback of Notre-Dame*, with a special emphasis on mass scenes. With an unusual realism (for a ballet), Gorsky showed the hungry crowds of impoverished people, the torturing of Quasimodo by the executioners, and Esmeralda's procession to the place of her death. Esmeralda herself, in her torn shirt, with her face covered in dirt and blood and a huge penitential candle in her thin, childlike hands, was quite different from the heroines of old ballets. The production caused heated discussions in the press; however, it did not become part of the permanent repertoire.

Gorsky's next big production, the multi-act ballet *Salammbô*, did not appear until 1910, but during the interval a few short one-act ballets were created by him. *Salammbô*, as compared with *Gudule's Daughter*, was a more traditional, though no less large-scale, production. It was a picturesque and exotic show, like Flaubert's novel itself. The crowd came again to the fore, featuring soldiers and mercenaries, beggars and slaves, as well as priests with their ritual ceremonies. Gorsky was thinking of a monumental dramatic performance with the popular masses as its centre, but the actual production fell short of his plans—primarily because of Andrei Arends's music, which was disappointingly traditional. Gorsky also had to put up with the performers' demands. The part of Salammbô was given to Ekaterina Geltser, whose wishes determined the ballet's choreography to a great extent, even though the leading male role, Mato, was performed by Gorsky's favourite dancer, Michail Mordkin, and not by Geltser's regular partner, Vasily Tikhomirov. Geltser was a talented actress and coped excellently with all the dramatic episodes, but she insisted on there being at least some classical dancing; she wanted to dance on pointe and to retain the pas de deux, sanctified by tradition and loved by spectators. Gorsky had to stage a duet of this kind for Geltser with Tikhomirov as Narravas, Salammbô's fiancé, which destroyed the ballet's stylistic continuity and was regarded by the choreographer himself as a deplorable compromise.

Most of Gorsky's works of 1912–17 have this feeling of compromise about them. During those years he revised many old productions and created some new one-act ballets; he made no more attempts to stage multi-act choreographic dramas.

Gorsky's ballet *Love is Quick!* (1913) reflected the general mood on the eve of a World War when people, frightened of the inevitable future, sought support in the images of wild nature, everyday work, and innocent love, with their healing and purifying effect on the human soul. So Gorsky created lyrical genre scenes of a young fisherman having a shipwreck and thus meeting a shepherd girl, the two falling in love with each other, and their engagement being celebrated in the village. He portrayed people untouched by civilization, rough and heavy like the rocks among which they live. Violating the rules of classic choreography, Gorsky made his characters move slowly, clumsily, with their flat feet turned inwards and their arms hanging down. In the years of the First World War Gorsky created several ballets giving expression to the feelings which then dominated his life. One of them, *The Genius of Belgium* (a dance for Ekaterina Geltser) was a demonstration of sympathy for that small country. Another, *Eunice and Petronius* (1915) was an elegiac ballet where admiration for beauty was mixed with grief, for people in their madness were destroying the beauty. At the same time, in 1916, Gorsky experimented with a new form, a ballet symphony, based on the Fifth Symphony by Aleksandr Glazunov.

All those years Gorsky continued revising old ballets, a practice which caused much dispute and often met with much opposition from the conservative members of his company. Still, his pupils, the dancers of the younger generation, supported him through thick and thin—and he, in his turn, promoted them.

It was then that Gorsky created his new version of *Swan Lake* and *Raymonda*, while in 1912 he staged *Le Corsaire* in a completely revised form (even Geltser and Tikhomirov, who used to be Gorsky's opponents, took part in that picturesque production and were a great success). In 1917, he revised *La Bayadère* thoroughly, trying to introduce Indian style dancing in the place of classical choreographic forms (including the famous "Shadows" act).

After the Socialist revolution of 1917, Gorsky continued his active work with the Bolshoi's young dancers. During the summer season of 1918, he did a number of new productions in the theatre of the Moscow Aquarium Gardens, where among others he staged the ballet *En Blanc* to the music of Tchaikovsky's Third Suite. In 1919, *The Nutcracker* was staged in Moscow for the first time, and it was choreographed by Gorsky. 1920 saw an entirely new production of *Swan Lake* where Odette and Odile were two different dancers and where the part of the Jester was first introduced. *Giselle*, also with a consistently modernized choreography, appeared in 1922.

However, Gorsky had too many opponents in his company. The dancers of the older generation demanded a return to the traditional versions of ballet productions and tried to prevent Gorsky from promoting younger people. The choreographer's health was deteriorating and signs of mental disorder were becoming increasingly evident. During the last years of his life, which were the years of severe economic crisis for Russia, he had to teach ballet in private schools and to stage dances for concert and even circus performances in order to earn his living. He died in 1924 in a mental hospital.

—Elizabeth Souritz

---

## GRADUATION BALL

**Choreography:** David Lichine

**Music:** Johann Strauss, arranged and orchestrated by Antal Dorati

**Design:** Alexandre Benois

**Libretto:** David Lichine

**First Production:** Original Ballet Russe, Sydney, Australia, 1 March 1940

**Principal Dancers:** Borislav Runanine (Headmistress), Tatiana Riabouchinska (Junior Girl), David Lichine (Junior Cadet), Igor Schwezoff (The Old General), Nicholas Orlov (The Drummer).

**Other productions include:** Ballet Theatre (staged Lichine; design Mstislav Doboujinsky), with Alpheus Koon (Headmistress), Tatiana Riabouchinska (Junior Girl), David Lichine (Junior Cadet), John Taras (Old General); Montreal, 26 September 1944. Borovansky Ballet (restaged Lichine); Sydney, 4 November 1955. Ballet Russe de Monte Carlo (staged Vladimir Dokoudovsky after Lichine), with Jean Yazvinsky (Headmistress), Yvonne Chouteau, Nina Novak (Junior Girls), Leon Danielian (Cadet), Igor Schwezoff (General); New York, 21 September 1949. Royal Danish Ballet (revival), with Frebjørn Bjørnsson (Junior Cadet), Inge Sand (Girl), Gerda Karstens (Headmistress); Copenhagen, 22 March 1952. London Festival Ballet (revival; design Benois); London, 24 May 1957.

### PUBLICATIONS

Beaumont, Cyril, *Supplement to Complete Book of Ballets*, London, 1942

***Graduation Ball*, as performed by London Festival Ballet, early 1970s**

Barnes, Clive, et al., "*Graduation Ball*", *Dance and Dancers* (London), September 1957

Anthony, Gordon, "A Hero of the 1930s: David Lichine", *Dancing Times* (London), November 1972

Anderson, Jack, *The One and Only: The Ballet Russe de Monte Carlo*, London, 1981

Denby, Edwin, *Dance Writings*, edited by Robert Cornfield and William Mackay, New York, 1986

* * *

*Graduation Ball* is a popular ballet with audiences worldwide, and although it is now 50 years old, its felicitous charm is timeless.

The light-hearted ballet was first created to replace the gap in the repertoire caused when Léonide Massine left Colonel de Basil's company, and went to choreograph for the rival company of Russian dancers run by René Blum, taking his *Le Beau Danube* with him. Anxious to acquire another popular Strauss ballet as soon as possible, de Basil commissioned David Lichine, a young dancer in his company, to create *Graduation Ball* to a collection of pieces composed by Johann Strauss and orchestrated by the company's conductor, Antal Dorati.

Set in a Viennese girls' finishing school (c. 1840), complete with chandeliers and gilt chairs, the ballet takes the form of a graduation ball to which cadets from a local military academy, led by their doddery old General, are duly invited. Opening to the tuneful strains of Strauss's Acceleration Waltz, the junior girls (traditionally dressed in white frocks with blue pinafores) creep on stage in two groups of four from each wing. One set boasts a vanity mirror and the other group fight over a powder puff. There is an air of excitement and expectation, as the young girls prepare for the ball. The senior girls enter, with a shade more decorum, but even they cannot resist bumping into the Headmistress "by accident".

Pinafores are discarded and order resumed to greet the cadets who march in with their General. After coy introductions and much heel-clipping, the comical tension is dispersed as the girls and boys form couples and a breathless waltz around the stage ensues. This lively romp immediately squashes any expectation that this could be a serious or technically loaded ballet.

Then the entertainment starts with a Drummer Boy variation—a virtuoso solo for a male dancer with multiple double tours as well as baton-twirling—and a quiet interlude is then furnished by a Sylphide and a kilted Scotsman. Mesmerized by the romantic couple, one of the junior girls edges her way, still seated on her chair, to the centre of the stage in order to gaze after the departing dancers at the end of their pas de deux. Her pert solo which follows, with kisses blown to all and sundry, shows her good nature, and is responsible for much of the ballet's subtle humour.

The lead junior girl, who plays Mistress of the Ceremonies, dances next. A dancer with strong ankles is needed for this role because the solo concludes with a long series of hops on one pointe. More virtuosity comes in the form of the Competition in which two soubrette dancers try to turn more fouettés than each other, but the contest is not especially earnest, and both competitors are declared winners.

A parlour game involving the writing of love letters then goes astray when an apparently passionate letter is delivered to the General by mistake. An innocent cadet gets reprimanded while the real culprit, the leading cadet, goes scot-free. Originally danced by Lichine himself, this role has attracted many great dancers early on in their careers. John Gilpin, in the London Festival Ballet's staging of the work, made "a feast of the tiny role", according to one critic in 1969.

After the divertissements, the General and Headmistress (usually played "en travestie" by a man) flirt clumsily with each other in a comic pas de deux, and a grand finale finishes with the discovery of the General and Headmistress in an amorous embrace behind the curtains.

Finally it is time to say goodbye and the young ladies dutifully give their young men ribbons from their hair. The lights dim and all are tearful; if the ballet has been well performed, and the subtlety not lost, the audience too experiences a sadness and sense of the ephemeral. But there is one last piece of comedy. When the coast is clear, the lead junior girl and the lead cadet keep an illicit rendezvous, only to be caught by the Headmistress, who chases the cadet away and hauls the junior girl back to her school.

The success or otherwise of a performance of *Graduation Ball* rests entirely with the cast. It is all too easy to destroy the subtle humour by over-acting, and in consequence, to ruin the ballet's charm. It is important that there remain a distinction between the junior and the senior girls, for example; the younger set have to be convincingly naive and gamine, while the older pupils need to be more aloof and elegant; mere coyness is not enough. Overall, Lichine's ballet is a light but delicate piece which, with the proper handling, has a sort of universal appeal. The American critic Edwin Denby put it best when he wrote:

> Lichine's *Graduation Ball* is in its type just an operetta to Strauss music, the stock item every company offers. But Lichine's piece, without visible effort to be special, turns out to be a pleasant surprise. You may think you are looking at the same old thing, but you don't feel as if you were. The very first waltz strikes you right away as a little human scene. And the show-off "Perpetuum Mobile," which is a feat of new steps and trick technique, doesn't impress you, it delights you as spontaneously as the best lindy-hop does. *Graduation Ball* has its weak spots too, but they do not seem important because you feel the piece directly as a whole; you feel its whole-hearted impulse before you judge its detail.

Without a doubt Lichine's ballet is, in Denby's words, "in the best class of comedy" when given the sensitive treatment it deserves.

—Emma Manning

---

## GRAHN, Lucile

Danish dancer and choreographer. Born Lucina Alexia Grahn in Copenhagen, 30 June 1819. Studied at the Royal Danish Theatre School, Copenhagen, pupil of Pierre Larcher and August Bournonville; later studied with Jean-Baptiste Barrez, Paris Opéra, 1834, 1838. Married singer Friedrich Young, 1856. Début at age of seven (in the role of Cupid), Royal Theatre, Copenhagen; dancer, Royal Theatre, Copenhagen, from 1829; official début, in a pas de deux inserted into *La Muette de Portici*, 1834; principal dancer, Royal Theatre, Copenhagen, 1837–39; Paris Opéra début, 1838, returning as soloist, 1839–40, and also performing as guest ballerina, Hamburg, 1839, St. Petersburg and Milan, 1843; ballerina, Her Majesty's Theatre, London, 1845–47, also performing at Drury Lane Theatre, London, 1844, 1848, Venice and Rome, 1846–47, and Théâtre de La Monnaie, Brussels, 1847; ballerina, touring Germany from 1848, including Dresden, Leipzig, Hamburg, Hanover, and Berlin; retired from the stage on marriage, 1856; also choreographer, staging many of the ballets in which she first danced; ballet mistress, Leipzig State Theatre, 1858–61, Munich Hofoper, 1869–75. Died in Munich, 4 April 1907.

### ROLES

1829 Zabi in *Danina; eller, Jocko, den brasilianske Abe* (Larcher after F. Taglioni), Royal Theatre, Copenhagen

1832 Marguerite in *Faust* (ballet; Bournonville), Royal Theatre, Copenhagen

1834 Pas de deux (cr; chor. Bournonville) added to *Den Stumme i Portici* (*La Muette de Portici*, opera; mus. Auber), Royal Theatre, Copenhagen

Solo variation (cr) in *Nina; eller, Den Vanvittige af Kaerlighed* (*Nina; ou, La Folle par amour*; Milon, Bournonville), Royal Theatre, Copenhagen

1835 Hannchen (cr) in *Tyrolerne* (Bournonville), Royal Theatre, Copenhagen

Astrid (cr) in *Valdemar* (Bournonville), Royal Theatre, Copenhagen

1836 Title role (cr) in *Sylfiden* (*La Sylphide*; Bournonville), Royal Theatre, Copenhagen

1837 Quitteria (cr) in *Don Quixote ved Camachos bryllup* (Bournonville), Royal Theatre, Copenhagen

1838 Hertha (cr) in *Herthas Offer* (divertissement; Bournonville), Royal Theatre, Copenhagen

The Queen of Fantasy (cr) in *Fantasiens Ø* (Bournonville), Royal Theatre, Copenhagen

Pas de deux (cr) added to *Le Carnaval de Venise* (Milon), Opéra, Paris

Dancer in *La Somnambule* (Aumer), Opéra, Paris

Dancer in *La Sylphide* (F. Taglioni), Opéra, Paris

1838/39 Solo (*La Cachucha*; as performed by Elssler) added to *Fiorella* (opera; mus. Auber), Royal Theatre, Copenhagen

1839 Solo (*El Jaleo de Xeres*; as performed by Elssler) added to *Robert af Normandiet* (*Robert le diable*, opera; mus. Meyerbeer), Royal Theatre, Copenhagen

Dancer in *La Muette de Portici* (opera; mus. Auber), Opéra, Paris

Pas de deux (cr; chor. Coralli) added to *Don Juan* (opera; mus. Mozart), Opéra, Paris

Title role in *La Sylphide* (Taglioni), Opéra, Paris

1843 Title role in *Giselle* (F. Taglioni), St. Petersburg

Title role in *L'Ombre* (F. Taglioni), St. Petersburg

Lauretta in *La Gitana* (F. Taglioni), St. Petersburg

Aglaë in *L'Elève de l'amour* (F. Taglioni), St. Petersburg

Title role (cr) in *Elda; ossia, Il Patto degli spiriti* (B. Vestris), La Scala, Milan

**Lucile Grahn**

1844 Pas de Vénus (cr) in *Lady Henrietta; or, The Statue Fair* (Varin after Mazilier), Drury Lane Theatre, London
1845 Title role (cr) in *Eoline; ou, La Dryade* (Perrot), Her Majesty's Theatre, London
Title role (cr) in *Kaya; ou, L'Amour voyageur* (Perrot), Her Majesty's Theatre, London
Zanetta in *Le Pêcheur napolitain* (*Die neapolitanischen Fischer* (Perrot), Her Majesty's Theatre, London
Title role (cr) in *La Bacchante* (divertissement; Perrot), Her Majesty's Theatre, London
Ballerina (cr) in *Pas de quatre* (Perrot), Her Majesty's Theatre, London
1846 Title role (cr) in *Catarina; ou, La Fille du bandit* (Perrot), Her Majesty's Theatre, London
A Goddess (cr) in *Le Jugement de Pâris* (Perrot), Her Majesty's Theatre, London
1846/47 Sarah Campbell in *La Gypsy* (also chor., after Mazilier), La Fenice, Venice
Mazourka in *Le Diable à quatre* (after Mazilier), Teatro Argentina, Rome
Principal dancer in *Bacchus et Ariadne* (divertissement; also chor.), Teatro Argentina, Rome
1848 Title role in *La Péri* (also chor., after Coralli), Berlin
Title role in *La Esmeralda* (also chor., after Perrot), Berlin
Dancer in *Tarantella napolitana* (solo), Berlin
1850 Principal dancer in *Le Rêve du peintre*, Darmstadt

## WORKS

1846/47 *Bacchus et Ariadne* (divertissement), Teatro Argentina, Rome
1873 *Ein Ball unter Ludwig XV*, Munich Court Opera, Munich
Bacchanale in *Tannhäuser* (opera; Wagner), Munich Court Opera, Munich

Also staged:
1846 *Il Folletto a quattro; o, La Capricciosa punita* (after Mazilier's *Le Diable à quatre*), Teatro Argentina, Rome
1846/47 *La Gypsy* (after Mazilier; mus. Benoist, Thomas, Marliani), Teatro La Fenice, Venice
1848 *La Péri* (after Coralli), Berlin
*La Esmeralda* (after Perrot), Berlin

## PUBLICATIONS

"A Great Danish Dancer: Lucile Grahn", *Dancing Times* (London), June 1921
Beaumont, Cyril, *The Complete Book of Ballets*, revised edition, London, 1951
Guest, Ivor, *The Romantic Ballet in England*, London, 1954
Kragh-Jacobsen, Svend, *The Royal Danish Ballet*, Copenhagen, London, 1955
Moore, Lillian, "Ballerina in Exile: The Mystery of Lucile Grahn", *Dance News* (New York), May 1956
Neiiendam, Robert, *Lucile Grahn: en skaebne i dansen*, Copenhagen, 1963
Guest, Ivor, *The Romantic Ballet in Paris*, London, 1966
Migel, Parmenia, *The Ballerinas*, New York, 1972
Aschengreen, Erik, "A Bournonville Ballerina Then and Now", *Danish Journal: The Royal Danish Ballet and Bournonville* (Copenhagen), 1979
Guest, Ivor, *Jules Perrot: Master of the Romantic Ballet*, London, 1984
*Gautier on Dance*, edited by Ivor Guest, London, 1986

Lucille Grahn, one of the great Romantic ballerinas, was the most important Danish dancer of her time, and the first to leave the Royal Danish Ballet to begin a successful international career. Grahn was gifted with great natural talent, and established herself early as a leading dancer on the Danish scene. She was appointed principal dancer in 1837, when she was just seventeen years old. Although her Danish career lasted only ten years (1829–39), she made history in her native land. Bournonville epitomized what she meant for him and the Romantic ballet when he wrote: "Lucille Grahn possesses all the qualities which distinguish a first-class dancer . . . she gave our audience their first idea of female virtuosity in dance, and her noble performance in *La Sylphide* and as Astrid in *Valdemar* created an epoch in the annals of ballet." Grahn set a very high standard for the Danish dancer, which is still maintained today.

It is often stated that Grahn left Denmark because Bournonville made advances towards her, and she did not reciprocate his feelings. But her departure was caused by more than a clash of feelings. During his tenure as ballet master Bournonville was preoccupied with promoting ballet to a status equal with opera and drama, and to raise the social status of the dancers. His aim was to create a uniform corps de ballet. Within this framework there was no room for an individual star with her own artistic ambitions. Grahn had studied with Jean-Baptiste Barrez in Paris, and added to the Bournonville style what she had learned there. From Paris she also brought back the two Fanny Elssler dances, *La Cachucha* and *El Jaleo de Xeres*, which were much more sensual than the chaste ideal Bournonville was striving for. Finally, she changed some of Bournonville's steps, which he found unacceptable. Grahn did not thrive under the Danish ballet master's dictatorial regime. She wanted more than he was willing to give.

Her international career began in Paris, where she was engaged as a soloist at the Opéra, and where among other things she excelled in *La Sylphide*. From there she appeared on all the major stages in Europe, to much acclaim. She reached the peak of her career in London in 1845, when she danced in the famous *Pas de quatre*. The ballet was highly praised by all critics, but more for the coming together of the four ballerinas than for the choreography. In 1846 Perrot choreographed *Le Jugement de Pâris*, featuring Grahn, Taglioni, and Cerrito, and he also choreographed *Eoline* and *Catarina; ou, La Fille du bandit* for Grahn.

Grahn's style was a mixture of what she learned from Bournonville and the French style. Contemporary descriptions give a flavour of what her dance looked like. She seems to have combined all the best qualities of the other four famous Romantic ballerinas. Benjamin Lumley, the director of Her Majesty's Theatre in London, where *Pas de quatre*'s premiere took place, wrote: "[She] combined the ideal school of Taglioni with the realistic school of Cerrito, and the sprightliness of Carlotta Grisi, adding something of the pantomimic art of Fanny Elssler." Most critics, however, compared her to Taglioni, and after her Paris début in *La Sylphide*, she was claimed to be the dancer closet to perfection, and the only worthy successor to Taglioni.

The features which the critics repeatedly praised were Grahn's natural grace, lightness, elevation, suppleness, energy, technical virtuosity, and the ease with which she danced. She transmitted in her dance a sense of innocence, modesty, and chasteness, which was so essential to the Romantics. But her greatest skill was in pantomime. A London critic wrote: "Her expressive pantomime inspires even more admiration than her wonderful flying leaps and apparent defiance of the laws of gravitation . . .", and "She not only executes [the poses] as danseuse, but understands the situation as an actress . . .".

In 1856 Grahn married the Austrian tenor Friedrich Young and her career as a dancer ended. She continued, however, to work as ballet mistress at the Leipzig State Theatre. Interestingly enough, she denies this in a letter of 6 October 1897, to the Danish Opera rehearser Levyson. She writes: "I am very eager to know who told you that I once was employed in Leipzig. There as everywhere else in the world I have given guest performances, voila tout!" From 1869 until 1875 she was ballet mistress at the Munich Court Opera, where she choreographed at least one ballet, *Ein Ball unter Ludwig XV* (1873), and where she staged many of the ballets in which she had danced. She also staged and choreographed a great number of ballets for the Opera, among others some of the first Wagner productions. In Munich she was praised for her efforts to raise ballet to the same level as opera and drama.

Lucile Grahn may have been the first dancer to leave Denmark and pursue an international career, but many have followed her since. The passing of time has caused slight changes in the Bournonville style, but the core is still the same. The Bournonville dancer of today is still praised for the same characteristics as was Grahn: lightness, elevation, apparent effortlessness, and strong mime.

—Jeannette Andersen

---

## LES GRANDS BALLETS CANADIENS

Canadian ballet company based in Montreal. Founded by Ludmilla Chiriaeff, with dancers from her television ballet productions, 1955; first performances as Les Ballets Chiriaeff, 1955, participating in Montreal Festival, 1956; performed as Les Grands Ballets Canadiens, from 1957. Associated school, L'Académie des Grands Ballets Canadiens, now known as L'École supérieure de danse du Québec, founded 1957. Current artistic director of Les Grands Ballets Canadiens (succeeding joint directors Linda Stearns and Jeanne Renaud): Lawrence Rhodes, from 1989.

### PUBLICATIONS

Maynard, Olga, "Ludmilla Chiriaeff and Les Grands Ballets Canadiens", *Dance Magazine* (New York), April 1971

Citron, Paula, "Montreal's Les Grands Ballets Canadiens", *Dance Magazine* (New York), April 1982

Crabb, Michael, "Les Grands Ballets Canadiens", *Dancing Times* (London), July 1982

"Out of the Box: The Improbable Adventure of Canada's French Ballet Company", *Dance and Dancers* (London), August 1982

Wyman, Max, *Dance Canada: An Illustrated History*, Vancouver/Toronto, 1989

* * *

Audiences and critics like a ballet company to have a clear identity, embodied in its repertoire and performance style. Les Grands Ballets Canadiens permits no such easy definition. From its foundation, in 1955, the company has performed in both classics and extremely modern works, ranging from Dolin's staging of *Giselle*, via Fokine, Balanchine, and a ballet version of The Who's rock opera *Tommy*, to Paul Taylor, Maurice Béjart, James Kudelka, and one of Canada's best-known choreographers, Brian Macdonald (an erstwhile artistic director and resident choreographer with the company).

The company's founder, Ludmilla Chiriaeff, began her career as a ballet director and choreographer in a Montreal television studio rather than on the stage, collaborating with a group of young producers in an attempt to bring ballet to a mass audience. By 1955, however, Les Ballets Chiriaeff (as the company was then known) had begun to make "live" appearances, and in 1958 it took the ambitious name of Les Grands Ballets Canadiens (though some pointed out that "grand" was an inappropriate adjective for a company with sixteen dancers and little else).

Despite Madame Chiriaeff's Russian origins and determination that her company should be based in the classical tradition, the company soon proved worthy of the name "Canadien". Madame Chiriaeff employed Canadian choreographers, composers, and designers whenever possible, as her successor Brian Macdonald would continue to do, and based some of her earliest works on French-Canadian folklore. The company's dancers, too, were to be predominantly Canadian, and for the purpose of cultivating home-grown talent Chiriaeff established her first school, l'Académie des Grands Ballets Canadiens, in 1957. A professional division, l'Ecole supérieure de danse, was established in 1970. Since 1974, when she retired as artistic director, Madame Chiriaeff has dedicated herself to increasing opportunities for ballet training in Quebec, and ballet classes now form part of the provincial school curriculum.

The history of Les Grands Ballets Canadiens has not been an easy one. In its early days, the company met with the disapproval of the Catholic church, a powerful influence in Quebec, which believed that dance led to immorality, and for the sake of which all female dancers had to cover their shoulders and ensure that they never pointed their bottoms towards the audience. Another recurrent problem was financial hardship. This was particularly prevalent during Linda Stearns's tenure as ballet mistress and artistic director in the early 1980s, when the company was beginning to concentrate on modern works at the expense of its classical repertoire, alienating its audience. The situation was remedied, however, when the company's former administrator and director of productions, Colin McIntyre, returned as director-general to oversee impressive new productions of such ballets as *Coppélia* and Nijinsky's *L'Après-midi d'un faune*. This tradition has continued in recent years, with Anna Markard's 1991 staging of Kurt Jooss's *The Green Table*.

It was evident, however, that the company's dancers lacked the star quality that would have made the new productions truly successful. The non-hierarchical structure and wide repertoire that gave the dancers their enthusiasm and vitality also resulted in wide variations in quality between productions, and even between the dancers themselves, with experienced performers such as Annette av Paul contrasting uncomfortably with less seasoned dancers. It was perhaps in an attempt to correct this discrepancy that Lawrence Rhodes, who succeeded Linda Stearns as artistic director in 1989, ended his first season by replacing a large number of the company's dancers.

Les Grands Ballets Canadiens has nurtured such talents as James Kudelka, who joined the company as a principal dancer in 1981 and was its resident choreographer, creating such successful works as *Le Sacre du printemps* and *In Paradisum*, until he turned freelance in 1990.

—Jessica Arah

---

**GRANT, Alexander**

New Zealand/Canadian dancer and ballet director. Born Alexander Marshall Grant in Wellington, New Zealand, 22 February 1925. Studied with Kathleen O'Brien and Jean Horne, New Zealand, and at the Royal Academy of Dancing (on scholarship), from 1945, and Sadler's Wells School, London, from 1946. Stage début (while still a student) with Sadler's Wells Theatre Ballet, 1946; dancer, Sadler's Wells Ballet (later the Royal Ballet), from 1946: soloist from 1949, becoming leading character dancer; principal dancer, 1950–76; also leading dancer with Margot Fonteyn World Tour, 1963; director, Ballet for All performing group of the Royal Ballet, 1971–76; artistic director, National Ballet of Canada, 1976–83; senior principal, London Festival Ballet (now English National Ballet), from 1985; has also performed as guest artist with the Joffrey Ballet, New York and Los Angeles, 1987, 1988, 1989, and with Royal Ballet, London, Christmas seasons 1985, 1986; has also appeared on television and films, including in *Steps of the Ballet* (1948); judge, International Ballet Competition, Jackson (Mississippi), Helsinki, and Moscow. Commander of the Order of the British Empire, 1965.

**ROLES**

1946 Popular song in *Façade* (Ashton), Sadler's Wells Theatre Ballet, London
Old Man (cr) in *Khadra* (Franca), Sadler's Wells Theatre Ballet, London
Child (cr) in *Les Sirènes* (Ashton), Sadler's Wells Ballet, London
A Savage (cr) in *The Fairy Queen* (masque; mus. Purcell, chor. Ashton), Sadler's Wells Ballet and Covent Garden Opera, London
Gravedigger in *Hamlet* (Helpmann), Sadler's Wells Ballet, London
1947 The Dandy in *The Three-Cornered Hat* (Massine), Sadler's Wells Ballet, London
The Barber in *Mam'zelle Angot* (Massine), Sadler's Wells Ballet, London
1948 Principal dancer (cr) in *Scènes de ballet* (Ashton), Sadler's Wells Ballet, London
The Clockmaker (cr) in *Clock Symphony* (Massine), Sadler's Wells Ballet, London
The Jester (cr) in *Cinderella* (Ashton), Sadler's Wells Ballet, London
1949 Tango: A Dago in *Façade* (Ashton), Sadler's Wells Ballet, tour
1950 Sancho Panza (cr) in *Don Quixote* (de Valois), Sadler's Wells Ballet, London
Principal dancer (cr) in *Ballabile* (Petit), Sadler's Wells Ballet, London
1951 Bryaxis (cr) in *Daphnis and Chloë* (Ashton), Sadler's Wells Ballet, London
Donald (cr) in *Donald of the Burthens* (Massine), Sadler's Wells Ballet, London
The Rake in *The Rake's Progress* (de Valois), Sadler's Wells Ballet, Tour
1952 Black King (cr) in *Bonne-Bouche* (Cranko), Sadler's Wells Ballet, London
Eros (cr) in *Sylvia* (Ashton), Sadler's Wells Ballet, London
Pas de six, Neopolitan Dance (cr; chor. Ashton) in *Swan Lake* (new production; Petipa, Ivanov; staged Sergeyev, de Valois, Ashton), Sadler's Wells Ballet, London
The Miller in *The Three-Cornered Hat* (Massine), Sadler's Wells Ballet, London
Franz in *Coppélia* (Petipa, Cecchetti; staged Sergeyev), Sadler's Wells Ballet, London
1953 Spirit of Fire (cr) in *Homage to the Queen* (Ashton), Sadler's Wells Ballet, London
Dance of the Furies (cr) in *Orpheus* (opera; mus. Gluck, chor. Ashton), Sadler's Wells Ballet and Royal Opera, London
1954 Can-Can in *La Boutique fantasque* (Massine), Sadler's Wells Ballet, London
Trepak (cr) from *The Nutcracker*, Act II (Ashton after Ivanov), Granada Festival, Granada
1955 Principal dancer (cr) in *Variations on a Theme of Purcell* (Ashton), Sadler's Wells Ballet, London
Pierre (cr) in *Madame Chrysanthème* (Ashton), Sadler's Wells Ballet, London
1956 Dancer (cr) in *Birthday Offering* (Ashton), Sadler's Wells Ballet, London
The Pimp (cr) in *The Miraculous Mandarin* (Rodrigues), Sadler's Wells Ballet, Edinburgh
Satan in *Job* (de Valois), Sadler's Wells Ballet, London
1957 Title role in *Petrushka* (Fokine; staged Grigoriev and Tchernicheva) Royal Ballet, London
1958 Tirrenio (cr) in *Ondine* (Ashton), Royal Ballet, London
Captain Belaye in *Pineapple Poll* (Cranko), Royal Ballet Touring Company, tour
1960 Alain (cr) in *La Fille mal gardée* (Ashton), Royal Ballet, London
1961 Mercury (cr) in *Persephone* (Ashton), Royal Ballet, London
Mr. Scratch, The Devil (cr) in *Jabez and the Devil* (Rodrigues), Royal Ballet, London
1962 The Young Man in *The Two Pigeons* (Ashton), Royal Ballet, London
Niccolo in *The Good-Humoured Ladies* (Massine), Royal Ballet, London
1964 Bottom (cr) in *The Dream* (Ashton), Royal Ballet, London
1968 Thursday (cr) in *Jazz Calendar* (Ashton), Royal Ballet, London
William Beath Baker (W.M.B.) (cr) in *Enigma Variations* (Ashton), Royal Ballet, London
1969 Dr. Coppélius in *Coppélia* (Petipa, Cecchetti; staged Sergeyev), Royal Ballet, London
1971 Peter Rabbit (cr) in *Tales of Beatrix Potter* (film; director, Reginald Mills, chor. Ashton)
1975 Stepsister in *Cinderella* (Ashton), Royal Ballet, London
1976 Yslaev (cr) in *A Month in the Country* (Ashton), Royal Ballet, London
1984 Corregidor in *The Three-Cornered Hat* (Massine), London Festival Ballet
1986 Tchaikovsky/Drosselmeyer, Master of Ceremonies (cr) in *The Nutcracker* (new production; Schaufuss), London Festival Ballet, Plymouth
1987 Drosselmeyer (cr) in *The Nutcracker* (new production; Joffrey, Arpino after Ivanov), Joffrey Ballet, Iowa City

**Other roles include:** for Sadler's Wells/Royal Ballet—One of Seven Sons and War, Pestilence, and Famine in *Job* (de Valois), Child of Darkness in *Dante Sonata* (Ashton), Poodles and Tarantella in *La Boutique fantasque* (Massine), dancer in *Symphonic Variations* (Ashton), Bridegroom in *A Wedding Bouquet* (Ashton), dancer in *Tritsch-Tratsch* (Cranko), Carabosse, Three Ivans, and Puss-in-Boots in *The Sleeping Beauty* (Petipa; staged Sergeyev, de Valois, Ashton), Drosselmeyer in

*The Nutcracker* (Wright); for London Festival/English National Ballet—Madge in *La Sylphide* (Schaufuss after Bournonville), Drosselmeyer in *The Nutcracker* (Hynd), Lord Capulet in *Romeo and Juliet* (Ashton), Lord Montague in *Romeo and Juliet* (Nureyev), the Monk in *Apparitions* (Ashton), the Inquisitor in *Cruel Garden* (Bruce, Kemp), Giacomo in *Napoli* (Schaufuss after Bournonville).

## PUBLICATIONS

By Grant:
Interview with Tobi Tobias, "Alexander Grant", *Dance Magazine* (New York), November 1976
Interview in Barbara Newman, *Striking a Balance*, Boston, 1982

About Grant:
Davidson, Gladys, *Ballet Biographies*, revised edition, London, 1954
Swinson, Cyril, *Six Dancers of the Sadler's Wells*, London, 1956
Percival, John, "Accent on the Male: Alexander Grant", *Dance and Dancers* (London), December 1957
Roberts, Sonia, "Men in Ballet: Alexander Grant", *Ballet Today* (London), May 1958
De Valois, Ninette, "Alexander Grant", *Dance Gazette* (London), February 1979

* * *

Alexander Grant was, and still is, one of the greatest character dancers of our time; indeed he is perhaps one of the finest of stylists to have been produced in British ballet. His gift is unique, and is still being appreciated by audiences around the world.

Having passed his Royal Academy of Dance examinations and won a number of competitions in his native New Zealand, Grant took up a Sadler's Wells scholarship in 1945 and became the first overseas student to join the school after the war. Although he had only been with the school for one year, he joined the Sadler's Wells Theatre Ballet in 1946 and enjoyed his first major success in Léonide Massine's *Mam'zelle Angot* in 1947.

Grant started his professional career as a "song and dance" man (the only one amongst eight girls), entertaining the men aboard the many troopships based in the Pacific during the war, so amongst his earliest and strongest influences were Gene Kelly and Fred Astaire. He has said that this teenage experience, performing to a non-specialist audience of hundreds, made him lose stage-fright at a very early age. Grant also believed that the easy-going contacts with those early audiences never left him, and his many admirers in the field of classical dance have always been aware of the immediacy of his performances. He is a superb actor, one of the rare breed who can bring an audience to the edge of tears or laughter during a single danced phrase.

Of all the many influences in a long career it was the great Polish dancer Leon Woizikowsky who the young Alexander Grant felt was nearest to a role-model. In fact, Grant was to follow in Woizikowsky's footsteps in several of Massine's ballets, performing (arguably with equal success) many of the roles that Woizikowsky had created or made his own. Another role in which Grant excelled was that of Petrushka—and it was a role which he continued to work on and to perfect throughout his long career.

Grant's range, from classical ballet to character dancing to straight comic acting, has always impressed both colleagues and critics. "To all of his roles", wrote John Percival in 1957, "Grant brings strength and precision of movement. The power, vigour and pace of his character dancing are unequalled in British ballet, and he brings the same qualities of exact timing and sharp attack to those classical parts which suit him best." But then, as Percival pointed out, "almost any of Grant's roles could be taken to illustrate his power of characterisation, even those which are merely divertissements".

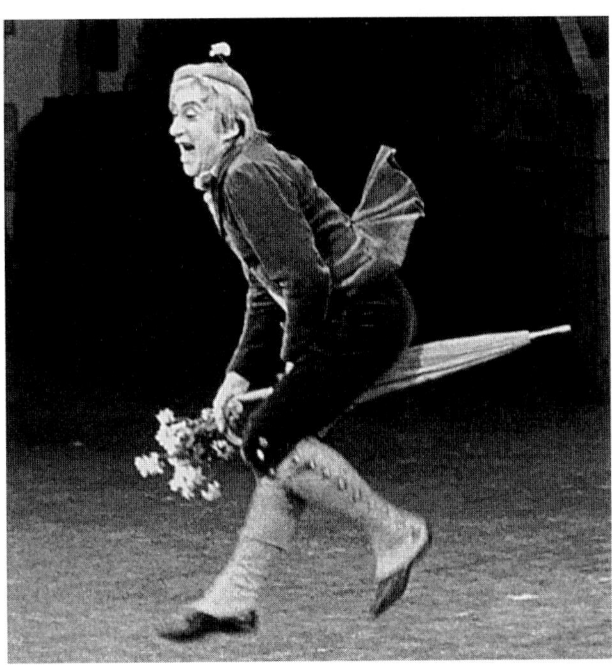

**Alexander Grant as Alain in *La Fille mal gardée*, 1968**

Grant firmly believes that every role in ballet is, or should be, a character role: "If Albrecht does not believe he is in love with this enchanting country girl, then what is *Giselle* all about?" He has said that his own favourite roles are hard to define but, despite the unexpected fact that at first he was not too keen to dance his famous and well-loved Alain in Ashton's *La Fille mal gardée*, he later called it "the happiest ballet I ever worked in".

Other great colleagues by whom he has been influenced include Robert Helpmann, Frederick Ashton, and Robert Joffrey, for whom he created the role of Drosselmeyer in the Joffrey Ballet acclaimed 1987 production of *The Nutcracker*.

For some, Alexander Grant might be the last great representative of a dying breed. Ninette de Valois called Grant ". . . that rare combination—a strong personality totally dedicated and disciplined to a true interpretation of the role": and it may well be a thing of the past. "It is considered old-fashioned to express character or emotion," Grant has said, but "today's dancers are in danger of becoming no more than tools of the choreographer—blank faces are considered to be the most modern". But still, "Diaghilev was the greatest modernist and innovator of all time—and his ballets are still produced—where there are good enough companies to present them." Perhaps it is time for a renaissance of good character dancing—particularly with the recent resurgence of interest in the Diaghilev ballets. As Grant repeatedly stresses, "A dancer is only as good as the character or role he or she is portraying."

—Sally Whyte

## THE GREEN TABLE

**Choreography:** Kurt Jooss
**Music:** Frederick Cohen
**Design:** Hein Heckroth
**Libretto:** Kurt Jooss
**First Production:** Folkwang Tanzbühne, "Concour international de chorégraphie en souvenir de Jean Börlin", organized by the Archives internationales de la danse, Théâtre des Champs-Elysées, Paris, 3 July 1932
**Principal Dancers:** Kurt Jooss (Death), Karl Bergeest (The Profiteer), Ernst Uthoff (The Standard Bearer), Elsa Kahl (Woman), Lisa Czobel (Young Girl)

**Other productions include:** Jooss Ballet (new name for Folkwang Tanzbühne; ballet restaged Jooss); New York, 31 October 1933. Chilean National Ballet (restaged and revised Jooss), International Festival of Music and Dance, Rio de Janeiro, Brazil, 11 September 1963. City Center Joffrey Ballet (restaged Jooss), New York, 9 March 1967. Northern Dance Theatre (staged Anna Markard); Manchester, England, 30 May 1973. Les Grands Ballets Canadiens (staged Markard); Montreal, May 1991. Birmingham Royal Ballet (staged Markard); Birmingham, 19 November 1992.

### PUBLICATIONS

Storey, A., "The Art of Kurt Jooss", *Dancing Times* (London), July 1940
Coton, A.V., *The New Ballet: Kurt Jooss and his Work*, London, 1946
Denby, Edwin, *Looking at the Dance*, New York, 1949
Beaumont, Cyril, *The Complete Book of Ballet*, revised edition, London, 1951
Ehrmann-Ewart, Hans, "On *The Green Table*'s 25th Anniversary", *Ballet Annual* (London), vol.12, 1958
Barnes, Clive, "The Constantly Set Table", *Dance and Dancers* (London), May 1967
Siegel, Marcia, *At the Vanishing Point*, New York, 1968
Siegel, Marcia, "*The Green Table*, Movement Masterpiece", *Arts in Society* (Madison, Wisconsin) Autumn/Winter 1968
Baril, Jacques, "Kurt Jooss", *Les Saisons de la danse* (Paris), November 1975
Markard, Anna, *Kurt Jooss*, Venice, 1981
Servos, Norbert, "The Green Table", *Ballett International* (Cologne), August 1982
Huxley, Michael, "*The Green Table*: A Dance of Death", *Ballett International* (Cologne), August/September 1982
Servos, Norbert, "*The Green Table*: A Piece Holds its Own", *Ballet International* (Cologne), August/September 1982
Whitney, M., "A Tragedy of War", *Ballet News* (London), December 1982
Jowitt, Deborah, *The Dance in Mind*, Boston, 1985
Marinari, Silvia, "*The Green Table* by Kurt Jooss", New York University, Doctoral Dissertation, 1985
Siegel, Marcia, "*The Green Table*: Sources of a Classic", *Dance Research Journal* (New York), Spring 1989
Sinclair, Janet, "*The Green Table*", *Dance and Dancers* (London), July 1992

* * *

*The Green Table* is the masterpiece of the German choreographer Kurt Jooss, and his most popular work. It is in the repertory of ballet companies worldwide, where it has been staged by Jooss himself. Since his death in 1979, his daughter Anna Markard has been responsible for stagings of the work. It was created in 1932 for the Concour international de chorégraphie in Paris, in which Jooss had been invited to participate. The originality of the piece won him the first prize and marked an important step in his career. He left Essen, where since 1927 he had directed the Volkwangschule's dance department and experimental dance group and, since 1930, the ballet company of the Opera as well. He founded the Ballet Jooss, a private company which toured Europe and performed his dances, including *The Green Table*.

Lasting about 30 minutes and subtitled "a dance of death in eight scenes", *The Green Table* is a commentary on the futility of war and the horrors it causes. It opens with a group of diplomats (the Gentlemen in Black) having a discussion around a rectangular table covered with a green cloth. They end up pulling guns from their pockets and shooting in the air, thus symbolizing the declaration of war. The next six scenes portray different aspects of wartime: the separation from loved ones in "The Farewells", war itself in "The Battle" and "The Partisan", loneliness and misery in "The Refugees", the emotional void and the atmosphere of forced entertainment in "The Brothel", and finally, the psychologically beaten and wounded survivors in "The Aftermath". Throughout these episodes the figure of Death is triumphant, portrayed as a skeleton moving in a forceful and robot-like way, relentlessly claiming its victims. The dance ends with a repeat of the opening scene, a device the choreographer uses to show his mistrust in the talks of the diplomats; completely indifferent to the ravages of war, they continue their hypocritical negotiations.

The inspiration for the dance, originally conceived as a solo, was provided by the medieval "Lübecker Totentanz", a sequence of pictures portraying different types of people dancing with Death. Jooss gave it a contemporary setting and added the political content which reflected his and many artists' concerns during Germany's Weimar Republic. He then worked closely with the designer, Hein Heckroth, and the composer, Frederick Cohen, to build the piece. Jooss, in fact, advocated a form of dance-theatre, in which the choreography is dramatic and develops from a libretto (often his own). Choreographer, composer, and designer combine their efforts to produce a coherent work in which all the elements, in harmony with each other, convey the feelings and ideas more powerfully.

This concept of a unified work of art, previously theorized by Richard Wagner and, in the eighteenth century, by Jean-Georges Noverre, was popular among German artists in the early twentieth century. Examples are found in the visual arts, for instance in the work of George Grosz and the Herzfelde brothers, or in the theatre of Erwin Piscator and his dramaturgical collective. *The Green Table* reflects a concern for social issues and the problems of that era (shared by many artists contemporary with Jooss) such as political corruption and militaristic policies. Its style, with its cutting irony, caricature, and boldness of language, has much in common with Expressionism, which flourished in the first decade of the twentieth century. The cyclical structure of the dance, for example, is a formal expression of this dry humour: the diplomats repeat their routine with total indifference to the real consequences of their decisions. The seriousness of their discussion is negated by the music that Jooss chose to accompany their scene: a playful tango. He also dressed the characters in masks, which give them a grotesque look, and created movements that are exaggerations of naturalistic movement, such as gesticulating while talking, or nervously pacing up and down while thinking.

The costumes and props were chosen for their symbolic

***The Green Table*, Ballets Jooss, 1935**

qualities: a flag for the hopeful soldier, a red scarf for the partisan, or the skeleton-like costume of Death. Jooss mastered the visual outlook of his compositions with great skill; again the scene of "The Gentlemen in Black" provides an example of how the choreographer directed the audience to focus on a particular point of interest, which may be a dancer located on a higher plane than the rest of the group, or someone keeping still while everybody else is moving (or vice versa), or simply a convergence of the compositional lines. His use of the space for expressive purposes, as well as the foundation of his technique, stemmed from his formative training as Rudolf Laban's student and assistant. Together they explored the interrelation between space and the body, with its various movement qualities reflecting different mental states and feelings. Jooss integrated Laban's findings and his free-style approach to dancing with the discipline of classical ballet training. The result was a new technique that emphasizes the use of the body as an expressive whole.

This technique was to be absorbed and further developed by Jooss's students, among whom were Birgit Cullberg and Pina Bausch. *The Green Table* is a mature example of this technique. It uses elements of classical ballet, such as turn-out, demi-pointe, extensions, turns, arabesques, and other ballet steps. However, there is no pointe work or any other feature that could suggest virtuoso display. The gracefulness, elegance, ethereal quality, and other affectations of classical ballet are eliminated. As with the choreography of Antony Tudor, every step is used, not for its formal look, but for its intrinsic expressive value, and the meaning it conveys is often reinforced by the position of the hands: rather than the relaxed wrists of ballet, Jooss uses stretched palms, fists, reaching hands, and so on. The focus of the dancers also varies, shifting towards the centre of drama, rather than being primarily towards the audience, as in ballet.

The resulting style, called by Jooss "essentialism", tries to capture the essence of each movement or pose, its inner motivation. Death, for instance, moves with sharp, direct, strong, and angular movements, cutting through space, advancing, or pacing with clockwork regularity. In contrast is the style of the Profiteer: he has a swift and agile way of moving, his back usually curved, his cunning nature further accentuated by the indirectness of his focus and his multidirectional spatial patterns. A third example of characterization through movement, in which the relationship between space and movement is very clear, is the part of the Old Mother. Her diminishing vitality is expressed in her lack of impact over the space around her: she advances and retreats with little tiptoe steps along a narrow path, holding her bent arms close to her curved body, with an almost crippled posture. The few expansive movements she does make, when she reaches upwards, end in collapses sideways, with an arm dangling lifeless. Such elements combine to make *The Green Table* a truly innovative work and the depth and universality of its humanistic content give it a timeless and meaningful quality.

—Silvia Marinari

---

**GREGORY, Cynthia**

American dancer. Born in Los Angeles, 8 July 1946. Studied with Michel Panaieff, Robert Rossellat, and Carmelita Maracci, and later at the San Francisco Ballet School, from 1961. Married (1) dancer Terry Orr, 1966 (div.); (2) John Hemminger, 1976 (d. 1984); (3) Hilary B. Miller, 1985: son born 1987. Début as apprentice, San Francisco Ballet, 1961: soloist, 1961–65, and principal dancer, 1964–65; dancer, American Ballet Theatre, New York, from 1965, becoming soloist, 1966, principal dancer, from 1967; left American Ballet Theatre for temporary retirement, 1975: returned to stage as principal dancer, American Ballet Theatre, from 1976; permanent guest artist, Cleveland/San José Ballet, from 1986; also ballerina in "Star" tours in South America, Australia, and Taiwan; international guest artist, including for Zurich Ballet, National Ballet of Cuba, San Francisco Ballet, Ballet West, Vienna State Opera Ballet, Stuttgart Ballet, Bavarian State Opera Ballet, Munich, German Opera Ballet, Berlin, and Teatro Colón in Buenos Aires. Recipient: *Dance Magazine* Award, 1975; Harkness Ballet Foundation's First Annual Dance Award, 1978; Dance Educators of America Achievement Award, 1983, 1987; Cyril Magnin Award for Outstanding Achievement in the Arts, San Francisco, 1986; Citation of Merit from the International Arts Club, 1991.

**ROLES**

1961 Arabian Dance in *The Nutcracker* (L. Christensen), San Francisco Ballet, San Francisco
Solo role in *Con Amore* (L. Christensen), San Francisco Ballet, San Francisco
1962 Principal dancer (cr) in *Biography* (Gladstein), San Francisco Ballet, San Francisco
Principal dancer (cr) in *Bach Concert* (L. Christensen), San Francisco Ballet, San Francisco
1963 Principal dancer (cr) in *Divertissement d'Auber* (L. Christensen), San Francisco Ballet, Phoenix, Arizona
Principal dancer (cr) in *Vivaldi Concerto* (Gladstein), San Francisco Ballet, San Francisco
The Woman (cr) in *Triptych* (Clarke), San Francisco Ballet, San Francisco
1964 Anna I in *The Seven Deadly Sins* (text: Weill, chor. L. Christensen after the staging of Balanchine), San Francisco Ballet, San Francisco
Sugar Plum Fairy in *The Nutcracker* (L. Christensen), San Francisco Ballet, San Francisco
Beauty in *Beauty and the Beast* (Christensen), San Francisco Ballet, San Francisco
1966 Principal dancer (cr) in *Kontraste* (Bolender), American Ballet Theatre, New York
1967 Principal dancer (cr) in *Harbinger* (Feld), American Ballet Theatre, Miami
Principal dancer in *Concerto* (MacMillan), American Ballet Theatre, Jacksonville, Florida
Ballerina in *Theme and Variations* (Balanchine), American Ballet Theatre, Orlando, Florida
Principal dancer (cr) in *At Midnight* (Feld), American Ballet Theatre, New York
Odette/Odile in *Swan Lake* (Petipa, Ivanov; staged Blair), American Ballet Theatre, San Francisco
1968 Myrtha in *Giselle* (Petipa after Coralli, Perrot; staged Blair), American Ballet Theatre, Washington, D.C.
Principal dancer (cr) in *Gartenfest* (Smuin), American Ballet Theatre, Brooklyn, New York
Title role in *Miss Julie* (Cullberg), American Ballet Theatre, New York
Swanilda in *Coppélia* (Fernandez after Petipa, Cecchetti), American Ballet Theatre, New York
1969 Principal dancer (cr) in *Brahms Quintet* (Nahat), American Ballet Theatre, Brooklyn, New York
Principal dancer (cr) in *The Eternal Idol* (pas de deux;

**Cynthia Gregory with David Anderson in *The Nutcracker*, San Francisco Ballet, 1964**

Smuin), American Ballet Theatre, Brooklyn, New York
Title role in *La Sylphide* (Bournonville; staged Lander), American Ballet Theatre, Chicago
1970 Lake (cr) in *The River* (Ailey), American Ballet Theatre, New York
1971 Principal dancer (cr) in *Schubertiade* (Smuin), American Ballet Theatre, New York
Principal dancer (cr) in *Mendelssohn Symphony* (Nahat), American Ballet Theatre, New York
Title role in *Paquita* (Nureyev after Petipa), American Ballet Theatre, New York
1972 Principal dancer in *Grand Pas Classique* (pas de deux; Gsovsky), American Ballet Theatre, New York
Principal dancer in *Intermezzo* (Feld), American Ballet Theatre, New York
Principal dancer in *Unfinished Symphony* (pas de deux; van Dijk), American Ballet Theatre, New York
Title role in *Giselle* (Petipa after Coralli, Perrot; staged Blair), American Ballet Theatre, Milwaukee
1973 Stella/ Olympia/ Antonia/ Giulietta in *Tales of Hoffmann* (Darrell), American Ballet Theatre, New York
1974 Nikiya in *La Bayadère* ("Kingdom of the Shades", Act IV; Makarova after Petipa), American Ballet Theatre, New York
The Fairy in *Le Baiser de la fée* (Neumeier), American Ballet Theatre, New York
1975 Title role in *Raymonda* (Nureyev after Petipa), American Ballet Theatre, Houston
Principal dancer in *Gemini* (Tetley), American Ballet Theatre, New York
Principal dancer in *La Ventana Pas de Trois* (Bruhn after Bournonville), American Ballet Theatre, New York
1976 Princess Aurora in *The Sleeping Beauty* (Petipa; staged Skeaping), American Ballet Theatre, Washington, D.C.
1977 Principal dancer in *Voluntaries* (Tetley), American Ballet Theatre, Cleveland
1978 Kitri in *Don Quixote* (*Kitri's Wedding*) (Baryshnikov after Petipa), American Ballet Theatre, Washington, D.C.
1979 The Accused in *Fall River Legend* (de Mille), American Ballet Theatre, Washington, D.C.
1980 The Siren in *Prodigal Son* (Balanchine), American Ballet Theatre, New York
1981 Gamzatti in *La Bayadère* (Makarova after Petipa), American Ballet Theatre, Washington, D.C.
1982 Principal dancer (cr) in *Clair de lune* (Anastos), American Ballet Theatre, New York
Hagar in *Pillar of Fire* (Tudor), American Ballet Theatre, New York
1983 Principal Dancer in *Symphonie Concertante* (Balanchine), American Ballet Theatre, Washington, D.C.
Principal dancer (cr) in *Interludes* (McFall), American Ballet Theatre, San Francisco
1984 Principal dancer (cr) in *Bach Partita* (Tharp), American Ballet Theatre, New York
1986 Title role in *Francesca da Rimini* (Taras), American Ballet Theatre, New York

**Other roles include:** Second Song in *Dark Elegies* (Tudor), Cybele and Medusa in *Undertow* (Tudor), Caroline and An Episode in His Past in *Jardin aux lilas* (Tudor), Desdemona in *The Moor's Pavane* (Limón), principal dancer in *Other Dances* (Robbins), principal dancer in *Undertow* (Tudor).

## PUBLICATIONS

By Gregory:
Interview in Maynard, Olga, "Conversations with Cynthia Gregory", *Dance Magazine* (New York), April 1975
Interview in Gruen, John, *The Private World of Ballet*, New York, 1975
Interview in Kendall, Elizabeth, *Dancing*, New York, 1983
*Ballet is the Best Exercise*, New York, 1986
Interview in Gruen, John, *People Who Dance*, Pennington N.J., 1988
*Cynthia Gregory Dances Swan Lake*, New York, 1990

About Gregory:
Goodman, Saul, "Cynthia Gregory: Brief Biography", *Dance Magazine* (New York), June 1965
Maynard, Olga, "Through a Glass, Brightly", *Dance Magazine* (New York), June 1970
Gruen, John, "Observing Dance: Cynthia Gregory", *Dance Magazine* (New York), September 1974
Hodgson, Moira, "Cynthia Gregory: In Search of Siegfried", *Dance News* (New York), March 1975
Greskovic, Robert, "Dancers at a Gathering", *Ballet Review* (Brooklyn, N.Y.), vol. 5, no. 1, 1975–76
Woodward, Robin, and Cook, Susan (photographer), *In a Rehearsal Room*, New York, 1976
Terry, Walter, "American Beauty", *Ballet News* (New York), May 1979
Gruen, John, "Gregory and Bujones", *Dance Magazine* (New York), September 1984
Gruen, John, "Celebrating Cynthia", *Dance Magazine* (New York), September 1985

* * *

Martha Graham has called the choreographic process a "divine unrest". Without being so sanctified, unrest has marked the performing career of American Ballet Theatre ballerina

Cynthia Gregory. By 1991, after 26 years with the company, she had three times left its employ and had each time returned in fairly short order. Why? The reason lies partially with Gregory's intrepid nature and partially with the company's tendency to give preferential billing to foreign guest stars. Cynthia Gregory is, for better or for worse, a thoroughly American performer.

She was born and trained in California. The most influential of her teachers was Carmelita Maracci, known for her ability to ferret out the innermost strengths and weaknesses of her students, and known as a performer/choreographer for her own iconoclastic style.

After a brief tenure with the San Francisco Ballet, Gregory joined American Ballet Theatre in 1965, and by 1967 had made her début as Odette/Odile in the full-length *Swan Lake* staged by David Blair. In the same season, she initiated the poignant role of the lone woman in *At Midnight*, the second (and finest) work of the young choreographer Eliot Feld. *At Midnight* was as contemporary in style as *Swan Lake* was traditional. Gregory understood the requirements of both.

By nature, she is what might be called the quintessential Californian. The residents especially of Southern California spend a good deal of their time living out of doors and driving on the freeways. There is a ranginess in the way they move, and in Gregory's case, an amplitude and decisiveness of gesture. To these traits might be added strength, aplomb, and a presence underscored by her above-average height and her clearly defined facial features. The minute she enters the stage, there is drama; her brilliant technique flows forth precisely and free of strain.

Purely classical roles like the ballerina in George Balanchine's *Theme and Variations* or the lead in Victor Gsovsky's *Grand Pas Classique* make full use of her coruscating attack and her sure musical phrasing. In some ways she is a dancer's dancer. But in suitable dramatic roles (usually those of twentieth-century ballets) she is equally convincing. Her guilt-ridden Miss Julie in the Birgit Cullberg ballet, and her tempestuous Medusa in Antony Tudor's *Undertow* were impressive because they were close to her essential presence. While she was also a commanding Myrtha, Queen of the Wilis, in *Giselle*, the more poetic role of the heroine lacked a romantic aura with Gregory, as did her portrayal of the even more romantic sylph in *La Sylphide*.

In 1985, American Ballet Theatre celebrated Cyntha Gregory's twentieth anniversary with the company. The gala performance at the Metropolitan Opera House consisted of excerpts from ballets in which she had danced leading roles. The variety was impressive. In addition to *Swan Lake, Act II*, there were excerpts from Alvin Ailey's *The River*, Eliot Feld's *At Midnight*, Twyla Tharp's *Bach Partita*, Dennis Nahat's *Brahms Quintet*, Michael Smuin's *Eternal Idol*, plus *La Sylphide*, *La Bayadère*, *Coppélia*, *Miss Julie*, *The Sleeping Beauty*, and *Raymonda*. Not many ballerinas can claim such range.

And yet in Gregory's eyes, there has been something missing in her career, something for which she holds the company responsible. But one might answer that it is Gregory who lacks mystery—that most indefinable of traits, which differentiates the fine artist from the great one. Most dancers conceal their minute flaws by selecting only those roles fully suited to them. Others choose to extend themselves beyond, sometimes with sacrifice. Cynthia Gregory is one of the latter. She impels us to thank her for her courage, if not always for her good sense.

—Doris Hering

---

## GREY, Beryl

British dancer and ballet director. Born Beryl Groom in London, 11 June 1927. Studied with Madeleine Sharp, Audrey de Vos, and at Sadler's Wells School, London, from 1937. Married Dr. Sven Gustav Svenson, 1953. Dancer, Sadler's Wells Ballet (later Royal Ballet), 1941–57: soloist, from 1942, with first ballerina role, Odette/Odile, in 1942; international guest artist, including for Royal Opera House, Stockholm, 1953, 1955, Opera House, Helsinki, 1954; first English dancer to appear as guest wtih Bolshoi Ballet, Moscow, 1957–58, and Beijing, 1964; other guest appearances include in South America, South Africa, Canada, New Zealand, and eastern Europe; also appeared in films, including in first stereoscopic ballet film, *Black Swan*, 1952; director general, Arts Educational School, 1965–68; artistic director, London Festival Ballet, 1968–79; trustee, London City Ballet, from 1978; vice-president, Royal Academy of Dancing, from 1980, becoming Executive Member, from 1982; chairman, Imperial Society of Teachers of Dancing, from 1984. Recipient: Honorary Doctorate in Music, Leicester University, 1970; Commander of the Order of the British Empire, 1973; Honorary Doctorate in Literature, City University, London, 1974; Dame of the Order of the British Empire, 1988.

### ROLES

1941 Waltz, Mazurka in *Les Sylphides* (Fokine), Sadler's Wells Ballet, London

1942 The Lady in *Comus* (Helpmann), Sadler's Wells Ballet, London

Sabrina in *Comus* (Helpmann), Sadler's Wells Ballet, London

The Nightingale (cr) in *The Birds* (Helpmann), Sadler's Wells Ballet, London

Children of Light in *Dante Sonata* (Ashton), Sadler's Wells Ballet, London

Polka in *Façade* (Ashton), Sadler's Wells Ballet, London

Serving Maid in *The Gods Go a-Begging* (de Valois), Sadler's Wells Ballet, Oxford

Odette/Odile in *Swan Lake* (Petipa, Ivanov; staged Sergeyev), Sadler's Wells Ballet, London

Love in *Orpheus and Eurydice* (de Valois), Sadler's Wells Ballet, London

Variations/Adagio of Lovers in *Les Rendezvous* (Ashton), Sadler's Wells Ballet, London

1943 Ophelia in *Hamlet* (Helpmann), Sadler's Wells Ballet, London

Rendezvous (cr) in *Promenade* (de Valois), Sadler's Wells Ballet, Edinburgh

Duessa (cr) in *The Quest* (Ashton), Sadler's Wells Ballet, London

1944 Young Girl in *Nocturne* (Ashton), Sadler's Wells Ballet, tour

1945 Spider in *Le Festin de l'araigneé* (Howard), Sadler's Wells Ballet, London

Chiarina in *Carnaval* (Fokine), Sadler's Wells Ballet, London

1946 Queen of Denmark in *Hamlet* (Helpmann), Sadler's Wells Ballet, London

Myrtha in *Giselle* (Petipa after Coralli, Perrot; staged Sergeyev), Sadler's Wells Ballet, London

Title role in *Giselle* (Petipa after Coralli, Perrot; staged Sergeyev), Sadler's Wells Ballet, London

A Child of Darkness in *Dante Sonata* (Ashton), Sadler's Wells Ballet, London

Lilac Fairy in *The Sleeping Beauty* (Petipa; staged

**Beryl Grey in *Swan Lake***

Sergeyev, Ashton, de Valois), Sadler's Wells Ballet, London
Countess Kitty (cr) in *Les Sirènes* (Ashton), Sadler's Wells Ballet, London
Princess Aurora in *The Sleeping Beauty* (Petipa; staged Sergeyev, Ashton, de Valois), Sadler's Wells Ballet, London
Echo dancer (cr) in *The Fairy Queen* (masque after Shakespeare; mus. Purcell, chor. Ashton), Covent Garden Opera and Sadler's Wells Ballet, London
1947 Black Queen in *Checkmate* (de Valois), Sadler's Wells Ballet, London
Pas de deux in *Les Patineurs* (Ashton), Sadler's Wells Ballet, London
Queen of Clubs in *La Boutique Fantasque* (Massine), Sadler's Wells Ballet, London
1948 Principal dancer in *Scènes de ballet* (Ashton), Sadler's Wells Ballet, London
The Fairy Winter (cr) in *Cinderella* (Ashton), Sadler's Wells Ballet, London
1949 Young Wife in *Don Juan* (Ashton), Sadler's Wells Ballet, London
The Aristocrat in *Mam'zelle Angot* (Massine), Sadler's Wells Ballet, London
La Morte amoureuse in *Don Juan* (Ashton), Sadler's Wells Ballet, London
1950 Second Ballerina in *Ballet Imperial* (Balanchine), Sadler's Wells Ballet, London
1951 Death (cr) in *Donald of the Burthens* (Massine), Sadler's Wells Ballet, London
1952 Title role in *Sylvia* (Ashton), Sadler's Wells Ballet, London
The Miller's Wife in *The Three-Cornered Hat* (*Le Tricorne*; Massine), Sadler's Wells Ballet, London
First Ballerina in *Ballet Imperial* (Balanchine), Sadler's Wells Ballet, London
1953 Queen of Fire (cr) in *Homage to the Queen* (Ashton), Sadler's Wells Ballet, London
1955 La Capricciosa (cr) in *The Lady and the Fool* (Cranko), Sadler's Wells Ballet, London
1956 Variation (cr) in *Birthday Offering* (Ashton), Royal Ballet, London

**Other roles include:** Queen of Clubs in *La Boutique fantasque* (Massine), Chiarina in *Carnaval* (Fokine), Aurora and "Prayer" Variation in *Coppélia* (Petipa, Cecchetti, Sergeyev), Myrtha in *Giselle* (Petipa after Coralli, Perrot; staged Sergeyev), Ophelia in *Hamlet* (Helpmann), Beatrice in *The Haunted Ballroom* (de Valois).

## PUBLICATIONS


By Grey:
"Ballet in Stockholm", *Dancing Times* (London), May 1953
*Red Curtain Up*, London, 1958
*Through the Bamboo Curtain*, London, 1965
*My Favorite Ballet Stories* (editor), Guildford, 1981
Interview in Newman, Barbara, *Stiking a Balance: Dancers Talk About Dancing*, Boston, 1982

About Grey:
Hall, Fernau, *Modern English Ballet*, London, 1950
"Beryl Grey", *Ballet* (London), January 1952
Alvarez, Elke, "Meet Sadler's Wells Ballerina Beryl Grey", *Ballet Today* (London), December 1952
Anthony, Gordon (photographer), *Beryl Grey*, London, 1952
Crowle, Pigeon, *Beryl Grey*, London, 1952
Barnes, Clive, "Fate Made her a Dancer", *Dance and Dancers* (London), December 1954
Davidson, Gladys, *Ballet Biographies*, revised edition, London, 1954
"Beryl Grey and the Strong Heart", *Ballet Today* (London), February 1955
Fisher, Hugh, *Beryl Grey*, London, 1955
Clarke, Mary, *The Sadler's Wells Ballet*, London, 1955
Gillard, David, *Beryl Grey: A Biography*, London, 1977


* * *

Legend has it that when Beryl Grey, aged nine, joined the Vic-Wells Ballet School in 1937, an alarmed teacher telephoned Ninette de Valois with the cry "I think you'd better come and look at this child, Miss de Valois". After watching class, de Valois enquired "Well, what's wrong with her?" to which the teacher replied "What's wrong with her? She can do everything, that's what's wrong!" Five years later, Beryl Grey, joining the Sadler's Wells Ballet (aged fourteen), turned out to be the English answer to the Russian "baby ballerinas" of the 1930s, quite capable of dancing the complete four-act *Swan Lake*, with the invaluable support of Robert Helpmann, on her fifteenth birthday. What luck for English ballet, struggling with the various disasters of the Second World War, that talented children were not then obliged to stay at school until sixteen and then expected to spend a further three years at a "vocational school". And what luck for Beryl Grey also, for had she been made to wait until she was nearly twenty to join a company, and then spent another two or three years in the corps de ballet, she might well have lost the limitless adolescent confidence which enabled her to sail through Odile's 32 fouettés, aged fifteen to the day.

If it were possible 50 years later to watch Beryl Grey's début performances all over again, one would surely be struck by the sweet, gauche innocence, the guileless naïveté which, at fourteen years old, she displayed. Her technique, however, was anything but gauche or naïve. Looking back, it is clear that the impression she created on stage, from her very first steps in the corps de ballet, was that which she continued to create throughout her career: a feeling of radiant warmth which stretched out, not only to the upper reaches of the New Theatre during the war years, but also, later, to the very back of the gallery at the Royal Opera House. She had a warmth which established immediate personal contact with every single member of the audience.

Beryl Grey's dancing career spanned 25 years, and it was remarkable in other ways beyond her extraordinary technical facility, the facility which set her free to develop her roles unpreoccupied by any physical strain. It also provided the clear evidence that it is quite possible to achieve an outstanding career and to form an unique link with the public, despite only two choreographers (in this case Helpmann and Massine) creating leading roles for one. This must have been a source of some disappointment to Grey, only partially balanced by the fact that in spite of her height (phenomenal for a ballerina at that time), she danced the lead and/or the supporting lead in every classical ballet in the repertoire—with only Swanilda outside her range—and that she excelled equally in the works of Fokine, de Valois, Ashton, Balanchine, Helpmann, and Cranko.

Dancers immediately following a great ballerina such as Fonteyn, Ulanova, or Alonso can have problems in dissociating themselves from the style and personality of their senior, and Grey was no exception. Indeed, at the period when she was still a child prodigy, every dancer in the company was at a disadvantage with the ballet audience, either because she looked like Fonteyn, or because she didn't. Like Fonteyn, Grey was dark-haired; she had a small, neat head, and her facial characteristics in no radical way differed from Fonteyn's. Her dance style at the time was lyrical, romantic, wistfully pleasing, in much the same way that her elder's was lyrical, romantic, wistfully pleasing. She could no more have avoided being influenced by Fonteyn than could Fonteyn herself, at the same age, have avoided being influenced by Markova.

Such an influence, inevitable as it is in a young artist in any sphere, must be controlled and translated into a personal individuality before that young person can reach artistic maturity. And over the years Grey did develop a style very clearly her own. By the time she attacked the role of the second ballerina in Balanchine's *Ballet Imperial*, Grey had shed the mannerisms which she had acquired simply from being on the same stage with Fonteyn for eight years, and showed the public the finished product: a ballerina with a technical mastery so effortless that the audience didn't even notice it. She had an ability to react in the nuances of her dancing to the emotional feel of the particular music to which she was dancing, instead of presenting every role in the same style, no matter who had written the music. There was a grandeur in her movements rare in English, or, indeed, any ballet—yet it was a grandeur which never caused her to appear condescending to her audience; she presented her performance for their approval and they were happy to give it.

Grey's career did not begin and end with her own dancing. She wrote three books on her dancing travels in foreign countries; she ran the Arts Educational School; and her eleven years as artistic director of Festival Ballet, where she not only improved standards of technique but also encouraged and developed many young English dancers, have been, some may well feel, undervalued. She was something of a pioneer at that time when, unlike the present day, ex-dancers were not in fashion as artistic directors of ballet companies, and such a situation was far from commonplace. Had she taken that position twenty years later, when the advantages of employing a director with personal experience of dancers' problems had become apparent, the length of her career with Festival Ballet might well have been doubled.

—Janet Sinclair

---

## GRIGORIEV, Serge

Russian dancer, ballet master, and rehearsal director. Born Sergei (Serge) Leonidovich Grigoriev in Tikhvin, 5 October 1883. Studied at the Imperial Theatre School, St. Petersburg; graduated in 1900. Married dancer Lubov Tchernicheva, 1909. Dancer, Maryinsky Theatre, 1900–12; appointed régisseur (stage manager and rehearsal director) by Diaghilev for the Ballets Russes, 1909, remaining in this post until Diaghilev's death and disbanding of company, 1929; also creator of several character roles, Diaghilev's Ballets Russes, from 1909; chief régisseur, de Basil's Ballets Russes de Monte Carlo (later becoming the Original Ballet Russe), 1929–51; producer, with wife Tchernicheva, of revivals of Fokine ballets for Sadler's Wells (later Royal) Ballet, London, 1954, 1955, also overseeing rehearsals for Massine ballets; also staged ballets for London Festival Ballet and La Scala, Milan. Died in London, 28 June 1968.

### ROLES

1910 Shah Shariar (cr) in *Schéhérazade* (Fokine), Diaghilev's Ballets Russes, Paris
1914 Guidone (cr) in *Le Coq d'or* (Fokine), Diaghilev's Ballets Russes, Paris
1919 Russian Merchant (cr) in *La Boutique fantasque* (Massine), Diaghilev's Ballets Russes, London

**Other roles include:** the Merchant in *Petrushka* (Fokine), Emperor in *Le Chant du rossignol* (Massine).

### WORKS

Staged:
1954 *The Firebird* (with Tchernicheva, after Fokine; mus. Stravinsky), Sadler's Wells Ballet, Edinburgh
1955 *Les Sylphides* (with Tchernicheva, after Fokine; mus. Chopin), Sadler's Wells Ballet, London
1956 *Petrushka* (with Tchernicheva, after Fokine; mus. Stravinsky), London Festival Ballet (staged for Royal Ballet, 1957)
*Schéhérazade* (with Tchernicheva, after Fokine; mus. Rimsky-Korsakov), London Festival Ballet

### PUBLICATIONS

By Grigoriev:
*The Diaghilev Ballet 1909–1929*, translated by Vera Bowen, London, 1953

About Grigoriev:
Johns, Eric, "Serge Grigoriev and Lubov Tchernicheva", *Dancing Times* (London), February 1964
Beaumont, Cyril, "Serge Grigoriev", *Dancing Times* (London), November 1968
Ostlere, Hilary, "Keepers of the Flame", *Dance Magazine* (New York), October 1975
Garafola, Lynn, *Diaghilev's Ballets Russes*, New York, 1989

* * *

It was Serge Diaghilev himself who once remarked, "No one is indispensible; Grigoriev almost". As "régisseur", or rehearsal director, to the Diaghilev Ballet, Serge Grigoriev was the loyalest of Diaghilev's colleagues, and he was the only one to remain with the company throughout the twenty years of its existence.

Originally a member of the Maryinsky Theatre in St. Petersburg, Grigoriev began his real career when Fokine suggested him to Diaghilev as régisseur for the first Russian Ballet seasons in Europe. For those first seasons, his post combined the duties of production and business manager, being mainly concerned with contracts, payment of salaries, and the transportation of the company from venue to venue. However, when Fokine left Diaghilev in 1912, Grigoriev assumed responsibility for company rehearsals as well.

While Diaghilev concerned himself with the creative side of the company and the production of new works, Grigoriev was responsible for carrying out Diaghilev's orders, upholding company discipline, and maintaining performance standards. As the link between Diaghilev and the company, he often had to carry out unpleasant tasks, of which the most disagreeable were undoubtedly to effect the dismissals of Vaslav Nijinsky and Léonide Massine.

**Serge Grigoriev demonstrating a step for members of the Original Ballet Russe**

The efficient day-to-day running of the company was in Grigoriev's hands, and he concerned himself with every aspect of the organization. He never missed a performance or a rehearsal. He was present at the creation of a new work, so that he could carry out the choreographer's wishes once the ballet had passed into the regular repertoire and he then staged revivals. He worked out rehearsal schedules and the individual coaching sessions for the dancers, supervising many of them himself; thus he knew each dancer's capabilities, and was, in consultation with Diaghilev, responsible for casting and understudying. Each night he checked that every dancer was in the theatre, and watched every ballet, meticulously noting any details that displeased him. He even regulated the curtain calls.

None of this would have been possible without his phenomenal memory—a necessary attribute at a time when there were no written records of ballets to help with revivals—and an eye for the minutest detail. Throughout the often turbulent daily life of the company, he remained impeturbable, calm, painstaking, and tactful; and he was completely loyal to Diaghilev and his aims—whether he agreed with them or not. But his responsibilities extended beyond the dancing. He adapted each production to the many different stages on which the company danced. He supervised the stage and wardrobe staff, keeping an eagle eye on the condition of scenery and costumes, and it was on his orders that repairs or replacements were effected, with a strict eye on the costs at the same time. Once Diaghilev had set the lighting, Grigoriev saw that his wishes were maintained. He also worked out the logistics of company travelling, even to the conversion of salaries into the currency of each country visited, and arranged for the storage of productions no longer in the repertory.

Grigoriev was not a regular performer, but he was a remarkable mime and his characterizations were memorable, notably the Russian Merchant in *La Boutique fantasque*, the Emperor in *Le Chant du rossignol* and the Shah in *Schéhérazade*.

After Diaghilev's death, Grigoriev tried to keep the company together, but when this proved impossible, he loyally ran the de Basil Ballets Russes de Monte Carlo in the same capacities as he had for Diaghilev, keeping the Diaghilev ballets that they inherited as fresh and exciting as ever and ensuring the smooth running of the company.

He was to prove an invaluable link with the past, and in later years, his extraordinary memory was put at the service of a number of companies, including London Festival Ballet and La Scala. In the 1950s and 1960s he and his wife, Lubov Tchernicheva, revived a series of Diaghilev ballets for the

Royal Ballet, notably *The Firebird* and *Petrushka*, and rehearsed the Massine ballets in their repertory. He had lost none of his eye for detail and the revivals were lovingly and scrupulously mounted.

Grigoriev's memoirs, *The Diaghilev Ballet 1909–1929*, are a model of information and discretion. They detail meticulously the history of the company, but loyally maintain silence upon anything that might be considered detrimental, and even the sensational is defused by his matter-of-fact approach. As in his work, Grigoriev's concern was with the public face of the company, and he maintained that he took no interest in the private lives of its members. It is unlikely that anyone will ever again be asked to play such a part with any company, combining as it did the roles of business manager, ballet master, producer, coach, company and business manager; in all categories, Grigoriev set standards that few could ever hope to equal.

—Sarah C. Woodcock

---

## GRIGOROVICH, Yuri

Russian dancer, choreographer, and ballet director. Born Yuri Nikolaevich Grigorovich in Leningrad, 2 January 1927. Studied at the Leningrad Choreographic School, pupil of Vladimir Ponomarev, Aleksandr Pushkin, Andrei Lopukhov, Boris Shavrov; graduated in 1946; also attended State Institute of Theatrical Art (GITIS), graduating in 1965. Married Bolshoi ballerina Natalia Bessmertnova. Soloist, Kirov Ballet, 1946–64, ballet master, 1961–64; artistic director and chief choreographer, Bolshoi Ballet, from 1964; artistic director and chief choreographer, Bolshoi Ballet Grigorovich Company, from 1990; also Professor of the Choreographers' Faculty, Leningrad Conservatory, 1973–80. Recipient: title of Honoured Artist of the Russian Federation, 1957; People's Artist of the Russian Federation, 1966; Lenin Prize, 1970; Honoured Artist of the USSR, 1973; State Prize, USSR, 1977, 1985; Hero of Socialist Labour, 1986.

### ROLES

1949 Soloist, "Russian Dance" (cr) in *The Bronze Horseman* (Zakharov), Kirov Ballet, Leningrad
1954 Harlequin (cr) in *The Nutcracker* (Vainonen), Kirov Ballet, Leningrad
1955 The Messenger (cr) in *Taras Bulba* (Fenster), Kirov Ballet, Leningrad
1956 Retiari in *Spartacus* (Yakobson), Kirov Ballet, Leningrad
1957 Severyan (cr) in *The Stone Flower* (also chor.), Kirov Ballet, Leningrad
1958 The Young Latino (cr) in *The Path of Thunder* (Sergeyev), Kirov Ballet, Leningrad
The Hunter (cr) in *The Red Flower* (Andreyev after Zakharov), Kirov Ballet, Leningrad

**Other roles include:** Lei-Shan-Fu in *The Red Flower* (Andreyev after Zakharov), Shurale in *Ali-Batyr* (Yakobson), Nikolai in *Tatyana* (Burmeister), Jérome in *The Flames of Paris* (Vainonen), Nur-Ali, the Youth in *The Fountain of Bakhchisarai* (Zakharov), the Golden Idol in *La Bayadère* (Petipa, Ponomarev, Chabukiani), Hans (Hilarion) in *Giselle* (Petipa after Coralli, Perrot), Jester in *Romeo and Juliet* (Lavrovsky), Jester in *The Bronze Horseman* (Zakharov), Puss-in-Boots in *The Sleeping Beauty* (Petipa, staged Sergeyev), Soloist, Ukrainian Dance in *The Little Humpbacked Horse* (Lopukhov after Gorsky), Polovotsian in *Polovotsian Dances* from *Prince Igor* (Fokine), Pan in *Walpurgis Night* from *Faust* (opera; mus. Gounod, chor. Lavrovsky).

### WORKS

1948 *Baby Stork* (mus. Klebanov), Children's Ballet Studio, Gorky Palace of Culture, Leningrad
1950 *Seven Brothers* (mus. Varlamova), Children's Ballet Studio, Gorky Palace of Culture, Leningrad
1956 *Valse Fantasia* (mus. Glinka), Graduation Performance of the Leningrad Choreographic School, Kirov Theatre, Leningrad
1957 *The Stone Flower* (mus. Prokofiev), Kirov Ballet, Leningrad (staged Bolshoi Ballet, Moscow, 1959)
1961 *The Legend of Love* (mus. Melikov), Kirov Ballet, Leningrad (staged Bolshoi Ballet, Moscow, 1965)
1968 *Spartacus* (mus. Khachaturian), Bolshoi Ballet, Moscow
1975 *Ivan the Terrible* (mus. Prokofiev), Bolshoi Ballet, Moscow (staged Paris Opéra, 1976)
1976 *Angara* (mus. Eshpai), Bolshoi Ballet, Moscow
1979 *Romeo and Juliet* (mus. Prokofiev), Bolshoi Ballet, Moscow
1982 *The Golden Age* (mus. Shostakovich), Bolshoi Ballet, Moscow

Also staged:
1963 *The Sleeping Beauty* (after Petipa; mus. Tchaikovsky), Bolshoi Ballet, Moscow
1966 *The Nutcracker* (after Ivanov; mus. Tchaikovsky), Bolshoi Ballet, Moscow
1969 *Swan Lake* (after Petipa, Ivanov; mus. Tchaikovsky), Bolshoi Ballet, Moscow
1984 *Raymonda* (after Petipa; mus. Glazunov), Bolshoi Ballet, Moscow
1986 *Giselle* (after Petipa, Coralli, Perrot; mus. Adam), Bolshoi Ballet, Moscow

### PUBLICATIONS

By Grigorovich:
"The Muse of Soviet Ballet", "Traditions and Innovations", in *The Music and Choreography of Soviet Ballet*, Leningrad, 1979
"Fedor Lopukhov", *Teatr* (Moscow), no. 7, 1965
"The Theatre of Virsaladze", *Sovietsky Balet* (Moscow), no. 4, 1982
Interview in Johnson, Robert, "Grigorovich Redux: Down but not Out", *Dance Magazine* (New York), February 1991

About Grigorovich:
Shostakovich, Dmitri, "Elevated Substance and Ideas", *Literaturnaya Gazeta* (Moscow), 12 March 1966
Lopukhov, Fedor, *Sixty Years in Ballet*, Moscow, 1966
Slonimsky, Yuri, *In Honour of Dance*, Moscow, 1967
Krasovskaya, Vera, *The Articles of Ballet*, Lenigrad, 1967
Goleizovsky, Kasyan, "The Handwriting of the Artist", *Teatr* (Moscow), no. 7, 1968
Vanslav, Viktor, *The Ballets of Grigorovich and the Problems of Choreography*, Moscow, 1971
Greskovic, Robert, "The Grigorovich Factor and the Bolshoi", *Ballet Review* (Brooklyn, N.Y.), vol. 5, no. 2, 1975–76

Demidov, Aleksandr, *The Russian Ballet Past and Present*, translated by Guy Daniels, London, 1978
Demidov, Aleksandr, "The Poetics of Grigorovich's Theatre", *Sovietsky Balet* (Moscow), no. 3, 1984
Demidov, Aleksandr, *Yuri Grigorovich*, Moscow, 1987
Alovert, Nina, "Yuri Grigorovich: An Appreciation", *Dance Magazine* (New York), July 1987
Alovert, Nina, "The Soviet Dance Theatre of Yuri Grigorovich", *Dance Magazine* (New York), December 1987
Percival, John, "Grigorovich of the Bolshoi", *Dance and Dancers* (London), September 1989

* * *

"His choreographic images are replete with genuine poetry . . . all the very best in the sphere of choreography, in the sense of the relationship between tradition and contemporary substance . . . is here. Everything is expressed, everything stated in his richest of languages—an original language of images that, I think, opens a new stage in the development of Soviet theatre" (Dmitri Shostakovich).

Yuri Grigorovich laid the foundation for a new stage in the development not only of Soviet choreography, but of twentieth-century ballet in general. He created a unique twentieth-century theatre, in which he moulded his choreographic, aesthetic, and philosophical ideas into living form. Grigorovich's theatre, coming together on the stage of the Bolshoi Theatre in Moscow, was nourished on the traditions of the Russian ballet. The work of Marius Petipa and, later, Mikhail Fokine and Fedor Lopukhov, marked the beginning of two traditions in the Russian ballet: theatrical, thematic ballet and abstract, athematic ballet. Grigorovich united these two strains in his work. At the base of his ballets there is always a clear drama, with a schema of conflict between character and situation. But the conflict and the characters and the ideas are given form only by means of dance—symbolic dance, Grigorovich's primary balletic form.

The sources for the appearance of this theatre include the greatest figures in Soviet art: the "grand old man" Fedor Lopukhov, drama theorist Yuri Slonimsky, and the painter Suleiko Virsaladze, a contemporary heir to the "World of Art" painters.

Grigorovich met them during his first year at the Kirov Theatre in Leningrad. He had completed his studies at the Leningrad School of Ballet and had been accepted into the Kirov Theatre corps de ballet. His first year at the theatre, he danced the Snowman and other corps de ballet roles in Lopukhov's production of *A Spring Fairy Tale*, to the music of Petr Tchaikovsky. Virsaladze did the artwork for the ballet and Slonimsky wrote the scenario. Thus the future ballet master's creative life had a happy beginning. Lopukhov's choreography stirred his fantasy of becoming a choreographer long before Lopukhov became his friend and teacher.

Grigorovich was a performer of note in the Kirov troupe, dancing grotesque character roles. His high leap, statuesque presence, and dynamic dancing style were combined with a refined grace and masculinity. Among his finest roles were Retiary in *Spartacus*, Shurale in *Ali-Batyr*, the Golden Idol in *La Bayadère*, and Severyan in *The Stone Flower*.

Grigorovich started choreographing while still a dancer at the Kirov. His first productions were the ballet *Aistenok* (*Baby Stork*), for a children's theatre, and dances for various operas. In 1957, Lopukhov, then artistic director of the Kirov Theatre, gave the budding ballet master the chance to stage the ballet *The Stone Flower*, to the music of Sergei Prokofiev. (In Leonid Lavrovsky's previous production of that ballet in Moscow, dance only illustrated plot, and the ballet was not successful.)

**Yuri Grigorovich**

Grigorovich's version of *The Stone Flower* created a revolution in the Russian ballet world and marked the beginning of a new phenomenon in that world—the theatre of Grigorovich. Little by little, the whole of Soviet ballet started to change under the influence of *The Stone Flower*, which pointed the way to a new alternative to stale "dram-ballet".

Grigorovich's second ballet, *The Legend of Love*, was another early masterpiece. Work on these ballets helped to form the future premier dancers of Grigorovich's troupe, such as Alla Osipenko, Irina Kolpakova, Aleksandr Gribov, Aleksandr Gridin, and Emma Minchenok, to name but a few.

Despite the success of these first two ballets, however, the administration of the Kirov Theatre was in no hurry to let Grigorovich work on any more new ballets. And it was then that the Bolshoi Theatre invited him to revive Petipa's *The Sleeping Beauty*. Grigorovich moved to Moscow and soon became the company's artistic director.

The Moscow ballet has its own traditions, separate from those of St. Petersburg–Leningrad, and naturally these had an influence on Grigorovich's new work, in terms of both the style and the substance of his choreography. His fidelity to the genre of ballet created purely by means of dance, however, remained unchanged, as did his concern for philosophical issues in dance and his unflagging creative energy. The philosophical problems in Grigorovich's ballets, however, do not just spring from his own creative interests; they reflect the atmosphere of the period when Grigorovich was coming into his own as a ballet master. The spirituality and the search for a moral ideal, which form the basis of Grigorovich's ballets, were always characteristic of Russia's best choreographers, regardless of their school. That is one of the reasons why the ballet is so popular in Russia: in the toughest and most spiritually deprived of times, the ballet, like a spring, quenched the thirst for beauty and spirituality.

Grigorovich's theatre arose during the temporary thaw of the 1950s and 1960s, a historical time for Russia. His questions constantly concerned such issues as the nature of man and the interrelationship of good and evil. The hero is confronted with a moral issue, a choice—often hopeless. Regardless of whether the hero sacrifices his duty for the sake of love (Danila) or sacrifices his love for the welfare of the people (Ferkhad), the outcome for the hero himself is unhappy. Whether Spartacus defends the slaves or Ivan the Terrible makes his subjects into slaves, the fate of anyone who takes power into his own hands is tragic; he pays for it with his love and with his life or with the loss of human dignity.

There are also the themes of the shattered dream (*The Nutcracker*) and the dream betrayed (*Swan Lake*). There is the tragedy of the mean-spirited man who tries to possess beauty—Severyan in *The Stone Flower*, Yashka in *The Golden Age*, and Abdurakhman in *Raymonda*. All of these are only brief outlines of the themes that Grigorovich addresses. One could say that Grigorovich's ballet is the theatre of great tragedy, and the ballets *Ivan the Terrible* and *Romeo and Juliet* attained the heights of Shakespearian tragedy during the period otherwise characterized by stagnation in Russia (the 1970s and 1980s).

In his productions, Grigorovich proceeds above all from the music, revamping the existing libretto if it does not fit the music completely. This was his approach to the musical content of Tchaikovsky's ballet *The Nutcracker*, and Prokofiev's *Romeo and Juliet*, which he staged on the basis of the complete scores, without the changes that had been made by his predecessors.

Grigorovich undoubtedly has been controversial, and in recent years especially many have claimed that his inspiration is failing him. But his importance to Russian/Soviet ballet is beyond question. The famous American ballet critic, Clive Barnes, wrote of Grigorovich: "He is a choreographer of enormous gifts—both in terms of theatricality, and fluency and authority of dance invention. Like all the great Russian choreographers of the past, he has a particular ability to create huge, flowing ensemble movements with his principals emerging from the rest like concertante soloists . . . I first saw his *Spartacus* at the Bolshoi and became fully convinced that here was a unique twentieth-century choreographer of genius."

—Nina Alovert

---

**GRISI, Carlotta**

Italian dancer. Born Caronne Adele Josephine Marie Grisi, in Visinada, Upper Istria, Italy, 28 June 1819. Studied at the Ballet School of Teatro alla Scala, Milan, from c. 1826, pupil of Claude Guillet; later studied under Jules Perrot, from 1833; also studied singing. Assumed name of Madame Perrot, 1836 (never married); daughter, Ernestine Grisi, by Prince Radziwill. Dancer, corps de ballet, La Scala, Milan, from 1829; leading dancer, touring Italy, 1833, and performing at Teatro San Carlo, Naples, 1834, 1835; leading dancer, performing with Perrot, London, 1836, thereafter touring Europe, including in Paris, Vienna, Milan, and Munich; Paris début, Théâtre de la Renaissance, 1840; engaged at Opéra, Paris, 1841, becoming leading ballerina; also appeared frequently in London, 1842–51, also making other guest appearances all over Europe; last season in Paris, 1849; ballerina, Imperial Theatres, Russia, 1850–53; retired from the stage, 1854. Died in St. Jean, Switzerland, 20 May 1899.

**ROLES**

1832 Principal dancer in *Sette reclute* (L. Astolfi), Teatro alla Canobbiana, Milan
1834 Dancer in *L'Ermita*, Teatro San Carlo, Naples
Principal dancer (cr) in *I Selvaggi della Florida* (Guerra), Teatro San Carlo, Naples
1835 Dancer in *Carlo di Borgogna* (opera; mus. Pacini), Teatro La Fenice, Venice
Amore (cr) in *Amore e Psiche* (S. Taglioni), Teatro San Carlo, Naples
Dancer in *Flore et Zéphire* (after Didelot), Teatro San Carlo, Naples
1836 Pas de deux inserted in *Le Rossignol* (Deshayes), Her Majesty's Theatre, London
Dancer in *Beniowsky* (Deshayes), Her Majesty's Theatre, London
Dancer in *Zéphir Berger* (Deshayes), Her Majesty's Theatre, London
Dancer (cr) in *Tarantella* (pas de deux; Perrot), Her Majesty's Theatre, London
Dancer (cr) in *Pas de deux* (Perrot), Théatre Français, Paris
Thisbe (cr) in *Die Nymphe und der Schmetterling* (Campilli; Grisi's and Perrot's dances by Perrot), Hofoper, Vienna
Dancer in *Liebe, stärker als Zaubernacht* (Campilli), Hofoper, Vienna
Lise (cr) in *Das Stelldichein* (Perrot), Hofoper, Vienna
1837 Title role in *La Sylphide* (F. Taglioni), Hofoper, Vienna
Dancer (cr) in *Pas de deux* (Perrot), Opéra-Comique, Paris
1838 Zanetta (cr) in *Die Neapolitanischen Fischer* (Perrot), Hofoper, Vienna
Iola (cr) in *Der Kobold* (Perrot), Hofoper, Vienna
Pas de deux (cr; Perrot) in *I Figli di Edoardo* (Cortesi), La Scala, Milan
1839 Pas de deux (cr; chor. Perrot) in *Il Rajah di Benares* (S. Taglioni), Teatro San Carlo, Naples
1840 Gianina (cr) in *Le Zingaro* (opera; mus. Fortuna, chor. Perrot), Théâtre de la Renaissance, Paris
1841 Pas de deux (cr; chor. Perrot) added to *La Favorite* (opera; mus. Donizetti), Opéra, Paris
Pas de deux (chor. Perrot) added to *La Juive* (opera; Halévy), Opéra, Paris
Pas de deux (cr) in *Don Juan* (opera; mus. Mozart, chor. Perrot), Opéra, Paris
Giselle (cr) in *Giselle; ou, Les Wilis* (Coralli, Perrot), Opéra, Paris
1842 Beatrix (cr) in *La Jolie Fille de Gand* (Albert), Opéra, Paris
1843 Title role (cr) in *La Péri* (Coralli), Opéra, Paris
1844 Title role (cr) in *La Esmeralda* (Perrot), Her Majesty's Theatre, London
Principal dancer in *Polka* (pas de deux; Perrot), Her Majesty's Theatre, London
1845 Ballerina (cr) in *Pas de quatre* (Perrot), Her Majesty's Theatre, London
Mazourka (cr) in *Le Diable à quatre* (Mazilier), Opéra, Paris
1846 Title role (cr) in *Paquita* (Mazilier), Opéra, Paris
1847 Fire (cr) in *Les Eléménts* (Perrot), Her Majesty's Theatre, London
1848 Principal dancer in *Griseldis* (Mazilier), Apollo Theatre, Rome

Summer (cr) in *Les Quatre Saisons* (Perrot), Her Majesty's Theatre, London
1849 Principal dancer (cr) in *Electra* (P. Taglioni), Her Majesty's Theatre, London
Ysaure (cr) in *La Filleules de fées* (Perrot), Opéra, Paris
1850 The Sprite (cr) in *Les Métamorphoses* (P. Taglioni), Her Majesty's Theatre, London
Ariel (mime role; cr) in *The Tempest* (opera; Halévy), Her Majesty's Theatre, London
1851 Naiad (cr) in *The Naiad and the Fisherman* (Perrot), Bolshoi Theatre, St. Petersburg
1852 Vlaida (cr) in *The War of the Women; or, The Amazons of the Ninth Century* (Perrot), Bolshoi Theatre, St. Petersburg
Principal dancer in *The Hungarian Hut* (revival; Didelot), Bolshoi Theatre, St. Petersburg
1853 Title role (cr) in *Gazelda; or, The Tziganes* (Perrot), Bolshoi Theatre, St. Petersburg
Principal dancer in *Amour et Psyché* (Le Picq), Bolshoi Theatre, St. Petersburg

**PUBLICATIONS**

Gautier, Théophile, *The Romantic Ballet as seen by Théophile Gautier*, compiled and translated by Cyril Beaumont, London 1932
Moore, Lillian, *Artists of the Dance*, New York, 1938
Lifar, Serge, *Carlotta Grisi*, Paris, 1941
Beaumont, Cyril, *Complete Book of Ballets*, revised edition, London, 1951
Pridden, D., *The Art of the Dance in French Literature*, London, 1952
Brillant, M., *Problèmes de la danse*, Paris, 1953
Guest, Ivor, *The Romantic Ballet in England*, London, 1954
Guest, Ivor, *The Romantic Ballet in Paris*, London, 1966
Migel, Parmenia, *The Ballerinas*, New York, 1972
Guest, Ivor, *The Ballet of the Second Empire*, London, 1974
Guest, Ivor, *Jules Perrot: Master of the Romantic Ballet*, London, 1984
*Gautier on Dance*, edited by Ivor Guest, London, 1986

* * *

Best remembered for her creation of the lead role in *Giselle*, the nineteenth-century ballerina Carlotta Grisi began dancing in her native Italy at an early age. By the time she was ten she had made her début in Milan, and she was already touring Italy at the age of fourteen. It was then that she met dancer and choreographer Jules Perrot, who was engaged in Naples. He took her under his wing—at first as his student, later as his mistress.

After performances in Italy and London, Grisi's elegant and poetic style earned her a contract at the Paris Opéra in 1841. Although Perrot was not offered a post, he arranged an agreement whereby he would create the choreography for Grisi at the Opéra. Théophile Gautier, the leading French critic of the period, was also a creator of several libretti for ballets. Inspired by tales from Heinrich Heine, he had written the scenario for *Giselle*, with the help of his friend Jules Vernoy de Saint-Georges, for presentation at the Opéra. With Grisi as the heroine and Lucien Petipa as Albrecht, the ballet was an immediate success. Although Jean Coralli was credited with the choreography, Perrot was later acknowledged to have created the choreography for Grisi's role. The ballet's success was due in no small part to Grisi's great talents as both dancer and actress. She and her partner Lucien Petipa, according to Gautier, made a "poem", a "choreographic elegy full of charm and tenderness" out of the now-famous second act, in which Giselle returns from her grave to protect Albrecht from the vengeance of the spirits, or Wilis. "[She] danced with a perfection, a lightness, a boldness, a chaste and refined seductiveness which place her in the first rank between Elssler and Taglioni," wrote Gautier, "in her miming she surpassed all expectations—not a conventional gesture, not a false movement—she is nature and artlessness personified." Grisi's contribution to the Romantic ballet in this landmark work cannot be underestimated. As historian Ivor Guest has put it, "*Giselle*, born of a poet's fancy, given music which reflected so faithfully the moods of its strange tale, and danced with lyrical sweetness by an entrancing ballerina whose steps had been dictated by a poet of choreography, was to be recognized as the master-work of the Romantic ballet."

A great admirer and friend of Grisi's after the success of *Giselle*, Gautier created another ballet for her, again with choreography by Coralli. This was *La Péri*, another Romantic tale of physical man in search of the ideal, the premiere of which took place at the Opéra in 1843. Once again Grisi's success was great, resulting in a renewal of her Paris Opéra contract. Once again, Gautier wrote movingly of Grisi's beauty and skill as a dancer, particularly in the *Pas du Songe* and *Pas de l'Abeille*, in which her light, "rose-leaf" delicacy made her seem not to touch the ground.

Between 1845 and 1848 ballet master Joseph Mazilier created several ballets for Grisi: *Le Diable à quatre* (1845), *Paquita* (1846), and *Griseldis* (1848). From 1842 until 1851 Grisi danced in London annually, presenting *Giselle* there for the first time in 1842. In 1844 she created the lead role in *La Esmeralda*—Perrot's ballet based on Victor Hugo's *Notre Dame de Paris*—at Her Majesty's Theatre, and joined three other leading Romantic ballerinas—Taglioni, Cerrito, and Grahn—for the historic divertissement *Pas de quatre*, created by Perrot in 1845.

Grisi danced in Paris for the last time in 1849. The ballet was *La Filleule de fées*, considered by many to be Perrot's greatest creation. Gautier was overwhelmed by the ballet, particularly the originality of the ensembles, and its heroine, whom he had never stopped worshipping. The Paris Opéra, in recognition of her artistry, placed a bust of Grisi alongside those of Marie Taglioni and Emma Livry as the great representatives of the Romantic ballet era.

Grisi and Perrot were reunited as dancing partners in St. Petersburg in 1850. Although Grisi had originally created the role of Giselle in Paris, Fanny Elssler's great success in the role in St. Petersburg earlier led to an initially lukewarm reception for Grisi. The public warmed to her, however, and by the time she left Russia after three years she was much loved.

Following her retirement at the age of 34, Grisi devoted the remainder of her life to her family, home, and friends. As with many of the dancers of the period, her contribution to dance was primarily an ephemeral one, based mainly on her performance and the memory of it as passed down by critics and by word-of-mouth. Her style of dancing was elegant, impressive also for its brilliance and suppleness. Although Grisi created many roles in great ballets, she was not considered necessarily the best interpreter of them, even in her own day. Nevertheless she remains one of the brightest legends in the golden age of ballet, the Romantic period.

—Carol Egan

**Carlotta Grisi in *La Péri***

**GSOVSKY** (Gsovska), **Tatjana**

Russian/German teacher, choreographer, and ballet director. Born Tatyana Issatchenko in Moscow, daughter of actress Claudia Issatchenko, 18 March 1901. Studied at the Isadora Duncan Studio, Petrograd; later studied ballet with Laurent Novikov, Matyatin, Nina Kirsanova, and Olga Preobrazhenska, and at the Dalcroze school, Hellerau. Married choreographer Victor Gsovsky (Gzovsky). Ballet mistress, Experimental Theatre, Moscow, 1914, and Krasnodar, c. 1918; left Russia, 1925: founder, with Gsovsky, and teacher, ballet school in Berlin, 1928; founder and choreographer, Gamiaun Ballet at the Wintergarden, Berlin; also choreographer in variety theatres and at the Opera Houses in Essen, Leipzig, and Dresden; ballet director and choreographer, State Opera House, (East) Berlin, 1945–52, Teatro Colón, Buenos Aires, 1950, 1952–53, and for the Municipal Opera (becoming the German Opera), West Berlin, 1954–66; also staged ballets for La Scala, Milan, 1953 and 1954; founder, with Gert Reinholm, and choreographer, Berlin Ballet, from 1955, becoming the touring section of the German Opera Ballet, 1961; ballet director, Frankfurt Opera, 1959–66; teacher at the school of the German Opera Ballet, Berlin.

**WORKS**

1936 *Landsknechte* (mus. Weismann), Essen Opera Ballet, Essen

1938 *Don Juan* (mus. Strauss), Berlin State Opera, Berlin

1940 *Goyescas* (mus. Granados), Berlin State Opera, Berlin

1942 *Romeo und Julia* (mus. Spies), Leipzig Opera Ballet, Leipzig
*Daphnis und Chloe* (mus. Ravel), Leipzig Opera Ballet, Leipzig

1943 Dances in *Catulli Carmina* (scenic cantata; mus. Orff), Leipzig Opera, Leipzig

1944 *Prinzessin Turandot* (mus. von Einim), Dresden Opera Ballet, Dresden

1946 *Don Juan* (mus. Gluck), Berlin State Opera, Berlin
*Daphnis und Chloe* (new version; mus. Ravel), Berlin State Opera Ballet, Berlin
*Bolero* (mus. Ravel), Berlin State Opera Ballet, Berlin
*Nobilissima Visione* (mus. Hindemith), Berlin State Opera Ballet, Berlin
*Petruschka* (mus. Stravinsky), Berlin State Opera Ballet, Berlin
*L'Oiseau de feu* (mus. Stravinsky), Berlin State Opera Ballet, Berlin
*Der Pfeil* (mus. Walter), Berlin State Opera Ballet, Berlin

1947 *Der Zauberladen* (mus. Rossini, Respighi), Berlin State Opera Ballet, Berlin
*Der Geist der Rose* (mus. Weber), Berlin State Opera Ballet, Berlin
*Goyescas* (new version; mus. Granados), Berlin State Opera Ballet, Berlin

1948 *Romeo und Julia* (mus. Prokofiev), Berlin State Opera Ballet, Berlin
*Die Geschöpfe des Prometheus* (*Prometheus-Ballett*; mus. Beethoven), Berlin State Opera Ballet, Berlin

1949 *Don Quixote* (mus. Spies), Berlin State Opera Ballet, Berlin

1950 *Hohe Schule* (mus. Tchaikovsky), Berlin State Opera Ballet, Berlin
*Juan de Zarissa* (*Joan von Zarissa*; ballet with chorus; mus. Egk) Teatro Colón, Buenos Aires

1951 *La Valse* (mus. Ravel), Berlin State Opera Ballet, Berlin
*Kindertraum* (mus. Bizet), Berlin State Opera Ballet, Berlin

1952 *Der Idiot* (mus. Henze), Berlin State Opera Ballet, Berlin
*Pulcinella* (mus. Stravinsky), Berlin Festival
*Apollon musagète* (mus. Stravinsky), Berlin Festival

1953 Dances in *Trionfo di Afrodite* (scenic concerto; mus. Orff), Teatro alla Scala, Milan
*Die chinesische Nachtigall* (mus. Egk), Bavarian State Opera Ballet, Munich
*Ajedrez* (mus. d'Esposito), Teatro Colón, Buenos Aires
*Hamlet* (mus. Blacher), Municipal Opera Ballet, (West) Berlin
*Choreomusica* (mus. Mozart), Municipal Opera Ballet, (West) Berlin

1954 *Les Noces* (mus. Stravinsky), La Scala Ballet, Milan
*Pelleas und Melisande* (mus. Baumann), Municipal Opera Ballet, Berlin
*Der rote Mantel* (mus. Nono), Municipal Opera Ballet, Berlin

1955 *Orphée* (mus. Liszt), Municipal Opera Ballet, Berlin
*Signale* (mus. Klebe), Berlin Ballet, Berlin Festival
*Souvenirs* (mus. Offenbach, Karlinsky), Berlin Ballet, Berlin Festival

1956 *Der Mohr von Venedig* (mus. Blacher), Municipal Opera Ballet, Berlin
*Fleurenville* (mus. Klebe), Berlin Ballet, Berlin
*Das Tor* (mus. Hartig), Berlin Ballet, Berlin
*Sinfonische Etuden* (mus. Schumann), Berlin Ballet, Berlin

1957 *Die Kameliendame* (mus. Sauguet), Berlin Ballet, Berlin
*Kain* (mus. Sandloff), Berlin Ballet, Berlin
*Labyrinth*, Berlin Ballet, Berlin Festival

1958 *Medusa* (mus. von Einem), Municipal Opera Ballet, Berlin
*Agon* (mus. Stravinsky), Municipal Opera Ballet, Berlin
*Die Letzte Blum* (mus. Nabokov), Municipal Opera Ballet, Berlin
*Menagerie* (mus. Klebe), Municipal Opera Ballet, Berlin
*Joan von Zarissa* (new production; mus. Egk), Municipal Opera Ballet, Berlin

1959 *Schwarze Sonne* (mus. Hartig), Municipal Opera Ballet, Berlin
*Undine* (mus. Henze), Municipal Opera Ballet, Berlin
*Orpheus Pas de deux* (mus. Lizst), Enghein Festival

1960 *Paean* (mus. Gassmann, Sala), Municipal Opera Ballet, Berlin
*The Seven Deadly Sins* (mus. Weill), Frankfurt Opera Ballet, Frankfurt

1961 *Etudes* (mus. Tchaikovsky), German Opera Ballet, Berlin
*Les Illuminations* (mus. Britten), German Opera Ballet, Berlin
*Der Tat* (mus. Heiss), Berlin Ballet, tour

1962 *Rätsel der Sphinx* (mus. Sauget), German Opera Ballet, Berlin
*Vier Nachstücke nach Goya* (mus. Granados), German Opera Ballet, Berlin
*Raskolnikoff* (mus. Heiss), Berlin Ballet

1963 *Abraxas* (mus. Egk), Teatro Colón, Buenos Aires

1964 *Labyrinth der Warheit* (mus. Varese), German Opera Ballet, West Berlin

1965 *Entrée* (mus. Tchaikovsky), German Opera Ballet, Berlin
*Capriccio* (mus. Liebermann), German Opera Ballet, Berlin
*Tristan* (mus. Blacher), German Opera Ballet, Berlin

Also staged:
1949 *The Sleeping Beauty* (*Dornröschen*, after Petipa; mus. Tchaikovsky), Berlin State Opera Ballet, East Berlin (staged Municipal Opera, later German Opera Ballet, West Berlin, 1955)

**Other works include:** *Till Eulenspiegel* (mus. Strauss), *Danze Slave* (mus. Dvořák), *Ballade*, *Les Climats*, *Mouvements*, *Pathetische Etude*.

## PUBLICATIONS

By Gsovsky:
With Enkelmann, S., *Ballet in Deutschland*, Berlin, 1954

About Gsovsky:
Moore, Lillian, "Ballet in Berlin", *Dance Magazine* (New York), March 1948
Bulow, Eva, "Tatjana Gsovsky", *Ballet Today* (London), January 1954
Korda, Margot, "Two Women Choreographers", *Dance Magazine* (New York), May 1954
Koegler, Horst, "Gsovsky and the Dance Theater—Berlin", *Dance Magazine* (New York), October 1955
Goth, Trudy, "The Dancing World: Berlin", *Ballet Today* (London), January 1962
Sorrell, Walter, "Tatjana Gsovsky: A Prayer to the Deity", *Dance Magazine* (New York), August 1965
Geitel, Klaus, "Hommage à Tatjana Gsovsky", in *Ballett: Chronik und Bilanz des Ballettjahrs* (Velber and Hanover), 1966
Garske, Rolf, "Das Leben ist ein ewiger Tanz—Drei Kronzeugen geben Auskunft: Martha Graham, Tatjana Gsovsky, Gret Palucca", *Ballett: Chronik und Bilanz des Ballettjahrs* (Velber and Hanover), 1985

* * *

Tatjana Gsovsky was the major influence on German ballet in the years from 1930 to 1960. In fact, her influence still continues, through the work of her pupils who have dispersed into the European dance community.

Coming to Berlin in 1925 from Russia, where she had studied with leading classical ballet teachers, as well as at the Isadora Duncan Studio, Gsovsky soon founded her own school. Ballet was not solidly rooted in Germany at that time; the "Ausdruckstanz" (modern, or literally expressionist, dance) of Mary Wigman, Harald Kreuzberg, Rudolf von Laban, and Kurt Jooss was at its height. Germany's historical past had favoured autonomous states, each with its own opera house, where ballet was a poor cousin. Still, Berlin was the cultural centre and here Gsovsky trained an exceptional generation of ballet dancers.

Among them was Peter van Dijk, an outstanding premier danseur of dramatic warmth, clean technique, and great musicality—and the first German dancer to be appointed premier danseur étoile at the Paris Opéra, where he created leading roles. He later became artistic director and choreographer of the Hamburg Opera, and also of the Wiesbaden and Hanover companies.

Gert Reinholm, acclaimed in his prime as Germany's leading "Gestaltungstanzer" as Gsovsky's Hamlet, Orestes, and in other roles, became ballet director of the German Opera in Berlin after Gsovsky stepped down to take over the school.

Gsovsky furnished dancers to many major companies: Natascha Trofimova, critically acclaimed as Germany's best dancer in the 1950s, was prima ballerina in Berlin and Munich; the exquisite Maria Fris created roles in Janine Charrat's company and was ballerina for the Hamburg Opera at the time of her tragic suicide. Gisela Deege excelled in the dramatic and demi-caractère roles created for her by Gsovsky.

Gsovsky's teaching style embodied the best of the Russian method: fluid port de bras, supple backs, and above all, flow. Barre work was not a series of mechanical exercises, but embued already with dance quality. Gsovsky paid attention also to the subtleties of head and body alignment. As a teacher, she had the mesmerizing ability to inspire and draw from her pupils feats and qualities beyond their expectations.

Passionately and almost mystically devoted to dance, "Tatjana" had the capacity to transform the classroom into a temple, where dancers, often underfed and ill-equipped in the wartime and post-war period, worked with fanaticism to master technique.

Gsovsky was a victim of historical circumstance. The upheavals of the Second World War and the subsequent partition of Berlin hindered the development of German ballet. However, in the aftermath, the pendulum of public taste swung from modern dance to ballet. People sought the comfort of the classical line, the orderliness of ballet and its idealism.

Tatjana Gsovsky was the leading German choreographer in the post-war period. She led first the German State Opera of East Berlin and was then associated with the West Berlin State Opera. Her reputation was international, cemented by a sojourn in Buenos Aires as ballet mistress for the Teatro Colón and a commission to choreograph for the Ballet of La Scala in Milan.

Still, it was only in 1955 that Gsovsky at last realized her dream and formed a chamber group, the Berlin Ballet. This company toured widely and publicized the existence of German ballet. Certainly, the pioneering work of the Berlin Ballet paved the way for the dance developments of the 1960s, fostered by John Cranko in Stuttgart and John Neumeier in Hamburg.

Gsovsky was a prolific choreographer, favouring literary or mythological themes. (She was the daughter of a Moscow actress and "almost born in the theatre".) Sometimes, she wrote her own scenarios, as in *Signale*, involving a dramatic triangle of a railway signalman and his erring wife, or in *Undine* (*Ondine*), where she adapted the plot (quite different from Ashton's version) to include novel and charming touches of her own. Critics commented on the original, dramatic, and sometimes surreal ideas in her ballets. Her premieres always caused sensation and controversy. She collaborated with avant-garde composers from various fields and was open to new forms of expression. Though solidly rooted in classical tradition, she melded the ballet vocabulary with German expressionism to create her own idiosyncratic style. Acclaimed by European audiences, Gsovsky's choreography was seen as melodramatic and restless by North American critics during tours by the Berlin Ballet, though the dancers were considered strikingly gifted.

Gsovsky was not much interested in abstract dances; she felt only Balanchine could raise them above gymnastic exercises. She acknowledged the influence of Wigman and Graham on her work. In an interview with Walter Sorell, she said, "There's a strong spiritual tie between modern dance and ballet. All Muses must be seen as a single Deity. And the artists, 'the dream-walkers', pray to it, and to it they sacrifice their lives."

—Alanna Matthew

**GSOVSKY, Victor**

Russian dancer, choreographer, and teacher. Born Viktor Gzovsky (Gsovsky) in St. Petersburg, 12 January 1902. Studied with Evgenia Sokolova, Petrograd, from 1914. Married dancer Tatyana Isatchenko (Tatjana Gsovsky, or Gsovska). Stage début, Petrograd, 1920; left Russia, 1925: ballet master, State Opera, Berlin, 1925–28, and choreographer for UFA Film Company, Berlin, 1930–33; ballet master, Markova–Dolin company, 1937; choreographer, Paris Opéra, 1946, Roland Petit's Ballets des Champs-Elysées, Paris, 1946–47, and again 1948, 1953, and Metropolitan Ballet, London, 1947; ballet director, State Opera, Munich, 1950–52; worked as choreographer and ballet master in numerous other European locations, including Berlin, 1950 and 1952, Bordeaux, 1952; choreographer for the Grand Ballet du Marquis de Cuevas, Théâtre de l'Empire, Paris, 1953; ballet master, Düsseldorf Ballet, 1964–67, and Hamburg Ballet, 1967–70; also choreographer for several French films, including *Vautrin* (1943), *Un Seul Amour* (1943), *Un Revenant* (1946), *Par Ordre du Tsar* (or *Ungarische Rhapsodie*, 1954), *Cadet Rousselle* (1954), and for German film *Dans letzte Rezept* (1952); also teacher: founder and director of own school in Berlin, from 1928, and Paris, from 1938: students include Colette Marchand, Yvette Chauviré, Irène Skorik, Violette Verdy, Serge Perrault, Vera Zorina; occasional teacher, Hamburg State Opera Ballet, from 1971. Died in Hamburg, 14 March 1974.

## WORKS

1947 *Dances of Galanta* (mus. Kodály), Metropolitan Ballet, London
*Pygmalion* (mus. Field), Metropolitan Ballet, London

1948 *Pas de quatre* (mus. Strauss), Ballets des Champs-Elysées, Paris
*Mascarade* (mus. Bizet, Weingartner), Ballets des Champs-Elysées, Paris
*Fête galante* (mus. Arrieu), Ballets des Champs-Elysées, Paris
*Nocturne* (mus. Mozart), Ballets des Champs-Elysées, Paris

1949 *Grand Pas classique* (mus. Auber), Ballets des Champs-Elysées, Paris

1950 *Hamlet* (mus. Blacher), Bavarian State Opera, Munich
*Der 13 Juli* (mus. Offenbach), Bavarian State Opera, Munich

1951 *Kain Innocentius* (mus. Loeper), Bavarian State Opera, Munich
*Eine Kleine Nachtmusik* (mus. Mozart), State Opera, Munich
*Couperinsuite* (mus. Strauss), Bavarian State Opera, Munich
*Castor und Pollux* (mus. Rameau), Bavarian State Opera, Munich
*Pas de deux* (mus. Auber), Bavarian State Opera, Munich
*Cinderella* (mus. Prokofiev), Bavarian State Opera, Munich

1952 *Josephslegende* (mus. Strauss), Bavarian State Opera, Munich
*Der Weg zum Licht* (*Chemin de Lumière*; mus. Auric), Bavarian State Opera, Munich
*Pas de coeur* (mus. Einem), Bavarian State Opera, Munich
*Pas de action* (mus. Henze), Bavarian State Opera, Munich
*Antinoüs* (mus. Nicolaou), Grand Ballet du Marquis de Cuevas, Bordeaux

1953 *Aigrette* (mus. Chachavadze), Grand Ballet du Marquis de Cuevas, Paris
*La Perle* (mus. Pascal), Ballets de Paris de Roland Petit, Paris

1954 *Cinderella* (mus. Prokofiev), Opéra, Paris
*Eugene Onegin* (mus. Tchaikovsky), Ballet Comique, Oxford

1955 *Antar* (mus. Rimsky-Korsakov), Théâtre du Casino, Enghien
*La Dryade* (mus. Jordania), Théâtre du Casino, Enghien

Also staged:

1945 *Le Lac des cygnes* (Act II, after Ivanov; mus. Tchaikovsky), Opéra, Paris

1946 *La Sylphide* (after Taglioni; as reconstructed by Petit and Kochno), Ballets des Champs-Elysées, Paris

1948 *Grand Pas de deux* (*Le Mariage d'Aurore*, after Petipa; mus. Tchaikovsky), Ballets des Champs-Elysées, Paris
*La Fôret* (suite from *The Sleeping Beauty*, after Petipa; mus. Tchaikovsky), Ballets des Champs-Elysées, Paris

## PUBLICATIONS

Regner, O.F., *Das Ballettbuch*, Frankfurt, 1954
Robinson, Jacqueline, "Persons déja aux vacances prochaines", *La Danse* (Paris), April 1956
Testa, Alberto, "Italie", *La Danse* (Paris), January 1956
Hering, Doris, "Violette Lunaire", *Dance Magazine* (New York), April 1962
Chauviré, Yvette, "Hommage à Victor Gsovsky", *Les Saisons de la danse* (Paris), May 1974
Huckenpahler, Victoria, *Ballerina: A Biography of Violette Verdy*, New York, 1978

* * *

Born in St. Petersburg right after the turn of the century, Victor Gsovsky began his early studies with Evgenia Sokolova, one of the great Imperial Russian ballerinas of the Petipa era. He himself began to teach at an early age—and his superb natural gift for teaching was acknowledged throughout his career—but he did not remain in St. Petersburg for long. In 1925 he left Russia, moving to Berlin with his colleague and newly-wed bride, Tatyana Isatchenko. Soon after he was appointed ballet master of the State Opera, a post he held until 1928; after this, he and his wife (also an experienced teacher) opened their own school in Berlin, which was to produce such excellent dancers as Natasha Trofimova, Gisela Deege, Helga Sommerkamp, Gert Reinholm, and Rainer Koechermann.

In 1930, Gsovsky began working as a choreographer for the German UFA (Universum-Film-Aktiengesellschaft) film company, one of the most important film production companies in Europe at the time. Here he undoubtedly absorbed some of the influences of a more "modern" art form and its diverse media, but his adherence to the principles of balletic classicism learned in St. Petersburg remained with him throughout both his teaching and his choreographic career. After his early work in Berlin, Gsovsky embarked on what remained essentially a freelance career as ballet master, teacher, choreographer, and authority on the Russian classical repertoire. He worked as ballet master for the Markova–Dolin Company and the Metropolitan Ballet in England, for the Paris Opéra and Petit's

Ballets des Champs-Elysées in Paris, and later for the Düsseldorf and Hamburg companies in Germany. For the most part his career remained centred in Paris during the late 1930s and 1940s, and his own classes, which he began teaching in 1938 in Paris, became the training ground for leading young French dancers of the day, including Irène Skorik, Colette Marchand, Violette Verdy, Serge Perrault, and Yvette Chauviré.

One ballerina who attributed a great deal of her success to Gsovsky was Violette Verdy. She first encountered Gsovsky's excellent teaching methods when an apprentice to the newly-formed Ballets de Champs-Elysées in 1946, and as she developed into a ballerina Gsovsky became her mentor and coach. It was he who first taught her the variations from the nineteenth-century classics, bringing not just a technical, academic background but an intuitive understanding of style and artistic nuance to his teaching of each role. In her biography of Verdy, Victoria Huckenpahler writes of these early sessions: "After warming up she would begin her hour-and-a-half sessions with Gsovsky during which he not only taught her the choreography, but also imparted the emotional overtones of each ballet. His lessons were particularly valuable for, having seen many of the classical roles portrayed by legendary artists, he was able to pass along first-hand recollections of their interpretations." Verdy herself paid tribute to Gsovsky's excellent teaching methods, explaining that in his classes "Gsovsky went beyond [pure academism], creating small enchaînments as he taught. His phrasing was remarkable." As for Gsvosky's own personal coaching of her, Verdy from the start acknowledged the Russian ballet master's hugely important part in her developing artistry.

Ultimately Gsovsky's career was uneven and largely peripatetic, perhaps due to his alcoholism—the result of which, writes Huckenpahler, being that he "tragically . . . never attained the heights of which he was capable". Despite this fundamental weakness, however, Gsovky still made a fundamental contribution to the development of classical ballet in Europe before and after the Second World War, and the fact that he held a number of different posts meant that his influence was widespread. His stagings of the classics, such as his important revival of *La Sylphide* for the Ballets des Champs-Elysées in 1946, meant that many of the traditions of a previous era in classical ballet were kept alive in the twentieth century. His famous *Grand Pas classique*, created for a single gala performance in 1949, is still in the repertoire of many modern ballet companies, and remains a true technical and artistic challenge for any pair of dancers that attempts it. As a teacher, whose expertise was brought to countless students in France, England, and Germany (where he returned for the last decade of his career), Gsovsky was always hugely admired, remembered by Horst Koegler as "one of the most internationally respected teachers of his generation."

—Amanda Chisnell

---

## GUGLIELMO EBREO

(also Guillaume le Juif, or William the Jew of Pesaro)

Italian dancing master, choreographer, and theoretician. Born in Pesaro, c. 1420. Studied with dancing master Domenico de Piacenza (also known as Domenico da Ferrara), most likely in Piacenza, c. 1440s. Travelled in Italy, teaching social dance, and performing and staging balli at various courts; was dancing master to Isabella d'Este in Ferrara; arranged, along with Domenico, dances for wedding of Constanzio Sforza and Camilla d'Aragon, 1465; wrote major treatise on dance, 1463. Recipient: Knighthood from Emperor Frederick III, Venice, 1469. Died c. 1481.

### PUBLICATIONS

By Ebreo:

*Guglielmi Hebraei pisauriensis de pratica seu arte tripudii vulgare opusculum*, 1463

About Ebreo:

Kinkeldey, Otto, "A Jewish Dancing Master of the Renaissance: Guglielmo Ebreo", in *Studies in Jewish Bibliography and Related Subjects in Memory of Abraham Solomon Freidus*, New York, 1929

Kirstein, Lincoln, *Dance: A Short History of Classic Theatrical Dancing*, New York, 1935

Dolmetsch, Mabel, *Dances of Spain and Italy 1400–1600*, London, 1954; reprinted New York, 1975

Brainard, Ingrid, "Bassedanse, Bassadanza and Ballo in the 15th Century", *Dance History Research: Perspectives from Related Arts and Disciplines*, New York, 1970

*The Art of Courtly Dancing in the Early Renaissance*, West Newton, Massachusetts, 1981

Sorrell, Walter, *Dance in its Time*, New York, 1981

*Guglielmo Ebreo da Pesaro e la danza nelle corti italiane del XV secolo*, Proceedings of International Conference, Pesaro (July 1987), Milan, 1990

* * *

The fifteenth-century Jewish Italian dancing master and choreographer Guglielmo Ebreo was born in Pesaro. He was a contemporary of Antonio Cornazano, and both were pupils of Domenico, probably at his school at Piacenza in the 1440s. It is now generally accepted that in about 1460 he became a Christian and took the name of Johannis (Giovanni) Ambrosio, possibly in order to advance his social and professional status. In 1469 he was knighted by the Emperor Frederick III in Venice. Guglielmo travelled extensively throughout the major courts of Italy, including Naples, Urbino, Milan, Pavia, and Ferrara (where he was dancing master to Isabella d'Este), teaching, performing, and choreographing court festivities. When the Sforza family of Pesaro sent Guglielmo to Milan in 1480, he was recommended as the finest dancer in Italy.

There are seven major versions of his treatise, *Guglielmi Hebraei pisauriensis de pratica seu arte tripudii vulgare opusculum* (1463)—two of which are lost (Pesaro and Urbino)—whereas only one copy each of those of Domenico and Cornazano is extant. Guglielmo Ebreo's treatise is divided into two main parts, the theoretical and the practical. Of the three major fifteenth-century dancing masters, Guglielmo writes with most eloquence about the importance of music in the art of dancing. The beginning of his treatise is concerned entirely with music, its antiquity and origin. He emphasizes the virtue of music in order to elevate the status of dancing to that of a liberal art rather than a mere pastime. He appears to be particularly anxious to give dignity to the art of dancing, and presents a spiritual vindication of dance by associating it inextricably with music—which he describes as a sublime and virtuous art more akin to human nature than the other arts, since it has the power to calm the passions, console the spirit, and delight the mind. Music is formed by four consonant voices which correspond to the four elements and the four humours, which must all harmonize perfectly with each other. The virtue of dancing, he writes, is nothing but the external manifestation of inner states of mind, inspired by the affective power of music to move the spirit, which in turn moves the body. The manner in which a person dances is a mirror of the state of the soul.

Guglielmo emphasizes the intellectual and moral aspects of dancing; dance theory is firmly based on reason with strict rules of deportment and decorum. He criticizes those who consider themselves to be masters of dancing but cannot tell the right foot from the left, and think they can become experts in three days.

He defends dance against attacks that it leads to immoral behaviour, by dissociating it from the abandoned and lascivious dancing of the common people who abuse the art to satisfy their lusts. He writes his treatise exclusively for an aristocratic circle of friends, maintaining a strong distinction between the noble and graceful dancing of the courtier and his lady, and the uncontrolled and vulgar dancing of the lower orders. He stresses that dancing is a virtuous art for those of gentle birth who have a natural aptitude for it. His treatise reflects strongly the growing segregation of court and country manners, and the exclusively of an art form which is strictly rule-governed, with new dances known only to an élite and courtly circle.

His treatise includes dances by Domenico, Lorenzo de' Medici, and Guiseppe Ebreo. His own dances are mainly the basic kinds of fifteenth-century courtly dances, the Bassa Danza and the Ballo. He gives helpful advice to aspiring choreographers and suggests ways in which the dance student can test his musical awareness.

—Françoise Carter

---

**GUILLEM, Sylvie**

French dancer. Born in Paris, 23 February 1965. Trained first as a gymnast; studied at the Paris Opéra Ballet School, from 1976. Dancer, Paris Opéra Ballet, from 1981: quadrille, from 1981; coryphée, from 1982; sujet, from 1983; promoted to premiere danseuse, and five days later to étoile, 1984; performed in Japan and New York with Paris Opéra Ballet, 1986; has appeared frequently as guest artist, including at Sofia Opera House, 1984, German Opera Ballet, Berlin, 1985, Teatro Comunale, Florence, and La Scala, Milan, and Lisbon, 1987, Kirov Ballet, Leningrad (now St. Petersburg), 1990; guest ballerina, Royal Ballet, 1988, returning as principal guest artist, various seasons, from 1989; principal guest artist, American Ballet Theatre, 1991; has also appeared on television, including in Natalia Makarova's *Ballerina* (BBC, 1988), and in French television documentary *Sylvie Guillem au travail* (1987). Recipient: Gold Medal, International Ballet Competition, Varna, 1983; Carpeaux Prize, 1984; Prix Andersen, Copenhagen, 1988; Commandeur des arts et des lettres, 1988; Grand Prix de la danse, Ministère de la Culture, France, 1988.

**ROLES**

1983 Queen of the Dryads in *Don Quixote* (Petipa; staged Nureyev), Paris Opéra Ballet, Paris
Pas Hongrois in *Raymonda* (Petipa; staged Nureyev), Paris Opéra Ballet, Paris
1984 Clemence, Henrietta in *Raymonda* (Petipa; staged Nureyev), Paris Opéra Ballet, Paris
Solo variation, "Kingdom of the Shades" in *La Bayadère* (Petipa; staged Nureyev), Paris Opéra Ballet, Paris
Principal dancer (cr) in *France/Dance* (Forsythe), Paris Opéra Ballet, Paris
Principal dancer in *Divertimento No. 15* (Balanchine), Paris Opéra Ballet, Paris
Odette/Odile in *Swan Lake* (Petipa, Ivanov; staged Nureyev), Sofia Opera Ballet, Sofia
Principal dancer (cr) in *No Man's Land* (van Dantzig), Paris Opéra Ballet, Paris
Principal dancer (cr) in *GV 10* (Armitage), Paris Opéra Ballet, Paris
Kitri in *Don Quixote* (Petipa; staged Nureyev), Paris Opéra Ballet, Paris
Principal dancer in *Bhakti* III (Béjart), Cuba Festival
1985 Juliet in *Romeo and Juliet* (Nureyev), Paris Opéra Ballet, Paris
Second Movement (Adagio) in *Le Palais de cristal* (*Symphony in C*; Balanchine), Paris Opéra Ballet, Paris
Pas de deux in *Agon* (Balanchine), Paris Opéra Ballet, Paris
Principal dancer (cr) in *Premier Orage* (Childs), Paris Opéra Ballet, Paris
Principal dancer (cr) in *Before Nightfall* (Christe), Paris Opéra Ballet, Paris
Pas de deux (cr) in *Mouvement—Rythme—Étude* (Béjart), Paris Opéra Ballet, Paris
Title role in *Giselle* (Petipa after Coralli, Perrot), Paris Opéra Ballet, Paris
Principal dancer in *Song of the Earth* (MacMillan), Paris Opéra Ballet, Paris
Principal dancer in *Continuo* (Tudor), Paris Opéra Ballet, Paris
Principal dancer in *Adagietto* (Araiz), German Opera Ballet, Berlin
1986 Title role (cr) in *Cendrillon* (*Cinderella*; Nureyev), Paris Opéra Ballet, Paris
Principal dancer (cr) in *Arepo* (Béjart), Paris Opéra Ballet, Paris
Principal dancer in *Le Corsaire* Pas de deux (after Petipa), Paris Opéra Ballet, Paris
Principal dancer in *Grand Pas classique* (also *Grand Pas d'Auber*; Gsovsky), French television
Title role in *Raymonda* (Nureyev after Petipa), Paris Opéra Ballet, New York
The Woman in *Bolero* (Béjart), Paris Opéra Ballet, Paris
Principal dancer in *Sonate à trois* (Béjart), Paris Opéra Ballet, Paris
Principal dancer in *In Memory of . . .* (Robbins), Paris Opéra Ballet, Paris
1987 "Cigarette" variation in *Suite en blanc* (Lifar), Paris Opéra Ballet, New York
Principal dancer (cr) in *In the Middle, Somewhat Elevated* (Forsythe), Paris Opéra Ballet, Paris
Principal dancer (cr) in *Magnificat* (Forsythe), Paris Opéra Ballet, Paris
Principal dancer in *Symphony in Three Movements* (Balanchine), Paris Opéra Ballet, Paris
Principal dancer in *Four Last Songs* (van Dantzig), Paris Opéra Ballet, Paris
Kitri (cr) in *Don Quixote* (new production; Nureyev after Petipa), La Scala, Milan
1988 Saint-Sebastien (cr) in *Le Martyre de Saint-Sebastien* (Wilson), Paris Opéra Ballet
Esmeralda in *Notre-Dame de Paris* (Petit), Paris Opéra Ballet, Paris

**Sylvie Guillem as Juliet in Macmillan's *Romeo and Juliet*, Royal Ballet**

Terpsichore in *Apollo* (Balanchine), Royal Ballet, London
1989 Gamzatti in *La Bayadère* (Makarova after Petipa), Royal Ballet, London
Nikiya in *La Bayadère* (Makarova after Petipa), Royal Ballet, London
Princess Aurora in *The Sleeping Beauty* (Petipa, Ashton; staged de Valois), Royal Ballet, London
1990 Juliet in *Romeo and Juliet* (MacMillan), Royal Ballet, London
Title role in *Cinderella* (Ashton), Royal Ballet, London
Natalia Petrovna in *A Month in the Country* (Ashton), Royal Ballet, London
Princess Rose in *The Prince of the Pagodas* (MacMillan), Royal Ballet, London
Principal dancer in *Other Dances* (Robbins), Royal Ballet, London
Manon in *L'Histoire de Manon* (*Manon*; MacMillan), Paris Opéra Ballet, Paris
1991 Lizzie Borden in *Fall River Legend* (de Mille), American Ballet Theatre, New York
Kitri in *Don Quixote* (Vasiliev after Petipa), American Ballet Theatre, New York

**PUBLICATIONS**

By Guillem:

Interview in Craine, Debra, "Tempestuous Talent", *The Times Saturday Review* (London), 23 June 1990
Interview, "Everybody Could Learn from Each Other", *Dance and Dancers* (London), December 1991

About Guillem:

Diénis, Jean-Claude, "La Bonne Étoile de Sylvie Guillem", *Danser* (Paris), February 1985
Passet, Dominique, "Sylvie Guillem", *Danser* (Paris), November 1986
Merrett, Sue, "Sylvie Guillem", *Dancing Times* (London), January 1988
"Personality of the Month: Sylvie Guillem", *Dance and Dancers* (London), April 1989

* * *

Sylvie Guillem's early career marked her as one of the greatest technicians of all time. A tall dancer, she possesses a phenomenal technique based on steel-hard virtuosity and elastic suppleness, with flamboyantly high extensions that recall her early gymnastic training. She has left critics straining for superlatives and box office managers eyeing their swollen coffers with glee. In demand around the world as a guest artist, she has also expanded the boundaries for other dancers. Ballet after Guillem will never be the same. But despite the accolade of world's greatest ballerina, she is clearly not a dancer for all seasons. Although her technical wizardry knows no limits, her dramatic ability does, and a tendency to overstate her physical prowess is perhaps her greatest flaw. Only time will tell if her early pyrotechnics will develop into a mature magic.

Sylvie Guillem was introduced to Covent Garden by Rudolf Nureyev, who spotted in his young protégée at the Paris Opéra Ballet the qualities that would make her an undoubted star. In her Royal Opera House début, he danced Albrecht to her Giselle, a role somewhat at odds with her naturally exhibitionist performing style, yet one she imbued with a coquettish grace and ethereal beauty. Her arrival at the Royal Ballet a year later as a permanent guest artist caused a sensation, her reputation as a prima donna attracting as much publicity as the novelty of her extraordinary extensions. But soon some critics began to complain of an emotional coolness and a studied approach to her dramatic interpretations, showing the application of intelligence rather than feelings.

Her Odette/Odile was a case in point. Whereas the languorous flexibility of her long limbs and the finesse of her attack were admirably suited to the role's contrasting physical demands, the classical proportions of Swan Lake did not sit well on her. Further, her dramatic response lacked warmth, and the remote imperiousness of her Odette failed to move the heart, despite the ballerina's forceful presence on stage and the exciting sense of timing she revealed in an ability to mould Tchaikovsky's score to her own particular lyricism. Her extroverted stage persona and competitive streak, rather, were at their finest in *La Bayadère*, especially in the first-act garden scene choreography for Gamzatti. In one especially delightful performance, Guillem and Russian star Faruk Ruzimatov literally battled it out in Olympic-style rivalry for the audience's affection. Yet even in the more spiritual role of Nikiya, Guillem shone with an inner sincerity and beauty.

Her attempts at the British repertoire provided the most interest, if not the most success. Tackling the role of Natalia Petrovna in Ashton's *A Month in the Country* was a brave decision. Although Guillem lacked the subtlety of gesture and the sheer acting skills required to make Ashton's ballet work, her effort revealed a new and humbler artist, one prepared to venture outside the established formula. Much happier in the ballets of Kenneth MacMillan, she triumphed as Juliet. From the girlish impetuosity of the early scenes to the luscious passion of her balcony pas de deux with Jonathan Cope, this was a performance that gave us glimpses of a dramatic richness which, if developed, could catapult Guillem into the ranks of the truly great ballerinas.

—Debra Craine

---

**GUIMARD, Marie-Madeleine**

French dancer. Born in Paris (baptized 27 December) 1743. Married dancer Jean-Etienne Despréaux (upon retiring from stage), 1789. Dancer, corps de ballet, Comédie-Française, from c.1753; official début, 1756; joined L'Académie royale de la musique (Paris Opéra), 1762, with début in *Les Caractères de la danse*; appointed première danseuse de demi-caractère, 1766; made many appearances before the court at Versailles and Fontainebleau; followed ballet master Noverre to London: guest dancer, King's Theatre and Covent Garden, London, 1789, retiring from the stage in the same year; also teacher: students include Opéra dancer Mlle. Gosselin; opened own theatre, Temple of Terpsichore, Paris, 1772; closed, for financial reasons (sold off by lottery tickets), 1785. Died in Paris, 4 May 1816.

**ROLES**

1762 Danseuse in *Les Caractères de la danse* (ballet; mus. Rebel), Opéra, Paris
Terpsichore in *Les Fêtes grecques et romaines* (ballet héroïque; mus. de Blamont), Opéra, Paris
Dancer in *La Guirlande* (ballet; mus. Rameau), Opéra, Paris
Dancer (cr) in *L'Opéra de société* (ballet; mus. Giraud), Opéra, Paris
1764 Ombre heureuse in *Castor et Pollux* (tragédie-lyrique; mus Rameau), Opéra, Paris
Eglé chanté et dansé in *Les Fêtes d'Hébé; ou, Les Talents lyriques* (ballet; mus. Rameau), Opéra, Paris
Flore in *Naïs* (ballet; mus. Rameau), Opéra, Paris
Amazone in *Tancrède* (tragédie-lyrique; mus. Campra), Opéra, Paris
Statue animée, "Pigmalion" entrée in *Les Triomphes des arts* (ballet; mus. de la Barre, de Sovot, Rameau), Opéra, Paris
1765 Dancer in *Le Devin du village* (intermède; mus. Rousseau), Opéra, Paris
Dancer in *Fêtes de l'Hymen et de l'Amour* (ballet; mus. Rameau), Opéra, Paris
Dancer in *Les Fêtes de Thalie* (ballet; mus. Mouret), Opéra, Paris
Dancer in *Erosine* (pastorale-héroïque; mus. Berton, chor. Laval, father and son), Court Theatre, Fontainebleau
Bergère in *Thésée* (tragédie-lyrique; mus. Mondonville, chor. Laval, father and son), Opéra, Paris
Nymphe and Venus (cr) in *Sylvie* (ballet; chor. Laval, father and son), Court Theatre, Fontainebleau
Dancer in *Thétis et Pelée* (tragédie-lyrique; mus. Colasse, chor. Laval, father and son), Court Theatre, Fontainebleau
Dancer in *La Fée Urgele* (comedy; mus. Duni, chor. Laval, father and son), Court Theatre, Fontainebleau
Dancer in ballet fragments from *Prologue des amours des dieux* (mus. Mouret), *L'Amour enjoue* (mus. Dauvergne), and *La Danse* (ballet; mus. Rameau, all chor. Laval, father and son), Court Theatre, Versailles
Dancer in Prologue and *Les Sauvages* from *Les Indes galantes* (ballet; mus. Rameau, chor. Laval, father and son), Court Theatre, Versailles
Dancer in *Intermèdes d'amour pour amour* (comedy; mus. Rameau, chor. Laval, father and son), Court Theatre, Versailles
Dancer in *Les Incas du Perou* (ballet; mus. Rameau, chor. Laval, father and son), Court Theatre, Versailles
Dancer in *Palmire* (ballet-héroïque; mus. de la Borde, Buni, chor. Laval, father and son), Court Theatre, Fontainebleau
Dancer in *Ballet d'Eglé* (ballet; mus. d'Auvergne, chor. Laval, father and son), Court Theatre, Fontainebleau

**Marie Guimard in *La Chercheuse d'esprit***

1766 Dancer in *Les Fêtes lyriques* (fragments from different ballets), Opéra, Paris
Sultan in *La Turquie* from *L'Europe galante* (ballet; mus. Campra), Opéra, Paris
Nymphe in *Zélindor, roi des sylphes* (ballet; mus. Rebel, Francoeur), Opéra, Paris
1767 Jardinière in *Le Carnaval du Parnasse* (ballet; mus. Mondonville), Opéra, Paris
Dancer in *Le Feu* and *La Terre* from *Les Éléments* (ballet; mus. Destouches), Opéra, Paris
Dancer (cr) in *Ernelinde* (tragédie-lyrique; mus. Philidor), Opéra, Paris
Bergère in *Hippolyte et Aricie* (tragédie-lyrique; mus. Rameau), Opéra, Paris
Dancer (cr) in *Theonis* (pastorale; mus. Berton, Trial), Opéra, Paris
1768 Chasseresse in *Daphne et Alcimadure* (pastorale; mus. Mondonville), Opéra, Paris
Dancer in *Dardanus* (tragédie-lyrique; mus. Rameau), Opéra, Paris
Dancer in *Tithon et l'Aurore* (pastorale; mus. Mondonville), Opéra, Paris
Dancer in *La Vénitienne* (comedy; new version, mus. Dauvergne), Opéra, Paris
Victorine in *Philosophe sans le savoir* (lib. Sedaine), Opéra, Paris
1769 Lycoris in *Anacreon* (ballet; mus. Rameau), Opéra, Paris
Dancer in *Les Amours de Ragonde* (*Le Mariage de Ragonde et de Colin; ou, La Veillée de village* (opéra-ballet; mus. Mouret), Opéra, Paris
Dancer in *Énée et Lavinie* (tragédie-lyrique; new version, mus. Dauvergne), Opéra, Paris
Dancer in *Erigone* from *Fêtes de Paphos* (ballet; mus. Mondonville), Opéra, Paris
Lucinde in *Zaïs* (ballet; mus. Rameau), Opéra, Paris
1770 Dancer in *Zoroastre* (tragédie-lyrique; mus. Rameau), Opéra, Paris
Créuse in *Jason et Médée* (ballet; G. Vestris after Noverre), Opéra, Paris
Grand Prêtresse de Junon in *Alcyone* (tragédie-lyrique; mus. Marais), Opéra, Paris
Dancer in *Aeglé* (ballet-héroïque; mus. de la Garde, chor. Laval), Court Theatre, Fontainebleau
1771 Dancer in *La Cinquantaine* (pastorale; mus. la Borde), Opéra, Paris
Dancer in *La Sybylle* from *Fêtes d'Euterpe* (ballet; mus. Dauvergne), Opéra, Paris
Esprit aérien in *Pyrame et Thisbé* (tragédie-lyrique; mus. Rebel, Francoeur), Opéra, Paris
Leading dancer in *Le Devin de village* (intermède; mus. Rousseau, chor. after Noverre), Opéra, Paris
1772 Dancer in *Adèle de Ponthieu* (tragédie-lyrique; mus. Berton), Opéra, Paris
Amante in *Aline, reine de Golconde* (ballet; mus. Monsigny), Opéra, Paris
Dancer (cr) in *Eglé* (ballet; mus. la Garde), Opéra, Paris
1773 Diane (cr) in *Endymion* (ballet; G. Vestris), Opéra, Paris
Dancer in *Ismène* (pastorale; mus. Rebel, Francoeur), Opéra, Paris
Dancer (cr) in *L'Union de l'amour et des arts* (ballet; mus. Floquet), Opéra, Paris
Dancer in *Céphale et Procris; ou, L'Amour conjugal* (tragédie-lyrique; mus. Grétry), Court Theatre, Versailles
Dancer in *Les Mélanges liriques* (ballet-héroïque; mus. Rebel, Francoeur), Opéra, Paris
1774 Ariane (cr) in *Azolan; ou, Le Serment indiscret* (ballet; mus. Floquet), Opéra, Paris
Dancer (cr) in *Iphigénie en Aulide* (tragédie-lyrique; mus. Gluck), Opéra, Paris
Dancer (cr) in *Orphée* (tragédie-lyrique; mus. Gluck), Opéra, Paris
Dancer (cr) in *Sabinus* (tragédie-lyrique; mus. Gossec), Opéra, Paris
1775 Dancer (cr) in *Alexis et Daphne* (pastorale; mus. Gossec), Opéra, Paris
Dancer (cr) in *Céphale et Procris* (new version; tragédie-lyrique; mus. Grétry), Opéra, Paris
Dancer (cr) in *Cythère assiègée* (ballet; mus. Gluck), Opéra, Paris
1776 Dancer in *L'Union de l'Amour et des arts* (opéra-ballet; mus. Floquet), Opéra, Paris
Campaspe (cr) in *Apelles et Campaspe* (ballet, revival; mus. Rodolphe, chor. Noverre), Opéra, Paris
Galathée in *Les Caprices de Galathée* (ballet; Noverre), Opéra, Paris
1777 Dancer in *Les Horaces* (ballet; Noverre), Opéra, Paris
Dancer (cr) in *Myrtil et Lycoris* (pastorale; mus. Desormery), Opéra, Paris
Dancer in *Tibule; ou, Les Saturnales*, entrée from *Les Fêtes grecques et romaines* (opéra; mus. Candeille), for Duc d'Orléans, Paris
Title role (cr) in *Ninette à la cour* (ballet d'action; M. Gardel), Court Theatre, Choisy
Nicette (cr) in *La Chercheuse d'esprit* (ballet; M. Gardel), Court Theatre, Choisy (revived at Opéra in same year)
1778 Bergère (cr) in *Les Petits Riens* (ballet; Noverre), Opéra, Paris
Dancer in *Momie* (opéra burlesque; lib. Despreaux), Court Theatre, Choisy
Dancer in *Phaon* (lyric drama mixed with song; M. Gardel), Court Theatre, Choisy
1779 Dancer in *Amadis* (tragédie-lyrique; new version, mus. Bach), Opéra, Paris
Bergère (cr) in *Echo et Narcisse* (pastorale; mus. Gluck), Opéra, Paris
Mirza (cr) in *Mirza et Lindor* (ballet; M. Gardel), Opéra, Paris
Divertissement (cr) in *Iphigénie en Tauride* (opéra; mus. Piccini), Opéra, Paris
1780 Dancer in *Andromaque* (tragédie-lyrique; Dauberval), Opéra, Paris
Divertissment from *Le Seigneur bienfaisant* (Dauberval, Noverre, M. Gardel), Opéra, Paris
1781 Mirza (cr) in *La Fête de Mirza* (ballet; M. Gardel), Opéra, Paris
1782 Terpsichore (cr) in *Apollon et Daphne* (ballet; mus. Mayer), Opéra, Paris
Paysanne (cr) in *La Double Épreuve; ou, Colinette à la cour* (opera; mus. Grétry), Opéra, Paris
Dancer (cr) in *L'Embarras de richesses* (comic opera; mus. Grétry, chor. M. Gardel), Opéra, Paris
Dancer in *Thésée* (tragédie-lyrique; new version, mus. Gossec), Opéra, Paris
1783 Dancer in *Atys* (tragédie-lyrique; new version, mus. Piccini), Opéra, Paris
Dancer (cr) in *Peronne sauvée* (opera; mus. Dezaides), Opéra, Paris
Bergère (cr) in *Renaud* (tragédie-lyrique; mus. Sacchini), Opéra, Paris
Surveillante (cr) in *La Rosière* (ballet; M. Gardel), Opéra, Paris

Divertissement from *Didon* (tragédie-lyrique; mus. Marmontel), Opéra, Paris
1784 Lucinde (cr) in *L'Oracle* (ballet; M. Gardel), Opéra, Paris
Dancer in *Tibulle*, entrée from *Fêtes grecques et romaines* (ballet; new version, mus. Mlle Beaumesnil), Opéra, Paris
Divertissement from *Chimène; ou, Le Cid* (tragédie-lyrique; mus. Sacchini), Opéra, Paris
Divertissement from *Les Danaïdes* (tragédie-lyrique; mus. Gluck, Salieri, chor. M. Gardel), Opéra, Paris
Divertissement from *Diane et Endymion* (opera; mus. Piccini), Opéra, Paris
Divertissement from *Dardanus* (tragédie-lyrique; mus. Sacchini), Opéra, Paris
1785 Dancer (cr) in *Panurge dans l'île des lanternes* (opera; mus. Grétry), Opéra, Paris
Dancer (cr) in *Pizarre* (opera; mus. Candeille), Opéra, Paris
Melite (cr) in *Le Premier Navigateur; ou, Le Pouvoir de l'amour* (ballet; M. Gardel), Opéra, Paris
1786 Dancer (cr) in *Rosine* (opera; mus. Gossec), Opéra, Paris
Dancer (cr) in *Les Sauvages* (ballet; M. and P. Gardel), Opéra, Paris
Dancer in *Syncope, reine de Mic-Mac* (parody by Despreaux), Court Theatre, Versailles
Louise (cr) in *Le Déserteur* (ballet; M. Gardel), Court Theatre, Fontainebleau
Dancer in *Phèdre* (tragédie-lyrique; mus. Lemoyne, chor. M. Gardel), Opéra, Paris
Dancer in *Oedipe à Colonne* (tragédie-lyrique; mus. Sacchini, chor. M. Gardel), Court Theatre, Versailles
1787 Dancer (cr) in *Alcindor* (opera; mus. Dezaides), Opéra, Paris
Maitresse du Garçon (cr) in *Le Coq du village* (ballet; M. Gardel), Opéra, Paris
Dancer in *Penelope* (tragédie-lyrique; mus. Piccini), Opéra, Paris
Divertissement from *Tarare* (opera; mus. Salieri, chor. P. Gardel), Opéra, Paris
1788 Dancer in *Armire et Evelina* (tragédie-lyrique; mus. Sacchini), Opéra, Paris
Dancer in *La Toison d'or; ou, Médée à Colchos* (tragédie-lyrique; mus. Vogel), Opéra, Paris
1789 Divertissement from *Aspasie* (opera; mus. Grétry, chor. P. Gardel), Opéra, Paris
Dancer (cr) in *Pas de deux Anacréontique* (Noverre), King's Theatre, London
Dancer in *Minuet de la cour*, King's Theatre, London
Anette (cr) in *Anette et Lubin* (ballet; Noverre), King's Theatre, London
Galathée in *Les Caprices de Galathée* (ballet; Noverre), King's Theatre, London
Ninette in *Ninette à la cour* (ballet; Gardel after Noverre), King's Theatre, London
Dancer in *Le Tuteur trompé* (ballet; Le Picq), King's Theatre, London
Dancer in *Les Folies d'Espagne* (ballet), King's Theatre, London
Dancer in *Pas de deux russe*, King's Theatre, London

## PUBLICATIONS


Noverre, Jean Georges, *Lettres sur la danse et les ballets*, Stuttgart, Lyons, 1760; translated as *Letters on Dancing and Ballets* by C.W. Beaumont, London, 1930

Jal, A., *Dictionnaire critique de biographie et d'histoire*, second edition, Paris, 1872

Campardon, Émile, *L'Académie royale de musique*, 2 volumes, Paris, 1881

Goncourt, Edmond de, *La Guimard*, Paris, 1893; reprinted Geneva, 1973

Beaumont, Cyril, *Three French Dancers of the Eighteenth Century*, London, 1934

Moore, Lillian, *Artists of the Dance*, New York, 1938

Lynham, Deryck, *The Chevalier Noverre: The Father of Modern Ballet*, London, 1950

Daniels, Diana, "The First Ballerina?", *Dance Magazine* (London), January 1960

Migel, Parmenia, *The Ballerinas*, New York, 1972


* * *

Marie-Madeleine Guimard, one of the most celebrated ballerinas of the Paris Opéra, was a great dramatic dancer who excelled in pantomime action combined with graceful exhibitions of terre-à-terre dancing. The *Mercure de France* described her as "this charming actress-dancer, who, through her artistry, can transform herself into whatever she wishes to be". In her 27 years of service to the Opéra, Guimard was so popular that she appeared before the public almost without respite, dancing the leading roles in over 100 ballets and operas. She danced in ballets choreographed by Laval, Noverre, and the two Gardels; she was featured in operas written by Gluck, Mozart, Rameau, and many of the great composers of the day.

Guimard first danced, as a child of ten, in the corps de ballet of the Comédie-Française, making her début in 1756. Four years after her Paris Opéra debut in Rebel's *Les Caractères de la danse* (1762), she was appointed first dancer of demi-caractere. In one of her earliest appearances at the Paris Opéra, she danced the part of Terpsichore in *Les Fêtes grecques et romaines* (1762). Her association with the muse of dancing was life-long: in 1772, she constructed an opulent new home, complete with her statue in the guise of Terpsichore at the front gate and with Fragonard's portrait of herself as Terpsichore in the grand salon, and named it the Temple of Terpsichore. Such pretensions encouraged some to mock the dancer, who was unfashionably thin, as "the Skeleton of the Graces".

In one of her greatest roles, she was cast as Nicette in Gardel's *La Chercheuse d'esprit*. She played a simpleton—naïve, graceful, and mischievous. The audience was astounded by Guimard's ability to play this character, because off-stage she was infamous as mistress of bishops and princes, known as a courtesan who revelled in luxury and performed pornographic ballets in her own private theatre. Grimm declared of her interpretation that never had he seen such a "gradation of nuances conveyed so finely, so accurately, so delicately, in such piquant style; only the most ingenious poetry could render such characters with so much spirit, delicacy, and truth". Even in her forties, the ever-youthful Guimard was famed for her heart-warming depictions of young women who resonated with innocence and goodness. Her characters were precursors, in some respects, of Romantic heroines, such as *Giselle* or *La Somnambule*. Even her dress in Gardel's *Le Premier Navigateur* anticipated the Romantic tutu: she wore a simple white muslin gown with blue sash; her hair flowed loosely about her shoulders; and her feet were shod in soft sandals rather than the usual high heels.

Guimard remained at the Paris Opéra until she retired in 1789, and then followed Noverre to London, where she appeared for one season. The English, she noted with some bemusement, adored her to the point of madness, and she seized the moment of triumph to retire at the height of her powers. Although she abjured the theatre for a Christian marriage to a dancer, Jean-Etienne Despréaux, her love of dance led her to devise strategies to continue. The couple occasionally invited friends to performances, using a curtained stage that revealed the aged ballerina's dancing feet or her fingers marking out steps on the tabletop. She also taught Mlle. Gosselin, the greatest French ballerina of the next generation.

In an age when women were generally denied access to positions of authority, Guimard was widely recognized as the power behind the scenes at the Paris Opéra and was feared by its administrators. Her nineteenth-century biographer, Goncourt, castigated her as a trouble-maker and leader of cabals, whereas modern feminist historians might be more inclined to interpret her actions as consistent with those of an early advocate of women's rights. Guimard challenged high salaries given to the male stars and dared to ask for parity. The institution was noted for its autocratic style of management, but Guimard agitated for a voice in its governance. She urged dancers to stand united in their demands rather than to fragment as had recently happened with Parlement. She persuaded so many dancers to follow her lead that M. de la Ferte reported to his superiors that "she was in effect the director" of the Opéra. Guimard was, he complained, "an enormous expense" to the Opéra because women dancers, by dint of her example, insisted upon higher pay.

Guimard was the interpreter par excellence of the rococo style of ballet, particularly the dramatic *ballets en action* that were characteristic of that period. Her dancing combined eloquent gestures with subtle coquetry, emphasizing the sentimental value of the naïve characters in which she specialized. Noverre, in his *Letters*, praised Guimard for the ease, balance, nimbleness, and precision of her dance, as well as the ability to make her gestures as expressive as her face. Her charm, he maintained, derived from a combination of "tenderness" and "voluptuousness", which conveyed an unusual "spiritual" quality to her dance. Noverre went so far as to say that her retirement signalled the end of an era: "La Guimard is inimitable, and when she left the theatre, she carried with her a genre of dance that was never more to be seen on the stage of the Paris Opéra." Her husband Despréaux, who called himself her "best friend", concurred with this judgement: the greatest period of French theatrical dance ran from 1770 to 1790, he insisted, and early nineteenth-century dancers, with their emphasis on multiple pirouettes and exaggerated extension of the legs, could not compete with the "simple, correct execution" and "spiritual grace" of La Guimard.

—Maureen Needham Costonis

---

## GUSEV, Petr

Russian/Soviet dancer, choreographer, and teacher. Born Petr Andreevich Gusev in St. Petersburg, 29 December (16 December old style) 1904. Studied at the Leningrad Choreographic School, pupil of Aleksandr Shiryaev, Vladimir Ponomarev; graduated in 1922. Married dancer Olga Mungalova. Dancer, State Academic Theatre for Opera and Ballet (GATOB, later the Kirov), 1922–35, also performing at the Leningrad Maly Theatre, 1932–35; one of founders and dancers, Young Ballet, Leningrad, 1922–24; soloist, Bolshoi Ballet, Moscow, 1935–45; artistic director and choreographer, Kirov Ballet, 1945–50, Leningrad Maly Theatre, 1960–62, and Novosibirsk Theatre, 1963–66; ballet director and head of Choreographers' School, Beijing, 1958–60, teaching and directing also in Shanghai and Guangzhou, until 1962; artistic director, Leningrad Chamber Ballet, 1967–69; also teacher: Leningrad Institute of Theatrical Art, 1922–30, Leningrad State Concert Organization, 1925–35, Leningrad Choreographic School, 1927–30, Leningrad Maly Theatre, 1930–35, 1960–62, and Bolshoi Ballet, 1935–40; teacher, Moscow Choreographic School, 1935–45, and director, 1935–41; teacher and coach, Stanislavsky and Nemirovich-Danchenko Theatre, 1950–57, Novosibirsk Theatre, 1963–66; director of Choreographers' Faculty, Leningrad Conservatory, from 1966, Professor, from 1973. Recipient: title of Honoured Artist of the Russian Federation, 1947; Honoured Arts Worker of the Russian Federation, 1966; People's Artist of the USSR, 1984. Died in Leningrad, 31 March 1987.

### ROLES

1921 Ivan Tsarevich in *Firebird* (Lopukhov), State Academic Theatre for Opera and Ballet (GATOB), Petrograd

1922 Dancer (cr) in *Solveig* (Petrov), GATOB, Petrograd
Principal dancer (cr) in *Waltz and Adagio* (pas de deux; Balanchivadze, later Balanchine), Petrograd Theatre School Graduation Performance, Petrograd (performed 1923 with the Young Ballet, Petrograd)

1923 Dancer (cr) in *The Magnificence of the Universe* (Lopukhov), Young Ballet and Dancers of GATOB, Petrograd

1925 Egyptian Acrobat (cr) in *Judith* (opera; mus. Serov, chor. Lopukhov), GATOB, Leningrad

1927 Asak (cr) in *The Ice Maiden* (Lopukhov), GATOB, Leningrad

1929 Title role (cr) in *The Nutcracker* (Lopukhov), GATOB, Leningrad

1930 Principal dancer (cr) in *Muszkowsky Waltz* (pas de deux; Vainonen), GATOB, Leningrad

1931 Boris (cr) in *Bolt* (Lopukhov), GATOB, Leningrad

1932 Jérome (cr) in *The Flames of Paris* (Vainonen), GATOB, Leningrad

1934 Franz (cr) in *Coppélia* (Lophukov after Petipa), Maly Theatre Ballet, Leningrad

1935 Petr (cr) in *The Bright Stream* (Lophukov), Maly Theatre Ballet, Leningrad

1936 Girei in *The Fountain of Bakhchisarai* (Zakharov), Bolshoi Ballet, Moscow

1937 Rothbart (cr) in *Swan Lake* (Gorsky, Petipa, Ivanov; staged Dolinskaya and Messerer), Bolshoi Ballet, Moscow

1940 Principal dancer (cr) in *Gypsies* (choreographic miniature; Yakobson), Bolshoi Ballet, Moscow

1942 Meners in *The Crimson Sails* (Radunsky, Popko, Pospekhin), Bolshoi Ballet, Moscow

1944 Hilarion in *Giselle* (Petipa after Coralli, Perrot; staged Lavrovsky), Bolshoi Ballet, Moscow

**Other roles include:** James in *La Sylphide* (Ponomarev after Bournonville), Lucien in *Paquita* (Petipa), Amoun in *Egyptian Nights* (Fokine), Abderakhman and Jean de Brienne in *Raymonda* (Gorsky after Petipa), Bluebird and Prince in *The Sleeping Beauty* (Petipa), Coolie in *The Red Poppy* (Tikhomirov, Lashchilin), Pas de deux in *Vain Precautions* (*La Fille mal gardée*; Petipa, Ivanov), Siberian and Ukranian Dances in *The Little Humpbacked Horse* (Gorsky after Petipa, Saint-Léon); also various concert pieces with Olga Mungalova and Tanya Vecheslova in Leningrad, and with Olga Lepeshinskaya in Moscow.

**Petr Gusev with Olga Mungalova in *Ice Maiden*, Leningrad, 1927**

## WORKS

1951 *The Seven Beauties* (mus. Karaev), Akhundov Theatre, Baku (staged Leningrad Maly Theatre, 1953)
1959 *The Magic Goldfish* (*The Maid of the Sea*; in collaboration with Chinese students; mus. Tzutsiang, Du Minsin), Beijing
1960 *The Flood* (in collaboration with Chinese students; mus. Minsin), Beijing
1966 *The Three Musketeers* (mus. Basnev), Novosibirsk Theatre, Novosibirsk

Also staged:
1955 *Le Corsaire* (after Petipa; mus. Adam, Minkus, Drigo, and others), Maly Theatre Ballet, Leningrad
1959 *Swan Lake* (after Petipa, Ivanov; mus. Tchaikovsky), Beijing
1960 *Giselle* (after Petipa, Coralli, Perrot), Maly Theatre Ballet, Leningrad (staged Beijing, 1958)
1964 *The Ice Maiden* (after Lopukhov; mus. Grieg), Novosibirsk Theatre, Novosibirsk
*Raymonda* (after Petipa; mus. Glazunov), Novosibirsk Theatre, Novosibirsk (staged Budapest, 1978)
1967 *Harlequinade* (after Petipa; mus. Drigo), Leningrad Chamber Ballet, Leningrad (staged Maly Theatre, Leningrad, 1975)
1968 *Cavalry Halt* (after Petipa; mus. Armsheimer), Chamber Ballet, Leningrad (staged Maly Theatre, Leningrad, 1975)
1972 *Paquita Grand Pas* (after Petipa; mus. Minkus), Stanislavsky and Nemirovich-Danchenko Theatre, Moscow (staged Kirov Ballet, Leningrad, 1978)
1978 *Chopiniana* (after Fokine; mus. Chopin), Novosibirsk Theatre, Novosibirsk
1984 *The Naiad and the Fisherman* (after Perrot, Petipa; mus. Pugni), Kirov Ballet, Leningrad
Pas de deux from *The Talisman* (after Petipa; mus. Drigo), Kirov Ballet, Leningrad
1987 *Le Corsaire* (after Petipa; mus. Adam, Pugni, Delibes, and others), Kirov Ballet, Leningrad

## PUBLICATIONS

By Gusev:
"The New *Nutcracker*", *Sovetskaya Muzyka* (Moscow), no. 7, 1966
"Ballets, Seminars, Doubts", *Teatr* (Moscow), no. 3, 1966
Preface to Slonimsky, Yuri, *In Honour of Dance*, Moscow, 1968
"*The Sleeping Beauty*", in *Marius Petipa*, Leningrad, 1971

About Gusev:
Slonimsky, Yuri, "Maestro's Jubilee", *Sovetskaya Muzyka* (Moscow), no. 12, 1964
Roslavleva, Natalia, *Era of the Russian Ballet*, London, 1966
Stanishevsky, Yuri, *Classics on Stage*, Kiev, 1969
Degen, Arsen, *The Leningrad Maly Ballet*, Leningrad, 1979
Chernova, Natalia, *From Geltser to Ulanova*, Moscow, 1979

Petr Gusev was an extremely influential figure in twentieth-century Soviet ballet, whose importance remains unrecognized in the West. Born in St. Petersburg in 1904, he was a pupil at the Imperial Theatre School, graduating one year after his schoolmate George Balanchine, then known as Georgi Balanchivadze. Gusev studied with Aleksandr Shiryaev and Vladimir Ponomarev, both dancers at the Maryinsky Theatre who were interested in reviving the old ballets which had been nearly forgotten. Because of this, Gusev, who, like any pupil of the Theatre School, participated in Maryinsky performances, learned ballets from the regular repertoire as well as excerpts from many others, including *The Magic Flute*, *Cavalry Halt*, *Graziella*, *The Talisman*, *The Naiad and the Fisherman* (the Russian title for *Ondine*), and *La Sylphide*. Dancing these works, many of which were originally created by Marius Petipa, would prove important for his future activities.

While in school, Gusev started a friendship with Balanchine and later became an active member of his Young Ballet group. Gusev frequently partnered a talented young dancer, Olga Mungalova, who became his wife. In addition to works by Balanchine, Gusev danced with Mungalova in many of Fedor Lopukhov's avant-garde productions, such as *Firebird*, the "dance symphony" *The Magnificence of the Universe*, the opera *Judith* by Aleksandr Serov, and Lopukhov's controversial version of *The Nutcracker*, a non-traditional interpretation which was constructivist in conception. In 1927, Lopukhov created one of his best ballets, *The Ice Maiden*, to music by Edvard Grieg, for Gusev and Mungalova. Both were outstanding performers of acrobatic feats: she, lithe and elastic; he, an excellent partner who could lift, throw, and catch the ballerina, turning her in all directions (including upside down) at tremendous speed. Throughout his career as a dancer, Gusev was called "the king of the *podderzhka*" (supported pas de deux work). Later, he taught pas de deux classes as well as ballet classes for boys.

Gusev was a man of various talents. As a dancer, he was a member of two Leningrad companies: the State Academic Theatre for Opera and Ballet (known as GATOB, and later, the Kirov) and the Maly Opera Theatre, where he danced in the Lopukhov ballet to Shostakovich, *The Bright Stream*, in 1935. The same year he moved to Moscow and became famous at the Bolshoi Theatre performing in numerous ballets where he proved himself an outstanding mime as well as a virtuoso dancer. He also partnered many famous ballerinas at recitals, especially Olga Lepeshinskaya.

Gusev was equally appreciated as a teacher and ballet master with a gift for administration and organization. He held many important posts, such as artistic director of the Kirov Ballet, the Maly Theatre Ballet, and the Novosibirsk Ballet (in central Russia). He also worked in Baku (in Azerbaijan), where he choreographed his own ballet, *The Seven Beauties*, to music by Kara Karaev.

Gusev was the principal Soviet architect of ballet in China and of the Chinese school of classical dance. He organized the first ballet academies in Beijing, Shanghai, and Guangzhou (Canton) from 1958 to 1962, taught the first Chinese dancers and choreographers, and helped them create their first classical ballets, such as *The Maid of the Sea*. In the 1970s and 1980s, he worked on many revivals in various theatres in the Soviet Union and abroad (in Budapest, for example), mounting *Giselle*, *Raymonda*, *Le Corsaire*, *Cavalry Halt*, *Harlequinade*, the grand pas from *Paquita*, and the pas de deux from *The Talisman*, among other works. Because of his excellent memory and knowledge of the Petersburg–Petrograd repertory, Gusev was by 1980 virtually the only authority on nineteenth-century choreography in Russia. This was especially important because the Moscow dancers of his generation (such as Asaf Messerer) never had the opportunity, as Gusev did, to study authentic Petipa choreography; they only knew the versions by Aleksandr Gorsky.

As head of the Choreography Faculty at the Leningrad Conservatory, Gusev taught many young choreographers, some of them now quite prominent: Nikolai Boyarchikov, director of Leningrad's Maly Theatre; Valentin Yelisariev, director of Minsk Ballet Theatre; Boris Eifman, director of Leningrad Contemporary Ballet Theatre; and Nikita Dolgushin, soloist at the Kirov and Maly Theatres and professor at the Leningrad Conservatory.

Gusev was also known as a writer on ballet. His articles in magazines and the introductions he wrote to various ballet books were always very personal, intelligent, and lively. He had a keen sense of humour and was an outstanding raconteur. It is a pity he left no written memoirs, but there is a tape recording deposited at the Union of Theatre Workers—many hours long—of him reminiscing about the past.

Gusev was always attracted by young people, new ideas, and new places and impressions. He appreciated a beautiful sight, a beautiful performance, a beautiful girl. In short, he loved life. A man of great vitality and wit, he always gave the impression of being young. When preparing for his eightieth birthday jubilee, he could be seen racing from the Bolshoi Theatre to his hotel and back, rehearsing at all hours, never tiring. One always felt Petr Gusev to be immortal, someone whom death dared not claim.

—Elizabeth Souritz

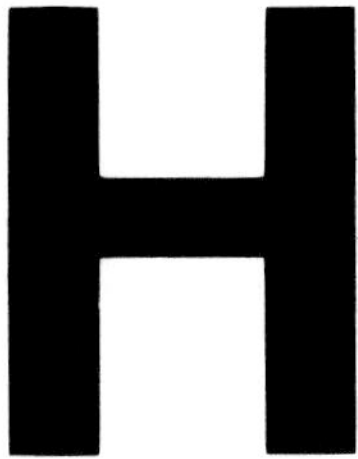

## HAMBURG BALLET

German ballet company based in Hamburg. Origins in ballets arranged at Hamburg Opera House from the seventeenth century; company associated throughout with opera company, with visits to Hamburg stage by leading Romantic ballerinas of the nineteenth century; company raised to international standard, with widened repertoire of modern ballets, under directorship of American choreographer John Neumeier. Offical school affiliated with company based in Ballettzentrum Hamburg since 1989. Current artistic director of Hamburg Ballet (succeeding Peter van Dyk): John Neumeier, from 1973.

### PUBLICATIONS


Anderson, Jack, "Neumeier in Hamburg", *Dancing Times* (London), August 1975

Garske, Rolf, "John Neumeier: A Vision of Continuity", *Ballett International* (Cologne), February 1983

Various authors, *Zehn Jahre: John Neumeier und das Hamburger Ballett 1973–1983* (with English essay by John Percival), Hamburg, 1983

Merrett, Sue, "John Neumeier and the Hamburg Ballet", *Dancing Times* (London), October 1988


* * *

In Hamburg, the name John Neumeier is synonymous with ballet. Since 1973 the American has led the Hamburg Opera Ballet, as it is officially named. As the Hamburg Ballet, it is known throughout the dance world.

John Neumeier's work in Hamburg began in 1973. Peter van Dyk had led the ensemble before him (1962–70), and had presented a number of Balanchine pieces (among them the first European performances of *Agon* and *Orpheus*) along with a few more conventional productions. Under van Dyk's leadership, however, the company was only ever of minor importance, and became even less notable in the three-year interim between van Dyk's departure and Neumeier's assumption of his post. It never reached the same level of importance as the Stuttgart Ballet under John Cranko's directorship in the same period. Only when John Neumeier took on the position of ballet director of the Hamburg Ballet, having previously led the Frankfurt am Main ballet company, did the Hamburg Ballet begin its rise to become a world-class ensemble.

From the beginning John Neumeier set himself the target of creating a company with an "unmistakable face". He has undoubtedly achieved this goal, if one takes the company repertoire as a gauge: it consists in the most part of Neumeier productions. Other choreographers, who are mostly represented by a single work, seldom performed, include Maurice Béjart, Rudi van Dantzig, Jiří Kylián, José Limón, Jerome Robbins, and Antony Tudor. Regularly-performed full-length ballets by John Cranko and several one-act pieces by George Balanchine extend the list of pieces by guest choreographers in the Hamburg repertoire.

John Neumeier's choreographic creativity is extremely varied. The Hamburg Ballet owes its well-balanced repertoire to that talent. The sixty-odd productions which Neumeier has presented in Hamburg since 1973 include full-length and single-act narrative ballets as well as abstract, symphonic, and religious pieces and even two musicals (Leonard Bernstein's *West Side Story* and *On the Town*). Along with the often radical new interpretations of the classics (such as the three Tchaikovsky ballets), Neumeier's own narrative ballets and his pieces choreographed to several Gustav Mahler symphonies and to church music by Johann Sebastian Bach and Wolfgang Amadeus Mozart give the Hamburg Ballet an unmistakable stamp.

Among the notable dance personalities who helped determine the shape of the company in the first years of Neumeier's engagement were Ray Barra, Beatrice Cordua, Truman Finney, François Klaus, Marianne Kruuse, Max Midinet, and Persephone Samaropoulo. Soon after these came Lynne Charles, Colleen Scott, and Ivan Liska (only the last of these is still one of the principals of the ensemble). Most of them had already worked under Neumeier in Frankfurt, or before that with him as a dancer in the Stuttgart Ballet. The outstanding artists of the company in recent times have included Anna Grabka, Gigi Hyatt, Bettina Beckmann, Gamal Gouda, Anders Hellstrom, and Jean Laban. Every year the Hamburg Ballet finishes its season with the so-called Nijinsky Gala, which is sometimes given over to a certain theme. More and more, world-famous dancers appear on the stage of the Hamburg Ballet as guest artists on this occasion.

A clever approach to performance programmes and "ballet workshops" held several times a year in which John Neumeier introduces themes specific to dance and, from time to time, develops new productions, have helped to create a faithful ballet-going public in Hamburg. John Neumeier, whose present contract runs until 1996, has also understood how to bind dancers to the Hamburg Ballet throughout their active lives—as ballet masters or educators for the next generation of dancers. Since 1978 there has been a training establishment for professional dancers attached to the Hamburg Ballet, which quickly earned a secure position among internationally recognized ballet schools under its educational leaders—initially Peter Appel, later Truman Finney.

Under John Neumeier's leadership, the Hamburg Ballet has developed into an important cultural institution of the Hanseatic town. This widely recognized status enjoyed by the company found its particular expression in 1989 in the completion of the "Ballettzentrum Hamburg—John Neumeier", a former school offering plenty of space in which the Hamburg Ballet is now housed, along with the administration, attached school, and accommodation for boarders.

—Horst Vollmer

---

HAMEL, Martine van *see* VAN HAMEL, Martine

---

### HAMLET

**Choreography:** Robert Helpmann
**Music:** Petr Ilyich Tchaikovsky
**Design:** Leslie Hurry (scenery and costumes)
**Libretto:** based on the play by William Shakespeare
**First Production:** Sadler's Wells Ballet, New Theatre, London, 19 May 1942
**Principal Dancers:** Robert Helpmann (Hamlet), Margot Fonteyn (Ophelia), Celia Franca (Queen of Denmark), David Paltenghi (King of Denmark), Leo Kersley (Gravedigger)

**Other productions include:** Royal Ballet Touring Company (restaged Helpmann); Sydney, 4 November 1958. Australian Ballet (restaged Helpmann), with Rudolf Nureyev (Hamlet), Josephine Jason (Ophelia); Adelaide, 23 March 1970.

**Other choreographic treatments of story:** Francesco Clerico (Venice, 1788), Louis Henry (Vienna, 1822), Bronislava Nijinska (with herself in title role, Paris, 1934), Victor Gsovsky (Munich, 1950), Tatiana Gsovsky (Berlin, 1953), Konstantin Sergeyev (Leningrad, 1970), Vakhtang Chabukiani (Tbilisi, 1971), L. Monreal (Boston, 1975), John Neumeier (New York, 1976, and Copenhagen, 1985), Jurek Makarowski (Hagen, 1989).

#### PUBLICATIONS

Williamson, Audrey, "Robert Helpmann as Choreographer", *Theatre World* (London), September 1942
Williamson, Audrey, "Shakespearean Ballet", *Dancing Times* (London), June 1943
*Hamlet and Miracle in the Gorbals*, London, 1949
Beaumont, Cyril, *Ballets Past and Present*, London, 1955
Clarke, Mary, *The Sadler's Wells Ballet*, London, 1955
Barnes, Clive, and Williams, Peter, "Helpmann's Return", *Dance and Dancing* (London), May 1958
Clarke, Mary, "Ballet in Wartime: Part III", *Dancing Times* (London), May 1990

* * *

There are two ways to treat Shakespeare's plays in ballet—either by a full-evening translation into dance and mime which follows the course of the story chronologically, interspersing dramatic scenes with incidental ensembles; or by a more condensed and selective form, as a one-act work. In his *Hamlet*, Robert Helpmann adopted the second method, exploiting it for an unforgettable, and brilliantly concise, dance drama.

The ballet grew out of his admiration and knowledge of the play. As he was a lover of Shakespeare from childhood, there was no question of his producing any facile or shallow adaptation of *Hamlet*. What he aimed at, and achieved, was a unique amalgam of essential incidents, treated impressionistically and incorporating ideas arising from Shakespearian scholarship of the late 1930s.

The music, suggested to him by Constant Lambert, was Tchaikovsky's short Fantasy Overture. The designer was Leslie Hurry, a young artist whose work Helpmann (always keenly interested in contemporary artists) had seen at the Redfern Gallery in London. For Hurry it was a first theatrical commission, and he made an outstanding contribution to the production. He provided a doom-laden décor, and costumes in sumptuous colours and richly fantastic detail, indications of the kind of duality Helpmann introduced into his choreography. The theme of Hamlet's dying thoughts and confused memories was expressed in his identification of Gertrude and Ophelia, of Claudius and the Ghost, and of the jester Yorick and the First Gravedigger.

Dance and mime, classically based but modern in mood, were completely integrated into a fluent, cinematic ebb and flow of incident, so closely fitted to the music that it might have been a commissioned score. A viewer had to be alert to follow the rapid succession of episodes. Lighting played an important part, and Helpmann's choice of his dancers was impeccable. Celia Franca as Gertrude, David Paltenghi as Claudius, and Margot Fonteyn as Ophelia were perfect interpretations, as of course was Helpmann's own central role of Hamlet, which utilized his powerful stage presence and dramatic sense. But the ballet was above all an example of fine choreographic integration—something which revivals, sadly, have usually failed to reproduce. Helpmann's *Hamlet* communicated instantly in theatrical terms to any audience, but also proved progressively illuminating to anyone who really knew the text of the play.

—Kathrine Sorley Walker

---

### HANKA, Erika

Austrian dancer, choreographer, and ballet director. Born in Vinkovci, Slavonia, 18 June 1905. Studied modern dance at the Vienna State Academy of Music and the Performing Arts, pupil of Gertrud Bodenwieser, 1923–24, and with Karin Schneider, Graz; studied ballet with Irmgard Thomas, Vienna. Début in dance recital with Fritz Kaiserfeld, Graz, 1927; founder, school of gymnastics and dance, Vienna, 1927; dancer, Düsseldorf Opera House, 1929–35, becoming assistant to the ballet director, 1931–35; dancer, Ballets Jooss, England, 1935–38; choreographer and ballet director, Apollo Theatre, Cologne, 1938–39, Essen Opera House, 1939–40, Hamburg State Opera House, 1940–42, and Vienna State Opera Ballet, 1942–58; also librettist, writing scenarios for many of her ballets. Recipient: Title of Professor, 1951. Died in Vienna, 15 May 1958.

#### WORKS

1939 *Kleines Liebesspiel* (*Les Petits Riens*; mus. Mozart), Essen Opera Ballet, Essen
*Spanisches Intermezzo* (mus. Rimsky-Korsakov), Essen Opera Ballet, Essen
1940 *Tänze nach klassischen Motiven* (*Antiche Danze ed Arie*; mus. Respighi), Essen Opera Ballet, Essen

**Margot Fonteyn and Robert Helpmann in *Hamlet*, Sadler's Wells Ballet, London, 1942**

*Fest und Erinnerung* (mus. Schumann), Essen Opera Ballet, Essen
*Andreasnacht* (mus. Schacht), Essen Opera Ballet, Essen
*Capriccio Espagnol* (mus. Rimsky-Korsakov), Hamburg Opera Ballet, Hamburg
*Joan von Zarissa* (mus. Egk), Hamburg Opera Ballet, Hamburg
1941 *Liebeszauber* (*El Amor Brujo*; mus. de Falla), Hamburg Opera Ballet, Hamburg
*Titus Feuerfuchs* (mus. J. Strauss Jr., arranged Brückner-Rüggeberg), Hamburg Opera Ballet, Hamburg
1942 *Der Dreispitz* (*Le Tricorne*; mus. de Falla), Vienna State Opera Ballet, Vienna
1943 *Florentiner Intermedien* (mus. ancient, arranged Paumgartner), Vienna State Opera Ballet, Vienna
*Colombinens Heirat* (*Columbine's Wedding*; mus. Mozart, arranged Paumgartner), Vienna State Opera Ballet, Vienna
*Sophonisbe* (mus. Varacini, arranged Paumgartner), Vienna State Opera Ballet, Vienna
*Divertimento* (mus. Starzer, arranged Paumgartner), Vienna State Opera Ballet, Vienna
*Karparthenhochzeit* (mus. Constantinescu), Vienna State Opera Ballet, Vienna
*Festa Romantica* (mus. Piccioli), Vienna State Opera Ballet, Vienna
*Capriccio Silvestre* (mus. Casella), Vienna State Opera Ballet, Vienna
1944 *Couperin-Suite* (mus. Couperin, arranged R. Strauss), Vienna State Opera Ballet, Vienna
1945 *Coppélia* (mus. Delibes), Vienna State Opera Ballet, Vienna
1947 *Bilder einer Ausstellung* (*Pictures at an Exhibition*; mus. Mussorgsky), Vienna State Opera Ballet, Vienna
*Nobilissima Visione* (mus. Hindemith), Vienna State Opera Ballet, Vienna
*Petruschka* (mus. Stravinsky), Vienna State Opera Ballet, Vienna
1949 *Höllische G'schicht'* (mus. J. Strauss, arranged Kattnigg, Paulik), Vienna State Opera Ballet, Vienna
*Don Juan* (mus. Gluck), Vienna State Opera Ballet, Vienna
*Josephslegende* (*La Légende de Joseph*; mus. R. Strauss), Vienna State Opera Ballet, Vienna
1950 *Der Feuervogel* (*L'Oiseau de feu*; mus. Stravinsky), Vienna State Opera Ballet, Vienna
*Homerische Symphonie* (mus. Berger), Vienna State Opera Ballet, Vienna
1952 *Ballettsuite Sylvia* (mus. Delibes), Vienna State Opera Ballet, Vienna
*Das Rondo vom goldenen Kalb* (mus. von Einem), Vienna State Opera Ballet, Vienna
*Scheherazade* (mus. Rimsky-Korsakov), Vienna State Opera Ballet, Vienna
1953 *Daphnis und Chloé* (mus. Ravel), Vienna State Opera Ballet, Vienna
*Abraxas* (mus. Egk), Vienna State Opera Ballet, Vienna
1954 *Symphonie classique* (mus. Prokofiev), Vienna State Opera Ballet, Vienna
*Orpheus* (mus. Stravinsky), Vienna State Opera Ballet, Vienna
*Der Zauberladen* (*La Boutique fantasque*; mus. Rossini, arranged Respighi), Vienna State Opera Ballet, Vienna
*Polowetzer Tänze* (*Polovtsian Dances from Prince Igor*; mus. Borodin), Vienna State Opera Ballet, Vienna
1955 *Der Mohr von Venedig* (mus. Blacher), Vienna State Opera Ballet, Vienna
1957 *Hotel Sacher* (mus. Hellmesberger, Schönherr), Vienna State Opera Ballet, Vienna
*Der Wunderbare Mandarin* (*The Miraculous Mandarin*; mus. Bartók), Vienna State Opera Ballet, Vienna
*Medusa* (mus. von Einem), Vienna State Opera Ballet, Vienna

**PUBLICATIONS**

By Hanka:

"Dramaturgisches Gespräch mit Erika Hanka", *Der Tanz: Die Deutsche Tanz-Zeitschrift* (Berlin), April 1942
"Bezaubernder Ballettabend in der Staatsoper", *Die Wiener Bühne* (Vienna), March 1946
"Probleme der Tanzkunst", *Die Wiener Bühne* (Vienna), March 1946
"Das Ballett der Wiener Staatsoper", *Almanach der Wiener Staatsoper 1945–54*, Vienna, 1954

About Hanka:

Moore, Lillian, "Viennese Choreographer", *Dance Magazine* (New York), September 1948
Regner, O. F., *Das Ballettbuch*, Frankfurt, 1954
Schüller, Gunhild, and Oberzaucher, Alfred, "Erika Hanka", *Tanzblätter* (Vienna), 6 parts: June 1978, October 1978, February 1979, April–June 1979

* * *

Erika Hanka's multi-faceted career as dancer, choreographer, and ballet director in Germany and Austria reflects the general development of dance within a larger cultural sphere during the first half of the twentieth century. In line with the prevailing trends of her time, Hanka found her artistic roots within the realm of "Ausdruckstanz". This movement, dominant after World War I, had had a decisive impact around the time of Hanka's birth through the performances of American modern dance pioneers. In the early 1920s, when Hanka studied with Gertrud Bodenwieser (an advocate of the teachings of François Delsarte and Émile Jaques-Dalcroze), Ausdruckstanz had already conquered the academic world in Vienna, in the form of a course given at the Vienna State Academy for Music and the Performing Arts. After completing this course, Hanka perfected her studies in Graz with Karin Schneider, a pupil of such Ausdruckstanz exponents as Rudolf Bode, Rudolf von Laban, and Mary Wigman. Thus well prepared, she started to perform, together with partner Fritz Kaiserfeld, competing with numerous other dancers who as soloists or as small groups gave dance recitals in various concert halls. Like many of her colleagues, she also opened a "Schule für Gymnastik und künstlerischen Tanz". At the same time, she herself took classes in classical dance with Irmgard Thomas, who, as a pupil of Carl Raimund Sen., taught classical ballet in the tradition of the Vienna Opera.

Hanka's theatrical career started at the time of the Weimar Republic, when representatives of Ausdruckstanz were frequently appointed as ballet directors in German theatres. This development was interrupted only later, when the National Socialists revealed a preference for a more classically orientated ballet technique at the centre of their cultural policy. Hanka was first engaged in Düsseldorf as a soloist and assistant to the former Laban colleague, Ruth Loeser. Hanka had met Laban himself in Vienna in 1929, when she was dancing in the "Festzug der Gewerbe" which he had arranged. When Loeser had to leave for political reasons, Hanka remained assistant—

first to Harald Kreutzberg, and later to Aurel Milloss—and she then went to England to join the Ballets Jooss in exile there. She stayed with them for three years, creating a leading role in Kurt Jooss's *The Mirror* in 1935. Returning to Germany, she started her career as choreographer and ballet director at the Apollo Theatre in Cologne.

After being engaged by the opera houses of Essen and Hamburg, Hanka was called to Vienna, where she headed the State Opera Company until her death. This ballet company, steeped in tradition, had almost entirely lost its prestigious name with the downfall of the monarchy. Although maintaining its classical foundation, it had, through the influence of choreographers like Sascha Leontjew, Grete Wiesenthal, Valeria Kratina, Margarete Wallmann, Rosalia Chladek, and Helga Swedlund, turned more and more towards Ausdruckstanz. Hanka had great success with Werner Egk's *Joan von Zarissa*, with Harald Kreutzberg as leading dancer. During the war years she continued her success with ballets bearing the imprint of Ausdruckstanz; yet the abrupt turn towards classical ballet after World War II (definitely prompted by guest appearances of the Sadler's Wells Ballet in central Europe) did not present any problems for Hanka. Her ballets, prepared and performed under difficult conditions in makeshift places (the State Opera building having been destroyed by bombs), were now more strongly orientated towards classical ballet, without losing the individual stamp of their formerly Ausdruckstanz-based creator. Ballets by contemporary composers like Boris Blacher and Gottfried von Einem formed the centre of the repertoire, with Blacher's *Der Mohr von Venedig* emerging as one of the highlights of the re-opening of the Staatsoper in 1955.

The repertoire also included ballets with Viennese themes, along with ballets of the Diaghilev era, which, according to the custom of that time, were produced with new choreography. Following the international example, and starting in the mid-1950s, productions of the classics were mounted, with the Australian Gordon Hamilton responsible for the stagings. At the same time, a change in the leading soloists took place with the stylistic shift: at the beginning of Hanka's era, Hedy Pfundmayr, Julia Drapal, Carl Raimund Jun., and Poldy and Erwin Pokorny were the leading dancers, whereas in the later years, Willy Dirtl, Edeltraud Brexner, Margaret Bauer, Christl Zimmerl, and the American dancer Richard Adama took the lead. The last premiere under Hanka's reign brought the first production for Vienna of a Balanchine work. With it, the Vienna ballet reached a new threshold, which was finally crossed only after Hanka's death—towards a ballet repertoire formed by international taste.

—Alfred Oberzaucher

---

## HARANGOZÓ, Gyula

Hungarian dancer, choreographer, and ballet director. Born in Budapest, 19 April 1908. Studied at the Budapest State Opera Ballet School, with Jan Cieplinski. Married (1) dancer Vera Ilona; (2) dancer Irén Hamala: son, dancer Gyula Harangozó, born 1956. Dancer, Hungarian State Opera Ballet, Budapest, from 1926: soloist from 1928, performing chiefly in character roles; début as choreographer, 1936: chief choreographer, Budapest State Opera Ballet, 1936–39, 1941–74; choreographer and ballet master, La Scala, Milan, 1939–41; also choreographer for film and theatre. Recipient: title of Merited Artist of the Hungarian Republic, 1950; Kossuth Prize, 1956; Eminent Artist of the Hungarian Republic, 1957; Gold Medal of Socialist Labour, 1966. Died in Budapest, 30 October 1974.

### WORKS

1936 *Scene in the Csárda* (mus. Hubay), Hungarian State Opera Ballet, Budapest
1937 *Sybil* (mus. Victor), Hungarian State Opera Ballet, Budapest
*Perhaps To-morrow!* (mus. Kenessey), Budapest Opera Theatre, Budapest
*Little Johnny in Top-Boots* (mus. Kenessey), Hungarian State Opera Ballet, Budapest
1938 *Francia saláta* (mus. Milhaud), Hungarian State Opera Ballet, Budapest
*Majális* (*May Picnic*; mus. Kenessey), Hungarian State Opera Ballet, Budapest
*Polovtsian Dances* (mus. Borodin), Hungarian State Opera Ballet, Budapest
1939 *The Wooden Prince* (mus. Bartók), Hungarian State Opera Ballet, Budapest
*Romeo and Juliet* (mus. Tchaikovsky), Hungarian State Opera Ballet, Budapest
*Polovtsian Dances* (in opera *Prince Igor*; mus. Borodin), Ballet of La Scala, Milan
1939/40 *Rainbow* (mus. Mirago, Liszt), Ballet of La Scala, Milan
1941 *The Jar* (*La Giarra*; mus. Casella), Hungarian State Opera Ballet, Budapest
1942 *Liebestraüme* (mus. Liszt), Hungarian State Opera Ballet, Budapest
1945 *The Miraculous Mandarin* (mus. Bartók), Hungarian State Opera Ballet, Budapest
1947 *Le Tricorne* (mus. de Falla), Hungarian State Opera Ballet, Budapest
1948 *Promenade Concert* (mus. J. Strauss), Hungarian State Opera Ballet, Budapest
1949 *Mischievous Students* (mus. Farkas), Hungarian State Opera Ballet, Budapest
1951 *The Kerchief* (mus. Kenessey), Hungarian State Opera Ballet, Budapest
1953 *Coppélia* (mus. Delibes), Hungarian State Opera Ballet, Budapest
1956 *The Miraculous Mandarin* (new version; mus. Bartók), Hungarian State Opera Ballet, Budapest
1958 *The Wooden Prince* (new version; mus. Bartók), Hungarian State Opera Ballet, Budapest
1959 *Schéhérazade* (mus. Rimsky-Korsakov), Hungarian State Opera Ballet, Budapest
1960 *Mattie the Gooseboy* (mus. Szabó), Hungarian State Opera Ballet, Budapest
1961 *Polovtsian Dances* (mus. Borodin), Hungarian State Opera Ballet, Budapest
1968 *Promenade Concert* (mus. Strauss, Kenessey), Hungarian State Opera Ballet, Budapest

### PUBLICATIONS

Beaumont, Cyril, *Complete Book of Ballets*, London, revised edition, London, 1951
Rey, Jan, "Change and Growth in Czechoslovakia", *Dance and Dancers* (London), October 1960
Körtvélyes, Géza, and Lórincz, G., *The Budapest Ballet*, in English, Budapest, 1971

Körtvélyes, Géza, "Remembering Gyula Harangozó", *Hungarian Dance News* (Budapest), 2 parts: nos. 3–4, 1983; nos. 5–6, 1983

* * *

Gyula Harangozó is considered Hungary's most important choreographer; one speaks today of what is called the "Harangozó tradition" in Hungarian ballet. Harangozó brought new accents to Hungarian choreography. He belonged to that group of dancers and choreographers who rejected pantomime in ballet: he insisted that each entrance, each story, be communicated entirely through dance steps, and that each of these must have sense and meaning. In doing this, he blended folk dance and the elements of classical choreography.

Harangozó's entry into the world of dance is legendary in Hungary. Upon graduating from school, he intended to embark upon a banking career. However, in his neighbourhood, he happened to meet several Russian prisoners of war, and became fascinated with their dancing. From this moment on, he devoted himself to dance. The choreography of a Trepak in the opera *Eugene Onegin*, which he also danced, first brought him to the attention of the Hungarian public. As a dancer his speed and musicality, coupled with a brilliant sense of humour, made him ideal for the character roles in which he was principally cast. The Doll in *The Wooden Prince*, the Old Man in *The Miraculous Mandarin*, Coppélius in *Coppélia*, and the Corregidor in *Le Tricorne* were among his most successful roles. In all these, the unusual articulation and placement of the legs and hips in his dancing were highly admired. In his sixties Harangozó was still dancing Coppélius, which, in his version, had many difficult variations. His choreography for *Coppélia* became the standard for Hungary, and is still performed there.

Even in his early ballets, Harangozó had already found his mature style. He was admired by audiences, and spoiled by the critics. He went from one success to the next. His international success is due principally to his two Bartók ballets, *The Wooden Prince* and *The Miraculous Mandarin*. The Hungarian premiere of the latter did not take place until 1945; it had been announced in 1941, but was cancelled for political reasons.

Harangozó worked from 1939 to 1941 in Italy. His *Polovtsian Dances* at La Scala in Milan were so successful that the director immediately hired him as ballet master. However, soon afterwards he returned to Hungary: his love for his country made him want to remain in his native land. At this time he met Massine, who wished to work with him; but the war prevented it.

Harangozó's choreographic career was indirectly influenced by the Soviet full-length ballet. Many of the Russian epics (*The Nutcracker*, *The Flames of Paris*, *Swan Lake*, and so on) began to enter the repertoire of the Hungarian theatres. Harangozó at that time was basing his programming on the model of Diaghilev's Ballets Russes. When asked to expand his one-act works to evening-length ballets, he made his legendary reply: "I wouldn't think of adding a litre of water to a small glass of French cognac in order to make it easier to drink." However, he did proceed to produce a series of outstanding full-length ballets (*Furfangos Diákok*, or *Mischievous Students*, *Keszkenö*, or *The Kerchief*, and *Coppélia*) which established his reputation as the creator of the Hungarian "dance-play".

Harangozó's private life was closely connected with his career. His first wife, the prima ballerina Vera Ilona, assisted him in the choreography of such works as *Romeo and Juliet*, while his second wife, Irén Hamala, was responsible for a great part of his most important works. She not only helped to create them but also rehearsed them, and is today responsible for preserving the Harangozó heritage. His son, who carries the same name, has embarked on an international dance career. He first stood on stage in his father's ballet, *Platzmusik*, at the age of twelve. Unfortunately, the father did not live to see his son's rise in the world of dance.

Privately, Harangozó was punctual, good-natured, and, when away from the theatre, did not speak of dance. He had many journalists as friends, but no critics. His hobby was painting; and he produced some very good impressionistic works. For over 40 years he ruled the Hungarian ballet scene, and, during that time, he set valid standards for Hungarian dance. His motto was: "Through teaching, we are taught".

—Evelyn Téri

---

## HARKARVY, Benjamin

American choreographer, ballet director, and teacher. Born in New York, 16 December 1930. Studied with George Chaffee, and at School of American Ballet, New York, pupil of George Balanchine, Anatole Obukhov, Pierre Vladimirov, Muriel Stuart, and Felia Doubrovska; also studied with Edward Caton, Elizaveta Anderson-Ivantzova, Alexandra Fedorova, Antony Tudor, and Margaret Craske. Dancer, Brooklyn Lyric Opera, 1949–50, also performing with various concert groups; teacher, Fokine School, 1951–55; founder and teacher, Benjamin Harkarvy Ballet School, New York, from 1955; choreographer for own concert group at Jacob's Pillow Dance Festival, 1955; director, choreographer, and teacher, Royal Winnipeg Ballet, 1957–58; choreographer, Netherlands Ballet, 1958–59; founder and artistic co-director, Netherlands Dance Theatre, 1959–69; artistic joint director, Harkness Ballet, New York, 1969–70, also acting as choreographer, Bat-Dor Company, and teacher, Bat Sheva Dance Company, Israel, from 1969; choreographer and co-director, Dutch National Ballet, 1970–71; associate director, Pennsylvania Ballet, 1972, becoming artistic director, 1973–82; permanent guest teacher, Les Grands Ballets Canadiens, 1986–90; teacher and choreographer, Juilliard School, New York, from 1990; also guest teacher, coach, and choreographer, including for Jacob's Pillow, various seasons, from 1986, Netherlands Dance Theatre, Royal Conservatory of the Hague, and National Ballet of Spain, Madrid, from 1990.

### WORKS

1955 *Three Lyric Dances* (mus. Vivaldi), Young Choreographers Evening, New York
*The Walk Between* (mus. Hindemith), Benjamin Harkarvy Ballet Company, Silvermine Festival, Connecticut
1956 *Four Times Six* (mus. Mourant), Royal Winnipeg Ballet, Canada
1957 *Twisted Heart* (mus. Wernick), Royal Winnipeg Ballet, Canada
*Fête Brillante* (mus. Mozart), Royal Winnipeg Ballet, Canada
1959 *Septet* (mus. Saint-Saëns), Netherlands Dance Theatre, Amsterdam
1960 *Primavera* (mus. Cimarosa), Netherlands Dance Theatre, The Hague
1961 *Sol y Sombra* (mus. Ohana), Netherlands Dance Theatre, The Hague

**Benjamin Harkarvy's ballet *Grand Pas Espagnol*, performed by Nederlands Dans Theater**

*Blues* (mus. Copland), Netherlands Dance Theatre, The Hague
1962 *Ballade* (mus. Fauré), Netherlands Dance Theatre, The Hague
1963 *Madrigalesco* (mus. Vivaldi), Netherlands Dance Theatre, The Hague
*Grand Pas espagnol* (mus. Moszkowski), Netherlands Dance Theatre, The Hague
1964 *Recital for Cello and Eight Dancers* (mus. Bach), Netherlands Dance Theatre, The Hague
*Kwartet* (mus. Van Delden), Netherlands Dance Theatre, The Hague
1965 *Partita* (mus. J. S. Bach), Netherlands Dance Theatre, The Hague
1966 *I Gelosi* (mus. Stravinsky), Netherlands Dance Theatre, The Hague
1967 *Visage* (mus. Berio), Netherlands Dance Theatre, The Hague
*Le Diable à quatre* Pas de deux (mus. Adam), Netherlands Dance Theatre, The Hague
1968 *Double Duet* (mus. Bartók), Netherlands Dance Theatre, The Hague
*Aswingto* (mus. Hindemith; 1969 version mus. Donizetti), Netherlands Dance Theatre, The Hague
1969 *La Favorita* (mus. Donizetti), Harkness Ballet, New York
1970 *Contrasts* (mus. Miramoglu), Bat-Dor Company, Tel Aviv
1972 *Quartet* (mus. Takemitsu), Pennsylvania Ballet, Philadelphia
1973 *Time Passed Summer* (mus. Tchaikovsky), Pennsylvania Ballet, Philadelphia
*Continuum* (mus. Kryzwieki), Pennsylvania Ballet, Philadelphia
1976 *Signatures* (mus. Kaplow), Pennsylvania Ballet, Philadelphia
1977 *From Gentle Circles* (mus. Dvořák), Pennsylvania Ballet, Philadelphia
1979 *Poems of Love and the Seasons* (mus. Nocella), Pennsylvania Ballet, Philadelphia
1983 *Pillow Sonata* (mus. Schubert), Jacob's Pillow Dance Festival, Lee, Massachusetts
1984 *Four Men Waiting* (mus. Saint-Saëns), Pennsylvania Ballet, Philadelphia
*Five Madrigals* (mus. Monteverdi), Jacob's Pillow Dance Festival, Lee, Massachusetts
*Mozart K.456* (mus. Mozart), Ballet British Columbia, Vancouver
1985 *Wind Dances* (mus. Mendelssohn), Peridance, New York
1986 *Bilitis* (mus. Debussy), Wake Forest Festival, Winston-Salem, North Carolina
1987 *Hothouse Dreams* (mus. Ravel), Jacob's Pillow Dance Festival, Lee, Massachusetts
1988 *Prom Story* (mus. Haydn), Juilliard Dance Theater, New York
*American Dancer* (mus. Debussy), Joyce Tristler Company, New York
1990 *Premonitions* (mus. Ravel), New American Ballet Ensemble, New York
1991 *Frames* (mus. Volinsky), New American Ballet Ensemble, New York
1992 *Three Debussy Duets* (mus. Debussy), Juilliard Dance Theater, New York

## PUBLICATIONS

Hall, Fernau, "American in Holland", *Dance Magazine* (New York), June 1962

Fatt, Amelia, "Reintroducing Benjamin Harkarvy", *Dance Magazine* (New York), November 1972
Gow, Gordon, "The Rebels of Netherlands Dance Theatre", *Dancing Times* (London), May 1973
Webster, Daniel, "Philadelphia Dance Alliance: Pennsylvania Ballet", *Dance Magazine* (New York), June 1978
"Reports: U.S., Philadelphia", *Ballet News* (New York), January–February 1980
Sandler, Ken, "Benjamin Harkarvy and the Pennsylvania Ballet", *Ballet News* (New York), June 1981
Meyers, Deborah, "Benjamin Harkarvy: Philosopher and Artist", *Vandance* (Vancouver), Summer 1984
Hunt, Marilyn, "Return of the Prodigal Mentor", *Dance Magazine* (New York), April 1992

* * *

Benjamin Harkarvy, a relatively unsung hero in his own country, has been a major figure on the international dance scene for the past 40 years. He spent ten years abroad building The Netherlands Dance Theatre, a company that bridged the new vocabulary of modern dance and ballet, and brought to The Hague the most vigorous and talented choreographers. He is notably responsible for bringing the American schools of choreography to the European continent.

In his work as ballet director, Harkarvy has always been interested in blending a serious and reverent attitude towards classical ballet tradition with the new and innovative. His own eloquent and poetic choreography reflects this coalescence. As a teacher of classical dancing, he is a purist, but his fascination with and appreciation for other forms of dance combine to give him a truly contemporary approach. His contribution to the art has not gone unnoticed: while artistic director of the Pennsylvania Ballet, the company was featured on national television (the "Dance in America" series). In addition, he has been the subject of a documentary series entitled *The Creative Person*.

Harkarvy's teaching skills have become legendary. His ballet classes are carefully prepared, with a definite purpose to each exercise and combination. Everyone in his classes receives attention and believes in his or her ability for improvement. "Harkarvy approaches genius as a breeder of dancers," wrote Tobi Tobias in 1982. "He teaches through compelling analysis and persuasion, demonstrating to his dancers how technique, musical sensitivity and a projected presence must be fused." Though demanding, he is never fussy. His combinations may look mightily difficult, yet he presents them with an intelligent clarity that eases and simplifies their execution. The tendency for famous ballet teachers to take over the dancer's personal way of moving is well known. "Harkarvy limits himself to improving the efficiency of their work," is the way Amelia Fatt has put it. Harkarvy states, "I'm very much against the nineteenth-century mannerisms encouraged by many teachers today ... Peek-a-boo heads and adorable hands are as impossible in *Concerto Barocco* as they are in *Pillar of Fire* or *The Moor's Pavane*. Let the choreographer determine the style."

Harkarvy's teaching methodology greatly affected his choices as a director of ballet companies. He built repertoires, especially at the Netherlands Dance Theatre, that would make use of fully trained classical dancers whose capabilities were "multi-purpose". He saw the dancer of the future as a dancer of marvellous virtuosity, exposed to many dance styles. As Fernau Hall explained in 1962, "Harkarvy felt that by experiencing the more adult emotional demands of modern choreographers ... his company would make a statement of importance, going beyond the merely decorative." One of the most serious and provocative dances produced during Harkarvy's tenure at the Netherlands Dance Theatre was modern dancer Anna Sokolow's *Rooms*, staged by the choreographer. Much to Harkarvy's credit, Sokolow relished the way the ballet-trained dancers reproduced her modern dance movements.

In Harkarvy's choreography are invariably "craft, intelligence, thematic cogency and above all, taste" (Tobi Tobias). One of his most ambitious and best realized works created for the Pennsylvania Ballet, *Time Passed Summer*, "depicts a small society of late Victorians placidly listening to Tchaikovsky songs at an outdoor concert; the music draws out of them reincarnations of critical events and profound feelings from their past lives". In another ballet, with a commissioned score by Peter Nocella, Harkarvy produced *Poems of Love and the Seasons* (1979). In four sections, its loose narrative concerns the relationship between a man and a woman in the context of their community, the death of the man, and the nobility the woman gains through mourning. As in Tudor's ballet *Dark Elegies*, the community represents strength and helps the woman to discover her own stability and spiritual integrity. Under Harkarvy's guidance, The Pennsylvania Ballet became famous for a sculpted style, and for robust and graceful dancing. Harkarvy's obvious gift—as teacher, director, choreographer, and coach—is one which should be well appreciated in the ballet world.

—Judith Chazin-Bennahum

---

## HARLEQUINADE

**Choreography:** George Balanchine
**Music:** Riccardo Drigo
**Design:** Rouben Ter-Arutunian (scenery, costumes, and lighting)
**Libretto:** based on *Les Millions d'Arlequin*, by Marius Petipa, after *commedia dell'arte* characters
**First Production:** New York City Ballet, New York State Theatre, 4 February 1965
**Principal Dancers:** Patricia McBride (Columbine), Edward Villella (Harlequin), Suki Schorer (Pierrette), Deni Lamont (Pierrot)

**Other productions include:** Hermitage Theatre (original production to Drigo score; chor. Marius Petipa), as *Les Millions d'Arlequin*; St. Petersburg, 1900. London Festival Ballet (new version; chor. David Lichine); London, 26 December 1950. Ballet Russe de Monte Carlo (new version; chor. Boris Romanov); Chicago, 27 December 1956. Royal Danish Ballet (chor. Hans Brenaa after Petipa); Copenhagen, 1 October 1958. London Festival Ballet (chor. Anton Dolin after Petipa); Monte Carlo, 19 November 1960. New York City Ballet (expanded version; restaged Balanchine, with complete Drigo score); New York, 14 January 1973.

### PUBLICATIONS

Balanchine, George, with Mason, Francis, *Balanchine's Complete Stories of the Great Ballets*, Garden City, N.Y., 1977
Reynolds, Nancy, *Repertory in Review*, New York, 1977
Atlas, Helen, "Reminiscences ... *Harlequinade*", *Dancing News* (New York), February 1978
Croce, Arlene, *Going to the Dance*, New York, 1982

The ballet George Balanchine created as *Harlequinade* for New York City Ballet in 1965 began life as *Les Millions d'Arlequin* in 1900 with the ballet company of the Imperial Theatre in St. Petersburg. The original staging, to a score by house composer Riccardo Drigo, was by Marius Petipa, then in the twilight of his long career in Russia. The plot, carefully arranged alongside its score, involved Harlequin, Columbine, Pierrot, and others of *commedia dell'arte* fame. These various rascally, toy theatre personages here live through one of their most classic episodes: Columbine is courted by Harlequin, who is rejected by her father in favour of a bloated, foppish swain with bags of money. Machinations by Pierrette, Columbine's maid, and counter-manoeuvrings by Pierrot, her father's man, complicate the battle of wills, until a Good Fairy intervenes, showering the cocky Harlequin with gold and making possible a happy union between him and his lady love.

Balanchine had appeared in a staging of this work in his youth, and in 1952 created *Harlequinade Pas de Deux* for André Eglevsky and Maria Tallchief, two of his New York City Ballet dancers. The two-act version he arranged some thirteen years later, in the year marking the ballet's 65th birthday, became the first full-scale version of the work outside Russia. (Various restagings had taken place over the years, but most were truncated ones in pantomime formulas for such venues as Copenhagen's Tivoli Theatre.) Balanchine's creation, led by Edward Villella and Patricia McBride as Harlequin and Columbine respectively, variously struck some dance journalists as thin in substance, hokey of music, and thick with empty dancing.

With its Italianate roots, its Frenchified characters, and its Russian formulas, Balanchine's ballet was a delicate hybrid in which the French side took precedence. (Petipa was French-born and the Russian court he worked for was deeply concerned with things French: the leading characters of *Harlequinade* had the look, in both Rouben Ter-Arutunian's costumes and in Balanchine's ballet plastique, of French porcelain figurines of Italian theatre types.) For Villella, the mischievous Harlequin was succinctly and illuminatingly defined by Balanchine, when he described him as a premier danseur. McBride in petal pink or baby blue tutu, was the picture of a Sèvres statuette. What early analysts saw as shallowness in the refined presentation of such stock characters was in fact Balanchine's intentional emphasis on formal elegance.

As in his version of *The Nutcracker*, and as he would later do with *Coppélia*, Balanchine respected the nineteenth-century art of pantomime in his *Harlequinade*, setting clear passages of formal, musical sign language wherever they were originally intended. The other nineteenth-century, and especially Russian, tradition that Balanchine honoured with this ballet was the one of showing off young dance pupils. Even before 1973, when he opened up the cuts he initially made in the score to include an entire suite of children's dances, the ballet master included a prominent retinue of little Harlequins to accompany the leading Harlequin on all his escapades.

Critical reaction to the ballet's first appearances was, in general, made with reference to Balanchine's twentieth-century slant on classicism. Thus, his *Harlequinade* was variously thought either a frivolous empty artifact or a dubious gloss on some more sound traditions. By the end of his lifetime, however, with more and more information and evidence filtered out of the Russia of his past, his staging of this late nineteenth-century classic was seen in an adjusted light. A telecast from the Maly Theatre of Leningrad in the late 1970s showed that the extant re-staging of Petipa's *Harlequin* work, largely the efforts of Petr Gusev, related most strongly and directly to what Balanchine had done. Both men, one-time classmates in the Imperial Theatre's ballet school, appeared to be remembering the same distinct source. Gusev's was presented with particular regard for the somewhat petrified state of Soviet ballet schooling, while Balanchine's was enlivened by the rather more advanced musical and physical expertise of his eagerly adept young dancers.

***Harlequinade*, performed by Edward Villella and Patricia McBride, New York City Ballet, 1965**

Villella's Harlequin was both contemporary and personal to his American outgoingness, but it was also grounded in plastic and dramatic notions that related strongly to what Michel Fokine undoubtedly retained for *Le Carnaval*, his recycling of Petipa's *commedia dell'arte* milieu. McBride's Columbine gave fresh and contemporary life to a far-reaching theatrical tradition of feminine finesse. Suki Schorer's Pierrette and Deni Lamont's Pierrot were both solidly classical and solidly demi-caractère in creating their roles. The ballet's crucial character roles—such as those of the father, the suitor, the suitor's lackey—were all played in carefully, yet colourfully arranged pantomime. Among the incidental highlights Balanchine put in his ballet were an amorous serenade for four couples of Scaramouches, a wittily tipsy forray for a sleepy police patrol, and a fluttering frolick for a flock of nine women.

Essentially Balanchine's *Harlequinade* is a fresh and shining example of a century-old pantomime-ballet tradition. It is revised Petipa, without being revisionist in slant.

—Robert Greskovic

**HART, Evelyn**

Canadian dancer. Born in Toronto, 4 April 1956. Studied with Victoria Carter, London, Ontario, from 1970, at National Ballet School, Toronto, 1971–72, and at Royal Winnipeg Ballet School, pupil of David Moroni, Jacqueline Weber, from 1973. Dancer (while still a student), Royal Winnipeg Ballet, from 1974; dancer in corps de ballet, from 1976; soloist from 1978; principal dancer from 1979; international guest artist, including for Dutch National Ballet, 1982, National Ballet of Canada, from 1983, Sadler's Wells Royal Ballet, 1984, and Bavarian State Opera Ballet, Munich, from 1990; also performed with Universal Ballet, Far East tour, 1985, in Odessa and Moscow with Andris Liepa, 1986, at World Ballet Festival, Japan, 1988 and 1991, and on Russian tour with Royal Winnipeg Ballet, 1988; has appeared on television and film, including with Peter Schaufuss in *Swan Lake* (1989). Recipient: Bronze Medal, World Ballet Concours, Osaka, Japan, 1980; Gold Medal and Certificate of Exceptional Artistic Achievement, International Ballet Competition, Varna, 1980; Actra Award for Best Variety Performer, Canada, 1981; title of Officer of the Order of Canada, 1983.

## ROLES

1977 Pas de deux from *The Sleeping Beauty* (after Petipa), Banff Festival, Banff

Louise in *The Nutcracker* (Neumeier), Royal Winnipeg Ballet, Vancouver

1978 Principal dancer in *Mahler Four: Eternity is Now* (Araiz), Royal Winnipeg Ballet, Winnipeg

**Evelyn Hart in Hans van Manen's *Five Tangos*, Royal Winnipeg Ballet**

1979 Principal dancer in *Songs without Words* (van Manen), Royal Winnipeg Ballet, Winnipeg

Prelude and Pas de deux in *Les Sylphides* (Fokine; staged Markova), Royal Winnipeg Ballet, Winnipeg

1979/80 Dancer in *Moments Shared* (pas de deux; van Dantzig), Royal Winnipeg Ballet, Winnipeg (also performed for Varna International Ballet Competition)

Dancer in *Belong* (pas de deux; Vesak), Royal Winnipeg Ballet, Winnipeg

1980 Principal dancer in *Four Last Songs* (van Dantzig), Royal Winnipeg Ballet, Winnipeg

Dancer in *Venus Pas de deux* (McKinnon), Royal Winnipeg Ballet, Winnipeg

Pas de deux from *Don Quixote* (after Petipa; staged Bogomolova), Royal Winnipeg Ballet, Winnipeg

Principal dancer in *Five Tangos* (van Manen), Royal Winnipeg Ballet, Winnipeg

Pas de deux from *Giselle* (after Petipa, Coralli, Perrot), International Ballet Competition, Varna

Dancer in *A Dance for You* (pas de deux; Nebrada), Royal Winnipeg Ballet, tour

Principal dancer in *Our Waltzes* (Nebrada), Royal Winnipeg Ballet, Winnipeg

1981 Principal dancer in *Meadow Dance* (Vesak), Royal Winnipeg Ballet, Winnipeg

Juliet in *Romeo and Juliet* (van Dantzig), Royal Winnipeg Ballet, Winnipeg

1982 Title role (cr) in *Firebird* (Nebrada), Royal Winnipeg Ballet, Winnipeg

Principal dancer in *Lento a Tempo e Appassionato* (Nebrada), Royal Winnipeg Ballet, Winnipeg

Odile in *Black Swan* Pas de deux (after Petipa), Royal Winnipeg Ballet, Winnipeg

Principal dancer in *Allegro Brillante* (Balanchine), Royal Winnipeg Ballet, Winnipeg

Title role in *Giselle* (Petipa after Coralli, Perrot; staged Wright), Royal Winnipeg Ballet, Winnipeg

1984 Principal dancer in *Elite Syncopations* (MacMillan), Sadler's Wells Royal Ballet, London

Princess Aurora in *The Sleeping Beauty* (Nureyev after Petipa), National Ballet of Canada, Toronto

Odette/Odile in *Swan Lake* (Petipa, Ivanov; staged Wright), Sadler's Wells Royal Ballet, Cambridge

1985 Pas de deux from *Proust* (Petit), Universal Ballet, Far East tour

1986 Dancer in *Nuages* (pas de deux; Kylián), Royal Winnipeg Ballet, Vancouver

Sanguinic in *The Four Temperaments* (Balanchine), National Ballet of Canada, Toronto

Second Movement in *Symphony in C* (Balanchine), National Ballet of Canada, Toronto

Principal dancer in *Serenade* (Balanchine), National Ballet of Canada, Toronto

1987 Valencienne in *The Merry Widow* (Hynd), National Ballet of Canada, Winnipeg

1988 Tatiana in *Onegin* (Cranko), National Ballet of Canada, Toronto

Principal dancer in *Adagio Hammerklavier* (van Manen), Royal Winnipeg Ballet, Winnipeg

Principal dancer in *Piano Variations III* (van Manen), Royal Winnipeg Ballet, Winnipeg

1989 Principal dancer in *Concerto Barocco* (Balanchine), Royal Winnipeg Ballet, Winnipeg

The Swan in *The Dying Swan* (after Fokine, Pavlova), Royal Winnipeg Ballet, Winnipeg

1990 Title role (cr) in *Cinderella* (Duse), Bavarian State Ballet, Munich

Title role in *La Sylphide* (Bjørn after Bournonville), Bavarian State Ballet, Munich
Nikiya in "The Kingdom of the Shades" from *La Bayadère* (Yordanova after Petipa), Royal Winnipeg Ballet, Winnipeg
Principal dancer in *Valse Triste* (Martins), Royal Winnipeg Ballet, Winnipeg
1991 Caroline in *Jardin aux lilas* (Tudor), Royal Winnipeg Ballet, Winnipeg

**Other roles include:** Ballerina in *Esmeralda Pas de deux* (mus. Pugni).

## PUBLICATIONS

Crabb, Michael, "Evelyn Hart's Giselle", *Dance Magazine* (New York), April 1983
Crabb, Michael, "Evelyn Hart of the Royal Winnipeg Ballet", *Dancing Times* (London), December 1983
Wyman, Max, "North Star", *Ballet News* (New York), April 1984
Crabb, Michael, "*Swan Lake* [in Manitoba]", *Dance Magazine* (New York), December 1987
Jenish, Darcy, and Willer, Brian, "Slaying the Dragons", *MacLeans* (Toronto), 25 December 1989
Wyman, Max, *Evelyn Hart: An Intimate Portrait*, Ontario, 1991

* * *

What makes Evelyn Hart one of Canada's finest ballerinas is her obvious stage presence. She has a natural lyricism and innate musicality which make her a dancer of extraordinary expressiveness. Her emotional nakedness makes her popular with audiences, showing her continued ability to imbue any role she tackles, whether classical or contemporary, with deep personal feeling. Beyond the technical demands of a given ballet, Hart always has something more to communicate with her body. Yet ironically it is a body that Hart herself often mistrusts. Her relatively late start in dance at the age of fourteen and a highly sensitive nature have combined to make Hart a nervous and insecure dancer. She suffers from tremendous stage fright and is self-critical to the point of self-deprecation, referring to her superb technique as her "achilles' heel". Yet these neuroses are in place as a result of Hart's unstinting quest for perfection. "I want so much to dance beautifully, to be the very best I can be," she has said. To see her is to believe her. Her performances are one-hundred-percent applications of selfless devotion to the dance.

"She's very individual. She loves the dramatic overtones," Canadian choreographer Brian Macdonald has said of her. "She loves to realize her personality through dancing rather than remain a musical abstraction." This means that her dancing is more visceral and generally more passionate than that of her Canadian counterparts. It is a very personal style that some have called idiosyncratic in its tendency to carry the dramatic nuances in a role to an extreme. Also, her vulnerable, emotional style often makes her a liability. She will only perform with companies she feels "comfortable" with and by that she means "comforting". She has stayed with the Royal Winnipeg Ballet despite the fact that her award-winning technical prowess could make her a star with any of the world's leading companies, and this is because the Winnipeg troupe has gone out of its way to make her happy, expanding its quirky, predominantly modern repertoire to house the classics and other works that show off Hart's polished line. The Winnipeg company's artistic director emeritus, Arnold Spohr, has called her "Little Miss Leningrad" because she dances in the Russian style. "I think Russian ballet focuses on the flow of movement. Everything is involved. It's not only the body; it's the head and the heart, with a lot of passion and drama rather than speed and technique," Hart has explained. In the past she has relied on adrenalin or instinct to get her through performances. But now she is resting on an assured technique and creating out of a new-found sense of confidence, something which has been increasingly evident in both her dancing and her attitude towards her art.

—Deirdre Kelly

---

## HART, John

British dancer and ballet director. Born in London, 4 July 1921. Studied with Judith Espinosa, and at the Royal Academy of Dancing (on student and choreographic scholarship), London, 1933–38. Served in the Royal Air Force, 1942–46. Dancer, Vic-Wells Ballet (later Sadler's Wells Ballet), soon becoming principal dancer, 1938–42, and 1946–63; also appeared on television, including in British Broadcasting Corporation (BBC) television series *Ballet for Beginners*, 1950, and on film *The Man Who Loved Redheads* (dir. French, 1955); ballet master and director of ballet staff, Sadler's Wells (later Royal) Ballet, from 1955; assistant director, Royal Ballet, 1962–70; director, U.S. International University of Performing Arts, San Diego, California, 1970–74; artistic director, PACT (Performing Arts Council of Transvaal) Ballet, Johannesburg, South Africa, 1971–75; artistic director, San Diego Ballet, California, 1980; dance director, San Diego Opera, 1985; artistic director, Ballet West, Salt Lake City, Utah, from 1985. Recipient: First Adeline Genée Gold Medal for male dancers, London, 1939; Queen Elizabeth II Coronation Award, Royal Academy of Dancing, 1970; title of Commander of the Order of the British Empire, 1971.

## ROLES

1938 Trepak in *The Nutcracker*, Act III (Sergeyev after Ivanov), Vic-Wells Ballet, London
The Porter (cr) in *Harlequin in the Streets* (Ashton), Vic-Wells Ballet, London
1940 Angel (cr) in *The Wise Virgins* (de Valois), Vic-Wells Ballet, London
Monsieur Vestris (cr) in *The Prospect Before Us* (de Valois), Vic-Wells Ballet, London
Popular Song in *Façade* (Ashton), Vic-Wells Ballet, London
Shepherd in *The Gods Go a-Begging* (de Valois), Vic-Wells Ballet, London
Elihu in *Job* (de Valois), Vic-Wells Ballet, London
1941 Dancer (cr) in *The Wanderer* (Ashton), Sadler's Wells Ballet, London
Peasant (cr) in *Orpheus and Eurydice* (de Valois), Sadler's Wells Ballet, London
Nutcracker Prince in *The Nutcracker* (Sergeyev after Ivanov), Sadler's Wells Ballet, London
Dr. Coppélius in *Coppélia* (Petipa, Ivanov, Cecchetti; staged Sergeyev), Sadler's Wells Opera Ballet, tour
Pas de deux in *Les Patineurs* (Ashton), Sadler's Wells Ballet, London

The Bridegroom in *The Wise Virgins* (Ashton), Sadler's Wells Ballet, London
Bluebird in *The Sleeping Princess* (Petipa; staged Sergeyev), Sadler's Wells Ballet, London
Mazurka, Pas de deux in *Les Sylphides* (Fokine), Sadler's Wells Ballet, London
1942 A Child of Light in *Dante Sonata* (Ashton), Sadler's Wells Ballet, London
Albrecht in *Giselle* (Petipa after Coralli, Perrot; staged Sergeyev), Sadler's Wells Ballet, London
Siegfried in *Swan Lake*, Act II (Ivanov; staged Sergeyev), Sadler's Wells Ballet, London
Orpheus in *Orpheus and Eurydice* (de Valois), Sadler's Wells Ballet, London
Variation, Adagio of Lovers in *Les Rendezvous* (Ashton), Sadler's Wells Ballet, London
A Lover in *The Wanderer* (Ashton), Sadler's Wells Ballet, London
Prince Florimund in *The Sleeping Princess* (Petipa; staged Sergeyev), Sadler's Wells Ballet, London
1946 Principal dancer in *Symphonic Variations* (Ashton), Sadler's Wells Ballet, tour
A Chinese Dancer (cr) in *The Fairy Queen* (masque after Shakespeare; mus. Purcell, chor. Ashton), Covent Garden Opera and Sadler's Wells Ballet, London
1947 A Child of Darkness in *Dante Sonata* (Ashton), Sadler's Wells Ballet, London
The Official in *Miracle in the Gorbals* (Helpmann), Sadler's Wells Ballet, London
The Governor in *The Three-Cornered Hat* (Massine), Sadler's Wells Ballet, London
A Government Official in *Mam' zelle Angot* (Massine), Sadler's Wells Ballet, London
1948 Can-Can dancer in *La Boutique fantasque* (Massine), Sadler's Wells Ballet, London
Prince in *Cinderella* (Ashton), Sadler's Wells Ballet, London
Principal dancer in *Scènes de ballet* (Ashton), Sadler's Wells Ballet, London
1949 Title role in *Don Juan* (Ashton), Sadler's Wells Ballet, London
King of Denmark in *Hamlet* (Helpmann), Sadler's Wells Ballet, London
Satan in *Job* (de Valois), Sadler's Wells Ballet, London
Bridegroom in *A Wedding Bouquet* (Ashton), Sadler's Wells Ballet, London
Principal dancer in *Symphonic Variations* (Ashton), Sadler's Wells Ballet, tour
1951 The Lover of Tiresias in *Tiresias* (Ashton), Sadler's Wells Ballet, London
1952 The Stranger (cr) in *A Mirror for Witches* (Howard), Sadler's Wells Ballet, London
A Rich Old Neighbour (cr) in *Bonne-Bouche* (Cranko), Sadler's Wells Ballet, London
Orion (cr) in *Sylvia* (Ashton), Sadler's Wells Ballet, London
1953 Consort to the Queen of the Waters (cr) in *Homage to the Queen* (Ashton), Sadler's Wells Ballet, London
1954 Franz in *Coppélia* (Petipa, Cecchetti; staged Sergeyev), Sadler's Wells Ballet, London
1955 Köstchei in *Firebird* (Fokine), Sadler's Wells Ballet, London

**Other roles include:** Laertes in *Hamlet* (Helpmann), Bread Boy in *Harlequin in the Street* (Ashton), Shopkeeper in *La Boutique fantasque* (Massine), Elder Brother in *Comus* (Helpmann).

**WORKS**

Staged:
1969 *Façade* (chor. Ashton; mus. Walton), City Center Joffrey Ballet, Chicago
*La Fille mal gardée* (chor. Ashton; mus. Hérold, arranged Lanchbery), PACT Ballet, Johannesburg (restaged San Francisco Ballet, 1978)
1971 *The Sleeping Beauty* (after Petipa; mus. Tchaikovsky), PACT Ballet, Johannesburg
*Les Rendezvous* (chor. Ashton; mus. Auber), PACT Ballet, Johannesburg
*The Dream* (chor. Ashton; mus. Mendelssohn), PACT Ballet, Johannesburg (restaged Joffrey Ballet, 1973, Ballet West, 1985)
1972 *Giselle* (after Petipa, Coralli, Perrot; mus. Adam), PACT Ballet, Johannesburg
*Cinderella* (chor. Ashton; mus. Prokofiev), PACT Ballet, Johannesburg
1974 *Les Patineurs* (chor. Ashton; mus. Meyerbeer), American Ballet Theatre (restaged Ballet West, 1985)
1985 *Monotones* (chor. Ashton; mus. Satie), Ballet West, Salt Lake City

**PUBLICATIONS**

By Hart:
*Ballet and Camera*, London, 1956
*The Royal Ballet in Performance at Covent Garden*, London, 1958
"Administrative Needs of Ballet", *Dancing Times* (London), May 1963

About Hart:
Davidson, Gladys, *Ballet Biographies*, revised edition, London, 1954
Anthony, Gordon, "John Hart, C.B.E.", *Dancing Times* (London), February 1971
"Personality of the Month: John Hart", *Dance and Dancers* (London), September 1975
Grut, Marina, *The History of Ballet in South Africa*, Cape Town, 1981
McLean, Adrienne, "Hart of the West", *Dancing Times* (London), October 1989

* * *

John Hart's career in ballet is marked less by public brilliance and self-aggrandizement than some, but it is nevertheless one of the most distinguished careers in the field. He is best known for his work with the Vic-Wells/Sadler's Wells/Royal Ballet, but since the 1970s he has lived in America and his career has been an essentially international one, as a teacher, administrator, and producer of Royal Ballet repertoire. Since 1985 he has been artistic director of Utah's Ballet West, which is one of the largest regional companies in America.

Hart began dancing professionally in 1938, when Ninette de Valois invited him to join her Vic-Wells Ballet. Given the general dearth of male dancers in ballet at the time, a dancer of Hart's good looks and talent was likely to begin assuming leading roles at a very early age, and before his twenty-first birthday Hart had danced the principal role in all five of the classic ballets then in the repertoire. As a partner, Hart was not only strong and reliable but gallant; and he took, as he put it later, "the greatest pleasure in making the girl look good". His versatility made him an asset of more value than gold when older male dancers began to be called up in World War II, but eventually Hart too reached enlistment age, and between 1942 and 1946 he served overseas with the Royal Air Force. Upon his return, he again became principal dancer with the Sadler's Wells, recovering much, if not all, of the "lost time" in his dancing career. It was a big chunk gone, but one he never regretted having to give up. In 1955 he agreed to become ballet master and principal of the ballet staff to the Sadler's Wells, while continuing to perform in character roles. (Also in 1955, Moira Shearer asked Hart to partner her in the third-act pas de deux from *The Sleeping Beauty* in the film *The Man Who Loved Redheads*, and their performance makes the film worth seeking out.) Upon de Valois's retirement in 1962, Hart became one of three assistant directors under Frederick Ashton, and was responsible for the day-to-day running of the company and for its overseas tours. Hart retired when Ashton did in 1971, and although it seemed for a time he might go into another business entirely—he had had virtually a second career as a dance photographer, and was also a philatelist and wine connoisseur—Hart's numerous offers from other companies kept him in ballet, where he remains.

Besides partnering, Hart delighted throughout his career in playing heavies, villains, and comic parts of all varieties, and his Dr. Coppélius, his Orion in Ashton's *Sylvia*, his Official in Robert Helpmann's *Miracle in the Gorbals*, his Governor (Corregidor) in *The Three-Cornered Hat*, and his Shopkeeper and Can-Can dancer in *La Boutique fantasque* (roles for the Sadler's Wells revivals of which he was hand-picked by Massine) will be forgotten by none who saw them. He was also incomparably an organizer, not only competent at juggling the myriad responsibilities, crises, and scheduling difficulties of a company of some 120 dancers, but also actively enjoying the process. For his service to British ballet Hart was awarded the Queen Elizabeth Award in 1970, and the following year he was made a Commander of the Order of the British Empire. If he was never the great performing superstar (few male dancers of his generation were), John Hart for more than 50 years has gone quietly and skillfully about the task of leaving every operation he has been involved in better than he found it.

—Adrienne L. McLean

---

**HARVEY, Cynthia**

American dancer. Born in San Rafael, California, 17 May 1957. Studied at the Novato School of Ballet, California, pupil of Christine Walton; also studied at the National Ballet of Canada School, San Francisco Ballet School, School of American Ballet, and American Ballet Theatre School. Dancer, American Ballet Theatre, New York, from 1974, becoming soloist from 1978, and principal dancer 1982–86; principal guest artist, Royal Ballet, London, 1986–88; returned to American Ballet Theatre, 1988, while continuing as guest artist for the Royal Ballet, 1988–90; performed with Baryshnikov and Company, various seasons 1980–86, and with Nureyev and Friends; has also appeared as guest artist with Northern Ballet Theatre in London, 1982, and Sadler's Wells Royal Ballet, various seasons 1987–90, and at international arts festivals, including the Spoleto Festival, 1981, and Aspen Festival, Colorado, 1983; has appeared on television, including British television special *Tchaikovsky's Women* (ITV, 1988).

**ROLES**

1979 Myrtha in *Giselle* (Petipa after Coralli, Perrot; staged Blair), American Ballet Theatre

1980 Gamzatti (cr) in *La Bayadère* (new production; Makarova after Petipa), American Ballet Theatre, New York
Principal dancer in *Theme and Variations* (Balanchine), American Ballet Theatre
Clara in *The Nutcracker* (Baryshnikov), American Ballet Theatre

1982 A Passer-by in *Fancy Free* (Robbins), American Ballet Theatre
Title role in *Giselle* (Petipa after Coralli, Perrot; staged Blair), American Ballet Theatre

1983 Scherzo (cr) in *Interludes* (McFall), American Ballet Theatre, San Francisco

1984 Fairy Godmother (cr) in *Cinderella* (Baryshnikov, Anastos), American Ballet Theatre, New York
Title role in *Cinderella* (Baryshnikov, Anastos), American Ballet Theatre
Solo variation in *Paquita* (Makarova after Petipa), American Ballet Theatre

1986 The Moon (cr) in *Beauty and the Beast* (Eagling), Royal Ballet, London
Princess Aurora in *The Sleeping Beauty* (Petipa, Ashton; staged de Valois), Royal Ballet, London
Bluebird in *The Sleeping Beauty* (Petipa, Ashton; staged de Valois), Royal Ballet, London
Principal dancer in *Opus 19/The Dreamer* (Robbins), Royal Ballet, London
Principal dancer in *Symphonic Variations* (Ashton), Royal Ballet, London
Title role in *Cinderella* (Ashton), Royal Ballet, London
Countess Marie Larisch in *Mayerling* (MacMillan), Royal Ballet, London

1987 The Woman (cr) in *Still Life at the Penguin Café* (Bintley), Royal Ballet, London
Title role in *Manon* (MacMillan), Royal Ballet, London
Odette/Odile in *Swan Lake* (Petipa, Ivanov, Ashton; staged Dowell), Royal Ballet, London
Title role in *The Firebird* (Fokine), Royal Ballet, London
Principal dancer in *Serenade* (Balanchine), Royal Ballet, London

1988 Title role in *Ondine* (Ashton), Royal Ballet, London
Principal dancer (cr) in *Quartet* (Tharp), American Ballet Theatre, Miami Beach, Florida

1989 First ballerina in *Ballet Imperial* (Balanchine), American Ballet Theatre
Mrs. Harriman's Daughter in *Everlast* (Tharp), American Ballet Theatre, San Francisco

1990 La Reine de la danse from Moscow in *Gala Performance* (Tudor), American Ballet Theatre
Principal dancer in *Sinfonietta* (Kylián), American Ballet Theatre
Swanilda in *Coppélia* (Martinez after Saint-Léon), American Ballet Theatre, New York
Principal dancer in *Brief Fling* (Tharp), American Ballet Theatre

1991 Principal dancer in *Birthday Offering* (Ashton), American Ballet Theatre

**Other roles include:** Sweetheart/Mother in *Billy the Kid* (Loring), Second Movement in *Bourrée fantasque* (Balanchine), Pas de deux from *Le Corsaire* (Nureyev after Petipa), principal dancer in *Donizetti Variations* (Balanchine), Kitri in *Don Quixote: Kitri's Wedding* (Baryshnikov after Petipa), principal

**Cynthia Harvey (left) in *La Bayadère*, with Anthony Dowell and Alicia Markova, American Ballet Theatre, 1974**

dancer in *Grand Pas Classique* (Bujones), title role in *Paquita* (Makarova after Petipa), principal dancer in *Raymonda Divertissements* (from Act II and Act III; Baryshnikov after Petipa), Lovers' Pas de deux from *Les Patineurs* (Ashton), Pas de trois from *The Guards of Amager* (Bournonville), Juliet in *Romeo and Juliet* (MacMillan), Odette in *Swan Lake* (Baryshnikov after Petipa, Ivanov), title role in *La Sylphide* (Bruhn after Bournonville), Waltz, Prelude, Mazurka in *Les Sylphides* (Fokine), principal dancer in *Bach Partita* (Tharp), principal dancer in *The Little Ballet* (Tharp), principal dancer in *Symphonie Concertante* (Balanchine), principal dancer in *Requiem* (MacMillan), principal dancer in (*Tchaikovsky*) *Pas de deux* (Balanchine).

## PUBLICATIONS

By Harvey:

Interview in Finch, Tamara, "Dance Portrait: Cynthia Harvey", *Dancing Times* (London), June 1988

"Working with Ashton", Cynthia Harvey in Conversation with David Vaughan, *Ballet Review* (New York), Fall 1989

About Harvey:

Laine, Barry, "Taking on Giselle", *Ballet News* (New York), March 1983

Laine, Barry, "Aiming High", *Ballet News* (New York), February 1986

Greco, Stephen, "Harvey's Royal Stint: 'Like Fonteyn in Overdrive'", *Dance Magazine* (New York), March 1987

* * *

Cynthia Harvey is one of the most versatile of contemporary ballerinas. The purity of her technique and her freedom from the kind of aggressive "personality" that is manifested through mannerism and flamboyant self-display enable her to adapt to many different styles and to identify with many different characters. She is equally at home in ballets by Frederick Ashton and George Balanchine, Kenneth MacMillan and Twyla Tharp, as well as in the classical repertory.

She joined American Ballet Theatre at the age of seventeen and remained with that company for twelve years, moving from corps de ballet through soloist rank to that of principal, and dancing ballerina roles in such nineteenth-century classics as *Giselle*, *La Sylphide*, and *La Bayadère*, in Balanchine's *Theme and Variations*, and in Mikhail Baryshnikov's versions of *The Nutcracker*, *Cinderella*, and *Don Quixote*, among other ballets.

A partnership with Anthony Dowell during the time that he danced with ABT from the late 1970s led to an invitation to Harvey to join the Royal Ballet as guest artist when Dowell returned to that company and was appointed director, in 1986. She danced Odette/Odile in the premiere of his new production of *Swan Lake* in the following year. The two years she spent with the Royal Ballet, though marred by an injury that kept her off the stage for part of the time, were important for her development as an artist.

Such a development was possible because she did not go to the company as a visiting star, determined to impose her own way of dancing on the roles she was given, but with a modest eagerness to learn from the experience of dancing a varied repertory of classic and modern ballets. In physique and temperament she was ideally suited to the Royal style, while at the same time bringing to it a welcome dash of American physicality. Her reward came when Ashton approved of her being cast in the leading role, created by Margot Fonteyn, in the revival of his masterpiece *Symphonic Variations*, absent from the repertory for many years. Ashton himself coached her in the role of Aurora in *The Sleeping Beauty* and in the title role of his *Ondine*; in his *Cinderella* and *Symphonic Variations* she was coached by Michael Somes. Although these roles are indelibly associated with Fonteyn at the Royal Ballet, Harvey was able to find her own interpretations of them, which won Ashton's approval.

Returning to her home company in 1988 as a senior ballerina, she displayed new authority in a variety of works, including Twyla Tharp's austere *Quartet*, Balanchine's *Ballet Imperial* (as the virtuoso first ballerina), and Antony Tudor's parody of different styles of dancing, *Gala Performance* (in which she portrayed the Russian Ballerina). She was even able to bring some conviction to two misguided stagings of nineteenth-century classics—Baryshnikov's new *Swan Lake* and Enrique Martinez's *Coppélia*, in which she gave some humanity to the role of Swanilda. When ABT added Ashton's *Birthday Offering* to its repertory in 1991, Harvey showed a real understanding of his combination of lyricism with technical strength.

Harvey has continued to appear as a guest with both the Royal Ballet and the Birmingham (formerly Sadler's Wells) Royal Ballet, each of which has its own version of the major classic ballets, and with other companies.

—David Vaughan

---

**HAYDÉE, Marcia**

Brazilian dancer and ballet director. Born Marcia Haydée Salaverry Pereira da Silva, in Niteroi, Brazil, 18 April 1939. Studied with Vaslev Veltchek, Rio de Janeiro, at Sadler's Wells Ballet School, pupil of Tatiana Leskova, London, and with Lubov Egorova and Olgo Preobrazhenska, Paris. Dancer, corps de ballet, Teatro Municipal in Rio de Janeiro, from 1951; dancer, Grand Ballet du Marquis de Cuevas, 1957–61; dancer, Stuttgart Ballet, from 1961, becoming principal dancer, from 1962; international guest artist, including for National Ballet of Canada, Boston Ballet, Royal Ballet, American Ballet Theatre, and English National Ballet; artistic director, Stuttgart Ballet, from 1976; has also appeared as Vera Baronova in *On Your Toes* (musical by Rogers and Hart; chor. Fuller), Forum Theatre, Stuttgart, 1990. Recipient: Étoile d'or, Paris, 1967; German Critics' Prize, 1971; Doctor Honoris Causa, Stuttgart University, 1981; German Honour of Merit, First Class, 1981; Golden Ballet Shoe Award, 1984; German Dance Prize, 1989; Title of Professor.

**ROLES**

1961 Title role in *Antigone* (Cranko), Stuttgart Ballet, Stuttgart
La Capricciosa in *The Lady and the Fool* (Cranko), Stuttgart Ballet, Stuttgart
Aurora in *The Sleeping Beauty* (Beriozoff, Cranko after Petipa), Stuttgart Ballet, Stuttgart
1962 Swanilda in *Coppélia* (Cranko after Petipa), Stuttgart Ballet, Stuttgart
The Year (cr) in *The Seasons* (Cranko), Stuttgart Ballet, Stuttgart
Principal dancer in *The Great Peacock* (Wright), Stuttgart Ballet, Stuttgart
Juliet (cr) in *Romeo and Juliet* (new version; Cranko), Stuttgart Ballet, Stuttgart
1963 Dancer Behind the Mirror (cr) in *The Mirror Walkers* (Wright), Stuttgart Ballet, Stuttgart
Waltz, Mazurka in *Les Sylphides* (Fokine; staged Wright), Stuttgart Ballet, Stuttgart
Zero (cr) in *Variations* (Cranko), Stuttgart Ballet, Stuttgart
The Eldest Sister (cr) in *Las Hermanas* (Cranko), Stuttgart Ballet, Stuttgart
Odette/Odile in *Swan Lake* (Cranko after Petipa, Ivanov), Stuttgart Ballet, Stuttgart
1964 Title role (cr) in *The Firebird* (Cranko), German Opera Ballet, Berlin
Principal dancer (cr) in *Bolshoi Pas de deux* (Cranko), Stuttgart Ballet, Stuttgart
1965 Nocturne (cr) in *Bouquet Garni* (Cranko), Stuttgart Ballet, Stuttgart
Principal dancer in *La Valse* (Balanchine), Stuttgart Ballet, Stuttgart
Tatiana (cr) in *Onegin* (Cranko), Stuttgart Ballet, Stuttgart Ballet, Stuttgart
Principal dancer (cr) in *Jeux de vagues* (pas de deux; Cranko), Stuttgart Ballet, Stuttgart
Principal dancer in *Danses Concertantes* (MacMillan), Stuttgart Ballet, Stuttgart
The Woman (cr) in *Das Lied von der Erde* (*Song of the Earth*; MacMillan), Stuttgart Ballet, Stuttgart
1966 Title role in *Giselle* (Petipa after Coralli, Perrot; staged Wright), Stuttgart Ballet, Stuttgart
Principal dancer (cr) in *Pas de quatre* (Cranko), Stuttgart Ballet, Stuttgart
Lene in *The Nutcracker* (Cranko), Stuttgart Ballet, Stuttgart
1967 The Human (cr) in *Oiseaux exotiques* (Cranko), Stuttgart Ballet, Stuttgart Ballet, Stuttgart
The Mermaid (cr) in *Quatre Images* (Cranko), Stuttgart Ballet, Stuttgart Ballet, Stuttgart
1968 Molly (cr) in *Présence* (Cranko), Stuttgart Ballet, Stuttgart
Title role (cr) in *The Sphinx* (MacMillan), Stuttgart Ballet, Stuttgart
1969 Katherina (cr) in *The Taming of the Shrew* (Cranko), Stuttgart Ballet, Stuttgart
1970 Title role (cr) in *Miss Julie* (MacMillan), Stuttgart Ballet, Stuttgart

**Marcia Haydée with Richard Cragun in *Onegin*, Stuttgart Ballet**

Principal dancer (cr) in *Raymonda Pas de deux* (Beale), Stuttgart Ballet, Stuttgart
Principal dancer (cr) in *Kommen und Gehen* (Kylián), Stuttgart Ballet, Stuttgart
1971 Title role (cr) in *Carmen* (Cranko), Stuttgart Ballet, Stuttgart Ballet, Stuttgart
1972 M. (=Marcia; cr) in *Initials R.B.M.E.* (Cranko), Stuttgart Ballet, Stuttgart
Title role in *Raymonda* (Nureyev after Petipa), Zürich Ballet, Zürich
Principal dancer (cr) in *Légende* (pas de deux; Cranko), Stuttgart Ballet, Munich
Principal dancer in *Trisch-Trasch* (pas de deux; Cranko), television performance
1973 The Woman (cr) in *Spuren* (*Traces*; Cranko), Stuttgart Ballet, Stuttgart
Principal dancer in *Concerto* (MacMillan), Stuttgart Ballet, Stuttgart
Principal dancer (cr) in *Voluntaries* (Tetley), Stuttgart Ballet, Stuttgart
1974 Principal dancer (cr) in *Ritual Album* (Berg), Stuttgart Ballet, Stuttgart
Principal dancer in *Gemini* (Tetley), Stuttgart Ballet, Stuttgart
Principal dancer (cr) in *Nacht* (Neumeier), Stuttgart Ballet, Stuttgart
1975 Principal dancer in *Laborintus* (Tetley), Stuttgart Ballet, Stuttgart
Principal dancer in *Intermezzo* (Feld), Stuttgart Ballet, Stuttgart
Chloe (cr) in *Daphnis and Chloe* (Tetley), Stuttgart Ballet, Stuttgart
Columbine in *Pierrot lunaire* (Tetley), Stuttgart Ballet, Stuttgart
Principal dancer (cr) in *Alegrias* (Tetley), Stuttgart Ballet, Stuttgart
1975/76 The Accused in *Fall River Legend* (de Mille), American Ballet Theatre, New York
Hagar in *Pillar of Fire* (Tudor), American Ballet Theatre, New York
1976 Title role in *Anastasia* (MacMillan), Stuttgart Ballet, Stuttgart
Gertrude (cr) in *Hamlet Connotations* (Neumeier), American Ballet Theatre, New York

Gertrude (cr) in *Der Fall Hamlet* (new version of *Hamlet Connotations*; Neumeier), Stuttgart Ballet, Stuttgart
Title role in *Medea* (pas de deux; Butler), American Ballet Theatre, New York
Sanctus, Pie Jesu (cr) in *Requiem* (MacMillan), Stuttgart Ballet
1977 Title role (cr) in *Daphne* (Forsythe), Stuttgart Ballet, Stuttgart
The Woman (cr) in *Mirage* (Helliwell), Stuttgart Ballet, Stuttgart
Principal dancer (cr) in *Innere Not* (Montagnon), Stuttgart Ballet, Stuttgart
1978 Principal dancer (cr) in *Glocken* (Montagnon), Stuttgart Ballet, Stuttgart
Principal dancer (cr) in *Concertino* (Helliwell), Stuttgart Ballet, Stuttgart
Marguerite Gautier (cr) in *Die Kameliendame* (*The Lady of the Camellias*; Neumeier), Stuttgart Ballet, Stuttgart
1979 Principal dancer in *Exsultate, Jubilate* (Lubovitch), Stuttgart Ballet, Stuttgart
Principal dancer (cr) in *Time Cycle* (Forsythe), Stuttgart Ballet, Stuttgart
Principal dancer in *Symphony of Psalms* (Kylián), Stuttgart Ballet, Stuttgart
1980 Principal dancer (cr) in *Forty Winters* (Anderson), Stuttgart Ballet, Stuttgart
Principal dancer (cr) in *Das Märchen* (Scholz), Stuttgart Ballet, Stuttgart
1981 Title role (cr) in *Hedda* (Helliwell), Stuttgart Ballet, Stuttgart
Principal dancer in *Leda* (Béjart), Stuttgart Ballet, Stuttgart
1982 Principal dancer in *Divine* (Béjart), Stuttgart Ballet, Stuttgart
Principal dancer (cr) in *Something Special Pas de deux* (Aschcar), Rio de Janeiro
1983 Title role (cr) in *Isadora* (new version; Béjart), Stuttgart Ballet, Stuttgart
Blanche du Bois (cr) in *A Streetcar Named Desire* (Neumeier), Stuttgart Ballet, Stuttgart
1984 Principal dancer (cr) in *Stabat Mater* (Scholz), Stuttgart Ballet, Stuttgart
The Woman in *The Chairs* (Béjart), Gala performance, Brussels
1985 Principal dancer (cr) in *Operette* (Béjart), Stuttgart Ballet, Stuttgart
Principal dancer (cr) in *Corps* (van Manen), Stuttgart Ballet, Stuttgart
1986 Principal dancer (cr) in *Fratres* (Neumeier), Stuttgart Ballet, Stuttgart
1987 Principal dancer in *Bits and Pieces* (van Manen), Stuttgart Ballet, Stuttgart
1988 Blind Seer (cr) in *Wie Antigone* (new version; Mats Ek), Stuttgart Ballet, Stuttgart
Principal dancer in *Chambre separée* (Béjart), Stuttgart Ballet, Stuttgart
Principal dancer (cr) in *Pas de Crackkkk* (van Manen), Stuttgart Ballet, Stuttgart
1990 Title role (cr) in *Medea* (Neumeier), Stuttgart Ballet, Stuttgart
Engel-Lilli in *Wien, Wien nur du allein* (Béjart), Stuttgart Ballet, Stuttgart

**Other roles include:** The Coquette in *Divertimento* (Cranko), Kitri in *Don Quixote Pas de deux* (after Petipa), the Girl in *Intermezzo* (Cranko), principal dancer in *L'Estro Armonico* (Cranko), principal dancer in *The Interrogation* (*Die Befragung*; Cranko), Belle Epine in *The Prince of the Pagodas* (Cranko), Die Schöne in *Poème de l'extase* (Cranko), principal dancer in *Ebony Concerto* (Cranko), principal dancer in *Allegro Brillante* (Balanchine), Terpsichore in *Apollo* (Balanchine), principal dancer in *Sonntag* (van Manen), the Melody in *Bolero* (Béjart), Madame in *Gaîté Parisienne* (Béjart), principal dancer in *Five Short Stories* (van Manen), principal dancer in *Twilight* (van Manen), principal dancer in *Five Tangos* (van Manen), Mathilde Wesendonck in *Träume* (Spoerli), principal dancer in *Adagio Hammerklavier* (van Manen), principal dancer in *Phèdre* (Lifar), principal dancer in *Composition abstracte* (Velczek), Coquette and Sleepwalker in *Night Shadow* (*La Somnambule*; Balanchine), principal dancer in *Suite en blanc* (Lifar), principal dancer in *Vierte Sinfonie von Gustav Mahler* (Neumeier).

## WORKS

1987 *ENAS* (pas de deux; mus. Vangelis), Stuttgart Ballet, Tokyo
1988 *Herbst* (pas de deux; mus. Glazunov), Stuttgart Ballet, Stuttgart
1990 *Beziehungen* (mus. Micus), Stuttgart Ballet, Stuttgart
1991 *The Planets* (mus. Holst), Stuttgart Ballet, Stuttgart

Also staged:
1987 *The Sleeping Beauty* (after Petipa; mus. Tchaikovsky), Stuttgart Ballet, Stuttgart
1989 *Giselle und die Wilis* (after Petipa, Coralli, Perrot; mus. Adam), Stuttgart Ballet, Ludwigsburg Festival

## PUBLICATIONS

By Haydée:
Interview in Gruen, John, *The Private World of Ballet*, New York, 1975
Interview with Kirchner, Birgit, "Marcia Haydée: Dance is Like Life", *Ballett International* (Cologne), March 1983
Interview with Robertson, Allen, "Fearless Flyer", *Ballet News* (New York), March 1985
"The Art of Being Properly Understood", *Ballett International* (Cologne), February 1986
*Dornröschen—Ein Balletraum von Marcia Haydée*, 1987

About Haydee:
Niehaus, Max, *Ballett Faszination*, Munich, 1972
Cranko, John, *Uber den Tanz*, Frankfurt, 1974
Austin, Richard, *Images of the Dance*, London, 1975
Gruen, John, "Stuttgart Profiles: Marcia Haydée and Richard Cragun", *Dance Magazine* (New York), August 1975
Kilian, Hannes, *Marcia Haydée: Portrait einer grossen Tänzerin*, 1975
Koegler, Horst, "Marcia Haydee", *Les Saisons de la danse* (Paris), November 1976
Robertson, Allen, "New Lease on Life", *Ballet News* (New York), September 1983
Gruen, John, "Marcia Haydée: Muse and Mentor", *Dance Magazine* (New York), January 1984
Crisp, Clement, "The Muse Observed", *Ballet News* (New York), March 1985
Woihsyk, Rainer, *Marcia Haydée*, Stuttgart, 1987

* * *

The Brazilian dancer, director, and choreographer Marcia Haydée is one of the great ballerinas and personalities of the late twentieth-century dance world. After her first small stage appearances when still a schoolgirl at the Teatro Municipal in Rio de Janeiro, she was taken on as part of the corps by the Marquis de Cuevas's Grand Ballet de Monte Carlo, and in 1961 she joined the Stuttgart Ballet under John Cranko's directorship, advancing to prima ballerina status by 1962. The great choreographer Cranko had sensed the artist in the dark-haired South American, whom one would have been tempted to think of as an average dancer, for her technique was far from brilliant. Marcia Haydée, none the less, became Cranko's great muse. Through his choreography and her strength of interpretative ability, Stuttgart became a world centre for ballet.

The quality particular to Haydée is her rare dual dramatic talent: she is equally as effective in the tragic as in the comic female roles. Her Tatiana in Cranko's Onegin (1965), her Marguerite in John Neumeier's *Kameliendame* (1978), her "Madame", the cranky old Russian ballet mistress, in Maurice Béjart's *Gaîeté parisienne* (1978)—all these different roles are interpreted with the same Haydée quality. Right into the late 1980s, she was as successful in the young maiden roles as she was in parts requiring a more mature woman.

If any exception to Haydée's great range is to be made, it must be in the classical or neo-classical ballets in the Balanchine mode. Haydée has, of course, danced the late nineteenth-century classics, as well as in the more romantic works of MacMillan and Balanchine. But fairy-tale figures or romantic ethereal creatures were never her speciality, nor were purely abstract classical works. Her great strength is historical or literary female characters, whose experiences contain a profound realism which Haydée, through the gifts of her great interpretitive art, is able to reflect with strength and power.

Yet Haydée was able also to shine like one of the best technicians in the company in Cranko's own abstract pieces, notably in his *Initialen R.B.M.E.*, Cranko's ode to friendship dedicated to his four soloists Richard (Cragun), Birgit (Keil), Marcia (Haydée), and Egon (Madsen). In these extremely rapid variations and pas de deux so typical of Cranko, with their constant changes of direction, stream of steps, and difficult lifts, she would glide in lightly and throw herself with her familiar, apparently careless courage into the high, twisting holds and lifts, often around her partner's body. Here she was at one with the dance vocabulary in which she moved; indeed, it continually recreated itself through her. With Haydée one felt, as rarely before, how great a role trust can play in partner work.

Her partners, above all Richard Cragun, felt honoured by this trust, and were consequently inspired to even greater care wherever possible. The various *Taming of the Shrew* pas de deux are perfect examples of this impressive pair work: when Richard Cragun hurled Haydée about like a puppet, twisted her arms in a firm grip, swept the ground from under her feet with a deft blow, and, in the final love pas de deux, raised her to his shoulders in a frantic action and let her fall away, it always looked effortless. It is only when one sees these almost stunt-like dances performed by a younger pair, unpractised and not yet fully at ease with each other, that the difficulties of this ballet become apparent.

But the mastery of the technical demands and character portrayal tend to be at odds with one another in this ballet, even with technically competent dancers. With Marcia Haydée, however, technique and expression, or—put another way—the dancer and the role, are never separate. One never watches and analyzes how Haydée links steps or performs a gesture. With her, there is never an idle "look at me"—in fact, often one does not remember at all the steps that she has danced in a particular ballet, but only her uniquely expressive face and gestures. And if one remembers movement, it is not the individual steps but a general impression which is left: a dynamic advance, an upward sweep, high flights supported by a partner, as in the balcony scene of *Romeo and Juliet*. In such "partner scenes" Haydée's dancing is a single flow: dance becomes the outward extension of inner movement, the metaphor for human emotion.

In 1976 Marcia Haydée assumed leadership of the Stuttgart company. She is valued by all its members as a sympathetic director who looks after her dancers individually with an almost motherly care. At the presentation of the German Tanzpreis in 1991 Richard Cragun described Haydée as "the heart of the company". She encourages new dancing talent at the John Cranko Ballet School as she does choreographic promise. In her first year as director she brought in William Forsythe and Uwe Scholz as choreographers. Recently she has given Daniela Kurz, an independent choreographer just 22 years old, the chance to choreograph for the company. By virtue of the fact that both John Neumeier and Maurice Béjart would like to work with her as leading dancer, she is also in a position to link them more closely to Stuttgart. Haydée has far greater opportunity than most ballet directors to rejuvenate the company's repertoire, with pieces frequently created by guest choreographers Hans van Manen, Jiří Kylián, and Uwe Scholz. She has also presented her own choreographic works, although not always with unanimously positive reactions from the critics. She is still young as a choreographer, however, and has every chance of developing with a committed company.

Haydée brings outstanding qualities to both her careers. As a dancer she brings the ability to give herself as a finely tuned instrument to the choreographer, while in the role of ballet director she brings from her South American home a sense of family, community, loyalty to her colleagues, and understanding. She will surely rank alongside the English pioneers Marie Rambert and Ninette de Valois, the Swede Birgit Cullberg, the Cuban Alicia Alonso, and the Germans Yvonne Georgi and Tatiana Gsovsky as an outstanding female ballet director and promoter of young choreographers.

—Malve Gradinger

---

**HAYDEN, Melissa**

Canadian/American dancer, teacher, and ballet director. Born Mildred Herman in Toronto, 25 April 1923. Studied with Boris Volkov, Toronto, at the Vilzak-Schollar School, New York, and at the School of American Ballet, pupil of George Balanchine. Married Donald Hugh Coleman, 1954: two children. Dancer, corps de ballet, Radio City Music Hall, 1945; dancer, soon becoming soloist, Ballet Theatre (later American Ballet Theatre), 1945–49; dancer, Ballet Alicia Alonso, touring South America, 1949; soloist, New York City Ballet, 1950–53; soloist, Ballet Theatre, 1953–54; principal dancer, New York City Ballet, 1955–73; frequent guest star with National Ballet of Canada; also guest artist with Royal Ballet in London, Chicago Opera Ballet, San Francisco Ballet, American Ballet Theatre, Ballet Alicia Alonso, and Boston Ballet; has also appeared on television and film: performed ballerina role in Charlie Chaplin's film *Limelight* (1952), title role in *The Countess Becomes the Maid* (chor. Balanchine, NBC television, 1953), and took part in "Great Moments of the Dance" film series, shown on television, 1957; artist-in-residence, Skidmore College, New York State, from 1973; founder and director of own dance school in Saratoga, New York, 1974; artistic director, Pacific Northwest Dance, Seattle, from 1976; on faculty of the Department of Dance, North Carolina School of the Arts, from 1983. Recipient: Merit Award, *Mademoiselle*, 1952; Albert Einstein Woman of Achievement Award; *Dance Magazine* Award, 1961; Honorary Doctorate, Skidmore College, New York, 1970; Handel Medallion, New York City, 1973.

**ROLES**

1945 Ensemble in *Interplay* (Robbins), Ballet Theatre, New York
1947 Solo (cr) in *Theme and Variations* (Balanchine), Ballet Theatre, New York
1949 Giannina (cr) in *Ondine* (Dollar), New York City Ballet, New York
1950 Clorinda (cr) in *The Duel* (Dollar), New York City Ballet, New York
Principal dancer (cr) in *The Age of Anxiety* (Robbins), New York City Ballet, New York
Profane Love (cr) in *Illuminations* (Ashton), New York City Ballet, New York
Sunday (cr) in *Jones Beach* (Balanchine), New York City Ballet, New York
The Fair Girl (cr) in *The Witch* (Cranko), New York City Ballet, London
1951 The Woman (cr) in *The Miraculous Mandarin* (Bolender), New York City Ballet, New York
Principal dancer (cr) in *The Pied Piper* (Robbins), New York City Ballet, New York
1952 Principal dancer (cr) in *Caracole* (Balanchine), New York City Ballet, New York
Leaves and Flowers (cr) in *Bayou* (Balanchine), New York City Ballet, New York
Principal dancer (cr) in *Kaleidoscope* (R. Boris), New York City Ballet, New York
1953 Principal dancer (cr) in *Valse-Fantaisie* (Balanchine), New York City Ballet, New York
The Fairy (cr) in *The Five Gifts* (Dollar), New York City Ballet, New York
Pas de deux in *The Combat* (Dollar), Ballet Theatre, New York
1955 Principal dancer (cr) in *Pas de Trois (II)* (Balanchine), New York City Ballet, New York
The Doll, Pas de deux (cr) in *Jeux d'enfants* (Balanchine, Milberg, Moncion), New York City Ballet, New York
1956 Principal dancer (cr) in *The Still Point* (new production; Bolender), New York City Ballet, New York
Second Variation (cr) in *Divertimento No. 15* (Balanchine), New York City Ballet, Stratford, Connecticut
1957 Young Woman in *The Masquers* (Bolender), New York City Ballet, New York
Second Pas de trois, Bransle Gay (cr) in *Agon* (Balanchine), New York City Ballet, New York
1958 Fourth Campaign (cr) in *Stars and Stripes* (Balanchine), New York City Ballet, New York
Title role in *Medea* (Cullberg), New York City Ballet, New York
1959 Ricercata (cr) in *Episodes* II (Balanchine), New York City Ballet, New York
1960 Princess of Persia (cr) in *The Figure in the Carpet* (Balanchine), New York City Ballet, New York
Principal dancer (cr) in *Variations from Don Sebastian* (later called *Donizetti Variations*; Balanchine), New York City Ballet, New York

**Melissa Hayden with Earle Sieveling in *Brahms-Schoenberg Quartet*, New York City Ballet**

Principal dancer (second couple) (cr) in *Liebeslieder Walzer* (Balanchine), New York City Ballet, New York
1961 Principal dancer (cr) in *Modern Jazz: Variants* (Balanchine), New York City Ballet, New York
1962 Titania (cr) in *A Midsummer Night's Dream* (Balanchine), New York City Ballet, New York
1964 Principal dancer (cr) in *Irish Fantasy* (d'Amboise), New York City Ballet, New York
1965 Valse Lente, Pas de Deux, Pizzicati (cr) in *Pas de Deux and Divertissement* (Balanchine), New York City Ballet, New York
1966 Allegro (cr) in *Brahms–Schoenberg Quartet* (Balanchine), New York City Ballet, New York
Second Young Girl (cr) in *Jeux* (Taras), New York City Ballet, New York
Principal dancer (cr) in *La Guirlande de Campra* (Taras), New York City Ballet, New York
1967 Principal dancer (cr) in *Trois Valses Romantiques* (Balanchine), New York City Ballet, New York
Jota Aragonese (cr) in *Glinkiana* (second movement later *Valse Fantaisie*; Balanchine), New York City Ballet, New York
1972 Eurydice in *Orpheus* (Balanchine), New York City Ballet, New York
Principal dancer (cr) in *Choral Variations on Bach's "Vom Himmel Hoch"* (Balanchine), New York City Ballet, New York
1973 Classical pas de deux (cr) in *Cortège Hongrois* (Balanchine), New York City Ballet, New York

**Other roles include:** for Ballet Theatre—Bird in *Peter and the Wolf* (Bolm), leading roles in *Pas de quatre* (Dolin), *Helen of Troy* (Lichine), *On Stage!* (Kidd), *Romeo and Juliet* (Tudor), *Undertow* (Tudor); for New York City Ballet—Sanguinic in

*The Four Temperaments* (Balanchine), principal dancer in *Symphonie Concertante* (Balanchine), First, Second, and Third Movements in *Symphony in C* (Balanchine), Odette in *Swan Lake* (one-act version; Balanchine after Ivanov), Sugar Plum Fairy in *The Nutcracker* (Balanchine), ballerina in *Tchaikovsky Pas de Deux* (Balanchine), title role in *Firebird* (Balanchine), principal dancer in *Concerto No. 2* (Balanchine), principal dancer in *Concerto Barocco* (Balanchine), principal dancer in *The Guests* (Robbins), Bearded Lady in *Jinx* (L. Christensen), Prelude in *Bourrée Fantasque* (Balanchine), principal dancer in *The Age of Anxiety* (Robbins), principal dancer in *Sylvia: Pas de Deux* (Balanchine), the Novice in *The Cage* (Robbins), principal dancer in *A La Françaix* (Balanchine), Wife in *Picnic at Tintagel* (Ashton), principal dancer in *Scotch Symphony* (Balanchine), principal dancer in *Afternoon of a Faun* (Robbins), principal dancer in *Gounod Symphony* (Balanchine), principal dancer in *Raymonda Variations* (Balanchine), divertissement in *A Midsummer Night's Dream* (Balanchine), Emeralds in *Jewels* (Balanchine), First Movement in *Tchaikovsky Suite No. 2* (d'Amboise), principal dancer in *Dances at a Gathering* (Robbins), principal dancer in *In the Night* (Robbins).

## PUBLICATIONS

By Hayden:

*Melissa Hayden, Off Stage and On*, New York, 1963

*Ballet Exercises for Figure, Grace and Beauty*, New York, 1969

Interview with Anastos, Peter, "Melissa Hayden on Ballet, Ballets, Balanchine", *Dance Magazine* (New York), August 1973

Interview in Gruen, John, *The Private World of Ballet*, New York, 1975

*Dancer to Dancer*, Garden City, N.Y., 1981

Interview in Tracy, Robert, *Balanchine's Ballerinas*, New York, 1983

About Hayden:

Chujoy, Anatole, *The New York City Ballet*, New York, 1953

Terry, Walter, "'H' is for Hayden, Ballerina", in *New York Herald Tribune*, 25 January 1959

Gustaitis, Rasa, *Melissa Hayden, Ballerina*, London and New York, 1967

Goodman, Saul, "Spotlight on Melissa Hayden and Jacques d'Amboise of the New York City Ballet", *Ballet Today* (London), May–June 1970

Goodman, Saul, "An Extraordinary Anniversary", *Dance Magazine* (New York), November 1970

Kirstein, Lincoln, "Melissa Hayden: A Tribute", *Dance Magazine* (New York), August 1973

Reynolds, Nancy, *Repertory in Review*, New York, 1977

* * *

Melissa Hayden performed as company member and later as guest artist with American Ballet Theatre. She was also guest artist with the Ballet Alicia Alonso, England's Royal Ballet, and Ruth Page's Chicago Opera Ballet. But the major portion of her career was spent with the New York City Ballet. When she retired in 1973, after 23 years with the company, its general director Lincoln Kirstein wrote that she was the nearest thing to a star in their "starless company", and artistic director George Balanchine created *Cortège Hongrois* as a farewell tribute to her during her final season.

Hayden's performing was marked by unusual physical endurance and by relentless professionalism. She was rarely injured and rarely missed a performance except when her two children were born. During much of her tenure, Balanchine was preoccupied with devising new roles for his wives, Maria Tallchief and then Tanaquil LeClercq. His primary attention then turned to Allegra Kent and subsequently Suzanne Farrell. Thus, while Melissa Hayden danced principal roles in approximately 50 ballets, they were often not initially made for her. At the outset of her career with the company, other choreographers were quicker to see her potential, especially when it came to her gifts as a dance actress. During her first seven years, her most notable portrayals included the striking yet vulnerable warrior-maiden Clorinda in William Dollar's *The Duel*, the tempestuous Profane Love in Sir Frederick Ashton's *Illuminations*, the Woman in Todd Bolender's *Miraculous Mandarin*, and the troubled girl in Bolender's *The Still Point*.

The first Balanchine role which exploited her individuality came in 1957 with *Agon*, in which she performed the "Bransle Gay" solo and the "Bransle Double de Poitou" with Roy Tobias and Jonathan Watts. In both of these she was called upon to execute feats of balance, all the while maintaining an easy sang-froid. As the two men seemed alternately to be testing her, she approached the challenge with a delicious wit culminating with an insouciant clap of the hands.

The following year Balanchine presented Hayden with an even greater challenge—the grand pas de deux in *Stars and Stripes*. Here he essentially threw the book at her. Partnered by the company's ranking premier danseur, Jacques d'Amboise, and accompanied by two rousing John Philip Sousa marches ("Liberty Bell" and "El Capitan"), she tossed off the gamut of bravura classical steps, all the while saluting, saucily cocking her head, or allowing herself to be literally thrown into the air by her partner. As the tempo steadily accelerated, it became evident that Melissa Hayden not only relished this kind of physical challenge, but was vastly exhilarated by it. Hers was the perfect balance between bravura and bravado.

This triumph did not confine Hayden to choreography which exploited her zest for technical display. Subtlety was also within her range. Balanchine's *A Midsummer Night's Dream* provided her with the sumptuous role of Titania. Here she was both feminine and imperious as the Queen of the Fairies, and in her pas de deux with Bottom disguised as a donkey, she again evinced the sense of humor which had sparked her interpretations in *Agon* and *Stars and Stripes*.

She was also radiant in purely classical works such as the *Sylvia: Pas de Deux*, *Swan Lake*, *The Nutcracker*, *Divertimento no. 15*, *Raymonda Variations*, and *Tchaikovsky Pas de Deux*. Throughout she remained true to the demands of the choreographer. Less consistent, however, was her musical sensitivity. Lyricism and the execution of cantilena did not come naturally to her.

Upon her retirement, Melissa Hayden tackled the demands of teaching with the same drive she had brought to her dancing. After a stint at Skidmore College in Saratoga, New York, she opened her own school in New York City. During this period, in 1981, she wrote an extremely valuable book called *Dancer to Dancer*. It drew upon her own practical experience during a long and well-spent career. She also served on the board of directors of the National Association for Regional Ballet.

Eventually she was invited to become both teacher and coach at the North Carolina School of the Arts in Winston-Salem, and she has also remained in demand as a guest teacher.

—Doris Hering

## HEART OF THE HILLS
(original Russian title: *Serdtse Gor*)

**Choreography:** Vakhtang Chabukiani
**Music:** Andrei Balanchivadze
**Design:** Simon Virsaladze (scenery)
**Libretto:** Georgi Leonidze and Nikolai Volkov
**First Production:** Kirov Ballet, Leningrad, 28 June 1938
**Principal Dancers:** Tatiana Vecheslova (Manizhe), Vakhtang Chabukiani (Dzhardzhi), Sergei Koren (Zaal)

**Other productions include:** Tbilisi Theatre of Opera and Ballet (earlier version; chor. Chabukiani), as *Mzechabuki* (*Sunny Youth*); Tbilisi, 27 December 1936. Kiev Theatre (new version; chor. S. Sergeyev); Kiev, 1940. Tashkent Theatre (new version; chor. E. Baranovsky); Tashkent, 1940.

### PUBLICATIONS

Beaumont, Cyril, *Supplement to Complete Book of Ballets*, London, 1942
Krasovskaya, Vera, *Vakhtang Chabukiani*, Moscow, 1956
Lawson, Joan, "*The Heart of the Hills*": A New Departure in Soviet Ballet", *Dancing Times* (London), July 1939
Lawson, Joan, "A Short History of Soviet Ballet", *Dance Index* (New York), June/July 1943
Roslavleva, Natalia, *Era of the Russian Ballet*, London, 1966

* * *

*The Heart of the Hills* was the first ballet choreographed by the outstanding Soviet dancer Vakhtang Chabukiani. At the centre of the story, devoted to the history of the choreographer's native Georgia and also in full agreement with the strict canons of Soviet art at that time, lay a protest against social inequality. The youthful hunter, Dzhardzhi, has fallen in love with the Prince's daughter, Manije, who is expected to marry another. The hero then leads a peasant rebellion, and, in bloody battle, the heroine sacrifices herself in order to defend her loved one, Dzhardzhi, now the living symbol of peasant revolt. It seems a fairly standard formula; however, the ballet was unusual for several reasons. As the historian of Soviet ballet, Natalia Chernova, noted, "Vakhtang Chabukiani brought into the Russian school of classical dance the traditions of Georgian folklore, united them with the academic laws of classicism, and yet, while subordinating himself to such canons, has not lost his independence. Chabukiani has put on the stage a people's hero, united by bonds of blood with the people's own style."

In *The Heart of the Hills*, as in his ballets which followed, Chabukiani thinks freely in terms of dance and not in terms of mimetic images. In this lies the essence of his choreographic vision. He said, "The folk dances of Georgia are striking for their grace, nobility, temperament, fluency, and lightness. The sun of Georgia, her mountains and fertile meadows, her woods and gardens, and all the richness and variety of nature, may be felt in Georgian dance".

Now, for the first time, the dancing hero became the centre of balletic action. This was undoubtedly helped by the fact that Chabukiani himself performed the role of Dzhardzhi. A contemporary critic wrote, "It was impossible to forget his powerful leaps, reminiscent of an eagle soaring in the clouds, impossible to forget his whirlwind turns, or the manly plastique of his arms. The artist was especially expressive in the dance revealing the depths of Dzhardzhi's feelings for his loved one, when, at the end of a fiery solo, the youth falls on his knees before her with wide-flung arms. In this movement was both passion and moral reverence towards woman."

***The Heart of the Hills*, with Vakhtang Chabukiani and Tatiana Vecheslova, Leningrad, 1938**

As for the music of the ballet, created by one of the founders of Soviet Georgian music, Andrei Balanchivadze (the brother of George Balanchine), Dmitri Shostakovich warmly commented shortly after the premiere: "In this production there is nothing petty; everything is very deeply and I would say nobly executed. There is much serious pathos proceeding from its high poetry." The ballet's success was also helped by Simon Virsaladze's décor. For Virsaladze, later an outstanding artist of the Soviet theatre, this was the first venture into scenic work for ballet. A participant in the premiere of *The Heart of the Hills*, Mikhail Mikhailov, remembers, "I sensed in the creative style of the artist a special spiritual nearness to the nature of music and choreography. The mountainous landscape and the severity of the medieval castle, with its massive walls and grey stone—all was as if real, and yet at the same time not real, as if appearing in a dream."

The first version of the ballet was shown in Chabukiani's native Georgia, at the Tblisi Theatre of Opera and Ballet, under the name of *Mzechabuki* (meaning *Sunny Youth*) with E. Mikoledze as director. The ballet now known as *The Heart of the Hills* (*Serdtse Gor*) received its Kirov premiere at the Leningrad Theatre of Opera and Ballet a year and a half later, in June 1938. In its three years of existence on the stage of the Kirov Theatre, *The Heart of the Hills* was shown to the public just 29 times, but it retains an undisputed place in the history of Soviet ballet.

—Arsen Degen

**HEATHCOTE, Steven**

Australian dancer. Born in Wagin, West Australia, 16 October 1964. Studied with Kira Bousloff and Shelley Rae, Perth, and at Australian Ballet School (scholarship award student), Melbourne; graduated in 1982. Married Kathleen Ann Reid, 1991. Dancer, Australian Ballet, from 1983: coryphée from 1984, soloist from 1985, senior artist from 1986, principal artist from 1987; touring wtih Australian Ballet to China, 1987, the Soviet Union, United Kingdom, and Greece, 1988, and Taiwan, Thailand, and Singapore, 1989; international guest artist, including with Sadler's Wells Royal Ballet, 1986, 1991, Ballet Nacional de Cuba, Havana, 1988, Kirov Ballet, Leningrad, Kiev Ballet and Riga Ballet, Soviet Union, 1989, American Ballet Theatre, New York season, 1992; has also made appearances in Tokyo and Osaka, Japan. Recipient: Order of Australia, 1991.

**ROLES**

1983 The Adolescent in *Beyond Twelve* (Graeme Murphy), Australian Ballet, Sydney
Mercutio in *Romeo and Juliet* (Cranko), Australian Ballet, Sydney
Benvolio in *Romeo and Juliet* (Cranko), Australian Ballet, Sydney

1984 Nathaniel in *The Tales of Hoffmann* (Darrell), Australian Ballet, Melbourne
Pas de trois in *Voluntaries* (Tetley), Australian Ballet, Sydney
Colas in *La Fille mal gardée* (Ashton), Australian Ballet, Newcastle
Alan Strang in *Equus* (Reiter-Soffer), Australian Ballet, Sydney
Lensky in *Onegin* (Cranko), Australian Ballet, Sydney
Copain in *Gaîté Parisienne* (Béjart), Australian Ballet, Sydney
Pas de trois, Mazurka in *Suite en blanc* (Lifar), Australian Ballet, Melbourne

1985 Franz in *Coppélia* (van Praagh after Petipa, Cecchetti), Australian Ballet, Melbourne
Principal dancer in *Webern Opus V* (Béjart), Australian Ballet, Sydney
Principal dancer in *In the Night* (Robbins), Australian Ballet, Sydney
Prince Siegfried in *Swan Lake* (Petipa, Ivanov; staged Woolliams), Australian Ballet, Melbourne
Siegfried in *Variations on a Nursery Theme* (Seregi), Australian Ballet, Sydney
Principal dancer in *Serenade* (Balanchine), Australian Ballet, Sydney
Title role (cr) in *The Sentimental Bloke* (Ray), Australian Ballet, Sydney
James in *La Sylphide* (Bournonville; staged Bruhn), Australian Ballet, Melbourne
Junior Cadet in *Graduation Ball* (Lichine), Australian Ballet, Melbourne

1986 Basil in *Don Quixote* (Nureyev after Petipa), Australian Ballet, Melbourne
Principal dancer in *Symphony in D* (Kylián), Australian Ballet, Sydney
Principal dancer in *Songs of a Wayfarer* (Béjart), Australian Ballet, Sydney
Albrecht in *Giselle* (Petipa after Coralli, Perrot; staged Gielgud), Australian Ballet, Melbourne
Principal dancer in *Études* (Lander), Australian Ballet, Sydney
Principal dancer in *Les Sylphides* (Fokine), Australian Ballet, Sydney
Red Knight in *Checkmate* (de Valois), Australian Ballet, Sydney
Black and White Pas de deux in *Forgotten Land* (Kylián), Australian Ballet, Sydney
Petruchio in *The Taming of the Shrew* (Cranko), Australian Ballet, Sydney
Solor in "The Kingdom of the Shades" (from *La Bayadère*; after Petipa), Australian Ballet, Sydney

1987 Romeo in *Romeo and Juliet* (Cranko), Australian Ballet, Melbourne
Principal dancer (cr) in *Orpheus* (Tetley), Australian Ballet, Melbourne
The Adult in *Beyond Twelve* (Murphy), Australian Ballet, Sydney
Prince Florimund in *The Sleeping Beauty* (Petipa; staged Gielgud), Australian Ballet, Perth
Principal dancer in *Song of the Earth* (MacMillan), Australian Ballet, Sydney
Statue Pas de deux (cr) in *Gallery* (Murphy), Australian Ballet, Melbourne
Principal dancer in *Sonata for 7* (Gordon), Australian Ballet, Sydney
Principal dancer in *The Concert* (Robbins), Australian Ballet, Sydney
Principal dancer in *Raymonda* (Nureyev after Petipa), Australian Ballet, Japan

1988 Aramis in *The Three Musketeers* (Prokovsky), Australian Ballet, Melbourne
Principal dancer in *Return to the Strange Land* (Kylián), Australian Ballet, Melbourne

1989 Title role in *Onegin* (Cranko), Australian Ballet, Melbourne
Principal dancer in *Transfigured Night* (Kylián), Australian Ballet, Melbourne
Principal dancer in *Four Last Songs* (Béjart), Australian Ballet, Sydney
Principal dancer in *Birthday Offering* (Ashton), Australian Ballet, Canberra

1990 Title role in *Spartacus* (Seregi), Australian Ballet, Melbourne
Danilo in *The Merry Widow* (Hynd), Australian Ballet, Melbourne
The Detective in *Le Concours* (*The Competition*; Béjart), Australian Ballet, Melbourne
Title role (cr) in *My Name is Edward Kelly* (Gordon), Australian Ballet, Sydney
Principal dancer (cr) in *Of Blessed Memory* (Welch), Australian Ballet, Melbourne

1992 The Prince in *The Sleeping Beauty* (MacMillan after Petipa), American Ballet Theatre, New York
Solor in *La Bayadère* (Makarova after Petipa), American Ballet Theatre, New York
Principal dancer in *Moondance* (Selya), American Ballet Theatre, New York

**PUBLICATIONS**

Laughlin, Patricia, "Making the Grade", *Dance Australia* (Melbourne), October–November 1987

Baum, Caroline, *Artists of the Australian Ballet*, Melbourne, 1989

Laughlin, Patricia, "Impressions of Russia", *Dance Australia* (Melbourne), June–July 1989

"The Australian Ballet: The Biographies", *Ballet in London Yearbook*, London, 1989/90

Laughlin, Patricia, "Australian Ballet", *Dance Magazine* (New York), August 1990

* * *

Steven Heathcote is one of the younger generation of Australian male dancers who has already demonstrated strength and versatility in a wide variety of roles. Heathcote is handsome and well built, and, although his body might be thought rather stiff and not ideally shaped for pure classicism, he performs the princely roles and always looks attractive in them. His real forte, however, lies in demi-caractère and contemporary works.

Technically, Heathcote is strong, if not in a purely classical way, and he is somewhat limited by his physique. His turns are instinctive rather than controlled, but his jump is good, with soft ballon. He is an excellent and considerate partner. Heathcote's greatest strength lies in his magnetic stage presence and in an exceptionally pleasant and likeable personality; and he tends to rely on these assets rather than in-depth characterizations when he performs classical roles. He looks more physically pleasing in neo-classical roles, largely as a result of a strongly modern element in his character, something which is somewhat at odds with a romantic approach.

It is significant that Heathcote was first noticed as the boy in Domy Reiter-Soffer's *Equus*. He had only recently graduated from the Australian Ballet School, but already he demonstrated a degree of understanding of this complex character. Soon afterwards he was able to give free rein to his delightful, friendly personality in a new Australian ballet by Robert Ray—*The Sentimental Bloke*—in which he had the title role. Another Australian ballet, *My Name is Edward Kelly*, by Timothy Gordon, gave him a chance to show fine understanding of the tormented outlaw of the title.

Although outstanding and highly praised for his performances in Maurice Béjart's *Songs of a Wayfarer*, and as the Man in Kenneth MacMillan's *Song of the Earth*, Heathcote leans most towards acting roles. He is a very good actor and has said "My preference is for roles that have a concrete character, a real person. I always use the analogy that you can jump into their suit and zip it up."

Among the characters whom he has most successfully inhabited are Lensky in Cranko's *Onegin*, whom he portrays as a sunny young man who cannot understand the betrayal, as he sees it, of Olga and Onegin; Romeo, in which he is youthfully ardent and convincing; and the title role in *Spartacus*, in which he suggests the tyrant is an essentially decent young man who is almost crushed by the brutality of his fate, and who is inspired to rise and revolt by the brutal deaths of his two friends.

Heathcote enjoyed great success when he guested with the Kirov Ballet in 1989, dancing Albrecht in *Giselle*, and he has created a favourable impression wherever he has danced, both at home in Australia and abroad. He is still young, and no doubt with maturity will develop even greater insights into those characters he has already successfully portrayed. It seems unlikely that Heathcote will ever develop into a classical danseur noble, but he could reach great heights in dramatic and contemporary ballet.

—Patricia Laughlin

---

**HEINEL, Anne** (Anna)

German dancer. Born Anna Friedrike (later appearing as Anne-Frédérique) Heinel (sometimes known as Heynel, or Ingle) in Bayreuth, 4 October 1753. Studied as a child under Lépy; later trained under Jean-Georges Noverre, Court of Württemberg, Stuttgart. Married (1) dancer Monsieur Fierville, 1773 (annulled); (2) dancer Gaetano Vestris, 16 June 1972: one son, Adolphe Vestris, b. 1791. Début, l'Académie royale de musique (Paris Opéra), 1767; dancer, Paris Opéra, 1767–71; left for England: leading dancer, King's Theatre, London, December 1771, opera seasons 1772, 1773, and as guest ballerina (while still under contract to the Opéra), 1773–76; returned to Paris Opéra 1776–82; retired from the stage in 1782. Died in Paris, 17 March 1808.

## ROLES

1767 Dancer in *Ernelinde* (opera; mus. Philidor), Opéra, Paris

1768 Dancer (cr) in *La Vénitienne* (ballet; new mus. Dauvergne), Opéra, Paris

Dancer in *Dardanus* (tragédie-lyrique; mus. Rameau), Opéra, Paris

Dancer in *Daphnis et Alcimadure* (pastorale; mus. Mondonville), Opéra, Paris

Dancer in *Sylvie* (ballet; mus. Berton, Trial), Opéra, Paris

Dancer in *Titon et l'Aurore* (pastorale; mus. Mondonville), Opéra, Paris

1769 Dancer (cr) in *Omphale* (tragédie-lyrique; mus. Cardonne), Opéra, Paris

Dancer in *Alix et Alexis* (mus. Poinsinet, chor. Laval), Royal Court, Choisy

Dancer in *Zélindor, roi des sylphes* (ballet; mus. Rebel, Francoeur; chor. Laval), Royal Court, Fontainebleau

Dancer (cr) in *La Rosière de Salency* (opera; mus. Philidor, Monsigny, van Swieten, chor. Laval), Royal Court, Fontainebleau

Dancer in *Iphis et Ianthe* (mus. Rebel, Francoeur, chor. Laval), Royal Court, Fontainebleau

Dancer in *Erosine* (pastorale-héroïque; mus. Berton, chor. Laval), Royal Court, Fontainebleau

Dancer in *Erigone* and *Psyché* (acts from *Les Fêtes de Paphos*, ballet; mus. Mondonville), Opéra, Paris

Dancer in *Enée et Lavinie* (tragédie-lyrique; new mus. Dauvergne), Opéra, Paris

Dancer (cr) in *Hippomène et Atalante* (ballet; mus. Vachon), Opéra, Paris

Dancer in *Sandomir* (tragédie-lyrique; mus. Philidor), Opéra, Paris

Dancer in *Zaïs* (ballet; mus. Rameau), Opéra, Paris

1770 Dancer in *Zaïde, reine de Grenade* (pastorale; mus. Royer, chor. Laval), Opéra, Paris

Dancer in *Zoroastre* (tragédie-lyrique; mus. Rameau), Opéra, Paris

Dancer in *Persée* (tragédie-lyrique; mus. Lully, chor. Laval), Royal Court, Versailles

Dancer in *Castor et Pollux* (tragédie-lyrique; mus. Rameau, chor. Laval), Royal Court, Versailles

Dancer in *Théonis; ou, Le Toucher* (pastorale; mus. Berton, Trial, chor. Laval), Royal Court, Fontainebleau

Dancer in *Alphée et Aréthuse* (ballet; mus. Campra, Dauvergne, chor. Laval), Royal Court, Fontainebleau

Dancer in *La Sybille* (mus. Dauvergne, chor. Laval), Royal Court, Fontainebleau

Dancer in *Ajax* (tragédie-lyrique; mus. Bertin), Opéra, Paris
Dancer in *Les Fêtes grecques et romaines* (ballet; mus. de Blâmont), Opéra, Paris
Dancer in *Hylas et Zélis* (pastorale; mus. Bury), Opéra, Paris

1771 Dancer in *Aline, reine de Golconde* (ballet-héroïque; mus. Monsigny, chor. Laval), Royal Court, Versailles
Dancer in *Les Projects de l'amour* (mus. Mondonville, chor. Laval), Royal Court, Versailles
Dancer (cr) in *Le Prix de la valeur* (mus. Dauvergne, chor. Vestris), Opéra, Paris
Dancer in *Alcione* (tragédie-lyrique; mus. Marais), Opéra, Paris
La Dame du village (cr) in *La Cinquantaine* (ballet; mus. Laborde), Opéra, Paris
Dancer in *Ixion* (act from *Les Eléments*, ballet; mus. Destouches), Opéra, Paris
Une Assyrienne in *Pyrame et Thisbé* (tragédie-lyrique; mus. Rebel, Francoeur), Opéra, Paris
Dancer in *New Grand Ballet*, King's Theatre, London

1772 Dancer in *Admète et Alceste* (ballet; Lépy, after Noverre), King's Theatre, London
Dancer in *Osiris* (ballet; mus. Rameau), Opéra, Paris
Dancer in *Tyrtée* (act from *Les Talents lyriques*, ballet; mus. Rameau), Opéra, Paris
Dancer in *Half-Comic Ballet* (Lepy), King's Theatre, London
Dancer (cr) in *A New Pastoral*, King's Theatre, London
Dancer (cr) in *Grand Turkish Dance*, King's Theatre, London
Dancer (cr) in *Le Triomphe du magie*, King's Theatre, London
Spanish divertissement (cr) in *Le Jaloux sans un rival*, King's Theatre, London
Dancer (cr) in *Adèle de Ponthieu* (tragédie-lyrique; mus. Laborde, Berton), Opéra, Paris

1773 Dancer (cr) in *Sabinus* (tragédie-lyrique; mus. Gossec), Royal Court, Versailles
Pas de deux and New Chacone in *New Grand Serious Ballet*, King's Theatre, London
Zelima (cr) in *L'Isle désert* (D'Auvigne), King's Theatre, London
Dancer in *Apollo and Venus*, King's Theatre, London
Minuet (cr) in *La Fête du village*, Benefit for Heinel, King's Theatre, London
Sauvage (cr) in *New Grand Ballet*, Benefit for Heinel, King's Theatre, London
Dancer in *Les Tartares*, Benefit for Heinel, King's Theatre, London
A Sultana in *Turkish Ballet*, Benefit for Heinel, King's Theatre, London

1774 Dancer (cr) in *Iphigénie en Aulide* (tragédie-lyrique; mus. Gluck), Versailles
Dancer in *Le Carnaval du Parnasse* (opera-ballet; mus. Mondonville), Opéra, Paris
Pas de trois, Act III (cr) in *Orphée et Eurydice* (tragédie-lyrique; mus. Gluck), Opéra, Paris
Dancer (cr) in *Azolan; ou, Les Serments indiscrets* (ballet-héroïque; mus. Floquet), Opéra, Paris

1775 Dancer (cr) in *Cythère assiégée* (ballet; Paris version, mus. Gluck), Opéra, Paris
Dancer (cr) in *Alexis et Daphné* (pastorale; mus. Gossec), Opéra, Paris

1776 Medée in *Medée et Jason* (ballet; Noverre), Opéra, Paris
Roxane (cr) in *Apelles et Campaspe* (ballet; Noverre), Opéra, Paris
Dancer (cr) in *Alceste* (tragédie-lyrique; Paris version, mus. Gluck), Opéra, Paris
Dancer in *Les Romans* (ballet; mus. Niel, Cambini), Opéra, Paris
Dancer (cr) in *Euthyme et Lyris* (ballet; mus. Desormery), Opéra, Paris

1777 Camille (cr) in *Les Horaces* (ballet; Noverre), Opéra, Paris
Dancer (cr) in *Armide* (tragédie-lyrique; mus. Gluck, chor. Noverre), Opéra, Paris
Dancer (cr) in *Myrtil et Lycoris* (pastorale; mus. Desormery), Opéra, Paris

1778 Dancer (cr) in *Annette et Lubin* (ballet; Noverre), Opéra, Paris
Dancer (cr) in *La Fête de village* (intermède; mus. Gossec), Opéra, Paris
Hébé in *Castor et Pollux* (tragédie-lyrique; mus. Rameau), Opéra, Paris

1779 Dancer (cr) in *Iphigénie en Tauride* (tragédie-lyrique; mus. Gluck), Opéra, Paris
Dancer (cr) in *Echo et Narcisse* (tragédie-lyrique; mus. Gluck), Opéra, Paris

1780 Dancer (cr) in *Atys* (tragédie-lyrique; new version, mus. Piccinni), Opéra, Paris
Dancer (cr) in *Andromaque* (tragédie-lyrique; mus. Grétry), Opéra, Paris
Dancer (cr) in *Persée* (tragédie-lyrique; new version, mus. Philidor), Opéra, Paris
Dancer (cr) in *Le Seigneur bienfaisant* (comédie-lyrique; mus. Floquet, chor. Dauberval, Noverre, M. Gardel), Opéra, Paris

1781 Dancer (cr) in *Iphigénie en Tauride* (tragédie-lyrique; new version, mus. Piccinni), Opéra, Paris
Dancer (cr) in *La Fête de Mirza* (ballet; chor. M. Gardel), Opéra, Paris
Title role in *Ninette à la Cour* (ballet; M. Gardel), Opéra, Paris

**PUBLICATIONS**


Grimm, Baron Melchior von, *Correspondance Littéraire, Philosophique et Critique de Grimm et de Diderot*, Paris, 1829
Campardon, Emile, *L'Académie royale de musique au XVIIIe siècle*, Paris, 1884
Capon, Gaston, *Les Vestris*, Paris, 1908
Lifar, Serge, *Auguste Vestris*, Paris, 1950
Beaumont, Cyril, *A Miscellany for Dancers*, London, 1954
Migel, Parmenia, *The Ballerinas*, New York, 1972
Lynham, Deryck, *The Chevalier Noverre: Father of Modern Ballet*, London, 1972


* * *

The German dancer Anne Heinel is often credited only with the invention of the multiple pirouette à la seconde, but in her own day she was also crowned "La Reine de la danse" both for her formidable technique and for her impressive dramatic abilities. Much of her success can be attributed to her initial training with Lépy and Jean-Georges Noverre at the renowned Court of Württemberg in Stuttgart, Germany. Under Noverre, the opera house became a mecca for the finest dance luminaries—Jean Dauberval, Charles Le Picq, and Gaetano Vestris among them. When Noverre left Stuttgart in 1767, just prior to Heinel's official début, she quickly followed his example and travelled to France to make her début at the Paris Opéra, or the Académie royale de musique.

Immediately, she attracted the public's attention. Baron Von Grimm, in his *Correspondence Littéraire*, described her in glowing terms, saying "Mademoiselle Heinel, burdened with seventeen or eighteen years, two large, well-set eyes, and two shapely legs which support an extremely pretty figure, arrived from Vienna for her debut at the Opéra in danse noble. It was conceded that she displayed precision, sureness, aplomb and nobility comparable to the talents of the great Vestris . . . two or three years from now Mademoiselle Heinel will be the greatest dancer in Europe. . . ." His observations proved correct, and praise continued to follow her.

Success also brought its share of problems, however, since the current Paris Opéra ballet master, Gaetano Vestris, was intensely jealous of anyone who captured public attention, and he attempted to quell her popularity by giving her only minor roles. Although public outcry squashed his selfish plans, and Vestris was forced to apologize to the dancer from the stage of the Paris Opéra, this squabble probably contributed to her decision to flee to England.

In London, her arrival was heralded by Horace Walpole, who wrote in a letter to Lord Strafford, "There is a finer dancer [than Mlle Guimard] whom Mr. Hobart is to transport to London; a Mademoiselle Heinel, or Ingle, a Fleming. She is tall, perfectly made, very handsome, and has a set of attitudes copied from the Classics; she moves as gracefully slow as Pygmalion's statue when it was coming to life, and moves her leg round as imperceptibly as if she was dancing in the Zodiac. But she is not Virgo." Heinel appeared at London's King's Theatre frequently from 1771 to 1776, performing mostly in short divertissements, often with Fierville, whom she married. There too she enchanted audiences, causing the playwright Oliver Goldsmith to pay tribute to her in his epilogue to *She Stoops to Conquer* by referring to his heroine as one who "Dotes upon dancing, and in all her pride, / Swims round the room, the Heinel of Cheapside".

Heinel was an ideal exponent of the "danse noble" style which suited her elegant stature, and she excelled in serious dances like the chaconne, loure, and gavotte. When she returned to Paris, she became a leading interpreter of Noverre's tragic ballets, dancing such heroines as Medée in *Jason et Medée*, Roxane in *Apelles et Campaspe*, and Camille in *Les Horaces*, in addition to appearing in ballets by Jean Dauberval and Maximilien Gardel.

Although nicknamed "La Belle Statue" for the reserved quality of her dancing, she was warm and amiable in her personal life and eventually succeeded in winning the admiration of the egotistical Gaetano Vestris during a strike at the Opéra. The couple were married in 1792. Heinel retired at the height of her career, leaving memories of a supreme dancer whom Burney remembered for her "grace and executions . . . so perfect as to eclipse all other excellence", and whom Noverre declared was "the most perfect example of the serious style of dancing".

—Mary Jane Warner

---

**HELPMANN, Robert**

Australian dancer, choreographer, and ballet director. Born in Mount Gambier, South Australia, 9 April 1909. Studied with Pavlova Company in Australia, pupil of Laurent Novikoff, 1926, and at Vic-Wells Ballet, London, from 1933; also studied with Olga Preobrazhenska and Nikolai Legat. Early stage career as principal dancer in musicals for J.C. Williamson, Ltd., Australia, 1927–32; dancer, Vic-Wells Ballet (later Sadler's Wells Ballet), London, 1933–50: principal dancer from 1934, becoming chief male dancer and partner to Fonteyn, and returning as guest artist from 1955; also dancer in theatre, revue, and opera productions, including in *Stop Press* (revue; Adelphi Theatre, 1935) and for Old Vic Company; choreographer, Sadler's Wells Ballet, 1942–46, Royal Ballet, 1963, Australian Ballet, 1964–76; joint artistic director, with Peggy van Praagh, Australian Ballet, Melbourne, from 1965, becoming artistic director, 1974–75; also leading actor, producer, and director of plays, musicals, and operas, from 1938; appeared in films, including *The Red Shoes* (also chor.; dir. Powell, 1948), *The Tales of Hoffmann* (dir. Powell, 1951), *Chitty Chitty Bang Bang* (dir. Hughes, 1968). Recipient: Order of the Star of the North, Sweden, 1954; Order of the Merit of the Cedars, Lebanon, 1957; Queen Elizabeth II Award, Royal Academy of Dancing, London, 1961; title of Commander of the Order of the British Empire, 1964; Knighthood, 1968. Died in Sydney, New South Wales, 28 September 1986.

**Robert Helpmann as Hamlet, 1942**

**ROLES**

1932 The Young Man (cr) in *Business à la Russe* (also chor.), Theatre Royal, Melbourne

1933 Bridegroom in *The Wise and Foolish Virgins* (de Valois), Vic-Wells Ballet, London
Satan in *Job* (de Valois), Vic-Wells Ballet, London
Title role in *The Lord of Burleigh* (Ashton), Vic-Wells Ballet, London
Georgie Porgie in *Nursery Suite* (de Valois), Vic-Wells Ballet, London
The Prince in *Nursery Suite* (de Valois), Vic-Wells Ballet, London
Vertumnus in *Pomona* (Ashton), Vic-Wells Ballet, London
Pas de trois (cr) in *Les Rendezvous* (Ashton), Vic-Wells Ballet, London
A Son, War in *Job* (de Valois), Vic-Wells Ballet, London
Florestan in *Carnaval* (Fokine), Vic-Wells Ballet, London
Harlequin in *Carnaval* (Fokine), Vic-Wells Ballet, London
Cook's Man in *Douanes* (de Valois), Vic-Wells Ballet, London
1934 The Nutcracker Prince in *The Nutcracker* (Ivanov; staged Sergeyev), Vic-Wells Ballet, London
Adagio, pas de deux in *Fête polonaise* (de Valois), Vic-Wells Ballet, London
Hilarion in *Giselle* (Petipa after Coralli, Perrot; staged Sergeyev), Vic-Wells Ballet, London
Albrecht in *Giselle* (Petipa after Coralli, Perrot; staged Sergeyev), Vic-Wells Ballet, London
Master of Treginnis (cr) in *The Haunted Ballroom* (de Valois), Vic-Wells Ballet, London
Don Lollo Zirafa (cr) in *The Jar* (de Valois), Vic-Wells Ballet, London
Prince Siegfried in *Swan Lake* (Petipa, Ivanov; staged Sergeyev), Vic-Wells Ballet, London
Variation, Adagio of Lovers in *Les Rendezvous* (Ashton), Vic-Wells Ballet, London
The Spirit of the Rose in *Le Spectre de la rose* (Fokine), Vic-Wells Ballet, London
Mazurka, Pas de deux in *Les Sylphides* (Fokine), Vic-Wells Ballet, London
1935 Pierrot in *Carnaval* (Fokine), Vic-Wells Ballet, London
Franz in *Coppélia*, Acts I and II (Petipa, Cecchetti; staged Sergeyev), Vic-Wells Ballet, London
The Rake in *The Rake's Progress* (de Valois), Vic-Wells Ballet, London
The Squire (cr; added), Scotch Rhapsody in *Façade* (Ashton), Vic-Wells Ballet, London
A Villager (cr) in *Le Baiser de la fée* (Ashton), Vic-Wells Ballet, London
1936 Leading Nobleman (cr) in *The Gods Go a-Begging* (de Valois), Vic-Wells Ballet, London
Principal dancer (cr) in *Siesta* (pas de deux; Ashton), Vic-Wells Ballet, London
The Poet (cr) in *Apparitions* (Ashton), Vic-Wells Ballet, London
Eusebius in *Carnaval* (Fokine), Vic-Wells Ballet, London
Principal dancer (cr) in *Music for Ballet* (de Valois), Cambridge Theatre Gala, London
Young man (cr) in *Nocturne* (Ashton), Vic-Wells Ballet, London
Title role (cr) in *Prometheus* (de Valois), Vic-Wells Ballet, London
The Prince in *The Sleeping Princess* Pas de deux (*Aurora Pas de deux*; after Petipa), Vic-Wells Ballet, London
1937 Principal dancer (cr) in *Perpetuum mobile* (pas de deux; Ashton), Vic-Wells Ballet, London
Pas de deux (cr) in *Les Patineurs* (Ashton), Vic-Wells Ballet, London
The Bridegroom (cr) in *A Wedding Bouquet* (Ashton), Vic-Wells Ballet, London
The Red King (cr) in *Checkmate* (de Valois), Vic-Wells Ballet, Paris
1938 The Emperor (cr) in *Le Roi nu* (*The Emperor's New Clothes*; de Valois), Vic-Wells Ballet, London
Paris (cr) in *The Judgment of Paris* (Ashton), Vic-Wells Ballet, London
A Personage in *Les Masques* (Ashton), Ballet Rambert, London
1939 Prince Florimund in *The Sleeping Princess* (Petipa; staged Sergeyev), Vic-Wells Ballet, London
Variation ("Blue Boy") in *Les Patineurs* (Ashton), Vic-Wells Ballet, London
1940 Title role in *Barabau* (de Valois), Vic-Wells Ballet, London
Leading Child of Darkness (cr) in *Dante Sonata* (Ashton), Vic-Wells Ballet, London
Mr. O'Reilly (cr) in *The Prospect Before Us* (de Valois), Vic-Wells Ballet, London
Foxtrot (cr) added to *Façade* (Ashton), Vic-Wells Ballet, London
Franz in *Coppélia* (3-act version; Petipa, Cecchetti staged Sergeyev), Vic-Wells Ballet, London
1941 Principal dancer (cr) in *The Wanderer* (Ashton), Sadler's Wells Ballet, London
Dr. Coppélius in *Coppélia* (3-act version; Petipa, Cecchetti, staged Sergeyev), Sadler's Wells Ballet, London
Tango: A Dago in *Façade* (Ashton), Sadler's Wells Ballet, London
Noche espagnola in *Façade* (Ashton), Vic-Wells Ballet, London
Orpheus (cr) in *Orpheus and Eurydice* (de Valois), Sadler's Wells Ballet, London
The Bridegroom in *The Wise Virgins* (Ashton), Sadler's Wells Ballet, London
Carabosse in *The Sleeping Princess* (Petipa; staged Sergeyev), Vic-Wells Ballet, London
1942 Title role (cr) in *Comus* (also chor.), Sadler's Wells Ballet, London
Title role (cr) in *Hamlet* (also chor.), Sadler's Wells Ballet, London
1943 St. George (cr) in *The Quest* (Ashton), Sadler's Wells Ballet, London
1944 The Stranger (cr) in *Miracle in the Gorbals* (also chor.), Sadler's Wells Ballet, London
1945 The Lepidopterist in *Promenade* (de Valois), Sadler's Wells Ballet, Paris
1946 The Principal Dancer (cr) in *Adam Zero* (also chor.), Sadler's Wells Ballet, London
Adelino Canberra (cr) in *Les Sirènes* (Ashton), Vic-Wells Ballet, London
1948 A Stepsister (cr) in *Cinderella* (Ashton), Sadler's Wells Ballet, London
Title role (cr) in *Don Juan* (Ashton), Sadler's Wells Ballet, London
1950 Title role (cr) in *Don Quixote* (de Valois), Sadler's Wells Ballet, London
"Spirits of the Air" pas de deux from *The Fairy Queen* (Ashton), Norwegian Ballet, Oslo
The Mariner (cr) in *Île des Sirènes* (A. Rodrigues), Sadler's Wells Ballet Concert Group, Tunbridge Wells
1958 Title role in *Petrushka* (Fokine), Royal Ballet, London

1964 Narrator in *A Wedding Bouquet* (Ashton), Royal Ballet, London
1970 Title role in *Don Quixote* (Nureyev after Petipa), Australian Ballet, Adelaide
1975 Sergeant Pepper in *The Fool on the Hill* (Lynne), Australian television

**Other roles include:** A God in *La Création du monde* (de Valois), Danse chinoise, Danse espagnol in *The Nutcracker* (Ivanov; staged Sergeyev), a Gendarme in *Douanes* (de Valois), a suitor in *The Sleeping Princess* (Petipa; staged Sergeyev).

## WORKS

1932 *Business à la Russe* (mus. various), Theatre Royal, Melbourne
1942 *Comus* (mus. Purcell, arranged Lambert), Sadler's Wells Ballet, London
*Hamlet* (mus. Tchaikovsky), Sadler's Wells Ballet, London
*The Birds* (mus. Respighi), Sadler's Wells Ballet, London
1944 *Miracle in the Gorbals* (mus. Bliss), Sadler's Wells Ballet, London
1946 *Adam Zero* (mus. Bliss), Sadler's Wells Ballet, London
1963 *Elektra* (mus. Arnold), Royal Ballet, London
1964 *The Display* (mus. Williamson), Australian Ballet, Adelaide
1965 *Yugen* (mus. Toyama), Australian Ballet, Adelaide
1968 *Sun Music* (mus. Sculthorpe), Australian Ballet, Sydney
1974 *Perisynthyon* (mus. Sibelius), Australian Ballet, Melbourne

Also staged:
1960 *The Sleeping Beauty* (with Nijinska, after Petipa; mus. Tchaikovsky), Grand Ballet du Marquis de Cuevas, Paris
1963 *Swan Lake* (Petipa, Ivanov, with alterations Sergeyev, de Valois; mus. Tchaikovsky), Royal Ballet, London
1975 *The Merry Widow* (chor. Hynd; mus. Lehár, arranged Lanchbery), Australian Ballet, Melbourne

## PUBLICATIONS

By Helpmann:
"The Function of Ballet", *Dancing Times* (London), September 1942
"An Informal Interview with Robert Helpmann", *Dancers' Digest* (San Jose), May/June 1957

About Helpmann:
Haskell, Arnold, "Robert Helpmann's Choreography", *Dancing Times* (London), September 1942
Williamson, Audrey, "Robert Helpmann as Choreographer", *Theatre World* (London), September 1942
Brahms, Caryl, *Robert Helpmann: Choreographer*, London, 1943
Anthony, Gordon, *Studies of Robert Helpmann*, London, 1946
Haskell, Arnold, *Miracle in the Gorbals*, London, 1946
Gourlay, J. Logan (ed.), *The Robert Helpmann Album*, Glasgow, 1948
Robertson, Marion, "*Hamlet* and *Miracle in the Gorbals*", London, 1949
Miller, Tatlock, "Chameleon of the Theatre", *Dance and Dancers* (London), May 1950
"Robert Helpmann: A Portrait", *Dancing Times* (London), June 1953
Davidson, Gladys, *Ballet Biographies*, revised edition, London, 1954
Clarke, Mary, *The Sadler's Wells Ballet*, London, 1955
Sorley Walker, Kathrine, *Robert Helpmann*, London, 1957
Anthony, Gordon, "Pioneers of the Royal Ballet: Robert Helpmann", *Dancing Times* (London), October 1970
Gow, Gordon, "Helpmann and the Australian Ballet", *Dancing Times* (London), October 1973
Salter, Elizabeth, *Helpmann: The Authorized Biography*, Brighton, 1978
Brysha, "A Man of the Theatre", *Dance Australia* (Melbourne), no. 27, 1987

* * *

Robert Helpmann's performances and productions grew from his belief in the basic importance of the dramatic element in theatre and his philosophy that "all art, no matter how highbrow, should be entertainment". After tasting success as a dancer in musicals and revue in Australia and New Zealand, he arrived in England in 1933 and was taken without audition into the Vic-Wells Ballet by Ninette de Valois, who said, "I can do something with that face". From a strictly technical, classical viewpoint he was a somewhat indifferent dancer, but he had extraordinary theatrical magnetism and mimetic powers; Haskell remarked that he could "act the role of a *danseur noble* so perfectly that he carried conviction from the moment he appeared on stage". His famous partnership with Fonteyn in classics like *Swan Lake*, *Giselle*, and *The Sleeping Beauty*, as well as in modern ballets, was a cornerstone of the development of British ballet. The dramatic range and energy which characterized his work, first seen when he took over Dolin's role of Satan in *Job* (1933), distinguished such roles as the Bridegroom (*A Wedding Bouquet*), Dr. Coppélius (*Coppélia*), a stepsister (*Cinderella*), the Rake (*The Rake's Progress*), Don Quixote, and his own Hamlet. His charismatic drawing power did much to popularize dance in Britain, and this influence extended more widely through *The Red Shoes*, the only ballet film to have been consistently revived.

Helpmann's own ballets were firmly theatrical, dramatic in narrative structure and usually spectacular in presentation. Always innovatory in ideas, if not choreographically, he chose for his first major work *Comus*, the presentation of a masque by the seventeenth-century poet John Milton; and as well as dance he used the spoken word and a great deal of mimetic movement. *Elektra*, based on Greek myth, contained extraordinary athleticism; *The Display* combined a bush picnic, Australian football, near-rape, and mysticism in a cogent, satisfying unity; *Yugen* fused through dance Japanese myth and Western theatricalism. His production of *The Merry Widow* became the most acclaimed ballet of its time in the Australian Ballet's repertoire.

In 1955, Helpmann made his first return to Australia, leading with Katharine Hepburn an Old Vic company directed by his close friend Michael Benthall in *The Merchant of Venice*, *Measure for Measure*, and *The Taming of the Shrew*; but it was not until a Royal Ballet tour of 1958 that he appeared there as a dancer. His links with dance in his home country became firm with his appointment as co-artistic director of the Australian Ballet with Peggy van Praagh in 1965. He stimulated the young company through his presence, his creativity, and a wide network of international contacts which led to visits by high calibre guest artists and smooth arrangements for overseas tours to Britain, Europe, and America. The film of *Don Quixote* (1972), which he co-directed and co-starred in with Nureyev, brought the company to an even wider audience, as he intended it should.

Helpmann was one of the great theatrical stars of his generation, but he was the first Australian male dancer to achieve recognition in the field of ballet, and his first and last loyalties were to dance. It was fitting that he should have died in Sydney, aged 77, during a season with the Australian Ballet in which he recreated his role of the Red King in de Valois' *Checkmate*.

—Alan Brissenden

---

**HENRY, Louis**

French dancer and choreographer. Born Louis Stanislas Xavier Henri Bonnachon in Versailles, 7 March 1784. Studied at L'Académie royale de musique (Paris Opéra), pupil of André Deshayes, Jean-François Coulon, and Pierre Gardel. Married dancer Mme Queriau, c.1820. Début as dancer, Paris Opéra, 1803; first choreography, *L'Amour à Cythère*, Paris Opéra, 1805; choreographer and producer of own ballets for Théâtre de la Porte-Saint-Martin, Paris, 1807; left for Milan, 1807: premier danseur, La Scala, Milan, Carnaval season, 1808, also choreographing pantomime dramas in the style of Viganò; choreographer, Milan, Naples, Vienna, 1808–34, returning to Théâtre de la Porte-Saint-Martin, 1816, 1822; ballet master, Théâtre Nautique, Paris, 1834; ballet master, Paris Opéra, producing *L'Ile des pirates* for Fanny Elssler, 1835; returned to Naples 1836, having choreographed over 125 ballets. Died in Naples, 4 November 1836.

**WORKS**

1805 *L'Amour à Cythère* (mus. Gaveux), Opéra, Paris
1807 *Les Sauvages de la Floride* (mus. Darondeau), Théâtre de la Porte-Saint-Martin, Paris
*Les Deux Petits Savoyards* (mus. Darondeau, Piccini), Théâtre de la Porte-Saint-Martin, Paris
1808 *Otello; ossia, Il Moro di Venezia* (mus. Gallenberg), Teatro San Carlo, Naples
1809 *Guillaume Tell* (mus. Gallenberg), Teatro San Carlo, Naples
*Robinson Crusoe* (mus. Gallenberg), Teatro San Carlo, Naples
1810 *Atala; o, Die Wilden von Florida* (*Les Sauvages de la Floride*; mus. Darondeau), Kärntnertor Theater, Vienna
*Venus und Adonis* (pantomime), Kärntnertor Theater, Vienna
1814 *Romeo e Giulietta* (mus. Gallenberg), Teatro del Fondo, Naples
1815 *Pandora*, Teatro San Carlo, Naples
1816 *Hamlet* (mus. Gallenberg), Théâtre de la Porte-Saint-Martin, Paris
*Le Rosier* (mus. Darondeau), Théâtre de la Porte-Saint-Martin, Paris
*Samson* (mus. Gallenberg), Théâtre de la Porte-Saint-Martin, Paris
*Le Chateau infernal*, Théâtre de la Porte-Saint-Martin, Paris
*Le Mariage rompu*, Théâtre de la Porte-Saint-Martin, Paris
1817 *Rinaldo e Armida*, La Scala, Milan
*Il Castello degli spiriti*, La Scala, Milan
1818 *La Belle Arsène*, Teatro San Carlo, Naples
1819 *Aladino; ossia, La Lampada maravigliosa* (mus. Gallenberg), Teatro San Carlo, Naples
*Ballo carnevalesco*, Teatro del Fondo, Naples
*Piramo e Tisbe*, Teatro del Fondo, Naples
1820 *Chao-Kang* (mus. Carlini), Teatro San Carlo, Naples
1821 *Gl 'Inca* (mus. Cartini), Teatro San Carlo, Naples
*Il Giudizio di Paride* (mus. Cartini), Teatro San Carlo, Naples
*Il Due Genii*, Teatro San Carlo, Naples
*L 'Orfano* (mus. Raimondi), Teatro San Carlo, Naples
1822 *Le Sacrifice indien* (pantomime; mus. Raimondi, Carafe, Carlini), Théâtre Porte-Saint-Martin, Paris
*Agnès et Fitz-Henri* (pantomime), Théâtre de la Porte-Saint-Martin, Paris
*La Fortune vient en dormant* (pantomime), Théâtre de la Porte-Saint-Martin, Paris
*Arsena*, Kärntnertor Theater, Vienna
1823 *Ismaens Grab* (mus. Gallenberg), Kärntnertor Theater, Vienna
*Die Amazonen*, Kärntnertor Theater, Vienna
*Meleagro*, Teatro San Carlo, Naples
1824 *La Caravana del Cairo*, Teatro San Carlo, Naples
1825 *Amenie* (mus. Gyrowetz), Kärntnertor Theater, Vienna
*Undine* (mus. Gyrowetz), Kärntnertor Theater, Vienna
*Il Combattimento delle chimera*, Teatro San Carlo, Naples
1826 *Dircea*, La Scala, Milan
*Elerz e Zulmida* (mus. Pugni), La Scala, Milan
*Selico; ossia, Il Buon Figlio* (mus. Carlini, Gallenberg, Mercadante), Teatro San Carlo, Naples
1827 *Edoardo III; ossia L'Assedio di Calais* (mus. Mozart, Rossini, Meyerbeer, Pugni), La Scala, Milan
1828 *Arminio* (mus. Brambilla), La Scala, Milan
*La Silfida* (mus. Carlini), La Scala, Milan
*Gengis-Kan; ovvero, L'Orfano della China* (mus. arranged Brambilla), La Scala, Milan
1829/ *Adelaide di Francia* (mus. Pugni), La Scala, Milan
30 *La Festa da ballo in maschera*, La Scala, Milan
*Macbetto* (*Macbeth*; mus. Pugni), La Scala, Milan
1830 *La Vedova nel giorno delle nozze*, Teatro Carcano, Milan
1831 *Tutto al contrario* (mus. Panizza), Teatro Carcano, Milan
*Orpheus und Euridice* (mus. Gallenberg), Kärntnertor Theater, Vienna
1832 *Adelheid von Frankreich* (mus. Pugni), Kärntnertor Theater, Vienna
*Camma* (mus. arranged Brambilla), La Scala, Milan
1833 *Guglielmo Tell* (mus. Pugni, Rossini, and others), La Scala, Milan
Dances in *Il Conte d'Essex* (melodrama; mus. Mercadante), La Scala, Milan
1834 *Les Ondines* (mus. Struntz), Théâtre Nautique, Paris
*Guillaume Tell* (new version of *Guglielmo Tell*; mus. Struntz et al.), Théâtre Nautique, Paris
*Chao-Kang* (ballet-pantomime; mus. Carlini), Théâtre Nautique, Paris
*La Dernière Heure d'un colonel* (pantomime), Théâtre Nautique, Paris
1835 *L'Ile des pirates* (mus. Gide, Carlini, Rossini, Beethoven), Opéra, Paris
1836 *Licaone* (mus. Pugni), Teatro San Carlo, Naples
*Le Tre Sultane* (mus. Gallenberg), Teatro San Carlo, Naples

**Other works include:** *La Colonie*, *L'Incendio di Troja*, *L'Isola della fortuna*, *Paul et Virginie*, *Phaeton*.

### PUBLICATIONS

Baron, M.A., *Lettres sur la danse*, Paris, 1825
Saint-Léon, Arthur, *La Sténochorégraphie*, Paris, 1852
d'Heylé, J., *Foyers et coulisses*, Paris, 1875
Guest, Ivor, *The Romantic Ballet in Paris*, London, 1966
Winter, Marian Hannah, *The Pre-Romantic Ballet*, London, 1974
Chapman, John, "August Vestris and the Expansion of Technique", *Dance Research Journal* (New York), Summer 1987

* * *

It is fitting that Louis Henry was brought up during the most cataclysmic revolution in French history, for he proved to be a rebel throughout much of his career. From his early days as a Paris Opéra dancer, he refused to be limited to the genre for which he was best suited, the regal "danse noble", and followed instead in the footsteps of Auguste Vestris and Louis Duport, who were popularizing a new, athletic style that merged the traditional genres (the sérieux, comique, and demi-caractère). Then in 1804 he joined with Jean Aumer and Louis Duport to fight the Paris Opéra administration to earn the right to create a ballet. The battle was a success, but the works that resulted were mediocre. Indeed, Henry's *L'Amour à Cythère* (1805) was derivative of the neo-classical anacreontic approach of the eighteenth century.

Determined to continue making ballets, however, Henry turned to the Théâtre de la Porte-Saint-Martin, where he produced works that displayed a remarkable creative imagination and a disdain for tradition, in particular *Les Sauvages de la Floride* (1807). Based on Chateaubriand's *Atala* (1801), this ballet was a fitting prelude to his future career. Its seriousness and first-rate literary source took ballet into previously unexplored territory. Intensely romantic, the ballet explored individual passion, religion, and natural grandeur, and ended with that most romantic of all human gestures, suicide. The more conservative spectators were shocked that ballet should deal with such a meaningful and highly respected story. However, most people were delighted. One critic wrote: ". . . it seems that one returns to the cradle of the world, and that one is transported far from the yoke of society, to all the primitive liberty of nature".

1807 was the year the yoke of Napoleon's society fell onto the Parisian theatres. The Porte-Saint-Martin, along with most Boulevard theaters, was closed. Henry fled France, spending most of the rest of his career in Milan, Naples, and Vienna, returning to Paris only rarely. In Milan he was introduced to the action-orientated approach of Salvatore Viganò, who drilled his chorus dancers to mime in unison to the music in ballets such as *The Creatures of Prometheus* (1801, to music by Beethoven). Bournonville, who was himself much influenced by Henry, wrote: "Henry, a most ingenious Frenchman, had absorbed the Italian style of ballet, but, by virtue of his originality, knew how to forge his own path. He employed the French style of pantomime in lyrical or idyllic subjects, and the Italian in heroic or historical ones. In this way he achieved a high degree of variety, and as he had great feeling for the picturesque, his groupings were excellent." Henry was famous enough in Italy to find his way into Dumas' *Le Comte de Monte-Cristo*, where his "whole corps de ballet, from the principal dancer to the humblest supernumerary, are all engaged on the stage at the same time; and a hundred and fifty persons may be seen exhibiting the same attitude, or elevating the same arm or leg with simultaneous movement". His highly disciplined corps de ballet danced works such as *Otello* (Naples, 1808), *Romeo e Giulietta* (Naples, 1814), *La Bella Arsene* (Naples, 1818), *Die Amazonen* (Vienna, 1823), and *Guglielmo Tell* (Milan, 1833). Such works placed Henry at the forefront of balletic romanticism, a rightful colleague to Victor Hugo, Eugène Delacroix, and Giocomo Rossini. But his brand of romanticism—intense, rebellious, often tragic—was not to the refined tastes of Paris Opéra audiences who preferred a sugar-coated version, a romanticism of dream-like poetic illusions and seductive exoticism.

Henry first returned to Paris in 1816 when the Porte-Saint-Martin reopened, and here he created further ballets that challenged traditional ideas of what a ballet could be. *Hamlet* and *Samson*, both deeply romantic subjects, made it clear that Henry believed that no theme was beyond the scope of his art. And though there were those who found it ridiculous to see "a man who strikes an entrechat, having a sword in hand", most audiences were convinced that ballet could tackle any subject. Henry was aided in his efforts by the brilliant pantomime dancer, Mme Queriau, who was said to draw tears from those who witnessed her touching performances. She worked closely with Henry in Paris and Europe, marrying him when she became a widow some time around 1820.

By the time Henry returned to Paris for the last time in 1834, many saw him as a foreign ballet master. He produced several works at the Théâtre Nautique, *Chao-Kang*, *Guillaume Tell*, and *Les Ondines* among them. In his Preface to the *Chao-Kang* scenario, Henry demonstrates his preoccupation with the dramatic, pantomimic aspect of ballet. Here he cites Roman pantomime as a model and explains various gestures from his ballet; for example the gesture for the Governor is the indication of five moustaches. But the French by 1834 were interested in dancing, not pantomime action. It is not surprising that when Henry finally got the opportunity to create a work for the Opéra stage, *L'Ile des pirates* (1835), it did not appeal to French tastes. Indicative of the problems were complaints by the dancers who disliked the rigid discipline imposed by the unison corps de ballet miming. Henry had spent too long in other European cities; he was out of tune with the Paris of the Romantic era. Nevertheless, his unwillingness to compromise the intensity of his vision merely to conform to conservative expectations meant that his works were among the most deeply romantic in the ballet genre.

—John Chapman

---

**HENZE, Hans Werner**

German composer. Born in Gütersloh, Westphalia, 1 July 1926. Studied in Heidelberg, student of Wolfgang Fortner, 1946. Work on propaganda films, 1944; répétiteur, Stadttheater, Bielefeld, 1945; music director, Heinz Hilpert's Deutsches Theater, Constance, 1948; artistic director and conductor, Ballet of Hessian State Theatre, Wiesbaden, 1950–52; first ballet, composed for Wiesbaden, performed 1951; resident in Italy, from 1953; professor of composition, Mozarteum, Salzburg, from 1961; professor of composition, Staatlichen Hochschule für Musik, Cologne, 1980; artistic director, Accademia Filarmonica Romana, 1982; International Professor of Composition, Royal Academy of Music, London, 1987–88. Recipient: Robert Schumann Prize, 1952; Prix d'Italia, 1954; Sibelius Gold Medal, 1956; Kunstpreis, Berlin, Niedersachischer Kunstpreis, 1962; honorary D. Mus., Edinburgh University, 1971; Ludwig-Spohr Preis, 1976.

**WORKS** (Ballets)

1951 *Jack Pudding* (chor. von Pelchrzim), Wiesbaden State Theatre
*Labyrinth* (concert version performed Darstadt, 1952)
1952 *Der Idiot* (chor. T. Gsovsky), Berlin State Opera Ballet, East Berlin
1954 *Pas d'action* (chor. V. Gsovsky), Bavarian State Opera Ballet, Munich
*Die schlafende Prinzessin* (*The Sleeping Beauty*, after Tchaikovsky; chor. Bortoluzzi), Essen State Theatre
1957 *Maratona di danza* (chor. Sanders), Berlin
1958 *Ballett-Variationen* (chor. Walter), Wuppertal
*Ondine* (chor. Ashton), Royal Ballet, London
*Rosa Silber* (chor. Kretschmar), Cologne (first performed as ballet-scenes for orchestra, Berlin, 1951)
1959 *L'Usignolo dell'Imperatore* (*Der Kaiser's Nachtigall*; pantomime), Giorgio Strehler's "Piccolo Teatro", La Fenice, Venice
1966 *Tancredi* (revised version of *Pas d'action*; chor. Nureyev), Vienna State Opera Ballet, Vienna
1979 *Orpheus* (chor. Forsythe), Stuttgart Ballet, Stuttgart

**Other ballets using Henze's music:** *Anrufung Apolls* (van Dyk, 1949; Walter, 1961), *Fragmente* (Cranko, 1968), *Undine* (Eck, 1969), *The Poppet* (Arpino, 1969), *Elektra* (Bolender, 1972), *Gemini* (Tetley, 1973), *Tristan* (Tetley, 1974), *Artus Sage* (with other composers; Neumeier, 1983), *Einhorn* (Neumeier, 1985).

**PUBLICATIONS**

By Henze:
*Undine, Tagebuch eines Balletts*, Munich, 1959
"Tanze und Musik/Dance and Music" (in German and English), *Das Ballett und die Künste*, Cologne, 1972
Interview in Garske, Rolf, "Compositions for Dance: Hans Werner Henze", *Ballett-International* (Cologne), November 1986

About Henze:
Herrman, Joachim, "Ballett: Henze, der Romantiker", *Musica* (Kassel-Wilhelmshoehe), March 1959
Geitel, Klaus, *Hans Werner Henze*, Berlin, 1968
Henderson, R., "Hans Werner Henze", *Musical Times* (London), cxxvii, 1976
Koegler, Horst, "At the End of a Partnership", *Ballet-International* (Cologne), December 1986
Petersen, Peter, *Hans Werner Henze*, Hamburg, 1988

* * *

Few composers of the avant-garde during the mid-twentieth century have devoted as much thought and energy to the problems of creating new music for dance, and developing dance forms through music, as Hans Werner Henze. Though Henze is best known to the wider public for his collaboration with Frederick Ashton on the traditional three-act fairy-tale ballet *Ondine*, his involvement with dance has been wide ranging and eclectic, encompassing plotless orchestral scores (such as *Ballett-Variationen* and *Rosa Silber*), the arrangement of classics to suit different performing circumstances (*Die schlafende Prinzessin* after Tchaikovsky), a series of one-act ballets on literary, fantasy, and mythological themes, and dance within other stage works (such as his opera *Boulevard Solitude*). An intrinsic balletic quality in others of his orchestral works have also led to their independent use by several choreographers—notably Symphony no. 3, used by van Dyk for *Anrufung Apolls* and by Tetley for *Gemini*, and the Tristan preludes, used by Tetley for *Tristan* and by Neumeier for *Artus Sage*.

Henze's earliest experience of dance (within a performance of Gluck's *Orfeo*) was paradoxically not a favourable one, though it seems to have formed several of the attitudes which can be distinguished as later constants in his work for the medium: it was "horrible", he has himself written; ". . . the new German dance one saw performed in those days—barefooted . . . I didn't feel that the style of the production had anything to do with the music." Throughout his subsequent involvement with dance, he has characteristically preferred to work with classical choreographers in all his various experiments. Henze has been far-reaching in his attempts to find new and authoritative ways to combine music and movement effectively, and has frequently made dance a significant structural component in what are ostensibly termed operas.

While maintaining strong inner links with "classical" traditions and classic material in the broadest sense, Henze has also been always deeply interested in revolutionizing the possibilities of "theatre" in dance. The lack of a positive dance environment in Germany in the 1950s, coupled with the absence of major companies with strong traditions at that time, undoubtedly helped shape the freedom of his development, while he in turn helped form the climate of innovation and experiment that spread among German companies in the years that followed. But it should be pointed out that any consideration of his many stage works is complicated by the unusual freedom with which Henze treats conventional boundaries between different forms.

The free rein he allows himself, especially where dance is involved, can be seen in the broad shift his works show, away from relatively orthodox ballet scores, and towards an increasingly complex interaction with other theatrical means of expression. In some works the interweaving of musical content, vocal elements, dance, mime, and "pantomime" is so marked that any traditional boundaries between what is a ballet and what is not become blurred. It is worthy of note, however, that Henze's large-scale involvement with ballet in any form, which was so strong in his early career, reached the peak of a long crescendo with *Tancredi*, and apart from the dance-pantomime *Orpheus—a Story in Six Scenes*, he has not set out since to write a predominantly "dance" score.

Initially, however, Henze regarded dance extremely highly, and the valuable experience he gained at the theatres in Bielefeld and at Constance, where he was briefly a répétiteur, fostered the swift development of his ideas about form. The preoccupations shown in many of his later, more mature, ballets can be related to practical observations made by him during this period: his earliest works, created in quick succession, proceed immediately from the relatively traditional plotless *Ballet-Variationen* and *Rosa Silber* to his first reworkings of traditional material in a personal form: *Jack Pudding* is a *commedia del'arte*-styled work, derived from themes in Molière's play *George Dandin*, while *Labyrinth* treats the minotaur myth in six movements combining classical solos, duets, and ensembles with less ballet-oriented "pantomime" sequences. The production of his second opera *Boulevard Solitudé* also saw the first of his substantial incorporations of dance into opera.

After Henze's taking up the post of artistic director and conductor for the ballet at the Hessischen Staatstheater in Wiesbaden, the pantomime element became more highly focused, notably in his treatment of Dostoyevsky's *The Idiot*, and emerging most fully in his treatment of *L'Usignolo dell' Imperatore*, where the title dance role was supported by a mime company at the first performances. The period of Henze's more recent preoccupation with revolutionary politics has seen only one major dance work, *Orpheus*, choreographed by William Forsythe, in which the elements of Greek myth are coloured by the text of its librettist, Edward Bond, to suggest analogies between the totalitarian control of Pluto and Persephone over the dead and the rulers of modern states.

Though the majority of Henze's dance scores have not yet found widespread acceptance with the public, and dance companies have been comparatively slow to incorporate them into ballet's mainstream repertoire, it remains significant that Henze has been a leader among the few contemporary composers to have addressed ballet as a profoundly serious rather than a relatively decorative medium. Even his provision of an apparently "traditional" score for Ashton's *Ondine* reveals a twentieth-century mind working out a contemporary approach to nineteenth-century Romanticism's obsession with the elusive nature of "the spirit". In recognizing the ability of dance to penetrate to the heart of archetypes still motivating human behaviour—as well as the complexity of levels on which it operates—and in attempting to provide music to renew them in contemporary form, Henze may yet emerge as one of the most important twentieth-century figures involved in the process of ballet's "growing up".

—Geoffrey Baskerville

---

## LAS HERMANAS

**Choreography:** Kenneth MacMillan
**Music:** Frank Martin
**Design:** Nicholas Georgiadis (scenery and costumes)
**Libretto:** Kenneth MacMillan (after the play *La Casa de Bernarda Alba*, by Federico García Lorca)
**First Production:** Stuttgart Ballet, Württemberg State Theatre, Stuttgart, 13 July 1963
**Principal Dancers:** Marcia Haydée (Eldest Sister), Helga Heinrich (Jealous Sister), Birgit Keil (Youngest Sister), Ray Barra (The Man)

**Other productions include:** Western Theatre Ballet; Cardiff, 22 June 1966. American Ballet Theatre, with Lupe Serrano (Eldest Sister), Eleanor D'Antuono (Jealous Sister), Ellen Everett (Youngest Sister) Royes Fernandez (The Man); New York, 29 November 1967. Royal Ballet New Group (touring company), with Lynn Seymour (Eldest Sister); London, 2 June 1971. Australian Ballet, with Marilyn Rowe (Eldest Sister); Sydney, 10 May 1979.

**Other choreographic treatments of story:** Alvin Ailey (New York, 1962), Ivan Sertic (Lübeck, 1964), Eleo Pomare (New York, 1967).

### PUBLICATIONS

Bayston, Michael, "MacMillan Ballet a TV Success", *Dancing Times* (London), April 1965

Williams, Peter, "*Las Hermanas*: Lorca/MacMillan and the Spanish Tragedy", *Dance and Dancers* (London), August 1966

Brinson, Peter, and Crisp, Clement, *Ballet for All*, London, 1970

Thorpe, Edward, *Kenneth MacMillan*: *The Man and his Ballets* London, 1985

* * *

*Las Hermanas* (*The Sisters*) came about as MacMillan's response to an invitation from John Cranko, his friend and former Royal Ballet colleague, to create a work for the Stuttgart Ballet which Cranko had been directing since 1961. The Spanish title is explained by the ballet's derivation from a play by Federico García Lorca, *The House of Bernarda Alba*. It was suggested to the choreographer by Nicholas Georgiadis, who then designed the austere, almost entirely black, grey, and white décor so evocative of the dramatic theme of sexual repression by entrenched social formality.

For music MacMillan chose the Concerto for Harpsichord and Small Orchestra (1952) by Frank Martin, the Swiss composer whose music had previously served MacMillan for *Laiderette* (1954) and the highly dramatic *The Burrow* (1958). As Edward Thorpe explained in his biography of MacMillan, "Despite the delicacy of the writing for the solo instrument he thought that the thematic ideas of the concerto were sufficiently dark-toned to illustrate the dramatic events of the ballet while the sound qualities of the harpsichord itself would do much to intimate the formalities of the feminine ménage."

The music's formal structure—consisting of an opening movement which winds down its initial tempo and tension, followed by a sombre, slow middle movement, running into a faster finale that incorporates an elaborate harpsichord cadenza—was put to ingenious choreographic purpose. In the theatre it is prefaced by the sight of a claustrophobic interior room with staircase, down which the mother makes halting progress, with her walking-stick thumping on each step as the only sound. She moves towards her five daughters who sit in separate rocking-chairs, gently moving them in aimless despondency. When the mother also sits, they gather themselves into a line sitting on each other's laps, as if springing from the mother's belly.

The contrast of character in the three principal sisters is revealed choreographically: the eldest neurotic and desperate, her arms making arcs of nervous movement, the middle sister jealous and malign, the youngest still having the spirit to try on the bridal veil intended for the eldest, who must be married as the first in age. The prospective husband calls, stiffly attired, but nevertheless sensuously provocative to the women around him. He escorts the eldest sister out, leaving the others to their rocking-chairs as the light fades.

The start of the middle movement brings a nocturnal assignation between the man and the eldest sister. Now coatless, he tries to importune an embrace for which she is both eager and afraid. Noticing the middle sister watching, she quickly kisses the man and goes within. The youngest sister takes her place, and dances an openly erotic duet with the man, culminating in a sexual embrace. The middle sister, again watching, rouses the household to mutual recriminations and the banishment of the man from the house.

After a solo of agonized suffering by the eldest sister, and her last look through the window at a freedom now lost, the Mother abruptly shuts and locks the door on the world outside, while the youngest daughter has rushed despairingly upstairs and through a curtain. Painfully the mother climbs the stairs in search of her; pulling back the curtain she reveals the girl's suicide, and the last image is of the girl hanging by the neck on a rope as the curtain falls on the final chord.

MacMillan's choreographic strength is in his characterization by means of arms, hands, and the upper torso, allied to steps which take their impetus from the musical rhythm and

*Las Hermanas*, performed by Sadler's Wells Royal Ballet, London

are adapted to suggest appropriate feelings at a particular moment. The two pas de deux, with the eldest followed by the youngest sisters, are similarly contrasted in different expressions of feelings aroused by the man. Lorca's portrayal of social and sexual tragedy is given almost verbal definition by dancing and mime, and emotional feeling by music.

Following the premiere at Stuttgart, *Las Hermanas* was first staged in Britain by Western Theatre Ballet, and has formed part of Sadler's Wells (now Birmingham) Royal Ballet repertory since 1971. It has also been staged by the Australian Ballet.

—Noël Goodwin

---

**HET NATIONALE BALLET** *see* **DUTCH NATIONAL BALLET**

---

## HIGHTOWER, Rosella

American dancer, teacher, and ballet director. Born in Ardmore, Oklahoma, 30 January 1920. Studied with Dorothy Perkins in Kansas City, and with Mikhail Fokine, Anatole Vilzak, and Pierre Vladimirov, New York. Married Jean Robier, 1952; one daughter, Dominique, b. 1955. Dancer, (Denham's) Ballet Russe de Monte Carlo, 1938–41; soloist, Ballet Theatre (later American Ballet Theatre), 1941–45, Massine's Ballets Russe Highlights, (de Basil's) Original Ballet Russe, 1945–46, and Markova-Dolin Company, 1946; principal dancer, becoming prima ballerina, Nouveau Ballet de Monte Carlo (becoming Grand Ballet du Marquis de Cuevas), 1947–62, also performing with American Ballet Theatre, 1955–56; appeared as international guest artist, including for concert group with Sonia Arova, Erik Bruhn, and Rudolf Nureyev, 1962, for Les Grand Ballets Canadiens, 1963, and with ensemble of French dancers, touring North Africa and South America, 1964; director, Nouveau Ballet Opéra de Marseille, 1969–72, Ballet de Nancy, 1975–78; also appeared in films and on television, including *Carosello Napoletano* (film; chor. Giannini, 1954); founder of own company, Cannes, 1976; artistic director, Paris Opéra Ballet, 1981–83; ballet director, La Scala, Milan, 1984; also teacher: founder and director, Centre de danse classique, Cannes, from 1962; director, International Academy of Dance at the Venice Festival, 1975; has also taught frequently for the Ballet du XXe Siècle, Brussels. Recipient: Grand Prix des critiques de danse, 1949; Médaille Universitaire de la danse, 1967; Chevalier de la Légion d'Honneur, 1975; Officier de la Légion d'Honneur, 1988; Grand Prix national de danse, France, 1990; Officier de l'Ordre National du mérite.

### ROLES

1938 A Fish, "The Creation", in *Seventh Symphony* (Massine), Ballet Russe de Monte Carlo

1939 Variation (cr) in *Devil's Holiday* (*Le Diable s'amuse*; Ashton), Ballet Russe de Monte Carlo, New York

1940 Pas de trois in *Swan Lake* (after Petipa, Ivanov), Ballet Russe de Monte Carlo
1941 One of the Philistines in *Carnaval* (Fokine), Ballet Russe de Monte Carlo
Carlotta Grisi in *Pas de quatre* (Dolin), Ballet Theatre, New York
Blanca, a wife of Bluebeard (cr) in *Bluebeard* (Fokine), Ballet Theatre, Mexico City
Pas de trois in *Aurora's Wedding* (divertissement from *The Sleeping Beauty*; Dolin after Petipa), Ballet Theatre, Mexico City
A Nymph in *L'Après-midi d'un faune* (Lazovsky after Nijinsky), Ballet Theatre, Mexico City
1942 A Lover-in-Experience (cr) in *Pillar of Fire* (Tudor), Ballet Theatre, New York
A Street dancer, A Bat (cr) in *Aleko* (Massine), Ballet Theatre, Mexico City
Hera (cr) in *Helen of Troy* (Lichine), Ballet Theatre, Detroit
1943 Aristocrat (cr) in *Mademoiselle Angot* (later *Mam'zelle Angot*; Massine), Ballet Theatre, New York
She Wore a Perfume (cr) in *Dim Lustre* (Tudor), Ballet Theatre, New York
Calliope in *Apollo* (Balanchine), Ballet Theatre, New York
White Witch (cr) in *Fair at Sorochinsk* (Lichine), Ballet Theatre, New York
1944 A Mother (cr) in *Barn Dance* (Littlefield), Ballet Theatre, New York
Dance Impromptu in *Graduation Ball* (Lichine), Ballet Theatre, Montreal
Odette in *Swan Lake*, Act II (Dolin after Ivanov), Ballet Theatre
Title role in *Giselle* (Petipa after Coralli, Perrot; staged Dolin), Ballet Theatre, New York
1946 The Courtesan in *Sebastian* (Caton), Original Ballet Russe, New York
Waltz, Mazurka in *Les Sylphides* (Fokine), Original Ballet Russe, New York
Larghetto in *Constantia* (Dollar), Original Ballet Russe, New York
Principal dancer in *Don Quixote* Pas de deux (after Petipa), Original Ballet Russe, New York
Principal dancer in *Black Swan* Pas de deux (from *Swan Lake*; after Petipa), Original Ballet Russe, New York
1947 Principal dancer (cr) in *Pas de trois* (Robbins), Original Ballet Russe, New York
Principal dancer in *Brahms Variations* (Nijinska), (de Cuevas's) Grand Ballet de Monte Carlo, Paris
1948 Ballerina in White in *Noir et blanc* (Lifar), (de Cuevas's) Grand Ballet de Monte Carlo, Monte Carlo
Principal dancer in *Concerto Barocco* (Balanchine), (de Cuevas's) Grand Ballet de Monte Carlo, London
Principal dancer (cr) in *Pas de trois classique* (Balanchine), London
1949 Principal dancer (cr) in *In Memoriam* (Nijinska), (de Cuevas's) Grand Ballet de Monte Carlo, Paris
The Street Dancer in *Le Beau Danube* (Massine), (de Cuevas's) Grand Ballet de Monte Carlo, Paris
Mariucca in *Les Femmes de bonne humeur* (Massine), (de Cuevas's) Grand Ballet de Monte Carlo, London
The Miller's Daughter, Jealousy (cr) in *Le Moulin enchanté* (Lichine), (de Cuevas's) Grand Ballet de Monte Carlo, Paris
The Miller's Wife in *Le Tricorne* (Massine), (de Cuevas's) Grand Ballet de Monte Carlo
1950 She in *Persephone* (Taras), (de Cuevas's) Grand Ballet de Monte Carlo, Monaco
The Ballerina in *Petrushka* (Nijinska), (de Cuevas's) Grand Ballet de Monte Carlo, Barcelona
1951 Principal dancer (cr) in *Les Saisons* (*Symphonie allégorique*; Massine), Grand Ballet du Marquis de Cuevas, Bordeaux
Principal dancer (cr) in *Tarasiana* (pas de deux; Taras), Grand Ballet du Marquis de Cuevas, Paris
The Young Wife (cr) in *Scaramouche* (also chor.), Grand Ballet du Marquis de Cuevas, Paris
Tcherkessian Maiden (cr) in *Le Prisonnier du Caucase* (Skibine), Grand Ballet du Marquis de Cuevas, Paris
1952 Title role (cr) in *Doña Iñes de Castro* (Ricarda), Grand Ballet du Marquis de Cuevas, Cannes
La Jeune Fille (cr) in *Coup de feu* (Milloss), Grand Ballet du Marquis de Cuevas, Paris
Principal dancer (cr) in *Scherzo* (Taras), Grand Ballet du Marquis de Cuevas, Paris
Principal dancer (cr) in *Rondo Capriccioso* (Nijinska), Grand Ballet du Marquis de Cuevas, Paris
The Queen of the Morphides (cr) in *Piège de lumière* (Taras), Grand Ballet du Marquis de Cuevas, Paris
1953 L'Aigrette/L'Ange blanc (cr) in *L'Aigrette* (first version; Bartholin), Grand Ballet du Marquis de Cuevas, Cannes
Title role (cr) in *La Sylphide* (new production; Lander after Bournonville), Grand Balled du Marquis de Cuevas, Paris
1956 La Désespérée (cr) in *Le Pont* (Starbuck), Grand Ballet du Marquis de Cuevas, Deauville
1957 Carmen in *Corrida* (Lichine), Grand Ballet du Marquis de Cuevas, Paris
Principal dancer (cr) in *Fiesta* (Martinez), Grand Ballet du Marquis de Cuevas, Paris
Principal dancer (cr) in *Soirée musicale* (Taras), Grand Ballet du Marquis de Cuevas, Paris
Principal dancer in *Aubade* (Lifar), Grand Ballet du Marquis de Cuevas, Paris
1958 The Glove Seller in *Gaîté parisienne* (Massine), Grand Ballet du Marquis de Cuevas, Paris
Principal dancer (cr) in *Le Mal du siècle* (Starbuck), Grand Ballet du Marquis de Cuevas, Brussels
Principal dancer (cr) in *Concerto d'Aranjuez* (Corelli), French television
1960 Le Rossignol (cr) in *Le Rossignol et l'Empereur de Chine* (Corelli), French television
The Annunciation (cr) in *Tryptique* (Caton), Grand Ballet du Marquis de Cuevas, Cannes
Princess Aurora in *The Sleeping Beauty* (Nijinska, Helpmann after Petipa), Grand Ballet du Marquis de Cuevas, Paris
1962 Principal dancer (cr) in *Toccata et fugue* (Bruhn), Nureyev/Bruhn Company, Cannes
Principal dancer (cr) in *Raymonda Pas de quatre* (Nureyev after Petipa), Nureyev/Bruhn Company, Cannes
Principal dancer (cr) in *Fantasie* (Bruhn), Nureyev/Bruhn Company, Cannes
Principal dancer (cr) in *Lamenti de Monteverdi*, Belgian television
Principal dancer in *Le Combat* (pas de deux; Dollar), Ballets de Paris
Principal dancer (cr) in *Le Violin* (pas de deux; Petit), Ballets de Paris, Paris
1963 Principal dancer in *Flower Festival at Genzano* (after Bournonville), Gala, Cannes
Principal dancer (cr) in *Fantasia par un gentilhomme*

**Rosella Hightower teaching class**

(Corelli), French television

1965 Principal dancer (cr) in *La Robe de plumes* (Lau-Siu-Ming), Théâtre des Champs-Elysées, Paris
Principal dancer (cr) in *Profile de silence* (Clouser), Théâtre des Champs-Elysées, Paris
Principal dancer (cr) in *Tzigane* (Tonin), Théâtre des Champs-Elysées, Paris

1969 Principal dancer (cr) in *Variations* (Béjart), in *Concert de danse*, Royan

1991 Maude (cr) in *Harold et Maude* (Frey), Sinopa

**Other roles include:** Leading role in *The House Party* (*Les Biches*; Nijinska), Bluebird Pas de deux in *The Sleeping Beauty* (Petipa), principal dancer in *Capriccio Espagnol* (Massine), Wife in *Tally-ho!* (de Mille), Myrtha in *Giselle* (after Petipa, Coralli, Perrot), Sugar Plum Fairy in *The Nutcracker Pas de deux* (after Ivanov), principal dancer in *Raymonda Pas de deux* (after Petipa), Desdemona in *Othello* (Adret), principal dancer in *Rouge et noir* (Massine), principal dancer in *Serenade* (Balanchine), Swanilda in *Coppélia* (Semenoff after Petipa).

## WORKS

1949 *Henry VIII* (mus. Rossini, Zeller), Markova–Dolin Ballet, New York
*Pleasuredrome* (mus. Lanchbery), Metropolitan Ballet, London

1950 *Salomé* (mus. Strauss), Grand Ballet du Marquis de Cuevas, Paris

1951 *Scaramouche* (mus. Sibelius), Grand Ballet du Marquis de Cuevas, Paris

1966 *Le Chauve-Souris* (mus. Strauss), Théâtre de la Monnaie, Brussels

1967 *Four Moons* (with Jasinsky, Skibine, and Terekoff), Oklahoma Indian Ballerina Festival, Tulsa

Also staged:

1977 *The Sleeping Beauty* (after Petipa, Nijinska; mus. Tchaikovsky), Stuttgart Ballet, Stuttgart

1985 *Swan Lake* (with Zeffirelli, after Petipa, Ivanov; mus. Tchaikovsky), La Scala, Milan

## PUBLICATIONS

By Hightower:

Interview in Gruen, John, *The Private World of Ballet*, New York, 1975

Interview in Merrill, Bruce, "Rosella Hightower", *Dance Magazine* (New York), July 1981

About Hightower:

Williams, Peter, "Rosella Hightower", *Dance and Dancers* (London), January 1950

Cadieu, Marlie, *Rosella Hightower*, Paris, 1951

Davidson, Glenys, *Ballet Biographies*, revised edition, London, 1954

"Portrait: Rosella Hightower", *Dance Magazine* (New York), August 1954

"Rosella Hightower", *Paris Théâtre* (Paris), October 1954

"Rosella Hightower", *Ballet Today* (London), October 1964

Lidova, Irène, "Rosella Hightower", *Les Saisons de la danse* (Paris), April 1968

Harris, Dale, "Modest Maîtresse", *Ballet News* (New York), December 1980

Brooks, V.G., "On the Riviera", *Ballet News* (New York), August 1985

* * *

Born in Oklahoma of Choctaw Indian descent and raised in Kansas City, Rosella Hightower established her reputation as a dancer of breathtaking technical virtuosity and lyricism in France with the Ballet Russe de Monte Carlo under ballet master Léonide Massine, and later with the Grand Ballet du Marquis de Cuevas, where she was prima ballerina until the company's demise in 1962.

As a member of the Ballet Russe de Monte Carlo during the war, Hightower learned the repertory while performing at American bases on company tours, eventually performing in such pieces as Edward Caton's *Sebastian*, William Dollar's *Constantia*, and the *Black Swan* pas de deux. Filling in for star Alicia Markova in the role of Giselle in New York, she was instantly acclaimed a full-ranking ballerina and was consequently invited by the Marquis de Cuevas to lead his newly-formed Grand Ballet de Monte Carlo, the reincarnation of the Nouveau Ballet de Monte Carlo.

In between Ballets Russes engagements in the 1940s, and then following the birth of her daughter in the 1950s, Hightower performed with American Ballet Theatre. Showing her mastery of the American repertoire, she appeared in ballets by Robbins, de Mille, and Tudor, performing in de Mille's *Tally-Ho*, and mastering such roles as the girl with perfume in Tudor's *Dim Lustre*, and the "Lover-In-Experience" in his *Pillar of Fire*. Her technique was cited by critics as "brilliant" and "meticulous" in such classics as *Giselle* and the *Black Swan Pas de deux*, where, partnered by André Eglevsky or Anton Dolin, she was always in control: her fouettés seemed unequalled in profusion and speed, and her strong point work made no step or combination seem impossible.

The favorite dancer of the Marquis de Cuevas, in whose company she toured Europe, Asia, and South America, Hightower found one of her most challenging roles in Taras's *Piège de lumière*. The ballet dealt with the theme of French prisoners seeking escape from a tropical island and their experience catching the butterflies which come out at night. In this work, Hightower's virtuosity was challenged by her role as "La Grande Morphide", in which she wore a heavy, wing-shaped costume, designed by Andre Levasseur, and danced a classical variation lasting for nearly fifteen minutes on stage.

By far the most profound influence on Hightower was Nijinska, teacher and coach with de Cuevas during her time as ballerina with the company. The choreographer's musicality was a challenge to Hightower; as she explained herself, "Nijinska approached everything from the point of view of 'accent–dynamics', 'music–dynamics' . . . you had to approach it musically, and eventually, by working it out in that way, it would happen . . . She was architectural, because, you see, music was architectural". In such ballets as *Rondo Capriccioso* and *Les Biches*, Hightower found continued development as an artist.

Although she danced until 1977, Hightower has also developed a reputation as a choreographer, beginning during her years with de Cuevas with small concert works such as *Pleasuredrome*, *Salomé*, and *Scaramouche*. In her choreography, she makes use of her extensive knowledge of the ballet repertoire to develop a style which is intended to challenge the expressive as well as the technical ranges of the dancer. In recent years, she has appeared as a guest for the Stuttgart Ballet, for whom she staged *The Sleeping Beauty*, and took part in staging the more recently acclaimed "modernized" *Swan Lake*, produced by Franco Zeffirelli at La Scala, Milan.

In France, where she continues to reside, Hightower's reputation as choreographer and teacher has spread—and she has become, since the establishment of her school, Le Centre de danse classique in Cannes in the early 1960s, a major force in the decentralization of ballet from Paris to the provinces. Through her establishment of a school for the training of professionals and her subsequent directorship of regional companies (such as Le Nouveau Ballet at the Opéra de Marseille and Le Ballet de Nancy), she has sought to introduce dancers and public to a variety of choreographic styles, providing opportunities to perform in many different idioms. Her philosophy is clear; she believes that the growth of regional companies will raise the quality of audience and of performance in dance everywhere.

In 1981, Hightower became the first American to direct the Paris Opéra Ballet. In this position she attacked the complex hierarchical system of the Opéra and aimed to surmount such administrative problems as the star system and lack of rehearsal time, while trying to develop a company policy which would permit all dancers to develop as performers. She wanted the Opéra not only to welcome guest artists, but also to permit its dancers opportunities to appear as guests with foreign troupes. Hightower's most controversial reform was the institution of a three-tiered system of programming, which allowed one segment of the company to perform in the opera house, a second to tour, and a third to perform as a voluntary "group de recherches" in modern works.

Hightower's first season as director included new creations by Douglas Dunn (*Pulcinella*) and Alwin Nikolais (*Schema*) as well as revivals of Béjart works (*L'Oiseau de feu* and *Le Sacre du printemps*). The premiere performance of *Hommage au ballet*, although critized by the Parisian press for problems of length and balance, nevertheless allowed the rare appearance of all company members together, focusing their efforts on their continued progress as a unified ballet company.

Hightower's direction of the Paris Opéra between 1981 and 1983 solidified her presence on the French ballet scene, defining her as an advocate not only of the dance, but also of the dancer, whom she feels still suffers from the lack of a truly structured dance education. "Of all people," she has said, "I think the most dedicated are dancers, and certainly with the sacrifices they make in society, they should have their place."

Today, Le Centre de danse in Cannes functions as a haven where dancers of major world companies as well as beginners can participate in classes, and are assured a year-round training center. Here, dance can be recognized as a profession that is at once intellectual, cultural, artistic, and technical; Hightower assures that dancers, in society, have their place.

—Pamela Gaye

---

**HILAIRE, Laurent**

French dancer. Born in 1963. Studied at the Paris Opéra Ballet School, pupil of J. Huriel and Alexandre Kalioujny; graduated in 1980. Dancer, Paris Opéra Ballet: quadrille, 1981; coryphée, 1982; sujet, 1983; étoile (promoted by Nureyev without first being named premier danseur), from 1985; also international guest artist, including in regular appearances for Royal Ballet, London, from 1988, as well as appearances in Sofia, 1984, New Zealand, 1987, Canada, 1991, Vienna, and for the Ballet of La Scala, Milan and American Ballet Theatre, New York; has also appeared on television, including in *Aurora Pas de deux* for television programme *Ballerina* (1987). Recipient: Prix Carpeaux, Paris Opéra Ballet School, 1984; Silver Medal (with Isabelle Guérin) for Best Couple, International Ballet Competition, Paris, 1984.

**ROLES**

1983 Principal dancer (cr) in *Marée de morte eau* (Wengerd), Opéra-Comique, Paris
Béranger and Bernard in *Raymonda* (new production; Nureyev after Petipa), Paris Opéra Ballet, Paris
Franz in *Coppélia* (Lacotte after Saint-Léon), Paris Opéra Ballet, Paris
1984 Pâris (cr) in *Romeo and Juliet* (Nureyev), Paris Opéra Ballet, Paris
Ferdinand in *The Tempest* (Nureyev), Paris Opéra Ballet, Paris
Demetrius in *A Midsummer Night's Dream* (Nureyev), Paris Opéra Ballet, Paris
Prince Siegfried in *Swan Lake* (Nureyev after Petipa, Ivanov), Sofia Opera Ballet, Sofia
Polichinelle in *Harlequin, magicien par amour* (Cramér), Paris Opéra Ballet, Paris
Eusebius in *Le Bourgeois Gentilhomme* (Balanchine), Paris Opéra Ballet, Paris
1985 Pas de deux des vendangeurs in *Giselle* (Petipa after Coralli, Perrot; staged Skeaping), Paris Opéra Ballet, Paris
Romeo in *Romeo and Juliet* (Nureyev), Paris Opéra Ballet, Paris
Morris in *Washington Square* (Nureyev), Paris Opéra Ballet, Paris

Pas de six in *Napoli* (extracts; Bournonville), Paris Opéra Ballet, Paris
Her Lover in *Jardin aux lilas* (Tudor), Paris Opéra Ballet, Paris
Title role in *Continuo* (Tudor), Paris Opéra Ballet, Paris
Principal dancer in *Dark Elegies* (Tudor), Paris Opéra Ballet, Paris
Principal dancer (cr) in *Before Nightfall* (Criste), Paris Opéra Ballet, Paris
Drosselmeyer / Prince (cr) in *The Nutcracker* (Nureyev), Paris Opéra Ballet, Paris
1986 Principal dancer (cr) in *Fantasia simplice* (Bagouet), Paris Opéra Ballet, Paris
Principal dancer in *Un Jour ou deux* (Cunningham), Paris Opéra Ballet, Paris
Leading role in *Manfred* (Nureyev), Paris Opéra Ballet, Paris
Basil in *Don Quixote* (Nureyev after Petipa), Paris Opéra Ballet, Paris
The Prince (cr) in *Cinderella* (Nureyev), Paris Opéra Ballet, Paris
1987 Principal dancer in *Symphony in Three Movements* (Balanchine), Paris Opéra Ballet, Paris
Principal dancer (cr) in *In the Middle, Somewhat Elevated* (Forsythe), Paris Opéra Ballet, Paris
Principal dancer in *Four Last Songs* (van Dantzig), Paris Opéra Ballet, Paris
Principal dancer in *In Memory of . . .* (Robbins), Paris Opéra Ballet, Paris
Principal dancer in *Magnificat* (Neumeier), Paris Opéra Ballet, Paris
Mazurka and Adage in *Suite en blanc* (Lifar), Paris Opéra Ballet, Paris
1988 Title role in *Études* (Lander), Paris Opéra Ballet, Paris
Prince in *The Sleeping Beauty* (Petipa; staged MacMillan), Royal Ballet, London
Abderam in *Raymonda* (Nureyev after Petipa), Paris Opéra Ballet, Paris
Jean de Brienne in *Raymonda* (Nureyev after Petipa), Paris Opéra Ballet, Paris
1989 Second Movement in *In the Night* (Robbins), Paris Opéra Ballet, Paris
Principal dancer in *Violin Concerto* (Balanchine), Paris Opéra Ballet, Paris
Title role in *Le Spectre de la rose* (Fokine), Paris Opéra Ballet, Paris
Principal dancer in *Les Présages* (Massine; staged Leskova), Paris Opéra Ballet, Paris
Ballet Master in *Tanz Schul* (Kylián), Paris Opéra Ballet, Paris
Frollo in *Notre Dame de Paris* (Petit), Paris Opéra Ballet, Paris
1990 Don José in *Carmen* (Petit), Paris Opéra Ballet, Paris
Solor in *La Bayadère* (Makarova after Petipa), Royal Ballet, London
Romeo in *Romeo and Juliet* (MacMillan), Royal Ballet, London
James in *La Sylphide* (Lacotte after Taglioni), Paris Opéra Ballet, Paris
Des Grieux in *L'Histoire de Manon* (*Manon*; MacMillan), Paris Opéra Ballet, Paris
Albrecht in *Giselle* (Petipa after Coralli, Perrot; staged Wright), Royal Ballet, London
Title role in *The Prince of the Pagodas* (MacMillan), Paris Opéra Ballet, Paris
1991 Principal dancer in *En Sol* (*In G Major*; Robbins), Paris Opéra Ballet, Paris
Dancer (cr) in *La Prisonnière* (pas de deux; Petit), Paris Opéra Ballet Gala, Paris
Principal dancer in *Sonatine* (Balanchine), Paris Opéra Ballet, Paris
Principal dancer in *Dances at a Gathering* (Robbins), Paris Opéra Ballet, Paris

**Other roles include:** Principal dancer in *Song of a Wayfarer* (Béjart), *Laurencia* Pas de Six (Nureyev after Chabukiani), *Other Dances* (Robbins).

## PUBLICATIONS

Clarke, Mary, "Royal and Sadler's Wells Royal Ballets", *Dancing Times* (London), June 1990
Hersin, André Philippe, "*Le Lac du cygnes*", *Les Saisons de la danse* (Paris), June 1990
Cournand, Gilberte, "Un Best-Seller", *Les Saisons de la danse* (Paris), February 1991
Sulcas, Roslyn, "*Manon* Revisited", *Dance and Dancers* (London), February–March 1991

* * *

Laurent Hilaire first danced at the Paris Opéra while still a student, in one of the few performances given each year by the Paris Opéra school at the Opéra–Comique, the Théâtre des Champs-Elysées, or the Opéra itself. Hilaire is tall and very good-looking with dark hair, long legs, and yet a skill for sharp, small batterie, which enables him to tackle a wide range of ballets in which he can display his assured technique.

While still a member of the corps de ballet, Hilaire was selected by Nureyev to dance the leading role of Franz in *Coppélia*. He was successful in this role, and for as long as Nureyev remained artistic director at the Paris Opéra, he continued to give Hilaire solo roles in the ballets he mounted.

Hilaire is particularly well suited to classical roles; critics have commented on his good looks, confident technique, and charm, pointing to his elegance in *Don Quixote*, his dramatic depth in *Romeo and Juliet*, and his courtliness in *Giselle*. Some have seen this noble elegance as limiting: French critic Irène Lidova, for example, commented that in the 1990 revival of Roland Petit's fiery *Carmen*, Hilaire was "a perfect classical cavalier, handsome and elegant, but he totally lacked the passion and fire which the role needs". However, he has made successful appearances in contemporary ballets, such as Forsythe's *In the Middle somewhat Elevated* (created for Hilaire and Sylvie Guillem) and Robbins's *In the Night*, *Dances at a Gathering*, and *Other Dances* (in which role Hilaire was praised by the critic John Percival for "the sharpness of his cabrioles, the firm control of his chaîné turns . . . and [his] assured personality"). In the role of Des Grieux in MacMillan's *Manon*, Hilaire not only displayed brilliant technique but also portrayed with great conviction the plight of the tragic hero who loses everything.

Hilaire's life is divided between the Opéra, guest appearances abroad, and his family—he is married with a young daughter. He does not discuss his private life. He has danced with many leading ballerinas of the day, including with Noëlla Pontois in *Giselle*, Claude de Vulpian in *Romeo and Juliet*, Elisabeth Platel in *Études*, and Isabelle Guérin, with whom he won a silver medal for the duet from Act III of *Giselle* in 1984. Abroad, he has danced with Alessandra Ferri in Italy, Karine Kain in Canada, and Yoko Morishita in Vienna in *Aurora's Wedding*. In recent years he has been a frequent guest at Covent Garden in London, where he has partnered not only fellow guest artist and compatriot Sylvie Guillem—with whom he has a strong stage rapport—but many other ballerinas of the Royal Ballet.

—Monique Babsky

---

**HILVERDING (van Wewen), Franz**

(also Hilferdin, Hilferding, Helwerding, Helferting, Helfferting) Austrian choreographer, dancer, ballet master, and teacher. Baptized Anton Christoph Hilverding in Vienna, son of theatre director Johann Baptist Hilverding, 17 November 1710. Studied at Imperial Court Dance School, Vienna; later studied with Michel Blondy in Paris, c. 1734–36. Court dancer, Vienna, from c. 1737; choreographer, arranging dances, ballets, and pantomimes for court operas, Vienna, from c.1740; ballet master, Kärntnertor Theater, from 1742; ballet master for both Kärntnertor Theater and Burgtheater, 1752–58; left Vienna for Russia: ballet master and choreographer, Imperial Theatres of St. Petersburg and Moscow, 1758–64; returned to Vienna, 1764; lessee of Kärntnertor Theater, from 1766; also leading teacher: students include Gaspero Angiolini and Eva Maria Veigl (known as Violetti; later wife of David Garrick); retired 1767. Recipient: noble title "van Wewen", c.1766. Died in Vienna, 30 May 1768.

**WORKS**

1742 *Die Abenteuer im Serrail* (in *La Fedeltà sin alla morte*), Kärntnertor Theater, Vienna

1744 Dances (mus. Holzbauer) in *Ipermestra* (opera; Hasse; mus. Holzbauer), Hoftheater am Tummelplatz, Vienna

1748 Dances in *Semiramide riconosciuta* (opera; mus. Gluck), Burgtheater, Vienna
Dances in *Leucippo* (opera; mus. Hasse), Burgtheater, Vienna

1752 *Orphée et Euridice*, Burgtheater, Vienna
*Les Amériquains*, Burgtheater, Vienna
*Les Jalousies du serrail*, Kärntnertor Theater, Vienna

1753 *La Fabrique de coton*, Kärntnertor Theater, Vienna
*Dom Quichot; ou, Les Noces de Gamache*, Kärntnertor Theater, Vienna
*Le Balet bleu*, Burgtheater, Vienna
*Le Ballet couleur de rose*, Burgtheater, Vienna

1754 *Les Bûcherons tirolois*, Kärntnertor Theater, Vienna

1755 *Les Quatre Parties du jour en quatre balets différens*, Burgtheater, Vienna
*La Noce de Bastien et Bastienne* (ballet in *Les Amours de Bastien et Bastienne*, mus. Starzer), Laxenburg

1758 *Le Turc généreux* (mus. Rameau), Kärntnertor Theater, Vienna

1759 *Virtue's Refuge* (opera-ballet; mus. Raupach, dance mus. Starzer), Court Theatre, St. Petersburg

1760 *La Victoire de Flore sur Borée* (mythological ballet; mus. Starzer), Winter Palace, St. Petersburg

1762 *Amour et Psyché* (pantomime-ballet; mus. Manfredini), Moscow
*Le Seigneur de village moqué* (*The Ridiculed Landowner*, with Angiolini; mus. Starzer), in *Olimpiade* (opera; mus. Manfredini), for Coronation of Catherine II, Court Theatre, Moscow

1763 *Le Vengeance du dieu de l'amour* (mus. Starzer), Court Theatre, Moscow
*Le Combat de l'amour et de la raison* (mus. D. Springer), for members of the court, Imperial Palace, Moscow
*Le Retour de la déesse du printemps*, Imperial Palace, Moscow
*Pygmalion; ou, La Statue animée* (mus. Starzer), St. Petersburg

1764 *Les Amours d'Acis et Galathée* (mythological ballet; mus. Starzer), St. Petersburg

1765 *Les Amans protégés par l'amour*, Burgtheater, Vienna
*Le Triomphe de l'amour* (mus. F.L. Gassmann), Schönbrunn Palace, Vienna

1766 *Der Triumph des Frühlings*, Kärntnertor Theater, Vienna

**Other works include:** heroic and pantomime ballets (almost all mus. Florian Deller and Ignaz von Holzbauer)—*Britannicus, Idomeneus, Alzire, Ulisses und Circe, Acis und Galathea, Orpheus und Euridice, Ariadne und Bacchus, Amor und Psyche, Venus und Adonis* (all c.1742–52), *The Lame Cavalier* (c. 1763).

**PUBLICATIONS**

*Répertoire des théâtres de la ville de Vienne depuis l'année 1752 à l'année 1757*, Vienna, 1757

Angiolini, Gaspero, *Lettere di Gaspero Angiolini a Monsieur Noverre sopra i balli pantomimi*, Milan, 1773

Arteaga, S., *Le rivoluzioni del teatro musicale italiano dalla sua origine fino al presente*, Bologna, 1783–88

von Weilen, A., and Teuber, O., *Die Theater Wiens*, Vienna, 1899

Haas, Robert, "Die Wiener Ballet-Pantomime im 18 Jahrhundert und Glucks *Don Juan*", *Studien zur Musikwissenschaft* (Leipzig and Vienna), 1923

Hass, Robert, *Gluck und Durazzo im Burgtheater*, Vienna, 1925

Beaumont, Cyril, *A History of Ballet in Russia*, London, 1930

Sandt, A., "Le Séjour de Noverre à Vienne", *Archives internationales de la danse*, Paris, 1933

Haas, Robert, "Der Wiener Bühnentanz von 1740 bis 1767", *Jahrbuch der Musikbibliothek Peters* (Leipzig), 1937

Artur, Michel, "The Ballet d'Action Before Noverre", *Dance Index* (New York), no. 6, 1947

Lynham, Deryck, *The Chevalier Noverre*, London, 1950

Mooser, R.A., *Opéras, intermezzos, ballets, cantates, oratorios joués en Russie durant le XVIIIe siècle*, Basle, 1964

Derra de Moroda, Friderica, "A Neglected Choreographer: Hilverding", *Dancing Times* (London), June 1968

Kirstein, Lincoln, *Movement and Metaphor: Four Centuries of Ballet*, New York, 1970

Winter, Marian Hannah, *The Pre-Romantic Ballet*, London, 1974

* * *

In 1803 the Viennese theatre historian Joseph Oehler wrote: "The first creator of a regular ballet was Hilverding. He it was who taught dancers an expressive play of gestures both facial and bodily. He was the first to reestablish in Europe that art of pantomime so highly esteemed and brought to such perfection by the ancient Greeks and Romans. What distinguished the Viennese ballet of his time from all other ballets in the world were the *figurants*. When Noverre succeeded Hilverding in 1767 he found a [gifted] assemblage . . . ." Oehler's claims for Hilverding are impressive and largely accurate: he pioneered the "ballet d'action" in Vienna and St. Petersburg, applied

**Franz Hilverding's revival of *Le Turc généreux*, a ballet-pantomime from Rameau's *Les Indes galantes*, Vienna (engraving by Bernardo Belotto, 1759)**

classical theory of pantomime to contemporary dance (although John Weaver had done this somewhat earlier in England), and developed, perhaps for the first time, a technique of integrated dance which made use of the entire body. To these might be added features which modern dance historians have cherished: his striking choreographic use of large groups on stage, his encouragement of national dance styles and native dancers, and his interest in what we would today call theatre realism. In spite of all this, Hilverding remains, as Derra de Moroda has said, a neglected choreographer, a state of affairs which began with the characteristic ingratitude of Noverre toward his predecessor, but which has been exacerbated by the scant and scattered state of the Viennese theatre records.

The earliest record of Hilverding's choreographic work suggests that he had already a sophisticated notion of the possibilities of the *ballet d'action*: Stefano Arteaga reports that in 1740 Hilverding produced a ballet of Racine's *Britannicus* using gesture alone. Unfortunately we know nothing else of this ballet, but it sounds like a self-conscious attempt to revive ancient tragic pantomime. Ballets of Crebillon's *Idomeneus* and Voltaire's *Alzire* soon followed, suggesting that Hilverding was attracted to current French drama for its historical realism and tight structure. In his experiments with dance drama, he had the advantage of working with two superb ballet composers, Florian Deller and Joseph Starzer, now better known for their collaborations with Noverre. Starzer's sense of tight dramatic structure no doubt suited Hilverding especially, for he even took Starzer with him to Russia.

Hilverding, however, was no mean musician himself, having earned a reputation as a serious student of all the arts, and for precision of execution in his choreography. He soon attracted dancers from all over Europe, and by 1752 he was already ballet master of both court theatres in Vienna, the Burgtheater (a French stage where serious mythological pieces were preferred) and the Kärntnertor Theater (a German stage for comic productions). Moreover, he was also responsible for performances in the palace theatres of Laxenburg and Schönbrunn.

We owe to Count Giacomo Durazzo, Italian manager of the Vienna court theatres, some of the best evidence we have of Hilverding's work, for he collected a number of illustrations of the ballet master's productions. One of the most intriguing drawings in the collection depicts the effects of a wind storm on a large ensemble of dancers, whose stances and gestures suggest a type of theatre realism in ensemble design unusual for the period. The picture is thought to represent Hilverding's *La Victoire de Flore sur Borée*, and most exciting is the centre stage image of one of Boreas's attacking minions performing a grand jeté of some elevation in the direction of a group of female dancers whose bodies are curved away from his blast. This suggests that Hilverding, who had trained in Paris in the 1730s when the transition from "terre á terre" to "danse haute" was in progress, had continued to develop this style in Vienna.

This scene, and another portraying his *Le Turc généreux*, leave little doubt that Hilverding's trademark was the development of a choreography which used the dancer's entire body, not just mimic gesture and footwork, to represent emotion. The illustration of *Le Turc généreux*, engraved by Bernardo Belotto, nephew of Canaletto, captures again a strong sense of movement and ensemble design: ladies of the harem rush in on one side, French soldiers spring in on the other, with the principals arranged in striking poses centre stage. This ballet was, according to his famous pupil and defender, Angiolini, one of Hilverding's masterpieces, although the story is now better known in Mozart's operatic version (*Die Entführung aus dem Serail*); it was produced on the occasion of Count Durazzo's state welcome of a special envoy from Turkey in April, 1758, and it was Hilverding's last major work before his departure for Russia in November of that year.

In vogue in Russia were the allegorical ballet and the traditional opera-ballet, both of which must have seemed rather outmoded to him, but he and Starzer collaborated on a number of well-received political allegorical pieces—such as the balletic sections of *Virtue's Refuge*, an early theatrical instance of Russian nationalism, which gave great scope for the kind of European folkdance which Hilverding had used so successfully in Vienna. The Russians also seem to have enjoyed his considerable skill with comic realism; titles like *The Ridiculed Landowner* or *The Lame Cavalier* hint at a robust inventiveness for capturing everyday life on stage. Upon his return to Vienna Hilverding's first task was *Le Triomphe de L'amour*, a ballet performed at the palace of Schönbrunn for the wedding of Emperor Joseph II and Maria Josepha of Bavaria. It is immortalized in a painting showing the young Marie Antoinette and her small brothers in an elegant configuration, flanked by an ensemble of courtiers; but as delightful as the demure little Marie Antoinette is, the scene lacks the vitality of the designs for Hilverding's public productions, a contrast which may suggest the limitations of choreographing for royalty.

The closure of the theatres in August 1765 on the death of Emperor Franz I, husband of Maria Theresa, seems to have dealt Hilverding a personal blow from which he never recovered. After the theatres reopened in 1766 he was granted the lease of the German Theatre, where he tried to raise standards and strengthen national traditions, an endeavour which aroused the opposition of the nobility who, in Winter's words, "were happier to pay tremendous sums to the Vestris family . . . than to aid Austrian dancers". This must have been frustrating for the ageing ballet master, who had trained many world-class dancers in Vienna. In his sense of the need for a strong national theatre Hilverding was only slightly ahead of his time: in the late 1770s Emperor Joseph would establish a national *Singspiel* company in Vienna, a crusade to which Mozart would contribute his *Entführung*, but the veteran ballet master did not live to see these changes. He died, apparently bankrupt, in May 1768.

His influence, however, did not die. Angiolini had as early as 1761 attacked Noverre for plagiarizing the ideas of his teacher, who, he asserted, had first recovered the dramatic potential of ballet from the Ancients. The extent of Noverre's knowledge of Hilverding has been a matter of much debate, but it is certain that when Maria Theresa appointed Noverre as Hilverding's successor in Vienna, Noverre found a superbly trained troop of dancers with a distinctive style and tradition, none of which he acknowledged. If Noverre's influence on mainline ballet history is best exemplified in his pupil Dauberval, Hilverding's can be traced though Angiolini, whose disciple Vicenzo Galeotti established the Royal Danish Ballet. Indeed, the nature of his criticisms of Noverre show the extent to which Angiolini remained an adherent of Hilverding's ideologies, especially in his championing of the Aristotelian theory of the Unities, representing the French theatrical ideology with which Hilverding had launched his own career decades earlier. Furthermore, the Russian choreographer Ivan Valberg self-consciously carried forth the work of Hilverding and Angiolini, producing ballets devoted to a new realism with dancers in contemporary costume.

If one had to describe the single most innovative yet influential quality of Hilverding's choreography it might be, to borrow a phrase from literary criticism, his magical realism. Lincoln Kirstein's description of Hilverding's famous *Pygmalion*, produced for the German stage in Vienna, captures this quality succinctly: "While the chief dancers wore traditional dancing dress, workmen turned grindstones . . . There was a combination of realism and opera-house magic—real ropes and pulleys to lift Pygmalion's marble, and (invisible) ropes and counterweights to bring Venus on her cloud. Throughout the seventeenth-century, the use of everyday occupational gesture . . . had been possible only as satire . . . [now] there was a new impulse toward the human scale, expressed on one hand by a theatricalization of daily life, on the other by borrowings from exotic lands and people." The strengths of the native *Singspiel* tradition were given a new dignity in Hilverding's work, paving the way ultimately for the century's greatest work of magic realism, Mozart's *Zauberflöte*.

One final question remains for speculation: how did Hilverding develop his early sophistication in the *ballet d'action*? Precedents in the *Singspiel* and in the ubiquitous eighteenth-century fashion for classical theory were obviously contributing factors, but equally important would have been the time that he spent, as a young dance student in Paris, the time during which Marie Sallé's experimental works and the balletic comedies of the Dutch choreographer de Hesse were being produced. Even more intriguing, however, is Hilverding's connection with his Paris teacher, Michel Blondy, who had as early as 1714 staged the dances for Jean-Joseph Mouret's *Les Festes de Thalie*, the first opera-ballet in contemporary costume. And Blondy was the favourite partner of Mlle. Prévost, who had danced in the historic 1715 production at Sceaux of the fourth act of Corneille's *Les Horaces*, one of the earliest *ballets d'action* on record. Perhaps it is no wonder that the young Hilverding returned to Vienna and immediately experimented with choreographing serious French drama, and, in his comic work, replacing *commedia dell'arte* stereotypes with characters from the Austrian streets. His choreographic achievements on both fronts deserve more attention.

—Katherine Kerby-Fulton

---

**HINDEMITH, Paul**

German/American composer. Born in Hanau, near Frankfurt, 16 November 1895. Studied violin with Anna Hegner, 1907–08; studied violin, 1908–17, and composition, 1912–17, under Arnold Mendelssohn and Bernard Seklesat, Hoch Conservatory, Frankfurt. Married Gertrud Rottenberg, 1924. Leader of Frankfurt Opera Orchestra, 1915–17 and 1919–23; founder and performer, Amar–Hindemith Quartet, 1921–29, and string trio, 1929–34; first public concert of compositions, 1919; first one-act operas, including *Mörder, Hoffnung der Frauen*, performed 1921; first ballet score, *Der Dämon*, performed 1923; member of administrative committee of the

Donaueschingen Festival, 1923–30; professor of composition, Hochschule für Musik Berlin, 1927–37; left Germany for Switzerland, as result of pressure from Nazi régime, 1938; travelled to United States, 1940; Professor of Theory of Music, Yale University, 1940–53; naturalized as American citizen, 1946; lectured and conducted in Europe for first time since war, 1947; took up appointment at University of Zurich, 1951; resident in Switzerland, from 1953; gave up regular teaching, 1955; several major concert tours in South America, Japan, U.S., and Europe, 1955–63. Died in Frankfurt, 28 December 1963.

**WORKS** (Ballets)

1923 *Der Dämon* (chor. Joseph), Landestheater, Darmstadt
1926 *Das Triadische Ballett* (new music; chor. Schlemmer), Donaueschingen
1938 *Nobilissima visione* (*St. Francis*; chor. Massine), Ballet Russe de Monte Carlo, London
1943 *Cupid and Psyche* (overture only; not performed)
1944 *Hérodiade* (chor. Graham), Martha Graham Company, Washington
1946 *The Four Temperaments* (chor. Balanchine), Ballet Society, New York (first concert performance, Boston, 1940)

**Other ballets using Hindemith's music:** *Der Dämon* (new version; Georgi, 1925), *Das seltsame Haus* (Georgi, 1928), *Der Antiquar* (Korty, 1933), *Nobilissima visione* (new version; Gsovsky, 1946), *Metamorphoses* (music originally written for Massine's *Vienna—1814* but not used; Balanchine, 1952; also Skibine, 1961), *Die vier Temperamente* (Georgi, 1952), *Four Temperaments* (Gore, 1959), *St. George and the Dragon* (L. Christensen, 1961), *Shadows* (L. Christensen, 1961), *Sextet* (Meyer, 1964), *Lucifer* (L. Christensen, 1965), *Five Sketches* (van Manen, 1966), *Aswingto* (Harkarvy, 1969), *Herodias* (Darrell, 1970), *Sinfonietta* (d'Amboise, 1975), *Chamber Music No. 1* (Seregi, 1976), *Kammermusik No. 2* (Balanchine, 1978), *Chicago Brass* (Alston, 1983), *Opening* (van Manen, 1986).

**PUBLICATIONS**

By Hindemith:
*A Composer's World*, Cambridge, Massachusetts, 1952

About Hindemith:
Hussey, Dyneley, "Paul Hindemith", *Dancing Times* (London), August 1947
Marks, Marcia, "Stage Works by Paul Hindemith", *Dance Magazine* (New York), May 1963
Kemp, I., *Hindemith*, Zurich, Mainz, 1971
Skelton, G., *Paul Hindemith: The Man Behind the Music*, London, 1975
Lampert, Vera, et al., *The New Grove Modern Masters: Bartók, Stravinsky, Hindemith*, New York, 1984
Neumeyer, David, *The Music of Paul Hindemith*, New Haven, 1986
"Celebrating *The Four Temperaments*" (based on Dance Critics' Association Seminar, 1985), *Ballet Review* (New York), Winter 1987

* * *

Hindemith's two important contributions to the ballet repertoire were both composed in the same period, between 1938 and 1940, and give an impression of the composer at a mature, central point in his long career. Despite Hindemith's strong attachment to German culture and musical traditions, these two ballets, like the bulk of his work both during and after the Nazi period, were created and first performed outside Germany.

Hindemith grew up in Frankfurt, and began his musical studies with the violin. He had a working-class background, and his obvious musical ability brought him into contact with more privileged elements in Frankfurt society. In 1908 he was accepted by the Conservatory, where he studied violin and composition. His talent brought him a place in the orchestra of the Frankfurt Opera before he was twenty, and he led the orchestra while still a student. His later concern with performing (on the viola), teaching, and practical music-making could be seen to have its origin in this hard-working background.

His first dramatic works were composed immediately after the First World War and have a typically expressionist idiom and aesthetic. One early instrumental piece, *Kammermusik No. 1*, suggests a more frivolous attitude, but the general trend of Hindemith's work during this time was towards neo-classicism, and the re-establishment of counterpoint as a key compositional tool. In historical terms Hindemith can thus be matched with his two contemporaries, Bartók and Stravinsky, in opposition to the drift of Schoenberg's theories of composition and the music of the Second Viennese School.

The appointment to teach composition at the Berlin Hochschule für Musik further developed the composer's interest in music for amateurs and in the current fashion for music with a practical purpose (*Gebrauchsmusik*). Hindemith then came into contact with the songs of the German Renaissance, and their influence on his subsequent style was enormous.

At the time of his removal from his Berlin post in 1937 Hindemith was at work on an opera on the subject of the painter Mathias Grünewald, with the background of the Reformation in Germany. This shares many aspects with the composer's first great ballet score, which followed immediately afterwards, *Nobilissima visione*.

According to Massine, the ballet sprang from a meeting between himself and Hindemith in Florence. The composer had just seen the Giotto frescoes of the life of St. Francis in the church of Santa Croce, and was inspired by them to create a ballet. *Nobilissima visione* was first performed in London with Massine's choreography in July 1938, and reached the United States under the title *St. Francis* in October of the same year. In this score Hindemith's move away from full chromaticism, his four-square rhythmic periods and underlying conventional structures (counterpoint, melody plus harmony) are strongly in evidence, and match the spirit of mortification and resignation inherent in the subject matter. The "straight-line" movement and frieze appearance of Massine's choreography show similar restraint and seriousness of intention.

The ballet is in five scenes, with a prelude based on the medieval troubadour song "Ce fut en Mai". The music proceeds in a sequence of numbers from which Hindemith was later able to assemble a suite (of three movements). If Hindemith in the 1920s shared Stravinsky's need to re-establish pre-Romantic values, by the time of this ballet he can be seen to have a quite different purpose from that of the Russian composer. Hindemith's desire is to convey a specifically Christian theme, forming a connection with the musical past, both in the use of old material and in the architecture of the music, which is designed to affirm faith and spirituality on the same principles as the works of Bach.

The second great ballet, *The Four Temperaments*, was written two years later. Hindemith had waited until 1938 before leaving Germany for Switzerland, but he stayed there only a short time before settling in the United States. With a teaching appointment at Yale (made permanent in 1941), he was able to survive financially in a way that was not available to another refugee from Europe, Béla Bartók.

The music was given a concert performance in 1940 by the Boston Symphony Orchestra (the prominent piano solo part makes it almost a piano concerto); but the ballet itself was not seen until November 1946, in New York, with choreography by Balanchine. The structure is a classical one of theme and variations, and the balance between the broadly descriptive (the various personalities) and structural coherence make the music ideal for Balanchine's artistry.

The "theme" consists of three themes, danced in sequence as three pas de deux by separate couples. The four variations are "Melancholic", "Sanguinic", "Phlegmatic", and "Choleric". All three themes are varied in each movement.

Hindemith's last piece of ballet music was *Hérodiade*, based on the poetry of Mallarmé, and choreographed by Martha Graham for performance in Washington, D.C. in October 1944. Hindemith's post-war music tends increasingly towards triadic harmony, his harmonic convictions exposed in his principles of a fixed hierarchy of intervals, and his philosophical convictions seen, perhaps, in the large-scale opera *Die Harmonie der Welt*, which deals with the Renaissance astronomer Kepler and his search for the harmony of the spheres.

—Kenneth Chalmers

---

**HONEGGER, Arthur**

Swiss composer. Born in Le Havre, 10 March 1892. Studied at the Zurich Conservatoire, from 1909, and at the Paris Conservatoire, with violin studies under L. Capet, counterpoint under Gédalge, orchestration under Widor, and conducting under d'Indy, 1911–15. Married pianist Andrée Vaurabourg, 1927. Became established in Paris musical world as member of "Les Six", group of French composers so named by Jean Cocteau at end of World War I; first important work, *Violin Sonata*, 1918; first stage work, *Le Dit des jeux du monde* (masque), performed at Théâtre du Vieux-Colombier, 1918; composed music, with other members of "Les Six", for Jean Börlin and Les Ballets Suédois, Paris, 1921–22; also composer of music for Ida Rubinstein Company, Paris Opéra, and Nouveau Ballet de Monte Carlo; composer of incidental music for theatre and of numerous film scores; lecturer, conductor, and accompanist, touring Europe, 1930s; elected to Institut de France, 1938; teacher at École Normale de Musique, Paris, during World War II. Recipient: Honorary doctorate, University of Zurich, 1948. Died in Paris, 27 November 1955.

**WORKS** (Ballets)

1920 *Horace victorieux* ("mimed symphony"; not staged), Concert Performance, Lausanne
*Vérité-Mensonge* (marionette ballet; lib. Hellé), Salon d'Automne, Paris
1921 *Les Mariés de la Tour Eiffel* (with Auric, Milhaud, Poulenc, Tailleferre; chor. Börlin), Les Ballets Suédois, Paris
1922 *Skating Rink* (chor. Börlin), Les Ballets Suédois, Paris
1925 *Sous-marine* (chor. Ari), Opéra-Comique, Paris
1928 *Les Noces de Psyché et de l'Amour* (Bach, arranged Honegger; chor. Nijinska), Ida Rubinstein Company, Paris
*Roses de Métal* (chor. de Grammont), Théâtre Xavier de Courville, Paris
1931 *Amphion* (chor. Massine), Ida Rubinstein Company, Paris
*Sémiramis* (chor. Fokine), Ida Rubinstein Company, Paris
1937 *Un oiseau blanc s'est envolé*, Salle Pleyel, Paris
1938 *Le Cantique des cantiques* (chor. Lifar), Paris Opéra Ballet, Paris
1941 *Le Mangeur de rêves*, Salle Pleyel, Paris
1945 *L'Appel de la montagne* (chor. Peretti), Paris Opéra Ballet, Paris
1946 *Chota Roustaveli* (*L'Homme à peau de léopard*; with Tcherepnin, Harsanyi; chor. Lifar), Nouveaux Ballets de Monte Carlo, Monte Carlo
1949 *La Naissance des couleurs* (chor. Lifar), Paris Opéra Ballet, Paris

**Other ballets using Honegger's music:** *Pacific 231* (Shawn, 1933), *Lady into Fox* (Howard, 1939), *Danse des morts* (Wallmann, 1955), *Pastorale d' été* (van Manen, 1958), *Von Unschuld und Erfahrung* (Neumeier, 1967), *Brainstorm* (van Manen, 1982).

**PUBLICATIONS**

By Honegger:
*Je suis compositeur*, Paris, 1951

About Honegger:
George, A., *Arthur Honegger*, Paris, 1925
Tappolet, W., *Arthur Honegger*, Zurich, 1933
Claudel, P., et al., *Arthur Honegger*, Paris, 1943
Evans, Edwin, "Les Six", *Dancing Times* (London), May 1944
Bruyr, J., *Honegger et son oeuvre*, Paris, 1947
Delannoy, Marcel, "Honegger et la danse", *La Danse* (Paris), January 1956
Gauthier, A., *Arthur Honegger*, London, 1957
Landowski, M., *Honegger*, Paris, 1957
Meylan, Pierre, *Honegger: Son Oeuvre et son message*, Lausanne, 1970
Harding, James, *The Ox on the Roof: Scenes from Musical Life in Paris in the 20s*, London, 1972
Spratt, Geoffrey K., *The Music of Arthur Honegger*, Cork, 1987

* * *

Arthur Honegger imposed his strong but well-balanced personality on the music world by adopting the technical preoccupations and innovations of his day, but at the same time never quite breaking with tradition. Both his flowing melodies and his jerky rhythms were natural: "the dissonant chords and the characteristic features of his style were not done self-consciously, but because they were to his liking", observed Ernst Ansermet.

Of Swiss origins but living in France, Honegger was able to balance the Swiss-German and Latin components of his nature, drawing certain of his characteristics from them, showing at once strength and clarity, refinement and dynamism. Beside his purely symphonic or chamber works, his works intended for the stage had a place already foreseen in his childhood preferences: at the age of nine he composed an opera, at fifteen he preferred Bach, and from 1911 onwards he went around with Debussy, Fauré, Ravel, Roussel, and Stravinsky. He became friendly with Milhaud and Auric, yet surprising all by the way in which "this revolutionary won over the people", he followed his own path without making any concessions, thus rallying the majority of the public.

Honegger owed his first contact with the dance world to the opera singer Jane Bathori and to Paul Méral's *Dit des jeux du monde*, whose ten dances were arranged by Jeanne Ronsay and whose strange costumes by Guy-Pierre Fauconnet caused a scandal when they were shown to the "tout-Paris" in 1918. Not long afterwards Jean Cocteau made him the centre of attraction in the "Groupe des Six" with Milhaud, Auric, Poulenc, and Germaine Tailleferre, and asked him on several occasions to collaborate with him. Friendship played an important role in the inception of Honegger's collaborations for the theatre, whether they were choreographic, musical, or dramatic, from the cheeky "Marche funèbre" in *Les Mariés de la Tour Eiffel* to Börlin's *Skating Rink*, overshadowed by Léger's costumes and sets. The death of Fauconnet prevented the creation of the tragic pantomime *Horace victorieux*, whose vitality showed Honegger himself ready to confront heroic subjects. So it was that René Morax's popular mystical oratorio *Le Roi David* was an immediate and thundering success. In a work which radiates a religious fervour, unusual for its time, the composer evokes warlike atmosphere, holy mystery, and ecstasy, culminating in the "dance in front of the arch". Replying to Cocteau that in order to make progress, it was essential that one should remain firmly attached to the past, Honegger composed the music for his play *Antigone*, which he later went on to develop rather belatedly into an opera, in 1943, in which Cocteau's hand movements were strikingly interpreted by Roland Petit.

In *Sous-marine* Honegger evoked the fluid movements of underwater flora for Carina Ari, whereas he made his first attempt at "electronic" music in *Roses de Métal* in 1928 at the request of the Duchess of Grammont. Another, more fruitful, liaison was with Ida Rubinstein, for whom he wrote the music for the ballet *Les Noces de Psyché et de l'Amour*, arranged by Nijinska and inspired by Bach. *Amphion* seemed to be very personal and allowed him to collaborate with Paul Valéry and Léonide Massine in creating a piece of words, music, dance, and décor combined to make an expressive and radiant brightness. *Sémiramis*, which was arranged by Fokine, was a failure due to verbal and decorative excess. But *Jeanne au Bûcher*, another of Rubinstein's enterprises, was an all-round success thanks to the text by Paul Claudel. This popular play combined unlikely burlesque farce with a sensuous naïveté and glowed with intense simplicity. The frequent dance interludes, arranged by Lifar in 1950, were perfectly in tune with the text and the score. Lifar had been attracted by Honegger's generosity and heroic feeling, and wanted to collaborate with a musician who showed such a predilection for the dynamic order and for the use of new instruments, such as Ondes Martenot.

As early as 1935, Lifar asked Honegger to orchestrate for percussion the rhythms he had conceived for *Icare*, a project that Honegger was unable to sign officially as he was under contract to Rubinstein. On the other hand he was able to compose the score for *Le Cantique des cantiques*, following Lifar's strict rhythmic framework. The ballet's emotional shading was not fully realized until the grand finale, and it was not until Jean-Louis Barrault's mimed interludes in Paul Claudel's *Le Soulier de satin* that this perfect synchronization of music and dance was found again. After the failure of *L'Appel de la montagne* as the result of indifferent choreography, Honegger used his inspiration to good effect, incorporating the rhythmic demands and Georgian tones into two acts of Lifar's dazzling epic, *Chota Roustaveli*.

Through his non-conformism, his dramatic sense, his infectious ardour, and his gift for rhythmic precision, which he was able to adapt to the needs of the choreographer, Honegger occupies a unique position in the history of the relationship between choreography and music.

—Marie-Françoise Christout

---

**HORSMAN, Greg**

Australian dancer. Born Gregory Brian Horsman in Geelong, Victoria, 29 August 1963. Studied at the Victoria College of the Arts, pupil of Alan Alder, Jan Stripling, and Anne Woolliams, and at the Peter Dickinson Dance Studio. Married dancer Lisa Pavane, 1988: one daughter, Cassandra (b. 1992). Dancer, Australian Ballet, from 1982: member of corps de ballet, 1982–84; coryphée, from 1984; soloist, from 1985; senior artist, from 1986; principal dancer, from 1987, touring internationally with Australian Ballet, including in London, Russia, and Greece, 1988, South East Asia, 1989, and London, 1992; also guest artist, including for Boston Ballet, 1987, Kirov Ballet, Leningrad (St. Petersburg), 1989, Royal Danish Ballet, 1990, Houston Ballet, 1991, and at Sixth World Festival of Ballet, Tokyo, 1991. Recipient: Ballet Society Scholarship, 1983; Green Room Award, 1989, 1990, 1991; Best Dance Performance Award, Australian Entertainment Industry, 1992.

**ROLES**

1982 Russian in *The Nutcracker* (Kozlovs), Australian Ballet, Sydney
1983 Pas de six in *Swan Lake* (Petipa, Ivanov; staged Woolliams), Australian Ballet, Brisbane
Neapolitan Cavalier in *Swan Lake* (Petipa, Ivanov; staged Woolliams), Australian Ballet, Brisbane
Benvolio in *Romeo and Juliet* (Cranko), Australian Ballet, Sydney
Crixus in *Spartacus* (Seregi), Australian Ballet, Melbourne
1984 Colas in *La Fille mal gardée* (Ashton), Australian Ballet, Sydney
Lensky in *Onegin* (Cranko), Australian Ballet, Sydney
Florestan (Bluebird) in *The Sleeping Beauty* (Petipa; staged Gielgud), Australian Ballet, Melbourne
Pas de trois in *Voluntaries* (Tetley), Australian Ballet, Sydney
1985 Franz in *Coppélia* (Van Praagh after Petipa, Cecchetti), Australian Ballet, Melbourne
Prince Siegfried in *Swan Lake* (Petipa, Ivanov; staged Woolliams), Australian Ballet, Melbourne
James in *La Sylphide* (Bournonville; staged Bruhn), Australian Ballet, Melbourne
Lead Cadet in *Graduation Ball* (Lichine), Australian Ballet, Sydney
Scotsman in *Graduation Ball* (Lichine), Australian Ballet, Sydney
Principal dancer in *In the Night* (Robbins), Australian Ballet, Sydney
Smithers (cr) in *The Sentimental Bloke* (Ray), Australian Ballet, Sydney

**Greg Horsman in *The Sleeping Beauty*, Australian Ballet**

The Bloke in *The Sentimental Bloke* (Ray), Australian Ballet, Sydney
Melancholic in *The Four Temperaments* (Balanchine), Australian Ballet, Melbourne
1986 Basilio in *Don Quixote* (Nureyev after Petipa), Australian Ballet, Melbourne
Peasant Pas de deux in *Giselle* (Petipa after Coralli, Perrot; staged Van Praagh), Australian Ballet, Melbourne
Albrecht in *Giselle* (Petipa after Coralli, Perrot; staged Gielgud), Australian Ballet, Adelaide
Hortensio in *The Taming of the Shrew* (Cranko), Australian Ballet, Melbourne
Lucentio in *The Taming of the Shrew* (Cranko), Australian Ballet, Melbourne
The Poet in *Les Sylphides* (Fokine), Australian Ballet, Sydney
Principal dancer in *Études* (Lander), Australian Ballet, Sydney
Red Knight in *Checkmate* (de Valois), Australian Ballet, Sydney
Principal dancer in *Forgotten Land* (Kylián), Australian Ballet, Sydney
The Young Man in *Songs of a Wayfarer* (Béjart), Australian Ballet, Sydney
The Double in *Songs of a Wayfarer* (Béjart), Australian Ballet, Sydney
1987 Solor in *La Bayadère* (Petipa; staged Popa), Australian Ballet, Sydney
D'Artagnan in *The Three Musketeers* (Prokovsky), Australian Ballet, Melbourne
Solo Boy in *Gallery* (Murphy), Australian Ballet, Melbourne
1988 Prince Florimund in *The Sleeping Beauty* (Petipa; staged Gielgud), Australian Ballet, Melbourne
Principal dancer (cr) in *Ballade* (Baynes), Australian Ballet, Melbourne
Romeo in *Romeo and Juliet* (Cranko), Australian Ballet, Sydney
Mazurka in *Suite en blanc* (Lifar), Australian Ballet, Sydney
Pas de deux in *Suite en blanc* (Lifar), Australian Ballet, Sydney
Principal dancer in *Return to the Strange Land* (Kylián), Australian Ballet, Sydney
Principal boy in *Paquita* (Petipa; staged Valukin), Australian Ballet, Melbourne
1989 Pas de deux in *Transfigured Night* (Kylián), Australian Ballet, Melbourne
Cavalier in *Birthday Offering* (Ashton), Australian Ballet, Canberra
Solo in *Four Last Songs* (Béjart), Australian Ballet, Sydney
Ivy in *Le Concours* (*The Competition*; Béjart), Australian Ballet, Melbourne
Solo in *Le Concours* (*The Competition*; Béjart), Australian Ballet, Melbourne
1990 Crassus in *Spartacus* (Seregi), Australian Ballet, Melbourne
Title role in *Spartacus* (Seregi), Australian Ballet, Melbourne
Principal dancer (cr) in *Catalyst* (Baynes), Australian Ballet, Sydney
Aaron (cr) in *My Name is Edward Kelly* (Gordon), Australian Ballet, Sydney
Camille in *The Merry Widow* (Hynd), Australian Ballet, Melbourne
Principal dancer in *The Leaves are Fading* (Tudor), Australian Ballet, Melbourne
Cavalier in *Gala Performance* (Tudor), Australian Ballet, Melbourne
1991 Title role in *Apollo* (Balanchine), Australian Ballet, Sydney
Dancer in *La Favorita Pas de deux* (Ashmole), World Festival of Ballet, Tokyo
Principal dancer in *Voluntaries* (Tetley), Australian Ballet, Melbourne
Principal dancer (cr) in *Of Blessed Memory* (Welch), Australian Ballet, Melbourne
Principal dancer in *Gemini* (Tetley), Australian Ballet, Melbourne
1992 The Prince (cr) in *The Nutcracker* (G. Murphy), Australian Ballet, Sydney

## PUBLICATIONS

Laughlin, Patricia, "Making the Grade", *Dance Australia* (Melbourne), October–November
Laughlin, Patricia, "Australian Dancers", *Dance Magazine* (New York), December 1987
Baum, Caroline, *Artists of the Australian Ballet*, Melbourne, 1989
Koch, Peta, "Strengths Highlighted", *Dance Australia*, February–March 1989
Sykes, Jill, "Reviews", *Dance Australia* (Keysborough), February–March 1989
Laughlin, Patricia, "Greg Horsman, a Hit", *Dance Magazine* (New York), May 1991

* * *

Greg Horsman is the most classical of the present generation of Australian male dancers. He has all the attributes which are generally considered prerequisites for a danseur noble, with one exception—he could be a little taller. At 175 centimetres in height, he is not short; but a few more centimetres would complete the picture.

Horsman has a very strong technique. His turns are brilliant and absolutely controlled, and he possesses fine line and ballon. He has beautiful feet and immaculate placement. His muscle structure is soft and pliable.

Despite his technical strength and purity, and the fact that he has scored great success in some showy, virtuoso roles such as Basilio in *Don Quixote*, Horsman's main interest appears to lie in dramatic interpretation. He is intelligent and always looking to explore a character in depth, rather than opting for a superficial approach. He is not interested in technique for its own sake or effect, but for its application to interpretation. Horsman is a musical dancer too and a fine partner, with a notable stage presence. Indeed, he has so many strengths and assets that his less-than-perfect height goes unnoticed most of the time.

Horsman has developed an outstanding partnership with his wife, Australian ballerina Lisa Pavane. Their understanding is such that they move as one, and can create a wonderful effect of flowing line in their perfectly synchronized movement. They both have beautiful feet and arms, and have added lustre to the many ballets they have danced together. These include *Giselle*—for which they were both coached by the great Galina Ulanova—*The Sleeping Beauty*, *Romeo and Juliet*, *La Sylphide*, *Don Quixote*, *Études*, and *Suite en blanc*.

There is an innate gentleness about Horsman's persona, which does not lend itself to the cold haughtiness of Onegin or the roistering, swaggering Petruchio in *The Taming of the Shrew*. However, in the latter ballet he was a charming Lucentio and also contributed an amusing performance as a mincingly effete Hortensio. Lensky, in *Onegin*, is one of his finest roles. This Lensky is idealistic and rather introverted, gently happy in his love for Olga. His over-reaction when provoked by Onegin in Act II is part of his idealism, a violent response to his perceived betrayal by his love and his friend. He dances Lensky's solos with lyrical softness, and there is aching despair in his final solo when he is going to what he knows will be his death.

Despite his quietly poetic style, Horsman is surprisingly good in the title role of *Spartacus*, achieving a rugged strength in his solos which indicates a further, perhaps as yet unexplored, facet of his ability. He has also demonstrated an excellent sense of movement in contemporary works. He has shown fine understanding of Jiří Kylián's choreography in *Forgotten Land*, *Return to the Strange Land* and *Transfigured Night*. He is also outstanding in Maurice Béjart's *Songs of a Wayfarer*.

Greg Horsman is still maturing, both as a dancer and artist, and it seems likely that he will develop equally as a classicist and an interpreter of contemporary choreography. His talent is such that, barring injuries, he could achieve recognition among the world's top male dancers.

—Patricia Laughlin

---

## HOUSTON BALLET

American ballet company based in Houston, Texas. Origins in the Houston Ballet Academy, established by the Houston Foundation for Ballet, 1955; first performances as independent ballet company (as separate from the opera company), directed by Nina Popova, 1968, eventually becoming official home company of the Houston Civic Theatre; has also toured successfully in regional United States and abroad. Current artistic director (succeeding James Clouser): Ben Stevenson, from 1976.

### PUBLICATIONS

Shelton, S., "Houston Ballet: Brainchild of a Community", *Dance Magazine* (New York), February 1975

Holmes, A., "Boom Town Ballet", *Ballet News* (New York), September 1979

Percival, John, "Dancing out of Texas", *Dance and Dancers* (London), March 1982

"Summer Invasion: On the Way from Texas", *Dance and Dancers* (London), June 1983

Trucco, Terry, "Ben Stevenson's Houston Ballet", *Dance Magazine* (New York), March 1992

* * *

During the early twentieth century, American arts institutions took great pride in their European roots, and favored foreign soloists over Americans. In dance, this reverse chauvinism centered on Russians. Often the expression "Russian ballet" became synonymous with "ballet".

When the wealthy and exceedingly conservative board of directors of the Houston Ballet was first established in 1955, it selected Ballet Russe de Monte Carlo alumna Tatiana Semenova as intended director. This did not materialize, and Nina Popova was engaged in 1967. By 1975 they named James Clouser. But his predilection for indigenous, even Southwestern, subject matter was too "American" for the board. So was his choreographic style, which had a modern dance dynamic. They then turned to Ben Stevenson, who is British.

This union, begun in 1976, has proved felicitous. Instead of a Russian expatriate company, they acquired a British one. As the seasons have gone by, British choreographers and designers have found a generous haven in Houston. Stevenson's artistic associate for several years was Sir Kenneth MacMillan, a former director of the Royal Ballet. His resident choreographer is the British Christopher Bruce. Dame Margot Fonteyn served as consultant during the staging of *The Sleeping Beauty*. Prominent among guest designers have been Peter Farmer, Desmond Heeley, Nadine Baylis, Peter Docherty, and David Walker, all from Britain.

In taking over the company, Stevenson quickly realized that the Houston audience was eager for the full-length, essentially fairy-tale ballets associated with the nineteenth century, and the board could afford to subsidize suitably lavish productions. In his very first season Stevenson staged a full-length *Cinderella*. Virtually every season since has contained three full-length ballets in addition to the annual performances of *The Nutcracker*, which are *de rigueur* in virtually every American ballet company. Among Stevenson's other full-length works have been *Swan Lake*, *Peer Gynt*—which the company first performed in Grieg's native land—*The Sleeping Beauty*, *Lady in Waiting*, a tribute to the women who remain at home while their men go to war, and *Romeo and Juliet*. He also engaged British choreographer Ronald Hynd to stage *Rosalinda*, based upon *Die Fledermaus*, *Papillon*, inspired by a ballet which Marie Taglioni created for her protégée Emma Livry, and *The Hunchback of Notre Dame*. Peter Wright, another British choreographer, has staged *Giselle*, and among the shorter British acquisitions have been Sir Frederick Ashton's *Les Deux Pigeons* and *Les Patineurs*, John Cranko's *The Lady and the Fool*, Walter Gore's *Eaters of Darkness*, Barry Moreland's *Prodigal Son in Ragtime*, Jack Carter's *Witchboy*, and Gillian Lynne's *Café Soir*.

The Houston Ballet has remained remarkably stable in its roster of dancers. Many of its soloists have grown through the ranks. In addition to being fond of their artistic director, the dancers enjoy generous salaries and a substantial performing season. The company also has its own specially built facility, as does the ballet academy. The latter is also on its way to acquiring dormitories.

Over the years, the roster of dancers has grown from 39 to nearly 60. Because many of them come from the Southwest, the spacious landscape in which they have been raised lends a characteristic warmth and ease to their dancing style. Among soloists of relatively long standing are Rachel Jonell Beard, Li Cunxin, Jeanne Doornbos, Kenneth McKombie, Mary McKendry, Janie Parker, and Dorio Perez.

Now and then company members are invited to create ballets. Among these have been William Pizzuto, Ken Kempe, Daniel Jamison, and Kristine Richmond. But the repertoire does not really encourage the experimental or the avant-garde. The Houston Ballet is a handsome company that cherishes stability over challenge.

—Doris Hering

---

**HOWARD, Andrée**

British dancer, choreographer, and ballet designer. Born in London, 3 October 1910. Studied with Marie Rambert, from 1924; also studied with Lubov Egorova, Olga Preobrazhenska, Vera Trefilova, and Mathilde Kshessinskaya. Dancer (also appearing as Louise Barton), Marie Rambert Dancers, from 1927; founder member of Ballet Club (later Ballet Rambert), 1930; dancer, (de Basil's) Ballets Russes de Monte Carlo, 1933 (leaving later the same year); first choreography, Ballet Club, 1933; guest dancer and choreographer, Ballet Theatre (now American Ballet Theatre), New York, 1940; choreographer for many companies including International Ballet, Sadler's Wells Ballet, Sadler's Wells Opera Ballet, Fortune Ballet, and Walter Gore Ballet; choreographer for films, including *Steps of the Ballet* (documentary; Crown Film Unit, 1948), and *The Secret People* (dir. Dickinson, 1951); also designer: designed sets and costumes for her own and other works, Ballet Club/Ballet Rambert, Turkish National Ballet, also collaborating with Sophie Fedorovitch. Died in London, 18 March 1968.

**ROLES**

1927 Dance of Fairies, Dance of Haymakers, Chaconne (cr) in *The Fairy Queen* (opera; mus. Purcell, chor. Rambert, Ashton), Pupils of Marie Rambert Dancers with Purcell Opera Society and Cambridge Amateur Dramatic Society, London
1928 Entrée de Cupidon, Gavotte joyeuse, Courante (cr) in *Nymphs and Shepherds* (Ashton), Pupils of Marie Rambert, London
A Naiad (cr) in *Leda* (Ashton, Rambert), Marie Rambert Dancers, London
1929 A Nymph (cr) in *The Ballet of Mars and Venus* in *Jew Süss* (play by Ashley Dukes; chor. Ashton), Opera House, Blackpool
1930 Entrée de Cupidon in Dances from *Les Petits Riens* (probably a revision of *Nymphs and Shepherds*; chor. Ashton), Marie Rambert Dancers, London
A Nymph (cr) in *Leda and the Swan* (new production of *Leda*; chor. Ashton), Marie Rambert Dancers, London
Tordion (cr) in *Capriol Suite* (Ashton), Marie Rambert Dancers, London
1931 Lover (cr) in *The Lady of Shalott* (Ashton), Ballet Club, London
1932 Lampito (cr) in *Lysistrata* (Tudor), Ballet Club, London
1933 The Lonely Lady (cr) in *Our Lady's Juggler* (second version; Salaman, Howard), Ballet Club, London
1935 An Ugly Sister (cr) in *Cinderella* (also chor.), Ballet Rambert, London
Ariel (cr) in *The Rape of the Lock* (also chor.), Ballet Rambert, London
1936 Muse (cr) in *La Muse s'amuse* (also chor.), Ballet Rambert, London
1937 The Maiden (cr) in *Death and the Maiden* (also chor.), Ballet Rambert, London
Principal dancer (cr) in *Suite of Airs* (Tudor), Ballet Rambert, London (originally for BBC television)
1938 Danse de Tendresse (cr) in *Croquis de Mercure* (also chor.), Ballet Rambert, London
1940 Mrs. Tebrick in *Lady into Fox* (also chor.), Ballet Theatre, New York
1960 A Stepsister in *Cinderella* (Ashton), Royal Ballet, London

**Other roles include:** for Ballet Club/Ballet Rambert—La Goulue in *Bar aux Folies-Bergère* (de Valois), Vamp de Luxe in *Le Boxing* (Salaman), Papillon and Estrella in *Carnaval* (Fokine), Fourth dance in *Dark Elegies* (Tudor), Milkmaid in *Façade* (Ashton), Étoile in *Foyer de danse* (Ashton), The Snake in *The Garden* (Salaman), Mermaid and Bride in *Mermaid* (Howard, Salaman), Young Girl in *Le Spectre de la rose* (Fokine), Mazurka in *Les Sylphides* (Fokine), The Lassie in *The Tartans* (first version; Ashton), Solange in *Valentine's Eve* (Ashton).

**WORKS**

1933 *Our Lady's Juggler* (mus. Respighi), Ballet Club, London
1934 *Mermaid* (with Salaman; mus. Ravel), Ballet Club, London
*Alcina Suite* (mus. Handel, Purcell), Ballet Club, London
1935 *Cinderella* (mus. Weber), Ballet Club, London
*The Rape of the Lock* (mus. Haydn), Ballet Club, London
1936 *La Muse s'amuse* (mus. Sévérac), Ballet Rambert, London
1937 *Death and the Maiden* (mus. Schubert), Ballet Rambert, London
1938 *Croquis de Mercure* (mus. Satie), Ballet Rambert, London
1939 *Lady into Fox* (mus. Honegger), Ballet Rambert, London
1940 *La Fête étrange* (mus. Fauré), London Ballet, Arts Theatre, London
1942 *Twelfth Night* (mus. Grieg), International Ballet, Liverpool
1943 *Carnival of Animals* (mus. Saint-Saëns), Ballet Rambert, London
*Water Music Suite* (mus. Handel), Royal Academy of Dancing Production Club, London
1944 *The Fugitive* (mus. Salzedo), Ballet Rambert, Bedford
*Le Festin de l'araignée* (mus. Roussel), Sadler's Wells Ballet, London
1946 *Elegy* (mus. Liszt), Fortune Ballet, Florence
*Assembly Ball* (mus. Bizet), Sadler's Wells Opera Ballet (later Sadler's Wells Theatre Ballet), London
*Mardi Gras* (mus. Salzedo), Sadler's Wells Opera Ballet, London
*Pygmalion* (mus. Field), Fortune Ballet, Florence
1947 *The Sailor's Return* (mus. Oldham), Ballet Rambert, London
1948 *Selina* (mus. Rossini), Sadler's Wells Theatre Ballet, London
1949 *Ballamento* (mus. Vivaldi), Metropolitan Ballet, London
1951 *Orlando's Silver Wedding* (mus. Benjamin), Festival of Britain, Pleasure Gardens Amphitheatre, London
1952 *A Mirror for Witches* (mus. ApIvor), Sadler's Wells Ballet, London
1953 *Veneziana* (mus Donizetti), Sadler's Wells Ballet, London
*Vis-à-vis* (mus. ApIvor), Walter Gore Ballet, London
1957 *Conte fantastique* (mus. Caplet), Ballet Rambert, London
1958 *La Belle dame sans merci* (mus. Goehr), Edinburgh Festival Ballet, Edinburgh
1963 *Les Baricades mystérieuses* (mus. Couperin), Turkish State Ballet, Ankara

**Andrée Howard with John Byron in *Death and The Maiden*, Ballet Rambert, London, 1937**

## PUBLICATIONS

Haskell, Arnold, *The Marie Rambert Ballet*, London, 1930
Rambert, Marie, "Andrée Howard: An Appreciation", *Dancing Times* (London), March 1943
Bradley, Lionel, *Sixteen Years of Ballet Rambert*, London, 1946
Hobbs, Tarquin, "Born Under Mercury", *Ballet* (London), July 1946
Hall, Fernau, *Modern English Ballet*, London, 1950
Franks, A.H., *Twentieth Century Ballet*, London, 1954
Davidson, Gladys, *Ballet Biographies*, revised edition, London, 1954
Clarke, Mary, *The Sadler's Wells Ballet*, London, 1955
Williams, Peter, "Creator of Characters", *Dance and Dancers* (London), May 1955
"Personality of the Month: Andrée Howard", *Dance and Dancers* (London), September 1957
Clarke, Mary, *Dancers of Mercury: The Story of Ballet Rambert*, London, 1962
Gilmour, Sally, "Remembering Andrée Howard", *Dance Research* (London), Spring 1989
Sorley Walker, Kathrine, "The Choreography of Andrée Howard", *Dance Chronicle* (New York), vol. 13, no. 3, 1990–91
Pritchard, Jane, "The Choreography of Andrée Howard: Some Further Information", *Dance Chronicle* (New York), vol. 15, no. 1, 1992

* * *

The hallmark of all Andrée Howard's choreography was her ability to create and sustain a mood. This quality is seen at its best in *La Fête étrange*, as the initial atmosphere of anticipation gradually modulates through one of joy, to the rapture of first love, before fading into the solitude of a shattered dream.

With remarkable economy of movement and exquisite taste, Howard was able to convey the most subtle of emotions. The ambiguities inherent in the character of a young woman, part-human, part-vixen, were conveyed with immense skill in the character of Mrs. Tebrick in *Lady into Fox*—a role strongly associated with its creator, Sally Gilmour, but which Howard herself danced in 1940, in New York, for the Ballet Theatre revival of this work.

Although she danced many important roles in the early 1930s for Rambert's Ballet Club, Howard's career as a performer was interrupted by illness shortly after joining Colonel de Basil's Ballets Russes. There were a number of later dance engagements, both at home and abroad, and as a mature artist Howard returned to the London stage in character roles in Ashton's *Cinderella* and in the Festival Ballet production of *The Nutcracker*. But it was as a choreographer that she made a unique and highly individual contribution to the development of British ballet between 1933 and the late 1950s.

As well as creating over twenty one-act works, Howard choreographed the first English two-act ballet, *The Sailor's Return* (1947). This was based on a novel by David Garnett, as was *Lady into Fox*. Howard often used literary sources but—as in the episode from Alain-Fournier's *Le Grand Meaulnes* which she moulded, with Ronald Crichton, into the scenario for *La Fête étrange*—she knew how to distil the essence of these novels into dance movement.

Andrée Howard shared the exquisite musical sensitivity that was characteristic of both Ashton and Tudor. Her lyrical use of classically based movement showed the influence of the former, and her insight into the psychological make-up of her characters echoed that of the latter. Yet her style was always intensely personal. In spite of their literary origins, her ballets were seldom overtly narrative: dramatic conflict was portrayed in dance movement symbolic of emotion. Drama and dance were always fully integrated: the mood of each ballet was carefully sustained and the unfolding of the narrative never obscured by the interpolation of extraneous dances. The two pas de trois in *La Fête étrange* may seem mere divertissements, yet both are essential to the dramatic continuity of the ballet, as much as to the creation of this work's intensely evocative mood.

Howard's choice of subject matter covered a wide range. From her witty satire of Romantic ballet in *Selina* to the stark tragedy of a prisoner's flight in *The Fugitive*, it encompassed such varied concerns as the fairy-tale simplicity of Andersen's *Mermaid* and the powerful social conflict in *A Mirror for Witches*, based on the novel by Esther Forbes. She could portray with equal skill the elegance and romantic intrigue of Venice at Carnival time (*Veneziana*), the drama of Death relentlessly claiming his young victim (*Death and the Maiden*), or the sheer joy of dance (*Assembly Ball*).

As well as arranging the dances for several important Shakespearean productions and other plays, Howard showed that she was also a gifted designer. She created the sets and costumes for several of her own ballets (although she also worked with artists such as Fedorovitch and Nadia Benois) and she designed *The Sleeping Beauty* for the Turkish State Ballet in Ankara, for whom she created *Les Baricades mystérieuses* (1963). This was the very first work specially choreographed for this company, and was also to be Howard's last ballet. Set to music by Couperin, it depicted a young woman bathing in a lake by moonlight, attended by her maid. In the ballet, the two women suddenly become aware of a gentleman fishing nearby, who, on seeing the young ladies, abandons his sport in the hope of a better catch. The wit and delicacy required to handle successfully a theme as simple and as tenuous as this were exactly the qualities possessed by Andrée Howard.

Tragically, hardly any of Howard's works have survived in the repertoire. *La Fête étrange* has enjoyed several revivals but even this, her most important ballet and one of the best created by an English choreographer, is now rarely performed. In these days of ever increasing athleticism and pyrotechnics in ballet, the delicate subtlety of Andrée Howard's work is not the stuff of popular box-office success. Yet British ballet is much the poorer for having all but forgotten this rare and highly sensitive artist. The contemporary ballet stage would benefit from a return to the poetic dimension to be found in Andrée Howard's ballets.

—Richard Glasstone

---

## HÜBBE, Nikolaj

Danish dancer. Born in Copenhagen, Denmark, 30 October 1967. Studied at the Royal Danish Ballet School, from 1978, and later in Paris and the United States. Dancer, Royal Danish Ballet, from 1986: solo dancer (principal), from 1988; guest artist, San Francisco Ballet, 1991, and New York City Ballet, 1992–93; has also appeared in Tokyo, Munich, Toronto, Montreal, Paris, and Buenos Aires. Recipient: Critics' Special Prize, International Ballet Competition, Paris, 1986; First Prize, Eurovision Competition for Young Dancers, 1987; Danish Theatre Critics' Prize, 1990.

**Nikolaj Hübbe in *La Sylphide*, Royal Danish Ballet, 1991**

## ROLES

1983 Ballet student in *Bournonville Exercises* (Bournonville; staged Ralov), Royal Danish Ballet, Copenhagen
Molynask dance in *The Life Guards on Amager* (Bournonville), Royal Danish Ballet, Copenhagen
1985 Second movement in *In the Glow of the Night* (Goh), Royal Danish Ballet, Copenhagen
Dancer in *Symphony in Three Movements* (Christe), Royal Danish Ballet, Copenhagen
Courtier/Soldier in *Amleth* (*Hamlet*; Neumeier), Royal Danish Ballet, Copenhagen
Pas de six, second male solo in *Napoli* (Bournonville), Royal Danish Ballet, Copenhagen
Ballabile in *Napoli* (Bournonville), Royal Danish Ballet, Copenhagen
Dancer in *Capriccio for Piano and Orchestra* ("Rubies" from *Jewels*; Balanchine), Royal Danish Ballet, Copenhagen
1986 Dancer in *Konservatoriet* (Bournonville), Royal Danish Ballet, The Royal Danish Ballet, Copenhagen
Assaulter in *The Miraculous Mandarin* (Flindt), Royal Danish Ballet, Copenhagen
Dancer in *Caverna Magica* (Ailey), Royal Danish Ballet, Copenhagen
The Prince in *The Nutcracker* (Flindt), Royal Danish Ballet, Copenhagen
Greek dance in *The Whims of Cupid and the Ballet Master* (Galeotti), Royal Danish Ballet, Copenhagen
Slave/Son of Ismael in *Abdallah* (T. Lander, Marks after Bournonville), Royal Danish Ballet, Copenhagen
Pas de deux from *Concertette* (Bruhn), Royal Danish Ballet, Copenhagen
Dancer in *Changing Images* (Goh), Royal Danish Ballet, Copenhagen
1987 Boy (cr) in *Draught* (Abildgaard), Royal Danish Ballet, Copenhagen
Romeo in *Romeo and Juliet* (Neumeier), Royal Danish Ballet, Copenhagen
Principal dancer in *Études* (Lander), Royal Danish Ballet, Copenhagen
Pas de sept in *A Folk Tale* (Bournonville), Royal Danish Ballet, Copenhagen
Principal dancer (cr) in *1-2-3—1-2* (Andersen), Royal Danish Ballet, Copenhagen
1988 Gennaro in *Napoli* (Bournonville), Royal Danish Ballet, Copenhagen
Principal dancer (cr) in *Das Lied von der Erde* (Patsalas), Royal Danish Ballet, Copenhagen
Title role in *Abdallah* (T. Lander, Marks after Bournonville), Royal Danish Ballet, Copenhagen
Dancer in *Songs Without Words* (van Manen), Royal Danish Ballet, Copenhagen

Carelis in *The Kermesse in Bruges* (Bournonville), Royal Danish Ballet, Copenhagen
Pas de deux in *The Kermesse in Bruges* (Bournonville), Royal Danish Ballet, Copenhagen
James in *La Sylphide* (Bournonville), Royal Danish Ballet, Copenhagen
Basil in *Don Quixote* (Petipa, Gorsky), Royal Danish Ballet, Copenhagen
Nilas in *Moon Reindeer* (Cullberg), Royal Danish Ballet, Copenhagen

1989 Principal dancer in *Afternoon of a Faun* (Robbins), Royal Danish Ballet, Copenhagen
Frantz in *Coppélia* (Brenaa after Saint-Léon), Royal Danish Ballet, Copenhagen
Title role in *Onegin* (Cranko), Royal Danish Ballet, Copenhagen
Apollo in *Apollon Musagète* (*Apollo*; Balanchine), Royal Danish Ballet, Copenhagen
Principal dancer in *Rhapsody in Blue* (Lubovitch), Royal Danish Ballet, Copenhagen
Principal dancer (cr) in *Fête galante* (Andersen), Royal Danish Ballet, Copenhagen
Principal dancer (cr) in *Manhattan Abstraction* (Lærkesen), Royal Danish Ballet, Copenhagen

1990 Albrecht in *Giselle* (Petipa after Coralli, Perrot; staged Kronstam), Royal Danish Ballet, Copenhagen
Pas de deux (cr) in *Birthday Dances* (Neumeier), Royal Danish Ballet, Copenhagen
Loke in *The Lay of Thrym* (Bournonville; staged von Rosen), Royal Danish Ballet, Copenhagen
The Man in *Serait-ce la mort?* (Béjart), Royal Danish Ballet, Copenhagen

1991 Struensee (cr) in *Caroline Mathilde* (Flindt), Royal Danish Ballet, Copenhagen
Junker Ove in *A Folk Tale* (Bournonville), Royal Danish Ballet, Copenhagen
Principal dancer in (*Tchaikovsky*) *Pas de deux* (Balanchine), New York City Ballet, New York

1992 Principal dancer in *Donizetti Variations* (Balanchine), New York City Ballet, Saratoga Springs, N.Y.
Principal dancer in *Theme and Variations* (Balanchine), Saratoga Springs, N.Y.
Principal dancer (cr) in *Zakouski* (pas de deux; Martins), New York City Ballet, New York
Principal dancer in *Andantino* (Robbins), New York City Ballet, New York

**PUBLICATIONS**

Hunt, Marilyn, "Bournonville Pas de Six: Those Dashing Young Danes", *Dance Magazine* (New York), June 1988
Johansen, Birthe, "Copenhagen", *Ballett International* (Cologne), November 1989
Reiter, Susan, "Nikolai Hübbe: The New Yorker", *Dance Magazine* (New York), November 1992
Tobias Tobi, "Dramatic Import", *The New York Magazine* (New York), 7 December 1992

* * *

"A young lyric poet", wrote a prominent Danish critic of Nikolaj Hübbe's James in *La Sylphide* in 1988. The year before, a pas de deux from this ballet had already won him and partner Rose Gad the first prize at the Eurovision contest for young dancers. Since then, Hübbe, appointed a principal dancer at the Royal Danish Ballet when he was only twenty years old, has leapt triumphantly through the company's entire repertory. Mastering the traditional Bournonville parts as well as the neoclassicism of Balanchine's *Apollo* and the impassioned dramas of Neumeier and Cranko, Hübbe has developed a range of expression almost incredible for his young age. Indeed, no other dancer at the Royal Danish Ballet has danced so many different roles in so short a time.

Tall and strong, swift-footed and high-jumping, Hübbe has an impressive classical technique which fits both the Bournonville style—one of quick, flexible turns and well-controlled épaulement—and the more extrovert athleticism of the Russian school, displayed in his sparklingly assured and cheerful Basil in *Don Quixote*. Hübbe's intense dramatic presence and, at times, almost aggressive dancing style made him a desperately loving, boyish Romeo in John Neumeier's *Romeo and Juliet*, as well as an extremely compelling character as the young and arrogant Onegin.

The second Bournonville Festival in Copenhagen in 1992 also became a personal triumph for Nikolaj Hübbe. He showed himself as a handsome Ove in *A Folk Tale*, a brave and tenderhearted Gennaro, the fisherman ardently fighting for his beloved Teresina, in *Napoli*; and he was heartbreakingly moving as James in *La Sylphide*. Hübbe made the unhappy romantic hero an intriguing modern type, a serious and passionate young dreamer sacrificing his bride and happiness for a fantasy of perfect beauty. The tragedy that his vision—in the Sylph's evanescent figure—cannot be possessed in real life also becomes a story of our own time, of the disillusionment of growing up in any age, when the most sensitive of us do not survive. Virtually exploding with talent and energy, the blond and handsome Hübbe extends his repertory at the New York City Ballet from 1992. After a successful début with the company in Saratoga Springs in the summer of 1992, he went on to create his first New York City Ballet role (the lead in a pas de deux by Peter Martins) in New York. Already compared by some American critics to the young Baryshnikov, Nikolaj Hübbe has been called "the most complete and most magnetic classical danseur on the international scene today".

—Marie-Louise Kjølbye

---

**HUMPBACKED HORSE, The** *see* **LITTLE HUMPBACKED HORSE, The**

---

**HUNGARIAN STATE OPERA BALLET (BUDAPEST BALLET)**

(also known as the Hungarian National Ballet)
Hungarian ballet company based in Budapest. Origins in ballet performances at both the Ofen Court Theatre and the National Theatre, Budapest; current company officially established at opening of State Opera House, Budapest, 1884; suffered decline during early twentieth century, but reestablished as the national ballet company (often known as Hungarian National Ballet), from 1930s; currently resident in two theatres, State Opera House and Erkel Theatre, sharing both with opera. Official school associated with company, the State Ballet Institute, founded under the direction of Ferenc Nádasi, 1950. Artistic director of the Hungarian State Opera Ballet: Gábor Keveházi, from 1990.

**PUBLICATIONS**

Körtvélyes, Géza, and Lörincz, Györg, *The Budapest Ballet* (in English), Budapest, 1971

Koegler, Horst, "The Hungarian State Ballet", *Dance and Dancers* (London), September 1975

Körtvélyes, Géza, *The Budapest Ballet 2*, translated by Lili Halápy and Elizabeth West, Budapest, 1981

Lidova, Irène, "Le Ballet National de Hongrie", *Les Saisons de la danse* (Paris), November 1981

Körtvélyes, Géza, "Remembering Ferenc Nádasi", *Hungarian Dance News* (Budapest), nos. 5–6, 1983

Kaposi (ed.), *The Art of the Dance in Hungary* (in English), Budapest, n.d.

* * *

The ballet ensemble of the State Opera House in Budapest is the leading classical dance company of the country. It has a history dating back over a hundred years. In Hungary, most dance and drama companies are identified by the theatre, or building, in which they are based; therefore, the birth of this particular company is linked with the opening of the State Opera House in 1884. There were classical ballet performances before this date by smaller companies, which were incorporated into the State Opera. However, it took a few more decades before the art of ballet reached the same dominant position as that which opera had occupied.

The company's early style evolved from two major influences: the national Hungarian folk dancing tradition, and the Russian ballet. The latter came through visiting companies. The first was the St. Petersburg ballet in 1899, displaying the work of artists like Fokine and Petipa. Its visit resulted in the demand for higher standards in the home-grown company and consequently the engagement of its first significant ballet master—the Italian Nicolas Guerra. His task was not easy, but he gave rigorous classical training to the dancers and created new ballets, always taking into account the standard his dancers had achieved at any particular point. During his artistic leadership (1902–15) he choreographed nineteen ballets.

After Guerra's departure the company went into a long decline, which lasted until after the First World War. It was only during the new regime of Miklos Radnai, general manager of the Opera House (1925–35), that attempts were made to raise the standard of Hungarian ballet. Several guest ballet masters and choreographers were invited, most notable among them being the Polish Jan Cieplinski, who created several ballets with Hungarian national themes, and the Hungarian-born Aurel Milloss, who was the first to use Kodály's music for ballet at the Budapest Opera.

The company's most significant development came about in the 1930s. It was due to two outstanding artists—Ferenc Nádasi, a ballet master who developed the company to a high artistic and technical level, and Gyula Harangozó, a very imaginative choreographer and character dancer with a unique talent. Nádasi eliminated the provincial, amateurish elements of classical dancing in the company, founded a school within the Opera House, and established professional standards.

If a date had to be named for the birth of the Hungarian National Ballet, 6 December 1936 is the obvious choice. It was the day of the premiere of Harangozó's first ballet on a national theme, the *Scene in the Czarda*. This was followed by his most fertile period (1936–41), during which he created a string of successful ballets; Bartok's *The Wooden Prince*, *Romeo and Juliet* (using Tchaikovsky's music), *La Giara* (music by Casella), and Bartók's *The Miraculous Mandarin* were but a few. Harangozó excelled in the fusion of dance and mime, classical and folk-dance elements mixed with his very own brand of humorous characterization. In his second period he created the ballets *Promenade Concert* (music by Johann Strauss), *Mischievous Students* (based on a well-known Hungarian short story, with original Hungarian music by Ferenc Farkas), *The Kerchief* (a full-length ballet with national dances including gypsy motifs), and, in the more classical vein, *Coppélia*. The fact that the dancers could rise to the challenge of Harangozó's inventive choreography was largely due to the efforts of Nádasi, who meanwhile trained an excellent line of star quality dancers and a highly professional corps de ballet.

This was confirmed by the Soviet ballet masters who arrived in Hungary in the 1950s to teach the company the great Russian classical repertoire. This was the time when every artistic endeavour was suppressed unless it originated in Russia. The dark Stalinist years had a disastrous effect on most other art forms, but of course ballet in Eastern Europe could benefit from the Russian influence. First, the authorities pushed aside Nádasi and Harangozó because only the Soviet masters were considered suitable for making artistic decisions, according to the doctrine of the day. However, when choreographers like Vasily Vainonen, Asaf Messerer, and Leonid Lavrovsky expressed their high regard for the local artists, the Hungarian practitioners were gradually reinstated in their former positions. A new generation of choreographers also emerged, notably Ernö Vashegyi and Imre Eck.

In the 1970s the major choreographer of the company was László Seregi. He created some ballets in the great epic Russian mould (*Spartacus*, *Romeo and Juliet*), while to others he added his individual wit (*Sylvia*) and intellect (*The Cedar Tree*, *Variation for a Children's Song*). Neo-classical and modern works are linked with the name of Antal Fodor, who stretched the company's technique towards the idioms of modern dance, hitherto not part of the dancers' training. His choreographies include *Eclogue*, *Outburst*, *Polymorphia*, and his most popular work, the rock ballet *The Rehearsal*.

The company's repertoire is now varied, due not only to the local talent but also to the staging of a number of foreign works during the last couple of decades, which greatly enriched the company with their different styles and perceptions. Outstanding examples were ballets by Frederick Ashton, Harald Lander, Maurice Béjart, George Balanchine, and Alvin Ailey.

The 120-strong company has toured regularly in Europe since the 1960s. The majority of the dancers come from the State Ballet Institute, which was created in 1950, and the teachers (often members of the company) keep close ties with the Opera House. Pupils of the Institute start appearing with the company from an early age.

The formation of a new Eastern Europe, where artistic freedom is much greater but funding is less secure, will constitute a new phase in the life of the company. It is hoped that all future governments will realize that the Hungarian State Opera Ballet is a great asset and a source of pride to the whole nation.

—Myrtill Nadasi

---

**HYND, Ronald**

British dancer, choreographer, and ballet director. Born Ronald Hens in London, 22 April 1931. Studied at the Rambert School, London, from 1945. Married dancer Annette Page. Dancer, Ballet Rambert, 1949–51, joining Sadler's Wells Ballet

**Ronald Hynd's *Dvořák Variations*, with Ben van Cauwenbergh and Andria Hall, London Festival Ballet**

(later Royal Ballet), 1952–70: soloist from 1954; also leading dancer, touring with Margot Fonteyn World Tour, 1963; choreographer, staging first work for Dutch National Ballet, 1968; ballet director, Bavarian State Opera, Munich, 1970–73, 1984–86; choreographer, London Festival Ballet, various seasons 1970, 1973–83; freelance choreographer, including in United States, Japan, South Africa, and Europe.

## ROLES

1947 A New Tenant (cr) in *The Sailor's Return* (Howard), Ballet Rambert, London

1949 Le Vieux Marcheur in *Bar aux Folies-Bergère* (de Valois), Ballet Rambert, London

Spanish Dance in *The Nutcracker Suite* (after Ivanov), Ballet Rambert, London

1950 The Man She Must Marry in *Jardin aux lilas* (Tudor), Ballet Rambert, London

Popular Song in *Façade* (Ashton), Ballet Rambert, London

1951 The Prince in *Swan Lake*, Act II (after Ivanov), Ballet Rambert, London

Albrecht in *Giselle* (after Petipa, Coralli, Perrot), Ballet Rambert, London

Death in *Death and the Maiden* (Howard), Ballet Rambert, London

The Prince in *The Nutcracker Suite* (after Ivanov), Ballet Rambert, London

The Prince in *Mermaid* (Howard), Ballet Rambert, London

Title role in *The Fugitive* (Howard), Ballet Rambert, London

1955 Gandolfo (cr) in *Rinaldo and Armida* (Ashton), Sadler's Wells Ballet, London

Principal dancer (cr) in *Variations on a Theme by Purcell* (Ashton), Sadler's Wells Ballet, London

1957 Pas de deux in *Solitaire* (MacMillan), Royal Ballet, New York

Title role in *The Prince of the Pagodas* (Cranko), Royal Ballet, London

Ivan Tsarevitch in *The Firebird* (Fokine), Royal Ballet, London

1958 Moondog in *The Lady and the Fool* (Cranko), Royal Ballet, London

Claudius, King of Denmark in *Hamlet* (Helpmann), Royal Ballet, London

Dorkon in *Daphnis and Chloë* (Ashton), Royal Ballet, London

Grand Pas classique (cr) in *Ondine* (Ashton), Royal Ballet, London

The Bridegroom in *La Fête étrange* (Howard), Royal Ballet, London

1959 Pas de deux in *Les Patineurs* (Ashton), Royal Ballet, London

Prince Florimund in *The Sleeping Beauty* (Petipa; staged Sergeyev, de Valois, Ashton), Royal Ballet, London
1960 Albrecht in *Giselle* (Petipa after Coralli, Perrot; staged Sergeyev), Royal Ballet, London
Prince Siegfried in *Swan Lake* (Petipa, Ivanov; staged Sergeyev, de Valois, Ashton), Royal Ballet, London
Creon in *Antigone* (Cranko), Royal Ballet, London
1962 Leonardo in *The Good-Humoured Ladies* (Massine), Royal Ballet, London
1963 Principal dancer in *Birthday Offering* (abridged version; Ashton), Margot Fonteyn World Tour, Athens
1968 The Husband in *The Invitation* (MacMillan), Royal Ballet, London

**Other roles include:** Mazurka in *Les Sylphides* (Fokine), Hypnotist, Rich Man in *Noctambules* (MacMillan), Tirrenio in *Ondine* (Ashton), Orion in *Sylvia* (Ashton).

## WORKS

1968 *Le Baiser de la fée* (mus. Stravinsky), Dutch National Ballet, The Hague
1969 *Pasiphäe* (mus. D. Young), Royal Ballet Choreographic Group, London
1970 *Dvořák Variations* (mus. Dvořák), London Festival Ballet, London
1972 *In a Summer Garden* (mus. Delius), Royal Ballet Touring Company, London
*Das Wendekreise* (mus. Moran), Bavarian State Opera Ballet, Munich
1973 *Mozartiana* (mus. Tchaikovsky), London Festival Ballet, London
1974 *Charlotte Brontë* (mus. Young), Royal Ballet New Group, Bradford
*Mozart Pas de deux* (mus. Mozart), London Festival Ballet, London
1975 *The Merry Widow* (mus. Lehár, arr. Lanchbery), Australian Ballet, Melbourne
*Marco Polo* (mus. Xenakis), Tokyo Ballet, Venice
*La Valse* (mus. Ravel), Slovenian National Ballet, Ljubljana
*Valses nobles et sentimentales* (mus. Ravel), New London Ballet
1976 *The Sanguine Fan* (mus. Elgar), London Festival Ballet, London
*The Nutcracker* (mus. Tchaikovsky), London Festival Ballet, Liverpool
1978 *La Chatte* (mus. Sauget), London Festival Ballet, London
*Rosalinda* (mus. J. Strauss), PACT Ballet, Johannesburg
1979 *Papillon* (mus. Offenbach), Houston Ballet, Houston
1981 *The Seasons* (mus. Glazunov), Houston Ballet, Houston
1982 *Scherzo Capriccioso* (mus. Dvořák), Les Grands Ballets Canadiens, Montreal
1984 *Le Diable à quatre* (mus. Adam), PACT Ballet, Pretoria
1985 *Fanfare for Dancers* (mus. Janáček), Bavarian State Opera Ballet, Munich
1986 *Ludwig—Fragments of a Puzzle* (mus. Young), Bavarian State Opera Ballet, Munich
1988 *The Hunchback of Notre Dame* (mus. Berlioz, arranged Lanchbery), Houston Ballet, Houston
*Ballade* (mus. Chopin), German Opera Ballet Gala, Berlin
1989 *Les Liaisons amoureuses* (mus. Offenbach, arranged Davis), Northern Ballet Theatre, Manchester

## PUBLICATIONS

By Hynd:
"The Battle of Munich", *Dance and Dancers* (London), June 1973
Interview with Otis Stuart, in "To Humanize the Classics", *Ballett-International* (Cologne), August 1984

About Hynd:
Barnes, Clive, "Dancer You Will Know: Ronald Hynd", *Dance and Dancers* (London), April 1953
Corathiel, Elisabeth, "Men in Ballet: Ronald Hynd", *Ballet Today* (London), August–September 1957
Boscawen, Penelope, "Bavarian State Ballet", *Dancing Times* (London), January 1985

* * *

Ronald Hynd was fortunate in that he was at the right age—fourteen years old—to begin studying at the Rambert School immediately after the end of the Second World War. Any young person at that period wishing to take up ballet professionally was lucky to start with Rambert, for in that establishment there was no rigid Union demarcation between different jobs—young dance students found themselves involved in stage management, in helping to make and paint scenery, and in all the thousand facets of theatrical production, experience of which was to stand Hynd in good stead during his later career, both as freelance choreographer and as company director.

After a distinguished, if not phenomenal, career as leading dancer with both the Ballet Rambert, where he danced in works by Tudor, Howard, Ashton, Staff, and Gore, and the Sadler's Wells (and Royal) Ballet, where he worked with Ashton, Cranko, and MacMillan, it was suggested to Hynd (by Leslie Edwards, the director of the Royal Ballet Choreographic Group) that he try his hand at choreography. Hynd, then in his mid-thirties with no previous interest in becoming a choreographer, took some persuading, but eventually he embarked upon Stravinsky's *Le Baiser de la fée*, in response to an invitation from Dutch National Ballet director Sonia Gaskell, for whom he had previously mounted Fokine's *Firebird*. During the following year (1969) he made his second ballet, *Pasiphäe*, for the Royal's Choreographic Group, using an original score by Douglas Young. Other work followed, both for the Sadler's Wells company and for Festival Ballet, and in 1975 he was invited by Robert Helpmann to produce a full-length ballet, *The Merry Widow*, for the Australian Ballet. Since then he has freelanced all over the world, including the United States, South Africa, Tokyo, Berlin, and Munich, where he was artistic director of the state ballet for two separate periods. His experience with the Munich company demonstrated to him, in common with many English choreographers who have worked in Germany, that if the Intendant does not really want an independent ballet company to stand on level terms artistically and financially with the opera, the life of the ballet director will not be worth living, however much he may succeed in raising technical dance standards.

If Hynd was perhaps not in the absolute first flight of premiers danseurs, he was versatile enough to dance almost every role in the repertory, ranging from the Princes of classical ballet, the Poet in *Les Sylphides*, or the "white" pas de deux in *Les Patineurs* to the dramatic roles of the Husband in *The Invitation*, The Man she must Marry in *Jardin aux lilas*, and Claudius in Helpmann's *Hamlet*. He was also a thoroughly reliable partner. This extremely varied experience working in the ballets of so many diverse choreographers must have been invaluable to him when he began to make ballets himself: he was never in any danger of getting into a choreographic rut, but varied his approach and his style according to the occasion. Few choreographers of today can have chosen to use such a catholic selection of composers for their works. Few too can have developed such a gift for the light touch and the combination of comedy with fluent, musical, and inventive steps. And few classical choreographers today have preferred to concentrate on original ballets inspired by ideas, and refrained from re-vamping the classics and the works of others. It must be sad for Hynd, and for those who have enjoyed watching the comparatively small section of his mature output which has been on view in his native England, to consider that the majority of his big successes have been created abroad, and remained there.

—Janet Sinclair

---

# I

## ICARE

**Choreography:** Serge Lifar
**Music:** Serge Lifar (rhythms), Georges Szyfer (orchestration)
**Design:** Paul Larthes (scenery and costumes)
**Libretto:** Serge Lifar
**First Production:** Paris Opéra Ballet, Théâtre de l'Opéra, Paris, 9 July 1935
**Principal Dancer:** Serge Lifar (Icare)

**Other productions include:** Ballet Russe de Monte Carlo (restaged Lifar; scenery and costumes Eugene Berman); New York, 28 July 1938. Original Ballet Russe (restaged Lifar); Sydney, 16 February 1940. Paris Opéra Ballet (revival; scenery and costume Pablo Picasso), with Attilio Labis; Paris, 5 December 1962.

**Other choreographic treatments of story:** Lucas Hoving (1964), Vladimir Vasiliev (Moscow, 1971), Aurel Milloss (Florence, 1972), Gerald Arpino (Lewiston, N.Y., 1974).

### PUBLICATIONS


Scheuer, L. Franc, "New Ballets in Paris: Lifar's *Icare*", *Dancing Times* (London), August 1935

Lifar, Serge, "The Path of Icarus", *Dancing Times* (London), January 1938

Howlett, J., "The Domination of Décor", *Dancing Times* (London), January 1950

Michaut, Pierre, *Le Ballet contemporain*, Paris, 1950

Beaumont, Cyril, *Complete Book of Ballets*, revised edition, London, 1951

Laurent, Jean, and Sazonova, Julie, *Serge Lifar: Rénovateur du ballet français*, Paris, 1960


* * *

From as far back as 1932, Serge Lifar had been haunted by the myth of Icarus: the struggle of man against gravity, the very foundation of classical dance. After some fruitless attempts at collaboration with Igor Markevitch and Salvador Dali, the choreographer felt the need to eliminate all superfluous and needlessly provocative elements from the central theme, and he tried to illustrate this by publishing a significant work, *Le Manifeste du Chorégraphe*, at the same time. In it he states: "Ballet linked to its natural base, dance, should not be the illustration of any other art; its rhythmic pattern must not be taken from music. It can exist free of any musical accompaniment; it must not be the designer's slave." These remarks, considered daring at the time, were approved by Honegger and Bérard and accepted by Jacques Rouché, the innovative director of the Paris Opéra. In two months, Lifar had composed the rhythms and movements of this short work, whose exceptional dramatic intensity and beautiful "plastique" first amazed the public, then fired its enthusiasm, becoming a milestone in ballet history. Dance had, in those twenty minutes, assumed the autonomy which until then had been held by the composer or the designer. *Icare* opened the way for more experimentation and foreshadowed the daring innovations of Lifar's successors.

In indirect homage to Diaghilev, the first scene showed the architect Daedalus encouraging the efforts of his son Icarus, surrounded by a group of eight young boys and girls. In order to solve the problem of gravity methodically, the hero first observes, then imitates, the flight of an arrow, and then that of a bird, to which end his father makes him a pair of wings. He gradually accustoms himself to their weight and to their length, which extend his arms; he tramples the ground which he yearns to leave in order to be able to circle freely in the sky. To achieve this in the ballet Lifar increased the number of sustained grands jetés, entrechats, and beats which would give him the necessary driving force. Suddenly he seemed able to launch himself into the air towards the sun. But, as dictated by the myth, his wings melt and suddenly, thrown off balance, Icarus appears rolling to the ground from the top of a huge gantry. He tries one last time to leap up before dying, with one leg pathetically stretched in arabesque towards the sky which has defeated him.

The perfect harmony of the myth of the dancer's flight, the magic of dance combined with the originality of Lifar's hand movements and rhythms, coincided with the contemporary preoccupation with aviation and the instinctive desire for the Unknown. The poet Paul Valéry perceived that the "choreoauthor" had created the ballet around a single rhythm: "In fact," he said, "I do not know to which abstract poem his body gives life without music being its necessary guide. I was struck by the idea behind *Icare* because it touches the truth."

Lifar gave physical beauty to the mythological hero, together with a dramatic intensity which changed the emotional content of the story and caught the imagination of his contemporaries. Lifar has been perpetuating the role for many years at the Musée Grévin (the waxwork museum in Paris) in recognition of his popularity and his contribution to dance.

—Marie-Françoise Christout

**Serge Lifar in *Icare*, Paris Opéra, 1936**

## THE ICE MAIDEN

(original Russian title: *Ledyanaya deva*)

**Choreography:** Fedor Lophukov
**Music:** Edvard Grieg (selections, mostly from *Peer Gynt*) arranged by Boris Asafiev
**Design:** Alexander Golovin
**Libretto:** Fedor Lopukhov
**First Production:** State Academic Theatre for Opera and Ballet (GATOB), Leningrad, 27 April 1927
**Principal Dancers:** Olga Mungalova (Ice Maiden), Petr Gusev (Asak)

**Other productions include:** GATOB (earlier production to score; chor. Pavel Petrov), as *Solveig*; Petrograd, 1992. Novosibirsk Theatre for Opera and Ballet (chor. Petr Gusev after Lopukhov); Novosibirsk, 1964.

### PUBLICATIONS

Beaumont, Cyril, *Ballets Past and Present*, London, 1955
Lopukhov, Fedor, *Sixty Years in Ballet*, Moscow, 1966
Roslavleva, Natalia, *Era of the Russian Ballet*, London, 1966
Krasovskaya, Vera, *Articles on Ballet*, Lenigrad, 1967
Dobrovolskaya, Galina, *Fedor Lopukhov*, Leningrad, 1976
Souritz, Elizabeth, *The Art of Choreography in the 1920s*, Moscow, 1979; as *Soviet Choreographers in the 1920s*, translated by Lynn Visson, Durham, N.C., and London, 1990

* * *

*The Ice Maiden*, by choreographer Fedor Lopukhov, had its premiere in Leningrad on 27 April 1927. The music was by Edvard Grieg, compiled in 1917 by Boris Asafiev for Boris Romanov (who never choreographed the ballet). In 1922 Pavel Petrov had staged the ballet at the Petrograd State Theatre of Opera and Ballet (the ex-Maryinsky, later called the Kirov Theatre). Aleksandr Golovine did beautiful sets and costumes, but the production was not a success. Later (1927), Lopukhov used both the music and the designs in his production.

Between 1922 and 1927 Lopukhov had produced many experimental works: *The Magnificence of the Universe* (to Beethoven's Fourth Symphony), *The Red Whirlwind* (a ballet about the Bolshevik revolution), and Stravinsky's *Renard* and *Pulcinella*. They were all closely related to the avant-garde art of the time. Now he was producing a fairy-tale ballet, traditional in structure and reminiscent of nineteenth-century ballets, and even featuring faeries. Lopukhov himself called his production "a classical ballet in a 1927 interpretation". *The Ice Maiden* did return to the traditions which had been abandoned in the heat of the debate during the 1920s; but at the same time, it revealed new possibilities.

The ballet was in three acts, like many nineteenth-century ballets. The first act depicted a forest in the mountains in Norway, where a hunter (Asak), wandering among mountain spirits, gnomes, monsters, and snowflakes, encounters the Mistress of this domain—the Ice Maiden—and is subjugated by her. The Ice Maiden disappears, but as spring comes to the mountains Asak meets a girl (Solveig) who greatly resembles the Ice Maiden. Asak leads Solveig to his village and the second act depicts quite realistically a very colourful Norwegian wedding. At the very end of the act, the young people play a game in which they daringly leap over bonfires. As Solveig leaps over the fire, however, she melts and disappears in the guise of a little cloud. Asak runs off to the mountains in the hope of finding her there. In the third act, the scenery is the same as in the first, but with an air of dark premonition. Asak, in his search, encounters not one Ice Maiden but twelve maidens that look alike; and among them he cannot distinguish his beloved. Before disappearing altogether, the Ice Maiden hands Asak to the vengeance of the whirlwinds, which toss him about until, dead, he is left hanging head downwards from a tree.

In the initial libretto (used by Petrov in 1922), there were, as in most Romantic ballets, two conflicting characters—the fantastical creature ruling the ice kingdom, and the human being, a sweet and naive maiden. Lophukov, instead, had one character: the Ice Maiden. Thus the traditional motif of dissonance between dream and reality, because it remains unexplained (what is the dream and what is the reality?), acquires the peculiar, almost bitter taste of an unrevealed secret. Lopukhov's Ice Maiden has become a mysterious being in an enchanted, deceptive world akin to some of the images of the Russian symbolist poets (Aleksandr Blok, for instance). This already distinguishes his ballet from the traditional nineteenth-century works of Petipa. Even more, however, the images of symbolist poetry in choreographic form acquired a different look, clearly belonging to the 1920s. Olga Mungalova and Petr Gusev were both famous as performers of athletic dance, in which the classical style merged with gymnastics. Lopukhov made use of Mungalova's extraordinary flexibility and Gusev's mastery of acrobatic lifts to create a new style of dance. There was a large duet in the first act, composed of an adagio in which a pose appeared, and became the leitmotiv of the Ice Maiden (a "ring", where the dancer's raised left leg was held behind by her right hand), a variation composed almost entirely of "splits", and another very intricate step, named "the step of the Ice Maiden". Mungalova was the only dancer able to perform it exactly as Lopukhov choreographed it.

In the second act Lopukhov unfolded the colourful pageant of a Norwegian wedding. This was a brilliant theatricalization of authentic national dances and games: Lopukhov borrowed from past tradition, for instance Fokine's *Jota Aragonesa*, where musical and choreographic image, along with décor, were strongly linked on the basis of national authenticity. But Lopukhov brought character dance even closer than Fokine to ethnically authentic ritual folk dance. This was also a sign of the times. National folklore started to enjoy success on the popular stage, and soon—in the 1930s—so-called "ensembles" of folk dance (the famous Moiseyev ensemble and others) were to appear in the Soviet Union.

*The Ice Maiden* was a ballet in which something new was born from the past, revived and reworked into a thing of the twentieth century. It revived the full-length ballet which was out of fashion during the 1920s. It reinstated the classical lexicon, while at the same time making it a language of modern art. And it pointed the way for the theatricalization of folklore,

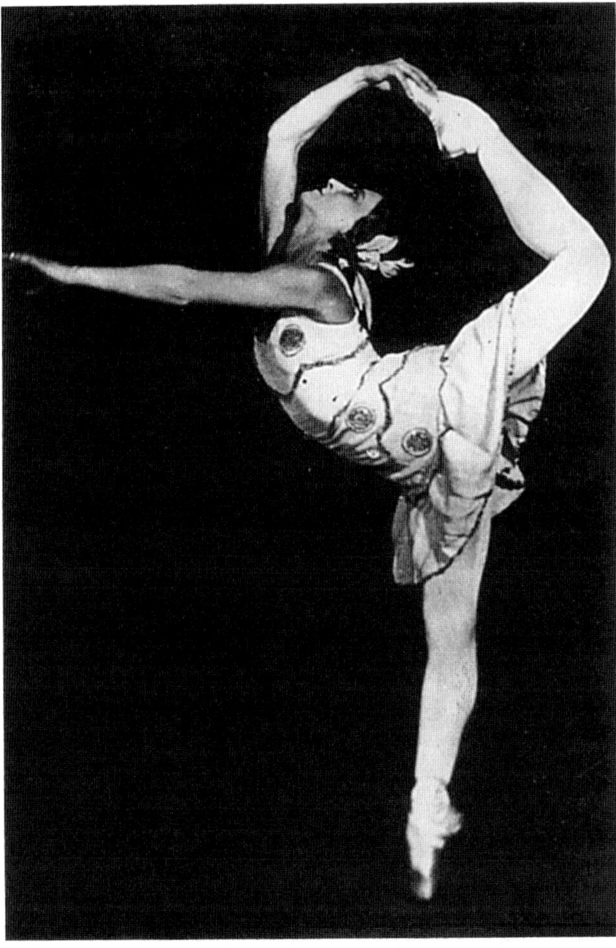

***The Ice Maiden*, with Olga Mungalova, Leningrad, 1927**

so promising for future Soviet choreography.

The ballet was in the repertory of the Leningrad Theatre of Opera and Ballet longer than any other Lopukhov ballet. It was revived (in a slightly different version) by Petr Gusev in Novosibirsk in 1964.

—Elizabeth Souritz

---

**IDZIKOWSKI, Stanislas**

Polish dancer and teacher. Born in Warsaw, 1894. Studied at the Ballet School of the Wielki Theatre, from 1904, pupil of Gillert, Walczak; later studied with Auguste Berger, Enrico Cecchetti. Début (as Ikowski), in musical *New York*, Empire Theatre, London, 1911; performed with Anna Pavlova's Company, London, 1912; soloist, Imperial Russian Ballet of Theodore and Alexis Kosloff, 1913; dancer, Diaghilev's Ballets Russes, from 1914, creating many roles in Massine ballets; also leading dances, performing with Lopokova at the Coliseum, London, 1924; principal dancer, Comte de Beaumont's "Soirées de Paris", 1924, rejoining Diaghilev, 1925–27; also performed regularly on the popular stage, especially at the Coliseum, London, and in own company, 1929–30; guest artist, Vic-Wells Ballet, London, 1933–34; also teacher, London, from 1933, and co-author of manual on ballet technique (Cecchetti method); ballet master, International Ballet, 1941. Died in London, 12 February 1977.

## ROLES

1912 Colin's friend in *La Fille mal gardée* (Shiryaev after Dauberval), Anna Pavlova's Company, London
Dancer in *Danse des Iroquois*, Anna Pavlova's Company, London
1913 Principal dancer in *Tarantelle* (*sic*; duet), Imperial Russian Ballet, British tour
Principal dancer in *Kosak Dance* (*sic*; solo), Imperial Russian Ballet, British tour
1914 Grand Pas de deux from *Faust* (Alexander Genée), various concert performances, Britain
1915 Harlequin in *Le Carnaval* (Fokine), Diaghilev's Ballets Russes, Geneva
1917 Battista (cr) in *Les Femmes de bonne humeur* (Massine), Diaghilev's Ballets Russes, Paris
The Cat (cr) in *Contes russes* (Massine), Diaghilev's Ballets Russes, Paris
1918 A Fish in *Sadko* (Bolm), Diaghilev's Ballets Russes
The Prince in *The Enchanted Princess* (Bluebird pas de deux from *The Sleeping Beauty*; Petipa), Diaghilev's Ballets Russes
1919 The Snob (cr) in *Le Boutique fantasque* (Massine), Diaghilev's Ballets Russes, London
The Dandy (cr) in *Le Tricorne* (Massine), Diaghilev's Ballets Russes, London
A Shepherd in *Narcisse* (Fokine), Diaghilev's Ballets Russes
Youth of the Polovtsi in *Polovtsian Dances from Prince Igor* (Fokine), Diaghilev's Ballets Russes
A Buffoon in *The Midnight Sun* (Massine), Diaghilev's Ballets Russes
A Youth in *Schéhérazade* (Fokine), Diaghilev's Ballets Russes
1920 Mechanical Nightingale (cr) in *Le Chant du rossignol* (Massine), Diaghilev's Ballets Russes, Paris
Caviello (cr) in *Pulcinella* (Massine), Diaghilev's Ballets Russes, Paris
Pas de deux and Finale (cr) in *Le Astuzi Femminili* (Massine), Diaghilev's Ballets Russes, Paris
The Spirit of the Rose in *Le Spectre de la rose* (Fokine), Diaghilev's Ballets Russes, Paris
Title role in *Petrushka* (Fokine), Diaghilev's Ballets Russes, Paris
1921 Waltz, Mazurka ("The Poet") in *Les Sylphides* (Fokine), Diaghilev's Ballets Russes, Lyons
Page to the Lilac Fairy, Bluebird (cr) in *The Sleeping Princess* (new production; Petipa, staged Sergeyev, with additional chor. Nijinska), Diaghilev's Ballets Russes, London
1922 The Cat (cr) in *Le Renard* (Nijinska), Diaghilev's Ballets Russes, Paris
1924 Lysandre in *Les Fâcheux* (Nijinska), Diaghilev's Ballets Russes, Paris
The Soldier in *Soldier and Grisette* (Legat), Coliseum, London
King of the Dandies in *Le Beau Danube* (Massine), Soirées de Paris, Paris
Principal dancer in *Premier Amour*, Soirées de Paris, Paris
Principal dancer in *Les Roses* (Massine), Soirées de Paris, Paris
Page in *Gigue* (Massine), Soirées de Paris, Paris
1925 Title role in *The Postman* (Legat), Coliseum, London
1926 The Puppet (cr) in *Jack in the Box* (Balanchine), Diaghilev's Ballets Russes, Paris
Principal dancer (cr) in *Les Contes d'Hoffmann* (opera; mus. Offenbach, chor. Balanchine), Diaghilev's Ballets Russes, Monte Carlo
Pas de trois in *Swan Lake* (after Petipa, Ivanov, with revisions by Fokine), Diaghilev's Ballets Russes
1927 Cupid (cr; new role added) in *The Triumph of Neptune* (new version; Balanchine), Diaghilev's Ballets Russes, Paris
1929/30 Principal dancer in divertissements *Valse d'amour*, *Mazurka fantastique*, *The Enchanted Princess* ("Bluebird" variation), *Johnny's Rendezvous*, *Galop finale* (all staged Idzikowski), Idzikowski's Company, tour
1933 Variations, Adagio (cr) in *Les Rendezvous* (Ashton), Vic-Wells Ballet, London
Prince in Act III pas de deux ("Aurora pas de deux") from *The Sleeping Beauty* (after Petipa), Vic-Wells Ballet, London
1934 A Devil (cr) in *Three Virgins and the Devil* (de Mille), in *Why Not Tonight?* (musical; chor. de Mille), Palace Theatre, London
The Wind, "Tourbillon", in *Why Not Tonight?* (musical; chor. de Mille), Palace Theatre, London

## PUBLICATIONS

By Idzikowski:
*A Manual of the Theory and Practice of Classical Theatrical Dancing* (Cecchetti method), in collaboration with Cyril Beaumont, London, 1922
"Renversée", *Dancing Times* (London), December 1935

About Idzikowski:
Beaumont, Cyril, *The Art of Stanislas Idzikowsky*, London, 1926
Beaumont, Cyril, *The Diaghilev Ballet in London*, London, 1940
Howlett, Jasper, "Stanislas Idzikowsky: An Appreciation", *Dancing Times* (London), April 1944
Lifar, Serge, *L'Histoire du ballet russe*, Paris, 1950
Grigoriev, Serge, *The Diaghilev Ballet*, translated by Vera Bowen, London, 1953
Greskovic, Robert, "Ballet, Barre and Center, on the Bookshelf", *Ballet Review* (Brooklyn, N.Y.), vol. 6, no. 2, 1977–78

* * *

Though Idzikowski's first claim to fame lay in the fact that he took over many of Nijinsky's roles and danced them with almost equal success, while also on occasion topping the variety bill at the London Coliseum, his importance to the dance world does not finish there. He was instrumental in the codification of the method of his teacher Cecchetti and collaborated with Cyril Beaumont on the first volume of the Cecchetti Manual, and his role as teacher irrevocably influenced all who attended his classes in London, including Jean Babilée, Erik Bruhn, Celia Franca, Derek Westlake (currently director of the Legat School), and Leo Kersley.

Though Idzikowski's short stature could have hampered him in finding a partner, and restricted him to solo work, he was lucky to become famous at a time when ballerinas such as Lopokova and Markova were dancing, both small enough to work with him without looking incongruous. He was a famous Bluebird, the role he danced for Diaghilev in *The Sleeping Princess* in 1921, and such choreographers as Nijinska, Balanchine, and Massine—who created many distinctive roles

**Stanislas Idzikowski with Lydia Lopokova in *The Enchanted Princess***

for him—were happy to use him in leading parts in their ballets, right through to Frederick Ashton, for whom he created the lead in *Les Rendezvous* in 1933. His collaboration, brief as it was, with the then Vic-Wells Ballet (where he also taught) made him one of the small valuable band of émigré dancers who, after Diaghilev's death, remained in England and contributed enormously, both as performers and teachers, to the birth of ballet in their adopted country.

In 1926, at the height of his fame, Beaumont wrote of him, "His torso and limbs are those of an athlete, the muscular development of his calves and thighs is extraordinary . . .". Today his physique would probably appear over-muscular, as would Nijinsky's; at the time, it caused Beaumont to write: "So agile, so easy are his leaps that one feels that if the puppet-master were to raise his controlling finger but a trifle more, Harlequin would spring upwards into the 'flies'. . . . All his movements, all his gestures radiate an effervescent humour, and as he dances one is reminded of the glittering bubbles that rise, fall and froth together when champagne is poured into a wine glass . . . to-day an academic dancer without equal."

In many ways, Idzikowski was the consummate craftsman; his dancing was prodigiously accomplished, polished, and correct in every minute detail: he had that infinite capacity for taking pains which is the mark of genius. To him, mastering a step was fun, and the precise execution of a jump or turn gave him enormous pleasure. Yet he was also far more than a mere technician. He always spoke of Nijinsky—the only dancer of the century in his class technically—with humility and admiration, for, he would say, though Nijinsky had unmatched technique, that technique was unimportant when he danced. "He began where the most of us left off", was his most telling comment: "He was an artist".

And so too was Idzikowski an artist. The many Massine ballets which he helped create were not simple divertissements in which to show off balletic virtuosity, but were brilliant displays of "character" dancing in the truest sense, requiring dramatic skill, a true understanding of human character, and a sense of humour as well. Some of his most famous and well-loved roles were as Battista in *The Good-Humoured Ladies*, the Snob in *La Boutique fantasque*, the Dandy in *Le Tricorne*—all Massine masterpieces which displayed Idzikowski's fine gifts to their fullest. Yet also in his inheritance of many of Nijinsky's roles from the Fokine repertoire, such as The Spirit of the Rose in *Le Spectre de la rose*, Harlequin in *Carnaval*, and the "Poet" in *Les Sylphides*, he proved himself a worthy successor to Nijinsky, both technically and artistically.

When teaching, Idzikowski was something of a martinet. He wasted no time (he could get through a barre in ten minutes, leaving the student well prepared to perform the most taxing steps in the centre) and rarely gave a correction more than once, for if the student was not sufficiently attentive to listen to what he was told, he would simply waste the time of others while he was told again, and probably not grasp the point even then. Idzikowski's classes never became the mode; he would never flatter his students, nor did he shout at them: they, and he, were in class solely to work, and to acquire the absolute discipline so vitally necessary if success is to be achieved in that most disciplined and hardworking of all branches of the theatrical profession, the classical ballet. He did not teach in accordance with the rigid syllabus devised by the Cecchetti Society: though all attending his classes had to be conversant with the "set pieces" of the System, he always insisted that Cecchetti's method of teaching was in no way rigid, but varied according to the needs of the individual and the occasion, and he gave his own classes accordingly.

—Leo Kersley

---

## ILLUMINATIONS

**Choreography:** Frederick Ashton
**Music:** Benjamin Britten *Les Illuminations*, (settings of poems by Arthur Rimbaud)
**Design:** Cecil Beaton (scenery and costumes)
**Libretto:** after the life and works of Arthur Rimbaud
**First Production:** New York City Ballet, City Center, 2 March 1950
**Principal Dancers:** Nicholas Magallanes (The Poet), Melissa Hayden (Profane Love), Tanaquil LeClercq (Sacred Love)

**Other productions include:** German Opera Ballet (new version; chor. Tatiana Gsovsky); Berlin, 1961. German Opera Ballet (new version; chor. Norman Walker); Berlin, 1969. Joffrey Ballet (staged John Taras after Ashton); New York, 28 October 1980. Royal Ballet (staged Taras, supervised by Ashton), with Ashley Page (The Poet), Jennifer Penney (Sacred Love), Genesia Rosato (Profane Love); London, 3 December 1981.

### PUBLICATIONS

Fern, Dale, "Frederick Ashton in New York", *Dance Magazine* (New York), April 1950
Barnes, Clive, "Sparkling Angels, Moving Jewels", *Dance and Dancers* (London), June 1967
Balanchine, George, with Mason, Francis, *Balanchine's Complete Stories of the Great Ballets*, Garden City, N.Y., 1977
Reynolds, Nancy, *Repertory in Review*, New York, 1977
Vaughan, David, *Frederick Ashton and his Ballets*, London, 1977
Aloff, Mindy, "Frederick Ashton's *Illuminations*", *Dance Magazine* (New York), November 1980
Goodwin, Noël, "Britten and the Ballet", *Dance and Dancers* (London), February 1982
Percival, John, "Lighting up the Stage", *Dance and Dancers* (London), February 1982
Jowitt, Deborah, *The Dance in Mind*, Boston, 1985

* * *

The ballet *Illuminations*, though choreographed by Sir Frederick Ashton—whose work was the embodiment of a distinctive "English" style of grace and refinement—was first performed by an American ballet company. In 1949, when Ashton, then principal choreographer of Sadler's Wells Ballet, had been in New York with his company, George Balanchine and Lincoln Kirstein asked him to choreograph a work especially for New York City Ballet. Both men regarded Ashton as a fine exponent of classical technique, with Balanchine particularly attracted to the Englishman's strong sense of musicality, and they both hoped that the British choreographer's association with the company would prove a major attraction for their forthcoming season in February–March 1950.

The premiere of *Illuminations* was a glittering occasion, opening the International Theater Month sponsored by UNESCO, and dedicated to the British ambassador. The event was important in the history of New York City Ballet, securing its position as a major dance company; but it was also a watershed in Ashton's career, since it marked the first time he had created a work for an American company. Furthermore, with its subject matter drawn from literature, *Illuminations* showed evidence of Ashton expanding the range of material from which his choreography drew inspiration.

During the Second World War, Ashton had read the poetry and biography of the nineteenth-century French poet Arthur

***Illuminations*, as performed by the New York City Ballet**

Rimbaud. Considered one of the first surrealist poets, Rimbaud wrote a body of work which is principally contained in two volumes, of which *Les Illuminations* is the first. This title indicates the purpose of Rimbaud's work, for he sought to enlighten his readers, providing fresh insights into everyday occurrences in an attempt to make some sense out of life's chaotic disorder. Ashton found this aspect of Rimbaud's writing fascinating and sympathized with the poet's tragic life, which included being jailed at the age of fifteen, spending time as a tramp, and almost being killed by the poet Verlaine.

For *Illuminations* Ashton used a series of Rimbaud's poems to provide the structure of the ballet, which would be accompanied by the score previously written by Benjamin Britten, *Les Illuminations*, also inspired by Rimbaud's writings. The ballet was divided into nine sections, each visualizing key aspects of the poems: Fanfare—"Alone, I hold the key to this savage sideshow"; Dreamtown—"Suburban Bacchantes Weep . . . barbarians dance nocturnal rites . . ."; Phrase—"I have hung golden chains from star to star . . . and I dance"; Antiquity—". . . Supple son of Pan"; Royalty and Anarchy—"A man and a woman claim they would be king and queen"; Being Beauteous; Sideshow and Farewell—"Departure amid sounds, and love". Interwoven with these segments were references to the poet's own life. Thus, in one ballet, Ashton sought to capture the spirit of Rimbaud's poetry and at the same time reveal something of the character and life of the man who wrote them.

In keeping with this intention, the central role of *Illuminations* is the poet, who wanders through all nine sections encountering moon creatures, evil soldiers, satin-clad pierrots, a king and queen, and sacred and profane love, until a shooting episode, reminiscent of Verlaine's attempt on Rimbaud's life, results in the poet's utter dejection.

A constant theme in the ballet is the artist's struggle to equate his sordid existence with his aspirations, recalling a central preoccupation of nineteenth-century Romanticism. But although the theme of the ballet harked back to the last century, Ashton's use of the classical vocabulary was decidedly different, as were the set and costumes.

In reviewing the premiere, Lillian Moore noted the inventiveness of Ashton's choreography, particularly praising a scene where Melissa Hayden (in the role of Profane Love, costumed as a bacchante) danced with one ballet shoe and one bare foot. Ashton had choreographed the dance in such a way that all the steps requiring the use of the full point occurred on one foot only.

Another article was devoted to the ballet's designs, noting "so seldom is ballet in America gifted with a background of costumes and decors of the richness, the sensual texture and dazzling colour provided by Cecil Beaton for the Frederick Ashton ballet, *Illuminations*". However, not all the dance critics responded favourably to the work. Many found the choreography too sexually explicit, especially the pas de deux of the Poet and Profane Love, which involved interwinings of arms and legs and bodies rolling on the floor. Others focused on the designs, regarding them as too fussy and elaborate.

Interestingly, the 1981 revival of *Illuminations* by the Royal Ballet received a similar mixed response. For example, John Percival of *The Times* referred to the "marvellously imaginative collaboration of Ashton and Cecil Beaton", while David Dougall of *The Sunday Times* highlighted conversations during the interval which featured views ranging from praise to outright criticism of overbearing designs hindering the choreography.

Such a contrasting reception may well have amused Ashton. Certainly he would rather his works prompted controversy than no reaction at all, and despite conflicting views, *Illuminations* is worthy of attention, for it marks a turning point in the choreographic career of Frederick Ashton, one of the most crucial figures in the history of British ballet.

—Martin Wright

---

## LES INDES GALANTES

**Choreography:** probably by Michel Blondy, with *Les Fleurs* probably by Marie Sallé
**Music:** Jean-Philippe Rameau
**Design:** Giovanni-Niccolò Servandoni
**Libretto:** Louis Fuzelier
**First Production:** Théâtre de l'Académie royale de musique (Paris Opéra), Paris, 23 August 1735 (prologue and two entrées: *Le Turc généreux*, and *Les Incas de Peru*, with *Les Fleurs* added 25 August 1735); Fourth entrée (*Les Sauvages*) added 1736
**Principal Dancers:** Mlle. Rabon, Louis Dupré, David Dumoulin, M. le Breton, M. Javellier, Marie Sallé

**Other productions include:** Kärntnertor Theater (first entrée only; chor. Franz Hilverding), as *Der Grossmutige Türke* (*Le Turc généreux*); Vienna, 26 April 1758. Paris Opéra Ballet (new version, staged Maurice Lehmann and Harald Lander: Prologue, chor. Albert Aveline, design Jacques Dupont; First entrée, chor. Aveline, design Georges Wakhevitch; Second entrée, chor. Serge Lifar, design Carzou; Third entrée, chor. Lander, design Maurice Moulène and Raymond Fost; Fourth entrée, chor. Lifar, design Roger Chapelain-Midy; Epilogue, chor. Lifar), with Nina Vyroubova, Lycette Darsonval, Christiane Vaussard, Liane Daydé, Micheline Bardin, Serge Lifar, Alexandre Kalioujny, Michel Renault; Paris, 18 June 1952.

### PUBLICATIONS

*Recueil général des opéras representés par l'Académie royale de musique depuis son établissement*, Tome 16, 1745

de la Laurencie, Lionel, *Le Goût musical en France*, Paris, 1905; Geneva, 1970

Kirstein, Lincoln, *Dance: A Short History of Classical Theatrical Dancing*, New York, 1935

Guest, Ivor, "*Les Indes Galantes*", *Dance and Dancers* (London), January 1953

Leclerc, Hélène, "Les Indes galantes (1735–1952)", *Revue d'histoire du théâtre* (Paris), no. 5, 1953

Kochno, Boris, *Le Ballet en France*, Paris, 1954

Fuzelier, Louis, *Livret et preludes parlés—Les Indes galantes*, Dole-du-Jura, 1956

Kirstein, Lincoln: *Movement and Metaphor: Four Centuries of Ballet*, New York, 1970

Masson, Paul-Marie, *Les Opéras de Rameau*, New York, 1970

Winter, Marian Hannah, *The Pre-Romantic Ballet*, London, 1974

Langellier-Bellevue, Richard, "Le Concept d'exotisme chez Rameau", *La Vie musicale en France sous les Rois Bourbons*, Second series, *Recherches sur la musique française*, Paris, vol. 21, 1983

* * *

The premiere of *Les Indes galantes* in Paris in 1735 reflected culturally the passion of France for the New World. In the music of Rameau, and in the libretto of Fuzelier, were fused the country's history, joined to a new understanding of the world derived from its conquests. Fusing the art of the court ballet at its apogée with the new genre of the opera ballet, *Les Indes galantes* expressed the enlightened concerns of eighteenth-century France.

The ballet was performed at the juncture of two aesthetic debates—in music, with the "Ramists", championed by Rameau, espousing dramatic chords and harmonies as opposed to the more evenly measured, lyrical chords of the Lullists; and in dance, with the advocates of "danse haute", favoring vertical choreography of "sautillage", opposing those of "danse basse", or dance composed of stately "à terre" formations.

In his libretto, Fuzelier, poet and manager of the Théątre royale de la foire and of L'Académie royale de la musique, states that he intends to please his public, one increasingly interested in ballet, and summons the muses of Erato and Terpsichore. Throughout his four entrées, he engages his readers in lively debates, which are of interest in being championed by the philosophers Rousseau, Diderot, and Voltaire. In the final entrée, he evokes in verse the presences of "Jean-Jacques", Diderot, and Voltaire to witness the peacefulness of the savage as example to a Europe fraught with discord.

In his correspondences of 11 September and 25 August 1735, following the ballet's 23 August premiere, Voltaire declares that the music of Rameau in *Les Indes galantes* embodies the spirit of France as a nation and must be heard. Although he questions whether the semi-quaverings of Rameau's dramatic musical chords will displease the Lullists, he predicts they will be remembered 150 years hence.

In Rameau's music, musicians and dancers worked together to evoke the characters of the libretto, who danced wearing masks, in alternating parts with the singers. Dancers were priests or warriors, dryads, nymphs, shepherds, Indians, Incan warriors, or savages. Unlike that of many of his contemporaries, his music was judged danceable, with danced segments serving to form a part of the action. In this he was ahead of his time, preceding the reforms indicated by Noverre in his treatise *Lettres sur la danse*.

The prologue of *Les Indes galantes* was based on the lyrical-tragic style of the previous century, and evoked the four peaceful nations of Italy, Poland, Spain, and France. It contained allegorical characters of nymphs and dryads, yet was followed by four distinct entrées with spoken preludes, each suggesting a different exotic terrain. Each entrée related as a unity to a central theme of love triumphing over war and exposed a single "galant" intrigue. Fuzelier wished to convince his public that love prevails, even in distant lands. Throughout his livret, actual events and persons are used to reveal a France acutely aware of geography, politics, and conquest.

For the first entrée, "Le Turc généreux", Fuzelier draws on a January 1734 account in *Mercure de France*. Since 1604 France had established commercial relations with India and had received accounts from merchants, missionaries, and ambassadors. Fuzelier uses the history of Grand Vizier Topal Osman for his character, Osman Pacha, whose generosity grants freedom to his slaves, Emilie and Valerie.

In the second entrée, "Les Incas de Perou", Fuzelier recommends to his public the writings of the Peruvian historian Garcilasso de la Vega, for details of the magnificent Incan "Temple du soleil". Conversely, he reveals details of its partial distruction by conquerers of the Americas. To an eighteenth-century reader aware of the increasing power of the church, he cautions, through the character of Huascar, against the priests whose power is as vast as that of monarchs. Huascar, who receives death at his own hands, brings forth the theme of a pagan conjurer, blinded by jealousy, whose evil is hidden beneath religion's sacred mantle.

The Asians are fond of flowers, Fuzelier admits candidly, and offers in the third entrée the character of a Persian Prince, who reveals to his harem a garden of flowers. It was in this entrée, less linked to the central intrigue, that Marie Sallé returned to the Parisian stage to dance the role of the Rose. The Rose here is also gallant. Pursued by hostile winds, she shelters her family of flowers. Aware of his public's taste, Fuzelier praises ballets which contain a "reasoned and picturesque design", appropriately for a century desirous of being enlightened in the sciences yet not lacking in grace.

In his fourth and final entrée, "Les Sauvages", written in 1736, Fuzelier succumbs to a fascination with France's colonies in the New World. Here he echoes Rameau who, in 1725, had witnessed two Louisianan Indians dance at the Théâtre Italien to the tune of their instruments, and had subsequently incorporated this melody in the "dance of the peace pipe", evoking a peaceful forest in the New World surrounded by Spanish and French colonies. The beautiful savage Zima, Fuzelier relates, will choose Adario, Chieftain of the Savage Warriors, over the rival French and Spanish colonial officers, Damon and Don Alvar.

Fuzelier's libretto brings to mind fantastic scenes, conjuring up onstage images of earthquakes and tempests. Scenic designs by the Italian, Giovanni-Niccolò Servandoni, were restricted to the third entrée; however, his experience with stage machinery, used to evoke the tempest of the second entrée, and his creation of sumptuous cradles and arcades of flowers, in which Sallé, in front of a rosebush surrounded by deities, posed centre stage, increased the work's popularity.

In early eighteenth century France, Oriental and philosophical literature were in vogue. Montesquieu's *Lettres Persanes* had appeared over a decade earlier, while the achievement of wisdom by "savage", primitive peoples of "Les Indes" and other exotic lands, along with the fascination of the eighteenth-century European for all which derived from the Orient, assured the appeal of Rameau's ballet. Although slight geographic inaccuracies in the libretto existed (such as "a Turkish isle in the Sea of India", as pointed out in the November 1735 account in *Mercure de France*), the work's exotic flavour won over realistic detail.

Sixteen editions of Fuzelier's livret were published. In the third, a reversal of the order of the first two entrées results in the entrée, "The Incas of Peru", coming first. By far the most popular entrée with the French public, "The Incas of Peru" was not officially returned by the Académie royale de la musique to its original position until 28 May 1743. As a result of the new possibilities of the opera-ballet, wherein each act could be detached from the central work while preserving its own unity, entrées of *Les Indes galantes* were sometimes performed separately, as before their Highnesses, the King and Queen of France at Fountainebleau in 1765.

Although Rameau's originally titled *Les Victoires galantes* was not performed until his 52nd year, his opera-ballet as a genre developed with his career, and consisted of a continual juxtaposition of singing and dance. This mélange, thought common in France, provoked criticism from foreign audiences. (Grimm lamented that song was incessantly interrupted by danced segments, and that art which imitated nature through dance had nothing in common with that which imitated through song). With Fuzelier, the genre became ballet-héroïque through the use of characters who were by nature heroic or divine. Like the pastoral of the preceding century, this genre included as characters dryads and nymphs, yet its arguments were interlaced with actual persons and events, fruits of a Europe possessed of an encyclopaedic thirst for knowledge.

—Pamela Gaye

---

## INTERPLAY

**Choreography:** Jerome Robbins
**Music:** Morton Gould
**Design:** Carl Kent (scenery)
**First Production:** Billy Rose's *Concert Varieties*, Ziegfeld Theatre, New York, 1 June 1945
**Principal Dancers:** John Kriza, Janet Reed, Jerome Robbins, Muriel Bentley, Bettina Rosay, Roszika Sabo, Michael Kidd, Erik Kristen

**Other productions include:** Ballet Theatre (scenery Oliver Smith, costumes Irene Schaff), with Janet Reed, John Kriza (pas de deux), Harold Lang (solo); New York, 17 October 1945. New York City Ballet (costumes Schaff), with Janet Reed, Todd Bolender, Michael Maule, Jacques d'Amboise; New York, 23 December 1952. City Center Joffrey Ballet; New York, 6 October 1972. Royal Danish Ballet; Copenhagen, 9 February 1977. Pennsylvania Ballet, 1977. San Francisco Ballet (staged Wilma Curley, 1989; restaged Christine Redpath); San Francisco, 3 April 1990.

### PUBLICATIONS

Foote, Horton, "Dance and Broadway", *Dance Observer* (New York), August 1945
Moore, Lillian, "Some Ballet Theatre Productions", *Dancing Times* (London), December 1945
Haskell, Arnold, "Ballet Theatre of New York", *Ballet Annual* (London), vol. 1, 1947
Brinson, Peter, and Crisp, Clement, *Ballet for All*, London, 1970
Balanchine, George, with Mason, Francis, *Balanchine's Complete Stories of the Great Ballets*, Garden City, N.Y., 1977
Siegel, Marcia, *The Shapes of Change*, Boston, 1979
Croce, Arlene, *Going to the Dance*, New York, 1982

* *

*Interplay* was Jerome Robbins' second ballet but was first presented in the context of the Broadway review, *Concert Varieties*, produced by Billy Rose. It marked Robbins's initial collaboration with composer Morton Gould, with whom he worked on a number of productions for the next 40 years. Later in the same year the work found its natural home within the repertory of Ballet Theatre (subsequently American Ballet

***Interplay*, performed by Ballet Theatre, London tour, 1946**

Theatre) and over the years in a variety of other companies.

From the start of his career, Robbins drew heavily on his New York City background for gesture and subject matter. In *Interplay* he imaginatively wove common street games into the fabric of the dance, as he had done the previous year in *Fancy Free*. There, the teasing game "saloogie" was employed by the sailors who were tossing a woman's handbag back and forth just out of her reach.

The competitive high energy of the eight boys and girls in *Interplay* is evident from the rise of the curtain. The first boy stands poised, then shows an exuberant eagerness to be the leader in his opening solo. He and the other three boys play "leap frog", crouching and vaulting over one another. After this they sprawl forward with legs folded up in the air.

Their attention is quickly caught by the entrance of the lead girl and her friends. With each imitating the actions of the person in front of them, the group plays "follow the leader". Couples form and dance in the jazzy fashion of the time. Down at the front of the stage they are seen in silhouette side by side in a horizontal line, jutting their arms and legs with similar abandon. To conclude the movement the boys bend forward as the girls hook arms with them and roll across their backs. The boys drop to sit immobile on the stage with one arm thrust upward. The girls stand quietly behind them resting a palm on the men's arms. It is the end of the "Free Play" section.

"Horseplay" indicates the spirit of the second movement. The couples array themselves around the stage to watch one boy's solo. He toys with and distorts (i.e. "horses around with") jumps, steps, and poses from the standard classical repertory. On two occasions he breaks the correctness of couronne arms to wave blatantly to the audience. He is briefly joined by others for a mock minuet. He feeds on his own high spirits while dashing about the stage and humorously stops in front of two girls, throwing open his arms to them.

The third movement is a romantic duet for one couple appropriately titled "Byplay". While the bluish lighting contributes to the aura of intimacy, the intensity of their dancing is relatively low. The other dancers retire to sit at the corners of the stage. Periodically some of them rise to crook arms and legs and snap fingers rhythmically. Their slow-motion gestures reflect the casual nature of the relationship between the romantic couple. They are interested in one another but at a playful level.

In the final movement high energy dominates. Two team captains "choose up sides" by pointing to individuals from the group who run over to stand by each. Both teams "huddle" separately, then issue "challenges" to the other side. The boys try to best one another in air turns, the girls in fouettés. Still full of energy, the group dashes to the back of the stage. The girls turn and run down to the front where they stop with legs firmly planted apart. They are followed closely by the boys who take a frontal "slide" such as one might see in a baseball game, to peer out at the audience while framed by the girls' legs.

The mixture of solid bright color costumes add to the work's lighthearted tone. Robbins, who has made historical allusions to ballet history throughout his career, might have had David Lichine's *Graduation Ball* competition in mind when he developed the "Team Play" section of his own work.

—Don McDonagh

---

## IN THE NIGHT

**Choreography:** Jerome Robbins
**Music:** Frédéric Chopin
**Design:** Joe Eula (costumes)
**First Production:** New York City Ballet, New York State Theatre, New York, 29 January 1970
**Principal Dancers:** Kay Mazzo, Anthony Blum, Violette Verdy, Peter Martins, Patricia McBride, Francisco Moncion

**Other productions include:** Royal Ballet (restaged Robbins; costumes Anthony Dowell), with Antoinette Sibley, Anthony Dowell, Monica Mason, Donald MacLeary, Merle Park, David Wall; London, 10 October 1973. Ballet Nacional de Cuba; Havana, 28 October 1978. San Francisco Ballet (staged Sara Leland); San Francisco, 2 April 1985. Australian Ballet, 1985. Houston Ballet (staged Leland); Houston, March 1986. Paris Opéra Ballet (restaged Robbins), with Monique Loudières, Jean-Yves Lormeau, Elisabeth Platel, Laurent Hilaire, Isabelle Guérin, Jean Guizerix; Paris, 26 November 1989.

### PUBLICATIONS

Barnes, Patricia, "Three Generations of Choreography", *Dance and Dancers* (London), May 1970
Sealy, Robert, "Mr. Robbins, Mr. Balanchine, Mr. Boelzner", *Ballet Review* (Brooklyn, N.Y.), vol. 3, no. 3, 1970
Balanchine, George, with Mason, Francis, *Balanchine's Complete Stories of the Great Ballets*, Garden City, N.Y., 1977
Reynolds, Nancy, *Repertory in Review*, New York, 1977

* * *

When Jerome Robbins's *In the Night* was first performed in 1970, less than one year after his *Dances at a Gathering*, it was considered to be an extension of that earlier work. Both were plotless; both were danced to the piano music of Chopin on a bare stage. As close as the two works appear on the surface, however, *In the Night* can easily stand on its own. It is a work distinctive in texture and mood.

Although Chopin did not invent the name and style of "Nocturne"—this is credited to the Irish composer John Field—he composed a total of twenty of these "night pieces", which have become standards of the concert piano repertoire. For his ballet, Robbins chose four Nocturnes: No. 1, Opus 27, Nos. 1 and 2 of Opus 55, and No. 2 of Opus 9.

Structurally, *In the Night* is quite simple: three couples dance three separate duets, then meet briefly for a final ensemble. The open stage is dominated by a starry sky with alternating shadows and shafts of light. One must not think of this ballet as a dreamy, "pretty" piece, however. The choreography mirrors the night music, shifting from moments of serenity and near silence to fervor and agitation. Each couple acts out its romantic intimacies in the night space. At various times, the dancers appear noble, shy, proud, ecstatic; no single emotion is exclusive to one episode.

The first duet, the most lyrical, presents two youthful lovers, tender and cautious one moment in their innocence, rapturous the next. In the second pas de deux, under a faint outline of chandeliers, a more mature, aristocratic couple dance, at times elegantly and courtly, at other times charmingly flirtatious. The third couple, dramatic and intense, appear to be in the midst of a quarrel or confrontation, as they part, then reconcile, never trying to hide their passion. The fourth section, danced to Chopin's most familiar Nocturne, the No.2 in E Flat, brings all six dancers together in a formal introduction, as they briefly greet each other, then part in pairs.

Robbins's choreography, firmly implanted in the academic style, calls for a strong technique in partnering to achieve the series of daring lifts, catches, and jumps that are performed with little preparation and with split-second timing. Each duet is brief but amplified with diverse movements and striking images. The challenge the dancer must accept is to incorporate the parts into the whole—the three pas de deux are not acrobatic show pieces. No better example is the moment in the second section when the ballerina is supported, upside down, her straight legs and pointed feet moving in tiny batterie. Beyond the technical difficulties, the dancers face the danger of trying to "act" a character or impose a personality with expressions and extraneous gestures. Robbins has made it clear in printed statements that there is no story for *In the Night*.

The premiere for the New York City Ballet took place in 1970, with costumes by Joe Eula. Later, when the Royal Ballet undertook the work, costumes were by Anthony Dowell, who also appeared in one of the duets. Many impressive performances have taken place, the mood and impact of the ballet changing with each cast, but it would be hard to duplicate the effect of the original cast with Kay Mazzo and Anthony Blum, Violette Verdy and Peter Martins, and Patricia McBride and Francisco Moncion. It also would be difficult to determine how much the dancers' bodies and personalities originally shaped the choreographer's creative efforts.

In addition to the Royal Ballet staging, the work has been a welcome addition to the Australian Ballet (1985) and more recently joined the repertory of the Paris Opéra Ballet.

—Richard Rutledge

---

## THE INVITATION

**Choreography:** Kenneth MacMillan
**Music:** Matyas Seiber
**Design:** Nicholas Georgiadis (scenery and costumes)
**Libretto:** Kenneth MacMillan (after Beatriz Guido's *The House of the Angel* and Colette's *Le Blé en herbe*)
**First Production:** Royal Ballet Touring Company, New Theatre, Oxford, 10 November 1960
**Principal Dancers:** Lynn Seymour (The Girl), Christopher Gable (Her Cousin), Anne Heaton (The Wife), Desmond Doyle (The Husband)

**Other productions include:** Royal Ballet, with same cast, except Donald MacLeary (Her Cousin), Anya Linden (The Wife);

***The Invitation*, with Lynn Seymour and Gary Sherwood, Royal Ballet, London, c.1970**

London, 13 December 1962. German Opera Ballet, with Lynn Seymour; Berlin, 30 November 1966.

## PUBLICATIONS

Currie, Jean, "*The Invitation*", *Dancing Times* (London), January 1961
Crisp, Clement, "*The Invitation*", *Musical Times* (London), February 1961
Barnes, Clive, Goodwin, Noël, and Williams, Peter, "*The Invitation*", *Dance and Dancers* (London), February 1961
Brinson, Peter, and Crisp, Clement, *Ballet for All*, London, 1970
Williams, Peter, "The Twenty-One Years That Changed British Ballet", *Dance and Dancers* (London), March 1971
Buckle, Richard, *Buckle at the Ballet*, London, 1980
Thorpe, Edward, *Kenneth MacMillan*, London, 1985

* * *

*The Invitation* was a landmark for British ballet in several respects. First, it reinforced the earlier successes of choreographer Kenneth MacMillan, and established his reputation for challenging and controversial work. Second, it confirmed the special magic of MacMillan's work with dancer Lynn Seymour, on whom he created the central character of the young girl. Seymour's special talents as a highly expressive, dramatic dancer were first fully realized in this role. Third, and perhaps most significantly, *The Invitation* represented a radical departure for British ballet in terms of subject matter.

The criticism that *The Invitation* received after its opening in Oxford and its subsequent transfer to Covent Garden delighted in the shock value of MacMillan's new ballet. It may not have been a great ballet, and most of the leading critics pointed to quite serious problems and flaws, but it was certainly something of a seminal work. "I'm sick to death of fairy-tales," said MacMillan in an interview about this work with *Dance and Dancers*. It seems that he was not alone. Richard Buckle, for example, wrote: "For years we have longed for a new wave in British ballet, comparable to that which has reanimated the spoken drama. Well, MacMillan has done something new: he has dealt with a real and tragic event. For this he deserves credit". Far from the genre of the fairy tale, *The Invitation* has as its subject matter the rape of a young girl by an older man, who takes advantage of her naiveté ruthlessly to destroy her innocence.

*The Invitation* developed the dramatic instincts MacMillan had previously explored with Lynn Seymour in *The Burrow* (1958). In her autobiography Seymour recalls that *The Burrow* (her first solo role) "... was the first British ballet to express the feelings of the post-war generation". This observation is probably one of the most significant factors in any appraisal of Kenneth MacMillan's work. At a time when choreographers such as Norman Morrice were turning to new forms as well as new subject matter, MacMillan recognized the need for ballet itself to widen its horizons, and he demonstrated that this was possible within the classical technique.

*The Invitation* was a ballet about sex and sexual initiation rather than romantic love, the more usual theme of ballets in the repertoire at that time. Its dramatic power derived from its contrasts as well as from its choreography. The disintegration of a marriage provides a stark contrast to the youthful hopes of the young couple; more vividly still, the relatively harmless seduction of the young man by the older woman contrasts powerfully with the destructive sexual violence of the man's rape of the young girl. The ballet was inspired by two novels, Beatriz Guido's *The House of the Angel* and Colette's *The Ripening Seed*, and it has been compared to the works of Tennessee Williams in its exploration of the seamy side of life.

In terms of its concerns with the dark side of human nature, with hypocrisy, frustration, and destructiveness, the ballet followed in the tradition of Antony Tudor, who was the first British choreographer to explore psychological states through dance. In terms of its subject matter it was often compared to Tudor's *Pillar of Fire* (1942), although the rape scene was more reminiscent of the seduction in Balanchine's *The Prodigal Son*. Clive Barnes pointed out, however, that whereas Tudor fused naturalistic gesture with classical dancing, in *The Invitation* MacMillan allowed the two to co-exist in a relationship of independence. Barnes felt that MacMillan's approach ran the risk of coming so close to the realm of drama that the audience would miss the spoken word. This was an important criticism that was to follow MacMillan throughout his career.

*The Invitation* was not a ballet of easy relationships in terms of its form or its subject matter. There were passages of realism that, critics found, sat uneasily within the whole. Buckle pointed to clichés, and Peter Williams found that the music and décor were in their different ways at odds with the ballet. The music was by Matyas Seiber and was his first ballet score; sadly, it was also his last, as he was killed in an accident shortly before the ballet opened. Williams considered the music to be particularly successful in evoking the quality of innocence and the shifting psychological states of the characters, but found that it lacked the imaginative and assertive qualities that could have given the ballet a greater dramatic impact. Williams also found that the designs by Nicholas Georgiadis (who had also designed *The Burrow*), with their rich use of colour and texture, were at odds with the harsh realism of the ballet's theme.

Despite the adverse criticisms that the work attracted, its importance was almost unanimously recognized. The critics agreed that MacMillan excelled in his choreographic passages for the young girl and that these were powerfully interpreted by Lynn Seymour. Alexander Bland described this role as "... a modern Giselle, fractured by lust instead of love". While MacMillan stood accused of seeing like a novelist or a dramatist in the overall construction of the work, his choreographic strengths were clearly acknowledged. Critics pointed to his vivid dramatic forms and images and his beautifully fluid movement phrases. In addition, MacMillan was creating roles for women that were in great contrast to the ethereal, charming, but insubstantial creatures of more traditional ballets—although it could be argued that MacMillan merely flipped the coin and turned the female image in ballet from an object engendering love into one engendering lust. Whatever the judgement on his use of women in ballet, he certainly expanded the range of British ballerinas with an increasingly dramatic, if acrobatic, dance vocabulary, and he set new limits in terms of the kinds of characters portrayed.

*The Invitation* was a radical departure from the ethos and concerns of the Ashton ballets and clearly demonstrated that the Royal Ballet had a choreographer whose works could form a strong and exciting alternative to the style of Ashton. *The Invitation*, if nothing else, was a stark contrast to the sublime decorum of Ashton's ballets and to the romanticism of both Ashton and the nineteenth-century classics.

Above all, *The Invitation* established Kenneth MacMillan as ballet's answer to the ethos of the "angry young man" that had revitalized the dramatic theatre since the success of John Osborne's play *Look Back in Anger* (1956). The mood of the time was for a theatre of social relevance. *The Invitation* was of undoubted importance in demonstrating that ballet could deal with "ugly" issues and, in the context of British ballet, it broadened the subject matter and aesthetic range of the classical technique.

—Lesley-Anne Sayers

---

## ISTOMINA, Avdotia

Russian dancer. Born Avdotia Ilinichna Istomina in St. Petersburg, 17 January (6 January old style) 1799. Studied at the St. Petersburg Theatre School, pupil of Ekaterina Sazonova and Charles-Louis Didelot, from 1805, also studying with Eugenia Kolosova, from 1811; graduated in 1815. Married actor Pavel Ekunin. Debut (in *Acis et Galathée*), Bolshoi Theatre, St. Petersburg, 1816, becoming leading dancer; created many roles for ballet master Didelot; also actress in comedies and vaudevilles, with début in vaudeville production *Phoenix; or, The Morning of the Journalist* (Shakhovskoi, 1821); retired from the stage in 1836. Died in St. Petersburg, 8 July (26 June old style) 1848.

### ROLES

1816 Galathée (cr) in *Acis et Galathée* (Didelot), Bolshoi Theatre, St. Petersburg

1817 Susanne (cr) in *Don Carlos and Rosalba; or, The Lover, the Doll, and the Model* (Didelot), Bolshoi Theatre, St. Petersburg

1818 Flore in *Zéphire et Flore* (Didelot), Hermitage Theatre, St. Petersburg

1820 Cora (cr) in *Cora and Alonso; or, The Virgin of the Sun* (Didelot), Bolshoi Theatre, St. Petersburg

Eucharis (cr) in *Euthyme and Eucharis; or, the Vanquished Shade of Libas* (Didelot), Bolshoi Theatre, St. Petersburg

Zetulba in *The Caliph of Baghdad; or, The Youthful Adventures of Harun Al-Rashid* (Didelot), Bolshoi Theatre, St. Petersburg

1821 Alcestis (cr) in *Alcestis; or, The Descent of Hercules into the Underworld* (Didelot), Bolshoi Theatre, St. Petersburg

Tisbe (cr) in *Pirame et Tisbe* (Didelot, Auguste), Bolshoi Theatre, St. Petersburg

1823 Heroine (cr) in *Lily of Narbonne; or, The Knight's Vow* (Didelot), Bolshoi Theatre, St. Petersburg
Circassian girl (cr) in *The Prisoner of the Caucasus; or, The Shade of the Bride* (Didelot), Bolshoi Theatre, St. Petersburg
1824 Lyudmila (cr) in *Ruslan and Lyudmila; or, The Overthrow of Chernomor the Evil Sorcerer* (Didelot), Bolshoi Theatre, St. Petersburg
1828 Nina in *Nina; or, Mad from Love* (Didelot after Milon), Bolshoi Theatre, St. Petersburg
Ariadne in *Theseus and Ariadne; or, The Defeat of the Minotaur* (Didelot), Bolshoi Theatre, St. Petersburg
1832 Sumbeka (cr) in *Sumbeka; or, The Subjugation of the Kazan Kingdom* (Blache after Didelot), Bolshoi Theatre, St. Petersburg

**Other roles include:** Izora in *Raoul Barbe-Bleue* (Didelot, Auguste), Inès in *Inès de Castro* (Didelot, Auguste), Albert in *Satan with all Devices* (Auguste), Lisa in *Lisa and Colin; or, Vain Precautions* (Didelot after Dauberval's *La Fille mal gardée*), Télémaque in *Télémaque dans l'isle de Calypso* (Blache after Dauberval), title role in *Zoraya* (Blache), Aglaya, Aminta in *Zéphire et Flore* (Didelot).

## PUBLICATIONS

Krasovskaya, Vera, *Russian Ballet Theatre from the Beginning to the Middle of the Nineteenth Century*, Leningrad and Moscow, 1958
Slonimsky, Yuri, *Didelot: Landmarks of Creative Biography*, Leningrad and Moscow, 1958
Roslavleva, Natalia, *Era of the Russian Ballet*, London, 1966
Eliash, Nikolai, *Avdotia Istomina*, Leningrad, 1971
Miguel, Parmenia, *The Ballerinas*, New York, 1972
Swift, Mary Grace, *A Loftier Flight: The Life and Accomplishments of Charles Louis Didelot, Balletmaster*, London, 1974
Schmidt, Paul, "Pushkin and Istomina: Ballet in Nineteenth-century Russia", *Dance Research Journal* (New York), Winter 1989

* * *

The nineteenth-century Russian ballerina Avdotia Istomina was the daughter of a low-ranking officer in the Russian army. In 1805, she entered the St. Petersburg Imperial Theatre School, and for two years she studied dance under Ekaterina Sazonova. Charles-Louis Didelot noticed the gifted little girl and took her into his class. Between 1811 and 1816, Didelot, as a French subject, was forced to leave Russia during its war with Napoleon, and Eugenia Kolosova replaced him as a teacher. So, at the beginning of her career, Istomina acquired from her two distinguished teachers both the principles of French virtuosity of the time and that soulful charm which belonged to the Russian style of dance. When Didelot came back to Russia, he took up his class again and had the girl-pupils dance in his ballets on the stage of St. Petersburg Imperial Bolshoi Theatre.

In December 1815, Istomina graduated and joined the ballet company of this theatre. In August 1816, she made her début in Didelot's anacreontic ballet *Acis et Galathée* with music by Caterino Cavos. *Acis et Galathée* was an example of the pre-romantic trend in ballet, of which Didelot was a great master. The nymphs and cupids, naiades and tritons of his mythological works preceded the sylphides and wilis of the romantic era in ballet. The plot of *Acis et Galathée* was simple: Cyclops Polyphemus falls in love with Galathée, is jealous of the shepherd Acis, and wants to destroy the happiness of the young couple. But Amour helps the lovers and all of Olympus come to celebrate their wedding.

The public was enraptured with this ballet. The part of the shepherd Acis, was entrusted to Anastasia Novitskaya: choreographer Adam Glushkovsky recalled in his memoirs that Novitskaya was "charming in spite of the fact that she played a man's character". Istomina's Galathée personified the ideas of Didelot. She looked like a young nymph, well-formed and blooming. Her dance had the special quality of seeming to glide over the earth. The great Russian poet, Aleksandr Pushkin, compared this dance in his novel *Eugene Onegin* with "a flight of down from the lips of Aeolus". And as there was a mise-en-scene in *Acis et Galathée* where Galathée-Istomina "stood surrounded by a throng of nymphs", it is reasonable to suppose that Pushkin wrote his inspired lines about Istomina after seeing her in this ballet. Her other famous character, Flore, in Didelot's ballet *Zéphire et Flore*, also lived in the joyful, sunny atmosphere of Didelot's early works.

The gilded youth of the Russian capital also admired the beautiful Istomina. In 1818, she was the cause of a tragic duel between four society men (one of them the famous Russian writer, Aleksandr Griboedov), in which her lover Vasily Sheremetev was killed. Not long before her death, in the middle of the 1840s, Istomina married a mediocre dramatic actor named Pavel Ekunin.

Istomina's whole artistic life was linked with the choreographic works of Didelot. He recognized and admired the versatile qualities of her talent and charged the young dancer with many varied roles. In 1817, she danced the part of Susanne in his comic ballet *Don Carlos and Rosalba; or, The Lover, the Doll, and the Model*, adapted from the French opera *Une Folie* by Mehul. Istomina incarnated the realistic character of Susanne—a mischievous girl who knew how to get out of the most embarrassing situations. By and by, roles appeared that demanded strong and experienced miming. Istomina successfully performed the parts of dramatic as well as comic heroines. To the first group belonged Cora in *Cora and Alonso; or, The Virgin of the Sun*, Eucharis in *Euthyme and Eucharis; or, The Vanquished Shade of Libas*, Alcestis in *Alcestis; or, The Descent of Hercules into the Underworld*, and Tisbe in *Pirame et Tisbe*. The second group included the above-mentioned Susanne, Zetulba in *The Caliph of Baghdad; or, The Youthful Adventures of Harun Al-Rashid*, and others.

Istomina also performed the roles of the Circassian girl in *The Prisoner of the Caucasus; or, The Shade of the Bride* and Lyudmila in *Ruslan and Lyudmila; or, The Overthrow of Chernomor the Evil Sorcerer*—both ballets were founded on subjects from the poems of Pushkin. In the first one, a Russian officer is captured by the Circassians. A beautiful Circassian girl falls in love with him and helps him to escape. The officer swims across the river, and, looking back, sees the rings in the water where the desolate girl has drowned herself. Didelot gave the sad story a happy ending—the officer married his beautiful deliverer. At the time of the première, Pushkin was living in exile. He wrote to his brother, "Write to me about Didelot, about that Circassian girl Istomina, whom I once courted like the prisoner of the Caucasus."

Towards the end of her career Istomina began to put on weight but her beautiful face was unchanged. Among her last creations was the role of the Tsaritsa Sumbeka, in a ballet composed on a theme from Russian history and entitled *Sumbeka; or, The Subjugation of the Kazan Kingdom*. This was a tragedy with battle scenes and many deaths. Such ballets were out of fashion in the 1830s, so critics were rather reserved about the whole, and only "the beautiful brow of Istomina under the crown of the Tartar tsaritsa" was rewarded by praise. In the same year, the Paris Opéra staged *La Sylphide*, which opened the era of Romantic ballet. Istomina retired in 1836, a year before Maria Taglioni came to Russia.

—Vera Krasovskaya

---

**IVANOV, Lev**

Russian dancer, choreographer, ballet master, and teacher. Born Lev Ivanovich Ivanov in Moscow, 2 March (18 February old style) 1834. Studied dance first in Moscow, then at the Imperial Theatre School, St. Petersburg, pupil of Emile Gredlu, Jean Petipa; graduated in 1852. Married (1) dancer Vera Lyadova, 1859 (d. 1870); (2) dancer Varvara Ivanova-Malchugina, 1877. Dancer, corps de ballet (while still a student), Imperial Theatres, St. Petersburg, from 1850, officially joining corps de ballet, 1852, and eventually becoming leading dancer and mime; premier danseur, from 1869; régisseur (succeeding Aleksei Bogdanov), Maryinsky Theatre, 1882, becoming second ballet master, 1885; first choreography, new version of *La Fille mal gardée*, 1885, thereafter working under chief ballet master Marius Petipa; also staged ballets at Tsar's private court theatre at Krasnoye-Selo, 1888–91, and invited to Warsaw to stage ballets and dances for opera, 1897; also teacher, lower school of the Imperial Theatre School, St. Petersburg, from 1858: students included Evgenia Sokolova, Ekaterina Vazem, Olga Preobrazhenskaya. Died, while collaborating with Pavel Gerdt on production of *Sylvia*, in St. Petersburg, 11 December 1901.

**ROLES**

1850 Pas de deux in *The Millers* (Gredlu), Bolshoi Theatre, St. Petersburg

Pas de deux in *La Péri* (Perrot), Bolshoi Theatre, St. Petersburg

1852 Pas de deux (with Maria Surovshchikova), Aleksandrovsky Theatre, St. Petersburg

1853 Ulrich in *The Hungarian Hut* (after Didelot), Bolshoi Theatre, St. Petersburg

Grand Pas in *La Fille mal gardée* (after Dauberval), Bolshoi Theatre, St. Petersburg

1858 Hans in *La Vivandière* (Saint-Léon), Bolshoi Theatre, St. Petersburg

Phoebus in *Esmeralda* (Perrot), Bolshoi Theatre, St. Petersburg

1862 Fisherman (cr) in *Pharaoh's Daughter* (Petipa), Bolshoi Theatre, St. Petersburg

**Lev Ivanov's *The Nutcracker*, Maryinsky Theatre, St Petersburg, 1892 (first production)**

1868 Guges (cr) in *King Candaule* (Petipa), Bolshoi Theatre, St. Petersburg
1871 Basil in *Don Quixote* (Petipa), Bolshoi Theatre, St. Petersburg
1872 Comte de Melun (cr) in *La Camargo* (Petipa), Bolshoi Theatre, St. Petersburg
1877 Solor (mime role; cr) in *La Bayadère* (Petipa), Bolshoi Theatre, St. Petersburg
1881 Ali-Ben-Tamarat (cr) in *Zoraya; or, The Lady Moor in Spain* (Petipa), Bolshoi Theatre, St. Petersburg

**Other roles include:** Valentin in *Faust* (Petipa), Conrad in *Le Corsaire* (Petipa after Perrot); leading dancing and mime roles in *Catarina* (Petipa after Perrot), *Esmeralda* (Perrot), *Le Diable à quatre* (Petipa after Mazilier), *Fiammetta* (Saint-Léon), *The Little Humpbacked Horse* (Saint-Léon), *Zoraya* (Petipa).

## WORKS

1885 *Vain Precautions* (*La Fille mal gardée*, after Dauberval; mus. Hertel), Maryinsky Theatre, St. Petersburg
1887 *The Enchanted Forest* (mus. Drigo), Maryinsky Theatre, St. Petersburg
*The Tulip of Haarlem* (mus. Schel), Maryinsky Theatre, St. Petersburg
*Fiametta* (with Petipa, after Saint-Léon; mus. Minkus), Maryinsky Theatre, St. Petersburg
1888 *La Belle de Séville* (mus. Sbornaya), Court Theatre, Krasnoye-Selo
1890 *Les Espiègleries de l'amour* (mus. Pugni, Friedmann), Court Theatre, Krasnoye-Selo
"Polovtsian Dances" in *Prince Igor* (opera; mus. Borodin), Maryinsky Theatre, St. Petersburg
1891 *Une Fête de bataliers* (mus. Friedman), Court Theatre, Krasnoye-Selo
1892 Dances in *Mlada* (opera; mus. Rimsky-Korsakov), Maryinsky Theatre, St. Petersburg
*The Nutcracker* (scenario devised by Petipa, chor. completed by Ivanov; mus. Tchaikovsky), Maryinsky Theatre, St. Petersburg
*Fiammetta* (new version, after Saint-Léon; mus. Minkus), Bolshoi Theatre, Moscow
1893 *The Magic Flute* (mus. Drigo), Imperial Ballet School, St. Petersburg
*Les Sacrifices à l'amour* (after Didelot), Maryinsky Theatre, St. Petersburg
*Cinderella* (with Petipa, Cecchetti; mus. Schel), Maryinsky Theatre, St. Petersburg
1894 *The Awakening of Flora* (with Petipa; mus. Drigo), Maryinsky Theatre, St. Petersburg
*Swan Lake*, Act II (mus. Tchaikovsky), Maryinsky Theatre, St. Petersburg
*Le Pâtre et les abeilles* (after Saint-Léon), Maryinsky Theatre, St. Petersburg
*Le Diable à quatre* (after Perrot, Mazilier; mus. Adam), Maryinsky Theatre, St. Petersburg
*Vain Precautions* (*La Fille mal gardée*; after Petipa, Dauberval), Maryinsky Theatre, St. Petersburg
1895 *Swan Lake* (complete ballet; with Petipa; mus. Tchaikovsky), Maryinsky Theatre, St. Petersburg
1896 *Acis and Galathea* (mus. Kadletz), Maryinsky Theatre, St. Petersburg
1897 *The Daughter of Mikado* (mus. Vrangel), Maryinsky Theatre, St. Petersburg
Dances in *The Demon* (opera; mus. Rubinstein), Maryinsky Theatre, St. Petersburg
*Halte de cavalerie* (after Petipa; mus. Armsheimer), Grand Theatre, Warsaw
*Le Marché des innocents* (after Petipa; mus. Pugni), Grand Theatre, Warsaw
1899 *Marcobomba* (after Perrot; mus. Pugni), Maryinsky Theatre, St. Petersburg
*Graziella* (after Saint-Léon), Maryinsky Theatre, St. Petersburg
1900 Czardas (mus. Liszt) added to *The Little Humpbacked Horse* (Saint-Léon), Maryinsky Theatre, St. Petersburg
1901 *Sylvia* (mus. Delibes; chor. completed by Pavel Gerdt), Maryinsky Theatre, St. Petersburg

## PUBLICATIONS

By Ivanov:
"Memoirs" (selections) in *Petersburgskaya Gazeta*, 13 January 1901

About Ivanov:
Slonimsky, Yuri, *Masters of the Ballet in the Nineteenth Century*, Leningrad, 1937
Borisoglebsky, Mikhail, *Materials on the History of Russian Ballet*, Leningrad, 1938
Beaumont, Cyril, *Complete Book of Ballets*, London, revised edition, 1951
Slonimsky, Yuri, "Writings on Lev Ivanov", translated by Anatole Chujoy, *Dance Perspectives* (New York), no. 2, 1959
Krasovskaya, Vera, *Russian Ballet Theatre of the Second Half of the Nineteenth Century*, Leningrad, 1963
Roslavleva, Natalia, *Era of the Russian Ballet*, London, 1966
Wiley, Roland John, *Tchaikovsky's Ballets*, Oxford, 1985

* * *

The fame of Lev Ivanov has been almost entirely posthumous. His service to ballet as the creator of the second and fourth acts—the "white acts"—of *Swan Lake*, which put him on the highest level of world choreography, received scant recognition in his life.

Partly this was because of his unassuming character, and partly it was because he was the first native Russian choreographer of note to practise in nineteenth-century St. Petersburg, where native Russians were at a disadvantage compared to the numerous foreign artists brought in from Europe. It was not until 30 years after his death that the pendulum began to swing the other way.

The reassessment could only begin in Russia, where the historical records were preserved. Moreover, it happened when revolutionary sentiment was asserting the equality of Slav genius with all others. Ivanov was hailed as the soul of Russian choreography. The West, hitherto largely ignorant of his contribution to a ballet which had been thought of as Petipa's, accepted his equal artistic responsibility at the cost of some lasting confusion.

Ivanov was born into an intelligent and affluent family in Moscow, though not of the upper class. Showing interest in ballet as a child, he was sent to attend the St. Petersburg Theatre School, where after a year he was sufficiently promising to be taken on as a state-supported pupil. Among his teachers was Jean Petipa, father of Marius, who like others of the Petipa family had come to St. Petersburg in the wake of his son's success.

From the age of sixteen, still at the Theatre School, Ivanov began to dance in the corps in productions such as *Catarina*,

*Esmeralda*, and *La Filleule des fées* (*The Fairies' Godchild*), all staged by Perrot for Fanny Elssler. In class, Ivanov was noticed by the Russian ballerina Tatiana Smirnova, who persuaded him to partner her in *La Fille mal gardée*.

From this time his career as a dancer was in the ascendant. He took opportunities to substitute for Petipa when the latter was ill. He partnered eminent visiting ballerinas. He became the premier danseur, but relinquished the position to Pavel Gerdt, appearing on the stage for the last time in 1893.

Ivanov had begun to teach early in his professional career, and later became régisseur. When Petipa was appointed chief ballet master, the 51-year-old Ivanov became second ballet master. He held this position until his death at 67, and in this post the work for which he is chiefly remembered was done.

For the most part, Ivanov's duties were to produce the many minor ballets required for the various stages of the Imperial Theatres. His first major enterprise was his staging of Dauberval's *La Fille mal gardée*. This was followed by *The Tulip of Haarlem*. In the 1890s he embarked upon *The Nutcracker*, *The Magic Flute*, and the white acts of *Swan Lake*.

The first of these, *The Nutcracker*, he took over as a result of Petipa's illness when the latter had already started upon this, his second collaboration with Tchaikovsky (the first being *The Sleeping Beauty*). *The Nutcracker* gave Tchaikovsky much trouble, and its choreography remains contentious. Tchaikovsky's brother Modest suggested that Ivanov was to blame for its shortcomings, but in the circumstances this can hardly be right. If there was a lack of overall artistic control, the fault must lie higher up than with a subordinate ballet master. And further, it must be remembered that one of the enduring successes of *The Nutcracker* is the dance of snowflakes. Its soft lyricism is characteristic of Ivanov, and its wintry theme is profoundly Russian.

*The Magic Flute* was a one-act ballet to the music of Drigo, originally produced for the private stage of the Theatre School, but eventually familiar to world audiences as part of the repertory of the Pavlova company.

Ivanov revived the second (lakeside) act of *Swan Lake* in his own choreography for the memorial concert following Tchaikovsky's death (the initial choreography having been by Reisinger). It was the success of this act that led to the full revival under the overall artistic direction of Petipa, who contributed the first and third acts, Ivanov adding the final lakeside act. The acts are typical of their respective creators, Ivanov's second and fourth showing his lyrical, elegiac, dreamlike style, keeping within the limits of traditional choreography, and Petipa's first and third glittering with the bravura feats of the Italian school and vivid national dances.

The appeal of *Swan Lake* as a complete ballet is owed to just this contrast, though Slonimsky's claim that *Swan Lake* ultimately owes its longevity to the lakeside scenes cannot be contested. This claim was made in the book *Masters of Ballet*, published in 1937, which marked the turning point in the assessment of Ivanov. Slonimsky's essay remains the definitive study. He drew on Ivanov's own memoirs, as well as the recollections of Ivanov's contemporary Shiryayev.

Of his own achievements, Ivanov simply said: "Although I do not possess such talent as Mr. Petipa, I nevertheless produce ballets no worse than many other balletmasters." Undoubtedly, this was a historic understatement.

—Tony Devereux

---

## IVAN THE TERRIBLE

(original Russian title: *Ivan Groznyi*)

**Choreography:** Yuri Grigorovich
**Music:** Sergei Prokofiev (arranged by Mikhail Chulaki)
**Design:** Simon Virsaladze (scenery and costumes)
**Libretto:** Yuri Grigorovich
**First Production:** Bolshoi Ballet, Moscow, 20 February 1975
**Principal Dancers:** Yuri Vladimirov (Ivan), Natalia Bessmertnova (Anastasia), Boris Akimov (Kurbsky)

**Other productions include:** Paris Opéra Ballet (restaged Grigorovich); Paris, 14 October 1976.

### PUBLICATIONS

Demidov, Aleksandr, "Fidelity", *Teatr* (Moscow), no. 10, 1975
Roslavleva, Natalia, "'Ivan' through Russian Eyes", *Dancing Times* (London), July 1975
Greskovic, Robert, "The Grigorovich Factor and the Bolshoi", *Ballet Review* (Brooklyn, N.Y.), vol. 5, no. 2, 1975–76
Barnes, Patricia, "*Ivan the Terrible*", *Dance and Dancers* (London), January 1976

* * *

Yuri Grigorovich's ballet, *Ivan the Terrible* is a powerful, dramatically disturbing work—a Russian epic set to Russian music about a pivotal period in Russian history. It tells of Tsar Ivan IV's struggle to unify the Russian state in the sixteenth century, despite attacks from the hostile Tartars and the plottings of the Boyars (nobles) in Ivan's own court. Grigorovich portrays Ivan as an absolute ruler who suffers from periods of mental illness, and who sinks into demonic cruelty and sadism after the Boyars poison his beloved wife Anastasia. He creates a secret police—the Oprichnina—to detect and destroy his enemies. He turns Russia into a land of unified but terrified people.

The ballet was Grigorovich's seventh full-length work and took him four years to complete. He says of this ballet that it "seeks to re-create an image of the period. The essential theme is the nature of the Russian character, the traditions of loyalty and heroism, the ethics and morals of the individual Russian . . .". The choreography includes elements of Russian folk-dancing and gesture, and to link the scenes he uses six bell-ringers, like town-criers, who alert the townsfolk to impending events.

The music was originally composed as the film score for Sergei Eisenstein's film, *Ivan the Terrible*, from which Grigorovich found the inspiration for his ballet. Lacking enough music for a full-length ballet, conductor A. L. Spasevich suggested to Grigorovich the possibility of adding other compositions by Prokofiev, but he died soon after work had begun. The initial idea was continued by Professor Mikhail Chulaki of the Moscow Conservatoire, an expert on Prokofiev, who created the ballet score by blending different compositions from other works by Prokofiev including his Third Symphony.

The ballet calls for both convincing interpretation and strong, athletic dancing from its principal character. Grigorovich establishes Ivan's terrifying sovereignty from the character's first appearance. Dressed in black and tightly gripping the sides of his throne, he stares menacingly at his court. Slowly he genuflects and, with exaggerated and deliberate strides, descends the staircase. The choreography for Ivan is sharp-edged yet brooding, full of passion and anger. It is only with his wife, Anastasia, that, for a few moments, a gentler nature is

***Ivan The Terrible*, with Natalia Bessmertnova and Irek Mukhamedov, Bolshoi Ballet, Moscow**

visible. Here Grigorovich shows us a man deeply in love, almost poet-like in his attentions, the weight of guarding his kingdom lifted from body as well as soul. When Anastasia dies, poisoned by Prince Kurbsky, the chief of the Boyars, the tortured Ivan lifts her corpse, swaying with it in anguish before giving it up to be buried. But the tenderness does not last long and he is soon back to his "terrible" ways, rounding up and punishing the Boyars. Dressed in a grotesque clown mask, he re-enacts the poisoning. He sadistically and enthusiastically kills a Boyar in place of his wife, then commands that all be slaughtered. To Prokofiev's ever-accelerating pace, Grigorovich wrings every drop of drama from the scene.

When Ivan leads his men into battle against the Tartar invaders, the choreography relies completely on physical strength and force. This confrontation (at Kazan in 1552) was Ivan's greatest victory. The colourful, nine-onion-domed St. Basil's Cathedral in Red Square was built to commemorate his success (and he then commanded that the architect be blinded lest he be tempted to build another like it). Grigorovich uses the event to show off the technical stamina of both company and leading dancer. Opposing sides charge after each other around the stage. Symbols of doom, depicted by scythe-wielding, corpse-like shapes, and trumpet-blowing heralds of victory in red wigs, rush in between the action to give progress reports. Into this furore, the lone Ivan comes hurtling diagonally across, then encircling, the stage in a collection of macho leaps and turns. The scene is typically Bolshoi, a spectacle of dramatic entertainment. Yet there are also memorable non-danced moments: Ivan throwing his spear-tipped staff into the midst of the scheming Boyars, or creeping up to surprise, then throttle, one who has dared to sit on his throne. In the final scene Ivan, showing supreme control over all Russia, grasps the bell-ringers' ropes around his hands and feet and swings out over his people.

Georgian-born Simon Virsaladze designed the action of the Court around three innovative revolving curtains—Ivan's throne, at the top of a steep flight of stairs, is flanked by the two "rooms" of the Boyars. Thus scenes flow in continuity, starting as the curtains begin to roll back and then spilling out onto the front stage.

The role of Ivan has been interpreted by some of the finest Bolshoi dancers. Each one has shown exemplary dancing and thoughtful characterization. Yuri Vladimirov, the original Ivan and exponent of the role in the film of the ballet, made him a formidable personality, blanketing the role with heaviness and emphasizing the Tsar's dark side and his mental illness. Vladimir Vasiliev presented, through convincing acting as well as dynamic dancing, the Tsar's deterioration from a dominating but humane ruler to a frenzied maniac who speedily exterminates without trial all who challenge his authority. Mikhail Lavrovsky, with a slighter physique than the other two, offered a wily and cunning interpretation, strong on classical technique and inner emotion, which finally spilled over into uncontrollable passion. Vyacheslav Gordeyev, a refined, exacting technician, stressed the paranoid aspect of the Tsar's nature, while Aleksei Fadeyechev, usually cast as a gentle, classical Prince, proved his domination over his enemies through an authoritative command and his own fear of survival. The latest Bolshoi superstar, Irek Mukhamedov, unleashed his extraordinary physical prowess and natural theatrical presence in the role of Ivan, terrorizing and conquering.

—Margaret Willis

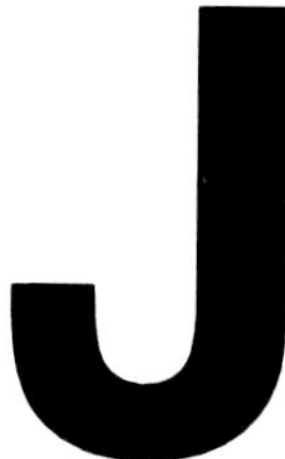

**JACOBSON, Leonid** *see* **YAKOBSON, Leonid**

---

**JAFFE, Susan**

American dancer. Born in Washington, D.C., 22 May 1962. Studied at the Maryland School of Ballet, pupil of Hortensia Fonseca, the School of American Ballet (scholarship student), and at American Ballet Theatre School, New York. Married conductor Paul Connelly, 1984. Dancer, American Ballet Theatre II, from 1978; joined American Ballet Theatre, 1980, becoming soloist, from 1981, and principal dancer, from 1983; also international guest artist, including for Kirov Ballet, Leningrad (now the St. Petersburg Ballet), and with Baryshnikov and Company, touring United States and Japan; also appeared in "Dancing for Life" Gala with the New York City Ballet at Lincoln Center, New York.

## ROLES

1980 Pas d'Esclave from *Le Corsaire* (after Petipa), American Ballet Theatre, Washington, D.C.

1981 Prélude in *Bourrée Fantasque* (Balanchine), American Ballet Theatre, Washington, D.C.

Principal dancer in *Symphonie Concertante* (Balanchine), American Ballet Theatre, Washington, D.C.

Gamzatti in *La Bayadère* (Makarova after Petipa), American Ballet Theatre, Chicago

The Coquette in *La Sonnambula* (Balanchine), American Ballet Theatre, Chicago

Second Movement in *Concerto* (MacMillan), American Ballet Theatre, Miami

Myrtha in *Giselle* (Petipa after Coralli, Perrot; staged Blair), American Ballet Theatre

1982 Pas de deux (cr) in *Great Galloping Gottschalk* (Taylor-Corbett), American Ballet Theatre, Miami

Pas de deux in *Variations on "America"* (Feld), American Ballet Theatre, Miami

Terpsichore in *Apollo* (Balanchine), American Ballet Theatre, Miami

Title role in *Giselle* (Petipa after Coralli, Perrot; staged Blair), American Ballet Theatre, New York

Principal dancer in *Duets* (Cunningham), American Ballet Theatre, New York

Principal dancer in *Afternoon of a Faun* (Robbins), American Ballet Theatre, Spoleto

Principal dancer in *Other Dances* (Robbins), American Ballet Theatre, Spoleto

Principal dancer in *N.Y. Export: Opus Jazz* (Robbins), American Ballet Theatre, Spoleto

Title role in *Carmen* (Petit), American Ballet Theatre, Washington, D.C.

Odette/Odile in *Swan Lake* (Petipa, Ivanov; staged Blair), American Ballet Theatre

1984 Nikiya in *La Bayadère* (Makarova after Petipa), American Ballet Theatre, New York

Kitri in *Don Quixote* (*Kitri's Wedding*) (Baryshnikov after Petipa), American Ballet Theatre, Chicago

1985 The Lady with Him in *Dim Lustre* (Tudor), American Ballet Theatre

Juliet in *Romeo and Juliet* (MacMillan), American Ballet Theatre, Chicago

1986 Principal dancer in *Requiem* (MacMillan), American Ballet Theatre, Chicago

1987 Princess Aurora in *The Sleeping Beauty* (Petipa; staged MacMillan), American Ballet Theatre, New York

Principal dancer in *Stravinsky Violin Concerto* (Balanchine), American Ballet Theatre, Miami

1988 Odette/Odile in *Swan Lake* (new production; Petipa, Ivanov; staged Baryshnikov), American Ballet Theatre, Orange County, California

An Episode in his Past in *Jardin aux lilas* (Tudor), American Ballet Theatre

La Déesse de la danse from Milan in *Gala Performance* (Tudor), American Ballet Theatre

Principal dancer in *Ballet Imperial* (Balanchine), American Ballet Theatre, Chicago

Glove Seller in *Gaîté Parisienne* (Massine), American Ballet Theatre, New York

1989 Principal dancer in *Birthday Offering* (Ashton), American Ballet Theatre, Houston

Mrs. Harriman's Daughter (cr) in *Everlast* (Tharp), American Ballet Theatre, San Francisco

1991 Title role in *Raymonda*, Act III (Bujones after Petipa), American Ballet Theatre

1992 Title role in *Firebird* (Fokine), American Ballet Theatre

Kitri in *Don Quixote* (complete ballet; Vasiliev after Petipa, Gorsky, Goleizovsky), American Ballet Theatre

Principal dancer (cr) in *Serious Pleasures* (Dove), American Ballet Theatre

Principal dancer in *Symphonic Variations* (Ashton), American Ballet Theatre

## PUBLICATIONS


Laine, Barry, "The Baby Ballerina Boom: Adolescent Terpsichore", *Dance Magazine* (New York), November 1982

Laine, Barry, "Taking on Giselle", *Ballet News* (New York), March 1983

Gruen, John, "ABT's New Generation: Susan Jaffe and Robert La Fosse", *Dance Magazine* (New York), May 1985

Tobias, Tobi, "Swan's Way", *New York* Magazine (New York), 5 June 1989

* * *

American Ballet Theatre in the 1980s was a stimulating company for young dancers to join, but a harsh, often harrowing showcase for displaying their talents. Mikhail Baryshnikov, who had returned after sixteen months as a principal at New York City Ballet to become artistic director at ABT, had decided to reduce its reliance on superstars by developing the dancers already on its roster. Those corps members and soloists he pushed into prominence, however, would often feel they had been shoved before audiences simmering with resentment at having to watch someone from the U.S. instead of the U.S.S.R.

Susan Jaffe, whose very home town is the nation's capital, has had a career that would have been typical of the Baryshnikov generation at ABT had she not developed into a ballerina of atypical distinction. She made her début at the age of eighteen within months of transferring to the corps from ABT II, the main company's junior troupe. As it so happened, that evening—10 December 1980—marked the company's first appearance anywhere under its new management. The setting, Washington's Kennedy Center, could not have been more glittering, nor the occasion more dramatic. Jaffe replaced a superstar, albeit an American (Gelsey Kirkland) in *Pas d'Esclave*, a Kirov fragment from *Le Corsaire*. She spent her opening moments swathed in a veil, but Arlene Croce, covering the occasion for *The New Yorker*, could nevertheless discern a "long, finely tempered body and easy extension", along with a sort of "wooden bravura".

Jaffe's advancement through the ranks was rapid. She was a principal dancer within three years, acquiring a heady mix of classic and contemporary roles along the way (although her reviews continued to follow what might be called the "yes, but" format). Confronted with such critical see-sawing, dancers usually make one of two choices: they either work harder to overcome weaknesses while refining their strengths, or they play it safe and concentrate on nothing but their strengths, until they become artistically and technically musclebound, turning a forte into something monotonous and predictable. Jaffe made the first choice. Happily, Baryshnikov had acquired the services of two Russian ballerinas, Elena Tchernichova and Irina Kolpakova, as ballet mistresses, so Jaffe had excellent guidance.

Kolpakova proved a particular inspiration. "When people ask me what it means to be a ballerina", Jaffe has said, "I just point to her as an example. She's someone who has to pass on this incredible desire to be your best—to pass on the joy of it, too." Kolpakova's gift is "to make you feel you're a part of something bigger than yourself", that is, to work at the service of art rather than personality.

Technical problems cleared up under such supervision. So did her reviews, which came to be dominated by unreservedly positive phrases such as "glittering", "brilliant", and even "womanly". Jaffe began to be hailed as a ballerina capable of bringing to classical roles an approach both modern and convincing. She was even singled out as one ABT dancer whose musicality and technique qualified her to dance Balanchine roles with the authority usually only found in Balanchine's own company, the New York City Ballet. In New York City a ballerina gets no higher, or rarer, praise.

Such an achievement instantly calls up the cliché of a long-stemmed American beauty, yet Jaffe, who is undeniably beautiful, is only five feet, five inches tall. Her much longer look is the happy result of a command of line, achieved by moving as if the legs do not stop at the hips but extend well up into the torso—a grand old Russian idea. In dramatic roles her dark good looks and expressive eyes come into play with added force, along with a genuine delight in interpreting character. Odile, for example, ". . . should be looked at from her point of view . . . she wants the prince to fall in love with her". As Jaffe perceives it, the character is "not just hard . . . but genuinely charming".

Of course, Jaffe knows which "story" ballets should be regarded with less respect than one should accord *Hamlet*, and how to respond accordingly. ABT's 1991 version of *Don Quixote*, for example, was restaged by Vladimir Vasiliev in a rather communal manner: choreography was credited to Petipa, Gorsky, and Goleizovsky as well. She and her partner, Julio Bocca, therefore felt no compunction about adding their own kinetic cadenzas when that ever-protean pas de deux came along. Here, bravura display was allowed, indeed called for.

ABT's 1992 season afforded Jaffe a typically varied choice of assignments. She returned to a classic, *Giselle*, for the first time in years; she carried the burden of starring in a demanding new work, Ulysses Dove's *Serious Pleasures* (Washington reviewers added "searing" to her collection of adjectives); and for good measure, she performed such disparate twentieth-century works as the complete Fokine *Firebird* and Ashton's *Symphonic Variations*.

—Harris Green

---

## JARDIN AUX LILAS
(also *Lilac Garden*)

**Choreography:** Antony Tudor
**Music:** Ernest Chausson (*Poème*)
**Design:** Hugh Stevenson (scenery and costumes)
**Libretto:** Antony Tudor and Hugh Stevenson
**First Production:** Ballet Rambert, Mercury Theatre, London, 26 January 1936
**Principal Dancers:** Maude Lloyd (Caroline), Hugh Laing (Her Lover), Antony Tudor (The Man She Must Marry), Peggy van Praagh (An Episode In His Past)

**Other productions include:** Ballet Theatre (restaged Tudor, design Raymond Sovey after Hugh Stevenson), with Viola Essen (Caroline), Hugh Laing (Her Lover), Antony Tudor (The Man She Must Marry), Karen Conrad (An Episode In His Past); New York, 15 January 1940. New York City Ballet (restaged Tudor, scenery Horace Armistead, costumes Barbara Karinska), as *Lilac Garden*, with Nora Kaye (Caroline), Hugh Laing (Her Lover), Antony Tudor (The Man She Must Marry), Tanaquil LeClercq (An Episode in His Past); New York, 30 November 1951. National Ballet of Canada (restaged Celia Franca, with Tudor, design Kay Ambrose); Toronto, 22 January 1953. Royal Ballet (scenery Tom Lingwood, costumes Hugh Stevenson), as *Lilac Garden*, with Svetlana Beriosova (Caroline), Donald MacLeary (Her Lover), Desmond Doyle (The Man She Must Marry), Georgina Parkinson (An Episode In His Past); London, 12 November 1968. Royal Ballet Touring Company, with Margaret Barbieri (Caroline), Desmond Kelly (Her Lover); Nottingham, 12 November 1970. Royal Danish Ballet; Copenhagen, 9 December 1970. Zurich Opera Ballet (staged Sallie Wilson after Tudor); Zurich, 1976. Les Grands Ballets Canadiens (staged Wilson); 1980. Royal Swedish Ballet (staged Wilson); Stockholm, 1985. Paris Opéra

*Jardin aux lilas*, with Maude Lloyd and Hugh Laing, Ballet Rambert, London, 1936

Ballet (staged Wilson); Paris, 18 February 1985. Ballet Nacional de Cuba (staged Alicia Alonso); Havana, 7 November 1986. Kirov Ballet (staged Airi Hynninen); Washington, D.C., 15 October 1991.

## PUBLICATIONS

Beaumont, Cyril, *The Complete Book of Ballets*, revised edition, London, 1951

Barnes, Clive, "*Jardin aux Lilas*", *Dance and Dancers* (London), June 1959

Clarke, Mary, *Dancers of Mercury: The Story of Ballet Rambert*, London, 1962

Percival, John, *Antony Tudor: A Young Man's Ballets*, Dance Perspectives New York, 1963

Kirstein, Lincoln, *Movement and Metaphor*, New York, 1970

Anderson, Jack, "The View from the House Opposite: Some Aspects of Tudor", *Ballet Review* (Brooklyn, N.Y.), vol. 4, no. 6, 1974

Jordan, Stephanie, "Antony Tudor: His Use of Music and Movement", *Eddy* (New York), no. 8, Spring/Summer 1976

Percival, John, "Years of Achievement", *Dance and Dancers* (London), April 1986

Perlmutter, Donna, *Shadowplay: Antony Tudor's Life in Dance*, London, 1991

* * *

It was with *Jardin aux lilas* that Antony Tudor first began to be referred to as the originator of the "psychological ballet". Tudor's interest in the underlying motivation and psychological experience of human beings had been growing and developing from the early days of his choreographic career. In other disciplines, in the arts and the sciences, much thought was being given to the darker, unknown reaches of the human psyche—and it was perhaps inevitable, looking back from the perspective of the 1990s, that at some point a choreographer would enter the field also. Modern dance choreographers were already exploring these areas, most obviously Martha Graham, but it is probably fairly safe to say that Tudor was the first to do this successfully coming from a classical background. Others have since followed his lead—perhaps most notably Kenneth MacMillan—although their methods of treatment and choreographic styles are vastly different.

On the surface, *Jardin aux lilas* is about a young woman, in whose honour a party is thrown on the eve of her marriage; all is Edwardian charm and restraint as couples dance together, in and out of the lilac glade. Underneath the surface, the ballet is about the inner experiences of four of the main characters, in particular Caroline, for whom the party is being given. Other guests provide a framework for the comings and goings, meetings and partings which take place during the course of the evening. All are individuals in their own right, with different relationships with one other and with Caroline; they show sympathy or curiosity, for example, or reveal petty rivalries within their own partnerships.

The ballet provides a glimpse beyond the façade of polite society and into the secret lives of the protagonists. There is a sense of the spectator being privy to otherwise hidden thoughts and motivations, and this is achieved through the tiniest nuances of movement and gesture which colour the choreography. After its appearance in Ballet Theatre's first season of 1940, John Martin wrote that "It would be difficult to recall another ballet that so thoroughly projects the inner being of its characters." The basic movement vocabulary used is classical, but Tudor was renowned for his skill in incorporating "natural" gesture into his choreography for the purposes of character delineation, and there is clear evidence of this in *Jardin aux lilas*. Small details, such as characters offering hands in greeting, or Caroline smoothing her dress and her hair in order to appear composed to meet her guests, are incorporated into more traditional ballet steps.

There is, of course, more to it than that. Many of the images in this and other ballets by Tudor seem to bear perhaps only a slight resemblance to any recognizable gestures, yet still have the power to evoke moods, atmospheres, and ideas most tellingly—existing, as Doris Hering wrote in 1952, in the "breathless realm between mime and pure dance". The former mistress of Caroline's fiancé (called "An Episode In His Past"), for example, dances a simple phrase of poses in attitude, on pointe, as she turns to leave the lilac garden, where Caroline and her Lover are hoping to snatch a few moments together. Her arm sweeps strongly but fluidly this way and that as she turns, as if she is holding an enormous ostrich-feather fan. Despite the apparent innocence of this phrase, it has a supremely chilling quality, a sense of foreboding, which is hard to explain but which is very much bound up with Tudor's particularly sensitive use of music as "partner".

Tudor, perhaps more than any other choreographer, has exploited the potential for music and dance to combine fruitfully for dramatic effect; music is allowed to give emotional colouring to dance, and vice versa, such that neither repeats the other but adds other layers of possible meaning. Structure, phrasing, rhythm, melody and tonality all interact with the movement and structure of the dance, often in unexpected ways. The most celebrated moment in *Jardin aux lilas* is the "frozen tableau" very near the end of the ballet when time, as it were, stands still for Caroline, and she confronts the inevitability of her future and the impossibility of her dreams. This happens just at the musical climax of the ballet, when Chausson's main theme is played fortissimo by the whole orchestra: the action on stage is arrested completely, in the most extreme contrast of music and dance possible.

In his excellent 1963 essay on Tudor's early career, John Percival wrote that, in watching the ballet, we feel that it *matters* what happens to the characters involved, despite the inevitability of it. This is perhaps because of the sense, on the part of the spectator, that he or she is possibly the only person to notice what is really going on. (Tudor himself wrote, in the notes at the beginning of the notated score, that the audience watches the action "clandestinely".) Hence precision and subtlety in performance are essential, as is the necessary sense of intimacy. Although the ballet has been transposed to the large stage, it has not always been done successfully, because to reach a larger audience, gestures must be made larger and will tend to lose that very sense of fragility and privacy which is so important to the ballet's effect. The American Ballet Theatre performance on video is a case in point: on the large San Francisco stage, the dancers are obliged to overplay their roles, with the result being an unfortunate tendency towards melodrama, even though the dramatic structure and interaction of music and dance are still clear. However, the Royal Swedish Ballet's performance, recorded in a staging made especially for film, is far more successful; the camera is able to come close enough to recapture the very intimacy of the action and the dancers without nuance being lost.

—Rachel S. Richardson

---

**JEANMAIRE, Zizi** (Renée)

French dancer and music-hall artist. Born Renée Jeanmaire in Paris, 24 April 1924. Studied at the Paris Opéra School, from 1933; later studied with Alexandre Volinine and Boris Kniaseff, Paris. Married dancer and choreographer Roland Petit, 1954: one daughter, Valentine. Dancer, Paris Opéra Ballet, 1939–44, also performing with Soirées de Paris, 1944; ballerina, Nouveau Ballet de Monte Carlo, 1946; appeared frequently in galas, including "Les Étoiles de la danse" at Salle Pleyel, and in recitals with Vladimir Skouratoff; principal dancer, Original Ballet Russe, London season, 1947; leading ballerina, Ballets de Paris de Roland Petit, 1948–53; dancer-actress in shows and revues, appearing on Broadway in *The Girl in Pink Tights* (chor. de Mille, 1953), and in musical comedy *Patron* (chor. Petit), Paris, 1959; co-director and star performer, in works choreographed by Petit, Casino de Paris (bought by Petit and Jeanmaire), from 1970; has also appeared in films, including *Hans Christian Andersen* (dir. Goldwyn, chor. Petit, 1951), *Anything Goes* (dir. Lewis, chor. Petit and others, 1956), *Charmants Garçons* (chor. Petit, 1957) *Folies Bergère* (chor. Petit, 1958), and *Les Collants noirs* (*Black Tights*; chor. Petit, 1960); guest artist, Paris Opéra Ballet, 1975 and 1979, and London Contemporary Dance Theatre Gala at Covent Garden, 1985; has appeared frequently on television. Recipient: Prix d'Interpretation (for *Carmen*), 1949; Prix du Disque (for *La Croqueuse de diamants*, 1950); Chevalier de la Legion d'honneur, 1974; Officier de l'Ordre national du mérite; Chevalier des arts et des lettres.

**ROLES**

1941 Dancer in *Le Chevalier et la demoiselle* (Lifar), Paris Opéra Ballet, Paris

1942 Principal dancer (cr) in *Les Pas, Abeilles, Sylphes* (Lifar), Gala, Paris

1943 Principal dancer (cr) in *Persée* (pas de deux; Lifar), Gala, Paris

1944 Swanilda in *Coppélia* (extracts; after Saint-Léon), Gala, Paris

Princess Aurora in *The Sleeping Beauty Adagio* (Petipa; staged Gsovsky), Gala, Paris

Principal dancer (cr) in *Syrinx Allégresse* (pas de deux; Lifar), Gala, Paris

Principal dancer (cr) in *Études* (Pas de trois; Fenonjois), Gala, Paris

Principal dancer (cr) in *Cakewalk* (also chor.), Gala, Paris

**Renée Jeanmaire in *Carmen*, 1949**

Principal dancer (cr) in *Lutins* (pas de deux; Fenonjois), Gala, Paris
Principal dancer (cr) in *Cakewalk* (also chor.), Gala, Paris
Principal dancer (cr) in *Lutins* (pas de deux; Fenonjois), Gala, Paris
Principal dancer (cr) in *Duo* (also chor.), Gala, Paris
Principal dancer (cr) in *La Bergère et le ramoneur* (Pas de trois; Fenonjois), Gala, Paris
Principal dancer (cr) in *Papillon* (Kniaseff), Gala, Paris
Principal dancer (cr) in *La Chatte* (Volinin), Gala, Paris
Dancer (cr) in *Arlequinade* (pas de deux; Fenonjois), Gala, Paris
Principal dancer (cr) in *Cakewalk* (Gsovsky), Gala, Paris

1945 Principal dancer (cr) in *Le Poète* (Petit), Théâtre Sarah Bernhardt, Paris
Principal dancer (cr) in *Quadrille* (Fenonjois), Gala, Paris

1946 Principal dancer (cr) in *Aubade* (Lifar), Nouveau Ballet de Monte Carlo, Monte Carlo
Title role (cr) in *La Péri* (Lifar), Nouveau Ballet de Monte Carlo, Monte Carlo
Galatée (cr) in *Pygmalion* (Lifar), Nouveau Ballet de Monte Carlo, Monte Carlo
Lise in *La Fille mal gardée* (Balachova), Nouveau Ballet de Monte Carlo, Monte Carlo
Principal dancer in *Noir et blanc* (*Suite en blanc*; Lifar), Nouveau Ballet de Monte Carlo, Monte Carlo

1947 Principal dancer (cr) in *Piccoli* (new version; Kniaseff), Original Ballet Russe, London
The Siren in *Prodigal Son* (Lichine), Original Ballet Russe, London
Waltz, Mazurka in *Les Sylphides* (Fokine), Original Ballet Russe, London
Divertissement in *Graduation Ball* (Lichine), Original Ballet Russe, London

1948 Principal dancer (cr) in *Que le Diable l'emporte* (Petit), Ballets de Paris, Paris
Principal dancer (cr) in *Études symphoniques* (Kniaseff), Ballets de Paris, Paris
Street dancer in *Le Beau Danube* (Massine), Ballets de Paris, Paris

1949 A Chicken (cr) in *L'Oeuf à la coque* (Petit), Ballets de Paris, London
Title role (cr) in *Carmen* (Petit), Ballets de Paris, London
Principal dancer (cr) in *Pas d'action* (pas de deux; Petit), Ballets de Paris, London
The Girl without Hair (cr) in *Le Rêve de Léonor* (Ashton), Ballets de Paris, London

1950 Title role (cr) in *La Croqueuse de diamants* (Petit), Ballets de Paris, Paris

1956 Principal dancer (cr) in *La Nuit* (Petit), Revue de Ballets de Paris, Paris
Leading role (cr) in *Valentine; ou, Le Vélo magique* (Petit), Revue de Ballets de Paris, Paris
Principal dancer (cr) in *La Peur* (Petit), Revue de Ballets de Paris, Paris

1957 Premiere danseuse (cr) in *Zizi au Music Hall* (Petit), Théâtre de l'Alhambra, Paris

1958 Sirène (cr) in *La Rose des vents* (Petit), Ballets de Paris, London
Principal dancer (cr) in *Contrepointe* (Petit), Ballets de Paris, London

1959 Roxane (cr) in *Cyrano de Bergerac* (Petit), Ballets de Paris, London

1960 Sadie Thompson (cr) in *Rain* (Petit), "Zizi à London", London
La Dame in *Deuil en vingt-quatre heures* (Petit), Ballets de Paris, Paris

1961 Principal dancer in *La Chaloupée* (Petit), Revue de Ballets de Paris, Paris
Principal dancer (cr) in *Mon Truc en plumes* (Petit), Revue de Ballets de Paris, Lyon
Principal dancer (cr) in *Zizirama*, Revue de Ballets de Paris
La Belle Endormie in *Les Forains* (Petit), French television

1963 Principal dancer (cr) in *La Silla* (Petit), Spectacle Zizi Jeanmaire, Italy
Principal dancer (cr) in *Les Gourmandises* (Petit), Spectacle Zizi Jeanmaire, Italy

1965 Principal dancer (cr) in *Les Chemins de la creation* (Petit), French television

1968 Principal dancer (cr) in *La Voix humaine* (Petit), Florence
Principal dancer (cr) in *Show Zizi Jeanmaire*, Olympia Theatre, Paris

1969 Principal dancer in *Zizi–Petit Show* (Petit), French television

1970 Principal dancer (cr) in *Revue de Roland Petit* (Petit), Casino de Paris

1972 Principal dancer (cr) in *Zizi je t'aime* (Petit), Casino de Paris

1974 Principal dancer in *Top à Zizi Jeanmaire* (Petit), French television

1975 Principal dancer in *Symphonie fantastique* (Petit), Paris Opera Ballet, Paris

1977 Principal dancer (cr) in *Perfume Suite* (Petit), Paris Opéra Ballet, Paris

1979 Bella (cr) in *La Chauve Souris* (Petit), Ballet de Marseille, Monte Carlo
Principal dancer (cr) in *Parisiana* (Petit), Ballet de Marseille, Marseille

1981 Principal dancer in *Can Can* (Petit), Broadway, New York

1984 Principal dancer (cr) in *Hollywood Paradise* (Petit), Ballet de Marseille, Marseille

1988 Principal dancer (cr) in *Spectacle recital au Théâtre des Bouffes du Nord* and *Java for Ever* (Petit), Opéra-Comique, Paris

1990 Carabosse (cr) in *The Sleeping Beauty* (Petit after Petipa), Ballet de Marseille, Marseille

## PUBLICATIONS

By Jeanmaire:

Interview in Vaughan, David, "Shop Talk with Roland Petit and Renée Jeanmaire", *Dance and Dancers* (London), November 1960

About Jeanmaire:

Lidova, Irène, "Quatre Visages de la danse française", *Ballet Today* (London), no. 3, 1949
Lidova, Irène, *17 Visages de la danse française*, Paris, 1953
Austin, Richard, "Renée Jeanmaire", *Ballet Today* (London), July 1954
Beaumont, Cyril, *Ballets of Today*, London, 1954
Davidson, Glenys, *Ballet Biographies*, revised edition, London, 1954
"Renée Jeanmaire et Roland Petit", *La Danse* (Paris), January 1956

"Personality of the Month: Renée Jeanmaire", *Dance and Dancers* (London), November 1960
Williams, Peter, "The New World of Renée Jeanmaire", *Dance and Dancers* (London), December 1960
Livio, Antoine, *Étoiles et ballerines*, Paris, 1965
Lidova, Irène, "Zizi Jeanmaire", *Les Saisons de la danse* (Paris), January 1975
Diénis, Jean Claude, "Renée Jeanmaire", *Les Saisons de la danse* (Paris), January 1975
Croce, Arlene, *Going to the Dance*, London, 1982

* * *

In a brief note for a 1990 Paris Opéra programme, covering a triple bill of Roland Petit ballets given there in the spring, the choreographer recalled not only the excited reception of the first performance of *Carmen* in 1949, but also Jeanmaire's fear of breaking down in the last scene. When she whispered to him that she could not stand any more, his reaction was brutal. She had no choice but to continue; the rest is history. As a result of the triumphant outcome of that evening at the Prince's Theatre in London, Renée Jeanmaire abandoned her career as a classical dancer, retained her gamine haircut, and was transformed into "Zizi".

A further metamorphosis took place when she sang on the stage for the first time, revealing an attractively husky voice in the witty lyrics of *La Croqueuse de diamants*. From then on, her second stage-persona, as a musical-hall performer, was written in her stars, although she continued for a while to appear in some of the repertory of the Ballets de Paris—for example as Roxane in Petit's *Cyrano de Bergerac*.

It would have been difficult to foresee this development at the beginning of Jeanmaire's career. She emerged from the Paris Opéra school with an admirable technique, but also with the impatience she shared with the group of "rebels" led by her husband-to-be. Although she was seen in the first programme put together by Petit, with the collaboration of Boris Kochno, she did not then join the newly formed Ballets des Champs-Elysées—for in 1946, Serge Lifar invited her to dance with the Nouveau Ballet de Monte-Carlo. Among the ballets she appeared in was *Suite en blanc*, the competitive virtuosity of which suited her as much as the less elegant but still enjoyable "fouetté competition" in David Lichine's *Graduation Ball* (which Londoners saw for the first time in 1947, during the de Basil season at Covent Garden). Noticed in that work for her charm, high spirits, and crisp technique, Jeanmaire showed in her performance as the Siren, in the same choreographer's reworking of *Prodigal Son*, that she was more than a likeable soubrette.

Because of her long career as an exponent of Roland Petit's works, it is easy to lose sight of the fact that Jeanmaire could perfectly well have made a niche for herself as a ballerina in a classical company, even if that might have involved the occasional compromise of her own special individuality. She might not have become so famous—but she did not change direction simply because no other road was open to her. Her short neck and body were less than perfect material for supreme success in a classical context, but other ballerinas have successfully overcome such drawbacks. Petit placed constant emphasis on her exceptionally lovely legs—slim and shapely—but he did not find much use for the grace and poetry that Cyril Beaumont, for one, remarked upon.

Once Jeanmaire had joined the Ballets de Paris, her legs, vivacity, charm, and skill in demi-caractère roles were first exploited by Petit in an engaging trifle to an amusing score by Maurice Thiriet, *L'Oeuf à la coque*. However, the impression that she had made previously was virtually eclipsed on that much-recorded evening in February 1949. The role of Carmen gave her the opportunity to display her interpretative versatility. While the ravishing (and for then shockingly revealing) costume which Antoni Clavé designed for the Lillas Pastia scene makes a beautiful figure and a certain degree of sensuality essential for this role, many other qualities are also required: sly mockery in the first scene, a vein of cruelty as she realizes Don José is her slave, and last, heightened dramatic power in the last scene when she taunts José to kill her. Unlike most of her successors, Jeanmaire was able to fulfil all these requirements.

Petit had been attracted to the music-hall since he was a child, and after the success of *L'Oeuf à la coque* he gradually weaned Jeanmaire away from classical dance into "showbiz". First she alternated between ballet and song-and-dance. Then came Petit's acquisition of the Casino de Paris, with a series of shows built around Jeanmaire. The interlude in Hollywood itself furnished material for a long sequence in one of the later shows, no longer quite so lavish, but still relying on Zizi's voice (speaking as well as singing), her generous and ebullient temperament, and her legs.

As recently as 1988, Jeanmaire was still performing her showpiece *Mon Truc en plumes*, in which she sang and moved, but did not exactly dance. She has retained the gift of immediately winning over any audience; in autumn 1990, she showed that she had lost none of her star quality, and was still amazingly secure standing on full pointe, when she performed the exacting role of Carabosse in her husband's reworking of *The Sleeping Beauty*, which the Ballet National de Marseille, with Jeanmaire as guest, toured round Italy for several weeks after a brief run in the company's home town. It must be the first production of the ballet in which Carabosse is the principal character; Jeanmaire sustained the chameleon-like role, which marked her return to classical ballet, with unimpaired charm and aplomb and considerable technical ability.

Jeanmaire has genuine warmth and charm, with none of the *hauteur* frequently met with in Parisian dancers. She is regularly to be seen in the audience—at home or abroad—watching her husband's ballets. By her own humorous admission, he bullied her as much as any member of his company, but she does not bear him a grudge on that account. It is impossible to know what her life would have been if she had not thrown in her lot with Petit. She may have lost other opportunities, but it is unlikely that anyone else would have made for her a role as memorable as that of Carmen.

—Freda Pitt

---

**JEFFERIES, Stephen**

British dancer. Born in Reintelm, West Germany, 24 June 1951. Studied at the Royal Ballet School, pupil of Walter Trevor, Peter Clegg, Keith Lester, Donald Britton, 1967–69. Married Rashna Hanji, 1972: two children. Dancer, Royal Ballet Touring Company (performing as Royal Ballet New Group, 1970–74, and also as the Royal Ballet on Tour), from 1969, becoming soloist, 1971–72; principal dancer, National Ballet of Canada, Toronto, 1976–77; principal dancer, Royal Ballet (at Covent Garden), from 1976; also guest artist, including for Northern Ballet Theatre, PACT Ballet in South Africa, Tokyo World Ballet Festival, and Stuttgart Ballet; has also appeared in opera and musicals, including in *An Actor's*

*Revenge* (opera by Minoru Miki; Old Vic, 1979), and in *Song and Dance* (mus. Lloyd Webber; Palace Theatre, 1982).

## ROLES

1969 Prince Florimund in *The Sleeping Beauty* (Petipa; staged Ashton, de Valois), Royal Ballet Touring Company, Leeds

1970 Satan in *Job* (de Valois), Royal Ballet Touring Company, London

Solo in *Danses concertantes* (MacMillan), Royal Ballet Touring Company, Leeds

The Rake in *The Rake's Progress* (de Valois), Royal Ballet Touring Company, Manchester

Dancer in *Field Figures* (Tetley), Royal Ballet Touring Company, Manchester

1971 The Steward (cr) in *The Grand Tour* (Layton), Royal Ballet New Group, Norwich

Principal dancer (Trois Gymnopédies) in *Monotones No. 2* (Ashton), Royal Ballet New Group, London

Popular Song in *Façade* (Ashton), Royal Ballet New Group, Wimbledon

No te escaparas in *Caprichos* (Ross), Royal Ballet New Group, Wimbledon

Principal dancer (cr) in *St. Thomas' Wake* (Drew), Royal Ballet New Group, London

Principal dancer in *Ante Room* (Cauley), Royal Ballet New Group, London

1972 Servant/Young Chap (cr) in *O.W.* (Layton), Royal Ballet New Group, London

Dancer in *The Mirror Walkers* (pas de deux; Wright), Royal Ballet New Group, Bournemouth

Principal dancer in *Grosse Fugue* (van Manen), Royal Ballet New Group, London

Principal dancer in *Laurentia Pas de six* (Nureyev after Chabukiani), Royal Ballet New Group, London

Principal dancer (cr) in *Ballade* (MacMillan), Royal Ballet New Group, Lisbon

The Brother in *Triad* (MacMillan), Royal Ballet New Group, Bournemouth

Solange in *The Maids* (Ross), Royal Ballet New Group, Bristol

Pas de deux in *Les Patineurs* (Ashton), Royal Ballet New Group, Norwich

Adagio of Lovers, Variation in *Les Rendezvous* (Ashton), Royal Ballet New Group, Bournemouth

Harlequin (cr) in *The Poltroon* (MacMillan), Royal Ballet New Group, London

Solo and pas de deux in *Solitaire* (MacMillan), Royal Ballet New Group, London

1973 Principal dancer in *Tilt* (van Manen), Royal Ballet New Group, London

The Joker in *Card Game* (Cranko), Royal Ballet New Group, London

Etienne (cr) in *Sword of Alcace* (Drew), Royal Ballet New Group, London

Principal dancer in *Twilight* (van Manen), Royal Ballet New Group, Leeds

1974 A Country Boy in *La Fête étrange* (Howard), Royal Ballet New Group, Leicester

Principal dancer in *Septet Extra* (Van Manen), Royal Ballet New Group, London

Title role in *The Prodigal Son* (Balanchine), Royal Ballet New Group, Leicester

Second Movement in *Concerto* (MacMillan), Royal Ballet New Group, Peterborough

The Cousin in *The Invitation* (MacMillan), Royal Ballet New Group, London

Captain Belaye in *Pineapple Poll* (Cranko), Royal Ballet New Group, London

Principal dancer (cr) in *Unfamiliar Playground* (Bruce), Royal Ballet on Tour

Albrecht in *Giselle* (Petipa after Coralli, Perrot; staged Wright), Royal Ballet on Tour, London

Guy in *A Wedding Bouquet* (Ashton), Royal Ballet on Tour, London

1975 A Brother (cr) in *Shukumei* (J. Carter), Royal Ballet on Tour, Stratford-upon-Avon

Dr. Coppélius (cr) in *Coppélia* (new production; Wright after Petipa, Cecchetti), Royal Ballet on Tour, London

Franz in *Coppélia* (new production; Wright after Petipa, Cecchetti), Royal Ballet on Tour, London

First Red Knight in *Checkmate* (de Valois), Royal Ballet on Tour, London

Oberon in *The Dream* (Ashton), Royal Ballet on Tour, Stratford-upon-Avon

Lysander in *The Dream* (Ashton), Royal Ballet on Tour, Stratford-upon-Avon

Tango: A Dago in *Façade* (Ashton), Royal Ballet on Tour, York

Jean de Brienne in *Raymonda*, Act III (Nureyev after Petipa), Royal Ballet on Tour, Manchester

The Ghost (cr) in *El Amor Brujo* (Wright), Royal Ballet on Tour, Edinburgh

1976 Zeus (cr) in *Pandora* (Morse), Royal Ballet on Tour, Stratford-upon-Avon

The Ringmaster/Jack the Ripper (cr) in *Lulu* (J. Carter), Royal Ballet on Tour, London

Principal dancer (cr) in *A Party* (Kudelka), National Ballet of Canada, Toronto

1976/77 Colas in *La Fille mal gardée* (Ashton), National Ballet of Canada, Toronto

Franz in *Coppélia* (Franca after Petipa, Cecchetti), National Ballet of Canada, Toronto

The Prince in *The Sleeping Beauty* (Nureyev after Petipa), National Ballet of Canada, Toronto

Romeo in *Romeo and Juliet* (Cranko), National Ballet of Canada, Toronto

Pas de deux from *Le Corsaire* (after Petipa), National Ballet of Canada, Toronto

Principal dancer in *Four Schumann Pieces* (van Manen), National Ballet of Canada, Toronto

Principal dancer in *Kettentanz* (Arpino), National Ballet of Canada, Toronto

1977 Morris (cr) in *Washington Square* (Kudelka), National Ballet of Canada, Toronto

Prince Siegfried in *Swan Lake* (Petipa, Ivanov, Ashton; staged Helpmann), Royal Ballet, London

Mercutio in *Romeo and Juliet* (MacMillan), Royal Ballet, London

Golden Hours in *Elite Syncopations* (MacMillan), Royal Ballet, London

Lescault in *Manon* (MacMillan), Royal Ballet, London

Petruchio in *The Taming of the Shrew* (Cranko), Royal Ballet, London

The Cousin in *The Invitation* (MacMillan), Royal Ballet, London

Prince Florimund in *The Sleeping Beauty* (new production; Petipa, Ashton; staged de Valois), Royal Ballet, London

1978 Crown Prince Rudolf in *Mayerling* (MacMillan), Royal Ballet, London

The Messenger of Death in *Song of the Earth* (MacMillan), Royal Ballet, London

1979 Principal dancer in *La Fin du jour* (MacMillan), Royal Ballet, London
Romeo in *Romeo and Juliet* (MacMillan), Royal Ballet, London
Chanson dansée ("Athlete") in *Les Biches* (Nijinska), Royal Ballet, London
Principal dancer in *Liebeslieder Walzer* (Balanchine), Royal Ballet, London

1980 The Shah (cr) in *Papillon* (Hynd), Sadler's Wells Royal Ballet, Leeds
Principal dancer in *Troy Games* (North), Royal Ballet, London
Principal dancer (cr) in *Adieu* (Bintley), Royal Ballet, London
Principal dancer (cr) in *Dances of Albion* (Tetley), Royal Ballet, London
The Brother in *My Brother, My Sisters* (MacMillan), Royal Ballet, London
Fifth Song in *Dark Elegies* (Tudor), Royal Ballet, London
Principal dancer in *Rhapsody* (pas de deux; Ashton), Royal Ballet, London
The Caricaturist in *Mam'zelle Angot* (Massine), Royal Ballet, London
Hilarion in *Giselle* (Petipa after Coralli, Perrot; staged Sergeyev, Ashton), Royal Ballet, London
Ivan Tsarevitch in *Firebird* (Fokine), Royal Ballet, London

1981 Bryaxis in *Daphnis and Chloë* (Ashton), Royal Ballet, London
Esenin (cr) in *Isadora* (MacMillan), Royal Ballet, London
Title role in *Hamlet* (Helpmann), Royal Ballet, London

1982 Principal dancer (cr) in *L'Invitation au voyage* (Corder), Royal Ballet, London

1983 Principal dancer (cr) in *Consort Lessons* (Bintley), Royal Ballet, London
The Prince in *Cinderella* (Ashton), Royal Ballet, London

1984 Drum Major (cr) in *Different Drummer* (MacMillan), Royal Ballet, London
Wozzeck in *Different Drummer* (MacMillan), Royal Ballet, London
Solor in *La Bayadère* ("Kingdom of the Shades"; Nureyev after Petipa), Royal Ballet, London
Aminta in *Sylvia* Pas de deux (Ashton), Ashton Gala, Royal Ballet, London

1985 Dr. Frankenstein (cr) in *Frankenstein, the Modern Prometheus* (Eagling), Royal Ballet, London
Hapi (cr) in *The Songs of Horus* (Bintley), Royal Ballet, London
The Young Man in *The Two Pigeons* (Ashton), Royal Ballet, London

1988 Tirrenio in *Ondine* (Ashton), Royal Ballet, London
Brazilian Woolly Monkey (cr) in *Still Life at the Penguin Café* (Bintley), Royal Ballet, London

1990 Uranus (cr) in *The Planets* (Bintley), Royal Ballet, London
Lead Wedding Guest in *Les Noces* (Nijinska), Royal Ballet, London

1991 Title role (cr) in *Cyrano* (Bintley), Royal Ballet, London

1992 Alain in *La Fille mal gardée* (Ashton), Royal Ballet, London
Widow Simone in *La Fille mal gardée* (Ashton), Royal Ballet, London

**Other roles include:** principal dancer in *Symphonic Variations* (Ashton), Bluebird in *The Sleeping Beauty* (Petipa, Ashton; staged de Valois), Summer Pas de deux in *The Seasons* (MacMillan), Solo and pas de deux in *Solitaire* (MacMillan), principal dancer in *Gloria* (MacMillan), Warrior Chief in *Polovtsian Dances from Prince Igor* (Fokine), principal dancer in *Konservatoriet* (Bournonville), principal dancer in *Birthday Offering* (Ashton).

## PUBLICATIONS

Cruickshank, Janet, "A Man with a Motive", *Dance and Dancers* (London), April 1983

"Pick of the Bunch", *Dance and Dancers* (London), November 1985

"The Royal Ballet: The Biographies", *Ballet in London Yearbook 1989/90*, London, 1990

Woodcock, Sarah, *The Sadler's Wells Royal Ballet*, London, 1991

* * *

Among the Royal Ballet dancers of the 1970s and 1980s, only Stephen Jefferies could be ranked with the legendary artists of previous generations. From his earliest performances with the Royal Ballet Touring Company in 1969, he was recognized as a performer of exceptional insight and intelligence, whose unequivocal virility, satisfying maturity, and incandescent personality appealed to balletomane and non-specialist audiences alike. By the mid 1970s, he was seen as the outstanding dramatic dancer of his generation, and, after the consolidation of his technique during a sabbatical with the National Ballet of Canada, he joined the Royal Ballet at Covent Garden as fine a dancer as he was actor.

Many speak of dancers "acting", but usually dancers are only actors within the narrow conventions of ballet. While remaining true to those conventions, Jefferies' performances can be measured within the wider context of the legitimate theatre, showing him creating characters with whom everybody, balletomane or sceptic, can identify. In every role he finds nuances and traits that breathe new life into the most familiar choreography, making the characters live anew so that audiences see them as though for the first time. The motivation is culled from everyday experience; his characters are recognizable individuals, who yet illuminate human emotion and behaviour. The most undistinguished choreography is performed by Jefferies with commitment and conviction, so that not until another dancer takes over the role can its worth be properly assessed.

The stage is Jefferies' natural world, but there is nothing "stagey" about his personality. Even in the most implausible choreographic creations, in the most conventional mime scenes, or as the most cardboard of ballet princes, he gives an impression of naturalness and a refreshing normality—he is a human being, not a "danseur". His whole body is used not just for movement's sake, but as a communicative medium. Gesture and movement illuminate thought, emotion, and character with startling clarity; his interpretations are memorable as true and real. No one but Nureyev himself has stepped so seamlessly and expressively into Prince Siegfried's elegiacally sorrowful Act I solo in Nureyev's *Swan Lake*; only Jefferies and Blair have made Mercutio's fiendishly difficult ballroom solo in MacMillan's *Romeo and Juliet* a natural outcome of character and situation. At the same time, Jefferies never attempts to copy his predecessors; he takes the character and choreography into himself, never distorting a role for novelty's sake, but finding his own equally valid approach.

His range is wide. A wicked sense of humour, given extra force by a God-given sense of timing, infuses such roles as the Joker in *Card Game*, Petruchio in *The Taming of the Shrew*, or the Shah in *Papillon*. At the other extreme is his matchless performance as the tortured Crown Prince Rudolf, whose intense anguish, sadistic cruelty, uninhibited sensuality, and world-weariness embodies not just the corruption of an individual but of any empire. Corruption of a subtly different kind is the keynote of Jefferies' violent but insouciantly amoral Lescault. In contrast is the personal grief of the bereaved father in *Dark Elegies*, a Romeo more passionately memorable than most who attempt the role, and, above all, the Prodigal Son, journeying from impetuous, rebellious youthful innocence to a tragically won maturity. No less moving is his Young Man learning the meaning of true love in *The Two Pigeons* or his Colas, whose cheerful optimism is tempered by the underlying sadness that he and Lise may never be united.

Jefferies' interpretative ability and theatricality make him a superb performer of the choreography of Ninette de Valois. For both, dance is a valid part of theatre, not a dilettante art for aesthetes or a branch of athletics. Jefferies was among the greatest exponents of the Rake and his Satan embodied the pure Blakean power and spirit of de Valois's vision.

Of course, with such a dancer there is always an unspoken suspicion that dramatic skills are developed to compensate for suspect technique; and indeed, Jefferies has never been guilty of show-stopping virtuosity. His impressive technique can be underrated because it is primarily used in the service of a role, to communicate character and emotion; for him there are no redundant movements, no step that is without motivation and meaning. His virtuosity lies in the subtle control of line, wondrous clarity of movement, and a breathtaking sense of phrasing. Even in abstract, pure dance works, every movement is redolent with mood and significance, finding its complete meaning in the overall dance patterns. A superb partner, Jefferies presents his ballerina with charm and tact, emphasizing her femininity and providing a perfect dramatic foil, while still remaining her equal in the partnership.

His appeal to the non-specialist audience has been seen in ventures beyond the ballet stage. As Yukinojo, the *onnegata* actor in Miki's opera *An Actor's Revenge*, for example, he gave one of his most astonishing, moving, and technically impressive performances. As the only non-singing performer, communicating with face and body only, he perfectly transmitted the meaning and emotion of the sung text (performed by his "other self"), as well as contending with the stylized Kabuki movements and subtly conveying the sexual complexities of the *onnegata* actor's situation.

Although one of the Royal Ballet's most admired dancers, especially by audiences old enough to remember what it means to be a great demi-caractère dancer, Jefferies has never received the recognition due to his outstanding talents, and, although he has often outclassed the dancers for whom many roles were originally made, no choreographer has created for him a great role worthy of his talents. He was unfortunate in establishing himself at Covent Garden at a time when Royal Ballet casting seemed to be dictated by hierarchy rather than suitability or talent, and by the time he had risen to the top of that hierarchy, media attention was focused on youth or guest dancers.

Nevertheless, Jefferies' performances were a breath of fresh air in the technically obsessed ballet world of the 1980s, when many works were stagnating through over-familiarity. His example may encourage younger dancers to explore the interpretative, and not just the technical, possibilities of a role, and he will certainly leave behind memories of an astonishing number of great performances that, if ballet is fortunate, may be equalled, but are unlikely to be surpassed.

—Sarah C. Woodcock

---

**JEPPESEN, Lis**

Danish dancer. Born in Copenhagen, 5 April 1956. Studied at the Royal Danish Ballet School, Copenhagen, from 1963. Married Jan Boris Pedersen: one daughter, b. 1987. Stage début, as child actress in Tivoli Festival, Copenhagen, 1962; Royal Theatre début, when still a student, 1973; dancer, Royal Danish Ballet, from 1974, becoming solo dancer (principal), from 1980, dancing character roles from 1991; also international guest artist, with appearances in London, New York, Dallas, and Chicago. Recipient: Pavlova Prize, 1979; Theatre Cup, Copenhagen, 1982.

## ROLES

1973 The White Girl in *Monument for a Dead Boy* (van Dantzig), Royal Danish Ballet, Copenhagen
Dancer in *Wednesday's School* (Bournonville; staged Ralov), Royal Danish Ballet, Copenhagen
Poul in *Far from Denmark* (Bournonville), Royal Danish Ballet, Copenhagen
1974 Bärbel's friend (cr) in *Chronicle* (Holm), Royal Danish Ballet, Copenhagen
Dancer (cr) in *Asylum* (Marks), Royal Danish Ballet, Copenhagen
Dancer (cr) in *Dreamland* (Flindt), Royal Danish Ballet, Copenhagen
Piccolo in *Fanfare* (Robbins), Royal Danish Ballet, Copenhagen
Emilia in *Romeo and Juliet* (Neumeier), Royal Danish Ballet, Copenhagen
1975 Dancer in *The Four Seasons* (Flindt), Royal Danish Ballet, Copenhagen
Dancer in *Triumph of Death* (Flindt), Royal Danish Ballet, Copenhagen
1976 Pastorale in *Night Shadow* (*La Sonnambula*; Balanchine), Royal Danish Ballet, Copenhagen
Moor in *The Whims of Cupid and the Ballet Master* (Galeotti), Royal Danish Ballet, Copenhagen
The Pupil in *The Lesson* (Flindt), Royal Danish Ballet, Copenhagen
Neapolitan dance in *Swan Lake* (Petipa, Ivanov; staged Flindt), Royal Danish Ballet, Copenhagen
Pas de trois in *Swan Lake* (Petipa, Ivanov; staged Flindt), Royal Danish Ballet, Copenhagen
Mrs. Bonacieux in *The Three Muskateers* (Flindt), Royal Danish Ballet, Copenhagen
1977 Fourth Junior Girl in *Graduation Ball* (Lichine), Royal Danish Ballet, Copenhagen
Dancer in *Septet Extra* (van Manen), Royal Danish Ballet, Copenhagen
Hilda in *A Folk Tale* (Bournonville), Royal Danish Ballet, Copenhagen
Spring in *The Four Seasons* (Flindt), Royal Danish Ballet, Copenhagen
Two of Diamonds in *Jeu de cartes* (Cranko), Royal Danish Ballet, Copenhagen

Friend of the Bride in *Les Noces* (Lubovitch), Royal Danish Ballet, Copenhagen
Theme in *The Four Temperaments* (Balanchine), Royal Danish Ballet, Copenhagen
Clara in *The Nutcracker* (Flindt), Royal Danish Ballet, Copenhagen
1978 Victorine in *Konservatoriet* (Bournonville), Royal Danish Ballet, Copenhagen
Pas de six and Tarantella in *Napoli* (Bournonville), Royal Danish Ballet, Copenhagen
Corella in *Napoli* (Bournonville), Royal Danish Ballet, Copenhagen
Dancer in *Serenade* (Balanchine), Royal Danish Ballet, Copenhagen
Céleste in *The Toreador* (Bournonville; staged Flindt), Royal Danish Ballet, Copenhagen
1979 Dancer in *Voluntaries* (Tetley), Royal Danish Ballet, Copenhagen
Eleonora in *The Kermesse in Bruges* (Bournonville), Royal Danish Ballet, Copenhagen
Title role in *Giselle* (Petipa after Coralli, Perrot; staged Bruhn), Royal Danish Ballet, Copenhagen
Title role in *La Sylphide* (Bournonville), Royal Danish Ballet, Copenhagen
1980 Dancer in *Songs Without Words* (van Manen), Royal Danish Ballet, Copenhagen
Hermia in *A Midsummer Night's Dream* (Neumeier), Royal Danish Ballet, Copenhagen
1981 Third song in *Four Last Songs* (van Dantzig), Royal Danish Ballet, Copenhagen
Fourth song in *Four Last Songs* (van Dantzig), Royal Danish Ballet, Copenhagen
Swanilda in *Coppélia* (Brenaa after Saint-Léon), Royal Danish Ballet, Copenhagen
1982 French dance in *The Whims of Cupid and the Ballet Master* (Galeotti), Royal Danish Ballet, Copenhagen
Little Pierrot in *Night with Waning Moon* (Bruce), Royal Danish Ballet, Copenhagen
Gavotte (cr) in *Dances from the Kingdom of the Pagodas* (Alston), Royal Danish Ballet, Copenhagen
1983 Pas de deux from *The Flower Festival at Genzano* (Bournonville), Royal Danish Ballet, Copenhagen
Soloist in *Bournonville Exercises* (Bournonville; staged Ralov), Royal Danish Ballet, Copenhagen
Juanita in *Don Quixote* (Petipa, Gorsky), Royal Danish Ballet, Copenhagen
Señorita in *La Ventana* (Bournonville), Royal Danish Ballet, Copenhagen
Dancer in *Arden Court* (Taylor), Royal Danish Ballet, Copenhagen
1984 Principal dancer in *Études* (Lander), Royal Danish Ballet, Copenhagen
The Shadow in *Transfigured Night* (Kylián), Royal Danish Ballet, Copenhagen
Venus in *Maskarade* (opera; mus. Nielsen, chor. Cullberg), Royal Danish Ballet, Copenhagen
Third movement in *In the Glow of the Night* (Goh), Royal Danish Ballet, Copenhagen
Ballerina in *Petrushka* (Fokine), Royal Danish Ballet, Copenhagen
1986 Lake in *The River* (Ailey), Royal Danish Ballet, Copenhagen
1987 Amra in *Siddharta* (opera; mus. Nørgaard, chor. Lander), Royal Danish Ballet, Copenhagen
Principal dancer (cr) in *Sextet* (Eliasson), Royal Danish Ballet, Copenhagen
1988 Machen in *The Kermesse in Bruges* (Bournonville), Royal Danish Ballet, Copenhagen
Principal dancer (cr) in *Das Lied von der Erde* (Patsalas), Royal Danish Ballet, Copenhagen
Queen of the Dryads in *Don Quixote* (Petipa, Gorsky), Royal Danish Ballet, Copenhagen
1989 Principal dancer in *Afternoon of a Faun* (Robbins), Royal Danish Ballet, Copenhagen
Tatiana in *Onegin* (Cranko), Royal Danish Ballet, Copenhagen
Polyhymnia in *Apollon Musagète* (*Apollo*; Balanchine), Royal Danish Ballet, Copenhagen
Teresina in *Napoli* (Bournonville), Royal Danish Ballet, Copenhagen
Principal dancer (cr) in *Fête galante* (Andersen), Royal Danish Ballet, Copenhagen
Principal dancer (cr) in *Manhattan Abstraction* (Laerkesen), Royal Danish Ballet, Copenhagen
1990 Kitri in *Don Quixote* (Petipa, Gorsky), Royal Danish Ballet, Copenhagen

**PUBLICATIONS**

By Jeppesen:
Interview in Mørk, Ebbe, "Danish Delight: Lis Jeppesen", *Ballet News* (New York), June 1982

About Jeppesen:
Duff, Helen, "Royal Danish Ballet", *Dancing Times* (London), August 1980
Macaulay, Alastair, "This World, and Others", *The New Yorker* (New York), 4 July 1988

* * *

Lis Jeppesen's career began early. At the age of six she had already performed on several television shows, and she had made a very successful appearance as Columbine in a play. In 1963, at the age of seven, she entered the Royal Danish Ballet School. She made her début with the Royal Danish Ballet in 1973 as the White Girl in Rudi van Dantzig's *Monument for a Dead Boy*, and in 1974 she became a full member of the company.

Her dramatic talents, which had been dormant through her years at the ballet school, were soon discovered and developed. Her first dramatic part was the Pupil in Flemming Flindt's *The Lesson* in 1976. At the beginning of her career she was mainly cast in demi-caractère parts. She turned Poul, one of the Naval Cadets in *Far from Denmark*, into an amusing rogue. When she danced Clara in *The Nutcracker* in 1977 she was praised for being as much an actress as a dancer. She reached her peak within this genre of comic, or light dramatic ballet in 1981, when she danced Swanilda in *Coppélia*. In the first act she danced as a light soubrette, while in the second she was a grand comedienne, as one Danish critic wrote. Another, recognizing her dramatic potential, called her a teenage Carla Fracci.

But Jeppesen's greatest career development came with the Bournonville repertoire, and in the two Romantic classics, *Giselle* and *La Sylphide*. By 1977 she had already danced Hilda in *A Folk Tale*, and had her performance described as a poetic wonder, full of youthful joy. She combined the innocence and purity of this changeling with elfin-light dancing that made her appear almost supernatural. This was followed in 1979 by *Giselle* and *La Sylphide*. She dances the first act of *Giselle* as an innocent, naïve peasant girl with the transition into insanity made compellingly realistic. The second act she turns into a tale of love which conquers all evil. Her love for Albrecht extends

**Lis Jeppesen with Nikolaj Hübbe in *La Sylphide***

beyond death. She does not seek revenge, but forgives him for his sin. Jeppesen's Giselle has been compared in dramatic intensity to Alicia Alonso's, although her technical abilities do not compare to those of the latter. As the Sylph of *La Sylphide*, she dances as an innocent, but at the same time seductive, creature of the air. With great musicality, lightness, elegance, and grace, as one Danish critic put it, she infuses the role with a poetic soul.

It was also in 1979 that Jeppesen became an international name. At the Bournonville Festival, many foreign critics saw the Royal Danish Ballet and the Bournonville repertoire for the first time. Jeppesen was singled out as the most talented female dancer in the company. She received many offers to join companies abroad, but chose to stay in Copenhagen.

Jeppesen's rare talent for acting and mime makes her the perfect Bournonville dancer, and she has danced in all the Bournonville ballets in the Royal Danish Ballet's repertoire. Although she danced all the female leads in *Napoli*, it was not until 1989 that she was given the central Bournonville role of Teresina. She dances this role with innocence, wit, and a contagious joy—and she is also one of the only dancers who has been able to make the second act credible, making the transition from an innocent country girl to a sensual, seductive naiad somehow believable. Although she is no great technician, she has natural feeling for the Bournonville style, and has been called a Bournonville dancer par excellence.

Up until the 1980s Jeppesen's most frequent partner was Arne Willumsen. They were called "the Romantic couple", because they were able to turn Romantic characters into living human beings, making their fates relevant for a contemporary audience. They seemed to believed in the Romantic universe and to identify genuinely with its characters. They also seemed to believe in the stories without any sense of irony or dissociation. Because of this, Jeppesen has also been described as the dancer of her generation who most approximates to the ideal of the Romantic, classical ballerina.

Still, although she has mostly been identified with the Romantic repertoire, Jeppesen has also danced in modern choreography by Flindt, Robbins, Neumeier, Balanchine, Lichine, van Manen, Cranko, Lubovitch, Tetley, Taylor, Lander, and Ailey, among others. In 1989 she made her début as Tatiana in Cranko's *Onegin* to much critical acclaim, with Nikolaj Hübbe as Onegin, and in 1990 she danced Kitri in *Don Quixote*.

Jeppesen is still dancing *La Sylphide* and *Giselle*, although not as often as before. The role of Hilda in *A Folk Tale* has been handed over to the younger generation; instead, she has progressed to the character role of Birthe in the same ballet in a new production mounted in 1991. The critics were disappointed with the traditional staging, but singled out Jeppesen's fabulous acting, saying that if nothing else she alone would be reason enough to see the ballet. This might be Jeppesen's first step into a successful second career as a character dancer within the Bournonville repertoire of the Royal Danish Ballet.

—Jeannette Andersen

## LE JEUNE HOMME ET LA MORT

**Choreography:** Roland Petit
**Music:** J.S. Bach
**Design:** Georges Wakhevitch (set), Jean Cocteau (costumes)
**Libretto:** Jean Cocteau
**First Production:** Ballets des Champs-Elysées, Paris, 25 June 1946
**Principal dancers:** Jean Babilée (Young Man), Nathalie Philippart (Death)

**Other productions include:** American Ballet Theatre (restaged Petit; performed without sets), with Babilée and Philippart; New York, 9 April 1951 (restaged American Ballet Theatre, with original sets restored, with Mikhail Baryshnikov and Bonnie Mathis, 1975). Ballet National de Marseille; Paris, May 1984. German Opera Ballet; Berlin, 13 February 1985. Paris Opéra Ballet (restaged Petit), with Kader Belarbi and Marie-Claude Pietragalli; April 1990.

### PUBLICATIONS

Beaumont, Cyril, "Les Ballets des Champs-Elysées", *Ballet* (London), November 1948
Beaumont, Cyril, *Ballets of Today*, London, 1954
Wildman, Carl, "Jean Cocteau and the Ballet", *Dance and Dancers* (London), October 1973
Percival, John, "Assembly of Stars", *Dance and Dancers* (London), March 1975
Aschengren, Erik, *Jean Cocteau and the Dance*, Copenhagen, 1986
Mannoni, Gérard, *Roland Petit, un chorégraphe et ses peintres*, Paris, 1990

* * *

Regarded by many of its earliest audiences as shocking because of its use of Bach to accompany what was then seen as a work of sordid eroticism, *Le Jeune Homme et la mort* totally succeeded in fulfilling the aims of its leading collaborator, Jean Cocteau. At the time it was produced, the repertory of Les Ballets des Champs-Elysées consisted of some very fashionable, vaudeville-style ballets, some rather elegantly mounted story ballets, and classical pas de deux. *Le Jeune Homme et la mort* provided a stark contrast to these.

The basic theme and conception were Cocteau's, based on a request by Boris Kochno for a contemporary *Spectre de la rose*, and stemming from Cocteau's knowledge that the need to shock an audience was an essential ingredient of a successful theatre piece. The original programme modestly states that he described the décor to the designer Wakhevitch, the steps to the choreographer Petit, and the costumes to the costume-maker Karinska; but Cocteau's involvement was more than this. It was his idea that the ballet deliberately be rehearsed to jazz music, without the dancers being aware of (or indeed without a final decision made about) the choice of the Bach Passacaglia until the day before the first performance. Chance and improvisation also played a considerable part in minor details. The artist became specifically a painter because Babilée chose to rehearse in overalls, which became his costume. The culmination of the ballet, when the attic set flies away to reveal the neon-lit rooftops of contemporary Paris, is both realistic and expressionistic. The flashing Parisian skyline was found by Cocteau in a television studio and adapted for the stage after the broadcast.

*Le Jeune Homme et la mort* certainly achieved Cocteau's aim of creating controversy, its mixture of violence and tenderness causing its admirers to claim it as the archetype of post-war French ballet and even of existentialist theatre, and its detractors to decry the use of Bach as a background to the violence. The ballet actually derives most of its impact from the contrast between the classical serenities of the Bach Passacaglia and the realistic, violent emotion of the stage action. *Le Jeune Homme* was one of Petit's earliest works and perhaps he played a relatively minor role in its creation. Cocteau always had an extremely clear idea of the movement he envisaged for any of his works, and he must have indicated much of the movement to Petit and to the dancers Jean Babilée and Nathalie Philippart. The steps Petit devised were in his own soon-to-be-familiar style of inwardly turned, classically based movement, interspersed with straight classical jumps and turns and everyday, natural gestures, such as lighting a cigarette or glancing at a watch, to heighten realism. The power of such movement can have considerable impact on stage but is very reliant on the personalities and the abilities of the performers to create characters. The lessons Petit learned about creating theatrical impact during the devising of *Le Jeune Homme et la mort* have formed the basis of his choreographic style ever since.

Both Nathalie Philippart and Jean Babilée are reputed to have disliked the ballet. Certainly at first the classical serenities of the music gave them very little assistance in building the violence and tension of the action, not even providing much in the way of cues for specific incidents. Yet, by a combination of personal magnetism and theatrical technique, they created two performances which are among the most memorable of the twentieth century. Babilée, as the desperate lover, used all his muscular beauty and sensuous movement to express the overwhelming desperation of sexual rejection; and he was able to use his classical technique and powerful physique to turn the acrobatic elements of the role—handstands balanced on the edge of the table, a balance on the back of a chair just before it falls—into an expression of his frustration. To balance this, Philippart created an enigmatic apparition, half-child, half-experienced woman, with an extreme element of feminine cruelty towards the male. "Vicious", "spiteful", "malevolent", and "humiliating" are some of the descriptions contemporary writers used to describe her performance.

The ballet still works in the theatre after nearly 50 years, and Baryshnikov's performance in it was featured in the film *White Nights*. Even more startling, and thereby following in the whole tradition of the ballet, was Babilée's triumphant return to it at the age of 61, the fire of his personality and characterization shocking a whole new generation of French audiences.

—Peter Bassett

---

## JEUX

**Choreography:** Vaslav Nijinsky
**Music:** Claude Debussy
**Design:** Léon Bakst
**Libretto:** Vaslav Nijinsky
**First Production:** Diaghilev's Ballets Russes, Théâtre des Champs-Elysées, Paris, 15 May 1913
**Principal Dancers:** Tamara Karsavina, Vaslav Nijinsky, Ludmilla Schollar

**Other productions include:** Les Ballets Suédois (new version;

***Le Jeune Homme et la mort*, with Jean Babilée and Natalie Philippart, Les Ballets des Champs-Elysées, 1947**

chor. Jean Börlin), with Carina Ari, Jean Börlin, Jenny Hasselquist; Paris, 25 October 1920. Ballet Theatre (new version; chor. William Dollar, scenery and costumes David Ffolkes), with Nora Kaye, Igor Youskevitch, Norma Vance; New York, 23 April 1950. Western Theatre Ballet (new version; chor. Peter Darrell); Glasgow, 7 March 1963. New York City Ballet (new version; chor. John Taras, design Raoul Pène DuBois), with Melissa Hayden, Edward Villella, Allegra Kent; New York, 28 April 1966. Rome Opera Ballet (new version; chor. Aurel Milloss), with Elisabetta Terabust, Alfredo Rainò, Giancarlo Vantaggio; Rome, 2 December 1967. Düsseldorf Opera Ballet (new version; chor. Erich Walter); Düsseldorf, 29 May 1973. Paris Opéra Ballet (new version; chor. Flemming Flindt); Paris, 12 April 1973. Dutch National Ballet (new version; chor. Toer Van Schayk), Amsterdam, 17 March 1977.

## PUBLICATIONS

Nijinsky, Vaslav, *The Diaries of Vaslav Nijinsky*, edited by Romola Nijinsky, London, 1933

Howe, Martin, "The Ballets of Nijinsky", *Ballet* (London), May 1947

Kirstein, Lincoln, *Movement and Metaphor*, New York, 1970

Buckle, Richard, *Nijinsky*, London, 1971

Balanchine, George, with Mason, Francis, *Balanchine's Festival of Ballet*, Garden City, N.Y., 1977

Krasovskaya, Vera, *Nijinsky*, Leningrad, 1974; translated by John E. Bowlt, New York, 1979

Nijinska, Bronislava, *Bronislava Nijinska: Early Memoirs*, New York, 1981

Nijinska, Bronislava, "Present at the Creation" (excerpt from memoirs), *Ballet News* (New York), September 1981

Barker, Barbara, "Nijinsky's *Jeux*", *The Drama Review* (New York), September 1982

Garafola, Lynn, *Diaghilev's Ballets Russes*, New York, 1989

* * *

*Jeux* was the second ballet that Vaslav Nijinsky, then premier danseur of Serge Diaghilev's Ballets Russes, composed for Diaghilev. It was performed on the opening night of the Ballets Russes's fifth season, about one year after Nijinsky's first choreographic effort, *L'Après-midi d'un faune* (1912), also to music by Claude Debussy.

*Jeux* was a modern ballet, one of the first to deal with athletics, which was then a new enthusiasm in Europe. (The Olympic Games had been revived at the turn of the century.) Ostensibly the theme of the ballet was tennis, but it also hinged on sexual ambiguity and desire, a socialized version of modern love. Nijinsky called it "my experiment in stylized gesture".

It may have been conceived by Nijinsky in England in July 1912, at Lady Otteline Morrell's garden in Bedford Square, where Nijinsky and Bakst observed a twilight game of tennis. The house which was depicted in the set resembled in architecture those of the Bloomsbury group, as if a version of a Bloomsbury square.

Another theory is that the ballet was created while Nijinsky was at a restaurant in the Bois de Boulogne lunching with Bakst, Debussy, Diaghilev, Reynaldo Hahn, Robert Brussel, Jean Cocteau, Jacques-Emile Blanche, and Hector Cahusac. The discussion was about ballet and modern art, specifically, cubism. The cubists, so the argument went, fragmented the world into separate elements, but in dance the human body for the choreographer should have only limited possibilities.

"Not so!" was Nijinsky's reputed reply. "The kind of man I see on stage is first and foremost a contemporary man. My dream is to create costumes, plastic movements that would be characteristic of our time. Undoubtedly a man's body contains elements that denote the era that he himself represents. If we watch the contemporary man walking, reading or dancing, we won't find anything in common with his gestures and those of—let's say a stroller in Louis XV's time." Nijinsky had evidently been giving a great deal of attention to such sports as polo, golf, and tennis, and became "convinced that these games are not simply healthy pastimes, but . . . also form a plastic beauty".

***Jeux*, with Vaslav Nijinsky, Diaghilev's Ballets Russes, 1913**

When asked about appropriate music, Nijinsky apparently replied, "There is no need to compose a theme. As a ballet progresses one shouldn't have to think any more profoundly than when one is looking at a painting or listening to a symphony. I wish to compose a score of movements in which everything will be defined by a bend of a finger, by the modulation of a muscle, and not by leaps and pirouettes; it will be a score that will reveal boundless possibilities for the human body . . ." Nijinsky then demonstrated without moving from his spot, but by flexing his muscles, and concentrating in his strained neck the burst of energy and fixed mad dash of the tennis player who deflects the ball. He retained his position, threw his head back, turned it from view and pretended to follow the slow flight of an aeroplane.

Diaghilev loved the idea of the aeroplane, which was later deleted. He commissioned Debussy to write an original score for the ballet. In 1924, twelve years later, Cocteau composed the scenario for the Bronislava Nijinska / Darius Mihaud ballet, *Le Train bleu*, which was close to Nijinsky's *Jeux*, incorporating athletics, an imaginary aeroplane, and so on.

Debussy's score, as set out by Diaghilev in 1920, was to deal with a flirtation on the tennis courts. The cast was two young women and a man who carries a tennis racquet, and the games were suggestively erotic as well as athletic. The characters in their three-way courtship suggested a ménage à trois. In his later diary (edited by Romola Nijinska in 1936), Nijinsky wrote, "It was a ballet about flirting, and unsuccessful as I had no feeling for it. I started it well but then people began to hurry me and I could not finish it properly. The story of this ballet is about three young men making love to each other."

Nijinsky complained, "Diaghilev likes to say he created the ballet, because he likes to be praised. I do not mind that Diaghilev says he composed the stories of *Faune* and *Jeux* because when I created them I was under the influence of 'my life' with Diaghilev. The Faune is me, and *Jeux* is the life of which Diaghilev dreamed. He wanted to have two boys as lovers. He often told me so, but I refused. In the ballet, the two girls represent the two boys and the young man is Diaghilev. I changed the characters as love between three men could not be represented on stage."

Nijinsky mounted the ballet in Monte Carlo with his sister, Bronislava Nijinska, as one of the leads. She soon became pregnant with her daughter Irina, however, and could not dance the part. Later, Ludmilla Schollar and Tamara Karsavina, recruited by Diaghilev from the St. Petersburg Imperial Ballet, joined Nijinsky for rehearsal. Nijinsky informed them that all three would be dancing on demi-pointe, and that they should wear soft shoes like his. The key position was to be frontal, on demi-pointe, with bent wrists and half-clenched fists to create angular and broken lines. He asked the two dancers not to smile or flirt in the dance but to keep their faces motionless. Expression was to come from plastic movements of the body. At this time Nijinsky was aware of the work of Gauguin, Cezanne, Modigliani, and Matisse, as well as of the sculpture of Rodin, Mailliol, and Renoir. The groupings of the three figures in his ballet seemed influenced by Gauguin's Tahitian paintings, and Nijinsky's pose—with the weight on his left leg and his right fist to his forehead—is reminiscent of Greco-Roman sculpture.

The ballet opened to a backdrop by Léon Bakst, a dense bank of trees lit by painted, stylized circles created by patches of electric lights, with a flat white house. The green floorcloth had four circular flowerbeds. In the ballet, the "action" was roughly as follows: A white ball comes flying onstage. Leaping after it is a young man holding a tennis racquet. He is dressed in a white shirt, with sleeves rolled up, and a red tie under a turned-down collar, with white flannel trousers loose above the knees. Two women then enter, apparently seeking a private place for conversation. They are dressed alike in white, tight-knitted tops and white skirts with the hemline just above the knees. The women are interrupted by the youth, who has been spying on them. He dances with one, and then the other, each time provoking the excluded one to jealousy. Finally the three dance together. Suddenly another ball falls on the stage, and the young people run away. The curtain comes down on an empty garden, lit, as at the beginning, by the moon and the electric lights.

Nijinsky seemed in the ballet to have aimed at compact, enclosed, scuptural forms, the very opposite of the extended arabesques, attitudes, and port de bras of classical ballet. He deliberately placed the ballet in a contemporary setting, the first Diaghilev ballet production of this kind. But *Jeux* was very coolly received. Debussy walked out of the first performance, and Diaghilev disliked it as well, leading to the ballet's being discarded after five performances. It is presently a "lost" ballet, though Kenneth MacMillan reconstructed parts of it for the 1980 Herbert Ross feature film *Nijinsky*.

Bronislava Nijinska, however, felt Nijinsky had shown new choreographic achievements and discoveries in the position of the arms and the body, and in the creation of the groupings for three dancers. Everything in the choreography was new. Nijinska states she was formed as a choreographer more by *Jeux* and *Sacre* than by *Faune*. The leitmotif for *Les Noces* was *Jeux*, which lived on in Bronislava. "The unconscious art of these ballets inspired my initial work. From them I sought to realize the potential of my brother's creativity in terms of neoclassical and modern dance," she said.

Nijinsky appears to have been a genius born before his time, and today his influence can be seen on Roland Petit and Maurice Béjart, among many others. And, although the music of *Jeux* by Debussy was barely appreciated in 1913, it subsequently has been recognized as one of Debussy's finest achievements.

—Rosaline George

---

## JEUX D'ENFANTS

**Choreography:** Léonide Massine
**Music:** Georges Bizet
**Design:** Joan Miró
**Libretto:** Boris Kochno
**First Production:** (de Basil's) Ballets Russes de Monte Carlo, Monte Carlo, 14 April 1932
**Principal Dancers:** Tatiana Riabouchinska (The Child), Tamara Toumanova (The Top), David Lichine (The Traveller)

**Other productions include:** Paris Opéra Ballet (new version; chor. Albert Aveline, design Cassandre); Paris, 16 July 1941. Ballet del Teatro Colón (restaged Massine); Buenos Aires, 1955. New York City Ballet (new version: chor. George Balanchine, Francisco Moncion, Barbara Milberg; design Esteban Francés); New York, 22 November 1955 (revised version, 1959). Ballet National de Marseilles (new version; chor. Roland Petit, design Pace); Marseille, 23 January 1974. New York City Ballet (new version; chor. Balanchine, design David Mitchell) as *The Steadfast Tin Soldier*, with Patricia McBride, Peter Schaufuss; Saratoga Springs, New York, 30 July 1975.

### PUBLICATIONS

Goodman, G.E., "Décor at the Alhambra: Les Ballets Russes de Monte Carlo", *Dancing Times* (London), 3 parts: September, October, November 1933
Hall, Fernau, "De Basil and Vic-Wells: Three Comparisons", *Dancing Times* (London), November 1937
Coton, A.V., *A Prejudice for Ballet*, London, 1938
Beaumont, Cyril, *Complete Book of Ballets*, revised edition, London, 1951
Massine, Léonide, *My Life in Ballet*, London, 1960
Sorley Walker, Kathrine, *De Basil's Ballets Russes*, London, 1982

**_Jeux d'enfants_, with Tamara Toumanova as the Top, Ballets Russes de Monte Carlo, 1932**

García-Márquez, Vicente, *Les Ballets Russes*, New York, 1990

* * *

At the distance of nearly 60 years from the event, it is not so hard to realize the fact that *Jeux d'enfants*, so much in line with the kind of work choreographers were producing for Diaghilev in the second decade of his company, had its premiere less than three years after the great impresario's death. At the time, the demise of Diaghilev and the resultant disbandment of the Ballets Russes was felt to be the death of the peripatetic ballet company as well. In the event, however, though the interim period must have seemed interminable to those involved, by early 1932 René Blum and Colonel de Basil had combined to form the Ballets Russes de Monte Carlo, one of the first actions of which was to engage Massine to produce *Jeux d'enfants* to Bizet's music, with the cooperation of the surrealist painter Joan Miró as designer.

Although *Jeux d'enfants* has not survived, it was in its time an exceedingly charming little ballet. The scenario by Boris Kochno, about a child and her toys coming to life in the nursery at night, was not much more than a peg on which to hang a series of dances; but they were inventive as only Massine's choreography could be, and displayed the dancers to good advantage. Tatiana Riabouchinska was especially well served, for her wide-eyed wonder and delight at the entire proceedings still lingers in the mind's eye after a passage of more than half a century. The other roles were all admirably characterized, from the two Spirits of the Toys—the beautiful Lyubov Rostova, with Roland Guérard—to the exuberant Traveller (originally David Lichine, danced subsequently from time to time by the choreographer himself), to the Top of Tamara Toumanova (and later, Irina Baronova), performing perfect fouettés, matched perfectly to the Bizet music.

Openers in ballet are hard to find; *Jeux d'enfants* was the ideal opener. The simple story was easy to understand, even without reference to the programme synopsis, and the tale of the small girl and her larger-than-life toys holds the universal appeal of every children's fable. When the story was illuminated by the standard of dancing provided by the Ballets Russes of the 1930s, delight was universal.

The only especial novelty of the ballet was provided by the surrealist Catalán painter Joan Miró, who designed two abstract structures by way of décor, and costumes which, while in no way hampering the dancers, yet encapsulated and developed the characters of child and toys in a picture always interesting and pleasant to the eye.

*Jeux d'enfants* is the sort of ballet which nowadays is completely out of fashion, and it probably would not bear revival, since classical dancers of strong individuality are rare today, and present-day performers might have few standards of reference from which to fathom out what the choreographer intended. The loss to contemporary ballet is all the greater, for *Jeux d'enfants* was a work with an atmosphere and a charm entirely its own, a different world into which we, the adult audience, were privileged to take an unobtrusive peep, rather like proud parents watching their children playing, unconscious of any grown-up presence. And even the technical side was fully developed, if unobtrusive, for in the dance of the Top, the fouettés today utilized by every choreographer who cannot think what to do next were presented in an entirely appropriate context. This was one of Massine's strengths as choreographer—the ability to know what to use, how and when, to produce exactly the effect at which he was aiming.

—Janet Sinclair

---

## JEWELS

**Choreography:** George Balanchine
**Music:** Gabriel Fauré, Igor Stravinsky, Peter Ilyich Tchaikovsky
**Design:** Barbara Karinska (costumes), Peter Harvey (scenery)
**First Production:** New York City Ballet, New York State Theatre, New York, 13 April 1967
**Principal Dancers:** Violette Verdy, Conrad Ludlow, Mimi Paul, and Francisco Moncion (Emeralds), Patricia McBride, Edward Villella, and Patricia Neary (Rubies), Suzanne Farrell and Jacques d'Amboise (Diamonds)

**Other productions include:** Paris Opéra Ballet (*Rubies* only, as *Capriccio*); Paris, 13 March 1974. Dutch National Ballet (*Rubies* only); Amsterdam, 1977. Zurich Opera Ballet (staged Patricia Neary); Zurich, 1980. Los Angeles Ballet, 1982. Royal Ballet (*Rubies* only); London, 9 October 1989.

### PUBLICATIONS

Balanchine, George, with Mason, Francis, *Balanchine's Complete Stories of the Great Ballets*, Garden City, N.Y., 1977
Reynolds, Nancy, *Repertory in Review*, New York, 1977
Croce, Arlene, *Going to the Dance*, New York, 1982
Jowitt, Deborah, *The Dance in Mind*, Boston, 1985

* * *

In 1967, the year of the premiere performance of George Balanchine's *Jewels*, something called a "dance boom" was gaining momentum in the United States. Ballet was leading the way, and discourse on the phenomenon frequently pitted the hugely popular imported ballet companies of Sol Hurok, with their respective "stars", against the so-called "no star" system of Balanchine's New York City Ballet. Underlying the surface analysis of these factors, there regularly ensued a debate over the merits of the full-length story ballet versus those of the shorter, "storyless" works. Balanchine and his work were more patronized than championed during this time by the populist press, and his *Jewels*, a full programme of dancing without literary reference of any kind, became tricky to evaluate—for everybody, that is, but the audience. *Jewels* was a big hit with the public of the dance boom.

Analyzing the work's powers and popularity the year after the premiere, Robert Garis, a champion of Balanchine's, wrote: "Though there's no important meaning in the fact that *Jewels* is the 'first abstract three-act ballet', there's a lot of good copy in the phrase." Garis identified *Jewels* as "a work of genius both as a work of art and as show-business". All Balanchine had really done was serve up a triple bill of ballet in the savvy guise of a "three-acter", as ballet shorthand would have it.

Playing along the "good copy" angle, Balanchine noted how his *Emeralds, Rubies*, and *Diamonds* creations—as the segments of *Jewels* were individually identified—were inspired by the beauty of gemstones. Specifically, he noted that he had admired these jewels in the collection of the famous Van Cleef and Arpels jewellery firm. However accurate all this was, Balanchine's real inspiration came from his very own dancers by way of music which he particularly admired.

*Emeralds* is set to sections of *Pelléas et Mélisande* and *Shylock* by Gabriel Fauré, and features two couples of principal dancers (one slightly more prominent) as well as a trio—two women and a man—all framed by a corps de ballet of ten women. In their sea-green, long tulle skirts, the women recall some nineteenth century ballet "vision scene". Graciously attended and intricately partnered by their cavaliers, the central women dominate the verdant visions like sister queens. The more dominant of the two, in the role originated by Violette Verdy, has the ballet's most striking solo: an iridescent reverie in which the arms purl and ripple like floral tendrils. The lesser queen is presented in a pas de deux designed like a lovers' stroll, steadily and delicately threading its way from the depth of the stage to the front. The trio is youthfully carefree. The work's epilogue, a sarabande-like dance, which Balanchine added in 1976, is a fateful, melancholy parting: the four women seem to float off into the depth of the stage while the three men pace forward and kneel, yearning in the opposite direction.

*Rubies*, to Stravinsky's *Capriccio* for piano and orchestra, is as outwardly directed as *Emeralds* is introspective. Arranged for a central couple (originally Patricia McBride and Edward Villella) and female soloist (originally Patricia Neary), with a little ensemble (eight women, four men), this ballet is a dashing game of wits. The man has as much to say here as his partner, and the secondary woman—generally a tall dancer's role—commands attention with prowess both majestic and teasing. The whole affair is notably a tart symphony of legs: there are no skirts on the women here; like the men's, their costumes are basically glorified tunics revealing their strong and showy legwork.

*Diamonds*, set to the last four movements of Tchaikovsky's Third Symphony, conjures up visions, especially in its capstone position here, of Imperial Russian splendour. Created around a single ballerina, originally the singular Suzanne Farrell, and a befitting cavalier, originally the partner-par-excellence Jacques d'Amboise, *Diamonds* represents the myriad colours refracted by the colourlessness of crystal. As he often did, Balanchine here created his central pas de deux first, even though it was meant as the ballet's second section. Its courtly manners, imperial mood, baroque configurations, and sometimes recklessly daring moments of interaction are all concentrated in the "Andante elegiaco" but they reverberate throughout the ballet's other three sections.

The opening segment sets the ballerina tone by displaying an ensemble for fourteen women as so many echoes of the central ballerina's plastique. The whirlwind scherzo for the ballet's third section introduces four demi-soloist couples and shows off an empowered danseur noble and his mercurially forceful mate. The finale, a polonaise in which the master of such climaxes arguably outdoes himself, regathers all forces and crests forward like a sea of frothing foam asparkle with glittering diamonds.

During Balanchine's lifetime only one production of the ballet existed. Besides its costume designs by Barbara Karinska, it had a minimal setting by Peter Harvey, which

*Jewels*, with Violette Verdy and Conrad Ludlow, New York City Ballet, 1967

gave the stage a surround of cement-coloured, textured draperies and a changeable splash of transparent gemstones to catch different and appropriately coloured light. After his death, in 1983, New York City Ballet presented *Jewels* with new settings (Karinska's costumes were retained). These new sets by Robin Wagner, reportedly based on sketches Balanchine made when imagining the sets for himself, were much more literal and more confining than the originals.

—Robert Greskovic

---

## JOB

**Choreography:** Ninette de Valois
**Music:** Ralph Vaughan Williams
**Design:** Gwendolen Raverat (scenery and costumes after William Blake), Hedley Briggs (wigs and masks)
**Libretto:** Geoffrey Keynes (based on William Blake's illustrations for *The Book of Job*)
**First Production:** Camargo Society, Cambridge Theatre, London, 5 July 1931
**Principal Dancers:** Anton Dolin (Satan), Stanley Judson (Elihu)

**Other productions include:** Vic-Wells Ballet, with same cast; London, 22 September 1931. Sadler's Wells Ballet (restaged de Valois, new scenery John Piper), with Robert Helpmann (Satan); London, 21 May 1948. Royal Ballet Touring Company; London, 23 April 1970.

**Other choreographic treatments of story:** Ted Shawn (New York, 1931).

### PUBLICATIONS

Goodman, G.E., "Notes on Decor: The Camargo Season, I", *Dancing Times* (London), July/August 1932
Hussey, Dyneley, "Vaughan Williams and the Masque of *Job*", *Dancing Times* (London), 2 parts: June, July 1948
Williams, Peter, and Goodwin, Noël, "*Job*", *Dance and Dancers* (London), June 1970
Brinson, Peter, and Crisp, Clement, *Ballet For All*, London, 1970
Howes, Frank, "The Music of *Job*", *Dancing Times* (London), July 1970
Ries, Frank W.D., "Sir Geoffrey Keynes and the Ballet *Job*", *Dance Research* (London), Spring 1984
Sorley Walker, Kathrine, *Ninette de Valois: Idealist without Illusions*, London, 1987
Clarke, Mary, "Ballet in Wartime: Part III", *Dancing Times* (London), June 1990

Dale, Margaret, "When the Morning Stars Sang Together", *Ballet Review* (New York), Spring 1991

* * *

*Job* is generally considered to be the first truly English ballet. Its initial performance was under the auspices of the Camargo Society, a short-lived group of ballet enthusiasts whose aim was to nurture English ballet following the cessation of the Ballets Russes. The inspiration for the work, Blake's illustrations to *The Book of Job* (1825), was likewise English and had been translated to the stage by Geoffrey Keynes (scenario) and Gwendolen Raverat (design). The ballet was choreographed to the music of one of the most English of composers of the era, Ralph Vaughan Williams, whose work encompassed elements of traditional English dance music and utilized in particular the form of the seventeenth-century English masque. Even at an early stage, when only the initial ideas of scenario, design, and music were in existence, Diaghilev,—to whom the notion was submitted with a view to the Ballets Russes choreographing and performing the work—rejected it as being too English in character. De Valois, although of Irish descent and trained in the French, Italian, and Russian styles of ballet, was wholly in sympathy with the nature of the piece and agreed to choreograph the ballet within the guidelines already established by its originators. The result not only brought together a number of the most able English collaborators, but also began to determine the identity of early English ballet.

The fusion of the different arts into a coherent whole was most important to the initial success of the ballet. On accepting the commission of the score, Vaughan Williams insisted that the ballet should not include pointe work and requested that it be described as a "masque for dancing". As well as being a reflection of his own personal taste this preference was also in keeping with the traditional roots of his music. De Valois, whose choreographic starting point was always musical, also wanted to take the focus away from academic ballet technique. She therefore responded by adjusting her movement vocabulary accordingly and by making a most imaginative and original use of groupings of dancers.

To highlight the biblical subject matter of the ballet, technique was adjusted to suit each individual role. The human characters used steps based on mime and folk dance while those from Heaven used balletic technique and some movement influenced by early Central European modern dance. This symbolic division of Heaven and Earth in dance was emphasized by the splitting of the stage into two levels for selected scenes, the upper being inhabited by Job's Spiritual Self and Satan, together with the Children of God and the Sons of the Morning, while Job and his family occupied the lower level. Within these realms, groupings of dancers were also of great importance, their static tableaux visually recalling the ballet's artistic origins. These added to the dramatic impact of the ballet by highlighting key moments in the narrative, such as the downfall of Satan, which became a dramatic plummet down the staircase linking Heaven and Earth, flanked by a statuesque grouping of the corps de ballet.

Although primarily a group work, relying on the moulding of the cast into a dramatically unified whole, de Valois' ballet created one role of particular significance—that of Satan, made for the talented Anton Dolin. At the time there were few male dancers of a high technical calibre and the role of Satan advanced the skills of dancers who undertook the part, such as the young Helpmann. De Valois' ability to reveal and excite the talents of male dancers was increased in her later creations, as in the role of the Rake in *The Rake's Progress*.

With *Job* de Valois confirmed her position as one of the most talented and mature choreographers working in Britain at the time. This early ballet drew together the two major threads of her previous dance experience: first, her work in the British repertory theatre creating movement and dance interludes for plays and, second, her dancing experience with the Ballets Russes under Diaghilev's umbrella of artistic collaboration. A marginal Central European influence was also identifiable, a characteristic noted by a number of contemporary critics. *Job* helped de Valois, through these three traditions, to develop the choreographic formula which she was to apply to her most successful future works. Simultaneously it established the guidelines for the now distinctive English style of dramatic ballet—ballets which have a sound theme, and often a narrative, and which use the elements of dance, design, and music collaboratively to achieve a dramatically effective whole. Such works also use dramatic characterization to great effect and in the early years they were usually British in origin.

De Valois' theatrical creations, with *Job* as the herald of this new form of English ballet, were originally the cornerstone of the Vic-Wells company's repertoire. They became the dramatic counterpart to the lyrical, fashionable, and witty works of Ashton in the late 1930s and 1940s, during which time she utilized her developing choreographic model with greater sophistication—as seen in ballets like *The Rake's Progress* (1935) and *Checkmate* (1937). Her dramatic tradition, epitomized and initiated by *Job*, is one which has passed down to later generations of British choreographers such as Cranko, MacMillan, and Bintley, whose work uses and extends de Valois' choreographic strengths.

—Kate King

---

***Job*, with Harold Turner as Satan in a 1949 revival**

**JOFFREY BALLET**

American ballet company based in New York and Los Angeles. Origins in performing groups directed by Robert Joffrey from 1954, beginning as Robert Joffrey Ballet Concert, then becoming Robert Joffrey Theatre Ballet, 1956, with financial backing of Rebekah Harkness, 1962–64; Harkness funding withdrawn to form the Harkness Ballet, 1964; new company established, with first performances as the Robert Joffrey Ballet, 1965; resident company of City Center, New York, performing as City Center Joffrey Ballet, 1966–77; has performed as Joffrey Ballet, from 1977, establishing second home in Los Angeles, 1982, and continuing major seasons in both cities. Official school associated with company, American Ballet Center (now the Joffrey Ballet School), founded by Robert Joffrey and based in New York from 1953; also a training company, Joffrey II, largely affiliated with school and based in New York. Current artistic director of the Joffrey Ballet (succeeding Robert Joffrey on his death): Gerald Arpino, from 1988.

**PUBLICATIONS**

Heitzig, R., "Culture in Kabul: Report on the Robert Joffrey Company Abroad", *Dance Magazine* (New York), April 1963

Roslavleva, Natalia, "The Most American? Russian Opinions about the Joffrey Ballet", *Dancing Times* (London), March 1964

Kriegsman, A.M., "The Joffrey Ballet: Small Size, Large Vision", *The Reporter* (New York), December 1966

Hering, Doris, "Company Rhythm", *Dance Magazine* (New York), May 1967

Hering, Doris, "The Maiden in the Cake of Ice", *Dance Magazine* (New York), November 1967

Fatt, A., "The Capricorn Combine", *Dance Magazine* (New York), October 1970

Maynard, Olga, "The Joffrey", *Dance Magazine* (New York), November 1974

Coe, Robert, *Dance in America*, New York, 1985

Dorris, George, "The Choreography of Robert Joffrey. A Preliminary Check List", *Dance Chronicle* (New York), 2 parts: vol. 12, no. 1, 1989; vol. 12, no. 3, 1989

Anawalt, Sasha, "Joffrey Perseveres", *Dance Magazine* (New York), August 1990

Anawalt, Sasha, "Gerald Arpino and Joffrey Ballet: No Compromise", *Dance Magazine* (New York), May 1992

* * *

On 2 October 1956, Robert Joffrey Theatre Ballet was launched with an early morning performance at State Teachers College in Frostburg, Maryland. One of the company's six dancers recalls the troupe receiving "a frosty reception in Frostburg". This did not cause great surprise because, until the company's first tour, which covered 23 destinations in five weeks (reached by the dancers in a borrowed station wagon), the primary American experience of ballet in remote cities had been Denham's Ballet Russe de Monte Carlo. Expectations therefore were for ballet on a grand scale, performed by glamorous foreign artists of the highest order.

Artistic director Robert Joffrey profoundly changed ballet's identity in the popular mind and experience. He envisioned his company as independently American, presenting dancers of exceptional skill but diverse background, in original works by young Americans. His group initially consisted of Gerald Arpino, Beatrice Tompkins, Glen Tetley, John Wilson, Dianne Consoer, and Brunilda Ruiz.

Although the early chamber ensemble performed only Joffrey's ballets—*Pas des Déesses* (1954), *The Ball*, *Within Four Walls*, and *Kaleidoscope* (all 1956)—his ambition was never to develop the company for his own aesthetic expression as a choreographer. The motor behind Joffrey Ballet (as it became officially known in 1977) was its dancers, who frequently defied the classical norm in appearance. With radically different heights and weights, they required a tailor-made repertory in which to excel.

Over time, the company evolved as a group of individuals noted for a dynamic sense of rhythm and spirited youthfulness—qualities Joffrey believed were the American dancer's true legacy. He accepted dancers from a modern dance training and instituted a democratic no-star, all-star system that continues to the present.

From the beginning Joffrey Ballet was based in New York City, where in 1953 Joffrey and co-founder Gerald Arpino opened the American Ballet Center school. Joffrey was a respected teacher. He hired many of his dancers from the school and, although as a choreographer he was noted for integrating ballet with modern dance discipline, he taught pure classical form in the studio. He was a perfectionist and an academic traditionalist, believing rules could be broken on stage only if rigorously practised in class. In this way Joffrey Ballet was able to compete with the more firmly established American companies, because its standards were just as high even if the scale was smaller, the financial resources severely limited, and the repertory contemporary and eclectic.

By 1960, Robert Joffrey Theatre Ballet had performed one-night stands in over 260 towns and cities across the United States on annual tours under Columbia Artists Management. The ensemble had expanded to twenty dancers with the advantage of a ten-member orchestra. Its repertoire included commissioned works by Job Sanders (*Contretemps*, 1958), Todd Bolender (*Whirligig*, 1958) and Dirk Sanders (*Yesterday's Papers*, 1959). An invitation to perform at Jacob's Pillow in Lee, Massachusetts, increased the company's prestige, and several Balanchine works were added to the repertory.

In 1961 Gerald Arpino contributed *Ropes* and *Partita for Four*, and their success paved the way for his future position as chief choreographer and associate director. Financial difficulties, however, threatened to prohibit further creative efforts, but in the summer of 1962 the Rebekah Harkness Foundation offered to underwrite the company's escalating costs and the company was invited for a twelve-week residency at Mrs. Harkness's estate in Watch Hill, Rhode Island. During this rehearsal period, Joffrey choreographed his suite of Eastern-inspired dances, *Gamelan*, and Arpino created his depiction of a young girl's nightmare, *Incubus*. Alvin Ailey's *Feast of Ashes* was also commissioned and the novel concept of having an established modern dance choreographer create works for a ballet troupe was introduced.

In 1962–63, under the auspices of the U.S. State Department (and sponsored by the Rebekah Harkness Foundation), the company toured the Near and Middle East, India, and Pakistan. In October, it appeared at the White House in an entertainment given by President Kennedy for Emperor Haile Selassie of Ethiopia. The first international tour's monumental success precipitated an invitation to perform in major cities of the Soviet Union in the winter of 1963.

The company was established as a mature artistic force; outside choreographers (Anna Sokolow, Glen Tetley, and Norman Walker) continued to broaden the repertoire. But in March 1964 support from the Harkness Foundation was terminated and Mrs. Harkness organized a new company as Harkness Ballet, employing most of the former Joffrey dancers.

**Robert Joffrey (left), with Gerald Arpino, late 1950s**

Robert Joffrey was asked to be its artistic director, but declined because the company would not have his name. He had lost everything—sets, costumes, dancers, and the vast majority of repertory.

In September 1965 he reconstituted his troupe as the Robert Joffrey Ballet, performing in public for the first time ever in New York City, in the borough of Manhattan at Central Park's Delacourte Theatre. Arpino's exuberant *Viva Vivaldi* had its premiere and became an instant hit. The company was again invited to the White House, performing for President Johnson as part of a Festival of Arts.

The following year, at the encouragement of his enthusiastic and faithful general director Alexander Ewing, Joffrey took a financial and artistic risk. He rented the theater at City Center of Music and Drama for a self-produced week-long engagement. This potential folly proved Joffrey's salvation: Morton Baum asked the company to become resident at City Center.

In the fall of 1966, City Center Joffrey Ballet held its first season, featuring Arpino's all-male *Olympics*. The company became known as a troupe in which men were not simply "sky caps", lifting women from one place to another. Men were liberated and often used with a confidence equal to that of the women. This heralded the image of Joffrey's company as reflecting its times, aware of the sexual revolution, Vietnam, flower power, and rock 'n' roll.

In 1967 Joffrey further revolutionized dance history with the revival of Kurt Jooss's 1932 anti-war ballet, *The Green Table*. Painstaking reconstructions of international masterpieces from the twentieth century became a goal in Joffrey's overall plan, allowing audiences to see signature works that might otherwise have been lost. At the other end of the spectrum, that same year he choreographed *Astarte*, a multi-media ballet which deepened the company's reputation for innovation and a "cutting-edge" aesthetic.

By 1970, the Joffrey Ballet was at the center of the so-called dance boom. Revivals of Ashton's *Façade*, Cranko's *Pineapple Poll*, Fokine's *Petrushka*, and Massine's *Le Tricorne* and *Le Beau Danube* had entered the repertory, setting the pace for future reconstructions, the most ambitious of which was Massine's *Parade* in 1973.

In 1973 Joffrey also commissioned a relatively unknown avant-garde choreographer, Twyla Tharp, who brought her own company to City Center and created *Deuce Coupe*. Her modern-dance-trained dancers appeared on stage with Joffrey's, moving to a Beach Boys' score against a backdrop painted by graffiti artists during the performance. It was the initiation of pop wedded to classical form, the first time that high- and low-concept art had been put before the theater-going public; Tharp's career hurtled forward.

In 1974 the company made a second trip to the Soviet Union,

receiving 42 curtain calls on closing night in Moscow for Arpino's rock ballet, *Trinity*. Joffrey Ballet's popularity waxed as it inaugurated the "Dance In America" series on television's Public Broadcasting System in 1976. Yet the next year, when a Ford Foundation grant ran out, the company's alarming deficit forced it to cancel the annual New York spring season. In 1979, a National Endowment for the Arts grant materialized and the company went back into action after having disbanded for six months.

The 1980s were a period of restitution and solidification that witnessed extensive tours throughout the U.S., and the acquisition of new ballets by Jiří Kylián, William Forsythe, James Kudelka, Mark Morris, and Laura Dean. Ever enterprising, Joffrey in 1982 signed a contract with the Music Center of Los Angeles County to become that theater's first resident ballet troupe. The Joffrey Ballet was now bi-coastal, having two homes and the privilege of a doubled board and twice the fund-raising opportunity.

In 1987 Joffrey attained his crowning achievement as a "collector" of ballets from the Diaghilev period. He directed a revival of Nijinsky's *Le Sacre du printemps* (1913), scrupulously researched and reconstructed by Millicent Hodson and Kenneth Archer. In the winter, Joffrey collaborated with Arpino, Scott Barnard, and George Verdak to stage his version of *The Nutcracker*, set in America during the Victorian era. It was his final ballet. On 25 March 1988 Robert Joffrey died.

Arpino was made artistic director of Joffrey Ballet, but in May 1990, board members voted to limit Arpino's responsibilities and he resigned, withdrawing his and Joffrey's ballets from the repertory. The takeover failed without Arpino in leadership. He returned at the end of the month and those who had contested him departed from the company.

In 1991 the Music Center of Los Angeles dropped its contract with Joffrey Ballet as resident, and Arpino responded by attaining a new residence status at Los Angeles' Wiltern Theater. Since then, he has concentrated on eliminating Joffrey Ballet's cash flow problems. He has rigorously commissioned works by Charles Moulton, Peter Pucci, Edward Stierle, Laura Dean, Alonzo King, and Margo Sappington. He is also responsible for the revival of Massine's *Les Présages* (1933), staged by Tatiana Leskova and Nelly Laporte first for the Paris Opera Ballet in 1989 and for the Joffrey Ballet in 1992.

Arpino looks toward securing a permanent institution for Joffrey Ballet's forty dancers, complete with its own theater and rehearsal studios. At present, Joffrey Ballet and its apprentice ensemble, Joffrey II, are still based in New York (as well as Los Angeles), renting office and theater space at City Center. The American Ballet Center school, now the Joffrey School, continues as the anchor, an important training ground for their dancers.

—Sasha Anawalt

---

**JOFFREY, Robert**

American dancer, choreographer, teacher, and ballet director. Born Anver Joffrey (legal name; some sources cite family name as Abdullah Jaffa Anver Bey Khan), in Seattle, Washington, 24 December 1930. Studied with Ivan Novikoff, from c. 1937, and Mary Ann Wells, from c. 1942, Seattle, and at the School of American Ballet (Summer School), New York, pupil of Anatole Obukhov, Pierre Vladimirov, Alexandra Fedorova; also studied modern dance with May O'Donnell and Gertrude Schurr. Dancer, Roland Petit's Ballets de Paris, 1949–50, May O'Donnell and Company, 1951–53; first choreography for own recital, Seattle, 1948; choreographer, concerts for YM-YWHA, New York, 1952–55, also staging works for Ballet Rambert, London, 1955, and for musicals and operas, including Chautauqua Opera and New York City Opera, 1957–62, 1968–69; founder, Robert Joffrey Ballet Concert, 1954, becoming Robert Joffrey Theatre Ballet, 1956–64 (later becoming Harkness Ballet under the direction and funding of Rebekah Harkness); founder, Robert Joffrey Ballet (new company), 1965, becoming City Center Joffrey Ballet, 1966, and Joffrey Ballet, 1977; founder, Joffrey II (training company), 1970; also teacher, High School of Performing Arts, New York, 1950–55; founder and teacher, American Ballet Center (now Joffrey Ballet School), New York, 1953; member, Dance Panel of the National Endowment for the Arts, and National Council on the Arts; served as co-president (with Yuri Grigorovich), dance section of the International Theatre Institute. Recipient: *Dance Magazine* Award, 1964; Capezio Award, 1974; Handel Medallion of the City of New York, 1981; Distinguished Service Award of the Dance Notation Bureau, 1985; Honorary Doctorate, Pacific Lutheran University, Tacoma, Washington. Died in New York, 25 March 1988.

**WORKS**

1948 *Vestris Suite* (mus. period music), *Two Studies* (mus. Hindemith), *Punch* (mus. Prokofiev), *Suite of Dances* (mus. Schubert), *Slavonic Dances* (mus. Bartok), *24 Hour Liberty* (mus. Bennet), Solo concert, Seattle

1952 *Persephone* (mus. Silverman), Choreographers' Workshop, YM-YWHA, New York

*Scaramouche* (also known as *Teen Age Scaramouche*; mus. Strauss), Students of the High School of Performing Arts, New York, 1952

1953 *Umpateedle* (mus. Strauss), Students of the High School of Performing Arts, New York

1954 *Pas de Déesses* (mus. Field, arranged Wilson), Robert Joffrey Ballet Concert, New York

*Le Bal masqué* (mus. Poulenc), Robert Joffrey Ballet Concert, New York

1955 *Harpsichord Concerto in B Minor* (mus. Falla), "An Evening of Original Ballets by Robert Joffrey", New York

*Pierrot Lunaire* (mus. Schoenberg), "An Evening of Original Ballets by Robert Joffrey", New York

*Workout* (mus. McBride), Ballet Theatre Workshop, New York

*Persephone* (revised version; mus. Vivaldi), Ballet Rambert, London

1956 *The Ball* (later *Le Bal*; mus. Chabrier), Robert Joffrey Theatre Dancers, Frostburg, Maryland

*Kaleidoscope* (mus. Gershwin), Robert Joffrey Theatre Dancers, Frostburg, Maryland

*Within Four Walls* (mus. Foster, Wilson), Robert Joffrey Theatre Dancers, Frostburg, Maryland

1959 *A la Gershwin* (revised version of *Kaleidoscope*; mus. Gershwin), Robert Joffrey Theatre Ballet, Frostburg, Maryland

1963 *Gamelan* (mus. Harrison), Robert Joffrey Ballet, Leningrad

1967 *Astarte* (mus. Syrcus), City Centre Joffrey Ballet, New York

1973 *Remembrances* (mus. Wagner), City Centre Joffrey Ballet, New York

1980 *Postcards* (mus. Satie), The Joffrey Ballet, Seattle

**Other works include:** Dances in musicals—*Oklahoma!* (mus. Rodgers; Seattle, 1954), *The Student Prince* (mus. Romberg; Seattle, 1954), *Carousel* (mus. Rodgers; Seattle, 1954), *Johnny Johnson* (mus. Weill; 1955), *High Button Shoes* (mus. Styne and Cahn; Seattle, 1955), *Call me Madam* (mus. Berlin; Seattle, 1956), *The King and I* (mus. Rodgers; Seattle, 1956), and *Brigadoon* (mus. Loewe; Chautauqua, N.Y., 1959); dances in operas — *Griffelkin* (mus. Foss; NBC Television, 1955), *La Traviata* (mus. Verdi; NBC Television, 1957), *Turandot* (mus. Puccini; 1957), *Susannah* (mus. Floyd; 1957), *Die Fledermaus* (mus. J. Strauss; 1957), *Carmen* (mus. Bizet; 1957), *Faust* (mus. Gounod; 1957, 1968), *Macbeth* (mus. Verdi; 1957), *Regina* (mus. Blitzstein; 1958), *The Good Soldier Schweik* (mus. Kurka; 1958), *The Voyage to the Moon* (mus. Offenbach; 1958), *La Cenerentola* (mus. Rossini; 1958), *Street Scene* (mus. Weill; 1959), *The Devil and Daniel Webster* (mus. Moore; 1959), *Wuthering Heights* (mus. Floyd; 1959), *The Bartered Bride* (mus. Smetana; 1959), *Orfeo* (mus. Monteverdi; 1960), *Rigoletto* (mus. Verdi; 1960, 1969), *Aida* (mus. Verdi; 1961, 1962), *Wings of the Dove* (mus. Moore; 1961), *The Marriage of Figaro* (mus. Mozart; 1961, 1968), *Aida* (mus. Verdi; Seattle, 1962), *La Traviata* (mus. Verdi; 1968), *Manon* (mus. Massenet; 1968), *Mefistofele* (mus. Boito), *Lucia di Lammermoor* (mus. Donizetti; 1969); dances in *Love's Labour's Lost* (play by Shakespeare; songs and mus. Morris, 1965).

## PUBLICATIONS

By Joffrey:

Interview in Gruen, John, *The Private World of Ballet*, New York, 1975

About Joffrey:

"Personality of the Month: Robert Joffrey", *Dance and Dancers* (London), August 1955

"Robert Joffrey", *Dance Magazine* (New York), March 1964

Fatt, Amelia, "The Capricorn Connection", *Dance Magazine* (New York), October 1970

Maynard, Olga, "The Joffrey", *Dance Magazine* (New York), November 1975

Coe, Robert, *Dance in America*, New York, 1985

Dorris, George, "The Choreography of Robert Joffrey: A Preliminary Checklist", *Dance Chronicle* (New York), 2 parts: vol. 12, nos. 1 and 2, 1989

* * *

Robert Joffrey began his career as a choreographer of unusual talent; then of necessity and finally by choice he largely abandoned choreography, becoming a director whose wide-ranging taste made his company excitingly youth-oriented and experimental. He gave early chances to Gerald Arpino, Alvin Ailey, Glen Tetley, Twyla Tharp, Laura Dean, Mark Morris, Moses Pendleton, and William Forsythe among others, while reviving important works by Ashton, Balanchine, Bournonville, Cranko, Fokine, Jooss, Massine, de Mille, Robbins, and Tudor. His own choreography was notably varied, one 1954 programme contrasting the neo-Romantic *Pas de Déesses* with Poulenc's hallucinatory *Le Bal masqué*. *Gamelan* (1963) evoked Balinese movement through modifications of academic steps, while *Astarte* (1967) epitomized the early rock and psychedelic generation through its rock score, dreamlike film against a pulsating set, and erotic pas de deux (it was featured on the covers of both *Time* and *Life*).

In the early years, most of his ballets were made for specific occasions and dancers (*Pierrot Lunaire* was given only once because of its musical demands, although considered by many the score's finest visual realization). His last ballets breathed a sense of longing for a more romantic, yet also wittier, age; his final production (which he planned and oversaw, but was too weak to choreograph) was a *Nutcracker* stressing nineteenth-century American family warmth. Regrettably, except for the pastiche *Pas de Déesses*, his other works have not remained in the repertoire, in part because of their musical requirements—such as a rock group for *Astarte* or a singer for *Remembrances*.

As a collector of ballets, Joffrey started the Jooss revival with a powerful *Green Table* (1967), the Massine revival with *Parade* (1973), then *Tricorne* and *Pulcinella*. The last program he planned (not living to see it) was a Nijinsky/Nijinska evening, adding to the carefully reproduced *L'Après-midi d'un faune* and the acclaimed Archer/Hodgson conjectural reconstruction of *Le Sacre du printemps*, and the sculptural *Les Noces*—a historic trio of twentieth-century masterpieces. Clearly in Diaghilev's legacy he found an approach to ballet to be emulated and a tradition to be reconstructed, without invading the territories of the New York City Ballet in abstract ballets or American Ballet Theatre in nineteenth-century spectacles. Fortunately the ten Ashton ballets, the Jooss evening, and the Ballets Russes repertoire (ranging from Fokine's *Petrushka* to Balanchine's long-unseen *Cotillon*) proved successful with the public as well as the critics.

The resilience that enabled him totally to rebuild a company and a repertoire after the Harkness débâcle (which won him the support of the dance community, beginning with Balanchine) and to keep afloat during difficult financial times, also enabled Joffrey to plan the future of the company when death was imminent from a physical deterioration (complicated by the asthma that had led him to take up dance as a child).

Just as his teaching stressed clarity and an understanding of tradition—early guest teachers at his school included Vera Volkova and Eric Bruhn—while at the same time acknowledging the athleticism of American modern and vernacular dance (which he knew first-hand), so his company aspired to the same range and eclecticism. It presented the acrobatics of Arpino, whose trendy ballets frequently emphasize physical agility and a rather murky eroticism, alongside the modern classics, while also introducing a challenging range of younger choreographers (limited only by the budgetary problems which effectively limited the company to around 40 dancers) to create Joffrey's ideal of a living gallery of dance, his own Museum of Modern Art.

This balancing of the up-to-date with the timeless was also reflected in his concern for promoting young dancers through workshops, regional festivals, and international competitions, his training (or "junior") company, and his interest in dance scholarship. Joffrey's teaching had soon attracted many leading dancers, but although always offering dancing on a high level, his companies always had a "no star" policy, putting the emphasis on the ballet rather than the personality of the performer. Many former company members and students have gone on to become teachers or company directors, thus passing on the traditions that Joffrey learned from the Ballets Russes and his own teachers, as well as those he established through his emphasis on developing an American style within the framework of academic classicism. This, together with the company that he shaped and the repertory that he gathered, remains his legacy.

—George Dorris

**JOHANSSON, (Per) Christian**

Swedish–Russian dancer and teacher. Born in Stockholm, 20 May 1817. Studied at Royal Theatre Ballet School, Stockholm, from 1829; later studied with August Bournonville, Royal Theatre, Copenhagen. Début, Stockholm Royal Theatre, 1836, becoming principal dancer, 1837; toured in Sweden, and performed with Marie Taglioni in Stockholm, 1837; staged Bournonville's *The Homecoming*, Copenhagen, 1838; went to Russia: début in St. Petersburg, 1841; partnered ballerinas Elena Andreyanova and Marie Taglioni; offered contract with the Imperial Theatres, October 1841: principal dancer, Imperial Theatres, 1841–69; teacher, St. Petersburg Imperial School, from 1860, with official appointment from 1869; credited as one of the most important teachers of his time: pupils include Praskovia Ledendeva, Platon Karsavin, Pavel Gerdt, Nikolai Legat, Agrippina Vaganova, Mathilde Kshessinskaya, Olga Preobrazhenskaya, Anna Pavlova, and Tamara Karsavina. Died in St. Petersburg, 25 January 1903.

## ROLES

1841 Pas de trois in *Le Lac des fées* (Taglioni), Bolshoi Theatre, St. Petersburg
- Pas de deux in *La Gitana* (Taglioni), Bolshoi Theatre, St. Petersburg

1848 Colin in *La Fille mal gardée* (also known as *Lise and Colin*; after Didelot, Dauberval), Bolshoi Theatre, St. Petersburg

1849 Pas d'action in *Esmeralda* (Perrot), Bolshoi Theatre, St. Petersburg
- Pas de trois (cr; chor. Perrot) added to *Lida; ou, La Laitière suisse* (J. Petipa), Bolshoi Theatre, St. Petersburg
- Salvator Rosa in *Catarina; ou, La Fille du bandit* (Perrot), Bolshoi Theatre, St. Petersburg
- Gringoire in *Esmeralda* (Perrot), Bolshoi Theatre, St. Petersburg

1850 Hugues in *La Filleule des fées* (Perrot), Bolshoi Theatre, St. Petersburg

1851 A Fisherman (cr) in *The Naiad and the Fisherman* (Perrot), Bolshoi Theatre, St. Petersburg

1852 Ulrich (cr) in *The War of the Women; or, The Amazons of the Ninth Century* (Perrot), Bolshoi Theatre, St. Petersburg

1853 Rodolf (cr) in *Gazelda; or, The Tziganes* (Perrot), Bolshoi Theatre, St. Petersburg

1854 Leading Peasant (cr) in *Marcobomba* (Perrot), Bolshoi Theatre, St. Petersburg

1855 Pas de tambourin, Pas de deux (cr; Perrot) added to *La Fille du marbre* (Saint-Léon; staged Perrot), Bolshoi Theatre, St. Petersburg
- Principal dancer in *La Vivandière* (Saint-Léon; staged Perrot), Coronation Gala, Moscow

1858 Count Edgar (cr) in *Eoline; ou, La Dryade* (Perrot), Bolshoi Theatre, St. Petersburg

1859 Barone in *Saltarello* (Saint-Léon), Bolshoi Theatre, St. Petersburg

1864 Mutcha (cr) in *The Little Humpbacked Horse* (Saint-Léon), Bolshoi Theatre, St. Petersburg

**Other roles include:** Akhmet in *La Péri* (Coralli), Albert (Albrecht) in *Giselle* (Coralli, Perrot), Colin in *La Fille mal gardée* (after Dauberval), Aleko in *Le Due Maghe* (Titus), François in *Pâquerette* (Saint-Léon), Conte Ulrich in *The Orphan Theolinda* (Saint-Léon), Altamirano in *Jovita; ou, Les Boucaniers* (Mazilier), Count Polinski in *Le Diable à quatre* (Mazilier), Alvarez in *Le Délire d'un peintre* (Perrot), Valentine in *Faust* (Perrot), Emar in *The Beauty of Lebanon* (Petipa), Koretto in *Florida* (Petipa), Duke of Mayenne in *Camargo* (Petipa), Rajah Dugmanta in *La Bayadère* (Petipa), Bojko in *Roxana* (Petipa).

## WORKS

Staged:

1838 *The Homecoming* ("pantomime idyll"; after Bournonville), Royal Theatre, Stockholm

## PUBLICATIONS

By Johansson:

"Letters from Johanssen", translated by Lulli Svedin, with commentary by John Gregory, *Dancing Times* (London), 6 parts: February–July 1986

About Johansson:

Legat, Nikolai, "The Making of a Dancer and Ballet Master", *Dancing Times* (London), March 1931
Legat, Nikolai, "Twenty Years with Marius Petipa and Christian Johansson", *Dancing Times* (London), April 1931
Legat, Nikolai, "'The Class of Perfection' of the Imperial Ballet School", *Dancing Times* (London), July 1931
Legat, Nikolai, *The Story of the Russian School* (translated by Sir Paul Dukes), London, 1932
Borioglebsky, M., *Materials for the History of Russian Ballet*, vol. 1, Leningrad, 1938
Karsavina, Tamara, *Theatre Street*, London, 1950
Lifar, Serge, *A History of the Russian Ballet*, London, 1954
Krasovskaya, Vera, *Russian Ballet Theatre in the First Half of the Nineteenth Century*, Leningrad and Moscow, 1958
Bruhn, Erik, and Moore, Lillian, *Bournonville and Ballet Technique*, London, 1961
Karsavina, Tamara, "Christian Petrovich Johansson: Family Album 2", *Dancing Times* (London), July 1964
Roslavleva, Natalia, *Era of the Russian Ballet*, New York, 1966
Bakhrushin, Yuri, *History of Russian Ballet*, Moscow, 1973
Gregory, John, "Christian Johansson", *Dancing Times* (London), February 1986

* * *

Christian Johansson is credited as being one of the principal architects of the Russian school. A Swedish dancer who also studied with August Bournonville in Copenhagen, Johansson left Stockholm at the age of 24 for St. Petersburg, where he became a leading male dancer with the Imperial Theatre. Despite Johansson's holding that position for over twenty years, his reputation as a dancer has been eclipsed by the respect and devotion he earned as a teacher. Johansson taught at the Imperial Ballet School in St. Petersburg for over 40 years. Those who studied with him include Pavel Gerdt, Nikolai Legat, Mathilda Kschessinskaya, Olga Preobrazhenskaya, and Anna Pavlova. In some instances, he taught two generations of dancers from the same family, including Platon Karsavin and his daughter Tamara Karsavina.

Ballet's declining status in Sweden, and the resultant frustrations experienced by Johansson at the Royal Swedish Ballet, influenced his decision to accept a position with the Imperial Theatre. Johansson's employment in Russia, beginning in 1841, was in keeping with an extensive tradition of European involvement in Russian ballet. From the founding of the Imperial School in 1738 and the appointment of Jean Baptiste Landé as its first ballet master, the Russians had consistently turned to foreigners to direct the Imperial Ballet. During the first half of the nineteenth century, Russian ballet was dominated by Charles-Louis Didelot, Jules Perrot, and Arthur Saint-Léon. Unlike many others who preceded him, Johansson did not enter Russia with an established reputation. His career was built in Russia, where he married and remained for the rest of his life.

Johansson's teaching is always cited as his greatest legacy. It is unfortunate that his contributions as a dancer are seldom acknowledged, for they were not insignificant. Johansson introduced the Russians to technical elements and skills associated with the Danish school developed by Bournonville. Blessed with outstanding elevation, Johansson was also renowned for his flawless batterie and pirouettes. The influence of Bournonville was apparent in both his technical abilities and performance philosophy. Unwilling to sacrifice expression to execution, Johansson was respected as a virtuoso dancer whose presentation was graced with elegance. He was an advocate of Bournonville's belief in the necessity of gender equality on the stage. While the role of the male dancer declined in Europe, Johansson helped preserve the male tradition in Russia. Most obviously, the respect he earned as a dancer had a positive impact on the young male Russian dancers. His skill in assembling enchaînements was another important factor. Marius Petipa, also considered an architect of the Russian school, was appointed first ballet master of the Imperial Theatres in 1862. He made female variations the focus of his choreography and had difficulty creating male solos. Frequently, male dancers who were dissatisfied with the variations composed for them by Petipa would turn to Johansson for advice and specific combinations. Petipa, too, considered Johansson a master of choreographic variety, and was known to observe his classes in search of inspiration and steps.

Christian Johansson assumed the post of principal teacher at the Imperial Ballet School in 1869 and is reputed to be one of the most revered ballet masters in its history. Johansson's teaching wove the brilliance of the Danish school into the softness of the French style that was so familiar to the Russian dancers. Technical elements introduced by Johansson included greater use of ballon, precise batterie, and brilliant pirouettes executed in a variety of positions. He accompanied his own classes, playing the violin, and rarely praised his students' efforts. According to Nikolai Legat, the highest compliment a student could hope to receive was a terse "Now you may perform in public".

Like those of his teacher and mentor, Bournonville, Johansson's classes refected the richness of his vocabulary. His combinations are frequently described as intricate, exceedingly complicated, and musically challenging. Renowned for his ability to invent enchaînements, Johansson is said never to have repeated an exercise. In contrast, the classes of Enrico Cecchetti followed a set weekly pattern with a specific daily focus. Cecchetti, an Italian, began to teach at the Imperial School in 1892. His assigned task was to impart to the Russians the virtuoso technical skills developed by the Italians. Cecchetti's methodology was based on continued repetition of material, the antithesis of Johansson's approach. Yet one section of Cecchetti's class broke with his preferred format: the daily unseen enchaînements. It is possible that this aspect of his teaching was inspired by Johansson's example. Both Johansson and Cecchetti designed ever-changing combinations to accommodate the needs of individual pupils. Their pedagogy differed in that Johansson approached his entire lesson in this manner; Cecchetti restricted his unseen combinations to the allegro portion of the class.

In his last years of teaching, Johansson led the Class of Perfection, restricted to the best graduates who were already performing on the stage of the Imperial Theatre. It would be this generation of Russian dancers who would herald the arrival of the Russian school: a hybrid of French, Danish, and Italian strengths. Interestingly, the three men who played vital roles in this development all left the employ of the Imperial Theatre within a two-year period. Cecchetti, guardian of the Italian technical tradition, left in 1902, while Petipa, the Frenchman, retired in 1903, the same year in which Johansson, who represented the Danish school, died. It was the end of an era. The Russian dancers and ballet masters who for so long had assimilated the styles of others were now on the threshold of having their own school perceived and respected as a separate entity. Christian Johansson, who influenced the Russians first as a performer and then as a teacher, was one of many involved in the evolutionary process which culminated in the establishment and recognition of the Russian school.

—Norma Sue Fisher-Stitt

---

**JOHNSON, Virginia**

American dancer. Born Virginia Alma Fairfax Johnson in Washington, D.C., 25 January 1950. Studied at the Washington School of Ballet, pupil of Therrell Smith and Mary Day, from 1953; later studied with Arthur Mitchell, Karel Shook, New York. Dancer, Dance Theatre of Harlem, from 1969, becoming soloist, and eventually leading company ballerina, with tours abroad including Festival of Two Worlds, Spoleto, Italy, from 1971, London, from 1974, U.S.S.R., 1988; also guest artist, including for Washington Ballet and Capitol Ballet, Washington, D.C., Stars of the World Ballet, touring Australia, 1979, Chicago Opera Ballet, 1975, Baltimore Civic Youth Ballet, Detroit Symphony, Cleveland Ballet, 1991, and Royal Ballet, 1992; has also appeared on television, including in Public Broadcasting Service (PBS) "Dance in America" series and as dancer and choreographer of television film *Ancient Voices of Children.* Recipient: Young Achiever Award, National Council of Women, 1985; Outstanding Young Woman of America, 1985; *Dance Magazine* Award, 1991.

**ROLES**

1970 Pas de trois (cr) in *Holberg Suite* (Mitchell), Dance Theatre of Harlem, New York
Pas de deux (cr) in *Tones* (Mitchell), Dance Theatre of Harlem, New York
Principal dancer (cr) in *Fun and Games* (Mitchell), Dance Theatre of Harlem, New York
1971 Principal dancer (cr) in *Rhythmetron* (Mitchell), Dance Theatre of Harlem, New York
Principal dancer (cr) in *Fête noire* (Mitchell), Dance Theatre of Harlem, New York
The Woman in *The Beloved* (Horton), Dance Theatre of Harlem, New York
1972 "Shout" solo in *Forces of Rhythm* (L. Johnson), Dance Theatre of Harlem, New York
1973 "Coo" in *Wings* (L. Johnson), Dance Theatre of Harlem, New York
Earth Goddess (cr) in *Haiku* (Raines), Dance Theatre of Harlem, New York

**Virginia Johnson as Giselle, Dance Theatre of Harlem**

Principal dancer (cr) in *Bélé* (Holder), Dance Theatre of Harlem, New York
Carmen in *Carmen and José* (Page), Dance Theatre of Harlem and Chicago Ballet
1974 Pas de deux in *Wings* (L. Johnson), Dance Theatre of Harlem
Woman in Green in *Dougla* (Holder), Dance Theatre of Harlem
Principal dancer in *Allegro Brillante* (Balanchine), Dance Theatre of Harlem, Manchester, England
1975 Ballerina in *Don Quixote Pas de deux* (Shook after Petipa), Dance Theatre of Harlem, New York
Glauce (cr) in After Corinth (Raines), Dance Theatre of Harlem, New York
1977 Principal dancer in *(Tchaikovsky) Pas de deux* (Balanchine), Dance Theatre of Harlem
1979 Principal dancer in *Serenade* (Balanchine), Dance Theatre of Harlem, New York
Sanguinic in *The Four Temperaments* (Balanchine), Dance Theatre of Harlem, New York
1981 Zobéïde in *Schéhérazade* (Franklin after Fokine), Dance Theatre of Harlem, New York
Principal dancer in *The Greatest* (Mitchell), Dance Theatre of Harlem, New York
1982 Blanche Dubois in *A Streetcar Named Desire* (Bettis), Dance Theatre of Harlem, New York
The dancer in *Songs of the Auvergne* (solo; Holder), Dance Theatre of Harlem, New York
Title role in *Firebird* (Taras), Dance Theatre of Harlem, New York
Desdemona in *Othello* (Butler), Dance Theatre of Harlem, Spoleto
1983 The Accused in *Fall River Legend* (de Mille), Dance Theatre of Harlem, New York
Adagietto ("La Garçonne") in *Les Biches* (Nijinska), Dance Theatre of Harlem, New York
Principal dancer in *Sylvia Pas de deux* (Franklin), Dance Theatre of Harlem, New York
1984 Title role (cr) in *Giselle* (new production; Mitchell, Franklin after Petipa, Coralli, Perrot), Dance Theatre of Harlem, London
Principal dancer in *Voluntaries* (Tetley), Dance Theatre of Harlem, New York
1986 Principal dancer (cr) in *Toccata a due Canzone* (McFall), Dance Theatre of Harlem, New York
Principal dancer (cr) in *Footprints Dressed in Red* (Fagan), Dance Theatre of Harlem, New York
1991 Principal dancer (cr) in *Ginastera* (Wilson), Dance Theatre of Harlem, New York
Principal dancer (cr) in *Dialogues* (Tetley), Dance Theatre of Harlem, Washington D.C.

**Other roles include:** Pas de trois from *Designs with Strings* (Taras), Swan Queen in *Swan Lake* (Act II; Franklin after Ivanov), principal dancer in *The Greatest Love of All* (pas de deux; Mitchell); leading roles in *Invasion* (Maldoom), *Mirage* (*The Games People Play*) (Wilson), principal dancer in *Concerto Barocco* (Balanchine), pas de deux in *Agon* (Balanchine), principal dancer in *Greening* (Tetley), ballerina in *Paquita* (pas de deux; Danilova, Franklin after Petipa), pas de dix from *Raymonda* (Petipa; staged Franklin, Danilova), principal dancer in *Bugaku* (Balanchine), Kitri in *Don Quixote* Pas de deux (after Petipa).

**PUBLICATIONS**

By Johnson:
Interview in Hunt, Marilyn, "Offstage View: Virginia Johnson as Herself", *Dance Magazine* (New York), October 1990

About Johnson:
Bakst, Fan Graf, "Virginia Johnson of the Dance Theatre of Harlem", *Dance News* (New York), January 1980
Vaughan, David, "Dance Theatre of Harlem", *Dance Magazine* (New York), April 1981
Finkel, Anita, "Dream Dancer", *Ballet News* (New York), January 1983
Kendall, Elizabeth, "Dance Theatre of Harlem at 20", *Dance Magazine* (New York), June 1989

* * *

When Virginia Johnson joined the Dance Theatre of Harlem in 1969, there were just four dancers in the company working with its founder, Arthur Mitchell, in the basement of a church. Therein began a long professional relationship which has demonstrated her loyalty to the company and to classical ballet itself. Johnson, who had been a student of dance at New York University at the time, has remained throughout her career with Dance Theatre of Harlem, gaining status as a major ballerina and exhibiting a range of roles that would be impossible to duplicate in any other company.

Virginia Johnson's early training in dance began at the Washington, D.C. School of Ballet, and her love for dance—and for ballet in particular—can be traced to her first instruction with the teacher and choreographer Mary Day.

For many years, before the existence of Dance Theatre, it was questionable whether a black dancer, no matter how talented, could be justly served in classical ballet. Opportunities in modern dance or jazz dancing were more frequent. The Dance Theatre of Harlem changed this considerably. As a charter member, Virginia Johnson became involved in building a serious company—a historic company that would make it possible for her to become a full-time dancer, and a professional one at that.

Dancing her first solo in 1974, she performed in works choreographed by Mitchell, John Taras, and Louis Johnson, moving from soloist to ballerina to prima ballerina. During her first decade with the company, many of the ballets were those of George Balanchine, for whom Mitchell had danced during his stay with the New York City Ballet. Tall (5′ 8″), elegant, and beautiful, with exceptionally long legs and arms, Johnson was seen to distinct advantage in the Balanchine pieces, bringing a clarity and sleekness to the difficulties of *Agon*, *The Four Temperaments*, and *Concerto Barocco*. Essentially a lyric dancer, she found it often necessary to expand and challenge her technique to meet the demands of other Balanchine ballets that were being added to the company's roster, such as the Tchaikovsky *Pas de deux* and *Allegro Brilliante*.

In the 1980s, the Dance Theatre of Harlem began to stress the theatre of its title and brought into its repertory several dance dramas. Wishing to be a dancer, as she put it, in "every part of myself", Johnson undertook several new roles. As the Accused in *Fall River Legend*, she was able to portray the repressed tension with an intensity that went beyond technique.

The role of Blanche Dubois in Valerie Bettis's *A Streetcar Named Desire* increased Johnson's extraordinarily diversified range. Johnson's Blanche was effective, if perhaps softened by a classic complacency, a restraint inherent in her dancing that has kept her at times from entering totally into the character.

She has danced the dramatic roles beautifully, but perhaps too beautifully to expose the true force of their emotions. This same restraint has sometimes inhibited other performances that call for pure flash and bravura, such as the *Don Quixote* Pas de deux. The contemporary choreography of Glen Tetley, John Butler, and Geoffrey Holder, however, have presented her at her best, as has Bronislava Nijinska's *Les Biches*. To complete the picture, Johnson has excelled as a romantic ballerina. The Dance Theatre's production of the full-length *Giselle* was an important milestone for the company—a full-length classic re-set in the Bayou country of Louisiana. This re-interpretation, admittedly a risky undertaking, proved a huge success, as did Johnson's Giselle. As a dancer, she showed new skill incorporating the nineteenth-century romantic style and technique into the "Creole" identity of her Giselle.

Part of Arthur Mitchell's original decree for his Dance Theatre was the stated belief that "we are artists who happen to be black—not a novelty". Virginia Johnson's dedication to that company for over twenty years has enabled her audience to see a ballerina develop, modify, and shape her own artistry to prove that credo.

—Richard Rutledge

---

**JONES, Marilyn**

Australian dancer, choreographer, ballet director, and teacher. Born in Newcastle, New South Wales, 14 February 1940. Studied with Tess Maunder, Lorraine Norton, and Peggy van Praagh, Australia; also studied at the Royal Ballet School, London, 1956. Married dancer Garth Welch (later div.): two sons, Stanton and Damien. Dancer, Royal Ballet, London, 1957; soloist, Beth Dean's Arts Council Ballet, touring Australia, 1957–58, also performing with Robert Pomie's Ballet Français; soloist, Borovansky Ballet, 1959–61; soloist, becoming étoile, International Ballet of the Marquis de Cuevas, 1961–62; ballerina, touring Angola, Mozambique, and Nice with small company led by Serge Golovine, 1962; prima ballerina, Australian Ballet, 1962–72; guest artist, London Festival Ballet, 1963; choreographer, producing *Sylvia* for Ballet Theatre of Queensland, 1974; guest artist, eventually returning as resident principal, Australian Ballet, 1974–78; artistic director, Australian Ballet, 1979–83; guest artist, Queensland Ballet, 1988 and 1991. Recipient: Order of the British Empire, 1972; Australian Artists Creative Fellowship, 1989; Honorary Doctorate in Music, University of Newcastle, New South Wales, 1992.

**ROLES**

1957 Garland Dance, Vision Scene in *The Sleeping Beauty* (Petipa; staged Sergeyev, Ashton, de Valois), Royal Ballet, New York

"Vision" Diana in *Sylvia* (Ashton), Royal Ballet, New York

1957/58 Mazurka, pas de deux in *Les Sylphides* (Fokine), Beth Dean company, Australian tour

Soloist in *Coppélia*, Act II (after Petipa), Beth Dean company, Australian tour

Marie Taglioni in *Pas de quatre* (Dean), Beth Dean company, Australian tour

Soloist in *Botany Bay* (Dean), Beth Dean company, Australian tour

Soloist in *G'Day Digger* (Dean), Beth Dean company, Australian tour

Principal dancer in *Le Surf* (Pomie), Robert Pomie's Ballet Français, Australian tour

Principal dancer in *Étude classique* (pas de deux; Pomie), Robert Pomie's Ballet Français, Australian tour

Principal dancer in *Death Cell* (Pomie), Robert Pomie's Ballet Français, Australian tour

Pas de deux in *Giselle*, Act II (after Petipa, Coralli, Perrot), Robert Pomie's Ballet Français, Australian tour

Grand pas de deux in *The Sleeping Beauty*, Act III (after Petipa), Robert Pomie's Ballet Français, Australian tour

1959 Princess Aurora in *The Sleeping Princess* (Petipa), Borovansky Ballet, Sydney

1960 Bonnie Sugarbun (cr) in *Journey to the Moon* (Grinwis), Borovansky Ballet, Sydney

Queen of the Wilis in *Giselle* (Petipa after Coralli, Perrot), Borovansky Ballet, Sydney

Love in *The Eternal Lovers* (Grinwis), Borovansky Ballet, Sydney

Odette in *Swan Lake*, Act II (after Ivanov), Borovansky Ballet, Sydney

Variation, Adagio des amoureux in *Les Rendezvous* (Ashton; staged van Praagh), Borovansky Ballet, Melbourne

1961 Lilac Fairy in *The Sleeping Beauty* (Petipa; staged Nijinska), Grand Ballet (International Ballet) du Marquis de Cuevas, Paris

Princess Aurora in *The Sleeping Beauty*, Act I (Petipa; staged Nijinska), Grand Ballet (International Ballet) du Marquis de Cuevas, Paris

Principal dancer in *Constantia* (Dollar), Grand Ballet (International Ballet) du Marquis de Cuevas, Israel

Title role in *The Dying Swan* (after Fokine), Grand Ballet (International Ballet) du Marquis de Cuevas, Hamburg

1962 Title role in *The Black Swan* Pas de deux (Petipa), Grand Ballet (International Ballet) du Marquis de Cuevas, Cannes

Principal dancer in *Suite en blanc* (Lifar), Grand Ballet (International Ballet) du Marquis de Cuevas, Cannes

Pas de deux from *The Nutcracker* (after Ivanov), Grand Ballet (International Ballet) du Marquis de Cuevas, Cannes

Odette/Odile in *Swan Lake* (after Petipa, Ivanov), Australian Ballet, Sydney

Female Clown in *One in Five* (Powell), Australian Ballet, Sydney

Swanilda in *Coppélia* (van Praagh after Petipa, Cecchetti), Australian Ballet, Sydney

Principal dancer in *Don Quixote* Pas de deux (after Petipa), Australian Ballet, Perth

La Capricciosa in *The Lady and the Fool* (Cranko), Australian Ballet, Sydney

1963 Ingrid in *Peer Gynt* (Orlikovsky), London Festival Ballet, London

Persian Princess in *Polovtsian Dances from Prince Igor* (Fokine), London Festival Ballet, London

Sugar Plum Fairy in *The Nutcracker* (Lichine), Australian Ballet, Melbourne

1964 Blue (cr) in *Jazz Spectrum* (Pounder), Australian Ballet, Adelaide Festival of the Arts, Adelaide
Title role in *Giselle* (Petipa after Coralli, Perrot; staged van Praagh), Australian Ballet, Perth
Pas de deux from *Flower Festival at Genzano* (Bournonville; staged Gnatt), Australian Ballet, Sydney
1965 Title role in *Esmeralda* Pas de deux (Welch after Petipa), Australian Ballet, Adelaide
Title role in *Raymonda* (Nureyev after Petipa), Australian Ballet, Birmingham, England
Principal dancer in *Le Corsaire* Pas de deux (Petipa), Australian Ballet, London
1966 Principal dancer (cr) in *Illyria* (Welch), Australian Ballet, Adelaide
1967 Lise in *La Fille mal gardée* (Ashton), Australian Ballet, Sydney
Principal dancer in *Ballet Imperial* (Balanchine), Australian Ballet, Sydney
1968 The Experienced in *Threshold* (Butler), Australian Ballet, Sydney
1970 Principal dancer in *Serenade* (Balanchine), Australian Ballet, Adelaide Festival, Adelaide
Pas de deux (Skater in White) in *Les Patineurs* (Ashton), Australian Ballet, Adelaide
Queen of the Dryads in *Don Quixote* (Nureyev after Petipa), Australian Ballet, Adelaide
Kitri in *Don Quixote* (Nureyev after Petipa), Australian Ballet, Sydney
Principal dancer in *Symphony in Gold* (Powell), Australian Ballet, Sydney
Desdemona in *Othello* (Welch), Australian Ballet, Adelaide
1971 Principal dancer in *Mam'zelle Angot* (Massine), Australian Ballet, Melbourne
1972 Principal dancer in *Woman of Andros* (Welch), Western Australian Ballet Company, Perth
1974 Juliet in *Romeo and Juliet* (Cranko), Australian Ballet, Sydney
1975 Principal dancer (cr) in *Night Encounter* (Butler), Australian Ballet, Sydney
Trois Gymnopédies in *Monotones* (Ashton), Australian Ballet, Brisbane
Eleanor Rigby (cr) in *The Fool on the Hill* (Lynne), Australian Ballet, Australian television
The Widow in *The Merry Widow* (Hynd), Australian Ballet, Melbourne
1976 Principal dancer in *Gemini* (Tetley), Australian Ballet, Brisbane
Titania in *The Dream* (Ashton), Australian Ballet, Melbourne
1977 Tatania in *Onegin* (Cranko), Australian Ballet, Melbourne
1978 Principal dancer in *Afternoon of a Faun* (Robbins), Australian Ballet, Sydney
1986 Carlotta Grisi in *Pas de quatre* (Dolin), Australian Ballet, Sydney
1988 Principal dancer (cr) in *Once Around the Sun* (Collins-Buckman), Queensland Ballet, Brisbane
1991 The Mother (cr) in *Of Blessed Memory* (Welch), Australian Ballet, Melbourne
Lady Capulet in *Romeo and Juliet* (Cranko), Australian Ballet, Sydney

**Other roles include:** principal dancer in *Monkeys in a Cage* (Asker), Elisa in *Konservatoriet* (*Le Conservatoire*; Bournonville), principal dancer in *Sacred Space* (Moreland), Débutante in *Melbourne Cup* (Reid).

## WORKS

1974 *Sylvia* (mus. Delibes), Ballet Theatre of Queensland, Brisbane

## PUBLICATIONS

Cook, Michael, *Swan Lake: The Making of a Ballerina*, Sydney, 1978
Laughlin, Patricia, *Marilyn Jones: A Brilliance All Her Own*, Melbourne, 1978
"Marilyn Jones, OBE", *Dance Gazette* (London), June 1979
Pask, Edward, H., *Ballet in Australia: The Second Act*, Melbourne, 1982
Munday, Rosemary, *The Australian Ballet: 25 Years*, Sydney, 1987
Baum, Caroline, *Artists of the Australian Ballet*, 1989

* * *

Marilyn Jones is generally considered to be Australia's finest classical dancer. A versatile ballerina who combined classic purity with natural interpretive ability, she excelled equally in traditional classics, intensely dramatic roles and, where necessary, works of light-hearted humour.

Physically, Jones was ideally suited to classical dance. Although a little taller than many ballerinas, her body was perfectly proportioned for a dancer, with long limbs and neck. This, combined with lovely, expressive face and eyes, and beautiful legs and feet, made a picture of classical perfection which has now become legendary.

Marilyn Jones's dancing career can be divided into four phases. The first was when she made her Australian professional début dancing with the Borovansky Ballet during its final tour. At the time she was nineteen years old—technically very strong, beautiful to look at, but still a little raw around the edges. In her first performance of the role of Princess Aurora in *The Sleeping Beauty*, these qualities were noted, and so was her instinctive musical understanding.

The second phase of the ballerina's career took her to Europe, where she danced with the International Ballet of the Marquis de Cuevas. The de Cuevas company was an exciting and glamorous one and numbered many famous dancers in its ranks. Arriving as a virtually unknown young Australian dancer, Jones received much acclaim when very soon she was given principal roles and was awarded the rank of étoile at the age of 21. This company occasionally cast different ballerinas in each act of *The Sleeping Beauty*, and Jones first danced Act I, and then the vision scene in Act II (partnered by Rudolf Nureyev, who had only recently arrived in the West), before essaying the full ballet. Also at this time she danced her first Odette in Act II of *Swan Lake*, as well as the *Black Swan* pas de deux from Act III.

The poise and maturity gained from this European experience was evident when Jones returned to Australia in 1962 to join the newly founded Australian Ballet. Beginning with a notable performance in the dual Odette/Odile role in *Swan Lake*, she gradually increased her repertoire and began to demonstrate her versatility.

Over the next ten years Jones became the undisputed "queen" of Australian ballet. She was a gentle, moving Giselle, but sparkled like a diamond in Balanchine's *Ballet Imperial*. Her performance as La Capricciosa in John Cranko's *The Lady and the Fool* will always be remembered, and during that decade she also acquired one of her finest roles—Lise, in Frederick Ashton's *La Fille mal gardée*. It was not in her nature to play this part as a straight soubrette. Although funny where she needed to be, her Lise had a gentle, sweet side as well, and this gave a special quality to the whole ballet which is missed when dancers interpret Lise as a pert soubrette.

It is this special quality that has always set Marilyn Jones apart from other fine dancers, and it reflects her honest and unassuming personality. Her interpretations are instinctive—it is acting that goes beyong acting. When performing, she becomes so totally immersed in a role that she is unaware of anything or anyone outside it. She has never embellished her dancing or interpretations with exaggerated flourishes, nor has she tried to milk applause from an audience. In her simple, modest way, she has darted away from individual curtain calls, almost embarrassed by cheers and applause.

The third—and finest—phase of Jones's career began in 1974, when she returned to dancing after two years in retirement. She had suffered great personal unhappiness during this period, and because of the instinctive nature of her artistry, her experience lent added emotional depth to her dramatic interpretations. Two of her greatest roles came at this time: Tatiana in Cranko's *Onegin* and Juliet in the same choreographer's version of *Romeo and Juliet*. She has not been equalled in Australia in either of these roles. On a lighter plane, she was delightful in Ronald Hynd's *The Merry Widow*.

Jones had a special gift for establishing partnerships; this was partly because she identified so completely with her character, and maintained such genuine eye contact with her partner, that she drew from him a similar commitment, and this led to some unforgettable performances. Three of these partnerships stand out—those with Garth Welch during the 1960s, and with John Meehan and Jonathan Kelly in the 1970s.

Marilyn Jones retired from dancing at the end of 1978 because of problems with her achilles tendons. Although teaching is now her principal occupation, a fourth phase of her dancing career has blossomed in recent years. She has made cameo appearances, as a guest artist, with the Australian Ballet in gala seasons and with the Queensland Ballet in several roles specially created for her. Her special quality is still evident and a new generation of dancers and audiences marvels at those legendary legs and feet.

One factor prevented Marilyn Jones from achieving the full recognition she deserved when dancing in her prime: no new ballets were created especially for her. Sadly, the Australian Ballet has not yet developed its own choreographer to utilize and develop the talent and style of its artists. Marilyn Jones deserved a choreographer who could have done for her what Frederick Ashton did for Margot Fonteyn, created roles with her unique qualities in mind and in which she left indelible memories. Jones has had a wonderful career, but because of this she was never given the opportunity to reach her full potential.

—Patricia Laughlin

---

## JOSEPH THE BEAUTIFUL

(Original Russian title: *Iosef Prekrasny*)

**Choreography:** Kasyan Goleizovsky
**Music:** Sergei Vassilenko
**Design:** Boris Erdman
**Libretto:** Kasyan Goleizovsky
**First Production:** Bolshoi Ballet, Experimental Theatre, Moscow, 3 March 1925

**Principal Dancers:** Lyubov Bank (Tayakh), Vasily Yefimov (Joseph)

**Other productions include:** Odessa Theatre for Opera and Ballet; Odessa, 1926. Kharkov Theatre for Opera and Ballet; Kharkov, 1926.

### PUBLICATIONS


Lawson, Joan, "A Short History of Soviet Ballet", *Dance Index* (New York), June/July 1943

Swift, Mary Grace, *The Art of Dance in the Soviet Union*, Notre Dame, Indiana, 1968

Banes, Sally, "Goleizovsky's Ballet Manifestos", *Ballet Review* (New York), Fall 1983

Manor, Giora, "Kasyan Goleizovsky's Russian Revolution", *Dance Magazine* (New York), February 1989

Souritz, Elizabeth, *The Art of Choreography in the 1920s*, Moscow, 1979; as *Soviet Choreographers in the 1920s*, translated by Lynn Visson, Durham, N.C. and London, 1990


* * *

*Joseph the Beautiful* was the most important ballet by Kasyan Goleizovsky, and was produced by the Bolshoi company in the Experimental Theatre (a theatre affiliated with the Bolshoi Theatre) in early 1925. It was a ballet in two acts. The first act took place in Canaan, the native land of Joseph. Joseph was shown as a poetic youth, a dreamer responsive to beauty and goodness. His brothers, appearing next to him in the first act, were shown as primitive and crude people whose weapons are deceit and physical force. In the story, the brothers abduct Joseph, and sell him to Egyptian slave-drivers. In the second act, in the court of the Pharaoh, Joseph is pitted against the unconquerable force of the despot: when the Pharaoh's wife Tayakh tries to seduce him, and he resists, she denounces him to her husband, declaring that he has offended her honour. Joseph is condemned to death. Into the abyss into which he is to be thrown he leaps of his own accord.

*Joseph the Beautiful* was the culmination of all the experiments Goleizovsky had conducted in his own studio and with its performing group, the Chamber Ballet, from 1921 on. The theme of protest against force, and the theme of freedom of feeling—repeatedly developed by Goleizovsky in dances and ballet miniatures at the Chamber Ballet—became the definitive element in this production. It showed the struggle for human dignity which, in its nobility, eventually undermines despotic power. Here, after the earth has swallowed Joseph, the entire pyramid of the Pharaoh's court is scattered into pieces.

Goleizovsky's ballet continued thematically from his earlier pieces, but it also developed further the formal experiments which had been occupying him. Goleizovsky had been the first choreographer to use, as early as 1922, a constructivist décor in his dances *The Faun* and *Salomé*. He insisted that the set design for dance should not be scenery, as such, but part of the dance composition itself, a way to amplify movement. In *Joseph the Beautiful*, Boris Erdman built several small platforms, positioned at various levels and connected by little bridges, as the setting for the first act. They suggested the hills of Canaan, but they also served, especially in the ensemble dances, to create fanciful patterns of dancers, with performers standing, sitting, or lying down, their lines stretching from one platform to the next. In the second act, the platforms were mounted in an absolutely symmetrical pyramid, its several levels suggesting the hierarchy of the court: in the centre of this enormous triangle towered the Pharaoh, with his numerous couriers frozen in sycophantic immobility below.

In *Joseph the Beautiful*, as in his earlier works, Goleizovsky used dance which had classical ballet as its basis; yet it was not made into the traditional (and somewhat stale) compositions which one was accustomed to see on the academic stage. Taking off from the ballet technique which the classical school had given him, Goleizovsky invented daring, even dangerous, movements not seen before in ballet. He looked at old dance forms in new ways, turned them in unexpected directions, and put them into unprecedented sequences. Many of the dancers performed movements while sitting or lying down (which gave the choreographer's opponents occasion to grumble about dancers "lolling about on the floor"). Goleizovsky also insisted that a dancer's costume should reveal as much of the body as possible, thus bringing about accusations of excessive, even pornographic, eroticism in his work.

*Joseph the Beautiful* caused a wide split at the Bolshoi Theatre. The younger dancers, headed by Lyubov Bank and Vasily Yemifov (who danced Tayakh and Joseph), as well as Mikhail Gabovich, Igor Moiseyev, and Asaf Messerer, were enthusiastic about the ballet. But those in control of the company—Vasily Tikhomirov, Ivan Smoltzov, Leonid Zhukov, and others—along with many of the older generation, conspired to throw the ballet out of the repertory. Dozens of letters still exist in the Bolshoi's archives, showing the struggle between Goleizovsky and the Directorate, forbidding dancers to appear in such revealing costumes, forcing them to wear knitted shirts and tights, ordering the choreographer to make changes in his dances. Goleizovsky, in turn, answered with threats and ultimata.

In May 1925 an episode occured at the Bolshoi which became known as the "revolt" of the younger generation, who were protesting more generally against the leadership of the company and its politics. Some of the dancers were fired, but later taken back into the company. This struggle lasted for a whole year, and ended in the spring of 1926 with Goleizovsky departing for the Ukraine. There, in Odessa, and later in Kharkov, he mounted his own productions of *Joseph the Beautiful*. By that time it was no longer produced at the Bolshoi and it was never produced again: throughout the 1930s and even up to the 1960s, Goleizovsky was a *persona non grata* in Soviet ballet—a "formalist" and an "aesthete" whose art was not consistent with official socialist realism.

—Elizabeth Souritz

## THE JUDGMENT OF PARIS

**Choreography:** Antony Tudor
**Music:** Kurt Weill (from *The Threepenny Opera*)
**Design:** Hugh Laing (scenery and costumes)
**Libretto:** Hugh Laing
**First Production:** London Ballet, Westminster Theatre, London, 15 June 1938 (originally performed for Solo Concert by Agnes de Mille)
**Principal Dancers:** Agnes de Mille (Venus), Thérèse Langfield (Juno), Charlotte Bidmead (Minerva), Antony Tudor (The Client), Hugh Laing (The Waiter)

**Other productions include:** Ballet Rambert (restaged Tudor); Arts Theatre, London, 1 October 1940. Ballet Theatre (restaged Tudor; design Hugh Laing), with Agnes de Mille (Venus), Viola Essen (Juno), Lucia Chase (Minerva), Antony Tudor (The Client), Hugh Laing (The Waiter); New York, 23 January 1940. Gala Benefit for Dance Collection of New York Public Library, with Agnes de Mille, Lucia Chase, Maria Karnilova; New York, 24 January 1972.

### PUBLICATIONS

Menuhin, Diana, "The Varying Moods of Tudor", *Dance and Dancers* (London), July 1955
Percival, John, *Antony Tudor: A Young Man's Ballets*, Dance Perspectives 17, New York, 1963
Maynard, Olga, "Souvenir of a Gala Performance", *Dance Magazine* (New York), April 1972
Balanchine, George, with Mason, Francis, *Balanchine's Complete Stories of the Great Ballets*, Garden City, N.Y., 1977
Clarke, Mary, "Rambert in Wartime", *Dancing Times* (London), July 1990
Perlmutter, Donna, *Shadowplay: Antony Tudor's Life in Dance*, London, 1991

* * *

*The Judgment of Paris* is a bitingly satirical treatment of the ancient Greek myth of the three goddesses competing for the golden apple, the award from Paris to the most beautiful. The story is altered almost beyond recognition, and indeed, without the title, the original myth might not come to mind at all, despite the fact that in essence there remains a strong connection with it. In a sleazy Parisian bar at the turn of the century, three ageing prostitutes (Juno, Minerva, and Venus), drag themselves through their tired routines in competition for the custom of the bar's one patron, who is rapidly descending into drunken oblivion. No prize is awarded in this sordid contest—but the three whores, as well as the waiter, fall upon the customer as soon as he lapses into unconsciousness, ridding him of all valuables.

Characteristically, Tudor disguised the true squalor of the whole story by means of perceptive and humorous comments on the three prostitutes, shown in their individual dances and in the details of their relationships with one other: they are competitors, but colleagues with more in common among themselves than with any passing customer. As in *Gala Performance*, which followed the year after *The Judgment of Paris*, the movement vocabulary and structure of dances demonstrate a keen perception of social conventions and character idiosyncracies which pertain to the setting—and this is allowed to introduce the leaven of humour into what would otherwise be a shockingly depressing story. All the same, shocking is what it surely intended to be; it is not a rollicking burlesque, properly sanitized and protective of audience sensibilities. The humour makes us laugh despite ourselves, even at the time when we are horrified by the sordid inevitability of it all.

The ballet was made at the request of Agnes de Mille, to form a curtain-raiser to her own solo recital; and it was later taken into the repertoire of Tudor's own company, the short-lived London Ballet. This company presented a season of fortnightly performances in the Toynbee Hall, London, during 1938 and 1939, with programmes almost exclusively of Tudor's own work. Lack of resources prevented the full realization of this aim, but even so it can be seen that with *The Judgment of Paris* alongside, for example, *Jardin aux lilas*, *Dark Elegies*, *Gala Performance*, and *Gallant Assembly*, Tudor could provide genuinely varied programmes of works. When the London Ballet merged with Ballet Rambert, *The Judgment of Paris*, in common with most other ballets, remained in the joint repertoire and has since been added to the repertoires of several companies, including American Ballet Theatre, for whom Tudor himself produced the ballet.

Tudor told Canadian students in the 1970s that it was "a rather evil take-off" of Ashton's "neo-classic" version, made very shortly before Tudor's. The music for Tudor's version, from Kurt Weill's *The Threepenny Opera*, provides in its seductive rhythms and thinly veiled irony the perfect partner.

As with all of Tudor's work, complete success requires dedicated devotion to choreographic detail and a sensitivity which eschews any temptation to exaggerate for the purpose of gaining a few easy laughs. This ballet can all too easily slip over the edge into burlesque—and once there, it loses its real power. Several subsequent productions of the ballet have failed to realize its promise, because ballerinas have overplayed their roles. The choreography speaks for itself, if allowed to do so.

—Rachel S. Richardson

---

## LE JUGEMENT DE PÂRIS

**Choreography:** Jules Perrot
**Music:** Cesare Pugni
**Design:** Charles Marshall
**First Production:** Her Majesty's Theatre, London, 23 July 1846
**Principal Dancers:** Marie Taglioni, Lucile Grahn, Fanny Cerrito (Goddesses), Arthur Saint-Léon (Pâris), Jules Perrot (Mercury)

**Other productions include:** Bolshoi Theatre (restaged and expanded Perrot), as *Le Soucis du maître de ballet*; St. Petersburg, 18 February 1851.

**Other choreographic treatments of story:** Jean-Georges Noverre (Marseilles, c. 1755, and Milan, 1775), Pierre Gardel (Paris, 1793).

### PUBLICATIONS


Michel, Artur, "*Pas de quatre* 1845–1945", *Dance Magazine* (New York), July 1945

Beaumont, Cyril, *Complete Book of Ballets*, revised edition, London, 1951

Guest, Ivor, *The Romantic Ballet in England*, London, 1954

Guest, Ivor, *Fanny Cerrito*, London, 1956

Guest, Ivor, *Jules Perrot: Master of the Romantic Ballet*, London, 1984


* * *

The tremendous success of Perrot's divertissement ballet of 1845, *Pas de Quatre*, made the creation of such works during ensuing years a season highlight. The purpose of divertisse-

***Le Jugement de Pâris*, with Fanny Cerrito, Marie Taglioni, Lucile Grahn, and Arthur Saint-Léon, Her Majesty's Theatre, London, 1846**

ments was to show off the talents of the star ballerinas present at Her Majesty's Theatre, London; however, they also offered Jules Perrot an opportunity to create dances pure and simple. It is a tribute to Perrot's outstanding skill as a ballet master that observers saw beyond the brilliance of the fabulously popular ballerinas to the high excellence of his choreography. "The pas is a vastly complicated affair," wrote one critic of *Le Jugement*, "and the combinations are unquestionably of a more attractive character than any Perrot has yet invented, the multiplicity of individuals concerned in it giving both breadth and originality to the groupings."

*Le Jugement de Pâris*, in which the shepherd Pâris presides over a beauty contest between three goddesses, was not a new ballet theme. Pierre Gardel had employed it to great effect at the Paris Opéra when classical themes were all the rage in 1793. It is curious that in the midst of the Romantic era, Perrot should have chosen such a theme. Perhaps the classical simplicity of the storyless format suggested a classical setting. Whatever the case, the story was a natural for ballet, since the beauty contest readily became a dance contest, in this instance between the reigning goddesses at Her Majesty's Theatre—Marie Taglioni, Lucile Grahn, and Fanny Cerrito as the Goddesses.

The most significant difference between *Le Jugement* and *Pas de quatre* was that the former ballet introduced a corps de ballet of seven, as well as two men, Jules Perrot as Mercury and Arthur Saint-Léon as Pâris. Thus the work opened with a series of tableaux consisting of statuesque poses by the corps dancers, "varied with great artistical taste, forming exquisite tableaux of irregular composition, sometimes scattered and sometimes compressed". Only after this choreographic hors d'oeuvre did the goddesses make their entrances, dancing solo and with one another, vying for the golden apple, symbol of victory. There was the "exquisite poetry of Taglioni", the "youthful fire of Cerrito", and the "graceful vigour of Grahn". The men too were impressive. At one point Taglioni, Cerrito, and Grahn enter holding hands "while St. Léon follows behind them, vaulting so high that his head and shoulders are . . . seen above them all . . .". Perrot for his part outdid himself in pirouetting. The finale presented snatches of earlier dances, ending with a statuesque group, Saint-Léon/Pâris standing in the middle holding up the apple. A shepherd of infinite tact, he wisely chose not to insult the goddesses by singling out one as the victor. The audience was left to make up its own mind as to the winner.

—John Chapman

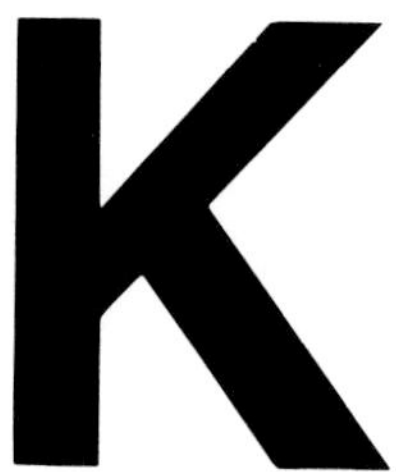

**KAIN, Karen**

Canadian dancer. Born in Hamilton, Ontario, 28 March 1951. Studied at the National Ballet of Canada School, Toronto. Married Ross Petty. Dancer, National Ballet of Canada, from 1969, becoming principal dancer, from 1970; also international guest artist, including for Roland Petit's Ballet National de Marseille, various seasons 1974–82, London Festival Ballet (now English National Ballet), touring Britain and Australia, 1975, Bolshoi Ballet, Soviet tour, 1977, Stuttgart Ballet, 1984, Eliot Feld Company, from 1984, and Vienna State Opera Ballet; also appeared with "Makarova and Company", 1980, on teaching and performance tour of China, 1981, and in numerous galas and concert tours, frequently partnered by Rudolf Nureyev; has also appeared on television, including in "Karen Kain Superspecial", Canadian television (CBC; 1979), and in "100th Anniversary of the Met", American public television (PBS; 1983). Recipient: Silver Medal, International Ballet Competition, Moscow, 1973; Companion of the Order of Canada, 1976; Honorary Doctorates, York University, McMaster University, Trent University, and University of British Columbia.

**ROLES**

1970 Principal dancer in *The Mirror Walkers* (Wright), National Ballet of Canada, Ottawa
1971 Odette/Odile in *Swan Lake* (Bruhn after Petipa, Ivanov), National Ballet of Canada, Arizona
Principal Dancer in *Fandango* (Tudor), National Ballet of Canada, North Bay, Ontario
Principal dancer in *Autumn Song* (Comelin), National Ballet of Canada, Sudbury, Ontario
1972 Principal dancer in *Intermezzo* (Feld), National Ballet of Canada, Windsor, Ontario
Juliet in *Romeo and Juliet* (Cranko), National Ballet of Canada, Toronto
Sugar Plum Fairy in *The Nutcracker* (Franca), National Ballet of Canada, Ottawa
Title role in *The Sleeping Beauty* (Nureyev after Petipa), National Ballet of Canada, Houston
1973 Principal dancer in *Solitaire* (MacMillan), National Ballet of Canada, Windsor, Ontario
Title role in *Giselle* (Petipa after Coralli, Perrot; staged Wright), National Ballet of Canada, Windsor, Ontario
Waltz, Mazurka in *Les Sylphides* (Fokine; staged Franca, Bruhn), National Ballet of Canada, Hamilton, Ontario
1974 The Lady in White in *Don Juan* (Neumeier), National Ballet of Canada, Toronto
Principal dancer (cr) in *Whispers of Darkness* (Vesak), National Ballet of Canada, Toronto
Principal dancer (cr) in *Inventions* (Patsalas), National Ballet of Canada, Toronto
Albertine (cr) in *Intermittences du coeur* (Petit), Ballet National de Marseille, Paris
Title role in *La Sylphide* (Bournonville; staged Bruhn), National Ballet of Canada, New York
1975 Swanilda (cr) in *Coppélia* (new production; Petit), Ballet de Marseilles, Paris
1976 Title role (cr) in *Nana* (Petit), Paris Opéra Ballet, Paris
Swanilda in *Coppélia* (Bruhn after Saint-Léon), National Ballet of Canada, Toronto
1977 Louise (cr) in *Mad Shadows* (Ditchburn), National Ballet of Canada, Toronto
1978 Chosen Maiden (cr) in *The Rite of Spring* (Patsalas), National Ballet of Canada, Toronto
Principal dancer in *Élite Syncopations* (MacMillan), National Ballet of Canada, Toronto
Titania in *The Dream* (Ashton), National Ballet of Canada, Toronto
1980 Lucrece (cr) in *The Rape of Lucrece* (Kudelka), National Ballet of Canada, Toronto
1981 Kitri in *Don Quixote* (Beriozoff after Petipa), National Ballet of Canada, Toronto
The Bride (cr) in *The Seven Daggers* (*Los Siete Punales*; Susana), National Ballet of Canada, Toronto
1982 Guilietta (cr) in *Les Contes d'Hoffman* (Petit), Ballet National de Marseille, Monte Carlo
Dancer in *Nelligan Pas de deux* (Ditchburn), Festival of Two Worlds, Spoleto
1983 Title role in *Sphinx* (Tetley), National Ballet of Canada, Toronto
1984 Tatiana in *Onegin* (Cranko), National Ballet of Canada, Toronto
Principal dancer (cr) in *Oiseaux exotiques* (Patsalas), National Ballet of Canada, Toronto
1986 Title role (cr) in *Alice* (Tetley), National Ballet of Canada, Toronto
Hanna in *The Merry Widow* (Hynd), National Ballet of Canada, Toronto
1987 Principal dancer in *Impromptu* (Feld), Feld Ballet, New York
The Actress (cr) in *La Ronde* (Tetley), National Ballet of Canada, Toronto
Second Movement in *Concerto* (MacMillan), National Ballet of Canada, Toronto
1988 Principal dancer in *Forgotten Land* (Kylián), National Ballet of Canada, Toronto
1989 Lykanion in *Daphnis and Chloë* (Tetley), National Ballet of Canada, Toronto

**Karen Kain in *Onegin*, National Ballet of Canada**

Principal dancer (cr) in *Tagore* (Tetley), National Ballet of Canada, Toronto

**Other roles include:** Desdemona in *The Moor's Pavane* (Limón), Teresina in *Napoli* (Bournonville; staged Schaufuss), ballerina in *Raymonda Pas de Dix* (Balanchine), principal dancer in *Serenade* (Balanchine), *The Four Temperaments* (Balanchine), and *Symphony in C* (Balanchine), ballerina in *Études* (Lander), the girl in *Afternoon of a Faun* (Robbins), Lise in *La Fille mal gardée* (Ashton), title role in *Carmen* (Petit), principal dancer in *Echo* (Feld), *At Midnight* (Feld), and *Straw Hearts* (Feld).

## PUBLICATIONS

Darling, C., and Frazer, J., *Karen Kain and Frank Augustyn*, Toronto, 1977

Street, David, *Karen Kain: Lady of the Dance*, New York, 1978

Zola, Meguido, *Karen Kain: Born to Dance*, Danbury, 1983

* * *

Karen Kain is the first Canadian ballerina to have won a significant international reputation without permanently leaving her homeland. In part this has been the result of circumstance. By the time Kain entered the National Ballet of Canada in 1969, the company was reaching a stage in its artistic development where it was possible for a talented dancer to achieve international recognition within its ranks. Unlike the Canadians Lynn Seymour and Jennifer Penney, who felt it necessary to build their careers in Britain, Kain found the National Ballet both a suitable and appreciative platform for her talent and a secure base to which she could return from her frequent guest engagements abroad.

However, Kain's celebrity, particularly within Canada—where she is a household name—is rooted firmly in a remarkable and distinctive gift for movement. Quite apart from her striking beauty and strong classical technique, Kain's sensitive musicality, dramatic intensity, and versatility has established her as one of the best dancers Canada has ever produced. Her range extends from authoritative interpretations of virtually all the full-length classics, through such Ashton ballets as *La Fille mal gardée* and *The Dream*, to a wide range of contemporary and neo-classical works by Balanchine, MacMillan, Kylián, Feld, and many others.

Kain's abilities had already been acknowledged by her rapid promotion to principal status even before Rudolf Nureyev arrived to stage *The Sleeping Beauty* for the National Ballet of Canada in 1972. Nevertheless, Kain herself credits Nureyev with accelerating her growth and reputation as an artist through his hard-driving encouragement and interest in her career. Although during the 1970s Kain had a very fruitful and popular partnership with her National Ballet colleague Frank Augustyn, her frequent appearances with Nureyev on company tours and in international guest engagements brought her to the attention of a worldwide audience. As a result, during the early part of her career Kain was often invited abroad to dance with such companies as the London Festival Ballet, the Bolshoi, and particularly Roland Petit's Ballet National de Marseille. Petit, in fact, created several major roles for Kain.

The pressure of all this attention, however, in addition to the heavy demands made on her at home, led to a personal crisis and temporary loss of confidence in her own abilities. Although she continued to be the darling of Canadian audiences and one of the National Ballet's most reliable box-office draws, Kain's performances were sometimes less spontaneous and expressive than before.

Fortunately, Kain broke through this difficult period to emerge in the mid-1980s as a mature ballerina of rare authority. Her dancing became more personal and intense, her dramatic interpretations more textured and convincing. Without losing their dynamic excitement, Kain's performances were bathed in a rich sensuality that attracted the particular attention of Glen Tetley, who, during his association with the National Ballet, created roles for her in *Alice*, *La Ronde*, and *Tagore*.

As she entered her third decade with the National Ballet, Kain had already chosen to relinquish certain full-length roles, but her almost undiminished technical powers, combined with an artistry fed by long experience, has continued to secure her place as the National Ballet's most popular ballerina.

—Michael Crabb

---

## KARINSKA, Barbara

Russian/American designer and costumer. Born Varvara Zhmoudska in Kharkov, Ukraine, 3 October 1886. Married (1) Russian newspaper editor in Kharkov; (2) Karinsky: one child, Irena, b. 1924. Left Russia in 1928; seamstress, executing designs by Christian Bérard, André Derain, Salvador Dali, Henri Matisse, Cecil Beaton, and others, Paris, from 1930; went to United States, 1938, working in New York and Hollywood; first independent design commission for George Balanchine, 1949, continuing both to design and to execute costumes for New York City Ballet; also worked as costumer for Ballet Russe de Monte Carlo, Ballet International, Ballet Society, Ballet Theatre, and Ballets des Champs-Elysées; principal costumer for New York City Ballet, 1963–83; also creator of costumes for theatre, including for *Too Many Girls* (1939), *Call Me Madam* (1950), *Can-Can* (1953), *The Girl in Pink Tights* (1954), *Silk Stockings* (1955), *Candide* (1956), and *Becket* (1960); executed costumes for opera, including for Metropolitan Opera, New York, and La Scala, Milan; also worked in Hollywood, executing costumes for films including *Gaslight* (dir. Cukor, 1944), *Frenchman's Creek* (dir. Leisen, 1944), *Joan of Arc* (dir. Fleming, 1948), and *Kismet* (dir. Minnelli, 1955). Recipient: Academy Award (for costumes in *Joan of Arc*), 1948; Capezio Award for Outstanding Contribution to the World of Dance, 1962. Died in New York, 18 October 1983.

**WORKS** (costume design)

1949 *Birthday* (chor. Chamié), Ballet Russe de Monte Carlo, New York
*Bourrée Fantasque* (chor. Balanchine), New York City Ballet, New York
1950 *Prima Ballerina* (chor. Chamié), Ballet Russe de Monte Carlo, Chicago
*Mazurka from "A Life for the Tsar"* (chor. Balanchine), New York City Ballet, New York
*Sylvia: Pas de Deux* (chor. Balanchine), New York City Ballet, New York
*Symphony in C* (chor. Balanchine), New York City Ballet, New York
1951 *Pas de Trois* (chor. Balanchine), New York City Ballet, New York
*La Valse* (chor. Balanchine), New York City Ballet, New York
*Capriccio Brillante* (chor. Balanchine), New York City Ballet, New York
*Lilac Garden* (chor. Tudor), New York City Ballet, New York
*Apollo, Leader of the Muses* (new production; Balanchine), New York City Ballet, New York
1952 *Scotch Symphony* (chor. Balanchine, costumes with Ffolkes), New York City Ballet, New York
*Harlequinade Pas de Deux* (chor. Balanchine), New York City Ballet, New York
*Concertino* (chor. Balanchine), New York City Ballet, New York
*Serenade* (new production; chor. Balanchine), New York City Ballet, New York
1953 *Valse Fantaisie* (chor. Balanchine), New York City Ballet, New York
1954 *Quartet* (chor. Robbins), New York City Ballet, New York
*The Nutcracker* (chor. Balanchine), New York City Ballet, New York
1955 *Western Symphony* (chor. Balanchine), New York City Ballet, New York (ballet premiere without costumes, 1954)
*(Glinka) Pas de Trois* (chor. Balanchine), New York City Ballet, New York
1956 *Divertimento No. 15* (chor. Balanchine), New York City Ballet, Stratford, Connecticut
*Allegro Brillante* (chor. Balanchine), New York City Ballet, New York
1958 *Gounod Symphony* (chor. Balanchine), New York City Ballet, New York
*Stars and Stripes* (chor. Balanchine), New York City Ballet, New York
*Waltz-Scherzo* (chor. Balanchine), New York City Ballet, New York
*Springtime* (chor. Novak), Ballet Russe de Monte Carlo, Chicago
1959 *Slavonic Dances* (chor. Novak), Ballet Russe de Monte Carlo, Seattle
*Episodes* (chor. Graham, Balanchine), New York City Ballet, New York
*Ballad* (chor. Cieplinski), Ballet Russe de Monte Carlo, Pittsburgh
1960 *Sinfonia No. 5* (chor. Balanchine), Part V of *Panamerica* (chor. Balanchine, Contreras, Moncion, Taras,

d'Amboise), New York City Ballet, New York
*(Tchaikovsky) Pas de Deux* (chor. Balanchine), New York City Ballet, New York
*Variations from "Don Sebastian"* (later *Donizetti Variations*; chor. Balanchine), New York City Ballet, New York
*Liebeslieder Walzer* (chor. Balanchine), New York City Ballet, New York
*Ragtime* I (chor. Balanchine), New York City Ballet, New York

1961 *Valses et Variations* (later *Raymonda Variations*; chor. Balanchine), New York City Ballet, New York

1962 *A Midsummer Night's Dream* (chor. Balanchine), New York City Ballet, New York

1963 *Bugaku* (chor. Balanchine), New York City Ballet, New York
*Meditation* (chor. Balanchine), New York City Ballet, New York
*The Chase; or, The Vixen's Choice* (chor. Balanchine), New York City Ballet, New York
*Meditations* (chor. Balanchine), New York City Ballet, New York

1964 *Tarantella* (chor. Balanchine), New York City Ballet, New York
*Ballet Imperial* (new production; staged Frederic Franklin after Balanchine), New York City Ballet, New York
*Irish Fantasy* (chor. d'Amboise), New York City Ballet, Los Angeles
*The Nutcracker* (new production; chor. Balanchine), New York City Ballet, New York

1965 *Pas de deux and Divertissement* (chor. Balanchine), New York City Ballet, New York

1966 *Brahms-Schoenberg Quartet* (chor. Balanchine), New York City Ballet, New York

1967 *Trois Valses Romantiques* (chor. Balanchine), New York City Ballet, New York
*Jewels* (chor. Balanchine), New York City Ballet, New York

1968 *La Source* (chor. Balanchine), New York City Ballet, New York
*Western Symphony* (restaging; chor. Balanchine), New York City Ballet, New York

1970 *Who Cares?* (chor. Balanchine), New York City Ballet, New York

1972 *Scherzo à la Russe* (chor. Balanchine), New York City Ballet, New York
*Scènes de Ballet* (chor. Taras), New York City Ballet, New York

1973 *Tchaikovsky Concerto no. 2* (new production of *Ballet Imperial*; chor. Balanchine), New York City Ballet, New York

1974 *Coppélia* (chor. Balanchine, Danilova), New York City Ballet, New York

1976 *Chaconne* (chor. Balanchine), New York City Ballet, New York

1977 *Vienna Waltzes* (chor. Balanchine), New York City Ballet, New York

## PUBLICATIONS

"Madame Karinska: Biography of a Designer", *Vogue* (London), 19 February 1936

Chujoy, Anatole, *The New York City Ballet*, New York, 1953

Martin, John J., "Karinska', *Center: A Magazine of the Performing Arts* (New York), February 1955

Rubin, J. Alleman, "Costumes by Karinska", *Dance Magazine* (New York), June 1967

Reynolds, Nancy, *Repertory in Review*, New York, 1977

Huckenpahler, Victoria, "Madame Barbara Karinska: Costumes to Delight", *Dance Magazine* (New York), January 1978

* * *

Dance critic Walter Terry called Karinska "ballet's most cherished sorceress, and artist of uncommon powers". Although she began her long career as the highly acclaimed interpreter of designs by such artists as Salvador Dali, Henri Matisse, and Marc Chagall, it was as principal costumer of the New York City Ballet that she made her name.

Karinska's talent as a designer first came to the fore when, as a child in Russia, she created costumes for the theatrical performances put on for her wealthy family's amusement. Already she showed a strong will and dramatic sense of colour. As she later said, "If someone criticized my choice of colour I was mad. I would say, 'I know what I am doing, and I do it'."

At first her career took a different path. She studied law in Moscow and worked with women in prisons, but was forced to return to the Ukraine as social unrest began in Russia. It seems—although Karinska never discussed this period in her life—that Karinska married the editor of a socialist paper in Kharkov. She took over editorship of the paper when her husband died but had to abandon it when it began to lose money. During World War I Karinska went to Moscow, where she met and married her second husband, a lawyer named Karinsky. In 1917 Karinska was on holiday in the Crimea when the Bolsheviks took power in Moscow. She could not return to Moscow for nearly a year, but stayed in the Crimea and studied painting. When she returned to Moscow to find her husband, she discovered that he had left the city to look for her. Karinska now had to earn her own living, teaching embroidery and running an embroidery and dress shop. She also exhibited several paintings in a gallery and was offered the title of commissar of art by the Bolsheviks. This gave her an excuse to leave Russia in 1928, ostensibly to study museum administration in Germany; in fact, she did not do so, but joined her father and brothers in Brussels, moving to Paris soon afterwards.

At first Karinska supported herself and her daughter Irena by embroidering scarves for Liberty of London—she was taught embroidery as a child—and making "paintings" from chiffon on cardboard. Her first costumes were made for nightclub performers and the Comédie-Française, but in 1932 she received a commission from ballet and opera directors Colonel de Basil and René Blum to make the costumes for Balanchine's ballet *Cotillon*, to designs by Christian Bérard. At that time Karinska knew nothing about the making of ballet costumes, and had to learn through trial and error, with the assistance of a Russian friend Toussia. Many more commissions followed, for theatre as well as ballet, and she became known as the only costumer able to translate an artist's sketches into fabric. Perhaps the most striking demonstration of this talent was in her execution of Dali's designs for *Bacchanale*, in which she turned his highly fantastic Surrealist sketches into costumes that were "well cut, well sewn and wearable—a masterpiece of artistic engineering".

Karinska left Paris for the United States in 1938 and worked in Hollywood for a short period, creating costumes for films. (Later, in 1948, she won an Academy Award for her designs for Ingrid Bergman in *Joan of Arc*. She had returned to Europe to research methods of clothing construction in Joan of Arc's time and the resulting costumes, both simple and historically authentic, were hand-woven and dyed.)

However, Karinska had not yet become a U.S. citizen, nor was she a member of the costumers' union, and she found herself unable to continue her work in Hollywood. She moved to New York and renewed her acquaintanceship with Balanchine, who gave her a room in his ballet school. She opened a dress shop for society women but it did not prove successful, so she decided to devote herself to making costumes for ballet, opera, and theatre, where the quality of her workmanship would be appreciated. Her tutus, consisting of six layers of tulle attached to a tight bodice with numerous elastic bands, became famous for permitting a full range of movement without "wilting". All Karinska costumes were hand-sewn and fitted their wearer to perfection, lasting up to eight years.

*Bourrée Fantasque* was the first Balanchine ballet for which Karinska created her own costume designs. These matched the choreography in their combination of wittiness and chic; the girls were elegantly dressed in crisp black with yellow, blue, or red, and held small black fans in their hands. The critic John Martin commented on the "extraordinary unity of artistic outlook" of Karinska and Balanchine: "Her dresses, like his dances, are classic abstractions, splendidly unreal, coolly sensuous, with a jeune fille elegance, their formalism airily tinged with waywardness."

In 1963 Balanchine appointed Karinska principal costumer of the New York City Ballet and used a Ford Foundation grant to establish a costume shop for her, full of the fine fabrics and trimmings she insisted upon using. These enabled her to create costumes that would inspire the performers, such as the prince costume worn by Jacques d'Amboise in *The Firebird*, which she constructed to Chagall's designs in Balanchine's 1970 restaging of the ballet. His purple velvet jacket, silk-lined and trimmed with mink, and his white kid boots would, she insisted, make him feel like (and dance like) a prince. Her own designs for *Jewels* reproduced the qualities of emeralds, rubies, and diamonds without their weight, which, as Balanchine said, would have rendered dancing impossible.

Karinska's costumes were not merely decorative; Walter Terry said that Karinska made "the garment part of dancing itself" and her designs captured the spirit of each ballet perfectly. Her designs for the 1973 production of *Ballet Imperial* evoked the riches of Imperial Russia, while her costumes for *Who Cares?*, set to Gershwin songs, were "1920s and mini-mod at the same time", according to Lincoln Kirstein (the women, in turquoise and lemon-yellow, wore pleated skirts, and the men black bellbottom trousers and striped necktie-belts, in homage to Fred Astaire and Coco Chanel).

In other ballets the costumes played an important symbolic role. In *Episodes I*, based on the final moments of Mary Queen of Scots, Mary first appeared in a stiff black dress that seemed both protective and imprisoning. As she remembered herself as a young girl going to meet her lover, she stepped free of the dress and revealed herself in white. Her empty black dress stood "like an empty cage" (in Balanchine's words). For her court tennis "duel" with Queen Elizabeth, Mary wore blood red and Elizabeth gold. At the end, when Mary was about to be executed, a red light shone on her discarded queenly dress. In *La Valse*, the dancers wore formal dress, the women in long white gloves and vivid red full skirts under slate-grey costumes. One wore white. At first, the women's costumes had a decorative function, providing a striking contrast with the black walls of the set, but later the colours took on a symbolic meaning when a figure in black appeared, changing the mood of the ballet to one of horror. Before her fatal dance with the man in black, the girl in white put on the long black gloves and black gown that he offered her.

In 1962 Karinska's achievements were publicly recognized when she received the Capezio Dance Award for costumes "of visual beauty for the spectator and complete delight for the dancer". A true perfectionist, she deserved the compliment paid her by Balanchine: "There is Shakespeare for literature and Madame Karinska for costumes."

—Jessica Arah

---

**KARSAVINA, Tamara**

Russian/British dancer and ballet mistress. Born Tamara Platonovna Karsavina in St. Petersburg, daughter of Maryinsky dancer and teacher Platon Karsavin, 9 March (25 February old style) 1885. Studied with father and at the Imperial Theatre School, St. Petersburg, pupil of Enrico Cecchetti, Pavel Gerdt, Christian Johansson; also studied with Caterina Beretta in Milan, 1904. Married British diplomat Henry J. Bruce (second husband), 1950: one son. Début, Maryinsky Theatre, 1902; dancer, Maryinsky Theatre, 1902–18, performing ballerina roles from 1907, and named prima ballerina, 1909; also performed with Lydia and Georgi Kyaksht (director), Warsaw, and on Russian provincial tour, 1905; engaged by Diaghilev for first Ballets Russes season, 1909: ballerina, Diaghilev's Ballets Russes, performing Paris, London, Monte Carlo, and other European cities, seasons 1910–13; also performed at the Coliseum (under manager Marinelli), London, 1910; left Russia to settle in London, 1918; guest ballerina, Diaghilev's Ballets Russes, Monte Carlo and London, 1926, Paris, 1928, 1929, and Ballet Club (later Ballet Rambert), London, 1930–31; also guest ballet mistress, staging ballets, including Fokine's *Carnaval*, *Le Spectre de la rose*, and *Les Sylphides* for Ballet Rambert, 1930, and serving as adviser to Royal Ballet productions; Vice-President, 1946–55, and Fellow, Royal Academy of Dancing, London. Recipient, Gold Medal of the Order of St. Valentin; Palme Académique, Paris, 1909; Order of the Red Cross; Royal Academy of Dancing Coronation Award, 1954. Died in Beaconsfield, 26 May 1978.

## ROLES

1902 The Pearl, Pas de deux added to *Javotta* (Petipa), Maryinsky Theatre, St. Petersburg
Friend of Swanilda in *Coppélia* (Petipa, Cecchetti), Maryinsky Theatre, St. Petersburg

1904 Flore in *Le Réveil de Flore* (Petipa), Maryinsky Theatre, St. Petersburg
Flower girl in *Don Quixote* (Gorsky after Petipa), Maryinsky Theatre, St. Petersburg
Emerald in *Bluebeard* (Petipa), Maryinsky Theatre, St. Petersburg

1906 A Wine (cr) in *La Vigne* (Fokine), Maryinsky Theatre, St. Petersburg
Gertrude (cr) in *Puss in Boots* (Legat), Maryinsky Theatre, St. Petersburg
Tsar-Maiden in *The Little Humpbacked Horse* (Petipa after Saint-Léon), Maryinsky Theatre, St. Petersburg

1907 Principal dancer (cr; solo) in *Dance with a Torch* (*Danse Assyrienne*; Fokine), Maryinsky Theatre, St. Petersburg
Solo variation (cr) in *The Night of Terpsichore* (Fokine), Maryinsky Theatre, St. Petersburg

**Tamara Karsavina as Giselle, 1910**

Princess Florine in *The Sleeping Beauty* (Petipa), Maryinsky Theatre, St. Petersburg

1908 Medora in *Le Corsaire* (Petipa), Maryinsky Theatre, St. Petersburg

Odette in *Swan Lake* (Petipa, Ivanov), Maryinsky Theatre, St. Petersburg

Principal dancer (cr) in *Danses sur la musique de Chopin* (Fokine), Maryinsky Theatre, St. Petersburg

Principal dancer (cr) in *Rêverie romantique: Ballet sur la musique de Chopin* (*Chopiniana*, second version; Fokine), Maryinsky Theatre, St. Petersburg

1909 Title role in *The Fairy Doll* (N. and S. Legat), Maryinsky Theatre, St. Petersburg

Title role in *Raymonda* (Petipa), Maryinsky Theatre, St. Petersburg

Nerilia in *The Caprices of the Butterfly* (Petipa), Maryinsky Theatre, St. Petersburg

Princess Florine in Bluebird pas de deux from *The Sleeping Beauty* (Petipa), Diaghilev's Ballets Russes, Paris

Friend of Armide (cr) in *Le Pavillon d'Armide* (new production; Fokine), Diaghilev's Ballets Russes, Paris

Principal dancer (cr) in *Le Festin* (Fokine and others), Diaghilev's Ballets Russes, Paris

Slave (cr) in *Cléopâtre* (new version of *Egyptian Nights*; Fokine), Diaghilev's Ballets Russes, Paris

Waltz (cr) in *Les Sylphides* (new version of *Chopiniana*; Fokine), Diaghilev's Ballets Russes, Paris

1910 Columbine (cr) in *Le Carnaval* (Fokine), Pavlov Hall, St. Petersburg

Nikiya in *La Bayadère* (Petipa), Maryinsky Theatre, St. Petersburg

Title role in *Giselle* (Petipa after Coralli, Perrot; staged Fokine), Diaghilev's Ballets Russes, Paris

Title role (cr) in *L'Oiseau de feu* (Fokine), Diaghilev's Ballets Russes, Paris

Principal dancer (cr) in *Les Orientales* (Fokine), Diaghilev's Ballets Russes, Paris

1911 Aurora in *The Sleeping Beauty* (Petipa), Maryinsky Theatre, St. Petersburg

The young girl (cr) in *Le Spectre de la rose* (Fokine), Diaghilev's Ballets Russes, Monte Carlo

Echo (cr) in *Narcisse* (Fokine), Diaghilev's Ballets Russes, Monte Carlo

Ballerina (cr) in *Petrushka* (Fokine), Diaghilev's Ballets Russes, Paris

Zobéïde in *Schéhérazade* (revised version; Fokine), Diaghilev's Ballets Russes, London

1912 Title role in *Paquita* (Petipa), Maryinsky Theatre, St. Petersburg

Indian girl (cr) in *Le Dieu Bleu* (Fokine), Diaghilev's Ballets Russes, Paris

Chloë (cr) in *Daphnis et Chloë* (Fokine), Diaghilev's Ballets Russes, Paris

Title role (cr) in *Thamar* (Fokine), Diaghilev's Ballets Russes, Paris

A Wife of the King (cr) in *Islamey* (Fokine), Maryinsky Theatre, St. Petersburg

Dancer (cr) in *Papillon* (Fokine), Maryinsky Theatre, St. Petersburg

1913 Soloist (cr) in *Preludes* (Fokine), Maryinsky Theatre, St. Petersburg

Principal dancer (cr) in *Jeux* (Nijinsky), Diaghilev's Ballets Russes, Paris

Salomé (cr) in *La Tragédie de Salomé* (Romanov), Diaghilev's Ballets Russes, Paris

1914 Queen of Shemakhan (cr) in *Le Coq d'or* (Fokine), Diaghilev's Ballets Russes, Paris

Queen (cr) in *Midas* (Fokine), Diaghilev's Ballets Russes, Paris

1915 Principal dancer (cr; solo) in *The Dream* (Fokine), Maryinsky Theatre, Petrograd

Lise in *Vain Precautions* (*La Fille mal gardée*; Petipa, Ivanov), Maryinsky Theatre, Petrograd

1917 Principal dancer (solo; cr) in *Ruslan and Lyudmila* (opera; mus. Glinka, chor. Fokine), Maryinsky Theatre, Petrograd

1919 The Miller's Wife (cr) in *Le Tricorne* (Massine), Diaghilev's Ballets Russes, London

1920 Rossignol (cr) in *Le Chant du Rossignol* (Massine), Diaghilev's Ballets Russes, Paris

Pimpinella (cr) in *Pulcinella* (Massine), Diaghilev's Ballets Russes, Paris

Principal dancer (cr) in *Le Astuzie femminili* (Massine), Diaghilev's Ballets Russes, Paris

1926 Juliet (cr) in *Romeo and Juliet* (Nijinska), Diaghilev's Ballets Russes, Monte Carlo

1931 Jenny (cr) in *Waterloo and Crimea* (Salaman), Ballet Club (later Ballet Rambert), London

Venus (cr) in *Mercury* (Ashton), Ballet Club (later Ballet Rambert), London

**Other roles include:** for the Maryinsky Theatre—Swanilda in *Coppélia* (Petipa, Cecchetti), Butterfly in *The Caprices of the Butterfly* (Petipa), Spanish doll in *The Fairy Doll* (N. and S. Legat), Berenice in *Eygptian Nights* (Fokine), title role in *Eunice* (Fokine).

## PUBLICATIONS

By Karsavina:

*Theatre Street* (memoirs), London, 1930

*Ballet Technique*, London, 1956

*Classical Ballet: The Flow of Movement*, London, 1962

Interview in Wildman, Carl, "Conversation with Karsavina" (from BBC interview), *Dancing Times* (London), June 1965

Numerous articles on ballet technique and history, in *Dancing Times* (London), 1927–68

About Karsavina:

Svetlov, Valerian, *Thamar Karsavina*, translated by H. Beauclerk and N. Evrevnov, London, 1922

Haskell, Arnold, *Tamara Karsavina*, London, 1931

Moore, Lillian, *Artists of the Dance*, New York, 1938

Lifar, Serge, *Le Histoire du Ballet Russe*, Paris, 1950

Grigoriev, Serge, *The Diaghilev Ballet 1909–1929*, translated by Vera Bowen, London, 1953

Lifar, Serge, *The Three Graces*, translated by G. Hopkins, London, 1959

Krasovskaya, Vera, *Russian Ballet Theatre at the Beginning of the Twentieth Century*, volume 2: Leningrad, 1972

Smakov, Gennady, *The Great Russian Dancers*, New York, 1984

Williams, Peter, "Celebrating Karsavina, 1885–1978", *Dance Gazette* (London), July 1985

Garafola, Lynn, *Diaghilev's Ballets Russes*, New York, 1989

* * *

Tamara Karsavina is best remembered for the many great roles she created for Diaghilev's Ballets Russes. Like her partner of the first few seasons, Vaslav Nijinsky, she was a product of the Imperial Theatre School and company of the Maryinsky

Theatre in St. Petersburg. Although she made her official début there seven years before the 1909 premiere of Diaghilev's company, her international reputation as a ballerina of great beauty, grace, and versatility was earned through her creation and interpretation of roles in such beloved ballets as *Petrushka*, *Firebird*, *Carnaval*, and *Le Spectre de la rose* for Diaghilev's Ballets Russes. Karsavina's most important contribution to dance history may well be in her serving as "muse" to Fokine for many of his earliest and most brilliant creations.

Karsavina was gifted not only with incredible talent but also with unusual intelligence and curiosity. She became one of Diaghilev's closest female friends and was the only woman allowed to participate in his "artistic committee" which helped plan the repertory works for the first few seasons.

Unlike Nijinsky and other members of the Ballets Russes, Karsavina did not sever relations with the Maryinsky until after the Revolution of 1917. Although this complicated her career and life enormously, it also made her a valuable link between the classical old guard and the experiments of Fokine, Nijinsky, and all who came under Diaghilev's wing. Karsavina's technical skill enabled her to interpret the most traditional roles of the great nineteenth-century classic ballets as well as the newest innovations of the Ballets Russes. As Robert Brussel, the music critic of *Le Figaro* at the time, claimed, she understood that a union between a tradition and a revolution was possible.

Like the legendary Nijinsky, Karsavina was able to personify many roles with an incredible display of versatility. Whereas Nijinsky, however, seemed to assume his characters instinctively, Karsavina applied her intelligence and talent to the task at hand, researching each role from the dancer's as well as the dramatic actress's point of view.

From the time she left Russia until Diaghilev's death in 1929, Karsavina continued to dance at intervals with the Ballets Russes, appearing successfully in Massine's and Nijinska's works created in the final years of the company. Finally she settled in London with her British husband and their son.

The remainder of her long life (she died in 1978 at age 93) was spent in England, where she was a valuable asset to the British dance community, even coming out of retirement to dance as guest artist with Ballet Rambert in its earliest days. Her lecture-demonstrations on the art of dance-mime were considered incomparable. Not only did she teach, coach, and lecture, but she also wrote a delightful autobiography, *Theatre Street*, which provides an excellent look at the life of the aspiring young dancer growing up in the Imperial Ballet School. In addition to her autobiography, she also wrote a textbook, *Classical Ballet: The Flow of Movement*.

Karsavina's expertise was also invaluable to the Royal Ballet on numerous occasions in its formative years. She helped reconstruct works such as *Le Spectre de la rose* and *Firebird*, and provided great assistance to Sir Frederick Ashton in remembering and restoring the mime scene in the second act of *La Fille mal gardée* for him. Margot Fonteyn, in her own autobiography, revealed the insight into the role of the Firebird she received through Karsavina's coaching and recall of Fokine's original directions.

—Carol Egan

---

**KAYE, Nora**

American dancer and ballet director. Born Nora Koreff in New York, 17 January 1920. Studied with Margaret Curtis at the Metropolitan Opera Ballet School, with Mikhail Fokine, Anatole Vilzak, Ludmilla Schollar, and at the School of American Ballet, New York. Married (1) Michael Van Buren, 1943 (annulled 1943); (2) Isaac Stern, 1948 (div. 1950); (3) choreographer and director Herbert Ross, 1959. Début in children's ballets, Metropolitan Opera House; dancer, George Balanchine's American Ballet, from 1935; dancer, corps de ballet, Ballet Theatre (later American Ballet Theatre), from 1939, becoming ballerina, 1942–1951, 1954–59; left Ballet Theatre to perform with New York City Ballet, 1951–54; also appeared in Broadway musicals, including *Virginia* (mus. Schwartz; 1937), *Great Lady* (mus. Loewe, chor. Balanchine-/Dollar; 1938), *Stars in Your Eyes* (mus. Schwartz, chor. Randall; 1939), Bette Davis revue *Two's Company* (mus. Duke, chor. Robbins; 1952); guest ballerina, touring Japan with Paul Szilard, 1953, 1955, 1956; performed at Festival of Two Worlds, Spoleto, Italy, 1960: co-founder (with Ross), Ballet of Two Worlds, touring Europe 1960–61; retired from dancing, 1961, becoming film producer with husband Ross: films produced include *Nijinsky* (dir. Ross, 1980), and *The Turning Point* (dir. Ross, 1977); member of board of directors, Ballet Theatre Foundation, from 1975; associate director, American Ballet Theatre, from 1977. Died in Santa Monica, 28 February 1987.

**ROLES**

1940 Ensemble in *Dark Elegies* (Tudor), Ballet Theatre, New York
Guest in *Jardin aux Lilas* (Tudor), Ballet Theatre, New York
Maja (cr) in *Goya Pastoral* (Tudor), Ballet Theatre, New York

1941 La Reine de la danse from Moscow in *Gala Performance* (Tudor), Ballet Theatre, New York
A Wife of Bluebeard (cr) in *Bluebeard* (Fokine), Ballet Theatre, Mexico City
Friend of Slavonika (cr) in *Slavonika* (Psota), Ballet Theatre, Mexico City

1941/42 The Bird in *Peter and the Wolf* (Bolm), Ballet Theatre
An Episode in His Past in *Jardin aux Lilas* (Tudor), Ballet Theatre
Carlotta Grisi in *Pas de quatre* (Dolin after Lester), Ballet Theatre
Myrtha in *Giselle* (Petipa after Coralli, Perrot; staged Dolin), Ballet Theatre
A Sister of Florestan in *Princess Aurora* (divertissements from *The Sleeping Beauty*; Dolin after Petipa), Ballet Theatre

1942 Hagar (cr) in Pillar of Fire (Tudor), Ballet Theatre, New York
Princess in *Bluebeard* (Fokine), Ballet Theatre

1943 Tarantella in *The Fantastic Toyshop* (*La Boutique fantasque*; Massine), Ballet Theatre, Omaha
Gypsy Scene and Asturian Fandango in *Capriccio Espagnol* (Massine, with La Argentinita), Ballet Theatre, San Francisco
Polyhymnia in *Apollo* (Balanchine), Ballet Theatre, New York
Caroline in *Jardin aux Lilas* (Tudor), Ballet Theatre
Title role in *Princess Aurora* (divertissements from *The Sleeping Beauty*; Dolin after Petipa), Ballet Theatre
The Swan Queen (Odette) in *Swan Lake*, Act II (Dolin after Ivanov), Ballet Theatre
The Lady with Him (cr) in *Dim Lustre* (Tudor), Ballet Theatre, New York

**Nora Kaye as Hagar in *Pillar of Fire***

Soubrette (cr) in *Mademoiselle Angot* (later *Mam'zelle Angot*; Massine), Ballet Theatre, New York
Juliet in *Romeo and Juliet* (Tudor), Ballet Theatre
Zemphira in *Aleko* (Massine), Ballet Theatre
1944 Pas de trois (cr) in *Waltz Academy* (Balanchine), Ballet Theatre, Boston
1945 The Girl in *Harvest Time* (Nijinska), Ballet Theatre
Russian Ballerina (cr) in *On Stage!* (Kidd), Ballet Theatre, Boston
Dela (cr) in *The Gift of the Magi* (S. Semenoff), Ballet Theatre, Boston
Principal dancer (cr) in *Graziana* (Taras), Ballet Theatre, New York
Title role in *Firebird* (Bolm), Ballet Theatre
The Black Swan (Odile) in *Black Swan Pas de deux* (from *Swan Lake*, Act III; Dolin after Petipa), Ballet Theatre
1946 Woman (cr) in *Facsimile* (Robbins), Ballet Theatre, New York
A Lover in *Les Patineurs* (Ashton), Ballet Theatre, New York
1947 La Déesse de la danse from Milan in *Gala Performance* (Tudor), Ballet Theatre
1948 The Accused (cr; though not at premiere) in *Fall River Legend* (de Mille), Ballet Theatre, New York
Ballerina in *Petrushka* (Fokine), Ballet Theatre
1949 Principal dancer (lead couple) in *Theme and Variations* (Balanchine), Ballet Theatre
Title role in *Giselle* (Petipa after Coralli, Perrot; staged D. Romanoff), Ballet Theatre, New York
1950 Principal dancer (cr) in *Jeux* (Taras), Ballet Theatre, New York
The Dreamer (cr) in *Nimbus* (Tudor), Ballet Theatre, New York
1951 Principal dancer in *Symphony in C* (Balanchine), New York City Ballet, New York
The Novice (cr) in *The Cage* (Robbins), New York City Ballet, New York
Prélude in *Bourrée Fantasque* (Balanchine), New York City Ballet, New York
Young Girl in *Mother Goose Suite* (Bolender), New York City Ballet, New York
1952 Principal dancer (cr) in *Ballade* (Robbins), New York City Ballet, New York
Title role (cr) in *La Gloire* (Tudor), New York City Ballet, New York
1955 Blanche in *A Streetcar Named Desire* (Bettis), Ballet Theatre, New York
Title role in *The Sphinx* (*La Rencontre*; Lichine), Ballet Theatre, New York
1956 Operetta Star in *Offenbach in the Underworld* (Tudor), Ballet Theatre, New York
Hostess (cr) in *The Rib of Eve* (de Mille), Ballet Theatre, New York
1957 Blind girl (cr) in *Winter's Eve* (MacMillan), Ballet Theatre, Lisbon
Bride in *Blood Wedding* (L. Rodrigues), Ballet Theatre Previews, New York
Principal dancer (cr) in *Journey* (MacMillan), Ballet Theatre Previews, New York
Principal dancer (cr) in *Paean* (Ross), Ballet Theatre, New York
Princess (cr) in *Sebastian* (de Mille), Ballet Theatre Previews, New York
Ballerina (cr) in *Paquita* (pas de deux; Fedorova after Petipa), Ballet Theatre, Washington, D.C.
1958 The Woman (cr) in *The Mirror* (Martinez), Ballet Theatre Workshop, New York
Principal dancer (cr) in *Concerto* (Ross), American Ballet Theatre, New York
Principal dancer (cr) in *Tristan* (pas de deux; Ross), American Ballet Theatre, New York
1959 Principal dancer (cr) in *Serenade for Seven* (later called *Dialogues*; Ross), American Ballet, Festival of Two Worlds, Spoleto
1960/61 Principal dancer (cr) in *Angel Head* (Ross), Ballet of Two Worlds, European tour
Principal dancer (cr) in *Within the Grove* (*Rashomon Suite*; Ross), Ballet of Two Worlds, European tour
Principal dancer (cr) in *The Dybbuk* (Ross), Ballet of Two Worlds, European tour

**Other roles include:** for New York City Ballet—Profane Love in *Illuminations* (Ashton).

**PUBLICATIONS**

By Kaye:
Interview in Chapin, Isolde, "Dressing Room Interview", *Dance Magazine* (New York), February 1947
"The American Ballerina" in Nadel, Myron Howard, editor, *The Dance Experience* (New York), 1970
"The Lure of Ballet Theatre", in Payne, Charles, *American Ballet Theatre*, New York, 1978
Interview in Newman, Barbara, "Character of Caring: Nora Kaye on Nora Kaye", *Dance Magazine* (New York), September 1987

About Kaye:
Amberg, George, *Ballet in America*, New York, 1949
Denby, Edwin, *Looking at the Dance*, New York, 1949
Chujoy, Anatole, *The New York City Ballet*, New York, 1953
Beaumont, Cyril, *Ballets of Today*, London, 1954
Rudko, Doris, "Walter Terry with Nora Kaye", *Dance Observer* (New York), June/July 1955
Terry, Walter, *The Dance in America*, New York, 1956
Todd, Arthur, "Kaye: Actress-Ballerina", *Dance and Dancers* (London), September 1956
Goodman, Saul, "Nora Kaye", *Dance Magazine* (New York), February/March 1969
Payne, Charles, *American Ballet Theatre*, New York, 1978
Manchester, Phyllis Winifred, "Remembering Nora Kaye", *Dance Magazine* (New York), May 1987
Taras, John, "Nora Kaye: A Tribute", *Ballet Review* (New York), Winter 1987

* * *

With the advent of Ballet Theatre, which established itself in 1940, a grand-scale opportunity befell American dancers inclined to greatness. Nora Kaye was one such—and not remotely in the European mold. She was of a new variety and came to define the category of "dramatic" ballerina, inspiring such native choreographers as Agnes de Mille and Jerome Robbins to create starring vehicles for her.

But this was not to happen before she developed under the all-seeing scrutiny of Antony Tudor. This British playwright of the dance was Svengali to her Trilby. She lent herself to him at the peak of his powers—the first five years of Ballet Theatre—with the reward of fame for both of them. As Hagar in *Pillar of Fire*, the first major work Tudor made in the United States, she managed to portray a social isolate and find the dimension of a fully realized literary character. It was a tour de force, one that brought the choreographer and his heroine on stage for 28 curtain calls. Commenting on the 1942 premiere of *Pillar*, which he attended, composer Leo Smit recalled: "I did not speak for a week." The New York public had witnessed an artistic phenomenon that would, from then, represent a standard.

For Tudor, finding such an instrument as Kaye in his adopted country and at Ballet Theatre was tantamount to rubbing sticks together to make fire. In England there had been Maude Lloyd, the heroine of his *Jardin aux lilas*. But until encountering Kaye he did not deign to attempt the ballet (*Pillar*) that had occupied his thoughts for three years. Through this young American he could see the flickerings of his autobiographical instincts come to life. Moreover, her depth and dedication to the cause spurred him on. She certainly boasted the right background; her actor-father had studied with Stanislavsky at the Moscow Art Theatre.

The role of Hagar, with its emblematic angst and yearning and loneliness, called upon Kaye's extraordinary strength as a dancer as well as her dramatic intensity. Indeed, Tudor conceived the steps based on those attributes. She had the wherewithal to stand flat-footed, for instance, and, on a staccato signal, rise to an accented full pointe; he encoded the psychological character of Hagar in such steps.

Others also seized on her powerful presence. Robbins, in *The Cage*, utilized it to portray a predatory female monster. But it took a Tudor again to grant Kaye a multi-layered persona: in *La Gloire* he gave her the role of a reigning actress threatened by rising ingenues, an instance of art imitating life that she danced with overwhelming sincerity.

De Mille also bequeathed a tragic role to Kaye—that of Lizzie Borden, called "The Accused", in *Fall River Legend*. All of the above-mentioned circumvented Kaye's less-than-perfect line and form. Luckily, she did not have to make her mark in the classical ballets for which she was not ideally suited. But that did not stop her from competing for such roles as the Swan Queen and even Tudor's Juliet, which the choreographer created for Alicia Markova.

Although she set herself against such rivals as Alicia Alonso—indeed, the two often fought for top billing at Ballet Theatre—Nora Kaye stood in a class alone. No one equalled her in the contemporary dramatic roles to which she brought towering, often terrible authority, principally because she refused to compromise her vision for that of the traditionally lyric, beauteous ballerina.

—Donna Perlmutter

---

**KCHESSINSKA, Mathilde** *see* **KSHESINSKAYA, Matilda**

---

## KEHLET, Niels

Danish dancer. Born in Copenhagen, 6 September 1938. Studied at the Royal Danish Ballet School, Copenhagen, 1948–57. Dancer, Royal Danish Ballet, from 1957, becoming solo dancer (principal), from 1961, and touring America, South Africa, and Europe with company; also international guest artist, including with Margot Fonteyn Gala, 1961, Grand Ballet du Marquis de Cuevas, 1961, London Festival Ballet, 1965, Stuttgart Ballet, 1965, Boston Ballet, 1966, San Diego Ballet at Jacob's Pillow Dance Festival, 1966, Geneva Ballet, 1968, and with Carla Fracci, Milan, 1971; also appeared frequently on television, including for Danish television, 1965, 1969, French television, 1962, 1963, and Swedish television, performing in Cullberg's *Cain and Abel*, 1964; producer of Bournonville repertoire, including *Napoli Pas de six*, Florence, 1988; director, "Stars and Soloists of the Royal Danish Ballet", 1991; teacher and mime artist, Royal Danish Ballet, Copenhagen, after retiring from principal roles.

### ROLES

1956 Eskimo Dance in *Far from Denmark* (Bournonville), Royal Danish Ballet, Copenhagen

1957 Bluebird in *The Sleeping Beauty* (Petipa; staged Ashton), Royal Danish Ballet, Copenhagen

Principal dancer in *Fever* (Schaufuss), Royal Danish Ballet, Copenhagen

Pas de deux from *Don Quixote* (Schaufuss after Petipa), Royal Danish Ballet, Copenhagen

1958 Anders in *Miss Julie* (Cullberg), Royal Danish Ballet, Copenhagen

1959 Nilas in *Moon Reindeer* (Cullberg), Royal Danish Ballet, Copenhagen

1960 Brigand in *Carmen* (Petit), Royal Danish Ballet, Copenhagen

Peter in *Peter and the Wolf* (Larsen), Royal Danish Ballet, Copenhagen

1961 Marquis in *Cyrano de Bergerac* (Petit), Royal Danish Ballet, Copenhagen

1962 Principal dancer in *Études* (Lander), Royal Danish Ballet, Copenhagen

1963 Gennaro in *Napoli* (Bournonville), Royal Danish Ballet, Copenhagen

Third Movement in *Symphony in C* (Balanchine), Royal Danish Ballet, Copenhagen

First Movement in *Bourrée fantasque* (Balanchine), Royal Danish Ballet, Copenhagen

1964 Colas in *La Fille mal gardée* (Ashton), Royal Danish Ballet, Copenhagen

Principal dancer in *Virgin Spring* (von Rosen), Royal Danish Ballet, Copenhagen

Jester in *Swan Lake* (Petipa, Ivanov; staged Anisimova), Royal Danish Ballet, Copenhagen

1965 Norwegian Dance in *The Whims of Cupid and the Ballet Master* (Galeotti), Royal Danish Ballet, Copenhagen

Franz in *Coppélia* (Beck, Lander after Saint-Léon), Royal Danish Ballet, Copenhagen

Principal dancer in *Concertette* (Bruhn), Danish television

Principal dancer in *Contredanse* (Holm), Danish television

1966 Principal dancer in *Afternoon of a Faun* (Robbins), Royal Danish Ballet, Copenhagen

Planchet (cr) in *The Three Musketeers* (Flindt), Royal Danish Ballet, Copenhagen

The Joker in *Jeu de cartes* (Cranko), Royal Danish Ballet, Copenhagen

Gert in *The Kermesse in Bruges* (Bournonville), Royal Danish Ballet, Copenhagen

1967 A Brigand (cr) in *The Miraculous Mandarin* (Flindt), Royal Danish Ballet, Copenhagen

Principal dancer in *Agon* (Eske Holm), Royal Danish Ballet, Copenhagen

Gracioso (cr) in *Don Juan* (von Rosen), Royal Danish Ballet, Copenhagen

Principal dancer in *Gala Variations* (Flindt), Royal Danish Ballet, Copenhagen
Title role in *Pierrot Lunaire* (Tetley), Royal Danish Ballet, Copenhagen
Title role in *The Prodigal Son* (Balanchine), Royal Danish Ballet, Copenhagen
Title role in *Orestes* (Eske Holm), Royal Danish Ballet, Copenhagen
Señor in *La Ventana* (Bournonville), Royal Danish Ballet, Copenhagen
1969 Diderik in *A Folk Tale* (Bournonville), Royal Danish Ballet, Copenhagen
Principal dancer in *Cicatricis* (Eske Holm), Royal Danish Ballet, Copenhagen
Principal dancer in *Pas de deux pour quatre* (Dolin), Danish television

**Other roles include:** James in *La Sylphide* (Bournonville), Junior Cadet and Drummer in *Graduation Ball* (Lichine), *Mercutio in Romeo and Juliet* (Neumeier), principal dancer in *Solitaire* (MacMillan), Dr. Tarantola in *Katharsis* (Cramer), principal dancer in *Tropismes* (Holm), title role in *Le Spectre de la rose* (Fokine), title role in *Petrushka* (Fokine), principal dancer in *Night with Waning Moon* (Bruce).

**Niels Kehlet in *Coppélia*, 1971**

## PUBLICATIONS

By Kehlet:
Interview in Hunt, Marilyn, "Dancing Bournonville Now", *Ballet News* (New York), November 1979
Interview in Hunt, Marilyn, "A Conversation with Niels Kehlet", *Ballet Review* (New York), Summer 1988

About Kehlet:
Goodman, Saul, "Niels Khelet: Brief Biography", *Dance Magazine* (New York), November 1965
Aschengreen, Erik, "Niels Kehlet", *Les Saisons de la danse* (Paris), March 1970
Niehaus, Max, *Ballett Faszination*, Munich, 1972
Cunningham, Katherine, "Soloists of the Royal Danish Ballet", *Dance News* (New York), October 1979

* * *

Niels Kehlet was one of the first members of the Royal Danish Ballet to achieve a truly international reputation. He followed Henning Kronstam and Erik Bruhn on to the world stage, yet, like Kronstam, he maintained his strong connection with his national company. Always a popular dancer with audiences, Kehlet showed natural good spirits and an ebullience which made him perfect for many demi-caractère roles.

A native of Copenhagen, Kehlet had joined the Royal Danish Ballet School by the time he was ten and was dancing with the Royal Danish Ballet nine years later. He was swiftly promoted to principal (known in Denmark as solo dancer) in 1961. He was a utility dancer who developed a large and varied repertoire, having the strong, polished technique for the major classical roles and yet the dramatic personality required for mime and demi-caractère roles; he was that rare thing, a demi-caractère virtuoso.

In the Bournonville canon he is remembered principally for James in *La Sylphide* and Gennaro in *Napoli*, in the former for his sincerity and depth as a tragic actor, and in the latter for his sunny charm and exuberance. His ability to encompass extremes of emotion was displayed to great advantage in such roles as Mercutio in Neumeier's *Romeo and Juliet*, the title role in Fokine's *Petrushka*, and the Jester in *Swan Lake*. Most memorable, perhaps, are Kehlet's interpretations of Franz in *Coppélia* and Colas in *La Fille mal gardée* (mounted by Ashton for the Royal Danish Ballet in 1964). In these parts Kehlet had the opportunity to display to his public a command of bravura technique combined with the finely tuned characterizations he brought to demi-caractère principal roles. In this he was a great exponent of what is effectively a dying art. The world of dance has had many successful Siegfrieds, but a dancer who understands the role of Franz is a rare artist. Recent generations have had little exposure to this tradition—hence the continuing presence of Kehlet and older performers like Niels Bjørn Larsen and Alexander Grant, who display a strength in character roles that is unmatched by dancers half their age.

Kehlet's created roles include those in von Rosen's *Don Juan* and Flemming Flindt's *The Three Musketeers* and *The Miraculous Mandarin*. Other modern roles have included *Night with Waning Moon* by Christopher Bruce and *Pierrot Lunaire* by Glen Tetley. Currently, he dances character roles and teaches at the school of the Royal Danish Ballet. He has danced as a guest with many companies, principally with the Marquis de Cuevas in the early 1960s, the Fracci–Menegatti–Gai company in Italy, and with many companies in the United States.

Possessed of a face that is round and expressive rather than handsome, along with a compact physique and a generous stage presence, Kehlet has the ability to make audiences warm to him immediately. As *The New Yorker* critic Arlene Croce put it, seeing Kehlet perform *Coppélia* during the company's U.S. tour, "As Frantz, marvelous Niels Kehlet—pumpkin face, button eyes, frayed hair, and eel-like sinuousness to his leaps—was the perfect folk tale hero." He has always been a true professional. In April 1974, when he was nearing the end of his career in purely bravura classical roles, the Royal Danish Ballet opened its season in London with Harold Lander's *Études* at a Royal Gala. Although Kehlet was nursing an injury, he wished to dance as announced in the Gala, and he performed alongside an inspired Peter Schaufuss in one of the two leading male roles. Kehlet suffered an uncomfortable evening, but delivered a performance of such honesty and goodwill in a technically fiendish part that he succeeded completely in giving a polished performance, and the audience acknowledged it with cheers. If a single performance had to characterize a dancer's career, this should have been Kehlet's: technically pure, abundantly warm, and full of commitment.

—Mike Dixon

---

**KEIL, Birgit**

German dancer. Born in Kowarschen, Sudetenland, 22 September 1944. Studied at the ballet school of the Württemberg State Theatre (Stuttgart Ballet School), and at the Royal Ballet School, London, 1962–63. Married principal dancer Vladimir Klos, 1968. Dancer, Stuttgart Ballet, from 1961, becoming soloist from 1964; international guest artist with companies including Eliot Feld Ballet, Vienna State Opera Ballet, La Scala Ballet, Milan, American Ballet Theatre, Royal Ballet in London, Paris Opéra Ballet, Zürich Ballet, and Basel Ballet, also appearing in Japan, Russia, and Australia; actress/dancer, performing the role of Vera Baronova in the musical *On Your Toes* (mus. Rodgers; chor. Fuller), Ludwigsburg, 1990; has also appeared on television, including in works (chor. MacMillan) for British television, 1983, 1984. Recipient: Baden-Württemberg Order of Merit, 1979; Order of Merit, First Class, of the German Federal Republic; German Critics' Award, 1982; Emmy Award for *A Lot of Happiness* (Granada Television programme), 1984; John Cranko Medal, 1985.

**ROLES**

1961 Wood Fairy, Meadow Fairy, and Pas de quatre in *The Sleeping Beauty* (Cranko after Petipa), Stuttgart Ballet, Stuttgart
1962 Principal dancer (cr) in *Scènes de ballet* (Cranko), Stuttgart Ballet, Stuttgart
1963 Youngest Sister (cr) in *Las Hermanas* (MacMillan), Stuttgart Ballet, Stuttgart
Pas de six, Leading Swan, and Russian Princess (cr) in *Swan Lake* (new production; Cranko after Petipa, Ivanov), Stuttgart Ballet, Stuttgart
1964 Principal dancer in *Diversions* (MacMillan), Stuttgart Ballet, Stuttgart
Tsarevna (cr) in *The Firebird* (Cranko), Stuttgart Ballet, Stuttgart
1965 Principal dancer in *La Valse* (Balanchine), Stuttgart Ballet, Stuttgart
Queen of Hearts (cr) in *Jeu de cartes* (Cranko), Stuttgart Ballet, Stuttgart
Odette/Odile in *Swan Lake* (Cranko after Petipa, Ivanov), Stuttgart Ballet, Stuttgart
Principal dancer (cr) in *Opus 1* (Cranko), Stuttgart Ballet, Stuttgart
Principal dancer (cr) in *Das Lied von der Erde* (*Song of the Earth*; MacMillan), Stuttgart Ballet, Stuttgart
1966 Queen of the Wilis in *Giselle* (Petipa after Coralli, Perrot; staged Wright), Stuttgart Ballet, Stuttgart
Russian Ballerina and Pas de quatre (cr) in *The Nutcracker* (Cranko), Stuttgart Ballet, Stuttgart
Title role in *Giselle* (Petipa after Coralli, Perrot; staged Wright), Stuttgart Ballet, Stuttgart
1967 Principal dancer in *Katalyse* (Cranko), Stuttgart Ballet, Stuttgart
Terpsichore in *Apollo* (Balanchine), Stuttgart Ballet, Stuttgart
Principal dancer (cr) in *Holberg Suite* (Cranko), Stuttgart Ballet, Stuttgart
Title role (cr) in *Namouna* (Wright), Stuttgart Ballet, Stuttgart
Swanilda in *Coppélia* (Keres), Hesse State Theatre Ballet, Wiesbaden
1968 Sugar Plum Fairy in *The Nutcracker* (Cranko), Stuttgart Ballet, Stuttgart
Juliet in *Romeo and Juliet* (Cranko), Stuttgart Ballet, Stuttgart
Principal dancer (cr) in *Kyrie Eleison* (Cranko), Stuttgart Ballet, Stuttgart
Principal dancer (cr) in *Salade* (Cranko), Stuttgart Ballet, Stuttgart
Principal dancer in *Concerto for Flute and Harp* (Cranko), Stuttgart Ballet, Stuttgart
1969 Bianca in *The Taming of the Shrew* (Cranko), Stuttgart Ballet, New York
1970 Olga in *Onegin* (Cranko), Stuttgart Ballet, Stuttgart
Footprints in the Snow (cr) in *Brouillards* (Cranko), Stuttgart Ballet
Kristin (cr) in *Miss Julie* (MacMillan), Stuttgart Ballet, Stuttgart
Principal dancer (cr) in *Adagio* (Clauss), Stuttgart Ballet, Stuttgart
Eurydice (cr) in *Orpheus* (Cranko), Stuttgart Ballet, Stuttgart
Katherine in *The Taming of the Shrew* (Cranko), Stuttgart Ballet, Stuttgart
1971 Title role in *Carmen* (Cranko), Stuttgart Ballet, Stuttgart
The Year (cr) in *Die Jahrzeiten* (*The Seasons*; new version; Cranko), Stuttgart Ballet, Stuttgart
1972 B. (cr) in *Initials R.B.M.E.* (Cranko), Stuttgart Ballet, Stuttgart
Pas de deux in *Agon* (Balanchine), Stuttgart Ballet, Stuttgart
Principal dancer (cr) in *Ariel* (pas de deux; Cranko), Stuttgart Ballet, Stuttgart
1973 Principal dancer (cr) in *Green* (Cranko), Stuttgart Ballet, Stuttgart
Principal dancer (cr) in *Voluntaries* (Tetley), Stuttgart Ballet, Stuttgart
1974 Tatiana in *Onegin* (Cranko), Stuttgart Ballet, Stuttgart
The Bride in *Les Noces* (Nijinska), Stuttgart Ballet, Stuttgart
Principal dancer (cr) in *Return to the Strange Land* (first version, pas de trois; Kylián), Stuttgart Ballet, Stuttgart
1975 Principal dancer in *Laborintus* (Tetley), Stuttgart Ballet, Stuttgart
Principal dancer in *Mythical Hunters* (Tetley), Stuttgart Ballet, Stuttgart
Lykanion (cr) in *Daphnis und Chloe* (Tetley), Stuttgart Ballet, Stuttgart
Principal dancer (cr) in *Greening* (Tetley), Stuttgart

**Birgit Keil in *Onegin*, Stuttgart Ballet**

Ballet, Stuttgart

1976 Principal dancer (cr) in *Nuages* (Kylián), Stuttgart Ballet

Principal dancer in *Le Sacre du printemps* (Tetley), Stuttgart Ballet, Stuttgart

Principal dancer (cr) in *Impromptu* (Feld), Eliot Feld Ballet, New York

Principal dancer in *At Midnight* (Feld), Eliot Feld Ballet, New York

Agnus Dei (cr) in *Requiem* (MacMillan), Stuttgart Ballet, Stuttgart

1977 Principal dancer (cr) in *Innere Not* (Montagnon), Stuttgart Ballet, Stuttgart

Princess Aurora in *The Sleeping Beauty* (Petipa, Nijinska; staged Hightower), Stuttgart Ballet, Stuttgart

1978 Principal dancer (cr) in *Glocken* (Montagnon), Stuttgart Ballet, Stuttgart

First Sister (cr) in *My Brother, My Sisters* (MacMillan), Stuttgart Ballet, Stuttgart

Manon (cr) in *The Lady of the Camellias* (Neumeier), Stuttgart Ballet, Stuttgart

Title role in *Undine* (Spoerli), Basel Ballet, Basel

1979 Marguerite Gautier in *The Lady of the Camellias* (Neumeier), Stuttgart Ballet, Stuttgart

Eurydice (cr) in *Orpheus* (Forsythe), Stuttgart Ballet, Stuttgart

Mathilde (cr) in *Träume* (Spoerli), Swiss television, Zürich

1980 The Beauty in *Poème de l'extase* (Cranko), Stuttgart Ballet, Stuttgart

The Queen (cr) in *Richard III (IV, 1)* (Scholz), Stuttgart Ballet, Stuttgart

Donna Belisa (cr) in *Der Rote Mantel* (Spoerli), Basel Ballet, Basel

1981 Principal dancer (cr) in *Forgotten Land* (Kylián), Stuttgart Ballet, Stuttgart

Augusta (cr) in *Childe Harold* (Spoerli), German Opera Ballet, Berlin

1982 Title role in *La Sylphide* (Bournonville; staged Schaufuss), Stuttgart Ballet, Stuttgart

1983 Trois Gnossiennes in *Five Short Stories* (van Manen), Stuttgart Ballet, Stuttgart

Principal dancer in *Wendung* (Neumeier), Stuttgart Ballet, Stuttgart

Principal dancer (cr) in *A Lot of Happiness* (MacMillan), British television

Principal dancer (cr) in *Fantasien* (Spoerli), Basel Ballet, Basel

1984 Principal dancer in *Wiegenlied* (Kylián), Vienna State Opera Ballet, Vienna

Principal dancer (cr) in *The Seven Deadly Sins* (MacMillan), British television

1985 Taglioni in *Pas de quatre* (Dolin), Paris Opéra Ballet, Paris

Principal dancer (cr) in *Pieces of Glass* (Vesak), Stuttgart Ballet, Stuttgart

Mother (cr) in *Abschied* (Spoerli), Stuttgart Ballet, Stuttgart

1986 Title role in *Raymonda*, Act III (Petipa; staged Lepeshinskaya), Stuttgart Ballet, Stuttgart

1987 Principal dancer in *Sarkasmen* (*Piano Variations I*; pas de deux; van Manen), Stuttgart Ballet, Stuttgart

Principal dancer (cr) in *ENAS* (pas de deux; Haydée), Stuttgart Ballet, Tokyo

Principal dancer (cr) in *Shaker Loops* (van Manen), Stuttgart Ballet, Stuttgart

1988 Title role (cr) in *Salomé* (Wyss), Stuttgart Ballet, Stuttgart

Title role (cr) in *Die Listige Witwe* (Kurz), Stuttgart Ballet, Stuttgart

1989 Principal dancer in *Herbst* (pas de deux; Haydée), Stuttgart Ballet, Stuttgart

Title role (cr) in *Giselle und die Wilis* (Haydée after Petipa, Coralli, Perrot), Stuttgart Ballet, Stuttgart

1991 Venus (cr) in *The Planets* (Haydée), Stuttgart Ballet, Stuttgart

**Other roles include:** for Stuttgart Ballet—principal dancer in *Concerto* (MacMillan), principal dancer in *Gemini* (Tetley), principal dancer in *Symphony in C* (Balanchine), Death in *Ist dies etwa der Tod?* (Béjart), principal dancer in *Gloria* (MacMillan), Lover in *Gaîté Parisienne* (Béjart), principal dancer in *Elegie für eine tote Liebe* (Vesak), principal dancer in *Mahler's Fourth Symphony* (Neumeier), principal dancer in *Adagio Hammerklavier* (van Manen); as guest artist—principal dancer in *Nachmittag* (Keres), principal dancer in *Atrées* (Gora), Clorinda in *Le Combat* (Menge), principal dancer in *Intermezzo* (Feld), principal dancer in *Gespalten* (Brannon), principal dancer in *Requiem* (Biagi), principal dancer in *Beethoven's Seventh Symphony* (Biagi), principal dancer in *Also Sprach Zarathustra* (Biagi), principal dancer in *Sonate* (pas de deux; Scholz), principal dancer in *Quartetto con maschera rossa* (Legey).

## PUBLICATIONS

Niehaus, Max, *Ballett Faszination*, Munich, 1972

Winkler-Betzendahl, Madeline, *John Cranko und das Stuttgarter Ballett*, revised edition, Pfullingen, 1975

Koegler, Horst, *Stuttgart Ballet*, London, 1978

Regitz, Hartmut, "Birgit Keil: Portrait einer Ballerina", *Das Tanzarchiv* (Cologne), October 1980

Various contributors, *Birgit Keil; Portrait einer Ballerina*, Pfullingen, 1980; revised edition, 1991

Schmidt, Jochen, "Birgit Keil, Beruf: Ballerina", *Ballett International* (Cologne), April 1981

* * *

Birgit Keil is undoubtedly the most famous German ballerina of her time. As a member of the Stuttgart Ballet since the beginning of John Cranko's directorship in 1961, she has found international recognition in Europe and overseas, both in world-wide company tours and through guest solo appearances. This recognition rests as much upon her flawless technique and perfect classical line as on her warm and, above all, feminine radiance and presence. The international standing that Birgit Keil enjoys is matched by the great respect in which her home audience in Stuttgart holds her, as both dancer and individual. Along with Marcia Haydée and Richard Cragun, she numbers among the personalities of the Stuttgart Ballet who have become synonymous with the name of the ensemble, through their art and long-standing work together.

Because of her height, Keil's brilliant technique and lyrical stage presence have made her into a very particular type of ballerina, with long arms and legs and beautifully soft port de bras. Her appearance, on stage as in real life, is distinguished by a stylish elegance. Birgit Keil is an excellent interpreter of the great leading roles of the classical repertoire, which she still dances. Her technique, like her appearance of ethereal beauty, has inspired choreographers again and again in a special way—from John Cranko, who paid her tribute in the second section of *Initialen R.B.M.E.*, a homage to the dancers Richard

Cragun, Birgit Keil, Marcia Haydée, and Egon Madsen, up to Marcia Haydée herself, who choreographed an unconventional version of *Giselle* expressly for her, which was described by Horst Koegler as "astral". In 1987, the first piece choreographed entirely by Marcia Haydée appeared for Birgit Keil (after *The Sleeping Beauty*, in the same year). In *Enas* (with music by Vangelis), Keil showed a quite different aspect of herself at the side of Richard Cragun, namely not only her human, even maternal warmth, but also the almost masculine coolness and severity of her irreproachable technique.

Birgit Keil's sheer, unshakeable bond with Stuttgart and her company undoubtedly counts among her human qualities. Somewhere other than Stuttgart, where she often stood in Marcia Haydée's shadow, an even more brilliant and spectacular career would have been possible. In the great full-length ballets of John Cranko (and also in the full-length pieces choreographed by John Neumeier for the Stuttgart Ballet in the 1970s), she usually danced supporting or secondary leading roles, before later taking over the part as female protagonist as understudy to Marcia Haydée, often at her husband Vladimir Klos's side. Only then could she bring her different yet no less impressive abilities as interpreter to the attention of others. Straight away, however, Cranko understood completely how to bring out the particular qualities of Birgit Keil the dancer on stage. Again and again he created roles for her in single-act pieces. In doing so, he had already sounded out the whole technical and artistic range at Birgit Keil's disposal by 1964 (the same year that she was named soloist with the Stuttgart Ballet): she was just as convincing in the abstract and mysteriously equivocal *Opus 1* as she was in the witty story ballet *Jeu de cartes*.

Birgit Keil has worked with numerous important choreographers, mainly in Stuttgart, where she took part in the opening performances of the first productions of works by Kenneth MacMillan, Peter Wright, Glen Tetley, Jiří Kylián, and Hans van Manen. Heinz Spoerli entrusted the role of Mathilde Wesendonk to Birgit Keil in his Richard Wagner ballet *Träume*, and in doing so exploited the many-faceted qualities of the dancer more fully than others (this was also the case in the filming of the work with the Basel Ballet), while William Forsythe had already presented Birgit Keil as Eurydice in the same year in his radically modernistic *Orpheus*. Although a symbiosis never came out of her work with various choreographers which could be compared to that of Cranko and Haydée or Ashton and Fonteyn, again and again Birgit Keil has interpreted roles in which she was at odds with her apparently fixed type. Examples of this are the nonchalantly feminine part in Hans van Manen's ironic pas de deux *Sarkasmen*, and the representation of a mad widow in a humorous one-act ballet by the young Stuttgart Ballet choreographer Daniela Kurz.

—Horst Vollmer

---

**KENT, Allegra**

American dancer. Born in Los Angeles, 11 August 1938. Studied with Bronislava and Irina Nijinska, and with Carmelita Maracci, Los Angeles; studied (as scholarship pupil) at the School of American Ballet, New York, from 1952. Married Bert Stern, 1959 (div.): 3 children. Dancer, New York City Ballet, from 1953: principal dancer, from 1957, touring Japan and Australia, 1958; appeared in Broadway musical, *Shinbone Alley*, 1957, and occasionally as guest artist, including for André Eglevsky's Ballet Divertissements, Bavarian State Opera Ballet, Munich, the Ravinia Festival, Chicago, and the Ballet of Los Angeles (also acting as associate director), 1990; has also worked as freelance coach and teacher, including for Royal Ballet staging of Balanchine's *Bugaku*, 1988; director, Stamford City Ballet, Stamford, Connecticut, after retiring from stage.

**ROLES**

1954 Violas in *Fanfare* (Robbins), New York City Ballet, New York
"The Unanswered Question" (cr) in *Ivesiana* (Balanchine), New York City Ballet, New York
1956 First Variation (cr) in *Divertimento No. 15* (Balanchine), New York City Ballet, Stratford, Connecticut
Wallflower in *Souvenirs* (Bolender), New York City Ballet, European tour
Dewdrop Fairy in *The Nutcracker* (Balanchine), New York City Ballet, New York
Principal dancer in *Serenade* (Balanchine), New York City Ballet, New York
1957 Principal dancer in *Valse Fantaisie* (Balanchine), New York City Ballet, New York
Pas de deux in *Interplay* (Robbins), New York City Ballet, New York
Principal dancer in *Concerto Barocco* (Balanchine), New York City Ballet, New York
Second Movement in *Symphony in C* (Balanchine), New York City Ballet, New York
Principal dancer (cr) in *Pastorale* (Moncion), New York City Ballet, New York
The Countess in *The Unicorn, The Gorgon and the Manticore* (Butler), New York City Ballet, New York
Principal dancer in *Afternoon of a Faun* (Robbins), New York City Ballet, New York
1958 First Campaign (cr) in *Stars and Stripes* (Balanchine), New York City Ballet, New York
Odette in *Swan Lake* (one-act version; Balanchine after Ivanov), New York City Ballet, tour
Anna II (cr) in *The Seven Deadly Sins* (new production; Balanchine), New York City Ballet, New York
1959 Concerto (cr) in *Episodes* II (Balanchine), New York City Ballet, New York
Terpsichore in *Apollo* (Balanchine), New York City Ballet, New York
The Novice in *The Cage* (Robbins), New York City Ballet, New York
Principal dancer in *Native Dancers* (Balanchine), New York City Ballet, New York
The Doll in *Jeux d'enfants* (Balanchine, Millberg, Moncion), New York City Ballet, New York
Principal dancer in *Waltz-Scherzo* (Balanchine), New York City Ballet, New York
1960 The Sleepwalker in *Night Shadow* (*La Sonnambula*; Balanchine), New York City Ballet, New York
Principal dancer (cr) in *Serenata Concertante* (Contreras) in *Panamerica* (Contreras, Balanchine, Taras, d'Amboise), New York City Ballet, New York
1963 Principal dancer (cr) in *Bugaku* (Balanchine), New York City Ballet, New York
The Vixen (cr) in *The Chase* (d'Amboise), New York City Ballet, New York
1964 Sugar Plum Fairy in *The Nutcracker* (new production; Balanchine), New York City Ballet, New York

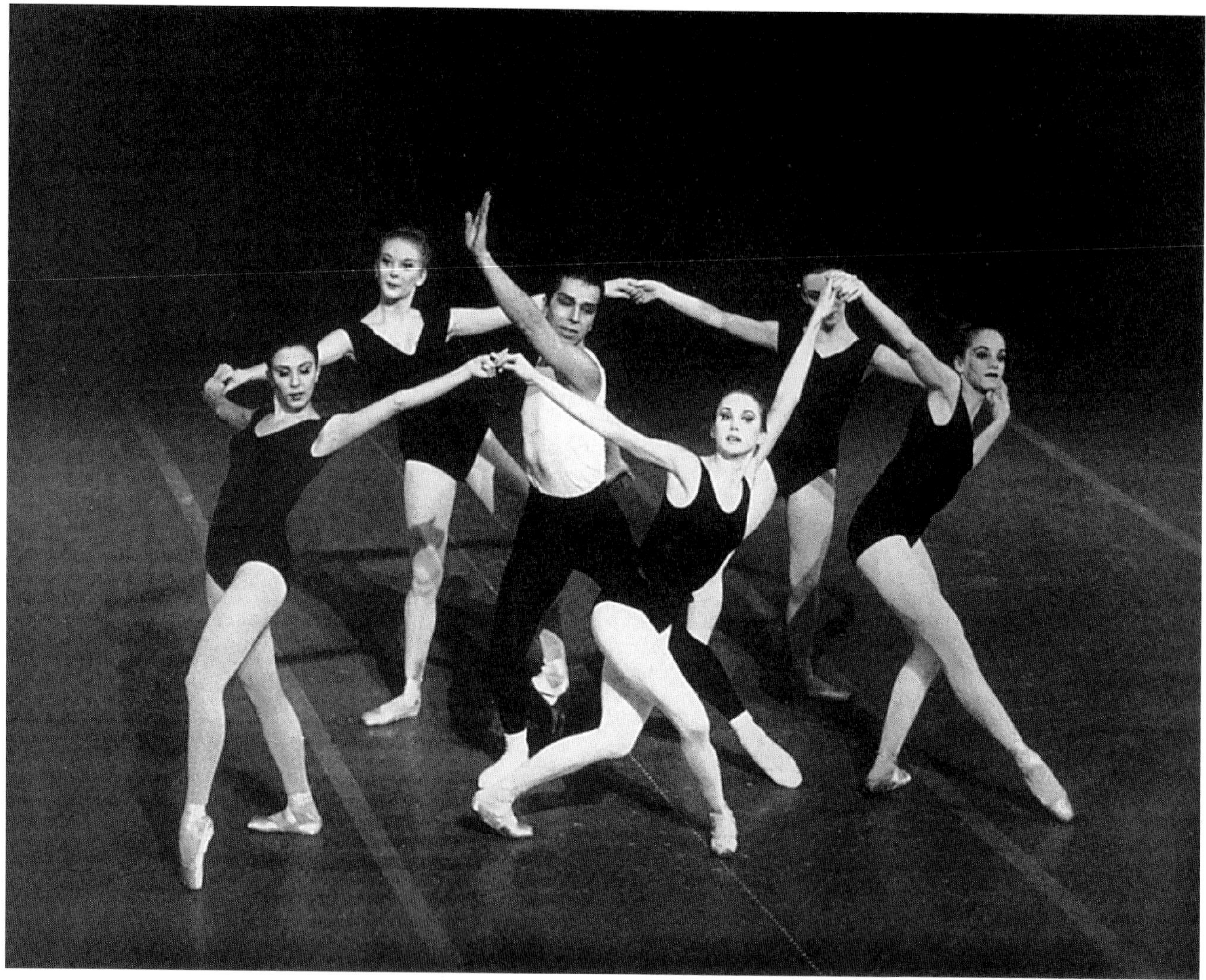

**Allegra Kent (centre front) with Nicholas Magallanes in *Episodes*, New York City Ballet**

1966 Andante (cr) in *Brahms–Schoenberg Quartet* (Balanchine), New York City Ballet, New York
First Young Girl (cr) in *Jeux* (Taras), New York City Ballet, New York
1969 Second Movement (cr) in *Tchaikovsky Suite* (d'Amboise), New York City Ballet, New York
Principal dancer (cr) in *Prelude, Fugue and Riffs* (Clifford), New York City Ballet, New York
Principal dancer (cr) in *Dances at a Gathering* (Robbins), New York City Ballet, New York
1972 Principal dancer (cr) in *Dumbarton Oaks* (Robbins), New York City Ballet, New York

**Other roles include:** Choleric in *The Four Temperaments* (Balanchine), Third Movement in *Symphony in C* (Balanchine), Leader of the Bacchantes in *Orpheus* (Balanchine), Ricercata in *Episodes* II (Balanchine), Prélude and Fête Polonaise in *Bourrée Fantasque* (Balanchine), principal dancer in *Sylvia: Pas de Deux* (Balanchine), principal dancer in *Scotch Symphony* (Balanchine), Pas de deux in *Agon* (Balanchine), principal dancer in *Gounod Symphony* (Balanchine), principal dancer in *Movements for Piano and Orchestra* (Balanchine), principal dancer in *Irish Fantasy* (d'Amboise), principal dancer in *Pas de Deux and Divertissement* (Balanchine), Intermezzo in *Brahms–Schoenberg Quartet* (Balanchine), Emeralds and Diamonds in *Jewels* (Balanchine), principal dancer in *Fantasies* (Clifford), principal dancer in *In the Night* (Robbins), Variations II in *The Goldberg Variations* (Robbins), principal dancer in *The Concert* (Robbins), principal dancer in *Allegro Brillante* (Balanchine), variation in *A Midsummer Night's Dream* (Balanchine).

**PUBLICATIONS**

By Kent:
Interview in Gruen, John, *The Private World of Ballet*, New York, 1975
*Allegra Kent's Water Beauty Book*, New York, 1976
Interview in Tracy, Robert, *Balanchine's Ballerinas*, New York, 1983
*The Dancer's Body Book*, New York, 1984
Interview in Newman, Barbara, "Speaking of Dance: Allegra Kent", *Dancing Times* (London), May 1988

About Kent:
Goodman, Saul, "Brief Biographies: Allegra Kent", *Dance Magazine* (New York), January 1957

Boroff, David Marion, "Group Portrait", *Dance Magazine* (New York), May 1957
Ginna, Robert Emmett, "Allegra Kent", *Horizon* (New York), November 1959
Greskovic, Robert, "Some Artists of the New York City Ballet", *Ballet Review* (New York), vol. 4, no. 4, 1973
Reynolds, Nancy, *Repertory in Review*, New York, 1977

* * *

Although American dancer Allegra Kent easily fits the category of the Balanchine ballerina, she has always maintained her own distinctive profile. It was George Balanchine who picked her from the corps and cast her in the premiere of "The Unanswered Question", a segment of his Ives ballet, in 1954. Held aloft by four boys, she was turned and manipulated in the air, never touching the floor. It was an auspicious solo for a young girl and introduced the image of a lyric dancer of great plasticity and precision, of innocence and mystery.

Like other great dancers, Kent was able to inject these unique qualities into many roles during her long engagement with the New York City Ballet. Kent's early training began in California, where she was a pupil of both Bronislava Nijinska and Carmelita Maracci. She moved to New York City, attended the School of American Ballet, apprenticed at the New York City Ballet, and at the age of fifteen became a permanent member of that company. Within the Balanchine canon, Kent amassed over twenty roles that encompassed a phenomenal musical range: Tchaikovsky's *Nutcracker* and *Allegro Brillante*, Stravinsky's *Agon*, Webern's *Episodes*, Bizet's *Symphony in C*, Hindemith's *Four Temperaments*, Mendelssohn's *A Midsummer Night's Dream* (not as Titania but in the second act pas de deux), the *Gounod Symphony*, Fauré's Emeralds (in *Jewels*). Balanchine chose Kent for the premieres of his *Divertimento No. 15* of Mozart, Sousa's *Stars and Stripes*, and the *Brahms–Schoenberg Quartet*. As Odette in the one-act *Swan Lake*, Kent garnered some of her most enthusiastic reviews for her musical phrasing. At the same time, she appeared a provocative but beautifully removed figure in Jerome Robbins's works, such as *Afternoon of a Faun*, *The Cage*, and *The Concert*.

In addition to Robbins's works, she has appeared in choreography by Bolender, Butler, d'Amboise, Dollar, Taras, Moncion, and Clifford, with many of the roles tailored especially to her supple body and musicality. Critic Walter Terry referred to Kent's "muscular lyricism", though she rarely undertook parts that were known for sheer strength and virtuosity. Despite her youth and femininity, she never became a true ingenue or soubrette, and she never challenged her company colleagues in balletic fireworks.

The figure Kent has presented to her audiences, combining elements mysterious, virginal, and poetic, was perhaps best seen in two Balanchine ballets: *Bugaku* and *La Sonnambula*. Kent's Bride in *Bugaku*, as she prepared for her wedding and later in an erotic pas de deux, appeared sexually enticing, yet coolly remote to her bridegroom and to the exacting demands of the choreography. The role of the Sleepwalker in *La Sonnambula* was rendered primarily through a long series of flowing bourrées. Again, Kent was able to go beyond the mere steps and, in their execution, to embody a figure of near-fantasy.

The ballerina's popularity was undoubtedly enhanced by her engagement in the Broadway musical, *Shinbone Alley*, dancing opposite Jacques d'Amboise, and further bolstered when Balanchine cast her in his new staging of the Weill/Brecht theater piece, *The Seven Deadly Sins* (1958), with Lotte Lenya. Kent, portraying Anna II, infused her character with a combination of innocence and exuberance that helped make the ballet a sell-out success.

Kent's long career with the New York City Ballet was broken by a series of absences, some explained—motherhood and school—others unexplained. At some performances one never knew if she would appear or not, which for many of her fans only added to the Kent mystique. Among her admirers was the artist Joseph Cornell, who dedicated several of his collages to her and to her children. She herself has written two books on physical therapy.

Never officially retired from the New York City Ballet, she left quietly during the mid-1980s but has remained active teaching and coaching. In 1990, she appeared as dancer and associate director of John Cliffords' Ballet of Los Angeles, where once more she displayed her remarkable talents.

—Richard Rutledge

---

## THE KERMESSE IN BRUGES
(Danish title: *Kermessen i Brügge*)

**Choreography:** August Bournonville
**Music:** Holger Simon Paulli
**Design:** Christian Ferdinand Christensen (scenery), Edvard Lehmann (costumes)
**Libretto:** August Bournonville
**First Production:** Royal Danish Ballet, Copenhagen, 4 April 1851
**Principal Dancers:** Juliette Price (Eleonora), Georg Brodersen (Adrian), Ferdinand Hoppensach (Geert), Ferdinand Hoppe (Carelis)

**Other productions include:** Royal Swedish Ballet (staged S. Lund); Stockholm, 30 December 1858. Royal Danish Ballet (staged Harald Lander and Valborg Borchsenius after Bournonville, with revisions and additional mus. Holm); Copenhagen, 5 May 1943. New York City Ballet (Act I Pas de deux only, staged Stanley Williams after Bournonville), as part of *Bournonville Divertissement*; New York, 1977. Royal Danish Ballet (two-act version; restaged Hans Brenaa, design Lars Juhl); Copenhagen, 1978. Pennsylvania Ballet (pas de deux only; staged E. Borne, J. Gribler after Stanley Williams); 19 May 1986. Bolshoi Ballet (pas de deux only; staged Jens Graff and Kirsten Ralov after Bournonville); Moscow, 10 May 1986.

### PUBLICATIONS

Bournonville, Auguste, *Mit Theater Liv*, 3 parts: Copenhagen, 1848, 1865, 1877; as *My Theatre Life*, translated by Patricia McAndrew, Middletown, Connecticut, 1979
Bruhn, Erik and Moore, Lillian, *Bournonville and Ballet Technique*, London, 1961
Ralov, Kirsten (ed.), *The Bournonville School*, New York, 1979
Terry, Walter, *The King's Ballet Master*, New York, 1979
Fridericia, Allan, *Auguste Bournonville*, Copenhagen, 1979
Aschengreen, Erik, *The Royal Danish Ballet and Bournonville*, Copenhagen, 1979
Clarke, Mary, "The Bournonville Festival", *Dancing Times*, London, January 1980
"The Ballet Poems of August Bournonville", (translated by Patricia McAndrew), *Dance Chronicle* (New York), vol. 4, no. 2, 1981

***The Kermesse in Bruges*, performed by the Royal Danish Ballet, Copenhagen, 1951**

Clarke, Mary, "Royal Danish Ballet", *Dancing Times*, June 1988

Hallar, Marianne, and Scavenius, Alette (eds.), *Bournonvilleana*, English edition, translated by Gaye Kynoch, Copenhagen, 1992

* * *

*The Kermesse in Bruges; or, The Three Gifts* is something of a rarity—it is both a comic and a "romantic" ballet, and it has been performed with great success for about 150 years at the Royal Theatre in Copenhagen. The choreographer, August Bournonville, gives us some details himself about how the ballet came into being. In his delightful autobiography, *My Theatre Life*, he writes about the fiasco of an unsuccessful serious ballet, and how he was told afterwards by an old theatre doorkeeper that "They want something to laugh at". Bournonville continues "I did owe my public some fun after my last trip to Olympus", referring to the ballet *Psyche* in 1850.

For inspiration Bournonville had studied the visual arts, and he was most attracted by the bourgeois painting of the seventeenth century, particularly the Flemish painter Gerard Dou and his 1663 painting *A Violin-player at the Window* (now in the Dresdner Gallery). Along with visual art, Bournonville was inspired by the magic of music, as exemplified by the Norwegian violin virtuoso Ole Bull. The dramatic structure of this bourgeois ballet is based on the fairy tale of the three gifts: the story of the nobleman Josias Rantzau's sword of victory, little Tove's magic ring, and of Gerard Dou's violin (or viola da gamba).

The action takes place in Bruges in the seventeenth century. A local festival in honour of the city's patron saint is underway in the marketplace. We are shown a spirited street scene, featuring dancing both in clogs and en pointe. The two older burgher sons, Adrian and Geert, have their sweethearts Johanna and Marchen with them, whereas the youngest brother, Carelis, is captivated by the young Eleonora, daughter of the alchemist Mirewelt. Some gypsies at the fair dance a spirited Slowanka (Mazurka) and Carelis and Eleonora dance a delicate pas de deux. A couple of noblemen flirt with Johanna and Marchen, which leads to the girls quarrelling with Adrian and Geert.

The latter are angered and decide to set out to see the world together with Carelis. Darkness falls, and just as the three youths are leaving, Mirewelt is attacked by noblemen who want to kidnap his young daughter. Carelis and his brothers come to their aid, and the young men save father and daughter. Mirewelt's housekeeper arrives and as thanks the three young men are rewarded by the alchemist with three gifts. Geert receives a ring which causes everyone to fall in love with its owner; Adrian receives a sword which brings victory in battle; and Carelis is given a viola da gamba, which forces everyone who hears its melody to dance.

In Act II, Johanna and Marchen seek out Mirewelt in his study, hoping to discover the fates of their sweethearts through his magic arts. They see a tableau with Adrian as a war hero, while Geert's tableau shows him enjoying himself with wine and beautiful women in happy luxury. The two girls are saddened, but Carelis encourages the sisters to set out to find his two brothers. Carelis, now alone with Eleonora, wins her over by the magic power of his playing; the music unites them and they declare their love.

Next we see Geert at the palace of the rich and beautiful widow, Mrs. van Everdingen, who because of the magic ring is wildly infatuated with the unpolished young commoner. At an aristocratic party, Geert is importuned by the ladies, while their companions hold the coarse fellow in contempt. Adrian, now a true hero, returns from the wars and comes visiting. Shortly after this, Johanna, Marchen, and their mother Trutje appear. The young people are reconciled while the magic ring makes the rounds, finally ending up on the old woman, who is now the object of the gentlemen's attention. Adrian defeats the noblemen with his sword. The family decides to get rid of the magic gifts, but no sooner have they done so than the authorities arrive. Adrian and Geert are carried away.

In Act III, the old alchemist is seen musing over the imaginary value of gold. Soon afterwards, he is arrested for practising witchcraft, but Carelis promises to help him. Meanwhile Mirewelt, along with Adrian and Geert, is condemned to be burned at the stake for sorcery.

In the final scene the condemned are already standing at the stake, but Carelis arrives with his viola da gamba, and he forces everyone to dance. The entire town jumps, hops, and dances until all collapse, exhausted and begging for mercy. The condemned men are freed, while in return the authorities receive the viola da gamba, which is locked in a chest only to be taken out at the yearly Kermesse.

The music for this lighthearted ballet was arranged by Bournonville's assistant of many years, H.S. Paulli. Bournonville always had precise requirements regarding music, and for this ballet he wanted Paulli to consult a number of popular operas which he had seen in Paris during the 1820s. Large sections of the music, therefore, are taken from Rossini's *Le Comte d'Ory* and *Le Siège de Corinthe*, while there are also sections from Hérold's *Zampa*.

Choreographically, we are presented with a ballet in typical Bournonville style, employing a large number of the choreographer's well-known effects. The burghers' heavy clog dance in Act I is set in relief against the tense and gypsy-like Slowanka, and in the pas de deux between Carelis and Eleonora in the same scene we find Bournonville's typical classical style with a beautiful and delicate use of pointe-work. The long mime passages are both musically and dramatically balanced with grander dance sections. The divertissement in the first scene of Act II shows the later and more difficult Bournonville style, while the concluding finale dance is extremely festive. The ballet bubbles with life and with humour.

It would seem that *The Kermesse in Bruges* is one of Bournonville's best-preserved ballets. It was continuously staged by Bournonville himself at the Royal Theatre in Copenhagen from 1851 until 1884; Emil Hansen followed with a staging in 1891, Hans Beck staged the ballet in 1900 and 1909–11, and Gustav Uhlendorff kept *Kermesse* on the stage from 1918 until 1926. Harald Lander, who (assisted by Borchsenius) staged *Kermesse* from 1943 until 1945, was the first to make cuts and changes to the original choreography. He cut the scene between Carelis and Eleonora (Act II, scene 4) heavily, and he removed the opening scene of the third act, which takes place in Mirewelt's laboratory. It was also Lander who introduced a grand divertissement in Act II, at the party of Mrs. van Everdingen. This divertissement has its musical origins in an addition first made to the opera *La Muette de Portici* (by Auber); the music for the divertissement was written by V.C. Holm and dates from 1873.

Since Lander's version, several other productions have been seen on the stage of the Royal Danish Theatre. Niels Bjørn Larsen, assisted by Hans Brenaa, was responsible for stagings in 1951–53, and 1957–59, while Brenaa himself collaborated in Flemming Flindt's 1966 production, which stayed in the repertory until 1969; this was followed in 1979 by a staging overseen by Brenaa and Anne Marie Vessel. As of 2 April 1992, *The Kermesse in Bruges* had been performed by the Royal Danish Ballet 303 times.

—Ole Nørlyng

---

**KHACHATURIAN, Aram**

Soviet composer. Born Aram Ilyich Khachaturian in Tbilisi, 6 June (24 May old style) 1903. Attended Gnesin Music Academy, learning cello, from 1922, and composition from 1925; studied at the Moscow Conservatory, studying composition with Myaskowsky, 1929–37. Married composer Nina Makarova, 1933. Composed first ballet, *Happiness*, 1939, incorporating music from its score into *Gayané*, 1942; music censured by Communist Party, 1948; teacher, Moscow Conservatory, from 1950; best-known work, *Spartacus*, performed in Leningrad, 1956 (revised 1968). Recipient: Order of Lenin, 1939; People's Artist of the USSR, 1954; Lenin Prize (for *Spartacus*), 1959. Died in Moscow, 1 May 1978.

**WORKS** (Ballets)

1939 *Happiness* (chor. Arbatov), Yerevan
1942 *Gayané* (expanded from *Happiness*; chor. Anisimova), Kirov Ballet, Perm
1956 *Spartacus* (chor. Yakobson), Kirov Ballet, Leningrad

**Other ballets using Khachaturian's music:** *Le Prisonnier du Caucase* (Skibine, 1951), *Spartacus* (new version; chor. Moiseyev, 1958; also Grigorovich, 1968; Yakobson, 1962; Seregi, 1968), *Movement Eternal* (Eifman, 1979).

**PUBLICATIONS**

Kaltat, L., *Khachaturian*, Moscow, 1946
Shneyerson, G. M., *Aram Khachaturian*, Moscow, 1956
Searle, Humphrey, *Ballet Music: An Introduction*, New York, 1958
*Music of the Soviet Ballet* (collection of articles), Moscow, 1962
Swift, Mary Grace, *The Art of the Dance in the U.S.S.R.*, Notre Dame, Indiana, 1968
Krebs, S.D., *Soviet Composers and the Development of Soviet Music*, London, 1970
Schwarz, B., *Music and Musical Life in Russia 1917–1970*, London, 1972
Dorris, George, "Music for Spectacle", *Ballet Review* (Brooklyn), vol. 6, no. 1, 1977

Yuzefovich, Viktor, *Aram Khachaturyan*, translated by Nicholas Kournokoff, and Vladimir Bobrov, New York, 1985

* * *

Aside from other musical works in concert form, it is principally Khachaturian's two works for the ballet stage which have secured his reputation with Western audiences both in and out of the theatre, and their popularity in purely musical terms—mainly through the concert suites derived from them—vies with their historical importance in the development of large-scale Soviet dramatic ballets.

In structural terms, both *Gayané* (several times reworked from an earlier ballet, *Happiness*) and *Spartacus*, in its various successive versions, are the first Soviet ballets to reconcile new subject matter—relating either in actuality or in symbolic form to life after the revolution—with the relatively traditional formulae of numbered pas d'action, pas de deux, solos, and character dances. They do this while at the same time allowing for a genuinely twentieth-century (if at times highly lyrical) musical idiom and more extended musical forms.

Khachaturian's nationality as an Armenian, rather than a Russian, not only broadened the range of orchestral sound with genuine (as opposed to imitated) "oriental" material, but also allowed an authentic marriage of regional folk dance material, in immediately appealing and vivid forms, to plot lines which could still reflect official Soviet principles. In this respect, though they were to go through several versions with different choreographers, Khachaturian's ballets have fared better than those of his principal contemporaries—especially Shostakovich. (Both Khachaturian and Shostakovich, however, lacked the cosmopolitan background of Prokofiev, who gained practical experience in the theatre while within the Diaghilev circle.)

In practice, Khachaturian's scores have presented choreographers with certain difficulties. While his character dances tend to be short and specific, his music for longer scenes d'action is frequently based on the culmulative repetition of undeveloped phrases, which, despite their individual attractiveness, often deny support for variety of pacing in the steps. Their need for space to accomplish the long-range working out of their balance frequently makes concise treatment of action a problem, and suggests that the composer does not possess an instinctive sense of broader choreographic logic. The changing versions of *Spartacus*, in particular (before Grigorovich's final version crystallized it into the form that has become famous), confirm this. It is the impact of Grigorovich's spectacularly athletic movement in ensembles and passionately sinuous line in solos and pas de deux which conveys the work's essential power to the audience; and the wider appreciation of Khachaturian's ballet's appears to rest on an unusual coincidence of great external charm supported by fortunate theatrical circumstance.

—Geoffrey Baskerville

---

**KIDD, Michael**

American dancer, choreographer, and director. Born Milton Greenwald in Brooklyn, New York, 12 August 1920. Educated at the School of Engineering, City College, New York, 1936–37; studied dance at the School of American Ballet, New York, pupil of Anatole Vilzak, Ludmila Schollar, and Muriel Stuart, 1937–39. Married dancer Mary Heater, 1940. Married Shelah Hackett, 1970. Début as dancer in musical *The Eternal Road*, Manhattan Opera House, 1937; dancer, American Ballet, Metropolitan Opera, New York, 1937; soloist, Ballet Caravan, 1937–40, also dancing at World's Fair, New York, 1939 and 1940, and Radio City Music Hall, 1941; soloist and assistant director, Eugene Loring's Dance Players, 1941–42; principal dancer, Ballet Theatre (later American Ballet Theatre), 1942–47; also choreographer, staging work for Ballet Theatre, *On Stage!*, 1945; choreographer and director for musical comedy and revue, including for *Wonderworld*, World's Fair, 1964; also choreographer for film, including *Where's Charley?* (after farce *Charley's Aunt* by Brandon Thomas; dir. Butler, 1952), *Band Wagon* (dir. Minnelli, 1953), *Knock on Wood* (dir. Panama, 1954), *Seven Brides for Seven Brothers* (dir. Donen, 1954), *Guys and Dolls* (dir. Mankiewicz, 1955), *It's Always Fair Weather* (dir. Kelly, Donen, 1955), *Star!* (dir. Wise, 1968), *Hello Dolly* (dir. Kelly, 1969), and *Movie Movie* (dir. Donen, 1978), and for television, including television special "Baryshnikov in Hollywood" (1982); has also appeared as actor in films. Recipient: Antoinette Perry Awards for choreography in musicals *Finian's Rainbow*, 1947, *Guys and Dolls*, 1951, *Can-Can*, 1953, *Li'l Abner*, 1956, and *Destry Rides Again*, 1959.

**ROLES**

1937 The Adversary's Follower in *The Eternal Road* (musical; mus. K. Weill, chor. Zemach), Manhattan Opera House, New York

A Sailor (cr) in *Yankee Clipper* (Loring), Ballet Caravan, Saybrook, Connecticut

1938 Solo (cr) in *Billy the Kid* (Loring), Ballet Caravan, Chicago

1938/39 Billy in *Billy the Kid* (Loring), Ballet Caravan

1941 The Son, The Drugstore Cowboy (cr) in *City Portrait* (Loring), Ballet Caravan, Mobile, Alabama

1941/42 Harlequin in *Harlequin for President* (Loring), Dance Players

Principal dancer in *The Man from Midian* (Loring), Dance Players

1942 Principal dancer in *Jinx* (Christensen), Dance Players, Schenechtady, New York

1942/45 Title role in *Petrushka* (Fokine), Ballet Theatre, New York

Devil in *Three Virgins and a Devil* (de Mille), Ballet Theatre, New York

1943 The Dandy in *Three-Cornered Hat* (Massine), Ballet Theatre, New York

Another Reflection (cr) in *Dim Lustre* (Tudor), Ballet Theatre, New York

Peddler (cr) in *Fair at Sorochinsk* (Lichine), Ballet Theatre, New York

Vagabond (cr) in *Mademoiselle Angot* (later *Mam'zelle Angot*; Massine), Ballet Theatre, New York

1944 First Sailor in *Fancy Free* (Robbins), Ballet Theatre, New York

The Barber in *Mademoiselle Angot* (*Mam'zelle Angot*; Massine), Ballet Theatre, New York

1945 One of the Satyrisci (cr) in *Undertow* (Tudor), Ballet Theatre, New York

Dancer (cr) in *Interplay* (Robbins), Billy Rose's "Concert Varieties", Ziegfeld Theatre, New York

Handyman (cr) in *On Stage!* (also chor.), Ballet Theatre, Boston

1946 The Transgressor in *Undertow* (Tudor), Ballet Theatre, New York

**Michael Kidd's *On Stage!*, Ballet Theatre tour, London, 1946**

1955 Angie (cr) in *It's Always Fair Weather* (musical; dir. Kelly, Donen; also. chor.), Hollywood film

**Other roles include:** roles in *Pillar of Fire* (Tudor), *Bluebeard* (Fokine), *Aurora's Wedding* (divertissements from *The Sleeping Beauty*; Dolin after Petipa), *Helen of Troy* (Lichine), *Romeo and Juliet* (Tudor), *Giselle* (Dolin after Petipa, Coralli, Perrot), *Coppélia* (Semenoff after Petipa, Cecchetti).

## WORKS

1945 *On Stage!* (mus. Dello Joio), Ballet Theatre, Boston

**Other works include:** dances in musicals and revues—*Finian's Rainbow* (lib. Harburg and Saidy, mus. Lane; 1947), *Hold It!* (lib. Brooks and Arthur, mus. Marks; 1948), *Love Life* (lib. Lerner, mus. Weill; 1948), *Pretty Penny* (lib. Rome and Chorodov; Boston, 1949), *Arms and the Girl* (lib. Fields and Mamoulian, mus. Gould; 1950), *Guys and Dolls* (lib. Swerling and Burrows, mus. Loesser; 1950), *Can-Can* (lib. and mus. Cole Porter; 1953), *Li'l Abner* (lib. Panama and Frank, mus. de Paul; 1956), *Destry Rides Again* (lib. Gershe, mus. Rome; 1959), *Wildcat* (lib. Leigh, mus. Coleman and Morris; 1960), *Subways are for Sleeping* (lib. Comden, mus. Styne; 1961), *Here's Love* (lib. Willson, mus. Willson, arranged Howard; 1963), *Ben Franklin in Paris* (lib. Michaels, mus. Sandrich, arranged Adams; 1964), *Cyrano* (lib. Burgess after Rostand; 1973), *The Music Man* (revival; lib. Willson, mus. dir. Heindorf), *The Sound of Music* (revival; lib. Lindsay and Crouse, mus. Rodgers), *Bells are Ringing* (lib. Comden, mus. Styne).

## PUBLICATIONS


Barzel, Ann, "Bright Young Men", *Dance Magazine* (New York), April 1946

Goodman, Ezra, "Broadway Choreographers", *Dance Magazine* (New York), March 1947

Denby, Edwin, *Looking at the Dance*, New York, 1949

Martin, J., "Kidd from Brooklyn", *New York Times* (New York), 13 July 1954

Martin, J., "Kidd on his Toes", *New York Times* (New York), 10 July 1955

Newnham, John K., "Kidd as an Actor", *Dancing Times* (London), November 1955

Coleman, E., "Dance Man Leaps to the Top", *New York Times Magazine* (New York), 19 April 1959

Payne, Charles, *American Ballet Theatre*, New York, 1978

de Mille, Agnes, *America Dances*, New York, 1980

Denby, Edwin, *Dance Writings*, edited by Robert Cornfield and William Mackay, New York, 1986


* * *

In the 1930s there emerged a new breed of American choreographer who translated into the ballet style some of the dynamics of the modern dance school, and made use of colloquial steps from both rural and urban American dance forms. Agnes de Mille was the first to exploit this mongrel heritage with her ballet *Rodeo* (1942), and Jerome Robbins followed her in 1944 with *Fancy Free*. Both choreographers spent their long and lively careers working in both the musical theatre and the ballet. Michael Kidd, who shared their diversified background in dance, created but one ballet in 1945 while a soloist with Ballet Theatre (*On Stage!*) and was never tempted to return to the medium again. Over five decades Kidd has continued to create winsome and imaginative dances for the Broadway stage and the Hollywood musical, dabbling occasionally in choreography for television. As he approached his sixtieth birthday, Kidd capped a vital career in the theatre with superb performances as a comic actor in three commercial motion pictures.

Of the three American ballet pioneers, Kidd was surely the most adaptable and dedicated performer in the works of others during his decade in American ballet troupes. A late starter, he trained with Anatole Vilzak and Lyudmila Schollar, who provided him with a sound classical base and a respect for Ballet Russe traditions. Short in stature, a natural comic, he found his forte in character roles, excelling in those in which his gamin characteristics were utilized. No major roles were created for his talents, but the ballet repertoire of the era offered him a vast range of portrayals, from Fokine's *Petrushka* to Eugene Loring's *Billy the Kid*. Léonide Massine cast him in all the ballets he staged for Ballet Theatre, and upon the choreographer's departure in 1944 Kidd took over his part as the Barber in *Mademoiselle Angot*. Equally effective in the Tudor repertoire, Kidd assumed Hugh Laing's powerful role as the Transgressor in *Undertow*. During Ballet Theatre's first London season in 1946, Kidd was seen in the full spectrum of his interpretive powers.

In 1947, he left the ballet world and entered the second phase of a bright career when he devised the dances and musical numbers for the Broadway play, *Finian's Rainbow*. This endeavour won him his first Tony (Antoinette Perry) Award and led him to a string of comparable successes over the next two decades, during which time he commuted between Broadway and Hollywood. Perhaps his most endearing creation over the years was the barn-raising ballet for the film, *Seven Brides for Seven Brothers* (1954), surely a classic of the genre.

Kidd's choreography for stage and screen has an amicable urgency about it and a sharp comic-strip look. From the classical ballet he has borrowed the spectacular lifts and the split-second timing required for his breezy partnerships. His vernacular concepts are tempered with the extroverted, full-out dancing style of ballet russe, a genre which he has successfully satirized on occasion. Invariably concerned with gender roles, never sentimental, fastidiously serving the music, his dances tell clear, touching, and frequently hilarious tales of American lives and manners.

—Leland Windreich

---

## KIRKLAND, Gelsey

American dancer and teacher. Born in Bethlehem, Pennsylvania, 29 December 1952. Studied at the School of American Ballet, New York, from 1961. Married Greg Lawrence, 1985. Début with New York City Ballet, when still a student, in child roles; dancer, corps de ballet, New York City Ballet, 1968, becoming soloist, 1969, and principal dancer, 1972–74, touring Russia with company, 1972; principal dancer, American Ballet Theatre, 1974–80, 1981–84; international guest artist, including with Royal Winnipeg Ballet, 1974, Paris Opéra, 1975, "Serato a Quattro", Venice, 1975, Boston Ballet, 1980, Stuttgart Ballet, 1980, Eglevsky Ballet, 1981, Pacific Northwest Ballet, 1981, Royal Ballet, London, 1980 and 1986; freelance teacher and coach, including for American Ballet Theatre, from 1992.

### ROLES

1968 Pas de deux from *Flower Festival at Genzano* (Bournonville; staged Williams), School of American Ballet Workshop Performance, New York
- Pas de trois from *Paquita* (Petipa; staged Danilova), School of American Ballet Workshop Performance, New York

1969 Principal dancer (cr) in *Reveries* (later *Tchaikovsky Suite No. 1*; Clifford), New York City Ballet, New York
- Dew Drop Fairy in *The Nutcracker* (Balanchine), New York City Ballet, New York
- Principal dancer in *Monumentum Pro Gesualdo* (Balanchine), New York City Ballet, New York
- Sugar Plum Fairy in *The Nutcracker* (Balanchine), New York City Ballet, New York

1970 Title role (cr) in *Firebird* (new production; Balanchine, Robbins), New York City Ballet, New York
- Tema con variazioni (cr) in *Suite No. 3* (later *Tchaikovsky Suite No. 3*; Balanchine), New York City Ballet, New York

1970/71 The Novice in *The Cage* (Robbins), New York City Ballet, New York
- Principal dancer in *Dances at a Gathering* (Robbins), New York City Ballet, New York

1971 Principal dancer (cr) in *Concerto for Two Solo Pianos* (R. Tanner), New York City Ballet, New York
- Variations (cr) in *The Goldberg Variations* (Robbins), New York City Ballet, New York

1971/72 Columbine in *Harlequinade* (Balanchine), New York City Ballet, New York
- Principal dancer in *Concerto Barocco* (Balanchine), New York City Ballet, New York
- Second Movement in *Symphony in C* (Balanchine), New York City Ballet, New York
- Rubies in *Jewels* (Balanchine), New York City Ballet, New York
- Dancer in *Tarantella* (pas de deux; Balanchine), New York City Ballet, New York
- Allegro in *Brahms-Schoenberg Quartet* (Balanchine), New York City Ballet, New York
- Pas de deux Mauresque in *Don Quixote* (Balanchine), New York City Ballet, New York
- Ballerina in *Theme and Variations* (Balanchine), New York City Ballet, New York

1972 Principal dancer (cr) in *Scherzo Fantastique* (Robbins), New York City Ballet, New York
- Principal dancer (cr) in *Symphony in E Flat* (Clifford), New York City Ballet, New York

1973 Principal dancer (cr; but did not dance premiere) in *An Evening's Waltzes* (Robbins), New York City Ballet, New York

1974 Nightingale (cr) in *The Son of the Nightingale* (Taras), New York City Ballet, New York
- Dancer (cr) in *Four Bagatelles* (pas de deux; Robbins), New York City Ballet, New York
- Principal dancer in *Variations pour une porte et un soupir* (Balanchine), New York City Ballet
- Dancer in *La Source* (pas de deux; Balanchine), New York City Ballet, New York
- Principal dancer in *In the Night* (Robbins), New York City Ballet, New York
- Principal dancer in *Irish Fantasy* (d'Amboise), New York City Ballet, New York

**Gelsey Kirkland as Giselle, American Ballet Theatre, London, c.1978**

Ballerina in (*Tchaikovsky*) *Pas de deux* (Balanchine), New York City Ballet, New York
Kitri in *Don Quixote* Pas de deux (after Petipa), Royal Winnipeg Ballet, Winnipeg
Swanilda in *Coppélia* (Martinez after Saint-Léon), American Ballet Theatre, Washington, D.C.
Nikiya in "The Kingdom of the Shades" from *La Bayadère* (Petipa; staged Makarova), American Ballet Theatre

1975 Principal dancer in *Le Corsaire* Pas de deux (after Petipa), American Ballet Theatre, New York
Lise in *La Fille mal gardée* (D. Romanoff after Petipa), American Ballet Theatre, New York
Title role in *La Sylphide* (Bournonville; staged Lander), American Ballet Theatre, New York
Waltz, Mazurka in *Les Sylphides* (Fokine), American Ballet Theatre, New York
Principal dancer in *Concerto* (MacMillan), American Ballet Theatre, New York
Lake in *The River* (Ailey), American Ballet Theatre, New York
Title role in *Giselle* (Petipa after Coralli, Perrot; staged Blair), American Ballet Theatre, Washington, D.C.
Principal dancer (cr) in *The Leaves are Fading* (Tudor), American Ballet Theatre, New York
Celestial in *Shadowplay* (Tudor), American Ballet Theatre, New York
Principal dancer (cr) in *A Promise* (pas de deux; R. Weiss), American Ballet Theatre, New York

1976 Ophelia (cr) in *Hamlet Connotations* (Neumeier), American Ballet Theatre, New York
Princess Aurora in *The Sleeping Beauty* (Petipa; staged Skeaping), American Ballet Theatre

1977 Principal dancer in *Other Dances* (pas de deux; Robbins), American Ballet Theatre, New York
Odette/Odile in *Swan Lake* (Petipa, Ivanov; staged Blair), American Ballet Theatre, New York
Clara in *The Nutcracker* (Baryshnikov), American Ballet Theatre, New York

1978 Kitri in *Don Quixote* (Baryshnikov after Gorsky, Petipa), American Ballet Theatre, Washington, D.C.
Principal dancer (cr) in *The Tiller in the Fields* (Tudor), American Ballet Theatre, Washington, D.C.
Principal dancer in *Voluntaries* (Tetley), American Ballet Theatre, New York

1979 Principal dancer (cr) in *Three Preludes* (Stevenson), American Ballet Theatre

1980 Juliet in *Romeo and Juliet* (Cranko), Stuttgart Ballet, Stuttgart
Juliet in *Romeo and Juliet* (MacMillan), Royal Ballet, London
Pas de deux from *The Dream* (Ashton), Royal Ballet Gala, London

1981 Adagio in *Les Rendezvous* (Ashton), American Ballet Theatre

1983 The Sleepwalker in *La Sonnambula* (Balanchine), American Ballet Theatre

1986 Princess Aurora in *The Sleeping Beauty* (Petipa, Ashton; staged MacMillan), Royal Ballet, London

**Other roles include:** for New York City Ballet—Andante in *Brahms–Schoenberg Quartet* (Balanchine), Polka in *Valse Fantaisie* (Balanchine), First and Third Movements in *Tchaikovsky Suite No. 2* (d'Amboise), Fourth Campaign in *Stars and Stripes* (Balanchine), principal dancer in *In the Night* (Robbins), principal dancer in *Divertimento from "Le Baiser de la Feé"* (Balanchine), Young Woman in the *Dybbuk Variations* (Robbins); for American Ballet Theatre—principal dancer in *Pavane* (pas de deux), Caroline in *Jardin aux lilas* (Tudor).

## PUBLICATIONS

By Kirkland:

*Dancing on my Grave* (autobiography), co-written with Greg Lawrence, New York, 1986

"Reflections on a Vanishing Art", *Dance Magazine* (New York), November 1986

*The Shape of Love* (autobiography), co-written with Greg Lawrence, London, 1990

About Kirkland:

Goodman, Saul, "Gelsey Kirkland: Brief Biography", *Dance Magazine* (New York), December 1971

Tobias, Toni, "Celebration", *Dance Magazine* (New York), December 1977

Croce, Arlene, *Afterimages*, New York, 1977

Sandler, Ken, "Her Own Best Friend", *Ballet News* (New York), October 1981

Fowler, Carol, *Dance*, Minneapolis, 1981

Croce, Arlene, *Going to the Dance*, New York, 1982

Horn, L., "On the Comeback Trail", *Ballet News* (New York), August 1982

Percival, John, "Back from the Living Dead", *Dance and Dancers* (London), February 1987

* * *

One of the most outstanding of twentieth-century ballerinas, Gelsey Kirkland has had a career that straddles both the heights of artistry, courage, and imagination and the depths of self-obsession and self-destruction. Born with unsurpassed gifts, she was singled out at the School of America Ballet, and began dancing solo roles shortly after joining the New York City Ballet. Her first solos, the Butterfly in George Balanchine's *A Midsummer Night's Dream*, and the Marzipan Shepherdess and Dew Drop Fairy in his *Nutcracker*, attracted attention because of her delicate strength, effortless jump, and breathtaking speed. Then, in the role of the Sugar Plum Fairy, she revealed both poise and authority. These were the qualities Balanchine explored when he created a new *Firebird* with her as the lead in 1970. He said he did not want a woman, but "one of God's natural creatures . . . I didn't want people. I wanted Chagall." Kirkland was compared to a hummingbird. For the next four years, she mastered major roles in the New York City Ballet repertory and yet, an independent spirit, she distanced herself from Balanchine by not attending his daily company class. He did not create anything further for her, but others (John Clifford, Jerome Robbins, Richard Tanner, John Taras) did.

At 5′ 4″, Kirkland's body is perfectly proportioned, her head elegantly poised on her long neck. Big blue eyes enhance her sweet, childlike face. Her feet are exquisite, beautifully arched and supple. Her ability to rise and descend on to her points, silently and effortlessly, has been frequently noted. Her long legs are well turned out and shapely. Kirkland's port de bras is delicate and textbook correct. In her years with the New York City Ballet, her port de bras was distinctly more refined and rounded than the prevailing style, which was much more extended, with the angle of the wrist somewhat exaggerated.

Technically, there was little that eluded her. She could be the mercurial sprite, leaping and darting with no regard for gravity. She turned with ease and precision. Her adagio work was fluid, perfectly placed and sensitive to musical innuendo. It was particularly gratifying to watch her in pas de deux work because the lightness of her body allowed for the maximum effect in lifts. It was with apparent ease that her partners lifted her from side to side, in the arc of arabesques in the second movement of *Concerto Barocco* and in the skimming developpés en avant in *Symphony in C*. She was particularly poignant in Robbins' *Dances at a Gathering*, for the fluidity of her dancing was perfectly suited to the lyricism of his choreography. Probably the only criticism, mild and infrequent, of Kirkland's dancing during her years at New York City Ballet was for lapses in portrayal of dramatic roles, such as Columbine in *Harlequinade*.

In 1974, Kirkland left City Ballet to join American Ballet Theatre, so that she could dance the nineteenth-century classics. (It was also no secret that Mikhail Baryshnikov, recently defected from the Kirov, had asked her to be his partner.) With Ballet Theatre, Kirkland, the quintessential soubrette, triumphed as Swanilda in *Coppélia* and Lise in *La Fille mal gardée*. The incredible lightness of her dancing was put to perfect effect in her portrayals of these playful young women. In *La Sylphide* she was able to turn that playfulness to touching melancholy. In this role, too, her delicate and expansive jump was the vehicle that convinced viewers she was a supernatural creature.

With her portrayal of *Giselle*, Kirkland reached a pinnacle of artistic and critical success. She was compared to the great Giselles of the century. Critics stated that this was the role she was born to dance. Her youthful vulnerability in the first act was real, the transition to madness, compelling. In the second act, her commitment to the choreography was total. The purity and depth of her dancing were the essence of Giselle's resolve. The same year that she did *Giselle*, Kirkland created the lead in Antony Tudor's *The Leaves are Fading*. It was through the lush, romantic choreography that she expressed the passion of love so eloquently.

But, as she achieved greatness, she failed to maintain it with consistency. As early as 1975 there were lapses. These were seldom technical, but rather suggested the intrusion of an attitude or a manner that was imposed unnecessarily upon her dancing. It was as though she put something between her dancing and the audience. She continued to give superb performances and to take on new roles, such as in *The Sleeping Beauty* and *Swan Lake*, which demanded greater maturity. But her dancing varied, not only from performance to performance but sometimes from act to act. She went through bouts of illness and dissatisfaction. She failed to honor contracts and rehearsal schedules. She left and returned to American Ballet Theatre many times between 1980 and 1984, resigning permanently in May 1984.

In 1986 Kirkland published a sensational account of her career which she had written with her husband Greg Lawrence. Entitled *Dancing on my Grave*, the book elucidated the trials of Kirkland's life (disappointments in art, love, and drugs) and managed to place blame on just about everyone except herself. It was an indictment of the world of ballet, not without some grains of truth, but dismally told. Most important to those who had watched her career, it answered some questions about the changes in her dancing which were so perplexing.

Since 1984, Kirkland has performed as a guest artist with many companies, most successfully with the Royal Ballet. She is also teaching, and coaching young dancers.

—Rose Anne Thom

---

**KIROV BALLET**

Russian ballet company based in Leningrad/St Petersburg. Origins in court performances, then in professional company (or Imperial Ballet) of the Bolshoi (Grand) Theatre, St. Petersburg, 1783–86, moving to Maryinsky Theatre (opened 1860, but not to ballet until after 1880), 1886–1917, State Maryinsky Theatre, 1917–20, State Academic Theatre for Opera and Ballet (GATOB), 1920–35, and Kirov Theatre, from 1935; established as official resident ballet company of the Leningrad Theatre for Opera and Ballet named after Kirov, known more commonly as the Kirov Ballet, until 1991, when theatre reverted to earlier title, the Maryinsky Theatre, with company named the St. Petersburg Ballet. School affiliated with the company has origins in school founded by French dancing master Jean-Baptiste Landé, St. Petersburg, 1738: became the Imperial Theatre School, St. Petersburg, then the Petrograd State Ballet School, and eventually the Leningrad Choreographic School; officially named after Aggripina Vaganova, and known also as the Vaganova School, from 1957. Current artistic director of the Kirov Ballet (from 1977): Oleg Vinogradov.

### PUBLICATIONS


Krasovskaya, Vera, *Russian Ballet Theatre from its Beginning to the Mid-Nineteenth Century*, Leningrad and Moscow, 1958

Bogdanov-Berezovsky, V., *The Leningrad Opera and Ballet Theatre Named after Kirov*, Leningrad and Moscow, 1959

Krasovskaya, Vera, *Leningrad's Ballet*, Leningrad, 1961

Slonimsky, Yuri, "Cradle of the Russian Ballet: The History of the Leningrad Ballet", *Ballet Annual* (London), vol. 15, 1961

Krasovskaya, Vera, *Russian Ballet Theatre of the Second Half of the Nineteenth Century*, Moscow, 1963

Roslavleva, Natalia, *Era of the Russian Ballet*, London, 1966

Lopukhov, Fedor, *Sixty Years in Ballet*, Moscow, 1966

Swift, Mary Grace, *The Art of Dance in the USSR*, Notre Dame, Ind., 1968

Krasovskaya, Vera, *Russian Ballet Theatre of the Early Twentieth Century*, 2 volumes: *Choreographers*, Leningrad, 1971; *Dancers*, Leningrad, 1972

Konnov, A., and Stupnikov, Igor, *The Leningrad Theatre of Opera and Ballet*, Leningrad, 1976

Mikhailov, M., *The Early Years of the Leningrad Ballet*, Leningrad, 1978

Gregory, John, and Ukladnikov, Alexander, *Leningrad's Ballet: Maryinsky to Kirov*, London, 1981

Degen, Arsen, and Stupnikov, Igor, *The Leningrad Ballet, 1917–1987*, Leningrad, 1988

Wiley, Roland John (ed. and trans.), *A Century of Russian Ballet: Documents and Eyewitness Accounts 1810–1910*, Oxford, 1990

Kendall, Elizabeth, "Reflections: The Kirov", *The New Yorker* (New York), 8 June 1992


* * *

The St. Petersburg Maryinsky Theatre, known for over a half-century as the Leningrad Opera and Ballet Theatre named after Kirov, is one of the oldest Russian theatres, famous throughout the world. Its ballet company was first part of the Petersburg Bolshoi, or Kamenny, Theatre (from 1783), and later of the Maryinsky (from 1880) and the State Maryinsky (from 1917), which in 1920 changed its name into the State Opera and Ballet Theatre. In 1935 it was named after Kirov to commemorate the Soviet political leader assassinated on Stalin's order a year before.

The history of the company begins with court performances given by professional male and female dancers, who appeared as soon as the Empress Anna Ioannovna established a School of Dance (now the Leningrad School of Choreography named after Agrippina Vaganova) in 1738. Supervised by the French ballet master Jean-Baptiste Landé, the dancers soon appropriated the elegant style of European ballet, while at the same time blending it with the freedom and fluidity of Russian folk dance.

Foreign choreographers and teachers who worked in St. Petersburg, such as Franz Hilverding, Gasparo Angiolini, Giuseppe Canziani, and Charles LePicq, introduced the Russian dancers to the best of European choreography. Nevertheless, the Russian ballet had an identity of its own from the very start. Classicism in the Russian interpretation was a patriotic style, based on lofty political ideas—such as, for instance, Angiolini's ballet *Semira* after a tragedy by the Russian poet and dramatist Aleksandr Sumarokov (1772). The best dancers of the time combined excellent professional skills with subtle emotional play and deep understanding of the characters.

In 1783 the Bolshoi (Kamenny) Theatre was built (it was rebuilt in 1836 by the architect A.K. Cavos). It was there that the dancer and teacher who was to become the first Russian choreographer, Ivan Valbergh, started to stage ballets on a grand scale. In his ballets, mime acting and elaborate dancing techniques no longer served to glorify emperors, military commanders, or deities: sentimentalism had by then brought new characters to the fore, dramatizing the lives of common people. Valbergh staged Russia's first ballet with a contemporary theme, *A New Werther* (1799), as well as one of the earliest ballets with a Shakespearean story, *Romeo and Juliet* (1809). In his divertissement *Russia's Triumph; or, The Russians in Paris* (1814) the choreographer celebrated Russia's victory in the 1812 war with Napoleon.

St. Petersburg's ballet was to a great extent moulded by Charles-Louis Didelot. Having been trained under Dauberval, the choreographer had witnessed Noverre's attempts to do away with the outdated conventions of the court ballet; he had an excellent knowledge of different European balletic traditions, and brought these to the imperial city of St. Petersburg. At the time when Didelot was working in Russia, there was a general flourishing of national culture, so that along with other things St. Petersburg's ballet grew to become one of the most advanced in Europe. Didelot produced mythological, historical, and genre ballets as well as divertissements featuring dances in various styles, while his "balletic poems" anticipated Romanticism. In those ballets the interaction of group and solo dancing, an important feature of the later style, was already noticeable.

The 1830s was the heyday of Romanticism, with its juxtaposition of dream and reality, and its artistic exploration of the world of visions. In 1837, the Italian choreographer Filippo Taglioni and his daughter, the famous ballerina Marie Taglioni, brought *La Sylphide* to the St. Petersburg stage. The Romantic style soon proved appealing to the Russian dancers. In 1842 Elena Andreyanova performed successfully in *Giselle*. A more down-to-earth trend in Romantic ballet was represented by Jules Perrot, who headed St. Petersburg's ballet from 1848 to 1859. In the ballets *Esmeralda*, *Catarina*, and *Faust*, the main dramatic conflict is between people's characters, passions, and circumstances. During this period the celebrated dancers Fanny Elssler, Carlotta Grisi, and Fanny Cerrito performed on the St. Petersburg stage, while the Russian ballerinas Nadezhda Bogdanova, Marfa Muravieva, and Marie Surovschikova Petipa were catching up with the foreign dancers in mastering the Romantic repertoire.

In 1860, the company moved into a new building, and the theatre was given the name of Maryinsky (though ballets continued to be performed at the Bolshoi Theatre of St. Petersburg until 1886). Perrot was succeeded as ballet master in 1859 by Arthur Saint-Léon, whose favoured genre was multi-act pageantry. In his ballets *The Little Humpbacked Horse* (1864) and *The Goldfish* (1867), the Russian subject matter was, in effect, just a pretext for staging long and colourful divertissements.

After Perrot and Saint-Léon came the choreographer and teacher Marius Petipa. He had himself been a ballet dancer since 1847, later becoming a choreographer, and from 1869 to 1903 he worked as the theatre's chief ballet master. At first, Petipa too had a predilection for large-scale ballet productions, such as *The Pharaoh's Daughter* (*La Fille du Pharaon*, 1862), *Le Roi Candaule* (1868), *Don Quixote* (1871), and *La Bayadère* (1877). However, already in these productions, to music by Pugni and Minkus, Petipa was beginning to develop his concept of "symphony ballet". Building on the achievements of his predecessors and developing them further, he created outstanding choreographic works which remain the pinnacle of choreographic achievement in ballet history: the "Kingdom of the Shades" scene in *La Bayadère*, the dryads scene in *Don Quixote*, and many others. Petipa invented new forms and techniques, constantly improving on the patterns of classical dance. It was his mastery of diverse expressive means used in ballet which enabled him to create, together with leading composers Tchaikovsky and Glazunov, the first true "symphony ballets": *The Sleeping Beauty* (1890), *Swan Lake* (in collaboration with Lev Ivanov, who choreographed the "Swan" acts, 1895), and *Raymonda* (1898).

Petipa's ballets demanded high professional skills from the whole of the company, and these were achieved with the help of gifted and committed teachers like Christian Johansson, Enrico Cecchetti, and others. The main dancers in Petipa's and Ivanov's ballets were Marie Surovschikova Petipa, Ekaterina Vazem, Eugenia Sokolova, Varvara Nikitina, Marius Petipa, Pavel Gerdt, Platon Karsavin, Nikolai Legat, Iosif Kshessinsky, and Aleksandr Shiryaev. Petipa's work was the consummation of the artistic achievements of the nineteenth century, and represented one of the most significant periods in the history of Russian ballet; and his masterpieces have become part of the classical heritage of world ballet. They are also respectfully preserved by the Soviet ballet theatre.

In the early twentieth century many prominent dancers, such as Olga Preobrazhenskaya, Mathilde Kshesinskaya, Vera Trefilova, Agrippina Vaganova, Lyubov Egorova, and Nikolai Legat kept up the classical tradition. However, after Petipa had retired, the aesthetics of the classical dance became increasingly conservative, turning classicism into simplistic dogma, which merely hampered creative thought. It was Mikhail Fokin (Fokine) who became the leader in the fight against old stereotypes. He used the innovations of contemporary graphic arts as a basis of his own search for new forms, thereby developing his own favourite genre, which was the one-act ballet with compressed non-stop action and distinctive stylistic colouring. Such were his early ballets *Le Pavillon d'Armide* (1907), *Chopiniana* (*Les Sylphides*, 1908), *Egyptian Nights* (1908), *Le Carnaval* (1910), *Petrushka* (1911), and the *Polovtsian Dances* from the opera *Prince Igor* (1909). The performers made famous by Fokine's ballets were Tamara Karsavina, Vaslav Nijinsky, and Anna Pavlova.

In the first years after the 1917 October revolution, the theatre faced a dual task: preserving the classical heritage and creating a new repertoire, consonant with the spirit of the time. The responsibility for carrying out this task was undertaken by the leading soloists of the company: Ekaterina Gerdt, Petr Gusev, Leonid Leontiev, Andrei Lopukhov, Elena Lyukom,

Olga Mungalova, Vladimir Ponomarev, Viktor Semenov, and Boris Shavrov. In 1922, Fedor Lopukhov became head of the company. Guided by him, the theatre kept up the best productions by Petipa and Ivanov, Fokine and Gorsky, as part of its repertoire. A truly innovative choreographer, Lopukhov created original productions in which he experimented in quite a daring way with various means of choreographic expression and balletic symphonism. During the 1920s Lopukhov created *The Magnificence of the Universe* to the music of Beethoven (1923), *Night on the Bare Mountain* to the music of Mussorgsky (1924), *Pulcinella* to the music of Stravinsky (1926), *The Ice Maiden* to the music of Grieg (1927), and *A Tale of the Fox* (*Le Renard*) to the music of Stravinsky (1927); and in 1931 he staged *Bolt* to the music of Shostakovich. His theory of ballet and his practical discoveries were the first important steps in the development of the Soviet ballet theatre.

In 1929, Lopukhov, Ponomarev, and Leontiev staged one of the first Soviet ballets, *The Red Poppy*, and in 1930 another ballet with a contemporary story, Shostakovich's *The Golden Age*, was produced by Vasily Vainonen, Leonid Yakobson, and Vladimir Chesnokov. During the 1930s and 1940s, when dramatic interpretations and approaches occupied the central place in all ballet productions, the best ballets of the time were created: *The Flames of Paris* (Vainonen, 1932), *The Fountain of Bakhchisarai* (Zakharov, 1934), *Laurencia* (Chabukiani, 1939), and *Romeo and Juliet* (Lavrovsky, 1940).

During the war, the artists who remained in besieged Leningrad formed a small ballet company headed by the remarkable ballerina Olga Iordan. The dancers of that company went on concert tours to the frontline, gave performances at factories, and visited hospitals. The main part of the Kirov company was evacuated to Perm, where old productions were kept on the stage and some new ones appeared (such as Anisimova's well-known *Gayané*).

More new productions appeared in the 1940s and 1950s. The ballets *Tatiana* (Burmeister) and *Militsa* (Vainonen), staged in 1947, were both based on the subject of war. The ballets *The Bronze Horseman* (Zakharov, 1949) and *Taras Bulba* (Fenster, 1955) continued the tradition of adapting literary works, such as those of Aleksandr Pushkin, to the stage. The fairy-tale ballets *Cinderella* (Sergeyev) and *Shurale* (Yakobson) made an extensive use of classical style.

The 1950s and 1960s were the years of a creative upswing. It was at that time that Yakobson incorporated his idea of ancient Roman postures and movements in his innovative choreography for *Spartacus* (1956). He also proved the versatility of choreographic expression in his programme of *Choreographic Miniatures* (1958), which featured a long series of pieces, diverse in style and potential, and ranging from "danse libre" to the purely classical. In his ballet *The Bedbug*, Yakobson managed to re-enact the creative work of the Soviet poet Mayakovsky with his scathing portrayals of contemporary vices. Yakobson's ballet *The Twelve* (1964) gave visual expression to the revolutionary sentiment of another Russian poet, Aleksandr Blok.

Productions by choreographers of a new generation were yet another breakthrough. The ballets *The Stone Flower* (1957), and *A Legend of Love* (1961), both by Yuri Grigorovich, as well as *The Coast of Hope* (1959) and *The Leningrad Symphony* (1961), both by Igor Belsky, gave new life to the tradition of symphonic ballet as started by Petipa and continued by Lopukhov. These productions also appropriated Fokine's experiences of balletic and musical continuity, and the young choreographers found new vehicles for their philosophical message. The new perspective on choreography helped to bring out new talents among dancers, among them Irina Kolpakova, Alla Osipenko, and later, Alla Sizova and Yuri Soloviov, to name but a few. The most important productions of the 1960s to the 1970s were Vinogradov's *Goryanka* (*Mountain Girl*, 1968) and *The Creation of the World* by Natalia Kasatkina and Vladimir Vasiliev (1971).

Since 1977, the company has been headed by Oleg Vinogradov, who has proven an innovative and daring choreographer. Along with his loyal stagings of the classics, Vinogradov has created *The Hussard Ballad* (1979), *The Fairy of the Rond Mountains* (1980), *The Government Inspector* (1980), *The Knight in Tigerskin* (1985), *Battleship Potemkin* (1986), a new *Petrushka* (1990), and many others. Many of his leading dancers, such as Altynai Asylmuratova, Farouk Ruzimatov, and Konstantin Zaklinsky, are known throughout the ballet world.

—Igor Stupnikov

---

**KIRSTEIN, Lincoln**

American ballet director, writer, and dance historian. Born in Rochester, New York, 4 May 1907. Educated at Harvard University: Bachelor of Arts, 1929, Master of Arts, 1930. Married Fidelma Cadmus, 1941. Served in U.S. Army, 1943–45. Co-founder and director (with Balanchine and Edward M.M. Warburg), School of American Ballet, 1934; co-founder and director, American Ballet, 1935; founder and director, Ballet Caravan, 1936–41; co-founder and secretary, Ballet Society, 1946, and general director of its successor, New York City Ballet, from its founding, 1948; founder, Dance Archives of the Museum of Modern Art, New York, 1940; founder and editor, *Dance Index* (New York), 1942–48; also sponsor of Japanese theatre in the United States, including Gagaku (dancers and musicians of Imperial Household), 1959, and The Grand Kabuki (Japanese classic dramatic theatre), 1960; also leading dance historian, publishing books on Fokine, Nijinsky, the New York City Ballet, and on history of theatrical dance, also assisting in writing of Romola Nijinsky's biography of Nijinsky, 1932–33; retired as President of the School of American Ballet and general director of New York City Ballet, 1989. Recipient: Capezio Award, 1953; Order of the Sacred Treasure, Fourth Class, Government of Japan, September 1960; Benjamin Franklin Medal of the Royal Society of the Arts, December 1981; National Medal of Arts, 1985; Handel Medallion, 1987.

**PUBLICATIONS**

By Kirstein:

*Fokine* (with introduction by Arnold Haskell), London, 1934

*Dance: A Short History of Classical Theatrical Dancing*, New York, 1935; published as *The Book of the Dance*, New York, 1942

*Blast at Ballet: A Corrective for the American Audience*, New York, 1938

*Ballet Alphabet: A Primer for Beginners*, New York, 1939

*The Classic Ballet*, New York, 1952

*Rhymes of a Pfc*, reprinted as *Rhymes and More Rhymes of a Pfc*, New York, 1964

*Movement and Metaphor: Four Centuries of Ballet*, New York, 1971; as *Four Centuries of Ballet: 50 Masterworks*, revised edition, New York, 1984

*The New York City Ballet*, New York, 1972

*Elie Nadelman*, New York, 1973

*Lay this Laurel*, New York, 1974
*Nijinsky Dancing*, New York, 1975
"Rationale of a Repertory" in Reynolds, Nancy, *Repertory in Review*, New York, 1977
*Thirty Years: Lincoln Kirstein's The New York City Ballet* (revised and expanded edition of 1972 book), New York, 1978
*Loomis: A Memoir*, New Brunswick, New Jersey, 1982
*Ballet, Bias and Belief*, New York, 1983
*Quarry: A Collection in Lieu of Memoirs*, Pasadena, 1987
*A Short History of Classic Theatrical Dancing*, Princeton, 1987
*The Poems of Lincoln Kirstein*, New York, 1987

About Kirstein:
Cohen, S.J., "Some Theories of Dance in Contemporary Society", *Journal of Aesthetics and Art Criticism* (New York), December 1950
Buckle, Richard, "The Adventures of a Ballet Critic", *Ballet* (London), 3 parts: December 1951, January 1952, February 1952
Reynolds, Nancy, *Repertory in Review*, New York, 1977
Chapman, John, "The Aesthetic Interpretation of Dance History", *Dance Chronicle* (New York), vol. 3, no. 3, 1979–80
Temin, Christine, "The Master Builder", *Ballet News* (New York), May 1982
Anderson, Jack, "Kirstein Reminisces", *Dance Chronicle* (New York), vol. 12, no. 1, 1989
Jackson, George, "Lincoln Kirstein", *Ballett International* (Cologne), December 1989

* * *

Brilliant, in some ways erratic, and endowed with consummate good taste, Lincoln Kirstein has often been likened to Serge Diaghilev. In many ways his gifts exceed those of Diaghilev. Or perhaps, astute scholar that he is, Kirstein early taught himself to avoid Diaghilev's mistakes. For example, in his founding and directing of the Ballets Russes, Diaghilev was not consistent in his aesthetic, nor was he constant in his artistic relationships with the choreographers whose careers he elected to foster. He was also seduced by trends in painting and music—sometimes to the detriment of the choreography.

Kirstein, on the other hand, was absolutely constant in creating a company setting for the choreography of George Balanchine. It was he who lured Balanchine to the United States with the promise of a company and school of his own. The promise was fully kept. Their relationship spanned more than half a century. And while the New York City Ballet, of which Kirstein was general director until 1989, has always remained on the highest level both musically and visually, the choreography and its needs have always been primary.

Diaghilev was a catalyst; Kirstein has been that and more. Of course, it must be remembered that Diaghilev died at 57, while Kirstein has had much more time. Until his retirement at 82, he worked unflaggingly to assure the economic stability of the New York City Ballet and the School of American Ballet through his own wealth and personal connections, through his friendship with W. McNeil Lowry, who steered generous Ford Foundation funding to the two projects, and through his awareness that arts organizations in the United States must develop a sound corporate structure in order to survive.

Although bedevilled by manic depression, Kirstein has also structured an unusually productive creative life for himself. During his school years he thought of being a painter, and he developed considerable skill in that direction. But like the young Diaghilev, who founded the magazine *Mir Iskusstva* (*The World of Art*), Kirstein, while still a Harvard undergraduate, founded the magazine *Hound and Horn* in 1927. He was its editor until 1934, when his energies were concentrated on establishing the School of American Ballet with George Balanchine and Vladimir Dimitriev. At this time he also began the early performing projects which eventually blossomed into the New York City Ballet.

**Lincoln Kirstein with George Balanchine**

Kirstein's writing career has been steadfast. A 1978 bibliography indicates 473 titles of books and articles on dance, drawing, painting, sculpture, architecture, photography, film, music, and literature. He has also written some intriguingly oblique autobiographical works. The first of these was *Flesh is Heir* (1932), a novel in which there is a memorable chapter about a young American tourist (Kirstein) who happens upon Diaghilev's funeral in Venice. His collection of ballads called *Rhymes of a Pfc* and reprinted in 1964 as *Rhymes and More Rhymes of a Pfc*, reveals Kirstein's affection for army life. (He served in the United States Army from 1943 to 1946.) This affection for military order was to remain with him. It became his metaphor for the School of American Ballet, which he decorated with prints of equestrian ballets and about which he said, "I am . . . very much interested in order—in the order of the military exercise."

Also of an autobiographical nature is his *Quarry* (1986), a journey through his art-filled New York home via photographs and text. Quickly revealed are his taste for grandeur, for depictions of the human figure (especially the male figure), and a total lack of interest in abstract and non-objective art, which he calls "expensive wall coverings".

Kirstein's *Dance* (1935), a history of Western theatrical dance, is still unrivalled in its incisiveness. His *Blast at Ballet* (1938) and *Ballet Alphabet* (1939) established his iconoclasm and his utter disdain for modern dance, which he terms a "simulacre of strain". Between 1942 and 1948 Kirstein founded and edited *Dance Index*, the first serious monograph in the dance field. And in 1952 he collaborated with School of American Ballet teacher Muriel Stuart on a lucid textbook called *The Classic Ballet: Basic Technique and Terminology*. Unlike most ballet manuals, which were often inadequately illustrated, this one had handsome line drawings by Kirstein's brother-in-law Paul Cadmus.

The quest for order which had led him to classical ballet and to the army also led Lincoln Kirstein to the Catholic Church, for which he foresook his German Jewish heritage. But it is safe to assume that his most fundamental allegiance is to ballet, for which, as choreographer Jerome Robbins has observed, "... he feels in the deepest possible way".

—Doris Hering

---

**KISTLER, Darci**
American dancer. Born Darci Anna Kistler in Riverside, California, 4 June 1964. Studied with Irina Kosmovska, Los Angeles, from 1976, and at the School of American Ballet, New York (scholarship student) from 1978; also coached by Alexandra Danilova and Stanley Williams. Married New York City Ballet dancer and director Peter Martins, 1991. Apprentice to New York City Ballet, 1979: début, as a student, in School of American Ballet Workshop performance, 1979; dancer, corps de ballet, New York City Ballet, 1980–81, becoming soloist, 1981–83, and principal dancer, from 1983; left stage following injury, 1983–85; returned to principal roles, 1985; has toured with New York City Ballet, including Edinburgh, Scotland, for the Edinburgh Festival, 1991; occasional guest artist, including for Princeton Ballet, New Jersey, 1981; has also appeared on U.S. television, including in Public Broadcasting Service (PBS) "Dance in America" series. Recipient: Capezio Dance Award, 1991; *Dance Magazine* Award, 1992.

## ROLES

1979 Principal dancer (cr) in *Haydn Concerto* (Bonnefoux), School of American Ballet Workshop Performance, New York
Pas de deux from *William Tell* (opera; mus. Rossini, chor. Williams after Bournonville), School of American Ballet Workshop Performance, New York
1980 Odette in *Swan Lake*, Act II (Danilova after Ivanov), School of American Ballet Workshop Performance, New York
Principal dancer in *Walpurgisnacht* (Balanchine), New York City Ballet, New York
Odette in *Swan Lake* (one-act version; Balanchine after Ivanov), New York City Ballet, New York
Scherzo in *Tchaikovsky Suite No. 3* (Balanchine), New York City Ballet, New York
Second Movement in *Symphony in C* (Balanchine), New York City Ballet, New York
1980/81 Principal dancer in *Brahms–Schoenberg Quartet* (Balanchine), New York City Ballet, New York
Principal dancer in *Divertimento No. 15* (Balanchine), New York City Ballet, New York
Principal dancer in *Raymonda Variations* (Balanchine), New York City Ballet, New York
Principal dancer in *Valse Fantaisie* (Balanchine), New York City Ballet, New York
Dewdrop Fairy in *The Nutcracker* (Balanchine), New York City Ballet, New York
Sugar Plum Fairy in *The Nutcracker* (Balanchine), New York City Ballet, New York
The Novice in *The Cage* (Robbins), New York City Ballet, New York
1981 Principal dancer (cr) in *Suite from "Histoire du Soldat"* (Martins), New York City Ballet, New York
Principal dancer (cr) in *Andantino* (Robbins), Tchaikovsky Festival, New York City Ballet, New York
Principal dancer (cr) in *Symphony No. 1* (Martins), New York City Ballet, New York
1981/82 Principal dancer in *Who Cares?* (Balanchine), New York City Ballet, New York
Principal dancer in *Chaconne* (Balanchine), New York City Ballet, New York
Principal dancer in *Afternoon of a Faun* (Robbins), New York City Ballet, New York
1982 Principal dancer (cr) in *Gershwin Concerto* (Robbins), New York City Ballet, New York
Principal dancer (cr) in *Piano-Rag-Music* (Martins), New York City Ballet, New York
Principal dancer (cr) in *Pastorale* (d'Amboise), New York City Ballet, New York
Lise in *The Magic Flute* (Martins), New York City Ballet, New York
1985 Titania in *A Midsummer Night's Dream* (Balanchine), New York City Ballet, New York
The Siren in *Prodigal Son* (Balanchine), New York City Ballet, New York
1986 Principal dancer (cr) in *Piccolo Balletto* (Robbins), New York City Ballet, New York
1988 Principal dancer (cr) in *The Chairman Dances* (Martins), American Music Festival, New York City Ballet, New York
Diamonds in *Jewels* (Balanchine), New York City Ballet, New York
1988/89 Terpsichore in *Apollo* (Balanchine), New York City Ballet, New York
Principal dancer in *Concerto Barocco* (Balanchine), New York City Ballet, New York
Principal dancer in *Serenade* (Balanchine), New York City Ballet, New York
"In the Inn" in *Ivesiana* (Balanchine), New York City Ballet, New York
1989 Strip Tease Girl in *Slaughter on Tenth Avenue* (Balanchine), New York City Ballet, New York
Principal dancer (cr) in *Echo* (Martins), New York City Ballet, New York
Principal dancer in *Danses Concertantes* (Balanchine), New York City Ballet, New York
Principal dancer in *Tchaikovsky Piano Concerto No. 2* (Balanchine), New York City Ballet, New York
Principal dancer in *Mozartiana* (Balanchine), New York City Ballet, New York
1989/90 Autumn in *The Four Seasons* (Robbins), New York City Ballet, New York
Principal dancer (third pas de deux) in *In the Night* (Robbins), New York City Ballet, New York
Principal dancer in *In Memory of ...* (Robbins), New York City Ballet, New York
Principal dancer in *Vienna Waltzes* (Balanchine), New York City Ballet, New York
Principal dancer in *Goldberg Variations* (Robbins), New York City Ballet, New York

Principal dancer in *Other Dances* (pas de deux; Robbins), New York City Ballet, New York
1991 Eighth Waltz and La Valse in *La Valse* (Balanchine), New York City Ballet, New York
Principal dancer (cr) in *Salute to Fred Astaire* (La Fosse), New York City Ballet, Edinburgh
Princess Aurora (cr) in *The Sleeping Beauty* (new production; Martins after Petipa), New York City Ballet, New York
1992 Principal dancer (cr) in *Delight of the Muses* (Martins), New York City Ballet, New York
Principal dancer (cr) in *Jeu de Cartes* (Martins), New York City Ballet, New York

**Other roles include:** the "Door" in *Variations pour une porte et un soupir* (Balanchine), the Sleepwalker in *La Sonnambula* (Balanchine), principal dancer in *In G Major* (Robbins), principal dancer in *The Concert* (Robbins), principal dancer in *Dances at a Gathering* (Robbins), principal dancer in *Allegro Brillante* (Balanchine), principal dancer in *(Tchaikovsky) Pas de deux* (Balanchine), principal dancer (lead couple) in *Theme and Variations* (Balanchine).

## PUBLICATIONS

By Kistler:
Interview in Tracy, Robert, *Balanchine's Ballerinas*, New York, 1983
Interview in Mason, Francis (ed.), *I Remember Balanchine*, New York, 1991
Interview with Trucco, Terry, "Darci Kistler", *Dance Magazine* (New York), February 1991

About Kistler:
Greskovic, Robert, "The Arrival of Darci Kistler", *Ballet Review* (New York), Summer 1981
"Dancer You Will Know: Darci Kistler", *Dance and Dancers* (London), July 1982
Laine, Barrie, "The Baby Ballerina Boom", *Dance Magazine* (New York), November 1982
Croce, Arlene, *Going to the Dance*, New York, 1982
Croce, Arlene, *Sightlines*, New York, 1987
Acocella, Joan, "Balanchine's Last Princess", *Connoisseur* (New York), June 1989
Croce, Arlene, "Different", *The New Yorker* (New York), 26 February 1990

* * *

At fifteen, Darci Kistler captured the imagination of George Balanchine as a latter-day baby ballerina, inspiring the great ballet master to cast her at her tender age in some of his most important roles. After bowling over the New York dance audience in the School of American Ballet Workshop performances of Bournonville's pas de deux from *William Tell* and *Swan Lake*, Act II (in which she had been coached by Alexandra Danilova), Kistler joined the New York City Ballet and was immediately cast in *Symphony In C* (second movement), giving a mature and richly articulated performance that was greeted with superlatives. The ballet served as a kind of annunciation: here was the successor to Suzanne Farrell.

Brimming with talent, youthful vigour, and the performing style of a full-fledged ballerina that belied her teenage years, Kistler assumed major roles in *Tchaikovsky Suite No. 3*, *The Nutcracker*, and *Brahms–Schoenberg Quartet*, and put her stamp on them. Her artistry was also evident in the ballets Jerome Robbins choreographed for her, *Andantino* and *Gershwin Concerto*, which ratified her stardom. Peter Martins followed with a part for her in *Histoire du Soldat* and *The Magic Flute*.

This segment of Kistler's career came to an end because of a serious foot injury which kept her off the stage for two years; she spent another two returning in fits and starts. It seemed for a time as if she would never recapture the magic of those first seasons, or fulfil the incredible promise she displayed as a young ballerina of distinctive and original gifts. Subsequent seasons put these fears to rest. Her dancing serves not only to state, in the boldest terms imaginable, "I'm back", but to express a vision of artistry that Balanchine himself could only have intuited from seeing her early work. Kistler now commands the stage of the New York State Theater as a ballerina of the first rank.

In the late 1980s and early 1990s she danced a series of important ballets, making débuts in Diamonds (*Jewels*), *Apollo* (as Terpsichore), *Concerto Barocco*, *A Midsummer Night's Dream* (as Titania), *Tchaikovsky Piano Concerto*, *Mozartiana*, and *Theme and Variations*. These are among the most exalted roles in the canon for a Balanchine ballerina, and Kistler danced them with attention to technical clarity and to the musical shape of the choreography. She dazzles in this repertory from her sense of the breadth of each ballet. Time will tell if her footwork is not as precise as some of her predecessors in these roles because of her injury, or because she is still developing this aspect of her technique. Her heroic assumption of so many roles in relatively few seasons is matched by the grand manner in which she performs them. Kistler dances "big".

Like so many tall, long-legged Balanchine dancers, Darci Kistler displays athletic grace and fresh-faced charm which transforms itself in Balanchine's style and repertory into a poetic quality that is at once romantic and classical. She is uniquely American and a sunniness imbues her dancing with a sheen. But Kistler is a sophisticated performer who can communicate the plastique of *Apollo* and Diamonds in *Jewels* no less tellingly than she can summon up the energy and tongue-in-cheek glamour of a Broadway showgirl in *Slaughter on Tenth Avenue*. Her bold, elongated, eternally fresh line is especially revelatory in the Balanchine/Stravinsky *Danses Concertantes*, which was revived by NYCB in 1989. This ballet was originally choreographed by Balanchine for the Ballet Russe and starred Danilova; Kistler's interpretation of Stravinsky's astringent score as expressed in Balanchine's sly ironies is a marvellous fusion of 1940s classic chic filtered through a stupendous present-day sensibility.

Kistler has also excelled in the City Ballet's Robbins repertory, nowhere more persuasively than in the Autumn section of *The Four Seasons*, a spoof of the grand Bolshoi style in which she reveals herself as a technician who can reel off a series of recklessly fast piqué turns with startling éclat, and then punctuate them with a fillip of fouettés. Although Martins' early ballets for Kistler captured some of her qualities, his recent works for her, *The Chairman Dances*, a bit of tacky nightclub chinoiserie, and *Echo*, a postmodern exercise in formalism, seemed to leave her stranded on the stage.

But these are minor setbacks. As Arlene Croce wrote in 1989, ". . . at twenty-five Kistler is at the peak of her physical beauty and her prowess . . . As a prima ballerina, she's just bursting into bloom; she's starting to open meanings to us. The meanings are unnameable; they're in the shimmer of the spell she casts, in the potency of an illusion. . . . Kistler has always been a beautiful, talented, unique dancer, but what she hasn't been until this season is someone whose absolute identification with the life of a ballet we never questioned. It's a power that goes beyond authority, and only true ballerinas have it."

—Larry Kaplan

---

**KNIASEFF** (Kniasev), **Boris**

Russian/French dancer, choreographer, and teacher. Born in St. Petersburg, 1 July 1900. Studied with Mikhail Mordkin, Lidiya Nelidova, and Kasyan Goleizovsky, Moscow, and with Orlov and Evgenia Sokolova, St. Petersburg. Married dancer Olga Spessivtseva. Début at Voronezh Opera, 1916; dancer and ballet master, Kharkov Opera, Kharkov, 1916/17; left Russia, 1917: first choreographed works staged in Constantinople, 1918; principal dancer and ballet master, Sofia Opera, 1919–20; dancer and choreographer, Casino di San Remo, and Gaîté-Lyrique, Paris, 1922; leading dancer, performing with Lyubov Egorova and Sophia Fedorova at the Théâtre des Champs-Elysées, Paris, from 1922; dancer, choreographer, and assistant to Léo Staats at Casino de Paris, 1924; choreographer, staging ballets for Théâtre de l'Exposition des arts décoratifs, 1925; founder, with Tamara Geva, and choreographer, Les Ballets Stylisés, 1926–28, touring South America, 1927; choreographer and producer of classical ballets for Olga Spessivtseva, Théâtre des Champs-Elysées, from 1928; founder, choreographer, and director, Ballets Russes de Boris Kniaseff, from 1930, also working as dancer and ballet master, Opéra de Monte Carlo, 1931, and Opéra-Comique, Paris, 1932; premier danseur, Théâtre de la danse Nijinska, 1932, also performing with Original Ballet Russe; founder of dance studio, presenting ballets at Théâtre de Marigny, 1940, and leading to founding of Ballets Russe de Paris, appearing at the Salle Pleyel, Paris, and touring Germany, 1943; also staged ballets for de Basil's Original Ballet Russe and Ballets de Paris, and worked as ballet master in Greece; ballet master, Buenos Aires, 1949; founder, Académie international de danse classique, Lausanne (transferred to Geneva, later to Rome, and finally to Paris as the Académie de Paris). Recipient: Second Choreographic Award, International Archives de la Danse (for *La Légende du Bouleau*), 1932. Died in Paris, 7 October 1975.

**ROLES**

1916 Pas de trois in *Swan Lake* (Petipa, Ivanov), Voronezh Opera, Voronezh
Principal dancer in *Les Sylphides* (Fokine), Kharkov Opera Ballet, Kharkov
Franz in *Coppélia* (after Saint-Léon), Kharkov Opera Ballet, Kharkov
Principal dancer in *The Enchanted Forest* (Petipa), Kharkov Opera Ballet, Kharkov
1919 Principal dancer in *Carnaval* (Fokine), Sofia Opera Ballet, Sofia
Title role in *Le Spectre de la rose* (Fokine), Sofia Opera Ballet, Sofia
The Faune in *L'Après-midi d'un faune* (Nijinsky), Sofia Opera Ballet, Sofia
1922 Principal dancer (cr) in *Fumées* (also chor.), Gaîté-Lyrique, Paris
Principal dancer (cr) in *Obsession* (new version; also chor.), Gaîté-Lyrique, Paris
1924 Principal dancer (cr) in *Aux Pieds des pyramides* (also chor.), Casino de Paris, Paris
1929 Chief Warrior in *Polovtsian Dances from Prince Igor* (Fokine), Opera Privé de Paris, Paris
1931 Leading role in *Paquita* (after Petipa), Pavlova Gala, Théâtre des Champs-Elysées, Paris
1932 Chanson dansée ("Athlete") in *Les Biches* (Nijinska), Théâtre de la danse Nijinska, Paris
Guidon in *La Princesse Cygne* (Nijinska), Théâtre de la danse Nijinska, Paris
Wedding Guest in *Les Noces* (Nijinska), Théâtre de la danse Nijinska, Paris
Principal dancer (cr) in *Bolero* (new version; Nijinska), Théâtre de la danse Nijinska, Paris
Principal dancer in *Étude* (Nijinska), Théâtre de la danse Nijinska, Paris
Principal dancer in *Variations* (Nijinska), Théâtre de la danse Nijinska, Paris
Count Anselmi in *Scuola di Ballo* (Massine), Ballets Russes de Monte Carlo
Principal dancer in *Les Rêveries*, Gala, Salle Pleyel, Paris
Principal dancer (cr) in *Jeux et couleurs* (Ari), Opéra-Comique, Paris
Principal dancer (cr) in *Valses de Brahms* (Quinault), Opéra-Comique, Paris

**WORKS**

1918 *La Rose rouge* (mus. Kreisler), Constantinople
*L'Allée des soupirs* (mus. Mozart), Constantinople
*Vision* (mus. Procrass), Constantinople
*Obsession* (first version), Constantinople
1919 *L'Amour de Polichinelle* (mus. Rachmaninov), Sofia Opera Ballet, Sofia
*Esclave d'Orient* (mus. Rubenstein), Sofia Opera Ballet, Sofia
1920 *The Four Seasons* (mus. Glazunov), Sofia Opera Ballet, Sofia
*L'Atlantide* (mus. Gerlin), Sofia Opera Ballet, Sofia
*Rhapsodie de Brahms* (mus. Brahms), Sofia Opera Ballet, Sofia
1922 *Fumées* (mus. Gerlin), Gaîté-Lyrique, Paris
*Obsession* (second version; mus. Tchaikovsky), Gaîté-Lyrique, Paris
1924 *Aux Pieds des pyramides* (mus. Arensky), Casino de Paris, Paris
1925 *Playing*, Théâtre du Palais Arts Décoratifs, Paris
*Jadis*, Théâtre du Palais Arts Décoratifs
*Egypte*, Théâtre du Palais Arts Décoratifs
1926 *Obsession* (third version; mus. Sibelius), Les Ballets Stylisés
*Esquisses* (mus. Tchaikovsky), Les Ballets Stylisés
*Étude d'Après Verlaine* (mus. Chopin), Les Ballets Stylisés
*La Soif* (mus. Arensky), Les Ballets Stylisés
*Le Feu sacré*, Les Ballets Stylisés
*Suggestion*, Les Ballets Stylisés
*Suite Egyptienne* (mus. Arensky), Les Ballets Stylisés
1928 *Vieille Chanson orientale* (mus. Kjui), Théâtre des Champs-Elysées, Paris
*Les Caprices de Papillon* (mus. Krotkov), Théâtre des Champs-Elysées, Paris
1930 *Au Temps des Tartares* (mus. Spendlarov), Ballets Russes de Boris Kniaseff
*Rêverie lunaire* (mus. Chopin), Ballets Russes de Boris Kniaseff
*Mascarade* (mus. Schumann), Ballets Russes de Boris Kniaseff

**Boris Kniaseff**

*Devant le Sphinx* (mus. Arensky), Ballets Russes de Boris Kniaseff
*Bouffonnerie romantique* (mus. Coppola), Ballet Russe de Boris Kniaseff
*Tziganes* (mus. popular songs, arranged Cluny), Ballet Russe de Boris Kniaseff
*La Légende de Berioska* (mus. Konstantinov, Tchaikovsky), Ballets Russes de Boris Kniaseff
*Le Rendezvous manqué* (mus. Debussy), Ballet Russes de Boris Kniaseff
1931 *La Temple abandonnée* (mus. M. d'Ollone), Opéra de Monte Carlo, Monte Carlo
1932 *La Légende du Bouleau* (also *Biroska*; new version of *La Légende de Berioska*, mus. Tchaikovsky), Ballets Léon Woizikowsky (staged Original Ballet Russe as *The Silver Birch*, 1940)
*Taras Bulba* (mus. Rousseau), Opéra-Comique, Paris
1937 *Endymion*, Belgrade Opera, Belgrade
1940 *Piccoli* (mus. Rossini), Théâtre Marigny, Paris
1941 *Eros*, Salle Pleyel, Paris
1944 *Papillon*, Gala, Paris
1948 *Études symphoniques* (mus. Schumann), Ballet de Paris, Paris
1949 *Per Aspara* (mus. Brahms), Politeama Theatre, Buenos Aires
*Fête tartare* (mus. Spendiasrov), Politeama Theatre, Buenos Aires
*La Veillée* (mus. Skriabin), Politeama Theatre, Buenos Aires
*La Vie d'un jour* (mus. Glazunov), Politeama Theatre, Buenos Aires
*Quid Pro Quo* (mus. Rimsky-Korsakov), Politeama Theatre, Buenos Aires
1954 Dances in *Mazeppa* (opera; mus. Tchaikovsky), Maggio Musicale Fiorentino, Florence
1955 Dances in *Fair at Sorochinsky* (opera; mus. Mussorgsky), La Scala, Milan
*Scènes de ballet* (mus. Stravinsky), La Scala, Milan

Also staged:
1919 *Swan Lake* (after Petipa, Ivanov; mus. Tchaikovsky), Sofia Opera Ballet, Sofia
1920 *Coppélia* (after Petipa, Cecchetti; mus. Delibes), Sofia Opera Ballet, Sofia

## PUBLICATIONS

By Kniaseff:
*25 Années de danse 1918–43*, Paris, 1943

About Kniaseff:
Hall, Fernau, *An Anatomy of Ballet*, London, 1953
Severn, G., *Teach Your Child Ballet, Based on Boris Kniaseff's New System*, London, 1958

* * *

The name of Boris Kniaseff is not very well known in the international dance world and yet he was one of the great teachers of the second half of the century, and an important dancer in his own right. Born in Russia, Kniaseff belonged above all to Parisian dance, and although he taught and danced in Italy, Latin America, Switzerland, and Greece, Paris was always his home port.

Kniaseff started dancing very young in Voronezh and Kharkov in pre-revolutionary Russia. His next stop was Constantinople and then Sofia in Bulgaria, where he first achieved success as both a dancer and a choreographer. His activity in Paris had both successes and failures. In 1924 he had a personal triumph at the Casino de Paris where, looking like an animated bas-relief, he danced *Aux Pieds des pyramides*. His beauty and seductive flexibility in this piece caused a sensation. Still, in the 1920s, he changed direction and performed with a classical group at the Edouard VII Theatre and then produced his outstanding works, *Obsession*, to music by Sibelius, and *Esquisses* (Tchaikovsky). He worked with well-known designers at this time, among them Nathalie Gontcharova.

Kniaseff's best years were the 1930s. He met and married the great romantic ballerina, Olga Spessivtseva. For her, he created *La Légende du Bouleau*, one of his great successes, but one which she never danced. The ballet was danced later on by other ballerinas, including Valentina Blinova and Yvette Chauviré. In 1932 Kniaseff was made ballet master and "étoile" at the Opéra-Comique, where his partner was Tamara Geva, Balanchine's first wife. By this time he had choreographed another of his successes, *Au Temps des Tartares*, with designs by Gontcharova. Also at this period he performed with the Opéra Russe de Paris, dancing the role of a barbarian chieftain, bursting with temperament, in the Polovtsian Dances from *Prince Igor*.

His teaching was at its height during the 1940s and 1950s. At class in his huge studio at the Salle Pleyel one could often see, all at the same time, dancers such as Yvette Chauviré, Zizi Jeanmaire, Liane Daydé, Ludmila Tcherina, Youly Algaroff, Vladimir Skouratoff, Igor Fosca, Milorad Miskovitch, and many other of the most brilliant young dancers then in Paris. He was an inspired teacher, passionate and capricious, a perfectionist who knew how to get the best out of his students and to go to the limit of their physical and emotional capabilities. He wanted to give his dancers soul, and his cutting remarks in picturesque French roused even the laziest student. He would not tolerate any weaknesses and avidly upheld the purity of classical dance style.

Kniaseff tried to launch his own company and found among his admirers some reliable sponsors, but his choreography was unoriginal and terribly conventional. He did, however, manage a short season at the Marigny Theatre with Yvette Chauviré as principal dancer, and in 1941 he presented a group under the name of "Ballets Russes de Paris". He spent the 1950s in Switzerland where, thanks to some solid backing, he opened a dance academy in Lausanne and then in Geneva, which was a decided success. It was here that he instigated his famous barre "par terre" (on the ground), classical exercises done lying on the floor, thus permitting the strengthening and lengthening of the muscles. This method was adopted by his many students, who still practise it today in France. After his activities in Switzerland, Kniaseff went to South America where he hoped to found a company with the help of one of his wealthy pupils. But his passionate, intractable character and the demands he made meant that this project never materialized.

The next stopping place for Kniaseff was Greece, where he tried to revive Greek dance from its dormant state, but his old fire and energy had gone. The last stage of his career was an engagement at the Teatro Colón in Buenos Aires, a traditional theatre where dance was still at a fairly elementary level and the innovations asked for by Kniaseff were denied. He returned to France empty-handed, discouraged and disappointed.

His funeral in 1975 was attended by many of his old students, most of whom owed their careers to him.

—Irène Lidova

**KOCHNO, Boris**

Russian/French ballet librettist and critic. Born in Moscow, 3 January 1904. Educated at the Imperial Lycée, Moscow. Left Russia for Paris, 1920: met Serge Diaghilev, becoming his secretary, from 1920; lyricist, composing verses for Igor Stravinsky's *Mavra*, 1922; librettist, writing first ballet scenario, for Auric's *Les Fâcheux* (chor. Nijinska), 1924, collaborating on numerous ballets (occasionally under pseudonym Sobeka) for Diaghilev's Ballets Russes, 1924–29; artistic advisor, Charles Cochran's 1931 Revue; librettist and artistic advisor, (de Basil's) Ballets Russes de Monte Carlo, 1932–33, and 1933–37; co-founder (with George Balanchine) and artistic organizer, Les Ballets 1933; artistic collaborator with Roland Petit, assisting in creation of *Les Forains*, 1945; co-founder, with Petit, and librettist, Les Ballets des Champs-Elysées, 1945–51; also librettist and advisor, Les Ballets de Janine Charrat; writer on ballet from 1954. Died in Paris, 8 December 1991.

**WORKS** (Ballet libretti)

1924 *Les Fâcheux* (after Molière; mus. Auric, chor. Nijinska, design Braque), Diaghilev's Ballets Russes, Monte Carlo
1925 *Zéphire et Flore* (mus. Dukelsky, chor. Massine, design Braque), Diaghilev's Ballets Russes, Monte Carlo
*Les Matelots* (mus. Auric, chor. Massine, design Pruna), Diaghilev's Ballets Russes, Paris
1926 *La Pastorale* (mus. Auric, chor. Balanchine, design Pruna), Diaghilev's Ballets Russes, Paris
1927 *La Chatte* (mus. Sauget, chor. Balanchine, design Gabo, Pevsner), Diaghilev's Ballets Russes, Monte Carlo
1928 *Ode* (mus. Nabokov, chor. Massine, design Tchelitchev), Diaghilev's Ballets Russes, Paris
*The Gods Go a-Begging* (mus. Handel, arranged Beecham, chor. Balanchine, design Bakst, Gris), Diaghilev's Ballets Russes, London
1929 *Le Bal* (after Count Vladimir Sologub; mus. Rieti, chor. Balanchine, design de Chirico), Diaghilev's Ballets Russes, Monte Carlo
*Le Fils prodigue* (mus. Prokofiev, chor. Balanchine, design Rouault), Diaghilev's Ballets Russes, Paris
1932 *Cotillon* (mus. Chabrier, chor. Balanchine, design Bérard), Ballets Russes de Monte Carlo, Monte Carlo
*Jeux d'enfants* (mus. Bizet, chor. Massine, design Miró), Ballets Russes de Monte Carlo, Monte Carlo
*Le Bourgeois Gentilhomme* (after Molière; mus. R. Strauss, chor. Balanchine, design Benois), Ballets Russes de Monte Carlo, Monte Carlo
1935 *Les Cent Baisers* (after Hans Christian Andersen; mus. d'Erlanger, chor. Nijinska, design Hugo), de Basil's Ballets Russes, London
1936 *Le Pavillon* (mus. Borodin, arranged Dorati, chor. Lichine, design Beaton), de Basil's Ballets Russes, London
1945 *Les Forains* (mus. Sauguet, chor. Petit, design Bérard), Théâtre des Champs-Elysées, Paris
*La Fiancée du diable* (mus. Hubeau after Paganini, chor. Petit, design Malclès), Ballets des Champs-Elysées, Paris
1946 *Les Amours de Jupiter* (mus. Ibert, chor. Petit, design Hugo), Ballets des Champs-Elysées, Paris
*Quadrille* (mus. Auric, chor. Fenonjois, design Hugo), Ballets des Champs-Elysées, Paris
*Le Bal des blanchisseuses* (mus. Duke, chor. Petit, design Lepri), Ballets des Champs-Elysées, Paris
1948 *La Rencontre; ou, Oedipe et le Sphinx* (mus. Sauget, chor. Lichine, design Bérard), Ballets des Champs-Elysées, Paris
*Mascarade* (mus. Bizet, orchestrated Weingartner, chor. V. Gsovsky, design Vertès), Ballets des Champs-Elysées, Paris
1949 *Devoirs de vacances* (mus. Walton, chor. Taras, design Beaton), Ballets des Champs-Elysées, Paris
*Le Peintre et son modèle* (mus. Auric, chor. Massine, design Balthus), Ballets des Champs-Elysées, Paris
*La Nuit* (mus. Sauget, chor. Charrat, design Bérard), Ballets des Champs-Elysées, Paris
1951 *Le Dernier Jugement* (mus. Sauget, chor. Charrat, design Kéogh), Ballets des Champs-Elysées, Paris
1964 *Pâris* (mus. Sauget, chor. Charrat), Les Ballets Janine Charrat, Paris

**PUBLICATIONS**

By Kochno:
*Le Ballet*, Paris, 1954
"Dialogue par la danse", with Serge Lifar, *La Danse* (Paris), January 1956
*Diaghilev et Les Ballets Russes*, Paris, 1970; as *Diaghilev and the Ballets Russes*, translated by Adrienne Foulke, New York, 1970

About Kochno:
Beaumont, Cyril, *Complete Book of Ballets*, revised edition, London, 1951
Beaumont, Cyril, *Ballets of Today*, London, 1954
Buckle, Richard, *In Search of Diaghilev*, London, 1955
Garafola, Lynn, "Diaghilev and the Ballets Russes", *Dance Magazine* (New York), May 1971
Spencer, Charles, *The World of Serge Diaghilev*, London, 1974
Buckle, Richard, *Diaghilev*, London, 1979
Percival, John, *The World of Diaghilev*, revised edition, 1979
Stéphant, Anne, "Ombre et lumière: Boris Kochno", *Danse* (Paris), February 1979
Garafola, Lynn, *Diaghilev's Ballets Russes*, New York, 1989

* * *

Boris Kochno's involvement with ballet began in 1921 when, at the age of seventeen, he accepted the position of secretary to Serge Diaghilev. He can hardly have minded that he would not receive a salary for his efforts; he had shown a keen interest in Diaghilev's Ballets Russes before he had even seen the company perform, eagerly following its successes in the newspapers. Born in Moscow, the son of a colonel in the Hussars, Kochno had been brought to Paris by his mother after the revolution, where he persuaded the painter Soudeikine to introduce him to Diaghilev.

Not long afterwards, Kochno made his first artistic contribution to the company, helping Diaghilev to find a subject for a new Stravinsky opera—a comic poem by Pushkin—and writing the lyrics for it himself. Two years after the 1922 premiere of this work, *Mavra*, Kochno wrote his first ballet libretto, *Les Fâcheux*, adapted from Molière and with music by Auric, choreography by Nijinska, and designs by Braque. A year later he wrote two works for Massine, *Zéphire et Flore* and *Les Matelots*, and in 1926 two works for Balanchine, *La Pastorale* and *La Chatte* (the latter under the pseudonym Sobeka, and performed in 1927). Although *Les Matelots* and *La Pastorale* received some criticism for their insubstantial plots, *La Chatte* (based on a fable by Aesop) was admired for its

**Alicia Nikitina and Serge Lifar in *La Chatte*, 1927, based on a libretto by Boris Kochno**

modernism. The following two years brought four more successful libretti—Massine's *Ode*, Balanchine's *The Gods Go a-Begging*, *Le Bal*, and most notably *Le Fils prodigue*.

Meanwhile, as Diaghilev's adviser, spokesman, and friend (though not, apparently, lover), Kochno helped to form and sustain collaborations between artists (Braque, de Chirico, Rouault, and Tchelitchev), composers (Auric, Nabokov, Prokofiev, and Sauguet), and choreographers (Nijinska, Massine, and Balanchine). Kochno's growing influence made him some enemies, however, among them Serge Lifar, who created a stir at Diaghilev's funeral by leaping at Kochno and falling with him into the open grave. Kochno's influential position enabled him to inherit some of Diaghilev's archives, to which he added the many documents and drawings he had collected over the years. In 1975 these were sold to the French government and are now housed in the Bibliothèque of the Paris Opéra Garnier.

After Diaghilev's death in 1929, it was hoped that Kochno would keep the company in operation, but it seems that Lifar's insistence on being joint director prevented this. Kochno would always regret the demise of the company. His next involvement with the stage was as adviser on ballet to C. B. Cochran's 1931 Revue and it was at this time that his lifelong friendship with the painter Christian Bérard began. The next year Kochno joined René Blum's and Colonel de Basil's Ballets Russes de Monte Carlo as artistic collaborator, writing the libretti for two successful works, Massine's *Jeux d'enfants* and Balanchine's *Cotillon*. He went on to join Balanchine in forming Les Ballets 1933, for which he commissioned scores from Milhaud and Sauguet, and staged Brecht and Weill's *The Seven Deadly Sins* with financial backing from Edward James. During the 1930s Kochno returned to the Monte Carlo company, where he remained until 1937.

It was not until 1945, however, that Kochno's next truly successful work was staged. This was *Les Forains*, co-produced with Bérard and choreographed by Roland Petit to Sauguet's score. The ballet's great success led directly to the founding of Les Ballets des Champs-Elysées, with Kochno as artistic director, Petit as first choreographer, and a list of eminent collaborators including Babilée, Charrat, Cocteau, and Milloss. Kochno's libretti for the new company included *Les Amours de Jupiter*, *La Fiancée du diable*, *Pâris*, and *Le Bal des blanchisseuses*. Les Ballets des Champs-Elysées was dissolved in 1951, although Kochno tried to revive it with the help of Jean Robin and Ruth Page.

In subsequent years Kochno succeeded in conquering a long-standing addiction to alcohol and went on to write two books on ballet: *Le Ballet* (Paris, 1954), and *Diaghilev et Les Ballets Russes* (1970), both containing illustrations from Kochno's archives.

—Jessica Arah

---

## KOLPAKOVA, Irina

Russian dancer and teacher. Born Irina Aleksandrovna Kolpakova in Leningrad, 22 May 1933. Studied at the Leningrad Choreographic School, pupil of Agrippina Vaganova; graduated in 1951. Married the dancer (and long-time stage partner) Vladilen Semenov. Dancer, soon becoming leading ballerina, Kirov Ballet, 1951–87; teacher and répétiteur (rehearsal director) from 1987; permanent guest coach, American Ballet Theatre, New York, from 1989; has also appeared frequently on Soviet television. Recipient: title of Honoured Artist of the Russian Federation, 1957; First Prize at the International Festival of Youth and Students, Vienna, 1959; titles of People's Artist of the Russian Federation, 1960, and People's Artist of the USSR, 1965; Prize of the Third International Festival of Dance, Paris, 1965; State Prize of the USSR, 1980; Hero of Socialist Labour, 1983.

### ROLES

1957 Katerina (cr) in *The Stone Flower* (Grigorovich), Kirov Ballet, Leningrad
1959 The Beloved (cr; with Osipenko) in *Coast of Hope* (Belsky), Kirov Ballet, Leningrad
1960 Desdemona (cr) in *Othello* (Kirov version; Chabukiani), Kirov Ballet, Leningrad (originally staged Tbilisi, 1957)
Nina (cr) in *Masquerade* (Fenster), Kirov Ballet, Leningrad
1961 Shirien (cr) in *The Legend of Love* (Grigorovich), Kirov Ballet, Leningrad
1966 Love (cr) in *Man* (Aleksidze), Kirov Ballet, Leningrad
1969 Ala (cr) in *Scythian Suite* (Aleksidze), Kirov Ballet, Leningrad
The Girl (cr) in *Two* (Vinogradov), Choreographic Evening for Kolpakova, Kirov Ballet, Leningrad
Julia in *Romeo and Julia* (Chernichov), Choreographic Evening for Kolpakova, Kirov Ballet, Leningrad
1971 Eve (cr) in *The Creation of the World* (Kasatkina, Vasiliev), Kirov Ballet, Leningrad
1974 Dream-Bird (cr) in *Icarus* (Belsky), Kirov Ballet, Leningrad

**Irina Kolpakova in *The Sleeping Beauty*, Kirov Ballet**

1977 Nelly (cr) in *Til Eulenspiegel* (Elezariev), Kirov Ballet, Leningrad
1979 Natalia Nicolayevna (cr) in *Pushkin* (Kasatkina, Vasiliev), Kirov Ballet, Leningrad
1980 The Fairy (cr) in *The Fairy of the Rond Mountains* (Vinogradov), Kirov Ballet, Leningrad

**Other roles include:** Title role in *Cinderella* (Sergeyev), Tao Hoa in *The Red Poppy* (Zakharov), Queen of the Dryads and Kitri in *Don Quixote* (Gorsky after Petipa), Maria in *The Fountain of Bakhchisarai* (Zakharov), title role in *La Sylphide* (von Rosen after Bournonville), Princess Aurora, Princess Florine, Fairies of Tenderness, Gold, and Sapphires in *The Sleeping Beauty* (Petipa, staged Sergeyev), title role, Myrtha, and Zulme in *Giselle* (Petipa after Perrot, Coralli), Masha and Little Doll in *The Nutcracker* (Vainonen), Juliet and Juliet's Friend in *Romeo and Juliet* (Lavrovsky), Raymonda, Raymonda's Friend, and Dream Scene Variation in *Raymonda* (Petipa, staged Sergeyev), Pannochka in *Taras Bulba* (Fenster), Syuimbike in *Ali Batyr* (*Shurale*; Yakobson), Beautiful Maiden in *Land of Miracles* (Yakobson), the Seventh Waltz and Mazurka in *Chopiniana* (Vaganova after Fokine), Menada in *Spartacus* (Yakobson), the Bird in *The Bird and the Hunter* and *Eternal Spring* (Choreographic Miniatures, Yakobson), Pas de Trois in *Swan Lake* (Petipa, Ivanov; staged Sergeyev), Variation and Dance of the Shades in *La Bayadère* (Petipa, Ponomarev, Chabukiani), Waltz in *Ivan Susasin* (opera; mus. Glinka, chor. Lopukhov, Koren), soloist in *Pas de quatre* (Dolin), title role in *Le Papillon* (Lacotte after Taglioni).

## PUBLICATIONS

By Kolpakova:
"The Last Graduation Class", in *Agrippina Vaganova*, Leningrad, 1958
Interview in Ilicheva, M., "Harmony Gives Birth to Dance", *Sovetsky Balet* (Moscow), no. 1, 1982
Interview with Janet and Leo Kersley, *Ballet Today* (London), October 1961

About Kolpakova:
Lvov-Anokin, Boris, "Irina Kolpakova", *Muzykalnaya Zhizn* (Moscow), no. 6, 1961
Demidov, Aleksandr, *The Russian Ballet Past and Present* translated by Guy Daniels, London, 1978
Grigoriev, A., "Irina Kolpakova", *Teatr* (Leningrad), no. 2, 1981
Mukhin, K., "Irina Kolpakova", *Sovetsky Balet* (Moscow), no. 3, 1983
Krasovskaya, Vera, and Ilicheva, M., *Irina Kolpakova*, Leningrad, 1984
Smakov, Gennady, *The Great Russian Dancers*, New York, 1984
Ilicheva, M., *Irina Kolpakova*, Leningrad, 1979, 1986
Finch, Tamara, "Vaganova's Pupil: Irina Kolpakova", *Dancing Times* (London), October 1988

* * *

Irina Kolpakova is a classical ballerina with a special gift for the lyrical repertoire. She has always had beautiful natural gifts: she is well-proportioned, with a slender and elegant figure, and her dancing was distinguished by a light, high jump, a nobility of manner, and great musicality. A representative of the strict academic style, with an impeccable command of virtuoso ballet technique, Kolpakova yet produced an impression of lightness and airiness when she danced. From the beginning she was a magnificent performer of the classical repertoire, and her best roles were in *The Sleeping Beauty* and *The Nutcracker* (she never danced the large ballets, such as *Swan Lake, Paquita*, or *La Bayadère*). She reminded one of a dainty figurine on stage, and Western audiences in particular admired the delicate, porcelain quality of her physical beauty.

Kolpakova's classical repertoire was perhaps rather limited in comparison to those of the great ballerinas, but within lyrical roles she represented classical perfection. Moreover, she also excelled in the contemporary repertoire. The collision of her career with that of choreographer Yuri Grigorovich opened the door to new possibilities in contemporary art; as the Soviet ballet historian Chistyakova wrote, "Kolpakova was in the crucible of creativity, exploration, and accomplishment. Her encounter with outstanding choreographers who were determining the course of contemporary Soviet ballet decided her destiny. In her expressiveness and ability to enter into the very pattern of a dance lay the secret of her rise and her success."

Kolpakova's appearance in the role of Katerina in Grigorovich's *The Stone Flower* attracted the attention of audiences, colleagues, and critics alike—and her future success in contemporary ballet was determined from then. As Shirien in *The Legend of Love* she demonstrated a fine mastery over the central role, creating both a living human character and a poetic image in her performance. Kolpakova was always close to, and in touch with, the art of her contemporaries, and she was able to infuse into the images of dance the poetry and pulse of the day. She had a fruitful and interesting working relationship with many contemporary choreographers, including Yakobson, Belsky, Kasatkina, and Vasiliev. "In the most unquiet of times artist are called, in defiance of the passions of their age, to concentrate on their individuality and to confirm with their creativity all that is harmonic and positive," wrote the Leningrad critic M. Ilicheva. "Such an artist was Kolpakova. . . . Her perfected art, without pathos or pressure, convinced one of the eternal ideals of good, love, and beauty."

Kolpakova stopped dancing in 1987, but has remained with the Kirov to work as a teacher and coach. She currently works with such outstanding young Kirov dancers as Larissa Lezhnina and Veronika Ivanova, dancers who in many ways resemble Kolpakova in shape and stature, and are proving themselves to be exciting and accomplished performers in the mould of their teacher. Kolpakova has also travelled abroad, and has worked with major international companies, such as American Ballet Theatre. She is acknowledged to be an excellent coach, because she is so clearly able to communicate her own profound understanding of the principles of the Russian Vaganova school—the foundation of the Kirov style, and the essence of her own dancing.

—Igor Stupnikov

---

**KØLPIN, Alexander**

Danish dancer. Born in Copenhagen, Denmark, 1 June 1965. Studied at the Royal Danish Ballet School, Copenhagen, from 1978. One son, Niclas, b. 1984. Apprentice (while still a student), Royal Danish Ballet, 1981: dancer, from 1985, principal dancer, from 1988, also touring internationally with soloists of the Royal Danish Ballet; international guest artist, including for Nijinsky Gala, Hamburg, 1987, with Boston Ballet, 1988, and Australian Ballet, performing in Tokyo and Sydney, 1991, and other guest appearances in Hong Kong,

Singapore, New York, Washington, Athens, Berlin, Paris, Beijing, Shanghai, Rio de Janeiro, and Sao Paulo; artistic director, Soloists and Principals of the Royal Danish Ballet (touring company), from 1991; also television host, Danish television, and occasional visiting lecturer on dance. Recipient: IBM Prize, 1986; Special Prize (for best couple), International Ballet Competition, Jackson, Mississippi, 1986; Bournonville Prize of Honours, 1987; Benois Dance Prize, 1992.

## ROLES

1984 Melancholic in *The Four Temperaments* (Balanchine), Royal Danish Ballet, Copenhagen
Principal dancer in *Arden Court* (Taylor), Royal Danish Ballet, Copenhagen
Principal dancer in *Memoria* (Ailey), Royal Danish Ballet, Copenhagen
1985 Pulcinella in *Pulcinella and Pimpinella* (Cullberg), Royal Danish Ballet, Copenhagen
Principal dancer in *Flower Festival in Genzano* (Bournonville), Royal Danish Ballet, Copenhagen
Principal dancer in *Tchaikovsky Pas de Deux* (Balanchine), Royal Danish Ballet, Copenhagen
Principal dancer in *Symphony in Three Movements* (Christe), Royal Danish Ballet, Copenhagen
Pas de deux from *William Tell* (opera; mus. Rossini, chor. Bournonville), Bournonville Ballet Competition, Copenhagen
1986 Principal dancer in *Capriccio* ("Rubies" from *Jewels*; Balanchine), Royal Danish Ballet, Copenhagen
Dancer in *The Miraculous Mandarin* (Flindt), Royal Danish Ballet, Copenhagen
Fifth Mourner in *Sad Songs* (Christe), Soloists of the Royal Danish Ballet, tour
Pas de deux from *William Tell* (Bournonville), International Ballet Competition, Jackson, Mississippi
Title role in *Abdallah* (Bournonville; staged Lander, Marks, Ryberg), Royal Danish Ballet, Copenhagen
1987 Principal dancer in *Études* (Lander), Royal Danish Ballet, Copenhagen
Mercutio in *Romeo and Juliet* (Neumeier), Royal Danish Ballet, Copenhagen
Norwegian Dance in *The Whims of Cupid and the Ballet Master* (Galeotti), Royal Danish Ballet, Copenhagen
Principal dancer in *Entre Dos Aguas* (North), Royal Danish Ballet, Copenhagen
Principal dancer in *Caverna Magica* (Ailey), Royal Danish Ballet, Copenhagen
Falls in *The River* (Ailey), Royal Danish Ballet, Copenhagen
James in *La Sylphide* (Bournonville; staged Kronstram, Weinreich), Royal Danish Ballet, Paris
Principal dancer in *Septet Extra* (van Manen), Soloists of the Royal Danish Ballet, tour
1988 Gennaro in *Napoli* (Bournonville), Royal Danish Ballet, Copenhagen
1989 Principal dancer in *Afternoon of a Faun* (Robbins), Royal Danish Ballet, Copenhagen
Lensky in *Onegin* (Cranko), Royal Danish Ballet, Copenhagen
Pas de trois in *Agon* (Balanchine), Royal Danish Ballet, Copenhagen
Title role in *Billy the Kid* (Loring), University of California 50th Anniversary Performance
1990 Basil in *Don Quixote* (Petipa), Royal Danish Ballet, Copenhagen
Principal dancer in *Jockey Dance Pas de deux* (Bournonville), Royal Danish Ballet, Copenhagen
Frantz in *Coppélia* (Brenaa after Saint-Léon), Royal Danish Ballet, Copenhagen
Variation in *France/Dance* (Forsythe), Royal Danish Ballet, Copenhagen
Principal dancer in *Serait-ce la mort?* (Béjart), Royal Danish Ballet, Copenhagen
1991 Puck/Philostret in *A Midsummer Night's Dream* (Neumeier), Royal Danish Ballet, Copenhagen
Principal dancer (lead couple) in *Theme and Variations* (Balanchine), Royal Danish Ballet, Copenhagen
The Ballet Master in *The Lesson* (Flindt), Rio de Janiero
Principal dancer in *Quartet for Two* (pas de deux; Flindt), Royal Danish Ballet, Stockholm
King Christian (cr) in *Caroline Mathilde* (Flindt), Royal Danish Ballet, Copenhagen
Principal dancer (cr) in *Sonata for 7* (Laerkesen), Soloists and Principals of the Royal Danish Ballet
Romeo in *Romeo and Juliet* (Cranko), Australian Ballet, Sydney

**Other roles include:** Soloist in *Konservatoriet* (Bournonville), the Prince in *The Nutcracker* (Flindt).

## PUBLICATIONS

Hunt, Marilyn, "Bournonville Pas de Six: Those Dashing Young Danes", *Dance Magazine* (New York), June 1988

* * *

Alexander Kølpin was recognized as a promising new star of the Royal Danish Ballet at an early age, establishing himself quickly as a leading dancer of the company in the brief period between 1985, when he joined, and 1988, when he was made a principal dancer at the age of just 22.

Continuing in the long line of Danish male dancers produced by the school of Copenhagen's Royal Theatre, Kølpin is a fine exponent of the Bournonville style. He brings life and energy to *Flower Festival at Genzano* which he performed with success in his first year as a full member of the Royal Danish Ballet, and his precise technique has suited him well in virtuoso solo roles in the Bournonville classroom classic, *Konservatoriet*. In 1986 Kølpin was awarded a special prize at the International Ballet Competition in Jackson, Mississippi, for his performance, with Henriette Muus, of the Bournonville pas de deux from *William Tell*. In the same year he scored an important success dancing the title role of *Abdallah*, a long lost Bournonville ballet restored to the modern stage by Toni Lander, Bruce Marks, and Flemming Ryberg.

Kølpin's first role as a principal dancer was as Gennaro in *Napoli*, that well-loved example of the Danish style brought to a southern Italian setting, to which he brought his usual energy and enthusiasm, showing the changing moods and vivid temperament of the fisherman-hero who is at the centre of the ballet's tale. On the other hand, in ethereal rather than earthy worlds, Kølpin is equally at home: in the tragic story of *La Sylphide* he gives a sensitive portrayal of James as a sincere and vulnerable lover, torn between the worlds of dream and reality in one of ballet's finest examples of nineteenth-century romanticism.

Kølpin is not just a Bournonville dancer, however; indeed, he has shown an impressive range in works by a variety of choreographers. It is perhaps not surprising, given his clean technique (and a brief period of study at the School of

**Alexander Kølpin**

American Ballet) that he has excelled in the Balanchine repertoire, performing with confidence in such neo-classical masterpieces as *The Four Temperamants*, *Tchaikovsky Pas de deux*, and *Agon*. He is a strong partner in all genres; seeing Kølpin perform Balanchine's *Theme and Variations* (first staged for the Danish company by Patricia Neary in 1991), critic Alexandra Tomalonis pointed to the Danish "instinct for intimate partnering [which] can work in Balanchine as well as Bournonville".

Beyond this, Kølpin has successfully performed in works by leading modern choreographers including Paul Taylor, Alvin Ailey, William Forsythe, and Maurice Béjart. As a dramatic dancer Kølpin has also won recognition, showing an ability to inhabit whatever character he is playing with conviction, bringing intelligence and sensitivity to roles ranging from the impassioned Lensky of Cranko's *Onegin* to the homocidal dancing teacher in Flemming Flindt's *The Lesson*. In Flindt's 1991 ballet for the Royal Danish Ballet, *Caroline Mathilde*, Kølpin danced the central role of the epileptic King Christian VII, giving us a vivid portrait of the crazed and desperate king whose wife, the Caroline of the title, has embarked on an affair with his physician. Greeted with enthusiasm by the home audience in Denmark, while rejected by some critics as banal and dull, *Caroline Mathilde* none the less established Kølpin as a dramatic dancer of ability and versatility.

In recent years Kølpin's career has been curtailed somewhat by injury; enthusiastic Royal Danish Ballet followers were disappointed by his absence, as one of the company's top dancers, from the Bournonville Festival in Copenhagen in 1992. But he has continued as a leading presence in Danish ballet, serving as director of the chamber group known as the Soloists and Principals of the Royal Danish Ballet, and demonstrating, if only in a small group, that he has a flair for effective programming and artistic direction.

—Eric Maier

---

## KONSERVATORIET
(*Conservatory*, or *The Dance School*)

**Choreography:** August Bournonville
**Music:** Holger Simon Paulli
**Libretto:** August Bournonville
**First Production:** Royal Danish Ballet, as *Konservatoriet; eller, Et Avisfrieri* (*Conservatory; or, A Proposal of Marriage by Newspaper*), Copenhagen, 6 May 1849

**Other Productions include:** Royal Swedish Ballet (restaged August Bournonville); Stockholm, 26 May 1857. Royal Danish Ballet (Act I only; restaged Harald Lander and Valborg Borchsenius), as *Konservatoriet*; Copenhagen, 1941. Royal New Zealand Ballet (one-act version; staged and designed Poul Gnatt); New Zealand, 23 May 1955. Australian Ballet (one-act version; staged Gnatt, design Desmond Digby); Adelaide, 5 February 1965. City Center Joffrey Ballet (one-act version; staged Hans Brenaa, design William Pitkin); New York, 20 February 1969. London Festival Ballet (one-act version; staged Mona Vangsaae, design Michael Stennett); London, 9 April 1973. Royal Swedish Ballet (one-act version; staged Fredbjørn Bjørnsson); Stockholm, 9 November 1973. Bonn Opera Ballet (one-act version; staged Hans Brenaa); Bonn, 1973. Paris Opéra Ballet (one-act version; staged Brenaa); Paris, 15 September 1976. Dallas Ballet (one-act version; staged Flemming Flindt, design William Pitkin); Dallas, 21 October 1982. Royal Ballet (one-act version; staged Dinna Bjørn, design David Walker); London, 2 December 1982. Bolshoi Ballet (one-act version; staged Kirsten Ralov, design Jens-Jacob Worsaae); Moscow, 10 May 1989.

### PUBLICATIONS

Bournonville, Auguste, *Mit Theater Liv* 3 parts: Copenhagen, 1848, 1865, 1877; as *My Theatre Life*, translated by Patricia McAndrew, Middletown, Connecticut, 1979
Kragh-Jacobsen, Svend, *The Royal Danish Ballet*, Copenhagen, 1955
Bruhn, Erik and Moore, Lillian, *Bournonville and Ballet Technique*, London, 1961
Ralov, Kirsten (ed.), *The Bournonville School*, New York, 1979
Terry, Walter, *The King's Ballet Master*, New York, 1979
Fridericia, Allan, *Auguste Bournonville*, Copenhagen, 1979
Aschengreen, Erik, "The Ballet Poems of August Bournonville", translated by Patricia McAndrew, *Dance Chronicle* (New York), vol. 4, no. 1, 1981
Hallar, Marianne, and Scavenius, Alette (eds.), *Bournonvilleana*, English edition, translated by Gaye Kynoch, Copenhagen, 1992

* * *

The ballet which Bournonville created in 1849 was in two acts, with the sub-title "A Proposal of Marriage by Newspaper". Inspired by the memory of his youthful studies in Paris under "my famous teacher, Auguste Vestris", Bournonville stated his intention to "give a little sketch of the fresh young life that in my day went on in one corner [of the Conservatoire] . . . namely, the Royal Ballet School". He also sought to remember his "French comrades" in their shared studies: "in the present ballet . . . I have attempted to describe the feelings that refined their gaiety and the joys that seasoned their strenuous work".

The *Konservatoriet* which survives today is the first act of that original work in a revised form, presenting the ballet class itself, which includes children, without the story complications. As such, it is a unique record of the early nineteenth-century French school of ballet, which formed the basis of Bournonville's own performing style. Bournonville had made notes at the time of his studies, and incorporated ideas and combinations from Vestris's classes in his own teaching from that time on. The ballet thus embodies both the homage of one choreographer/dancer to his mentor, and the display of significant aspects of that choreographer's own teaching methods and style. A number of the variations in *Konservatoriet*, indeed, appear in "Friday's class" (in the weekly Bournonville syllabus) as described by Kirsten Ralov in her 1979 text.

Bournonville as a dancer understood how to exploit his own strengths and camouflage his weaknesses—and this is apparent not simply in the fact that all his ballets give demanding roles to the male dancers at a time when, elsewhere in Europe, the male dancer was all but eclipsed by the female, but also is shown in aspects of what is now recognized as the "Bournonville style". He knew how to disguise, for example, his own limited demi-plié facility in landing from jumps, and arranged sequences so that the landings would be fleeting, themselves the preparation for further jumps or different steps (frequently with an unexpected change of direction), such that a unique quality of "balon" was given to the movement—and all of this is clearly shown in *Konservatoriet*.

Pirouettes, also, were not a strong point, but Bournonville recognized the importance and potential of these, and set many

***Konservatoriet*, with Antoinette Sibley, Royal Ballet, London, 1982**

variations on the basic type. Erik Bruhn remembered dreading the difficult pirouettes in second position in *Konservatoriet*. However, pirouettes again tend to be part of the whole rather than a final flourish. They often do not end in fifth position, but lead, via fondu, into another turn, perhaps in attitude, after an initial turn in second position. In the female variation (which also appears as number seven in Friday's class) a pirouette will end in a dégagé before leading directly into another step. Even the last pirouette in this variation is not allowed to become a flourish of virtuosity; after the turn, the leg extends, but closes into a decorous soutenu turn, so that the final image is of the dancer in fifth position sur les pointes, arms in open fifth—contained and composed, after a demonstration of typical Bournonville neatness and aplomb. This example also highlights the role of "linking steps" such as dégagés, pas de bourrées, soutenus; always part of the overall phrasing, they frequently seem even to take precedence over the more "important" steps. Lillian Moore made the point that in Bournonville's work—and this is especially true in *Konservatoriet*—we can see how classical technique has altered its focus during the last century and a half; we realize how the emphasis has shifted towards high, strong extensions and spectacular leaps and pirouettes, to the detriment, sometimes, of neat, precise footwork and alignment, and with the result that many of the smaller, more intricate but less "showy" steps have all but disappeared.

Pas de bourrées are used flexibly with component steps going in different directions, according to the requirements of the phrase as a whole. The importance of the step is quietly stressed in the Finale, which begins with pas de bourrées and jetés. With a nice touch familiar to countless ballet students, the class is brought gradually to a close in reverse direction, as it were; grands battements appear again, followed by a slow grand plié, before the final dégagé and lift into attitude effacée. This is itself a fitting final picture, and surely the true signature of Bournonville, appearing, as it does, in so many buoyant jetés and sustained adagio combinations.

Boys and girls have similar variations and share almost all steps and combinations, showing the basic equality of the sexes championed by Bournonville, but each show a greater emphasis on a particular range of steps; the girls tend to have more fast, intricate strings of steps terre-à-terre, for example, whereas the boys will have more jetés, assemblés, tours en l'air, and pirouettes.

Ports de bras, in comparison with footwork, is simple and understated, but used in such a way as to allow attention to focus on different aspects at a given time. Sometimes, the arms are held quietly; at other times, the arms complete the picture and complement the shape made by feet and legs, for example in the favourite attitude, whether it be in an adagio pivot turn, a pirouette, or a grand jeté. Like the ports de bras, the floor patterns tend to be clear, and alignment precise, allowing the dance to be shown to best effect without being predictable; a straight path across the stage may also incorporate many turns and changes of focus.

*Konservatoriet* presents audiences with a familiar picture; the female dancers like Degas models in their full-skirted, frothy white dresses; dancers relaxing at the sides of the studio at different times, leaning on the barre, or adjusting ribbons on shoes. Throughout, the movements themselves, performed for their own sake—or, rather, as part of the unending quest for perfection which underpins classical ballet study—resonate with latent significance echoing down the ages through all the ballets ever made with classical technique as their basis. Bournonville's love for his art is clearly manifested here, where enchaînements become celebrations, and one sees again, in each new generation of Bournonville dancers, "the feelings that refined their gaiety and the joys that seasoned their strenuous work" in the Paris Conservatoire of 1820.

—Rachel S. Richardson

---

## LA KORRIGANE

**Choreography:** Louis Mérante
**Music:** Charles Marie Widor
**Design:** J.-B. Lavastre, Auguste Rubé, Chaperon, and Eugène Lacoste
**Libretto:** François Coppée and Louis Mérante
**First Production:** Théâtre National de l'Opéra, Paris, 1 December 1880
**Principal Dancers:** Rosita Mauri (Yvonette), Marie Sanlaville (Queen of the Korriganes), Louis Mérante (Lilèz)

## PUBLICATIONS

Coppée, François, *La Korrigane*, Paris (no date)
Beaumont, Cyril, *Complete Book of Ballets*, revised edition, London, 1951

* * *

The action of *La Korrigane* is set in Brittany during the seventeenth century, taking place over a single day and night. The village square is full of people on the Day of Pilgrimage. Yvonette, the penniless tavern maid, repulses the advances of Pascou, the hunchbacked town crier. She feeds Janik, the beggar boy, as the sound of the *biniou* (bagpipes) is heard. Its player is Lilèz, most handsome man in the village. Yvonette tries to win his attention, but he goes into church with the other villagers.

During the service, an old woman coming into the square falls, and Yvonette goes to her assistance. The woman reveals herself to be the Queen of the Korriganes, and offers Yvonette a bargain: jewels and beautiful clothes are hers to keep if she can win Lilèz's affections before the Angelus rings. If she fails, Yvonette must herself become a korrigane.

The jealous Pascou, who has stolen from Lilèz a magic rosary that repels korriganes, overhears the Queen's proposal to which Yvonette has agreed. Yvonette dresses herself in the magnificent clothes, and during the village festival attracts the attentions of Lilèz. Just as he is about to propose, Pascou moves the hands of the town clock forward, and the Angelus strikes. Yvonette is borne away by the Queen's dwarfs and korriganes as the first act curtain falls.

On the heath at midnight, Pascou, now drunk, falls asleep, and is relieved of the magic rosary by Janik. Korriganes and other mysterious creatures arrive for a midnight frolic. The Queen queries Yvonette's sadness, and is told that the hunchback had altered the clock. Dwarfs drag him in, and he is forced to dance until he drops.

Lilèz arrives, searching for Yvonette. The Queen offers to free the girl if Lilèz can find her among the korriganes, but then uses her magic to prevent this. Yvonette is suddenly inspired: she repeats the dance steps of their first meeting, which the korriganes cannot imitate, and Lilèz claims his love. The korriganes attempt to part them, but Janik appears with the magic rosary, the korriganes scatter as dawn approaches, and Lilèz and Yvonette are united.

The plot of *La Korrigane*, inspired by a Breton legend, was devised by François Coppée with the ballet's choreographer Louis Mérante, who also danced Lilez. The music by Charles Widor—his first stage score—elicited much critical praise for its evocative use of folk rhythm and orchestral tone colour. Coppée, in an interview published some fifteen years later, recalled the composer's effortless ability to produce a "page of exquisite melody" inspired by a choreographic idea, and his readiness to re-write whenever required.

The Breton setting was something of a novelty for a public which relished the exotic and unusual. Traditional dances for the sabot-shod peasants, and show pieces like the *Sabotière* and *Gigue bretonne* for Yvonette, together with the ethnic costuming, gave the ballet a vivid sense of place. This folkloric flavour made a telling contrast with the more fantastic dances of the Queen of the Korriganes' ethereal minions. Mérante won critical praise for the "picturesque and animated scenes" he had devised.

Rosita Mauri, who created the role of Yvonette, was described in glowing terms by Coppée in the same interview: "After soaring in the air, [she] returned to the stage so lightly, so delicately, that you could not hear a sound . . . she whinnied and darted like a young foal; she soared and glided in space like a young bird."

*La Korrigane* was an immediate success, and was performed over one hundred times at the Opéra.

—Louise Stein

---

**KRIGER** (Krieger), **Viktorina**

Russian/Soviet dancer and critic. Born Viktorina Vladimirovna Kriger in St. Petersburg, 9 April (28 March old style) 1893. Studied at the Moscow Theatre School, pupil of Maria Stanislavskaya and Vasily Tikhomirov, 1903–10. Married Soviet musical theatre director and producer Ilya M. Shlugleit. Ballerina, Bolshoi Theatre, Moscow, 1910–20, 1925–48; toured abroad, first with Anna Pavlova's company, 1921, then with Mikhail Mordkin, United States, 1923–25; artistic director, Moscow Art Ballet, 1929–39 (becoming company of the Stanislavsky and Nemirovich-Danchenko Theatre, from 1939); director of the Bolshoi Theatre Museum, 1955–63; also dance critic and writer, Moscow, from 1926. Recipient: title of Honoured Artist of the Russian Federation, 1929; Honoured Arts Worker of the Russian Federation, 1951. Died in Moscow, 23 December 1978.

## ROLES

1911 The Fairy of Canaries in *The Sleeping Beauty* (Petipa, staged Gorsky), Bolshoi Ballet, Moscow
Little Red Riding Hood in *The Sleeping Beauty* (Petipa, Gorsky), Bolshoi Ballet, Moscow
1912 The White Cat in *The Sleeping Beauty* (Petipa, Gorsky), Bolshoi Ballet, Moscow
1915 Tsar-Maiden in *The Little Humpbacked Horse* (Gorsky after Saint-Léon), Bolshoi Ballet, Moscow
1917 Kitri in *Don Quixote* (Gorsky), Bolshoi Ballet, Moscow
Swanilda in *Coppélia* (Gorsky after Petipa), Bolshoi Ballet, Moscow
1919 Soloist, "Tea" (cr) in *The Nutcracker* (Gorsky), Bolshoi Ballet, Moscow
1925 Odette/Odile in *Swan Lake* (Gorsky after Petipa, Ivanov), Bolshoi Ballet, London
1927 Tao-Hoa in *The Red Poppy* (Lashchilin, Tikhomirov), Bolshoi Ballet, Moscow
Ballerina (cr) in *Petrushka* (Ryabtsev after Fokine), Bolshoi Ballet, Moscow
1932 Concita in *The Comedians* (Bolotov, Virsky), Moscow Art Ballet, Moscow
Tao-Hoa in *The Red Poppy* (Kholfin after Lashchilin, Tikhomirov), Moscow Art Ballet, Moscow
Jeanne (cr) in *La Carmagnole* (Bolotov, Virsky), Moscow Art Ballet, Moscow
1933 Lise in *The Rivals* (new version of *La Fille mal gardée*; Kholfin, Markov), Moscow Art Ballet, Moscow
1935 Therèse in *The Flames of Paris* (Vainonen), Bolshoi Ballet, Moscow
1936 Zarema in *The Fountain of Bakhchisarai* (Zakharov), Moscow Art Ballet, Moscow
Carabosse (cr) in *The Sleeping Beauty* (Messerer, Chekrygin after Petipa), Bolshoi Ballet, Moscow
1945 Stepmother (cr) in *Cinderella* (Zakharov), Bolshoi Ballet, Moscow

**Other roles include:** numerous concert programmes, including such dances as the *Bacchanal* (own choreography for dance in Fokine ballet; mus. Glazunov), the *Caucasian Lezginka* and the *Comic Jewish Dance* (also chor.), *Lizst's Second Rhapsody* (also chor.), *Street Urchin* (also chor.), Miller's Wife in *Le Tricorne* (Kholfin).

## PUBLICATIONS

By Kriger:
*My Notes*, Moscow, 1930
Numerous articles on dance, including—
"Watching People Dance", *Novy Zritel*, no. 8, 1925
"My Teacher" (about Vassily Tikhomirov), *Muzykalnaya Zhizn* (Moscow), no. 10, 1966
"Masters of Concert Dancing", *Muzykalnaya Zhizn* (Moscow), no. 8, 1969
"The French Ballet in Moscow", *Kultura i Zhizn* (Moscow), no. 6, 1970
"The Unique One" (about Galina Ulanova), *Sovetskaya Muzyka* (Moscow), no. 5, 1976

About Kriger:
Volynsky, Akim, "Choreographic Arabesques: The Guests from Moscow", *Zhizn Iskusstva*, no. 45, 1923.
Brodersen, Y., "Viktorina Kriger's Guest Performance", *Rabochi i Teatr* (Leningrad), no. 47, 1925
Cherepin, A., "Viktorina Kriger in *Swan Lake*", *Programmy Gosudarstvennykh Akademicheskikh Teatrov*, no. 53, 1926
Iving, Viktor, *Viktorina Kriger*, Moscow, 1928
Raffé, W.G., "What the Russians are Trying to Do in Ballet", *Dance Magazine* (New York), March 1948
Chudnovski, Mikhail, *Viktorina Kriger*, Moscow, 1964
Roslavleva, Natalia, *Era of the Russian Ballet*, London, 1966
Borel, L., "Viktorina Kriger", *Sovetsky Balet*, no. 2, 1983

* * *

Viktorina Kriger was not just one of the Moscow Bolshoi ballerinas; she was among the best-known personalities of the Moscow artistic world of the time, renowned as a concert dancer, the organizer of a new ballet company, a prolific journalist, and a director of the Bolshoi Theatre Museum.

Viktorina Kriger was born into an artistic family: her father was an actor, her mother an actress and the author of many plays for children. As a student of the Moscow School of Theatre, she studied under Vasily Tikhomirov, who was famous for developing excellent technical skills in his trainees. The girl mastered classical dance rapidly, while her liveliness, charm, and confidence enabled her to perform children's roles, not only in ballets but in drama as well.

During her early years in the Bolshoi, Kriger had danced many small solo parts, both character and classical, but soon she was offered her first major roles: the Tsar-Maiden, Kitri, and Swanilda. In those parts one could already see her technical sophistication, vivacity, and gift for comic acting.

From 1921 to 1923, Kriger went abroad. She made a big concert tour of Europe, then danced in North America with Anna Pavlova's company and later gave solo concerts in New York for an entire season. The ballet *The Fairy Doll* was staged exclusively for her in a Broadway theatre. American critics wrote favourably of Kriger; they were particularly impressed by the virtuosity and the dynamic style of her performance.

After coming back to Moscow, Kriger started to combine her work in the Bolshoi (resumed in 1925) with tireless concert touring and did so almost to the very end of her theatrical career. She gave performances not just in the capitals but all over the USSR: in quiet provincial towns, at frontier posts, on warships, and so on. Those concerts brought the dancer wide publicity and great success with audiences. She made ballet accessible to the broadest public. Kriger's emotional, joyful dancing was consonant with the general mood of the time and was easily understood by the new audience, whose democratic tastes were then emerging.

Kriger was one of the most skilful dancers of her time. She had an enormous leap, and was famous for her turns as well as for her "bouncy" pointe work. Her particular forte was fouettés, which she performed with amazing skill and, according to witnesses, at a giddy speed. Kriger did not conceal from the public how difficult dancing was, but she let everyone see the skill and enthusiasm with which she overcame those difficulties.

A true Moscow dancer, she was never too strict in observing the laws of classical choreography; on the contrary, her movements could be impetuous and even slightly "rough" in quite an unorthodox way. She had very vivid gestures and facial expressions too.

Kriger's energy and passion for all things new brought forth yet another undertaking: in 1929, she started a ballet company, the Moscow Art Ballet, together with her husband Ilya Shlugleit. This company, which was to merge with the famous Stanislavsky and Nemirovich–Danchenko Lyric Theatre, did much to promote the new genre of choreographic drama in the USSR. As the leader of the Moscow Art Ballet, Kriger performed a number of parts which required, besides perfect technique, deep psychological penetration; such were the parts of Zarema (*The Fountain of Bakhchisarai*), Tao-Hoa (*The Red Poppy*), and Jeanne (*La Carmagnole*).

At the Bolshoi Theatre Kriger continued dancing her old roles, ever improving on them. Her pièce de résistance was the part of Kitri; she was considered the best Kitri that had ever appeared on the Moscow stage. Her artistic temperament mingled the liveliness and sincerity of character dancing with the refined correctness of classical choreography.

Kriger also created several new roles, such as the Ballerina in Ryabtsev's *Petrushka* and several character parts, among which can be numbered the evil fairy Carabosse in *The Sleeping Beauty* and the grotesque Stepmother in *Cinderella*, which were perhaps her best achievement.

Viktorina Kriger started writing on ballet in 1926 and continued her work as a journalist to the end of her life. During that period, several hundred of her reviews of touring performances and new productions, as well as her portrayals of individual dancers and humorous short stories, appeared in the press. As with all her activities, there was much vigour and sincere emotion in Kriger's journalism. Thus, in the 1930s she called for a popular art, urging the artists to give as many performances in villages as possible and even to open theatres in the countryside. Later, when "dram–ballet" (balletic drama) was the only officially approved genre, Kriger was also brave enough to defend in her articles the dancer's right to dance. She always did her best to promote young talent, and was undoubtedly a strong influence on those who succeeded her in Moscow ballet.

—Irina Gruzdeva

---

**KRIZA, John**

American dancer. Born in Berwyn, Illinois, 15 January 1919. Studied with Mildred Prchal in Berwyn, with Bentley Stone and Walter Camryn at Stone-Camryn School, Chicago, and with Anton Dolin and Antony Tudor at School of American Ballet, New York. Début in W.P.A. Federal Project and Chicago City Civic Opera Ballet (ballet director Ruth Page), 1939; dancer, Page–Stone Ballet, 1939/40; dancer, Ballet Theatre (later American Ballet Theatre) from its inception, 1940, becoming principal dancer until 1966; also leading dancer, performing with Lincoln Kirstein's American Ballet Caravan, touring South America, 1941; guest artist, New York City Ballet, 1948, also performing as guest with Chicago Opera Ballet, and Sociedad Pro-Arte, Havana; appeared in musical comedies, including in *Kiss Me, Kate* (mus. Cole Porter), and *Brigadoon* (mus. Loewe), Cohasset, Massachusetts, 1952, and in films, including in Mexican films *Yo Bailé con Don Porfiro* (1942), *Yolanda* (1943), and *The Three Muskateers* (1943); assistant director, administration and stage revivals, American Ballet Theatre, from 1966. Died in Naples, Florida, 18 August 1975.

**ROLES**

1941 A Marine (cr) in *Time Table* (Tudor), American Ballet Caravan, Rio de Janeiro
The Hermit (cr) in *Pastorela* (L. Christensen, Fernandez), American Ballet Caravan, Rio de Janeiro
Polka: Couple in Black and White (cr) in *Divertimento* (Balanchine), American Ballet Caravan, Rio de Janeiro

1942 Harlequin (cr) in *Coppélia* (new production; Semenoff after Saint-Léon), Ballet Theatre, Mexico City
The Faun (cr) in *Romantic Age* (Dolin), Ballet Theatre, New York

1943 Dancing Poodle in *The Fantastic Toyshop* (*La Boutique fantasque*; Massine), Ballet Theatre, Omaha
It Was Spring (cr) in *Dim Lustre* (Tudor), Ballet Theatre, New York
A Gypsy (cr) in *Fair at Sorochinsk* (Lichine), Ballet Theatre, New York
The Old Official's Confidant (cr) in *Mademoiselle Angot* (later *Mam'zelle Angot*; Massine), Ballet Theatre, New York

1944 Second Sailor (cr) in *Fancy Free* (Robbins), Ballet Theatre, New York

**John Kriza (centre) in *Fancy Free*, Ballet Theater, 1940s**

Drummer in *Graduation Ball* (Lichine), Ballet Theatre, Montreal
Pas de trois (cr) in *Waltz Academy* (Balanchine), Ballet Theatre, Boston
1945 The Shepherd (cr) in *Harvest Time* (Nijinska), Ballet Theatre, New York
Pollux (cr) in *Undertow* (Tudor), Ballet Theatre, New York
Jim (cr) in *Gift of the Magi* (Semenoff), Ballet Theatre, Boston
Pas de deux (cr) in *Interplay* (Robbins), Billy Rose's "Concert Varieties", Ziegfeld Theater, New York (restaged Ballet Theatre, same year)
The Ballerina's Partner (cr) in *On Stage!* (Kidd), Ballet Theatre, Boston
1946 Another Man (cr) in *Facsimile* (Robbins), Ballet Theatre, New York
Boy in Green in *Les Patineurs* (Ashton), Ballet Theatre, New York
1947 Principal dancer in *Summer Day* (pas de deux; Robbins), Ballet Theatre, New York
1948 The Pastor (cr) in *Fall River Legend* (de Mille), Ballet Theatre, New York
Principal dancer (cr) in *Shadow of the Wind* (Tudor), Ballet Theatre, New York
1950 Pas de deux (III) in *Caprichos* (Ross), Ballet Theatre, New York
Champion Roper in *Rodeo* (de Mille), Ballet Theatre, Wiesbaden, Germany
1951 Young musician in *Les Demoiselles de la nuit* (Petit), Ballet Theatre, New York
Thief in *The Thief who Loved a Ghost* (Ross, Ward), Ballet Theatre, New York
1953 Principal dancer (Tancredi) in *The Combat* (*Le Combat*, also *The Duel*; Dollar), Ballet Theatre, London
1956 His Imperial Excellency in *Offenbach in the Underworld* (Tudor), Ballet Theatre, New York
Stanley in *A Streetcar Named Desire* (Bettis), Ballet Theatre
1957 Young Man (cr) in *Winter's Eve* (MacMillan), Ballet Theatre, London
The Lover in *Annabel Lee* (Skibine), Ballet Theatre Previews, New York
Leonardo in *Blood Wedding* (Rodrigues), Ballet Theatre Previews, New York
Principal dancer (cr) in *Journey* (MacMillan), Ballet Theatre, New York
Title role (cr) in *Sebastian* (de Mille), Ballet Theatre Previews, New York
Principal dancer (cr) in *Paean* (Ross), Ballet Theatre Previews, New York
1958 Principal dancer (cr) in *Concerto* (Ross), American Ballet Theatre, New York
Principal dancer in *Variations for Four* (Dolin), American Ballet Theatre, New York
1962 Principal dancer in *The Taming* (pas de deux; Sanders), American Ballet Theatre, New York
1963 First intruder (cr) in *L'Inconnue* (Bentley Stone), Stone-Camryn Ballet, Chicago

**Other roles include:** Principal dancer in *Les Sylphides* (Fokine), title role in *Bluebeard* (Fokine), principal dancer in *Black Swan Pas de deux* (from *Swan Lake*, Act III; Dolin after Petipa), title role in *Billy the Kid* (Loring), Colin in *La Fille mal gardée* (D. Romanoff), Hermes in *Helen of Troy* (Lichine), Jean in *Miss Julie* (Cullberg), principal dancer in *Romeo and Juliet* (Tudor), principal dancer in *Tally-Ho!* (de Mille), Cavalier in *Gala Performance* (Tudor), principal dancer in *Jardin aux lilas* (Tudor), Hermes in *Helen of Troy* (Lichine).

## PUBLICATIONS

Owen, Walter, "Meet John Kriza", *Dance Magazine* (New York), December 1945
Amberg, George, *Ballet in America*, New York, 1949
Coleman, Emily, "Hallmark: American" *Dance News Annual* (New York), 1953
Lansdale, Nelson, "Versatile John Kriza", *Dance Magazine* (New York), July 1954
Payne, Charles, *American Ballet Theatre*, New York, 1978

* * *

John Kriza tops the list of under-appreciated American dancers. He was the first American-born, American-trained premier danseur in a major ballet company and had a relatively large personal following. But the major part of his career spanned a period (the mid-1930s through the 1950s) when the majority of Americans ranked ballet close to the bottom among the performing arts.

Earlier in the century, Anna Pavlova and Vaslav Nijinsky familiarized Americans with ballet and sparked an interest that evolved into dance's popularity today. And in the late 1950s, the Soviets created a mild balletomania with their dancers-cum-athletes. In the years between, native companies were born, and they established ballet as a viable art form.

Kriza, as one of Ballet Theatre's mainstays, was part of that development. Conditions were ideal. Sol Hurok had presented the Ballet Russe de Monte Carlo in New York and in regional urban centers with sufficient financial success to continue. The Ballet Russe, however, represented Europe. The company capitalized on its Russian, faintly imperial provenance to the extent that dancers Russianized their names; and the repertoire was primarily adaptations of nineteenth-century works and more recent pieces which Serge Diaghilev had commissioned a decade earlier.

The time was right for change, which American choreographers provided. Their ballet style was freer in movement than that of the Russians, completely purged of mime and often set to contemporary scores. This demanded a new breed of dancers. Among the men who met the requirements and joined the American companies were Herbert Bliss, Todd Bolender, William Dollar, Harold Lang, Nicholas Magallanes, Francisco Moncion, and Kriza.

Kriza had the added advantage of theater training, from dancing in the W.P.A. projects of the late 1930s. His eclectic background, youth (he was barely 20), and enthusiasm attracted the attention of Ruth Page, director of the Chicago Civic Opera Ballet.

Page was well qualified as a mentor. She had studied with Bolm and Cecchetti, toured with Pavlova, danced for Diaghilev, and toured the Orient with her own chamber ballet ensemble. Under her tutelage, Kriza developed the formidable technique and adaptability that served him well in the classics and learned the Page style of "Made in America" dance.

After a season with the opera company, Kriza danced with the Page–Stone company in a tour of the American midwest. When the still unknown Ballet Theatre was named the official company at the Chicago opera house for one season, he was invited to join the fledgling group.

For the next two decades, Kriza and Ballet Theatre were closely associated. The company had abolished the rigid classification of dancers and had only two categories: principals and "company". Kriza began in the lower rank but advanced quickly to principal.

Kriza perfected his technique while working with Page. Ballet Theatre allowed him to develop the stage personality that made him popular. He was of medium height, well-built but not conspicuously muscular, and had the reflexes and coordination of an athlete. He projected an image of non-threatening masculinity, the "kid next door" grown to young adulthood.

The public identified this Just Folks American quality in *Fancy Free* (1941), in which he danced the sentimental Second Sailor. (Jerome Robbins and Harold Lang were his shipmates.) He wore a gob's hat pushed back on tousled curls, and smiled with a hint of something even funnier held back—he was the epitome of American youth.

The same quality applied to the role of Champion Roper in *Rodeo* and the title role in *Billy the Kid*, though in neither was he the original creator. Eugene Loring choreographed *Billy* for himself and danced the premiere performance. He then sold the rights to Ballet Theatre, where Kriza made the role his own. The ballet is an enduring example of choreographic Americana, a folk tale of the Old West in a blend of classic and theatre dance styles. Aaron Copland composed the score. The titular hero is a skewed Horatio Alger character, the wronged youth whose first killing is a reflexive act of vengeance. The role fit Kriza's persona like a second skin, but he made more of it. In the long solo for adult Billy, Kriza transcended charisma and image to create a believable character in a series of spins, elevations, and pirouettes.

Kriza did not confine himself to the American idiom. The male lead in *Les Sylphides*, Colin in *La Fille mal gardée*, and Tancredi in *Le Combat* were among his roles. In 1951, when Britain's Royal Ballet and Ballet Theatre were on the same touring circuit, Kriza and Nora Kay's version of the "Black Swan" pas de deux received better reviews than that of their British counterparts, Margot Fonteyn and Robert Helpmann.

One of Kriza's surprising triumphs was as Bluebeard. Anton Dolin, who danced the role first, made the king something of a spoiled brat, world-weary and easily bored. Kriza's Bluebeard was a tongue-in-cheek villain, having a terrific time.

Kriza's boy-next-door image was not an act. He was the same off stage. He answered to "Johnny", and had a lively sense of humor along with genuine modesty. When asked about the ovations he received at the Bolshoi Theatre during Ballet Theatre's tour of the Soviet Union in 1953, he said, "It was all right."

Kriza retired early. He left Ballet Theatre to rejoin Page's Chicago Opera Ballet for a tour of the United States, appeared in clubs and on television, and played summer stock.

Soon after he left Ballet Theatre, the company dropped *Billy the Kid* from its active repertoire. So strong was the identification of Kriza with the role that it never had a major revival for 30 years.

His final activity was teaching ballet, which he did successfully. He was thorough, patient, and willing to give individual attention despite a tight class schedule. He returned to dancing for an American Ballet Theatre anniversary gala, in which he danced the familiar role of Youth in *Three Virgins and the Devil*.

Even before Kriza's death in 1975, American ballet companies and dancers stood tall in international dance. But some who knew Kriza's contribution to this success remembered. American-born and -trained Edward Villella, premier danseur for New York City Ballet said, "We all owe him. He was the first."

—William E. Fark

---

**KRONSTAM, Henning**

Danish dancer, teacher, and ballet director. Born in Copenhagen, 29 June 1934. Studied at the Royal Danish Ballet School, Copenhagen, pupil of Vera Volkova, from 1941. Début, while still a student, Royal Theatre, Copenhagen, 1948; dancer, Royal Danish Ballet, from 1952, becoming solo dancer (principal), from 1956; also international guest artist, including in Oslo, 1957, Britain, 1959, 1960, with Grand Ballet du Marquis de Cuevas, 1961, and with Chicago Opera Ballet; director, Royal Danish Ballet School, from 1966; artistic director, Royal Danish Ballet, 1978–85. Recipient: title of Knight of the Order of Dannebrog, 1964.

## ROLES

1948 Dancer in *Episode de la vie d'un artiste* (*Symphonie fantastique*; Massine), Royal Danish Ballet, Copenhagen
Street-sweeper in *Le Beau Danube* (Massine), Royal Danish Ballet, Copenhagen
1950 Dancer in *Concerto* (Theilade), Royal Danish Ballet, Copenhagen
Chinaman in *The Shepherdess and the Chimney Sweeper* (Lander), Royal Danish Ballet, Copenhagen
Dancer in *Romeo and Juliet* (Bartholin), Royal Danish Ballet, Copenhagen
1951 Dancer in *Desire* (Larsen), Royal Danish Ballet, Copenhagen
1952 Senior Cadet in *Graduation Ball* (Lichine), Royal Danish Ballet, Copenhagen
Drummer in *Graduation Ball* (Lichine), Royal Danish Ballet, Copenhagen
Dancer in *Idolon* (Schaufuss), Royal Danish Ballet, Copenhagen

1953 Artist in *Parisiana* (Bartholin), Royal Danish Ballet, Copenhagen
1954 Moor in *The Whims of Cupid and the Ballet Master* (Galeotti), Royal Danish Ballet, Copenhagen
Arlechino/Najade (cr) in *Capricious Lucinda* (Larsen), Royal Danish Ballet, Copenhagen
Violinist (cr) in *Behind the Curtain* (Bjørnsson), Royal Danish Ballet, Copenhagen
1955 The Poet in *Night Shadow* (*La Sonnambula*; Balanchine), Royal Danish Ballet, Copenhagen
June, The Lover in *Twelve by the Post* (B. Ralov), Royal Danish Ballet, Copenhagen
Romeo (cr) in *Romeo and Juliet* (Ashton), Royal Danish Ballet, Copenhagen
1956 Principal dancer in *Les Sylphides* (Fokine), Royal Danish Ballet, Copenhagen
Vilhelm in *Far from Denmark* (Bournonville), Royal Danish Ballet, Copenhagen
Chinese dance in *Far from Denmark* (Bournonville), Royal Danish Ballet, Copenhagen
Pas de trois in *La Ventana* (Bournonville), Royal Danish Ballet, Copenhagen
James in *La Sylphide* (Bournonville), Royal Danish Ballet, Copenhagen
Orpheus (cr) in *Myth* (Hansen), Royal Danish Ballet, Copenhagen
1957 Apollo in *Apollon musagète* (*Apollo*; Balanchine), Royal Danish Ballet, Copenhagen
Prince Florimund in *The Sleeping Beauty* (Petipa; staged Ashton), Royal Danish Ballet, Copenhagen
Prince Siegfried in *Swan Lake* (one-act version; Petipa, Ivanov; staged Lander), Royal Danish Ballet, Copenhagen
Nilas (cr) in *Moon Reindeer* (Cullberg), Royal Danish Ballet, Copenhagen
1958 Second movement in *Symphony in C* (Balanchine), Royal Danish Ballet, Copenhagen
Quaker dance in *The Whims of Cupid and the Ballet Master* (Galeotti), Royal Danish Ballet, Copenhagen
The Husband (cr) in *Secrets* (Cranko), Edinburgh International Ballet, Edinburgh
Principal dancer (cr) in *Octet* (Taras), Edinburgh International Ballet, Edinburgh
Principal dancer (cr) in *Opus 13* (Schaufuss), Royal Danish Ballet, Copenhagen
Yellow man (cr) in *Spectrum* (Vangsaae), Royal Danish Ballet, Copenhagen
Harlequin in *Les Millions d'Arlequin* (Walbom), Royal Danish Ballet, Copenhagen
Boss (cr) in *Happiness on Journey* (Bjørnsson), Royal Danish Ballet, Copenhagen
1959 Albrecht in *Giselle* (Petipa after Coralli, Perrot; staged Bruhn), Royal Danish Ballet, Copenhagen
Jean in *Miss Julie* (Cullberg), Royal Danish Ballet, Copenhagen
Jason in *Medea* (Cullberg), Royal Danish Ballet, Copenhagen
1960 Toreador in *Carmen* (Petit), Royal Danish Ballet, Copenhagen
Bridegroom in *Blood Wedding* (Rodrigues), Royal Danish Ballet, Copenhagen
The Learned Man (cr) in *The Shadow* (Bartholin), Royal Danish Ballet, Copenhagen
1961 Title role in *Cyrano de Bergerac* (Petit), Royal Danish Ballet, Copenhagen
Pas de deux from *The Nutcracker* (Brenaa after Ivanov), Royal Danish Ballet, Copenhagen
The Seaman in *The Lady from the Sea* (Cullberg), Royal Danish Ballet, Copenhagen
Principal dancer in *Danses concertantes* (MacMillan), Royal Danish Ballet, Copenhagen
1962 Señor in *La Ventana* (Bournonville), Royal Danish Ballet, Copenhagen
1963 Pas de deux from *Don Quixote* (after Petipa), Royal Danish Ballet, Copenhagen
First movement in *Symphony in C* (Balanchine), Royal Danish Ballet, Copenhagen
Phlegmatic in *The Four Temperaments* (Balanchine), Royal Danish Ballet, Copenhagen
Second movement in *Bourrée fantasque* (Balanchine), Royal Danish Ballet, Copenhagen
Melancholic in *The Four Temperaments* (Balanchine), Royal Danish Ballet, Copenhagen
Danilo in *The Merry Widow* (Page), Chicago Opera Ballet, Chicago
Daphnis in *Daphnis und Cloé* (Cranko), Stuttgart Ballet, Stuttgart
The principal dancer in *Irene Holm* (von Rosen), Royal Danish Ballet, Copenhagen
The Host (cr) in *Garden Party* (Schaufuss), Royal Danish Ballet, Copenhagen
1964 Principal dancer (cr) in *Sentiments* (Brenaa), Royal Danish Ballet, Copenhagen
Ballet master in *The Lesson* (Flindt), Royal Danish Ballet, Copenhagen
Prince Siegfried in *Swan Lake* (Petipa, Ivanov; staged Lander), Royal Danish Ballet, Copenhagen
1965 The Fool in *The Lady and the Fool* (extracts; Cranko), Copenhagen Summer Ballet, The New Theatre, Copenhagen
1966 Don José in *Carmen* (Petit), Royal Danish Ballet on tour, Aarhus
Pas de deux in *The Kermesse in Bruges* (Bournonville), Royal Danish Ballet, Copenhagen
d'Artagnan in *The Three Musketeers* (Flindt), Royal Danish Ballet, Copenhagen
1967 Principal dancer (cr) in *Gala Variations* (Flindt), Royal Danish Ballet, Copenhagen
The principal in *Aimez-vous Bach?* (Macdonald), Royal Danish Ballet, Copenhagen
Gennaro in *Napoli* (Bournonville), Royal Danish Ballet, Copenhagen
Title role in *Don Juan* (von Rosen), Royal Danish Ballet, Copenhagen
Principal dancer in *Ballet Royal* (Flindt), Royal Danish Ballet, Copenhagen
1968 Principal dancer in *Aureole* (Taylor), Royal Danish Ballet, Copenhagen
Alexis in *Konservatoriet* (Bournonville), Royal Danish Ballet, Copenhagen
Principal dancer in *Donizetti Variations* (Balanchine), Royal Danish Ballet, Copenhagen
Brighella in *Pierrot Lunaire* (Tetley), Royal Danish Ballet, Copenhagen
Jester in *Fresco* (Theilade), Royal Danish Ballet, Copenhagen
1969 Junker Ove in *A Folk Tale* (Bournonville), Royal Danish Ballet, Copenhagen
Franz Pander in *Bagage* (Tomaszewski), Royal Danish Ballet, Copenhagen
1970 Edouard in *The Life Guards on Amager* (Bournonville), Royal Danish Ballet, Copenhagen
The Man in *Jardin aux lilas* (Tudor), Royal Danish Ballet, Copenhagen

1972 Green in *Prism* (Kølgaard), Royal Danish Ballet, Copenhagen
The Man in *Winter's Court* (Feld), Royal Danish Ballet, Copenhagen
Principal dancer in *Dichterliebe* (Marks), Royal Danish Ballet, Copenhagen
1973 The Father in *Monument for a Dead Boy* (van Dantzig), Royal Danish Ballet, Copenhagen
Iago in *The Moor's Pavane* (Limón), Royal Danish Ballet, Copenhagen
Alvar in *Far from Denmark* (Bournonville), Royal Danish Ballet, Copenhagen
1974 Confessor in *Chronicle* (Holm), Royal Danish Ballet, Copenhagen
Patient in *Asylum* (Marks), Royal Danish Ballet, Copenhagen
Principal dancer in *Dreamland* (Flindt), Royal Danish Ballet, Copenhagen
Lord Capulet in *Romeo and Juliet* (Neumeier), Royal Danish Ballet, Copenhagen
1975 Peppo in *Napoli* (Bournonville), Royal Danish Ballet, Copenhagen
The Father in *The Young Man must Marry* (Flindt), Royal Danish Ballet, Copenhagen
Clown in *Hoopla* (Louis), Royal Danish Ballet, Copenhagen
1976 Caesar (cr) in *Cleopatra* (Louis), Royal Danish Ballet, Copenhagen
Richelieu in *The Three Musketeers* (Flindt), Royal Danish Ballet, Copenhagen
1977 The General in *Graduation Ball* (Lichine), Royal Danish Ballet, Copenhagen
1978 Mr. William in *The Toreador* (Bournonville/Flindt), Royal Danish Ballet, Copenhagen
1979 Duke of Kurland in *Giselle* (Petipa after Coralli, Perrot; staged Bruhn), Royal Danish Ballet, Copenhagen
1980 Starveling in *A Midsummer Night's Dream* (Neumeier), Royal Danish Ballet, Copenhagen
1982 Orpheus in *Letters to Orpheus* (Weinreich), Royal Danish Ballet, Copenhagen
1983 Title role in *Don Quixote* (Gorsky after Petipa), Royal Danish Ballet, Copenhagen
1986 Sheik Ismael in *Abdallah* (Bournonville; staged Marks), Royal Danish Ballet, Copenhagen

**PUBLICATIONS**


Goodman, Saul, "Ballet Biographies: Henning Kronstam", *Dance Magazine* (New York), May 1958

Kragh-Jacobsen, Svend, *Twenty Solo Dancers of the Royal Danish Ballet*, Copenhagen, 1965

Aschengreen, Erik, "Henning Kronstam", *Les Saisons de la danse* (Paris), February 1977

Näslund, Erik, "Kronstam", *Dance News* (New York), February 1979

Duff, Helen, "Kronstam and the Royal Danish Ballet", *Dancing Times* (London), August 1982


* * *

The year 1955 was the turning point in Henning Kronstam's career. Only 21 years old, he had danced within one spring season the Poet in Balanchine's *Night Shadow* and Romeo in Frederick Ashton's *Romeo and Juliet*, created especially for the Royal Danish Ballet. A great romantic dancer was born. Young, handsome, sensitive, and poetic with a touch of melancholy, Henning Kronstam was perfectly suited to these roles, which started off one of the great Danish dancing careers of this century.

Henning Kronstam's domain was the classical ballet. Brought up by Harald Lander, he belonged to the first generation of Danish dancers taught by the great Russian-English pedagogue Vera Volkova, who had a particular interest in Kronstam's talent. She trained Kirsten Simone and Henning Kronstam and made them into an international couple.

When the great Russian ballets *The Sleeping Beauty*, *Swan Lake*, and *The Nutcracker* were performed in extenso for the first time in Denmark, Kronstam was the natural prince, with his perfect looks and brilliant technique. For over fifteen years he was the incarnation of the romantic hero, from the poet in *Chopiniana* (*Les Sylphides*) to Albrecht in *Giselle*, and he interpreted more Bournonville roles, from young heroes to character parts, than any other Danish dancer of his generation. Few dancers have made us share so strongly as Henning Kronstam in the longings, hopes, and fears in the soul of James in Bournonville's *La Sylphide*.

When international choreographers in great numbers began to appear in Copenhagen in the 1950s and 1960s to work with the Royal Danish Ballet, Henning Kronstam was the preferred male dancer—and indeed he showed a remarkable ability to change from one role and style to another. He mastered Balanchine's neo-classical style in *Apollo*, which he danced with dignity and majesty, and he danced other Balanchine ballets with success, but he was also a modern dancer, excelling in Glen Tetley and Paul Taylor works. His triumph in the modern repertoire was as Iago in José Limón's *The Moor's Pavane*, where he gave a many-faceted portrait of the complex, diabolic character. Kronstam was thus far more than a classical "danseur noble et sérieux". He was a marvellous character dancer in roles as varied as Jean in Birgit Cullberg's *Miss Julie*, the title role in Roland Petit's *Cyrano de Bergerac*, the dancing master in Flindt's *The Lesson*, and the clown in John Cranko's *The Lady and the Fool*. His most powerful character portrait was perhaps that of Franz Pander in Henryk Tomaszewski's *Bagage*, based upon a short story by the Danish writer Herman Bang. He was unforgettable in this role as the hotel waiter who commits suicide because he cannot stand the brutality and ugliness of this world. To this role Henning Kronstam brought his artistic authority, balancing the pain of the martyr with the perverse pleasure Franz Pander also feels in his own misery and suffering.

As artistic director of the Royal Danish Ballet, Henning Kronstam saw his main task as protecting the classical repertory while at the same time striving to keep dancers and repertory open to the currents of the day. After resigning as artistic director he has become invaluable as teacher, ballet master, and coach in the theatre, knowing the repertory and the tradition better than any and always demonstrating a highly refined taste.

—Erik Aschengreen

---

**KSHESINSKAYA** (Kschesinska), **Matilda**

Russian dancer and teacher. Born Matilda (Mathilde) Maria Feliksovna Kshesinskaya, daughter of Polish character dancer Felix Krzesinski, in Ligovo, near Peterhof (Petrodvorets), 31 August (19 August old style), 1872. Studied at the Imperial Theatre School, St. Petersburg, pupil of Lev Ivanov, Enrico Cecchetti, and Christian Johansson; graduated in 1890.

Married the Grand Duke Andrei of Russia, 1921. Début, Maryinsky Theatre, 1890; appointed ballerina, 1892, prima ballerina, 1893, and prima ballerina assoluta, 1895, performing as leading dancer of the company until 1904, and continuing as guest ballerina afterwards; guest ballerina, Paris Opéra, 1909; ballerina, Diaghilev's Ballets Russes, 1911–12, performing at Covent Garden, London, 1911, and in Monte Carlo, Vienna, and Budapest, 1912; left Russia, 1920; also teacher, opening own school in Paris, from 1929: pupils included André Eglevsky, Tatiana Riabouchinska, Yvette Chauviré, Margot Fonteyn. Died in Paris, 6 December 1971.

**ROLES**

1893 Princess Aurora in *The Sleeping Beauty* (Petipa), Maryinsky Theatre, St. Petersburg
1894 Flore (cr) in *Le Réveil de Flore* (Petipa), Maryinsky Theatre, St. Petersburg
1896 The Shadow of Mlada in *Mlada* (Petipa), Maryinsky Theatre, St. Petersburg
1897 Gotaru-Gime (cr) in *The Daughter of Mikado* (Petipa), Maryinsky Theatre, St. Petersburg
1898 Aspicia, Mummy in *Pharaoh's Daughter* (Petipa), Maryinsky Theatre, St. Petersburg
Title role in *Fiametta* (Saint-Léon), Maryinsky Theatre, St. Petersburg
1899 Title role in *Esmeralda* (Petipa after Perrot), Maryinsky Theatre, St. Petersburg
1900 Corn (cr) in *Les Saisons* (Petipa), Hermitage Theatre, St. Petersburg (produced Maryinsky Theatre, St. Petersburg, same year, for Kshesinskaya benefit performance)
Columbine (cr) in *Harlequinade* (*Les Millions d'Arlequin*; Petipa), Hermitage Theatre, St. Petersburg
Leading dancer (cr) in *The Pupils of Monsieur Dupré* (Petipa), Maryinsky Theatre, St. Petersburg
Nikiya in *La Bayadère* (Petipa), Maryinsky Theatre, St. Petersburg
1901 Title role in *Camargo* (Petipa), Maryinsky Theatre, St. Petersburg
1902 Kitri (cr) in *Don Quixote* (new production, St. Petersburg version; Gorsky after Petipa), Maryinsky Theatre, St. Petersburg
1903 Princess (cr) in *The Magic Mirror* (Petipa), Maryinsky Theatre, St. Petersburg
Title role (cr) in *The Fairy Doll* (N. and S. Legat), Maryinsky Theatre, St. Petersburg
1907 Title role in *Eunice* (Fokine), Maryinsky Theatre, St. Petersburg
"Reverie" (cr) in *The Blood-Red Flower* (Legat), Maryinsky Theatre, St. Petersburg
1908 Nisia in *King Candaule* (Petipa), Maryinsky Theatre, St. Petersburg
1909 Swanilda in *Coppélia* (Saint-Léon), Opéra, Paris
1910 Butterfly in *The Caprices of the Butterfly* (Petipa, staged N. Sergeev), Maryinsky Theatre, St. Petersburg
Niriti in *The Talisman* (N. Legat after Petipa), Maryinsky Theatre, St. Petersburg
Isora (cr) in *Bluebeard* (Legat after Petipa), Maryinsky Theatre, St. Petersburg
1911 Odette/Odile in *Swan Lake* (Petipa, Ivanov; staged Fokine), Diaghilev's Ballets Russes, London
Mazurka and Waltz in *Les Sylphides* (Fokine), Maryinsky Theatre, St. Petersburg
1912 Papillon in *Les Papillons* (Fokine), Maryinsky Theatre, St. Petersburg
Columbine in *Le Carnaval* (Fokine), Diaghilev's Ballets Russes, European tour
Girl in *Le Spectre de la rose* (Fokine), Diaghilev's Ballets Russes, European tour
1915 The Girl (cr) in *Eros* (Fokine), Maryinsky Theatre, St. Petersburg

**Other roles include:** at the Maryinsky Theatre—title role in *Cinderella* (Ivanov, Cecchetti), Sugar Plum Fairy in *The Nutcracker* (Ivanov), Lise in *Vain Precautions* (*La Fille mal gardée*; Petipa, Ivanov after Dauberval), title role in *Giselle* (Petipa after Coralli, Perrot), title role in *Sylvia* (Ivanov, Gerdt), title role in *Raymonda* (Petipa), Fenella in *La Muette de Portici* (opera; mus. Auber, chor. Petipa), Marietta in *Kalkabrino* (Petipa), Teresa in *Cavalry Halt* (Petipa), Catarina in *Catarina; or, La Fille du bandit* (Petipa after Perrot).

**PUBLICATIONS**

By Kshesinskaya:
*Souvenirs de la Kschessinska*, Paris, 1970; as *Dancing in St. Petersburg*, translated by Arnold Haskell, New York and London, 1970

About Kshesinskaya:
Tugat, Pierre, "A Witness of a Glorious Past: Mathilde Kshessinska", *Dancing Times* (London), January 1953
O'Connor, Eileen, "Portrait of an Era", *Dance Magazine* (New York), March 1961
Maynard, Olga, "Kschessinska at Ninety-nine", *Dance Magazine* (New York), November 1971
Macdonald, Nesta, "Kshessinska with Diaghilev in 1911", *Dancing Times* (London), November 1971
Krasovksaya, Vera, *Russian Ballet Theatre at the Beginning of the Twentieth Century*, vol. 2, 1972
Smakov, Gennady, *The Great Russian Dancers*, New York, 1984

* * *

Matilda Kshesinskaya graduated from the Imperial Theatre School and made her début at the Maryinsky Theatre, St. Petersburg, at the age of eighteen. Two years later (1892) she was made ballerina, the following year prima ballerina, and at the age of 23 she was accorded the official (and very seldom bestowed) rank of prima ballerina assoluta. This meteoric rise to success was vindicated by a sustained stage career lasting over a quarter of a century, and an enduring reputation as the last great Imperial Russian ballerina.

Kshesinskaya's career was undoubtedly advanced by two associations in particular, one professional and one personal. The chief ballet master and choreographer of the Imperial Ballet in St. Petersburg during Kshesinskaya's reign was Marius Petipa, and his ballets were the ideal vehicles for her specific talents. It was as the exemplary executant of Petipa's typically academic, technically demanding variations that she was most valued, and is most remembered. At the same time, her close links with the Russian royal family, especially her long love affair with the Tsarevich Nikolai (who became Tsar Nikolai II, last tsar of Russia), and later, her liason with the Grand Duke Andrei (whom she married in France in 1921), did nothing to hinder her eminence.

On the other hand, that very closeness to royalty which helped her career before the Revolution caused Kshesinskaya's reputation to be denigrated by Soviet ballet historians. Her reputation also suffered by her having reached the peak of her

**Mathilde Kshesinskaya in *Esmeralda***

career just as fashions in ballet began to change, and as the taste for the rather academic classicism that sustained Petipa's career for so long began to give way to a desire for greater expressiveness and naturalism in dance, best exemplified perhaps by the ballets of Mikhail Fokine. It is in fact difficult to gain a clear picture of just what kind of dancer she was, given that most contemporary reviewers suffered an excess of respect, and many later writers, an insufficiency. The photographs that survive are of little assistance to the modern eye, accustomed to spontaneous action photography; Kshesinskaya (like many of her contemporaries), obliged to hold poses for some minutes, appears lifeless and affected. Such images offer no impression of the formidable technician that she is universally held to have been, even by those to whom virtuosity was almost irrelevant or worse.

As early as 1891, before she became powerful enough to influence the critics, a certain Bezobrazov was remarking on Kshesinskaya's "perfect command of the whole set of Italian choreographic means," commenting that "her torso is powerful, her pointes are precise and firm: she executes impeccable glissades and even triple pirouettes on pointe". The 1880s and 1890s were dominated by Italian virtuoso ballerinas like Carlotta Brianza and Pierina Legnani, whom few Russian ballerinas could rival for technique, so Kshesinskaya's reputation was all the more hard-won. In her memoirs (*Dancing in St. Petersburg*) she names Legnani and Virginia Zucchi, a great dramatic ballerina, as her two ideals: there is nothing to suggest that she ever approached Zucchi's remarkable histrionic gifts, but she clearly developed a strength of technique that could more than hold its own with her Italian rivals. Such characterization as she attempted in her roles derived from her attention to detail of step, rather than any psychological development. She is remembered best for her performances in the ballerina role of such Petipa ballets as *The Sleeping Beauty*, *Swan Lake*, *La Bayadère*, *Esmeralda*, and *Pharaoh's Daughter*, ballets ideally suited to the display of her bravura classical technique. Even in such an essentially demi-caractère role as Esmeralda, Kshesinskaya evidently danced in her accustomed, impersonally classical manner. André Levinson wrote of her Esmeralda, "In her portrayal the national coloration is hardly perceived", and he noted that, for all her strict classicism, "her technical tricks seem exaggerated". Levinson, a great adherent of Pavlova's more expressive and lyrical style, concluded this honest description (rather unconvincingly) ". . . but this spectacular display stirs our feelings deeply".

Bronislava Nijinska, in her memoirs, makes no such concession: in her view, Kshesinskaya was "vulgar and brusque in all her movements", her style "essentially that of the old classical acrobatic technique". The overwhelming impression is that Kshesinskaya's most successful role was as herself; whether dancing Aurora, Odette, Nikiya, or any other of her great roles, she was always and above all the ballerina. As Vera Krasovskaya writes:

> Her image in photographs does not change from role to role. Her head is slightly tilted, her hair is carefully curled; a string of large diamonds adorns her décolletage. Her waist is tightly corseted; the precise port de bras is perfect; the turnout of her feet impeccably demonstrates the fourth or fifth position. She conveys the aesthetic standards of her era as if frozen in its elaborate, immutable forms.

The essence of Kshesinskaya's greatness, and also the inevitability of her decline in popularity, are contained in Krasovskaya's description. The twentieth century brought profound social and artistic changes, and the era of Duncan and Fokine could not easily accommodate a dancer so inflexibly in the nineteeth-century mould as Kshesinskaya. Her association with Serge Diaghilev, such an important influence in changing tastes in ballet in the second decade of this century, was disastrous, her increasingly old-fashioned approach to roles contrasting unfavourably with Anna Pavlova's and Tamara Karsavina's greater artistry and expressiveness. Moreover, Pavlova's extreme lightness and fleetness of movement cruelly emphasized Kshesinskaya's one significant technical weakness, her lack of elevation.

Her last created role was that of the girl in Fokine's ballet *Eros* in 1915: according to her brother Jozeph, in his memoirs, the part was conceived by Fokine in a satirical spirit, a fact entirely lost upon Kshesinskaya, who fell unerringly into the trap thus devised by Fokine to punish (according to Jozeph) his "wolf in sheep's clothing". Her career came to a sadly ignoble end on this sour note, and for a long period thereafter she was ignored or even vilified in Soviet Russia. Nevertheless, the spirit of this indomitable ballerina remains unextinguished. Isadora Duncan, an important contributor to the changing artistic climate that helped to eclipse Kshesinskaya, commented that she was "more like a lovely bird or butterfly than a human being", and she was, in however limited a way by modern standards, a singular monument to classical schooling. It was her misfortune that the peak of her career coincided with the decline of the particular school of nineteenth-century Imperial Russian ballet which she so grandly epitomized, but her reputation within that school is firmly and permanently established.

—Penelope Jowitt

---

**KUDELKA, James**

Canadian dancer and choreographer. Born in Newmarket, Ontario, 10 September 1955. Studied at the National Ballet School, Toronto. Dancer, National Ballet of Canada, Toronto, from 1972: soloist, from 1976, company choreographer, 1980–82; principal dancer, 1981–86, and resident choreographer, Les Grands Ballets Canadiens, Montreal, 1984–91; has also staged ballets for Joffrey Ballet, San Francisco Ballet, Montreal Danse, Toronto Dance Theatre, Margie Gillis and Peggy Baker; freelance choreographer, based in Montreal, from 1991. Recipient: Chalmers Award, National Ballet of Canada, 1975; Isadora Duncan Award, San Francisco, 1988; Dora Mavor Moore Award, 1992.

## WORKS

1973 *Sonata* (*Moods of Intimacy*) (mus. Franck), National Ballet of Canada, Toronto

1974 *Apples* (mus. Tchaikovsky), National Ballet of Canada, Niagara-on-the-Lake, Ontario
*Sonata* (mus. Franck), National Ballet of Canada, Toronto

1976 *A Party* (mus. Britten), National Ballet of Canada, Toronto

1977 *Washington Square* (mus. Baker), National Ballet of Canada, Toronto

1979 *Bach Pas de deux* (mus. Bach), National Ballet of Canada, Toronto
*Windsor Pas de deux* (mus. Copland), National Ballet of Canada, Toronto

*Washington Square* (new version; mus. Baker), National Ballet of Canada, Toronto
1980 *The Rape of Lucrece* (mus. Martin), National Ballet of Canada, Toronto
*Playhouse* (mus. Shostakovich), National Ballet of Canada, St. John's, Newfoundland
1981 *All Night Wonder* (mus. Britten), National Ballet of Canada, Toronto
*Passage* (mus. Tallis), American Ballet Theatre, Tampa, Florida
*Intimate Letter* (mus. Janáček), Susan MacPherson, Montreal
1982 *Genesis* (mus. Stravinsky), Les Grands Ballets Canadiens, Montreal
*Dido and Aeneas* (with David Earle and others; mus. Purcell), Toronto Dance Theatre, Stratford, Ontario
1983 *Hedda* (mus. Beecroft), National Ballet of Canada, Toronto
*In Paradisium* (mus. Baker), Les Grands Ballets Canadiens, Montreal
*Court of Miracles* (with David Earle, Christopher House, and others), Toronto Dance Theatre, Toronto
1984 *Alliances* (mus. Brahms), Les Grands Ballets Canadiens, Quebec City
*unfinished business* (mus. Baker), Dancemakers, Toronto
1985 *Dracula* (mus. Baker), Les Grands Ballets Canadiens, Montreal
*Death of an Old Queen* (mus. Tallis), Fortier Danse Création, Montreal
*Diversion* (mus. Britten), Les Grands Ballets Canadiens, Gala, Montreal
1986 *The Heart of the Matter* (mus. Prokofiev), Joffrey Ballet, Iowa City, Iowa
*Vers la glace* (with Margie and Christopher Gillis; mus. Friesen), Margie Gillis Dance Foundation, New York
*Collisions* (mus. Kucharzyk), Les Grands Ballets Canadiens, Vancouver
1987 *Soudain l'hiver dernier* (mus. Bryars), Montréal Danse, Ottawa
*Dreams of Harmony* (mus. Schumann), San Francisco Ballet, San Francisco
*Le Sacre du printemps* (mus. Stravinsky), Les Grands Ballets Canadiens, Montreal
*"the wakey nights"* (mus. Baker), Joyce Trisler Company, New York
1988 *Concerto Grosso* (mus. Papineau-Couture), Joffrey Ballet, Calgary
*In Camera* (mus. Volans), Dancemakers, Toronto
*La Salle des pas perdus* (mus. Brahms), Les Grands Ballets Canadiens, Montreal
*Signatures* (mus. Beethoven), National Ballet School, Toronto
1989 *Love, Dracula* (mus. Baker), Les Grands Ballets Canadiens, Montreal
*The Comfort Zone* (mus. Beethoven), San Francisco Ballet, San Francisco
*Ouverture Russe* (mus. Glinka), Les Grands Ballets Canadiens, Montreal
*There, Below* (mus. Vaughan Williams), BalletMet, Columbus, Ohio
*Divertissement Schumann* (mus. Schumann), Les Grands Ballets Canadiens, Montreal
*Schéhérazade* (with David Earle; mus. Rimsky-Korsakov), Les Grands Ballets Canadiens, Montreal
1990 *Romance* (mus. Dvořák), Les Grands Ballets Canadiens, Montreal
*C.V.* (mus. Baker), Montréal Danse, Montreal
*Pastorale* (mus. Beethoven), National Ballet of Canada, Toronto
*Romeo and Juliet Before Parting* (mus. Prokofiev), Canada Dance Festival, Ottawa
*Violin Concerto (Misfits)* (mus. Prokofiev), Les Grands Ballets Canadiens, Winnipeg
1991 *The Kiss of Death* (sound: Oswald), Pat Fraser, Quebec City
*This Isn't the End* (sound: Oswald), Peggy Baker, New York
*Musings (Fare Well)* (mus. Mozart), National Ballet of Canada, Toronto
*Mirror* (mus. Mozart), Hamburg Ballet and National Ballet of Canada, Hamburg
*Mixed Program* (mus. Schubert, arranged Baker), National Ballet School, Toronto
*Fifteen Heterosexual Duets* (mus. Beethoven), Toronto Dance Theatre, Waterloo, Ontario
*Désir* (mus. Prokofiev), Les Grands Ballets Canadiens, Montreal
1992 *The End* (mus. Brahms), San Francisco Ballet, San Francisco

**PUBLICATIONS**

By Kudelka:
Interview in Doob, Penelope, "Spotlight on James Kudelka", *Dance Magazine* (New York), March 1977

About Kudelka:
Shearer, Ellen, "James Kudelka", *Dance in Canada* (Toronto), Summer 1979

* * *

James Kudelka began to choreograph while still a student of the National Ballet School in Toronto. Although he was a technically accomplished demi-caractère dancer—fast, clean, and expressive—who became a principal dancer at Montreal's Les Grands Ballets Canadiens, Kudelka's importance derives from his choreography.

Unlike many ballet choreographers who have abandoned a whole range of steps (particularly beats and terre-à-terre work) to create a more streamlined neo-classical style, Kudelka remains open to the full classical vocabulary. His expressive and often complex use of the arms, particularly in turns, is sometimes reminiscent of Ashton, whose ballets he danced most capably with the National Ballet of Canada. At the same time, by exposing himself to a range of modern dance idioms, Kudelka has opened his imagination to fresh movement possibilities which have enabled him to work with both ballet and modern dance troupes. The resulting creative versatility can be seen in such predominantly classical works as *Alliances* (to Brahms) and *Divertissement Schumann*, while his *Sacre du printemps* reflects a blending of influences. Unusually too for his generation, Kudelka has not been afraid to use ballet as a narrative form, although his approach in recent years has become increasingly oblique and allusive.

Even such an early work as *A Party* revealed Kudelka's gift for defining character in movement. This youthful unravelling of the human dynamics of a social gathering showed Kudelka's extreme sensitivity to the delicate shadings of human emotion. This gift began to mature in *Washington Square*, his adaptation of the Henry James novel, and again in the more abstract Ibsen-inspired *Hedda*, demonstrating Kudelka's understanding of the pain of human anguish. Themes of love and death recur in his work and emerged in almost elegaic form in *In Paradisium*, a non-narrative ballet that nevertheless resonates with deep emotional themes. It was Kudelka's second work for Les Grands Ballets Canadiens, which he joined in 1981 after almost nine years with the National Ballet.

Kudelka, who claimed to find the atmosphere of the Toronto company stultifying, was clearly liberated by his move to Montreal. Not only did he use his new dancers superbly but he appeared to find them ideally suited to his expressive needs. Kudelka's work began to exhibit greater confidence, and although he has produced inferior ballets, notably *Dracula* (to which he returned, with no greater success, four years later in the revised *Love, Dracula*), the majority of his later ballets have demonstrated a strong grasp of the choreographic craft, always tinged by Kudelka's inherent musical sense, his wry wit, and his often ironical turn of mind.

After a seven-year absence, Kudelka returned to the National Ballet in 1990 to create *Pastorale*, to Beethoven's sixth symphony. Here his gift for narrative and emotional expressiveness flowered in a remarkable response to a powerful and familiar score. Without rejecting Beethoven's mood of almost arcadian reverie, Kudelka managed to suggest less a story than a mysterious dramatic atmosphere, in which a visit to the country by a group of aristocrats in period costume provides opportunity for comment on social behavior and emotional repression.

Not surprisingly, Kudelka's growing maturity as a choreographer has attracted attention outside his homeland. He is one of very few Canadian ballet choreographers to have established a strong reputation in the United States, where he has created works for the Joffrey Ballet and San Francisco Ballet, among others.

—Michael Crabb

---

**KUN, Zsuzsa**

Hungarian dancer and teacher. Born in Budapest, 9 December 1934. Studied at the Ballet School of the Hungarian State Opera House, Budapest, pupil of Ferenc Nádasi, 1943–49; also studied at the Moscow Choreographic School and the Bolshoi Theatre, pupil of Marina Semenova, Elisaveta Gerdt, Asaf Messerer, Moscow, 1950. Married (1) dancer Viktor Fülöp (div.); (2) dancer Levente Sipeke. Dancer, State Opera Ballet, Budapest, from 1949, becoming soloist, from 1952; international guest artist, including with Bolshoi Ballet, Moscow, 1960, 1962, 1968, and 1969, Tbilisi, 1960, London Festival Ballet, various seasons 1961–65, Novosibirsk, Ufa, and Perm, 1962, Jerevan and Baku, 1965, Zurich, 1966, Odessa and Tallin, 1968, Yugoslavia, 1968, 1972, Basel, 1968, Berlin, Prague, and Sydney, 1972; director, Hungarian State Ballet Institute, 1972–79; teacher, from 1979; also editor, presenter, and contributor to the television programme *Ballet Shoes* on Hungarian television. Recipient: Second Prize, World Youth Meeting, 1953; First Prize, World Youth Meeting, 1955; Liszt Prize, 1960; Kossuth Prize, 1962; Knight of the White Rose Award, Finland, 1965; title of Merited Artist of the Republic of Hungary, 1968; Critics' Prize, Paris, 1969; title of Outstanding Artist, 1971, and Outstanding Teacher, 1985.

**ROLES**

1948 Snowflake Solo in *The Nutcracker* (Vainonen), Hungarian State Opera Ballet, Budapest
1952 Masha in *The Nutcracker* (Vainonen), Hungarian State Opera Ballet, Budapest
Jeanne in *The Flames of Paris* (Vainonen), Hungarian State Opera Ballet, Budapest
Zarema in *The Fountain of Bakhchisarai* (Zaharov), Hungarian State Opera Ballet, Budapest
1953 Sári in *Handkerchief* (Harangozó), Hungarian State Opera Ballet, Budapest
1958 Juliet in *Romeo and Juliet* (Lavrovsky), Hungarian State Opera Ballet, Budapest
Title role in *Giselle* (Petipa after Coralli, Perrot; staged Lavrovsky), Hungarian State Opera Ballet, Budapest
Leading role (cr) in *Csongor and Tünde* (Eck), Hungarian State Opera Ballet, Budapest
1959 Title role in *Schéhérazade* (Harangozó), Hungarian State Opera Ballet, Budapest
Title role in *Gayané* (Anisimova), Hungarian State Opera Ballet, Budapest
1960 Odette/Odile in *Swan Lake* (Messerer), Hungarian State Opera Ballet, Budapest
Waltz, Mazurka in *Chopiniana* (*Les Sylphides*; Fokine), Hungarian State Opera Ballet, Budapest
The Actress in *The Flames of Paris* (Vainonen), Hungarian State Opera Ballet, Budapest
1963 Human (cr) in *Le Sacre du printemps* (Eck), Hungarian State Opera Ballet, Budapest
1964 Prostitute in *The Miraculous Mandarin* (Harangozó), Hungarian State Opera Ballet, Budapest
1965 Principal dancer (cr) in *Music for Strings, Percussion, and Celesta* (Eck), Hungarian State Opera Ballet, Budapest
1967 Princess Aurora in *The Sleeping Beauty* (Gusev after Petipa), Hungarian State Opera Ballet, Budapest
1968 Flavia (cr) in *Spartacus* (Seregi), Hungarian State Opera Ballet, Budapest
1971 Lise in *La Fille mal gardée* (Ashton), Hungarian State Opera Ballet, Budapest
1972 Title role (cr) in *Sylvia* (Seregi), Hungarian State Opera Ballet, Budapest
1973 Title role in *La Sylphide* (Bournonville), Hungarian State Opera Ballet, Budapest

**WORKS**

1964 *Mario and the Magician* (with Fülöp), Hungarian State Opera Ballet, Budapest

**PUBLICATIONS**

By Kun:
"The Bolshoi's *Rite of Spring*", *Dancing Times* (London), February 1966
"A Subjective Comment after a Budapest Ballet Night", *Hungarian Music News*, no. 1, 1978

About Kun:
Clarke, Mary, "Sugar Plums and Cinders", *Dancing Times* (London), February 1961
Herf, Estelle, "Zsuzsa Kun: Ballerina from Budapest", *Ballet*

*Today* (London), March 1964
"Zsu Zsu Kun: Profile", *Dancing Times* (London), March 1969
Körtvélyes, G., and Lörinc, B., *Budapest Ballet* (in English), Budapest, 1971

* * *

Zsuzsa Kun was the greatest Hungarian ballerina of the post-war years. At the height of her career, she had danced virtually all the significant roles that were in the ballet repertoire at the State Opera House at the time. She entered the profession very young, and played an important role in the Hungarian dance scene throughout her career. "She seems fragile like porcelain, but in reality she is like steel," a contemporary critic wrote about her.

When asked about the major influence on her career, Kun mentioned simply, and with spontaneity, Ferenc Nádasi (her first teacher) and the Russian Ballet. As a young girl she had danced to Béla Bartók's *Allegro Barbaro* in a Nádasi ballet for a school performance, and here everybody noticed her outstanding dynamism and a dramatic power which belied her young age. Later, these characteristics were enriched by assured technique, lyricism, and musicality. As a member of the Budapest Opera company she soon caught the attention of critics and choreographers, and in the 1950s various visiting Russian choreographers cast her in leading roles. She became a soloist and the latest "discovery" of the choreographers—but she also discovered that there was still a lot to learn. Accordingly, Kun went to Moscow for a year. She studied with the best teachers and laid the foundation for her future as one of the most significant exponents of Hungarian classical ballet.

Her Giselle was unforgettable. What was her secret? Zsuzsa Kun was never satisfied with the achievement of technical brilliance in a given part, and she never imitated anybody. She found inspiration in humanity and in the world, and she brought to the stage the struggle of a human being for purity and goodness. She re-created, virtually gave new birth to, each role at every single new performance, and she strove constantly for perfection. She once said in an interview, ".. passion, suffering, work, this is ballet. One is gnawing oneself to find the right movement, to store it, to make it embedded in one's blood and sinews, and then the music and the dance can find each other. It seldom succeeds to make me utterly satisfied."

Kun's superb technique enabled her to create her roles with freedom. In her Juliet the innocent cheerful girl matured into the ill-fated loving woman through a subtle, delicate process. As the actress in the ballet *The Flames of Paris* she showed the pain which brings this darling of the French Court to the side of the revolutionaries. In her great classical roles in *Swan Lake* and *The Sleeping Beauty* she gave a memorable experience not only to Hungarian but to foreign audiences as well. She revealed Odette's character with great harmonious care, first showing her humiliation and then her desire for freedom. As Odile she was fascinating and mesmerising; but she did not rely simply on sensuality: she became part of Rothbart's evil plan, and she was calculating and cruel. In *The Sleeping Beauty* she created a delicate fairy-tale character with brilliant technique, while her Flavia in *Spartacus* encompassed both the gentle woman at her husband's side and the determined fighter—and her mourning dance over the body of Spartacus was heart-rending. In *The Miraculous Mandarin* her every gesture was that of a victim, whose verdict on the age and the circumstances in which she lived was expressed not only through her body but facially as well. She showed her sense of humour in the role of Lise in Ashton's *La Fille mal gardée* and in the title role of *Sylvia*.

On foreign tours, Kun's preoccupation was not only with her own performance; she also tried to see as much as possible. She discovered foreign choreographers and modern experiments, and returned home under new influences. MacMillan's *The Invitation* made such an impression on her that she persuaded the company's leadership to enrich the repertoire with new modern ballets, and asked to take part in them. As a result she danced in two new ballets by Imre Eck, *Le Sacre du printemps* and *Music for Strings, Percussions, and Celesta*—and in these she showed herself in a new light. The artist who matured on the classical idiom felt at home in the alien movement-language as well. She became renowned in Hungarian and foreign official circles; she received many awards; but the greatest prize for Kun was always the applause of a grateful audience.

After many physical injuries, Zsuzsa Kun gave up dancing and started working as a teacher, transferring her rich experience to a younger generation. She said herself "I believe I was born only to dance, and I would not have been able to do anything else well".

—Agnes Roboz

---

**KYASHT, Lydia**

Russian/British dancer, choreographer, and teacher. Born Lidiya Georgievna Kyaksht (Kyasht) in St. Petersburg, sister of Maryinsky dancer and ballet master Georgi Kyaksht, 25 March (13 March old style) 1885. Studied at the Imperial Theatre School, St. Petersburg, pupil of Pavel Gerdt, from 1893; graduated in 1902; later studied with Evgenia Sokolova, Enrico Cecchetti, St. Petersburg, and Aleksandr Gorsky, Moscow. Married Colonel Aleksis Ragosin: one daughter, Lydia (b. 1921). Début as child, Mikhailovsky Theatre, St. Petersburg, 1896; dancer, soon becoming soloist, Maryinsky Theatre, St. Petersburg, 1902–08: second dancer, 1905, first dancer, 1908; also soloist, Bolshoi Theatre, Moscow, season 1903–04; performed (with Karsavina) in Warsaw and on Russian provincial tour, under direction of brother Georgi Kyaksht, 1905; first performer (according to own claims) of Fokine's *Dying Swan* (*Le Cygne*), 1905; ballerina, appearing with Adolph Bolm, Empire Theatre, London, 1908, and performing at the Empire various seasons through 1913; dancer with Diaghilev's Ballets Russes, touring France, Germany, Austria, 1912; U.S. début, Winter Garden Theatre, New York, 1914, also performing at the Coliseum, London, 1914, and again in 1917, 1918; returned to Russia during World War I, performing mostly in concerts, St. Petersburg, 1914–17; ballerina, Diaghilev's Ballets Russes, London season, 1919; toured with "The 7:30 Cabaret", 1924, with own show, *A La Russe*, 1925–26, and own company, Cabaret Entertainment Gala Nights, 1926–29; performed with Picadilly Cabaret, 1930–31, and Spring-Time Cabaret, 1933; appeared with Anton Dolin in play *Ballerina* (Eleanor Smith), 1933; founder, Ballet de la Jeunesse Anglaise, 1939, touring England, 1939, Europe, 1944; founder, Lydia Kyasht Russian Ballet, 1940; also teacher: director of own school, Lydia Kyasht Dancing Academy, London, from 1919, and Cirencester, from 1948; teacher, Legat School of Dancing, Tunbridge Wells, from 1953. Member, Branch Committee of the Classic Ballet, U.K. Died in London, 11 January 1959.

**ROLES**

1896 Cupid in *Don Quixote* (Petipa), Coronation of Nicholas II, Mikhailovksy Theatre, Moscow

**Lydia Kyasht in *Sylvia*, Empire Theatre, London, c.1911**

1902 Solo variation in *Le Corsaire* (Petipa), Maryinsky Theatre, St. Petersburg
Solo variation in *Pharaoh's Daughter* (Petipa), Maryinsky Theatre, St. Petersburg
Butterfly, first variation (cr) in *La Source* (Coppini after Saint-Léon), Maryinsky Theatre, St. Petersburg
1903 Swanilda in *Coppélia* (Petipa, Cecchetti), Maryinsky Theatre, St. Petersburg
Pas de deux in *The Magic Flute* (Ivanov), Maryinsky Theatre, St. Petersburg
Solo variation in *Cavalry Halt* (Petipa), Maryinsky Theatre, St. Petersburg
1904 Lise in *Vain Precautions* (*La Fille mal gardée*; Petipa, Ivanov), Bolshoi Theatre, Moscow
1906 Champagne (cr) in *La Vigne* (Fokine), Maryinsky Theatre, St. Petersburg
1908 Pas de deux from *The Little Humpbacked Horse* (Gorsky after Saint-Léon), Empire Theatre, London
Swanilda in *Coppélia* (Alexander Genée), Empire Theatre, London
Pas Seul, Pas Russe, Monte Carlo scene (cr) in *A Day in Paris* (revue by Lt.-Col. Newnham-Davis; chor. Alexander Genée), Empire Theatre, London
Princess Florine in Bluebird pas de deux from *The Sleeping Beauty* (Petipa), Maryinsky Theatre, St. Petersburg
1909 Elena in "The Ballet of the Nuns" (chor. F. Farren) from *Robert le Diable* (opera; mus. Meyerbeer), Empire Theatre, London
"Dance Tzigane" (cr) in *Round the World* (Farren), Empire Theatre, London
1910 Princess (cr) in *Fantasie Choreographique* (*Dance Idylls*; Bolm), Empire Theatre, London
Mimi, the Débutante, in *The Dancing-Master* (Farren after *The Débutante*), Empire Theatre, London
Italian Flower Girl (cr) in *The Faun* (Farren), Empire Theatre, London
French danseuse (cr) in *Ship Ahoy* (Farren), Empire Theatre, London
Pas de deux, "Les Papillons de l'Orient" (cr) in *East and West* (new version of *Round the World*; Farren), Empire Theatre, London
1911 Title role in *Sylvia* (one act version; C. Wilhelm after Ivanov, Gerdt), Empire Theatre, London
Russian Ballerina (cr) in *New York* (Farren), Empire Theatre, London
1912 Naiad (cr) in *The Water Nymph* (also chor.), Empire Theatre, London
Principal dancer (cr) in *First Love* (also chor.), Empire Theatre, London
Columbine in *Le Carnaval* (Fokine), Diaghilev's Ballets Russes, Monte Carlo

Title role in *L'Oiseau de feu* (Fokine), Diaghilev's Ballets Russes, Monte Carlo
Young girl in *Le Spectre de la rose* (Fokine), Diaghilev's Ballets Russes, European tour
Principal dancer in *Les Sylphides* (Fokine), Diaghilev's Ballets Russes, Vienna
1913 Spirit of the Wheatsheaf (cr) in *The Reaper's Dream* (also chor.), Empire Theatre, London
Title role in *Titania* (or *A Midsummer Night's Dream*; also chor.), Empire Theatre, London
Pas de Deux, "The Gambler" (also chor.) in *All the Winners* (revue), Empire Theatre, London
1914 Bluebird in *The Whirl of the World* (revue; Shubert), Winter Garden Theatre, New York
Principal dancer in *The Enchanted Isle* (revue), Coliseum, London
1915 The Daughter in *Javotte* (extract; staged Kyasht), Coliseum, London
Psyche in *Cythera* (also chor.), Coliseum, London
1916 Maria in *Somewhere in France* (also chor.), Coliseum, London
1918 Principal dancer in *Cupid's Conspiracy*, Coliseum, London
Principal dancer in *Les Elégantes*, Lyric Theatre, London
1933 Retiring Ballerina (cr) in *Ballerina* (comedy; Eleanor Smith), Gaiety Theatre, London

**Other roles include:** at the Maryinsky Theatre, St. Petersburg—Tsar-Maiden in *The Little Humpbacked Horse* (Petipa after Saint-Léon), title role in *Sylvia* (Ivanov, Gerdt), Teresa in *Cavalry Halt* (Petipa).

## WORKS

1912 *The Water Nymph* (mus. Pugni), Empire Theatre, London
*First Love* (mus. Glinka, Clarke), Empire Theatre, London
1913 *The Reaper's Dream* (mus. Tchaikovsky, Delibes), Empire Theatre, London
*"The Gambler"* (mus. Drigo) in *All the Winners* (revue), Empire Theatre, London
*Titania* (mus. Mendelssohn; additional music Clarke), Empire Theatre, London
1915 *Javotte* (extract; possibly after Gerdt), Coliseum, London
*Cythera*, Coliseum, London
1916 *Somewhere in France*, Coliseum, London

## PUBLICATIONS

By Kyasht:
Interview in Richardson, Philip, "The First of the Russians", *Dancing Times* (London), December 1921
*Romantic Recollections*, edited by Erica Beale, New York, 1978

About Kyasht:
Karsavina, Tamara, *Ballets Russes*, Paris, 1931
Beaumont, Cyril, *The Diaghilev Ballet in London*, London, 1940
Lifar, Serge, *Histoire du ballet russe*, Paris, 1950
Grigoriev, Serge, *The Diaghilev Ballet*, translated by Vera Bowen, London, 1953
Davidson, Gladys, *Ballet Biographies* (revised edition), London, 1954
Bedells, Phyllis, "Lydia Kyasht", *Dancing Times* (London), March 1959
Guest, Ivor, "Russian Dancers in London before Diaghileff", *Ballet Annual* (London), 1960
Guest, Ivor, *The Empire Ballet*, London, 1962

* * *

Lydia Kyasht was the first of the Russian dancers to be seen in London, and her success at the Empire Theatre in 1908 helped pave the way for her compatriots Pavlova and Karsavina, and, eventually, for Diaghilev's Ballets Russes. It was not only the first time that the Russian classical style had been seen in England, but also the first time that London had a chance to see a classical pas de deux, for the male dancer had long fallen out of favour in England, and the developments that had taken place elsewhere in pas de deux were entirely unknown. Her success was so great that she was invited to succeed Adeline Genée as ballerina at the Empire Theatre, and along with Genée, Kyasht helped to restore ballet in London to something of the eminence it had enjoyed in the Romantic era.

It was only with the coming of Kyasht that the word "choreography" came into general use on London programmes. At first she only appeared in isolated solos in the Empire Ballets, but from 1912 she began to arrange her own choreography and to create works more akin to the integrated ballets that Diaghilev had introduced to London the previous year.

Kyasht lacked the dazzling technique and ecstatic abandon of some of her Russian contemporaries, displaying rather a statuesque purity of style and a flawless, flowing lyricism unbroken by any hint of athleticism or acrobatics. As a formal and decorative dancer she was unsurpassed. She made no concessions to public taste, nor was she seduced by any extreme developments in dance, maintaining the purity of the classical style in which she had been trained and an "almost hieratic concentration to achieve physical grace". Her main fault lay in a lack of imagination and interpretative ability, which meant that she was at her best in roles such as Sylvia, the chaste nymph of Diana, Titania, the fairy queen, or as the living automaton Swanilda impersonating the doll Coppélia.

As her dancing career came to an end in the 1920s, Kyasht turned to teaching and, for a time in the 1930s and 1940s, had her own ballet companies—notably Ballet de la Jeunesse Anglaise and the Lydia Kyasht Russian Ballet. As a teacher, she was remembered for her charming mime classes, and the way in which she could make the old Russian ballets come alive for pupils. She had a facility for devising attractive, danceable enchaînements, but she was no mere technician and laid particular stress upon the expressive importance of each movement.

—Sarah C. Woodcock

---

### KYLIÁN, Jiří

Czechoslovakian dancer, choreographer, and ballet director. Born in Prague, 21 March 1947. Studied at the National Ballet School, Prague Conservatory, pupil of Zora Semberova, from 1962, and at the Royal Ballet School, London, from 1967. Married dancer Sabine Krupferberg. Dancer, becoming soloist, Stuttgart Ballet, 1968–75; choreographer, with first work for Stuttgart Ballet, 1970; co-artistic director, Nederlands Dans Theater, 1975, becoming artistic director and choreo-

**Jiří Kylián rehearsing *No More Play* with Beatriz Almeida and Tamas Detrich**

grapher from 1977. Recipient: Carina Ari Medal, Stockholm; West End Theatre Award, London; Nederlandse Choreografie Prijs, Amsterdam; Hans Christian Andersen Ballet Award, Copenhagen; Grand Prix International Video-Danse, Nimes; Sonia Gaskellprijs, Amsterdam; Dutch Theatre Critics' Prize, 1991.

## WORKS

1970 *Paradox* (mus. Kylián), Noverre Society Gala, Stuttgart
*Kommen und Gehen* (mus. Bartók), Stuttgart Ballet, Stuttgart
1971 *Incantations* (mus. Jolivet), Stuttgart Ballet, Stuttgart
1972 *Der Einzeiganger* (mus. Kylián), Stuttgart Ballet, Stuttgart
*Der Stumme Orpheus* (mus. Takemitsu), Stuttgart Ballet, Stuttgart
1973 *Viewers* (mus. Martin), Nederlands Dans Theater, The Hague
1974 *Blue Skin* (mus. traditional), Stuttgart Ballet, Stuttgart
*Der Morgen Danach* (mus. Bartók), Stuttgart Ballet, Stuttgart
*Rückkehr ins fremde Land* (*Return to the Strange Land*; first version, pas de trois; mus. Janáček), Stuttgart Ballet, Stuttgart
*Stoolgame* (*The Odd One*; mus. Nordheim), Nederlands Dans Theater, Amsterdam
1975 *La Cathédrale engloutie* (mus. Debussy), Nederlands Dans Theater, The Hague
*Rückkehr ins fremde Land* (*Return to the Strange Land*; extended version; mus. Janáček), Stuttgart Ballet, Stuttgart
*Verklärte Nacht* (*Transfigured Night*; mus. Schoenberg), Nederlands Dans Theater, The Hague
*Torso* (mus. Takemitsu), Nederlands Dans Theater, Groningen
1976 *Nuages* (mus. Debussy), Stuttgart Ballet, Stuttgart
*Elegia* (mus. Shostakovich), Nederlands Dans Theater, Scheveningen
*Symfonie in D* (two-part version; mus. Haydn), Nederlands Dans Theater, Scheveningen
1977 *November Steps* (mus. Takemitsu), Nederlands Dans Theater, The Hague
*Ariadne* (mus. Nordheim), Nederlands Dans Theater, Scheveningen
*Symfonie in D* (three-part version; mus. Haydn), Nederlands Dans Theater, Schweinfurt
1978 *Kinderspelen* (*Children's Games*; mus. Mahler, Carpenter), Nederlands Dans Theater, Amsterdam
*Sinfonietta* (mus. Janáček), Nederlands Dans Theater, Spoleto Festival, Charleston, South Carolina

*Intimate Pages* (mus. Janáček), Swedish television
*Rainbow Snake* (mus. Norby), Nederlands Dans Theater, Scheveningen
*Symphony of Psalms* (mus. Stravinsky), Nederlands Dans Theater, Scheveningen
1979 *Glagolitic Mass* (mus. Janáček), Nederlands Dans Theater, Florence
*Dream Dances* (mus. Berio), Nederlands Dans Theater, Scheveningen
1980 *Soldier's Mass* (also called *Field Mass*; mus. Martinů), Nederlands Dans Theater, Scheveningen
*Overgrown Path* (mus. Janáček), Nederlands Dans Theater, Scheveningen
1981 *Forgotten Land* (mus. Britten), Stuttgart Ballet, Stuttgart
*Nomaden* (mus. Stravinsky), Nederlands Dans Theater, Scheveningen
*Symfonie in D* (four-part version; mus. Haydn), Nederlands Dans Theater, The Hague
1982 *Svadebka* (*Les Noces*; mus. Stravinsky), Nederlands Dans Theater, Scheveningen
*Lieder eines fahrenden Gesellen* (mus. Mahler), Nederlands Dans Theater, Scheveningen
1983 *Stamping Ground* (mus. Chavez), Nederlands Dans Theater, Scheveningen
*Dreamtime* (mus. Takemitsu), Nederlands Dans Theater, Scheveningen
*Curses and Blessings* (with Christopher Bruce; mus. Eben), Nederlands Dans Theater, Scheveningen
*Wiegelied* (mus. Berg), Nederlands Dans Theater, Scheveningen
1984 *Valencia* (mus. Padilla), Nederlands Dans Theater, Scheveningen
*L'Enfant et les sortilèges* (mus. Ravel), Nederlands Dans Theater, Scheveningen
*Heart's Labyrinth I* (mus. Schoenberg, Webern, Dvořák), Nederlands Dans Theater, Amsterdam
1985 *Heart's Labyrinth II* (mus. Schoenberg, Webern, Lutoslawski), Nederlands Dans Theater, Scheveningen
*Piccolo Mondo* (mus. Praetorius), Scapino Ballet, Amsterdam
1986 *Silent Cries* (mus. Debussy), Nederlands Dans Theater, Scheveningen
*L'Histoire du Soldat* (mus. Stravinsky), Nederlands Dans Theater, Scheveningen
*Six Dances* (mus. Mozart), Nederlands Dans Theater, Amsterdam
1987 *Heart's Labyrinth* (new version; mus. Schoenberg, Webern, Dvořák), Nederlands Dans Theater, Scheveningen
*Frankenstein!!* (mus. Gruber), Nederlands Dans Theater, Scheveningen
*Sint Joris rijdt uit* (mus. Debussy, Minkus, Mellnäs, Villa-Lobos, Stravinsky), Nederlands Dans Theater, The Hague
*Evenings Songs* (mus. Dvořák), Nederlands Dans Theater, The Hague
1988 *Kaguyahime* (mus. Ishii), Nederlands Dans Theater, The Hague
*No More Play* (mus. Webern), Nederlands Dans Theater, The Hague
1989 *Tantz-Schul* (mus. Kagel), Nederlands Dans Theater, The Hague
*Falling Angels* (mus. Reich), Nederlands Dans Theater, The Hague
1990 *Sweet Dreams* (mus. Webern), Nederlands Dans Theater, The Hague
*Sarabande*, Nederlands Dans Theater, The Hague
*Feuillets d'automne* (mus. Mozart), "La Soirée carte blanche" for Jean Guizerix, Paris
1991 *Un Ballo* (mus. Ravel), Nederlands Dans Theater 2, The Hague
*Petite Mort* (mus. Mozart), Nederlands Dans Theater, Salzburg
*Obscure Temptations* (mus. Cage), Nederlands Dans Theater 3, The Hague
*Stepping Stones* (mus. Cage), Stuttgart Ballet, Stuttgart

## PUBLICATIONS

By Kylián:
Interview in Merret, Sue, "Spotlight on Jiri Kylián", *Dancing Times* (London), May 1991

About Kylián:
Stoop, Norma McLain, "Jiří Kylián of the Netherlands Dance Theatre", *Dance Magazine* (New York), October 1979
Barnes, Patricia, "New Faces: Jiří Kilián", *Dance News* (New York), December 1979
Manor, Giora, "Modern Dance, Ballet and Folk Dance", *Israel Dance* (Tel Aviv), 1981
Stoop, Norma McLain, "Midsummer Nights' Dreams", *Dance Magazine* (New York), July 1982
Croce, Arlene, *Going to the Dance*, New York, 1982
Monaghan, James, "Amsterdam and Kylián", *Dancing Times* (London), May 1984
Garske, Rolf, "In Love with Music and Movement", *Ballett International* (Cologne), March 1987
Moffett, Luisa, "Kylián Changes Keys", *Dance Magazine* (New York), May 1987
Anderson, Jack, *Choreography Observed*, Iowa City, 1987
Koegler, Horst, "Pledged to the Spirit of our Times: Nederlands Dans Theater, 1959–1989", *Ballett International* (Cologne), May 1989
Garske, Rolf, "At the Crossroads: NDT—1989", *Ballett International* (Cologne), May 1989
Mannoni, Gerard, *Kylián* (in French), Arles, 1989
Sinclair, Janet, "Choreographer's Luck", *Dance and Dancers* (London), June/July 1991

* * *

"Perhaps the factors most likely to impress the newcomer to Jiří Kylián's choreography," wrote British critic Janet Sinclair in 1991, "are, first, his own obvious enjoyment in what he is doing, secondly, the effortlessness of his invention, thirdly the fact that his steps do not derive from those of any other choreographer. Many choreographers are made, through their own determination and the encouragement of others: very few are born." Jiří Kylián is one of those rare few who falls into the latter category.

Jiří Kylián was born and educated in Prague, where he received a sound classical ballet training at the Conservatory; this was augmented in 1967 by study at the Royal Ballet School, which he attended on a British Council grant. In addition to classical dance and music (both theory and practice), Kylián also studied modern dance (Graham technique) and folk dance, both later to be important influences in his work. In 1968 Kylián was engaged by John Cranko as a dancer for the Stuttgart Ballet, where he progressed to soloist, dancing Lucentio in Cranko's *The Taming of the Shrew*. Kylián made his first choreography for Stuttgart's Noverre Society in 1970, and this was followed by *Kommen und Gehen*, for the Stuttgart company, in the same year.

In 1973 Kylián choreographed his first ballet for the Nederlands Dans Theater, the company with which he was to become so closely identified for the next 20 years; by 1975 he was named co-artistic director. In 1978 of the company made its first trip to the United States, and as a consequence Kylián became an international name on the dance scene. Performing at the Spoleto Festival in South Carolina, the Netherlands company made a particularly strong impression with Kylián's tribute to Janáček, *Sinfonietta*, made especially for the festival. The ballet has since become a classic of the modern repertoire, universally praised for its inventiveness of movement and for its sympathetic and intuitive relationship with the music. Kylián himself explained his motivation in simple terms, saying, "I had no other ambition but of making a physical expression of the music, where motion and emotion go hand in hand with the music."

Kylián was recognized from the very beginning of his career as an important talent. His early work may have been influenced by the choreography of John Cranko and Glen Tetley at Stuttgart, but within a relatively short time he had developed his own special dance vocabulary. He has created a unique synthesis, blending classical ballet technique and Graham technique, making his ballets extremely emotive and moving experiences. His ballets can express in a poignant way feelings of fear, sadness, and anger—as in *Field Mass* and *Heart's Labyrinth*—and a tremendous joy, love, and happiness, as in the glorious *Sinfonietta*. This ballet, along with *Svadebka* and *Dream Dances*, shows Kylián's additional interest in movement derived from Slavonic folk dance. Religiously inspired feelings of hope and trust are expressed in devout ballets such as *Symphony of Psalms* and *Glagolitic Mass*, made to the music of his compatriot Janáček—one of his favourite composers, along with Stravinsky, Schoenberg, and Webern. Especially characteristic of these works are the impassioned duets using fluent, whirling movements, a complicated use of space, as in high-speed group crossings, and a close, flowing relationship with the music.

In 1981 Kylián was searching for new sources of inspiration, and travelled to Australia to attend the Aboriginal dance festivals. Afterwards he choreographed the ballets *Nomaden* and *Stamping Ground*, employing a supple and athletic vocabulary which can be traced throughout his later work. A sense for grotesque humour can also be found in Kylián's work, as in *Symfonie in D*, *L'Enfant et les sortilèges*, and *Six Dances*. In his later work, *No More Play*, *Falling Angels*, and *Sweet Dreams*, Kylián can again be seen renewing himself. A Kafkaesque absurd realism is expressed in choreographic parables; fluent, rounded movements become more angular, the timing even more precise, and the theatrical possibilities of light, space, set, and costumes continually expanded.

Kylián can express joy in movement and reveal in his work the delight and ease of being a fluent dance-maker; but he is equally attracted to difficult subjects and seemingly intractable scores; he has never choreographed a throw-away piece, and as Sinclair has written, "Kylián has never compromised". Within the positive and creative environment of the Nederlands Dans Theater this choreographer has continued to develop and build upon his unique talent, such that a critic can sum it up in 1991 with the words, "Jiří Kylián, 44-year-old Prague-born polyglot, artistic director of a company embracing more than a dozen nationalities, in a small country where the history of ballet spans less than fifty years, could well be classed the most important choreographer working today".

—Helma Kloos